W9-DAZ-332

THE
ALMANAC
OF
AMERICAN
POLITICS
1984

THE ALMANAC OF AMERICAN POLITICS 1984

The President, the Senators,
the Representatives, the Governors:
Their Records and Election Results,
Their States and Districts

Michael Barone
and
Grant Ujifusa

Photographs by Shepard Sherbell

National Journal

Washington, D.C.

Photographs by Shepard Sherbell, Washington, D.C. All rights reserved. For information regarding photographs contact: Picture Group, Inc., 5 Steeple Street, Providence, Rhode Island 02903. Telephone (401) 273-5473.

Printing by R.R. Donnelley & Sons Company, Chicago, Illinois.

Text design by Lee E. Fischer, Fine Print & Production, Inc., Cambridge, Massachusetts.

Typesetting by Unicorn Graphics, Washington, D.C.

ISSN 0362-076X
ISBN 0-89234-030-4 (Cloth)
ISBN 0-89234-031-2 (Paper)

ACKNOWLEDGMENTS

The authors owe a special debt of gratitude to Tony Stout and John Fox Sullivan at *National Journal*. Without their faith and commitment to the *Almanac*, it would not exist.

A very special thanks to executive editors John Ross and Julie Romero, who guided the *Almanac* project. Their commitment to excellence, attention to detail, and willingness to work long hours were indispensable to the publication of this edition. And to Sally Roffman of Creative Strategy who contributed imagination and good humor to the marketing of this book.

The authors would like to thank Kevin Chaffee, who using his considerable energy and intelligence, developed and researched the new campaign finance section of the book; Lisa Cherubini, who edited the master file and compiled the name and geographical indexes; and Jeff Ingraham, who assisted with the FEC and demographic data. We are also immensely grateful to those people whose long hours of work went into making this *Almanac* possible: Robin Gradison; Lee Fischer; Greg Dobie; Jim Ross; Cindy Kennedy, Jean Gallagher and Craig Millett at Unicorn Graphics; Carson Connor at Creative Strategy; Priscilla Totten; and Jake Welch.

We wish to acknowledge gratefully ABC News and the Republican National Committee for their contributions of data on the 1980 presidential vote by new congressional district. In addition, we thank the National Governors Association for their contribution of additional photographs.

For

Joan S. Barone
and
Amy B. Ujifusa

CONTENTS

THE POLITICS OF CULTURAL VARIETY

No other nation has a political system whose basic character has remained unchanged for so long as the United States. We have been holding presidential and congressional elections for 195 years now, and in that time just 39 men have held our highest office. The senior senator from New Hampshire still sits at Daniel Webster's desk; the inkwell is kept filled and sand is provided for blotting. Our political parties, though not mentioned in the Constitution, are nearly as old. The Democratic Party was formed in the early 1830s, under Andrew Jackson's aegis, by that master politician Martin Van Buren; the Republican Party sprung up almost spontaneously in reaction to Stephen Douglas's Kansas-Nebraska Act of 1854 and won the congressional elections that year. The two have remained our major parties ever since. The winners of the Democratic presidential and vice presidential nominations in 1984 will be part of an unbroken string going back to Jackson and Van Buren, and the Republican nominees will be part of a string beginning with John C. Fremont and William Dayton. No other nation's political system comes close to matching this continuity.

Beneath the veneer of continuity, American politics—and American life—have of course changed. The nation of 3 million mostly English colonists who chose the first president in 1790—that is, the white males with sufficient property to vote—is a very different place from the continental nation of 228 million which votes in 1984. More to the point, the United States of 1984 is a very different nation from the United States that launched the D-Day invasion of 1944 or the United States that was unknowingly about to embark on the Vietnam war in 1964. The nation today is larger in population, vastly richer (despite the protracted recession that began in 1979), more tolerant of diversity, economically more intertwined with the rest of the world. Its politics has changed as well.

But in recent history there has been no clear divide, no one date you can point to—no 1789, no 1865, no 1914—when everything changed. Yet it is apparent that the rules which governed American politics in the 1940s or even as recently as the middle 1960s no longer obtain. Examples:

- It used to be assumed that there was a natural Democratic majority in presidential elections, a majority which would give the Democrats victory absent unusual circumstances like raging inflation or war. But in the last four presidential elections Democrats have averaged 43% of the vote.
- It used to be assumed that the American people would overwhelmingly reject deviations from moral norms. As recently as 1963, remarriage cost Nelson Rockefeller his lead in polls for the Republican presidential nomination. Since 1981 the nation has had a president—a Republican who proclaims himself a conservative—who has been divorced and remarried. In the middle 1960s, it was unheard of for issues like abortion, marijuana, pornography, or homosexuality to arise in politics; everyone was against them. Today all have been explicitly or implicitly legalized, and those who want to see those decisions reversed have been continually frustrated.
- It used to be assumed that the American people were united in support of a bipartisan foreign policy and would rally unanimously to the flag in time of war. That, after all, had been the experience of World War II (though not of previous wars) and the postwar years. But that was not how Americans reacted to the Vietnam war.

- It used to be assumed that the average American thought of himself as "the little guy," as an average person, a working person far below the top levels of society, a person whose basic tastes and morality nonetheless typified the nation. Americans prided themselves on being normal, average, ordinary. Today that is far less often the case. People celebrate their differentness, not their sameness; their distinction, not their normality. Politically, there is this effect: a decline in the confidence that working class Democrats and middle class Republicans had that they represented the solid middle majority of Americans. Instead, we have developed a politics of cultural variety, a politics in which cultural and social characteristics which used to be thought irrelevant to politics are increasingly determining political attitudes.
- It used to be assumed that virtually all Americans lived in nuclear families with several children. That pattern is no longer universal. Because of rising divorce rates and lower birth rates, 26% of households no longer contain families, and a majority of households—61%—contain no children.

This politics of cultural variety has developed in a nation where people have, gradually, become more *alike* economically, more *alike* ethnically and regionally, but more *different* culturally. Since these changes are not obvious, let us look at each in turn.

Americans have become more alike economically. Leftish critics of the American economic system like to point out that the income distribution—the percentage of income going to the highest, lowest, and middle-income groups—has not changed much since 1945. True enough. But real incomes have grown enormously—more than at any other time in American history. Real income per person was 2½ times in 1980 what it was 40 years before. This still understates the change, since a larger percentage of Americans were children in 1940: real income per adult has increased more than 2½ times in 40 years.

Such a vast increase in real income does not obliterate income differentials. Some people are still a lot richer than others. But it makes income disparities much easier to tolerate—and less relevant to daily life. Most Americans of 1945 had incomes below the poverty levels of today. Most Americans today have real incomes at levels the Americans of 1945 would have regarded as near the top of the scale. In 1960, just 19% of American families had incomes over $25,000 in 1980 dollars; in 1980, 39% did. And the percentage with incomes under $10,000, in 1980 dollars, fell from 28% to 19%. That means, roughly, that twice as many Americans have incomes that provide a comfortably secure standard of living, and that the proportion of low income families has dropped vastly. That doesn't mean that Americans universally regard themselves as affluent. But it does mean, for all his complaints about the economy, the ordinary American today takes for granted an access to necessities and many luxuries which his counterpart a long generation ago would have considered utterly beyond his means. Even unemployed Americans today need not worry about sending their children to bed hungry, as many did 40 years ago. Americans may complain, but the urgency of their complaints is surely much less than those of 40 or even 20 years ago, when many people feared they could not afford necessities.

Real income rises have other politically significant effects. Despite the model showing a stable distribution of income, there is a vast amount of social mobility in the United States, both upward and downward. In times of growing real incomes, the possibilities for upward mobility are great, and the rewards are often greater than people ever dreamed. And rising real income levels cushion downward social mobility. In such times you can hold a job several notches below your father's occupational level and still enjoy the same income. So in politically significant terms, Americans in 1945–75 came to be more alike: more alike in the sense that they became, apparently securely, part of a large, affluent middle-income segment of the population. The sense of deprivation that helped to cement many people in the New Deal Democratic coalition, the sense of precarious privilege that helped to keep many others solidly Republican—these have both tended to fade, silently and gradually, in the long generation after World War II.

One way to measure the narrowing income gap between parts of the country is to show each state's per capita income as a percentage of the national average. The following table does this for 1940, 1960, and 1980. To some extent it still overstates regional differences, since a larger percentage of residents of southern states are children; they count the same for per capita income figures as single householders in New York or California, who absorb much higher incomes in just basic living expenses.

State Per Capita Income as Percentage of National Average

	1940	1960	1980		1940	1960	1980
EAST				**WEST**			
DC	202	129	126	AK	—	124	134
CT	149	129	123	CA	141	123	115
NJ	138	123	115	WY	102	100	114
MD	120	105	110	NV	150	127	113
DE	173	124	109	WA	111	107	108
NY	147	123	108	HI	—	104	106
MA	132	111	106	CO	92	102	105
RI	125	99	99	OR	104	100	98
PA	109	102	99	AZ	85	91	92
NH	96	99	96	MT	96	90	90
ME	87	83	83	ID	76	82	85
VT	85	85	82	NM	63	82	82
				UT	81	89	80
				SOUTH			
				TX	73	86	100
MIDWEST				VA	77	86	99
IL	127	119	111	OK	62	84	96
KS	71	95	105	FL	86	89	94
MI	114	106	105	LA	61	75	89
MN	89	94	102	GA	57	75	85
OH	111	105	99	NC	55	72	82
NE	74	91	98	WV	68	72	82
IA	85	89	98	TN	56	72	81
WI	93	99	98	KY	54	72	80
MO	88	95	94	AL	47	69	79
IN	93	98	94	AR	43	62	76
ND	57	76	92	SC	51	63	76
SD	61	80	82	MS	36	54	69

Thus the gap between New York and Mississippi was 147–36 in 1940 and 108–69 in 1980—still considerable, but also offset in considerable part by the lower cost of living in Mississippi. Northeastern states are regressing toward the mean, though we should remember that in the period on the table, the national per capita income, in real dollars, roughly tripled, and 99% of a tripled income is a lot more than 123% of the original amount. Metropolitan areas typically have higher incomes than rural ones, but the gap again has narrowed. Local events, like the collapse of the textile industry in Massachusetts and Rhode Island in the postwar years, are readily apparent. So is the continuing rise in southern incomes. It should not have been so surprising that they would rise in time of war; that usually happens in backward parts of a country. But their rise in the 1960–80 period is an extraordinary event, and one cause may have been the civil rights revolution, which made the South more attractive to talented blacks, reduced black outmigration, and gave blacks more opportunity to be economically productive.

Political preferences in the America of the 1940s correlated to a fair degree with income. Republican strength was greater than average in high income states like New York, Connecticut, New Jersey, and Delaware (all of which Thomas Dewey carried over Harry Truman in 1948), while Roosevelt and Truman carried virtually every state with incomes below the national level (the exceptions were rock-ribbed Republican since the Civil War: Maine and Vermont, Nebraska and Kansas). But today there is virtually no correlation between income level and political preference. Utah, with one of the lowest per capita incomes, was the nation's most Republican state in 1980; its low per capita income reflects the large number of children in the state, and family ties and the presence of children began to be correlated with Republican preference by 1980. In the Midwest high income Illinois is more Democratic than low income Indiana; in the East New Hampshire is the most Republican and one of the lowest income states. Only in the South does the old correlation of economic situation and political preference still hold, to some extent: the oil-rich states of Texas, Louisiana, and Oklahoma all had fast-rising incomes in the late 1970s and trended sharply to Ronald Reagan's Republicans in 1980. Even so, economic factors seem less and less to explain political preference, and cultural variety seems to do it more and more.

Americans have tended to become more alike ethnically and regionally. Because writers of the history of racial and ethnic groups have concentrated on discrimination and oppression, we lose sight of how tolerant and welcoming the United States has been. Comparison with other countries is illuminating: almost every other country with a multiracial population has a worse race problem, and few countries have been as open to immigrants as we have during most of our existence (and are today in fact, if not in legal theory). Certainly it is clear that ethnic and religious origin have become much less important as barriers to advancement. It is clear as well that being a Catholic or a Jew, being of Italian or Polish descent, is simply a less distinctive experience in the America of the 1980s than it was in the America of, say, the 1950s. Religious practice is far less likely to set one apart; contact between various groups is greater; intermarriage is so common that many people fear these groups will lose their distinctiveness entirely. Ethnic festivals and ethnic studies programs show that people are still interested in their diverse origins. But even if their origins are different, their present lives are rather like those of other Americans.

Racial differences still matter much more. But we should not lose sight of the fact that the civil rights revolution of the 1960s changed the lives of black—and many white—Americans more than any other peaceful change in any other nation's history. To understand that, you only have to recall that many serious and well-informed people, of both races, said that southern whites would never accept blacks on the job or in the polling booth, in restaurants or in their neighborhoods or in their children's schools. Now outward resistance to any of these forms of integration has just about vanished. It is true that racial discrimination in housing still seems the rule, although even here some progress is being made: small numbers of blacks now live in hundreds of suburbs and city neighborhoods across the nation which, a generation ago, would have been all white. And there will always be some concentration of blacks in neighborhoods, by choice, for the same reason there is some clustering of whites of particular ethnic backgrounds or cultural preferences: people like to live in neighborhoods with others of similar tastes. In the meantime, there is no question that there has been a vast change in white attitudes and black opportunities, just as there is no question that it is difficult for blacks to overcome the handicaps imposed by generations of slavery and segregation.

Regional differences have also become muted. This is not just because announcers on Dallas TV have the same accents as those on Boston TV; local accents have some vitality left. A more important reason is that the income gap between the regions has narrowed. In 1940 New York's per capita income was four times Mississippi's; today New York's per capita income is about 50% higher, but much of the difference is eaten up by a higher cost of living. The South and West now have metropolitan areas as rich and cosmopolitan as any in the Northeast and universities as learned and well endowed. The South is no longer set apart from the rest of the country by virtue of racial segregation or the presence of blacks.

Many of the historically important divisions in American politics have been regional and ethnic. Democrats could once count on carrying a Solid South, and blacks used to vote (where they could) almost unanimously for the party of Lincoln. The Irish immigrants of the 1840s, encountering Whig and later Republican Yankees, found they were welcomed into the minority Democratic Party—to the point where it wasn't a minority any more. Some later immigrants, shut out of politics by the Irish, responded by becoming Republicans or even Socialists. Franklin Roosevelt's New Deal brought disparate and sometimes hostile groups together into the Democratic Party: blacks and southern whites, most of the products of 1840–1924 immigration. The result was a majority party made up of self-conscious minorities, just as the popular base of the minority Republican Party were the white Anglo-Saxon Protestants who considered themselves, inaccurately, as a majority group.

The FDR coalition didn't last. For some years its breakup was considered the result of quarrels that might be patched up. Southern whites abandoned Democratic presidential and many local candidates in the middle 1960s, in protest of the national party's support of civil rights laws. By 1970 in state races and 1976 in the presidential race, many southern whites voted Democratic again. But as the 1980 election showed, this was not an invariable loyalty. The real reason the Democratic coalition could not last was that the ethnic and economic consciousness of its members—or their children—was fading. The minorities, whether they were Jews or southern whites, blacks or Irish or Italians or Poles, weren't very self-conscious any more. They were much less often the object of discrimination or persecution. They needed less from government or politics. They were becoming much more like other Americans— and other Americans much more like them.

Americans are becoming more different culturally. In vivid contrast to the era of conformism, Americans value themselves now for how they are different from each other more than for how they are alike. What has happened is this. In an increasingly affluent and tolerant nation, people have been able to choose their own identity. Distinctiveness is no longer something determined by birth, but something you can choose. A once economically and ethnically heterogeneous people have become culturally heterogeneous.

The result is that increasingly we have a politics of cultural variety. This has been replacing the politics of economic class which was inspired by the New Deal and the politics of ethnic, racial, and regional rivalries which was never entirely eradicated by the New Deal, and important vestiges of which survived the Roosevelt years. Such a process is never total, not at least in a country at peace and untouched by economic cataclysm.

The emergence of the politics of cultural variety is further camouflaged by the fact that many cultural differences have not become politically significant. In a tolerant country, why should they? In recent years, we have seen a great divergence in eating habits: we have steak-eaters and vegetarians, devotees of European cuisines and lovers of soul food and barbecue, martini drinkers and teetotalers and sippers of mineral water. The old predilection for almost all Americans to eat and drink the same things—processed cheese and Cokes, eggs for breakfast and meat and potatoes for dinner—is changing. Yet no one makes a political issue of this. The only time choice of food became a political issue in recent years was when a Reagan administration official suggested classifying ketchup as a vegetable in school lunch programs. The proposal was promptly denounced by, among others, Senator John Heinz.

So we have tended to treat cultural issues as if they are nuisances—as if they ought not to be political issues at all. If you could poll working politicians on abortion, for example, you would find that most hope the controversy would just go away. Gun control is seen as a nuisance by most of its supporters—a means the opposition uses to divert the voters who would support them on "real issues." School prayer, marijuana legislation, the nuclear freeze, environmental protection, homosexual rights—all are derisively called "peripheral" issues or denounced as "single issues," on which voters should not base their decisions. Politicians, particularly Democrats who still think their party has a "natural majority," want elections decided on New Deal economic issues and along the old ethnic and regional lines.

But for most voters, those economic issues are largely settled, and the old ethnic and regional loyalties are no longer compelling. Political events of 1977–82 clarified where Americans stand on the big macroeconomic issue. They do not want to dismantle the makeshift welfare state this country has constructed, and they do not want it increased much in size or scope. The political process, acting in response to public opinion, flatly rejected Carter administration proposals for a guaranteed minimum income ("welfare reform") and for massive government jobs programs. Just as surely, the political process rejected Reagan administration proposals to cut scheduled Social Security benefit increases and rejected as well proposals to pare down aid programs for the disadvantaged. While no one in early 1983 seemed to have a fiscal policy they seemed confident would promote economic growth and still hold down inflation, almost everyone, silently, seemed to agree on the question, more important in the long run, of how to balance the public and private sectors.

The most striking aspect of cultural variety is not the personal styles people affect, but the personal lives they choose to live. Membership in a nuclear family is still the pattern that guides most people's lives. But belonging to one does not guide them as rigidly as it once did. The divorce level is much higher than ever before, and so is the remarriage rate. Women are much more likely to enter, and stay in, the work force. People are much more likely to live to-gether, and to have sex, before marriage. Homosexual lifestyles are becoming more common. Young people are choosing to have many fewer children than they were a generation ago. This is not quite the departure from historical norm most of us suppose: the birth rates of the baby boom generation of 1947–62 were unprecedentedly high for an advanced, affluent country. What is odd is not that the birth rate fell, but that it stayed high for so long. Still, the current low birth rate represents a change from expectations.

The effect of all these changes on expectations may be greater than the immediate effect on behavior. A woman getting married today cannot count, as her mother probably did, on her husband supporting her for life. That, as well as changing attitudes toward children and home, may be pushing her to get a job. Affluence and tolerance have combined to give Americans an unprecedented freedom of choice. But they have also given them what inevitably accompanies that freedom—uncertainty and insecurity.

The most important manifestation of the politics of cultural variety, more important than the emergence here and there of cultural issues like abortion and gun control, is the increasing correlation of voting behavior with personal circumstances. Analysts of the 1980 election found a "gender gap," a significant difference in voting behavior between men and women. Such differences before had been on the order of 1% or 2%. But in 1980 men favored Ronald Reagan 57%–39%—over an incumbent president!—while women favored Reagan by the narrow margin of 47%–43%. The difference between the two sexes was almost as great as the difference between union and non-union households, and greater than the difference between North and South. Moreover, the gender gap in 1980 applied not just to Reagan but to Republican candidates generally.

And gender was not the only—perhaps not the main—personal characteristic correlated with political choice. CBS's Martin Plissner identified what he called the "marriage gap": in 1982 married people gave the Democrats only a 4% margin in congressional elections, while unmarried people—singles, divorced persons, widows and widowers—gave the Democrats a 24% margin. Young voters continue to vote differently from their elders, though the patterns are not always linear: the most liberal, on issues like foreign policy and cultural matters, are the Vietnam generation, people in their 30s in 1984; those in their 20s seem more liberal on some economic issues and on nuclear power. Voters over 55, typically more conservative on cultural issues, responded very negatively to suggestions that the Reagan administration would reduce Social Security benefits. And in each case there seem to be sharp differences between men and women.

Plausible reasons can be advanced to explain these differences. Women tend to be more fearful of war and therefore more cautious on foreign policy; younger women, at least, tend to be more liberal on cultural issues like abortion and the Equal Rights Amendment; women generally tend to have less economic security (if only because their husbands can always leave them) and therefore to be more fearful of the consequences of cutting Social Security; and they tend, perhaps, to be more compassionate and less eager for efficiency, and thus to be more reluctant to cut programs intended to help the disadvantaged. Single voters, less tied to communities and less likely to be regularly employed, are more likely to be liberal on cultural and economic issues than are married people, who tend to have much higher incomes. For the differences between men and women, between married and single people, may be cultural, but they have economic consequences. We live in a day when the difference, for many Americans, between economic security and the insecurity of living from payday to payday, is the difference between living in a one-paycheck and a two-paycheck household. Single people, and a disproportionate number of women, live in one-paycheck households. Married people, and a disproportionate number of men (who die younger and remarry earlier) live in two-paycheck households.

We are not accustomed to dividing the electorate and analyzing election results along these lines. They do not correspond to the geographic units in which election results are reported, although increasingly in metropolitan areas you find neighborhoods that are identifiably family or single areas. We come from a nation in which it was assumed that everyone would get and stay married, and that husbands and wives would usually have similar opinions on political matters. Today men and women, married and single people live increasingly in different Americas, as well as different households. It should not be surprising that, increasingly, they have different politics. So it becomes important to know to what extent Americans are still living in familiar family patterns and to what extent they are not. To the old politically relevant statistics—income levels, blue collar/white collar, racial and ethnic origin—must now be added the percentage of households containing families, containing children, and containing married couples. Fortunately, they are available for each state and congressional district; the state figures are provided in the table below. Some 74% of American households contain families, a figure below historic precedent, and only 39% contain children, a much lower figure than previously in our history. And 61% contain married couples, leaving at least 13% of the families not headed by a married couple.

1980 Households: Families, Children and Married Couples

	Families	Children	Married Couples		Families	Children	Married Couples
UNITED STATES	74%	39%	61%	WEST			
EAST				UT	78	50	69
NJ	76	39	61	HI	77	45	63
MD	75	42	59	ID	76	44	67
DE	75	41	61	NM	75	45	62
ME	74	41	63	AZ	74	39	62
NH	74	40	63	AK	73	49	61
CT	74	38	61	WY	73	43	65
PA	74	38	61	MT	72	40	63
VT	72	40	61	CO	70	39	59
RI	72	37	59	WA	70	38	59
MA	71	36	57	OR	70	37	60
NY	70	37	54	CA	69	37	55
DC	53	29	30	NV	68	36	56
				SOUTH			
				SC	78	46	63
MIDWEST				MS	78	46	62
IN	76	42	64	KY	78	44	65
MI	75	42	61	NC	77	43	63
OH	74	41	62	AL	77	43	63
ND	73	40	65	WV	77	42	65
SD	73	40	64	TN	77	42	63
WI	73	40	63	AR	77	41	65
IA	73	39	64	LA	76	45	60
MO	73	39	62	GA	76	44	61
KS	73	38	63	TX	75	43	63
MN	72	40	62	VA	75	42	62
IL	72	39	59	OK	74	40	63
NE	72	38	63	FL	72	33	59

Non-family populations, it is clear, tend to be concentrated in big metropolitan areas and in Florida. The South remains distinctly more family-oriented than the rest of the country, but with low marriage rates, which are held down by the low marriage rate in black households. Other family-oriented states include heavily Mormon Utah and Idaho, the frontier states of Hawaii and Alaska, New Mexico with its large Hispanic population, and Indiana, which seems to live largely untouched by the changes in behavior and attitudes which are more noticeable even in its midwestern neighbors—and whose voting patterns seemed surprisingly unaffected by the recession of 1982.

* * *

The growth of a politics of cultural variety has been a long process—the product of a long period of affluence and tolerance, though the emergence of voting behavior based on personal circumstances seems to have been quite sudden. It could, however, be overshadowed at any time. Cultural issues can fade in importance if the society as a whole seems threatened with military or economic destruction. Or the nation itself can change.

There are two possible changes that can give us a different politics. One is a continuation of the 1979–83 economic doldrums, in which the nation essentially had zero economic growth. That, it should be emphasized, is not the same as the experience of the Great Depression, when GNP dropped by nearly 50%. But should this prove to be the beginning of a protracted period of no-growth, then our politics is likely to come to resemble the New Deal model more closely than it has in recent years. That is true even if we continue, as we have since 1979, to live in the great majority of cases in what is in any historic perspective great affluence. For the absence of real income growth changes everyone's view of society. There is less upward mobility, and those who do move upward are not rewarded so lavishly. There is more downward mobility, and those who move downward suffer, as they did not in 1945–75, losses in real income. For those who don't move, there is frustration: because the common expectation is that almost everybody rises in real income. And for those who are, unexpectedly, unemployed or uprooted, there is something more than frustration. The first reaction may be dazed disbelief. Later comes anger against the economic system and resentment against those who have, for no apparent good reason, done better.

Thus we could have a self-conscious working class bloc once again, and a kind of New Deal economic politics—if large numbers of people become convinced economic growth is not going to return, and that they had better fight to get their share of a pie that is not growing and may be shrinking. Evidence of such thinking exists in the 1982 election results, in the victories of Democrats in Michigan and Ohio, states where the major industries seem to have collapsed and people live in dazed uncertainty about their futures, and in the victories of some Democratic candidates, notably legal services lawyers, in blue collar constituencies which had been trending Republican on cultural issues. The history of the 1930s suggests, however, that it takes a long time for Americans to give up on the possibility of economic growth; the economic voting blocs did not really emerge until 1936 and 1938, long after the 1929 crash. For the 1980s, the question is whether 1983 and 1984 will see the recovery being predicted as this is written.

The other change which could alter the course of our politics is what seems to be a third major wave of American immigration. Curiously, immigration into this country seems to have occurred almost entirely within limited periods. The first wave came to America mostly in 1640–1720, and consisted primarily of Englishmen, Scots, Welsh, and African blacks; by ancestry this first wave accounts for almost precisely half of Americans today. The other half are accounted for by the second wave of immigration, in 1840–1924, which included large numbers of British (working class), Irish, German, Italian, Polish, and Jewish migrants. The first wave immigrants provided the historic base for the post-Civil War Republican Party majority, the second wave immigrants for the post-New Deal Democratic Party majority.

Now we may be at the beginning of a third wave of immigration, beginning for reasons no one is quite clear about around 1970. Its prime constituents are Latin Americans and Asians. In the 1970s, Spanish origin persons rose from 4% to 6% of the national total, and Asians from ½% to 1½%. These sound like small numbers, but they are striking increases. So far these changes have had minimal effect on politics. Sudden influxes of immigrants—like the Cuban refugees of 1980 in Miami and Fort Chaffee, Arkansas—evoke angry reactions, though most of the immigrants have encountered very little prejudice. Meanwhile, they have entered the voting stream in uneven numbers. Cubans in Florida, though they have mostly become U.S. citizens, seem hesitant to vote. Mexican-Americans vote frequently in California and somewhat less frequently in Texas (where they meet more resistance), but both groups seem to be moving up the socioeconomic ladder so fast that their voting habits are not so different as we would expect from those of the Anglo majority. Migrants from some other Latin countries don't participate in U.S. politics at all, just as Puerto Ricans vote hardly at all in New York; their allegiance and their interests remain back home, where they hope to return soon—if they are not already flying back and forth. Socioeconomically, the Asians are the fastest rising immigrants, and if they vote somewhat more Democratic than average, the difference does not seem overwhelming.

What seems fairly clear is that most of these immigrants, unlike the Irish of 1840–1924 or the black migrants to northern cities after 1945, do not see a better way of life coming through politics. They may live at first in identifiable ethnic neighborhoods, but they are moving outward to working and middle class neighborhoods most people think of as white: from East Los Angeles to the San Fernando Valley or Orange County. Evidently they encounter less housing discrimination than do blacks, and otherwise have fewer problems which government might plausibly address. Their basic attitude toward this country, after all, is positive; they decided affirmatively to come here, to leave a familiar culture, friends, family, and everything they knew for a chance in the United States. So perhaps they are less likely to be an identifiable, protest-minded voting bloc; and are more likely to fit in, quietly and without too much fuss, into affluent and tolerant middle class America—and to the politics of cultural variety it has developed.

THE PRESIDENCY

The American presidency is the most important public office in the world and the one whose holder is chosen by the world's most intricate and protracted process. No other major democratic nation reposes so much power in a single elected official, and no other nation spends so much time and energy determining who its next leader is to be. Prime ministers in Japan and Western Europe, leaders in dictatorships like Russia and China—each is one in a crowd of many politicians struggling for power. But the president stands alone. The Constitution sets him apart, and his at least theoretical control over the huge executive branch gives him power far outweighing that of any member of Congress. The most important powers of the presidency are not necessarily formal; he is circumscribed by law and custom and can seldom achieve his major goals by command. What the president does have is the spotlight. More than any other American, or any other world leader, he has the power and ability to frame issues, to set the terms of discussion, to dominate the public dialogue, and to set a national agenda. The president can set the tone of our public life.

And inevitably he does—for better or worse. Franklin Roosevelt, entering office in 1933, had few specific ideas of how to extricate the nation from economic catastrophe. But from the time he told Americans that they had nothing to fear but fear itself, he made people believe that something would be done and that it would work. Roosevelt was one of only two Americans nominated for national office by a major political party five times; the other was Richard Nixon. Roosevelt set a positive tone for his generation and the one after; Nixon set a very different tone for our own times. So did other presidents who seemed to fail, again and again, to deliver on their promises. Lyndon Johnson ran in 1964 promising not to send American boys to fight where Asian boys should fight and then did just what he said he wouldn't do; Richard Nixon ran in 1968 promising to uphold middle class morality and then was forced out of office for breaking the law. Vietnam, Watergate, the new experience of persistent inflation, wildly rising energy prices—these all contributed to a negative climate of opinion, a climate none of the presidents since 1965 has been able to alter.

Nor have they had much luck running for reelection. Americans in the early 1960s assumed that in the ordinary course of things a president would win two terms; since then only one president has, and he resigned because of excesses committed by officials of his campaign. In the 1970s we adjusted and tinkered with our presidential selection system, in the hope of getting better results. But the new process became so complicated and the primary season so long that it seems that only politicians who can campaign full time—politicians with no governmental responsibilities—can win. But no system guarantees good results. The nation also needs luck, which it seemed to have until recently. One president after another has been ousted—Johnson in 1968, Nixon in 1974, Ford in 1976, Carter in 1980. Each time we were surprised, and never more than by the size of Ronald Reagan's plurality over Jimmy Carter in 1980, and by the fact that the Republicans won control of the Senate that year for the first time since 1952. Our knowledge of the political process, and the care with which it is covered by the press, has increased vastly in the past 20 years. But the results surprise us more than ever.

Will we be surprised again in 1984? In early 1983 the two frontrunners for their parties'

nominations are Ronald Reagan and Walter Mondale. But it has been a long time since a
frontrunner at this point in the race has been inaugurated as president two years later. It is not
possible in early 1983 to predict anything about the 1984 elections. But it may be useful to
look at the election calendar and the distribution of national delegates to both parties'
conventions, to get a sense of the range of things that might happen.

The path to the nomination: the Democrats. The rules for the presidential selection process
are not yet set as this is written. State legislatures or political parties can change primary
dates, alter caucus procedures, scuttle primaries in favor of caucuses, or vice versa. So it is
safest to begin with a look backward, at how the process worked in 1980.

For the Democrats, the nomination was essentially decided by March 18, when Edward
Kennedy lost the Illinois primary 65%–30%. In January Carter had won by a 59%–31%
margin the precinct caucuses in Iowa, a state where liberal activists had scheduled the

1980 Democratic Presidential Primaries: Leading Candidates

Date	State	Carter	Kennedy	Brown	Others
February 26	NH	47	37	10	6
March 4	MA	29	65	3	3
	VT	73	26	—	1
March 11	FL	61	23	5	11
	GA	88	8	2	2
	AL	82	13	4	1
March 18	IL	65	30	3	2
March 25	NY	41	59	—	—
	CT	41	47	3	9
April 1	WI	56	30	12	2
	KS	57	32	5	7
April 5	LA	56	23	5	17
April 22	PA	45	46	2	7
May 3	TX	56	23	3	19
May 6	NC	70	18	3	9
	IN	68	32	—	—
	TN	75	18	2	5
	DC	37	62	—	1
May 13	MD	47	38	3	12
	NE	49	38	4	12
May 20	OR	57	31	9	3
	MI	—	—	29	71
May 27	AR	60	18	—	22
	KY	67	23	—	10
	NV	38	29	—	34
	ID	62	22	4	12
June 3	CA	38	45	4	14
	OH	51	44	—	5
	NJ	38	56	—	6
	WV	62	38	—	—
	NM	42	46	—	12
	MT	51	37	—	12
	SD	45	49	—	6
	RI	26	68	1	5
	TOTAL	51	37	3	9

caucuses early to increase their own influence; in February Carter had won 47%–37% in New Hampshire, next door to Kennedy's home state, and among a primary electorate mostly Catholic; in early March Carter had won overwhelming victories in the South, taking most black as well as most white votes. His victory in Illinois—a large midwestern industrial state, with just about every kind of voter—suggested strongly that even if Kennedy's win in Massachusetts were repeated in other East Coast states, Carter would still win the nomination. And so it turned out. Kennedy did better than he had in Illinois in some primaries when it seemed he had little chance to win the nomination (Pennsylvania, California) and even won a couple of states in the interior of the country (New Mexico, South Dakota). But the race was decided in Illinois.

What does this tell us about the Democratic presidential delegate selection process? That it has no necessary bias toward the political left or toward insurgents. It also shows that how people vote depends very much on what they consider at stake. In the New Hampshire primaries of 1972 and 1976, Democrats voted for George McGovern and Jimmy Carter in unanticipated numbers not so much because they wanted them to be president; they didn't really know much about them. But they did want to give them a chance. They figured that if these candidates could motivate clean-cut college students or homey fellow Georgians to canvass door-to-door, they might be worth looking at; and that voters in later primaries would have a chance to accept or reject them. Yet such is the power of the publicity generated by New Hampshire and other early tests that both candidates were given a tremendous boost and ended up with the Democratic nomination. In 1980, in contrast, voters in the early primaries voted as if the presidency depended on their choice; only after March 18 were they willing to cast protest votes—send them a message, in George Wallace's old phrase. Both candidates' advisers admitted that the strongest argument for their candidate was that the other man might win.

For 1984, then, an important question in the early tests in Iowa, New Hampshire, other New England and southern states, and Illinois, is whether voters think they are making a final choice or whether they can be persuaded to help elevate one of the lesser-known candidates—Alan Cranston or Ernest Hollings or Reubin Askew—out of the pack and into further consideration. The best-known candidates—presumably Walter Mondale and John Glenn—will have an incentive to persuade voters they are making a final choice. The lesser-known candidates, struggling to win attention, will ask to be given a chance.

The process itself puts a premium on certain strategies and tactics. Often those that help a candidate in the primaries hurt in the general election; the strategies and tactics that help win the general election can make it more difficult to govern. The preconvention campaign process puts a premium on stressing the current hot issue, although it may not continue to be a major issue when the candidate is inaugurated. It puts a premium on novelty, especially for the little-known candidate, although novel policies (McGovern's $1,000-a-year plan) often turn out to be poorly thought out and politically damaging. It puts a premium on the negative, particularly for those candidates (Glenn, Hollings, Askew) not strongly associated with partisan Democratic appeals, even though ultimately a president must present a positive vision of the future rather than carping about the past. And it puts a premium on making lots of separate appeals to diverse pressure groups, although many of the most successful Democratic policies have been those (like Social Security, federal mortgage guarantees, Medicare) that affect the great mass of people in pretty much the same way. This pressure will be great in 1983 if, as promised, the AFL-CIO decides whether to endorse a candidate (by a two-thirds vote) in November and if the National Education Association does likewise. The frontrunner for these endorsements, Walter Mondale, will be pressed to back certain positions unpopular with the general electorate (like strengthening unions' powers) or with opinion leaders (like trade restrictions); other candidates will have an incentive to denounce him for his backing.

Much has been made of the fact that the Democrats' Hunt Commission reserved some 561 of the seats at the Democratic National Convention for elected officials and others chosen without public participation. This may be a salutary reform, but it is not likely to have as great an effect as the ballyhooing suggests. The great majority of delegates will still be bound to vote as determined in the primaries. Elected officials are unlikely to be a solid bloc, even if the convention deadlocks. Will there be a deadlock and the kind of brokering and dealmaking that aficionados of H. L. Mencken's coverage of ancient conventions would love to see again? Not likely. The primary process tends to determine the outcome; and if it doesn't produce an obvious nominee, there will be lots of time for everyone to learn that—and to make their deals over the telephone. We are far from those innocent days when delegates arrived at the convention city and no one had any idea how many votes each candidate had. So the conventions are likely to be what they have been for at least 20 years: television broadcasts that, if skillfully managed by the party's leaders and nominee, can help them appeal to voters for the general election.

At this writing it simply does not make sense to list the sequence of presidential primaries for 1984. They are considered certain to change, and likely to change enough so that setting down any specific list would be misleading. The following should, however, be noted. The Hunt Commission tried to set up a "window" from March to June in which primaries could be held or the caucus selection process begun. But it specifically allowed the Iowa precinct caucuses and the New Hampshire primary to be conducted before the window. New Hampshire's state law requires that its primary be conducted a week before any other state's; no one has speculated on what would happen if another state wrote a law saying its primary would be held on the same day as New Hampshire's. Anyway, there seems almost certain to be a plethora of primaries within one or two weeks of New Hampshire's: one set in New England, with Massachusetts the flagship, another in the South, where Florida would be the largest state but not the most typical. It is quite possible that, by the middle of March, even before Illinois, the nominee could be determined. There will not be much time for little known candidates to get better known or for candidates who falter to recover.

The path to the nomination: the Republicans. It is not known, as this is written, whether President Reagan will run for reelection; if he does, he will surely win the Republican nomination without difficulty. Republican primary voters and party activists are less numerous than Democrats, and more ideological; most have waited for years for a leader like Reagan and would not abandon him now. As a non-incumbent, he won 63% of the primary votes in 1980; as an incumbent he will surely do much better.

If Reagan is not a candidate, all bets are off. The Republican convention constituency wants a Reagan-like candidate. But there is no clear heir apparent. Vice President George Bush, a loyal supporter of administration policies and a vice president who, like Walter Mondale, has found a way to use the office constructively, nonetheless is distrusted by a large part of the Reagan constituency. Senate Majority Leader Howard Baker, who by his early announcement of retirement from the Senate made clear he would be a candidate in 1984 if the

1980 Republican Presidential Primaries: Leading Candidates

Date	State	Reagan	Bush	Anderson	Baker	Others
February 26	NH	50	23	10	13	5
March 4	MA	29	31	31	5	5
	VT	30	22	29	12	7
March 8	SC	55	15	—	1	30
March 11	FL	56	30	9	1	3
	AL	70	26	—	1	3
	GA	73	13	8	1	5
March 18	IL	48	11	37	1	3
March 25	CT	34	39	22	1	4
April 1	WI	40	30	27	0	2
	KS	63	13	18	1	5
April 5	LA	75	19	—	—	6
April 22	PA	43	50	2	2	2
May 3	TX	51	47	—	—	2
May 6	IN	74	16	10	—	—
	TN	74	18	4	—	3
	NC	68	22	5	2	4
	DC	—	66	27	—	7
May 13	NE	76	15	6	—	3
	MD	48	41	10	—	1
May 20	MI	32	57	8	—	3
	OR	54	35	10	—	1
May 27	ID	83	—	10	4	3
	KY	82	7	5	—	5
	NV	83	6	—	—	10
June 3	CA	80	5	14	—	1
	OH	81	19	—	—	—
	NJ	81	17	—	—	2
	WV	84	14	—	—	2
	SD	88	4	—	—	8
	MT	87	10	—	—	4
	NM	64	10	12	—	14
	MS	89	8	—	—	2
	RI	72	19	—	—	9
	TOTAL	61	23	12	1	3

president were not, is even more distrusted; he is the man, after all, who helped push cultural issues like abortion to the back burner and who played the crucial part in approving the Panama Canal Treaties. Senate Finance Chairman Robert Dole is known to be skeptical of supply side economics and is one of the architects of the food stamp program. As for possible candidates with more solid Reagan credentials, Paul Laxalt and Jack Kemp in early 1983 were not prepared, organizationally at least, to run. Jesse Helms is openly disliked even by many on the right, and his standing in his home state of North Carolina is, to say the least, shaky. Senator William Armstrong, an effective legislative leader on economic issues, is not well known nationally.

Obviously someone has to win the nomination. The outlook is for something like the 1980 pattern, with essentially two sets of primaries in the beginning to determine the field. One is in the northern tier of the country—the Iowa caucuses, the primaries in New Hampshire, Massachusetts, and Vermont; the other is in the South. Some candidates (Reagan in 1980, probably Bush in 1984) can compete in both; others are likely to try to establish themselves mainly in the northern tier (Anderson and Bush in 1980, perhaps Baker or Dole in 1984) and others mainly in the South (Connally in 1980, perhaps Helms in 1984). The contest then proceeds probably with three candidates in the big states of Illinois, New York, Pennsylvania, and Texas.

1984 National Conventions: Delegate Apportionment

	Democratic	Republican		Democratic	Republican
UNITED STATES	3,923	2,234	CO	51	35
			NM	28	24
EAST	982 (25%)	524 (23%)	AZ	39	32
ME	27	20	UT	27	26
NH	22	22	NV	20	22
VT	17	19	CA	345	176
MA	116	52	OR	50	32
RI	27	14	WA	70	43
CT	60	35	AK	14	18
NY	285	136	HI	27	14
NJ	122	64			
PA	195	98	SOUTH	1,090 (28%)	641 (29%)
DE	18	19	WV	44	19
MD	74	31	VA	78	50
DC	19	14	NC	88	53
			SC	48	35
MIDWEST	1,042 (27%)	566 (25%)	GA	82	37
OH	175	89	FL	143	82
IN	88	52	AL	62	38
IL	194	93	MS	43	30
MI	155	77	TN	76	46
WI	89	46	KY	63	37
MN	86	32	AR	42	29
IA	58	37	LA	68	41
MO	86	47	TX	200	109
KS	44	32	OK	53	35
NE	30	24			
SD	19	19	OTHERS	76 (2%)	22 (1%)
ND	18	18	Democrats Abroad	5	—
			Guam	7	4
WEST	733 (19%)	481 (22%)	Latin America	5	—
MT	25	20	Puerto Rico	53	14
ID	22	21	Virgin Islands	6	4
WY	15	18			

The third men. In our last four presidential elections two different independent candidates, with almost entirely non-overlapping constituencies, together won more than 20% of the vote. That should not be surprising in a country where few voters feel an attachment to either major party so strong as to obligate them to support a presidential nominee about whom they have some reservations. Nor should it be surprising, since voters divide along several types of issues, cultural and foreign as well as economic, and along different lines than most politicians. Thus there is a substantial body of Americans liberal on cultural issues but conservative on at least some economic issues; concentrated in the northern tier of the country, in university communities, high-income suburbs, and old Yankee redoubts, they were the base constituency for John Anderson in 1980. There is another body of Americans, probably larger, who are conservative on cultural issues and liberal on at least some economic issues; concentrated in the South and in the Midwest below U.S. 40, they were the base constituency for George Wallace in 1968.

One likely third candidate in 1984 is John Anderson. His 7% showing in 1980 apparently entitles him to federal matching funds for 1984; and so he seems likely to run. Yet he has not taken an active part in either politics or government since 1980; having left Congress, after 20 years, he made his living lecturing. Anderson's strong point is his willingness—sometimes it seems eagerness—to ignore political shibboleths and advocate policies considered politically impossible. In 1980, for example, in the Iowa caucus campaign, he advocated a 50¢ per gallon gas tax, backed the grain embargo, and said that the only way you could do what Reagan and others were promising—balance the budget, cut taxes, and increase defense—was with mirrors. Anderson was featured prominently in *Doonesbury* and became the favorite of a young, affluent constituency; failing to win a single Republican primary (although he came close in a few), he ran as an independent.

Yet the Anderson candidacy has obvious weaknesses. He is not the perfect candidate to appeal to the constituency that seems available: as a congressman, he was pretty much a foreign policy hawk and a consistent backer of nuclear power. His liberalism on cultural issues could be matched by a Democratic nominee, and his track record—the fact that he won just 7% in 1980—leaves his candidacy vulnerable to the argument that supporting Anderson is throwing your vote away. Many of his potential supporters would tolerate many deficiencies in a Democrat if they thought he could beat Reagan or a Reagan-like Republican. Anderson has promised to produce a book before the 1984 campaign, and perhaps there he will come forward with compelling reasons for his candidacy. In 1982 and 1983 he talked, in somewhat confusing terms, about improving the political process; he has a good record on such issues (especially campaign finance reform), but if he wants to talk, as he sometimes does, about strengthening political parties, he is going to have to explain what running an independent presidential campaign does to achieve that.

Another third candidate could come from the New Right. By the end of 1981, the proprietors of the vast New Right mailing lists—Senator Jesse Helms, National Conservative PAC head Terry Dolan, direct mail expert Richard Viguerie—were expressing dissatisfaction with the Reagan administration. If George Bush or Howard Baker is the Republican nominee in 1984, that dissatisfaction could turn to opposition. The funding is available: both Helms and NCPAC raised about $10 million for the 1982 campaigns. One possible candidate is Helms, who otherwise faces a difficult race for reelection in North Carolina. Could such a candidacy compete for the electoral votes of some states? At least as well as John Anderson's movement—although it would attract almost entirely different voters and would compete in different states.

The Libertarian Party has made brave efforts to stimulate support; and it might have done better than 1% nationally in 1980 had not Ronald Reagan attracted the votes of many who are sympathetic to its views (it opposes almost all domestic government programs, as well as moral prohibitions and foreign entanglements). The Libertarian ticket was able to advertise heavily on television not because its presidential candidate, Ed Clark, raised much money, but because its vice presidential candidate, David Koch, is very rich and could spend money on his own behalf. The Koch family has been influential in this small party for some time, and presumably will be able to afford ads again in 1984. The Libertarians' greatest strength is in Alaska, where the Clark–Koch ticket won 12% of the vote, and where Libertarian Dick Randolph ran a respectable third in the race for governor in 1982.

The general election. In his 1980 debate with Jimmy Carter, Ronald Reagan asked voters to answer several questions when they made their choice for president.

> Are you better off than you were four years ago? Is it easier for you to go and buy things in the stores than it was four years ago? Is there more or less unemployment in the country than there was four years ago? Is America as respected throughout the world as it was? Do you feel that our security is as safe, that we're as strong as we were four years ago?

Those are the basic questions: the issues of peace and prosperity. You will be able to tell a lot about the outcome of the 1984 election by noticing which party asks these questions, which party refers specifically to this quotation. If you had concentrated on these questions throughout the 1980 campaign, you would have noticed that President Carter, though his job

1980 General Election: Total Percentage Vote Won by Reagan, Carter & Anderson
(including number of electoral votes in 1980 and 1984)

	Reagan %	Carter %	Anderson %		Reagan %	Carter %	Anderson %
UNITED STATES (538)	51	41	7	WEST (102, 111)	54	34	9
				MT (4)	57	32	8
EAST (138, 129)	47	42	9	ID (4)	66	25	6
ME (4)	46	42	10	WY (3)	63	28	7
NH (4)	58	28	13	CO (7, 8)	55	31	11
MA (14, 13)	42	42	15	NM (4, 5)	55	37	6
RI (4)	37	48	14	AZ (6, 7)	61	28	9
CT (8)	48	39	12	UT (4, 5)	73	21	5
NY (41, 36)	47	44	8	NV (3, 4)	64	27	7
NJ (17, 16)	52	39	8	CA (45, 47)	53	36	9
PA (27, 25)	50	42	6	OR (6, 7)	48	39	10
DE (3)	47	45	7	WA (9, 10)	50	37	11
MD (10)	44	47	8	AK (3)	55	27	7
DC (3)	13	75	9	HI (4)	43	45	11
				SOUTH (153, 161)	52	44	3
				WV (6)	45	50	4
MIDWEST (145, 137)	51	41	7	VA (12)	53	40	5
OH (25, 23)	52	41	6	NC (13)	49	47	3
IN (13, 12)	56	38	5	SC (8)	49	48	2
IL (26, 24)	50	42	7	GA (12)	41	56	2
MI (21, 20)	49	42	7	FL (17, 21)	56	39	5
WI (11)	48	43	7	AL (9)	49	47	1
MN (10)	43	47	9	MS (7)	49	48	1
IA (8)	51	39	9	TN (10, 11)	49	48	2
MO (12, 11)	51	44	4	KY (9)	49	48	2
KS (7)	58	33	7	AR (6)	48	48	3
NE (5)	66	26	7	LA (10)	51	46	2
SD (4, 3)	61	32	7	TX (26, 29)	55	41	2
ND (3)	64	26	8	OK (8)	60	35	2

rating was temporarily inflated by the response to the Iran hostage crisis, was receiving poor marks on the basic issues of handling the economy and foreign policy. Many of the fall campaign voters in effect waited to see whether Ronald Reagan would in some way disqualify himself. After the Carter–Reagan debate, just a week before the election, they were finally ready to decide. The 51%–41% Reagan margin was not an accident: it did not happen just because Carter had a bad weekend, or because by coincidence election day was the exact anniversary of the taking of the hostages. The potential was there all along for the result.

The 1980 election result also disabused those who thought that there is still a natural Democratic majority in presidential elections. The figures tell a different story.

1968–80 Presidential Vote: Percentage Democratic, Republican and Major Third Candidate

	1968	1972	1976	1980	Average
Democratic	43%	38%	50%	41%	43%
Republican	43	61	48	51	51
Third candidate	14	—	—	7	5

At the same time, there is no warrant for saying that the Republicans have become a natural majority party; their average is a bare majority and only once in four elections did they exceed it. Meanwhile, only once—after the Republicans produced the worst presidential scandal in American history—were the Democrats able to win even a bare majority, and overall they averaged only 43% of the vote. It may be objected that each of the Democratic losses was, in some way, a special case. Of course each presidential election is unique. But continued failure over an extended period raises the presumption that something is seriously wrong. The results suggest that neither major party has a natural majority, and that we are not likely to see one again soon, in this age of weak party allegiances. And they suggest that the Democrats, coming from a more diverse and less united party, have more difficulty in building a national coalition than the Republicans.

But the Democrats' predicament is a result, not of their failures, but of their success. For 40 years they won almost every important political battle. Their ideas prevailed. In 1930 most Americans did not believe that the federal government had a responsibility to maintain a strong economy with low unemployment and to provide sustenance for those who could not find it for themselves; by 1964 most Americans did. In 1930 most Americans did not believe that the federal government should guarantee the civil rights of blacks; by 1970 most Americans did. Democrats have, in effect, written the history books: most Americans believe that Franklin Roosevelt was a good president and Richard Nixon a bad one, and they believe that John Kennedy was the best of all. They believe that isolationism before World War II was wrong and they believe that the Vietnam war was wrong too.

On the surface the political dialogue of the 1980s seems dominated by conservatives, people who call for less domestic spending, a stronger defense, lower taxes, and less government interference in business. But just beneath that surface dialogue are values that represent a liberal consensus. Voters want government spending controlled, in the abstract; but they also want continuation of just about every specific government spending program they can think of. They want a tougher foreign policy, but after Vietnam they are hesitant indeed to risk any American military involvement abroad. So the Reagan administration in its first two years proved unable to pare down entitlements programs like Social Security; it faced severe challenges of its policies on nuclear arms and in El Salvador; it had little success when it finally got around to trying to pass constitutional amendments and legislation on the cultural issues so important to many of its voters.

After the 1980 election it seemed that, for the first time in 15 years, the nation's surface political dialogue and the basic impulses of the president and his administration were in harmony rather than at cross-purposes. Richard Nixon came to office in 1969 in a nation still determined to expand the role of government, inclined to liquidate the American commitment in Vietnam, and eager to get rid of traditional moral restraints. Against all his personal inclinations, Nixon presided over a government that saw domestic spending increase and defense spending decrease, that saw the development of a youth culture, the legalization of abortion, and the effective legalization of pornography, prostitution, and marijuana. Ideas moved the nation more than the administration did. Then the Carter administration came to office, staffed by people determined to continue in the direction the nation was moving around 1970, only to see the tide change. Now people wanted less government and lower taxes, higher defense spending and an aggressive, truculent foreign policy.

The Reagan administration, in its first months, was moving in the direction people said they wanted. But it found soon enough that they wanted to move only so far. The recession that was, at the very least, exacerbated by the Reagan economic policies, placed the administration on the defensive and forced it to support programs and ideas—jobs programs, deficit spending—many of its leaders would prefer to repudiate. But even apart from the recession, the Reaganites found there were limits on how far the public wanted anti-government rhetoric taken. It is too soon to say we are entering a period when the power of ideas will work directly against the administration's own desires. But we have at least uncovered, below the surface dialogue, the more fundamental beliefs Americans share—beliefs in the welfare state as well as free enterprise, in cautious approaches to nuclear weapons as well as opposition to the Soviet Union. To the extent that these underlying beliefs—this basic liberal consensus—works against what the administration wants to do, we will see a continuing movement and change in direction of policy from what it was in the Reaganites' halcyon days of 1981, even if the administration's policies produce, or seem to produce, the peace and prosperity that will likely keep Ronald Reagan or his Republican successor in the White House in 1984.

THE SENATE

Howard Baker's Senate. For the 20 years before 1980, the Senate was technically controlled by the Democrats; actually, it was controlled by no one. The majority leader during 16 of those 20 years was Mike Mansfield; he took a laissez-faire approach and let the powers in the Senate try to bend it, on issues that they cared about, to their will. And powers there were. They may not be remembered as giants of the magnitude of Clay, Calhoun, and Webster, but they were nonetheless formidable men: James Eastland, chewing silently on his cigar, maintaining iron control of his Judiciary Committee as long as he had a one-vote margin and sometimes when he didn't; Warren Magnuson, spawning consumer legislation at Commerce and handing out goodies at Appropriations; Henry Jackson, the ruler of the Interior Committee; Russell Long, the master of Finance; J. William Fulbright, the skeptical, scholarly head of Foreign Relations; Jacob Javits, with no great titles, no close friends, nothing going for him but brains and hard work, and a power on issues ranging from civil rights to labor law to the regulation of Wall Street.

In the early 1980s, however, there was just one giant in the Senate, Howard Baker. Elevated quite to his surprise to the majority leadership when the Republicans gained 12 Senate seats in 1980, Baker became the strongest and most creative Senate majority leader since Lyndon Johnson, and maybe since a long time before. His committee chairmen, with only a few exceptions, were either inexperienced or unaggressive; his back benches were filled with fire-breathing New Rightists ready to filibuster and obstruct if they could not immediately get their way; and the few moderates disenchanted from the beginning with Ronald Reagan's Republicanism still were necessary to maintain the thin Republican majority.

Baker took this unwieldy Republican majority and forged it into a united party that won victory after victory. He worked hard, keeping in touch with all of his 53 constituents (54 since 1982); he listened to their complaints and catered to the particular problems they and their states had. He spoke directly and carefully and kept his word. He took particular care to keep in friendly contact with Republicans inclined to go off the reservation, like Lowell Weicker; and he made sure that they had party support in their elections, even against Reaganite primary opponents. From the beginning Baker seems to have made the decision that he would control the Senate with Republican votes—the same partisan way Tip O'Neill operates with Democratic votes in the House. If Baker got some Democratic votes, that would be lagniappe; but he would make little effort to seek them out. He would make his Republicans, every one of them, feel wanted—not left out when their leadership woos members of the opposition.

Baker also decided, apparently, to support his committee chairmen—but also to move in when they needed help. Old pros like Strom Thurmond at Judiciary could take care of themselves. But Pete Domenici at Budget, whose highest office before the Senate was the Albuquerque City Commission, got assistance from Baker at crucial points. At Finance, Bob Dole blossomed into a strong and creative leader himself, the only senator besides Baker to take a major initiative on a central issue; Dole also moved in to rescue Agriculture Chairman Jesse Helms when his farm bill fell apart. There were also some bravura performances, like Robert Stafford's on the Clean Air Act renewal and Alan Simpson's on immigration law reform.

But on every big issue, on the budget cuts of 1981 and the tax cuts later that year; on the tax bill that came out of Bob Dole's Finance Committee in 1982 and on the gas and road tax bill in the lame duck session, Howard Baker won the support of a united—in some instances, unanimous—Republican Party in the Senate. In negotiations with other leaders in government, whether with the White House on raising taxes or with Speaker O'Neill on the gas and roads tax, everyone understood that Howard Baker could deliver the Senate. There is no doubt about it: this is Howard Baker's Senate.

This will not last long. Baker announced in early 1983 that he would not seek reelection to the Senate in 1984, and he made it clear that he would run for president if Ronald Reagan retires, in which case he will probably relinquish the majority leadership early. One can imagine several reasons for Baker's decision to bow out at the top of his powers. First, there is a good chance Republicans will lose control of the Senate in 1984, regardless of the performance of the head of the ticket. Republicans have 19 seats up while Democrats have only 14; and many of the Republicans seem vulnerable indeed. Baker served four years as minority leader and apparently has no desire to hold that job again. Second, Baker himself, in increasingly Democratic Tennessee, could not have taken reelection entirely for granted; he would have had to put on a major campaign. Third, Baker concluded from his unsuccessful presidential campaign in 1980—and from the fact that Jimmy Carter and Ronald Reagan won while not holding public office—that a candidate for the highest office is best off if he doesn't have to tend to the duties of any other office at all.

Who will succeed Howard Baker? That obviously depends on many factors. Will the Republicans still have a majority? Will Ronald Reagan, or another Republican, be president? Neither of the Republicans who hold leadership positions, Ted Stevens of Alaska or James McClure of Idaho, can expect to win the position automatically; Paul Laxalt of Nevada has many friends and admirers, but he will do what his friend Ronald Reagan wants if Reagan is still president; Pete Domenici of New Mexico may have antagonized some by his actions on the Budget Committee and could face a tough 1984 race at home; Richard Lugar is close to Baker but won the campaign chairmanship by only a small margin; William Armstrong of Colorado has impressed many but cannot expect to win if the New Right loses many Senate seats in 1984.

Other sources of power. A notoriously large percentage of the work in any legislature is done in committee, and in the Senate that is still true, even given the tremendous influence Howard Baker has exerted on major issues and minor. What follows are thumbnail sketches of the committees, in rough order of their likely importance in the 98th Congress.

Budget. So long as what President Reagan calls the "structural deficit" remains a feature of American government, the struggle over the budget will be at the center of our politics every year, and the Budget Committee will be the central focus of the Senate much of the year. Chairman Pete Domenici, who stepped into the job with little practice, has performed ably, and under terrific pressures. With Howard Baker's help, and in the absence of politically viable administration proposals, he has fashioned budget proposals that could unite Republicans and carry the Senate. The new ranking Democrat, Lawton Chiles, is more conciliatory than his predecessor, Ernest Hollings. But it is easier to deal with the Republicans: except for Bill Armstrong, they were all new to the committee in 1981, and they still remain docile to the Domenici–Baker leadership.

Finance. Chairman Bob Dole's construction and management of the tax bill of 1982 was one of the bravura performances of recent legislative history. In his own way, Dole has proved as competent as his predecessor (and perhaps successor), Russell Long. Dole's achievement is all the more impressive, because his committee includes quite liberal Republicans and tribunes of the New Right. Long, shorn of the chairmanship, cannot wheel and deal as much as he used to (although on minor tax bills, his support is still very helpful), and other Democrats played a more public role. Pat Moynihan spoke out against any Social Security cuts quite early in 1981; Bill Bradley has been fashioning economic alternatives.

Appropriations. Its power eclipsed by Budget, its capacity for detail traditionally much more limited than that of its House counterpart, with a bright chairman, Mark Hatfield, but one who is not aggressive and not in the mainstream of his party, Senate Appropriations is not in its best years. In the past, it typically was more generous than House Appropriations; subcommittee chairmen got to add what goodies they liked to their programs. In stringent fiscal times that is much harder to do. Still, Appropriations members can still exert vast influence over the conduct of government if they want to.

Armed Services. Here, in one small committee, is the forum for debate on what may turn out to be the major issue of our times: American military policy. Almost all sides are represented. Chairman John Tower is a strong Pentagon man, Barry Goldwater is loyal to the Air Force, Warner of Virginia to the Navy. Scoop Jackson never trusts the Russians; Carl Levin and new member Edward Kennedy back the kind of arms agreements of which the Reagan administration disapproves. Gary Hart of Colorado, seconded by William Cohen of Maine, call themselves military reformers: they want more money spent, but on smaller rather than larger ships, on less sophisticated, less breakdown-prone equipment. John Stennis has decades of experience in these matters, and Sam Nunn of Georgia may be the most thoughtful and knowledgeable of them all. The Pentagon usually has the votes here, but this is a fast track.

Foreign Relations. A committee so deeply riven, with a chairman who sits roughly in the middle but has few allies, that it hardly ever reaches a consensus. Almost all the Democrats are avid arms controllers and advocates of restraint, the current equivalent of Vietnam doves; the Republicans tend to be hawkish, with Jesse Helms taking care to disapprove any nominee whose faith seems insufficiently pure or whose name seems a little too exotic. Chairman Charles Percy has performed better than expected, by playing issues carefully and straight, and hiring a competent and nonpolitical staff.

Select Committee on Intelligence. As improbable as it may seem, Barry Goldwater and Pat Moynihan have developed a partnership and have made this a useful body.

Commerce, Science, and Transportation. This body handles most of the regulated industries, but the change in party control and other committee membership changes have disrupted some longstanding relationships. Chairman Bob Packwood seems to defer to his subcommittee chairmen on many matters, which is sensible given the committee's diverse jurisdiction. Ernest Hollings took the ranking minority position on this committee rather than on Budget—to give him time to run for president in 1983 and 1984, and perhaps, if that effort doesn't succeed, to give him a comfortable position in 1985.

Judiciary. Ruled over with an iron hand by Strom Thurmond, in the old James Eastland tradition. Thurmond took the trouble to bump Charles Mathias from the ranking minority position in 1979, and lets Mathias have little say. This is the committee that votes out—or pigeonholes—constitutional amendments, but unlike some members of the New Right Thurmond is not champing at the bit to have the Senate consider them. He goes along and gets along. Other senators want to make sure to get along with him, since Judiciary handles nominations for federal judgeships—matters of great importance to many senators.

Environment and Public Works. Chairman Robert Stafford did a brilliant job of reporting out a Clean Air Act revision in 1982. It was not exactly what anti-regulation ideologues and some affected businessmen wanted, but opposition on the committee was led by Steven Symms of Idaho, a specialist in lost causes. The Clean Air Act will likely be the committee's major focus in 1983.

Labor and Human Resources. Chairman Orrin Hatch, first elected to the Senate as recently as 1976, is tantalizingly close to control of this committee that handles labor law and many welfare and education programs. But he's not quite there. Republicans Robert Stafford and Lowell Weicker deserted him on many issues in 1981–82 and, having been reelected with help from labor, probably will again in 1983–84; and without their votes Hatch loses 10–8. The Democratic members, led by Edward Kennedy, are all solidly pro-labor and supportive of generous spending on education and welfare. So Hatch has failed to report out such measures as the youth minimum wage or repeal of the Davis–Bacon Act.

Agriculture, Nutrition, and Forestry. Chairman Jesse Helms is one of the Senate's more controversial members, not because of his views, but because of how he goes about advocating them. He raises huge sums ($10 million in 1981–82) and spends them in campaigns against other senators; he filibusters measures that have near-unanimous support and to which he does not seem to be opposed in principle. But what he did that probably irritated more people than anything else was to fail to manage the farm bill as senators expected. The farm bill is a sort of glue, cementing together different interests from all over the country. But Helms is overtly hostile to one important Ag program, food stamps, and in managing the farm bill he seemed unprepared or unable to defend any programs but those covering peanuts and tobacco—the major crops in his native North Carolina. Bob Dole had to come in to rescue him. It is entirely possible that senators will vote down the minuscule tobacco subsidy in 1983 or 1984, just to show Helms's constituents how effective he is. As for other farm programs, it may be a matter of leaving every senator for himself, and hoping that things get straightened out in conference.

Energy and Natural Resources. A committee with an important jurisdiction, but a chairman, James McClure of Idaho, who seems reluctant to do much. In early 1983, when the administration advanced a complex gas deregulation bill, the response coming from the Senate was that the committee wasn't interested in working on it. Two years before, McClure had ducked the same issue. The committee also superintends the affairs of the Interior Department; McClure, perhaps because he is pleased with the stewardship of James Watt, has done little here too. This committee used to be run actively and more or less singlehandedly by Henry Jackson, but he is ranking minority member now on Armed Services. If the Democrats win control, the new chairman will be Bennett Johnston of Louisiana, an advocate of energy price decontrol and an expert on the intricacies of such legislation.

Banking, Housing, and Urban Affairs. Issues relating to banks, savings institutions, and financial institutions generally are of great importance but make deadly dull reading, and so little is generally known of them. This committee is led by Jake Garn, a brainy senator but one with a hair-trigger temper who sometimes spars with colleagues. On these tough issues, though, he may be the right man: rigorous, demanding, careful, aggressive. A lot of the committee's jurisdiction has been dormant lately (housing, price controls, federal loan guarantees).

Governmental Affairs. This committee will probably have more leeway on reorganization bills, since Paul Laxalt gave up a Judiciary subcommittee that competed with William Roth's Governmental Affairs for jurisdiction. But how much does organizational chart stuff really matter? This committee also has a license to investigate just about anything. But Roth is a team-playing Republican and is not likely to risk embarrassing a Republican administration.

Veterans' Affairs. A committee of quite limited jurisdiction. The fight internally is mostly over levels of funding, with the Democrats more generous; there is less heard here about the special problems of Vietnam era veterans than in the House. Chairman Alan Simpson is personally highly popular, but is likely to spend most of his time in 1983 on the immigration bill, which passed with 80 votes in the Senate but got stalled in the House in 1982.

Rules and Administration. Not an important committee, unless you're a vice presidential nominee waiting for confirmation. This is the chairmanship the Republicans gave Charles Mathias, whose seniority dates to 1968 but who has never taken the trouble to conceal his lack of enthusiasm about the Reagan administration.

Small Business. This is the subcommittee headed by the Republicans' most voluble renegade, Lowell Weicker. Its jurisdiction is limited, as is the loaning authority of the Small Business Administration, the regulation of which is the committee's main legislative responsibility.

Select Committee on Ethics. A body every member hopes will have little to do. One reason Adlai Stevenson left a safe Senate seat in 1980 is that he hated having to spend months looking into Herman Talmadge's personal finances. In 1982, Malcolm Wallop led the committee in recommending the expulsion of Harrison Williams, who resigned just before the final vote; Wallop has now left the committee, undoubtedly with relief. It's easier to handle these things in the House, where you have 434 colleagues, than in the tight and highly publicized confines of the Senate. It is chaired now by Ted Stevens of Alaska.

Special Committee on Aging. This body has no legislative jurisdiction but, when Social Security is such a lively issue, it has some potential influence.

Select Committee on Indian Affairs. Ordinarily this would be a subcommittee. Here it's notable for the fact that it includes both of Arizona's senators, who take different views of the controversy there between the Navajo, the nation's most populous tribe, and the Hopi.

The most influential senators. Which senators are likely to be the most powerful on the issues that are likely to be most important in 1983 and 1984? After Howard Baker, and a few other obvious names, what you come up with largely are the chairmen of key committees. In some cases that is because they have their own goals on important issues and have proved they have the political skills to achieve them (Stafford on the Clean Air Act, for example). In some cases their power is really negative: they can stall a bill, hold up a nomination, or bollix up a bill on the floor. In some cases (notably Jesse Helms) the senator's goal is not to pass legislation but to propagate ideas and to nurture grievances; it is little wonder that he is not legislatively productive, although he still can stop nominations and delay things he doesn't like. Here is a list, then, of the senators likely to be most powerful in the Senate in the 98th Congress, with all the caveats appropriate to such an enterprise. We show each senator's primary leadership or committee positions, the year he is up for reelection, and his percentage margin over his major party opponent in the most recent election.

Senate Leadership

Senator	Party/State	Committee	Term Exp.	%
Howard Baker	R-TN	Majority Leader	1984	56–42
Robert Dole	R-KS	Chmn., Finance	1986	64–36
Pete Domenici	R-NM	Chmn., Budget	1984	53–47
Paul Laxalt	R-NV	Gen. Chmn., Repub. Party	1986	59–37
John Tower	R-TX	Chmn., Armed Services	1984	50–49
Bill Armstrong	R-CO	Chmn., Soc. Sec. Subc.	1984	59–40
Mark Hatfield	R-OR	Chmn., Appropriations	1984	62–38
Bob Packwood	R-OR	Chmn., Commerce	1986	52–44
Robert Byrd	D-WV	Minority Leader	1988	69–31
Jesse Helms	R-NC	Chmn., Agriculture	1984	55–45
Charles Percy	R-IL	Chmn., Foreign Relations	1984	53–46
Robert Stafford	R-VT	Chmn., Environment	1988	51–48

What is striking is how much of this list could change in 1984, and not just because the Democrats might win control of the Senate then. Seven of these 12 senators are up for reelection in 1984; one, Baker, has announced his retirement, and none of the others can be assured of reelection. Two had solid percentages in 1978, but Hatfield had an exceedingly weak opponent and Armstrong has taken on the Social Security issue. Tower won by only a hairsbreadth in a state Democrats swept in 1982; Domenici did not show overwhelming strength in a state with a Democratic trend; Helms has been trailing far behind Governor Jim Hunt in polls; Percy showed in 1978 that his support, while potentially broad, is not deep, and he may well have a strong opponent in the primary as well as the general election. So these men will be under great pressure to make themselves popular at home. But some, like Baker, may choose to retire; and others are men of strong beliefs and steely backbones. They came to Washington to move the country in a certain direction, they are determined to take advantage of it, and they will do their best to win reelection only after that.

The Democratic minority. Democratic senators still get some publicity, and they still can affect legislative outcomes sometimes. But to a man they are not very powerful today—far less powerful than many Republicans were in the less tightly controlled Democratic Senate of the 1980s. There are several reasons for this. First, the 1980 Republican takeover cost the Democratic senators most of their staffs. Many had come to rely heavily on staff to keep them abreast of all their subcommittee assignments and of legislation on the floor; without the staff, some of these things—some of the programs the staff helped develop—have just been let slide. Second, Baker's reliance on Republicans to carry his programs has meant that it hardly matters how Democrats vote. No longer subject to the discipline of legislating, they can just drift, or let themselves go where it seems politically useful to be. Such reactions account for the diverse directions Senate Democrats went off in when called on to respond to the Reagan budget and tax cuts of 1981.

Finally, the leadership provided by Democratic Leader Robert Byrd has not succeeded in coalescing the party. Byrd's style is well suited to the loosely knit majority party that he served as leader in the Carter years: he tends carefully to the details of housekeeping, he knows the rules, he is punctilious about doing favors, and except when he has studied a subject personally and in close detail he does not try to impose his policy views on his colleagues. So the Democrats, naturally fractious, have had trouble uniting in response to Reagan programs or providing initiatives of their own; their House counterparts have done better in both respects. Their mastery of the rules has led some Democrats to stage filibusters and otherwise delay legislation they don't like—the prime example in 1982 was Howard Metzenbaum, whose politics is almost diametrically the opposite of that of the old southern filibusterers. But they have not done much legislating.

The 1982 elections. The 1982 elections were something of a triumph for Baker. While Republicans were losing seats in the House and the governorships, they held onto their 54 seats in the Senate. In fact, there was one more Republican senator in 1983 than 1981, because one of the 54 seats Republicans held in 1982 was in New Jersey, where Democrat Harrison Williams resigned and was replaced by the appointee of a Republican governor. It is true that Republicans held onto Senate control only narrowly: they came within 2% of losing five seats. But the fact that they won them cannot be regarded as accidental. It is, instead, the result of Republican Party campaign efforts: the party raises money that enables it to contribute the maximum amount allowable to every Senate candidate, and it follows the races closely with tracking polling. When there is a problem, the Republicans are ready to help pour money in, and solve it. As a result, in 1980 and 1982 the Republicans have won 14 out of 17 races decided by 2% or less. With those victories, they have 54–46 control of the Senate. If they had just split those races evenly with Democrats, they would be out of power, and if the Democrats had swept them *they* would have Senate control 60–40, about the same margin they held the Senate during most of the 1970s.

The 1982 Senate elections provided fewer surprises than 1980, when the Republicans won 12 seats and captured control of the Senate for the first time since 1952. What was more important in 1982 is what didn't happen. Although the Republicans had more targets—20 of the 33 seats up were held by Democrats—they failed to make the gains they had been hoping for in 1981. This means that the Republicans will have a much harder time holding onto control in 1984 and 1986, when most of the Senate seats at risk will be theirs. The second thing that didn't happen is that the Democrats did not gain control. A switch of just 1% of the vote in each of five states—Vermont, Rhode Island, Virginia, Missouri, and Nevada—would have given the Democrats a 51–49 edge. But the Republicans have the campaign tools—and money—to make the difference in most such close races.

The third thing that did not happen was not quite so apparent, but in the long run may be more important; and that was that most incumbents were reelected. It was not always so. In 1976, 1978, and 1980 most senators who had serious opposition were defeated. A Senate seat, for years seen as a secure place from which to contemplate a presidential bid, had suddenly become insecure; senators had become the point men of American politics. When voters had complaints or were just angry, they retaliated by voting against their senators. But in 1982 by and large they didn't. Only two incumbent senators, Cannon of Nevada and Schmitt of New Mexico, were defeated, while another, Hayakawa of California, retired facing unfavorable political odds. Some Republicans in this recession year were given harder races than they expected but only one went down. Does this mean that voters, despite the recession, are emerging from the negative, anti-incumbent mood that characterized the politics of the late 1970s? Perhaps. But it does mean that no one can take for granted the 1984 Senate elections. Many Republicans up in 1984 have looked shaky for years now, but they will not fall automatically—particularly if their party brings a record of peace and prosperity to the election.

The 1984 elections. It's easy predicting the outcome of the presidential election—compared to predicting the outcome of the Senate contests. That's because there are 33 different Senate races, and all sorts of local and personal factors can make a difference. Still, some things can be said about the 1984 Senate elections.

First, it seems clear that the Republicans will be on the defensive, even if Ronald Reagan is steaming ahead to a glorious reelection victory. Senate elections are held on a six-year cycle, and senators elected on a surge of negative feeling when a party is out of power (*e.g.,* Republicans in 1978) come up for reelection when the president swept in by that same surge is running too. The problem is—and this is definitely true in this case—that some of the senators elected in 1978 were not, on their personal characteristics alone, very strong candidates. They were the flotsam and jetsam, to adapt Hymie Shorenstein's phrase, who were swept into the harbor by the ferryboat of "less government." Five of the 19 Republicans won in 1978 with 51% or less. Even some of the Republicans' strongest legislators—Pete

1984 Senate Elections

State	Senator	Age 1982	Year App'd or Elected	%
Democrats				
EAST				
DE	Joseph Biden	41	1972	58–41
MA	Paul Tsongas	43	1978	55–45
NJ	Bill Bradley	41	1978	56–43
RI	Claiborne Pell	65	1960	75–25
MIDWEST				
MI	Carl Levin	51	1978	52–48
NE	James Exon	63	1978	68–32
WEST				
MT	Max Baucus	42	1978	56–44
SOUTH				
AL	Howell Heflin	63	1978	94–0
AR	David Pryor	50	1978	77–16
GA	Sam Nunn	46	1972	83–17
KY	Dee Huddleston	58	1972	61–37
LA	Bennett Johnston	52	1972	59–41
OK	David Boren	43	1978	65–33
WV	Jennings Randolph	82	1958	50–50
Republicans				
EAST				
ME	William Cohen	44	1978	57–34
NH	Gordon Humphrey	44	1978	51–49
MIDWEST				
IL	Charles Percy	65	1966	53–46
IA	Roger Jepsen	55	1978	51–48
KS	Nancy Kassebaum	52	1978	54–42
MN	Rudy Boschwitz	54	1978	57–40
SD	Larry Pressler	42	1978	67–33
WEST				
AK	Ted Stevens	60	1968	76–24
CO	William Armstrong	47	1978	59–40
ID	James McClure	59	1972	68–32
NM	Pete Domenici	52	1972	53–47
OR	Mark Hatfield	62	1966	62–38
WY	Alan Simpson	53	1978	62–38
SOUTH				
MS	Thad Cochran	46	1978	45–32
NC	Jesse Helms	63	1972	55–45
SC	Strom Thurmond	81	1956	56–44
TN	Howard Baker	58	1966	56–42
TX	John Tower	59	1961	50–49
VA	John Warner	57	1978	50–50

Domenici, John Tower, William Armstrong—do not seem assured of easy races. Howard Baker in early 1983 announced his retirement and the Democrats became favored to win the seat; the same could happen if, as rumored, Mark Hatfield of Oregon retires too.

You have to look hard to find, in 1983, Republican senators who seemed assured of safe seats. Cohen in the East; Kassebaum and Pressler in the Midwest; Stevens, McClure, and Simpson in the West—these names would probably lead the list. Note that few are associated with the New Right; these are Republicans much more comfortable with Howard Baker's style of leadership than that of Jesse Helms. The Helms wing of the party will be under particular siege in 1984, with few targets among the Democrats and many of its own paragons— notably Helms himself—under heavy attack. These senators—Helms, McClure, Jepsen, Humphrey, Armstrong—have been a major force since the Panama Canal Treaties fight in 1978; now they look like an endangered species.

Moreover, the Republicans' brilliant campaign apparatus has relatively few targets this year. Nineteen Republicans are up for reelection, and few are safe; 14 Democrats are up, seven from the South. You could write scenarios for the defeat of some of these southern Democrats, but it seems highly unlikely that more than one or two will have serious challenges. Unencumbered by the responsibilities of power, they will be able to avoid unpopular stands and associations, like the Canal Treaties and Jimmy Carter. And in any case the South is becoming increasingly Democratic, as its black percentages rise and its blue collar whites rejecting what they increasingly regard as the country club economics of Ronald Reagan's Republicans.

As for the seven northern Democrats, few look terribly vulnerable. Three are from heavily Democratic states (Pell, Tsongas, Levin), and one is a former governor who remains personally popular (Exon). Two are bright activists of great political acumen in industrial states (Bradley, Biden); the last (Baucus) is from a state that hasn't elected a Republican senator since 1946 (although it has come close).

This is a young class of senators. Only two will be over 65 on election day 1984. These are two durable octogenarians, Jennings Randolph of West Virginia and Strom Thurmond of South Carolina. Randolph was first elected to Congress in 1932, and is the only member today who served during Franklin Roosevelt's Hundred Days. He is in good health, and scarcely graying, but he had a close race in 1978 and announced in early 1983 he would retire. His likely successor is Democrat Jay Rockefeller, who cannot seek a third term as governor. Thurmond, the State's Rights Democratic presidential candidate, was elected governor of South Carolina in 1946 and won election to the Senate as a write-in candidate in 1954 and then, after resigning, again in 1956. A longtime believer in physical fitness, he is in fine physical shape; in winning against a strong opponent in 1978 he showed a base of strong support that probably exceeds 50%. So he just might run again, and, if he doesn't, could sponsor a race by his wife Nancy. Otherwise, Democrats will be favored to capture the seat.

THE HOUSE

Tip O'Neill's House. There was no formal change of control. But on election night, when it became apparent that the Democrats were going to gain 26 House seats, it also became apparent that a change in effective control of the House was taking place. On television Tip O'Neill made a gracious statement, and talked about how the nation's problems were too important to play politics with. But he also made it plain who was in charge of the House. There would be no Social Security bill in the lame duck session, he said. There wasn't. A few weeks later Senate Majority Leader Howard Baker paid O'Neill the compliment of coming over to his office, and together they agreed to support a gas and roads tax bill in the lame duck session. The administration moved quickly and supported it a day later. It passed. Tip O'Neill will certainly not win every legislative battle in the House in 1983 and 1984. He will occasionally stumble and make mistakes. As a Democratic leader, he will be outshone sooner or later by the party's presidential candidates and its nominee.

But in the meantime Thomas P. O'Neill, Jr., of North Cambridge, Massachusetts, is the effective leader of the national Democratic Party and the undisputed leader of the House of Representatives. He rules not because he has some mechanism for manipulating Democratic House members, but because he has their support; he leads them not against their own inclinations, but in the directions they would choose, on reflection and sometimes with hindsight, to go. The House he leads is a complex institution. It has several dozen major committees and subcommittees and literally hundreds of less important subcommittees with overlapping jurisdictions and, often, ambitious chairmen. It has more than its share of talented people and not all that many backbench hacks. Increasingly, it does not cleave neatly into two organized blocs; members have varying sets of opinions on economic and cultural issues, foreign and domestic policy. Lobbying—and concomitant campaign contributions through political action committees—are carried on with a sophistication and urgency unprecedented in history.

Yet for all that the House works. It decides, with reasonable dispatch and under fair procedures, the major questions posed for it each year. It reflects, with seismic accuracy, changes in the direction of public opinion. And it gives voters clear choices on election day not only between candidates but between parties that in almost all cases stand for reasonably coherent philosophies and policies. It was not always so. Just a decade ago, the House seemed unable to handle its most difficult business; it never voted, for example, on the merits of the Vietnam war until after it was really over. Committee leaders chosen years before, and accountable to no one but their home district voters, made policy that no one could change. The Democratic Party was a collection of politicians with almost no common beliefs and no discipline. Even the Republicans had their own mavericks who won their elections not because they voted like Republicans but because on most occasions they did not.

All this was altered by a few apparently simple changes in the rules—and by Tip O'Neill. Teller—that is, unrecorded—voting was abolished. Democratic committee assignments were removed from the party's Ways and Means Committee members—a group historically weighted to the South, in order to preserve the oil depletion allowance—and given to a Steering and Policy Committee. Members of the Rules Committee, which determines procedure on the floor, were chosen by the speaker. Most important, committee and leading subcommittee chairmanships were made truly elective, and chairmen were thereby made accountable to the Democratic Caucus. It happened this way. In 1974, a new rule allowed a chairman to be challenged if enough members signed a petition requiring it. Phil Burton of California announced that he would secure enough signatures to challenge every single chairman, even though he himself would support most of them personally. When that happened, the old guard capitulated, and now every two years elections, by secret ballot, are held routinely. Policy is affected. An instructive example is that of Jamie Whitten of Mississippi, the dean of the House. Before 1974 he had a solidly conservative voting record and ran the Agriculture Appropriations Subcommittee as a personal fiefdom. After 1974 his labor voting record went up 40%, and he became one of the strongest supporters of the food stamp program. He wanted to succeed to the chairmanship of the Appropriations Committee when it became vacant, and he did in 1978. Even then, a switch of 35 votes would have defeated him—a warning that he cannot get too far out of line. So Whitten and most senior Democrats with a good position to lose did not support the major Reagan programs in 1981. The Boll Weevils were mostly junior members, with little to lose.

Tip O'Neill has used the tools these reforms provided and forged a strong Democratic Party. And he achieved, even while losing, more party unity than the great Sam Rayburn. Of the 243 Democrats elected in 1980, O'Neill held all but 48 on the key budget vote—and he could have held more if it had been closer. By comparison, in the fight to pack the Rules Committee in 1961, in which the speaker had the all-out support, not opposition, of the administration, Rayburn suffered 64 defections out of 262 Democrats. He won only because he had the support of 22 Republicans. Since he became speaker in 1977, O'Neill has not sought Republican votes. He chooses instead to win or lose with Democrats, and any Republicans who might tag along; and if he loses he hopes the voters will have the good sense to elect more Democrats. That's what happened in 1982. And because some Republicans from industrial states lost because of their support for Reagan's policies, their counterparts who remain are likely to vote with the Democrats more often, unbidden.

O'Neill has the image of generosity or, in the language of a former Republican congressman, he is "just like the federal budget—fat, bloated, and out of control." He does feel strongly that government should help the unfortunate. But at the same time, he has not tried to force Democrats to support budgets and all the measures he, as a congressman from Massachusetts, might support personally. On the contrary, the budget alternatives he has supported have been attacked by many liberal Democrats as too stingy. But O'Neill understands that the fulcrum of his Democratic Party has been moving south and west with the people. Of the Democrats' 26-seat gain in 1982, 14 came in the South and six more in California (thanks largely to Phil Burton's redistricting). The House that O'Neill leads now has notably fewer Democrats from the Northeast and the industrial heartland that stretches from the Appalachian mountains to Missouri and Wisconsin.

1975–83 Democratic Caucus: Regional Composition

Area	1975	1977	1979	1981	1983
TOTAL	290	292	276	243	269
Northeast	66	68	65	56	57
Industrial Heartland	67	66	65	59	59
Farm Belt	11	12	10	9	12
Rocky Mountains	10	10	9	7	8
Pacific Northwest & Hawaii	12	12	12	10	10
California	28	29	25	22	28
South	96	95	90	80	95

So as a result largely of population movements, there are fewer Democrats from constituencies that demand big government and more from constituencies that are at least a little wary of it. It is true that southern Democrats are not so conservative, on civil rights or economic issues, as were their counterparts in Sam Rayburn's time. But they are more cautious both on economic and on cultural issues, and O'Neill tries to tailor policies they—and their constituents—can support. On important issues, like the energy bill of 1977 or the budget in 1981 and 1982, he has appointed special committees or worked closely with the Budget Committee (with its temporary membership, a kind of *ad hoc* committee itself) to get the result that can command a majority of Democratic votes. And he has not mentioned what some might regard as the unfinished business of the Carter years—national health insurance, a guaranteed annual income, progressive tax reform.

At the same time, O'Neill has a nose for long-range strategy. He spotted the Social Security issue early in 1981, killed efforts in the House to compromise it that year and the next, heated it up for the 1982 election, and then worked to compromise it in 1983. When it was apparent he lacked effective control of the House in 1981, he worked to build a record for the next election; when he had effective control, he worked to achieve compromise on issues like jobs and Social Security. House Democrats were positioned to take advantage of the dismal results of the Reagan economic program in 1982 and, as a part of the government, they may be positioned to take their share of the credit if there is an economic upturn by 1984.

In effect, we have something like what the Europeans call a national government or a grand coalition. Tip O'Neill's House Democrats and Howard Baker's Senate Republicans are yoked together to the wagon of government, and sometimes they choose a path, as they did on the gas and roads tax, while the wagonmaster seems to doze.

Other sources of power. Tip O'Neill is clearly in command of the House on major issues. But he cannot keep in close touch with everything, and the House, much more than the Senate, is full of active legislators who make their own imprint on the nation's laws and life. Some observers have attacked the proliferation of subcommittees in the House, and it is a nuisance for administration officials who may have to testify regularly before half a dozen of them. But in practice some subcommittees are much more equal than others; in a given session, only a couple of dozen really matter. What follows is a brief description of each of the major committees, listed in rough order of importance.

Budget. Given the continuing fiscal problems of the government—"the structural deficit," as President Reagan calls it, Budget will continue to be a key committee. Its chairman, Jim Jones of Oklahoma, is able and articulate. But he comes from a district that on issues is really Republican, and he is not fully trusted by the speaker. O'Neill wants to keep in close touch with this committee, and Jim Wright is there to keep an eye on things. Important actors include such younger Democrats as Tim Wirth, Leon Panetta, Richard Gephardt, and Les Aspin. Panetta is the Democrats' real workhorse, and a possible candidate for David Stockman's job should the Democrats win the presidency. The Republicans, under tough partisan Delbert Latta, do not have the votes to do much on committee. After his experiences with Phil Gramm—who resigned from Congress in 1983 and won reelection as a Republican—O'Neill put up a "No Boll Weevils need apply" sign.

Ways and Means. Chairman Dan Rostenkowski, having lost the tax fight in 1981, wants to put his stamp on this committee, and will probably succeed. Not strongly anchored to any issue position, Rostenkowski is comfortable dealing with lobbyists, but he also wants to come up with positions on big issues his fellow Democrats will like; he wouldn't mind being speaker some day. On little issues, they need him; Ways and Means handles all those little tax and trade bills that mean so much to specific businesses and communities and are ignored by everyone else. Ways and Means has a free trade tilt, but not one that can't be turned around.

The committee benefits from highly competent Republican members like Barber Conable on taxes and trade and Bill Archer on Social Security.

Energy and Commerce. The most sought after assignment for young Democrats, because it handles important regulatory issues—and can generate large campaign contributions from regulated industries. Natural gas deregulation, the Clean Air Act, toxic waste cleanup are all on its agenda. Chairman John Dingell is acerbic and competent, but does not always prevail; he is an environmentalist but, coming from Michigan, also a strong advocate of auto industry positions. A major power is Henry Waxman, chairman of the Health Subcommittee, who controlled the pace of the Clean Air bill in his subcommittee although he was outvoted 12–8 on the merits, and who also took great pains to get the new committee members he wanted. Most of the Republicans take a Chamber of Commerce point of view.

Appropriations. Technically this committee controls everything, and bright subcommittee chairmen, if so inclined, can effectively control a department of government for years: Jamie Whitten and Agriculture. But Appropriations has lost some of its clout to the Budget Committee, although budget resolutions are not technically binding; and some subcommittees have been unable to pass their bills on the floor and have seen their agencies funded year after year in the catchall continuing resolution. Appropriations had a reputation for years of caution and conservatism. But Joseph Addabbo, a dove on defense issues, chairs the Defense Subcommittee; and David Obey, perhaps the most politically competent young liberal, may emerge as the power on the full committee soon. Ranking Republican Silvio Conte is an adept and thoughtful politician.

Rules. Rules controls the flow of legislation to the floor, the time it can be debated, the amendments that can be offered—all with certain exceptions. In the 1950s and 1960s a conservative Rules Committee bottled up liberal legislation; Speaker Rayburn and the Kennedy administration increased its size in 1961 to stop that, with limited success. Now its nine Democratic members are appointed and controlled by the speaker, and always outvote the four Republicans. Chairman Claude Pepper is temperamentally inclined to go along with the speaker, except if he thinks Tip is giving away too much on Social Security.

Judiciary. A committee, chaired by Peter Rodino and dominated by liberals, that spends much of its time trying to kill legislation it thinks bad—various constitutional amendments, anti-abortion and busing laws, and the like. Its major product is likely to be an immigration bill, shepherded by Romano Mazzoli.

Interior. Chairman Morris Udall has been arguably the most legislatively productive member of Congress in the last decade, and his Interior Committee continues to have plenty of work to do. Its jurisdiction includes government lands, mining, irrigation and reclamation, many environmental laws, Indians. It has a majority strongly opposed to Interior Secretary James Watt, and on occasion Udall has had to step in to stop a subcommittee chairman from ridiculing Watt.

Education and Labor. Back in 1959, organized labor was beaten in this committee on labor law, and its leaders vowed that never again would a bill come out of this committee that it strongly opposed. None has. Labor and the Democratic leadership have allowed only pro-labor Democrats on the committee, and it has a solid liberal Democratic majority, and some of the Republicans started off or grew sympathetic to their views. It favors generous aid to education, school lunch, and welfare laws. Chairman Carl Perkins is a canny politician who has solid control over the committee proceedings; his heir in the long term is probably William Ford, a competent and solidly pro-labor legislator.

Foreign Affairs. A committee whose chairman, Clement Zablocki, has had to cede effective control over its proceedings to subcommittee chairmen. These include young liberals (Stephen Solarz, Don Bonker, Michael Barnes, Howard Wolpe) and some highly competent veterans (Dante Fascell, Lee Hamilton). This is a less important committee than its Senate counterpart since its approval is not needed for ratification of treaties or confirmation of State Department and ambassadorial appointees and it has never had much to say about appropriations. But it could be the forum for major clashes with Reagan administration policy in Latin America, Africa, or elsewhere.

Public Works and Transportation. Its finest hour in recent years was the passage of the gas and roads tax in the 1982 lame duck session; Transportation Secretary Drew Lewis worked closely with Chairman James Howard on this. Public Works used to be important because members desperately wanted rivers and harbors projects and government buildings in their districts; some still do, but most don't care.

Armed Services. With exceedingly important jurisdiction, Armed Services is not as powerful as it could be, because issues usually reach it long after decisions have effectively been made. Committee membership, moreover, is heavily tilted to backers of the Pentagon; accordingly, it can't count on floor approval of its decisions on controversial issues. A few liberals are inching upward in seniority, and there was a move—squelched—to keep them off subcommittee chairmanships. The Chairman, Melvin Price, turns 79 in 1984.

Agriculture. Farm programs are the glue that keeps the Democratic coalition together these days. Northern big city representatives want food stamps (as do representatives from the Deep South, now that blacks and poor whites vote). Rural congressmen from the South and Midwest want price supports. They support each others' bills and everyone is happy, except those (often liberal Republicans) who attack the subsidy bills or those (doctrinaire conservatives) who hate the food stamps program. This coalition, in trouble in the Senate, is alive and well in the House. That's not because Agriculture has a strong chairman, but its number two Democrat, Thomas Foley, used to be chairman before he became majority whip, and he keeps a close eye on Ag issues; and some of the subcommittee chairmen are highly competent. Also, there is considerable cooperation with farm state Republicans on specific programs.

House Administration. An unimportant committee, unless campaign finance becomes a hot issue. That's why Majority Whip Thomas Foley and Democratic Campaign Chairman Tony Coelho are on it this year. Ranking Republican Bill Frenzel is an articulate opponent of public financing of campaigns.

Post Office and Civil Service. Even the title sounds deadly, yet there is important business to be done here—but probably not in this Congress. Chairman William Ford is competent, very pro-union, but he was also willing to compromise intelligently on the Carter era civil service reform. The Democratic leadership had to scrape around to get enough members for this committee. Ranking Republican Gene Taylor is an earthy, practical-minded conservative.

Science and Technology. Support for scientific education and research may be a big issue for the 98th Congress, and if so the Science Committee will be an interesting body to watch. It also handles the space program and issues like the Clinch River Breeder Reactor.

Government Operations. Theoretically, Government Operations has a license to investigate every corner of government. In practice, it is always criticized for doing too little. The problem is probably not leadership: it has had a number of competent, politically knowledgeable chairmen, and none more so than the incumbent, Jack Brooks of Texas. Every so often a Gov. Ops. subcommittee makes headlines. Perhaps the committee's accomplishments are too subtle for journalists and other Washington observers to understand.

Banking, Finance, and Urban Affairs. This committee referees the endless fights between banks and savings institutions; it authorizes housing programs (although it hasn't authorized many for a while). Its membership is large; in part because committee members can help steer HUD funds to their districts, as Banking's chairman does in Rhode Island. Certainly there's nothing nicer than a Fernand J. St Germain Housing for the Elderly when you're running for reelection. All members of Congress are concerned about whether ordinary people can afford houses any more, and Democrats would like the federal government to help them; their problem is that when they investigate they find that current government programs are quite generous. The problem is that interest rates are high and many people in their 20s are expecting to buy a 3,300 square foot house with all the trimmings.

Veterans' Affairs. New members on this committee may change the balance of power between those who champion programs aimed at World War II era veterans, like Chairman Sonny Montgomery, and those who champion special programs for Vietnam era veterans, like Bob Edgar. Whoever wins on committee prevails, since the Rules Committee never allows veterans' bills to be amended on the floor.

Merchant Marine and Fisheries. Its main work will be passage of the Maritime Act that went through in 1982 but was stalled in the Senate. The committee's function over the years has been to funnel federal subsidies to U.S. shipbuilders, ship owners, and seamen; almost every member of the committee favors them and is on the committee primarily to perpetuate them. Exceptions are the few opponents of subsidies and the few members from fishing districts, notably Gerry Studds, who have established our 200-mile limit.

Small Business. This committee has a very limited jurisdiction, mostly over the SBA, an agency that loans out relatively small sums to relatively few businesses in very limited circumstances. But nearly one-tenth of the House belongs, because every congressional district likes small businessmen and the Small Business credential is handy in election season.

District of Columbia. This committee, under John McMillan of South Carolina, superintended D.C. government the way a plantation overseer supervised slaves. Then McMillan was beaten in his primary, and the new committee voted home rule for the District. That leaves the D.C. Committee with very little to do.

Standards of Official Conduct. This is the House Ethics Committee, of importance only when there is a scandal or major impropriety. It is the only committee with equal numbers from both parties. Most current members are not regarded as overly indulgent to their colleagues, but they tend not to be as rigorous and demanding as some colleagues might have been.

The most influential congressmen. When we get into substantive issues we move from the realm of committees to subcommittees, from the nominal chairmen of the committees to the men and women (and sometimes they are the chairmen) who really make things happen. At this point, there is really no substitute for considering matters issue by issue and committee by committee, as we do in the rest of the book. It is possible here, however, to attempt to indicate who the most important players are likely to be on the issues most likely to be important over the next two years. Many of them are subcommittee chairmen—a reflection of the power that subcommittees really have. This is not so much an unintended consequence of House reforms as it is a reflection of how the House has always worked. The House has many more members than the Senate and, much more than in the Senate, House members actually work personally on legislation. They depend much less on staff; most of their staff time is devoted to casework. Detail work on legislation, given the large size of the full committees, is often done in subcommittee. And the fact that subcommittee chairmen are elected, usually by the Democrats on the full committee, means that most important subcommittees have chairmen of considerable competence who enjoy the confidence of most of the committee's Democrats—not, as in the past, a member who simply has a few years more seniority than anyone else or who won a coin toss with fellow freshmen years ago.

In that spirit, let us present this list of powerful congressmen, with their parties and districts, their committee or subcommittee chairmanships or memberships, the year they were first elected, and their percentage of the total vote in 1982.

House Leadership

Congressman	Party/ State/District	Committee/ Subcommittee	Year App'd or Elected	%
Thomas O'Neill	D-MA 8	Speaker	1952	75
Dan Rostenkowski	D-IL 8	Chmn., Ways & Means	1958	84
James Jones	D-OK 1	Chmn., Budget	1972	55
James Wright	D-TX 12	Majority Leader	1954	68
Thomas Foley	D-WA 5	Majority Whip	1964	64
Leon Panetta	D-CA 16	Mbr., Budget	1976	85
Claude Pepper	D-FL 18	Chmn., Rules	1962	71
John Dingell	D-MI 16	Chmn., Energy & Com.	1955	74
Henry Waxman	D-CA 24	Chmn., Health Subc.	1974	68
Carl Perkins	D-KY 7	Chmn., Educ. & Labor	1948	79
Jamie Whitten	D-MS 1	Chmn., Appropriations	1941	71
Morris Udall	D-AZ 2	Chmn., Interior	1961	72
Robert Michel	R-IL 18	Minority Leader	1956	52
Timothy Wirth	D-CO 2	Chmn., Telec. Subc.	1974	63
Richard Gephardt	D-MO 3	Mbr., Budget	1976	78
Barber Conable	R-NY 30	Rank., Ways & Means	1964	68
Sam Gibbons	D-FL 7	Chmn., Trade Subc.	1962	74
Richard Cheney	R-WY a-l	Chmn., Repub. Policy	1978	71
Trent Lott	R-MS 5	Minority Whip	1972	79
Don Edwards	D-CA 10	Chmn., Const. Subc.	1962	65
Jake Pickle	D-TX 10	Chmn., Soc. Sec. Subc.	1963	93
Romano Mazzoli	D-KY 3	Chmn., Immigrat. Subc.	1970	67
Michael Barnes	D-MD 8	Chmn., Inter-Am. Subc.	1978	71
Tony Coelho	D-CA 15	Chmn., Dem. Campaign	1978	65

There are quite a few House veterans on the list. But what is striking is how many junior members there are. Election of committee and subcommittee chairmen has made the House more of a meritocracy, and every individual on this list has earned rather than inherited his position.

The 1984 elections. Every member of the House must face the voters every two years. So there is no way of handicapping the House races by saying that this candidate is up next year and that one is not. Redistricting could have some effect on the outcome, notably in California, where the plan adopted by the Democratic legislature in December 1982 and signed by outgoing Governor Jerry Brown may be challenged by the Republicans. But for the most part we will see the same congressmen running in the same districts. The overall outcome can be seen as the total of the different outcomes in each of the 435 districts, or it can be seen as the verdict of the nation's voters, expressed in national polls and translated through the medium of votes into 435 separate results. The 1982 results suggest that the former view is a little more accurate: if you had just been projecting off the national polls, and off the high unemployment rates in some parts of the country, you would have predicted a significantly larger Democratic gain than actually occurred. In either case, the result cannot be projected from things we know now or without resort to the minutiae and details that are described later in this book.

THE GOVERNORS AND BIG-CITY MAYORS

Does it really matter to residents of one state who is governor of another? Often it seems the answer is no. Citizens of Virginia, even well-informed ones, spend their whole lives knowing nothing of what the governor of North Dakota does and are none the worse for it. Yet there are reasons to give at least some attention to the governors and the state governments they head. After all, our incumbent president and his predecessor served as governors—and had never been in the federal government at all before they were elected, except as members of the military service. Governors are executives, in charge of an administration—something senators and congressmen cannot claim for themselves. Governors even have command of military forces—a technical responsibility in most circumstances, but a vital one when a riot breaks out in a big city or on a large campus. Our most eminent political writer, David Broder, has argued that a governorship, at least of a large state, provides training for the presidency at least as good as a seat in the Senate; there is no way to duplicate the requirements of executive responsibility. Some of our greatest presidents have served as governors but not as members of Congress—Thomas Jefferson, Theodore Roosevelt, Woodrow Wilson, Franklin Roosevelt.

And it can matter to the rest of us what the governor of North Dakota does. North Dakota, as it happens, sits atop huge strata of low sulphur coal. Decisions that its state government makes—the amount of severance tax, regulations of strip mining, whether to allow a slurry pipeline—can make as much difference to national energy supplies as many provisions of the federal energy laws. Moreover, over the past 20 years, the government spending that has been rising most rapidly is state and local government spending. Most of the government services we enjoy—or disparage—are actually delivered by state or local governments.

So the states really do matter—even still. Critics are fond of pointing out that state boundaries don't make any sense. Many of our major metropolitan areas sit astride state boundaries—New York, Philadelphia, Washington, Chicago, Cincinnati, St. Louis, Kansas City, Portland. Others are astride international boundaries—Detroit, Buffalo, San Diego, El Paso. Nevertheless states continue to have political and governmental personalities; traditional ways of conducting political business still shape the way decisions are reached. With surprisingly few exceptions, most Americans feel some sort of allegiance to or bond with their state. We are not where we were early in the 19th century, when if someone was asked what country he was from, he would say Pennsylvania or Virginia. But the states do mean something and do merit attention in an almanac of American politics.

The 1982 elections. The most important thing the 1982 state elections did was to confer on Democrats the power—and the responsibility—for the conduct of state government in most of the large and financially troubled industrial states. They include Massachusetts, New York (although it still has a Republican Senate), Ohio, Michigan, Wisconsin, and Minnesota; Democrats, and below the level of governor mostly liberal Democrats, won a striking victory in Texas, and by 1983 they held the governor's office in every state in the South but Tennessee and Louisiana.

But the Democratic triumph was not national. They lost California, by far the largest state; the major reason seems to have been their nominee's support of a gun control initiative that was resoundingly defeated. Their margins in New York and Michigan, heavily Democratic and hurt by recession, were smaller than expected. They lost Illinois and Pennsylvania, by smaller margins than expected, but still lost; they failed to oust Republican governors in recession-afflicted states like Oregon and Iowa. Democrats now hold all the governorships in the Rocky Mountain states, though they are heavily Republican in national elections; the key in most cases is the personal performance of the incumbent.

Still, if you want to get an idea of how the Democrats would govern if they were to win the White House and the Congress in the 1984 elections, you would be wise to focus, not on the Democratic presidential candidates (who have no governmental responsibilities now) nor on the House Democrats (who make decisions knowing Republicans control the Senate), but on the big-state governors and their legislative leaders. They are the ones who must make the tough decisions—to raise taxes, to cut services, or both. They are the ones who cannot, ultimately, shift the blame to someone else.

Who bears these responsibilities? What follows is a list of the governors, by regions, with their parties, the years they were elected, their percentage of the total vote in the most recent election, and the parties in control of each house of the legislature. All states but four—Arkansas, New Hampshire, Rhode Island, and Vermont—now elect governors for four-year terms. Nebraska has a one-house legislature; we have uniformly listed the number of Democrats first in each house.

Governors and Legislative Control

State	Governor	Party	Year(s)	%	State Senate	State House
EAST						
ME	Joseph Brennan	D	1978, 1982	62	23–10	92–59
NH	John Sununu	R	1982	51	9–15	159–238
VT	Richard Snelling	R	1976, 1978, 1980, 1982	55		
MA	Michael Dukakis	D	1974, 1982	60	33–7	131–29
RI	J. Joseph Garrahy	D	1976, 1978, 1980, 1982	76	45–5	85–15
CT	William O'Neill	D	1982	53	23–13	89–62
NY	Mario Cuomo	D	1982	51	26–35	97–52
NJ	Thomas Kean	R	1981		21–19	43–37
PA	Richard Thornburgh	R	1978, 1982	52	23–26	103–100
DE	Pierre du Pont IV	R	1976, 1980	71	13–8	25–16
MD	Harry Hughes	D	1978, 1982	62	41–6	124–17

State	Governor	Party	Year(s)	%	State Senate	State House
MIDWEST						
OH	Richard Celeste	D	1982	60	17–16	63–36
IN	Robert Orr	R	1980	58	18–32	43–57
IL	James Thompson	R	1976, 1978, 1982	51	33–26	70–48
MI	James Blanchard	D	1982	52	20–18	63–47
WI	Anthony Earl	D	1982	57	17–14	59–40
MN	Rudy Perpich	D	1982	59	42–25	77–57
IA	Terry Branstad	R	1982	53	28–22	60–40
MO	Christopher Bond	R	1972, 1980	53	22–12	110–53
KS	John Carlin	D	1978, 1982	54	16–24	53–72
NE	Robert Kerrey	D	1982	51	16–32	
SD	William Janklow	R	1978, 1982	71	9–26	16–54
ND	Allen Olson	R	1980	54	21–32	55–51
WEST						
MT	Ted Schwinden	D	1980	55	24–26	55–45
ID	John Evans	D	1978, 1982	51	14–21	19–51
WY	Ed Herschler	D	1974, 1978, 1982	63	11–19	25–38
CO	Richard Lamm	D	1974, 1978, 1982	67	14–21	25–40
NM	Toney Anaya	D	1982	53	23–19	46–24
AZ	Bruce Babbitt	D	1978, 1982	62	12–18	21–39
UT	Scott Matheson	D	1976, 1980	55	5–24	16–59
NV	Richard Bryan	D	1982	54	17–4	23–19
CA	George Deukmejian	R	1982	50	25–15	48–32
OR	Victor Atiyeh	R	1978, 1982	63	21–9	36–24
WA	John Spellman	R	1980	57	26–23	54–44
AK	Bill Sheffield	D	1982	46	9–11	19–21
HI	George Ariyoshi	D	1974, 1978, 1982	45	20–5	43–8
SOUTH						
WV	John D. Rockefeller	D	1976, 1980	54	31–3	87–13
VA	Charles Robb	D	1981		31–9	66–33
NC	James Hunt	D	1980	62	44–6	102–18
SC	Richard Riley	D	1978, 1982	70	40–6	104–20
GA	Joe Frank Harris	D	1982	63	49–7	156–24
FL	Bob Graham	D	1978, 1982	65	32–8	84–36
AL	George Wallace	D	1962, 1970, 1974, 1982	60	35–0	98–7
MS	William Winter	D	1979	61	47–5	116–4
TN	Lamar Alexander	R	1978, 1982	59	22–11	60–38
KY	John Y. Brown	D	1979	59	29–9	76–24
AR	Bill Clinton	D	1978, 1982	55	32–3	93–7
LA	David Treen	R	1979	50	38–1	96–9
TX	Mark White	D	1982	54	26–5	114–36
OK	George Nigh	D	1978, 1982	62	34–13	76–25

The governorships up in 1984 are an odd lot. The biggest states in contention are North Carolina, Indiana, Missouri, and Washington. The first is held now by the Democrats, the other three by the Republicans; the prospect, considering Republican weakness in North Carolina, is for at least one Democratic gain. More interesting, perhaps, and more turbulently contested, are those up in 1983: Kentucky, Mississippi, and Louisiana. In Kentucky and Louisiana the powers of the governor are great, and the race in each case is the focus of state politics for years; in oil-rich, scandal-indifferent Louisiana the spending is lavish, on a scale not seen outside the oil republic of Venezuela. It should be apparent that, in these circumstances, results of these elections do not serve as a barometer of national opinion.

State and major local governments. The magnitude of state and local governments has grown far beyond expectations 20 years ago. By 1980 state governments were spending some $257 billion, or $1,138 for each person in the nation. Local governments were spending more—often doubling the state total in major cities. Politics is a game played for stakes, and to understand the stakes it is helpful to know the magnitude of the spending of each of the state governments and of the relatively few local governments whose magnitude of spending is similar. The table below shows spending by states and by nine big city governments in 1980, and spending per capita—a figure which varies, but not as widely as it did in the past. It is highest still in the East and lowest in the South (the two vote bases, incidentally, of the national Democratic Party).

Among the highest per capita spenders are New York and Rhode Island, both of which lost population in the 1970s. A major portion of the expenditures of any state or local government are wages, salaries, and fringe benefits (especially pensions). Since government workers almost never can be fired or laid off, their numbers tend not to decrease, even if population does. By the same token, they do not necessarily increase as fast as population in areas with high private sector growth and population gain. Two of the lowest per capita state spending figures are those of Texas and Florida, the two booming Sun Belt states which, between them, accounted for 26% of U.S. population growth in the 1970s.

It is interesting to set beside the state figures those for the largest cities. Note that none of the Sun Belt cities outside California is among them. Houston is the fourth largest city in the country now, or will be soon, counting just within city limits, but it does not spend as much money as any but the smallest of states, which have many fewer people. The cities with the largest per capita spending are those with the longest-established big-city governments—New York and Boston—plus Washington, D.C., which fills the functions of both city and state and has part of its budget supplied by the federal government. The impact of high state and local spending can be judged by combining the per capita figures for New York state and city. They total $3,668 per person—a pretty heavy load for taxpayers to carry. The figures for residents of Chicago and Los Angeles, in contrast, are not much more than half that.

1980 State and Major City Government Expenditures

State or City	$m	$ per cap.	State or City	$m	$ per cap.
EAST	**$67,409**	**$1,108**	**MIDWEST**	**$65,523**	**$1,113**
NY	24,978	1,423	MI	12,634	1,365
PA	12,644	1,065	IL	12,429	1,089
NJ	8,537	1,159	OH	11,397	1,056
MA	7,336	1,279	WI	6,074	1,291
MD	5,435	1,289	MN	5,418	1,329

State or City	$m	$ per cap.	State or City	$m	$ per cap.
CT	3,341	1,075	IN	4,867	887
RI	1,361	1,437	MO	3,996	813
ME	1,326	1,180	IA	3,412	1,171
NH	889	965	KS	2,254	954
DE	886	1,489	NE	1,392	887
VT	676	1,323	ND	910	1,394
			SD	642	1,072
New York City	15,872	2,245			
Washington	2,110	3,307	Chicago	1,778	592
Philadelphia	2,066	1,224	Detroit	1,391	1,156
Baltimore	1,118	1,421			
Boston	945	1,679			
WEST	**58,558**	**1,357**	**SOUTH**	**66,325**	**949**
CA	32,812	1,386	TX	11,487	807
WA	5,715	1,384	FL	7,387	758
OR	3,456	1,313	NC	5,733	976
CO	2,805	971	VA	5,393	1,009
AZ	2,637	970	GA	4,901	897
AK	2,033	5,083	LA	4,887	1,162
UT	1,755	1,201	KY	4,569	1,248
NM	1,744	1,342	AL	4,002	1,029
HI	1,660	1,720	TN	3,874	844
NV	1,098	1,374	SC	3,325	1,066
ID	1,041	1,103	OK	3,249	1,074
MT	1,005	1,277	MS	2,691	1,067
WY	797	1,692	WV	2,679	1,374
			AR	2,148	940
Los Angeles	2,668	899			
San Francisco	1,123	1,654			

The Big-City Mayors. Only a few big-city mayors are that important any more in national politics, and not because they control blocs of votes in presidential elections or national conventions, but because they help to set the agenda and the tone for public life in important constituencies, and can determine trends in the spending of large sums of public monies. The 1982 election year did not seem a good one for such mayors: Edward Koch of New York was defeated in the gubernatorial primary, and by a man he defeated for mayor of the city in 1977, and Thomas Bradley of Los Angeles was beaten for governor of California by 1% of the vote. But in Koch's case it was the gubernatorial candidacy which was uncharacteristic. As mayor, he has continued to set a feisty tone to public life in New York—but also one that celebrates the city's many strengths. Koch is criticized by black politicians and some white liberals for his opposition to racial quotas, and he is urged to be more conciliatory; but seldom do his critics try to argue he is wrong on the merits. The fact is that under his leadership the New York City government has put its fiscal affairs in much better order, has reduced crime, and has improved the basic education of the city's public school pupils, most of whom are black and Puerto Rican.

Other big-city mayors who have done outstanding jobs include Donald Schaefer of Baltimore, Coleman Young of Detroit, and, despite recent scandals and seeming political megalomania, Kevin White of Boston. Bradley in Los Angeles has an easier job in most respects: his city is thriving economically and generating plenty of revenues. But he, more than any other mayor, has to accommodate the third wave of immigration breaking on our shores. For since 1970 the greatest port of entry for Latin American and Asian immigrants has been Los Angeles; it is to the United States today what New York was in 1913.

The 1983 elections saw the defeat of Chicago Mayor Jane Byrne in the Democratic primary and the election of Harold Washington. The highlight of the race was Washington's strategy of campaigning almost exclusively for black support and then attacking national Democrats—who demonstrably lack the power to swing votes in Chicago—for the fact that few whites were planning to vote for him. This election was treated by some black leaders as if it were the first time a black had sought a major mayoralty, and as if it were a test of white America's tolerance. But there were plenty of non-racist reasons to vote against Washington, and white America has already proved many times it will support black candidates. Majority-white constituencies elected Edward Brooke senator in 1966, Carl Stokes mayor of Cleveland in 1967, Ron Dellums congressman from California in 1970, Andrew Young congressman from Georgia in 1972, and Thomas Bradley mayor of Los Angeles in 1973. California—93% non-black—came within 1% of electing Bradley governor in 1982.

The real story in mayors' races is that voters of both races are willing to support candidates of both races, if they think they will do a good job. Thus majority-white Los Angeles reelects Bradley and majority-black Baltimore reelects Schaefer, both without significant opposition. In Washington, D.C., candidates for mayor and other office regularly seek support from both black and white voters. Voters of one race no longer assume that only a member of their race can serve their interests. In that context, Chicago is not a harbinger of the future, but a reminder of an unpleasant past.

1984 STATE ELECTION CALENDAR

1984 State Election Calendar. What follows is a calendar of primary and runoff election dates scheduled, as of early 1983, for 1984 *state* elections. They are not necessarily, or even usually, the same dates as those of presidential primaries, though in some states they are. The reader should be aware that states can change their primary dates for any reason and sometimes do; therefore, these should not be regarded as final. They are particularly likely to be changed if they are linked with a presidential primary, since many states may change their primary dates. Primaries are held on Tuesdays, except in Texas, Delaware, and Hawaii, where they are held on Saturdays, and in Utah, where they are held on Monday.

March 20	Illinois
April 24	Pennsylvania
May 5	Texas
May 8	North Carolina, Indiana, Maryland, Nebraska
May 15	Oregon
May 22	Idaho
May 29	Arkansas
June 2	Texas runoff
June 5	Ohio, New Jersey, Iowa, Mississippi, West Virginia, New Mexico, Montana, South Dakota
June 12	California, Virginia, South Carolina, Arkansas runoff, Maine, North Dakota
June 26	South Carolina runoff, Mississippi runoff
August 2	Tennessee
August 7	Michigan, Missouri, Kansas
August 14	Georgia
August 28	Kentucky, Oklahoma, Alaska
September 4	Alabama, Georgia runoff
September 8	Delaware
September 11	New York, Florida, Wisconsin, Minnesota, Connecticut, Colorado, Arizona, Utah, Rhode Island, New Hampshire, Nevada, Vermont, Wyoming, District of Columbia
September 18	Massachusetts, Washington, Oklahoma runoff
September 22	Hawaii
September 25	Alabama runoff
October 2	Florida runoff, Louisiana

THE PEOPLE AND THE REGIONS

American Demographics in the 1980s. No sooner do we feel we are catching up with demographic changes in America than we find ourselves falling behind. In the early 1980s the Census Bureau was still tabulating the results of the 1980 Census, which presented a magnificent and wondrously accurate picture of the nation as it was in 1980 and as it changed over the 1970s. But it was already becoming apparent that the nation was changing again. Consider the case of Michigan, which had one of the more robust rates of growth, high income levels, and young age structures of all the major industrial states. Yet beginning in 1979, its auto industry collapsed and its population began to decline, the income level dropped, and the age structure rose. That is only the most egregious example, but it is an instructive one, of the post-census changes that have occurred and to which attention must be paid.

Such changes are apparent from the 1982 Census estimates of state populations that are presented below, together with 1970 and 1980 Census tabulation results.

1970–82 State and Regional Population: Total and Percentage Change
(in thousands)

State	1982 Prov. Est.	1980 Census	1970 Census	1980– 82 ± %	1970– 82 ± %
UNITED STATES	**231,534**	**226,546**	**203,302**	**2**	**14**
EAST	**54,954**	**54,584**	**54,289**	**1**	**1**
ME	1,133	1,125	994	1	14
NH	951	921	738	3	29
VT	516	511	445	1	16
MA	5,781	5,737	5,689	1	2
RI	958	947	950	1	1
CT	3,153	3,108	3,032	1	4
NY	17,659	17,558	18,241	1	−3
NJ	7,438	7,365	7,171	1	4
PA	11,865	11,864	11,801	0	1
DE	602	594	548	1	10
MD	4,265	4,217	3,924	1	9
DC	631	638	757	−1	−17
MIDWEST	**58,927**	**58,866**	**56,590**	**0**	**4**
OH	10,791	10,798	10,657	0	1
IN	5,471	5,490	5,195	0	5
IL	11,448	11,427	11,110	0	3
MI	9,109	9,262	8,882	−2	3
WI	4,765	4,706	4,418	1	8
MN	4,133	4,076	3,806	1	9
IA	2,905	2,914	2,825	0	3
MO	4,951	4,917	4,678	1	6
KS	2,408	2,364	2,249	2	7
NE	1,586	1,570	1,485	1	7
SD	691	691	666	0	4
ND	670	653	618	3	8

State	1982 Prov. Est.	1980 Census	1970 Census	1980– 82 ± %	1970– 82 ± %
WEST	**45,015**	**43,172**	**34,838**	**4**	**29**
MT	801	787	694	2	15
ID	965	944	713	2	35
WY	502	470	332	7	51
CO	3,045	2,890	2,210	5	38
NM	1,359	1,303	1,017	4	34
AZ	2,860	2,718	1,775	5	61
UT	1,554	1,461	1,059	6	47
NV	881	800	489	10	80
CA	24,724	23,668	19,971	4	24
OR	2,649	2,633	2,092	1	27
WA	4,245	4,132	3,413	3	24
AK	438	402	303	9	45
HI	994	965	770	3	29
SOUTH	**72,638**	**69,923**	**57,584**	**4**	**26**
WV	1,948	1,950	1,744	0	12
VA	5,491	5,347	4,651	3	18
NC	6,019	5,882	5,084	2	18
SC	3,203	3,122	2,591	3	24
GA	5,639	5,463	4,588	3	23
FL	10,416	9,746	6,791	7	53
AL	3,943	3,894	3,444	1	14
MS	2,551	2,521	2,217	1	15
TN	4,651	4,591	3,926	1	18
KY	3,667	3,661	3,221	0	14
AR	2,291	2,286	1,923	0	19
LA	4,362	4,206	3,645	4	20
TX	15,280	14,229	11,199	7	36
OK	3,177	3,025	2,559	5	24

The picture that emerges is a good bit more complex than the rule used hastily (and not entirely accurately) to sum up the demographic changes of 1970–80, that the Sun Belt or the South and the West gained at the expense of the East and the Midwest. It is true that even in 1980–82 only 7% of the nation's population growth occurred in the East and only 1% in the Midwest, as compared to 37% in the West and 54% in the South. But growth and decline are not evenly distributed over each region.

In the East, for example, New England showed relatively robust growth in the 1980s. The migration to northern New England—part of a national trend of movement to north woods and other resort areas—continued, as did the migration to Cape Cod. Massachusetts's high tech industries and Connecticut's big defense contractors provided a solid base for economies that suffered far less from the 1979–83 recession than the national average. You get quite a different picture farther south. New York in the early 1970s experienced a virtual explosion of outmigration in response to extremely high tax rates and middle class antipathy to policies of John Lindsay's administration. That slowed in the late 1970s, as New York City's financial crisis slowed the growth of government; the simultaneous real decline in welfare payments, however, cut New York City's poverty population. Now New York seems stabilized, in much the same pattern as New Jersey.

From New York west to Missouri and Michigan—an area roughly coincident with what Joel Garreau in *The Nine Nations of North America* called "the Foundry"—there was essentially no population growth in 1980–81 and, given the condition of the auto and steel industries, there has probably been an absolute drop in population since. Garreau claims that this is the one part of the country that is genuinely economically sick. But it is important to keep in perspective what is happening. The auto and steel labor forces are suffering, inadvertently, from what the coal labor force suffered from deliberately 20 years ago: a decision to force higher wages even if that meant a vastly reduced number of jobs. The damage to particular communities—to a Flint, Michigan, or a Youngstown, Ohio—is vast: housing values fall to zero, civic institutions are dismantled, young residents with initiative and ambition leave and those left behind are dispirited. There is the possibility of revival (as in Lowell, Massachusetts, in the 1970s, 50 years after the textile industry there collapsed). But the more likely outcome is for what was a high-wage, growing town to become a low-wage, stagnant town. You can see that today in Scranton, Pennsylvania, where apparel mills have replaced anthracite mines as the biggest employer. We are not talking about suffering here in the absolute sense—not about people starving or putting their children to bed hungry. But we may be seeing an irreversible loss of enterprise and initiative—of embers burning out slowly in a grate—not only in small factory cities but in huge metropolises like Detroit and Cleveland.

The likelihood of that occurring is increased by another, unrelated trend: the movement to less settled areas. This is a product not of recession, but of affluence; and the Census data suggests it has at least slowed up in the 1980s. But it was a major factor in the 1970s, when metropolitan areas grew less rapidly than non-metropolitan areas, when thousands of young people migrated to formerly rural and small town counties 50 miles out from a central city, or moved altogether away to Rocky Mountain cities or resort areas from Maine to northern Michigan to the Ozarks of Arkansas and the Sierras of California. Polls have shown for years that most Americans would prefer to live in small towns; they like the rural landscape, the greater friendliness, and the conservative cultural tone of life, especially in churches and schools. In the 1970s, many more could afford to seek this life, using extra income for long commutes, or forgoing larger salaries in return for a preferred lifestyle. People with young children—the family voters in our politics of cultural variety—were especially likely to move to such places.

The recession of 1979–83 seems to have slowed this migration down, in northern New England, northern Michigan and Wisconsin, the hills of Arkansas, and even in some of the Rocky Mountain states—although not perceptibly in Florida. The largest population gains in 1980–81, in percentage terms, were in the oil states of the South (Texas, Oklahoma, and Louisiana), California, and some of the Rocky Mountain states (Nevada with its gambling, Utah with its large families, and Wyoming with its oil and coal). These seem to represent Americans—and immigrants from abroad—seeking job opportunities, responding to economic incentives, not seeking leisure or using their affluence to improve their lifestyle. Such migration is oriented to production, while the migrations of the 1970s were oriented to consumption.

Will consumption-oriented migration resume if and when economic recovery occurs in the 1980s? That is a question of the most profound significance. For it will serve as a signal to tell us whether Americans have been chastened by this extended downturn and have become convinced they must work to enhance production, or whether the lengthy recession will just seem a brief interruption and they will once again take affluence and prosperity for granted. On that basic psychology, more than on tax incentives or oil shocks, will depend the economic course of the next couple of decades.

Minorities, ethnics, and immigration. This nation has been shaped—created, actually—by successive waves of immigration. The first, from about 1640 to about 1720, came mostly from the British Isles and, involuntarily, West Africa, with smatterings from Germany and the Netherlands as well. The second wave, from 1840 to 1924, came first from Ireland, then Germany, then southern, northern, and eastern Europe, with substantial numbers from the British Isles throughout. A third wave of immigration seems to have begun around 1970, and comes mainly from Latin America and East Asia, with smaller numbers from the eastern Mediterranean and other parts of Europe. Between the second and third waves, there was a massive movement within the United States of black Americans, from the rural South to the big industrial cities of the North and, later, to cities in the South itself. The northward migration was most numerous between 1942 (when the demand for wartime labor led many blacks to move north) and about 1972; the migration to urban centers in the South itself continues.

What is surprising about all these migrations—and it bears thinking about as we revise our immigration laws—is not so much why these people came over when they did, but why others didn't come over then, and why those who came over later didn't come sooner. It seems to be a rule that a nation or area does not produce mass migration to a more advanced or affluent nation unless it has itself reached a certain plateau, a point within striking distance as it were. There was no American immigration to speak of from the peasantry of Ireland or Germany before the 1840s, virtually none from Italy until the 1880s, or from the Russian Empire until the 1890s. American blacks did not migrate north in very large numbers in 1890–1924, even though they, unlike the European migrants of the same period, were already American citizens and lived much closer to the big industrial cities. Blacks faced discrimination in the North, but so did many migrants, and it is not at all clear that blacks could not have gotten jobs in much larger numbers; as for discrimination, the system of legal segregation was being established in the South at this time, giving blacks a strong incentive to leave. Yet they did not, in large numbers, until the advent of war, which disrupts so many patterns of life at home.

Today we speak of immigration from Latin America as if it were obvious why it occurs: they're poorer down there, and they come up here to get rich. If that's all there were to it, we would have had huge Latin American immigration for 150 years: Latin countries have been poorer than the U.S. all that time, and immigration laws have never restricted them more than they do today. In fact, Latin America—like the European donor countries, like the South the blacks were leaving in the 1940s and 1950s—is experiencing quite rapid economic growth, growth that by its nature is disorderly and that produces people with ambitions and talents their native country seems unable to accommodate. So they move. That movement, even from Latin America, is not easy: Mexico may look close to California on the map, but it is more than 1,000 miles, across desert, from any populated part of Mexico except the border towns to Los Angeles. Emma Lazarus called on other nations to give us their tired, their poor, their huddled masses yearning to breathe free; but what they seem to give us rather are those with initiative and ambition, skills or the strong desire to obtain them, adaptability to new and different cultures. Otherwise, how would a set of rejects, mostly from second- and third-rank countries, have built the strongest and most productive nation in the world?

No one knows today just how our most recent immigrants—the internal black migrants of 1942–72 and the mostly Spanish origin and Asian (the Census Bureau's current terms) of the post-1970 years will change America. But we can at least count them. The following table shows the percentages, first of the adult population of each state and then of its under 18 or child population for blacks, those of Spanish origin, Asians, and those non-immigrants the American Indians. The latter are almost always higher. Remember that in 1916, when Henry Cabot Lodge, Sr., beat John F. "Honey Fitz" Fitzgerald for the U.S. Senate in Massachusetts, most of the adult residents of that commonwealth were Protestants but most of the children were Catholics. Thirty-six years later their two grandchildren ran against each other, and this time the younger Henry Cabot Lodge was beaten by John Fitzgerald Kennedy. The figures on the child population do not tell us much about our politics today, but they do give us a hint of the shape of things to come.

1980 Minority Population: Adult (18+ Years) and Children

State	Black %		Spanish %		Asian %		Am. Ind.%	
	Adult	Child	Adult	Child	Adult	Child	Adult	Child
UNITED STATES	11%	15%	6%	9%	2%	2%	1%	1%
EAST	11	15	4	7	—	1	—	—
ME	—	—	—	1	—	—	—	1
NH	—	—	—	1	—	—	—	—
VT	—	—	1	1	—	—	—	—
MA	3	5	2	4	1	1	—	—
RI	2	5	2	3	1	—	—	—
CT	6	10	3	6	1	1	—	—
NY	12	17	8	13	2	2	—	—
NJ	11	17	6	9	1	2	—	—
PA	8	11	1	2	—	1	—	—
DE	14	21	1	2	1	1	—	—
MD	21	28	1	2	1	2	—	—
DC	66	85	3	3	1	1	—	—
MIDWEST	8	11	2	3	1	1	—	1
OH	9	12	1	2	—	—	—	—
IN	7	9	1	2	—	—	—	—
IL	13	19	5	8	1	2	—	—
MI	12	16	1	3	1	1	—	1
WI	3	6	1	2	—	—	1	1
MN	1	2	1	1	1	1	1	1
IA	1	2	1	1	—	1	—	—
MO	9	13	1	1	—	1	—	—
KS	5	7	2	4	1	1	1	1
NE	3	4	1	3	—	—	—	1
SD	—	—	—	1	—	—	5	11
ND	—	1	—	1	—	1	2	5
WEST	5	6	12	20	5	5	1	2
MT	—	—	1	2	—	—	4	7
ID	—	—	3	6	1	1	1	2
WY	1	1	4	7	—	1	1	2
CO	3	4	10	17	1	1	1	1
NM	2	2	33	44	1	—	7	11
AZ	2	3	13	23	1	1	4	9
UT	1	1	4	5	1	1	1	2
NV	5	9	6	9	2	2	1	2
CA	7	9	16	28	5	6	1	1
OR	1	2	2	4	1	1	1	1
WA	2	3	2	4	2	3	1	2
AK	3	4	2	2	2	2	14	21
HI	2	1	6	11	60	62	—	—

State	Black %		Spanish %		Asian %		Am. Ind.%	
	Adult	Child	Adult	Child	Adult	Child	Adult	Child
SOUTH	**16**	**23**	**6**	**8**	**1**	**1**	**—**	**1**
WV	3	4	1	1	—	—	—	—
VA	17	22	1	2	1	1	—	—
NC	20	28	1	1	—	—	1	2
SC	27	37	1	1	—	—	—	—
GA	24	33	1	1	—	—	—	—
FL	11	21	9	10	1	1	—	—
AL	23	32	1	1	—	—	—	—
MS	31	44	1	1	—	—	—	—
TN	14	20	1	1	—	—	—	—
KY	7	8	1	1	—	—	—	—
AR	14	22	1	1	—	—	—	—
LA	27	35	2	3	1	1	—	—
TX	11	14	18	29	1	1	—	—
OK	6	9	2	3	1	1	5	8

The following table shows the ancestry of Americans by state. The Census Bureau simply asked people what their ancestry was; this table shows the percentage that responded that they were members of this group and only this group. It provides a useful index of ethnicity: not precise numbers, because that is really impossible in a country where there has been so much intermarriage between ethnic groups; but a number suggesting the percentage who feel an identification with a certain ancestry. That is probably the relevant number politically anyway.

Consider the percentages identifying themselves as of English ancestry. There are plenty of people of this ethnic stock in every state. But they appear in the largest numbers here in northern New England and the South, where conflicts between people of English descent and those of another large ethnic group, either French Canadians or blacks, have structured politics for years, and in Utah, a state whose Mormon majority is particularly knowledgeable about its ancestry.

Other politically notable features include: the large Irish percentage in Massachusetts; the large German percentages in Pennsylvania and most of the Midwest (much of the Midwest was a kind of Mitteleuropa in the 19th century); the concentrations of Scandinavians in the Upper Midwest; the concentration of Italians in the East and the Great Lakes states; the small concentrations of later European immigrants like Greeks in the northeast and Portuguese in southern New England, California, and Hawaii. The Census Bureau unfortunately has not made available state-by-state figures for most other ancestries, nor has it provided these figures for congressional districts.

Self-Described Single-Group Ancestry: 1980 Census

State	English	Scottish	Irish	French	Dutch	German	Norw.	Swedish	Polish	Hung.	Italian	Portug.	Greek
EAST													
ME	23	1	5	13	—	2	—	1	1	—	1	—	—
NH	14	1	6	12	—	2	—	1	2	—	2	—	1
VT	15	1	5	11	—	2	—	—	1	—	2	—	1
MA	8	—	12	5	—	2	—	1	3	—	8	3	1

State	English	Scottish	Irish	French	Dutch	German	Norw.	Swedish	Polish	Hung.	Italian	Portug.	Greek
RI	8	1	8	8	—	1	—	1	2	—	13	7	—
CT	7	1	6	3	—	3	—	1	5	1	11	1	1
NY	5	—	6	1	—	5	—	—	3	1	11	—	1
NJ	4	1	6	—	1	6	—	—	4	1	11	1	1
PA	6	—	5	—	1	15	—	—	3	1	6	—	—
DE	13	1	6	1	—	6	—	—	2	—	4	—	—
MD	10	—	4	1	—	9	—	—	2	—	2	—	—
DC	4	—	2	—	—	2	—	—	—	—	1	—	—
MIDWEST													
OH	9	—	4	1	—	13	—	—	2	1	2	—	—
IN	12	—	4	1	1	13	—	—	1	—	1	—	—
IL	6	—	4	1	1	10	—	1	4	—	3	—	1
MI	8	1	3	2	2	8	2	1	4	1	2	—	—
WI	3	—	2	1	1	24	3	1	4	—	1	—	—
MN	3	—	2	1	1	17	7	4	—	—	1	—	—
IA	7	—	4	1	2	21	2	1	—	—	—	—	—
MO	11	—	5	1	1	13	—	—	1	—	1	—	—
KS	11	—	4	1	1	15	—	1	—	—	—	—	—
NE	6	—	4	1	1	22	5	2	2	—	1	—	—
SD	4	—	3	1	2	26	7	2	—	—	—	—	—
ND	2	—	2	1	—	26	15	2	1	—	—	—	—
WEST													
MT	7	1	5	1	1	14	5	2	1	—	1	—	—
ID	18	1	4	1	1	10	1	2	—	—	1	—	—
WY	11	1	5	1	1	13	1	2	1	—	1	—	—
CO	9	1	4	1	1	11	1	1	1	—	2	—	—
NM	9	1	3	1	—	5	—	—	—	—	1	—	—
AZ	10	1	4	1	1	7	1	1	1	—	2	—	—
UT	28	1	2	1	1	4	1	1	—	—	1	—	—
NV	10	1	4	1	1	7	1	1	1	—	4	—	—
CA	8	1	3	1	1	5	1	1	1	—	2	1	—
OR	10	1	4	1	1	9	2	1	—	—	1	—	—
WA	9	1	3	1	1	8	3	2	1	—	1	—	—
AK	9	1	4	2	1	8	2	1	1	—	1	—	—
HI	3	—	1	—	—	2	—	—	—	—	1	3	—
SOUTH													
WV	20	—	5	1	1	7	—	—	1	—	2	—	—
VA	20	1	4	1	—	5	—	—	1	—	1	—	—
NC	23	1	4	1	—	5	—	—	—	—	—	—	—
SC	19	1	5	1	—	4	—	—	—	—	—	—	—
GA	21	—	5	1	—	3	—	—	—	—	—	—	—
FL	12	1	4	1	1	6	—	—	1	—	3	—	—
AL	22	—	6	1	—	3	—	—	—	—	—	—	—
MS	20	—	6	1	—	2	—	—	—	—	—	—	—
TN	23	—	6	1	—	4	—	—	—	—	—	—	—
KY	25	—	6	1	—	7	—	—	—	—	—	—	—
AR	18	—	6	1	—	4	—	—	—	—	—	—	—
LA	10	—	3	11	—	3	—	—	—	—	2	—	—
TX	12	—	4	1	—	5	—	—	—	—	1	—	—
OK	13	—	5	1	1	6	—	—	—	—	—	—	—

ALABAMA

Alabama is, once again, George Wallace country. Twenty years after he was first elected governor, Wallace won again. But this time his appeal was different. The man who promised in 1962 to stand in the schoolhouse door to preserve "segregation forever"—and who stood futilely at the entrance to the University of Alabama in 1963—ran this time as a supporter of equal treatment for citizens of all races. The man who campaigned all over the nation as the symbol of opposition to civil rights won this time in Alabama only because he had the support of black voters—about one-third of them in the Democratic runoff, the overwhelming majority in the general election. There is no way to be sure whether Wallace really changed his views or whether he simply adapted to the biracial politics of a new South. But either way, George Wallace's victory in 1982, and the way he won, symbolized the vast changes that have transformed the South during the last twenty years.

In the early 1960s it was by no means certain that the civil rights revolution would prevail in Alabama or the other states of the Deep South. Alabama's vibrant populist tradition seemed to be in eclipse. Alabama politics had never been dominated by an economically conservative planter elite; there were too many small independent white farmers who saw the banks, railroads, and cotton factories as their adversaries. They elected men like Sen. Hugo Black, later a Supreme Court justice, Sens. Lister Hill and John Sparkman, and half a dozen congressmen who supported New Deal economic programs. It was this kind of politics which George Wallace championed when he ran to succeed populist Kissin' Jim Folsom as governor in 1958; but he was, as he put it,"out-segged" in that contest, and he campaigned four years later as the state's most determined foe of integration.

Wallace did not get much of what he said he wanted. The university was integrated and Bull Connor's police dogs brought shame to Alabama in Wallace's first years in office. But his politics prospered. The almost all-white electorates of Alabama and its neighbors deserted the national Democratic Party in 1964; populist congressmen lost or, like Hill, prudently retired; and George Wallace became unbeatable. In 1966 he persuaded voters to elect his wife to a term he was ineligible for himself; in 1970 he beat an interim governor who succeeded to office after Mrs. Wallace died, in a campaign with strong racial overtones; in 1974, he was reelected without effective opposition. Nationally, he scored well in several Democratic presidential primaries in 1964, captured 13% of the nation's vote in the 1968 general election, and was on his way to winning the 1972 Maryland and Michigan primaries when he was shot and left paralyzed.

While Wallace was railing against court-ordered busing and pointy-headed bureaucrats, life in Alabama was changing. Alabama whites accepted integration in schools, on the job, in restaurants, and while shopping. They no longer minded that blacks voted and, by the late 1970s, black support was no longer a kiss of death costing a candidate all white support. Alabama voters no longer split along racial lines; rather, the main lines of cleavage once again seemed to be economic. Life on the hardscrabble hill farms or in the factories of Birmingham and the state's smaller cities has become more pleasant, but in the presidential election and in partisan contests the Democrats carry the bulk of the blue collar vote, white and black, while the Republicans overwhelmingly win the white collar and country club vote. That does not mean the Democrats have an urban vote base: Birmingham, once a great factory town, has lost so many steel jobs that the university medical center, not U.S. Steel, is now the city's largest employer, and in elections the city leans Republican and anti-Wallace. The mostly white hill areas now join the majority-black Black Belt as the most Democratic part of the state.

The upshot is that Alabama is one of the South's most Democratic states, especially on economic issues, even as it continues to favor an assertive defense policy and to be skeptical of non-traditional stands on cultural issues. Alabama was one of Jimmy Carter's strongest states in 1976, and in 1980 as well, although Ronald Reagan carried it narrowly; in 1982, with one of the nation's highest unemployment rates, it was solidly Democratic. Alabama has not had the economic growth in recent decades of other Sun Belt states: Atlanta, not Birmingham, became the capital of the South, and the steel industry, which gave Alabama above-average growth 1900-50 now is costing it jobs. People are not starving in Alabama, as they were in the 1930s, but this remains a low-skill, mostly low-wage state which is having trouble competing with those neighbors traditionally more friendly to business.

Governor. Turning that around is the first priority of George Wallace. Wallace achieved his narrow victory over racially more liberal Lt. Gov. George McMillan in the Democratic runoff and his somewhat more comfortable margin over militantly anti-crime Montgomery Mayor Emory Folmar in the general election, by arguing that his international contacts could bring jobs to the state. Actually Wallace is regarded as notorious rather than famed by most foreign leaders, and his health does not seem likely to permit him to make the kind of internatonal job-seeking tours which seem part of the standard routine of a southern governor these days. Alabama is going to have to create new jobs on its own. As for the state government's fiscal problems, they are manageable only because this historically poor state has not been ambitious in expanding spending. In his most recent years as governor, Wallace seemed unable or unwilling to spend needed time with legislators and administrators. Will he do so now?

Wallace does seem likely, however, to contrast favorably with his predecessor, Fob James. Former Auburn football star, inventor of the high-density plastic barbell, a Republican party leader as recently as 1976, James spent his way to victory in the multi-candidate contest to succeed Wallace in 1978. He promised a new era, but was not able to deliver. He prudently decided not to run for reelection in 1982. Given the state of Wallace's health, there is likely to be a ghoulish preoccupation with the succession in state politics. The new lieutenant governor, Bill Baxley, had Wallace's support in the 1978 runoff against James, even though Baxley was identified with civil rights. His greatest achievement as attorney general was the prosecution of the men who bombed the black church in Birmingham in 1963. Baxley was embarrassed that year by the revelation of his six-figure gambling debts; but he could be governor some day. So perhaps could George McMillan, another young politician with a similar base, or Joe McCorquodale, the legislator who finished third in the 1982 primary; so, perhaps, could Mayor Folmar, should his brand of politics become more popular.

In the meantime, has George Wallace really changed? There are many skeptics, including thousands who voted for him. But he did go to the length, unusual for a politician, of admitting he had been wrong on a major issue, and of claiming to have changed; and that counts for something. The intriguing question is what George Wallace, with his instinctive understanding of opinion, in the North as well as South, might have done had he not allowed his career to be tied to the issue of racial segregation.

Senators. In the 1950s Alabama had, in Hill and Sparkman, a pair of senators with as much clout as any state's. No one would claim that today. Howell Heflin, elected in 1978, is a man of substance; but as a freshman member of the minority party, and as a man whose adult career has been in the more rarified heights of the legal profession rather than in politics, he can hardly be called powerful. Jeremiah Denton, the junior senator, was elected in 1980 after a series of unlikely events; he has taken positions and taken on causes no politically prudent senator would have anything to do with. On taking office, he told staffers he expected to serve only one six-year term.

Heflin is, first and foremost, a legal craftsman, a man who prides himself on his scrupulous regard for and sensitive understanding of the rule of law. He served in the 1960s as president of the state bar and in 1970, as an anti-Wallace candidate, was elected chief justice of the state Supreme Court. Despite his pedigree (his uncle, "Cotton Tom" Heflin, was a fierce segregationist who served in the Senate from 1920 to 1931), this was his first elective office. When he ran for the Senate in 1978, he expected Wallace to be his opponent; but Wallace, less popular then than he is today, declined to run. Heflin beat Rep. Walter Flowers in the primary by running against "the Washington crowd"—a slogan used by Alabama candidates of all political stripes.

Probably Heflin's most important assignment—certainly his most unpleasant in his first four years—was his role as ranking Democrat on the Ethics Committee, in making the case against Abscam defendant Sen. Harrison Williams. He strongly and successfully backed the expulsion of Williams. On fiscal issues, he is inclined to budget-cutting; on the proposed constitutional convention and the constitutional amendment to ban abortion, his lawyerlike caution takes over and he opposes what he considers precipitous action. He has spent much time on Judiciary Committee matters, particularly on the regulatory reform act and on deregulation of broadcasting. He is interested in anti-crime and drug legislation as well. As an Agriculture Committee member, he has tended to oppose Reagan administration measures. Heflin is up for reelection in 1984, in a state where Senate candidates have had great success running against "the Washington crowd" and in which no incumbent senator has won since 1974. The threshold question is whether Heflin will have serious opposition. If he does, his chief weakness seems likely to be not his stands on issues—which are basically in line with those of most Alabama voters—but rather the fact that he does not like to pitch his appeal in the feisty, contentious, outsider's tone which George Wallace was far from the first to use in Alabama politics.

The state's other Senate seat had four occupants in five years: James Allen, the conservative master of the Senate rules, who died suddenly in 1978 after leading the unsuccessful fight against the Panama Canal Treaties; Maryon Allen, his unexpectedly spunky widow who was appointed to the seat and upset in the 1978 primary; Donald Stewart, a populist young lawyer who held the seat for two years and was upset in the 1980 runoff by Public Service Commissioner Jim Folsom, Jr.; and Admiral Jeremiah Denton, a prisoner of war in Vietnam for seven years, who surprised almost everyone by winning the seat in 1980.

Denton is an authentic hero—a prisoner of war who blinked out the word "torture" in Morse code when being filmed in North Vietnam, the first POW to return, a man whose story became a made-for-television movie. He is a person of strong beliefs: very religious (a Catholic, not a Moral Majority Protestant) and concerned about problems that senators do not ordinarily consider solvable. This has made him something of the butt of jokes in sophisticated Washington. Denton would like to do something to diminish sexual promiscuity; and to understand why, you need only reflect on the difference of tone in American life between 1965, when he left home, and 1972, when he returned. During that time, prostitution, pornography, abortion, and marijuana were effectively, if not explicitly, legalized; the divorce rate soared; living together without marriage became commonplace; restrictions against sexual explicitness in movies and television were relaxed. Denton would like to change all that, although as a conservative he is reluctant to use the power of the federal government to achieve his ends. He has taken some positive, workable initiatives, however—supporting adoption, sponsoring the measure to allow Amerasians (children of U.S. servicemen and Asian women) to enter the U.S. His efforts to set up a new internal security investigation have come to very little.

Denton seems to eschew the constant campaigning and concentration on issues of local importance which help keep so many senators in office. Accordingly, almost everyone will be surprised if he wins a second term—including the senator himself. However, given the unusual, if not bizarre, turns of fate in recent Alabama elections, almost anything can happen.

Presidential politics. With a populist tradition and, in the 1981-82 recession, the highest unemployment in the South, Alabama seems likely to be one of the most Democratic states in its region—more so than in 1980, when it was about as Democratic as the Carolinas, Kentucky, Tennessee, Arkansas, and Mississippi. George Wallace used to dominate the presidential politics of this state, as a candidate or, as in 1976, an endorser; the tenuousness of his own victories, however, suggests that, as in most states, voters in Alabama will make their own decisions in what is the most personal of political choices.

Alabama has a presidential primary scheduled for March 19, the same day as those in Florida and Georgia. The national focus is usually on Florida, the largest and least southern of these states; Alabama is usually regarded as a gimme for one candidate. That will not necessarily be true in 1984. Florida increasingly seems *sui generis* and may have a former governor in the race, while Alabama and Georgia are arguably more typical of opinion in at least half the South. Alabama does not have party registration, and usually the overwhelming majority of voters, whatever their national preference, vote in the Democratic primary; in some years more votes are cast in that contest than in the general election. The Republican primary, then, is likely to be a battle for a small number of mostly country club votes.

Congressional districting. The state's seven congressional districts were changed only slightly for 1982. The legislature did make the 6th district more black and more Democratic—which helped to beat a Republican incumbent.

The People Est. Pop. 1982: 3,943,000; Pop. 1980: 3,890,061, up 1.3% 1980–82 and 13.1% 1970–80; 1.7% of U.S. total, 22d largest; voting age pop. 2,731,640; 23% Black, 1% Spanish origin. Single ancestry: 22% English, 6% Irish, 3% German, 1% French. Registered voters (1982): 2,103,900 Total. No party registration. 13% with 1-3 yrs. col., 13% with 4+ yrs. col. 17.9% below poverty level. 27% housing units rented; median house value: $33,900; median monthly rent: $119. Households: 77% family, 43% with children, 63% married couples.

1982 Share of Federal Tax Burden $7,583,200,000; 1.27% of U.S. total, 25th largest.

1982 Share of Federal Expenditures

	Total		Non-Defense		Defense	
Total Expend	$9,668m	(1.60%)	$7,250m	(1.71%)	$2,417m	(1.35%)
St/Lcl Grants	1,429m	(1.62%)	1,427m	(1.62%)	2m	(5.56%)
Salary/Wages	1,863m	(2.39%)	718m	(2.62%)	1,145m	(2.26%)
Ind Payments	5,026m	(1.76%)	4,376m	(1.70%)	650m	(2.27%)
Procurement	1,294m	(0.89%)	349m	(1.11%)	945m	(0.83%)
Other Programs	56m	(1.03%)	51m	(0.95%)	5m	(11.63%)
Loan/Insurance	1,032m	(1.61%)	1,007m	(1.63%)	25m	(1.14%)

Political Lineup   Governor, George C. Wallace (D). Senators, Howell Heflin (D) and Jeremiah Denton (R). Representatives, 7 (5 D and 2 R). State Senate, 35 D; State House of Representatives, 105 (98 D and 7 R).

Presidential Vote

1980	Reagan (R)	654,192	(49%)
	Carter (D)	636,730	(47%)
	Anderson (I)	16,481	(1%)
1976	Ford (R)	504,070	(43%)
	Carter (D)	659,170	(56%)

1980 Democratic Presidential Primary			*1980 Republican Presidential Primary*		
Carter	193,734	(82%)	Reagan	147,352	(70%)
Kennedy	30,667	(13%)	Bush	54,730	(26%)
Three others	10,678	(4%)	Six others	9,271	(4%)
Uncommitted	1,670	(1%)			

SENATORS

Sen. Howell Heflin (D) Elected 1978, seat up 1984; b. June 19, 1921, Lovina, Georgia; home, Tuscumbia; Birmingham-Southern College, B.A., U. of AL, J.D. 1948; United Methodist.

Career USMC, WWII; Practicing atty., 1948–71. Pres., AL State Bar, 1965–68; Chief Justice, AL Supreme Court, 1971–77.

Offices 728 HSOB, 202-224-4124. Also P.O. Box 3294, Montgomery 36101, 205-832-7287.

Committees *Agriculture, Nutrition, and Forestry* (8th). Subcommittees: Soil and Water Conservation; Agricultural Credit and Rural Electrification; Agricultural Research and General Legislation. *Commerce, Science, and Transportation* (7th). Subcommittees: Merchant Marine; Science, Technology and Space. *Judiciary* (8th). Subcommittees: Administrative Practice and Procedure; Courts; Immigration and Refugee Policy. *Select Committee on Ethics* (Vice-Chairman).

Group Ratings

	ADA	ACLU	COPE	CFA	LCV	LWV	NTU	NSI	COC	ACA	CSFC
1982	25	39	59	50	7	50	47	100	75	62	61
1981	35	—	58	29	6	—	41	—	61	57	58
1980	39	47	63	27	20	40	39	80	63	50	50

National Journal Ratings

	Economic		Foreign		Cultural	
1982	60%	(LIB)	3%	(LIB)	30%	(LIB)
	39%	(CONS)	84%	(CONS)	69%	(CONS)
1981	53%	(LIB)	45%	(LIB)	56%	(LIB)
	46%	(CONS)	54%	(CONS)	43%	(CONS)

Key Votes

1) Reagan 81 Budget	FOR	5) $ to El Salvador	FOR	9) Poor Pay Food Stamps	AGN
2) Reagan 81 Tax Cut	FOR	6) Saudi AWACS Sale	AGN	10) Ban Crt Busing Order	AGN
3) Bal Budget Amend	FOR	7) Ban Abortion	FOR	11) Clinch Riv Brdr Rctr	FOR
4) Gas & Road Tax	AGN	8) Nerve Gas Prod	FOR	12) Legal Services Corp	FOR

Election Results

1978 general	Howell Heflin (D)	547,054	(94%)	($1,059,113)
	Jerome B. Couch (ProL)	34,951	(6%)	
1978 runoff	Howell Heflin (D)	556,685	(65%)	
	Walter Flowers (D)	300,654	(35%)	($755,259)
1978 primary	Howell Heflin (D)	369,270	(48%)	
	Walter Flowers (D)	236,894	(31%)	
	John Baker (D)	101,110	(13%)	($179,388)
	Four others (D)	56,179	(8%)	
1972 general	John Sparkman (D)	654,491	(62%)	($702,109)
	Winton M. Blount (R)	347,523	(33%)	($764,961)

Campaign Contributions and Expenditures

1977–78			PACS brkdwn	
Receipts	$1,107,015	Agr	$7,250	Ideo	$4,700
Expend.	$1,059,113	Bus	$52,150	Lbr	$43,000
Unspent	$47,900	Hlth	$13,100	Prof	$5,300

Sen. Jeremiah Denton (R) Elected 1980, seat up 1986; b. July 15, 1924, Mobile; home, Mobile; Spring Hill Col., 1942–43, U.S. Naval Acad., B.A. 1946, Geo. Wash. U., M.A. 1964; Roman Catholic.

Career U.S. Naval Officer, 1946–77; Rear Admiral, 1973; Commandant, Armed Forces Staff Col., Norfolk, VA 1974–77.

Offices 516 HSOB, 202-224-5744. Also 3280 Dauphin St., Su. B121, Mobile 36616, 205-690-3222; and Daniel Bldg., 15-20th St., S., Su. 1701, Birmingham 35233, 205-254-0806.

Committees *Judiciary* (9th) Subcommittees: Juvenile Justice; Separation of Powers; Security and Terrorism (Chairman). *Labor and Human Resources* (6th). Subcommittees: Education, Arts and Humanities; Aging; Family and Human Services (Chairman); Labor. *Veterans' Affairs (*6th).

Group Ratings

	ADA	ACLU	COPE	CFA	LCV	LWV	NTU	NSI	COC	ACA	CSFC
1982	5	7	6	10	7	9	87	100	71	88	84
1981	0	—	11	14	6	—	75	—	100	80	87

National Journal Ratings

	Economic		Foreign		Cultural	
1982	8%	(LIB)	2%	(LIB)	4%	(LIB)
	91%	(CONS)	97%	(CONS)	95%	(CONS)
1981	2%	(LIB)	22%	(LIB)	28%	(LIB)
	88%	(CONS)	77%	(CONS)	71%	(CONS)

Key Votes

1) Reagan 81 Budget	FOR	5) $ to El Salvador	FOR	9) Poor Pay Food Stamps	FOR
2) Reagan 81 Tax Cut	FOR	6) Saudi AWACS Sale	FOR	10) Ban Crt Busing Order	FOR
3) Bal Budget Amend	FOR	7) Ban Abortion	FOR	11) Clinch Riv Brdr Rctr	FOR
4) Gas & Road Tax	AGN	8) Nerve Gas Prod	FOR	12) Legal Services Corp	AGN

Election Results

1980 general	Jeremiah Denton (R)	650,362	(50%)	($855,346)
	Jim Folsom, Jr. (D)	617,175	(47%)	($356,647)
1980 primary	Jeremiah Denton (R)	73,708	(64%)	
	Armistead Selden (R)	41, 825	(36%)	($269,965)
1978 general	Donald W. Stewart (D)	401,852	(55%)	($816,456)
	James D. Martin (R)	316,170	(43%)	($552,504)
1978 runoff	Donald W. Stewart (D)	502,346	(57%)	
	Mrs. Jim Allen (D)	375,894	(43%)	($305,498)
1978 primary	Mrs. Jim Allen (D)	334,758	(46%)	
	Donald W. Stewart (D)	259,795	(35%)	
	Two others (D)	137,583	(19%)	
1974 general	Jim Allen (D)	501,541	(96%)	($37,328)

Campaign Contributions and Expenditures

1979–80		*PACS brkdwn*			
Receipts	$862,057	Agr	$8,850	Ideo	$42,634
Expend.	$855,343	Bus	$177,571	Lbr	$6,000
Unspent	$6,712	Hlth	$5,500	Prof	$1,000

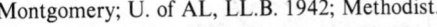

GOVERNOR

Gov. George C. Wallace (D) Elected 1982, term expires Jan. 1987; b. Aug. 15, 1919, Clio; home, Montgomery; U. of AL, LL.B. 1942; Methodist.

Career Army Air Corps, WWII: Asst. Atty. Gen. of AL, 1946; AL House of Reps., 1947–53; Judge, AL 3d Judicial Circuit, 1953–62; Candidate for Dem. Nomination for Gov., 1958; Gov. of AL, 1963–67, 1970–79; Amer. Indep. Party Nominee for Pres., 1968.

Offices Executive Dept., Montgomery 36104, 205-834-3022.

Election Results

1982 gen.	George C. Wallace (D)	650,538	(58%)
	Emory Folmar (R)	440,815	(39%)
1982 runoff	George C. Wallace (D)	512,203	(51%)
	George McMillan (D)	488,444	(49%)
1982 prim.	George C. Wallace (D)	425,469	(43%)
	George McMillan (D)	296,262	(30%)
	Joe C. McCorquodale (D) ...	250,614	(25%)
1978 gen.	Forrest (Fob) James, Jr. (D) ..	551,886	(73%)
	Guy Hunt (R)	196,963	(26%)

FIRST DISTRICT

The Tombigbee and Alabama Rivers flow south from Alabama's Black Belt—named for the fertility of its black cotton-growing soil—to the port of Mobile and the Gulf of Mexico. This is a part of America that for many years had little economic growth. The great planters and small farmers had established its economy, and their descendants continued to produce crops in fields alongside the slow, sluggish rivers which drained this damp, low land. The port of

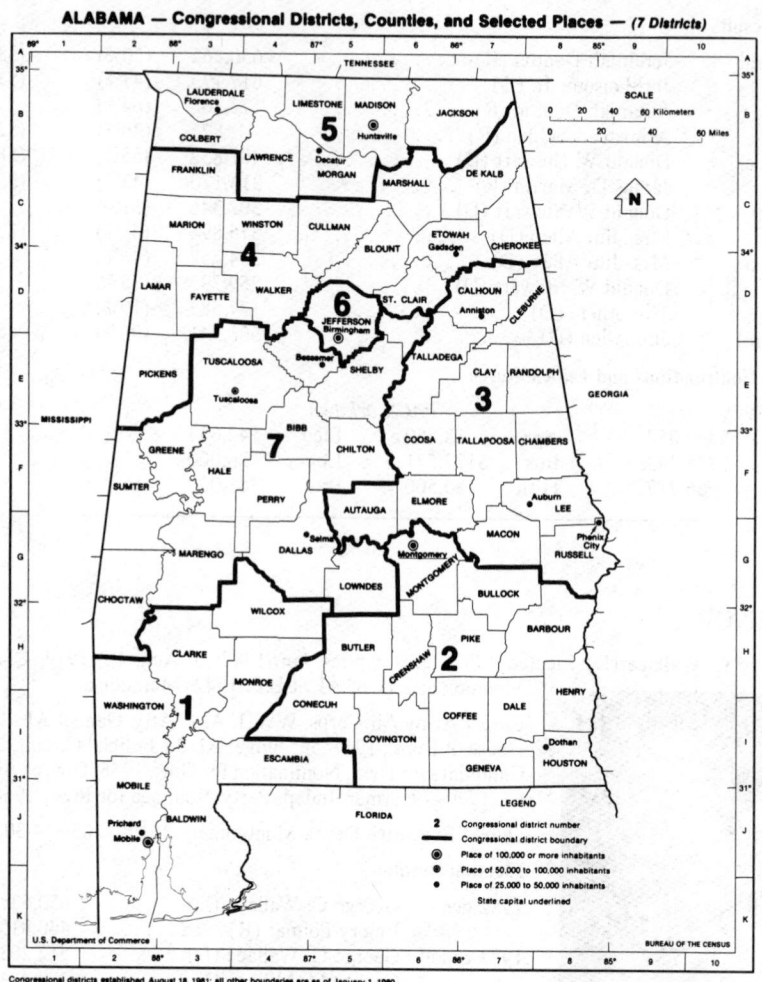

ALABAMA — Congressional Districts, Counties, and Selected Places — *(7 Districts)*

Mobile—with a Creole past but a prosaic industrial present, connected this unchanging hinterland to the outside world.

One thing that kept it unchanging was the South's system of legally enforced racial segregation. No one can say for sure how much, but certainly to some extent segregation prevented blacks from achieving economic success. The end of legal segregation in the 1960s was accompanied by a sharp drop in the black migration northward (which meant that Alabama quit losing a congressional district every ten years) and by a sharp rise in the state's economic growth. One reason must have been black success—not the splashy success of a few millionaires, but the unheralded incremental successes of hundreds and thousands of ordinary people. Businessmen who dislike unions and government regulation like to see the recent growth of the South as an example of free enterprise in action. Yet the growth of places like the Tombigbee and Alabama valleys and the Mobile metropolitan area owes much to intrusive federal civil rights laws and heavily subsidized federal projects like the still unfinished Tennessee-Tombigbee Waterway.

Still, this area, which makes up Alabama's 1st congressional district, remains one of the more Republican parts of the state. The suburbs and beach resorts south and east of Mobile are affluent and solidly Republican; Mobile itself, like so many southern cities, has more residents who identify with entrepreneurs and achievers than with proletarians and the downtrodden. The 1st went heavily Republican for the first time in 1964, when few blacks voted and most whites supported Barry Goldwater; it went Republican not only in the 1980 presidential election but in 1976 as well.

Congressman Jack Edwards was first elected in the 1964 Goldwater landslide. He was 36 then, a lawyer who had not held political office: he is an example of the bright, public-minded pillar of the community who would not have reached public office except for unusual circumstances. Once in, he has commanded considerable respect. He is third-ranking Republican on the House Appropriations Committee, and ranking minority member on the Defense Appropriations Subcommittee. That last assignment is likely to give him plenty of exposure. The chairman, Joseph Addabbo, wants to slow down the rate of increase in defense spending, while Edwards tends to support the administration and favor more spending. Edwards is respected as thoughtful and not a knee-jerk vote for every defense proposal; he is motivated by national concerns, not a desire to aggrandize his own district. He has a good command of the arcana of defense policy, but even the most conscientious congressman is at a disadvantage here: the Executive Branch has the data and tends to structure the choices and make the decisions, leaving Congress to decide up or down—when neither decision is satisfactory to thoughtful members. Should the administration's defense budget requests continue to seem as extravagant to Congress as they did in late 1982, Edwards is in for some unpleasant duty in the 98th Congress.

Edwards is also a member of the House Republican leadership, as vice-chairman of the House Republican Conference—a post more symbolic of the regard in which he is held than it is of any clout he may have. He does not seem aggressive or ambitious enough to seek a higher leadership post, and there was talk that he would retire from office in 1982. That would allow him to begin another career while still in the prime of life, and to avoid the grind of campaigning and the frustrations of deliberating the defense budget. Edwards has had no trouble winning reelection, but his percentage in 1982 was his lowest since 1974. This is a district the Democrats might choose to contest if he retires, and possibly even if he doesn't.

The People Pop. 1980: 563,905, up 14.7% from 1980; voting age pop. 384,289; 28% Black, 1% Span. orig. 27% housing units rented. Median owner $35,600; renter $119. Households: 78% family, 46% with children, 62% married couples.

Presidential Vote

1980	Reagan (R)	107,679	(57%)
	Carter (D)	77,758	(41%)
	Other	1,969	(1%)

Rep. **Jack Edwards** (R) Elected 1964; b. Sept. 20, 1928, Birmingham; home, Mobile; U. of AL, B.S. 1952, LL.B. 1954; Presbyterian.

Career USMC, 1946–48, 1950–51; Instructor in Business Law, U. of AL, 1954; Practicing atty., 1954–64.

Offices 2369 RHOB, 202-225-4931. Also 8011 Fed. Ofc. Bldg., 109 St. Joseph St., Mobile 36602, 205-690-2811.

Committee *Appropriations* (3d). Subcommittees: Defense; Transportation.

Group Ratings

	ADA	ACLU	COPE	CFA	LCV	LWV	NTU	NSI	COC	ACA	CSFC
1982	10	25	15	20	11	33	59	89	76	87	57
1981	20	—	14	12	14	—	52	—	95	63	59
1980	17	30	11	14	22	25	42	83	84	83	66

National Journal Ratings

	Economic		Foreign		Cultural	
1982	32%	(LIB)	12%	(LIB)	4%	(LIB)
	68%	(CONS)	84%	(CONS)	87%	(CONS)
1981	4%	(LIB)	37%	(LIB)	59%	(LIB)
	79%	(CONS)	62%	(CONS)	41%	(CONS)

Key Votes

1) Reagan 81 Budget	FOR	5) Incr SS Rtmt Age	FOR
2) Reagan 81 Tax Cut	FOR	6) Saudi AWACS Sale	FOR
3) Bal Budget Amend	FOR	7) $ for MX Missile	FOR
4) Gas & Road Tax	—	8) Nerve Gas Prod	FOR

9) Poor Pay Food Stamps	FOR
10) Ban Crt Busing Order	FOR
11) Auto Local Content	AGN
12) Nuclear Arms Freeze	AGN

Election Results

1982 general	Jack Edwards (R)	87,901	(61%)	($123,760)
	Steve Gudac (D)	54,315	(38%)	($59,032)
1982 primary	Jack Edwards (R) unopposed			
1980 general	Jack Edwards (R)	111,089	(95%)	
	Steve Smith (Libertarian)	6,130	(5%)	

Campaign Contributions and Expenditures

1982-82		*Direct Cont. 81-82*		*PACS brkdwn*			
Receipts	$136,475	Indiv	$70,471	Agr	$—	Ideo	$2,100
Expend.	$123,760	Party	$4,644	Bus	$49,150	Lbr	$1,000
Unspent	$38,562	PACS	$55,738	Hlth	$3,250	Prof	$—

SECOND DISTRICT

It was not until some years after Alabama was admitted to the Union that southern planters, their soil in Virginia and the Carolinas grown tired, discovered the Black Belt of Alabama. The fertile black soil gave the region its name and almost cried out for the crop that came to characterize the Confederacy: King Cotton. As every schoolchild knows, cotton was a crop that required cheap, abundant labor, and Alabama's Black Belt became slave territory; before the Civil War slaves outnumbered whites by as much as 10-1 in some counties. For years after the Civil War most of the Black Belt's citizens were the descendants of slaves. But as black migration to the North continued, the black percentage here diminished, and by the time the 1965 Voting Rights Act gave blacks the ballot, only a handful of small rural counties were left with black majorities.

The 2d district of Alabama, which covers the southeast corner of the state, includes part of the Black Belt, and, although it has only one black-majority county, it has many landmarks of the nation's racial history. Its largest city is Montgomery, the Cradle of the Confederacy, the rebels' capital before Richmond. Montgomery was also the city where a young black minister, Martin Luther King Jr., led a bus boycott in 1956, and proved that blacks could effectively seek their rights in the South. In the late 1960s, voting in this part of Alabama broke down pretty much along racial lines; the congressional district lines were drawn to prevent blacks from dominating one. Today, when black support no longer dooms a white candidate, the district lines may end up enabling blacks to have a noticeable effect on more congressmen in the 1980s than they would if black voters were concentrated in a couple of districts.

The 2d has been the scene of as many vigorously contested two-party races as any district in Alabama. It surprised everyone by electing a Republican, Bill Dickinson, in 1964, when Barry Goldwater swept the state (few blacks voted in Alabama then) and Republicans won five House seats and wiped out 87 years of Democratic seniority. Redistricting after the 1970 census added some rural counties, which caused Dickinson problems; his strength has always been in urban Montgomery. Dickinson had tough races in 1972, 1976, and 1978. In 1980 he won easily, as Ronald Reagan carried the district; in 1982, although redistricting made no changes in the district lines, he nearly lost.

One reason was changing attitudes to national issues. In 1980 most voters here were confident that Ronald Reagan could balance the government's budget and strengthen America's defense. By 1982 they had given up on the first and were a little skeptical about the second. In state elections in 1982, George Wallace swept this district over Montgomery's tough-line Mayor, Emory Folmar; the Democratic nominee, Public Service Commission President Billy Joe Camp, used to be Wallace's press secretary and, like the former governor, managed to appeal both to lower-income whites and to blacks. He carried all the smaller counties except around Fort Rucker. He was helped by turnout, which rose from 107,000 in 1978 to 165,000; black turnout in particular seems to have risen, which hurt Republicans up and down the ticket.

What is surprising is that Dickinson was in so much trouble. Since the 1980 election, he has been ranking Republican on the House Armed Services Committee. His support generally for more defense spending is highly popular in southern Alabama; his continued support of Montgomery's Maxwell Air Force Base and of Fort Rucker, near Dothan, is of even greater importance to many voters. Apparently, however, Dickinson has failed to make the most of his strategic committee post; or else he simply has not impressed constituents as the sort of solid congressman who should be kept in office despite trends on national issues. Dickinson, who is nearing 60, will be torn between the demands of his committee position and his need to keep in close touch with his district, unless he should decide to retire from Congress. In the meantime he seems likely to attract serious opposition in the 1980s as he did in the 1970s.

The People Pop. 1980: 549,505, up 11.7% 1970–80; voting age pop. 383,150; 27% Black, 1% Span. orig.

29% housing units rented. Median owner $29,400; renter $103. Households: 76% family, 43% with children, 61% married couples.

Presidential Vote

1980	Reagan (R)	99,283	(54%)
	Carter (D)	83,720	(45%)
	Other	1,991	(1%)

Rep. William L. Dickinson (R) Elected 1964; b. June 5, 1925, Opelika; home, Montgomery; U. of AL, A.B. 1948, LL.B. 1950; United Methodist.

Career Navy, WWII; Practicing atty., 1950–63; Judge, Opelika City Court, Lee Cnty. Court of Common Pleas, and Juvenile Court, 5th Judicial Circuit; Asst. V.P., Southern Rlwy. System.

Offices 2406 RHOB, 202-225-2901. Also 401 Fed. Court Bldg., Montgomery 36104, 205-832-7292.

Committees *Armed Services* (Ranking Member). Subcommittees: Research and Development; Military Installations and Facilities; Readiness. *House Administration* (2d). Subcommittees: Sevices; Office Systems

Group Ratings

	ADA	ACLU	COPE	CFA	LCV	LWV	NTU	NSI	COC	ACA	CSFC
1982	0	12	10	10	8	10	76	100	84	95	71
1981	5	—	11	7	0	—	72	—	100	76	70
1980	11	23	10	14	17	33	59	100	81	83	80

National Journal Ratings

	Economic		Foreign		Cultural	
1982	4%	(LIB)	15%	(LIB)	22%	(LIB)
	96%	(CONS)	85%	(CONS)	78%	(CONS)
1981	4%	(LIB)	2%	(LIB)	40%	(LIB)
	79%	(CONS)	97%	(CONS)	60%	(CONS)

Key Votes

1) Reagan 81 Budget	FOR	5) Incr SS Rtmt Age	FOR	9) Poor Pay Food Stamps	AGN
2) Reagan 81 Tax Cut	FOR	6) Saudi AWACS Sale	FOR	10) Ban Crt Busing Order	FOR
3) Bal Budget Amend	FOR	7) $ for MX Missile	FOR	11) Auto Local Content	AGN
4) Gas & Road Tax	—	8) Nerve Gas Prod	FOR	12) Nuclear Arms Freeze	AGN

Election Results

1982 general	William L. Dickinson (R)	83,290	(50%)	($287,346)
	Billy Joe Camp (D)	81,904	(50%)	($141,373)
1982 primary	William L. Dickinson (R) unopposed			
1980 general	William L. Dickinson (R)	104,796	(61%)	($116,504)
	Cecil Wyatt (D)	63,447	(37%)	($27,952)

Campaign Contributions and Expenditures

1981-82		Direct Cont. 81-82		PACS brkdwn			
Receipts	$300,183	Indiv	$140,323	Agr	$2,950	Ideo	$11,400
Expend.	$287,396	Party	$5,539	Bus	$108,300	Lbr	$—
Unspent	$111,788	PACS	$129,235	Hlth	$2,250	Prof	$500

Indep Expend: For: $1,868 (NRA)

THIRD DISTRICT

The 3d district of Alabama extends from the cotton-growing Black Belt in the southern part of the state to the red clay hills of the north. In the south is Tuskegee, a black-majority town in a black-majority county, and the home of Booker T. Washington's Tuskegee Institute. Also in the southern part is Phenix City, a onetime Alabama "sin city" across the Chattahoochee River from Georgia's huge Fort Benning. A mid-1950s cleanup of Phenix City propelled a young prosecutor, John Patterson, into the governor's chair in 1958; he beat George Wallace in the Democratic primary, the one time Wallace allowed himself to be "out-segged." In the northern part of the district is the small industrial city of Anniston, home of a distinguished small newspaper and of the Army's Fort McClellan.

Outside the Black Belt counties in the south, the 3d is mostly white, and the whites living in the district's small factory towns and rugged farm country were for years the heart of George Wallace's constituency. The current congressman, Bill Nichols, was a Wallace floor leader in the Alabama Senate in the 1960s, and it was as a Wallace Democrat that in 1966 he captured the district by beating a Republican elected in the Goldwater landslide two years before. Since then Nichols has been sent back to Washington every two years without difficulty; he has not had a Republican opponent since 1972. On economic issues, he tended to vote with Republicans in the 1970s, but he was not a supporter of Reagan economic policies; and coming from the economically distressed Alabama of the 1980s he seems likely to continue opposing them.

Nichols is now the fourth-ranking Democrat on the House Armed Services Committee. This sounds like a position of great influence, but that is not always the case. The fact is that the great debates over military policy take place mostly within the Executive Branch, and the Pentagon tends to structure the alternatives Congress must choose between. A member like Nichols, whose personal beliefs and political interest both lead him to favor more rather than less defense spending, is left in the position of approving what has been offered up. On interservice disputes, he tends to favor the Army over its rivals. He has had some potential clout as chairman of the subcommittee handling military pay since 1977. But even there the real decision—the total amount to be spent—is big enough to be determined by the Budget Committee. In 1983 he got the chairmanship of the Investigations Subcommittee. This is potentially a powerful tool, but it is not clear to what extent Nichols will use it. It may provide a useful forecast of the kind of full committee chairman Nichols would be—and he does have a good chance for the post; given his record of supporting House leadership positions, he probably wouldn't be denied that position by the Democratic Caucus. The guessing is that he would not be a particularly assertive or aggressive leader, but would fit into the mold of the present chairman, Mel Price of Illinois.

The People Pop. 1980: 555,321, up 15.5 % 1970–80; voting age pop. 390,418; 25% Black, 1% Span. orig.

27% housing units rented, Median owner $29,400, renter $103. Households, 77% family, 43% with children, 62% married couples.

Presidential Vote

1980	Reagan (R)	80,051	(47%)
	Carter (D)	86,753	(51%)
	Other	2,048	(1%)

Rep. Bill Nichols (D) Elected 1966; b. Oct. 16, 1918, near Becker; home, Sylacauga; Auburn U., B.S. 1939, M.S. 1941; United Methodist.

Career Army, 1941–47; V.P., Parker Fertilizer Co., Pres., Parker Gin Co., 1947–66; AL Senate, 1963–67.

Offices 2407 RHOB, 202-225-3261. Also Fed. Bldg., P.O. Box 2042, Anniston 36201, 205-236-5655.

Committee *Armed Services* (4th). Subcommittees: Investigations (Chairman); Readiness.

Group Ratings

	ADA	ACLU	COPE	CFA	LCV	LWV	NTU	NSI	COC	ACA	CSFC
1982	5	4	29	20	26	0	50	97	48	68	50
1981	10	—	29	28	7	—	46	—	67	78	63
1980	17	13	25	14	17	22	44	97	67	59	63

National Journal Ratings

	Economic		Foreign		Cultural	
1982	39%	(LIB)	16%	(LIB)	4%	(LIB)
	60%	(CONS)	82%	(CONS)	87%	(CONS)
1981	48%	(LIB)	3%	(LIB)	24%	(LIB)
	52%	(CONS)	87%	(CONS)	76%	(CONS)

Key Votes

1) Reagan 81 Budget	FOR	5) Incr SS Rtmt Age	AGN	9) Poor Pay Food Stamps	AGN
2) Reagan 81 Tax Cut	FOR	6) Saudi AWACS Sale	FOR	10) Ban Crt Busing Order	FOR
3) Bal Budget Amend	FOR	7) $ for MX Missile	FOR	11) Auto Local Content	FOR
4) Gas & Road Tax	AGN	8) Nerve Gas Prod	FOR	12) Nuclear Arms Freeze	AGN

Election Results

1982 general	Bill Nichols (D)	100,864	(96%)	($21,458)
	Richard Landers (R)	3,920	(4%)	($7,203)
1982 primary	Bill Nichols (D) unopposed			
1980 general	Bill Nichols (D)	107,654	(99%)	($33,572)

Campaign Contributions and Expenditures

1981-82		Direct Cont. 81-82		PACS brkdwn			
Receipts	$86,764	Indiv	$13,695	Agr	$2,250	Ideo	$2,500
Expend.	$21,458	PACS	$55,590	Bus	$38,500	Lbr	$3,200
Unspent	$135,007			Hlth	$7,950	Prof	$1,050

FOURTH DISTRICT

Nowhere have the shifting fortunes of Alabama politics during the past two decades been more apparent than in the 4th congressional district. We think of the civil rights revolution as something that changed the lives of blacks, as of course it did. But it probably changed attitudes even more among southern whites, and these changes are particularly plain in the 4th district, which is 93% white. Situated between Birmingham on the south and the Tennessee River on the north, the 4th is part of the Alabama hills—the southernmost extension of the Appalachian chain. There's iron in these hills, iron ore that brought the steel industry to Birmingham; and some of the little cities—Gadsden, Cullman, Jasper—are factory towns. But the area was first settled, and given its political tone, by small farmers from Andrew Jackson's Tennessee, and this has been Jacksonian Democratic country ever since.

As such, it has supported such economic liberals as Sens. Hugo Black, Lister Hill, and John Sparkman. It produced Alabama populists like Kissin' Jim Folsom, who dominated the state's politics until drink brought him down; he still appears on the ballot and gets a few votes. It even produced its own national Democratic dynasty (with a theatrical offshoot), the Bankheads: Sen. John H. Bankhead 2d (1931-46) and Rep. William B. Bankhead (1917-40), who was Speaker 1936-40, were both New Deal supporters.

But when civil rights became *the* major issue in Alabama, voters here repudiated their populist past and supported the advocates of segregation. The local congressman, Carl Elliott—considered a reliable enough national Democrat to have been one of Speaker Rayburn's choices to "pack" the Rules Committee in 1961—lost his seat. Barry Goldwater swept the area, and a Republican congressman was elected in 1964. The district went 71% for George Wallace in 1968, 78% for Richard Nixon in 1972.

In retrospect, this appears to have been only a temporary deviation from the district's basic populist politics. When the national Democratic party nominated a southerner, the 4th went 65% Democratic in a national election; and it stayed with Jimmy Carter in 1980 as well. In state politics, the 4th has followed George Wallace from his loud—and ineffective—opposition to segregation to a politics that endorses racial equality and seeks black votes. In congressional politics, the district has continued to support Tom Bevill, a Democrat first elected in 1966 as a Wallace supporter who has made a career in the House as a national Democrat. It is as if the segregation issue never existed; and, as a practical matter, in the mostly-white 4th district, it really did not. It was just one of a series of symbolic political issues—one with greater emotional impact than others, to be sure—which served as vehicles for expression of the feelings of people whose politics has always been pitched in the tones of complaint. Those complaints may be addressed to Washington bureaucrats or to Wall Street bankers, producing very different voting patterns; in either case, the basic tone remains the same, and sooner or later the district returns to the party it has backed most of the time since the days of Andrew Jackson.

Tom Bevill is an old-fashioned kind of Democratic politician. He chairs the Appropriations Subcommittee on Energy and Water Development—a fancy name for public works, or the pork barrel. He adheres to the philosophy that government should spend liberally on projects to build dams and public buildings and, in the process, to provide public service jobs. In a low-wage, rural area like the 4th district, such programs, historically at least, were an unalloyed good: local communities desperately needed the facilities, and local people needed the jobs. Bevill's stands on economic issues generally are as close to those of northern Democrats as any member of the Alabama delegation, and he tends to cooperate with the party leadership. He tends to favor high defense spending and has little sympathy for liberal positions on most cultural issues.

In the late 1970s, Bevill's philosophy seemed out of fashion in Washington. Environmentalists and the Carter administration were skeptical about many of his water projects; fiscal conservatives and believers in the free market didn't think government should be involved in them at all. The recession of the early 1980s made his views more fashionable; in late 1982 and early 1983 Republicans were vying with Democrats to create jobs-and-public-works programs. Bevill, as might be expected, had a list of projects ready. Bevill has been reelected without difficulty, and without Republican opposition since 1976.

The People Pop. 1980: 562,088, up 19.7% 1970–80; voting age pop. 397,076; 6% Black, 1% Span. orig. 21% housing units rented. Median owner $28,000; renter $92. Households: 83% family, 44% with children, 70% married couples.

Presidential Vote

1980	Reagan (R)	94,371	(47%)
	Carter (D)	106,474	(53%)
	Other	NA	

Rep. Tom Bevill (D) Elected 1966; b. Mar. 27, 1921, Townley; home, Jasper; U. of AL, B.S. 1943; Baptist.

Career Army, WWII; Practicing atty., 1949–67; AL House of Reps., 1958–66.

Offices 2302 RHOB, 202-225-4876. Also 600 Broad St., Gadsden 35901, 205-546-0201.

Committee Appropriations (11th). Subcommittees: Military Construction; Energy and Water Development (Chairman).

Group Ratings

	ADA	ACLU	COPE	CFA	LCV	LWV	NTU	NSI	COC	ACA	CSFC
1982	20	0	53	60	49	36	13	100	47	48	40
1981	25	—	52	50	23	—	10	—	28	43	52
1980	22	7	42	36	31	38	35	89	68	35	46

National Journal Ratings

	Economic		Foreign		Cultural	
1982	54%	(LIB)	16%	(LIB)	43%	(LIB)
	45%	(CONS)	82%	(CONS)	57%	(CONS)
1981	64%	(LIB)	18%	(LIB)	33%	(LIB)
	35%	(CONS)	73%	(CONS)	67%	(CONS)

Key Votes

1) Reagan 81 Budget	AGN	5) Incr SS Rtmt Age	AGN	9) Poor Pay Food Stamps	AGN
2) Reagan 81 Tax Cut	AGN	6) Saudi AWACS Sale	AGN	10) Ban Crt Busing Order	FOR
3) Bal Budget Amend	FOR	7) $ for MX Missile	FOR	11) Auto Local Content	FOR
4) Gas & Road Tax	AGN	8) Nerve Gas Prod	FOR	12) Nuclear Arms Freeze	AGN

Election Results

1982 general	Tom Bevill (D)	118,595	(100%)	($63,927)
1982 primary	Tom Bevill (D) unopposed			
1980 general	Tom Bevill (D)	129,365	(98%)	($16,495)

Campaign Contributions and Expenditures

1981-82		Direct Cont. 81-82				PACS brkdwn		
Receipts	$163,675	Indiv	$75,812	Agr	$2,500	Ideo	$2,000
Expend.	$63,927	PACS	$59,050	Bus	$42,500	Lbr	$7,750
Unspent	$185,865			Hlth	$1,500	Prof	$2,700

Indep Expend: For: $250

FIFTH DISTRICT

Fifty years ago the Tennessee River coursed through the northern counties of Alabama and every spring flooded the farm country and small towns along its banks. Then the Tennessee Valley Authority, TVA, was created in the 1930s. The agency dammed the wild river for most of its length, controlled the flooding, and produced cheap public power. This part of Alabama has had a populist streak since it was first settled in the time of Andrew Jackson, and since the coming of TVA it has been the part of the state most likely to support generous federal spending. It has also consistently elected congressmen inclined to support such programs, including John Sparkman, who represented what now is the 5th congressional district 1937-46 before spending 32 years in the Senate, and Bob Jones, who represented the 5th from 1946 until his retirement in 1976 and ended up chairing the House Public Works Committee.

These men helped to bring to the 5th benefits from the federal government, and the changes in the district have been striking. In 1950 Huntsville, considered a big town in these parts, was just a sleepy hill town of 14,000. Today its population is more than ten times that, and growing. The principal agent of change has been the Redstone Missile Arsenal, the home of hundreds of Army and NASA rocket engineers and technicians. In recent years the Pentagon and NASA have pumped about $400 million a year into the seven counties that make up the 5th district.

The federal government, most visibly through TVA and the missile program but also through other, more broadly targeted programs, has in 50 years transformed this backward, impoverished area into a place whose standard of living and level of sophistication is up to or above the national average. This change has been symbolized by a recent decision made by the district's congressman, Ronnie Flippo. Elected in 1976, Flippo had embarked on a predictable course: membership on the Public Works and Science Committees, a voting record leaning toward national Democrats on economic issues, solid support of defense spending. But after the 1982 election Flippo sought and won a seat on Ways and Means, whose jurisdiction is much broader and less parochial (although it can still be useful to local interests). That suggests that he regards the 5th district's economy as developed and self-sustaining, not requiring constant infusions of federal money.

The People Pop. 1980: 549,844, up 12.3% 1970–80; voting age pop. 397,076; 13% Black, 1% Span. orig. 26% housing units rented. Median owner $37,400; renter $143. Households: 80% family, 46% with children, 68% married couples.

Presidential Vote

1980	Reagan (R)	72,831	(41%)
	Carter (D)	96,169	(54%)
	Other	3,746	(2%)

Rep. Ronnie G. Flippo (D) Elected 1976; b. Aug. 15, 1937, Florence; home, Florence; U. of N. AL, B.S. 1965; U. of AL, M.A. 1966; Churches of Christ.

Career CPA, 1966–77; AL House of Reps., 1971–75; AL Senate, 1975–77.

Offices 405 CHOB, 202-225-4801. Also 122 Hilton Ct., Florence 35630, 205-766-7692.

Committee *Ways and Means* (21st). Subcomittees: Oversight; Select Revenue Measures.

Group Ratings

	ADA	ACLU	COPE	CFA	LCV	LWV	NTU	NSI	COC	ACA	CSFC
1982	20	17	51	40	39	44	10	100	55	45	41
1981	20	—	47	43	23	—	26	—	38	55	54
1980	28	20	40	36	31	30	35	100	70	42	49

National Journal Ratings

	Economic		Foreign		Cultural	
1982	55%	(LIB)	8%	(LIB)	4%	(LIB)
	45%	(CONS)	91%	(CONS)	87%	(CONS)
1981	58%	(LIB)	2%	(LIB)	41%	(LIB)
	42%	(CONS)	97%	(CONS)	59%	(CONS)

Key Votes

1) Reagan 81 Budget	AGN	5) Incr SS Rtmt Age	FOR	9) Poor Pay Food Stamps	AGN
2) Reagan 81 Tax Cut	AGN	6) Saudi AWACS Sale	FOR	10) Ban Crt Busing Order	FOR
3) Bal Budget Amend	FOR	7) $ for MX Missile	FOR	11) Auto Local Content	FOR
4) Gas & Road Tax	—	8) Nerve Gas Prod	FOR	12) Nuclear Arms Freeze	AGN

Election Results

1982 general	Ronnie G. Flippo (D)	108,807	(81%)	($197,401)
	Leo Yambrek (R)	24,593	(18%)	($32,888)
1982 primary	Ronnie G. Flippo (D) unopposed			
1980 general	Ronnie G. Flippo (D)	117,626	(94%)	($77,827)
	Betty Benson (Libertarian)	7,341	(6%)	($0)

Campaign Contributions and Expenditures

1981-82		Direct Cont. 81-82		PACS brkdwn			
Receipts	$210,472	Indiv	$70,975	Agr	$11,450	Ideo	$3,500
Expend.	$197,401	PACS	$109,670	Bus	$73,950	Lbr	$13,500
Unspent	$139,348			Hlth	$5,300	Prof	$1,800

SIXTH DISTRICT

Standing above the city of Birmingham, atop Red Mountain, is a statue of Vulcan, the Roman god of fire and metal working. It is an appropriate place and symbol. The mountain is red because it is made of iron ore, and Birmingham, a city that lies in a curving valley between two mountain chains, would not exist without iron and steel. This is one of the few major southern cities that did not exist during the Civil War. It was founded a few years later, named after the British manufacturing city, and intended from the beginning to be the industrial center of a New South. It has, in the sense that no other southern city has anything like this concentration of heavy industry. But Birmingham has not become what its founders must have hoped, the economic center of the South: that role has gone to Atlanta, which is a great commercial and transportation rather than manufacturing center. And Birmingham has not since the 1950s shared proportionately in the growth of the South.

The city began that period well ahead of the rest of the region, with its industrial base, comparatively advanced attitudes, and relatively high incomes. But its industry has not grown, and its performance during the civil rights revolution in the early 1960s made it an object of opprobrium around the world. As Atlanta was billing itself the city too rich to hate, Birmingham's Police Commissioner Bull Connor set dogs and firehoses against civil rights demonstrators. That same year, 1963, Connor seemed unperturbed when someone set off a bomb in a black church and killed four young girls. Those events supplied some of the momentum that produced the Civil Rights Act of 1964 and they also damaged the city's economy. Investors usually shun commotion and uncertainty: during the 1960s metropolitan Atlanta grew 37% and metropolitan Birmingham 3%.

Now Birmingham is long since rid of segregation and has established a fair degree of racial harmony; the city even has a black mayor, Richard Arrington. But its economy is ailing—and changing—as never before. Steel mills here, as in Pennsylvania and the Midwest, are closing and laying off workers; the air that hovers over the valley is no longer evil-looking, but clear, partly because of the antipollution laws, but also because the mills are idle. The University of Alabama Medical Center has replaced U.S. Steel as Birmingham's biggest employer; the city has become more white collar and less blue collar. Birmingham has an image of being a rough workingman's town, but politically the more important impulse has been a white collar, upscale distaste for populist-tone politics. In the early days the steel mills were manned mainly by blacks, and even today there is a smaller white working class, proportionately, than in the big steel manufacturing centers of the North. Birmingham is the part of Alabama least hospitable to George Wallace—it voted against him again in the 1982 primary and general election—and it did not go for Jimmy Carter in 1980 or 1976. The white collar and professional population of Alabama is heavily concentrated in this one urban center, and it votes heavily against the blue collar and farm electorates of the small counties.

Birmingham and most of its Jefferson County suburbs form Alabama's 6th congressional district, a seat which has elected three different congressmen in the last three elections. The current incumbent, Ben Erdreich, is the first Democrat elected here in 20 years; he was helped by redistricting (which added some industrial and heavily black suburbs west of the city), by high turnout among blacks, and by division among the Republicans. The district's longtime Republican congressman, John Buchanan, could probably have won general elections as long as he wanted; he was beaten in the 1980 Republican primary, however. A Baptist minister elected in the Goldwater landslide, he became increasingly sympathetic to blacks and voted with them on a variety of issues—after several primary challenges, he finally lost. The winner, Albert Lee Smith, was one of the most faithful supporters of Reaganomics—a position he never abandoned, even as one after another of Birmingham's steel mills closed down. Smith attracted a well-known opponent in the person of County Commissioner Erdreich, who as a state legislator sponsored Alabama's Clean Air Act.

Although Smith heavily outspent the Democrat, he was unable to prevent the high turnout among blacks and blue collar whites that went heavily Democratic. The high income areas stayed Republican, but the turnout was enough to change the 1980 result.

Erdreich is one of those Democrats who may set the tone of the 1983-84 House. He represents a Sun Belt district unsympathetic to traditional economic programs but terribly eager for an economic upturn. His own politics have no roots in the old segregationist South, but neither is he likely to support the kind of Democratic politics that has been standard in the North. Politically, he cannot be regarded as safe; any kind of economic upturn could restore Birmingham's usual Republican majority, and the Republicans may be able to find a more adept candidate than Smith. Finally, turnout will be important. Will Erdreich and the Democrats be able to inspire the kind of turnout in 1984 which helped them in 1982?

The People Pop. 1980: 554,156, up 3.3% 1970–80; voting age pop. 404,782; 32% Black, 1% Span. orig. 36% housing units rented. Median owner $40,000; renter $151. Households: 73% family, 39% with children, 56% married couples.

Presidential Vote

1980	Reagan (R)	112,479	(55%)
	Carter (D)	93,205	(45%)
	Other	NA	

Rep. Ben Erdreich (D) Elected 1982; b. Dec. 9, 1938, Birmingham; home, Birmingham; Yale U., B.A. 1960; U. of AL Law Sch., J.D. 1963; Jewish.

Career U.S. Army, 1963–65; Practicing atty., 1965–73; AL House of Reps., 1970–74; Jefferson Cnty. Comm., 1974–82.

Offices 512 CHOB, 202-225-4921. Also 105 Fed. Ct. Hse., Birmingham 35203, 205-254-0956.

Committees *Banking, Finance and Urban Affairs* (27th). Subcommittees: Economic Stabilization; Financial Institutions Supervision, Regulation and Insurance; Housing and Community Development. *Government Operations* (27th).Subcommittees: Financial Institutions Supervision; Housing and Community Development. *Select Committee on Aging* (31st). Subcommittee: Human Services.

Group Ratings and Key Votes: Newly Elected

Election Results

1982 general	Ben Erdreich (D)	88,029	(53%)	($214,886)
	Albert Lee Smith (R)	76,726	(46%)	($537,935)
1982 primary	Ben Erdreich (D) unopposed			
1980 general	Albert Lee Smith (R)	95,019	(51%)	($264,199)
	W. B. (Pete) Clifford (D)	87,536	(47%)	($41,812)

Campaign Contributions and Expenditures

1981-82		Direct Cont. 81-82*		PACS brkdwn			
Receipts	$232,602	Indiv	$96,483	Agr	$3,000	Ideo	$11,400
Expend.	$214,886	Party	$11,687	Bus	$12,000	Lbr	$53,400
Unspent	$17,712	PACS	$91,050	Hlth	$1,000	Prof	$—
		Cand	$35,000				

*Indirect Party Expend: $120   *Non-Cand Loans: $5,500*

SEVENTH DISTRICT

The 7th congressional district of Alabama contains a virtual cross-section of the state. It includes a significant part of metropolitan Birmingham, including the steel mill suburb of Bessemer, with its black majority, and Black Belt counties with the highest black percentages and lowest incomes in Alabama. Here is Selma, the old small city where the black majority was not allowed to vote as recently as 1965; that sparked the demonstrations and the march on Montgomery that led to the Voting Rights Act. Between Birmingham and the Black Belt is Tuscaloosa, the geographical center of the district, a reasonably prosperous middle-sized city, home of the University of Alabama.

For years the 7th district had the largest black percentage of any Alabama district; that is no longer so, because of black outmigration and because some black Birmingham suburbs were added to the 6th district to make it more Democratic. But it still has a politics redolent of the Black Belt—not a politics which dotes on black constituents, but one which is responsive to the well-to-do whites who run local businesses and governments and consider themselves the only people in the community competent to do so. They live in the prominent houses of their towns, with Early American furniture and old rugs; they eat off good china and with real silver; they travel to Europe now, and shop in Atlanta and New York. They don't consider themselves responsible for the poverty of their communities; they credit themselves, rather, for whatever the community has achieved. Without their talents and skills, they ask, what would the rest of these people do?

Such people have had only a tenuous hold on the politics of the post-Voting Rights Act 7th district. Their candidates have been voted out of local office here and there, and blacks have won some elections. But in congressional elections the local elites have prevailed. The most recent serious contest was the 1978 Democratic primary. State legislator Chris McNair, a black from the Birmingham area, ran a good campaign; he won 38% in the first primary and 41% in the runoff. The winner was Richard Shelby, a state legislator and former law partner of Congressman Walter Flowers (who was running, unsuccessfully, for the U.S. Senate). Flowers was a Democrat so attuned to the views of his local elite that he was surprised when his vote for the impeachment of Richard Nixon turned out to be a political asset rather than liability in his district. Shelby appears to be a man with a similar perspective; he is parsimonious on domestic spending, aggressive on defense spending, and tradition-minded on cultural issues. He serves on the Energy and Commerce Committee, a body with jurisdiction over some of the most important regulatory issues; he is one of the committee Democrats most open to persuasion from regulated interests. Since 1978 he has not had a really serious challenge in the 7th district, but it is worth noting that rival Jack Kartus got 35% in the 1982 primary. This is a district that may not always choose the kind of representation it has received from Shelby and Flowers.

The People Pop. 1980: 559,069, up 15.5% 1970–80; voting age pop. 386,537; 30% Black, 1% Span. orig. 26% housing units rented. Median owner $34,400; renter $108. Households: 78% family, 45% with children, 62% married couples.

Presidential Vote

1980	Reagan (R)	87,498	(49%)
	Carter (D)	92,651	(51%)
	Other	NA	

Rep. Richard C. Shelby (D) Elected 1978; b. May 6, 1934, Fairfield; home, Tuscaloosa; U. of AL, A.B. 1957, LL.B. 1963; Presbyterian.

Career Practicing atty., 1963–; AL Senate, 1971–79.

Offices 1705 LHOB, 202-225-2665. Also P.O. Box 2627, Tuscaloosa 35401, 205-752-3578.

Committees *Energy and Commerce* (15th). Subcommittees: Fossil and Synthetic Fuels; Health and the Environment. *Veterans' Affairs* (7th). Subcommittees: Housing and Memorial Affairs (Chairman); Compensation, Pension, and Insurance.

Group Ratings

	ADA	ACLU	COPE	CFA	LCV	LWV	NTU	NSI	COC	ACA	CSFC
1982	10	0	28	10	21	9	64	100	67	74	58
1981	0	—	30	29	7	—	75	—	89	83	69
1980	11	17	20	7	17	30	45	100	76	67	64

National Journal Ratings

	Economic		Foreign		Cultural	
1982	36%	(LIB)	16%	(LIB)	15%	(LIB)
	64%	(CONS)	82%	(CONS)	83%	(CONS)
1981	4%	(LIB)	18%	(LIB)	15%	(LIB)
	79%	(CONS)	73%	(CONS)	84%	(CONS)

Key Votes

1) Reagan 81 Budget	FOR	5) Incr SS Rtmt Age	FOR	9) Poor Pay Food Stamps	AGN
2) Reagan 81 Tax Cut	FOR	6) Saudi AWACS Sale	AGN	10) Ban Crt Busing Order	FOR
3) Bal Budget Amend	FOR	7) $ for MX Missile	FOR	11) Auto Local Content	FOR
4) Gas & Road Tax	AGN	8) Nerve Gas Prod	FOR	12) Nuclear Arms Freeze	AGN

Election Results

1982 general	Richard C. Shelby (D)	124,070	(97%)	($298,232)
1982 primary	Richard C. Shelby (D)	80,265	(65%)	
	Jack Kartus (D)	44,060	(35%)	($131,938)
1980 general	Richard C. Shelby (D)	122,505	(73%)	($126,936)
	James E. Bacon (R)	43,000	(26%)	($0)

Campaign Contributions and Expenditures

1981-82		*Direct Cont. 81-82**		*PACS brkdwn*			
Receipts	$451,636	Indiv	$110,928	Agr	$6,750	Ideo	$2,750
Expend.	$298,232	PACS	$168,526	Bus	$137,860	Lbr	$1,700
Unspent	$153,403			Hlth	$17,375	Prof	$2,250

*Non-Cand Loans: $135,000

ALASKA

Alaska is the nation's largest state (586,000 square miles) and its smallest (412,000 residents in 1981—and one-quarter of that growth since 1970). Alaskans live in the land of the midnight sun and of darkness at noon; of winter wind-chill factors that reach 100 below and of muggy, mosquito-filled summers; of the tallest mountains in North America and thousands of miles of rugged seacoast. Life in Alaska may be the closest thing we can experience to living on the moon: people live in protected urban environments, travel on airplanes, and otherwise protect themselves from a natural environment which in most places and most times is inhospitable to human life.

It is hard for someone from the "Lower 48" to comprehend the physical size of Alaska. More than twice as large as Texas, the state spans four different time zones. If Alaska were superimposed on a map of the Lower 48, the Panhandle would reach Jacksonville, Florida, the last Aleutian Island would touch Los Angeles, and the North Slope would reach to Lake Superior. But for all its expanse, Alaska has only one railroad (federally owned) and a few paved highways; the only way to get around is by airplane. Even the most isolated villages in the interior have an airstrip cleared in the bush or along a frozen river. Politicians especially have to fly a lot, and crashes are not uncommon; one killed Congressman Nick Begich and House Majority Leader Hale Boggs in 1972, and another seriously injured Senator Ted Stevens and killed his wife in 1978.

Most of Alaska still belongs to nature; it remains the home of the caribou and perhaps an occasional Eskimo hunter. Most of the population is clustered in a few small urban areas, with 43% of the people living in greater Anchorage. Dreams of sudden riches still bring men to Alaska (and this is one state that has more men than women), but riches are hard to find and harder, given the high cost of living, to keep. But the lone trapper or miner or the laid-off pipeline worker are not the typical Alaskans; this is a state with a high birth rate and lots of young families with small children. Public life is conducted by men who have been far more successful than they dreamed possible, and Alaska's politicians—like its businessmen and labor leaders—are men with the self-assurance and optimism of the newly rich. Yet life here is hard: one measure of that is the fact that there are fewer people over 65 living here, by a wide margin, than in any other state. So however much people love Alaska, after a while things get too rough, and they tend to move back south.

The familiar image of Alaska is one of uncharted wilderness. Yet Alaska, like most western states, is essentially an urban place for people who live and work there. Anchorage, the state's metropolis, owes its prominence to its good natural port, even though it is not the terminus of the oil pipeline nor is it anywhere near where the oil is found. Anchorage continues to grow because it is the one place where services and amenities are generally available and is the site of the major airport that connects Alaska to the Lower 48 and the Orient. In a 200-mile arc around Anchorage, in southern Alaska, there are smaller settlements, places where boomers from the Lower 48 came up to make their fortunes: the Matanuska Valley, one of the few places in Alaska where farming is possible; Willow, the on-again-off-again proposed site for the new state capital; Seward; the Kenai peninsula; the little port of Valdez, the southern terminus of the pipeline.

The other major city, with about one-seventh the state's population, is Fairbanks. Located in the interior, unprotected from the Arctic winds as Anchorage is by the towering Alaska Range, Fairbanks is exceedingly hot during its brief summer and terrifyingly cold during its long winter. Economically, Fairbanks is primarily a service town for the pipeline and other mineral enterprises in the interior, and it has suffered from high unemployment since the pipeline was completed. Vast beds of coal and other minerals as well lie under Fairbanks, but the environment puts up formidable obstacles to commercial development of these resources—obstacles quite unfamiliar to most Americans, who take technological achievements for granted.

There is an older Alaska as well, in the fishing towns of the Panhandle and the old capital of Juneau, located on an inlet of the Pacific up against a steep mountain. There is the Alaska of the Bush, the villages where Alaska's Natives—Indians, Aleuts, Eskimos—live, often in poverty. Natives make up 16% of Alaska's population, and 70% in the vast lands north and west of Anchorage and Fairbanks. But we are talking here of some 51,000 people, living in an area larger than the Northeast United States. Almost all of Alaska remains physically vacant, devoid of human habitation, perhaps unseen by human eyes. What to do with this vast expanse and with the oil and other minerals which are or may be there is the continuing and dominant question of Alaska politics.

For years Alaska longed for statehood, for control of its own affairs and release from the economic thrall of Seattle and the political control of Washington, D.C. Alaska has succeeded in generating a boom economy—thanks largely to the North Slope oil find of the late 1960s, which was finally put into production when the Trans-Alaska Pipeline System began operation in 1977. The North Slope now provides 17% of the United States's oil and, because it is pumped on state-owned lands, generates 90% of Alaska's revenues. But Alaska still has had to endure decisions imposed by the federal government that will shape its future as surely as the Northwest Ordinance did Ohio's or the Homestead Act Nebraska's.

Many of these decisions were made during the 1970s and in 1980, and in no case was the outcome what most Alaskans would have preferred. The first of these decisions concerned the basic question of the ownership of Alaska's land. The Statehood Act of 1959 promised Alaska the right to select 103 million acres (of 375 million total) as the state share, but that right was subordinated to the claims of the Natives, which had never been surrendered to anyone. In 1966 the federal government imposed a freeze, refusing to allow Alaska to select any more land until the Native claims were settled. Most Alaskans, aware of oil discoveries, wanted the state to claim as much land with mineral potential as it could. But the Alaska Native Claims Act of 1971 forced them to wait until 12 regional Native corporations selected their own 44 million acres; these corporations were also given $962 million.

The process took time. By 1982, some 23 million acres were distributed to the Native corporations; final transfers to the corporations and to the state were expected to occur in 1986. The Native corporations are fascinating entities, operating on uncharted waters. With various management strategies, some have tried to promote traditional though uneconomic activities, others have sought a higher return. One is already on the Fortune 1000 list. Stock in them will become transferable in 1991, and some fear that Natives will no longer own or run them. The end of the land freeze does seem to have stanched some anti-Native feeling, although Natives have quite distinctive (heavily Democratic) voting patterns.

Even more frustrating to development-minded Alaskans than the need to settle Native land claims was the delay in building the oil pipeline. Proposed in the early 1970s, the pipeline was the only feasible way to get North Slope oil out to civilization. Environmentalists charged that the pipeline as originally designed would destroy the permafrost (land that remains frozen year round except for a few inches at the top), would interfere with caribou migrations, and would otherwise irreparably injure Alaska's unique and fragile environment. The environmentalists went to court and in 1973 got a ruling halting pipeline construction. Alaskans could have taken their chances on the Supreme Court, but they preferred to overturn the lower court decision by congressional action. So in 1973, by a one-vote margin in the Senate, the pipeline was exempted from submitting an environmental impact statement; in return, its builders agreed to an expensive and time-consuming redesign, including building the pipeline on platforms above ground level. Construction was not completed until ten years after the oil was found, and after monstrous cost overruns. But in the long run the outcome has pleased everyone: the oil was pumped when the price was highest, which helped the state; the pipeline is a model of environmental regard, and environmentalists have had no complaints about it. Missing, amid all the clamor and controversy, was the awe Americans used to feel in the face of such vastly difficult projects.

The third major decision of the 1970s affecting Alaska determined which lands should be set aside as wilderness or otherwise protected by the federal government from use and development. Under the Native Claims Act, the Carter Interior Department withdrew some 80 million acres from development, pending congressional decision on how much should be protected. Environmentalists from the Lower 48 rallied around the issue; they knew the nation would never again have the opportunity to protect so much wilderness. They had the sympathy of the Carter administration, the support of most congressional Democrats, and they also enlisted such conservative conservationists as ex-Senator James Buckley and Ford administration Interior officials. The result was the Alaska Lands Act of 1980, which protected 159 million acres; altogether, 49% of Alaska's land is protected in some way. This was the single major victory of liberal-oriented groups in the 96th Congress, and it may turn out to be the last major achievement of the environmental movement of the late 1960s and 1970s. Certainly Alaska will be affected for years to come. President Reagan would never have signed such a bill, but it is unlikely to be repealed or substantially altered for many years.

None of these major decisions made by Congress would have come out the same way if Alaskans had decided them. White Alaskans would never have been as generous to the Natives as Congress was; the pipeline would have been built much earlier, without environmental safeguards; nothing like the Alaska Lands Act would have come out of the Alaska legislature. The major forces in Alaska politics, the *Anchorage Times* and Jesse Carr's Teamsters Union, are strongly in favor of development. Most of the state's politicians, like the new governor, Bill Sheffield, are more equivocal, but only a little. Every indication is that the overwhelming majority of voters are boomers (backers of development) rather than greenies (environmentalists). Alaskans, after all, have a high-wage and high-cost economy in a forbidding physical environment (it enrages them to hear it described as fragile). Alaskans may concede now that the decisions made worked out well. But they would never have made them themselves.

Now Alaskans have the chance to make more decisions for themselves. The focus of the state's politics has shifted from Washington to Juneau and Anchorage. One problem—if it can be called that—is that Alaska has so much money. Its oil revenues allowed it to repeal its income and sales taxes; they mounted up so much that in June 1982 the state sent every resident of more than six months a check for $1,000. (Alaska wanted to give longtime residents more than others, but the U.S. Supreme Court said no.) That money came from the Alaska Permanent Fund, set up under Governor Jay Hammond, which in early 1983 contained more than $3 billion. Further payments were forecast: $350 in 1983, $250 in 1984. But in 1982 oil prices declined, and the schedule seemed uncertain. What does seem clear is that Alaska could have frittered away a lot of that money if it had not been set aside.

One possible expenditure is on a new state capital. Juneau is not, for many Alaskans, a convenient place: it is two time zones away from Anchorage, it is reachable only by air or sea, and its airport is often closed because of bad weather. It has only 19,000 people, isolated from everyone else—not an ideal atmosphere for thoughtful deliberations. In 1978 Alaskans voted to establish a new capital near Anchorage, and eventually they chose a site at Willow; extensive plans have been made for building a new city. Perhaps too extensive: in 1982 voters in another referendum decided to keep the capital in Juneau. The issue is expected to go to the people again.

Governor. The state capital issue played an important role in the 1982 election in which a record number of voters chose a new governor. Jay Hammond, after eight years of handling important and unanticipated decisions, left office to become a bush pilot again in Naknek; the lieutenant governor, Keith Miller, a Republican with a moderate reputation and experience in state government, was expected to win.

But Miller was beaten in Alaska's unusual primary (you can vote for a gubernatorial candidate of one party and a legislative candidate of another). Tom Fink, a former speaker of the state House and avid supporter of unfettered development, won the Republican nomination in an upset. Fink, who wants the capital in Willow, beat Miller in Anchorage and the nearby south by 35,000 to 13,000. Miller, who wants to keep the capital in Juneau, carried the Panhandle over Fink 11,344 to 730, but it was not enough.

Regional variations were even more striking in the general election, in which the major contenders were Sheffield, a pro-Juneau hotel chain owner, Fink, and Dick Randolph, a state legislator from Fairbanks elected under the banner of the Libertarian Party. Statewide Sheffield won with 46% to Fink's 37% and Randolph's respectable 15%. Fink got almost all his votes in Anchorage and the nearby South; he won more than 50% in both. But Sheffield carried the Panhandle with 81% of the vote and got 68% in the mostly Native Bush. The Fairbanks area was heavily contested: Randolph got 26% there, better than Fink's 25%; Sheffield carried the area, however, with 46%.

Outsiders might argue that if the votes for Fink and Randolph, candidates similarly placed on the ideological spectrum, were combined, they would have prevailed. Perhaps; no one doubts that Alaskans resent government interference and want more free enterprise. But this is a small state, and if the voters don't necessarily meet all the candidates personally, all the major political actors know each other well. Sheffield seems well liked, and his party label does not seem to matter much in a state which in national elections is one of the most Republican in the country. He personifies the kind of entrepreneurial success typical of Alaska politicians, and he does not seem far out of line from the consensus on issues. He and his legislature, cooped up in Juneau in the dark months, will have to make some big money decisions in the years ahead.

Presidential politics. Alaska's reaction against the environmental movement has made it one of the most Republican states in presidential politics. In the very close elections of 1960 and 1968, Alaska came very close to the national average in its preferences. In 1976 and

1980, however, it was one of the most Republican—or least Democratic—states. In 1980 Jimmy Carter got only 26% here, and in some places Carter ran behind Libertarian Party candidate Ed Clark. This was the Libertarians' strongest state: they took 12% of the vote, and have elected state legislators since 1978. The success of this small, rough-and-ready party in Alaska makes a certain amount of sense. A strong desire for untrammeled development plus an equally strong desire to be left alone characterize Alaska politics. The state hates federal regulations and has decriminalized marijuana; in 1982 it rejected, by similar margins, ballot measures to limit state funding of abortions and to prohibit subsistence fishing and hunting. Just as various parts of Alaska seem to vote increasingly their parochial interests, so Alaska as a whole seems to vote on the basis of its special issues rather than national ones. Alaska has no presidential primary; what presidential candidate is going to take time off to campaign way up here?

Senators. Because so many basic decisions affecting Alaska have been made in Congress, being a senator from Alaska is a different kind of job from being a senator from any other state. Alaska senators sometimes get involved in issues of national scope. But necessarily much of their time and energy are consumed in dealing with parochial Alaska issues. That has been the case, since 1968, for the senior senator, Ted Stevens. His job was complicated further by the fact that he approached issues differently from, and did not get along with, his colleague for 12 years, Mike Gravel. Stevens's instinct on Alaska issues is to work hard with all the interested groups and then reach a compromise. Gravel's instinct was to grandstand alone. It paid off once, in 1973, when he persuaded the Senate to approve the pipeline by one vote; that was probably enough to reelect him in 1974. But in 1978 and 1980 Gravel's efforts to filibuster the Alaska Lands bill only resulted in far more land being tied up than would have been the case if Stevens's compromise had passed. Alaska voters pay close attention to these things. In the summer of 1980, just before the primary, the Senate voted cloture on a Gravel filibuster by a scathing 63 to 25 margin. It was as if senators were trying to send a signal to Alaska; if so, it was received. Gravel was defeated by Clark Gruening, a young lawyer and grandson of the senator Gravel had beaten 12 years before. Gruening was defeated in turn by Frank Murkowski, a Republican with a pleasant personality and unobjectionable issue stands.

That left Stevens as indisputably Alaska's leading spokesman on Capitol Hill. He has had a lot of training for that position: he was U.S. attorney in Alaska 30 years ago, served in the Interior Department in the Eisenhower administration, and was a member of the Alaska legislature. He probably knows the details of Alaska legislation better than anyone else. And he does more than represent local interests. He is Senate Majority Whip, the number two man in the leadership; he chairs the Defense Appropriations Subcommittee. He has taken a leading and constructive role on civil service issues. Stevens is a good example of a senator who is a work horse, not a show horse.

Yet in some ways the results have been disappointing. On Alaska issues his compromises, laboriously negotiated and based on thoughtful and knowledgeable understanding of the issues, are not automatically accepted. His version of the Alaska Lands bill was rejected, for instance; and, on a much less important matter, Howard Metzenbaum of Ohio prevented the Senate from passing in 1982 a bill to give the federally owned Alaska Railroad to the state government. Stevens is hurt sometimes by his temper; having spent months and months negotiating these issues, he has a tendency to explode when a colleague or a lobbyist new to the issue comes along and attacks his plans. However justified his irritation, it does not persuade his colleagues that they ought to support automatically his resolution of a difficult and technical issue.

On national issues Stevens is also frustrated sometimes. His Defense Subcommittee chair forces him to deal with what most of his colleagues by 1983 regarded as the extravagant defense budgets of the administration; he risks either losing his credibility in the Senate or antagonizing the administration on many issues. He seems unlikely to be elected Republican Leader if Howard Baker should retire or run for president in 1984. Stevens's voting record on many issues—abortion, for example, or some labor issues—makes him anathema to many right-wing colleagues, and his occasional outbursts have not helped him with others.

"God forbid that anyone will ever tell me that the city of Washington is my home," he told the Senate in 1982. "It is not. I detest it. I really do. I cannot think of another place to have a nation's capital in the world that is a worse place to live." By 1984, when his seat is up, Stevens will have spent most of his time in Washington for 21 of the past 28 years; but few people expect him to retire to Alaska. As frustrating as his job has sometimes been, it seems clear he wants to keep it; and past election returns suggest he will have no trouble doing so. But nothing is for certain in Alaska politics. Stevens had weak opposition in 1972 and 1978; nothing guarantees him that in 1984. The 1982 elections show how a popular middle-of-the-road Republican, with plenty of experience and endorsements, could nonetheless be beaten. Could the same thing happen to Ted Stevens? Perhaps the toughest manuevering will come in 1983, when in the tight-knit world of Alaska politics potential strong opponents decide whether they will make this race. If they don't, Stevens will be reelected easily; if they do, he may have to fight hard for his seat.

Stevens has, as predicted, worked comfortably with Alaska's junior senator, Frank Murkowski. A banker who favors opening up and developing Alaska's resources, Murkowski is not part of the group of New Right senators elected in 1980; like many Alaskans, he is skeptical of government interference in personal as well as economic life. In his first term he served on the bread-and-butter committees of Energy (the old Interior) and Environment (the old Public Works). In 1983 he left Environment to go to Foreign Relations, in hope of serving on the Far East Subcommittee. Alaska trades a lot with Japan and other rapidly growing nations in East Asia; it is one state with a natural interest in opposing the forms of trade protection which seem so attractive to states in the industrial East and Midwest. Murkowski is not up for reelection until 1986; he takes issue positions which are pretty closely in line with the views of most of his constituents; he is a member of the majority party who has gone along with the leadership. He is thus in an excellent position to be legislatively productive and to stake out claims on two or three issues that can provide the basis for a long Senate career.

Congressman. Congressman Don Young also tends to work well with Stevens. First elected after Nick Begich was killed in a plane crash, Young is a Republican from the Bush. A teacher in the winter and riverboat captain in the summer, he is a man of directness, fluent in the salty language in which much of Alaska politics is conducted. He serves on the Interior Committee and is ranking Republican on the Public Lands and National Parks Subcommittee, the body which handles any revisions of the Alaska Lands Act. It is chaired by John Seiberling, one of the authors of the present law, and he is likely to have a majority over Young on this issue. Young has faced both strong and weak opposition; the last time he faced the former, in the person of state Senator Patrick Rodey in 1978, he won with just 55% of the vote. He has done much better against weaker candidates.

ALASKA — Congressional District, Boroughs, Census Areas, and Selected Places — *(1 At Large)*

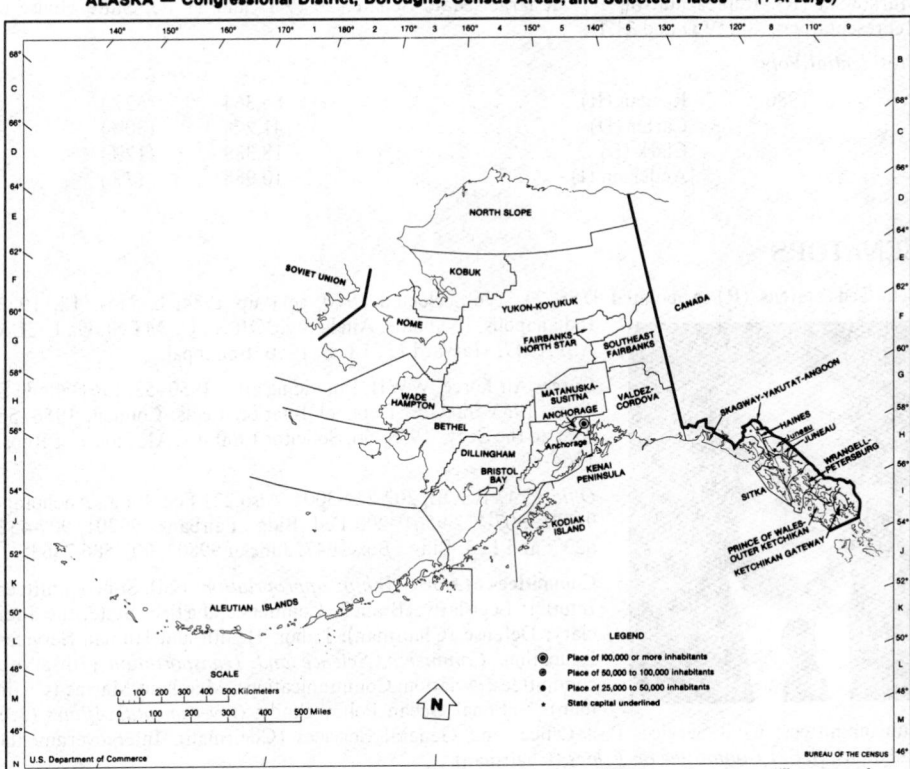

The People   Est. Pop. 1982: 438,000; Pop. 1980: 400,481, up 8.9% 1980–82 and 32.8% 1970–80; .19% of U.S. total, 51st largest; voting age pop. 271,106; 14% American Indian, 3% Black, 2% Spanish origin, 2% Asian origin. Single ancestry: 9% English, 8% German, 4% Irish, 2% Norwegian, French, 1% Swedish, Scottish, Italian, Dutch, Polish. Registered voters (1982): 266,407 Total. 22% with 1–3 yrs. col., 22% with 4+ yrs. col. 10.1% below poverty level. 34% housing units rented; median house value: $75,200; median monthly rent: $338. Households: 73% family, 49% with children, 61% married couples.

1982 Share of Federal Tax Burden $1,679,100,000; .28% of U.S. total, 47th largest.

1982 Share of Federal Expenditures

	Total		Non-Defense		Defense	
Total Expend	$1,868m	(0.31%)	$1,006m	(0.24%)	$861m	(0.48%)
St/Lcl Grants	422m	(0.48%)	422m	(0.48%)	0m	(0%)
Salary/Wages	703m	(0.90%)	214m	(0.78%)	489m	(0.96%)
Ind Payments	277m	(0.10%)	216m	(0.08%)	61m	(0.21%)
Procurement	449m	(0.31%)	121m	(0.38%)	328m	(0.29%)
Other Programs	16m	(0.30%)	13m	(0.24%)	3m	(6.98%)
Loan/Insurance	101m	(0.16%)	81m	(0.13%)	20m	(0.91%)

Political Lineup Governor, William Sheffield (D). Senators, Ted Stevens (R) and Frank H. Murkowski (R). Representative, 1 R at large. State Senate, 20 (9 D and 11 R); State House of Representatives, 40 (19 D and 21 R).

Presidential Vote

1980	Reagan (R)	85,364	(62%)
	Carter (D)	41,228	(30%)
	Clark (L)	18,389	(12%)
	Anderson (I)	10,988	(7%)

SENATORS

Sen. Ted Stevens (R) Appointed Dec. 23, 1968, elected 1970, seat up 1984; b. Nov. 18, 1923, Indianapolis, IN; home, Anchorage; OR St. U., MT St. U., UCLA, A.B. 1947, Harvard U., LL.B. 1950; Episcopal.

Career Air Force, WWII; Practicing atty., 1950–53, 1961–68; U.S. Atty., 1953-56; U.S. Dept. of Interior, Legis. Council, 1956–58, Asst. to the Secy., 1958–60, Solicitor 1960–61; AK House of Reps., 1964–68.

Offices 147 RSOB, 202-224-3004. Also 221 Fed. Bldg., Anchorage 99501, 907-272-9561; 200 Fed. Bldg., Fairbanks 99701, 907-452-6227; and Fed. Bldg., Box 1647, Juneau 99802, 907-586-7463.

Committees *Majority Whip: Appropriations* (2d). Subcommittees: Interior; Legislative Branch; Commerce, Justice, State, the Judiciary; Defense (Chairman); Labor, Health and Human Services, Education. *Commerce, Science and Transportation* (7th). Subcommittees: Aviation; Communications; Merchant Marine (Chairman); National Ocean Policy Study. *Governmental Affairs* (3d). Subcommittees: Civil Service, Post Office, and General Services (Chairman); Intergovernmental Relations. *Select Committee on Ethics* (Chairman).

Group Ratings

	ADA	ACLU	COPE	CFA	LCV	LWV	NTU	NSI	COC	ACA	CSFC
1982	15	36	48	10	15	45	56	100	76	67	70
1981	15	—	50	14	12	—	54	—	100	61	76
1980	39	37	50	7	5	25	39	89	86	71	67

National Journal Ratings

		Economic		Foreign		Cultural	
1982	27%	(LIB)	16%	(LIB)	32%	(LIB)	
	72%	(CONS)	68%	(CONS)	67%	(CONS)	
1981	14%	(LIB)	32%	(LIB)	52%	(LIB)	
	85%	(CONS)	67%	(CONS)	47%	(CONS)	

Key Votes

1) Reagan 81 Budget	FOR	5) $ to El Salvador	FOR	9) Poor Pay Food Stamps	AGN
2) Reagan 81 Tax Cut	FOR	6) Saudi AWACS Sale	FOR	10) Ban Crt Busing Order	FOR
3) Bal Budget Amend	FOR	7) Ban Abortion	AGN	11) Clinch Riv Brdr Rctr	FOR
4) Gas & Road Tax	FOR	8) Nerve Gas Prod	FOR	12) Legal Services Corp	FOR

Election Results

1978 general	Ted Stevens (R)	92,783	(76%)	($346,837)
	Donald W. Hobbs (D)	29,574	(24%)	($21,234)
1978 primary	Ted Stevens (R) unopposed			
1972 general	Ted Stevens (R)	74,216	(77%)	($195,123)
	Gene Guess (D)	21,791	(23%)	($47,131)

Campaign Contributions and Expenditures

1977–78			PACS brkdwn		
Receipts	$366,895	Agr	$3,400	Ideo	$8,150
Expend.	$346,837	Bus	$98,649	Lbr	$43,350
Unspent	$87,547	Hlth	$12,700	Prof	$900

Sen. Frank H. Murkowski (R) Elected 1980, seat up 1986; b. Mar. 28, 1933, Seattle, WA; home, Fairbanks; Seattle U., B.A. 1955; Roman Catholic.

Career U.S. Coast Guard, 1955–56; Pres., AK Natl. Bank of the North, 1971; AK Commissioner of Econ. Devel., 1967–70; Pres., AK Chamber of Comm., 1977.

Offices 317 HSOB, 202-224-6665. Also Fed. Bldg, 701 C St., Box 1, Anchorage 99513, 907-271-3735; and 101 12th Ave., Box 7, Fairbanks 99701, 907-586-7463.

Committees Energy and Natural Resources (7th). Subcommittees: Energy and Mineral Resources; Water and Power; Energy Regulation (Chairman). *Foreign Relations* (9th). Subcommittees: East Asian and Pacific Affairs (Chairman); International Economic Policy; Western Hemisphere Affairs. *Veterans' Affairs* (4th). *Select Committee on Indian Affairs* (4th).

Group Ratings

	ADA	ACLU	COPE	CFA	LCV	LWV	NTU	NSI	COC	ACA	CSFC
1982	10	18	18	0	16	42	81	90	70	70	75
1981	15	—	24	14	12	—	58	—	93	65	80

National Journal Ratings

	Economic		Foreign		Cultural	
1982	20%	(LIB)	3%	(LIB)	25%	(LIB)
	79%	(CONS)	84%	(CONS)	74%	(CONS)
1981	27%	(LIB)	44%	(LIB)	40%	(LIB)
	72%	(CONS)	55%	(CONS)	59%	(CONS)

Key Votes

1) Reagan 81 Budget	FOR	5) $ to El Salvador	FOR	9) Poor Pay Food Stamps	FOR
2) Reagan 81 Tax Cut	FOR	6) Saudi AWACS Sale	FOR	10) Ban Crt Busing Order	AGN
3) Bal Budget Amend	FOR	7) Ban Abortion	FOR	11) Clinch Riv Brdr Rctr	FOR
4) Gas & Road Tax	FOR	8) Nerve Gas Prod	FOR	12) Legal Services Corp	FOR

Election Results

1980 general	Frank H. Murkowski (R)	84,159	(54%)	($697,387)
	Clark Gruening (D)	72,007	(46%)	($507,445)
1980 primary	Frank H. Murkowski (R)	16,292	(59%)	
	Art Kennedy (R)	5,527	(20%)	($97,530)
	Four others (R)	5,813	(21%)	
1974 general	Mike Gravel (D)	54,361	(58%)	($469,300)
	C. R. Lewis (R)	38,914	(42%)	($353,701)

Campaign Contributions and Expenditures

1979–80			PACS brkdwn		
Receipts	$712,837	Agr	$9,250	Ideo	$20,903
Expend.	$697,387	Bus	$250,768	Lbr	$12,000
Unspent	$13,649	Hlth	$4,750	Prof	$7,300

GOVERNOR

Gov. William Sheffield (D) Elected 1982, term expires Dec. 1986; b. June 26, 1928, Spokane WA; home, Anchorage; DeForest Training School of Radio Broadcasting and Engineering; Protestant.

Career Army Air Corps, 1946–49; Sears, Roebuck and Co., 1952–62; Bd. Chmn., Sheffield Enterprises, 1962–82.

Offices Pouch A, State Capitol, Juneau 99811, 907-465-3500.

Election Results

1982 gen.	William Sheffield (D)	89,259	(46%)
	Thomas A. Fink (R)	71,949	(37%)
	Richard L. Randolph (L)	28,981	(15%)
1982 prim.	William Sheffield (D)	21,940	(40%)
	Steve Cowper (D)	21,680	(39%)
	Four others (D)	11,695	(21%)
1978 gen.	Jay S. Hammond (R)	49,580	(39%)
	Walter J. Hickel (write-in) ...	33,555	(26%)
	Chancy Croft (D)	25,656	(20%)
	Tom Kelly (I)	15,656	(12%)

Rep. Don Young (R) Elected Mar. 6, 1973; b. June 9, 1933, Meridian, CA; home, Fort Yukon; Chico St. Col., B.A. 1956; Episcopal.

Career Construction work, 1959; Teacher, 1960–69; Riverboat capt.; Fort Yukon City Cncl., Mayor of Fort Yukon; AK House of Reps., 1966–70; AK Senate, 1970–73.

Offices 2331 RHOB, 202-225-5765. Also 115 Fed. Bldg., Anchorage 99501, 907-279-1587.

Committees *Interior and Insular Affairs* (2d). Subcommittees: Mining, Forest Management, and BPA; Public Lands and National Parks. *Merchant Marine and Fisheries* (4th). Subcommittees: Coast Guard and Navigation; Fisheries and Wildlife, Conservation and the Environment; Merchant Marine; Panama Canal and Outer Continental Shelf.

Group Ratings

	ADA	ACLU	COPE	CFA	LCV	LWV	NTU	NSI	COC	ACA	CSFC
1982	10	33	39	30	17	33	56	100	57	82	57
1981	10	—	40	14	23	—	54	—	88	65	68
1980	22	40	31	14	6	33	55	100	67	70	69

National Journal Ratings

	Economic		Foreign		Cultural	
1982	34%	(LIB)	11%	(LIB)	29%	(LIB)
	66%	(CONS)	89%	(CONS)	71%	(CONS)
1981	35%	(LIB)	43%	(LIB)	26%	(LIB)
	64%	(CONS)	56%	(CONS)	74%	(CONS)

Key Votes

1) Reagan 81 Budget	FOR	5) Incr SS Rtmt Age	FOR	9) Poor Pay Food Stamps	AGN
2) Reagan 81 Tax Cut	FOR	6) Saudi AWACS Sale	AGN	10) Ban Crt Busing Order	—
3) Bal Budget Amend	FOR	7) $ for MX Missile	FOR	11) Auto Local Content	—
4) Gas & Road Tax	—	8) Nerve Gas Prod	FOR	12) Nuclear Arms Freeze	AGN

Election Results

1982 general	Don Young (R)	127,558	(71%)	($270,154)
	Dave Carlson (D)	51,740	(29%)	($0)
1982 primary	Don Young (R)	95,313	(100%)	
1980 general	Don Young (R)	114,089	(74%)	($285,594)
	Pat Parnell (D)	39,922	(26%)	($51,065)

Campaign Contributions and Expenditures

1981–82		*Direct Cont. 81-82*		*PACS brkdwn*			
Receipts	$276,542	Indiv	$156,349	Agr	$4,000	Ideo	$3,750
Expend.	$270,154	Party	$20,382	Bus	$58,737	Lbr	$11,000
Unspent	$9,167	PACS	$88,198	Hlth	$7,500	Prof	$2,900

ARIZONA

Arizona, the last of the 48 contiguous states to be admitted to the Union, was for years *terra incognita* to most Americans: a vast expanse of thinly populated desert, with almost as many Indians as whites, a place that impinged very little on the national consciousness. People had heard stories about the fierce Apache and the sheepherding Navajo, and they knew about Arizona's tourist attractions, especially the Grand Canyon and those Saguaro cactuses behind which the sun set in movies. In the 1930s, as farmers from the Dust Bowl of Oklahoma and Kansas sought a better life in California, they drove across northern Arizona on Route 66, a road celebrated in song and which was the setting of the play *The Petrified Forest*. Americans knew vaguely that Arizona had copper mines and that it had had its share of western outlaws and lawmen (such as Wyatt Earp). Meanwhile, economically and politically, Arizona was a sleepy state, a constituency that sent to Washington conservative Democrats who concentrated on aiding the state (the most famous of whom was Carl Hayden) and wealthy mine owners (Lewis Douglas).

All this was changed by two inventions that became commercially practical in the years after World War II—the passenger airplane and the air conditioner. The airplane made it possible for tourists to visit Arizona in the winter, and so Midwesterners got the idea that this state, with its warm winters and hot but dry summers, might be a good place to retire, or even make a living. Air service made Arizona a practical place to do business, and today booming Phoenix is the central focus of major corporations like Greyhound and Motorola. Air conditioning made Arizona's summer heat bearable. People here like to say that the dry heat is not so bad, but the fact is that for three or four months of the year it is hot enough to be unbearable to most Americans. Airline service and air conditioning became commonplace in the decade after World War II, and that is when Arizona began to be transformed by population growth. In 1940 this state had 550,000 people, mostly scattered in small towns. In the early 1960s it passed the one million mark, and by 1981 there were 2.8 million Arizonans.

These newcomers inhabit an almost entirely new Arizona. There are still remnants of the older Arizona: mining towns like Bisbee, pleasant country towns like Prescott that but for the mountains could be in the midwestern plains, and sun-baked agricultural centers like Yuma. But today most Arizonans live in metropolitan areas: 56% of the state's population is in Phoenix and surrounding Maricopa County and another 21% is in Tucson and Pima County. The new Arizonans like to think of themselves as upholders of traditional values, but Phoenix has little of the stability or tradition found in politically more liberal places like Boston or Philadelphia. Phoenix proclaims itself, with the glare of chrome and glass catching the sunlight, new and contemporary. The main streets proceed straight north and south or east and west, separated one mile apart on the remorseless grid transplanted from the Midwest, until mountains stop them from going any farther. Inside an automobile with the windows up and the air conditioning on, Phoenix seems to be an exceedingly silent city, quiet and orderly as cities where you get around by walking never are.

Yet there is something vibrant and chaotic about life in Phoenix—the absence of an established order and, often, of established standards of legality and fair play. The establishment occupies a very thin layer atop local society; there are no really old families here, and the men who have guided the destiny of the city and state are businessmen and lawyers whose names are not widely known. Underneath that top layer, there is plenty of money but there are few standards. The lures of Arizona have brought in big corporations, and there has been little unemployment; contrary to popular impression, Arizona is not just a retirement haven and has a percentage of elderly near the national average. Arizona has also lured many unscrupulous con men and fast-buck artists: drifters and grifters who would have been at home in Raymond Chandler's Los Angeles (though not in the most stable and sophisticated Los Angeles of today). This side of life in Phoenix was revealed a few years ago by the Don Bolles murder case. Bolles, an investigative reporter looking into land-selling scandals, was murdered by a bomb that exploded in his car; a group of substantial businessmen and a small-time hoodlum were accused of the crime and convicted, although that verdict was overturned by the state Supreme Court.

Arizona's sudden growth literally transformed the state's politics. The change—from an old-fashioned Democratic state to a sleek and brash conservative one—is best illustrated by contrasting the careers of the men who have so far been the state's best-known politicians: Carl Hayden and Barry Goldwater. Hayden began his political career as a councilman in Tempe (formerly Hayden's Crossing) in 1902, when Phoenix was just a hot, sleepy depot on the Southern Pacific Railroad. He was a Democrat in a state much of whose small population came from the South and which was both conservative and Democratic. Although Arizona occasionally went Republican in national elections (it never supported a losing candidate until 1960), Hayden and most Arizona Democrats seldom were seriously challenged. Hayden's career was built around bringing federal money and Colorado River water into Arizona, and he used all his seniority—he represented Arizona in Congress from statehood in 1912 until his retirement in 1969—to that end. His monument was the Central Arizona Project, finally approved in 1968, when he was 91 years old. Interestingly, most of this water goes not to residential Phoenix, but to the large farms in the otherwise parched Gila River valley around the city. Jimmy Carter tried to phase out the CAP, but Arizona politicians of all stripes—liberal Democrat Morris Udall and conservative Republicans John Rhodes and Barry Goldwater—rallied to protect Hayden's legacy.

The birth of Arizona's dominant conservative Republicanism can de dated with some precision to the year 1949, when Barry Goldwater, then proprietor of his family's department store, was elected to the Phoenix city council. The next year Goldwater helped a Republican win the governorship, and in 1952 Republicans swept the state, and Goldwater himself was elected to the Senate. (The man he beat, Ernest MacFarland, was then Senate majority leader, and his defeat set the stage for Lyndon Johnson's ascent to that post.) Goldwater won reelection by a large margin in 1958, and in a bad year for Republicans generally he distinguished himself as the only successful conservative Republican. His frank, often blunt and impolitic articulation of his beliefs brought him so much devotion and volunteer support from all over the country that he won the 1964 Republican presidential nomination despite his malapropisms, his modesty, and his evident distaste for running.

Goldwater's resolute conservatism—he said he wanted to repeal federal programs, not start new ones—was vastly appealing to the new Arizonans of the 1950s and 1960s. These people were mostly white collar workers, professionals, and technicians, from traditional cultural backgrounds in the Midwest and South. Their desire for stability in a patently unstable cultural environment and their affection for the free enterprise system that enabled them to be more successful and more productive than most of them had ever dreamed: these basic impulses were given detail and thrust in Goldwater's politics. The older "pinto" Democrats were unappealing—dusty, rural, old, and more concerned about a few federal dollars when the real growth of the local economy seemed to come from private business. Some of these young Arizonans became prominent in Washington: John Rhodes, William Rehnquist, Richard Kleindienst, Sandra Day O'Connor. Their contemporaries made all of metropolitan Phoenix more Republican in the last three presidential elections than Orange County, California. The years 1958 to 1972 were almost entirely Republican in Arizona—the only state which has gone Republican in every presidential election since 1948, a state where Republicans held the governorship for all but two years in the 1958-74 period, whose congressional delegation was, with the exception of Morris Udall, entirely Republican during the entire Nixon and Ford administrations.

Arizona Republicans have not controlled all the top offices lately, however. They lost the governorship in 1974 and have not regained it since. They lost one of the state's Senate seats in 1976 and did not come close to winning it back in 1982. Democrats hold several statewide offices. Yet overall this is still a very Republican state. That is evident in presidential elections, it is evident from the Republican majorities in the legislature, from the success of Republican candidates in local elections in the big counties. Republicans set the agenda in Arizona, they dominate the political discussion, and they dominate the middle and lower layers of government. Their failure to win the top offices is due in part to the talent of the Democrats who hold them, but it can be ascribed as well to a kind of abdication. Successful young men and women of Republican views here do not see high office as the way to success or achievement: accomplishment comes through private enterprise. For these free market philosophers of the desert, government and politics are not where it's at.

Senators. Barry Goldwater, more than 30 years after he was first elected to the Senate, is the grand old man of Arizona politics, but he is not ready yet to be placid or noncontroversial. He has seen his views vindicated more than most politicians ever do, but he is not necessarily treated as a prophet with honor at home or in Washington. He calls himself the granddaddy of the conservative movement, but Republicans of the New Right do not consider him their leader. Goldwater's conservatism is bottomed on two beliefs: that the government should not interfere with private economic matters and that the nation needs a strong and aggressive defense. This salty-tongued veteran, whose religious beliefs are not of the evangelical type, is reluctant to support attempts by self-styled conservatives to regulate or reform citizens' morals. Abortion, for example, is a side issue for Goldwater, something he is not at all sure is the federal government's business; it is certainly not the kind of thing that got this businessman, civic leader, and tinkerer with gadgets into politics.

Goldwater's most visible responsibility is the chairmanship of the Select Committee on Intelligence. He still bristles with indignation at what he regards as disastrous disclosures of intelligence and weakening of the intelligence agencies in the 1970s, but he works comfortably on a bipartisan basis with the committee's ranking Democrat, Daniel Patrick Moynihan. Goldwater is also counted as something of a critic of CIA Director William Casey; he is an admirer of former CIA Deputy Director Bobby Inman and was sorry to see him leave government. Goldwater would surely love to chair the Armed Services Committee, but because his current Senate service dates only from 1969 he is outranked by John Tower and Strom Thurmond. Goldwater is, as everyone knows, a hawk on defense and foreign policy issues, and he is in particular a partisan of the Air Force: he is a pilot and became an Air Force major general.

It is fair to say that Goldwater is less interested in domestic issues. He serves as chairman of the Commerce Communications Subcommittee, which has jurisdiction over such important fields as broadcasting, the breakup of AT&T, and telecommunications. He pays some attention to Arizona issues, but not as much as Hayden used to; and for Arizona voters, many of whom were not alive and most of whom were not Arizonans when his political career began, he is a remote rather than familiar figure. That was apparent from the results of the 1980 election, which he barely won. Part of the reason was his health: he had a painful hip injury, and he appeared on crutches at the 1980 Republican National Convention, visibly more irritable and distracted than usual. His Democratic opponent, Phoenix apartment owner Bill Schulz, ran on the slogan "Energy for the '80s," and spent more than $2 million on the race. In the most Republican election year in a generation, in one of the nation's most Republican states, he came within 1% of winning. It should be added that Schulz did not campaign as an old-fashioned liberal; he stressed his West Point background and his advocacy of a strong defense. Goldwater's term comes up again in 1986, when he turns 76; he speaks wistfully of the pleasures of living in Phoenix, and no one expects him to run again.

Arizona's other senator, Democrat Dennis DeConcini, came to office in 1976 after one of the state's liveliest elections and was reelected after what turned out to be one of its most somnolent campaigns. DeConcini entered statewide politics with solid assets: his family had been active politically for years, he had served creditably as the local prosecutor in Tucson, and he had a solid base in that usually Democratic city. He was helped, however, by a vitriolic primary fight between two Republican congressmen, born-again Christian John Conlan and short-tempered Sam Steiger, whose shooting of a burro in unclear circumstances was a campaign issue. Steiger won the Republican nomination, but in the general election could do no better than break even in Maricopa County; so DeConcini won easily.

In his first years in the Senate DeConcini proved to be a swing vote on many issues, and by no means an automatic Democratic or liberal vote. On the Judiciary Committee he supports tough sentencing and crackdowns on organized crime, and claims success in cracking down on drug smuggling through the Arizona–Mexico border; as ranking Democrat on the Constitution Subcommittee, he supports measures to mandate a balanced budget. His moment in history, so far, came as the Senate considered the Panama Canal Treaties in 1978.

DeConcini suddenly became the center of national attention when he advanced his own understanding that the treaties did not bar the United States from using military force to keep the canal open in the future. The Carter administration had to negotiate carefully with DeConcini, then with Panama's Omar Torrijos, then with DeConcini again, in order to get the treaties through. DeConcini's vote turned out to be crucial—and threatened, for a while, to cause him trouble in Arizona: some Arizonans started to circulate recall petitions. If he had been up for reelection in 1980, when so many Canal Treaties supporters were defeated, he might have been in real trouble.

But by 1982 he was in very strong shape in Arizona. This was not simply the result of a Democratic surge nationally; Arizona remained in pretty good shape economically, and no one imagined it would support a Democrat over Ronald Reagan. But DeConcini did establish his own, personal record on issues; and he raised substantial enough sums to discourage some strong opposition. By the time legislator Pete Dunn emerged as the winner of the September Republican primary, the race was effectively over. Dunn was not well known, but more important was the fact that voters had no real complaint with DeConcini. DeConcini is not likely to be as much of a swing vote as he was in the Carter years as long as the Republicans control the Senate; but if they lose control in 1984 he could be a critical vote again. DeConcini has said in the past that he will seek no more than two terms in the Senate, and his chances of winning a third in Republican Arizona despite his good showings are problematical; but after the 1982 election he could look forward to at least six politically secure years. One of his major goals is to see the Central Arizona Project through to completion; he is well placed to help it along as a member of the Appropriations Committee.

Governor. Arizona has traditionally had one of the most parsimonious and smallest state governments: it was the only state for years that did not participate in the Medicaid program, and its governor has what most of his peers would regard as no staff at all. Yet Arizona today has one of the nation's brainiest governors, and one of its most original; all the more surprising, he is a Democrat elected to his second full term at age 44. Babbitt succeeded to the governorship in 1978, having served most of one term as attorney general (in which capacity he personally prosecuted the Bolles case); Governor Raul Castro resigned in 1977 to become ambassador to Argentina and his successor, Wesley Bolin, died suddenly in March 1978, making Babbitt, to everyone's surprise, governor. He performed creditably enough to win the endorsement of the usually archconservative *Arizona Republic* and to win a full term with 52% of the vote. That was not an overwhelming endorsement, particularly since his opponent, a onetime state senator and Pontiac dealer, was not impressive; but in 1982, after 4½ years in office, Babbitt did much better (62%) against a stronger Republican, former state Senate president Leo Corbet.

Babbitt likes to stress his Arizona roots: he comes from an old Flagstaff family, he goes backpacking with his family in the Grand Canyon, he remains unpretentious and unflappable despite his political success. And if he is from the old, pre-air conditioning Arizona, he is also respectful of the new Arizona built up since World War II. He understands that it represents a good life for hundreds of thousands of people; he does not see it as just a blot on the environment. And he understands that free enterprise and the profit motive are responsible for a lot of what is right about Arizona as well as for some of what is wrong. Babbitt is a severe man: severe in his approach to crime (he favors capital punishment, and has a theoretical argument ready to back his position) and severe in his reaction to intellectual shoddiness. In his first years as governor, he attacked federal programs for requiring too much paperwork—not simply, one suspects, because of the burden imposed on the state, but because so much of the paperwork was mindless or plainly unnecessary. At governors' conferences, Babbitt has come forward with proposals for new divisions of government responsibilities between the federal and state governments—alternatives which have not been adopted, one suspects, simply because they are so austerely rational.

Babbitt's performance in the 1982 election suggests he could be a strong candidate for the Senate, either in 1986 for Goldwater's seat or in 1988 for DeConcini's. He has even been mentioned as a possible presidential candidate. That is looking ahead too far: presiding over Arizona's small state government is quite a different enterprise from presiding over just the Executive Office of the President, not to mention the rest of the federal government. He does have some important qualifications for national office: intellectual ability, candor, energy, a lack of the cynicism that seems to affect some of the more perceptive of veteran senators.

Presidential politics. If any state is likely to go Republican in the 1984 presidential election, Arizona is: don't look for general election candidates to spend much time there, even with a Udall nomination. Arizona has one of the earliest delegate selection processes: its presidential preference is registered in precinct elections in February. Unaccountably, these are ignored by the national press and hence by the candidates. Maybe the reason is that the one upset winner in this process was John Lindsay in 1972: it was his only electoral success in his brief career as a Democratic presidential candidate.

Congressional districting. Arizona gained one congressional district from the 1980 census, as it has in each of the last four decades, giving it five. The Republican legislature, with enough votes to override Governor Babbitt's veto, enacted a plan which split the Phoenix metropolitan area among four, three of them solidly Republican. Tucson—as it happens, the perfect size for one district—was also split, giving Morris Udall the choice of running in a district combining the most Democratic parts of Tucson and Phoenix (connected by a strip of desert) or in a district containing the Republican parts of Tucson and the copper country which Udall failed to carry in 1978 and 1980. Udall chose the Democratic district, which he won easily; the other district, the new 5th, contrary to the legislature's expectations went Democratic as well, by a narrow margin. It will likely be the most closely contested of these districts in 1984.

The People Est. Pop. 1982: 2,860,000; Pop. 1980: 2,717,866, up 5.3% 1980–82 and 53.1% 1970–80; 1.24% U.S. total, 29th largest; voting age pop. 1,926,728; 13% Spanish origin, 4% American Indian, 3% Black, 1% Asian origin. Single ancestry: 10% English, 7% German, 4% Irish, 2% Italian, 1% Polish, French, Swedish, Scottish, Dutch, Norwegian. Registered voters (1982): 1,142,159 Total. 508,606 R (45%), 535,530 D (47%), 94,302 others (8%). 21% with 1–3 yrs. col., 17% with 4+ yrs. col. 12.4% below poverty level. 27% housing units rented; median house value: $56,600; median monthly rent: $228. Households: 74% family, 39% with children, 62% married couples.

1982 Share of Federal Tax Burden $6,661,700,000; 1.11% of U.S. total, 28th largest.

1982 Share of Federal Expenditures

	Total		Non-Defense		Defense	
Total Expend	$7,465m	(1.23%)	$5,017m	(1.18%)	$2,448m	(1.37%)
St/Lcl Grants	799m	(0.91%)	799m	(0.91%)	0m	(0%)
Salary/Wages	1,013m	(1.30%)	377m	(1.38%)	636m	(1.26%)
Ind Payments	3,774m	(1.32%)	3,187m	(1.24%)	587m	(2.05%)
Procurement	1,814m	(1.24%)	351m	(1.11%)	1,463m	(1.28%)
Other Programs	65m	(1.20%)	64m	(1.19%)	1m	(2.33%)
Loan/Insurance	656m	(1.03%)	593m	(0.96%)	63m	(2.86%)

Political Lineup Governor, Bruce E. Babbitt (D). Senators, Barry Goldwater (R) and Dennis DeConcini (D). Representatives, 5 (3 R and 2 D). State Senate, 30 (18 R and 12 D); State House of Representatives, 60 (39 R and 21 D).

Presidential Vote

1980	Reagan (R)	529,688	(61%)
	Carter (D)	246,843	(28%)
	Anderson (I)	76,952	(9%)
1976	Ford (R)	418,642	(56%)
	Carter (D)	295,602	(40%)

SENATORS

Sen. Barry Goldwater (R) Elected 1968, seat up 1986; b. Jan. 1, 1909, Phoenix; home, Phoenix; U. of AZ, 1928; Episcopal.

Career Maj. Gen., USAFR, 1937–67; Phoenix City Cncl., 1949–51; U.S. Sen., 1952–64; Repub. Nominee for Pres., 1964.

Offices 353 RSOB, 202-224-2235. Also 5429 Fed. Bldg., Phoenix 85025, 602-261-4086; and Fed. Bldg., Su. 7-G, Tucson 85701, 602-792-6334.

Committees *Armed Services* (3d). Subcommittees: Tactical Warfare (Chairman); Strategic and Theater Nuclear Forces; Preparedness. *Commerce, Science and Transportation* (2d). Subcommittees: Aviation; Communications (Chairman); Science, Technology, and Space. *Select Committee on Indian Affairs* (2d). *Select Committee on Intelligence* (Chairman).

Group Ratings

	ADA	ACLU	COPE	CFA	LCV	LWV	NTU	NSI	COC	ACA	CSFC
1982	10	39	9	0	7	33	92	88	86	76	75
1981	0	—	9	0	13	—	89	—	92	86	82
1980	0	13	18	7	12	29	63	86	83	100	83

National Journal Ratings

	Economic		Foreign		Cultural	
1982	1%	(LIB)	40%	(LIB)	53%	(LIB)
	98%	(CONS)	59%	(CONS)	46%	(CONS)
1981	28%	(LIB)	20%	(LIB)	0%	(LIB)
	71%	(CONS)	78%	(CONS)	99%	(CONS)

Key Votes

1) Reagan 81 Budget	FOR	5) $ to El Salvador	FOR	9) Poor Pay Food Stamps	FOR
2) Reagan 81 Tax Cut	FOR	6) Saudi AWACS Sale	FOR	10) Ban Crt Busing Order	—
3) Bal Budget Amend	FOR	7) Ban Abortion	AGN	11) Clinch Riv Brdr Rctr	FOR
4) Gas & Road Tax	—	8) Nerve Gas Prod	FOR	12) Legal Services Corp	—

Election Results

1980 general	Barry Goldwater (R)	432,371	(50%)	($949,992)
	Bill Schulz (D)	422,972	(49%)	($2,073,232)
1980 primary	Barry Goldwater (R)	140,765	(100%)	
1974 general	Barry Goldwater (R)	320,396	(58%)	($394,042)
	Jonathan Marshall (D)	229,523	(42%)	($129,260)

Campaign Contributions and Expenditures

	1981–82		*PACS brkdwn*		
Receipts	$979,055	Agr	$14,100	Ideo	$25,240
Expend.	$949,992	Bus	$223,738	Lbr	$4,700
Unspent	$29,062	Hlth	$16,550	Prof	$6,800

Sen. Dennis DeConcini (D) Elected 1976, seat up 1988; b. May 8, 1937, Tucson; home, Tucson; U. of AZ, B.A. 1959, LL. B. 1963; Roman Catholic.

Career Army Adjutant General Corps, 1959–60; Practicing atty., 1963–65, 1968–73; Special Counsel, A. A. to Gov. Samuel P. Goddard, 1965–67; Pima Cnty. Atty., 1973–76.

Offices 328 HSOB, 202-224-4521. Also AZ Bank Bldg., 101 N. 1st St., Su. 1634, Phoenix 85003, 602-261-6756; and 301 W. Congress, Tucson 85701, 602-792-6831.

Committees Appropriations (13th). Subcommittees: Foreign Operations; Interior; Treasury, Postal Service, and General Government. *Judiciary* (5th). Subcommittees: Constitution; Courts; Patents, Copyrights and Trademarks. *Rules and Administration* (5th). *Veterans' Affairs* (4th). *Select Committee on Indian Affairs* (3d). *Joint Committee on the Library* (5th).

Group Ratings

	ADA	ACLU	COPE	CFA	LCV	LWV	NTU	NSI	COC	ACA	CSFC
1982	45	43	59	70	62	70	47	78	53	50	58
1981	45	—	56	43	31	—	43	—	53	61	51
1980	67	37	67	20	34	33	40	60	56	39	40

National Journal Ratings

	Economic		*Foreign*		*Cultural*	
1982	66%	(LIB)	37%	(LIB)	45%	(LIB)
	33%	(CONS)	62%	(CONS)	54%	(CONS)
1981	60%	(LIB)	57%	(LIB)	30%	(LIB)
	39%	(CONS)	42%	(CONS)	69%	(CONS)

Key Votes

1) Reagan 81 Budget	FOR	5) $ to El Salvador	AGN	9) Poor Pay Food Stamps	—
2) Reagan 81 Tax Cut	FOR	6) Saudi AWACS Sale	AGN	10) Ban Crt Busing Order	FOR
3) Bal Budget Amend	FOR	7) Ban Abortion	FOR	11) Clinch Riv Brdr Rctr	AGN
4) Gas & Road Tax	FOR	8) Nerve Gas Prod	AGN	12) Legal Services Corp	FOR

Election Results

1982 general	Dennis DeConcini (D)	413,951	(59%)	($2,086,401)
	Pete Dunn (R)	292,638	(41%)	($884,517)
1982 primary	Dennis DeConcini (D)	140,328	(84%)	
	Caroline P. Killeen (D)	25,909	(16%)	
1976 general	Dennis DeConcini (D)	400,334	(54%)	($597,405)
	Sam Steiger (R)	321,236	(43%)	($679,384)
1976 primary	Dennis DeConcini (D)	121,423	(53%)	
	Carolyn Warner (D)	71,612	(32%)	
	Wade Church (D)	34,266	(15%)	

Campaign Contributions and Expenditures

1979–82		Direct Cont. 81-82		PACS brkdwn			
Receipts	$2,093,816	Indiv	$1,406,258	Agr	$40,075	Ideo	$47,575
Expend.	$2,086,401	Party	$17,500	Bus	$237,711	Lbr	$107,450
Unspent	$107,324	PACS	$541,585	Hlth	$30,500	Prof	$18,950

Indirect Party Expend: $37,500 *Indep Expend:* For: $4,414 (NRA) Agn: $26,592 (NCPAC)

GOVERNOR

Gov. Bruce E. Babbitt (D) Elected 1978, term expires Jan. 1987; b. June 27, 1938, Flagstaff; home, Phoenix; Notre Dame U., B.S. Marshall Scholar, U. of Newcastle, England, M.S. 1963, Harvard U., J.D. 1965; Roman Catholic.

Career Spec. Asst. to the Dir. of VISTA, 1965-67; Practicing atty., 1967–74; Atty. Gen. of AZ, 1974–78.

Offices Capitol West Wing, 9th Flr., Phoenix 85007, 602-255-4331.

Election Results

1982 gen.	Bruce E. Babbitt (D)	455,760	(62%)
	Leo Corbet (R)	236,857	(32%)
	One other	36,680	(5%)
1982 prim.	Bruce E. Babbitt (D)	142,559	(86%)
	Steve Jancek (D)	23,492	(14%)
1978 gen.	Bruce E. Babbitt (D)	282,605	(52%)
	Evan Mecham (R)	241,093	(45%)

FIRST DISTRICT

Phoenix is the archetype of the Sun Belt city, an almost instant metropolis created not in response to geographical imperative but in spite of it. Phoenix is almost totally the product of the air-conditioned years after World War II. In 1940 Phoenix had 65,000 residents; in 1950, 106,000; by 1970 the metropolitan area had nearly one million and in 1980 1½ million. There is little evidence of tradition or heritage here: almost every building is new, and the concessions to Indian or Mexican styles are clearly in the idiom of the 1970s. Many people think Phoenix is a giant retirement village, and there is one huge retirement development, Del Webb's Sun City, nearby. But statistically, metropolitan Phoenix is a young city, full of energetic young people with growing families, eager to work their way up from whatever level of society they came from. There are all kinds of opportunities: top-level executive and professional jobs, white collar and engineering opportunities in many high tech industries, including the giants of the semiconductor business, Motorola and Intel. There are also lots of low-wage jobs for immigrants from south of the border.

Technologically advanced, Phoenix is politically conservative. Not conservative in the Burkean sense, however: this is not a place that seeks to maintain ancient institutions, tightly knit communities, or webs of interlocking relationships that go back generations. On the contrary, most Phoenix residents have left these behind. Here conservatism means devotion to abstract principle, to the ideal of the untrammeled free market, opposition to unionization

ARIZONA — **Congressional Districts, Counties, and Selected Places** — *(5 Districts)*

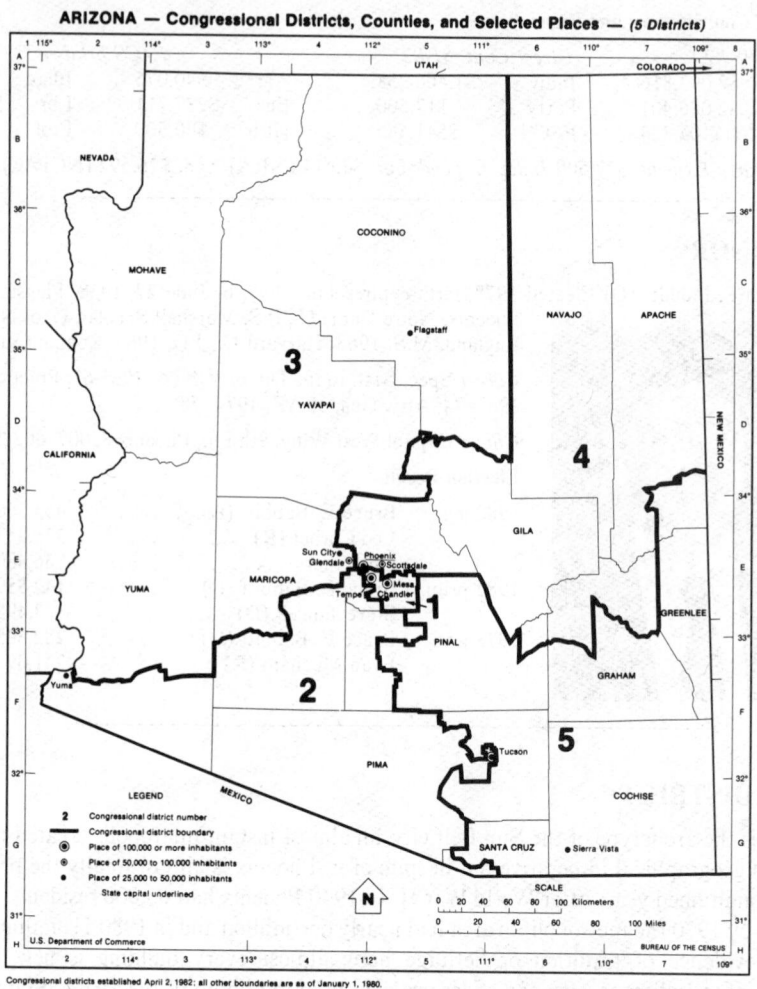

and minimum wages, abhorrence of government welfare programs. Of all the nation's states, Arizona probably comes closest to this conservative ideal, but it is still that, an ideal; Phoenix, reluctantly, is part of the American welfare state. Such an abstract politics comes naturally, it seems, to engineers and technicians, whose work it is to make unruly nature conform to concrete principle and abstract rule, and to upwardly mobile migrants, who have staked their lives on change and movement and who believe—or want to—that the system works fairly.

The 1st congressional district of Arizona is the only one wholly within the Phoenix metropolitan area. It includes some of the comfortable neighborhoods east of downtown Phoenix and north of Sky Harbor Airport. The district dips south of the Salt River and includes some black and low- income neighborhoods, but it also extends to the high- income areas near the Arizona Biltmore and takes in the southern half of high-income Scottsdale. To the south and east it includes two suburbs, each with its own distinctive character, of more than 100,000 people. One is Tempe, home of Arizona State University. Here are dozens of 1960s and 1970s subdivisions with curved streets and cul-de-sacs; income levels are high, although you won't find many members of Phoenix's establishment. To the east, along the old U.S. 60 and 89 that leads to Tucson, is Mesa, a city whose central focus is a Mormon temple. This is very much a family-oriented suburb, except for some of the trailer parks in the east where the city gives way to desert. The 1st includes a corner of desert, as well as the old desert town of Chandler, becoming part of suburbia now that freeways bring it within easy driving distance of Phoenix.

Although the 1st does include a few Democratic precincts in Phoenix, this is a solidly Republican district. Incumbent John Rhodes, after 30 years in the House and with a residence in Mesa, could have held this seat if he wanted to. But he relinquished the position of minority leader in 1980, after seven years, in frank recognition of the fact that many aggressive young Republicans wanted a more pugnacious style of leadership than he was inclined to provide. Having given that up, he decided to retire from the House altogether in 1982. That meant the new congressman would be chosen in the Republican primary. The result was a close four-way primary. Donna Carlson-West, the candidate identified by some as a moderate, finished fourth, but with a respectable 20%. The winner, John McCain, had 32%.

McCain is the son of a distinguished admiral, was a career Navy man himself, and spent six years in a North Vietnamese prisoner of war camp. As a Pentagon lobbyist he became friendly with senators like John Tower and William Cohen; on retirement from the Navy he moved to Tempe. He was attacked during the campaign as a carpetbagger—an odd charge, since it would disqualify most Arizonans and most retired military officers from running for political office. He had the support of other retired military men, and in Washington he can be expected to be friendly to increased defense spending.

The People Pop. 1980: 543,747, up 47.8% 1970–80; voting age pop. 399,698; 9% Span. orig., 3% Black, 1% Am. Ind., 1% Asian orig. 31% housing units rented. Median owner $60,600; renter $228. Households: 69% family, 35% with children, 58% married couples.

Presidential Vote

1980	Reagan (R)	111,319	(65%)
	Carter (D)	43,340	(25%)
	Anderson (I)	15,557	(9%)

Rep. John McCain (R) Elected 1982; b. Aug. 29, 1936, Panama Canal Zone; home, Tempe; U.S. Naval Acad., 1958, National War College, 1973–74; Episcopal.

Career Naval Officer, 1954–81.

Offices 1123 LHOB, 202-225-2635. Also 1255 W. Baseline Rd., Su. 151, Mesa 85202, 602-897-0892.

Committees *Interior and Insular Affairs* (13th). Subcommittees: Energy and the Environment; Water and Power Resources; Mining, Forest Management and BPA. *Select Committee on Aging* (18th). Subcommittee: Health and Long-Term Care.

Group Ratings and Key Votes: Newly Elected

Election Results

1982 general	John McCain (R)	89,116	(66%)	($569,545)
	William E. Hegarty (D)	41,261	(31%)	($20,620)
1982 primary	John McCain (R)	15,363	(32%)	
	Ray Russell (R)	12,500	(26%)	($251,722)
	James A. Mack (R)	10,675	(22%)	($179,978)
	Donna Carlson-West (R)	9,736	(20%)	($120,399)
1980 general	John J. Rhodes (R)	136,961	(73%)	($191,809)
	Steve Jancek (D)	40,045	(21%)	($0)

Campaign Contributions and Expenditures

1981–82		*Direct Cont. 81-82*				*PACS brkdwn*		
Receipts	$579,481	Indiv	$295,302	Agr	$4,800	Ideo	$14,400
Expend.	$569,545	Party	$17,280	Bus	$68,967	Lbr	$—
Unspent	$9,934	PACS	$105,286	Hlth	$6,550	Prof	$3,375
		Cand	$167,100				

SECOND DISTRICT

The 2d congressional district of Arizona is an object lesson in creative redistricting. It owes its shape to the determination of a partisan legislature. Yet it failed to achieve its framers' goals—as happens with many redistricting plans. Arizona Republicans, in solid control of the legislature, wanted to put about as many Democrats into this one district as they could, so the others would be Republican. Yet another district, the newly created 5th, ended up electing a Democrat as well. The 2d contains almost all the Democratic precincts of Phoenix with the Democratic parts of the often Democratic city of Tucson, 120 miles away. Also included is Yuma, 180 miles across the desert on the other side of Phoenix, an agricultural center on the Colorado River and, on a given day, usually one of the hottest places in the United States. The few towns connecting these three points have mostly been excised from the 2d, leaving a few Indian reservations and a lot of desert. That leaves a district in which 30% of the adults are of Spanish origin, 5% Black, and 4% Indian.

The three urban segments are only superficially similar. Nearly half the district's population is in Phoenix, and it includes the city's downtown and the state Capitol. Even so, this is in many ways a peripheral part of Phoenix. There are low and middle income neighborhoods on the west side of town, where there is less grass (water is expensive) and fewer palm trees than in most parts of Phoenix; the vacant lots between the small stucco houses and the gaudy roadside establishments grow easily back into small patches of desert. South of downtown and the Capitol is an industrial zone, where the railroad tracks run; on the other side of the tracks and the Salt River are Phoenix's small all-black neighborhoods and mostly Mexican-American areas. Here the atmosphere is almost rural: jerry-built houses with no grass, old cars strewn here and there. Tucson is different: here the 2d includes not just the downtown, but most of the city except for its high-income periphery. Tucson, overshadowed demographically by Phoenix, has always been the more Democratic of the two cities; it is somewhat more blue collar, more Mexican-American, less high-tech, not blessed with so many corporate headquarters. Copper, though not actually mined in Tucson, is important; most of the U.S. copper supply comes from within a 100-mile radius, and many of the services ancillary to the copper industry are here. The 2d's portion of Tucson includes the University of Arizona; it has few blacks, but 42% of its residents are of Spanish origin.

The congressman from the 2d district is Morris Udall, who has been both a presidential candidate and one of the most legislatively productive members of the House. First elected to Congress in 1961, to fill the place of his brother Stewart who became Secretary of the Interior, Mo Udall has many legislative accomplishments. One is our current campaign finance law, the source of much carping, but a measure which has substantially improved the political process. Another is the civil service reform of 1978. Udall labored for years in the dull vineyards of the Post Office and Civil Service Committee; this bill moves, finally, at least a little toward making government employees more accountable. Udall's most noted efforts have been in the environmental field. Since 1977 he has chaired the Interior Committee, which has jurisdiction over national parks, mining and mineral exploration, government land, Indian tribes, and American overseas possessions. He has always been counted as a friend, though not an automatic vote, by environmentalists. During the Carter years, when the committee and the administration were of similar views, he had a number of accomplishments, most notably a comprehensive strip mining law and the Alaska Lands Act. In the Reagan years, Udall and his committee have been at odds with Interior Secretary Watt. But their differences have not made headlines so often as they might: Udall is temperamentally disinclined to harsh controversy, and on occasion (as when Watt's religious views were mocked) he has insisted that his own allies conduct themselves more civilly. His perseverance paid off in at least some victories, as in early 1983 when Watt said he would no longer encourage mineral exploration of wilderness lands.

Udall has also had his disappointments. He was unable to persuade even a heavily Democratic Congress to pass postcard voter registration. His proposals for public financing of congressional elections languished in the late 1970s. He encountered spirited opposition at home on his proposals for mining reform, and though he backed down, he failed to carry copper-mining Cochise County in 1978 or 1980 (it is now in the 5th district). His national stature seems to have hurt rather than helped him at home, and he had an uncomfortably close call in the 1978 election. Only after extensive personal campaigning and expensive TV advertising was he able to win convincingly in 1980. For 1982 he had his choice of districts. Choosing the 2d would clearly produce an easy win, though he complained he would have to buy TV time in Phoenix (where he had never run before) as well as Tucson. Choosing the 5th would have been risky: even in 1980 he had lost most of the high-income parts of Tucson and the mining country which, together, make up most of the new district. As it happens, Cochise County lawyer James McNulty was able to win the 5th—and probably ran more strongly than Udall could have.

Following the 1982 elections and Edward Kennedy's announcement that he would not run, Udall considered becoming a presidential candidate again. His first candidacy, in 1976, was inspired by fellow House members, who thought he would make a good president—at least as good as many of the senators who were running. He described himself then as the leading progressive in the race, and he ran creditable—and sometimes heartbreakingly close—seconds in primaries from New Hampshire at the beginning of the season to Ohio at the end. But he never finished first, and some of his strongest showings were achieved when it seemed clear that Jimmy Carter had already clinched the nomination.

But Udall declined to run again, and even his admirers admit he has handicaps. First is his reputation—not entirely deserved—for standing on the left of his party. Voters in 1982 were clearly distressed by the results of Reaganomics, but they were just as clearly not in favor of some of the big government and other programs Udall has been associated with in the past. His second handicap is health: he has Parkinson's disease and promised that he would not run if doctors did not approve; but some voters may be dubious even so. His third handicap is a quality that has helped make him a great legislator: his good nature. Udall is a man who listens to his adversaries' arguments, who instinctively concedes their good faith, who works hard to reach a sensible middle ground between views. He has strong beliefs, but also a willingness to compromise. His friends and admirers include many, like Barry Goldwater, who share his views on few issues. In the House, this helps him forge legislation that can win majority support. On the presidential campaign trail, however, he may lack the driving ambition that keeps winning candidates chipper 20 hours a day and that leads them to attack their opponents' jugulars when they are exposed. He has, finally, a finely honed comic delivery and a sense of humor directed as often against himself as against his adversaries.

If Udall chooses to remain in the House, he should be able to win reelection without difficulty. And, given Arizona's late filing date, he can compete in the presidential primaries and even at the national convention without giving up his chance to run for reelection. Should he not run in the 2d, the district will surely go Democratic, presumably after a vigorous primary that could produce Arizona's first Mexican-American congressman.

The People   Pop. 1980: 543,187, up 21.9% 1970–80; voting age pop. 372,734; 30% Span. orig., 5% Black, 4% Am. Ind., 1% Asian orig. 36% housing units rented. Median owner $40,300; renter $185. Households: 71% family, 42% with children, 56% married couples.

Presidential Vote

1980	Reagan (R)	64,211	(48%)
	Carter (D)	55,877	(42%)
	Anderson (I)	13,765	(10%)

Rep. Morris K. Udall (D) Elected May 2, 1961; b. June 15, 1922, St. Johns; home, Tucson; U. of AZ, J.D. 1949; Mormon.

Career Air Force, WWII; Pro basketball player, Denver Nuggets, 1948–49; Practicing atty., 1949–61; Pima Cnty. Atty., 1952–54.

Offices 235 CHOB, 202-225-4065. Also 301 W. Congress, Tucson 85701, 602-792-6404.

Committees *Interior and Insular Affairs* (Chairman). Subcommittees: Energy and the Environment (Chairman); Mining, Forest Management and BPA; Water and Power Resources. *Post Office and Civil Service* (2d). Subcommittees: Civil Service; Investigations.

Group Ratings

	ADA	ACLU	COPE	CFA	LCV	LWV	NTU	NSI	COC	ACA	CSFC
1982	85	87	85	90	73	70	11	40	25	17	28
1981	75	—	85	71	76	—	19	—	17	14	39
1980	61	77	67	50	61	67	16	25	61	14	32

National Journal Ratings

	Economic		Foreign		Cultural	
1982	88%	(LIB)	76%	(LIB)	99%	(LIB)
	12%	(CONS)	23%	(CONS)	0%	(CONS)
1981	81%	(LIB)	60%	(LIB)	81%	(LIB)
	15%	(CONS)	40%	(CONS)	19%	(CONS)

Key Votes

1) Reagan 81 Budget	AGN	5) Incr SS Rtmt Age	FOR	9) Poor Pay Food Stamps	AGN
2) Reagan 81 Tax Cut	AGN	6) Saudi AWACS Sale	AGN	10) Ban Crt Busing Order	AGN
3) Bal Budget Amend	AGN	7) $ for MX Missile	AGN	11) Auto Local Content	FOR
4) Gas & Road Tax	FOR	8) Nerve Gas Prod	AGN	12) Nuclear Arms Freeze	FOR

Election Results

1982 general	Morris K. Udall (D)	29,391	(71%)	($840,142)
	Roy B. Laos (R)	28,407	(27%)	($134,619)
1982 primary	Morris K. Udall (D)	29,391	(100%)	
1980 general	Morris K. Udall (D)	127,786	(58%)	($763,650)
	Richard H. Huff (R)	88,653	(40%)	($696,954)

Campaign Contributions and Expenditures

1981–82		Direct Cont. 81-82		PACS brkdwn			
Receipts	$794,533	Indiv	$667,500	Agr	$2,850	Ideo	$15,000
Expend.	$840,142	Party	$1,750	Bus	$26,975	Lbr	$54,140
Unspent	$487	PACS	$113,458	Hlth	$1,000	Prof	$6,050

Indep Expend: Agn: $50

THIRD DISTRICT

Like three other Arizona districts, the 3d is a hybrid—a combination of part of metropolitan Phoenix with sparsely populated non-metropolitan counties. Like the 4th, unlike the 2d, this was designed to be, and is, a Republican district. It extends north to the Grand Canyon and the Utah border, west to the Colorado River and newly built towns like Lake Havasu City, the incongruous site of the transplanted London Bridge. This huge expanse of land is almost entirely desert, punctuated by just a few of these fast-growing developments. But not all of rural Arizona is desert. The 3d also covers the mountains around Prescott and Flagstaff, high ground, some of which is tree-covered if not verdant.

But most of the people, 60%, of the 3d district live in Maricopa County, in or near Phoenix. The district includes part of the city itself, a strip along the northwest side that is affluent, although not fashionable; next door is the sociologically similar suburb of Glendale, with nearly 100,000 people. Interestingly, about 13% of the residents of these areas are of Spanish origin: it is a mistake to picture Mexican-Americans in Phoenix as huddled in an impoverished ghetto, for most live in rather pleasant, and diverse, neighborhoods like this. Northwest Phoenix and Glendale are young, populated mainly by families with children—a reminder of the suburbia that was so common in the 1950s. In terms of age, the next suburb out—Sun City—is a vivid contrast: it allows no residents under 50, three-fourths of its residents are over 65, and has its own cemetery and hospital as well as eight golf courses. In terms of attitudes, however, the differences are not necessarily so stark. For 30 years ago Sun City residents were living a life not so very different—except for the climate—as their neighbors are now.

Politically, the 3d district is not, theoretically, as heavily Republican as the 4th on the east side of Phoenix. The people here are of humbler socioeconomic origins and still vote for occasional Democrats. But on all the major issues—economic, foreign, cultural—their instincts go with the Republicans on the national level.

Congressman Bob Stump has similar leanings. He started off as a cotton and grain farmer, in the rich irrigated lands west of Phoenix: the green splotches you see from the air as you bank toward Sky Harbor. He was elected to the state legislature in 1958 as a Democrat, when they were still the majority party; he was state Senate president in 1975-76, when the 1974 election gave them a majority again. His politics have been solidly conservative; although his farm benefited from generous federal water policies, he has been a foe of government spending generally. When the 3d district's Sam Steiger ran for the Senate in 1976, Stump won a close race for the Democratic nomination and won the general election easily.

Stump's record in the House, from the beginning, was much closer to most Republicans than most Democrats. Electorally, his only problems were in the Democratic primary. He was one of the few non-southern Democrats to support the Reagan budget and tax proposals in 1981. So it was not much of a surprise when he announced in 1982 that he would run for re-election as a Republican. This was one of only two such party switches, although the administration hoped for many more; and the other convert, Eugene Atkinson of Pennsylvania, was defeated in 1982. Stump also drew significant opposition in the person of Democrat Pat Bosch, who had run Steiger a close race in 1974; but even in the Democratic year of 1982 Stump won by a very comfortable margin. As a Republican, Stump does not have much seniority of course, but he is in a position, politically and legislatively, where he will feel comfortable.

The People   Pop. 1980: 544,870, up 90.8% 1970–80; voting age pop. 389,150; 9% Span. orig., 4% Am. Ind., 1% Black, 1% Asian orig. 20% housing units rented. Median owner $58,3000; renter $222. Households: 78% family, 39% with children, 69% married couples.

Presidential Vote

1980	Reagan (R)	126,418	(69%)
	Carter (D)	45,051	(24%)
	Anderson (I)	12,412	(7%)

Rep. Bob Stump (R) Elected 1976; b. Apr. 4, 1927, Phoenix; home, Tolleson; AZ St. U., B.S. 1951; Seventh Day Adventist.

Career Navy, WWII; Cotton and grain farmer; AZ House of Reps., 1958–66; AZ Senate, 1967–76, Senate Pres., 1975–76.

Offices 211 CHOB, 202-225-4576. Also 5001 Fed. Bldg., Phoenix 85025, 606-261-6923.

Committees *Armed Services* (7th). Subcommittees: Investigations; Research and Development. *Select Committee on Intelligence* (4th). Subcommittee: Program and Budget Authorization.

Group Ratings

	ADA	ACLU	COPE	CFA	LCV	LWV	NTU	NSI	COC	ACA	CSFC
1982	0	8	10	0	3	10	96	100	89	95	83
1981	0	—	12	7	0	—	95	—	95	91	80
1980	0	17	17	14	13	0	73	100	71	83	82

National Journal Ratings

	Economic		Foreign		Cultural	
1982	7%	(LIB)	4%	(LIB)	14%	(LIB)
	92%	(CONS)	92%	(CONS)	86%	(CONS)
1981	4%	(LIB)	3%	(LIB)	0%	(LIB)
	79%	(CONS)	87%	(CONS)	100%	(CONS)

Key Votes

1) Reagan 81 Budget	FOR	5) Incr SS Rtmt Age	FOR	9) Poor Pay Food Stamps	FOR
2) Reagan 81 Tax Cut	FOR	6) Saudi AWACS Sale	FOR	10) Ban Crt Busing Order	FOR
3) Bal Budget Amend	FOR	7) $ for MX Missile	FOR	11) Auto Local Content	AGN
4) Gas & Road Tax	AGN	8) Nerve Gas Prod	FOR	12) Nuclear Arms Freeze	AGN

Election Results

1982 general	Bob Stump (D)	101,198	(63%)	($296,458)
	Pat Bosch (R)	58,644	(37%)	($89,608)
1982 primary	Bob Stump (D)	42,008	(100%)	
1980 general	Bob Stump (D)	141,448	(64%)	($88,979)
	Bob Croft (R)	65,845	(30%)	($2,799)

Campaign Contributions and Expenditures

1981–82		*Direct Cont. 81-82*				*PACS brkdwn*		
Receipts	$280,712	Indiv	$103,293	Agr	$5,600	Ideo	$17,105
Expend.	$296,458	Party	$17,205	Bus	$96,400	Lbr	$—
Unspent	$43,418	PACS	$128,536	Hlth	$7,350	Prof	$1,250

Indirect Party Expend: $14,745 *Indep Expend:* For: $17,026 (AMA, NRA)

FOURTH DISTRICT

In the northeast part of the Phoenix metropolitan area, in the shadow of and behind Camelback Mountain and Squaw Peak, live most of the city's richest and most prominent citizens. Their neighborhoods spill over municipal boundaries and include parts of Phoenix, Scottsdale, and Paradise Valley (where the median house value in 1980, according to the Census Bureau, was $190,000). The sunlight falls on the desert with a kind of hush here; the careful landscaping of houses and estates contrasts with the bluff stone of the mountains that punctuate Phoenix's plain and with the brown earth and vagrant cactus plants on the land that has been left undeveloped. Shopping centers affect western decor here, and galleries are full of paintings depicting the Old West; but inside the houses you can find furniture of just about any period you want. The planting of such a comfortable and secure civilization in such an inhospitable environment—it seldom rains, but when it does anything near a usually dry creek bed can get washed away—is one of the generally unappreciated triumphs of American civilization.

This corner of greater Phoenix is the heart of Arizona's 4th congressional district. It includes just about all of Phoenix north of Camelback Road and east of 35th Avenue—square mile after square mile of affluent, new neighborhoods and subdivisions. For people here the life style of the Phoenix elite is something of a model; they are people to be admired, imitated, identified with. The most affluent and the most heavily Republican part of Arizona, this part of Phoenix and Maricopa County accounts for 71% of the 4th district.

The rest of the district could not be more different. It is familiar enough terrain for affluent Phoenix: they see it in every edition of *Arizona Highways* on their coffee tables. But conditions of life in the pictures and around the coffee tables are in stark contrast. The 4th hops northeast over the Mazatzal and Sierra Ancha Mountains to pick up the copper mining towns of Globe and Miami; the Fort Apache Indian Reservation; the dusty Route 66 towns of Holbrook and Winslow, lined with gas stations; and the Navajo and Hopi Reservations to the north. The Navajo are by far the nation's largest organized tribe; they have an active politics, fiercely contested tribal elections, disputes over whether and on what terms they should allow strip mining of coal and the burning of it in the giant Four Corners power plants; and in 1982 they elected a new tribal chairman. The Navajo also have a burning dispute with the much less numerous Hopi, whose reservation they surround. Barry Goldwater, long a friend of the Navajo, took the Hopi's side, opposing Navajo leasing of Hopi land, and lost a lot of Navajo votes in 1980; Dennis DeConcini and New Mexico's Pete Domenici take the other side.

This part of the 4th district is, to varying degrees, poor—certainly in comparison with affluent Phoenix. Hundreds of workers have been laid off in the copper mines, and it is not clear when, if ever, American production will be economically competitive with foreign operations. The Indians are still, by white standards, desperately poor, though their economic condition has improved. Only in the last dozen years have they come onto the voter rolls in large numbers; the result has been that Apache County (misnamed: it is mostly Navajo) is now a solid Democratic bastion. Overall, however, this is a solidly Republican district. In 1972, when it was newly created, and in 1976, when incumbent John Conlan ran for the Senate, it was seriously contested by high-spending Democrats.

Since then, it has been won easily by Republican Eldon Rudd. After a career in the FBI and local government, he seemed a safe and solid conservative, and he has not disappointed his backers. He is a quiet, faithful member of the Republican Conference, a member of the Appropriations Committee. Past 60, he is not one of the young Republican firebrands of the House, but he often votes with them on substantive issues. With no serious primary opposition since he was first elected in 1976, Rudd must be considered to have a safe seat.

The People Pop. 1980: 543,493, up 65.9% 1970–80; voting age pop. 375,192; 12% Am. Ind., 5% Span. orig., 1% Asian orig., 1% Black. 23% housing units rented. Median owner $66,200; renter $267. Households: 76% family, 42% with children, 64% married couples.

Presidential Vote

1980	Reagan (R)	121,224	(68%)
	Carter (D)	42,325	(24%)
	Anderson (I)	13,841	(8%)

Rep. Eldon Rudd (R) Elected 1976; b. July 15, 1920, Camp Verde; home, Scottsdale; AZ St. U., B.A. 1947, U. of AZ, J.D. 1949; Roman Catholic.

Career USMC, WWII; Practicing atty., 1949; Spec. Investigator, FBI, 1950–70; Maricopa Cnty. Bd. of Supervisors, 1972–76.

Offices 2244 RHOB, 202-225-3361. Also 6009 Fed. Bldg., 230 N. 1st Ave., Phoenix 85025, 602-261-4803.

Committee *Appropriations* (14th). Subcommittees: Energy and Water Development; Treasury, Postal Service, and General Government.

Group Ratings

	ADA	ACLU	COPE	CFA	LCV	LWV	NTU	NSI	COC	ACA	CSFC
1982	5	0	9	10	3	9	90	100	89	95	77
1981	0	—	9	7	0	—	75	—	94	81	72
1980	6	13	11	7	17	20	59	100	71	95	84

National Journal Ratings

	Economic		Foreign		Cultural	
1982	6%	(LIB)	1%	(LIB)	4%	(LIB)
	94%	(CONS)	99%	(CONS)	87%	(CONS)
1981	21%	(LIB)	18%	(LIB)	4%	(LIB)
	79%	(CONS)	73%	(CONS)	90%	(CONS)

Key Votes

1) Reagan 81 Budget	FOR	5) Incr SS Rtmt Age	FOR
2) Reagan 81 Tax Cut	FOR	6) Saudi AWACS Sale	AGN
3) Bal Budget Amend	FOR	7) $ for MX Missile	FOR
4) Gas & Road Tax	—	8) Nerve Gas Prod	FOR

9) Poor Pay Food Stamps	FOR
10) Ban Crt Busing Order	FOR
11) Auto Local Content	AGN
12) Nuclear Arms Freeze	AGN

Election Results

1982 general	Eldon Rudd (R)	95,620	(66%)	($248,536)
	Wayne O. Earley (D)	44,182	(30%)	($110,878)
1982 primary	Eldon Rudd (R)	31,918	(100%)	
1980 general	Eldon Rudd (R)	142,565	(63%)	($228,663)
	Les Miller (D)	85,046	(37%)	(153,345)

Campaign Contributions and Expenditures

1981–82		Direct Cont. 81-82		PACS brkdwn			
Receipts	$299,854	Indiv	$162,997	Agr	$3,800	Ideo	$2,655
Expend.	$248,536	Party	$10,150	Bus	$67,710	Lbr	$—
Unspent	$159,347	PACS	$85,585	Hlth	$4,950	Prof	$2,950

FIFTH DISTRICT

Every ten years, with each new census, congressional districts are reapportioned among the states. Every ten years since 1950, Arizona has gained one new seat, and now it has five. Most of Arizona's growth has been Republican, and Republicans gained the new seats after the 1950 and 1970 censuses, and in 1966 they won the new seat created after the 1960 census. They expected as well to win the new 5th district created for the 1982 election. It was designed by a Republican legislature, and within its boundaries Republican candidates had won margins over Democrats in 1978 and 1980—which is all the more notable since the Democrat then running in most of this area was Arizona's most durable liberal, Morris Udall. Yet the Republicans failed to carry the 5th district and, unless they win it back soon, may have lost it for a decade.

The 5th district is split between two roughly equal halves: the Tucson area and the rural counties to the north and east. The 5th's portion of Tucson is very carefully defined. It includes the eastern part of the city, newer, more prosperous, and less Mexican-American than Tucson as a whole; the affluent neighborhoods in the hills and mountainsides overlooking the city from the north; Davis-Monahan Air Force Base; and the community of Green Valley to the south. This is Republican territory, though not so heavily Republican as corresponding areas of Phoenix; it went Republican in the close 1982 election.

The rural parts of the district are a collection of the older, pre-air conditioning Arizona.

They include the little Pinal County towns of Coolidge, Casa Grande, and Eloy, oases on or near the main highway between the two metropolises; the mining towns of San Manuel, Safford, Clifton, and Morenci, cleft between mountains, with large Mexican-American populations; the Cochise County mining towns of Bisbee and Douglas, and Sierra Vista near giant Fort Huachuca. The southern part of the district sits squarely on the Mexican border; and although there is much local concern over illegal immigration, in fact the percentage of Mexican-Americans is less than in some other parts of the state. The bigger problem locally is the apparent demise of the American copper mining industry: mines are being closed and workers, accustomed to generous wages and fringe benefits, are at a loss what to do. The copper mining areas voted against Morris Udall in 1978 and 1980, but they went Democratic in 1982.

One reason was anger at Reaganomics. Another was the local popularity of the Democratic nominee, James McNulty. Although he has more than a trace of his native Massachusetts in his accent, McNulty has lived all his adult life in Arizona and practiced law in Bisbee. He served in the legislature, started to run for Congress in 1976 when it looked as though Morris Udall might be nominated for president, ran for the Senate himself in 1980 and lost the primary to Phoenix apartment house millionaire Bill Schulz, and then ran for Congress in 1982 with little primary opposition. The Republican nominee, Tucson legislator Jim Kolbe, helped to draw the district lines himself and won the primary easily. The general election presented a sharp, if not stark, contrast in philosophy. McNulty called for a balanced budget, but in general he is not far out of line with national Democrats. He can be almost certain of serious competition again in 1984; he will have the advantages of incumbency, but in a good Republican year it will be hard to prevent a creditable Republican candidate from running up sizable margins in the affluent parts of Tucson.

The People   Pop. 1980: 542,918, up 55.6% 1970–80; voting age pop. 389,954; 14% Span. orig., 2% Black, 1% Asian orig., 1% Am. Ind. 27% housing units rented. Median owner $57,800; renter $216. Households: 75% family, 39% with children, 64% married couples.

Presidential Vote

1980	Reagan (R)	106,516	(57%)
	Carter (D)	60,250	(32%)
	Anderson (I)	21,377	(11%)

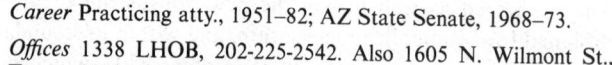

Rep. James F. McNulty (D) Elected 1982; b. Oct. 18, 1925, Boston, MA; home, Tucson; U. of AZ, B.A. 1948, U. of AZ Col. of Law, J.D. 1951; Roman Catholic.

Career Practicing atty., 1951–82; AZ State Senate, 1968–73.

Offices 1338 LHOB, 202-225-2542. Also 1605 N. Wilmont St., Tucson 85712, 602-629-6030.

Committees *Interior and Insular Affairs* (27th). Subcommittees: Water and Power Resources; Mining, Forest Management and BPA. *Public Works and Transportation* (21st). Subcommittee: Surface Transportation; Water Resources.

Group Ratings and Key Votes: Newly Elected

Election Results

1982 general	Jim McNulty (D)	82,938	(50%)	($343,318)
	Jim Kolbe (R)	80,531	(48%)	($532,588)
1982 primary	Jim McNulty (D)	41,670	(83%)	
	Soleng Tom (D)	8,789	(17%)	($16,647)
1980 general	Newly created district			

Campaign Contributions and Expenditures

1981–82		*Direct Cont. 81-82*			*PACS brkdwn*			
Receipts	$350,868	Indiv	$217,225	Agr	$3,200	Ideo	$11,000
Expend.	$343,318	Party	$5,500	Bus	$11,300	Lbr	$57,700
Unspent	$7,548	PACS	$91,401	Hlth	$1,000	Prof	$2,050
		Cand	$28,800				

ARKANSAS

Two decades ago the outlook for Arkansas was bleak. The state pretty much deserved the Dogpatch reputation it had across the nation. Since the days of the Great Depression, its young people had left by the thousands, looking for jobs elsewhere. The state's population peaked at nearly 2 million in 1940 and fell 163,000 over the next 20 years. Arkansas's reputation as a tolerant border state was shattered by the machinations of Governor Orval Faubus, who blocked enforcement of a federal court integration order and forced President Eisenhower to send federal troops into Little Rock's Central High. (The Little Rock episode, however, enabled Faubus to become the first Arkansas governor to win a third term.) Throughout, Arkansas's income and education levels were among the lowest in the nation. By any measure Arkansas was in trouble in the early 1960s.

Today Arkansas is in much better shape. Its income levels are still below the national average, but the gap has narrowed greatly, and increasing differentials in the cost of living have made Arkansas's relatively low wages and salaries worth much more than they would be in a big northeastern metropolitan area. Segregation has long since been left behind, and education and other services have been improved. Much of the credit for these developments must go to the late Governor Winthrop Rockefeller, who served only four years (1966-70), but who turned the state around in that short time. Rockefeller, like many southern governors, worked hard at attracting jobs, especially in small factories that could be located out near where people had grown up; he repudiated segregation and in effect liberated every politician from the race issue ever since. He increased spending and improved the quality of government services—steps that, contrary to supply side doctrine, aided rather than discouraged economic growth. And he established a more positive attitude toward Arkansas, a sense that the state was more than a backwater, that it could advance and provide good livelihoods for its citizens.

The other reason for the change in Arkansas's fortunes is a basic change in American patterns of migration. In the 20 years after World War II, the great internal migrations were from the rural areas of the South and Midwest to the giant metropolitan areas and their expanding economies. People pursued opportunity anywhere they could find it in a time of economic growth. But in the 1970s a contrary trend became apparent. Americans, now at a level of prosperity and with a standard of living much higher than a generation before, no longer felt as much of an urge to leave their home towns to make a living. The end of segregation made southern home towns more attractive to many blacks. Finally, the growth of truck transportation made many once isolated areas accessible. Americans became willing to pay a price—to forego higher wages or commute 50 miles over freeways—in order to live in rural areas or small towns, with their slower pace of life and more traditional cultural atmosphere.

The result was a gigantic migration that didn't take place: people in rural southern and plains states stayed put rather than move, and the population of states like Arkansas, after plummeting for 20 years, began to grow again. Arkansas stopped losing most of its talented young people, and during the 1970s there was net migration into, not out of, the state. In fact, there was a countermigration—a migration of people from northern cities and suburbs and from Arkansas's own urban areas to the rural, mountainous counties of the northern part of the state. The Ozarks are one of those resort areas that attracted thousands of new year-round residents in the 1970s. In all, that decade saw the fastest population growth in Arkansas since the 1900-10 decade. Net migration into Arkansas stopped in the recession of the early 1980s; will it begin again if prosperity returns?

For all of Winthrop Rockefeller's success as a governor, he was not much of a success as a Republican politician: almost all the state's leading politicians since have been Democrats, and for much of the 1970s this was one of the nation's most Democratic states. Then there was a sharp shift to the Republicans in the late 1970s, plain for all to see in 1980 election results; in 1982, the state seemed to go back to its Democratic ways, but to what extent is not yet clear. The Democratic strength was heralded by the victory of country lawyer Dale Bumpers over Rockefeller in 1970; Bumpers was a racial moderate and economic liberal who acknowledged that his own success would not have been possible without Rockefeller's trailblazing example. By 1974, when Bumpers beat William Fulbright in the Senate primary, Democratic dominance seemed established: the state's own Republican congressman was nearly defeated. Arkansas seemed to have a glut of talented young Democratic politicians: Bumpers, his successor as governor David Pryor, Attorney General and Congressman Jim Guy Tucker, Congressman Ray Thornton, Attorney General and Governor Bill Clinton. Inevitably, their ambitions collided, and talk of their national potential did not necessarily do them good at home. In 1980 Democrats faced several unpopular issues. Governor Clinton was criticized for raising license plate fees and for spending too much time on national issues.

Democrats were also hurt by the decision to house Cuban refugees in Fort Chaffee, near the state's second largest city, Fort Smith. This was one of two major entry points for the Cubans, chosen because the base was available and, perhaps, because it seemed unlikely to cause much political trouble for President Carter, who had won 65% of Arkansas's votes in 1976. Such a calculation, if it was made, overlooked the fear people in a homogeneous area can feel about alien creatures in their midst. Lurid stories, mostly apocryphal, began circulating about crimes committed by the internees and about homosexual refugees. Arkansans, like most Americans called on to make sacrifices these days, were quick to believe they had been unfairly singled out. The Fort Smith area and, to a lesser extent, the entire state turned against the Democrats. Jimmy Carter lost Arkansas to Ronald Reagan, Dale Bumpers's percentage was reduced from 85% in 1974 to 59%, and Bill Clinton lost in one of the nation's biggest upsets to Little Rock businessman Frank White.

By 1982, the refugees were gone, and the Democrats rebounded. Clinton, after a primary fight with Lieutenant Governor Joe Purcell and Jim Guy Tucker, beat White in a rematch (Arkansas is one of four states that elects its governor every two years), and one of the state's two Republican congressmen came much closer to defeat than expected. But the Democratic majorities did not match those of the middle 1970s, and Arkansas is by no means certain to be a one-party state.

Governor. The 1982 election was a contest between two governors, each with their weaknesses. Clinton's background—Yale Law, Rhodes Scholar, a lawyer wife who used her maiden name and had her own successful career—helped bring him to the notice of the national media when he first took office (some, absurdly, mentioned this 32-year-old incoming governor of a small state as a possible president); that same background, and his attention to national issues, hurt him when he got into trouble over license plate fees and Cuban refugees. Frank White's background as a businessman showed in the blunt, sometimes embarrassing way he defended his actions. He got in trouble for raising costs for prescriptions for the elderly, allowing utility rate increases and then taking a free trip on the utility's airplane, and signing the bill requiring "balanced treatment" in public school science classes of the theory of evolution and the Biblical theory of creation. That led to a nationally publicized trial in which the law was declared unconstitutional—and which made Arkansas look more backward and silly than it is.

In his 1982 campaign Clinton made a point of admitting errors and his personal demeanor was different: his hair was cut shorter and his wife called herself Hilary Clinton. He presumably will avoid his earlier mistakes and not seek the national spotlight. He had his chance in 1981, when he was mentioned as a candidate for the Democratic national chairmanship; he declined to run, and in effect committed himself to an Arkansas political career. Since neither of the state's Senate seats is likely to be open soon, and both are held by politicians of similar outlook, Clinton will likely try to remain governor. There is no constitutional limit on the number of terms he can serve.

Senators. For 30 years Arkansas had the same two senators, John McClellan and William Fulbright. McClellan, nearly beaten by David Pryor in the 1972 primary, was preparing to retire when he died in 1978; Fulbright was beaten in the 1974 primary by Dale Bumpers. Men of different views and interests, they both were men of substance and left a mark. Bumpers and Pryor are more similar in background and views: both are from small towns, both served two years as governor, both are quite different from the old Dixiecrat stereotype.

Dale Bumpers sprang from a small town law practice straight to the governorship, with an assist from political consultant Deloss Walker, who specializes in finding such candidates. But it would be a mistake to see him simply as the product of political packaging. Bumpers is pleasant, fluent, sincere but not cloying, able to master difficult issues easily. In general his voting record resembles that of many northern Democrats—not those who take their lead from organized labor, to be sure, but like many of those recently elected who oppose Reagan positions on many but not all issues. On the Energy Committee he has taken positions opposed by the oil companies (there is some oil in Arkansas, but far less than in Louisiana or even Mississippi) and has backed a federal role in matters like energy conservation. He is not ready to trust the unalloyed workings of the free market. Yet he is suspicious enough of government to have been the main sponsor of a bill to remove the presumption in federal courts that federal regulations are valid—a measure some think would produce government-by-litigation.

In the Republican Senate, Bumpers does not often make headlines, as he did in the Democratic Senate when he declined to be the 60th vote to break the filibuster against the AFL-CIO's labor law reform. In 1982 his greatest national notice came when he rose to answer Jeremiah Denton's charge that his wife was working with Communists in support of nuclear disarmament. But he has other distinctions. He was one of three senators (Bradley and Hollings were the others) to support President Reagan's 1981 spending cuts and oppose his tax cuts—a set of positions which, if adopted, would have trimmed the deficit to near nothing. He was the only southern senator willing to vote against an antibusing measure, because he had doubts about its constitutionality.

Bumpers was mentioned in 1983, as he has been in the past, as a presidential candidate; but after much consultation he decided in April 1983 not to make the race. He cited the difficulties of fundraising and his own preference for the life of being a senator; he seems to have the confidence that he has answers for the nation's problems, but it is not clear whether he has the fire and ambition to run a campaign. Bumpers was reelected in 1980 against a weak opponent by a much smaller margin than expected. Most people ascribe this to the reaction to the Cuban refugees at Fort Chaffee and do not regard it as evidence of a permanent loss of popularity at home. But no one expects him to be defeated, or even to be in major trouble, when he seeks reelection in 1986.

David Pryor, first elected to Congress at age 32 as a small town lawyer and editor, made a name for himself as one of the most liberal of southern representatives. That was in 1966 and 1967. It was news then when Pryor worked in a nursing home himself and then set up informal hearings in a trailer when he was denied subcommittee hearings on the subject; it was news when, coming from a district that supported Goldwater and Wallace for president, he voted for civil rights legislation; it was news when he voted at the 1968 national convention against the seating of the regular Mississippi delegation. Given that record, it is striking how close Pryor came to beating John McClellan in 1972 and how easily he won the governorship in 1974 and 1976.

Now Pryor is no longer counted as one of the most liberal southern members. During his years as governor, he seemed to grow distinctly skeptical of the value of some government programs, and in the Senate his voting record on economic issues is far to the right of Bumpers's. On foreign policy issues, he is inclined to favor cuts in the Reagan defense budget and a cautious approach overseas, but he rather seldom takes non-traditional views on cultural issues. As a freshman Democrat in a Republican Senate, he has not taken a lead role on major national issues. Instead he has concentrated on issues affecting the aging, and on matters too small to win national headlines but still important enough to affect peoples' lives. Examples include consumer mail order protection and Social Security disability procedures.

Pryor had to win a tough three-way primary for his Senate seat in 1978. The first primary was a nearly even three-way contest with then-Congressmen Jim Guy Tucker and Ray Thornton; in the runoff he beat Tucker largely by citing Tucker's labor support. The general election was effectively uncontested. The question for 1984 is whether Pryor will encounter serious opposition in either the primary or the general election.

Presidential politics. If the Cuban refugee issue is given credit for Ronald Reagan's victory in Arkansas in 1980, then it is likely that this will be, with West Virginia, one of the most Democratic states in the South in 1984. Democratic incumbents Clinton and Pryor will presumably have an incentive to swell Democratic turnout in the general election. Arkansas has a presidential primary scheduled for May 29, late in the season. This seems unlikely to be seriously contested; the state has a small delegation, and strategists will likely assume that it will be carried by any candidate who dominates the southern primaries. That is how Arkansas's primaries have worked out in the past.

Congressional districting. Only minor changes were made in redistricting. The city of Hot Springs, sometimes Republican, was shifted from the 3d district to the 4th.

The People Est. Pop. 1982: 2,291,000; Pop. 1980: 2,286,435, up .2% 1980–82 and 18.9% 1970–1980; .99% of U.S. total, 33d largest; voting age pop. 1,615,061; 14% Black, 1% Spanish origin. Single ancestry: 18% English, 6% Irish, 4% German, 1% French. Registered voters (1982): 1,116,082 Total. 11% with 1–3 yrs. col., 10% with 4+ yrs. col. 18.7% below poverty level. 27% housing units rented; median house value: $31,100; median monthly rent: $129. Households: 77% family, 41% with children, 65% married couples.

1982 Share of Federal Tax Burden $4,137,100,000; .69% of U.S. total, 33d largest.

1982 Share of Federal Expenditures

	Total		Non-Defense		Defense	
Total Expend	$5,100m	(0.84%)	$4,115m	(0.97%)	$985m	(0.55%)
St/Lcl Grants	844m	(0.96%)	842m	(0.95%)	2m	(5.56%)
Salary/Wages	466m	(0.60%)	183m	(0.67%)	283m	(0.56%)
Ind Payments	3,116m	(1.09%)	2,680m	(1.04%)	436m	(1.53%)
Procurement	610m	(.42%)	94m	(0.30%)	516m	(0.45%)
Other Programs	64m	(1.18%)	63m	(1.17%)	1m	(2.33%)
Loan/Insurance	1,464m	(2.29%)	1,458m	(2.36%)	6m	(0.27%)

Political Lineup Governor, Bill Clinton (D). Senators, Dale Bumpers (D) and David Pryor (D). Representatives, 4 (2 D and 2 R). State Senate, 35 (32 D and 3 R); State House of Representatives, 100 (93 D and 7 R).

Presidential Vote

1980	Reagan (R)	....	403,164	(48%)
	Carter (D)	....	398,041	(48%)
	Anderson (I)	....	22,468	(3%)
1976	Ford (R)	....	267,903	(35%)
	Carter (D)	....	498,604	(65%)

1980 Democratic Presidential Primary

Carter	269,290	(60%)
Kennedy	78,503	(18%)
One other	19,459	(4%)
Uncommitted	80,940	(18%)

SENATORS

Sen. Dale Bumpers (D) Elected 1974, seat up 1986; b. Aug. 12, 1925, Charleston; home, Charleston; U. of AR, Northwestern U., LL. B. 1951; United Methodist.

Career USMC, WWII; Practicing atty., 1951–70; Charleston City Atty.; Gov. of AR, 1970–74.

Offices 3229 DSOB, 202-224-4843. Also 2527 Fed. Bldg., 700 W. Capitol, Little Rock 72201, 501-378-6286.

Committees *Appropriations* (14th). Subcommittees; District of Columbia, Interior; Legislative Branch; Commerce, Justice, State, the Judiciary. *Energy and Natural Resources* (3d). Subcommittees: Energy and Mineral Resources; Energy Research and Development; Public Lands and Reserved Water. *Small Business* (3d). Subcommittees: Capital Formation and Retention; Government Procurement.

Group Ratings

	ADA	ACLU	COPE	CFA	LCV	LWV	NTU	NSI	COC	ACA	CSFC
1982	85	79	61	90	77	91	24	22	21	28	33
1981	95	—	60	57	79	—	21	—	24	15	32
1980	56	50	53	27	58	75	35	33	41	35	38

National Journal Ratings

	Economic		Foreign		Cultural	
1982	98%	(LIB)	81%	(LIB)	75%	(LIB)
	1%	(CONS)	18%	(CONS)	24%	(CONS)
1981	82%	(LIB)	81%	(LIB)	78%	(LIB)
	17%	(CONS)	18%	(CONS)	21%	(CONS)

Key Votes

1) Reagan 81 Budget	FOR	5) $ to El Salvador	AGN	9) Poor Pay Food Stamps	AGN
2) Reagan 81 Tax Cut	AGN	6) Saudi AWACS Sale	AGN	10) Ban Crt Busing Order	AGN
3) Bal Budget Amend	AGN	7) Ban Abortion	AGN	11) Clinch Riv Brdr Rctr	AGN
4) Gas & Road Tax	AGN	8) Nerve Gas Prod	FOR	12) Legal Services Corp	FOR

Election Results

1980 general	Dale Bumpers (D)	477,905	(59%)	($220,861)
	Bill Clark (R)	330,576	(41%)	($119,196)
1980 primary	Dale Bumpers (D) unopposed			
1974 general	Dale Bumpers (D)	461,056	(85%)	($335,874)
	John Harris Jones (R)	82,026	(15%)	($18,651)

Campaign Contributions and Expenditures

1979–80		PACS brkdwn			
Receipts	$299,465	Agr	$2,650	Ideo	$1,000
Expend.	$220,861	Bus	$33,875	Lbr	$2,000
Unspent	$79,499	Hlth	$6,800	Prof	$6,000

Sen. David Pryor (D) Elected 1978, seat up 1984; b. Aug. 29, 1934, Camden; home, Camden; U. of AR, B.A. 1957, LL.B. 1964; Presbyterian.

Career Ed. and Publisher, *Ouachita Citizen*, Camden, 1957–61; Practicing atty., 1964–66; U.S. House of Reps., 1967–72; Candidate for Dem. Nomination for U.S. Senate, 1972; Gov. of AR, 1975–78.

Offices 248 RSOB, 202-224-2353. Also Fed. Bldg., Su. 3030, Little Rock 72201, 501-387-6336.

Committees *Agriculture, Nutrition, and Forestry* (5th). Subcommittees: Agricultural Research and General Legislation; Nutrition; Rural Development, Oversight, and Investigations. *Finance* (9th). Subcommittees: Energy and Agricultural Taxation; Savings, Pensions and Investment Policy; Social Security and Income Maintenance Programs. *Special Committee on Aging* (4th). *Select Committee on Ethics* (2d).

Group Ratings

	ADA	ACLU	COPE	CFA	LCV	LWV	NTU	NSI	COC	ACA	CSFC
1982	70	57	52	80	66	70	45	20	45	39	46
1981	75	—	49	36	44	—	37	—	53	48	44
1980	44	53	42	7	33	67	38	44	59	46	42

National Journal Ratings

	Economic		Foreign		Cultural	
1982	69%	(LIB)	90%	(LIB)	58%	(LIB)
	30%	(CONS)	3%	(CONS)	41%	(CONS)
1981	54%	(LIB)	84%	(LIB)	51%	(LIB)
	45%	(CONS)	12%	(CONS)	48%	(CONS)

Key Votes

1) Reagan 81 Budget	FOR	5) $ to El Salvador	AGN	9) Poor Pay Food Stamps	AGN
2) Reagan 81 Tax Cut	FOR	6) Saudi AWACS Sale	AGN	10) Ban Crt Busing Order	FOR
3) Bal Budget Amend	FOR	7) Ban Abortion	AGN	11) Clinch Riv Brdr Rctr	AGN
4) Gas & Road Tax	AGN	8) Nerve Gas Prod	AGN	12) Legal Services Corp	—

Election Results

1978 general	David Pryor (D)	395,506	(77%)	($774,824)
	Thomas Kelly, Jr. (R)	84,308	(16%)	($16,208)
	John G. Black (I)	37,211	(7%)	($32,863)
1978 runoff	David Pryor (D)	265,525	(55%)	
	Jim Guy Tucker (D)	218,026	(45%)	($1,019,659)
1978 primary	David Pryor (D)	198,039	(34%)	
	Jim Guy Tucker (D)	187,568	(32%)	
	Ray Thornton (D)	184,095	(32%)	($1,004,515)
	One other (D)	8,166	(1%)	
1972 general	John L. McClellan (D)	386,398	(61%)	($516,573)
	Wayne H. Babbitt (R)	248,238	(39%)	

Campaign Contributions and Expenditures

1977–78		PACS brkdwn			
Receipts	$802,861	Agr	$11,400	Ideo	$2,700
Expend.	$774,824	Bus	$62,280	Lbr	$500
Unspent	$28,037	Hlth	$15,900	Prof	$5,000

GOVERNOR

Gov. Bill Clinton (D) Elected Nov. 82, term expires Jan. 1985; b. Aug. 19, 1946, Hope; home, Little Rock; Georgetown U., B.A. 1968, Rhodes Scholar, Oxford U., 1969–70, Yale U., J.D. 1973; Baptist.

Career Law Professor, U. of AR, 1973–76; Dem. Nominee for U.S. House of Reps., 1974; Atty. Gen. of AR, 1977–78; Gov. of AR, 1978–80.

Offices State Capitol, Little Rock 72201, 501-371-2345.

Election Results

1982 gen.	Bill Clinton (D)	431,855	(55%)
	Frank D. White (R)	357,496	(45%)
1982 runoff	Bill Clinton (D)	239,209	(54%)
	Joe Purcell (D)	206,358	(46%)
1982 prim.	Bill Clinton (D)	236,961	(42%)
	Joe Purcell (D)	166,066	(29%)
	Jim Guy Tucker (D)	129,362	(23%)
1980 gen.	Frank D. White (R)	435,684	(52%)
	Bill Clinton (D)	403,241	(48%)

FIRST DISTRICT

Eastern Arkansas—the flat, fertile, cotton-growing plains that line the west bank of the Mississippi River—is economically more tied to Mississippi or to Memphis, Tennessee, than to the hilly regions of central Arkansas or the Ozark Mountains. Like the Delta in Mississippi and the Bootheel in Missouri, eastern Arkansas is occupied by large farms and even plantations where, until the last two decades, whites imposed a life of segregation on the large black population. This part of the state seldom favored any form of upcountry populism, but it has always retained at least a nominal Democratic allegiance. Today, with segregation gone and other old antagonisms forgotten, eastern Arkansas remains the most Democratic part of the state. It went solidly for Jimmy Carter in 1980, and on the basis of the 1982 results seems solidly 2-1 Democratic today.

Eastern Arkansas forms about half of Arkansas's 1st congressional district. The district also includes some hill counties to the northwest, added after the 1970 and 1980 censuses. Nonetheless, this is basically an agricultural area. Its largest cities are West Memphis, a tiny hamlet staring across the levees and the river, barely able to make out the towers of Memphis in the distance; and Jonesboro, home of Arkansas State University.

The 1st district's congressman, Bill Alexander, is the House's Assistant Majority Whip, the

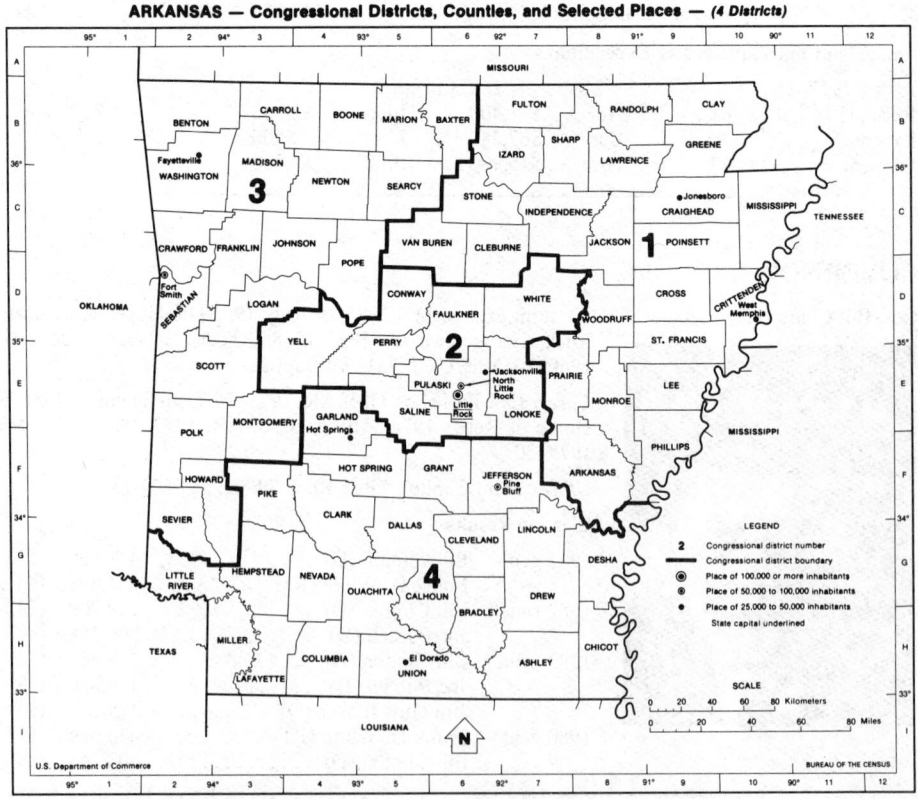

ARKANSAS — Congressional Districts, Counties, and Selected Places — (4 Districts)

Congressional districts established February 25, 1982 ; all other boundaries are as of January 1, 1980.

number four man in the Democratic Party leadership. He was chosen for that position by Speaker O'Neill and Majority Leader Jim Wright after the 1980 election. Oddly, in a House that elects committee and subcommittee chairmanships, this high post is appointive; the reason, apparently, is that that procedure allows the Democrats to balance their leadership, regionally and ideologically. Alexander's selection seems designed to do that. He is indisputably from the Deep South, from a district represented for years by a Dixiecrat—quite a contrast from Tip O'Neill's Massachusetts 8th, Whip Thomas Foley's Washington 5th, or even Jim Wright's Texas 12th, in the gritty, cowpoke's city of Fort Worth. Alexander's voting record on economic issues has for some time been not too far distant from those of northern Democrats; on foreign and cultural issues, he has little tint of liberalism.

All this, and his basic competence, makes him an acceptable member of the leadership. But some think he holds the position more because he is not seen as a threat by others who are in the leadership or would like to be some day than because he is a strong candidate for a higher leadership position himself. His chances were not helped when he deserted the Democrats on a difficult vote on the Appropriations Committee in 1982, voting to report to the floor a measure the leadership opposed. Alexander might be a good choice, again as a kind of ticket-balancer, for majority leader; it seems unlikely that anything like the present Democratic Caucus would make him speaker. He retains a fairly high ranking on the Appropriations Committee and is in line to be chairman of the Commerce, Justice, State, and Judiciary Subcommittee.

Back home, he may have become used to winning reelection unopposed, but after he won the leadership post, Republicans targeted him and poured money into the race. That forced him to raise money and campaign, but in retrospect it seems that he was never in danger of losing: he won at least 58% in each of the district's counties. It seems unlikely the Republicans will try again soon, unless Alexander gets in trouble on some specific issue.

The People Pop. 1980: 573,551, up 9.5% 1970–80; voting age pop. 396,107; 16% Black, 1% Span. orig. 29% housing units rented. Median owner $28,000; renter $99. Households: 78% family, 43% with children, 65% married couples.

Presidential Vote

1980			
	Reagan (R)	88,732	(45%)
	Carter (D)	103,906	(53%)
	Other	4,049	(2%)

Rep. Bill Alexander (D) Elected 1968; b. Jan 16, 1934, Memphis, TN; home, Osceola; U. of AR, Southwestern U. at Memphis, B.A. 1957, Vanderbilt U., LL.B. 1960; Episcopal.

Career Army, 1951–53; Practicing atty., 1960–69.

Offices 233 CHOB, 202-225-4076. Also Fed. Bldg., Jonesboro 72401, 501-972-1550.

Committee *Appropriations* (13th). Subcommittees: Agriculture, Rural Development; Commerce, Justice, State and Judiciary; Military Construction.

Group Ratings

	ADA	ACLU	COPE	CFA	LCV	LWV	NTU	NSI	COC	ACA	CSFC
1982	40	42	62	60	45	55	7	75	42	22	34
1981	45	—	60	50	40	—	5	—	24	38	44
1980	44	40	56	43	31	70	15	25	80	33	31

National Journal Ratings

	Economic		Foreign		Cultural	
1982	66%	(LIB)	56%	(LIB)	60%	(LIB)
	34%	(CONS)	43%	(CONS)	40%	(CONS)
1981	66%	(LIB)	0%	(LIB)	50%	(LIB)
	34%	(CONS)	99%	(CONS)	50%	(CONS)

Key Votes

1) Reagan 81 Budget	AGN	5) Incr SS Rtmt Age	FOR	9) Poor Pay Food Stamps	AGN
2) Reagan 81 Tax Cut	AGN	6) Saudi AWACS Sale	FOR	10) Ban Crt Busing Order	—
3) Bal Budget Amend	AGN	7) $ for MX Missile	—	11) Auto Local Content	FOR
4) Gas & Road Tax	FOR	8) Nerve Gas Prod	FOR	12) Nuclear Arms Freeze	FOR

Election Results

1982 general	Bill Alexander (D)	124,208	(65%)	($504,281)
	Chuck Banks (R)	67,427	(35%)	($236,462)
1982 primary	Bill Alexander (D) unopposed			
1980 general	Bill Alexander (D) unopposed			($50,289)

Campaign Contributions and Expenditures

1981–82		Direct Cont. 81–82*			PACS brkdwn		
Receipts	$447,210	Indiv	$237,444	Agr	$22,100	Ideo	$8,050
Expend.	$504,281	Party	$3,525	Bus	$73,450	Lbr	$36,800
Unspent	$43,785	PACS	$144,719	Hlth	$1,700	Prof	$2,250

Indep Expend: For: $1,556 (NRA) Agn: $2,150 (NTLPAC) *Non-Cand Loans:* $40,000

SECOND DISTRICT

The 2d congressional district of Arkansas is the center of the state—geographically and politically as well. A little more than half its population lives in Pulaski County, including the state capital of Little Rock, with its large black and affluent white neighborhoods, and North Little Rock, a kind of industrial suburb across the Arkansas River known informally for years as Dog Town, because at the turn of the century Little Rock officials, peeved that North Little Rock was allowed to incorporate separately, dumped all its stray dogs there. The district also includes several hill counties to the north and, in the southeast, part of the flat, cotton-growing Mississippi plain. Little Rock made an international name for itself forcibly resisting integration of Central High School in 1957; President Eisenhower had to send in federal troops when Governor Orval Faubus refused to enforce the court order. But Little Rock has since overcome this reputation and has become one of the politically more progressive cities in the South. It supported Republican Governor Winthrop Rockefeller and his three Democratic successors, Dale Bumpers, David Pryor, and Bill Clinton; it has elected progressive candidates at about every level. Unlike most southern cities, Little Rock is not the Republican bastion of the state; in 1980 it gave Jimmy Carter a hefty plurality even as he was losing Arkansas as a whole.

In congressional elections, the 2d district has been a reasonably faithful example of recent changes in Arkansas's congressional representation. Once this small, poor state specialized in allowing its representatives to accumulate great seniority: for example, an Arkansas district, ultimately the 2d, elected longtime Ways and Means Committee Chairman Wilbur Mills every two years from 1938 to 1974. (The margin in that last election was close: that was the year of the Fanne Fox scandal.) More recently, Arkansas politicians seem to regard a congressional seat, like the office of state attorney general, as a sort of political launching pad. Both David Pryor and Ray Thornton gave up the 4th district seat to seek statewide office, and so, after serving only one term, did Mills's successor in the 2d, Jim Guy Tucker.

The present incumbent, Republican Ed Bethune, seems to want to stay in Washington for a while. But it is not clear if he will be able to do so. He surprised just about everyone when he won this usually Democratic seat in 1978, and he won by a huge margin in 1980, even while Jimmy Carter carried the district. But he got only 54% of the vote in 1982 against an opponent who was underfinanced because no one thought Bethune was vulnerable. Bethune used to work for Winthrop Rockefeller and does not have a background of being sympathetic to segregation that some southern Republicans do. But in the House, starting with his service as chairman of the freshman Republican class of 1978 and continuing with his service on the Budget Committee, he has been an aggressive and faithful partisan. He must be more than that—or he must count on a strong national Republican trend in 1984—in order to win another term.

The People Pop. 1980: 569,116, up 24.5% 1970–80; voting age pop. 401,104; 15% Black, 1% Span. orig. 30% housing units rented. Median owner $37,300; renter $160. Households: 76% family, 43% with children, 63% married couples.

Presidential Vote

1980	Reagan (R)	90,488	(46%)
	Carter (D)	98,096	(50%)
	Other	7,110	(4%)

Rep. Ed Bethune (R) Elected 1978; b. Dec. 19, 1935, Pocohontas; home, Searcy; Little Rock Jr. Col., 1957–58, U. of AR, B.S. 1961, J.D. 1963; United Methodist.

Career USMC, 1954–57; Randolph Cnty. Dpty. Prosecuting Atty., 1963–64; FBI Agent, 1964–68; Practicing atty., 1968–.

Offices 1535 LHOB, 202-225-2506. Also 1527 New Fed. Ofc. Bldg., Little Rock 72201, 501-378-5941.

Committees Banking, Finance and Urban Affairs (6th). Subcommittees: Economic Stabilization; Financial Institutions Supervision, Regulation and Insurance; Housing and Community Development. Budget (5th). Task Forces: Budget Process; Economic Policy and Growth.

Group Ratings

	ADA	ACLU	COPE	CFA	LCV	LWV	NTU	NSI	COC	ACA	CSFC
1982	10	25	18	10	35	36	83	89	86	87	65
1981	15	—	21	50	29	—	72	—	89	79	68
1980	11	20	11	29	17	30	54	100	69	74	76

National Journal Ratings

	Economic		Foreign		Cultural	
1982	13%	(LIB)	32%	(LIB)	24%	(LIB)
	86%	(CONS)	68%	(CONS)	75%	(CONS)
1981	33%	(LIB)	18%	(LIB)	37%	(LIB)
	66%	(CONS)	73%	(CONS)	63%	(CONS)

Key Votes

1) Reagan 81 Budget	FOR	5) Incr SS Rtmt Age	FOR	9) Poor Pay Food Stamps	FOR
2) Reagan 81 Tax Cut	FOR	6) Saudi AWACS Sale	AGN	10) Ban Crt Busing Order	—
3) Bal Budget Amend	AGN	7) $ for MX Missile	FOR	11) Auto Local Content	AGN
4) Gas & Road Tax	—	8) Nerve Gas Prod	AGN	12) Nuclear Arms Freeze	AGN

Election Results

1982 general	Ed Bethune (R)	96,775	(54%)	($229,050)
	Charles George (D)	82,913	(46%)	($345,360)
1982 primary	Ed Bethune (R) unopposed			
1980 general	Ed Bethune (R)	159,148	(79%)	($193,207)
	James Reid (D)	42,278	(21%)	($14,919)

Campaign Contributions and Expenditures

1981–82		Direct Cont. 81-82		PACS brkdwn			
Receipts	$172,370	Indiv	$100,239	Agr	$2,000	Ideo	$1,100
Expend.	$229,050	Party	$4,893	Bus	$41,695	Lbr	$—
Unspent	$12,903	PACS	$48,263	Hlth	$3,750	Prof	$500

Indirect Party Expend: $4,808

THIRD DISTRICT

The 3d district of Arkansas is the northwest and western part of the state—a region of green hills rising to mountains, of historic poverty but recent prosperity. The new economic climate comes in part from retirees and young people attracted by the area's mild climate, its scenic mountains and reservoirs, by its jobs in small industries, by its low-keyed pace of life, and by its fidelity to traditional values. The cities of the 3d are medium-sized, the kind of place most Americans say they would like to live in. Among them are Fort Smith, on the Oklahoma border, which erupted in anger and fear when nearby Fort Chaffee was filled with Cuban refugees in 1980; Fayetteville, site of the University of Arkansas; Bentonville, up near the Missouri border. The last is the headquarters of the Wal-Mart discount chain whose success has made its owner, Sam Walton, and his family worth some $690 million. Despite his success, he still lives in Bentonville and, according to *Forbes,* drives a beat-up Chevrolet with dog-teeth marks on the steering wheel.

The hills of northwestern Arkansas have always harbored more Republicans than any other part of the state, and for most of the 20th century this was the only part of Arkansas with two party politics. The Republicanism here was the ornery type, often encountered in southern hill country, a vestige of opposition to slavery and the Civil War. In Iowa people are Republicans because they identify with established authority; here they are Republicans because they defy it. In 1966 the Republicans were finally successful here. They helped to elect Winthrop Rockefeller, and in the 3d district they elected Republican State Chairman John Paul Hammerschmidt as their congressman.

As a congressman Hammerschmidt has been a reliable member of the Republican Conference and on the Public Works Committee he has tended to support pork barrel projects. It is the record one would expect of the representative of a rural district whose lakes were mostly created by federally built dams and whose barge industry depends on federal navigation projects. Hammerschmidt is ranking Republican on the House Veterans Affairs Committee and tends to take the point of view of the traditional veterans' organizations, which—more oriented to World War II era veterans—are skeptical about increasing benefits for Vietnam era veterans and oppose cuts in or elimination of the separate system of VA hospitals.

Hammerschmidt's issue positions and constituency work have been a recipe for political success. He has had tough opposition only once, in 1974, when Bill Clinton, then a 28-year-old law professor at the University of Arkansas, ran a vigorous campaign here. In that Watergate year Clinton held him to 52% of the vote. Hammerschmidt had no such trouble in 1982. Recent population increases seem to have strengthened the Republicans, although the Cuban refugee issue no longer works for them in the Fort Smith area and the new party followers are probably less feisty than traditional Arkansas Republican voters. Hammerschmidt won reelection with 66% of the vote and seems unlikely to be challenged seriously in the future.

The People Pop. 1981: 572,937, up 33.3% 1970–80; voting age pop. 414,806; 2% Black, 1% Span. orig., 1% Am. Ind. 24% housing units rented. Median owner $32,200; renter $147. Households: 77% family, 39% with children, 68% married couples.

Presidential Vote

1980	Reagan (R)	134,908	(60%)
	Carter (D)	84,426	(37%)
	Other	7,229	(3%)

Rep. John Paul Hammerschmidt (R) Elected 1966; b. May 4, 1922, Harrison; home, Harrison; The Citadel, OK A&M Col., U. of AR; Presbyterian.

Career Army Air Corps, WWII; Bd. Chmn., Hammerschmidt Lumber Co.; Chmn., Repub. State Central Comm., 1964–66.

Offices 2207 RHOB, 202-225-4301. Also Fed. Bldg., Fayetteville 72701, 501-442-5215.

Committees *Public Works and Transportation* (2d). Subcommittees: Aviation (Ranking Member); Surface Transportation; Water Resources. *Veterans' Affairs* (Ranking Member). Subcommittees: Compensation, Pension and Insurance; Hospitals and Health Care. *Select Committee on Aging* (2d). Subcommittee: Housing and Consumer Interests.

Group Ratings

	ADA	ACLU	COPE	CFA	LCV	LWV	NTU	NSI	COC	ACA	CSFC
1982	5	17	16	30	16	33	63	100	86	65	62
1981	5	—	16	7	0	—	57	—	89	83	68
1980	6	27	10	14	17	30	49	100	73	77	72

National Journal Ratings

	Economic		Foreign		Cultural	
1982	25%	(LIB)	19%	(LIB)	4%	(LIB)
	75%	(CONS)	80%	(CONS)	87%	(CONS)
1981	4%	(LIB)	3%	(LIB)	25%	(LIB)
	79%	(CONS)	87%	(CONS)	74%	(CONS)

Key Votes

1) Reagan 81 Budget	FOR	5) Incr SS Rtmt Age	FOR	9) Poor Pay Food Stamps	FOR
2) Reagan 81 Tax Cut	FOR	6) Saudi AWACS Sale	FOR	10) Ban Crt Busing Order	FOR
3) Bal Budget Amend	FOR	7) $ for MX Missile	FOR	11) Auto Local Content	AGN
4) Gas & Road Tax	FOR	8) Nerve Gas Prod	FOR	12) Nuclear Arms Freeze	AGN

Election Results

1982 general	John Paul Hammerschmidt (R) ...	133,909	(66%)	($262,003)
	Jim McDougal (D)	69,089	(34%)	($121,540)
1982 primary	John Paul Hammerschmidt (R) unopposed			
1980 general	John Paul Hammerschmidt (R) unopposed			($42,307)

Campaign Contributions and Expenditures

1981–82		Direct Cont. 81-82		PACS brkdwn			
Receipts	$252,335	Indiv	$155,082	Agr	$6,850	Ideo	$3,050
Expend.	$262,003	Party	$5,446	Bus	$58,495	Lbr	$—
Unspent	$33,997	PACS	$76,536	Hlth	$5,700	Prof	$2,100
		Cand	$1,948				

Indep Expend: For: $735 (NRA)

FOURTH DISTRICT

The 4th congressional district of Arkansas is, geographically, the southern third of the state. It stretches from the flat Delta lands along the Mississippi River, west across rolling hills to the resort town of Hot Springs and to Texarkana, a city situated so squarely on the Texas-Arkansas border that the state line runs through City Hall. The principal towns in the district are, with the exception of Hot Springs (once home to a major illegal gambling industry), quiet places: El Dorado (with a long A, please), just north of Louisiana and a center of oil production; Camden, the home of Senator David Pryor and of the late Senator John McClellan; Arkadelphia; and Pine Bluff, an old agricultural center with a large black population on the flat banks of the Arkansas River. Southern Arkansas, together with the flatlands west of the Mississippi to the north, is the section of Arkansas most clearly part of the Deep South. In racial makeup (24% black), economic base (cotton, oil, rice), mores (traditional Dixie), and political leanings (solidly Democratic for years, interrupted by enthusiasm for candidates like Barry Goldwater and George Wallace), the 4th district is the most indisputably southern part of Arkansas.

For a dozen years, even at the height of anti-civil rights feeling, the 4th district elected congressmen who seemed far out of the Dixiecrat tradition: David Pryor (1966-72, later governor and now senator) and Ray Thornton (1972-78, who voted to impeach Richard Nixon). Now its representation is more conservative in tone. Beryl Anthony, a lawyer who was a prosecutor for most of his career, edged veteran Secretary of State Winston Bryant (now lieutenant governor) in the 1978 runoff when Thornton ran for the Senate. Anthony seemed temperamentally inclined to work with other young conservatives first elected in 1978 and is a member of the group known informally as the Boll Weevils.

But he is also a practical politician representing a partisan Democratic constituency and eager to make a successful career in the House. A Budget Committee member, he voted with the Democrats, not the Republicans on the 1981 budget and tax issue, although he does not have as liberal a record on economic issues generally as many southern Democrats with similar districts. Anthony's stand proved to be good politics in 1982 and 1983. Republicans had not run a candidate in this district since 1966; they did in 1982, but Anthony got 66% of the vote. The district went solidly as well for Bill Clinton for governor. With the race issue almost entirely forgotten, and national Democrats no longer identified with avant garde positions on cultural issues, the 4th district looks like a more dangerous place for a Republican, not a Democrat.

Meanwhile, back in Washington, Anthony won a much-coveted place on the Ways and Means Committee—something he could not have hoped for had he voted with the Reaganites in 1981. Anthony's fate is likely to be a lesson to southern Democrats in the future—a lesson that it pays to play ball with the Democratic leadership.

The People   Pop. 1980: 570,831, up 11% 1970–80; voting age pop. 403,044; 25% Black, 1% Span. orig. 25% housing units rented. Median owner $26,200; renter $102. Households: 76% family, 40% with children, 63% married couples.

Presidential Vote

1980	Reagan (R)	89,036	(43%)
	Carter (D)	111,613	(54%)
	Other	4,080	(2%)

Rep. Beryl F. Anthony, Jr. (D) Elected 1978; b. Feb. 21, 1931, El Dorado; home, El Dorado; U. of AR, B.S., B.A. 1961, J.D. 1963; Lutheran.

Career Asst. Atty. Gen. of AR, 1964–65; Dpty. Union Cnty. Prosecutor, 1966–70; Prosecuting Atty., 13th Judicial Dist., 1971–76; Legal Counsel, Anthony Forest Products Co., 1977; Practicing atty., 1977–.

Offices 1117 LHOB, 202-225-3772. Also Fed. Bldg., P.O. Box 2021, El Dorado 71730, 501-863-0121.

Committee *Ways and Means* (20th). Subcommittees: Social Security; Oversight.

Group Ratings

	ADA	ACLU	COPE	CFA	LCV	LWV	NTU	NSI	COC	ACA	CSFC
1982	40	42	54	50	40	60	31	90	56	65	39
1981	30	—	50	7	23	—	7	—	33	50	47
1980	22	37	44	36	26	30	29	56	76	36	43

National Journal Ratings

	Economic		Foreign		Cultural	
1982	55%	(LIB)	58%	(LIB)	47%	(LIB)
	45%	(CONS)	42%	(CONS)	52%	(CONS)
1981	56%	(LIB)	2%	(LIB)	46%	(LIB)
	43%	(CONS)	97%	(CONS)	54%	(CONS)

Key Votes

1) Reagan 81 Budget	AGN	5) Incr SS Rtmt Age	FOR	9) Poor Pay Food Stamps	AGN
2) Reagan 81 Tax Cut	AGN	6) Saudi AWACS Sale	FOR	10) Ban Crt Busing Order	FOR
3) Bal Budget Amend	FOR	7) $ for MX Missile	AGN	11) Auto Local Content	AGN
4) Gas & Road Tax	FOR	8) Nerve Gas Prod	FOR	12) Nuclear Arms Freeze	FOR

Election Results

1982 general	Beryl F. Anthony, Jr. (D)	121,256	(66%)	($351,472)
	Bob Leslie (R)	63,661	(34%)	($186,180)
1982 primary	Beryl F. Anthony, Jr. (D)	115,540	(78%)	
	William Cain Lyon (D)	33,108	(22%)	
1980 general	Beryl F. Anthony, Jr. (D) unopposed			($101,235)

Campaign Contributions and Expenditures

1981-82		Direct Cont. 81-82		PACS brkdwn			
Receipts	$337,956	Indiv	$151,649	Agr	$16,100	Ideo	$7,400
Expend.	$351,472	Party	$3,946	Bus	$105,600	Lbr	$17,950
Unspent	$330	PACS	$167,921	Hlth	$16,600	Prof	$2,300
		Cand	$19,000				

CALIFORNIA

California is almost a nation by itself. During the 1980 presidential campaign, Ronald Reagan liked to say that California, if it stood alone, would have the seventh largest gross national product in the world. This was an attempt to inflate the importance of his experience as governor; but it also brought home the magnitude of this state, its affluence, and its separateness from the rest of the nation. Twenty-four million Americans live in California, the large majority in just a few urban agglomerations; they are separated by almost two thousand miles of desert and mountain, punctuated by a few other California-like metropolitan areas, from the places where the large majority of Americans still live.

Moreover, they live in a nation-state whose affluence can hardly be overstated. Yet no one is entirely sure just why California's economy is so productive. Economists of the right, supply siders like Arthur Laffer, argue that Proposition 13 and other tax cuts in the late 1970s stimulated growth—and migration—here that was more vigorous than in the rest of the nation and that continued, albeit slowly, during the recessionary years of the early 1980s. But in any broader perspective, the supply side theory explains nothing. California has been a high tax state since at least the 1940s, when Earl Warren deliberately kept taxes high during World War II. He anticipated vast population growth after the war, and wanted to be able to build schools, highways, and water mains for the new residents; seldom has a public official been so right. California thus did not grow as a tax haven, as a giant New Hampshire. It grew despite high taxes and in part because of what the taxes bought: a vast freeway system, an awe-inspiring water delivery system, a higher educational system that every year nonchalantly takes in more than half the state's young people.

Leftist critics are no more helpful than supply siders in explaining California's affluence. They ascribe it to the spasmodic growth of single industries, such as entertainment (first the movies, later TV and records, now such offshoots as video games) and defense (first aircraft, then aerospace). But over the long term California has grown rapidly despite wide oscillations in the health of these industries. The prime example is cited by Jane Jacobs in *The Economy of Cities*. In 18 months at the end of World War II, metropolitan Los Angeles lost 230,000 jobs in defense industries. Every sign pointed to vast depression and depopulation of the Los Angeles Basin in the postwar years. Exactly the opposite happened. In 1945-55 Los Angeles was the fastest growing metro area in the nation and generated one out of eight new jobs in the United States. Standard economic analysis tells us that growth comes where there are basic resources and access to markets. But California is thousands of miles away from any other significant market, and its basic resources are limited. It has been a net importer of oil since the 1950s (although it is a significant producer as well), it is hundreds of miles from basic fuels like coal and raw materials like iron ore; southern California is always in danger of running short of water. California has only one basic industry from its physical endowment: agriculture (although that depends on irrigation as well). The conclusion is unavoidable that the only reason a major thriving economy exists in California is because people want it to.

And that has continued, even in recession. For the past decade, California has been the goal of vast migrations, mostly of Mexicans and Asians. Government statistics are unable to keep up with the rapid social mobility of these people: they begin their life in America in what look to journalists like ghetto neighborhoods, but they quickly begin to make comfortable livings and to move up in the world—not to Beverly Hills, but to the San Fernando Valley and Orange County (the comparative absence of upwardly mobile migrants on the west side of Los Angeles makes them invisible to people in the entertainment business, and thus we don't see much of them on television or in movies). Los Angeles is to the nation today what New York was in 1913: the great entry port for people seeking—and finding—opportunity. Nor is this the result of simple geographic proximity. Los Angeles is close to the Mexican border, to be sure, but it is 1000 miles away from any significant concentration of population in Mexico except for the border towns. And while it is true that the West Coast is the part of the continental United States closest to Asia, that is not what makes Asian migrants stay here: they fly in, and could just as easily fly to the Midwest or the South. In California and in Washington, immigration is treated as a problem and immigrants are considered people in distress. But the continuing large immigration to California is a sure sign that its economy is buoyant and for the immigrants themselves the move is their big opportunity. Why else would they come?

Opportunity is what California has always represented to migrants, and this is a state largely built by outsiders. They may have been attracted, initially, by the climate, which for most Americans is well-nigh perfect (or was, until smog became a plague in the Los Angeles Basin in the 1950s). For post-1945 migrants from the Midwest and South, the cultural atmosphere was good: except for San Francisco, all California then had the small-town atmosphere most Americans consider ideal. Today it is far more cosmopolitan: Los Angeles produced Rodeo Drive just as New York in 1913 had Fifth Avenue. Many Californians find such an atmosphere unfriendly; they have moved farther out, to suburbs in Orange County, and increasingly to small towns and subdivisions 50 and 80 miles from the large metro areas or even, in the late 1970s, to the foothills of the Sierras. As California grew more affluent, its cultural habits grew more diverse: it supports not only Rodeo Drive, but decorated vans and weekend skydiving and skiing and surfing and Jacuzzi thermal baths. The new migrants will pioneer—are already pioneering—other cultural styles.

It is against this background of continual migration and constantly rising affluence that California politics must be understood. Government has played an important part in California's growth, from the time the United States went to war with Mexico to win it. Water programs, subsidies to the first railroads, the freeways, schools and universities—all are examples of government spending without which it seems unlikely that California would be nearly as affluent or productive as it is. But support for these measures has usually been bi-partisan, and many of the most important—the Los Angeles Aqueduct, Earl Warren's and Pat Brown's support of higher education—were pushed through without much debate.

Politics in California has revolved around national issues, and around cultural issues, often symbolic struggles between various cultural groups to validate their own moral principles. California, more affluent than most other states, and because most of its residents have come from somewhere else and are less fettered by traditions rooted in old communities, has been a kind of national trend-setter. It will happen first in California, we are told, whether it be hang gliders or the latest campaign technique; maybe so. But California is not inevitably a trend-setter; it is a part of the United States with certain characteristics that have produced a politics that sometimes appears elsewhere later.

So in the 1970s California produced a politics that is the exact reverse of the politics produced by the New Deal in most parts of America. That traditional New Deal politics— you can find it best exemplified in a Pennsylvania factory town—is liberal on economic issues and conservative on cultural issues, because most people in that community regard them-selves as economically deprived and as part of a deep-rooted cultural community. Affluent, shallow-rooted California produced a politics that tends to be conservative on economic issues and liberal on cultural issues. It is American politics turned upside down, with this added fil-lip, that politics is not so central to people's lives or essential to their well-being in California as it has been for most Americans in the post-New Deal years.

California politics thus presents us with a series of paradoxes and countercyclical trends. It is a young, culturally liberal state, yet it is also the home of our most tradition-minded and oldest president—who has won elections here three times by large margins. Politically, California moved to the left in the early 1970s as the nation was moving to the right; now it seems to be moving right in the early 1980s—a movement symbolized by the replacement of Governor Jerry Brown with conservative Republican George Deukmejian—as the nation is moving to the left. Involved in each case was Ronald Reagan. In 1966 and 1970 he was elected governor by wide margins, but during his term in office he was frustrated in attempts to achieve many of his goals. He wanted to make California like Disneyland's Main Street, but it ended up in some respects looking more like Haight-Ashbury. He came to office in 1967 preaching against the drug culture and student rioting. He left the governorship in 1974 with marijuana, abortion, and pornography essentially legalized and the values of the student generation being propagated by the media and spreading to all groups. He came to office as an opponent of civil rights legislation. Yet when he left office there was a black mayor of Los Angeles, elected over conservative opposition. He came to office as a champion of traditional values. Yet as he left office the birth rate was at an all-time low, divorce was growing ever more common, and people were struggling to come up with a convenient name for the practice of living with a partner without being married. This politician who always called for limited government in the late 1960s proclaimed the ambitious goal of using government to encourage one lifestyle and discourage others. The inevitable failure led to some loss of popularity. It is not generally recalled now that Reagan's margin was cut in half in his second gubernatorial election and that if he had run for the Senate when he left office he might have met the same fate—defeat—that his successor, Jerry Brown, did eight years later. This experience may have been instructive for Reagan. In his 1980 campaign and his first years in office he downplayed the cultural issues that were so important to some of his followers. The Ronald Reagan of the early 1980s was a mellower politician than the Reagan of the late 1960s.

Ironically, Reagan's ideas seem to have become more influential in California since he left the governorship than they were when he held that office. He has always preached economy in government. But the state budget grew rapidly during his governorship, just as the federal budget grew rapidly during the overlapping Nixon-Ford years. In 1973 Reagan failed to persuade Californians to support a ballot proposition to limit state spending. But by June 1978 Californians voted 2–1 in favor of Proposition 13, to limit local property taxes. That vote set the agenda for California's fiscal politics during the rest of Jerry Brown's governorship. The state's prosperity generated vast revenues for several years, but the cap on taxes forced government to eliminate some services, cut back on others, and charge users for many. The surprising success of Proposition 13 crystallized a national mood and marked a turning point in public attitudes and public policy, between the time people were happy to have government grow faster than GNP and a time when they demanded its growth be slowed. That change not only made possible the 1980 election result, but shaped national policy both before and after the Reagan victory.

So by 1978 Reagan and his allies seized control of the public dialogue from Reagan's successor, Jerry Brown. In Brown's first years he had captivated the nation, both by his austere lifestyle and by his unusual ideas. For a Democrat everyone called a liberal, he was surprisingly skeptical about many government programs; and he surprised many by supporting the space program. He was proud of appointing women, blacks, and Mexican-Americans to high positions and judgeships, where they performed sometimes brilliantly and sometimes just controversially. He essentially solved the state's farm labor problems, not in a way the growers especially liked, but one they accepted in practice. (Although the real solution is mechanization: if farm workers get good wages, it's cheaper to use machines.) He accepted the analyses and prescriptions of advanced environmentalists, even when that got him into trouble, as it did in 1981 when he refused to use spray against the Mediterranean fruit fly until forced to at the last minute. His personal habits were, in a word, weird: he worked late at night, seldom dealt directly with legislators, went on safari in Africa with Linda Ronstadt. He openly scorned his father, former Governor Pat Brown, although the latter worked hard for him in each of his campaigns.

In many ways Brown personified the style and beliefs of what is loosely called the Vietnam generation: young people who came of age after or during the 1960 election. That accounts for much of his appeal during his 1976 presidential campaign and in his early years in office. But Proposition 13 destroyed voters' belief that he was a different, more candid type of politician. It was not so much that he flip-flopped on the issue after the proposition passed as that he opposed it in the first place, echoing the arguments that the defenders of things-as-they-are put forward. The man who won 59% in California's Democratic presidential primary won only 4% four years later. Brown's passion for innovation came to seem only a reflex against the past, an echo of his desire not to replicate his father's policies (although in so many ways he has replicated his father's career); his rigorous skepticism came to seem only corrosive cynicism. He was reelected in 1978 against an opponent whose mistakes he shrewdly and cynically exploited. His rejection in the 1982 Senate election was no fluke and certainly not the result of enthusiasm for his opponent; it was a good indication of where he stands in voters' regard.

The 1982 gubernatorial election tells us a good deal less about the tone of politics in the state than do the results of some ballot propositions. George Deukmejian virtually sneaked into the governor's office, winning both the primary and the general election by carefully planned last minute blitzes. He actually lost the vote at the polls to Los Angeles Mayor Thomas Bradley but won the election because of a vast (and expensive) Republican drive to encourage absentee ballots.

More important, in the long run, may be the result in the election for superintendent of public instruction. The incumbent, Wilson Riles, was beaten by San Francisco lawyer Donald Honig. Riles's original victory, in 1970 over ultraconservative Max Rafferty, was hailed at the time as a rejection of Rafferty's philosophy. Honig's victory will have the effect of changing California's bilingual education programs. Under Riles and Governor Jerry Brown's appointees, bilingual programs were designed to hold children into Spanish-language classes; Hispanic organization leaders argued that Spanish should not be regarded as a second class language. But under Honig and Governor Deukmejian's appointees, bilingual programs will probably be changed to shift children into English-language instruction as soon as possible. The theory behind this change is obvious, and has the additional advantage of having been tried for over 100 years in this country and of having worked: the business and public life of the United States is conducted in English, and the only fair way to educate children is to make sure that they are completely proficient in English.

California pioneered the ballot propositions, and the results over the years provide great insight into changing political opinions, on issues from open housing (1964), coastal preservation (1972), marijuana (1972), spending limitation (1973), and property tax limits (1978). The big issues in 1982 were the nuclear freeze and handgun registration. Much ballyhooed nationally, the freeze had enthusiastic supporters, an organized campaign, and momentum from the fears aroused by saber-rattling statements by President Reagan and subordinates. But in October, freeze opponents started running TV ads, and the 2-1 poll leads for the freeze started to melt. In the end, it won with 52% of the vote. California, although more Republican than the national average, was the home of much of the earliest public protest—and voter feeling—against the Vietnam war. Now, judging from this result, voters here are more likely to see military issues as ambiguous and as requiring the resolution of conflicting considerations.

Gun control was really the central issue in California in 1982 and the main reason why this state moved to the right while the nation was moving to the left. Gun control opponents spent some $5 million opposing the mild handgun registration Proposition 15; its advocates raised less than $1 million, most of it late in the campaign. Opinion, initially favorable to gun control, shifted sharply; in the end it got majorities only in San Francisco, trendy Marin County, some parts of central Los Angeles, and in university towns. Outside the big metro areas it lost 3-1, and overall 63% voted against it. This badly hurt Thomas Bradley, who supported Prop. 15, and helped George Deukmejian, who opposed it. It brought to the polls probably several hundred thousand new voters, many who had left the big metro areas, physically or in spirit, and sought out rural and small town atmospheres and values. The marijuana and coastal zone propositions ten years before helped to bring college-educated young people of the baby boom generation into the California electorate—and helped them set the agenda and tone for that electorate for several years to come. The handgun registration proposition seems to have brought into the electorate the other side of the baby boom, the people who did not necessarily graduate from college, who do not share the values of people who grew up protesting the Vietnam war and seeking women's liberation. These new voters are more likely to be family people (although they undoubtedly include many divorcees); despite their lack of college degrees they tend to be affluent (who else buys those vans and snowmobiles?); they tend to be more fascinated by consumers technology rather than revolted by it, devotees of country and western music rather than progressive rock. Drawn to the polls by their opposition to gun control, they probably voted for Deukmejian, but may have supported Democrats for other offices; many voted for the nuclear freeze. By no means automatic Reagan votes, they are not automatic anti-Reagan votes either.

The Deukmejian victory and the defeat of Proposition 15 overshadow the fact that Democrats won at just about every other level in California. They retained the wide margins they have held in the legislature since they recaptured it from Reagan's Republicans in 1970; they have a wide edge in the congressional delegation that is not due entirely to Phil Burton's redistricting plan. They don't dominate all local governments (Republicans control the Los Angeles County Board of Supervisors), but for the most part Californians, like most Americans, have decided to entrust the humdrum administration of their welfare state to Democrats. That was not always so: the post-1945 migrants to California naturally tended to favor Republicans for lesser office, and it was a great and daring departure from tradition when Democrats first captured the legislature in 1958. Now that is the norm. The Democrats are the practical men of business who can be trusted to administer the status quo; the Republicans are the impractical theorists who may be called in to set things right occasionally but who usually end up bollixing things up. The Democrats do not have untrammeled control in Sacramento: Deukmejian has the veto and administrative appointments, and anyway it takes a two-thirds vote to adopt a budget under the state constitution. Sacramento has become a kind of smaller Washington: a city where competent legislators not only work year-round but live, flying back to their districts from time to time; a city full of lawyers and lobbyists who raise most of the campaign money for legislators and in turn are well-positioned to ask for their support. It has become a cynical place, but the legislature deserves its high reputation, and the state government is highly competent.

Congressional districting. California's House delegation of 45 is the largest since New York had that many districts in the 1940s; it is lopsidedly (28-17) Democratic. That is a result largely of a redistricting plan designed by the late San Francisco Congressman Phillip Burton and Michael Berman, an aide to Congressman Henry Waxman and brother of former Assembly Majority Leader and now Congressman Howard Berman. Republicans howled and yelped when the legislature passed this plan, with its grotesquely shaped districts; Phil Burton, unwisely, gloated in public. It was voted down in referendum in 1982, although voters also denied Republicans the nonpartisan commission they wanted and Democrats, with Burton orchestrating, passed another, similar plan in time for Jerry Brown to sign before he left office.

Republicans actually have themselves to blame for their plight. In 1981 Burton was ready to negotiate a bipartisan plan with Republican Congressman Bill Thomas, but Thomas refused. Republicans had visions of making a combination with Mexican-American legislators and passing their own plan, despite the fact that the Democrats controlled both the legislature and the governorship. But those visions, if they were ever realistic, should have vanished when Burton came up with a plan which included as many Mexican-majority districts as the Republicans were promising. (Actually, it's hard to draw Mexican-majority districts, because of the dispersal of the Mexican-American population—the same reason it's hard to draw Italian-majority districts on Long Island.) The Republicans, with no bargaining chips, hung tough; they were lucky that Burton decided to spare as many incumbent Republicans as he did.

The history of redistricting in California tells us, in any case, that the Republicans will have a few last laughs before the 1990 census forces the lines to be totally redrawn again. The Republicans redistricted in 1952; Democrats ended up representing most of the districts by 1959. Democrats redistricted in 1962; Republicans ended up holding half the delegation anyway by 1968. The 1972 redistricting was a bipartisan incumbent protection deal, engineered by Burton and Republican Charles Gubser; nonetheless, some incumbents had a hard time. So will some apparent beneficiaries of the 1982 redistrictings, before the decade is up. For there is one factor which will always work against incumbents from California: distance from Washington, D.C. To get back and forth to the capital and still get some work done, Californians have to fly the red-eye (the overnight plane that leaves California around midnight and arrives back east around 7 a.m.); repeated red-eyes leave legislators so groggy they are vulnerable to defeat or choose to retire.

Senators. California's most experienced officeholder today (and, in early 1983, its only avowed presidential candidate) is Senator Alan Cranston. His career in public affairs goes back a long time: as a young journalist in the 1930s he published an unexpurgated version of Hitler's *Mein Kampf*, and in the years after World War II he was a founder of the California Democratic Council, the leading liberal political force in the state. Cranston was elected state controller in 1958 and 1962 and U.S. senator in 1968, 1974, and 1980—the last time with the most votes any senator has ever received in any state. His career has had its ups and downs: he was defeated for controller in the 1966 Reagan landslide, and he won the Senate seat only when the incumbent, Thomas Kuchel, was defeated in the primary by right-winger Max Rafferty. It is a measure of the strength of the Reagan movement then that even after certain facts about Rafferty's past came out—he sat out World War II with an alleged injury and then threw away his crutches on VJ Day—Cranston still won with only 52%. Six years later, opinion turned, and Cranston would probably have beaten Reagan had he run.

Cranston is not an easy politician to define: part dreamy idealist, part shrewd political operator. His manner is quiet and cool; he is so thin he looks older than he is and not as fit (he holds the world record for the 100-yard dash for his age group). Cranston got into politics, in the 1930s and 1940s, as an opponent of fascism and an advocate of world government. He remains more interested in arms control than any other issue. He eagerly supported the nuclear freeze and is always ready to discuss the arcana of disarmament. He favors some form of national service, not necessarily military, for young people. Concern about foreign policy issues, more than anything else, probably explains best his presidential candidacy.

But he is also anything but an innocent about the world. For 15 years his colleagues in the Senate have been men with rather abstract interests or limited attention spans, and so California interests—farmers, aerospace companies, banks and savings and loans, labor unions, the entertainment industry, the new Silicon Valley industries—have gone to Cranston when they needed help in the Senate. Cranston has delivered. When Lockheed needed a federal loan guarantee to stay in business, Cranston produced the critical vote on the floor by persuading a colleague who later admitted a drinking problem to change his mind. He has no bias against business; he was a successful real estate developer himself. Perhaps more than anyone else in Washington, Cranston understands how the incredibly productive economy of California works, and who the major players are. That knowledge has paid off at reelection time, when he has gathered huge campaign treasuries from a wide range of donors, including many Republicans.

And he understands Washington as well. From the beginning of his service in the Senate, he has nurtured friendships with a wide variety of senators; he seems to have paid attention particularly to those who aren't stars. That helped to make him one of the Senate's ablest vote-counters. That skill, in turn, made him the easy favorite for the Democratic whip position when Robert Byrd moved up to the majority leadership in 1977. Unfortunately for Cranston, Byrd is not a man inclined to delegate; his success is based on attention to detail, and he is not about to leave those details to anyone else. So Cranston had less to do than he might have in the Carter years and, after Republicans won control of the Senate to Howard Baker's Republicans, even less in the Reagan years. That is probably another reason he is running for president.

How well can he do? Cranston's prowess at fund-raising was shown when he qualified for matching funds before other candidates, but by early 1983 he had not yet become known to many voters or a favorite of the press. The conventional wisdom is that he is too old (he turns 70 in 1984, which makes him a little older than Ronald Reagan was in 1980), too boring (although one could argue that oratorical skill is not what voters look for in a candidate), and too unaggressive (although he has taken big risks and won big victories in his career) to win. Probably the chemistry isn't there, and he won't make it. Even then, he still looks like a strong candidate for reelection in California in 1986—and a much more important senator in 1985 if Democrats regain control.

Pete Wilson is Cranston's fourth colleague, a man with no Washington experience and whose election resulted more from his opponent's unpopularity than his own assets. Still, he has some. He was a competent member of the California Assembly, a body full of skilled legislators; he was a very successful mayor of San Diego, a rapidly growing city that decided under his leadership to control its growth a little more strictly than it had in the past. He was bold enough to endorse Gerald Ford over Ronald Reagan in the 1976 presidential campaign—an endorsement that left Reagan so cool that he could hardly bear to pronounce Wilson's name when he made a speech in his behalf in 1982.

Wilson, however, is not at all a Jacob Javits Republican. He endorsed the Reagan program warmly in 1982, and even went the President one better by opposing the tax rise produced by the Republican Senate and reluctantly accepted by Reagan. For a while it seemed that blunders would defeat him: he talked about making Social Security voluntary for people under 45, and it turned out that he lived in a friend's fancy apartment for free while getting a divorce. Jerry Brown's campaign ran a series of ads in which vividly anti-Brown voters said they would "take another look at Jerry Brown." Wilson forces responded with an old Linda Ronstadt song title: "Just One Look Is All It Took."

As a senator, Wilson is dead last in seniority among Republicans; he is not likely to make a big splash in his first years in office, and he may be prevented from doing so later if

Democrats win back control. His problem is that of all California senators: how do you establish yourself in a good position on a couple of key issues over the long term, when your audience is 24 million people 2,500 miles away who don't care much about government, dislike politicians, and see politics as a means of displaying their cultural identities?

Governor. California voters had their choice in 1982 of electing the nation's first black or its first Armenian-American governor; they chose the latter. Deukmejian is a Sacramento veteran, with four years as attorney general and 16 years in the legislature; he is a vehement supporter of the death penalty and a tough approach to crime; he is a strong family man, a believer in pomp and ceremony, and in general a contrast to Jerry Brown. He has gathered around him a group of talented aides, many of Armenian descent, who may feel beleaguered in the capital. Sacramento is a city full of Democratic politicians and of talented bureaucrats who regard Republican campaign rhetoric as hogwash—they saw Ronald Reagan fail to live up to his promises, and they expect the same of Deukmejian. In practice, compromise with the legislature is necessary, but the Democrats have to compromise with Deukmejian too. That is what happened in the first big struggle between them, over the budget in early 1983. The Democrats wanted a tax increase to close the huge state deficit; Deukmejian insisted on none. The 11th hour compromise: no new tax increases this year, with this year's deficit to be paid off with money expected to come in next year. It is similar to differences between congressional Democrats (and many Senate Republicans) and the Reagan White House: the Democrats assume that new taxes will be necessary sooner or later, and might as well be adopted now, a long way away from the election; the Republicans believe that something will turn up—a stronger economy, pressure to cut spending—that will make new taxes unnecessary. What is odd is that this leaves the party historically associated with fiscal probity taking grave risks with government's fiscal stability.

The other statewide offices in California have duties of varying importance; politically, their function is to give their occupants the visibility and name identification necessary to make a run for a really important office like governor or senator. Every governor since the 1940s except Reagan has come from one of these offices. Among the current occupants, all Democrats, most likely to run for governor in the future are Lieutenant Governor Leo McCarthy, a former Speaker who solved many of Jerry Brown's legislative problems while the Governor stayed up late at night and worried about space; Attorney General John Van de Kamp, formerly Los Angeles County District Attorney; and Controller Ken Cory, a 6'7" former Orange County Assemblyman who came close to running for governor in 1980. Another possible candidate, and one with substantial governmental responsibilities, is Mayor Bradley, though he will be 68 in 1986.

Presidential politics. Conservative on economic issues, but perhaps getting more liberal if conditions are like those in 1982; liberal on cultural issues, but getting more conservative if 1982's votes on gun control and the nuclear freeze are an indication—California's leanings on national issues are a puzzle. In close presidential elections—1960, 1968, 1976—it has ended up Republican by small margins, but it has otherwise not followed, or established, national trends. It was notably less enthusiastic than average for Richard Nixon in 1972, but gave Ronald Reagan a larger than average percentage in 1980. The native son factor may play some role here, but just what that role is is unclear. Nixon, after all, lost a California state election in 1962, and Reagan is still hated by some members of the numerous baby boom generation for his policies as governor.

Californians were able to vote—or to decide not to vote—knowing the likely result. Political scientists will debate forever whether this shapes the outcome, but it does seem clear there is no bandwagon effect: California almost always produces a higher percentage than the rest of the nation for the *loser* of the presidential election. There is probably no way, in this day of exit polls, to suppress information about who is ahead back East, except perhaps by holding the polls open nationwide for the same 24-hour period.

California's presidential primaries have selected many presidential candidates. They cinched the nominations for Barry Goldwater in 1964 and George McGovern in 1972; their winner-take-all feature gave McGovern one-fifth of the votes he needed for the nomination, in one fell swoop. More recently the California primary has become less important. It was conceded to native sons Ronald Reagan (1976, 1980) and Jerry Brown (1976). The Republican electorate here is much smaller than the Democratic, and more conservative probably than Republican primary electorates nationally; since the primary is held late in the season, it will likely be won by the candidate who is clearly more conservative. Ronald Reagan will win it if he runs in 1984. How it would go in a primary between George Bush, Howard Baker, and Jesse Helms is unclear; each has his liabilities for this constituency (Bush and Baker as too liberal, Helms as too much the southern fundamentalist).

As for the Democrats, Alan Cranston bases much of the argument for the plausibility of his candidacy on his possible strength in the California primary (and Jerry Brown has promised not to run). But while Democratic primary voters certainly know and respect Cranston, it is not certain that they have the enthusiasm for him or the confidence that he would make a good president that would guarantee him a strong finish here. Other Democrats may have problems if they concentrate too hard on appealing to the sunset industries of the Northeast and Midwest, or if they seem too far out of line with the liberal cultural attitudes that still dominate at least the Democratic primary electorate here. If there is a close contest, no candidate will come away with all of California's delegates, as the winner did under the old winner-take-all system: now most are apportioned by congressional district, in proportion to the percentages won there by candidates who win at least a certain threshold percentage.

The People   Est. Pop. 1982: 24,724,000; Pop. 1980: 23,667,902, up 4.5% 1980–82 and 18.5% 1970–80; 10.68% of U.S. total, 1st largest; voting age pop. 17,278,944; 1% American Indian, 7% Black, 16% Spanish origin, 5% Asian origin. Single ancestry: 8% English, 5% German, 3% Irish, 2% Italian, 1% French, Russian, Portuguese, Polish, Swedish, Dutch, Scottish, Norwegian. Registered voters (1982): 11,559,099 Total. 6,150,716 D (53%); 4,029,684 R (35%); 1,083,031 Declined to state (9%). 23% with 1–3 yrs. col., 20% with 4+ yrs. col. 11.3% below poverty level. 41% housing units rented; median house value: $84,700; median monthly rent: $253. Households: 69% family, 37% with children, 55% married couples.

1982 Share of Federal Tax Burden $70,716,700,000; 11.84% of U.S. total, 1st largest.

1982 Share of Federal Expenditures

	Total		Non-Defense		Defense	
Total Expend	$75,014m	(12.43%)	$42,685m	(10.05%)	$32,329m	(18.08%)
St/Lcl Grants	9,016m	(10.22%)	9,014m	(10.22%)	2m	(5.56%)
Salary/Wages	9,925m	(12.72%)	1,946m	(7.11%)	7,979m	(15.75%)
Ind Payments	28,274m	(9.88%)	25,033m	(9.72%)	3,241m	(11.34%)
Procurement	27,257m	(18.69%)	4,855m	(15.40%)	22,402m	(19.60%)
Other Programs	542m	(10.01%)	542m	(10.28%)	0m	(0%)
Loan/Insurance	3,938m	(6.16%)	3,746m	(6.07%)	192m	(8.73%)

Political Lineup   Governor, George Deukmejian (R). Senators, Alan Cranston (D) and Pete Wilson (R). Representatives, 45 (29 D and 16 R). State Senate, 40 (25 D and 15 R); State Assembly, 80 (48 D and 32 R).

Presidential Vote

1980	Reagan (R)	4,524,835	(53%)
	Carter (D)	3,083,652	(36%)
	Anderson (I)	739,832	(9%)
1976	Ford (R)	3,882,244	(49%)
	Carter (D)	3,742,284	(48%)

1980 Democratic Presidential Primary			*1980 Republican Presidential Primary*		
Kennedy	1,507,142	(45%)	Reagan	2,057,923	(80%)
Carter	1,266,276	(38%)	Anderson	349,315	(14%)
Unpledged delegation	382,759	(11%)	Bush	125,113	(5%)
Brown	135,962	(4%)	Two others.........	31,707	(1%)
One other	71,779	(2%)			

SENATORS

Sen. Alan Cranston (D) Elected 1968, seat up 1986; b. June 19, 1914, Palo Alto; home, Los Angeles; Pomona Col., 1932–33, U. of Mexico, 1935, Stanford U., B.A. 1936; Protestant.

Career Foreign Correspondent, Internatl. News Svc., 1936–38; Lobbyist, Common Cncl. for American Unity, 1939; Army, WWII; Real estate business, 1947–67; Pres., United World Federalists, 1949–52; State Comptroller of CA, 1958–66.

Offices 112 HSOB 202-224-3553. Also 10960 Wilshire Blvd., Los Angeles 90024, 213-824-7641; and One Hallidie Plaza, Su. 301, San Francisco 94102, 415-556-8440.

Committees *Minority Whip: Banking, Housing and Urban Affairs* (2d). Subcommittees: Housing and Urban Affairs; Financial Institutions; Economic Policy; Rural Housing and Development. *Foreign Relations* (7th). Subcommittees: Arms Control, Oceans and International Operations, and Environment; Western Hemisphere Affairs. *Veterans' Affairs* (Ranking Member).

Group Ratings

	ADA	ACLU	COPE	CFA	LCV	LWV	NTU	NSI	COC	ACA	CSFC
1982	95	93	92	100	71	91	2	33	11	6	24
1981	85	—	91	50	80	—	0	—	13	6	26
1980	83	97	88	67	78	78	25	0	22	5	25

National Journal Ratings

	Economic		Foreign		Cultural	
1982	81%	(LIB)	90%	(LIB)	93%	(LIB)
	18%	(CONS)	3%	(CONS)	4%	(CONS)
1981	92%	(LIB)	78%	(LIB)	–%	(LIB)
	7%	(CONS)	21%	(CONS)	–%	(CONS)

Key Votes

1) Reagan 81 Budget	AGN	5) $ to El Salvador	AGN	9) Poor Pay Food Stamps	AGN
2) Reagan 81 Tax Cut	FOR	6) Saudi AWACS Sale	AGN	10) Ban Crt Busing Order	AGN
3) Bal Budget Amend	AGN	7) Ban Abortion	AGN	11) Clinch Riv Brdr Rctr	AGN
4) Gas & Road Tax	—	8) Nerve Gas Prod	AGN	12) Legal Services Corp	—

Election Results

1980 general	Alan Cranston (D)	4,705,399	(57%)	($2,823,462)
	Paul Gann (R)	3,093,426	(37%)	($1,705,523)
1980 primary	Alan Cranston (D)	2,608,746	(80%)	
	Richard Morgan (D)	350,394	(11%)	
	Two others (D)	305,476	(9%)	
1974 general	Alan Cranston (D)	3,693,160	(61%)	($1,336,202)
	H.L. Richardson (R)	2,210,267	(36%)	($702,767)

Campaign Contributions and Expenditures

1979-80			*PACS brkdwn*	
Receipts	$3,144,094	Agr $36,937	Ideo	$22,037
Expend.	$2,823,607	Bus $203,226	Lbr	$128,450
Unspent	$320,741	Hlth $18,591	Prof	$9,075

Sen. Pete Wilson (R) Elected 1982, seat up 1988; b. Aug. 23, 1933, Lake Forest, IL; home, San Diego; Yale U., B.A. 1955, U. of CA at Berkeley, J.D. 1962; Protestant.

Career Practicing atty., 1965–66; CA Assembly, 1966–71, Minor. Whip, 1968–69; Mayor of San Diego, 1971–83.

Offices 720 HSOB, 202-224-3841. Also Fed. Bldg., 880 Front St., Rm. 6-S-9, San Diego 92188, 619-230-0366; Fed. Bldg., 1130 O St., Fresno 93721, 209-487-5727; Fed. Bldg., 450 Golden Gate Ave., San Francisco 94102, 415-556-4307; and Fed. Bldg., 11000 Wilshire Blvd., Los Angeles 90017.

Committees *Agriculture, Nutrition and Forestry* (9th). Subcommittees: Agricultural Research and General Legislation; Foreign Agricultural Policy; Soil and Water Conservation. *Armed Services* (10th). Subcommittees: Sea Power and Force Projection; Tactical Warfare; Preparedness. *Select Committee on Aging* (8th).

Group Ratings and Key Votes: Newly Elected
Election Results

1982 general	Pete Wilson (R)	4,022,565	(52%)	($7,082,651)
	Edmund G. Brown, Jr. (D)	3,494,968	(45%)	($5,367,931)
1982 primary	Pete Wilson (R)	851,292	(38%)	
	Paul N. (Pete) McCloskey, Jr. (R)	577,267	(26%)	($2,143,253)
	Barry Goldwater, Jr. (R)	408,308	(18%)	($2,686,985)
	Robert K. Dornan (R)	181,970	(8%)	($1,132,228)
	Maureen E. Reagan (R)	118,326	(5%)	($138,023)
1976 general	S.I. Hayakawa (R)	3,748,973	(50%)	($1,184,624)
	John Tunney (D)	3,502,862	(47%)	($1,940,988)

Campaign Contributions and Expenditures

1981-82		*Direct Cont. 81-82*		*PACS brkdwn*			
Receipts	$7,190,985	Indiv	$5,894,693	Agr	$127,944	Ideo	$73,115
Expend.	$7,082,651	Party	$28,796	Bus	$855,795	Lbr	$16,450
Unspent	$108,080	PACS	$1,182,432	Hlth	$32,850	Prof	$20,750

Indirect Party Expend: $1,311,272 *Indep Expend:* For: $2,718

GOVERNOR

Gov. George Deukmejian (R) Elected 1982, seat up 1986; b. June 6, 1928, Menands, NY; home, Long Beach; Sienna Col., B.A. 1949, St. Johns U. Law Sch., J.D. 1952; Episcopal.

Career Practicing atty., 1952–53, 1958–62; Army, 1953–55; Texaco Inc., 1955–58; CA Assembly, 1962–66; CA Senate, 1966–78; Atty. General, 1978–82.

Offices State Capitol, Sacramento 95814, 916-445-2841.

Election Results

1982 gen.	George Deukmejian (R)	3,881,014	(49%)
	Tom Bradley (D)	3,787,669	(48%)
1982 prim.	George Deukmejian (R)	1,165,266	(51%)
	Mike Curb (R)	1,020,935	(45%)
1978 gen.	Edmund G. Brown, Jr. (D) ..	3,878,812	(56%)
	Evelle J. Younger (R)	2,526,534	(37%)
	Ed Clark (Libertarian)	377,960	(5%)

FIRST DISTRICT

For more than 300 miles north out of San Francisco, the California coast stands in massive grandeur. This is an isolated part of the country, cut off from the interior by the Coast Range and bounded by the cold, often stormy Pacific. The first white settlers here were Russians, who left little behind them but interesting place names (the Russian River, Sebastopol). They were followed, in the years after the California Gold Rush, by lumbermen and fishermen. The damp, foggy climate here—the rainfall is higher than just about anywhere else in the United States, except the Oregon and Washington coasts—helps to grow giant trees, Douglas firs and majestic redwoods. By the late 19th century great fortunes had been made in lumber, as the Victorian mansions still standing in Eureka attest. This area is called the Redwood Empire, and it occupies most of California's 1st congressional district.

This is not a thickly populated area, however, and most of the population of the district is in its southern portion, in Sonoma County. Here are several valleys, sheltered from the ocean by small mountains, with relatively sunny and gentle climates; the Sonoma Valley is one of California's leading wine-producing areas. Attracted by the scenery, the unaffected atmosphere, migrants have been moving up from the San Francisco Bay area: rich people buying ranches, counterculture veterans seeking a quieter, but still tolerant atmosphere (and, in some cases, a place to harvest an economically significant marijuana crop), and just plain suburbanites looking for the next subdivision.

Sonoma County has the high income levels and housing prices associated with the Bay Area; the Redwood Empire operates on a lower dollar level, and shakier, economy. The lumber industry is very responsive to high interest rates: they discourage homebuilding and other construction and reduce demand for lumber and depress lumber prices. The record high interest rates of the early 1980s have resulted in depression levels of unemployment in much of the Redwood Empire. Resentment is increased by the fact that the Redwood National Park, never popular locally, was enlarged under the parks bill pushed through by

CALIFORNIA — Congressional Districts, Counties, and Selected Places — (45 Districts)

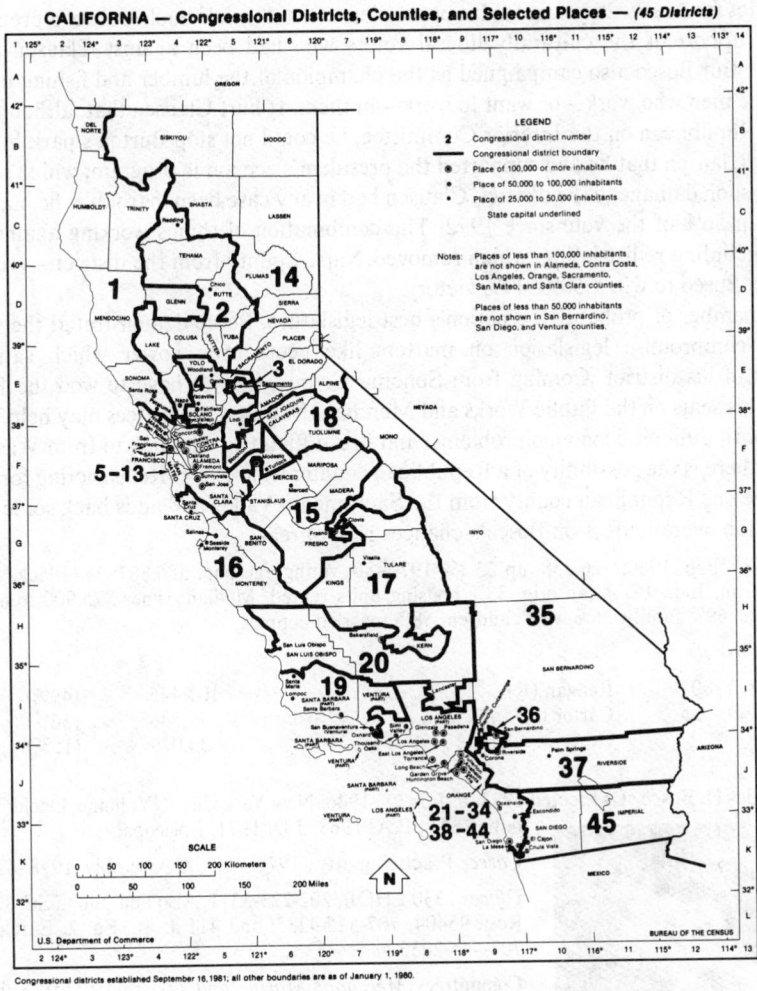

LEGEND

2   Congressional district number
—   Congressional district boundary
●   Place of 100,000 or more inhabitants
●   Place of 50,000 to 100,000 inhabitants
•   Place of 25,000 to 50,000 inhabitants
       State capital underlined

Notes: Places of less than 100,000 inhabitants
          are not shown in Alameda, Contra Costa,
          Los Angeles, Orange, Sacramento,
          San Mateo, and Santa Clara counties.

          Places of less than 50,000 inhabitants
          are not shown in San Bernardino,
          San Diego, and Ventura counties.

SCALE

0   50   100   150   200 Kilometers
0   50   100   150   200 Miles

N

U.S. Department of Commerce   BUREAU OF THE CENSUS

Congressional districts established September 16,1981; all other boundaries are as of January 1, 1980.

San Francisco Congressman Phillip Burton. That probably had only a minimal economic effect, but it symbolized the gulf between the continuously prosperous Bay Area and the economically troubled Redwood Empire.

The 1st district consists of Sonoma County and the Redwood Empire north to the Oregon border; it also hops over the Coast Range to include two small counties in the northern Sacramento Valley. The political heritage here is progressive Republican: these counties were strong for Teddy Roosevelt in 1912 and Bob LaFollette in 1924. Since the 1950s, their partisan preferences have been closely divided and unstable: cultural attitudes and economic issue stands have pulled many voters in opposite directions.

In 1982, however, both worked for the Democratic congressional candidate, Assemblyman Douglas Bosco. Bosco attacked incumbent Republican Don Clausen, who had represented the district for nearly 20 years, for his opposition to California's nuclear freeze proposal, and got the support of the culturally liberal voters who had been against Clausen in recent elections. But Bosco also campaigned as the champion of the lumber and fishing industries, and of the men who work—or want to work—in them. It hurt Clausen that, although he was ranking Republican on the Interior Committee, he could not stop Burton's park bill. And it also hurt Clausen that he had supported the president's economic program, which seemed to be doing such damage to the district. Clausen had in any case been in trouble: he had not won more than 56% of the vote since 1972. The combination of things working against him in 1982—including redistricting, which removed Napa County from the district—was enough to enable Bosco to win a 50%–47% victory.

As a member of probably the nation's best legislature, Bosco demonstrated the ability to produce compromise legislation on matters like geothermal power which satisfied all elements in his district. Coming from Sonoma County, he will have to woo the Redwood Empire; his seats on the Public Works and Merchant Marine Committees may help. This is a district with difficult economic problems, and it is difficult to get back to from Washington, D.C.; so there is the possibility of a Republican counterattack here. Redistricting for 1984 removes the one Republican county from the Sacramento Valley and adds back some of Napa County; the overall effect on Bosco's chances is not great.

The People   Pop. 1980: 526,358, up 33.1% 1970–80; voting age pop. 386,887; 1% Black, 5% Span. orig., 2% Am. Ind., 1% Asian orig. 33% housing units rented. Median owner $75,900; renter $232. Households: 69% family, 36% with children, 58% married couples.

Presidential Vote

1980	Reagan (R)	107,445	(49%)
	Carter (D)	79,246	(36%)
	Other	34,029	(15%)

Rep. Douglas H. Bosco (D) Elected 1982; b. July 28, 1946, New York City, NY; home, Occidental; Willamette U., B.A. 1968, J.D. 1971; Episcopal.

Career Practicing atty., 1971–78; CA Assembly, 1978–82.

Offices 1330 LHOB, 202-225-3311. Also Fed. Bldg., Su. 329, Santa Rosa 95404, 707-525-4235; and 411 J. St., Su. 2, Eureka 95501, 707-445-2055.

Committees *Merchant Marine and Fisheries* (22d). Subcommittees: Fisheries and Wildlife Conservation and the Environment; Panama Canal and Outer Continental Shelf. *Post Office and Civil Service* (15th). Subcommittees: Compensation and Employee Benefits; Human Resources. *Public Works and Transportation* (20th). Subcommittees: Aviation; Economic Development; Surface Transportation.

Group Ratings and Key Votes: Newly Elected

Election Results

1982 general	Douglas H. Bosco (D)	107,749	(50%)	($271,990)
	Don H. Clausen (R)	102,043	(47%)	($539,448)
1982 primary	Douglas H. Bosco (D)	57,504	(74%)	
	Mike Koepf (D)	20,758	(27%)	($11,826)
1980 general	Don H. Clausen (R)	141,698	(54%)	($451,056)
	Norma K. Bork (D)	109,789	(42%)	($190,689)

Campaign Contributions and Expenditures

1981-82		Direct Cont. 81-82*		PACS brkdwn			
Receipts	$275,053	Indiv	$108,398	Agr	$1,000	Ideo	$54,750
Expend.	$271,990	Party	$7,242	Bus	$10,900	Lbr	$51,350
Unspent	$3,062	PACS	$125,271	Hlth	$1,250	Prof	$1,500
		Cand	$10,300				

Indirect Party Expend: $39,233   *Indep Expend*: Agn: $2,718   *Non-Cand Loans*: $9,500

SECOND DISTRICT

The great valley of California extends not only south from Sacramento but north. This Sacramento Valley is less heavily populated than the Central Valley in the south; it does not cultivate so many different kinds of agricultural products. But it is wonderfully productive. And it does have the most plentiful supply of what may be California's most precious resource: water. The Sacramento Valley is hemmed in on three sides by mountains: the Coast Range on the west, the Sierra Nevada on the east, and the gigantic volcanoes, Mount Lassen and Mount Shasta, on the north. From their slopes flow the waters that become the Sacramento River and are distributed over an ingenious set of canals and aqueducts to the Central Valley and the Los Angeles Basin, where they sustain the most productive part of western civilization. The Sacramento Valley has always guarded its water jealously and in the days before one-person-one-vote it had enough seats in the California Senate to veto water decisions it didn't like; today it still retains a plentiful supply for its own use.

In fact, the Sacramento Valley turned out to be one of the fastest growing parts of California in the 1980s. Young people from the big metropolitan areas came up here to be closer to nature; young families came here to raise their children in a small town atmosphere, where people still go to neighborhood churches and you don't have to worry about drugs in the schools.

The 2d congressional district of California occupies most of the Sacramento Valley. Its rather jagged boundaries follow county lines, but it includes most of the larger towns north of Sacramento: Yuba City, Marysville, Oroville, Chico, Red Bluff, Redding. Partisan traditions here vary: some counties are heavily Republican, some heavily Democratic. The 2d district also includes, west over a small range of mountains, Napa and Lake Counties. Napa is America's premier wine-growing valley, an area with a pleasant climate and fine soil that seems to be perfect for producing many premium wines. Lake, the next county to the north, is largely uninhabited. Politically, these two counties lean Republican.

The political trend in both parts of the district is Republican. The new migrants seem to lean definitely to the right. Turnout here was at record levels in 1982, in large part to register opposition to the gun control proposition on the ballot; anti-gun control voters stuck with the Republicans, who shared their views on this issue, in partisan races. Most of this area was represented for years by Harold Johnson, a bluff Democrat who specialized in bringing public works projects into the district. But Johnson was defeated in 1980 by a Republican who seems to have a lock on the district.

He is Eugene Chappie, a 16-year veteran of the California legislature. Chappie's home area is actually in the foothills of the Sierras; redistricting changed his constituency, 41% of which was new to him. He won easily nevertheless. A good humored man of legislative competence, he sits on the Agriculture Committee. This is a district that now needs protection of its major industry more than it does subsidization through federal public works projects. Chappie has been a loyal Reagan Republican on most issues.

84 CALIFORNIA

Redistricting for 1984 removes Napa County and part of Lake and adds Democratic territory up around Mount Shasta. Given Chappie's strength, however, this is unlikely to affect the outcome of the election.

The People   Pop. 1980: 526,015, up 32.5% 1970–80; voting age pop. 388,986; 1% Black, 6% Span. orig., 2% Asian orig., 1% Am. Ind. 32% housing units rented. Median owner $61,100; renter $196. Households: 71% family, 36% with children, 60% married couples.

Presidential Vote

1980	Reagan (R)	117,948	(57%)
	Carter (D)	66,608	(32%)
	Other	23,079	(11%)

Rep. Eugene A. Chappie (R) Elected 1980; b. Mar. 28, 1920, Sacramento; home, Roseville; Roman Catholic.

Career Army, WWII; El Dorado Cnty. Sprvsr., 1950-64; CA Assembly, 1965-80.

Offices 1730 LHOB, 202-225-3076. Also 270 E. 4th St., Chico 95926, 916-893-8365.

Committees *Agriculture* (14th). Subcommittees: Cotton, Rice and Sugar; Forests, Family Farms and Energy. *Small Business* (13th). Subcommittees: Antitrust and Restraint of Trade Activities Affecting Small Business; Export Opportunities and Special Small Business Problems. *Select Committee on Narcotics Abuse and Control* (7th).

Group Ratings

	ADA	ACLU	COPE	CFA	LCV	LWV	NTU	NSI	COC	ACA	CSFC
1982	10	4	7	20	6	33	87	100	75	91	69
1981	0	—	0	21	17	—	87	—	100	90	73

National Journal Ratings

	Economic		Foreign		Cultural	
1982	30%	(LIB)	18%	(LIB)	14%	(LIB)
	70%	(CONS)	82%	(CONS)	86%	(CONS)
1981	1%	(LIB)	27%	(LIB)	11%	(LIB)
	97%	(CONS)	73%	(CONS)	89%	(CONS)

Key Votes

1) Reagan 81 Budget	FOR	5) Incr SS Rtmt Age	FOR	9) Poor Pay Food Stamps	FOR
2) Reagan 81 Tax Cut	FOR	6¹ Saudi AWACS Sale	AGN	10) Ban Crt Busing Order	—
3) Bal Budget Amend	FOR	7) $ for MX Missile	FOR	11) Auto Local Content	AGN
4) Gas & Road Tax	—	8) Nerve Gas Prod	—	12) Nuclear Arms Freeze	AGN

Election Results

1982 general	Eugene A. Chappie (R)	116,172	(58%)	($426,905)
	John Newmeyer (D)	81,314	(41%)	($95,195)
1982 primary	Eugene A. Chappie (R)	59,603	(100%)	
1980 general	Eugene A. Chappie (R)	145,585	(54%)	($375,721)
	Harold T. Johnson (D)	107,993	(40%)	($378,764)
	Jim McClarin (Libertarian)	17,497	(6%)	($0)

Campaign Contributions and Expenditures

1981-82		Direct Cont. 81-82*			PACS brkdwn		
Receipts	$453,397	Indiv	$280,356	Agr	$31,050	Ideo	$9,016
Expend.	$426,905	Party	$11,386	Bus	$54,250	Lbr	$5,250
Unspent	$34,118	PACS	$105,496	Hlth	$8,600	Prof	$1,050
		Cand	$30,000				

*Non-Cand Loans: $5,750

THIRD DISTRICT

Sacramento is perhaps America's purest political city. Even more than Washington, it depends on politics and government for its livelihood. And more than Washington, it operates out of the day-to-day scrutiny of the constituents it serves. Sacramento has been an important urban center since gold was discovered at Sutter's mill in 1849. In the Gold Rush, it was the natural choice to be California's capital, situated as it was halfway between the Mother Lode country in the foothills of the Sierras and San Francisco Bay, and in the middle of California's vast valley. Sacramento has been an important agricultural and food processing center, like the other cities in the valley; but government has been its main business. California's gleaming Capitol is as impressive as any in the nation; its state government generally is conducted with a competence and often with an esprit that should be the envy of most other governments in the world.

And, in the past few decades—and despite the intentions of Ronald Reagan—it has gotten vastly bigger. In the 1940s Sacramento was a hangout for a few fabled lobbyists; in the 1980s it is headquarters for a vast army of lobbyists, lawyers, and consultants exceeded in size only by those in Washington, D.C. California's highly competent legislators and their large staffs in effect live year-round in Sacramento, although they usually keep legal residences elsewhere; so good a job do they do in keeping in touch with both constituents and lobbyists that the best way to get elected to the legislature now is to have been a staffer. Legislators control much of the flow of information to their constituents through free mail and expensive campaigns, and so Sacramento has become an almost self-contained engine of government, situated in a huge valley, serving primarily two hugely populous metropolitan areas situated in niches between mountains and ocean.

Oddly, as government has become a bigger and bigger business in Sacramento, its voting habits have become more Republican. Historically, this has always been a Democratic city; it even went for McGovern in 1972. Its large government work force and the Democratic *Sacramento Bee* helped sustain those attitudes. But the increasingly affluent and literate citizens of Sacramento voted for Proposition 13 in 1978 and for Ronald Reagan in 1980. The work force here, as in Washington, is increasingly well educated and highly paid—and, perhaps, increasingly skeptical about the value of some of its own work. Jerry Brown, the dominant figure here for eight years, may have encouraged such attitudes. So a sort of liberal guilt may be making Sacramento more conservative.

The 3d congressional district of California consists of the main part of the city of Sacramento and its suburbs east of the Sacramento River and south of the American River. It includes the Capitol, downtown, and most of the more affluent parts of the Sacramento area. Historically, it is heavily Democratic; in recent elections, somewhat less so. The congressman from the 3d, Robert Matsui, is a Democrat, first elected in a close contest in

1978, returned easily since then. Matsui is a loyal member of the Democratic Caucus, with strong liberal records on most issues except foreign ones; like many Japanese-American politicians, he is something of a hawk on military and national security matters. He is a member of the Ways and Means Committee and sits on the sensitive subcommittee on Social Security and unemployment compensation. He seems to have become firmly entrenched in the district and is not threatened by its Republican trending in other elections.

The People   Pop. 1980: 525,784, up 23.2% 1970–80; voting age pop. 390,358; 7% Black, 8% Span. orig., 6% Asian orig., 1% Am. Ind. 38% housing units rented. Median owner $67,100; renter $217. Households: 67% family, 35% with children, 53% married couples.

Presidential Vote

1980	Reagan (R)	97,853	(47%)
	Carter (D)	86,632	(41%)
	Other	25,736	(12%)

Rep. Robert T. Matsui (D) Elected 1978; b. Sept. 17, 1941, Sacramento; home, Sacramento; U. of CA, B.A. 1963, Hastings Col. of Law, J.D. 1966; Presbyterian.

Career Practicing atty., 1967–; Sacramento City Cncl., 1971–78.

Offices 231 CHOB, 202-225-7163. Also 8058 Fed. Bldg., Sacramento 95814, 916-440-3543.

Committees *Ways and Means* (19th). Subcommittees: Social Security; Public Assistance and Unemployment Compensation. *Select Committee on Narcotics Abuse and Control* (8th).

Group Ratings

	ADA	ACLU	COPE	CFA	LCV	LWV	NTU	NSI	COC	ACA	CSFC
1982	85	83	88	80	83	83	1	60	14	22	27
1981	70	—	85 79	57	—	1	—	17	17	33	
1980	94	93	79	71	76	100	11	20	58	13	23

National Journal Ratings

	Economic		Foreign		Cultural	
1982	83%	(LIB)	75%	(LIB)	79%	(LIB)
	15%	(CONS)	24%	(CONS)	21%	(CONS)
1981	74%	(LIB)	46%	(LIB)	85%	(LIB)
	25%	(CONS)	52%	(CONS)	14%	(CONS)

Key Votes

1) Reagan 81 Budget AGN	5) Incr SS Rtmt Age FOR	9) Poor Pay Food Stamps AGN
2) Reagan 81 Tax Cut AGN	6) Saudi AWACS Sale AGN	10) Ban Crt Busing Order AGN
3) Bal Budget Amend AGN	7) $ for MX Missile AGN	11) Auto Local Content FOR
4) Gas & Road Tax FOR	8) Nerve Gas Prod AGN	12) Nuclear Arms Freeze FOR

Election Results

1982 general	Robert T. Matsui (D)	194,680	(90%)	($140,652)
	Bruce A. Daniel (Libertarian)	16,222	(8%)	($916)
1982 primary	Robert T. Matsui (D)	71,813	(100%)	
1980 general	Robert T. Matsui (D)	170,670	(71%)	($211,981)
	Joseph Murphy (R)	64,215	(26%)	($0)

Campaign Contributions and Expenditures

1981-82		*Direct Cont. 81-82*				*PACS brkdwn*		
Receipts	$267,641	Indiv	$120,455	Agr	$19,800	Ideo	$800
Expend.	$140,652	PACS	$124,590	Bus	$63,500	Lbr	$28,850
Unspent	$163,617			Hlth	$8,850	Prof	$2,500

FOURTH DISTRICT

The low, flat delta lands where the Sacramento and San Joaquin Rivers empty into San Francisco Bay; the rich fruit-growing land of the lower Sacramento Valley; the northern and southern suburbs of Sacramento, and a part of the city itself—these make up the 4th congressional district of California. The delta is the district's central geographical focus, although it is scarcely inhabited: the river byways bend around curves and irrigate rice fields, whose farmers wonder if the California water system is going to divert too much water from the delta. The delta and the 4th district generally are separated from the weather—and the cultural ambience—of the San Francisco Bay area by a ridge of mountains only barely interrupted by the river making its way to the sea. The farmlands and suburbs here are one part of California with large numbers of young families with children, a kind of Middle America set off near Baghdad. The district's major university, California at Davis, made headlines when its medical school was sued by Alan Bakke, a white applicant rejected because of racial quotas; it has lapsed now into less controversial times, concerned again with its agricultural research, its bikepaths thronged with bicycles.

The 4th district is and has been Democratic country for many years. Half its population is in Sacramento County, traditionally heavily Democratic though recently less so; the 4th district has some of the lower income, less elite parts of the county—the industrial suburbs north of the American River, the heavily Mexican–American towns on the flatlands across the Sacramento River from the city's historic landing. Davis and the agricultural area around it are Democratic, though for different reasons; so is the area farther west, around Fairfield and Suisun.

It is appropriate that this Sacramento area district be represented by a man who is, in effect, a professional legislator. Vic Fazio used to serve in the California Assembly; before that, he was an Assembly staffer and founder of the estimable *California Journal*. That means that he was learning the legislative business from some of the best teachers in the country, in one of the best schools. He won the 4th district House seat in 1978, when incumbent Robert Leggett prudently retired (it was revealed that he had been maintaining two families for years, and he nearly lost in 1976). And Fazio brought to Washington the lessons he learned in Sacramento.

He has a good position to apply them: he is chairman of the Legislative Appropriations Subcommittee. This is an obscure body, sometimes even to congressmen; but it is an important one for those who wish to accomplish something legislatively. It controls the budgets of House members, committees, and their staffs, and so has a lot to say about what work they can get done. It also handles the politically difficult matter of the congressional salary. In the late 1970s the House tried a supposedly automatic mechanism to increase its pay, but it was always defeated by members who took the matter to the floor; some members feared voting for any pay increase, and others didn't want to be recorded for something that looked sneaky. Fazio decided to attack the problem head on in 1982. In the lame duck session, he persuaded 303 members of the House to go on record for a higher salary. It was only the second time since 1976 that House members got a raise.

Fazio also serves on an Energy and Water Development Subcommittee—a body more politically useful to him, considering how much water flows into, around, down, and under his district. Despite the salary issue, he has been reelected with solid margins.

The People Pop. 1980: 525,754, up 32.2% 1970–80; voting age pop. 374,274; 5% Black, 10% Span. orig., 5% Asian orig., 1% Am. Ind. 36% housing units rented. Median owner $64,200; renter $216. Households: 73% family, 42% with children, 60% married couples.

Presidential Vote

1980	Reagan (R)	89,728	(50%)
	Carter (D)	73,533	(41%)
	Other	17,743	(10%)

Rep. Vic Fazio (D) Elected 1978; born Oct. 11, 1942, Winchester, MA; home, Sacramento; Union Col., B.A. 1965; Episcopal.

Career Aide to U.S. Rep. Ronald Cameron; Consultant, CA Assembly, 1967; Founder, *The California Journal*; Dir., Ofc. of Assembly Major., Consultant and Asst. to Assembly Spkr., 1971; CA Assembly, 1975-78.

Offices 1421 LHOB, 202-225-5716. Also 823 Marin St., Rm. 8, Vallejo 94590, 707-552-0720.

Committees *Appropriations* (25th). Subcommittees: Energy and Water Development; Legislative (Chairman); Military Construction. *Budget* (20th). Task Forces: Energy and Technology; Entitlements, Uncontrollables, and Indexing; International Finance and Trade. *Standards of Official Conduct* (5th).

Group Ratings

	ADA	ACLU	COPE	CFA	LCV	LWV	NTU	NSI	COC	ACA	CSFC
1982	80	83	85	80	77	83	3	56	14	22	28
1981	80	—	81	64	45	—	0	—	17	5	35
1980	89	80	79	71	58	90	12	22	59	23	26

National Journal Ratings

	Economic		Foreign		Cultural	
1982	83%	(LIB)	68%	(LIB)	70%	(LIB)
	15%	(CONS)	31%	(CONS)	29%	(CONS)
1981	75%	(LIB)	61%	(LIB)	91%	(LIB)
	24%	(CONS)	39%	(CONS)	9%	(CONS)

Key Votes

1) Reagan 81 Budget	AGN	5) Incr SS Rtmt Age	AGN	9) Poor Pay Food Stamps	AGN
2) Reagan 81 Tax Cut	AGN	6) Saudi AWACS Sale	AGN	10) Ban Crt Busing Order	AGN
3) Bal Budget Amend	AGN	7) $ for MX Missile	AGN	11) Auto Local Content	FOR
4) Gas & Road Tax	FOR	8) Nerve Gas Prod	FOR	12) Nuclear Arms Freeze	FOR

Election Results

1982 general	Vic Fazio (D)	118,476	(64%)	($314,033)
	Roger B. Canfield (R)	67,047	(36%)	($62,176)
1982 primary	Vic Fazio (D)	61,095	(100%)	
1980 general	Vic Fazio (D)	133,853	(65%)	($185,300)
	Albert Dehr (R)	60,935	(30%)	($5,517)
	Robert J. Burnside (Libertarian) ..	10,267	(5%)	($0)

Campaign Contributions and Expenditures

1981-82		Direct Cont. 81-82		PACS brkdwn			
Receipts	$336,964	Indiv	$133,278	Agr	$32,800	Ideo	$5,550
Expend.	$314,033	Party	$69	Bus	$51,200	Lbr	$48,700
Unspent	$51,265	PACS	$151,687	Hlth	$6,700	Prof	$1,450

FIFTH DISTRICT

San Francisco is a special city, named over and over as the city most Americans would like to live in and most tourists would like to visit. It has a unique climate (or climates: they vary all over the city), physical beauty, a psychological atmosphere that some people find enchanting and some don't. It is a quintessentially American city: founded and built into major city status in a single year, 1850; built in indigenous American styles, both before and after the 1906 earthquake; for all its claims to be cosmopolitan, still a city that dotes on itself and has little interest in foreign modes.

Yet San Francisco is also one of our most polyglot cities, and not in any familiar pattern. For all the Irish and Italian families who still live within the city limits, there are more Mexican–Americans and blacks. And the largest minority group, if you count them altogether, are the Asians. Actually, they are as diverse as Europeans: the Japanese tend to be upwardly mobile; the Chinese still rather insular, as if they all lived still in Chinatown, although many are well educated and economically successful now; the Filipinos concentrated in low wage jobs. And there are the gays. If you credited some accounts, you would suppose that everyone in San Francisco is homosexual, which of course is not the case. But as anyone who has been there lately knows, there is a large, self-conscious gay community, full of professionally successful and, increasingly, politically active people.

How do you explain all this diversity? One way is by realizing that the city of San Francisco is just one part, and a rather small part at that, of a much larger metropolitan area. Some 5.1 million people live in the counties around San Francisco Bay; only 678,000 of them, or 13%, live in the city of San Francisco. It is a physically small area as well, its neighborhoods squeezed into valleys or spread on steep hillsides at the end of a small bony peninsula that separates the Bay from the Ocean. No one has much of a yard in San Francisco—which is one reason, wholly apart from the presence of gays, that you find one of the nation's smallest percentages of households with children here (21% in the 5th district). The city's population is in fact a skewed sample of the Bay Area, just as the Bay Area is a skewed sample of California. San Francisco has the cultural extremes—the rich and poor, the ethnic and gay—because they tend to cluster, in most cases by preference, here in the central city.

In some ways, San Francisco is probably less distinctive than it was—or likes to think of itself. In the late 19th century, it was set off by itself so far from other urban centers—days of railroad travel, weeks of ocean voyage from any other large city—that it developed its own traditions and styles. It spawned its own radical Workingman's Party, whose leader, Denis Kearney, wanted to prohibit Chinese immigration; it had its own local political boss, Abe Ruef, who was thrown out by the progressive reformer Hiram Johnson. It developed its own literary heroes—Jack London, Frank Norris, Ambrose Bierce—and its own arts and crafts style. It also fostered one of the strongest union movements in the land. Underneath this turbulence and efflorescence, San Francisco enjoyed an economy based on that most prosaic of commodities, food. It was through San Francisco's ports and rail facilities, its canneries and packers, that most of California's incredibly rich harvest of vegetables, fruits, and other agricultural products made its way to the rest of the world. This is the mouth of the Central Valley cornucopia.

San Francisco's political tradition was progressive Republican until the 1930s—pro-union, anti-corruption, pro-regulation. In the New Deal period it switched to the party of Franklin D. Roosevelt, and San Francisco today is one of the most Democratic constituencies in California or the nation. Yet it is an uneasy coalition, of those who like the Democrats for their economic redistributionist programs and those who like them for their liberality on cultural issues. San Francisco was always an economically comfortable city and didn't suffer as much in the Depression as much of the nation. But in the 1960s and 1970s it became incredibly affluent. Its downtown is the largest in the nation, after Chicago's and New York's; its metropolitan area has spawned the high tech industry, in which its only rival is Boston; the food business goes on. Housing prices have risen vastly in the city and its suburbs; in effect San Franciscans with good jobs have performed the trick of persuading the rest of the world to support them so generously that they can afford an affluent lifestyle the rest of the world envies. True, there are poor people here; but many of them appear to be moving upward rapidly, especially the Asians who are, after all, the city's largest minority.

The 5th congressional district of California takes in three-fourths of the people of the city of San Francisco. Although its boundaries were changed for 1984 by the December 1982 redistricting, its basic character will remain the same. It includes all the rich areas of the city: Nob Hill, Russian Hill, and Pacific Heights overlooking the Bay; the Marina district down by the water's edge; Presidio Heights with its leafy palms and Sea Cliff with its enormous vistas of the Ocean and the Golden Gate; St. Francis Wood, below Twin Peaks, the home of the city's Catholic elite. It includes the city's middle income residential areas, with their older houses amid unburied telephone and electric wires: Richmond, with its many Chinese families, Sunset, stretching out on grid streets toward the Ocean. And it includes lower income areas: the sunny Mission District, shielded from the Ocean clouds by Twin Peaks; Portrero Hill, with restored houses overlooking downtown; the farther reaches of the city, with their varicolored pastel houses strewn out along grid streets hugging the steep hills.

The 5th district was the district represented by the late Phillip Burton, one of the two or three most important congressmen in the last 20 years. Although he failed, by one vote, to be elected House majority leader in 1976, he still did more to change the way business is done in the House, and channeled more money and benefits to poor people than any other congressman. Richard Bolling, his longtime rival and in the end an ally, can claim to have done more for reform; Morris Udall passed more environmental legislation; but no one else came close to doing all the different things Burton did.

Burton's contributions were often undervalued outside the House—partly because he didn't care about publicizing himself. He was not an easy man to like: he was loud, he had a hot temper, he was a fighter whose persistence and vehemence are legendary. There was nothing subtle or ingratiating about him. Yet from his seats on the Interior and Education and Labor Committees, and his subcommittee chairmanships (the Interior subcommittee on insular affairs and parks, the Education and Labor subcommittee on labor laws), his legislative output was immense. His achievements include:

- Vastly expanding the number and size of the national parks, including the Redwood National Park in California. His 1978 bill created or expanded 34 parks, 12 wilderness areas, eight scenic rivers, and four national trails.
- Helping to establish the Supplemental Security Income (SSI) program. This augments the income of four million aged, blind, and disabled people—a kind of welfare program on top of Social Security.
- Making strikers eligible for food stamps.
- Establishing the Black Lung Compensation program for coal miners.
- Increasing the minimum wage in 1978 from $2.30 to $3.35.
- Extending the food stamp program to Puerto Rico, the Virgin Islands, Guam, and American Samoa.
- Engineering the abolition in 1975 of what had been the House Un-American Activities Committee. Richard Nixon, running for governor of California in 1962, called on Pat Brown to repudiate Burton, then an assemblyman, because he wanted to abolish HUAC.
- Establishing the rule that all House committee chairmen must be elected by the Democratic Caucus, by secret ballot, every two years.

On some of these other legislators played major roles. But few if any would have been accomplished without Burton. In some cases he shaped the legislation himself; in others he forged the alliance without which they wouldn't have passed. A typical Burton move was to gather liberal votes for cotton subsidies in return for southern votes for black lung legislation. Burton was known for his bombastic speaking style and forceful personality. But his secret on all these matters—and on California redistricting as well—was detailed knowledge of the legislation and the facts. He did not depend on staff: he liked to boast that he knows more about welfare or parks legislation than anyone else, and he probably did.

He had his shortcomings as a legislator and his disappointments. He had a taste for the unexpected alliance: he liked to befriend southern members or certain conservatives, and cosponsor measures with them, or get their support on procedural matters. But one such alliance—with Wayne Hays, then one of the leading powers in the House—cost him dearly. Hays was forced to leave the House by the Elizabeth Ray scandal in 1976, and Burton lost the election for House majority leader by one vote a few months later; he lost a number of votes because of his closeness to Hays. He also had a taste for obtaining results surreptitiously. He got HUAC abolished by persuading most of the Democrats on the committee to resign and by getting others disqualified from membership by a rules change—an elaborate procedure, when the Caucus might very well have voted to abolish it outright. His aversion to publicity led Washington observers to undervalue his productivity and undoubtedly left many constituents wondering what he was up to in Washington.

He finally had to tell them in 1982, when he faced his first serious Republican opponent in a congressional election. It was sparked by Republican outrage over the redistricting plan he engineered and which inflicted more damage on the Republicans than they thought possible. Burton had also taken care to carve out a safe, but grotesquely shaped, district for his brother, John Burton, who had represented a San Francisco-Marin County district since 1974. John Burton had serious personal problems and surprised everyone, including his brother, by retiring. But in the meantime the Republicans had persuaded state Senator Milton Marks to run against Phil. Marks is the most popular Republican in the city: he has won citywide races several times (including once against John Burton), and in this race the city's most heavily Democratic precincts (mostly black) would be in the other district, put there to help John. Moreover, Marks had spent a lot of time cultivating local groups, notably the gays, and attending to their problems; Phil Burton spent most of the time in Washington, concentrating on national legislation.

That turned out, in the end, to be an asset. Burton raised huge amounts of money—he was the number one beneficiary of labor funds in 1982—and attracted hundreds of volunteers, based on his national record. In the end Burton ended up winning, 59%–41%, and proved conclusively that there was no district in San Francisco in which he could not beat the strongest posssible opponent.

In 1983 Burton was as busy as ever. He and Henry Waxman of Los Angeles were the dominant forces in the Democratic Steering Committee's assignment of committee positions; he was helping John Seiberling of Ohio with a new parks bill; he was revelling in his 1982 victory. Then he died suddenly in April. The special election for his seat has been scheduled for June 21, 1983. His widow, Sala Burton, has announced her candidacy. She is an astute politician herself, a strong believer in the programs Burton backed, and knows both the district and Washington well. She has more surface charm, but is just as unyielding. She may have strong competition, from Milton Marks, or from Supervisor Quentin Kopp, a conservative in city issues, or City Administrator Roger Boas. But Sala Burton, in touch with the large organization she helped her husband assemble in 1982, seems the favorite.

The People   Pop. 1980: 525,914, dn. 3.1% 1970–80; voting age pop. 435,713; 7% Black, 11% Span. orig., 20% Asian orig. 58% housing units rented. Median owner $107,000; renter $285. Households: 50% family, 21% with children, 37% married couples.

Presidential Vote

1980	Reagan (R)	59,018	(33%)
	Carter (D)	91,579	(51%)
	Other	30,007	(17%)

Rep. Phillip Burton (D) Died April 10, 1983. Special election scheduled for June 21, 1983.

Election Results

1982 general	Phillip Burton (D)	103,268	(59%)	($779,801)
	Milton Marks (R)	72,139	(41%)	($837,440)
1982 primary	Phillip Burton (D)	61,230	(100%)	
1980 general	Phillip Burton (D)	93,400	(69%)	($140,812)
	Tom Spinosa (R)	34,500	(26%)	($6,906)
	Roy Childs (Libertarian)	6,750	(5%)	($0)

SIXTH DISTRICT

Marin County—it is a place that has assumed a significance in the national mind out of all proportion to its size. It is a county of just 222,000 people, packed into a string of suburbs tucked between mountains and the northern reaches of San Francisco Bay. In a nation in which politics is increasingly based on cultural attitudes, Marin occupies an extreme on a spectrum. It is, all at the same time, trendy and affluent, liberal if not totally permissive on cultural issues, conservative if not downright parsimonious and selfish on economic matters. "Trendy Marin" in the 1970s has been captured for history in Cyra McFadden's *The Serial*, but life goes on there pretty much as it was; people in Marin may be me-centered, but they do not seem very self-conscious. In their Volvo-filled parking lots, in their rustic redwood-sided contemporary homes, in their evergreen-shaded Jacuzzi thermal baths, Marin Countians continue to keep up with the latest fads and fashions and to believe almost devoutly in their own virtue for doing so.

Marin's combination of attitudes has not taken the country by storm. Even if it is true that the nation has become more liberal on cultural issues and more conservative on economics, it has not done so in the rigorous way Marin has. In presidential elections, in fact, Marin seems almost precisely countercyclical. A longtime Republican stronghold, it came within a hairsbreadth of going for George McGovern in 1972. Then it turned around and voted solidly for Gerald Ford in 1976. In 1980 it refused to give Ronald Reagan a majority and gave John Anderson one of his highest percentages in the nation.

Marin County forms about half of California's 6th congressional district. The other half, for the 1982 elections, was made up of an odd combination: the waterfront edge of San Francisco, together with most of its black neighborhoods; the working class suburb of Daly City, south of the city; the working class city of Vallejo, far on the other side of San Francisco. This odd combination was intended by Congressman Phillip Burton, who drew the plan, to re-elect his brother John; but John, citing personal problems and a desire to get out of public office, retired instead. There was obviously some kind of personal tragedy here, and a failure to live up to expectations. John Burton seemed a misfit in Congress, but in the early 1970s he had been one of the leading legislators in Sacramento. When he came to Washington he probably expected to be a leader again, when Phil became majority leader; but Phil lost that race by one vote in 1976, and John Burton ended up without much to do.

Burton's withdrawal probably enhanced Democratic chances and certainly changed the plans of Dennis McQuaid, the Republican who gave him a close race in 1980 and looked forward to beating him in 1982. The five-candidate Democratic primary was won by Marin County Supervisor Barbara Boxer with an even 50%—just enough to have kept her out of a runoff in the South. Boxer seems to personify, in a more serious way, the Marin approach to politics, but she got her support from outside Marin as well as in. Indeed, in the general election, McQuaid, who is from the northern, not particularly trendy Marin town of Novato, actually carried Marin; he stressed his support of the nuclear freeze and environmental measures. Boxer won by virtue of a huge margin in San Francisco and small margins in Daly City and Vallejo. The revised boundaries for 1984 are not quite so favorable to a Democrat, and so there is the possibility of a seriously contested general election again.

The People Pop. 1980: 525,724, up 1.1% 1970–80; voting age pop. 408,694; 13% Black, 7% Span. orig., 12% Asian orig., 1% Am. Ind. 51% housing units rented. Median owner $114,200; renter $261. Households: 57% family, 29% with children, 43% married couples.

Presidential Vote

1980	Reagan (R)	72,949	(37%)
	Carter (D)	89,964	(47%)
	Other	33,367	(17%)

Rep. Barbara Boxer (D) Elected 1982; b. Nov. 11, 1940, Brooklyn, NY; home, Greenbrae; Brooklyn Col., B.A. 1962; Jewish.

Career Stockbroker, researcher, 1962–65; Journalist, *Pacific Sun*; District aide to U.S. Rep. Phillip Burton; Marin Cnty. Bd. of Sprvsrs., 1976–82, President, 1980–81.

Offices 1517 LHOB, 202-225-5161. Also 450 Golden Gate Ave., Box 36024, San Francisco 94102, 415-556-1333; 823 Marin, Rm. 8, Vallejo 94590, 707-552-0720; and 901 Irwin St., San Rafael 94901, 415-457-7272.

Committees *Government Operations* (17th). Subcommittees: Government Information, Justice, and Agriculture; Environment, Energy and Natural Resources. *Merchant Marine and Fisheries* (25th). Subcommittees: Merchant Marine; Coast Guard and Navigation; Oceanography. *Select Committee on Children, Youth, and Families* (11th).

Group Ratings and Key Votes: Newly Elected

Election Results

1982 general	Barbara Boxer (D)	96,379	(52%)	($531,401)
	Dennis McQuaid (R)	82,128	(45%)	($621,477)
1982 primary	Barbara Boxer (D)	40,199	(51%)	
	Louise H. Renne (D)	23,340	(30%)	($334,394)
	Three others	14,817	(19%)	
1980 general	John L. Burton (D)	101,105	(51%)	($369,237)
	Dennis McQuaid (R)	89,624	(45%)	($484,140)

Campaign Contributions and Expenditures

1981-82		*Direct Cont. 81-82*		*PACS brkdwn*			
Receipts	$519,313	Indiv	$339,974	Agr	$4,000	Ideo	$39,810
Expend.	$531,401	Party	$11,500	Bus	$1,645	Lbr	$60,687
Unspent	$2,384	PACS	$114,333	Hlth	$2,350	Prof	$950
		Cand	$29,445				

Indirect Party Expend: $58   *Indep Expend:* For: $460

SEVENTH DISTRICT

The 7th congressional district of California is the northernmost of four East Bay districts. The East Bay is not nearly so well known nationally as San Francisco, yet just as many people live on the east side of the Bay as the west—nearly two million if you count all the way down to San Jose. The 7th district, entirely within Contra Costa County and reasonably regular in shape on the map, actually jumps over several rugged chains of mountains that separate successive strings of East Bay communities. Facing the Bay in the 7th is Richmond; much of this was an instant town, housing put up for the workers at the Kaiser Shipyard here in World War II. Employers have changed, but Richmond and nearby San Pablo still have the hard look of shipyard towns. About half of Richmond's residents are black, and the area is heavily Democratic.

Separated from Richmond by the Berkeley Hills and the San Pablo Ridge are several industrial towns on the Bay (Pinole, Hercules, Rodeo); they are in turn separated by more hills from the county seat of Martinez, on the Bay where it becomes an arm of the Sacramento River, and the inland suburbs of Concord and Pleasant Hill. These are white collar in character, politically marginal in elections; they are far enough out from the Bay—nearly 20 miles from downtown San Francisco by freeway or BART—to have housing prices that are affordable for young couples; this is where many, hoping to move some place more fashionable later, start out. Another ridge separates Concord from the industrial towns of Pittsburg and Antioch, near the Sacramento River delta.

The 7th leans Democratic, but not overwhelmingly so. Its congressman is George Miller, one of the more important members of the Democratic class of 1974. His father was a powerful state senator, and he got his legislative training in Sacramento; in the House he was a protege and ally of San Francisco's Phillip Burton. Miller is not burdened with the doubts some members of the class of 1974 express about the wisdom of government spending programs; he generally supports them, and with some enthusiasm and skill. Like many older Democrats, he seems to regard his duty as preventing the rich from getting too greedy and seeing that the poor and middle class enjoy economic security and get their share of society's wealth.

Miller has been the House's leading opponent of Central Valley farmers and tried to prevent them from repealing the law that limits the recipients of federally subsidized water to 160 acres; it has never been enforced, but big landowners are worried that it will. Miller has been forced to compromise on this issue, but not so much so as to constitute a defeat; and had he not been raising the issue the valley growers would have had their way completely in the House.

Miller sits on the Education and Labor and Budget Committees; he gave up his seat on Interior in 1983 to take Budget. There he will likely be one of the chief backers of generous spending on domestic programs and relatively low increases in defense spending. He chairs the Subcommittee on Labor Standards, which considers such controversial matters as the proposal for a youth subminimum wage, which as of 1983 the Reagan administration had not dared to advance; it will not go far in Miller's subcommittee.

In 1983 Miller picked up an additional, and potentially fascinating, assignment, as chairman of a new Select Committee on Children, Youth, and Families. Politicians of both right and left like to talk of family issues. The right usually talks about strengthening belief in traditional morality and encouraging traditional cultural attitudes; the left sometimes talks about somehow reducing the inequalities between families that leave one child with less of a chance to ascend to the top levels of society than another. As a practical matter, however, liberals usually end up talking about providing government aid and services to disadvantaged families and in particular to single parents—while conservatives rage that these very programs provide incentives for families to split up and fathers to shirk their family responsibilities. Both sides miss the point. In the United States, as in the world generally, poor people usually have more children than rich people. That means that at any given time, the income levels of children are lower than the income levels of adults, and so every generation has the task of upgrading the skills and abilities of its children, so that they can rise not only above the level of their parents but above the even higher level occupied by the generation of adults ahead of them. Every generation the United States has been successful at doing this, despite the pauses in economic growth during major depressions in the 1890s and 1930s. Now many Americans doubt that there is a better economic future for today's children. The lesson of history is that there can be. But will this committee help? It could easily degenerate into a forum for stereotyped liberal and conservative arguments from Miller and the ranking Republican, Dan Marriott of Utah. But Miller seems to have an original enough mind to ask how government, which has helped upgrade children in the past, can do so in the rather different environment we face today. This select committee has no power to mark up legislation but, if it is led properly, can help Congress and the country to focus on ways to solve what too many people now are dismissing as insoluble problems.

Miller has won reelection by wide margins since 1976. He was helped by Burton's redistricting plan: Ronald Dellums of the next door 8th district would surely have liked to have Richmond in his district, but Burton made sure that its heavy Democratic margins would go to his friend Miller.

The People   Pop. 1980: 525,334, up 15.2% 1970–80; voting age pop. 387,842; 10% Black, 8% Span. orig., 4% Asian orig., 1% Am. Ind. 33% housing units rented. Median owner $84,600; renter $261. Households: 72% family, 40% with children, 59% married couples.

Presidential Vote

1980	Reagan (R)	96,765	(47%)
	Carter (D)	84,516	(41%)
	Other	24,793	(12%)

Rep. George Miller (D) Elected 1974; b. May 17, 1945, Richmond; home, Martinez; Diablo Valley Col., San Fran. St. Col., B.A. 1968, U. of CA at Davis, J.D. 1972; Roman Catholic.

Career Leg. Aide to CA Senate Major. Ldr., 1969–74.

Offices 2422 RHOB, 202-225-2095. Also 367 Civic Ctr., Pleasant Hill 94523, 415-687-3260.

Committees *Budget* (14th). Task Forces: Budget Process; Education and Employment; Tax Policy. *Education and Labor* (10th). Subcommittees: Elementary, Secondary and Vocational Education; Labor Standards (Chairman); Select Education; Human Resources.

Group Ratings

	ADA	ACLU	COPE	CFA	LCV	LWV	NTU	NSI	COC	ACA	CSFC
1982	95	100	90	80	91	91	31	0	20	5	22
1981	100	—	90	93	100	—	46	—	11	9	27
1980	94	100	88	93	88	100	25	0	65	27	29

National Journal Ratings

	Economic		Foreign		Cultural	
1982	82%	(LIB)	96%	(LIB)	98%	(LIB)
	18%	(CONS)	1%	(CONS)	1%	(CONS)
1981	81%	(LIB)	92%	(LIB)	92%	(LIB)
	15%	(CONS)	2%	(CONS)	8%	(CONS)

Key Votes

1) Reagan 81 Budget AGN	5) Incr SS Rtmt Age AGN	9) Poor Pay Food Stamps AGN
2) Reagan 81 Tax Cut AGN	6) Saudi AWACS Sale AGN	10) Ban Crt Busing Order AGN
3) Bal Budget Amend AGN	7) $ for MX Missile AGN	11) Auto Local Content FOR
4) Gas & Road Tax —	8) Nerve Gas Prod AGN	12) Nuclear Arms Freeze FOR

Election Results

1982 general	George Miller (D)	126,952	(67%)	($139,512)
	Paul E. Vallely (R)	56,960	(30%)	($120,089)
1982 primary	George Miller (D)	73,904	(100%)	
1980 general	George Miller (D)	142,044	(63%)	($132,477)
	Giles St. Clair (R)	70,479	(31%)	($38,434)

Campaign Contributions and Expenditures

1981-82		Direct Cont. 81-82		PACS brkdwn			
Receipts	$207,101	Indiv	$126,932	Agr	$850	Ideo	$3,531
Expend.	$139,512	Party	$2,106	Bus	$6,113	Lbr	$46,411
Unspent	$88,704	PACS	$61,120	Hlth	$950	Prof	$2,170

Indirect Party Expend: $4,075

EIGHTH DISTRICT

The closest thing we have in the United States to a self-consciously radical congressional district is the 8th district of California. This is where the first great student rebellion of the 1960s broke out, the Free Speech Movement at the University of California's Berkeley campus. Berkeley itself has a unique sort of politics: it is one of the few places in the nation where an elected school board imposed a busing program for integration, to bring together black children from the flatlands near San Francisco Bay and affluent whites from the professional neighborhoods in the hills above the campus. Berkeley no longer sees the kind of disturbances and riots it had in the early 1970s, when Governor Ronald Reagan sent in troops to quell them; its political activists are a little older now, the students more quiescent. But there is, among these highly educated, often not very well-paid professionals, a kind of simmering resentment against the order of things, a sense that they, and not the old white males in the Bank of America tower across the Bay, should be running society, a search for causes to champion and sores to rub raw.

That spirit still seems to dominate the politics of the 8th district, even though it animates a relatively small percentage of its voters. About one-quarter of the district's residents live in Berkeley and three similar suburbs (Albany, Kensington, El Cerrito); about half live in Oakland; and another quarter live over the Berkeley Hills, in highly affluent suburbs. Oakland is very much a divided city: 43% of its residents in the 8th district are black, living again on the flatland spreading north and south from the city's downtown; most of the rest are affluent whites, living on curving streets in the hills or in the enclave suburb of Piedmont.

There are fewer professors and liberals, more conservatives like Edwin Meese, the top Reagan aide who grew up in Oakland and whose father and grandfather were active in its civic affairs. The suburbs over the hills—whether woodsy and rustic like Orinda, Moraga, and Lafayette, or full of newly minted subdivisions like Alamo, Danville, and San Ramon— are not sympathetic at all to anything smacking of radical politics.

Nonetheless, the district is represented by a self-styled radical, Democrat Ronald Dellums. A former social worker and Berkeley councilman, he won the seat in 1970, beating a Democrat with a near-perfect liberal record by charging that he was not anti-war and anti-establishment enough. Dellums's stance infuriated California Reagan Republicans, and they made serious attempts to defeat him, to no avail: he ran 8% or more behind the standard Democratic vote, but in this very Democratic district that still left him with enough votes to win easily. That has been the story in elections here ever since. The radical Berkeley movement that gave Dellums his first primary victory has petered out, and the district would not *ab initio* pick someone like him as its congressman today. But the opposition he aroused among some Democrats has also quieted down, and he has not had serious opposition in the primary. As for the general, in 1982 he lost the suburbs east of the hills by a 3–1 margin, but still managed to hold the seat comfortably. He will not be helped there by charges made in 1983 that he and members of his staff used cocaine and other illegal drugs; but it should be remembered that congressmen in the early 1980s became targets for totally unsubstantiated accusations, and in any case this is one of the districts in the country least likely to punish an elected official for use or tolerance of recreational drugs.

In the House Dellums has succeeded, by seniority, to the chairmanship of the District of Columbia Committee. This is not a particularly important body any more, since Congress a decade ago granted the District home rule; and Dellums is not inclined to interfere in its affairs. His more important position, at least potentially, is as a subcommittee chairman on the House Armed Services Committee. Dellums has always been an odd man out on this hawkish panel, but its members decided not to tinker with the operation of the seniority rule they (but not Dellums) always championed, and let him become a subcommittee chairman in 1983. The subcommittee is Military Installations and Facilities; and some historian 100 years hence may argue that Dellums sought this position for years to protect the interests of Oakland's big military bases. Of course that's nonsense, and the big decisions in these matters are usually taken by the Appropriations subcommittees anyway. Nonetheless, there are some new, unknown members on this subcommittee, and it may be willing to approve the deactivation of some military bases that both Dellums and Pentagon bureaucrats would agree are unnecessary. That would be a delicious outcome and a reminder that the seniority system brings to positions of power men whose careers are impelled by ardent positions on the issues of 15 and 20 years before.

The People   Pop. 1980: 525,927, up .5% 1970–80; voting age pop. 409,493; 24% Black, 6% Span. orig., 8% Asian orig. 49% housing units rented. Median owner $108,000; renter $218. Households: 57% family, 29% with children, 42% married couples.

Presidential Vote

1980	Reagan (R)	74,370	(33%)
	Carter (D)	116,652	(52%)
	Other	34,946	(15%)

Rep. Ronald V. Dellums (D) Elected 1970; b. Nov. 24, 1935, Oakland; home, Berkeley; Oakland City Col., A.A. 1958, San Fran. St. Col., B.A. 1960, U. of CA, M.S.W. 1962; Protestant.

Career USMC, 1954–56; Psychiatric Social Worker, CA Dept. of Mental Hygiene, 1962–64; Program Dir., Bayview Community Ctr., 1964–65; Dir., Hunter's Pt. Bayview Youth Opp. Ctr., 1965–66; Assoc. Dir., San Fran. Econ. Opp. Council's Concentrated Empl. Program, 1967–68; Berkeley City Cncl., 1967–71.

Offices 2136 RHOB, 202-225-2661. Also 2490 Channing Way, Rm. 202, Berkeley 94704, 415-548-7767.

Committees *District of Columbia* (Chairman). Subcommittee: Fiscal Affairs and Health. *Armed Services* (8th). Subcommittees: Research and Development; Military Installations and Facilities (Chairman).

Group Ratings

	ADA	ACLU	COPE	CFA	LCV	LWV	NTU	NSI	COC	ACA	CSFC
1982	85	100	91	90	99	75	46	0	18	0	23
1981	95	—	91	71	100	—	52	—	0	10	26
1980	100	100	89	100	92	100	31	0	36	23	22

National Journal Ratings

	Economic		Foreign		Cultural	
1982	79%	(LIB)	96%	(LIB)	88%	(LIB)
	21%	(CONS)	1%	(CONS)	11%	(CONS)
1981	89%	(LIB)	89%	(LIB)	95%	(LIB)
	3%	(CONS)	10%	(CONS)	1%	(CONS)

Key Votes

1) Reagan 81 Budget	AGN	5) Incr SS Rtmt Age	AGN	9) Poor Pay Food Stamps	AGN
2) Reagan 81 Tax Cut	AGN	6) Saudi AWACS Sale	AGN	10) Ban Crt Busing Order	AGN
3) Bal Budget Amend	AGN	7) $ for MX Missile	AGN	11) Auto Local Content	FOR
4) Gas & Road Tax	AGN	8) Nerve Gas Prod	AGN	12) Nuclear Arms Freeze	FOR

Election Results

1982 general	Ronald V. Dellums (D)	121,537	(56%)	Est.–($944,089)
	Claude B. Hutchison, Jr. (R)	95,694	(44%)	($555,155)
1982 primary	Ronald V. Dellums (D)	67,613	(76%)	
	Andreas Vamis (D)	21,193	(24%)	
1980 general	Ronald V. Dellums (D)	108,380	(56%)	($312,128)
	Charles V. Hughes (R)	76,580	(39%)	($82,500)
	Tod Mikuriya (Libertarian)	10,465	(5%)	($0)

Campaign Contributions and Expenditures*

1981-82		Direct Cont. 81-82		PACS brkdwn			
Receipts	$944,089 est.	PACS	$46,010	Agr	$650	Ideo	$5,650
Expend.	$868,705 est.			Bus	$5,750	Lbr	$32,830
				Hlth	$800	Prof	$250

Indirect Expend: Agn: $840   *As of May 1, 1983 candidate had not yet provided final figures to F.E.C.

NINTH DISTRICT

As you look out on the East Bay from the skyscrapers of downtown San Francisco, your eyes go first to the Bay Bridge, then to the big Navy and Army bases and the port of Oakland, up a little to the skyscrapers of Oakland behind, then over to the left of the Bridge to see if you can make out the towers of the campus in Berkeley. Those are the landmarks: you don't look much to the right, or south, of downtown Oakland, to see the expanse of East Bay neighborhoods and suburbs spreading out down to where the Bay itself spreads out to the width of a miniature sea and is spanned by the mostly causeway-like San Mateo Bridge. If you were looking there, though, what you would be seeing is most of the 9th congressional district of California.

The 9th district includes the old city of Alameda, resolutely middle class despite its proximity to Navy bases and the Oakland ghetto; it includes some mostly black neighborhoods in Oakland itself; it passes south and includes the modest working class suburbs of San Leandro, San Lorenzo, and Hayward. The terrain here is not much different from other places in the Bay Area; the houses are built of the same materials, mostly stucco; the shopping centers to outward appearances are what you see all over. But there are discount chains rather than Saks, bargain drugstores rather than boutiques. Housing prices here are among the least unreasonable in the Bay Area, and this is where working people, mostly white but many Mexican–Americans as well, live. Over the mountains, where you can't see if you are looking from San Francisco, it includes the upper middle income suburbs of Pleasanton and Livermore, situated in a peaceful valley outside the Bay Area orbit.

This is a Democratic district in most elections, but its Democratic margins are not inflated by the presence of a large black community, and it sometimes goes Republican. The congressman here is Fortney (Pete) Stark, first elected in 1972 when he beat an elderly incumbent. Stark is by nature a kind of insurgent: he started a bank in nearby Walnut Creek and attracted deposits from all over the Bay Area by putting a giant peace symbol atop his headquarters and peace symbol motifs on all the checks. He spent liberally on his own campaign and, reversing what was then the usual practice, got rid of his bank stock before taking a seat on the House Banking Committee; other members used to acquire bank stock, often for nominal amounts, at that point.

Stark is part of the solidly liberal contingent in the Bay Area delegation. He is ready to admit that business needs incentives in order to produce economic growth, but he is inclined to think the incentives today are more than sufficient; after all, his experience has been that it's easy to make money. He serves now on the Ways and Means Committee and chairs one of its most important subcommittees, Select Revenue Measures. This is the body that approves or disapproves all those terribly minor and boring changes in the tax code, each one of which, however, can mean a great deal to certain taxpayers. This committee is endlessly lobbied, by business representatives and by other congressmen, and most of its work never engages the attention of the public or the press. Stark is now in a position of great power, but it is also one that imposes considerable responsibility and involves some political risks too.

In 1982 Stark spent much time and effort as the chief sponsor of a measure that would have given Apple Computer a tax deduction for donating computers to every high school in the nation. Everyone these days wants to promote computer literacy, and the measure won wide support in the House; it was prevented from coming to a vote in the Senate, however.

Undoubtedly the Apple bill generated favorable publicity in his district, and it will probably be one of his major projects in the 98th Congress. Stark has not had really tough competition at the polls since 1972, although there is a Republican base over the hills and this is a hard district to keep in touch with. But redistricting, thanks to Phil Burton, didn't hurt Stark, and he seems likely to keep winning reelection easily in the 1980s.

The People   Pop. 1980: 524,649, up 2.4% 1970–80; voting age pop. 387,387; 10% Black, 6% Span. orig., 6% Asian orig., 1% Am. Ind. 39% housing units rented. Median owner $82,600; renter $258. Households: 71% family, 38% with children, 57% married couples.

Presidential Vote

1980	Reagan (R)	82,368	(46%)
	Carter (D)	75,939	(42%)
	Other	21,393	(12%)

Rep. Fortney H. (Pete) **Stark** (D) Elected 1972; b. Nov. 11, 1931, Milwaukee, WI; home, Oakland; MIT, B.S. 1953, U. of CA, M.B.A. 1959; Unitarian.

Career Air Force, 1955–57; Founder, Beacon Savings and Loan Assn., 1961; Founder and Pres., Security Natl. Bank, Walnut Creek, 1963–72.

Offices 1034 LHOB, 202-225-5065. Also 7 Eastmont Mall, Oakland 94605, 415-635-1092.

Committees District of Columbia (4th). Subcommittees: Fiscal Affairs and Health; Government Operations and Metropolitan Affairs. *Ways and Means* (5th). Subcommittees: Public Assistance and Unemployment Compensation; Select Revenue Measures (Chairman). *Select Committee on Narcotics Abuse and Control* (3d).

Group Ratings

	ADA	ACLU	COPE	CFA	LCV	LWV	NTU	NSI	COC	ACA	CSFC
1982	95	100	91	80	90	92	24	10	11	5	23
1981	95	—	90	86	99	—	52	—	11	8	27
1980	94	100	83	93	87	100	24	11	53	17	25

National Journal Ratings

	Economic		Foreign		Cultural	
1982	96%	(LIB)	95%	(LIB)	99%	(LIB)
	2%	(CONS)	5%	(CONS)	1%	(CONS)
1981	89%	(LIB)	80%	(LIB)	95%	(LIB)
	3%	(CONS)	19%	(CONS)	1%	(CONS)

Key Votes

1) Reagan 81 Budget	AGN	5) Incr SS Rtmt Age	FOR
2) Reagan 81 Tax Cut	AGN	6) Saudi AWACS Sale	AGN
3) Bal Budget Amend	AGN	7) $ for MX Missile	AGN
4) Gas & Road Tax	—	8) Nerve Gas Prod	AGN

9) Poor Pay Food Stamps	AGN
10) Ban Crt Busing Order	AGN
11) Auto Local Content	FOR
12) Nuclear Arms Freeze	FOR

Election Results

1982 general	Fortney H. (Pete) Stark (D)	104,393	(61%)	($344,759)
	Bill Kennedy (R)	67,702	(39%)	($290,442)
1982 primary	Fortney H. (Pete) Stark (D)	51,506	(78%)	
	John O'Donnell (D)	14,151	(22%)	($39,488)
1980 general	Fortney H. (Pete) Stark (D)	90,504	(53%)	($62,905)
	Bill Kennedy (R)	67,265	(41%)	($28,806)

Campaign Contributions and Expenditures

1981-82		Direct Cont. 81-82		PACS brkdwn			
Receipts	$340,470	Indiv	$89,638	Agr	$3,000	Ideo	$10,730
Expend.	$344,759	Party	$2,000	Bus	$35,024	Lbr	$56,050
Unspent	$917	PACS	$121,496	Hlth	$4,000	Prof	$1,550
		Cand	$116,158				

TENTH DISTRICT

Just beyond the south end of San Francisco Bay lies the city of San Jose. At the end of World War II it was a sleepy, medium-sized town, the commercial and marketing center for the fertile farms of the Santa Clara Valley. It had, even then, a significant Mexican-American population (as other California farm towns, like Salinas and Hollister, do today). Few people anticipated then what was about to happen: that San Jose would become the focus of the most massive population growth in the San Francisco Bay Area. It made a certain amount of sense: the San Jose area had the largest supply of level land facing the Bay. But San Jose was 60 miles from San Francisco—part of another world. And how would people make a living down there?

The answer is, in the widest variety of ways. San Jose's growth came from two directions. From the east, people moved down from working class East Bay neighborhoods. Factories were built on vacant land, and employees flocked to the new subdivisions nearby. The east side of San Jose is thus largely blue collar, as are the East Bay suburbs to the north: Fremont, Newark, Union City. The other stream of migration to San Jose came from the northwest. Here, along U.S. 101 and Interstate 280, is the Silicon Valley, the heart of the nation's microelectronics industry. People here are highly educated, affluent, addicted to Perrier, bicycling, and jogging. The heart of the Silicon Valley is a dozen miles or so up the freeways from downtown San Jose, but the entire area has benefited from the prosperity and growth it has generated. On both sides, the flat land has now been pretty well filled in, and the hillsides are thick with the houses of affluent residents. Santa Clara County, which includes San Jose and many of the Silicon Valley towns, has increased in population from 290,000 in 1950 to 1.3 million in 1980.

California's 10th congressional district consists of eastern and central San Jose, suburban areas nearby, and the East Bay cities just to the north. It spans the southern edge of the Bay from Hayward to the border between San Jose and Sunnyvale. The 10th has the largest Spanish origin population in the Bay Area (28%), some concentrated in old Mexican neighborhoods in San Jose, but many scattered about the district, as are many products of earlier waves of immigration. This is a solidly Democratic district, solid enough to have voted for George McGovern in 1972 though not for Jimmy Carter in 1980.

For more than 20 years this part of California has been represented by Democratic Congressman Don Edwards. He has a conservative background: he was once an FBI agent, and he got rich because his family owned the only title company in Santa Clara County during its years of great expansion. But by the time he was elected to Congress in 1962, he was one of its most liberal members: one of the early opponents of the Vietnam war and an advocate of abolition of the House Un-American Activities Committee. And today he continues to be one of its most liberal members—and also a competent and accomplished legislator.

Edwards is the fourth ranking Democrat on the Judiciary Committee, and chairman of its Civil and Constitutional Rights Subcommittee. This is a hot seat: the committee has jurisdiction over all constitutional amendments, to ban abortion and to enforce school prayer, to declare that Congress must balance the budget and to ban school busing. Edwards opposes all these amendments, and has used his 4–3 margin on the subcommittee to make sure that they are not reported out to the full Judiciary Committee (although the balanced budget amendment did come to a vote in 1982). In effect, he takes the heat for killing attractive sounding measures that a majority of the House in most cases would oppose on a secret ballot but doesn't want to vote on. Edwards's chief adversary on most of these measures is Henry Hyde, the ranking Republican on the subcommittee, and the House's most effective foe of abortion. They are worthy adversaries: both idealistic men and accomplished practical politicians as well.

Edwards does more than stop measures he doesn't like. He was the chief sponsor of the renewal of the Voting Rights Act in 1982 and succeeded in getting his measure passed despite opposition from the Reagan administration on important provisions; this was one of the chief liberal legislative achievements of the 98th Congress. Edwards also sponsored the Fair Housing Act that passed the House in 1980, and he is ready to press a similar measure if the Reagan administration will give it bipartisan support. Edwards has a deserved reputation for being scrupulously fair when it comes to procedure, and he is pleasant on a personal level; a good athlete and scratch golfer, he can relate to conservatives through shared interests in sports. But he also fights hard for what he believes in and does not make concessions easily.

In the 10th district he is reelected routinely without significant opposition.

The People Pop. 1980: 527,278, up 37.4% 1970–80; voting age pop. 361,394; 5% Black, 24% Span. orig., 10% Asian orig., 1% Am. Ind. 36% housing units rented. Median owner $88,800; renter $276. Households: 76% family, 48% with children, 61% married couples.

Presidential Vote

1980	Reagan (R)	61,657	(45%)
	Carter (D)	57,207	(41%)
	Other	18,894	(14%)

Rep. Don Edwards (D) Elected 1962; b. Jan. 6, 1915, San Jose; home, San Jose; Stanford U. Law School; Unitarian.

Career FBI Agent, 1940–41; Navy, WWII; Pres., Valley Title Co., San Jose.

Offices 2307 RHOB, 202-225-3072. Also 1625 The Alameda, San Jose 95126, 408-292-0143.

Committees *Judiciary* (4th). Subcommittees: Civil and Constitutional Rights (Chairman); Criminal Justice; Monopolies and Commercial Law. *Veterans' Affairs* (2d). Subcommittee: Oversight.

Group Ratings

	ADA	ACLU	COPE	CFA	LCV	LWV	NTU	NSI	COC	ACA	CSFC
1982	100	100	93	100	100	92	27	0	9	13	21
1981	95	—	93	86	91	—	44	—	12	9	24
1980	100	97	89	100	96	100	21	0	63	17	21

National Journal Ratings

	Economic		Foreign		Cultural	
1982	96%	(LIB)	92%	(LIB)	93%	(LIB)
	2%	(CONS)	6%	(CONS)	3%	(CONS)
1981	89%	(LIB)	92%	(LIB)	95%	(LIB)
	3%	(CONS)	2%	(CONS)	1%	(CONS)

Key Votes

1) Reagan 81 Budget	AGN	5) Incr SS Rtmt Age	AGN	9) Poor Pay Food Stamps	AGN
2) Reagan 81 Tax Cut	AGN	6) Saudi AWACS Sale	AGN	10) Ban Crt Busing Order	AGN
3) Bal Budget Amend	AGN	7) $ for MX Missile	AGN	11) Auto Local Content	FOR
4) Gas & Road Tax	—	8) Nerve Gas Prod	AGN	12) Nuclear Arms Freeze	FOR

Election Results

1982 general	Don Edwards (D)	77,263	(63%)	($162,680)
	Bob Herriott (R)	41,506	(34%)	($141,520)
1982 primary	Don Edwards (D)	30,486	(100%)	
1980 general	Don Edwards (D)	102,231	(62%)	($29,151)
	John M. Lutton (R)	45,987	(28%)	($1,542)
	Joseph Fuhrig (Libertarian)	11,904	(7%)	($0)

Campaign Contributions and Expenditures

1981-82		*Direct Cont. 81-82*				*PACS brkdwn*		
Receipts	$162,864	Indiv	$79,505	Agr	$1,600	Ideo	$8,978
Expend.	$162,680	Party	$200	Bus	$13,250	Lbr	$36,200
Unspent	$3,081	PACS	$62,814	Hlth	$550	Prof	$1,850
		Cand	$5,000				

ELEVENTH DISTRICT

The Peninsula is the bony finger of land south of San Francisco that connects the city to the rest of California. Almost down the middle of the Peninsula runs the San Andreas Fault, which some experts believe will shift again in the next 20 years or so. On top of the Fault are San Francisco's reservoirs; to the west the land is mountainous enough to have prevented development south of the suburb of Pacifica, which clings to the foggy mountainsides above the Ocean, a few miles south of San Francisco. Most of the Peninsula's population is packed into neat little suburbs between the Fault and the salt flats and industrial parks on the landfill along San Francisco Bay.

There are two distinct sets of Peninsula suburbs. In the north, adjacent to the city and encircling San Bruno Mountain, are towns that, demographically and politically, are extensions of the city neighborhoods just to the north. Daly City, at the southern extension of the BART lines, has substantial numbers of Mexican-Americans and Asians as well as whites of varying descent; South San Francisco proclaims itself "the industrial city" in big letters on San Bruno Mountain near the Bayshore Freeway; the streets lined with boxy houses in Pacifica and San Bruno wind over sweeping hillsides facing the cemeteries where so many San Franciscans and veterans of Pacific wars have been buried. People in these neighborhoods are mostly from working class backgrounds, although most are upwardly mobile; they are ancestral Democrats, although they sometimes vote Republican; their orientation is to the urban pace of San Francisco, not the life of the Peninsula suburbs south of the airport.

There the atmosphere is different. For one thing, the weather is warmer and sunnier, because the towns are protected from the ocean clouds and fogs by mountains. The people here are more likely to have white collar jobs, to be college educated, to be from backgrounds both Protestant and Republican. The weather is perfect for outdoor sports, and there are more jogging and bicycle paths and tennis courts here, in the string of suburbs south from Millbrae to Los Altos, than anywhere else in the United States. Cultural attitudes here tend to be liberal; people want to save the environment, oppose Vietnam-like wars, and in some cases even legalize marijuana. On economic issues, however, they are not especially interested in redistributing income nor much concerned with unemployment. The federal government is as much a threat as a helper.

Most of the Peninsula makes up California's 11th congressional district. In the 1982 elections it included all of the Peninsula but Daly City in the north and the very high income suburbs near the San Andreas Fault: Hillsborough, Woodside, Portola Valley, Atherton, Menlo Park. But Palo Alto, the solidly Democratic home of Stanford University, was included for 1982; for 1984 Palo Alto is not included, but all of Daly City is; the result is a district with similar Democratic percentages but more of a leaning toward San Francisco and less toward the Silicon Valley. The total district in both cases leans Democratic, but not by overwhelming margins. The Peninsula, under various district boundaries, has been the scene of some closely contested elections; the 11th was picked up by the Republicans in a 1979 election after the death of Congressman Leo Ryan in Jonestown, Guyana, and was recaptured by the Democrats in 1980—one of only four Republican districts they picked up that year.

The congressman is Tom Lantos, an economist and sometime Senate staffer. Lantos was born in Hungary and fought as a teenager in the underground against the Nazis; he was one of the Jews saved by the Swedish diplomat Raoul Wallenberg. A member of the Foreign Affairs Committee, he tried to persuade the Swedes to use the leverage they gained by trapping a Soviet submarine in their waters to get more information about Wallenberg, who many think has been a Soviet prisoner since 1945. Temperamentally, Lantos seems akin to other liberals in the Bay Area delegation; his voting record is somewhat different, however. He is not always as willing to give government a greater role in the economy and regulation. And as a strong supporter of Israel and one who has at first hand opposed dictatorships in Eastern Europe, he is not so critical of American foreign policy or so skeptical about every challenged defense program. On the Foreign Affairs Committee, he specializes not in Third World countries, where liberals are inclined to criticize American policy, but in European, Middle East, and East Asian problems, in which they tend to be more sympathetic with American aims.

Lantos has faced the same Republican, Bill Royer, twice now, and in 1982 substantially increased his 1980 margin. This will still be a tempting district for the right kind of Republican, however, and Lantos cannot count on a free ride in 1984.

The People Pop. 1980: 525,102, up 2.0% 1970–80; voting age pop. 404,129; 5% Black, 10% Span. orig., 7% Asian orig. 41% housing units rented. Median owner $124,300; renter $315. Households: 66% family, 32% with children, 54% married couples.

Presidential Vote

1980	Reagan (R)	92,520	(45%)
	Carter (D)	79,707	(39%)
	Other	34,267	(17%)

Rep. Tom Lantos (D) Elected 1980; b. Feb. 1, 1928, Budapest, Hungary; home, Hillsborough; U. of WA, B.A. 1949, M.A. 1950, U. of CA at Berkeley, Ph.D. 1953; Jewish.

Career Econ.-Foreign Policy Adviser to Sen. Joseph R. Biden, Jr., DE, 1978–79; Consultant to Senate Foreign Relations and Judiciary Committees; Member, Pres. Task Force on Defense and Foreign Policy; Faculty, San. Fran. St. U., 1950–80.

Offices 1707 LHOB, 202-225-3531. Also 520 S. El Camino Real, Su. 800, San Mateo 94402, 415-342-0300.

Committees *Foreign Affairs* (15th). Subcommittees: Asian and Pacific Affairs; Europe and the Middle East; Human Rights and International Organizations. *Government Operations* (14th). Subcommittees: Environment, Energy, and Natural Resources; Government Activities and Transportation; Legislation and National Security. *Select Committee on Aging* (23d). Subcommittee: Human Services.

Group Ratings

	ADA	ACLU	COPE	CFA	LCV	LWV	NTU	NSI	COC	ACA	CSFC
1982	80	71	85	80	73	73	11	40	11	18	29
1981	70	—	71	64	76	76	26	—	24	29	43

National Journal Ratings

	Economic		Foreign		Cultural	
1982	81%	(LIB)	78%	(LIB)	79%	(LIB)
	19%	(CONS)	22%	(CONS)	21%	(CONS)
1981	67%	(LIB)	72%	(LIB)	72%	(LIB)
	33%	(CONS)	26%	(CONS)	27%	(CONS)

Key Votes

1) Reagan 81 Budget	AGN	5) Incr SS Rtmt Age	AGN	9) Poor Pay Food Stamps	AGN
2) Reagan 81 Tax Cut	AGN	6) Saudi AWACS Sale	AGN	10) Ban Crt Busing Order	AGN
3) Bal Budget Amend	AGN	7) $ for MX Missile	AGN	11) Auto Local Content	FOR
4) Gas & Road Tax	—	8) Nerve Gas Prod	AGN	12) Nuclear Arms Freeze	FOR

Election Results

1982 general	Tom Lantos (D)	109,812	(57%)	($1,192,394)
	Bill Royer (R)	76,462	(40%)	($508,907)
1982 primary	Tom Lantos (D)	59,330	(100%)	
1980 general	Tom Lantos (D)	85,823	(46%)	($514,718)
	Bill Royer (R)	80,100	(43%)	($781,795)
	Wilson Branch (Peace and Freedom)	13,723	(7%)	($0)

Campaign Contributions and Expenditures

1981-82		Direct Cont. 81-82		PACS brkdwn			
Receipts	$1,220,529	Indiv	$922,365	Agr	$1,350	Ideo	$25,200
Expend.	$1,192,394	Party	$12,200	Bus	$24,340	Lbr	$114,953
Unspent	$30,701	PACS	$200,363	Hlth	$13,950	Prof	$1,300

Indirect Party Expend: $14,050   *Indep Expend:* For: $243

TWELFTH DISTRICT

The 12th congressional district of California is the High Tech district, indisputably the center of the computer and microchip industries, the now famous Silicon Valley. The district's boundaries even follow the admittedly hazy geographical boundaries of the Silicon Valley. In the north, nearest San Francisco, it includes the center of the Peninsula, taking in Hillsborough, Woodside, Portola Valley, and Atherton—the highest income suburbs of San Francisco, the places where successful Silicon Valley entrepreneurs buy houses for as much as seven figures. Farther south, where Interstate 280 dips below the hills to the string of towns on the flatlands below, it reaches the town of Cupertino, next to San Jose; with only 34,000 people, Cupertino is nonetheless the center of the microcomputer industry, the headquarters of Apple Computer and many other firms less known to the general public but important nonetheless in the growth and development of the industry that has become perhaps the fastest-growing segment—although not as large a segment as is often suggested—of our economy. The 12th district includes also the high income hillside suburbs of Los Altos, Saratoga, and Monte Sereno. In 1982, it then curved around San Jose, avoiding the city and its east side Mexican-American suburban fringe, and climbed over the Coast Range to include enough of Stanislaus County in the Central Valley to meet the population standard. Under the more elegant plan drawn by Phillip Burton for 1984, the 12th avoids the valley and includes instead a part of Santa Cruz County, over the mountains toward the coast.

Why did this area become the center of American high tech? It could, after all, have happened anywhere: it is not an industry tied down by the need for raw materials or requiring ready access to certain energy sources. No one is quite sure of the answer. Some point to the presence of Stanford University, which has encouraged its faculty to experiment with—and profit from—high tech breakthroughs. Others cite the presence in Palo Alto (Stanford's home, and almost surrounded by, but not within, the 12th district) of the pioneering and continually innovative Hewlett-Packard company. These contributed to, but do not explain, the result. You don't find high tech industries clustering around the great midwestern universities.

There seems to be another reason: this part of the country has a natural attraction for innovative, creative people. Not, it should be added, for those who regard themselves as part of the vanguard of the latest proletarian revolution: you'll find them in Berkeley, not around Stanford, and anyway most of them are looking for fellow believers, not for some new insight of their own. The Silicon Valley attracts tinkerers, wonderers, people who are several years ahead of the latest fad. Their offices and factories are set in unpretentious lots on what was, 20 or 40 years ago, exceedingly fertile fruit and vegetable croplands, on the flat Peninsula lands radiating southeast from what was once Leland Stanford's farm. More attractive to the innovators were the hillside communities. The oldest settlements here were in the hills, not the valleys, and some of the buildings still stand: dark frame buildings, huddled under huge live oak and eucalyptus trees, shady and green and cool in the moist air. The mountains that separate the Peninsula communities from the coast rise up behind; nearby are fields where horses graze or are ridden. There are even hitching posts: the Western author Wallace Stegner is quite comfortable living in what outsiders might assume is an effete area.

The hillside communities were rustic but never poor, rural but never bigoted, country-like but still easily accessible to all the luxuries of civilization. The ancient social hierarchies of San Francisco, the ethnic stereotypes you find on the East Coast, the preoccupation with current politics you find in Washington—none of them are important to people here. The people who live here were ahead of the rest of the nation in fighting to preserve the environment, in favoring natural over processed foods, in indulging in systematic exercise, and in appreciating the possibilities of computers and microcircuitry. Unfettered by tradition, they have been ready to accept—and anticipate—the latest fashion as well as the latest innovation.

In congressional representation this district has also been ahead of the curve. For 15 years, beginning in 1967, it was represented by Pete McCloskey, a Republican who won his first election primarily on environmental issues and became known later as an opponent of the Vietnam war and Richard Nixon; his views on economic issues, however, were closer to conventional Republicanism. McCloskey ran unsuccessfully for the Senate in 1982, and his successor in the House, Ed Zschau (the z is silent), is almost the personification of high tech.

Elected at 42, Zschau already has had successful careers in business and in politics. In 1969, as a business school professor, he founded a company that became one of the largest manufacturers of disc storage systems. He also had political success. Builders of rapidly growing and innovative businesses seldom have time for, or interest in, lobbying government. That's usually left for the chief executives of declining companies—leaving a built-in bias in our system against economic growth. Zschau went up and down the Silicon Valley building a lobbying group, and went to Washington in 1978. At that time the House was considering the tax reform package proposed by the Carter administration. More heavily Democratic than it is today, the House was expected to vote higher taxes on the rich. Zschau argued for exactly the opposite. High capital gains taxes, he said, were reducing investment in innovative companies and therefore were retarding economic growth. He supported the move led by Wisconsin's William Steiger to cut the capital gains tax in half. Against the odds, it succeeded: a classic example of Congress being persuaded by argument, against its political instincts, to support a policy no one would have predicted it would pass. It also marked a turning point for the Democrats and the nation. Previously they had taken economic growth for granted, and argued about how to redistribute the wealth. Afterward they concentrated on how to increase wealth and productivity, and left redistribution for later. Today almost no one advocates returning to higher taxation of capital gains. Zschau and others argue that the change spurred investments of millions into new high tech companies. That may or may not be true; but no politician is willing to take the chance that it is not.

Zschau's abilities were evident in that effort and in the 1982 campaign. In this heavily Republican district—Phil Burton put the most Republican parts of the Bay Area in it, to keep them out of Democrats' districts—Zschau won the Republican primary without opposition and won the general election by a wide margin. He surely has a safe seat. But he has more than that: he is in a fine position to influence policy. He is a member of the Foreign Affairs Committee, which seems to have no close relation to his expertise, but he has taken to working closely on the International Economic Policy and Trade Subcommittee, although he is not a member of it. High tech fascinates everyone in Congress now, and he is a high tech success representing the premier high tech district. Other members of both parties, seeking to encourage similar growth elsewhere, will naturally look to him for advice just as members look to former fighter pilots in Congress for advice on the flightworthiness of the latest military aircraft. Will he use this position as productively as he has used his opportunities in the past?

The People   Pop. 1980: 525,271, up 18.1% 1970–80; voting age pop. 389,448; 1% Black, 12% Span. orig., 6% Asian orig., 1% Am. Ind. 36% housing units rented. Median owner $137,500; renter $298. Households: 61% family, 36% with children, 61% married couples.

Presidential Vote

1980	Reagan (R)	109,355	(54%)
	Carter (D)	61,024	(30%)
	Other	32,493	(16%)

Rep. Ed Zschau (R) Elected 1982; b. Jan. 6, 1940, Omaha, NE; home, Los Altos; Princeton U., B.A. 1963, Stanford U., M.B.A. 1963, M.S. 1964, Ph.D. 1967; Protestant.

Career Asst. Prof., Stanford U. Grad. Bus. Sch., 1965–69; Visiting Asst. Prof., Harvard Bus. Sch., 1967–68; Pres., Systems Industries, Inc., 1968–82.

Offices 429 CHOB, 202-225-5411. Also 505 West Olive, Su. 125, Sunnyvale, CA 94086, 408-730-8555.

Committee *Foreign Affairs* (13th). Subcommittees: Africa; Europe and the Middle East; Human Rights and International Organizations.

Rating Groups and Key Votes: Newly Elected

Election Results

1982 general	Ed Zschau (R)	115,365	(63%)	($630,570)
	Emmett Lynch (D)	61,372	(34%)	($60,950)
1982 primary	Ed Zschau (R)	46,184	(100%)	
1980 general	Paul N. McCloskey, Jr. (R)	143,817	(72%)	($84,141)
	Kirsten Olsen (D)	37,009	(19%)	($128,953)
	Bill Evers (Libertarian)	15,073	(8%)	($26,963)

Campaign Contributions and Expenditures

1981-82		Direct Cont. 81-82			PACS brkdwn			
Receipts	$647,780	Indiv	$488,858	Agr	$6,750	Ideo	$1,250
Expend.	$630,570	Party	$17,624	Bus	$97,781	Lbr	$—
Unspent	$17,011	PACS	$123,181	Hlth	$11,500	Prof	$5,500

Indep Expend: For: $25,736

THIRTEENTH DISTRICT

Twenty-five years ago, most of what is now the 13th congressional district of California was acres of vineyards and fruit orchards below the mountains of the Coast Range near San Jose. This was one of the richest agricultural areas in the country, but it was also in the path of some of the most explosive suburban growth the country has ever seen. Santa Clara County, which includes San Jose and the 13th district, grew from 290,000 people in 1950 to 1,064,000 in 1970 and 1,297,000 in 1980. In the 1960s and 1970s the 13th district just about tripled in population—a rate of growth exceeded by only a few other districts in the United States.

Two-thirds of the people in the district live within the city limits of San Jose, but that covers a pretty wide stretch of ground. San Jose's boundaries have been extended, in jagged fashion, hundreds of times; growth was so rapid that for a while someone had to paste on top of the city government's own map inserts adding new streets and subdivisions. The 13th includes the southern and southwestern parts of the city, areas basically suburban, white Anglo, and white collar in character. They are farther out than some of the more expensive Silicon Valley suburbs, though similar in outward appearances. Most of the rest of the people in the 13th live in Santa Clara, an old suburban town just west of downtown San Jose, with its own mission and university. The 13th also includes the suburb of Campbell, surrounded by and indistinguishable from San Jose, and Los Gatos, a higher income town going up into the hills.

The congressman from the 13th is Norman Mineta, one of the most active and effective of the large class of Democrats first elected in 1974. Mineta made a name in San Jose in the early 1970s for slowing up the development that had transformed a market town of 95,000 to a city of 445,000 in 20 years; he was popular enough to succeed a Republican congressman when he retired in 1974. The district is actually not all that Democratic; Jimmy Carter lost it twice and Democrats seldom carry it in statewide elections. Nevertheless, Mineta has consistently won by wide margins.

Mineta was one of the high-ranking Budget Committee members who set strategy and hammered out alternative budgets for the Democrats in 1981 and 1982; his term on the committee has now expired. He is a high ranking member of the Public Works Committee and chairman of its Aviation Subcommittee; he is fourth ranking Democrat on the Select Committee on Intelligence; in 1983, he joined the Science and Technology Committee, important for this Silicon Valley district. Mineta's importance is not limited to his committee positions. He is the kind of member who is singled out for important assignments, like the Intelligence post, by the leadership, because many members rely on his judgment and opinions. He continues to win reelection easily.

The People   Pop. 1980: 526,579, up 21.5% 1970–80; voting age pop. 380,351; 2% Black, 10% Span. orig., 6% Asian orig., 1% Am. Ind. 38% housing units rented. Median owner $104,800; renter $331. Households: 71% family, 41% with children, 58% married couples.

Presidential Vote

1980	Reagan (R)	96,893	(50%)
	Carter (D)	66,607	(34%)
	Other	31,883	(16%)

Rep. Norman Y. Mineta (D) Elected 1974; b. Nov. 12, 1931, San Jose; home, San Jose; U. of CA, B.S. 1953; Methodist.

Career Army, 1953–56; Owner/Agent, Mineta Ins. Agcy.; San Jose City Cncl., 1967–71, Vice Mayor, 1968–71, Mayor, 1971–74.

Offices 2350 RHOB, 202-225-2631. Also Golden Pacific Ctr., 1245 S. Winchester Blvd., Su. 310, San Jose 95128, 408-984-6045.

Committees *Public Works and Transportation* (5th). Subcommittees: Aviation (Chairman); Surface Transportation. *Science and Technology* (14th). Subcommittees: Science, Research and Technology; Space Science and Applications. *Select Committee on Intelligence* (4th). Subcommittee: Program and Budget Authorization.

Group Ratings

	ADA	ACLU	COPE	CFA	LCV	LWV	NTU	NSI	COC	ACA	CSFC
1982	80	92	87	80	75	83	3	40	23	17	31
1981	80	—	86	64	61	—	8	—	32	4	34
1980	83	87	68	71	72	80	15	21	59	35	24

National Journal Ratings

	Economic		Foreign		Cultural	
1982	83%	(LIB)	80%	(LIB)	68%	(LIB)
	15%	(CONS)	20%	(CONS)	31%	(CONS)
1981	74%	(LIB)	70%	(LIB)	91%	(LIB)
	25%	(CONS)	29%	(CONS)	8%	(CONS)

Key Votes

1) Reagan 81 Budget	AGN	5) Incr SS Rtmt Age	AGN	9) Poor Pay Food Stamps	AGN
2) Reagan 81 Tax Cut	AGN	6) Saudi AWACS Sale	AGN	10) Ban Crt Busing Order	AGN
3) Bal Budget Amend	AGN	7) $ for MX Missile	AGN	11) Auto Local Content	FOR
4) Gas & Road Tax	FOR	8) Nerve Gas Prod	AGN	12) Nuclear Arms Freeze	FOR

Election Results

1982 general	Norman Y. Mineta (D)	110,805	(66%)	($346,293)
	Tom Kelly (R)	52,806	(31%)	($20,858)
1982 primary	Norman Y. Mineta (D)	39,188	(100%)	
1980 general	Norman Y. Mineta (D)	132,246	(59%)	($221,552)
	W. E. (Ted) Gagne (R)	79,766	(35%)	($9,439)

Campaign Contributions and Expenditures

1981-82		Direct Cont. 81-82		PACS brkdwn			
Receipts	$369,874	Indiv	$207,656	Agr	$9,200	Ideo	$3,650
Expend.	$346,293	Party	$2,817	Bus	$61,119	Lbr	$35,133
Unspent	$86,046	PACS	$118,650	Hlth	$5,800	Prof	$2,550
		Cand	$19,000				

FOURTEENTH DISTRICT

Although no one predicted it, the Mother Lode country became one of the fastest-growing parts of California in the 1970s. The Mother Lode country is the name for the land where the Central Valley of California starts getting hilly and rises until it becomes the Sierra Nevada. The fast-flowing creeks and rivers here were the focus of the Gold Rush of 1849; good-sized towns complete with opera houses sprang up in places that a year before no white man had seen. Placerville, Nevada City, Angels Camp, Poker Flat—the names recall a way of life made immortal by Mark Twain and Bret Harte and that then quickly disappeared. The mining towns were abandoned quickly when the ore gave out; some parts of the Mother Lode country had more people in 1850 than they have had ever since. They left behind Victorian houses and commercial buildings, set amidst beautiful hills and mountains.

But until the 1970s there seemed to be no reason why anyone would want to move there.

There weren't any new jobs and industries in the Mother Lode country; there weren't convenient shopping centers or supermarkets; television reception was bad. Suddenly, in the 1970s, the population here began to rise—not as rapidly as it did in 1849, but startlingly nonetheless. The new migrants came mostly from California's metropolitan areas, and they were looking for something more than the jobs, shopping centers, supermarkets, and TV reception they had in abundance there. They liked the rural atmosphere and the physical beauty of the region. They liked the old Victorian buildings, which seemed to have so much more character than the stucco subdivisions and shopping centers of metropolitan California. And they liked the traditional cultural patterns and moral values of its small towns. In metropolitan California, children grew up as parts of vast peer groups, taught by teachers who wanted them to rebel more than anything else, interested in everything from drugs to cult religions. In the Mother Lode country, migrants felt they could keep an eye on their children's upbringing and have more say in how they grew up.

So this has proved to be more a conservative than a liberal migration. By 1980 the effect was plain in partisan elections: these traditionally Democratic counties were swinging to the Republicans. In 1982, the gun control referendum brought to the polls thousands of people who had not voted before: young fathers in plaid flannel shirts and down-filled jackets, who strongly opposed gun control and voted for Republicans up and down the ballot. These may turn out to be a permanent feature of the political landscape now. In any case, many younger and some older people in California seem to be re-creating in the Sierra foothills the kind of communities their parents or grandparents left behind in the Midwest.

The Mother Lode country is large enough now to rate a congressional district of its own. Under Phil Burton's 1981 redistricting plan, part of the Mother Lode area and sparsely populated rural counties in the northeast corner of the state account for 76% of the population of California's 14th congressional district. The rest is in the Central Valley, and includes the more Republican parts of the city of Stockton and Lodi, a Republican town settled almost entirely by North Dakotans. Burton's plan for 1984 removes the northwestern edge of the district, but otherwise it is similar.

This is a Republican district, designed for Congressman Norman Shumway. Shumway was a member of the board of supervisors in Stockton in 1978 when he beat John McFall, who had been House Democratic whip from 1972 to 1976; McFall made the mistake in 1974 of taking $3,000 from Korean lobbyist Tongsun Park, depositing it in his office account, and using it for personal business. Shumway's reelection since then, in two quite different-shaped districts, shows the Republican trend in the Mother Lode country distinctly. He is a faithful conservative Republican who seldom strays from the party line in the House.

The People   Pop. 1980: 525,893, up 57.5% 1970–80; voting age pop. 383,299; 1% Black, 6% Span. orig., 2% Asian orig., 1% Am. Ind. 25% housing units rented. Median owner $71,200; renter $221. Households: 75% family, 38% with children, 65% married couples.

Presidential Vote

1980	Reagan (R)	117,495	(58%)
	Carter (D)	62,509	(31%)
	Other	22,946	(11%)

Rep. Norman D. Shumway (R) Elected 1978; b. July 28, 1934, Phoenix, AZ; home, Stockton; U. of UT, B.S. 1960, Hastings Col. of Law, J.D. 1963; Mormon.

Career Practicing atty., 1964–74; San Joaquin Cnty. Bd. of Sprvsrs., 1974–78, Chmn., 1978.

Offices 1203 LHOB, 202-225-2511. Also 1045 N. El Dorado, Stockton 95202, 209-464-7612.

Committees *Banking, Finance and Urban Affairs* (7th). Subcommittees: Economic Stabilization; Financial Institutions Supervision, Regulation and Insurance; International Trade, Investment and Monetary Policy. *Merchant Marine and Fisheries* (5th). Subcommittees: Fisheries and Wildlife Conservation and the Environment; Merchant Marine; Oceanography. *Select Committee on Aging* (4th). Subcommittee: Retirement Income and Employment.

Group Ratings

	ADA	ACLU	COPE	CFA	LCV	LWV	NTU	NSI	COC	ACA	CSFC
1982	0	0	8	0	16	18	97	100	85	96	80
1981	5	—	10	14	7	—	94	—	94	92	80
1980	0	3	7	14	17	0	65	100	69	95	86

National Journal Ratings

	Economic		Foreign		Cultural	
1982	2%	(LIB)	3%	(LIB)	28%	(LIB)
	98%	(CONS)	96%	(CONS)	71%	(CONS)
1981	4%	(LIB)	30%	(LIB)	2%	(LIB)
	79%	(CONS)	68%	(CONS)	97%	(CONS)

Key Votes

1) Reagan 81 Budget	FOR	5) Incr SS Rtmt Age	FOR	9) Poor Pay Food Stamps	FOR
2) Reagan 81 Tax Cut	FOR	6) Saudi AWACS Sale	FOR	10) Ban Crt Busing Order	FOR
3) Bal Budget Amend	FOR	7) $ for MX Missile	FOR	11) Auto Local Content	AGN
4) Gas & Road Tax	AGN	8) Nerve Gas Prod	FOR	12) Nuclear Arms Freeze	AGN

Election Results

1982 general	Norman D. Shumway (R)	134,225	(63%)	($323,702)
	Baron Reed (D)	77,400	(37%)	($54,663)
1982 primary	Norman D. Shumway (R)	63,257	(100%)	
1980 general	Norman D. Shumway (R)	133,979	(61%)	($235,364)
	Ann Cerney (D)	79,883	(36%)	($65,486)

Campaign Contributions and Expenditures

1981-		Direct Cont. 81-82		PACS brkdwn			
Receipts	$324,319	Indiv	$155,432	Agr	$21,844	Ideo	$8,225
Expend.	$323,702	Party	$13,191	Bus	$109,379	Lbr	$1,000
Unspent	$1,774	PACS	$157,963	Hlth	$11,225	Prof	$1,150

Indirect Party Expend: $20,734 *Indep Expend:* For: $1,327 (NRA)

FIFTEENTH DISTRICT

The Central Valley of California is the greatest swath of farmland in the world—and a great creative achievement as well. When white men first came here it seemed barren, almost a desert—a vast flat expanse between the Sierra Nevada and the Coast Range, extending up and down the state from Tehachapi, north of Los Angeles, almost to the Oregon border. Today the Valley is incredibly productive, the nation's leading producer of vegetables and fruits, and a major cotton producer as well. It has been a joint effort: the Valley as it is today is the creation of man, of free enterprise, and of government.

Nowhere is that more evident than in the 15th congressional district of California. Here, between Modesto and Fresno, are some of the Valley's most productive farmlands and some of its larger cities. Fresno, the largest next to Sacramento, is mostly in other districts; Modesto, at the other end, may be familiar as the setting of the movie *American Graffiti*. But it is not in the string of towns along Route 99 that one sees the Valley's greatest riches, nor in the towns on the straight roads that criss-cross the foothills between Modesto and Fresno and the Sierras. The Westlands are the real agricultural heart of the Valley. Vast, largely unpopulated, the site of huge corporate farms, the Westlands are exceedingly productive and profitable. But they would be worth nothing without the water which the federal and state governments provide. Federal reclamation projects and the California Aqueduct channel the plentiful waters that flow down from the Sierras into the Westlands, from channels that begin as far away as the northern Sacramento River, 300 miles away.

Politically, the 15th district is Democratic, but rather conservative on cultural issues. Some 22% of the residents are of Spanish origin, and probably about the same number are of white southern ancestry; both groups tend to be predisposed to the Democrats. But the 15th and the neighboring 17th districts are also the most family- and children-oriented parts of California, except for a couple of suburban Los Angeles districts; the 15th has a higher than national average percentage of children, married couples, and families. Voters here have never been very positive toward the liberal referenda promoted by coastal Californians, from gun control (1982) to marijuana (1972) and coastal zone preservation (also 1972).

The congressman from the 15th district is Tony Coelho, who has deep roots in the Central Valley but has quickly become a power in Washington as well. Coelho was an aide to Fresno Congressman B. F. Sisk for 15 years, and learned water politics at a master's knee. Elected in his own right in 1978, when Sisk retired, Coelho got seats on the Agriculture and Interior Committees and fought hard for Valley and Westlands water interests. Their problem was a 1902 law limiting users of cheap federal water to 160 acres. This is an absurdly low acreage for efficient farming in the Valley and, relying on a 1932 interior secretary's opinion that said the 1902 law didn't really mean what it seemed to say, the owners amassed huge holdings. But in the 1970s liberals and Bay Area Congressman George Miller sought to enforce the 160-acre limit, and the owners sought to protect themselves by getting new legislation. The liberals had the votes; the owners had much at stake; Coelho produced the compromise under which owners would pay a higher price for the water and still keep their land. It was a sensible move: whatever you may want to say about the evils of corporate farmers or the sanctity of the free market, it is apparent that American agriculture is a great success story *because* both government and private business are involved. No one has a good theory for it: it just works. Coelho is one of the people who keeps it doing so.

But this is not what has made this young congressman a major force on the national political scene. He is that because of his work as chairman of the House Democratic Campaign Committee. It seemed a thankless post when he got it in 1980: his predecessor had just been defeated. But Coelho made something of it. He raised unprecedented sums of money. He developed the ongoing direct mail fundraising that the Democrats desperately needed but had neglected in the 1970s. He provided unprecedented kinds of aid to candidates. He modeled much of his operation after the successful work of Republicans, and unblushingly. The Democrats picked up 26 House seats in 1982, his first election year as chairman.

As campaign chairman, Coelho has also been a *de facto* member of the Democratic leadership; in early 1983 he was trying to make the committee chairman an official part of the leadership. His own politics are not nearly so liberal as those of some of his fellow Californians, nor as conservative as Sisk's views sometimes were; he matches his constituency—more liberal than some would suppose, especially on economics, but less liberal than much of coastal California. But Coelho is not one to pick fights with other Democrats. His instincts are for compromise and accomplishment, for accommodation within the party and tough, hard opposition to its adversaries.

The Republicans, to harass Coelho, made a point of putting $100,000 into the campaign of his opponent in 1982. But he was bothered much less than were some leading Republicans, like Minority Leader Robert Michel, and won easily. He should have no greater trouble in the 1980s in the 15th district, which, as redistricted, includes all of Stanislaus County around Modesto and is about as solidly Democratic as before.

The People Pop. 1980: 525,888, up 33.8% 1970–80; voting age pop. 359,314; 2% Black, 22% Span. orig., 2% Asian orig., 1% Am. Ind. 35% housing units rented. Median owner $58,400; renter $191. Households: 77% family, 45% with children, 65% married couples.

Presidential Vote

1980	Reagan (R)	78,040	(50%)
	Carter (D)	62,240	(40%)
	Other	14,724	(10%)

Rep. Tony L. Coelho (D) Elected 1978; b. June 15, 1942, Los Banos; home, Merced; Loyola U., L.A., B.A. 1964; Roman Catholic.

Career Staff of U.S. Rep. B. F. Sisk, 1965–78, A. A., 1970–78.

Offices 403 LHOB, 202-225-6131. Also Fed. Bldg., 415 W. 18th St., Merced 95340, 209-383-4455.

Committees *Agriculture* (15th). Subcommittees: Cotton, Rice and Sugar; Department Operations, Research, and Foreign Agriculture; Livestock, Dairy, and Poultry. *House Administration* (11th). Subcommittees: Accounts; Personnel. *Interior and Insular Affairs* (18th). Subcommittees: Public Lands and National Parks; Water and Power Resources.

Group Ratings

	ADA	ACLU	COPE	CFA	LCV	LWV	NTU	NSI	COC	ACA	CSFC
1982	65	62	78	50	78	67	7	70	33	23	30
1981	55	—	73	57	50	—	5	—	32	22	36
1980	72	73	71	71	45	57	14	40	60	9	29

National Journal Ratings

	Economic		Foreign		Cultural	
1982	74%	(LIB)	62%	(LIB)	46%	(LIB)
	26%	(CONS)	38%	(CONS)	53%	(CONS)
1981	65%	(LIB)	65%	(LIB)	67%	(LIB)
	34%	(CONS)	34%	(CONS)	33%	(CONS)

Key Votes

1) Reagan 81 Budget	AGN	5) Incr SS Rtmt Age	AGN	9) Poor Pay Food Stamps	AGN
2) Reagan 81 Tax Cut	AGN	6) Saudi AWACS Sale	AGN	10) Ban Crt Busing Order	AGN
3) Bal Budget Amend	AGN	7) $ for MX Missile	AGN	11) Auto Local Content	FOR
4) Gas & Road Tax	FOR	8) Nerve Gas Prod	AGN	12) Nuclear Arms Freeze	FOR

Election Results

1982 general	Tony Coelho (D)	86,022	(64%)	($767,953)
	Ed Bates (R)	45,948	(34%)	($107,543)
1982 primary	Tony Coelho (D)	46,223	(100%)	
1980 general	Tony Coelho (D)	108,072	(72%)	($140,382)
	Ron Schwartz (R)	37,895	(25%)	($5,136)

Campaign Contributions and Expenditures

1981-82		Direct Cont. 81-82		PACS brkdwn			
Receipts	$744,808	Indiv	$412,018	Agr	$95,205	Ideo	$13,250
Expend.	$767,953	PACS	$305,765	Bus	$104,775	Lbr	$53,458
Unspent	$16,987	Cand	$1,161	Hlth	$15,450	Prof	$12,800

Indep Expend: For: $11,941 (AMAPAC, NRA)

SIXTEENTH DISTRICT

The 16th congressional district of California boasts some of the nation's most spectacular scenery, from the Monterey cypresses at Carmel's Pebble Beach, through the mountainous wild Big Sur coast, to William Randolph Hearst's San Simeon. It extends altogether from Santa Cruz in the north down to Morro Bay in San Luis Obispo County. Just a few miles from the Ocean is some of the nation's richest farmland: the lettuce fields of the Salinas Valley, the artichoke fields around Castroville. This is John Steinbeck country: he grew up in Salinas, and the Cannery Row he described in Monterey still exists, even if only as a tourist attraction.

These coastal areas over the years have tended to vote Republican. Landowners in Salinas and the townspeople who sympathize with them, retirees in Santa Cruz and the Monterey peninsula—these older residents all tended to vote Republican. But in the 1970s the coastal areas moved notably to the left. One reason was the change in focus from economic to cultural issues. On the latter, opinion here tends to be tolerant of deviations from tradition and very interested in preserving a unique and magnificent environment. Another reason for the shift was a change in population. The coast seems to attract migrants who, while affluent, subscribe to liberal magazines and buy Sierra Club calendars. Also, the branch of the

University of California at Santa Cruz is so liberal (97% for McGovern in 1972) that it changed the political balance of the whole county.

The 16th district elects a Democratic congressman, and one who, although he holds no high-ranking position, is in fact one of the most influential and powerful members of the House. He is Leon Panetta, and he, like many in his district, was once a Republican—a Nixon administration appointee, in fact, who resigned over policy as head of the Office of Civil Rights at HEW in 1970. Panetta is a member of the Budget Committee, the fifth ranking Democrat. But he is, in combination with Chairman James Jones, the main strategist for the Democrats. Why? Because of his detailed knowledge of the budget, for one thing; he is the closest thing the House Democrats have to David Stockman. Because of his own ability to work with his colleagues, for another. And, finally, because of his own views that, while being recognizably Democratic, are not so liberal as to be out of line with many members of the Caucus, northern as well as southern, who are no longer convinced that heavy domestic spending is the answer to every program. He could easily be Budget chairman in a future Congress or director of the Office of Management and Budget in a future Democratic administration.

Panetta also has a seat on the Agriculture Committee. Like other Democrats who represent farming districts, he does not see himself as the adversary of the big growers; he refused to embrace, as a previous unsuccessful Democratic candidate in this district did, all the works of Cesar Chavez's United Farm Workers. Panetta's standing in the district is strong, and he seems likely to continue winning reelection by wide margins.

The People Pop. 1980: 525,893, up 30.6% 1970–80; voting age pop. 385,887; 4% Black, 18% Span. orig., 5% Asian orig., 1% Am. Ind. 40% housing units rented. Median owner $88,800; renter $264. Households: 70% family, 38% with children, 58% married couples.

Presidential Vote

1980	Reagan (R)	87,639	(49%)
	Carter (D)	64,704	(36%)
	Other	27,777	(15%)

Rep. Leon E. Panetta (D) Elected 1976; b. June 28, 1938, Monterey; home, Carmel Valley; U. of Santa Clara, B.A. 1960, J.D. 1963; Roman Catholic.

Career Army, 1964–66; Legis. Asst. to U.S. Sen. Thomas Kuchel, 1966–69; Dir., U.S. Ofc. of Civil Rights, HEW, 1969–70; Exec. Asst. to the Mayor of New York City, 1970–71; Practicing atty., 1971–76.

Offices 339 CHOB, 202-225-2861. Also 380 Alvorado, Monterey 93940, 408-649-3555.

Committees *Agriculture* (11th). Subcommittees: Department Operations, Research, and Foreign Agriculture; Forests, Family Farms, and Energy. *Budget* (5th). Task Forces: Budget Process (Chairman); Education and Employment.

Group Ratings

	ADA	ACLU	COPE	CFA	LCV	LWV	NTU	NSI	COC	ACA	CSFC
1982	75	83	70	80	71	92	27	40	18	22	33
1981	90	—	67	64	71	—	30	—	16	21	39
1980	67	80	58	50	63	80	24	10	79	29	24

National Journal Ratings

	Economic		Foreign		Cultural	
1982	65%	(LIB)	80%	(LIB)	84%	(LIB)
	35%	(CONS)	20%	(CONS)	15%	(CONS)
1981	75%	(LIB)	67%	(LIB)	75%	(LIB)
	24%	(CONS)	32%	(CONS)	25%	(CONS)

Key Votes

1) Reagan 81 Budget	AGN	5) Incr SS Rtmt Age	AGN	9) Poor Pay Food Stamps	AGN
2) Reagan 81 Tax Cut	AGN	6) Saudi AWACS Sale	AGN	10) Ban Crt Busing Order	AGN
3) Bal Budget Amend	AGN	7) $ for MX Missile	AGN	11) Auto Local Content	AGN
4) Gas & Road Tax	AGN	8) Nerve Gas Prod	AGN	12) Nuclear Arms Freeze	FOR

Election Results

1982 general	Leon E. Panetta (D)	....	142,630	(85%)	($75,936)
	G. Richard Arnold (R)	....	24,448	(15%)	($0)
1982 primary	Leon E. Panetta (D)	....	61,549	(100%)	
1980 general	Leon E. Panetta (D)	....	153,360	(71%)	($55,475)
	W.A. Jack Roth (R)	....	54,675	(25%)	($11,995)

Campaign Contributions and Expenditures

1981-82		Direct Cont. 81-82		PACS brkdwn			
Receipts	$138,063	Indiv	$71,564	Agr	$15,450	Ideo	$1,550
Expend.	$75,936	Party	$1,550	Bus	$20,650	Lbr	$9,900
Unspent	$117,118	PACS	$55,439	Hlth	$6,800	Prof	$300

SEVENTEENTH DISTRICT

The 17th congressional district of California occupies some of the richest agricultural land in the world. Here in the southern part of the Central Valley, between Fresno and Bakersfield, are grown an impressive variety of crops: grapes, cotton, alfalfa, cantaloupes, plums, peaches, lima beans, tomatoes, sugar beets, walnuts, olives, poultry, and dairy products. It is almost all produced by very large farming operations that, even if not run by large corporations, bear little resemblance to the family farm of memory: they are serious, large businesses. The producers pride themselves on their success through free enterprise, but like most entrepreneurs they are happy to have the government provide safety nets, in the form of crop subsidies, agricultural research, irrigation systems, and subsidized water. It's hard to make a theoretical case for such a mixed system, and no one person would have designed it from scratch. But it works. It has made Central Valley agriculture exceedingly productive; and if it has helped some producers get rich, surely they deserve no less for the contribution they make to the wealth and strength of the entire country.

So much of the business of a congressman from this area is to influence government and maintain its part in this system. That, it appears has been the main occupation in his congressional career for 17th district Congressman Chip Pashayan. He serves on the Interior Committee and its Water Subcommittee, a vital one here; he also serves on the Parks

Subcommittee, which regulates the district's national parks (Sequoia, Kings Canyon). On most issues Pashayan votes as you would expect a Republican from Ronald Reagan's home state to vote. But his greatest energy is probably saved for local matters.

Pashayan won this district, when it included much of Fresno, in an upset in 1978 and retained it easily in 1980. Redistricting appeared to help him, moving the district south. It includes now just the higher income parts of Fresno, all of the Valley counties of Tulare (half the district's population and heavily Republican) and Kings (much smaller and heavily Democratic) and dips down into Kern County almost to Bakersfield. That last area, which includes Delano, the headquarters of Cesar Chavez's United Farm Workers, is usually Republican; the UFW is rather unpopular, in the manner of insurgent unions, except with its own membership. But in 1982, Kern County Supervisor Gene Tackett ran as the Democratic candidate against Pashayan, and with home area support, and despite a large financial disadvantage, held Pashayan to 54%. This is a good example of how the Republican advantage in fund-raising has helped them hold Democratic gains down. Pashayan is a competent candidate, but without his larger campaign treasuries he might not have been able to capture this seat in 1978 or retain it in 1980. Quite possibly the Democrats will try to beat him again in 1984.

The People Pop. 1980: 524,790, up 39.4% 1970–80; voting age pop. 355,077; 3% Black, 24% Span. orig., 3% Asian orig., 1% Am. Ind. 35% housing units rented. Median owner $54,300; renter $191. Households: 78% family, 46% with children, 65% married couples.

Presidential Vote

1980	Reagan (R)	80,523	(56%)
	Carter (D)	53,235	(37%)
	Other	9,861	(7%)

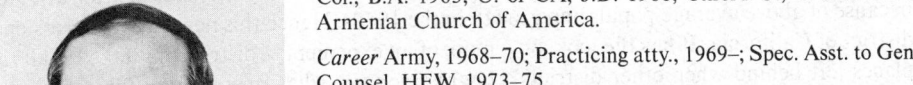

Rep. Charles (Chip) Pashayan, Jr. (R) Elected 1978; b. Mar. 27, 1941, Fresno; home, Fresno; Pomona Col., B.A. 1963, U. of CA, J.D. 1968, Oxford U., B. Litt. 1977; Armenian Church of America.

Career Army, 1968–70; Practicing atty., 1969–; Spec. Asst. to Gen. Counsel, HEW, 1973–75.

Offices 129 CHOB, 202-225-3341. Also 4114 Fed. Bldg., 1130 'O' St., Fresno 93721, 209-487-5487.

Committees *Interior and Insular Affairs* (7th). Subcommittees: Public Lands and National Parks; Water and Power Resources. *Post Office and Civil Service* (5th). Subcommittees: Civil Service; Postal Operations.

Group Ratings

	ADA	ACLU	COPE	CFA	LCV	LWV	NTU	NSI	COC	ACA	CSFC
1982	15	42	26	30	7	11	74	100	76	91	65
1981	5	—	25	14	14	—	67	—	94	77	71
1980	11	20	21	7	28	22	52	100	75	77	73

National Journal Ratings

	Economic		Foreign		Cultural	
1982	31%	(LIB)	21%	(LIB)	15%	(LIB)
	69%	(CONS)	79%	(CONS)	83%	(CONS)
1981	23%	(LIB)	18%	(LIB)	24%	(LIB)
	76%	(CONS)	73%	(CONS)	75%	(CONS)

Key Votes

1) Reagan 81 Budget	FOR	5) Incr SS Rtmt Age	FOR	9) Poor Pay Food Stamps	FOR
2) Reagan 81 Tax Cut	FOR	6) Saudi AWACS Sale	AGN	10) Ban Crt Busing Order	FOR
3) Bal Budget Amend	FOR	7) $ for MX Missile	FOR	11) Auto Local Content	AGN
4) Gas & Road Tax	FOR	8) Nerve Gas Prod	FOR	12) Nuclear Arms Freeze	AGN

Election Results

1982 general	Charles (Chip) Pashayan, Jr. (R) ..	80,271	(54%)	($433,229)
	Gene Tackett (D)	68,364	(46%)	($151,530)
1982 primary	Charles (Chip) Pashayan, Jr. (R) ..	36,482	(100%)	
1980 general	Charles (Chip) Pashayan, Jr. (R) ..	129,159	(71%)	($55,475)
	Willard H. Johnson (D)	53,780	(29%)	($11,995)

Campaign Contributions and Expenditures

1981-82		Direct Cont. 81-82		PACS brkdwn			
Receipts	$427,259	Indiv	$256,133	Agr	$42,900	Ideo	$7,850
Expend.	$433,229	Party	$20,762	Bus	$69,235	Lbr	$7,205
Unspent	$7,293	PACS	$140,485	Hlth	$11,650	Prof	$1,300

Indirect Party Expend: $1,000   *Indep Expend:* For: $904 (NRA) Agn: $4,378 (Freeze PAC)

EIGHTEENTH DISTRICT

Northern California outside the San Francisco Bay Area—the Central Valley and the Mother Lode country in the Sierras—was entitled to a new congressional district in 1982, because of above average population growth in the 1970s. Hence this new 18th congressional district of California. It has the look, on a map, of an expedient: a district that takes in all the places left behind when other districts' congressmen got what they wanted (or, rather, got what Phil Burton wanted them to have). It is actually a little more complicated than that: this grotesquely shaped district was crafted for a specific California assemblyman, and drawn so as not to discommode other nearby Democrats.

The district consists of two sections of the Central Valley, connected only by largely uninhabited land on the other side of the Sierra Nevada. There is no road entirely within the district that will take you from Stockton, in the north, to Fresno, in the south; they are only 120 miles apart on Interstate 99, you have to go through two or three other districts to get between them. The two parts of the valley are quite different. The northern part includes most of the city of Stockton and southern San Joaquin County. It is the less affluent part of the city, and even this far north you find substantial numbers of Mexican-Americans and blacks. Still, it is pretty closely divided politically.

The southern portion includes most of the city of Fresno and the agricultural town of Sanger, home of the new congressman, Richard Lehman. Fresno, at the edge of rolling foothill country, is the home of the nation's largest Armenian community; it was celebrated by author William Saroyan. It also has a large number of Mexican-Americans, most pretty thoroughly mixed in with the rest of the population. Aside from Sacramento, it is consistently the most Democratic part of the Central Valley. That Democratic preference also exists in Sanger and in many Fresno County towns just outside the current bounds of the 18th district; rather abruptly, when you cross the Tulare County line, almost all the towns become Republican. The Fresno and Stockton portions of the 18th are connected by a strip of Mother Lode country in the hills above Stockton and, on the eastern side of the Sierras, the bleak territory around Mono Lake and the upper Owens Valley, the ultimate source of most of Los Angeles's water.

Richard Lehman is one of those young idealistic political manueverers that the California legislature seems to nurture in such abundance. The description sounds contradictory, yet it is accurate. Lehman wants to move society at least a little further in the direction of welfare state and environmental protection. Yet he has also proved himself extremely adept in protecting and advancing the interests of the agricultural business which is almost the sole basis of the economies of both halves of his district. He would probably tell you that he sees no contradiction; his own legislative work has, creatively, pointed to ways in which public policy can work toward both goals harmoniously. At 34, he was such a clear beneficiary of Phil Burton's handiwork in drawing the 18th district's boundaries as they are that he won the Democratic primary without opposition and, with huge home town support from Fresno County, won the general election easily. In the House he won assignment to the Interior Committee, which handles issues relating to water, which is so precious to the Valley. Whatever new districting plan is in effect for 1984 will probably smooth out the boundaries and give Lehman some new territory, but he seems likely to win easily.

The People Pop. 1980: 527,348, up 13.4% 1970–80; voting age pop. 376,599; 6% Black, 20% Span. orig., 4% Asian orig., 1% Am. Ind. 36% housing units rented. Median owner $54,200; renter $184. Households: 71% family, 38% with children, 56% married couples.

Presidential Vote

1980	Reagan (R)	75,812	(48%)
	Carter (D)	68,985	(43%)
	Other	14,817	(9%)

Rep. Richard H. Lehman (D) Elected 1982; b. July 20, 1948, Sanger; home, Fresno; Fresno City College, 1967–68, CA State U., Fresno, 1969; U. of CA at Santa Cruz, 1970; Lutheran.

Career A. A. to CA State Senator George N. Zenovich, 1969–76; CA Assembly, 1976–82.

Offices 1319 LHOB, 202-225-4540. Also 1900 Mariposa Mall, Su. 301, Fresno 93721, 209-487-5760; and 808 Center St., Stockton 95202, 209-946-6353.

Committees *Banking, Finance, and Urban Affairs* (23d). Subcommittees: Financial Institutions Supervision, Regulation and Insurance; Housing and Community Development; International Trade, Investment and Monetary Policy. *Interior and Insular Affairs* (28th). Subcommittees: Water and Power Resources; Public Lands and National Parks.

Group Ratings and Key Votes: Newly Elected

Election Results

1982 general	Richard Lehman (D)	92,762	(60%)	($169,107)
	Adrian C. Fondse (R)	59,664	(38%)	($68,246)
1982 primary	Richard Lehman (D)	55,424	(100%)	
1980 general	Newly created district			

Campaign Contributions and Expenditures

1981-82		*Direct Cont. 81-82*		*PACS brkdwn*			
Receipts	$173,752	Indiv	$94,683	Agr	$12,125	Ideo	$14,250
Expend.	$169,107	PACS	$71,151	Bus	$14,300	Lbr	$26,000
Unspent	$4,644			Hlth	$1,700	Prof	$1,100

NINETEENTH DISTRICT

With only a narrow strip of land for towns and the wilderness nearby, the Santa Barbara Coast still boasts the climate and beauty that brought so many people here in the 1940s and 50s. Santa Barbara has always been a resort town, a home for rich retirees; it has also, on a flat strip of sand out of town alongside the Ocean, what was in the early 1970s one of the most radical branches of the University of California. Santa Barbara, ancestrally Republican, had its consciousness raised by the hideous oil spill in the Santa Barbara Channel. It was a nightmare in paradise: matrons and hippies went down to the beach and washed oil from sea birds; Interior Secretary Walter Hickel went out to view the damage from a helicopter and ordered drilling stopped. Voters here trended Democratic in state and national elections and elected Democrats to the legislature. Now such a spill is treated as more routine, and the oil more valued; Santa Barbara did not protest too loudly when Interior Secretary James Watt ordered bids taken for drilling in coastal waters all up and down California.

West of Santa Barbara the mountains fall directly into the Ocean; above are the misty Santa Ynez Mountains, the site of Ronald Reagan's Rancho del Cielo. The four-lane road bends and twists over the mountains, to find the valley where Vandenberg Air Force Base and Lompoc Federal Prison are situated; farther north is the town of Santa Maria, one of those rural California towns where voter turnout was swelled by opponents of gun control in 1982. East of Santa Barbara, toward Los Angeles, the atmosphere also changes. Beyond the pleasant small city of Ventura is industrial Oxnard, the busy oil harbor of Port Hueneme, and Mugu Naval Air Station.

These areas, altogether, make up California's 19th congressional district, a constituency historically Republican that trended Democratic for a while in the 1970s. Its congressman, Robert Lagomarsino, is an adept and intelligent veteran politician who won the district under difficult circumstances and has held it with seeming ease. He was the only Republican in a 1974 special election to hold a district for his party, despite Watergate; he was shrewd enough to say that he would not support Richard Nixon if he deserved to be impeached.

Lagomarsino serves now on the Interior and Foreign Affairs Committees. On Interior he is ranking minority member on the Insular Affairs Subcommittee, a body of great importance to Puerto Rico, the Virgin Islands, Guam, and American Samoa, but of virtually no interest to anyone who votes in congressional elections—a workhorse assignment. On Foreign Affairs in 1983 he became ranking Republican on the Inter-American Affairs Subcommittee. This could be a hot seat. Chairman Michael Barnes and the committee's Democrats are, at the least, skeptical about Reagan administration policy in El Salvador and inclined to oppose it; Lagomarsino's job will likely be to present the administration's case to a skeptical House—or, another frustrating role, to be the messenger of bad news back to the administration. He has been under attack back home for his opposition to the nuclear freeze resolution (which, however, in November 1982 ballot initiative form, only barely carried the 19th district). None of these things caused Lagomarsino great trouble in 1982, but his percentage was sharply down, against a not particularly strong opponent—a sign that this old pro may need to use all his skills in 1984 if the big issues with which he is involved do not break his way.

The People   Pop. 1980: 526,068, up 17.3% 1970–80; voting age pop. 384,040; 3% Black, 21% Span. orig., 3% Asian orig., 1% Am. Ind. 43% housing units rented. Median owner $88,200; renter $268. Households: 70% family, 38% with children, 57% married couples.

Presidential Vote

1980	Reagan (R)	100,387	(53%)
	Carter (D)	63,939	(34%)
	Other	24,910	(13%)

Rep. Robert J. Lagomarsino (R) Elected Mar. 5, 1974; b. Sept. 4, 1926, Ventura; home, Ventura; U. of CA at Santa Barbara, B.A. 1950, Santa Clara Law Sch., LL.B. 1953; Roman Catholic.

Career Navy, WWII; Practicing atty., 1954–74; Ojai City Cncl., 1958, Mayor, 1958–61; CA Senate, 1961–74.

Offices 2332 RHOB, 202-225-3601. Also 814 State St., Studio 121, Santa Barbara 93102, 805-963-1708.

Committees *Foreign Affairs* (4th). Subcommittee: Western Hemisphere Affairs. *Interior and Insular Affairs* (3d). Subcommittees: Insular Affairs; Public Lands and National Parks.

Group Ratings

	ADA	ACLU	COPE	CFA	LCV	LWV	NTU	NSI	COC	ACA	CSFC
1982	5	0	13	29	42	33	84	100	77	91	68
1981	5	—	13	21	29	—	—	—	100	92	75
1980	11	27	16	7	43	30	59	100	79	83	79

National Journal Ratings

	Economic		Foreign		Cultural	
1982	18%	(LIB)	12%	(LIB)	36%	(LIB)
	82%	(CONS)	84%	(CONS)	64%	(CONS)
1981	4%	(LIB)	14%	(LIB)	4%	(LIB)
	79%	(CONS)	84%	(CONS)	90%	(CONS)

Key Votes

1) Reagan 81 Budget	FOR	5) Incr SS Rtmt Age	FOR	9) Poor Pay Food Stamps	FOR
2) Reagan 81 Tax Cut	FOR	6) Saudi AWACS Sale	FOR	10) Ban Crt Busing Order	FOR
3) Bal Budget Amend	FOR	7) $ for MX Missile	FOR	11) Auto Local Content	AGN
4) Gas & Road Tax	AGN	8) Nerve Gas Prod	FOR	12) Nuclear Arms Freeze	AGN

Election Results

1982 general	Robert J. Lagomarsino (R)	112,486	(61%)	($233,356)
	Frank Frost (D)	66,042	(36%)	($54,958)
1982 primary	Robert J. Lagomarsino (R)	52,669	(100%)	
1980 general	Robert J. Lagomarsino (R)	162,854	(78%)	($97,504)
	Carmen Lodise (D)	36,990	(18%)	($0)
	Jim Trotter (Libertarian)	9,765	(5%)	($0)

Campaign Contributions and Expenditures

1981-82		Direct Cont. 81-82		PACS brkdwn			
Receipts	$236,607	Indiv	$150,281	Agr	$7,000	Ideo	$2,250
Expend.	$233,356	Party	$9,690	Bus	$33,525	Lbr	$—
Unspent	$89,799	PACS	$54,096	Hlth	$11,250	Prof	$—

Indep Expend: For: $410 Agn: $3,177 (Freeze PAC)

TWENTIETH DISTRICT

The Central Valley of California stands out clearly on a relief map—a swath of green down the middle of the state, surrounded by brown: a vast, flat expanse bounded by rugged mountains. The Valley's heavily irrigated plains are probably the world's most productive farmland. In the south, the mountains form a kind of semicircle, separating the Valley from the desert on the east, the Los Angeles Basin over 50 miles to the south, and from the valleys of San Luis Obispo to the west. The 20th congressional district of California includes parts of three of these regions: most of the southern end of the Valley around Bakersfield, a portion of the desert, and most of San Luis Obispo County all the way to the ocean.

Half the district's population, and its center of political gravity, is in the Valley around Bakersfield. In the 1930s, Bakersfield was a kind of promised land: the first green land that the Dust Bowl migrants from Oklahoma and Kansas saw after 1,500 miles of travel in rickety cars across the desert on U.S. 66. This is still the part of California where you are likely to find the most southern accents; Bakersfield is even a country music center, the home of Merle Haggard. As in Oklahoma, the political heritage here is Democratic, voting habits increasingly Republican since the late 1960s.

A surprisingly large number of people—about 140,000—live in the 20th district east of the Tehachapi Pass, in the desert. Here you find giant military installations, first put out here because of the dry climate and to keep them isolated and out of sight: the China Lake Naval Weapons Center and Edwards Air Force Base, where most of the space shuttles have landed. South of Edwards—in northern Los Angeles County, but in the desert, not the Los Angeles Basin—are the fast-growing towns of Lancaster and Palmdale. In subdivisions and shopping centers sprouting quickly from the desert, young people with families have been moving here, to work at Lockheed or other local businesses, or even to commute the 35 freeway miles to the San Fernando Valley. Political attitudes here are ultraconservative: strongly pro-defense, for the free market and traditional family values.

About the same number of people live in the 20th district's portion of San Luis Obispo County. Ranching is still important in these hills (President Reagan's National Security Adviser William Clark has a ranch here), and the small towns have not been transformed into outposts of advanced cultural values even by the presence of students at California Polytechnic. San Luis Obispo County is, as it has been for many years, mildly Republican.

The 20th district's congressman, Bill Thomas, was elected after the incumbent died quite suddenly in the summer of 1978. A former college teacher and four-year veteran of the California Assembly, he seems to be one of those people who instinctively know how to go about being a legislator. He got a seat on the Agriculture Committee in his first term—a plum assignment for a Bakersfield representative—and now sits on the Ways and Means Committee. Thomas was the leading strategist for California House Republicans on redistricting. He was entrusted with a seat on the House Ethics Committee, and now is a member of House Administration, ordinarily a housekeeping committee, but one which passes on the campaign finance laws.

Thomas has a pretty solid Reagan Republican voting record on most national issues. He won reelection by a very solid margin in 1982, despite the Democratic trend and a considerable shift in district boundaries. For 1984 the boundaries have been shifted again, to include Inyou County along the Nevada border, but Thomas still has a pretty safe seat.

The People Pop. 1980: 525,894, up 21.7% 1970–80; voting age pop. 379,934; 4% Black, 10% Span. orig., 2% Asian orig., 1% Am. Ind. 33% housing units rented. Median owner $64,600; renter $224. Households: 73% family, 39% with children, 62% married couples.

Presidential Vote

1980	Reagan (R)	110,892	(62%)
	Carter (D)	51,337	(29%)
	Other	17,170	(10%)

Rep. William M. Thomas (R) Elected 1978; b. Dec. 6, 1941, Wallace, ID; home, Bakersfield; Santa Ana Comm. Col., San Fran. St. U., B.A., M.A. 1965; Baptist.

Career Prof., Bakersfield Comm. Col., 1965–74; CA Assembly, 1974–78.

Offices 324 CHOB, 202-225-2915. Also 800 Truxtun, Bakersfield 93301, 805-323-8322.

Committees *House Administration* (5th). Subcommittees: Accounts; Office Systems. *Ways and Means* (12th). Subcommittees: Social Security; Oversight; Public Assistance and Unemployment Compensation.

Group Ratings

	ADA	ACLU	COPE	CFA	LCV	LWV	NTU	NSI	COC	ACA	CSFC
1982	5	21	8	10	11	18	77	100	85	100	71
1981	5	—	10	14	15	—	52	—	100	75	69
1980	0	13	17	7	13	0	56	100	86	91	77

National Journal Ratings

	Economic		Foreign		Cultural	
1982	17%	(LIB)	21%	(LIB)	24%	(LIB)
	83%	(CONS)	79%	(CONS)	76%	(CONS)
1981	21%	(LIB)	14%	(LIB)	32%	(LIB)
	78%	(CONS)	84%	(CONS)	68%	(CONS)

Key Votes

1) Reagan 81 Budget	FOR	5) Incr SS Rtmt Age	FOR	9) Poor Pay Food Stamps	FOR
2) Reagan 81 Tax Cut	FOR	6) Saudi AWACS Sale	FOR	10) Ban Crt Busing Order	—
3) Bal Budget Amend	FOR	7) $ for MX Missile	FOR	11) Auto Local Content	AGN
4) Gas & Road Tax	FOR	8) Nerve Gas Prod	FOR	12) Nuclear Arms Freeze	AGN

Election Results

1982 general	William M. Thomas (R)	123,312	(68%)	($178,320)
	Robert J. Bethea (D)	57,769	(32%)	($7,166)
1982 primary	William M. Thomas (R)	55,923	(100%)	
1980 general	William M. Thomas (R)	126,046	(71%)	($192,111)
	Mary (Pat) Timmermans (D)	51,415	(29%)	($13,183)

Campaign Contributions and Expenditures

1981-82		Direct Cont. 81-82		PACS brkdwn			
Receipts	$198,775	Indiv	$105,477	Agr	$30,500	Ideo	$1,500
Expend.	$178,320	Party	$8,498	Bus	$40,800	Lbr	$500
Unspent	$94,759	PACS	$83,000	Hlth	$9,500	Prof	$—

TWENTY-FIRST DISTRICT

Demographically, Los Angeles has become a city very much like those back east, with population concentrations of the elderly and minorities, the very rich and the very poor. This trend is apparent even in the San Fernando Valley, the huge 12-by-20 mile expanse that is a Los Angeles synonym for suburbia (and the inspiration for the phrase "Valley girls"). Twenty years ago, the Valley was filled, or filling up, with young families: working fathers, homemaker mothers, two or three or four kids walking every day to the local public school. These were almost entirely white Anglo people, few of them Jewish or members of any self-conscious minority group. Today, as the Valley has aged, it has become a very different place. Erstwhile young parents are now living alone—often divorced. Young married couples both work, and have few if any children. The whites who have remained have often withdrawn their children from public schools, because of a busing order, although it was overturned in 1981. Substantial numbers of Mexican-Americans and some blacks live in the Valley now, as well as large numbers of Jews.

What most resembles the Valley of 20 years ago is the collection of communities that form the 21st congressional district of California. This includes the fringes of the Valley: parts of Woodland Hills on the west, Northridge and Granada Hills on the north and, separated by mountains but still within the Los Angeles city limits, the communities of Sunland and Tujunga on the east. These comprise only about one-third of the district's population, however. More than 60% live in a series of communities enclosed by mountains and connected with the northern San Fernando Valley by freeway: Simi Valley, Moorpark, Thousand Oaks (known locally as T.O.), and Camarillo. These areas have grown fast; there were very few people here in 1960. They are filled now with young families, the kind of people who used to settle in the Valley. The district also includes, farther north in Ventura County, the more established communities of Fillmore and Ojai.

Fully 80% of the households in this district are occupied by families, 69% by married couples, and 47% have children. These figures are well above the national average and are exceeded in California only by the predominantly Mexican-American 34th district, on the other side of the Los Angeles Basin. While the divorce rate may be higher here than it was in the Valley 20 years ago, otherwise life has probably undergone less change than you would guess judging by outward appearances. Politically, this is an area that in a politics of cultural variety is one of the most conservative. Its young parents are more affluent than average, but they vote much more Republican than do people in different family circumstances who have considerably more money.

They are represented, appropriately, by a woman who got her political start crusading on a family issue. She is Bobbi Fiedler, who as a San Fernando Valley housewife, led a movement against the Los Angeles busing order and got herself elected to the citywide school board. In 1980 she ran against and beat James Corman, a high ranking Ways and Means member and chairman of the House Democratic Campaign Committee, primarily because of the busing issue; ironically, Corman had first been elected in 1960 in a surge of Democratic enthusiasm among the young voters in the Valley. The difference in 1980 may have been Jimmy Carter: he conceded while the polls were still open in California, people were seen leaving the lines, and Corman lost by 752 votes.

San Francisco Congressman Phillip Burton, drawing the new district lines, constructed a new Valley district for Democratic legislator Howard Berman; Fiedler prudently moved out to the 21st, most of which was represented by Barry Goldwater, Jr., who was running for the Senate. In this family-oriented district, this family-oriented candidate (who is, however, divorced) won easily. Fiedler, as it happens, is the California Republican most likely to vote against the Reagan administration, although she certainly does not belong in the ranks of northeastern liberals. Ironically, it is on cultural and foreign issues that her views are more moderate.

The People Pop. 1980: 524,977, up 37.4% 1970–80; voting age pop. 367,512; 1% Black, 9% Span. orig., 3% Asian orig., 1% Am. Ind. 24% housing units rented. Median owner $114,400; renter $330. Households: 80% family, 47% with children, 69% married couples.

Presidential Vote

1980			
	Reagan (R)	129,662	(65%)
	Carter (D)	50,364	(25%)
	Other	20,803	(10%)

Rep. Bobbi Fiedler (R) Elected 1980; b. Apr. 22, 1937, Santa Monica; home, Northridge; Santa Monica City Col.; Jewish.

Career Housewife; Drugstore owner; Interior decorator; Organizer of BUSTOP, L.A. antibusing group, 1976; L.A. Sch. Bd., 1977–80.

Offices 1607 LHOB, 202-225-5811. Also 14600 Roscoe Blvd., Su. 506, Panorama City 91402, 213-787-1776.

Committee *Budget* (7th). Task Forces: Capital Resources and Development; Tax Policy; International Finance and Trade.

Group Ratings

	ADA	ACLU	COPE	CFA	LCV	LWV	NTU	NSI	COC	ACA	CSFC
1982	0	29	21	20	34	30	67	100	82	78	61
1981	10	—	25	29	31	—	72	—	100	83	68

National Journal Ratings

	Economic		Foreign		Cultural	
1982	21%	(LIB)	10%	(LIB)	4%	(LIB)
	79%	(CONS)	89%	(CONS)	87%	(CONS)
1981	39%	(LIB)	57%	(LIB)	45%	(LIB)
	61%	(CONS)	42%	(CONS)	55%	(CONS)

Key Votes

1) Reagan 81 Budget	FOR	5) Incr SS Rtmt Age	FOR	9) Poor Pay Food Stamps	FOR
2) Reagan 81 Tax Cut	FOR	6) Saudi AWACS Sale	AGN	10) Ban Crt Busing Order	FOR
3) Bal Budget Amend	FOR	7) $ for MX Missile	FOR	11) Auto Local Content	AGN
4) Gas & Road Tax	AGN	8) Nerve Gas Prod	FOR	12) Nuclear Arms Freeze	AGN

Election Results

1982 general	Bobbi Fiedler (R)	138,474	(72%)	($285,171)
	George H. Margolis (D)	46,412	(24%)	($0)
1982 primary	Bobbi Fiedler (R)	59,588	(86%)	
	Herb Cruse (R)	9,511	(14%)	
1980 general	Barry M. Goldwater, Jr. (R)	199,681	(79%)	($193,063)
(CA 20)	Matt Miller (D)	43,025	(17%)	($15,420)
1980 general	Bobbi Fiedler (R)	74,843	(49%)	($560,492)
(CA 21)	James C. Corman (D)	74,091	(48%)	($905,231)

Campaign Contributions and Expenditures

1981-82		Direct Cont. 81-82		PACS brkdwn			
Receipts	$337,811	Indiv	$211,312	Agr	$4,050	Ideo	$2,500
Expend.	$285,171	Party	$15,746	Bus	$69,850	Lbr	$5,250
Unspent	$55,303	PACS	$90,066	Hlth	$12,500	Prof	$450

Indep Expend: For: $749 (NRA)

TWENTY-SECOND DISTRICT

The 22d congressional district of California consists of three distinct parts of Los Angeles County, united by political affiliation but separated by the awesome San Gabriel Mountains. One is centered on Glendale, an old suburb nestled just below the mountains and almost directly north of downtown Los Angeles. The population here tends to be elderly, WASPy, Republican. So too the surrounding towns: a jagged-demarked section of Burbank and the mountain-surrounded suburbs of La Canada and La Crescenta.

The second section, which also includes about 40% of the district's voters, is demographically similar. This is a string of towns running east from Los Angeles beneath the mountains. These started off as stations on the Santa Fe Railroad line, then became separate little towns, then finally high income suburbs: Monrovia (starting from the east), Arcadia, Sierra Madre, Temple City, San Marino, Pasadena (except for a portion in the 25th district), South Pasadena. These suburbs have relatively low numbers of Mexican-Americans (though in many cases more than 10%) than the suburbs farther south from the mountains; their incomes are high, though with the exception of San Marino not the highest in the Los Angeles metropolitan area; their residents tend to be older than average, with grown rather than young families.

The third part of the district includes the communities of Saugus and Newhall nestled in the mountains north of the San Fernando Valley. This has a much younger population, but all three parts of the district are heavily Republican.

When the 22d's lines were drawn, two Republican congressmen lived in the district. One, John Rousselot, in an act of unusual political unselfishness moved to the Democratic 30th district, where he nearly won. The other, Carlos Moorhead, who had represented Glendale and Pasadena for 10 years, ran here and won easily. Moorhead, a high ranking member of the Judiciary and Energy and Commerce Committees, is not a particularly assertive or articulate politician. He is a solid Republican vote on most issues, however, and seems unlikely to encounter any trouble in this district.

The People Pop. 1980: 526,566, up 7.3% 1970–80; voting age pop. 403,454; 2% Black, 11% Span. orig., 4% Asian orig., 1% Am. Ind. 41% housing units rented. Median owner $110,600; renter $268. Households: 67% family, 32% with children, 55% married couples.

Presidential Vote

1980	Reagan (R)	147,114	(68%)
	Carter (D)	50,520	(23%)
	Other	20,260	(9%)

Rep. Carlos J. Moorhead (R) Elected 1972; b. May 6, 1922, Long Beach; home, Glendale; UCLA, B.A. 1943, USC, J.D. 1949; Presbyterian.

Career Army, WWII; Practicing atty., 1950–72; CA Assembly, 1966–72.

Offices 2346 RHOB, 202-225-4176. Also 420 N. Brand Blvd., Rm. 404, Glendale 91203, 213-247-8445.

Committees *Energy and Commerce* (4th). Subcommittees: Energy Conservation and Power; Telecommunications, Consumer Protection and Finance. *Judiciary* (2d). Subcommittees: Courts, Civil Liberties, and the Administration of Justice; Monopolies and Commercial Law.

Group Ratings

	ADA	ACLU	COPE	CFA	LCV	LWV	NTU	NSI	COC	ACA	CSFC
1982	0	0	9	0	25	33	92	100	90	96	76
1981	5	—	10	21	29	—	95	—	94	100	80
1980	11	27	16	7	35	20	60	100	71	96	80

National Journal Ratings

	Economic		Foreign		Cultural	
1982	3%	(LIB)	4%	(LIB)	4%	(LIB)
	96%	(CONS)	92%	(CONS)	87%	(CONS)
1981	3%	(LIB)	3%	(LIB)	2%	(LIB)
	97%	(CONS)	87%	(CONS)	98%	(CONS)

Key Votes

1) Reagan 81 Budget	FOR	5) Incr SS Rtmt Age	FOR	9) Poor Pay Food Stamps	FOR
2) Reagan 81 Tax Cut	FOR	6) Saudi AWACS Sale	FOR	10) Ban Crt Busing Order	FOR
3) Bal Budget Amend	FOR	7) $ for MX Missile	FOR	11) Auto Local Content	AGN
4) Gas & Road Tax	AGN	8) Nerve Gas Prod	FOR	12) Nuclear Arms Freeze	AGN

Election Results

1982 general	Carlos J. Moorhead (R)	145,831	(74%)	($107,690)
	Harvey L. Goldhammer (D)	46,521	(24%)	($0)
1982 primary	Carlos J. Moorhead (R)	81,246	(100%)	
1980 general	Carlos J. Moorhead (R)	115,241	(64%)	($124,297)
(CA 22)	Pierce O'Donnell (D)	57,477	(32%)	($171,977)
1980 general	John H. Rousselot (R)	116,715	(71%)	($92,824)
(CA 26)	Joseph Louis Lisoni (D)	40,099	(24%)	($41,082)
	William J. (B.J.) Wagener (Lib.) ..	7,700	(5%)	($1,120)

Campaign Contributions and Expenditures

1981-82		*Direct Cont. 81-82*			*PACS brkdwn*		
Receipts	$208,741	Indiv	$114,273	Agr	$2,600	Ideo	$2,050
Expend.	$107,690	Party	$8,900	Bus	$63,700	Lbr	$—
Unspent	$196,958	PACS	$83,197	Hlth	$6,450	Prof	$1,750

TWENTY-THIRD DISTRICT

The 23d congressional district of California consists of two halves, with roughly equal population, one north and one south of the Santa Monica Mountains that separate the San Fernando Valley from the Los Angeles Basin. The southern, Los Angeles, part is easily the more famous. It includes Beverly Hills, whose exorbitantly priced real estate and shops on Rodeo Drive keep show business personalities all atwitter and hence are common knowledge to the rest of us; the UCLA campus, in a neighborhood now far too expensive for most faculty members or students to live in; the Century City development, Westwood, the rather modest neighborhood of West Los Angeles, the high rises along Wilshire Boulevard, the pleasant rich neighborhood of Brentwood, and the very pleasant and grand Bel Air, where it seems that every house has its own tennis court and manicured garden, with a view overlooking the whole Los Angeles Basin.

The San Fernando Valley side is much more modest. It does have its hillside communities, Encino and Woodland Hills, but the view of the Valley is considered much less desirable. The Valley neighborhoods themselves, spread out along the mile-square grid avenues, vary widely, from modest to affluent. Twenty years ago these streets were filled with children; now more often they are quiet. The boundaries at the edge of the district are jagged so as to include the maximum number of Democratic votes.

The more affluent and famous part of this district is also the more Democratic; in fact, supporters of Congressman Anthony Beilenson reportedly complained that the district went out too far into the Valley. But Beilenson was not a favorite of redistricter Phillip Burton, and so in 1982, 60% of the district's population was on the Valley side; for 1984, Burton was kind enough to reverse the proportions. Beilenson got serious competition here in 1982, from academic busing opponent David Armor, and the incumbent was held to 60% of the vote.

Possibly a Republican could do even better, in a better year; but it seems likely that Beilenson would still have enough votes to defeat him, and so he is unlikely to attract another strong challenger soon.

Beilenson, a veteran of the California legislature, is a competent legislative strategist who has taken on tough assignments for the leadership. He is a member of the Rules Committee—a position that goes only to those who are loyal to the Democratic leadership and Speaker O'Neill.

The People Pop. 1980: 526,007, up 2.8% 1970–80; voting age pop. 426,336; 2% Black, 8% Span. orig., 4% Asian orig. 52% housing units rented. Median owner $134,000; renter $337. Households: 58% family, 25% with children, 46% married couples.

Presidential Vote

1980	Reagan (R)	107,985	(49%)
	Carter (D)	83,686	(38%)
	Other	28,416	(13%)

Rep. Anthony C. Beilenson (D) Elected 1976; b. Oct. 26, 1932, New Rochelle, NY; home, Sacramento; Harvard U., B.A. 1954, LL.B. 1957; Jewish.

Career Practicing atty., 1957–59; Counsel, CA Assembly Comm. on Finance and Insurance Fund, 1961–62; CA Assembly, 1963–66; CA Senate, 1971–77.

Offices 1025 LHOB, 202-225-5911. Also 11000 Wilshire Blvd., Los Angeles 90024, 213-824-7801.

Committee *Rules* (5th). Subcommittee: Rules of the House.

Group Ratings

	ADA	ACLU	COPE	CFA	LCV	LWV	NTU	NSI	COC	ACA	CSFC
1982	95	96	79	90	90	100	11	0	19	17	26
1981	90	—	78	71	93	—	30	—	6	4	26
1980	94	90	68	86	99	100	29	0	39	21	22

National Journal Ratings

	Economic		Foreign		Cultural	
1982	86%	(LIB)	85%	(LIB)	99%	(LIB)
	14%	(CONS)	12%	(CONS)	0%	(CONS)
1981	89%	(LIB)	99%	(LIB)	94%	(LIB)
	3%	(CONS)	0%	(CONS)	6%	(CONS)

Key Votes

1) Reagan 81 Budget	AGN	5) Incr SS Rtmt Age	FOR	9) Poor Pay Food Stamps	AGN
2) Reagan 81 Tax Cut	AGN	6) Saudi AWACS Sale	AGN	10) Ban Crt Busing Order	AGN
3) Bal Budget Amend	AGN	7) $ for MX Missile	AGN	11) Auto Local Content	AGN
4) Gas & Road Tax	FOR	8) Nerve Gas Prod	AGN	12) Nuclear Arms Freeze	FOR

Election Results

1982 general	Anthony C. Beilenson (D)	120,788	(60%)	($278,414)
	David Armor (R)	82,031	(40%)	($260,679)
1982 primary	Anthony C. Beilenson (D)	71,124	(100%)	
1980 general	Anthony C. Beilenson (D)	126,020	(63%)	($61,194)
	Robert Winckler (R)	62,742	(32%)	($9,865)
	Jeffrey P. Lieb (Libertarian)	10,623	(5%)	($0)

Campaign Contributions and Expenditures

1981-82		Direct Cont. 81-82				PACS brkdwn		
Receipts	$248,290	Indiv	$233,357	Agr	$—	Ideo	$1,000
Expend.	$278,414	PACS	$2,092	Bus	$—	Lbr	$—
Unspent	$5,225			Hlth	$—	Prof	$—

TWENTY-FOURTH DISTRICT

For the past 50 years, the heart of the entertainment world has been located on the West side of Los Angeles—either in Hollywood, on Sunset Strip, in Beverly Hills and downtown Burbank or over the mountains in Universal City. The offices that house the men and women who run the entertainment business are mostly modest and anonymous; they themselves dress in tennis shirts and slacks (and perhaps a few gold chains). Most of this territory lies within the 24th congressional district of California, whose boundaries go from near Dodgers Stadium in downtown Los Angeles west to Beverly Hills, and north from near Wilshire Boulevard over the mountains and into the San Fernando Valley to Hollywood Burbank Airport.

Within this area you will find Hollywood itself—a rather disappointing Hollywood Boulevard and tawdry stucco side streets. To the north, their precipitous rise dominating smogless days, are the Santa Monica Mountains, on their face the Hollywood sign. Among the mountains are picturesque houses built in steep canyons or on flat-topped mountains, yet from Hollywood these urban hillsides look surprisingly desolate and wild. To the north, in the San Fernando Valley, are the modest and heavily Jewish residential sections of North Hollywood and Studio City. To the south, below Wilshire Boulevard and east of Western Avenue are the burgeoning Koreatown neighborhood and pleasant districts with largely Mexican-American populations.

Show business is in many ways a Jewish industry, and this part of Los Angeles includes the heart of its Jewish community in the Fairfax district and many Jewish residents. But the population is diverse, and getting more so. Gay rights activists have become an important political force here, and their strongest areas are in Hollywood and West Hollywood. The district includes some neighborhoods of large elegant houses, the home less of the show business elite than of the businessmen and lawyers who earn their livings in downtown Los Angeles. Its Korean and Mexican-American residents have not yet become much involved in politics, but when they do they will affect it in ways yet unknown. Today some 22% of the district's adult residents are of Spanish origin and 11% are Asian (the latter the highest figure in southern California); but of the district's children, 44% are of Spanish origin and 15% Asian.

The congressman from this district, Henry Waxman, has become one of the most powerful members of the House, although he was first elected as recently as 1974. He was not even then a legislative novice, however. Elected to the California Assembly at age 29, in his second term he was entrusted with the chair of the Redistricting Committee—not an assignment for political innocents (but it was a court and not his committee which created this district). Waxman's big break came after the 1978 election, when he was elected chairman of the Energy and Commerce Committee's Health Subcommittee. This is one of the half dozen most important subcommittees in the House, and Waxman did not just inherit it. He was elected by Commerce Committee members and had to beat Richardson Preyer of North Carolina, a popular and highly competent member. Waxman questioned Preyer's pharmaceutical holdings, argued that he would have to do the will of the tobacco industry, and (an entirely legal practice) gave campaign contributions to committee Democrats; he won their support 15–12.

The campaign contributions was no accident. Waxman and several allies—notably former Assembly Majority Leader and now Congressman Howard Berman—have built a political machine of their own in Los Angeles. It is based not on its ability to give workers public jobs, but on its ability to raise money for candidates, and it draws on rich and liberal contributors in and near the 24th district.

In the House Waxman has been adept at building power in similar ways. After the 1983 elections he was instrumental in getting Berman elected to the Democratic Steering and Policy Committee, which makes committee assignments, and he was largely (though not completely) successful in getting people he wanted on Energy and Commerce—which, as it happens, was the most sought after committee assignment. In effect Waxman had become, after eight years in the House, a central power broker in the process that determines the course of dozens of House careers. It would be wrong to suggest that Waxman is just a wheeler-dealer, however. On the contrary, he cares about—and knows more than just anyone about—important areas of public policy. His performance on the Clean Air Act in 1981 and 1982 was a clear example. He favored reauthorization of the Clean Air Act pretty much as is, while committee Chairman John Dingell of Michigan, most committee Republicans, and the Reagan administration wanted it significantly relaxed. Waxman's own subcommittee was against him on the issue, 12–8. Yet for 15 months he prevented any vote on Clean Air, until the climate of public opinion had changed and there was strong pressure for strengthening rather than weakening it. He did that through exploiting his opponents' mistakes and lack of preparation, leaking administration proposals which aroused a storm of protest, getting his adversaries to agree to request jointly more information before they acted, and, in the summer of 1982 in full committtee, simply using stalling tactics. He rounded up the votes to defeat the provisions, to help the auto companies, that Dingell wanted most of all; at that point Dingell stopped markup of the bill.

Through all this Waxman was well prepared, cheerful, calm, and polite to his opponents. He is used to getting along personally with people he disagrees with philosophically, and he takes care to understand why they take their positions; that gives him the opportunity sometimes to suggest a compromise that gives them something of what they want without giving away much of what he considers important. He is one of those people who thinks legislatively, always aware of parliamentary procedure, and who has difficulty only in understanding why others don't do what is best calculated to achieve their ends. Waxman's career shows how the House has changed in the last dozen years. It is more of a meritocracy now; important positions are given not just to senior members, but to those most capable of using them in the way the majority wants.

At home Waxman, not surprisingly, had no trouble with redistricting; he and Howard Berman were in fact key figures in making sure that Phillip Burton's redistricting plans had the votes to pass the legislature.

134   CALIFORNIA

The People Pop. 1980: 525,909, up 13.5% 1970–80; voting age pop. 429,058; 6% Black, 22% Span. orig., 11% Asian orig. 73% housing units rented. Median owner $112,600; renter $235. Households: 47% family, 22% with children, 34% married couples.

Presidential Vote

1980	Reagan (R)	62,749	(42%)
	Carter (D)	67,571	(45%)
	Other	18,473	(12%)

Rep. Henry A. Waxman (D) Elected 1974; b. Sept. 12, 1939, Los Angeles; home, Los Angeles; UCLA, B.A. 1961, J.D. 1964; Jewish.

Career Practicing atty., 1965–68; CA Assembly, 1968–74.

Offices 2418 RHOB, 202-225-3976. Also 8425 W. 3d St., Los Angeles 90048, 213-651-1041.

Committees *Energy and Commerce* (4th). Subcommittees: Health and the Environment (Chairman); Telecommunications, Consumer Protection and Finance. *Government Operations* (8th). Subcommittees: Legislation and National Security; Commerce, Consumer, and Monetary Affairs. *Select Committee on Aging* (18th). Subcommittee: Retirement Income and Employment.

Group Ratings

	ADA	ACLU	COPE	CFA	LCV	LWV	NTU	NSI	COC	ACA	CSFC
1982	95	75	89	90	96	92	10	10	14	18	25
1981	85	—	87	79	99	—	19	—	11	15	27
1980	83	77	89	71	94	90	19	13	50	22	26

National Journal Ratings

	Economic		Foreign		Cultural	
1982	86%	(LIB)	74%	(LIB)	86%	(LIB)
	14%	(CONS)	26%	(CONS)	14%	(CONS)
1981	81%	(LIB)	77%	(LIB)	79%	(LIB)
	15%	(CONS)	21%	(CONS)	21%	(CONS)

Key Votes

1) Reagan 81 Budget	AGN	5) Incr SS Rtmt Age	AGN	9) Poor Pay Food Stamps	—
2) Reagan 81 Tax Cut	AGN	6) Saudi AWACS Sale	AGN	10) Ban Crt Busing Order	FOR
3) Bal Budget Amend	AGN	7) $ for MX Missile	AGN	11) Auto Local Content	AGN
4) Gas & Road Tax	FOR	8) Nerve Gas Prod	AGN	12) Nuclear Arms Freeze	FOR

Election Results

1982 general	Henry A. Waxman (D)	88,516	(65%)	($95,012)
	Jerry Zerg (R)	42,133	(31%)	($113,841)
1982 primary	Henry A. Waxman (D)	49,894	(100%)	
1980 general	Henry A. Waxman (D)	93,569	(64%)	($32,391)
	Roland Cayard (R)	39,744	(27%)	($8,288)

Campaign Contributions and Expenditures

1981-82		Direct Cont. 81-82		PACS brkdwn			
Receipts	$118,639	Indiv	$37,939	Agr	$1,200	Ideo	$5,000
Expend.	$95,012	PACS	$90,920	Bus	$29,400	Lbr	$27,650
Unspent	$34,761			Hlth	$25,350	Prof	$1,100

TWENTY-FIFTH DISTRICT

The 25th district includes the state's largest number of Mexican-Americans concentrated on the East side of Los Angeles and in the incorporated suburb of East Los Angeles. This area is portrayed, typically, as a barrio or a ghetto, into which Mexican-Americans are condemned to live by discrimination; and its population is portrayed as desperately poor, without opportunity, and, politically, as deprived of their rightful share of power. For the most part, this picture is false; in East Los Angeles and the 25th district we can see why.

In the first place, there is little evidence that Mexican-Americans are prevented by discrimination from living pretty much anywhere they want. Every congressional district in the Los Angeles metropolitan area, every suburb and enclave of Los Angeles, has a significant Spanish origin population, of 3% or more. The evidence of the 1980 Census suggests that Mexican-Americans are dispersing themselves around the metropolitan area—to the San Fernando Valley, to Orange County, as well as in the suburbs east and southeast of East Los Angeles—more rapidly than demographers and magazine article writers can keep up with them. True, there are Mexican-American concentrations. Fully 95% of the people in East Los Angeles are of Spanish origin, and so are 67% of those in the Los Angeles portion of the 25th district—basically, the city east of downtown, from Boyle Heights next to East Los Angeles north to the increasingly middle class neighborhoods of Highland Park and Eagle Rock. But these essentially serve the same function as the old Italian neighborhoods of New York or Philadelphia. They are where the immigrants first come in, where they are received by relatives or friends, live doubled up in houses or apartments, find their first jobs. People are not permanently stuck here: these are way stations. Soon enough they move out to more comfortable and not always identifiably Mexican-American neighborhoods.

As for being desperately poor, Mexican-Americans might well answer, compared to what? Compared to peasants in central Mexico, almost everyone in East Los Angeles is affluent indeed. But even by U.S. standards, people here aren't desperately poor. A drive through the area shows not empty storefronts, but busy shops with new signs; not housing riddled with vandalism and neglect, but houses newly painted and with carefully tended gardens. Americans are used to seeing their lowest income neighborhoods nearly abandoned, but East Los Angeles is thronged with people, and especially with children. Housing prices tell an interesting story. According to the Census Bureau, housing prices in 1980 in mostly black Watts were about $42,000. But in East Los Angeles they were $53,000 and in the Los Angeles portion of the 25th, $65,000 (the same as prices in the comfortable suburbs of Philadelphia). You can't afford to buy or rent housing of that price, even if two families act together, on welfare payments or the minimum wage. What we are seeing in these areas are not people who are failures but people who are in the process of becoming successes.

The rather low number of Mexican-Americans in high public office in California is often cited as evidence that they are deprived of political power. But it probably just means that in the process of moving up in the world they don't have time to exercise it. They would not be the first ethnic group in America to move up mainly through private sector jobs, largely ignoring politics. The 1982 redistricting did increase the number of Mexican-Americans elected from California from one to three and made for corresponding increases in the legislative races. But the real question is whether Mexican-Americans are getting what they want from politics and government. The answer seems to be yes. Moving up rapidly economically, they don't need as much from government as do blacks, hobbled by segregation and discrimination.

The 25th district includes, besides the east side of Los Angeles and East Los Angeles, the northeast quadrant of highish income Pasadena, an area with significant numbers of blacks and Mexican-Americans, and a black-majority part of the suburb of Altadena just to the north. It is a safely Democratic district, although it should not be assumed that Mexican-Americans will vote as heavily or faithfully Democratic as blacks have since 1964. The district is represented in the House by Edward Roybal, who is of Spanish but not Mexican origin; he is from northern New Mexico, where the Spanish-speaking community dates back from before Plymouth Rock.

Roybal has had his problems in the House. In 1978 the Ethics Committee recommended that he be censured for having lied about a $1,000 campaign contribution from Tongsun Park that he converted to his own use. Roybal admitted taking the money, but his supporters persuaded the House that he should be reprimanded rather than censured. Some observers believe he would have been censured but for his minority status. On the Appropriations Committee he chairs the Treasury, Postal Service, General Government Subcommittee, ordinarily one of the less controversial units. He has a solidly liberal voting record. Although nearing 70, he has shown no sign of retiring.

The People   Pop. 1980: 525,411, up 6.6% 1970–80; voting age pop. 357,889; 10% Black, 58% Span. orig., 8% Asian orig., 1% Am. Ind. 59% housing units rented. Median owner $65,300; renter $176. Households: 70% family, 45% with children, 49% married couples.

Presidential Vote

1980	Reagan (R)	30,850	(34%)
	Carter (D)	52,120	(57%)
	Other	8,462	(9%)

Rep. Edward R. Roybal (D) Elected 1962; b. Feb. 10, 1916, Albuquerque, NM; home, Los Angeles; UCLA, Southwestern U.; Roman Catholic.

Career Army, WWII; Dir. of Health Educ., L.A. Cnty. Tuberculosis & Health Assn., 1945–49; L.A. City Cncl., 1949–62, Pres. Pro Tem, 1961–62.

Offices 2211 RHOB, 202-225-6235. Also New Fed. P. O. Bldg., 300 N. Los Angeles St., Los Angeles 90012, 213-688-4870.

Committees *Appropriations* (9th). Subcommittees: Labor, Health and Human Services, Education; Treasury, Postal Service, General Government (Chairman). *Select Committee on Aging* (Chairman). Subcommittee: Housing and Consumer Interests (Chairman).

Group Ratings

	ADA	ACLU	COPE	CFA	LCV	LWV	NTU	NSI	COC	ACA	CSFC
1982	95	100	94	90	86	75	39	0	9	0	20
1981	95	—	93	71	79	—	26	—	5	4	24
1980	89	83	89	93	61	89	16	0	50	14	21

National Journal Ratings

	Economic		Foreign		Cultural	
1982	87%	(LIB)	96%	(LIB)	93%	(LIB)
	12%	(CONS)	1%	(CONS)	3%	(CONS)
1981	89%	(LIB)	83%	(LIB)	91%	(LIB)
	3%	(CONS)	16%	(CONS)	9%	(CONS)

Key Votes

1) Reagan 81 Budget	AGN	5) Incr SS Rtmt Age	AGN	9) Poor Pay Food Stamps	AGN
2) Reagan 81 Tax Cut	AGN	6) Saudi AWACS Sale	AGN	10) Ban Crt Busing Order	AGN
3) Bal Budget Amend	AGN	7) $ for MX Missile	AGN	11) Auto Local Content	FOR
4) Gas & Road Tax	FOR	8) Nerve Gas Prod	AGN	12) Nuclear Arms Freeze	FOR

Election Results

1982 general	Edward R. Roybal (D)	71,106	(85%)	($40,336)
	Daniel John Gorham (L)	12,060	(15%)	($0)
1982 primary	Edward R. Roybal (D)	39,667	(100%)	
1980 general	Edward R. Roybal (D)	49,080	(66%)	($44,411)
	Richard E. Ferraro, Jr. (R)	21,116	(28%)	($14,757)
	William D. Mitchell (Libertarian)	4,169	(6%)	($367)

Campaign Contributions and Expenditures

1981-82		Direct Cont. 81-82		PACS brkdwn			
Receipts	$110,105	Indiv	$52,271	Agr	$2,700	Ideo	$2,425
Expend.	$40,336	PACS	$48,236	Bus	$9,050	Lbr	$30,900
Unspent	$111,490			Hlth	$2,450	Prof	$100

TWENTY-SIXTH DISTRICT

The movie *Chinatown* tells the story, with some artistic license. The San Fernando Valley, 20 miles east to west and 12 north to south, was vacant, arid land, surrounded by mountains, at the turn of the century. Then civic leaders (including Harry Chandler of the *Los Angeles Times*) encouraged city engineer William Mulholland to build a huge aqueduct from the Owens Valley to give Los Angeles water and got the city to annex most of the San Fernando Valley, large chunks of which they had, with foresight, already acquired. The land is just about all built up now, except for movie ranches and flood control areas, and is changing slowly from suburban to urban in character. Its population is becoming older and consists more frequently of identifiable minorities; it is more liberal politically. The San Fernando Valley now has more than one million people, enough to constitute the major part of two congressional districts and minor parts of three others. One of them is the 26th congressional district of California.

This is a district created for and by a particular congressman, Howard Berman. It begins in the Hollywood Hills, above West Hollywood and Beverly Hills. Here expensive houses are built off the roads that twist up hillsides; nestled under steep overhangs or looking out, from atop a scraped-off hillside, on the whole city. Two decades ago, the Hollywood Hills were affluent, family-oriented, and Republican, primarily because of economic issues; today they are affluent, singles- (and sometimes gay-) oriented, and Democratic, primarily because of cultural issues. The politician who first perceived and acted on the change was Howard Berman. In 1972, supposedly a terrible year for Democrats, at age 27, he ran for in the Hollywood Hills district represented by the Assembly Republican Leader—and won handily.

Berman showed himself to be ambitious to do more than represent the hills. In 1974, he supported Leo McCarthy for speaker against Willie Brown—and became Assembly majority leader when McCarthy won. He was the chief sculptor of California's farm labor law, one of the most sensitive measures passed by the legislature in recent years. In 1980, he made a misstep, trying to oust McCarthy in mid-session; Willie Brown, now a McCarthy ally, was elected speaker instead. But after the 1980 elections, Phil Burton came to Sacramento, got Berman and McCarthy together, and got them and Brown to support a set of redistricting plans that, among other things, was designed to send Berman and his friends Mel Levine and Richard Lehman to Congress.

The 26th district created for Berman proceeds directly north from the Hollywood Hills into the heart of the San Fernando Valley. It includes the Democratic middle class neighborhoods of Van Nuys and Panorama City, goes northwest to take in, within a jagged boundary, the more Democratic parts of Granada Hills, takes in the black neighborhood of Pacoima and the mostly Mexican-American neighborhoods on either side of the Golden State Freeway, and dips a little south to include a carefully selected set of precincts in Burbank. With this district Berman had only nominal primary opposition and won the general election with 60% of the vote.

In the House Democratic Caucus Berman executed something of a coup by beating John Bryant of Texas for a seat on the Democratic Steering and Policy Committee, the body that makes Democratic committee assignments. This was a reprise of the battle in which Jim Wright of Texas beat Phil Burton for the majority leadership in 1976 by one vote; this time California won. Berman has seats on the Judiciary and Foreign Affairs Committees, and, while still in his early 40s, apparently has a bright future as well as a distinguished past as a legislator.

The People   Pop. 1980: 526,118, up 2.1% 1970–80; voting age pop. 392,935; 4% Black, 21% Span. orig., 3% Asian orig., 1% Am. Ind. 43% housing units rented. Median owner $95,400; renter $280. Households: 67% family, 34% with children, 53% married couples.

Presidential Vote

1980	Reagan (R)	94,136	(51%)
	Carter (D)	70,376	(38%)
	Other	20,598	(11%)

Rep. Howard Berman (D) Elected 1982; b. Apr. 15, 1941, Los Angeles; home, Los Angeles; UCLA, B.A. 1962, LL.B. 1965; Jewish.

Career Practicing atty., 1966–72; CA Assembly, 1973–82.

Offices 1022 LHOB, 202-225-4695. Also 14600 Roscoe Blvd., Su. 506, Panorama City 91402, 213-891-0543.

Committees Foreign Affairs (19th). Subcommittees: Africa; International Economic Policy and Trade. *Judiciary* (20th). Subcommittees: Courts, Civil Liberties, and the Administration of Justice; Administrative Law and Government Relations; Criminal Justice.

Group Ratings and Key Votes: Newly Elected

Election Results

1982 general	Howard L. Berman (D)	....	97,383	(60%)	($308,949)
	Hal Phillips (R)	....	66,072	(40%)	($291,996)
1982 primary	Howard L. Berman (D)	....	51,625	(83%)	
	Barry D. Gorelick (D)	....	10,417	(17%)	
1980 general	Newly created district				

Campaign Contributions and Expenditures

1981-82		Direct Cont. 81-82*				PACS brkdwn		
Receipts	$309,328	Indiv	$200,125	Agr	$1,000	Ideo	$22,391
Expend.	$308,949	PACS	$106,201	Bus	$15,900	Lbr	$53,850
Unspent	$378			Hlth	$5,200	Prof	$600

Non-Cand Loans: $7,000

TWENTY-SEVENTH DISTRICT

The 27th congressional district of California is a long, thin swath of land along the Pacific Coast, from Malibu in the north almost to Palos Verdes in the south: Los Angeles's beachfront, plus some fingers of land inland. The cool ocean breezes give the area its own special climate, cooler than the rest of Los Angeles in the summer, a little less cool but damper in the winter. The beach communities are about as diverse as can be imagined, and there is no simple way you can describe the 27th district. The beach cottages of Malibu, huddled against each other and facing a beach that was eroded seriously by storms in 1983, are nonetheless incredibly expensive. Santa Monica and Venice, full of young people living in cheap housing and fearful that they will be expelled for higher-paying tenants or condominium buyers, have generated in Santa Monica's case an indigenous leftish political movement (Tom Hayden's Committee for Economic Democracy which, however, lost the 1983 mayor's race) and in

Venice's case a countercultural lifestyle full of enthusiasm for the latest crazes. Below Venice is Marina Del Rey, full of sailboats and contemporary apartments where young single executives live near restaurants with dimly lit bars and picture window views of the harbor from the dining room. Next is Los Angeles International Airport (known by its three letter code, LAX), followed by the beach suburbs of El Segundo (named after Socal's second refinery), Manhattan Beach, Hermosa Beach, and Redondo Beach. The tightly packed frame houses here were originally the homes of elderly retirees; by the 1970s they were inhabited more often by groups of young singles.

Politically, the beach communities do have some things in common: a Republican heritage, dating from their original settlement by midwestern retirees, and liberal cultural attitudes, brought in by the suntanned, pot-smoking residents of the 1970s. To this should be added the atmosphere created by CED's successful capture of the Santa Monica city government, based primarily on the rent control issue: young renters celebrating themselves as proletarians because they are denied the right to rent apartments a few blocks from the beach for $175 a month. But altogether the 27th would be a politically marginal district—as it was before 1982—without the addition of some inland territory: an odd-shaped finger of land some five miles inland into some of Los Angeles's Jewish and black neighborhoods, the mostly Mexican–American suburbs of Lennox behind the airport and Lawndale behind the South Bay beach towns. These areas, heavily Democratic, made this a safe district for Assemblyman Mel Levine.

Levine presents a vivid contrast with the district's most recent congressman, Robert K. Dornan, a fiery conservative who ran for the Senate when he saw that Phil Burton took Torrance and Palos Verdes away from his district and added the inland territory; Dornan had won three close elections, and knew there was no way he could win in the new 27th. Everyone else apparently felt the same way. Tom Hayden ran, not for Congress but for the California Assembly, and won by somewhat less than the usual Democratic percentage after spending something like a million dollars.

Levine had no competition in the Democrat primary and won the general election easily with 59% of the vote. He did not succeed in getting a seat on the Energy and Commerce Committee with his friend Henry Waxman, but he does serve on Foreign Affairs and Government Operations. On issues Levine is, if not as liberal as Dornan was conservative, still noticeably to the left of most incoming Democratic freshmen, a man who seems to have a burning desire to use government to improve the lot of ordinary people and who has—perhaps sensibly—less skepticism that this can be done than most young Democrats do today. He seems to have a safe seat and a good platform from which to try.

The People   Pop. 1980: 525,758, up 1.5% 1970–80; voting age pop. 416,355; 10% Black, 14% Span. orig., 6% Asian orig., 1% Am. Ind. 60% housing units rented. Median owner $126,200; renter $302. Households: 54% family, 26% with children, 40% married couples.

Presidential Vote

1980	Reagan (R)	88,457	(45%)
	Carter (D)	80,577	(41%)
	Other	26,087	(13%)

Rep. Mel Levine (D) Elected 1982; b. June 7, 1943, Los Angeles; home, Los Angeles; U. of CA at Berkeley, B.A. 1964, Princeton U., M.P.A. 1966, Harvard Law Sch., J.D. 1969; Jewish.

Career Practicing atty., 1969–71, 1973–77; Legis. Asst. to Senator John V. Tunney, 1971–73; CA Assembly, 1977–82.

Offices 502 CHOB, 202-225-6451. Also 5250 W. Century Blvd., Su. 447, Los Angeles 90045, 213-642-3935.

Committees *Foreign Affairs* (21st) Subcommittees: Asian and Pacific Affairs; Europe and the Middle East; Human Rights and International Organizations. *Government Operations* (20th). Subcommittees: Environment, Energy, and Natural Resources; Manpower and Housing.

Group Ratings and Key Votes: Newly Elected

Election Results

1982 general	Mel Levine (D)	108,347	(60%)	($431,931)
	Bart W. Christensen (R)	67,479	(37%)	($126,419)
1982 primary	Mel Levine (D)	59,311	(100%)	
1980 general	Robert K. Dornan (R)	109,807	(51%)	($1,947,209)
	Carey Peck (D)	100,061	(47%)	($559,315)

Campaign Contributions and Expenditures

1981-82		*Direct Cont. 81-82*			*PACS brkdwn*		
Receipts	$464,190	Indiv	$406,271	Agr	$600	Ideo	$3,191
Expend.	$431,931	PACS	$45,922	Bus	$10,462	Lbr	$26,120
Unspent	$32,259			Hlth	$3,160	Prof	$100

TWENTY-EIGHTH DISTRICT

The 28th district includes much of the historic heart of Los Angeles's black community—yet overall a majority of the district's citizens are not black. The district goes nearly to downtown Los Angeles and MacArthur Park; it includes the campus of the University of Southern California, which has produced so many prominent Republicans and which is surrounded by mostly black neighborhoods. The district proceeds southwest, to the long-integrated Crenshaw, View Park, and Ladera Heights areas, and the integrated suburb of Inglewood, as well as to mostly white Culver City and the Westchester area—a classic 1950s suburban enclave within the Los Angeles city limits—just north of the airport.

Someone looking at this area in 1970, when its population was about 38% black and 12% Spanish origin, might have predicted a rapid increase in the black percentage in the next decade. But actually it has not increased much at all; it is the Spanish origin that has risen (but no one is sure by quite how much, since the categories in the two censuses are not commensurate). The Mexican-Americans do not seem to be concentrated in just a few neighborhoods; neither, to a surprising extent considering our history of neighborhood segregation, do blacks. Culver City, once virtually all white, is now 8% black; but there is no established ghetto there. Inglewood is now 57% black, but there are no signs that the whites there are about to move out en masse. This slower, more relaxed pace of change seems to have prevented the sort of feverish politics and wildly fluctuating housing prices often seen in racially changing neighborhoods. In any case, this is a solidly Democratic area: not only the blacks, but a majority of the whites, regularly vote Democratic. With relatively little fuss the mostly white voters have elected black Democrats: first Yvonne Brathwaite Burke and, since 1978, Julian Dixon.

Dixon, who served six years in the California Assembly, is considered a competent and politically shrewd politician. In his first term he won a seat on the Appropriations Committee; in his second he became chairman of the District of Columbia Appropriations Subcommittee. This is a body of not much importance nationally, and indeed of somewhat less importance to Washingtonians since they got home rule, but of some interest nonetheless. Every year the District still gets a sizable federal payment, in lieu of the property taxes that would be paid if government buildings were privately owned; and that payment, which keeps Washington's budget from being hopelessly unbalanced, goes through Dixon's subcommittee. He can be sure that his phone calls to Washington Mayor Marion Barry will be speedily returned.

Dixon is politically safe in his district. He has not had primary opposition since 1978, and the district is heavily Democratic in the general election.

The People   Pop. 1980: 525,682, up 6.3% 1970–80; voting age pop. 385,847; 42% Black, 26% Span. orig., 6% Asian orig. 60% housing units rented. Median owner $79,800; renter $192. Households: 61% family, 36% with children, 39% married couples.

Presidential Vote

1980	Reagan (R)	35,398	(26%)
	Carter (D)	91,477	(68%)
	Other	8,565	(6%)

Rep. Julian C. Dixon (D) Elected 1978; b. Aug. 8, 1934, Washington, D.C.; home, Los Angeles; CA St. U. at L.A., B.S. 1962, Southwestern U., LL.B. 1967; Episcopal.

Career Army, 1957–60; Practicing atty., 1960–73; CA Assembly, 1973–78.

Offices 423 CHOB, 202-225-7084. Also One La Brea Ave., Inglewood 90301, 213-678-5424.

Committees *Appropriations* (24th). Subcommittees: District of Columbia (Chairman); Foreign Operations. *Standards of Official Conduct* (4th).

Group Ratings

	ADA	ACLU	COPE	CFA	LCV	LWV	NTU	NSI	COC	ACA	CSFC
1982	85	83	95	80	69	83	15	22	32	5	26
1981	80	—	94	50	61	—	3	—	16	9	217
1980	94	97	88	86	62	100	11	0	54	10	21

National Journal Ratings

	Economic		Foreign		Cultural	
1982	81%	(LIB)	89%	(LIB)	85%	(LIB)
	18%	(CONS)	11%	(CONS)	14%	(CONS)
1981	89%	(LIB)	83%	(LIB)	86%	(LIB)
	3%	(CONS)	17%	(CONS)	14%	(CONS)

Key Votes

1) Reagan 81 Budget	AGN	5) Incr SS Rtmt Age	AGN	9) Poor Pay Food Stamps	AGN
2) Reagan 81 Tax Cut	AGN	6) Saudi AWACS Sale	AGN	10) Ban Crt Busing Order	AGN
3) Bal Budget Amend	AGN	7) $ for MX Missile	AGN	11) Auto Local Content	FOR
4) Gas & Road Tax	FOR	8) Nerve Gas Prod	AGN	12) Nuclear Arms Freeze	FOR

Election Results

1982 general	Julian C. Dixon (D)	103,469	(79%)	($53,807)
	David Goetz (R)	24,473	(19%)	($0)
1982 primary	Julian C. Dixon (D)	59,500	(100%)	
1980 general	Julian C. Dixon (D)	108,725	(79%)	($63,882)
	Robert Reid (R)	23,179	(17%)	($14,919)

Campaign Contributions and Expenditures

1981-82		Direct Cont. 81-82		PACS brkdwn			
Receipts	$58,043	Indiv	$22,719	Agr	$900	Ideo	$2,500
Expend.	$53,807	PACS	$35,020	Bus	$12,700	Lbr	$14,550
Unspent	$23,723			Hlth	$3,400	Prof	$100

TWENTY-NINTH DISTRICT

Watts has been a familiar American place name since the 1965 riot there put it in the national headlines. Although no longer in the headlines, Watts remains the focus of Los Angeles's black community, directly south of downtown. As official Los Angeles found out after 1965, despite its central location, Watts has few community institutions—no hospitals, few parks, and few bus lines. Indeed, much of the territory around Watts isn't part of the city of Los Angeles at all, and the city has no intention of annexing it. The area's most distinctive feature is the Watts Tower, a weird sculpture of bits of broken glass and scrap metal, assembled over 30 years by Italian immigrant Simon Rodia; he gave it to the city free, while other cities spend tens of thousands for similar but less attractive pieces. New York journalists sent to Watts in the wake of the riot were quick to write that the place didn't look like a ghetto. Actually more blacks live in places like Watts—with its small frame double- or single-family houses along quiet streets—than in places like Harlem, with its five-story turn-of-the-century tenements.

Watts is also the center of California's 29th congressional district, and the almost unanimously Democratic voting habits of the black areas inevitably place the district in the Democratic column. But there is another part of the 29th district, across Alameda Street, the unofficial eastern boundary of Watts, which has been changing rapidly. Alameda used to be an impenetrable racial barrier, separating blacks from working class whites. In the 1970s, however, most of the working class whites moved out (or died: the area was elderly) and were replaced by Mexican–Americans in industrial suburbs like Huntington Park and South Gate. So the Mexican-American population of the district rose by more than 100,000. At the same time, the black population of the district actually declined. As Watts's population aged, there were fewer children, and as it grew more affluent there were fewer people per housing unit; many blacks simply moved away, to more pleasant neighborhoods to the west and south.

None of this neighborhood change (nor the addition, for the 1982 election only, of the relatively affluent white suburb of Downey) has had much effect on congressional politics in the 29th, at least not yet. Congressman Augustus Hawkins, who turned 75 in 1982, was reelected easily. Hawkins is now the senior black legislator in the nation and the senior member of the Congressional Black Caucus. For 28 years, from 1934 to 1962, he served in the California Assembly, for most of the time as its only black member; in 1959 he was nearly elected speaker. But California was apparently not ready for that then, and so Hawkins had to settle for a seat in Congress.

Hawkins's experience has not disposed him to verbal militance or oratorical pyrotechnics. He is more interested in building support, over a period of years, for legislation he believes in. A prime example is the Humphrey–Hawkins full employment act, which in its original form required the government to create jobs at prevailing wage rates until unemployment dropped to a specified figure. In the 1976 presidential campaign Humphrey–Hawkins became a kind of litmus test for Democratic candidates; Jimmy Carter eventually endorsed it, but in lukewarm terms, leaving little doubt he considered it impractical. For most candidates, it was a cynical exercise; even then, they knew they could never persuade Congress to authorize the open-ended spending that the bill would require. But Hawkins was serious: he wanted to attack the problems of high unemployment among blacks and others and wanted government to move in here as it had, with such success, in other areas. Eventually, after Humphrey's death, a bill was passed that gave lip service to this idea; but a real full employment program is a dream Hawkins would still like to pursue.

Hawkins is now the second ranking Democrat on the House Education and Labor Committee; he is five years older than the chairman, Carl Perkins of Kentucky. He is a committee chairman himself, however, of the House Administration Committee. Most of its business in 1981–82 was routine housekeeping, although even that, in hands more aggressive than Hawkins's, can make a chairman powerful, as it did Wayne Hays in the middle 1970s. House Administration is also the committee that handles campaign finance law, an issue of extreme importance to congressmen that may arise in 1983–84. Hawkins's views on this are apparently in line with those of the Democratic leadership, which is to say that he is vaguely sympathetic but certainly not committed to public financing of congressional elections and would like to reduce the influence of business and right wing ideological PACs.

Hawkins can be reelected from this district as long as he likes.

The People   Pop. 1980: 525,795, up 2.1% 1970–80; voting age pop. 346,664; 46% Black, 28% Span. orig., 1% Asian orig. 55% housing units rented. Median owner $57,400; renter $174. Households: 71% family, 45% with children, 45% married couples.

Presidential Vote

1980	Reagan (R)	34,792	(27%)
	Carter (D)	86,438	(68%)
	Other	5,038	(4%)

Rep. Augustus F. Hawkins (D) Elected 1962; b. Aug. 31, 1907, Shreveport, LA; home, Los Angeles; UCLA, A.B. 1931; USC Institute of Govt.; Methodist.

Career Real estate business; CA Assembly, 1935–62.

Offices 2371 RHOB, 202-225-2201. Also 936 W. Manchester St., Los Angeles 90044, 213-750-0260.

Committees *House Administration* (Chairman). *Education and Labor* (2d). Subcommittees: Elementary, Secondary and Vocational Education; Employment Opportunities (Chairman). *Joint Printing Committee* (Chairman). *Joint Library Committee* (Vice-Chairman). *Joint Economic Committee* (4th). Subcommittees: Economic Goals and Intergovernmental Policy; International Trade, Finance, and Security Economics.

Group Ratings

	ADA	ACLU	COPE	CFA	LCV	LWV	NTU	NSI	COC	ACA	CSFC
1982	70	83	95	70	77	75	7	30	29	5	27
1981	85	—	95	71	79	—	14	—	11	4	28
1980	89	100	88	79	70	100	11	11	59	6	24

National Journal Ratings

	Economic		Foreign		Cultural	
1982	80%	(LIB)	79%	(LIB)	85%	(LIB)
	20%	(CONS)	20%	(CONS)	14%	(CONS)
1981	87%	(LIB)	79%	(LIB)	94%	(LIB)
	12%	(CONS)	21%	(CONS)	5%	(CONS)

Key Votes

1) Reagan 81 Budget	AGN	5) Incr SS Rtmt Age	AGN	9) Poor Pay Food Stamps	AGN
2) Reagan 81 Tax Cut	AGN	6) Saudi AWACS Sale	AGN	10) Ban Crt Busing Order	AGN
3) Bal Budget Amend	AGN	7) $ for MX Missile	AGN	11) Auto Local Content	FOR
4) Gas & Road Tax	—	8) Nerve Gas Prod	AGN	12) Nuclear Arms Freeze	FOR

Election Results

1982 general	Augustus F. Hawkins (D)	97,028	(80%)	($27,679)
	Milton R. Mackaig (R)	24,568	(20%)	($0)
1982 primary	Augustus F. Hawkins (D)	56,615	(100%)	
1980 general	Augustus F. Hawkins (D)	80,095	(86%)	($33,711)
	Michael Arthur Hirt (R)	10,282	(11%)	($0)

Campaign Contributions and Expenditures

1981-82		Direct Cont. 81-82		PACS brkdwn			
Receipts	$44,645	Indiv	$12,788	Agr	$950	Ideo	$250
Expend.	$27,679	Party	$100	Bus	$4,630	Lbr	$26,500
Unspent	$40,516	PACS	$33,979	Hlth	$450	Prof	$200

THIRTIETH DISTRICT

The 30th congressional district of California is one of two suburban Los Angeles County districts running from northeast to southwest, in the valley east of downtown Los Angeles. Both the 30th and the 34th are considered Mexican-American districts, though in neither is a majority of the adult population of Spanish origin, and in both Mexican-American voters are not just concentrated in a couple of enclosed ghettos, but in fact are dispersed through a wide variety of neighborhoods. The heaviest Mexican-American concentrations, on the order of 60%, in the 30th district are in industrial suburbs: young Mexican families have replaced aging whites in the factory and warehouse suburbs of Vernon, Maywood, Commerce, Bell, and Bell Gardens directly south of Boyle Heights, on either side of the usually dry, cement-channeled Los Angeles River. The towns directly adjacent to East Los Angeles have lower Mexican percentages. In some cases, as in Montebello and Monterey Park, this is because they also have sizable numbers of Korean and other Asian inhabitants. In others, like Alhambra and San Gabriel, the economic level is a little higher. But even here the population in 1980 was 38% Spanish origin. From there the 30th sweeps far northeast, through the valley blue collar suburb of El Monte to Azusa, at the foot of the giant San Gabriel Mountains.

This has always been a solidly Democratic area, even when there were few Mexican-Americans there. The steady dispersal of Mexican-Americans outward, in a kind of Brownian movement, from the East Los Angeles and Boyle Heights concentrations, has not changed the political percentages as much as some might expect. Mexican-Americans, it is plain, vote more like preceding white immigrant groups, which is to say about 60% to 65% Democratic, than like blacks (85% to 90% Democratic).

This means that elections in this area can theoretically be closely contested, and in fact the 1982 election in the 30th district was. The reason was that incumbent Republican John Rousselot, rather than run against a copartisan in the 22d district where his residence was, decided to run against Democrat Matthew Martinez in the 30th instead. The district did not look auspicious for Rousselot, a longtime member of the John Birch Society who is considered one of the most conservative of Republicans. But he campaigned gamely and good-humoredly, and evidently won a considerable share of Mexican-American as well as Anglo votes.

The Democrat, Martinez, was not well established here. He won a July special election with only 51% of the vote to replace longtime incumbent George Danielson, who had been appointed to a judgeship. Martinez had served less than a full term in the Assembly; his chief political asset was financial support engineered by 24th district Congressman Henry Waxman and former Assembly majority leader and now 26th district Congressman Howard Berman. In the end, he won because of Democratic strength here, with 54% of the vote. It seems unlikely that a Republican will make as great an effort or do as well in future elections as Rousselot did in 1982.

The People   Pop. 1980: 524,883, up 9% 1970–80; voting age pop. 360,162; 1% Black, 54% Span. orig., 9% Asian orig. 51% housing units rented. Median owner $73,600; renter $234. Households: 74% family, 45% with children, 56% married couples.

Presidential Vote

1980	Reagan (R)	57,866	(49%)
	Carter (D)	50,316	(43%)
	Other	9,587	(8%)

Rep. Matthew G. Martinez (D) Elected 1982; b. Feb. 14, 1929, Walsenburg, CO; home, Monterey Park; Roman Catholic.

Career Monterey Park Planning Comm., 1971–74; Monterey Park City Cncl., 1974–76; Mayor of Monterey Park, 1976–80; CA Assembly, 1980–82.

Offices 1714 LHOB, 202-225-5464. Also 1712 West Beverly Blvd., Montebello 90640, 213-722-7231.

Committees *Education and Labor* (18th). Subcommittees: Elementary, Secondary and Vocational Education; Employment Opportunities; Labor-Management Relations; Labor Standards. *Veterans' Affairs* (11th). Subcommittee: Compensation, Pension and Insurance.

Group Ratings and Key Votes: Newly Elected

Election Results

1982 general	Matthew G. (Marty) Martinez (D)	60,905	(54%)	($300,744)
	John H. Rousselot (R)	52,177	(46%)	($990,236)
1982 primary	Matthew G. (Marty) Martinez (D)	17,618	(35%)	
	Dennis S. Kazarian (D)	17,206	(34%)	($66,059)
	Olga E. Moreno (D)	8,875	(18%)	($70,636)
	Rose Ochi (D)	6,985	(14%)	($88,688)
1982 special	Matthew G. (Marty) Martinez (D)	14,566	(51%)	($112,372)
	Ralph Ramirez (R)	13,828	(48%)	($57,927)
1980 general	George Danielson (D)	74,119	(72%)	($79,852)
	J. Arthur (Art) Platten (R)	24,136	(24%)	($5,006)

Campaign Contributions and Expenditures

1981-82		Direct Cont. 81-82*				PACS brkdwn		
Receipts	$308,682	Indiv	$72,655	Agr	$3,600	Ideo	$65,975
Expend.	$300,744	Party	$16,500	Bus	$910	Lbr	$137,630
Unspent	$7,946	PACS	$126,923	Hlth	$1,000	Prof	$500
		Cand	$40,000				

Indirect Party Expend: $15,806   *Indep Expend*: Agn: $1,465   *Non-Cand Loans*: $5,000

THIRTY-FIRST DISTRICT

The 31st congressional district of California is a patch of fairly typical 1940s and 1950s Los Angeles County suburban territory, on both sides of the Harbor Freeway between downtown Los Angeles and the port at San Pedro. Most of it is made up of neat single-family stucco houses, in natural tan or different pastels, often with an above-ground swimming pool and some slightly shabby lawn furniture. There are parcels of still vacant land here and newly laid out subdivisions, and next to them the overgrown lots of factory workers' widows who are just getting by on Social Security. The 31st also contains sparkling steel-and-glass shopping centers and the fading pink stucco commercial strips of the 1940s. Undergirding the economy are huge defense plants and other factories spread out along the Harbor and San Diego Freeways.

The 31st sits directly south of the Watts black neighborhood, and over the past few decades some of its suburbs—Willowbrook, Compton—have changed from white to black. But in the 1970s and 1980s the pace of racial change has been less than the other ethnic changes. The suburbs of Lynwood and Paramount, southeast of Watts, have become more Mexican than black; Bellflower, directly north of Long Beach, is still mostly white Anglo. Gardena, just west of the Harbor Freeway, has the most varied mix, with roughly equal parts white Anglo, black, Spanish, and Japanese. (Gardena has another distinction: it is permitted by California law to license poker clubs at which some of the most cutthroat poker in the country is played.)

This part of Los Angeles County has been solidly Democratic since the 1930s, when it was almost entirely white. It is not, however, a coherent political community. The 31st is the kind of congressional district where people can get elected to legislative office by putting up billboards that say "Charles Wilson is a good guy." Charles Wilson is the name of a congressman who was elected here for 18 years and finally left after it was revealed that he lied about a $600 wedding gift from Tongsun Park (he got only 15% in his last primary).

The current congressman is a more vivid political figure, former Lieutenant Governor Mervyn Dymally. He has a distinctive speaking style and accent from his native Trinidad. But his reputation was damaged by allegations (subsequently never proved) and he lost his statewide office in 1978. He made a striking comeback by winning 49% of the vote in a primary against four other candidates (including Wilson and former 34th district Congressman Mark Hannaford) in 1980, in a district no more than one-third of whose voters were black. The redrawn district lines decrease rather than increase the black percentage, but Dymally won in 1982 by overwhelming margins. He seems to regard his 1978 loss as resulting from racism, but his record in congressional elections shows he can overcome any racist tendencies in this mixed, Democratic electorate. He sits on the Foreign Affairs, Science and Technology, and District of Columbia Committees.

The People   Pop. 1980: 526,129, up 2.1% 1970–80; voting age pop. 353,829; 31% Black, 22% Span. orig., 9% Asian orig., 1% Am. Ind. 45% housing units rented. Median owner $68,600; renter $238. Households: 75% family, 47% with children, 54% married couples.

Presidential Vote

1980	Reagan (R)	45,544	(35%)
	Carter (D)	76,459	(59%)
	Other	7,697	(6%)

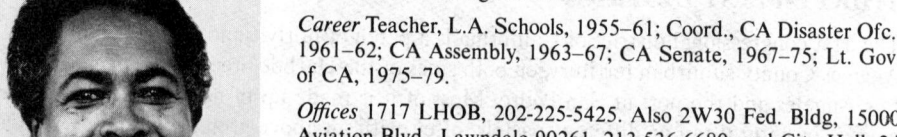

Rep. Mervyn M. Dymally (D) Elected 1980; b. May 12, 1926, Trinidad, British West Indies; home, Compton; CA St. U., B.A. 1954, M.A. 1969, U.S. Internatl. U., Ph.D. 1978; No religious affiliation.

Career Teacher, L.A. Schools, 1955–61; Coord., CA Disaster Ofc., 1961–62; CA Assembly, 1963–67; CA Senate, 1967–75; Lt. Gov. of CA, 1975–79.

Offices 1717 LHOB, 202-225-5425. Also 2W30 Fed. Bldg, 15000 Aviation Blvd., Lawndale 90261, 213-536-6680; and City Hall, 2d Fl., 4455 W. 126th St., Hawthorne 90250, 213-536-6772.

Committees *Foreign Affairs* (14th). Subcommittees: Asian and Pacific Affairs; Europe and the Middle East. *Science and Technology* (17th). Subcommittees: Science, Research and Technology; Transportation, Aviation and Materials; Space Science and Applications. *District of Columbia* (8th). Subcommittee: Judiciary and Education (Chairman).

Group Ratings

	ADA	ACLU	COPE	CFA	LCV	LWV	NTU	NSI	COC	ACA	CSFC
1982	65	92	95	50	69	90	15	33	30	11	23
1981	55	—	91	43	69	—	7	—	21	10	27

National Journal Ratings

	Economic		Foreign		Cultural	
1982	93%	(LIB)	82%	(LIB)	74%	(LIB)
	6%	(CONS)	18%	(CONS)	25%	(CONS)
1981	99%	(LIB)	71%	(LIB)	85%	(LIB)
	0%	(CONS)	29%	(CONS)	15%	(CONS)

Key Votes

1) Reagan 81 Budget	AGN	5) Incr SS Rtmt Age	AGN	9) Poor Pay Food Stamps	AGN
2) Reagan 81 Tax Cut	AGN	6) Saudi AWACS Sale	AGN	10) Ban Crt Busing Order	AGN
3) Bal Budget Amend	AGN	7) $ for MX Missile	AGN	11) Auto Local Content	FOR
4) Gas & Road Tax	—	8) Nerve Gas Prod	AGN	12) Nuclear Arms Freeze	FOR

Election Results

1982 general	Mervyn W. Dymally (D)	86,718	(72%)	($294,434)
	Henry C. Minturn (R)	33,043	(28%)	($0)
1982 primary	Mervyn M. Dymally (D)	43,498	(77%)	
	Craig J. Mitchell (D)	7,146	(13%)	($5,636)
	Colin K. O'Brien (D)	5,631	(10%)	
1980 general	Mervyn M. Dymally (D)	69,146	(64%)	($617,007)
	Don Grimshaw (R)	38,203	(36%)	($3,750)

Campaign Contributions and Expenditures

1981-82		Direct Cont. 81-82		PACS brkdwn			
Receipts	$290,366	Indiv	$209,963	Agr	$950	Ideo	$1,891
Expend.	$294,434	PACS	$59,322	Bus	$20,600	Lbr	$33,625
Unspent	$244	Cand	$12,750	Hlth	$1,000	Prof	$250

THIRTY-SECOND DISTRICT

The focus of the 32d congressional district of California is on the busy port area of metropolitan Los Angeles. That is so even though the port itself is technically outside the district; it is part of the 42d district, connecting two disparate Republican areas into a single district and preventing them from contaminating districts which are, like the 32d, Democratic. The port area is one of the recognizably working class areas of Los Angeles, where someone nostalgic for the ethnic neighborhoods of the northeast might, amid scruffy palm trees and stucco storefronts, still feel at home. You can find a Yugoslav-American community here in San Pedro, or groups of Italian-American families who still send husbands and fathers out in fishing boats. The 32d district includes relatively few blacks and Mexican-Americans, though the 1980s will likely see them move in in fair numbers; the district's boundaries fence off, in jagged lines, the Democratic parts of the Los Angeles port area, Long Beach, and, to the northeast, the suburbs of Lakewood (mostly white Anglo), Cerritos (until quite recently dairying country), and Hawaiian Gardens (mostly Mexican-American).

Yet if this port area district is demographically reminiscent of northeastern cities, the development of the port itself is a pure Los Angeles story. In the beginning there was no port at all—no geographic reason for Los Angeles to be anything but a farming community betwixt ocean and mountain. But the city fathers of Los Angeles, who went to so much trouble to bring enough water into the parched basin to keep millions wet, wanted a port too. So they built one, or rather two. Near where the usually dry Los Angeles River empties into the Ocean, on both sides of Terminal Island, both the city of Los Angeles and the city of Long Beach (not an inconsiderable unit, by the way, with more than 350,000 residents) dredged and built their own port facilities. These combined have become the biggest port on the West Coast, a triumph of man-made channels and breakwaters over the superb harbors nature sculpted in San Francisco, San Diego, and Seattle.

Most of the residents of the 32d district are traditional Democrats, union members who supported the economic programs of Franklin D. Roosevelt and John F. Kennedy, people whose livelihoods depend in many cases directly or indirectly on the port. Occasionally this district goes Republican in statewide contests; once in a while, in state elections. But not recently in congressional races.

The 32d has a congressman who seems to fit it like a glove, though his political base used to be in other Los Angeles suburbs. He is Glenn Anderson, a Democrat and strong union supporter who is now one of the ranking Democrats on the Public Works and Transportation and the Merchant Marine and Fisheries Committees. These are the perfect assignments for a member of a port district who wants to help his constituents: Anderson can see that federal monies go to the port, that construction projects around it are funded, that the interests of shipping companies, seamen, and fishermen are protected and subsidized. Anderson is best known in California outside his district for his role as lieutenant governor during the Watts riots of 1965, when some charged he was tardy at sending in the National Guard. He is best known in Washington as a supporter of most public works projects, both because of what they do for local communities and because they put people to work. But in the 32d district he is probably far better known for what he has done for the port and other local interests.

Certainly that seems to have helped him in 1982. His district had been moved considerably east, to include much of Long Beach he had never represented; Anderson was not a particular favorite of Phil Burton, who gave him a district that presented more difficulties than other Democratic incumbents had. And his opponent, 28-year-old Brian Lungren, had a recognizable name since his brother Dan had been representing Long Beach (in what now is the 42d district) and an attractive credential as a former policeman. But the 69-year-old Anderson beat him soundly—soundly enough to suggest that this district will remain in Democratic hands for the next decade.

The People   Pop. 1980: 527,814, up 8.3% 1970–80; voting age pop. 376,303; 8% Black, 19% Span. orig., 7% Asian orig., 1% Am. Ind. 47% housing units rented. Median owner $83,000; renter $225. Households: 69% family, 39% with children, 53% married couples.

Presidential Vote

1980	Reagan (R)	82,728	(52%)
	Carter (D)	60,535	(38%)
	Other	14,590	(9%)

Rep. Glenn M. Anderson (D) Elected 1968; b. Feb. 21, 1913, Hawthorne; home, Harbor City; UCLA, B.A. 1936; Episcopal.

Career Mayor of Hawthorne, 1940–43; CA Assembly, 1943, 1945–51; Army, WWII; Lt. Gov. of CA, 1958–67.

Offices 2329 RHOB, 202-225-6676. Also 300 Long Beach Blvd., Long Beach 90801, 213-548-2721.

Committees *Merchant Marine and Fisheries* (3d). Subcommittees: Fisheries and Wildlife Conservation and the Environment; Merchant Marine; Panama Canal and Outer Continental Shelf. *Public Works and Transportation* (2d). Subcommittees: Aviation; Surface Transportation (Chairman); Water Resources.

Group Ratings

	ADA	ACLU	COPE	CFA	LCV	LWV	NTU	NSI	COC	ACA	CSFC
1982	55	58	84	60	67	50	41	70	64	35	43
1981	50	—	83	64	64	—	30	—	17	38	48
1980	72	83	64	64	44	60	23	40	53	33	35

National Journal Ratings

	Economic		Foreign		Cultural	
1982	51%	(LIB)	57%	(LIB)	49%	(LIB)
	48%	(CONS)	42%	(CONS)	51%	(CONS)
1981	71%	(LIB)	53%	(LIB)	71%	(LIB)
	29%	(CONS)	45%	(CONS)	28%	(CONS)

Key Votes

1. Reagan 81 Budget	AGN	5) Incr SS Rtmt Age AGN	9) Poor Pay Food Stamps AGN
2) Reagan 81 Tax Cut	AGN	6) Saudi AWACS Sale AGN	10) Ban Crt Busing Order FOR
3) Bal Budget Amend	FOR	7) $ for MX Missile AGN	11) Auto Local Content AGN
4) Gas & Road Tax	FOR	8) Nerve Gas Prod AGN	12) Nuclear Arms Freeze FOR

Election Results

1982 general	Glenn M. Anderson (D)	84,663	(58%)	($443,879)
	Brian Lungren (R)	57,863	(40%)	($214,027)
1982 primary	Glenn M. Anderson (D)	42,870	(77%)	
	Ed Tuttle (D)	8,792	(16%)	
	Richard H. Hallowell (D)	4,327	(8%)	
1980 general	Glenn M. Anderson (D)	84,057	(66%)	($153,001)
	John R. Adler (R)	39,260	(31%)	($33,878)

Campaign Contributions and Expenditures

1981-82		Direct Cont. 81-82		PACS brkdwn			
Receipts	$444,603	Indiv	$189,330 (Est.)	Agr	$2,050	Ideo	$7,700
Expend.	$443,879	Party	$9,079	Bus	$84,975	Lbr	$67,400
Unspent	$8,175	PACS	$164,700	Hlth	$900	Prof	$1,700
		Cand	$68,000				

Indirect Party Expend: $5,961

THIRTY-THIRD DISTRICT

The 33d congressional district of California, in its present lines, is pretty much the lineal descendant of the 12th district that ousted Democrat Jerry Voorhis and elected 33-year-old Republican Richard Nixon in the 1946 election. It is the eastern end of Los Angeles County, far enough east that the percentage of Mexican-Americans is not much higher than in Nixon's time. One part of the district, with about one-third of its population, is centered around Nixon's home town of Whittier, a onetime Quaker settlement and now a pleasant suburban town with its own civic institutions and colleges, above average housing prices, and a Mexican-American population of 23%. The other heavily populated part of the district, separated from the Whittier area by the low Puente Hills, is centered on another old college town, Pomona, laid out in the flat lands directly east of Los Angeles, on the last leg of the Santa Fe Railroad on its long trek from Chicago. Just north are the Claremont colleges, which are among other things a center for conservative scholarship, and the above average income suburbs of LaVerne, San Dimas, Covina, and Glendora, above the valley floor and not far below the glaring San Gabriel Mountains.

All parts of this district are solidly Republican, and in 1982 there was a Republican primary, featuring two incumbent congressmen, which probably determined the representation here for several elections to come. Neither had much seniority, but Wayne Grisham, a 59-year-old veteran of local government in his home town of La Mirada, thought the district was rightly his, and that his opponent, 30-year-old David Dreier, should have moved out to the 37th district in Riverside County, which had no incumbent. Dreier, who had represented more of the district himself, said no dice. The two men had voting records which looked identical. But their priorities were probably a little different. Grisham, with long experience in local affairs, seemed to approach matters as a traditional small town conservative would, mistrustful of government because of its practical effects, interested in fostering traditional values. Dreier, with a little experience in private business, had spent most of his adult life on the Claremont campus; he seems opposed to government action on an intellectual, theoretical basis. Dreier seems to have been anything but theoretical when it came to raising money for the race. Grisham could raise only $84,000, while Dreier raised $422,000; he was confident enough to spend only $275,000 and still win a 57%–43% primary victory.

Dreier is one of those conservatives who came to Washington less to pass bills than to repeal them. He was part of the hard core of 1980 Republican freshmen who supported the Reagan program wholeheartedly and exerted pressure on the Republican leadership to be aggressive and advance cultural as well as economic issues. The failure of the Reagan economic programs to live up to expectations had little effect on the 33d district's general election results (Dreier won easily), but it would be interesting to know what effects they had on his morale. Do they raise doubts in his mind about the worth of the program? Does he dismiss them as the result of Congress's unwillingness to adopt *all* the needed measures? Or does he think that the recession of 1982 was a time of testing, to see who has the nerve and the strength to sit tight without panicking and wait for the program to work?

The People   Pop. 1980: 526,296, up 15.3% 1970–80; voting age pop. 370,644; 4% Black, 16% Span. orig., 4% Asian orig., 1% Am. Ind. 27% housing units rented. Median owner $87,400; renter $263. Households: 78% family, 45% with children, 66% married couples.

Presidential Vote

1980	Reagan (R)	118,017	(64%)
	Carter (D)	49,694	(27%)
	Other	16,514	(9%)

Rep. David Dreier (R) Elected 1980; b. July 5, 1952, Kansas City, MO; home, La Verne; Claremont Men's Col., B.A. 1973, M.A. 1975; Christian Science.

Career Dir. of Corp. Relations, Claremont Men's Col., 1975–79; Repub. Nominee for U.S. House of Reps., 1978; Dir. of Pub. Affairs, Industrial Hydrocarbons, 1979–80.

Offices 410 CHOB, 202-225-2305. Also 917 Village Oaks Dr., Covina 91724, 213-339-9078 and 714-592-2857.

Committees *Banking, Finance and Urban Affairs* (14th). Subcommittees: Housing and Community Development; General Oversight and Renegotiation; International Trade, Investment and Monetary Policy. *Small Business* (10th). Subcommittees: Tax, Access to Equity Capital and Business Opportunities; General Oversight and the Economy.

Group Ratings

	ADA	ACLU	COPE	CFA	LCV	LWV	NTU	NSI	COC	ACA	CSFC
1982	0	0	0	0	11	25	97	100	95	90	84
1981	5	—	0	29	21	—	95	—	95	96	82

National Journal Ratings

	Economic		Foreign		Cultural	
1982	0%	(LIB)	26%	(LIB)	4%	(LIB)
	98%	(CONS)	73%	(CONS)	87%	(CONS)
1981	4%	(LIB)	18%	(LIB)	4%	(LIB)
	79%	(CONS)	73%	(CONS)	90%	(CONS)

Key Votes

1) Reagan 81 Budget	FOR	5) Incr SS Rtmt Age	FOR	9) Poor Pay Food Stamps	FOR
2) Reagan 81 Tax Cut	FOR	6) Saudi AWACS Sale	AGN	10) Ban Crt Busing Order	FOR
3) Bal Budget Amend	FOR	7) $ for MX Missile	FOR	11) Auto Local Content	AGN
4) Gas & Road Tax	—	8) Nerve Gas Prod	FOR	12) Nuclear Arms Freeze	AGN

Election Results

1982 general	David Dreier (R)	112,362	(65%)	($275,464)
	Paul Servelle (D)	55,514	(32%)	($0)
1982 primary	David Dreier (R)	35,137	(57%)	
	Wayne Grisham (R)	26,145	(43%)	($85,312)
1980 general	Wayne Grisham (R)	122,439	(71%)	($103,423)
(CA 33)	Fred L. Anderson (D)	50,365	(29%)	($0)
1980 general	David Dreier (R)	100,743	(52%)	($379,325)
(CA 35)	Jim Lloyd (D)	88,279	(45%)	($237,886)

Campaign Contributions and Expenditures

1981-82		Direct Cont. 81-82		PACS brkdwn			
Receipts	$422,789	Indiv	$257,945	Agr	$2,600	Ideo	$5,400
Expend.	$275,464	Party	$20,471	Bus	$100,350	Lbr	$—
Unspent	$183,287	PACS	$115,849	Hlth	$7,000	Prof	$—

Indep Expend: For: $682 (NRA)

THIRTY-FOURTH DISTRICT

If you want to see the shape of the future of much of California, the place to come to is the 34th congressional district. This is a barbell-shaped hunk of suburban Los Angeles County, on either side of the San Gabriel River, south and southeast of downtown Los Angeles. It includes the middle income suburb of West Covina and the working class suburbs of Baldwin Park, La Puente, and Industry in its northern section; the basically blue collar suburbs of Pico Rivera, Santa Fe Springs, South Whittier, and Norwalk, all strung out along the Santa Ana Freeway, on the southern section. Connecting them is a narrow corridor through the industrial town of South El Monte.

This area provides a preview of the future of California because it has the largest number of children of any congressional district in the state. The white middle class children of the 1950s, educated in the schools that burgeoned in every new suburb and finally on the culturally liberal campuses of the University of California, are the adults of California today: technologically capable, relatively high income, culturally liberal if not liberated. They take affluence and economic growth for granted; they concentrate much of their psychic energy on making life pleasant for themselves and, compared to their parents, little of it on having children.

The children of the 34th district, growing up on some of the same terrain, have a different background. Some 59% of them are of Spanish origin; they come from parents or grandparents who are immigrants from another culture. They are part of large families—not a sign of their parents' ignorance, but of the same optimism which brought them to America, and out to the suburbs of eastern Los Angeles County—the same optimism which produced the large white Anglo families of the baby boom years. Some of them start off speaking little else but Spanish, but most know English, and they are entirely capable of absorbing instruction in it provided that the political authorities (and Mexican-American lobbying groups) don't keep them confined in classes where the instruction is in a language which will not prepare them for most good jobs. People here are not impoverished: the median house price, according to the Census, was $69,000 in 1980; people have jobs and very few live below the poverty level. You will see some of the youths here parading down avenues on Friday night in souped-up cars, just as you would have seen white teenagers doing the same thing, with similar cars, 25 years ago; that doesn't mean, in either case, that they won't grow up to hold solid and even high level jobs. The history of America is largely a history of the rapid progress of children of immigrant groups. Why should the history of the Mexican-American residents of California be any different from the history of the Italian-American residents of New York?

The 34th district was newly created by Congressman Phillip Burton from the results of the 1980 Census. It was Burton's *piece de resistance*. The Republicans had hoped to get crucial Mexican-American votes in the California Assembly and pass a districting plan that had more Mexican-American districts than the Democrats could come up with—and of course more Republican districts as well. But Burton, by creating this district which is 48% Spanish origin, in addition to the 54% Spanish origin 30th and the 64% Spanish origin 25th, did the Republicans one better. From that point there was nothing to stop the Democratic legislature and governor from approving Burton's plans.

And, as it turned out, there was not much that anyone could do to stop Democrat Esteban

Torres from being elected to Congress. Torres had tried once before, in 1974, against George Danielson in the old 30th district, and fallen short; Mexican-Americans do not invariably vote for Mexican-Americans, presumably because they do not feel deprived of fair representation when they have an Anglo congressman. But Torres does have a positive appeal. He rose from an auto assembly line, through the ranks of the United Auto Workers, to head an antipoverty program in East Los Angeles; in the Carter administration he was a White House aide and ambassador to UNESCO. He had financial support from the local "machine" of Henry Waxman and Howard Berman. He won a solid primary victory against former Congressman Jim Lloyd, whose base is in West Covina, and won the general election by a 57%–43% margin. Torres's positions on economic issues are likely to be what you would expect from a UAW veteran; he is, however, opposed to abortion. He represents, after all, the number one family district in Los Angeles, a place where people have committed themselves to family patterns and where their large hopes for the future depend on the progress of their children in schools and in jobs. They are interested in having a secure government safety net, but they seem to believe that their children will get somewhere—as their parents or grandparents emerged from rural Mexico—largely through their own efforts.

Torres, having captured the district, seems likely to hold onto it. He serves on the Banking and the Small Business Committees.

The People Pop. 1980: 526,321, up 3.9% 1970–80; voting age pop. 348,369; 2% Black, 42% Span. orig., 4% Asian orig., 1% Am. Ind. 29% housing units rented. Median owner $68,600; renter $275. Households: 83% family, 53% with children, 68% married couples.

Presidential Vote

1980	Reagan (R)	69,299	(52%)
	Carter (D)	52,982	(40%)
	Other	10,923	(8%)

Rep. Esteban E. Torres (D) Elected 1982; b. Jan. 27, 1930, Miami, AZ; home, W. Covina; E. Los Angeles Comm. Col., 1959, State Univ. of Los Angeles, B.A. 1963, U. of MD, 1965, American U., 1966; No religious affiliation.

Career Assembly-line worker, Chrysler Corp., 1954–63; Chief Steward, Local 230 UAW, 1961–63; UAW Internatl. Rep., Region 6, 1963–64, Inter-Am. Rep., 1965–68, Asst. Dir., Internatl. Affairs Dept., 1974–77; Dir., E. Los Angeles Community Union, 1968–74; U.S. Permanent Rep., UNESCO, 1977–79; Special Asst. to the Pres., 1979–81; Pres., Internatl. Enterprise Develop. Corp., 1981–82.

Offices 1740 LHOB, 202-225-5256. Also 12440 Fireside Blvd., Saddleback Square, Su. 117, Norwalk 90650, 213-929-2711; and Home Savings and Loan Bldg., 1400 Covina Pkwy., Su. 201, W. Covina 91790, 213-814-1557.

Committees *Banking, Finance and Urban Affairs* (30th). Subcommittees: Housing and Community Development; International Development Institutions and Finance; Economic Stabilization. *Small Business* (21st). Subcommittees: Energy, Environment and Safety Issues Affecting Small Business; Export Opportunities and Special Small Business Problems.

Goup Ratings and Key Votes: Newly Elected

Election Results

1982 general	Esteban E. Torres (D)	68,316	(57%)	($274,613)
	Paul R. Jackson (R)	51,026	(43%)	($13,824)
1982 primary	Esteban E. Torres (D)	27,271	(51%)	
	Jim Lloyd (D)	19,951	(37%)	($179,246)
	Fred L. Anderson (D)	6,881	(13%)	
1980 general	Newly created district			

Campaign Contributions and Expenditures

1981-82		Direct Cont. 1981-82		PACS brkdwn			
Receipts	$275,619	Indiv	$115,244	Agr	$1,250	Ideo	$24,625
Expend.	$274,613	Party	$5,593	Bus	$9,800	Lbr	$70,200
Unspent	$1,004	PACS	$111,386	Hlth	$3,000	Prof	$1,700
		Cand	$30,000				

THIRTY-FIFTH DISTRICT

The 35th congressional district of California includes most of the geographically largest county in the United States, the highest point in the coterminous 48 states and the lowest point in North America, an enormous expanse of desert and the primary source of water for the 11 million citizens of greater Los Angeles. It extends as far north as Bishop, in the Owens Valley, where the Los Angeles Aqueduct begins; not far south is Mount Whitney, and off to the east, beyond sight range in the harsh desert light, is Death Valley. Most of the people of this 35th district are concentrated in the southwest corner of San Bernardino County, in the eastern end of the Los Angeles Basin. Even so, more than 150,000 people live in the desert— in tiny gas station towns, now swelled with people who have left the city behind; in trailer parks scattered a few miles away; in military bases and the neat geometrical towns that grow up beside them.

The 35th was designed to be a Republican district. It bypasses the heavily Democratic towns in the flatlands often choked with smog at the eastern end of the Los Angeles Basin, and includes those up higher, near the mountains, or with higher real estate prices: Upland, Montclair, and Chino in western San Bernardino County, Redlands, Highland, and Loma Linda (a Seventh Day Adventist town) east of the city of San Bernardino.

The congressman from the 35th is Jerry Lewis (no relation to the comedian), a former insurance agent and California Assemblyman with the blow-dry hair look of a stereotypical candidate. Actually, Lewis is an independent-minded Republican, whose stand on cultural and foreign issues sometimes diverges from orthodoxy. He won the district (with rather different boundaries) in 1978 with not much problem, and has retained it easily ever since. Legislatively, he is rather quiet, since he works as a minority member on the Appropriations Committee, not usually a good place to win headlines.

The People Pop. 1980: 526,398, up 40.4% 1970–80; voting age pop. 372,537; 3% Black, 11% Span. orig., 2% Asian orig., 1% Am. Ind. 23% housing units rented. Median owner $68,600; renter $232. Households: 77% family, 42% with children, 66% married couples.

Presidential Vote

1980	Reagan (R)	112,232	(65%)
	Carter (D)	46,323	(27%)
	Other	14,821	(8%)

Rep. Jerry Lewis (R) Elected 1978; b. Oct. 21, 1934, Seattle, WA; home, Highland; UCLA, B.A. 1956; Presbyterian.

Career Life insurance agent, 1959–78; Field Rep. to U.S. Rep. Jerry Pettis, 1968; CA Assembly, 1968–78.

Offices 326 CHOB, 202-225-5861. Also 101 6th St., Redlands 92373, 714-862-6030.

Committee *Appropriations* (19th). Subcommittees: HUD-Independent Agencies; Foreign Operations; Legislative.

Group Ratings

	ADA	ACLU	COPE	CFA	LCV	LWV	NTU	NSI	COC	ACA	CSFC
1982	5	37	13	10	7	58	74	100	100	91	68
1981	5	—	0	7	7	—	64	—	100	68	72
1980	11	20	21	14	40	33	52	90	61	75	70

National Journal Ratings

	Economic		Foreign		Cultural	
1982	22%	(LIB)	4%	(LIB)	27%	(LIB)
	77%	(CONS)	92%	(CONS)	72%	(CONS)
1981	4%	(LIB)	46%	(LIB)	41%	(LIB)
	79%	(CONS)	52%	(CONS)	59%	(CONS)

Key Votes

1) Reagan 81 Budget	FOR	5) Incr SS Rtmt Age	FOR	9) Poor Pay Food Stamps	FOR
2) Reagan 81 Tax Cut	FOR	6) Saudi AWACS Sale	AGN	10) Ban Crt Busing Order	FOR
3) Bal Budget Amend	FOR	7) $ for MX Missile	FOR	11) Auto Local Content	AGN
4) Gas & Road Tax	—	8) Nerve Gas Prod	AGN	12) Nuclear Arms Freeze	AGN

Election Results

1982 general	Jerry Lewis (R)	112,786	(68%)	($86,679)
	Robert E. Erwin (D)	52,349	(32%)	($56,495)
1982 primary	Jerry Lewis (R)	46,202	(100%)	
1980 general	Jerry Lewis (R)	166,640	(72%)	($54,448)
	Donald M. Rusk (D)	58,462	(25%)	($47,882)

Campaign Contributions and Expenditures

1981-82		Direct Cont. 81-82		PACS brkdwn			
Receipts	$147,175	Indiv	$42,295	Agr	$10,600	Ideo	$2,800
Expend.	$86,679	Party	$8,997	Bus	$42,750	Lbr	$1,750
Unspent	$138,674	PACS	$69,052	Hlth	$10,550	Prof	$500

Indirect Party Expend: $3,000

THIRTY-SIXTH DISTRICT

At the far east end of the Los Angeles Basin, where the smog almost piles up against the mountains, are two cities with their own historical beginnings but that are now near the eastern end of the strip city that goes more than 50 miles to Los Angeles and beyond. These are San Bernardino and Riverside, county seats of the counties with the same names, old agricultural towns and railroad stops. Parts of each city and of several suburbs in the immediate vicinity and to the east make up the 36th congressional district of California. The district includes industrial suburbs—Colton, Rialto, and Fontana with its once thriving Kaiser Steel plant—and the city of Ontario, west toward Los Angeles, which has its own airport where you can catch a jet to Chicago. Riverside is still a major center for the citrus industry, and the University of California branch there is one of the leading sources of research on citrus.

Surrounded by Republican territory, the 36th district is nonetheless Democratic. There is a substantial Mexican-American population in each of these towns, totaling almost one-fourth of the district's population; there are a fair number of blacks in each town as well. Union membership is higher in some of these precincts than in most of southern California, and working class consciousness is perhaps fed by the poor air quality: if you felt you could afford to move to a higher and more expensive area, you probably would.

The 36th district was designed for, and is represented by, a congressman with a long career now that has benefited, stage by stage, from redistricting. George Brown was a councilman from Monterey Park (now in the 30th district) when he was first elected to the California Assembly in 1958; he had the good fortune to be placed on the Redistricting Committee, and when California gained eight House seats in 1962, he was elected to one of them. He ran for the Senate in 1970 and almost beat John Tunney in the primary; if he had, this longtime peacenik—a scientist with a Quaker upbringing, he cares deeply about arms control issues—might have beaten George Murphy and made his way to the Senate. As it is, he found a new district in 1972, here in the eastern part of the valley, and in redistricting it has been altered and shaped for him.

Brown's committee assignments would seem to be useful ones for the district—Agriculture, Science and Technology. But his very liberal politics has helped attract serious Republican competition. In 1980 and 1982 Brown was challenged by a young religious fundamentalist who held him to 53% and 54% of the vote respectively. The first time neither candidate spent much money; in 1982 the Republican spent more than $250,000, and Brown, raising money through peace and liberal contacts, spent more than $400,000. The results do not look impressive for the incumbent, particularly since redistricting probably helped him; and he can expect serious competition again in 1984.

The People   Pop. 1980: 528,091, up 19.4% 1970–80; voting age pop. 363,372; 7% Black, 20% Span. orig., 1% Asian orig., 1% Am. Ind. 34% housing units rented. Median owner $58,800; renter $213. Households: 74% family, 44% with children, 59% married couples.

Presidential Vote

1980	Reagan (R)	74,870	(51%)
	Carter (D)	58,253	(40%)
	Other	14,142	(10%)

Rep. George E. Brown, Jr. (D) Elected 1972; b. Mar. 6, 1920, Holtville; home, Colton; UCLA, B.A. 1946; Methodist.

Career Army, WWII; Monterey Park City Cncl., Mayor, 1954–58; Personnel, Engineering, and Management Consultant, City of Los Angeles, 1957–61; CA Assembly, 1959–62; U.S. House of Reps., 1962–70; Candidate for Dem. Nomination for U.S. Senate, 1970.

Offices 2256 RHOB, 202-225-6161. Also 552 N. LaCadena St., Colton 92324, 714-825-2472.

Committees *Agriculture* (5th). Subcommittees: Department Operations, Research and Foreign Agriculture (Chairman); Forests, Family Farms and Energy. *Science and Technology* (3d). Subcommittees: Natural Resources, Agriculture, Research and Environment; Science, Research and Technology; Space Science and Applications.

Group Ratings

	ADA	ACLU	COPE	CFA	LCV	LWV	NTU	NSI	COC	ACA	CSFC
1982	75	92	90	70	78	90	3	22	29	5	21
1981	85	—	89	64	82	—	12	—	12	5	28
1980	94	100	82	64	72	100	14	13	52	10	23

National Journal Ratings

	Economic		Foreign		Cultural	
1982	95%	(LIB)	76%	(LIB)	89%	(LIB)
	5%	(CONS)	24%	(CONS)	8%	(CONS)
1981	97%	(LIB)	84%	(LIB)	91%	(LIB)
	3%	(CONS)	16%	(CONS)	9%	(CONS)

Key Votes

1) Reagan 81 Budget	AGN	5) Incr SS Rtmt Age	AGN
2) Reagan 81 Tax Cut	AGN	6) Saudi AWACS Sale	AGN
3) Bal Budget Amend	AGN	7) $ for MX Missile	AGN
4) Gas & Road Tax	FOR	8) Nerve Gas Prod	AGN

9) Poor Pay Food Stamps	AGN
10) Ban Crt Busing Order	AGN
11) Auto Local Content	—
12) Nuclear Arms Freeze	FOR

Election Results

1982 general	George E. Brown, Jr. (D)	76,546	(54%)	($419,947)
	John Paul Stark (R)	64,361	(46%)	($189,534)
1982 primary	George E. Brown, Jr. (D)	38,054	(74%)	
	Jimmy Pineda (D)	7,382	(14%)	
	Ron Hibble (D)	5,742	(11%)	
1980 general	George E. Brown, Jr. (D)	88,634	(53%)	($66,917)
	John Paul Stark (R)	73,252	(43%)	($38,094)

Campaign Contributions and Expenditures

1981-82		Direct Cont. 81-82		PACS brkdwn			
Receipts	$409,173	Indiv	$242,227	Agr	$9,450	Ideo	$23,260
Expend.	$419,947	Party	$12,623	Bus	$11,850	Lbr	$66,538
Unspent	$688	PACS	$124,632	Hlth	$2,100	Prof	$2,050
		Cand	$10,000				

Indep Expend: Agn: $7,858 (incl. NCPAC)

THIRTY-SEVENTH DISTRICT

In the 1920s, when California first became a major retirement haven, most older people moving out were looking for homes near the ocean. If they were poor they retired in Long Beach or one of the smaller beach towns near Los Angeles; if they were rich, they might move to Santa Barbara or La Jolla. Retirees made up a larger share of California's population before World War II than they have since; the state is now younger than the national average. But in absolute numbers there are still plenty of retirees. Increasingly, though, they avoid the ocean areas, which tend to be crowded, smoggy, and annoyingly damp, and move instead to the desert, where there is more room, cleaner air, and a drier climate.

You find a lot of retirees in the country east of Riverside that makes up most of the 37th congressional district. In the geologically fascinating valleys immediately east of Riverside there are a series of towns, some rather affluent, some noticeably threadbare, which have large numbers of retirees. Altogether, nearly 200,000 people live here now—a vast increase even over 1970.

Farther east, through the San Gorgonio Pass, you come to the desert proper, with a year-round population, in the 37th district, of 145,000 people. Here the days are almost always crystal clear, the sky usually blue and cloudless. The desert can be fertile farmland, as it is in the Coachella Valley; almost all of America's dates are produced near Indio, east of Palm Springs. But constant irrigation is necessary for most crops; without daily doses of water almost any plant will wilt and die in the heat. The first white settlers in the desert were prospectors, and some ghost towns still stand. They are quite a contrast with Palm Springs and Palm Desert, which are outposts of affluence (Palm Springs is more show business, Palm Desert more WASPy). It is too hot here in the summer for most people, even though the heat is dry, but the winter weather is almost ideal. Two presidents have retired within the confines of the 37th district, Eisenhower in Palm Desert for the winters, Ford in nearby Rancho Mirage—which is also the home of Frank Sinatra and Spiro Agnew.

The third part of the district includes the more affluent and Republican parts of the city of Riverside, plus the towns of Norco and Corona immediately to the east. Overall, this is a Republican district; the most Democratic parts of the Riverside area were cropped off carefully and put into the 36th. Still, there have been Democrats elected to the legislature from the desert, and both parties' primaries were seriously contested when no incumbent congressman chose to run in this district in 1982. In the eight-candidate Democratic primary, Indio police chief Sam Cross won with 28% of the vote; in the nine-candidate Republican primary, County Supervisor Al McCandless of Palm Desert won with 25%.

So the district had to choose between two candidates from the desert. Given its views on national issues, it's not surprising that a solid majority of the voters chose the Republican. True, the Republicans were under attack on the Social Security issue. But most of the people who can afford to retire in California, even in a trailer park, are from backgrounds affluent or comfortable enough to commend Republican views. McCandless appears now to have a safe seat, and is expected to be a pretty reliable supporter of administration and House Republican leadership policy. He is a member of the Government Operations and Science and Technology Committees.

The People Pop. 1980: 524,963, up 55.3% 1970–80; voting age pop. 383,312; 3% Black, 15% Span. orig., 1% Asian orig., 1% Am. Ind. 23% housing units rented. Median owner $69,400; renter $236. Households: 74% family, 35% with children, 64% married couples.

1980	Reagan (R)	113,631	(61%)
	Carter (D)	56,492	(31%)
	Other	14,963	(8%)

Rep. Alfred A. (Al) McCandless (R) Elected 1982; b. July 23, 1927, Brawley; home, Palm Desert; U. of CA at Los Angeles, B.A. 1951; Protestant.

Career USMC, Korea, 1945–46, 1950–52; Automobile dealer, 1959–82; Riverside Cnty. Sprvsr., 1970–82.

Offices 510 CHOB, 202-225-5330. Also 6529 Riverside Ave., Su. 165, Riverside 92506, 714-682-7127.

Committees *Government Operations* (12th). Subcommittees: Government Activities and Transportation; Intergovernmental Relations and Human Resources. *Science and Technology* (14th). Subcommittees: Transportation, Aviation and Materials; Investigations and Oversight.

Group Ratings and Key Votes: Newly Elected

Election Results

1982 general	Alfred A. (Al) McCandless (R) ...	105,065	(59%)	($196,516)
	Curtis R. (Sam) Cross (D)	68,510	(39%)	($40,291)
1982 primary	Alfred A. (Al) McCandless (R) ...	15,349	(25%)	
	Ken Calvert (R)	14,481	(24%)	($75,997)
	Raymond P. Horspool, Jr. (R)	11,340	(19%)	($37,150)
	Benjamin F. Davis (R)	8,855	(15%)	($18,787)
	William B. Wiley (R)	4,624	(8%)	($19,885)
	Four others (R)	5,870	(10%)	
1980 general	Newly created district			

Campaign Contributions and Expenditures

1981-82		*Direct Cont. 81-82*			*PACS brkdwn*		
Receipts	$203,286	Indiv	$136,210	Agr	$1,000	Ideo	$8,850
Expend.	$196,516	Party	$21,600	Bus	$32,750	Lbr	$—
Unspent	$6,768	PACS	$50,928	Hlth	$6,000	Prof	$—

Indirect Party Expend: $33,156

THIRTY-EIGHTH DISTRICT

"Orange County" has become a synonym for "conservative" in political discourse. Thirty years ago, Orange County, California, had all the political notoriety of a few thousand acres of citrus trees; its population in 1950 was 216,000. But that prime agricultural real estate, was part of the Los Angeles Basin, that mass of flat land surrounded by mountains and sea that was growing vastly in population, and one natural path of settlement, unimpeded by natural barriers, was southeast into Orange County. Population increased ninefold in 30 years: by 1960 there were 703,000 people there; in 1970, 1,421,000; in 1980, 1,931,000. And most of that migration was, politically, Republican. In the 1960s and 1970s Orange County consistently turned in the highest Republican percentages of any major California county and, in the 1980 election, gave Ronald Reagan his largest majority, in terms of actual votes, of any county in the country. Yet Orange County is not as uniformly affluent or as monolithically conservative and Republican as is supposed. There is actually a robust two-party competition in many elections. Democrats have elected as many as three of the county's six assemblymen, and since 1962 Democrats have held the congressional district currently numbered the 38th.

Roughly speaking, the 38th district includes that portion of Orange County between the Santa Ana and San Diego Freeways, bounded by the Los Angeles County border on the west and the Newport Freeway on the east. Actually, the boundary is more jagged: Democratic redistricters for 20 years have become adept at cutting heavily Republican precincts out of this district and pasting on precincts willing to vote for an Orange County Democrat. In national terms, this is an above average income district, with median house prices, according to the Census, of $85,700 and median rents at $310 per month. Yet these are on the modest end of the scale in Orange County. Certainly as you zoom by on the freeways or drive more slowly on the straight avenues that intersect every mile, the stucco houses and apartment complexes you see tightly packed in each of these subdivisions do not look grand. Comfortable, to be sure: and many have swimming pools, even if they do take up the whole backyard.

Orange County is usually portrayed as unrelievedly white; actually the 38th district in particular, and the whole county to some extent, are ethnically more various. Some 26% of the residents of the 38th district are of Spanish origin, and another 6% are Asian, and except for a concentration of Mexican-Americans in Santa Ana, they are scattered, it seems almost randomly, throughout the district. In political terms, they probably are more Democratic than other Orange Countians, but it's not clear by how much. After all, they seem to move pretty much unimpeded into these neighborhoods; they have good enough jobs to be able to afford them. Altogether they don't seem to be suffering from—or at least can rather easily evade—the kind of discrimination whose sting can make a voter oppose bitterly a party or candidate identified with it. In many statewide and national contests this district has gone so solidly Republican that it seems certain that its Mexican-American voters have voted Republican as well. Presumably these new residents share many of the values and attitudes of the people they have chosen as neighbors.

The Democratic congressman from the 38th district is Jerry Patterson, a former mayor of Santa Ana, who first won the district in 1974. He serves on the Banking Committee, where he tends to be one of the strongest supporters of savings institutions in their fights with commercial banks. Savings and loans in California, contrary to the law in most states, may be investor-owned, and some of the great fortunes in the state have been made by S&L founders. S&Ls directed and greatly profited from the transformation of Orange County from citrus farms to suburbs, and, as is natural in such things, they have always been deeply involved in politics. In local matters it served their interests well to back Republicans. But Sacramento and Washington have been controlled by Democrats for most of the last 25 years, and so the Orange County S&Ls have been careful to back sympathetic Democrats, like Senator Alan Cranston and Congressman Patterson and his predecessor, Richard Hanna. Patterson has concentrated on more than S&Ls; he chairs a subcommittee on International Development Institutions and serves on another with jurisdiction over international policies.

When there is a national Republican trend, a congressman in this district can be in trouble. Patterson's percentage slipped against weak competition in 1980, and in 1982 the Republicans for the first time since 1974 raised and spent more than $100,000 here and held Patterson to a 56%–43% margin. This is a seat that a Democrat can never feel completely secure in, and Patterson may have a significant struggle in 1984.

The People Pop. 1980: 525,560, up 11.4% 1970–80; voting age pop. 367,088; 2% Black, 22% Span. orig., 5% Asian orig., 1% Am. Ind. 42% housing units rented. Median owner $85,700; renter $310. Households: 76% family, 45% with children, 62% married couples.

Presidential Vote

1980	Reagan (R)	99,697	(63%)
	Carter (D)	45,316	(28%)
	Other	14,191	(9%)

Rep. Jerry M. Patterson (D) Elected 1974; b. Oct. 25, 1934, El Paso, TX; home, Santa Ana; Long Beach St. U., B.A. 1960, UCLA, J.D. 1966; United Church of Christ.

Career Coast Guard, 1953–57; Practicing atty., 1967–74; Santa Ana City Cncl., 1967–73, Mayor, 1973–74.

Offices 2238 RHOB, 202-225-2965. Also 34 Civic Ctr. Plaza, Su. 921, Santa Ana 92701, 714-835-3811.

Committees *Banking, Finance, and Urban Affairs* (8th). Subcommittees: Housing and Community Development; International Development Institutions and Finance (Chairman); International Trade, Investment and Monetary Policy. *Interior and Insular Affairs* (15th). Subcommittees: Energy and the Environment; Public Lands and National Parks. *Select Committee on Children, Youth, and Families* (6th).

Group Ratings

	ADA	ACLU	COPE	CFA	LCV	LWV	NTU	NSI	COC	ACA	CSFC
1982	65	83	85	70	81	82	18	22	45	17	32
1981	70	—	85	71	76	—	30	—	18	13	35
1980	72	87	72	64	67	75	15	40	56	18	27

National Journal Ratings

	Economic		Foreign		Cultural	
1982	59%	(LIB)	65%	(LIB)	93%	(LIB)
	41%	(CONS)	35%	(CONS)	3%	(CONS)
1981	86%	(LIB)	82%	(LIB)	83%	(LIB)
	14%	(CONS)	18%	(CONS)	17%	(CONS)

Key Votes

1) Reagan 81 Budget	AGN	5) Incr SS Rtmt Age	AGN
2) Reagan 81 Tax Cut	AGN	6) Saudi AWACS Sale	AGN
3) Bal Budget Amend	AGN	7) $ for MX Missile	AGN
4) Gas & Road Tax	—	8) Nerve Gas Prod	—

9) Poor Pay Food Stamps	AGN
10) Ban Crt Busing Order	AGN
11) Auto Local Content	FOR
12) Nuclear Arms Freeze	FOR

Election Results

1982 general	Jerry M. Patterson (D)	73,914	(52%)	($278,994)
	William F. Dohr (R)	61,279	(43%)	($248,425)
1982 primary	Jerry M. Patterson (D)	36,076	(100%)	
1980 general	Jerry M. Patterson (D)	91,880	(56%)	($199,521)
	Art Jacobson (R)	66,256	(40%)	($39,195)

Campaign Contributions and Expenditures

1981-82		Direct Cont. 81-82		PACS brkdwn			
Receipts	$265,722	Indiv	$59,995	Agr	$10,700	Ideo	$12,965
Expend.	$278,994	Party	$5,500	Bus	$88,210	Lbr	$68,425
Unspent	$5,704	PACS	$189,800	Hlth	$1,700	Prof	$2,850

Indirect Party Expend: $37,960   *Indep Expend:* Agn: $564 (NTLPAC)

THIRTY-NINTH DISTRICT

The 39th congressional district of California is the northern section of the heavily populated part of Orange County, one of three districts wholly within this jurisdiction whose name has become synonymous with conservatism. It includes some of Orange County's most important landmarks. In Anaheim, there is Disneyland, the amusement park whose opening here in 1955 introduced millions to Orange County, and Anaheim Stadium, where the former Los Angeles Angels and the former Los Angeles Rams now play. In tiny Yorba Linda, where the subdivisions end and the scrubby hills begin, is the birthplace of Richard Nixon, a man whose career moved back and forth in and out of Orange County for several decades.

What kind of communities are these? It's a mistake to think of Orange County as just a collection of suburbs, although they would not have the economic vitality they do were they not part of a larger metropolitan expanse. In their grid street patterns and square moral outlooks, in their comfortable but far from showy affluence and their industriousness, in their apparent ethnic homogeneity and their adherence to traditional family patterns, they resemble those midwestern towns 40 and 60 miles away from Chicago, which are classed as part of the Chicago metropolitan area by the Census Bureau but in their own residents' minds are places apart. These places also share a strong allegiance to the Republican Party and a conviction that they represent the typical American community—although, in political terms at least, that is patently wrong, since the Republicans haven't been the national majority party for more than 50 years. Many of the people here actually come from towns like these in the Midwest and Illinois, at the other end of the Santa Fe Railroad and U.S. 66, and have brought their attitudes with them. And if their view of themselves and America is statistically not accurate, there is a sense in which almost all Americans believe it to be true: this is, for more than Orange Countians, how typical Americans live.

And so you have a county, and especially the 39th district, that may not be the most affluent part of the country but is certainly one of the most Republican; its residents' children may be grown, and many more of them than expected may have gotten divorces, but they still believe fiercely in family values; there may be more renters here, in the apartment complexes that line the main streets behind painted cement block walls, but they believe in the kind of strong communities that are nurtured by homeownership. The 39th is, in election after election, one of the strongest Republican districts in the country.

The current Congressman, William Dannemeyer, was once, oddly enough, a Democrat; he served in the California Assembly as such, and switched parties only when he lost a race for the state Senate. You would never know it from his current voting record, which is solidly conservative on just about all issues. After another term in the Assembly, as a Republican, he won the Republican primary unopposed in 1978 when Charles Wiggins, Richard Nixon's brilliant defender in the House Judiciary Committee impeachment hearings, decided to retire. Dannemeyer is a member of the important Energy and Commerce Committee, where he favors reducing regulation on business, and of the Post Office and Civil Service Committee.

The People Pop. 1980: 526,004, up 32.4% 1970–80; voting age pop. 380,905; 1% Black, 13% Span. orig., 3% Asian orig., 1% Am. Ind. 39% housing units rented. Median owner $100,300; renter $311. Households: 73% family, 40% with children, 61% married couples.

Presidential Vote

1980	Reagan (R)	155,576	(69%)
	Carter (D)	46,580	(22%)
	Other	23,109	(9%)

Rep. William E. Dannemeyer (R) Elected 1978; b. Sept. 22, 1929, Long Beach; home, Fullerton; Valparaiso U., B.A. 1950, Hastings Col. of Law, J.D. 1952; Lutheran.

Career Army, Korea; Practicing atty.; Dpty. Fullerton Dist. Atty.; CA Assembly, 1963–66, 1976–78.

Offices 1032 LHOB, 202-225-4111. Also 1370 Brea Blvd., Su. 108, Fullerton 92632, 714-992-0141.

Committees *Energy and Commerce* (7th). Subcommittees: Fossil and Synthetic Fuels; Health and the Environment. *Post Office and Civil Service* (6th). Subcommittees: Compensation and Employee Benefits; Census and Population.

Group Ratings

	ADA	ACLU	COPE	CFA	LCV	LWV	NTU	NSI	COC	ACA	CSFC
1982	5	0	7	0	21	20	97	100	86	87	85
1981	10	—	7	29	36	—	95	—	100	100	84
1980	6	13	10	14	31	22	80	90	70	100	87

National Journal Ratings

	Economic		Foreign		Cultural	
1982	22%	(LIB)	26%	(LIB)	4%	(LIB)
	78%	(CONS)	73%	(CONS)	87%	(CONS)
1981	4%	(LIB)	32%	(LIB)	4%	(LIB)
	79%	(CONS)	67%	(CONS)	90%	(CONS)

Key Votes

1) Reagan 81 Budget	FOR	5) Incr SS Rtmt Age	FOR	9) Poor Pay Food Stamps	FOR
2) Reagan 81 Tax Cut	FOR	6) Saudi AWACS Sale	FOR	10) Ban Crt Busing Order	FOR
3) Bal Budget Amend	FOR	7) $ for MX Missile	FOR	11) Auto Local Content	AGN
4) Gas & Road Tax	AGN	8) Nerve Gas Prod	FOR	12) Nuclear Arms Freeze	AGN

Election Results

1982 general	William E. Dannemeyer (R)	129,539	(72%)	($162,829)
	Frank G. Verges (D)	46,681	(26%)	($7,512)
1982 primary	William E. Dannemeyer (R)	57,262	(100%)	
1980 general	William E. Dannemeyer (R)	175,228	(76%)	($154,849)
	Leonard L. Lahtinen (D)	54,504	(24%)	($16,369)

Campaign Contributions and Expenditures

1981-82		Direct Cont. 81-82			PACS brkdwn		
Receipts	$229,880	Indiv	$137,750	Agr	$950	Ideo	$950
Expend.	$162,829	Party	$4,164	Bus	$54,195	Lbr	$—
Unspent	$98,838	PACS	$73,610	Hlth	$15,565	Prof	$1,200

FORTIETH DISTRICT

During the past 20 years, no congressional district in the country has had the kind of population growth that has been seen in the 40th district of California. In the early 1960s, this was vacant land: between Santa Ana and the mountains that form the eastern end of the Los Angeles Basin here, there was literally almost nothing. The Santa Ana and San Diego Freeways joined here, on their way to San Diego; there was an artsy settlement on the coast in Laguna Beach, locked in by hills, and farther north on the coast there was the yachtsy suburb of Newport Beach. But the shopping malls and subdivisions had not made their way to Newport yet, and the vast Irvine Ranch, stretching 15 miles from the coast to the mountains and six miles wide, was the largest undeveloped urban property in the world and would be kept that way until a dispute between the Irvine heirs was settled.

Today much, although not all, of this territory has filled in, and it houses enough people—525,000 in 1980—to make a full congressional district. This 40th district includes some of the older parts of Santa Ana, but most of it still seems almost brand new. The subdivisions are walled off from the surrounding roads and freeways, with access limited to a few roads; the old grid street patterns do not provide enough privacy and security for the affluent residents here. The underlying street patterns however, are geometrical, as if people were trying to impose a predictable order on the lush and unpredictable California landscape of mountain, coast, and desert. Such attempts do not always succeed, just as the efforts of the conservative Republicans whom voters here inevitably prefer do not always succeed: Richard Nixon retired in disgrace and Ronald Reagan has not been able to (did he really want to?) dismantle the welfare state.

The 40th district is the most Republican part of Orange County and hence one of the most Republican districts in the nation. It has been represented since 1976 by Robert Badham, a solidly conservative Republican. A legislator now for two decades—he was in the California Assembly for 14 years—Badham is one of those Republican politicians who has devoted his work life to reducing the influence of the very government that is inevitably his preoccupation. He is a member of the Armed Services Committee and an advocate of large increases in defense spending. He is in no conceivable trouble for reelection.

The People   Pop. 1980: 525,521, up 50.6% 1970–80; voting age pop. 399,141; 1% Black, 7% Span. orig., 4% Asian orig. 37% housing units rented. Median owner $132,200; renter $365. Households: 66% family, 33% with children, 55% married couples.

Presidential Vote

1980	Reagan (R)	155,576	(69%)
	Carter (D)	46,580	(21%)
	Other	23,109	(10%)

Rep. Robert E. Badham (R) Elected 1976; b. June 9, 1929, Los Angeles; home, Newport Beach; Occidental Col., 1947–48, Stanford U., B.A. 1951; Lutheran.

Career Navy, Korea; Secy. and V.P., Hoffman Hardware, Los Angeles, 1954–69; CA Assembly, 1963–77.

Offices 2438 RHOB, 202-225-5611. Also 1649 Westcliff, Newport Beach 92660, 714-631-0040.

Committees *Armed Services* (6th). Subcommittees: Procurement and Military Nuclear Systems; Research and Development. *House Administration* (3d). Subcommittee: Accounts.

Group Ratings

	ADA	ACLU	COPE	CFA	LCV	LWV	NTU	NSI	COC	ACA	CSFC
1982	5	4	12	0	6	27	88	100	85	100	78
1981	0	—	13	14	15	—	79	—	100	79	77
1980	0	10	11	7	12	14	66	89	74	95	83

National Journal Ratings

	Economic		Foreign		Cultural	
1982	11%	(LIB)	4%	(LIB)	4%	(LIB)
	88%	(CONS)	92%	(CONS)	87%	(CONS)
1981	3%	(LIB)	30%	(LIB)	10%	(LIB)
	97%	(CONS)	70%	(CONS)	89%	(CONS)

Key Votes

1) Reagan 81 Budget	FOR	5) Incr SS Rtmt Age	FOR	9) Poor Pay Food Stamps	FOR
2) Reagan 81 Tax Cut	FOR	6) Saudi AWACS Sale	—	10) Ban Crt Busing Order	FOR
3) Bal Budget Amend	FOR	7) $ for MX Missile	FOR	11) Auto Local Content	AGN
4) Gas & Road Tax	FOR	8) Nerve Gas Prod	FOR	12) Nuclear Arms Freeze	AGN

Election Results

1982 general	Robert E. Badham (R)	144,228	(72%)	($126,582)
	Paul Haseman (D)	52,546	(26%)	($9,921)
1982 primary	Robert E. Badham (R)	73,027	(100%)	
1980 general	Robert E. Badham (R)	213,999	(70%)	($123,492)
	Michael P. Dow (D)	66,512	(22%)	($15,863)
	Dan Mahaffey (Libertarian)	24,486	(8%)	($34,285)

Campaign Contributions and Expenditures

1981-82		Direct Cont. 81-82		PACS brkdwn			
Receipts	$147,439	Indiv	$64,055	Agr	$1,000	Ideo	$2,200
Expend.	$126,582	Party	$9,049	Bus	$51,720	Lbr	$—
Unspent	$82,079	PACS	$66,913	Hlth	$9,100	Prof	$650

FORTY-FIRST DISTRICT

Before World War II, San Diego was a sleepy resort town with a fine natural harbor and a few Navy installations. Then the United States fought a war in the Pacific, and San Diego was forever changed. It became the Navy's West Coast headquarters and naval installations proliferated. Later its pleasant climate—perhaps the most pleasant in the continental United States—made it a favorite retirement place for Navy officers and for others as well. But San Diego, like most Sun Belt cities, is far more than a collection of retirement villages. It has developed a significant industrial base, largely on high-skill businesses; its metropolitan area population has reached nearly two million.

San Diego was evenly divided politically before 1945, split between the well-to-do Republican north side and the more modest and sometimes working class south side. In the years following the war, the heavy immigration gave both the city and county of San Diego a very Republican, conservative complexion. Richard Nixon for years regarded this as his "lucky city"—until the unfolding ITT scandal caused him to cancel plans to have the 1972 Republican National Convention here.

Since Watergate San Diego has seen a more competitive two-party politics; for a while Democrats even managed to hold most of the county's Assembly seats. The dominant figure in the area's politics, however, was Pete Wilson during his years as mayor. Bringing a conservative record from the legislature, he nonetheless challenged big developers and insisted on regulating growth; he became one of the most popular politicians around and carried the city easily in general elections. He also made it easier for his kind of Republicans to win the votes of young, affluent voters who were conservative on economic issues but liberal on cultural matters. In the middle 1970s they were trending Democratic; by 1980 they seemed pretty solidly Republican.

Or so one might conclude from the election of 41st district Congressman Bill Lowery. The 41st district takes in the part of San Diego—basically the north side of the city—where Wilson's politics was most popular. The north side includes affluent beach communities (La Jolla, Pacific Beach, Mission Bay) as well as inland, comfortable sections of San Diego and the suburb of La Mesa. It has a very small Mexican–American population, despite the proximity of Mexico, lower in percentage than in even affluent Los Angeles area districts. Its congressman since 1952 was an old San Diego figure, Bob Wilson, who looked after the naval bases from a seat on the Armed Services Committee. Lowery was 5 years old when Bob Wilson was first elected to Congress and entered the race as a former councilman and Pete Wilson's deputy mayor. He won a close primary over the son of Bob Wilson's Republican predecessor, Dan McKinnon, who went on to become chairman of the Civil Aeronautics Board in 1981. In the general election Lowery faced a different, Democratic Bob Wilson, a state senator who took more conservative positions on some cultural issues. With economic issues predominating, Lowery won an easier-than-expected victory. He was reelected without difficulty in a district not vastly changed in 1982.

Befitting his background in city government, Lowery sits on the Banking Committee and also on Science and Technology. Curiously, his record on foreign issues is less stridently conservative than one expects from a San Diego area Republican.

The People   Pop. 1980: 526,012, up 48.8% 1970–80; voting age pop. 397,122; 2% Black, 6% Span. orig., 4% Asian orig. 38% housing units rented. Median owner $99,500; renter $301. Households: 67% family, 35% with children, 55% married couples.

Presidential Vote

1980	Reagan (R)	139,435	(60%)
	Carter (D)	60,346	(26%)
	Other	32,524	(14%)

Rep. Bill Lowery (R) Elected 1980; b. May 2, 1947, San Diego; home, San Diego; San Diego St. Col.; Roman Catholic.

Career Pub. Rel./Adv.; San Diego City Cncl., 1977–80, Dpty. Mayor, 1980.

Offices 1440 LHOB, 202-225-3201. Also 880 Front St., Rm. 6-S-15, San Diego 92188, 714-231-0957.

Committees *Banking, Finance, and Urban Affairs* (12th). Subcommittees: Domestic Monetary Policy; Financial Institutions Supervision, Regulation and Insurance; Housing and Community Development. *Science and Technology* (10th). Subcommittees: Energy Research and Production; Space Science and Applications; Energy Development and Applications.

Group Ratings

	ADA	ACLU	COPE	CFA	LCV	LWV	NTU	NSI	COC	ACA	CSFC
1982	0	4	4	10	30	42	73	100	100	91	69
1981	5	—	0	29	56	—	72	—	100	71	71

National Journal Ratings

	Economic		Foreign		Cultural	
1982	12%	(LIB)	12%	(LIB)	4%	(LIB)
	87%	(CONS)	84%	(CONS)	87%	(CONS)
1981	4%	(LIB)	49%	(LIB)	17%	(LIB)
	79%	(CONS)	50%	(CONS)	82%	(CONS)

Key Votes

1) Reagan 81 Budget	FOR	5) Incr SS Rtmt Age	FOR	9) Poor Pay Food Stamps	FOR
2) Reagan 81 Tax Cut	FOR	6) Saudi AWACS Sale	AGN	10) Ban Crt Busing Order	FOR
3) Bal Budget Amend	FOR	7) $ for MX Missile	FOR	11) Auto Local Content	AGN
4) Gas & Road Tax	FOR	8) Nerve Gas Prod	FOR	12) Nuclear Arms Freeze	AGN

Election Results

1982 general	Bill Lowery (R)	140,130	(69%)	($399,486)
	Tony Brandenburg (D)	58,677	(29%)	($23,862)
1982 primary	Bill Lowery (R)	61,780	(100%)	
1980 general	Bill Lowery (R)	123,187	(53%)	($213,099)
	Bob Wilson (D)	101,101	(43%)	($362,792)

Campaign Contributions and Expenditures

1981-82		*Direct Cont. 81-82*		*PACS brkdwn*			
Receipts	$402,742	Indiv	$201,701	Agr	$4,500	Ideo	$9,360
Expend.	$399,486	Party	$9,737	Bus	$119,705	Lbr	$4,250
Unspent	$6,264	PACS	$159,030	Hlth	$12,650	Prof	$700
		Cand	$10,000				

Indep Expend: For: $769 (NRA)

FORTY-SECOND DISTRICT

The 42d congressional district of California is the descendant of several districts based in the city of Long Beach, a sort of mini-central city near directly south of downtown Los Angeles, that is large enough to constitute most of a district by itself. But less than one-fifth of the residents of the current 42d live in Long Beach or the nearby harbor area of Los Angeles. Rather, Long Beach and the harbor area are just a kind of land bridge, tying together two heavily Republican areas that redistricter Phillip Burton wanted to keep out of Democratic districts.

One is centered on the Palos Verdes Peninsula and the suburb just to the north. Palos Verdes is a mountainous peninsula jutting up above the flat plain of the Los Angeles Basin and staring out over the ocean to Santa Catalina Island; all but its most seismically active parts are filled with spacious ranch houses built on, for the Los Angeles area, generous-sized lots. The population here is affluent and highly Republican; perhaps Palos Verdes's best-known resident is Arthur Laffer, the inventor, on a paper napkin, of the now-famous Laffer Curve. Torrance, down on the plain, is much more prosaic in appearance and is criss-crossed by railroads, with warehouses and factories. Nonetheless, it is a higher than average income (and Republican) suburb.

The other part of the district, connected by a thin strip of waterfront going inland a distance in Long Beach, is in Orange County: the retirement development of Rossmoor and nearby Seal Beach, the spread-out suburb of Huntington Beach, affluent but with many renters as well as homeowners.

The congressman from the 42d district is Dan Lungren, as enthusiastic a young Republican as one could find. His father was Richard Nixon's personal physician; he worked on the staffs of Senators George Murphy and Bill Brock. After a few years of law practice in Long Beach, he challenged a Democrat elected in 1974, lost in 1976, then came back and won in 1978. Lungren jammed down his opponent's throat his opposition to Proposition 13 and won rather easily. He has been reelected easily in 1980 and 1982, although he must have been disappointed in the latter year when his brother, former policeman Brian Lungren, fell far short of unseating Democrat Glenn Anderson in the 32d district, which now includes most of the Lungrens' ancestral home of Long Beach.

Lungren is easily one of the most conservative members of the House. He serves on the Judiciary Committee. In 1983 he switched from the Civil and Constitutional Rights Subcommittee—a hair-shirt assignment for one of his beliefs, since it is the graveyard of conservatives' favorite constitutional amendments—to the ranking Republican position on Immigration, Refugees, and International Law. Subcommittee chairman Romano Mazzoli's major immigration law was prevented from coming to the floor in late 1982 because of delaying tactics by Mexican-American congressmen, but Mazzoli won sympathy and respect in the process, and will be working hard to pass a bill. Lungren, by working with him or opposing him, can play a major role in either advancing or impeding this legislation, whose main Senate sponsor is Wyoming Republican Alan Simpson.

The People   Pop. 1980: 524,346, up 7.9% 1970–80; voting age pop. 403,473; 1% Black, 6% Span. orig., 6% Asian orig., 1% Am. Ind. 40% housing units rented. Median owner $130,700; renter $332. Households: 66% family, 32% with children, 55% married couples.

Presidential Vote

1980	Reagan (R)	149,988	(65%)
	Carter (D)	57,371	(25%)
	Other	23,901	(10%)

Rep. Daniel E. (Dan) Lungren (R) Elected 1978; b. Sept. 2, 1946, Long Beach; home, Long Beach; Notre Dame U., B.A. 1964, USC, Georgetown U., J.D. 1971; Roman Catholic.

Career Staff of U.S. Sen. George Murphy, 1969–70; Staff of U.S. Sen. Bill Brock, 1971; Spec. Asst., Repub. Natl. Comm., 1971–72; Practicing atty., 1973–78.

Offices 328 CHOB, 202-225-2415. Also 5514 Britton Dr., Long Beach 90815, 213-594-9761.

Committees *Judiciary* (6th). Subcommittees: Immigration, Refugees and International Law; Monopolies. *Select Committee on Aging* (6th). Subcommittees: Health and Long-Term Care; Human Services. *Joint Economic Committee* (3d). Subcommittees: Investment, Jobs, and Prices; Trade Productivity (Vice-Chairman).

Group Ratings

	ADA	ACLU	COPE	CFA	LCV	LWV	NTU	NSI	COC	ACA	CSFC
1982	0	8	6	0	25	33	92	90	90	95	80
1981	20	—	7	29	36	—	95	—	89	87	79
1980	6	13	10	7	31	20	65	100	74	100	82

National Journal Ratings

	Economic		Foreign		Cultural	
1982	12%	(LIB)	12%	(LIB)	4%	(LIB)
	87%	(CONS)	84%	(CONS)	87%	(CONS)
1981	24%	(LIB)	3%	(LIB)	34%	(LIB)
	68%	(CONS)	87%	(CONS)	66%	(CONS)

Key Votes

1) Reagan 81 Budget	FOR	5) Incr SS Rtmt Age	FOR	9) Poor Pay Food Stamps	FOR
2) Reagan 81 Tax Cut	FOR	6) Saudi AWACS Sale	FOR	10) Ban Crt Busing Order	FOR
3) Bal Budget Amend	FOR	7) $ for MX Missile	FOR	11) Auto Local Content	AGN
4) Gas & Road Tax	AGN	8) Nerve Gas Prod	FOR	12) Nuclear Arms Freeze	AGN

Election Results

1982 general	Daniel E. (Dan) Lungren (R)	142,845	(69%)	($232,084)
	James P. Spellman (D)	58,690	(28%)	($19,250)
1982 primary	Daniel E. (Dan) Lungren (R)	59,811	(81%)	
	Tom Heinsheimer (R)	13,716	(19%)	($42,469)
1980 general	Daniel E. (Dan) Lungren (R)	138,024	(72%)	($235,834)
	Simone (D)	46,351	(24%)	($12,082)

Campaign Contributions and Expenditures

1981-82		Direct Cont. 81-82		PACS brkdwn			
Receipts	$246,176	Indiv	$158,813	Agr	$1,450	Ideo	$4,050
Expend.	$232,084	Party	$5,981	Bus	$50,350	Lbr	$—
Unspent	$20,279	PACS	$70,639	Hlth	$9,466	Prof	$3,200

Indirect Party Expend: $16,452   *Indep Expend:* For: $619 (GOA)

FORTY-THIRD DISTRICT

One of America's most comfortable environments, and one largely undiscovered by the mass media, is the country north of San Diego. The coastline was pretty well settled, all the way from the Marine Corps's Camp Pendleton south to La Jolla several decades ago, but it is only in the last dozen years that there has been major settlement inland. Here, amid dry but not desert landscape, you can see miles of rolling hills, with occasional surrealistic trees and sagebrush-like bushes; mountains clump up not in ridges but here and there, almost at random. Here developers have planted, rather than standard subdivisions, whole little communities, existing alone in the mountains. Many but by no means all their residents are retirees; and while some may miss the urbanity and busyness of big cities (or even a metropolitan area like Orange County) most don't. The climate is close to ideal, the air remains clear, there is little fear of crime.

Yet condominiums and houses here cost less—roughly 50% less—than in the more regimented developments like Mission Viejo in southern Orange County. Northern San Diego County is one of the real bargains left in the United States. Why do the media ignore it (except for the Teamsters' luxurious La Costa development)? Partly because it is outside the ambit of one of our really big metropolitan areas, partly because it is not fashionable in the way Malibu or the Hamptons are. And partly, perhaps, because the very existence of such a place, and the fact that quite ordinary people can afford to live here, contradicts the pessimistic picture of America in which so many in the media have a psychological stake.

Most of northern San Diego County, plus the southern tip of Orange County (including San Clemente and San Juan Capistrano of Nixon and swallows fame, respectively) form the 43d congressional district of California. The people who have moved here are, by a large margin, heavily Republican: affluent enough to identify with the party of property, conventional enough in their personal lives to identify with what identifies itself as the party of the family, unscarred enough by ethnic identities to identify with the party that fancies it is made up of an unethnic majority.

The 43d district was a new creation, in effect half of the old 43d, represented by Clair Burgener, who was retiring; even a Democratic redistricter as creative as Phillip Burton could not avoid drawing a new Republican district in the San Diego area, given its recent growth. The new congressman, it was confidently assumed, would be determined in the Republican primary that attracted no less than 18 entrants (which made it theoretically possible for a candidate to win with 6%). But it turned out to be more complicated than that.

The reason was that the winner of the Republican primary, Johnnie Crean, struck most of the other contenders—and many others—as a despicable candidate. Crean spent some $500,000 of his own money on television advertising that implied that he was the choice of President Reagan and on direct mail that charged one of his opponents, spuriously, with vote fraud. He won the primary by only 92 votes out of 83,000 cast, and the second place finisher,

Carlsbad Mayor and sometime dentist Ron Packard, ran as a write-in candidate. This was not as quixotic as it sounds: this is a highly literate district, and a lot of voters are over 65 and regularly vote on absentee ballots, on which write-ins are easy. However, it was also risky: Democrat Roy Archer tried to launch a serious campaign and must have dreamed of becoming, though presumably for only one term, the Democratic congressman from what is arguably the most Republican district in the country. Republican officials seeemed to think it was worth a gamble. Theoretically they supported Crean, but with enough winks and nudges that it was apparent that they really preferred Packard.

It turned out to be that rarity: a real three-way race. Democrat Archer, with 32%, actually came in ahead of Republican Crean, with 31%; but the winner was write-in Packard, with 37%. Of course Packard joined the Republican Conference, of which he is expected to be a loyal member; he had no trouble winning acceptance or getting seats on the Education and Labor and Public Works Committees. He surely hopes to win a noncontroversial and conventional Republican primary and general election in 1984.

The People Pop. 1980: 528,086, up 103.2% 1970–80; voting age pop. 387,512; 2% Black, 1% Am. Ind. 31% housing units rented. Median owner $110,900; renter $290. Households: 76% family, 39% with children, 66% married couples.

Presidential Vote

1980	Reagan (R)	141,259	(71%)
	Carter (D)	38,525	(20%)
	Other	18,046	(9%)

Rep. Ronald C. Packard (R) Elected 1982; b. Jan. 31, 1931, Meridian, ID; home, Carlsbad; Brigham Young U., 1948–50, Portland State U., 1952–53, U. of OR, D.M.D. 1957; Mormon.

Career USN, 1957–59; Dentist, 1960–; Carlsbad Sch. Cncl., 1962–72; Carlsbad City Cncl., 1976–78; Mayor of Carlsbad, 1978–82.

Offices 511 CHOB, 202-225-3906. Also 2121 Palomar Airport Rd., Su. 105, Carlsbad 92008, 619-438-0443.

Committees *Education and Labor* (10th). Subcommittees: Elementary, Secondary and Vocational Education; Labor Standards. *Public Works and Transportation* (17th). Subcommittees: Aviation; Water Resources.

Group Ratings and Key Votes: Newly Elected

Election Results

1982 general	Ronald C. Packard (R-write in) ...	66,444	(37%)	($366,711)
	Roy (Pat) Archer (D)	57,995	(32%)	($36,072)
	Johnnie Crean (R)	56,297	(31%)	($1,140,863)
1982 primary	Johnnie Crean (R)	13,761	(16.6%)	
	Ronald C. Packard (R)	13,669	(16.5%)	
	Bill McColl (R)	13,297	(15.8%)	($401,376)
	Fifteen others	42,478	(51.1%)	($1,214,652)
1980 general	Clair W. Burgener (R)	299,037	(87%)	($175,009)
	Tom Metzger (D)	46,383	(13%)	($26,003)

Campaign Contributions and Expenditures

1981-82		Direct Cont. 81-82		PACS brkdwn			
Receipts	$368,511	Indiv	$236,273	Agr	$—	Ideo	$2,000
Expend.	$366,711	Party	$10,000	Bus	$3,950	Lbr	$10,000
Unspent	$1,802	PACS	$40,836	Hlth	$4,000	Prof	$—
		Cand	$80,925				

FORTY-FOURTH DISTRICT

Like most Sun Belt cities, San Diego has its second side. To many, San Diego evokes images of La Jolla, its shopping streets lined with boutiques and stockbrokers' offices, or Mission Bay, with its comfortable homes of retired Navy officers, or the magnificent Balboa Park Zoo. But just a short distance away is another San Diego, down by the harbor, along the hills running inland, and on the flat, dusty land going down to Tijuana. This is the south side where the city's blacks live in neighborhoods stretching east from the city's gleaming downtown and where Mexican-Americans are scattered in various parts of the city, from Encanto and Chollas Park in the east down through the blue collar suburbs of National City and Chula Vista to the south. They live also, unobtrusively and here and there, in mostly Anglo neighborhoods like East San Diego and suburbs like Lemon Grove. Indeed, the Mexican-American percentage here is not as large as most people would guess, given the proximity of Mexico. One reason is that immigrants come to the United States less to get residency and qualify for welfare than they do to get jobs; and Mexicans in the San Diego area can live in Tijuana, which is cheaper and culturally more comfortable, and cross the border each day as thousands do to commute to jobs in San Diego.

This central and southern part of San Diego, enclosed by a jagged line drawn by Phil Burton, makes up California's 44th congressional district. Its boundaries were very carefully sculpted, because most of its precincts were in the old 42d district that surprised everyone and elected a Republican congressman, Duncan Hunter, last time. Heavily Republican areas, like the old beach resort of Coronado, were split off and put into a new 45th district, safe for Hunter; the rest, with some new parts added, was made a safe Democratic seat.

This left a district ripe for San Diego County Supervisor Jim Bates. A onetime Republican with 11 years in local government, he was well known. His record and his campaign as well were rather conservative on economic issues and more liberal on cultural and economic issues; indeed, he first became a Democrat because he supported Eugene McCarthy in 1968. He is now a strong environmentalist. Bates won both the primary and the general election by wide margins. He was adroit enough to win a seat on the Energy and Commerce Committee, beating in the process a Los Angeles freshman backed by Health Subcommittee Chairman Henry Waxman; he takes a special interest in telecommunications and sits on Tim Wirth's subcommittee. He serves on House Administration as well. Bates seems to be a competent politician with every prospect of continuing to represent this part of San Diego for some years.

The People   Pop. 1980: 525,906, up 15% 1970–80; voting age pop. 381,563; 7% Black, 13% Span. orig., 4% Asian orig. 51% housing units rented. Median owner $69,600; renter $226. Households: 68% family, 40% with children, 51% married couples.

Presidential Vote

1980	Reagan (R)	63,521	(48%)
	Carter (D)	54,114	(41%)
	Other	15,575	(12%)

Rep. Jim Bates (D) Elected 1982; b. July 21, 1941, Denver, CO; home, San Diego; San Diego State, B.A. 1975; Congregationalist.

Career San Diego City Cncl., 1971–74; Member, Cnty. Board of Sprvsrs., 1975–82.

Offices 1632 LHOB, 202-225-5452. Also 880 Front St., Rm. 5S35, San Diego 92188, 619-234-2766.

Committees *Energy and Commerce* (27th). Subcommittees: Oversight and Investigations; Telecommunications, Consumer Protection, and Finance. *House Administration* (12th). Subcommittees: Accounts; Office Systems.

Group Ratings and Key Votes: Newly Elected

Election Results

1982 general	Jim Bates (D)	78,474	(65%)	($251,486)
	Shirley M. Gissendanner (R)	38,447	(32%)	($63,667)
1982 primary	Jim Bates (D)	32,155	(72%)	
	Michael J. Aguirre (D)	12,578	(28%)	($75,378)
1980 general	Newly created district			

Campaign Contributions and Expenditures

1981-82		Direct Cont. 81-82*			PACS brkdwn		
Receipts	$251,585	Indiv	$172,849	Agr	$1,250	Ideo	$7,250
Expend.	$251,486	Party	$2,000	Bus	$3,550	Lbr	$37,900
Unspent	$319	PACS	$61,683	Hlth	$4,500	Prof	$100

Non-Cand Loans: $14,905

FORTY-FIFTH DISTRICT

One of the fastest-growing metropolitan areas in the United States in the 1970s was San Diego, and as a result of its fast growth its predominantly suburban 43d congressional district had to be split in two. One part makes up most of the current 43d district, the other most of the current 45th; the 45th also includes certain parts of the old 42d district, a longtime Democratic seat that surprised almost everyone by electing a Republican congressman in 1980. The 45th appears quite regularly shaped on the map, but actually its population concentrations are oddly dispersed. One is right on the coast: it includes the relatively high income Ocean Beach area of San Diego, plus the comfortable neighborhoods just north of the Balboa Park Zoo inland.

This area is connected only by water to the rest of the district, which begins on the old beach suburb of Coronado, with its delightful Victorian hotel, a favorite of retired Navy officers. The 45th also sweeps around the southern end of San Diego and includes the more affluent half of Chula Vista. Then it runs along the eastern edge of suburban settlement: these are pleasant suburbs nestled between mountains, not terribly high income, but conservative on both economic and cultural issues. The 45th includes the sparsely populated interior of San Diego County, with its small Indian reservations—some of the last traces of the people who populated the state, very lightly, before Junipero Serra set up his missions along the coast. Farther inland still, outside San Diego County, is the Imperial Valley, an agricultural area in the desert created entirely by irrigation; the majority of the people here are Mexican, with many more huddling in Mexicali, right on the border; the political power is in the hands of the growers.

This is a solidly Republican district, created to entice freshman Duncan Hunter out of the otherwise Democratic 44th, most of which he had been representing and which he, alone of San Diego area Republicans, might have won. The strategy worked. Hunter may have had some misgivings: before his election he was a storefront lawyer in a low income neighborhood, and he was proud of his ability to win votes, often through door-to-door campaigning, among Democrats. But the prospect of having to court a basically contrary constituency indefinitely must have been daunting. So Hunter ran in the 45th and won easily.

Hunter is also a Vietnam veteran and a believer in strong national defense. Over his fellow 1980 San Diego freshman Bill Lowery, he won a seat on the Armed Services Committee. Its jurisdiction remains important, although not as crucial to San Diego's economy, as it once was; and to Hunter it is important for its national policy responsibilities as well. An upset winner, he now seems firmly established in Congress and in San Diego.

The People   Pop. 1980: 525,906, up 27.0% 1970–80; voting age pop. 387,456; 2% Black, 18% Span. orig., 3% Asian orig., 1% Am. Ind. 43% housing units rented. Median owner $90,300; renter $241. Households: 67% family, 36% with children, 55% married couples.

Presidential Vote

1980	Reagan (R)	115,923	(62%)
	Carter (D)	50,729	(27%)
	Other	21,357	(11%)

Rep. Duncan L. Hunter (R) Elected 1980; b. May 31, 1948, Riverside; home, Coronado; U. of MT, 1967–68, U. of CA at Santa Barbara, 1968–69, Western St. U., J.D. 1976; Baptist.

Career Army, Vietnam; Practicing atty., 1976–80.

Offices 415 CHOB, 202-225-5672. Also 2530 Highland Ave., National City 92050, 714-474-8554.

Committees *Armed Services* (12th). Subcommittees: Procurement and Military Nuclear Systems; Seapower and Strategic and Critical Materials. *Select Committee on Narcotics Abuse and Control* (8th).

Group Ratings

	ADA	ACLU	COPE	CFA	LCV	LWV	NTU	NSI	COC	ACA	CSFC
1982	5	25	19	10	12	25	81	100	82	100	73
1981	10	—	27	14	21	—	72	—	89	75	70

National Journal Ratings

	Economic		Foreign		Cultural	
1982	25%	(LIB)	4%	(LIB)	28%	(LIB)
	75%	(CONS)	92%	(CONS)	72%	(CONS)
1981	24%	(LIB)	18%	(LIB)	16%	(LIB)
	68%	(CONS)	73%	(CONS)	83%	(CONS)

Key Votes

1) Reagan 81 Budget	FOR	5) Incr SS Rtmt Age	FOR	9) Poor Pay Food Stamps	FOR
2) Reagan 81 Tax Cut	FOR	6) Saudi AWACS Sale	AGN	10) Ban Crt Busing Order	—
3) Bal Budget Amend	FOR	7) $ for MX Missile	FOR	11) Auto Local Content	FOR
4) Gas & Road Tax	—	8) Nerve Gas Prod	FOR	12) Nuclear Arms Freeze	AGN

Election Results

1982 general	Duncan L. Hunter (R)	117,771	(69%)	($425,864)
	Richard Hill (D)	50,148	(29%)	($0)
1982 primary	Duncan L. Hunter (R)	53,491	(100%)	
1980 general	Duncan L. Hunter (R)	79,713	(53%)	($208,596)
	Lionel Van Deerlin (D)	69,936	(47%)	($140,557)

Campaign Contributions and Expenditures

1981-82		Direct Cont. 81-82		PACS brkdwn			
Receipts	$432,373	Indiv	$258,824	Agr	$6,490	Ideo	$13,569
Expend.	$425,864	Party	$12,284	Bus	$102,175	Lbr	$7,000
Unspent	$18,726	PACS	$143,978	Hlth	$12,000	Prof	$1,750

Indep Expend: For: $16,617 (AMAPAC, NRA)

COLORADO

For anyone driving across the country, there are few sights more thrilling than coming over an incline and seeing, suddenly, in the distance the Front Range of the Rocky Mountains towering over an ocean-like expanse of dry, brown, flat plateau. The base of these mountains is an improbable place for an advanced civilization. The High Plains, to the east of the Front Range, are parched and without dependable water supplies. The rivers are mere trickles, except in flood season, and even the Plains Indians had a hard time here. The mountains behind the Front Range—the Western Slope—get plenty of precipitation, but their terrain is forbidding. There are dozens of peaks over 10,000 feet and scarcely a patch of level ground, but nothing much grows anyway at these altitudes.

Yet Colorado thrives, and the 3 million people who live in the 30-mile margin just east of the Front Range are the largest population cluster between the Missouri River and San Francisco Bay. The civilization they have built is not just comfortable, but affluent; and Colorado has been hailed as a trend-setter, one of the first places where you'll find the ideas and fads that will sweep the nation.

Colorado's economy has been based on mining and minerals: extracting resources from the vast Rocky Mountain region Joel Garreau, in *The Nine Nations of North America* called "the Empty Quarter." The first settlements here were in gold mining towns in the mountains; Denver, on the South Platte River just a few miles east of the Front Range, was established as a kind of supply depot. It became something more. A U. S. Mint (still operating) was built there. The railroad came. Banks were set up, law offices, wholesale firms, meatpacking plants. When ore petered out, the mining settlements became ghost towns. But Denver grew into the undisputed metropolis of the Rocky Mountains.

Today Denver lives, not on gold or silver, but on oil. Like Houston or Dallas, Denver is an energy center where one can find the services and hardware necessary to drill for oil or process shale or extract uranium. For many of the majors and hundreds of independent oil companies, Denver is the hub of exploration and production activities for the Rocky Mountains and the Great Plains, as far east as Kansas and as far north as Alberta. The surge in oil prices in the 1970s produced a vast office-building boom in Denver, and increased the already high rate of population growth along the Front Range. The growth here also owes something to high technology, with lots of little new companies no one has ever heard of but which, taken together, add up to a critical mass of national importance. Finally, people come to Denver for the physical environment. Not so much in the city itself—Denver has some of the smoggiest air in the country—but in the nearby mountains. For two or three decades now, well educated young people who fancy backpacking, skiing, fishing, and mountain climbing have been moving to Denver. The successive waves of young migrants have added immeasurably to the area's economy—they are bright and full of initiative, energetic—and they have changed Colorado's politics every decade or so.

Historically, Colorado politics revolved around water, which the Western Slope had and the Eastern Slope (*i.e.,* Denver and other cities on the Front Range) wanted. The Eastern Slope's success was memorialized when Denver's airport was named for Ben Stapleton, who got Western Slope water for the city. Water issues remain important—Colorado protested angrily when President Carter cancelled some water projects in 1977, and there is a dispute between Denver and its suburbs now—but do not divide the state along partisan lines. Those splits have developed, suddenly, on rather abstract economic issues or on the basis of cultural attitudes.

So Colorado voters, unfettered by pressing economic need, with no deep roots in the community, seem to swing wildly from right to left and back again. In the early 1960s, affluent Coloradans, resentful of a distant federal government, went heavily Republican. In the early 1970s, affluent Coloradans, eager to preserve their environment from overdevelopment, voted against having the 1976 Winter Olympics in Denver and elected a series of liberal Democrats to Congress and state office. Their appeal was very much targeted to the younger generation, as indicated by Gary Hart's 1974 slogan, "They've had their turn; now it's our turn." In the late 1970s, affluent Coloradans seemed once again resentful of a federal government that appeared to penalize, not honor, Colorado's contributions to the national economy; in 1980 they voted heavily against Jimmy Carter and nearly ousted Senator Gary Hart despite a very weak Republican campaign. Yet in 1982 they elected Democratic

Governor Dick Lamm to a third term by a wide margin. These results cannot be explained any longer simply as partisan trends, but must be seen as responses to specific choices and issue stances.

Governor. In a state like Colorado, with great population and economic growth, a governor can set an agenda and a tone in a way not usually possible in more settled and stable states. Colorado's current governor, Dick Lamm, came to office in 1974 determined to change things greatly. He was only 39 then, a backpacker and mountain climber, a migrant from Wisconsin and California, part of the generation of young Democrats who had stopped the Olympics and wanted to limit growth. Lamm had a stormy first term and a much more successful second one. He won reelection in 1978 largely because his opponent made mistakes; he won in 1982 on his own popularity.

Lamm has clearly changed perspective in his years in office. He evinces as great a mistrust of the federal government as any conservative Republican these days; he talks about how the problems of the West are unique, and not understood by folks back East. He is not so ready to spend money, nor is he as inclined to regard growth as a blight. Colorado has seen what happened to Oregon when its timber industry collapsed, and the oil business in the middle 1980s was not as robust as it had been a few years before. He thinks Denver should share its water—it owns most of the water rights on the Front Range—with its suburbs. He wants to build a strong educational system and a kind of research park so that Colorado can keep attracting high tech industry. Thus he seems to personify the maturing of a young electorate. Yet he has not been able to persuade the voters to restore Democratic majorities to the state legislature since the Republicans captured both houses in 1976. It is too soon to guess whether Lamm will run for reelection in 1986; if he doesn't, there will surely be vigorous competition for the post. In the meantime Lamm is likely to remain an important national spokesman for the western states.

Senators. Colorado has two senators, both in their 40s, who are in quite different ways important national politicians. Each was first elected in a year when enthusiasm for his party's ideas was surging; one ran for reelection in a tough year, and nearly lost, and the other may find himself running, in 1984, in a tough year also.

Gary Hart is probably the better known of the two, and he hopes to become far better known: on February 17, 1983 he announced his presidential candidacy for 1984. He is campaigning as the candidate of new ideas, which is appropriate enough, but he could also run as the candidate with a strategic approach to issues. It was as a strategist, after all, that he first achieved national prominence: as much as anyone, he devised the strategy that made George McGovern the 1972 Democratic presidential nominee. This was a considerable achievement, against the odds, and seems unlikely to hurt Hart too much: with a record of ten years in the Senate, he should not be vulnerable to accusations that he is a carbon copy of McGovern.

It was as a strategist—this time as a military thinker—that Hart first established his credentials as a new ideas politician. As a candidate and senator from Colorado, he had taken some positions unusual for a Democrat, backing western water projects and opposing price controls on oil and gas. But he startled almost everyone by taking a seat on the Armed Services Committee and delving deeply into military policy. He supported the SALT II and Panama Canal Treaties, like most Democrats, but he also spent time on combat readiness and strengthening the Navy. He argues that the military relies too much on sophisticated weaponry and not enough on maneuverable, simple airplanes and ships. He wants a larger

Navy composed of many smaller ships—unlike Navy Secretary John Lehman, who wants big carriers and reactivated World War II battleships. Hart is the major proponent of the theory of warfare that emphasizes throwing the enemy's commanders off guard by harrying them constantly and attacking them where they least expect it—the strategy of Hitler's Panzer divisions when they overran Poland and France. He believes that soldiers should spend less time on bureaucratic duties and more time reading military history. He questions whether soldiers should rotate from one unit to another rather than stay with one unit for years and build cohesion and morale. Hart obviously really cares about these issues: after the 1980 campaign he took the unusual step of signing up, at age 43, in the Naval Reserve.

In other policy areas, Hart has taken a similar tack, although with less dazzling results. When the Democrats controlled the Senate, he chaired a subcommittee on nuclear power; he acted cautiously and fair-mindedly after the Three Mile Island accident. In the last Carter year he chaired a commission to monitor the Clean Air Act, and again produced thoughtful results. On issues that he studies closely he thinks originally and clearly, avoids stereotyped responses, and does not indulge in cheap shots. On issues he has not studied closely, however, he has gotten into trouble by trying to take stands that please everyone but which turn out to be contradictory. Some of his critics wonder whether he takes positions sheerly for the sake of novelty. A better criticism, and one that cuts against his presidential candidacy, is that he has not thought through all the issues on which a president needs clear views.

No one should underrate Hart's ability as a campaign strategist. Yet his 1980 campaign for reelection in Colorado nearly failed. He underestimated the Republican trend of the year, failed to stress some of his strongest issues, and underestimated his opponent. As it happened, the Republican primary victor, Mary Estill Buchanan, won for the silliest of reasons: voters had sympathy for her because she had failed to win the 20% support at the Republican state convention needed to get on the primary ballot. But what politician doesn't want to get on the ballot? Buchanan was unprepared to discuss national issues, yet in a Republican year she came close to upsetting Hart. He owes his victory less to what he did in 1980 than to his hard work cultivating the state and, to a large extent, reflecting its views on issues for the six years before the election.

For 1984, Hart seems determined to stake out the "new ideas" vote for himself, to be the one candidate with a strong appeal to the younger generation of voters, those who came of political age during the Vietnam era. There may be an opening here: do Walter Mondale or John Glenn have any special appeal to this group? Yet Americans under, say, 40 are no longer quite as special as they were, as Americans under 28, in 1972. The passions ignited by Vietnam have faded; their view of themselves as society's victims, especially in the case of the affluent college educated, has grown thin. This group is more liberal on cultural and foreign issues than their elders; they do have a different perspective. But the differences may not be so great—and they do not have a good record of turning out to vote. Yet on something like this base the Hart candidacy depends. He has no real strength among those blocs that comprised virtually the whole Democratic Convention which nominated John Kennedy in 1960. It is hard to see how he will appeal much to old-line union members or urban ethnics, nor does he have close ties to big state governors or big city mayors; his reputation for cultural liberalism and his lack of identification with civil rights seems to leave him little chance to win many primary votes in the South. Yet ideas are the wild cards of American presidential politics. Hart understood, when no one else did, how certain ideas about Vietnam could make a rather pedestrian senator from South Dakota the master, for a moment anyway, of the Democratic Party. Now he insists that he is campaigning at his own pace and on his own issues; and in matters of pace and issues American politics has few more perceptive practitioners.

Colorado's junior senator, William Armstrong, is less well known, but in 1981 and 1982 at least he was much more influential. At age 45, Armstrong already had 20 years' experience as a legislator; he was first elected to the Colorado House in 1962. He was later majority leader of the state Senate, and helped to draw the new congressional district, the 5th, which he was the first to represent, in 1972. For most of his House career, he was aiming for the Senate; and in 1978, a good Republican year, he was able to soundly beat Floyd Haskell, a Democrat who won an unexpected victory in 1972 and did not return as often to the state later as voters have come to expect.

With the Republican capture of the Senate in 1980, Armstrong catapulted out of obscurity into exceedingly important positions. He became second ranking Republican on the Budget Committee; he chaired the Social Security Subcommittee on Finance; he served on the President's Social Security Commission. Armstrong brought to these positions firm convictions. Although he has served for years in government, and made his money in a heavily regulated industry (broadcasting), he wants to cut the size of government and increase the strength and vitality of the private sector. And unlike many other young Republican senators, he has shown that he knows how to get what he wants.

One example, which could prove to be the most important, came in the fight over the Reagan tax bill in August 1981. Without fanfare, Armstrong introduced and got the Senate to adopt an indexing provision. This means that after 1985, unless Congress repeals it, progressive income tax rates will be adjusted downward to take account of inflation. This is a change in our system of potentially far-reaching effect, and no one knows exactly how it will work. Armstrong makes the attractive argument that the government shouldn't let inflation push people with the same real incomes into higher tax brackets. But others question whether any one index factor can reflect inflation accurately and fairly (the Consumer Price Index overstated inflation in the late 1970s—one of the reasons why Social Security, which is indexed, got into financial trouble). And in early 1983 the revenue that would be lost through indexing became very attractive to politicians—not all of them advocates of big government—who saw otherwise the prospect of never-ending deficits. Armstrong can be counted on to defend indexing vigorously, but he may have a difficult fight.

And if it comes to that, he will fight. Armstrong demonstrated that in 1981 on the budget and in 1983 on Social Security. On taxes, Armstrong led a group of Republican conservatives against the Reagan budget in 1981, arguing presciently that the administration was not providing long-term savings and cuts needed to hold down deficits. Their unexpected defection forced the administration—and the Democrats—to fashion a compromise closer to their position. It was a classic example of a well-timed maneuver forcing the center to move toward an extreme. On Social Security, Armstrong led three dissenters on the Commission. He objected, reasonably given his perspective, that the commission closed the Social Security gap mostly by raising taxes rather than cutting promised future benefits; and he argued, that in a recession particularly, the tax burden is simply too high. Although Armstrong does not want Social Security dismantled, it seems clear that he thinks society would be better off with more savings in the private sector (i.e., in investments, pensions, etc., which could provide capital), and less in the public sector (i.e., in Social Security). He has had the courage to take a stand, in what for him is an election year, on this very sensitive issue—rather than just writing an article about it.

Still, there is reason for Armstrong to approach 1984 with confidence. In national contests,

Colorado still seems pretty solidly Republican; Reagan carried the state easily in 1980, and party registration moved toward the Republicans in 1982. Armstrong himself is a vigorous campaigner who has kept up with Colorado issues.

Like Gary Hart, who at a similar stage in the Carter years had made a name for himself on national issues, Armstrong may have national ambitions. Already in 1983 he was being mentioned by a few conservatives as a vice presidential nominee on some ticket if Ronald Reagan doesn't run again. And some see him as a presidential candidate in 1988.

Presidential politics. For all its trend-setting reputation, Colorado does not bulk large in presidential campaigning. Its national convention delegates are chosen by party caucuses. The Republicans are dominated by conservatives like Joseph Coors of the beer family; this group has given the nation such officials as Interior Secretary James Watt and former EPA Administrator Anne Gorsuch Burford. The Democrats are dominated by liberals of the Vietnam generation; they have given us Carter administration Peace Corps Director (and former Colorado state Treasurer) Sam Brown. In close general elections over the past 40 years Colorado has been Republican. It was the only western state to go against FDR twice (1940, 1944); it went easily for Nixon in 1960 and 1968, and for Ford in 1976. Even now it has only eight electoral votes, and seems unlikely to be a target for the Democrats in 1984—unless, of course, Gary Hart is on the ticket.

Congressional districting. Control over congressional districting was split between the Republican legislature and Democratic Governor Lamm. After lengthy argument, they couldn't agree, and a federal court came up with one of the more sensible plans around the country—and a vast improvement from what Colorado had before. Virtually the whole Western Slope was placed in one district (the 3d), instead of being split in two. Ditto for most of the eastern plains, which were combined with Front Range towns outside the Denver metropolitan area, places with which they have more in common than with Denver. The new 6th district was placed entirely in the Denver suburbs. The three Democratic incumbents were strengthened or left in similar condition; the two Republican incumbents were left with safe districts, and the new district seemed safely Republican.

The People   Est. Pop. 1982: 3,045,000; Pop. 1980: 2,889,964, up 5.3% 1980–82 and 30.8% 1970–80; 1.3% of U.S. total, 27th largest; voting age pop. 2,081,151; 9.8% Spanish origin, 3% Black, 1% Asian origin, 1% American Indian. Single ancestry: 11% German, 9% English, 4% Irish, 2% Italian, 1% Swedish, French, Dutch, Polish, Scottish, Norwegian. Registered voters (1982): 1,464,549 Total. 536,146 unaffiliated (37%); 465,566 D (32%); 462,837 R (32%). 21% with 1–3 yrs. col., 23% with 4+ yrs. col. 10.2% below poverty level. 32% housing units rented; median house value: $64,600; median monthly rent: $225. Households: 70% family, 39% with children, 59% married couples.

1982 Share of Federal Tax Burden $8,270,700,000; 1.38% of U.S. total, 23d largest.

1982 Share of Federal Expenditures

	Total		Non-Defense		Defense	
Total Expend	$7,613m	(1.26%)	$5,194m	(1.22%)	$2,419m	(1.35%)
St/Lcl Grants	967m	(1.10%)	967m	(1.10%)	0m	(0%)
Salary/Wages	1,600m	(2.05%)	631m	(2.31%)	969m	(1.91%)
Ind Payments	3,105m	(1.09%)	2,531m	(0.98%)	574m	(2.01%)
Procurement	1,828m	(1.25%)	756m	(2.40%)	1,071m	(0.94%)
Other Programs	114m	(2.11%)	112m	(2.08%)	2m	(4.65%)
Loan/Insurance	976m	(1.53%)	874m	(1.42%)	102m	(4.64%)

Political Lineup   Governor, Richard D. Lamm (D). Senators, Gary W. Hart (D) and William L. Armstrong (R). Representatives, 6 (3 D and 3 R). State Senate, 35 (21 R and 14 D); State House of Representatives, 65 (40 R and 25 D).

Presidential Vote

1980	Reagan (R)	652,264	(55%)
	Carter (D)	368,009	(31%)
	Anderson (I)	130,633	(11%)
1976	Ford (R)	584,278	(54%)
	Carter (D)	460,801	(43%)

SENATORS

Sen. Gary W. Hart (D) Elected 1974, seat up 1986; b. Nov. 28, 1937, Ottawa, KS; home, Denver; Bethany Col., Yale U., LL.B. 1964; Protestant.

Career Atty., U.S. Dept. of Justice; Special Asst. to U.S. Secy. of Interior; Practicing atty., 1967–74; Natl. Campaign Dir., McGovern for Pres., 1971–72.

Offices 237 RSOB, 202-224-5852. Also 1748 High St., Denver 80218, 303-837-4421; and 303 Fed. Bldg., Pueblo 81003, 303-544-5277, ext. 355.

Committees *Armed Services* (4th). Subcommittees: Military Construction; Strategic and Theater Nuclear Forces; Sea Power and Force Projection. *Budget* (6th). *Environment and Public Works* (4th). Subcommittees: Environmental Pollution; Nuclear Regulation; Toxic Substances and Environmental Oversight.

Group Ratings

	ADA	ACLU	COPE	CFA	LCV	LWV	NTU	NSI	COC	ACA	CSFC
1982	95	96	79	90	66	83	9	30	40	15	32
1981	95	—	77	64	72	—	5	—	11	17	31
1980	61	83	47	53	73	75	48	30	39	36	36

National Journal Ratings

	Economic		Foreign		Cultural	
1982	78%	(LIB)	90%	(LIB)	89%	(LIB)
	21%	(CONS)	3%	(CONS)	10%	(CONS)
1981	87%	(LIB)	88%	(LIB)	81%	(LIB)
	12%	(CONS)	9%	(CONS)	18%	(CONS)

Key Votes

1) Reagan 81 Budget	AGN	5) $ to El Salvador	AGN	9) Poor Pay Food Stamps	AGN
2) Reagan 81 Tax Cut	AGN	6) Saudi AWACS Sale	AGN	10) Ban Crt Busing Order	AGN
3) Bal Budget Amend	AGN	7) Ban Abortion	AGN	11) Clinch Riv Brdr Rctr	AGN
4) Gas & Road Tax	FOR	8) Nerve Gas Prod	AGN	12) Legal Services Corp	—

Election Results

1980 general	Gary W. Hart (D)	590,501	(50%)	($1,142,304)
	Mary Estill Buchanan (R)	571,295	(49%)	($1,099,945)
1980 primary	Gary W. Hart (D)	105,592	(100%)	
1974 general	Gary W. Hart (D)	471,691	(57%)	($352,557)
	Peter H. Dominick (R)	325,508	(39%)	($502,343)

Campaign Contributions and Expenditures

	1979-80		*PACS brkdwn*		
Receipts	$1,184,979	Agr	$1,800	Ideo	$40,738
Expend.	$1,142,304	Bus	$53,770	Lbr	$147,762
Unspent	$320,741	Hlth	$3,750	Prof	$7,950

Sen. William L. Armstrong (R) Elected 1978, seat up 1984; b. Mar. 16, 1937, Fremont, NE; home, Aurora; Tulane U., U. of MN; Lutheran.

Career Pres., KOSI Radio, Aurora; CO House of Reps., 1963–64; CO Senate, 1965–72, Major. Ldr., 1969–72; U.S. House of Reps., 1973–78.

Offices 528 DSOB, 202-224-5941. Also 1450 S. Havana, Su. 736, Aurora 80012, 303-837-2655.

Committees *Banking, Housing and Urban Affairs* (4th). Subcommittees: Federal Credit Programs; Financial Institutions (Chairman); International Finance and Monetary Policy. *Budget* (2d). *Finance* (9th). Subcommittees:Taxation and Debt Management; International Trade; Social Security and Income Maintenance Programs (Chairman). *Governmental Affairs* (10th). Subcommittees: Civil Service, Post Office, and General Services; Intergovernmental Relations; Permanent Subcommittee on Investigations.

Group Ratings

	ADA	ACLU	COPE	CFA	LCV	LWV	NTU	NSI	COC	ACA	CSFC
1982	10	11	1	10	31	36	92	100	67	100	86
1981	5	—	2	21	26	—	93	—	94	90	88
1980	17	30	5	0	27	20	75	90	88	92	84

National Journal Ratings

	Economic		Foreign		Cultural	
1982	4%	(LIB)	3%	(LIB)	7%	(LIB)
	94%	(CONS)	84%	(CONS)	92%	(CONS)
1981	17%	(LIB)	27%	(LIB)	1%	(LIB)
	79%	(CONS)	71%	(CONS)	98%	(CONS)

Key Votes

1) Reagan 81 Budget	FOR	5) $ to El Salvador	FOR	9) Poor Pay Food Stamps	FOR
2) Reagan 81 Tax Cut	FOR	6) Saudi AWACS Sale	FOR	10) Ban Crt Busing Order	FOR
3) Bal Budget Amend	FOR	7) Ban Abortion	FOR	11) Clinch Riv Brdr Rctr	AGN
4) Gas & Road Tax	AGN	8) Nerve Gas Prod	FOR	12) Legal Services Corp	AGN

Election Results

1978 general	William L. Armstrong (R)	480,596	(59%)	($1,081,944)
	Floyd K. Haskell (D)	330,247	(40%)	($664,249)
1978 primary	William L. Armstrong (R)	109,021	(73%)	
	Jack Swigert (R)	39,415	(27%)	($321,545)
1972 general	Floyd K. Haskell (D)	457,545	(49%)	($176,234)
	Gordon Allott (R)	447,957	(48%)	($308,305)

Campaign Contributions and Expenditures

1977–1978				PACS brkdwn	
Receipts	$1,163,790	Agr	$11,550	Ideo	$28,229
Expend.	$1,081,944	Bus	$258,251	Lbr	$—
Unspent	$111,165	Hlth	$19,000	Prof	$5,400

GOVERNOR

Gov. Richard D. Lamm (D) Elected 1974, term expires Jan. 1987; b. Aug. 3, 1935, Madison, WI; home, Denver; U. of WI, B.A. 1957, U. of CA, LL.B. 1961; Unitarian Universalist.

Career CPA, 1961–62. Atty., CO Anti-Discrimination Comm., 1962–63; Practicing atty., 1963–75; CO House of Reps., 1966–75, Asst. Minor. Ldr., 1971–74; Assoc. Prof. of Law, U. of Denver, 1969–75.

Offices State Capitol, Rm. 136, Denver 80203, 303-866-2471.

Election Results

1982 gen.	Richard D. Lamm (D)	627,960	(66%)
	John Fuhr (R)	302,740	(32%)
1982 prim.	Richard D. Lamm (D)	107,872	(100%)
1978 gen.	Richard D. Lamm (D)	483,885	(59%)
	Ted Strickland (R)	317,232	(39%)

FIRST DISTRICT

The city of Denver is the center, the focus, of the entire Rocky Mountain region. The old gold dome on the state Capitol, the gleaming new skyscrapers pushing up—these are the tangible symbols of Denver's riches, first from mining, more recently from oil. Surrounded by hundreds of miles of mountains on one side and High Plains on the other, Denver has become one of the nation's major metropolises. In the process, development has spread far beyond its original city limits, and the city itself, and the 1st congressional district, which is almost precisely coterminous, contains less than one-third of the metropolitan area's 1.6 million people.

To many easterners, Denver doesn't look like a central city at all. It does have stockyards, some grimy old warehouses, and light manufacturing plants in its industrial corridor along the (usually dry) South Platte River. It does have some unpleasant slums—and nasty brawls between blacks, Mexicans, and even Vietnamese. But for the most part Denver looks like a carefully manicured suburb, with small, pleasant houses on almost miniature lots on neatly maintained streets. The orderliness and the lack of spaciousness here are characteristically Western, even though less than 20 miles away there are acres and acres of vacant plains. The water supply is limited, and you can build only where there is water. So Denver is closely settled, and the High Plains are not littered with jerry-built suburbs.

That same environment is what has attracted so many young people to the Denver area—producing great population growth and a quiet transformation of the central city. Fifteen years ago, Denver, outside its slums, was not much different demographically from its

COLORADO — Congressional Districts, Counties, and Selected Places — (6 Districts)

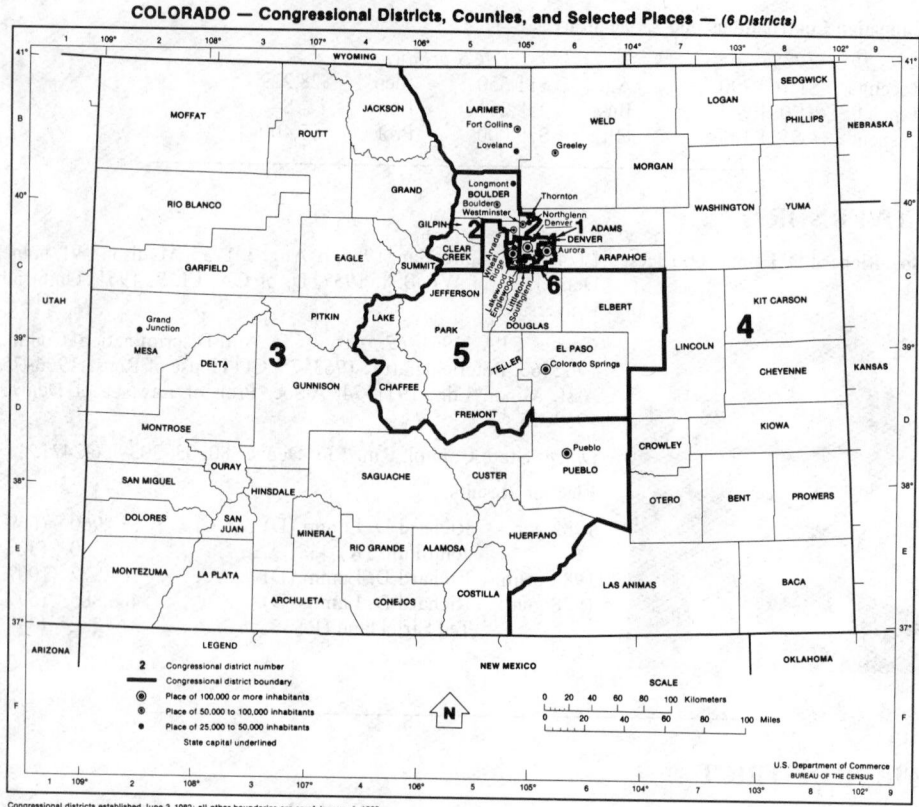

suburbs: a city full of middle class white families. But young families in recent years have moved mostly to the suburbs, and the city itself has attracted a disproportionate number of young singles. They, and the older residents whose children have grown and left, account for the fact that only one in four households here has children, and that less than half include a married couple. Demographically, Denver has come to look a little like San Francisco.

That has produced important political changes. Denver has always been a little more Democratic than its suburbs, but as recently as 1970 the 1st congressional district elected a Republican congressman, in part because his Democratic opponent favored a controversial school busing order. Now Denver's attitudes tend to be liberal on both economic and non-economic issues, and it is one of the most safely Democratic parts of Colorado (the others are the industrial city of Pueblo and the Spanish counties in the south). The businessmen who built the huge skyscrapers and the oil company managers who work in them may believe in unregulated free enterprise and economic growth, in traditional family values and a strong military. But the young whites of Denver, and to some extent its Mexican-Americans and blacks, who live in the neighborhoods in the skyscrapers' shadows, tend to have different values and beliefs.

Those values and beliefs are represented with fair accuracy by Congresswoman Patricia Schroeder. She was first elected in 1972, in an upset, at a time when not many women ran for

Congress: this was one of those victories for young, anti-Vietnam war, pro-environmentalist Democrats that set the tone for Colorado in the early 1970s. It was a textbook campaign, and a victory that irritated conservatives for years; they consider Schroeder flaky and have spent large sums trying to beat her even though her Denver district gets safer and safer. By 1982 they seem to have given up. The legislature left Denver as a single district, making no attempt to dilute its votes; and the Republicans ran only a desultory campaign against her.

In Washington Schroeder won a seat on the Armed Services Committee, over the heated objection of then Chairman F. Edward Hebert, who did not like the idea of an anti-war woman on the committee, and did his best to make Schroeder uncomfortable. It was unavailing: she was not going to be embarrassed off the committee. She is now the 9th ranking Democrat on Armed Services, just below the level that would, by seniority, entitle her to a subcommittee chairmanship. She has been active on personnel matters, particularly pensions and various regulations affecting women in the service; she has worked to get chemical weaponry out of the Rocky Mountain Arsenal near Denver; she has opposed most controversial weapons systems.

Such opposition is never successful on the committee, most of whose members believe in high defense spending and tend to trust the Pentagon's recommendations. But Schroeder's views have, in the middle 1970s and perhaps again in the middle 1980s, found support on the floor. Schroeder is not one of the weightiest of Pentagon opponents when it comes to swaying opinion on the floor, but she is well enough prepared not to be disregarded either. She also serves on the Judiciary Committee, where she is a solid vote against an anti-abortion constitutional amendment and for the Equal Rights Amendment. And she chairs a Post Office and Civil Service Subcommittee, in which capacity she is likely to be a champion of federal workers; Denver is one of the federal government's major regional centers, and has a large number of well-organized federal employees.

The People Pop. 1980: 481,672, dn. 5.5% 1970–80; voting age pop. 373,579; 15% Span. orig., 11% Black, 1% Asian orig., 1% Am. Ind. 47% housing units rented. Median owner $63,600; renter $214. Households: 55% family, 26% with children, 42% married couples.

Presidential Vote

1980			
	Reagan (R)	80,698	(41%)
	Carter (D)	81,547	(42%)
	Other	32,761	(17%)

Rep. Patricia Schroeder (D) Elected 1972; b. July 30, 1940, Portland, OR; home, Denver; U. of MN, B.S. 1961, Harvard U., J.D. 1964; United Church of Christ.

Career Field Atty., Natl. Labor Relations Bd., 1964–66; Practicing atty.; Lecturer and Law Instructor, Comm. Col. of Denver, 1969–70, U. of Denver, Denver Ctr., 1969, Regis Col., 1970–72; Hearing Officer, CO Dept. of Personnel, 1971–72; Legal Counsel, CO Planned Parenthood.

Offices 2410 RHOB, 202-225-4431. Also Denver Fed. Bldg., 1767 High St., Denver 80218, 303-837-2354.

Committees *Armed Services* (9th). Subcommittees: Research and Development; Military Personnel and Compensation. *Judiciary* (11th). Subcommittee: Civil and Constitutional Rights. *Post Office and Civil Service* (4th). Subcommittee: Civil Service (Chairwoman). *Select Committee on Children, Youth and Families* (3d).

Group Ratings

	ADA	ACLU	COPE	CFA	LCV	LWV	NTU	NSI	COC	ACA	CSFC
1982	90	83	74	90	95	90	56	0	25	9	31
1981	95	—	73	93	91	—	81	—	6	26	38
1980	94	100	56	71	85	88	30	0	55	25	44

National Journal Ratings

	Economic		Foreign		Cultural	
1982	82%	(LIB)	84%	(LIB)	93%	(LIB)
	18%	(CONS)	16%	(CONS)	3%	(CONS)
1981	80%	(LIB)	83%	(LIB)	88%	(LIB)
	20%	(CONS)	16%	(CONS)	11%	(CONS)

Key Votes

1) Reagan 81 Budget	AGN	5) Incr SS Rtmt Age	AGN	9) Poor Pay Food Stamps	AGN
2) Reagan 81 Tax Cut	AGN	6) Saudi AWACS Sale	AGN	10) Ban Crt Busing Order	AGN
3) Bal Budget Amend	AGN	7) $ for MX Missile	AGN	11) Auto Local Content	—
4) Gas & Road Tax	AGN	8) Nerve Gas Prod	AGN	12) Nuclear Arms Freeze	FOR

Election Results

1982 general	Patricia Schroeder (D)	94,969	(60%)	($210,420)
	Arch Decker (R)	59,009	(37%)	($251,406)
1982 primary	Patricia Schroeder (D)	21,553	(100%)	
1980 general	Patricia Schroeder (D)	107,364	(60%)	($181,299)
	Naomi Bradford (R)	67,804	(38%)	($118,417)

Campaign Contributions and Expenditures

1981-82		Direct Cont. 81-82		PACS brkdwn			
Receipts	$247,391	Indiv	$140,985	Agr	$300	Ideo	$14,325
Expend.	$210,420	Party	$1,500	Bus	$19,125	Lbr	$44,080
Unspent	$90,407	PACS	$86,452	Hlth	$2,650	Prof	$2,800

SECOND DISTRICT

The 2d congressional district of Colorado is one of the suburban Denver districts. Republican in national elections, it appears to be solidly Democratic in congressional contests. This is testimony to the political strength of Congressman Timothy Wirth, who has represented the 2d since 1974. But, since the 1982 redistricting, this has become a more Democratic district. It includes the high income suburb of Arvada, northwest of Denver, but here also now are the suburbs directly north of the city where voters, while generally affluent, are more likely to come from blue collar backgrounds and make their living in blue collar jobs—Westminster, Thornton, Northglenn. There are also more Mexican-Americans here, not isolated in a small ghetto, but moving, mostly unnoticed, into various middle class neighborhoods in upwardly mobile fashion, like similar immigrant groups before them.

The 2d district also proceeds north along the Front Range to Longmont, a small city that is culturally beyond the Denver orbit, and into the mountains, to onetime mining boom towns like Central City which now, thanks to Interstate 80, are just about within commuting time of Denver. The biggest and most distinctive city in the district, however, is Boulder, the home of the University of Colorado. Before students got the vote, in 1972, this was a Republican town: affluent, comfortable, satisfied with the status quo. The student voters changed that: they opposed the Vietnam war, wanted to choke off population growth and economic development, sought approval of diverse lifestyles. They made Boulder more Democratic—and sparked a series of bitter town vs. gown local elections. Sometimes the student voters received setbacks, but on balance their views and values have ended up influencing even those voters who have fought their efforts. Boulder and the working class suburbs, in their different ways, provide a voting base for an adept Democrat, which Tim Wirth has proved to be.

One of the stars of the large Democratic freshman class of 1974, Wirth is arguably one of the most powerful and important members of the House today. Handsome, educated in elite schools despite a modest economic background, well connected around Washington after stints as a White House Fellow and at the old HEW Department, Wirth helped organize the freshmen to press for good committee assignments and for ouster of some committee chairmen. He also attracted notice because he did not always take stereotyped positions. One of the continuing battles of the 1970s was the struggle over price controls on oil and gas. Most traditional northern Democrats backed controls, as protection for the ordinary citizen. But Wirth and some other younger Democrats, many from traditionally Republican districts, argued that controls were ineffective in holding down prices of commodities traded in a world market, and served only to diminish supplies by reducing incentives for exploration. This was a popular argument in his constituency, which then included high income suburbs like Lakewood and Golden rather than Westminster and Northglenn; many residents there were in the oil business themselves. In the long run, Wirth's argument and position seem to have prevailed: price controls are being phased out, and despite concern about natural gas prices in 1983 controls have little political or intellectual support any more.

Wirth's power in the House comes not just from his organizing ability and the strength of his arguments. He also has perhaps the choicest committee assignments of any young member. He is one of the high ranking Democrats on the Budget Committee; and given his position on issues, one of the key bloc of middle votes. He is a member of the Energy and Commerce Committee, a body not particularly glamorous in 1974 but the most sought after assignment in 1982. The reason: Commerce has jurisdiction over most of the regulatory agencies, over important regulatory issues like clean air, over many health issues. It is a committee to which lobbyists pay close attention and whose members can expect contributions from a whole raft of political action committees. Many lobbyists are happy just to get Commerce members to return their phone calls.

Wirth has played an important role on clean air issues in the Health Subcommittee, but he is even more important as the Chairman of the old Communications Subcommittee (now Telecommunications, Consumer Protection and Finance). This body has jurisdiction over all broadcasting regulation and over the rapidly expanding field of telecommunications. The decisions it makes may do more to affect the quality and substance of American life 40 years from now than any other subcommittee. Wirth has backed some deregulation of broadcasting, a position not universally popular with broadcasters, some of whom prefer protection of their franchises. In 1982, after the Justice Department settled its antitrust suit against AT&T, Wirth wrote a bill regulating the way in which the telephone company should be split up. It is hard to overstate the importance, or complexity, of this issue; and it is a testimony to his legislative skill that he was able to get unanimous approval of his bill in his subcommittee. But AT&T decided that it didn't like Wirth's terms and found a member of the full Commerce Committee—Tom Corcoran of Illinois—willing to advance its cause. More important, it sent out mailings to AT&T's hundreds of thousands of shareholders, urging them to oppose Wirth's bill. Before that kind of lobbying force—something AT&T had never brought into play before—support for Wirth's bill wilted, and he withdrew it from consideration himself. It was, nonetheless, testimony to his skill as a legislator and his in-depth knowledge of an important field. Advanced technology is relentlessly changing the telecommunications business, and Tim Wirth is almost sure to be a major—perhaps the major—figure in determining government's response to that change in the years ahead.

The 1982 redistricting tends to ensure that: it makes Wirth's district significantly safer. He won reelection by only narrow margins in 1976 and 1978, and after massive campaign efforts that included not only television advertising but also a series of election- and non-election-year Washington seminars for interested constituents. He labored hard to identify himself with the interests of his skilled, high tech constituency. By 1980, it paid off, and he won more easily; in 1982, in the new district, he won with 62% of the vote. Such victories do not come cheap: Wirth raised and spent more than $700,000 in 1982. The ability to raise that kind of money, and the new arithmetic of the district, are likely to scare off strong opponents. But as long as he represents the Denver suburbs, Wirth can never take reelection for granted.

It has been suggested that Wirth might want to run for the Senate. But that seems unlikely. Colorado already has two strongly entrenched senators. And how could Wirth expect to have more clout and influence on legislation as a junior senator than he has now?

The People Pop. 1980: 481,617, up 50.4% 1970–80; voting age pop. 339,617; 5% Span. orig., 1% Black, 1% Asian orig., 1% Am. Ind. 29% housing units rented. Median owner $70,500; renter $266. Households: 73% family, 44% with children, 62% married couples.

Presidential Vote

1980	Reagan (R)	95,800	(51%)
	Carter (D)	60,882	(32%)
	Other	31,156	(17%)

Rep. Timothy E. Wirth (D) Elected 1974; b. Sept. 22, 1939, Santa Fe, NM; home, Denver; Harvard U., A.B. 1961, M. Ed. 1964, Stanford U., Ph.D. 1973; Episcopal.

Career White House Fellow, Spec. Asst. to Secy. of HEW, 1967–68; Dpty. Asst. Secy. of Educ., HEW, 1969–70; Businessman, Great Western United Corp.; Mgr., Rocky Mt. Ofc., Arthur D. Little, Inc., consultants.

Offices 2454 RHOB, 202-225-2161. Also 9485 W. Colfax, Lakewood 80215, 303-234-5200.

Committees *Budget* (4th). Task Forces: Energy and Technology (Chairman); Education and Employment; International Finance and Trade. *Energy and Commerce* (5th). Subcommittees: Health and the Environment; Telecommunications, Consumer Protection and Finance (Chairman).

Group Ratings

	ADA	ACLU	COPE	CFA	LCV	LWV	NTU	NSI	COC	ACA	CSFC
1982	95	83	74	90	89	83	31	11	14	22	25
1981	85	—	73	93	73	—	35	—	21	10	34
1980	78	87	50	71	79	100	19	0	67	22	31

National Journal Ratings

	Economic		Foreign		Cultural	
1982	71%	(LIB)	85%	(LIB)	93%	(LIB)
	29%	(CONS)	12%	(CONS)	3%	(CONS)
1981	63%	(LIB)	85%	(LIB)	88%	(LIB)
	36%	(CONS)	13%	(CONS)	11%	(CONS)

Key Votes

1) Reagan 81 Budget	AGN	5) Incr SS Rtmt Age	AGN	9) Poor Pay Food Stamps	AGN
2) Reagan 81 Tax Cut	AGN	6) Saudi AWACS Sale	AGN	10) Ban Crt Busing Order	AGN
3) Bal Budget Amend	AGN	7) $ for MX Missile	AGN	11) Auto Local Content	FOR
4) Gas & Road Tax	FOR	8) Nerve Gas Prod	AGN	12) Nuclear Arms Freeze	FOR

Election Results

1982 general	Timothy E. Wirth (D)	101,194	(62%)	($750,295)
	John Buechner (R)	59,580	(36%)	($125,547)
1982 primary	Timothy E. Wirth (D)	72,874	(100%)	
1980 general	Timothy E. Wirth (D)	153,550	(56%)	($548,261)
	John McElderry (R)	111,868	(41%)	($193,072)

Campaign Contributions and Expenditures

1981-82		Direct Cont. 81-82		PACS brkdwn			
Receipts	$791,458	Indiv	$546,764	Agr	$12,300	Ideo	$19,900
Expend.	$750,295	Party	$900	Bus	$129,500	Lbr	$41,650
Unspent	$42,175	PACS	$220,629	Hlth	$800	Prof	$7,350

Indep Expend: For: $371

THIRD DISTRICT

The 3d congressional district of Colorado consists of two geographically and politically distinct parts. The first is just east of the Rockies, around and including the industrial city of Pueblo. This is not one of Colorado's glamour spots: its biggest industries historically have been steel (it has one of the few major steel plants west of the Mississippi) and meatpacking. It is, however, a pleasant community that has managed to remain stable and prosperous despite the general condition of steelmaking and meatpacking. Pueblo is heavily Democratic, and so are the Hispanic counties just to the south. Hispanic, not Mexican-American: the Spanish-speaking people here, like those in northern New Mexico, have been living here for generations. Altogether, this part of the 3d casts about one-fourth of its votes.

The other part of the district is almost the entire Western Slope—that is, the mountainous region west of the Front Range. Interspersed among the mountains are, literally, all sorts of communities: ghost towns suddenly rendered accessible by plane and fashionable to affluent outsiders who renovate their old buildings and erect new ski lifts (Aspen is the prototype), Hispanic villages where people live in poverty much as they have for hundreds of years, mining camps thrown up more recently by explorers for uranium, oil, and natural gas, and would-be extractors of oil shale. Where miners once built Victorian gingerbread houses and, in some towns, ornate opera houses, today they tend to favor trailers or prefabricated dwellings, small steel and glass stores and restaurants; 19th century miners undoubtedly left their garbage and tailings lying around, but were they as unsightly as the detritus of today's mining camps? The largest city on the Western Slope, Grand Junction, is a sort of large mining camp itself; it woke up one day in the 1970s to find that the uranium tailings it had been using as fill dirt were radioactive.

Except in enclaves like Aspen or Vail, the fashionable environmentalism of metropolitan Denver has little appeal in either segment of the 3d district. Election contests here tend to be struggles between labor-backed Democrats and Republicans who favor untrammeled development of mineral resources. That was the case in 1982, when Ray Kogovsek, a Pueblo Democrat first elected in 1978, managed to hold onto this sharply changed seat. Kogovsek lost a lot of territory east of the Rockies, some of which he was probably glad to see go (part of Republican Colorado Springs, some Republican plains counties), but some of which backed him heavily (Hispanic Las Animas County). And he gained several counties in the northern part of the Western Slope where mining exploration has been fiercest: the oil shale country in far northwest Colorado, now fearful because of Exxon's sudden abandonment of its shale project; the uranium country around Grand Junction, unhappy with the drop in uranium prices.

Republican Tom Wiens, a young businessman from the Western Slope, tried to capitalize on these apprehensions, and carried the Western Slope counties, which cast 73% of the district's votes. But Kogovsek won 70% of the vote in Pueblo and adjoining counties, which gave him nearly a 20,000-vote margin; in this recession year, turnout in Pueblo was hardly down from the 1980 presidential year. But this should not be considered a safe seat for Kogovsek. His percentage in three elections has not risen above the marginal level, and he has yet to prove that he can carry the Western Slope counties. He cannot necessarily count on a high turnout from Pueblo; and Republicans, who apparently did not target this district in 1982, could direct a lot more money to their nominee.

In the House, Kogovsek is Colorado's most labor-oriented and traditional Democrat. He serves on Education and Labor, where he is a solid labor vote, and on Interior, where he supports many environmental causes and can also attend to local interests—mining, water, wilderness designations. A veteran legislator—he served 10 years in Denver before his election to Congress—he is not yet a leader in Congress.

The People Pop. 1980: 481,854, up 29.5% 1970–80; voting age pop. 345,175; 15% Span. orig., 1% Black, 1% Am. Ind. 24% housing units rented. Median owner $48,900; renter $198. Households: 72% family, 40% with children, 62% married couples.

Presidential Vote

1980	Reagan (R)	104,676	(57%)
	Carter (D)	60,099	(33%)
	Other	19,331	(10%)

Rep. Ray Kogovsek (D) Elected 1978; b. Aug. 19, 1941, Pueblo; home, Pueblo; Pueblo Jr. Col., 1960–62, Adams St. Col., B.S. 1964; Roman Catholic.

Career Pueblo Cnty. Chief Dpty. Clerk, 1964–72; CO House of Reps., 1969–71; CO Senate, 1971–78, Minor. Ldr., 1973–78.

Offices 430 CHOB, 202-225-4761. Also United Bank Bldg., Rm. 425, Pueblo 81003, 303-544-5277, ext. 313.

Committees Education and Labor (16th). Subcommittees: Employment Opportunities; Post Secondary Education. *Interior and Insular Affairs* (16th). Subcommittees: Mining, Forest Management, and BPA; Public Lands and National Parks; Water and Power Resources.

Group Ratings

	ADA	ACLU	COPE	CFA	LCV	LWV	NTU	NSI	COC	ACA	CSFC
1982	70	71	83	70	62	58	18	20	30	22	32
1981	80	—	83	64	57	—	12	—	16	9	33
1980	56	43	72	50	44	56	25	20	55	22	38

National Journal Ratings

	Economic		Foreign		Cultural	
1982	79%	(LIB)	81%	(LIB)	64%	(LIB)
	20%	(CONS)	19%	(CONS)	35%	(CONS)
1981	77%	(LIB)	68%	(LIB)	81%	(LIB)
	21%	(CONS)	32%	(CONS)	19%	(CONS)

Key Votes

1) Reagan 81 Budget	AGN	5) Incr SS Rtmt Age	AGN
2) Reagan 81 Tax Cut	AGN	6) Saudi AWACS Sale	AGN
3) Bal Budget Amend	AGN	7) $ for MX Missile	AGN
4) Gas & Road Tax	FOR	8) Nerve Gas Prod	AGN

9) Poor Pay Food Stamps	AGN
10) Ban Crt Busing Order	AGN
11) Auto Local Content	FOR
12) Nuclear Arms Freeze	FOR

Election Results

1982 general	Ray Kogovsek (D)	92,384	(53%)	($329,557)
	Tom Wiens (R)	77,409	(45%)	($142,463)
1982 primary	Ray Kogovsek (D)	34,952	(100%)	
1980 general	Ray Kogovsek (D)	105,820	(55%)	($301,626)
	Harold L. McCormick (R)	84,292	(44%)	($255,896)

Campaign Contributions and Expenditures

1981-82		Direct Cont. 81-82		PACS brkdwn			
Receipts	$325,423	Indiv	$113,280	Agr	$20,650	Ideo	$13,050
Expend.	$329,557	Party	$11,435	Bus	$38,100	Lbr	$106,675
Unspent	$1,502	PACS	$189,185	Hlth	$3,200	Prof	$2,400

Indep Expend: Agn: $7,521 (NCPAC)

FOURTH DISTRICT

The 4th congressional district of Colorado includes most of the state's High Plains—the brown, dusty western edge of the great American flatlands that are the world's single richest stretch of agricultural land. Out here, however, it's not easy to wrest a living from the plains. Rainfall is scarce, the rivers most of the year are just a trickle, and in many places groundwater is scarce: it's hard to find enough water to irrigate wheatlands or swab out a feedlot. Nonetheless, Coloradans try; and when hard times hit the plains, they are among the first to cry out. The American Agricultural Movement, for example, had its beginnings in this part of Colorado.

The High Plains contain most of the 4th district's land; a thin strip of settlement along the Front Range, north of Denver, contains most of the district's people. The major cities here, Greeley and Fort Collins, have universities, but they are not so liberal culturally or politically as Boulder; in most years, in most elections they, like the High Plains, vote Republican. So do the string of towns along Interstate 25 running south from Fort Collins to Denver. The only Democratic part of the 4th is its small segment of the Denver metropolitan area, the working class suburb of Commerce City and once completely agricultural Brighton, both with large Mexican-American populations.

The 4th is a solidly Republican district, and has a solidly Republican congressman, Hank Brown. A veteran of the Colorado legislature, and a former manager in the giant Monfort feedlot operation, Brown was an easy winner in 1980 when the incumbent retired; he didn't even have any competition in the Republican primary. By any definition he has a safe seat. On economic issues Brown is a solid conservative; on foreign and cultural issues he leans somewhat towards Colorado's more liberal attitudes. He serves on the Interior Committee, and has been active on difficult issues, like the disposal of nuclear waste. He is thought highly of by his colleagues and the Republican leadership and has a seat on the House's Ethics Committee.

The People Pop. 1980: 481,512, up 29.6% 1970–80; voting age pop. 342,745; 11% Span. orig., 1% Black, 1% Asian orig. 29% housing units rented. Median owner $54,000; renter $191. Households: 73% family, 41% with children, 64% married couples.

Presidential Vote

1980	Reagan (R)	104,036	(58%)
	Carter (D)	52,431	(29%)
	Other	21,945	(12%)

Rep. Hank Brown (R) Elected 1980; b. Feb. 12, 1940, Denver; home, Greeley; U. of CO, B.S. 1961, J.D. 1969; Congregationalist.

Career Navy, 1962–66; CO Senate, 1972–76, Asst. Major. Ldr., 1974; Rep. Nominee for Lt. Gov. of CO, 1978; Greeley City Planning Commission, 1979; V.P., Monfort of CO, Inc., 1969–80.

Offices 1510 LHOB, 202-225-4676. Also 1015 37th Ave. Ct., Su. 101A, Greeley 80631, 303-352-4112; 203 Fed. Bldg., Ft. Collins 80521, 303-493-9132; 230 Main St., Rm. 9, Ft. Morgan 80701, 303-867-8909; and Post Ofc. Bldg., La Junta 81050, 303-384-7370.

Committees *Interior and Insular Affairs* (9th). Subcommittees: Energy and the Environment; Water and Power Resources; Insular Affairs. *Standards of Official Conduct* (5th).

Group Ratings

	ADA	ACLU	COPE	CFA	LCV	LWV	NTU	NSI	COC	ACA	CSFC
1982	20	17	7	0	25	42	99	80	91	83	71
1981	20	—	13	43	50	—	98	—	89	75	69

National Journal Ratings

	Economic		Foreign		Cultural	
1982	0%	(LIB)	48%	(LIB)	18%	(LIB)
	98%	(CONS)	52%	(CONS)	80%	(CONS)
1981	24%	(LIB)	68%	(LIB)	42%	(LIB)
	68%	(CONS)	31%	(CONS)	58%	(CONS)

Key Votes

1) Reagan 81 Budget	FOR	5) Incr SS Rtmt Age	FOR	9) Poor Pay Food Stamps	FOR
2) Reagan 81 Tax Cut	FOR	6) Saudi AWACS Sale	AGN	10) Ban Crt Busing Order	FOR
3) Bal Budget Amend	FOR	7) $ for MX Missile	FOR	11) Auto Local Content	AGN
4) Gas & Road Tax	FOR	8) Nerve Gas Prod	AGN	12) Nuclear Arms Freeze	AGN

Election Results

1982 general	Hank Brown (R)	105,542	(70%)	($120,475)
	Charles L. (Bud) Bishopp (D)	45,750	(30%)	($15,126)
1982 primary	Hank Brown (R)	14,009	(100%)	
1980 general	Hank Brown (R)	178,221	(68%)	($233,857)
	Polly Baca Barragan (D)	76,849	(30%)	($116,186)

Campaign Contributions and Expenditures

1981-82		Direct Cont. 81-82				PACS brkdwn		
Receipts	$196,344	Indiv	$104,439	Agr	$3,450	Ideo	$550
Expend.	$120,475	Party	$18,494	Bus	$43,375	Lbr	$550
Unspent	$116,214	PACS	$52,462	Hlth	$3,950	Prof	$500

Indep Expend: For: $1,274 (NRA, Co-Housing PAC)

FIFTH DISTRICT

Colorado Springs is the second largest city in Colorado, standing almost precisely at the base of Pike's Peak. Far smaller than Denver, and once just a small town, it is now the center of a metropolitan area of 300,000 people. It is known as a tourist attraction: people come to drive the Pike's Peak road, to see the Garden of the Gods, to stay at the Broadmoor, one of America's grand old resort hotels. But the real economic mainstay of Colorado Springs for many years has been the military. Colorado Springs has been the home for years of the Army's Fort Carson, and just to the north is the Air Force Academy, its striking modern buildings silhouetted against the mountains. The military atmosphere probably strengthens Colorado Springs's disposition to Republicanism, a disposition that draws as well from the affluence and midwestern small town roots of many of its residents. Just as Pueblo, one county to the south, is solidly Democratic, so is Colorado Springs solidly Republican.

Colorado Springs is the heart and geographical center of Colorado's 5th congressional district. It goes north to the Denver metropolitan area and includes some of its suburbs: Golden, west of the city, an old mining town with a mining school and the Coors brewery, and some of the new suburbs at the southern edge of settlement. Both Denver and Colorado Springs stop quite abruptly, and the arid plains begin, where the water lines have not yet penetrated. Much of the 5th district that is now vacant will probably be developed as the Denver area continues to expand in the 1980s. The 5th district also proceeds east across the High Plains to the gas station junction of Limon and west into the Rockies to the old mining town of Leadville.

The 5th district's congressman is Ken Kramer, a native of Chicago who is a New Right Republican. In the Colorado legislature he was part of a group known as "the crazies"; he has had the satisfaction since of seeing many of his ideas being accepted as ordinary common sense. Kramer was first elected in 1978, when William Armstrong ran for the Senate; he has not had trouble winning reelection since. Not a man afraid of a fight, he serves on the Education and Labor Committee, one of the most liberal panels in the House, where he is almost always in the minority, and on Armed Services, where he must find other members' views more congenial, if not always aggressive enough.

The People Pop. 1980: 481,627, up 60.6% 1970–80; voting age pop. 335,156; 6% Span. orig., 5% Black, 1% Asian orig., 1% Am. Ind. 28% housing units rented. Median owner $66,100; renter $209. Households: 76% family, 46% with children, 66% married couples.

Presidential Vote

1980	Reagan (R)	106,216	(64%)
	Carter (D)	41,377	(25%)
	Other	19,367	(11%)

Rep. Ken Kramer (R) Elected 1978; b. Feb. 19, 1942, Chicago, IL; home, Colorado Springs; U. of IL, B.A. 1963, Harvard U., J.D. 1966; Jewish.

Career Army, 1967–70; Dpty. Dist. Atty., 4th Judicial Dist., Colorado Springs, 1970–72; Practicing atty., 1972–78; CO House of Reps., 1973–78.

Offices 114 CHOB, 202-225-4422. Also 1520 N. Union Blvd., Su. C & D, Colorado Springs 80909, 303-632-8555.

Committee *Armed Services* (11th). Subcommittees: Military Installations and Facilities; Procurement and Military Nuclear Systems.

Group Ratings

	ADA	ACLU	COPE	CFA	LCV	LWV	NTU	NSI	COC	ACA	CSFC
1982	0	17	17	10	21	36	83	100	82	78	72
1981	0	—	14	36	14	—	86	—	94	87	76
1980	0	13	12	7	22	13	68	100	72	91	82

National Journal Ratings

	Economic		Foreign		Cultural	
1982	16%	(LIB)	4%	(LIB)	18%	(LIB)
	84%	(CONS)	92%	(CONS)	80%	(CONS)
1981	4%	(LIB)	27%	(LIB)	12%	(LIB)
	79%	(CONS)	72%	(CONS)	86%	(CONS)

Key Votes

1) Reagan 81 Budget	FOR	5) Incr SS Rtmt Age	FOR
2) Reagan 81 Tax Cut	FOR	6) Saudi AWACS Sale	AGN
3) Bal Budget Amend	FOR	7) $ for MX Missile	FOR
4) Gas & Road Tax	FOR	8) Nerve Gas Prod	FOR

9) Poor Pay Food Stamps	FOR
10) Ban Crt Busing Order	FOR
11) Auto Local Content	AGN
12) Nuclear Arms Freeze	AGN

Election Results

1982 general	Ken Kramer (R)	84,479	(60%)	($395,286)
	Thomas E. Cronin (D)	57,392	(40%)	($173,907)
1982 primary	Ken Kramer (R) unopposed	25,193		
1980 general	Ken Kramer (R)	177,319	(72%)	($247,756)
	Ed Schreiber (D)	62,003	(25%)	($3,152)

Campaign Contributions and Expenditures

1981-82		Direct Cont. 81-82		PACS brkdwn			
Receipts	$390,383	Indiv	$247,730	Agr	$6,550	Ideo	$7,882
Expend.	$395,286	Party	$19,319	Bus	$87,400	Lbr	$650
Unspent	$22,348	PACS	$108,374	Hlth	$4,000	Prof	$750

Indirect Party Expend: $10,000   *Indep Expend:* For: $1,256 (NRA, Co-Housing PAC)

SIXTH DISTRICT

From the results of the 1980 Census it was apparent that the Denver suburbs were entitled to another congressional seat: hence the new 6th district. It forms a kind of U around the city of Denver. In the south, at the bottom of the U, are Englewood and Littleton, directly south of downtown Denver. These were the city's main high income suburbs in the 1940s and 1950s; today they are older, still pleasant but no longer the place where you expect to find Denver's elite. Farther to the south and east are newer suburbs and subdivisions, with names like Columbine Valley, Dream House Acres, and Cherry Knolls. West of Denver are Lakewood and Wheat Ridge, creations of the 1960s, high income but for the most part not elite suburbs with winding streets and, stuck incongruously on a highway in Lakewood, the gigantic Denver Federal Center. East of Denver, just beyond Stapleton Airport and Lowry Air Force Base, is Aurora. Bisected by the garish signs of the East Colfax strip, Aurora is the creation of the 1960s and 1970s. On the socioeconomic scale it does not rank as high as, say, Lakewood or Englewood; but in its voting habits it is comfortably Republican.

In fact, all of the 6th district is comfortably Republican in most elections. These are regions of upward mobility, places people usually not from Denver have worked their way up to. Their occupations tend to be technical or managerial, their moral values and family patterns traditional; they may pride themselves on their concern for the environment, but they also respect the need for economic growth. Their experience has persuaded them that orderliness and predictability are important virtues, all the more so in a new environment where neither they nor anyone else has deep roots. The politics of Reagan Republicanism—disciplining domestic spending, giving obeisance to traditional family patterns—seems to provide some of this orderliness, and voters here seem to accept it.

In 1982 the 6th district voted for a man who exemplified many of these virtues, former astronaut Jack Swigert. A jaunty bachelor in private life, Swigert was disciplined and courageous enough to bring a disabled Apollo capsule back to earth—and without much fuss or bother. He ran for the Senate in 1978, lost the primary to Bill Armstrong, and ended up his close friend. He won both the Republican primary and the general election handily despite his announcement that he had cancer; he campaigned with only the most minor interruptions for chemotherapy treatments. But in December 1982 his condition grew worse and he died days before he would have taken office.

Governor Lamm set a March 29 special election. Under Colorado law, local party conventions selected the candidates. The clear favorite, given the district's partisan tilt, was the Republican nominee, state Senator Dan Schaefer. And despite some talk about an upset, Schaefer was an easy winner. As number 435 out of 435 in seniority, at least for a moment, Schaefer got assigned to the Government Operations and Small Business Committees; he may well try to shift after the 1984 election. He is certainly the solid favorite to win that; this should prove to be a safe Republican seat.

The People   Pop. 1980: 481,682, up 43% 1970–80; voting age pop. 344,879; 5% Span. orig., 3% Black, 1% Asian orig. 30% housing units rented. Median owner $73,200; renter $261. Households: 73% family, 41% with children, 62% married couples.

Presidential Vote

1980	Reagan (R)	115,316	(60%)
	Carter (D)	51,098	(26%)
	Other	27,542	(14%)

Rep. Daniel (Dan) **Schaefer** (R) Elected March 29, 1982; b. Jan. 25, 1936, Guttenberg, IA; home, Lakewood; Niagara U., B.A. 1961; Roman Catholic.

Career Teacher, NY Sch. Sys., 1961–64; Construction business, 1964–67; Public relations consultant, 1967–82; CO House of Reps., 1976–78; CO Senate, 1978–82.

Offices 1631 LHOB, 202-225-7882. Also 730 West Hampden Ave., Su. 40, Engelwood 80110, 303-762-8890.

Committees *Government Operations* (39th). Subcommittees: Government Activities and Transportation; Manpower and Housing. *Small Business* (15th).

Group Ratings and Key Votes: Newly Elected

Election Results

1983 special	Daniel Schaefer (R)	49,101	(63%)	($299,895)
	Steve Hogan (D)	27,560	(36%)	($80,563)
1982 general	Jack Swigert (R) died Dec. 27, 1982	98,909	(62%)	($330,681)
	Steve Hogan (D)	56,598	(36%)	($98,355)
1982 primary	Jack Swigert (R)	18,423	(100%)	
1980 general	Newly created district			

Campaign Contributions and Expenditures

1981-82		*Direct Cont. 81-82*	
Receipts	$327,790	Indiv	$181,174
Expend.	$299,895	Party	$19,035
Unspent	$27,895	PACS	$124,855

Indirect Party Expend: $7,419   *(PACS Breakdown Not Available)*

CONNECTICUT

Connecticut in the 1980s seems a little out of place: a pocket of prosperity in the economically depressed Northeast, a state with one of the lowest unemployment rates outside the Sun Belt, yet a state that seems entirely to accept the politics of the welfare state. The reasons are apparent if you study current budget and ethnic history. The budget tells you that Connecticut is a major beneficiary of the surge in defense spending that began late in the Carter administration and accelerated in the Reagan budgets. United Technologies, one of the nation's largest and best managed defense contractors, has its headquarters here and major plants as well. Moreover, Connecticut, like neighboring Massachusetts, has not suffered as many jobs lost in this recession as in earlier ones. Many low-wage, low-skill jobs vanished long ago, as the textile industry moved south. And another major Connecticut business, insurance, is largely recession-proof. Connecticut's income levels dipped from the top of the list in the 1970s; they are back up there now.

Connecticut's political history, like that of most eastern states, is one in which ethnic conflicts and rivalries were played out in the political arena. Some people still cherish a "Connecticut Yankee" tradition, celebrated by Mark Twain; and if you drive around the state, you still see towns with saltbox colonial houses, tourist attraction whaling ships, and low green mountains, and you can still talk to old Yankees with slightly dry New England accents (though not nearly so distinctive as those in Massachusetts). But Yankees are no longer the majority in Connecticut, and haven't been for years. The Republican Party, which they championed after the demise of the Federalists and the Whigs, is no longer the majority party it was in 1932, when the state went for Hoover despite the Depression. Connecticut has become solidly, if not safely, Democratic.

This happened even as the state grew more affluent. You can understand why if you look back to 1932, when a majority of the state's adults were Protestant, but a majority of its children were Catholic. Catholics had been Democrats since they settled here and found the Republican Party dominated by WASPs; their allegiance was cemented by the Al Smith candidacy in 1928. From there it was only a matter of time. The Catholic/Democratic dominance of the state's politics was speeded up by the skill of John Bailey, Democratic State Chairman from 1946 to 1975. He was a master legislative strategist and ticket-balancer, and Connecticut's strong party and straight ticket voting traditions enabled him to exercise more clout than he could have in Massachusetts or New York. He had brilliant timing: he endorsed, early, the state's first Jewish governor, Abraham Ribicoff, in 1954 and the nation's first Catholic president, John Kennedy. Bailey and his Democrats also gave the state honest and thrifty government; Connecticut does not have a state income tax nor a big bureaucracy like those of its neighbors.

Since the 1950s, Connecticut has had its seizures of Republican enthusiasm, but they have passed. In 1970 Democrats were split by strife between ethnic Democrats with traditional views on cultural issues and young affluent activists who opposed the Vietnam war. That election produced, among others, Senator Lowell Weicker. In 1976 and 1980 Connecticut went Republican for president, the first time apparently cool to the appeal of a southern Baptist (as were other states in the Northeast), the second time in line with the national trend. But Connecticut has had Democratic governors for all but four of the last 30 years. It has one Democratic senator, elected in 1980, and a Republican who ostentatiously opposes the Reagan administration on all manner of issues. It has a congressional delegation with no strong Reagan Republicans. In 1982 Connecticut did not produce a Democratic landslide. But it returned to office a Democratic governor with serious weaknesses, and in the close Senate contest between Weicker and Congressman Toby Moffett gave only 3% of its votes to the one candidate, an independent conservative, who wholeheartedly backed Reagan policies. It elected a moderate Republican to fill Moffett's place, but ousted another moderate Republican who seemed to have a safe seat. At the lower levels Connecticut was solidly Democratic.

Senators. Lowell Weicker is now Connecticut's senior official, but he remains very much a maverick and a loner. His politics seems well suited to this state: an aggressive, independent Republicanism, which gives him high marks from organized labor and Common Cause. But Weicker does not have much patience for cultivating constituents or local politicians. That, more than anything else, was why he was in trouble at the beginning of 1982. His reelection was against the odds: the denouement of a perils of Pauline saga. He seemed vulnerable in the Republican convention or, if not there, certainly in the primary, to the candidacy of Prescott Bush, Jr., son of a former senator and brother of the Vice President. But Bush proved to be a naive candidate, given to embarrassing statements; he had a hard time understanding that not everyone lives in Greenwich. After qualifying for the ballot, he abruptly withdrew from the primary; apparently the White House got him to do so. If so, it was a sensible move: he might have won the primary, but both the polls and his performance on the stump indicated he would have been a disaster in the general election.

Bush's withdrawal still left Weicker with a formidable opponent, Toby Moffett. First elected to the House in 1974, Moffett personified the energy and elan of the post-Watergate crop of young Democrats. A onetime Ralph Nader assistant, he attacked oil companies vociferously and built a crackerjack staff to provide constituency service. But by 1982 Moffett had a problem. He had built his career in large part around a policy discredited by events, oil price controls. In the early 1980s he was still assailing the oil companies, but the 1979 oil crisis had demonstrated that controls couldn't hold the price down—and that the allocation of gasoline by bureaucrats was a mistake. By 1980 Congress voted to phase out controls; Moffett lost his biggest issue. He was still formidable in 1982 and ended up with 46% of the vote; but he wasn't able to carry much of the state outside its central cities, and in mostly suburban Connecticut this simply wasn't enough.

Weicker has the committee posts—Appropriations, Energy, Labor—to be an important senator, and his vote is sometimes crucial. On the Labor Committee, for example, he is one of the Republicans who keeps Chairman Orrin Hatch from having a working majority on most issues—something organized labor didn't forget in 1982. But Weicker is so much the maverick that he does more denouncing than legislating. His colleagues regard him as someone who refuses to play ball. He was one of the few Republicans, and the only one not identified with the right, who refused to support Bob Dole's tax bill in 1982, for example. He owed his first election to the Nixon administration (which may have helped persuade Thomas Dodd to run as an independent, splitting the Democratic vote) and he owed much in 1982 to the Reagan administration (for yanking Bush) and to Howard Baker (who came in to campaign for him despite his uncooperativeness on many issues). But Weicker apparently refuses to acknowledge, much less to honor, these debts. Often his refusal is based on high principle, as in his critical attitude toward Richard Nixon when he served on the Senate Watergate Committee. But sometimes it seems based simply on peevishness or political selfishness.

Connecticut's other senator is more popular with his colleagues. Christopher Dodd was first elected to Congress in 1974, from the eastern part of the state. In 1980, when Abraham Ribicoff retired, he faced down Toby Moffett and got the Democratic nomination uncontested. He easily beat his Republican opponent, former New York Senator James Buckley. Dodd's father served Connecticut in the Senate for two terms, and was even mentioned as a vice presidential candidate by Lyndon Johnson in 1964; he was notably conservative on some foreign and cultural issues and had a following among the state's more tradition-minded voters. He was censured by the Senate for misuse of campaign funds in 1967 and left the Senate a broken man; Chris Dodd's election was a much happier moment for the family.

Dodd ran for the Senate expecting to be part of the majority party and ended up part of the minority instead. He has made his most visible mark so far on foreign policy issues; his record is generally in line with other northern Democrats. He is the Senate's leading spokesman critical of Reagan administration policy in Latin America. He is pleasant and good-humored, and easy to deal with while still adhering to principles. There has been little talk about what will happen when he comes up for reelection in 1986; the general assumption is that he will win a second term.

Governor. Connecticut's governor, William O'Neill, is a man with a very traditional Democratic background. A bar owner in the town of East Hampton, on the lower Connecticut River, he got active in local Democratic politics in the 1950s when he returned from the Air Force. In 1966 he was elected to the legislature—not a difficult feat since Connecticut's lower house has many seats and a district is about the size of a neighborhood. He got his current job less for his leadership ability than for his loyalty. Governor Ella Grasso made him chairman of the state Democratic Party when John Bailey died, and when her lieutenant governor ran against her in the 1978 primary, she chose the faithful O'Neill as his successor. A popular and forceful leader, Grasso was expected to win a third term in 1982, but she developed cancer and turned the governorship over to O'Neill at the end of 1980, just before her death.

O'Neill won the job in his own right in 1982, but not without difficulty. He had to withstand a primary challenge from legislative leader Ernest Abate and then won with only 53% against Republican legislator Lewis Rome in the general election. O'Neill's background and basic impulses seem similar to those of John Dempsey, who succeeded to the governorship when Abraham Ribicoff became Secretary of HEW in 1961 and held the office up through 1970. But Dempsey had two advantages O'Neill lacks: support from a strong state chairman who was also the state's premier legislative lobbyist, and a growing economy that generated plenty of revenue. O'Neill operates on his own and, despite Connecticut's relative prosperity, must hold down spending or raise taxes.

Presidential politics. Connecticut has now gone Republican in the last three presidential elections, despite Democrats' strength here. In a close presidential race, Connecticut is likely to be more closely contested than most northeastern states; but it has only eight electoral votes and so sees little personal campaigning by the candidates. Connecticut has a presidential primary, and the comparatively small number of voters who have taken the trouble to register in either party—a vestige of the strong organization days—makes these contests almost similar to the Iowa caucuses. The party organizations end up having more to say about the outcome than in most primary states.

Congressional districting. The boundaries of Connecticut's six congressional districts received only marginal adjustments for the 1980s.

The People   Est. Pop. 1982: 3,153,000; Pop. 1980: 3,107,576, up 1.5% 1980–82 and 2.5% 1970–80; 1.36% of U.S. total, 26th largest; voting age pop. 2,284,657; 6% Black, 3% Spanish origin, 1% Asian origin. Single ancestry: 11% Italian, 7% English, 6% Irish, 5% Polish, 3% French, German, 1% Russian, Portuguese, Swedish, Hungarian, Scottish, Greek. Registered voters (1982): 1,645,454 Total. 661,181 D (40%); 435,374 R (27%); 547,943 unaffiliated (33%). 16% with 1–3 yrs. col., 21% with 4+ yrs. col. 8.7% below poverty level. 34% housing units rented; median house value: $67,400; median monthly rent: $203. Households: 74% family, 38% with children, 61% married couples.

1982 Share of Federal Tax Burden $10,945,200,000; 1.83% of U.S. total, 19th largest.

1982 Share of Federal Expenditures

	Total		Non-Defense		Defense	
Total Expend	$11,967m	(1.98%)	$5,658m	(1.33%)	$6,309m	(3.53%)
St/Lcl Grants	1,120m	(1.27%)	1,120m	(1.27%)	0m	(0%)
Salary/Wages	447m	(0.57%)	118m	(0.43%)	329m	(0.65%)
Ind Payments	3,650m	(1.28%)	3,426m	(1.33%)	224m	(0.78%)
Procurement	6,672m	(4.58%)	785m	(2.49%)	5,887m	(5.15%)
Other Programs	79m	(1.46%)	79m	(1.47%)	0m	(0%)
Loan/Insurance	328m	(0.51%)	307m	(0.50%)	21m	(0.95%)

Political Lineup Governor, William A. O'Neill (D). Senators, Lowell P. Weicker, Jr. (R) and Christopher J. Dodd (D). Representatives, 6 (4 D and 2 R). State Senate, 36 (23 D and 13 R); State House of Representatives 151 (89 D and 62 R).

Presidential Vote

1980	Reagan (R)	677,210	(48%)
	Carter (D)	541,732	(39%)
	Anderson (I)	171,807	(12%)
1976	Ford (R)	719,261	(52%)
	Carter (D)	647,895	(47%)

1980 Democratic Presidential Primary			*1980 Republican Presidential Primary*		
Kennedy	98,662	(47%)	Bush	70,367	(39%)
Carter	87,207	(41%)	Reagan	61,735	(34%)
Others	11,003	(5%)	Anderson	40,354	(22%)
Uncommitted	13,403	(6%)	Five others.........	5,572	(3%)
			Uncommitted	4,256	(2%)

SENATORS

Sen. Lowell P. Weicker, Jr. (R) Elected 1970, seat up 1988; b. May 16, 1931, Paris, France; home, Greenwich; Yale U., B.A. 1953, U. of VA, LL.B. 1958; Episcopal.

Career Army, 1953–55; Practicing atty.; CT Gen. Assembly, 1962–68; U.S. House of Reps., 1969–71.

Offices 303 HSOB, 202-224-4041. Also 102 U.S. Court House, 915 Lafayette Blvd., Bridgeport 06603, 203-579-5830.

Committees *Appropriations* (3d). Subcommittees: Defense; HUD-Independent Agencies; Labor, Health and Human Services, Education (Chairman); Commerce, Justice, State, Judiciary; Interior. *Energy and Natural Resources* (3d). Subcommittees: Energy Conservation and Supply (Chairman); Energy Research and Development; Energy Regulation. *Labor and Human Resources* (7th). Subcommittees: Education, Arts, and Humanities; Handicapped (Chairman); Family and Human Services. *Small Business* (Chairman). Subcommittees: Urban and Rural Economic Development; Entrepreneurship and Special Problems Facing Small Business.

Group Ratings

	ADA	ACLU	COPE	CFA	LCV	LWV	NTU	NSI	COC	ACA	CSFC
1982	75	86	67	50	29	70	12	33	31	17	36
1981	55	—	65	43	48	—	34	—	60	17	54
1980	72	73	81	73	87	90	27	38	44	43	36

National Journal Ratings

	Economic		Foreign		Cultural	
1982	97%	(LIB)	75%	(LIB)	83%	(LIB)
	2%	(CONS)	24%	(CONS)	15%	(CONS)
1981	70%	(LIB)	79%	(LIB)	86%	(LIB)
	29%	(CONS)	20%	(CONS)	6%	(CONS)

Key Votes

1) Reagan 81 Budget	FOR	5) $ to El Salvador	AGN	9) Poor Pay Food Stamps	AGN
2) Reagan 81 Tax Cut	FOR	6) Saudi AWACS Sale	AGN	10) Ban Crt Busing Order	AGN
3) Bal Budget Amend	AGN	7) Ban Abortion	AGN	11) Clinch Riv Brdr Rctr	FOR
4) Gas & Road Tax	FOR	8) Nerve Gas Prod	AGN	12) Legal Services Corp	FOR

Election Results

1982 general	Lowell P. Weicker, Jr. (R)	545,987	(50%)	($2,306,615)
	Anthony Toby Moffett (D)	499,146	(46%)	($1,368,147)
1982 primary	Lowell P. Weicker, Jr. (R) unopposed			
1982 pre-primary	Prescott S. Bush, Jr. (R)			($1,503,209)
1976 general	Lowell P. Weicker, Jr. (R)	785,683	(58%)	($480,709)
	Gloria Schaffer (D)	561,018	(41%)	($306,104)

Campaign Contributions and Expenditures

1980-82		*Direct Cont. 80-82*			*PACS brkdwn*			
Receipts	$2,308,888	Indiv	$1,474,396	Agr	$10,250	Ideo	$57,975
Expend.	$2,306,615	Party	$36,748	Bus	$216,744	Lbr	$110,825
Unspent	$2,273	PACS	$444,954	Hlth	$26,100	Prof	$3,300
		Cand	$236,000				

Indirect Party Expend: $171,930   *Indep Expend:* For: $21,248 Agn: $200,508 (NCPAC)

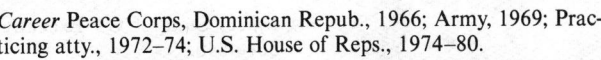

Sen. Christopher J. Dodd (D) Elected 1980, seat up 1986; b. May 27, 1944, Willimantic; home, Norwich; Providence Col., B.A. 1966, U. of Louisville, J.D. 1972; Roman Catholic.

Career Peace Corps, Dominican Repub., 1966; Army, 1969; Practicing atty., 1972–74; U.S. House of Reps., 1974–80.

Offices 324 HSOB, 202-224-2823. Also 60 Washington St., Hartford 06106, 203-224-3470.

Committees *Banking, Housing and Urban Affairs* (5th). Subcommittees: Consumer Affairs; Economic Policies; Securities. *Foreign Relations* (8th). Subcommittees: International Economic Policy; African Affairs; Western Hemisphere Affairs. *Labor and Human Resources* (8th). Subcommittees: Education, Arts, and Humanities; Family and Human Services; Handicapped. *Special Committee on Aging* (7th).

Group Ratings

	ADA	ACLU	COPE	CFA	LCV	LWV	NTU	NSI	COC	ACA	CSFC
1982	100	82	100	100	57	80	4	11	16	11	23
1981	90	—	100	86	88	—	3	—	0	0	26

National Journal Ratings

	Economic		Foreign		Cultural	
1982	74%	(LIB)	99%	(LIB)	91%	(LIB)
	25%	(CONS)	0%	(CONS)	8%	(CONS)
1981	98%	(LIB)	91%	(LIB)	76%	(LIB)
	1%	(CONS)	8%	(CONS)	23%	(CONS)

Key Votes

1) Reagan 81 Budget	AGN	5) $ to El Salvador	AGN	9) Poor Pay Food Stamps	AGN
2) Reagan 81 Tax Cut	AGN	6) Saudi AWACS Sale	AGN	10) Ban Crt Busing Order	AGN
3) Bal Budget Amend	AGN	7) Ban Abortion	AGN	11) Clinch Riv Brdr Rctr	AGN
4) Gas & Road Tax	FOR	8) Nerve Gas Prod	AGN	12) Legal Services Corp	FOR

Election Results

1980 general	Christopher J. Dodd (D)	763,969	(56%)	($1,403,672)
	James L. Buckley (R)	581,884	(43%)	($1,652,672)
1980 primary	Christopher J. Dodd (D) nominated by convention			
1974 general	Abraham A. Ribicoff (D)	690,820	(64%)	($435,985)
	James H. Brannen III (R)	372,055	(34%)	($66,162)

Campaign Contributions and Expenditures

1980–1981		*PACS brkdwn*			
Receipts	$1,400,991	Agr	$9,000	Ideo	$26,663
Expend.	$1,495,674	Bus	$77,425	Lbr	$137,050
Unspent	$1,149	Hlth	$14,500	Prof	$3,750

GOVERNOR

Gov. William A. O'Neill (D) Appointed Jan. 1, 1981, term expires Jan. 1987; b. Aug. 11, 1930, Hartford; home, East Hampton; New Britian Teachers Col., U. of Hartford; Roman Catholic.

Career USAF, 1950–53; Dem. East Hampton Town Committee, 1954–80; CT House of Reps., 1966–76; Chmn., CT Dem. Central Committee, 1975–78; Lt. Gov. of CT, 1978–80.

Offices State of CT Executive Chambers, Hartford 06115, 203-566-4840.

Election Results

1982 gen.	William A. O'Neill (D)	578,264	(53%)
	Lewis B. Rome (R)	497,773	(46%)
1982 prim.	William A. O'Neill (D) unopposed		
1978 gen.	Ella T. Grasso (D)	613,109	(59%)
	Ronald A. Sarasin (R)	422,316	(41%)

FIRST DISTRICT

Hartford is Connecticut's first city, the center of its largest urban area, the state capital, and its economic capital as well. Hartford's history and location resemble those of many bedraggled mill towns, but over the years it has proved economically adaptable and productive. Like all of southern New England, this was a land of tinkerers in the early 1800s—tinkerers who built machines and factories to produce things like the Colt revolver, whose big factory still stands on the Connecticut River south of downtown Hartford. These precision mass-production industries gave Hartford its growth and prosperity in the early 19th century. The insurance companies came later, growing naturally in the part of the country with the most surplus capital. Their steady business remains an important contribution to Hartford's well-being. More recently, Hartford became the center of one of the nation's leading defense contractors, United Technologies, which produces a large percentage of the world's jet engines in the Pratt & Whitney plant in East Hartford. State government also provides Hartford with a stable employment base, but not a large one in thrifty Connecticut.

CONNECTICUT — Congressional Districts, Counties, County Subdivisions (Towns), and Places — *(6 Districts)*

We are speaking here of metropolitan Hartford, for this city has long since outgrown the limits it had as a colonial town. Metropolitan Hartford is, give or take a few suburbs, coterminous with Connecticut's 1st congressional district. Politically, this is the most Democratic part of the state, less because of the leanings of an industrial proletariat than because of its ethnic history and local political leadership. Hartford's Irish-, Italian-, French Canadian-, Polish-, and Jewish-Americans far outnumber its Yankees (and its small black community); they were enrolled in the Democratic Party early, and they and their children have stayed with it pretty much ever since. They were strengthened in their resolve by John Bailey, longtime state (1946-75) and national (1961-68) Democratic chairman, an old-fashioned political boss who had a career free of scandal and who promoted a raft of first-class candidates.

It is fitting that today the 1st district is represented in Congress by Bailey's daughter, Barbara Kennelly. She first won in a special election in 1980, to fill the vacancy caused by the death of William Cotter, who had held the seat nearly 10 years. Kennelly's Republican opponent, Ann Uccello, former Hartford mayor, had given Cotter his only close run in his first election; she seriously contested this one too, but with more meager results. By

November 1980 the Republicans gave up on this district, and Kennelly won by a 2-1 margin. She seems now to have a safe seat.

Kennelly is a professional politician in her own right, and she showed her mettle when she won a seat on the Ways and Means Committee in early 1983. This was a prized position: Ways and Means has jurisdiction over taxes—a matter of concern to virtually every economic interest—and the unpopularity of the results of the Reagan economic programs made a major revision of tax laws seem likely for 1983 or 1984. Hartford's insurance industry, for one, would like a sympathetic ear should that happen; so, presumably, would other Hartford interests. Kennelly shrewdly made a combination with Alabama's Ronnie Flippo, a politician of somewhat different views and very different cultural attitudes; they both won seats on Ways and Means. Kennelly can be counted on as a down-the-line Democratic vote; her background does not incline her to apostasy. But she by no means regards herself as an enemy of business interests and will presumably pay close attention to those in her constituency.

The People Pop. 1980: 516,232, dn. 1.7% 1970–80; voting age pop. 383,559; 10% Black, 5% Span. orig., 1% Asian orig. 41% housing units rented. Median owner $65,700; renter $205. Households: 71% family, 36% with children, 56% married couples.

Presidential Vote

1980	Reagan (R)	93,750	(39%)
	Carter (D)	109,702	(46%)
	Other	34,942	(15%)

Rep. Barbara B. Kennelly (D) Elected 1982; b. July 10, 1930, Hartford; home, Hartford; Trinity Col.(DC), B.A. 1958, Trinity Col.(Hartford), M.A. 1971; Roman Catholic.

Career Vice Chmn., Hartford Comm. on Aging, 1971–75; Hartford Court of Common Cncl., 1975–79; Sec. of State, 1979–82.

Offices 1228 LHOB, 202-225-2265. Also Abraham Ribicoff Fed. Bldg., 450 Main St., Su. 618, Hartford 06103, 203-722-2383.

Committee *Ways and Means* (23d). Subcommitttees: Select Revenue Measures; Public Assistance and Unemployment Compensation.

Group Ratings and Key Votes: Newly Elected

Election Results

1982 general	Barbara B. Kennelly (D)	126,798	(68%)	($144,808)
	Herschel A. Klein (R)	58,075	(31%)	($17,119)
1982 primary	Barbara B. Kennelly (D) unopposed			
1982 special	Barbara B. Kennelly (D)	51,795	(59%)	($196,202)
	Antonina P. Uccello (R)	36,043	(41%)	($109,083)
1980 general	William R. Cotter (D)	137,849	(63%)	($127,447)
	Marjorie D. Anderson (R)	80,816	(37%)	($27,713)

Campaign Contributions and Expenditures

1981-82		Direct Cont. 81-82				PACS brkdwn		
Receipts	$173,335	Indiv	$104,676	Agr	$—	Ideo	$4,050
Expend.	$144,808	Party	$2,378	Bus	$19,950	Lbr	$43,152
Unspent	$51,409	PACS	$55,105	Hlth	$1,525	Prof	$925

Indep Expend: For: $9,968 (AMAPAC)

SECOND DISTRICT

The 2d district is the eastern half, geographically, of Connecticut. The district has Yankee villages and high-income summer and retirement colonies with names like Old Saybrook and Old Lyme. But its political character and personality come more from its small industrial cities and mill towns—the cities of New London and Norwich, mill towns like Danielson, Putnam, Jewett City, and Willimantic. The port of New London and Norwich, up the river, were among the largest cities in the 13 colonies in the revolutionary period; had history taken different turns, they might have turned out to be the centers of large metropolitan areas, like Providence or Newark or Wilmington. Instead, they remain a size the Founding Fathers would have found comprehensible—about as big as New York City was in 1790.

Their population has, of course, changed, as have their economies. New London lives more off General Dynamics' Electric Boat Company, which builds nuclear submarines, and off its Navy base than it does off fishing or trading with England; ethnically, most residents are the offspring of migrants of the 1840-1924 wave, not of the Yankees who lived here during the Revolution. That is even more the case with the mill towns, which were at most farmer's market towns in 1790. They grew because the rapidly flowing rivers were the major energy source of early 19th century America and because ingenious local entrepreneurs figured out things to make and how to make them here. Although their original industries have long since left, their populations are almost entirely the offspring of the immigrants who came here years ago, and they have fanned out to populate some of the once all-Yankee rural towns between the rivers.

This mixture of mostly Protestant Yankees and mostly Catholic immigrants has produced a politics in which neither party has enjoyed a clear edge in this district. Over the last 25 years it has been represented by both Republicans and Democrats, although none has actually lost an election: they usually have run for other office. The most recent example of this was Senator Christopher Dodd. He had a well-known name to begin and, after representing the 2d district for six years, he became well enough known on Hartford and New Haven television (each of which covers part of the district) to be a formidable statewide candidate.

The current congressman, Sam Gejdenson, started off with a name not only not well-known, but difficult to pronounce (gay-den-son). A young liberal running in a Republican year, a not-at-all affluent son of World War II refugees running at a time when campaigns cost a great deal of money—he did not seem like a particularly hot prospect. But he turned out to have assets not apparent on his resume: an ability to organize a campaign, an instinctive feel for communicating issues to voters, a wry sense of humor, and the willingness to campaign hard personally. In the 1980 primary he beat John Dempsey, son of a former governor; in the general election he beat a Republican of Italian descent with 53% of the vote. Against the same candidate he won with 56% in 1982.

Gejdenson is part of that generation of Democratic politicos who came of age during the Vietnam war. He is a shade less liberal on economic issues than many older northern Democrats (although far from being a Reaganite); he is solidly liberal on foreign policy and cultural issues. His committee assignments—Foreign Affairs and Interior—suggest that the latter are what engage his attention. He cannot be said to hold a safe seat yet, and statewide office will probably have to wait for some time.

The People Pop. 1980 518,244, up 6.4% 1970–80, voting age pop. 378,132; 3% Black, 1% Span. orig., 1% Asian orig. 32% housing units rented. Median owner $56,800; renter $202. Households: 74% family, 40% with children, 63% married couples.

Presidential Vote

1980	Reagan (R)	103,603	(47%)
	Carter (D)	85,537	(39%)
	Other	31,954	(14%)

Rep. Samuel Gejdenson (D) Elected 1980; b. May 20, 1948, Eshwege, Germany; home, Bozrah; Mitchell Col., A.S., U. of CT, B.A. 1970; Jewish.

Career CT House of Reps., 1974–78; Coal Co. Consultant, 1978; Legislative Liaison to Gov. of CT, 1979–80.

Offices 1404 LHOB, 202-225-2076. Also P.O. Box 2000, Norwich 06360, 203-886-0139; and 29 Court St., Middletown 06457, 203-346-1123.

Committees *Foreign Affairs* (13th). Subcommittees: International Economic Policy and Trade; Western Hemisphere Affairs. *Interior and Insular Affairs* (21st). Subcommittees: Energy and the Environment; Oversight and Investigations; Public Lands and National Parks.

Group Ratings

	ADA	ACLU	COPE	CFA	LCV	LWV	NTU	NSI	COC	ACA	CSFC
1982	100	100	89	80	84	92	3	10	23	13	24
1981	95	—	80	86	86	—	12	—	5	4	28

National Journal Ratings

	Economic		Foreign		Cultural	
1982	73%	(LIB)	85%	(LIB)	89%	(LIB)
	27%	(CONS)	12%	(CONS)	8%	(CONS)
1981	70%	(LIB)	79%	(LIB)	95%	(LIB)
	30%	(CONS)	21%	(CONS)	1%	(CONS)

Key Votes

1) Reagan 81 Budget	AGN	5) Incr SS Rtmt Age	AGN	9) Poor Pay Food Stamps	AGN
2) Reagan 81 Tax Cut	AGN	6) Saudi AWACS Sale	AGN	10) Ban Crt Busing Order	AGN
3) Bal Budget Amend	AGN	7) $ for MX Missile	AGN	11) Auto Local Content	FOR
4) Gas & Road Tax	FOR	8) Nerve Gas Prod	AGN	12) Nuclear Arms Freeze	FOR

Election Results

1982 general	Samuel Gejdenson (D)	95,254	(56%)	($538,679)
	Tony Guglielmo (R)	74,294	(44%)	($311,570)
1982 primary	Samuel Gejdenson (D) unopposed			
1980 general	Samuel Gejdenson (D)	119,176	(53%)	($217,721)
	Tony Guglielmo (R)	104,107	(47%)	($141,682)

Campaign Contributions and Expenditures

1981-82		Direct Cont. 81-82		PACS brkdwn			
Receipts	$542,706	Indiv	$334,150	Agr	$5,500	Ideo	$43,492
Expend.	$538,679	Party	$14,965	Bus	$18,575	Lbr	$62,890
Unspent	$5,508	PACS	$146,152	Hlth	$4,000	Prof	$2,000
		Cand	$31,722				

Indep Expend: For: $1,585 (NTLPAC)

THIRD DISTRICT

The 3d congressional district of Connecticut centers on the city of New Haven, once the state's largest and most industrialized major city and the home of one of Connecticut's best known institutions, Yale University. At the turn of the century, New Haven was the most important factory town in Connecticut, and it attracted thousands of Irish, Italian, and Polish immigrants. Today their descendants have spread out, from the old neighborhoods of frame houses, huddled within walking distance of the factories, to the close-in suburbs and beyond. New Haven for years was very much an ethnic town, with barriers erected here and there to keep people of various ancestry out or in. The resentments caused by such barriers led to political alignments: the Irish became Democrats because the Yankee Republicans would have nothing to do with them; the Italians became Republicans because the Democratic Party was controlled by the Irish. In all this Yale played only a minor part: despite its national reputation, it has a relatively small enrollment and, except for a few blocks near the campus, New Haven is not really a college town.

For years ethnic loyalties and enmities structured politics; now that seems to be diminishing. Ethnic origin has, after all, come to matter less. There are probably still clubs and social circles Italian-Americans cannot aspire to; but they certainly have the opportunity to make a good living, join a profession, build a strong business, even go to Yale. As real incomes rose in the 1950s, 1960s, and 1970s, people of various ethnic backgrounds moved to suburbs where they would have felt unwelcome before and married into families that would have been reluctant to have them a generation before. Some were left behind. In the old houses in New Haven and the relatively low-income suburbs of East Haven and West Haven live those of varying ethnic backgrounds who, for whatever reason, have not achieved economic success.

The declining importance of ethnic status in economic and political life helps to explain how, in this very ethnic—and especially Italian-American—congressional district, represented for 30 years by men named DeNardis, Giaimo, and Cretella, was captured in a kind of populist uprising by a man named Morrison. It helped, of course, that the new congressman, Bruce Morrison, was a Democrat running in a year when Republican economic policies supported by his opponent seemed to have produced high unemployment; but in Connecticut unemployment was lower than average, at levels that people in some other parts of the country found tolerable a few years ago. Moreover, Morrison was not given the Democratic nomination. He had to win it by beating the New Haven Democratic organization and the president of the New Haven City Council in the primary. And in the general election he had to beat a Republican, Lawrence DeNardis, with strong local ties and a deserved reputation as a critic of at least some of the Reagan economic policies, who received plenty of publicity as one of the leaders of the Gypsy Moths.

Morrison did this by stressing his record as the head of New Haven Legal Services. He is a prime example of how legal service lawyers have been elected in several congressional districts, usually as the champion of economic policies designed to aid the kind of low-income people who have been their clients. We are in an age when voters want representatives with educational credentials, and about the only such people who are in close and non-adversary contact with relatively low income people, day in and day out, are legal services lawyers. The clients they have helped can turn out to be extremely effective political workers, because they are strongly motivated and, usually, so new to politics, that they are not caught in a web of interlocking relationships which cause them to commit themselves less than fully to any particular candidate. Morrison in his job had been energetic in promoting just those kinds of test cases and class action lawsuits that Ronald Reagan would like to stop; and in his campaign he proved that a network based on legal services clients can be more effective than a larger, but less motivated network of people involved in an existing Democratic machine.

His general election victory, then, must be counted as more than just a knee-jerk reaction against Reaganomics. It was a vote for a rather different kind of politics from what we have seen recently. Morrison does not share the kind of upper income, *noblesse oblige* perspective from which so many of the Democratic politicians of the baby boom generation view the world below. He sees it more from the point of view of the crowd. Other Democratic congressmen his age, with more elite credentials, have been dubious about government spending and aid programs. Morrison seems more likely to be the kind of true believer in them that most liberal Democrats were 15 years ago.

If that is the kind of politics he develops, it remains to be seen how it is received over the long run in the New Haven area. Morrison, after all, did not carry the district in a landslide; he ran close, but did not carry, all the major suburbs outside East Haven and West Haven. He ran only even with Joseph Lieberman, the more elite-minded Democrat who lost to DeNardis in 1980, in high-income suburbs like Woodbridge and Guilford; but he made significant gains in New Haven and in the close-in suburbs of Hamden and East Haven. The question for 1984 is whether the Republicans will seriously contest this district. DeNardis was stunned and surprised by his defeat, and may not venture into elective politics again; without him, Republicans are unlikely to make a major effort unless the economy improves and they go on the offensive in many districts.

The People   Pop. 1980: 518,677, up 1.6% 1970–80; voting age pop. 387,740; 9% Black, 2% Span. orig., 1% Asian orig. 35% housing units rented. Median owner $65,400; renter $212. Households: 73% family, 36% with children, 59% married couples.

Presidential Vote

1980	Reagan (R)	118,469	(51%)
	Carter (D)	91,123	(39%)
	Other	23,400	(10%)

Rep. Bruce A. Morrison (D) Elected 1982; b. Oct. 8, 1944, New York City; home, Hamden; MIT, B.A. 1965, U. of IL, M.S. 1970, Yale U., J.D. 1973; Lutheran.

Career Practicing atty. 1973–.

Offices 437 CHOB, 202-225-3661. Also 85 Church St., New Haven 06510, 203-773-2325.

Committees *Banking, Finance and Urban Affairs* (24th). Subcommittees: Housing and Community Development; Domestic Monetary Policy; Economic Stabilization. *Judiciary* (17th). Subcommittees: Courts Civil Liberties and the Administration of Justice; Crime. *Select Committee on Children, Youth and Families* (13th).

Group Ratings and Key Votes: Newly Elected

Election Results

1982 general	Bruce A. Morrison (D)	....	90,638	(50%)	($313,517)
	Lawrence J. DeNardis (R)	......	88,951	(49%)	($330,644)
1982 primary	Bruce A. Morrison (D)	....	13,275	(55%)	
	Stephen Wareck (D)	....	10,668	(45%)	($0)
1980 general	Lawrence J. DeNardis (R)	....	117,024	(52%)	($185,799)
	Joseph I. Lieberman (D)	....	103,903	(46%)	($302,054)

Campaign Contributions and Expenditures

1981-82		Direct Cont. 81-82*				PACS brkdwn		
Receipts	$312,141	Indiv	$127,738	Agr	$—	Ideo	$15,535
Expend.	$313,517	Party	$500	Bus	$—	Lbr	$45,500
		PACS	$70,254	Hlth	$—	Prof	$1,400
		Cand	$70,520				

Non-Cand Loans: $37,300

FOURTH DISTRICT

If Hartford County is the traditional base of Connecticut's Democrats, then Fairfield County is bedrock for the state's Republicans. Fairfield is one of the most affluent counties in the nation, a land of broad, well-manicured lawns sweeping down to Long Island Sound, of woodsy New Canaan and artsy-craftsy Westport, of commuters driving down to the station to take the bedraggled New Haven Railroad into Manhattan. Unlike the rest of Connecticut, Fairfield County is in many ways an extension of the New York metropolitan area, economically and culturally. People watch New York, not New Haven or Hartford, TV stations; they are Yankees, not Red Sox, fans; and their political attitudes, more than in other parts of the state, are shaped by what is happening in the City. Many people here have little idea what is happening in politics or government in Connecticut; Hartford is a lot farther away than Grand Central Station.

Most of the people of Fairfield County live in the 4th congressional district—a string of high-income, traditionally Republican towns along Long Island Sound: Greenwich, Stamford, Darien, Norwalk, Westport, Fairfield. But it would be inaccurate to say that the harried advertising executive on the commuter train is the typical 4th district voter. For one thing, these towns are not identical: Westport is more liberal on cultural issues than the others, Stamford has sprouted its own downtown and its set of corporate headquarters and has a little slum section to boot, Norwalk is partly industrial. Also, the 4th district goes a little farther along the Sound and takes in the industrial city of Bridgeport. Bridgeport is nothing like the South Bronx: it has a bounteous system of parks and its old ethnic neighborhoods are pleasant and unimperiled. But it is a medium-sized industrial city, quite separate from the commuter towns, and people here are not nearly so likely to think of themselves as part of metropolitan New York.

The two segments of the 4th—Bridgeport and the Republican towns—perform a kind of political counterpoint. Westport, for example, which went 36% for Kennedy in 1960, was 41% for McGovern in 1972, and back down to 30% for Carter in 1980 (with 14% for John Anderson). Bridgeport moved in the opposite direction: Kennedy, the first Catholic president, got 61% here, the culturally liberal McGovern only 45%, Carter an in-between 56% in 1976 and 51% in 1980.

Either way, this counterpoint tends to produce a Republican majority. That has been true in congressional elections, in which this district has chosen such worthies as Lowell Weicker (in 1968) and Clare Boothe Luce (1942, 1944). Its current congressman, Stewart McKinney, was first elected in 1970 and has been reelected, mostly with comfortable margins, ever since. McKinney is one of those Gypsy Moth Republicans who, although he supported the Reagan budget and tax programs in 1981, has looked out carefully for what he regards as the region's interests and is dubious about pure free market or supply side economics. He has also devoted considerable attention to the thankless task of overseeing District of Columbia affairs and has worked to keep Congress from usurping the authority of the elected District government.

McKinney is only one slot down from occupying the ranking Republican position on the Banking Committee, a body with a jurisdiction over the rapidly changing banks and savings institutions, and over housing programs as well, over wage and price controls, and over loan guarantees to ailing companies like Chrysler and ailing governments like New York City. Historically, the committee has spent much of its time refereeing disputes between the banks and the savings institutions; McKinney believes there are likely to be less of these in the future, and that the tough issues will be how to protect both types of depository institutions, which are heavily regulated and tied down to their headquarters, against the competition of mostly unregulated and unfettered financial institutions like Merrill Lynch, American Express, and Sears. Sensibly, he is afraid of the consequences of a sudden and complete deregulation. McKinney is ranking Republican on the Housing Subcommittee, a body less active now than in the 1960s, because of the effective demise of so many federal subsidy programs.

McKinney's opponent in 1980 and 1982 was the young man who, as a Princeton undergraduate, produced a design for an atom bomb. In what most Washington observers of his party consider a hopelessly Republican district with a congressman who has no serious weaknesses, John Phillips won one upset primary victory, raised $150,000 twice, and increased his percentage from 37% in 1980 to 43% in the more Democratic year of 1982. Will he try again? If so, McKinney will have another race he must take seriously; otherwise, he may draw a bye, as Republicans in this district often do.

The People   Pop. 1980: 518,577, dn. 4.8% 1970–80; voting age pop. 384,352; 10% Black, 6% Span. orig., 1% Asian orig. 37% housing units rented. Median owner $98,500; renter $230. Households: 74% family, 37% with children, 59% married couples.

Presidential Vote

1980	Reagan (R)	125,523	(54%)
	Carter (D)	82,475	(36%)
	Other	23,405	(10%)

Rep. Stewart B. McKinney (R) Elected 1970; b. Jan. 30, 1931, Pittsburgh, PA; home, Fairfield; Princeton U., 1949–51, Yale U., B.A. 1958; Episcopal.

Career Air Force, 1951–55; Pres., CMF Tires, Inc.; Real estate development; CT House of Reps., 1967–70.

Offices 106 CHOB, 202-225-5541. Also Fed. Bldg., Lafayette Blvd., Bridgeport 06604, 203-384-2286.

Committees *Banking, Finance and Urban Affairs* (2d). Subcommittees: Economic Stabilization; Financial Institutions Supervision, Regulation and Insurance; Housing and Community Development. *District of Columbia* (Ranking Member). Subcommittee: Government Operations and Metropolitan Affairs.

Group Ratings

	ADA	ACLU	COPE	CFA	LCV	LWV	NTU	NSI	COC	ACA	CSFC
1982	80	75	59	50	73	75	53	20	50	38	41
1981	70	—	58	57	68	—	59	—	78	30	47
1980	78	80	57	42	62	75	28	13	57	41	40

National Journal Ratings

	Economic		Foreign		Cultural	
1982	58%	(LIB)	70%	(LIB)	74%	(LIB)
	41%	(CONS)	30%	(CONS)	26%	(CONS)
1981	40%	(LIB)	80%	(LIB)	88%	(LIB)
	59%	(CONS)	20%	(CONS)	12%	(CONS)

Key Votes

1) Reagan 81 Budget	FOR	5) Incr SS Rtmt Age	FOR	9) Poor Pay Food Stamps	AGN
2) Reagan 81 Tax Cut	FOR	6) Saudi AWACS Sale	AGN	10) Ban Crt Busing Order	AGN
3) Bal Budget Amend	AGN	7) $ for MX Missile	AGN	11) Auto Local Content	FOR
4) Gas & Road Tax	FOR	8) Nerve Gas Prod	AGN	12) Nuclear Arms Freeze	FOR

Election Results

1982 general	Stewart B. McKinney (R)	93,660	(56%)	($285,910)
	John Aristotle Phillips (D)	71,110	(43%)	($152,616)
1982 primary	Stewart B. McKinney (R) unopposed			
1980 general	Stewert B. McKinney (R)	124,285	(63%)	($220,183)
	John Aristotle Phillips (D)	74,326	(37%)	($155,631)

Campaign Contributions and Expenditures

1981-82		Direct Cont. 81-82				PACS brkdwn		
Receipts	$293,340	Indiv	$187,757	Agr	$—		Ideo	$3,250
Expend.	$285,910	Party	$16,704	Bus	$66,537		Lbr	$15,500
Unspent	$11,696	PACS	$85,793	Hlth	$3,150		Prof	$1,250

FIFTH DISTRICT

The 5th congressional district of Connecticut is a slice of the state that takes in some of its prettiest rural towns, some of its most affluent suburbs, and some of those small industrial cities where ingenious Connecticut Yankees built factories and businesses that made—and in some case make—the state one of the nation's most prosperous. The biggest of these cities, Waterbury, has long been the nation's largest producer of brass products and one of its major clockmakers. Danbury, near the New York border, was known for years for its hats. The towns of the Naugatuck Valley, along a fast-flowing river, made a variety of products. All of these small cities in the late 19th and early 20th centuries attracted an immigrant population, and by the 1940s they had Catholic majorities.

This changed their political complexion. Originally, this part of Connecticut, between New Haven and Long Island Sound on one side and Hartford and Litchfield County on the other, was contrary Yankee country. Its voters—first Federalists, later Whigs, then Republicans—were men who wanted to stop foolish populists from putting into effect their newfangled ideas, even as they themselves, in their factories, were putting into production newfangled machines and products. By the 1940s they were in a political minority, replaced by Democrats who went to Mass, lived in traditional ethnic neighborhoods, supported the New Deal, and, when he came along, revered John F. Kennedy (who spoke, in the closing days of the 1960 campaign, to a huge and hugely enthusiastic crowd in Waterbury—after midnight). The 5th district ends up being pretty closely divided politically. The Democratic factory towns are balanced off by the smaller, still Yankee rural towns and by the wide Republican margins in the high income woodsy suburbs of Weston, Wilton, and Ridgefield.

So this has been a close district in many elections. Party control changed twice in the 1970s, most recently when Democrat William Ratchford was elected in 1978. His credentials were good: he was Speaker of the Connecticut House for four years, he was a department head under Governor Ella Grasso, he nearly beat the incumbent in this district in 1974. But Ratchford won by an uninspiring margin in 1978, when Grasso was sweeping the state, and by an even smaller margin two years later. If Republicans had been as much on the offensive in 1982 as they had hoped in 1981, this is a district they would have targeted; and they ended up with a creditable candidate in former legislative leader Neal Hanlon.

But circumstances proved good for Ratchford. Redistricting helped a little by removing the heavily Republican commuter town of New Canaan. The Republicans split over the nomination (the near-winner in 1980 wanted it), making it harder for Hanlon to raise funds for the general election. Around the country, Republicans were on the defensive, and so the national party's funds went more to incumbents than to challengers like Hanlon. In the high income towns Ratchford's percentages were very close to what he had in 1980. But he made big gains in the smaller towns in and near the working class Naugatuck Valley (Shelton, Seymour, Monroe, and Derby)—big enough to raise his overall percentage to a comfortable 58%. This should not be regarded as a safe seat, however.

Ratchford, as a relatively junior member of the Education and Labor and House Administration Committees, does not make headlines. As a former speaker, he has a bias toward party regularity, and he generally follows the Democratic leadership.

The People   Pop. 1980: 518,700, up 8.2% 1970–80; voting age pop. 372,002; 4% Black, 3% Span. orig. 31% housing units rented. Median owner $70,200; renter $179. Households: 78% family, 42% with children, 66% married couples.

Presidential Vote

1980	Reagan (R)	122,662	(54%)
	Carter (D)	79,940	(35%)
	Other	25,348	(11%)

Rep. William R. Ratchford (D) Elected 1978; b. May 24, 1934, Danbury; home, Danbury; U. of CT, B.A. 1956, Georgetown U., LL.B. 1959; Unitarian.

Career CT House of Reps., 1962–74, Spkr., 1969–72, Minor. Ldr., 1972–74; Dem. Nominee for U.S. House of Reps., 1974; Chmn., CT Blue Ribbon Commission to Investigate Nursing Home Industry, 1975–76; Commissioner, CT Dept. of Aging, 1977–78.

Offices 432 CHOB, 202-225-3822. Also 135 Grand St., Waterbury 06701, 203-573-1418.

Committees *Appropriations* (32d). Subcommittees: Interior; Transportation. *Select Committee on Aging* (16th). Subcommittee: Health and Long-Term Care.

Group Ratings

	ADA	ACLU	COPE	CFA	LCV	LWV	NTU	NSI	COC	ACA	CSFC
1982	90	83	85	70	79	92	24	10	38	4	29
1981	90	—	83	86	93	—	26	—	11	9	30
1980	83	97	72	75	87	100	18	0	61	19	31

National Journal Ratings

	Economic		Foreign		Cultural	
1982	70%	(LIB)	99%	(LIB)	89%	(LIB)
	30%	(CONS)	1%	(CONS)	8%	(CONS)
1981	81%	(LIB)	85%	(LIB)	82%	(LIB)
	15%	(CONS)	13%	(CONS)	18%	(CONS)

Key Votes

1) Reagan 81 Budget	AGN	5) Incr SS Rtmt Age	AGN	9) Poor Pay Food Stamps	AGN
2) Reagan 81 Tax Cut	AGN	6) Saudi AWACS Sale	AGN	10) Ban Crt Busing Order	AGN
3) Bal Budget Amend	AGN	7) $ for MX Missile	AGN	11) Auto Local Content	FOR
4) Gas & Road Tax	FOR	8) Nerve Gas Prod	AGN	12) Nuclear Arms Freeze	FOR

Election Results

1982 general	William R. Ratchford (D)	101,362	(58%)	($272,568)
	Neal B. Hanlon (R)	70,808	(41%)	($161,532)
1982 primary	William R. Ratchford (D) unopposed			
1980 general	William R. Ratchford (D)	117,316	(50%)	($150,570)
	Edward M. Donahue (R)	115,614	(50%)	($52,740)

Campaign Contributions and Expenditures

1981-82		Direct Cont. 81-82		PACS brkdwn			
Receipts	$283,446	Indiv	$168,025	Agr	$1,950	Ideo	$17,091
Expend.	$272,568	Party	$8,975	Bus	$15,000	Lbr	$81,750
Unspent	$11,093	PACS	$124,602	Hlth	$500	Prof	$1,550

Indep Expend: Agn: $6,066 (NCPAC)

SIXTH DISTRICT

Some congressional districts seem to be made up of territory left over after everyone else has constructed his own constituency. Such a district is the 6th of Connecticut. Its population concentrations are widely dispersed, at just about opposite ends of the district. Enfield and Windsor Locks, in the far northeast corner, are predominantly Italian-American and part of the Hartford-to-Springfield, Massachusetts, industrial corridor along the Connecticut River. In the southeast corner are New Britain and Bristol, old mill towns, the latter predominantly Polish-American. In the north central part of the district, amid the mountains, are the much smaller mill towns of Torrington and Winsted, the latter the hometown of Ralph Nader. These Democratic areas are separated by much larger (geographically) and much smaller (in population) Yankee Republican towns, like Litchfield, whose proud houses witness its prosperity in the Revolutionary era, and Sharon, home of the Buckley clan. The 6th also includes several high income suburbs of Hartford: Farmington (site of the famous Miss Porter's School), Avon, and Simsbury.

The 6th district was created in the 1960s to elect a Democrat, but in fact it has proved to be a bipartisan district: in its 20 years of existence it has elected two Republicans and three Democrats. An unusual number of them have gone on to win, or run for, statewide office: Republican Thomas Meskill was elected governor in 1970, Democrat Ella Grasso was elected governor in 1974 and 1978, and Democrat Toby Moffett ran a close but unsuccessful race for the Senate in 1982.

The 6th district was the scene of one of the most strenuously contested congressional races in 1982, and was one district Republicans ended up capturing from Democrats despite the general Democratic trend. Everyone knew it would be a close race: there were serious primaries in both parties. One reason for the outcome was money. State Senator Nancy Johnson, the Republican nominee, ended up spending over $400,000, and was able to buy Hartford and New Haven TV time. Her opponent, state Senator Bill Curry, spent only about half as much and could not afford a TV buy. Another reason was issues. Curry tried to portray Johnson as a down-the-line Reagan supporter. But the fact that she had won three terms in the state Senate, most recently by a 2-1 margin, in heavily Democratic New Britain cast doubt on this charge; and she emphasized her support of measures like aid for the elderly, the Equal Rights Amendment, and domestic content legislation for autos. In the end the party label did not help Curry as much as he must have hoped: Toby Moffett was expected to carry his old district in the Senate contest, but actually lost it by 1,000.

The final factor may have been the personal contrast between the candidates. Curry is one of those young men always fascinated by politics and who has made it his whole career: he was elected to the state Senate (from a Republican-leaning district) at age 26. Johnson, in contrast, had a full and busy life before running for office. She raised three children and was active in charitable and community affairs—the kind of activities that, if approached sensitively, teach people more about the fabric of life in a community than do a few campaigns of canvassing and caucusing. The fact that Johnson ran so well in New Britain (she didn't carry it in the congressional race, but did well for a Republican) suggests that she learned a great deal more from these experiences than Curry, in his much briefer adult life, ever had a chance to. In the 1970s voters seemed eager to take chances on eager, energetic, bright, young, hyperpolitical candidates. Does the result in the 6th district suggest they are looking for something else now?

Johnson can expect good committee assignments and gingerly treatment from the Republican leadership: this is a seat they would like to keep, and she is obviously the strongest candidate to keep it.

The People   Pop. 1980: 517,146, up 6.4% 1970–80; voting age pop. 378,872; 2% Black, 2% Span. orig. 29% housing units rented. Median owner $63,300; renter $185. Households: 77% family, 39% with children, 65% married couples.

Presidential Vote

1980	Reagan (R)	113,203	(47%)
	Carter (D)	92,955	(39%)
	Other	32,748	(14%)

Rep. Nancy L. Johnson (R) Elected 1982; b. Jan. 5, 1935, Chicago, IL; home, New Britain; Radcliffe Col., B.A. 1957, U. of London, 1957–58; Unitarian.

Career Teacher, New Britain Mus. of Art, 1968–71; CT State Senate, 1976–82.

Offices 119 CHOB, 202-225-4476. Also 40 South High St., New Britain, 203-223-8412.

Committees *Public Works and Transportation* (17th). Subcommittees: Economic Development; Investigations and Oversight. *Veterans' Affairs* (11th). Subcommittees: Oversight and Investigations; Hospitals and Health Care. *Select Committee on Children, Youth and Families* (7th).

Group Ratings and Key Votes: Newly Elected

Election Results

1982 general	Nancy L. Johnson (R)	99,703	(52%)	($420,578)
	William E. Curry, Jr. (D)	92,178	(48%)	($233,284)
1982 primary	Nancy L. Johnson (R)	13,570	(70%)	
	Nicholas Schaus (R)	5,808	(30%)	($255,582)
1980 general	Anthony Toby Moffett (D)	142,685	(59%)	($190,266)
	Nicholas Schaus (R)	98,331	(41%)	($125,137)

Campaign Contributions and Expenditures

1981-82		*Direct Cont. 81-82**		*PACS brkdwn*			
Receipts	$425,832	Indiv	$192,501	Agr	$2,500	Ideo	$22,275
Expend.	$420,578	Party	$33,363	Bus	$116,835	Lbr	$—
Unspent	$5,252	PACS	$148,806	Hlth	$6,000	Prof	$1,000
		Cand	$1,000				

Indirect Party Expend: $38,273   *Indep Expend*: For: $1,227 (NRA)   **Non-Cand Loans*: $55,000

DELAWARE

Delaware is not a state anybody would design today: a small chunk of the eastern United States not much larger, in population or area, than the average congressional district. Most of the people live in one medium-sized metropolitan area, Wilmington; but downstate you could almost imagine yourself in the rural South. Delaware owes its existence to a footnote in American history. In colonial times, America was settled by ship, and these three counties along the Delaware River split away from William Penn's Pennsylvania over some dispute. Little Delaware became the "First State," as it still boasts on its license plates, because it beat Pennsylvania and New Jersey to become, by a few days, the first state to ratify the new Constitution in 1787.

Since then Delaware has managed to make itself one of the nation's more prosperous states. One reason is the liberal incorporation laws it passed in the 19th century; these allowed the owners or managers of a corporation to do pretty much what they pleased, without worrying much about stockholders. Delaware today is still, technically, the home of many of the nation's leading corporations: they exist because of a few sheets of paper in a Georgian state office building in the small state capital of Dover. Delaware is also the home, this time in a real sense, of the Du Pont Company. It is by far the state's largest employer, and of course its size dwarfs state government. Du Pont was founded by a French emigre, an impractical inventor whose sons had an aptitude for business. For years it grew by monopolizing the gunpowder trade, and later by pioneering new plastics and other synthetics. In the 1980s it branched out in another direction, acquiring Conoco for its oil reserves and a source of cheap chemical feedstock; this loaded Du Pont with expensive debt and may turn out to be a bad deal if oil prices don't climb from 1982 levels.

Wealthy members of the du Pont family—there are about 2,000 of them—and corporate executives of course have considerable influence in Delaware. The current governor is Pierre du Pont IV, a Republican elected in 1976 and 1980. A few years ago some Naderites wrote a book breathlessly charging that du Ponts, family and corporation, were powerful in Delaware. How could it be otherwise? What does not follow from this is that the corporation or the more politically troglodytic of the du Pont cousins always get their way. In fact Governor du Pont has made his career by opposing the company on some environmental issues, and the company was headed through most of the 1970s by a prominent Democrat, Irving Shapiro. Public officials who do not pay attention to big employers and rich and potentially useful citizens are not doing their job, any more than they would if they followed their orders on everything.

The politics of this small state (49th in area, 47th in population) has seldom engaged the attention of commentators. Technically Delaware has as much clout in the U.S. Senate as California or New York. But even when its senators have considerable seniority and respectable talents, as is the case today, they do not seem to attract much attention. Over the years Delaware has had a hardy two-party competition, with the du Ponts (the company owned the Wilmington newspapers for years) involved in both parties. In the 1960s the Republicans seemed to gain an edge, as the state became increasingly suburban and affluent—a result of the national rise in real incomes as well as the prosperity of Du Pont. But in the 1980s Delaware seems, if anything, leaning Democratic. It ousted its Republican congressman in 1982, albeit in special circumstances, and it came very close to going for Jimmy Carter in the 1980 election. It is almost as if the state were becoming more southern, even as the South has shed its heritage of racism. This is one state where the black percentage is rising, to 16% of all residents and 14% of adults in 1980—figures notably higher than in states farther northeast.

Senators. Delaware's senior statewide official is Senator William Roth, a Republican first elected to the House in 1966 and to the Senate in 1970. Roth is a party stalwart, a man who came to national politics as the Republicans were ruing their failure to stop Lyndon Johnson's Great Society legislation. He is not the sort to strike observers as a deep thinker, but in fact he sponsored in the late 1970s several of the major initiatives against what he considers negative trends: a case in point for the proposition that Republicans seized the legislative initiative and were winning the battle of ideas even before they won the presidency and control of the Senate in the 1980 elections. Roth's initiatives include the tuition tax credit (of $250 per student) for college tuitions, an antibusing proposal, and the Roth-Kemp bill (as it is known in the Senate) to cut tax rates 10% per year for three straight years.

These ideas came not only from intellectuals in think tanks, but in response to conditions in Delaware. Some 58% of this state's voters live in suburban New Castle County, outside the city of Wilmington (which once cast about one-third of the state's votes and now casts only 11%). There is a wide range of suburbs, from Greenville where du Ponts live on vast estates, to working class areas where people live in small frame houses and trailers nearly in the shadows of chemical plants and oil tank farms. But on the average people here are affluent and upwardly mobile. They want their children to do at least as well as they have, and so they resent it when they are ordered bused to what they consider, often rightly, inferior schools; they feel threatened by high tuition fees; they resent high tax rates that seem to take away money they desperately need. Of course Roth's proposals are open to serious criticism. The tax cut, largely enacted, by early 1983 had not produced the prosperity its backers promised; the antibusing measure is of dubious constitutionality; ditto for tuition tax credits, which can also be attacked as a very generous subsidy for the relatively rich.

Despite this productivity in ideas, Roth is not much stronger politically than when he came to the Senate. Legislatively, he occupies important positions on the Finance Committee and chairs Governmental Affairs. But he has not been the man to frame tax proposals; Bob Dole clearly is. And Governmental Affairs, theoretically a good place to gain visibility, always seems mired in issues of government organization that turn out to matter very little; Roth, as a loyal Republican, is not likely anyway to stage lurid hearings on the wrongdoings of the Reagan administration.

Electorally, Roth came up for reelection in 1982, not a particularly good year for Republicans. It was a heavy-spending campaign. In Delaware, which has no VHF TV stations of its own, candidates didn't used to go to the expense of buying Philadelphia TV time; Roth and his opponent, David Levinson, did. Levinson, who spent considerable sums of his own money, began the campaign unknown and did not prove to be a strong campaigner. Nonetheless he held Roth to 55% of the vote—a lower percentage than he received in either 1970 or 1976, in the latter case against a better-known opponent. That percentage does not add to Roth's clout in the Senate over the next few years.

Delaware's junior senator, Joseph Biden, is seen by many, and especially by himself, as one of the Democratic Party's brightest future leaders. He may in time become the first Delaware

Democrat since James Bayard (Cleveland's first secretary of state) to be a serious candidate for president. Biden was elected to the Senate in 1972 when he was 29 (although he turned 30 by the time the term began); he campaigned against an incumbent who, the voters sensed accurately, would have preferred to retire. Biden had the advantages of energy, a skillful handling of the issues, and an attractive extended family; tragically his first wife and daughter died in an auto accident just after the election.

Biden is considered brash and aggressive, unashamed of his own ambitions and intelligent enough to realize them. He owed his initial election in large part to his acute ear: he is quick to sense what is troubling the public and to come up with plausible ways to attack the problem. He was the first incumbent senator to back Jimmy Carter in 1976, and he was one of the first to criticize Carter later when things were not working out well. Early in his Senate career he won seats on the committees that seemed most important at the time—Foreign Relations and Judiciary—and has used their platforms ably. On the former, he stands behind only Claiborne Pell in seniority and may become chairman some day if Democrats regain a Senate majority; on the latter he is already ranking member, since Edward Kennedy relinquished that position to take it on the Labor Committee in 1981.

On economic issues Biden follows the mainstream of his party, although he expresses some doubts about the effectiveness of government action. On foreign policy, he is very much a child of the era he entered politics: a skeptic about American military involvement abroad, a critic of many American allies (but a supporter of Israel), an opponent of some military spending programs. In the Carter years he became an authentic expert on and supporter of the SALT II Treaty. In the Reagan years he has not taken a lead role on the major foreign policy issues, although he has the potential to be a force on less publicized ones.

On cultural issues, he often does not support positions associated with liberal Democrats. He has joined with Roth in sponsoring measures to limit the ability of federal courts to issue busing orders and has supported them if anything more vociferously. But he is with the Senate majority against a constitutional amendment to ban abortion.

Biden's Senate seat is up in 1984. Everyone assumes he will run for reelection, and it is possible that he will have formidable opposition—perhaps Governor Pete du Pont. Even so, Biden will be a strong candidate, and against any other opponent the solid favorite. He must be a little disappointed, however, that by early 1983 no one was mentioning him as a possible presidential candidate. He has time to wait; he will be only 42 in 1984. But will his politics be out of date in some future election? Biden is a master of the kind of campaigning that was so important in the 1970s: direct interaction with voters, close identification with their complaints about government and the system generally. It is an approach well suited to the outsider. But the Democratic Party seems to be moving toward selecting fewer of its delegates in primaries and more by the choice of professional politicians; it is not clear how well Biden can do at gathering the support of his peers. Temperamentally he is a man who runs against the establishment, yet he will also have to run, presumably, as a relatively senior senator who has helped run things for many years. It is not clear whether he can make the transition to this kind of politics.

Congressman. Delaware's House seat was held securely by Republican Thomas Evans until March 1981. A pleasant man who had the additional advantage of being a close friend of the Ronald Reagans, Evans was strong in Delaware until it was revealed that he had an "association" with Paula Parkinson, a lobbyist whose picture appeared in *Playboy* and who was rumored (incorrectly) to have videotaped affairs with 17 congressmen. This revelation put a stop to Evans's White House invitations and made him an inviting target for Democrats.

Yet not until late in the game did Democrats come up with a strong candidate, state Treasurer Thomas Carper. He won his previous job also after entering the race at the last minute; he won this one fairly handily. He was helped by the economy and his own strength, but no one supposes that he would have won—or run—without the Parkinson affair. Having captured the seat, however, Carper is a good bet to hold onto it. He has proved himself as a vote-getter, and his Democratic label is not a serious handicap.

Governor. Delaware's Governor Pierre S. du Pont IV understandably prefers to be called Pete. Despite the majesty of the name, he is not an offshoot of the richest part of the family and never came close to running (though he did work in) the Du Pont company. He was elected to Congress in 1970 when Roth ran for the Senate and was easily reelected in 1972 and 1974; he ran for governor in 1976 when both Senate seats seemed taken for some time. Governor du Pont has an interest in environmental laws, on which he has opposed the company on occasion. But he is by no means anti-business. One of his major achievements is a revision of Delaware's banking laws to encourage out-of-state banks to move some of their operations here. In personal style du Pont is straight from *The Preppy Handbook,* with his frayed button down collars. He has worn well with the voters and was reelected with 71% of the vote in 1980. He is a possible candidate for the Senate in 1984.

Presidential politics. Delaware chooses its small number of national convention delegates by caucus. In the general election, it is one of the nation's most closely contested states, and in close elections it has gone with the winner since 1948. Yet Delaware voters are not heavily wooed in presidential elections, for the good reason that there are not very many of them. Commercials on Philadelphia TV stations reach almost all the state, so there is not much reason for a candidate to come here in a day when most voters have no desire to see a candidate in person anyway.

The People Est. Pop. 1982: 602,000; Pop. 1980: 594,338, up 1.3% 1980–82 and 8.4% 1970–80; .26% of U.S. total, 47th largest; voting age pop. 427,743; 14% Black, 1% Spanish origin, 1% Asian origin. Single ancestry: 13% English, 6% Irish, German, 4% Italian, 2% Polish, 1% French, Scottish. Registered voters (1982): 285,736 Total. 127,385 D (45%); 93,873 R (33%); 64,299 other (22%). 14% with 1–3 yrs. col., 16% with 4+ yrs. col. 11.9% below poverty level. 27% housing units rented; median house value: $44,600; median monthly rent: $202. Households: 75% family, 41% with children, 61% married couples.

1982 Share of Federal Tax Burden $1,711,400,000; .29% of U.S. total, 46th largest.

1982 Share of Federal Expenditures

	Total		Non-Defense		Defense	
Total Expend	$1,491m	(0.25%)	$1,059m	(0.25%)	$432m	(0.24%)
St/Lcl Grants	279m	(0.32%)	279m	(0.32%)	0m	(0%)
Salary/Wages	164m	(0.21%)	11m	(0.04%)	153m	(0.30%)
Ind Payments	732m	(0.26%)	660m	(0.26)	72m	(0.25%)
Procurement	309m	(0.21%)	70m	(0.22%)	239m	(0.21%)
Other Programs	7m	(0.13%)	7m	(0.13%)	0m	(0%)
Loan/Insurance	73m	(0.11%)	67m	(0.11%)	6m	(0.03%)

Political Lineup Governor, Pierre S. du Pont IV (R). Senators, William V. Roth, Jr. (R) and Joseph R. Biden, Jr. (D). Representative, 1 (D) at large. State Senate, 21 (13 D and 8 R); State House of Representatives, 41 (25 D and 16 R).

Presidential Vote

1980	Reagan (R)	111,252	(47%)
	Carter (D)	105,754	(45%)
	Anderson (I)	16,754	(7%)
1976	Ford (R)	109,780	(47%)
	Carter (D)	122,559	(52%)

SENATORS

Sen. William V. Roth, Jr. (R) Elected 1970, seat up 1988; b. July 22, 1921, Great Falls, MT; home, Wilmington; U. of OR, B.A. 1944, Harvard U., M.B.A. 1947, LL.B. 1947; Episcopal.

Career Army, WWII; Practicing atty.; Chmn., DE Repub. State Comm., 1961-64; U.S. House of Reps., 1967-71.

Offices 3215 DSOB, 202-224-2441. Also 3021 Fed. Bldg., 844 King St., Wilmington 19801, 302-573-6291; and 200 U.S.P.O. Bldg., Georgetown 19947, 302-856-7690.

Committees *Finance* (3d). Subcommittees: International Trade; Savings, Pensions, and Investment Policy; Economic Growth, Employment, and Revenue Sharing. *Governmental Affairs* (Chairman). Subcommittee: Permanent Subcommittee on Investigations (Chairman). *Select Committee on Intelligence* (7th). Subcommittee: Analysis and Production; Budget Authorization. *Joint Economic Committee* (2d). Subcommittees: Agriculture and Transportation; Trade, Productivity, and Economic Growth (Chairman). *Joint Committee on Taxation* (3d).

Group Ratings

	ADA	ACLU	COPE	CFA	LCV	LWV	NTU	NSI	COC	ACA	CSFC
1982	50	36	19	30	49	55	88	56	67	55	70
1981	20	—	19	36	44	—	89	—	78	70	71
1980	22	23	21	0	65	40	69	90	80	73	70

National Journal Ratings

	Economic		Foreign		Cultural	
1982	35%	(LIB)	47%	(LIB)	48%	(LIB)
	64%	(CONS)	52%	(CONS)	51%	(CONS)
1981	57%	(LIB)	43%	(LIB)	2%	(LIB)
	42%	(CONS)	56%	(CONS)	82%	(CONS)

Key Votes

1) Reagan 81 Budget	FOR	5) $ to El Salvador	FOR	9) Poor Pay Food Stamps	FOR
2) Reagan 81 Tax Cut	FOR	6) Saudi AWACS Sale	AGN	10) Ban Crt Busing Order	FOR
3) Bal Budget Amend	FOR	7) Ban Abortion	AGN	11) Clinch Riv Brdr Rctr	AGN
4) Gas & Road Tax	FOR	8) Nerve Gas Prod	AGN	12) Legal Services Corp	AGN

Election Results

1982 general	William V. Roth, Jr. (R)	105,472	(56%)	($797,516)
	David N. Levinson (D)	83,722	(44%)	($1,247,054)
1982 primary	William V. Roth, Jr. (R) unopposed			
1976 general	William V. Roth, Jr. (R)	125,454	(56%)	($322,080)
	Thomas Maloney (D)	98,042	(44%)	($211,258)

Campaign Contributions and Expenditures

1979-82		Direct Cont. 81-82		PACS brkdwn			
Receipts	$843,047	Indiv	$423,656	Agr	$3,200	Ideo	$38,600
Expend.	$797,516	Party	$18,066	Bus	$261,870	Lbr	$7,500
Unspent	$48,019	PACS	$353,444	Hlth	$26,250	Prof	$14,250

Indirect Party Expend: $73,760

Sen. Joseph R. Biden, Jr. (D) Elected 1972, seat up 1984; b. Nov. 20, 1942, Scranton, PA; home, Wilmington; U. of DE, B.A. 1965, Syracuse U., J.D. 1968; Roman Catholic.

Career Practicing atty., 1968–72; New Castle Cnty. Cncl., 1970–72.

Offices 456 RSOB, 202-224-5042. Also 6021 Fed. Bldg., Wilmington 19801, 302-573-6345.

Committees *Budget* (3d). *Foreign Relations* (2d). Subcommittees: International Economic Policy; European Affairs. *Judiciary* (Ranking Member). Subcommittee: Criminal Law. *Select Committee on Intelligence* (3d). Subcommittee: Collection and Foreign Operations.

Group Ratings

	ADA	ACLU	COPE	CFA	LCV	LWV	NTU	NSI	COC	ACA	CSFC
1982	80	57	79	90	74	82	24	22	38	29	32
1981	80	—	77	79	99	—	21	—	28	33	34
1980	67	63	76	67	71	80	35	33	31	18	22

National Journal Ratings

	Economic		Foreign		Cultural	
1982	86%	(LIB)	72%	(LIB)	68%	(LIB)
	13%	(CONS)	27%	(CONS)	31%	(CONS)
1981	84%	(LIB)	93%	(LIB)	58%	(LIB)
	15%	(CONS)	5%	(CONS)	41%	(CONS)

Key Votes

1) Reagan 81 Budget	AGN	5) $ to El Salvador	AGN	9) Poor Pay Food Stamps	FOR
2) Reagan 81 Tax Cut	FOR	6) Saudi AWACS Sale	AGN	10) Ban Crt Busing Order	FOR
3) Bal Budget Amend	AGN	7) Ban Abortion	FOR	11) Clinch Riv Brdr Rctr	AGN
4) Gas & Road Tax	AGN	8) Nerve Gas Prod	AGN	12) Legal Services Corp	FOR

Election Results

1978 general	Joseph R. Biden, Jr. (D)	93,930	(58%)	($494,718)
	James H. Baxter, Jr. (R)	66,479	(41%)	($206,250)
1978 primary	Joseph R. Biden, Jr. (D) nominated by convention			
1972 general	Joseph R. Biden, Jr. (D)	116,006	(50%)	($260,699)
	J. Caleb Boggs (R)	112,844	(49%)	($167,657)

Campaign Contributions and Expenditures

1977-78		PACS brkdwn			
Receipts	$494,851	Agr	$2,600	Ideo	$2,000
Expend.	$494,718	Bus	$21,750	Lbr	$92,350
Unspent	$556	Hlth	$3,300	Prof	$6,300

GOVERNOR

Gov. Pierre S. du Pont IV (R) Elected 1976, term expires Jan. 1985; b. Jan. 22, 1935, Wilmington; home, Wilmington; Princeton U., B.S.E. 1956, Harvard U., LL.B. 1963; Episcopal.

Career Navy, 1957–60; Business exec., Photo Products Div., E.I. Du Pont Co., 1963–70: DE House of Reps., 1968–70; U.S. House of Reps., 1971–77.

Offices Legislative Hall, Dover 19001, 302-736-4101.

Election Results

1980 gen.	Pierre S. du Pont IV (R)	159,004	(71%)
	William J. Gordy (D)	64,217	(29%)
1980 prim.	Pierre S. du Pont IV (R) nominated by convention		
1976 gen.	Pierre S. du Pont IV (R)	130,531	(57%)
	Sherman W. Tribbitt (D)	97,480	(42%)

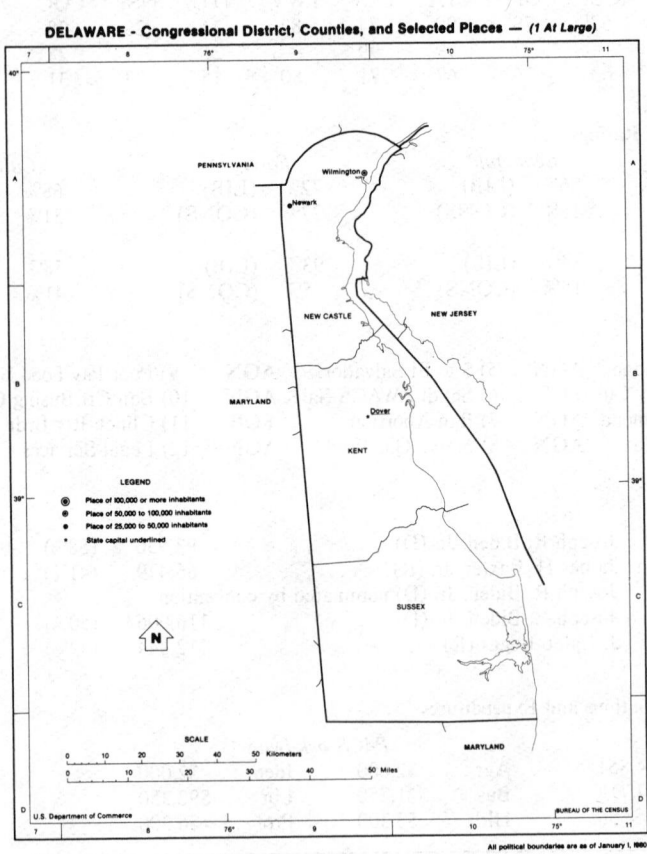

DELAWARE - Congressional District, Counties, and Selected Places — *(1 At Large)*

Rep. Thomas R. Carper (D) Elected 1982; b. Jan. 23, 1947, Beckley, WV; home, Wilmington; OH State University, B.A. 1968, U. of DE, M.B.A. 1975; Presbyterian.

Career Naval flight ofcr., 1968–73; Treas., James R. Soles for Congress Cmpgn., 1974; Industrial develop., DE Div. of Econ. Develop., 1975–76; State Treas., 1976–82.

Offices 1020 LHOB, 202-225-4165. Also 5021 J. Caleb Boggs Fed. Ofc. Bldg., 844 King St., Wilmington 19801, 302-573-6181;

Committees *Banking, Finance and Urban Affairs* (29th). Subcommittees: Financial Institutions Supervision, Regulation and Insurance; Housing and Community Development; Domestic Monetary Policy. *Merchant Marine and Fisheries* (21st). Subcommittees: Fisheries and Wildlife Conservation and the Environment; Coast Guard and Navigation.

Group Ratings and Key Votes: Newly Elected

Election Results

1982 general	Thomas R. Carper (D)	98,533	(52%)	($146,451)
	Thomas B. Evans (R)	87,153	(46%)	($340,383)
1982 primary	Thomas R. Carper (D) unopposed			
1980 general	Thomas B. Evans (R)	133,842	(62%)	($340,383)
	Robert L. Maxwell (D)	81,227	(38%)	($86,038)

Campaign Contributions and Expenditures

1981-82		*Direct Cont. 81-82*				*PACS brkdwn*		
Receipts	$148,340	Indiv	$43,313	Agr	$3,000	Ideo	$5,250
Expend.	$146,451	Party	$15,000	Bus	$1,550	Lbr	$67,000
Unspent	$1,887	PACS	$82,724	Hlth	$500	Prof	$500

Indirect Party Expend: $1,500

FLORIDA

By 1990 Florida will almost surely be the nation's fourth most populous state, behind only California, New York, and Texas—and ahead of such industrial giants as Pennsylvania, Ohio, and Illinois. To some that may seem unremarkable. But put in any kind of historic—or geographic—perspective it is astonishing. Florida is not the kind of place nature intended for dense human habitation. It is mostly swamp; its highest point is 345 feet above sea level, and much of it is really below water level. The climate, its greatest attraction today, was considered intolerable by most Americans until air conditioning became common. Florida does not have any important mineral resources (except phosphates in the central part of the state), and its agricultural potential (except for citrus) went unrecognized for years. The state is not close to much of anything, except the farmlands of south Georgia and, across 90 miles of sea, Cuba. Considering the length of its shoreline, it has surprisingly few natural ports.

So it's hardly remarkable that for most of its history Florida was a steamy, sparsely populated backwater, one of the more backward parts of the rural South. What is remarkable is Florida's recent development, in the years after World War II, and its position as one of the nation's most rapidly growing—and most diverse—states.

For Florida in the 1980s is a place that has seen repeated collisions of one culture against another. The old, pre-migration Florida, located almost entirely within the northern part of the state and extending a little way down the peninsula, saw a typically southern collision between white Anglo–Saxons and blacks forcibly imported from Africa. To that mix was added, beginning in the 1920s but in significant numbers starting in the 1950s, Anglo-Saxons from the northern states—many but by no means all of them retirees. At about the same time Florida became home for hundreds of thousands of people from the second (1840-1924) wave of American migration. Jews moving from New York to Miami were the most visible part of this migration, but it also included many others, Catholic and Protestant as well, from the big metropolitan areas of the Northeast and Great Lakes. Now Florida is becoming the home for much of what appears to be a third wave of migration to this country: not only the Cubans who came here first in the 1960s and then again in 1980 as refugees from Castro's dictatorship, but also people from all over Latin America: Haiti and Nicaragua, Colombia and Jamaica. All of them came looking for the opportunity and freedom that the United States still promises.

These cultural collisions have produced friction and set off a lot of sparks—not least because most were unexpected. Miami has become *the* center for Latin American commerce and trade—and also for a vicious drug importing business that dwarfs most legal enterprises. Blacks have rioted in Miami, in part because of resentment over the more rapid economic progress of the Cubans and other Latins. Meanwhile, within Florida's big metropolitan areas, there have been major population movements as one group flees another it dislikes. There are vast potential differences between elderly retirees who dominate most of south Florida and the young parents with large numbers of children in northern and central Florida. But in all, what is remarkable is not that there has been friction, but that there has not been much more. Florida has seen almost as many cultural collisions as the Hapsburg empire in the late 19th century, with conflict between Germans and Czechs, Hungarians and Poles, Serbs and Croats, and among Slovenes and Slovaks and Jews. In Mitteleuropa the resulting turmoil led directly to World War I; in Florida the results, as unpleasant as they may be for Americans, have been much less dire.

What those collisions have given Florida is an especially chaotic and unstable politics. One reason is the diverse origin of Florida's residents and the fact that they have little or no connection with the civic culture of the state. There is especially rapid turnover among the elderly population. The elderly Republican voters of, say, St. Petersburg of 20 years ago are, mostly, not with us any more. Today's elderly voters are from different backgrounds, have different political opinions and different perspectives, and have no institutional memory for Florida politics. Most of them know nothing of the antics of Governor (1967-70) Claude Kirk or the fact that the legislature was dominated for years by conservatives from north Florida called the Pork Chop Gang.

The other reason for the instability of Florida politics is the physical size of the state. There is no dominant metropolitan area here, like New York or Chicago. Instead, there are eight major TV markets. Miami's Dade County, the state's largest, casts only 13% of its votes; the three Gold Coast counties together—Dade, Broward, Palm Beach—cast only 33%. Another major metropolitan area has two central cities that could not be more unlike: working-class Tampa and retiree haven St. Petersburg. Jacksonville is big enough to be significant in the state's economy and politics, and so is Orlando, the home of Disney World and its Epcot Center as well as the center of the state's citrus industry. There are literally dozens of small communities, from Pensacola to Naples and Key West that, for most of their residents, are Florida. With no dominant newspapers or TV stations, this is a hard state to grasp. Meanwhile, state government and politics are not usually matters of major interest. The capital, Tallahassee, is a small (though growing) city tucked away almost in a corner of the state, more than a comfortable drive from where most Floridians live.

All these factors make Florida elections unpredictable and subject to startling fluctuations. In presidential races it trended Republican after 1945, then went for Jimmy Carter in 1976, then turned sharply against him in 1980. The Republicans seemed on the verge of becoming seriously competitive in the late 1960s when they elected a senator and a governor. But except for a narrow victory in the 1980 Senate election, they haven't won a major statewide contest since. The most enduring politicians have been little-known state legislators with moderate reputations, who have finished second to well-known candidates in the first Democratic primary and then have beaten them in runoffs; then, a month later, they have beaten Republicans in general elections. This scenario—one that produces unpredictable results—describes the careers of Governors Reubin Askew (first elected 1970) and Bob Graham (1978) and Senator Lawton Chiles (1970). Florida, represented by the same two U.S. senators in the 1950s and 1960s, has retired senators often since; only one of them, Chiles, has been reelected since 1964. The state's House delegation had only six members, all conservative Democrats, in 1950; now it has 19, of all political descriptions.

Presidential politics. Is Florida Democratic or Republican in national elections? Arguments can be made both ways. In 1976 it was solidly Democratic, voting for Jimmy Carter of neighboring south Georgia. Carter cultivated this state carefully, first for the early Florida presidential primary, then for the general election; and it paid off. Then in 1980, Florida went solidly Republican. The main reason was the influx, within 10 weeks, of 125,000 Cuban refugees into Miami. Lurid stories were being told everywhere: these refugees (unlike earlier Cubans) were mostly criminals, they were organizing into gangs that were stopping cars and assaulting people on the streets, they were bringing in diseases—the sort of thing you surely could have heard about immigrants in New York in 1907, when 1.7 million of them landed. The uncertain response of the Carter administration—first welcoming the refugees, then sternly promising that no more would be allowed in, then declining to turn them back—made a difficult situation worse. The refugee influx, coming on top of the growth of the drug business in Miami, with attendant killings and floods of $100 bills, and accompanied by a riot in black Liberty City, profoundly shook many south Florida voters. Largely as a result, usually Democratic south Florida, with its many migrants from New York and the Northeast, went for Ronald Reagan in 1980; Carter would have lost the state anyway, but by 50%–44%, not 56%–39%.

Given that volatility, it is hard to say anything about the 1984 presidential election here. The Democratic primary, one of the nation's earliest, will probably feature the attempt of former Governor Askew to carry his home state. His popularity remained high through eight years in office, despite his unpopular stands on some issues (busing) and his support of proposals to raise taxes. The national media may tend to ignore the primary here or discount a solid showing; but isn't the testimony of people who have watched a politician make decisons under stress for nearly a decade worth more than that of people who have shaken his hands, watched his TV ads and listened to his door-to-door canvassers for eight weeks? Of course a weak showing by Askew here will sink his candidacy.

The presidential primary here is a more southern accented primary than many think— something that became clear when George Wallace won it easily in 1972. But the Florida primary is peculiar not because it is southern, but because it is held in Florida. No other state comes close to duplicating the electorate here. So while having little precedental value, it is important nonetheless: Florida has 21 electoral votes.

There are actually quite a few registered Republicans here (up to 31% of the total, a new high, in 1982), but they are still concentrated in those parts of the state—the Gulf Coast, the Gold Coast north of Dade County—with lots of migrants from the WASP suburbs of the Northeast and Midwest. They tend to favor more conservative candidates.

As for the general election, the only certainty is that it will be fiercely contested. Issues and events of little importance to voters elsewhere—the Caribbean Basin Initiative, Latin American rebellions which produce refugees—can surely affect the outcome of Florida's election, as 1980 showed. Otherwise, Florida is a balanced state: probably Republican-leaning on cultural issues, and on many economic issues—except for Social Security. And if the affluent retirees add to the Republican base, then the increasing number of working class retirees help the Democrats.

Senators. Florida's senior senator is Lawton Chiles, a Democrat whose origin and politics are part of an old Florida tradition. Chiles is from Lakeland, an old community in the central part of the state; his politics can be described as small town Democratic. He is a very religious man, and an earnest one, but even enough in temperament not to be cloying. When Chiles first ran, as an unknown in 1970, he had the advantages of not having held high office: he was not associated with the cynical and in some cases corrupt legislators who ran things in Tallahassee; he was not associated with the policies of the Johnson administration; and he was not encumbered with a record of opposition to civil rights either. Chiles was the originator that year of the walking campaign. He walked the length of the state—more than 1,000 miles—attracting little notice at first and then, more and more often, being recognized by drivers and fellow pedestrians. It worked not simply as a gimmick, but because it symbolized something genuine about Chiles: his openness (he switched from Vietnam hawk to dove in the course of his walk), his good humor, his strength, his lack of ties to the old politics (although it didn't hurt, in some quarters, that he won the support of his Polk County neighbor, retiring Senator Spessard Holland).

Chiles won an upset victory in the runoff that year against a former governor, and he beat, with surprising ease, the Republican, St. Petersburg Congressman William Cramer, who expected to win the seat easily. Since then he has won two more terms against weak opposition. Republicans in 1981 hoped to give Chiles a harder fight; they suspected that, after 11 years in office in this large, unstable state, he was not really very well known by most voters. But the lateness of Florida's state primary and runoff made it very hard for the eventual Republican nominee, Fort Lauderdale legislator Van Poole, to make any headway in what turned out to be a Democratic year.

Chiles's major position in the Senate in 1983 and 1984 is as ranking minority member of the Budget Committee. It is a post that would have conferred much power five years ago, when Budget was run on a bipartisan basis and leaders of both parties sought consensus. But Majority Leader Howard Baker and Budget Chairman Pete Domenici have tried to fashion Republican budgets, and in 1981 and 1982 they succeeded. They did not consult Chiles's predecessor, Ernest Hollings, much then, and they will not consult Chiles much more unless Senate Republicans become visibly and hopelessly split. That is true even though Chiles and Domenici are friends and respect each other's moral beliefs. If the Republicans are split, however, Chiles will be calling the shots—if he can fashion a consensus among often fractious Senate Democrats. Chiles is also a member of the Appropriations and Governmental Affairs Committees. These posts give him an opportunity to get involved in the nitty-gritty operation of government, which he did, for example, when the Government Services Agency was under attack. But most such work wins no headlines and, even to participants, headway is hard to gauge. Chiles has the potential to serve many more years in the Senate. But he has a constituency difficult to keep in touch with and has not yet succeeded in establishing a high profile in Washington.

Paula Hawkins, Florida's junior senator, has different problems. In state politics she performed the difficult feats, for a Republican, of winning statewide office (public service commissioner) and gaining a reputation as a consumer advocate. This enabled her to beat an Orlando area congressman in the 1980 Republican Senate primary and to edge, by a narrow margin, state Insurance Commissioner Bill Gunter in the general election. The Hawkins-Gunter contest was one of those close races in which the national Republican Party's expertise—and ability to channel in big money—made the difference: Gunter spent more, but most of it was consumed in his primary and runoff fights. So Hawkins found herself in the uncharacteristic position of being in the majority party.

Hawkins found herself in some uncomfortable positions as well. In 1981 she wanted publicity for her proposals to cut the food stamp program, so she gave a lunch—and served sirloin steak. Television news had a lot of fun with that. She had a taste for the too clever maneuvers—stealing colleagues' ideas and reneging on commitments. Now probably very few of her colleagues trust her. She serves on committees with jurisdiction over some very important Florida interests: Agriculture and Banking. But while she has steadfastly supported major Reagan programs, she may be something of a freewheeling maverick on other issues—or may not be very effective on them. Her strategy for winning reelection seems clear: to portray herself as a maverick fighting for the (somewhat comfortable) little guy. Whether that strategy will prove successful, in mostly Democratic Florida, is unclear.

Governor. The state's governor, Bob Graham, was reelected by a wide margin in 1982 after several turbulent Florida political years, and that says something about his popularity and political strength. True, his opponent, Congressman Skip Bafalis, was little known outside his outsized south Florida district, but the fact is that Graham ran much better than Jimmy Carter had in 1980, although Graham had been one of Carter's most vocal supporters. Moreover, Graham, like Carter, had been fiercely criticized for the state's handling of the Cuban refugees. Graham benefited from other accomplishments. He presides over the rapidly expanding government of a rapidly expanding state, but has been able to avoid an income tax, which even Florida liberals shun (the theory is that a sales tax gets a lot of revenues from tourists). Like his predecessor, Reubin Askew, he likes to emphasize his rural and small town roots, although in Graham's case the small town is Miami Lakes, once his family's farm and now a sprawling suburb northwest of Miami. He will not be eligible for a third term in 1986, but he seems a logical candidate for Paula Hawkins's Senate seat.

Congressional districting. Florida gained four House seats in the 1980 Census—more than any other state. The Democratic legislature took most of 1981 and 1982 to draw the lines, but in the end two of the four new seats went Republican. One in south Florida (either the 12th or 13th, since both together essentially made up one district in the 1970s) was easily Republican, and the Republicans narrowly beat the state House speaker in a new seat in the Tampa Bay area. The north central Florida seat went easily to one Democratic legislator; a new Gold Coast seat was solidly Democratic. Of incumbent congressmen, the one with the toughest race turned out to be Bill Chappell, a Boll Weevil with a seemingly safe conservative Democratic district, who almost lost his primary.

The People Est. Pop. 1982: 10,416,000; Pop. 1980: 9,746,324, up 6.9% 1980–82 and 43.5% 1970–80; 4.5% of U.S. total, 7th largest; voting age pop. 7,386,688; 11% Black, 9% Spanish origin, 1% Asian origin. Single ancestry: 12% English, 6% German, 4% Irish, 3% Italian, 1% Polish, Russian, French, Scottish, Dutch. Registered voters (1982): 4,865,636 Total. 3,066,351 D (63%); 1,500,031 R (31%); 299,254 other (6%). 17% with 1–3 yrs. col., 15% with 4+ yrs. col. 13.0% below poverty level. 27% housing units rented; median house value: $45,300; median monthly rent: $209. Households: 72% family, 33% with children, 59% married couples.

1982 Share of Federal Tax Burden $25,895,700,000; 4.33% of U.S. total, 7th largest.

1982 Share of Federal Expenditures

	Total		Non-Defense		Defense	
Total Expend	$28,460m	(4.72%)	$20,730m	(4.88%)	$7,731m	(4.32%)
St/Lcl Grants	2,859m	(3.24%)	2,857m	(3.24%)	2m	(5.56%)
Salary/Wages	2,935m	(3.76%)	630m	(2.30%)	2,305m	(4.55%)
Ind Payments	17,652m	(6.17%)	15,329m	(5.95%)	2,323m	(8.13%)
Procurement	4,954m	(3.40%)	878m	(2.78%)	4,077m	(3.57%)
Other Programs	60m	(1.11%)	57m	(1.06%)	3m	(6.98%)
Loan/Insurance	1,333m	(2.08%)	1,186m	(1.92%)	147m	(6.68%)

Political Lineup Governor, Robert (Bob) Graham (D). Senators, Lawton Chiles (D) and Paula Hawkins (R). Representatives, 19 (13 D and 6 R). State Senate, 40 (32 D and 8 R); State House of Representatives, 120 (84 D and 36 R).

Presidential Vote

1980	Reagan (R)	2,046,951	(56%)
	Carter (D)	1,419,475	(39%)
	Anderson (I)	189,692	(5%)
1976	Ford (R)	1,469,531	(47%)
	Carter (D)	1,636,000	(52%)

1980 Democratic Presidential Primary			*1980 Republican Presidential Primary*		
Carter	666,321	(61%)	Reagan	345,699	(56%)
Kennedy	254,727	(23%)	Bush	185,996	(30%)
Two others.........	72,634	(7%)	Anderson	56,636	(9%)
No preference.......	104,321	(10%)	Six others	26,664	(4%)

SENATORS

Sen. Lawton Chiles (D) Elected 1970, seat up 1988; b. Apr. 3, 1930, Lakeland; home, Lakeland; U. of FL, B.S. 1952, LL.B. 1955; Presbyterian.

Career Army, Korea; Practicing atty., 1955–71; Instructor, FL Southern Col., 1955–57; FL House of Reps., 1958–66; FL Senate, 1966–70.

Offices 450 RSOB, 202-224-5274. Also Fed. Bldg., Lakeland 33801, 813-688-6681; and 931 Fed. Bldg., P.O. Box 79, 51 S.W. First Ave., Miami 33130, 305-350-4891.

Committees Appropriations (7th). Subcommittees: Agriculture, Rural Development; Defense; Labor, Health and Human Services, Education; Transportation. *Budget* (Ranking Member). *Governmental Affairs* (3d). Subcommittees: Governmental Efficieny and the District of Columbia; Information Management and Regulatory Affairs; Permanent Subcommittee on Investigations. *Special Committee on Aging* (2d).

Group Ratings

	ADA	ACLU	COPE	CFA	LCV	LWV	NTU	NSI	COC	ACA	CSFC
1982	50	29	46	60	62	75	35	90	67	57	56
1981	45	—	45	36	50	—	25	—	44	55	49
1980	50	43	52	13	33	50	41	40	50	38	41

National Journal Ratings

	Economic		Foreign		Cultural	
1982	55%	(LIB)	48%	(LIB)	50%	(LIB)
	44%	(CONS)	51%	(CONS)	49%	(CONS)
1981	67%	(LIB)	54%	(LIB)	38%	(LIB)
	32%	(CONS)	45%	(CONS)	60%	(CONS)

Key Votes

1) Reagan 81 Budget	FOR	5) $ to El Salvador	AGN	9) Poor Pay Food Stamps	AGN
2) Reagan 81 Tax Cut	FOR	6) Saudi AWACS Sale	AGN	10) Ban Crt Busing Order	FOR
3) Bal Budget Amend	FOR	7) Ban Abortion	FOR	11) Clinch Riv Brdr Rctr	AGN
4) Gas & Road Tax	FOR	8) Nerve Gas Prod	AGN	12) Legal Services Corp	AGN

Election Results

1982 general	Lawton Chiles (D)	1,636,857	(62%)	($806,629)
	Van B. Poole (R)	1,014,551	(38%)	($472,505)
1982 primary	Lawton Chiles (D) unopposed			
1976 general	Lawton Chiles (D)	1,799,518	(63%)	($362,235)
	John Grady (R)	1,057,886	(37%)	($394,574)

Campaign Contributions and Expenditures

1981-82		Direct Cont. 81-82		PACS brkdwn			
Receipts	$848,266	Indiv	$821,117	Agr	$200	Ideo	$1,600
Expend.	$806,629	Party	$ 5,813	Bus	$5,758	Lbr	$2,100
Unspent	$41,646	PACS	$10,158	Hlth	$100	Prof	$600

Indep Expend: For: $2,754 (LCV) Agn: $10,168 (NCPAC, LIFEPAC)

Sen. Paula Hawkins (R) Elected 1980, seat up 1986; b. Jan. 24, 1927, Salt Lake City, UT; home, Winter Park; UT St. U.; Mormon.

Career Repub. Natl. Committee, 1968; Spec. Advis. Committee, Consum. Affairs, Fed. Energy Admin., 1968; Pres. Commission on White House Fellowships, 1968; FL Pub. Svc. Commissioner, 1973–79.

Offices 313 HSOB, 202-224-3041. Also 701 Semoran Blvd., Rm. 200, Altamonte Springs 32701, 305-339-1980; and 604 Lewis State Bank Bldg., Tallahassee 32301, 904-224-5748.

Committees *Agriculture, Nutrition and Forestry* (7th). Subcommittees: Agricultural Credit and Rural Electrification (Chairwoman); Foreign Agricultural Policy; Nutrition. *Banking, Housing and Urban Affairs* (7th). Subcommittees: Consumer Affairs (Chairwoman); Housing and Urban Affairs; Insurance; Securities. *Labor and Human Resources* (10th). Subcommittees: Aging; Employment and Productivity; Handicapped.

Group Ratings

	ADA	ACLU	COPE	CFA	LCV	LWV	NTU	NSI	COC	ACA	CSFC
1982	10	25	29	40	46	75	53	90	60	57	71
1981	15	—	28	43	26	—	54	—	94	62	79

National Journal Ratings

	Economic		Foreign		Cultural	
1982	49%	(LIB)	1%	(LIB)	47%	(LIB)
	50%	(CONS)	98%	(CONS)	52%	(CONS)
1981	43%	(LIB)	41%	(LIB)	2%	(LIB)
	56%	(CONS)	58%	(CONS)	82%	(CONS)

Key Votes

1) Reagan 81 Budget	FOR	5) $ to El Salvador	FOR	9) Poor Pay Food Stamps	AGN
2) Reagan 81 Tax Cut	FOR	6) Saudi AWACS Sale	AGN	10) Ban Crt Busing Order	—
3) Bal Budget Amend	FOR	7) Ban Abortion	FOR	11) Clinch Riv Brdr Rctr	FOR
4) Gas & Road Tax	AGN	8) Nerve Gas Prod	—	12) Legal Services Corp	AGN

Election Results

1980 general	Paula Hawkins (R)	1,822,460	(52%)	($696,969)
	Bill Gunter (D)	1,705,409	(48%)	($2,164,560)
1980 runoff	Paula Hawkins (R)	293,600	(62%)	
	Lou Frey, Jr. (R)	182,911	(38%)	($320,489)
1980 primary	Paula Hawkins (R)	209,856	(48%)	
	Lou Frey, Jr. (R)	119,834	(27%)	
	Ander Crenshaw (R)	54,767	(13%)	($71,626)
	Three others (R)	51,505	(12%)	
1974 general	Richard (Dick) Stone (D)	781,031	(43%)	($919,787)
	Jack Eckerd (R)	736,674	(41%)	($421,169)
	John Grady (AI)	282,659	(16%)	($148,495)

Campaign Contributions and Expenditures

1979-80		PACS brkdwn			
Receipts	$888,986	Agr	$22,850	Ideo	$74,860
Expend.	$795,968	Bus	$119,165	Lbr	$1,000
Unspent	$92,042	Hlth	$12,600	Prof	$5,000

GOVERNOR

Gov. Robert (Bob) **Graham** (D) Elected 1978, term expires Jan. 1987; b. Nov. 9, 1936, Miami; home, Tallahassee; U. of FL, B.A. 1959, Harvard U., J.D. 1962; United Church of Christ.

Career V.P., Graham Co., cattle and dairy production; Chmn. of Bd., Sengra Development Corp., land developers; FL House of Reps., 1967–71; FL Senate, 1971–78.

Offices The Capitol, Tallahassee 32304, 904-488-1234.

Election Results

1982 gen.	Robert (Bob) Graham (D) ...	1,739,553	(65%)
	Lewis A. Bafalis (R)	949,023	(35%)
1982 prim.	Robert (Bob) Graham (D) ...	839,320	(85%)
	Two others (D)	154,214	(16%)
1978 gen.	Robert (Bob) Graham (D) ...	1,406,580	(56%)
	Jack M. Eckerd (R)	1,123,888	(44%)

FIRST DISTRICT

When John Quincy Adams persuaded Spain to sell Florida to the United States in 1819, the main prize was the part of what we now call the Florida Panhandle around the city of Pensacola. This was, so far as Americans knew, the only decent harbor in Florida, and the Panhandle about the only part of the area not covered by swamp. Today Pensacola and the Panhandle do not typify Florida to many people. Economically, culturally, politically, they are really part of the Deep South, more akin to neighboring Mobile, Alabama, than to Miami, 1,000 miles away.

You will not hear many Yankee accents in this part of Florida; it is settled almost entirely by southerners. Nor will you find many retirees. In the Panhandle, and in that part of north Florida that stretches east to Jacksonville, nearly half the households contain children: this is young family country. People here live in small houses, not stucco condominium villages; they shop, at least sometimes, on old main streets as well as in air-conditioned shopping malls. There are not many beachcombers here: most of the Gulf Coast is swampy, not sandy, and except for a few areas around Pensacola and Panama City there has been little beach development.

This was poor country historically: the tag end of the poor dirt farm country of the Deep South. But in the post-1945 period it has prospered. For much of that time the prime engine of development was military spending. Pensacola has a naval station, and nearby is giant Eglin Air Force Base, which spreads over the lion's share of three counties. Later, starting probably in the mid-1960s, the Panhandle seemed to generate economic development on its own. This was part of a broader trend, not so much a migration of people and jobs to this area as an end to the time when people and jobs were migrating out. One reason may have been the civil rights revolution, which made the South more attractive to talented blacks; another may have been developments in transportation and communications (truck transport, cheap long distance phone calls) that made it easier to run a business from a small city.

The 1st congressional district of Florida covers the western end of the Panhandle, including

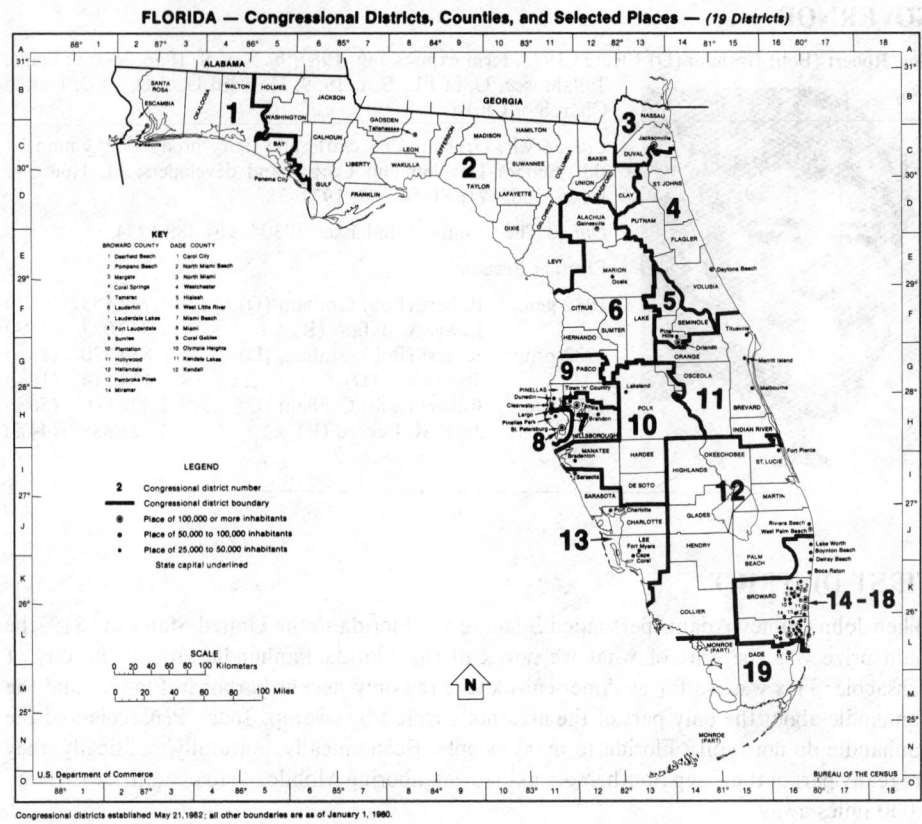

FLORIDA — Congressional Districts, Counties, and Selected Places — *(19 Districts)*

Congressional districts established May 21,1982; all other boundaries are as of January 1, 1980.

Pensacola and Panama City. For many years it was inclined to attribute its economic success to its Congressman, Bob Sikes, who was first elected in 1940 and for years chaired the Military Construction Appropriations Subcommittee. Sikes eventually left office under a cloud, after he was reprimanded formally by the House for unethical practices in 1976 and stripped of his chairmanship by the Democratic Caucus in 1977. But the 1st district seems not to have suffered. Internal forces within the military establishment keep the big bases here, and the strength of the private economy here has become increasingly apparent.

When Sikes retired, the Republicans made a major effort to win the district, and quite sensibly so. It had shown no allegiance to the national Democratic Party: it was solidly for George Wallace in 1968, 84% for Richard Nixon in 1972, and for Gerald Ford over south Georgia neighbor Jimmy Carter in 1976. But the Democratic primary proved to be the decisive contest still, and it produced a winner, Earl Hutto, a Panama City legislator, who could not be portrayed as a squishy-soft liberal. The Republicans tried again in 1980 to beat him, to no avail; in 1982, he won without serious opposition.

Hutto is the member of the Florida delegation most closely associated with Boll Weevil Democrats; he supported the Reagan budget and tax programs in 1981 and has joined liberals on few issues. He serves on what have historically been bread-and-butter committees for this district: Armed Services and Merchant Marine and Fisheries. He seems to be close to an Armed Services subcommittee chairmanship, either on Military Installations and Facilities (of obvious local importance) or Seapower (of both local and national significance).

The People   Pop. 1980: 512,821, up 22.6% 1970–80; voting age pop. 362,491; 12% Black, 2% Span. orig., 1% Asian orig., 1% Am. Ind. 28% housing units rented. Median owner $35,500; renter $162. Households: 78% family, 44% with children, 64% married couples.

Presidential Vote

1980	Reagan (R)	87,425	(62%)
	Carter (D)	52,620	(38%)

Rep. Earl Dewitt Hutto (D) Elected 1978; b. May 12, 1926, Midland City, AL; home, Panama City; Troy St. U., B.S. 1949, Northwestern U., 1951; Baptist.

Career Navy, WWII; Pres., Earl Hutto Advertising Agency; FL House of Reps., 1972–78.

Offices 330 CHOB, 202-225-4136. Also Fed. Bldg., Panama City 32401, 904-234-8933.

Committees *Armed Services* (15th). Subcommittees: Research and Development; Readiness; Military Installations and Facilities. *Merchant Marine and Fisheries* (12th). Subcommittees: Fisheries and Wildlife Conservation and the Environment; Coast Guard and Navigation.

Group Ratings

	ADA	ACLU	COPE	CFA	LCV	LWV	NTU	NSI	COC	ACA	CSFC
1982	10	25	42	30	51	36	33	100	71	55	47
1981	10	—	42	29	21	—	33	—	78	63	56
1980	22	0	50	36	35	40	36	100	81	48	49

National Journal Ratings

	Economic		Foreign		Cultural	
1982	33%	(LIB)	12%	(LIB)	4%	(LIB)
	67%	(CONS)	84%	(CONS)	87%	(CONS)
1981	44%	(LIB)	28%	(LIB)	31%	(LIB)
	56%	(CONS)	71%	(CONS)	69%	(CONS)

Key Votes

1) Reagan 81 Budget	FOR	5) Incr SS Rtmt Age	FOR	9) Poor Pay Food Stamps	AGN
2) Reagan 81 Tax Cut	FOR	6) Saudi AWACS Sale	AGN	10) Ban Crt Busing Order	FOR
3) Bal Budget Amend	FOR	7) $ for MX Missile	FOR	11) Auto Local Content	AGN
4) Gas & Road Tax	FOR	8) Nerve Gas Prod	FOR	12) Nuclear Arms Freeze	AGN

Election Results

1982 general	Earl Dewitt Hutto (D)	82,482	(74%)	($93,371)
	J. Terryl Bechtol (R)	28,285	(26%)	($23,596)
1982 primary	Earl Dewitt Hutto (D) unopposed			
1980 general	Earl Dewitt Hutto (D)	119,829	(61%)	($63,541)
	Warren Briggs (R)	75,939	(39%)	($227,563)

Campaign Contributions and Expenditures

1981-82		Direct Cont. 81-82		PACS brkdwn			
Receipts	$129,548	Indiv	$—	Agr	$550	Ideo	$2,200
Expend.	$93,371	PACS	$43,070	Bus	$31,300	Lbr	$3,000
Unspent	$59,522			Hlth	$5,500	Prof	$—

SECOND DISTRICT

The 2d congressional district of Florida is the part of the state most like the Deep South. It is really the southernmost extension of Dixie (the name of a county here, incidentally, on the Suwanee River). For years there was little here to distinguish this part of Florida from neighboring south Georgia, and in some respects they are still similar. The 2d district, for example, has one of the highest black percentages of any Florida district, and for years it elected nobody but conservative Democrats. It was the one part of Florida that remained politically faithful to Jimmy Carter in 1980. There are few Yankees here, few retirees; lots of catfish farms, lots of young families.

There are also lots of state institutions. In the 19th century the state capital was situated at Tallahassee, centrally located between Jacksonville and Pensacola (almost no one lived in the Florida peninsula then). Tallahassee is still small, but growing: no longer among the sleepiest of state capitals. It has a major university, Florida State; another, Florida, is in Gainesville, which was in the 2d until the 1982 redistricting. The 2d even has the state prison, in Raiford.

The 2d district has been represented for more than 20 years by the same congressman, Don Fuqua. His reputation is conservative, but his voting record is more in line with those of northern Democrats than one might expect. On economic issues he often lines up with other Democrats, and sometimes does so on cultural issues as well. Two political factors lead him in this direction. The first is the fact that he has something to lose in the House if he does not stay with the leadership. He is chairman of the Science and Technology Committee, and chairmanships can be taken away by the Democratic Caucus. The second is that his district is not so Dixiecratic as it might seem. The only real threat to his tenure comes in the Democratic primary; Republicans virtually never carry this district. Fuqua had one political scare, back in 1976, when two opponents came within 355 votes of forcing him into a runoff; his weaknesses then were in Tallahassee and Gainesville, with their black and university voters. In 1982, he had two primary opponents again, neither strong; he won with 65%, but was slightly weaker (59%) in Tallahassee.

Science and Technology for some years did not seem an important committee: the space program was in eclipse, and Americans seemed to be losing their sense of wonderment at scientific achievements. But in the middle 1980s the committee suddenly shaped up as an important body. It handles certain nuclear energy projects, notably the Clinch River Breeder Reactor; Fuqua supports this controversial project, but a bipartisan majority on the committee voted against it as long ago as May 1981, and prevailed on the floor of the House;

the breeder was kept going only by a one-vote margin in the Senate and some parliamentary legerdemain. The Science Committee also has jurisdiction over scientific education—now, given the vogue of high tech, as politically important as it was in the wake of the Sputnik launching in 1957. So this hitherto obscure body, and its not nationally prominent chairman, could become important as the nation seeks more scientists, engineers, and inventors of high technology devices.

The People   Pop. 1980: 513,127, up 33.5% 1970–80; voting age pop. 363,447; 22% Black, 1% Span. orig. 25% housing units rented. Median owner $30,700; renter $142. Households: 74% family, 42% with children, 60% married couples.

Presidential Vote

1980	Reagan (R)	79,069	(44%)
	Carter (D)	100,962	(56%)

Rep. Don Fuqua (D) Elected 1962; b. Aug. 20, 1933, Jacksonville; home, Alta; U. of FL, B.S. 1957; Presbyterian.

Career Army, Korea; FL House of Reps., 1958–62.

Offices 2269 RHOB, 202-225-5235. Also 100 P.O. Bldg., Tallahassee 32302, 904-224-1152.

Committees *Science and Technology* (Chairman). Subcommittee: Energy Development and Applications (Chairman). *Government Operations* (3d). Subcommittee: Legislation and National Security.

Group Ratings

	ADA	ACLU	COPE	CFA	LCV	LWV	NTU	NSI	COC	ACA	CSFC
1982	25	46	35	30	60	55	44	88	67	52	44
1981	20	—	36	50	36	—	14	—	56	36	51
1980	33	37	44	57	26	22	32	63	73	29	42

National Journal Ratings

	Economic		Foreign		Cultural	
1982	24%	(LIB)	40%	(LIB)	25%	(LIB)
	76%	(CONS)	60%	(CONS)	75%	(CONS)
1981	50%	(LIB)	34%	(LIB)	53%	(LIB)
	50%	(CONS)	63%	(CONS)	47%	(CONS)

Key Votes

1) Reagan 81 Budget	AGN	5) Incr SS Rtmt Age	FOR	9) Poor Pay Food Stamps	AGN
2) Reagan 81 Tax Cut	FOR	6) Saudi AWACS Sale	AGN	10) Ban Crt Busing Order	FOR
3) Bal Budget Amend	FOR	7) $ for MX Missile	AGN	11) Auto Local Content	AGN
4) Gas & Road Tax	FOR	8) Nerve Gas Prod	FOR	12) Nuclear Arms Freeze	—

Election Results

1982 general	Don Fuqua (D)	79,096	(62%)	($235,566)
	Ron McNeil (R)	49,084	(38%)	($241,480)
1982 primary	Don Fuqua (D)	76,678	(65%)	
	Sherrill (Pete) Skinner (D)	22,892	(19%)	($31,896)
	Allen Cox (D)	18,963	(16%)	($42,614)
1980 general	Don Fuqua (D)	138,252	(71%)	($131,165)
	John R. LaCapra (R)	57,588	(29%)	($47,786)

Campaign Contributions and Expenditures

1981-82		Direct Cont. 81-82			PACS brkdwn			
Receipts	$237,482	Indiv	$70,530	Agr	$7,100	Ideo	$4,000
Expend.	$235,566	Party	$2,400	Bus	$90,420	Lbr	$2,600
Unspent	$8,021	PACS	$122,590	Hlth	$9,950	Prof	$5,350
		Cand	$40,185				

THIRD DISTRICT

Jacksonville is a border city, on the border between the Old South and the new boom lands of central Florida. It was long Florida's largest city and, technically, it still is because it annexed almost all of surrounding Duval County. But Jacksonville's metropolitan population, though considerable, has been eclipsed by Miami, Fort Lauderdale, St. Petersburg, Tampa, and even Orlando. Jacksonville remains an important port, paper manufacturer, and banking and insurance center; and if the central city did not grow much in the 1970s, the surrounding areas within commuter distance have. Because of its coolish winter climate, Jacksonville has not attracted as many retirees or northern migrants as have Florida cities and towns farther south. It has the largest black percentage of any major Florida city and a large population of southern white origin. It was the largest city in Florida to be carried by George Wallace in 1968 and came close to going for Jimmy Carter in 1980.

The 3d congressional district of Florida includes almost all of Jacksonville and one small county to the north. It has one of the most senior congressmen in the House, Charles Bennett, a Democrat first elected in 1948. Bennett set a record for consecutive roll calls—a record that symbolizes but does not fully illustrate his punctilious character. His probity and attention to detail are second to none in the House. He served on the House's Ethics Committee (its official name is a mouthful: the Committee on Standards of Official Conduct) but was not made chairman for years, because House leaders feared, justifiably, that he would not be understanding of members' difficulties. He is a stickler for propriety, a man who is reluctant to think badly of others but who insists that all rules must be followed. In 1978, with the Koreagate scandal looming and Bennett the committee's senior member, the chair could no longer be denied him. He oversaw the Abscam investigation and headed the 10–2 majority that recommended and secured the expulsion of Congressman Ozzie Myers from the House. He relinquished the chair in the 97th Congress after serving the allowable two terms.

Bennett holds a potentially much more influential position now, as number two Democrat on the House Armed Services Committee and chairman of its Seapower Subcommittee. Jacksonville, as it happens, is one of the major Navy towns in the United States; the giant base at nearby Mayport is second in importance only to Norfolk for the Atlantic Fleet. And Bennett is considered a very strong supporter of the Navy, its most important advocate in the House. But no one thinks that Bennett does this to help his constituency; his views would be the same if he represented a district in Kansas. Over the years he has been a backer of most military spending programs; after all, he is part of the generation that can remember vividly how costly it was to be militarily unprepared. But his support for weapons systems is by no means automatic. He opposed the Densepack basing mode for the MX missile in 1982, for example—a stand which probably convinced many members that this was a responsible position to take.

Yet Bennett's influence is not as great as his position would imply. In 1983, he sought another subcommittee chairmanship, the Procurement post already held by New York's Samuel Stratton. In the old days, when no one challenged the rule of seniority, Bennett would have had his choice. In the 1980s, however, the decision was made by the Democratic members of Armed Services, and in secret ballot they chose Stratton. Nor is Bennett a man who, in general, aggressively sets out to make military policy. He is not the kind of aggressive legislator who reaches out and tries to make events go his way. Rather, he seems to see his role as something more like that of a judge: to sit back, reflect, apply sound principles, and decide. Given the complexity of military policy, perhaps that is all a legislator can do. There is no reason to believe that the Democratic Caucus would refuse to elect Bennett chairman of Armed Services should Mel Price retire; Bennett is widely respected and has a fairly middle-of-the-road voting record on domestic issues.

The People Pop. 1980: 512,692, up 4.7% 1970–80; voting age pop. 362,272; 25% Black, 2% Span. orig., 1% Asian orig. 33% housing units rented. Median owner $29,900; renter $165. Households: 73% family, 42% with children, 55% married couples.

Presidential Vote

1980	Reagan (R)	83,360	(48%)
	Carter (D)	88,595	(52%)

Rep. Charles E. Bennett (D) Elected 1948; b. Dec. 2, 1910, Canton, NY; home, Jacksonville; U. of FL, B.A., J.D. 1934; Disciples of Christ.

Career Practicing atty., 1934–42, 1947–48; FL House of Reps., 1941–42; Army, WWII.

Offices 2107 RHOB, 202-225-2501. Also Fed. Ofc. Bldg., 400 W. Bay St., Su. 352, Jacksonville 32202, 904-791-2587.

Committee *Armed Services* (2d). Subcommittees: Research and Development; Compensation; Seapower and Strategic and Critical Materials (Chairman).

Group Ratings

	ADA	ACLU	COPE	CFA	LCV	LWV	NTU	NSI	COC	ACA	CSFC
1982	40	42	43	60	46	42	51	100	64	74	52
1981	25	—	43	64	29	—	50	—	58	58	56
1980	22	13	42	21	30	20	42	70	62	42	51

National Journal Ratings

	Economic		Foreign		Cultural	
1982	46%	(LIB)	35%	(LIB)	38%	(LIB)
	54%	(CONS)	65%	(CONS)	62%	(CONS)
1981	53%	(LIB)	43%	(LIB)	55%	(LIB)
	47%	(CONS)	56%	(CONS)	44%	(CONS)

Key Votes

1) Reagan 81 Budget	AGN	5) Incr SS Rtmt Age	FOR	9) Poor Pay Food Stamps	FOR
2) Reagan 81 Tax Cut	AGN	6) Saudi AWACS Sale	AGN	10) Ban Crt Busing Order	FOR
3) Bal Budget Amend	FOR	7) $ for MX Missile	AGN	11) Auto Local Content	AGN
4) Gas & Road Tax	FOR	8) Nerve Gas Prod	FOR	12) Nuclear Arms Freeze	AGN

Election Results

1982 general	Charles E. Bennett (D)	73,713	(84%)	($38,289)
	George Grimsley (R)	13,921	(16%)	($18,975)
1982 primary	Charles E. Bennett (D) unopposed			
1980 general	Charles E. Bennett (D)	104,672	(77%)	($39,318)
	Harry Racliffe (R)	31,208	(23%)	($0)

Campaign Contributions and Expenditures

1981-82		Direct Cont. 81-82		PACS brkdwn			
Receipts	$90,699	Indiv	$42,806	Agr	$650	Ideo	$1,000
Expend.	$38,289	Party	$200	Bus	$27,900	Lbr	$3,950
Unspent	$56,958	PACS	$40,870	Hlth	$5,700	Prof	$1,250

FOURTH DISTRICT

The 4th congressional district is part of transitional Florida. Its roots are in Dixie, but its residents, increasingly, are from somewhere else. Geographically, the 4th follows the Atlantic Coast from Jacksonville (it includes 70,000 of the city's residents) down to a point near the Kennedy Space Center. Here are scores of condominiums, and huge developments like Palm Coast; here also is St. Augustine, Florida's oldest city. The district also extends some 20 miles inland, taking in much of Florida's prime citrus land. In the middle, roughly, is Daytona Beach, famous for its rock-hard sand beach. Daytona and surrounding Volusia County track Florida statewide political results pretty closely: this is a town that could vote for George Wallace and elect black councilmen in the same year.

The 4th district has a congressman who is straight out of an older Florida politics. Bill Chappell was speaker of the Florida House back in the early 1960s when the legislature was still dominated by Dixie conservatives—the Pork Chop Gang—from the northern part of the state. Perhaps anticipating the changes that redistricting would make in the legislature, Chappell ran for Congress in 1968, and won; he had some close early races, but won easily beginning in 1974. Like many southern Democrats, he gravitated naturally to military affairs, and a seat on the Defense Appropriations Subcommittee. He is a solid Navy man, as befits the representative of the giant Mayport Naval Base; he is also a solid supporter generally of increased defense spending and new weapons systems. By virtue of his subcommittee position, Chappell has been the House's chief sponsor of such weapons systems as the B-1 bomber and the nuclear aircraft carrier. On domestic issues, Chappell is a Boll Weevil with as conservative a record as any Florida Democrat.

For years this appeared to be a successful political strategy. Chappell's subcommittee position seemed to protect him against primary competition; his conservative record made it hard for Republicans to attack him. Redistricting cut back the size of his growing district, which made it all the easier to defend. Yet in 1982 Chappell was nearly beaten in the Democratic primary. His opponent, Reid Hughes, spent his own money liberally. He ran television ads accusing Chappell of voting 15 times to cut Social Security and featuring an endorsement of the challenger by Congressman Claude Pepper. Chappell, outspent and unused to television campaigning, led by only 47% to 45% in the first primary. Usually such a result means that the incumbent is beaten in the runoff. But Chappell rallied. He raised plenty of money (undoubtedly his defense industry friends helped) and counterattacked. With a smaller turnout he won 54%–46%.

But that is not much of a showing for a 14-year incumbent. In all likelihood Chappell will attract serious opposition in 1984—if he runs. And his close call shows that, at present, the Dixiecrat strategy is no longer the safe course in politics, at least in Florida.

The People Pop. 1980: 512,672, up 56.8% 1970–80; voting age pop. 385,967; 10% Black, 2% Span. orig. 25% housing units rented. Median owner $41,800; renter $196. Households: 72% family, 33% with children, 60% married couples.

Presidential Vote

1980	Reagan (R)	85,881	(59%)
	Carter (D)	59,138	(41%)

Rep. Bill Chappell, Jr. (D) Elected 1968; b. Feb. 3, 1922, Kendrick; home, Ocala; U. of FL, B.A. 1947, LL.B. 1949; Methodist.

Career Navy, WWII; Marion Cnty. Prosecuting Atty., 1950–54; FL House of Reps., 1955–64, 1967–68, Spkr., 1961–63.

Offices 2468 RHOB, 202-225-4035. Also Fed. Bldg., Rm. 258, Ocala 32670, 904-629-0039.

Committee *Appropriations* (12th). Subcommittees: Defense, Energy and Water Development; Military Construction.

Group Ratings

	ADA	ACLU	COPE	CFA	LCV	LWV	NTU	NSI	COC	ACA	CSFC
1982	20	0	31	20	34	30	41	89	73	72	50
1981	5	—	31	7	6	—	44	—	79	67	60
1980	6	10	26	7	13	20	43	88	76	63	55

National Journal Ratings

	Economic		Foreign		Cultural	
1982	22%	(LIB)	3%	(LIB)	32%	(LIB)
	78%	(CONS)	97%	(CONS)	67%	(CONS)
1981	44%	(LIB)	18%	(LIB)	24%	(LIB)
	56%	(CONS)	73%	(CONS)	76%	(CONS)

Key Votes

1) Reagan 81 Budget	FOR	5) Incr SS Rtmt Age	FOR	9) Poor Pay Food Stamps	AGN
2) Reagan 81 Tax Cut	FOR	6) Saudi AWACS Sale	AGN	10) Ban Crt Busing Order	FOR
3) Bal Budget Amend	FOR	7) $ for MX Missile	FOR	11) Auto Local Content	AGN
4) Gas & Road Tax	—	8) Nerve Gas Prod	FOR	12) Nuclear Arms Freeze	AGN

Election Results

1982 general	Bill Chappell, Jr. (D)	83,830	(67%)	($600,029)
	Larry Gaudet (R)	41,399	(33%)	($33,052)
1982 runoff	Bill Chappell, Jr. (D)	32,478	(54%)	
	Reid Hughes (D)	27,756	(46%)	($604,173)
1982 primary	Bill Chappell, Jr. (D)	33,163	(48%)	
	Reid Hughes (D)	31,410	(45%)	
	David Lee Davis (D)	5,189	(7%)	($12,921)
1980 general	Bill Chappell, Jr. (D)	147,775	(66%)	($100,668)
	Barney E. Dillard, Jr. (R)	76,924	(34%)	($8,750)

Campaign Contributions and Expenditures

1981-82		Direct Cont. 81-82			PACS brkdwn		
Receipts	$561,840	Indiv	$257,381	Agr	$5,550	Ideo	$36,100
Expend.	$600,029	Party	$200	Bus	$211,350	Lbr	$7,500
Unspent	$1,471	PACS	$284,416	Hlth	$13,600	Prof	$750

Indep Expend: For: $30,332 (Realtors, NRA)

FIFTH DISTRICT

Looking ahead from 1945, say, few people would have picked Orlando to become a major American metropolis. Orlando was a pleasant town of some 40,000 and the major citrus processing center of central Florida. It was not a resort area—at most, just a place where people stopped for gas on their way to the beaches of south Florida. Yet by 1980 Orlando had become one of the state's larger metropolitan areas, with over 700,000 people, and one of the most well known. The growth is all the more extraordinary, because very little of it can be attributed to retirees. The Orlando area ranks behind only northern Florida in the percentage of households with children. The people who have moved here have come probably more from the South than the North, more from other small cities than from farms. In sum, the citrus center has become a widely diversified and high-skill economic center.

And, of course, Orlando is the home of Walt Disney World which has made Orlando Airport one of the nation's busiest. Indeed, the complex has made the Orlando metropolitan area arguably the nation's number one tourism center. Actually, Disney World is several miles southwest of the city, set amid thousands of acres that the Disney organization accumulated years ago; it is perhaps the world's most fascinating example of urban planning, among other things. In this case, as in California's Disneyland, Disney picked a site in a politically conservative area; both in fact are in Orange County. But Orlando is Southern enough to be, in most elections, a two-party area; and the two congressional districts centered on Orlando, the 5th and the 11th, are represented by a Republican and a Democrat.

The 5th includes most of the city and its suburbs. In the north, into Seminole County, are high income suburbs in a string leading to the citrus town of Sanford; to the west, across the lakes that dot central Florida, is Winter Garden. The 5th on balance is basically Republican; it went only narrowly for Democrats Bob Graham and Lawton Chiles when they carried the state by wide margins in 1982.

The 5th's congressman is Bill McCollum, a Republican first elected in 1980. His record is one of solid loyalty to the Reagan administration, but he does not seem to be one of those self-assured darlings of the New Right elected in the Reagan landslide. He owes his seat more to special circumstances than to any great change in the national or local mood. His predecessor was none other than Richard Kelly, the Abscam defendant who stuffed his pockets with money before the hidden cameras and then pleaded later that he was conducting his own investigation. Kelly got a pitiful 18% in the 1980 Republican primary; McCollum had to beat another candidate in the runoff and then won the general election by a decisive but not overwhelming margin. He increased his margin in 1982. His performance is more impressive than at first appears. The district lines were not set until late in the season, and McCollum, whose previous district covered most of two new seats, was not sure where he was running. And the Democratic nominee, Dick Batchelor, was a popular local legislator. So despite McCollum's failure to run much ahead of his party's basic strength, he seems in good political shape.

In the House McCollum serves on the Banking and Judiciary Committees. The former is an assignment of considerable importance in a district with lots of home-building and savings institutions; McCollum is one Republican who can be expected to be more sympathetic to them than to commercial banks. He has worked to limit circumstances in which a bank can obtain an S&L. Banking rather than Judiciary seems to be his major focus of actions. That makes sense, because McCollum's instincts are conservative, and Judiciary is one of the most liberal committees in Congress.

The People Pop. 1980: 513,005, up 47% 1970–80; voting age pop. 373,987; 12% Black, 2% Span. orig., 1% Asian orig. 31% housing units rented. Median owner $45,400; renter $200. Households: 73% family, 38% with children, 59% married couples.

Presidential Vote

1980	Reagan (R)	94,378	(64%)
	Carter (D)	53,371	(36%)

Rep. Bill McCollum (R) Elected 1980; b. July 12, 1944, Brooksville; home, Altamonte Springs; U. of FL, B.A. 1965, J.D. 1968; Episcopal.

Career Navy, 1969–72; Practicing atty., 1973–80; Chmn., Seminole Cnty. Repub. Exec. Committee, 1976.

Offices 1507 LHOB, 202-225-2176. Also 5800 U.S. Hwy. 19 N., Su. 224, Holiday 33590, 813-937-4231; and 701 E. Altamonte Dr., Su. 345, Altamonte Springs 32701, 305-830-6655.

Committees *Banking, Finance and Urban Affairs* (9th). Subcommittees: Domestic Monetary Policy; Financial Institutions Supervision, Regulation and Insurance; International Trade, Investments and Monetary Policy; Housing and Community Development. *Judiciary* (12th). Subcommittees: Criminal Justice; Immigration, Refugees and International Law; Administrative Law and Government Relations.

Group Ratings

	ADA	ACLU	COPE	CFA	LCV	LWV	NTU	NSI	COC	ACA	CSFC
1982	10	17	14	20	42	25	83	100	82	87	69
1981	0	—	13	43	30	—	79	—	94	86	72

National Journal Ratings

	Economic		Foreign		Cultural	
1982	27%	(LIB)	26%	(LIB)	34%	(LIB)
	73%	(CONS)	73%	(CONS)	66%	(CONS)
1981	4%	(LIB)	18%	(LIB)	29%	(LIB)
	79%	(CONS)	73%	(CONS)	71%	(CONS)

Key Votes

1) Reagan 81 Budget	FOR	5) Incr SS Rtmt Age	FOR	9) Poor Pay Food Stamps	FOR
2) Reagan 81 Tax Cut	FOR	6) Saudi AWACS Sale	AGN	10) Ban Crt Busing Order	FOR
3) Bal Budget Amend	FOR	7) $ for MX Missile	FOR	11) Auto Local Content	AGN
4) Gas & Road Tax	FOR	8) Nerve Gas Prod	FOR	12) Nuclear Arms Freeze	AGN

Election Results

1982 general	Bill McCollum (R)	69,939	(59%)	($335,186)
	Dick Batchelor (D)	49,042	(41%)	($208,607)
1982 primary	Bill McCollum (R) unopposed			
1980 general	Bill McCollum (R)	177,603	(56%)	($278,664)
	David Best (D)	140,903	(44%)	($187,121)

Campaign Contributions and Expenditures

1981-82		Direct Cont. 81-82		PACS brkdwn			
Receipts	$422,974	Indiv	$257,945	Agr	$7,150	Ideo	$14,175
Expend.	$335,186	Party	$26,900	Bus	$137,882	Lbr	$200
Unspent	$104,512	PACS	$131,415	Hlth	$13,550	Prof	$2,450

Indirect Party Expend: $37,095   *Indep Expend*: For: $478

SIXTH DISTRICT

The 6th congressional district is one of the four new districts created by the Florida legislature after the 1980 Census. Its existence reflects the growth of central Florida, the slow march up Florida's peninsula of in-migrants seeking sun and pleasant places to retire—or to make their livings. The 6th includes Gainesville, the small city which is the home of the University of Florida; Ocala and the pleasant horse country in surrounding Marion County; a slice of the Gulf Coast, where the swamps are being drained to accommodate the march of condominiums north from St. Petersburg, Clearwater, and New Port Richey; and part of the lake country of central Florida around Leesburg.

The political tradition here, particularly in the northern counties, is mostly Democratic; and it has been supplemented in the last decade by rather liberal voting behavior in Gainesville; the new migrants, more prosperous than those in the older neighborhoods of St. Petersburg, tend to be Republican. But this district was drawn by a Democratic legislature, with the firm intention of creating a Democratic district; and for once the aim was realized.

The new congressman is a man who came tantalizingly close to being elected U.S. senator from this state which, in that term, will probably become the nation's fourth largest. He is Kenneth "Buddy" MacKay, a 12-year veteran of the Florida legislature who ran for the Senate in 1980 against incumbent Richard Stone. MacKay nearly duplicated the scenario that made obscure state legislators like Reubin Askew, Lawton Chiles, and Bob Graham into statewide candidates: finish a rather distant second in the first primary, overtake the better known but not universally popular front-runner in the runoff, and then win the general election as a fresh face. MacKay's problem was that he finished third in the first primary;

edging him out, by a narrow margin, was Insurance Commissioner Bill Gunter. Had MacKay won 3% more of the vote in that first primary, he probably would be a senator now, in Paula Hawkins's place.

That MacKay's 1980 showing was not just a fluke was demonstrated in 1982 when, in this new Democratic district, he was unopposed in the Democratic primary, and then won comfortably the general election. In the Florida legislature MacKay championed "sunshine" and "sunset" laws. Florida has the nation's most comprehensive disclosure (sunshine) measures, which prevent public business from being done in private; it also originated the idea that government programs should have a specific expiration (sunset) date. MacKay seems likely to stick with national Democrats on most issues, though not to have an entirely liberal voting record. He has the potential for a long House career, although in 1986 he might choose to run for the Senate seat he has some reason to regard as "his."

The People Pop. 1980: 512,950, up 70.9% 1970–80; voting age pop. 394,134; 12% Black, 2% Span. orig. 22% housing units rented. Median owner $37,500; renter $174. Households: 73% family, 31% with children, 62% married couples.

Presidential Vote

1980	Reagan (R)	91,678	(55%)
	Carter (D)	73,593	(45%)

Rep. Kenneth H. (Buddy) **MacKay** (D) Elected 1982; b. March 22, 1933, Ocala; home, Ocala; U. Of FL, B.A. 1954, J.D. 1961; Presbyterian.

Career Practicing atty., 1961–82.

Offices 503 CHOB, 202-225-5744. Also P.O. Box 160, Ocala 32678, 904-351-8777; 401 S.E. First Ave., Gainesville 32601, 904-372-0382; and 111 S. Sixth St., Leesburg 32748, 904-326-8285.

Committees Government Operations (19th). Subcommittees: Government Information, Justice and Agriculture; Intergovernmental Relations and Human Resources. *Science and Technology* (22d). Subcommittees: Natural Resources, Agriculture Research and Environment; Science, Research and Technology; Space Science and Applications. *Select Committee on Aging* (33d). Subcommittee: Human Services.

Group Ratings and Key Votes: Newly Elected

Election Results

1982 general	Buddy MacKay (D)	85,799	(61%)	($228,413)
	Ed Havill (R)	54,058	(39%)	($53,946)
1982 primary	Buddy MacKay (D) unopposed			
1980 general	Newly created district			

Campaign Contributions and Expenditures

1981-82		*Direct Cont. 81-82*			*PACS brkdwn*		
Receipts	$228,720	Indiv	$165,135	Agr	$2,750	Ideo	$1,500
Expend.	$228,413	Party	$4,450	Bus	$16,600	Lbr	$7,950
Unspent	$307	PACS	$37,870	Hlth	$9,200	Prof	$100
		Cand	$11,900				

SEVENTH DISTRICT

Tampa is one of Florida's lesser known cities, a metropolis of more than 250,000 in a metropolitan area of more than one million—most of whose residents don't think of themselves as part of greater Tampa at all. Across the bay from St. Petersburg, Tampa is glaringly different. Tampa is the closest thing in Florida to a manufacturing city, the kind of industrial center so many Floridians moved here to get away from.

It is not the kind of industrial center it used to be, however. Its port is still important, but it is a lot more containerized and less picturesque than it once was. The cigar industry is pretty small potatoes here now, and the Cuban community that once seemed so large—and dated from pre-Castro days—is now eclipsed by Miami's. Nor does Tampa have a particularly large black population. This is largely a white working class town, with a population derived mostly from the South—a city with lots of children, and lots of divorced parents.

Tampa and most of the Hillsborough County suburbs and rural crossroads—the 7th congressional district of Florida— have had the same congressman since 1962: Sam Gibbons. Tampa is basically Democratic, though it has supported George Wallace and given Republicans majorities in national elections; and Gibbons is, and always has been, a national Democrat. He supported civil rights and progressive tax reform in the 1960s, and sometimes clashed with Ways and Means Chairman Wilbur Mills. In 1972 he ran briefly for House majority leader against Tip O'Neill. In the 1970s, he anticipated some of the changes the House seems to have made, moving from advocacy of higher taxes on the rich to lower taxes on capital gains.

His major role in Congress, however, is on trade issues. Gibbons is the number two Democrat on Ways and Means now, and chairman of its Trade Subcommittee. He is very much a supporter of free trade when it is threatened, on many fronts and on many pretexts. Since Ways and Means Chairman Dan Rostenkowski seems to have no strong views on these issues but is disposed to support his subcommittee chairmen, Gibbons is in a good position to lead the committee in opposition to all sorts of trade barriers and restrictions, the more so because Ways and Means's ranking Republican, Barber Conable, is a staunch free trader too. His major problem is that groups seeking trade restrictions are smart enough to try to avoid his subcommittee or to line up enough votes on the floor (as the United Auto Workers did on the "domestic content" legislation in 1982). But Gibbons is politically shrewd, and armed with the determination of a man fighting for a cause he believes in. At home, he has had no significant opposition for years and seems unlikely to encounter any in this district whose views he reflects pretty accurately.

The People Pop. 1980: 512,905, up 25.3% 1970–80; voting age pop. 376,478; 13% Black, 11% Span. orig., 1% Asian orig. 32% housing units rented. Median owner $35,800; renter $188. Households: 71% family, 37% with children, 56% married couples.

Presidential Vote

1980	Reagan (R)	91,659	(53%)
	Carter (D)	80,725	(47%)

Rep. Sam Gibbons (D) Elected 1962; b. Jan. 20, 1920, Tampa; home, Tampa; U. of FL, LL.B. 1947; Presbyterian.

Career Army, WWII; Practicing atty., 1947–62; FL House of Reps., 1952–58; FL Senate, 1958–62.

Offices 2204 RHOB, 202-225-3376. Also 510 Fed. Bldg., 500 Zack St., Tampa 33602, 813-228-2101.

Committees *Ways and Means* (2d). Subcommittees: Oversight; Trade (Chairman). *Joint Committee on Taxation* (2d).

Group Ratings

	ADA	ACLU	COPE	CFA	LCV	LWV	NTU	NSI	COC	ACA	CSFC
1982	50	29	56	20	62	70	46	60	48	67	48
1981	30	—	57	36	15	—	30	—	50	50	56
1980	39	23	50	50	26	50	27	56	67	30	39

National Journal Ratings

	Economic		Foreign		Cultural	
1982	39%	(LIB)	54%	(LIB)	65%	(LIB)
	61%	(CONS)	45%	(CONS)	35%	(CONS)
1981	54%	(LIB)	44%	(LIB)	36%	(LIB)
	45%	(CONS)	55%	(CONS)	64%	(CONS)

Key Votes

1) Reagan 81 Budget	AGN	5) Incr SS Rtmt Age	FOR	9) Poor Pay Food Stamps	FOR
2) Reagan 81 Tax Cut	AGN	6) Saudi AWACS Sale	AGN	10) Ban Crt Busing Order	FOR
3) Bal Budget Amend	FOR	7) $ for MX Missile	AGN	11) Auto Local Content	AGN
4) Gas & Road Tax	FOR	8) Nerve Gas Prod	FOR	12) Nuclear Arms Freeze	FOR

Election Results

1982 general	Sam Gibbons (D)	85,317	(74%)	($93,494)
	Ken Ayers (R)	29,624	(26%)	($13,274)
1982 primary	Sam Gibbons (D) unopposed			
1980 general	Sam Gibbons (D)	132,529	(72%)	($43,410)
	Charles P. Jones (R)	52,138	(28%)	($56)

Campaign Contributions and Expenditures

1981-82		Direct Cont. 81-82			PACS brkdwn		
Receipts	$118,106	Indiv	$50,220	Agr	$4,000	Ideo	$2,650
Expend.	$93,494	Party	$2,100	Bus	$52,036	Lbr	$500
Unspent	$104,176	PACS	$66,386	Hlth	$7,000	Prof	$500

EIGHTH DISTRICT

When somebody mentions St. Petersburg, almost everyone has an image of elderly retirees sitting on park benches in the Florida sun. The cliche has considerable validity. To be sure, St. Petersburg and its suburbs to the north and west do have some light manufacturing, and there are some young families here with children. But not many. In the 8th congressional district, which includes St. Petersburg and Pinellas County suburbs as far north as Clearwater, only 23% of households contain children; 34% of adults are 65 or older—the highest percentage in any congressional district in the country. There are more than 40,000 people over 65 living alone here, accounting for one out of every six households.

Most of these people were not born in St. Petersburg, which had very few residents 65 years ago. They are immigrants from some other part of the South or, more frequently, from the North. The large Yankee concentration here produced Florida's first center of Republican strength. The migrants of the 1940s and 1950s were people of at least modest affluence— blue collar workers at the time didn't get much in the way of pensions—and the new residents continued to vote in St. Petersburg as they had back in Oak Park or Garden City. They carried Pinellas County for Eisenhower, and in 1954 elected a Republican congressman.

More recently, St. Petersburg has been trending Democratic in national and state elections. In 1976 Pinellas County almost went for Carter and in 1980 its Reagan percentage was less than the statewide average. In 1982, while affluent retirement communities like Sarasota and Naples went Republican, St. Petersburg was going Democratic. Why? Inevitably there is a turnover in this area's elderly population; very few of the elderly voters who made this area Republican are still alive today. In the 1960s and 1970s people with blue collar—and Democratic—backgrounds increasingly could afford to retire in Florida. They settled in St. Petersburg, while their more affluent counterparts went to the newer, more glittery retirement towns.

This trend has not changed the 8th district's representation in Congress, however. Bill Young—ironic name—has been representing St. Petersburg for more than 25 years, first as an aide to its first Republican congressman, then as a legislator in Tallahassee, and finally as congressman since 1970. Yet he is still only approaching his voters' median age. Through careful attention to the district, and devotion to the Social Security system, Young has gained a reputation for political strength, and has encountered no serious challenges.

In Washington he has been able to concentrate on national problems. For some years he worked on the Foreign Operations Appropriations Subcommittee, a body with the unpleasant task of managing the foreign aid bill. In 1981 he switched to Defense Appropriations. On national issues Young is an orthodox Republican, with an approach more similar to that of Gerald Ford, for example, than to the New Right. Despite occasional rumors, he has not run for statewide office.

The People   Pop. 1980: 512,909, up 30.3% 1970–80; voting age pop. 413,853; 7% Black, 1% Span. orig. 32% housing units rented. Median owner $39,600; renter $201. Households: 65% family, 23% with children, 54% married couples.

Presidential Vote

1980	Reagan (R)	110,858	(54%)
	Carter (D)	93,446	(46%)

Rep. C. W. Bill Young (R) Elected 1970; b. Dec. 16, 1930, Harmarsville, PA; home, Seminole; Methodist.

Career Aide to U.S. Rep. William C. Cramer of FL, 1957–60; FL Senate, 1960–70, Minor. Ldr., 1966–70.

Offices 2266 RHOB, 202-225-5961. Also 627 Fed. Bldg., 144 First Ave. S., St. Petersburg 33701, 813-893-3191.

Committees *Appropriations* (8th). Subcommittees: Defense; Labor-Health and Human Services-Education. *Permanent Select Committee on Intelligence* (3d). Subcommittees: Oversight and Evaluation; Program and Budget Authorization.

Group Ratings

	ADA	ACLU	COPE	CFA	LCV	LWV	NTU	NSI	COC	ACA	CSFC
1982	10	0	14	33	31	25	67	109	80	73	64
1981	5	—	17	21	23	—	75	—	94	83	70
1980	11	20	10	14	30	40	54	100	76	88	76

National Journal Ratings

	Economic		Foreign		Cultural	
1982	13%	(LIB)	18%	(LIB)	33%	(LIB)
	87%	(CONS)	82%	(CONS)	67%	(CONS)
1981	4%	(LIB)	18%	(LIB)	10%	(LIB)
	79%	(CONS)	73%	(CONS)	90%	(CONS)

Key Votes

1) Reagan 81 Budget	FOR	5) Incr SS Rtmt Age	FOR	9) Poor Pay Food Stamps	FOR
2) Reagan 81 Tax Cut	FOR	6) Saudi AWACS Sale	AGN	10) Ban Crt Busing Order	FOR
3) Bal Budget Amend	FOR	7) $ for MX Missile	FOR	11) Auto Local Content	AGN
4) Gas & Road Tax	AGN	8) Nerve Gas Prod	FOR	12) Nuclear Arms Freeze	AGN

Election Results

1982 general	C.W. Bill Young (R) unopposed	($52,322)
1982 primary	C.W. Bill Young (R) unopposed	
1980 general	C.W. Bill Young (R) unopposed	($61,313)

Campaign Contributions and Expenditures

1981-82		Direct Cont. 81-82		PACS brkdwn			
Receipts	$131,188	Indiv	$75,358	Agr	$250	Ideo	$150
Expend.	$52,322	Party	$7,503	Bus	$27,150	Lbr	$1,000
Unspent	$122,374	PACS	$32,250	Hlth	$6,700	Prof	$500

NINTH DISTRICT

In the early 1950s you could have driven U.S. 19 north from St. Petersburg and never noticed much more than the swamp. The road passed through intersections marked by gas stations, and every so often there was a sleepy little town, with low brick buildings constructed in some northern style, baking in the Florida sun. There weren't many people here. The coastline that looks so tempting on the map was then mostly swamp. Any large development would have required investment in what we call infrastructure today—water and sewer lines, underground electricity—that would have seemed hopelessly uneconomical.

Today all that investment has been made, and the Gulf Coast for 50 miles north of St. Petersburg is home now to half a million people (and that doesn't include the 350,000 right around St. Petersburg). Most of this area is in the 9th congressional district, one of the four new districts created by the Florida legislature after the 1980 Census. The district begins in Largo and Clearwater, some eight miles from St. Petersburg, and continues up past the old resort of Tarpon Springs to the new condominium communities of New Port Richey in Pasco County. It also sweeps inland, circling Tampa and including the agricultural center of Plant City inland; but more than two-thirds of its population is along the coast.

The district lies in a Republican part of the state, but its lines were drawn by a Democratic legislature: the result is one of the most evenly balanced districts in the state. Democratic legislator George Sheldon, of Tampa, had been eyeing the district for a long time. He won the Democratic nomination with 55% in a field of four in the first primary; in this district where 30% of the eligible voters are over 65, he planned to stress his opposition to any cuts in Social Security. He probably expected to face an experienced Republican politician, either state House Minority Leader Curt Kiser or Clearwater Mayor Charles LeCher. But to almost everyone's surprise the leader in the first Republican primary and the winner in the runoff was Michael Bilirakis, a 52-year-old businessman who had been a judge but never a legislator.

Even more surprising to many, Bilirakis won the general election. His key weapon seems not so much to have been issues—he campaigned as a routine endorser of Reagan Republicanism, and as a firm opponent of Social Security cuts—as personality. Like many other candidates of Greek descent, he raised money from successful businessmen of similar background. Sheldon, younger, more political, saddled with liberal positions on issues like capital punishment, coming from Tampa, which is outside the district's borders, was not able to win despite the Democratic year and the Social Security issue. It was Florida's closest House race, and the Democrat managed to carry Pasco County as well as the Tampa area. But Bilirakis won big margins in Clearwater and Pinellas County and gained a 51% victory. In Washington, as a freshman member of the minority party, he does not seem likely to be a key legislator. And he can hardly expect to hold the seat in 1984 without facing formidable competition—although he has already shown the ability to capture it against the odds.

The People   Pop. 1980: 513,191, up 91.6% 1970–80; voting age pop. 404,361; 3% Black, 2% Span. orig. 19% housing units rented. Median owner $44,600; renter $208. Households: 74% family, 27% with children, 65% married couples.

Presidential Vote

1980	Reagan (R)	119,478	(59%)
	Carter (D)	82,697	(41%)

Rep. Michael Bilirakis (R) Elected 1982; b. July 16, 1930, Tarpon Springs; home, Palm Harbor; U. of Pittsburgh, B.S. 1959, U. of FL, J.D. 1963; Eastern Orthodox.

Career Air Force, 1951–55; Steelworker, 1955–59; Govt. contract negotiator, 1959–60; Petroleum engineer, 1960–63; Practicing atty., 1969–83.

Offices 319 CHOB, 202-225-5755. Also 1100 Cleveland St., Su. 1103, Clearwater 33515, 813-441-3721.

Committees *Veterans' Affairs* (10th). Subcommittees: Hospitals and Health Care; Housing and Memorial Affairs. *Small Business* (15th). Subcommittees: General Oversight and the Economy; Export Opportunities and Special Small Business Problems. *Select Committee on Aging* (20th). Subcommittees: Health and Long-Term Care; Human Services.

Group Ratings and Key Votes: Newly Elected

Election Results

1982 general	Michael Bilirakis (R)	94,993	(51%)	($299,558)
	George H. Sheldon (D)	90,673	(49%)	($379,692)
1982 runoff	Michael Bilirakis (R)	16,952	(54%)	
	Curt Kiser (R)	14,517	(46%)	
1982 primary	Michael Bilirakis (R)	17,033	(45%)	
	Curt Kiser (R)	14,394	(38%)	
	Charles F. LeCher (R)	6,349	(17%)	
1980 general	Newly created district			

Campaign Contributions and Expenditures

1981-82		Direct Cont. 81-82				PACS brkdwn		
Receipts	$309,414	Indiv	$134,900	Agr	$—	Ideo	$21,650
Expend.	$299,558	Party	$33,947	Bus	$28,475	Lbr	$—
Unspent	$9,854	PACS	$69,143	Hlth	$6,400	Prof	$—
		Cand	$77,065				

Indirect Party Expend: $34,244   *Indep Expend:* For: $3,888 (NRA)

TENTH DISTRICT

If you want to see what Florida looked like before the huge growth of the last 30 years, the best way is to drive inland from the coast and look at the parts of the state that have changed least. One such is the citrus country of central Florida, south of Orlando. Of course there has been growth here: the population figures have grown by percentages unheard of in the Northeast; new shopping malls have sprung up on four-lane highways leading out of the old downtowns, and most people live in small, air-conditioned stucco houses or apartments built since 1950.

Yet a visitor from that year would not find utterly unrecognizable Lakeland or Winter Haven or Lake Wales or the citrus fields lying between these towns and the dozens of lakes of central Florida. None of these towns has grown to metropolitan size. None has reclaimed and built on hundreds of acres of swamp, as has been done in so many other parts of Florida. Nor would attitudes here be totally unrecognizable to our hypothetical visitor. Racial segregation, once firmly embedded in central Florida, is of course gone. But political attitudes associated with rural southern Democrats are not. People here tend to be southern in origin, faithful churchgoers in religion, believers in traditional mores, sympathetic to the idea of government intervention in the economy to help the ordinary person (though not always the poor). They still register Democratic and, even though not as often, vote for Democrats.

This is the country that forms most of Florida's 10th congressional district. Most of its people are in Polk County; it also extends to the Gulf Coast, taking in Bradenton, one of the more modest and least Yankeefied towns on the Gulf Coast. Before 1982 this district also included high income, heavily Republican Sarasota; now that city is in the heavily Republican 13th district. Republicans failed in several efforts to win this district in the 1970s. Now it is held firmly by Andy Ireland, a Democrat with a record that seems much in accord with central Florida's traditions. First elected in 1976, he has not been seriously challenged since.

Ireland is by profession a banker, and he has, on non-economic as well as economic issues, one of the most conservative records among Florida Democrats. He was, for example, one of the Democrats who supported the Reagan budget and tax cuts in 1981. He serves on Foreign Affairs and on its International Operations Subcommittee (one of three Florida Democrats on that body); he is next in line for the chair of the latter, after Miami's Dante Fascell.

The People Pop. 1980: 512,890, up 44.3% 1970–80; voting age pop. 381,628; 11% Black, 3% Span. orig. 23% housing units rented. Median owner $38,100; renter $170. Households: 75% family, 35% with children, 63% married couples.

Presidential Vote

1980	Reagan (R)	106,226	(60%)
	Carter (D)	70,983	(40%)

Rep. Andy Ireland (D) Elected 1976; b. Aug. 23, 1930, Cincinnati, OH; home, Winter Haven; Yale U., B.S. 1952, Columbia Business Sch., 1953–54, LA St. U.; Episcopal.

Career Chmn. of the Bd., Barnett Banks of Winter Haven, Cypress Gardens, and Auburndale; Mbr., Winter Haven City Commission, 1966–68.

Offices 2446 RHOB, 202-225-5015. Also 519 W. Central Ave., Winter Haven 33880, 813-299-4041.

Committees *Foreign Affairs* (8th). Subcommittees: Asian and Pacific Affairs; Europe and the Middle East. *Small Business* (9th). Subcommittee: Export Opportunities and Special Small Business Problems (Chairman).

Group Ratings

	ADA	ACLU	COPE	CFA	LCV	LWV	NTU	NSI	COC	ACA	CSFC
1982	10	25	18	20	24	33	69	89	80	84	58
1981	5	—	20	14	8	—	57	—	100	74	65
1980	6	17	11	21	31	33	43	88	73	46	53

National Journal Ratings

	Economic		Foreign		Cultural	
1982	23%	(LIB)	27%	(LIB)	29%	(LIB)
	77%	(CONS)	73%	(CONS)	71%	(CONS)
1981	4%	(LIB)	34%	(LIB)	26%	(LIB)
	79%	(CONS)	63%	(CONS)	73%	(CONS)

Key Votes

1) Reagan 81 Budget	FOR	5) Incr SS Rtmt Age	FOR	9) Poor Pay Food Stamps	AGN
2) Reagan 81 Tax Cut	FOR	6) Saudi AWACS Sale	AGN	10) Ban Crt Busing Order	FOR
3) Bal Budget Amend	FOR	7) $ for MX Missile	FOR	11) Auto Local Content	AGN
4) Gas & Road Tax	—	8) Nerve Gas Prod	FOR	12) Nuclear Arms Freeze	AGN

Election Results

1982 general	Andy Ireland (D) unopposed			($161,853)
1982 primary	Andy Ireland (D) unopposed			
1980 general	Andy Ireland (D)	151,613	(69%)	($221,103)
	Scott Nicholson (R)	61,820	(28%)	($12,460)

Campaign Contributions and Expenditures

1981-82		Direct Cont. 81-82		PACS brkdwn			
Receipts	$196,143	Indiv	$109,107	Agr	$5,275	Ideo	$2,300
Expend.	$161,853	PACS	$74,795	Bus	$59,400	Lbr	$150
Unspent	$88,136			Hlth	$7,150	Prof	$400

ELEVENTH DISTRICT

In the 1940s, Cape Canaveral was chosen as the site for the nation's rocket tests for two reasons: it was on the Atlantic coast (rockets have to be launched eastward, and if they fail it's better that they sink in the ocean) and it was in a virtually unpopulated area. There were only 20,000 people living then in all of Brevard County, which stretches along 60 miles of the coast and includes the Cape. Florida's attraction to a generation of affluent Americans, plus the special attraction of the Cape, have produced such rapid growth that today, although there is no major city in Brevard County, there are about 300,000 people living there. They live mostly not on the beach (a lot of that, after all, is restricted government property), but in towns west of the channel (here called the Indian River) that separates all of Florida's Atlantic coastal barrier islands from the mainland.

Brevard County forms the heart of Florida's 11th congressional district. The district also extends westward into metropolitan Orlando; it actually includes Walt Disney World, although that hardly matters politically since few voters are registered there. To the south, it extends as far as Vero Beach, an old Dixie town with a large black community and a gaggle of new, high-priced condominium developments. In the 1960s, these areas trended Republican. Apparently they were not grateful to the Kennedy administration for putting the space shots here, and instead resented increased federal spending for the poor. Brevard and Orlando's Orange County, then a single district, elected a Republican congressman as long ago as 1962 (he was Edward Gurney, later of Senate Watergate Committee fame). In the 1970s, however, this area seemed to get more Democratic—or at least became less unequivocally Republican. It supported Democrats in statewide elections and, when the incumbent didn't run, elected a Democratic congressman in 1978.

He is Bill Nelson, a man typical in many ways of his generation's politicians. He is handsome, well educated, and from a background rich enough that he can afford to finance much of his own campaign. He was elected at age 30 to the Florida legislature; by the time he won his seat in Congress, at 36, he was a political veteran. He is also not freighted with the baggage of old political ideologies—or deep political convictions. Unlike the liberal Democrats of the 1950s, he does not see politics as inevitably a struggle between rich and poor, or between business and labor; nor does he see a large federal government as the answer to every problem. In his first term in office, he was politically shrewd enough to win appointment to the Budget Committee. But once there he seemed in a quandary when the Reagan budget and tax cut proposals were advanced.

Reagan administration lobbyists, in a document later leaked, described Nelson as a member they could muscle. His instinct seemed to be to stay with his fellow Democrats, and in committee he supported the budget draft sponsored by Chairman James Jones. But on the floor he found the Reagan budget cuts attractive—and the Reagan lobbyists persistent. Eventually he ended up supporting the administration and providing it with one of its key votes on this major issue.

By 1982 Nelson was attacking the economic strategy he had, at the crucial moment, supported; and the Reaganites surely knew they did not have his vote any more. He voted faithfully enough with the Democratic leadership to keep his Budget Committee post in 1983, and in fact is now one of the more senior Democrats on that body (to which members can belong for three terms at a time).

At home, Nelson won reelection without difficulty in 1982; with a strong Brevard County base, he has a safe seat. He has been mentioned as a candidate for statewide office, but an opening is not likely soon. He could conceivably run for governor in 1986, though that doesn't seem likely; he might run for Senate that year, but he might have to face Governor Bob Graham or some other better-known Democrat in the primary. Another possibility is one of the several state elective offices. Probably Nelson will remain in the House, where he has a chance for a long career.

The People   Pop. 1980: 512,691, up 39.8% 1970–80; voting age pop. 380,011; 6% Black, 3% Span. orig., 1% Asian orig. 27% housing units rented. Median owner $47,400; renter $219. Households: 76% family, 37% with children, 64% married couples.

Presidential Vote

1980	Reagan (R)	104,787	(64%)
	Carter (D)	58,649	(36%)

Rep. Bill Nelson (D) Elected 1978; b. Sept. 29, 1942, Miami; home, Melbourne; Yale U., B.A. 1965, U. of VA, J.D. 1968; Episcopal.

Career Army, 1968–70; Practicing atty.; FL House of Reps., 1972–78.

Offices 307 CHOB, 202-225-3671. Also Goldfield Bldg., 65 E. NASA Blvd., Su. 202, Melbourne 32901, 305-724-1978.

Committees *Budget* (7th). Task Forces: Energy and Technology; Federalism/State-Local Relations (Chairman). *Science and Technology* (13th). Subcommittees: Energy Development and Applications: Space Science and Applications.

Group Ratings

	ADA	ACLU	COPE	CFA	LCV	LWV	NTU	NSI	COC	ACA	CSFC
1982	20	17	39	50	71	75	34	100	45	61	43
1981	10	—	35	43	33	—	26	—	68	54	53
1980	33	27	37	43	48	50	28	78	82	46	46

National Journal Ratings

	Economic		Foreign		Cultural	
1982	46%	(LIB)	4%	(LIB)	50%	(LIB)
	54%	(CONS)	92%	(CONS)	50%	(CONS)
1981	44%	(LIB)	34%	(LIB)	43%	(LIB)
	56%	(CONS)	63%	(CONS)	56%	(CONS)

Key Votes

1) Reagan 81 Budget	AGN	5) Incr SS Rtmt Age	AGN	9) Poor Pay Food Stamps	AGN
2) Reagan 81 Tax Cut	FOR	6) Saudi AWACS Sale	AGN	10) Ban Crt Busing Order	FOR
3) Bal Budget Amend	FOR	7) $ for MX Missile	FOR	11) Auto Local Content	AGN
4) Gas & Road Tax	—	8) Nerve Gas Prod	FOR	12) Nuclear Arms Freeze	AGN

Election Results

1982 general	Bill Nelson (D)	101,625	(71%)	($176,878)
	Joel Robinson (R)	42,323	(29%)	($31,151)
1982 primary	Bill Nelson (D) unopposed			
1980 general	Bill Nelson (D)	139,468	(70%)	($267,457)
	Stan Dowiat (R)	58,734	(30%)	($268,979)

Campaign Contributions and Expenditures

1981-82		Direct Cont. 81-82		PACS brkdwn			
Receipts	$215,376	Indiv	$125,982	Agr	$1,550	Ideo	$2,750
Expend.	$176,878	Party	$600	Bus	$61,125	Lbr	$500
Unspent	$34,498	PACS	$74,120	Hlth	$7,500	Prof	$1,300

TWELFTH DISTRICT

The history of the settlement of Florida's Gold Coast is one that begins in south Florida, in Miami, and, contrary to intuition, marches north, along the Atlantic coast. At each step, this northward migration has encountered and then eclipsed the small southern towns it finds in its way. Thus Fort Lauderdale, once a sleepy southern crossroads, is now the center of a Yankee metropolis; ditto, West Palm Beach. Now the migration is moving north of Palm Beach, into what is now Florida's 12th congressional district. The north side of West Palm and neighboring Riviera Beach include most of that area's black population. Farther north, surrounding the old aristocratic resort of Hobe Sound, are several major condominium developments, ranging from high to very high income. They are reaching up past Stuart, in Martin County, to St. Lucie County, where Fort Pierce, a good-sized town with a black near-majority, has as its neighbors developments filled with affluent Yankees. The same is true of Vero Beach, farther north. This stretch of coast includes three-fourths of the 12th district's population.

The rest is spread over a much vaster expanse of land, all the way across to Naples on the Gulf Coast. The district also takes in the town of Sebring, in whimsically named Highlands County, where a Grand Prix car race is held yearly. In the middle is Lake Okeechobee, not so much a resort area as the center of an agricultural empire. In cleared and drained swampland, acres of crops are planted, raised, sprayed, and finally harvested, mostly by blacks and Mexican-Americans whose wages and working conditions have long been among America's worst.

This is essentially a Republican district, certainly in national elections; but its boundaries were crafted by a Democratic legislature in the wistful—and, as it happened, almost realized—hope that it would elect a Democrat. The Republican candidate, Tom Lewis, had many assets: as a state senator, he had represented most of the new 12th and had won high ratings for competence; he steadfastly professed his opposition to Social Security cuts. Democrat Brad Culverhouse spent liberally of his own money and had labor endorsement; he carried Palm Beach County (with its big black votes) and the interior counties. But Lewis had enough votes in the coastal counties north of Palm Beach and in Naples to win. Literally, this was a triumph for Republican Yankees.

Lewis has backgrounds both in the military and in local government. He served in the Air Force for 11 years and was an executive for Pratt & Whitney, the jet engine manufacturers. His career in local government goes back almost 20 years. Neither is likely to make him an insurgent or a believer in lost causes: he is a man who has worked his way up through competent organizations, and seems likely to believe in orderly, sober conservatism. Nor do his committee assignments—Government Operations, Science and Technology—suggest a high profile. Lewis's major concern will probably be to strengthen his position in the district, and to deter significant opposition. If he does so, he should be able to make this a safe Republican seat.

The People   Pop. 1980: 513,121, up 67% 1970–80; voting age pop. 384,221; 16% Black, 4% Span. orig. 24% housing units rented. Median owner $47,700; renter $190. Households: 73% family, 32% with children, 61% married couples.

Presidential Vote

1980	Reagan (R)	102,321	(60%)
	Carter (D)	68,315	(40%)

Rep. Tom Lewis (R) Elected 1982; b. Jan. 26, 1924, Philadelphia, PA; home, North Palm Beach; Palm Beach Jr. Col., 1956–57, U. of FL, 1957–58; Methodist.

Career Corp. Exec., Pratt & Whitney Aircraft, 1957–73; Real estate and investments, 1973–; FL Legislature, 1972–82.

Offices 1313 LHOB, 202-225-5792. Also 8895 N. Military Trail, Su. 304-B, Palm Beach Gardens 33410, 305-627-6192.

Committees *Government Operations* (11th). Subcommittees: Government Information, Justice, and Agriculture; Commerce, Consumer, and Monetary Affairs. *Science and Technology* (15th). Subcommittees: Energy Development and Application; Natural Resources, Agriculture Research and Environment. *Select Committee on Narcotics Abuse and Control* (9th).

Group Ratings and Key Votes: Newly Elected

Election Results

1982 general	Tom Lewis (R)	81,864	(53%)	($346,124)
	Brad Culverhouse (D)	73,886	(47%)	($289,570)
1982 primary	Tom Lewis (R)	17,509	(62%)	
	Al Worden (R)	10,883	(38%)	($95,797)
1980 general	L. A. (Skip) Bafalis (R)	272,393	(79%)	($128,953)
	Richard D. Sparkman (D)	72,646	(21%)	($26,963)

Campaign Contributions and Expenditures

1981-82		*Direct Cont. 81-82*				*PACS brkdwn*		
Receipts	$347,888	Indiv	$190,644	Agr	$1,250	Ideo	$22,450
Expend.	$346,124	Party	$28,523	Bus	$59,650	Lbr	$—
Unspent	$1,762	PACS	$103,445	Hlth	$13,000	Prof	$2,000
		Cand	$25,000				

Indirect Party Expend: $35,371   *Indep Expend:* For: $2,011 (NRA)

THIRTEENTH DISTRICT

Florida's Gulf Coast is probably the closest thing there is in the continental United States to a tropical paradise. The weather, hot and humid in the summer, is pleasant most of the rest of the year. The geography here is more varied than on the Atlantic coast, with its monotonous barrier islands. There are barrier islands on the Gulf, too; but there are also major gaps between them, wide estuaries, and places where the swampy lowlands seem to proceed directly into the ocean. The beaches face west, to the sunset, or south, to the midday sun. And, perhaps most important, the sea is not fenced off here by miles of high-rise apartments. There are, to be sure, some high-rises on the Gulf Coast; but the favored building height here is only two stories, and the favored community is not the high-rise, but the sprawling, city-sized development like Cape Coral or Port Charlotte.

The Gulf Coast, Sarasota south to Naples, is Florida's 13th congressional district. It is, like much of America's Sun Belt, the creature of the air conditioner: 40 years ago, before air conditioning was widely available, some 45,000 people lived here; in 1980, 513,000 did. The population here is heavily tilted toward retirees: only 24% of households include children, and 33% of the adults are over 65—one of the highest percentages in the country. The population is almost entirely white and usually affluent. These are the people who populated the WASPy suburbs of Chicago and New York and Detroit and Philadelphia in the 1950s and 1960s. Not surprisingly, this is the most Republican congressional district in Florida, perhaps one of the most solidly Republican in the nation.

So it was appropriate that the 13th's congressman was selected in the Republican primary in 1982. The incumbent, Skip Bafalis (whose district included most of the 13th and most of what is now the 12th), was running for governor; and in the 13th five local notables contested for the seat. The winner was the man with the most notable name, Connie Mack III. The grandson of the longtime manager and owner of the Philadelphia Athletics, Mack was a banker in Cape Coral with a record of civic involvement but no experience in elective office. Bankers are often important men in these new Florida towns, and not just because they help manage the money of rich widows. In a climate of economic growth, they help determine who gets the money to start a business or build a condominium. It is their business to know everyone in town who has money and to know how they made it.

Mack led the first primary and survived the runoff against a state legislator who attacked him for his support of the Equal Rights Amendment and legal abortion. Like many of the 1982 freshman Republicans—and in vivid contrast to those of 1980—he seems more interested in orthodox economic conservatism (a balanced federal budget, for example) than in either supply side economics or New Right cultural issues. Apparently that pleases the Republican leadership: he won a seat on the Budget Committee. With a safe seat and safe views, he has the potential for a long and perhaps important House career.

The People Pop. 1980: 513,048, up 86.5% 1970–80; voting age pop. 413,477; 4% Black, 2% Span. orig. 18% housing units rented. Median owner $53,700; renter $233. Households: 73% family, 24% with children, 65% married couples.

Presidential Vote

1980	Reagan (R)	159,302	(71%)
	Carter (D)	66,205	(29%)

Rep. Connie M. Mack III (R) Elected 1982; b. Oct. 29, 1940, Philadelphia; home, Cape Coral; U. of FL, B.S. 1966; Roman Catholic.

Career Sunbank 1966–68, 1971–75; First Natl. Bank, Fort Myers, 1968–71; President, FL Bank of Lee Cnty., 1975–82.

Offices 504 CHOB, 202-225-2536. Also Fed. Bldg., Rm. 106, Fort Myers 33901, 813-334-4424.

Committees *Budget* (10th). Task Forces: Energy and Technology; Education and Employment; Entitlements, Uncontrollables, and Indexing. *Post Office and Civil Service* (9th). Subcommittees: Postal Operations and Services; Compensation and Employee Benefits.

Group Ratings and Key Votes: Newly Elected

Election Results

1982 general	Connie Mack III (R)	132,906	(65%)	($496,829)
	Dana N. Stevens (D)	71,206	(35%)	($35,974)
1982 runoff	Connie Mack III (R)	36,408	(58%)	
	Ted Ewing (R)	26,130	(42%)	($237,571)
1982 primary	Connie Mack III (R)	19,962	(29%)	
	Ted Ewing (R)	15,233	(22%)	
	Hugh Paul Nuckolls (R)	13,717	(20%)	($100,622)
	Jim Gardner (R)	10,545	(15%)	($326,668)
	Richard T. Nelson (R)	10,490	(15%)	($178,456
1980 general	L. A. (Skip) Bafalis (R)	272,393	(79%)	($128,953)
	Richard D. Sparkman (D)	72,646	(21%)	($26,963)

Campaign Contributions and Expenditures

1981-82		Direct Cont. 81-82		PACS brkdwn			
Receipts	$501,482	Indiv	$380,135	Agr	$700	Ideo	$4,050
Expend.	$496,829	Party	$20,515	Bus	$27,400	Lbr	$—
Unspent	$4,652	PACS	$50,200	Hlth	$6,750	Prof	$1,500
		Cand	$46,510				

FOURTEENTH DISTRICT

Palm Beach is a place that has intrigued Americans for more than 50 years. The very idea of a town inhabited entirely by the very rich, and just in one season of the year, fascinates—as do pictures of the marble palaces the rich of previous generations built for themselves in the 1920s. Then Palm Beach was just about the only resort in south Florida: Miami was just being developed, Fort Lauderdale was a crossroads, the Gulf Coast was still swamp. And in those days almost no one but the very rich could afford to go to Florida—much less the Caribbean or Mexico!—in the wintertime. Today there are many who are still fascinated by Palm Beach, including many of its own residents and the millions who devoured news of the 1982 Pulitzer divorce trial. But Palm Beach has lost most of its uniqueness. Its ethnic barriers, happily, are mostly gone; its quiet streets are lined less often by palaces than by tasteful condominiums; and it is only one of several dozen very high income winter resorts scattered across the southern part of the country.

Palm Beach is just a small part, but the part you inevitably begin with, of Florida's 14th congressional district. This is a strip of Florida's Gold Coast. In the north is Palm Beach and, across Lake Worth, the more ordinary city of West Palm Beach. To the south are the newer towns of Boynton Beach and Delray Beach, and Boca Raton, a place whose residents' wealth rivals that of Palm Beach. Along this stretch of coast, land has been reclaimed from swamp to about 12 miles inland, and inland is where the growth of the 1980s will take place, in places like Florida Gardens, Country Club Acres, and, to the south in Broward County, in Margate and Tamarac. The 14th was one of the nation's most rapidly growing congressional districts in the 1970s and will probably be again in the 1980s.

Historically, Palm Beach County's voting habits have been more Democratic than Broward County's (Fort Lauderdale, Hollywood) and more Republican than Dade County's (Miami). Recent migrations have made these rules of thumb a little unreliable, however: it is better to note that Palm Beach County was split about evenly in the 1976 presidential election, was solidly Republican in 1980, and gave Democrats Lawton Chiles and Bob Graham percentages similar to their statewide averages in 1982. In congressional elections, the 14th and its predecessors have always gone Democratic, though not for lack of Republican trying. The key election recently was in 1978, when 25-year incumbent Paul Rogers retired. Republicans made a major effort here, but Dan Mica, an assistant to Rogers who won an upset victory in the Democratic primary, won anyway. Against well-financed opposition in 1980 Mica increased his percentage; he won easily in 1982.

Mica's great advantage in his first elections was his experience doing constituency work, first for Rogers and then for himself. On issues, Mica took a cautious course, as Rogers had, supporting national Democratic positions often but by no means always. For many years, such a strategy served southern Democrats well: it made reelection easy and acceptance by other Democrats was not a problem. But for Mica it has been. In 1981 he was the senior member of two Foreign Affairs subcommittees, on Latin America and Africa, but he was beaten for the chairs by two other Democrats, Michael Barnes and Howard Wolpe, who take more liberal positions. True, Mica had seniority only because he had beaten the others in a coin toss; nonetheless, he was understandably bitter about the losses. He supported the Reagan budget and tax cuts in 1981. But on most issues he has not been too far out of line with national Democrats. And he has had the satisfaction of seeing Barnes unable to command a majority on his subcommittee on some major issues. Mica seems clearly able to keep his seat; the question is what this young man can make out of his congressional career in a Democratic Caucus that is not especially sympathetic to members of his views.

The People   Pop. 1980: 512,803, up 126.3% 1970–80; voting age pop. 406,873; 3% Black, 4% Span. orig. 18% housing units rented. Median owner $62,200; renter $278. Households: 74% family, 27% with children, 65% married couples.

Presidential Vote

1980	Reagan (R)	106,816	(64%)
	Carter (D)	61,201	(36%)

Rep. Daniel (Dan) **Mica** (D) Elected 1978; b. Feb. 4, 1944, Binghamton, NY; home, West Palm Beach; U. of FL, 1961–62, Miami Dade Jr. Col., A.A., 1965, FL Atlantic U., B.A. 1966; Roman Catholic.

Career Pub. sch. teacher, 1966–68; A. A. to U.S. Rep. Paul Rogers, 1968–78.

Offices 131 CHOB, 202-225-3001. Also 321 Fed. Bldg., West Palm Beach 33401, 305-832-6424.

Committees *Foreign Affairs* (9th). Subcommittees: International Security and Scientific Affairs; International Economic Policy and Trade. *Veterans' Affairs* (8th). Subcommittees: Hospitals and Health Care; Housing and Memorial Affairs; Compensation, Pension and Insurance. *Select Committee on Aging* (17th). Subcommittee: Retirement Income and Employment.

Group Ratings

	ADA	ACLU	COPE	CFA	LCV	LWV	NTU	NSI	COC	ACA	CSFC
1982	45	42	51	60	62	55	18	80	52	39	38
1981	30	—	46	43	30	—	14	—	53	50	51
1980	33	27	41	36	42	44	36	80	81	52	51

National Journal Ratings

	Economic		Foreign		Cultural	
1982	57%	(LIB)	48%	(LIB)	56%	(LIB)
	43%	(CONS)	51%	(CONS)	44%	(CONS)
1981	53%	(LIB)	52%	(LIB)	39%	(LIB)
	47%	(CONS)	48%	(CONS)	61%	(CONS)

Key Votes

1) Reagan 81 Budget	FOR	5) Incr SS Rtmt Age AGN	9) Poor Pay Food Stamps AGN
2) Reagan 81 Tax Cut	FOR	6) Saudi AWACS Sale AGN	10) Ban Crt Busing Order FOR
3) Bal Budget Amend	FOR	7) $ for MX Missile AGN	11) Auto Local Content FOR
4) Gas & Road Tax	—	8) Nerve Gas Prod AGN	12) Nuclear Arms Freeze FOR

Election Results

1982 general	Daniel (Dan) Mica (D)	128,627	(73%)	($268,170)
	Steve Mitchell (R)	47,542	(27%)	($30,630)
1982 primary	Daniel (Dan) Mica (D)	42,364	(81%)	
	John D. Fleckner, Jr. (D)	9,677	(19%)	
1980 general	Daniel (Dan) Mica (D)	201,713	(59%)	($265,177)
	Al Coogler (R)	137,520	(41%)	($201,217)

Campaign Contributions and Expenditures

1981-82		Direct Cont. 81-82				PACS brkdwn		
Receipts	$290,558	Indiv	$204,811 (est.)	Agr	$4,350	Ideo	$3,950
Expend.	$268,170	PACS	$70,900	Bus	$44,500	Lbr	$10,000
Unspent	$22,540	Cand	$12,274	Hlth	$7,850	Prof	$900

FIFTEENTH DISTRICT

Just about smack in the middle of Florida's Gold Coast—the strip of Atlantic Coast from somewhere south of Miami to somewhere north of Palm Beach, with 3.3 million people—is the city of Fort Lauderdale. In its rather short life, it has gone through a number of transformations. As late as 1950, when it had 36,000 people with 83,000 in Broward County altogether, almost no one had heard of it. Ten years later it was famous nationally for its college spring sand-and-beer vacations—*Where the Boys Are,* in the book and movie title. Among a more select company it had won a reputation as a pleasant place to retire or, perhaps, make a living: a city cosmopolitan but small, with interesting canals and (with air conditioning) a pleasant climate. Here also were wide beaches and good shopping and at least some of the cultural attractions you would expect in a big metropolitan area.

Most of Fort Lauderdale's early residents were from the high income suburbs of the East and Midwest, the Locust Valleys and Winnetkas of America. Through the middle 1960s, Fort Lauderdale tended to exclude Jews: this was the WASPy part of south Florida. Its politics was straight out of the old *Chicago Tribune:* solidly Republican, conservative, unchanging. Then in the late 1960s restrictions against Jews eased in Broward County. Hollywood, just south of Fort Lauderdale, became a mostly Jewish city; Fort Lauderdale itself had many Jewish residents. At the same time, there was vast growth, in beach towns to the north and especially in the newly created cities west in reclaimed swampland. All this made the Fort Lauderdale area culturally more varied and politically more closely—and sometimes bitterly—contested. In 1964 Broward County went for Barry Goldwater, in 1976 for Jimmy Carter—the first time it had gone Democratic for president since 1944.

Now Broward County is split into essentially two congressional districts. The 15th district includes Fort Lauderdale: on the coast it goes past Pompano Beach and Deerfield Beach up to the Palm Beach County line; inland it includes golf-course-laden suburbs like Plantation, Lauderhill, and Lauderdale Lakes. The 16th, a new district, includes Hollywood and much of Dade County to the south. The 16th is very solidly Democratic, and is represented by a Jewish Democrat who grew up in Brooklyn. The 15th is marginally Republican, and is represented by a Republican who made a career in local government in Fort Lauderdale.

He is Clay Shaw, and his involvement in city government goes back to 1968, when he was not yet 30; he served as mayor from 1975 to 1980. Shaw won the seat after a series of tumultuous contests. J. Herbert Burke, a *Tribune* Republican first elected in 1966, was defeated in 1978 following an arrest for disorderly behavior; Ed Stack, the 68-year-old Broward County Sheriff who won was in turn beaten in the Democratic primary in 1980; the primary winner, Miami area legislator Alan Becker, was not even from Broward County and had other problems, and lost to Shaw. Redistricting seems to have cooled things down. Shaw won in 1982 over Ed Stack, though by a 57%–43% margin which, in the circumstances, is not overly impressive. Shaw appears to be a thoughtful legislator and a regular Republican as well. He serves on the nuts-and-bolts Public Works Committee and in 1983 took a seat on Judiciary as well.

The People   Pop. 1980: 512,950, up 34% 1970–80; voting age pop. 411,582; 13% Black, 3% Span. orig. 28% housing units rented. Median owner $59,900; renter $261. Households: 65% family, 24% with children, 53% married couples.

Presidential Vote

1980	Reagan (R)	111,599	(62%)
	Carter (D)	68,107	(38%)

Rep. E. Clay Shaw (R) Elected 1980; b. Apr. 19, 1939, Miami; home, Ft. Lauderdale; Stetson U., B.A. 1961, U. of AL, M.A. 1963, Stetson U., J.D. 1966; Roman Catholic.

Career Practicing atty., 1966–68; Ft. Lauderdale Chf. City Prosecutor, 1968–69, Assoc. Munic. Judge, 1969–71, City Commissioner, 1971–73, Vice Mayor, 1973–75, Mayor, 1975–80; Pres., Natl. Conf. of Repub. Mayors, 1979–80.

Offices 322 CHOB, 202-225-3026. Also Broward Fed. Bldg., 299 E. Broward Blvd., Ft. Lauderdale 33301, 305-527-7253.

Committees *Judiciary* (9th). Subcommittees: Administrative Law; Crime. *Public Works and Transportation* (8th). Subcommittees: Oversight and Investigations; Public Buildings and Grounds; Surface Transportation. *Select Committee on Narcotics Abuse and Control* (3d).

Group Ratings

	ADA	ACLU	COPE	CFA	LCV	LWV	NTU	NSI	COC	ACA	CSFC
1982	15	0	11	20	33	42	73	100	82	78	63
1981	10	—	0	21	36	—	87	—	89	92	75

National Journal Ratings

	Economic		Foreign		Cultural	
1982	24%	(LIB)	36%	(LIB)	50%	(LIB)
	76%	(CONS)	64%	(CONS)	50%	(CONS)
1981	24%	(LIB)	18%	(LIB)	16%	(LIB)
	68%	(CONS)	73%	(CONS)	84%	(CONS)

Key Votes

1) Reagan 81 Budget	FOR	5) Incr SS Rtmt Age	FOR	9) Poor Pay Food Stamps	FOR
2) Reagan 81 Tax Cut	FOR	6) Saudi AWACS Sale	AGN	10) Ban Crt Busing Order	FOR
3) Bal Budget Amend	FOR	7) $ for MX Missile	FOR	11) Auto Local Content	AGN
4) Gas & Road Tax	FOR	8) Nerve Gas Prod	FOR	12) Nuclear Arms Freeze	AGN

Election Results

1982 general	E. Clay Shaw, Jr. (R)	89,128	(57%)	($302,070)
	Edward J. Stack (D)	67,058	(43%)	($99,138)
1982 primary	E. Clay Shaw, Jr. (R) unopposed			
1980 general	E. Clay Shaw, Jr. (R)	128,561	(55%)	($423,603)
	Alan S. Becker (D)	107,164	(45%)	($117,264)

Campaign Contributions and Expenditures

1981-82		Direct Cont. 81-82		PACS brkdwn			
Receipts	$296,906	Indiv	$195,283	Agr	$700	Ideo	$11,050
Expend.	$302,070	Party	$13,934	Bus	$53,085	Lbr	$1,050
Unspent	$4,367	PACS	$77,166	Hlth	$10,000	Prof	$—

Indep Expend: For: $17,889

SIXTEENTH DISTRICT

The 16th congressional district of Florida is one of the four new districts the state won after the 1980 Census, and the one that is most strongly Democratic. It is made up of two geographically and ethnically distinct parts. The first is in Broward County: the city of Hollywood, Pembroke Pines to the west, Hallandale to the south, and Miramar to the southwest. These are places which are predominantly Jewish. Perhaps not a majority of their residents is Jewish, but Jews give the area its cultural and political tone. Twenty years ago, it was almost unheard of for Jews to live north of the Dade-Broward line, but there has been steady migration since then, particularly since large numbers of Cubans have settled in Miami neighborhoods which, but for their presence, might have turned out to be Jewish. Condominium activists are the big political force here. Large high-rise condominiums bring into one handy location, to which access can be controlled, hundreds and sometimes even thousands of voters. In many cases, they are articulate people with organizational literacy, interest in issues, a knack for politics, and plenty of time on their hands. Properly organized, a condominium can give an endorsed candidate a margin of hundreds of votes—a huge advantage in a closely contested primary where most ordinary precincts are carried by 10 or 20 votes.

The second part of the 16th district is in Miami's Dade County, not directly south of the Broward County portion of the 16th, but to the west. There it stretches south past the Tamiami Trail, also known as Southwest 8th Street or, to Cubans, Calle Ocho. This does not include the most ethnically vivid parts of the Cuban community, but it is clearly a Cuban area. Between 60% and 80% of the residents here are of Spanish origin, living, around and behind Miami International Airport, in houses not altogether alien in style to those in other middle class neighborhoods. Here Cuban-Americans move when they achieve modest success. Altogether the Dade County portion of the 16th district is 60% Spanish, and has 41% of the district's residents.

Yet so far their impact on the political process seems limited. The real contest for this district was in the 1982 Democratic primary. There were only two candidates: Alan Becker, a former legislator who had run unsuccessfully for Congress and attorney general; and Larry Smith, a two-term member of the Florida House from Hollywood. Both are Jewish, and both concentrated their campaigns on Broward County. That made sense: 83% of the primary votes were cast there. The Dade County portion of the district, with 150,000 residents, cast less than 8,000 votes in the primary. Becker, whose base is in Dade County, carried that portion; but Smith, who won solidly in Broward, prevailed, with a solid 55%.

Smith was brought up in Brooklyn and Long Island, and approaches life and politics with a brash New York style. The culture shock when he and others like him went to Tallahassee can be imagined—and must have been something like the same shock that occurred when Jews and other ethnics from New York City first went up to Albany and confronted Yankee Upstate legislators.

Smith can be counted on to vote in line with national Democrats on most issues, though he doesn't share all the tastes of some liberals: he is interested in anti-crime legislation. That makes sense when you realize that his key constituents are elderly residents of large highrises, people who were terrified of street criminals back in New York and are fearful of encountering them again in Florida. He serves on Judiciary, where he will be able to work on anti-crime bills, and on Foreign Affairs, where he undoubtedly will be a strong champion of Israel. Given his performance in the 1982 election, Smith appears to have a safe seat.

The People   Pop. 1980: 513,365, up 74.6% 1970–80; voting age pop. 396,409; 4% Black, 20% Span. orig., 1% Asian orig. 23% housing units rented. Median owner $62,500; renter $273. Households: 74% family, 33% with children, 63% married couples.

Presidential Vote

1980	Reagan (R)	85,995	(62%)
	Carter (D)	52,955	(38%)

Rep. Lawrence J. (Larry) **Smith** (D) Elected 1982; b. Apr. 25, 1941, Brooklyn, NY; home, Hollywood; NYU, Brooklyn Law Sch., LL.B. 1964, J.D. 1967; Jewish.

Career Broward Cnty. Dem. Exec. Comm., 1973–78; Hollywood Planning and Zoning Board, 1974–77, Chmn., 1976–77; Broward Cnty. Advisory Board, 1978; FL House of Reps., 1978–82; Governor's Task Force on Criminal Justice Systems, 1980–81.

Offices 113 CHOB, 202-225-7931. Also 4747 Hollywood Blvd., Hollywood 33021, 305-987-6484.

Committees Foreign Affairs (18th). Subcommittees: International Operations; Europe and the Middle East. *Judiciary* (19th). Subcommittees: Immigration, Refugees, and International Law; Crime. *Select Committee on Narcotics Abuse and Control* (15th).

Group Ratings and Key Votes: Newly Elected

Election Results

1982 general	Laurence J. (Larry) Smith (D)	91,869	(68%)	($317,088)
	Maurice Berkowitz (R)	43,343	(32%)	($104,319)
1982 primary	Laurence J. (Larry) Smith (D)	25,275	(55%)	
	Alan S. Becker (D)	20,401	(45%)	($127,453)
1980 general	Newly created district			

Campaign Contributions and Expenditures

1981-82		*Direct Cont. 81-82*				*PACS brkdwn*		
Receipts	$318,892	Indiv	$146,473	Agr	$8,600	Ideo	$5,525
Expend.	$317,088	Party	$6,525	Bus	$64,274	Lbr	$61,475
Unspent	$1,803	PACS	$151,939	Hlth	$10,300	Prof	$1,200
		Cand	$1,500				

Indirect Party Expend: $6,000

SEVENTEENTH DISTRICT

Florida's 17th congressional district is the northern part of Dade County—an almost square portion between the beach above Bal Harbour to the new town suburb of Miami Lakes developed by Governor Bob Graham in the west. The district includes only a small part of the city of Miami itself, but in many ways is the heart of the metropolitan area. It is about one-quarter Cuban: the once white working class suburb of Hialeah, around the race track, is now mostly Cuban. The 16th is also about one-quarter black: just as Cubans move out from Miami along S.W. 8th Street, blacks tend to move north in a corridor between N.W. 7th and 27th Avenues. Yet the dominant political tone in the 17th is set by a group less numerous than either: the Jews, who tend to live in the communities along Biscayne Bay, especially North Miami and North Miami Beach (which is not on the beach at all). They turn out in Democratic primaries, which are tantamount to election here; they organize in condominium and neighborhood associations, which can deliver large margins to candidates.

The congressman from the 17th is William Lehman. He was first elected in 1972, when the district was newly created; he had been active on the school board. Before that he had had a long and successful career selling, of all things, used cars. Lehman entered Congress when he was almost 60, and in 1982 he was ill with cancer, from which he recovered. He serves rather quietly on the Appropriations Committee, and on the sudden death in 1982 of Adam Benjamin he became chairman of the Transportation Subcommittee. This is a position of potentially vast influence, but Lehman, a pleasant man, does not seem to have the aggressiveness and ambition to make high policy. At home, he is safe, and has not had serious competition since his first campaign.

The People Pop. 1980: 513,048, up 25.6% 1970–80; voting age pop. 385,199; 22% Black, 14% Span. orig., 1% Asian orig. 36% housing units rented. Median owner $46,700; renter $237. Households: 72% family, 35% with children, 55% married couples.

Presidential Vote

1980	Reagan (R)	77,578	(56%)
	Carter (D)	61,776	(44%)

Rep. William Lehman (D) Elected 1972; b. Oct. 5, 1913, Selma, AL; home, North Miami Beach; U. of AL, B.S. 1934, U. of Miami, Teaching Cert. 1963. Additional studies at Oxford U., Cambridge U., U. of Edinburgh, Harvard U., and Middlebury Col.; Jewish.

Career Auto dealer, 1936–42, 1946–72; Army Air Corps, WWII; Teacher, Pub. Schools, 1963, Miami Dade Jr. Col., 1964–66; Dade Cnty. Sch. Bd., 1964–70, Chmn., 1971.

Offices 2347 RHOB, 202-225-4211. Also 2020 N.E. 163rd St., Su. 108, N. Miami Beach 33162, 305-945-7518.

Committees *Appropriations* (21st). Subcommittees: District of Columbia; Foreign Operations; Transportation (Chairman). *Select Committee on Children, Youth, and Families* (2d).

Group Ratings

	ADA	ACLU	COPE	CFA	LCV	LWV	NTU	NSI	COC	ACA	CSFC
1982	89	79	85	78	87	88	24	10	15	23	27
1981	85	—	84	57	68	—	14	—	18	0	31
1980	83	93	72	71	54	70	14	0	61	17	26

National Journal Ratings

	Economic		Foreign		Cultural	
1982	90%	(LIB)	84%	(LIB)	—	(LIB)
	10%	(CONS)	16%	(CONS)	—	(CONS)
1981	79%	(LIB)	85%	(LIB)	92%	(LIB)
	20%	(CONS)	13%	(CONS)	8%	(CONS)

Key Votes

1) Reagan 81 Budget	AGN	5) Incr SS Rtmt Age	AGN	9) Poor Pay Food Stamps	AGN
2) Reagan 81 Tax Cut	AGN	6) Saudi AWACS Sale	AGN	10) Ban Crt Busing Order	—
3) Bal Budget Amend	AGN	7) $ for MX Missile	AGN	11) Auto Local Content	—
4) Gas & Road Tax	—	8) Nerve Gas Prod	AGN	12) Nuclear Arms Freeze	FOR

Election Results

1982 general	William Lehman (D) unopposed			
1982 primary	William Lehman (D)	48,092	(88%)	($116,762)
	R. (Dan) Conoley (D)	6,844	(12%)	($0)
1980 general	William Lehman (D)	127,828	(75%)	($208,900)
	Alvin E. Entin (R)	42,830	(25%)	($63,434)

Campaign Contributions and Expenditures

1981-82		*Direct Cont. 81-82*				*PACS brkdwn*		
Receipts	$169,826	Indiv	$107,951	Agr	$1,250	Ideo	$2,750
Expend.	$116,762	PACS	$57,088	Bus	$24,650	Lbr	$25,000
Unspent	$59,078			Hlth	$1,750	Prof	$1,300

EIGHTEENTH DISTRICT

Miami is one of America's most troubled cities and yet one of its most vibrant; and if we are to understand its troubles, we must also understand its potential. For Miami—technically a city of 350,000 people, but also the major metropolis in Florida's Gold Coast, with almost ten times that population—is not withering. Its civic discords are basically growing pains. Since its abrupt beginnings in the 1920s, Miami has always been on its way to becoming something else, and today the transformation is particularly striking—and painful. Miami, once a tourist and retirement center, then a major Yankee-and-Jewish subtropical metropolis, is now becoming the economic capital of all of Latin America.

Almost no one expected this to happen. But Miami had several unappreciated assets. The first was its airport. It has long had flights to all parts of Latin America and the Caribbean. As businessmen sought to open Latin American offices, they found that the best location was Miami: it is easier to fly to most parts of Latin America from here than from any other place. The second major asset was its tourist facilities. If no longer attractive to successful Americans, they could be made attractive to Europeans. First charter flight operators and then regular airlines found that they could fill planes from Heathrow and Frankfurt to Miami. The third asset is Miami's Cuban-American population. More than 600,000 people of Spanish origin live in the area. Most are refugees from Castro's Cuba, many of middle class background; they worked in menial jobs when they first arrived, but by now they have built businesses or gotten good jobs. The result is a large, Spanish-speaking business and professional community—unique in the United States. The fourth asset is Latin America's political instability. Property in Miami is not about to be confiscated; businessmen or travellers are not about to be jailed; taxes of 100% and 200% are not exacted on sales of imported consumer products; the currency is not about to be devalued or bank accounts frozen. All these things *could* happen (some of them have, repeatedly) in Mexico City or Caracas or Lima or Rio de Janeiro. But not in Miami.

And so Miami has had vibrant growth. Its downtown has sprouted new office buildings galore, even when new construction was off in other U.S. cities in 1982. Its retail sales, buoyed by Latin customers, have been strong. Tourism here is doing better than ever. But there have been negative effects. One of the biggest new businesses here is illegal drugs—the number one export from Colombia and an important product in a number of Latin economies. So there have been wars among drug dealers and wholesalers, decrepit planes full of drugs crashing in the Everglades or ditched in the ocean. Miami's prosperity has also attracted Latins who are not always welcome. The Cuban refugees of 1980 were brought over in boats financed by Miami's Cuban community, and were welcomed at first. But as lurid tales circulated, resentment toward the new migrants grew. There has also been resentment—and there have been fewer patrons—of the Haitians who have struggled in tiny boats to reach south Florida. Miami's black community, jealous of the progress of the Cubans, resentful of bad treatment from white and Cuban policemen, erupted in riots in 1980 and 1982.

Underlying these events is the most pervasive streak of cynicism about politics and government in the United States. Voter participation is low (the large majority of Cubans don't vote), and even among the few voters cynicism is high. Perhaps it makes sense: Miami's prosperity owes more to governments' (usually Latin governments') misdeeds than to governments' achievements. The Cubans, in particular, owe government little for their advance. The crime rate is high, and it seems that little can be done about it. Tallahassee and Washington seem far away, and uninterested in Miami.

Florida's 18th congressional district covers most of the city of Miami; all of Miami Beach, Bal Harbour, and Key Biscayne; the high income suburb of Coral Gables. Its center is S.W. 8th Street—Calle Ocho—which extends west from downtown and becomes the Tamiami Trail; this is the main street of the Cuban community. There are still many Jewish residents here, though perhaps more in Miami Beach than on the mainland; there are blacks in the ghetto running north from downtown. But the overall ethnic flavor is distinctly Cuban. Fully 50% of the district's residents are of Spanish origin, almost all of them Cuban.

The 18th is represented by the oldest man in Congress, Claude Pepper, a man with a glorious political past who became one of the most powerful and popular politicians in the nation in 1981 and 1982. Pepper was born in 1900, and went to the Senate in 1936; he is one of two men in Congress who served during the New Deal years (the other is West Virginia's Jennings Randolph). He was known for his old-fashioned southern oratory and his up-to-date New Deal views; he was a stalwart as well of Franklin Roosevelt's anti-isolationist foreign policy. For these stands he became known as "Red Pepper," and was subject to scurrilous attacks in the 1950 primary which he lost to George Smathers.

Today Smathers has long since (1968) retired, and Claude Pepper is again one of the most senior members of Congress. When Miami got a second House seat after the 1960 Census, Pepper was the obvious man to fill it, and he won easily. His constituency then tended to be elderly, with many Jewish and Catholic migrants from the Northeast; it has changed since, but he continues to win reelection easily. In the House, Pepper was a supporter of the Democratic leadership; but he was also floundering about, looking for a major issue. He tried to promote a sort of theme park in Miami, which never got off the ground; he chaired a special subcommittee on crime, which made some recommendations and finally died. Then he got a seat on, and eventually became chairman of, the Select Committee on Aging. Here he finally found a good match of conviction and position. Pepper is still a New Dealer: he believes that government should do more to help the aged and infirm and to give them options to lead their lives as they wish. Thus he pushed to passage the bill changing the minimum mandatory retirement age for most jobs from 65 to 70—allowing people to work longer. And he has opposed most vigorously proposals to cut back Social Security benefits—allowing people to retire earlier in comfort.

Pepper does not seem much interested in arguments that society can't afford to be so generous, or that there might not be enough jobs for everyone if the elderly want to keep working. Like a good New Dealer, he sees these as clever obfuscations by those who serve the interests of the rich and the selfish. He seems serenely confident that society will find a way to pay for the benefits he supports.

Technically, Pepper has no great legislative power on these issues: the Aging Committee has no power to initiate legislation. The head of the House's Social Security Subcommittee, Jake Pickle, is of different views; he concedes that there should be some cuts in future benefits. For a time it appeared that Pepper, as a member of the Social Security Commission President Reagan established, would have an effective veto over any compromise, since Republicans would be reluctant to support any plan Pepper publicly opposed. But on the floor of the House Pickle, who stayed off the commission, prevailed on the key issue of raising the retirement age in the 21st century. Pepper strongly opposed this; he wants to give people the option to work longer, but he doesn't want to force them to do so. But Pickle, who is no Boll Weevil on economic issues, got enough Democratic votes to combine with Republicans and make a majority on this issue.

Pepper's had great clout in the 1982 campaign, when his was one of the most sought-after endorsements in House races, and he was one of the most active campaigners for Democrats around the country. Interestingly, Robert Caro's book on Lyndon Johnson, published in 1982, showed how Pepper as a young senator was one of the most sought-after speakers for Democratic candidates in the 1940 campaign. Is there another example of a member of Congress who has been a major campaigner in elections 42 years apart?

In 1983 Pepper relinquished his Aging Committee chair to become Chairman of the House Rules Committee. Theoretically, that makes him more powerful; in fact, his power remains, based not on position but on forcefully articulated principle. As Rules chairman, Pepper will act as a good right arm to Speaker O'Neill; both remember serving on the committee when conservatives used it to bottle up liberal legislation, and neither wants to be an obstructionist. It is understood, however, that he will allow no tampering with Social Security.

Pepper's lead role on Social Security obviously doesn't hurt him politically in a district where 30% of the adults are 65 or over, and many of the rest are Cubans who don't vote. The long-term political trend here may be toward the Republicans, whose support of free enterprise and hardline opposition to Communism appeals to many Cubans; but that trend is by no means clear, and so far Cubans have yet to become a major political force. An attractive Cuban candidate, supported generously by the Republican Party, could manage to win only 37% of the vote against Pepper in 1978. On occasion some Miamians have urged Pepper to retire; but that call seems unlikely to be heeded, by him or the voters. For all of Miamians' cynicism about politics and government, they don't seem to be cynical about this least cynical of politicians.

The People   Pop. 1980: 513,250, up 6.4% 1970–80; voting age pop. 416,969; 13% Black, 50% Span. orig., 1% Asian orig. 58% housing units rented. Median owner $53,500; renter $210. Households: 62% family, 25% with children, 46% married couples.

Presidential Vote

1980	Reagan (R)	77,578	(56%)
	Carter (D)	61,776	(44%)

Rep. Claude Pepper (D) Elected 1962; b. Sept. 8, 1900, near Dudleyville, AL; home, Miami; U. of AL, A.B. 1921, Harvard U., LL.B. 1924; Baptist.

Career Instructor in Law, U. of AR, 1924–25; Practicing atty., 1925–36, 1951–62; FL House of Reps., 1929–30; FL Bd. of Pub. Welfare, 1931–32; FL Bd. of Law Examiners, 1933–34; U.S. Senate, 1937–51; Candidate for Dem. Nomination for U.S. Senate, 1950, 1958.

Offices 2239 RHOB, 202-225-3931. Also 823 Fed. Bldg., 51 S.W. 1st Ave., Miami 33130, 305-350-5565.

Committees *Rules* (Chairman). *Select Committee on Aging* (2d). Subcommittee: Health and Long-Term Care (Chairman).

Group Ratings

	ADA	ACLU	COPE	CFA	LCV	LWV	NTU	NSI	COC	ACA	CSFC
1982	60	62	93	90	66	70	0	88	22	16	29
1981	55	—	93	64	53	—	0	—	22	19	35
1980	61	67	95	57	29	70	8	33	74	19	27

National Journal Ratings

	Economic		Foreign		Cultural	
1982	96%	(LIB)	57%	(LIB)	83%	(LIB)
	2%	(CONS)	43%	(CONS)	16%	(CONS)
1981	87%	(LIB)	46%	(LIB)	78%	(LIB)
	12%	(CONS)	52%	(CONS)	21%	(CONS)

Key Votes

1) Reagan 81 Budget	AGN	5) Incr SS Rtmt Age	AGN	9) Poor Pay Food Stamps	AGN
2) Reagan 81 Tax Cut	AGN	6) Saudi AWACS Sale	AGN	10) Ban Crt Busing Order	AGN
3) Bal Budget Amend	AGN	7) $ for MX Missile	AGN	11) Auto Local Content	FOR
4) Gas & Road Tax	FOR	8) Nerve Gas Prod	—	12) Nuclear Arms Freeze	FOR

Election Results

1982 general	Claude Pepper (D)	72,137	(71%)	($218,455)
	Ricardo Nunez (R)	29,156	(29%)	($193,822)
1982 primary	Claude Pepper (D) unopposed			
1980 general	Claude Pepper (D)	95,820	(75%)	($211,659)
	Evelio S. Estrella (R)	32,027	(25%)	($50,620)

Campaign Contributions and Expenditures

1981-82		Direct Cont. 81-82		PACS brkdwn			
Receipts	$243,947	Indiv	$122,063	Agr	$1,650	Ideo	$4,200
Expend.	$218,455	PACS	$99,835	Bus	$24,550	Lbr	$61,500
Unspent	$26,564	Cand	$13,399	Hlth	$4,500	Prof	$1,450

NINETEENTH DISTRICT

Not so long ago U.S. 1 south of Miami was a narrow ribbon of highway passing between acres of Everglades swamp. It was a road for tourists: every so often there was a tourist attraction (the Serpenterium, Monkey Jungle, Coral Castle) as the road made its way toward the miraculous series of causeways that take it all the way to Key West. In the past 30 years much of this land has been reclaimed, filled in, and paved with subdivisions. It has become the part of the Miami area closest to the typical middle class American ideal. This is Florida's 19th congressional district, which starts in Miami's Coconut Grove area and passes through Coral Gables to new suburbs like Kendall, Olympia Heights, Richmond Heights, and Perrine. In one way this area is not typical: 22% of its population is of Spanish origin. But if the Cubans still speak Spanish at home and at work, they also are upwardly striving, young, and family-oriented (40% of the households here contain children, one of the highest figures in Florida). More than many Americans whose immigrant ancestors are more remote, they are believers in the American dream.

The political tone here, it should be added, is still set mainly by Anglos; Cubans have not yet entered the electorate in massive numbers. And while this area is definitely middle class, it is also definitely Democratic. There are exceptions, notably in 1980, when furor over the Cuban refugees delivered Dade County to Ronald Reagan.

The south Dade County district has, since 1954, regularly elected and reelected Congressman Dante Fascell. He does not have as liberal a reputation as his neighbor Claude Pepper, nor is he as famous; but insiders know he is a congressman of national Democratic views and national rank. On cultural and foreign policy issues, Fascell's views are probably to the left of Pepper's, on economic issues slightly to the right. He is the second ranking Democrat on the Foreign Affairs Committee, and for years chaired the Inter-American Subcommittee—of obvious importance to Miami, now that it is the center of Latin American trade. Now he has a subcommittee (International Operations) that gives him *carte blanche* to investigate foreign policy matters—and the responsibility to floor manage some difficult items, like the State Department authorization bill. Fascell is in line to succeed Chairman Clement Zablocki, whose views on some issues (Israel, for one) combined with his mild temperament makes his hold on the chair a little shaky. In effect Zablocki has allowed subcommittee chairmen, most of them young liberals, to take the lead. Fascell is unlikely to do so—unless they lead where he would like to go. On Latin American issues in particular he takes a somewhat different stand. While he is wary of American involvement there, he is also under no illusions about the nature of Castro's regime or that of his Sandinista allies in Nicaragua. He strongly backs Radio Marti and is against a cutoff of aid to El Salvador.

Fascell is also number two on Government Operations, and while he is not going to overwhelm the chairman, Jack Brooks of Texas, he is not afraid to stand up to Brooks when he disagrees with him. Indeed, Fascell is one of the most fearless members of the House and will not run away from a fight with the most formidable opponent. He took on Brooks when Brooks opposed Jimmy Carter's government reorganization bill; he took on Wayne Hays during his heyday on campaign finance. Fascell is regarded by some observers of the House as one of its most competent and sensitive legislative craftsmen—a man who can put together a piece of legislation, explain it, and get it passed without major change.

The People   Pop. 1980: 512,886, up 45% 1970–80; voting age pop. 373,329; 10% Black, 21% Span. orig., 1% Asian orig. 29% housing units rented. Median owner $69,900; renter $263. Households: 73% family, 40% with children, 60% married couples.

Presidential Vote

1980	Reagan (R)	95,584	(59%)
	Carter (D)	66,890	(41%)

Rep. Dante B. Fascell (D) Elected 1954; b. Mar. 9, 1917, Bridgehampton, L.I., NY; home, Miami; U. of Miami, J.D. 1938; Protestant.

Career Practicing atty., 1938–42, 1946–54; Army, WWII; Legal Attache, Dade Cnty. St. Legislative Del., 1947–59; FL House of Reps., 1950–54; Mbr., U.S. Delegation to U.N., 1969.

Offices 2354 RHOB, 202-225-4506. Also 904 Fed. Bldg., 51 S.W. 1st Ave., Miami 33130, 305-350-5301.

Committees *Foreign Affairs* (2d). Subcommittees: International Operations (Chairman); International Security and Scientific Affairs. *Government Operations* (2d). Subcommittee: Legislation and National Security.

Group Ratings

	ADA	ACLU	COPE	CFA	LCV	LWV	NTU	NSI	COC	ACA	CSFC
1982	75	79	82	70	69	83	15	20	25	30	32
1981	80	—	81	79	91	—	35	—	21	5	33
1980	83	83	83	79	43	90	13	10	59	25	25

National Journal Ratings

	Economic		Foreign		Cultural	
1982	76%	(LIB)	67%	(LIB)	64%	(LIB)
	24%	(CONS)	33%	(CONS)	36%	(CONS)
1981	73%	(LIB)	72%	(LIB)	92%	(LIB)
	26%	(CONS)	26%	(CONS)	8%	(CONS)

Key Votes

1) Reagan 81 Budget	AGN	5) Incr SS Rtmt Age	AGN	9) Poor Pay Food Stamps	AGN
2) Reagan 81 Tax Cut	AGN	6) Saudi AWACS Sale	AGN	10) Ban Crt Busing Order	AGN
3) Bal Budget Amend	AGN	7) $ for MX Missile	AGN	11) Auto Local Content	FOR
4) Gas & Road Tax	—	8) Nerve Gas Prod	AGN	12) Nuclear Arms Freeze	FOR

Election Results

1982 general	Dante B. Fascell (D)	74,274	(59%)	($466,502)
	Glenn Rinker (R)	51,925	(41%)	($233,716)
1982 primary	Dante B. Fascell (D) unopposed			
1980 general	Dante B. Fascell (D)	132,952	(65%)	($73,971)
	Herbert J. Hoodwin (R)	70,433	(35%)	($34,172)

Campaign Contributions and Expenditures

1981-82		Direct Cont. 81-82		PACS brkdwn			
Receipts	$529,625	Indiv	$293,373	Agr	$1,500	Ideo	$75,322
Expend.	$466,502	Party	$10,500	Bus	$27,950	Lbr	$80,000
Unspent	$71,446	PACS	$191,411	Hlth	$5,800	Prof	$2,200

Indirect Party Expend: $3,645   *Indep Expend:* For: $8,982 (NCFC)

GEORGIA

Georgia is the center of the South—the New South and the Old South, the Deep South and the civil rights South, the South of the poor white and of the black elite. It is the center partly because of its geographic position—it is the pivot point between the Atlantic coastal South and the Mississippi Valley South, between the lowlands and the Piedmont and the mountains—and partly because of the success of Atlanta as a commercial and transport center. (Atlanta's airport, the busiest in the nation, is the key to that; it really *is* hard to fly from one place in the South to another without going through Atlanta.)

Georgia has given the nation the Rev. Martin Luther King, Jr., and Jimmy Carter—and Lester Maddox. It is the home of the South's black intellectual and economic elite, and it was the home base of dedicated supporters of segregation like Senator Richard Russell. It was once the most Democratic state in the "solid South"; it led the South in switching to the Republicans over the race issue in 1964. And Georgia has become the center without any noted aristocracy. It was the last of the 13 colonies, founded as a home for convicts; it never had an aristocracy like those in Virginia or South Carolina. Georgia remembers the Civil War, but Georgians were more often foot soldiers and victims of Sherman's Army than Confederate leaders. Georgia was the place where the term New South was first coined—in the 1870s—but it was also a state where the fundamental issue in politics was race, and where racial segregation prevailed until it was abolished by a determined federal government.

Georgia's progress beyond racial politics was symbolized in the moment in 1976 when Jimmy Carter, freshly nominated by the Democratic Party, called the Rev. Martin Luther King, Sr., to the podium to give the benediction. The father of the greatest leader of the civil rights movement gave his blessing to the first white from the Deep South nominated for the presidency in a century. There was irony here: Carter had at points in his career suggested that he was less favorable to civil rights than his opponents, and King, Sr., spent most of his career accommodating to segregation rather than protesting it. But for all that, the moment did signify a real—and valuable—change. It meant something when Jimmy Carter put a picture of Martin Luther King, Jr., on the wall of the Georgia Capitol in 1971, just as it meant something when he was elected governor in 1970 despite his support for blacks. That year was the watershed in Georgia—and southern—politics, the first time after the civil rights revolution that candidates supported by blacks did not automatically forfeit white support. (Atlanta blacks used to send out endorsements in letters to arrive on election day, so that white voters wouldn't know whom they were backing.) And Carter's victory in 1976 marked the first time since the civil rights revolution that a presidential candidate supported by blacks was able to win substantial numbers of white votes in the Deep South.

Politics in post-civil rights revolution Georgia and the South is, inevitably, less momentous. There is less to be decided. In the days before Jimmy Carter, Georgia elections were almost always a matter of black versus white and, as a variation on this theme, metropolitan Atlanta versus the vast expanse of rural Georgia. Atlanta tended to favor candidates who favored civil rights, who were close to their national parties, whose accents were broadcaster-neutral and whose clothes and bearing reflected the sophistication which Atlanta prides itself on. Rural Georgia tended to oppose such candidates and, being more numerous (especially in

Democratic primaries) tended to beat them. Jimmy Carter won the 1970 Democratic primary by campaigning as a "redneck" from south Georgia; the only candidate who lived in Atlanta and won a major office was Lester Maddox, who symbolized rural values.

But by the late 1970s the dichotomy between Atlanta and rural Georgia was fading. Carter's successor as governor, George Busbee, was a Democrat with a base around Albany, in the same part of the state as Plains. But Busbee was also a businesslike executive, a man perfectly at home at governors' conferences or speaking on management techniques. He knew how to work the legislature—better than Carter, many observers said—and he won reelection handily (he was the first governor eligible to seek it) in 1978. Busbee retired from office popular (though he roused some resentment by seeking a higher pension than most people assumed he was entitled to), and after setting a new tone to political life.

The race for governor in 1982 showed how much Georgia politics had changed. For this time there simply were not the sharp differences between Atlanta and the rural counties, between blacks and whites which characterized Georgia elections in the past. True, in the Democratic primary, black voters did tend to support one candidate, Savannah area Congressman Bo Ginn, whose record on economic issues was more liberal than those of his opponents. But Ginn did not have monolithic support from blacks, only a somewhat larger percentage than his rivals. The Atlanta area gave somewhat larger percentages to the more cosmopolitan candidates, notably former White House aide Jack Watson, than did the rural counties. But again the difference was not huge, and Watson was the choice of only 20% in the Atlanta area in the first primary. The runoff featured a choice more stylistic than ideological, between the businesslike, efficient Ginn and the deeply religious, moralistic state legislator Joe Frank Harris. Harris won, 55%–45%, running about the same in all parts of the state, except for Ginn's home district. The general election was anticlimactic: a Republican, unless some special factor is in play, does not really have a chance in Georgia, which was the number one Democratic state in 1980 and in 1956 and earlier elections as well.

So Georgia seems to have moved from the politics of race to the politics of style. The vast differences over civil rights and between metropolitan and rural areas seem to have disappeared, as desegregation has been accepted and the cultural styles of city and country blend—or at least coexist in the same geographical areas. As the metropolitan area expands, it is possible to live in a neighborhood whose physical and cultural setting resembles a small town; and it is possible, even in south Georgia, to enjoy many of the pleasures and share many of the attitudes of sophisticated big city residents. The result is a politics based not on race or residence, but on inner attitudes—a politics where choices correlate better with magazine subscriptions (*New York* versus *Popular Mechanics*) or leisure time behavior (jogging versus churchgoing) than with standard political categories.

Ironically, the two most visible political executives in Georgia today, Governor Joe Frank Harris and Atlanta Mayor Andrew Young owe their rise to their religiosity: Harris emphasized his strong Christian views on issues and his abstemious personal behavior; Young is a minister whose understanding of the gospel directly influenced his political stands. For that matter, Jimmy Carter owes much of his rise to religion as well, for it was religious conviction, apparently, that led him to repudiate segregation—without which he never could have been a national candidate. In sum, absent overriding issues like race, Georgia voters evidently are looking for candidates who share their outlook on matters they consider important, like religion or making money.

Governor. Joe Frank Harris entered office a largely unknown quantity. He served 18 years in the legislature and chaired the House Appropriations Committee, but as a candidate he was attacked for being dominated by House Speaker Tom Murphy; after winning the primary, he secured the nomination of a strong Democratic state chairman, former federal Budget Director Bert Lance. Will he be dominated by stronger men or is he showing the confidence of a leader not afraid to surround himself with first-raters? In either case, Harris's strong religious views will surely color the tone of political life in the state and his no-new-tax pledge will affect his approach to issues.

Senators. The senior member of Georgia's congressional delegation, Senator Sam Nunn, does not play an active role in the state's politics; he doesn't have to. He was first elected in 1972, at age 34, as a young legislator from a south Georgia town campaigning against Atlanta-based opponents. A better clue to his Senate career than his first campaign is his lineage: he is the grandnephew of former Congressman (1914–65) Carl Vinson, the longtime Chairman of the House Armed Services Committee; and in his first year in the Senate he inherited the seat on Armed Services of former Senator (1933–71) and Armed Services Chairman Richard Russell. Nunn very soon made himself one of the Senate's most respected experts on military policy. His background and basic leanings make him sympathetic to increases in defense spending, but he approaches all issues in depth and on his own. He is thoughtful, candid, and never given to cheap shots; he respects authority but questions all assumptions and does not hesitate to voice his dissent from any one of them. He has worked hard on such arcana as NATO deployments as well as on major weapons systems; he is not one of the group of "military reformers" like Colorado's Gary Hart, but he shares some of their views.

Nunn will probably some day be Armed Services chairman, but his influence depends on his knowledge and fairmindedness, not on his position. Even in a Republican Senate, he may be the single most influential senator on military matters; and if he throws himself into a fight on a military issue, he is likely to prevail. He is, it should be added, not a reliable ally for any president. Nunn criticizes some of the Reagan administration's defense plans, and he made no secret of the fact that he thought his fellow Georgian Jimmy Carter (with whom he was not close) was cutting defense spending dangerously.

On non-military issues Nunn takes a similar approach. His basic instincts are conservative, particularly on cultural issues; and on many matters his voting record looks like that of an old Dixiecrat. But he is not a knee-jerk vote for anything, and he is open to persuasion on most domestic matters. Should the Democrats regain control of the Senate, he would probably chair the Permanent Investigations Subcommittee, for years one of the showcases of Capitol Hill. But Nunn, whose capacity for national office no one who knows him doubts, does not seem to have any ambition to become well known nationally. He seems content to operate in the old southern—and Georgia—tradition of the experienced, hard-working, knowledgeable legislative insider, the man who affects national policy quietly and with very few people outside Capitol Hill knowing it.

Nunn is up for reelection in 1984, and he is sure to win easily; it is highly unlikely that he will have serious competition. He got 80% of the vote in the 1978 primary and 83% in the general election.

Georgia's other senator is a Republican elected in an upset in 1980; and his victory cannot be ascribed to Jimmy Carter's weakness, since Georgia was the one state where Carter had an absolute majority. He won by beating four-term Senator Herman Talmadge, a man of great abilities but serious weaknesses, who was "denounced" by the Senate for financial improprieties. Mack Mattingly is a pleasant man, a Yankee migrant who worked for IBM, a Republican state chairman; he lives on St. Simon's Island, and epitomizes the wealthy country club crowd which remains the heart of Georgia's Republican Party. Mattingly did have good financial support: the national Republican Party appreciated Talmadge's weakness, and contributed the maximum to his little-known opponent. And Talmadge, who campaigned hard in metropolitan Atlanta and among blacks, could not overcome a whole career of seeming to run against both. Outside Georgia's metropolitan areas Talmadge won 61% of the vote. But in the 12 counties within a 60-mile circle around Atlanta, where 40% of the state's votes are cast, 63% voted for Mattingly. Mattingly also carried the state's minor metropolitan areas by a small margin; almost everyone there has seen enough economic activity to generate a significant country club class—from the Chattanooga suburbs in the north to Valdosta in the south—Mattingly carried.

Mattingly has one of the most conservative records in the Senate; he was one of the Republicans most reluctant to vote for Bob Dole's tax bill in 1982 for example. But he shows little of the fervor of New Right and Moral Majority politicians; he supports their stands, but not as if his life depends on it. He has a seat on the Appropriations Committee, but among the crowd of new Republicans has not emerged as a leader.

Mattingly must expect serious competition when he comes up for reelection in 1986. His best hope is that the Democrats have such a confusing and acrimonious primary that the winner comes out badly scarred—a real possibility, particularly since Georgia's runoff is held just before Labor Day.

Presidential politics. Will Georgia remain one of the most Democratic states without Jimmy Carter on the ticket? No one is sure, but the state seems likely to remain as heavily Democratic as Alabama, say, or Tennessee or the Carolinas, all of which were about 8% less Democratic in 1980. Georgia's presidential primary, held early, has never been decisive for either party: the Democratic result has been taken for granted (Wallace, Carter); the Republican contest has a small, country club electorate.

Congressional redistricting. The Georgia legislature did a workmanlike job of adjusting the state's congressional district lines outside the Atlanta area. There is no way to build a black-majority rural district, and so the issue does not arise. But in Atlanta, a federal court intervened and redrew the district lines to increase the black percentage in the 5th district to 65%, and the election was not held until late in November. This was the district once represented by Andrew Young (who won it when it had a white majority); it is now represented by a white, Wyche Fowler, who did not have any competition, black or white, in the 1982 Democratic primary. This is not, of course, because blacks in Atlanta are somehow suppressed, but because Fowler had done a good job representing his black constituents.

The People   Est. Pop. 1982: 5,639,000; Pop. 1980: 5,463,105, up 3.2% 1980–82 and 19% 1970–80; 2.4% of U.S. total, 12th largest; voting age pop. 3,816,975; 24% Black, 1% Spanish origin, 1% Asian origin. Single ancestry: 21% English, 5% Irish, 3% German, 1% French. Registered voters (1982, pri.): 2,284,184 Total. 13% with 1–3 yrs. col., 15% with 4+ yrs. col. 16.4% below poverty level. Housing units rented, 32%; median house value: $36,900; median monthly rent: $153. Households: 76% family, 45% with children, 61% married couples.

1982 Share of Federal Tax Burden $11,818,700,000; 1.98% of U.S. total, 16th largest.

1982 Share of Federal Expenditures

	Total		Non-Defense		Defense	
Total Expend	$12,766m	(2.12%)	$8,660m	(2.04%)	$4,106m	(2.30%)
St/Lcl Grants	2,185m	(2.48%)	2,184m	(2.48%)	1m	(2.78%)
Salary/Wages	2,618m	(3.35%)	685m	(2.50%)	1,933m	(3.81%)
Ind Payments	6,021m	(2.10%)	5,092m	(1.98%)	929m	(3.25%)
Procurement	1,870m	(1.28%)	190m	(0.60%)	1,680m	(1.47%)
Other Programs	71m	(1.31%)	68m	(1.27%)	3m	(6.98%)
Loan/Insurance	2,230m	(3.49%)	2,170m	(3.51%)	60m	(2.73%)

Political Lineup Governor, Joe Frank Harris (D). Senators, Sam Nunn (D) and Mack Mattingly (R). Representatives, 10 (9 D and 1 R); State Senate, 56 (49 D and 7 R); State House of Representatives, 180 (156 D and 24 R).

Presidential Vote

1980	Reagan (R)	654,168	(41%)
	Carter (D)	890,733	(56%)
	Anderson (I)	36,055	(2%)
1976	Ford (R)	483,743	(33%)
	Carter (D)	979,409	(67%)

1980 Democratic Presidential Primary			*1980 Republican Presidential Primary*		
Carter	338,772	(88%)	Reagan	146,500	(73%)
Kennedy	32,315	(8%)	Bush	25,293	(13%)
Four others	9,986	(3%)	Anderson	16,853	(8%)
Uncommitted	3,707	(1%)	Six others	11,525	(6%)

SENATORS

Sen. Sam Nunn (D) Elected 1972, seat up 1984; b. Sept. 8, 1938, Perry; home, Perry; Emory U., A.B. 1960, LL.B. 1962; United Methodist.

Career Coast Guard, 1959–60; Legal Counsel, U.S. House of Reps., Armed Services Comm., 1962–63; Farmer; Practicing atty., 1963–72.

Offices 335 DSOB 202-224-3521. Also 275 Peachtree St. N.E., Rm. 430, Atlanta 30303, 404-221-4811; and 915B Main St., Perry 31069, 912-987-1458.

Committees *Armed Services* (3d). Subcommittees: Strategic and Theater Nuclear Forces; Sea Power and Force Projection; Manpower and Personnel. *Governmental Affairs* (4th). Subcommittees: Permanent Subcommittee on Investigations; Intergovernmental Relations. *Small Business* (Ranking Member). Subcommittee: Small Business; Family Farm.

Group Ratings

	ADA	ACLU	COPE	CFA	LCV	LWV	NTU	NSI	COC	ACA	CSFC
1982	45	29	38	80	46	67	49	90	67	65	61
1981	35	—	35	43	46	—	45	—	72	71	57
1980	56	27	26	7	40	60	48	60	58	54	51

National Journal Ratings

	Economic		Foreign		Cultural	
1982	62%	(LIB)	45%	(LIB)	46%	(LIB)
	37%	(CONS)	54%	(CONS)	53%	(CONS)
1981	51%	(LIB)	48%	(LIB)	34%	(LIB)
	48%	(CONS)	51%	(CONS)	64%	(CONS)

Key Votes

1) Reagan 81 Budget	FOR	5) $ to El Salvador	FOR	9) Poor Pay Food Stamps	FOR
2) Reagan 81 Tax Cut	FOR	6) Saudi AWACS Sale	FOR	10) Ban Crt Busing Order	FOR
3) Bal Budget Amend	FOR	7) Ban Abortion	AGN	11) Clinch Riv Brdr Rctr	AGN
4) Gas & Road Tax	FOR	8) Nerve Gas Prod	FOR	12) Legal Services Corp	AGN

Election Results

1978 general	Sam Nunn (D)	536,320	(83%)	($548,814)
	John W. Stokes (R)	108,808	(17%)	
1978 primary	Sam Nunn (D)	525,703	(80%)	
	Five others (D)	131,584	(20%)	
1972 general	Sam Nunn (D)	635,970	(54%)	($567,968)
	Fletcher Thompson (R)	542,331	(46%)	($444,635)

Campaign Contributions and Expenditures

1977-78		PACS brkdwn			
Receipts	$708,417	Agr	$12,750	Ideo	$2,500
Expend.	$548,814	Bus	$96,130	Lbr	$2,600
Unspent	$160,844	Hlth	$15,000	Prof	$5,500

Sen. Mack Mattingly (R) Elected 1980, seat up 1986; b. Jan. 7, 1931, Anderson, IN; home, St. Simon; IN U., B.A. 1957; Episcopal.

Career Air Force, 1955; IBM Sales, 1960–80; Pres., Mattingly's Office Products, 1965–80; Member, Repub. Natl. Comm. Econ. Affairs Cncl., 1977–78, Energy Advisory Committee, 1978–79, Foundation for Defense Analysis, 1979–80.

Offices 320 HSOB, 202-224-3643. Also 260 Capitol Ave. S.E., Atlanta 30334, 404-221-3898.

Committees *Appropriations* (12th). Subcommittees: Agriculture, Rural Development; District of Columbia; Energy and Water Development; Military Construction (Chairman); Treasury, Postal Service, and General Government. *Banking, Housing, and Urban Affairs* (8th). Subcommittees: Internatl. Finance and Monetary Policy; Rural Housing and Development (Chairman); Securities. *Joint Economic Committee* (5th). Subcommittees: Internatl. Trade, Finance, and Security Economics; Monetary and Fiscal Policy.

Group Ratings

	ADA	ACLU	COPE	CFA	LCV	LWV	NTU	NSI	COC	ACA	CSFC
1982	0	0	9	0	23	25	90	90	90	86	83
1981	5	—	11	29 6	—	86	—	100	86	84	

National Journal Ratings

	Economic		Foreign		Cultural	
1982	28%	(LIB)	3%	(LIB)	16%	(LIB)
	71%	(CONS)	84%	(CONS)	83%	(CONS)
1981	2%	(LIB)	18%	(LIB)	2%	(LIB)
	88%	(CONS)	80%	(CONS)	82%	(CONS)

Key Votes

1) Reagan 81 Budget	FOR	5) $ to El Salvador	FOR	9) Poor Pay Food Stamps	FOR
2) Reagan 81 Tax Cut	FOR	6) Saudi AWACS Sale	FOR	10) Ban Crt Busing Order	FOR
3) Bal Budget Amend	FOR	7) Ban Abortion	FOR	11) Clinch Riv Brdr Rctr	FOR
4) Gas & Road Tax	AGN	8) Nerve Gas Prod	FOR	12) Legal Services Corp	AGN

Election Results

1980 general	Mack Mattingly (R)	803,677	(51%)	($504,016)
	Herman E. Talmadge (D)	776,025	(49%)	($2,213,289)
1980 primary	Mack Mattingly (R)	28,191	(60%)	
	Five others (R)	18,947	(40%)	
1974 general	Herman E. Talmadge (D)	627,376	(72%)	($65,207)
	Jerry Johnson (R)	246,866	(28%)	($12,856)

Campaign Contributions and Expenditures

1979-80			PACS brkdwn		
Receipts	$790,266	Agr	$2,750	Ideo	$28,656
Expend.	$735,875	Bus	$75,005	Lbr	$1,000
Unspent	$45,296	Hlth	$8,658	Prof	$350

GOVERNOR

Gov. Joe Frank Harris (D) Elected 1982, term expires Jan. 1987; b. Feb. 16, 1936, Atco, Bartow County; home, Atlanta; U. of GA, B.A. 1958; Methodist.

Career Army, 1953–64; Concrete business; GA House of Reps., 1964–80.

Offices State Capitol, Atlanta 30332, 404-656-1776.

Election Results

1982 gen.	Joe Frank Harris (D)	732,686	(63%)
	Robert H. Bell (R)	434,204	(37%)
1982 runoff	Joe Frank Harris (D)	500,765	(55%)
	Bo Ginn (D)	410,259	(45%)
1982 prim.	Bo Ginn (D)	316,019	(35%)
	Joe Frank Harris (D)	223,545	(25%)
	Norman Underwood (D)	147,536	(16%)
	Jack Watson (D)	114,533	(12%)
	Six others (D)	98,457	(11%)
1978 gen.	George Busbee (D)	534,572	(81%)
	Rodney M. Cook (R)	128,139	(19%)

GEORGIA — Congressional Districts, Counties, and Selected Places — (10 Districts)

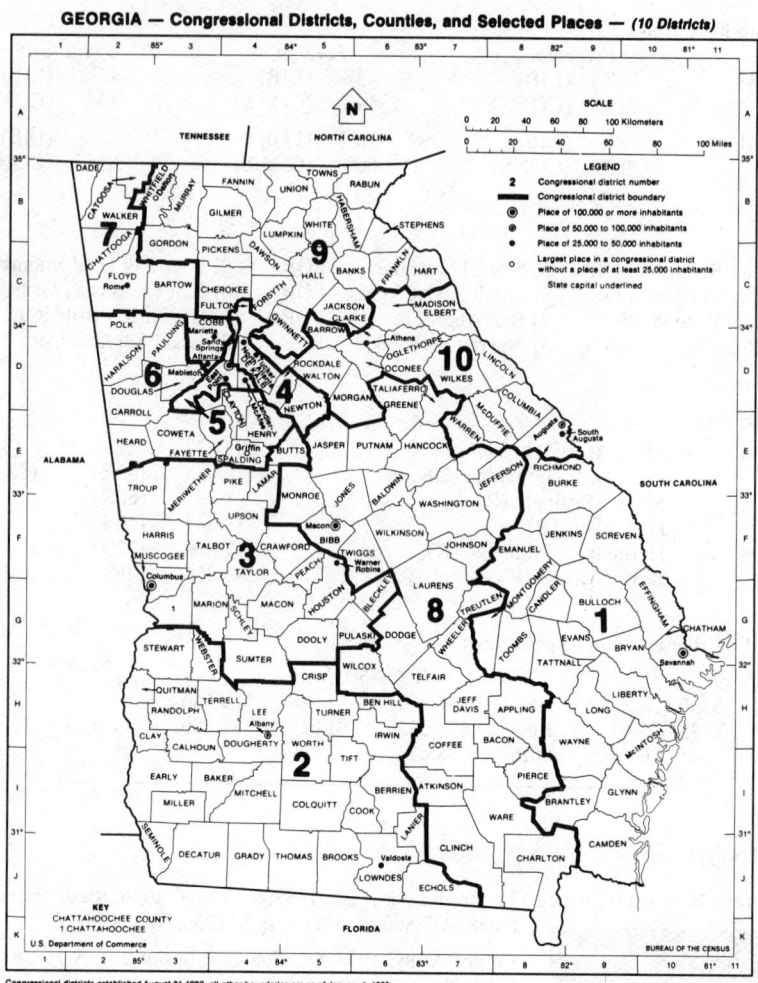

Congressional districts established August 24, 1982; all other boundaries are as of January 1, 1980.

FIRST DISTRICT

The 1st congressional district of Georgia is the southeastern corner of the state. This part of Georgia was first settled by Englishmen, in James Oglethorpe's attempt to establish an orderly and closely regulated life for convicts and other misfits from the home country. The attempt failed; settlers refused, sensibly, to follow detailed instructions from London. But something of Oglethorpe's vision remains: the rectangular street plan of Savannah, with its 19 parks. In the early 1960s, most of old Savannah—once Georgia's largest and richest city— was looking pretty bedraggled; the cotton factors and bankers and scions of old families had mostly moved out, and their grand old mansions, some dating from the 18th century, were slum dwellings or rooming houses. But one of the nation's most active restoration movements has restored most of old Savannah to pristine condition, or better. With its variety of architectural styles, its occasional pastel buildings, its trees hanging with Spanish moss, Savannah suggests the tropics; and the kind of social structure it has developed over the years is almost tropical. There are a few rich people, while the great majority of the population has income levels as low as anywhere in the United States; there are beautiful mansions, but most people live in modest dwellings within sight or smell of the Union Camp paper mills and the chemical plants outside the city. Savannah, which once made its living shipping cotton, now processes paper pulp from the fast-growing pine trees which are Georgia's biggest crop.

Savannah and surrounding Chatham County comprise 37% of the 1st congressional district; the rest consists of mostly rural counties, a few running down the coast (and including Georgia's resort-and-retirement islands) and most inland. Politically, there seems to be an antipathy, or at least a lack of perceived common interest, between Savannah and its hinterland. It is as if the small farmers, black and white, of the rural counties suppose that everyone in Savannah lives in a grand mansion, enjoying the profits made from the sweat of their own brows. The real division in elections here then is between town and country, not—as it seemed likely to be 15 years ago—between black and white.

That geographic division was never more apparent than in the 1982 race to succeed Congressman Bo Ginn. Ginn was running for governor and, although he lost the runoff primary, he carried the 1st district handsomely—testimony to his work on the Military Construction Appropriations Subcommittee, channeling military bases to southeast Georgia, and to his somewhat liberal voting record on economic issues. Ginn left no heir apparent, and eight candidates entered the Democratic primary to succeed him. One, Charles Wessels, was from a prominent Savannah family. The other leading contenders were from rural counties, including Lindsay Thomas, the leader in the first primary with 27%. Thomas had been a banker in Savannah eight years before he bought a farm in Wayne County in 1973. Active in civic affairs, he had never run for office; he was perfectly positioned to run as the citizen farmer, champion of the rural counties against Savannah.

That's what Thomas did. Rich enough to help finance his own campaign, he put on TV ads appealing for rural votes. In the Democratic runoff he carried all the rural counties, most with more than 80%, while losing Savannah to Wessels. In the general election, against a Republican legislator, he won huge margins in the rural counties, while getting just 51% in Chatham County. Thomas does not seem to be an entirely orthodox rural conservative, however: he called for holding down defense spending—something unheard of previously in these parts, and evidence of the strong feeling that the Reagan administration had already raised defense spending enough. His major committee assignment, Agriculture, suggests a different approach to emphasizing local issues from Ginn's. It will be interesting to see how Thomas votes on the major national issues in his first term. After his convincing victories, he seems unlikely to encounter a serious challenge in 1984.

The People   Pop. 1980: 541,180, up 16% 1970–80; voting age pop. 375,257; 30% Black, 1% Span. orig., 1% Asian orig. 32% housing units rented. Median owner $32,900; renter $125. Households: 77% family, 45% with children, 61% married couples.

Presidential Vote

1980	Reagan (R)	NA
	Carter (D)	NA
	Anderson (I)	NA

Rep. Lindsay Thomas (D) Elected 1982; b. Nov. 20, 1943, Waycross; home, Screven; U. of GA, B.A. 1965; Methodist.

Career Investment banker, 1965–71; Farmer, 1971–82.

Offices 427 CHOB, 202-225-5831. Also P.O. Box 10074, Savannah 31412, 912-944-4074.

Committees *Agriculture* (24th). Subcommittee: Tobacco and Peanuts. *Merchant Marine and Fisheries* (23d). Subcommittees: Coast Guard and Navigation; Merchant Marine.

Group Ratings and Key Votes: Newly Elected

Election Results

1982 general	Lindsay Thomas (D)	65,625	(64%)	($355,120)
	Herb Jones (R)	36,799	(36%)	($192,194)
1982 runoff	Lindsay Thomas (D)	28,835	(61%)	
	Charles Wessels (D)	18,239	(39%)	($221,534)
1982 primary	Lindsay Thomas (D)	22,188	(28%)	
	Charles Wessels (D)	16,583	(21%)	
	Rene D. Kemp (D)	16,529	(20%)	($158,617)
	Bobby L. Hill (D)	8,474	(11%)	
	Matt Schaffer (D)	7,333	(9%)	($95,800)
	Three others (D)	9,728	(12%)	
1980 general	Bo Ginn (D)	82,145	(100%)	($32,902)

Campaign Contributions and Expenditures

1981-82		Direct Cont. 81-82				PACS brkdwn		
Receipts	$364,910	Indiv	$234,118	Agr	$3,100	Ideo	$250
Expend.	$355,120	Party	$5,459	Bus	$26,150	Lbr	$3,750
Unspent	$8,849	PACS	$39,064	Hlth	$1,000	Prof	$—
		Cand	$81,000				

SECOND DISTRICT

The 2d congressional district is the southwest corner of Georgia. This is one of the lowest income parts of the United States, and statistically one of the most rural and backward. It is an area that became familiar to many Americans when Jimmy Carter was elected president in 1976. Carter lives just one county north of the 2d district, in Sumter County; and if you know about life in Plains, you know a lot about life in the rural and small town communities where most of the people of south Georgia live. There are usually a few rich white families, like the Carters, who own the local businesses, go on to college, and harbor a few family eccentrics; there are poor white farmers and workers; there are many blacks, with their own separate churches, most of whom never make much money. Such towns are as stratified as any in

America, yet in the past 20 years they have undergone vast change. Legal segregation has disappeared, despite predictions that whites would never tolerate integration; schools, restaurants, and shops are integrated; old forms of address are no longer required, though the sometimes elaborate politeness of the Deep South has not altogether vanished.

The breakup of a once solid social pattern has been reflected, perhaps, in the breakup of a once solid political pattern. South Georgia was once almost unanimously Democratic, and in the habit of returning to office indefinitely the men they selected as youngsters and kept as oldsters to represent them. Giving their representatives seniority gave them power in Washington (from such veterans as Carl Vinson, who served 49¾ years in Congress) and in Atlanta (where south Georgia was represented by the likes of George Busbee, a legislator for 18 years and governor for eight, elected in 1974 and 1978). A man of similar background, but whose tenure has been threatened by the area's recent fickleness, is Congressman Charles Hatcher.

Hatcher was first elected to the legislature in 1972, at 33; he represented Albany, the largest city in the 2d district, but he is from an elite family in a small town, like the Carters. He became an assistant floor leader with the help of his south Georgia neighbor, Busbee; with Busbee's patronage, he was elected to Congress in 1980 the when 2d district incumbent, Dawson Mathis, ran for the Senate.

Here the scenario veers from the old pattern. Hatcher, a member of the Agriculture Committee and with a conservative record, would have encountered no serious opposition in the old days. But his predecessor, Mathis—no ally of the Busbee-Hatcher Democrats—ran against him in the primary, and almost won. Mathis captured the eastern half of the district; Hatcher won the western half, by a margin enough larger to give him a 52% victory overall.

Why such turmoil? One reason was the end of subsidies for peanuts, an important crop in the district. Voters had reason to be angry with both men: Mathis had left the chairmanship of the Tobacco and Peanuts Subcommittee to run for the Senate; Hatcher served on that subcommittee, but was unable to preserve the subsidy. The two men's records on national issues seem similar, judging from their ratings from different groups. But their approaches actually are quite different. Mathis was an ally of California Congressman Phil Burton on the House floor, voting with him on procedural and leadership matters and sometimes voting liberal on key substantive votes as well. Hatcher, in contrast, was a Boll Weevil, one of the southern Democrats who supported Reaganomics in 1981. It may be coincidence, but of the four Georgia Democrats who supported the administration, two had rough primaries and one (Billy Lee Evans) lost. The conclusion any practical politician would draw from this is that support of conservative economic measures is no longer a safe political course in the increasingly unstable politics of south Georgia.

The People Pop. 1980: 549,977, up 13.7% 1970–80; voting age pop. 369,606; 32% Black, 1% Span. orig. 33% housing units rented. Median owner $30,200; renter $100. Households: 78% family, 47% with children, 61% married couples.

Presidential Vote

1980	Reagan (R)	NA
	Carter (D)	NA
	Anderson (I)	NA

Rep. Charles F. Hatcher (D) Elected 1980; b. July 1, 1939, Colquitt; home, Albany; GA Southern Col., B.S. 1965, U. of GA, J.D. 1969; Episcopal.

Career Air Force, 1958–62; Practicing atty.; GA House of Reps., 1973–80, Asst. Flr. Ldr.

Offices 1726 LHOB, 202-225-3631. Also 225 Pine Ave., Albany 31701, 912-439-8067.

Committees *Agriculture* (19th). Subcommittees: Cotton, Rice and Sugar; Livestock, Dairy and Poultry; Tobacco and Peanuts. *Small Business* (14th). Subcommittee: Energy, Environment and Safety Issues Affecting Small Business.

Group Ratings

	ADA	ACLU	COPE	CFA	LCV	LWV	NTU	NSI	COC	ACA	CSFC
1982	25	42	68	50	40	45	36	90	65	55	41
1981	25	—	57	36	15	—	14	—	63	55	49

National Journal Ratings

	Economic		Foreign		Cultural	
1982	50%	(LIB)	19%	(LIB)	26%	(LIB)
	50%	(CONS)	81%	(CONS)	73%	(CONS)
1981	49%	(LIB)	28%	(LIB)	51%	(LIB)
	51%	(CONS)	71%	(CONS)	49%	(CONS)

Key Votes

1) Reagan 81 Budget	AGN	5) Incr SS Rtmt Age	FOR	9) Poor Pay Food Stamps	AGN
2) Reagan 81 Tax Cut	FOR	6) Saudi AWACS Sale	AGN	10) Ban Crt Busing Order	FOR
3) Bal Budget Amend	FOR	7) $ for MX Missile	FOR	11) Auto Local Content	FOR
4) Gas & Road Tax	—	8) Nerve Gas Prod	FOR	12) Nuclear Arms Freeze	AGN

Election Results

1982 general	Charles F. Hatcher (D)	73,897	(100%)	($286,430)
1982 primary	Charles F. Hatcher (D)	53,553	(52%)	
	Dawson Mathis (D)	48,768	(48%)	($145,514)
1980 general	Charles F. Hatcher (D)	92,264	(74%)	($242,960)
	Jack E. Harrell, Jr. (R)	33,107	(26%)	($23,478)

Campaign Contributions and Expenditures

1981-82		Direct Cont. 81-82		PACS brkdwn			
Receipts	$282,541	Indiv	$143,970	Agr	$22,100	Ideo	$2,200
Expend.	$286,430	Party	$300	Bus	$59,125	Lbr	$4,950
Unspent	$3,300	PACS	$102,391	Hlth	$7,950	Prof	$500

THIRD DISTRICT

The 3d congressional district of Georgia is Jimmy Carter's home district—a fact which tells you a lot about the sociology of the district but very little about its politics. This is a part of rural and small town south Georgia; it was once cotton land, with big plantations and plenty of small farmers too. Now it is devoted to other crops: soybeans, peanuts, and the softwood pine trees which grow almost as fast as cotton bolls in the warm, humid South. Since the Civil War, this has been a poor area, with a few rich families in each town, but the large majority living on incomes northern city-dwellers would regard as pathetically low. Actually, their living standards were not quite as low as those figures suggest; they could eat vegetables grown in their gardens and barter for some goods. But until the 1970s this was still one of the more economically backward parts of the country.

That changed, for several reasons. One was the civil rights revolution, which made life in the South more attractive for blacks: in the 1960s black outmigration slowed significantly, and income levels rose very rapidly. The second reason is the spread of (mostly low-wage) industry, particularly textiles and apparel mills, into the Southeast. The third reason is the boost military installations have given to this area. The 3d district is home to Fort Benning, the giant Army training base which takes up most of a county; and to the Warner Robins Air Materiel Command. For none of these developments can Jimmy Carter (or most other area politicians) claim major credit. Carter, though more sympathetic to the civil rights revolution than most southern whites, had no major part in it; as a local official and businessman, he may have encouraged some industries to move to south Georgia, but again his efforts were marginal. And, because he never served in Congress, he never took much role in keeping the military bases here.

Of course the very fact that Carter was not burdened down with such tasks is one of the reasons he was able to become president. Carter, as a young state senator, could probably have had the Democratic nomination for Congress in 1966. But if he had taken it, he probably would have compiled the same kind of record as the man who did, Jack Brinkley. He voted against civil rights measures, supported military spending, and parted company with the Democratic Party on most major national issues. Such a record would have made Carter unacceptable to the people who determine national Democratic nominations. And the high committee posts Brinkley held—he became Chairman of the Military Installations Subcommittee—which were important to 3d district voters would have meant little to others.

Brinkley retired in 1982. Usually an open seat would trigger a fiercely contested Democratic primary. But in the 3d district, one candidate easily dominated the contest: Richard Ray. Ray had more than ten years experience as administrative assistant to Senator Sam Nunn, who is probably the most popular politician in Georgia, and is from the 3d district himself. That credential, plus his own contacts (he ran a successful pesticide business), gave him an easy victory in the first primary. That background—like Nunn he believes in increased defense spending, and he knows the farming business as well—is well tailored to this district. In his first term Ray won a seat on the Armed Services Committee. He appears to have a safe seat.

The People Pop. 1980: 540,865, up 8.9% 1970–80; voting age pop. 376,128; 31% Black, 2% Span. orig., 1% Asian orig. 33% housing units rented. Median owner $30,200; renter $117. Households: 78% family, 46% with children, 61% married couples.

Presidential Vote

1980	Reagan (R)	NA
	Carter (D)	NA
	Anderson (I)	NA

Rep. Richard B. Ray (D) Elected 1982; b. Feb. 2, 1927, Fort Valley; home, Perry; Methodist.

Career Navy, WWII; Owner, Ray Services Inc., 1950–62; Southeastern Manager, Getz Inc., 1962–72; Cnclmn. of Perry, 1962–64; Mayor of Perry, 1964–70; Pres., GA Municipal Assoc., 1969; A.A. to Sen. Sam Nunn, 1972–82.

Offices 514 CHOB, 202-225-5901. Also P.O. Box 2057, Columbus 31902, 404-324-0292; and 200 Carl Vinson Pkwy., Warner Robins 31056, 912-929-2764.

Committees *Armed Services* (24th). Subcommittees: Investigations; Procurement and Military Nuclear Systems. *Small Business* (26th). Subcommittee: General Oversight and the Economy.

Group Ratings and Key Votes: Newly Elected

Election Results

1982 general	Richard Ray (D)	74,626	(71%)	($444,368)
	Tyron Elliott (R)	30,537	(29%)	($222,421)
1982 primary	Richard Ray (D)	50,346	(63%)	
	James N. Cantrell (D)	23,677	(30%)	($27,985)
	E.J. Bagley (D)	5,733	(7%)	
1980 general	Jack Brinkley (D)	89,040	(100%)	($29,043)

Campaign Contributions and Expenditures

1981-82		Direct Cont. 81-82		PACS brkdwn			
Receipts	$467,291	Indiv	$191,567	Agr	$7,950	Ideo	$2,500
Expend.	$444,368	Party	$8,950	Bus	$66,050	Lbr	$3,450
Unspent	$22,922	PACS	$102,012	Hlth	$5,870	Prof	$—
		Cand	$135,000				

FOURTH DISTRICT

The Atlanta metropolitan area, largest in the Deep South, increasingly is coming to resemble northern metropolises—as they were a decade or two ago. The central city now has a black majority, and the large majority of whites now live in suburbs, or even in outlying counties that a few years ago everyone considered completely rural. The 4th congressional district of Georgia is a large part of suburban Atlanta, with just a sliver of the city's rich north side; its lines are drawn carefully to keep blacks in the neighboring 5th district and out of the 4th. This is the most Republican part of Georgia: the white collar and middle to high income suburbs of DeKalb County have been electing Republicans to the Georgia legislature for years; from 1966 to 1974, they elected a Republican congressman as well. This was the Georgia district which gave Jimmy Carter the lowest plurality in 1976 and 1980.

The Republican preference in suburbs like DeKalb County is often attributed to Yankee migrants; but actually most of the people here were born in the South. Their willingness to vote Republican indicates changes in their own lives: they have, through private enterprise, become much more affluent than most of them ever dreamed; they live in a culture which, while it prizes some southern traditions, nevertheless prides itself even more on being cosmopolitan and up to date. These are people who for vacations fly directly from Atlanta to Europe; they want no part of heavily accented politicians who emphasize their rural origins and campaign, as Jimmy Carter did in 1970, as the "redneck" candidate. To them, Republicanism stands for modernity, sophistication, erudition, and good taste.

The Democrats, as it happened, recaptured the 4th district in 1974 and have held it with a candidate who exemplifies these qualities. He is Elliott Levitas, Rhodes Scholar, legislator from DeKalb County, successful lawyer. Levitas was a southern liberal on issues like civil rights, and when he was first elected he was called a national Democratic liberal. As it has turned out, however, he has become identified with skepticism about the efficacy of government. He has been a major sponsor of legislative vetoes, provisions allowing Congress to overturn administrative decisions; the idea is to get bureaucracy off citizens' backs, although in practice what sometimes happens is that politically adept businesses and professions in effect buy, through campaign contributions, favorable decisions from Congress. Levitas also was a major backer of deregulation of the airlines, and his record on economic issues generally is not so very different from those of rural Georgia Democrats—or of northern moderate Republicans who represent similar suburban districts.

On cultural and foreign issues Levitas does have a record somewhat to the left of his rural Georgia colleagues, although even so he is by no means a left winger. He offered several critical amendments to the nuclear freeze resolution in 1983, for example. In 1982 and 1983 he was the point man in the House's effort to subpoena documents from former EPA Administrator Anne Gorsuch Burford and to enforce the subpoena by criminal process if necessary. Levitas is not an easy man to deal with: he is prickly, well informed, and a stickler for what he considers the proper course.

He has remained popular in his district. The 1982 election in the 4th and 5th districts was held in late November because of the time it took to resolve whether the 5th district boundaries were allowable under the Voting Rights Act. Despite the chance this gave Republicans to win one more seat, Levitas won in a landslide. Although the district might go Republican were he not a candidate, he seems to have made a safe seat for himself.

The People Pop. 1980: 542,368, up 24% 1970–80; voting age pop. 399,703; 11% Black, 2% Span. orig., 1% Asian orig. 37% housing units rented. Median owner $57,100; renter $253. Households: 71% family, 38% with children, 58% married couples.

Presidential Vote

1980	Reagan (R)	NA
	Carter (D)	NA
	Anderson (I)	NA

Rep. Elliott H. Levitas (D) Elected 1974; b. Dec. 26, 1930, Atlanta; home, Atlanta; Emory U., B.S. 1952, J.D. 1956, Rhodes Scholar, Oxford U., M.A. 1953, U. of MI; Jewish.

Career Practicing atty.; 1955–75; Air Force; GA House of Reps., 1965–75.

Offices 2416 RHOB, 202-225-4272. Also 141 E. Trinity Pl., Decatur 30030, 404-377-1717.

Committees *Government Operations* (7th). Subcommittees: Commerce, Consumer, and Monetary Affairs; Legislation and National Security. *Public Works and Transportation* (6th). Subcommittees: Aviation; Investigations and Oversight (Chairman); Public Buildings and Grounds.

Group Ratings

	ADA	ACLU	COPE	CFA	LCV	LWV	NTU	NSI	COC	ACA	CSFC
1982	15	42	49	40	75	58	55	90	50	61	47
1981	35	—	49	64	64	—	35	—	42	52	51
1980	28	47	41	43	63	44	40	90	79	48	50

National Journal Ratings

	Economic		Foreign		Cultural	
1982	42%	(LIB)	24%	(LIB)	55%	(LIB)
	57%	(CONS)	76%	(CONS)	45%	(CONS)
1981	52%	(LIB)	52%	(LIB)	58%	(LIB)
	48%	(CONS)	48%	(CONS)	42%	(CONS)

Key Votes

1) Reagan 81 Budget	AGN	5) Incr SS Rtmt Age	FOR
2) Reagan 81 Tax Cut	FOR	6) Saudi AWACS Sale	—
3) Bal Budget Amend	FOR	7) $ for MX Missile	—
4) Gas & Road Tax	—	8) Nerve Gas Prod	FOR

9) Poor Pay Food Stamps	AGN
10) Ban Crt Busing Order	FOR
11) Auto Local Content	FOR
12) Nuclear Arms Freeze	AGN

Election Results

1982 general	Elliott H. Levitas (D)	....	38,758	(65%)	($229,667)
	Dick Winder (R)	....	20,418	(35%)	($245,447)
1982 spec. primary	Elliott H. Levitas (D)	....	42,616	(100%)	
1980 general	Elliott H. Levitas (D)	....	117,091	(69%)	($142,342)
	Barry Billington (R)	....	51,546	(31%)	($84,355)

Campaign Contributions and Expenditures

1981-82		Direct Cont. 81-82		PACS brkdwn			
Receipts	$230,755	Indiv	$104,852	Agr	$3,520	Ideo	$4,250
Expend.	$229,667	Party	$6,925	Bus	$74,150	Lbr	$8,325
Unspent	$2,830	PACS	$114,960	Hlth	$9,700	Prof	$6,300

FIFTH DISTRICT

Stuck smack in the Deep South—and, by just about any definition, the capital of the region—is Atlanta, "the city," it used to boast, "too busy to hate." Atlanta owes some of its prosperity to its central position, to its role as a transportation hub (it was a key railroad junction, and not much else, during the Civil War, and now has the nation's busiest airport), and to the success of some local businesses (notably Coca-Cola). But, ironically, it owes much of its status as capital of the South to its longstanding reputation for tolerance and its central importance to the civil rights movement. Under longtime Mayors William Hartsfield and Ivan Allen, Atlanta avoided resistance to integration, and thereby became the kind of peaceful, uncontroversial environment which investors and big corporations like. With the nation's largest black middle class and long-established black institutions, Atlanta was a natural choice as the headquarters for Martin Luther King, Jr., and other leaders of the civil rights movement. That brought the media and, when the movement was successful, Atlanta seemed the natural center for a New South. So ironically Atlanta owes its status as the center of the South to its own refusal to join whites in the region in resisting integration.

Yet today Atlantans, white and black, are not quite as smug about their success as they used to be. The city's business district continues to be important, but it was overbuilt during most of the 1970s; growth has continued, but aside from the rich north side, Atlanta has been left with mostly low-income residents. More sadly, this city which once prided itself on a degree of neighborhood integration—with blacks living in close proximity to whites—is now mostly all-black. Whites have moved to almost all-white suburbs leaving blacks with a central city on whose government increasing demands are made with fewer resources left to meet them. One of Atlanta's most distinguished blacks, Andrew Young—former congressman, former ambassador to the United Nations—was elected mayor in 1981. His election was marred by blatantly racial appeals by his partisans, including outgoing Mayor Maynard Jackson, and he was criticized afterwards for his extensive travels and his business interests. Young remains an important national figure, and was the chief skeptic in 1983 toward proposals for a symbolic black presidential candidacy in the Democratic primaries.

The 5th congressional district of Georgia includes most of Atlanta, and some diverse suburban territory, from posh Sandy Spring in the north; to middle class East Point, where blacks have been moving in the 1970s; to the rural precincts of southwest Fulton and mostly black southwest DeKalb Counties. Its current boundaries were set by a federal court, which decided that the Georgia legislature's district did not contain enough blacks to satisfy the Voting Rights Act. The Justice Department standard, requiring that a district be 65% black to be counted as black, is pretty silly; if blacks are allowed to vote, as they have been for years now in Atlanta, then a majority black district should be one where the majority of adult residents are black. In any case, the result was ironic. A 5th district with a white majority elected Andrew Young congressman in 1972; ten years later a 5th district with a court-augmented black majority elected Wyche Fowler, who is white.

Actually, what this shows is a maturing of Atlanta's black voters. Fowler, first elected in 1977 when Young went off to Turtle Bay, has always supported civil rights and worked hard for black voters. His position on national issues is not much different from Young's, though his rhetoric is different; he would not suggest carelessly that there are "hundreds, perhaps thousands" of political prisoners in the United States. On local matters, Fowler was tested in the crucible of the presidency of the Atlanta Council; one can presume that 5th district voters know him well. So it is significant that even after the district's black percentage was increased, no black so much as filed to run against Fowler. Julian Bond, the state senator who achieved national notice when he was nominated for vice president at the 1968 Democratic National Convention at age 28, made soundings, but decided not to make the race. He said he couldn't raise enough money; since Atlanta has plenty of affluent blacks, this can mean only that people in the know concluded he had no reason to win or were satisfied with Fowler's representation. This can hardly be called a safe seat for Fowler, yet it is entirely possible that he can hold it indefinitely, as Peter Rodino has held the majority black New Jersey 10th.

Fowler early in his House career won a seat on the Ways and Means Committee, a position of importance to Atlanta business interests. He is considered a leadership man, one who makes few waves for fellow Democrats and supports them on virtually all major issues. His record is by far the most liberal in the Georgia delegation.

The People Pop. 1980: 550,070, dn. 6.4% 1970–80; voting age pop. 390,138; 60% Black, 1% Span. orig. 49% housing units rented. Median owner $34,500; renter $154. Households: 66% family, 40% with children, 41% married couples.

Presidential Vote

1980	Reagan (R)	NA
	Carter (D)	NA
	Anderson (I)	NA

Rep. Wyche Fowler, Jr. (D) Elected Apr. 5, 1977; b. Oct. 6, 1940, Atlanta; home, Atlanta; Davidson Col., B.A. 1963, Emory U., LL.B. 1969; Presbyterian.

Career Army, 1963–65; Chief Asst. to U.S. Rep. Charles Weltner, 1965–66; Night Mayor for the City of Atlanta, 1966–69; Mbr., Atlanta Bd. of Aldermen, 1969–73; Pres., Atlanta City Cncl., 1973–77; Practicing atty., 1970–77.

Offices 1210 LHOB, 202-225-3801. Also 32 Peachtree St., Rm. 425, Wm. Oliver Bldg., Atlanta 30303, 404-688-8207.

Committees Ways and Means (16th), Subcommittees: Oversight; Select Subcommittee on Revenue Measures. *Select Committee on Intelligence* (6th). Subcommittees: Legislation; Oversight and Evaluation.

Group Ratings

	ADA	ACLU	COPE	CFA	LCV	LWV	NTU	NSI	COC	ACA	CSFC
1982	65	67	64	46	84	75	15	70	35	41	36
1981	80	—	62	79	79	—	19	—	17	36	44
1980	61	53	71	50	80	75	28	50	71	48	44

National Journal Ratings

	Economic		Foreign		Cultural	
1982	67%	(LIB)	61%	(LIB)	60%	(LIB)
	33%	(CONS)	39%	(CONS)	40%	(CONS)
1981	70%	(LIB)	64%	(LIB)	70%	(LIB)
	30%	(CONS)	35%	(CONS)	30%	(CONS)

Key Votes

1) Reagan 81 Budget	AGN	5) Incr SS Rtmt Age	AGN	9) Poor Pay Food Stamps —
2) Reagan 81 Tax Cut	AGN	6) Saudi AWACS Sale	—	10) Ban Crt Busing Order AGN
3) Bal Budget Amend	AGN	7) $ for MX Missile	AGN	11) Auto Local Content FOR
4) Gas & Road Tax	FOR	8) Nerve Gas Prod	AGN	12) Nuclear Arms Freeze FOR

Election Results

1982 general	Wyche Fowler, Jr. (D)	53,264	(81%)	($226,592)
	J. E. McKinney (I)	9,049	(14%)	($17,701)
	Paul Jones (R)	3,633	(5%)	($11,290)
1982 special	Wyche Fowler, Jr. (D)	53,440	(83%)	
primary	Paul Jones (R)	4,365	(7%)	
	Doug Steele (R)	3,750	(6%)	
	Jack Hester (R)	3,037	(5%)	
1980 general	Wyche Fowler, Jr. (D)	101,646	(74%)	($141,037)
	F. William Dowda (R)	35,640	(26%)	($48,856)

Campaign Contributions and Expenditures

1981-82		Direct Cont. 81-82		PACS brkdwn			
Receipts	$334,360	Indiv	$152,510	Agr	$7,000	Ideo	$5,800
Expend.	$226,592	Party	$5,000	Bus	$84,825	Lbr	$24,750
Unspent	$178,998	PACS	$138,338	Hlth	$4,950	Prof	$4,350

SIXTH DISTRICT

The 6th congressional district of Georgia, the lineal descendant of a rural and small town district, is today almost entirely within the metropolitan ambit of Atlanta. About 40% of the district's population is directly south of Atlanta: the increasingly black suburbs of College Park and Hapeville, near the Atlanta Airport, and nearly all-white Clayton County just to the south. This is politically conservative country, but not in the same way as DeKalb County, to the northeast. In DeKalb live the somewhat older, somewhat more affluent, more well-established business executives and professionals of the Atlanta area. Clayton is full of younger men and women with young families, lower on the business and professional ladder, though not without hopes of climbing higher. The difference is suggested by some political results: in 1968 DeKalb went for Richard Nixon, Clayton for George Wallace.

Farther out, you can almost see metropolitan Atlanta fanning out along the freeways; the counties within a 50-mile radius of Fulton and DeKalb Counties increased their population 74% in the 1970s. Small towns and rural counties which were once a full day's travel from the capital are now within 60 minutes' drive of I-285 around Atlanta; so you can work in Atlanta or a close-in suburb and live in Newnan or Griffin or Carroll County. Many people do. They like the homier, culturally more conservative atmosphere of the smaller counties, where most people still attend church and the high school kids don't use drugs. The political preference out here remains Democratic, and conservative on cultural issues, although like rural Georgia voters generally they have accepted some ideas that seemed overly liberal and Atlanta-based in the 1960s. And they are willing to vote Republican on occasion, given a good reason.

Giving them good reasons has been the work of Congressman Newt Gingrich, Georgia's only Republican in the House. Gingrich is an improbable congressman for this district: a transplanted Yankee, a college professor, a Republican, a man of intellectual originality. He is temperamentally a gadfly in a state which has valued in its representatives a kind of dull faithfulness to duty. He ran for the district twice before he finally won; against a gray-haired Dixiecrat, John Flynt, he almost won in both the heavily Democratic year of 1974 and the Carter Georgia sweep of 1976. Flynt retired in 1978, and Gingrich beat a woman state senator. He was reelected with respectable, though not overwhelming margins in 1980 and 1982; the addition of blacks in the district in the latter year did not seem to hurt him.

In the House, Gingrich was one of those young Republicans who, with David Stockman and Jack Kemp, set the tone for the new members of their party in the late 1970s and early 1980s. Gingrich believes in harassing the Democratic leadership, in bringing up votes which will embarrass them and unite the Republicans. But he believes in more than tactics. A history professor, he would like to reverse trends he believes have damaged the nation: trends toward higher government spending and taxes, towards a greater Soviet military advantage. In these causes he is not afraid to move away from orthodoxy. Gingrich championed the Kemp-Roth tax cut as a means to discipline federal spending (and, incidentally, to unite Republicans), and he is sympathetic to military reformers who are skeptical that just accepting Pentagon plans will increase our military strength. In 1981 he was a vocal supporter of Reaganomics; in late 1982 and early 1983 he was one of those who helped persuade President Reagan that changes needed to be made in his planned fiscal policy to hold down deficits. Gingrich has rather humdrum committee assignments, and is probably no more a favorite of the Republican leadership than he is of Tip O'Neill. But he is one young congressman who, by force of character and ideas, has already had a major impact on national policy—and may have more in the future.

The People   Pop. 1980: 548,959, up 41% 1970–80; voting age pop. 375,209; 14% Black, 1% Span. orig. 28% housing units rented. Median owner $38,200; renter $177. Households: 80% family, 49% with children, 67% married couples.

Presidential Vote

1980	Reagan (R)	NA
	Carter (D)	NA
	Anderson (I)	NA

Rep. Newt Gingrich (R) Elected 1978; b. June 17, 1943, Harrisburg, PA; home, Carrollton; Emory U., B.A. 1965, Tulane U., M.A. 1967, Ph.D. 1970; Baptist.

Career Prof., West GA Col.; Repub. Nominee for U.S. House of Reps., 1974, 1976.

Offices 1005 LHOB, 202-225-4501. Also 1635 Phoenix Blvd., Su. 9, College Park 30349, 404-221-3854.

Committees *House Administration* (4th). Subcommittees: Contracts and Printing; Personnel and Police. *Public Works and Transportation* (5th). Subcommittees: Aviation; Investigations and Oversight; Surface Transportation. *Joint Committee on the Library* (Ranking Member).

Group Ratings

	ADA	ACLU	COPE	CFA	LCV	LWV	NTU	NSI	COC	ACA	CSFC
1982	5	12	5	30	66	45	75	90	75	96	65
1981	10	—	4	36	29	—	61	—	100	74	66
1980	11	23	10	14	50	40	50	100	79	91	74

National Journal Ratings

	Economic		Foreign		Cultural	
1982	15%	(LIB)	2%	(LIB)	48%	(LIB)
	85%	(CONS)	98%	(CONS)	52%	(CONS)
1981	35%	(LIB)	56%	(LIB)	18%	(LIB)
	65%	(CONS)	44%	(CONS)	81%	(CONS)

Key Votes

1) Reagan 81 Budget	FOR	5) Incr SS Rtmt Age	FOR	9) Poor Pay Food Stamps	—
2) Reagan 81 Tax Cut	FOR	6) Saudi AWACS Sale	FOR	10) Ban Crt Busing Order	FOR
3) Bal Budget Amend	FOR	7) $ for MX Missile	FOR	11) Auto Local Content	FOR
4) Gas & Road Tax	AGN	8) Nerve Gas Prod	FOR	12) Nuclear Arms Freeze	AGN

Election Results

1982 general	Newt Gingrich (R)	62,352	(55%)	($363,041)
	Jim Wood (D)	50,459	(45%)	($154,210)
1982 primary	Newt Gingrich (R)	8,170	(100%)	
1980 general	Newt Gingrich (R)	96,071	(59%)	($397,557)
	Dock H. Davis (D)	66,606	(41%)	($72,962)

Campaign Contributions and Expenditures

1981-82		Direct Cont. 81-82				PACS brkdwn	
Receipts	$367,621	Indiv	$241,503 (est.)	Agr	$1,550	Ideo	$12,200
Expend.	$363,041	Party	$11,725	Bus	$82,628	Lbr	$1,700
Unspent	$1,886	PACS	$111,179	Hlth	$13,650	Prof	$800

SEVENTH DISTRICT

Running northwest from Atlanta, toward Chattanooga and ultimately to Chicago, is U.S. 41. Its four lanes go up and down the red hills of northern Georgia, which are part of the southern end of the Appalachian chain. This is a part of Georgia which never saw a plantation culture and to this day is almost all white. Nonetheless, it is also an area which, historically, was strongly attached to racial segregation. Starting 60 years ago, this was one of the first industrialized parts of Georgia: textile mills and carpet factories moved here, near swift-flowing rivers, major railroads, U.S. 41, and a plentiful low-wage labor supply. In recent decades industry here has been upgraded. Marietta, now really an Atlanta suburb, is the home of Lockheed's giant plant; and in surrounding Cobb County you now see many of those office parks and high-skill employers whose similar modern offices can be seen off Route 128 near Boston or the Capital Beltway around Washington. Farther out U.S. 41 and Interstate 75, which runs parallel, the Atlanta metropolitan area has been marching into what were once entirely rural areas and small towns: to Cartersville, the home of churchish Governor Joe Frank Harris, and Calhoun, the home of Democratic State Chairman and former U.S. Budget Director Bert Lance. To the north is the mill town of Dalton and, finally, the Georgia suburbs of Chattanooga, Tennessee.

Most of this part of northwest Georgia is the 7th congressional district. Its boundary is a little irregular; because of fast population growth in the 1970s it had to shed some territory to meet the one-person-one-vote standard. By demographic measurements, this district should be represented by one of Georgia's most sophisticated and up-to-date congressmen. But that has not been the case for at least 20 years. For 14 years the seat was held by a Democrat with a severe drinking problem. In 1974, he was beaten by Larry McDonald, a member of the John Birch Society, who has held the district ever since.

McDonald has fine credentials: a good education, a successful career as a urologist. But his views on issues are so far out, and his political skill so limited, that he has little impact. His voting record is unremarkable, as solidly conservative as you might suppose. But, as his Birch membership suggests, McDonald seems to regard his colleagues as something close to Communists. One mystery is why he remains in the Democratic Party. Although the Democratic Caucus is not about to take away his seat on Armed Services, it is pretty sure to see that he will never hold a subcommittee chairmanship or other position of power. Years ago, the Caucus abolished the successor of the House Un-American Activities Committee out from under him. The Republicans, in 1981 when they had visions of taking over the House by a combination of election victories and party switches, might have offered McDonald a choice committee post in return for changing parties; but he vehemently denies that he was ever interested. Instead, with the very few like-minded members, he plots strategies which have virtually no chance of success.

Back home in the 7th district, he has fared better of late than he did earlier in his career. He nearly lost the 1974 general, the 1976 primary and general, and the 1978 primary and runoff. In 1980 he had 68% in both primary and general election; in 1982 he had 66% in the primary and 61% in the general. Nevertheless, he shows some weakness. He runs best in the Chattanooga area, where his race probably receives less coverage in local media; he had bare majorities in the carpet town of Dalton in the 1982 primary and in Cobb County in the 1982 general. In neither case did he have strong opposition. How would he fare against tougher competition?

The People   Pop. 1980: 545,913, up 32% 1970–80; voting age pop. 385,552; 6% Black, 1% Span. orig. 28% housing units rented. Median owner $41,200; renter $207. Households: 78% family, 45% with children, 67% married couples.

Presidential Vote

1980	Reagan (R)	NA
	Carter (D)	NA
	Anderson (I)	NA

Rep. Larry P. McDonald (D) Elected 1974; b. Apr. 1, 1935, Atlanta; home, Marietta; Davis Col., Emory U., M.D. 1957; Methodist.

Career U.S. Navy Physician and Overseas Flight Surgeon; Residency, Grady Mem. Hosp., Atlanta, and U. of MI Hosp., Ann Arbor; Jr. Mbr., McDonald Urology Clinic, Atlanta.

Offices 103 CHOB, 202-225-2931. Also 100 Cherokee St., Marietta 30060, 404-422-4480.

Committee *Armed Services* (12th). Subcommittees: Readiness; Research and Development.

Group Ratings

	ADA	ACLU	COPE	CFA	LCV	LWV	NTU	NSI	COC	ACA	CSFC
1982	5	0	6	0	17	18	98	100	82	91	93
1981	5	—	7	14	37	—	99	—	100	100	93
1980	6	13	5	7	39	20	86	100	56	100	92

National Journal Ratings

	Economic		Foreign		Cultural	
1982	8%	(LIB)	4%	(LIB)	4%	(LIB)
	92%	(CONS)	92%	(CONS)	87%	(CONS)
1981	4%	(LIB)	2%	(LIB)	2%	(LIB)
	79%	(CONS)	97%	(CONS)	98%	(CONS)

Key Votes

1) Reagan 81 Budget	FOR	5) Incr SS Rtmt Age	FOR	9) Poor Pay Food Stamps	FOR
2) Reagan 81 Tax Cut	FOR	6) Saudi AWACS Sale	FOR	10) Ban Crt Busing Order	FOR
3) Bal Budget Amend	FOR	7) $ for MX Missile	FOR	11) Auto Local Content	AGN
4) Gas & Road Tax	AGN	8) Nerve Gas Prod	FOR	12) Nuclear Arms Freeze	AGN

Election Results

1982 general	Larry P. McDonald (D)	71,647	(61%)	($246,656)
	Dave Sellers (R)	45,569	(39%)	($200,708)
1982 primary	Larry P. McDonald (D)	47,232	(66%)	
	Sadie Jenkins (D)	13,229	(19%)	
	Jack Bade (D)	10,818	(15%)	
1980 general	Larry P. McDonald (D)	115,892	(68%)	($276,449)
	Richard Castellucis (R)	54,242	(32%)	($6,292)

Campaign Contributions and Expenditures

1981-82		Direct Cont. 81-82				PACS brkdwn		
Receipts	$247,164	Indiv	$175,624	Agr	$500	Ideo	$5,350
Expend.	$246,656	Party	$5,000	Bus	$42,260	Lbr	$—
Unspent	$1,720	PACS	$67,342	Hlth	$6,800	Prof	$350

Indep Expend: For: $6,994 (SSPAC)

EIGHTH DISTRICT

South Georgia—the part of the state with a large black population and thousands of poor white farmers, with a history that features Sherman's march through Georgia and remembers dimly better times—this south Georgia is not so much a geographical location as it is a state of mind. In that sense, the state's 8th congressional district is very much a part of south Georgia, even though it reaches almost as far north as Atlanta and its portion of the southern edge of the state is only a few counties wide. The 8th district's northernmost counties are in fact part of Georgia's Black Belt: most of their residents are black, and have been since there were large plantations here in antebellum times. The black percentages are high also in and around Macon, the district's largest city, a place which despite its technical urban status remains very much country at heart. To the south there are fewer blacks, as the district makes its way south to the Okefenokee Swamp.

The 8th district is a lesson in point for those who thought that the safest political course for a southern Democrat was to support the Reagan administration. That was the strategy followed by 8th district Congressman Billy Lee Evans, and it was one which came naturally: he served as a Republican in the Georgia legislature before he was elected to Congress as a Democrat in 1976. Yet, against conventional wisdom, his support for Reagan ended up causing him a lot of political trouble—and helped defeat him in the 1982 Democratic primary. That was not his only problem: he was also hurt when he was fined for accepting illegal contributions and loans in his 1980 campaign. It didn't help either that his chief opponent, Roy Rowland, was the picture of rectitude, a gray-haired doctor who served in the legislature, or that a minor opponent spent most of his energy attacking Evans. Rowland insisted he was a conservative, but he attacked Evans for supporting the Reagan budget and tax programs, and called for reducing the deficit instead.

Evans was not only forced into a runoff; he actually trailed Rowland in the first primary, 47%–42%. Rowland carried almost all the counties in the northern part of the district, with particularly large margins in those near his home town. In the runoff he even carried some of the southern counties as well, for a solid 58%–42% victory. Rowland serves on the same major committee as Evans (Public Works). It is far too early to say how solid a hold the new incumbent has on this district.

The People Pop. 1980: 541,723, up 10.6% 1970–80; voting age pop. 372,727; 32% Black, 1% Span. orig. 29% housing units rented. Median owner $27,300; renter $94. Households: 78% family, 45% with children, 61% married couples.

Presidential Vote

1980	Reagan (R)	NA
	Carter (D)	NA
	Anderson (I)	NA

Rep. J. Roy Rowland (D) Elected 1982; b. Feb. 3, 1926, Wrightsville; home, Dublin; Emory U., S. GA Col., U. of GA, Medical Col. of GA, M.D. 1952; Methodist.

Career Practicing physician 1952–, GA House of Reps. 1977–83.

Offices 513 CHOB, 202-225-6531. Also P.O. Box 6258, Macon 31208; Fed. Bldg., Tebeau St., Rm. 207, Waycross 31501, 912-285-8420; and Franklin St., Courthouse Sq., Rm. 203/204, Dublin 31021, 912-275-0024.

Committees *Public Works and Transportation* (30th). Subcommittees: Investigations and Oversight, Public Buildings and Grounds, Water Resources. *Veterans' Affairs* (18th). Hospitals and Health Care, Oversight and Investigations. *Select Committee on Children, Youth, and Families* (14th).

Group Ratings and Key Votes: Newly Elected

Election Results

1982 general	J. Roy Rowland (D)	. . . .	75,009	(100%)	($222,032)
1982 runoff	J. Roy Rowland (D)	. . . .	45,016	(58%)	
	Billy Lee Evans (D)	. . . .	32,709	(42%)	($306,006)
1982 primary	J. Roy Rowland (D)	. . . .	52,602	(48%)	
	Billy Lee Evans (D)	. . . .	46,474	(42%)	
	Ed Wheeler (D)	. . . .	10,936	(10%)	($20,492)
1980 general	Billy Lee Evans (D)	. . . .	91,103	(75%)	($107,743)
	Darwin Carter (R)	. . . .	31,033	(25%)	($44,034)

Campaign Contributions and Expenditures

1981-82		*Direct Cont. 81-82*			*PACS brkdwn*		
Receipts	$225,984	Indiv	$109,130	Agr	$1,500	Ideo	$1,000
Expend.	$222,032	Party	$14,074	Bus	$13,900	Lbr	$2,200
Unspent	$3,954	PACS	$32,838	Hlth	$9,738	Prof	$—
		Cand	$55,200				

NINTH DISTRICT

The 9th congressional district of Georgia is the northeastern part of the state, where the rolling hills of the Piedmont meet the southernmost extension of the Appalachian chain. This was a backwater in the antebellum period, a part of the South never covered by large plantations and with very few slaves; it continues to have a low black percentage today. Indeed, some of the mountain counties here resisted secession in 1861 and supported the Union; for decades afterwards they regularly returned Republican majorities in heavily

Democratic Georgia. Two waves of prosperity have swept over the 9th district in the last 40 years. The first was the growth of the textile industry along what is now Interstate 85, the highway which runs from Raleigh, North Carolina, to Atlanta, and along the way is within a few miles of perhaps half the textile producing capacity in the United States. There are no big textile cities in this part of Georgia; mills are strung out along the Interstate and main highways, within an hour's driving distance of the large supply of low-wage labor.

The other wave of prosperity comes from the expansion of metropolitan Atlanta outward, along the interstates and into the mountain country. The most striking example is in Gwinnett County, just outside Atlanta, where the population doubled in the 1970s; the increase was so great that part of the county was removed from the 9th in redistricting. But even the mountain counties showed rates of increase not recorded since they were first settled. The reason: they have become the year-round home for retirees from Atlanta and the North or for people who have decided to forego the high dollar incomes of the metropolitan area for the less obvious attractions of the mountains. Doubtless this immigration leaves some of the mountain folk bewildered and unhappy, though they are compensated by the rapid rise in their property values.

The Dixie Democrats of the Piedmont and the foothills far outnumber the remnants of the mountain Republicans in the 9th. Even the spreading prosperity, which makes people more willing to consider Republicans in national elections, leaves them pretty satisfied with the Democrats in state and local contests. Congressional elections in this district have mostly been uncontested, and the district has been represented for 30 years by congressmen closely attuned to the textile industry. One was Phil Landrum, whose name remains attached to the Landrum-Griffin Act of 1959, the last major piece of labor law Congress passed. The other is Ed Jenkins, the current congressman, who was elected when Landrum retired in 1976.

Jenkins, like Landrum, sits on the House Ways and Means Committee, and is regarded there as a leading champion of the textile industry. Its main concern in legislation is trade protection. The textile industry, from its beginnings in the mills of Lancashire and New England, has been a low-wage industry; and existing textile mills have always been vulnerable to competition from lower-wage areas. The Interstate 85 corridor thus took most of the textile industry away from New England, beginning in the 1920s; now the Piedmont finds competition from Taiwan, South Korea, and Hong Kong. Some day those countries will be undercut by lower-wage Indonesia and (who knows?) mainland China. But existing southern textile interests are fighting back through the trade laws, seeking restrictions on imports, tariff, duties—whatever mechanism they can to keep the U.S. market insulated against foreign competition. In the short run, this protects jobs and investment; in the long run, of course, this approach tends to make this country economically inefficient and decrepit. On Ways and Means Jenkins works hard for all these measures.

Jenkins had to fight hard to win the district in 1976, and he even had a significant primary in 1978. His major problem then was Gwinnett County, and his seat has been made safer by the removal of part of it from the 9th. In personal style and background, he seems much more at home among the older parts of the 9th than in what amounts to expanding metropolitan Atlanta. He has won general elections easily, and in 1982 he had no trouble at all winning reelection.

The People   Pop. 1980: 551,782, up 35.1% 1970–80; voting age pop. 384,558; 5% Black, 1% Span. orig. 21% housing units rented. Median owner $36,400; renter $122. Households: 82% family, 47% with children, 71% married couples.

Presidential Vote

1980	Reagan (R)	NA
	Carter (D)	NA
	Anderson (I)	NA

Rep. Ed Jenkins (D) Elected 1976; b. Jan. 4, 1933, Young Harris; home, Jasper; Young Harris Col., A.A. 1951, Emory U., U. of GA, LL.B. 1959; Baptist.

Career Coast Guard, 1952–55; A.A. to U.S. Rep. Phil Landrum, 1959–62; Asst. U.S. Atty., N. Dist. of GA., 1962–64; Practicing atty., 1964–76; Jasper City Atty.; Pickens Cnty. Atty.

Offices 217 CHOB, 202-225-5211. Also P.O. Box 70, Jasper 30143, 404-692-2022.

Committees *Ways and Means* (9th). Subcommittees: Select Revenue Measures; Trade. *Standards of Official Conduct* (3d).

Group Ratings

	ADA	ACLU	COPE	CFA	LCV	LWV	NTU	NSI	COC	ACA	CSFC
1982	30	17	36	40	61	44	60	100	57	52	51
1981	10	—	34	57	24	—	49	—	60	63	62
1980	6	7	33	29	41	38	56	80	68	60	61

National Journal Ratings

	Economic		Foreign		Cultural	
1982	43%	(LIB)	38%	(LIB)	28%	(LIB)
	57%	(CONS)	62%	(CONS)	71%	(CONS)
1981	48%	(LIB)	2%	(LIB)	38%	(LIB)
	52%	(CONS)	97%	(CONS)	62%	(CONS)

Key Votes

1) Reagan 81 Budget	AGN	5) Incr SS Rtmt Age	FOR	9) Poor Pay Food Stamps	AGN
2) Reagan 81 Tax Cut	AGN	6) Saudi AWACS Sale	FOR	10) Ban Crt Busing Order	FOR
3) Bal Budget Amend	FOR	7) $ for MX Missile	AGN	11) Auto Local Content	FOR
4) Gas & Road Tax	—	8) Nerve Gas Prod	AGN	12) Nuclear Arms Freeze	AGN

Election Results

1982 general	Ed Jenkins (D)	86,514	(77%)	($194,007)
	Charles Sherwood (R)	25,907	(23%)	($46,430)
1982 primary	Ed Jenkins (D)	64,037	(78%)	
	Jim Boyd (D)	18,176	(22%)	
1980 general	Ed Jenkins (D)	115,576	(68%)	($115,012)
	David Ashworth (R)	54,341	(32%)	($0)

Campaign Contributions and Expenditures

1981-82		Direct Cont. 81-82		PACS brkdwn			
Receipts	$210,455	Indiv	$77,336	Agr	$7,200	Ideo	$2,800
Expend.	$194,007	Party	$5,100	Bus	$88,050	Lbr	$4,200
Unspent	$69,348	PACS	$110,785	Hlth	$7,950	Prof	$1,100
		Cand	$500				

TENTH DISTRICT

The 10th congressional district is a group of 14 counties, and part of another, in the northern part of Georgia. The district is anchored by three urbanized areas. The first is around Augusta, the home of the Masters Golf Tournament. Although Augusta has always had a large black population (or perhaps because of that), the Masters was long all-white; election returns from Augusta and Richmond County, however, have often reflected black preferences. In the middle of the district is Athens, the home of the University of Georgia, famous for its football team and also as the retirement home of former Secretary of State Dean Rusk, a Georgia native. At the western end of the district, added in the 1982 redistricting, is part of Gwinnett County, which is very much a part of the Atlanta metropolitan area. This is one of those rather high income, but not elite, suburban areas whose population expanded rapidly in the 1970s. These three urban areas give a certain cast to election results here: not exactly liberal, since they favored Senator Mack Mattingly, one of the most conservative senators elected in 1980, but more anti-rural, since at the same time they opposed that longtime champion of rural Georgia, Herman Talmadge. In the 1982 gubernatorial primary, where there was no perceptible urban-rural split, the results here approximated those of the state as a whole.

The congressman from the 10th, Doug Barnard, was first elected in 1976 and, like his predecessor in the House, is a banker by trade; although why an area like this should favor bankers is unclear. Barnard also has a political background: he was once an aide to Governor Carl Sanders, who was elected in 1962 and was considered a moderate in his time, and who was Jimmy Carter's opponent in the 1970 runoff for governor. To win the seat, Barnard had to beat a former aide to Governor Lester Maddox. So by background Barnard is a moderate and, like other members of the Georgia delegation, was more likely to be an old political opponent rather than an ally of Jimmy Carter.

Barnard is a Boll Weevil and supported the Reagan economic program in 1981. On economic issues he is among the most conservative in the Georgia delegation, and by no means is he liberal on cultural or foreign issues. But unlike other Georgia Boll Weevils, he encountered no opposition in the 1982 primary. In fact, he has been reelected without effective opposition since 1976. He has a chance to succeed to a subcommittee chairmanship on the Banking Committee in a few years, although it cannot be considered completely certain that Banking Committee Democrats will vote him into a position which, in the old days, would have been his automatically by virtue of seniority.

The People   Pop. 1980: 550,268, up 32% 1970–80; voting age pop. 388,067; 23% Black, 1% Span. orig., 1% Asian orig. 32% housing units rented. Median owner $39,200; renter $153. Households: 76% family, 45% with children, 62% married couples.

Presidential Vote

1980	Reagan (R)	....	NA
	Carter (D)	....	NA
	Anderson (I)	....	NA

Rep. Doug Barnard, Jr. (D) Elected 1976; b. March 20, 1922, Augusta; home, Augusta; Augusta Col., Mercer U., B.A. 1943, LL.B. 1948; Baptist.

Career Army, WWII; Banker, GA Railroad Bank and Trust, 1948–49, Fed. Res. Bank of Atlanta, 1949–50; Exec. Secy., to the Gov. of GA, 1963–66.

Offices 236 CHOB, 202-225-4101. Also Fed. Bldg., Athens 30603, 404-546-2194.

Committees *Banking, Finance and Urban Affairs* (15th). Subcommittees: Domestic Monetary Policy; Financial Institutions Supervision, Regulation and Insurance. *Government Operations* (12th). Subcommittee: Commerce, Consumer, and Monetary Affairs (Chairman).

Group Ratings

	ADA	ACLU	COPE	CFA	LCV	LWV	NTU	NSI	COC	ACA	CSFC
1982	10	17	17	30	46	30	52	100	63	64	54
1981	0	—	16	21	6	—	50	—	94	73	64
1980	11	3	16	14	17	22	41	75	86	63	59

National Journal Ratings

	Economic		Foreign		Cultural	
1982	18%	(LIB)	30%	(LIB)	30%	(LIB)
	81%	(CONS)	70%	(CONS)	70%	(CONS)
1981	36%	(LIB)	13%	(LIB)	15%	(LIB)
	62%	(CONS)	87%	(CONS)	84%	(CONS)

Key Votes

1) Reagan 81 Budget	FOR	5) Incr SS Rtmt Age	FOR	9) Poor Pay Food Stamps	AGN
2) Reagan 81 Tax Cut	FOR	6) Saudi AWACS Sale	—	10) Ban Crt Busing Order	FOR
3) Bal Budget Amend	FOR	7) $ for MX Missile	AGN	11) Auto Local Content	AGN
4) Gas & Road Tax	—	8) Nerve Gas Prod	FOR	12) Nuclear Arms Freeze	AGN

Election Results

1982 general	Doug Barnard, Jr. (D)	80,311	(100%)	($69,764)
1982 primary	Doug Barnard, Jr. (D)	38,535	(100%)	
1980 general	Doug Barnard, Jr. (D)	102,177	(80%)	($57,866)
	Bruce J. Neubauer (R)	25,194	(20%)	($4,431)

Campaign Contributions and Expenditures

1981-82		Direct Cont. 81-82		PACS brkdwn			
Receipts	$147,763	Indiv	$35,095	Agr	$3,050	Ideo	$2,661
Expend.	$69,764	PACS	$85,001	Bus	$73,150	Lbr	$600
Unspent	$175,646			Hlth	$4,900	Prof	$—

HAWAII

Hawaii is unique: of all the tropical islands acquired by western powers in the late 19th century, it is the only one which has become an integral part of the nation that acquired it. This outcome was far from obvious in the 1890s, when the last Hawaiian monarch, Queen Liliuokalani, was ousted from power and the Islands were annexed by the United States. One reason Hawaii developed as it has is that there were close ties between the United States and Hawaii long before these events. American missionaries had been proselytizing in the Islands since the 1820s, and missionary families, as readers of James Michener know, had also become profitably involved in trade. They came, as the saying goes, intending to do good and instead did well. Most Americans today think of Hawaii as a tropical vacation paradise, not realizing that these volcanic islands have incredibly rich and quite extensive farmland. Well before annexation Hawaii was a major producer of sugar and later of pineapple for the American market.

But intensive farming and trade with the mainland U.S. are not enough to develop the kind of advanced society and affluent standard of living Hawaii has today. If that were the case, there would not be much poverty left in the world. An economy also needs creative, hardworking people to establish businesses and provide labor. Hawaii has gotten most of its citizens from successive waves of immigration. The missionary families built the big trading companies—the Big Five—which have dominated shipping and commerce here; with the estate of the last surviving member of the royal family, the old Yankee families and their companies still control a huge percentage of Hawaii's land. But there were never enough native Hawaiians—particularly after their numbers were reduced by disease—to provide the hard labor these operations needed. So labor was imported. People were brought in systematically, first from Japan, then later from China, the Philippines, Korea, Spain, and Portugal. Native Hawaiians were outnumbered as early as the turn of the century (although their percentage of the Islands' population is increasing today because of their high birth rate).

So Hawaii has become one of the most polyglot places in the world. Although there is plenty of intermarriage among groups and no overt segregation, many of the traditions and ways of each group remain evident. The Japanese, the largest single migrant group after whites (who are sometimes called haoles), are by most measures the most successful, doing well in the professions and in organizations such as unions, government, and the Democratic Party. But they have not developed as many big entrepreneurs and businessmen as the Chinese community has; notable examples are the millionaire Chin Ho and former Senator Hiram Fong. Whites still tend to have the highest incomes; many come to Hawaii after they have been successful on the Mainland. Filipinos are more likely to be manual laborers. Native Hawaiians, from a culture that lived easily and well off a bounteous physical environment, also tend toward the lower end of the income scale, and some have mounted protest movements similar to those launched in the 1960s by American Indians.

Hawaii's ethnic mix seems a recipe for discord, and in ethnic differences do play some part in political conflicts here. But on the whole Hawaii is a good example of how people from diverse origins can live together. A distinctive form of pidgin is spoken here, and there is as well a special kind of Hawaiian cultural provinciality—not an uncommon phenomenon on islands throughout the world. Hawaiians are proud of their tradition of tolerance (one meaning of the word aloha), and any form of racial segregation or discrimination is considered repugnant. Those attitudes delayed Hawaii's admission into the Union for some time; southern Democrats objected so much that Hawaii voted Republican for many years.

Hawaii has a standard of living today that matches the Mainland states. Its economy is still not self-sufficient, however; even today, after three decades of explosive growth, the Islands still have fewer than one million people, not really enough of a market to justify many capital expenditures. Agriculture continues to be very important to the economy here, but is not always dependable. Changes in the Sugar Act meant that Hawaiian cane producers could no longer count on selling their sugar at a guaranteed price; production plummeted. Another major industry is tourism. The jet plane has done amazing things for Hawaii's economy but has made the state dependent in the process, producing a sense of near-calamity when, for the first time in years, the number of tourists dropped in 1980 because of sharp increases in jet fuel prices and airfares. Yet despite these setbacks, Hawaii has a lower than average unemployment rate and was not hurt as badly as most of the Mainland by the 1979–83 recession.

Another major component of the Hawaiian economy, one that also leaves the state economically dependent, is the military. The Navy built fortifications and a huge drydock at Pearl Harbor as long ago as 1919, and since then Hawaii has been the center of American military power in the Pacific; the Japanese attack on Pearl Harbor in 1941 struck not a peripheral outpost but the heart of the U.S. Navy. There are now more than 44,000 military personnel stationed in Hawaii, and this is not a state where antimilitary or antiwar attitudes ever made much headway. Finally, Hawaii, where the cost of living is very high, remains dependent on the Mainland for much of its food and manufactured products; shipping and warehousing remain major industries, and the powerful unions—the International Long-shoremen's and Warehousemen's Union (ILWU) and the Teamsters—are those associated with these industries.

Demographically, Hawaii is basically a city-state, with about three-fourths of its population concentrated in and near Honolulu, on the island of Oahu. The other islands have distinct personalities. Hawaii, the Big Island, is large enough to boast huge cattle ranches and has in Mauna Kea the highest mountain in the world if you count from its base far under the ocean to the peak, that rises in a seemingly slow, endless slant from Hilo or the Kona (western) Coast. On the north shore, with heavy rainfall and tropical foliage, are the old port of Hilo and Hawaii's macadamia nut industry; this is a blue collar, heavily Democratic area. On the Kona Coast, where there is little rainfall and the landscape is dominated by lava flows, there are retirement condominiums and a higher-income, more Republican population. Maui, in the early 1980s, was the fastest-developing island, with dozens of luxury condominiums and rapidly rising real estate prices. Kauai, west of Oahu, is the least-developed and most agricultural of the main islands; its large farm work force makes it the most Democratic of the islands.

Oahu itself has about the same land area as the city of Los Angeles, and perhaps more diversity. The tourist usually sees Waikiki, with its 40-story hotels rising within a few feet of one another, its restaurants and souvenir shops—a place more to the taste of conventioneers, one would think, than to people looking for a place to relax. It is a favorite of Japanese tourists, and much property in Waikiki is now owned by Japanese investors.

There are high-income neighborhoods past Waikiki, around Diamond Head and out to the Kohala and Koko Head beach areas; these places delivered large enough majorities for Ronald Reagan in 1980 to enable him almost to carry this ordinarily Democratic state. Honolulu's other neighborhoods are politically more Democratic and ethnically diverse; there are no real slums here, but incomes are lower near the city's downtown and the military bases and airport to the west. The area around Pearl Harbor is middle class, with many military families; farther out the island, between the two jagged chains of mountains that lift it out of the sea, is some of Hawaii's best farmland. Over the mountains to the west is the Leeward Coast, calm, sultry, and lightly populated; over the mountains to the northeast is the Windward Coast, windy as its name implies, with many prosperous and spanking new subdivisions.

Hawaii, the only state that was once a monarchy, had no trouble accepting the Mainland parties. For the first couple of years after statehood, which came in 1960, Hawaii tended to vote Republican. But soon a remarkable Democratic organization took control of the state's politics—and, despite internal feuds and bitter challenges, still holds it today. One of its leaders was John Burns, who was elected governor in 1962 and remained in office until he retired because of illness in 1974. Another was Daniel Inouye, the state's first congressman-at-large and senator since 1962. Inouye was a distinguished member of the group of Japanese-Americans who served in the all-Nisei (segregated) 442d Infantry Regimental Command Team, the most decorated and perhaps the most celebrated American military unit in World War II. The fighting skill and courage of these Nisei, along with their mainland counterparts who volunteered out of the infamous Japanese-American internment camps, produced acceptance of the Japanese-Americans as part of the nation's mainstream. Japanese immigrants to both Hawaii and the mainland were denied naturalization rights and American citizenship until 1952. Returning to Hawaii after the war, Inouye and other 442d veterans, like the state's other senator, Spark Matsunaga, moved into the empty ranks of the territorial Democratic Party—and soon came to dominate it. The other major component of Hawaii's Democratic organization has been the ILWU, the largest union in Hawaii and an organization with a stormy radical past; its president for years was Harry Bridges, who used to be denounced as a Communist and later dealt amicably with the shipowners. The ILWU's clout in Hawaiian politics became legendary: for 12 years (1960–72) no candidate endorsed by the union lost a major election, and few have since.

Senators. Daniel Inouye is now Hawaii's senior elected official, the only person who has held major statewide office throughout the 2½ decades since statehood. Probably the most popular politician in Hawaii, he won more than 80% of the vote in his last three elections. He has also achieved national prominence, as keynoter at the Democratic National Convention in 1968 and as a dignified, low-key member of the Senate Watergate Committee in 1973.

Inouye probably owed both positions to his reputation as a party loyalist. He is known in the Senate as a strong and steadfast Democrat, and as a believer in policies historically associated with Democratic presidents. He steadfastly supported President Johnson's domestic and Vietnam war policies; and on defense issues, unlike most other non-Dixie Democrats, he has always supported strong defense policies. Inouye combines this party loyalty with a reputation for being well prepared and intellectually rigorous. He does not make arguments he cannot fully support, and he does not choose to fight fights he is not ready to wage in intellectually honest fashion. Sometimes grim and severe, he does not play favorites; on defense issues, for example, he is one of the few important members not known as a partisan of a particular service. He is an important supporter also of federal maritime subsidy programs and is not eager to deregulate industries. He believes in what the history of Hawaii teaches—the need for centralized control, planning, generous spending. On spending issues, foreign and domestic, Inouye is consistently one senator who favors higher rather than lower figures.

Inouye's party loyalty and intellectual capacity have led Democrats to give him important committee positions: Appropriations and Commerce. He is not, however, in line to chair either of them should the Democrats regain control in 1984; he stands behind John Stennis and William Proxmire on Appropriations and behind Ernest Hollings on Commerce. There is another possibility, whispered about in Washington in 1982 and early 1983, that if the Democrats win control, they would elect Inouye to a leadership position. Perhaps this just represents grumbling about the party's current leader, Robert Byrd. Yet should there be a vacancy, Inouye might be a strong contender for the leadership. He has many friends and admirers among all wings of the party. One major asset is his reputation for loyalty. In 1981, he was the only senator willing to stand up and defend Harrison Williams against expulsion for his part in Abscam; few senators agreed publicly with Inouye's stand, but many must have admired his willingness to stand by a colleague—and may have wondered how many other senators would stand by them if they were in serious trouble. It is out of character, however, for Inouye to be an insurgent; and Byrd, ever attentive to detail, has many assets and many strong backers. Yet Inouye is capable of surprise: in early 1983 he surprised many observers, and probably the Reagan administration, by opposing the administration's policy in El Salvador. This was an abrupt and agonizing change of mind for Inouye—and one which probably affected other senators' opinions.

Hawaii's other senator, Spark Matsunaga, is less senior and less well known, although he is older than Inouye. Matsunaga sat in the House for 14 years, and he won his Senate seat in a 1976 primary fight with his House colleague Patsy Mink. Matsunaga, like Inouye, is a party loyalist who makes little trouble for the leadership. In the House he sat on the Rules Committee, in the Senate on Finance and Energy. Rating groups list him as one of the most liberal members of the Senate, yet he is anything but a boat-rocker. Second-ranking Democrat on the Trade Subcommittee, he is basically a free trader but is concerned about protecting Hawaii's pineapples and macadamia nuts. Reelected without serious opposition at age 66 in 1982, he may be serving his last term—although no one knows for sure.

Governor. George Ariyoshi became acting governor in 1973 and has been elected in his own right three times now; counting his terms and those of his predecessor John Burns together, the same group has won control of the governorship for 24 years. That is a tenure not matched in any other state. But it has been hard won. Ariyoshi had tough primary challenges from Frank Fasi, then Honolulu mayor, in 1974 (Ariyoshi led 36%–31%) and 1978 (Ariyoshi won 51%–49%). Fasi lost his office to an Ariyoshi candidate, Eileen Anderson, in the 1980 primary. But the Governor had tough opposition in 1982 anyway. In the primary he won just 54% of the vote against his lieutenant governor, Jean King. In the general election, he won 51% against Fasi, running as an Independent, and Andy Anderson, the Republican leader of the state Senate. Analysis of the returns shows Ariyoshi with strong backing from Japanese-Americans and union voters. But he is strongly opposed by middle income white voters on Oahu (who went for Fasi in the general election) and by upper income voters in Honolulu and the Windward Coast (who went for Anderson).

Some of the contrast between Ariyoshi and his opponents is a matter of style. Fasi is flashy and in 1977 he was charged with accepting bribes (but never convicted); Ariyoshi once ran with the campaign slogan "quiet but effective," an attempt to make the best of his stolid demeanor. Ariyoshi is not closely associated with specific policies: when Hawaii was booming, he advocated limits on growth; when the tourist industry slumped, he claimed credit for the Islands' still low unemployment rate. Can a governor and a political organization remain in power forever if they win every four years by such tenuous margins? Ariyoshi might test that proposition, once again, in 1986.

Congressmen. Hawaii has two congressional districts: the 1st consists of the historic city of Honolulu (though the mayor's election includes all of Oahu) and extends westward to Pearl Harbor; the 2d includes the rest of Oahu and the Neighbor Islands. Hawaii has never elected a Republican to the House. It came closest in 1976, when Matsunaga and Mink relinquished their seats, and the Republicans made a serious attempt in the 1st district, which has a larger high income and haole population and is slightly more Republican (it went for Reagan in 1980, for example, while the 2d and the state as a whole went for Carter). The winner in the 1st district was Cecil Heftel, a millionaire broadcaster who had nearly beaten Senator Hiram Fong in 1970. Heftel spent more than $300,000 of his own money (then a large sum for a House race); he had a bitter primary, supported by Inouye but fiercely opposed by Ariyoshi; he had a close race in the general election. In the 2d district, the contest was determined in the Democratic primary, which was won by Daniel Akaka, an Ariyoshi appointee. Neither has had significant opposition for reelection since.

Both Akaka and Heftel are pretty solid Democratic loyalists. Heftel serves on the Ways and Means Committee and thus has a voice on national issues of taxes, trade, and health care. His voting record is generally, but not exceedingly, liberal.

Akaka serves on Appropriations and its Agriculture Subcommittee—bodies with practical concerns that are especially important to Hawaii. His voting record on economic and cultural issues is extremely liberal; but on foreign policy issues he is inclined to support defense increases.

Presidential politics. Hawaii was one of only six states carried by President Carter in 1980, and the only one west of Minnesota. Two factors seem to have combined to produce the Carter victory and to make Hawaii so atypical of the rest of the nation: a strong leaning toward Democrats generally, combined with a strong inclination to support presidential candidates of the party in power. These two factors explain Hawaii's other presidential results, its narrow margin for winning Democratic candidates when Republicans were in power (1960, 1976), its landslide margins for incumbents of different parties (1964, 1972), and its far higher than average percentages for Democrats when they were in power (1968, 1980). The predilection for incumbents may be explained by the fact that this is a state that takes its patriotism very seriously, in part because the patriotism of so many of its citizens was, unjustly, doubted within living memory, and in part because this is the only state whose population center came under direct foreign attack since the War of 1812. If this analysis is right, Republicans should have a chance of carrying Hawaii in 1984, even though the state—with no major senatorial or gubernatorial race—is likely to remain solidly Democratic in elections for other offices.

The People   Est. Pop. 1982: 994,000; Pop. 1980: 964,691, up 3% 1980–82 and 25.3% 1970–80; .43% of U.S. total, 39th largest; voting age pop. 689,108; 60% Asian origin, 6% Spanish origin, 2% Black. Single ancestry: 3% Portuguese, English, 2% German, 1% Irish, Italian. Registered voters (1982): 201,789 Total. 18% with 1–3 yrs. col., 20% with 4+ yrs. col. 10.0% below poverty level. 43% housing units rented; median house value: $119,400; median monthly rent: $273. Households: 77% family, 45% with children, 63% married couples.

1982 Share of Federal Tax Burden $2,595,900,000; .43% of U.S. total, 38th largest.

1982 Share of Federal Expenditures

	Total		Non-Defense		Defense	
Total Expend	$3,433m	(0.57%)	$1,501m	(0.35%)	$1,932m	(1.08%)
St/Lcl Grants	408m	(0.46%)	408m	(0.46%)	0m	(0%)
Salary/Wages	1,554m	(1.99%)	52m	(0.19%)	1,502m	(2.96%)
Ind Payments	1,106m	(0.39%)	939m	(0.36%)	167m	(0.58%)
Procurement	350m	(0.24%)	38m	(0.12%)	312m	(0.27%)
Other Programs	15m	(0.28%)	14m	(0.26%)	1m	(2.33%)
Loan/Insurance	126m	(0.20%)	120m	(0.19%)	6m	(0.27%)

Political Lineup Governor, George R. Ariyoshi (D). Senators, Daniel K. Inouye (D) and Spark M. Matsunaga (D). Representatives, 2 D. State Senate, 25 (20 D and 5 R); State House of Representatives, 51 (43 D and 8 R).

Presidential Vote

1980	Reagan (R)	130,112	(43%)
	Carter (D)	135,879	(45%)
	Anderson (I)	32,021	(11%)
1976	Ford (R)	139,969	(48%)
	Carter (D)	147,351	(51%)

SENATORS

Sen. Daniel K. Inouye (D) Elected 1962, seat up 1986; b. Sept. 7, 1924, Honolulu; home, Honolulu; U. of HI, B.A. 1950, Geo. Wash. U., J.D. 1952; United Methodist.

Career Army, WWII; Honolulu Asst. Prosecuting Atty., 1953–54; Practicing atty., 1954–59; HI Territorial Senate, 1958–59; U.S. House of Reps., 1959–63.

Offices 722 HSOB, 202-224-3934. Also 300 Ala Moana Blvd., Honolulu 96850, 808-546-7550.

Committees *Appropriations* (4th). Subcommittees: Defense; Foreign Operations; Labor, Health and Human Services, Education; Military Construction; Commerce, Justice, State, the Judiciary. *Commerce, Science and Transportation* (3d). Subcommittees: Aviation; Communications; Merchant Marine; National Ocean Policy Study. *Rules and Administration* (4th). *Select Committee on Indian Affairs* (2d). *Select Committee on Intelligence* (4th). Subcommittees: Budget Authorization (Vice Chairman); Collection and Foreign Operations. *Joint Committee on the Library* (4th).

Group Ratings

	ADA	ACLU	COPE	CFA	LCV	LWV	NTU	NSI	COC	ACA	CSFC
1982	70	75	88	30	71	83	0	30	22	32	27
1981	70	—	87	43	66	—	1	—	44	26	32
1980	67	50	75	60	33	67	24	14	34	23	30

National Journal Ratings

	Economic		Foreign		Cultural	
1982	95%	(LIB)	71%	(LIB)	71%	(LIB)
	4%	(CONS)	28%	(CONS)	28%	(CONS)
1981	78%	(LIB)	73%	(LIB)	95%	(LIB)
	21%	(CONS)	26%	(CONS)	4%	(CONS)

Key Votes

1) Reagan 81 Budget	FOR	5) $ to El Salvador	AGN	9) Poor Pay Food Stamps	AGN
2) Reagan 81 Tax Cut	FOR	6) Saudi AWACS Sale	AGN	10) Ban Crt Busing Order	AGN
3) Bal Budget Amend	AGN	7) Ban Abortion	AGN	11) Clinch Riv Brdr Rctr	AGN
4) Gas & Road Tax	AGN	8) Nerve Gas Prod	AGN	12) Legal Services Corp	FOR

Election Results

1980 general	Daniel K. Inouye (D)	224,485	(78%)	($480,113)
	Cooper Brown (R)	53,068	(18%)	($14,382)
1980 primary	Daniel K. Inouye (D)	198,467	(88%)	
	Two others (D)	28,291	(12%)	
1974 general	Daniel K. Inouye (D)	207,454	(83%)	($205,265)
	James D. Kimmel (People's Party) .	42,767	(17%)	

Campaign Contributions and Expenditures

1979-80		PACS brkdwn			
Receipts	$747,213	Agr	$5,500	Ideo	$8,500
Expend.	$480,113	Bus	$92,192	Lbr	$52,280
Unspent	$281,511	Hlth	$9,200	Prof	$2,200

Sen. Spark M. Matsunaga (D) Elected 1976, seat up 1988; b. Oct. 8, 1916, Kukuiula; home, Honolulu; U. of HI, B.Ed. 1941, Harvard U., J.D. 1951; Episcopal.

Career Pub. sch. teacher, 1941; Army, WWII; Vet. Counselor, Surplus Prop. Ofc., U.S. Dept. of Interior, 1945–47; Chf., Asst. Pub. Prosecutor, 1952–54; Practicing atty., 1954–63; HI Territorial House of Reps., 1954–59, Major. Ldr.; U.S. House of Reps., 1963–77.

Offices 109 HSOB, 202-224-6361. Also 300 Ala Moana Blvd., Honolulu 96850, 808-546-7555.

Committees *Energy and Natural Resources* (6th). Subcommittees: Energy Conservation and Supply; Energy and Mineral Resources; Public Lands and Reserved Water. *Finance* (3d). Subcommittees: Taxation and Debt Management; International Trade; Savings, Pensions, and Investment Policy. *Labor and Human Resources* (7th). Subcommittees: Alcoholism and Drug Abuse; Handicapped; Labor. *Veterans' Affairs* (3d).

Group Ratings

	ADA	ACLU	COPE	CFA	LCV	LWV	NTU	NSI	COC	ACA	CSFC
1982	85	79	85	80	62	90	2	0	21	21	27
1981	80	—	85	57	66	—	13	—	44	21	31
1980	78	77	83	53	51	89	21	14	33	13	25

National Journal Ratings

	Economic		Foreign		Cultural	
1982	85%	(LIB)	90%	(LIB)	69%	(LIB)
	14%	(CONS)	3%	(CONS)	30%	(CONS)
1981	79%	(LIB)	92%	(LIB)	86%	(LIB)
	20%	(CONS)	7%	(CONS)	6%	(CONS)

Key Votes

1) Reagan 81 Budget	FOR	5) $ to El Salvador	—	9) Poor Pay Food Stamps	AGN
2) Reagan 81 Tax Cut	FOR	6) Saudi AWACS Sale	AGN	10) Ban Crt Busing Order	AGN
3) Bal Budget Amend	AGN	7) Ban Abortion	AGN	11) Clinch Riv Brdr Rctr	AGN
4) Gas & Road Tax	FOR	8) Nerve Gas Prod	AGN	12) Legal Services Corp	FOR

Election Results

1982 general	Spark M. Matsunaga (D)	245,386	(80%)	($655,713)
	Clarence J. Brown (R)	52,071	(17%)	($0)
	One other (I)	8,953	(3%)	
1982 primary	Spark M. Matsunaga (D)	187,708	(100%)	
1976 general	Spark M. Matsunaga (D)	162,305	(54%)	($435,130)
	William Quinn (R)	122,724	(41%)	($415,138)
	Tony Hodges (People's Party)	14,223	(5%)	

Campaign Contributions and Expenditures

1979-82		*Direct Cont. 79-82*		*PACS brkdwn*			
Receipts	$969,999	Indiv	$561,758				
Expend.	$655,713	Party	$17,500	Agr	$9,525	Ideo	$16,300
Unspent	$338,524	PACS	$289,770	Bus	$158,460	Lbr	$63,090
				Hlth	$28,800	Prof	$12,475

Indep Expend: Agn: $3,184 (NCPAC)

GOVERNOR

Gov. George R. Ariyoshi (D) Elected 1974, after serving as Acting Gov. since Oct. 1973, term expires Dec. 1986; b. Mar. 12, 1926, Honolulu; home, Honolulu; U. of HI, U. of MI, B.A. 1949, J.D. 1952; United Church of Christ.

Career Army, WWII; Practicing atty., 1953–70; HI Territorial House of Reps., 1954–58; HI Territorial Senate, 1958–59, HI Senate, 1959–70, Major. Ldr., 1965–66, Major. Flr. Ldr., 1969–70; Lt. Gov. of HI, 1970–74.

Offices Executive Chambers, State Capitol, Honolulu 96813, 808-548-5420.

Election Results

1982 gen.	George R. Ariyoshi (D)	141,043	(45%)
	D.G. Anderson (R)	81,507	(26%)
	Frank F. Fasi (I)	89,303	(29%)
1982 prim.	George R. Ariyoshi (D)	128,993	(54%)
	Jean King (D)	106,935	(45%)
1978 gen.	George R. Ariyoshi (D)	153,394	(55%)
	John R. Leopold (R)	124,610	(44%)

FIRST DISTRICT

The People Pop. 1980: 482,344, up 15.2% 1970–80; voting age pop. 362,790; 64% Asian orig., 5% Span. orig., 1% Black. 47% housing units rented. Median owner $139,400; renter $277. Households: 72% family, 39% with children, 58% married couples.

Presidential Vote

1980	Reagan (R)	NA
	Carter (D)	NA
	Anderson (I)	NA

HAWAII — Congressional Districts, Counties, and Selected Places — *(2 Districts)*

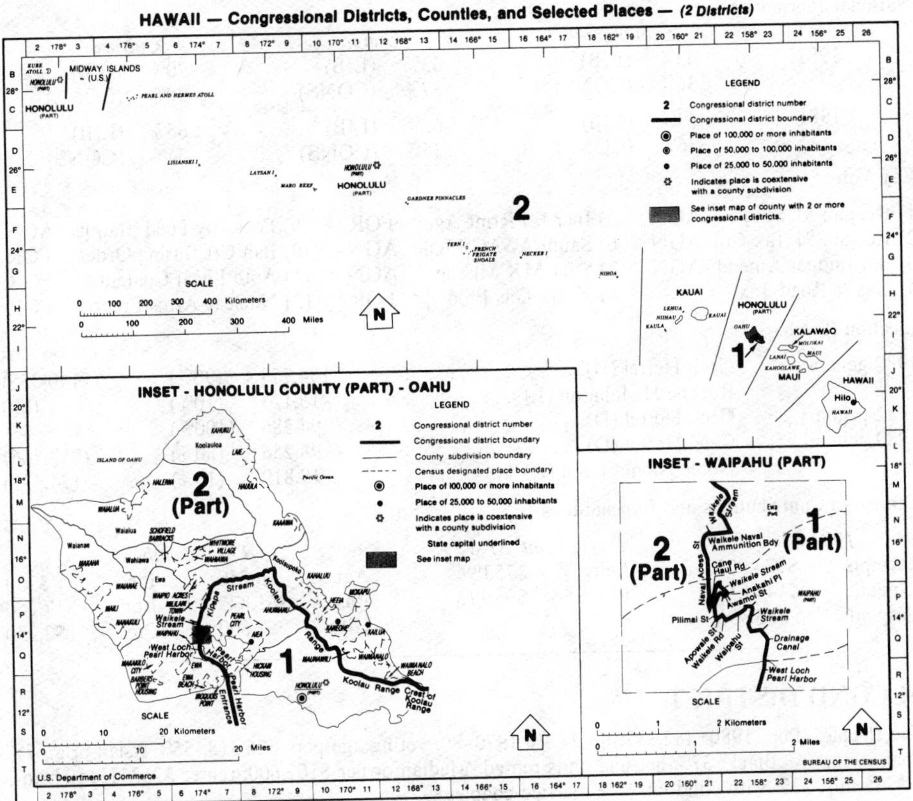

Congressional districts established July 16, 1982; all other boundaries are as of January 1, 1980.

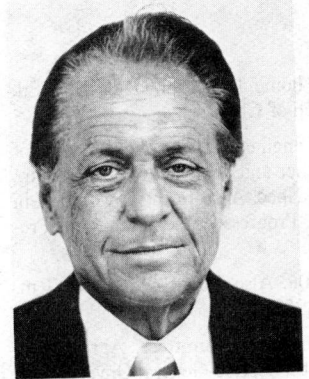

Rep. Cecil (Cec) **Heftel** (D) Elected 1976; b. Sept. 30, 1924, Cook Cnty., IL; home, Honolulu; AZ St. U., B.S. 1951, U. of UT, NYU; Baptist.

Career Army, WWII; Pres., Heftel Broadcasting, 1964–; Dem. Nominee for U.S. Senate, 1970.

Offices 1030 LHOB, 202-225-2726. Also 300 Ala Moana Blvd., Rm. 4104, Honolulu 96850, 808-546-8997.

Committee *Ways and Means* (12th). Subcommittees: Select Revenue; Trade.

Group Ratings

	ADA	ACLU	COPE	CFA	LCV	LWV	NTU	NSI	COC	ACA	CSFC
1982	60	46	70	70	71	75	18	60	15	27	33
1981	50	—	69	64	71	—	8	—	32	26	41
1980	50	47	67	64	49	67	21	40	57	29	37

National Journal Ratings

	Economic		Foreign		Cultural	
1982	63%	(LIB)	63%	(LIB)	70%	(LIB)
	36%	(CONS)	37%	(CONS)	30%	(CONS)
1981	63%	(LIB)	65%	(LIB)	65%	(LIB)
	36%	(CONS)	35%	(CONS)	34%	(CONS)

Key Votes

1) Reagan 81 Budget	AGN	5) Incr SS Rtmt Age	FOR	9) Poor Pay Food Stamps	AGN
2) Reagan 81 Tax Cut	AGN	6) Saudi AWACS Sale	AGN	10) Ban Crt Busing Order	FOR
3) Bal Budget Amend	AGN	7) $ for MX Missile	AGN	11) Auto Local Content	FOR
4) Gas & Road Tax	—	8) Nerve Gas Prod	FOR	12) Nuclear Arms Freeze	FOR

Election Results

1982 general	Cecil Heftel (D)	134,779	(90%)	($140,055)
	Rockne H. Johnson (L)	15,123	(10%)	($0)
1982 primary	Cecil Heftel (D)	94,386	(100%)	
1980 general	Cecil Heftel (D)	98,256	(80%)	($57,866)
	Noble Aloma Keen (R)	19,819	(16%)	($4,431)

Campaign Contributions and Expenditures

1981-82		Direct Cont. 81-82		PACS brkdwn			
Receipts	$174,905	Indiv	$75,096	Agr	$6,250	Ideo	$750
Expend.	$140,055	PACS	$96,115	Bus	$61,875	Lbr	$17,250
Unspent	$55,996			Hlth	$7,600	Prof	$2,350

SECOND DISTRICT

The People Pop. 1980: 482,347, up 37.4% 1970–80; voting age pop. 326,318; 55% Asian orig., 7% Span. orig., 2% Black. 37% housing units rented. Median owner $102,600; renter $268. Households: 82% family, 53% with children, 68% married couples.

Presidential Vote

1980	Reagan (R)	NA
	Carter (D)	NA
	Anderson (I)	NA

Rep. Daniel K. Akaka (D) Elected 1976; b. Sept. 11, 1924, Honolulu; home, Honolulu; U. of HI, B.Ed. 1952, M.Ed. 1966; United Church of Christ.

Career Welder, mechanic, and engineer, U.S. Army Corps of Engineers, WWII; Pub. sch. teacher and principal, 1953–71; Dir., HI Ofc. of Econ. Opp., 1971–74; Spec. Asst. to the Gov. of HI in Human Resources, 1975–76; Dir., Progressive Neighborhoods Program, 1975–76.

Offices 2301 RHOB, 202-225-4906. Also Kuhio Fed. Bldg., Rm. 5104, Honolulu 96813, 808-546-8952.

Committees *Appropriations* (28th). Subcommittees: Agriculture, Rural Development; Treasury-Postal Service-General Government. *Select Committee on Narcotics Abuse and Control* (6th).

Group Ratings

	ADA	ACLU	COPE	CFA	LCV	LWV	NTU	NSI	COC	ACA	CSFC
1982	65	58	83	90	64	58	1	80	21	19	33
1981	65	—	80	64	50	—	2	—	16	30	41
1980	72	57	74	71	35	78	14	25	67	25	31

National Journal Ratings

	Economic		Foreign		Cultural	
1982	89%	(LIB)	51%	(LIB)	73%	(LIB)
	11%	(CONS)	49%	(CONS)	27%	(CONS)
1981	77%	(LIB)	18%	(LIB)	74%	(LIB)
	21%	(CONS)	73%	(CONS)	26%	(CONS)

Key Votes

1) Reagan 81 Budget	AGN	5) Incr SS Rtmt Age	AGN	9) Poor Pay Food Stamps	AGN
2) Reagan 81 Tax Cut	AGN	6) Saudi AWACS Sale	AGN	10) Ban Crt Busing Order	AGN
3) Bal Budget Amend	AGN	7) $ for MX Missile	AGN	11) Auto Local Content	FOR
4) Gas & Road Tax	AGN	8) Nerve Gas Prod	FOR	12) Nuclear Arms Freeze	FOR

Election Results

1982 general	Daniel K. Akaka (D)	132,072	(89%)	($108,910)
	Greg Mills (No party)	9,080	(6%)	($0)
	Amelia Fritts (L)	6,856	(5%)	($0)
1982 primary	Daniel K. Akaka (D)	96,385	(100%)	
1980 general	Daniel K. Akaka (D)	141,477	(90%)	($96,774)
	Smith D. Gordon (R)	15,903	(10%)	

Campaign Contributions and Expenditures

1981-82		Direct Cont. 81-82		PACS brkdwn			
Receipts	$86,237	Indiv	$41,176	Agr	$3,250	Ideo	$1,050
Expend.	$108,910	PACS	$38,240	Bus	$18,690	Lbr	$13,400
Unspent	$24,423			Hlth	$1,750	Prof	$—

IDAHO

Idaho, like most of the other Rocky Mountain states, came into existence because of mining. In 1890, when it became a state, its major product was silver, and it was one of the strongest supporters of William Jennings Bryan's free silver platform. But beginning early in the 20th century, Idaho became predominantly an agricultural state. The fertile lands along the Snake River were irrigated, often thanks to federal reclamation projects, to the point that Idaho now uses more water per capita than any other state. So Idaho's agriculture prospered, and the Idaho potato became famous across the nation. As a result, Idaho today is different from the other fast-growing Rocky Mountain states. The population is not concentrated here as Colorado's is in metropolitan Denver or Arizona's in metropolitan Phoenix. People are spread fairly evenly across Idaho, from the Panhandle in the north, with its grimy mining towns and lumber mills, through the Snake River valley, from Boise and Nampa in the west to Pocatello and Idaho Falls in the east. Boise, which in 1980 for the first time reported a population over 100,000, is a city of some dynamism—the home of such important companies as Boise Cascade (lumber and paper) and Morrison Knudsen (construction). The city's several gleaming towers and its proud older high-rises shine against the backdrop of the mountains; its tree-shaded streets and Spanish-style railroad station bespeak a comfort that contrasts sharply with the arid expanse of plains beyond the city.

Idaho's economic growth and its physical attractions and lifestyle have made it one of the fastest-growing states in the nation. Its population rose by one-third in the 1970s, and continued rising in the early 1980s as well. But with the exception of a few places, like the resort town of Sun Valley, the influx has not been like Colorado's—environmentalists with liberal attitudes on cultural issues—but has been of family people interested in a less hurried but still affluent way of life in a place with a small town atmosphere where traditional values are accorded more respect than they are in big metropolitan areas. There are few trendy singles here; among all states, Idaho has the second highest percentage of households occupied by married people. For every Carole King (the singer who moved to Idaho because she loves the physical environment) there are a dozen new Idahoans who left California because they thought Orange County was not conservative enough.

The great influx of the 1970s strengthened a trend that was already in evidence when the decade began: a decided shift from the Democratic to the Republican Party. Idaho favored Bryan at the turn of the century, Wilson a few years later, and was solidly for Franklin Roosevelt and Harry Truman. As late as 1960 John Kennedy was able to win 46% of the vote here. But in the 1960s attitudes changed. Idahoans began to think of themselves less as downtrodden employees of big corporations who need a generous federal government on their side and more as pioneering entrepreneurs who need to get a bloated, bossy federal government off their backs. The federal government is a real presence here, as it is in most western states, and when it blocks the exploitation of local resources, as it frequently does in order to protect the environment, it often arouses stronger resentment in the community directly affected than it does gratitude in the broader constituency more indirectly benefited. One of the most popular Idaho politicians in recent years was Governor (1970–77) Cecil Andrus, who became President Carter's Interior secretary. But Andrus's policies stirred great resentment, and his boss was able to win only 25% of the vote here in 1980. Yet Idahoans are not ready to accept the program of the Sagebrush Rebellion, which wants all federal lands turned over to the states, nor have the policies of Interior Secretary James Watt proved as popular as the 1980 results would suggest. One might even say that resentment in Idaho ends up being directed at Washington—whoever is in office.

Governor. The Republicans have not won a gubernatorial election here since 1966. The Democrats's secret has been good candidates—and weak opposition. Cecil Andrus's successor, John Evans, has now won two full terms on his own, the first against a Mormon from the heavily Mormon southeastern part of the state, who campaigned on imposing Mormon strictures on the whole population; the second time against the lieutenant governor, Phil Batt, who campaigned as an opponent of farm workers' unions and a backer of right-to-work laws. The name is appealing, and speakers at gatherings of small employees can always get a cheer when they urge that workers be allowed not to join a union that bargains for them. Yet in major referenda right-to-work laws have been defeated, notably in Ohio and California in 1958 and in Missouri in 1978. Governor Evans vetoed right-to-work measures several times, and publicly accepted union support—usually a liability in Idaho politics. But on election day 1982 he was able to win. Right-to-work, like the Sagebrush Rebellion, turned out to be more attractive as a slogan and a rallying cry than as a concrete program.

Senators. The most powerful member of Idaho's congressional delegation these days is Senator James McClure. He was first elected to the House in 1966 and to the Senate in 1972; he has unusual seniority for a member whose views are associated with the New Right. Yet McClure does not appear to be a leader of the conservative wing of the Republican Party. He supports its positions rather than advancing them; he is cautious where he might be bold. In 1981 he inherited the chair of the Energy and Natural Resources Committee—the old Interior Committee—which has jurisdiction over major environmental laws. But he never pushed legislation to enact the platform of the Sagebrush Rebellion, about which he had spoken sympathetically. Nor was he willing, as some in the Reagan administration urged, to put through a bill advancing deregulation of natural gas ahead of schedule. McClure could reply that there was little for the committee to do: oil and gas price deregulation had already been set in motion, and with the Interior Department in the hands of James Watt, there was little need for legislative oversight initiative or oversight.

McClure's caution is joined to a reputation, in some quarters, for sleight of hand. In the 1972 election—his closest campaign—he suggested that his opponent supported a potato boycott, a suggestion for which the only evidence offered was the man's support of a resolution endorsing Cesar Chavez's boycott against non-union lettuce. More recently, McClure was accused by Vermont Senator Patrick Leahy and others of telling the Senate that a bill was noncontroversial and getting it passed—when in fact the bill contained provisions many senators wanted to oppose. Leahy announced that he would put a hold on any measure advanced by McClure—an unusual move, which means no such bills could be considered without notifying Leahy.

McClure is nonetheless a competent senator, of generally dependable views; and few people doubt that he will be reelected in 1984. He has been elected secretary of the Senate Republican Conference and has been mentioned as a possible successor to Majority Leader Howard Baker. Idaho is, after all, one of the most Republican states in the nation.

Idaho's junior senator, Steven Symms, is a more controversial and flamboyant man. First elected to the House in 1972, he defeated Frank Church in the 1980 Senate race, one of those fiercely contested, exceedingly close elections which everyone remembers for a generation afterward. Symms is one of the closest things to a libertarian in Congress: he opposes practically every kind of government program, and for a while, before he sought the support of New Rightists and Mormons, he even toyed with voting against government regulation of abortion. He likes to portray himself as a simple apple-grower, arrayed against the powers in Washington; but he is also a big plunger in the futures markets, speculating heavily in silver when Nelson Bunker Hunt was trying to squeeze short-sellers in the silver market. Symms later introduced bills which would have benefited Hunt, who claimed that the nation's elite financial institutions changed the rules on him in the middle of the game.

In any case, the 1980 election was a battle of opposites: the ultraconservative, flamboyant Symms versus the liberal, reserved Frank Church. Church had survived his opposition to the Vietnam war and won reelection (in 1968, against George Hansen, now 2d district congressman); his chairmanship of a key water subcommittee had helped produce the economic growth that most Idahoans like to think flowed from their efforts alone. But during his last year he seemed to be reeling, yanking the SALT II Treaty from consideration after he announced, dramatically in Boise, the appearance of a Soviet combat brigade in Cuba; he ended up losing by the narrowest of margins.

Symms has good committee assignments: Budget, Finance, Environment and Public Works. But he is usually not a leader on issues and, when he is, his reputation for slapdash work and oddball ideas makes it difficult for him to win much support. He led the fight on the Environment Committee to relax the terms of the Clean Air Act; the result was near-unanimous passage of a bill backed by Chairman Robert Stafford that not only reaffirmed the terms of the original law but strengthened them.

Symms comes up for reelection in 1986. In a less Republican state, he would be a prime Democratic target; even in Idaho, he can expect spirited opposition. Still, it would be a significant upset for a Republican to lose an Idaho Senate seat unless there is a major shift of opinion in the state.

Congressmen. Idaho has one of the weakest House delegations. The 1st district congressman, Larry Craig, was first elected in 1980. A young bachelor, he went on the air after initial reports that male pages had been solicited by congressmen and denied any wrongdoing. But nobody had—or has—accused Craig of any misconduct. The 2d district congressman, George Hansen, has more seniority. He was first elected in 1964 (one of only two Republicans to capture a Democratic seat outside the South that year) and reelected in 1966, lost a Senate race to Church in 1968, beat another Congressman Hansen in the 1974 primary, and has been in the House ever since. He is one of Congress's authentic zanies. He has been found out in one bit of misconduct after another. In 1975 he pleaded guilty to violating the campaign finance laws and was sentenced to two months in jail—a sentence changed to a fine after his lawyer argued that Hansen had behaved stupidly rather than viciously. He has also admitted filing late income tax returns. In the late 1970s he got around an Ethics Committee prohibition by having his wife, who also acts as his assistant, solicit some $200,000 from political contributors to pay off his personal debts. And in 1982, the *Wall Street Journal* reported that he may have violated federal laws by failing to report a $50,000 loan from Nelson Bunker Hunt to his wife and an $87,000 gain she made from a silver futures transaction with Hunt's guidance.

Moreover, Hansen does not even seem to be able to follow his conservative principles consistently. In 1979, after American embassy personnel were taken hostage in Tehran, Hansen went there twice and tried to negotiate their release, offering to set up a congressional committee to inquire into American misconduct—a more craven alternative than the Carter administration ever considered.

Yet Craig and Hansen, with virtually identical ultraconservative voting records, seem able to overcome any qualms Idaho voters may have about other aspects of their records. In 1982 both survived challenges of some seriousness. The 1st district, which includes the Panhandle and Canyon County around Nampa, as well as most of Boise, is marginally the more Democratic of the two districts; but Craig was marginally the stronger of the two congressmen. Craig survived a challenge from former Church aide Larry LaRocco, who carried the Panhandle and, very narrowly, the whole district north of Boise. But Craig won the Boise area and Canyon County by solid margins. This was one of those races where the Republican edge in campaign finance probably played a role; Craig simply was much better able to communicate his message.

The 2d district contains some of the most family- and morals-minded voters in the nation, particularly in the southeastern end, which is mostly Mormon. The only Democratic concentration is in the old railroad town of Pocatello, but the Democratic margin there is almost always overshadowed by Republican edges in Twin Falls and Idaho Falls. Altogether, this is one of the dozen or so most Republican districts in the nation. Nonetheless Hansen was hard pressed in 1982. It was not that his opponent, history professor Richard Stallings, had much money; he did not. The problem was Hansen's own checkered record. Hansen lost the 2d district's portion of the Boise area; he lost Pocatello by a large margin; he lost Sun Valley. But he managed to carry almost everything else. Stallings ran essentially even with the percentages Governor Evans had in his successful reelection race. But Evans did not carry this more Republican half of the state, and neither did Stallings.

Craig sits on the Education and Labor and Interior Committees; as a junior member of the minority party, he is not likely to be a major legislator. Nor is Hansen, for all his seniority and the vehemence with which he states his views. There is nothing in the 1982 election results or in their likely legislative output in 1983 and 1984 which suggests that these two congressmen will be immune from serious challenges in 1984.

Presidential politics. Idaho has a presidential primary late in the season, which both media and candidates tend to ignore. It is usually predictable, and the number of delegates elected is very small. In general elections, Idaho is just as predictable: one of the nation's three or four most Republican states.

The People   Est. Pop. 1982: 965,000; Pop. 1980: 943,935, up 2.3% 1980–82 and 32.4% 1970–1980; .42% of U.S. total, 40th largest; voting age pop. 637,270; 3% Spanish origin, 1% American Indian, 1% Asian origin. Single ancestry: 18% English, 10% German, 4% Irish, 2% Swedish, 1% French, Norwegian, Scottish, Dutch, Italian. Registered voters (1982): 541,164 Total. 21% with 1–3 yrs. col., 16% with 4+ yrs. col. 12.7% below poverty level. 24% housing units rented; median house value: $45,900; median monthly rent: $172. Households: 76% family, 44% with children, 67% married couples.

1982 Share of Federal Tax Burden $1,923,600,000; .32% of U.S. total, 44th largest.

1982 Share of Federal Expenditures

	Total		Non-Defense		Defense	
Total Expend	$2,102m	(0.35%)	$1,866m	(0.44%)	$236m	(0.13%)
St/Lcl Grants	350m	(0.40%)	350m	(0.40%)	0m	(0%)
Salary/Wages	290m	(0.37%)	171m	(0.62%)	119m	(0.23%)
Ind Payments	1,030m	(0.36%)	910m	(0.35%)	120m	(0.42%)
Procurement	393m	(0.27%)	340m	(1.08%)	53m	(0.05%)
Other Programs	39m	(0.72%)	39m	(0.73%)	0m	(0%)
Loan/Insurance	389m	(0.61%)	385m	(0.62%)	4m	(0.18%)

Political Lineup   Governor, John V. Evans (D). Senators, James A. McClure (R) and Steven D. Symms (R). Representatives, 2 R. State Senate, 35 (21 R and 14 D); State House of Representatives, 70 (51 R and 19 D).

Presidential Vote

1980	Reagan (R)	290,699	(66%)
	Carter (D)	110,192	(25%)
	Anderson (I)	27,058	(6%)
1976	Ford (R)	204,151	(59%)
	Carter (D)	126,549	(37%)

1980 Democratic Presidential Primary			*1980 Republican Presidential Primary*		
Carter	31,383	(62%)	Reagan	111,868	(83%)
Kennedy	11,087	(22%)	Anderson	13,130	(10%)
Uncommitted	5,934	(12%)	Uncommitted	3,441	(3%)
One other	2,078	(4%)	Two others.........	6,440	(5%)

SENATORS

Sen. James A. McClure (R) Elected 1972, seat up 1984; b. Dec. 27, 1924, Payette; home, Payette; U. of ID, J.D. 1950; Presbyterian.

Career Practicing atty., 1950–66; Payette Cnty. Atty., 1950–56; Payette City Atty., 1953–66; ID Senate, 1960–66; U.S. House of Reps., 1967–73.

Offices 361 DSOB, 202-224-2752. Also 304 N. 8th. St., Rm. 434, Boise 83708, 208-384-1560; and 305 Fed. Bldg., Coeur d'Alene 83814, 208-664-3086.

Committees *Appropriations* (4th). Subcommittees: Agriculture, Rural Development; Defense; Energy and Water Development; Interior (Chairman). *Energy and Natural Resources* (Chairman). *Rules and Administration* (4th).

Group Ratings

	ADA	ACLU	COPE	CFA	LCV	LWV	NTU	NSI	COC	ACA	CSFC
1982	5	7	10	10	15	0	81	80	80	59	80
1981	10	—	11	0	19	—	87	—	94	74	84
1980	17	30	11	0	6	30	64	100	89	92	82

National Journal Ratings

	Economic		Foreign		Cultural	
1982	17%	(LIB)	41%	(LIB)	0%	(LIB)
	82%	(CONS)	58%	(CONS)	96%	(CONS)
1981	25%	(LIB)	37%	(LIB)	2%	(LIB)
	74%	(CONS)	62%	(CONS)	82%	(CONS)

Key Votes

1) Reagan 81 Budget	FOR	5) $ to El Salvador	FOR
2) Reagan 81 Tax Cut	FOR	6) Saudi AWACS Sale	FOR
3) Bal Budget Amend	FOR	7) Ban Abortion	FOR
4) Gas & Road Tax	FOR	8) Nerve Gas Prod	—

9) Poor Pay Food Stamps	FOR
10) Ban Crt Busing Order	FOR
11) Clinch Riv Brdr Rctr	FOR
12) Legal Services Corp	AGN

Election Results

1978 general	James A. McClure (R)	194,412	(68%)	($434,871)
	Dwight Jensen (D)	89,635	(32%)	($55,163)
1978 primary	James A. McClure (R) unopposed			
1972 primary	James A. McClure (R)	161,804	(52%)	($405,788)
	William E. Davis (D)	140,913	(47%)	($204,878)

Campaign Contributions and Expenditures

1977-78		*PACS brkdwn*			
Receipts	$427,419	Agr	$7,000	Ideo	$18,527
Expend.	$434,871	Bus	$116,346	Lbr	$2,500
Unspent	$26,444	Hlth	$10,500	Prof	$5,500

Sen. Steven D. Symms (R) Elected 1980, seat up 1986; b. Apr. 23, 1938, Nampa; home, Caldwell; U. of ID, B.S. 1960; Free Methodist.

Career USMC, 1960–63; Personnel and Production Mgr., V.P., Symms Fruit Ranch, Inc., 1963–72, Mbr. Bd. of Dirs., 1967–; U.S. House of Reps., 1972–80.

Offices 509 HSOB, 202-224-6142. Also P.O. Box 1190, Boise 83701, 208-334-1776; 401 2d St., #108, Twin Falls 83301, 208-734-2515; Lewiston, 208-743-1492; Moscow, 208-882-5560; Coeur d'Alene, 208-664-5490; and Idaho Falls, 208-522-9779.

Committees *Budget* (8th). *Environment and Public Works* (6th). Subcommittees: Transportation (Chairman); Nuclear Regulation; Environmental Pollution. *Finance* (10th). Subcommittees: International Trade; Energy and Agricultural Taxation; Estate and Gift Taxation (Chairman). *Joint Economic Committee* (4th). Subcommittees: International Trade, Finance and Security Economics; Monetary and Fiscal Policy (Chairman).

Group Ratings

	ADA	ACLU	COPE	CFA	LCV	LWV	NTU	NSI	COC	ACA	CSFC
1982	5	7	3	10	15	8	91	100	80	85	84
1981	0	—	6	14	19	—	92	—	100	81	89

National Journal Ratings

	Economic		Foreign		Cultural	
1982	12%	(LIB)	3%	(LIB)	0%	(LIB)
	87%	(CONS)	84%	(CONS)	96%	(CONS)
1981	22%	(LIB)	1%	(LIB)	2%	(LIB)
	77%	(CONS)	85%	(CONS)	82%	(CONS)

Key Votes

1) Reagan 81 Budget	FOR	5) $ to El Salvador	FOR	9) Poor Pay Food Stamps	FOR
2) Reagan 81 Tax Cut	FOR	6) Saudi AWACS Sale	FOR	10) Ban Crt Busing Order	FOR
3) Bal Budget Amend	FOR	7) Ban Abortion	FOR	11) Clinch Riv Brdr Rctr	FOR
4) Gas & Road Tax	FOR	8) Nerve Gas Prod	FOR	12) Legal Services Corp	AGN

Election Results

1980 general	Steven D. Symms (R)	218,701	(50%)	($1,780,777)
	Frank Church (D)	214,439	(49%)	($1,931,487)
1980 primary	Steven D. Symms (R)	108,813	(100%)	
1974 general	Frank Church (D)	145,140	(56%)	($300,300)
	Robert L. Smith (R)	109,072	(42%)	($127,926)

Campaign Contributions and Expenditures

1979-80		PACS brkdwn			
Receipts	$1,793,429	Agr	$11,150	Ideo	$58,726
Expend.	$1,780,777	Bus	$541,641	Lbr	$2,000
Unspent	$12,651	Hlth	$21,430	Prof	$5,200

GOVERNOR

Gov. John V. Evans (D) Succeeded Gov. Cecil D. Andrus, Jan. 24, 1977, term expires Jan. 1987; b. Jan. 18, 1925, Malad; home, Malad; ID St. U., Stanford U., B.A. 1951; Mormon.

Career Army, WWII; Rancher and banker; ID Senate, 1953–57, 1967–73, Major. Ldr., 1957, Minor. Ldr., 1969–74; Mayor of Malad City, 1960–66.

Offices State House, Boise 83720, 208-334-2100.

Election Results

1982 gen.	John V. Evans (D)	165,365	(51%)
	Phil Batt (R)	161,157	(49%)
1982 prim.	John V. Evans (D)	40,613	(100%)
1978 gen.	John V. Evans (D)	169,540	(59%)
	Allan E. Larsen (R)	114,149	(40%)

FIRST DISTRICT

The People   Pop. 1980: 472,412, up 40.5% 1970–80; voting age pop. 324,509; 3% Span. orig., 1% Am. Ind., 1% Asian orig. 24% housing units rented. Median owner $47,400; renter $173. Households: 77% family, 43% with children, 67% married couples.

Presidential Vote

1980	Reagan (R)	132,917	(63%)
	Carter (D)	62,327	(30%)
	Anderson (I)	15,292	(7%)

Rep. Larry Craig (R) Elected 1980; b. July 20, 1945, Council; home, Midvale; U. of ID, B.A. 1969, Geo. Wash. U., M.A. 1971; Methodist.

Career Natl. Guard, 1970–74; Chmn., State Senate Races, ID Repub. Party, 1976–78; ID Senate, 1973–81.

Offices 1318 LHOB, 202-225-6611. Also 304 N. 8th St., Rm. 134, Boise 83702, 208-334-9046; 903 D St., Lewiston 83501, 208-743-0792; and 305 Fed. Bldg., Coeur d'Alene 83814, 208-667-6130.

Committees *Government Operations* (13th). Subcommittees: Intergovernmental Relations and Human Resources; Environment, Energy and Natural Resources. *Interior and Insular Affairs* (8th). Subcommittees: Energy and the Environment; Mining, Forest Management, BPA; Public Lands and National Parks. *Select Committee on Aging* (11th). Subcommittee: Health and Long-Term Care.

Group Ratings

	ADA	ACLU	COPE	CFA	LCV	LWV	NTU	NSI	COC	ACA	CSFC
1982	5	0	12	20	16	17	94	100	90	91	77
1981	0	—	13	29	14	—	92	—	95	88	81

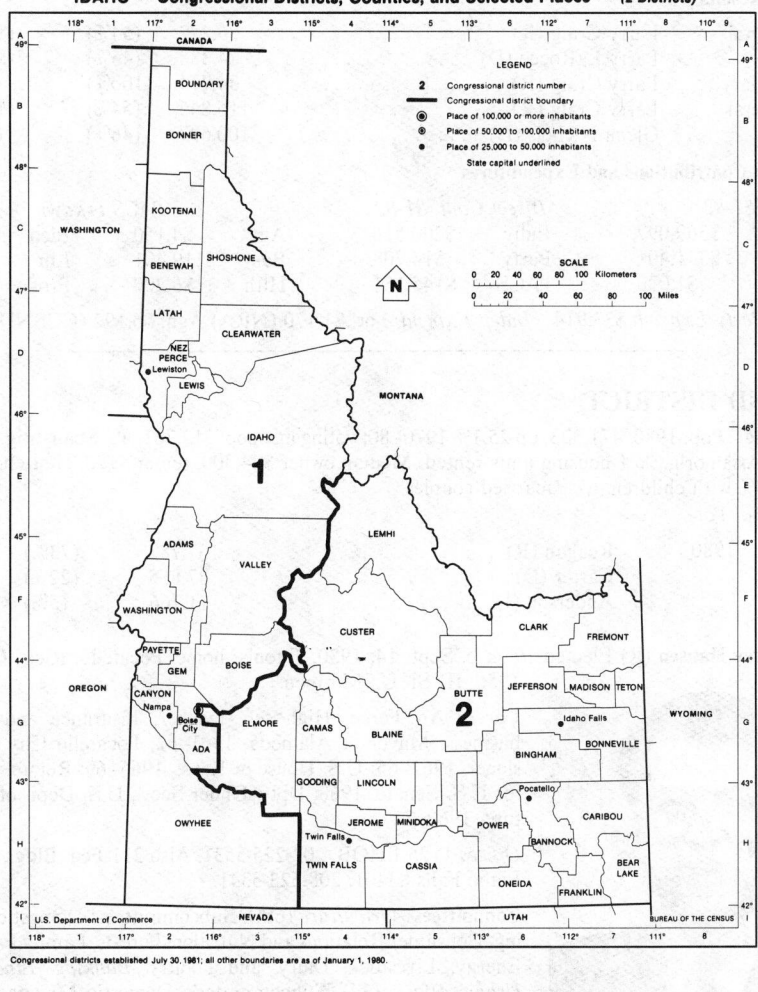

IDAHO — Congressional Districts, Counties, and Selected Places — (2 Districts)

National Journal Ratings

	Economic		Foreign		Cultural	
1982	12%	(LIB)	36%	(LIB)	4%	(LIB)
	88%	(CONS)	63%	(CONS)	87%	(CONS)
1981	4%	(LIB)	3%	(LIB)	4%	(LIB)
	79%	(CONS)	87%	(CONS)	90%	(CONS)

Key Votes

1) Reagan 81 Budget	FOR	5) Incr SS Rtmt Age	FOR	9) Poor Pay Food Stamps	FOR
2) Reagan 81 Tax Cut	FOR	6) Saudi AWACS Sale	FOR	10) Ban Crt Busing Order	FOR
3) Bal Budget Amend	FOR	7) $ for MX Missile	FOR	11) Auto Local Content	AGN
4) Gas & Road Tax	AGN	8) Nerve Gas Prod	AGN	12) Nuclear Arms Freeze	AGN

Election Results

1982 general	Larry Craig (R)	86,277	(54%)	($371,401)
	Larry LaRocco (D)	74,388	(46%)	($211,149)
1982 primary	Larry Craig (R)	34,774	(100%)	
1980 general	Larry Craig (R)	116,845	(54%)	($306,910)
	Glenn Nichols (D)	100,697	(46%)	($92,914)

Campaign Contributions and Expenditures

1981-82		*Direct Cont. 81-82*				*PACS brkdwn*		
Receipts	$369,097	Indiv	$200,516	Agr	$4,150	Ideo	$7,250
Expend.	$371,401	Party	$14,708	Bus	$119,401	Lbr	$3,000
Unspent	$1,020	PACS	$145,181	Hlth	$6,200	Prof	$1,400

Indirect Party Expend: $33,914   *Indep Expend:* For: $1,170 (NRA) Agn: $6,192 (CCSND)

SECOND DISTRICT

The People   Pop. 1980: 471,523, up 25.1% 1970–80; voting age pop. 312,761; 4% Span. orig., 1% Am. Ind., 1% Asian orig. 25% housing units rented. Median owner $44,300; renter $170. Households: 76% family, 44% with children, 67% married couples.

Presidential Vote

1980	Reagan (R)	157,782	(73%)
	Carter (D)	47,865	(22%)
	Anderson (I)	11,766	(5%)

Rep. George Hansen (R) Elected 1974; b. Sept. 14, 1930, Tetonia; home, Pocatello; Ricks Col., B.A. 1956, ID St. U.; Mormon.

Career Air Force; High sch. teacher; Insurance and retailing business; Mayor of Alameda, 1961–62; Pocatello City Commissioner, 1962–65; U.S. House of Reps., 1965–69; Repub. Nominee for U.S. Senate, 1968; Dpty. Under Secy., U.S. Dept. of Agriculture, 1969–71.

Offices 1125 LHOB, 202-225-5531. Also 211 Fed. Bldg., Box 740, Idaho Falls 83401, 208-523-5341.

Committees *Agriculture* (6th). Subcommittees: Domestic Marketing, Consumer Relations and Nutrition; Forests, Family Farms, and Energy; Livestock, Dairy, and Poultry. *Banking, Finance and Urban Affairs* (3d). Subcommittees: Domestic Monetary Policy; Financial Institutions Supervision, Regulations and Insurance; International Trade, Investment and Monetary Policy.

Group Ratings

	ADA	ACLU	COPE	CFA	LCV	LWV	NTU	NSI	COC	ACA	CSFC
1982	0	0	8	0	7	9	95	100	90	95	84
1981	0	—	8	14	7	—	93	—	94	100	83
1980	6	17	18	14	5	13	73	100	74	95	88

National Journal Ratings

	Economic		Foreign		Cultural	
1982	3%	(LIB)	4%	(LIB)	15%	(LIB)
	96%	(CONS)	92%	(CONS)	83%	(CONS)
1981	22%	(LIB)	3%	(LIB)	4%	(LIB)
	77%	(CONS)	87%	(CONS)	90%	(CONS)

Key Votes

1) Reagan 81 Budget	FOR	5) Incr SS Rtmt Age	FOR	9) Poor Pay Food Stamps	FOR
2) Reagan 81 Tax Cut	FOR	6) Saudi AWACS Sale	FOR	10) Ban Crt Busing Order	FOR
3) Bal Budget Amend	FOR	7) $ for MX Missile	FOR	11) Auto Local Content	AGN
4) Gas & Road Tax	AGN	8) Nerve Gas Prod	FOR	12) Nuclear Arms Freeze	AGN

Election Results

1982 general	George Hansen (R)	83,873	(52%)	($185,727)
	Richard Stallings (D)	76,608	(48%)	($116,931)
1982 primary	George Hansen (R)	42,296	(100%)	
1980 general	George Hansen (R)	116,196	(59%)	($222,447)
	Daniel Bilyeu (D)	81,364	(41%)	($32,355)

Campaign Contributions and Expenditures

1981-82		Direct Cont. 81-82				PACS brkdwn		
Receipts	$180,523	Indiv	$115,885	Agr	$1,650	Ideo	$4,150
Expend.	$185,727	Party	$9,139	Bus	$47,975	Lbr	$—
Unspent	$230	PACS	$55,710	Hlth	$1,550	Prof	$200

Indirect Party Expend: $33,883   *Indep Expend:* For: $925 (NRA)

ILLINOIS

The tone of Illinois politics these days—the brawling and name-calling, the bitter personal feuds and lack of debate on issues—is jarringly out of kilter with the state's high levels of income, education, of all the things that are supposed to elevate the spirit and nourish the mind. A campaign between candidates as cerebral as Governor James Thompson and former Senator Adlai Stevenson III turns into a flurry of charges: one candidate gets his friends to buy him expensive antiques, another belongs to an all-male lunch club. The mayoral race between a little-known congressman and an even less-known businessman threatened to polarize race relations across the country. The tone and content of Illinois politics seems even to have visibly declined since the early 1970s, and even then it never was very elevating.

To understand why, you have to realize that Illinois is one of those states whose growth and prosperity are the result, not of governmental action or political imagination, but almost entirely of the strength and growth of its private economy. Illinois likes to boast of Abraham Lincoln, the most important politician Illinois has produced; but Lincoln's greatest contribution to Illinois (dwarfed, to be sure, by his contributions to the nation), was his work as a railroad lawyer, helping the lines connect East and West.

When white men first came to Illinois, they saw a vast, treeless prairie, an incredibly rich land where the topsoil can still be measured in feet. This vacant, flat land occupied an important geographic position—it connected the Mississippi Valley and the Great Lakes and lay on the direct level route from the American West to the East Coast and the outer world. Illinois was the natural focus for the nation's railroad network, and the natural place also for processing the agricultural products of the Midwest for use in the East and in Europe. Chicago was a frontier village in the 1830s; by 1890 it was a city of millions, one of the greatest metropolises of the world, with a huge immigrant population drawn from all quarters of the world, and cultural institutions of the first magnitude. Downstate Illinois, in which Lincoln as a young man had seen an Indian uprising, was by the same time well established as one of the richest agricultural regions in the world.

This bustling and muscular Illinois has never been hospitable to political idealists. Instead, politics has always been a business here; politicians have had the unglamorous job of managing the governmental institutions and, for the most part, seeing that they stay out of the way of commerce and industry. Chicago has had a political machine since before the turn of the century, a machine whose function has been to modulate the demands of the city's many ethnic groups and to maintain municipal services in the city. For their part, businesses have always felt that a certain amount of inefficiency and graft was a reasonable price to pay for these services, particularly since it has usually been possible to arrange for low property tax assessments. Of course most of Chicago's business leaders have been Republicans and boosters of the free enterprise system, but most of them also supported the late Mayor (1955–76) Richard J. Daley, because he did his job efficiently and because he built great structures, from McCormick Place to O'Hare Airport, which helped Chicago maintain its status as a national center of commerce and world class city. The Democrats are not the only party to practice machine politics here; the Republicans, while not as picturesque, are also hardheaded professionals with little time for sentimentality or idealism. Politics has always been a business in Illinois, and while it is by no means the most important business in the state it is still pursued seriously and with practical ends clearly in mind. *Don't Back No Losers* is the title of a recent book on Illinois politics.

Yet today, even as the tone of the state's politics has become more raucous, less and less seems to be at stake. The change can be dated to 1972. That was the year the McGovernites in control of the Democratic National Convention refused to seat the Daley delegation from Illinois—which had been selected, defiantly, with no regard to the new reform rules. It was also the year the Better Government Association and the *Chicago Tribune* pretty well stamped out ballot box stuffing on the West Side of Chicago. A series of indictments in the early 1970s—many brought by Thompson, then U.S. Attorney in Chicago—thinned the top ranks of the machine. And it was around that time that the patronage jobs which had been the lifeblood of both parties' machines became less numerous and less attractive. One reason was inroads by civil service; another was a 1976 Supreme Court decision, which gravely spoke of how the right of free expression of Republican sheriff's deputies would be chilled if they could be fired by a newly elected Democratic sheriff. But more important was the fact that patronage jobs were no longer so attractive when wages and salaries in the private sector were rising rapidly and job security seemed assured. Who wants an $8,500 job which requires you to work nights and weekends keeping track of voters in your precinct, when you can make two or three times the money in a factory or office? Mayor Daley's personal talents and reputation made it easy to imagine there was still a huge, united political machine in Chicago. But after his death, and with the defeat of his chosen successor Michael Bilandic in the 1979 primary, it became clear that the machine was simply a collection of an admittedly large number of local political operatives, most of whom sought a few patronage jobs and worked hard themselves for incomes most LaSalle Street lawyers would have regarded with scorn. Harold Washington's election as mayor in 1983 presumably opened up several dozen $50,000 jobs to blacks. But its effect on city services and broad policies was less clear.

So now that politics is no longer needed in Chicago to deliver bread, it delivers circuses. It has heady competition: in 1981 and 1982 the raging debate over Cardinal Cody's stewardship of the Roman Catholic Archdiocese of Chicago (did he divert money to a favorite cousin?) vied with the shenanigans of Mayor Jane Byrne for coverage in the 1920s-style newspaper war between the *Tribune* and the *Sun-Times*. The papers took sides, on their news as well as their editorial pages: the *Tribune* backed the Cardinal and opposed the Mayor, the *Sun-Times* savaged the prelate (who died at a dramatic moment in the controversy) and applauded Her Honor. The 1982 governor's race and the 1983 mayor's race lent themselves to the same kind of coverage. Thompson and Stevenson conducted campaigns that came alive only when one or the other was caught in some blunder; Byrne and her competitors, Cook County State's Attorney Richard M. Daley (the late Mayor's son) and black Congressman Harold Washington, attacked each other brutally; and that was nothing next to the vituperation in the general election race between Washington and Republican Bernard Epton. So much for Illinois's tradition of blue ribbon candidates at the top of the ticket (Adlai Stevenson and Paul Douglas in 1948, Charles Percy in 1966, candidates Stevenson and Thompson themselves in 1970 and 1976).

What is at stake in all this? Less than meets the eye. Illinois has a stronger—because more white collar—economy than other Great Lakes states, but in straitened economic circumstances the range of choices before its state government is not great. Chicago has large bureaucracies that conduct city government's business, with a tolerable level of graft; and it appears that its tribes of patronage politicians will stay in business, fewer of them each year, but still a factor in local affairs for decades to come. The strengths of the state exist despite politics and its weaknesses do not seem susceptible to quick cure by government. It should be added that, despite all this, Illinois has been sending distinguished congressional delegations to Washington, highly qualified members of both parties who grapple intelligently with national issues.

Presidential politics. In national politics Illinois comes very close to the national average. It has backed only one losing presidential candidate since 1916 (Gerald Ford in 1976) and in 1980 came within 1% of the national results. Illinois is, arguably, a kind of national microcosm: Cairo, at its southern tip, is closer to Mississippi than to Chicago; and Chicago itself has hundreds of thousands of black residents whose family roots are in Mississippi and other states in the South. There is a line across central Illinois that marks the division between Democratic and Republican counties in Lincoln's day and almost exactly separates counties carried by Jimmy Carter and by Gerald Ford in the close 1976 election. Metropolitan Chicago, with its yeasty ethnic composition, contrasts with Downstate Illinois, where most people are of Yankee and German descent. With 24 electoral votes, Illinois is always closely contested in presidential races—a key state for any candidate.

Illinois also has an important presidential primary—the first on the calendar of any northern state outside New England. (Illinois has its primary for state offices at the same time; the early date was chosen to favor the machines, which are ready to move any time, and to handicap reformers and insurgents, who must organize for each election.) The Republican primary electorate is conservative, in two senses of the word. In the old *Tribune* tradition, most Republican voters are suspicious of the old East Coast internationalists in the party. But they are also wary of insurgents. Ronald Reagan, who lost the 1976 primary to an incumbent president, carried the 1980 primary over the standard-bearer of the party's liberal wing, Illinois's Congressman John Anderson; George Bush, with his East Coast origins, and Congressman Philip Crane, with his insurgent right wing backing, got nowhere.

The Democratic primary electorate was, a decade ago, considered the property of Mayor Daley; and about half the Democratic primary votes are still cast in Chicago. But no one thinks the mayor can deliver them. Jane Byrne endorsed Edward Kennedy in 1980; he lost by more than 2–1. The evidence suggests that Democratic presidential primary voters in Illinois, like those in other states, make up their minds on the basis of their own information and preference, not because of the endorsement of some politico. Still, they are not typical of other major states. There may still be a bias against insurgents: primary voters here showed an antipathy for Kennedy he encountered in no other major nonsouthern state. Carter's primary campaign, by the way, was managed by staffers of Vice President Mondale, who must be considered to have a head start in Illinois for 1984.

Governor. National reporters covering the 1982 gubernatorial race insisted on speculating that the winner would become a presidential candidate. Why anyone would suppose that either one of these obviously neurotic, though admittedly able, men would make a good president is unclear. Stevenson's distaste for national politics became obvious even before he quit the Senate in 1980; he thinks original thoughts about major issues, but he seems largely devoid of the political skills needed to translate those thoughts into action. Thompson had dazzled Illinois voters as federal prosecutor in the early 1970s, and he has a forceful personality. But he also has the habit of rushing into unnecessary controversy. As a Republican with a middle-of-the-road reputation, he should not have been in political trouble in 1982, but he came within 5,034 votes of losing. Among the reasons were the strength of Stevenson's name and some of his ideas and increased Democratic turnout among blacks and other strong Democrats in Chicago; if turnout had been at 1980 levels, Thompson would have won by about 75,000 votes—without the lengthy recount that took place. But the fact that the race was so close showed comparative weakness. Visiting reporters should concentrate on how Thompson is governing Illinois before they run him for president again. It is a long time until 1986, but the early favorite for the Democratic nomination is Neil Hartigan, now attorney general and former (1972–76) lieutenant governor. Hartigan easily beat Thompson appointee Tyrone Fahner, though Fahner was getting lots of publicity at the time as the coordinator of the poisoned Tylenol investigation. Hartigan grew up as a machine loyalist and is counted as one of its most competent products.

Senators. Another Illinois politician who has run for president several times is Senator Charles Percy. He started off in politics as a boy wonder: head of Bell & Howell at age 30, head of the platform committee at the Republican National Convention at age 41, much ballyhooed (but unsuccessful) candidate for governor at 45. Elected to the Senate in 1966, at 47, he is now one of the most senior Republicans there, and after the 1980 elections became Chairman of the Foreign Relations Committee. Yet Percy does not enjoy the respect his seniority would suggest. His portentous demeanor, self-righteousness, and lack of humor, combined with the presidential ambitions he nurtured for years, made him few friends or admirers among his fellow politicians. He has never really labored over a piece of major legislation and gotten it through the Senate; many observers regard him as a good example of a showhorse, not a workhorse. He has been all over the lot on issues. Despite his aspirations to leadership, his record, on economic issues particularly, seems to have been a creature of fashion. For much of the 1970s he supported big government programs and was dovish on foreign policy; in the late 1970s, after his scare in 1978 and especially after 1980, he has been more conservative on economic issues and more aggressive on foreign policy. On cultural issues he maintains a somewhat liberal stance.

That made a number of Republicans uneasy. They remembered that Percy had come forward, in the 1960s, with a plan to end the Vietnam war, and that he had supported antiwar measures in the early 1970s. He was regarded as a skeptic toward some defense spending. He has been sympathetic to the Palestine Liberation Organization's claims and is regarded as an opponent of aid to Israel. But even before Reagan's victory, Percy was taking a harder line. He chairs a sharply split committee: most of its Democrats are onetime Vietnam doves, devotees of disarmament, and strong supporters of Israel; most of its Republicans are hardliners. They include intellectual heavyweights like Howard Baker and Richard Lugar and political heavyweights like Jesse Helms, who has blocked several foreign policy appointments he didn't like. Percy has responded to these competing pressures by playing things pretty straight. After some embarrassing statements in late 1980 and early 1981 he has been more discreet on touchy issues, and he has allowed consensus to emerge on the committee rather than try to force it. Administration strategists probably do not entirely trust him, however, on issues like disarmament; and it can be argued that he has done little to make the committee a force in itself, as chairmen like William Fulbright and Frank Church did.

But it is certain that Percy will be emphasizing his importance as a national leader when—few people expect him to retire—he runs for reelection in 1984. He is no longer a boy wonder (not at age 65) nor does he have plausible presidential ambitions. And his concentration on national issues has made him a remote figure in Illinois—a state so large it is difficult for any senator to remain in close touch. Going into the 1978 campaign, Percy was thought to be a strong candidate; he had won previous races with large percentages, and as a liberal Republican he seemed well positioned at the center of a closely divided electorate. But unknown Democrat Alex Seith was able to take a lead over Percy and lost it only when Percy dug into his own pocket for campaign funds and found mistakes of Seith's he could exploit. So in 1984 Percy is likely to have serious competition.

He may even have primary opposition. In early 1983 Congressman Tom Corcoran was considering running; he was bold enough to hold a fundraiser on the same day President Reagan was appearing at a fundraiser for Percy. Majority Leader Howard Baker has a policy of supporting incumbent Republicans, of whatever stripe; and Reagan's support of Percy is in that spirit. It may prove enough to deter Corcoran. But Corcoran has shown political skills and aggressiveness, and as a member of the Energy and Commerce Committee, who has led some successful fights on behalf of business interests like AT&T, he can probably raise plenty of money. Moreover, Percy is if anything weaker in the Republican primary than in the fall. Back in 1964, he was trailing a more conservative candidate in the gubernatorial primary, and won only after the man died during the campaign. As for the general election, there is almost sure to be a primary to choose the Democratic nominee. We are probably past the stage when such a nomination could be delivered by organization endorsement, and the chances are too good—against Percy or Corcoran—for any politician ambitious to be a senator to sit this one out.

Illinois's other senator is almost unknown nationally, and is probably not known in much depth even in Illinois. Yet Alan Dixon was one of the nation's leading vote-getters in the 1980 Senate races, and one of the few Democrats to win convincingly in that Republican year. A Downstate Democrat, Dixon made satisfactory records as state treasurer and secretary of state; he won the Democratic nomination with competition only from Alex Seith, and in the general election faced Lieutenant Governor (and onetime sheriff) Dave O'Neal, a candidate so rough-hewn and prone to damaging statements that victory was a matter of keeping his mouth shut. It helped that Dixon did not have a record on national issues in a year when most Democrats' national records were unpopular.

In the Senate Dixon did not emerge from anonymity in his first two years. He sits on the Agriculture and the Banking, Housing and Urban Affairs Committees—something for Downstate, something for Chicago. But as a junior member of the minority party, and as a man without experience in the federal government, he has not been a major legislative actor. His voting record, on all types of issues, must be classed as moderate.

Congressional districting. One sign of the deterioration of Illinois's hardnosed partisan politics is the 1982 congressional redistricting. The Republicans held the governorship and the state House, the Democrats the Senate; but they could not manage to compromise. The issue went to a federal court made up of two Republicans and one Democrat—yet they chose a partisan Democratic plan! The strategy of the redistricting is to extend Chicago districts out into the suburbs, adding enough territory to meet the population standard but not enough to tilt the district Republican. In the process, two Republican suburban districts were squeezed out of existence—even though the suburbs have gained more population than any other part of the state. Downstate the boundaries were carefully crafted to help incumbent Democrats and unseat incumbent Republicans. Republicans held a 14–10 edge in the old congressional delegation; Democrats have a 12–10 edge now. But at least one of those seats must be considered shaky, and so the balance may change again in 1984.

The People   Est. Pop. 1982: 11,448,000; Pop. 1980: 11,426,518, up .2% 1980–82 and 2.8% 1970–80; 4.9% of U.S. total, 5th largest; voting age pop. 8,183,481; 13% Black, 5% Spanish origin, 1% Asian origin. Single ancestry: 10% German, 6% English, 4% Irish, Polish, 3% Italian, 1% Swedish, Russian, Dutch, French, Greek. Registered voters (1982): 5,965,514 Total. 15% with 1–3 yrs. col., 15% with 4+ yrs. col. 11.5% below poverty level. 35% housing units rented; median house value: $53,900; median monthly rent: $201. Households: 72% family, 39% with children, 59% married couples.

1982 Share of Federal Tax Burden $34,788,100,000; 5.82% of U.S. total, 4th largest.

1982 Share of Federal Expenditures

	Total		Non-Defense		Defense	
Total Expend	$22,353m	(3.70%)	$19,584m	(4.61%)	$2,770m	(1.55%)
St/Lcl Grants	4,103m	(4.65%)	4,103m	(4.65%)	0m	(0%)
Salary/Wages	2,068m	(2.65%)	871m	(3.18%)	1,197m	(2.36%)
Ind Payments	13,919m	(4.87%)	13,271m	(5.15%)	648m	(2.27%)
Procurement	2,053m	(1.41%)	709m	(2.25%)	1,344m	(1.18%)
Other Programs	211m	(3.90%)	209m	(3.89%)	2m	(4.65%)
Loan/Insurance	2,537m	(3.97%)	2,448m	(3.96%)	89m	(4.05%)

Political Lineup   Governor, James R. Thompson (R). Senators, Charles H. Percy (R) and Alan J. Dixon (D). Representatives, 22 (12 D and 10 R). State Senate, 59 (33 D and 26 R); State House of Representatives, 118 (70 D and 48 R).

Presidential Vote

1980	Reagan (R)	2,358,094	(50%)
	Carter (D)	1,981,413	(42%)
	Anderson (I)	346,754	(7%)
1976	Ford (R)	2,384,269	(50%)
	Carter (D)	2,271,295	(48%)

1980 Democratic Presidential Primary			*1980 Republican Presidential Primary*		
Carter	780,787	(65%)	Reagan	547,355	(48%)
Kennedy	359,875	(30%)	Anderson	415,193	(37%)
Two others & write-ins	60,405	(5%)	Bush	124,057	(11%)
			Five others & write-ins	43,476	(4%)

SENATORS

Sen. Charles H. Percy (R) Elected 1966, seat up 1984; b. Sept. 27, 1919, Pensacola, FL; home, Wilmette; U. of Chicago, B.A. 1941; Christian Science.

Career Navy, WWII; Corp. Exec., Bell & Howell Co., Pres. and Chf. Exec. Officer, 1949–61, Bd. Chmn., 1961–66; Rep. of Pres. Eisenhower to pres. inaugurations in Peru and Bolivia, 1956; Repub. Nominee for Gov., 1964.

Offices 443 DSOB, 202-224-2152. Also 230 Dearborn St., Rm. 3859, Chicago 60604, 312-353-4952; and 117 P.O. Bldg., Springfield 92701, 217-515-4442.

Committees *Foreign Relations* (Chairman). Subcommittees: African Affairs; European Affairs; Near Eastern and South Asian Affairs. *Governmental Affairs* (2d). Subcommittees: Permanent Subcommittee on Investigations; Information Management and Regulatory Affairs; Energy, Nuclear Proliferation, and Government Processes (Chairman). *Special Committee on Aging* (3d).

Group Ratings

	ADA	ACLU	COPE	CFA	LCV	LWV	NTU	NSI	COC	ACA	CSFC
1982	45	68	53	0	57	67	77	60	65	56	62
1981	35	—	56	29	38	—	71	—	82	43	74
1980	39	70	41	40	77	67	48	50	63	64	49

National Journal Ratings

	Economic		Foreign		Cultural	
1982	24%	(LIB)	58%	(LIB)	70%	(LIB)
	75%	(CONS)	41%	(CONS)	29%	(CONS)
1981	48%	(LIB)	42%	(LIB)	66%	(LIB)
	51%	(CONS)	57%	(CONS)	33%	(CONS)

Key Votes

1) Reagan 81 Budget	FOR	5) $ to El Salvador	AGN	9) Poor Pay Food Stamps	AGN
2) Reagan 81 Tax Cut	FOR	6) Saudi AWACS Sale	FOR	10) Ban Crt Busing Order	AGN
3) Bal Budget Amend	FOR	7) Ban Abortion	AGN	11) Clinch Riv Brdr Rctr	AGN
4) Gas & Road Tax	FOR	8) Nerve Gas Prod	AGN	12) Legal Services Corp	FOR

Election Results

1978 general	Charles H. Percy (R)	1,698,711	(53%)	($2,417,155)
	Alex R. Seith (D)	1,448,187	(46%)	($1,371,478)
1978 primary	Charles H. Percy (R)	401,409	(84%)	
	One other (R)	74,739	(16%)	
1972 general	Charles H. Percy (R)	2,867,078	(62%)	($1,408,822)
	Roman Pucinski (D)	1,721,031	(37%)	($335,482)

Campaign Contributions and Expenditures

1977-78		PACS brkdwn			
Receipts	$2,438,753	Agr	$15,550	Ideo	$6,825
Expend.	$2,417,155	Bus	$138,835	Lbr	$43,000
Unspent	$25,116	Hlth	$15,200	Prof	$950

Sen. Alan J. Dixon (D) Elected 1980, seat up 1986; b. July 7, 1927, Belleville; home, Belleville; U. of IL, B.S. 1949, Washington U., St. Louis, LL.B. 1949; Presbyterian.

Career Belleville Police Magistrate, 1948; IL House of Reps., 1951–63; IL Senate, 1963–71; Treas. of IL, 1971–77; Secy. of State of IL, 1977–81.

Offices 316 HSOB, 202-224-2854. Also 230 S. Dearborn St., Chicago 60604, 312-353-5420; 108 P.O. Bldg., Springfield 62701, 217-492-4126; and 227 Fed. Bldg., Mt. Vernon 62864, 618-224-6703.

Committees *Agriculture, Nutrition, and Forestry* (7th). Subcommittees: Agricultural Production, Marketing, and Stabilization of Prices; Foreign Agricultural Policy; Nutrition. *Banking, Housing and Urban Affairs* (6th). Subcommittees: Financial Institutions; International Finance and Monetary Policy; Consumer Affairs. *Small Business* (8th). Subcommittee: Urban and Rural Economic Development.

Group Ratings

	ADA	ACLU	COPE	CFA	LCV	LWV	NTU	NSI	COC	ACA	CSFC
1982	80	71	77	70	46	83	35	70	33	28	40
1981	65	—	61	21	56	—	34	—	61	48	48

National Journal Ratings

	Economic		Foreign		Cultural	
1982	80%	(LIB)	76%	(LIB)	86%	(LIB)
	19%	(CONS)	23%	(CONS)	12%	(CONS)
1981	63%	(LIB)	66%	(LIB)	59%	(LIB)
	36%	(CONS)	33%	(CONS)	40%	(CONS)

Key Votes

1) Reagan 81 Budget	FOR	5) $ to El Salvador	AGN	9) Poor Pay Food Stamps	AGN
2) Reagan 81 Tax Cut	FOR	6) Saudi AWACS Sale	AGN	10) Ban Crt Busing Order	AGN
3) Bal Budget Amend	FOR	7) Ban Abortion	AGN	11) Clinch Riv Brdr Rctr	AGN
4) Gas & Road Tax	FOR	8) Nerve Gas Prod	FOR	12) Legal Services Corp	FOR

Election Results

1980 general	Alan J. Dixon (D)	2,565,302	(56%)	($2,346,897)
	David C. O'Neal (R)	1,946,296	(42%)	($1,293,991)
1980 primary	Alan J. Dixon (D)	671,746	(67%)	
	Alex R. Seith (D)	190,339	(19%)	($146,402)
	Three others & write-ins (D)	142,289	(14%)	
1974 general	Adlai E. Stevenson III (D)	1,811,496	(62%)	($757,329)
	George M. Burditt (R)	1,084,884	(37%)	($488,556)

Campaign Contributions and Expenditures

1979-80			PACS brkdwn		
Receipts	$2,396,908	Agr	$20,375	Ideo	$5,500
Expend.	$2,346,897	Bus	$99,479	Lbr	$139,600
Unspent	$58,109	Hlth	$15,700	Prof	$6,500

GOVERNOR

Gov. James R. Thompson (R) Elected 1976, term expires Jan. 1985; b. May 8, 1936, Chicago; home, Chicago; U. of IL, Chicago, Washington U., St. Louis, Northwestern U., J.D. 1959; Presbyterian.

Career Prosecutor for Cook Cnty. States Atty., 1959–64; Assoc. Prof., Northwestern Law Sch., 1964–69; Chief, Dept. of Law Enforcement and Pub. Protection, IL Atty. Gen's Ofc., 1969; 1st Asst. U.S. Atty., N. Dist. of IL, 1970; U.S. Atty., 1971–75.

Offices State House, Springfield 62706, 217-782-6830.

Election Results

1982 gen.	James R. Thompson (R)	1,816,101	(49%)
	Adlai E. Stevenson III (D) ...	1,811,027	(49%)
1982 prim.	James R. Thompson (R)	507,893	(84%)
	John E. Roche (R)	54,858	(9%)
	V.A. Kelley (R)	43,627	(7%)
1978 gen.	James R. Thompson (R)	1,859,684	(59%)
	Michael J. Bakalis (D)	1,263,134	(40%)

FIRST DISTRICT

The most stable, longest-lived—the prototypical—urban black community in the United States is on the South Side of Chicago. Here, as long ago as 1900, was a large community of blacks centered around the corner of 63d and Cottage Grove. There have always been poor people in the South Side ghetto, but there have always been middle class and prosperous blacks as well: this is the home of the nation's first black bourgeoisie. The South Side has been a center of black culture since before the jazz age, and there are twice as many blacks here—some 800,000—as in New York's Harlem.

The South Side has also furnished political leadership for blacks. Illinois's 1st congressional district, more than 90% black today, includes the larger part of the South Side black community. It covers a wide sociological range, from the mansions of Kenwood, once the home of the city's Jewish aristocracy and more recently the headquarters of the Black Muslims, to the high-rise housing projects that line the Dan Ryan Expressway for what seems like miles. The 1st also includes the University of Chicago and the intellectual Hyde Park neighborhood around it, but the typical neighborhood here is one where the straight streets are lined with modest well-kept houses built around the turn of the century, in neighborhoods which have been entirely black for decades.

The 1st district has the longest continuous tradition of black representation in the nation. It elected its first black congressman, Oscar DePriest in 1928. DePriest was a Republican, for in those days blacks were still faithful to the party of Lincoln; they even stayed with Herbert Hoover in the depths of the Depression in 1932. But the New Deal and the racial liberalism of Eleanor Roosevelt attracted blacks to the Democratic Party in the 1930s. DePriest was beaten by a black Democrat, Arthur Mitchell, in 1934; Mitchell was succeeded in 1942 by another black Democrat, William Dawson.

Just about forgotten today, Dawson was the first American black since Reconstruction to be a major force in electoral—and patronage—politics. He was the undisputed political boss

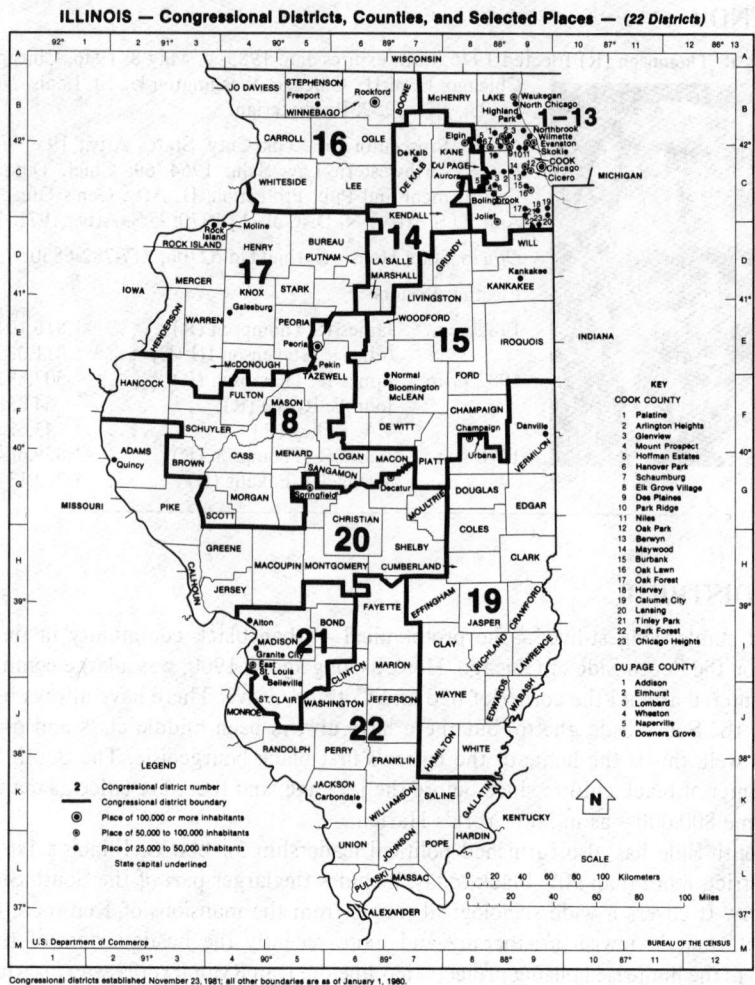

ILLINOIS — Congressional Districts, Counties, and Selected Places — (22 Districts)

KEY

COOK COUNTY

1 Palatine
2 Arlington Heights
3 Glenview
4 Mount Prospect
5 Hoffman Estates
6 Hanover Park
7 Schaumburg
8 Elk Grove Village
9 Des Plaines
10 Park Ridge
11 Niles
12 Oak Park
13 Berwyn
14 Maywood
15 Burbank
16 Oak Lawn
17 Oak Forest
18 Harvey
19 Calumet City
20 Lansing
21 Tinley Park
22 Park Forest
23 Chicago Heights

DU PAGE COUNTY

1 Addison
2 Elmhurst
3 Lombard
4 Wheaton
5 Naperville
6 Downers Grove

LEGEND

2 Congressional district number
— Congressional district boundary
◉ Place of 100,000 or more inhabitants
◉ Place of 50,000 to 100,000 inhabitants
● Place of 25,000 to 50,000 inhabitants
State capital underlined

U.S. Department of Commerce   BUREAU OF THE CENSUS

Congressional districts established November 23, 1981; all other boundaries are as of January 1, 1980.

of the South Side, and he was consulted regularly by Mayor Daley and his predecessors, just like the ward leaders of other ethnic groups. Dawson for his part was not a boat-rocker. He endorsed civil rights measures, but in contrast to such leaders as A. Philip Randolph—who pressed hard for fair employment measures in the midst of World War II—Dawson was firmly committed to working within the conventional political system. His goals were to provide patronage jobs, Democratic nominations, and public services to the South Side's blacks, and to make sure that everyone knew they came courtesy of William Dawson. In turn he delivered for the machine. Turnout on the South Side was—and is—always high. And as other ethnic groups became less loyal to the Democrats, the black wards provided Chicago's largest Democratic margins. Dawson's black constituency kept Mayor Daley in office in 1963, when he was nearly beaten by a Polish Republican.

Today the Democratic margins are still huge, but the politics of William Dawson is a thing of the past. Dawson's successor in Congress, Ralph Metcalfe, broke with Mayor Daley in 1972 when the Mayor refused to come to Metcalfe's office to discuss the beating of two black dentists by a policeman. Later that year, half the South Side's votes went to Republicans, Senator Charles Percy and Cook County State's Attorney Bernard Carey; the South Side declared independence from the machine. Machine Democrats did gain control of the House seat when Metcalfe died in October 1978, but their hold was short-lived; the machine incumbent, Bennett Stewart, was able to win only 17% in the 1980 primary.

The winner then was the district's most recent congressman, Harold Washington. Suddenly in 1983, when he upset Jane Byrne and Richard Daley and won the Democratic nomination for mayor, he became one of the nation's most famous politicians. His strengths and weaknesses in the general election race could have been forecast from his career. He is intellectually distinguished: he was a top law student at Northwestern (at a time when few blacks attended such schools) and a state legislator who could draft a bill. But he also had the weaknesses you might expect in a man active in South Side and hence machine politics for many years before and after 1972: the sloppiness of a pol confident the machine will protect him, the pride of a black politician suddenly made independent because he has the support of an autonomous black constituency.

The sloppiness resulted in his conviction for failing to file income tax returns, even though the amounts he owed were trifling; the stiff-necked pride resulted in his disbarment when he refused to appear at a hearing on trivial charges made against him. When he refused after his primary victory to meet with Democratic ward leaders who endorsed other candidates and refused to take repeated phone calls from Walter Mondale, he may have been remembering Metcalfe's refusal to go down to City Hall to meet Daley; but he was forgetting that the constituency he was seeking to represent was the whole city, more than 60% of it white. If that was a sin of pride, it was a sin of sloppiness for him to have allowed Jesse Jackson—a pariah among Chicago whites—to appear on his platform on primary night.

It is unlikely that Washington supposed that Democratic voters would automatically support him after he won the primary, as he maintained; he is shrewder than that. His refusal to court ward leaders, or to do enough until the last minute to calm white voters' fears, was probably part of a high-risk strategy. He would risk losing the race, but if he won it he would have done so his way—without owing anything to County Chairman Edward Vrdolyak or former Congressman Roman Pucinski, probably the two most powerful aldermen. Having won, his program is to give blacks better city services, and access to the relatively few high-paid jobs at the top levels of city government; to do so, he will probably have to make deals with enough aldermen to command a majority on the council.

Washington's replacement in Congress will be another black Democrat who will have a liberal voting record in Washington, but who will probably be more concerned about affairs in Chicago. He will almost surely be a Washington backer.

The People Pop. 1980: 519,045, dn. 18.9% 1970–80; voting age pop. 358,925; 90% Black, 5% Span. orig., 1% Asian orig. 67% housing units rented. Median owner $37,300; renter $183. Households: 63% family, 39% with children, 32% married couples.

Presidential Vote

1980	Reagan (R)	NA
	Carter (D)	NA
	Anderson (I)	NA

Rep. Harold Washington (D) vacated seat April 29, 1983. Elected Mayor of Chicago on April 12 and sworn in April 29. Special elections held at discretion of Governor within 60 days of swearing in.

Election Results

1982 general	Harold Washington (D)	172,641	(97%)	($105,857)
1982 primary	Harold Washington (D)	69,799	(100%)	
1980 general	Harold Washington (D)	119,562	(95%)	($72,716)
	George Williams (R)	5,660	(5%)	($0)

SECOND DISTRICT

Chicago has a strikingly well-rounded economy: it is one of the nation's leading white collar employment centers, perhaps its most important transportation center, and also one of its major manufacturing centers. The heavy industry is concentrated on the far south side of town, around the city's artificial port in Lake Calumet. Standing on the 92d Street bridge across the Calumet River, which connects Lake Calumet and Lake Michigan, you are within sight of the largest concentration of steel plants in the United States. To this part of Chicago, late in the 19th century, immigrants began coming from economically backward parts of Europe—from Sicily and Galicia, Bohemia and Lithuania—to work in the steel mills and in George Pullman's model factory town. Some of their descendants live there still, in neighborhoods with names like Slag Valley and the Island, places described colorfully in Ron Grossman's *Guide to Chicago Neighborhoods*. In this area also is the home of Eddie Vrdolyak, 10th Ward Alderman, Mayor Jane Byrne's choice as chairman of the Cook County Democratic Party, and the leader of the anti-Harold Washington majority on the Chicago city council. In a modest working class neighborhood, Vrdolyak lives in a lavish house—a kind of lord living in a castle among the people he rules.

Lake Calumet and the steel mills are the central focus of Illinois's 2d congressional district. But despite the remaining pockets of white ethnics here, this is a black congressional district. The 2d forms a kind of U around the 1st district. The upper left hand side of the U is an almost entirely black neighborhood, mostly Irish at the beginning of the 1960s, and the scene of some of the most rapid neighborhood racial change in the nation during the last 20 years. The bottom left part of the U is almost entirely black now as well, the result of more recent neighborhood change. There has been some black movement southward as well, into the suburbs directly south of Lake Calumet; some of that has been into a well-established black community in Markham and Harvey, some is just scattered around into neighborhoods of the kind which, 20 years ago, always remained all white. The 2d district's boundaries extend down into these suburbs, crossing the city line but following the natural migration of its ethnic groups outward.

The 2d district is represented by Gus Savage, who has made a career as an opponent of Mayor Daley's Democratic machine. He ran against Congressman Morgan Murphy in 1970, in a district whose white majority was just then vanishing; when Murphy retired in 1980, Savage ran again. For 25 years before that he ran a community newspaper and attacked the powers that be. Savage is a temperamental rebel, a man whose reaction, when his son was stopped for driving without a license, was to call up the police chief and protest. In appearance and temperament he reminds some observers of the television character George Jefferson.

Some Illinois politicians wanted to get rid of Savage by eliminating his district in redistricting, which would have been possible; the federal court instead gave him a seat 66% of whose adults and 78% of whose children are black. His seat is nonetheless anything but safe. In the 1982 primary, against two candidates, he won only 39% of the vote; a major issue was the charge that he had been absent for a large number of votes. He can expect similar, and perhaps more successful, opposition in 1984.

In the House Savage has a solid liberal voting record, as one might expect. He has not had a major impact on legislation. Chicago is the center of his political world and, with a seat in jeopardy in Illinois's early 1984 primary, he will likely devote most of his attention to his home district in 1983.

The People Pop. 1980: 518,931, dn. 1.9% 1970–80; voting age pop. 340,827; 66% Black, 7% Span. orig. 42% housing units rented. Median owner $37,700; renter $190. Households: 78% family, 50% with children, 50% married couples.

Presidential Vote

1980	Reagan (R) .... NA	
	Carter (D) .... NA	
	Anderson (I) .... NA	

Rep. Gus Savage (D) Elected 1980; b. Oct. 30, 1925, Detroit, MI; home, Chicago; Roosevelt U., B.A. 1951; Kent Col. of Law, 1952–53; Baptist.

Career Army, WWII; Community newspaper publisher, 1954–79; Cofounder, Chicago League of Negro Voters, 1958.

Offices 1121 LHOB, 202-225-0773. Also 1743 E. 87th St., Chicago 60617, 312-374-5000.

Committees *Public Works and Transportation* (17th). Subcommittees: Public Buildings and Grounds; Surface Transportation; Water Resources. *Small Business* (17th). Subcommittees: SBA and SBIC Authority, Minority Enterprise and General Small Business Problems; Export Opportunities and Special Small Business Problems.

Group Ratings

	ADA	ACLU	COPE	CFA	LCV	LWV	NTU	NSI	COC	ACA	CSFC
1982	75	79	95	70	83	70	48	0	26	0	23
1981	65	—	100	64	91	—	19	—	0	0	19

National Journal Ratings

	Economic		Foreign		Cultural	
1982	77%	(LIB)	94%	(LIB)	84%	(LIB)
	23%	(CONS)	5%	(CONS)	16%	(CONS)
1981	98%	(LIB)	91%	(LIB)	87%	(LIB)
	2%	(CONS)	9%	(CONS)	13%	(CONS)

Key Votes

1) Reagan 81 Budget	AGN	5) Incr SS Rtmt Age	AGN	9) Poor Pay Food Stamps —
2) Reagan 81 Tax Cut	AGN	6) Saudi AWACS Sale —		10) Ban Crt Busing Order AGN
3) Bal Budget Amend	AGN	7) $ for MX Missile	AGN	11) Auto Local Content FOR
4) Gas & Road Tax	FOR	8) Nerve Gas Prod	AGN	12) Nuclear Arms Freeze FOR

Election Results

1982 general	Gus Savage (D)	140,827	(87%)	(*)
	Kevin Walker Sparks (R)	20,670	(13%)	($0)
1982 primary	Gus Savage (D)	24,777	(39%)	
	Eugene M. Barnes (D)	22,466	(35%)	($20,746)
	Monica Faith Stewart (D)	12,950	(20%)	($30,076)
	Bruce Crosby (D)	3,740	(6%)	
1980 general	Gus Savage (D)	129,771	(88%)	($80,213)
	Marsha A. Harris (R)	17,428	(12%)	($11,033)

Campaign Contributions and Expenditures

*As of May 1, 1983, the candidate has failed to file year end reports with the Federal Election Commission.

THIRD DISTRICT

The 3d congressional district of Illinois consists of the southwest edge of the city of Chicago and Cook County suburbs adjacent to the south and west. It is an artfully designed district, one intended to reelect the current congressman, Democrat Marty Russo. The Chicago portion of the district has 40% of its people and in 1980 was 96% white, although the area just to the east is heavily black; the district line, running near Western Avenue and the Rock Island tracks, was the 1980 boundary of westward black expansion. Most of the people here are of Irish or Eastern European descent, family-oriented but with their children grown up now in many cases; they cover a broad economic spectrum, from the gritty neighborhoods around Midway Airport to the mansions and Prairie architecture homes of Beverly Hills and Morgan Park, old rich neighborhoods that sit atop one of Chicago's few perceptible hills.

This part of Chicago is only marginally Democratic in close state elections; the old ancestral Democratic preference is balanced by a dislike of programs that seem overly generous to the poor and by fear of the heavily Democratic blacks. But these areas provide solid support for local Democrats, like Marty Russo, whose politics is geared to their attitudes. The 1980s will probably see blacks move into these neighborhoods in large numbers, as they moved into the neighborhoods just to the east in the 1970s. But the district lines seem drawn adroitly enough that such movement will only increase Democratic margins in the general election without adding enough black votes to provide a basis for a challenge of a white candidate like Russo in the primary.

The suburban part of the district can be divided into two sections. Running west along 95th Street are predominantly white collar suburbs, centered on Oak Lawn, a comfortable but not lavish product of the 1950s populated mainly by descendants of the immigrants who lived on Chicago's South Side. To the south, from Blue Island to Markham, are suburbs with a little more of a working class cast to them, and with significant black populations in some cases. The 3d also swings east to take in parts of the comfortable white collar suburbs of Homewood and South Holland (Russo's district residence). The suburban territory goes Republican in close statewide elections. But Russo has represented much of this territory since 1974, and has worked it hard, and he seems in little jeopardy.

Russo is part of the 1974 class of Democrats, but he is less typical of them than he is of traditional Chicago area politicians. His earlier career was in patronage jobs, and he came to Congress less interested in any abstract issue than he did in making a successful career. He has. He has attracted particular notice as a young Democrat with whom important interests usually associated with Republicans can and do work. As a member of the Energy and Commerce Committee, he cast decisive votes against the Carter administration's hospital cost containment proposals. He was the leader in the House of the move to veto Federal Trade Commission regulation of funeral homes. He is a close ally of Ways and Means Chairman Dan Rostenkowski, and in 1979 won a seat on that committee. He supports his chairman and has a seat on the Select Revenue Measures Subcommittee—the body which must pass on all the specialized tax legislation, and tax breaks, sought by interests all over the country. Russo's willingness to listen to various pleas has probably helped him collect the $200,000-plus campaign treasuries he has every two years.

As a result, Russo has deterred serious opposition. Although he took this seat from a Republican congressman, he has not had serious opposition since 1976. It appears likely that he will remain an important—for many, a strategic—member of Congress through the 1980s.

The People Pop. 1980: 519,040, dn. 2% 1970–80; voting age pop. 379,396; 5% Black, 3% Span. orig. 25% housing units rented. Median owner $55,600; renter $238. Households: 78% family, 39% with children, 65% married couples.

Presidential Vote

1980	Reagan (R) .... NA	
	Carter (D) .... NA	
	Anderson (I) .... NA	

Rep. Martin A. (Marty) **Russo** (D) Elected 1974; b. Jan. 23, 1944, Chicago; home, S. Holland; De Paul U., B.S. 1965, J.D. 1967; Roman Catholic.

Career Law Clerk for IL Appellate Ct. Judge John V. McCormack, 1967–68; Cook Cnty. Asst. States Atty., 1971–73; Practicing atty., 1974.

Offices 206 CHOB, 202-225-5736. Also 12526 S. Ashland Ave., Calumet Park 60643, 312-353-0439.

Committee *Ways and Means* (16th). Subcommittees: Health; Select Revenue Measures; Trade.

Group Ratings

	ADA	ACLU	COPE	CFA	LCV	LWV	NTU	NSI	COC	ACA	CSFC
1982	80	42	77	80	90	58	55	30	27	13	34
1981	55	—	76	71	86	—	72	—	25	26	42
1980	50	23	68	64	72	40	44	10	66	39	47

National Journal Ratings

	Economic		Foreign		Cultural	
1982	62%	(LIB)	78%	(LIB)	71%	(LIB)
	38%	(CONS)	21%	(CONS)	29%	(CONS)
1981	65%	(LIB)	76%	(LIB)	61%	(LIB)
	34%	(CONS)	23%	(CONS)	39%	(CONS)

Key Votes

1) Reagan 81 Budget AGN	5) Incr SS Rtmt Age AGN	9) Poor Pay Food Stamps AGN
2) Reagan 81 Tax Cut AGN	6) Saudi AWACS Sale AGN	10) Ban Crt Busing Order FOR
3) Bal Budget Amend AGN	7) $ for MX Missile AGN	11) Auto Local Content FOR
4) Gas & Road Tax —	8) Nerve Gas Prod AGN	12) Nuclear Arms Freeze FOR

Election Results

1982 general	Martin A. (Marty) Russo (D)	137,391	(74%)	($270,600)
	Richard D. Murphy (R)	48,268	(26%)	($0)
1982 primary	Martin A. (Marty) Russo (D)	54,646	(100%)	
1980 general	Martin A. (Marty) Russo (D)	137,283	(69%)	($211,989)
	Lawrence C. Sarsoun (R)	61,955	(31%)	($0)

Campaign Contributions and Expenditures

1981-82		Direct Cont. 81-82		PACS brkdwn			
Receipts	$270,648	Indiv	$132,843				
Expend.	$270,600	Party	$1,075	Agr	$11,000	Ideo	$850
Unspent	$137	PACS	$135,139	Bus	$61,465	Lbr	$51,774
				Hlth	$8,400	Prof	$1,200

FOURTH DISTRICT

The 4th congressional district is the southern edge of metropolitan Chicago, where the suburbs generated by the growth of the great city began to thin out and the vast prairies, punctuated by neat rectangular-block towns, begin. The eastern end of the district is anchored in suburbs directly south of Chicago's Lake Calumet industrial district: Calumet City, Lansing, Chicago Heights. In the center, west and south of the Cook County line, is Joliet; in the northwest, Aurora. Joliet and Aurora are urban centers with histories of their own: Downstate cities, really, the market towns for the surrounding rich farmland. Settled by Yankees and Germans, they are hard working and prosperous, orderly and pious. Historically they saw Chicago—with its rapid, disorderly growth, its tolerance of graft and vice, its vast peasant immigrant populations—as a cultural enemy; and, as solid Republicans, after the New Deal era they saw Democratic Chicago as a political enemy as well.

Joliet and Aurora are now part of the Chicago metropolitan area, as much as Chicago Heights. People commute back and forth from these towns to Cook County and even the Loop; they tune into Chicago radio and TV stations. Politically, they are part of a vast suburban belt which outvotes Democratic Chicago and almost always delivers solid Republican margins. Demographically, the 4th is out on Chicago's frontier, a district where 46% of the households contain children (one of the highest figures in Illinois) and 66% contain married couples (ditto).

The relative youth of the district may help to explain the 1982 election result. This was drawn as a Republican district, and contained the homes of two incumbent Republican congressmen. One, Edward Derwinski, had 24 years of seniority and cut an important figure in Washington. As ranking member of the Post Office and Civil Service Committee, he put together the compromise civil service reform legislation of 1978; as second ranking Republican on the Foreign Affairs Committee, he worked hard to build consensus for a bipartisan, anti-Communist foreign policy. Derwinski's base was in southern Cook County; more of the new 4th district had been represented by George O'Brien of Joliet, when it had been part of the old 17th. A pleasant man, and a friend of Derwinski, O'Brien was a quiet junior member of the Appropriations Committee, and not a major force on legislation.

Yet Derwinski, who was both younger and more senior, lost. Still only in his 50s, he had gotten out of the habit of campaigning because he had had a safe district so long; his gruff manner and pithy replies were not well suited to the politics of the television age. O'Brien won 83% and a 10,000-vote margin in Joliet and Will County; Derwinski won 72% and an 8,000-vote margin in Cook County. The general election was anticlimactic. O'Brien at 65 won another term, although by a smaller margin than anyone anticipated; Derwinski, in early 1983, was nominated to be Counselor of the State Department.

The People Pop. 1980: 519,049, up 13.9% 1970–80; voting age pop. 356,524; 87% Black, 5% Span. orig., 1% Asian orig. 27% housing units rented. Median owner $54,400; renter $221. Households: 79% family, 46% with children, 66% married couples.

Presidential Vote

1980	Reagan (R)	NA
	Carter (D)	NA
	Anderson (I)	NA

Rep. George M. O'Brien (R) Elected 1972; b. June 17, 1917, Chicago; home, Joliet; Northwestern U., A.B. 1939, Yale U., J.D. 1947; Roman Catholic.

Career Air Force, WWII; Will Cnty. Bd. of Sprvsrs., 1956–64; Practicing atty., 1966-74; IL House of Reps., 1971–72.

Offices 2262 RHOB, 202-225-3635. Also 101 N. Joliet St., Joliet 60431, 815-740-2040.

Committee *Appropriations* (11th). Subcommittees: Commerce, Justice, State and Judiciary; Labor-Health and Human Sevices-Education.

Group Ratings

	ADA	ACLU	COPE	CFA	LCV	LWV	NTU	NSI	COC	ACA	CSFC
1982	25	21	21	30	33	25	61	88	63	67	53
1981	20	—	18	50	14	—	49	—	94	65	60
1980	22	27	23	21	28	38	55	75	86	77	64

National Journal Ratings

	Economic		Foreign		Cultural	
1982	44%	(LIB)	47%	(LIB)	1%	(LIB)
	56%	(CONS)	52%	(CONS)	99%	(CONS)
1981	35%	(LIB)	61%	(LIB)	33%	(LIB)
	64%	(CONS)	39%	(CONS)	67%	(CONS)

Key Votes

1) Reagan 81 Budget	FOR	5) Incr SS Rtmt Age	FOR	9) Poor Pay Food Stamps	FOR
2) Reagan 81 Tax Cut	FOR	6) Saudi AWACS Sale	FOR	10) Ban Crt Busing Order	FOR
3) Bal Budget Amend	FOR	7) $ for MX Missile	AGN	11) Auto Local Content	FOR
4) Gas & Road Tax	FOR	8) Nerve Gas Prod	FOR	12) Nuclear Arms Freeze	AGN

Election Results

1982 general	George M. O'Brien (R)	79,842	(55%)	($309,393)
	Michael A. Murer (D)	66,323	(45%)	($81,840)
1982 primary	George M. O'Brien (R)	19,353	(53%)	
	Edward J. Derwinski (R)	17,292	(47%)	($146,705)
1980 general	Edward J. Derwinski (R)	152,377	(68%)	($108,597)
(IL 4)	Richard S. Jalovec (D)	71,814	(32%)	($63,686)
1980 general	George M. O'Brien (R)	125,806	(66%)	($132,147)
(IL 17)	Michael A. Murer (D)	65,305	(34%)	($29,724)

Campaign Contributions and Expenditures

1981-82		Direct Cont. 81-82		PACS brkdwn			
Receipts	$293,839	Indiv	$140,259	Agr	$550	Ideo	$5,500
Expend.	$309,393	Party	$19,434	Bus	$79,925	Lbr	$2,000
Unspent	$1,912	PACS	$109,155	Hlth	$12,275	Prof	$625
		Cand	$8,800				

FIFTH DISTRICT

The South Branch of the Chicago River is the site of one of western civilization's astonishing engineering feats: here in 1900 the course of the river was turned backward, so that sewage flowed Downstate through a canal rather than out into Lake Michigan. The river wards—the old name for the neighborhoods along the river—performed an historic function as important for Chicago as the Sanitary and Ship Canal: they provided a home for successive waves of immigrants from almost every quarter of Europe, the Mediterranean, and, more recently, Latin America. Work could be found nearby on the docks, in warehouses and factories, on the railroads, or on the canal itself. So the Jews came to Maxwell Street, the Czechs to Pilsen, the Irish to Bridgeport, the Italians near Halsted Street, where Jane Addams built Hull House.

These neighborhoods were the real heart of the Chicago Democratic machine. Their residents needed the patronage jobs or even the buckets of coal and turkeys at Christmas the precinct committeeman or ward leader would supply; and in return they were happy to give the Democratic ticket their votes. And more—or so some people charged, since the river wards tended to report their vote totals late, and had a habit of supplying the Democratic ticket with almost exactly the margin it needed to prevail.

Now most of the old residents are gone, particularly on the north side of the river. On the south side Bridgeport and the Back of the Yards (the stockyards) area remain mostly white and Irish; they are still neighborhoods full of young families and freckle-faced kids. And of course Bridgeport's 11th ward was the home of Mayor Richard J. Daley and of a succession of mayors, from 1933 to 1979; part of Daley's strength was that he always remained in Bridgeport, living in a modest bungalow on South Lowe, three blocks from where he was born. Most of the 5th district south of the canal has a distinct Irish flavor; Archer Avenue, a diagonal that heads out toward Midway Airport, was historically the path of outward migration for Chicago's South Side Irish population.

The north side of the river has changed, however—or, rather, is serving again the function it did for so many years. This time the group being welcomed is Chicago's Mexican-Americans. The 5th congressional district, which includes wards on both sides of the river and extends into suburban communities on both sides of the canal out to the Cook County line, has an adult population 21% of Spanish origin in 1980. More strikingly, fully 40% of the children in the district are of Spanish origin; most of the non-Spanish population here is relatively old, and it is not hard to see who will inherit the future. The Mexican-Americans are not an important factor in the 5th district's politics today; the machine is not able to help them get ahead as it did their predecessors, nor do they seem convinced—as the Irish and blacks tended to be—that politics was the way up for them. But by the 1990s it seems clear the Mexican-Americans will transform the politics of the river wards, and no one is sure how.

It could be quite a change, however, since today the 5th district is Chicago's strongest machine area. The current congressman, William Lipinski, was slated by the Cook County Democratic Committee in 1982 and beat the incumbent, John Fary, by a 61%–36% margin in the primary. The surprise is that Fary bothered to run at all: the story goes that he got the seat when he was summoned into Mayor Daley's office, expecting to be told that he was retiring from the legislature, and instead was told he would replace a deceased congressman.

The 5th district, extended into the suburbs in 1982, includes some Republican territory, notably the suburbs of Cicero and Berwyn. Cicero is an oddity, a Bohemian town with an old-fashioned Republican machine, famous for welcoming Al Capone's operations in the 1920s. More recently it made a big point of excluding blacks and was the site of a march by Martin Luther King, Jr. But most of the suburbs along the canal are modest, working class places which do not cast large Republican majorities; and overall the district is safely Democratic. Certainly that is the case in congressional contests. Lipinski was elected by a 3–1 margin and can be assumed to have a safe seat—so long as he continues to be slated.

In Washington, the 5th district's congressmen have taken little legislative initiative. One, John Kluczynski, rose in seniority to chair a highways subcommittee, but he was not an initiator of legislation; Fary was almost inert. Lipinski, younger, politically more adept, may do more; he serves on nuts-and-bolts committees (Public Works, Merchant Marine) which presumably reflect his interests. But no one expects him to do much more than have a solid Democratic voting record.

The People Pop. 1980: 518,971, dn. 2.7% 1970–80; voting age pop. 377,195; 21% Span. orig., 3% Black, 2% Asian orig. 45% housing units rented. Median owner $52,600; renter $161. Households: 73% family, 37% with children, 56% married couples.

Presidential Vote

1980	Reagan (R) .... NA	
	Carter (D) .... NA	
	Anderson (I) .... NA	

Rep. William O. Lipinski (D) Elected 1982; b. Dec. 22, 1937, Chicago; home, Chicago; Loras Col., 1957–58; Roman Catholic.

Career Chicago City Alderman, 1975–83.

Offices 1222 LHOB, 202-225-5701. Also 5832 Archer Ave., Chicago 60638, 312-668-0481.

Committees *Merchant Marine and Fisheries* (18th). Subcommittees: Merchant Marine; Oceanography. *Public Works and Transportation* (27th). Subcommittees: Aviation; Investigations and Oversight; Surface Transportation.

Group Ratings and Key Votes: Newly Elected

Election Results

1982 general	William O. Lipinski (D)	110,351	(75%)	($101,178)
	Daniel J. Partyka (R)	35,970	(25%)	($0)
1982 primary	William O. Lipinski (D)	43,195	(61%)	
	John G. Fary (D)	25,312	(36%)	($69,564)
	One other (D)	2,644	(4%)	
1980 general	John G. Fary (D)	106,142	(80%)	($67,214)
	Robert V. Kotowski (R)	27,136	(20%)	($6,925)

Campaign Contributions and Expenditures

1981-82		Direct Cont. 81-82			PACS brkdwn		
Receipts	$100,866	Indiv	$73,877	Agr	$3,000	Ideo	$1,000
Expend.	$101,178	PACS	$24,484	Bus	$7,100	Lbr	$7,000
Unspent	$313			Hlth	$5,000	Prof	$100

SIXTH DISTRICT

North and west of O'Hare Airport, one to two dozen miles away from Chicago's Loop, is the 6th congressional district of Illinois. This is one of the newer parts of the Chicago metropolitan area. Back in the 1950s, when Mayor Richard J. Daley first got the idea of making O'Hare into one of the major transportation centers in the world, this land was mostly cornfields and apple orchards. There were strings of suburbs along railroad commuter lines: Park Ridge, Des Plaines, and Mount Prospect on the Chicago and Northwestern line running directly northwest from the Loop; Elmhurst, Villa Park, Lombard, and Glen Ellyn on the lines running directly west. In the last 30 years, the land in between has been filled in with one suburb and subdivision after another, and the result is the current 6th district.

This is high income, almost all white, mostly WASP suburbia, and, as one might expect, heavily Republican. It represents an almost entirely new constituency for Congressman Henry Hyde; his old territory, closer in to Chicago, is now split between several Chicago-based districts. But this new constituency has not posed any problems for him.

That is fitting, for Hyde is one of the Republicans' most competent legislators. And, even though he is from the hard-bitten world of Illinois politics, he is also one of the more idealistic. His name is attached to a series of Hyde Amendments, prohibiting the use of federal funds to pay for abortions in various circumstances. Most congressmen regard these measures as a time-wasting diversion from what they consider their real legislative duties. Hyde, who deeply opposes abortion and considers it equivalent to murder, believes the issue goes to the heart of what government is about. He has been ingenious in finding programs to which he can attach his amendments and in devising procedures that require them to be considered. By the early 1980s the House was routinely passing Hyde Amendments; and while some were rejected by the Senate, abortions can no longer be federally financed in the vast majority of cases.

Hyde has been less successful in passing a constitutional amendment to outlaw abortion (or any other amendment, for that matter). He is the ranking Republican on the Civil Liberties Subcommittee, but he is outvoted, by straight party votes, by the chairman, Don Edwards of California. Yet he has also worked amicably enough with Edwards on other issues, most notably on the Voting Rights Act extension in 1981. Hyde originally was against reenacting the important preclearance sections, then changed his mind, after hearing testimony, and finally just barely missed reaching a compromise with Edwards. Hyde also sits on the Banking Committee. He is a man with skills worthy of the House leadership, though he apparently does not have the inclination to seek a top leadership post.

The People Pop. 1980: 519,015, up 19.4% 1970–80; voting age pop. 367,916; 1% Black, 3% Span. orig., 2% Asian orig. 23% housing units rented. Median owner $76,000; renter $293. Households: 79% family, 44% with children, 70% married couples.

Presidential Vote

1980	Reagan (R)	NA
	Carter (D)	NA
	Anderson (I)	NA

Rep. Henry J. Hyde (R) Elected 1974; b. Apr. 18, 1924, Chicago; home, Park Ridge; Georgetown U., B.S. 1947, Loyola U., J.D. 1949; Roman Catholic.

Career Navy, WWII; Practicing atty., 1950–75; IL House of Reps., 1967–74, Major. Ldr., 1971–72.

Offices 2104 LHOB, 202-225-4561. Also Oak Park P.O. Bldg., Rm. 220, 901 Lake St., Oak Park 60301, 312-383-6881.

Committees *Foreign Affairs* (9th). Subcommittees: Western Hemisphere Affairs; International Security and Scientific Affairs. *Judiciary* (3d). Subcommittees: Courts, Civil Liberties, and the Administration of Justice; Monopolies and Commercial Law.

Group Ratings

	ADA	ACLU	COPE	CFA	LCV	LWV	NTU	NSI	COC	ACA	CSFC
1982	15	8	20	33	34	42	77	100	81	86	62
1981	10	—	20	43	36	—	61	—	94	74	67
1980	28	13	26	21	43	60	38	80	79	74	62

National Journal Ratings

	Economic		Foreign		Cultural	
1982	16%	(LIB)	3%	(LIB)	29%	(LIB)
	84%	(CONS)	96%	(CONS)	70%	(CONS)
1981	24%	(LIB)	14%	(LIB)	40%	(LIB)
	68%	(CONS)	84%	(CONS)	60%	(CONS)

Key Votes

1) Reagan 81 Budget	FOR	5) Incr SS Rtmt Age	FOR	9) Poor Pay Food Stamps	AGN
2) Reagan 81 Tax Cut	FOR	6) Saudi AWACS Sale	FOR	10) Ban Crt Busing Order	FOR
3) Bal Budget Amend	FOR	7) $ for MX Missile	FOR	11) Auto Local Content	AGN
4) Gas & Road Tax	—	8) Nerve Gas Prod	FOR	12) Nuclear Arms Freeze	AGN

Election Results

1982 general	Henry J. Hyde (R)	97,918	(68%)	($226,205)
	Le Roy E. Kennel (D)	45,237	(32%)	($52,591)
1982 primary	Henry J. Hyde (R)	32,499	(100%)	
1980 general	Henry J. Hyde (R)	123,593	(67%)	($144,469)
	Mario Raymond Reda (D)	60,951	(33%)	($30,049)

Campaign Contributions and Expenditures

1981-82		Direct Cont. 81-82				PACS brkdwn		
Receipts	$267,971	Indiv	$156,864	Agr	$1,500	Ideo	$7,365
Expend.	$226,205	Party	$10,199	Bus	$49,750	Lbr	$500
Unspent	$110,235	PACS	$70,116	Hlth	$4,100	Prof	$1,750

Indirect Party Expend: $16,978   *Indep Expend:* For: $3,892 (LIFEPAC)

SEVENTH DISTRICT

The Loop is usually the first thing you think of when you think of Chicago. Here, where high-rise construction was pioneered, stand the city's great skyscrapers, including the Sears Tower, the world's tallest. Chicago also means the luxury shopping and office district along North Michigan Avenue; the vast parks (and the railroad lines they all but conceal) along Lake Michigan. This is the face Chicago likes to present to the world: the giant buildings rising where the prairies meet the water, a vast concentration of brains and muscle, the nerve center of the nation.

But not all of Chicago is so dazzling. Behind the lakefront, there is virtually every kind of neighborhood. Directly west of the Loop you find the nation's largest skid row on West Madison and, beyond that, the West Side black ghetto. This is much less organized, less of a community, than the South Side; blacks who do well may stay on the South Side, but West Side blacks, when they do well, tend to get out as fast as they can. Farther west more contrasts: cross Austin Boulevard and you come to the suburb of Oak Park, middle class since Ernest Hemingway grew up there 80 years ago, though now integrated. Just beyond is River Forest, with grander streets and bigger lots; both Oak Park and River Forest contain a number of Frank Lloyd Wright houses. Still further are Maywood, a black-majority suburb, and the modest working class suburb of Bellwood.

Taken together, these disparate areas make up Illinois's 7th congressional district. Chicago accounts for three-fourths of its population, and the West Side ghetto for most of that. This is a black majority district, extended into the suburbs for the first time in 1982. That was done for political reasons, to maximize the number of Democratic and black districts; but it also recognized that the Chicago area's blacks are moving, slowly but to an increasing extent, to the suburbs when they want to.

The 7th district is represented in the House by Cardiss Collins. She cuts a different figure than she did when she was first elected in 1973. She was elected to fill the seat vacated when her husband died in a plane crash; he had been a routine machine backer and she was expected to be the same. But as the years went by she became more independent and articulate. She chaired the Black Caucus creditably and chairs a subcommittee with investigative power over housing programs; she also sits on Energy and Commerce, in 1983 the most sought after assignment for House Democrats. While not a legislative powerhouse, she has proved to be far more the cipher that some had expected.

The court-chosen Democratic redistricting plan treated her well, and she seems likely to continue representing the 7th district as long as she wants.

The People Pop. 1980: 519,034, dn. 15.8% 1970–80; voting age pop. 343,964; 60% Black, 4% Span. orig., 2% Asian orig. 57% housing units rented. Median owner $54,500; renter $184. Households: 65% family, 42% with children, 36% married couples.

Presidential Vote

1980	Reagan (R)	NA
	Carter (D)	NA
	Anderson (I)	NA

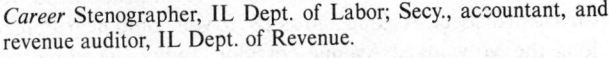

Rep. Cardiss Collins (D) Elected June 5, 1973; b. Sept. 24, 1931, St. Louis, MO; home, Chicago; Northwestern U.; Baptist.

Career Stenographer, IL Dept. of Labor; Secy., accountant, and revenue auditor, IL Dept. of Revenue.

Offices 2264 RHOB, 202-225-5006. Also 230 S. Dearborn St., Chicago 60604, 312-353-5754.

Committees *Energy and Commerce* (16th). Subcommittees: Fossil and Synthetic Fuels; Telecommunications, Consumer Protection and Finance. *Government Operations* (5th). Subcommittee: Government Activities and Transportation (Chairwoman). *Select Committee on Narcotics Abuse and Control* (5th).

Group Ratings

	ADA	ACLU	COPE	CFA	LCV	LWV	NTU	NSI	COC	ACA	CSFC
1982	90	100	93	90	87	83	33	0	33	4	24
1981	85	—	93	93	91	—	35	—	6	5	25
1980	89	93	94	64	81	100	18	13	48	20	23

National Journal Ratings

	Economic		Foreign		Cultural	
1982	92%	(LIB)	96%	(LIB)	81%	(LIB)
	7%	(CONS)	1%	(CONS)	18%	(CONS)
1981	87%	(LIB)	92%	(LIB)	99%	(LIB)
	12%	(CONS)	2%	(CONS)	0%	(CONS)

Key Votes

1) Reagan 81 Budget	AGN	5) Incr SS Rtmt Age	AGN	9) Poor Pay Food Stamps	AGN
2) Reagan 81 Tax Cut	AGN	6) Saudi AWACS Sale	AGN	10) Ban Crt Busing Order	AGN
3) Bal Budget Amend	AGN	7) $ for MX Missile	AGN	11) Auto Local Content	FOR
4) Gas & Road Tax	FOR	8) Nerve Gas Prod	AGN	12) Nuclear Arms Freeze	FOR

Election Results

1982 general	Cardiss Collins (D)	133,978	(86%)	($47,454)
	Dansby (Dan) Cheeks (R)	20,994	(14%)	($2,515)
1982 primary	Cardiss Collins (D)	50,104	(100%)	
1980 general	Cardiss Collins (D)	80,056	(85%)	($19,409)
	Ruth R. Hooper (R)	14,041	(15%)	($7,255)

Campaign Contributions and Expenditures

1981-82		Direct Cont. 81-82				PACS brkdwn		
Receipts	$62,035	Indiv	$23,685	Agr	$4,900	Ideo	$4,360
Expend.	$47,454	PACS	$48,210	Bus	$15,800	Lbr	$18,250
Unspent	$36,171			Hlth	$500	Prof	$750

EIGHTH DISTRICT

The 8th congressional district of Illinois is a large chunk of the North Side of Chicago, with a couple of square miles of suburbs added to meet the one-person-one-vote standard. This is one of the most polyglot places in the nation, a part of Chicago which for more than 100 years has been home to immigrants and refugees from around the world. It is, particularly, a Polish–American district. As long ago as 1876, you could hear Polish spoken more often than English along the Milwaukee Avenue corridor. Today the same is true. In Chicago, ethnic groups tend to move out radial avenues, and the Polish have moved out along Milwaukee Avenue, which parallels the Kennedy Expressway and the North Branch of the Chicago River; Italians tended to move out along Grand Avenue, to the point that there are now more in the suburbs than in the city; Ukrainians have their main churches and community in between. Following roughly in the same footsteps have been Mexican–Americans. The 8th district's adult population in 1980 was 25% of Spanish origin; its under 18 population was 48% of Spanish origin. There are, by the way, virtually no blacks here. The boundary between the 7th and 8th districts pretty closely tracks neighborhood racial barriers, and Mexican–Americans, here as elsewhere, seem to seek out white working class rather than black neighborhoods.

In a comfortable but modest house in the southern part of the 8th district lives 32d Ward Committeeman Dan Rostenkowski, who has also served as the 8th district's congressman for a quarter-century. Rostenkowski has been careful to keep his local party post in a city which considers sending an alderman to Congress a demotion. Rostenkowski holds one of the most important positions in Washington, the chairmanship of the House Ways and Means Committee, and he has been mentioned as a possible speaker of the House. Back home it matters more that he has been mentioned as a possible mayor of Chicago. But at age 56 in 1984, in a city with a new black mayor, Rostenkowski seems certain to focus his ambitions on Capitol Hill—and perhaps to realize them.

Like most Chicago organization Democrats, Rostenkowski is anything but an ideologue on issues. His friends would say he is thoughtful and flexible; his critics would say he is open to persuasion by any high-powered lobbyist. More than accomplishing any one thing, Rostenkowski seems interested in staying on top—in maintaining his institutional position. The ship of state, he seems instinctively to feel, will sail on reasonably well, whatever happens; the important thing is whether you're captain or swabbing the decks. Rostenkowski's gut convictions on issues seem to be rather mild Democratic ones: he would like to help the little guy, but as one of the big guys who runs major institutions, he is also sympathetic to the problems that other big guys face.

But there have been at least changes of emphasis in Rostenkowski's strategies during the Reagan years. In 1981, Rostenkowski seemed most interested in passing his own program, and establishing his institutional role as chairman. So he tried to outbid the Reagan administration for lobbyists' support. The winners in such a bidding contest are those whose support is sought; this was the moment, David Stockman told William Greider, when "the hogs were really feeding." In the end, Rostenkowski was beaten on his first major tax bill out of Ways and Means; but the bill that was passed had far more goodies in it than either the chairman's or the president's original measure.

Rostenkowski heard a lot of criticism of his position from fellow Democrats later, after it became apparent that the tax cuts had not stimulated growth as Reagan predicted. His course in 1982 was to lie low. The Democratic House waited for the Republican Senate to come forward with what was called, for a season, a revenue enhancement bill. This, despite the constitutional requirement that revenue bills originate in the House—one of the legal bases for Ways and Means's institutional power.

By 1983 Rostenkowski's attitude seemed to have changed again. He was involved in the thick of major issues, managing the Social Security rescue measure and supporting a Democratic budget resolution that would require Ways and Means to come up with new taxes. Rostenkowski himself seemed interested in repealing the third year of the president's tax cut and perhaps in repealing income tax indexing; the latter, by eliminating the need for tax cuts in inflationary times, tends to reduce Ways and Means's power.

In general, it seems that Rostenkowski's guiding principles are institutional rather than theoretical or ideological. Some see a conservative pattern in his pre–1980 initiatives: helping kill the Carter administration's hospital cost containment bill (which the hospital lobby opposed; hospital costs since have soared) and supporting some trade restrictions when Chicago area industry is hurt (like Zenith, which used to make TVs). But his institutional interest now is as chairman of Ways and Means; and he seems to have become very responsive to its Democratic members, particularly the subcommittee chairmen. On Social Security, for example, he backed subcommittee Chairman Jake Pickle when he sought and won an increase in the retirement age; this was contrary to the votes of most Democrats, and was definitely not the policy of Tip O'Neill or Claude Pepper. If Rostenkowski continues to follow this course on other important subcommittees, it will mean he will stand behind free trader Sam Gibbons on trade issues, tax reformer Pete Stark on Select Revenue Measures, and Harold Ford on welfare and unemployment compensation. The really big issues, of major tax law, are reserved to the full committee and here presumably Rostenkowski will be expecting some reciprocity from the committee barons he has been backing up. Here his own views are flexible, and he is available to lobbyists; he wants to represent the little guy, but he also wants to nurture the geese that lay the golden eggs.

Rostenkowski could be a very serious candidate for speaker should the post become vacant; in 1983, before Tip O'Neill announced his intention to run for reelection, the scuffling was becoming noticeable. Rostenkowski's core constituency in the Democratic Caucus are the old-line big city representatives from states like Illinois and Pennsylvania, to which he would hope to add Ways and Means members and their allies, pragmatic southerners, and a few liberals. That does not sound like a majority of the Democratic Caucus by itself, which leads one to suspect that he is hoping to profit by any opponent's weaknesses as well as his own strengths. No one questions that Rostenkowski is politically skillful, fully capable of taking command of the floor, a forceful and competent parliamentarian. But is he what House Democrats want as a long-term political strategist? Or as a political symbol? There is something attractive about the way Rostenkowski keeps his roots and his family in Chicago; he boasts that he has spent only a few weekends in Washington in 25 years in Congress. But, as *The Washington Post* reported, Rostenkowski also spends much of the year—even when Congress is in session—roving about the country giving speeches to business and trade groups, for generous honoraria and with sometimes lavish expenses paid, and almost always at a place where he can get in a few rounds of golf. While others are slaving in Washington, the Chairman is conducting business by placing a few phone calls between the first and second nines. No one should begrudge a man of considerable achievements some moments of luxury and recreation. But is Rostenkowski really giving the many serious problems someone in his position must address deep enough consideration?

Rostenkowski holds the safest of seats. The 8th district is, understandably, proud of its congressman and his eminence; so are prominent members of the Polish–American community; so are businessmen in Chicago and leaders of industries all over America who have dealt with him. It is no accident that he amasses and holds onto one of the largest campaign treasuries of any congressman, even though he has never had serious opposition. Should Rostenkowski ever have a serious challenge in the district, he would have unparalleled resources to fight it. But that is unlikely. More likely, Dan Rostenkowski, in his early 70s, will observe the turn of the century as the Chairman of the House Ways and Means Committee.

The People Pop. 1980: 519,034, dn. 9.3% 1970–80; voting age pop. 375,186; 3% Black, 25% Span. orig., 2% Asian orig. 57% housing units rented. Median owner $51,500; renter $174. Households: 68% family, 36% with children, 49% married couples.

Presidential Vote

1980	Reagan (R)	NA
	Carter (D)	NA
	Anderson (I)	NA

Rep. Dan Rostenkowski (D) Elected 1958; b. Jan. 2, 1928, Chicago; home, Chicago; Loyola U., 1948–51; Roman Catholic.

Career Army, Korea; IL House of Reps., 1953–55; IL Senate, 1955–59.

Offices 2111 RHOB, 202-225-4061. Also 2148 N. Damen Ave., Chicago 60647, 312-431-1111.

Committees *Ways and Means* (Chairman). Subcommittee: Trade. *Joint Committee on Taxation* (Chairman).

Group Ratings

	ADA	ACLU	COPE	CFA	LCV	LWV	NTU	NSI	COC	ACA	CSFC
1982	85	50	88	70	73	83	24	60	35	13	31
1981	55	—	88	79	45	—	7	—	26	22	37
1980	50	37	87	79	27	67	17	25	56	17	33

National Journal Ratings

	Economic		Foreign		Cultural	
1982	62%	(LIB)	64%	(LIB)	73%	(LIB)
	38%	(CONS)	36%	(CONS)	26%	(CONS)
1981	65%	(LIB)	59%	(LIB)	62%	(LIB)
	34%	(CONS)	40%	(CONS)	37%	(CONS)

Key Votes

1) Reagan 81 Budget AGN	5) Incr SS Rtmt Age FOR	9) Poor Pay Food Stamps AGN
2) Reagan 81 Tax Cut AGN	6) Saudi AWACS Sale AGN	10) Ban Crt Busing Order AGN
3) Bal Budget Amend AGN	7) $ for MX Missile AGN	11) Auto Local Content AGN
4) Gas & Road Tax FOR	8) Nerve Gas Prod AGN	12) Nuclear Arms Freeze FOR

Election Results

1982 general	Dan Rostenkowski (D)	124,318	(83%)	($248,744)
	Bonnie Hickey (R)	24,666	(17%)	($0)
1982 primary	Dan Rostenkowski (D)	62,017	(91%)	
	Carl C. Lodico (D)	6,281	(9%)	
1980 general	Dan Rostenkowski (D)	98,524	(85%)	($170,056)
	Walter F. Zilke (R)	17,845	(15%)	($0)

Campaign Contributions and Expenditures

1981-82		*Direct Cont. 81-82*				*PACS brkdwn*		
Receipts	$519,438	Indiv	$144,628	Agr	$16,700	Ideo	$7,800
Expend.	$248,744	Party	$100	Bus	$213,650	Lbr	$30,750
Unspent	$494,894	PACS	$290,425	Hlth	$12,050	Prof	$6,450

Indep Expend: Agn: $57,507 (NCPAC)

NINTH DISTRICT

Along Chicago's Lake Shore Drive, overlooking Lake Michigan, are more classic buildings of the International School than are collected anywhere else in the world. Interspersed with older, more traditional and evocative buildings, they present to the world the face Chicago likes to show: affluent, elegant, massive. Behind the apartment towers, however, is another Chicago—messier, grimier, but also more vibrant and various. This is the Chicago of Studs Terkel's Division Street, a city full of life's losers and winners; the Chicago of Saul Bellow, a city of successful small businessmen and irrationally vengeful hoodlums; the Chicago of Nelson Algren, a city of drug addicts and drifters. You can find all these Chicagos just a few short blocks from each other, within a mile or so of the lakefront, where the only threat to this funkiness is the continued march north and west of young affluent Chicagoans in their renovated and restored old houses.

This is the Chicago of Illinois's 9th congressional district which begins at the Near North Side and follows the lakefront, and the varied neighborhoods just to the west, to Chicago's northern city limits and beyond. It is the one large part of the city where the dominant political tone is intellectual and where voters' gut preference is for reform over the machine. Demographically, this is a singles district, more like Manhattan than most parts of the Chicago metropolitan area; fewer than one-fourth of the households contain children, and less than half house families. The dominant ethnic bloc is Jewish: affluent Jews in high rises, older ethnic Jews in the Rogers Park neighborhood near the northern city limit.

They are joined by many Jewish voters in the suburban portions of the 9th district added for the 1982 elections. These include Evanston, which with Northwestern University and a large black community has thrown off a Republican heritage and now votes Democratic; most of Skokie, the most heavily Jewish of Chicago's suburbs, where a handful of Nazis wanted to stage a march; Glenview and Northbrook, more Protestant and Republican, but not enough to tip the district's balance. Altogether, about three-fifths of the district's votes are cast in the city, two-fifths in the suburbs.

The 9th district's congressman, Sidney Yates, has represented the Chicago lakefront wards a long time; he has steered a course between machine and reform by refraining from getting involved in local politics. His interests are national. He chairs the Appropriations Interior Subcommittee, and is counted an advocate of environmental causes; he is particularly active in sponsoring federal support of the arts and humanities. He was in the 1970s an advocate of ending American involvement in Vietnam; he has a solidly liberal voting record on economic issues. He also has long tenure in the Congress. He was first elected to the House in 1948, and could have held the seat for life; he gave it up to run for the Senate in 1962, against Everett Dirksen, and came closer to winning than is generally remembered. Yates then went back to the House in 1964, from which his current seniority dates. Had he not run for the Senate, he would be the number two Democrat on Appropriations today.

For years Yates has had no trouble winning reelection. He was nervous in 1982: he had never before represented the suburbs, and Republican Catherine Bertini was running a well-financed campaign. But Yates won with 67%. He carried Skokie and Evanston easily and did not lose the other suburbs badly; after all, he used to represent a lot of these people when they lived in the city. The question ahead is whether, at age 75 in 1984, he will choose to retire.

The People   Pop. 1980: 519,120, dn. 8.9% 1970–80; voting age pop. 407,592; 9% Black, 8% Span. orig., 5% Asian orig. 60% housing units rented. Median owner $88,100; renter $251. Households: 48% family, 22% with children, 37% married couples.

Presidential Vote

1980	Reagan (R)	83,852	(39%)
	Carter (D)	108,237	(50%)
	Anderson (I)	23,410	(11%)

Rep. Sidney R. Yates (D) Elected 1964; b. Aug. 27, 1909, Chicago; home, Chicago; U. of Chicago, Ph.D. 1931, J.D. 1933; Jewish.

Career Practicing atty.; Asst. Atty. for IL St. Bank Receiver, 1935–37; Asst. Atty. Gen. attached to IL Commerce Comm., 1937–40; Navy, WWII; U.S. House of Reps., 1949–63; Dem. Nominee for U.S. Senate, 1962.

Offices 2234 RHOB, 202-225-2111. Also 230 S. Dearborn St., Chicago 60604, 312-353-4596.

Committee *Appropriations* (7th). Subcommittees: Foreign Operations; Interior (Chairman).

Group Ratings

	ADA	ACLU	COPE	CFA	LCV	LWV	NTU	NSI	COC	ACA	CSFC
1982	75	96	92	100	96	100	18	0	13	6	23
1981	100	—	91	93	100	—	41	—	11	4	27
1980	100	100	83	100	79	100	22	0	48	17	23

National Journal Ratings

	Economic		Foreign		Cultural	
1982	99%	(LIB)	92%	(LIB)	92%	(LIB)
	1%	(CONS)	8%	(CONS)	7%	(CONS)
1981	89%	(LIB)	92%	(LIB)	95%	(LIB)
	3%	(CONS)	2%	(CONS)	1%	(CONS)

Key Votes

1) Reagan 81 Budget	AGN	5) Incr SS Rtmt Age	AGN	9) Poor Pay Food Stamps	AGN
2) Reagan 81 Tax Cut	AGN	6) Saudi AWACS Sale	AGN	10) Ban Crt Busing Order	AGN
3) Bal Budget Amend	AGN	7) $ for MX Missile	AGN	11) Auto Local Content	—
4) Gas & Road Tax	FOR	8) Nerve Gas Prod	AGN	12) Nuclear Arms Freeze	FOR

Election Results

1982 general	Sidney R. Yates (D)	114,083	(67%)	($353,712)
	Catherine Bertini (R)	54,851	(32%)	($305,998)
1982 primary	Sidney R. Yates (D)	36,315	(84%)	
	John B. McCauley (D)	7,113	(16%)	
1980 general	Sidney R. Yates (D)	106,543	(73%)	($63,024)
	John D. Andrica (R)	39,244	(27%)	($12,212)

Campaign Contributions and Expenditures

1981-82		Direct Cont. 81-82		PACS brkdwn			
Receipts	$343,414	Indiv	$270,787	Agr	$—	Ideo	$16,935
Expend.	$353,712	Party	$3,478	Bus	$6,442	Lbr	$35,500
Unspent	$14,230	PACS	$66,678	Hlth	$2,650	Prof	$1,475

TENTH DISTRICT

The North Shore suburbs of Chicago are where the elite of this metropolitan area mostly live. Running north from Evanston, a whole series of towns along Lake Michigan—Wilmette, Winnetka, Glencoe, Highland Park, Lake Forest—each has a slightly different personality and character, but all are basically alike sociologically. Here is where you will find the Chicago area's highest housing prices: up to $181,000 median (according to the 1980 Census) in Lake Forest. Here is also where you will find New Trier Township High School, which has long prided itself as the academically most distinguished public school in the nation. These suburbs were settled long ago, pioneered by riders on one of Chicago's commuter railroad lines. The large houses and shady streets have a comfortable, lived-in look, and not a trace of shabbiness. This is the land of the book and movie *Ordinary People*, a place where pleasant, affluent people live in an environment which seems very far away from the clamorous ethnic neighborhoods of Chicago.

The 10th congressional district of Illinois covers the North Shore, starting above Evanston and reaching north, past the rich suburbs, to the industrial city of Waukegan (once famous as the home of Jack Benny) and the Wisconsin border beyond. The 10th district also goes inland. As you move away from the Lake, housing prices fall, but slowly. Northbrook and

Deerfield, just west of Glencoe and Highland Park, are still among the most affluent of Chicago suburbs. Politically they are if anything more Republican than the lakefront towns; there is less hint here of fashionable liberalism or radical chic, and more unalloyed devotion to the free market system and opposition to the party of the Chicago machine. Farther inland you pass over land that was cornfields not long ago (some still is) to suburbs like Arlington Heights, developed in the 1950s and 1960s on the Northwestern railroad line, and Wheeling, developed in the 1960s and 1970s along Interstate 294. The 10th district is mostly urbanized now, and does not really reach out to the more modest, sparkling clean towns where you meet the mentality of Downstate Illinois; except for Waukegan and the towns around it, this district is very much within the Chicago orbit.

The 10th district was designed by Democrats to force two Republican congressmen to run against each other. Robert McClory had represented Waukegan and some of the inland towns, as well as suburban territory to the west and south, since 1962; he was ranking Republican on the Judiciary Committee. But at age 74 he decided to retire rather than contest a primary. That left the field to John Porter, a junior congressman first elected in a January 1980 special election. Porter had lost much of his district to the 6th, 9th, and 10th districts, and he had to move his district residence north from Evanston. But he had far fewer problems politically than ever before. In 1978 he lost the race to represent the district to Abner Mikva, a liberal Democrat first elected from the South Side of Chicago in 1970 and then the winner, by the narrowest of margins, in the North Shore in 1974, 1976, and 1978. When Mikva was appointed a federal judge in 1979, Porter ran for the seat in the general election and this time won, though by a narrow margin; he prevailed by a wider margin in the 1980 general election. In the course of those three elections he spent more than $1.2 million— an unusually high amount for a Chicago area district. The 10th is one of the few districts here where candidates, in the absence of old-fashioned party organizations and wary of the strength of party loyalty, have felt obliged to advertise on television. In a district shorn of almost all Democratic precincts, Porter did not have such a serious contest in 1982, but the Democratic nature of the year is indicated by the fact that he won with an unspectacular 59%.

Porter on issues is a good match for his constituents: solidly conservative on economic matters, skeptical of foreign involvements and highly touted defense systems, and mildly liberal on cultural issues. He is part of a Republican tradition that is pretty well extinct in most districts: the patrician moderate. In the House, he sits on the Appropriations subcommittees which handle foreign aid, health and welfare programs, and the District of Columbia. He seems in solid shape for reelection during the 1980s.

The People Pop. 1980: 519,660, up 5.7% 1970–80; voting age pop. 368,611; 5% Black, 4% Span. orig., 2% Asian orig. 25% housing units rented. Median owner $92,100; renter $275. Households: 79% family, 45% with children, 69% married couples.

Presidential Vote

1980	Reagan (R)	NA
	Carter (D)	NA
	Anderson (I)	NA

Rep. John E. Porter (R) Elected 1980; b. June 1, 1935, Evanston; home, Evanston; Northwestern U., B.A. 1957, U. of MI, J.D. 1961; Presbyterian.

Career Atty., U.S. Dept. of Justice, 1961–63; Practicing atty., 1963–80; IL House of Reps., 1972–78.

Offices 1530 LHOB, 202-225-4835. Also Evanston Civic Cntr., 2100 Ridge Ave., Evanston 60204, 312-491-0101; and Des Plaines Civic Cntr., 1420 Miner St., Des Plaines 60016, 312-655-8787.

Committee *Appropriations* (20th). Subcommittees: Commerce, Justice, State and Judiciary; Labor-Health and Human Services-Education; Legislative.

Group Ratings

	ADA	ACLU	COPE	CFA	LCV	LWV	NTU	NSI	COC	ACA	CSFC
1982	35	50	15	20	59	67	69	67	81	70	53
1981	30	—	12	50	64	—	67	—	89	63	63
1980	39	—	20	21	74	50	—	100	71	71	67

National Journal Ratings

	Economic		Foreign		Cultural	
1982	18%	(LIB)	63%	(LIB)	54%	(LIB)
	82%	(CONS)	37%	(CONS)	46%	(CONS)
1981	24%	(LIB)	75%	(LIB)	55%	(LIB)
	68%	(CONS)	25%	(CONS)	45%	(CONS)

Key Votes

1) Reagan 81 Budget	FOR	5) Incr SS Rtmt Age	FOR	9) Poor Pay Food Stamps	FOR
2) Reagan 81 Tax Cut	FOR	6) Saudi AWACS Sale	AGN	10) Ban Crt Busing Order	FOR
3) Bal Budget Amend	FOR	7) $ for MX Missile	AGN	11) Auto Local Content	AGN
4) Gas & Road Tax	FOR	8) Nerve Gas Prod	AGN	12) Nuclear Arms Freeze	FOR

Election Results

1982 general	John E. Porter (R)	90,750	(59%)	($296,156)
	Eugenia S. Chapman (D)	63,115	(41%)	($151,512)
1982 primary	John E. Porter (R)	34,591	(100%)	
1980 general	John E. Porter (R)	137,707	(61%)	($650,248)
	Robert A. Weinberger (D)	89,008	(39%)	($263,680)

Campaign Contributions and Expenditures

1981-82		Direct Cont. 81-82		PACS brkdwn			
Receipts	$298,966	Indiv	$184,294	Agr	$550	Ideo	$7,100
Expend.	$296,156	Party	$11,633	Bus	$75,336	Lbr	$—
Unspent	$3,313	PACS	$92,607	Hlth	$5,600	Prof	$900

Indirect Party Expend: $23,364

ELEVENTH DISTRICT

The 11th congressional district of Illinois is the northwest corner of Chicago and adjacent suburban areas. Demographically, the 11th is a family district, but one without children; this is a part of the metropolitan area filled with older people, their children grown and gone. People here are in a sense in transit: from the old ethnic neighborhoods where so many of them grew up, halfway out the radial highways to the new suburban neighborhoods where so many of their children live. At its southeastern corner the 11th contains Chicago's new Greek Town, where its Greek community moved after its old neighborhood was torn down. The northeastern corner, around Rogers Park, is a mostly Jewish neighborhood, though its longtime ward committeeman is Neil Hartigan, now Illinois's attorney general, a machine politician of Irish descent.

The 11th's northern suburbs, Lincolnwood and a part of Skokie, are mostly Jewish, and the highest income and most Democratic part of the district; to the west are Polish and Italian and Irish and German neighborhoods and suburbs. The half of the district west of North Cicero Avenue is no longer reliably Democratic in statewide contests, though all the wards here have gotten into the habit of electing Democratic aldermen. The western suburbs, regular rectangular-blocked old neighborhoods south of O'Hare Airport, interspersed with factories and warehouses, have an increasing Mexican–American population; the Mexicans are in effect following the footsteps of Italians and other earlier immigrant groups. These suburbs, historically Republican, have been trending Democratic.

But generally the political tradition in the 11th district is Democratic: many immigrants and their children bought houses in these modest but pleasant neighborhoods with their hard-won savings. Now, while they may find the Republicans more attractive in national and state contests, they stay Democratic when the issue is local and the real struggle is between yeasty Chicago and the flat plains beyond.

The congressman from the 11th district, Frank Annunzio, has the look of a hack politician: he talks like you would imagine an old ward politician from Chicago would talk; all his political ties and loyalties are to the old machine; he seems possessed by no overriding ideology. Yet on the Banking Committee and the subcommittee he chairs, Annunzio has not always taken the cooperative, cozy approach toward the businesses he is regulating; he has instead been something of a consumer advocate. His greatest moment in the limelight, so far, was when he killed a measure that would have allowed Armand Hammer's Occidental Petroleum to make money minting Olympic commemorative coins; and if that sounds like a trivial matter, the fact is that there are very few politicians in any country who have succeeded in frustrating one of Dr. Hammer's projects.

Ralph Nader's followers come by their consumerism by abstract economic analysis and an idealized love of the average person; Annunzio, needless to say, comes by his positions quite differently. He represents, in effect, not the Loop or even City Hall, but the neighborhoods of Chicago. In banking that has peculiar results, since Illinois allows banks to have only one office. The big banks in the Loop don't have branches in the 11th district; banks and S&Ls out there are locally owned and managed. Some reformers charge that these little local banks give their depositors lower interest and fewer services than big banks would; one suspects, however, that they also are more willing to grant loans to people with roots in the neighborhood.

Annunzio is also the second ranking Democrat on the House Administration Committee, a likely future chairman, and therefore a potential power on issues of campaign finance reform. He is not, as his background suggests, an early backer of the public financing of congressional elections or other major changes that have been proposed.

The People Pop. 1980: 518,995, dn. 7.8% 1970–80; voting age pop. 409,539; 5% Span. orig., 4% Asian orig. 39% housing units rented. Median owner $69,400; renter $239. Households: 72% family, 30% with children, 59% married couples.

Presidential Vote

1980	Reagan (R)	NA
	Carter (D)	NA
	Anderson (I)	NA

Rep. Frank Annunzio (D) Elected 1964; b. Jan. 12, 1915, Chicago; home, Chicago; De Paul U., B.S. 1940, M.A. 1942; Roman Catholic.

Career Pub. sch. teacher, 1935–43; Legis. and Ed. Dir., United Steel Workers of Amer., Chicago, Calumet Region Dist. 31, 1943–49; Dir., IL Dept. of Labor, 1949–52; Private businessman, 1952–64.

Offices 2303 RHOB, 202-225-6661. Also 4747 W. Peterson Ave., Su. 201, Chicago 60646, 312-736-0700.

Committees Banking, Finance and Urban Affairs (4th). Subcommittees: Consumer Affairs and Coinage (Chairman); Financial Institutions Supervision, Regulation and Insurance; General Oversight and Renegotiation. *House Administration* (2d). Subcommittees: Accounts (Chairman); Personnel and Police.

Group Ratings

	ADA	ACLU	COPE	CFA	LCV	LWV	NTU	NSI	COC	ACA	CSFC
1982	65	50	91	100	69	58	3	70	24	23	34
1981	45	—	91	79	50	—	3	—	21	25	42
1980	56	27	79	79	26	56	13	33	69	18	31

National Journal Ratings

	Economic		Foreign		Cultural	
1982	74%	(LIB)	45%	(LIB)	63%	(LIB)
	25%	(CONS)	55%	(CONS)	36%	(CONS)
1981	71%	(LIB)	46%	(LIB)	60%	(LIB)
	28%	(CONS)	52%	(CONS)	40%	(CONS)

Key Votes

1) Reagan 81 Budget	AGN	5) Incr SS Rtmt Age	FOR	9) Poor Pay Food Stamps	AGN
2) Reagan 81 Tax Cut	AGN	6) Saudi AWACS Sale	AGN	10) Ban Crt Busing Order	FOR
3) Bal Budget Amend	AGN	7) $ for MX Missile	AGN	11) Auto Local Content	FOR
4) Gas & Road Tax	—	8) Nerve Gas Prod	FOR	12) Nuclear Arms Freeze	FOR

Election Results

1982 general	Frank Annunzio (D)	134,755	(73%)	($112,371)
	James F. Moynihan (R)	50,967	(27%)	($26,750)
1982 primary	Frank Annunzio (D)	55,433	(100%)	
1980 general	Frank Annunzio (D)	121,166	(70%)	($59,436)
	Michael R. Zanillo (R)	52,417	(30%)	($0)

Campaign Contributions and Expenditures

1981-82		Direct Cont. 81-82		PACS brkdwn			
Receipts	$131,216	Indiv	$69,755	Agr	$2,000	Ideo	$100
Expend.	$112,371	Party	$100	Bus	$20,050	Lbr	$16,200
Unspent	$98,257	PACS	$39,650	Hlth	$1,000	Prof	$—

TWELFTH DISTRICT

Somewhere in the Chicago metropolitan area there is an invisible line, between the two different Chicagos. One is the Chicago dominated by blacks and the products of the vast immigration of 1840-1924: a Chicago where loyalty to ethnic group, church (usually the Catholic Church, but often with an ethnic prefix), and party (almost always the Democratic Party, but occasionally, as in Cicero, the Republicans) are taken for granted. This Chicago is a gritty city, where occasional acts of cheerfulness and courtesy lighten up days otherwise as cold and behavior as impersonal as the Chicago sky is gray during most of the winter. This part of Chicago sees the city not only as the center of life, but as the whole of it; people for whom there is not much life outside of Chicago and perhaps a little beach house somewhere on Lake Michigan.

The other Chicago is the Chicago of the Great Plains, a white Anglo-Saxon Protestant Chicago, a place whose residents are products of the first great wave of immigration to America. The tone of this Chicago is cheerier, its streets and highways cleaner and neater, its daily life somehow free from evidence of unpleasantness and deprivation. This is the Chicago of dozens of suburban and Downstate towns, all laid out on neat geometric grids on the flatness of the prairie, the Chicago which extends hundreds of miles out from the city and seems separate from it. People in this Chicago think of themselves as the typical Americans, and their geographical vision takes in the vast plains. This is the Chicago of Colonel McCormick's *Chicago Tribune* and Don McNeill's *Breakfast Club,* of Paul Harvey and Sears Roebuck catalogues. It is an optimistic world which knows personal, but not social, tragedy; a world in which all things are possible and most things are for the best. Ronald Reagan grew up in Downstate Illinois within the orbit of this kind of Chicago, and it can be seen in his optimism today. His migration to southern California, incidentally, is not atypical: you can see in the geometric grids and Republican voting patterns of Orange County or Phoenix almost precise replicas of the grids and patterns in Chicago's suburban "collar counties," transported out on the Atchison, Topeka & Santa Fe or U.S. 66 from their beginnings in Chicago's Loop to the vast and once empty southwest.

The line between these two Chicagos passes somewhere near the southern end of the 12th congressional district of Illinois. This is part of metropolitan Chicago, beginning at the northwest corner of Cook County, taking in the western half of Lake County and most of McHenry County just to the west. And it contains many descendants of the second wave of immigrants, moved out from Chicago one or two generations ago. But the cultural style of this area is very much that of the second, Great Plains Chicago.

That is apparent from the 12th district's voting habits, which are very much Republican. This is not just a function of income, though this area does have one of the highest income levels of any district in the Midwest or the nation; but the 10th district, along Lake Michigan, has higher housing prices and lower Republican percentages. The difference is cultural instead. The North Shore suburbanites are part of an urbane tradition, lineal descendants of the merchant princes who amassed great fortunes and patronized advanced arts and letters. The suburbanites inland are descendants of small town burghers, who uphold the traditions and observe the courtesies that are the fabric of life in cozy, affluent communities.

The 12th district is represented in Congress by a man who personifies many of the qualities of the kind of Chicago he represents. Philip Crane is the son of Dr. George Crane, who broadcast a medical advice radio program on Chicago's WGN for years and was a pillar of conservative thought; he raised an attractive family which includes two congressmen from Illinois and a nearly successful candidate in Indiana. Phil Crane is handsome, congenial, loyal to his beliefs but full of good-hearted camaraderie. He seems a kind of innocent in Washington. In an era when others of similar views have shaped national policies, he continues as a spokesman—and little else. He was one of the first announced presidential candidates for 1980, and one of the least successful; his strategy depended on picking up support when the Reagan candidacy faded, but even when it looked, after the Iowa caucuses, that that might happen, Crane made little headway. He has had a little more influence as head of the American Conservative Union, but only a little. The problem is that, for all his other assets, Phil Crane does not seem to have a particularly original mind. Although he is a Ph.D. he represents more a small town attitude that prides itself more on geniality than on intellectual achievement.

In the House Crane is a member of the Ways and Means Committee, but does not play an important part in its deliberations. His vote is predictable, and his arguments change few minds. In the 12th district, he is reelected by huge margins in what are for all practical purposes uncontested elections. Having emerged strong from redistricting, Crane seems assured of another decade in Congress.

The People   Pop. 1980: 519,181, up 39% 1970–80; voting age pop. 345,939; 1% Black, 3% Span. orig., 1% Asian orig. 24% housing units rented. Median owner $71,900; renter $300. Households: 79% family, 47% with children, 69% married couples.

Presidential Vote

1980	Reagan (R)	NA
	Carter (D)	NA
	Anderson (I)	NA

Rep. Philip M. Crane (R) Elected Nov. 25, 1969; b. Nov. 3, 1930, Chicago; home, Mt. Prospect; De Pauw U., Hillsdale Col., B.A. 1952, IN U., M.A. 1961, Ph.D. 1963, U. of MI, U. of Vienna; Methodist.

Career Instructor, IN U., 1960–63; Asst. Prof., Bradley U., 1963–67; Dir. of Schools, Westminster Acad., 1967–68.

Offices 1035 LHOB, 202-225-3711. Also 1450 S. New Wilke Rd., Su. 101, Arlington Heights 60005, 312-394-0790.

Committee *Ways and Means* (5th). Subcommittees: Social Security; Trade.

Group Ratings

	ADA	ACLU	COPE	CFA	LCV	LWV	NTU	NSI	COC	ACA	CSFC
1982	0	4	7	10	26	27	98	100	85	96	91
1981	10	—	7	36	30	—	99	—	89	100	90
1980	6	33	5	7	20	0	87	100	64	95	92

National Journal Ratings

	Economic		Foreign		Cultural	
1982	0%	(LIB)	4%	(LIB)	25%	(LIB)
	98%	(CONS)	92%	(CONS)	74%	(CONS)
1981	24%	(LIB)	14%	(LIB)	0%	(LIB)
	68%	(CONS)	86%	(CONS)	99%	(CONS)

Key Votes

1) Reagan 81 Budget	FOR	5) Incr SS Rtmt Age	FOR	9) Poor Pay Food Stamps	FOR
2) Reagan 81 Tax Cut	FOR	6) Saudi AWACS Sale	—	10) Ban Crt Busing Order	FOR
3) Bal Budget Amend	FOR	7) $ for MX Missile	FOR	11) Auto Local Content	AGN
4) Gas & Road Tax	AGN	8) Nerve Gas Prod	FOR	12) Nuclear Arms Freeze	AGN

Election Results

1982 general	Philip M. Crane (R)	86,487	(66%)	($334,720)
	Daniel G. DeFosse (D)	40,108	(31%)	($3,881)
1982 primary	Philip M. Crane (R)	39,073	(100%)	
1980 general	Philip M. Crane (R)	185,080	(74%)	($191,160)
	David McCartney (D)	64,729	(26%)	($9,424)

Campaign Contributions and Expenditures

1981-82		Direct Cont. 81-82				PACS brkdwn		
Receipts	$379,289	Indiv	$329,662	Agr	$—	Ideo	$250
Expend.	$334,720	Party	$8,930	Bus	$—	Lbr	$—
Unspent	$201,592	PACS	$250	Hlth	$—	Prof	$—

THIRTEENTH DISTRICT

The radial avenues that fan out from Chicago's Loop are the routes taken by the city's various ethnic groups—immigrants who came to Chicago and their descendants who have moved up and out as they prospered over the years. One of these routes runs almost straight west from the Loop, and the group that has trod it include many of the Chicago area's white Anglo-Saxon Protestants. From anonymous clerks in Loop offices to the aristocratic Colonel Robert Rutherford McCormick, proprietor of the *Chicago Tribune*, they have made their way westward, past the Chicago city limits and the Bohemian suburbs of Cicero and Berwyn, to the westernmost suburbs of Cook County and past to almost entirely affluent DuPage County.

This is the land of Illinois's 13th congressional district. It begins, if you start nearest to Chicago, in the turn-of-the-century suburb of Riverside; with its curved streets and Frank Lloyd Wright houses, it was an elite place in the days of *art nouveau* and still is today. Farther west are affluent railroad commuter suburbs: the string of LaGrange, Western Springs, and Hinsdale, more middle income Downers Grove, and the newer suburb of Oak Brook which is the headquarters of McDonald's, among other enterprises. The boundaries of the 13th district were carefully crafted to exclude Democratic suburbs (the Democrats who drew the plan wanted them to pad the Chicago-based Democratic districts); the district has a salient into southwest Cook County, in somewhat different socioeconomic country (affluent Irish), to meet the population standard. People from elsewhere may think of Chicago as Democratic, but this part of the Chicago metropolitan area is almost unanimously hostile to the city's Democratic machine, both for its reputed corruption and for its support of big government programs over the years. The 13th is, election after election, one of the most Republican districts in the nation.

It elects a Republican congressman, John Erlenborn, who personifies its views. Like 13th district residents who go into Chicago to work each day, Erlenborn is not afraid to crawl into the lion's mouth: he is ranking Republican on the House Education and Labor Committee. The committee's Democratic majority is solidly pro-organized labor, and Erlenborn's chances of gaining a working majority are slim, short of a Republican takeover of the House. Yet Erlenborn has had his successes on the floor. The common situs picketing and labor law reform bills the AFL-CIO hoped to pass during the Carter administration were killed instead, and do not seem likely to be resurrected soon. Education and Labor's Democrats have had to fight rearguard battles, to protect programs they passed 12 or 20 years ago; Republicans like Erlenborn in the early 1980s have been on the offensive intellectually and politically.

How long that can go on is unclear. But Erlenborn certainly can hold this seat for as long as he likes. Redistricting altered his seat somewhat; he had represented virtually all of DuPage County and none of Cook for 10 years. But he adjusted to the new boundaries easily and had no trouble winning another term in 1982.

The People   Pop. 1980: 519,441, up 33.5% 1970–80; voting age pop. 370,153; 1% Black, 2% Span. orig., 2% Asian orig. 23% housing units rented. Median owner $78,500; renter $291. Households: 79% family, 42% with children, 71% married couples.

Presidential Vote

1980	Reagan (R)	NA
	Carter (D)	NA
	Anderson (I)	NA

Rep. John N. Erlenborn (R) Elected 1964; b. Feb. 8, 1927, Chicago; home, Elmhurst; U. of Notre Dame, 1944, IN St. Teachers Col., 1944–45; Loyola U., LL.B. 1949; Roman Catholic.

Career Navy, WWII; Practicing atty., 1949–50, 1952–64; Asst. States Atty., DuPage Cnty., 1950–52; IL House of Reps., 1957–65.

Offices 2206 RHOB, 202-225-3515. Also DuPage Cnty. Ctr., 421 N. County Farm Rd., Wheaton 60187, 312-668-1417.

Committees *Education and Labor* (Ranking Member). Subcommittee: Labor Standards. *Government Operations* (2d). Subcommittees: Legislation and National Security; Manpower and Housing.

Group Ratings

	ADA	ACLU	COPE	CFA	LCV	LWV	NTU	NSI	COC	ACA	CSFC
1982	10	37	11	0	17	50	83	89	89	100	71
1981	20	—	11	43	38	—	67	—	95	68	66
1980	11	27	11	7	39	56	54	44	90	85	68

National Journal Ratings

	Economic		Foreign		Cultural	
1982	23%	(LIB)	31%	(LIB)	45%	(LIB)
	76%	(CONS)	69%	(CONS)	55%	(CONS)
1981	4%	(LIB)	39%	(LIB)	62%	(LIB)
	79%	(CONS)	60%	(CONS)	38%	(CONS)

Key Votes

1) Reagan 81 Budget	FOR	5) Incr SS Rtmt Age	FOR	9) Poor Pay Food Stamps	FOR
2) Reagan 81 Tax Cut	FOR	6) Saudi AWACS Sale	FOR	10) Ban Crt Busing Order	AGN
3) Bal Budget Amend	FOR	7) $ for MX Missile	FOR	11) Auto Local Content	AGN
4) Gas & Road Tax	FOR	8) Nerve Gas Prod	FOR	12) Nuclear Arms Freeze	AGN

Election Results

1982 general	John N. Erlenborn (R)	113,423	(70%)	($253,855)
	Robert Bily (D)	49,105	(30%)	($0)
1982 primary	John N. Erlenborn (R)	26,380	(62%)	
	Mark Q. Rhodes (R)	10,633	(25%)	($59,195)
	Two others (R)	5,767	(13%)	
1980 general	John N. Erlenborn (R)	202,583	(77%)	($66,340)
	LeRoy E. Kennel (D)	61,224	(23%)	($0)

Campaign Contributions and Expenditures

1981-82		Direct Cont. 81-82		PACS brkdwn			
Receipts	$240,406	Indiv	$74,427	Agr	$1,600	Ideo	$1,300
Expend.	$253,855	Party	$17,174	Bus	$103,074	Lbr	$700
Unspent	$35,734	PACS	$111,444	Hlth	$2,900	Prof	$500

Indirect Party Expend: $4,368

FOURTEENTH DISTRICT

The 14th congressional district is, numerically, the first of the Downstate Illinois districts. Technically, most of its people live in the metropolitan Chicago area, in some of the so-called "collar counties"; in the residents' own minds, however, they are very far indeed from Chicago, in the clean—physically clean, politically clean—and neat towns of Downstate Illinois. The 14th district gets as close as 30 miles to Chicago's Loop, in western DuPage County, where the subdivisions now are almost as built up and densely populated as they are in Cook County. The 14th contains the industrial city of Elgin and part of Aurora, both on the Fox River that runs parallel to Lake Michigan, 35 miles away. Past the Fox River, the subdivisions start thinning out and you see more cornfields; soon the cornfields devoted to producing fresh corn for suburbanites in the summer give way to serious commercial farming operations. By the time you get as far west as DeKalb, site of Northern Illinois University, or as far southwest as the industrial towns of Ottawa, LaSalle, and Peru on the Illinois River, you are unmistakably in the midst of some of the richest and most productively cultivated agricultural land in the world.

You are also in the midst of one of the most heavily Republican belts of territory in the country. Northern Illinois was settled, when Chicago was just one of thousands of frontier villages, by Yankees from Ohio, Indiana, Upstate New York, and New England, by people who formed the heart of the Republican Party from the year it was founded, in 1854, just as they would form the core of the Grand Army of the Republic a few years later. Their descendants remain mostly loyal to the Republican Party today. That does not mean that there are not parts of Illinois, either first settled by southerners or by immigrants from Europe, which are not Democratic; the major example is of course Chicago, and there are much smaller examples, like LaSalle and Ottawa. But on the whole this is Republican territory, and very seldom elects anything but Republican congressmen.

The current representative from the 14th district is Tom Corcoran. He has lived on the margins of politics and business for a long time: he was aide to a top state legislator, head of the Illinois state government office in Washington, a vice president of the Chicago & Northwestern Railroad. In other words, he knows how to put a lobbying operation together. As a member of the House he demonstrated that most visibly on the AT&T issue in 1982. Corcoran is a member of the Energy and Commerce Committee, one of the most prized assignments in the House; although he didn't serve on the Telecommunications Subcommittee, he led the opposition to the AT&T breakup bill for which Chairman Tim Wirth had won unanimous support. AT&T sent letters to its millions of stockholders, asking them to write their congressmen; after the deluge of letters, Wirth withdrew his bill, and Corcoran's bill prevailed.

Up through 1983 Corcoran has been mostly an insider. He did, of course, win elections in the 14th district and its predecessors, but without stimulating much attention elsewhere. But in 1983 Corcoran announced that he might run for Charles Percy's Senate seat, and he even held a fundraiser on the same day Percy had one. President Reagan, supporting all incumbent Republicans, appeared at Percy's fundraiser; Corcoran, faced with such opposition, has to decide whether to run as an insurgent in a state whose Republican as well as Democratic Party has always valued regularity. It would not necessarily be an easy campaign. Percy's popularity is not deep, and he is heartily disliked by many Republican primary voters. But can Corcoran get the enthusiastic support of those conservative voters whose fervor is directed toward cultural issues, when his own record has been concentrated on economic and business issues? Can he raise money from interests who like to be with the winner when Percy is supported by the administration? His decision must be made early: Illinois has a March primary and a filing date in December of the odd-numbered year. If he decides not to make the statewide race, he can easily win reelection in the 14th district.

The People Pop. 1980: 521,909, up 17.7% 1970–80; voting age pop. 367,441; 2% Black, 3% Span. orig., 1% Asian orig. 27% housing units rented. Median owner $63,200; renter $220. Households: 77% family, 44% with children, 67% married couples.

Presidential Vote

1980	Reagan (R)	NA
	Carter (D)	NA
	Anderson (I)	NA

Rep. Tom Corcoran (R) Elected 1976; b. May 23, 1939, Ottawa; home, Ottawa; U. of Notre Dame, B.A. 1961, U. of IL, U. of Chicago, Northwestern U.; Roman Catholic.

Career Army, 1963–65; Staff Dir., IL Senate Pres. Pro Tem, W. Russell Arrington, 1966–69; Dir., State of IL Ofc., Wash., DC, 1969–72; A.A. to IL Senate Pres., William C. Harris, 1972–74; V.P., Chicago and Northwestern Transportation Co., 1974–76.

Offices 2447 RHOB, 202-225-2976. Also 436 N. Lake St., Aurora 60506, 312-897-2220.

Committees *Energy and Commerce* (6th). Subcommittee: Fossil and Synthetic Fuels. *Post Office and Civil Service* (3d). Subcommittee: Postal Operations and Services.

Group Ratings

	ADA	ACLU	COPE	CFA	LCV	LWV	NTU	NSI	COC	ACA	CSFC
1982	0	33	10	0	29	42	85	100	100	87	73
1981	20	—	9	50	37	—	75	—	100	86	67
1980	6	30	5	7	36	11	54	100	83	96	79

National Journal Ratings

	Economic		Foreign		Cultural	
1982	12%	(LIB)	4%	(LIB)	4%	(LIB)
	87%	(CONS)	92%	(CONS)	87%	(CONS)
1981	4%	(LIB)	48%	(LIB)	28%	(LIB)
	79%	(CONS)	51%	(CONS)	72%	(CONS)

Key Votes

1) Reagan 81 Budget	FOR	5) Incr SS Rtmt Age	FOR	9) Poor Pay Food Stamps	FOR
2) Reagan 81 Tax Cut	FOR	6) Saudi AWACS Sale	AGN	10) Ban Crt Busing Order	FOR
3) Bal Budget Amend	FOR	7) $ for MX Missile	FOR	11) Auto Local Content	AGN
4) Gas & Road Tax	FOR	8) Nerve Gas Prod	FOR	12) Nuclear Arms Freeze	AGN

Election Results

1982 general	Tom Corcoran (R)	98,262	(65%)	($332,658)
	Dan McGrath (D)	53,914	(35%)	($28,226)
1982 primary	Tom Corcoran (R)	33,355	(79%)	
	Two others (R)	8,851	(21%)	
1980 general	Tom Corcoran (R)	150,898	(77%)	($97,859)
	John P. Quillin (D)	45,721	(23%)	($0)

Campaign Contributions and Expenditures

1981-82		Direct Cont. 81-82		PACS brkdwn			
Receipts	$276,631	Indiv	$136,471	Agr	$1,300	Ideo	$2,075
Expend.	$332,658	Party	$10,735	Bus	$97,850	Lbr	$5,200
Unspent	$17,644	PACS	$117,023	Hlth	$7,550	Prof	$1,650

FIFTEENTH DISTRICT

South from Chicago the Illinois Central Railroad heads, the roadbed elevating its tracks slightly above the level of some of the nation's richest farmland. If the IC tracks were to lie on the earth below the topsoil, they would be several feet—not inches—lower than they are; so deep is this marvelous black soil. This land was settled, 150 years ago, by Yankee farmers, but it is not really family farm country any more. Cultivating this soil has become a big business: choosing the right crops (soybeans and corn are the current favorites), maximizing yields, selecting proper pesticides, making marketing decisions. Farm owners here typically hold thousands, not hundreds, of acres; while they may lease some to farmers who cannot afford to buy land, they of course keep close control over the major decisions. There is no room for sentimentality in these matters, not with land values (and taxes) rising and interest rates sky high; no room, either, for producing vegetables and fruits for the family to eat. The land is too valuable to be put to anything but its highest economic use.

Secretary of Agriculture John Block comes from this kind of Illinois farm country; it is the heart as well of the constituency of the American Farm Bureau Federation. Block is a Republican and the Farm Bureau usually supports Republicans; both are convinced farming can be more efficient and productive by cutting down on government subsidies and interference and by letting the free market entrepreneurs who own farms make their own decisions. Such thinking commands majority support in the rich prairie lands through which the IC tracks cut, places which have been heavily Republican since the party was founded in 1854.

Such a place is the 15th congressional district of Illinois. It begins not quite 40 miles from Chicago, where the Illinois Central heads toward Kankakee and moves over 150 miles of prairie to the courthouse towns of Lincoln and Monticello. Its largest city is Bloomington, whose best-known citizen was the first Adlai Stevenson, grandfather of the presidential candidate and one-term vice president of the United States; he was a Democrat, but a *laissez faire* Cleveland Democrat, and his philosophy would not be too out of step today from that of many local Republicans.

The congressman from the 15th is Edward Madigan, a successful businessman in Lincoln and onetime Republican state legislator. Madigan saw his district much changed in redistricting (it used to be numbered the 21st), but he did not have much trouble winning in 1982. He has always been personally popular, and has usually run ahead of his majority party.

In the House Madigan is a member of the Energy and Commerce Committee, and ranking Republican on one of the House's most important subcommittees, Health and the Environment. That makes him potentially a pivotal force on such issues as the Clean Air Act, which was supposed to have been revised in 1981; but actually Madigan, whose convictions seem a little more equivocal than those of some of his colleagues, has deferred to the more senior James Broyhill of North Carolina when it comes to leading the subcommittee's Republicans. Madigan himself spends more time on smaller issues, which affect fewer people, but which are nonetheless of great importance—and on which he is more likely to make an original contribution.

The People Pop. 1980: 518,995, up 8.4% 1970–80; voting age pop. 370,509; 5% Black, 1% Span. orig. 29% housing units rented. Median owner $44,900; renter $182. Households: 75% family, 42% with children, 65% married couples.

Presidential Vote

1980	Reagan (R)	139,373	(64%)
	Carter (D)	65,732	(30%)
	Anderson (I)	13,711	(6%)

Rep. Edward R. Madigan (R) Elected 1972; b. Jan. 13, 1936, Lincoln; home, Lincoln; Lincoln Col.; Roman Catholic.

Career Owner, taxi and car leasing co.; Lincoln Bd. of Zoning Appeals; IL House of Reps., 1967–72.

Offices 2312 RHOB, 202-225-2371. Also 202 W. Church St., Champaign 61820, 217-398-5516.

Committees *Agriculture* (Ranking Member). *Energy and Commerce* (3d). Subcommittee: Health and the Environment.

Group Ratings

	ADA	ACLU	COPE	CFA	LCV	LWV	NTU	NSI	COC	ACA	CSFC
1982	20	0	29	20	45	33	64	100	68	76	57
1981	5	—	29	21	15	—	67	—	100	80	67
1980	11	47	23	14	39	38	49	78	68	76	70

National Journal Ratings

	Economic		Foreign		Cultural	
1982	34%	(LIB)	28%	(LIB)	53%	(LIB)
	65%	(CONS)	72%	(CONS)	47%	(CONS)
1981	4%	(LIB)	–%	(LIB)	19%	(LIB)
	79%	(CONS)	–%	(CONS)	81%	(CONS)

Key Votes

1) Reagan 81 Budget	FOR	5) Incr SS Rtmt Age	FOR	9) Poor Pay Food Stamps	FOR
2) Reagan 81 Tax Cut	FOR	6) Saudi AWACS Sale	AGN	10) Ban Crt Busing Order	FOR
3) Bal Budget Amend	FOR	7) $ for MX Missile	FOR	11) Auto Local Content	FOR
4) Gas & Road Tax	FOR	8) Nerve Gas Prod	FOR	12) Nuclear Arms Freeze	AGN

Election Results

1982 general	Edward R. Madigan (R)	105,038	(66%)	($263,859)
	Tim L. Hall (D)	53,303	(34%)	($1,658)
1982 primary	Edward R. Madigan (R)	42,509	(85%)	
	James J. O'Connell (R)	7,661	(15%)	
1980 general	Edward R. Madigan (R)	132,186	(68%)	($148,147)
	Penny L. Severns (D)	63,476	(32%)	($27,577)

Campaign Contributions and Expenditures

1981–82		Direct Cont. 81-82		PACS brkdwn			
Receipts	$275,859	Indiv	$97,632	Agr	$9,100	Ideo	$1,250
Expend.	$263,859	Party	$11,114	Bus	$92,827	Lbr	$7,250
Unspent	$52,290	PACS	$126,090	Hlth	$13,860	Prof	$1,500

SIXTEENTH DISTRICT

The northwest corner of Illinois, which forms its 16th congressional district, is not entirely like the rest of the state. A little like Wisconsin or Iowa, this part of Illinois has a larger number of Scandinavian-Americans and a stronger good government tradition than the patronage-rich precincts of Chicago or the businesslike precincts of the rest of Downstate Illinois. The political tradition here is, if anything, more Republican than that farther Downstate; but it is a Republicanism inclined to maverick tendencies on occasion. The 16th district includes the town of Freeport, site of the most famous of the Lincoln–Douglas debates, and Galena, the home of President U. S. Grant, once a thriving commercial center with its old houses and commercial buildings now being restored. The largest city here is Rockford, which is technically the second largest city in Illinois; but its metropolitan area population is under 300,000, which is pretty insignificant next to Chicago's six million.

The 16th has another distinction, as the birthplace and boyhood home of two of the major candidates in the 1980 presidential election and, quite possibly, the 1984 election as well. Ronald Reagan was born in Tampico and grew up in Dixon, a prosperous county seat on the Rock River; and although he left in 1929 for Eureka College (in the 18th district), the small Illinois towns of his youth still seem very real places for him. The other candidate from this district was John Anderson, who began the race as a Republican and then became an Independent for the general election. Anderson represented the 16th district for 20 years, and during most of that time was a more conventional Republican than his 1980 rhetoric would lead one to expect; he was a staunch supporter of the Vietnam war effort, for example, and he did not dissent much from Republican economic policies.

Where he did differ was on non-economic, cultural issues: campaign finance reform in particular. He displayed an independent streak on Watergate issues as well; he left little doubt that he felt Richard Nixon was guilty of improprieties. This kind of apostasy, and his self-righteousness, nearly got him ousted from the leadership post (chairman of the House Republican Conference) his parliamentary talents earned him. As his chief staffer, incidentally, in 1970 he hired a young divinity student named David Stockman. Anderson's political attitudes pretty well mirrored those of his district, enabling him to win general elections easily; nevertheless, he got into trouble in the Republican primary and won by only 58%–42% in 1978. That ended his appetite for a House career, despite his legislative output (most notably, the 1974 campaign finance law he helped write).

Ironically, the current representative, Lynn Martin, is a Republican in the Anderson mold, an advocate of the Equal Rights Amendment and often a liberal on cultural (but not economic or foreign) issues. But she never aroused the same fury Anderson did, perhaps because of her less stentorian manner, and the same right winger who got 42% of the vote against Anderson in the 1978 primary could manage only 26% in the 1980 primary against her. She had no primary opposition in 1982, and was reelected with a solid 57%, despite the fact that Rockford, hurt by the collapse of the market for agricultural machinery, had one of the highest unemployment rates in the nation.

Martin has two committee assignments of importance not to her district's parochial interests but for national issues. She sits on the Budget Committee where, despite her liberal reputation, she has not dissented notably from Reagan economic policies. And she sits on House Administration, an unimportant housekeeping committee except when issues of campaign finance reform arise. But that may happen in 1983 or 1984, and for those who support public financing of congressional campaigns Martin offers the best chance to get a Republican vote on the key committee.

The People   Pop. 1980: 519,035, up 2.8% 1970–80; voting age pop. 364,824; 4% Black, 2% Span. orig. 28% housing units rented. Median owner $42,300; renter $175. Households: 76% family, 42% with children, 65% married couples.

Presidential Vote

1980	Reagan (R)	117,600	(56%)
	Carter (D)	60,910	(29%)
	Anderson (I)	33,015	(16%)

Rep. Lynn M. Martin (R) Elected 1980; b. Dec. 26, 1939, Chicago; home, Rockford; U. of IL, B.A. 1960; Roman Catholic.

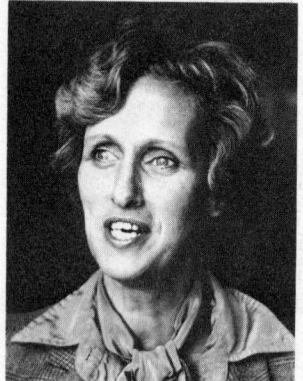

Career High sch. teacher, 1960–69; Mbr., Winnebago Cnty. Bd., 1972–76; IL House of Reps., 1977–79; IL Senate, 1979–81.

Offices 1208 LHOB, 202-225-5676. Also 416 E. State St., Rockford 61114, 815-987-4326; and 320 Ave. A, Sterling 61081, 815-626-1615.

Committees *Budget* (7th). Task Forces: Capital Resources and Development; Education and Employment; Tax Policy. *House Administration* (6th). Subcommittees: Accounts; Contracts and Printing.

Group Ratings

	ADA	ACLU	COPE	CFA	LCV	LWV	NTU	NSI	COC	ACA	CSFC
1982	30	50	26	20	63	45	82	67	59	70	53
1981	30	—	29	57	40	—	84	—	88	65	66

National Journal Ratings

	Economic		Foreign		Cultural	
1982	37%	(LIB)	65%	(LIB)	59%	(LIB)
	63%	(CONS)	34%	(CONS)	40%	(CONS)
1981	4%	(LIB)	41%	(LIB)	63%	(LIB)
	96%	(CONS)	58%	(CONS)	37%	(CONS)

Key Votes

1) Reagan 81 Budget	FOR	5) Incr SS Rtmt Age	FOR	9) Poor Pay Food Stamps	AGN
2) Reagan 81 Tax Cut	FOR	6) Saudi AWACS Sale	AGN	10) Ban Crt Busing Order	—
3) Bal Budget Amend	FOR	7) $ for MX Missile	AGN	11) Auto Local Content	FOR
4) Gas & Road Tax	—	8) Nerve Gas Prod	AGN	12) Nuclear Arms Freeze	FOR

Election Results

1982 general	Lynn M. Martin (R)	89,405	(57%)	($198,810)
	Carl R. (Skip) Schwerdtfeger (D) .	66,877	(43%)	($61,461)
1982 primary	Lynn M. Martin (R)	37,263	(100%)	
1980 general	Lynn M. Martin (R)	132,905	(67%)	($318,791)
	Douglas R. Aurand (D)	64,224	(33%)	($17,257)

Campaign Contributions and Expenditures

1981-82		*Direct Cont. 81-82*			*PACS brkdwn*		
Receipts	$225,565	Indiv	$132,510 (est.)	Agr	$5,450	Ideo	$900
Expend.	$198,810	Party	$14,021	Bus	$67,219	Lbr	$300
Unspent	$41,711	PACS	$77,490	Hlth	$4,400	Prof	$500

Indirect Party Expend: $78,940   *Indep Expend:* For: $486 (NRA)

SEVENTEENTH DISTRICT

The 17th congressional district of Illinois is a fairly representative cross-section of Downstate. It has one major industrial center, around the cities of Rock Island and Moline on the Mississippi River. It has other, smaller industrial centers on the Illinois River, including some suburbs of Peoria, and the small city of Galesburg, the birthplace of Carl Sandburg. And it has hundreds of square miles of Illinois prairie—the flat grasslands, which the white man found unforested and converted, after the difficult task of turning the soil, into some of the most productive farmland in the world. The 17th is an agricultural district; although only a handful of its residents are actually farmers, the economy of this part of Illinois depends almost entirely on agriculture. The main product of the industrial centers is agricultural equipment: tractors and backhoes and plows and harrows; the main business of the white collar sector is financing the production, storing, and transportation of agricultural commodities.

This land was first settled by Yankees coming overland from northern Indiana and Ohio and Upstate New York, and, after 1848, by Germans who left their homeland in search of better opportunities in a land that in so many ways resembles the flat, orderly plains of northern Germany. Their politics has been Republican since the 1850s. The only variation, this far north in Illinois, is the Democratic leaning of the working class, drawn mostly from a later wave of immigration and now mostly members of the United Auto Workers in John Deere plants, in Rock Island and Moline. But on balance this is a Republican district.

And on balance, over the years, it has been a prosperous one. After all, the history of American agriculture is a history of fabulous increases in productivity. Yet farming is also unstable. Farmers are the largest class of entrepreneurs we still have, a multitude who depend on profits rather than salaries and wages. And profits, as any economist knows, vary much more widely than revenues. In the early 1980s farm profits plummeted, as interest rates and other costs rose and commodity prices fell. The decline in profits broke the market for farm machines and caused a serious depression in the agricultural economy of the 17th district. As a result the usually Republican 17th district elected a Democratic congressman in 1982— only the second time that had happened since the great depression.

The story was a little more complicated than that, however. The incumbent congressman, Tom Railsback, would probably have won easily in ordinary circumstances. First elected in 1966, he had a record of liberalism on cultural and foreign issues; he even won the support of the United Auto Workers on occasion. As second ranking Republican on the Judiciary Committee, he was a *de facto* leader of the group of Republicans and southern Democrats who caucused together and provided the crucial votes for the impeachment of Richard Nixon. Later he was a lead sponsor of the Obey-Railsback bill to limit the amounts political action committees could give to candidates. As a result, Railsback was not a favorite of orthodox Republicans, and in 1982 he attracted significant primary opposition in the person of state Senator Kenneth McMillan. Yet McMillan certainly would not have won had it not been for the Paula Parkinson scandal. Parkinson, a lobbyist, admitted to having affairs with unnamed congressmen; Railsback admitted having spent the weekend in a small Florida apartment with Parkinson and two other House members. Another factor also hurt Railsback: redistricting, which shuffled Downstate Illinois counties around and gave him a lot of unfamiliar territory. For all these reasons McMillan defeated Railsback, 51%-49%, in the March 1982 primary. Railsback carried the parts of the district he had represented in the 1980s, 53%–47%, but lost the new counties, 58%–42%.

McMillan's reputation as a hard-right conservative, in a year when the local economy was ailing, gave Democrats their chance. Their candidate, Lane Evans, was not a powerhouse: a legal aid lawyer from Rock Island with limited experience and a youthful appearance (he parts his hair almost in the center). Evans was not particularly articulate and could not discuss national issues as well as McMillan. But McMillan's articulateness turned out to be a disadvantage. He campaigned as a wholehearted supporter of the Reagan economic policies, and his positions on issues like capital punishment, gun control, and school prayer made little difference. Evans's affiliations with the ACLU, NAACP, and the 1980 Kennedy campaign did not seem to hurt him. McMillan carried most of the rural counties, but Evans broke even around Peoria, carried the Galesburg area, and got a whopping 63% in Rock Island County, for a 53% victory overall.

The 17th is likely to be the scene of a major battle again in 1984. The Democrats would dearly like to hold this district; they would like to get Republicans like Railsback to defy their party's leadership on important issues. McMillan's defeat tends to show that it is counterproductive for Reaganites to try to apply discipline in the Republican Party. Evans was given a seat on the Agriculture Committee and, as a Vietnam era veteran, on Veterans' Affairs as well. But it will take more than steady attendance for Evans to win another term, especially if good times return to the farm. Republicans lost this district once before in a good Democratic year, 1964, and then regained it because the Democrat did not have the campaign skills and ability to use the perquisites of office demonstrated by Democrats first elected in 1974. Does Evans?

The People   Pop. 1980: 519,333, up 4.0% 1970–80; voting age pop. 372,502; 2% Black, 2% Span. orig. 26% housing units rented. Median owner $42,500; renter $172. Households: 75% family, 40% with children, 65% married couples.

Presidential Vote

1980	Reagan (R)	124,053	(57%)
	Carter (D)	79,928	(36%)
	Anderson (I)	15,196	(7%)

Rep. Lane Evans (D) Elected 1982; b. Aug. 4, 1951, Rock Island; home, Rock Island; Augustana Col., B.A. 1974, Georgetown U. Law Sch., J.D. 1978; Roman Catholic.

Career U.S. Marine Corps; Atty., Community Legal Clinic of Rock Island, 1978–82.

Offices 1427 LHOB, 202-225-5905. Also 3727 Blackhawk Rd., Rock Island 61201, 309-793-5760; and 125 E. Main St., Galesburg 61401, 309-342-4411.

Committees *Agriculture* (23d). Subcommittees: Conservation, Credit and Rural Development; Wheat, Soybeans, and Feed Grains. *Veterans' Affairs* (12th). Subcommittees: Education, Training and Employment; Hospitals and Health Care; Oversight and Investigations.

Group Ratings and Key Votes: Newly Elected

Election Results

1982 general	Lane Evans (D)	94,483	(53%)	($238,155)
	Kenneth G. McMillan (R)	84,347	(47%)	($295,044)
1982 primary	Lane Evans (D)	19,027	(99%)	
1980 general	Tom Railsback (R)	142,616	(73%)	($78,384)
	Thomas J. Hand (D)	51,753	(27%)	($0)

Campaign Contributions and Expenditures

1981-82		*Direct Cont. 81-82*		*PACS brkdwn*			
Receipts	$237,891	Indiv	$67,146	Agr	$5,250	Ideo	$21,696
Expend.	$238,155	Party	$7,220	Bus	$4,400	Lbr	$81,697
Unspent	$2,153	PACS	$124,918	Hlth	$1,000	Prof	$900
		Cand	$28,300				

EIGHTEENTH DISTRICT

"How will it play in Peoria?" is a question that became familiar to Americans during the Watergate crisis, as Richard Nixon's defenders argued that, however menacing the President's problems looked in Washington, they didn't matter much to people in Peoria. As events proved, their judgment was wrong. Peoria is a reasonable facsimile of the typical Middle American town; an industrial city with a metropolitan area of 365,000, it is often used as a test market for commercial products. What the Nixon defenders failed to realize was that Watergate was taken more seriously in the Peorias of the nation, once the scandal began to unfold, than it was in Washington. The capital, after all, is always awed by the power of the president; people in Peoria are not. And while politicians can be dragooned to support an unpopular position if it helps their party, ordinary voters cannot. Peoria was not sorry to see Richard Nixon go, and it gave Ronald Reagan and his House Republican Leader, Peoria area Congressman Robert Michel, a rough rap on the knuckles in 1982.

The main reason for Peoria's anger at this president—who had attended Eureka College just across the Illinois River—was the state of Peoria's biggest employer, the Caterpillar earth-moving and farm machinery company. It was reeling from two blows. The first was the collapse of the construction industry and the drop in farm profits and the resulting collapse in demand for Caterpillar products. The second was the cancellation of Caterpillar contracts abroad when the President decided to prohibit American companies from participating in the building of a natural gas pipeline from the Soviet Union to western Europe. The virtual shutdown of Caterpillar cast a pall over Peoria, one that not even a late campaign appearance by the President could dispel.

Michel had other problems as well. Redistricting changed his 18th district, removing some territory he had carried for years (Peoria suburbs, Illinois River counties) and adding unfamiliar territory (suburbs of the state capital of Springfield and the factory town of Decatur, whose unemployment was higher than Peoria's). And Michel himself, used to a hard schedule in Washington, found he had to spend more time campaigning in the district than he had in years. He must have been particularly rueful, because he was almost unopposed; Democrat G. Douglas Stephens, a 31-year-old attorney, won his nomination in a write-in campaign. Stephens was not a particularly strong candidate. But Michel, in a televised debate, lost his cool and interrupted the moderator—a performance that almost suggested panic and belied the image of calm, competent leadership he was trying to establish.

The end result was a 52%–48% victory for Michel. He carried Peoria, very narrowly, and carried the new parts of the district as well. But his campaign cost him nearly $700,000, and the closeness of the race seemed to shake him for weeks afterwards. Michel had begun the term hoping that Republicans could capture a majority in the House and elect him speaker. He ended it just barely reelected himself and not included in the negotiations in which Speaker O'Neill and Senate Majority Leader Baker agreed to back a gas-tax-and-highways bill. Even in the lame duck session, when he still had the 26 seats the Republicans had lost in the election, Michel was effectively shorn of the power he had exercised through most of 1981 and into 1982.

The irony is that the calm, competent image Michel sought to convey was accurate as a portrayal of his performance in the 97th Congress. He won the Republican leadership smoothly, beating Campaign Committee Chairman Guy VanderJagt 103–87, despite VanderJagt's closer contacts with new members and his more aggressive advocacy of Reaganite policies. He overcame charges that he was part of a comfortable leadership that was too close to O'Neill. In the first eight months of 1981, Michel showed himself a strong as well as competent leader, effectively managing what turned out to be a working majority of the House on budget and tax issues. Michel was capable of showing, in the well of the House, indignation at the tactics or proposals of the Democrats; and he could orate loudly, and sincerely, against what he regarded as the failure of their policies to work. But he was also capable of keeping in working communication with Tip O'Neill during most of these struggles, and no one accused him of going back on his word or using unfair tactics. Michel proved himself again and again a talented, decent leader who worked hard—and successfully—for policies that he believed in and for the party which he has worked so long for.

So from his perspective, you can understand why encountering such a tough challenge in usually Republican Peoria was such a shock for him. He had just been doing, ably, what he supposed his constituents elected him to do. Why were they trying to punish him for events— low farm prices, high interest rates, the Soviet embargo—which were beyond his control?

Michel continues now as Republican Leader (a title he prefers to Minority Leader) in the House, amid rumors that he will retire in 1984. But they may prove to be as unfounded as was the speculation that Republicans would win enough seats to make him speaker in 1983. Michel, first elected in 1956 and an aide to a Republican congressman as long ago as 1949, has seen the political tides ebb and flow half a dozen times. He is a resilient man who must resent his virtual exclusion from decision-making in early 1983, but who is also professional enough to understand that it happened because of the election results of 1982. If the tide turns again, he is likely to be a major factor once more.

The People   Pop. 1980: 519,026, up 8.3% 1970–80; voting age pop. 368,659; 4% Black, 1% Span. orig. 26% housing units rented. Median owner $44,400; renter $185. Households: 75% family, 41% with children, 65% married couples.

Presidential Vote

1980	Reagan (R)	136,648	(62%)
	Carter (D)	72,145	(33%)
	Anderson (I)	12,864	(6%)

Rep. Robert H. Michel (R) Elected 1956; b. Mar. 2, 1923, Peoria; home, Peoria; Bradley U., B.S. 1948; Apostolic Christian.

Career Army, WWII; A.A., U.S. Rep. Harold Velde, 1949–56.

Offices 2112 RHOB, 202-225-6201. Also 1007 1st Natl. Bank Bldg., Peoria 61602, 309-673-6358.

Committee *Minority Leader.*

Group Ratings

	ADA	ACLU	COPE	CFA	LCV	LWV	NTU	NSI	COC	ACA	CSFC
1982	5	17	12	10	16	45	77	100	80	87	67
1981	10	—	12	21	15	—	72	—	100	86	72
1980	6	27	10	14	22	22	63	89	74	82	78

National Journal Ratings

	Economic		Foreign		Cultural	
1982	32%	(LIB)	28%	(LIB)	4%	(LIB)
	67%	(CONS)	72%	(CONS)	87%	(CONS)
1981	4%	(LIB)	38%	(LIB)	20%	(LIB)
	79%	(CONS)	61%	(CONS)	80%	(CONS)

Key Votes

1) Reagan 81 Budget	FOR	5) Incr SS Rtmt Age	FOR	9) Poor Pay Food Stamps	FOR
2) Reagan 81 Tax Cut	FOR	6) Saudi AWACS Sale	FOR	10) Ban Crt Busing Order	FOR
3) Bal Budget Amend	FOR	7) $ for MX Missile	FOR	11) Auto Local Content	AGN
4) Gas & Road Tax	FOR	8) Nerve Gas Prod	FOR	12) Nuclear Arms Freeze	AGN

Election Results

1982 general	Robert H. Michel (R)	97,406	(52%)	($687,875)
	G. Douglas Stephens (D)	91,281	(48%)	($166,928)
1982 primary	Robert H. Michel (R)	38,657	(100%)	
1980 general	Robert H. Michel (R)	125,561	(62%)	($134,540)
	John L. Knoppel (D)	76,471	(38%)	($43,483)

Campaign Contributions and Expenditures

1981-82		Direct Cont. 81-82		PACS brkdwn			
Receipts	$697,084	Indiv	$191,786	Agr	$15,500	Ideo	$36,650
Expend.	$687,875	Party	$18,756	Bus	$363,707	Lbr	$11,000
Unspent	$76,531	PACS	$476,637	Hlth	$19,350	Prof	$11,125

Indirect Party Expend: $39,541   *Indep Expend:* For: $1,015(NRA) Agn: $9,692 (CCSND)

NINETEENTH DISTRICT

For 200 years the Englishmen and their descendants who settled the eastern United States had to clear their land before they planted their crops. The Eastern Seaboard, the Appalachian Mountains, and the Ohio River Valley were all covered with forests. But when the first white settlers got as far west as the Wabash River, they suddenly encountered the prairie: a vast sea of flat, unforested land that stretched much farther than the eye could see, all the way to the Mississippi River and beyond. It was hard land to tame at first: the soil resisted the plow and the old stump-clearing methods were inapplicable. But the settlers learned to make plows that would pierce the surface and bring up the wonderful topsoil.

White men came to the prairie of Illinois from two directions. The northern half of the state was settled originally by Yankees coming overland from Ohio, Upstate New York, and New England, people who soon formed the bedrock of the new Republican Party. The southern part was settled by people we would now call southerners, people who grew up in Kentucky (like Abraham Lincoln) or Virginia or Tennessee. The rough boundary between these two migrations runs through the middle of the 19th district, along the old National Road—now U.S. 40, paralleled by Interstate 70. North of this the accents are hard and the politics traditionally Republican; Danville, in the northern end of the district, used to elect Joseph Cannon, the speaker of the House against whom the progressives rebelled in 1909. South of the National Road, the accents are softer and more drawling and the politics traditionally Democratic. Voters here have had little use for national Democrats, but as late as 1976 they regularly reelected a Democratic congressman.

The current incumbent, Daniel Crane, is a Republican whose political roots are more in the national New Right movement than in the politics of this district. The brother of Chicago area Congressman Phil Crane, Dan Crane is a dentist who ran for Congress once in Indiana and then, after some years in Danville, ran in this district when the incumbent retired in 1978. His main campaign asset was money, almost $500,000, most of it raised by direct mail from New Right mailing lists from all over the nation. Against weak opposition he was easily reelected in 1980. He had more problems in 1982. The cities of Champaign and Urbana, home of the University of Illinois, were added to the 19th by redistricting, and Champaign-based Democrat John Gwinn ran a serious campaign. He won 61% in Champaign County, carried the Danville area, and got more than 40% of the vote in most of the rural counties, north and south of the National Road. Had Gwinn's race been targeted by national Democrats, he might have raised more money and changed the result.

One asset Gwinn had is that Crane's legislative record does not mark him as a major shaper of national policy. Like his brother, he is more a voice speaking out for conservative positions than he is a legislative leader or craftsman changing the way government works. His committee assignments are odd and not particularly helpful politically: Post Office and Civil Service, although his district contains few federal employees; Armed Services, even though there is not much military spending in Downstate Illinois. An economic upturn would probably put this district out of the Democrats' reach in 1984, but a serious challenge to Dan Crane cannot be ruled out.

The People   Pop. 1980: 518,350, up 4.9% 1970–80; voting age pop. 386,732; 3% Black, 1% Span. orig., 1% Asian orig. 28% housing units rented. Median owner $35,100; renter $161. Households: 75% family, 36% with children, 61% married couples.

Presidential Vote

1980	Reagan (R)	131,504	(58%)
	Carter (D)	78,422	(35%)
	Anderson (I)	16,800	(7%)

Rep. Daniel B. Crane (R) Elected 1978; b. Jan. 10, 1936, Chicago; home, Danville; Hillsdale Col., A.B. 1958, IN U., D.D.S. 1963, U. of MI, 1964–65; Methodist.

Career Army, Vietnam; Dentist, Dir., Crane Clinic, 1963–67.

Offices 115 CHOB, 202-225-5001. Also 426 Whittle Ave., Olney 62450, 618-395-2171.

Committees *Armed Services* (14th). Subcommittees: Investigations; Readiness. *Post Office and Civil Service* (7th). Subcommittees: Human Resources; Postal Operations and Services.

Group Ratings

	ADA	ACLU	COPE	CFA	LCV	LWV	NTU	NSI	COC	ACA	CSFC
1982	0	0	8	0	21	25	98	100	85	96	92
1981	10	—	8	43	43	—	99	—	88	96	90
1980	11	20	10	7	39	20	86	100	61	96	90

National Journal Ratings

	Economic		*Foreign*		*Cultural*	
1982	0%	(LIB)	4%	(LIB)	25%	(LIB)
	98%	(CONS)	92%	(CONS)	74%	(CONS)
1981	32%	(LIB)	18%	(LIB)	4%	(LIB)
	67%	(CONS)	73%	(CONS)	90%	(CONS)

Key Votes

1) Reagan 81 Budget	FOR	5) Incr SS Rtmt Age	FOR	9) Poor Pay Food Stamps	FOR
2) Reagan 81 Tax Cut	FOR	6) Saudi AWACS Sale	AGN	10) Ban Crt Busing Order	FOR
3) Bal Budget Amend	FOR	7) $ for MX Missile	FOR	11) Auto Local Content	AGN
4) Gas & Road Tax	—	8) Nerve Gas Prod	FOR	12) Nuclear Arms Freeze	AGN

Election Results

1982 general	Daniel B. Crane (R)	94,833	(52%)	($305,850)
	John Gwinn (D)	87,231	(48%)	($164,470)
1982 primary	Daniel B. Crane (R)	34,708	(100%)	
1980 general	Daniel B. Crane (R)	146,014	(69%)	($165,236)
	Peter M. Voelz (D)	66,065	(31%)	($19,691)

Campaign Contributions and Expenditures

1981-82		*Direct Cont. 81-82*		*PACS brkdwn*			
Receipts	$328,330	Indiv	$224,122	Agr	$2,500	Ideo	$9,400
Expend.	$305,850	Party	$15,179	Bus	$57,762	Lbr	$500
Unspent	$51,443	PACS	$83,232	Hlth	$11,050	Prof	$450

Indirect Party Expend: $10,378 *Indep Expend:* For: $896 (NRA)

TWENTIETH DISTRICT

The 20th district of Illinois is a descendant of the district that sent Abraham Lincoln, then a 37-year-old Springfield lawyer and Whig politician, to the House of Representatives in 1846. The western part of the district, to outward appearances, hasn't changed much since the 19th century. It remains a land of fertile prairies, the bottomlands of the Mississippi and Illinois Rivers, farm marketing towns and courthouse villages. The river port of Quincy on the Mississippi River looks pretty much the way it did at the turn of the century, as does the little village of Nauvoo, from which the Mormons were expelled in 1846 and led by Brigham Young to their promised land of Utah.

The largest city in the district is Springfield, with 99,000 people. It must have been a bustling, perhaps even a gracious town in Abe Lincoln's and Mary Todd's time. Today it is a typical state capital: a middle-sized city with an old Capitol building, several not-so-elegant hotels, a small black ghetto, a little bit of industry, and a few shopping centers on the edge of town. Next to state government, the Lincoln tourist business seems to be the mainstay of the local economy. That leaves Springfield in better shape, during recessions, than Decatur, the 20th's second largest city, added in the 1982 redistricting. Decatur is an industrial town, home of the Archer-Daniels-Midland soybean combine and of large Caterpillar plants. Unemployment in Decatur topped 18% in 1982—one of the highest rates in the country. Voters blamed Reagan economic policies and its sanctions on trade with the Soviet Union.

And, apparently, they blamed their congressman, Republican Paul Findley. A House member since 1960, Findley for many years seemed to have a safe seat; and if he was beaten finally by his support for a Republican administration, it was ironic, because most of his political strength—and weakness—came from his own distinctive record. For many years Findley specialized in agriculture issues, which helped him in the district. Then, in the late 1970s, he got interested in the Middle East. He met Yasir Arafat, head of the Palestine Liberation Organization, and became convinced that solution of the Middle East's problems required acceptance of many of the PLO's goals. He was happy to characterize himself as Arafat's best friend in Congress. He advanced these views as a senior member of the Foreign Affairs Committee, though not necessarily an influential one. On this issue, as on many others, Findley presented his views articulately, but seemed to lack that ability many politicians instinctively have of being able to persuade their colleagues to support positions they advocate. On the PLO, and on farm policy as well, Findley ended up a loner.

He also, predictably, attracted enemies. Jews and other advocates of U.S. support for Israel were infuriated by Findley's stands—his support for a pro-Soviet terrorist organization, as they saw it—and were determined to defeat him. There are few Jewish voters in the 20th district, but many ambitious politicians. In 1980 Findley was challenged in the Republican primary and received only 56% of the vote; against the serious campaign mounted by David Robinson he had the same percentage in the general election. Robinson raised and spent nearly $700,000, mostly from contributors opposed to Findley's Middle East stands.

Such contributors also helped Richard Durbin, the Democrat who beat Findley in 1982, to raise some $750,000. But by 1982 the Middle East had faded as an issue in the 20th district debate; the PLO was still unpopular, but Menachem Begin's Israel was probably a little less popular too. Instead Durbin campaigned heavily on economic issues. He was helped by the fact that Findley, so often a maverick, had—like almost all of his Republican colleagues—supported the Reagan program faithfully in the House in 1981. He was also helped by the

Democratic-drawn redistricting plan, which removed some Republican Springfield suburbs and added Decatur. Findley carried the old part of his district with 53%—only a little below his 1980 percentage. But Durbin carried the new part of the district 58%–42%. That was enough to give him a 1,410–vote victory.

Durbin is a professional politician who has spent most of his career in Springfield. There he worked for Democrats in the state Senate and for 22d district Congressman Paul Simon when he was lieutenant governor (1969–73). Durbin ran for office twice before, unsuccessfully, but in 1982 he was able to win the nomination to oppose a clearly vulnerable congressman and to raise and spend a large campaign budget intelligently. He won a seat on the Agriculture Committee and on Science and Technology as well; he will have the chance to do something toward the goals of upgrading the district's economy which he discussed in his campaign. Durbin can be almost certain of a serious Republican challenge in 1984. But he appears to be the kind of talented politician who can build enough loyalty among his constituents to withstand it.

The People Pop. 1980: 519,015, up 3.2% 1970–80; voting age pop. 375,764, 4% Black. 26% housing units rented. Median owner $37,200; renter $162. Households: 72% family, 38% with children, 61% married couples.

Presidential Vote

1980			
	Reagan (R)	131,970	(57%)
	Carter (D)	88,895	(38%)
	Anderson (I)	11,299	(5%)

Rep. Richard J. Durbin (D) Elected 1982; b. Nov. 21, 1944; E. St. Louis; home, Springfield; Georgetown U., B.S.F.S. 1966, J.D. 1969; Roman Catholic.

Career Practicing atty., 1969–.

Offices 417 CHOB, 202-225-5271. Also 1307 S. 7th St., Springfield 62703, 217-522-7733; 363 S. Main St., Decatur 62523, 217-428-4745; and 531 Hampshire, Quincy 62301, 217-228-1042.

Committees *Agriculture* (22d). Subcommittees: Conservation, Credit, and Rural Development; Wheat, Soybeans and Feed Grains. *Science and Technology* (20th). Subcommittees: Investigations and Oversight; Science, Research and Technology.

Group Ratings and Key Votes: Newly Elected

Election Results

1982 general	Richard J. Durbin (D)	100,758	(50%)	($777,043)
	Paul Findley (R)	99,348	(50%)	($780,105)
1982 primary	Richard J. Durbin (D)	33,956	(75%)	
	John L. Knuppel (D)	11,119	(25%)	($26,757)
1980 general	Paul Findley (R)	123,427	(56%)	($530,568)
	David Robinson (D)	96,950	(44%)	($674,974)

Campaign Contributions and Expenditures

1981-82		Direct Cont. 81-82		PACS brkdwn			
Receipts	$777,043	Indiv	$549,601	Agr	$9,000	Ideo	$91,825
Expend.	$780,052	Party	$7,145	Bus	$16,850	Lbr	$76,795
Unspent	$3,007	PACS	$206,225	Hlth	$1,750	Prof	$1,000
		Cand	$9,000				

Indirect Party Expend: $142

TWENTY-FIRST DISTRICT

The 21st congressional district of Illinois is the area across from St. Louis's Gateway Arch, where you can see East St. Louis, Belleville, and Granite City through the smoggy air across the Mississippi River. These are not the verdant St. Louis suburbs, but grimy industrial towns criss-crossed by miles of railroad tracks. They have all the problems associated with core city areas: air pollution, inadequate housing, crime, and a declining tax base. East St. Louis became a black majority city in the 1960s, but when blacks took over city hall they found the treasury virtually bare, and the city without resources to fill it. The Illinois side of the St. Louis metropolitan area has a disproportionate share of its poor and low-income working class residents; the rich stay on the Missouri side of the river.

The 21st proceeds north and inland from the river enough to take in territory more typical of Downstate Illinois. There is Alton, home of the antislavery martyr Elijah Lovejoy and, later, of Robert Wadlow, at 8'11" the world's tallest man, and Phyllis Schlafly. And there are the flat farmlands of southern Illinois, alive with the latest miracle plant, soybeans, a crop exported in great quantities to Japan. Yet politically this district is very much different from others in this part of the state; it is heavily Democratic, a kind of big city constituency in the middle of the prairie. The last time a Republican was elected to Congress here was in 1942.

He was defeated in 1944 by Democrat Mel Price, who has been the congressman from this district (renumbered at various times) ever since. A onetime newspaperman and congressional aide, Price became a pillar of the military and atomic energy establishments in the years after World War II. He served for years on the Joint Committee on Atomic Energy, which worked closely and productively with the Atomic Energy Commission to develop both nuclear weapons and nuclear power plants. He was one of the authors of the Price–Anderson Act which, by limiting the liability of nuclear plant operators in the event of accidents, helped encourage the development of nuclear power. When the AEC was broken up, the Joint Committee was abolished, and Price is no longer active on these issues.

Since 1975 Price has been chairman of the House Armed Services Committee. He got the job in a kind of uprising: the Democratic Caucus, after the 1974 elections, ousted Chairman Edward Hebert and voted in Price, the next ranking Democrat, although Price himself supported Hebert and backed most of the same policies. Price does not share the younger Democrats' skepticism toward military spending; the history that made an impression on him was the unpreparedness of the United States in the years before Pearl Harbor. His tendency is to defer to the advice of the military services. Unlike Hebert, he has been fortunate to serve as chairman in years when support for military spending has grown, not declined. Yet this very success has meant that Price, who has served longer as Armed Services chairman than anyone since Carl Vinson retired in 1964, has not made much of a personal imprint on military policy. Armed Services, alone of major legislative committees, listens to testimony from only one point of view, the Pentagon's and, given the choice of going along or dissenting, it almost always chooses to go along. That tendency is natural given its membership, drawn mostly from the ranks of conservative Republicans and southern Democrats. The real choices are almost always made elsewhere.

Price is the second most senior member of the House and one of the oldest; he turns 79 in 1984. He is still capable of serving, but he has also been less active and aggressive than he must have been in the great years of the Joint Committee. He has not been seriously challenged in his district for years, and could probably go on winning if he wants to run.

The People Pop. 1980: 521,036, dn. 2.0% 1970–80; voting age pop. 367,291; 12% Black, 1% Span. orig. 27% housing units rented. Median owner $36,700; renter $155. Households: 76% family, 42% with children, 62% married couples.

Presidential Vote

1980	Reagan (R)	104,414	(51%)
	Carter (D)	93,309	(45%)
	Anderson (I)	8,437	(4%)

Rep. Melvin Price (D) Elected 1944; b. Jan. 1, 1905, E. St. Louis; home, E. St. Louis; St. Louis U., 1923–25; Roman Catholic.

Career Newspaper correspondent, E. St. Louis *Journal*, St. Louis *Globe-Democrat*; Sports ed., E. St. Louis *News-Review*; St. Clair Cnty. Bd. of Sprvsrs., 1929–31; Secy. to U.S. Rep. Edwin M. Schaefer, 1933–43; Army, WWII.

Offices 2110 RHOB, 202-225-5661. Also Fed. Bldg., 690 Missouri Ave., E. St. Louis 62201, 618-274-2200.

Committee *Armed Services* (Chairman). Subcommittees: Research and Development (Chairman); Seapower and Strategic and Critical Materials.

Group Ratings

	ADA	ACLU	COPE	CFA	LCV	LWV	NTU	NSI	COC	ACA	CSFC
1982	55	50	96	60	64	73	0	89	35	32	35
1981	50	—	96	71	50	—	1	—	32	27	41
1980	56	33	89	86	44	70	8	22	67	13	27

National Journal Ratings

	Economic		Foreign		Cultural	
1982	73%	(LIB)	10%	(LIB)	62%	(LIB)
	27%	(CONS)	90%	(CONS)	38%	(CONS)
1981	77%	(LIB)	38%	(LIB)	67%	(LIB)
	23%	(CONS)	61%	(CONS)	33%	(CONS)

Key Votes

1) Reagan 81 Budget	AGN	5) Incr SS Rtmt Age	AGN	9) Poor Pay Food Stamps	AGN
2) Reagan 81 Tax Cut	AGN	6) Saudi AWACS Sale	FOR	10) Ban Crt Busing Order	AGN
3) Bal Budget Amend	AGN	7) $ for MX Missile	FOR	11) Auto Local Content	FOR
4) Gas & Road Tax	—	8) Nerve Gas Prod	FOR	12) Nuclear Arms Freeze	AGN

Election Results

1982 general	Melvin Price (D)	89,500	(64%)	($64,788)
	Robert H. Gaffner (R)	46,764	(33%)	($19,544)
1982 primary	Melvin Price (D)	39,318	(81%)	
	Two others (D)	8,946	(19%)	
1980 general	Melvin Price (D)	107,786	(64%)	($42,718)
	Ronald L. Davinroy (R)	59,644	(36%)	($23,683)

Campaign Contributions and Expenditures

1981-82		Direct Cont. 81-82			PACS brkdwn		
Receipts	$72,988	Indiv	$31,957	Agr	$500	Ideo	$525
Expend.	$64,788	PACS	$32,575	Bus	$20,150	Lbr	$9,650
Unspent	$22,363			Hlth	$250	Prof	$1,000

TWENTY-SECOND DISTRICT

Little Egypt is the name given to the southernmost part of Illinois—the flat, fertile farmland where the Ohio River joins the Mississippi. This is low, alluvial land, subject to floods almost as often as ancient Egypt itself. The countryside is protected by giant levees that rise above the fields and hide any view of the waters. There is more than a touch of Dixie here: the southern tip of Illinois is closer to Jackson, Mississippi, than to Chicago. The unofficial capital of Little Egypt is Cairo (pronounced KAYroh), a declining town at the exact confluence of the two rivers. Not so many years ago Cairo was the scene of a virtual war between its white majority and its large black minority; it must surely be one of the grimmest small towns in the United States.

There are no official boundaries to Little Egypt, but it is safe to say that the 22d congressional district goes north considerably beyond them. The district takes in the coal mining area around West Frankfort and Marion—one of the most heavily strip-mined areas in the United States—and it includes Carbondale, site of Southern Illinois University. Following the 1982 redistricting, it even has a salient that goes north on the Mississippi River to the city limits of heavily industrial East St. Louis. Nearly all this territory is Democratic in most elections, because of ancestral southern preference (this is southern drawl, not midwestern hard R territory) or because of the Democratic leanings of coal miners and industrial workers. But it has not been reliably Democratic in national elections. The 21st went against the Catholic John Kennedy in 1960 and the Great Society's Hubert Humphrey in 1968; it gave southerner Jimmy Carter a majority in 1976 but turned sharply against him, as did many border areas, in 1980.

The 22d district's congressman is Paul Simon, a Democrat who, on first glance, looks miscast for his job. A cerebral liberal in rough-hewn Little Egypt, a temperamental reformer in an area where politics has always been conducted by regulars—Simon is not the typical southern Illinois politician. But he is a successful one. As a small town newspaper editor, he was elected to the legislature where he became known both for his support of reform and his effectiveness—attributes not usually found in the same person in Illinois. He was elected lieutenant governor in 1968 and ran for governor in 1972 with Daley machine support; he lost the primary to Daniel Walker, when the courts suddenly opened the primary to voters who were not registered Democrats. He was elected to Congress in 1974, and his only close call since came in 1980, when his views on national issues (and his support of Edward Kennedy in the Illinois primary) nearly elected an underfinanced Republican. After harder campaigning, and with a little help from redistricting, Simon raised his majority to his usual 2–1 levels in 1982.

Actually, Simon's positions on issues do not put him at the extreme left of the rating charts. He is too thoughtful—and busy—for that. On the Education and Labor Committee, he supports the AFL-CIO position on labor issues and backs most of the big money education programs. But he seems most interested in special issues like adoption and special programs like aid to the arts, libraries, and museums—things that can arguably make a great deal of difference in the quality of national life with minimal spending by federal standards. He is troubled by Americans' increasing inability to speak and read foreign languages, and in 1981 published *The Tongue-Tied American: Confronting the Foreign Language Crisis*. In 1982 he came out with *The Once and Future Democrats: Strategies for Change*; that was his eighth published book. Simon also worked on the Budget Committee, but his term there, in accordance with the rules, expired in 1983. Simon cannot be classed as a legislative power, but he has the power to make a difference on issues he cares about; and if he has not been a leader in some of the major fights before Congress, he has the ability to raise—and make a difference on—issues which might otherwise be neglected were he not working on them.

The People Pop. 1980: 521,303, up 9.3% 1970–80, voting age pop. 381,684; 6% Black, 1% Span. orig. 23% housing units rented. Median owner $29,500; renter $131. Households: 73% family, 37% with children, 62% married couples.

Presidential Vote

1980	Reagan (R)	126,362	(54%)
	Carter (D)	99,441	(42%)
	Anderson (I)	8,432	(4%)

Rep. Paul Simon (D) Elected 1974; b. Nov. 29, 1928, Eugene, OR; home, Carbondale; U. of OR, 1945–46, Dana Col., 1946–48; Lutheran.

Career Editor-Publisher, Troy *Tribune*, and weekly newspaper chain owner, 1948–66; Army, 1951–53; IL House of Reps., 1955–63; IL Senate, 1963–69; Lt. Gov. of IL, 1969–73; Candidate for Dem. Nomination for Gov., 1972; Instructor, Sangamon St. U., 1973.

Offices 343 CHOB, 202-225-5201. Also 107 Glenview Dr., Carbondale 62901, 618-457-4171.

Committee *Education and Labor* (9th). Subcommittees: Employment Opportunities; Postsecondary Education (Chairman); Select Education.

Group Ratings

	ADA	ACLU	COPE	CFA	LCV	LWV	NTU	NSI	COC	ACA	CSFC
1982	75	71	81	80	83	80	3	10	15	25	23
1981	75	—	79	71	65	—	7	—	12	0	31
1980	78	77	72	64	72	100	18	0	59	24	26

National Journal Ratings

	Economic		Foreign		Cultural	
1982	88%	(LIB)	70%	(LIB)	83%	(LIB)
	12%	(CONS)	30%	(CONS)	17%	(CONS)
1981	80%	(LIB)	88%	(LIB)	74%	(LIB)
	19%	(CONS)	12%	(CONS)	25%	(CONS)

Key Votes

1) Reagan 81 Budget	AGN	5) Incr SS Rtmt Age	AGN	9) Poor Pay Food Stamps	AGN
2) Reagan 81 Tax Cut	AGN	6) Saudi AWACS Sale	AGN	10) Ban Crt Busing Order	—
3) Bal Budget Amend	AGN	7) $ for MX Missile	AGN	11) Auto Local Content	FOR
4) Gas & Road Tax	FOR	8) Nerve Gas Prod	AGN	12) Nuclear Arms Freeze	AGN

Election Results

1982 general	Paul Simon (D)	123,693	(66%)	($563,301)
	Peter G. Prineas (R)	63,279	(34%)	($27,517)
1982 primary	Paul Simon (D)	46,847	(100%)	
1980 general	Paul Simon (D)	112,134	(49%)	($217,098)
	John T. Anderson (R)	110,176	(48%)	($42,494)

Campaign Contributions and Expenditures

1981-82		Direct Cont. 81-82		PACS brkdwn			
Receipts	$580,893	Indiv	$411,738	Agr	$7,650	Ideo	$12,840
Expend.	$563,301	Party	$5,000	Bus	$23,565	Lbr	$82,400
Unspent	$17,016	PACS	$136,492	Hlth	$3,100	Prof	$1,450
		Cand	$19,000				

Indep Expend: Agn: $8,483 (NCPAC, LIFEPAC)

INDIANA

Politics in Indiana in the 1980s is out of sync with politics in the rest of the country. In an era when most political machines have long since crumbled, Indiana is the home of one of the most successful machines of the 20th century, the state Republican organization; and in a year in which a recession helped Democrats beat incumbent Republicans across the nation, Indiana continued its solidly Republican voting habits. Badly hit by the decline of the auto and steel industries, heavily industrial Indiana, you would think, would have swung sharply to the Democrats, as it did in the 1930s or the recession year of 1958. But this time it didn't. Democrats picked up only one House seat here, and that in the least industrial part of the state and in a race in which the incumbent was charged with drunk driving in October; the Democratic Senate candidate lost all of the state's auto factory counties and carried only Gary, South Bend (by 21 votes) and some small southern counties. Republicans remain in control of the governorship, which they have held since 1968, all the top state offices, both U.S. Senate seats and large majorities in the state legislature. They hold the mayoralty in Indianapolis, the state's largest city and capital, and patronage-rich county offices in most of the state's large counties.

Yet Indiana doesn't *look* different from surrounding states. Physically it is part of the limestone-bottomed plain that starts where the hills west of Pittsburgh level off and moves west across the Mississippi River and ultimately to the Rocky Mountains. The land is well watered and fertile, but as long as 100 years ago Indiana became more industrial than agricultural. The state sits astride the great east–west transportation routes, accessible to the Great Lakes and the Mississippi and Ohio River systems. Its boundaries to the east and west are nothing more than dotted lines on the map, but in people's minds Indiana has been a separate and distinct place for many years now. Few other states have as unusual a word as "Hoosier" to describe their residents, few others have had a writer who becomes a kind of state poet laureate like James Whitcomb Riley. Indiana's political traditions have contributed to its clearly perceived identity. Its heavy partisanship, going back to Civil War divisions; its practice of requiring patronage employees to contribute 2% of their salaries to political parties—these were commonplace in all the older midwestern states in the 1890s, but only in Indiana have they survived in such uninhibited fashion.

Indiana's political distinctiveness is ultimately due not to the persistence of custom, but to the underlying fact that life in this state has changed less than in other places. The cultural and ethnic patterns in Indiana today are not much different from what they were in the 1920s, and that is not true in other states of similar size. Ethnically, Indiana remains mostly the product of the first wave of American immigration, of people whose ancestors came over between 1640 and 1720, and moved overland—down from New England, up from Kentucky and Virginia—to these plains. So today the basic political geography of the state remains much the same as it was just after the Civil War. South of the old National Road, or U.S. 40, people speak with something like a southern drawl and tend to vote Democratic. North of the National Road (which goes right through Indianapolis) people talk with midwestern hard Rs and flat As and vote heavily Republican. Except for the steel area around Gary—really an extension of the Chicago metropolitan area—Indiana has relatively few ethnics from the second wave (1840–1924) of immigration, and no major metropolitan areas. True, metropolitan Indianapolis technically has a population over 1 million now, but no one would mistake it for a smaller Chicago or Cleveland.

The other way in which Indiana has not changed is in its cultural patterns. Again, the lack of major metropolitan areas is critical: nowhere in Indiana will you find large neighborhoods or significant political constituencies made up of young singles, much less gays. The divorce rate is lower than the American average, the percentage of households occupied by families and married people higher. The percentage of households with children is high and, were not the population a little older than the national average, would be among the highest in the United States. These patterns have important political consequences in a time when there may be less difference in voting habits between union members and non-union members than between married and single persons. The swing against Ronald Reagan's Republicans in 1982 was most accentuated among unmarried people, especially women; Indiana has relatively few of them. The swing against the Republicans was less noticeable, despite the economic bad times, among married blue collar workers. Hence Republican Senator Richard Lugar, a supporter of the Reagan programs and an unapologetic believer in something that can easily be depicted as trickle-down economics, nonetheless carried the factory towns of Kokomo and Anderson, Muncie and Fort Wayne—despite some of the highest unemployment rates in the nation.

The comparative absence of the politics of cultural variety which has been so important in most of the rest of the nation has left the Republican Party in virtually unchallenged command of Indiana politics. For many years politics here was competitive, and power roughly equally, if grudgingly, shared between the parties (there is little or no camaraderie between members of the two parties in Indiana). As other states struggle with the difficult problem of paying for generous services with declining revenues, Indiana Republicans continue to deliver low levels of spending and promise generous attractions to new business; and they have produced some genuinely talented leaders as well, notably Governor Otis Bowen (1972–80). On national issues, Indiana is seldom attracted to liberal positions on economic issues and never to liberal positions on cultural issues. As for foreign policy, it is enough to know that Indianapolis is the national headquarters of the American Legion: Indiana wants an assertive foreign policy and solid support of the military, but it still has a suspicion, dating perhaps to the days before World War II, of embroilment in foreign quarrels.

Presidential politics. In presidential elections Indiana is solidly Republican, except for landslide Democratic years when the Democrats don't need the votes anyway. To paraphrase A. J. Liebling, Indiana is more Republican than any state that is larger and is larger than any state that is more Republican. Indiana has a presidential primary that was once one of the earlier contests: in 1968, for example, it was the scene of an epic battle between Robert Kennedy, Eugene McCarthy, and Roger Branigin, the hapless governor who was a stand-in for President Johnson. As of early 1983, Indiana's primary was scheduled for May 8, 1984— a relatively late date chosen in part because state and congressional primaries, if any, take place then too. As a result, it seems unlikely to be a pivotal contest.

Senators. Indiana's two senators are men of very similar voting records but sharply different temperaments. Richard Lugar's success in politics must be seen as a triumph of intellect: he lacks most of the character traits usually associated with politicians. He is not gregarious, he has little sense of humor, his appearance is not striking. His manner seems overly pious and sometimes smirky. But he is undeniably bright: a Rhodes Scholar who has worked his way up through brains and hard work. His brilliance led Republican Party leaders to slate him for mayor of Indianapolis in 1967, when he was 35; he won and made a record of some note, consolidating the city and county, which added tax resources to the city and had the happy side effect of adding more Republican votes to city elections. Lugar bucked fashion among big city mayors and called for fewer rather than more federal programs; even so, he beat New York's John Lindsay for the vice presidency of the National League of Cities in 1969. That helped make him Richard Nixon's favorite mayor, and he played a prominent role, which he would probably rather forget, at the 1972 Republican National Convention. Lugar ran for the Senate twice before he won: in the Democratic year of 1974 he nearly beat Birch Bayh, and in 1976 he whipped the by then unpopular Vance Hartke. He won reelection in 1982 with a percentage lower than expected, an unimpressive 54%. Yet he carried virtually every large county in a state hard hit by recession, and outperformed almost every other Republican seeking reelection in that year.

On most issues Lugar is an ally of the New Right, yet he approaches issues far differently. Members of that group see themselves as insurgents whose cause, they secretly suspect, will fail; Lugar sees himself as one of the people who, in the natural course of events, run things, and who will succeed in stamping their imprint on history in the long run. Lugar has become a major Republican spokesman on both foreign and domestic affairs. On the Foreign Relations Committee, he sits below Chairman Charles Percy, Majority Leader Howard Baker, and North Carolina's Jesse Helms; because Baker is preoccupied with other duties and Percy and

Helms often go off on tangents, Lugar is often the leader of the committee's mainstream Republican forces. Liberals should not assume that, because he is bright, he is sympathetic to their positions. Quite the contrary. He believes in more defense spending, a more aggressive confrontation of the Soviets all over the world; he was an opponent of the Carter administration's SALT II and Panama Canal Treaties.

Lugar has not been involved deeply in budget matters, but he has had an impact on domestic issues. He also won the chairmanship of the Senate Republican Campaign Committee in 1983, after a fight with Bob Packwood and with White House support; for that he gave up his seat on the Banking Committee. Lugar is an unabashed admirer of free enterprise economics, but in line with authentic American tradition he does not interpret that as excluding an occasional intervention by government. Thus in 1979 he ended up as a sponsor of the bill to provide loan guarantees to Chrysler—a major Indiana employer—but only after changing the original bill to require some wage concessions by workers. In 1982, the year he was seeking reelection, he produced with much fanfare a bill to lower interest rates, in some circumstances, for home-buyers. A pure free market analyst would probably say Americans have too heavily subsidized home ownership for too many years; Lugar might reply that home ownership is an important ingredient in the glue that binds ordinary people to their society.

Lugar has probably had national political ambitions since the days he first received national publicity as a young mayor. In 1980 he sought the Republican vice presidential nomination, without much success. It could not have helped that he was an early supporter of Howard Baker for the presidency, and chaired Baker's campaign. Lugar genuinely admires Baker, and will probably back him strongly again if he runs in 1984 or 1988; their politics, despite Baker's somewhat different reputation, is similar. Baker's announced retirement from the Senate in 1984 gives Lugar a chance to seek a leadership position, perhaps the majority leadership itself. But he probably won't win it: all those qualities of a politician he lacks are just what a man needs to win support for a leadership position.

If Lugar is a kind of class intellectual and valedictorian, Indiana's other senator, Dan Quayle, is the class athlete and student body president—one the favorite of the teachers, the other the favorite of the students. Quayle came to the Senate at an early age (35) without much political experience (two terms in the House). He comes from a family prominent in publishing; his grandfather was Eugene Pulliam, proprietor of the *Indianapolis Star* and the *Arizona Republic*. Quayle himself seemed destined for the life of a small town grandee, something like a character in an early John O'Hara novel—successful business ventures, community service organizations, a nice family and pleasant vacations, Saturday night dinners at the country club, and plenty of golf. Quayle owes his Senate seat to lucky breaks: in 1976 he challenged a Democratic congressman everyone else considered unbeatable; he got the Republican Senate nomination in 1980 because the very popular governor didn't want to run for personal reasons; he ran against one of the nation's best instinctive political campaigners, Birch Bayh, in a year in which Bayh's views on issues, never terribly popular in Indiana, were a crushing liability.

Thrust near the national spotlight, with seats on the Budget, Armed Services, and Labor and Human Resources Committees, Quayle has at first behaved predictably and stayed out of trouble. He supported the President's economic program stalwartly. He voted solidly with his committee chairmen and gave them little trouble; occasionally, notably on the 1982 budget negotiations, he would get some concession for Indiana. But as the recession continued, Quayle began to show interest in and even propose jobs programs, and expressed sympathy for some of the existing federal programs. Less intellectual than Lugar, he seems also not closely tied to ideology, and he would probably defend his record by saying that he has been doing what the voters of Indiana elected him to do. Bayh, a gifted politician often out of step with his constituency, and Vance Hartke, who reveled in the reputation of a wheeler-dealer, each lasted three terms as Indiana senators; what is there to keep Quayle, who seems more in line with the state on issues, from doing the same? It should be added, however, that no one of either party has won a fourth Senate term from this state.

Governor. Indiana's Governor, Robert Orr, served as lieutenant governor under Otis Bowen and ran in 1980 as his disciple. It is a measure of the strength of the Republican organization that he won the primary without opposition and the general election with 58% of the vote. He has not proved as popular as his predecessor, however, and in 1983 Democrats had some hopes of beating him. One likely candidate is state Senator Wayne Townsend, who has strong labor backing and nearly beat the generously self-financed 1980 nominee, John Hillenbrand, in the Democratic primary. But it would be a major reversal of form for Indiana to elect a labor-oriented governor in 1984 or any other year.

Congressional districting. Indiana's 1981 redistricting was the most partisan Republican plan in the nation. Passed early in 1981 by Indiana's organization-dominated legislature, it may have been counterproductive nationally, since it convinced many Democrats that they should demand maximum political advantage from redistricting where they controlled the process, to compensate for Indiana. But Indiana has only 10 congressional districts (down one from the 1970s) and 1982 proved to be a good enough Democratic year that the Democrats lost only two seats and held onto another (Phil Sharp's) that seemed in jeopardy. The power of redistricting to affect congressional delegations is, after all, limited; Indiana's districts for more than a dozen years have been drawn by partisan Republicans but have elected mostly Democrats.

The People   Est. Pop. 1982: 5,471,000; Pop. 1980: 5,490,224, dn. 0.4% 1980–82 and up 5.7% 1970–80; 2.4% of U.S. total, 14th largest; voting age pop. 3,871,906; 7% Black, 1% Spanish origin. Single ancestry: 13% German, 12% English, 4% Irish, 1% Polish, French, Dutch, Italian. Registered voters (1982): 2,936,978 Total. 12% with 1–3 yrs. col., 15% with 4+ yrs. col. 9.8% below poverty level. 26% housing units rented; median house value: $37,200; median monthly rent: $166. Households: 76% family, 42% with children, 64% married couples.

1982 Share of Federal Tax Burden $13,386,100,000; 2.24% of U.S. total, 12th largest.

1982 Share of Federal Expenditures

	Total		Non-Defense		Defense	
Total Expend	$10,111m	(1.68%)	$7,522m	(1.77%)	$2,589m	(1.45%)
St/Lcl Grants	1,558m	(1.77%)	1,556m	(1.76%)	2m	(5.56%)
Salary/Wages	741m	(0.95%)	242m	(0.88%)	499m	(0.98%)
Ind Payments	5,603m	(1.96%)	5,205m	(1.39%)	398m	(1.02%)
Procurement	2,122m	(1.46%)	168m	(0.53%)	1,954m	(1.71%)
Other Programs	87m	(1.61%)	86m	(1.60%)	1m	(2.33%)
Loan/Insurance	1,257m	(1.97%)	1,230m	(1.99%)	27m	(1.23%)

Political Lineup   Governor, Robert Orr (R). Senators, Richard G. Lugar (R) and J. Danforth (Dan) Quayle (R). Representatives, 10 (5 D and 5 R). State Senate, 50 (32 R and 18 D); State House of Representatives, 100 (57 R and 43 D).

Presidential Vote

1980	Reagan (R)	1,255,656	(56%)
	Carter (D)	844,197	(38%)
	Anderson (I)	111,639	(5%)
1976	Ford (R)	1,183,958	(53%)
	Carter (D)	1,014,714	(46%)

1980 Democratic Presidential Primary			*1980 Republican Presidential Primary*		
Carter	398,949	(68%)	Reagan	419,016	(74%)
Kennedy	190,492	(32%)	Bush	92,955	(16%)
			Anderson	56,344	(10%)

SENATORS

Sen. Richard G. Lugar (R) Elected 1976, seat up 1988; b. Apr. 4, 1932, Indianapolis; home, Indianapolis; Denison U., B.A. 1954, Rhodes Scholar, Oxford U., B.A., M.A. 1956; United Methodist.

Career Navy, 1957–60; V.P. and Treasurer, Thomas L. Green & Co., banking equip., 1960–67, Pres., 1968–77; Treasurer, Lugar Stock Farms, Inc., 1960–77; Mayor of Indianapolis, 1968–76; Repub. Nominee for U.S. Senate, 1974.

Offices 306 HSOB, 202-224-4814. Also 447 Fed. Bldg., Indianapolis 46204, 317-269-5555.

Committees Agriculture, Nutrition, and Forestry (3d). Subcommittees: Agricultural Research and General Legislation (Chairman); Foreign Agricultural Policy; Nutrition. *Foreign Relations* (4th). Subcommittees: International Economic Policy; European Affairs (Chairman); Western Hemisphere Affairs. *Select Committee on Intelligence* (4th). Subcommittees: Analysis and Production (Chairman); Collection and Foreign Operations.

Group Ratings

	ADA	ACLU	COPE	CFA	LCV	LWV	NTU	NSI	COC	ACA	CSFC
1982	15	11	8	30	54	67	67	100	70	63	74
1981	5	—	6	29	31	—	84	—	94	76	83
1980	17	20	11	7	30	50	53	80	86	83	72

National Journal Ratings

	Economic		Foreign		Cultural	
1982	25%	(LIB)	16%	(LIB)	38%	(LIB)
	73%	(CONS)	68%	(CONS)	61%	(CONS)
1981	30%	(LIB)	1%	(LIB)	2%	(LIB)
	69%	(CONS)	85%	(CONS)	82%	(CONS)

Key Votes

1) Reagan 81 Budget	FOR	5) $ to El Salvador	FOR	9) Poor Pay Food Stamps	FOR
2) Reagan 81 Tax Cut	FOR	6) Saudi AWACS Sale	FOR	10) Ban Crt Busing Order	FOR
3) Bal Budget Amend	FOR	7) Ban Abortion	FOR	11) Clinch Riv Brdr Rctr	AGN
4) Gas & Road Tax	FOR	8) Nerve Gas Prod	FOR	12) Legal Services Corp	AGN

Election Results

1982 general	Richard G. Lugar (R)	978,301	(54%)	($2,987,573)
	Floyd Fithian (D)	828,400	(46%)	($870,023)
1982 primary	Richard G. Lugar (R) unopposed ..	404,050		
1976 general	Richard G. Lugar (R)	1,275,833	(59%)	($727,720)
	Vance Hartke (D)	868,522	(40%)	($654,729)

Campaign Contributions and Expenditures

1980-82		Direct Cont. 81-82				PACS brkdwn	
Receipts	$3,041,685	Indiv	$2,120,643	Agr	$33,400	Ideo	$32,100
Expend.	$2,987,573	Party	$55,457	Bus	$603,371	Lbr	$2,000
Unspent	$53,814	PACS	$715,139	Hlth	$26,960	Prof	$10,250

Indirect Party Expend: $287,145   Indep Expend: For: $130

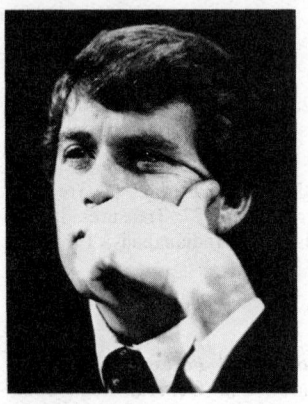

Sen. J. Danforth (Dan) Quayle (R) Elected 1980, seat up 1986; b. Feb. 4, 1947, Indianapolis; home, Huntington; DePauw U., B.A. 1969, IN U., J.D. 1974; Bible Church.

Career A. A. to the Gov. of IN, 1971–73; Dir. IN Inheritance Tax Div., 1973; Practicing atty.; Gen. Mgr. and Assoc. Publ., *Huntington Herald-Press*, 1974–76; U.S. House of Reps., 1976–80.

Offices 524 HSOB, 202-224-5623. Also 46 E. Ohio St., Rm. 447, Indianapolis 46204, 317-269-5555; and 5530 Fohl Ave., Hammond 46320, 219-932-5500, ext. 3801.

Committees *Armed Services* (8th). Subcommittees: Strategic and Theater Nuclear Forces; Sea Power and Force Projection; Military Construction. *Budget* (11th). *Labor and Human Resources* (3d). Subcommittees: Alcoholism and Drug Abuse; Education, Arts, and the Humanities; Employment and Productivity (Chairman).

Group Ratings

	ADA	ACLU	COPE	CFA	LCV	LWV	NTU	NSI	COC	ACA	CSFC
1982	25	29	6	10	46	67	72	78	70	75	73
1981	10	—	0	29	32	—	89	—	89	81	84

National Journal Ratings

	Economic		Foreign		Cultural	
1982	25%	(LIB)	38%	(LIB)	49%	(LIB)
	73%	(CONS)	61%	(CONS)	50%	(CONS)
1981	17%	(LIB)	27%	(LIB)	2%	(LIB)
	79%	(CONS)	71%	(CONS)	82%	(CONS)

Key Votes

1) Reagan 81 Budget	FOR	5) $ to El Salvador	FOR	9) Poor Pay Food Stamps	FOR
2) Reagan 81 Tax Cut	FOR	6) Saudi AWACS Sale	FOR	10) Ban Crt Busing Order	FOR
3) Bal Budget Amend	FOR	7) Ban Abortion	FOR	11) Clinch Riv Brdr Rctr	AGN
4) Gas & Road Tax	FOR	8) Nerve Gas Prod	FOR	12) Legal Services Corp	AGN

Election Results

1980 general	J. Danforth (Dan) Quayle (R)	1,182,414	(54%)	($2,430,878)
	Birch E. Bayh, Jr. (D)	1,015,922	(46%)	($2,773,254)
1980 primary	J. Danforth (Dan) Quayle (R)	397,453	(77%)	
	Roger Marsh (R)	118,273	(23%)	($173,712)
1974 general	Birch E. Bayh, Jr. (D)	889,269	(51%)	($1,024,486)
	Richard G. Lugar (R)	814,117	(46%)	($619,678)

Campaign Contributions and Expenditures

1979-80				PACS brkdwn		
Receipts	$2,308,194	Agr	$21,900	Ideo	$40,243
Expend.	$2,289,838	Bus	$536,626	Lbr	$1,000
Unspent	$18,366	Hlth	$14,500	Prof	$1,900

GOVERNOR

Gov. Robert Orr (R) Elected 1980, term expires Jan. 1985; b. Nov. 17, 1917, Ann Arbor, MI; homes, Indianapolis and Evansville; Yale U., B.A. 1940, Harvard U. Bus. Sch., 1940–42; Presbyterian.

Career Army, WWII; Businessman, Orr Iron Co., 1946–73; Chmn., Vandenburgh Cnty. Repub. Party, 1965–69; IN Senate, 1968–72; Lt. Gov. of IN, 1972–80.

Offices Rm. 206 State House, Indianapolis 46204, 317-633-4567.

Election Results

1980 gen.	Robert Orr (R)	1,257,383	(58%)
	John A. Hillenbrand (D)	913,116	(42%)
1980 prim.	Robert Orr (R)	483,952	(100%)
1976 gen.	Otis R. Bowen (R)	1,236,555	(57%)
	Larry A. Conrad (D)	927,243	(43%)

FIRST DISTRICT

Anyone who has driven west on the Indiana East–West Toll Road has seen it. Between the highway and the unseen shores of Lake Michigan is some of the most impressive and most polluted industrial landscape in the country. These are some of the nation's largest steel mills: from their chimneys and smokestacks come sulphurous fumes by day and the flare of flames at night. This is the heart of the 1st congressional district of Indiana, the northwest corner of Hoosier America.

Many of the steel mills are closed today, or working at frighteningly low levels of capacity; and their troubles have grave implications for this area. For steel is its lifeblood. The district's largest city, Gary, was founded in 1906 by J. P. Morgan's colossal United States Steel Corporation and named for one of Morgan's partners, Chicago Judge Elbert Gary. The site chosen was ideal. Iron ore from the Lake Superior ranges could be carried on Great Lakes freighters to the huge man-made port at the southern tip of Lake Michigan. Coal from West Virginia and Pennsylvania could be shipped in by rail on the great east–west rail lines that pass through Gary, Hammond, and East Chicago on their way to Chicago. The local political environment was favorable, too. Indiana has always been a low-tax state, and for years the Lake County Assessor was pleased to let the steel company's own auditors set their assessments and therefore their own property taxes.

For nearly 70 years the steel mills attracted a diverse work force to this corner of Indiana— Irish, Poles, Czechs, Ukrainians, and blacks from the American South. These groups live in uneasy proximity, and much of the politics in the area is about ethnic and racial rivalries. Gary has been a mostly black city since the 1960s, while Hammond and the suburbs south of

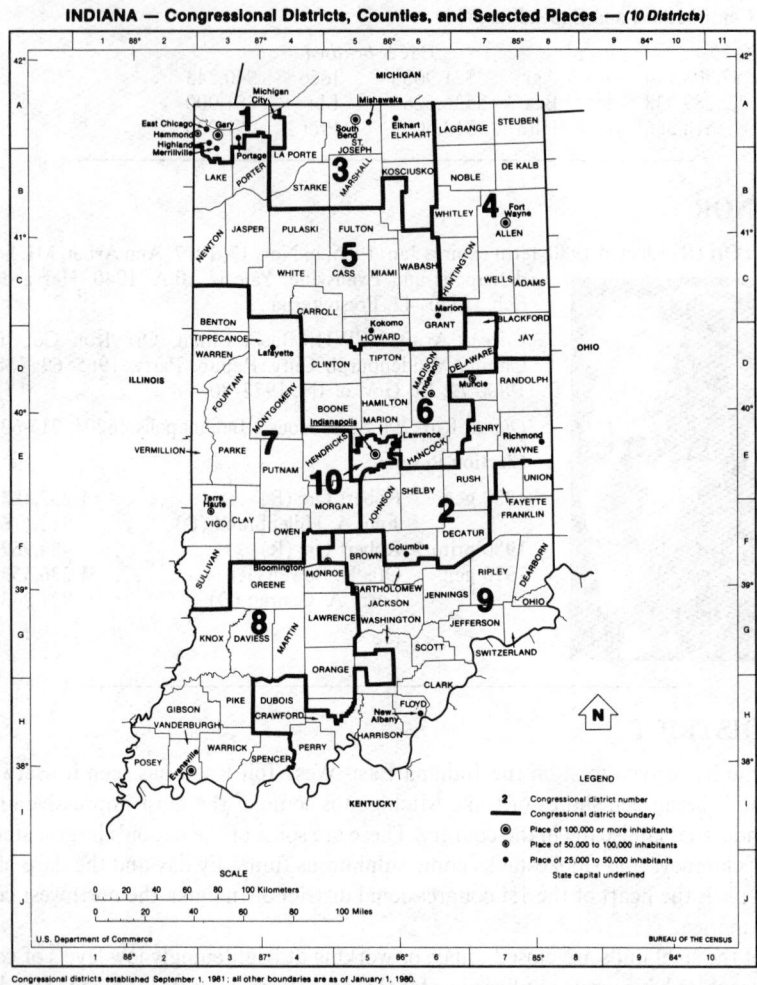

INDIANA — Congressional Districts, Counties, and Selected Places — *(10 Districts)*

Gary remain virtually all white. The often corrupt ethnic politicians who ran things in Lake County were displeased when Richard Hatcher, a black, was elected mayor of Gary in 1967; that job controlled important patronage, and Hatcher, though a canny politician, did not play their games. White homeowners also disliked the new mayor, and voted against him; as Gary's black population has increased, but Hatcher's margins in primaries have sometimes been tenuous, since as an incumbent he is easy to blame for all the city's various problems. He won his fifth primary by a rather narrow margin in 1983.

Racial animosities did not play much role in congressional politics, however, until 1982. The 1st district was represented for 34 years by Ray Madden, a labor-backed Democrat who spent his last four years as chairman of the House Rules Committee; unfortunately, by that time he was too old to be an effective chairman. Madden was beaten in 1976 by Adam Benjamin, a politically adept and hard-working state senator. Madden had all the endorsements—Lake County Democratic Party, Mayor Hatcher, labor—because of his position;

Benjamin was shrewd enough not to hold that against anyone, because he knew that, once in, he would inherit all that support himself. He rose quickly to become Chairman of the Transportation Appropriations Subcommittee; he worked 18 hours a day and mastered both the details and big picture of his legislative work. It was too much for him: he was found dead in his office of a heart attack in September 1982.

Under Indiana law, the Democratic nomination—tantamount to election in this Democratic district—in these circumstances goes to the choice of the 1st District Democratic Chairman. The 1st district, under its new boundaries, extended east along Lake Michigan beyond Lake County, to the old industrial town of Michigan City (Hatcher's home town, incidentally); and the Democratic chairmanship of this unit, ordinarily an unimportant post, was held by Richard Hatcher. To fill the spot he named not Benjamin's widow, but state Senator Katie Hall, a black—much to the fury of Lake County Democratic Chairman Robert Pastrick and other white leaders. But there was nothing they could do. The courts would not overturn Hatcher's choice, the Republican candidate was pathetically weak, and the 1st district went Democratic in the general election, as usual (although there were some defections in the congressional race). Hall was elected not only to the 98th Congress, but also to fill the unexpired portion of Benjamin's term.

Pastrick's chance—and Hall's real challenge—will come in the congressional primary in May 1984. Hall's voting record is likely to be solidly liberal and pro-labor, and she may be able to do something for this economically distressed district on the Public Works and Transportation Committee. But her real battle is to convince the white majority in the primary that she will give them constituency services and aggressive representation. Can that be done in a district with as racially divisive a political history as the 1st? Against a single white challenger she must be considered vulnerable; her best chance is for the opposition to be split among several candidates.

The People   Pop. 1980: 547,100, dn. 5.9% 1970–80; voting age pop. 375,863; 22% Black, 7% Span. orig. 31% housing units rented. Median owner $40,100; renter $170. Households: 77% family, 45% with children, 60% married couples.

Presidential Vote

1980	Reagan (R)	100,349	(46%)
	Carter (D)	109,917	(50%)
	Anderson (I)	9,186	(4%)

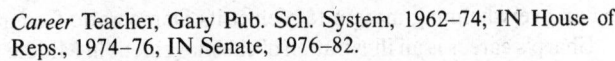

Rep. Katie Hall (D) Elected 1982; b. Apr. 3, 1938, Mound Bayou, MS; home, Gary; MS Valley State U., B.A. 1960, IN U., M.S. 1966; Protestant.

Career Teacher, Gary Pub. Sch. System, 1962–74; IN House of Reps., 1974–76, IN Senate, 1976–82.

Offices 132 CHOB, 202-225-2461. Also 215 W. 35th Ave., Gary 46408, 219-884-1177.

Committees *Post Office and Civil Service* (10th). Subcommittees: Civil Service; Postal Operations and Services. *Public Works and Transportation* (19th). Subcommittees: Aviation; Public Buildings and Grounds.

Group Ratings and Key Votes: Newly Elected

Election Results

1982 general	Katie Hall (D)	87,369	(56%)	($38,306)
	Thomas Krieger (R)	66,921	(43%)	($10,526)
1982 primary	Katie Hall (D) appointed			
1980 general	Adam Benjamin, Jr. (D)	112,016	(72%)	($73,867)
	Joseph Douglas Harkin (R)	43,537	(28%)	($0)

Campaign Contributions and Expenditures

1981-82		Direct Cont. 81-82				PACS brkdwn		
Receipts	$43,446	Indiv	$11,697	Agr	$—	Ideo	$7,625
Expend.	$38,306	Party	$1,110	Bus	$1,800	Lbr	$18,900
Unspent	$5,139	PACS	$30,675	Hlth	$—	Prof	$200

SECOND DISTRICT

When Robert and Helen Lynd published *Middletown* in the 1930s, they challenged the conventional wisdom that assumed small midwestern cities were tightly knit, homogeneous communities. They studied Muncie, Indiana—then as now a town with few ethnic minorities—and found a factory town divided sharply along class lines. The business elite—local bankers, merchants, executives at the Ball family's glass company and at the General Motors plants—saw themselves as typical Muncie citizens, and ran community affairs in what they believed was the common interest. The working class did not always agree, but was unable to do much about it. That picture has changed, massively, in the 50 years since. The workers unionized (in sometimes violent struggles with the companies), real incomes tripled for just about everyone, working class consciousness declined. The recent problems of the auto industry—the most important constituent part of Muncie's economy—should not obscure the vast improvement in economic conditions the auto industry, among others, helped to create.

Echoes remain of the Lynds' class-conscious Middletown, however, in Muncie and the other, similar towns which make up the bulk of Indiana's 2d congressional district. Voting patterns still tend to cleave the community along white collar/blue collar lines; and overall, Muncie is closer to being a marginal town than the Republican bastion some suppose. But the bitterness of the struggles of the 1930s seems gone. In 1982, with very high unemployment, the Muncie area still voted to reelect Senator Richard Lugar. And, at the same time, it voted by an overwhelming margin to reelect its Democratic Congressman, Phil Sharp.

Sharp's career is an illustration of the movement in Middle America from a class-conscious politics to something rather different. When he first ran for Congress here, in 1970, it was assumed that, if elected, he would vote a straight liberal-labor line on economic issues, as did virtually every non-southern Democrat in the House. But Sharp won the seat on non-economic as much as economic issues; Republican economic policies were unpopular in 1974, when he beat Republican David Dennis, but as important a factor was Dennis's opposition, on the House Judiciary Committee, to the impeachment of Richard Nixon. And even on economic issues, his position was not always orthodox. It was assumed, in the middle 1970s, that Democrats from non-oil-producing states would oppose any relaxation of price controls on oil and gas—indeed, this was a big campaign issue for many Democrats. But Sharp, as chairman of a special task force appointed by Speaker O'Neill, helped fashion a compromise energy program, which passed the House, and which phased out the price controls over several years. Sharp had become convinced of what now seems obvious: that attempts to hold down prices below market-clearing levels were reducing supplies and causing more problems than they were solving.

Sharp's appointment to that task force, and his concentration on energy issues, were typical of his career. He was one of the 1974 freshmen trusted by the leadership to do a solid job on a difficult issue which had great potential for dividing the Democratic Caucus. He now chairs the subcommittee on Fossil and Synthetic Fuels of the Energy and Commerce Committee whose work is not quite so crucial but is nonetheless important. Its most important issue seems likely to be deregulation of natural gas. Sharp tends to think there should be decontrol at some point, but he also wants to insure low prices and is not sure whether decontrol or revised controls would be the best way to do that in current circumstances. He also wants to continue stocking the strategic petroleum reserve—which is expensive, and tends to be a low priority item for many congressmen when oil prices are low.

On economic issues Sharp is generally, but not always, liberal; on foreign and cultural issues, as befits a representative from Indiana, he tends toward the conservative positions.

Sharp seemed likely to be one of the Democratic victims of the 1981 Republican redistricting in Indiana. His district (which used to be numbered the 10th) lost territory he carried easily and gained part of Indianapolis—the southern fringe suburbs, not the highest income part of the city, but leaning Republican on cultural issues—and heavily Republican Shelby and Johnson Counties. His Republican opponent, Ralph Van Natta, was well-financed and had experience in the legislature and as the head of the patronage-rich state motor vehicles department. Yet Sharp won, with a solid percentage. Van Natta carried Indianapolis and Johnson County. But Sharp carried some of the new territory, including the small city of Columbus (headquarters of Cummins Engine, which pays leading architects to design local public buildings). He had a near-unanimous 69% in Muncie's Delaware County, far more than he could expect from a class-conscious appeal, and 61% in Richmond, the district's second largest city, an old Quaker community (of the strain of Quakers who are strongly Republican).

It is too soon to say that Sharp has this district sewn up for the balance of the 1980s. Changes in the economy or the opposition could reverse the result one of these years, and Sharp, who by age 40 had fought seven fiercely contested congressional races, surely does not expect to win forever in Republican Indiana. But in the meantime he has the capacity and the position to be an accomplished legislator.

The People   Pop. 1980: 553,510, up 7.8% 1970–80; voting age pop. 390,981; 2% Black, 1% Span. orig. 26% housing units rented. Median owner $38,200; renter $165. Households: 77% family, 43% with children, 66% married couples.

Presidential Vote

1980	Reagan (R)	137,739	(61%)
	Carter (D)	76,210	(34%)
	Anderson (I)	10,082	(5%)

Rep. Philip R. Sharp (D) Elected 1974; b. July 15, 1942, Baltimore, MD; home, Muncie; DePauw U., Georgetown Sch. of Foreign Svc., B.S. 1964, Oxford U., 1966, Georgetown U., Ph.D. 1974; Methodist.

Career Legis. Aide to U.S. Sen. Vance Hartke, 1964–69; Asst. and Assoc. Prof. of Poli. Sci., Ball St. U., 1969–74; Dem. Nominee for U.S. House of Reps., 1970, 1972.

Offices 2452 RHOB, 202-225-3021. Also Fed. Bldg., 401 S. High St., Muncie 47305, 317-289-7948.

Committees *Energy and Commerce* (6th). Subcommittee: Fossil and Synthetic Fuels (Chairman). *Interior and Insular Affairs* (8th). Subcommittees: Energy and the Environment; Oversight and Investigations.

Group Ratings

	ADA	ACLU	COPE	CFA	LCV	LWV	NTU	NSI	COC	ACA	CSFC
1982	80	58	69	60	83	75	46	20	41	22	37
1981	65	—	68	79	86	—	41	—	21	33	47
1980	50	53	63	57	61	60	38	33	76	29	48

National Journal Ratings

	Economic		Foreign		Cultural	
1982	62%	(LIB)	77%	(LIB)	68%	(LIB)
	38%	(CONS)	23%	(CONS)	32%	(CONS)
1981	68%	(LIB)	65%	(LIB)	61%	(LIB)
	30%	(CONS)	35%	(CONS)	38%	(CONS)

Key Votes

1) Reagan 81 Budget	AGN	5) Incr SS Rtmt Age	AGN	9) Poor Pay Food Stamps	FOR
2) Reagan 81 Tax Cut	AGN	6) Saudi AWACS Sale	AGN	10) Ban Crt Busing Order	FOR
3) Bal Budget Amend	AGN	7) $ for MX Missile	AGN	11) Auto Local Content	FOR
4) Gas & Road Tax	FOR	8) Nerve Gas Prod	AGN	12) Nuclear Arms Freeze	FOR

Election Results

1982 general	Philip R. Sharp (D)	107,298	(56%)	($372,331)
	Ralph Van Natta (R)	83,593	(44%)	($285,770)
1982 primary	Philip R. Sharp (D)	33,039	(85%)	
	Two others	5,731	(15%)	
1980 general	Philip R. Sharp (D)	103,083	(53%)	($165,181)
	William C. Frazier (R)	90,051	(47%)	($279,789)

Campaign Contributions and Expenditures

1981-82		Direct Cont. 81-82		PACS brkdwn			
Receipts	$394,372	Indiv	$181,550	Agr	$5,825	Ideo	$16,250
Expend.	$372,331	Party	$6,250	Bus	$86,125	Lbr	$61,832
Unspent	$27,705	PACS	$188,150	Hlth	$6,900	Prof	$7,850
		Cand	$318				

Indep Expend: Agn: $2,446 (NCPAC)

THIRD DISTRICT

South Bend is one of those industrial cities set incongruously into the flat landscape of the limestone-bottomed plains of the Midwest. Surrounded by farm counties whose origins—and Republican allegiance—go back to the days when they served as northern terminals on the Underground Railroad, South Bend has a different origin. It is mostly the creation of the early 20th century, when its factories attracted an ethnic population here, which has always voted Democratic. Half a century ago South Bend was a boom town, like some place in Texas today; since World War II it has frequently been in trouble. It saw the collapse of its auto industry long before Detroit or Flint did: in the 1960s Studebaker went out of the auto business, and South Bend lost its largest employer. More recently its economy has suffered from other, less dramatic shutdowns and layoffs, to the point that its most vibrant economic institution is probably the University of Notre Dame. Interestingly, rural northern Indiana, which South Bend once threatened to overshadow, has done pretty well in recent decades. Its agricultural economy has generally been strong, and its small towns have attracted factories and mills even as those in cities like South Bend have been closing.

The 3d congressional district of Indiana has centered for years on South Bend; but it has mattered a great deal what other territory is included, particularly as South Bend, stagnant in population, has comprised a smaller and smaller percentage of the total district. Democrats have joined South Bend with the similar industrial city of Michigan City, to the west; Republicans have joined it with Elkhart, a higher income and heavily Republican city to the east, and with the rural counties directly south (one of which, however, Starke, often votes Democratic). The current redistricting plan was designed by Republicans and follows predictable outlines.

But it was only barely enough to reelect Republican Congressman John Hiler in 1982. Hiler had achieved one of the nation's notable upsets in 1980 when he beat John Brademas, for 22 years South Bend's congressman and the House Democratic Whip as well. Brademas's increasing prominence on national issues, and the unpopularity of the Carter administration with which he was increasingly associated, worked to beat him. Elected at 27, Hiler was a particularly pure Reagan Republican. Most congressmen, of whatever views, make a great show of bringing federal money to their districts. Hiler declines to do so. He announced publicly that he would not help local governments or businesses get federal assistance. Most congressmen make a big point of having a voting record that can be called independent. Hiler declines to do so. Instead he emphasized his lockstep support of Reagan administration programs. Nor is Hiler particularly articulate or personally engaging. He relies politically on what he believes.

In the redrawn 3d district it proved to be enough—just enough—in 1982. The Democratic nominee was a local legislator, but he proved unable to raise the kind of big money needed to win most congressional races these days. He carried South Bend's St. Joseph County with 58%, but Hiler got 63% in Elkhart County and an even higher percentage in one of the rural counties. Still, without redistricting Hiler would have lost; there was about a 6% swing against him. His fate for 1984 depends on the strength of his opposition and the state of the economy; his refusal to employ the tactics most congressmen use to make themselves popular, regardless of their party's popularity, leave him vulnerable to anti-Republican swings of opinion on national issues.

In the House, Hiler is part of the disciplined body of Republicans rather than a leader. He switched in 1983 from the Government Operations Committee—not a plum for someone of his views—to Banking, Finance, and Urban Affairs, and remains on the Small Business Committee, whose political attractiveness is much greater than its legislative importance.

The People Pop. 1980: 558,100, up 5.5% 1970–80; voting age pop. 395,121; 4% Black, 1% Span. orig. 22% housing units rented. Median owner $35,600; renter $168. Households: 76% family, 41% with children, 65% married couples.

Presidential Vote

1980	Reagan (R)	119,796	(57%)
	Carter (D)	78,214	(37%)
	Anderson (I)	13,242	(6%)

Rep. John P. Hiler (R) Elected 1980; b. Apr. 24, 1953, Chicago, IL; home, LaPorte; Williams Col., B.A. 1975, U. of Chicago, M.B.A. 1977; Roman Catholic.

Career Foundry exec., family business; LaPorte Repub. City Chmn.; Delegate, White House Conf. on Small Business.

Offices 316 CHOB, 202-225-3915. Also 120 River Glenn Ofc. Plaza, 501 E. Monroe, South Bend 46601, 219-234-4431.

Committees *Banking, Finance, and Urban Affairs* (15th). Subcommittees: Consumer Affairs and Coinage; Domestic Monetary Policy; General Oversight and Renegotiation. *Small Business* (5th). Subcommittee: Energy, Environment and Safety Issues Affecting Small Business.

Group Ratings

	ADA	ACLU	COPE	CFA	LCV	LWV	NTU	NSI	COC	ACA	CSFC
1982	5	25	11	20	38	58	91	100	86	82	72
1981	25	—	13	29	43	—	93	—	95	92	75

National Journal Ratings

	Economic		Foreign		Cultural	
1982	8%	(LIB)	27%	(LIB)	40%	(LIB)
	92%	(CONS)	72%	(CONS)	59%	(CONS)
1981	24%	(LIB)	41%	(LIB)	32%	(LIB)
	68%	(CONS)	59%	(CONS)	67%	(CONS)

Key Votes

1) Reagan 81 Budget	FOR	5) Incr SS Rtmt Age	FOR	9) Poor Pay Food Stamps	FOR
2) Reagan 81 Tax Cut	FOR	6) Saudi AWACS Sale	FOR	10) Ban Crt Busing Order	FOR
3) Bal Budget Amend	FOR	7) $ for MX Missile	FOR	11) Auto Local Content	AGN
4) Gas & Road Tax	FOR	8) Nerve Gas Prod	FOR	12) Nuclear Arms Freeze	AGN

Election Results

1982 general	John P. Hiler (R)	86,958	(51%)	($356,239)
	Richard Clay Bodine (D)	83,046	(49%)	($113,831)
1982 primary	John P. Hiler (R) unopposed	30,839		
1980 general	John P. Hiler (R)	103,972	(55%)	($407,979)
	John Brademas (D)	85,136	(45%)	($744,068)

Campaign Contributions and Expenditures

1981-82		Direct Cont. 81-82			PACS brkdwn		
Receipts	$354,045	Indiv	$206,401	Agr	$4,200	Ideo	$7,450
Expend.	$356,239	Party	$20,262	Bus	$86,800	Lbr	$—
Unspent	$36,123	PACS	$112,518	Hlth	$7,990	Prof	$—

Indirect Party Expend: $9,194   *Indep Expend:* For: $1,012 (NRA)

FOURTH DISTRICT

The 4th congressional district of Indiana centers on Fort Wayne, technically the state's second largest city, but actually just the largest of several small industrial cities; the metropolitan areas that rival Indianapolis are Indiana's overflows from Chicago and Louisville. Fort Wayne cannot be mistaken for that kind of metropolis: it is a typical medium-sized midwestern community, with a small black ghetto and nondescript frame houses that belong to people who work—or used to—in the factories and small businesses. Like many other such cities, Fort Wayne faced rough times in the early 1980s: double-digit unemployment, plant closings like that at International Harvester which wiped out 4,500 jobs in one fell swoop. Nor was the agricultural economy of the region around it doing well.

Yet these economic hard times did not seem to have much effect on the 4th district's politics. Ancestrally, this part of northern Indiana is heavily Republican: people here speak with hard R accents, and their ancestors supported and fought for the Union in the Civil War. In the years following the New Deal and the unionization of many plants here, Fort Wayne and the surrounding area would turn to the Democrats in times of economic trouble; this was especially pronounced in the recession years of 1958 and 1970, and up to 1976 the 4th district was represented by a Democrat. But the Democrats' nomination of a southerner in 1976 seemed to stimulate a residual regional Republicanism here, and the increasing importance of cultural patterns in voting has helped the Republicans in this corner of America where traditional family patterns still prevail.

The current congressman is Dan Coats. He served as an aide to Dan Quayle, the young newspaper scion who captured the district from the Democrats in 1976 and was elected to the Senate in 1980. Coats won the House seat that year easily, and had even less trouble winning reelection in 1982—despite the Fort Wayne area's economic problems.

In the House Coats sits on the Energy and Commerce Committee, one of the most sought after assignments; its jurisdiction includes most of the federal regulatory agencies and air pollution regulations. Coats does not have much seniority on any subcommittee, and is not a major actor in the foreground. But Energy and Commerce is closely divided on a number of important issues, and every vote is important. Coats usually takes the view that businesses have been overregulated, that the economy as a result has been hurt, and that consumers and the public would be better off with less onerous restriction of economic activity.

The People   Pop. 1980: 553,698, up 7.2% 1970–80; voting age pop. 382,150; 4% Black, 1% Span. orig. 22% housing units rented. Median owner $38,100; renter $168. Households: 76% family, 43% with children, 66% married couples.

Presidential Vote

1980	Reagan (R)	128,189	(59%)
	Carter (D)	73,699	(34%)
	Anderson (I)	16,699	(8%)

Rep. Daniel R. Coats (R) Elected 1980; b. May 16, 1943, Jackson, MI; home, Fort Wayne; Wheaton Col., B.A. 1965, IN U., J.D. 1971; Christian Reformed.

Career Army, 1966–68; Econ. consult. firm, 1968–70; Legal Intern, American Fletcher Natl. Bank, 1970–72; Asst. V.P. & Legal Counsel, Mutual Security Life Ins. Co., 1972–76; Dist. Rep. for U.S. Rep. J. Danforth (Dan) Quayle, 1976–80.

Offices 1417 LHOB, 202-225-4436. Also 326 Fed. Bldg., Fort Wayne 46802, 219-424-3040.

Committees *Energy and Commerce* (11th). Subcommittees: Energy Conservation and Power; Fossil and Synthetic Fuels. *Select Committee on Children, Youth, and Families* (3d).

Group Ratings

	ADA	ACLU	COPE	CFA	LCV	LWV	NTU	NSI	COC	ACA	CSFC
1982	30	25	21	30	47	58	87	100	73	77	65
1981	10	—	20	50	50	—	90	—	100	79	73

National Journal Ratings

	Economic		Foreign		Cultural	
1982	28%	(LIB)	52%	(LIB)	38%	(LIB)
	72%	(CONS)	48%	(CONS)	62%	(CONS)
1981	34%	(LIB)	34%	(LIB)	16%	(LIB)
	65%	(CONS)	63%	(CONS)	83%	(CONS)

Key Votes

1) Reagan 81 Budget	FOR	5) Incr SS Rtmt Age	FOR	9) Poor Pay Food Stamps	FOR
2) Reagan 81 Tax Cut	FOR	6) Saudi AWACS Sale	AGN	10) Ban Crt Busing Order	FOR
3) Bal Budget Amend	FOR	7) $ for MX Missile	AGN	11) Auto Local Content	AGN
4) Gas & Road Tax	FOR	8) Nerve Gas Prod	AGN	12) Nuclear Arms Freeze	AGN

Election Results

1982 general	Daniel R. Coats (R)	110,155	(64%)	($170,828)
	Roger Miller (D)	60,054	(35%)	($12,289)
1982 primary	Daniel R. Coats (R) unopposed	44,861		
1980 general	Daniel R. Coats (R)	120,055	(61%)	($223,695)
	John D. Walda (D)	77,542	(39%)	($126,520)

Campaign Contributions and Expenditures

1981-82		Direct Cont. 81-82		PACS brkdwn			
Receipts	$196,619	Indiv	$88,506	Agr	$3,350	Ideo	$400
Expend.	$170,828	Party	$18,285	Bus	$65,645	Lbr	$—
Unspent	$42,768	PACS	$82,744	Hlth	$13,000	Prof	$—

Indep Expend: For: $19,420 (AMAPAC)

FIFTH DISTRICT

People in the flatlands of northern Indiana think of themselves as living in the heartland of America, and for many good reasons. They live on the divide between the Great Lakes and

Mississippi River systems, on the major east–west railroads and highways that connect the nation's greatest metropolitan and industrial areas. They also live in small cities and large towns whose geometric regularity and neatness bespeak the virtues we think of as peculiarly American; and if those same cities and towns contain a few criminals, or if they suffer now from layoffs and unemployment, people there remain confident that most Americans—the typical resident and the men in charge of things—are competent, decent, sensible people who will do the right thing in time of crisis. This is a part of America with little immigrant heritage, where most people have ordinary (*i.e.,* Anglo–Saxon) names and white skins, and where most people vote Republican, as they have in most elections since the turbulent years before the Civil War.

This is the land of the 5th congressional district of Indiana, which extends most of the way across northern Indiana from the suburbs of Gary to the factory town of Marion and the much smaller town of North Manchester, home of Thomas R. Marshall, Woodrow Wilson's vice president. There are notes of discord here and there: echoes in the northwest corner of the racial animosities that dominate Gary politics, very high unemployment rates in Kokomo, where the Chrysler plant closed down. But basic values have not been shaken so much here as in many other parts of the nation: fully 79% of the households here contain families and 69% married couples—among the highest figures in the Midwest—and 45% have children, a high percentage given the rather old age structure. And the Republican Party held onto most of its ancestral support in the 1982 elections, despite the recession.

The 5th district, under the current redistricting, combines most of the old 2d and 5th districts. It was expressly designed to ease out of Congress Floyd Fithian, a Democrat elected against an unrepentently pro-Nixon Republican in 1974 and reelected three times; his home town was placed in the 7th district and most of the rest of his 2d district in the 5th, where he would have to face incumbent Republican Elwood Hillis. Fithian chose to run for statewide office instead: first for secretary of state, then, when things began looking better for Democrats, for the U.S. Senate. He ended up winning 46% of the vote against Republican Richard Lugar.

But Fithian didn't carry any of the counties in the 5th, and the Democrats did not make a serious campaign against Hillis. First elected in 1970, Hillis has had a record slightly more favorable to organized labor than most Indiana Republicans. But in 1981 he solidly supported the Reagan economic program, and in 1982 he carried Kokomo and Marion anyway.

For a representative of an inland district, Hillis has unusual committee assignments, Armed Services and Veterans' Affairs. This district does not have substantial military installations nor much in the way of defense contracts (the same is true of Indiana generally); one must conclude that Hillis serves on these bodies because he is interested in their work. A veteran of the Army, he is considered a partisan of the Army when the interests of the services collide, and he generally backs increased defense spending.

The People   Pop. 1980: 548,257, up 13.2% 1970–80; voting age pop. 380,248; 2% Black, 1% Span. orig. 22% housing units rented. Median owner $40,300; renter $166. Households: 79% family, 45% with children, 69% married couples.

Presidential Vote

1980	Reagan (R)	140,368	(64%)
	Carter (D)	68,760	(31%)
	Anderson (I)	9,677	(4%)

Rep. Elwood R. Hillis (R) Elected 1970; b. Mar. 6, 1926, Kokomo; home, Kokomo; IN U., B.S. 1949, J.D. 1952; Presbyterian.

Career Army, WWII; Practicing atty., 1952–71; IN House of Reps., 1967–71.

Offices 2336 RHOB, 202-225-5037. Also 518 N. Main St., Kokomo 46901, 317-457-4411.

Committees *Armed Services* (5th). Subcommittees: Military Personnel and Compensation; Seapower and Strategic and Critical Materials. *Veterans' Affairs* (3d). Subcommittees: Hospitals and Health Care; Oversight and Investigations.

Group Ratings

	ADA	ACLU	COPE	CFA	LCV	LWV	NTU	NSI	COC	ACA	CSFC
1982	10	25	35	20	33	50	72	100	67	83	62
1981	10	—	36	14	22	—	64	—	94	73	65
1980	22	13	35	29	27	22	39	88	78	70	66

National Journal Ratings

	Economic		Foreign		Cultural	
1982	27%	(LIB)	35%	(LIB)	39%	(LIB)
	73%	(CONS)	64%	(CONS)	61%	(CONS)
1981	22%	(LIB)	34%	(LIB)	14%	(LIB)
	77%	(CONS)	63%	(CONS)	85%	(CONS)

Key Votes

1) Reagan 81 Budget	FOR	5) Incr SS Rtmt Age	FOR
2) Reagan 81 Tax Cut	FOR	6) Saudi AWACS Sale	AGN
3) Bal Budget Amend	FOR	7) $ for MX Missile	FOR
4) Gas & Road Tax	—	8) Nerve Gas Prod	FOR

9) Poor Pay Food Stamps	FOR
10) Ban Crt Busing Order	FOR
11) Auto Local Content	FOR
12) Nuclear Arms Freeze	AGN

Election Results

1982 general	Elwood R. Hillis (R)	105,469	(61%)	($186,117)
	Allen Maxwell (D)	67,238	(39%)	($28,206)
1982 primary	Elwood R. Hillis (R) unopposed ...	43,232		
1980 general	Elwood R. Hillis (R)	129,474	(62%)	($185,414)
	Nels J. Ackerson (D)	80,378	(38%)	($115,086)

Campaign Contributions and Expenditures

1981-82		Direct Cont. 81-82		PACS brkdwn			
Receipts	$190,048	Indiv	$95,983	Agr	$4,050	Ideo	$1,900
Expend.	$186,117	Party	$10,682	Bus	$54,075	Lbr	$1,100
Unspent	$4,394	PACS	$75,739	Hlth	$10,575	Prof	$400
		Cand	$250				

Indep Expend: For: $937 (NRA)

SIXTH DISTRICT

If you want to find solidly Republican suburbs in the United States, you can do no better than to come to the suburbs of Indianapolis, Indiana. Thirty years ago, Indianapolis was a compact city; most of its residents lived within four or five miles of the Soldiers' and Sailors' Monument downtown. There were a few rich neighborhoods, mostly on the streets directly north of downtown, beyond the home of Benjamin Harrison, Indiana's one president; but most of Indianapolis consisted of modest neighborhoods of frame houses with clapboard shutters where most people voted Republican in most elections. In the years since, real incomes have risen here as elsewhere, and people have moved out. The old central neighborhoods have populations more Democratic and sometimes more black. And the once vacant flat fields and small hills 10 to 20 miles from downtown have become filled with people seemingly self-selected as strong Republicans.

For there is little radical chic in Indianapolis. People who have made money pride themselves on being brighter than other people. To them it seems natural that those they consider not-so-bright—people with low incomes, union members, and the like—will be Democrats and that bright people will usually be Republicans. After all, almost all the articulate sources of opinion in Indianapolis—the newspapers, the mayor and the governor, leading businessmen and civic leaders—are Republicans. They are, moreover, unabashed boosters of the free enterprise system, and sometimes even mystic devotees of free market economics.

The 6th congressional district of Indiana covers most of the Indianapolis suburbs. It includes some 120,000 people in Indianapolis itself, in the affluent north side, where gracious new suburbs are laid out on the hills near the White River; Hamilton County, a once mostly rural and now very affluent county, which gave Senator Richard Lugar 80% of its votes in the 1982 Senate race; the only slightly less Republican suburbs of Boone and Hancock Counties; and, incongruously, the industrial city of Anderson. With its General Motors plants, its strong United Auto Workers locals, and its high unemployment rate, Anderson would have seemed sure to go Democratic in 1982; yet it too went Republican, though much more narrowly than the rest of the district.

Before the 1982 redistricting, two Democrats represented the Indianapolis area in the House. The Republican legislature made the 6th a safe Republican district by keeping all Democratic territory in the 10th and in effect conceding it to the opposition. The 6th was so obviously hostile that Congressman David Evans, who had represented a different-shaped district with the same number for eight years, decided to run in the 10th against fellow incumbent Democrat Andrew Jacobs instead of here.

So the real battle was in the Republican primary. The district's boundaries were reportedly designed by state Republican Chairman Bruce Melchert, and he was a candidate. He ran with endorsements from Indianapolis Mayor (and former Congressman) William Hudnut and former Governor Otis Bowen and as an organization Republican—a strong supporter of Reagan economic programs, and but a less enthusiastic supporter of conservative positions on cultural issues. His main opponent was Dan Burton, at 44 already a veteran wheelhorse in Indianapolis politics. A hearty, backslapping type of politician, an enthusiastic conservative on cultural as well as economic issues, Burton has been running for office every two years, with one exception, since 1966. He was elected to the Indiana House in 1966, 1976, and 1978, and to the Indiana Senate in 1968 and 1980; he lost elections for the U.S. House in 1970 (to Andrew Jacobs) and 1972 (in the primary to William Hudnut). This time he finally won a congressional race, by winning the primary with 28% of the vote. Melchert was able to carry only Indianapolis, and two other candidates—one of them a perennial challenger to Democrat Philip Sharp in the old 10th district—had only regional strength. Assuming that he can consolidate his Republican base and avoid serious primary opposition, Burton will likely hold a safe seat for at least 10 years.

Burton should be one of the heartiest conservatives in the House. The 1982 election results may have chastened other Republicans; this one, who finally won a congressional race after years of trying, was probably emboldened. Burton serves as a junior member of the Government Operations and Veterans' Affairs Committees. Should he win attention for his role on specific legislation, it will be the result of some personal initiative, rather than the result of tending to committee duties.

The People   Pop. 1980: 540,939, up 16.1% 1970–80; voting age pop. 381,833; 3% Black, 1% Span. orig. 26% housing units rented. Median owner $45,600; renter $200. Households: 77% family, 43% with children, 67% married couples.

Presidential Vote

1980	Reagan (R)	136,596	(64%)
	Carter (D)	65,813	(31%)
	Anderson (I)	9,884	(5%)

Rep. Dan Burton (R) Elected 1982; b. June 21, 1938, Indianapolis; home, Indianapolis; IN U., 1958–59, Cincinnati Bible Seminary, 1959–60; Protestant.

Career Army, 1956–57; Founder, Dan Burton Ins. Agency; IN Senate, 1969–70, 1981–82; IN House of Reps., 1967–68, 1977–80.

Offices 120 CHOB, 202-225-2276. Also 8900 Keystone Crossing, Su. 1110, Indianapolis 46240, 317-848-0201; and 922 Meridian Plaza, Anderson 46016, 317-649-6887.

Committees *Government Operations* (9th). Subcommittees: Government Information, Justice, and Agriculture; Legislation and National Security; Manpower and Housing. *Veterans' Affairs* (9th). Subcommittees: Compensation, Pension, and Insurance; Oversight and Investigation. *Select Committee on Children, Youth, and Families* (6th).

Group Ratings and Key Votes: Newly Elected

Election Results

1982 general	Dan Burton (R)	131,100	(65%)	($407,718)
	George Grabianowski (D)	70,764	(35%)	($36,226)
1982 primary	Dan Burton (R)	23,640	(28%)	
	Bruce Melchert (R)	18,380	(22%)	($189,918)
	Four others	41,903	(50%)	($322,883)
1980 general	David W. Evans (D)	99,089	(50%)	($311,007)
	David G. Crane (R)	98,302	(50%)	($595,637)

Campaign Contributions and Expenditures

1981-82		Direct Cont. 81-82		PACS brkdwn			
Receipts	$422,747	Indiv	$177,741	Agr	$7,350	Ideo	$17,350
Expend.	$407,718	Party	$18,772	Bus	$79,625	Lbr	$2,500
Unspent	$15,938	PACS	$128,014	Hlth	$8,200	Prof	$1,100
		Cand	$76,012				

Indirect Party Expend: $35,355   *Indep Expend:* For: $930 (NRA)

SEVENTH DISTRICT

Like the old Wabash Cannonball—one of the most famous of the vanished passenger trains—the Wabash River flows across the rolling farmland of western Indiana on its way to the Ohio and Mississippi Rivers. And in a nearly straight line from Indianapolis to St. Louis runs the old National Road, now U.S. 40, closely paralleled by Interstate 70. The river and the road intersect in Terre Haute, which with fewer than 100,000 people is still the largest city in Indiana's 7th congressional district. Despite its elegant French name, Terre Haute is a rough and crude place, once known for its gambling and vice; it has long had the look of a run-down factory town. Politically Terre Haute has long had a strong Democratic machine (although it was the home town of the great Socialist leader Eugene Debs), which more often than not has controlled the Vigo County Courthouse.

The Wabash Cannonball traversed, in its day, both Republican and Democratic territory. The dividing line, roughly, was Terre Haute and the National Road. To the north people speak with the hard-edged accent of the Midwest; to the south they drawl in a manner reminiscent of Dixie. The counties to the north are traditionally Republican, those to the south traditionally Democratic. You can see the demarcation in maps of voting behavior in the 1860s. And more than a century later, although these preferences were hard to detect in the late 1960s and early 1970s, when the whole area went Republican, they surfaced again when Jimmy Carter, of Plains, Georgia, ran against Gerald Ford, of Grand Rapids, Michigan, in 1976. Carter carried the southern part of the district in 1976 and 1980 as well.

The 7th district was created basically in its present form by a Democratic legislature in 1966 with the intention of electing a Democratic congressman. Instead it has elected Republican John Myers ever since. He has benefited from weak opposition and from the 1982 redistricting, which added two suburban Indianapolis counties, and substituted for Bloomington and liberal arts Indiana University the city of Lafayette and technical Purdue. Myers was not seriously opposed and won easily.

That makes Myers one of the more senior House Republicans. Like so many of the midwestern Republicans who served in the House for years, Myers is quiet and uncontroversial. Younger Republicans seek to expose Democratic wrongdoing and to throw the House into turmoil; Myers does his duty by opposing what the Democrats propose and does not think of obstructing anything. He is fourth ranking Republican on the Appropriations Committee, and ranking Republican on the Energy and Water Development Subcommittee, which parcels out money for rivers and harbors projects. Such a post would once have made Myers potentially one of the most powerful members of the House. But today, when few voters care much about dams or new post offices, and Appropriations has lost much of its decision-making power to the budget process, Myers has far less chance to exert clout. In any case, he does not seem inclined to do so.

The People   Pop. 1980: 555,192, up 9.2% 1970–80; voting age pop. 403,139; 2% Black, 1% Span. orig., 1% Asian orig. 24% housing units rented. Median owner $36,400; renter $159. Households: 75% family, 40% with children, 66% married couples.

Presidential Vote

1980	Reagan (R)	136,445	(60%)
	Carter (D)	77,802	(34%)
	Anderson (I)	12,080	(5%)

Rep. John T. Myers (R) Elected 1966; b. Feb. 8, 1927, Covington; home, Covington; IN St. U., B.S. 1951; Episcopal.

Career Army, WWII; Cashier and Trust Officer, Foundation Trust Co., 1954–66.

Offices 2372 RHOB, 202-225-5805. Also Fed. Bldg., Terre Haute 47808, 812-238-1619.

Committees *Appropriations* (4th). Subcommittees: Agriculture, Rural Development; Energy and Water Development; Legislative. *Standards of Official Conduct* (3d).

Group Ratings

	ADA	ACLU	COPE	CFA	LCV	LWV	NTU	NSI	COC	ACA	CSFC
1982	5	0	17	30	8	17	73	100	86	78	63
1981	0	—	17	0	0	—	61	—	83	88	71
1980	11	20	14	14	13	20	55	100	70	75	75

National Journal Ratings

	Economic		Foreign		Cultural	
1982	19%	(LIB)	41%	(LIB)	4%	(LIB)
	81%	(CONS)	59%	(CONS)	87%	(CONS)
1981	4%	(LIB)	3%	(LIB)	4%	(LIB)
	79%	(CONS)	87%	(CONS)	90%	(CONS)

Key Votes

1) Reagan 81 Budget	FOR	5) Incr SS Rtmt Age	FOR	9) Poor Pay Food Stamps	FOR
2) Reagan 81 Tax Cut	FOR	6) Saudi AWACS Sale	FOR	10) Ban Crt Busing Order	FOR
3) Bal Budget Amend	FOR	7) $ for MX Missile	FOR	11) Auto Local Content	AGN
4) Gas & Road Tax	AGN	8) Nerve Gas Prod	FOR	12) Nuclear Arms Freeze	AGN

Election Results

1982 general	John T. Myers (R)	115,884	(62%)	($154,205)
	Stephen Bonney (D)	70,249	(38%)	($21,883)
1982 primary	John T. Myers (R) unopposed	48,355		
1980 general	John T. Myers (R)	137,604	(66%)	($142,908)
	Patrick D. Carroll (D)	69,051	(33%)	($51,232)

Campaign Contributions and Expenditures

1981-82		Direct Cont. 81-82				PACS brkdwn		
Receipts	$153,837	Indiv	$70,898	Agr	$3,900	Ideo	$950
Expend.	$154,205	Party	$10,751	Bus	$36,370	Lbr	$—
Unspent	$70,146	PACS	$48,723	Hlth	$7,100	Prof	$400

EIGHTH DISTRICT

The 8th congressional district of Indiana covers the southwest portion of the state. Its boundaries are as irregular as pieces of a jigsaw puzzle: the result of a partisan redistricting by the Republican legislature. The district extends eastward to take in a hunk of Republican Washington County and has a piece taken out of it in the west to remove Democratic Dubois. Similarly, only part of the university city of Bloomington—not all that Democratic a town anyway—is included. The largest city in the district remains Evansville; it would have been hard to remove the Democratic precincts of this usually closely divided industrial city, because it sits right on the Ohio River across from Kentucky. Oddly, this corner of Indiana was the first part of the state settled by white men. Vincennes, now a small town on the banks of the Wabash River, was once the metropolis of Indiana, and Robert Owen, the Scottish philanthropist and visionary, established the town of New Harmony downstream. Owen's son was the first congressman from the area, elected in 1842 and 1844.

Much of southwestern Indiana was settled by German Catholics, who have traditionally voted Democratic. During the Civil War most of this area was copperhead country, friendly to the South and hostile to Mr. Lincoln's war. Today, although the issues have changed, the 8th remains one part of Indiana within the Democrats' reach. It went for Jimmy Carter in 1976, and for Birch Bayh as late as 1980; even with its current borders, it came close to going for Democrat Floyd Fithian over Senator Richard Lugar in 1982.

The clash of local Democratic heritage with state and national Republican trends has made the 8th one of the nation's premier marginal congressional districts. It elected four different congressmen in four election years in the 1970s—the only district in the nation to do so. It ousted incumbents of varying parties in 1958, 1966, 1974, 1978, and 1982. The last incumbent to be defeated was Joel Deckard, a Republican whose resume reads like a list of fads (solar heating one year, cable TV another). Elected in 1978, Deckard had an occasionally maverick record (he opposed nuclear power), but he also had the capacity to get himself in trouble. In October 1982 he was charged with drunk driving when he missed a turn and crashed into a tree, and that was effectively the end of his congressional career.

The current congressman is Frank McCloskey, who for 11 years was mayor of Bloomington. McCloskey came to that office in 1971 as the champion of students and liberals; he stayed in office by attracting out-of-state industry to Bloomington and by improving services to elderly citizens. At 43, McCloskey is just a little older than the baby boom generation whose attitudes were shaped by Vietnam and Watergate; he served in the Air Force in the 1950s and, unlike some slightly younger congressmen who are just starting families, has a college-age daughter. He has been an adaptable enough politician to win three elections in a quickly changing Bloomington, and to win the 1982 congressional election even though he lost the relatively high income part of Bloomington which is in the 8th district. McCloskey campaigned on economic issues; in the House his major committee assignment is Armed Services.

This district has been closely contested so many times—in every election since 1974—and the Indiana Republican Party is so capable of financing a strong challenge that it seems almost certain that McCloskey will face a tough fight here in 1984.

The People   Pop. 1980: 546,744, up 9.3% 1970–80; voting age pop. 395,151; 2% Black. 24% housing units rented. Median owner $34,700; renter $154. Households: 74% family, 39% with children, 64% married couples.

Presidential Vote

1980	Reagan (R)	127,417	(54%)
	Carter (D)	95,823	(41%)
	Anderson (I)	10,846	(5%)

Rep. Francis X. McCloskey (D) Elected 1982; b. June 12, 1939, Philadelphia, PA; home, Bloomington; IN U., B.A. 1968, J.D. 1971; Roman Catholic.

Career   USAF; Newspaper reporter; Mayor of Bloomington, 1971–82.

Offices   116 CHOB, 202-225-4636. Also 210 S.E. 6th St., Evansville 47713, 812-425-6111.

Committees   *Armed Services* (26th). Subcommittees: Military Personnel and Compensation; Research and Development. *Small Business* (20th). Subcommittee: Antitrust and Restraint of Trade Activities Affecting Small Business.

Group Ratings and Key Votes: Newly Elected

Election Results

1982 general	Francis X. McCloskey (D)	100,592	(51%)	($157,223)
	H. Joel Deckard (R)	94,127	(48%)	($286,682)
1982 primary	Francis X. McCloskey (D) unopposed	36,698		
1980 general	H. Joel Deckard (R)	119,415	(55%)	($222,543)
	Kenneth C. Snider (D)	97,059	(45%)	($137,761)

Campaign Contributions and Expenditures

1981–82		Direct Cont. 81-82		PACS brkdwn			
Receipts	$157,501	Indiv	$67,422	Agr	$—	Ideo	$5,750
Expend.	$157,223	Party	$12,403	Bus	$1,000	Lbr	$58,442
Unspent	$277	PACS	$68,265	Hlth	$750	Prof	$1,000
		Cand	$110				

Indirect Party Expend: $500   *Indep Expend:* For: $1,451 (CACPAC)

NINTH DISTRICT

The Ohio River Valley was the first part of Indiana settled by white men. Most of them were southerners, from across the river in Kentucky or over the mountains in Virginia; they came here in the first two decades of the 19th century and established a new state. Their old city of Madison, on the Ohio, still has many of its marvelous old buildings from the days when it was one of the busiest ports on the Ohio River; but it has been a backwater since the middle of the 19th century. Farther down the river is Corydon, from 1816 to 1825 the state capital. Many other towns have well preserved 19th century buildings—well preserved, because since the railroads replaced Ohio River steamers as the main form of transportation in the 19th century, there has been little economic or population growth in this area.

The settlers in this part of Indiana retained their affection for things southern into the Civil War and beyond; one of their number, Jesse Bright, was expelled from the Senate in 1862 because of his Confederate sympathies. The hills along the Ohio typically deliver Democratic majorities, at least in elections that are close on the statewide level; even more Democratic are the working class Indiana suburbs of Louisville.

Most of Indiana's Ohio River counties, and an oddly shaped collection of lightly populated counties inland form Indiana's 9th congressional district. The irregularity of the boundaries results from the desire of the Republican legislature to pack as much Democratic territory into this district as possible. In effect, they were conceding it to Democratic Congressman Lee Hamilton, as well they might.

Hamilton was first elected in the 1964 landslide and has become one of the more senior Democrats in the House. His major attention is devoted to foreign affairs. He is third ranking Democrat on the Foreign Affairs Committee, behind two considerably older men; he chairs the Europe and the Middle East Subcommittee. On Middle Eastern issues, he is one of the few members of Congress or the administration who is genuinely respected on all sides. Hamilton painstakingly approaches difficult issues cautiously, hears out all sides, reaches decisions or makes recommendations judiciously and on the merits. He is one of those relatively rare members who can sway a vote in committee or on the floor just because members, of both parties, respect his judgment and fairness.

The Middle East is not the only touchy issue Hamilton has dealt with. He is involved in European foreign policy issues—the latest NATO problem, missile deployment, trade barriers. He is one of the House's leading experts on international lending institutions. He served on the Ethics Committee during its investigation of South Korea's lobbying; and advocates of tough enforcement of ethics codes see him as the strongest possible leader in any such effort. He is likely to chair the House Foreign Affairs Committee some day, and may well be able to elevate it to a more influential position than it currently occupies.

The redistricters actually removed Hamilton's home town of Columbus from the 9th district, but that did not stop him from running and easily winning in the new district. He has had his chances to run for statewide office (notably against Senator Vance Hartke in the 1976 primary) and passed them by; he seems certain to win reelection indefinitely in this district.

The People Pop. 1980: 544,873, up 14.2% 1970–80; voting age pop. 383,018; 2% Black, 1% Span. orig. 23% housing units rented. Median owner $36,500; renter $158. Households: 77% family, 44% with children, 67% married couples.

Presidential Vote

1980	Reagan (R)	112,578	(53%)
	Carter (D)	92,941	(43%)
	Anderson (I)	8,747	(4%)

Rep. Lee H. Hamilton, Jr. (D) Elected 1964; b. Apr. 20, 1931, Daytona Beach, FL; home, Columbus; DePauw U., B.A. 1952, Goethe U., Frankfort, Germany, 1952–53, IN U., J.D. 1956; Methodist.

Career Practicing atty., 1956–64; Instructor, Amer. Banking Inst., 1960–61.

Offices 2187 RHOB, 202-225-5315. Also U.S.P.O., Columbus 47201, 812-372-2571.

Committees *Foreign Affairs* (3d). Subcommittees: Europe and the Middle East (Chairman); International Security and Scientific Affairs. *Joint Economic Committee* (Vice Chairman). Subcommittees: Economic Goals and Intergovernmental Policy (Chairman); Monetary and Fiscal Policy. *Permanent Select Committee on Intelligence* (6th). Subcommittee: Oversight and Evaluation.

Group Ratings

	ADA	ACLU	COPE	CFA	LCV	LWV	NTU	NSI	COC	ACA	CSFC
1982	70	50	67	60	79	75	41	60	45	30	38
1981	65	—	66	71	64	—	19	—	28	33	44
1980	44	47	47	57	61	90	25	22	76	46	43

National Journal Ratings

	Economic		Foreign		Cultural	
1982	58%	(LIB)	65%	(LIB)	62%	(LIB)
	42%	(CONS)	35%	(CONS)	38%	(CONS)
1981	68%	(LIB)	69%	(LIB)	56%	(LIB)
	30%	(CONS)	30%	(CONS)	44%	(CONS)

Key Votes

1) Reagan 81 Budget	AGN	5) Incr SS Rtmt Age	FOR	9) Poor Pay Food Stamps	AGN
2) Reagan 81 Tax Cut	AGN	6) Saudi AWACS Sale	AGN	10) Ban Crt Busing Order	FOR
3) Bal Budget Amend	AGN	7) $ for MX Missile	AGN	11) Auto Local Content	FOR
4) Gas & Road Tax	FOR	8) Nerve Gas Prod	AGN	12) Nuclear Arms Freeze	FOR

Election Results

1982 general	Lee H. Hamilton, Jr. (D)	121,094	(67%)	($182,049)
	Floyd Coates (R)	58,532	(32%)	($232,749)
1982 primary	Lee H. Hamilton, Jr. (D) unopposed	66,312		
1980 general	Lee H. Hamilton, Jr. (D)	136,574	(64%)	($122,674)
	George Meyer, Jr. (R)	75,601	(36%)	($0)

Campaign Contributions and Expenditures

1981–82		Direct Cont. 81–82		PACS brkdwn			
Receipts	$161,022	Indiv	$83,798	Agr	$5,740	Ideo	$2,250
Expend.	$182,049	Party	$9,820	Bus	$25,725	Lbr	$20,400
Unspent	$447	PACS	$57,755	Hlth	$3,000	Prof	$350

TENTH DISTRICT

Indianapolis is Indiana's largest city, its capital and one of the few cities that indisputably sets the tone—and a distinctive tone—for an entire state. That tone can best be described as businesslike. Indianapolis has its factories, but it is not really an industrial city; it is more an office town, with major banks, insurance companies, and state government. Nor does it have the yeasty ethnic mix of most midwestern cities. There are some blacks here and some identifiable ethnics, but the dominant tone is very much white Protestant. Indianapolis did not share in the dynamic growth of the industrial Great Lakes cities in the 1900–30 period; it is not sharing today in their sharp and precipitous decline.

As in all of Indiana, politics is just one more everyday business here. Of the two major banks, for example, one is Republican and the other Democratic; naturally both are interested to know which party will win the state treasurer's office. Patronage is an integral part of politics and civil service virtually unheard of. Most state, county, and city employees traditionally "contribute" 2% of their paychecks to the party that got them their jobs. The national headquarters of the American Legion stares down toward the federal building and the state capital; the Republican and Democratic banks glare at each other across the Soldiers' and Sailors' Monument; this is a serious town, without much sense of humor.

Yet stern, usually Republican Indianapolis is represented in Congress by a Democrat with a puckish sense of humor. Andrew Jacobs has been a member of Congress for all but two years since 1964, but he refuses to take things too seriously. He has a fatalistic approach: in 1975 he refused to board an Indianapolis–Washington plane because only first class seats were available; it crashed, killing all aboard. He flouted tradition later that year when he married Congresswoman Martha Keys of Kansas. They met in that most unromantic of environments, the House Ways and Means Committee room; and although their voting records were not identical, they decided to marry. On weekends Jacobs flew to Indianapolis and Keys took the same plane on to Kansas City, until she was defeated for reelection in 1978.

Jacobs owed his initial election to the Democratic sweep in 1964 and his first reelections to a Democratic redistricting in 1966 and 1968. Because 1970 was a recession year, it was a good Democratic year in Indiana; in 1972 he was defeated by William Hudnut, now Indianapolis's mayor. Returned to office in the Watergate year of 1974, Jacobs has developed a record that has made him close to unbeatable. He has grown less enthusiastic and more skeptical about federal spending programs over the years, and more skeptical; his labor voting record declined in the 1970s to the point that local Democratic activists were grumbling. As a member of the Ways and Means Committee, he is one reason why there was no progressive tax reform during the Carter years; he is dubious about the worth of oil and gas price controls. On all economic issues his views are not notably more conservative than those of other Indiana Democrats. He brought to the Reagan economic program the same bemused skepticism he brought to Democratic panaceas. But particularly on issues where he has had a chance to be pivotal, Jacobs has made a difference often in a direction few would have predicted in the 1960s.

Jacobs brings the same bemusement to his own ambitions. He chairs Ways and Means's Health Subcommittee, a position less important than it sounds. It has jurisdiction over only Medicare, and its only likely task is to prop up the weakening financial position of the program. Characteristically, Jacobs announced he took that chairmanship only because a better one was not available.

His constituents don't seem to mind. The Republican legislature, despairing of beating both of Indianapolis's Democratic congressmen, made one district so Republican and one, the 10th, so Democratic, that they both decided to run in the latter. The 10th took in basically all of Indianapolis inside the Interstate 465 loop, except for the rich precincts directly north of downtown. It included most of Indianapolis's black voters, the white working class precincts out around the suburb of Speedway (the site of the Indianapolis 500), and the middle class areas east and south of town.

The two candidates presented quite a contrast. David Evans, at 36, had been campaigning assiduously since he first ran for the House 10 years before and since he first won in 1974; he was one of those earnest, if not particularly cerebral, young Democrats who had molded his record to his district and had used all the advantages of incumbency to win reelection. Jacobs, at 50, his eccentricities well known, declined to spend much money and won the primary anyway. He won the general election with a greater percentage than he had ever received in the less Democratic districts he represented in the 1960s and 1970s. For the first time in his career he has a truly safe district; the question is whether he will become more creative or more eccentric.

The People Pop. 1980: 541,811, dn. 12.4% 1970–80; voting age pop. 384,402; 25% Black, 1% Span. orig. 39% housing units rented. Median owner $28,400; renter $164. Households: 68% family, 39% with children, 51% married couples.

Presidential Vote

1980	Reagan (R)	....	116,179	(50%)
	Carter (D)	....	105,018	(45%)
	Anderson (I)	....	11,216	(5%)

Rep. Andrew Jacobs, Jr. (D) Elected 1974; b. Feb. 24, 1932, Indianapolis; home, Indianapolis; IN U., B.S. 1955, LL.B. 1958; Roman Catholic.

Career USMC, Korea; Practicing atty., 1958–65, 1973–74; IN House of Reps., 1959–60; U.S. House of Reps., 1965–73.

Offices 1533 LHOB, 202-225-4011. Also 441 A Fed. Bldg., 46 E. Ohio St., Indianapolis 46204, 317-269-7331.

Committee *Ways and Means* (7th). Subcommittees: Health (Chairman); Social Security.

Group Ratings

	ADA	ACLU	COPE	CFA	LCV	LWV	NTU	NSI	COC	ACA	CSFC
1982	85	67	70	70	80	83	56	20	41	14	38
1981	90	—	68	100	93	—	64	—	16	25	41
1980	50	53	53	50	48	40	67	44	58	63	66

National Journal Ratings

	Economic		Foreign		Cultural	
1982	67%	(LIB)	91%	(LIB)	77%	(LIB)
	33%	(CONS)	8%	(CONS)	22%	(CONS)
1981	67%	(LIB)	76%	(LIB)	80%	(LIB)
	33%	(CONS)	24%	(CONS)	20%	(CONS)

Key Votes

1) Reagan 81 Budget AGN	5) Incr SS Rtmt Age AGN	9) Poor Pay Food Stamps AGN
2) Reagan 81 Tax Cut AGN	6) Saudi AWACS Sale AGN	10) Ban Crt Busing Order AGN
3) Bal Budget Amend FOR	7) $ for MX Missile AGN	11) Auto Local Content FOR
4) Gas & Road Tax FOR	8) Nerve Gas Prod AGN	12) Nuclear Arms Freeze FOR

Election Results

1982 general	Andrew Jacobs, Jr. (D)	114,674	(67%)	($112,683)
	Michael Carroll (R)	56,992	(33%)	($177,176)
1982 primary	Andrew Jacobs, Jr. (D)	30,696	(60%)	
	Dave Evans (D)	17,654	(35%)	($184,351)
1980 general	Andrew Jacobs, Jr. (D)	105,468	(57%)	($39,581)
	Sheila Suess (R)	78,743	(43%)	($437,871)

Campaign Contributions and Expenditures*

1981-82		Direct Cont. 81-82	
Receipts	$109,779	Indiv	$105,665
Expend.	$112,683	Party	$100
Unspent	$870	Cand	$1,000

*Received no PAC contributions

IOWA

When you think of Iowa you think of farms—some of the greenest, most fertile, best-tended farms known to man. Iowa has more acreage in cropland than any other state; its crop production is greater in dollar terms than any other state but California's. Iowa was first settled in the years before the Civil War and filled up rapidly afterwards. It has never grown rapidly since and has sent many of its young people off to make their livings in the East or West. Superficially, there has been little change here in many respects since the turn of the century. Most Iowans still live on farms or in small towns, not in large cities or surrounding suburbs. They live in families; the divorce rate is among the nation's lowest. Iowa has no military installations and very little defense industry—few reminders that this heartland of America has become more entangled with the outside world since the days of the Spanish–American War. Iowa has never experienced rapid urbanization nor has it been home to many immigrants more exotic than German Catholics or Scandinavians; and the state is not known for its exotic lifestyles.

Yet in this century Iowa has changed a great deal—more dramatically in many ways than many parts of urban America. The key change has been in the productivity of agriculture. Technology in the late 19th century—the railroads, refrigeration—made possible the market agriculture we know today, and Iowa has been a leader in making it more productive. It is hard to overstate how great that gain in productivity has been. At the turn of the century, when the railroad network was complete and food processing was already a big industry, nearly half of all Americans lived on farms and produced enough among them to feed a nation of 76 million and export some besides. Today only 3% of Americans are farmers, but they produce enough to feed a nation of 226 million much better and export enough to feed millions more around the world besides.

Iowa is responsible for much of that, not only because it has some of America's richest farmland, but also because it has produced some of the most important crop hybrids and improved management and marketing techniques. This is a state where people's houses and personal values seem old-fashioned, but where people are innovators in business life. Far from being closed to the outside world, Iowans are more open to it than many residents of the insular urban villages which, together, make up most of New York City. Unlike most Americans, Iowans are export-conscious: they know that their prosperity depends in large part on exports and world markets; they are aware as well of the importance to their own lives of USDA regulations made in Washington and price fluctuations on the Chicago Board of Trade. Iowans are served by sophisticated newspapers, led by the *Des Moines Register & Tribune,* one of the few papers in the nation with genuine statewide circulation; the state also has advanced university communities in Iowa City, Ames, and many small college towns. Back in 1900 most Iowans seldom left their home counties and only on rare occasions left the state. Now the farthest reaches of the world are only a few hours' plane ride away through connections at O'Hare Airport.

The changes that have come to Iowa have come largely because of changes in agriculture, and the prosperity of Iowa remains very dependent on the success of agriculture— particularly corn, hogs, barley, oats, soybeans, wheat, dairy and beef cattle. Farmers are the nation's largest class of entrepreneurs, and on their revenues—not their profits—depends the whole fabric of Iowa's economic life. It is subject, therefore, to violent ups and downs, since small changes in prices, small increases in costs, or simply a break in the weather can have huge effects on farmers' incomes. So Iowa feels very vulnerable to downturns in agricultural prices, very dependent on trends it cannot control. But it tries to control them: when prices fall, Iowa demands that the government prop them up in various complicated ways; when interest rates rise, Iowa demands that they be forced back down; when presidential candidates come to Iowa's precinct caucuses in January, as they did in droves in 1980, Iowa forces most of them to pledge that they will not interrupt the flow of grain to the Soviet Union just because the Soviets invade another country.

Over the long run Iowa agriculture has been prosperous as well as productive; and in the late 1970s farmers were reduced to complaining about the high price of farmland, which made it hard for young men to buy a farm but of course just reflected high prices and profits. On the whole, agriculture has been one of the healthiest segments of the American economy, one that continues to grow more productive while heavy industry stagnates, one that produces exports and foreign exchange while much of the nation is worried about competition from imports. Yet in the early 1980s, Iowa's farmer-entrepreneurs suffered severe setbacks, and the state's economy reeled; sales of agricultural machinery—Iowa's main manufactured products—virtually stopped. The very fact that so many Iowans practice as well as preach free enterprise, that they are entrepreneurs and small businessmen, makes them seek government aid and work for government programs in any period of threatened bad times, because they, like other Americans, seek the economic security which we feel government should provide— and which entrepreneurs, by definition, don't have.

Political attitudes in Iowa have been shaped by the state's experience; and while they are less parochially concerned with agricultural issues than they used to be, they are still distinctive. Iowa has a certain orneriness, born perhaps in the vulnerability of its farm economy, and nurtured in the heritage of the Germans and Scandinavians and Yankees who came here precisely because they were unwilling to conform to the traditions of their native lands.

So Iowa is a politically countercyclical state. It seems to react, often harshly, against every national administration and its party, not only angrily denouncing its farm programs but often sternly denouncing its foreign and domestic policies as well. Iowa is particularly severe toward corruption. It was one of a handful of states that gave Richard Nixon in 1972 a lower percentage than 1968; Watergate was only a minor issue elsewhere then, but it cut in Iowa. And at the same time Iowa, skeptical about the Vietnam war, elected a raft of liberal Democrats, including Senators Dick Clark and John Culver. Then in the late 1970s Iowa turned sharply against the Democrats. Carter, who nearly carried Iowa in 1976, lost the state badly four years later. Democrats lost both Senate seats, one House seat, and control of the state legislature. One factor in that turnaround was agricultural issues, particularly Carter's grain embargo. But an issue many Iowans thought a moral one also played a role: abortion. Opponents of abortion helped defeat Clark and Culver and elect Iowa's current senators, Republicans Roger Jepsen and Charles Grassley.

Then, once the Reagan administration was installed and its programs put in place, Iowa began moving in the other direction. Democrats did not do so well at the top of the ticket in Iowa. Their candidate for governor, Roxanne Conlin, lost, in part because she avoided (entirely legally) paying state income taxes one year, and Democrats did not pick up any House seats. But they did win over control of both houses of the legislature, and they captured some of the minor statewide offices, including lieutenant governor. The income tax issue did cost Conlin considerable momentum, and gave her a liability more damaging than the reputation of the Republican candidate, Terry Branstad, as an ultraconservative, out of line with popular 14–year Governor Robert Ray. But the election returns suggest another problem: Conlin seemed unable to win majorities in traditionally Democratic Catholic areas, both cities like Dubuque and rural places like Carroll County—although they went for Democrats in other 1982 races. Was this the abortion issue again, or was it a less focused aversion to a candidate liberal on cultural issues on the part of an electorate which still lives by traditional moral values? In either case, it seems that the pendulum may not be swinging quite as widely in Iowa in the 1980s as it did, both ways, in the 1970s. Iowa, usually conservative on non-farm economic issues, tended to be liberal on non-economic issues when the focus was on the Vietnam war. But as we get more of a politics of cultural variety, Iowa's traditional family patterns make it more conservative on non-economic issues and, in 1982, provide a brake on its Democratic trend. Will this be the case again in 1984, both in the presidential contest and in the Senate race? Iowa Democrats have been confidently expecting to beat Roger Jepsen, whatever the national issues in 1984. But the 1982 results suggest that that outcome will not be automatic.

Presidential politics. Iowa does not have a presidential primary, but it does have what has become the first real race in the primary season each year: the Democratic and Republican precinct caucuses. On a frigid January night, Iowans gather in designated schools, public buildings, or usually just someone's house, and caucus. They divide into groups according to presidential preference (or non-preference) and elect delegates to their county conventions; those delegates are obliged to elect delegates to the state convention in accordance with the presidential preference expressed at the county level, which is then finally translated into presidential convention delegates. So you can get a fair—not quite a precise—idea of the composition of Iowa's delegations from the initial caucus results, if you keep in mind that candidates' withdrawals can have varying effects.

More important, you can get an idea of how candidates strike particular voters and how they respond to the pressures of a campaign in Iowa. Caucus turnout is high—almost as high as primary turnout in some states—and by 1980 the contest for support was treated by both national and Iowa media, and by the candidates, as a real campaign. The Iowa debates between Republican candidates were nationally televised: Ronald Reagan was hurt by his refusal to appear, and John Anderson's distinctive message helped him appeal to the non-Republican constituency which eventually supported his independent candidacy. It was in Iowa that Mary McGrory asked the candidates how they could cut taxes, increase defense spending, and balance the budget all at once, and Anderson replied, "You can only do it with mirrors."

But even conceding the sophistication of the Iowa electorate—the most literate in the nation—what do the results really mean? Jimmy Carter won the 1976 caucuses here and thereby became a more credible candidate; he won again in 1980, in large part because of Edward Kennedy's unpopularity. But Carter's standing in Iowa deteriorated to the point that he lost the state badly in 1980. George Bush won the 1980 Republican caucuses here in a brilliant organizational campaign, and because Reagan refused to debate; but when Reagan finally did debate, on his own terms, in New Hampshire, Bush was beaten. One gets the impression that Iowa caucus participants, like early primary voters, prize novelty overmuch. They are ready to make judgments on the basis of slim evidence, because they know those judgments can be reversed later on; and eventually they usually are. But in the meantime, they can have the profound effect of giving a candidate his party's nomination and even the White House. Many observers have criticized the advantage this system gives to the non-officeholder who can campaign full time; it also seems to have a built-in bias toward novel candidates and against familiar ones.

In presidential general elections, Iowa, despite its Republican tradition, usually tracks pretty closely to the national average, as it did in 1976 and 1980. With only eight electoral votes, it usually does not see much of the major party candidates after the precinct caucuses are over in January.

Senators. Iowa's two senators do not have a very good reputation in Washington, partly because of the good reputations their predecessors had, partly because their victories were attributed to "single-issue" anti-abortion campaigns waged against their opponents. But part of the reason is that by early 1983 neither had yet exceeded the rather low expectations people had for them.

The senior senator, Roger Jepsen, is up for reelection in 1984. More than just about any of his colleagues, he *looks* like a senator. He is handsome, with a fine head of white hair, and an expression that is both distinguished and grave. He insists on the dignity due the office; in 1983 he commuted to work, alone, in the highway lane reserved otherwise for cars with four commuters, arguing correctly that as a senator going to perform his official duties he is constitutionally exempt from being stopped. If his political career before the Senate was not particularly distinguished—he served a term as lieutenant governor and disagreed with the very popular governor, Robert Ray—it is similar to the experience many senators brought to their jobs. Nor are Jepsen's convictions out of line with those in the Senate generally. He profited in 1978 from his opposition to abortion. Critics pointed out that his stand differed from the position he took in the state legislature some years before, but Jepsen backers argued that the change resulted from a genuine conversion, from strong religious beliefs he and his wife shared. On foreign issues, Jepsen proclaimed himself a strong believer in increased defense spending and a strong supporter of Israel as well; on economic issues an advocate of cutting the size and power of the federal government; on cultural issues a believer in having government endorse traditional values.

Yet in the crunch Jepsen proved less steadfast than his rhetoric suggested. When the Senate in 1981 voted on selling AWACS planes to Saudi Arabia, Jepsen was counted from the beginning as a staunch opponent of the sale. Yet at the last minute he was persuaded by White House lobbyists to switch. "We just beat his brains out," a White House aide was quoted as saying. "We stood him up in front of an open grave and told him he could jump in if he wanted to." The *Des Moines Register* ran two front-page stories outlining the pros and cons of the AWACS sales, and leading off each with a quote from Jepsen. The episode suggested not so much hypocrisy—it was a close issue, and reasonable people could change their minds—as it does a lack of steadfastness of will; if it hurts Jepsen, it will be by convincing voters that behind his stately, sure facade is a man who cannot stand up to pressure. Evidently he thought it was damaging; he spent four days of detective work identifying the aide, Ed Rollins, and then demanded, unsuccessfully, that he be fired.

Jepsen can count on a tough race in 1984. His opponent is likely to be 5th district Congressman Tom Harkin, a proven vote-getter in one of the more Republican parts of the state. If you add Harkin's 1982 vote to Governor Terry Branstad's winning performance in the rest of the state, you have a Democratic majority. But no victory in this race will be automatic. The candidates will clash on foreign policy: Harkin has been a longtime human rights advocate and a strong critic of U.S. involvement in El Salvador and Guatemala, while Jepsen advocates more defense spending and a more assertive foreign policy. They will differ on farm policy: Harkin backs subsidies and price supports, while Jepsen emphasizes his stands in favor of the payment-in-kind program and international grain sales, programs backed by the Reagan administration. They will differ on macroeconomic issues: Jepsen supports Reaganomics, while Harkin opposes it. And they will differ in personal style: Jepsen is formal, serious, stern, an upholder of staid conservative tradition; Harkin younger, more informal, earnest, an advocate of liberal concern.

If Roger Jepsen looks dignified, his colleague Charles Grassley looks homespun. Grassley likes to bill himself as a simple farmer, and affects a hayseed manner. He is, however, a long-time and successful politician. He has a record of impressive electoral successes: he was elected to the Iowa legislature in the Democratic year of 1958, to the U.S. House in the Democratic year of 1974, and he won his Senate seat by beating a strong incumbent, John Culver.

Grassley's first two years in the Senate were spent as a backbencher. With low seniority seats on the Budget and Finance Committees, he was a foot-soldier rather than a general in the army supporting the Reagan administration's economic policies. He also serves on the Special Committee on Aging, and has made issues relating to the elderly one of his main political themes. His seat is up in 1986—too far away for any predictions in volatile Iowa.

Governor. For 14 years Robert Ray served as governor of Iowa, to the general satisfaction of voters. His 58% reelection victories suggested more the size of the minimum Democratic vote than they did any limit on his own high standing. Ray is always classed as a moderate Republican, cautious on economic matters, liberal on some cultural issues. He took the lead, for example, in welcoming Vietnamese refugees to Iowa when politicians from most states were ducking the problem. Ray could have been reelected in 1982, but decided to retire, and, like many moderate Republicans, did not really leave an heir.

The new governor, Terry Branstad, did serve as lieutenant governor during Ray's last term, but he won the 1978 Republican primary as a conservative, on the basis of his record in the legislature. Branstad was trailing Roxanne Conlin in the polls until her tax problem became an issue; then he led all the rest of the way. Branstad tried to campaign on Ray's coattails and argued that he had moderated his views. In practice, he will have to, to some extent: Iowa elected a Democratic legislature in 1982, and the new governor will have to work with them. Branstad is, incidentally, only 35, one of the nation's first baby boom governors, although he comes from a very different political tradition than that which seemed characteristic of that age cohort when they first became politically active in the anti-Vietnam movement in the late 1960s. For 1986, there are lots of potential rivals for Branstad, including Democrats Lieutenant Governor Bob Anderson and Attorney General Tom Miller.

Congressional districting. The redistricting process in Iowa was controlled by Republicans but, in line with state tradition, it was conducted in a relatively nonpartisan manner. A state commission presented plans, which the legislature could vote up or down; the plan finally accepted actually weakened the state's one shaky Republican incumbent and did not hurt any of the three Democrats.

The People   Est. Pop. 1982: 2,905,000; Pop. 1980: 2,913,308, dn. 0.3% 1980–82 and up 3.1% 1970–80; 1.24% of U.S. total, 28th largest; voting age pop. 2,087,935; 5% American Indian. Single ancestry: 21% German, 7% English, 4% Irish, 2% Dutch, Norwegian, 1% Swedish, French. Registered voters (1982): 1,608,196 Total. 554,922 D (34%); 510,050 R (32%); 543,224 no party (34%). 14% with 4+ yrs. col. 9.4% below poverty level. 26% housing units rented; median house value: $40,600; median monthly rent: $176. Households: 73% family, 39% with children, 64% married couples.

1982 Share of Federal Tax Burden $1,397,000,000; .23% of U.S. total, 50th largest.

1982 Share of Federal Expenditures

	Total		Non-Defense		Defense	
Total Expend	$5,196m	(0.86%)	$4,716m	(1.11%)	$480m	(0.27%)
St/Lcl Grants	893m	(1.01%)	893m	(1.01%)	0m	(0%)
Salary/Wages	224m	(0.29%)	154m	(0.56%)	70m	(0.14%)
Ind Payments	3,509m	(1.23%)	3,285m	(1.28%)	224m	(0.78%)
Procurement	427m	(0.29%)	77m	(0.24%)	350m	(0.31%)
Other Programs	143m	(2.64%)	143m	(2.66%)	0m	(0%)
Loan/Insurance	4,965m	(7.76%)	4,957m	(8.03%)	8m	(0.36%)

Political Lineup   Governor, Terry E. Branstad (R). Senators, Roger W. Jepsen (R) and Charles E. Grassley (R). Representatives, 6 (3 D and 3 R). State Senate, 50 (28 D and 22 R); State House of Representatives, 100 (60 D and 40 R).

Presidential Vote

1980	Reagan (R)	....	676,026	(51%)
	Carter (D)	....	508,672	(39%)
	Anderson (I)	....	115,633	(9%)
1976	Ford (R)	....	632,863	(49%)
	Carter (D)	....	619,931	(48%)

1980 Democratic Presidential Caucuses		*1980 Republican Presidential Caucuses*		
Carter	(59%)	Bush	33,530	(32%)
Kennedy	(31%)	Reagan	31,348	(29%)
Uncommitted	(10%)	Baker..............	16,216	(15%)
		Connally	9,861	(9%)
		Crane..............	7,135	(7%)
		Two others.........	6,161	(6%)
		Undecided..........	1,800	(2%)

SENATORS

Sen. Roger W. Jepsen (R) Elected 1978, seat up 1984; b. Dec. 23, 1928, Cedar Falls; home, Davenport; U. of N. IA, 1945–46, AZ St. U., B.S. 1950, M.A. 1953; Lutheran.

Career Army, 1946–47; Counselor, AZ St. U., 1950–53; Farmer and insurance agent, 1954–55; Branch Mgr., CT General Life Ins. Co., 1956–72; Scott Cnty. Supervisor, 1962–65; IA Senate, 1966–68; Lt. Gov of IA, 1968–72; Exec. V.P., Agridustrial Electronics Co., 1973–76; Pres., Marketing Co., 1976–78.

Offices 120 RSOB, 202-224-3254. Also 1416 W. 16th St., Davenport 52804, 319-322-0120.

Committees *Agriculture, Nutrition and Forestry* (6th). Subcommittees: Soil and Water Conservation (Chairman); Agricultural Credit and Rural Electrification; Foreign Agricultural Policy. *Armed Services* (7th). Subcommittees: Tactical Warfare; Preparedness; Manpower and Personnel (Chairman). *Joint Economic Committee* (Chairman). Subcommittee: International Trade, Finance, and Security Economics.

Group Ratings

	ADA	ACLU	COPE	CFA	LCV	LWV	NTU	NSI	COC	ACA	CSFC
1982	20	21	8	10	31	67	70	100	70	76	78
1981	5	—	7	7	26	—	80	—	94	81	85
1980	22	13	16	7	41	67	58	100	85	77	80

National Journal Ratings

	Economic		Foreign		Cultural	
1982	31%	(LIB)	16%	(LIB)	27%	(LIB)
	68%	(CONS)	68%	(CONS)	71%	(CONS)
1981	17%	(LIB)	1%	(LIB)	2%	(LIB)
	79%	(CONS)	85%	(CONS)	82%	(CONS)

Key Votes

1) Reagan 81 Budget	FOR	5) $ to El Salvador	FOR
2) Reagan 81 Tax Cut	FOR	6) Saudi AWACS Sale	FOR
3) Bal Budget Amend	FOR	7) Ban Abortion	FOR
4) Gas & Road Tax	FOR	8) Nerve Gas Prod	FOR

9) Poor Pay Food Stamps	FOR
10) Ban Crt Busing Order	FOR
11) Clinch Riv Brdr Rctr	FOR
12) Legal Services Corp	AGN

Election Results

1978 general	Roger W. Jepsen (R)	421,598	(51%)	($728,268)
	Dick Clark (D)	395,066	(48%)	($860,774)
1978 primary	Roger W. Jepsen (R)	87,397	(57%)	
	Maurice Van Nostrand (R)	54,189	(36%)	($68,594)
	One other (R)	10,860	(7%)	
1972 general	Dick Clark (D)	662,637	(55%)	($241,803)
	Jack Miller (R)	530,525	(44%)	($328,263)

Campaign Contributions and Expenditures

1977-78		PACS brkdwn			
Receipts	$738,581	Agr	$15,600	Ideo	$40,817
Expend.	$728,268	Bus	$92,515	Lbr	$—
Unspent	$10,313	Hlth	$8,940	Prof	$200

414　IOWA

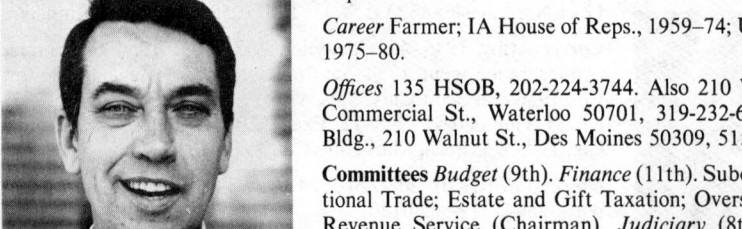

Sen. Charles E. Grassley (R) Elected 1980, seat up 1986; b. Sept. 17, 1933, New Hartford; home, New Hartford; U. of N. IA, B.A. 1955, M.A. 1956, U. of IA, 1957–58; Baptist.

Career Farmer; IA House of Reps., 1959–74; U.S. House of Reps., 1975–80.

Offices 135 HSOB, 202-224-3744. Also 210 Waterloo Bldg., 531 Commercial St., Waterloo 50701, 319-232-6657; and 721 Fed. Bldg., 210 Walnut St., Des Moines 50309, 515-284-4890.

Committees *Budget* (9th). *Finance* (11th). Subcommittees: International Trade; Estate and Gift Taxation; Oversight of the Internal Revenue Service (Chairman). *Judiciary* (8th). Subcommittees: Administrative Practice and Procedure (Chairman); Constitution; Immigration and Refugee Policy. *Labor and Human Resources* (8th). Subcommittees: Aging (Chairman); Employment and Productivity; Family and Human Services; Labor. *Special Committee on Aging* (7th).

Group Ratings

	ADA	ACLU	COPE	CFA	LCV	LWV	NTU	NSI	COC	ACA	CSFC
1982	30	21	8	20	38	42	88	100	62	76	78
1981	5	—	6	7	31	—	93	—	94	90	83

National Journal Ratings

	Economic		Foreign		Cultural	
1982	29%	(LIB)	43%	(LIB)	27%	(LIB)
	70%	(CONS)	56%	(CONS)	71%	(CONS)
1981	12%	(LIB)	23%	(LIB)	2%	(LIB)
	86%	(CONS)	74%	(CONS)	82%	(CONS)

Key Votes

1) Reagan 81 Budget	FOR	5) $ to El Salvador	FOR	9) Poor Pay Food Stamps	FOR
2) Reagan 81 Tax Cut	FOR	6) Saudi AWACS Sale	FOR	10) Ban Crt Busing Order	FOR
3) Bal Budget Amend	FOR	7) Ban Abortion	FOR	11) Clinch Riv Brdr Rctr	FOR
4) Gas & Road Tax	FOR	8) Nerve Gas Prod	AGN	12) Legal Services Corp	AGN

Election Results

1980 general	Charles E. Grassley (R)	683,014	(53%)	($2,183,028)
	John C. Culver (D)	581,545	(46%)	($1,750,680)
1980 primary	Charles E. Grassley (R)	170,120	(66%)	
	Tom Stoner (R)	89,409	(34%)	($1,895,551)
1974 general	John C. Culver (D)	462,947	(52%)	($470,970)
	David M. Stanley (R)	420,546	(47%)	($336,067)

Campaign Contributions and Expenditures

1979-80			PACS brkdwn		
Receipts	$2,217,229	Agr	$28,450	Ideo	$96,586
Expend.	$2,183,028	Bus	$597,117	Lbr	$1,000
Unspent	$34,200	Hlth	$22,853	Prof	$1,550

GOVERNOR

Gov. Terry E. Branstad (R) Elected 1982, term expires Jan. 1987; b. Nov. 17, 1947, Leland; home, Lake Mills; U. of IA, B.A. 1969, Drake U. Law Sch., J.D. 1974; Roman Catholic.

Career Army, 1969–71; Practicing atty., 1974–82; Farmer, 1974–.

Offices State Capitol, Des Moines 50319, 515-281-5211.

Election Results

1982 gen.	Terry E. Branstad (R)	548,313	(53%)
	Roxanne Conlin (D)	483,291	(47%)
1982 prim.	Terry E. Branstad (R)	128,314	(100%)
1978 gen.	Robert D. Ray (R)	491,713	(58%)
	Jerome Fitzgerald (D)	345,519	(41%)

FIRST DISTRICT

The 1st congressional district of Iowa is the southeast corner of the state. About one-third of the district's people live in and around Davenport, its largest city. Davenport, together with the Illinois cities of Rock Island, Moline, and East Moline, across the Mississippi River, are known as the Quad Cities. Davenport contains a disproportionate part of the affluent population of the Quad Cities. The Illinois cities lie on a thin wedge of flat land between the Mississippi and Rock Rivers, while there are pleasant hills on the Iowa side where well-off people tend to live. So in 1982 Rock Island County, Illinois, went heavily Democratic in both state and congressional elections, while Davenport's Scott County was Republican in both— narrowly Republican for governor, heavily Republican for Congress.

South of Davenport are several Mississippi River towns: Muscatine, heavily Protestant and Republican; Burlington, the namesake of the railroad which became the nucleus of the giant Burlington Northern, and which tends to vote Democratic; Fort Madison and Keokuk in the south, where the influence of the early southern-accented settlers from Missouri is apparent in Democratic voting preferences. Inland from the Mississippi River are the heavily Republican farm counties and the Democratic factory town of Ottumwa on the Des Moines River.

In all, the 1st is closely divided politically, and from 1964 to 1976 it was one of the few districts in the nation seriously contested by the parties in every election. In 1982 it went Republican for governor, Democratic for lieutenant governor. But in recent elections it has gone solidly for Republican Congressman Jim Leach. Although his percentage declined in 1982, there is nothing to indicate that he will have a hard time holding onto this district.

Leach's positions on issues are well suited to the district. On economic issues, he is pretty solidly conservative, as one might expect from a man who once headed his family's propane gas business. On cultural issues he is not an orthodox Republican, but he is careful not to get too far out of line with traditional opinion here. He concentrates not on lifestyle issues, but on

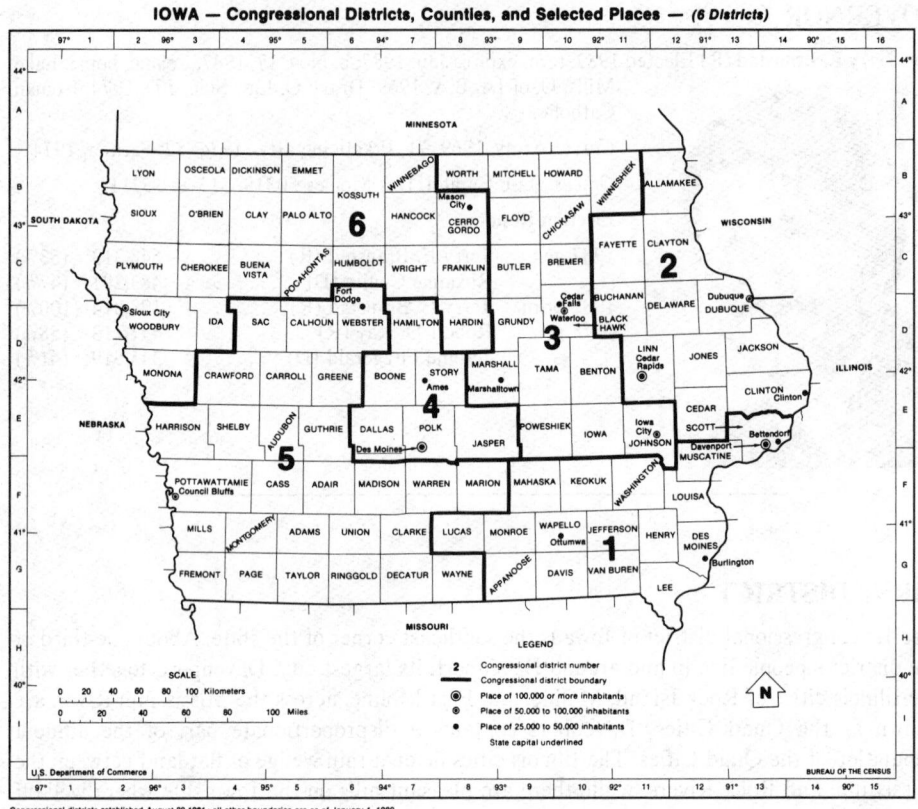

IOWA — Congressional Districts, Counties, and Selected Places — (6 Districts)

those relating to the political process: he is one of the leaders in the fight to reduce the importance of political action committees in financing campaigns. (Interestingly, another such leader was Tom Railsback, for 16 years congressman from Rock Island, across the river.) Opposition to anything that reeks of corruption or undue influence seems deeply rooted in this part of the country.

Finally, on foreign policy issues Leach is one of the few Republicans who has long been skeptical of defense spending increases and who supports a more accommodating, rather than more assertive, foreign policy generally. He was skeptical in early 1983 of U.S. involvement in El Salvador and opposed to U.S. covert action in Nicaragua. This again is in line with Iowa's rather dovish tradition. Leach serves on the Foreign Affairs Committee, but he is one of those congressmen who exerts influence as much through public leadership as through committee work. He is also chairman of the Ripon Society, a once influential group of liberal Republicans. It seems less intellectually rigorous today, though: in early 1983 Leach as its leader denounced the influence of the Rev. Sun Myung Moon in New Right movements but, when challenged, couldn't produce facts to support his charges. Usually he is better prepared, and more effective, although on the issues in which he gets the most attention he is very much a minority in his party.

The People Pop. 1980: 485,961, up 5% 1970–80; voting age pop. 345,540; 2% Black, 1% Span. orig. 25% housing units rented. Median owner $39,600; renter $178. Households: 74% family, 40% with children, 64% married couples.

Presidential Vote

1980	Reagan (R)	104,062	(51%)
	Carter (D)	85,545	(42%)
	Anderson (I)	14,763	(7%)

Rep. James A. S. (Jim) **Leach** (R) Elected 1976; b. Oct. 15, 1942, Davenport; home, Davenport; Princeton U., B.A. 1964, Johns Hopkins U., M.A. 1966, London Sch. of Econ., 1966–68; Episcopal.

Career Staff Mbr., U.S. Rep. Donald Rumsfeld of IL, 1965–66; U.S. Foreign Svc., 1968–69; 1971–72; A. A. to Dir. of OEO, 1969–70; Pres., Flamegas Co., Inc., propane gas marketers, 1973–; Repub. Nominee for U.S. House of Reps., 1974.

Offices 1514 LHOB, 202-225-6576. Also 234 Fed. Bldg., 322 W. 3rd St., Davenport 52801, 319-326-1841.

Committees *Banking, Finance and Urban Affairs* (4th). Subcommittees: Housing and Community Development; Financial Institutions Supervision, Regulation and Insurance; International Trade, Investment and Monetary Policy. *Foreign Affairs* (6th). Subcommittee: Human Rights and International Organizations.

Group Ratings

	ADA	ACLU	COPE	CFA	LCV	LWV	NTU	NSI	COC	ACA	CSFC
1982	65	58	31	80	75	67	59	20	45	32	37
1981	55	—	29	79	71	—	75	—	79	54	54
1980	61	63	37	57	63	70	38	40	76	58	59

National Journal Ratings

	Economic		Foreign		Cultural	
1982	48%	(LIB)	82%	(LIB)	78%	(LIB)
	52%	(CONS)	17%	(CONS)	22%	(CONS)
1981	40%	(LIB)	85%	(LIB)	62%	(LIB)
	59%	(CONS)	13%	(CONS)	38%	(CONS)

Key Votes

1) Reagan 81 Budget	FOR	5) Incr SS Rtmt Age	FOR	9) Poor Pay Food Stamps	AGN
2) Reagan 81 Tax Cut	FOR	6) Saudi AWACS Sale	AGN	10) Ban Crt Busing Order	FOR
3) Bal Budget Amend	FOR	7) $ for MX Missile	AGN	11) Auto Local Content	FOR
4) Gas & Road Tax	FOR	8) Nerve Gas Prod	AGN	12) Nuclear Arms Freeze	FOR

Election Results

1982 general	James A. S. (Jim) Leach (R)	89,585	(59%)	($231,594)
	William E. Gluba (D)	61,734	(41%)	($104,667)
1982 primary	James A. S. (Jim) Leach (R) unopposed	18,841		
1980 general	James A. S. (Jim) Leach (R)	133,349	(64%)	($235,933)
	Jim Larew (D)	72,602	(35%)	($46,834)

Campaign Contributions and Expenditures*

	1981-82		Direct Cont. 81-82
Receipts	$230,092	Indiv	$199,080
Expend.	$231,594	Party	$14,761
Unspent	$1,000	Cand	$13,802

Received no PAC contributions

SECOND DISTRICT

The 2d congressional district of Iowa is the northeastern corner of the state. Almost half its population lives in the counties along the Mississippi River. Farther south, the river's banks are monotonously flat; here they are pleasantly hilly—the hilliest part of the state, in fact. The landscape here is reminiscent of southern and central Germany, and the early settlers here included, besides many Yankees, many Germans as well. They have left their imprint on its political geography. The river town of Clinton, settled by German Protestants, still tends to be Republican. Dubuque, farther upriver, is almost entirely German Catholic, and is heavily Democratic in most, though these days not quite all, elections. (This city, made famous by Harold Ross's remark that his *New Yorker* was not edited for "the little old lady in Dubuque," produced a large margin for George McGovern in 1972.) The knobby hills that flank the Mississippi are less suitable for corn, hogs, wheat, and cattle than are the rolling plains farther west, but this part of Iowa provided the inspiration for much of the work of Grant Wood and its scenery is some of the most beautiful in the Midwest.

The other half of the district lives west of the Mississippi, on the plains of Iowa, with most clustered in and around Cedar Rapids. This is Iowa's second largest city, and has one of its more diversified economies: its big employers include not only agricultural implement manufacturers, but Collins Radio, a high tech firm. Politically, Cedar Rapids is very marginal, split closely between the parties. The surrounding rural counties usually go Republican.

The 2d district for two decades has voted close to national and state averages; it just missed going for Jimmy Carter in 1976 and was within 2% of the national percentages in the 1980 presidential election. In House elections it has been seriously contested as often as not over the last 20 years, and was held by Democrats for most of that period. But in the past several years, the politics of the 2d district has been affected by unusual local factors, and it has gone Republican in most elections, though not always for the same reasons. In 1978, Dubuque deserted Democratic Senator Dick Clark on the abortion issue, and helped defeat him; two years later it gave only a small margin to Senator John Culver, though he had represented this district in the House for 10 years.

Also in 1978 the district's present congressman, Tom Tauke, was first elected. He was only 28 then, a veteran of four years in the Iowa legislature, a Republican elected from Democratic Dubuque, and one of those instinctive politicians who are found more often among the Democrats than the Republicans. Tauke spent some $250,000 in that election, and has not stinted since. He knows how to raise money, and has fundraisers who work political action committees so aggressively that he puts ceilings on the amounts they may raise. Tauke is well situated to raise that kind of money: he sits on the Energy and Commerce Committee, which handles most federal regulatory and air pollution laws; practically every business (and labor) interest in the country is affected, and they are all willing to contribute to ensure they get a hearing. Tauke, whose votes on regulatory issues are not always predictable, is a key member of the committee, and advocates of all positions seek him out.

Generally speaking, Tauke is conservative on economic issues, but not always; he is not a doctrinaire free market advocate. On non-economic issues, he seems in line with Iowa opinion: cautiously conservative on cultural issues, liberal on foreign policy. The Democrats have run serious candidates against Tauke, but he raises far more money and manages to win even in Dubuque County. In 1982, despite the Democratic trend, he won his largest percentage ever. It is risky to say he has a safe seat, but he is clearly hard to beat.

The People   Pop. 1980: 485,708, up 2.9% 1970–80; voting age pop. 338,272; 1% Black. 25% housing units rented. Median owner $43,200; renter $180. Households: 74% family, 41% with children, 65% married couples.

Presidential Vote

1980	Reagan (R)	106,157	(50%)
	Carter (D)	86,085	(41%)
	Anderson (I)	19,774	(9%)

Rep. Thomas J. (Tom) **Tauke** (R) Elected 1978; b. Oct. 11, 1950, Dubuque; home, Dubuque; Loras Col., B.A. 1972, U. of IA, J.D. 1974; Roman Catholic.

Career Practicing atty.; IA House of Reps., 1975–78.

Offices 435 CHOB, 202-225-2911. Also 222 Fed. Bldg., Dubuque 52001, 319-557-7740.

Committees *Energy and Commerce* (9th). Subcommittees: Fossil and Synthetic Fuels; Telecommunications, Consumer Protection and Finance. *Select Committee on Aging* (7th). Subcommittee: Health and Long-Term Care.

Group Ratings

	ADA	ACLU	COPE	CFA	LCV	LWV	NTU	NSI	COC	ACA	CSFC
1982	60	42	24	40	70	82	69	60	70	52	46
1981	45	—	20	50	58	—	87	—	83	57	61
1980	33	53	—	36	59	57	49	60	71	61	71

National Journal Ratings

	Economic		Foreign		Cultural	
1982	48%	(LIB)	82%	(LIB)	78%	(LIB)
	52%	(CONS)	17%	(CONS)	22%	(CONS)
1981	42%	(LIB)	81%	(LIB)	50%	(LIB)
	58%	(CONS)	19%	(CONS)	49%	(CONS)

Key Votes

1) Reagan 81 Budget	FOR	5) Incr SS Rtmt Age	FOR	9) Poor Pay Food Stamps	FOR
2) Reagan 81 Tax Cut	FOR	6) Saudi AWACS Sale	FOR	10) Ban Crt Busing Order	AGN
3) Bal Budget Amend	FOR	7) $ for MX Missile	AGN	11) Auto Local Content	AGN
4) Gas & Road Tax	FOR	8) Nerve Gas Prod	AGN	12) Nuclear Arms Freeze	FOR

Election Results

1982 general	Thomas J. Tauke (R)	99,478	(59%)	($374,667)
	Brent Appel (D)	69,539	(41%)	($129,961)
1982 primary	Thomas J. Tauke (R) unopposed ..	15,433	(100%)	
1980 general	Thomas J. Tauke (R)	117,631	(57%)	($307,972)
	Steve Sovern (D)	87,131	(42%)	($129,815)

Campaign Contributions and Expenditures

1981-82		Direct Cont. 81-82		PACS brkdwn			
Receipts	$386,442	Indiv	$181,043	Agr	$22,870	Ideo	$6,500
Expend.	$374,667	Party	$24,871	Bus	$115,167	Lbr	$500
Unspent	$30,575	PACS	$160,769	Hlth	$10,250	Prof	$1,100

Indirect Party Expend: $6,490   *Indep Expend:* For: $885 (NRA)

THIRD DISTRICT

Iowa's 3d congressional district cuts a swath through the central part of the state, from the university town of Iowa City in the south all the way to the Minnesota border. This is prime agricultural land, but the population is not all rural. Iowa City, home of the State University of Iowa, is the liberal bastion of the state politically, a town that prides itself far more on its writers' workshop than on the fact that Herbert Hoover's birthplace is nearby. Waterloo, the district's largest city, is quite different. It is an industrial town, and an ailing one; its Rath meatpacking plant was taken over by the workers a few years ago, because no one else was willing to keep it running. Waterloo is not, however, a Democratic town; it is more evenly divided politically.

The rural counties have their touches of color, most notably the Amana Colonies, near Iowa City, with their old habits and new appliance factories. But mostly people here like to think of their Iowa as just plain farmland, a place as typically American as anywhere in the United States. Politically, these rural areas are Republican, and some of the most Republican parts of the state; they reacted rather negatively to Watergate and Richard Nixon's prosecution of the Vietnam war, but on most other issues they have stayed true to their ancestral party.

Demographically and therefore politically, the rural areas dominate the district; the 3d therefore has been a Republican seat since the 1930s. But not always securely: Charles Grassley won the seat very narrowly in the Democratic year of 1974, and when Grassley ran for the Senate in 1980, Republican Cooper Evans won only narrowly, despite spending more than $500,000 (most of it his own) in the race. Going into 1982, Evans looked very vulnerable. His 1980 opponent, Black Hawk County (Waterloo) Commissioner Lynn Cutler had become vice-chairman of the Democratic National Committee and was able to raise much more money; she spent more than $500,000 this time too. Also redistricting subtracted Republican Mason City and added Democratic Iowa City instead. Evans, a 50ish farmer and commodities trader with solidly conservative records on economic and cultural issues, seemed certain to lose Iowa City heavily and seemed in trouble in Waterloo and the rural counties as well.

Yet Evans won, and by an increased majority. He increased his percentage in the old part of the district from 51% to 58%, and in the new parts got large enough majorities in rural counties to offset Cutler's majority in Iowa City. The key was Waterloo. Cutler could not carry her old town. There was talk that her efforts to convince voters of her national importance backfired; she may have talked too much about how to get things done in Washington and too little about problems in Iowa.

Evans likes to talk more about cutting budgets and about agriculture programs. He serves on the Agriculture Committee, and his victory in 1982 shows that even in a time of falling farm prices advocacy of Republican farm programs is not necessarily a liability. It was not clear in 1983 whether Evans would draw strong opposition in 1984.

The People Pop. 1980: 485,529, up 3.9% 1970–80; voting age pop. 352,455; 2% Black. 28% housing units rented. Median owner $43,500; renter $185. Households: 72% family, 38% with children, 64% married couples.

Presidential Vote

1980	Reagan (R)	111,226	(49%)
	Carter (D)	91,217	(40%)
	Anderson (I)	23,484	(10%)

Rep. Cooper Evans (R) Elected 1980; b. May 26, 1924, Cedar Rapids; home, Grundy Center; IA St. U., B.S. 1949, M.S. 1954, Oak Ridge Sch. of Reactor Technology, Degree in Nuc. Engineering, 1956; Methodist.

Career Army, 1947–65; Corn farmer, 1965–80; Commodities trader, 1968–80; IA House of Reps., 1974–79.

Offices 127 CHOB, 202-225-3301. Also 162 W. 4th., Waterloo 50704, 319-234-3295; 309 P.O. Bldg., Mason City 50401, 515-424-3613; and 13 W. Main St., Marshalltown 50158, 515-753-3172.

Committees *Agriculture* (13th). Subcommittees: Department Operations, Research, and Foreign Agriculture; Wheat, Soybeans and Feed Grains. *Select Committee on Aging* (13th). Subcommittee: Retirement Income and Employment.

Group Ratings

	ADA	ACLU	COPE	CFA	LCV	LWV	NTU	NSI	COC	ACA	CSFC
1982	50	42	36	50	60	67	64	70	60	48	42
1981	30	—	27	29	21	—	81	—	84	71	68

National Journal Ratings

	Economic		Foreign		Cultural	
1982	46%	(LIB)	67%	(LIB)	68%	(LIB)
	54%	(CONS)	32%	(CONS)	31%	(CONS)
1981	35%	(LIB)	55%	(LIB)	39%	(LIB)
	64%	(CONS)	45%	(CONS)	61%	(CONS)

Key Votes

1) Reagan 81 Budget	FOR	5) Incr SS Rtmt Age	FOR	9) Poor Pay Food Stamps	AGN
2) Reagan 81 Tax Cut	FOR	6) Saudi AWACS Sale	AGN	10) Ban Crt Busing Order	AGN
3) Bal Budget Amend	FOR	7) $ for MX Missile	AGN	11) Auto Local Content	AGN
4) Gas & Road Tax	FOR	8) Nerve Gas Prod	AGN	12) Nuclear Arms Freeze	FOR

Election Results

1982 general	Cooper Evans (R)	104,072	(55%)	($585,044)
	Lynn G. Cutler (D)	83,581	(45%)	($532,440)
1982 primary	Cooper Evans (R)	22,657	(100%)	
1980 general	Cooper Evans (R)	107,869	(51%)	($575,496)
	Lynn G. Cutler (D)	101,735	(48%)	($227,543)

Campaign Contributions and Expenditures

1981-82		*Direct Cont. 81-82*				*PACS brkdwn*		
Receipts	$586,210	Indiv	$263,178	Agr	$21,325	Ideo	$22,300
Expend.	$585,044	Party	$33,477	Bus	$174,476	Lbr	$500
Unspent	$1,800	PACS	$236,574	Hlth	$7,750	Prof	$5,500
		Cand	$36,753				

Indirect Party Expend: $35,468   *Indep Expend:* For: $8,643

FOURTH DISTRICT

The 4th congressional district of Iowa is the geographical center of the state. It includes Ames, the home of Iowa State University, and the small manufacturing towns of Webster City, Boone, and Newton. But most of its votes are cast in and around Des Moines, Iowa's capital and largest city. Des Moines is the largest financial and commercial center of Iowa; it is a significant manufacturing center as well, whose main product is farm machinery. It is also the home of the *Des Moines Register & Tribune,* one of the nation's few newspapers with statewide circulation and one that is in many ways a leader of opinion in the state. Des Moines is a Democratic city in an historically Republican state, the most Democratic part of Iowa in most elections except for Dubuque and scattered Catholic rural counties.

Representing the 4th district in the House is Neal Smith, a Democrat first elected in 1958, and the senior member of the Iowa delegation. Smith is an old-fashioned farm belt Democrat, one whose liberalism is tempered by a moderate temperament and by a constituency which seems reluctant to go overboard in any direction. Caught on the wrong side of a generation gap, he began to enjoy significant seniority just as seniority was being devalued by the 1974 freshmen. In 1975 he sought to be the first chairman of the Budget Committee; he lost that post to Brock Adams, who became Jimmy Carter's first Secretary of Transportation. In running, Smith may have recognized that the Appropriations Committee, on which he serves, would inevitably lose influence to Budget—which is exactly what has happened—but since he lost that contest he has spent most of his time on Appropriations.

Now Smith is the number four Democrat on Appropriations, behind three other men a decade older. But he didn't get a subcommittee chairmanship until 1980, and the body he chairs—Commerce, Justice, State and Judiciary—was much more powerful in the hands of a ruthless chairman like John Rooney than it is in the hands of a man as scrupulous and fair-minded as Smith. The budgets it handles are not large, and a chairman not determined to interfere in operations will have relatively little influence in policymaking. Incidentally, Smith gave up the chair of the Small Business Committee to take the Appropriations subcommittee chair. That's a good indication of the importance of Small Business, a committee with a very limited jurisdiction which maintains a separate existence only because so many members like to tell voters that they sit on it.

Smith has a fair chance of becoming chairman of the full Appropriations Committee some day, and his Democratic colleagues would probably be happy to see him in that position: he is hard-working and capable but not overbearing or dictatorial, and his views on issues are in line with those of most Democrats. His popularity at home seemed great for years, and he never attracted serious opposition. In the Republican year of 1980, however, he received serious opposition from Dr. Don Young and was held to 54% of the vote. Dr. Young decided not to run again in 1982; redistricting had strengthened Smith somewhat by giving him Ames, and the trend of opinion seemed Democratic. Young's decision turned out to be a pretty good indicator of the results of the 1982 election, both here, where Smith won easily, and nationally.

The People   Pop. 1980: 485,480, up 6.6% 1970–80; voting age pop. 356,227; 3% Black, 1% Span. orig., 1% Asian orig. 30% housing units rented. Median owner $46,900; renter $144. Households: 70% family, 37% with children, 60% married couples.

Presidential Vote

1980	Reagan (R)	105,044	(46%)
	Carter (D)	95,948	(42%)
	Anderson (I)	27,252	(12%)

Rep. Neal Smith (D) Elected 1958; b. Mar. 23, 1920, Hedrick; home, Altoona; U. of MO, 1945–46, Syracuse U., 1946–47, Drake U., LL.B. 1950; Methodist.

Career Farmer; Army Air Corps, WWII; Practicing atty., 1950–58; Chmn., Polk Cnty. Bd. of Social Welfare; Asst. Polk Cnty. Atty., 1951.

Offices 2373 RHOB, 202-225-4426. Also 544 Insurance Exchange Bldg., Des Moines 50309, 515-284-4634.

Committees *Appropriations* (4th). Subcommittees: Agriculture, Rural Development and Related Agencies; Commerce, Justice, State and Judiciary (Chairman); Labor-Health and Human Services-Education. *Small Business* (2d). Subcommittee: SBA and SBIC Authority, Minority Enterprise and General Small Business Problems.

Group Ratings

	ADA	ACLU	COPE	CFA	LCV	LWV	NTU	NSI	COC	ACA	CSFC
1982	80	58	81	90	68	73	18	50	45	13	29
1981	55	—	81	79	33	—	14	—	18	22	36
1980	72	53	61	57	44	56	20	13	59	14	31

National Journal Ratings

	Economic		Foreign		Cultural	
1982	65%	(LIB)	79%	(LIB)	73%	(LIB)
	35%	(CONS)	21%	(CONS)	27%	(CONS)
1981	60%	(LIB)	67%	(LIB)	63%	(LIB)
	39%	(CONS)	33%	(CONS)	37%	(CONS)

Key Votes

1) Reagan 81 Budget AGN	5) Incr SS Rtmt Age AGN	9) Poor Pay Food Stamps AGN
2) Reagan 81 Tax Cut AGN	6) Saudi AWACS Sale AGN	10) Ban Crt Busing Order AGN
3) Bal Budget Amend AGN	7) $ for MX Missile AGN	11) Auto Local Content AGN
4) Gas & Road Tax —	8) Nerve Gas Prod AGN	12) Nuclear Arms Freeze FOR

Election Results

1982 general	Neal Smith (D)	118,849	(66%)	($134,158)
	Dave Readinger (R)	60,534	(34%)	($140,055)
1982 primary	Neal Smith (D)	40,940	(100%)	
1980 general	Neal Smith (D)	117,896	(54%)	($87,813)
	Donald C. Young (R)	100,335	(46%)	($240,518)

Campaign Contributions and Expenditures

1981-82		Direct Cont. 81-82		PACS brkdwn			
Receipts	$145,562	Indiv	$48,391	Agr	$10,150	Ideo	$5,200
Expend.	$134,158	Party	$2,898	Bus	$26,850	Lbr	$38,470
Unspent	$32,312	PACS	$91,365	Hlth	$5,835	Prof	$700

Indep Expend: Agn: $7,389

FIFTH DISTRICT

The 5th congressional district of Iowa is the southwestern quarter of the state. This is where the plains, as they roll toward the Missouri River, become browner and less green than they are farther east; the towns become less frequent and less thickly settled; the spaces become more wide open. In eastern Iowa farmers raise corn and feed grains to fatten hogs; farther west you begin to see more cattle and wheat.

There are also some political differences between this part of Iowa and the rest of the state, for the 5th district is one of the most Republican parts of Iowa. Its largest city, Council Bluffs, directly across the Missouri River from Omaha, Nebraska, is ordinarily Republican and has gone Republican in every presidential election since 1964. Fort Dodge, the district's only other city of any size, is more Democratic; but this is not a district where big urban majorities are going to elect a Democrat. Any Democrat has to win in the small towns and farm counties. The rural counties are more varied politically than they are agriculturally. The Catholic counties are Democratic (but did not back Roxanne Conlin in 1978), the more numerous Yankee Protestant counties Republican. The counties along the Missouri border have some affinity for the kind of southern Democrats rural Missourians favor; that was evident in their support of Jimmy Carter in 1976, and in their above-state-average support for Democrats in state elections up through 1982.

The 5th district is a good example of why the House remained Democratic through the Republican trends of 1978 and 1980. In fact, it has continued to elect a congressman who is considered one of the liberal leaders of the House on both foreign and domestic issues. This is Tom Harkin, one of those Democrats first elected in 1974 and who has been reelected since with large margins. One of Harkin's secrets is hard work. He first ran in this district in 1972, and in that year of the Nixon landslide got 49% against a Republican incumbent. Since then he has worked the district virtually nonstop. Another reason for his victories is that he identified himself with the way of life of the people in the district. In his 1974 campaign he set aside one day a week to work at some ordinary menial job. These "work days" got him positive television coverage and provided good footage for television commercials, one of which showed Harkin literally shoveling manure.

A third secret of Harkin's success is that he has continued to focus on the cultural and farm issues which got him elected in the first place. He continues to serve on the Agriculture Committee, where he backs price support programs and food stamps. In 1981 he became chairman of the Livestock, Dairy, and Poultry Subcommittee—a post of obvious importance to the 5th district and which will likely be a political asset for years to come. In this capacity he has been the leader in the fight for high dairy price supports—a losing battle sometimes, since the Reagan administration and some liberals have been working together to cut them, but one which is appreciated by the well organized dairy lobby when it comes time to make political contributions. Historically, farm subsidies are the glue that has held the Democratic Party together, uniting representatives of districts like Harkin's to those from urban districts in the Northeast, Great Lakes, and West Coast. Harkin has been one of the leaders in maintaining this important alliance, without which Democrats will lose working control of the House in the 98th Congress.

Harkin has also taken lead roles on other issues. He favors tougher requirements for labeling imported meat and opposed Reagan administration efforts to cut meat inspections. He was the main sponsor of legislation to prevent international banks from lending money to nations which violate human rights. He moved to cut military aid to South Korea because of such violations, during the Koreagate scandal; he went to El Salvador in 1981, and argued strongly against U.S. support of the government there. Neither stand hurts in a state where voters abhor scandals and are wary of foreign involvements. Harkin strongly opposed the Clinch River breeder reactor. Not all of these moves have been successful, but they have succeeded in highlighting Harkin's legislative agenda—and have shifted attention away from the Republican issues of cutting domestic spending and increasing defense.

Harkin is considered likely to run against Senator Roger Jepsen in 1984, and is given a good chance of winning. He has proved to be a strong vote-getter in his usually Republican district, and has the capacity to raise enough money to get his message across to the rest of the state. His percentage in the 5th district declined in 1982, but that was due to redistricting: in the counties he represented both years, his percentage rose from 57% to 58% in 1980–82. The decline resulted from the loss of Ames, home of Iowa State University, and several other counties, where he got 68% of the vote in 1980, and the addition of the area around Fort Dodge, where he got 61% in 1982.

The People Pop. 1980: 485,639, up 1.5% 1970–80; voting age pop. 346,800; 1% Span. orig. 24% housing units rented. Median owner $33,400; renter $144. Households: 75% family, 39% with children, 67% married couples.

Presidential Vote

1980	Reagan (R)	123,622	(58%)
	Carter (D)	74,675	(35%)
	Anderson (I)	14,128	(7%)

Rep. Tom Harkin (D) Elected 1974; b. Nov. 19, 1939, Cumming; home, Ames; IA St. U., B.S. 1962, Catholic U., J.D. 1972; Roman Catholic.

Career Navy, 1962–67; Staff Aide to U.S. Rep. Neal Smith, 1969–70; Dem. Nominee for U.S. House of Reps., 1972; Atty., Polk Cnty. Legal Aid Society, 1973–74.

Offices 2411 RHOB, 202-225-3806. Also P.O. Box 264, 213 P.O. Bldg., Ames 50010, 515-232-6111.

Committees *Agriculture* (8th). Subcommittees: Livestock, Dairy and Poultry (Chairman); Wheat, Soybeans and Feed Grains. *Science and Technology* (6th). Subcommittees: Energy Development and Applications; Natural Resources, Agriculture Research and Environment; Transportation, Aviation and Materials.

Group Ratings

	ADA	ACLU	COPE	CFA	LCV	LWV	NTU	NSI	COC	ACA	CSFC
1982	95	75	73	100	95	91	41	10	24	9	26
1981	85	—	71	71	93	—	46	—	5	27	31
1980	78	57	47	71	94	80	23	0	64	33	35

National Journal Ratings

	Economic		Foreign		Cultural	
1982	73%	(LIB)	92%	(LIB)	93%	(LIB)
	27%	(CONS)	6%	(CONS)	3%	(CONS)
1981	75%	(LIB)	92%	(LIB)	71%	(LIB)
	24%	(CONS)	2%	(CONS)	29%	(CONS)

Key Votes

1) Reagan 81 Budget	AGN	5) Incr SS Rtmt Age AGN	9) Poor Pay Food Stamps AGN
2) Reagan 81 Tax Cut	AGN	6) Saudi AWACS Sale AGN	10) Ban Crt Busing Order AGN
3) Bal Budget Amend	AGN	7) $ for MX Missile AGN	11) Auto Local Content FOR
4) Gas & Road Tax	—	8) Nerve Gas Prod AGN	12) Nuclear Arms Freeze FOR

Election Results

1982 general	Tom Harkin (D)	93,333	(59%)	($312,776)
	Arlyn E. Danker (R)	65,200	(41%)	($153,804)
1982 primary	Tom Harkin (D)	26,785	(100%)	
1980 general	Tom Harkin (D)	127,895	(60%)	($314,334)
	Cal Hultman (R)	84,472	(40%)	($309,325)

Campaign Contributions and Expenditures

1981-82		Direct Cont. 81-82		PACS brkdwn			
Receipts	$335,088	Indiv	$159,008	Agr	$35,339	Ideo	$4,475
Expend.	$312,776	Party	$4,108	Bus	$30,550	Lbr	$52,900
Unspent	$34,687	PACS	$135,031	Hlth	$1,000	Prof	$1,725

Indep Expend: Agn: $453

SIXTH DISTRICT

The 6th congressional district of Iowa is the northwestern part of the state, where the water and trees start to get scarce and the sky seems to get bigger. Except for Sioux City, an old river city that is larger than its neighbor, Sioux Falls, South Dakota, and Mason City, a manufacturing town in the eastern end of the 6th added in the 1981 redistricting, the 6th is almost entirely rural in character, with small farm market towns and grain elevators towering here and there over the flat or gently rolling landscape. The district has traditionally been Republican, as most of Iowa has been, but with notable exceptions—the kind of political divergences from the normal that dot the political maps of the Great Plains states. These arise from settlement by various ethnic groups. A colony of German Catholics or Norwegians, to name only one usually Democratic and one usually Republican group, would send encouraging letters back to the Old Country, and sometimes would forward steamship passage and railroad fare so that relatives and friends could make their way to new homes in Iowa or Kansas or the Dakotas. Such history makes sense of the Republican preference of Sioux County, Iowa (settled by Dutch Protestants and 79% for Ronald Reagan in 1980) or the Democratic leanings of nearby Palo Alto County (settled by German Catholics and 55% for Jimmy Carter in 1976). Palo Alto has a further distinction: it is one of three American bellwether counties that has never voted for the loser of a presidential election; the others are Coos County, New Hampshire, and Crook County, Oregon.

The 6th district currently has a Democratic congressman, elected in that surge of Democratic enthusiasm in Iowa in the early 1970s and strong enough to hold the seat although it has become the most Republican district in the state in most elections. He is Berkley Bedell, an attractive candidate wholly apart from partisan considerations. He grew up a fishing enthusiast in the town of Spirit Lake, near the Minnesota border. World War II intervened and he never finished college, but he started his own business manufacturing fishing tackle. This was not ordinary stuff: it was the monofilament line that revolutionized fishing habits, and Bedell became a millionaire. A deeply religious man, he also became a friend of Governor and Senator Harold Hughes, and Hughes—himself from a small town in the 6th district—convinced Bedell to enter politics. He became a Democrat, ran for Congress in 1972 and won 48% of the vote against Republican incumbent Wiley Mayne. Bedell ran again in 1974. In the meantime, Mayne voted against the impeachment of Richard Nixon, an act of political courage for which he never received credit; and Bedell easily won the general election.

Bedell has proved to be a popular congressman. He has seats on the Agriculture and Small Business Committees, both of importance to the district, although only Agriculture has an important legislative jurisdiction. He is chairman of an artfully named subcommittee: Energy, Environment and Safety Issues Affecting Small Business, which holds hearings on such matters as gasoline marketing practices and gasohol production. He has in effect an almost unlimited license to investigate hot issues—though not much legislative authority to deal with them. Bedell has proved to be very popular in his district. Some thought he might be in trouble in 1980 because his fishing tackle company was being investigated for importing products from its Taiwan subsidiary at artificially low prices to avoid duty. But nothing adverse was ever proved, and Bedell's reputation for probity and honesty did not suffer. He was reelected in 1980 and 1982 with 64%—despite his district's Republican leanings and despite a redistricting which shuffled quite a few counties into and out of the district.

The People Pop. 1980: 485,491, dn. 0.8% 1970–80; voting age pop. 348,641; 1% Span. orig. 25% housing units rented. Median owner $36,600; renter $152. Households: 74% family, 38% with children, 66% married couples.

Presidential Vote

1980			
	Reagan (R)	125,915	(58%)
	Carter (D)	75,202	(35%)
	Anderson (I)	16,232	(7%)

Rep. Berkley Bedell (D) Elected 1974; b. Mar. 5, 1921, Spirit Lake; home, Spirit Lake; IA St. U., 1940–42; Methodist.

Career Army Air Corps, WWII; Founder and Chmn., Berkley & Co., fishing tackle mfrs.; Dem. Nominee for U.S. House of Reps., 1972.

Offices 2459 CHOB, 202-225-5476. Also 406 Fed. Bldg., Fort Dodge 50501, 515-573-7169.

Committees *Agriculture* (9th). Subcommittees: Conservation, Credit and Rural Development; Forests, Family Farms and Energy; Wheat, Soybeans and Feed Grains. *Small Business* (6th). Subcommittees: Energy, Environment and Safety Issues Affecting Small Business; General Oversight and the Economy (Chairman).

Group Ratings

	ADA	ACLU	COPE	CFA	LCV	LWV	NTU	NSI	COC	ACA	CSFC
1982	85	71	63	80	95	100	44	13	36	22	26
1981	70	—	61	71	91	—	44	—	13	16	32
1980	72	57	44	64	88	75	27	0	62	13	35

National Journal Ratings

	Economic		Foreign		Cultural	
1982	61%	(LIB)	85%	(LIB)	77%	(LIB)
	38%	(CONS)	12%	(CONS)	22%	(CONS)
1981	66%	(LIB)	–%	(LIB)	77%	(LIB)
	33%	(CONS)	–%	(CONS)	22%	(CONS)

Key Votes

1) Reagan 81 Budget	AGN	5) Incr SS Rtmt Age	FOR	9) Poor Pay Food Stamps	AGN
2) Reagan 81 Tax Cut	AGN	6) Saudi AWACS Sale	AGN	10) Ban Crt Busing Order	AGN
3) Bal Budget Amend	AGN	7) $ for MX Missile	AGN	11) Auto Local Content	AGN
4) Gas & Road Tax	FOR	8) Nerve Gas Prod	AGN	12) Nuclear Arms Freeze	FOR

Election Results

1982 general	Berkley Bedell (D)	101,690	(64%)	($161,750)
	Al Bremer (R)	56,487	(36%)	($98,679)
1982 primary	Berkley Bedell (D)	17,506	(100%)	
1980 general	Berkley Bedell (D)	129,460	(64%)	($200,428)
	Clarence S. Carney (R)	71,866	(36%)	($250,335)

Campaign Contributions and Expenditures

1981-82		Direct Cont. 81-82		PACS brkdwn			
Receipts	$191,543	Indiv	$99,534	Agr	$17,400	Ideo	$3,350
Expend.	$161,750	Party	$1,160	Bus	$25,345	Lbr	$20,100
Unspent	$62,102	PACS	$75,555	Hlth	$2,000	Prof	$1,900

Indep Expend: Agn: $322

KANSAS

The political history of Kansas began with a rush in the 1850s, and the outcome of that decade's struggle has shaped the state's politics ever since. The land here was almost empty in 1850, and under the terms of the Kansas–Nebraska Act of 1854 the question of whether Kansas would be a free or a slave state would be determined by its voters—a system known as popular sovereignty to its backers and as squatter sovereignty to its detractors. Everyone assumed that Nebraska would be free soil, but Kansas—just west of slaveholding Missouri— was up for grabs. Almost immediately pro-slavery southerners and abolitionist New Englanders were financing likeminded settlers and moving them to Kansas. Soon armed fighting broke out between Democratic "bushwhackers" and free soil "jayhawkers." Pro-slavery raiders from Missouri rode into the territory, and John Brown massacred anti-abolitionists at Pottawatomie Creek. This was "Bleeding Kansas"—a major national issue and one of the direct causes of the Civil War. When the South seceded in 1861, Kansas was admitted to the Union as a free state, with a solid Republican majority. It has remained pretty solidly Republican ever since.

The major exception to Republican hegemony came during the depression of the 1890s— the Populist revolt. The 1880s were years of high rainfall on the plains, when Kansas attracted hundreds of thousands of new settlers. Suddenly the rain all but stopped, and world wheat prices plummeted; it became apparent that the Kansas plains could no longer support all who had come to depend on them. Kansas's boom went bust; some Kansas counties have never again reached the population levels recorded in the 1890 Census.

Suddenly Populists were beating Republicans in Kansas elections. They were politicians like Mary Ellen Lease ("What you farmers should do is to raise less corn and more hell") and "Sockless Jerry" Simpson, who served as an impoverished congressman. Lease, Simpson, and the farmers of the Populist Party became advocates of arcane doctrines of free silver and commodity credit programs. William Jennings Bryan, the lion of the prairies, was their man, and he swept Kansas in 1896. The period of Populist dominance—colorful, revivalist, desperate—was soon over. Soon after 1896 the nation began to enjoy an extended period of agricultural prosperity so great that parity prices are still based on those years. With small town Republicans back in the majority, Bryan failed to carry Kansas in 1900 and 1908. William Allen White, the progressive Republican editor of the *Emporia Gazette,* was the closest thing in state politics to a radical.

But echoes of the farm revolt of the 1890s can still be heard in Kansas politics. Fewer Kansans than ever are actually farmers, but the state's economy still depends heavily on agriculture. For years agriculture has been one of the most heavily regulated and subsidized businesses in the nation, the very definition of a special interest; yet there remains an assumption, shared by many who are not farmers, that any government action that helps farmers is in the public interest. America's largest class of entrepreneurial businessmen, farmers, evidently need the security government guarantees can bring; agricultural commodities are traded on the world market and are subject to wild swings in prices. For the past four or five years many farmers have been caught in a cost-price squeeze.

But even if the system of subsidies and price supports can't be defended on logical grounds, this can be said for it: it works. American agriculture is so productive that this country can feed millions abroad, and agriculture is now our biggest foreign exchange earner. Yet, for the people who conduct it and depend on it, this very successful business is also an insecure one. The populist tradition lives on, ready to be triggered by any downturn, real or perceived, in farmers' fortunes. Kansas voters are ready to react against the party in power and have done so often. There were farm revolts here against the Republicans in the late 1950s and again in the early 1970s; there were farm revolts against the Democrats in the late 1960s and again in the late 1970s.

Kansas's basic leanings are so Republican, however, that even revolts against a Republican administration do not necessarily produce Democratic victories. This is a state—the only one—that has not elected a Democratic senator since the 1930s. It elects few Democrats to the House. Only at the state level is it more bipartisan. By 1986 Kansas will have had Democratic governors for 20 of the last 30 years, and the Democrats had a majority in the state House of Representatives between 1976 and 1978. Lest there be any doubt of Kansas's preference in national elections, consider this: in the 1960, 1968, and 1980 elections, Democratic presidential candidates carried either one or two of the state's 105 counties.

Senators. Kansas's leading politician, and one of the towering political figures in America today, is Senator Robert Dole. Chairman of the Senate Finance Committee, architect of the 1982 tax bill eventually endorsed by President Reagan, the leading force in the Senate on agricultural issues, possible presidential candidate—Dole by 1982 was being hailed as a national leader by many who had scorned him a few years before. They treated him as if he had undergone some sort of metamorphosis, from the nasty partisan Bob Dole who was Nixon's Republican National Chairman and Gerald Ford's running mate/hatchet man to Chairman Dole, the statesmanlike friend of the poor and upholder of the system. Actually, Dole has not changed much at all; even his sharp, sometimes caustic wit is still very much with him. He remains the kind of politician he has been for nearly two decades now: a man whose values and beliefs remain very deeply rooted in Kansas, but who is also a Washington insider, a politician who knows the Senate, the lobbyists, the media—and has been around long enough to see the individual senators, lobbyists, and reporters come and go.

To understand Dole's politics, you have to understand that he is a Kansas Republican. He comes from a state where Republicanism is the natural affiliation of the majority, and where the Republican Party's base is broad. It includes not just rich people and country club members, but the mechanic at the garage and the clerk at the feed store; not just the banker and the lawyer, but the farmer and the minister. Kansas Republicanism believes in free enterprise, but it also understands that the untrammeled operation of the free market is going to hurt a lot of people. Kansas's populist past, and its frequent farm revolts, reinforce that lesson: Republicans as well as Democrats here believe in some sort of safety net. And, living in small towns where everyone knows, or knows something about, everyone else, they see the problems of the poor, not as theoretical, but as practical and personal.

Add to that background Bob Dole's grievous war injuries, and you can understand why he is one of the few Republicans who seems to have a gut feeling that something should be done to help the poor and victims of circumstance. Dole was seriously injured in World War II; his recovery was long and painful; he does not have use of his right hand, suffers considerable pain, and has difficulty dressing himself. The note of bitterness in his reference to "Democrat wars" in his 1976 debate with Walter Mondale comes from the same experiences that have made him one of the leading congressional advocates of the handicapped (well before his colleagues began putting sign language interpreters in the corners of their ads) and made him, with George McGovern, the architect of the food stamp program—the one form of aid to the really poor that grew in the 1970s.

The food stamp program, it should be added, is popular in Kansas: its constituency in Congress includes representatives of the urban and rural southern poor plus representatives of the farm states that produce food surpluses that the food stamp program helps use up. (That's why the Reagan administration wanted food stamps taken over by the states: neither of these constituencies is strong in most state legislatures.) The building of the food stamp program, and its preservation in the Reagan years, is a good example of Bob Dole the capable Washington insider. For he was not working from a position of strength. In the 1970s it was McGovern, not Dole, who belonged to the majority party in Congress; in the 1980s it was Jesse Helms, not Dole, who nominally chaired the Agriculture Committee. Yet Dole in each case has been a driving force—and a skilled legislative craftsman—behind the program.

Dole's legislative abilities were shown most dazzlingly in the summer of 1982, on the tax bill. Dole has always been skeptical about supply side economics, and he doubted, even as he supported them, that the 1981 tax cuts would prove a good idea. In 1982 he became alarmed at the size of the resulting deficit; Kansas Republicans have a visceral abhorrence of debt, and are willing even to raise taxes rather than to run a deficit. Most observers said there was no way to raise enough revenue to cut the deficit $100 billion without eliminating the third year of the Reagan tax rate cut—something the president said he would never accept. But Dole came up with a package that did the job—withholding of 10% of interest, dividend, and tip income, a tobacco tax, and a telephone users' tax. He did a masterful job of managing the bill on the floor, keeping the various provisions in with bipartisan majorities and then orchestrating the passage of the bill itself—it had belatedly been endorsed by the administration—with Republican votes only. At one point he lost tip withholding; he immediately rallied a majority in favor of cutting business deductions for meals, a provision he knew the restaurant industry would oppose so vehemently that it would accept tip withholding to avoid it. In all, Dole had taken responsibility for tax policy in 1982 and exercised it ably.

And he had exercised it in line with Kansas Republican principles. Not Keynesian economics, but an old-fashioned abhorrence of deficits was behind his general approach; the vehemence with which he supports withholding comes from a conviction that without it a lot of people are evading taxes they should rightfully pay. Unlike his predecessor as Finance chairman, Russell Long, Dole has no taste for passing out goodies to lobbyists and organized interests; Long's Louisiana taste for the politics of moneyed interests has never been shared by people in more austere and upright Kansas. Dole could not have secured passage of his bill without the skills he developed in 22 years as a national legislator; but he would not have put forward the bill he did without the values he acquired in Kansas.

Dole's prominence in 1982 and 1983 led naturally to speculation that he would run for president. His earlier excursions into national politics have not been auspicious. His aggressive performance as Richard Nixon's Republican National Chairman in 1971 and 1972 nearly led to his defeat in the 1974 election, though he had nothing to do with Watergate. His selection, late at night and after a canvassing of many other possibilities, as Gerald Ford's running mate in 1976 put Dole in a spotlight in which his acerbic wit and rhetorical aggressiveness were more on display than his more attractive qualities. In 1980 he ran a presidential campaign with virtually no staff, no money, and no on-the-ground support; he wanted to run as the candidate with Washington experience, in a year when Republican primary voters were happy to support a citizen-broadcaster from Pacific Palisades. Better known today, much more widely respected, Dole may still have trouble positioning himself for a candidacy appealing to Republican primary voters. Some of his major legislative achievements—the food stamp program, the 1982 tax bill—are not at all what these voters find attractive. They want a candidate who will rail against government, not one who is proud that he has served in it many years. He is knowledgeable about foreign affairs, but less experienced in foreign policy than George Bush or even Howard Baker. Baker, moreover, is likely to be a candidate if Dole is, and these two men—who have been genuine working partners since the Republicans took over the Senate—draw from the same constituencies. There is no reason to believe that Dole would be a candidate if Ronald Reagan runs again; Kansas Republicans are seldom insurgents. And even if Dole doesn't, he may find that the qualities and beliefs which have made him a superb legislator will not necessarily make him a successful president or, more to the point, a presidential candidate.

In Kansas, Dole stands for reelection in 1986. Given his national prominence, and even if the Republicans lose control of the Senate, it seems unlikely he will attract serious opposition.

Kansas's other senator, Nancy Landon Kassebaum, has a fine Kansas heritage, for she is the daughter of Alf Landon, onetime governor and the Republican nominee against FDR in 1936. Landon, more progressive than his 1930s reputation, still an active observer of politics, had the pleasure of seeing his daughter elected to the Senate in his 90s; as of 1983, he is still in good health, and has a chance to see her reelected in 1984. When she ran in 1978, Kassebaum had little political experience (she served on a local school board), but she won a nine-candidate Republican primary with 31%; and in the process of that upset victory gained precious momentum in her race against Bill Roy, the former congressman and doctor-and-lawyer who nearly beat Bob Dole in 1974.

Kassebaum has impressive committee assignments: Commerce, Foreign Relations, Budget. On foreign policy issues she is less hawkish and aggressive than most Republicans. As chairman of the Africa subcommittee, she wants to maintain aid to black African countries and is unsympathetic to South Africa; in central America she led the team monitoring El Salvador's elections and tends to favor negotiated rather than military solutions. On economic issues, she is counted as somewhat more moderate than the median Senate Republicans; on cultural issues, she is conservatively inclined. On none of these issues has she emerged as a leader yet. For one thing, she seems not to have that aggressive ambitiousness that moves so many of her colleagues, and she is one who appreciates arguments on both sides of an issue. These very traits, however, make her a potential swing vote on many important issues in the 98th Congress, and she is respected in the Senate for learning her job quietly rather than in the full glare of publicity.

As a generally popular Republican senator in a Republican state, Kassebaum should have little trouble winning reelection—unless she is opposed by a strong Democrat. There is no indication that Governor Carlin will run, but Wichita Congressman Dan Glickman, who has a strong legislative record on a wide variety of issues, was considering the race in early 1983. Well known in about half the state, he could be a formidable opponent—and might even be the first Democrat to win a Senate election in Kansas since 1930.

Governor. Kansas's current Governor, John Carlin, seems to violate all the rules: he is a Democrat, serving his second term, first elected at age 38, then divorced not long after. He bucked his own party's president by coming out for the major rules change sought by the Kennedy forces at the 1980 Democratic National Convention. Carlin has also gotten himself in trouble on Kansas issues: he vowed to sign a capital punishment law, then changed his mind and vetoed it.

But he also has had his political luck. He was elected in 1978 with lots of rural support against a Republican incumbent from the rich Johnson County Kansas City suburbs whose citified ways alienated many Kansans. In 1982, against rough-hewn oil millionaire Sam Hardage, Carlin won by carrying the more urbanized, eastern part of the state—including Johnson County. The key issue turned out not to be capital punishment, but oil severance taxes; Carlin favored them, Hardage was against. Kansas, as it happens, was one of the few oil-producing states without such a tax, and apparently voters didn't see any reason why the oil operators shouldn't pay something.

Congressional districting. Kansas redistricted its congressional seats, after some tussling between Carlin and the Republican legislature, with only a few significant changes. Democrats now hold two seats: one because of the personal popularity of an incumbent, the other largely because Republicans always seem to field weak candidates in the Topeka district.

The People Est. Pop. 1982: 2,408,000; Pop. 1980: 2,363,679, up 1.9% 1980–82 and 5.1% 1970–80; 1.0% of U.S. total, 32d largest; voting age pop. 1,714,644; 5% Black, 2% Spanish origin, 1% Asian origin, 1% American Indian. Single ancestry: 15% German, 11% English, 4% Irish, 1% Swedish, French, Dutch. Registered voters (1982): 1,186,513 Total. 454,894 R (38%); 345,395 D (29%); 386,224 unaffiliated (33%). 17% with 1–3 yrs. col., 16% with 4+ yrs. col. 10.2% below poverty level. 27% housing units rented; median house value: $37,800; median monthly rent: $168. Households: 73% family, 38% with children, 63% married couples.

1982 Share of Federal Tax Burden $6,363,700,000; 1.07% of U.S. total, 30th largest.

1982 Share of Federal Expenditures

	Total		Non-Defense		Defense	
Total Expend	$6,334m	(1.05%)	$4,167m	(0.98%)	$2,168m	(1.21%)
St/Lcl Grants	706m	(0.80%)	705m	(0.80%)	1m	(2.78%)
Salary/Wages	792m	(1.01%)	197m	(0.72%)	595m	(1.17%)
Ind Payments	3,009m	(1.05%)	2,737m	(1.06%)	272m	(0.95%)
Procurement	1,580m	(1.08%)	142m	(0.45%)	1,438m	(1.26%)
Other Programs	247m	(4.56%)	247m	(4.60%)	0m	(0%)
Loan/Insurance	1,727m	(2.70%)	1,715m	(2.78%)	12m	(0.55%)

Political Lineup Governor, John W. Carlin (D). Senators, Robert Dole (R) and Nancy Landon Kassebaum (R). Representatives, 5 (3 R and 2 D). State Senate, 40 (24 R and 16 D); State House of Representatives, 125 (72 R and 53 D).

Presidential Vote

1980	Reagan (R)	566,812	(58%)
	Carter (D)	326,150	(33%)
	Anderson (I)	68,231	(7%)
1976	Ford (R)	502,752	(52%)
	Carter (D)	430,421	(45%)

1980 Democratic Presidential Primary			*1980 Republican Presidential Primary*		
Carter	109,807	(57%)	Reagan	179,739	(63%)
Kennedy	61,318	(32%)	Anderson	51,924	(18%)
Brown	9,434	(5%)	Bush	35,838	(13%)
Four others	2,196	(1%)	Nine others	11,171	(4%)
None	11,163	(6%)	None	6,726	(2%)

SENATORS

Sen. Robert Dole (R) Elected 1968, seat up 1986; b. July 22, 1923, Russell; home, Russell; U. of KS, 1941–43, Washburn Municipal U., B.A., LL.B. 1952; Methodist.

Career Army, WWII; KS House of Reps., 1951-53; Russell Cnty. Atty., 1953-61; U.S. House of Reps., 1961–69; Chmn., Repub. Natl. Comm., 1971–73; Repub. Nominee for V.P., 1976.

Offices 141 HSOB, 202-224-6521. Also 4601 State Ave., Kansas City 66102, 913-287-4545; and 444 S.E. Quincy St., Fed. Ofc. Bldg., Topeka 66683, 913-295-2745.

Committees *Agriculture, Nutrition and Foresty* (2d). Subcommittees: Agricultural Production, Marketing, and Stabilization; Foreign Agricultural Policy; Nutrition (Chairman). *Finance* (Chairman). Subcommittees: Health; Social Security and Income Maintenance Programs; Oversight of the Internal Revenue Service. *Judiciary* (5th). Subcommittees: Courts (Chairman); Criminal Law; Patents, Copyrights and Trademarks. *Rules and Administration* (7th). *Joint Committee on Taxation* (Vice-Chairman).

Group Ratings

	ADA	ACLU	COPE	CFA	LCV	LWV	NTU	NSI	COC	ACA	CSFC
1982	15	21	18	0	23	50	72	80	62	71	69
1981	5	—	18	15	13	—	64	—	100	70	83
1980	22	33	28	20	49	33	44	100	90	77	65

National Journal Ratings

	Economic		Foreign		Cultural	
1982	2%	(LIB)	44%	(LIB)	31%	(LIB)
	97%	(CONS)	55%	(CONS)	68%	(CONS)
1981	2%	(LIB)	1%	(LIB)	36%	(LIB)
	88%	(CONS)	85%	(CONS)	63%	(CONS)

Key Votes

1) Reagan 81 Budget	FOR	5) $ to El Salvador	FOR	9) Poor Pay Food Stamps	AGN
2) Reagan 81 Tax Cut	FOR	6) Saudi AWACS Sale	FOR	10) Ban Crt Busing Order	FOR
3) Bal Budget Amend	FOR	7) Ban Abortion	FOR	11) Clinch Riv Brdr Rctr	FOR
4) Gas & Road Tax	FOR	8) Nerve Gas Prod	FOR	12) Legal Services Corp	AGN

Election Results

1980 general	Robert Dole (R)	598,686	(64%)	($1,224,494)
	John Simpson (D)	340,271	(36%)	($323,792)
1980 primary	Robert Dole (R)	201,484	(82%)	
	One other (R)	44,674	(18%)	
1974 general	Robert Dole (R)	403,983	(51%)	($1,110,024)
	Bill Roy (D)	390,451	(49%)	($836,927)

Campaign Contributions and Expenditures

1979-80		PACS brkdwn			
Receipts	$1,327,384	Agr	$39,610	Ideo	$16,655
Expend.	$1,224,494	Bus	$311,666	Lbr	$1,150
Unspent	$102,186	Hlth	$41,950	Prof	$11,500

Sen. Nancy Landon Kassebaum (R) Elected 1978, seat up 1984; b. July 29, 1932, Topeka; home, Wichita; U. of KS, B.A. 1954, U. of MI, M.A. 1956; Episcopal.

Career Staff of U.S. Sen. James B. Pearson, 1975.

Offices 302 RSOB, 202-224-4774. Also 444 S.E. Quincy St., Fed. Ofc. Bldg., Box 51, Topeka 66683, 913-295-2888.

Committees *Budget* (3d). *Commerce, Science, and Transportation* (4th). Subcommittees: Aviation (Chairwoman); Science, Technology and Space; Surface Transportation. *Foreign Relations* (6th). Subcommittees: Arms Control, Oceans, International Operations, and Environment; African Affairs (Chairwoman); Western Hemisphere Affairs. *Special Committee on Aging* (4th).

Group Ratings

	ADA	ACLU	COPE	CFA	LCV	LWV	NTU	NSI	COC	ACA	CSFC
1982	50	50	16	0	32	58	77	50	53	62	71
1981	35	—	17	36	25	—	66	—	88	67	73
1980	44	77	25	7	48	56	44	60	74	70	62

National Journal Ratings

	Economic		Foreign		Cultural	
1982	14%	(LIB)	65%	(LIB)	61%	(LIB)
	85%	(CONS)	34%	(CONS)	38%	(CONS)
1981	41%	(LIB)	69%	(LIB)	34%	(LIB)
	58%	(CONS)	30%	(CONS)	64%	(CONS)

Key Votes

1) Reagan 81 Budget	FOR	5) $ to El Salvador	AGN	9) Poor Pay Food Stamps	AGN
2) Reagan 81 Tax Cut	FOR	6) Saudi AWACS Sale	FOR	10) Ban Crt Busing Order	FOR
3) Bal Budget Amend	AGN	7) Ban Abortion	AGN	11) Clinch Riv Brdr Rctr	AGN
4) Gas & Road Tax	FOR	8) Nerve Gas Prod	AGN	12) Legal Services Corp	AGN

Election Results

1978 general	Nancy Landon Kassebaum (R) ...	405,354	(54%)	($856,644)
	Bill Roy (D)	317,602	(42%)	($813,754)
1978 primary	Nancy Landon Kassebaum (R) ...	67,324	(31%)	
	Wayne Angell (R)	54,161	(25%)	($388,334)
	Sam Hardage (R)	30,248	(14%)	($489,983)
	Jan Meyers (R)	20,933	(10%)	($72,307)
	Five others (R)	47,476	(22%)	
1972 general	James B. Pearson (R)	622,591	(71%)	($109,651)
	Arch O. Tetzlaff (D)	200,764	(23%)	($6,742)

Campaign Contributions and Expenditures

1977-78		*PACS brkdwn*			
Receipts	$864,288	Agr	$7,700	Ideo	$7,499
Expend.	$856,644	Bus	$99,722	Lbr	$150
Unspent	$7,361	Hlth	$5,000	Prof	$100

GOVERNOR

Gov. John W. Carlin (D) Elected 1978, term expires Jan. 1987; b. Aug. 3, 1940, Salina; home, Topeka; KS St. U., B.S. 1962; Lutheran.

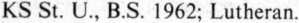

Career Dairy farmer, cattle sales mgr.; KS House of Reps., 1971–79, Minor. Ldr., 1975–77, Spkr., 1977–79.

Offices State Capitol, 2d Flr., Topeka 66612, 913-296-3232.

Election Results

1982 gen.	John W. Carlin (D)	405,309	(53%)
	Sam Hardage (R)	339,700	(44%)
1982 prim.	John W. Carlin (D)	103,780	(79%)
	Jimmy Montgomery (D)	27,785	(21%)
1978 gen.	John W. Carlin (D)	363,835	(49%)
	Robert F. Bennett (R)	348,015	(47%)

FIRST DISTRICT

The 1st congressional district of Kansas covers more than half the state's land area. It contains more counties (58) than any other congressional district in the country except three directly to the north, the 3d of Nebraska and the at-large districts of North and South Dakota. That fact is more than just a bit of trivia; it tells us a good deal about the expectations of the people who first settled this part of Kansas. Most of them came here in the 1880s from states like Illinois and Iowa and Missouri. When they organized counties, as they quickly did, they made them 30 or 36 miles square, just as they had in the states of the old Northwest Territory. Misled by a few years of unusually high rainfall, the settlers expected the new counties would eventually contain as many people as the ones they came from; hence it made sense to make them the same size. Not only the small size of the counties, but the grandiose place names (Concordia, Minneapolis, Montezuma) testify to the settlers' hopes, dreams, and ambitions.

But they never materialized. Out here past 98° longitude, rainfall is normally half what it is in Illinois. In the early years of the 19th century, this part of the country was called the Great American Desert—a howling wilderness of arid, treeless land and blowing soil, harder to cross than a stormy ocean. The early settlers worked hard to prove this image wrong, but never entirely succeeded. There are prosperous towns out here on the plains, particularly where cattle are raised or oil is pumped, but making a living here has proved difficult, and sometimes impossible. Since the 1890s, the population flow here has been out: tens of thousands of young people have left to make their fortunes elsewhere. The thousands more who were expected by the early settlers never arrived; today the average population of the district's 58 counties is only a little over 8,000.

Most are far less populous because the average is inflated by the district's "urban" concentrations. The largest city, Salina, has only 41,000 people; Dodge City, terminus of the old cattle drives and once the home of Wyatt Earp, has 18,000 residents; Holcomb, made famous by Truman Capote's *In Cold Blood,* has exactly 816. Hays, a German Catholic town

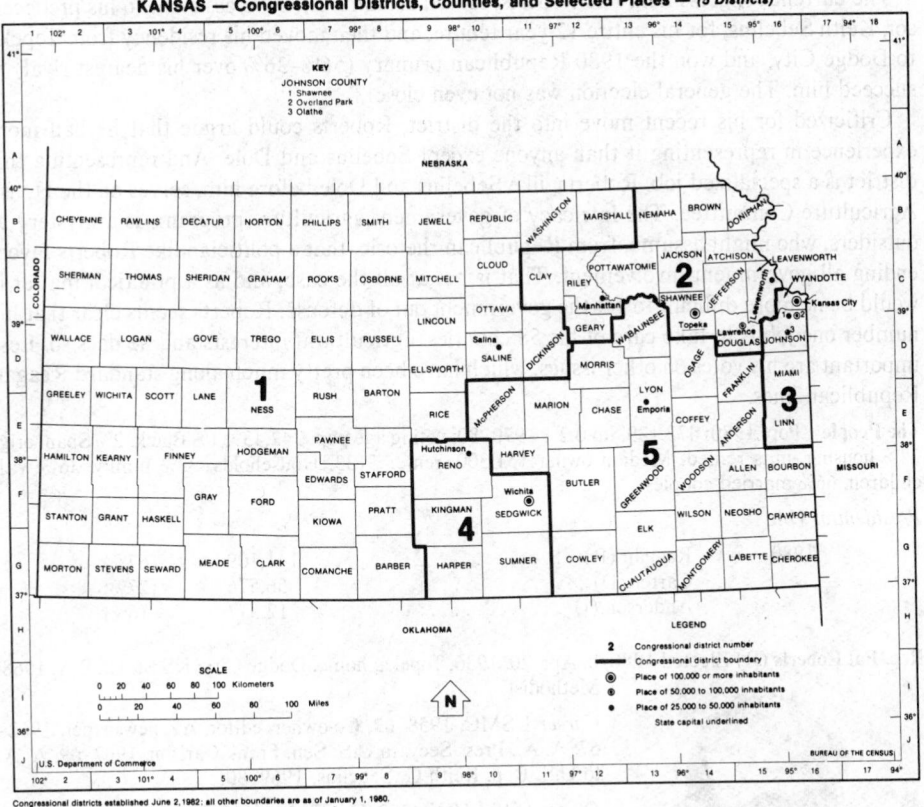

KANSAS — Congressional Districts, Counties, and Selected Places — (5 Districts)

of 16,000, is the one part of the district that usually goes Democratic; so too sometimes do some counties along the Arkansas River first settled by southerners. But the real 1st district cannot be found in the towns. This is livestock and wheat country, one of the most agricultural districts in the nation. For miles on end you can see nothing but rolling brown fields, sectioned off here and there by barbed wire fence, and in the distance a grain elevator towering over a tiny town and its miniature railroad depot. The winds and rain and tornadoes that come suddenly out of the sky remind you that the original settlers likened this part of Kansas to an ocean and thought themselves in their wooden wagons almost as helpless as passengers at sea in a wooden rowboat. And you can see why Dorothy's flight to Oz did not seem so improbable to turn-of-the-century Kansans.

The 1st district is basically Republican, but like most of the agricultural Great Plains it has a tendency to vote against the party in power. It has not swung heavily against the Republicans for some time, though. The last time it elected a Democratic congressman was in 1960; his district was combined with another represented by Bob Dole in 1962, and Republicans have won here ever since. In 1980 its two political tendencies worked in tandem to produce a huge margin for Ronald Reagan over Jimmy Carter.

The current congressman, Pat Roberts, served as administrative assistant to his predecessor, Keith Sebelius, for his entire 12-year tenure, and then moved his residency from Topeka to Dodge City, and won the 1980 Republican primary (56%–36% over his nearest rival) to succeed him. The general election was not even close.

Criticized for his recent move into the district, Roberts could argue that he had more experience in representing it than anyone except Sebelius and Dole. And representing this district is a specialized job. Roberts, like Sebelius and Dole before him, serves on the House Agriculture Committee. The intricacy of government agriculture programs is a mystery to outsiders, who might assume, from Republican rhetoric, that a politician like Roberts favors ending all government involvement. That is not at all the case, and as a practical matter it would be no more difficult to get the government out of defense. Roberts seems clear that his number one job is to take care of his 58 counties' agricultural interests and he does so. Less important are his votes on other issues, which have been pretty much along standard Reagan Republican lines.

The People   Pop. 1980: 472,139, up 0.2% 1970–80; voting age pop. 342,439; 1% Black, 2% Span. orig. 22% housing units rented. Median owner $31,300; renter $133. Households: 73% family, 36% with children, 66% married couples.

Presidential Vote

1980	Reagan (R)	141,109	(67%)
	Carter (D)	56,576	(27%)
	Anderson (I)	12,577	(6%)

Rep. Pat Roberts (R) Elected 1980; b. Apr. 20, 1936, Topeka; home, Dodge City; KS St. U., B.A. 1968; Methodist.

Career USMC, 1958–62; Co-owner, editor, AZ newspaper, 1962–67; A. A., Press Secy. to U.S. Sen. Frank Carlson, 1967–69; A. A. to U.S. Rep. Keith G. Sebelius, 1969–80.

Offices 1519 LHOB, 202-225-2715. Also P.O. Box 550, Dodge City 67801, 316-227-2244; P.O. Box 28, Norton 67654, 913-877-2454; and P.O. Box 1224, Salina 67401, 913-825-5409.

Committees Agriculture (8th). Subcommittees: Department Operations, Research and Foreign Agriculture; Tobacco and Peanuts; Wheat, Soybeans, and Feed Grains. *Select Committee on Aging* (12th). Subcommittee: Health and Long-Term Care.

Group Ratings

	ADA	ACLU	COPE	CFA	LCV	LWV	NTU	NSI	COC	ACA	CSFC
1982	15	17	0	20	14	36	88	100	90	87	68
1981	10	—	0	29	22	—	81	—	84	83	71

National Journal Ratings

	Economic		Foreign		Cultural	
1982	12%	(LIB)	53%	(LIB)	15%	(LIB)
	88%	(CONS)	47%	(CONS)	83%	(CONS)
1981	4%	(LIB)	3%	(LIB)	23%	(LIB)
	79%	(CONS)	87%	(CONS)	77%	(CONS)

Key Votes

1) Reagan 81 Budget	FOR	5) Incr SS Rtmt Age	FOR	9) Poor Pay Food Stamps	FOR
2) Reagan 81 Tax Cut	FOR	6) Saudi AWACS Sale	FOR	10) Ban Crt Busing Order	FOR
3) Bal Budget Amend	FOR	7) $ for MX Missile	AGN	11) Auto Local Content	AGN
4) Gas & Road Tax	AGN	8) Nerve Gas Prod	AGN	12) Nuclear Arms Freeze	AGN

Election Results

1982 general	Pat Roberts (R)	115,591	(68%)	($143,301)
	Kent Roth (D)	51,032	(30%)	($20,542)
1982 primary	Pat Roberts (R)	46,929	(86%)	
	Charles J. Sellens (R)	7,669	(14%)	
1980 general	Pat Roberts (R)	121,545	(62%)	($229,593)
	Phil Martin (D)	73,586	(38%)	($63,232)

Campaign Contributions and Expenditures

1981-82		Direct Cont. 81-82			PACS brkdwn			
Receipts	$184,218	Indiv	$91,810	Agr	$17,000	Ideo	$1,811
Expend.	$143,301	Party	$11,000	Bus	$44,125	Lbr	$400
Unspent	$64,915	PACS	$76,086	Hlth	$11,850	Prof	$500

SECOND DISTRICT

Topeka is the capital of Kansas and one of those prosperous, progressive midwestern cities that have provided much of the dynamism of the region. The economy is based first on state government, but Topeka is also an important agricultural center. There are a few big new buildings downtown; clean-cut, pleasant neighborhoods in all directions. This is the home town of Alf Landon, the still vigorous and progressive Republican who carried Maine and Vermont in the 1936 Roosevelt landslide; and the home as well of the Menninger Psychiatric Clinic. And although Topeka does not like to remember it, this is the city where the lawsuit *Brown v. Board of Education* was filed, the case in which the Supreme Court outlawed segregation in public schools.

The 2d congressional district of Kansas is centered on Topeka, which with its surrounding county casts about 40% of the district's votes. The district also contains the state's two major universities, Kansas State in Manhattan and the University of Kansas in Lawrence; two major military installations, Fort Riley near Manhattan and the Army's Leavenworth Prison, high on the bluffs overlooking the Missouri River; and even some Indian reservations. But otherwise the district is mostly agricultural. West of the Missouri the rolling hills flatten out to gently rolling, fertile plains. Rainfall here in the eastern part of the state is almost always sufficient to produce a good crop.

Politically, the 2d district has a Republican heritage. Lawrence was the Republicans' capital in the Bleeding Kansas days, the rival to the pro-slavery forces' Lecompton; Topeka has produced the longest-lived Republican presidential candidate. Yet for the last dozen years the Democrats have dominated congressional elections here—not always won, but dominated. Doctor-lawyer Bill Roy won in 1970 and 1972 and lost the seat only when he ran against Bob Dole. Martha Keys, his successor, won in 1974 and 1976, and when she finally lost in 1978 one factor seemed to be negative reaction to her marriage to Indiana Congressman Andrew Jacobs. The 1978 winner, Republican Jim Jeffries, proved to be one of the weakest congressmen politically, a man considered a flake by many of his colleagues; targeted for defeat, he retired in 1982.

That should have produced a two-party battle. Instead, Democrat Jim Slattery won rather easily, with 57% of the vote. Redistricting was not crucial: his percentage in his new territory, Lawrence, was no higher than his district average. Morris Kay, a 34% winner of a five-candidate Republican primary, was not considered a strong candidate; but he was far more presentable and experienced than Jeffries. The fact is that the Topeka area has just gotten used to voting Democratic for Congress; it gave Slattery 61% of its votes.

Slattery is one of those young Democrats who seems to have a knack for politics. Elected at 24 to the Kansas legislature, he was speaker pro tem at 28, after the Democrats won control in 1976. He seems to have an instinct for timing: he retired from the legislature, to make money in the real estate business, when the Democrats lost control in 1978; he passed up a chance to run against Jeffries in the Republican year of 1980 and chose 1982 instead. His strength is indicated by the fact that he was unopposed in his primary. His political acumen is apparent from the fact that he won a much coveted seat on the Energy and Commerce Committee. Slattery insists that he is a fiscal conservative and, like the other Democrats who have represented the district, he will undoubtedly stop short of a record of support for every big government measure. At the same time, there seems little doubt that he will take the side supported by most Democrats on most Energy and Commerce and macroeconomic issues.

It is too soon to say that Democrat Slattery, in Kansas, has a safe seat. But his commanding performance in 1982, at age 34, suggests that he will be hard indeed to beat.

The People   Pop. 1980: 472,988, up 5.8% 1970–80; voting age pop. 348,994; 7% Black, 3% Span. orig., 1% Asian orig., 1% Am. Ind. 33% housing units rented. Median owner $40,600; renter $176. Households: 71% family, 38% with children, 61% married couples.

Presidential Vote

1980	Reagan (R)	100,343	(56%)
	Carter (D)	61,150	(34%)
	Anderson (I)	16,303	(9%)

Rep. Jim Slattery (D) Elected 1982; b. Aug. 4, 1948, Good Intent; home, Topeka; Washburn U., B.S. 1970, J.D. 1974, Netherlands Sch. of Interntl. Econ. and Bus., 1969–70; Roman Catholic.

Career KS House of Reps., 1972–78, Chmn. of Dem. Policy Group, 1975–79, Spkr. Pro Tem, 1977–79; KS Acting Secy. of Revenue, 1979; Real estate and development, Brosius, Slattery and Meyer, Inc., 1973–82.

Offices 1729 LHOB, 202-225-6601. Also 444 S.E. Quincy, Su. 280, Topeka 66683, 913-295-2811.

Committees *Energy and Commerce* (24th). Subcommittees: Fossil and Synthetic Fuels; Oversight and Investigations. *Veterans' Affairs* (19th). Subcommittees: Education, Training and Employment; Hospitals and Health Care.

Group Ratings and Key Votes: Newly Elected

Election Results

1982 general	Jim Slattery (D)	86,075	(57%)	($263,873)
	Morris Kay (R)	64,164	(43%)	($312,459)
1982 primary	Jim Slattery (D)	22,675	(100%)	
1980 general	Jim Jeffries (R)	92,107	(54%)	($249,144)
	Sam Keys (D)	78,859	(46%)	($117,796)

Campaign Contributions and Expenditures

1981-82		Direct Cont. 81-82		PACS brkdwn			
Receipts	$265,987	Indiv	$166,091	Agr	$1,000	Ideo	$7,781
Expend.	$263,873	Party	$19,249	Bus	$7,200	Lbr	$53,000
Unspent	$2,113	PACS	$79,191	Hlth	$2,250	Prof	$2,400
		Cand	$10,000				

THIRD DISTRICT

Everyone thinks of Kansas as an agricultural, Great Plains state. Yet part of the eastern edge of Kansas is part of one of the nation's larger metropolitan areas, Kansas City. The big Kansas City, the one with the big office buildings, the one that hosted the 1976 Republican National Convention, is in Missouri; but it is separated from Kansas on the north by the Missouri River and to the south by only a rather minor residential street. Directly west of downtown Kansas City is Kansas City, Kansas, an industrial, meatpacking town. This is the Democratic bastion of Kansas: working class, middle income with a few slummy looking streets and the largest black neighborhood in the state.

To the south is Johnson County, adjoining high income neighborhoods in Missouri. Johnson County is basically white collar, middle to upper income; it contains some of metro Kansas City's newest and fastest-growing suburbs, with gleaming office parks and cul-de-sac streets; it is easily the highest income county in Kansas. It is also, in a Republican state, one of the most Republican; in fact, it has contributed to making Kansas more Republican in statewide elections. Yet when an issue pits metropolitan areas against rural Kansas—as liquor by the drink did in 1970 or the oil severance tax did in 1982—Johnson County votes metropolitan; thus it voted to reelect Democratic Governor John Carlin in 1982. Johnson County was once politically overshadowed by Kansas City and Wyandotte County; now, after rapid population growth, it casts about twice as many votes as Wyandotte.

That, more than anything else, accounts for the persistence of Republican margins in races in the 3d congressional district, which includes both metropolitan counties and two small rural counties just to the south. Congressman Larry Winn, first elected in 1966, is one of the more senior Republicans in the House. He is ranking minority member on the Science and Technology Committee, and second ranking Republican on Foreign Affairs. Yet he is not known as a legislative craftsman or indeed as one who is particularly active on legislation. The Science Committee is one whose subject matter sounds politically attractive but which has been, compared to many standing committees, underworked. It may have a busier agenda in the years ahead, because so many members want to do something to improve scientific and technical education. On Foreign Affairs Winn's tendency, like that of ranking Republican William Broomfield, is to go along with the administration, especially when it is a Republican one. Winn seems to be one of the less active, less aggressive members of the House, a man who has made little impact on legislation or government. He votes reliably with the Republican majority, although on occasion his attendance record has been low.

Even in a district as Republican as the 3d, that record has gotten Winn into some trouble. He had an aggressive challenger in 1980 who, in that Republican year, held Winn to 55% of the vote. In 1982, without effective opposition, Winn raised his percentage to 59%. But he still lost Wyandotte County, and overall the result is not particularly impressive. This is a district which may see a serious challenge to the incumbent, or his retirement, in an election soon.

The People Pop. 1980: 472,456, up 8.9% 1970–80; voting age pop. 334,153; 8% Black, 2% Span. orig., 1% Asian orig. 27% housing units rented. Median owner $52,000; renter $216. Households: 76% family, 42% with children, 64% married couples.

Presidential Vote

1980	Reagan (R)	108,207	(56%)
	Carter (D)	70,201	(36%)
	Anderson (I)	14,436	(7%)

Rep. Larry Winn, Jr. (R) Elected 1966; b. Aug. 22, 1919, Kansas City, MO; home, Overland Park; U. of KS, A.B. 1941; Disciples of Christ.

Career Radio announcer, WHB, Kansas City, MO; North Amerian Aviation; Pub. Rel. Dir., Amer. Red Cross, Kansas City, MO; V.P., Winn-Rau Corp., 1950–.

Offices 2308 RHOB, 202-225-2865. Also 204 Fed. Bldg., Kansas City 66101, 913-621-0832.

Committees *Foreign Affairs* (2d). Subcommittee: Europe and the Middle East. *Science and Technology* (Ranking Member).

Group Ratings

	ADA	ACLU	COPE	CFA	LCV	LWV	NTU	NSI	COC	ACA	CSFC
1982	0	17	17	20	9	36	74	100	80	78	65
1981	5	—	17	21	14	—	54	—	94	74	66
1980	11	17	14	14	26	22	45	100	83	79	71

National Journal Ratings

	Economic		Foreign		Cultural	
1982	10%	(LIB)	34%	(LIB)	15%	(LIB)
	90%	(CONS)	66%	(CONS)	83%	(CONS)
1981	4%	(LIB)	34%	(LIB)	18%	(LIB)
	79%	(CONS)	63%	(CONS)	82%	(CONS)

Key Votes

1) Reagan 81 Budget	FOR	5) Incr SS Rtmt Age	FOR	9) Poor Pay Food Stamps	FOR
2) Reagan 81 Tax Cut	FOR	6) Saudi AWACS Sale	AGN	10) Ban Crt Busing Order	FOR
3) Bal Budget Amend	FOR	7) $ for MX Missile	FOR	11) Auto Local Content	AGN
4) Gas & Road Tax	—	8) Nerve Gas Prod	FOR	12) Nuclear Arms Freeze	AGN

Election Results

1982 general	Larry Winn, Jr. (R)	82,007	(59%)	($140,007)
	Bill Kostar (D)	53,218	(38%)	($34,518)
1982 primary	Larry Winn, Jr. (R)	29,087	(82%)	
	John O. Stewart (R)	6,374	(18%)	
1980 general	Larry Winn, Jr. (R)	109,294	(55%)	($199,677)
	Dan Watkins (D)	82,414	(42%)	($123,494)

Campaign Contributions and Expenditures

1981-82		Direct Cont. 81-82				PACS brkdwn		
Receipts	$154,831	Indiv	$64,109	Agr	$3,650	Ideo	$1,850
Expend.	$140,007	Party	$9,042	Bus	$67,370	Lbr	$1,000
Unspent	$36,707	PACS	$80,198	Hlth	$3,400	Prof	$2,600

FOURTH DISTRICT

Before World War II, Wichita, Kansas, was a small city, a trading center for farm commodities, depending for its livelihood on the agricultural yield of the surrounding counties. Today Wichita is a substantial city, with a metropolitan population over 400,000; in many ways it is a Sun Belt city a little farther north than you would expect. Wichita owes most of its growth and prosperity to the general aviation industry. During World War II and the years immediately after, aircraft factories sprouted up here, on the Kansas plains. Today Boeing has a major plant here, its only one outside Washington state; so do Cessna, Beechcraft, and Piper. Wichita is far and away the nation's leading center for producing small airplanes—everything short of jetliners. This has been a prosperous business, but one not free from wild fluctuations. When the corporations and small businesses which buy most of the small planes run into profit squeezes, one of the easiest ways to economize is not to buy a small plane, or to sell the one you have; the market for small planes collapses; and Wichita falls on hard times. But when these businesses prosper, so does Wichita. During most of the 1970s Wichita did very well: the market for small planes was robust, and the rise in oil prices made the stripper wells around Wichita economically attractive once again. Wichita did less well in the 1980s, but it was not hit as badly as some places; the decline in basic industries like autos and steel has little impact on the general aviation business.

Wichita's politics is the product of two conflicting tendencies. On the one hand, this is a newly prosperous city that believes in free enterprise and economic growth and is suspicious of government regulation; such feelings tend to make Wichita Republican, and it has gone Republican in most state and national elections. But at the same time Wichita is a city that seems more than half southern, with many residents from Arkansas, Oklahoma, and southern Kansas. Many people here speak with a southern drawl, and Wichita would just as soon look south to Dallas as north to Kansas City. This kind of background inclines Wichita toward the Democrats. So in state elections like the 1978 and 1982 gubernatorial race, or in the 1976 presidential election, Wichita gave majorities or near-majorities to the Democrats.

The 4th congressional district of Kansas includes all of Wichita and Segdwick County; the much smaller city of Hutchinson to the northwest; and rural areas like Sumner County, usually the number one wheat-producing county in Kansas. The 4th district is represented by a man with an unusual background for a Kansas congressman. Dan Glickman was first elected in 1976, at age 31, when he beat a Republican incumbent; he emphasized his close ties to Wichita at a time when voters were suspicious of Washington. From the beginning, he was more skeptical about government programs than most Democrats and more inclined to hold down spending. Since the Carter years, when many of the creative ideas in politics came from Republicans, Glickman has been coming forth with many ideas on how government can be made to work better—or can be done without.

Glickman won seats on the Agriculture and Science and Technology Committees—both of obvious economic importance to this district. On science, he heads the Transportation, Aviation and Materials Subcommittee that handles research and development funds for the Federal Aviation Commission and NASA, and he has pushed hard for an increased government role in aeronautical research. On Agriculture he has been particularly attentive to wheat programs and as an expert on regulation of the futures markets pushed to passage in 1982 a bill tightening up regulation of them. He also serves on the Judiciary Committee. He gets involved in issues outside his committees as well: trying to hold down natural gas prices, for example, or limiting campaign contributions by political action committees.

He is already one of the most popular congressmen the Wichita area has ever had, and he is reelected by overwhelming margins. He has been a possible statewide candidate for some time now, and in 1983 was exploring the possibility of a race against Senator Nancy Landon Kassebaum in 1984. She is generally popular and has made few enemies, and has the party label advantage as well. But Glickman is already well known in much of the state—Wichita TV reaches almost all of western and central Kansas—and is more aggressively involved in more issues, and might be a formidable challenger.

The People Pop. 1980: 473,180, up 4.7% 1970–80; voting age pop. 341,718; 6% Black, 2% Span. orig., 1% Asian orig., 1% Am. Ind. 32% housing units rented. Median owner $40,100; renter $192. Households: 72% family, 38% with children, 61% married couples.

Presidential Vote

1980	Reagan (R)	100,023	(54%)
	Carter (D)	70,604	(38%)
	Anderson (I)	13,401	(7%)

Rep. Dan Glickman (D) Elected 1976; b. Nov. 24, 1944, Wichita; home, Wichita; U. of MI, B.A. 1966, Geo. Wash. U., J.D. 1969; Jewish.

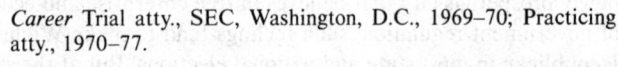

Career Trial atty., SEC, Washington, D.C., 1969–70; Practicing atty., 1970–77.

Offices 1507 LHOB, 202-225-6216. Also Box 403, Wichita 67201, 316-262-8396.

Committees *Agriculture* (13th). Subcommittees: Conservation, Credit and Rural Development; Domestic Marketing, Consumer Relations, and Nutrition; Wheat, Soybeans and Feed Grains. *Judiciary* (12th). Subcommittee: Courts, Civil Liberties, and the Administration of Justice. *Science and Technology* (9th). Subcommittee: Transportation, Aviation and Materials (Chairman).

Group Ratings

	ADA	ACLU	COPE	CFA	LCV	LWV	NTU	NSI	COC	ACA	CSFC
1982	70	58	59	90	77	91	46	40	24	30	37
1981	75	—	57	64	68	—	52	—	26	30	46
1980	56	63	37	50	81	60	32	56	73	33	47

National Journal Ratings

	Economic		Foreign		Cultural	
1982	58%	(LIB)	64%	(LIB)	77%	(LIB)
	42%	(CONS)	36%	(CONS)	23%	(CONS)
1981	58%	(LIB)	80%	(LIB)	67%	(LIB)
	42%	(CONS)	20%	(CONS)	33%	(CONS)

Key Votes

1) Reagan 81 Budget	AGN	5) Incr SS Rtmt Age FOR	9) Poor Pay Food Stamps AGN
2) Reagan 81 Tax Cut	FOR	6) Saudi AWACS Sale AGN	10) Ban Crt Busing Order FOR
3) Bal Budget Amend	AGN	7) $ for MX Missile AGN	11) Auto Local Content AGN
4) Gas & Road Tax	AGN	8) Nerve Gas Prod AGN	12) Nuclear Arms Freeze FOR

Election Results

1982 general	Dan Glickman (D)	106,157	(74%)	($148,875)
	Gerald Caywood (R)	35,311	(25%)	($39,774)
1982 primary	Dan Glickman (D)	25,523	(100%)	
1980 general	Dan Glickman (D)	124,014	(69%)	($122,894)
	Clay Hunter (R)	55,899	(31%)	($42,466)

Campaign Contributions and Expenditures

1981-82		Direct Cont. 81-82		PACS brkdwn			
Receipts	$151,353	Indiv	$97,358	Agr	$6,250	Ideo	$1,200
Expend.	$148,875	Party	$1,000	Bus	$23,325	Lbr	$5,140
Unspent	$40,962	PACS	$39,091	Hlth	$1,600	Prof	$2,350

FIFTH DISTRICT

The southeastern corner of Kansas has been nicknamed "the Balkans"—a reference to the Eastern European origin of some of the residents and to its low hill country, the outer fringe of the Ozarks. The hills here contain some coal, and the main town was named Pittsburg—another example of the unrealistic optimism of the people who first settled Kansas. This part of the state never became a notable coal or manufacturing center, and for many years it was in unmistakable decline. Only in the 1970s did its population increase slightly, and that largely because of retirees and others moving to small towns near the hills. This southeastern part of Kansas forms a little less than half of the state's 5th congressional district, which stretches north to a point near Topeka and west almost to Wichita.

Emporia is one of the larger towns in the district, and the home of William Allen White, the newspaper editor whose name was a household word 40 years ago but draws blank stares today. White was the voice of progressive midwestern Republicanism. Horrified by the Populists of his youth, as were most townspeople in the Midwest, White was enchanted by Theodore Roosevelt and came to care about the plight of society's unfortunates. Although a native of one of the nation's most isolationist regions, White was a leading spokesman for American aid to the British during the ominous days before Pearl Harbor.

The 5th district's politics has been pretty consistently Republican, although the Balkans, near the borders of Missouri and Oklahoma, sometimes vote Democratic. The 5th has never had a congressman who attracted national attention. In 1978, when incumbent Joe Skubitz retired, there was a spirited competition for the seat, with five Democrats and six Republicans running. The Republican primary was won by a dark horse, optometrist Robert Whittaker. A friendly man who served one term in the Kansas legislature, Whittaker went door to door talking with voters and worked at various jobs around the district for a day at a time. He won with 57% in the 1978 general election and has been reelected easily ever since.

He has a pretty solidly conservative record in the House; he seems a little more strongly conservative on economic issues than on cultural matters. He sits on the Energy and Commerce Committee, which has jurisdiction over all kinds of federal regulations, and generally supports easing regulations and reducing government interference in business.

The People   Pop. 1980: 472,916, up 6.2% 1970–80; voting age pop. 347,340; 2% Black, 1% Span. orig., 1% Am. Ind. 23% housing units rented. Median owner $28,600; renter $128. Households: 73% family, 36% with children, 65% married couples.

Presidential Vote

1980	Reagan (R)	117,130	(60%)
	Carter (D)	67,619	(34%)
	Anderson (I)	11,514	(6%)

Rep. Robert (Bob) Whittaker (R) Elected 1978; b. Sept. 18, 1939, Eureka; home, Augusta; IL Col. of Optometry, B.S. 1961, Dr. of Optometry 1962; Disciples of Christ.

Career Optometrist; KS House of Reps., 1975–77.

Offices 332 CHOB, 202-225-3911. Also 109 W. 5th St., Pittsburg 66762, 316-323-2320.

Committee *Energy and Commerce* (8th). Subcommittees: Health and the Environment; Oversight and Investigations.

Group Ratings

	ADA	ACLU	COPE	CFA	LCV	LWV	NTU	NSI	COC	ACA	CSFC
1982	15	17	9	20	23	36	87	90	90	78	65
1981	15	—	9	36	29	—	81	—	89	70	69
1980	11	7	10	14	48	50	53	100	82	88	79

National Journal Ratings

	Economic		Foreign		Cultural	
1982	10%	(LIB)	49%	(LIB)	55%	(LIB)
	90%	(CONS)	50%	(CONS)	45%	(CONS)
1981	4%	(LIB)	41%	(LIB)	31%	(LIB)
	79%	(CONS)	58%	(CONS)	69%	(CONS)

Key Votes

1) Reagan 81 Budget	FOR	5) Incr SS Rtmt Age	FOR	9) Poor Pay Food Stamps	FOR
2) Reagan 81 Tax Cut	FOR	6) Saudi AWACS Sale	AGN	10) Ban Crt Busing Order	FOR
3) Bal Budget Amend	FOR	7) $ for MX Missile	AGN	11) Auto Local Content	AGN
4) Gas & Road Tax	AGN	8) Nerve Gas Prod	AGN	12) Nuclear Arms Freeze	AGN

Election Results

1982 general	Robert (Bob) Whittaker (R)	102,910	(67%)	($144,988)
	Lee Rowe (D)	48,371	(32%)	($18,472)
1982 primary	Robert (Bob) Whittaker (R)	43,593	(89%)	
	Terry R. Miller (R)	5,551	(11%)	
1980 general	Robert (Bob) Whittaker (R)	141,029	(74%)	($113,716)
	David L. Miller (D)	45,676	(24%)	($1,204)

Campaign Contributions and Expenditures

1981-82		*Direct Cont. 81-82*				*PACS brkdwn*		
Receipts	$181,848	Indiv	$69,721	Agr	$4,150	Ideo	$2,100
Expend.	$144,988	Party	$8,960	Bus	$58,750	Lbr	$1,500
Unspent	$103,354	PACS	$87,221	Hlth	$19,850	Prof	$1,250

KENTUCKY

In 1775 Daniel Boone made his way through the Cumberland Gap in the Appalachian Mountains and came upon what we now know as Kentucky—a fertile, virgin land of gently rolling hills. After the Revolutionary War, streams of people from Virginia traveled Boone's Wilderness Road and settled in the hills and countryside around Lexington. The exodus was the new nation's first frontier boom and, up to that time, one of the most extensive mass migrations in western history. No more than a few dozen whites lived in Kentucky before the war; the 1790 Census counted 73,000; by 1820 there were 564,000 Kentuckians, and the state was the sixth largest in the nation. In those days Kentucky was the frontier, its communities full of opportunity and unburdened by the hierarchies that structured the societies of coastal America. Henry Clay, to take the most famous example, came to Kentucky from Virginia as a penniless youth. By the time he was 30 he had done well enough in law and land speculation to build a mansion with silver doorknobs and well enough in politics to become a United States senator.

In some respects Kentucky has not changed much since Clay's time. The state is still largely nonurban: only 21% of its residents live in metropolitan Louisville and only 7% in the Kentucky suburbs of Cincinnati, the state's only major metropolitan areas. During the 1950s and 1960s thousands of young people left the state; Kentuckians looking for jobs left the hills for the industrial cities of the Midwest, California, and Texas. In the 1970s the trend was reversed, and most young Kentuckians now remain in the state and find jobs here. Kentuckians remain very family-oriented: the percentage of households occupied by families and married couples are among the highest in the nation. But the percentage of households with children, while above the national average, is not so high relatively, because the population tends to be older than average—the product of decades of migration.

Recent prosperity has not changed the local landscape—or local attitudes—very much. The tobacco fields, the thoroughbred horse country of the Blue Grass region, and the flat fields of western Kentucky look the same as they have for years, though they are more likely to be planted in soybeans than cotton now. The coal industry, important 50 years ago, is important again, after tough times in the 1960s. Underground mining is, however, less common, and there is more strip mining than before. Coal towns are still isolated amid the mountains and the hills, but they are less grimy than they used to be and the work is less hazardous; more work is done by machines and less by union miners. Small companies find it easier to enter the business, and by the late 1970s the coal counties of Kentucky were filled with new millionaires and fleets of Rolls-Royces, plentiful jobs at good wages, and, since the state does not regulate strip mining strictly, ugly scars across the hills and valleys.

Politics in Kentucky also seems, with some few exceptions, stuck in a kind of time warp. As in other border states, in Kentucky political divisions are still based on the splits caused by the Civil War. Kentucky was a slave state, but it voted to stay with the Union, and there were strong feelings on both sides. Most of the hill country was pro-Union and remains Republican today; the major exceptions are counties where coal miners joined the United Mine Workers in the 1930s and became Democrats. The Blue Grass region and the western part of the state, areas called the Jackson Purchase and the Pennyrile, were more likely to be slaveholding territory, and today remain mostly Democratic, except for the rapidly growing city of Lexington. Louisville, influenced from its early days by German immigrants, was an antislavery river town, and for years supported a strong Republican organization. These patterns, which have prevailed now for more than 100 years, were as apparent as ever in the last two presidential elections. Both times Jimmy Carter lost by a narrow margin the county that contains Louisville, lost the Cincinnati suburbs and the mountain counties in the southeast, and carried the mining counties in the east, the Blue Grass country around Lexington, and Jackson Purchase and the Pennyrile. Slightly smaller margins in the rural areas in 1980 transformed Carter's fairly comfortable 1976 victory in Kentucky to a razor's edge defeat four years later, but the basic patterns of support were the same—and not all that much different from the patterns in the elections of 1960, 1940, or 1920.

In most Kentucky elections over the years, Democrats have outvoted Republicans, although not by the overwhelming margins found for years farther south. Still, in most elections the basic decision was produced in the Democratic primary. The most famous figure to come out of this era was Alben Barkley, who was congressman from Paducah (1913–27), U.S. senator (1927–49) and Senate majority leader, vice president under Harry Truman, and senator again until his death in 1956. In the 1950s and 1960s, Kentucky slowly became more Republican, until during one four-year period (1967–71) Republicans held the governorship and both Senate seats.

The first Republican victories were won by moderates from the Louisville area and the Cumberland Plateau, men like John Sherman Cooper and Thruston Morton whose politics came out of the Civil War tradition (and included support of civil rights). The Democrats they beat were southern in style and, in contrast to Barkley, well to the right of the party on national issues. Then, in the 1960s, Kentucky began to fit more into the national pattern. The Republicans, under Governor Louie Nunn, were conservative on economics and civil rights (a symbolic issue in Kentucky: only 7% of Kentuckians are black and most areas of the state are all white). The Democrats, under Governor (1959–63) Bert Combs and his successors, put in programs to help the poor.

Now the same contrasts in issue positions remain, but the old patterns of support—and the old Democratic majorities—have reasserted themselves. The key election was in 1971, when Wendell Ford beat Louie Nunn's choice in the election for governor. Ford's opposition to the sales tax on food and support of aid to education gave him the support of organized labor and teachers' groups; his Owensboro accent and conservative attitude on cultural issues made him acceptable to the rural voters who were deserting the party's national candidates. Ford's victory was followed by other Democratic victories: Dee Huddleston's election to the Senate in 1972, Ford's own election to the Senate in 1974, Julian Carroll's elevation to the governorship and election to the office in his own right in 1975. In none of these major races, nor in any contest up through the 1983 gubernatorial race, were the Republicans serious competitors: winning the Democratic primary once again became tantamount to election.

Governor. There is no question who stands at the apex of Kentucky politics: the governor. The governor's appointment powers are wide; this is not a state with a vibrant civil service tradition. The legislature is allowed to meet only 60 days every two years; after that, the governor can shift around line items in the budget as he likes. The governor is also the undisputed leader of his state party. These are powers rooted in tradition and history, and so are the restrictions on governors: they cannot serve consecutive terms and they must swear that they have never participated in a duel.

So, as this is written, Kentucky's Governor, John Y. Brown, Jr., is preparing to leave office. He came to office famous as the Kentucky Fried Chicken millionaire (he bought out Colonel Sanders and promoted the Colonel and the product brilliantly) and as the husband of sportscaster Phyllis George. But at the end of his term he was tarnished by controversy around his firing of his top state law enforcement officer for taping a conversation between a Brown appointee and a highway contractor at the Governor's own Florida vacation home. Brown has also been frustrated in his national ambitions. He hoped to win approval from voters of a constitutional amendment allowing him to run for a second term, as popular governors have in North Carolina, Georgia, Alabama, West Virginia, Tennessee, and Louisiana. But the amendment was defeated 64%–36%; it carried Louisville and Jefferson County but lost the other 119 counties. Strong governors in the past have tried and sometimes succeeded in installing proteges in the office: Combs succeeded in 1963, and Nunn and Carroll came close in 1971 and 1979. But Brown has no protege; less interested in power in Frankfort than in attention from the national media, he has no place to go, at least for a time. His $2 million, spent in a six-week campaign in 1979, has failed to catapult him quite as high as he apparently wanted.

The competition in the May 1983 primary was between Louisville Mayor Harvey Sloane, Lieutenant Governor Martha Layne Collins, and former secretary of human resources Grady Stumbo. Sloane, who nearly beat Brown in the 1979 primary, now has the support of Julian Carroll, Bert Combs, and many of their allies; Collins has the support of many who were close to Wendell Ford. Collins is not the first woman to run a major race in Kentucky: her predecessor Thelma Stovall ran, unsuccessfully, for governor in 1979, and Katherine Peden was nearly elected to the Senate in 1968. But Collins, if elected, would be the first woman to win—just as Sloane would be the first Louisville governor in living memory. Sloane's home town support in 1979, when he was not in office, was testimony to his deep popularity; his walking campaign made him fairly well known throughout the state.

In the Republican primary the favorite was late entrant Jim Bunning, a legislator from the Cincinnati suburbs and former major league baseball pitcher. But Bunning's experience in Kentucky politics is limited, and to win in November he would need a really acrimonious split among the Democrats and some major breaks.

Senators. One index of the power of the governorship in Kentucky is the fact that Wendell Ford was reluctant to give up the last year of his term in order to take what could turn out to be a lifetime Senate seat. Ford has not been a particularly visible senator, but he has been an important insider. On the Commerce Committee, which handles many issues of federal regulation, Ford is often a swing vote. On economic issues generally he usually votes with most other Democrats. But he is willing to listen to business lobbyists and to support them when persuaded. And, as longtime chairman of the Senate Democratic Campaign Committee, he has specialized in raising money from business as well as labor sources. At the same time this committee, like other national Democratic organizations, neglected for years to build the base of thousands of direct mail contributions—the kind of base which has enabled the Republicans to raise huge amounts of money and to put it so intelligently into crucial races that they won almost every close Senate race in 1980 and 1982.

Ford is ranking minority member on the Senate Rules Committee, a body with only one important subject matter, campaign finance reform. He is likely to approach the issue from a partisan and practical standpoint. Ford does have convictions on issues, and he does seem to identify with the little guy and want to help him; but like most Kentucky politicians he is a practical man whose idealism seldom gets in the way as he goes about his business from day to day.

Ford beat incumbent Republican Marlow Cook in 1974, in a close and bitter race; he was effectively unopposed in 1980 and got the highest percentage ever won by a candidate in a Senate election in Kentucky (65%). Whether he is likely to be in trouble in 1986 may be indicated by the fate in 1984 of his colleague, Dee Huddleston, whose voting record is similar.

Huddleston first won in 1972 as Ford's protege, though he is now the state's senior senator. He is ranking Democrat on the Agriculture Committee and also serves on Appropriations. If anything, he is less obtrusive than Ford. He has taken on some difficult legislative chores, like revising the intelligence laws, and he has gotten involved in issues like immigration (he wants tough restrictions) and bilingual education (he doesn't want programs which keep children speaking a native language). But his chief job is on agricultural issues. If the Democrats take over the Senate and he is reelected, he will chair the Agriculture Committee—an assignment of importance both to his party and the nation. For farm bills are the glue which have kept Democratic coalitions together in Congress, and under Jesse Helms's chairmanship that glue has been diluted. Huddleston, whose instinct is to cooperate with his party's leadership, is likely to try to restore these programs, both for idealistic and political reasons. Appropriations is an assignment usually given in the Senate to cooperative insiders. Huddleston's record on economic and foreign issues is somewhere between liberal and mildly conservative. He is not unwilling to take a chance on occasion: he voted for the Panama Canal Treaties in 1978 when he was up for reelection. On cultural issues he and Ford are both pretty conservative—which makes sense, since Kentucky is a state where new cultural patterns have made little headway.

Huddleston drew a bye in 1978: he easily beat an underfinanced Republican. But in the 1980s few, if any, Republican Senate candidates are underfinanced any more. And Huddleston may face serious competition. One possible candidate is Jefferson County Judge (*i.e.*, county executive) Mitch McConnell, Kentucky's most successful Republican vote-getter in recent years. McConnell was reelected by only a narrow margin last time, but that may make him only more eager to run. With plenty of exposure on Louisville TV, McConnell is already known in much of the state. If he does not run, other possible candidates include 1983 gubernatorial hopeful Jim Bunning or Lexington Congressman Larry Hopkins.

Any Republican candidate will try to put Huddleston on the defensive on foreign and cultural issues, and to tie him to the most unpopular parts of the Democratic platform. It will be an uphill battle unless economic recovery and international circumstances enable President Reagan or another Republican nominee to run as the candidate of peace and prosperity. But all bets will be off if Republicans upset the oddsmakers and capture the governorship in 1983. In that case the new governor will pick the party's nominee and assure him of satisfactory financing. And a Republican victory in 1983 would probably signal a shift away from the Democratic habits which have prevailed now for a dozen years.

Presidential politics. Kentucky, which used to have a presidential primary, abolished it; candidates didn't come to campaign much, and it was not seriously contested in 1980. For 1984 national convention delegates will be chosen by party caucuses. The Democrats will be influenced, though not completely controlled, by the new governor, if he or she is a Democrat; the Republicans are likely to be pretty solidly conservative on all issues.

In the general election, the big question for 1984 is whether Kentucky will be, as it was before the civil rights revolution and the Great Society and as it was again in 1976 and 1980, one of the more Democratic of states. It was one of Jimmy Carter's stronger states in both elections, especially 1980. Was that just a friendly response to a fellow southerner, or was it a reassertion of the historical patterns which have prevailed in state elections since 1971? We will know relatively soon: Kentucky's polls close early and it is one of the first states to report results.

Congressional districting. Kentucky's Democrats redrew its congressional district lines without major change and without much controversy. No incumbent was greatly helped or hurt.

The People Est. Pop. 1982: 3,667,000; Pop. 1980: 3,660,777, up 0.2% 1980–82 and 13.7% 1970–80; 1.6% of U.S. total, 23d largest; voting age pop. 2,578,047; 7% Black, 1% Spanish origin. Single ancestry: 25% English, 7% German, 6% Irish, 1% French. Registered voters (1982): 1,826,590 Total. 1,245,083 D (68%); 521,494 R (29%); 59,203 no party (3%). 11% with 1–3 yrs. col., 11% with 4+ yrs. col. 18.4% below poverty level. 28% housing units rented; median house value: $34,200; median monthly rent: $151. Households: 78% family, 44% with children, 65% married couples.

1982 Share of Federal Tax Burden $7,239,100,000; 1.21% of U.S. total, 27th largest.

1982 Share of Federal Expenditures

	Total		Non-Defense		Defense	
Total Expend	$7,747m	(1.28%)	$6,407m	(1.51%)	$1,340m	(0.75%)
St/Lcl Grants	1,424m	(1.61%)	1,423m	(1.61%)	1m	(2.78%)
Salary/Wages	1,198m	(1.54%)	276m	(1.01%)	922m	(1.82%)
Ind Payments	4,423m	(1.55%)	4,006m	(1.56%)	417m	(1.46%)
Procurement	679m	(0.47%)	411m	(1.30%)	268m	(0.23%)
Other Programs	23m	(0.42%)	23m	(0.43%)	0m	(0%)
Loan/Insurance	1,106m	(1.73%)	1,091m	(1.77%)	15m	(0.68%)

Political Lineup Governor, John Y. Brown, Jr. (D). Senators, Walter D. (Dee) Huddleston (D) and Wendell H. Ford (D). Representatives, 7 (4 D and 3 R). State Senate, 38 (29 D and 9 R); State House of Representatives, 100 (76 D and 24 R).

Presidential Vote

1980	Reagan (R)	635,274	(49%)
	Carter (D)	617,417	(48%)
	Anderson (I)	31,127	(2%)
1976	Ford (R)	531,852	(46%)
	Carter (D)	615,717	(53%)

1980 Democratic Presidential Primary			*1980 Republican Presidential Primary*		
Carter	106,819	(67%)	Reagan	78,072	(82%)
Kennedy	55,167	(23%)	Bush	6,861	(7%)
Uncommitted	19,219	(8%)	Anderson	4,791	(5%)
Two others..........	5,126	(2%)	Uncommitted	3,084	(3%)
			Two others..........	1,987	(2%)

SENATORS

Sen. Walter D. (Dee) Huddleston (D) Elected 1972, seat up 1984; b. Apr. 15, 1926, Cumberland Cnty.; home, Elizabethtown; U. of KY, B.A. 1949; United Methodist.

Career Army, WWII; Sports and Program Dir., WKCT Radio, Bowling Green, 1949–52; Gen. Mgr., WIEL Radio, Elizabethtown, 1952–72; Partner and Dir., WLBN Radio, Lebanon, 1957–72; KY Senate, 1965–72, Major. Flr. Ldr., 1970, 1972.

Offices 2121 DSOB, 202-224-2451. Also 600 Federal Pl., 13-C New Fed. Bldg., Louisville 40202, 502-582-6304; and 220 W. Dixie Ave., Elizabethtown 42701, 502-769-6316.

Committees *Agriculture, Nutrition, and Forestry* (Ranking Member). Subcommittees: Foreign Agricultural Production; Agricultural Production, Marketing, and Stabilization of Prices; Agricultural Research and General Legislation. *Appropriations* (9th). Subcommittees: Defense; Energy and Water Development; HUD-Independent Agencies; Interior. *Small Business* (2d). Subcommittees: Government Regulation and Paperwork; Export Promotion and Market Development. *Select Committee on Intelligence* (2d). Subcommittees: Legislation and the Rights of Americans; Collection and Foreign Operations (Vice-Chairman).

Group Ratings

	ADA	ACLU	COPE	CFA	LCV	LWV	NTU	NSI	COC	ACA	CSFC
1982	50	43	71	80	32	64	18	56	67	47	46
1981	65	—	71	57	46	—	27	—	61	33	45
1980	44	30	61	13	19	29	29	44	46	26	32

National Journal Ratings

	Economic		Foreign		Cultural	
1982	71%	(LIB)	68%	(LIB)	39%	(LIB)
	27%	(CONS)	31%	(CONS)	60%	(CONS)
1981	68%	(LIB)	70%	(LIB)	57%	(LIB)
	31%	(CONS)	29%	(CONS)	42%	(CONS)

Key Votes

1) Reagan 81 Budget	FOR	5) $ to El Salvador	AGN	9) Poor Pay Food Stamps	AGN
2) Reagan 81 Tax Cut	FOR	6) Saudi AWACS Sale	FOR	10) Ban Crt Busing Order	FOR
3) Bal Budget Amend	FOR	7) Ban Abortion	FOR	11) Clinch Riv Brdr Rctr	FOR
4) Gas & Road Tax	FOR	8) Nerve Gas Prod	AGN	12) Legal Services Corp	FOR

Election Results

1978 general	Walter D. (Dee) Huddleston (D) ..	290,730	(61%)	($461,808)
	Louie Guenthner, Jr. (R)	175,766	(37%)	($76,445)
1978 primary	Walter D. (Dee) Huddleston (D) ..	89,333	(76%)	
	Three others (D)	28,808	(24%)	
1972 general	Walter D. (Dee) Huddleston (D) ..	528,550	(51%)	($658,590)
	Louis B. Nunn (R)	494,337	(48%)	($603,649)

Campaign Contributions and Expenditures

1977-78			PACS brkdwn		
Receipts	$400,933	Agr	$21,900	Ideo	$250
Expend.	$461,808	Bus	$71,364	Lbr	$31,150
Unspent	$26,460	Hlth	$21,100	Prof	$5,450

Sen. Wendell H. Ford (D) Elected 1974, seat up 1986; b. Sept. 8, 1924, Davies Cnty.; home, Owensboro; U. of KY, MD School of Insurance; Baptist.

Career Army, WWII; Family insurance business; Chf. A. A. to Gov. Bert Combs; KY Senate, 1965-67; Lt. Gov. of KY, 1967–71; Gov. of KY, 1971–74.

Offices 363 RSOB, 202-224-4343. Also 600 Federal Pl., 172-C New Fed Bldg., Louisville 40202, 502-528-6251.

Committees *Commerce, Science and Transportation* (4th). Subcommittees: Aviation; Communications; Consumer. *Energy and Natural Resources* (4th). Subcommittees: Energy Regulation; Energy Research and Development; Water and Power. *Rules and Administration* (Ranking Member). *Joint Committee on Printing* (Ranking Member).

Group Ratings

	ADA	ACLU	COPE	CFA	LCV	LWV	NTU	NSI	COC	ACA	CSFC
1982	70	39	71	90	54	58	16	30	55	29	43
1981	70	—	70	50	50	—	17	—	50	40	42
1980	78	30	73	40	33	67	29	70	44	27	37

National Journal Ratings

	Economic		Foreign		Cultural	
1982	84%	(LIB)	78%	(LIB)	41%	(LIB)
	15%	(CONS)	21%	(CONS)	58%	(CONS)
1981	66%	(LIB)	80%	(LIB)	53%	(LIB)
	33%	(CONS)	19%	(CONS)	44%	(CONS)

Key Votes

1) Reagan 81 Budget	FOR	5) $ to El Salvador	AGN	9) Poor Pay Food Stamps	AGN
2) Reagan 81 Tax Cut	FOR	6) Saudi AWACS Sale	AGN	10) Ban Crt Busing Order	FOR
3) Bal Budget Amend	AGN	7) Ban Abortion	FOR	11) Clinch Riv Brdr Rctr	AGN
4) Gas & Road Tax	AGN	8) Nerve Gas Prod	AGN	12) Legal Services Corp	FOR

Election Results

1980 general	Wendell H. Ford (D)	720,891	(65%)	($491,522)
	Mary Louise Foust (R)	386,029	(35%)	($7,406)
1980 primary	Wendell H. Ford (D)	188,047	(87%)	
	Flora T. Stuart (D)	28,202	(13%)	
1974 primary	Wendell H. Ford (D)	399,406	(54%)	($1,006,670)
	Marlow W. Cook (R)	328,982	(44%)	(524,569)

Campaign Contributions and Expenditures

1979-80			PACS brkdwn		
Receipts	$596,866	Agr	$8,100	Ideo	$1,850
Expend.	$491,522	Bus	$152,025	Lbr	$44,250
Unspent	$112,861	Hlth	$17,550	Prof	$6,400

GOVERNOR

Gov. John Young Brown, Jr. (D) Elected 1979, term expires Dec. 1983; b. Dec. 28, 1933, Lexington; home, Lexington; U. of KY, B.A. 1957, J.D. 1960; Baptist.

Career Businessman; Practicing atty.; Hon. Treas., Dem. Party, 1972; Chmn., Dem Natl. Comm. Young Ldrshp. Cncl.; Chmn., Natl. Gov. Assn. Task Force on Small Business, 1980.

Offices Office of the Governor, State Capitol, Frankfort 40601, 502-564-2611.

Election Results

1979 gen.	John Young Brown, Jr. (D) ...	588,088	(59%)
	Louie B. Nunn (R)	381,278	(41%)
1979 prim.	John Young Brown, Jr. (D) ...	165,158	(29%)
	Harvey Sloane (D)	139,713	(25%)
	Terry McBrayer (D)	131,530	(23%)
	Carroll Hubbard, Jr. (D)	68,577	(12%)
	Thelma L. Stovall (D)	47,633	(8%)
	Four others (D)	14,175	(3%)
1975 gen.	Julian M. Carroll (D)	470,159	(63%)
	Robert E. Gable (R)	277,998	(37%)

FIRST DISTRICT

The western end of Kentucky, known historically as the Jackson Purchase, almost seems to be part of another state—of west Tennessee or the lowlands of the Bootheel of Missouri or even the Mississippi Delta. This is low-lying land, protected from the great muddy river by levees and cut off from the rest of Kentucky by the dammed-up Tennessee and Cumberland Rivers. Economically and politically, the area resembles the Deep South. It was the northernmost point of extensive cotton cultivation, although tobacco and soybeans are more important crops now. There are a considerable number of blacks here, in contrast to the rest of Kentucky, where there are few outside Louisville. And the political patterns are traditional southern: for Jimmy Carter in 1976 and 1980 as well, for George Wallace in 1968.

Just to the east of the Tennessee and the Cumberland Rivers is a region called the Pennyrile (after pennyroyal, a prevalent variety of wild mint). Here you find a land of low hills and small farms. It is also where you find the west Kentucky coal fields, the site of much

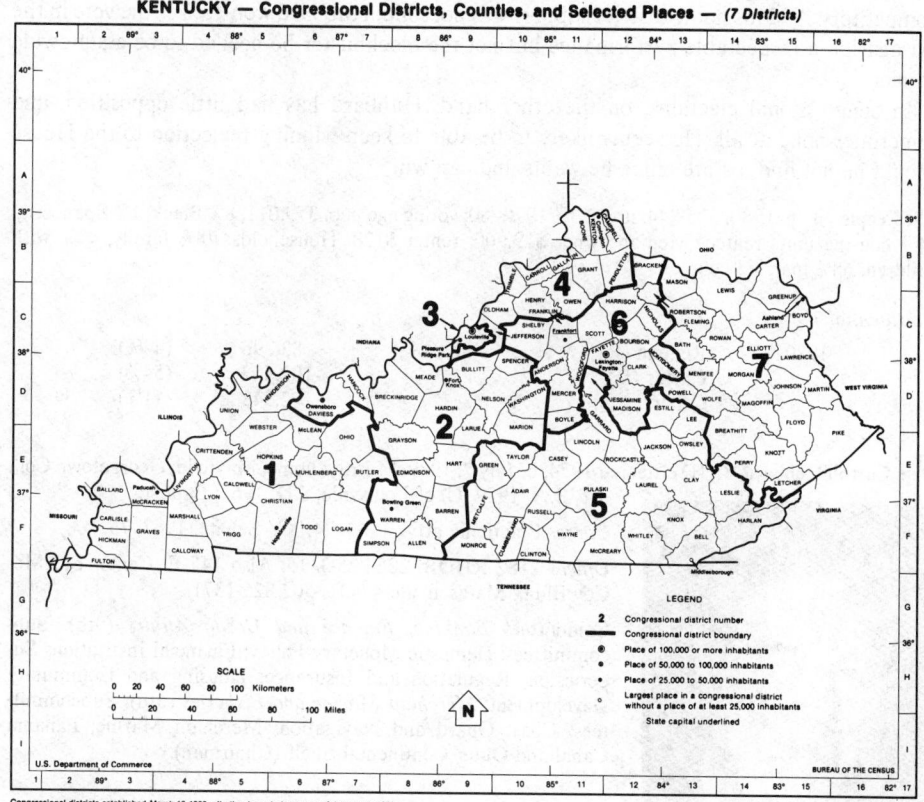

KENTUCKY — Congressional Districts, Counties, and Selected Places — (7 Districts)

strip mining in recent years. Like the Jackson Purchase, the Pennyrile is ancestrally Democratic, but not as much so; most counties vote Democratic, but with lower percentages.

These two parts of Kentucky form the state's 1st congressional district, the area that first elected Alben Barkley to Congress back in 1912. It has elected Democrats ever since. The current incumbent, Carroll Hubbard, was first elected in 1974 after he had the foresight to challenge a weak incumbent in the primary. On arrival in Washington, Hubbard was chosen chairman of the Freshman Caucus, the very existence of which was something of an innovation. Actually Hubbard turned out to be very far from typical of the Democrats first elected that year. His record on noneconomic issues is almost entirely conservative; on economic issues he calls for a balanced budget and for lower interest rates. He lacks the fluency—some might call it glibness—that characterizes so many of the 1974 freshmen.

And his ambitions do not center on Capitol Hill. He is not considered a particularly active legislator. He ran for governor of Kentucky in 1979 and, in early 1983, seemed interested in a statewide race again. But not necessarily governor. In 1979, after a fast start, he finished with just 12% of the vote—fourth of the five serious candidates. He was—and is—not aligned with any of the state's major political factions, nor was he able to raise money as well as some of his competitors. And his home district support was not solid: Hubbard won 33% of the vote in the 1st district, a respectable performance but not the blockbuster he needed to be a statewide winner.

In congressional elections, on the other hand, Hubbard has had little opposition, and sometimes none at all. He seems likely to be able to keep winning reelection to the House should he not find a state office he wants and can win.

The People Pop. 1980: 525,844, up 12.3% 1970–80; voting age pop. 379,011; 8% Black, 1% Span. orig. 24% housing units rented. Median owner $29,900; renter $128. Households: 78% family, 42% with children, 68% married couples.

Presidential Vote

1980	Reagan (R)	....	83,296	(44%)
	Carter (D)	....	102,503	(54%)
	Other	....	2,543	(1%)

Rep. Carroll Hubbard, Jr. (D) Elected 1974; b. July 7, 1939, Murray; home, Mayfield; Georgetown Col., KY, B.A. 1959, U. of Louisville, J.D. 1962; Baptist.

Career Practicing atty., 1962–74; KY Senate, 1967–75.

Offices 2182 RHOB, 202-225-3115. Also 145 E. Center St., Mc-Coy Bldg., Madisonville 42431, 502-825-1371.

Committees *Banking, Finance and Urban Affairs* (9th). Subcommittees: Domestic Monetary Policy; Financial Institutions Supervision, Regulation and Insurance; Housing and Community Development. *Merchant Marine and Fisheries* (6th). Subcommittees: Coast Guard and Navigation; Merchant Marine; Panama Canal and Outer Continental Shelf (Chairman).

Group Ratings

	ADA	ACLU	COPE	CFA	LCV	LWV	NTU	NSI	COC	ACA	CSFC
1982	25	17	58	50	30	30	60	100	71	65	55
1981	25	—	58	36	36	—	35	—	37	61	60
1980	22	10	58	29	31	40	44	70	82	46	55

National Journal Ratings

	Economic		Foreign		Cultural	
1982	49%	(LIB)	34%	(LIB)	15%	(LIB)
	51%	(CONS)	66%	(CONS)	83%	(CONS)
1981	56%	(LIB)	3%	(LIB)	38%	(LIB)
	44%	(CONS)	87%	(CONS)	61%	(CONS)

Key Votes

1) Reagan 81 Budget	AGN	5) Incr SS Rtmt Age	AGN	9) Poor Pay Food Stamps	AGN
2) Reagan 81 Tax Cut	FOR	6) Saudi AWACS Sale	FOR	10) Ban Crt Busing Order	FOR
3) Bal Budget Amend	FOR	7) $ for MX Missile	AGN	11) Auto Local Content	FOR
4) Gas & Road Tax	AGN	8) Nerve Gas Prod	FOR	12) Nuclear Arms Freeze	AGN

Election Results

1982 general	Carroll Hubbard, Jr. (D)	48,342	(100%)	($94,172)
1982 primary	Carroll Hubbard, Jr. (D) unopposed			
1980 general	Carroll Hubbard, Jr. (D)	118,565	(100%)	($95,581)

Campaign Contributions and Expenditures

1981-82		Direct Cont. 81-82				PACS brkdwn		
Receipts	$144,968	Indiv	$15,880	Agr	$10,400	Ideo		$900
Expend.	$94,172	PACS	$103,386	Bus	$64,086	Lbr		$18,050
Unspent	$129,442			Hlth	$4,700	Prof		$900

SECOND DISTRICT

The 2d congressional district of Kentucky is a sprawling, largely rural area extending from the Blue Grass country to the hilly Pennyrile area around Bowling Green. Its largest city is the factory town of Owensboro on the Ohio River, which has only 54,000 people. The best-known features of the district are Fort Knox, where the nation's gold bullion is kept, and Bardstown, where you can find Stephen Collins Foster's "Old Kentucky Home." Bardstown suffered more from the Vietnam war, proportionately, than almost any other place in America: 16 of its sons died there, five within one week of each other. It is from towns like these, where incomes are relatively low, respect for the flag and the family remain high, and few young people go on to college, that the armed forces of the Vietnam era—and today's volunteer army—are disproportionately drawn. Also in the district is the birthplace and boyhood home of Abraham Lincoln.

Kentucky was a slave state that was sharply divided when the South seceded; for a while it said that it was remaining neutral, but finally sided with the Union. But not much of Kentucky was enthusiastic for Mr. Lincoln's cause; Lincoln himself had negligible support in his native state in the 1860 election. The current 2d district was divided: the map shows splotches of counties pro-South and splotches pro-Union. On balance, it was sympathetic to the South, and since then it has voted Democratic in most elections.

William Natcher, one of the House's most hard-working and conscientious members, has represented this district since he won a special election in 1953. He is now the third ranking Democrat on the House Appropriations Committee. In Washington much of his reputation comes from his years of service as chairman of the District of Columbia Appropriations Subcommittee. He was attacked bitterly for being tightfisted and for imposing his own will on the city; some called him a racist. The progress of the D.C. government since it gained home rule in 1972 suggests that Natcher was acting responsibly, at least according to his own lights. He is above all meticulous and attentive to detail; he abhors waste and disorder; he is appalled by anything that smacks of corruption. And he insists on doing what he regards as his duty. If he sometimes seemed autocratic and ready to substitute his own judgment for that of Washington's residents (as when he insisted, unsuccessfully, on the building of an unwanted freeway), he also imposed some discipline on the city budget in the process.

Now Natcher is chairman of the Labor-HHS-Education Appropriations Subcommittee, a position of great influence and potential power. Potential because, despite Natcher's attention to duty, the subcommittee's appropriation has not passed the Senate since 1979. The bill is the target for a wide variety of amendments, particularly those to limit abortion; it takes a long time to consider, and instead of passing it the Senate has been content to let these appropriations be taken care of by the continuing resolution, which essentially continues previous funding. That doesn't mean that Natcher cannot wield influence; a telephone call from him to the secretary of any of these departments will be returned speedily. And if he hints that a particular program should be conducted in a different way, his suggestion may very well be followed, regardless of administration or party. But Natcher, as a stickler for propriety, is not going to exert any influence he thinks might in any way be improper. It is not that he is tightfisted. Actually, on economic issues he often takes the national Democratic position, and he is not a complete conservative on cultural issues either.

Natcher's influence may also be limited, ironically, by his attention to duty. He prides himself on never having missed a roll call vote or quorum call since he was elected in 1953— the all-time attendance record. Natcher also, in the old-fashioned manner, resists relying on staff; he does his own reading and research and prides himself on being well prepared. But a lot of the roll call votes on the House floor are on trivial matters or are delaying tactics. Natcher's presence on the floor cuts into his study time; and he has a jurisdiction which cannot be mastered by any single person anyway. Still, there is something awesome about his stubborn devotion to duty.

Natcher brings the same old-fashioned attitudes to elections in the 2d district. He refuses to spend any money but his own on campaigns and, in an age when voters will not pay attention to politicians unless they slip their messages into the middle of television shows, he ends up not communicating very effectively with his constituents. His attitude is like that of John Quincy Adams when he served in the House: he will do his duty, and his constituents can vote for him if they want to. So far this has been a winning formula. Four primary opponents in 1982 held him to 60% of the vote, but Kentucky does not have runoffs and so this seems like a comfortable showing. He turns 75 in 1984, but in 1983 showed no sign of abandoning his single-minded devotion to what he considers his duty.

The People   Pop. 1980: 520,634, up 17.5% 1970–80; voting age pop. 361,229; 6% Black, 1% Span. orig. 25% housing units rented. Median owner $34,500; renter $150. Households: 80% family, 47% with children, 69% married couples.

Presidential Vote

1980	Reagan (R)	83,861	(51%)
	Carter (D)	78,356	(47%)
	Other	3,009	(2%)

Rep. William H. Natcher (D) Elected Aug. 1, 1953; b. Sept. 11, 1909, Bowling Green; home, Bowling Green; W. KY St. Col., B.A. 1930, OH St. U., LL.B. 1933; Baptist.

Career Fed. Conciliation Commissioner, W. Dist. of KY, 1936–37; Warren Cnty. Atty., 1937–49; Navy, WWII; Commonwealth Atty., 8th Judicial Dist. of KY, 1951–53.

Offices 2333 RHOB, 202-225-3501. Also 414 E. 10th St., Bowling Green 42101, 502-842-7376.

Committee *Appropriations* (3d). Subcommittees: Agriculture, Rural Development; District of Columbia; Labor-Health and Human Services-Education (Chairman).

Group Ratings

	ADA	ACLU	COPE	CFA	LCV	LWV	NTU	NSI	COC	ACA	CSFC
1982	55	42	71	60	58	50	18	80	55	26	39
1981	35	—	70	64	36	—	5	—	26	33	48
1980	50	33	47	50	30	40	31	60	74	29	45

National Journal Ratings

	Economic		Foreign		Cultural	
1982	60%	(LIB)	54%	(LIB)	39%	(LIB)
	40%	(CONS)	46%	(CONS)	60%	(CONS)
1981	64%	(LIB)	18%	(LIB)	46%	(LIB)
	35%	(CONS)	73%	(CONS)	53%	(CONS)

Key Votes

1) Reagan 81 Budget	AGN	5) Incr SS Rtmt Age	AGN	9) Poor Pay Food Stamps	AGN
2) Reagan 81 Tax Cut	AGN	6) Saudi AWACS Sale	AGN	10) Ban Crt Busing Order	FOR
3) Bal Budget Amend	FOR	7) $ for MX Missile	AGN	11) Auto Local Content	FOR
4) Gas & Road Tax	FOR	8) Nerve Gas Prod	AGN	12) Nuclear Arms Freeze	FOR

Election Results

1982 general	William H. Natcher (D)	49,571	(74%)	($13,768)
	Mark T. Watson (R)	17,561	(26%)	($30,193)
1982 primary	William H. Natcher (D)	19,994	(60%)	
	H.S. (Harry) Spalding (D)	6,838	(21%)	($239,362)
	Three others (D)	6,239	(19%)	($175,520)
1980 general	William H. Natcher (D)	99,670	(66%)	($3,145)
	Mark T. Watson (R)	52,110	(34%)	($7,425)

Campaign Contributions and Expenditures

1981-82		Direct Cont. 81-82	
Receipts	$13,768	Cand	$13,499
Expend.	$13,768		
Unspent	$0		

Received No PAC Contributions Indep Expend: $11,757 (NCPAC, LIFEPAC)

THIRD DISTRICT

The 3d congressional district of Kentucky is made up of the city of Louisville and a few of its suburbs to the south and west. Despite the local pronunciation (LOOuhv'l) and southern traditions—Alistair Cooke calls Kentucky the most self-consciously southern of states, although it never seceded—Louisville is really less a southern town than it likes to think. It is closer in spirit to other old river ports, like Cincinnati and St. Louis, which though larger sprang up at about the same time in similar locations. All three cities, and particularly their large German communities, were hostile to the southern-leaning politics of their slaveholding rural neighbors at the time of the Civil War, and all three had long-standing Republican traditions, among blacks as well as whites. St. Louis turned Democratic in the 1930s, Cincinnati is still decidedly Republican, and Louisville moves back and forth.

The 1970s was a good decade for Democrats here, as the 1960s was for Republicans; which the 1980s will be good for is not entirely clear. The two major offices here are the mayoralty of Louisville and the Jefferson County judgeship, the administrative position at the head of county government. In the early 1980s the mayor was Harvey Sloane, a doctor elected first in 1973, then forced by the one-term limit to leave office, a nearly successful candidate for governor in 1979, elected mayor again in 1981, and a likely candidate for governor again in 1983. The county judge was Mitch McConnell, a Republican first elected in 1978, reelected by a small margin in 1982, but still expected to be a candidate for U.S. senator against Dee Huddleston in 1984. Local politics—and the ambitions of local politicians—dominate the political news. Relatively little is said about, or heard from, its congressman.

That is ironic, because the 3d district's congressman, Romano Mazzoli, played a pivotal role in the 97th Congress and seems sure to play a similar role in the 98th on an issue that will probably do more to shape the future of the country than any other: immigration. Mazzoli, first elected in 1970, went on the Judiciary Committee too late to be recorded on the impeachment of Richard Nixon; in 1981 he became chairman of the Immigration, Refugees and International Law Subcommittee. Since the last major revision of immigration laws, in 1965, Congress has just been tinkering with them. But the sharp increases in immigration, legal and illegal, in the 1970s, coupled with the influx of Cuban refugees in 1980, led to many demands for action. Unfortunately many of those demands were contradictory.

Working closely with Alan Simpson, the chairman of the corresponding subcommittee in the Senate, Mazzoli came up with a bill which did several things. It provided amnesty for immigrants who arrived before 1977, essentially legalizing all pre-1977 immigration. It attempted to discourage illegal immigration by imposing stiff penalties on employers that hire illegal immigrants. It liberalized refugee laws and increased the number of legal immigrants allowed in each year, but included in those quotas close relatives of U.S. citizens—people now allowed in without limit. A lot can be said for and against this legislation, but everyone must concede it is an impressive legislative achievement. Simpson managed to push his bill through the Senate in 1982. Mazzoli seemed on the verge of getting his bill through the House in the lame duck session, after the election, when Hispanic congressmen announced they would employ delaying tactics against it; they thought it would lead to prejudice against Hispanics. Nevertheless, on the day it was withdrawn, Mazzoli received a round of applause on the floor of the House—an extremely unusual accolade, recognition of his skillful and responsible handling of a difficult issue.

In 1983 Mazzoli starts over again. He hopes to bring forward the same bill and, if he can get it considered when there is more time, he will probably get it through the House. Understandably he spends less time on other issues. His record on economic issues in the late 1970s and in 1981 was moderate; in 1982 he started sounding more like a conventional Democrat. On cultural and foreign issues he is likely to line up with other urban northern Democrats.

In Louisville he has not had difficulty winning reelection. A busing controversy in the middle 1970s caused him some rough going, especially when he refused to support certain anti-busing constitutional amendments. His recent concentration on immigration hasn't hurt him directly, since Louisville is not much affected: it has relatively few new immigrants and few residents from the 1840–1924 wave of immigration who want to bring their relatives over. But his concentration on the issue may have distracted him enough to enable a 1982 primary opponent to get more than one-third of the vote. The addition in redistricting of new suburban territory, most in the moderate income south and west suburbs, did not have any effect on the race in the general election, despite a ballyhooed Republican challenge.

The People   Pop. 1980: 522,252, dn. 9.3% 1970–80; voting age pop. 381,792; 18% Black, 1% Span. orig. 36% housing units rented. Median owner $33,100; renter $162. Households: 70% family, 37% with children, 53% married couples.

Presidential Vote

1980	Reagan (R)	87,243	(46%)
	Carter (D)	103,315	(54%)
	Other	NA	

Rep. Romano L. Mazzoli (D) Elected 1970; b. Nov. 2, 1932, Louisville; home, Louisville; Notre Dame U., B.S. 1954, U. of Louisville, J.D. 1960; Roman Catholic.

Career Army, 1954–56; Law Dept., L & N Railroad Co., 1960–62; Practicing atty., 1962–70; KY Senate, 1967–71.

Offices 2246 RHOB, 202-225-5401. Also 600 Federal Pl., 551 New Fed. Bldg., Louisville 40202, 502-582-5129.

Committees *District of Columbia* (3d). Subcommittee: Judiciary and Education. *Judiciary* (7th). Subcommittees: Administrative Law and Governmental Relations; Courts, Civil Liberties, and the Administration of Justice; Immigration, Refugees and International Law (Chairman). *Small Business* (12th). Subcommittee: Antitrust and Restraint of Trade Activities Affecting Small Business. *Permanent Select Committee on Intelligence* (3d). Subcommittee: Legislation (Chairman).

Group Ratings

	ADA	ACLU	COPE	CFA	LCV	LWV	NTU	NSI	COC	ACA	CSFC
1982	70	62	70	70	69	83	24	30	41	22	35
1981	60	—	68	64	56	—	49	—	44	29	48
1980	33	57	46	43	54	40	31	33	62	33	41

National Journal Ratings

	Economic		Foreign		Cultural	
1982	69%	(LIB)	62%	(LIB)	75%	(LIB)
	31%	(CONS)	37%	(CONS)	25%	(CONS)
1981	55%	(LIB)	80%	(LIB)	66%	(LIB)
	44%	(CONS)	20%	(CONS)	34%	(CONS)

Key Votes

1) Reagan 81 Budget	AGN	5) Incr SS Rtmt Age	FOR	9) Poor Pay Food Stamps	AGN
2) Reagan 81 Tax Cut	FOR	6) Saudi AWACS Sale	AGN	10) Ban Crt Busing Order	AGN
3) Bal Budget Amend	AGN	7) $ for MX Missile	AGN	11) Auto Local Content	FOR
4) Gas & Road Tax	AGN	8) Nerve Gas Prod	AGN	12) Nuclear Arms Freeze	FOR

Election Results

1982 general	Romano L. Mazzoli (D)	92,849	(65%)	($192,344)
	Carl Brown (R)	45,900	(32%)	($121,917)
1982 primary	Romano L. Mazzoli (D)	43,951	(64%)	
	Mark D. O'Brien (D)	25,037	(36%)	($18,183)
1980 general	Romano L. Mazzoli (D)	85,873	(64%)	($94,674)
	Richard Cesler (R)	46,681	(35%)	($18,449)

Campaign Contributions and Expenditures

1981-82		Direct Cont. 81-82		PACS brkdwn			
Receipts	$185,491	Indiv	$67,250	Agr	$1,250	Ideo	$9,872
Expend.	$192,344	Party	$10,750	Bus	$38,650	Lbr	$27,690
Unspent	$3,202	PACS	$92,066	Hlth	$8,650	Prof	$250
		Cand	$5,000				

FOURTH DISTRICT

The 4th congressional district of Kentucky is the state's only suburban district. It consists of two separate suburban areas, connected by a strip of rural Kentucky extending 120 miles along the Ohio River. In effect, the district combines some of the newest with some of the oldest parts of the state. Redistricting changed the balance of the district: it lost many middle income precincts in Louisville's Jefferson County. Now about half its residents live in the suburban counties directly across the river from Cincinnati, Ohio. These are not necessarily bucolic: they include the gritty towns of Covington and Newport (once a noted sin city) on the lowlands by the river, as well as old affluent suburbs like Fort Thomas and new middle income suburbs like Florence and Erlanger on the heights which overlook Cincinnati. Historically these counties, like Cincinnati, have leaned Republican; and so they go in most Kentucky elections. But, with media oriented more to Ohio than Kentucky, people here seem to have political attitudes less anchored to a traditional party preference, and so they are often swing areas.

The Louisville suburbs, on the other hand, which include 36% of the 4th district's population and more of its voters, are Republican both by heritage and current inclination. The 4th goes right up to the city limits on Louisville's more affluent east side; it includes the farther out, more Republican suburbs on the less affluent south and west sides.

The central, connecting corridor of the district is quite different. Here you find tobacco fields along the Ohio River bottomlands and small farms with wooden fences in the knobby hills a few miles inland. This part of Kentucky was settled more than 150 years ago, and it has been heavily—often almost unanimously—Democratic since the Civil War. It casts only 11% of the 4th district's votes, but those are heavily Democratic.

Redistricting and economic conditions put veteran 4th district Congressman Gene Snyder on the defensive. Snyder's base is in the Louisville suburbs, and some of his best precincts were transferred by the Democratic legislature to Romano Mazzoli's 3d district. The Cincinnati suburbs, a more important part of the district, are the base of his opponent, Democratic state legislator Terry Mann. First elected in 1962, when he represented all of Louisville, defeated in 1964 and then returned to office in 1966 and ever since, Snyder was not used to tough competition. He and Mann denounced each other in violent terms. Mann carried the Cincinnati suburbs and the connecting counties. But Snyder won by nearly 2–1 in the Louisville suburbs and prevailed. Having survived a tough challenge in a Democratic year, he is not likely to have such a tough race again.

Snyder has the reputation of being an ultraconservative, but in fact his record is rather different. He used to be ranking Republican on the Merchant Marine Committee and now is ranking Republican on Public Works, and on neither of these bodies is he a dissenter from the consensus that government should spend generously to develop waterways, build various construction projects, and subsidize the American merchant fleet. On such issues he is a spender; and even on economic issues generally he is far less parsimonious than most Republicans you would call conservatives. He has been hailed, notably by Jack Anderson, as one of the most effective congressmen; and effective in his case means effective in old-fashioned pork barrel terms. On cultural and foreign issues he votes with the right. Tying his record together is a contentious and aggressive personality, which served him well in the 1982 campaign as it has in Congress.

The People Pop. 1980: 523,090, up 18.6% 1970–80; voting age pop. 363,792; 2% Black. 25% housing units rented. Median owner $43,400; renter $175. Households: 79% family, 46% with children, 68% married couples.

Presidential Vote

1980	Reagan (R)	105,355	(59%)
	Carter (D)	74,535	(41%)
	Other	NA	

Rep. Gene Snyder (R) Elected 1966; b. Jan. 26, 1928, Louisville; home, Jefferson Cnty.; Jefferson School of Law, LL.B. 1950; Lutheran.

Career Practicing atty., 1950–67; Realtor and builder; Jeffersontown City Atty., 1954–58; Jefferson Cnty. 1st Dist. Magistrate, 1957–65.

Offices 2188 RHOB, 202-225-3465. Also 125 Chenoweth Ln., St. Matthews 40207, 502-895-6949.

Committees *Merchant Marine and Fisheries* (2d). Subcommittees: Coast Guard and Navigation; Merchant Marine. *Public Works and Transportation* (Ranking Member).

Group Ratings

	ADA	ACLU	COPE	CFA	LCV	LWV	NTU	NSI	COC	ACA	CSFC
1982	10	17	21	20	30	25	85	80	81	74	72
1981	20	—	21	21	29	—	75	—	79	79	68
1980	11	20	21	21	13	20	60	100	70	71	76

National Journal Ratings

	Economic		Foreign		Cultural	
1982	24%	(LIB)	46%	(LIB)	34%	(LIB)
	76%	(CONS)	54%	(CONS)	66%	(CONS)
1981	49%	(LIB)	30%	(LIB)	18%	(LIB)
	51%	(CONS)	68%	(CONS)	82%	(CONS)

Key Votes

1) Reagan 81 Budget	FOR	5) Incr SS Rtmt Age	AGN	9) Poor Pay Food Stamps	FOR
2) Reagan 81 Tax Cut	FOR	6) Saudi AWACS Sale	FOR	10) Ban Crt Busing Order	FOR
3) Bal Budget Amend	FOR	7) $ for MX Missile	AGN	11) Auto Local Content	FOR
4) Gas & Road Tax	FOR	8) Nerve Gas Prod	FOR	12) Nuclear Arms Freeze	AGN

Election Results

1982 general	Gene Snyder (R)	74,109	(54%)	($303,653)
	Terry L. Mann (D)	61,937	(45%)	($201,217)
1982 primary	Gene Snyder (R)	17,583	(90%)	
	Dempsey Merrell (R)	2,030	(10%)	
1980 general	Gene Snyder (R)	126,049	(67%)	($83,015)
	Phil M. McGary (D)	62,138	(33%)	($38,005)

Campaign Contributions and Expenditures

1981-82		Direct Cont. 81-82		PACS brkdwn			
Receipts	$310,438	Indiv	$105,568	Agr	$ 5,737	Ideo	$7,500
Expend.	$303,653	Party	$9,000	Bus	$99,122	Lbr	$22,050
Unspent	$155,845	PACS	$146,825	Hlth	$6,500	Prof	$3,025

FIFTH DISTRICT

If you wanted to find the congressional district most consistently and solidly Republican over the entire course of the 20th century, you would do well to look not in the high income suburbs of Houston or in central Utah (they voted Democratic not too long ago) nor in the high income suburbs of Westchester County, New York, or the North Shore outside Chicago (they have trended Democratic in some recent elections). You would be well advised to avoid the Sun Belt and high income areas all together, and go to the Cumberland Plateau in the south central part of Kentucky. There, in an area with some of the lowest income levels in the United States, is the 5th congressional district of Kentucky, one of the most Republican parts of the nation.

It is Republican because it got that way during the Civil War, and not much has changed there ever since. The small farmers in these hill counties were always hostile to the richer, slaveholding aristocrats of the Blue Grass region; and so the Blue Grass, in northern Kentucky, favored secession, while the Cumberland Plateau, to the south, was faithful to the Union.

Since that time, these hills have seen little immigration; the people living there now are descendants of the people who were there then, living in the same communities, attending the same churches, farming the same land, and voting the same party. In some mountain counties, including a few in the eastern end of the 5th district, the United Mine Workers organized the miners in the 1930s and the vote shifted from Republican to New Deal Democrat. But not in most of these counties, which have little coal and very few union members. The 5th district is actually a little lukewarm about Reagan Republicanism; the Republicans here, with their low incomes, have always been willing to spend a little government money to help people in trouble. But they remain solidly Republican nevertheless.

The congressional election in this district is determined in the Republican primary. When Dr. Tim Lee Carter retired in 1980 after 16 years in the House, there were 11 candidates in the field, and the winner was Harold Rogers. His party's lieutenant governor candidate in 1979 and a supporter of Dr. Carter's, he was associated more with the Ford than the Reagan wing of his party. He dissents occasionally from conservative positions on economic issues. But he is reliable enough to have won in 1983 a seat on the Appropriations Committee. He has no need to worry about reelection—or raising money for future campaigns—and he has a district which will accept a wide variety of views on the regulatory issues which come before the committee.

The People   Pop. 1980: 523,664, up 22.4% 1970–80, voting age pop. 359,513; 2% Black, 1% Span. orig. 24% housing units rented. Median owner $25,000; renter $100. Households: 82% family, 47% with children, 70% married couples.

Presidential Vote

1980	Reagan (R)	115,982	(62%)
	Carter (D)	69,645	(38%)
	Other	NA	

Rep. Harold (Hal) **Rogers** (R) Elected 1980; b. Dec. 31, 1937, Barrier; home, Somerset; U. of KY, B.A. 1962, J.D. 1964; Baptist.

Career Natl. Guard, 1956–64; Newsman, radio announcer, 1955–62; Practicing atty., 1964–69; KY States Atty., Pulaski and Rockdale Cntys., 1969–81; Repub. Nominee for Lt. Gov. of KY, 1979.

Offices 1028 LHOB, 202-225-4601. Also 210 E. Mt. Vernon St., Somerset 42501, 606-679-8346.

Committee *Appropriations* (21st). Subcommittees: Agriculture, Rural Development; District of Columbia; Treasury-Postal Service-General Government.

Group Ratings

	ADA	ACLU	COPE	CFA	LCV	LWV	NTU	NSI	COC	ACA	CSFC
1982	15	0	36	30	25	17	63	100	77	68	59
1981	10	—	40	36	21	—	61	—	84	79	67

National Journal Ratings

	Economic		Foreign		Cultural	
1982	34%	(LIB)	24%	(LIB)	18%	(LIB)
	66%	(CONS)	75%	(CONS)	80%	(CONS)
1981	42%	(LIB)	30%	(LIB)	15%	(LIB)
	58%	(CONS)	68%	(CONS)	84%	(CONS)

Key Votes

1) Reagan 81 Budget	FOR	5) Incr SS Rtmt Age	FOR	9) Poor Pay Food Stamps	AGN
2) Reagan 81 Tax Cut	FOR	6) Saudi AWACS Sale	FOR	10) Ban Crt Busing Order	FOR
3) Bal Budget Amend	FOR	7) $ for MX Missile	FOR	11) Auto Local Content	FOR
4) Gas & Road Tax	—	8) Nerve Gas Prod	FOR	12) Nuclear Arms Freeze	AGN

Election Results

1982 general	Harold (Hal) Rogers (R)	52,928	(65%)	($281,315)
	Doye Davenport (D)	28,285	(35%)	($6,439)
1982 primary	Harold (Hal) Rogers (R)	10,239	(94%)	
	Thurman J. Hamlin (R)	671	(6%)	
1980 general	Harold (Hal) Rogers (R)	112,093	(67%)	($313,974)
	Ted R. Marcum (D)	54,027	(33%)	($4,788)

Campaign Contributions and Expenditures

1981-82		Direct Cont. 81-82		PACS brkdwn			
Receipts	$326,928	Indiv	$188,114	Agr	$7,150	Ideo	$2,750
Expend.	$281,315	Party	$8,782	Bus	$89,350	Lbr	$5,250
Unspent	$45,780	PACS	$116,056	Hlth	$5,750	Prof	$750

SIXTH DISTRICT

The 6th congressional district of Kentucky, though geographically compact, can be divided into two politically distinct parts. The first is the Blue Grass country. This is the traditional picture of Kentucky: the rolling green meadows where, behind the white wooden fences, thoroughbreds graze; the stately white mansion on the hillock overlooking the fields; the colonel sitting on the mansion's front porch, dressed in a white suit and sipping a mint julep. There actually are places like this in the 6th district, for it contains most of the beautiful horse country around Lexington, and it was the residence of the late Colonel Harland Sanders himself.

But few of the residents of the Blue Grass are so rich. More typical are the small towns with houses built as long ago as the 1810s—this part of Kentucky was the first part of America settled by migrants from across the Appalachians—or the small, poorer farms with their frame houses. The spiritual capital of this part of the 6th district is not Lexington, but Frankfort, the small and surprisingly gritty capital city. Frankfort and Franklin County lead the district in Democratic allegiance (it was 63% for Carter in 1980); the town's usual preference is strengthened by the fact that Kentucky is a patronage state and the Democrats have held the governor's office for all but eight of the last 50 years. Overall, the traditional Blue Grass part of the 6th district almost always delivers Democratic majorities—enough to enable Jimmy Carter to carry this district in both 1976 and 1980.

The other part of the 6th district is modern Lexington. This is a far bigger town than the city Henry Clay knew, although it retains a few historic structures. Its downtown is hardly picturesque, but it is a place of real prosperity, largely because of the main IBM typewriter plant located there. IBM's presence has made Lexington a major center for high technology industry and white collar employment. The Lexington area's population grew 18% in the 1970s, and in 1982 its unemployment rate was only 6%—one of the lowest in the nation. The city's new population has been filling up Fayette County (now consolidated with Lexington) with prosperous neighborhoods and spilling over into hitherto rural counties. These affluent, technology-minded voters find rural-oriented Democrats or the patronage politicians of Frankfort entirely uncongenial. While the 6th as a whole went for Carter in 1980, Lexington delivered a nearly 5,000-vote margin for Ronald Reagan.

The fact that the congressman from the 6th is a Republican shows the low priority practical Kentucky politicians place on congressional representation; in fact, one 6th district congressman, William Curlin, left Washington after less than two years to return to a more rewarding career in Frankfort. The current congressman, Larry Hopkins, was not even the Republican nominee in 1978 when the incumbent, a Democrat with the fine old Kentucky name of John C. Breckinridge, was beaten in the primary. The Republicans dumped their nominee, 68-year-old Marie Louise Foust, and named Hopkins instead; gave him a $300,000 campaign budget; helped him campaign against the Democrat as a backer of big government, big labor, and big spending. That was enough to give him a solid victory. He got a 2–1 margin in Lexington and a 51%–46% districtwide victory. In 1980, against the same opponent, Hopkins won Lexington better than 2–1 and got 49% in the Blue Grass counties. In 1982, he beat by a similar margin a Democrat who featured his endorsement by Governor John Y. Brown, Jr., and two predecessors. Hopkins slipped a little in Lexington but carried the Blue Grass counties. The Democrat carried Franklin County by exactly one vote.

Hopkins's major issue in the campaign was tobacco. Kentucky is the second largest tobacco state, and much is produced or processed here. Hopkins is ranking Republican on the Tobacco and Peanuts Subcommittee, and of course he opposes any changes in the small tobacco subsidy or cozy tobacco allotment programs. The 1982 tax bill, which included a doubling of the excise on tobacco, gave him a medium in which to trumpet his devotion to the crop; he was able to back tobacco and oppose a tax rise, all in one convenient vote which had no conceivable effect on the outcome. For 1983 and 1984 it may be more difficult to prevent further erosion of tobacco's position; the House may very well contain 218 anti-tobacco votes, and many senators are eager to hurt tobacco in order to injure North Carolina's Jesse Helms.

Hopkins also sits on the Armed Services Committee. The tax bill was not the only occasion when he parted company with Republican positions on economic issues; like other Kentucky Republicans he is more generous on spending bills than are Republicans from, say, Iowa. On other issues he is a solid conservative vote.

The People Pop. 1980: 519,009, up 18.5% 1970–80; voting age pop. 377,249; 9% Black, 1% Span. orig. 36% housing units rented. Median owner $43,800; renter $174. Households: 74% family, 41% with children, 61% married couples.

Presidential Vote

1980	Reagan (R)	83,127	(46%)
	Carter (D)	90,271	(50%)
	Other	8,031	(4%)

Rep. Larry J. Hopkins (R) Elected 1978; b. Oct. 25, 1933, Winyo; home, Lexington; Murray St. U., S. Meth. U., Purdue U.; Methodist.

Career USMC, Korea; Stockbroker; KY House of Reps., 1972–77; KY Senate, 1978.

Offices 331 CHOB, 202-225-4706. Also 400 E. Main, Lexington 40507, 606-233-2848.

Committees *Agriculture* (5th). Subcommittees: Livestock, Dairy and Poultry; Tobacco and Peanuts. *Armed Services* (9th). Subcommittees: Investigations; Research and Development.

Group Ratings

	ADA	ACLU	COPE	CFA	LCV	LWV	NTU	NSI	COC	ACA	CSFC
1982	20	33	30	40	33	42	77	90	68	70	64
1981	20	—	27	43	37	—	61	—	76	79	68
1980	6	20	22	14	31	50	56	100	73	87	76

National Journal Ratings

	Economic		Foreign		Cultural	
1982	34%	(LIB)	24%	(LIB)	18%	(LIB)
	66%	(CONS)	75%	(CONS)	80%	(CONS)
1981	45%	(LIB)	3%	(LIB)	24%	(LIB)
	54%	(CONS)	87%	(CONS)	76%	(CONS)

Key Votes

1) Reagan 81 Budget	FOR	5) Incr SS Rtmt Age	FOR	9) Poor Pay Food Stamps	AGN
2) Reagan 81 Tax Cut	FOR	6) Saudi AWACS Sale	FOR	10) Ban Crt Busing Order	FOR
3) Bal Budget Amend	FOR	7) $ for MX Missile	AGN	11) Auto Local Content	FOR
4) Gas & Road Tax	—	8) Nerve Gas Prod	AGN	12) Nuclear Arms Freeze	AGN

Election Results

1982 general	Larry J. Hopkins (R)	68,418	(57%)	($453,076)
	Don Mills (D)	49,839	(41%)	($105,000)
1982 primary	Larry J. Hopkins (R) unopposed			
1980 general	Larry J. Hopkins (R)	105,376	(59%)	($300,296)
	Tom Easterly (D)	72,473	(40%)	($79,344)

Campaign Contributions and Expenditures

1981-82		*Direct Cont. 81-82*			*PACS brkdwn*		
Receipts	$489,597	Indiv	$252,135	Agr	$15,875	Ideo	$14,000
Expend.	$453,076	Party	$23,434	Bus	$140,700	Lbr	$500
Unspent	$116,182	PACS	$189,217	Hlth	$13,250	Prof	$2,000

Indep Expend: For: $886

SEVENTH DISTRICT

The 7th congressional district of Kentucky is part—perhaps the heart—of Appalachia. There is hardly a flat acre of land anywhere in this mountainous district, and no city of any size: the largest is Ashland, with 27,000 people. Yet driving on the twisting roads, up and down hills and through hollows, you are never out of sight of a house: this is one of the most densely populated rural areas of the country. Many of the people here are descendants of original settlers, people who came here with or not long after Daniel Boone, in the years after the Revolution. But others came here much later, from other places in the hills or from the flatlands. They were attracted in the early 20th century by coal, the major energy source of its day; and many, though not all, of the counties that now make up the 7th district found that they were sitting on top of beds of coal.

Coal is a difficult mistress. Conditions in underground mines were usually dreadful; the old songs probably understate the miners' misery and dependence and isolation. Then, in the 1930s, the United Mine Workers moved in and organized most of eastern Kentucky's mines, but this was no easy task; there was violence, bloodshed, something approaching civil war. Mostly the union won, and in the short run raised wages and built hospitals for the miners and its families; in the longer run, the UMW planned to and did phase out jobs in the mines, as coal was replaced by oil as our major fuel. There was a steady outflow of people from these hills in the 1940s, 1950s, and 1960s: the counties which made up the 7th district had 579,000 people, and people with large families, in 1940; by 1970 the population was down to 459,000. There was another, political change. Historically, the hills had been solidly Republican, because they supported the Union during the Civil War. But the UMW organizing drives and the New Deal converted many miners and their families to the Democratic Party, raising Democratic percentages as much as 40%—a vast change in Kentucky, where political allegiances otherwise have mostly stayed the same for a century.

The plight of the 7th district and other parts of Appalachia like it inspired in the 1960s many of the nation's antipoverty programs; and one of the architects of those programs was the district's congressman since 1948, Carl Perkins. Perkins is still a believer in an active and compassionate government; he is not much for rethinking the old Democratic agenda. During the days when the Great Society bills were passed, Perkins was the number two Democrat on the House Education and Labor Committee, which reported most of them out; when Adam Clayton Powell was thrown out of the House in 1967, Perkins became chairman. He holds that position today, tenaciously. He guards his programs jealously, fights against cuts proposed by OMB's David Stockman or by the House's own Budget Committee. He is one of the few really strong committee chairmen left. One reason is that he—and organized labor—have made sure that only Democrats sympathetic to the committee's programs get on Education and Labor. Another is Perkins's own strength of character. Far from fashionable, he is one of those old-fashioned liberals—Sam Rayburn was another—who know their legislation cold, negotiate like master poker players, and refuse to compromise their principles.

Perkins believes his programs work, and he can cite the 7th district as evidence for that proposition. For the fact is that the Appalachia program, the various aid to education programs, the more generous welfare programs of the 1960s, have improved life in the 7th district and made it more prosperous and more comfortable. Also playing a role has been the relative prosperity of the coal industry in the 1970s: strip mining activity increased vastly, with many well paying and relatively safe jobs available. As a result, the outflow of people from the 7th district stopped, and the population rose by 1980 almost to the 1940 level. It should be added that most of the new coal jobs are nonunion, and the UMW is no longer the force it was in this area. That mirrors problems labor has encountered elsewhere; the labor law reform bill Perkins's committee reported out in the Carter years would have strengthened the unions, but it never passed. Still, the voters in the 7th district continue to believe in the programs which Carl Perkins pushed to passage and has been protecting in the Reagan years. This part of Kentucky votes solidly for Democrats in national elections, and solidly for Perkins, and there is no sign that he is ready to retire.

The People Pop. 1980: 526,284, up 23.4% 1970–80; voting age pop. 356,178; 1% Black, 1% Span. orig. 23% housing units rented. Median owner $27,900; renter $113. Households: 83% family, 49% with children, 71% married couples.

Presidential Vote

1980	Reagan (R)	....	76,410	(44%)
	Carter (D)	....	97,782	(56%)
	Other	....	NA	

Rep. Carl D. Perkins (D) Elected 1948; b. Oct. 15, 1912, Hindman; home, Hindman; Caney Jr. Col., Lees Jr. Col., U. of Louisville, Jefferson School of Law, LL.B. 1935; Baptist.

Career Practicing atty., 1935–48; KY House of Reps., 1940; Knott Cnty. Atty., 1941–48; Army, WWII.

Offices 2328 RHOB, 202-225-4935. Also P.O. Bldg., Ashland 41101, 606-325-8530.

Committee *Education and Labor* (Chairman). Subcommittee: Elementary, Secondary and Vocational Education (Chairman).

Group Ratings

	ADA	ACLU	COPE	CFA	LCV	LWV	NTU	NSI	COC	ACA	CSFC
1982	70	50	90	70	58	50	15	70	45	22	33
1981	60	—	89	64	36	—	3	—	11	33	42
1980	56	50	83	64	39	50	21	60	63	29	38

National Journal Ratings

	Economic		Foreign		Cultural	
1982	33%	(LIB)	47%	(LIB)	47%	(LIB)
	66%	(CONS)	53%	(CONS)	53%	(CONS)
1981	77%	(LIB)	41%	(LIB)	54%	(LIB)
	21%	(CONS)	58%	(CONS)	46%	(CONS)

Key Votes

1) Reagan 81 Budget	AGN	5) Incr SS Rtmt Age	AGN	9) Poor Pay Food Stamps	AGN
2) Reagan 81 Tax Cut	AGN	6) Saudi AWACS Sale	AGN	10) Ban Crt Busing Order	AGN
3) Bal Budget Amend	AGN	7) $ for MX Missile	AGN	11) Auto Local Content	FOR
4) Gas & Road Tax	—	8) Nerve Gas Prod	AGN	12) Nuclear Arms Freeze	FOR

Election Results

1982 general	Carl D. Perkins (D)	82,463	(79%)	($19,214)
	Tom Hamby (R)	21,436	(21%)	($6,333)
1982 primary	Carl D. Perkins (D) unopposed			
1980 general	Carl D. Perkins (D)	117,665	(100%)	($0)

Campaign Contributions and Expenditures

1981-82		Direct Cont. 81-82		PACS brkdwn			
Receipts	$23,564	Indiv	$2,255	Agr	$0	Ideo	$500
Expend.	$19,214	Party	$230	Bus	$6,150	Lbr	$14,750
Unspent	$4,399	PACS	$21,700	Hlth	$500	Prof	$200

Indirect Party Expend: $1,000

LOUISIANA

No state has seen a more dramatic change in its standard of living over the past generation, and in the single decade of the 1970s, than Louisiana. Forty years ago its income level was about 60% of the national average; as late as 1970 it was about 75%. In the early 1980s it reached 90% and, when you account for differences in local taxes and the cost of living, income levels in Louisiana have essentially risen to the national average, and when that average itself was rising. The reason can be summed up in one word: oil. Louisiana has long been the nation's number two oil producing state, after Texas, and it has also been one of the major refiners; the giant Exxon refinery in Baton Rouge is at the center of the nation's number one company's web of operations and for years has produced Exxon's top executives. The rapid increases in oil prices in the 1970s, which damaged so many states' economies, did wonderful things for Louisiana's. This is one state which does not see itself as a victim of economic trends and in which big economic institutions are regarded with affection rather than mistrust.

But if Louisiana's economic condition has been transformed, the basic quality of life here has not changed; the sudden influx of money has, if anything, helped preserve it. Louisiana remains, as A. J. Liebling described it two decades ago, an outpost of the Levant along the Gulf of Mexico. There is something foreign in the state's culture and physical environment. While most of the United States faces east toward the Atlantic Ocean or west toward the Pacific, Louisiana faces resolutely south, to the Gulf of Mexico and the steamy heat and volatile societies of Latin America beyond. New Orleans is our one major city that preserves the look and feel it had as a Spanish outpost in the New World, and Louisiana is the only state whose legal system comes not from British common law but from the Napoleonic Code of continental Europe.

Louisiana was not easy land to settle. About half of it is delta land, soil deposits brought downstream by the Mississippi River and accumulated at its mouth. Once, the Mississippi emptied into the Gulf in what is now northern Louisiana, and the land below is soggy, swampy delta, laced with tributaries and offshoots of the Mississippi, bayous and major rivers like the Atchafalaya. The Mississippi itself is held between giant levees, high above the surrounding land. It is possible to farm some of this land, but most is nearly under water; from a distance it's hard to tell where the land ends and water begins. At the edge of settlement of New Orleans, the swamp abruptly begins; people in nearby subdivisions sometimes find alligators in their yards. Houses don't have basements, and in New Orleans even the cemeteries, with their ornate 19th century headstones, are above ground.

Louisiana was the site of an advanced civilization when almost all the rest of the South was still Indian territory (although some of the Indians were pretty advanced themselves). At the outbreak of the Civil War New Orleans was one of the nation's five largest cities and the only significant urban center in the Confederacy. Yet in the years after the Civil War Louisiana became one of the poorest of states. There was always a large black population here, because the sugar, rice, and cotton plantations required many slaves. War and emancipation destroyed the wealth of the plantations, and while New Orleans remained a great port—its position at the mouth of the Mississippi and as the terminus of the Illinois Central Railroad guaranteed that—it was also very much a low-wage labor town. In its rickety frame houses, not always strong enough to keep the rain out and never tight enough to keep out the summer humidity or the damp winter chill, lived New Orleans's working class, blacks often living close by whites. New Orleans was one of the most corrupt of American cities in the years of Reconstruction, when its votes were regularly bid for and purchased; and like other southern cities it became rigidly segregated after 1890.

The Louisiana of the 1920s had enough vitality to give jazz to America and the world, but it also remained desperately poor: a kind of underdeveloped nation, with an impoverished rural hinterland and a single metropolis, where a small number of people managed to become (or remain) very rich and the large majority scratched out a living in low wage jobs. As in underdeveloped countries, public spending was negligible and public services very limited. One out of four Louisianans was illiterate, and most were poorly educated; while there were streetcar scandals in New Orleans, most of the parishes (the Louisiana name for counties) of the state had not a single paved road. That was the situation when Huey P. Long became governor in 1928. Probably no other politician has had as great and enduring an effect on the life of the state as the Kingfish: he is still regarded with the kind of awe and affection that underdeveloped countries reserve for their national liberators and caudillos.

Long was governor for only four years and senator for three more. But in that time he ruled

Louisiana with an iron hand. If his political enemies were willing to bribe and cheat, so would he—and he beat them at their own game. Long built Louisiana's skyscraper Capitol and Louisiana State University; he built a network of concrete roads; he passed an old age pension program. He was a serious national figure as well. His nebulous "share the wealth" program generated enough interest to pressure Franklin Roosevelt to support Social Security and the National Labor Relations Act in 1935. Roosevelt believed that Long would have been his most dangerous opponent in 1936, and many Americans believed it was only a matter of time before Long became president. Instead he was assassinated in the halls of the Capitol in Baton Rouge in 1935 at age 42.

Ever since, proteges of Huey and members of the Long family have held high political office in Louisiana; elections for 30 years split on pro- and anti-Long lines. Huey Long built a coalition of the poor, including some blacks, against the rich and better off; he never, however, did well in New Orleans, even in its poor neighborhoods. What is so amazing is that this structure of politics was superimposed on a state already divided in two other ways. First was division by race. Although Louisiana has always had a large black population (in 1980 the third highest black percentage among states), many blacks, especially in New Orleans, were always allowed to vote.

The other division was between Catholic and Protestant, Cajun and Baptist. The Cajun population of Louisiana is descended from the Acadians, French settlers of Nova Scotia driven out when the British took over the territory in 1755. They settled in Louisiana, and, except for some New England textile mill towns, they are the only major settlements of French-speaking people in the United States. About one of every six Louisianans today speaks French as his native tongue, and at least as many more have French names or (as in the case of former Governor Edwin Edwards) French blood. More than one-third of Louisianans are Catholic. Catholicism is the prevalent religion in the New Orleans area, but the real Cajun country is farther west, among the bayous and crawfish-laden swamps of southern Louisiana. There is a different culture here, valued more since the Cajun revival of the 1970s than it was in the past. French is used widely and English is spoken with a peculiar accent; the cuisine, spicy and laden with shellfish, is unique. In short, there are many cultural differences between the teetotaling Baptists of northern Louisiana and the beer-drinking Cajuns of the south, and those differences emerge from time to time in politics, usually in no more threatening form than a preference for a candidate of one religious background or another.

Louisiana's rapid economic growth has smoothed over some of these old divisions: elections are not referenda on the Longs any more (except when Russell Long is running), racial issues are submerged if not gone, and cultural hostilities between Cajuns and Baptists are of little importance. Louisianans are family people, with lots of children; the politics of cultural variety is not yet a major factor here. After a decade of rapid economic growth, Louisianans support and approve of their big institutions, though they do not particularly respect or admire them—the exact opposite of prevailing attitudes in most of the rest of the country. As for politicians, they judge them by results, not the process by which they achieve them: the political ends justify the means. Louisiana politics combines a Levantine tolerance of the means by which the world's business must be done with a Latin American gaudiness and fondness for display.

Governor. Never was this more apparent than in the 1979 race for governor. Louisiana chooses its state officials in an unusual manner at an unusual time. Every candidate, of whatever party, runs in a single primary in October 1983. If someone gets 50%, he is the winner; if not, there is a runoff between the two top vote-getters, regardless of party, in December. (The system was instituted by Edwards, who thought it unfair that he as a Democrat had to run in a primary, a runoff, and a general election, while his 1972 Republican opponent, and ultimate successor, David Treen, ran in just one election. The same method is used for electing congressmen and senators, and in most cases the primary, held in this case in September, has produced a winner.) In 1979 Edwards could probably have been elected, but he was not eligible for a third consecutive term; six serious candidates ran. The top competitors spent something on the order of $4 million, the low finishers over $1 million—a level of spending unmatched in state elections. Louisiana allows both individuals and corporations to make contributions in any amount in state elections; reporting is required for contributions over $1,000. Its campaign finance practices are closer to what you find in Venezuela, that other commonwealth across the Gulf and the Caribbean, whose standard of living has been raised rapidly by oil, and in whose presidential elections more money is spent than in presidential contests in the United States.

The winner of the 1979 election, by only 10,000 votes, was David Treen, a Republican. He has been an active politician for years: he ran for Congress twice unsuccessfully before he was elected in 1972; he ran for governor once before his winning race in 1979. Treen has been more flexible in office than his ultraconservative congressional voting record would suggest; he was proud, for example, of his environmental record and advocated a separate department of environmental quality. Nonetheless, as the 1983 election season approached, he faced a tough reelection challenge from his predecessor, Edwin Edwards—a politician in classic Louisiana style, a swashbuckling leader who gets things done, and who responds to charges of scandal without apology. He was not even embarrassed when it was learned that his wife (briefly, by his appointment, a United States senator) had taken $10,000 in cash from Korean lobbyist Tongsun Park; nor does he mind that people know he likes to buy flashy expensive suits and gamble for big stakes in Las Vegas. During his years out of office Edwards has held court and acted like a governor in exile; his entry was no surprise, and made it a two-man race.

Edwards beat Treen by a 57%–43% margin in 1972. Now both men are far better known and have been tested under fire. Edwards began the race with a big lead, but Treen made some headway with the corruption issue; Edwards's commissioner of administration, Charles Roemer, was convicted of bribery and conspiracy in federal court, along with reputed Mafia boss Carlos Marcello.

Senators. Louisiana's senior senator, and the second most senior member of the Senate, is Russell Long. He was first elected in 1948, at age 30, as Huey's son; but he has made a very strong record in his own right. He was elected Senate majority whip in 1965, by a coalition of outsiders from the left and the South; he lost the post to Edward Kennedy in 1969. He became chairman of the Senate Finance Committee in late 1965, and held that post until the Republicans won control of the Senate in the 1980 elections. Finance has an impressive jurisdiction, including taxes, Social Security and Medicare, and international trade; and it has had a tradition of strong chairmen. Long is very much part of that. He began in the old-fashioned manner by monopolizing staff resources and conducting secret sessions. By the late 1980s, however, he was dominating Finance by his mastery of its subject matter and by strategic scheduling. It was standard practice for Long to convene the committee when a deadline was near and to keep working most of the night. He delighted particularly in doling out tax cuts during those halcyon days of the 1970s, when inflation was thrusting people into higher tax brackets and Congress, in response, was voting tax cuts of various kinds. Russell

Long to a very large extent determined who got how much of a cut—and that was real power.

Long also succeeded in pushing to passage some of his pet ideas, including employee stock option plans (ESOPs) and the $1 tax checkoff for financing presidential campaigns. He also used his power negatively, to kill the Nixon administration's family assistance plan, a form of guaranteed annual income. It is hard to categorize Long as right or left according to conventional criteria; on economic issues he ends up around the middle of everyone's rating. But he does have very definite views; they simply run skew to the issues that receive the most attention. Thus Long is convinced that workers should be able to own stock in the corporations they work for so that they will have a greater stake in profits and productivity; he insisted on tough work requirements in the family assistance plan, so tough that lobbyists for the black and the poor scuttled the program rather than accept them. Through both positions runs the thread of a single idea: that society is best served when people work for their income, and know that there is a connection between effort and reward, between performance and pay. It is a lesson that life in Louisiana has not always taught, but it is one which Long thinks a just society should teach, and will do well by teaching. And he is quite possibly right in thinking that legislation which promotes these goals is much more important, in the long run, than the bits of fiscal and revenue tinkering which get most of the headlines and have absorbed a great deal of his own and his committee's attention.

It is not, of course, his committee, as of early 1983. Finance has a very capable Republican chairman, and a man with very different ideas and approach, Bob Dole. While Long was temperamentally indulgent to lobbyists seeking tax breaks, Dole tends to bristle at their approach; where Long enjoyed handing out goodies, Dole would like to hear an argument for why they *ought* to be given. Long and Dole respect each other and get along amicably, but their relationship can never be entirely easy. Long surely looks forward to becoming chairman again, as he will if, as many expect, Democrats win control of the Senate in 1984.

On other issues, which he doesn't care as much about, Long casts a nervous eye on his constituency. He agonized long and hard, for example, before voting for the Panama Canal Treaties; he takes almost uniformly conservative positions on cultural issues. He was an early and influential co-sponsor of extending the Voting Rights Act in 1981; but by now that is probably a popular position in Louisiana. Though he usually supports free trade, he is careful to tend the interests of Louisiana's rice and sugar producers. As the representative of America's second largest port, he staunchly supports subsidies for the merchant marine. And he is probably right in thinking that his electoral position in Louisiana is not as strong as most people in Washington think. In 1980, against state Senator Woody Jenkins, a Democrat running on a Reaganish platform, Long won by a 58%–39% margin in the first primary. Given that he had the near-unanimous support of the 23% of Louisiana voters who are black, that is not a particularly impressive margin. Louisiana's newly affluent white voters are in fact ready to reject a senator who is demonstrably powerful and whose voting records is one of the more conservative in the Senate. Everyone expects Long to be reelected in 1986, and he probably will be; he certainly will be able to raise the money for a good campaign. But it may not happen automatically.

Louisiana's other senator, Bennett Johnston, is almost unknown nationally, but is potentially a power in the Senate. Actually, Johnston was probably a busier legislator in the late 1970s, when Democratic control of the Senate was taken for granted and assumed to last forever. On the Interior Committee (now called Energy and Natural Resources) Johnston was the leading representative of the oil-producing states, and it was he who hammered out the incredibly complex provisions of the bills partially deregulating oil and natural gas. These were big money decisions, made under great pressure and time constraints; Johnston performed so competently that even adversaries had to ask him to tell them what was going on. Now that deregulation has proceeded apace, all those details are of less (or no) importance; and the current committee chairman, James McClure, seems determined to take on no major legislative tasks. So Johnston is in a waiting position: he will chair the committee if the Democrats win back control of the Senate in 1984. He is also in line to chair either the Interior or the Energy and Water Development Appropriations Subcommittee; he will be the man to see in a Democratic Senate on environmental issues. His voting record on them is what you might expect from a Louisianan: much more sympathetic to the need for economic growth than for environmental protection.

Johnston also has seats on the Appropriations Committee, and for a time he chaired the Senate Democratic Campaign Committee. Although his voting record is well to the right of most Democratic senators, he seems to be trusted by his colleagues. He has the pleasant sense of humor and easy charm that so many southern politicians seem born with; he is trustworthy and sympathetic to his colleagues' situations.

But before Johnston can succeed to these positions, he must win reelection to the Senate. That will not be entirely automatic. In 1978 he won 59% against conservative Democrat Woody Jenkins, the same man who ran against Russell Long, with similar results, two years later. Will Johnston's race draw a larger field this time? Louisiana voters must first get over the 1983 gubernatorial race, on which much more money will be spent than the Senate contest; and typically unsuccessful candidates in the race for governor run for the Senate. That is what Johnston did in 1972, when he barely lost in the Democratic runoff to Edwin Edwards. He was the only major challenger to Senator Allen Ellender, a Huey Long protege who had held the seat since 1936; Ellender died between the filing deadline and the primary, and Johnston won the nomination essentially unopposed and the general election against weakened opposition.

Congressional districting. Louisiana's congressional redistricting occupied quite a bit of the legislators' time but ended up strengthening all eight House incumbents. Lindy Boggs and Gillis Long, who vote with national Democrats on most issues, got new black precincts in New Orleans and Baton Rouge; the Republicans who lost those precincts were helped as well. The entire delegation was reelected in the September 1982 primary.

Presidential politics. Louisiana has been a closely divided state in the last two presidential elections: Jimmy Carter won by a small margin in 1976 and lost by a small margin in 1982. There is a general assumption that a non-southern Democrat cannot do so well here; and the fact that this is an oil state works against most Democrats who in 1983 were seeking their party's nomination. But there is a large black vote here, and the Cajun vote has gone Democratic in national contests; so Louisiana just might be competitive in 1984.

The People Est. Pop. 1982: 4,362,000; Pop. 1980: 4,205,900, up 3.7% 1980–82 and 15.4% 1970–80; 1.9% of U.S. total, 18th largest; voting age pop. 2,875,432; 27% Black, 2% Spanish origin, 1% Asian origin. Single ancestry: 11% French, 10% English, 3% Irish, German, 2% Italian. Registered voters (1982): 1,958,929 Total. 1,676,803 D (86%); 158,872 R (8%); 123,254 other (6%). 13% with 1–3 yrs. col., 13% with 4+ yrs. col. 18.9% below poverty level. 31% housing units rented; median house value: $43,000; median monthly rent: $156. Households: 76% family, 45% with children, 60% married couples.

1982 Share of Federal Tax Burden $10,313,100,700; 1.73% of U.S. total, 21st largest.

1982 Share of Federal Expenditures

	Total		Non-Defense		Defense	
Total Expend	$9,575m	(1.59%)	$6,439m	(1.52%)	$3,135m	(1.75%)
St/Lcl Grants	1,591m	(1.80%)	1,591m	(1.80%)	0m	(0%)
Salary/Wages	917m	(1.17%)	287m	(1.05%)	630m	(1.24%)
Ind Payments	4,274m	(1.49%)	3,771m	(1.46%)	503m	(1.76%)
Procurement	2,731m	(1.87%)	456m	(1.45%)	2,275m	(1.99%)
Other Programs	60m	(1.11%)	59m	(1.10%)	1m	(2.33%)
Loan/Insurance	1,104m	(1.73%)	1,074m	(1.74%)	30m	(1.36%)

Political Lineup   Governor, David C. Treen (R). Senators, Russell B. Long (D) and J. Bennett Johnston, Jr. (D). Representatives, 8 (6 D and 2 R). State Senate, 39 (38 D and 1 R); State House of Representatives, 105 (96 D and 9 R).

Presidential Vote

1980	Reagan (R)	792,853	(51%)
	Carter (D)	708,453	(46%)
	Anderson (I)	26,345	(2%)
1976	Ford (R)	587,446	(46%)
	Carter (D)	661,365	(52%)

1980 Democratic Presidential Primary			*1980 Republican Presidential Primary*		
Carter	199,956	(56%)	Reagan	31,212	(75%)
Kennedy	80,797	(23%)	Bush	7,818	(19%)
Brown	16,774	(5%)	Four others	432	(1%)
Four others	19,600	(5%)	Uncommitted	2,221	(5%)
Uncommitted	41,614	(12%)			

SENATORS

Sen. Russell B. Long (D) Elected 1948, seat up 1986; b. Nov. 3, 1918, Shreveport; home, Baton Rouge; LA St. U., B.A. 1941, LL.B. 1942; United Methodist.

Career Navy, WWII; Practicing atty., 1945–57.

Offices 217 RSOB, 202-224-4623. Also 200 Fed. Bldg., 750 FL Blvd., Baton Rouge 70801, 504-387-0181 ext. 445.

Committees *Commerce, Science and Transportation* (2d). Subcommittees: Merchant Marine; Surface Transportation; National Ocean Policy Study. *Finance* (Ranking Member). Subcommittees: Taxation and Debt Management; Social Security and Income Maintenance Programs; Oversight of the Internal Revenue Service. *Joint Committee on Taxation* (4th).

Group Ratings

	ADA	ACLU	COPE	CFA	LCV	LWV	NTU	NSI	COC	ACA	CSFC
1982	15	11	50	40	43	45	32	90	72	58	56
1981	15	—	49	14	6	—	46	—	78	61	65
1980	28	23	50	27	7	25	35	83	73	29	49

National Journal Ratings

	Economic		Foreign		Cultural	
1982	53%	(LIB)	33%	(LIB)	26%	(LIB)
	46%	(CONS)	64%	(CONS)	73%	(CONS)
1981	46%	(LIB)	16%	(LIB)	31%	(LIB)
	53%	(CONS)	83%	(CONS)	68%	(CONS)

Key Votes

1) Reagan 81 Budget	FOR	5) $ to El Salvador	FOR	9) Poor Pay Food Stamps	FOR
2) Reagan 81 Tax Cut	FOR	6) Saudi AWACS Sale	FOR	10) Ban Crt Busing Order	FOR
3) Bal Budget Amend	FOR	7) Ban Abortion	FOR	11) Clinch Riv Brdr Rctr	FOR
4) Gas & Road Tax	FOR	8) Nerve Gas Prod	FOR	12) Legal Services Corp	—

Election Results

1980 primary	Russell B. Long (D)	484,770	(58%)	($2,166,838)
	Louis (Woody) Jenkins (D)	325,922	(39%)	($237,242)
	Three others (D, R, No party)	30,321	(4%)	
1974 general	Russell B. Long (D)	434,643	(100%)	($498,774)

Campaign Contributions and Expenditures

1979-80			PACS brkdwn		
Receipts	$2,035,347	Agr	$31,100	Ideo	$1,750
Expend.	$2,166,838	Bus	$405,875	Lbr	$28,550
Unspent	$15,932	Hlth	$30,550	Prof	$20,100

Sen. J. Bennett Johnston, Jr. (D) Elected 1972, seat up 1984; b. June 10, 1932, Shreveport; home, Shreveport; Wash. & Lee U., LA St. U., LL.B. 1956; Baptist.

Career Army, 1956–59; Practicing atty.; LA House of Reps., 1964–68, Flr. Ldr.; LA Senate, 1968–72.

Offices 421 RSOB, 202-224-5824. Also Hale Boggs Fed. Bldg., 500 Camp St., Rm. 1010, New Orleans 70130, 504-589-2427; and New Fed. Bldg. and Courthouse, 500 Fannin St., Rm. 7A12, Shreveport 71102, 318-226-5085.

Committees *Appropriations* (8th). Subcommittees: Defense; Energy and Water Development; Foreign Operations; Interior. *Budget* (4th). *Energy and Natural Resources* (Ranking Member).

Group Ratings

	ADA	ACLU	COPE	CFA	LCV	LWV	NTU	NSI	COC	ACA	CSFC
1982	35	18	41	50	31	64	35	90	67	53	59
1981	25	—	39	36	26	—	40	—	82	48	63
1980	33	27	41	7	13	50	35	60	56	29	43

National Journal Ratings

	Economic		Foreign		Cultural	
1982	53%	(LIB)	33%	(LIB)	26%	(LIB)
	46%	(CONS)	64%	(CONS)	73%	(CONS)
1981	47%	(LIB)	50%	(LIB)	49%	(LIB)
	52%	(CONS)	49%	(CONS)	49%	(CONS)

Key Votes

1) Reagan 81 Budget	FOR	5) $ to El Salvador	AGN	9) Poor Pay Food Stamps	AGN
2) Reagan 81 Tax Cut	FOR	6) Saudi AWACS Sale	FOR	10) Ban Crt Busing Order	FOR
3) Bal Budget Amend	FOR	7) Ban Abortion	—	11) Clinch Riv Brdr Rctr	FOR
4) Gas & Road Tax	AGN	8) Nerve Gas Prod	FOR	12) Legal Services Corp	FOR

Election Results

1978 primary	J. Bennett Johnston, Jr. (D)	498,773	(59%)	($857,860)
	Louis (Woody) Jenkins (D)	340,896	(41%)	($327,340)
1972 general	J. Bennett Johnston, Jr. (D)	598,987	(55%)	($511,616)
	John J. McKeithen (I)	250,161	(23%)	($394,510)
	Ben C. Toledano (R)	206,846	(19%)	($116,347)

Campaign Contributions and Expenditures

1977-78			PACS brkdwn		
Receipts	$983,343	Agr	$18,000	Ideo	$900
Expend.	$857,860	Bus	$161,355	Lbr	$11,800
Unspent	$125,483	Hlth	$7,700	Prof	$6,500

GOVERNOR

Gov. David C. Treen (R) Elected 1979, term expires March 1984; b. July 16, 1928, Baton Rouge; home, Metairie; Tulane U., B.A. 1948, LL.B. 1950; United Methodist.

Career Air Force, 1950–52; Practicing atty., 1950–51, 1957–72; V.P. and Legal Counsel, Simplex Manufacturing Corp., 1952–57; Repub. Nominee for U.S. House of Reps., 1962, 1964, 1968; Repub. Nominee for Gov., 1972; U.S. House of Reps., 1972–80.

Offices P.O. Box 44004, Baton Rouge 70804, 504-342-7015.

Election Results

1979 gen.	David C. Treen (R)	690,691	(50%)
	Louis Lambert (D)	681,134	(50%)
1979 prim.	David C. Treen (R)	297,469	(22%)
	Louis Lambert (D)	283,266	(21%)
	James E. Fitzmorris (D)	280,760	(20%)
	Paul Hardy (D)	227,026	(17%)
	E. L. (Bubba) Henry (D)	135,769	(10%)
	Edgar G. Mouton, Jr. (D)	124,333	(9%)
	Three others (D, D, I)	17,052	(1%)
1975 gen.	Edwin W. Edwards (D)	430,095	(100%)
1975 prim.	Edwin W. Edwards (D)	750,107	(62%)
	Robert G. Jones (D)	292,220	(24%)
	Wade O. Martin, Jr. (D)	146,368	(12%)
	Three others (D)	14,309	(1%)

FIRST DISTRICT

The 1st district of Louisiana includes most of the parts of New Orleans the tourist never sees—and the parts that most tourists would feel most at home in if they had to live here. Some 61% of the district's residents are in New Orleans, in an area bounded by a jagged line, designed to keep the most Democratic parts of the city (most of them with black majorities) in Lindy Boggs's 2d district, and leaving the first, which has been represented by Republican

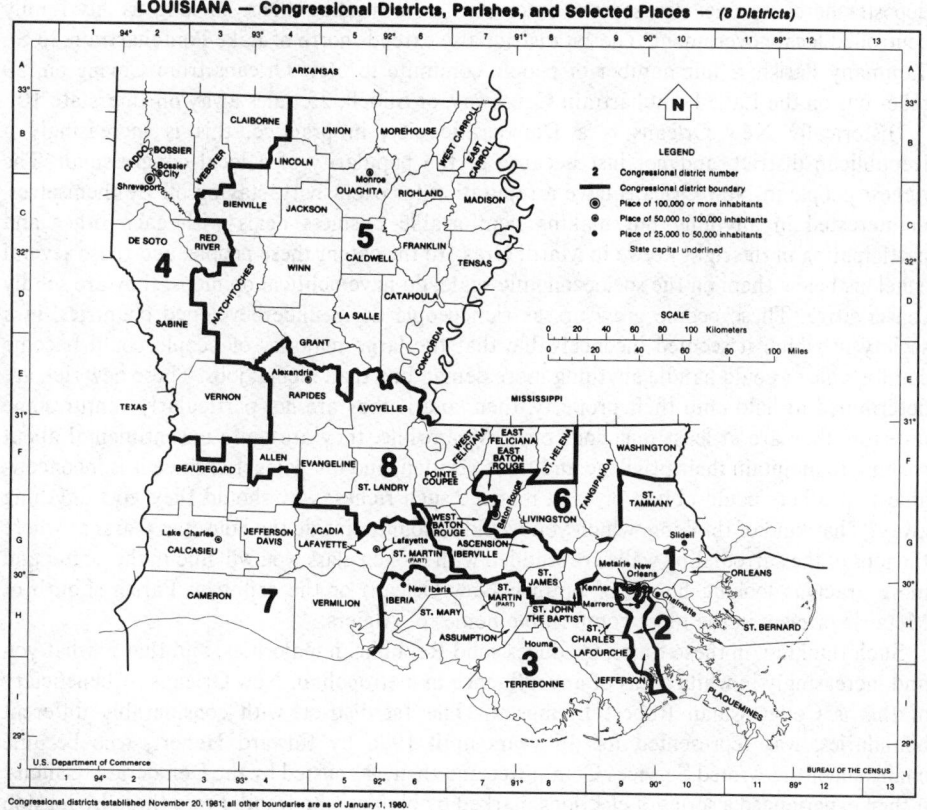

LOUISIANA — Congressional Districts, Parishes, and Selected Places — *(8 Districts)*

Bob Livingston since 1977, with the rest. Yet because New Orleans's black population is large and geographically dispersed, over 40% of the residents of these parts of the city are black. The 1st includes the uptown high income residential district around Tulane University; the neat, 1950s neighborhoods on straight streets headed out to Lake Pontchartrain on both sides of City Park; and new subdivisions along Interstate 10, on land only recently reclaimed from swamp. It also includes some of the old port area, with its rickety frame houses down the street from giant cranes and the hulls of huge ships. On the other side of the Mississippi is the New Orleans neighborhood of Algiers, less picturesque than its name suggests but still a typical New Orleans neighborhood, its flat streets with exotic names stretching into the distance, a mixture of frame and brick houses of indeterminate architecture, the air smelling faintly of industrial wastes and spicy foods.

Immediately downriver from New Orleans is St. Bernard Parish, once a tightly controlled fiefdom but now a part of suburbia; closer in, as you get near the Gulf, is Plaquemines Parish, where the Perez family held sway for decades. The late Leander Perez, Sr., once a Huey Long lieutenant, was excommunicated from the Catholic Church for his opposition to desegregation, but was still able to deliver a virtually unanimous vote for any candidate he chose. He also managed to make vast sums—no one knows how much—off the oil and sulfur deposits here; no one else seemed interested in extracting them so long as his family controlled local government. The 1st district also extends north of Lake Pontchartrain, to St. Tammany Parish; a fair number of people commute to New Orleans from Covington, 30 miles out on the Lake Pontchartrain Causeway, or Slidell, 25 miles away on Interstate 10.

Historically New Orleans is a Democratic city; in practice, this is increasingly a Republican district, and not just because of the popularity of a local congressman. The richest people in New Orleans have a reputation for exclusivity, staying off by themselves, uninterested in anything but making comfortable business deals with each other and participating in the right krewe in Mardi Gras. To the extent these people, and those several echelons below them on the socioeconomic scale, do have political opinions, they are solidly conservative. These people grew up, as rich people do in underdeveloped countries, in a society in which it seemed inconceivable that the large majority of people could become comfortable or could handle anything more demanding than menial jobs. These new rich are determined to hold onto their property, then, and if they are not particularly venturesome investors they are at least tenacious ones. Meanwhile, they are quite unsentimental about wishing to maintain their privilege and their position, and unapologetic: since it is inconceivable that others could obtain or even manage such riches, why should they give anything away? That kind of thinking, which you would encounter inside the houses in Caracas where the tops of the surrounding walls are studded with broken glass, you will find in the neater and more gracious looking homes of uptown New Orleans or the Jefferson Parish suburb of Metairie or even in the more comfortable homes of Algiers.

Such thinking, in these times, produces solid Republican majorities, and that is what you find increasingly in white areas of any affluence in metropolitan New Orleans. A beneficiary of this is Congressman Robert Livingston. The 1st district, with considerably different boundaries, was represented for 36 years until 1976 by Edward Hebert, who became chairman of the Armed Services Committee and then was ousted by the Democratic Caucus; it then experienced a series of elections marked by blatant vote fraud. From these Livingston emerged victorious and entirely innocent of any misconduct. He has won subsequent elections by huge margins against nuisance candidates.

Livingston bears a proud old New Orleans name; the family were originally Jeffersonians from New York, who settled in New Orleans after Mr. Jefferson purchased Louisiana. Livingston styles himself a conservative and usually votes that way. But he is a little quirky. His record on foreign policy issues, of all things, is a little mild. He spent most of his professional life as a prosecutor, but he seems to be a careful upholder of the law rather than a flamboyant one. He seems to be a stickler for what he regards as propriety: he stood up and opposed a measure to repeal a District of Columbia ordinance decriminalizing some sexual conduct on the grounds that the District had a competent legislature and could decide these matters itself. He has a seat on the Appropriations Committee—a good place for someone inclined to careful detail work.

The People Pop. 1980: 524,961, up 14.9% 1970–80; voting age pop. 367,614; 26% Black, 4% Span. orig., 1% Asian orig. 36% housing units rented. Median owner $55,400; renter $181. Households: 74% family, 42% with children, 57% married couples.

Presidential Vote

1980	Reagan (R)	112,165	(55%)
	Carter (D)	84,245	(42%)
	Anderson (I)	4,692	(2%)

Rep. Robert L. (Bob) Livingston (R) Elected Aug. 27, 1977; b. Apr. 30, 1943, Colorado Springs, CO; home, New Orleans; Tulane U., B.A. 1967, J.D. 1968; Episcopal.

Career Practicing atty.; Asst. U.S. Atty., 1970–73; Chf. Spec. Prosecutor, Orleans Parish Dist. Atty.'s Ofc., 1974–75; Chf. Prosecutor, LA Atty. Gen.'s Ofc., Organized Crime Unit, 1975–76.

Offices 306 CHOB, 202-225-3015. Also F. Edward Hebert Bldg., 610 South St., Rm. 742, New Orleans 70130, 504-589-2753.

Committee *Appropriations* (16th). Subcommittees: Foreign Operations; Military Construction.

Group Ratings

	ADA	ACLU	COPE	CFA	LCV	LWV	NTU	NSI	COC	ACA	CSFC
1982	5	29	13	8	34	42	77	89	82	100	65
1981	20	—	15	14	22	—	54	—	94	62	66
1980	11	23	5	36	35	50	47	90	84	83	71

National Journal Ratings

	Economic		Foreign		Cultural	
1982	5%	(LIB)	4%	(LIB)	41%	(LIB)
	94%	(CONS)	92%	(CONS)	59%	(CONS)
1981	35%	(LIB)	53%	(LIB)	42%	(LIB)
	64%	(CONS)	47%	(CONS)	57%	(CONS)

Key Votes

1) Reagan 81 Budget	FOR	5) Incr SS Rtmt Age	FOR	9) Poor Pay Food Stamps	AGN
2) Reagan 81 Tax Cut	FOR	6) Saudi AWACS Sale	AGN	10) Ban Crt Busing Order	FOR
3) Bal Budget Amend	FOR	7) $ for MX Missile	FOR	11) Auto Local Content	AGN
4) Gas & Road Tax	—	8) Nerve Gas Prod	FOR	12) Nuclear Arms Freeze	AGN

Election Results

1982 primary	Robert L. (Bob) Livingston (R) ...	77,102	(86%)	($138,464)
	Two others (I)	12,719	(14%)	
1980 primary	Robert L. (Bob) Livingston (R) ...	81,777	(88%)	($138,724)
	Two others (D, No party)	10,778	(12%)	

Campaign Contributions and Expenditures

1981-82		Direct Cont. 81-82		PACS brkdwn			
Receipts	$242,556	Indiv	$170,317	Agr	$1,500	Ideo	$450
Expend.	$138,464	Party	$221	Bus	$31,450	Lbr	$3,105
Unspent	$241,537	PACS	$39,615	Hlth	$2,000	Prof	$750

SECOND DISTRICT

Since New Orleans fell into American hands with the Louisiana Purchase of 1803, it has been one of the nation's most distinctive cities. The heritage of the city's French and Spanish past can still be seen in the French Quarter, where carefully preserved old houses with their iron balconies stand amid the squalor of tourist-packed bars and some of the nation's finest restaurants. New Orleans is our second busiest port, adding the new functions of shipping out Louisiana's oil and petroleum products in huge tankers to its historic role as the outlet of the Mississippi Valley's agriculture and the entrepot of Latin American trade.

Louisiana's 2d congressional district is made up of some of the older, more distinctive parts of New Orleans plus some of its older, more industrial suburbs. It includes all of the French Quarter, its 19th century homes still intact because the Americans who moved here after 1803 wanted to stay away from the snobbish creoles and built a new downtown west of Canal Street. Just above the Quarter is the site of Storyville, where prostitution was legal before 1918 and where jazz was probably first played; the old frame houses have long since been torn down, and replaced by housing projects. But many similar neighborhoods remain, inhabited mostly but not always by blacks, in the vividly named streets that go north from the river wharves east of the Quarter. In the other direction, you go through the downtown—full of particularly cold and severe skyscrapers—past the old slum known as the Irish Channel—a reminder that New Orleans had more foreign immigrants than any other part of the South— to the Garden district. This was the home of the rich early American settlers, and its antebellum homes are still covered with vines and Spanish moss. The country's last trolley cars still roll out St. Charles Avenue, passing out of the 2d district in the affluent uptown area and back into it when they reach a poor black neighborhood beyond. The district's boundaries were designed to produce a Democratic district, and the 2d's portion of New Orleans is 75% black.

The majority of the district's residents live in suburban Jefferson Parish. The 2d includes relatively little of Metairie, the affluent suburb out toward the lake; but it takes in all of the little communities clustered along the Mississippi. Those on the right side—Gretna, Harvey, Marrero, Westwego—are working class towns, hemmed in by the swamps and the river and by the giant grain elevators which flank it; New Orleans is the biggest grain-exporting port in the United States. These are the elevators you saw burning on national newscasts; the operators are none too scrupulous about cleaning them and keeping down the level of potentially explosive grain dust. On the north side of the river, too, west of the city there are industrial working class suburbs, whose lifeblood is the river and the railroad tracks that parallel it. Some 80% of the people in this part of the district are white, but they are more likely to be Democrats than the voters in the affluent neighborhoods just outside the district's boundaries.

This is the district represented by Lindy Boggs; its current boundaries were drawn pretty much to her specifications. She came to Congress, as many women do, as widows replacing their husband; but she has been more than the typical widow just as her husband, Hale Boggs, was more than the typical congressman. He was House majority leader when he was lost in a plane crash in 1972 while campaigning in Alaska; he had a congressional career that went back to 1940, which was distinguished by his courageous, and nearly politically fatal, support of the Civil Rights Acts of 1965 and 1968. Had he lived, Boggs would have been speaker of the House.

Lindy Boggs will not be speaker, but she has achieved distinction on her own. For years she was considered one of the most knowledgeable of congressional wives and she managed her husband's campaigns in New Orleans—not a job for a political innocent. She has the manners of a girl raised on a plantation (which she was), the panache of someone with an elegant old house in the French Quarter (which she has), and the political savvy of one who has managed tough campaigns and moved in the highest circles of Washington for years (which she has). Her talents were on view to the nation when she served as permanent chairwoman of the 1976 Democratic National Convention.

In the House she serves on the Appropriations Committee and on the HUD-Independent Agencies and Energy and Water Development Subcommittees. On major issues she is inclined to support the House Democratic leadership: she tends to be somewhat generous on economic issues, cautious on cultural issues, and supportive of defense spending. Her closest race in the 2d district was in 1980, when she won 61% against two candidates in the September primary and was thereby reelected. The 1982 redistricting strengthened her, although the district is more suburban, by removing some heavily Republican precincts in New Orleans. She seems to have a safe seat for the 1980s if she wants it.

The People Pop. 1980: 527,264, up 1.4% 1970–80; voting age pop. 364,679; 41% Black, 3% Span. orig., 1% Asian orig. 49% housing units rented. Median owner $46,700; renter $154. Households: 69% family, 41% with children, 48% married couples.

Presidential Vote

1980	Reagan (R)	67,856	(42%)
	Carter (D)	89,512	(55%)
	Anderson (I)	3,151	(2%)

Rep. Lindy (Mrs. Hale) **Boggs** (D) Elected Mar. 20, 1973; b. Mar. 13, 1916, Brunswick Plantation; home, New Orleans; Sophie Newcomb Col. of Tulane U., B.A. 1935; Roman Catholic.

Career Pub. sch. teacher; Gen. Mgr., campaigns of U.S. Rep. Hale Boggs; Cochwmn., Presidential Inaugural Balls, 1961, 1965; Chwmn., 1976 Dem. Natl. Convention.

Offices 2353 RHOB, 202-225-6636. Also Hale Boggs Bldg., 500 Camp St., Rm. 1012, New Orleans 70130, 504-589-2274.

Committees *Appropriations* (18th). Subcommittees: Energy and Water Development; HUD-Independent Agencies; Legislative. *Select Committee on Children, Youth, and Families* (3d).

Group Ratings

	ADA	ACLU	COPE	CFA	LCV	LWV	NTU	NSI	COC	ACA	CSFC
1982	50	50	71	62	67	58	1	70	36	33	33
1981	45	—	70	50	43	—	0	—	32	29	41
1980	50	47	50	71	40	70	11	44	70	30	29

National Journal Ratings

	Economic		Foreign		Cultural	
1982	82%	(LIB)	53%	(LIB)	36%	(LIB)
	18%	(CONS)	46%	(CONS)	64%	(CONS)
1981	60%	(LIB)	46%	(LIB)	59%	(LIB)
	39%	(CONS)	52%	(CONS)	41%	(CONS)

Key Votes

1) Reagan 81 Budget	AGN	5) Incr SS Rtmt Age	AGN	9) Poor Pay Food Stamps	AGN
2) Reagan 81 Tax Cut	AGN	6) Saudi AWACS Sale	AGN	10) Ban Crt Busing Order	FOR
3) Bal Budget Amend	AGN	7) $ for MX Missile	AGN	11) Auto Local Content	FOR
4) Gas & Road Tax	FOR	8) Nerve Gas Prod	AGN	12) Nuclear Arms Freeze	FOR

Election Results

1982 primary	Lindy Boggs (D)	44,968	(77%)	($464,594)
	Roger C. Johnson (D)	13,404	(23%)	($4,400)
1980 primary	Lindy Boggs (D)	45,091	(61%)	($571,673)
	Rob Couhig (R)	25,521	(34%)	($130,210)
	One other (D)	3,571	(5%)	

Campaign Contributions and Expenditures

1981-82		Direct Cont. 81-82*		PACS brkdwn			
Receipts	$476,779	Indiv	$79,589	Agr	$4,500	Ideo	$2,300
Expend.	$464,594	PACS	$63,924	Bus	$39,574	Lbr	$9,100
Unspent	$14,331	Cand	$257,050	Hlth	$2,100	Prof	$5,050

*Non-Cand Loans: $50,000

THIRD DISTRICT

The 3d congressional district is made up of two quite different parts of southern Louisiana. Most of the physical expanse of the district, and 70% of its population, is part of Louisiana's Cajun country—miles of bayou and swamp giving way from time to time to little ribbons of highway pavement and crossroads towns where French remains the first language and roadside diners feature crawfish etouffe. But Cajun country looks not just to tradition. It has become one of the nation's major oil-producing areas, and many of the people here work in local oil production or on offshore rigs. The oil industry indirectly and inadvertently may be responsible for preserving Cajun culture, for people here, unlike those in many southern rural areas, have not had to move somewhere else to find well-paying jobs and opportunities for advancement.

The Cajun country is traditionally Democratic, but the influence of the oil industry—not heavyhanded propaganda by the oil companies, but rather the example of success and prosperity oil production has brought here—has made this area more Republican in recent years. In the 1980 presidential election the Cajun counties of the 3d district, on balance, went for Ronald Reagan over Jimmy Carter.

The other 30% of the 3d district's residents live in suburban Jefferson Parish outside New Orleans. They live in on land laboriously reclaimed from swamp and criss-crossed by canals. On the north is the expanse of Lake Pontchartrain, on the west, as soon as you pass the Jefferson Parish line, the interstate rides on stilts above the swamp. The 3d includes most of Metairie, the upper income suburb of New Orleans, and much of Kenner, around the airport. Metairie is the home not of New Orleans's elite, but of its comfortable upper middle class, people who are proud of their own accomplishments and determined, in an unsentimental and unforgiving environment, to hold on to what they have. In national and statewide elections, this part of Jefferson Parish typically delivers the largest Republican margins in the state.

These two disparate parts of the state were thrown together by the one-person-one-vote doctrine. In the past decade, the district has elected congressmen who typify the different parts of the district. David Treen, now governor, is a Jefferson Parish Republican who proudly proclaimed his conservatism and had near-perfect conservative voting records in Congress. Billy Tauzin, from Thibodaux in Lafourche Parish, is a congenial Cajun who had the support of outgoing Governor Edwin Edwards (a Cajun himself) to succeed Treen in the May 1980 special election. Tauzin won that contest narrowly and has not been seriously challenged since.

Tauzin, unlike Treen, seems more interested in congressional issues than in running for governor. He serves on the Merchant Marine and Fisheries Committee, where he can protect local interests; they include wildlife preservation, since the Cajun country is full of sportsmen. He is also a member of the Energy and Commerce Committee. That is the body with jurisdiction over oil and gas price controls, and Tauzin of course can be counted on to oppose them (except that things get more complicated, since differently situated oil producers end up with different interests). On other regulatory issues, Tauzin combines generally conservative instincts with a willingness to support some form of regulation. He is, accordingly, a key vote on any number of critical regulatory issues, and one which cannot be predicted with certainty.

The People   Pop. 1980: 526,269, up 29.1% 1970–80; voting age pop. 351,768; 13% Black, 3% Span. orig., 1% Asian orig. 30% housing units rented. Median owner $53,800; renter $230. Households: 79% family, 49% with children, 67% married couples.

Presidential Vote

1980	Reagan (R)	105,491	(58%)
	Carter (D)	71,407	(39%)
	Anderson (I)	4,061	(2%)

Rep. Wilbert J. (Billy) **Tauzin** (D) Elected May 22, 1980; b. June 14, 1943, Chackbay; home, Thibodaux; Nicholls St. U., B.A. 1964, LA St. U., J.D. 1967; Roman Catholic.

Career Legis. Aide, LA Senate, 1964–68; Practicing atty., 1968–80; LA House of Reps., 1971–79.

Offices 222 CHOB, 202-225-4051. Also 4900 Veterans Memorial Blvd., Metairie 70002, 504-889-2303; Fed. Bldg., Su. 107, Houma 70360, 504-876-3033; and 210 E. Main St., New Iberia 70560, 318-367-8231.

Committees Energy and Commerce (18th). Subcommittees: Fossil and Synthetic Fuels; Commerce, Transportation, and Tourism. *Merchant Marine and Fisheries* (13th). Subcommittees: Coast Guard and Navigation; Fisheries and Wildlife Conservation and the Environment; Oceanography; Panama Canal and Outer Continental Shelf.

Group Ratings

	ADA	ACLU	COPE	CFA	LCV	LWV	NTU	NSI	COC	ACA	CSFC
1982	5	29	23	23	42	17	72	100	73	73	57
1981	0	—	29	43	21	—	52	—	79	64	60
1980	—	—	67	25	20	—	23	100	79	42	52

National Journal Ratings

	Economic		Foreign		Cultural	
1982	29%	(LIB)	33%	(LIB)	21%	(LIB)
	71%	(CONS)	66%	(CONS)	76%	(CONS)
1981	44%	(LIB)	18%	(LIB)	34%	(LIB)
	55%	(CONS)	73%	(CONS)	66%	(CONS)

Key Votes

1) Reagan 81 Budget	FOR	5) Incr SS Rtmt Age	FOR	9) Poor Pay Food Stamps	AGN
2) Reagan 81 Tax Cut	AGN	6) Saudi AWACS Sale	AGN	10) Ban Crt Busing Order	FOR
3) Bal Budget Amend	FOR	7) $ for MX Missile	FOR	11) Auto Local Content	FOR
4) Gas & Road Tax	AGN	8) Nerve Gas Prod	FOR	12) Nuclear Arms Freeze	AGN

Election Results

1982 general	W.J. (Billy) Tauzin (D) unopposed		
1982 primary	W.J. (Billy) Tauzin (D) unopposed		($286,358)
1980 primary	W.J. (Billy) Tauzin (D)	80,455 (85%)	($684,431)
	One other (D)	14,074 (15%)	

Campaign Contributions and Expenditures

1981-82		Direct Cont. 81-82*				PACS brkdwn		
Receipts	$415,797	Indiv	$226,526	Agr	$2,750	Ideo	$1,550
Expend.	$286,358	Party	$400	Bus	$61,217	Lbr	$5,000
Unspent	$139,939	PACS	$83,127	Hlth	$5,500	Prof	$5,500
		Cand	$50,000				

Non-Cand Loans: $50,000

FOURTH DISTRICT

Northern Louisiana is part of the Deep South, with none of the Creole ambience of New Orleans or the French accents of the Cajun country. For 150 years Baptist farmers have worked the upcountry hills around Shreveport, the commercial center of northwestern Louisiana and the adjacent part of Texas and the largest city in Louisiana's 4th congressional district. Shreveport and the adjacent suburban areas in Caddo and Bossier Parishes form about half the district, but in recent years these two segments have diverged in political attitude. The rural parishes remain wedded to the traditional Deep South attachment to the Democratic Party. They supported George Wallace in 1968 and Richard Nixon in 1972, but went back to Jimmy Carter in both 1976 and 1980.

Shreveport started off with the same tradition; it was just another market town for the surrounding agricultural parishes. But in the 1940s oil was found in the area, and Shreveport's population grew rapidly. Now Shreveport is more like the small oil cities of east Texas than the rural territory that surrounds it. The newly rich are closely acquainted with the virtues of the free enterprise system (and give little attention to the ways the government subsidized the oil business for years), and they bring doctrinaire free market ideas to politics. Traditional Democratic allegiance means nothing to them, though they are willing to support likeminded Democrats. Just as they are economically more conservative than their neighbors they are culturally more advanced and urbane. They wait not only for the latest edition of *Human Events* but for the current Neiman Marcus catalogue. So in presidential elections Caddo and Bossier Parish have gone Republican in recent years.

This district, with its split personality, had a turbulent congressional politics when longtime Congressman Joe Waggoner retired in 1978. Waggoner was a leader of the conservative bloc of southern Democrats and small town Republicans; a country boy, he worked hard and shrewdly to protect the interests of the district's oil operators. There followed two elections in which three competitors spent a total of $2.6 million—a huge amount, considering that the Shreveport TV stations cover almost all the district and not much else. Republican Jimmy Wilson carried the Shreveport area but lost in 1978 to Democrat Claude (Buddy) Leach by 266 votes. He charged vote fraud and Leach, in the second vote fraud case in Louisiana in two years, was indicted. Ultimately he was acquitted, and, though he edged Wilson out in the 1980 primary, he was defeated in the general by a large margin.

The winner and current congressman is Buddy Roemer. He looks like the Louisiana version of a liberal, or at least a city slicker—young, Harvard-educated, and well connected. His father was a leading operative for Governor Edwin Edwards (and had legal problems of his own). Roemer has built some kind of political base in Shreveport; he has raised and spent more than $2 million in the last three elections, and he had a solid vote base there in the 1980 runoff.

Roemer seems to echo Shreveport's views on issues. His voting record betrays little hint of any sympathy to the liberalism fashionable with many in his age group. He even threatened in 1981 to vote against Tip O'Neill for speaker, until someone pointed out that that could cost him membership in the Democratic Caucus and all committee assignments; he supported O'Neill. He has hip-hopped from Public Works to Banking without really getting his first choice assignment, Budget: he was one of those Boll Weevil supporters of President Reagan's budget and tax cuts in 1981 who did not fare well when committee assignments were made in 1983.

Roemer was unopposed in 1982; the 4th district got a breather from fiercely contested elections. He probably has a good hold on the district now. The only mystery of his career is why he has fought so hard, and spent so much money, to win such a small plum. Perhaps he intends to run for statewide office, and perhaps like many politicians in this state he sees in the mirror each morning a future governor of Louisiana. But one cannot help but think that the attraction for him and his opponents has been the fight itself. Next to professional football (and Shreveport is the home town of a disproportionate number of NFL quarterbacks), Louisiana politics with its uninhibited money-raising and its charges of vote-stealing and fraud are the closest things to armed conflict our society sanctions; the pull of battle may simply be irresistible. If so, look for Buddy Roemer to seek horizons wider than the 4th congressional district soon.

The People Pop. 1980: 525,194, up 11.3% 1970–80; voting age pop. 363,684; 29% Black, 2% Span. orig. 28% housing units rented. Median owner $34,900; renter $139. Households: 76% family, 44% with children, 60% married couples.

Presidential Vote

1980	Reagan (R)	99,526	(54%)
	Carter (D)	81,619	(44%)
	Anderson (I)	2,040	(1%)

Rep. Buddy Roemer (D) Elected 1980; b. Oct. 4, 1943, Shreveport; home, Bossier City; Harvard U., B.A. 1964, M.B.A. 1967; Methodist.

Career Businessman, farmer, banker, 1967–80; Delegate, LA Const. Conv., 1972.

Offices 1725 LHOB, 202-225-2777. Also P.O. Drawer 5100, Bossier City 71111, 318-797-9000.

Committees *Banking Finance and Urban Affairs* (22d). Subcommittees: Domestic Monetary Policy; Economic Stabilization; General Oversight and Renegotiation; International Trade, Investment and Monetary Policy. *Small Business* (18th). Subcommittee: Access to Equity Capital and Business Opportunities.

Group Ratings

	ADA	ACLU	COPE	CFA	LCV	LWV	NTU	NSI	COC	ACA	CSFC
1982	15	33	14	23	58	33	91	90	59	83	64
1981	5	—	20	43	50	—	89	—	79	67	69

National Journal Ratings

	Economic		Foreign		Cultural	
1982	20%	(LIB)	46%	(LIB)	56%	(LIB)
	80%	(CONS)	53%	(CONS)	43%	(CONS)
1981	38%	(LIB)	18%	(LIB)	38%	(LIB)
	62%	(CONS)	73%	(CONS)	62%	(CONS)

Key Votes

1) Reagan 81 Budget	FOR	5) Incr SS Rtmt Age	FOR	9) Poor Pay Food Stamps	AGN
2) Reagan 81 Tax Cut	FOR	6) Saudi AWACS Sale	AGN	10) Ban Crt Busing Order	FOR
3) Bal Budget Amend	FOR	7) $ for MX Missile	AGN	11) Auto Local Content	FOR
4) Gas & Road Tax	FOR	8) Nerve Gas Prod	FOR	12) Nuclear Arms Freeze	AGN

Election Results

1982 primary	Buddy Roemer (D) unopposed			($732,825 est.)
1980 general	Buddy Roemer (D)	103,625	(64%)	($693,859)
	Claude (Buddy) Leach (D)	58,705	(36%)	($643,639)

Campaign Contributions and Expenditures

1981-82		Direct Cont. 81-82		PACS brkdwn			
Receipts	$741,311 (est.)	Indiv	$485,341	Agr	$—	Ideo	$2,300
Expend.	$732,825 (est.)	Party	$20,350	Bus	$14,000	Lbr	$500
Unspent	$13,458 (est.)	PACS	$27,000	Hlth	$10,200	Prof	$—
		Cand	$200,000				

Estimated totals include fundraising to retire previous campaign debt.

FIFTH DISTRICT

The upcountry 5th congressional district of Louisiana, the state's most rural, is part of the Deep South. Aside from the small city of Monroe, the 5th has no urban center of any note. The agricultural establishments in this cotton and piney woods country range from large plantations along the Mississippi River to small, poor hill farms in places like Winn Parish, the boyhood home of Huey P. Long. Politics here was all white as recently as 20 years ago, and some figures suggest that blacks are still excluded today: 31% of the district's residents but only 25% of its registered voters are black. But that 25% is not much lower than the 28% of the district's over 18 population which is black; the differential is no greater than what you find in northern states. And fully 38% of the district's children are black. At a time when black outmigration from the South seems to have ended, that is the statistic that matters most to the future: black voters will almost certainly be more numerous and more powerful in districts like this 20 years from now than they are today.

The congressman from the 5th district is Jerry Huckaby, a dairy farmer and former Western Electric management employee, who had the shrewdness to challenge 30-year incumbent Otto Passman in 1976 and beat him. He has held the district ever since, against serious competition in 1978 and nuisance candidates in 1980 and 1982. Now he seems likely to hold it forever, or at least as long as Passman did.

The reason: in 1983 he succeeded to the chairmanship of the Agriculture Committee's Subcommittee on Cotton, Rice, and Sugar. That may sound like an obscure post to you, but those are Louisiana's three main crops, and historically producers of all three have depended on heavy subsidies, support programs, or import restrictions. The care and maintenance of such programs will be Huckaby's main work, and he can be counted on to further the interests of Louisiana farmers and middlemen. On other issues he will take a quieter role. His instincts are to the political right; he was one of the Boll Weevil Democrats who supported the Reagan budget and tax cut bills in 1981, and he seems to feel no particular obligation to go along with the Democratic leadership. But that does not jeopardize his subcommittee chairmanship. That position is bestowed by the Democratic members of the Agriculture Committee; more than half of them are southerners and most of them are sympathetic to Huckaby's stands.

The People   Pop. 1980: 527,220, up 12.6% 1970–80; voting age pop. 360,687; 28% Black, 1% Span. orig. 24% housing units rented. Median owner $29,400; renter $96. Households: 76% family, 44% with children, 61% married couples.

Presidential Vote

1980	Reagan (R)	98,777	(53%)
	Carter (D)	83,505	(45%)
	Anderson (I)	1,753	(1%)

Rep. Jerry Huckaby (D) Elected 1976; b. July 19, 1941, Jackson Parish; home, Ringgold; LA St. U., B.S. 1963, GA St. U., M.B.A. 1968; Methodist.

Career Mgmt. position, Western Electric, 1963–73; Dairy farmer, 1963–76.

Offices 2444 RHOB, 202-225-2376. Also 1200 N. 18th St., Monroe 71201, 318-387-2244.

Committees *Agriculture* (12th). Subcommittees: Cotton, Rice, and Sugar (Chairman); Forests, Family Farms, and Energy; Domestic Marketing, Consumer Relations, and Nutrition. *Interior and Insular Affairs* (14th). Subcommittees: Energy and the Environment; Mining, Forest Management, and BPA.

Group Ratings

	ADA	ACLU	COPE	CFA	LCV	LWV	NTU	NSI	COC	ACA	CSFC
1982	25	33	28	31	59	42	53	100	45	64	46
1981	10	—	25	14	15	—	57	—	76	78	61
1980	11	3	21	14	39	40	36	100	84	58	54

National Journal Ratings

	Economic		Foreign		Cultural	
1982	42%	(LIB)	44%	(LIB)	51%	(LIB)
	58%	(CONS)	55%	(CONS)	48%	(CONS)
1981	36%	(LIB)	3%	(LIB)	36%	(LIB)
	62%	(CONS)	87%	(CONS)	63%	(CONS)

Key Votes

1) Reagan 81 Budget	FOR	5) Incr SS Rtmt Age	AGN	9) Poor Pay Food Stamps	AGN
2) Reagan 81 Tax Cut	FOR	6) Saudi AWACS Sale	FOR	10) Ban Crt Busing Order	—
3) Bal Budget Amend	FOR	7) $ for MX Missile	AGN	11) Auto Local Content	AGN
4) Gas & Road Tax	AGN	8) Nerve Gas Prod	—	12) Nuclear Arms Freeze	AGN

Election Results

1982 primary	Jerry Huckaby (D)	71,571	(84%)	($106,208)
	Two others (D)	9,163	(11%)	
	One other (I)	4,771	(6%)	
1980 primary	Jerry Huckaby (D)	93,519	(89%)	($60,316)
	One other (D)	11,748	(11%)	

Campaign Contributions and Expenditures

1981-82		Direct Cont. 81-82		PACS brkdwn			
Receipts	$261,734	Indiv	$142,571	Agr	$15,500	Ideo	$1,200
Expend.	$106,208	Party	$100	Bus	$60,200	Lbr	$2,500
Unspent	$217,698	PACS	$83,131	Hlth	$1,750	Prof	$1,250

SIXTH DISTRICT

When Governor-elect Huey P. Long moved himself and his baggage to Baton Rouge in 1928, Louisiana's capital was a small, sleepy southern town of 30,000 people. Today Baton Rouge is a bustling city of 219,000, with a population up 32% in the 1970s. The change has been brought about by both to the Kingfish and his bitterest political enemies. Long built a major university in Baton Rouge (Louisiana State) and vastly increased the size and scope of state government. His old enemies, the oil companies, primarily Standard Oil of New Jersey (now Exxon), built the big refineries and petrochemical plants that are the other basis of Baton Rouge's prosperity. For Exxon, now the nation's largest industrial corporation, Baton Rouge is especially important; managing the big refinery here is a key job for Exxon, and many of the company's chief executives have held that post.

Baton Rouge (except for a small portion) and its suburban fringe make up about two-thirds of Louisiana's 6th congressional district. The remainder of the district is to the east, in farming and piney woods country, stretching northeast to the Mississippi border. This area is known as the Florida Parishes, because it was acquired by the United States when West Florida was annexed in 1810.

The district is traditionally Democratic but has been moving Republican in recent years. It favored Jimmy Carter by a solid margin in 1976 but went for Ronald Reagan in 1980. Carter's southern origin and his ambiguity on oil issues probably helped him win here the first time; four years later he was identified as an opponent of decontrol (although he finally favored it) and lost Baton Rouge quite heavily. In congressional politics, the 6th district has been a Republican district since 1975 and perhaps 1974. The reason for the ambiguity is that the 1974 election had to be rerun, because the results from one heavily Democratic precinct were not recorded; most likely the Democratic nominee, a young liberal who had beaten right wing incumbent John Rarick in the primary, actually had got the most votes. But in the January 1975 rerun the Republican, Henson Moore, ran a strong campaign and was elected. He has won easily ever since. Redistricting helped him by removing some black precincts in Baton Rouge and some heavily black rural parishes, but even without such aid he can expect no problems.

Moore has represented the district ever since. He is one of those handsome young southern

Republicans, but he is more than that too: he is an articulate and aggressive advocate of free enterprise principles. He is Louisiana's only member of the Ways and Means Committee, which writes the tax laws so important to the oil industry; there he harries the Democrats and protests vigorously if he thinks they are trying to stack subcommittees. He can be counted on to defend and advance the interests of oil producers, and he was a strong defender of the Reagan administration's economic programs. He is an ardent free trader, interested in agricultural exports; Baton Rouge is one of the nation's largest ports in tonnage, and ships not only oil and petrochemicals but also cotton and various grains brought down the Mississippi Valley in barges.

Moore has been mentioned as a possible statewide candidate. He could run for the Senate against Bennett Johnston in 1984 or Russell Long in 1986. Either race would be chancy. But there is a Republican base now in Louisiana of perhaps 35% or 40% of the vote, and Moore may be able to count on a geographical base in Baton Rouge and the Florida Parishes as well. It would still be very risky for him, however, and he may well decide to hold onto his safe seat in the House.

The People Pop. 1980: 524,770, up 29.5% 1970–80; voting age pop. 362,252; 23% Black, 2% Span. orig. 30% housing units rented. Median owner $50,800; renter $194. Households: 75% family, 45% with children, 61% married couples.

Presidential Vote

1980	Reagan (R)	105,491	(53%)
	Carter (D)	87,838	(44%)
	Anderson (I)	4,218	(2%)

Rep. W. Henson Moore (R) Elected Jan. 7, 1975; b. Oct. 4, 1939, Lake Charles; home, Baton Rouge; LA St. U., B.A. 1961, J.D. 1965, M.A. 1973; Episcopal.

Career Army, 1965–67; Practicing atty., 1967–74.

Offices 2404 RHOB, 202-225-3901. Also Fed. Bldg., 750 FL Blvd., Rm. 236, Baton Rouge 70801, 504-344-7679.

Committee *Ways and Means* (10th). Subcommittees: Health (Ranking Member); Public Assistance and Unemployment Compensation; Select Revenue Measures.

Group Ratings

	ADA	ACLU	COPE	CFA	LCV	LWV	NTU	NSI	COC	ACA	CSFC
1982	0	8	8	15	38	33	85	100	82	87	69
1981	10	—	9	21	50	—	79	—	84	75	69
1980	11	20	0	14	30	44	49	100	81	79	70

National Journal Ratings

	Economic		Foreign		Cultural	
1982	3%	(LIB)	39%	(LIB)	34%	(LIB)
	96%	(CONS)	61%	(CONS)	65%	(CONS)
1981	24%	(LIB)	18%	(LIB)	26%	(LIB)
	68%	(CONS)	73%	(CONS)	74%	(CONS)

Key Votes

1) Reagan 81 Budget	FOR	5) Incr SS Rtmt Age	FOR	9) Poor Pay Food Stamps	AGN
2) Reagan 81 Tax Cut	FOR	6) Saudi AWACS Sale	AGN	10) Ban Crt Busing Order	FOR
3) Bal Budget Amend	FOR	7) $ for MX Missile	FOR	11) Auto Local Content	AGN
4) Gas & Road Tax	AGN	8) Nerve Gas Prod	FOR	12) Nuclear Arms Freeze	AGN

Election Results

1982 primary	W. Henson Moore (R)	65,269	(77%)	($233,096)
	James D. Agnew (I)	19,354	(23%)	($0)
1980 primary	W. Henson Moore (R)	118,540	(91%)	($88,376)
	One other (D)	12,149	(9%)	

Campaign Contributions and Expenditures

1981-82		*Direct Cont. 81-82*				*PACS brkdwn*		
Receipts	$366,899	Indiv	$185,836	Agr	$9,550	Ideo	$1,250
Expend.	$233,096	Party	$9,944	Bus	$93,137	Lbr	$250
Unspent	$331,562	PACS	$110,087	Hlth	$4,200	Prof	$1,700

SEVENTH DISTRICT

The 7th congressional district of Louisiana is one of the very few in the nation where nearly half the population grew up speaking a language other than English. Here the language is French, Cajun style, and it is the mother tongue of more than 40% of the 7th district's residents. This district covers the southwestern part of Louisiana, hugging the Gulf Coast, from the swamps along the Atchafalaya River west to Lake Charles and the Texas border. In the middle is the city of Lafayette, unofficial capital of the Cajun country, and the center of oil exploration in the Tuscaloosa Trend; that formation here may have produced more millionaires in Lafayette than in any other small city in the country.

Many other rural backwaters like this have died in the years since World War II; not so the Cajun country of Louisiana. What has kept people here is petroleum, in plentiful quantities under the swampy soil and in even greater amounts below the Gulf of Mexico a few miles out to sea. Oil and attendant industries have generated money to keep right there all the Cajuns who wish to stay in their homeland. Cajun culture—language, music, cuisine—remains healthy as well. For years the use of French was discouraged, and seemed to be dying out; but in the 1970s, people here worked to keep the language alive—even while making sure, sensibly, that their children learned to become completely proficient in English.

The congressman from the 7th district, John Breaux, is a practical-minded legislator who has a substantial effect on serious legislation. When he was first elected in September 1972, to replace his former boss, Edwin Edwards, who had just been elected governor, Breaux was the youngest member of Congress. But he was never part of the legions who opposed the Vietnam war or tried to build programs to help the poor. Breaux was interested in more mundane things. He got seats on the Public Works and Merchant Marine and Fisheries Committees, which handled matters like dredging swamps, building levees, and subsidizing shipping companies. In the old days his function for his district would have been to funnel federal money in. In the oil-prosperous 1970s his function was to keep federal regulators out.

Breaux, like many others who grew up in impoverished districts, tends to favor economic growth over environmental considerations. He was the major sponsor of an amendment to relax federal control over landfill and dumping operations in marshes and swamps. He worked to change oil leasing procedures on the continental shelf, to encourage exploration. On Merchant Marine he tends to favor subsidies, but looks out for oil first; he opposed the oil cargo preference bill. Breaux is also the leading critic in the House of the law-of-the-sea treaty negotiated by the Carter administration and scuttled by the Reagan administration.

Breaux found himself on the side of the Reagan administration also on the budget and tax fights of 1981. The President invited him to the White House to seek his support on the budget bill, and Breaux got him to promise to reinstate sugar price supports. "We got the best deal," Breaux told a reporter. "Does that mean your vote is for sale?" he was asked. "No, but it's available for rent." That position made perfect sense to a constituency which sees politics as a struggle for economic advantage over other regions and interests in the country: you get the best deal you can. Breaux is respected as a wily and shrewd negotiator, one who gets good deals, and one who is articulate and effective as well. Yet he did pay a price for his support of the other party: the Democratic Steering Committee in 1983 did not give him the committee post he wanted.

Will that hurt Breaux in future elections? Not likely. He repelled a serious Republican challenge in the September 1978 election by a 60%–33% margin, and has been reelected easily since. He remains competent and devoted to the economic interests of the district and, unless he decides to run for statewide office, he seems likely to represent this district for many years.

The People Pop. 1980: 525,361, up 19.6% 1970–80; voting age pop. 355,571; 18% Black, 2% Span. orig. 26% housing units rented. Median owner $41,500; renter $154. Households: 78% family, 47% with children, 66% married couples.

Presidential Vote

1980	Reagan (R)	101,241	(50%)
	Carter (D)	94,697	(47%)
	Anderson (I)	4,182	(2%)

Rep. John B. Breaux (D) Elected Sept. 30, 1972; b. Mar. 1, 1944, Crowley; home, Crowley; U. of S.W. LA, B.A. 1964, LA St. U., J.D. 1967; Roman Catholic.

Career Practicing atty., 1967–68; Legis. Asst., Dist. Mgr. to U.S. Rep. Edwin W. Edwards, 1968–72.

Offices 2113 RHOB, 202-225-2031. Also 2530 P.O. and Fed. Bldg., Lake Charles 70601, 318-433-1122.

Committees Merchant Marine and Fisheries (4th). Subcommittees: Fisheries and Wildlife Conservation and the Environment (Chairman); Merchant Marine; Panama Canal and Outer Continental Shelf. *Public Works and Transportation* (4th). Subcommittees: Surface Transportation; Water Resources; Investigations and Oversight.

Group Ratings

	ADA	ACLU	COPE	CFA	LCV	LWV	NTU	NSI	COC	ACA	CSFC
1982	15	29	35	8	37	45	50	100	67	71	49
1981	0	—	36	14	31	—	41	—	84	55	53
1980	11	13	28	21	22	50	28	80	77	48	49

National Journal Ratings

	Economic		Foreign		Cultural	
1982	33%	(LIB)	16%	(LIB)	33%	(LIB)
	67%	(CONS)	84%	(CONS)	67%	(CONS)
1981	44%	(LIB)	44%	(LIB)	34%	(LIB)
	55%	(CONS)	56%	(CONS)	66%	(CONS)

Key Votes

1) Reagan 81 Budget	FOR	5) Incr SS Rtmt Age	FOR
2) Reagan 81 Tax Cut	AGN	6) Saudi AWACS Sale	AGN
3) Bal Budget Amend	FOR	7) $ for MX Missile	FOR
4) Gas & Road Tax	FOR	8) Nerve Gas Prod	FOR

9) Poor Pay Food Stamps	AGN
10) Ban Crt Busing Order	FOR
11) Auto Local Content	AGN
12) Nuclear Arms Freeze	AGN

Election Results

1982 primary	John B. Breaux (D)	62,722	(79%)	($171,244)
	Johnny Myers (D)	16,688	(21%)	($0)
1980 primary	John B. Breaux (D) unopposed			($89,822)

Campaign Contributions and Expenditures

1981-82		Direct Cont. 81-82		PACS brkdwn			
Receipts	$253,646	Indiv	$106,632	Agr	$17,862	Ideo	$1,350
Expend.	$171,244	PACS	$118,122	Bus	$87,620	Lbr	$6,050
Unspent	$179,534			Hlth	$800	Prof	$2,550

EIGHTH DISTRICT

Most of the people in Louisiana's 8th congressional district are members of one of the state's visible minorities: blacks or Cajuns. The district begins about where the real delta lands—the silting up of the Gulf of Mexico—begin, about 150 miles inland from the current Gulf coast. Here the Red River joins the Mississippi and, almost immediately the Mississippi's waters run into dozens of channels, from small bayous to the Atchafalaya and the lower Mississippi River itself. The Mississippi is enclosed by levees here and its flow carefully restricted; it is an avenue of commerce, no longer just a pathway of nature. There are large black populations in the parishes along the river, vestiges of the days when this was Louisiana's great plantation country, and the planters walked down the lane from the mansion and supervised the loading of sugar and rice onto river ships for the trip to New Orleans and the world. Inland you find a large Cajun population: the 8th district includes the northern part of Louisiana's Cajun country.

The presence of the blacks and Cajuns makes this an atypical Louisiana district politically; aside from the 2d district in the New Orleans area, this is the closest thing in the state to a constituency which supports national Democratic policies. Oil is less important here than it is in other districts (though the 8th includes a small part, almost all black, of Baton Rouge), and the civil rights revolution seems to have met less resistance here than elsewhere in the state.

The 8th district elects a national Democratic congressman, Gillis Long. A distant cousin of Huey Long, he first won in 1962, then was beaten in 1964, by a cousin, Speedy Long; Gillis was deemed too liberal for the district then. But times changed, Speedy retired in 1972, and Gillis won again. Since then he has had some competition in elections but has not really been pressed. The minor changes made in redistricting, by adding black areas, have helped him marginally.

Gillis Long is now second ranking Democrat on the Rules Committee. This was once a major roadblock to liberal legislation; during Tip O'Neill's years as speaker, it has served as a loyal working arm of the Democratic leadership. Rules schedules legislation for debate, determines the extent to which it can be amended, and thus does much to determine the outcome. O'Neill, Rules Chairman Claude Pepper, and Long can remember the bad old days when Rules simply refused to let measures its members disliked come to the floor, and they have a strong bias against obstruction; they are not unwilling, however, to use Rules's powers to help the leadership in some circumstances.

Long holds another position which has been honorific in the past, but which he has made important: the chairmanship of the House Democratic Caucus. In that capacity he spent considerable time in 1981 and 1982 getting a committee of House Democrats to write a series of papers articulating new Democratic policies. It produced more than many expected; especially notable was the paper on long-term economic policy authored by Tim Wirth, Richard Gephardt, and Long himself. But some of its other contributions were only tired rehashes of old programs. Long seemed to think its greatest accomplishment was getting Democrats from diverse regions to agree on a single document, even if a somewhat general one. But for one who remembers the political history Long remembers, and who has suffered some of the defeats he has, that is a significant achievement.

Long obviously has a good chance to be Rules Chairman some day. In 1979 he abandoned a longtime dream and declined to run for governor of Louisiana; shortly afterward he suffered a heart attack and seems unlikely to undertake a statewide race. His current district seems entirely pleased, however, to reelect him indefinitely.

The People Pop. 1980: 524,861, up 10.4% 1970–80; voting age pop. 349,177; 36% Black, 1% Span. orig. 26% housing units rented. Median owner $32,600; renter $93. Households: 80% family, 49% with children, 63% married couples.

Presidential Vote

1980			
	Reagan (R)	84,264	(42%)
	Carter (D)	112,429	(56%)
	Anderson (I)	2,386	(1%)

Rep. Gillis W. Long (D) Elected 1972; b. May 4, 1923, Winnfield; home, Alexandria; LA St. U., B.A. 1959, J.D. 1951; Baptist.

Career Army, WWII; Legal Counsel, U.S. Senate Comm. on Small Business, 1951; Chf. Counsel, U.S. House of Reps. Spec. Comm. on Campaign Expenditures; U.S. House of Reps., 1963–65; Asst. Dir., U.S. Ofc. of Econ. Opp., 1965–66; Legis. Counsel, Natl. Commission on Urban Growth Policy, 1968–69; Practicing atty., 1970–72.

Offices 2185 RHOB, 202-225-4926. Also P.O. Box 410, Alexandria 71301, 318-487-4595.

Committees *Rules* (2d). Subcommittee: The Legislative Process (Chairman). *Joint Economic Committee* (Chairman). Subcommittee: International Trade, Finance and Security Economics (Chairman).

Group Ratings

	ADA	ACLU	COPE	CFA	LCV	LWV	NTU	NSI	COC	ACA	CSFC
1982	45	46	60	69	57	55	3	78	36	32	34
1981	40	—	58	50	64	—	51	—	33	29	39
1980	50	27	63	79	39	60	13	60	73	21	28

National Journal Ratings

	Economic		Foreign		Cultural	
1982	67%	(LIB)	53%	(LIB)	57%	(LIB)
	32%	(CONS)	47%	(CONS)	43%	(CONS)
1981	64%	(LIB)	57%	(LIB)	52%	(LIB)
	36%	(CONS)	42%	(CONS)	47%	(CONS)

Key Votes

1) Reagan 81 Budget	AGN	5) Incr SS Rtmt Age AGN
2) Reagan 81 Tax Cut	AGN	6) Saudi AWACS Sale AGN
3) Bal Budget Amend	AGN	7) $ for MX Missile AGN
4) Gas & Road Tax	—	8) Nerve Gas Prod AGN

9) Poor Pay Food Stamps   AGN
10) Ban Crt Busing Order   FOR
11) Auto Local Content   FOR
12) Nuclear Arms Freeze   —

Election Results

1982 primary	Gillis W. Long (D)	71,103	(60%)	($516,321)
	Edward G. Randolph, Jr. (D)	46,656	(39%)	($365,327)
1980 primary	Gillis W. Long (D)	75,433	(69%)	($223,493)
	Clyde C. Holloway (R)	27,816	(25%)	($44,635)
	One other (R)	6,243	(6%)	

Campaign Contributions and Expenditures

1981-82		Direct Cont. 81-82		PACS brkdwn			
Receipts	$476,954	Indiv	$232,949	Agr	$15,500	Ideo	$3,350
Expend.	$516,321	PACS	$155,915	Bus	$83,485	Lbr	$39,100
Unspent	$311,426			Hlth	$4,250	Prof	$8,500

MAINE

"As Maine goes, so goes the nation," our best-known political rule of thumb, has also long since proved one of the least accurate. For years everyone knew James A. Farley's now nearly 50-year-old response, after the 1936 Roosevelt landslide, "As Maine goes, so goes Vermont." The saying got started not because Maine was a bellwether but because up through the 1950s the state held its elections in September, on the sensible theory that they should not be held when the weather is likely to be inclement and the sky is certain to be dark before five o'clock. In those days before polls and projections, the early results from Maine were the closest thing we had to a forecast of the election outcome.

Actually, Maine's political behavior has been almost perfectly countercyclical in recent years. It is the only state to have voted for the losers in the last four close presidential elections; if Maine had had its way, Dewey would have won in 1948, Nixon in 1960, Humphrey in 1968, and Ford in 1976. And, although no one noticed it in the Republican landslide, it came close to going for the loser again in 1980, giving Reagan only a 46%–42% margin over Carter. In local elections as well, Maine has produced countercyclical results. Democrats captured the governorship and both the state's House seats in 1966, a Republican year elsewhere; and in Democratic 1974 Maine elected two Republican congressmen and the Democrats lost the governorship to a Republican running as an Independent. In 1978 Maine followed the national pattern and elected a Republican senator, but it also elected a Democratic governor; in 1982 the Democrats held their Senate seat but Republicans held the House seat their Senate candidate left open.

Maine has a demographic history something like that of Illinois. It was a frontier state much later than most people think: settlers moved not only west but northeast in search of new land and more space, and they found it—can still find it—in Maine, which has as much land area as the rest of New England put together. Set far east and north of the rest of the country, Maine was not admitted to the Union until 1820 (it was part of Massachusetts before that) and did not experience its greatest growth until the 1830s. Like the midwestern states settled at the same time, Maine has been a significant agricultural state; although the lands in the southern part of the state are stony and not very productive, Aroostook County in northern Maine is still one of our major producers of potatoes.

There were limits ultimately to the settlement of Maine, however—limits imposed more by the land than anything else. The growing season is too short, the weather too cold, and the products Maine can easily produce—lumber and potatoes—do not require large settlements of people. Maine never developed huge urban centers as the midwest (or Massachusetts) did. Maine reached a population of 600,000 before 1860, 700,000 about 1905, and 800,000 in the 1930s—extraordinarily low population growth that resulted from the outmigration of people and a steady aging of a once young population.

Since 1970 Maine has had its highest rate of population growth since the 1840s. But this growth has not really resulted in—or reflected—a buoyant local economy. Rather, it is part of a nationwide movement of retirees and younger people willing to settle for low dollar incomes into what used to be resort and vacation areas. The fastest population growth in Maine has come in counties along the coast, not in inland farming areas or the old mill towns; the people who come in are looking more for the physical environment and cultural attitudes they expect in Maine than they are for some chance at quick and substantial money. When you take into account local taxes and cost of living (which includes the very high cost of oil here), Maine arguably has the lowest level of disposable income of any state.

In its frontier days, Maine was settled mostly by Yankees from farther south in New England, and that accounts for the Republican preference that has characterized most of the state's political history. Later, in the 20th century, as the Yankee stock aged, Maine had other immigrants: French Canadians from Quebec especially, Irish from Ireland and Boston, Greeks attracted perhaps from their own rocky coasts to the much colder rocky coasts of Maine. As the years went by, Maine became increasingly less Protestant and less Republican, until finally the Democrats became competitive here. That time was reached when Edmund Muskie was elected governor in 1954 and senator in 1958—the first time Maine voters ever elected a Democratic senator. Muskie probably accelerated the process by which Maine became a two-party state: his craggy honesty, his braininess, his fervor made him something considerably more than the run-of-the-mill ethnic politician, and he proved attractive to Yankee as well as non-Yankee voters. And of course he was the symbol of the Democratic

Party here, through his years as senator (1959–80) and his emergence as vice presidential nominee (1968) and, for a moment, front-running presidential candidate (1971–72).

During the Muskie years Maine voters, in large numbers, also got into the habit of splitting their tickets. In 1972, for example, Maine voted heavily for Nixon but voted against longtime Republican Senator Margaret Chase Smith. In 1974 a plurality split off from both parties and voted for an Independent for governor. These ticket-splitting habits help account for Maine's volatility in presidential elections. Yankees are still generally Republican, and Catholics are still generally Democratic. But on a given day, almost anyone will vote the opposite side. So in 1982 Maine voters went 61% Democratic for senator and 58% Republican for its congressmen.

Governor. Maine's governor, Joseph Brennan, is a Democrat who won his second term in 1982. The issue which first brought him to voters' attention was Indian claims; as the state's attorney general, he resolutely opposed them and was against a compromise. On economic issues, however, he is far enough to the left that it seemed quite natural when he became the only governor to endorse Edward Kennedy's presidential candidacy in 1982. He is, in whatever direction, a pugnacious man who has made some enemies—but, apparently, more friends. Brennan boasted in 1982 of his record of no income tax increases; his Republican opponent called for income tax indexing. The Maine electorate voted 56% for indexing but 60% for Brennan.

Senators. Maine has two freshman senators, one Democrat and one Republican. The more senior is William Cohen, Republican, elected in 1978, up for reelection in 1984. He first became well known as a young congressman, when he was one of the Republicans on the House Judiciary Committee who voted for the impeachment of Richard Nixon. From that and the high percentage ratings he had from liberal rating groups, many concluded that he was one of those Republican liberals who, on most issues, are indistinguishable from Democrats. But in 1978 he took on a Democratic incumbent, beat him, and has seemed reasonably well at home in the Republican Senate of the 1980s.

The fact is that Cohen's issue positions are more complicated than single rating percentages suggest. On economic issues, he stands pretty well between the orthodoxies of the two parties. On the one hand he shares with most Republicans a faith in the free market mechanism. On the other, his experience growing up in modest circumstances and then serving as mayor in Bangor, a small city where most people live in straitened circumstances, inclines him to believe that government should help people out. On cultural issues, he is one of those East Coast Republicans who take positions which are generally considered liberal. But sometimes cultural issues are more complicated too. Consider the Lincoln-Dickey Dam, a local issue of great controversy in Maine for more than 20 years. Democrats and unions want to build the dam, to generate cheap hydroelectric power and provide jobs. Most Republicans, including Cohen, tend to oppose it, to keep government out of the utility business and to protect the environment. Which is the liberal or conservative position?

On foreign and military issues Cohen began his career when young Eastern Republicans were assumed to be skeptical of U.S. entanglements abroad and interested in cutting the defense budget. But when the Carter administration began cutting defense spending, Cohen came to have very different views. His 1978 opponent, William Hathaway, charged him with a politically convenient conversion and pointed out he had never served in the military. But in the years since Cohen has followed through on his campaign talk. He has served on the Armed Services Committee and has supported defense buildups. He is, however, not a rubber stamp for the Pentagon. He chairs the Seapower Committee and, with Gary Hart of Colorado, has argued for building more smaller ships rather than fewer big ones. He is also concerned, as any senator from Maine would be, to see that the Bath Iron Works in Bath, Maine, gets its share of shipbuilding contracts. The Navy likes to shift contracts to southern yards, like the inefficient Litton Shipyards in Pascagoula, Mississippi; Cohen insists on pointing out that Bath does better work.

Cohen also serves on the Governmental Affairs Committee, and chairs a Select Committee on Indian Affairs. Indian issues are important in Maine, where a small local tribe sued, claiming they still owned most of the state, and held out for large payments in return for relinquishing their claims; Cohen made a point in 1978 of opposing the Carter administration's offer as too generous.

Cohen runs for reelection in 1984. Unless the economy is in noticeably better shape than it was in 1982, he may be on the defensive for his support of major Reagan administration economic programs. It is possible as well that he will be attacked as too hawkish. Otherwise his issue positions seem popular in the state, and at 44 he should be a vigorous and attractive campaigner.

Nothing, however, should be taken for granted about a Maine Senate race. At the beginning of 1982, the Democratic senator universally regarded as having the least chance for reelection was George Mitchell of Maine. He was appointed to the seat (when Muskie resigned in 1980 to become secretary of state), not elected; he had never won an election (he was the Democrat who lost the governorship to Independent James Longley in 1974); he had a wooden speaking style and no ethnic appeal. And he was running against a proven vote-getter, former 1st district Congressman David Emery. Yet Mitchell ended up winning, with 61% of the vote.

One reason for that result was Mitchell's steady, judicial (he used to be a judge) conduct of the campaign. Another was a set of mistakes by the 34-year-old Emery and his campaign staff. The Emery campaign circulated a comparison of the ratings of each candidate by various groups. Mitchell's low ratings, however, resulted from the fact that he was not yet a senator in the period in question. But probably most important was the trend of opinion on national issues. Emery, a member of the House Armed Services Committee, specialized in military issues; but by the fall of 1982, Maine voters wanted defense spending held in check, not increased. Emery's record on environmental issues was highly rated by environmental groups; but he was running as the candidate of the party of James Watt, and they rallied to Mitchell's support. Most of all, in this economically depressed state, Mitchell could point to his support, in the Environment and Public Works Committee and on the floor, of measures to relieve unemployment and its effects, and could attack Emery as a supporter of Reaganomics. All these things came together and gave Mitchell the kind of majority his longtime patron, Edmund Muskie, used to enjoy.

In the Senate Mitchell has neither the seniority nor the requisite number of likeminded colleagues to be a really influential senator. He has the potential to make a mark, however. The very qualities which seemed to make him a weak candidate—his plodding, detailed approach to issues—gives him a natural advantage in a legislature most of whose members make pronouncements on matters to which they have devoted only a fleeting moment's study.

1st congressional district. The new congressman from the 1st district is Republican John McKernan. The district stretches from Democratic York County and the area around Portland, the state's largest city, to the craggy-shored ancestrally Republican counties farther east. The 1982 campaign there was a vivid contrast in the old-fashioned New England style. The Democratic candidate, John Kerry, of Irish descent, a state legislator and bar owner, favored more active government economic programs, and wanted to curb abortions. The Republican, John McKernan, a Yankee lawyer with an Ivy League education, and former legislator, favored less government, and opposed restrictions on abortions. Kerry carried the mill towns but ran far behind the Democrats at the top of the ticket; McKernan made inroads among culturally liberal Democrats without losing many Republicans.

McKernan is a member of the Merchant Marine and Fisheries and Government Operations Committees; he didn't get his first choice, Armed Services. And as of the beginning of 1983, the 34-year-old divorced McKernan and the 35-year-old widowed Snowe were social companions—the first time to anyone's recollection that members of a state delegation enjoyed such a relationship.

2d congressional district. Maine has two Republican House members. Olympia Snowe was elected in 1978 to replace Bill Cohen in the 2d district. Geographically the district covers the northern three-quarters of the state; in the more thickly populated part of Maine, however, the boundary line is actually rather jagged, and it takes in the heavily Democratic mill town of Lewiston as well as some more Republican coastal area down east. Snowe is a visceral partisan Republican, and her voting record reflects considerable fidelity to the Reagan economic programs. On cultural issues, she is more to the center; on foreign and defense issues, cautiously conservative. It is in the last that her committee work, as a member of the Foreign Affairs Committee, is concentrated. She is of Greek descent, and is one of the Congress's leading advocates of cutting military aid to Turkey.

Congressional districting. Maine's current redistricting was put through by Republicans who wanted to split Democratic strength between the two districts. Given the ticket-splitting propensity of Maine voters, it hasn't much mattered: the districts have on occasion elected two Democrats and, as at present, two Republicans. Technically, the state should have redistricted for the 1982 elections, since the 1st district is now 6% larger than the 2d. But no one forced the issue. Now the legislature and the governorship are both controlled by the Democrats, and so there is a chance for a partisan districting—perhaps putting Lewiston into the 1st district.

Presidential politics. Maine has no presidential primary and casts four electoral votes. Therefore it attracts little national attention in presidential years. Democrats and Republicans here did try to stage a non-binding state convention vote on the candidates before the New Hampshire primary and Iowa caucus, and attracted some attention. In the Republican contest, the failure of Howard Baker to prevail and the good showing of George Bush (in a state where he and his family have summered for years) helped to make Bush a major candidate and to shunt Baker aside. Even so, Maine didn't attract overwhelming attention; everyone knew the votes could, and would, change as the field got winnowed out and candidates won or lost the early primaries.

The People   Est. Pop. 1982: 1,133,000; Pop. 1980: 1,124,660, up 0.8% 1980–82 and 13.2% 1970–80; .49% of U.S. total, 38th largest; voting age pop. 803,273. Single ancestry: 23% English, 13% French, 5% Irish, 2% German, Scottish, 1% Italian, Polish, Swedish. Registered voters (1982): 766,285 Total. 15% with 1–3 yrs. col., 14% with 4+ yrs. col. 12.9% below poverty level. 23% housing units rented; median house value: $37,900; median monthly rent: $173. Households: 74% family, 41% with children, 63% married couples.

1982 Share of Federal Tax Burden $2,218,900,000; .37% of U.S. total, 42d largest.

1982 Share of Federal Expenditures

	Total		Non-Defense		Defense	
Total Expend	$3,100m	(0.51%)	$2,039m	(0.48%)	$1,060m	(0.59%)
St/Lcl Grants	527m	(0.60%)	527m	(0.60%)	0m	(0%)
Salary/Wages	257m	(0.33%)	56m	(0.20%)	201m	(0.40%)
Ind Payments	1,495m	(0.52%)	1,324m	(0.51%)	171m	(0.60%)
Procurement	810m	(0.56%)	25m	(0.08%)	785m	(0.69%)
Other Programs	11m	(0.20%)	11m	(0.20%)	0m	(0%)
Loan/Insurance	206m	(0.32%)	196m	(0.32%)	10m	(0.45%)

Political Lineup   Governor, Joseph E. Brennan (D). Senators, William S. Cohen (R) and George J. Mitchell (D). Representatives, 2 R. State Senate, 33 (23 D and 10 R); State House of Representatives, 151 (92 D and 59 R).

Presidential Vote

1980	Reagan (R)	238,522	(46%)
	Carter (D)	220,974	(42%)
	Anderson (I)	53,450	(10%)
1976	Ford (R)	236,320	(49%)
	Carter (D)	232,279	(48%)

SENATORS

Sen. William S. Cohen (R) Elected 1978, seat up 1984, b. Aug. 28, 1940, Bangor; home, Bangor; Bowdoin Col., B.A. 1962, Boston U., LL.B. 1965; Unitarian Universalist.

Career Practicing atty., 1965–72; Asst. Penobscot Cnty. Atty., 1968; Instructor, Husson Col., 1968; U. of ME, 1968–72; Bangor City Cncl., 1969–72, Mayor of Bangor, 1971–72; U.S. House of Reps., 1973–78.

Offices 530 HSOB, 202-224-2523. Also Fed. Bldg., Bangor 04401, 207-947-6504.

Committees *Armed Services* (6th). Subcommittees: Strategic and Theater Nuclear Forces; Sea Power and Force Projection (Chairman); Manpower and Personnel. *Governmental Affairs* (5th). Subcommittees: Permanent Subcommittee on Investigations; Energy, Nuclear Proliferation, and Government Processes; Oversight of Government Management (Chairman). *Select Committee on Intelligence* (8th). *Special Committee on Aging* (5th).

Group Ratings

	ADA	ACLU	COPE	CFA	LCV	LWV	NTU	NSI	COC	ACA	CSFC
1982	55	86	31	30	69	92	57	89	42	57	60
1981	35	—	31	50	72	—	43	—	76	61	70
1980	33	73	22	20	82	88	46	80	70	68	60

National Journal Ratings

	Economic		Foreign		Cultural	
1982	46%	(LIB)	3%	(LIB)	81%	(LIB)
	53%	(CONS)	84%	(CONS)	18%	(CONS)
1981	59%	(LIB)	1%	(LIB)	77%	(LIB)
	40%	(CONS)	85%	(CONS)	22%	(CONS)

Key Votes

1) Reagan 81 Budget	—	5) $ to El Salvador	FOR	9) Poor Pay Food Stamps	AGN
2) Reagan 81 Tax Cut	FOR	6) Saudi AWACS Sale	FOR	10) Ban Crt Busing Order	AGN
3) Bal Budget Amend	AGN	7) Ban Abortion	AGN	11) Clinch Riv Brdr Rctr	AGN
4) Gas & Road Tax	AGN	8) Nerve Gas Prod	FOR	12) Legal Services Corp	FOR

Election Results

1978 general	William S. Cohen (R)	212,294	(57%)	($648,739)
	William D. Hathaway (D)	127,327	(37%)	($423,027)
	Hayes Gahagan (I)	27,824	(7%)	($115,901)
1978 primary	William S. Cohen (R) unopposed			
1972 general	William D. Hathaway (D)	224,270	(53%)	($202,208)
	Margaret Chase Smith (R)	197,040	(47%)	($14,950)

Campaign Contributions and Expenditures

1977-78			*PACS brkdwn*		
Receipts	$658,254	Agr	$3,700	Ideo	$4,829
Expend.	$648,739	Bus	$124,772	Lbr	$6,100
Unspent	$9,514	Hlth	$12,900	Prof	$5,250

Sen. George J. Mitchell (D) Appointed May 1980, seat up 1988; b. Aug. 20, 1933, Waterville; home, Waterville; Bowdoin Col., B.A. 1954, Georgetown U., J.D. 1960; Roman Catholic.

Career Army Counterintelligence, 1954–56; U.S. Dept. of Justice, 1960–62; Asst. Atty., Cumberland Cnty., 1971; U.S. Atty. for ME, 1977–79; U.S. Dist. Judge for ME, 1979–80.

Offices 344 RSOB, 202-224-5344. Also P.O. Box 8300, 151 Forest Ave., Portland 01401, 207-722-1226; 5 Washington St., Biddeford 04005, 207-282-4144; 8 Lisbon St., Lewiston 04240, 207-784-0163; P.O. Box 1237, 202 Harlow St., Bangor 04401, 207-945-6024; P.O. Box 786, Fed. Bldg., 33 College Ave., Waterville 04901, 207-873-3361; 387 Main St., Rockland 04841, 207-596-0311; and 6 Church St., Presque Isle 04769, 207-833-7313.

Committees *Environment and Public Works* (6th). Subcommittees: Environmental Pollution; Nuclear Regulation; Regional and Community Development. *Finance* (8th). Subcommittees: Employment and Revenue Sharing; Health; International Trade. *Veterans' Affairs* (5th).

Group Ratings

	ADA	ACLU	COPE	CFA	LCV	LWV	NTU	NSI	COC	ACA	CSFC
1982	95	86	93	80	85	92	31	20	30	33	34
1981	90	—	89	57	72	—	30	—	35	19	36
1980	67	—	78	80	69	—	38	80	48	18	27

National Journal Ratings

	Economic		Foreign		Cultural	
1982	92%	(LIB)	70%	(LIB)	93%	(LIB)
	7%	(CONS)	29%	(CONS)	4%	(CONS)
1981	85%	(LIB)	84%	(LIB)	82%	(LIB)
	14%	(CONS)	12%	(CONS)	17%	(CONS)

Key Votes

1) Reagan 81 Budget	FOR	5) $ to El Salvador	AGN	9) Poor Pay Food Stamps	AGN
2) Reagan 81 Tax Cut	FOR	6) Saudi AWACS Sale	AGN	10) Ban Crt Busing Order	AGN
3) Bal Budget Amend	AGN	7) Ban Abortion	AGN	11) Clinch Riv Brdr Rctr	AGN
4) Gas & Road Tax	AGN	8) Nerve Gas Prod	AGN	12) Legal Services Corp	FOR

Election Results

1982 general	George J. Mitchell (D)	279,819	(61%)	($1,209,599)
	David F. Emery (R)	179,882	(39%)	($1,081,122)
1982 primary	George J. Mitchell (D)	68,169	(100%)	
1976 general	Edmund S. Muskie (D)	199,954	(60%)	($320,427)
	Robert A.G. Monks (R)	193,489	(40%)	($598,490)

Campaign Contributions and Expenditures

1981-82		*Direct Cont. 81-82*			*PACS brkdwn*		
Receipts	$1,218,350	Indiv	$619,439	Agr	$7,350	Ideo	$117,050
Expend.	$1,209,599	Party	$20,134	Bus	$164,620	Lbr	$209,547
Unspent	$8,523	PACS	$563,836	Hlth	$16,100	Prof	$21,280

Indirect Party Expend: $66,045   *Indep Expend*: For: $850   Agn: $7,168 (NCPAC, LIFEPAC)

GOVERNOR

Gov. Joseph E. Brennan (D) Elected 1978, term expires Jan. 1987; b. Nov. 2, 1934, Portland; home, Augusta; Boston Col., B.A., U. of ME, J.D.; Roman Catholic.

Career Practicing atty., ME House of Reps., 1965–71; Cumberland Cnty. Atty., 1971–73; ME Senate, 1973–75, Dem. Flr. Ldr.; Atty. Gen. of ME, 1975–78.

Offices State Capitol, Augusta 04330, 207-289-3531.

Election Results

1982 gen.	Joseph E. Brennan (D)	281,066	(61%)
	Charles L. Cragin (R)	172,949	(38%)
1982 prim.	Joseph E. Brennan (D)	56,990	(77%)
	Georgette B. Berube (D)	17,219	(23%)
1978 gen.	Joseph E. Brennan (D)	176,493	(48%)
	Linwood E. Palmer, Jr. (R) ...	126,862	(34%)
	Herman C. Frankland (I)	65,889	(18%)

FIRST DISTRICT

The People Pop. 1980: 581,185, up 17.2% 1970–80; voting age pop. 418,360; 24% housing units rented. Median owner $41,700; renter $185. Households: 73% family, 40% with children, 62% married couples.

Presidential Vote

1980	Reagan (R)	126,274	(46%)
	Carter (D)	117,613	(43%)
	Anderson (I)	30,889	(11%)

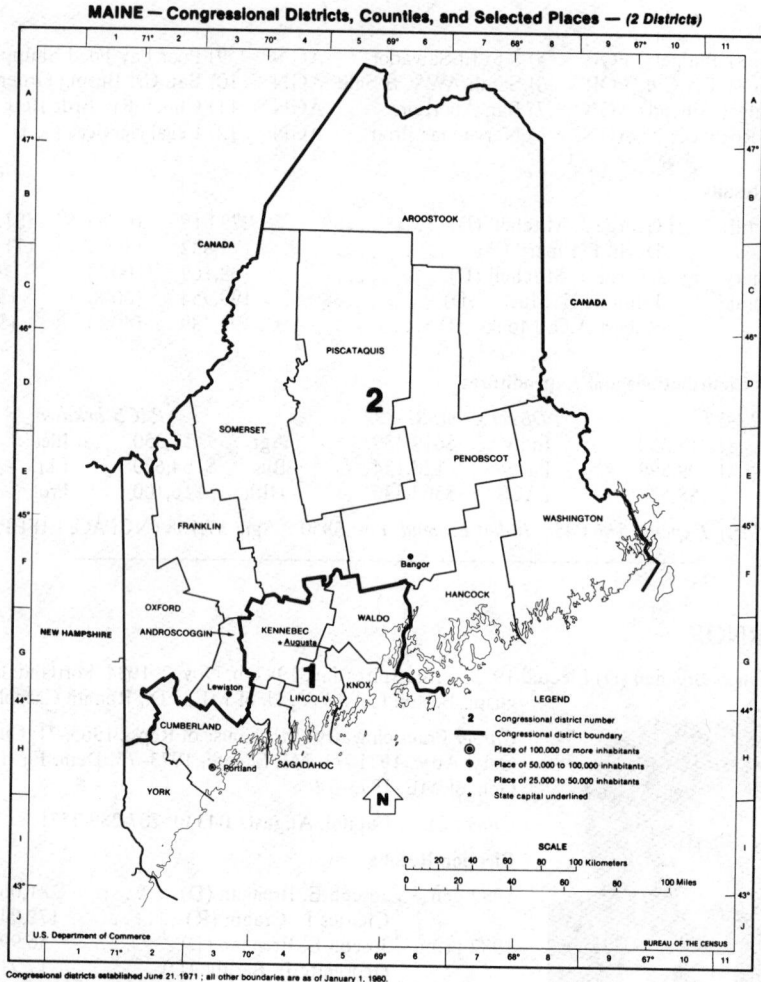

MAINE — Congressional Districts, Counties, and Selected Places — *(2 Districts)*

Rep. John R. McKernan, Jr. (R) Elected 1982; b. May 20, 1948, Bangor; home, Portland; Dartmouth Col., B.A. 1970, U. of ME, LL.B. 1974; Protestant.

Career ME House of Reps., 1972–76, Asst. Repub. Flr. Ldr., 1974–76; Practicing atty., 1976–82.

Offices 1428 LHOB, 202-225-6116. Also P.O. Box 10240, Portland 04104, 207-780-3381.

Committees *Government Operations* (10th). Subcommittee: Manpower and Housing. *Merchant Marine and Fisheries* (13th). Subcommittees: Fisheries and Wildlife Conservation and the Environment; Merchant Marine. *Select Committee on Children, Youth, and Families* (8th).

Group Ratings and Key Votes: Newly Elected

Election Results

1982 general	John R. McKernan, Jr. (R)	124,850	(50%)	($384,594)
	John M. Kerry (D)	118,884	(48%)	($288,924)
1982 primary	John R. McKernan, Jr. (R)	34,162	(77%)	
	Oram R. Lawry III (R)	9,968	(23%)	($34,319)
1980 general	David F. Emery (R)	188,667	(68%)	($247,509)
	Harold C. Pachios (D)	86,819	(32%)	($141,864)

Campaign Contributions and Expenditures

1981-82		Direct Cont. 81-82			PACS brkdwn			
Receipts	$387,073	Indiv	$206,733	Agr	$700	Ideo	$20,696
Expend.	$384,594	Party	$23,030	Bus	$83,974	Lbr	$—
Unspent	$2,479	PACS	$114,360	Hlth	$1,550	Prof	$4,500
		Cand	$41,196				

Indirect Party Expend: $34,300   *Indep Expend:* For: $2,397 (NRA)

SECOND DISTRICT

The People   Pop. 1980: 543,475, up 9.1% 1970–80; voting age pop. 384,913; 22% housing units rented. Median owner $33,700; renter $161. Households: 76% family, 42% with children, 64% married couples.

Presidential Vote

1980	Reagan (R)	112,248	(47%)
	Carter (D)	103,361	(43%)
	Anderson (I)	22,438	(9%)

Rep. Olympia J. Snowe (R) Elected 1978; b. Feb. 21, 1947, Augusta; home, Auburn; U. of ME, B.A. 1969; Eastern Orthodox.

Career Dist. Ofc. Mgr. for U.S. Rep. William S. Cohen, 1973; ME House of Reps., 1973–76; ME Senate, 1977–78.

Offices 133 CHOB, 202-225-6306. Also Fed. Bldg., Rm. 232, Bangor 04401, 207-942-4198.

Committees *Foreign Affairs* (14th). Subcommittees: Africa; Europe and the Middle East. *Small Business* (7th). Subcommittee: Tax, Access to Equity Capital and Business Opportunities. *Select Committee on Aging* (9th). Subcommittee: Human Services.

Group Ratings

	ADA	ACLU	COPE	CFA	LCV	LWV	NTU	NSI	COC	ACA	CSFC
1982	50	42	44	69	61	83	61	80	57	43	44
1981	45	—	45	50	43	—	67	—	89	67	60
1980	28	47	33	36	57	67	37	67	82	75	64

National Journal Ratings

	Economic		Foreign		Cultural	
1982	41%	(LIB)	62%	(LIB)	83%	(LIB)
	58%	(CONS)	38%	(CONS)	17%	(CONS)
1981	40%	(LIB)	48%	(LIB)	58%	(LIB)
	59%	(CONS)	51%	(CONS)	42%	(CONS)

Key Votes

1) Reagan 81 Budget	FOR	5) Incr SS Rtmt Age	FOR	9) Poor Pay Food Stamps	AGN
2) Reagan 81 Tax Cut	FOR	6) Saudi AWACS Sale	AGN	10) Ban Crt Busing Order	—
3) Bal Budget Amend	FOR	7) $ for MX Missile	AGN	11) Auto Local Content	AGN
4) Gas & Road Tax	AGN	8) Nerve Gas Prod	AGN	12) Nuclear Arms Freeze	FOR

Election Results

1982 general	Olympia J. Snowe (R)	136,075	(67%)	($182,701)
	James Patrick Dunleavy (D)	68,086	(33%)	($29,221)
1982 primary	Olympia J. Snowe (R)	33,562	(100%)	
1980 general	Olympia J. Snowe (R)	186,406	(79%)	($187,934)
	Harold J. Silverman (D)	51,026	(21%)	($20,947)

Campaign Contributions and Expenditures

1981-82		Direct Cont. 81-82		PACS brkdwn			
Receipts	$179,693	Indiv	$101,747	Agr	$1,200	Ideo	$3,300
Expend.	$182,701	Party	$14,572	Bus	$32,400	Lbr	$3,500
Unspent	$2,699	PACS	$42,862	Hlth	$2,150	Prof	$—
		Cand	$12,000				

MARYLAND

Looking at Maryland on a map of the United States, you would hardly think that this small state was so diverse; you might even wonder how such an attenuated bit of land could end up in the same state at all. Maryland owes its shape to the fact that it was settled when the chief form of transportation was by water, not land; Maryland's first white settlers moved up the Chesapeake and the broad tidal rivers that flow into it. Its borders were extended westward to the headwaters of one of the largest of those rivers, the Potomac; and so today you can drive 350 miles wholly within a state which ranks only 42d in area. In that distance you move from the south-of-the-Mason–Dixon-Line Eastern Shore, through the booming suburbs (and some dreary ones) of Baltimore and Washington, and up into the Appalachian Mountains. Tiny Maryland has just about every kind of people—northerners and southerners, blacks and ethnics, civil servants and Chesapeake Bay watermen—almost all the diversity of the United States compressed into one small package.

The very diversity of this state has made it hard to establish a single identity. It was most successful at doing this 50 years ago, when H. L. Mencken was extolling the virtues of the pleasant life of his native city in the *Baltimore Sun*. Maryland was then a kind of city-state: 49% of its residents lived in the closely packed, rowhouse-lined streets of Baltimore, with most of the rest spread in two distinct hinterlands, the southern-oriented counties of both shores of the Chesapeake and the northern-accented wheat-growing country around the antique small cities of Frederick and Hagerstown and the mountain-bound industrial city of Cumberland. Maryland was then a place tolerant of regional eccentricities: Prohibition was enforced only laxly in Baltimore; slot machines were legal in the rural counties of the Western Shore; the state's old law guaranteeing blacks equal access to public accommodations specifically excluded the Eastern Shore.

Today Maryland is quite different. Only 19% of its people live in the city of Baltimore, and the Eastern Shore and western counties have a much smaller share of the state's population than they did 50 years ago. Most Marylanders now live in suburban communities, 52% in suburban counties around Baltimore and 29% in the two suburban counties around Washington, D.C. Just 40 miles apart, these two metropolitan areas could hardly be more different. Baltimore is a major port with big shipbuilding companies and the nation's largest steel mill. Its heavy industries attracted a large number of America's second wave (1840–1924) immigrants like other big East Coast cities, as well as a large black migration from southern states and rural Maryland; yet Baltimore today is, for reasons no one entirely understands, economically more vibrant than most other industrial, heavily ethnic northeastern cities. Washington, whose economy has always been based on government, was a boom town in the 1960s and 1970s, and much of its growth has taken place in the Maryland suburbs, where high-rise office buildings and apartment complexes stand in what was pasture land a few years ago. As civil service salaries rose, the Washington suburbs in Montgomery County came to have the highest median incomes in the country; as government grew bigger, Washington developed a vigorous private economy of lawyers, lobbyists, consultants, trade associations, government contractors (including the so-called Beltway bandits), all paying high professional salaries. With the Reagan budget cuts of the early 1980s, growth in the Washington area perceptibly slowed, but income levels still remained among the highest in the nation.

Maryland's diversity made the state a good indicator of trends in presidential elections; from 1960 to 1976 it came as close as any state to duplicating the national results. Then in 1980 it was one of only six states to go for Jimmy Carter. One reason was the southern white vote, not only on the Eastern Shore but in many suburban areas as well; while Carter did not get enough such votes to carry more than one rural county, he did better here than among similar voters of more northerly origins in other East Coast cities. A second reason for Carter's better showing here is Maryland's relatively large number of blacks. Now nearly one in four Marylanders (23% in 1980) are black, largely because many Washington area blacks have moved out from the District of Columbia to Prince George's County and, though much less often, to Montgomery County as well. The black percentage will likely increase, even if that migration slows down, because 27% of Maryland's under-18 population in 1980 was black. Finally, there is still a working-class vote in Baltimore and its suburbs that went for Carter in 1976 and 1980. It is worth noting, finally, one fact that apparently was not of great help to Carter: Maryland's large number of federal employees. There is little evidence in the election returns that Reagan's advocacy of spending cuts repelled these voters: Reagan carried Montgomery County and the white vote in Prince George's County as well.

In state politics Maryland's growth, and the lack of local roots for so many of its citizens, have made this a state volatile in its partisan preferences and one which has produced more than its share of political corruption. Maryland typically votes heavily Democratic in statewide races, as it did in 1982. But when the Democrats have a particular problem, or when a liberal Republican like Senator Charles Mathias is running, the state is quite ready to go for the minority party. As for corruption, two successive governors—Spiro Agnew and Marvin Mandel—ended their political careers in disgrace, as have numerous county executives and some state legislators. The evidence suggests, however, that paying off local and state officials is no longer standard operating procedure in Maryland.

Governor. Maryland's governor, Harry Hughes, is one of the nation's most experienced state politicians. Yet he came to office in most voters' eyes as a novice and a new face, and he retains a nonpolitical image which works to his advantage. Hughes served in the legislature in the 1950s and 1960s and, as a representative of the Eastern Shore had the courage to support civil rights measures. He was transportation secretary in Marvin Mandel's administration, but left it before scandal broke. He entered the 1978 gubernatorial race as an unknown, with little money, running against Acting Governor Blair Lee III, Mandel's lieutenant governor and member of an old aristocrat family, and Baltimore County Executive Ted Venetoulis. When the *Baltimore Sun* endorsed Hughes, he suddenly took the lead; voters wanted a change from Lee, and Venetoulis's own constituents disliked him. It was one of the few instances of a newspaper editorial changing the outcome of an election, and it happened because Hughes was running in effect in a vacuum.

As governor, Hughes has been mostly uncontroversial. In his first few years, he had some rocky moments over budget and prison issues, but by the time he ran for reelection in 1982 things were running smoothly. Some of the credit for that should go to the legislature, especially Speaker Benjamin Cardin of Baltimore, one of the most talented young legislative leaders in the nation. Hughes had opposition in the primary from some disgruntled politicians and in the general from Anne Arundel County Executive Robert Pascal; his greatest potential problem was the fact that Baltimore Mayor Donald Schaefer—who is very popular both inside and beyond his city—dislikes him. But Schaefer, one of the nation's most effective mayors, knows that he is typecast for his current office not the governorship. And since there was little popular discontent with Hughes, he was reelected easily.

Senators. Also reelected easily in 1982 was Maryland's Democratic Senator Paul Sarbanes. That his victory would be so easy was not always predicted. Sarbanes, a hard worker in the Senate, has disdain for using the advantages of incumbency to get favorable publicity. He declines to introduce bills with attractive titles which will never get anywhere; he doesn't send videotape cassettes of his comments on the issues of the day to all local television stations; although he prides himself on continuing to live in Baltimore, where he served three terms as congressman, and commutes there every day, he does not have a high profile in the city. His voting record on issues is among the most liberal in the Senate, although by nature he is a cautious and careful man, averse to making a decision until he has studied an issue closely. So he was a natural target in early 1981 for the National Conservative Political Action Committee, still buoyant from the results of the 1980 elections. NCPAC hoped that, by running negative, anti-Sarbanes ads on Washington television, it could put him on the defensive and also put the fear of Reagan if not God into other Democratic officeholders up for reelection in 1982.

The result was almost precisely the opposite. Sarbanes, loath to start up a campaign early, suddenly found himself the recipient of contributions from NCPAC opponents all over the country. He himself considered the very tactic of negative advertising an illegitimate one, and made NCPAC—which in some races had been careless with facts—the real focus of the campaign. Rather than weakening Sarbanes's campaign, NCPAC strengthened him, to the point that his eventual Republican opponent, Prince George's County Executive Larry Hogan, was surely sincere when he said he wished NCPAC had not entered the race. By the time the general election campaign started Sarbanes was so far ahead it was no contest; moreover, Hogan's controversial nature and the Democratic strength in Prince George's meant he did not even have a reliable home base.

Sarbanes remains part of the minority in the Senate. He has a seat on the Banking Committee and is ranking minority member on one of its intellectually most demanding and politically least rewarding subcommittees, Securities. He receives more notice on Foreign Relations, where he is an intellectual leader of the usually outnumbered liberals wary of increased arms spending and U.S. military involvement abroad. Of Greek descent, Sarbanes was a leader in the long effort to impose an arms embargo on Turkey because of its invasion of Cyprus.

Maryland's senior senator is Charles (Mac) Mathias. From an old family in Frederick County, he was a liberal Republican congressman from a district including Montgomery County in the 1960s and was elected to the Senate in 1968. Mathias is the old-fashioned kind of Republican for whom one of the party's main attractions is its historic record on civil rights; he also, for a man who is skeptical of government involvement in the free market, comes down a large percentage of the time in favor of economic measures supported by most Democrats and the labor movement. Mathias was not a part of the Republican unity otherwise so apparent in 1980. His perfunctory endorsement of Ronald Reagan and his evident distaste for Reagan's cause made him the least pro-Reagan of Republican senators, except perhaps Lowell Weicker.

As a result, Mathias does not have the kind of committee positions one would expect of a senator of his seniority. Back before the Republicans got a Senate majority, Strom Thurmond made a point of giving up his ranking seat on Armed Services and taking it on Judiciary instead, to keep Mathias out; in 1981 Thurmond even abolished the Antitrust Subcommittee Mathias would have headed. Mathias was persuaded to give up a third-ranking seat on Appropriations to take a middle-rank position on Foreign Relations. Even there he has caused the administration some problems, as when he voted against the nomination of Kenneth Adelman to be arms negotiator in early 1983. Mathias chairs the Rules and Administration Committee, a body ordinarily of little importance. It does, however, handle campaign finance legislation, which may become important by 1984, and it passes on nominees to fill vacancies in the vice presidency. He also chairs the subcommittee with jurisdiction over the District of Columbia—a politically useful post for a Maryland senator, although Mathias believes in letting the District government conduct its own affairs.

During the Nixon administration, Mathias was a key senator on any number of issues, and his views were regularly sought and widely respected. In the first part of the Reagan administration, he seemed out of the mainstream of events. In all, he seems temperamentally more attuned to the role of judicious, careful critic than to the job of advocate for any administration; and if the Senate becomes more closely divided on issues, if Howard Baker's ability to muster a disciplined Republican majority fades, then Mathias may find his vote and his advice crucial again.

Congressional districting. Because of population loss in the inner city of Baltimore, Maryland had to change its district lines considerably, though the nucleus of each district stayed the same. The one incumbent really hurt was Clarence Long of Baltimore County, but his problem may be more age (76 in 1984) than partisan tilt.

Presidential politics. Maryland for some years was a close battleground in presidential general elections, and much hinged on the turnout in Baltimore, where providing "walking around money" to local politicos was and is standard practice. But now the best way to win votes is to advertise on Baltimore and Washington TV, and in any case Maryland seems to be leaning heavily toward the Democrats.

Maryland does, however, have a presidential primary in May. In the past, because of its late filing date, it has been the beginning of a kind of second round of contests. George Wallace did well here in 1964 and won (the day after he was shot) in 1972; Jerry Brown won his first primary here in 1976. Why these odd results? Perhaps because, by the time the candidates reached Maryland, it was already pretty apparent who was going to win; people could vote freely for any oddball candidate, and not worry that he actually might win the nomination itself. It has become a primary then for sending a message, not for selecting a presidential candidate.

The People   Est. Pop. 1982: 4,265,000; Pop. 1980: 4,216,975, up 1.1% 1980–82 and 7.5% 1970–80; 1.9% of U.S. total, 19th largest; voting age pop. 3,049,445; 21% Black, 1% Spanish origin, 1% Asian origin. Single ancestry: 10% English, 9% German, 4% Irish, 2% Italian, Polish, 1% Russian, French. Registered voters (1982): 1,968,498 Total. 1,360,233 D (69%); 463,761 R (24%); 144,504 others (7%). 15% with 1–3 yrs. col., 20% with 4+ yrs. col. 9.9% below poverty level. 35% housing units rented; median house value: $59,200; median monthly rent: $222. Households: 75% family, 42% with children, 59% married couples.

1982 Share of Federal Tax Burden $12,478,100,000; 2.09% of U.S. total; 14th largest.

1982 Share of Federal Expenditures

	Total		Non-Defense		Defense	
Total Expend	$15,065m	(2.50%)	$9,961m	(2.35%)	$5,104m	(2.85%)
St/Lcl Grants	1,793m	(2.03%)	1,793m	(2.03%)	0m	(0%)
Salary/Wages	3,622m	(4.64%)	1,949m	(7.12%)	1,673m	(3.30%)
Ind Payments	5,463m	(1.91%)	4,880m	(1.90%)	583m	(2.04%)
Procurement	4,086m	(2.80%)	1,016m	(3.22%)	3,070m	(2.69%)
Other Programs	101m	(1.87%)	101m	(1.88%)	0m	(0%)
Loan/Insurance	592m	(0.93%)	523m	(0.85%)	69m	(3.14%)

Political Lineup   Governor, Harry R. Hughes (D). Senators, Charles McC. Mathias, Jr. (R) and Paul S. Sarbanes (D). Representatives, 8 (7 D and 1 R). State Senate, 47 (41 D and 6 R); State House of Delegates, 141 (124 D and 17 R).

Presidential Vote

1980	Reagan (R)	680,606	(44%)
	Carter (D)	726,161	(47%)
	Anderson (I)	119,537	(8%)
1976	Ford (R)	672,661	(47%)
	Carter (D)	759,612	(53%)

1980 Democratic Presidential Primary			*1980 Republican Presidential Primary*		
Carter	226,528	(47%)	Reagan	80,557	(48%)
Kennedy	181,091	(38%)	Bush	68,389	(41%)
Three others	23,592	(5%)	Anderson	16,244	(10%)
Uncommitted	45,879	(10%)	Crane..............	2,113	(1%)

SENATORS

Sen. Charles McC. Mathias, Jr. (R) Elected 1968, seat up 1986; b. July 24, 1922, Frederick; home, Frederick; Haverford Col., B.A. 1944, U. of MD, LL.B. 1949; Episcopal.

Career Navy, WWII; Asst. Atty. Gen. of MD, 1953–54; Frederick City Atty., 1954–59; MD House of Delegates, 1959–60; U.S. House of Reps., 1961–69.

Offices 387A RSOB, 202-224-4654. Also 1616 Fed. Ofc. Bldg., 31 Hopkins Plaza, Baltimore 21201, 301-962-4850.

Committees *Foreign Relations* (5th). Subcommittees: International Economic Policy (Chairman); African Affairs; European Affairs. *Governmental Affairs* (4th). Subcommittees: Permanent Subcommittee on Investigations; Governmental Efficiency and the District of Columbia (Chairman); Civil Service, Post Office, and General Services. *Judiciary* (2d). Subcommittees: Immigration and Refugee Policy; Juvenile Justice; Patents, Copyrights and Trademarks (Chairman). *Rules and Administration* (Chairman). *Joint Committee on the Library* (Chairman). *Joint Committee on Printing* (Vice-Chairman).

Group Ratings

	ADA	ACLU	COPE	CFA	LCV	LWV	NTU	NSI	COC	ACA	CSFC
1982	65	82	75	30	43	82	27	33	33	14	40
1981	50	—	77	36	71	—	21	—	46	14	53
1980	72	80	100	60	62	71	18	33	46	8	28

National Journal Ratings

	Economic		Foreign		Cultural	
1982	45%	(LIB)	98%	(LIB)	83%	(LIB)
	54%	(CONS)	1%	(CONS)	15%	(CONS)
1981	80%	(LIB)	67%	(LIB)	99%	(LIB)
	19%	(CONS)	32%	(CONS)	0%	(CONS)

Key Votes

1) Reagan 81 Budget	FOR	5) $ to El Salvador	AGN
2) Reagan 81 Tax Cut	AGN	6) Saudi AWACS Sale	FOR
3) Bal Budget Amend	AGN	7) Ban Abortion	AGN
4) Gas & Road Tax	FOR	8) Nerve Gas Prod	AGN

9) Poor Pay Food Stamps	AGN
10) Ban Crt Busing Order	AGN
11) Clinch Riv Brdr Rctr	FOR
12) Legal Services Corp	—

Election Results

1980 general	Charles McC. Mathias, Jr. (R)	850,970	(66%)	($841,446)
	Edward T. Conroy (D)	435,118	(34%)	($46,456)
1980 primary	Charles McC. Mathias, Jr. (R)	82,430	(55%)	
	John M. Brennan (R)	24,848	(17%)	($73,338)
	V. Dallas Merrell (R)	23,073	(13%)	($71,448)
	Three others (R)	19,622	(13%)	
1974 general	Charles McC. Mathias, Jr. (R)	503,223	(57%)	($329,845)
	Barbara A. Mikulski (D)	374,563	(43%)	($74,311)

Campaign Contributions and Expenditures

1979-80		PACS brkdwn			
Receipts	$867,986	Agr	$4,825	Ideo	$13,924
Expend.	$841,446	Bus	$114,160	Lbr	$142,050
Unspent	$26,538	Hlth	$8,800	Prof	$8,625

Sen. Paul S. Sarbanes (D) Elected 1976, seat up 1988; b. Feb. 3, 1933, Salisbury; home, Baltimore; Princeton U., B.A. 1954, Rhodes Scholar, Oxford U., B.A. 1957, Harvard U., LL.B. 1960; Eastern Orthodox.

Career Law Clerk to Judge Morris A. Soper, U.S. 4th Circuit Ct. of Appeals, 1960–61; Practicing atty., 1961–62, 1965–71; A. A. to Chmn. Walter W. Heller of the Pres. Cncl. of Econ. Advisers, 1962–63; Exec. Dir., Baltimore Charter Revision Comm., 1963–64; MD House of Delegates, 1969–70; U.S. House of Reps., 1971–77.

Offices 237 DSOB, 202-224-4524. Also 1518 Fed. Ofc. Bldg., Baltimore 21201, 301-962-4436; and 344 E. 33d St., Baltimore 21218, 301-962-4436.

Committees *Banking, Housing and Urban Affairs* (4th). Subcommittees: Housing and Urban Affairs; Insurance; Securities. *Foreign Relations* (4th). Subcommittees: International Economic Policy; European Affairs; Near Eastern and South Asian Affairs. *Joint Economic Committee* (4th). Subcommittees: Investment, Jobs, and Prices; Monetary and Fiscal Policy.

Group Ratings

	ADA	ACLU	COPE	CFA	LCV	LWV	NTU	NSI	COC	ACA	CSFC
1982	85	86	97	93	91	100	4	13	15	19	29
1981	95	—	97	64	88	—	8	—	11	10	28
1980	83	90	94	87	85	90	16	10	36	0	20

National Journal Ratings

	Economic		Foreign		Cultural	
1982	96%	(LIB)	82%	(LIB)	96%	(LIB)
	3%	(CONS)	17%	(CONS)	3%	(CONS)
1981	90%	(LIB)	84%	(LIB)	82%	(LIB)
	8%	(CONS)	12%	(CONS)	17%	(CONS)

Key Votes

1) Reagan 81 Budget	AGN	5) $ to El Salvador	AGN	9) Poor Pay Food Stamps	AGN
2) Reagan 81 Tax Cut	FOR	6) Saudi AWACS Sale	AGN	10) Ban Crt Busing Order	AGN
3) Bal Budget Amend	AGN	7) Ban Abortion	AGN	11) Clinch Riv Brdr Rctr	AGN
4) Gas & Road Tax	AGN	8) Nerve Gas Prod	—	12) Legal Services Corp	FOR

Election Results

1982 general	Paul S. Sarbanes (D)	707,356	(63%)	($1,623,533)
	Lawrence J. Hogan (R)	407,334	(37%)	($90,976)
1982 primary	Paul S. Sarbanes (D)	432,931	(81%)	
	Eight others (D)	100,985	(19%)	
1976 general	Paul S. Sarbanes (D)	772.101	(57%)	($891,533)
	J. Glenn Beall, Jr. (R)	530,439	(39%)	($572,016)
	Bruce Bradley (I)	62,750	(5%)	

Campaign Contributions and Expenditures

1979-82		*Direct Cont. 81-82*		*PACS brkdwn*			
Receipts	$1,632,112	Indiv	$1,089,539	Agr	$16,275	Ideo	$64,383
Expend.	$1,623,533	Party	$17,500	Bus	$80,590	Lbr	$274,906
Unspent	$8,637	PACS	$463,287	Hlth	$4,700	Prof	$5,600

Indirect Party Expend: $45,000   *Indep Expend:* For: $30,351 (ProPAC, DEM80s) Agn: $697,763 (NCPAC, LIFEPAC)

GOVERNOR

Gov. Harry R. Hughes (D) Elected 1978, term expires Jan. 1987; b. Nov. 13, 1926, Easton; home, Annapolis; U. of MD, B.S. 1949, Geo. Wash. U., LL.B. 1952; Episcopal.

Career Navy Air Corps, WWII; Practicing atty.; MD House of Delegates, 1955–58; MD Senate, 1959–70, Major. Ldr., 1965-70; Chmn., Dem. Party of MD., 1969–70; Dir., MD Dept. of Transportation, 1971–77.

Offices Executive Dept., State House, Annapolis 21404, 301-269-3591.

Election Results

1982 gen.	Harry R. Hughes (D)	705,910	(62%)
	Robert A. Pascal (R)	432,826	(38%)
1982 prim.	Harry R. Hughes (D)	393,244	(67%)
	Harry J. McGuirk (D)	129,049	(22%)
	Harry W. Kelley (D)	61,271	(10%)
1978 gen.	Harry R. Hughes (D)	718,328	(71%)
	J. Glenn Beall, Jr. (R)	293,635	(29%)

FIRST DISTRICT

The Chesapeake Bay is unique among American waterways. It is as if the lower part of a large river were flooded—and stayed flooded. The Chesapeake is, in effect, the lower part of Pennsylvania's Susquehanna River, and the Bay's tidal waters turn small streams like the Patuxent and the Choptank into wide estuaries. The rivers leading off from the Chesapeake, on either side, were the most thickly settled part of the American colonies in the 17th century; the Bay was the avenue by which the rich tobacco crops of Maryland and Virginia reached the world. On the Western Shore of the Chesapeake and its branch river the Potomac have grown two of America's metropolises, Baltimore and Washington. But on the lower part of the Western Shore, and on the whole Eastern Shore, life in many respects has not changed for many years.

Neither had many immigrants since the first wave of American immigration (1640–1720) was over; both sent many of their children west to make their livings. There are a surprisingly small number of family names here, and population growth was low, scarcely more than doubling on the Eastern Shore between 1790 and 1970. The Western Shore was first settled by the Catholics for whom Maryland was founded as a religious haven, and there still is a Catholic influence here; also, the area has its own peculiarities, such as the slot machines which were legal for many years. The Eastern Shore was southern segregationist country and still has many blacks. It remains a region of southern drowsiness, chicken farms, fishing villages, and, on the necks of land that jut into the bay, big estates of some of the nation's richest families. It is also an area that has produced more than its share of Maryland's politicians, including Governor Harry Hughes and Senator Paul Sarbanes.

The 1st congressional district of Maryland includes the whole Eastern Shore, the Western Shore counties below Annapolis and the Washington suburbs, and part of suburban Baltimore's Harford County. These areas have a reputation for being Democratic; actually, in congressional and national elections, they have been voting mostly Republican since the 1950s. In the last few years the 1st district has been the scene of some of the nation's least ele-

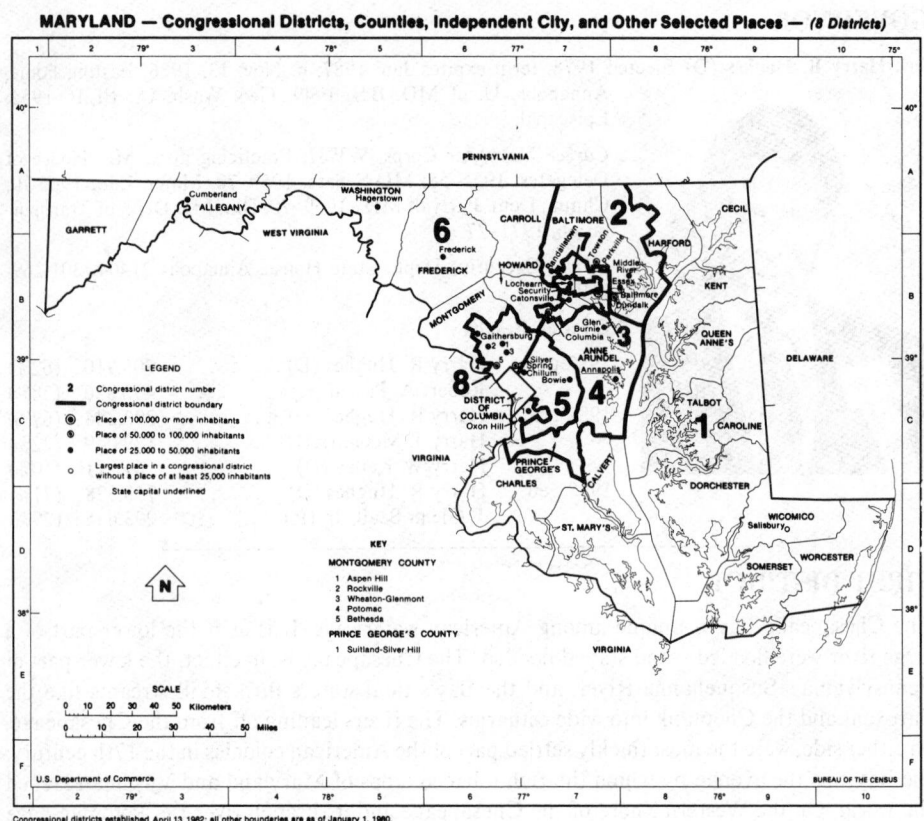

Congressional districts established April 13, 1982; all other boundaries are as of January 1, 1980.

vating congressional races. The district seemed securely represented by Robert Bauman, a brilliant parliamentarian and acerbic critic of the House Democratic leadership; he won elections here easily, and seemed destined for a place in the Republican leadership. But in October 1980 he was charged in Washington with soliciting sex from a 16-year-old boy. Bauman, who had ridiculed supporters of "gay rights" legislation, said his acts resulted from acute alcoholism, and sought professional help. However, he had never been known to have a drinking problem, he had been acting in a way that seemed to court discovery, and he behaved after his exposure with the look of a man somehow liberated.

Bauman's quandary split conservative activists and cost him enough votes to elect Roy Dyson, a Maryland legislator who had run for the seat before with poor results. In 1982, Bauman again dominated the headlines, by filing for the Republican nomination; he withdrew after the deadline, charging that the eventual nominee, Porter Hopkins, was making "scurrilous personal attacks." Hopkins's aggressive campaign got nowhere against Dyson, whose record on cultural and foreign issues was solidly conservative and whose record on economic issues was only liberal enough to give him a good basis for attacking Reaganomics. Given the odd circumstances attending each of his two victories, Dyson cannot be assured of having a safe seat. Dyson sits on two committees where his views are in line with those of solid majorities: Armed Services, where he tends to support Pentagon requests, and Merchant Marine and Fisheries, where he supports maritime subsidies.

The People Pop. 1980: 526,206, up 21.7% 1970–80; voting age pop. 369,721; 17% Black, 1% Span. orig., 1% Asian orig. 23% housing units rented. Median owner $49,500; renter $159. Households: 78% family, 45% with children, 65% married couples.

Presidential Vote

1980	Reagan (R)	86,525	(52%)
	Carter (D)	71,907	(43%)
	Anderson (I)	8,879	(5%)

Rep. Roy Dyson (D) Elected 1980; b. Nov. 15, 1948, Great Mills; home, Great Mills; U. of Baltimore, 1970, U. of MD, 1971; Roman Catholic.

Career Legis. Asst., Agr. Labor Subcom., U.S. House of Reps., 1973–74; MD House of Delegates, 1974–80; Dem. Nominee for U.S. House of Reps., 1976.

Offices 224 CHOB, 202-225-5311. Also 20 E. Fulford Ave., Bel Air 21014, 301-838-2063; 1 Plaza E., Su. 703, Salisbury 21801, 301-742-9070; Waldorf Five Ctr., Su. 105, Rte. 5, Waldorf 20601, 301-645-4844.

Committees Armed Services (20th). Subcommittees: Procurement and Military Nuclear Systems; Seapower and Strategic and Critical Materials. *Merchant Marine and Fisheries* (17th). Subcommittees: Merchant Marine; Fisheries and Wildlife Conservation and the Environment.

Group Ratings

	ADA	ACLU	COPE	CFA	LCV	LWV	NTU	NSI	COC	ACA	CSFC
1982	35	25	79	54	64	33	27	100	43	39	41
1981	30	—	80	43	29	—	19	—	47	58	52

National Journal Ratings

	Economic		Foreign		Cultural	
1982	50%	(LIB)	46%	(LIB)	36%	(LIB)
	50%	(CONS)	54%	(CONS)	64%	(CONS)
1981	59%	(LIB)	18%	(LIB)	39%	(LIB)
	41%	(CONS)	73%	(CONS)	60%	(CONS)

Key Votes

1) Reagan 81 Budget	AGN	5) Incr SS Rtmt Age	AGN	9) Poor Pay Food Stamps	AGN
2) Reagan 81 Tax Cut	FOR	6) Saudi AWACS Sale	AGN	10) Ban Crt Busing Order	FOR
3) Bal Budget Amend	FOR	7) $ for MX Missile	AGN	11) Auto Local Content	FOR
4) Gas & Road Tax	FOR	8) Nerve Gas Prod	FOR	12) Nuclear Arms Freeze	AGN

Election Results

1982 general	Roy Dyson (D)	89,503	(69%)	($195,330)
	C. A. Porter Hopkins (R)	39,656	(31%)	($222,472)
1982 primary	Roy Dyson (D) unopposed			
1980 general	Roy Dyson (D)	97,743	(52%)	($162,017)
	Robert E. Bauman (R)	91,143	(48%)	($358,926)

Campaign Contributions and Expenditures

1981-82		Direct Cont. 81-82				PACS brkdwn		
Receipts	$204,992	Indiv	$62,318	Agr	$5,400		Ideo	$3,000
Expend.	$195,330	Party	$9,965	Bus	$37,674		Lbr	$76,140
Unspent	$10,589	PACS	$134,382	Hlth	$9,100		Prof	$1,400

SECOND DISTRICT

Baltimore County, as almost anyone who lives there can tell you, is entirely separate from the city of Baltimore. Most of its people still live in neighborhoods we would all classify as suburban, but there remains a bucolic ideal in their residents' mind, one that owes something to the fact that some of Baltimore's richest and socially most exclusive families live on huge estates in the horse country only a few miles north of the county line. Actually, Baltimore County demographically is almost as heterogeneous as Baltimore itself; and its different suburbs are, in a sense, extensions out radial avenues of different ethnic and economic neighborhoods in Baltimore.

Directly east of the city, you have the working class suburbs of Dundalk and Middle River, with many people of Eastern European descent; this is where people from the old Highlandtown neighborhood move, out near the giant Bethlehem Steel mill at Sparrows Point. Just northeast of Baltimore, out Harford Road and the Pulaski Highway, are middle income, mostly Catholic neighborhoods. Towson, directly north of Baltimore's highest income neighborhoods, is WASPy and affluent; Pikesville, just beyond the northwest Baltimore Jewish neighborhood, is predominantly Jewish.

The 2d congressional district of Maryland includes most of these parts of Baltimore County; Pikesville was, however, removed in the 1982 redistricting. The district now goes beyond the Baltimore County line, however, to take in the old courthouse town of Bel Air and to the Edgewood Arsenal and Aberdeen Proving Ground in Harford County. This is an area, with its small town atmosphere, which has attracted people in search of neighborhoods with more traditional values and high schools without a drug problem, family people who, in these days of a politics of cultural variety, tend to vote Republican, and who have made this part of the Baltimore area more Republican than it has ever been. The historical background of the 2d district is Democratic, and it has been represented by Democratic congressmen since 1958. But in national and even statewide elections, it is increasingly Republican.

That fact, and the inexorable advance of age, cast a shadow over the congressional career of 2d district Representative Clarence Long; yet in 1983 Long was, on one major issue, the most powerful man in Congress. He was first elected more than 20 years ago, a blue ribbon candidate in a year when the Baltimore County Democratic organization was beset by the scandal that helped a Republican attorney named Spiro Agnew get elected county executive. Long was then a professor of economics at Johns Hopkins and a former staffer for the President's Council of Economic Advisers. In the 1960s he was a staunch supporter of the Kennedy and Johnson administrations. One of the few members of Congress whose son served in Vietnam, he switched from hawk to dove on the war. He got a seat on the Appropriations Committee, and in 1977 became Chairman of the Foreign Operations Subcommittee.

This is not a plum assignment. The chairman's main job is to steer to passage the foreign aid appropriation, which is the target of all kinds of amendments. Some members want to stop aid to Communist countries or international organizations; others want to stop aid to countries that violate human rights. Long has not always been successful in getting his bills through on the floor, and he is regarded as an eccentric and given to odd statements by many colleagues. He does not have a working majority on the subcommittee on all issues; in 1981, it voted 8–7 to continue military aid to El Salvador against his opposition. But in 1983 he had the votes on El Salvador, in the full house if not on subcommittee, and the Reagan administration was forced to accede to his demand that a special envoy be appointed, to put pressure on the Salvadorian government; in return, Long reluctantly supported continued aid.

For years Long was reelected without difficulty; he worked the district hard back in the 1960s, when most members didn't, and has always commuted every night to his home in Baltimore County. But in 1980 and 1982 he had trouble at the polls. It was not so much that his opponent, Helen Delich Bentley, former *Baltimore Sun* maritime reporter and Federal Maritime Administration head, outspent him, though she did; she still didn't spend nearly as much as candidates in districts targeted by the national Republican Party. But she increased her percentage in 1982—contrary to the national trend. Redistricting hurt Long, true; but a longtime congressman who can manage only 53% is in trouble. In 1984 Long's age (75) may work against him; his prominence on national and international issues may work in his favor. No one would be terribly surprised, however, if he chooses to retire. In that case, the contest will be a tough one, with Bentley probably running but perhaps getting competition in the Republican primary and almost certainly a wide open primary on the Democratic side.

The People Pop. 1980: 526,354, up 13.6% 1970–80; voting age pop. 388,788; 5% Black, 1% Span. orig., 1% Asian orig. 33% housing units rented. Median owner $57,100; renter $227. Households: 78% family, 41% with children, 66% married couples.

Presidential Vote

1980	Reagan (R)	105,283	(50%)
	Carter (D)	89,037	(42%)
	Anderson (I)	15,484	(7%)

Rep. Clarence D. Long (D) Elected 1962; b. Dec. 11, 1908, South Bend, IN; home, Ruxton; Wash. and Jeff. Col., B.A. 1932, Princeton U., M.A. 1935, Ph.D. 1938; Presbyterian.

Career Navy, WWII; Prof. of Econ., Johns Hopkins U., 1946–64; Sr. Staff Mbr., Pres. Cncl. of Econ. Advisers, 1953–54, 1956–57; Acting Chmn., MD Dem. St. Central Comm., 1961–62.

Offices 2405 RHOB, 202-225-3061. Also P.O. Bldg., Rm. 200, Towson 21204, 301-828-6616.

Committee *Appropriations* (6th). Subcommittees: Foreign Operations (Chairman); Treasury-Postal Service-General Government; Military Construction.

Group Ratings

	ADA	ACLU	COPE	CFA	LCV	LWV	NTU	NSI	COC	ACA	CSFC
1982	70	75	71	69	90	73	36	60	23	30	35
1981	75	—	71	86	45	—	23	—	32	4	40
1980	83	80	53	79	60	67	22	30	61	25	34

National Journal Ratings

	Economic		Foreign		Cultural	
1982	60%	(LIB)	60%	(LIB)	71%	(LIB)
	40%	(CONS)	40%	(CONS)	29%	(CONS)
1981	71%	(LIB)	66%	(LIB)	90%	(LIB)
	29%	(CONS)	33%	(CONS)	10%	(CONS)

Key Votes

1) Reagan 81 Budget	AGN	5) Incr SS Rtmt Age	AGN	9) Poor Pay Food Stamps	AGN
2) Reagan 81 Tax Cut	AGN	6) Saudi AWACS Sale	AGN	10) Ban Crt Busing Order	AGN
3) Bal Budget Amend	AGN	7) $ for MX Missile	AGN	11) Auto Local Content	FOR
4) Gas & Road Tax	FOR	8) Nerve Gas Prod	AGN	12) Nuclear Arms Freeze	FOR

Election Results

1982 general	Clarence D. Long (D)	83,318	(53%)	($162,435)
	Helen Delich Bentley (R)	75,062	(47%)	($209,059)
1982 primary	Clarence D. Long (D)	62,341	(84%)	
	Blaine Taylor (D)	12,227	(16%)	
1980 general	Clarence D. Long (D)	121,017	(57%)	($153,619)
	Helen Delich Bentley (R)	89,961	(43%)	($252,871)

Campaign Contributions and Expenditures

1981-82		Direct Cont. 81-82		PACS brkdwn			
Receipts	$186,959	Indiv	$97,092	Agr	$—	Ideo	$29,350
Expend.	$162,439	Party	$7,850	Bus	$11,050	Lbr	$28,450
Unspent	$30,164	PACS	$72,350	Hlth	$1,250	Prof	$1,200
		Cand	$5,000				

THIRD DISTRICT

A dozen years ago, Baltimore seemed to be a city in trouble. Like other big cities farther up the East Coast, its housing was aging, its population declining, and its economy seemed to be sagging. But the last dozen years have turned out to be good ones for Baltimore. Its diversified economy has not collapsed but rather has kept up with inflation and kept at least even with the rest of the nation during the recession. Both high- and low-wage jobs have been generated, and the city's downtown and some of its neighborhoods have been revitalized with new building that is also respectful of the old. The city government under Mayor Donald Schaefer—now generally acclaimed as the best big city mayor in the nation—has managed to work well in the estimation of both black and white Baltimoreans. The fact that Schaefer has been reelected without serious opposition by a majority black electorate says volumes about life in the city. And, if Baltimore's population is growing smaller, that is mostly because people are having fewer children and its white population is relatively old—neither a development that suggests the city is collapsing.

The 3d congressional district of Maryland is centered on Baltimore, though you would hardly know it to look at its convoluted boundaries. Actually there is a very easy explanation for them: the district includes most of the white majority precincts in the city, plus adjacent parts of Baltimore County, plus—added on to meet the population standard—most of the "new town" of Columbia, 15 miles from downtown Baltimore. The central focus is Baltimore's harbor, with the handsome Harborplace development overlooking the city's busy harbor; across the bay, not far away, is Fort McHenry, where Francis Scott Key stood and watched the star-spangled banner yet wave. Going counterclockwise from downtown, the district moves east to include the most Polish Highlandtown neighborhood, the political base of Congresswoman Barbara Mikulski; the middle-class northeastern corner of the city; upper income WASPy neighborhoods north of Johns Hopkins University and in the Baltimore County suburb of Towson; and the mostly Jewish area around the Pimlico Race Track and the suburb of Pikesville. West of downtown, this time clockwise, the 3d takes in the old ethnic neighborhoods overlooking the harbor; the modest suburbs of Arbutus and Catonsville; and goes out to Howard County and Columbia. This is a much heralded "new town" whose architecture is less distinctive than one might think, but which has attracted a population of nearly 40,000 which is by suburban standards unusually well integrated (20% black) and politically liberal.

The 3d district elects one of Congress's most distinctive members. She is Barbara Mikulski, who got her start in local politics in Polish east Baltimore. She was chosen head of the national Democratic Party's commission on delegate selection in 1973, but she never lost touch with her Baltimore Council constituency. She ran for the Senate in 1974, and got a respectable percentage against Charles Mathias; when Paul Sarbanes ran for the other Senate seat in 1976, Mikulski ran for his 3d district seat and won. She is still more comfortable in east Baltimore than in Georgetown, and she still retains the support of old politicos who are a little puzzled by her national prominence.

Though she has the liberal views on cultural and foreign issues that characterize many so-called Atari Democrats, Mikulski is not one of those Democrats with doubts about her party's traditional economic policies. She believes in a generous government, spending money to aid those in need and to help ordinary people maintain their dignity; she is not suspicious but scathingly denouncing of programs that purport to help the average person by cutting taxes on the rich. While her constituency has flirted with Republicans—the 3d went more than 2–1 for Nixon in 1972 and within its current boundaries gave Carter no edge in 1976—she has not. She has been probably the most active House member directing attention at problems faced largely by women, whether they be single women who are heads of families or battered spouses or mothers whose children are no longer eligible for free school lunches. She serves on the Energy and Commerce Committee, the key committee on most regulatory issues. Mikulski is a strong advocate of continuing regulation, despite the complaints of owners of some of the big factories which employ many of her constituents.

Anything but quiet, Mikulski has one of the best senses of humor, and comic deliveries, in the Congress. But she is also capable of sustained indignation and of genuine eloquence, which is why Edward Kennedy selected her to give his (as it turned out, undelivered) nominating speech at the 1980 national convention. With a safe seat, she has the potential to be one of the outstanding advocates in the House.

The People Pop. 1980: 527,699, dn. 3.3% 1970–80; voting age pop. 399,019; 14% Black, 1% Span. orig., 1% Asian orig. 37% housing units rented. Median owner $43,500; renter $197. Households: 71% family, 35% with children, 54% married couples.

Presidential Vote

1980	Reagan (R)	88,612	(40%)
	Carter (D)	112,520	(51%)
	Anderson (I)	20,473	(9%)

Rep. Barbara A. Mikulski (D) Elected 1976; b. July 20, 1936, Baltimore; home, Baltimore; Mt. St.

Agnes Col., Baltimore, B.A. 1958, U. of MD, M.S.W. 1965; Roman Catholic.

Career Admin., Baltimore Dept. of Soc. Svcs.; Caseworker; Teacher; Adjunct Prof., Loyola Col., 1972–76; Chwmn., Dem. Natl. Comm. Commission on Delegate Selection and Party Structure, 1973; Dem. Nominee for U.S. Senate, 1974.

Offices 407 CHOB, 202-225-4016. Also 1414 Fed. Bldg., Baltimore 21201, 301-962-4510.

Committees *Energy and Commerce* (12th). Subcommittees: Commerce, Transportation and Tourism; Health and the Environment. *Merchant Marine and Fisheries* (11th). Subcommittees: Coast Guard and Navigation; Merchant Marine; Oceanography; Panama Canal and Outer Continental Shelf. *Select Committee on Children, Youth, and Families* (6th).

Group Ratings

	ADA	ACLU	COPE	CFA	LCV	LWV	NTU	NSI	COC	ACA	CSFC
1982	90	75	90	85	87	83	15	11	19	13	29
1981	100	—	88	93	100	—	35	—	16	17	29
1980	89	73	83	71	74	90	16	20	56	27	26

National Journal Ratings

	Economic		Foreign		Cultural	
1982	77%	(LIB)	83%	(LIB)	85%	(LIB)
	22%	(CONS)	17%	(CONS)	14%	(CONS)
1981	89%	(LIB)	92%	(LIB)	84%	(LIB)
	3%	(CONS)	2%	(CONS)	15%	(CONS)

Key Votes

1) Reagan 81 Budget	AGN	5) Incr SS Rtmt Age	AGN
2) Reagan 81 Tax Cut	AGN	6) Saudi AWACS Sale	AGN
3) Bal Budget Amend	AGN	7) $ for MX Missile	AGN
4) Gas & Road Tax	FOR	8) Nerve Gas Prod	AGN

9) Poor Pay Food Stamps	AGN
10) Ban Crt Busing Order	AGN
11) Auto Local Content	FOR
12) Nuclear Arms Freeze	FOR

Election Results

1982 general	Barbara A. Mikulski (D)	110,042	(74%)	($123,460)
	H. Robert Scherr (R)	38,259	(26%)	($22,834)
1982 primary	Barbara A. Mikulski (D)	73,455	(81%)	
	Debra Hanania Freeman (D)	17,033	(19%)	($56,246)
1980 general	Barbara A. Mikulski (D)	102,293	(76%)	($39,353)
	Russell T. Schaffer (R)	32,074	(24%)	($0)

Campaign Contributions and Expenditures

1981-82		Direct Cont. 81-82			PACS brkdwn			
Receipts	$118,345	Indiv	$36,492	Agr	$700	Ideo	$9,875
Expend.	$123,460	Party	$100	Bus	$17,350	Lbr	$41,750
Unspent	$17,798	PACS	$74,737	Hlth	$4,200	Prof	$1,100

FOURTH DISTRICT

The 4th congressional district of Maryland runs from the Baltimore city limit to the District of Columbia line. It includes all of Anne Arundel County (Annapolis and Baltimore suburbs) and part of Prince George's County (near Washington). In the middle of the district is

Annapolis, the quaint 18th century town that contains Maryland's State House—the oldest capitol in the nation still in use—and the United States Naval Academy. Between Annapolis and Baltimore are a series of not-so-fashionable suburbs of Baltimore where about half the 4th district's residents live: Linthicum, Glen Burnie, Severna Park. The Prince George's County portion is shaped oddly, like a fishhook, and includes, in addition to Andrews Air Force Base, several mostly black suburbs.

Party registration in the 4th district is Democratic, but this is a place where Republicans often win national and sometimes even local elections. The voters here, many of them one generation removed from small Baltimore rowhouses, are proud of their accomplishments and resent politicians who do not seem to respect them. The major exception is in Prince George's County, where the black suburbanites vote almost as heavily Democratic as do their friends and relatives they left behind in the city.

The 4th district was created in basically its present form in 1972, and the only congressman it has ever had is Republican Marjorie Holt. She held local office in Anne Arundel County, and when that jurisdiction for the first time dominated a congressional district she was its favorite. She has been elected with ease against liberal and conservative Democratic opponents, and did handily in 1982 despite the national Democratic trend and the addition of black areas in Prince George's. One reason she wins is that she has a reputation for good constituency services—vital in a district where there are many federal employees.

Mrs. Holt has easily the most conservative record in the Maryland delegation. As a member of the Budget Committee in the 1970s, she was lead sponsor of measures to cut nonmilitary spending; but she had already served the allowed number of terms by 1980, and so was not on Budget when Republicans had working control of the floor on this issue in 1981. Mrs. Holt is a member of Armed Services, where she has pretty consistently supported defense spending increases. She is not flashy, but has a certain dogged persistence that one might expect from a woman who entered law school in 1946, a year that professional schools were flooded with male veterans returning from war.

The People   Pop. 1980: 525,453, up 17.7% 1970–80; voting age pop. 372,900; 19% Black, 1% Span. orig., 1% Asian orig. 33% housing units rented. Median owner $66,200; renter $261. Households: 78% family, 47% with children, 64% married couples.

Presidential Vote

1980			
	Reagan (R)	85,657	(50%)
	Carter (D)	71,762	(42%)
	Anderson (I)	12,512	(7%)

Rep. Marjorie S. Holt (R) Elected 1972; b. Sept. 17, 1920, Birmingham, AL; home, Severna Park; Jacksonville U., B.A. 1946, U. of FL, J.D. 1949; Presbyterian.

Career Practicing atty., 1950–66; Anne Arundel Cnty. Spvr. of Elections, 1963–65; Anne Arundel Cnty. Clk. of Circuit Ct., 1966–72.

Offices 2412 RHOB, 202-225-8090. Also 95 Aquahart Rd., Glen Burnie 21061, 301-768-8050.

Committees *Armed Services* (4th). Subcommittees: Military Personnel and Compensation; Procurement and Military Nuclear Systems (Ranking Member). *District of Columbia* (4th). Subcommittees: Fiscal Affairs and Health (Ranking Member); Judiciary and Education. *Joint Economic Committee* (2d). Subcommittees: Investment, Jobs, and Prices; Monetary and Fiscal Policy.

Group Ratings

	ADA	ACLU	COPE	CFA	LCV	LWV	NTU	NSI	COC	ACA	CSFC
1982	10	25	17	8	31	36	76	100	81	76	66
1981	10	—	17	14	15	—	75	—	84	82	72
1980	6	7	16	0	38	40	60	100	72	86	78

National Journal Ratings

	Economic		Foreign		Cultural	
1982	19%	(LIB)	19%	(LIB)	4%	(LIB)
	81%	(CONS)	80%	(CONS)	87%	(CONS)
1981	35%	(LIB)	3%	(LIB)	18%	(LIB)
	64%	(CONS)	87%	(CONS)	82%	(CONS)

Key Votes

1) Reagan 81 Budget	FOR	5) Incr SS Rtmt Age	FOR	9) Poor Pay Food Stamps	FOR
2) Reagan 81 Tax Cut	FOR	6) Saudi AWACS Sale	FOR	10) Ban Crt Busing Order	FOR
3) Bal Budget Amend	FOR	7) $ for MX Missile	FOR	11) Auto Local Content	AGN
4) Gas & Road Tax	AGN	8) Nerve Gas Prod	FOR	12) Nuclear Arms Freeze	AGN

Election Results

1982 general	Marjorie S. Holt (R)	75,617	(61%)	($178,514)
	Patricia O'Brien Aiken (D)	47,947	(39%)	($9,169)
1982 primary	Marjorie S. Holt (R) unopposed			
1980 general	Marjorie S. Holt (R)	120,985	(72%)	($147,170)
	James J. Riley (D)	47,375	(28%)	($9,225)

Campaign Contributions and Expenditures

1981-82		Direct Cont. 81-82		PACS brkdwn			
Receipts	$193,877	Indiv	$104,330	Agr	$—	Ideo	$42,590
Expend.	$178,514	Party	$9,311	Bus	$42,590	Lbr	$3,740
Unspent	$7,048	PACS	$50,419	Hlth	$3,740	Prof	$1,000

FIFTH DISTRICT

The 5th congressional district of Maryland includes most of Prince George's County, the largest suburban county in the state. Situated just north and east of Washington, D.C., Prince George's is somewhat less white collar and less affluent than neighboring Montgomery County, and it is regarded by many Washington area residents as a kind of working-class community. Actually, by national standards, Prince George's is far more affluent and well educated than average. One reason is the high salaries and wages paid by the federal government. In 1970 some 38% of the work force here was employed by Uncle Sam—the highest figure for any congressional district in the nation—and the figure today (not yet available from the Census Bureau) is probably similar. Defenders of government pay scales point out that the government has a work force more tilted to white-collar and professional positions than do most private businesses; and they would add that in the early 1980s, with recessions and Reagan spending cuts, job security is no longer absolute and pay is not rising as rapidly as it used to.

What should also be mentioned is that Prince George's is the nation's premier black suburban county. In 1980 37% of the Prince George's population was black, as compared to

14% in 1970. There are some all black suburbs, like those along Capital Avenue just east of the District, some still almost entirely white suburbs, like Bowie, out in the hills at the eastern edge of the county; but most are, at least for a time, integrated. Prince George's is the product of two successive waves of migration out from the District: whites came out in the 1950s and 1960s and built subdivisions on old Maryland farmland, and the population rose from 194,000 to 661,000; blacks came out in the late 1960s and throughout the 1970s, when the overall population stayed about the same, and the black percentage rose from 15% to 37%. Demographically, in terms of income and other indicia, Prince George's blacks are very similar to Prince George's whites: above average in income and education, likely to be family people interested in good public schools for their children. Only politically are they different: Prince George's whites are Democrats nominally and in many but not all elections; Prince George's blacks are almost unanimously Democrats.

The racial change has provoked some local conflict, over the police department and school busing. The county has developed, however, an up-to-date Democratic machine which includes politicians of both races; it lost the county executive post in 1978 but an ally regained it in 1982.

The rising black percentage has made the 5th district safely Democratic. As late as 1972 it elected Republican Lawrence Hogan, a law-and-order advocate who surprised almost everyone by voting for the impeachment of Richard Nixon. His successor was Gladys Spellman, a Democrat known for her hard work and devotion to government employees (she gave out a Beautiful Bureaucrat award). Spellman had a heart attack in October 1980, fell into a coma, and was still reelected easily; but her seat was declared vacant and a special election held in May 1981.

The Reagan administration was widely popular then, and the Republicans made a real effort to capture the district. But it was held for the Democrats by Steny Hoyer, who is one of those instinctive politicians who fill the ranks of young Democrats in Congress. That was not his first goal: he was elected to the Maryland Senate at age 27 and was Senate president from 1974 to 1978; he was the lieutenant governor on the ticket with Acting Governor Blair Lee III in the 1978 primary. When Lee lost, so did Hoyer, and his elective career seemed ended, or at least stalled, at age 39. The congressional race gave him an opening; he edged out Spellman's husband and several other Democrats in the primary and beat a well financed, competent Republican candidate in the general. Reelection in 1982 was no problem.

Congressmen in the Washington suburbs typically hang onto their seats by providing extensive constituency services, especially for federal employees who are constantly having problems with the government. Hoyer has followed this pattern. But he seems interested in national as well as local problems: he left the Post Office and Civil Service Committee in 1983 for a seat on Appropriations. On most national issues he is among the more liberal of Democrats.

The People Pop. 1980: 527,469, up .5% 1970–80; voting age pop. 374,737; 31% Black, 2% Span. orig., 2% Asian orig. 42% housing units rented. Median owner $64,100; renter $282. Households: 74% family, 45% with children, 56% married couples.

Presidential Vote

1980	Reagan (R)	65,497	(41%)
	Carter (D)	80,061	(51%)
	Anderson (I)	12,630	(8%)

Rep. Steny H. Hoyer (D) Elected May 19, 1981; b. June 14, 1939, New York City; home, Berkshire; U. of MD, B.S. 1963, Georgetown U., J.D. 1966; Baptist.

Career Practicing atty., 1966–80; MD Senate, 1966–79, Pres., 1975–79; Mbr., MD Bd. for Higher Education, 1978–.

Offices 1513 LHOB, 202-225-4131. Also 4351 Garden City Dr., Su. 625, Landover 20785, 301-436-5510.

Committee *Appropriations* (34th). Subcommittees: Labor-Health and Human Services-Education; Treasury-Postal Service-General Government.

Group Ratings

	ADA	ACLU	COPE	CFA	LCV	LWV	NTU	NSI	COC	ACA	CSFC
1982	75	96	96	85	92	83	1	50	32	13	28
1981	72	—	92	71	74	—	8	—	12	11	31

National Journal Ratings

	Economic		Foreign		Cultural	
1982	93%	(LIB)	57%	(LIB)	87%	(LIB)
	6%	(CONS)	43%	(CONS)	12%	(CONS)
1981	75%	(LIB)	61%	(LIB)	86%	(LIB)
	25%	(CONS)	39%	(CONS)	13%	(CONS)

Key Votes

1) Reagan 81 Budget	AGN	5) Incr SS Rtmt Age	AGN	9) Poor Pay Food Stamps	AGN
2) Reagan 81 Tax Cut	AGN	6) Saudi AWACS Sale	AGN	10) Ban Crt Busing Order	AGN
3) Bal Budget Amend	AGN	7) $ for MX Missile	AGN	11) Auto Local Content	FOR
4) Gas & Road Tax	FOR	8) Nerve Gas Prod	AGN	12) Nuclear Arms Freeze	FOR

Election Results

1982 general	Steny H. Hoyer (D)	83,937	(80%)	($168,889)
	William P. Guthrie (R)	21,533	(20%)	($0)
1982 primary	Steny H. Hoyer (D)	44,099	(92%)	
	Michael I. Sprague (D)	3,724	(8%)	
1981 special	Steny H. Hoyer (D)	42,573	(55%)	($317,751)
	Audrey Scott (R)	33,708	(44%)	($235,824)
1980 general	Gladys Noon Spellman (D)	106,035	(80%)	($96,646)
	Kevin R. Igoe (R)	25,693	(20%)	($24,333)

Campaign Contributions and Expenditures

1981-82		Direct Cont. 81-82		PACS brkdwn			
Receipts	$205,363	Indiv	$94,437	Agr	$4,950	Ideo	$8,350
Expend.	$208,782	Party	$1,379	Bus	$25,745	Lbr	$54,890
Unspent	$72,063	PACS	$94,085	Hlth	$9,050	Prof	$1,500

Indirect Party Expend: $11,627

SIXTH DISTRICT

West of Baltimore and Washington a series of gentle Maryland hills rise to the low mountains of the Catoctins and the Appalachian ridges. Here is a land known for its fertile valleys and its antique cities, like Frederick, where Barbara Fritchie supposedly reared her old gray head. Also here are the small industrial cities of Hagerstown and, nestled in the mountains, Cumberland. This is, traditionally, the most Republican part of Maryland. Some of the mountain folk and Pennsylvania Dutch who settled western Maryland have a long Republican tradition. Thus western Maryland went solidly for Ronald Reagan in 1980, though he lost the state; and western Maryland went Republican in the 1982 Senate race, although statewide Democrat Paul Sarbanes had a solid victory.

The 6th congressional district of Maryland takes in all of western Maryland and touches on Washington and Baltimore suburbs besides. In the Washington area, it takes in very high income Potomac all the way to the Capital Beltway; in the Baltimore area it includes a little bit of the new town of Columbia. For the most part, however, this is a rural not a cosmopolitan district, a place where family patterns are traditional and family values important.

Beverly Byron, the representative from the 6th district, is the fourth Byron elected to Congress in western Maryland. Her husband's father and mother served in the 1940s, and her husband, Goodloe Byron, was elected in 1970 and served until he died while jogging in October 1978. Mrs. Byron, who had no political record of her own, got the nomination then. Some might have expected her to be a caretaker congresswoman. But she seems comfortably ensconced. She continues her husband's general voting pattern: conservative on most issues, little different really from many Republicans elected from similar districts. Her pro-environment record on the Interior Committee—including support of the Alaska Lands Act of 1980—helped her avoid the primary opposition which gave her husband close races in the 1976 and 1978 primaries. On Armed Services she is part of the solid committee majority sympathetic to requests for military spending; this may come naturally, since her father, Harry Butcher, was an important aide to Dwight Eisenhower during World War II.

The People Pop. 1980: 528,168, up 24.3% 1970–80; voting age pop. 376,405; 4% Black, 1% Span. orig., 1% Asian orig. 25% housing units rented. Median owner $58,100; renter $167. Households: 80% family, 45% with children, 70% married couples.

Presidential Vote

1980	Reagan (R)	112,532	(59%)
	Carter (D)	66,934	(35%)
	Anderson (I)	12,651	(7%)

Rep. Beverly B. Byron (D) Elected 1978; b. July 27, 1932, Baltimore; home, Frederick; Hood Col., 1963–64; Episcopal.

Career Campaign Asst., U.S. Rep. Goodloe E. Byron.

Offices 1216 LHOB, 202-225-2721. Also Fredericktown Mall, Frederick 21701, 301-662-8622.

Committees *Armed Services* (13th). Subcommittees: Military Personnel and Compensation; Procurement and Military Nuclear Systems. *Interior and Insular Affairs* (19th). Subcommittees: Mines and Mining, and BPA; Public Lands and National Parks. *Select Committee on Aging* (15th). Subcommittee: Housing and Consumer Interests.

Group Ratings

	ADA	ACLU	COPE	CFA	LCV	LWV	NTU	NSI	COC	ACA	CSFC
1982	30	37	45	31	43	36	55	100	52	50	50
1981	15	—	42	43	17	—	35	—	65	62	62
1980	22	13	32	14	67	33	41	78	73	65	58

National Journal Ratings

	Economic		Foreign		Cultural	
1982	37%	(LIB)	42%	(LIB)	18%	(LIB)
	62%	(CONS)	57%	(CONS)	82%	(CONS)
1981	49%	(LIB)	18%	(LIB)	46%	(LIB)
	50%	(CONS)	73%	(CONS)	54%	(CONS)

Key Votes

1) Reagan 81 Budget	FOR	5) Incr SS Rtmt Age	FOR	9) Poor Pay Food Stamps	AGN
2) Reagan 81 Tax Cut	FOR	6) Saudi AWACS Sale	AGN	10) Ban Crt Busing Order	FOR
3) Bal Budget Amend	FOR	7) $ for MX Missile	AGN	11) Auto Local Content	AGN
4) Gas & Road Tax	AGN	8) Nerve Gas Prod	FOR	12) Nuclear Arms Freeze	AGN

Election Results

1982 general	Beverly B. Byron (D)	102,596	(74%)	($122,439)
	Roscoe Bartlett (R)	35,321	(26%)	($0)
1982 primary	Beverly B. Byron (D)	35,110	(74%)	
	William B. McMahon (D)	11,506	(24%)	($16,148)
1980 general	Beverly B. Byron (D)	146,101	(70%)	($163,168)
	Raymond E. Beck (R)	62,913	(30%)	($73,203)

Campaign Contributions and Expenditures

1981-82		Direct Cont. 81-82		PACS brkdwn			
Receipts	$152,609	Indiv	$75,316	Agr	$5,300	Ideo	$1,150
Expend.	$122,439	PACS	$76,450	Bus	$59,975	Lbr	$3,300
Unspent	$48,547			Hlth	$4,750	Prof	$1,850

SEVENTH DISTRICT

Baltimore in 1980 joined the list of major American cities with a black majority. It was a development a long time coming: this almost-southern city has had a large black community since before the Civil War, augmented by more or less continual migration for 100 years or so. The natural increase of population over the generations, plus the refusal of most Baltimore suburbs until the 1970s to accept black residents, has meant that Baltimore would, sooner or later, become majority black. The west side of the city—except for the northern edge which is still mostly Jewish—is largely black; so is much of the area just northeast of downtown, stretching out northward to a point east of Johns Hopkins University.

This demographic milestone has had less effect on the politics of Baltimore than one might think. The city has not elected a black mayor or even had a strong black candidate run against Mayor Donald Schaefer—not, presumably, because there are no ambitious black politicians here, but because everyone thinks that Schaefer has solid black support and can't be beaten. That is probably right: Schaefer, a bachelor, has lived with his mother in a rowhouse for years in a mostly black neighborhood, and his genius at providing city services and improvements is expended with racial impartiality. The city's cynical political traditions—the black vote is still courted, almost certainly ineffectively, with "walking around money" on election day— may also dampen blacks' ambitions. There are, it should be added, numerous black legislators and one black congressman, from the 7th district of Maryland.

The 7th district includes almost all of the mostly black neighborhoods and not much more of the city of Baltimore (though it does include most of Hopkins and the old patrician neighborhood of Bolton Hill). It also extends out directly west into the Baltimore County suburbs of Lochearn and Milford Mill, both of which have black majorities. It seems likely that the natural movement of black Baltimoreans in the next 10 years will be in this direction.

If so, that will only strengthen 7th district Congressman Parren Mitchell. He is a member of a distinguished political family: his older brother, Clarence Mitchell, was for many years the canny Washington lobbyist for the NAACP; his nephew served in the Maryland Senate. Parren Mitchell himself was a novice when he won his first term in Congress in 1970: he beat a white incumbent in a white majority district by just 38 votes; and in 1972 he faced serious black primary opposition. Since then he has been reelected without difficulty.

Mitchell is a senior member now on the Banking, Finance, and Urban Affairs Committee, a body with a diverse jurisdiction: it handles housing programs, price control legislation, and superintends the Federal Reserve, as well as refereeing the continuing fights between banks and savings institutions. Mitchell also serves as chairman of the House Small Business Committee, a body that by virtue of its name and jurisdiction attracts a large membership but in fact has a very constricted legislative jurisdiction. Mostly it deals with the Small Business Administration, which gives below-market-interest-rate loans to some small businesses; but the SBA is not calculated to stimulate a vast surge of entrepreneurial activity, and it is hard to see how any government agency could. Mitchell represents a constituency with a small number of entrepreneurs, and he would like to do something about this; but what? On economic, foreign, and cultural issues he has solidly liberal voting records, which is to say that he wants to see more government programs to solve most of these problems. He has been an articulate leader of the Black Caucus and a competent committee member, but he has not found—nor has he claimed to find—solutions to the problems he decries.

The People Pop. 1980: 527,590, dn. 11.2% 1970–80; voting age pop. 376,566; 70% Black, 1% Span. orig., 1% Asian orig. 54% housing units rented. Median owner $28,300; renter $158. Households: 67% family, 40% with children, 37% married couples.

Presidential Vote

1980			
	Reagan (R)	23,696	(14%)
	Carter (D)	135,170	(82%)
	Anderson (I)	6,462	(4%)

Rep. Parren J. Mitchell (D) Elected 1970; b. Apr. 29, 1922, Baltimore; home, Baltimore; Morgan St. Col., B.A. 1950, U. of MD, M.A. 1952, U. of CT, 1960; Episcopal.

Career Army, WWII; Prof. and Asst. Dir. of the Urban Studies Institute, Morgan St. Col.; Exec. Secy., MD Comm. on Interracial Problems and Relations, 1963–65; Exec. Dir., Baltimore Community Action Agcy., 1965–68.

Offices 2367 RHOB, 202-225-4741. Also Geo. Fallon Fed. Ofc. Bldg., 31 Hopkins Plaza, Rm. 1018, Baltimore 21201, 301-962-3223.

Committees *Banking, Finance and Urban Affairs* (5th). Subcommittees: General Oversight and Renegotiation; Housing and Community Development. *Small Business* (Chairman). Subcommittee: SBA and SBIC Authority, Minority Enterprise and General Small Business Problems (Chairman). *Joint Economic Committee* (3d). Subcommittees: Investment, Jobs, and Prices (Chairman); Trade, Productivity, and Economic Growth.

Group Ratings

	ADA	ACLU	COPE	CFA	LCV	LWV	NTU	NSI	COC	ACA	CSFC
1982	75	96	94	92	87	90	41	0	25	0	23
1981	95	—	94	86	97	—	46	—	11	5	21
1980	89	93	93	93	84	100	20	11	61	9	16

National Journal Ratings

	Economic		Foreign		Cultural	
1982	90%	(LIB)	96%	(LIB)	92%	(LIB)
	9%	(CONS)	1%	(CONS)	8%	(CONS)
1981	97%	(LIB)	92%	(LIB)	93%	(LIB)
	3%	(CONS)	2%	(CONS)	7%	(CONS)

Key Votes

1) Reagan 81 Budget	AGN	5) Incr SS Rtmt Age	AGN	9) Poor Pay Food Stamps	AGN
2) Reagan 81 Tax Cut	AGN	6) Saudi AWACS Sale	AGN	10) Ban Crt Busing Order	AGN
3) Bal Budget Amend	AGN	7) $ for MX Missile	AGN	11) Auto Local Content	FOR
4) Gas & Road Tax	FOR	8) Nerve Gas Prod	AGN	12) Nuclear Arms Freeze	FOR

Election Results

1982 general	Parren J. Mitchell (D)	103,496	(88%)	($135,521)
	M. Leonora Jones (R)	14,203	(12%)	($0)
1982 primary	Parren J. Mitchell (D)	75,224	(85%)	
	Lawrence K. Freeman (D)	7,652	(9%)	
	Elizabeth C. Gray (D)	5,847	(7%)	($14,130)
1980 general	Parren J. Mitchell (D)	97,104	(88%)	($104,567)
	Victor Clark, Jr. (R)	12,650	(12%)	($0)

Campaign Contributions and Expenditures

1981-82		Direct Cont. 81-82		PACS brkdwn			
Receipts	$129,019	Indiv	$90,089	Agr	$500	Ideo	$1,200
Expend.	$135,521	PACS	$31,726	Bus	$11,470	Lbr	$17,530
Unspent	$9,653			Hlth	$750	Prof	$300

EIGHTH DISTRICT

By most measures you might care to use, the 8th congressional district of Maryland is one of the two or three richest in the nation. It includes most of Maryland's Montgomery County—the hunk of valuable suburban real estate immediately northwest of Washington, D.C. Montgomery County experienced a vast population increase in the 1950s and 1960s, rising from 164,000 to 522,000 in those 20 years. The increase continued, much less rapidly, to 579,000 in 1980. Most of that came in new subdivisions in the outer reaches of the metropolitan area, like Gaithersburg, Montgomery Village, and Olney. The migrants are almost all affluent, highly educated, upscale in demographers' language. The typical resident of the 8th district is a high-ranking GS-15 civil servant, a lawyer in private practice, or, increasingly, a professional employee of a firm that does consulting for the government. He (or she) is as likely as not to have a graduate degree and to belong to a liberal-oriented Protestant church or a Reform Jewish temple. He is sympathetic to the striving nations of the Third World, to efforts to clean up political campaigns, to environmentalists. On his coffee table you will find *Smithsonian* rather than *National Geographic*, the *New Yorker* rather than

People. He professes a vaguely liberal sort of politics. Montgomery County voters are usually willing to support Democrats, but for years their favorite kind of candidate was the liberal Republican who cares deeply about the political process, like Senator Charles Mathias.

Such politicians are becoming scarcer, however. The district had just such a congressman in Gilbert Gude, who retired in 1976 and eventually became head of Congress's Legislative Research Service, as nonpolitical a position as it is within Congress's power to bestow. The current congressman, Michael Barnes, is a Democrat who has been able to win as wide support—and perhaps deeper—than any of his Republican predecessors.

Barnes's success has come against the odds. He beat an apparently popular Republican in 1978, not a very Democratic year, and then increased his percentage in the even less Democratic year of 1980. In 1982 he expected to face Marian Greenblatt, an articulate conservative who with several allies had controlled the County School Board for several years; but Greenblatt's allies lost control in the same September primary that Greenblatt was upset by school board adversary Elizabeth Spencer. Mrs. Spencer, who spent little money, was simply not visible in the general election, and Barnes won with an unprecedented 71%.

Barnes owes some of his success to a strong constituency service operation and just plain hard work. But he is more than punctilious; he is also thoughtful. He has some experience in state government and with local matters; he does not consider them beneath his dignity. Yet in 1981 he won what became one of the key subcommittee chairmanships of the 97th Congress, that of Inter-American Affairs. The incumbent, Gus Yatron of Pennsylvania, was voted out because most committee Democrats considered him too conservative on human rights and too inactive generally. Barnes has a strong background in Latin American affairs and a commitment to human rights stances most committee Democrats support; he was able to beat Dan Mica of Florida though Mica, by virtue of a coin toss, was more senior. The Inter-American Subcommittee put Barnes in the spotlight. He has opposed the Reagan administration's calls for military aid to the government of El Salvador and has counseled caution on American involvement there. Barnes is part of that generation of Democrats who came of political age during the Vietnam war, and he seems to worry that in El Salvador we may repeat our Vietnam mistakes. But his approach is not mechanical; he has taken care to visit El Salvador, and has not grandstanded or treated the Reagan administration contemptuously.

So for the first time Montgomery County has a congressman with a powerful committee position and real clout—if only on remote issues—in Congress. This is an unusual experience for, and may mark a maturing of, an electorate which has always regarded politics with distaste and has seemed to wonder whether there wasn't somehow some way we could do without it. Now they seem pleased with a congressman who does not apologize for his political actions; he is comfortable using the political system because he does so (as do many of his political adversaries) because he believes government should do certain things.

The People   Pop. 1980: 528,036, up 7.3% 1970–80; voting age pop. 391,309; 8% Black, 4% Span. orig., 4% Asian orig. 36% housing units rented. Median owner $96,900; renter $332. Households: 72% family, 38% with children, 60% married couples.

Presidential Vote

1980	Reagan (R)	112,804	(47%)
	Carter (D)	98,770	(41%)
	Anderson (I)	30,446	(13%)

Rep. Michael D. Barnes (D) Elected 1978; b. Sept. 3, 1943, Washington, DC; home, Kensington; U. of NC, B.A. 1965, Inst. of Higher Internatl. Studies, Geneva, Switz., 1965–66, Geo. Wash. U., J.D. 1972; Protestant.

Career Spec. Asst. to U.S. Sen. Edmund S. Muskie of ME, 1970–72; Practicing atty., 1972–; MD Pub. Svc. Comm., 1975–78; Vice-Chmn., Wash. Metro Area Transit Comm., 1976–78.

Offices 401 CHOB, 202-225-5341. Also 11141 Georgia Ave., Su. 302, Wheaton 20902, 301-946-6801.

Committees *District of Columbia* (7th). Subcommittees: Government Operations and Metropolitan Affairs; Judiciary and Education. *Foreign Affairs* (10th). Subcommittees: Western Hemisphere Affairs (Chairman); International Economic Policy and Trade.

Group Ratings

	ADA	ACLU	COPE	CFA	LCV	LWV	NTU	NSI	COC	ACA	CSFC
1982	75	100	91	85	100	92	10	30	30	9	27
1981	95	—	88	100	100	—	10	—	5	4	30
1980	94	100	82	86	91	90	17	0	50	13	29

National Journal Ratings

	Economic		Foreign		Cultural	
1982	90%	(LIB)	96%	(LIB)	92%	(LIB)
	9%	(CONS)	1%	(CONS)	8%	(CONS)
1981	97%	(LIB)	92%	(LIB)	93%	(LIB)
	3%	(CONS)	2%	(CONS)	7%	(CONS)

Key Votes

1) Reagan 81 Budget	AGN	5) Incr SS Rtmt Age	AGN	9) Poor Pay Food Stamps	AGN
2) Reagan 81 Tax Cut	AGN	6) Saudi AWACS Sale	AGN	10) Ban Crt Busing Order	AGN
3) Bal Budget Amend	AGN	7) $ for MX Missile	AGN	11) Auto Local Content	FOR
4) Gas & Road Tax	FOR	8) Nerve Gas Prod	—	12) Nuclear Arms Freeze	FOR

Election Results

1982 general	Michael D. Barnes (D)	121,761	(71%)	($243,457)
	Elizabeth W. Spencer (R)	48,910	(29%)	($27,630)
1982 primary	Michael D. Barnes (D) unopposed			
1980 general	Michael D. Barnes (D)	148,301	(59%)	($349,924)
	Newton I. Steers, Jr. (R)	101,659	(41%)	($565,952)

Campaign Contributions and Expenditures

1981-82		Direct Cont. 81-82		PACS brkdwn			
Receipts	$285,204	Indiv	$205,897	Agr	$—	Ideo	$13,300
Expend.	$243,457	Party	$1,268	Bus	$5,924	Lbr	$51,350
Unspent	$41,748	PACS	$75,028	Hlth	$1,800	Prof	$1,700

Indep Expend: For: $6,002 (Sheet Metal Workers)

MASSACHUSETTS

Massachusetts is one of our most Democratic states and yet, in a period of recession, it has one of our lowest unemployment rates. It has some of the highest levels of government spending, but is also one of the two leading states—the other is California—for scientific research and technological innovation. In politics Massachusetts says it wants security, yet in business it lives—and lives pretty well—on ingenuity. To understand these paradoxes, you have to understand that politics and economic life in Massachusetts don't have much to do with each other. Business in Massachusetts has had its ebbs and flows pretty much independently of politics. But politics, a lusty and contentious politics, has developed out of differences in ethnic origin and cultural style.

That politics goes far back in history, back not to the Civil War, as is the case in so many states, but to the Irish potato famine of the 1840s. That blight forced hundreds of thousands of Irish to immigrate to the United States, to the point that there are far more people of Irish descent here than in Ireland today. Nowhere did these new Americans make a greater impact than in Boston and Massachusetts. They found a thriving Yankee economy and political culture whose hostility was symbolized by "No Irish need apply" signs. And ever since, politics in Massachusetts has usually been a struggle between Yankee and Irish. Sometimes the stakes have been concrete—control of patronage jobs, command of the Boston Police Department—and sometimes they have just been symbolic. But anyone who doubts the strength of the feelings behind these struggles should spend an evening in a Boston bar or private club.

This ethnic conflict was very much reflected in party politics. The Yankees of the 1840s, not long removed from federalism, were solid Whigs and would become one of the bulwarks of the Republican Party when it was formed a decade later. The Whigs and Republicans backed policies that appealed to Yankees: promoting public works (the current word is "infrastructure") to help business, protective tariffs, sympathy for suitably distant oppressed people like the blacks of the South and for uplifting (and productivity-enhancing) social movements like temperance. The Irish knew from the beginning that they were not going to get very far in the party of the Yankees, and they found the Democrats of the 19th century more congenial. We now think of the Democrats as a party promoting government action, but in those days the Democrats represented laissez faire. That was fine with the Irish. They came from a place where the government was the enemy; they didn't want government spending money to help the rich or to stimulate commerce (with which they had little acquaintance in agricultural Ireland); they didn't want government to restrict immigration; they didn't want it to advance the blacks who might compete with them in the labor market; and they didn't want it to prohibit the consumption of liquor. They were people familiar with competing hierarchies—the hierarchy of the hated English lords and the hierarchy of their own, often suppressed, Roman Catholic Church. The Democratic Party, with its ward organization and rituals, seemed like a sympathetic hierarchy. So the Irish went into politics, determined to beat the Protestants.

And that is pretty much the story of a century of Massachusetts politics. Throughout, the Irish share of the population continually rose—and there were other immigrants, who usually became Democrats too—while the Yankee share of the population declined. Yankees had smaller families, they moved out west, they intermarried with people of immigrant stock and lost their Yankee identity. The Irish mostly stayed put, raised large families, and eventually ruled as Massachusetts very slowly moved from being one of our most Republican states to becoming one of the most Democratic. The state's economy waxed and waned several times, thriving in the early 19th century as the leading maritime center of a trading nation and then falling as the country turned inward to the frontier; thriving again later in the 19th century and in the early 20th as a manufacturing center, then falling as employers sought lower wage workers elsewhere; thriving now in the late 20th century as a center of high technology.

Through all these changes, politics followed its own rhythms. Massachusetts gave Republicans majorities in every presidential election from the Civil War to 1924, when that quintessential Massachusetts Yankee, Calvin Coolidge, was elected. In 1928, when the Democrats nominated an Irish Catholic, Al Smith, Massachusetts went Democratic. In 1918 the state elected a Democratic senator, but Republicans won as many congressional seats as Democrats for three decades. In the 1920s, 1930s, 1940s, and 1950s, a pretty close balance existed between Yankee Republicans and Irish Democrats; the Democrats were making headway, but the Republicans fielded candidates who were smarter or more honest. The state's preference in presidential elections shifted very little in this period. While the nation oscillated between Roosevelt and Eisenhower, in Massachusetts it was the balance between Yankee and Irish, not the programs of the New Deal nor the popularity of individual candidates that usually made the difference.

Thus political conflict in Massachusetts never really fell into the liberal-versus-conservative lines of the New Deal. The Republicans retained a Yankee interventionism, an urge to tinker: they strongly favored civil rights, pushed an anti-isolationist foreign policy, opposed the excesses of Joe McCarthy. Massachusetts Democrats, on the other hand, like the Republic of Ireland were hostile to the British and cheered Joe McCarthy as one of their own. (Joseph Kennedy used to invite him to Hyannisport.) The Republicans promised to root out corruption. The Democrats had the complacent attitude typical of an ethnic group only recently able to aspire to public office and the public payroll.

In the 1960s and 1970s, for the first time in Massachusetts history, the Irish Democrats and the Yankee Republicans began moving in the same direction. The key figure is Senator Edward Kennedy. More even than his brother the president, he has by personal example helped to shape attitudes in the state in which he has been the leading public figure for 20 years. On a whole series of issues, Kennedy and the national Democratic Party took positions that in Massachusetts had been more typical of interventionist Yankees than laissez faire Irish. Kennedy strongly supported civil rights even during the Boston busing controversy, he favored helping people who were impoverished or starving, he opposed the war in Vietnam, he stood against corruption generally and the excesses of Watergate in particular. Kennedy's stands made such positions respectable, even mandatory, among Democratic politicians and among the Catholic majority of voters in Massachusetts. And his stands led the Yankee minority to vote more and more often for the Democratic Party. It was no accident, and not simply the result of a local recession, that Massachusetts voted for George McGovern in 1972. It represented a kind of reconciliation here, which saw the upper-crust Yankee suburb of Lincoln and the lower-income Irish city of Somerville going for the same candidate.

Governor. But that does not mean that Yankee and Irish conflicts have ended. They emerged in classic—though somewhat updated—form in the 1978 and 1982 gubernatorial elections. The real contest, both times, was in the Democratic primary, between Edward King, who favored massive tax cuts, opposed abortion, favored capital punishment, and wanted to attract business to the state, and Michael Dukakis, who opposed the tax cuts, favored abortion, opposed capital punishment, and wanted to continue the state's tradition of generous public services.

In effect both won. King upset Dukakis in 1978, a victory which, with the victory of Proposition 13 in California a few months earlier, signified a clear change in the public mood; and King beat blue blood Republican Francis Hatch, who had much the same base of support as Dukakis, in an unusually close general election a few months later. Dukakis beat King, rather narrowly, in the 1982 primary and won the general election with ease. During King's years, Massachusetts maintained its tradition of tolerance of diversity and King himself was, rhetorically and politically, on the defensive during most of his term in office. Yet on major policies he prevailed. His tax cuts at the very least coincided with, and in all probability stimulated, Massachusetts's economy to the point that it was the healthiest of big states during the recession of the early 1980s. Dukakis himself in effect accepted that change in a campaign that prided itself on being issue-oriented but in fact discussed specific issues almost not at all. It was designed to persuade the increasingly upscale Massachusetts electorate that the cerebral, parsimonious Dukakis was much more "our sort" than the painfully inarticulate, expense account entertainer King.

Senators. Edward Kennedy, who won a fourth full term in 1982, is now the state's most enduring politician and, by any reasonable measure, its most deeply popular. Yet the year must have been disappointing for him and many of his followers: he won with his smallest reelection margin yet and, shortly afterward, he bowed out of the presidential race. There is no reason to believe that there is any connection between the events: Kennedy's explanation, that he gave up the presidential race for family reasons, rings true. But that does not mean that the race would not have been chancy or that the issue which has bothered many voters about Kennedy since 1969—Chappaquiddick—would have disappeared. Kennedy made a point, in his 1982 Senate race, of emphasizing his closeness to his family—something he had never done before. Kennedy is in fact a more devoted father and uncle than most politicians who talk constantly about family values or appear in campaign photos with seemingly intact families; but his ads, supposedly aimed at the 1984 presidential election, failed to help him much in the 1982 Senate race. His lower percentage does not necessarily represent lower standing among the voters; his majority is still very loyal, and respect for his performance as a senator is high. His opponent Raymond Shamie's high-spirited, self-financed campaign was directed ostensibly at getting Kennedy to debate, and finally succeeded; Kennedy donated to a Catholic school the $10,000 Shamie promised to whoever could get him to debate.

Kennedy's withdrawal from the presidential race seems likely to make him a more influential senator. He is not only one of the most senior Democrats but over the years has been one of the hardest working. As long ago as 1965 he shepherded to passage a major immigration reform package. In the years since he has sponsored such diverse laws as airline deregulation and reform of the criminal code. In general he votes to expand the government domestically, but he is correct in pointing out that not all the measures on which he has taken the initiative move in this direction.

Kennedy succeeded James Eastland as Chairman of the Judiciary Committee in 1979, and probably expected to last as long in that post as Eastland did (24 years); instead he stayed only two. When the Democrats lost control of the Senate, Kennedy relinquished ranking place on Judiciary—and the headaches of upholding the liberal positions on issues like abortion, capital punishment, busing, the balanced budget constitutional amendment—and took the ranking minority position on Labor and Human Resources instead. This committee has jurisdiction over many programs Kennedy would like to expand and the Reagan administration would like to kill, and over the labor laws, about which organized labor is very worried indeed. Kennedy must have resented the fact that Utah's Orrin Hatch took over as chairman after only four years in the Senate, but he could take satisfaction from the fact that on many important issues he—with the help of two Republicans, Stafford of Vermont and Weicker of Connecticut—foiled Hatch and the administration. Kennedy's many successes as a legislator result from the fact that he is a hard worker, prepares well, and chooses his openings carefully; he does not always succeed immediately on his efforts (he has never gotten very far on national health insurance, a favorite goal), but he does lay the groundwork for what may be a working law one day.

Hard work is, usually, the secret of a successful career in the Senate; so many senators are busy running for president or spread themselves so thin over so many issues that the ones who concentrate on a few issues, master them, and have the good sense to try to persuade rather than bludgeon their colleagues are usually the most legislatively productive. Kennedy, who for two years (1969–71) was Democratic whip in the Senate, has been mentioned as a possible candidate for the Democratic leadership should discontent with Robert Byrd develop. Kennedy and Byrd are old adversaries; Byrd beat Kennedy for the whip position after Chappaquiddick. It is possible that the Democrats, if they win control in 1984, will decide that they want a non-presidential Kennedy as their national spokesman rather than Byrd.

Massachusetts's junior senator is Paul Tsongas, who was first elected in 1978. He was expected to tend to local issues and to faithfully support Kennedy's positions. Instead, he has made a national name for himself as a supporter of new ideas in the Democratic Party. His 1980 speech to the ADA Convention and the book that followed, *The Road From Here,* expressed doubts about many government programs. Actually, Tsongas's voting record is, according to rating groups, pretty solidly liberal; and if as an author he makes a good case against energy price controls, as a senator from oil-poor Massachusetts he has voted for them. His key experiences, which have clearly shaped his thinking on all issues, are as a local official in Lowell and a Peace Corps volunteer in Ethiopia. He is sympathetic to attitudes articulated by Third World leaders and very hostile to the Reagan foreign and defense policies—an attitude that came out in his strong opposition to administration El Salvador policy and to the nomination of Kenneth Adelman as disarmament negotiator. On the Foreign Relations Committee Tsongas is a champion of these positions—and is usually on the minority on them.

Tsongas grew up in Lowell, an 1830s model textile mill town which has been in bad economic shape since the 1920s; he helped develop a partnership of government and local businesses which has revitalized the city, both downtown and in many neighborhoods, and has made it economically buoyant. Lowell also owes much of its success to its location on the edge of Massachusetts's high technology belt and to the decision of An Wang to locate his corporate headquarters there. From his Lowell experience Tsongas draws general lessons about the need for cooperation between government and business.

Tsongas won his seat in a rough-and-tumble contest in which his ads featured voters struggling to pronounce his name. He won a five-candidate Democratic primary and then beat Senator Edward Brooke, who was hurt by revelations stemming from a messy divorce.

Tsongas must run for reelection in 1984, and as of early 1983 little opposition had surfaced. The real threat would probably come in a Democratic primary, but voters have no real animus against him. It seems unlikely that anyone would relish a one-on-one race, or that enough opponents would run to make it a multi-candidate contest, in which he might be more vulnerable. As for Republicans, none is apparent who could make a serious race.

Presidential politics. Despite 1980, Massachusetts is still one of the most Democratic states in national elections. Ronald Reagan won here because the anti-Reagan vote was split between Jimmy Carter (42%) and John Anderson (15%). Reagan's 42% was actually his lowest percentage in any state except Rhode Island and Georgia. Massachusetts is not a state where either party tends to campaign much: if the Democrats can't carry Massachusetts, they've already lost and the Republicans have already won without it.

Massachusetts does have one of the earliest primaries, a week after New Hampshire; and since most of New Hampshire is covered by Boston TV, campaigning for Massachusetts goes on well before the one-week interval between them. This is the first of the wholesale, as opposed to retail, states—the constituencies so large that presidential candidates can't possibly meet or canvass a significant percentage of voters personally and so must appeal to them through the mass media of television, radio, and direct mail. Massachusetts surprised a lot of people by going for Henry Jackson in 1976, but that seems less startling today; it is a diverse state and in a multi-candidate race almost any candidate can win. But it does seem to bridle at southerners, and never gave Jimmy Carter much of a vote. On the Republican side, this is the only state where George Bush and John Anderson finished ahead of Ronald Reagan—a pretty accurate picture of the small Massachusetts Republican electorate.

Congressional districting. With one notable exception, the Massachusetts legislature redrew the congressional district boundaries by expanding the current congressmen's constituencies out a little farther, and with no perceptible effect on their chances. But the Census reduced the number of districts from 12 to 11, and so freshman Democrat Barney Frank and veteran Republican Margaret Heckler were placed together in a new 4th district. That produced a bitter, expensive race, and a Frank victory; Heckler was appointed Secretary of Health and Human Services.

The People Est. Pop 1982: 5,781,000; Pop. 1980: 5,737,037, up 0.8% 1980–82 and 0.8% 1970–80; 2.5% of U.S. total, 11th largest; voting age pop. 4,246,648; 3% Black, 2% Spanish origin, 1% Asian origin. Single ancestry: 12% Irish, 8% English, Italian, 5% French, 3% Portuguese, Polish, 2% German, 1% Russian, Swedish, Greek, Scottish. Registered voters (1982): 3,048,180 Total. 1,388,543 D (46%); 442,522 R (15%); 1,217,115 unenrolled (40%). 16% with 1–3 yrs. col., 20% with 4+ yrs. col. 9.8% below poverty level. 39% housing units rented; median house value: $48,500; median monthly rent: $197. Households: 71% family, 36% with children, 57% married couples.

1982 Share of Federal Tax Burden $15,960,400,000; 2.67% of U.S. total, 10th largest.

1982 Share of Federal Expenditures

	Total		Non-Defense		Defense	
Total Expend	$17,313m	(2.87%)	$11,334m	(2.67%)	$5,980m	(3.34%)
St/Lcl Grants	2,745m	(3.11%)	2,745m	(3.11%)	0m	(0%)
Salary/Wages	1,050m	(1.35%)	508m	(1.86%)	542m	(1.07%)
Ind Payments	7,579m	(2.65%)	6,937m	(2.69%)	642m	(2.25%)
Procurement	5,627m	(3.86%)	377m	(1.20%)	5,250m	(4.59%)
Other Programs	311m	(5.74%)	311m	(5.79%)	0m	(0%)
Loan/Insurance	502m	(0.78%)	479m	(0.78%)	23m	(1.05%)

Political Lineup   Governor, Michael S. Dukakis (D). Senators, Edward M. Kennedy (D) and Paul E. Tsongas (D). Representatives, 11 (10 D and 1 R). State Senate, 40 (33 D and 7 R); State House of Representatives, 160 (131 D and 29 R).

Presidential Vote

1980	Reagan (R)	1,056,223	(42%)
	Carter (D)	1,053,802	(42%)
	Anderson (I)	382,539	(15%)
1976	Ford (R)	1,030,276	(40%)
	Carter (D)	1,429,475	(56%)

1980 Democratic Presidential Primary			*1980 Republican Presidential Primary*		
Kennedy	590,393	(65%)	Bush	124,365	(31%)
Carter	260,401	(29%)	Anderson	122,987	(31%)
Others	36,866	(4%)	Reagan	115,334	(29%)
No preference	19,663	(2%)	All others...........	35,897	(9%)
			No preference	2,243	(0%)

SENATORS

Sen. Edward M. Kennedy (D) Elected 1962, seat up 1988; b. Feb. 22, 1932, Boston; home, Boston; Harvard U., B.A. 1956, Acad. of Internatl. Law, The Hague, The Netherlands, 1958, U. of VA, LL.B. 1959; Roman Catholic.

Career Army, 1951–53; Asst. Dist. Atty., Suffolk Cnty., 1961–62.

Offices 113 RSOB, 202-224-4543. Also JFK Fed. Bldg., Rm. 2400A, Boston 02203, 617-223-2826.

Committees *Armed Services* (7th). Subcommittees: Manpower; Preparedness; Tactical Warfare. *Judiciary* (2d). Subcommittees: Immigration and Refugee Policy; Juvenile Justice. *Labor and Human Resources* (Ranking Member). Subcommittees: Labor; Education, Arts, and Humanities; Employment and Productivity. *Joint Economic Committee* (3d). Subcommittees: Investment, Jobs, and Prices (Vice-Chairman); Monetary and Fiscal Policy.

Group Ratings

	ADA	ACLU	COPE	CFA	LCV	LWV	NTU	NSI	COC	ACA	CSFC
1982	75	89	93	90	92	100	9	0	0	21	25
1981	100	—	92	93	97	—	2	—	6	17	26
1980	33	73	100	27	77	100	21	0	20	20	15

National Journal Ratings

	Economic		Foreign		Cultural	
1982	79%	(LIB)	85%	(LIB)	93%	(LIB)
	20%	(CONS)	14%	(CONS)	4%	(CONS)
1981	99%	(LIB)	96%	(LIB)	83%	(LIB)
	0%	(CONS)	2%	(CONS)	16%	(CONS)

Key Votes

1) Reagan 81 Budget	AGN	5) $ to El Salvador	AGN	9) Poor Pay Food Stamps	AGN
2) Reagan 81 Tax Cut	AGN	6) Saudi AWACS Sale	AGN	10) Ban Crt Busing Order	AGN
3) Bal Budget Amend	AGN	7) Ban Abortion	AGN	11) Clinch Riv Brdr Rctr	AGN
4) Gas & Road Tax	AGN	8) Nerve Gas Prod	AGN	12) Legal Services Corp	FOR

Election Results

1982 general	Edward M. Kennedy (D)	1,247,084	(61%)	($2,470,473)
	Raymond Shamie (R)	784,602	(38%)	($2,305,996)
1982 primary	Edward M. Kennedy (D)	869,985	(100%)	
1976 general	Edward M. Kennedy (D)	1,726,657	(69%)	($896,196)
	Michael S. Robertson (R)	722,641	(29%)	($168,854)

Campaign Contributions and Expenditures

1981-82		Direct Cont. 81-82		PACS brkdwn			
Receipts	$2,609,514	Indiv	$2,149,499	Agr	$2,200	Ideo	$27,612
Expend.	$2,470,473	Party	$19,000	Bus	$35,675	Lbr	$225,150
Unspent	$139,041	PACS	$305,082	Hlth	$6,500	Prof	$2,250

Indirect Party Expend: $37,500 *Indep Expend:* For: $1,350 Agn: $1,078,434 (Citiz. Org. to Replace Kennedy, LIFEPAC, NCPAC, ADEPT)

Sen. Paul E. Tsongas (D) Elected 1978, seat up 1984; b. Feb. 14, 1941, Lowell; home, Lowell; Dartmouth Col., B.A. 1962, Yale U., LL.B. 1967, Harvard U., 1973; Eastern Orthodox.

Career Peace Corps Volunteer, Ethiopia, 1962–64, Trng. Coord., West Indies, 1967–68; Mbr., Governor's Comm. on Law Enforcement, 1968–69; MA Dpty. Asst. Atty. Gen., 1969–71; Practicing atty., 1971–74; U.S. House of Reps., 1975–78.

Offices 392 RSOB, 202-224-2742. Also JFK Fed. Bldg., Rm. 2003, Boston 02203, 617-223-1890.

Committees *Energy and Natural Resources* (8th). Subcommittees: Energy Conservation and Supply; Energy Research and Development; Water and Power. *Foreign Relations* (6th). Subcommittees: African Affairs; Near Eastern and South Asian Affairs; Western Hemisphere Affairs. *Small Business* (7th). Subcommittee: Productivity and Competition.

Group Ratings

	ADA	ACLU	COPE	CFA	LCV	LWV	NTU	NSI	COC	ACA	CSFC
1982	95	86	91	80	82	100	4	0	15	6	24
1981	95	—	89	71	84	—	9	—	13	13	30
1980	89	83	84	93	82	75	22	0	28	12	20

National Journal Ratings

	Economic		Foreign		Cultural	
1982	87%	(LIB)	83%	(LIB)	97%	(LIB)
	12%	(CONS)	16%	(CONS)	2%	(CONS)
1981	86%	(LIB)	95%	(LIB)	86%	(LIB)
	13%	(CONS)	4%	(CONS)	6%	(CONS)

Key Votes

1) Reagan 81 Budget	AGN	5) $ to El Salvador	AGN	9) Poor Pay Food Stamps	AGN
2) Reagan 81 Tax Cut	AGN	6) Saudi AWACS Sale	AGN	10) Ban Crt Busing Order	AGN
3) Bal Budget Amend	AGN	7) Ban Abortion	AGN	11) Clinch Riv Brdr Rctr	AGN
4) Gas & Road Tax	FOR	8) Nerve Gas Prod	AGN	12) Legal Services Corp	FOR

Election Results

1978 general	Paul E. Tsongas (D)	1,093,283	(55%)	($768,383)
	Edward W. Brooke (R)	890,584	(45%)	($1,284,855)

1978 primary	Paul E. Tsongas (D)	296,915	(36%)	
	Paul Guzzi (D)	258,960	(31%)	($301,747)
	Kathleen Sullivan Alioto (D)	161,036	(19%)	($143,777)
	Two others (D)	117,861	(14%)	
1972 general	Edward W. Brooke (R)	1,505,932	(64%)	($368,038)
	John J. Droney (D)	823,278	(35%)	($82,888)

Campaign Contributions and Expenditures

1981-82		*PACS brkdwn*			
Receipts	$772,513	Agr	$11,400	Ideo	$2,500
Expend.	$768,383	Bus	$19,550	Lbr	$20,256
Unspent	$4,128	Hlth	$150	Prof	$—

GOVERNOR

Gov. Michael S. Dukakis (D) Elected 1982, term expires Jan. 1987; b. Nov. 3, 1933, Brookline; home, Brookline; Swarthmore Col., B.A. 1955, Harvard U., LL.B. 1960; Greek Orthodox.

Career Army, Korea; Practicing atty.; MA House of Reps., 1963–71; Dem. Nominee for Lt. Gov., 1970; Moderator, "The Advocates," Natl. TV show; Governor, 1974–78.

Offices State House, Rm. 360, Boston 02133, 617-727-3600.

Election Results

1982 gen.	Michael S. Dukakis (D)	1,219,109	(59%)
	John W. Sears (R)	749,679	(37%)
1982 prim.	Michael S. Dukakis (D)	631,911	(53%)
	Edward J. King (D)	549,335	(47%)
1978 gen.	Edward J. King (D)	1,030,294	(53%)
	Francis W. Hatch, Jr. (R)	926,072	(47%)

FIRST DISTRICT

The 1st congressional district of Massachusetts is the western end of the state: the Berkshire Mountains and most of the Massachusetts portion of the Connecticut River valley. The Berkshires are known as a summer resort and for picturesque towns like Lenox, home of the Tanglewood Music Festival, and Stockbridge, home of Alice's Restaurant. This part of the state has the look of a wilderness about it, but its status as a resort is only the latest in a series of transformations. If you walk in the forests, you will come on stone walls, running up and down the hills; these were the boundary walls erected by Yankee farmers 150 and even 200 years ago. But the land that produced so many stones for walls never yielded much to the plow, and the farms were abandoned, their owners moving west or to the new factory towns in the valleys. This was the second, industrial, transformation of western Massachusetts. Waterpower was the chief energy source of the day, and the fast-flowing streams of the Berkshires were harnessed to waterwheels and millraces. Railroads wended their way through the hills to the factory towns of Pittsfield and North Adams, and this became a prosperous high-wage area.

There are still some farms and factories in western Massachusetts, but there is a third economy as well. Retirees and counterculture veterans have moved into the hills here, as they have in other parts of the country. Colleges and universities have sprung up, especially in the

MASSACHUSETTS — Congressional Districts, Counties, County Subdivisions (Towns), and Places — *(11 Districts)*

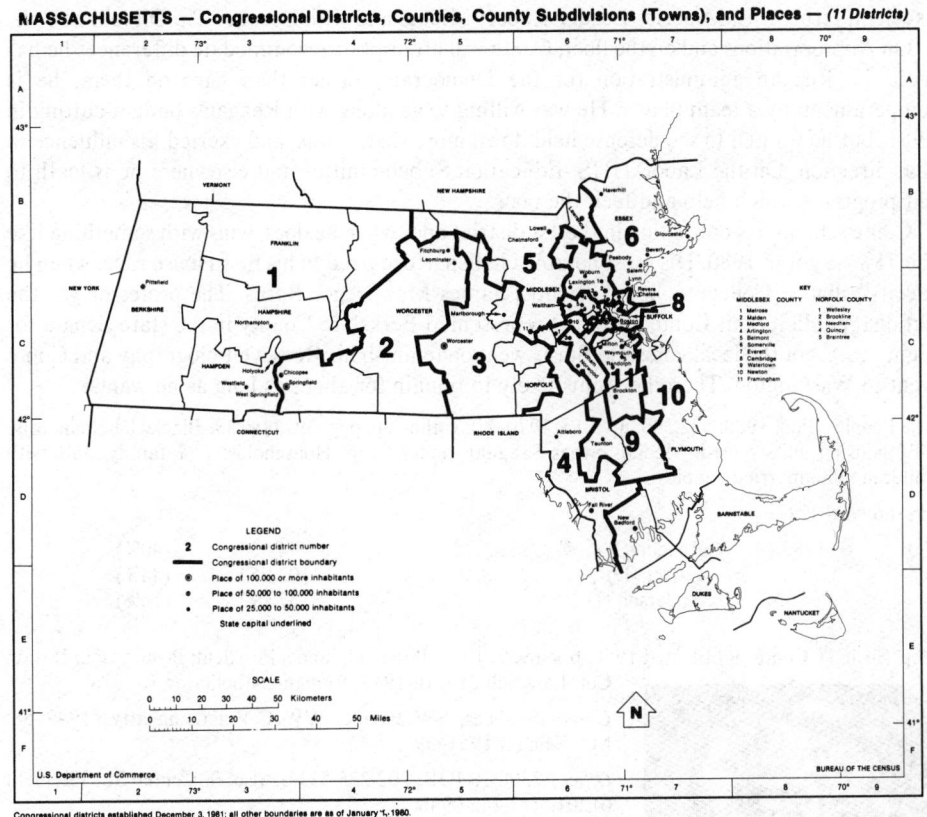

Congressional districts established December 3, 1981; all other boundaries are as of January 1, 1980.

Pioneer Valley (the Massachusetts name for the Connecticut River valley), with Amherst and the University of Massachusetts at Amherst and Smith at Northampton. Just to the south is the old industrial town of Holyoke and the middle class suburbs of Westfield and West Springfield, across the Connecticut River from Springfield.

The 1st congressional district is Democratic territory in national elections. Protestant Yankees were in the majority here when those stone walls were built, but they aren't any longer, and the Republican votes of some of the small towns are offset by the heavily Democratic votes usually coming out of the Pioneer Valley college towns. But in congressional races this is still a Republican—a very Republican—district. That is because of the popularity of Congressman Silvio Conte, one of the most senior of House Republicans.

Conte is also one of the shrewdest and, at the same time, most candid politicians among House Republicans. His positions on issues, from the time he first won the seat in 1958, have been to the left of most Republicans; and there was some talk in 1979 among conservatives of not letting him be ranking minority member of the Appropriations Committee in line with his seniority. But Conte does not antagonize his Republican colleagues as a John Lindsay used to do. He is self-righteous, but in the hearty, competitive way most politicians are; he can roar in indignation with the best of them. But he is not offended when others, of different views, do the same. He is shrewd enough to advance his views and his district's interests with considerable success, but he is not devious or underhanded. Friendly and garrulous, he is on excellent terms with Minority Leader Robert Michel and with Speaker Tip O'Neill as well.

On Appropriations and on the floor, Conte will attempt to accommodate differences he has with the Reagan administration (or the Democrats) rather than harp on them; he is temperamentally a team player. He was willing to go along with Reagan's budget-cutting in 1981, but he wanted to see defense held down more than it was, and exerted his influence in that direction. On the Labor–HHS–Education Subcommittee and elsewhere he is loath to cut programs which help and feed the poor.

Conte seldom has opposition in the 1st district and, when he does, wins with something like the 75% he got in 1980. His most notable challenge occurred in his first House race, when he faced Williams College political scientist James MacGregor Burns. The professor got the national publicity but Conte, who had represented Berkshire County in the state Senate for eight years, got the local votes. So Burns went on to finish his Roosevelt biography and Conte went to Washington. There he seems likely to remain for about as long as he wants.

The People   Pop. 1980: 522,540, up 4.1% 1970–80; voting age pop. 391,008; 1% Black, 1% Span. orig. 34% housing units rented. Median owner $38,600; renter $176. Households: 71% family, 36% with children, 58% married couples.

Presidential Vote

1980	Reagan (R)	94,850	(40%)
	Carter (D)	102,952	(44%)
	Anderson (I)	37,192	(16%)

Rep. Silvio O. Conte (R) Elected 1958; b. Nov. 9, 1921, Pittsfield; home, Pittsfield; Boston Col., Boston Col. Law Sch., LL.B. 1949; Roman Catholic.

Career Seabees, SW Pacific, WWII; Practicing atty., 1949–58; MA Senate, 1951–59.

Offices 2300 RHOB, 202-225-5335. Also 78 Center St., Pittsfield 01201, 413-442-0946.

Committees *Appropriations* (Ranking Member). Subcommittees: Labor-Health and Human Services-Education; Legislative; Transportation. *Small Business* (2d). Subcommittee: General Oversight and the Economy.

Group Ratings

	ADA	ACLU	COPE	CFA	LCV	LWV	NTU	NSI	COC	ACA	CSFC
1982	80	71	61	62	75	73	51	30	41	30	40
1981	55	—	61	64	64	—	46	—	67	35	49
1980	83	60	68	71	76	70	23	30	62	30	43

National Journal Ratings

	Economic		Foreign		Cultural	
1982	54%	(LIB)	79%	(LIB)	81%	(LIB)
	46%	(CONS)	21%	(CONS)	19%	(CONS)
1981	49%	(LIB)	70%	(LIB)	71%	(LIB)
	51%	(CONS)	29%	(CONS)	29%	(CONS)

Key Votes

1) Reagan 81 Budget	FOR	5) Incr SS Rtmt Age	AGN	9) Poor Pay Food Stamps	AGN
2) Reagan 81 Tax Cut	FOR	6) Saudi AWACS Sale	AGN	10) Ban Crt Busing Order	AGN
3) Bal Budget Amend	AGN	7) $ for MX Missile	AGN	11) Auto Local Content	FOR
4) Gas & Road Tax	FOR	8) Nerve Gas Prod	AGN	12) Nuclear Arms Freeze	FOR

Election Results

1982 general	Silvio O. Conte (R) unopposed	145,417		($52,867)
1982 primary	Silvio O. Conte (R) unopposed	11,665		
1980 general	Silvio O. Conte (R)	156,415	(75%)	($80,126)
	Helen Poppy Doyle (D)	52,457	(25%)	($14,464)

Campaign Contributions and Expenditures

1981-82		*Direct Cont. 81-82*				*PACS brkdwn*		
Receipts	$102,518	Indiv	$24,126	Agr	$700	Ideo	$1,900
Expend.	$52,867	Party	$8,948	Bus	$41,750	Lbr	$5,650
Unspent	$111,702	PACS	$54,700	Hlth	$3,000	Prof	$1,700

SECOND DISTRICT

The 2d congressional district of Massachusetts includes the city of Springfield, many of its suburbs, and a collection of rural and small industrial towns to the east. Springfield and Chicopee, which together have about half the district's population, are its Democratic bastions, although most of the rest of the 2d often produces Democratic margins as well. The image of the small New England town is of a clapboard village peopled by taciturn Yankees. But in fact many of the old Protestants have died off, moved west, or married into immigrant families, and in the towns they once lived in most people consider themselves to be of Irish, Italian, or Polish background. The storefronts may have New England Yankee facades, but hanging above are signs with names of Italian or Polish proprietors. You will see them not only in the industrial towns of Fitchburg, Leominster, and Gardner, at the northeast corner of the district, but also in the smaller towns that dot the stony hillsides of central Massachusetts between Fitchburg and Springfield.

Springfield is a hilly, industrial city, distinguished as the hometown of several diverse political pros, including Lawrence O'Brien, the Democratic national chairman whose telephone was the target of the Watergate burglars, and political consultant Joseph Napolitan, who still has his main office here. Another Springfield political pro is 2d district Congressman Edward Boland, a Democrat with 30 years service in the House. For many years Boland, long a bachelor, roomed with Tip O'Neill, whose wife remained in Cambridge; they have ended that arrangement but remain close. Like O'Neill, Boland was for many years a politician who could bridge the gap between the senior big city politicians—a group to which he temperamentally belongs—and the younger, more ideological liberals in the Democratic Caucus. Now the situation is different: not many of the old big city pols are left, and the young upstarts are as often skeptical about big government programs as they are enthusiastic supporters of them. But Boland remains an important and competent legislative leader.

One sensitive assignment he has is chairing the Permanent Select Committee on Intelligence in the House. Boland has supported some defense budget cuts and questioned some intelligence practices, but he does not share the suspicion of national security bureaucracies which is endemic to many of the younger Democrats who came into politics during the Vietnam war. But neither does he have the kind of total faith in the executive branch that many big city Democrats had years ago. Boland authored the amendment which, in somewhat delphic language, prohibited the government from supporting efforts to overthrow the Sandinista regime in Nicaragua; and in 1983 he charged that the Reagan administration was violating it. But unlike some younger liberals, his dislike of that policy does not lead him to a visceral championing of the Sandinistas, about whom he has few illusions.

Boland's other major position is on the Appropriations Committee. He is second ranking Democrat, and in 1979 there was a move to elect him chairman. He refused to support it but got 88 votes to 157 for Jamie Whitten of Mississippi—a smaller margin than it looks, because only 35 switches would have elected Boland. Whitten in recent years has had a record of supporting most national Democratic initiatives and of obstructing none; he and Boland are both temperamentally team players, and though their records look different to ratings groups they seldom work at cross purposes.

On both intelligence matters and on the appropriations bills his HUD–Independent Agencies Subcommittee reports, Boland has a reputation for getting bills and resolutions he manages adopted without major change. They are reported on time, he is prepared to answer queries, and the bills are usually passed without much challenge: he is one of the strongest Appropriations subcommittee chairmen (the group long referred to as "the college of cardinals").

Boland has not had serious opposition in many years and seems to be in solid political shape back home.

The People   Pop. 1980: 521,949, dn. 2.2% 1970–80; voting age pop. 377,798; 4% Black, 3% Span. orig. 36% housing units rented. Median owner $37,100; renter $158. Households: 74% family, 39% with children, 60% married couples.

Presidential Vote

1980	Reagan (R)	89,365	(42%)
	Carter (D)	93,997	(44%)
	Anderson (I)	29,306	(14%)

Rep. Edward P. Boland (D) Elected 1952; b. Oct. 1, 1911, Springfield; home, Springfield; Boston Col. Law Sch.; Roman Catholic.

Career MA House of Reps., 1935–41; Hampton Cnty. Register of Deeds, 1941–42, 1946–49; Army, WWII; Military Aide to Gov. Paul A. Dever, 1949–52.

Offices 2426 RHOB, 202-225-5601. Also 1883 Main St., Springfield 01103, 413-733-4127.

Committees *Appropriations* (2d). Subcommittees: HUD-Independent Agencies (Chairman); Interior; Treasury-Postal Service-General Government. *Permanent Select Committee on Intelligence* (Chairman). Subcommittee: Program and Budget Authorization (Chairman).

Group Ratings

	ADA	ACLU	COPE	CFA	LCV	LWV	NTU	NSI	COC	ACA	CSFC
1982	80	75	89	85	82	92	13	38	27	22	30
1981	80	—	88	93	91	—	5	—	6	17	36
1980	78	53	63	86	63	80	18	20	64	21	30

National Journal Ratings

	Economic		Foreign		Cultural	
1982	74%	(LIB)	70%	(LIB)	62%	(LIB)
	25%	(CONS)	29%	(CONS)	38%	(CONS)
1981	81%	(LIB)	82%	(LIB)	73%	(LIB)
	15%	(CONS)	17%	(CONS)	27%	(CONS)

Key Votes

1) Reagan 81 Budget	AGN	5) Incr SS Rtmt Age —	9) Poor Pay Food Stamps	AGN
2) Reagan 81 Tax Cut	AGN	6) Saudi AWACS Sale AGN	10) Ban Crt Busing Order	FOR
3) Bal Budget Amend	AGN	7) $ for MX Missile AGN	11) Auto Local Content	FOR
4) Gas & Road Tax	—	8) Nerve Gas Prod AGN	12) Nuclear Arms Freeze	FOR

Election Results

1982 general	Edward P. Boland (D)	118,215	(73%)	($32,187)
	Thomas P. Swank (R)	44,544	(27%)	($0)
1982 primary	Edward P. Boland (D)	62,597	(100%)	
1980 general	Edward P. Boland (D)	120,711	(67%)	($28,553)
	Thomas P. Swank (R)	38,672	(22%)	($0)
	John B. Aubuchon (I)	20,247	(11%)	

Campaign Contributions and Expenditures

1981-82		Direct Cont. 81-82		PACS brkdwn			
Receipts	$30,398	Indiv	$7,349	Agr	$—	Ideo	$—
Expend.	$32,187	PACS	$10,500	Bus	$8,900	Lbr	$1,500
Unspent	$55,738			Hlth	$—	Prof	$—

THIRD DISTRICT

Worcester, pronounced locally as if it had no Rs, is the second largest city in Massachusetts and is roughly in the geographical center of the state. But it is far smaller than Boston and bulks much smaller in the consciousness of the state. It is basically a small manufacturing town which has maintained reasonable prosperity over the years; it has always had a high-skill, high-wage labor market, and was not one of those New England cities that was devastated by the flight of the textile mills decades ago. Now metropolitan Boston has been growing out toward Worcester, and the computer and electronics industries are beginning to concentrate now along Interstate 495, some 20 miles east of Worcester, as they did around the circumferential highway closer to Boston, Route 128, 20 years ago. The biggest such company is Digital, one of the giants of the industry, a kind of junior IBM. The movement of this high tech industry brings with it prosperity, new residents, and higher housing prices to the towns and suburbs along I495 and toward Worcester itself.

The Worcester area, and the 3d congressional district with which it is roughly coincident, have been Democratic strongholds politically as long as anyone can remember. This is nitty gritty New England, where political attitudes are bred into people and remain almost as rock-solid as the stony terrain in these parts. The 3d district spreads north from Worcester to the mill town of Lunenburg, south to the Rhode Island border, east to Interstate 95, and west just beyond Worcester.

The congressman from this district is Joseph Early, a Democrat first elected in 1974. Unlike many other members of that freshman Democratic class, Early did not get his political start canvassing against the Vietnam war or trying to save sea birds from an oil spill. His district is a town, not a gown, district, and he is very much a product of town politics: a teacher and coach who won a seat in the Great and General Court (that is, the legislature) in 1962, at age 29, and was strong enough after 12 years to win the House seat in a seriously contested primary and against a serious Republican in a general election complicated by an independent candidate. Early's voting record looks a lot like those of his Massachusetts colleagues, but he is not one to make a public issue of our policy toward Chile, to take one example. He is, rather, an insider, a member of the Appropriations Committee who seldom gets publicity but has a chance to make policy. That seems to suit his constituents fine: since 1974, he has had no difficulty winning reelection, and seems unlikely to have any in the near future.

The People   Pop. 1980: 521,354, up 2.2% 1970–80; voting age pop. 376,641; 1% Black, 2% Span. orig. 37% housing units rented. Median owner $46,800; renter $175. Households: 75% family, 40% with children, 62% married couples.

Presidential Vote

1980	Reagan (R)	98,115	(43%)
	Carter (D)	97,053	(42%)
	Anderson (I)	33,336	(15%)

Rep. Joseph D. Early (D) Elected 1974; b. Jan. 31, 1933, Worcester; home, Worcester; Col. of the Holy Cross, B.S. 1955; Roman Catholic.

Career Navy, 1955–57; High sch. teacher and coach, 1959–63; MA House of Reps., 1963–74.

Offices 2349 RHOB, 202-225-6101. Also 34 Mechanic St., Rm. 203, Worcester 01608, 617-752-6718.

Committee *Appropriations* (16th). Subcommittees: Commerce, Justice, State and Judiciary; Labor-Health and Human Services-Education.

Group Ratings

	ADA	ACLU	COPE	CFA	LCV	LWV	NTU	NSI	COC	ACA	CSFC
1982	80	75	83	77	87	80	36	17	17	10	29
1981	85	—	81	86	90	—	35	—	0	27	36
1980	67	43	71	86	79	75	30	20	53	20	43

National Journal Ratings

	Economic		Foreign		Cultural	
1982	79%	(LIB)	71%	(LIB)	82%	(LIB)
	21%	(CONS)	28%	(CONS)	18%	(CONS)
1981	81%	(LIB)	90%	(LIB)	72%	(LIB)
	15%	(CONS)	9%	(CONS)	28%	(CONS)

Key Votes

1) Reagan 81 Budget	AGN	5) Incr SS Rtmt Age	AGN	9) Poor Pay Food Stamps	AGN
2) Reagan 81 Tax Cut	AGN	6) Saudi AWACS Sale	AGN	10) Ban Crt Busing Order	FOR
3) Bal Budget Amend	AGN	7) $ for MX Missile	AGN	11) Auto Local Content	FOR
4) Gas & Road Tax	—	8) Nerve Gas Prod	AGN	12) Nuclear Arms Freeze	FOR

Election Results

1982 general	Joseph D. Early (D)	142,611	(100%)	($110,878)
1982 primary	Joseph D. Early (D)	72,560	(100%)	
1980 general	Joseph D. Early (D)	141,560	(72%)	($71,210)
	David G. Skehan (R)	54,213	(28%)	($0)

Campaign Contributions and Expenditures

1981-82		Direct Cont. 81-82			PACS brkdwn		
Receipts	$86,794	Indiv	$69,605	Agr	$500	Ideo	$—
Expend.	$110,878	PACS	$16,350	Bus	$7,950	Lbr	$4,600
Unspent	$7,895			Hlth	$2,500	Prof	$700

FOURTH DISTRICT

The 4th congressional district was the scene of one of 1982's most heralded and bitterly fought congressional races, and the most expensive in the entire nation. The contest occurred because the Massachusetts Great and General Court (the official name of the legislature), forced to reduce the number of the commonwealth's congressional districts, put Democrat Barney Frank and Republican Margaret Heckler in the same district. Looking at the 4th district's boundaries on the map, you would have a hard time thinking of it as a cohesive unit. It has examples of almost every kind of Massachusetts community. They include:

- *Brookline and Newton.* These are old, close-in suburbs of Boston, with large Jewish populations, middle to upper income, and low percentages of families and children and large numbers of university students. Physically, they are places with comfortable old houses and huge overhanging trees, intersections with shops built in the 1920s but stocked and decorated in the chicest 1980s style. Politically, they are self-consciously liberal, particularly on cultural issues. They were the political base of Robert Drinan, the Jesuit priest and former Boston College law dean, who represented the 4th district for 10 years until forced to retire by a papal decree, and of Barney Frank, the former Boston legislator who moved to Newton and won the 4th district when Drinan retired in 1980. Altogether, Brookline and Newton cast 30% of the new 4th district's votes.
- *Wellesley and Dover.* These are the rich, WASPy suburbs which for many people typify suburban Boston but are in fact demographically rather unusual, and Wellesley and Dover cast only 7% of the 4th district's votes. If you want to see pure preppy style—from Weejuns to sensible hairdos—these are the places to go. Economically and physically, Wellesley looks a lot like Newton, which it adjoins; politically,

Wellesley has always been a Republican stronghold. But it is Massachusetts WASPy Republican, with roots in the old Yankee interventionist tradition; Republicans here tend to look to the League of Women Voters and Common Cause for advice, and they look askance at anything that reminds them of bigotry. This is the political base of Margaret Heckler, who was elected the only Republican on the Governor's Council in 1962; in Democratic Massachusetts, which seemed rife with corruption and cronyism, she proclaimed "I'm a Heckler," and got elected. Four years later she took on the 81-year-old Joseph Martin, former speaker of the House, and beat him in the Republican primary.

- *The middle suburbs.* From almost working class Natick in the north, down through newly built and upper middle income Medfield, Sharon with its large Jewish population; down through Foxboro, the home of the New England Patriots; to Attleboro and Norton, pleasant old New England towns of mixed ethnic background, there are a series of suburbs within range of Boston TV, but of widely different cultural character. This is the part of the district with the largest proportion of children and young families; subdivisions here, handy to the interstates, have been sprouting up more than in most other parts of Massachusetts. The middle suburbs cast more than one-third of the 4th district's votes.

- *Fall River.* You could hardly find a more working class town than Fall River. Once a textile center, it has adapted now; once full of Yankee farm girls and Irish immigrants, it now has a population with many Portuguese. Fall River is ancestrally very Democratic, and the Fall River area was the only part of the 4th to give Jimmy Carter an absolute majority of its votes in 1980. But Margaret Heckler, an indefatigable campaigner and strong constituency service congressman, had carried it with large margins. The Fall River area casts one-fourth of the new 4th district's votes.

Neither Frank nor Heckler wanted this fight, and both manuevered to get safe districts. But neither had many friends in the legislature. Frank, as a legislator with more wit than tact, had antagonized the House speaker and Senate president; Heckler, as a Republican, had few friends in the State House. Initially it seemed that the new district favored Heckler: Frank had represented only 30% of its voters, and only for one term; Heckler had represented 70% for 16 years. But Frank's base in Brookline and Newton was very solid; he ultimately won 77% of the vote there. And Heckler's base turned out to be considerably less solid than thought.

Some saw this campaign as a classic liberal versus conservative battle, but it was really a battle between a liberal Democrat with a consistent record and a Republican who likes to style herself liberal but has difficulty making up her mind on issues. Heckler was famous on Capitol Hill for her indecision, for agonizing between the demands of her conservative Republican leadership and her Massachusetts constituency. On the Reagan budget and tax programs of 1981 she supported the administration all the way; Frank used that to attack her hard in the Fall River area. The economic issues put Frank even in the early fall, and in the end he won 58% of the vote in the Fall River area.

Heckler tried to distance herself from the administration on economic issues by stressing cultural issues. But here she went too far. She ran ads which showed pictures of Frank with words like "supported prostitution" superimposed, because of a bill he had supported to limit vice to an area called "the combat zone" in Boston. Frank turned those ads against her, charging her with unfair tactics, and costing her lots of votes both in Brookline and Newton and in Wellesley and Dover. Heckler got only 23% in the former, 10% less than Reagan had in 1980; and she got only 57% in Wellesley and Dover, her home base, only slightly better than Reagan's performance there.

So Frank, after spending more than $1 million, ended up winning with 60% of the vote. Given that performance, he seems likely to have a safe seat for the 1980s. He may very well have the deadliest wit in Congress: commenting on the New Right's opposition to abortion and to child-feeding programs, he said "Sure, they're pro-life. They believe that life begins at conception and ends at birth." He is an unapologetic backer of liberal causes of almost all kinds, and he is also one of those natural politicians who has an instinct for how to frame an issue and how to get things done. Frank does not yet have any powerful committee posts, but the abilities he has shown already on his feet and on the campaign trail make him one of the most formidable Democrats in the House.

The People   Pop. 1980: 521,995, up 1.8% 1970–80; voting age pop. 386,245; 1% Black, 1% Span. orig., 1% Asian orig. 38% housing units rented. Median owner $58,900; renter $202. Households: 74% family, 38% with children, 61% married couples.

Presidential Vote

1980	Reagan (R)	95,429	(40%)
	Carter (D)	101,534	(43%)
	Anderson (I)	38,947	(17%)

Rep. Barney Frank (D) Elected 1980; b. Mar. 31, 1940, Bayonne, NJ; home, Newton Highlands; Harvard Col., B.A. 1962; Harvard U., 1962–67, J.D. 1977; Jewish.

Career Chf. of Staff to Boston Mayor Kevin White, 1967–76; A. A. to U.S. Rep. Michael Harrington, 1971–72; MA House of Reps., 1973–80; Lecturer on Pub. Policy, Harvard JFK Sch. of Gov., 1979–80.

Offices 1317 LHOB, 202-225-5931. Also 400 Totten Pond Rd., Waltham 02154, 617-890-9455; and Philip T. Philbin Fed. Bldg., 881 Main St., Fitchburg 01420, 617-342-8722.

Committees *Banking, Finance and Urban Affairs* (19th). Subcommittees: Financial Institutions Supervision, Regulation and Insurance; Housing and Community Development. *Government Operations* (13th). Subcommittee: Manpower and Housing. *Judiciary* (14th). Subcommittees: Administrative Law and Governmental Relations; Courts, Civil Liberties and the Administration of Justice; Immigration, Refugees and International Law. *Select Committee on Aging* (22d). Subcommittee: Retirement Income and Employment.

Group Ratings

	ADA	ACLU	COPE	CFA	LCV	LWV	NTU	NSI	COC	ACA	CSFC
1982	90	100	93	85	92	91	33	10	30	9	33
1981	100	—	87	93	93	—	40	—	11	4	27

National Journal Ratings

	Economic		Foreign		Cultural	
1982	90%	(LIB)	80%	(LIB)	93%	(LIB)
	9%	(CONS)	20%	(CONS)	3%	(CONS)
1981	89%	(LIB)	92%	(LIB)	95%	(LIB)
	3%	(CONS)	2%	(CONS)	1%	(CONS)

Key Votes

1) Reagan 81 Budget AGN	5) Incr SS Rtmt Age AGN	9) Poor Pay Food Stamps AGN
2) Reagan 81 Tax Cut AGN	6) Saudi AWACS Sale AGN	10) Ban Crt Busing Order AGN
3) Bal Budget Amend AGN	7) $ for MX Missile AGN	11) Auto Local Content FOR
4) Gas & Road Tax —	8) Nerve Gas Prod AGN	12) Nuclear Arms Freeze FOR

Election Results

1982 general	Barney Frank (D)	121,802	(60%)	($1,502,581)
	Margaret M. Heckler (R)	82,804	(40%)	($966,921)
1982 primary	Barney Frank (D)	82,079	(100%)	
1980 general	Barney Frank (D)	103,446	(52%)	($446,826)
(MA 4)	Richard A. Jones (R)	95,898	(48%)	($53,481)
1980 general	Margaret M. Heckler (R)	131,794	(61%)	($264,688)
(MA 10)	Robert E. McCarthy (D)	85,629	(39%)	($158,110)

Campaign Contributions and Expenditures

1981-82		Direct Cont. 81-82				PACS brkdwn		
Receipts	$1,509,239	Indiv	$1,212,576	Agr	$—		Ideo	$69,348
Expend.	$1,502,581	Party	$9,517	Bus	$41,727		Lbr	$98,247
Unspent	$7,354	PACS	$223,266	Hlth	$650		Prof	$4,035
		Cand	$64,000					

Indirect Party Expend: $145   *Indep Expend*: Agn: $1,368

FIFTH DISTRICT

The 5th congressional district, northwest of Boston, is a part of the state which has been the engine for more than one of the commonwealth's spurts of economic growth. In the early 19th century, when Massachusetts was a kind of maritime republic, with a few farmers struggling to scratch a living from the stony soil, a few ingenious Yankees decided to tame the rapidly flowing Merrimack River and build cotton spinning mills. They created the cities of Lowell and Lawrence, built model housing for the local farm girls and, later, the Irish and French Canadian immigrants they used as their work force. When the maritime trading business faded, Massachusetts continued to grow because of the textile industry; it lasted here for nearly 100 years. Then, in the 1920s, the price of labor rose in New England and newly built mills in the Carolinas, nearer the cotton supply, essentially ended the businesses Lawrence and Lowell built. Yet many in the work force, by then rather elderly, waited forlornly for some upturn in the local economy.

It came from an unexpected source. Starting in Cambridge, around MIT and Harvard, moving out to the Route 128 circumferential highway, and more recently locating also along Interstate 495, which passes through Lowell and Lawrence, high tech has become the engine of growth for Massachusetts. The computer, microchip, and defense industries here have had their ups and downs; but in the early 1980s, when the rest of the country was in recession, Massachusetts had one of the nation's lowest unemployment rates and continued to enjoy economic growth.

The 5th congressional district's main urban centers are Lowell and Lawrence, which with surrounding suburbs account for about half its population. They have been much transformed since the 1950s, however. High tech, exemplified by Wang Laboratories, has moved into Lowell; the city also, thanks in large part to Senator and former Congressman Paul

Tsongas, has a national historical restoration project in its old mill area. Moreover, when you factor in the suburbs immediately adjacent, these two old mill towns are actually rather prosperous places and, politically, not necessarily Democratic (they went for Reagan over Carter in 1980). There are still evidences of their working class origins, however. There was not much enthusiasm here for John Anderson, and Congressman James Shannon was thrown on the defensive in 1980 when he was opposed by Boston's Cardinal Medeiros for his opposition to curbs on abortion.

Attitudes are considerably different in the southern part of the district, along and below Route 2, where 37% of the 5th's residents live. Old New England towns like Concord, Lincoln, Littleton, and Harvard have become high income WASPy (but not discriminatory) suburbs; their old New England houses and stone walls recall earlier times, but their residents often make their livings in the latest high tech industries and pride themselves on their contemporary attitudes. Politically, they tend toward the most liberal of Republicanisms, in the old Yankee interventionist tradition. This was one of the strongest parts of the country for John Anderson; he got 28% of the vote in Lincoln, for example, a town which went for McGovern in 1972 and then Ford in 1976.

The congressman from the 5th district is James Shannon, a Democrat whose political base is in Lawrence but who has proved an attractive candidate in the southern part of the district as well. He was first elected in 1978, at age 26, as the survivor (and only Lawrence candidate) in a six-man primary and the 52% winner in a three-man general election. He only scraped by, with 54%, in the 1980 primary after the cardinal opposed him, but won the general election easily. In 1982, he was helped by redistricting; he may not carry the new southern towns that were added by much in the general election (except for working class Framingham) but he is likely to win big margins in them in the primary, which is where the greater threat is.

Shannon is one of those natural politicians who can convince you that the Irish have an in-born aptitude for the business. Early on, he caught Tip O'Neill's eye and won a seat on the Ways and Means Committee. He sits on two key subcommittees, Social Security and Trade, and on both faces fascinating choices. Massachusetts's declining industries—shoes, textiles—for years have backed protectionist measures, and Shannon's Bay State predecessor on Ways and Means, James Burke, was instinctively for trade restrictions. But Shannon represents a district which is the home of some of the nation's fastest growing industries—industries generally too busy growing to seek government favors or protection (although some are worried about the Japanese challenge in microchips). On Social Security, he is expected to support the Democratic leadership position, which is to have minimal cuts, if any, in scheduled benefit increases and no raising of the retirement age. But are the tax increases, which will be necessary to support that position, going to stifle the economic growth that is so apparent in the 5th district? Jim Shannon, in his early 30s, may have an important political future, but he also has to grapple directly, as few members of Congress do, with questions which affect the future of the nation and of the especially productive district he represents.

The People Pop. 1980: 518,313, up 3.3% 1970–80; voting age pop. 368,925; 1% Black, 3% Span. orig., 1% Asian orig. 38% housing units rented. Median owner $61,100; renter $207. Households: 75% family, 42% with children, 62% married couples.

Presidential Vote

1980	Reagan (R)	100,189	(44%)
	Carter (D)	89,068	(40%)
	Anderson (I)	35,942	(16%)

Rep. James M. Shannon (D) Elected 1978; b. Apr. 4, 1952, Lawrence; home, Lawrence; Johns Hopkins U., B.A. 1972, Geo. Wash. U., J.D. 1975; Roman Catholic.

Career Aide to U.S. Rep. Michael Harrington, 1973–75; Practicing atty., 1975–78.

Offices 229 CHOB, 202-225-3411. Also 325 Merrimack St., Lowell 01852, 617-459-0101.

Committee *Ways and Means* (15th). Subcommittees: Health; Social Security.

Group Ratings

	ADA	ACLU	COPE	CFA	LCV	LWV	NTU	NSI	COC	ACA	CSFC
1982	95	96	89	92	90	91	18	0	10	9	26
1981	90	—	87	79	100	—	26	—	6	8	26
1980	94	93	89	93	88	100	19	10	59	14	24

National Journal Ratings

	Economic		Foreign		Cultural	
1982	96%	(LIB)	84%	(LIB)	88%	(LIB)
	2%	(CONS)	16%	(CONS)	11%	(CONS)
1981	74%	(LIB)	81%	(LIB)	99%	(LIB)
	25%	(CONS)	19%	(CONS)	1%	(CONS)

Key Votes

1) Reagan 81 Budget	AGN	5) Incr SS Rtmt Age	AGN	9) Poor Pay Food Stamps	AGN
2) Reagan 81 Tax Cut	AGN	6) Saudi AWACS Sale	AGN	10) Ban Crt Busing Order	AGN
3) Bal Budget Amend	AGN	7) $ for MX Missile	AGN	11) Auto Local Content	FOR
4) Gas & Road Tax	FOR	8) Nerve Gas Prod	AGN	12) Nuclear Arms Freeze	FOR

Election Results

1982 general	James M. Shannon (D)	140,177	(85%)	($144,504)
	Angelo Louis Laudani (L)	25,224	(15%)	($5,443)
1982 primary	James M. Shannon (D)	80,533	(100%)	
1980 general	James M. Shannon (D)	136,758	(66%)	($326,587)
	William C. Sawyer (R)	70,547	(34%)	($110,365)

Campaign Contributions and Expenditures

1981-82		Direct Cont. 81-82		PACS brkdwn			
Receipts	$215,700	Indiv	$112,802	Agr	$1,250	Ideo	$2,900
Expend.	$144,504	PACS	$83,520	Bus	$40,900	Lbr	$28,900
Unspent	$75,362			Hlth	$4,900	Prof	$3,350

Indep Expend: For: $300

SIXTH DISTRICT

The 6th congressional district of Massachusetts is the North Shore district. Along and just behind the rocky coast north of Boston are the estates of some of the commonwealth's oldest families, including—to name some active politically in recent years—the Saltonstalls, the Lodges, and the Hatches. These are the descendants of the daring plungers who in the late 18th and early 19th centuries sent sailing ships from the small ports of Boston and, on the North Shore itself, Salem (then not much smaller), to China. The ships were gone often for a year, often forever; but if and when they returned, their owners made profits in the hundreds of percents. Their descendants, ironically, have been known for decades as investors who sought the safest harbors for their money, putting them in low interest railroad bonds and blue chip stocks. But some of them are still plungers as well. The Boston area is full of management consultants and venture capitalists who have financed and organized many of the high tech companies which have contributed so much to the growth of Massachusetts; quietly, behind their estate walls on the North Shore or in their colonial era houses in Lincoln or Dover, they have profited as greatly from their foresight as did their ancestors.

But the North Shore is not just estates. It includes the old fishing village of Gloucester, whose smells and atmospheres are probably closer to the Salem of the clipper ships than are the manicured estates of today. Salem itself, where 20 witches were once hanged and pressed to death, is now a town filled mostly with people of immigrant stock, as is the newer suburb of Peabody next door. Nearby are the boating suburbs of Marblehead and Swampscott, which WASPs now share with Jews, and Lynn, whose troubled shoe industry pressed for years for protection against imports. The Merrimack River flows through the northern edge of the district, just below New Hampshire, past the old mill towns of Haverhill and Newburyport.

This is, in other words, a varied area, and politically it is as well. High income WASPs tend to be Republicans, but self-consciously liberal ones; Lynn, Salem, and Peabody are basically Irish working class Democratic, as are the Merrimack mill towns. On balance it is a Democratic district, but Republicans have a base here; they represented the district in Congress until 1969 and made serious attempts to win it in the last several elections. This is, by the way, the site of the original gerrymander, named because its architect, Elbridge Gerry, a Jeffersonian, wanted to corral all the area's Federalist towns into one grotesquely shaped district. Ironically, the current 6th district's boundaries are about as regular and politically unobjectionable as those of any district in the country.

The district's current congressman, Nicholas Mavroules, in 1982 seemed finally to get a secure hold on the seat. He has deep roots in local politics, and was mayor of Peabody for 11 years; he planned in 1978 to challenge incumbent Michael Harrington in the Democratic primary and then got the nomination when Harrington retired. Harrington was one of the most acerbic critics of administration policy in Vietnam and made a major cause of the Nixon administration's support of the overthrow of the Allende regime in 1973; he had a tougher than expected challenge in 1976, which ended his statewide ambitions.

Ironically, Mavroules, who came to office as a critic of Harrington's preoccupation with distant and dubious causes, won his first solid victory largely because of his own liberal position on a foreign policy issue, the nuclear freeze. He won in 1978 with 54% and in 1980 with 51%, when he was under heavy challenge from Republican Tom Trimarco; during the campaign he was investigated and cleared of charges of influence peddling while mayor. Mavroules inherited Harrington's seat on the Armed Services Committee, probably intending to concentrate on keeping business in General Electric's jet engine plant in Lynn; but in

1981 he became the body's leading supporter of the nuclear freeze resolution. That may not have sparked genuine enthusiasm for him among the district's antiwar activists, most of whom come from a far different social background and speak with different accents; but they decided they must support him against Trimarco's 1982 challenge. They did, and Mavroules's percentage rose most in the upper income towns where the freeze had its greatest support and at the northern edge of the district to which he apparently gave more attention. Given the solidness of his victory, and the continuing salience of issues like the freeze as long as Ronald Reagan is in office, Mavroules looks comfortable politically for the first time.

The People   Pop. 1980: 518,841, dn. 0.8% 1970–80; voting age pop. 383,191; 1% Black, 1% Span. orig. 36% housing units rented. Median owner $55,000; renter $216. Households: 72% family, 37% with children, 59% married couples.

Presidential Vote

1980	Reagan (R)	109,933	(45%)
	Carter (D)	94,549	(38%)
	Anderson (I)	41,896	(17%)

Rep. Nicholas Mavroules (D) Elected 1978; b. Nov. 1, 1929, Peabody; home, Peabody; MIT, night courses; Eastern Orthodox.

Career Sprvsr. of Personnel, Sylvania Electronics Corp., 1949–67; Peabody Ward Cncl., 1958–61; Councillor-at-Large, 1964–65; Mayor of Peabody, 1967–78.

Offices 1204 LHOB, 202-225-8020. Also 99 Washington St., Salem 01970, 617-745-5800.

Committees *Armed Services* (14th). Subcommittees: Investigations; Procurement and Military Nuclear Systems. *Small Business* (13th). Subcommittee: Energy, Environment and Safety Issues Affecting Small Business.

Group Ratings

	ADA	ACLU	COPE	CFA	LCV	LWV	NTU	NSI	COC	ACA	CSFC
1982	80	75	89	85	75	82	7	30	19	13	32
1981	80	—	87	79	71	—	12	—	16	17	38
1980	72	47	77	58	85	78	18	50	61	15	32

National Journal Ratings

	Economic		Foreign		Cultural	
1982	90%	(LIB)	67%	(LIB)	76%	(LIB)
	9%	(CONS)	33%	(CONS)	24%	(CONS)
1981	77%	(LIB)	72%	(LIB)	65%	(LIB)
	21%	(CONS)	26%	(CONS)	35%	(CONS)

Key Votes

1) Reagan 81 Budget	AGN	5) Incr SS Rtmt Age	AGN
2) Reagan 81 Tax Cut	AGN	6) Saudi AWACS Sale	AGN
3) Bal Budget Amend	AGN	7) $ for MX Missile	AGN
4) Gas & Road Tax	FOR	8) Nerve Gas Prod	AGN

9) Poor Pay Food Stamps	AGN
10) Ban Crt Busing Order	—
11) Auto Local Content	FOR
12) Nuclear Arms Freeze	FOR

Election Results

1982 general	Nicholas Mavroules (D)	117,723	(58%)	($438,713)
	Thomas H. Trimarco (R)	85,849	(42%)	($289,261)
1982 primary	Nicholas Mavroules (D)	75,788	(79%)	
	James Carritte (D)	20,025	(21%)	
1980 general	Nicholas Mavroules (D)	111,393	(51%)	($360,960)
	Thomas H. Trimarco (R)	103,192	(47%)	($250,061)

Campaign Contributions and Expenditures

1981-82		Direct Cont. 81-82		PACS brkdwn			
Receipts	$439,474	Indiv	$219,381	Agr	$1,500	Ideo	$13,975
Expend.	$438,713	Party	$5,000	Bus	$48,283	Lbr	$75,220
Unspent	$3,747	PACS	$142,425	Hlth	$1,500	Prof	$1,100
		Cand	$40,534				

Indep Expend: For: $2,317 (MA LIFEPAC)

SEVENTH DISTRICT

The history of many Boston area families is the story of movement outward from Boston harbor, from a dockside where bewildered immigrants landed, seasick perhaps and squinting to find friends and relatives or anyone who spoke their language, to a comfortable suburb, with a New England white frame house with red or bright blue shutters, furnished in Early American, with a view out the paned windows of a large tree in the side or back yard. You can see this kind of history just by traveling through the 7th congressional district of Massachusetts. This is not the territory well known to tourists: the city of Boston, with all its sights, is almost entirely south of Boston harbor, while the 7th district is north.

A good place to start is Chelsea, long a disembarkation point for immigrants, a grim industrial place now with some of the lowest income levels in Massachusetts. It is host now to the newest immigrants, Puerto Ricans; with Boston and Lawrence, it is the only part of the state with a significant Hispanic population. Next you come to Everett, still a working class town; then out to Malden and Medford, which still have the look they did when they were inhabited mostly by ethnic-conscious Yankees in the 1920s. About here the streetcars stop and bus lines thin out. Some of the towns farther out remain Yankee strongholds, like Melrose; others are solidly high income, like Winchester; but just beyond is working class Woburn (pronounced as if it had two Os); and to the side the high tech suburb of Lexington, with its proud revolutionary heritage. Added to the 7th district in 1981, to meet the population standard, are Billerica (from an old English name that has a Celtic ring) and Tewksbury, which are really suburbs of Lowell.

Political attitudes have changed as families have moved up from the dockside and fanned out through this area. Up through the 1950s, this was a Republican district; only Chelsea and Everett were dependably Democratic. Now it is so solidly Democratic that it is never seriously contested by Republicans. In 1976, when the district's congressman died, 12 Democrats filed to run in the primary—and no Republican.

The winner of that free-for-all was Edward Markey, a young state legislator (30 then) who like Jimmy Stewart in *Mr. Smith Goes to Washington* had never been in the nation's capital. Markey stands among the most liberal young congressmen, with few doubts about the wisdom of traditional Democratic economic programs and a mistrust, bred in the Vietnam era, of American military adventures abroad. He was one of the leaders—and perhaps the most fervent of the leaders—in the battle for the nuclear freeze resolution in the House. Markey has a more mixed record on cultural issues, however; it should be remembered that he is a product of Boston College, not Harvard, and of Malden, not Newton.

Markey has seats on two important committees, Energy and Commerce and Interior. On the latter in 1981 he got the chairmanship of the Oversight and Investigations Subcommittee. This gives him an opportunity to look into what he regards as the misdeeds of the Reagan administration on environmental policy, and he has done so to some extent. But his greatest interest seems to be in nuclear power. Markey is one of the House's strongest opponents of nuclear power: he believes it is in its present form dangerous, uneconomical, and environmentally damaging, and he pursues the subject with grim determination. Markey got through redistricting in good shape, and seems unlikely to have serious competition for this seat in the 1980s.

The People   Pop. 1980: 523,982, dn. 3.7% 1970–80; voting age pop. 387,217; 1% Black, 1% Span. orig., 1% Asian orig. 38% housing units rented. Median owner $58,100; renter $220. Households: 75% family, 38% with children, 61% married couples.

Presidential Vote

1980	Reagan (R)	103,704	(42%)
	Carter (D)	103,876	(43%)
	Anderson (I)	36,425	(15%)

Rep. Edward J. Markey (D) Elected 1976; b. July 11, 1946, Malden; home, Malden; Boston Col., B.A. 1968, J.D. 1972; Roman Catholic.

Career MA House of Reps., 1973–76.

Offices 205 CHOB, 202-225-2836. Also JFK Fed. Bldg., Rm. 2100A, Boston 02203, 617-223-2781.

Committees *Energy and Commerce* (8th). Subcommittees: Fossil and Synthetic Fuels; Oversight and Investigations; Telecommunications, Consumer Protection and Finance. *Interior and Insular Affairs* (9th). Subcommittees: Energy and the Environment; Oversight and Investigations (Chairman).

Group Ratings

	ADA	ACLU	COPE	CFA	LCV	LWV	NTU	NSI	COC	ACA	CSFC
1982	100	75	86	92	90	83	24	10	9	9	25
1981	90	—	84	86	100	—	35	—	5	21	27
1980	83	80	84	93	100	90	23	0	63	22	27

National Journal Ratings

	Economic		Foreign		Cultural	
1982	83%	(LIB)	96%	(LIB)	86%	(LIB)
	15%	(CONS)	1%	(CONS)	13%	(CONS)
1981	81%	(LIB)	92%	(LIB)	67%	(LIB)
	15%	(CONS)	2%	(CONS)	32%	(CONS)

Key Votes

1) Reagan 81 Budget AGN	5) Incr SS Rtmt Age AGN	9) Poor Pay Food Stamps AGN
2) Reagan 81 Tax Cut AGN	6) Saudi AWACS Sale AGN	10) Ban Crt Busing Order AGN
3) Bal Budget Amend AGN	7) $ for MX Missile AGN	11) Auto Local Content FOR
4) Gas & Road Tax FOR	8) Nerve Gas Prod AGN	12) Nuclear Arms Freeze FOR

Election Results

1982 general	Edward J. Markey (D)	151,305	(78%)	($182,162)
	David M. Basile (R)	43,063	(22%)	($57,663)
1982 primary	Edward J. Markey (D)	103,936	(100%)	
1980 general	Edward J. Markey (D)	155,759	(100%)	($67,173)

Campaign Contributions and Expenditures

1981-82		*Direct Cont. 81-82*			*PACS brkdwn*		
Receipts	$234,307	Indiv	$140,339	Agr	$250	Ideo	$500
Expend.	$182,162	PACS	$68,553	Bus	$19,500	Lbr	$45,250
Unspent	$97,808			Hlth	$2,000	Prof	$—

Indep Expend: For: $562 (MA LIFEPAC)

EIGHTH DISTRICT

The 8th congressional district of Massachusetts is a district with a number of distinctions. It is the home of no less than two national universities—Harvard and MIT—and of dozens of other universities and colleges; altogether, about 15% of its adults are students, one of the two or three highest proportions in congressional districts nationwide. It is the home of some of the nation's greatest historic sites: Bunker Hill and the frigate *Constitution* in the Charlestown section of Boston, the gold-domed State House overlooking the Boston Common and, on the side, townhouse-bedecked Beacon Hill. The district contains literally dozens of distinctive neighborhoods, from the stately grandeur of Boston's Back Bay, built in high Victorian times, to the insular Irish community in Charlestown, the Portuguese in East Cambridge and the Armenians in Watertown, the elderly Jews in Brighton, and the upper income Yankees and professors in Belmont.

It is also distinctive in congressional representation. This heavily Democratic part of heavily Democratic Massachusetts has been represented successively by a president of the United States, John F. Kennedy, and by a speaker of the House, Thomas P. O'Neill, Jr., universally known as Tip. Kennedy was a rich man who had only a nominal residence in the district and spent his six years in the House waiting to run for the Senate. O'Neill (who was born five years before Kennedy) was different. He is a product of local politics, with deep roots in his constituency, and he is a professional legislator—and one of the most proficient and successful speakers in the history of the House. To understand why, you need to know where he comes from.

• *North Cambridge.* O'Neill is from Cambridge—but not the Cambridge of Harvard Square or the gray-painted frame mansions on Brattle Street. He is from a mixed Irish-Italian neighborhood in North Cambridge, where his family was involved in local politics. Until he became speaker, O'Neill really lived in North Cambridge, and just kept a bachelor apartment in Washington; even now he returns frequently. The people he sees—the barber, the old lady down the street, the young family starting off whose grandparents he knew—personify the nation for him. It is a different America from what Ronald Reagan remembers of

Downstate Illinois of 50 years ago. In North Cambridge it's not unusual to hold a public job, one you got because some politician recommended you; and your neighbors understand that you'll be coming around to see them to ask them to vote for your friend on election day. And you have to ask. O'Neill likes to remember the story of a former teacher who didn't vote for him when he first ran for office, and he asked her why she didn't automatically support him even though he hadn't been by. "People always like to be asked, Thomas," she said. Tip O'Neill is the kind of politician who keeps in touch with his colleagues, his neighbors, and his adversaries, asking them for what he wants and listening to find out what they care about.

O'Neill also knows, from the North Cambridge of today, that Americans live their lives relying on a web of interlocking institutions—family, church, employer, union, clubs, personal friendships, government. In Ronald Reagan's Hollywood relationships were always tentative, subject to cancellation in the next contract; and anyway people always did very well by themselves. But in North Cambridge people need—rely on—these different institutions. He likes to use as an example the government program to aid dwarfs—an odd choice, considering O'Neill's own impressive size. But he knows personally parents whose children are dwarfs or handicapped or retarded, and he believes deeply that an affluent society can afford to help them. O'Neill comes by his support of government programs not from some abstract theory but because he has seen how people need them. He is always called a liberal, but you can almost see him as a Burkean conservative, unwilling to rip up part of the web of social relationships we have constructed over a great many years.

• *The Great and General Court.* O'Neill's opponents have labeled him as old and out of touch, but he is actually sympathetic to younger Democratic members—partly because he was a young legislator himself. He was elected to Congress when he was 40; but he had already been a legislator for 16 years. And he was elected speaker of the Great and General Court of Massachusetts—the first Democratic speaker in the legislature's history—after the 1948 elections, at the age of 36. State legislatures then were very different from the Congress. Members of the majority party voted for speaker, and then the speaker had all power: he named committee chairmen and all committee members, he determined the order of business on the floor, he determined who got patronage jobs and who didn't. It sounds autocratic, but in practice it's less autocratic than the strict seniority system that prevailed in the House until the 1970s, because the speaker is elected, usually after a series of deals, and he can be ousted as well. The majority of the majority rules, and if the voters don't like what they do, they can vote them out at the next election.

So when O'Neill came to the speakership in a House which had just chucked the strict rule of seniority and adopted a rule requiring a vote by the Democratic Caucus on all committee chairmen, he found himself in a familiar situation. Not that his powers were as strong as they were on Beacon Hill. But as the genuine choice of a majority of the Democratic Caucus, he was in a position to put pressure on committee chairmen if need be—which means that there was very seldom need, as long as he kept in touch and kept things moving. On some occasions O'Neill has issued what seemed like orders: he told Social Security Subcommittee Chairman Jake Pickle in 1981 to stop pursuing a bipartisan compromise on Social Security, and so helped the Democrats retain it as a campaign issue for 1982. Pickle obeyed because he is a loyal party man—and because it seemed that O'Neill had a majority of the caucus behind him.

At the same time, O'Neill has not tried to force old-fashioned big government programs down a lot of reluctant throats. In the 1981 budget fight, for example, he worked with Budget

Chairman Jim Jones to produce a Democratic plan which many liberals attacked as pallid—however, he commanded a larger proportion of Democratic votes, on a more difficult issue, than Sam Rayburn had been able to summon with the aid of an aggressive administration on the crucial 1961 Rules Committee packing vote. O'Neill is aware that 95 of the 269 Democrats elected to the current Congress are from the South, and that many of the northerners do not automatically back programs associated with liberal Democrats like energy price controls or massive jobs programs; the jobs program he was backing in early 1983 was considerably smaller than those proposed by candidates Carter and Kennedy in much more prosperous 1980. In the early 1980s O'Neill has been helped in his efforts to unite Democrats by the absence of emotionally divisive issues like civil rights or the Vietnam war. But there are many intellectually divisive issues which O'Neill has managed to slough over in search of party unity.

And he is looking for Democratic Party unity. When O'Neill became speaker in 1977, there were 290 Democrats in the House; whether he has that many or whether he has 241, as in 1981, or 269, as in 1983, he makes no effort to win Republican votes. This is quite the opposite of what Rayburn and the brilliant labor lobbyists of the 1950s and 1960s did; they always counted on 20 or so industrial and northeastern Republicans. O'Neill lost the budget and tax cut battles in 1981 when these Republicans, with almost no exceptions, stuck with the Reagan program; but he won the war, because half a dozen of them were defeated in 1982, and in the future he will likely get several Republican votes without asking for them.

• *The House Rules Committee.* As a legislatively experienced, loyal Democrat with a safe district and no overwhelming interest in any specific issue, O'Neill was a natural choice for membership in the House Rules Committee, which is supposed to provide for orderly conduct of business on the floor of the House. In the 1950s and 1960s that body was the burial ground of liberal legislation. Chairman Howard Smith of Virginia, William Colmer of Mississippi, and all of its Republicans regularly refused to clear to the floor legislation of which they disapproved, or granted rules that insured its defeat; when all else failed, Judge Smith would go tend to his farm in Virginia and not call any meetings of the committee for weeks.

These must have been frustrating years for O'Neill, and they seem to have made an imprint. Today he steadfastly refuses to use procedure and rules to obstruct the legislative process. Some Republicans would quarrel with that, and cite the procedures the Rules Committee (now solidly controlled by O'Neill) supported on the major votes on the Reagan tax cuts in 1981. But the very fact that the vote took place at all that year is a tribute to O'Neill's sense of fairness: he kept the legislative process on schedule—not an easy task—and kept his word to the president that the House would vote on his program. It did, beating O'Neill on the rule and then on the substantive vote as well.

O'Neill's years on the Rules Committee, examining the product of substantive committees, may also have given him the approach he uses on matters of the highest importance. Many have criticized the House for its proliferation of subcommittees, but O'Neill is aware that the character of the chairman and perhaps a few leading members is critical to getting legislation through committee and then passed on the floor. So he sets up what amount to *ad hoc* supercommittees when the importance of the issues warrants it and the existing committee leadership is inadequate or the existing committee jurisdiction is unclear. He did this on the Carter energy plan in 1977 and, despite serious sectional splits, passed the bill promptly in the House, with more than the 218 majority needed supplied by Democrats. He did it in effect on the Budget Committee in 1981; not entirely trusting Budget Chairman Jim Jones, he delegated Rules Chairman Richard Bolling to superintend the process and see that a viable Democratic alternative emerged. On Social Security, he pushed Pickle aside and helped Claude Pepper, then chairman of the Select (*i.e.,* nonlegislative) Committee on Aging, to get the spotlight and, with his opposition to almost any diminution of benefits, speak for the Democratic Party. When multiple subcommittees began investigating the Environmental Protection Agency in early 1983, O'Neill moved in to consolidate the probes, hoping to lessen chaos—and perhaps provide a Democratic campaign issue.

• *Forty years of history.* In the 1980 campaign, the Republican Party ran a television ad with an O'Neill lookalike carefreely driving a car until it ran out of gas. It was a successful ad, and it capitalized on the feeling that O'Neill *looked* like an old-fashioned politician. "He's just like the federal budget—" freshman Republican John LeBoutillier said in 1981, "fat, bloated, and out of control." House Democrats fretted that O'Neill was not a telegenic representative of their cause, and there was talk of replacing him with someone crisper and more up-to-date. There was little of that talk in 1982, and there was only one Republican ad—quickly yanked—with the O'Neill lookalike. It seems that as the American people got to know Tip O'Neill better, as they saw him operate under stress, in defeat and in victory, they got to respect and like him more. They began to understand the character that has made him a successful legislator rather than the features that make him easy to caricature.

And they have seen that O'Neill has, as a politician should, a sense of the flow of history which sees ahead of the politics of the moment. Being in the minority—as he was, effectively, in 1981—is not a new experience for O'Neill. The Massachusetts legislature and the first Congress he entered were under Republican control. He understands that there are ebbs and flows in politics and life, and he believes that Republican economic policies tend to produce depressions and recessions. His long-term strategy in 1981 and 1982 was to put the Republicans on record in favor of the Reagan program and against a Democratic alternative, not only on budget and taxes, but particularly on Social Security, and then to jam those votes down their throats in the 1982 elections. His long-term strategy for 1983 and 1984 seems more conciliatory. On election night he sounded a cooperative note; in December he got together with Howard Baker and produced a gas tax and highway building bill; in January he helped produce a bipartisan agreement on Social Security. He has been around long enough to have seen Republican administrations, in trouble because of the economy in the off-year, rebound in the presidential year when the economy recovers. Perhaps he expects that again, and wants to leave House Democrats in a position to claim credit for whatever good that happens just as they were able to profit from the bad that happened in 1982. He knows, and the country knows, that Tip O'Neill and the Democrats have working control of the House; and he knows, as he learned from years when the Democrats had working control in Massachusetts and in Congress, that they will be held responsible for what happens. At the same time, he is positioned to jump and make a strong party record if the recovery fails to develop.

Tip O'Neill has been underestimated as a strategist and political thinker, because he doesn't look or talk like one. But he performs like one. He made his way up in the House quietly, winning the Rules Committee slot as a team player, becoming whip because he helped swing key big city votes to Hale Boggs in the majority leader fight in 1971. His rise from there seemed automatic, in the old seniority tradition: he became majority leader after Boggs was lost in a plane crash in 1972 and speaker after Carl Albert retired in 1976. But there is no question that he holds his position today because his constituency, the House Democrats, want him there, not because of inertia. In early 1983 there was speculation all over Washington that O'Neill would retire in 1984, when he turns 72. Perhaps. But he shows every sign of enjoying his work, and House Democrats, as they think about the alternatives, discover, often to their surprise, that they would very much like him to stay. So, one suspects, would all the Democratic presidential candidates, and perhaps Ronald Reagan and the Republicans who would like to succeed him as well. For he has done more than win victories for his party: he has shown how to make the system work, fairly and efficiently, and in a way that gives the voters a chance to make an informed final choice.

The People Pop. 1980: 521,548, dn. 7.1% 1970–80; voting age pop. 434,109; 4% Black, 3% Span. orig., 3% Asian orig. 65% housing units rented. Median owner $60,600; renter $236. Households: 50% family, 22% with children, 37% married couples.

Presidential Vote

1980	Reagan (R)	67,209	(32%)
	Carter (D)	106,217	(51%)
	Anderson (I)	33,656	(16%)

Rep. Thomas P. (Tip) O'Neill, Jr. (D) Elected 1952; b. Dec. 9, 1912, Cambridge; home, Cambridge; Boston Col., A.B. 1936; Roman Catholic.

Career Insurance business; MA House of Reps., 1936–52, Minor. Ldr., 1947–48, Spkr., 1948–52; Cambridge Sch. Comm., 1946–47.

Offices 2231 RHOB, 202-225-5111. Also JFK Fed. Bldg., 2200A, Boston 02203, 617-223-2784.

Committees *The Speaker of the House.*

Group Ratings and Key Votes: Speaker does not usually vote

Election Results

1982 general	Thomas P. O'Neill, Jr. (D)	123,296	(75%)	($554,971)
	Frank Luke McNamara, Jr. (R) ...	41,370	(25%)	($817,422)
1982 primary	Thomas P. O'Neill, Jr. (D)	87,901	(78%)	
	Robert Meany Cappucci (D)	24,213	(22%)	($64,370)
1980 general	Thomas P. O'Neill, Jr. (D)	128,689	(78%)	($62,837)
	William A. Barnstead (R)	35,477	(22%)	($4,829)

Campaign Contributions and Expenditures

1981-82		*Direct Cont. 81-82*	
Receipts	$539,464	Indiv	$280,741
Expend.	$554,971	PACS	$257,426
Unspent	$27,322		

PACS Breakdown Not Available   Indep Expend: Agn: $301,055 (NCPAC)

NINTH DISTRICT

Boston is the most political of cities. In a conversation in a working class bar, even over lunch at the Somerset Club, there is a shared assumption that people use government to shape political ends, as well as the other way around; that politics pervades everything. And so it may, in a city where building contractors and Ph.D. candidates are both looking to government to enrich them, in the knowledge that political connections will determine whether they succeed or fail.

Politics has been in the air in Boston throughout its history. Boston malcontents were starting the American revolution when the burghers of Philadelphia and New York were still concentrating on getting rich, and Boston was the hotbed for the abolitionist movement that had much to do with igniting the Civil War. Boston is also, and this is no coincidence, the nation's most Irish city; for the Irish seem to have some magical aptitude for politics. The Irish have been here a long time now—since the 1840s in many cases—but they retain their ethnic consciousness. You can still find little ladies in Boston who will tell you that they don't know much about the candidates but "I always vote for all the good Irish names"; and you will find people who, when asked about discrimination, say, "Oh, yes. You mean 'No Irish need apply.' " Even in the majority, in a city governed by a series of Irish mayors since 1906, the Irish still feel beleaguered, resentful of the privileges and connections Boston's Brahmins seem to enjoy, disdainful of what they consider the disrespectful behavior of many blacks, confused by the denunciations of their neighborhoods during the busing crisis by intellectuals from Boston's universities and writers for the *Boston Globe*.

You can understand the pessimism of the Irish a little better if you consider the career of Boston's longtime mayor, Kevin White. From an Irish political background, he is as talented a politician as there is around, a man who can hold his own with Harvard graduate students or with a patronage employee who works his precinct. He was first elected mayor in 1967, and celebrated nationally as a foe of busing foe Louise Day Hicks. In his first terms he was widely popular, and was almost offered the vice presidential nomination by George McGovern in 1972—until he was vetoed by John Kenneth Galbraith and Edward Kennedy. But after 15 years in office, White has turned sour. He has unabashedly built a political machine, requiring city workers to contribute money and work their precincts; some of his appointees, at least, have gone farther and asked city contractors to give expensive birthday presents to Mrs. White. Estranged from the press, alone with his retainers in City Hall, White was reported to be interested in seeking a fifth term in 1983. However, in a press conference shrouded in mystery, White announced his retirement from politics. Few of the city's Irish voters have any warm feeling toward him; and perhaps he illustrates for them the fact that circumstances will always, sooner or later, hold you down. No matter how successful you may seem, ultimately you are tied down by your roots, and still must stand out in the cold, windy, dark streets of Boston on election day looking for votes.

Once you get outside the northern edge of Boston, away from the downtown skyscrapers, Back Bay and Beacon Hill, you are likely to be in an Irish neighborhood, or in a black neighborhood which was, not too many years ago, mostly Irish. Most of these neighborhoods—the geographic heart of Boston—are part of the 9th congressional district of Massachusetts. It stretches from the Italian North End and the refurbished Quincy Market, near Faneuil Hall and the modern City Hall, out Washington Street, past mostly black Roxbury and mostly white South Boston, to the rolling hills lined with three-decker houses of Jamaica Plain, Forest Hills, Roslindale, and West Roxbury. Once this area formed all of a district. But over the years, Boston's population has been declining: young people move out to newer neighborhoods with their families, houses which once held half a dozen families now hold just a few old people, some neighborhoods decay and are filled with empty houses.

So the 9th district, to meet the one-person-one-vote standard without robbing the neighboring 11th district of Democratic votes in the Dorchester section of Boston, moves out in Massachusetts far beyond where most of the people who grew up in Boston went. It includes the well-to-do suburbs of Needham and Westwood, more modest towns like Stoughton, the small industrial city of Taunton, far south of Boston, and several small rural towns roundabout. Less than half the district's population is now in Boston.

This has not had any political consequences for Congressman Joe Moakley. He has not had serious competition for ten years, and the suburban territory has enough solid Democratic votes that, combined with Boston, the district is highly unattractive to a Republican. As for competition within the party, that seems unlikely: Moakley is a solid party man, a member of the Rules Committee who is fully responsive to Speaker Tip O'Neill and who has caused himself no problems on issues. He is solidly liberal on economic and foreign issues, but not on cultural ones—an attractive combination in Boston and many of the 9th district suburbs.

Curiously, considering his party regularity, Moakley was first elected, in 1972, as an Independent; he was running against Louise Day Hicks, the busing opponent who had won the Democratic nomination and the seat in 1970 with minority votes. Before that, the 9th district and its predecessors were represented since 1925 by John McCormack, who served as speaker during his last nine years in the House. Moakley won't be speaker, but he is an experienced legislator (he served in both houses in Massachusetts and on the Boston Council) and competent parliamentarian and, as third ranking Democrat on Rules, a possible future chairman of that committee.

The People Pop. 1980: 519,226, dn. 5.2% 1970–80; voting age pop. 380,987; 14% Black, 4% Span. orig., 1% Asian orig. 47% housing units rented. Median owner $49,400; renter $172. Households: 68% family, 36% with children, 49% married couples.

Presidential Vote

1980	Reagan (R)	82,352	(43%)
	Carter (D)	85,583	(44%)
	Anderson (I)	26,051	(13%)

Rep. John Joseph (Joe) **Moakley** (D) Elected 1972 as Independent, seated in Congress as Democrat, Jan. 3, 1973; b. Apr. 27, 1927, Boston; home, Boston; U. of Miami, Suffolk U., LL.B. 1956; Roman Catholic.

Career Navy, WWII; MA House of Reps., 1953–65, Major. Whip, 1957; Practicing atty., 1957–72; MA Senate, 1965–69; Boston City Cncl., 1971.

Offices 221 CHOB, 202-225-8273. Also JFK Fed. Bldg., Rm. 1900C, Boston 02203, 617-223-5715.

Committee *Rules* (3d). Subcommittee: Rules of the House (Chairman).

Group Ratings

	ADA	ACLU	COPE	CFA	LCV	LWV	NTU	NSI	COC	ACA	CSFC
1982	75	46	91	85	90	82	7	22	18	22	27
1981	55	—	90	64	88	—	19	—	6	16	34
1980	72	40	82	79	69	89	10	20	68	10	28

National Journal Ratings

	Economic		Foreign		Cultural	
1982	86%	(LIB)	78%	(LIB)	66%	(LIB)
	14%	(CONS)	22%	(CONS)	33%	(CONS)
1981	89%	(LIB)	84%	(LIB)	57%	(LIB)
	3%	(CONS)	16%	(CONS)	43%	(CONS)

Key Votes

1) Reagan 81 Budget	AGN	5) Incr SS Rtmt Age	AGN	9) Poor Pay Food Stamps	AGN
2) Reagan 81 Tax Cut	AGN	6) Saudi AWACS Sale	AGN	10) Ban Crt Busing Order	FOR
3) Bal Budget Amend	AGN	7) $ for MX Missile	AGN	11) Auto Local Content	FOR
4) Gas & Road Tax	FOR	8) Nerve Gas Prod	AGN	12) Nuclear Arms Freeze	FOR

Election Results

1982 general	John Joseph (Joe) Moakley (D) ...	102,665	(64%)	($420,241)
	Deborah R. Cochran (R)	55,030	(34%)	($159,521)
1982 primary	John Joseph (Joe) Moakley (D) ...	75,181	(100%)	
1980 general	John Joseph (Joe) Moakley (D) ...	104,010	(100%)	($81,938)

Campaign Contributions and Expenditures

1981-82		Direct Cont. 81-82		PACS brkdwn			
Receipts	$378,164	Indiv	$248,514	Agr	$2,200	Ideo	$1,550
Expend.	$420,241	PACS	$96,403	Bus	$43,203	Lbr	$42,450
Unspent	$36,634			Hlth	$5,250	Prof	$2,600

Indep Expend: For: $812 (MA Citiz. for Life)

TENTH DISTRICT

The 10th district of Massachusetts is the southeastern corner of the state—though corner is scarcely the word, since this part of Massachusetts stretches out to the Atlantic. Fifty years ago, the only thickly populated part of this district was New Bedford and the towns right around it. This onetime whaling port, from which Melville's Captain Ahab sailed in search of Moby Dick, is still a fishing port and the home of our largest Portuguese-American (actually, mostly Azorean-American) community.

Today, however, the New Bedford area contains only 28% of the district's population. About the same number live, year round, now on Cape Cod and the islands of Martha's Vineyard and Nantucket. Half a century ago, the Cape was entirely vacation country, only recently opened up to highways; the old industries there had long since vanished. Now it is sprouting new subdivisions all the time, and has the highest population growth rate in Massachusetts. Some of the new residents are retirees, some are rich people who can afford to live where they want; but many are just ordinary people who now, in a more affluent America than they grew up in, can make a living out where they would really like to live rather than where they used to feel they had to.

The remainder of the district's population is in the towns scattered on the South Shore of Boston, from Hingham and Hull down through Plymouth and the towns on Buzzards Bay. This is also a fast-growing area; some of the towns near Boston are affluent, while some are simply comfortably middle class.

On any quantitative scale, the 10th is the most Republican district in Massachusetts: it is the only district which did not go for George McGovern in 1972, for example, and the only one to give Ronald Reagan a substantial margin, though not an absolute majority, in 1982. The Cape continues to vote Republican in most elections, as it has for years; the South Shore is mostly Republican; the New Bedford area ordinarily is not heavily enough Democratic to counterbalance them.

In congressional elections, however, the district has gone Democratic since 1972. The winner then, and the congressman now, is Gerry Studds, a onetime prep school teacher who was one of Eugene McCarthy's key organizers in 1968. Studds ran in 1970 and lost, ran in 1972 and won, each time with the support of the usually diffident McCarthy. His opposition to the Vietnam war was his greatest asset in his early campaigns, but as congressman he has developed others. He learned Portuguese and has learned all about the local fishing industry. He serves on the Foreign Affairs Committee, where he is free to oppose sales of weapons systems to various countries and to assert the cause of human rights. But he also serves on Merchant Marine and Fisheries, and it is there he has his subcommittee chairmanship (Coast Guard and Navigation). In his first term he succeeded in pushing through to passage a bill extending the territorial waters of the United States to 200 miles off the shoreline; since then he has been looking out for the interests of small fishermen, and trying to keep their waters free from foreign trawlers and oil spills. To some this may seem humdrum work, but surely it has some fascination, and it helped Studds win reelection without substantial opposition for years.

His work on both committees paid off when he encountered serious competition in 1982. He carried every city and town in the district and won 81% of the votes in New Bedford, for an overall district total of 69%. That will probably discourage Republican aspirants in the future; Studds seems to have a safe seat for as long as he wishes to keep it.

The People   Pop. 1980: 522,200, up 26.6% 1970–80; voting age pop. 377,639; 1% Black, 1% Span. orig. 22% housing units rented. Median owner $48,800; renter $161. Households: 75% family, 38% with children, 62% married couples.

Presidential Vote

1980			
	Reagan (R)	118,065	(48%)
	Carter (D)	86,913	(35%)
	Anderson (I)	40,715	(17%)

Rep. Gerry E. Studds (D) Elected 1972; b. May 12, 1937, Mineola, NY; home, Cohasset; Yale U., B.A. 1959, M.A.T. 1961; Protestant.

Career U.S. Foreign Svc., 1961–63; Exec. Asst. to William R. Anderson, Pres. Consultant for a Domestic Peace Corps, 1963; Legis. Asst. to U.S. Sen. Harrison J. Williams of NJ, 1964; Prep. sch. teacher, 1965–69.

Offices 1501 LHOB, 202-225-3111. Also 243 P.O. Bldg., New Bedford 02740, 617-999-1251.

Committees *Foreign Affairs* (7th). Subcommittees: Western Hemisphere Affairs; International Security and Scientific Affairs. *Merchant Marine and Fisheries* (5th). Subcommittees: Coast Guard and Navigation (Chairman); Fisheries and Wildlife Conservation and the Environment; Oceanography.

Group Ratings

	ADA	ACLU	COPE	CFA	LCV	LWV	NTU	NSI	COC	ACA	CSFC
1982	95	100	90	92	100	92	33	0	23	13	25
1981	100	—	89	100	100	—	46	—	11	8	26
1980	100	100	84	86	96	100	22	0	67	17	23

National Journal Ratings

	Economic		Foreign		Cultural	
1982	76%	(LIB)	85%	(LIB)	93%	(LIB)
	24%	(CONS)	12%	(CONS)	3%	(CONS)
1981	89%	(LIB)	92%	(LIB)	95%	(LIB)
	3%	(CONS)	2%	(CONS)	1%	(CONS)

Key Votes

1) Reagan 81 Budget	AGN	5) Incr SS Rtmt Age	FOR	9) Poor Pay Food Stamps	AGN
2) Reagan 81 Tax Cut	AGN	6) Saudi AWACS Sale	AGN	10) Ban Crt Busing Order	AGN
3) Bal Budget Amend	AGN	7) $ for MX Missile	AGN	11) Auto Local Content	FOR
4) Gas & Road Tax	AGN	8) Nerve Gas Prod	AGN	12) Nuclear Arms Freeze	FOR

Election Results

1982 general	Gerry E. Studds (D)	....	138,418	(69%)	($119,911)
	John E. Conway (R)	....	63,014	(31%)	($184,829)
1982 primary	Gerry E. Studds (D)	....	72,567	(100%)	
1980 general	Gerry E. Studds (D)	....	195,791	(73%)	($78,937)
	Paul V. Doane (R)	....	71,620	(27%)	($47,490)

Campaign Contributions and Expenditures

1981-82		Direct Cont. 81-82			PACS brkdwn		
Receipts	$137,926	Indiv	$93,645	Agr	$300	Ideo	$6,000
Expend.	$119,911	PACS	$42,551	Bus	$3,450	Lbr	$32,300
Unspent	$25,771			Hlth	$100	Prof	$200

ELEVENTH DISTRICT

The 11th congressional district of Massachusetts includes the southern third of Boston, most of the city's South Shore suburbs, and more suburban territory stretching to the shoe manufacturing city of Brockton and the towns just beyond. This is the lineal descendant of the district whose Yankee voters elected John Quincy Adams to the House for the last years of his life (1831–48), despite his refusal to campaign; but it is not a district Yankee in tone today. With few exceptions, the 11th district's suburban cities and towns—Quincy, Braintree, and the newer Holbrook, Stoughton, and Randolph, away from the Shore—are filled with the grandsons and granddaughters of Irish, Italian, and Jewish immigrants; the Hyde Park and Dorchester wards of Boston are a mixture of old Irish and younger blacks. These are not grand places; except for Milton, housing values here are below the metropolitan average. Politically, this is Democratic country—much as that might surprise the staunchly anti-Jacksonian John Quincy Adams.

The congressman from the 11th is Brian Donnelly, a young man with political roots in Boston. He won the seat in 1978, when James Burke retired; Burke and other local politicos backed him, in pique over a challenger who opposed and nearly beat the incumbent in 1976 when he was sick. Donnelly has a more moderate attitude on cultural issues than most of the Massachusetts delegation; on economic and foreign issues, he is in line with them. He serves on the practical-minded Public Works and Transportation Committee and on Budget; he is expected to be responsive to the leadership, which is another way of saying he will usually do what Tip O'Neill wants. He has been reelected easily since he first won, and he can hold this seat for years, as Burke did, unless he should run for and win another office; he has been mentioned occasionally as a candidate for mayor of Boston.

The People   Pop. 1980: 525,089, dn. 2.8% 1970–80; voting age pop. 382,888; 7% Black, 1% Span. orig., 1% Asian orig. 41% housing units rented. Median owner $42,600; renter $211. Households: 73% family, 38% with children, 56% married couples.

Presidential Vote

1980	Reagan (R)	98,420	(45%)
	Carter (D)	92,060	(42%)
	Anderson (I)	29,073	(13%)

Rep. Brian J. Donnelly (D) Elected 1978; b. Mar. 2, 1946, Boston; home, Boston; Boston U., B.S. 1970; Roman Catholic.

Career Dir. of Youth Activities, Dorchester YMCA, 1968–70; High sch. and trade sch. teacher and coach, 1969–72; MA House of Reps., 1973–79.

Offices 438 CHOB, 202-225-3215. Also 47 Washington St., Quincy 02169, 617-472-1314.

Committees *Budget* (11th). Subcommittees: Budget Process; Entitlements, Uncontrollables, and Indexing (Chairman); Tax Policy. *Merchant Marine and Fisheries* (26th). Subcommittees: Fisheries and Wildlife Conservation and the Environment; Merchant Marine.

Group Ratings

	ADA	ACLU	COPE	CFA	LCV	LWV	NTU	NSI	COC	ACA	CSFC
1982	80	46	83	85	76	73	18	22	30	22	33
1981	65	—	78	71	71	—	30	—	0	15	31
1980	72	47	71	50	76	63	18	50	63	24	31

National Journal Ratings

	Economic		Foreign		Cultural	
1982	75%	(LIB)	75%	(LIB)	65%	(LIB)
	24%	(CONS)	25%	(CONS)	35%	(CONS)
1981	81%	(LIB)	75%	(LIB)	59%	(LIB)
	15%	(CONS)	25%	(CONS)	40%	(CONS)

Key Votes

1) Reagan 81 Budget	AGN	5) Incr SS Rtmt Age	AGN	9) Poor Pay Food Stamps	AGN
2) Reagan 81 Tax Cut	AGN	6) Saudi AWACS Sale	AGN	10) Ban Crt Busing Order	FOR
3) Bal Budget Amend	AGN	7) $ for MX Missile	AGN	11) Auto Local Content	AGN
4) Gas & Road Tax	FOR	8) Nerve Gas Prod	AGN	12) Nuclear Arms Freeze	FOR

Election Results

1982 general	Brian J. Donnelly (D)	144,132	(100%)	($49,077)
1982 primary	Brian J. Donnelly (D)	94,332	(100%)	
1980 general	Brian J. Donnelly (D)	137,066	(100%)	($60,806)

Campaign Contributions and Expenditures

1981-82		Direct Cont. 81-82					PACS brkdwn		
Receipts	$108,557	Indiv	$78,115	Agr	$200	Ideo	$575
Expend.	$49,077	Party	$25	Bus	$12,050	Lbr	$10,550
Unspent	$67,860	PACS	$24,425	Hlth	$1,250	Prof	$—
		Cand	$1,500				

MICHIGAN

Michigan is one state which seemed, in the early 1980s, to be at a turning point in its history. The collapse of the auto industry in 1979–82 has convinced almost everyone that Michigan's golden years of auto-propelled prosperity will never return again. A new era is beginning— whether of great prosperity again or of more straitened circumstances, no one is sure. The state's politics and its public life generally have been knocked akilter by the suddenness of Michigan's economic crisis: the state's major institutions no longer work as they used to; the rules of the game seem permanently changed. A state which seemed for years to be governed admirably by talented and well-motivated representatives of the political center found itself suddenly faced with a crisis it seemed unable to handle. But in fact this is not the first, but is rather the third, of the major turning points Michigan has experienced; and the strengths the state built up in response to the earlier turning points suggest that it has strengths which will enable it to capitalize on, rather than be crushed by, the turning point signalled by the collapse of the auto industry. And each of these turning points produced, in time, a characteristic political response, with reverberations all over the country. Will that be true again?

The first turning point in Michigan's history was in the years of its early settlement. At the beginning of the 1830s, Michigan was mostly populated by Indians; its Lower Peninsula, between Lakes Huron and Michigan, was off to the side of the major east-west settlement routes. But in the 1830s and 1840s, settlers poured into southern Michigan, most of them from Upstate New York; this was part of the vast Yankee migration westward, which transferred the values of the sons of the Puritans west from New England (where they have long been a minority) through Upstate New York, lower Michigan, northern Illinois, Iowa, and Kansas. They brought with them the Yankee urge for improvement. Not only were they successful farmers and good businessmen. They were also lovers of learning, setting up plenty of public schools and colleges (some of which made a point of accepting women and blacks), and instinctive reformers. Michigan by the 1850s had a large temperance movement, it was the first state to prohibit capital punishment, it had active supporters of the underground railway, and it became one of the birthplaces of the Republican Party, which was founded in Jackson in 1854 and swept the state in the elections later that year.

In those days the Democratic Party was the advocate of laissez faire, in both economics and on issues like slavery; the Republicans were the busybodies who wanted government to act to improve society. And in Michigan they were generally successful. As the 19th century wore on, Michigan was a successful commonwealth. Still mainly a farm state, it also had a major lumber industry (until a series of fires swept across the state from Lake Huron to Lake Michigan in the 1870s and 1880s) and several of its cities became significant manufacturing centers. Its civic institutions were of high quality—its higher education system was already one of the nation's best—and its quality of life high.

But until the development of the automobile industry in the 30 years after 1900 Michigan remained something of a backwater. This sudden growth of the auto industry was of course the second major turning point in Michigan's history. The fact that Michigan became a center of the industry happened almost by accident. Detroit was a much smaller city than Cleveland or Chicago in 1900, and it was only one of a dozen (including places like Dayton, home of the Wright brothers) which were buzzing with engineering innovations at the time. But Detroit's bankers were more venturesome than Cleveland's, and among the hundreds of auto pioneers the most successful was Henry Ford, who was based in the Detroit area. The three-county area around Detroit had 426,000 people in 1900; in 1930, it had 2,177,000. Detroit was the Houston of its day, the nation's fastest-growing major metropolitan area in 1900–30 except for Los Angeles. A few outstate cities—Flint, Lansing—with auto factories grew at similar rates, though on a much smaller scale. The auto industry drew immigrants into Detroit and Michigan from all over: from rural Michigan and southern Ontario, from the farms of Ohio and Indiana, whites from the mountains of Kentucky and Tennessee and (mostly after 1940) blacks from Alabama and Mississippi. Michigan had had relatively few European immigrants before this: some Germans in the southwestern part of the state, a Dutch colony (the nation's largest) around Grand Rapids and Holland, Finns in the mining towns of the Upper Peninsula. But Detroit attracted Poles and Italians, Hungarians and Serbs, Greeks and Jews.

This sudden influx of a polyglot proletariat also changed Michigan's politics, in time. The catalyst was the great depression of the 1930s, but the impetus came not so much from actual privation, as from the fact that the auto companies paid relatively good wages but treated their employees mechanically and with great distrust. Henry Ford and other assembly line pioneers had made production very efficient, but they also made the factory a place of adversary confrontation. So in 1937, when it began to appear that the economy wouldn't grow much any more, the workers supported the sit-in strikes organized by the new United Auto Workers; in effect, management and labor were fighting, sometimes in the literal sense of the word, for shares of what both sides thought was a static-sized pie. The UAW won those strikes and organized the companies, in large part because Governor Frank Murphy, a Democrat, declined to send in troops to break them, even though they were entirely illegal.

The success of the union organizing drives set the tone of Michigan politics for at least 25 years. The union won, but it did not carry all before it; much of the rest of the state resented its tactics and feared they would be the losers. As evidence, consider that Murphy's Democrats lost the 1938 elections, not only statewide but in factory towns like Flint; and Republicans won most contests for a decade-and-a-half afterwards. Demographics finally worked for the Democrats: the auto workers and post–1900 immigrants were producing more children than outstate Yankees and management personnel. Following Walter Reuther's election as UAW president in 1947, they elected G. Mennen Williams, then a young liberal, governor in 1948, and by 1954 the Democrats, closely allied to and heavily supported by the UAW, seemed to have become the natural majority in the state. The class-warfare atmosphere of Michigan politics continued up through 1962, when Republican George Romney only barely was elected governor. But in office Romney and his successor William Milliken made it clear that they accepted the welfare state policies which were the goal of the UAW leadership and the liberal Democrats. In the 1970s, as auto wages rose to levels unsurpassed by those in any other industry but steel, and as Michigan's standard of living surged ahead of those of other states, this seemed to be a state that had built an exemplary standard of living and had reached a solid political consensus.

Then Michigan suffered a sudden and devastating economic collapse. As late as 1979, Michigan had income levels at least 10% above the national average, it had the nation's highest blue collar wages, its residents had one of the highest rates of ownership of second homes and pleasure boats. The state government was one of the nation's most generous, to the poor and the unemployed and to others as well: it supported one of the nation's most distinguished and extensive systems of higher education; it had a fine system of state parks and recreation areas; it had been a pioneer in many efforts to end racial discrimination.

The problem—and one which was apparent, under the prosperous surface, for years—was overdependence on the auto industry. The American Big Three auto companies, all headquartered in the Detroit area, had watched their shares of the market slip for years; in 1979, after the Iranian revolution led to a sharp rise in the price of oil, the Big Three were entirely unprepared for the sudden drop in demand for big cars. Sales slumped, hundreds of thousands of auto workers were laid off, and unemployment in Michigan approached 20% by 1982. Chrysler nearly went bankrupt, Ford was in financial difficulty, and even General Motors had its first losses in years.

The temptation in Michigan is to blame it all on a few bad months, a few lousy decisions, unfair Japanese competition and the Ayatollah Khomeini. But the problem is endemic. Autos turned out to be a classic boom-and-bust industry. Before World War II, the auto industry converted the nation from other forms of transportation to the automobile. After World War II, it converted the one-car family to the two-car family. Each of these transformations kept the auto industry growing faster than the total economy. No one foresaw—despite the industry's extensive market research—that this kind of growth would come to an end. But it did, even before the crash of the late 1970s. Auto company management, apparently confident that they had a lock on the domestic auto market, agreed to UAW demands for wages that made auto workers' pay far out of line with other industrial workers here and abroad. Auto workers, egged on perhaps by journalists who hailed their alienation, did shoddy work and produced cars far below the quality of the Japanese imports.

And, most important, the American consumer had ended his romance with the auto. In the first, unexpectedly flush years after World War II, getting a new car was one of the thrills of American life, and the new models were awaited each September with such anticipation that showrooms papered over the windows so that no one could see them too soon. But with the proliferation of consumer goodies and with the increasing variety of cultural styles of the affluent years, cars increasingly had competition for Americans' leisure dollars. By the early 1980s auto analysts were blaming "sticker shock" for lower sales; new American cars typically sold for over $10,000. But in real dollars cars cost the same in 1955, when Americans had much lower real incomes. The difference is that what was once the object of romance is now a utilitarian tool. Domestic auto sales may rebound from the low points of the early 1980s. But now that half of American households have two or more cars, and now that few people feel any longer any romantic desire for a new car, auto sales are never going to grow faster than the economy again. Yet, as Jane Jacobs has pointed out, the Big Three for years, as successful, efficient giant firms, have squeezed out innovative small businesses and created a climate hostile to economic innovation.

Not all of Michigan was devastated, nor was every part of the state dependent on the auto industry. But most of it was: not only metropolitan Detroit, but also Flint, a GM town with the nation's highest unemployment during much of the early 1980s, Lansing, and Saginaw. Suppliers and small manufacturers depended on the Big Three as customers; retailers made their livings off auto wages. Even before 1979, there was sluggish growth in the Detroit metro area, which had had net outmigration since 1960. Outstate Michigan has been more buoyant. But one industry which helped outstate was state government—the capital at Lansing and the big state universities in Ann Arbor, East Lansing, and many other smaller towns—which had been hit hard by the collapse of the auto industry. The state's deficit as Governor James Blanchard took office in 1983 loomed up at nearly $1 billion, and its unemployment fund seemed hopelessly in debt to the federal government. Blanchard and the legislature eliminated the deficit by raising the state income tax from 4.6% to 6.35% and by cutting $225 million in education and social services, and the state has kept up its payments on the unemployment fund by cutting benefits. But the losses to beneficiaries of state programs seem more than temporary. Tenured professors found themselves out of jobs; whole departments were abolished. State employees took pay cuts deeper than those of Chrysler workers. Detroit's city government was in similarly desperate shape, and the Wayne County government had an accumulated deficit of $130 million, almost half the amount of its $300 million budget. In an America that had become used to receiving wage increases equal to the Consumer Price Index plus a couple of percentage points more, many people in Michigan found themselves taking pay cuts. In a very short time the state's income was cut back from a level well above the national average to a level roughly even with it.

That left Michigan demoralized, and without any obvious remedy. It was clear that both Big Three management and the UAW leaders had made mistakes—and ironic that in the 1970s these men were hailed as enlightened, liberal-minded community leaders. But it was not clear what the auto companies could do to rebound. Michigan's natural tendency, as a sort of welfare state, was to look to the federal government for help, and Michigan's representatives in Congress were able to work with Chrysler President Lee Iacocca and get an emergency loan guarantee for Chrysler in 1979. But for the long term, it seems unlikely that citizens of below-average-income states can be persuaded to send their tax dollars to Michigan to help it retain its above-average incomes. If Michiganders want them, they are going to have to earn them. But how? Despite its fine universities, Michigan is not a high tech state, and in the early 1980s failed to attract much new business of this sort. Its attractive physical environment has not drawn the kind of innovative people you find in New England or northern California. Michigan likes to brag about its water supply: one-quarter of the world's fresh water is in the Great Lakes, and all but one of them touch Michigan. But people are still moving from Michigan to Arizona. The long-range future of Michigan probably lies less in to-day's glamour industries and more in upgrading the heavy manufacturing and engineering skills Michigan already has. The auto industry's large core of engineers for years chafed at having little more to do than design different tail fins to cover the same machine; morale picked up when engineers were presented with truly difficult tasks, like complying with federal emissions and gas mileage standards. Perhaps Michigan will find other challenges of this sort, this time in enterprises not limited to the auto industry.

In the meantime, Michigan has a politics of turmoil. Voters have been knocked loose from their moorings, and have not necessarily rallied around their old flags. Some expected Michigan, long considered a Democratic state, to move closer to the Democrats on the theory that they would be more generous with government aid. But this is not what happened in 1980 or 1982. In 1980, Michigan went for Ronald Reagan by more than a hairsbreadth margin. The old working class Democratic vote did not come back: the three-county Detroit metro area, which went for John Kennedy over Richard Nixon by a 62%–38%, 379,000-vote margin in 1960, went for Jimmy Carter over Ronald Reagan by only a 49%–44%, 84,000-vote margin. In 1982, the Democrats won the governorship, but by a narrower margin than expected, and against a Republican who talked about cutting government financial aid permanently and was all but disowned by the retiring and still-popular incumbent, William Milliken. Voters seemed to have been shaken out of their old voting habits, and were willing to listen to almost any kind of proposal. The politics of the middle—of following the lead of enlightened big business and big labor—seemed to have failed, and no one is at all sure yet what will be the political response to this third turning point in Michigan's history.

Governor. The departure of William Milliken, after 14 years as governor, symbolized the shift in direction. Milliken was a kind of consensus governor, a Republican who transcended the old business-labor split that structured Michigan politics for so many years. Under his leadership state government expanded, as it did in states like New York and Massachusetts with liberal Republican governors and Democratic legislatures. Personally popular, he nonetheless won the 1970 and 1974 elections by only small margins; he won bigger in 1978. A pleasant man, he was also steely on occasion: he vetoed measures to eliminate Medicaid abortions several times in October just before elections. Until the economy collapsed, the biggest blot on his record was the state's sluggish response to the PBB disaster, when a chemical mistakenly fed to dairy cattle permeated the state's food chain. Milliken retired personally popular, but not as politically strong as he had been; despite his popularity his policies had not prevented economic disaster.

The new governor, James Blanchard, entered office a relatively unknown quantity. In eight years in Congress he performed creditably, and sometimes very well indeed: he piloted the Chrysler loan guarantee through a skeptical House. He got the Democratic nomination in a crowded field largely because he was endorsed by the UAW and most party leaders, and by Lee Iacocca as well. In the general election he was an overwhelming favorite against Republican Richard Headlee, and ended up winning with 51%. Among his first acts in office was to call for a tax increase. Blanchard understands that higher taxes may make the state less attractive to business. But with the state's huge deficit, he apparently feels he has no choice. The real test is ahead: can he help inspire a state that knows now that, to become economically sound and stable, it must change its way of life?

Senators. Michigan has two Democratic senators, both strong opponents of the Reagan administration, but with different backgrounds and personalities. Donald Riegle, just beginning his second term, has already had a long career—nearly 20 years in Washington—and a colorful one. He was first elected to Congress in 1966 as a Republican from Flint; he won UAW support for his record, supported Pete McCloskey against Richard Nixon in 1972, and became a Democrat in 1973. He won a close race in 1976 distinguished by a particularly nasty story in the *Detroit News,* featuring extracts from tapes of Riegle and a woman he had an affair with; a backlash against the often harshly partisan *News* probably helped elect Riegle.

The highlight of his first term was probably the Chrysler loan guarantee, which he as a member of the Senate Banking, Housing and Urban Affairs Committee managed. On the Labor Committee he is a solid pro-labor vote these days (though he graduated from Harvard Business School and once worked in IBM management), and on Commerce he tends to favor liberal positions, whether regulatory or deregulatory. Riegle voted for most of the Reagan economic plan, but he soon became one of the harshest critics of Reaganomics. In fact, he makes the national newscasts periodically with virtiolic denunciations of administration witnesses like Caspar Weinberger. Critics of Riegle see him as a grandstander or even a demagogue, a senator whose denunciations, as one source told the *Washington Post,* routinely empty out the Senate chamber. His defenders see him as an articulate and farsighted advocate of the right policies, even when those policies stand little chance of immediate passage. His tendency to denunciation can be explained partly by the fact that he, unlike most other congressional Democrats, has been in the minority party (and often the minority faction of the minority party) during most of what is now a rather long congressional career. But it is also a genuine reflection of his character. Like most politicians, he is ambitious (early in his career he talked about becoming president) and likes to be the center of attention; and he has probably been genuinely affected by what he has seen in the early 1980s as a representative of Michigan. He seems now to have as safe a seat as most senators from large states ever get, which is not very safe; he has yet to persuade his constituents that he is a workhorse with real accomplishments as well as an articulate tribune of the people. He may have his chance if the Democrats win control of the Senate in 1984.

Riegle had a rather easy time winning reelection in 1982. His record plus Michigan's economic depression made him the solid favorite, and his Republican opponent, Philip Ruppe—also a member of the Republican congressional class of 1966, and husband of Peace Corps director Lorett Ruppe—never made much headway with his charges that Riegle was ineffective. Still, Riegle's percentage was well below that of many of his Democratic colleagues.

Michigan's junior senator, Carl Levin, has a background mostly in local, not national, politics; he is not often given to grandstanding; he is more self-effacing than ambitious. In racially torn Detroit in the years just after the 1967 riots, he won elections to the City Council—and led the field in 1973—with support from both black and white voters. His election to the Senate in 1978 came in large part because the incumbent, Robert Griffin announced he would retire and proceeded to miss dozens of roll call votes, and then reentered the race. Levin attacked him for absenteeism as much for his Republican stands on issues; and Griffin, who through most of his career was a hard-working advocate and an effective partisan, lost.

Levin is a member of the Armed Services Committee, a body with a wide range of opinion on foreign and military issues. He takes sides sometimes with the so-called military reformers, led by Gary Hart and William Cohen, who emphasize the need for creative strategy and simple, reliable weapons. But Levin is also a strong arms controller and a believer in eliminating many weapons systems altogether. His record on domestic issues is, according to the rating groups, one of the most liberal in the Senate. He supports relatively generous funding of most domestic programs, but is also receptive to arguments that things need to be done differently. He is a man of passionate convictions who is also capable of understanding the passions of others—which is to say a naturally effective legislator.

Levin is anything but a perfectly packaged candidate—rumpled, balding, inclined to speak his mind when it might be more prudent to be silent. But these are the qualities, together with a quiet but intense empathy, which have made him genuinely attractive. In the rather Republican year of 1978, against a strong opponent, he did nearly as well in outstate Michigan as Riegle did in 1982. No major opponent has appeared against him in 1984, and his must be counted one of the Democrats' safer Senate seats.

Congressional districting. James Blanchard's decision to run for governor simplified Michigan's congressional redistricting process. The state lost one seat, and one district in the Detroit metropolitan area had to go; Blanchard's was the obvious choice. The adjustments made to other district lines were not necessarily elegant. Republicans bargained to save their chances in some of the outstate districts; they were not uniformly successful in 1982, but they have a chance to regain some seats some time in the decade.

Presidential politics. Michigan surprised just about everyone by the size of the margin it gave Ronald Reagan in 1980. Nothing like it would have been possible in 1982, but the state's movement away from its traditional labor-versus-management politics, and its movement away from traditional solutions at a time when they seemed not to be working, mean that it cannot be taken for granted—quite—by the Democrats in 1984. Michigan has had a presidential primary since 1972, when George Wallace won. In 1980 the Democrats had a complex delegate selection process and a nonbinding primary in which only those signed up to participate could vote; this was done because national party rules prohibit binding the delegate when, as in Michigan, there is no voter registration by party and anyone can vote in the Democratic primary. The Democratic delegation at the New York convention was split between Carter and Kennedy advocates; UAW operatives played major roles on both sides, as they usually do. The Republicans had a primary, won by George Bush, who had Governor Milliken's endorsement; their primary electorate here is probably one of the most liberal constituencies in the whole Republican delegate selection process.

The People   Est. Pop. 1982: 9,109,000; Pop. 1980: 9,262,078, dn. 1.7% 1980–82 and up 4.3% 1970–80; 4.0% of U.S. total, 8th largest; voting age pop. 6,510,092; 12% Black, 1% Spanish origin, 1% Asian origin. Single ancestry: 8% German, English, 4% Polish, 3% Irish, 2% Dutch, Italian, French, 1% Scottish, Swedish, Hungarian. Registered voters (1982): 5,624,573 Total. 16% with 1–3 yrs. col., 15% with 4+ yrs. col. 11.1% below poverty level. 24% housing units rented; median house value: $39,000; median monthly rent: $197. Households: 75% family, 42% with children, 61% married couples.

1982 Share of Federal Tax Burden $24,031,900,000; 4.02% of U.S. total, 10th largest.

1982 Share of Federal Expenditures

	Total		Non-Defense		Defense	
Total Expend	$18,016m	(2.98%)	$15,798m	(3.72%)	$2,217m	(1.24%)
St/Lcl Grants	3,634m	(4.12%)	3,633m	(4.12%)	1m	(2.78%)
Salary/Wages	889m	(1.14%)	392m	(1.43%)	497m	(0.98%)
Ind Payments	11,546m	(4.04%)	10,954m	(4.25%)	592m	(2.07%)
Procurement	1,840m	(1.26%)	276m	(0.88%)	1,565m	(1.37%)
Other Programs	106m	(1.96%)	105m	(1.95%)	1m	(2.33%)
Loan/Insurance	8.88m	(1.44%)	856m	(1.39%)	32m	(1.45%)

Political Lineup   Governor, James J. Blanchard (D). Senators, Donald W. Riegle, Jr. (D) and Carl Levin (D). Representatives, 18 (12 D and 6 R). State Senate, 38 (20 D and 18 R); State House of Representatives, 110 (63 D and 47 R).

Presidential Vote

1980	Reagan (R)	. . . .	1,915,225	(49%)
	Carter (D)	. . . .	1,661,532	(42%)
	Anderson (I)	. . . .	275,223	(7%)
1976	Ford (R)	. . . .	1,893,742	(52%)
	Carter (D)	. . . .	1,696,714	(46%)

1980 Democratic Presidential Primary		
This primary did not affect delegate selection.		
Brown	23,043	(29%)
Others	18,996	(24%)
Uncommitted	36,385	(46%)

1980 Republican Presidential Primary		
Bush	341,998	(57%)
Reagan	189,184	(32%)
Anderson	48,947	(8%)
Two others & scattering	4,782	(1%)
Uncommitted	10,265	(2%)

SENATORS

Sen. Donald W. Riegle, Jr. (D) Elected 1976, seat up 1988; b. Feb. 4, 1938, Flint; home, Flint; Flint Jr. Col., W. MI U., U. of MI, B.A. 1960, MI St. U., M.B.A. 1961, Harvard U. Grad. Sch., 1964–66; United Methodist.

Career Consultant, IBM Corp., 1961–64; Faculty Mbr., MI St. U., Boston U., Harvard U., U.S. House of Reps., 1967–77, first elected as Repub., switched to Dem. Party Feb. 27, 1973.

Offices 1207 DSOB, 202-224-4822. Also 477 Michigan Ave., 18th Flr., Detroit 48226, 313-226-3188; and Genesee Towers, 1st and Harrison Sts., Flint 48502, 313-234-5621.

Committees *Banking, Housing and Urban Affairs* (3d). Subcommittees: Housing and Urban Affairs; Financial Institutions; Securities. *Budget* (8th). *Commerce, Science and Transportation* (5th). Subcommittees: Business, Trade, and Tourism; Science, Technology and Space; Surface Transportation. *Labor and Human Resources* (5th). Subcommittees: Labor; Alcoholism and Drug Abuse; Employment and Productivity.

Group Ratings

	ADA	ACLU	COPE	CFA	LCV	LWV	NTU	NSI	COC	ACA	CSFC
1982	80	93	94	80	92	100	18	11	16	32	30
1981	90	—	93	79	86	—	18	—	22	15	29
1980	83	93	100	67	96	90	20	0	40	4	24

National Journal Ratings

	Economic		Foreign		Cultural	
1982	91%	(LIB)	97%	(LIB)	85%	(LIB)
	8%	(CONS)	2%	(CONS)	14%	(CONS)
1981	83%	(LIB)	98%	(LIB)	94%	(LIB)
	16%	(CONS)	1%	(CONS)	5%	(CONS)

Key Votes

1) Reagan 81 Budget	AGN	5) $ to El Salvador	—	9) Poor Pay Food Stamps	AGN
2) Reagan 81 Tax Cut	FOR	6) Saudi AWACS Sale	AGN	10) Ban Crt Busing Order	AGN
3) Bal Budget Amend	AGN	7) Ban Abortion	AGN	11) Clinch Riv Brdr Rctr	AGN
4) Gas & Road Tax	AGN	8) Nerve Gas Prod	AGN	12) Legal Services Corp	FOR

Election Results

1982 general	Donald W. Riegle, Jr. (D)	1,728,793	(58%)	($1,583,439)
	Philip E. Ruppe (R)	1,223,286	(41%)	($1,045,545)
1982 primary	Donald W. Riegle, Jr. (D)	633,028	(100%)	
1976 general	Donald W. Riegle, Jr. (D)	1,831,031	(52%)	($795,821)
	Marvin L. Esch (R)	1,635,087	(47%)	($809,564)

Campaign Contributions and Expenditures

	1978-82	Direct Cont. 81-82			PACS brkdwn		
Receipts	$1,845,680	Indiv	$1,044,110	Agr	$48,600	Ideo	$56,701
Expend.	$1,585,439	Party	$37,005	Bus	$220,853	Lbr	$240,621
Unspent	$274,240	PACS	$610,646	Hlth	$9,030	Prof	$14,950

Indirect Party Expend: $71,163   *Indep Expend:* For: $899 Agn: $3,278

Sen. Carl Levin (D) Elected 1978, seat up 1984; b. June 28, 1933, Detroit; home, Detroit; Swarthmore Col., B.A. 1956, Harvard U., LL.B. 1959; Jewish.

Career Practicing atty.; Asst. Atty. Gen. of MI and Gen. Counsel for the MI Civil Rights Comm., 1964–67, Spec. Asst. Atty. Gen. of MI and Chief Appellate Defender for the City of Detroit, 1968–69; Detroit City Cncl., 1969–78, Pres., 1973–78.

Offices 140 RSOB, 202-224-6221. Also McNamara Bldg., 18th Flr., Detroit 48226, 313-226-6020.

Committees *Armed Services* (6th). Subcommittees: Sea Power and Force Projection; Tactical Warfare; Preparedness. *Governmental Affairs* (7th). Subcommittees: Energy, Nuclear Proliferation, and Government Processes; Oversight of Government Management; Intergovernmental Relations. *Small Business* (6th). Subcommittee: Government Procurement.

Group Ratings

	ADA	ACLU	COPE	CFA	LCV	LWV	NTU	NSI	COC	ACA	CSFC
1982	95	82	97	80	92	92	16	20	14	29	27
1981	100	—	96	85	94	—	3	—	0	10	24
1980	94	90	94	80	80	80	16	10	38	12	24

National Journal Ratings

	Economic		Foreign		Cultural	
1982	82%	(LIB)	77%	(LIB)	86%	(LIB)
	17%	(CONS)	22%	(CONS)	12%	(CONS)
1981	95%	(LIB)	88%	(LIB)	96%	(LIB)
	4%	(CONS)	9%	(CONS)	2%	(CONS)

Key Votes

1) Reagan 81 Budget	AGN	5) $ to El Salvador	—	9) Poor Pay Food Stamps	AGN
2) Reagan 81 Tax Cut	AGN	6) Saudi AWACS Sale	AGN	10) Ban Crt Busing Order	AGN
3) Bal Budget Amend	AGN	7) Ban Abortion	AGN	11) Clinch Riv Brdr Rctr	AGN
4) Gas & Road Tax	FOR	8) Nerve Gas Prod	AGN	12) Legal Services Corp	—

Election Results

1978 general	Carl Levin (D)	1,484,193	(52%)	($971,775)
	Robert P. Griffin (R)	1,362,165	(48%)	($1,681,550)
1978 primary	Carl Levin (D)	226,584	(39%)	
	Phil Power (D)	115,117	(20%)	($943,500)
	Richard Vander Veen (D)	89,257	(15%)	($264,217)
	Anthony Derezinski (D)	53,696	(9%)	($63,917)
	John Otterbacher (D)	50,860	(9%)	($152,498)
	Paul Rosenbaum (D)	46,896	(8%)	($153,189)
1972 general	Robert P. Griffin (R)	1,781,065	(52%)	($1,394,927)
	Frank J. Kelley (D)	1,577,178	(47%)	($547,819)

Campaign Contributions and Expenditures

1977-78				PACS brkdwn		
Receipts	$994,439	Agr	$500	Ideo	$11,522
Expend.	$971,775	Bus	$15,994	Lbr	$169,225
Unspent	$22,662	Hlth	$3,600	Prof	$5,100

GOVERNOR

Gov. James J. (Jim) **Blanchard** (D) Elected 1982, term expires Jan. 1987; b. Aug. 8, 1942, Detroit; home, Pleasant Ridge; MI St. U., B.A. 1964, M.B.A. 1965, U. of MN, J.D. 1968; Unitarian Universalist.

Career Practicing atty., 1968–74; Legal Aide, MI St. Election Bureau, 1968–69; A. A. to MI Atty. Gen. Frank J. Kelley, 1970–71, Asst. Atty. Gen. of MI; Legal Advisor to MI Depts. of Licensing and Regulation, Commerce and Agriculture; U.S. House of Reps., 1974–1982.

Office State Capitol, Box 30013, Lansing 48909, 517-373-3430.

Election Results

1982 gen.	James J. (Jim) Blanchard (D) .	1,561,291	(51%)
	Richard H. Headlee (R)	1,369,582	(45%)
1982 prim.	James J. (Jim) Blanchard (D) .	406,941	(50%)
	William B. Fitzgerald (D)	138,453	(17%)
	David A. Plawecki (D)	95,805	(12%)
	Zolton Ferency (D)	85,088	(11%)
	Edward C. Pierce (D)	44,894	(6%)
1978 gen.	William G. Milliken (R)	1,628,485	(57%)
	William B. Fitzgerald (D)	1,237,256	(43%)

FIRST DISTRICT

The 1st congressional district of Michigan is a part of the city of Detroit and the close-in suburb of Highland Park—an area where you can see, graphically, the rise and the fall of Michigan's auto industry over the last 80 years. This was vacant land—flat farmland and scrubby swamp on the northern and western edges of urban settlement, when the automakers first started to build big factories near Detroit. They built them out here, at the city's outskirts, where factories are usually built. Railroad tracks were laid, to bring in steel and coal, and neighborhoods were laid out, on straight streets.

The houses sprang up rapidly, with whole square miles being built up within a single year: workingmen's cottages for the Polish and other immigrants on the city's east side, larger and more comfortable houses for the rapidly growing middle class on the northwest side as one got farther away from the factories themselves. The factories today still form a kind of ring about five miles from downtown Detroit—a line that coincides with the southern limits of the 1st district. But the plants are mostly vacant now. Most of Henry Ford's Highland Park plant— where he offered to pay workers $5 a day in 1914—has been torn down; the old DeSoto as-

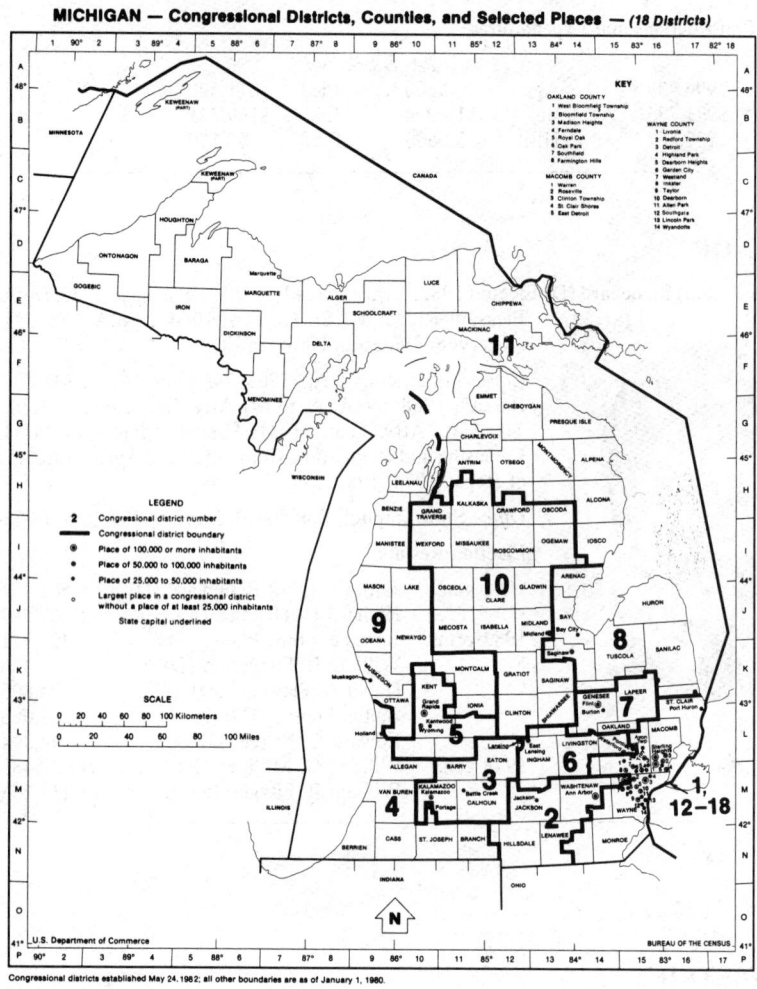

MICHIGAN — Congressional Districts, Counties, and Selected Places — *(18 Districts)*

Congressional districts established May 24, 1982; all other boundaries are as of January 1, 1980.

sembly plant is long gone; even the Cadillac plant is due to be phased out, to be replaced by a new facility out near today's edge of urban settlement.

Just as the auto industry and the neighborhoods were built quickly, so they changed quickly, and each time the change surprised people. The most noticeable movement was racial change. At the end of World War II, the area that is now the 1st district, extending westward almost all the way to Detroit's city limits, was almost fully built up, with a population somewhat larger than today's—and virtually all white. That changed rapidly. Thousands of blacks who came to Detroit during the war left the small ghettos where they had been confined, while whites fled to the outer limits of the city or the FHA-financed suburbs. Whole square miles of Detroit changed racial composition within a year or two— just as rapidly as they had been built. That process continued into the 1960s and was accelerated by the riots of 1967; that was when most of Detroit's Jewish population moved to the suburbs. Even the city's most affluent areas, just north of Highland Park, were opened up to blacks; today some of the most elegant housing in the Detroit area—the kind they don't build any more—can be found in black or integrated neighborhoods.

The 1st district is now the home of most of Detroit's successful black middle and upper classes, and they seem likely to remain here; the formerly all-white areas farther to the west in the city are mostly less desirable housing. Evidence of social disorganization—depopulation, high crime, lack of voter participation—are much lower here than in the neighboring 13th district; this is an area with relatively stable households and families with children. The district's boundaries go out beyond currently all black neighborhoods, evidently intending to include those areas which will become mostly black by 1990; even so, ⅔ of its current voters are black, and for all practical purposes it may be regarded as a black district.

The 1st district is one of the most heavily Democratic districts in the country—almost a unanimously Democratic district in national elections. Its voters are articulate, active in civic and political affairs, upwardly mobile—but none of these qualities has tended to make them, as some conservatives hoped, more Republican. On the contrary, they seem more fiercely anti-Republican than lower income blacks in less pleasant neighborhoods.

The 1st district's congressman is John Conyers, a Democrat who reflects its basic attitudes though not always its political sophistication. In 1964, when he was first elected to the House, there were only four other blacks there, and he was by far the most militant. From the beginning he spoke and voted against the Vietnam war; he made no efforts to get along personally with his adversaries on issues. He was instrumental in setting up the Congressional Black Caucus, in part to get around the mellow ways of the older black members; now it is some of the younger blacks who are more inclined to work quietly within the system and Conyers and some other senior blacks who want to be out front denouncing it. That does not prevent him from doing a competent job of managing floor legislation when it comes his turn, as a subcommittee chairman, to do so. But it does prevent him from having much influence on most issues beyond his single vote.

Conyers seems to believe his duty is to express his point of view—which usually means expressing his disgust at what is going on. He denounced the Carter administration, and made a point of walking out of a White House meeting in 1979, to protest its budget cuts; his relations with the Reagan administration are as distant as those of any member of Congress. Conyers's father was part of the left wing faction defeated by Walter Reuther in the UAW election of 1947, and Conyers himself seems to have the outlook shared by many of those rebels. In Conyers's view America is still a land and Congress an institution permeated by racism; he seems to view the white majority as basically malevolent. Given that view, there is little reason to compromise; and the most important thing may be to bear witness and to wait for the rare opportunity to change things a little.

Conyers is the fifth ranking Democrat on the House Judiciary Committee, with a real prospect of becoming chairman some day: he has a safe seat and nearly 20 years of seniority while still in his early 50s. Some of his colleagues might feel uncomfortable with such a firebrand in such a visible and important position, but there seems no likelihood he would be denied it. He chairs a subcommittee on Criminal Justice, a body which must handle matters of technical difficulty and arousing considerable ardor on occasion; he has performed competently.

The People   Pop. 1980: 514,560, dn. 10.0% 1970–80; voting age pop. 349,182; 66% Black, 2% Span. orig. 31% housing units rented. Median owner $21,400; renter $166. Households: 73% family, 44% with children, 44% married couples.

Presidential Vote

          1980   Reagan (R) .... NA
                        Carter (D) .... NA
                        Anderson (I) .... NA

Rep. John Conyers, Jr. (D) Elected 1964; b. May, 16, 1929, Detroit; home, Detroit; Wayne St. U., B.A. 1957, LL.B. 1958; Baptist.

Career Army, Korea; Legis. Asst. to U.S. Rep. John D. Dingell, 1958–61; Practicing atty., 1959–61; Referee, MI Workmen's Comp. Dept., 1961–63.

Offices 2313 RHOB, 202-225-5126. Also 305 Fed. Bldg., 231 W. Lafayette St., Detroit 48226, 313-226-7022.

Committees *Government Operations* (4th). Subcommittees: Commerce, Consumer and Monetary Affairs; Intergovernmental Relations and Human Resources. *Judiciary* (5th). Subcommittees: Civil and Constitutional Rights; Criminal Justice (Chairman).

Group Ratings

	ADA	ACLU	COPE	CFA	LCV	LWV	NTU	NSI	COC	ACA	CSFC
1982	80	96	91	92	93	60	52	0	6	12	31
1981	90	—	91	79	91	—	59	—	0	5	25
1980	78	90	89	86	81	90	26	0	59	25	21

National Journal Ratings

	Economic		Foreign		Cultural	
1982	76%	(LIB)	89%	(LIB)	98%	(LIB)
	23%	(CONS)	11%	(CONS)	1%	(CONS)
1981	89%	(LIB)	89%	(LIB)	99%	(LIB)
	3%	(CONS)	10%	(CONS)	1%	(CONS)

Key Votes

1) Reagan 81 Budget	—	5) Incr SS Rtmt Age AGN	9) Poor Pay Food Stamps AGN
2) Reagan 81 Tax Cut AGN	6) Saudi AWACS Sale AGN	10) Ban Crt Busing Order AGN
3) Bal Budget Amend AGN	7) $ for MX Missile AGN	11) Auto Local Content FOR
4) Gas & Road Tax AGN	8) Nerve Gas Prod AGN	12) Nuclear Arms Freeze FOR

Election Results

1982 general	John Conyers, Jr. (D)	125,517	(97%)	($22,876)
	Two others (LIB, WL)	4,328	(3%)	
1982 primary	John Conyers, Jr. (D)	62,295	(100%)	
1980 general	John Conyers, Jr. (D)	123,286	(95%)	($20,543)
	William M. Bell (R)	6,244	(5%)	($0)

Campaign Contributions and Expenditures

1981-82		Direct Cont. 81-82		PACS brkdwn			
Receipts	$20,177	Indiv	$4,432	Agr	$—	Ideo	$1,000
Expend.	$22,876	PACS	$15,643	Bus	$1,300	Lbr	$9,275
Unspent	$856			Hlth	$1,350	Prof	$1,200

Indep Expend: For: $568 (UAW)

SECOND DISTRICT

The 2d congressional district of Michigan is an odd amalgam: a part of Michigan which considers itself culturally and otherwise advanced, a part which is proud of its historic roots and traditions, and a part of the Detroit metropolitan area which prides itself on its importance even while it dislikes many aspects of life in the metropolis itself. The first and second each make up roughly ¼ of the district's population, the last about ½. They are, in order:

- *The Detroit suburbs of Livonia, Plymouth, and Northville.* Between the latter two and Detroit in 1945 was nothing but rolling farmland; in the next 20 years Livonia filled up with more than 100,000 people. Mostly they were affluent, but not exceedingly so; young, with large families; from Democratic backgrounds in many cases, but increasingly Republican over time. Plymouth and Northville, built around the nucleus of old villages, are similar, with slightly higher income levels.
- *Ann Arbor, the home of the University of Michigan.* Historically this is a Republican town, with many descendants of the German immigrants of 1848, who embraced the antislavery party of Union. But it also has, proportionately, one of the largest student electorates in the nation, and in the early 1970s became Democratic. It went for George McGovern in 1972, U of M alumnus Gerald Ford in 1976, and gave John Anderson a big vote in 1980.
- *South central Michigan.* Here, where the glacier stopped moving south, amidst the Irish Hills, is farmland settled in the 1830s and towns whose oldest buildings date from that era. Jackson, an old industrial town and the site of Michigan's huge prison, is here; it was one of the two towns which claims to have been the birthplace of the Republican Party in 1854. To the south is Hillsdale, a picture book old town, preserved through its prosperity. Hillsdale College presents a nice contrast to Ann Arbor: it was founded about the same time as the Republican Party, by likeminded people; it was one of the first colleges to admit women and blacks, but refuses government aid because it doesn't want equal opportunity investigators around; its students still wear traditional clothes, always sported short hair, and never protested against the Vietnam war. In the same spirit, Hillsdale embraces temperance (it is the home of E. Harold Munn, longtime Prohibition Party presidential candidate) and continues to believe in Michigan's longstanding (since 1855) ban on capital punishment.

This rather disparate district was assembled to suit the political needs of Congressman Carl Pursell and, so far, has done so. Pursell is a Republican, and Livonia, Plymouth, and Northville are his political base. Republican strength in Jackson and Hillsdale are down somewhat because of Michigan's economic problems; but this area is not dominated by the auto industry, and Pursell still carried them easily in 1982, even though they were new to him. As for Ann Arbor, its voting patterns have proved less responsive to the collapse of the auto industry than almost any other part of the state. Even if the university's prosperity depends finally on the auto industry, the focus politically here is on cultural issues and cultural style. Pursell lost Ann Arbor heavily to a local doctor and liberal activist in 1976. But his record on cultural issues is pretty solidly liberal, and he carried Ann Arbor against strong competition in 1980 and in 1982 as well. His more conservative record on economic issues is not so detrimental, in any part of the district; and in any case he has been a leader of the Northeast-Midwest Conference, a credential which he could have used had working class Ypsilanti, just east of Ann Arbor, remained in the district.

In the House and on the Appropriations Committee, Pursell has been a competent legislator, and in connection with the Northeast-Midwest Conference a voluble one. As one of the Republicans on the Appropriations Subcommittee on Labor-HHS-Education, he has helped to make that body more sympathetic to many grant and individual payment programs than many in the Reagan administration would like.

The People Pop. 1980: 514,560, up 10.1% 1970–80; voting age pop. 375,911; 5% Black, 1% Span. orig., 1% Asian orig. 28% housing units rented. Median owner $52,200; renter $251. Households: 73% family, 40% with children, 62% married couples.

Presidential Vote

1980	Reagan (R)	NA
	Carter (D)	NA
	Anderson (I)	NA

Rep. Carl D. Pursell (R) Elected 1976; b. Dec. 19, 1932, Imlay City; home, Plymouth; E. MI U., B.A. 1957, M.A. 1962; Protestant.

Career Army, 1957–59, Army Reserve, 1959–65; Teacher; Businessman; Mbr., Wayne Cnty. Bd. of Comm., 1969–70; MI Senate, 1971–76.

Offices 1414 LHOB, 202-225-4401. Also 15273 Farmington Rd., Livonia 48154, 313-427-1081.

Committee *Appropriations* (14th). Subcommittees: Labor-Health and Human Services-Education; Transportation.

Group Ratings

	ADA	ACLU	COPE	CFA	LCV	LWV	NTU	NSI	COC	ACA	CSFC
1982	45	67	55	31	46	60	67	13	71	35	41
1981	65	—	58	79	57	—	81	—	76	42	44
1980	89	67	71	64	77	90	25	25	72	36	45

National Journal Ratings

	Economic		Foreign		Cultural	
1982	41%	(LIB)	73%	(LIB)	69%	(LIB)
	59%	(CONS)	26%	(CONS)	31%	(CONS)
1981	46%	(LIB)	85%	(LIB)	72%	(LIB)
	53%	(CONS)	15%	(CONS)	28%	(CONS)

Key Votes

1) Reagan 81 Budget	FOR	5) Incr SS Rtmt Age	FOR	9) Poor Pay Food Stamps	AGN
2) Reagan 81 Tax Cut	FOR	6) Saudi AWACS Sale	AGN	10) Ban Crt Busing Order	FOR
3) Bal Budget Amend	FOR	7) $ for MX Missile	AGN	11) Auto Local Content	—
4) Gas & Road Tax	—	8) Nerve Gas Prod	AGN	12) Nuclear Arms Freeze	FOR

Election Results

1982 general	Carl D. Pursell (R)	106,960	(65%)	($137,108)
	George W. Sallade (D)	53,040	(32%)	($15,667)
1982 primary	Carl D. Pursell (R)	28,674	(82%)	
	Walt Long (R)	6,175	(18%)	($5,145)
1980 general	Carl D. Pursell (R)	115,562	(57%)	($143,576)
	Kathleen F. O'Reilly (D)	83,550	(41%)	($129,805)

Campaign Contributions and Expenditures

1981-82		Direct Cont. 81-82				PACS brkdwn		
Receipts	$146,475	Indiv	$64,131	Agr	$9,400	Ideo	$1,350
Expend.	$137,108	Party	$9,028	Bus	$32,300	Lbr	$4,450
Unspent	$47,730	PACS	$60,098	Hlth	$12,150	Prof	$400

THIRD DISTRICT

The 3d congressional district of Michigan is in the south central part of the state—a place first settled by migrants from New England and Upstate New York in the 1830s and a quiet, prosperous part of the nation ever since. Its economy is in better shape than in many parts of Michigan. Battle Creek's largest industry is not autos, but cereal: it's the headquarters of both Kellogg's and Post. Kalamazoo, the largest city, has a diversified industrial base; pharmaceuticals are a major employer as well as autos. Courthouse towns like Marshall and Charlotte look like museum pieces, with early Victorian homes and old-fashioned miniature downtowns. But these are not economically somnolent communities: people here have started small businesses, built them up, and made them significant employers for miles around. It's money from these innovations which has enabled people to keep the old building preserved; it would have been cheaper, after all, to tear them down or put aluminum siding all over them.

The one economically ailing part of the district is in and around Lansing. For political reasons, Lansing was split between this district and the 6th; the 3d got most of the city of Lansing and its eastern suburbs—the Capitol, the Oldsmobile plant, and most of its black population.

Historically, this is all Republican territory, and has been since the party was founded nearby in Jackson in 1854. It was the kind of place where America seemed to work just fine, with no New Deal tinkering needed, thank you: people took care of each other, economic innovation and growth seemed to happen every generation, traditional morals and community institutions continued strong. The Republican Party represented all these things to the mostly Yankee stock people here (with some even more conservative Dutch in Kalamazoo); the Democrats represented the kind of corruption, ethnic discord, labor unrest, and exotic socialistic theories you got in Detroit. As long as the Detroit area voted heavily Democratic, this part of outstate Michigan stayed heavily Republican.

By the late 1960s, however, Detroit stopped voting so monolithically Democratic, the student vote became, briefly at least, important here, and local attitudes started to change. Culturally, people became more open to variety and tolerant of change; the old racially liberal traditions of outstate Republicanism, dating from Underground Railroad days, may have played a role here. On economic issues, the makeshift American welfare state came to be taken for granted, and even welcomed. State government and education were big employers in this part of Michigan, and people who believed in them found the Democrats more generous and more likeminded.

These changes paved the way for the election and continued reelection of a Democratic congressman, Howard Wolpe. He came to the district from the West Coast and Washington as a teacher at Western Michigan University in Kalamazoo; he was elected to the city council and the state legislature; and he ran for Congress in 1976. His opponent was typical of the old Republican leadership here: Garry Brown, an aggressive, hard-driving young man who believed in increasing business's productivity and fighting hard against the Democrats. Wolpe lost the first battle, was hired as a staffer in Lansing by Senator Donald Riegle, ran again and beat Brown in a bitter race in 1978. He has increased his percentages since, but not vastly; and it is too soon to say that he has a safe seat.

But Wolpe has become an important member of the House. After only two years' service, in 1981, he won a major subcommittee chairmanship, on the Africa Subcommittee of Foreign Affairs. He lived for two years in Nigeria, and has a natural empathy for the emerging nations of the continent and for their leaders. He sees more aid, rather than a turn to free enterprise, as providing the best chance for economic growth; he strongly opposes South Africa's apartheid policy and has urged the United States to call on South Africa to withdraw from Namibia. With such views Wolpe is likely to be a critic of Reagan administration policy frequently; and if some crisis should develop in Africa he would be in effect the House's leading spokesman on the issue.

The People   Pop. 1980: 514,560, up 3.7% 1970–80; voting age pop. 367,512; 8% Black, 2% Span. orig. 30% housing units rented. Median owner $35,800; renter $199. Households: 71% family, 40% with children, 58% married couples.

Presidential Vote

1980	Reagan (R)	NA
	Carter (D)	NA
	Anderson (I)	NA

Rep. Howard E. Wolpe (D) Elected 1978; b. Nov. 2, 1939, Los Angeles, CA; home, Lansing; Reed Col., B.A. 1960, M.I.T., Ph.D., 1967; Jewish.

Career Consultant, U.S. Peace Corps, 1966–67; U.S. State Dept. Foreign Svc. Inst., 1967–72; Prof., W. MI U., 1967–72; Kalamazoo City Cncl., 1969–73; MI House of Reps., 1973–76; Dem. Nominee for U.S. House of Reps., 1976; Regional Rep. and State Liaison to U.S. Sen. Donald W. Riegle, Jr., 1977–78.

Offices 1527 LHOB, 202-225-5011. Also 142 N. Kalamazoo Mall, Kalamazoo 49007, 616-385-0039.

Committees *Budget* (18th). Task Forces: Capital Resources and Development; Education and Employment; Federalism/State-Local Relations. *Foreign Affairs* (11th). Subcommittees: Africa (Chairman); International Economic Policy and Trade.

Group Ratings

	ADA	ACLU	COPE	CFA	LCV	LWV	NTU	NSI	COC	ACA	CSFC
1982	100	92	87	85	100	92	27	10	18	13	27
1981	95	—	83	93	100	—	81	—	11	8	24
1980	94	100	79	79	99	100	18	0	71	30	29

National Journal Ratings

	Economic		Foreign		Cultural	
1982	96%	(LIB)	96%	(LIB)	89%	(LIB)
	2%	(CONS)	1%	(CONS)	8%	(CONS)
1981	73%	(LIB)	92%	(LIB)	88%	(LIB)
	26%	(CONS)	2%	(CONS)	12%	(CONS)

Key Votes

1) Reagan 81 Budget	AGN	5) Incr SS Rtmt Age AGN	9) Poor Pay Food Stamps AGN
2) Reagan 81 Tax Cut	AGN	6) Saudi AWACS Sale AGN	10) Ban Crt Busing Order AGN
3) Bal Budget Amend	AGN	7) $ for MX Missile AGN	11) Auto Local Content FOR
4) Gas & Road Tax	FOR	8) Nerve Gas Prod AGN	12) Nuclear Arms Freeze FOR

Election Results

1982 general	Howard E. Wolpe (D)	96,842	(56%)	($373,924)
	Richard L. Milliman (R)	73,315	(43%)	($480,182)
1982 primary	Howard E. Wolpe (D)	22,895	(100%)	
1980 general	Howard E. Wolpe (D)	113,080	(52%)	($341,910)
	James S. Gilmore (R)	102,591	(47%)	($702,649)

Campaign Contributions and Expenditures

1981-82		Direct Cont. 81-82			PACS brkdwn		
Receipts	$376,669	Indiv	$191,167	Agr	$8,925	Ideo	$32,030
Expend.	$373,924	Party	$27,545	Bus	$14,950	Lbr	$77,317
Unspent	$3,293	PACS	$144,050	Hlth	$505	Prof	$1,625
		Cand	$2,800				

Indirect Party Expend: $1,500

FOURTH DISTRICT

The 4th congressional district of Michigan is the southwest corner of the state, a part of Michigan quite out of sympathy with the prevailing trends of political opinion in Michigan generally. It has no notable cities, but has produced one of the most notable—and politically powerful—figures of the younger generation in American politics. The southern part of the district, along the Indiana border, was settled like most of southern Michigan by settlers of Yankee stock from Upstate New York and New England in the 1830s and 1840s. Its towns like to recall their heritage as stations on the Underground Railroad, and there is even a small rural black community in Cass County, dating from those days; these areas have stayed pretty solidly Republican over the years.

To the north are several counties along the shore of Lake Michigan, which the early settlers tended to avoid. The shoreline here is protected by dunes, the soil is sandy, and before the coming of industry to the Great Lakes—and of the fruit crops which are now important—this did not seem like productive land. So the towns here were settled by many Germans and, from South Haven north to Muskegon, by the Dutch. The Dutch brought with them tulip bulbs, wooden shoes, native costumes and a determination to preserve their rigorous

Christian Reformed religion; and to a considerable extent they have. They have built small businesses and prospered, but have kept their mores very much the same, and are proud of it. The center of Dutch settlement is Grand Rapids, in the 5th district, but its spiritual capital is in Holland, most of which is in the 4th. The Dutch areas are heavily Republican, and Holland's Ottawa County is often the most Republican in Michigan.

Neither half of the 4th district has much use for the welfare state which most of Michigan accepts and demands. For four decades the district was represented in the House by crusty men who railed against the New Deal and all its works: Clare Hoffman and Edward Hutchinson; the latter will be remembered as the ranking Republican on the House Judiciary Committee who woodenly defended Richard Nixon in the impeachment hearings. Then, in 1976, the 4th district elected a congressman who was determined to do something about what he called the "social pork barrel"—and knew how to do so. This was David Stockman. Although a staffer from Washington, he had solid roots in the district, and in 1976 he effectively forced Hutchinson to retire. Stockman came to the House a minor celebrity for his writings; he spent four years as a gadfly to the Democratic leadership and as one of those who tried to unite Republicans around interesting programs. Then his moment came. He helped Ronald Reagan to prepare for his debate by serving as a stand-in for his former Hill boss, John Anderson; able to recognize an effective performance, Reagan took to him, and after the election made him Director of the Office of Management and Budget. Most congressmen and top appointees just study briefing books and staff papers quickly. But Stockman had spent years poring through the budget and knew it himself. He was able to put together a package of budget cuts and get it through Congress before anyone else in the administration knew much about the subject. Stockman's power ebbed suddenly when his *Atlantic* interview was published, but it would have waned anyway: his monopoly on information and initiative could not have continued. But he remained, up through 1983 at least, a powerful figure in the administration and a feared and respected, though by no means loved, figure on Capitol Hill.

In the 1981 special election to replace Stockman, the 4th district seems to have gone back to its old kind of representation. In a seven-candidate primary, Stockman's choice was edged out, 38%–36%, by Mark Siljander, a 29-year-old state legislator who was backed by fundamentalist Christian groups and who was known for his support of an unsuccessful tax limit referendum. Siljander's is the politics of expressing attitudes rather than achieving results or shaping ideas; he serves on the Foreign Affairs Committee, but does not seem to have a major effect on policy. He was reelected in 1982, but won a two-candidate primary with only 56% of the vote—a low result indeed for an incumbent. He was stronger in the southern part of the district and only barely carried the Dutch areas.

The People   Pop. 1980: 514,560, up 12.8% 1970–80; voting age pop. 355,746; 6% Black, 1% Span. orig. 21% housing units rented. Median owner $35,600; renter $178. Households: 77% family, 43% with children, 66% married couples.

Presidential Vote

1980	Reagan (R)	NA
	Carter (D)	NA
	Anderson (I)	NA

Rep. Mark Siljander (R) Elected April 21, 1981; b. June 11, 1951, Chicago, IL; home, Three Rivers; W. MI U., B.A. 1972, M.A. 1973; Protestant.

Career Franchise for home building firm, 1973–76; Bonanza Restaurants, Inc., 1974–76; MI House of Reps., 1976–80.

Offices 137 CHOB, 202-225-3761. Also 325 Main St., Adrian 49221, 517-265-1511; 815 Main St., Su. 3A, St. Joseph 49085, 616-982-0722; and 15788 W. Michigan Ave., Three Rivers 49093, 616-279-7125.

Committee *Foreign Affairs* (12th). Subcommittees: Europe and the Middle East; International Operations.

Group Ratings

	ADA	ACLU	COPE	CFA	LCV	LWV	NTU	NSI	COC	ACA	CSFC
1982	5	12	8	15	26	33	90	100	89	87	73
1981	10	—	7	36	40	—	90	—	89	90	76

National Journal Ratings

	Economic		Foreign		Cultural	
1982	14%	(LIB)	10%	(LIB)	0%	(LIB)
	86%	(CONS)	90%	(CONS)	99%	(CONS)
1981	32%	(LIB)	37%	(LIB)	14%	(LIB)
	68%	(CONS)	63%	(CONS)	86%	(CONS)

Key Votes

1) Reagan 81 Budget	FOR	5) Incr SS Rtmt Age	FOR	9) Poor Pay Food Stamps	FOR
2) Reagan 81 Tax Cut	FOR	6) Saudi AWACS Sale	AGN	10) Ban Crt Busing Order	FOR
3) Bal Budget Amend	FOR	7) $ for MX Missile	FOR	11) Auto Local Content	FOR
4) Gas & Road Tax	—	8) Nerve Gas Prod	FOR	12) Nuclear Arms Freeze	AGN

Election Results

1982 general	Mark Siljander (R)	87,489	(60%)	($184,245)
	David A. Masiokas (D)	56,877	(39%)	($15,852)
1982 primary	Mark Siljander (R)	29,709	(56%)	
	Harold Schuitmaker (R)	23,030	(44%)	($64,046)
1981 special	Mark Siljander (R)	36,046	(73%)	($104,109)
	Johnie A. Rodebush (D)	12,461	(25%)	($29,647)
1980 general	David A. (Dave) Stockman (R)	148,950	(75%)	($90,721)
	Lyndon G. Furst (D)	47,777	(24%)	($14,235)

Campaign Contributions and Expenditures

1981-82		Direct Cont. 81-82		PACS brkdwn			
Receipts	$175,926	Indiv	$76,999	Agr	$1,600	Ideo	$35,442
Expend.	$184,245	Party	$13,982	Bus	$28,050	Lbr	$250
Unspent	$810	PACS	$69,092	Hlth	$3,250	Prof	$—
		Cand	$8,200				

Indirect Party Expend: $2,866   *Indep Expend:* For: $116 (MI LIFEPAC)

FIFTH DISTRICT

The 5th congressional district of Michigan is the seat that gave the nation our 40th vice president, Gerald Ford, and which, by electing a member of the opposite party as his successor in the House, helped to make Ford our 38th president. The center of the district is Grand Rapids, long the second largest city in Michigan and one which, despite the fact that it is far smaller than Detroit, has bulked large in the state's civic affairs. Unlike Detroit, it has always been a solidly Republican town, faithful to the party through all the New Deal years.

It had a heritage of Yankee Republicanism and, more recently, of Dutch conservatism. Grand Rapids is the heart of the nation's largest concentration of Dutch-Americans, as a glance at the phone book's list of Vander . . . s will show. The Dutch in the Netherlands are staunch supporters of the welfare state, advocates of departures from tradition in their Catholic and Protestant churches, sympathizers with an almost neutralist, pacifist foreign policy. But the Dutch who migrate, whether to South Africa or western Michigan, are rigidly conservative, in cultural style and political views. The Christian Reformed church in the Grand Rapids area still frowns on drinking, smoking, and dancing; its fierce Calvinist theology is not leavened by any sort of liberation theology.

The most eminent politician produced by the Grand Rapids Dutch community was Arthur Vandenberg, senator from Michigan 1928–51, a strong isolationist for many years who announced his conversion to internationalism in a famous speech in 1945, and as chairman of the Foreign Relations Committee helped set up the Marshall Plan and formulate the bipartisan foreign policy of the postwar years. Embarrassed that the 5th district seat was still held by an isolationist, in 1948 Vandenberg supported a 35-year-old lawyer in the Republican primary, Gerald Ford. Ford delayed his marriage to his fiancee Betty, who had been divorced, until after the primary.

Ford was stunned when Democrat Richard VanderVeen was elected to succeed him—which showed that Ford was out of touch with national opinion on Richard Nixon and that he had failed to notice that his Republican percentages in Grand Rapids had been growing smaller. The working class vote, in southern Grand Rapids and the blue collar suburb of Wyoming, was growing more Democratic; antipathy to the big city was growing less; the specter of corruption over the Nixon administration bothered the Dutch. The peculiarity of that election was shown by the fact that VanderVeen lost the seat in 1976 to Republican Harold Sawyer. But the change in Grand Rapids's attitudes is apparent from the fact that Sawyer has not won reelection by a convincing margin since: he had 49% in 1978 and 53% in 1980 and 1982. Almost certainly he will receive a serious challenge if he runs for reelection in 1984.

Sawyer's record on issues is probably not far out of line from what the 5th district, which includes Grand Rapids, its suburbs, and some rural territory roundabout, wants. But he has an explosive and sometimes profane temperament which seems out of line with local mores—and with what people remember about Gerald Ford. Sawyer serves on the House Judiciary Committee and, as a former Kent County prosecutor, has been active on reforming criminal law; his concentration on Washington activities may have hurt him in the 5th district, however.

The People   Pop. 1980: 514,560, up 9.5% 1970–80; voting age pop. 359,611; 5% Black, 2% Span. orig. 25% housing units rented. Median owner $38,400; renter $188. Households: 75% family, 43% with children, 63% married couples.

Presidential Vote

1980	Reagan (R)	132,020	(56%)
	Carter (D)	82,265	(35%)
	Anderson (I)	19,786	(8%)

Rep. Harold S. Sawyer (R) Elected 1976; b. Mar. 21, 1920, San Francisco, CA; home, Rockford; U. of CA, LL.B. 1945; Episcopal.

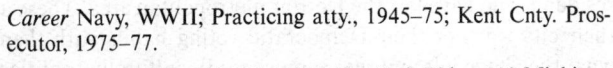

Career Navy, WWII; Practicing atty., 1945–75; Kent Cnty. Prosecutor, 1975–77.

Offices 301 CHOB, 202-225-3831. Also Fed. Bldg., 110 Michigan N.W., Grand Rapids 49503, 616-451-8383.

Committee *Judiciary* (5th). Subcommittees: Courts, Civil Liberties and the Administration of Justice; Crime; Monopolies and Commercial Law.

Group Ratings

	ADA	ACLU	COPE	CFA	LCV	LWV	NTU	NSI	COC	ACA	CSFC
1982	10	33	20	31	53	55	66	90	76	74	55
1981	15	—	20	50	36	—	49	—	94	67	59
1980	11	20	24	21	52	50	49	78	79	83	70

National Journal Ratings

	Economic		Foreign		Cultural	
1982	24%	(LIB)	34%	(LIB)	28%	(LIB)
	76%	(CONS)	66%	(CONS)	71%	(CONS)
1981	32%	(LIB)	38%	(LIB)	48%	(LIB)
	68%	(CONS)	61%	(CONS)	52%	(CONS)

Key Votes

1) Reagan 81 Budget	FOR	5) Incr SS Rtmt Age	FOR	9) Poor Pay Food Stamps	FOR
2) Reagan 81 Tax Cut	FOR	6) Saudi AWACS Sale	FOR	10) Ban Crt Busing Order	FOR
3) Bal Budget Amend	FOR	7) $ for MX Missile	FOR	11) Auto Local Content	AGN
4) Gas & Road Tax	—	8) Nerve Gas Prod	FOR	12) Nuclear Arms Freeze	AGN

Election Results

1982 general	Harold S. Sawyer (R)	98,650	(53%)	($422,129)
	Stephen C. Monsma (D)	87,229	(47%)	($269,339)
1982 primary	Harold S. Sawyer (R)	41,453	(100%)	
1980 general	Harold S. Sawyer (R)	118,061	(53%)	($366,147)
	Dale R. Sprik (D)	101,737	(46%)	($201,895)

Campaign Contributions and Expenditures

1981-82		*Direct Cont. 81-82*		*PACS brkdwn*			
Receipts	$422,725	Indiv	$244,044	Agr	$4,150	Ideo	$7,800
Expend.	$422,129	Party	$24,335	Bus	$114,905	Lbr	$100
Unspent	$3,147	PACS	$141,775	Hlth	$3,300	Prof	$3,500

Indirect Party Expend: $34,955   *Indep Expend:* For: $1,392 (MI LIFEPAC)

SIXTH DISTRICT

The 6th congressional district of Michigan cuts a swath through the southern part of the state between two cities whose major employers have been auto plants: Lansing (Oldsmobile) and Pontiac. The land between is full of hills and lakes deposited and carved out there centuries ago by Ice Age glaciers. It is marginal farmland and was sparsely settled for years; in the last two decades, it has sprouted subdivisions, trailer parks, and rows of lakeside cottages for new residents who have left the Detroit metropolitan area. These are not people who have brought their city ways or their Democratic voting habits with them; on the contrary, they dislike what they have left and seek a more rural, culturally traditional environment in which to live and raise their children. This migration is symbolic of the affluence of Michigan in the 1960s and 1970s, which enabled people with quite ordinary jobs to make such choices.

Now that affluence is threatened, and nowhere so obviously as in the auto towns. Lansing had a 20-year boom based on Oldsmobile and state government; in the 1970s the Olds Cutlass was America's number one selling make and state government and giant Michigan State University in East Lansing grew rapidly. The collapse of the auto industry at the end of the decade cut auto employment and state government payrolls and salaries as well; for once, a government or teaching job wasn't secure. The 6th district includes the eastern part of Lansing and the city of East Lansing as well, the more affluent parts of the metropolitan area; but they still have been hit hard by the recession.

Hit even harder has been Pontiac and its lake-studded suburb of Waterford Township. Though part of affluent suburban Oakland County, Pontiac has never really been in the Detroit orbit; it has always had its own newspaper and radio station, and is really the beginning of outstate Michigan. Its major employers were the Pontiac and GMC Truck & Coach plants; its population was drawn mostly from the South, blacks from the Black Belt of Alabama, whites from Appalachian Kentucky and Tennessee. They remain separated on opposite sides of town, though there was a large white flight to Waterford during the long pendency of a bitter school busing suit.

The three areas were joined for the first time in decades in the same congressional district in 1982, but the election was a rematch between Democrat Bob Carr, elected in a Lansing-based district in 1974, 1976, and 1978, and Republican Jim Dunn, who beat Carr in 1980. They took diametrically opposed positions on most issues. Carr was a Vietnam dove who, in his first term, got the Democratic Caucus to vote against military aid to Cambodia as the Khmer Rouge were closing in on Phnom Penh; serving on the Armed Services Committee, he was regarded as a dove and stressed spending on readiness rather than elaborate weapons systems. On economics he was a conventional pro-labor Democrat. Dunn in 1980 attacked Carr for cutting our defense forces too much, and in a year dominated by news of Western reverses in Afghanistan and Iran, that proved a popular appeal.

Dunn was also a supporter of Reaganomics; only on cultural issues, where both had rather liberal records, did the two come close to agreement. In his first campaign Dunn's economic stands had some appeal; in his second, with unemployment somewhere around 28% in Pontiac and the economy of Lansing staggering, they did not. Carr won the rematch by a 51%–48% margin. He serves now on the Appropriations Committee, but not on the Defense Subcommittee; despite his expertise, he seems to be steering clear of such issues.

The 6th district will almost certainly be the scene of another closely contested race in 1984. It was not designed by the Democratic legislature to be a Democratic district; they took solidly Democratic parts of Lansing and put them in the 3d district represented by Howard Wolpe, when Carr was out of office. But Carr knows how to campaign: he has run six times now, losing in 1972 and 1980 but winning four times; and Dunn, who could afford to finance much of his own campaign, may not run again. Moreover, even if the national economy improves vastly, it is not at all clear that the Olds and Pontiac factories will ever again employ as many people as they did so recently as 1979, nor that Michigan's state government will ever have payrolls as big and salaries as large in real terms as it did then.

The People Pop. 1980: 514,559, up 19% 1970–80; voting age pop. 360,961; 6% Black, 2% Span. orig., 1% Asian orig. 28% housing units rented. Median owner $46,700; renter $234. Households: 74% family, 45% with children, 62% married couples.

Presidential Vote

1980	Reagan (R)	107,405	(51%)
	Carter (D)	80,203	(38%)
	Anderson (I)	22,006	(10%)

Rep. Robert (Bob) Carr (D) Elected 1982; b. Mar. 27, 1943, Janesville, WI; home, East Lansing; U. of WI, B.S. 1965, J.D. 1968, U. of MI, 1968–69; Baptist.

Career Staff Asst. to U.S. Sen. Gaylord Nelson of WI, 1967; Staff Mbr., MI Senate Minor. Ldr.'s Ofc., 1968–69; A. A. to Atty. Gen. of MI, 1969–70; Asst. Atty. Gen. of MI, 1970–72; Counsel to MI Legislature Special Comm. on Legal Educ., 1972; Dem. Nominee for U.S. House of Reps., 1972, 1980; U.S. House of Reps., 1974–80.

Offices 2439 RHOB, 202-225-4872. Also P.O. Box 1552, E. Lansing 48823, 517-484-3363; and 91 N. Saginaw, Pontiac 48053, 313-332-2510.

Committee *Appropriations* (35th). Subcommittees: Commerce, Justice, State and the Judiciary; Transportation.

Group Ratings and Key Votes: Newly Elected

Election Results

1982 general	Robert (Bob) Carr (D)	84,778	(51%)	($388,057)
	Jim Dunn (R)	78,388	(48%)	($405,862)
1982 primary	Robert (Bob) Carr (D)	27,165	(100%)	
1980 general	Jim Dunn (R)	111,272	(51%)	($345,127)
	Robert (Bob) Carr (D)	108,548	(49%)	($146,725)

Campaign Contributions and Expenditures

1981-82		*Direct Cont. 81-82*			*PACS brkdwn*			
Receipts	$387,632	Indiv	$176,497	Agr	$8,740	Ideo	$34,575
Expend.	$388,057	Party	$36,963	Bus	$7,600	Lbr	$103,921
Unspent	$1,120	PACS	$164,374	Hlth	$2,100	Prof	$2,100

Indirect Party Expend: $2,500

SEVENTH DISTRICT

Flint, Michigan, with a metropolitan population of 500,000 and five major General Motors plants, is probably the nation's largest company town. Before the auto industry collapse of 1979, some 60% of metropolitan Flint's wage earners were on the GM payroll; and although there is some white collar employment here, this is mainly the Chevrolet and Buick factory town. Flint has no five o'clock rush hour; its traffic jams come at three thirty, when the shifts break. Even the management is factory-oriented: the plushest residential district here has a panoramic view of a Chevrolet plant. For years civic life in Flint was dominated by Charles Stewart Mott, a member of the General Motors board of directors for 60 years and for most of that time the largest individual shareholder in the corporation; as a very old man he continued to run the Mott Foundation, one of the nation's largest, out of Flint and concentrated on local projects until his death several years ago at age 97.

In the early 1980s Flint seemed about to become an ex-factory town. For much of 1981 and 1982 it had the nation's highest unemployment rate, close to 20%. General Motors, though not in as bad financial shape as Ford or Chrysler, had to lay off thousands of workers, and in a town as undiversified as Flint the impact was soon felt. Stores were forced to close, local businesses went bankrupt, and in most neighborhoods the bidding price for houses fell to zero. Flint has gotten used to layoffs over the years, but it has also gotten used to the nation's most generous unemployment benefits—and to coming back to work. Young workers, with no memory of the hard times of the 1930s, were particularly likely to be laid off; and when their benefits expired, usually after 65 weeks, they were stunned. Their faces showed mute disbelief, as if it never occurred to them that they would fall below society's safety net. The companies always seemed secure; the United Auto Workers, established after the bitter sitdown strikes of the 1930s in Flint, bargained for higher and higher wages and seemed to have accounted for every contingency—except the collapse of the industry. They had a hard time believing that something would not turn up at home. Flint was settled, mostly between 1910 and 1930, by migrants, from local rural areas, the American South, and Eastern Europe. But although some people left Flint in the early 1980s, many stayed, anchored to the place where their grandparents, after so much travel, had set down roots.

Oddly, such turmoil has had little effect on Flint's voting habits. Flint and the ring of suburbs around it, which together with Lapeer County to the east make up Michigan's 7th congressional district, have been solidly Democratic in most elections for years. Despite heavy campaigning by Ronald Reagan here in 1980, they remained so; but there was no huge Democratic bulge, except for Flint native Senator Donald Riegle, in the 1982 elections. It is as if Flint as a whole is stunned, responding mutely and in accordance with custom, to a disastrous change in its way of life which no one seems able to prevent.

The 7th district's congressman, Dale Kildee, is politically strong in any case. In 1976, when Riegle left the House seat to run for the Senate, Kildee won the Democratic primary and the general election easily. He had served 12 years in the legislature and in a 1974 Senate race had campaigned through most of Flint door to door. This is one of the few congressional districts which coincides almost precisely with a television media market; so Kildee, as congressman and even as state senator, got plenty of free air time. Earnest, austere, inclined to liberal views on most issues but not on cultural matters like abortion, Kildee is an opponent of the Reagan administration on most issues. He sits on the Education and Labor Committee and, since 1981, on Interior as well. His efforts to change committees in 1983 were reportedly nixed by the Democratic leadership because he opposed the congressional pay raise the year before. In Flint he has maintained high popularity and has not had serious opposition since 1976.

The People Pop. 1980: 514,560, up 5% 1970–80; voting age pop. 346,868; 14% Black, 1% Span. orig. 23% housing units rented. Median owner $36,800; renter $209. Households: 77% family, 47% with children, 61% married couples.

Presidential Vote

1980	Reagan (R)	NA
	Carter (D)	NA
	Anderson (I)	NA

Rep. Dale E. Kildee (D) Elected 1976; b. Sept. 16, 1929, Flint; home, Flint; Sacred Heart Sem., Detroit, B.A. 1952, U. of MI, M.A. 1961, Rotary Fellow, U. of Peshawar, Pakistan; Roman Catholic.

Career High sch. teacher, 1954–64; MI House of Reps., 1965–75; MI Senate, 1975–77.

Offices 2432 RHOB, 202-225-3611. Also 444 Church St., Flint 48502, 313-239-1437.

Committees *Education and Labor* (13th). Subcommittees: Elementary, Secondary and Vocational Education; Labor-Management Relations. *Interior and Insular Affairs* (17th). Subcommittees: Insular Affairs; Public Lands and National Parks.

Group Ratings

	ADA	ACLU	COPE	CFA	LCV	LWV	NTU	NSI	COC	ACA	CSFC
1982	95	83	90	92	96	92	15	10	23	9	25
1981	90	—	89	86	93	—	30	—	5	17	27
1980	89	80	84	71	83	100	15	10	62	21	26

National Journal Ratings

	Economic		Foreign		Cultural	
1982	92%	(LIB)	88%	(LIB)	86%	(LIB)
	7%	(CONS)	12%	(CONS)	13%	(CONS)
1981	89%	(LIB)	92%	(LIB)	70%	(LIB)
	3%	(CONS)	2%	(CONS)	30%	(CONS)

Key Votes

1) Reagan 81 Budget	AGN	5) Incr SS Rtmt Age	AGN	9) Poor Pay Food Stamps	AGN
2) Reagan 81 Tax Cut	AGN	6) Saudi AWACS Sale	AGN	10) Ban Crt Busing Order	AGN
3) Bal Budget Amend	AGN	7) $ for MX Missile	AGN	11) Auto Local Content	FOR
4) Gas & Road Tax	FOR	8) Nerve Gas Prod	AGN	12) Nuclear Arms Freeze	FOR

Election Results

1982 general	Dale E. Kildee (D)	118,538	(75%)	($60,806)
	George R. Darrah (R)	36,303	(23%)	($11,667)
1982 primary	Dale E. Kildee (D)	31,488	(100%)	
1980 general	Dale E. Kildee (D)	147,280	(93%)	($32,391)
	Dennis L. Berry (Libertarian)	11,507	(7%)	($0)

Campaign Contributions and Expenditures

1981-82		Direct Cont. 81-82		PACS brkdwn			
Receipts	$64,150	Indiv	$16,775	Agr	$325	Ideo	$1,475
Expend.	$60,806	PACS	$47,053	Bus	$5,300	Lbr	$36,175
Unspent	$7,237			Hlth	$1,750	Prof	$250

Indep Expend: For: $153

EIGHTH DISTRICT

To understand the geography of the 8th congressional district of Michigan, you have to understand that Michigan's Lower Peninsula is shaped like a mittened left hand. The 8th district includes most of the Thumb (as it actually is called locally) and the bottom part of the index finger. The Thumb is almost entirely agricultural, tilled by descendants of the Yankee, German, and Canadian farmers who settled it a little more than a century ago. Life's rhythms have changed little since then, although agriculture has become immensely more productive; the area's chief products are navy beans (used in Senate bean soup) and sugar beets.

Where the index finger extends from the palm (this is not local nomenclature) are the old industrial cities of Saginaw and Bay City. Both have been important since the 19th century when Michigan was the nation's leading lumber producer and these cities were, briefly, its major lumber ports. Today their economy is based in large part on the auto industry; Saginaw is, even still, the biggest producer of power steering equipment in the world.

Both the Thumb and the Saginaw area were mainstays for many years of the Republican Party. Their impact on national politics, however, was slight, except for the time a Saginaw congressman coauthored the Fordney-McCumber tariff, until 1974. That was when the 8th district saw the second special election that year in which Richard Nixon was the central issue. And for the second time, an historically Republican outstate Michigan district rejected the president and voted Democratic.

The victor in that race, Bob Traxler, is still congressman today. His local political base is Bay City, the one traditionally Democratic part of the district. But in recent years, even before the collapse of the auto industry, he carried Saginaw easily, and he has run well in the Thumb also. Traxler has specialized in agriculture issues, and he is now second ranking Democrat on two Appropriations subcommittees, Agriculture and HUD-Independent Agencies. Since the chairmen of these were born in 1910 and 1911 respectively, Traxler's chance of joining the "college of cardinals"—the old name for the chairmen of the appropriations subcommittees—is excellent. Of the two posts, the more powerful is probably Agriculture, through which Jamie Whitten has had a major hand in shaping American farm and food policy for more than 30 years; on that subcommittee Traxler has been a major supporter of the food stamp program. At home Traxler has not had serious competition since 1976 and did not even have a Republican opponent in 1982; he appears to have a safe seat.

The People   Pop. 1980: 514,560, up 8.3% 1970–80; voting age pop. 350,577; 6% Black, 3% Span. orig. 20% housing units rented. Median owner $35,600; renter $189. Households: 78% family, 45% with children, 65% married couples.

Presidential Vote

1980	Reagan (R) .... NA
	Carter (D) .... NA
	Anderson (I) .... NA

Rep. Bob Traxler (D) Elected Apr. 1974; b. July 21, 1931, Kawkawlin; home, Bay City; MI St. U., B.A. 1953, Detroit Col. of Law, LL.B. 1959; Episcopal.

Career Army, 1953–55; Asst. Bay Cnty. Prosecutor, 1960–62; MI House of Reps., 1963–74, Major. Flr. Ldr., 1965.

Offices 2448 RHOB, 202-225-2806. Also 62 New Fed. Bldg., 100 S. Warren, Saginaw 48606, 517-753-6444.

Committee *Appropriations* (15th). Subcommittees: Agriculture, Rural Development; HUD-Independent Agencies; Legislative.

Group Ratings

	ADA	ACLU	COPE	CFA	LCV	LWV	NTU	NSI	COC	ACA	CSFC
1982	75	50	84	69	84	73	24	25	19	10	29
1981	65	—	83	71	79	—	23	—	17	18	37
1980	56	47	79	79	43	50	14	29	58	17	36

National Journal Ratings

	Economic		Foreign		Cultural	
1982	79%	(LIB)	85%	(LIB)	65%	(LIB)
	21%	(CONS)	15%	(CONS)	35%	(CONS)
1981	67%	(LIB)	77%	(LIB)	57%	(LIB)
	32%	(CONS)	23%	(CONS)	42%	(CONS)

Key Votes

1) Reagan 81 Budget	AGN	5) Incr SS Rtmt Age	AGN	9) Poor Pay Food Stamps	AGN
2) Reagan 81 Tax Cut	AGN	6) Saudi AWACS Sale	AGN	10) Ban Crt Busing Order	FOR
3) Bal Budget Amend	AGN	7) $ for MX Missile	AGN	11) Auto Local Content	FOR
4) Gas & Road Tax	—	8) Nerve Gas Prod	AGN	12) Nuclear Arms Freeze	FOR

Election Results

1982 general	Bob Traxler (D)	113,515	(91%)	($84,209)
	Sheila M. Hart (Libertarian)	11,219	(9%)	($0)
1982 primary	Bob Traxler (D)	34,564	(100%)	
1980 general	Bob Traxler (D)	124,155	(61%)	($88,798)
	Norman R. Hughes (R)	77,009	(38%)	($25,075)

Campaign Contributions and Expenditures

1981-82		Direct Cont. 81-82		PACS brkdwn			
Receipts	$87,038	Indiv	$23,045	Agr	$10,550	Ideo	$1,500
Expend.	$84,209	Party	$35	Bus	$14,700	Lbr	$17,950
Unspent	$66,849	PACS	$46,900	Hlth	$2,000	Prof	$1,250

Indirect Party Expend: $1,000   *Indep Expend:* For: $151 (MI LIFEPAC)

NINTH DISTRICT

Michigan's 9th congressional district covers most of the eastern shore of Lake Michigan. Unlike the western shore, which from the steel mills of Gary north past Chicago and

Milwaukee to Sheboygan, Wisconsin, is heavily urban and industrial, the Michigan shore seems bucolic these days. It was not always so: its small industrial towns got their starts as lumber ports, when Michigan was the number one lumber state in the country; and until several disastrous fires in the late 19th century, huge numbers of logs were floated down the rivers to Muskegon, Ludington, and Manistee. Each of these harbors lies at a river mouth and behind the sand dunes which, at varying heights, line the eastern shore of the Lake. These dunes, and the peculiar climatic conditions produced by the Lake, have made this northern part of the country one of its major fruit and vegetable producers, specializing particularly in the tart cherries for which Traverse City (right at the base of the ring finger on Michigan's hand-shaped Lower Peninsula) holds a festival every year. The 9th district also extends inland, to lake and resort country in the northern end and to farm country in the southern end, around Grand Rapids.

The 9th is an ancestrally Republican district. Although Muskegon and the other lumber towns retain a trace of Democratic populism from their rougher days, they have become more Republican in recent years as their economic base shifts from low-skill to high-skill jobs; at the southern end of the district is part of Michigan's heavily Republican Dutch community.

The 9th's congressman is one of the leading Republican partisans in the House, Guy Vander Jagt. He has a diverse background: he was a television newscaster and a state senator, and is both an attorney and an ordained minister. He prides himself on his speaking ability, and he is not one of those new-fashioned orators who speaks conversationally to the television camera. Vander Jagt thunders out his speeches, which he likes to practice while walking through the woods, and which he insists on delivering extemporaneously.

His major success in the House has been as chairman of the House Republican Campaign Committee. He can claim credit for much of the Republican gains in 1978 and 1980, and for holding the party's losses in 1982 to 26 seats in a recession year. Vander Jagt has been in charge when the committee built up huge mailing lists and developed sophisticated media and polling techniques which enable it to step in and put massive resources—including prepared TV ads—into any campaign which shows signs of needing them, literally within 24 hours. No one can say for sure how many seats this capability has produced for the Republicans, but surely the number is over a dozen—and they may have made the difference in the passage of President Reagan's budget and tax cuts in 1981.

Vander Jagt also sits on the Ways and Means Committee and is ranking Republican on its Trade Subcommittee. But he is not known as a legislative detail man, nor one who is terribly interested in issues which are not central in campaigns, nor is he much concerned about subtleties or nonpartisan approaches. His skill is in painting the broad picture in bright colors and vivid contrasts. Perhaps for that reason Vander Jagt lost the 1981 Republican leadership race to Robert Michel, who is more of a nuts-and-bolts legislator. But Vander Jagt has worked loyally with Michel since then, and may again be a candidate for the leadership should Michel retire.

The People   Pop. 1980: 514,560, up 13.9% 1970–80; voting age pop. 356,896; 4% Black, 1% Span. orig. 17% housing units rented. Median owner $33,500; renter $163. Households: 77% family, 43% with children, 67% married couples.

Presidential Vote

1980	Reagan (R)	NA
	Carter (D)	NA
	Anderson (I)	NA

Rep. Guy Vander Jagt (R) Elected 1966; b. Aug. 26, 1931, Cadillac; home, Cadillac; Hope Col., B.A. 1953, Yale U., B.D. 1955, Rotary Fellow, Bonn U., Germany, 1956, U. of MI, LL.B. 1960; Presbyterian.

Career Practicing atty., 1960–64; MI Senate, 1965–66.

Offices 2409 RHOB, 202-225-3511. Also 950 W. Norton Ave., Muskegon 49441, 616-733-3131.

Committee *Ways and Means* (4th). Subcommittees: Select Revenue Measures; Trade.

Group Ratings

	ADA	ACLU	COPE	CFA	LCV	LWV	NTU	NSI	COC	ACA	CSFC
1982	15	17	17	23	51	45	59	100	65	70	54
1981	10	—	17	21	22	—	57	—	100	86	66
1980	22	30	11	14	35	44	48	100	84	79	69

National Journal Ratings

	Economic		Foreign		Cultural	
1982	35%	(LIB)	40%	(LIB)	20%	(LIB)
	65%	(CONS)	59%	(CONS)	79%	(CONS)
1981	0%	(LIB)	51%	(LIB)	10%	(LIB)
	99%	(CONS)	48%	(CONS)	90%	(CONS)

Key Votes

1) Reagan 81 Budget	FOR	5) Incr SS Rtmt Age	FOR	9) Poor Pay Food Stamps	FOR
2) Reagan 81 Tax Cut	FOR	6) Saudi AWACS Sale	AGN	10) Ban Crt Busing Order	FOR
3) Bal Budget Amend	FOR	7) $ for MX Missile	FOR	11) Auto Local Content	AGN
4) Gas & Road Tax	FOR	8) Nerve Gas Prod	AGN	12) Nuclear Arms Freeze	AGN

Election Results

1982 general	Guy Vander Jagt (R)	112,504	(65%)	($392,396)
	Gerald D. Warner (D)	69,932	(35%)	($34,450)
1982 primary	Guy Vander Jagt (R)	42,070	(100%)	
1980 general	Guy Vander Jagt (R)	168,713	(97%)	($185,491)

Campaign Contributions and Expenditures

1981-82		Direct Cont. 81-82		PACS brkdwn			
Receipts	$348,925	Indiv	$152,820	Agr	$8,200	Ideo	$4,000
Expend.	$392,396	Party	$9,709	Bus	$137,682	Lbr	$8,900
Unspent	$52,571	PACS	$176,430	Hlth	$9,050	Prof	$7,950

Indep Expend: For: $145

TENTH DISTRICT

When Michigan's Lower Peninsula was first settled by Yankees from Upstate New York and New England in the 1830s, they didn't go very far north in the state. They sensed, perhaps from their experience in the land they came from, that if you got too far north, the land thawed too late in the spring to plow and the frost came too soon in the fall for you to harvest your crops. So they left the forests of the northern half of the Lower Peninsula in place; and instead of moving north in Michigan, if they wanted to leave they sought lands farther west in Iowa or Nebraska. So later in the 19th century these lands were waiting for the lumber barons to cut them down and make vast sums of money. There was no nonsense about scientific harvesting of trees then; and what wasn't clear-cut in lower Michigan was mostly destroyed by a disastrous fire in 1871, which is supposed to have burned clear across from Holland on Lake Michigan to Saginaw Bay and Lake Huron. To this day, the timber growth along the inland lakes of the northern Lower Peninsula is new forest, only barely regenerated since that terrific pillage.

Michigan's 10th congressional district crosses the line between the state's historic farm and forest land, staying almost entirely inland, away from Lake Michigan and Lake Huron. In the south it goes as far as the Lansing city limits, and includes the old small city of Owosso, boyhood home of Thomas E. Dewey. To the north are the towns of Alma, Mount Pleasant, Big Rapids, agricultural centers originally, and now important as college towns as well. The district goes on, to take in most of the northern part of the Lower Peninsula.

This is the resort country. In the 1950s and 1960s, hundreds of thousands of Michiganders escaped each weekend from industrial cities and went up north. They stayed in log cabins or knotty pine cottages on the hundreds of inland lakes, getting up at dawn to fish or sleeping late and watching the children swim in the icy green waters or cut through the lakes in boats. In the fall there were traffic jams as thousands of men drove up north to hunt; in the winter increasing numbers of young people came north to ski. Rapidly rising incomes in auto-affluent Michigan made this resort country accessible not just to white collar and professional families, but increasingly to blue collar families as well. And, as everyone got even more affluent and economically secure in the 1970s, they began moving up here as well. Many came as retirees, planning to spend the worst of the winter in Florida; others came to live here year round, willing to give up the larger paychecks they could take home in suburban Detroit, happy to live in an area of physical beauty, available recreation, and freedom from some of the social problems (crime, large numbers of blacks) they felt existed in Detroit. In the 1970s, this part of Michigan had, for the first time ever, the state's most rapid population growth.

This migration has changed the political complexion of the 10th district. The farm and the resort country were both once among the most Republican parts of the state. But the new migrants were disproportionately Democratic, and if in Detroit they were trending Republican because of hostility to local blacks and their demands, in the north country that seemed no longer to operate. The 10th district trended Democratic in statewide elections (although it usually gives Republicans a small margin) and in 1978 it surprised almost everybody by ousting a 26-year incumbent Republican congressman—one of the most senior Republicans in the House—and electing Democrat Don Albosta.

Albosta is not the typical Michigan Democrat. He is a successful farmer who first came to public notice protesting the state's handling of the PBB contamination; he is a voluble, if not fluent man, one well suited to a time when political discourse seems to be a recitation of complaints. His committee assignments are practical (Public Works, Post Office and Civil Service). His positions on economic issues are liberal, on cultural issues quite conservative—the opposite of many other successful outstate Michigan Democrats, and a reflection of the fact that his key constituency comes ultimately from metropolitan Detroit rather than from the outstate communities themselves. That pattern is apparent from the 1982 election results: Albosta ran strongest in his home territory around Saginaw and in the northern resort counties, where he got more than 60%; he fell below 60% in the old farm counties, and failed to carry Midland, the home of Dow Chemical Company, which votes like a high-income suburb. He was reelected in 1980 against strong opposition with 52% and against a less well-financed opponent in 1982 with 60%. That latter figure suggests he has a safe district, but it would be wise to be cautious in saying so about an area that has changed so much in recent years.

The People Pop. 1980: 514,560, up 23.5% 1970–80; voting age pop. 357,369; 1% Black, 1% Span. orig. 14% housing units rented. Median owner $34,400; renter $170. Households: 78% family, 44% with children, 68% married couples.

Presidential Vote

1980	Reagan (R)	NA
	Carter (D)	NA
	Anderson (I)	NA

Rep. Donald Joseph (Don) **Albosta** (D) Elected 1978; b. Dec. 5, 1925, Saginaw Cnty.; home, St. Charles; Delta Col.; Roman Catholic.

Career Navy, WWII; Farmer; Saginaw Cnty. Comm., 1970–74; MI House of Reps., 1974–76.

Offices 1434 LHOB, 202-225-3561. Also 419 S. Saginaw Rd., Midland 48640, 517-839-0790.

Committees *Post Office and Civil Service* (7th). Subcommittees: Human Resources (Chairman); Postal Personnel and Modernization. *Public Works and Transportation* (15th). Subcommittees: Investigations and Oversight; Surface Transportation; Water Resources. *Select Committee on Aging* (25th). Subcommittee: Human Services.

Group Ratings

	ADA	ACLU	COPE	CFA	LCV	LWV	NTU	NSI	COC	ACA	CSFC
1982	75	33	79	69	67	70	27	56	32	9	28
1981	40	—	74	57	61	—	14	—	22	33	47
1980	28	37	68	21	30	40	22	25	81	42	41

National Journal Ratings

	Economic		Foreign		Cultural	
1982	73%	(LIB)	88%	(LIB)	48%	(LIB)
	26%	(CONS)	11%	(CONS)	51%	(CONS)
1981	62%	(LIB)	63%	(LIB)	33%	(LIB)
	37%	(CONS)	36%	(CONS)	67%	(CONS)

Key Votes

1) Reagan 81 Budget	AGN	5) Incr SS Rtmt Age	AGN	9) Poor Pay Food Stamps	AGN
2) Reagan 81 Tax Cut	AGN	6) Saudi AWACS Sale	AGN	10) Ban Crt Busing Order	FOR
3) Bal Budget Amend	AGN	7) $ for MX Missile	AGN	11) Auto Local Content	FOR
4) Gas & Road Tax	—	8) Nerve Gas Prod	AGN	12) Nuclear Arms Freeze	FOR

Election Results

1982 general	Donald Joseph (Don) Albosta (D) .	102,048	(60%)	($315,522)
	Lawrence W. Reed (R)	66,080	(39%)	($171,019)
1982 primary	Donald Joseph (Don) Albosta (D) .	25,606	(100%)	
1980 general	Donald Joseph (Don) Albosta (D) .	126,962	(52%)	($355,147)
	Richard J. Allen (R)	111,496	(46%)	($410,995)

Campaign Contributions and Expenditures

1981-82		*Direct Cont. 81-82*				*PACS brkdwn*		
Receipts	$307,745	Indiv	$105,142	Agr	$19,140	Ideo	$7,500
Expend.	$315,522	Party	$18,677	Bus	$38,779	Lbr	$60,450
Unspent	$2,078	PACS	$140,321	Hlth	$11,150	Prof	$900
		Cand	$33,000				

Indirect Party Expend: $13,367   *Indep Expend:* For: $1,409 (NRA, MI LIFEPAC)
Agn: $3,087 (NTLCPAC)

ELEVENTH DISTRICT

Michigan's Upper Peninsula (or the UP, as it is called here) is a world unto itself. It is isolated most of the year from the rest of the world by the elements, and for years travel here was discouraged by the high tolls ($3.75) on the Mackinac Straits Bridge. The UP was first settled around the turn of the century, when the iron and copper mines were booming, and the place had a Wild West air about it. The population influx was polyglot: Irish, Italians, Swedes, Norwegians, and Finns. The Finns remain the largest ethnic group here, and this land, so reminiscent of Finland with its lakes and its cold, has the largest concentration of Finnish-Americans. Some of the mine workers picked up radical or even socialist ideas, and many developed Democratic voting habits; their descendants, those who are left, retain the latter.

Forty or 50 years ago, the mines petered out, leaving the UP's economy stagnant and dependent on summer tourists and fall hunters. Farming has never been important here: it sometimes snows in July and the growing season is too short for most crops. Lumber was once an important industry, but production is easier in the Pacific Northwest and the Southeast, where the forests aren't covered with snow half the year. After World War II the young people of the Upper Peninsula left for Detroit, Chicago, and the West Coast. From 1940 to 1970, the UP's population has hovered around 300,000 (it was 332,000 in 1920). Even in the 1970s, the substantial migration from the metropolitan areas to the northern part of the Lower Peninsula did not cross the Mackinac Straits and reach the UP. Most of the migrants, after all, do not want to leave behind entirely those aspects of civilization—shopping centers, fast food and sitdown restaurants, convenient sporting goods stores—which they can find easily in the resort country of the Lower Peninsula but which are scarce in the summer and virtually nonexistent in the winter in the UP. By 1980 its population was up only to 318,000; the closest thing to a city was Marquette, with 23,000 people.

The Upper Peninsula forms about 60% of Michigan's 11th congressional district. The 11th altogether is a vast expanse, with 40% of Michigan's land area but only 6% of its population. In the Lower Peninsula, it includes the upper income resort towns of Petoskey and Charlevoix on the Lake Michigan side, the factory town of Alpena on Lake Huron, and the Tawas-Oscoda resort area, an area favored by Flint residents. From Tawas City to the western tip of the Upper Peninsula is 477 miles. The Lower Peninsula portion of the 11th is more prosperous than the UP; its Lake Michigan side remains Republican, but the central and Lake Huron counties have been trending Democratic. Overall, this is an evenly divided district; but since 1966 it has elected nothing but Republican congressmen.

This reflects the strength of successive incumbents: Philip Ruppe, scion of a Upper Peninsula brewing family, and Robert Davis, a mortician and experienced state legislator who represented a district on both sides of the bridge. Davis won a closely contested race here in 1978, to hold the seat for the Republicans; he has not been seriously challenged since. Davis is not a doctrinaire Reagan Republican, but his basic instincts are against high taxes and heavy regulation of business. His committee assignments suggest a legislator who is interested primarily in protecting the direct economic interests of a district characteristically uncertain of its economic future. On Armed Services he can protect the interests of K. I. Sawyer Air Force Base in Marquette County; on Merchant Marine and Fisheries he can protect the interests of the huge Great Lakes freighters—and their crews—which ship iron ore and cement from some ports in the district and nearby.

The People Pop. 1980: 514,560, up 10.9% 1970–80; voting age pop. 367,779; 1% Black. 15% housing units rented. Median owner $30,800; renter $160. Households: 75% family, 40% with children, 65% married couples.

Presidential Vote

1980	Reagan (R)	120,408	(51%)
	Carter (D)	100,291	(42%)
	Anderson (I)	15,706	(7%)

Rep. Robert W. (Bob) Davis (R) Elected 1978; b. July 31, 1932, Marquette; home, Gaylord; N. MI U., 1950, 1952, Hillsdale Col., 1951–52, Wayne St. U., B.S. 1954; Episcopal.

Career Mortician, 1954–66; St. Ignace City Cncl., 1964–66; MI House of Reps., 1966–70; MI Senate, 1970–78, Minor. Whip, 1970–74, Minor. Ldr., 1974–78.

Offices 1124 LHOB, 202-225-4735. Also Fed. Bldg., Rm. 102, Alpena 49707, 517-356-2028.

Committees Armed Services (10th). Subcommittees: Procurement and Military Nuclear Systems; Research and Development. *Merchant Marine and Fisheries* (6th). Subcommittees: Coast Guard and Navigation; Merchant Marine; Panama Canal and Outer Continental Shelf.

Group Ratings

	ADA	ACLU	COPE	CFA	LCV	LWV	NTU	NSI	COC	ACA	CSFC
1982	35	33	54	46	45	45	36	100	40	52	43
1981	15	—	47	50	30	—	41	—	74	74	63
1980	39	23	67	50	41	60	38	89	68	55	63

National Journal Ratings

	Economic		Foreign		Cultural	
1982	52%	(LIB)	29%	(LIB)	17%	(LIB)
	48%	(CONS)	71%	(CONS)	82%	(CONS)
1981	43%	(LIB)	3%	(LIB)	35%	(LIB)
	56%	(CONS)	87%	(CONS)	65%	(CONS)

Key Votes

1) Reagan 81 Budget FOR	5) Incr SS Rtmt Age AGN	9) Poor Pay Food Stamps AGN
2) Reagan 81 Tax Cut FOR	6) Saudi AWACS Sale FOR	10) Ban Crt Busing Order FOR
3) Bal Budget Amend FOR	7) $ for MX Missile FOR	11) Auto Local Content FOR
4) Gas & Road Tax AGN	8) Nerve Gas Prod FOR	12) Nuclear Arms Freeze AGN

Election Results

1982 general	Robert W. (Bob) Davis (R)	106,039	(60%)	($89,738)
	Kent Bourland (D)	69,181	(40%)	($23,901)
1982 primary	Robert W. (Bob) Davis (R)	36,345	(100%)	
1980 general	Robert W. (Bob) Davis (R)	146,205	(66%)	($121,198)
	Dan Dorrity (D)	75,515	(34%)	($42,578)

Campaign Contributions and Expenditures

1981-82		Direct Cont. 81-82			PACS brkdwn		
Receipts	$101,242	Indiv	$30,419	Agr	$8,000	Ideo	$750
Expend.	$89,738	Party	$12,528	Bus	$32,450	Lbr	$2,200
Unspent	$43,274	PACS	$47,520	Hlth	$3,950	Prof	$200

Indep Expend: For: $104 (MI RTLPAC)

TWELFTH DISTRICT

East and northeast of Detroit, just beyond the city limits, is Lake St. Clair, the smallest and shallowest of the Great Lakes. It is really just a place where the huge volume of water in the Great Lakes—one-quarter of the fresh water in the world—funneled through the St. Clair River, spreads out over the extremely flat, swampy lands of southern Michigan and Ontario before they are channeled again in the Detroit River. Few major cities have a recreational facility as useful as Lake St. Clair: it is large enough to accommodate many boats, but not so large as to be very dangerous; its waters are warm enough for swimming in the summer (and have been cleaned up greatly in recent years); it provides fishing in the summer and ice fishing in the winter.

As recently as the late 1940s, there was little settlement along Lake St. Clair. Between the Grosse Pointes, still Detroit's most exclusive high income suburbs, and the old industrial city of Port Huron, where Lake Huron empties into the St. Clair River, the only urban settlement was the old spa town of Mount Clemens. Otherwise the roads stretched out on empty flat farmland, with an occasional rustic lakeshore restaurant or beach shack. In the years since, this part of Michigan has filled up with people moving out of Detroit. It was a migration seen only in post-1945 America: predominantly blue collar and relatively affluent. High auto wages helped families finance large homes in the new subdivisions which sprouted in Macomb County, in suburbs along Lake St. Clair (St. Clair Shores, Harrison Township) and a little inland (East Detroit, Roseville, Warren, Clinton Township). Commercial strips went up, followed by shopping malls, and even by some office buildings, in land which just a few years before had been farmfields.

This is the heart of Michigan's 12th congressional district, which continues along Lake St. Clair from St. Clair Shores and Roseville in the south on past Port Huron in the north. In the process, it moves inland as much as 25 miles, but most of the population is concentrated along the lake. Before 1950, this was mostly Republican country; the new migrants made it, for a while, heavily Democratic; now they have moved more toward the Republicans, and it is politically marginal. President Kennedy won 63% of the vote in Macomb County in 1960, when it was the most Democratic major suburban county in the United States. But it moved against the Democrats on a number of issues: busing in the early 1970s (Macomb County was spiritedly against a busing decision which would have sent many of its children to dangerous schools in Detroit 25 miles away), aid to parochial schools and tuition tax credits later in the decade (Macomb is heavily Catholic), and high taxes late in the 1970s (high wages and upward social mobility made Macomb one of the highest income counties in the nation for a while). Now, with the collapse of the auto industry, the prosperity of the area along Lake St. Clair is threatened for many, and Democrats have done marginally better in recent elections. Even so, Democrat James Blanchard got just 51% of the vote here in the 1982 gubernatorial election—far from what Democrats won a dozen years before. What is striking is how little voting behavior has really changed after the collapse of the auto industry, as if no one has been persuaded that either party has an answer for the industry's and Michigan's problems.

The 1982 election did see an uncharacteristically easy victory for 12th district Democratic Congressman David Bonior. First elected in 1976, when longtime Macomb incumbent James O'Hara ran for the Senate, Bonior had three tough elections. In personal style, he seems a little out of place for Macomb—he wears a beard, and he handed out tiny trees as a symbol in one of his campaigns. But that is to take a stereotypical view of the Lake St. Clair suburbs: people here may have grandparents who live in old Polish neighborhoods and frown on what they consider faithlessness to traditional values, but in their affluence people here are themselves pursuing a variety of leisure time activities and in effect living, on their own time, different lifestyles. Bonior's political survival is pretty good evidence of this trend.

Bonior's voting record receives high ratings from liberal organizations; he is particularly concerned about problems of Vietnam era veterans (of which he is one) and environmental issues. Since 1981 he has been a member of the Rules Committee. That body is less pivotal than it once was, mainly because it is firmly controlled by Democrats who, like Bonior, are responsive to the leadership of Speaker O'Neill.

The People Pop. 1980: 514,560, up 9.4% 1970–80; voting age pop. 362,035; 2% Black, 1% Span. orig. 21% housing units rented. Median owner $47,200; renter $243. Households: 78% family, 44% with children, 66% married couples.

Presidential Vote

1980	Reagan (R)	NA
	Carter (D)	NA
	Anderson (I)	NA

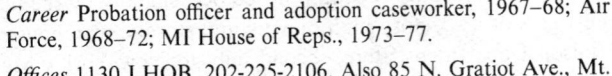

Rep. David E. Bonior (D) Elected 1976; b. June 6, 1945, Detroit; home, Mt. Clemens; U. of IA, B.A. 1967, Chapman Col., M.A. 1972; Roman Catholic.

Career Probation officer and adoption caseworker, 1967–68; Air Force, 1968–72; MI House of Reps., 1973–77.

Offices 1130 LHOB, 202-225-2106. Also 85 N. Gratiot Ave., Mt. Clemens 48043, 313-469-3232.

Committee *Rules* (7th). Subcommittee: Rules of the House.

Group Ratings

	ADA	ACLU	COPE	CFA	LCV	LWV	NTU	NSI	COC	ACA	CSFC
1982	70	71	91	85	99	83	18	11	5	6	26
1981	90	—	90	79	98	—	23	—	5	17	25
1980	83	80	89	79	88	100	20	0	52	18	25

National Journal Ratings

	Economic		Foreign		Cultural	
1982	88%	(LIB)	81%	(LIB)	74%	(LIB)
	11%	(CONS)	19%	(CONS)	26%	(CONS)
1981	97%	(LIB)	92%	(LIB)	75%	(LIB)
	3%	(CONS)	2%	(CONS)	24%	(CONS)

Key Votes

1) Reagan 81 Budget	AGN	5) Incr SS Rtmt Age	AGN	9) Poor Pay Food Stamps	AGN
2) Reagan 81 Tax Cut	AGN	6) Saudi AWACS Sale	AGN	10) Ban Crt Busing Order	FOR
3) Bal Budget Amend	AGN	7) $ for MX Missile	AGN	11) Auto Local Content	FOR
4) Gas & Road Tax	AGN	8) Nerve Gas Prod	AGN	12) Nuclear Arms Freeze	FOR

Election Results

1982 general	David E. Bonior (D)	103,851	(66%)	($177,767)
	Ray Contesti (R)	52,312	(33%)	($106,652)
1982 primary	David E. Bonior (D)	41,240	(100%)	
1980 general	David E. Bonior (D)	112,698	(55%)	($105,574)
	Kirk Walsh (R)	90,931	(45%)	($54,170)

Campaign Contributions and Expenditures

1981-82		Direct Cont. 81-82		PACS brkdwn			
Receipts	$175,505	Indiv	$66,316	Agr	$9,470	Ideo	$2,825
Expend.	$177,767	Party	$8,155	Bus	$11,680	Lbr	$60,300
Unspent	$2,255	PACS	$91,872	Hlth	$1,700	Prof	$2,600

Indep Expend: For: $86 (MI LIFEPAC)

THIRTEENTH DISTRICT

The 13th congressional district of Michigan is made up mostly of what is referred to as the inner city of Detroit, the heart of that troubled city. The physical dimensions of Detroit tell a story by themselves, of a community which had visions of becoming a world class city, and which didn't make it. The major avenues which radiate outward from Detroit's downtown are nine lanes wide; they stretch out over the flat land, lined by two and three story commercial buildings, now mostly vacant, relieved occasionally by the hulk of an empty movie palace of the 1920s or a six-story high moving and storage warehouse. Downtown was the giant J. L. Hudson Department Store, second only to New York's Macy's in size; a money loser for years, it was finally closed down in 1983. From Hudson's you can see Detroit's office skyscrapers, most built in the exuberant style of the 1920s, several in the expansionist 1960s, and, off down by the river, the Renaissance Center of the 1970s—forbidding on the outside, luxuriously pleasant on the inside—now near bankruptcy. Detroit's great auto factories and the headquarters of the Big Three are scattered several miles away from downtown, often hidden from the main avenues, alongside railroad tracks; the great avenues have been superseded in importance by the expressways named for, among others, Walter P. Chrysler, Edsel B. Ford, and the Fisher Brothers of General Motors.

The residential areas of Detroit, between these avenues, expressways, and factories, were mostly built up fast and, to a depressing extent, have been abandoned fast. The 13th district was expanded after the 1980 Census to take in about 40% of Detroit's population and land area. That added 200,000 to the old, depopulated 13th district—an area that had 576,000 people in 1960, 465,000 in 1970, and 291,000 in 1980, the biggest population decline in any congressional district in the United States.

Population loss does not always hurt a community. It may reflect only the fact that people are having fewer children or that single people can afford to live by themselves. But the population loss in inner city Detroit obviously goes far beyond that. It is not only a waste of valuable housing stock; it is evidence of social ills far more grievous, and which antedate the problems the city has suffered from the collapse of the auto industry. In Detroit for 50 years there was rapid population movement out from the central city. In the exuberance of boom times middle class people moved farther out the great avenues; in the racially troubled 1950s and 1960s, whites moved out the expressways to get away from blacks. In each case they were replaced by new, often lower-wage residents. But in the 1970s, there were fewer low-wage jobs in Detroit. High wages in the auto factories meant that few jobs were available except in boom years; the wages helped longtime workers, but not those who couldn't get or keep a job. The departure of so many people from inner city Detroit in 1960–80 was in line with the historic pattern. What was not was the fact that they were not replaced by anybody else. This kind of population loss turned out to have grim results. Inner city neighborhoods have lost their natural leaders, the kind of people who nurture and maintain community institutions. Left were the violent young men who commit the lion's share of Detroit's crime. After the 1967 riot, gun ownership became virtually universal in Detroit, and the city's murder rate was the highest in the country.

So the 1979 collapse of the auto industry hit a community that was already in grave trouble. Unemployment figures in inner city Detroit have been extremely high for years— and obviously conceal a considerable cash and crime economy. The wide avenues and the huge buildings which the city fathers built in the 1920s—when Detroit was what Houston is today—look down on a city in grave trouble; the white collar people who work downtown almost all live far out the freeways in the suburbs. Politically, the reflexive cry in Detroit is for more federal aid, government jobs, more social programs—but no one seems to know just how these would help cure the problems which are obvious.

The history of the 13th district is reflected in the career of Charles Diggs, congressman for 26 years, a man of considerable abilities but relatively few achievements; he left Congress after affirmance of his conviction for diverting $60,000 in staff salaries to himself. The 12-candidate primary in 1980 to replace him attracted only 21,000 voters. The winner was George Crockett, who became a freshman congressman at age 71. Crockett is something of a folk hero in Detroit's black community. A veteran of left-wing politics, he was elected to Detroit's Recorder's Court (a criminal bench) in the 1960s; he aroused great controversy when in the late 1960s he went down to the courthouse in the middle of the night, held hearings, and released on bail men arrested for killing a policeman. Whites launched a movement to recall him; but he had solid black support and was never defeated. Judge Crockett was probably the 1980 freshman least sympathetic to the new Reagan administration. He is a man of steely self-assurance and has done what he considers his duty in much less friendly environments than the House of Representatives.

Judge Crockett is a member of the Foreign Affairs Committee and its Africa Subcommittee and of the Judiciary Committee. His voting record is one of the most liberal in Congress. It is unlikely that he will attract serious competition in this district as long as he chooses to run.

The People Pop. 1980: 514,560, dn. 30.8% 1970–80; voting age pop. 360,241; 67% Black, 3% Span. orig., 1% Asian orig. 52% housing units rented. Median owner $17,900; renter $143. Households: 60% family, 36% with children, 31% married couples.

Presidential Vote

1980	Reagan (R) ....NA	
	Carter (D) ....NA	
	Anderson (I) ....NA	

Rep. George W. Crockett, Jr. (D) Elected 1980; b. Aug. 10, 1909, Jacksonville, FL; home, Detroit; Morehouse Col., A.B. 1931, U. of MI, J.D. 1934; Baptist.

Career Practicing atty., 1934–39, 1947–65; Sr. Atty., U.S. Dept. of Labor, 1939–43; Founder-Dir., UAW Fair Practices Dept., 1944–46; Judge, Recorder's Ct., 1966–78; Visiting Judge, MI Ct. of Appeals, 1979; Acting Corp. Counsel, Detroit, 1980.

Offices 1531 LHOB, 202-225-2261. Also 8401 Woodward Ave., Su. 106, Detroit 48202, 313-874-4900; and 2866 E. Grand Blvd., Detroit 48202, 313-875-4225.

Committees *Foreign Affairs* (12th). Subcommittees: Africa; International Operations. *Judiciary* (15th). Subcommittees: Immigration, Refugees, and International Law; Monopolies and Commercial Law. *Select Committee on Aging* (26th). Subcommittee: Housing and Consumer Interests.

Group Ratings

	ADA	ACLU	COPE	CFA	LCV	LWV	NTU	NSI	COC	ACA	CSFC
1982	80	92	95	92	90	82	39	11	20	0	22
1981	70	—	91	57	80	—	26	—	0	5	17

National Journal Ratings

	Economic		Foreign		Cultural	
1982	95%	(LIB)	96%	(LIB)	93%	(LIB)
	5%	(CONS)	4%	(CONS)	3%	(CONS)
1981	88%	(LIB)	89%	(LIB)	93%	(LIB)
	11%	(CONS)	11%	(CONS)	7%	(CONS)

Key Votes

1) Reagan 81 Budget	AGN	5) Incr SS Rtmt Age	AGN	9) Poor Pay Food Stamps	AGN
2) Reagan 81 Tax Cut	AGN	6) Saudi AWACS Sale	AGN	10) Ban Crt Busing Order	AGN
3) Bal Budget Amend	AGN	7) $ for MX Missile	AGN	11) Auto Local Content	FOR
4) Gas & Road Tax	FOR	8) Nerve Gas Prod	AGN	12) Nuclear Arms Freeze	FOR

Election Results

1982 general	George W. Crockett, Jr. (D)	108,351	(88%)	($56,039)
	Letty Gupta (R)	13,732	(11%)	($0)
1982 primary	George W. Crockett, Jr. (D)	54,488	(100%)	
1980 general	George W. Crockett, Jr. (D)	79,719	(92%)	($43,619)
	M. Michael Hurd (R)	6,473	(7%)	($0)

Campaign Contributions and Expenditures

1981-82		Direct Cont. 81-82				PACS brkdwn		
Receipts	$74,199	Indiv	$49,544	Agr	$1,000	Ideo		$500
Expend.	$56,039	Party	$1,030	Bus	$5,575	Lbr		$8,895
Unspent	$22,175	PACS	$17,747	Hlth	$—	Prof		$1,125

FOURTEENTH DISTRICT

You could almost call Michigan's 14th congressional district the Polish Corridor—a ring around the inner city of Detroit where the grandchildren of the Polish immigrants who came to work in the auto plants now live. Not everyone in the district is Polish, of course; there are plenty of Americans of Italian, German, Irish, and British descent as well. Nor is every neighborhood particularly ethnic. The 14th extends east to include most of the Grosse Pointes, the posh and exclusive suburbs on Lake St. Clair; it extends as far north as suburban Sterling Heights, indistinguishable physically from any one of a hundred shopping center suburbs which went up in the 1960s and 1970s; it extends as far west as the suburbs of Hazel Park and Madison Heights, most of whose residents are of Appalachian stock. The Polish heart of the district is Hamtramck, a tiny industrial town surrounded by Detroit. Here thousands of immigrants flocked to get jobs in the Dodge Main, Plymouth, and Packard auto plants; during the 1910s Hamtramck was the fastest growing city in the nation. As many as 56,000 people—mostly young parents with large families—lived there in 1930. Today the population is down to 21,000, mostly old people, and Dodge Main has been torn down. Hamtramck has been the butt of dozens of Polish jokes, but anybody who takes the trouble to visit the town will find freshly painted houses and carefully tended lawns—evidence of the pride of ownership that still flourishes here and in neighborhoods where younger Polish-Americans live.

The congressman from the 14th is Dennis Hertel, a Democrat who was popular enough as a state legislator to win an eight-candidate primary in 1980 with 62% of the vote. Republicans sometimes carry this district in statewide races, and they made a serious effort here in 1980, just as they had in 1972 (when busing was an issue) and in a 1961 special election. But each time they lost narrowly. The district was represented for nearly 20 years by Lucien Nedzi, one of the few Vietnam doves on the House Armed Services Committee; Hertel has a similar approach on issues, and also serves on Armed Services, but with less seniority has attracted less attention. In the 97th Congress Hertel's record was liberal on economic issues, moderate on cultural issues; this district may be aging, but it is still definitely family, not singles, country, and traditional on many cultural matters. Hertel, having survived redistricting, should be in strong shape to hold this district during the 1980s.

The People   Pop. 1980: 514,559, dn. 1.2% 1970–80; voting age pop. 372,422; 4% Black, 1% Span. orig., 1% Asian orig. 20% housing units rented. Median owner $39,000; renter $223. Households: 76% family, 39% with children, 62% married couples.

Presidential Vote

1980	Reagan (R)	NA
	Carter (D)	NA
	Anderson (I)	NA

Rep. Dennis M. Hertel (D) Elected 1980; b. Dec. 7, 1948, Detroit; home, Detroit; E. MI U., B.S. 1971, Wayne St. U., J.D. 1974; Roman Catholic.

Career Practicing atty.; MI House of Reps., 1974–80.

Offices 218 CHOB, 202-225-6276. Also 20491 Van Dyke, Detroit 48234, 313-892-4010.

Committees *Armed Services* (21st). Subcommittees: Military Installations and Facilities; Readiness; Research and Development. *Merchant Marine and Fisheries* (16th). Subcommittees: Fisheries and Wildlife Conservation and the Environment; Merchant Marine; Panama Canal and Outer Continental Shelf. *Select Committee on Aging* (29th). Subcommittee: Health and Long-Term Care.

Group Ratings

	ADA	ACLU	COPE	CFA	LCV	LWV	NTU	NSI	COC	ACA	CSFC
1982	75	50	88	77	93	75	31	40	15	14	30
1981	80	—	79	79	86	—	35	—	6	29	36

National Journal Ratings

	Economic		Foreign		Cultural	
1982	71%	(LIB)	82%	(LIB)	66%	(LIB)
	29%	(CONS)	18%	(CONS)	33%	(CONS)
1981	97%	(LIB)	72%	(LIB)	61%	(LIB)
	3%	(CONS)	26%	(CONS)	39%	(CONS)

Key Votes

1) Reagan 81 Budget	AGN	5) Incr SS Rtmt Age	AGN	9) Poor Pay Food Stamps	AGN
2) Reagan 81 Tax Cut	AGN	6) Saudi AWACS Sale	AGN	10) Ban Crt Busing Order	FOR
3) Bal Budget Amend	AGN	7) $ for MX Missile	AGN	11) Auto Local Content	FOR
4) Gas & Road Tax	—	8) Nerve Gas Prod	AGN	12) Nuclear Arms Freeze	FOR

Election Results

1982 general	Dennis M. Hertel (D)	116,421	(95%)	($81,326)
	Harold H. Dunn (Libertarian)	6,175	(5%)	($0)
1982 primary	Dennis M. Hertel (D)	52,826	(100%)	
1980 general	Dennis M. Hertel (D)	90,362	(53%)	($160,000)
	Vic Caputo (R)	78,395	(46%)	($211,590)

Campaign Contributions and Expenditures

1981-82		Direct Cont. 81-82		PACS brkdwn			
Receipts	$102,771	Indiv	$41,849	Agr	$1,155	Ideo	$605
Expend.	$81,326	Party	$915	Bus	$13,575	Lbr	$44,530
Unspent	$23,192	PACS	$68,607	Hlth	$2,400	Prof	$1,250

Indep Expend: For: $694 (MI RTL)

FIFTEENTH DISTRICT

When Henry Ford built the Ford Rouge plant in Dearborn in 1920, almost all of the land that is now the 15th congressional district of Michigan was vacant: an expanse of flat, swampy land stretching farther than the eye could see west across southern Michigan almost all the way to the college town of Ann Arbor. Crisscrossed early on by railroads and later by freeways, this is industrial land, a natural site for many of the auto factories built in the 1940s and 1950s. One of the most famous in its time was Willow Run, in the western end of the district, which Henry Ford made into the nation's biggest aircraft factory during World War II. The area was so empty then that the government built an expressway so that workers from Detroit could drive (with extra gas rations) the 35 miles to Willow Run in reasonable time. The expressway still stands and connects Detroit's airport to the city; it's the road on which you see a giant tire and billboards with digital meters showing the year's American car production.

Since the Willow Run expressway was built, the area that is now the 15th district has been filled up with mostly working class suburbs. Some are gleaming and carefully trimmed, like Westland (named after a shopping center) and Canton Township (the only part of the district with rapid population growth in the 1970s). Others like Romulus have the look of places where people with not much money worked a little at a time to build their own houses, on land so flat that the drainage is dubious and the ground oozes with water after even a slight rain. The biggest employer in these parts is the Ford Motor Company, but its Michigan payrolls have not grown significantly since before the 1957–58 recession. Lately they have been growing smaller. Unemployment in this part of Michigan is not quite as high as in some other places, such as Flint; but a comfortable way of life, which people had come to take for granted, now seems not just threatened but for many people conclusively ended.

This southwestern segment of the Detroit metropolitan area has a tradition of going solidly Democratic in most elections. But it flirted with George Wallace in several elections—there are a lot of white southerners here, and only a small percentage of blacks—and had no truck with George McGovern. In 1976 it did not give Jimmy Carter a large margin and in 1980 went for Ronald Reagan. In 1982 it went Democratic again, but not by the overwhelming margins it once did. If there is discontent with Reagan and his Republicans, there is also little confidence that national Democrats have solutions.

The congressman from the 15th district is William Ford, a Democrat first elected in 1964 (and no relation to Henry or Gerald Ford). Although he is not well known in most parts of Washington, he is one of the workhorses in the House of Representatives, and is likely to become a more visible legislator in the future. Ford has a political faith considered a little old-fashioned in some quarters: he is a believer in labor unions, and in strengthening them; he believes in the Great Society programs he voted for as a freshman; he believes in a generous, active federal government, helping people who cannot help themselves. On cultural and foreign issues he also has a liberal voting record. But his real fervor and energy seems concentrated on economic issues, in the broad sense of the term.

Ford is now chairman of the Post Office and Civil Service Committee, an often thankless job. He is not encumbered, as some committee members are, with a constituency loaded with government workers. He is a strong supporter of unions for government workers, but he is not about to change the federal government's longstanding and successful refusal to tolerate strikes. He is more concerned to protect the ordinary employee's rights more than most Democrats are these days. But he is also willing to compromise. He was one of the committee leaders who fashioned the compromise civil service reform bill in the Carter years—a major and difficult legislative achievement.

This is not really Ford's main committee assignment, however, nor the one which will probably be the most important in the future. He is now the third ranking Democrat on the

Education and Labor Committee, notably younger than the two who outrank him (Chairman Carl Perkins and Californian Augustus Hawkins). When Ford came to Washington, this was the glamour committee of the House, with jurisdiction over all the antipoverty programs; now it is a very practical body, on which organized labor and the education community are counting to protect the gains they have won in the past and which have been threatened by the Reagan budget cuts. It took a beating in the first year of Reagan budget cuts, when David Stockman and the administration were able to ram cuts through the budget process. Since then Education and Labor has managed to hold the line pretty well. Ford relinquished his subcommittee chairmanship to take Post Office and Civil Service, but he is still one of the *de facto* leaders of Education and Labor, and helped fashion the canny manuevers by which Chairman Perkins tried, mostly successfully, to prevent further budget cuts after 1981.

On the committee Ford has specialized in the big money education bills (elementary and secondary, or ESEA) and also sits on the main labor subcommittee. Since the early 1960s, organized labor has insisted, successfully, that none but strongly pro-labor Democrats be assigned seats on Education and Labor. As a result, this committee is as much the advocate of the programs it superintends as Armed Services is of the Pentagon's. Ford wins reelection easily in Michigan, usually with no significant opposition. Education and Labor has had a succession of strong chairmen who held the job many years—Perkins has had it since 1967— and Ford quite likely will be next on that list.

The People   Pop. 1980: 514,560, up 11.1% 1970–80; voting age pop. 356,253; 5% Black, 1% Span. orig., 1% Asian orig. 28% housing units rented. Median owner $46,400; renter $258. Households: 78% family, 48% with children, 65% married couples.

Presidential Vote

1980	Reagan (R) .... NA
	Carter (D) .... NA
	Anderson (I) .... NA

Rep. William D. Ford (D) Elected 1964; b. Aug. 6, 1927, Detroit; home, Taylor; NE Teachers Col., 1946, Wayne St. U., 1947–48, U. of Denver, B.S. 1949, J.D. 1951; United Church of Christ.

Career Practicing atty., 1951–64; Taylor Twnshp. J.P., 1955–57; Melvindale City Atty., 1957–59; MI Senate, 1963–65.

Offices 239 CHOB, 202-225-6261. Also Wayne Fed. Bldg., Wayne 48184, 313-722-1411.

Committees *Education and Labor* (3d). Subcommittees: Elementary, Secondary and Vocational Education; Health and Safety; Labor-Management Relations; Postsecondary Education. *Post Office and Civil Service* (Chairman). Subcommittee: Investigations (Chairman).

Group Ratings

	ADA	ACLU	COPE	CFA	LCV	LWV	NTU	NSI	COC	ACA	CSFC
1982	85	71	96	85	87	50	7	0	14	9	23
1981	70	—	96	43	61	—	7	—	6	13	28
1980	78	73	95	79	53	89	10	11	59	5	22

National Journal Ratings

	Economic		Foreign		Cultural	
1982	96%	(LIB)	95%	(LIB)	84%	(LIB)
	2%	(CONS)	4%	(CONS)	15%	(CONS)
1981	87%	(LIB)	75%	(LIB)	74%	(LIB)
	12%	(CONS)	24%	(CONS)	26%	(CONS)

Key Votes

1) Reagan 81 Budget	AGN	5) Incr SS Rtmt Age	AGN	9) Poor Pay Food Stamps	AGN
2) Reagan 81 Tax Cut	AGN	6) Saudi AWACS Sale	AGN	10) Ban Crt Busing Order	AGN
3) Bal Budget Amend	AGN	7) $ for MX Missile	AGN	11) Auto Local Content	FOR
4) Gas & Road Tax	FOR	8) Nerve Gas Prod	AGN	12) Nuclear Arms Freeze	FOR

Election Results

1982 general	William D. Ford (D)	94,950	(73%)	($212,709)
	Mitchell Moran (R)	33,904	(26%)	($12,579)
1982 primary	William D. Ford (D)	34,721	(82%)	
	Gerald R. Carlson (D)	7,486	(18%)	
1980 general	William D. Ford (D)	113,492	(68%)	($83,295)
	Gerald R. Carlson (R)	53,046	(32%)	($0)

Campaign Contributions and Expenditures

1981-82		Direct Cont. 81-82*			PACS brkdwn			
Receipts	$216,442	Indiv	$60,168	Agr	$2,450	Ideo	$2,500
Expend.	$212,709	Party	$1,050	Bus	$23,740	Lbr	$92,235
Unspent	$11,099	PACS	$135,235	Hlth	$5,950	Prof	$2,900

Indep Expend: For: $568 (UAW)   *Non-Cand Loans:* $15,000

SIXTEENTH DISTRICT

The 16th congressional district of Michigan is one of the nation's most heavily industrial areas. From the Interstate 75 bridge over the Rouge River, the 16th spreads out before you: on the right you can see the Ford Rouge plant, built in Dearborn by Henry Ford, on what amounts to an inlet off the Detroit River, as a single unit in which he could convert iron ore, coal, and other raw materials into an automobile within 48 hours; on the left, stretching out to the horizon are the steel mills, chemical plants, stamping plants, and auto assembly plants of the downriver suburbs. It is one of the premier industrial landscapes in America, ranking with the view of the Gary and Chicago steel mills from the Indiana Turnpike and the spectacle of northern New Jersey from the Pulaski Skyway. This is also a natural location for industry: the Detroit River, flowing into Lake Erie, provides a natural avenue for bulky raw materials like iron ore and limestone; the railroad lines along the flat, originally swampy shores, bring in coal and ship out finished products, connecting easily with the nation's main east-west rail lines, a few miles to the south.

Almost flush up against the older factories and well within range of their sulphurous odors are the neat, tightly packed houses of the old ethnic neighborhoods—some still mostly Polish, Hungarian, and Italian, some now black, Mexican, or Arab (the 16th district probably has the nation's largest proportion of Arab-Americans). There are a few high income enclaves, in west Dearborn and on Grosse Ile in the Detroit River. And the 16th does extend not only south across the industrial flatlands to Toledo, Ohio, but also west into the old Yankee town of Adrian. But for the most part it is working class vintage Democratic country. Even in

Republican years it has still gone Democratic (it was even for McGovern in 1972), and in recession years like 1982 you can find very little support for Republicans. But the response is not merely partisan. Here, as in other parts of industrial Michigan, there is a kind of desperation, a sense not just that these are bad times to get through, but that a way of life—a way of life people belatedly regard as comfortable and pleasant—has come to an end, and a desire somehow to bring it back. That places great pressures on politicians, even one like the 16th's congressman, John Dingell, whose standing in the district seems unlikely to be threatened.

Dingell is now one of the most senior Democrats in the House and one of the most important legislators in Congress. Since 1981, he has chaired the House Energy and Commerce Committee, a body with jurisdiction over major regulatory legislation which became by 1983 the most sought after committee assignment by Democrats. That is not because Dingell is easy to get along with: he has a notorious temper and is not inclined to share the spotlight. But he is also an able legislator, with strong beliefs, who runs his committee strongly and aggressively, but never underhandedly—a force by any measure to be reckoned with. One of his subcommittee chairmen called him "the best legislator in the House," and while there might be a little flattery in that estimate there are disinterested observers who might well agree.

Even so, in the early 1980s, Dingell found himself frustrated more often than he—and others—expected, both when he worked in alliance with, and when he opposed, the Reagan administration. One of his top priorities was revising the Clean Air Act, which he believes sets undue limitations on automobiles and has contributed to the collapse of the auto industry. He allied himself with the administration and businesses other than autos that wanted relief, but the administration failed to produce a draft bill itself and, when it did, could not hold support on the committee for each of its provisions. Fearing that measures he believes are needed by the auto industry would not pass, Dingell yanked the bill from the calendar, and so the terms of the old Clean Air Act stayed in effect.

Dingell's fight on Clean Air placed him at odds with many, like Health Subcommittee Chairman Henry Waxman, who are his allies on most other issues. Dingell was an opponent of deregulation of oil and natural gas—one of the major issues before this committee in the late 1970s, with gas becoming an issue again in 1983. He has a reputation, earned over many years, as a conservationist; he is an enthusiastic hunter (and opponent of gun controls) and an avid outdoorsman, and he has fought to maintain natural habitats and environments long before it was fashionable. For years he stayed on the Merchant Marine and Fisheries Committee not, as most members do, to funnel subsidies to the maritime industry, but to advance conservation. Dingell was one of the chief congressional adversaries of former EPA Administrator Anne Gorsuch Burford; his Oversight and Investigations Subcommittee investigated her stewardship and helped to promote the controversy over subpoenaed documents and executive privilege.

Overall, Dingell cannot be classified as a simple pro-industry or pro-regulation chairman. He can be classified as pro-auto industry, but he would probably reject the categorization and insist that he favors changes in the Clean Air Act on the merits and not simply because the industry (and the United Auto Workers) favors them. He is a kind of force by himself, and if he has been severely frustrated on matters very important to him in the early 1980s he has also had his successes—and will have more.

Dingell's seat is safe. His father was elected to Congress in 1932, and he was elected after his father's death in 1955; he had one serious fight, because of redistricting, in 1964. Then he beat a fellow Democrat who opposed the Civil Rights Act, even though most of the district was new to Dingell; he has been reelected easily since. He is the most powerful and formidable member of the Michigan delegation, and the heavily industrial—and distressed—16th district would not want to be represented by anyone else.

The People Pop. 1980: 514,560, dn. 0.7% 1970–80; voting age pop. 367,589; 3% Black, 2% Span. orig. 23% housing units rented. Median owner $44,000; renter $208. Households: 77% family, 41% with children, 65% married couples.

Presidential Vote

1980	Reagan (R)	NA
	Carter (D)	NA
	Anderson (I)	NA

Rep. John D. Dingell (D) Elected Dec. 13, 1955; b. July 8, 1926, Colorado Springs, CO; home, Trenton; Georgetown U., B.S. 1949, J.D. 1952; Roman Catholic.

Career Army, WWII; Practicing atty., 1952–55; Research Asst. to U.S. Dist. Judge Theodore Levin, 1952–53; Wayne Cnty. Asst. Prosecuting Atty., 1953–55.

Offices 2221 RHOB, 202-225-4071. Also 4917 Schaefer Rd., Dearborn 48126, 313-846-1276.

Committee Energy and Commerce (Chairman). Subcommittee: Oversight and Investigations (Chairman).

Group Ratings

	ADA	ACLU	COPE	CFA	LCV	LWV	NTU	NSI	COC	ACA	CSFC
1982	80	58	92	77	84	70	3	30	18	22	28
1981	70	—	92	50	81	—	23	—	21	17	33
1980	67	27	76	43	58	56	14	13	63	18	25

National Journal Ratings

	Economic		Foreign		Cultural	
1982	74%	(LIB)	69%	(LIB)	66%	(LIB)
	25%	(CONS)	31%	(CONS)	34%	(CONS)
1981	73%	(LIB)	72%	(LIB)	66%	(LIB)
	27%	(CONS)	26%	(CONS)	33%	(CONS)

Key Votes

1) Reagan 81 Budget	AGN	5) Incr SS Rtmt Age	AGN	9) Poor Pay Food Stamps	AGN
2) Reagan 81 Tax Cut	AGN	6) Saudi AWACS Sale	AGN	10) Ban Crt Busing Order	AGN
3) Bal Budget Amend	AGN	7) $ for MX Missile	AGN	11) Auto Local Content	FOR
4) Gas & Road Tax	FOR	8) Nerve Gas Prod	FOR	12) Nuclear Arms Freeze	FOR

Election Results

1982 general	John D. Dingell (D)	114,006	(74%)	($262,247)
	David K. Haskins (R)	39,227	(25%)	($0)
1982 primary	John D. Dingell (D)	43,652	(100%)	
1980 general	John D. Dingell (D)	105,844	(70%)	($115,821)
	Pamella A. Seay (R)	42,735	(28%)	($1,541)

Campaign Contributions and Expenditures

1981-82		Direct Cont. 81-82		PACS brkdwn			
Receipts	$265,249	Indiv	$71,463	Agr	$2,350	Ideo	$4,350
Expend.	$262,247	Party	$1,325	Bus	$114,740	Lbr	$46,615
Unspent	$28,916	PACS	$183,089	Hlth	$5,100	Prof	$7,650

Indep Expend: For: $1,235 (NRA, UAW)

SEVENTEENTH DISTRICT

The 17th congressional district of Michigan forms almost a semicircle around the city of Detroit—at a point just beyond, in most cases, where significant numbers of blacks live. Most Detroit's blacks are in the 1st and 13th districts, whose boundaries were drawn to make safe black constituencies; what is left over, on the far northwest side of Detroit, and in its near western and northwestern suburbs, is the 17th. That means that the 17th has plenty of variety. Some of its suburbs, like Ferndale and Royal Oak, along Woodward Avenue in Oakland County, or Redford Township just west of Detroit, are aging now: originally mixed Protestant and Catholic, and leaning Republican, Royal Oak has become more Democratic and older, as young families move farther out. Southfield, once empty swampland, has now become the main high-rise office center of the Detroit area, with almost as much square footage as downtown Detroit. The 17th's portion of Detroit includes what was once one of the metropolitan area's high income neighborhoods, Rosedale Park, as well as miles of straight streets lined by frame and white aluminum siding workingmen's houses from the 1940s. Blacks have been moving westward in Detroit, and the 17th's portion of the city is already one-third black; there are also a significant number of blacks in the mostly Jewish suburbs of Oak Park and Southfield. To the south the 17th takes in white working class Dearborn Heights and, just next door, the mostly black suburb of Inkster.

The 17th district has a freshman congressman, Sander Levin, who has a wealth of political experience. Twice he came within a hairsbreadth of beating William Milliken and becoming Michigan's governor, in 1970 and 1974; before that he was an important state legislator and Michigan's Democratic chairman in the turbulent year of 1968. In the Carter administration he was in charge of population control programs in AID—not a noncontroversial job. He is the older brother of Senator Carl Levin, and came to Congress later; but he was the first in his family to run for office, and the two brothers seem to have an entirely comfortable relationship.

Levin had not been expecting to run for Congress: the 17th district had a young (40 in 1982), competent Democratic congressman, William Brodhead, who seemed to have a long career ahead of him. Brodhead was head of the Democratic Study Group and a member of the Ways and Means Committee; he was generally counted a liberal, but he was also the one who put into the 1981 tax cut the provision cutting the maximum tax on "unearned" income from 70% to 50%—a provision the Reagan administration did not dare to advance. Then Brodhead surprised practically everyone in 1982 by announcing he would retire and go back to Detroit. Being a congressman—traveling back and forth to the district, working long hours, having little time you can call your (or your family's) own—was just not such an attractive life.

Sander Levin has always been a hard worker, a man who is less interested in trumpeting his own opinions than he is in working out compromise and agreement among everyone involved in an issue. He had to fight for the seat, and in a spirited primary beat one of his successors in the state Senate and a Detroit councilwoman; he will presumably have to work this diverse district to deter any future primary opposition (it is pretty safely Democratic in general elections). He is the only Michigan member of the Banking Committee—an important post, since this is the body which handled the Chrysler loan guarantee, and which will superintend any similar or related legislation in the future.

The People Pop. 1980: 514,560, dn. 11.7% 1970–80; voting age pop. 382,414; 10% Black, 1% Span. orig., 1% Asian orig. 25% housing units rented. Median owner $41,200; renter $268. Households: 73% family, 36% with children, 60% married couples.

Presidential Vote

1980	Reagan (R)	NA
	Carter (D)	NA
	Anderson (I)	NA

Rep. Sander Levin (D) Elected 1982; b. Sept. 6, 1932, Detroit; home, Southfield; U. of Chicago, B.A. 1952, Columbia U., M.A. 1954, Harvard U. Law Sch., LL.B. 1957; Jewish.

Career Practicing atty., 1957–64, 1971–74, 1981–82; MI Senate, 1964–70; Dem. Cand. for Gov., 1970 and 1974; Fellow, Harvard U., Kennedy Sch. of Govt., 1975; Asst. Admin., Agency for Internatl. Development, 1977–81.

Offices 323 CHOB, 202-225-4961. Also 17117 West Nine Mile Rd., Su. 1120, Southfield 48075, 313-559-4444.

Committees Banking, Finance and Urban Affairs (28th). Subcommittees: Economic Stabilization; Housing and Community Development; International Development Institutions and Finance; International Trade, Investment and Monetary Policy. *Government Operations* (18th). Subcommittee: Intergovernmental Relations and Human Resources. *Select Committee on Children, Youth, and Families* (12th).

Group Ratings and Key Votes: Newly Elected

Election Results

1982 general	Sander Levin (D)	116,901	(66%)	($213,600)
	Gerald E. Rosen (R)	55,620	(32%)	($105,542)
1982 primary	Sander Levin (D)	31,663	(44%)	
	Doug Ross (D)	18,526	(26%)	($107,331)
	Maryann Mahaffey (D)	10,380	(14%)	($58,118)
	Patrick F. O'Hara (D)	5,375	(7%)	($2,206)
	Agnes Mary Mansour (D)	4,146	(6%)	($20,682)
1980 general (MI 17)	William M. Brodhead (D)	127,525	(73%)	($18,539)
	L. Patterson (R)	44,313	(25%)	($0)
1980 general (MI 18)	James J. (Jim) Blanchard (D)	135,705	(65%)	($101,378)
	Betty J. Suida (R)	68,575	(33%)	

Campaign Contributions and Expenditures

1981-82		Direct Cont. 81-82		PACS brkdwn			
Receipts	$215,094	Indiv	$140,270	Agr	$500	Ideo	$3,500
Expend.	$213,600	Party	$958	Bus	$5,750	Lbr	$45,300
Unspent	$1,490	PACS	$57,262	Hlth	$650	Prof	$1,200
		Cand	$8,750				

EIGHTEENTH DISTRICT

Northwest of Detroit, which is situated on some of the flattest land in the nation, is a line of hills and lakes, beginning about 20 miles from downtown. This line runs from northeast to southwest, from northern Macomb County, down toward Ann Arbor. It marks the southern-most advance of an Ice Age glacier, which dug up the hills and valleys here and deposited un-usual soil and moraine. The advance of the glacier also marks the beginning, roughly, of Detroit's affluent suburbs. Since World War II, Detroiters with money have sought this hillier, more picturesque part of the metropolitan area in preference to the flat, more cramped affluent areas closer in; they didn't mind the long commutes, and by the 1970s many of the offices and most of the fancy shops had moved northwest anyway.

This affluent belt is approximately coincident with the 18th congressional district of Michigan. In the center are Birmingham and Bloomfield Hills, the former once a small outstate Michigan town and now a major shopping and office center, the latter the highest in-come suburb in the Detroit area. To the northeast are the affluent parts of Troy, Rochester, and, across the Macomb County line, Shelby Township. Southwest of Birmingham are Farmington Hills and the new suburb of Novi; the 18th proceeds west, across hilly country not yet thickly settled, almost all the way to Ann Arbor. This is not only the most affluent, but also the most heavily Republican district in Michigan; it was designed to take in the most heavily Republican parts of the metropolitan area, leaving safe Democratic constituencies for its other congressmen.

The congressman here is William Broomfield, one of the senior Republicans in the House. First elected in 1956, he is not a man who seeks the spotlight or looks particularly comfortable in it. Nonetheless, he is a professional politician, first elected to the Michigan legislature in 1948, and a solid party man, who wants never to embarrass his party or its administration. He is the ranking Republican on the Foreign Affairs Committee, and in that capacity acts as the administration's spokesman on such unpopular issues as aid to El Salvador. Broomfield is old enough to remember when the phrase "bipartisan foreign policy" was more than a cliche, and his instinct is to cooperate with administrations of either party, to present a united front abroad. His views on issues over the years have thus become less rather than more distinctive; he is, institutionally, a deeply conservative man. The one major exception to this procedure has come on Middle East policy. He is a strong supporter of aid to Israel, and he opposed the Reagan administration's proposal to sell the AWACS planes to Saudi Arabia.

Broomfield once had to fight hotly contested general elections, when his district included the tough working class town of Pontiac and the affluent suburbs were not so populous. He survived the Democratic year of 1958 nimbly and beat another Republican incumbent in the 1972 primary when they were redistricted together. Now he has a safe seat for as long as he wants, and, just past 60, may stay in Congress for many years to come.

The People   Pop. 1980: 514,560, up 31.4% 1970–80; voting age pop. 360,726; 1% Black, 1% Span. orig., 1% Asian orig. 21% housing units rented. Median owner $80,500; renter $314. Households: 79% family, 45% with children, 70% married couples.

Presidential Vote

1980	Reagan (R) .... NA
	Carter (D) .... NA
	Anderson (I) .... NA

Rep. William S. Broomfield (R) Elected 1956; b. Apr. 28, 1922, Royal Oak; home, Birmingham; MI St. U., B.A. 1951; Presbyterian.

Career MI House of Reps., 1949–55, Spkr. Pro Tem, 1953; MI Senate, 1955–57; Mbr., U.S. Delegation to U.N., 1967.

Offices 2306 RHOB, 202-225-6135. Also 430 N. Woodward St., Birmingham 48011, 313-642-3800.

Committees *Foreign Affairs* (Ranking Member). Subcommittee: International Security and Scientific Affairs. *Small Business* (3d). Subcommittee: Export Opportunities and Special Small Business Problems.

Group Ratings

	ADA	ACLU	COPE	CFA	LCV	LWV	NTU	NSI	COC	ACA	CSFC
1982	10	21	22	8	26	45	69	100	77	78	64
1981	20	—	22	36	57	—	81	—	94	70	68
1980	11	27	17	14	57	50	50	89	76	75	73

National Journal Ratings

	Economic		Foreign		Cultural	
1982	30%	(LIB)	37%	(LIB)	18%	(LIB)
	70%	(CONS)	62%	(CONS)	80%	(CONS)
1981	24%	(LIB)	62%	(LIB)	30%	(LIB)
	68%	(CONS)	37%	(CONS)	70%	(CONS)

Key Votes

1) Reagan 81 Budget	FOR	5) Incr SS Rtmt Age	FOR	9) Poor Pay Food Stamps	FOR
2) Reagan 81 Tax Cut	FOR	6) Saudi AWACS Sale	AGN	10) Ban Crt Busing Order	FOR
3) Bal Budget Amend	FOR	7) $ for MX Missile	FOR	11) Auto Local Content	FOR
4) Gas & Road Tax	—	8) Nerve Gas Prod	AGN	12) Nuclear Arms Freeze	AGN

Election Results

1982 general	William S. Broomfield (R)	132,902	(73%)	($62,599)
	Allen J. Sipher (D)	46,545	(26%)	($0)
1982 primary	William S. Broomfield (R)	52,264	(88%)	
	Roger A. Hall (R)	7,147	(12%)	
1980 general	William S. Broomfield (R)	168,530	(73%)	($83,608)
	Wayne E. Daniels (D)	60,100	(26%)	($9,608)

Campaign Contributions and Expenditures

1981-82		Direct Cont. 81-82		PACS brkdwn			
Receipts	$166,705	Indiv	$98,002	Agr	$—	Ideo	$1,250
Expend.	$62,599	Party	$9,212	Bus	$16,700	Lbr	$—
Unspent	$193,929	PACS	$21,966	Hlth	$4,000	Prof	$—

Indep Expend: For: $188 (MI LIFEPAC)

MINNESOTA

Over the years Minnesota has been one of the nation's leading exporters of iron ore, wheat, flour, and political talent. In the past two decades this not especially populous and geographically peripheral state has given us Hubert Humphrey, Walter Mondale, Eugene McCarthy, Orville Freeman, Warren Burger, and Harry Blackmun. There are still people who remember Minnesota in the 1930s when it produced such national figures as Harold Stassen (a very real presidential contender in 1940 and 1948) and Floyd Olson, the talented Farmer–Labor governor who died prematurely in 1936. No other state of this size—or any size—has produced so many presidential candidates in recent years, and few have had congressional delegations of similar distinction.

To understand how Minnesota developed this political culture we need to go back to its beginnings. Minnesota was far north of the nation's great paths of east–west migration: Minneapolis and St. Paul are as far north as Bangor, Maine, or Vancouver, Washington. In the mid-19th century the Yankee immigrants who pushed into Iowa, Nebraska, and Kansas mostly bypassed Minnesota, and left it to the Norwegians, Swedes, and Germans who were not deterred by its icy lakes and ferocious winters. They wanted to set up communities that would retain at least some of the characteristics of their native lands. The nation was knit together in those days by the great east–west railroads, and the twin cities of Minneapolis and St. Paul sprang up almost at once at the confluence of the Mississippi and Minnesota Rivers as the nerve center of a great agricultural empire stretching west from Minnesota through the Dakotas and eventually into Montana and beyond. The railroad magnates of St. Paul and the giant millers of Minneapolis seem to absolutely govern the economic life of the vast Scandinavian–German province of America.

The various rebellions against this dominance have given the politics of Minnesota a Scandinavian flavor. As in Wisconsin and North Dakota, a strong third party developed here in the years after the Populist era; and that organization, the Farmer–Labor Party, dominated Minnesota politics in the 1930s. Even in the 1940s the Farmer–Labor Party was still at least as important as the state's historically negligible Democrats when they merged to form the Democratic–Farmer–Labor Party (DFL) in 1945. Hubert Humphrey was one of the architects of the merger. He was then mayor of Minneapolis and was already helping the DFL attract dozens of talented young men and women; early volunteers included Walter Mondale and Minneapolis's current mayor, Donald Fraser. The DFL, led by Humphrey, swept the 1948 elections here and since then has been the most important political force in the state. Even when the DFL has lost elections, as in 1966 and 1978, its own mistakes or internal discord, as much as the Republicans' strength, have determined the outcome.

Today the DFL is once again on top. It suffered serious losses in 1978, in large part because voters resented Governor Wendell Anderson having himself appointed to the Senate vacancy created when Mondale became vice president. The Republicans won both Senate seats, the governorship, and one house of the legislature. Today the DFL has the governorship again, it controls the legislature solidly, and it gained two congressional seats (but not the two everyone expected) in the 1982 elections. But its success is not quite complete. Both Senate seats are still in Republican hands, though one is threatened in 1984; and although the party will undoubtedly do well if Mondale is the Democratic presidential nominee in 1984, it may be demoralized if he does not win the nomination.

So the product of an insurgent tradition survives and thrives in a state which has today one of the stablest and most dynamic economies in the Midwest. The stability comes from the food business: there is not much change in the demand for food from year to year, regardless of the strength or weakness of the economy. True, farmers are in a volatile business, because they depend on profits, not revenues, but the grain millers, cereal manufacturers, food processors, and food distributors who make up a major proportion of Minnesota's economy can count on pretty steady business. Thus you find bigger political fluctuations in rural Minnesota congressional districts than you do in the Twin Cities metro area, where political preference is stable and highly correlated to economic status.

Coupled with the rather old-fashioned food business are Minnesota's high-tech industries (a combination you also see in the San Francisco Bay area). Giant firms like Control Data, Honeywell, and the innovation-minded 3M company are headquartered here, and the Twin Cities metro area—with its lakes, its access to recreational facilities, its cultural lifestyle—have attracted many of the talented young people who are the critical ingredient in any recipe for economic growth.

Minnesota's Scandinavian heritage and the rapidly growing highly educated population it has attracted have made it a state tolerant of diversity and open to innovation. It is a state that makes a point of endorsing homosexual rights and of banning smoking in public places. Yet it is also a state where people live their personal lives mostly in traditional patterns, and Minnesotans are stern opponents of any form of corruption. This liberality on cultural issues is matched by a liberal approach to foreign issues. To some extent, this has its roots in isolationism. Minnesota, with its Scandinavian and German immigrants, harbored much opposition—overt and covert—to World War I, and even, as Samuel Lubell demonstrated, resentment of World War II. In the Vietnam war years this was echoed by a dislike of American military involvement in southeast Asia.

Presidential politics. Minnesota has been one of the most Democratic states in the nation in presidential elections since 1968. One reason may be that a Minnesotan has been on every Democratic ticket but one in that time. Yet even then, in 1972, Minnesota was the second most Democratic state, after only Massachusetts. It was one of only six states to favor the Carter–Mondale ticket in 1980.

Minnesota's two parties pride themselves on their distinctive identities; the Republicans took the trouble after the 1974 elections to rename themselves the Independent Republican Party, so now Minnesota elections are a contest of DFL vs. IR. They also pride themselves on having strong party organizations, based on volunteers; they select presidential delegates through caucuses, not in primaries. That means that in 1984 the DFL delegation will be solidly for Walter Mondale, while the IR delegation will be one of the more liberal at the Republican National Convention.

Senators. Minnesota continues to have two Republican senators, because David Durenberger was reelected in 1982. It was a closer contest than expected. Durenberger is in many ways about as strong a candidate as a Republican could be in Minnesota. On economic issues his record is mixed; on cultural issues he is to the left of the Senate, and not at all sympathetic to Moral Majority lobbyists. Their unwillingness to believe in the good faith of their adversaries is something foreign to Durenberger. Yet he shares their views on abortion. On foreign policy, he has called for smaller increases in defense spending than the administration has proposed.

On economic matters, he serves on Robert Dole's Finance Committee, and tends to take positions similar to Dole's. He is a specialist in health care legislation and has successfully backed a plan to encourage offering employees a choice of insurers; he draws on the experience of Minnesota's many health maintenance organizations as well as his own basic preference for market solutions. Durenberger has also chaired the Intergovernmental Relations Subcommittee of Governmental Affairs; once an aide to a Minnesota governor, he is the key legislator in the Senate on "new federalism" issues, and is critical of the Reagan administration approach.

Durenberger had two close races in four years, both against millionaires who self-financed their campaigns. In 1978 he resoundingly beat Bob Short, who had antagonized many liberal DFLers by the way he beat Donald Fraser in the primary. In 1982 he was expected to win easily over Mark Dayton, a 34-year-old Democrat with limited government experience. But Dayton spent upward of $7 million; he is a member of Minnesota's Dayton department store family, and his wife is the sister of West Virginia Governor Jay Rockefeller. Dayton is a classic example of the guilty rich liberal; he wants to redistribute income away from people like himself, and is sympathetic to just about every kind of policy advocated by those who style themselves as the representatives of the poor. Dayton's campaign was surprisingly effective, given his lack of experience; and he was helped, surely, by the recession. Durenberger raised some $2 million in self-defense, and was obviously unhappy to have to do so; he ended up winning 53%–47%. Dayton carried economically distressed Duluth and the Iron Range by 2–1 margins, but only broke even in the Twin Cities. Durenberger, a Catholic, ran well ahead of his party in rural Catholic areas like the counties around St. Cloud.

Dayton is likely to run against Senator Rudy Boschwitz in 1984. He may have competition for the DFL nomination, as he did, from no less than Eugene McCarthy, in 1982; but with his money he is expected to win and will surely be a strong candidate in the general.

Boschwitz has his own strengths, however. He has an unusual background: born in Germany, he came to the United States as a child; he moved to Minnesota and made a fortune (though not nearly as large as Dayton's) in the plywood business. Boschwitz is a booster of free-market principles in economics, though not an uncritical supporter of Reaganomics; he is a strong backer of Israel in foreign policy; he is one of the Senate's most passionate opponents of nuclear power. His interests—and his political needs—are reflected in his committee assignments. He chairs the Near Eastern and South Asian Subcommittee of Foreign Affairs. He serves on the Budget Committee. He is also on the Agriculture Committee—a matter of considerable concern to Minnesota. Minnesota is a major farm state, and food and farming are the businesses which ultimately undergird the solid economy of Minneapolis.

Governor. The 1982 elections were bad news for Minnesota's strong party system. For years state party conventions nominated statewide candidates, and their choices were seldom challenged in the primaries. In 1982, however, both parties had gubernatorial primaries, and in both the challenger won. Republican Wheelock Whitney's well-financed campaign overwhelmed the candidate backed by outgoing Governor Albert Quie. Former Governor Rudy Perpich beat Attorney General Warren Spannaus in the DFL primary; Spannaus carried the Twin Cities area and southern Minnesota, but Perpich won with huge majorities in his home area, the economically hard-hit Iron Range. The central focus of the general election was on the financial condition of the state government. Quie's major achievement was to index the state income tax; but state revenues fell far below expectations, and on five separate occasions the legislature had to revise the budget and raise other taxes. Quie claimed the main problem was a faltering economy; but his backers also admit that taxes were initially overindexed. The experience points to a real problem with indexing: how can you devise a fair and accurate *single* number to reflect how inflation affects a complex economy? After all that turbulence, Quie decided early in the year to retire.

In the general election, Perpich liked to contrast the flush condition of the state treasury when he left office and its depleted condition four years later. He won the 1982 DFL primary with overwhelming support in the Iron Range and Duluth; in the general election he carried most of the state. A dentist from a large political family in the Iron Range, Perpich has a distinctive sense of humor and an unusual political style. He engages in controversy with the zest of someone whose early career in politics came in a rough-and-tumble environment; in early 1983, for example, he exchanged denunciations with South Dakota Governor William Janklow. He and the DFL legislature, for all their unhappiness over how indexing has worked, do not want to repeal it outright.

Congressional districting. Minnesota's House districts were redrawn by a federal court, which adopted a Democratic plan. The Twin Cities metropolitan area now has four complete districts, and none of the four outstate districts now reaches far into the Twin Cities area. The surprise in 1982 was that the DFL picked up the 1st district, but lost the 7th; all the betting was the other way. The DFL also picked up the 6th, a new district in the northern Twin Cities suburbs which leaned Democratic. Four of Minnesota's eight districts were seriously contested in 1982, and that many may be seriously contested again in 1984—good evidence of how closely divided most of the state is outside the Twin Cities metro area and the Iron Range.

The People Est. Pop. 1982: 4,133,000; Pop. 1980: 4,075,970, up 1.4% 1980–82 and 7.1% 1970–80; 1.8% of U.S. total, 21st largest; voting age pop. 2,904,162; 1% American Indian, 1% Black, 1% Spanish origin, 1% Asian origin. Single ancestry: 17% German, 7% Norwegian, 4% Swedish, 3% English, 2% Irish, Polish, 1% French, Dutch, Italian. Registered voters (1982): 2,428,543 Total. 17% with 1–3 yrs. col., 17% with 4+ yrs. col. 9.3% below poverty level. 25% housing units rented; median house value: $54,300; median monthly rent: $212. Households: 72% family, 40% with children, 62% married couples.

1982 Share of Federal Tax Burden $10,761,400,000; 1.80% of U.S. total, 20th largest.

1982 Share of Federal Expenditures

	Total		Non-Defense		Defense	
Total Expend	$8,560m	(1.42%)	$6,874m	(1.62%)	$1,685m	(0.94%)
St/Lcl Grants	1,769m	(2.01%)	1,768m	(2.00%)	1m	(2.78%)
Salary/Wages	406m	(0.52%)	276m	(1.01%)	130m	(0.26%)
Ind Payments	4,580m	(1.60%)	4,252m	(1.65%)	328m	(1.15%)
Procurement	1,601m	(1.10%)	141m	(0.45%)	1,460m	(1.28%)
Other Programs	203m	(3.75%)	201m	(3.74%)	2m	(4.65%)
Loan/Insurance	3,569m	(5.58%)	5,517m	(5.69%)	52m	(2.36%)

Political Lineup Governor, Rudy Perpich (DFL). Senators, David Durenberger (IR) and Rudy Boschwitz (IR). Representatives, 8 (5 DFL and 3 IR). State Senate, 67 (42 DFL and 25 IR); State House of Representatives, 134 (77 DFL and 57 IR).

Presidential Vote

1980	Reagan (R)	873,268	(43%)
	Carter (D)	954,173	(47%)
	Anderson (I)	174,997	(9%)
1976	Ford (R)	819,395	(42%)
	Carter (D)	1,070,440	(55%)

SENATORS

Sen. David Durenberger (IR) Elected 1978, seat up 1988; b, Aug. 19, 1934, St. Cloud; home, Minneapolis; St. John's U., 1955, U. of MN, J.D. 1959; Roman Catholic.

Career Army, 1956; Practicing atty., 1959–66; Exec. Secy. to Gov. Harold LeVander, 1969–71; Counsel for Legal & Community Affairs, Corporate Secy., Mgr. Internatl. Licensing Div., H.B. Fuller Co., 1971–78.

Offices 353 RSOB, 202-224-3244. Also 174 Fed. Cts. Bldg.,110 S. 4th St., Minneapolis 55401, 612-725-6111.

Committees *Environment and Public Works* (8th). Subcommittees: Environmental Pollution; Toxic Substances (Chairman); Water Resources. *Finance* (8th). Subcommittees: Energy and Agricultural Taxation; Health (Chairman); Social Security and Income Maintenance Programs. *Governmental Affairs* (6th). Subcommittees: Energy, Nuclear Proliferation, and Government Processes; Information Management and Regulatory Affairs; Intergovernmental Relations (Chairman). *Select Committee on Intelligence* (6th). Subcommittees: Budget Authorization; Legislation and the Rights of Americans (Chairman). *Select Committee on Ethics* (3d).

Group Ratings

	ADA	ACLU	COPE	CFA	LCV	LWV	NTU	NSI	COC	ACA	CSFC
1982	70	57	43	40	67	100	35	63	28	32	49
1981	40	—	42	57	63	—	47	—	72	52	68
1980	44	47	33	20	75	89	35	70	77	72	57

National Journal Ratings

	Economic		Foreign		Cultural	
1982	51%	(LIB)	67%	(LIB)	76%	(LIB)
	48%	(CONS)	32%	(CONS)	23%	(CONS)
1981	52%	(LIB)	59%	(LIB)	65%	(LIB)
	47%	(CONS)	40%	(CONS)	34%	(CONS)

Key Votes

1) Reagan 81 Budget	FOR	5) $ to El Salvador	FOR	9) Poor Pay Food Stamps	AGN
2) Reagan 81 Tax Cut	FOR	6) Saudi AWACS Sale	AGN	10) Ban Crt Busing Order	AGN
3) Bal Budget Amend	FOR	7) Ban Abortion	FOR	11) Clinch Riv Brdr Rctr	AGN
4) Gas & Road Tax	FOR	8) Nerve Gas Prod	AGN	12) Legal Services Corp	FOR

Election Results

1982 general	David Durenberger (IR)	949,207	(53%)	($4,189,619)
	Mark Dayton (DFL)	840,401	(47%)	($7,172,312)
1982 primary	David Durenberger (IR)	287,651	(93%)	
	Mary Jane Rachner (IR)	20,401	(7%)	($12,197)
1978 general	David Durenberger (IR)	957,908	(61%)	($1,062,271)
	Robert E. Short (DFL)	538,675	(35%)	($1,972,060)

Campaign Contributions and Expenditures

1981-82		Direct Cont. 81-82		PACS brkdwn			
Receipts	$4,268,602	Indiv	$3,093,425	Agr	$54,100	Ideo	$100,100
Expend.	$4,189,619	Party	$27,861	Bus	$748,725	Lbr	$17,250
Unspent	$89,846	Cand	$50,000	Hlth	$67,675	Prof	$12,275
		PACS	$1,078,954				

Indirect Party Expend: $217,517   *Indep Expend:* For: $9,681 (NRA)

Sen. Rudy Boschwitz (IR) Elected 1978, seat up 1984; b. 1930, Berlin, Germany; home, Plymouth; Johns Hopkins U., N.Y.U., B.S. 1950, LL.B. 1953; Jewish.

Career Army, 1953–55; Practicing atty.; Founder and Pres., Plywood Minnesota, 1963–78.

Offices 2317 DSOB, 202-224-5641. Also 210 Bremer Bldg., St. Paul 55101, 612-221-0905.

Committees *Agriculture, Nutrition, and Forestry* (5th). Subcommittees: Agricultural Production, Marketing, and Stabilization of Prices; Nutrition; Foreign Agricultural Policy (Chairman). *Budget* (4th). *Foreign Relations* (7th). Subcommittees: European Affairs; International Economic Policy; Near Eastern and South Asian Affairs (Chairman). *Small Business* (4th). Subcommittees: Capital Formation and Retention; Export Promotion and Market Development (Chairman). *Veterans' Affairs* (7th).

Group Ratings

	ADA	ACLU	COPE	CFA	LCV	LWV	NTU	NSI	COC	ACA	CSFC
1982	30	64	12	10	46	83	60	70	60	71	62
1981	25	—	12	43	44	—	59	—	89	47	70
1980	28	67	10	7	67	90	53	89	86	96	69

National Journal Ratings

	Economic		Foreign		Cultural	
1982	11%	(LIB)	16%	(LIB)	64%	(LIB)
	88%	(CONS)	68%	(CONS)	35%	(CONS)
1981	29%	(LIB)	53%	(LIB)	67%	(LIB)
	70%	(CONS)	46%	(CONS)	32%	(CONS)

Key Votes

1) Reagan 81 Budget	FOR	5) $ to El Salvador	AGN	9) Poor Pay Food Stamps	AGN
2) Reagan 81 Tax Cut	FOR	6) Saudi AWACS Sale	AGN	10) Ban Crt Busing Order	AGN
3) Bal Budget Amend	FOR	7) Ban Abortion	FOR	11) Clinch Riv Brdr Rctr	AGN
4) Gas & Road Tax	FOR	8) Nerve Gas Prod	FOR	12) Legal Services Corp	FOR

Election Results

1978 general	Rudy Boschwitz (IR)	894,092	(57%)	($1,872,443)
	Wendell Anderson (DFL)	638,375	(40%)	($1,154,351)
1978 primary	Rudy Boschwitz (IR)	185,393	(87%)	
	Harold Stassen (IR)	28,170	(13%)	($139,230)
1972 general	Walter F. Mondale (DFL)	981,320	(57%)	($536,532)
	Phil Hansen (R)	742,121	(43%)	($304,750)

Campaign Contributions and Expenditures

1977-78			PACS brkdwn		
Receipts	$1,905,141	Agr	$24,050	Ideo	$13,973
Expend.	$1,872,443	Bus	$192,735	Lbr	$5,000
Unspent	$32,694	Hlth	$22,500	Prof	$5,200

GOVERNOR

Gov. Rudy Perpich (DFL) Elected 1982, term expires Jan. 1987; b. June 27, 1928, Carson Lake; home, Hibbing; Hibbing Jr. Col., Marquette U., DDS 1954; Roman Catholic.

Career Army, 1946–48; Dentist; MN Senate, 1963–71; Lt. Gov., 1971–76; Gov., 1976–79; Vice Pres., World Tech, Inc., 1979–82.

Offices 130 State Capitol Bldg., St. Paul 55155, 612-296-3391.

Election Results

1982 gen.	Rudy Perpich (DFL)	1,049,104	(59%)
	Wheelock Whitney (IR)	711,796	(40%)
1982 prim.	Rudy Perpich (DFL)	275,920	(51%)
	Warren Spannaus (DFL)	248,218	(46%)
1974 gen.	Albert H. Quie (IR)	830,019	(54%)
	Rudy Perpich (DFL)	718,244	(46%)

FIRST DISTRICT

The 1st congressional district of Minnesota, the southeastern corner of the state, is a region of farms and small pleasant cities. This is the Minnesota district with the most in common with the rural Midwest farther south. It was settled, as was neighboring Iowa, mainly by Germans and Yankees; the Scandinavians who have done so much to shape Minnesota usually went farther north. The Yankees were drawn by the farmland, rolling country that smooths out as you go farther west; the Germans, especially Catholics from southern Germany, must have felt at home in the cities they built on high hills overlooking the gorge of the Mississippi. Politically, this has always been the most Republican part of Minnesota. The rainfall is more regular, and farming as a business more secure here than in western Minnesota; there was little populism, little Scandinavian insurgency here.

Today that political picture is a little more complicated. The largest city in the 1st district is Rochester, home of the Mayo Clinic; with its large population of doctors and other professionals (Supreme Court Justice Harry Blackmun lived here as the Mayo Clinic's chief counsel, for many years) is heavily Republican. The agricultural machine factory towns of Austin and Albert Lea, so similar to Iowa's small cities, tend to be Democratic. Mankato, an old German town in picturesquely named Blue Earth County on the Minnesota River, is more Republican, as are the even older Mississippi River towns of Winona and Red Wing.

The 1st district was the scene of one of the closest contests, with one of the least expected results, in the 1982 elections. Two Republican congressmen were defeated here. Arlen Erdahl, a moderate Republican who represented 72% of the people in the newly drawn 1st district, was beaten at the Republican convention by 2d district incumbent Tom Hagedorn; Erdahl moved to the 6th district, ran, and was defeated there in the general election. Hagedorn had represented 28% of the new district, although his residence was just outside its boundaries. He won the convention's endorsement as a Reagan loyalist, on the theory that the voters should be given a real choice. On paper, it looked like no contest, given the historic Republican leanings of the district, Hagedorn's heavy fund-raising advantage, and his advan-

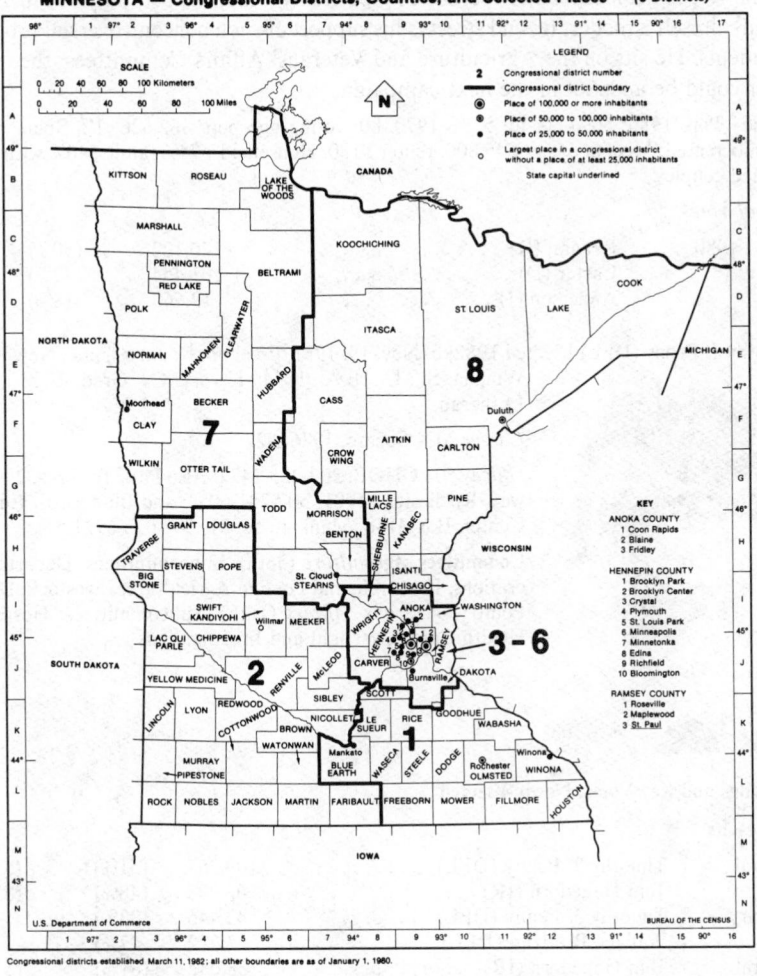

MINNESOTA — Congressional Districts, Counties, and Selected Places — *(8 Districts)*

Congressional districts established March 11, 1982; all other boundaries are as of January 1, 1980.

tage in having represented a part of the district likely to be the strongest base for a DFL challenger.

That challenger, and the new congressman, is Timothy Penny. A six-year veteran of the Minnesota Senate, Penny was only 30, and looked considerably younger; he had little money and was generally unknown. But he was able to raise more than $160,000, and to capitalize on Erdahl's popularity. Hagedorn still carried the area Erdahl used to represent, but by less than 1,000 votes, while Penny, who is from the area Hagedorn used to represent, won a 56%–43% advantage there. Hagedorn (only 38 and young in appearance himself) had indeed allowed the voters a choice, although presumably not the one he intended.

Penny is no stranger to legislative responsibilities, nor to the idea of representing an historically Republican constituency in a legislative body dominated by liberal Democrats. He can be almost sure of tough competition next time, and may not be blessed by the internecine Republican strife nor the flagging economy which helped him win in 1982. He likes to call himself a moderate, and stresses his support of such noncontroversial programs as aid to students. He sits on the Agriculture and Veterans' Affairs Committees; the former in particular could be an asset in the next campaign.

The People   Pop. 1980: 509,460, up 5.2% 1970–80; voting age pop. 362,626; 1% Span. orig. 23% housing units rented. Median owner $45,800; renter $180. Households: 74% family, 40% with children, 66% married couples.

Presidential Vote

1980	Reagan (R)	120,122	(50%)
	Carter (D)	101,454	(42%)
	Anderson (I)	19,660	(8%)

Rep. Timothy J. Penny (DFL) Elected 1982; b. Nov. 19, 1951, Freeborn County; home, New Richland; Winona St. U., B.A. 1974; U. of MN Grad. Sch., 1974–76; Lutheran.

Career MN Senate, 1976–82.

Offices 501 CHOB, 202-225-2472. Also Park Towers, 22 N. Broadway, Rochester 55901, 507-281-6053; and Blue Earth Cnty. Govt. Center, Box 3148, Mankato 56001, 507-625-6921.

Committees *Agriculture* (26th). Subcommittees: Department Operations, Research, and Foreign Agriculture; Livestock, Dairy, and Poultry. *Veterans' Affairs* (16th). Subcommittees: Hospitals and Health Care; Oversight and Investigations.

Group Ratings and Key Votes: Newly Elected

Election Results

1982 general	Timothy J. Penny (DFL)	109,257	(51%)	($182,226)
	Tom Hagedorn (IR)	102,298	(48%)	($390,795)
1982 primary	Timothy J. Penny (DFL)	42,446	(93%)	
	Wallace Brattrud (DFL)	3,272	(7%)	
1980 general	Tom Hagedorn (IR)	158,082	(61%)	($196,870)
	Harold J. Bergquist (DFL)	102,586	(39%)	($31,651)

Campaign Contributions and Expenditures

1981-82		*Direct Cont. 81-82*				*PACS brkdwn*		
Receipts	$191,373	Indiv	$81,647	Agr	$2,150	Ideo	$5,500
Expend.	$182,226	Party	$28,715	Bus	$3,550	Lbr	$52,175
Unspent	$9,533	PACS	$80,671	Hlth	$1,800	Prof	$200

Indirect Party Expend: $90

SECOND DISTRICT

The 2d congressional district of Minnesota is the southwest quadrant of the state. Most of this land is drained by the Minnesota River. In the eastern part of the district, the land is relatively green; it was once heavily forested, and is still verdant, especially in the hilly land near the river banks. This area was settled by German Lutherans and Scandinavians, nononsense folk who farmed its land profitably. Farther west, there were fewer trees and less rainfall. This is part of the vast grain-growing Great Plains. Politically, the difference can be summed up thus: the eastern counties are Republican, in some cases very heavily Republican, a preference dating back to their first settlement; the western counties are politically volatile, swinging usually away from the party in power in protest against any depression or threatened depression of farm profits.

The 2d district is represented in Congress by one of Minnesota's most successful—and youngest—politicians, Vin Weber. He helped manage Senator Rudy Boschwitz's successful campaign in 1978, at age 26; two years later, he ran for Congress in a seat held by the Democrats for six years and won. In the process he raised and spent nearly $500,000. In 1982 the Democratic redistricting plan placed much of Weber's old territory (the former 6th district) in the 2d district where fellow Republican Tom Hagedorn, but not Weber, had his residence. Weber persuaded Hagedorn, for whom he once worked, to challenge the more moderate Arlen Erdahl in the 1st district instead, and Weber himself won the Republican nomination in the 2d district without difficulty. He then raised and spent nearly $500,000 again in the general election. In a recession year, in a district prone to farm revolts, opposed by a DFL former-state senator who loves to denounce banks, Weber nonetheless won comfortably. He carried the eastern part of the district and the southern counties along the Iowa border; he balanced his opponent's margins in farm counties with a solid margin in the farm town of Alexandria.

What is fascinating about this is that Weber is actually not an orthodox Reaganite. He seems in fact to be temperamentally disinclined to orthodox positions of either right or left. On economic issues he tends to be against government regulation and involvement, and on many cultural matters he favors endorsement of traditional values. On foreign policy, he supports the administration on El Salvador and the nuclear freeze, but opposes it on the MX missile, chemical warfare, and the AWACS sale to Saudi Arabia. He is an opponent of nuclear power, and he was the leader on the Science and Technology Committee of the almost-successful fight to stop the Clinch River Breeder Reactor. The reactor's leading congressional champion is none other than Senator Howard Baker, and it has enthusiastic endorsement from the nuclear industry and the Reagan administration. Weber opposes it as a waste of money and as possibly damaging to the environment. On foreign policy he is also a bit of a maverick, tending to oppose interventionist policies. In all these areas he shows the energy and verve for combat that have made this conservative Republican a force to contend with in the liberal Democratic House. While he may well have serious DFL opposition in 1984, he should be considered the favorite to win.

The People Pop. 1980: 509,500, up 2.1% 1970–80; voting age pop. 363,087; 21% housing units rented. Median owner $37,300; renter $142. Households: 74% family, 38% with children, 67% married couples.

Presidential Vote

1980	Reagan (R)	135,644	(53%)
	Carter (D)	102,903	(40%)
	Anderson (I)	17,645	(7%)

Rep. Vin Weber (IR) Elected 1980; b. July 24, 1952, Slaton; home, St. Cloud; U. of MN, 1970–73; Roman Catholic.

Career Pres., Weber Publ. Co., family business; Press Secy.-Researcher for U.S. Rep. Tom Hagedorn, 1974; Campaign Mgr., Chief MN Aide for Sen. Rudy Boschwitz, 1978–80.

Offices 318 CHOB, 202-225-2331. Also 720 St. Germain, Rm. 135, St. Cloud 56301, 612-252-7580; and 208 College Dr., Marshall 56258, 507-532-9611.

Committees *Public Works and Transportation* (14th). Subcommittees: Aviation; Water Resources. *Small Business* (6th). Subcommittee: Antitrust and Restraint of Trade Activities Affecting Small Business.

Group Ratings

	ADA	ACLU	COPE	CFA	LCV	LWV	NTU	NSI	COC	ACA	CSFC
1982	20	25	7	15	75	58	94	70	77	78	63
1981	30	—	7	43	71	—	95	—	74	71	68

National Journal Ratings

	Economic		Foreign		Cultural	
1982	15%	(LIB)	50%	(LIB)	48%	(LIB)
	84%	(CONS)	49%	(CONS)	51%	(CONS)
1981	24%	(LIB)	67%	(LIB)	30%	(LIB)
	68%	(CONS)	32%	(CONS)	70%	(CONS)

Key Votes

1) Reagan 81 Budget	FOR	5) Incr SS Rtmt Age	FOR
2) Reagan 81 Tax Cut	FOR	6) Saudi AWACS Sale	AGN
3) Bal Budget Amend	FOR	7) $ for MX Missile	AGN
4) Gas & Road Tax	AGN	8) Nerve Gas Prod	AGN

9) Poor Pay Food Stamps	FOR
10) Ban Crt Busing Order	FOR
11) Auto Local Content	AGN
12) Nuclear Arms Freeze	AGN

Election Results

1982 general	Vin Weber (IR)	123,508	(54%)	($565,465)
	James W. (Jim) Nichols (DFL) ...	103,243	(45%)	($151,635)
1982 primary	Vin Weber (IR)	43,157	(88%)	
	James Kanne (IR)	5,659	(12%)	
1980 general	Vin Weber (IR)	140,402	(53%)	($498,304)
	Archie Baumann (DFL)	126,173	(47%)	($188,181)

Campaign Contributions and Expenditures

1981-82		Direct Cont. 81-82		PACS brkdwn			
Receipts	$574,386	Indiv	$343,429	Agr	$34,200	Ideo	$10,475
Expend.	$565,465	Party	$30,329	Bus	$122,451	Lbr	$5,000
Unspent	$8,251	PACS	$185,451	Hlth	$11,900	Prof	$2,300

Indirect Party Expend: $35,137   *Indep Expend:* For: $824 (NRA)

THIRD DISTRICT

The 3d congressional district of Minnesota can be called the southern suburban district. This is the most affluent, most highly educated, most Republican district in Minnesota. You get little sense, though, as you drive around these suburbs that they are the home of an elite. Even in Edina, the highest income town in the district, the houses, streets, and cars do not proclaim themselves as extraordinary; there is nothing showy or extravagant about these neighborhoods. They are places where people can enjoy their success without bragging about it, where they can enjoy the pleasure (and endure the pain) of Minnesota's environment without ostentation.

The 3d altogether has quite a combination of suburbs. Besides Edina and other high income suburbs like Eden Prairie, Minnetonka, and Plymouth, there is predominantly Jewish St. Louis Park, and the newer, younger suburbs of Burnsville, Eagan, and Inver Grove Heights south of the Minnesota River. To the south and west the suburbs thin out, and you come to farmlands; the district extends as far as 30 miles outward from the Twin Cities.

In the Twin Cities, political preference correlates highly with economic status, and this is a Republican district in most elections. Sometimes it supports DFL candidates in statewide contests; and in a favorable year, with no incumbent running, a Democrat might even get elected to the House from the 3d. But that is not likely to happen so long as Bill Frenzel keeps on running.

First elected by a narrow margin in 1970, Frenzel has won big ever since. Loud and brainy, partisan and thoughtful, he puts his stamp on every debate he participates in. He has a raft of important committee assignments: Budget, Ways and Means, House Administration. With long experience in a family-owned business, he is a strong supporter of free enterprise, and looks with suspicion on government interference in the marketplace. He is a member of the Ways and Means Committee, and one of the leaders there in efforts to cut taxes. He takes that position not only on regulatory issues but also on trade matters: he sits on the Trade Subcommittee, knows a lot about the subject, and often takes the lead in opposing trade restrictions.

On cultural and foreign issues Frenzel has a mixed record. He is the ranking Republican on the House Administration Committee, where he has a lot to say about any revision of the campaign finance laws. Frenzel is a vigorous, even vitriolic, opponent of public financing of campaigns, and of limitations on political action committees. He is in effect the Republican Party's lead player on these issues, which are of such great personal importance to so many of his colleagues.

Over the years Frenzel has become more partisan and increasingly hostile to government interference in business. He retains, however, a reputation as a moderate Republican, justified because of some of his stands on other issues, and a political asset in a district of this nature, where even strong Republican voters like to think of themselves as moderate and thoughtful.

The People Pop. 1980: 509,499, up 25.3% 1970–80; voting age pop. 352,682; 1% Black, 1% Asian orig. 24% housing units rented. Median owner $73,900; renter $289. Households: 77% family, 46% with children, 67% married couples.

Presidential Vote

1980	Reagan (R)	137,894	(48%)
	Carter (D)	118,344	(41%)
	Anderson (I)	30,111	(11%)

Rep. Bill Frenzel (IR) Elected 1970; b. July 31, 1928, St. Paul; home, Golden Valley; Dartmouth Col., B.A. 1950, M.B.A. 1951; No religious affiliation.

Career Navy, Korea; Pres., MN Terminal Warehouse Co.; MN House of Reps., 1962–70.

Offices 1026 LHOB, 202-225-2871. Also 120 Fed. Bldg., 110 S. 4th St., Minneapolis 55401, 612-881-4600.

Committees *Budget* (3d). Task Forces: Budget Process; Federalism/State-Local Relations; International Finance and Trade; Tax Policy. *House Administration* (Ranking Member). Subcommittee: Accounts. *Ways and Means* (6th). Subcommittees: Public Assistance and Unemployment Compensation; Trade.

Group Ratings

	ADA	ACLU	COPE	CFA	LCV	LWV	NTU	NSI	COC	ACA	CSFC
1982	25	37	17	8	38	55	91	78	81	91	65
1981	30	—	19	14	33	—	86	—	100	71	65
1980	22	43	12	7	31	33	57	50	77	70	67

National Journal Ratings

	Economic		Foreign		Cultural	
1982	11%	(LIB)	56%	(LIB)	51%	(LIB)
	88%	(CONS)	44%	(CONS)	49%	(CONS)
1981	1%	(LIB)	61%	(LIB)	56%	(LIB)
	97%	(CONS)	39%	(CONS)	44%	(CONS)

Key Votes

1) Reagan 81 Budget	FOR	5) Incr SS Rtmt Age	FOR	9) Poor Pay Food Stamps	FOR
2) Reagan 81 Tax Cut	FOR	6) Saudi AWACS Sale	AGN	10) Ban Crt Busing Order	AGN
3) Bal Budget Amend	FOR	7) $ for MX Missile	AGN	11) Auto Local Content	AGN
4) Gas & Road Tax	FOR	8) Nerve Gas Prod	AGN	12) Nuclear Arms Freeze	AGN

Election Results

1982 general	Bill Frenzel (IR)	166,891	(72%)	($243,611)
	Joel Alexander Saliterman (DFL) .	60,993	(26%)	($0)
1982 primary	Bill Frenzel (IR)	44,994	(100%)	
1980 general	Bill Frenzel (IR)	179,393	(76%)	($112,308)
	Joel Alexander Saliterman (DFL) .	57,868	(24%)	($0)

Campaign Contributions and Expenditures

1981-82		Direct Cont. 81-82		PACS brkdwn			
Receipts	$280,854	Indiv	$102,721	Agr	$4,650	Ideo	$2,000
Expend.	$243,611	Party	$6,000	Bus	$102,110	Lbr	$—
Unspent	$176,695	PACS	$122,460	Hlth	$12,250	Prof	$2,900
		Cand	$150				

FOURTH DISTRICT

St. Paul, the smaller of Minnesota's Twin Cities, is an old river town with a history somewhat like that of St. Louis, hundreds of miles farther down the Mississippi River. Settled before Minneapolis, St. Paul was for some years the larger of the two and has always been the state capital. While Minneapolis was attracting Swedes and Yankees, St. Paul got more Irish and German Catholics; while Minneapolis was becoming the nation's largest grain milling center, St. Paul was becoming a major transportation hub, a railroad center and river port. Long before the Democratic–Farmer–Labor Party was formed, St. Paul was one of the few places in Minnesota where Democrats sometimes won elections, and through all the changes that have occurred since, the city and its suburbs have remained staunchly Democratic ever since.

St. Paul and its close-in suburbs make up Minnesota's 4th congressional district. A compact unit, the 4th includes all but a few precincts of St. Paul's Ramsey County and several towns in Dakota County just across the Mississippi River from St. Paul's downtown. These are basically working class, DFL suburbs, as are the towns just east and northeast of the city; directly north you get into more white collar suburbs and into an occasional rich enclave, like the all-private-streets suburb of North Oaks where Walter Mondale bought a house in 1983. St. Paul's elite lived for years in town, in grand mansions on Summit Avenue; they made their way downtown past, on two facing hills, Archbishop Ireland's Cathedral and the state Capitol.

The 4th district has been held by the DFL since 1948, when Eugene McCarthy won it. McCarthy, incidentally, was a fine congressman: a hardworking member of Ways and Means who was both a favorite of Speaker Sam Rayburn and one of the founders of the liberal Democratic Study Group. The current congressman, Bruce Vento, was first elected in 1976; he was a successful state legislator who won party endorsement at the district DFL convention, and then won the primary easily.

Vento has not yet made vast waves in the House of Representatives. He is a member of the Banking and Interior Committees, but has not reached a subcommittee chairmanship. His voting record on practically all issues is among the more liberal of younger Democrats. Republican candidates held him below 60% of the vote in 1978—the big IR year in Minnesota—and 1980, but he won by a nearly 3–1 margin in 1982 and should be considered to have a safe seat.

The People Pop. 1980: 509,532, dn. 3.4% 1970–80; voting age pop. 375,922; 2% Black, 2% Span orig., 1% Asian orig. 36% housing units rented. Median owner $60,700; renter $226. Households: 67% family, 36% with children, 55% married couples.

Presidential Vote

1980			
	Reagan (R)	78,607	(35%)
	Carter (D)	124,624	(55%)
	Anderson (I)	23,144	(10%)

Rep. Bruce F. Vento (DFL) Elected 1976; b. Oct. 7, 1940, St. Paul; home, St. Paul; U. of MN, A.A. 1962; WI St. U., River Falls, B.S. 1965; Roman Catholic.

Career Jr. high sch. teacher, 1965–76; MN House of Reps., 1971–77, Asst. Major. Ldr., 1974–76.

Offices 2433 RHOB, 202-225-6631. Also Fed. Cts. Bldg., Rm. 544, St. Paul 55101, 612-725-7724.

Committees *Banking, Finance and Urban Affairs* (14th). Subcommittees: Consumer Affairs and Coinage; Economic Stabilization; Financial Institutions Supervision, Regulation and Insurance; Housing and Community Development. *Interior and Insular Affairs* (13th). Subcommittees: Energy and the Environment; Public Lands and National Parks. *Select Committee on Aging* (21st). Subcommittee: Health and Long-Term Care.

Group Ratings

	ADA	ACLU	COPE	CFA	LCV	LWV	NTU	NSI	COC	ACA	CSFC
1982	100	83	90	92	87	91	15	10	14	13	27
1981	90	—	89	79	96	—	19	—	13	4	29
1980	100	71	84	86	90	100	19	0	59	9	26

National Journal Ratings

	Economic		Foreign		Cultural	
1982	83%	(LIB)	96%	(LIB)	78%	(LIB)
	15%	(CONS)	1%	(CONS)	22%	(CONS)
1981	81%	(LIB)	87%	(LIB)	90%	(LIB)
	15%	(CONS)	13%	(CONS)	10%	(CONS)

Key Votes

1) Reagan 81 Budget	AGN	5) Incr SS Rtmt Age	AGN	9) Poor Pay Food Stamps	AGN
2) Reagan 81 Tax Cut	AGN	6) Saudi AWACS Sale	AGN	10) Ban Crt Busing Order	AGN
3) Bal Budget Amend	AGN	7) $ for MX Missile	AGN	11) Auto Local Content	FOR
4) Gas & Road Tax	FOR	8) Nerve Gas Prod	AGN	12) Nuclear Arms Freeze	FOR

Election Results

1982 general	Bruce F. Vento (DFL)	153,494	(73%)	($140,328)
	Bill James (IR)	56,248	(27%)	($43,223)
1982 primary	Bruce F. Vento (DFL)	61,918	(100%)	
1980 general	Bruce F. Vento (DFL)	119,182	(59%)	($128,032)
	John Berg (IR)	82,537	(41%)	($318,545)

Campaign Contributions and Expenditures

1981-82		Direct Cont. 81-82		PACS brkdwn			
Receipts	$154,579	Indiv	$43,269	Agr	$5,900	Ideo	$2,800
Expend.	$140,328	PACS	$98,203	Bus	$29,400	Lbr	$58,302
Unspent	$31,856			Hlth	$850	Prof	$300

FIFTH DISTRICT

Minneapolis is Minnesota's largest city, known both for its grain milling industry and for the sophisticated companies which are headquartered here. The Falls of St. Anthony make Minneapolis the head of navigation of the Mississippi River, and provided power for the early grain mills; but you will have a hard time today finding the falls, for Minneapolis seems not much interested today in the energy source which gave birth to the city. Minneapolis itself is just a part of the Twin Cities metropolitan area, and a rather peculiar part. To judge just from its population figures—521,000 in 1950, 370,000 in 1980—you might say it is a city in decay, and you can in fact find some decaying neighborhoods here and there.

But for the most part Minneapolis is thriving. In its older working-class neighborhoods, the small frame houses on grid streets which once held large families now typically hold just one or two old people; but they have enough money to live on comfortably, and their children are living in bigger houses and on larger lots in the suburbs. The large old houses along the chain of lakes in western and southern Minneapolis, which once held the large families of some of the city's richest citizens, now hold young professional couples who like being close to their work. In northeastern Minneapolis, behind the railroad and warehouse district along the Mississippi, is an old working-class neighborhood which has become the new home of many

Hmongs from Indochina. Minneapolis, once a place where many people had to live, is now a city where fewer people, with fewer children, choose to live.

Politics in Minneapolis sometimes features conflicts between the city's older and younger residents (only 8% of its residents are black, and hence racial divisions are not the basis of politics); the older people supported former Mayor Charles Stenvig, a law 'n' order advocate, while the younger tend to support the current mayor, Donald Fraser, a former congressman.

The 5th congressional district of Minnesota now consists of Minneapolis, several working-class suburbs just to the northwest (Robbinsdale, Crystal, Brooklyn Center), and some middle-income suburbs directly south of the city (Richfield, part of Bloomington). It is a solidly DFL district, and its congressman has solid DFL credentials. Martin Olav Sabo was elected to the Minnesota House of Representatives at age 22; at 30 he was the minority leader (members were elected without party labels then, putting the DFL at a disadvantage); and at 34 speaker. When Fraser ran, unsuccessfully, for the Senate in 1978, Sabo ran for the U.S. House, and easily won despite the fact that it was a Republican year. Sabo got a seat on the Appropriations Committee in his first year; Tip O'Neill, who was speaker of the Massachusetts House before he came to Congress, seems to have a soft spot in his heart for former speakers. Sabo is not a particularly voluble legislator, but he doesn't have to be: he has an important committee position, he has the trust of his party's leadership, and he has a safe seat and an appreciative constituency back home in Minneapolis. His record on all issues is one of the most liberal in the House.

The People Pop. 1980: 509,506, dn. 15.3% 1970–80; voting age pop. 401,381; 5% Black, 1% Span. orig., 1% Asian orig., 1% Am. In. 44% housing units rented. Median owner $57,800; renter $220. Households: 56% family, 27% with children, 44% married couples.

Presidential Vote

1980	Reagan (R)	84,499	(32%)
	Carter (D)	150,037	(56%)
	Anderson (I)	31,341	(12%)

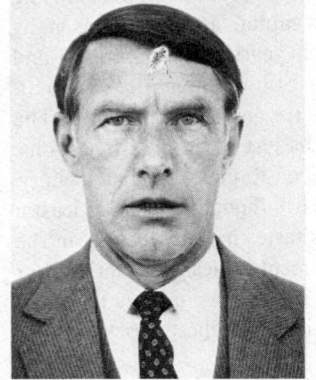

Rep. Martin Olav Sabo (DFL) Elected 1978; b. Feb. 28, 1938, Crosby, ND; home, Minneapolis; Augsburg Col., B.A. 1959, U. of MN; Lutheran.

Career MN House of Reps., 1961–78, Minor. Ldr., 1969–73, Spkr., 1973–78.

Offices 436 CHOB, 202-225-4755. Also 110 S. 4th St., Rm. 166, Minneapolis 55401, 612-725-2081.

Committee *Appropriations* (23d). Subcommittees: District of Columbia; HUD-Independent Agencies; Transportation.

Group Ratings

	ADA	ACLU	COPE	CFA	LCV	LWV	NTU	NSI	COC	ACA	CSFC
1982	100	96	90	85	80	82	18	0	29	14	22
1981	90	—	87	86	86	—	23	—	5	4	25
1980	94	93	79	79	74	100	18	0	58	9	21

National Journal Ratings

	Economic		Foreign		Cultural	
1982	88%	(LIB)	85%	(LIB)	98%	(LIB)
	12%	(CONS)	12%	(CONS)	1%	(CONS)
1981	89%	(LIB)	92%	(LIB)	99%	(LIB)
	3%	(CONS)	2%	(CONS)	1%	(CONS)

Key Votes

1) Reagan 81 Budget	AGN	5) Incr SS Rtmt Age	AGN	9) Poor Pay Food Stamps	AGN
2) Reagan 81 Tax Cut	AGN	6) Saudi AWACS Sale	AGN	10) Ban Crt Busing Order	AGN
3) Bal Budget Amend	AGN	7) $ for MX Missile	AGN	11) Auto Local Content	FOR
4) Gas & Road Tax	FOR	8) Nerve Gas Prod	AGN	12) Nuclear Arms Freeze	FOR

Election Results

1982 general	Martin Olav Sabo (DFL)	136,634	(66%)	($92,914)
	Keith W. Johnson (IR)	61,184	(29%)	($15,419)
	Two others	10,634	(5%)	
1982 primary	Martin Olav Sabo (DFL)	57,388	(100%)	
1980 general	Martin Olav Sabo (DFL)	126,451	(70%)	($83,547)
	John Doherty (IR)	48,200	(27%)	($0)

Campaign Contributions and Expenditures

1981-82		Direct Cont. 81-82		PACS brkdwn			
Receipts	$104,700	Indiv	$38,358	Agr	$5,350	Ideo	$1,800
Expend.	$92,914	PACS	$54,180	Bus	$18,700	Lbr	$26,100
Unspent	$29,431			Hlth	$1,000	Prof	$950

SIXTH DISTRICT

The 6th congressional district of Minnesota can be called the northern suburban Twin Cities district. It is an entirely new seat, created by court decree, designed to produce a Democratic congressman. The 6th forms a kind of semicircle around Minneapolis, St. Paul, and their closest in suburbs. Its oldest part is the town of Stillwater, facing Wisconsin on hills looking down at the St. Croix River; Stillwater was nearly Minnesota's capital, and it contains many Victorian commercial buildings and houses which date from its years as a lumber port and contender for the status of the new state's leading city. Outside Stillwater, on the road to St. Paul, is a more typical example of the architecture of this district: a new shopping center. The most thickly populated part of the 6th district are the suburbs just north of Minneapolis: Brooklyn Park in Hennepin County and Fridley, Blaine, and Coon Rapids in Anoka County. These are working-class suburbs, affluent by any historic standard, though pinched at least a bit in the 1979–83 recession. You can tell a lot about people's tastes here by looking in the shopping centers: you won't find much gourmet cooking equipment or designer clothes, but you will find elaborate tools, camping gear, and comfortable, inexpensive clothes for small children. The 6th district has Minnesota's—and one of the nation's—highest percentages of households with families, married couples, and children.

To the west the 6th extends almost all the way to St. Cloud and to Hubert Humphrey's lakeside home in Waverly. Closer to Minneapolis, it includes the very high-income Minneapolis suburbs around Lake Minnetonka.

When the 6th district's boundaries were announced, it had no incumbent congressman. It soon got one: Arlen Erdahl, rejected by the 1st district Republican convention as too liberal, moved his residence to Fridley in the 6th district, part of which (Washington County, which includes some St. Paul suburbs and Stillwater) he already represented. The DFL nominee was Gerry Sikorski, a resident of Stillwater and six-year veteran of the state Senate at age 34. This race was a rematch of a contest that took place in the 1st district in 1978, when Erdahl won; this time Sikorski was the winner. Sikorski ran on his record of opposing Governor Quie's budget cuts, and denounced Reagan Republicans' support of bankers and dress designers; Erdahl pleaded that he was a moderate Republican, but that was not enough. It was essentially a partisan contest: Sikorski got most of his margin in Anoka County, and just broke even in Washington County. Active, aggressive, ambitious, representing a district marginal enough that he needs to get attention, Sikorski may prove to be a notable congressman. He was able to win a seat on the Energy and Commerce Committee, the most sought after committee assignment in 1983; there he will likely be a voluble opponent of moves to ease the burden of regulation on business. He could have significant opposition in 1984, but he is likely to be a strong favorite to win reelection.

The People Pop. 1980: 509,446, up 38.8% 1970–80; voting age pop. 332,303; 1% Am. In. 18% housing units rented. Median owner $65,000; renter $249. Households: 75% family, 42% with children, 66% married couples.

Presidential Vote

1980	Reagan (R)	98,639	(43%)
	Carter (D)	112,410	(49%)
	Anderson (I)	20,006	(9%)

Rep. Gerry Sikorski (DFL) Elected 1982; b. Apr. 26, 1948, Breckenridge, ND; home, Stillwater; U. of MN, B.A. 1970, J.D. 1973; Roman Catholic.

Career Practicing atty., 1974–80; MN Senate, 1976–82, Major. Whip, 1980–82.

Offices 414 CHOB, 202-225-2271. Also 8535 Central Ave., N.E., Blaine 55434, 612-780-5801.

Committees *Energy and Commerce* (25th). Subcommittees: Health and the Environment; Oversight and Investigations. *Post Office and Civil Service* (11th). Subcommittees: Civil Service; Postal Operations and Services. *Select Committee on Children, Youth, and Families* (15th).

Group Ratings and Key Votes: Newly Elected

Election Results

1982 general	Gerry Sikorski (DFL)	109,246	(51%)	($245,136)
	Arlen Erdahl (IR)	105,734	(49%)	($432,497)
1982 primary	Gerry Sikorski (DFL)	40,645	(83%)	
	Les Betts (DFL)	4,806	(10%)	
	Phil Ratte (DFL)	3,645	(7%)	
1980 general	Arlen Erdahl (IR)	171,099	(72%)	($100,621)
	Russell V. Smith (DFL)	67,279	(28%)	($0)

Campaign Contributions and Expenditures

1981-82		Direct Cont. 81-82			PACS brkdwn		
Receipts	$256,613	Indiv	$69,983	Agr	$1,700	Ideo	$18,494
Expend.	$245,136	Party	$14,443	Bus	$8,700	Lbr	$109,415
Unspent	$10,051	PACS	$170,223	Hlth	$6,500	Prof	$1,100

Indirect Party Expend: $1,363

SEVENTH DISTRICT

The 7th congressional district of Minnesota consists of two segments, distinctive both geographically and physically. They lie successively along the highways and rail lines that extend northwest from Minneapolis and St. Paul toward North Dakota and the Pacific Northwest. The first of these areas, as you leave Minneapolis, is the farm country around St. Cloud. This is an area settled largely by German Catholics, dotted with farm villages with saints' names; it is densely populated, productive farmland. It was also the boyhood home of Sinclair Lewis, and his *Main Street* is set in a thinly disguised Sauk Centre. This was one of the most isolationist parts of Minnesota in both world wars—and one of the politically most volatile. Among these German-Americans there was an underlying sympathy for Germany, which most were reluctant to admit, but which, as Samuel Lubell found, was expressed in huge margins against the Democrats associated with those wars. Yet these same areas, when they are in agrarian distress, will on occasion swing heavily to the Democrats.

The other portion of the district, with 62% of its population, is the northwest corner of the state. Along the Red River of the North, which separates Minnesota from North Dakota, are vast fields of wheat and sugar beets; the farmers here are primarily of Norwegian descent. To the east are acres of forests, lakes, and occasional resort areas. This is the country of the legendary Paul Bunyan and his blue ox Babe, whose statues stand together in Bemidji, a small town on the shores of one of Minnesota's 10,000 lakes. Not far away is Lake Itasca, the headwaters of the Mississippi River. The lake country tends to be Democratic, the wheat country marginal, and responsive to discontent on the farms.

The 7th has a rather colorful political history. It made national headlines in 1958, when Coya Knutson was congresswoman here; her husband Andy issued a plaintive statement urging her to come home and, among other things, make his breakfast again. Apparently many voters considered the request reasonable; Knutson was the only Democratic incumbent to lose in the heavily Democratic year of 1958. The man who beat her, ultraconservative Republican Odin Langen, never built up much popularity, and was beaten by Bob Bergland in 1970. Bergland became very popular in the district and was appointed Jimmy Carter's Secretary of Agriculture in 1977; in the special election to fill it the winner was Republican Arlan Stangeland.

Stangeland had marvelous credentials: he was a bona fide farmer himself, and of Norwegian descent. Yet he, like Langen, has never taken firm hold of the district. His record on just about all issues is the most conservative in Minnesota; on the Agriculture Committee, however, he favors some price supports and other government interference with the marketplace. In three successive races against former legislator Gene Wenstrom, Stangeland has been held to victories of 52%–45%, 52%–48%, and 50.3%–49.7%. Given the volatility of this area, that is striking continuity. Although Wenstrom carried the St. Cloud area, most of which was added to the district in 1982, he might have won in 1982 but for redistricting: more

DFL territory was excised from the district than added to it. Will he try again? In all likelihood someone will, and this constantly contested district will see a serious race again in 1984.

The People Pop. 1980: 509,521, up 10.8% 1970–80; voting age pop. 355,632; 1% Am. In. 18% housing units rented. Median owner $39,300; renter $168. Households: 75% family, 42% with children, 66% married couples.

Presidential Vote

1980	Reagan (R)	123,462	(51%)
	Carter (D)	102,737	(42%)
	Anderson (I)	16,487	(7%)

Rep. Arlan Stangeland (IR) Elected Feb. 22, 1977; b. Feb. 8, 1930, Fargo, ND; home, Barnesville; Lutheran.

Career Farmer; MN House of Reps., 1966–74.

Offices 1526 LHOB, 202-225-2165. Also 403 Center Ave., Moorhead 56560, 218-233-8631.

Committees *Agriculture* (7th). Subcommittees: Cotton, Rice and Sugar; Wheat, Soybeans and Feed Grains. *Public Works and Transportation* (4th). Subcommittees: Aviation; Public Buildings and Grounds; Water Resources.

Group Ratings

	ADA	ACLU	COPE	CFA	LCV	LWV	NTU	NSI	COC	ACA	CSFC
1982	10	0	13	23	12	33	76	100	90	71	61
1981	0	—	13	29	7	—	59	—	95	78	69
1980	0	20	21	29	22	30	54	100	76	79	76

National Journal Ratings

	Economic		Foreign		Cultural	
1982	19%	(LIB)	39%	(LIB)	1%	(LIB)
	79%	(CONS)	61%	(CONS)	98%	(CONS)
1981	4%	(LIB)	14%	(LIB)	4%	(LIB)
	79%	(CONS)	84%	(CONS)	90%	(CONS)

Key Votes

1) Reagan 81 Budget	FOR	5) Incr SS Rtmt Age	FOR	9) Poor Pay Food Stamps	FOR
2) Reagan 81 Tax Cut	FOR	6) Saudi AWACS Sale	FOR	10) Ban Crt Busing Order	FOR
3) Bal Budget Amend	FOR	7) $ for MX Missile	FOR	11) Auto Local Content	AGN
4) Gas & Road Tax	—	8) Nerve Gas Prod	FOR	12) Nuclear Arms Freeze	AGN

Election Results

1982 general	Arlan Stangeland (IR)	108,254	(50%)	($441,649)
	Gene Wenstrom (DFL)	107,062	(50%)	($329,298)
1982 primary	Arlan Stangeland (IR)	37,740	(100%)	
1980 general	Arlan Stangeland (IR)	135,084	(52%)	($267,705)
	Gene Wenstrom (DFL)	124,026	(48%)	($253,893)

Campaign Contributions and Expenditures

1981-82		Direct Cont. 81-82		PACS brkdwn			
Receipts	$404,281	Indiv	$201,802	Agr	$21,200	Ideo	$13,850
Expend.	$441,649	Party	$24,038	Bus	$103,975	Lbr	$3,000
Unspent	$4,480	PACS	$154,709	Hlth	$11,850	Prof	$800

Indirect Party Expend: $35,248   *Indep Expend:* For: $1,866 (NRA)
Agn: $11,373 (PROPAC CCSND)

EIGHTH DISTRICT

The 8th congressional district of Minnesota is the northeast corner of the state. Physically, most of the acreage here is taken up by lakes and forests. There are few farmers: the soil is not adaptable to agriculture, the forests too entrenched, and most of all it is simply too cold for too much of the year. Most of the population here is clustered into what amount to two urban areas.

The first is called the Iron Range: the string of towns and settlements along the Mesabi Range. This is the largest single source of iron ore in the United States; altogether about 100,000 people live in the punishing physical environment of the Iron Range, and have for years. Immigrants came here in the years before World War I from Italy, Poland, Serbia and Croatia, Hungary, and Finland. Life was rough: the work was hard, the hours long, pay low. There was little time and few facilities for recreation, back in those days when working people couldn't afford special winter sports clothes or summer gear; the churches, a separate one for each ethnic group, were the main community institution. There was never much of an elite up in the Iron Range: the men who owned these mines never went to see them, and their top executives governed them from afar, through local foremen. As a result, there is a rough-hewn tone to life in the Iron Range even today. Living conditions improved vastly in the decades of great economic growth after World War II, but not as much as in the rest of the country; even as the unions got pay raised vastly, there were fewer jobs on the Iron Range, and many young people left for other places.

The other cluster of population is around Duluth, the Lake Superior port which contains 93,000 people after having almost exactly 100,000 for 50 years. Rail cars take the iron ore down to Duluth, where it is loaded into giant freighters and sent down to Great Lakes ports. Most of Duluth sits high on bluffs overlooking the frigid or, during much of the year, frozen waters of the lake—another aspect of the forbidding physical environment, which would never have attracted more than a handful of people, but for the iron ore of the Mesabis.

Now the demand for that ore has been declining. Domestic steel production plummeted in the 1979–83 recession, and layoffs were common on the Iron Range. Unemployment zoomed to record figures; whole towns seemed to be laid off. The Iron Range and Duluth had always been Democratic, so heavily Democratic that they literally dominated the rest of the 8th district, most of which is Democratic farms-and-lakes country. But in 1982 voter turnout and Democratic percentages here rose sharply. In the gubernatorial primary, Rudy Perpich, scion of a successful political family in the Iron Range, carried the 8th district by an overwhelming margin, and upset the candidate endorsed by the DFL convention; in the general election, Perpich beat Wheelock Whitney by better than a 3–1 margin in the 8th.

The congressman from the 8th, James Oberstar, seems to reflect district opinion closely. He supports government programs to help the poor, the unemployed, and distressed areas. Oberstar used to be an aide to John Blatnik, congressman from the 8th for 28 years and ultimately Chairman of the House Public Works Committee; Oberstar is a member of the same committee as well as Merchant Marine and Fisheries. He chairs the Economic Development Subcommittee of Public Works and Transportation, and helped to save the EDA program from complete destruction by the Reagan administration; Oberstar responded to David Stockman's arguments against EDA's rationale with photographs of the projects it helped build in Duluth. He has broader interests as well, as indicated by his proposal to allow tax deductions for expenses in adopting a child.

Oberstar inherited not only Blatnik's seat but his feuds. Politics in the Iron Range and Duluth is a personal business, one of the few ways to move up in the world; it is fought out largely in Democratic–Farmer–Labor Party conventions and primaries. With Blatnik's support Oberstar won a narrow victory in the primary over DFL convention winner Tony Perpich, Rudy Perpich's brother, and state Senator Florian Chmielewski. In 1980 Oberstar had another close primary again, beating Thomas Dougherty 56%–44%. His work on EDA seems to haved helped him avoid such opposition in 1982, but with Rudy Perpich as governor again, there is always the possibility of opposition.

The People   Pop. 1980: 509,506, up 10.7% 1970–80; voting age pop. 360,529; 1% Am. In. 16% housing units rented. Median owner $38,100; renter $166. Households: 74% family, 40% with children, 65% married couples.

Presidential Vote

1980	Reagan (R)	94,401	(37%)
	Carter (D)	141,664	(56%)
	Anderson (I)	16,603	(7%)

Rep. James L. Oberstar (DFL) Elected 1974; b. Sept. 10, 1934, Chisholm; home, Chisholm; Col. of St. Thomas, B.A. 1956, Col. of Europe, Bruges, Belgium, M.A. 1957; Roman Catholic.

Career A. A. to U.S. Rep. John A. Blatnik, 1965–74; Administrator, U.S. House of Reps. Comm. on Pub. Works, 1971–74.

Offices 2351 RHOB, 202-225-6211. Also 231 Fed. Bldg., Duluth 55802, 218-727-7474.

Committees *Merchant Marine and Fisheries* (9th). Subcommittees: Coast Guard and Navigation; Fisheries and Wildlife Conservation and the Environment. *Public Works and Transportation* (7th). Subcommittees: Aviation; Economic Development (Chairman); Water Resources.

Group Ratings

	ADA	ACLU	COPE	CFA	LCV	LWV	NTU	NSI	COC	ACA	CSFC
1982	100	75	92	92	93	82	18	10	14	13	25
1981	85	—	91	79	86	—	23	—	5	4	26
1980	83	67	89	86	70	90	12	10	59	17	25

National Journal Ratings

	Economic		Foreign		Cultural	
1982	89%	(LIB)	96%	(LIB)	78%	(LIB)
	11%	(CONS)	1%	(CONS)	22%	(CONS)
1981	89%	(LIB)	92%	(LIB)	77%	(LIB)
	3%	(CONS)	2%	(CONS)	23%	(CONS)

Key Votes

1) Reagan 81 Budget	AGN	5) Incr SS Rtmt Age	AGN	9) Poor Pay Food Stamps	AGN
2) Reagan 81 Tax Cut	AGN	6) Saudi AWACS Sale	AGN	10) Ban Crt Busing Order	AGN
3) Bal Budget Amend	AGN	7) $ for MX Missile	AGN	11) Auto Local Content	FOR
4) Gas & Road Tax	FOR	8) Nerve Gas Prod	AGN	12) Nuclear Arms Freeze	FOR

Election Results

1982 general	James L. Oberstar (DFL)	176,392	(77%)	($137,747)
	Marjory L. (Marnie) Luce (IR) ...	53,467	(23%)	($22,285)
1982 primary	James L. Oberstar (DFL)	94,377	(87%)	
	Bernard Sydow (DFL)	14,497	(13%)	
1980 general	James L. Oberstar (DFL)	182,228	(70%)	($188,096)
	Edward Fiore (IR)	72,350	(28%)	($18,673)

Campaign Contributions and Expenditures

1981-82		Direct Cont. 81-82		PACS brkdwn			
Receipts	$161,460	Indiv	$59,189	Agr	$3,800	Ideo	$1,775
Expend.	$137,747	Party	$1,345	Bus	$28,425	Lbr	$58,345
Unspent	$33,234	PACS	$94,344	Hlth	$500	Prof	$1,300

MISSISSIPPI

Mississippi is the quintessential southern state, the place you think of when you come across southern cliches, from the magnolia blossom-strewn lawn of the antebellum mansion to the tarpaper shacks of black sharecroppers. Historically, Mississippi is the product of several streams of migration: land-hungry Jacksonian farmers settled the northeastern and central parts of the state, which are still heavily white and largely rural and small town; wealthy planters settled the Mississippi River valley, together with their slaves. Mississippi has a mystique about it, thanks to the work of two of its great writers, William Faulkner and Eudora Welty. Mississippi has also been known for years as the state with the largest percentage of blacks and as the state with the lowest incomes and standards of living.

The overwhelming fact about Mississippi is that it has changed immeasurably over the last 20 and 40 years—changed more than any other state in the union. In the 1940s Mississippi still seemed like another country to most Americans. Along its dusty roads leading from market towns were loose-jointed frame farmhouses, where people, white as well as black, lived without automobiles and farmed without machines; they had no electricity and no leisure time to speak of; their isolation was more like the life of farmers in the early 19th century than like the life of Americans about to enter the freeway age. Many Mississippians were still sharecroppers, living outside the money economy; and many others considered themselves lucky to make $100 a month. Mississippi's per capita income was just 36% of the national average. There were successful businesses and plantations in Mississippi, but somehow the wealth here never seemed to trickle down. The families who had money had mostly had it for generations; they considered it inconceivable that most other Mississippians could make much money or, if they did, would know how to spend it. Mississippi was more like what we now call an underdeveloped country than it was like most of the rest of the United States.

In that era, Mississippi politics had no match in the nation for crudity and, on occasion, savagery. There was always an economic division, between the rich white planters of the Delta and the River valley and the poor white farmers of the hillier north and east. But even more important was the division between the races. In 1940, 49% of Mississippians were black, and white supremacy was maintained by a system as rigid and severe as South Africa's is today. Blacks were not allowed to vote; they could not mingle with whites in schools or public accommodations; they had to address whites with particular phrases. Infractions were sometimes punished with death; lynchings were not uncommon in the 1940s and occurred up through the 1950s; as late as 1964 three civil rights workers were murdered in the town of Philadelphia.

With this grim background, Mississippi's economy languished and its politics attracted few topnotch people. The state had as governor and senator Theodore Bilbo, who liked to compare blacks with monkeys, and Ross Barnett, the buffoonish governor who served when the University of Mississippi was integrated by federal troops in 1963. In national politics, Mississippi increasingly diverged from the rest of the country. In 1960, it backed an independent slate of electors—the only state to do so—and in 1964, when virtually no blacks voted, it went 87% for Goldwater. In 1968, with many blacks voting, it was still 63% for Wallace, and in 1972 it went for the winner, Richard Nixon, but gave him a larger percentage than any other state. In national elections, the candidacy of Jimmy Carter brought Mississippi back into the mainstream; Carter narrowly carried the state in 1976 and narrowly lost it in 1980.

But other factors were much more important than the presence of a southerner on the national Democratic ticket in changing the way people live in Mississippi. The first was the civil rights laws, particularly the Voting Rights Act of 1965, which gave blacks the right to vote and forever changed Mississippi politics. It did not, as some rural blacks hoped, give blacks majority control, because in the post-World War II era the black percentage of Mississippi's population has been declining rapidly: from 49% before the war to 35% in 1980. Moreover, only 31% of Mississippi's adult population is black; even if blacks registered and voted in the same proportion as whites, they could still be outvoted 2–1.

Nevertheless, being a part of the electorate can make a difference. Blacks will not win many races in Mississippi where all blacks vote one way and all whites another. But a state legislator or city council member with a 10% or 20% or 30% black constituency is likely to be interested in what black voters want; no sensible politician likes to write off permanently a constituency that large. Mississippi blacks have become more adroit at exerting political pressure and they have, quietly and out of the national spotlight, been getting more of what they want out of government. It is this kind of change more than the much-publicized election of black mayors (like Charles Evers) in tiny hamlets that is producing a real change in how blacks live in Mississippi.

Moreover, since the beginning of the 1970s, black out-migration has slowed way down, and the long-term trend, for the first time since the 1870s, is for the black percentage to increase. After all, 44% of the state's under-18 population is black. The primary reason for the slowdown in out-migration is that the state's economy has taken off; the state's per capita income, 36% of the national average in 1940 and 54% in 1960, is 69% of a much higher national average today, when living costs and taxes are much lower in Mississippi than in most states.

Is this economic growth a result of integration? No one is sure, but it is apparent that the economy got a boost just as Mississippi was forced to get rid of segregation. One reason is that investors are more willing to put up money in a state with no racial strife; another is that Mississippians have become better educated and more skilled; another may be that wage and tax levels in many northern states became so much higher than those in the South that states like Mississippi became more attractive. Still another reason—not mentioned by those who focus only on the motives of white businessmen and the performance of politicians—is that Mississippi's blacks themselves, finally free to express themselves and to make their livings as they wish, have been more likely, if they are skilled, to stay in Mississippi and more likely, whether skilled or not, to work harder and put out more effort than they were in the days when it seemed that anything they might accomplish could be taken away by whites.

Governor. Another factor that has changed life in Mississippi for the better—and has altered the state's politics—has been the performance of Governor William Winter. Mississippi had not elected an outspoken segregationist governor since 1967, but it did not elect an explicit supporter of integration until Winter won in 1979; he lost two earlier races, in 1967 and 1975, because of his reputation for racial moderation. Winter's role in changing Mississippi is ironic, since by temperament he is comfortable with tradition and stability; but he also believes strongly that state government can affect the future course of Mississippians' lives.

Winter's proudest accomplishment was an education package he got the legislature, finally, to pass in 1982. Some changes would seem unremarkable in other states—state-supported kindergartens, raising the school leaving age to 14. But the legislature agreed to raise taxes specifically for education, in a Mississippi where 50% of the public school students are black. Winter believes that Mississippi must improve its citizens' basic skills if it is to keep rising economically; that is surely right, for there will always be cheaper unskilled labor abroad. Some of his opponents don't want to spend money to improve blacks' skills, and so maintain traditional cultural patterns; now that view has been forcefully and explicitly repudiated in the state where it held sway for so long.

Winter also changed the course of the state's politics by bringing blacks into the Democratic Party. Democrats lost a number of races—and at least one Senate and one House seat—because of independent black candidacies. Winter concentrated on getting Democratic nominees who would be acceptable to blacks and getting enough black support for them that independent candidacies would not surface. He also increased black registration enough to show up in the 1980 election returns: the drop in Jimmy Carter's percentage between 1976 and 1980 was lower in Mississippi than in any other state, and the Carter percentage in Jackson and Hinds County actually went up, from 38% to 44%. Winter's work paid off when 81-year-old Senator John Stennis was reelected, for the first time with active black support, in 1982, and was almost rewarded when state Representative Robert Clark, a black, came heartbreakingly close to winning a seat in the House of Representatives.

Winter cannot seek a second term in 1983, and a host of candidates are running; there is nothing more difficult to predict than a Mississippi gubernatorial race. But it does seem clear that the educational and political changes Winter has set in motion will continue regardless of who is in office. Winter himself has been mentioned as a possible candidate for the Senate against Thad Cochran in 1984 or as a top-level appointee should there be a Democratic national administration in 1985.

Presidential politics. In 1980 Mississippi went for Ronald Reagan over Jimmy Carter by only a 49%–48% margin. On the basis of that result, Mississippi ranks with several other southern states as strongly Democratic, provided that the Democratic nominee is not repellent to white southerners. Mississippi selects national convention delegates by caucus.

Senators. Mississippi in 1982 reelected the oldest member of the Senate, John Stennis, but did it in a manner never seen before. Stennis had not had a serious challenge since 1947, when he was elected to replace Bilbo; this time he had a well-financed, 34-year-old Republican opponent, Haley Barbour. Stennis had never before sought or received much support from blacks; this time he voted for extension of the Voting Rights Act and won the lion's share of the black vote. Stennis had never had any contacts with national campaigns; this time, under Winter's tutelage, he hired national political consultants and spent $944,054. Everything ended up clicking. Barbour forces' efforts to point up Stennis's age (including a birthday party they staged) ended up backfiring; Barbour himself did not make a strong positive impression; Stennis proved an able campaigner. In the 2d congressional district, where Clark was running, the electorate seemed polarized by race, and there and in high-income parts of Jackson Barbour carried the white vote. But Stennis got overwhelming percentages in the mostly white eastern and central parts of the state. He carried all but two counties in the state and earned the right to remain in the Senate until 1989, when he will be 87.

With Republicans in control of the Senate, Stennis is not as powerful as he was, but he still has influence. In 1983 he took the ranking minority position on Appropriations, which means he will chair that committee if the Democrats regain control. Appropriations has lost some of its power to the new congressional budget process, but it still can steer amounts of money which are small in the government's eyes but can mean a lot to a politician. It is also a position from which Stennis can fight for the Tennessee–Tombigbee Waterway, one of his favorite causes. Stennis relinquished the ranking position on Armed Services, but he still has influence on arms policy. Armed Services is a talented committee now, and not all the members share Stennis's inclination to trust incumbent administrations of both parties and the Pentagon leadership. But he will continue to be a force to counter outright rebellion against this or any other administration.

Mississippi's other senator, Thad Cochran, is a Republican. Elected to fill James Eastland's seat in 1978, he has not attracted much notice nationally, but seems to be popular in Mississippi. In personal demeanor more than in political attitudes, Cochran personifies the upwardly mobile urban elite—found in Jackson, along the Gulf Coast, and in small numbers in other Mississippi cities—which until William Winter forged the Democratic Party into a strong instrument seemed to be the dominant force in Mississippi's politics. Cochran is less doctrinaire than many well-off Mississippians, however, and more inclined to accommodate his own views to the system. On any ideological scale Cochran is a solid conservative and supporter of the Reagan administration. But in terms of basic political instincts, as well as personal style, he seems closer to Majority Leader Howard Baker. He has seats on the Agriculture, Appropriations, and Governmental Affairs Committees.

It is not clear how strong Cochran will be when he runs for reelection in 1984. He has few political enemies, has made a generally good impression, and has some popularity even among blacks. Yet he was elected in 1978 as a minority candidate, with 45% of the vote; Democrat Maurice Dantin got 32% and Charles Evers 23%. In 1984 it is likely—though not certain—that there will not be a significant independent black candidate; black voters may still be solidly anti-Republican because of their attitude toward the Reagan administration. So there exists a potential majority against Cochran. But it will be hard for anyone, even for

William Winter, to assemble. The jockeying for the Democratic nomination, absent a Winter candidacy, will not really begin until after the 1983 gubernatorial campaign.

Congressional districting. The Mississippi legislature's congressional districting plan was thrown out under the Voting Rights Act, and a plan with a majority black 2d district was substituted. Actually, just 48% of the new 2d's adult citizens are black, and the Democratic nominee, black legislator Robert Clark, barely lost the race. The shapes of the other districts were either not much changed or were changed with little political effect.

The People Est. Pop. 1982: 2,551,000; Pop. 1980: 2,520,638, up 1.2% 1980–82 and 13.7% 1970–80; 1.1% of U.S. total, 31st largest; voting age pop. 1,706,441; 31% Black, 1% Spanish origin. Single ancestry: 20% English, 6% Irish, 2% German, 1% French. Registered voters (1982): 1,507,669 Total. 14% with 1–3 yrs. col., 14% with 4+ yrs. col. 24.5% below poverty level. 26% housing units rented; median house value: $31,400; median monthly rent: $113. Households: 78% family, 46% with children, 62% married couples.

1982 Share of Federal Tax Burden $4,238,200,000; .71% of U.S. total, 32d largest.

1982 Share of Federal Expenditures

	Total		Non-Defense		Defense	
Total Expend	$6,562m	(1.09%)	$4,408m	(1.04%)	$2,154m	(1.20%)
St/Lcl Grants	1,091m	(1.24%)	1,090m	(1.24%)	1m	(2.78%)
Salary/Wages	857m	(1.10%)	236m	(0.86%)	621m	(1.23%)
Ind Payments	3,073m	(1.07%)	2,680m	(1.04%)	393m	(1.37%)
Procurement	1,469m	(1.01%)	103m	(0.33%)	1,366m	(1.20%)
Other Programs	73m	(1.35%)	73m	(1.35%)	0m	(0%)
Loan/Insurance	1,591m	(2.49%)	1,580m	(2.56%)	11m	(0.50%)

Political Lineup Governor, William F. Winter (D). Senators, John C. Stennis (D) and Thad Cochran (R). Representatives, 5 (3 D and 2 R). State Senate, 52 (47 D and 5 R); State House of Representatives, 122 (116 D, 4 R and 2 I).

Presidential Vote

1980	Reagan (R)	441,089	(49%)
	Carter (D)	429,281	(48%)
	Anderson (I)	12,036	(1%)
1976	Ford (R)	366,846	(48%)
	Carter (D)	381,309	(50%)

SENATORS

Sen. John C. Stennis (D) Elected 1947, seat up 1988; b. Aug. 3, 1901, Kemper Cnty.; home, De Kalb; MS St. U., B.S. 1923, U. of VA, LL.B. 1928; Presbyterian.

Career MS House of Reps., 1928–32; Dist. Prosecuting Atty., 16th Judicial Dist., 1931–37; Circuit Judge, 1937–47.

Offices 205 RSOB, 202-224-6253. Also 303 P.O. Bldg., Jackson 39205, 601-353-5494.

Committees *Appropriations* (Ranking Member). Subcommittees: Agriculture, Rural Development; Energy and Water Development; Defense; HUD-Independent Agencies; Transportation. *Armed Services* (2d). Subcommittees: Military Construction; Sea Power and Force Projection; Strategic and Theater Nuclear Forces.

Group Ratings

	ADA	ACLU	COPE	CFA	LCV	LWV	NTU	NSI	COC	ACA	CSFC
1982	25	14	24	40	25	44	40	90	72	50	62
1981	15	—	24	14	19	—	47	—	93	67	65
1980	17	13	37	33	0	13	47	50	57	43	49

National Journal Ratings

	Economic		Foreign		Cultural	
1982	61%	(LIB)	42%	(LIB)	14%	(LIB)
	38%	(CONS)	57%	(CONS)	85%	(CONS)
1981	32%	(LIB)	35%	(LIB)	20%	(LIB)
	67%	(CONS)	64%	(CONS)	76%	(CONS)

Key Votes

1) Reagan 81 Budget	FOR	5) $ to El Salvador	AGN	9) Poor Pay Food Stamps	FOR
2) Reagan 81 Tax Cut	FOR	6) Saudi AWACS Sale	FOR	10) Ban Crt Busing Order	FOR
3) Bal Budget Amend	FOR	7) Ban Abortion	FOR	11) Clinch Riv Brdr Rctr	FOR
4) Gas & Road Tax	FOR	8) Nerve Gas Prod	FOR	12) Legal Services Corp	AGN

Election Results

1982 general	John C. Stennis (D)	414,099	(64%)	($944,054)
	Haley Barbour (R)	230,927	(36%)	($1,133,384)
1982 primary	John C. Stennis (D)	145,817	(75%)	
	Charles Pittman (D)	33,651	(17%)	($5,490)
	Colon Johnson (D)	14,696	(6%)	($19,956)
1976 general	John C. Stennis (D)	554,433	(100%)	($119,852)

Campaign Contributions and Expenditures

1981-82		Direct Cont. 81-82		PACS brkdwn			
Receipts	$949,213	Indiv	$584,834	Agr	$14,000	Ideo	$8,800
Expend.	$944,054	Party	$37,500	Bus	$188,550	Lbr	$6,500
Unspent	$5,156	PACS	$232,300	Hlth	$12,350	Prof	$1,750
		Cand	$50,000				

Indirect Party Expend: $57,700

Sen. Thad Cochran (R) Elected 1978, seat up 1984; b. Dec. 7, 1937, Pontotoc; home, Jackson; U. of MS, B.A. 1959, J.D. 1965, Rotary Fellow, Trinity Col., Dublin, Ireland, 1963–64; Baptist.

Career Navy, 1959–61; Practicing atty., 1965–72; U.S. House of Reps., 1973–78.

Offices 321 RSOB, 202-224-5054. Also Fed. Bldg., Rm. 316, Jackson 39205, 601-969-1353.

Committees *Agriculture, Nutrition, and Forestry* (4th). Subcommittees: Soil and Water Conservation; Agricultural Production, Marketing, and Stabilization of Prices (Chairman); Foreign Agricultural Policy. *Appropriations* (7th). Subcommittees: Agriculture, Rural Development (Chairman); Defense; Energy and Water Development; Interior; Transportation. *Governmental Affairs* (9th). Subcommittees: Governmental Efficiency and the District of Columbia; Intergovernmental Relations; Permanent Subcommittee on Investigations.

Group Ratings

	ADA	ACLU	COPE	CFA	LCV	LWV	NTU	NSI	COC	ACA	CSFC
1982	10	14	14	10	16	45	60	100	63	79	75
1981	10	—	16	14	6	—	51	—	94	62	79
1980	22	17	16	13	19	30	46	100	85	88	75

National Journal Ratings

	Economic		Foreign		Cultural	
1982	30%	(LIB)	36%	(LIB)	18%	(LIB)
	69%	(CONS)	63%	(CONS)	81%	(CONS)
1981	31%	(LIB)	23%	(LIB)	43%	(LIB)
	68%	(CONS)	74%	(CONS)	56%	(CONS)

Key Votes

1) Reagan 81 Budget	FOR	5) $ to El Salvador	FOR	9) Poor Pay Food Stamps	AGN
2) Reagan 81 Tax Cut	FOR	6) Saudi AWACS Sale	FOR	10) Ban Crt Busing Order	FOR
3) Bal Budget Amend	FOR	7) Ban Abortion	FOR	11) Clinch Riv Brdr Rctr	FOR
4) Gas & Road Tax	AGN	8) Nerve Gas Prod	AGN	12) Legal Services Corp	AGN

Election Results

1978 general	Thad Cochran (R)	263,089	(45%)	($1,052,303)
	Maurice Danton (D)	185,454	(32%)	($873,518)
	Charles Evers (I)	133,646	(23%)	($135,119)
1978 primary	Thad Cochran (R)	50,857	(69%)	
	Charles Pickering (R)	22,880	(31%)	($187,565)
1972 general	James O. Eastland (D)	375,102	(58%)	($410,221)
	Gil Carmichael (R)	249,779	(39%)	($154,913)

Campaign Contributions and Expenditures

1977-78		PACS brkdwn			
Receipts	$1,201,259	Agr	$9,700	Ideo	$15,500
Expend.	$1,052,303	Bus	$135,925	Lbr	$7,750
Unspent	$148,955	Hlth	$14,100	Prof	$5,200

GOVERNOR

Gov. William F. Winter (D) Elected 1979, term expires Jan. 1984; b. Feb. 21, 1923, Grenada Cnty.; home, Jackson; U. of MS, B.A. 1943, J.D. 1949; Presbyterian.

Career Army, WWII; MS House of Reps., 1948–56; MS Tax Collector, 1956–64, Treasurer, 1964–68; Dem. Nominee for Gov., 1967, 1975; Practicing atty., 1968–72, 1976–79; Lt. Gov. of MS, 1972–76.

Offices The Capitol, Jackson 39205, 601-354-7575.

Election Results

1979 gen.	William F. Winter (D)	413,620	(61%)
	Gil Carmichael (R)	263,702	(39%)
1979 runoff	William F. Winter (D)	386,174	(57%)
	Evelyn Gandy (D)	295,835	(43%)
1979 prim.	Evelyn Gandy (D)	224,746	(30%)
	William F. Winter (D)	183,944	(25%)
	John Arthur Eaves (D)	143,411	(19%)
	Jim Herring (D)	135,812	(18%)
	Two others (D)	49,250	(7%)
1975 gen.	Cliff Finch (D)	369,568	(54%)
	Gil Carmichael (R)	319,632	(46%)

MISSISSIPPI — Congressional Districts, Counties, and Selected Places — (5 Districts)

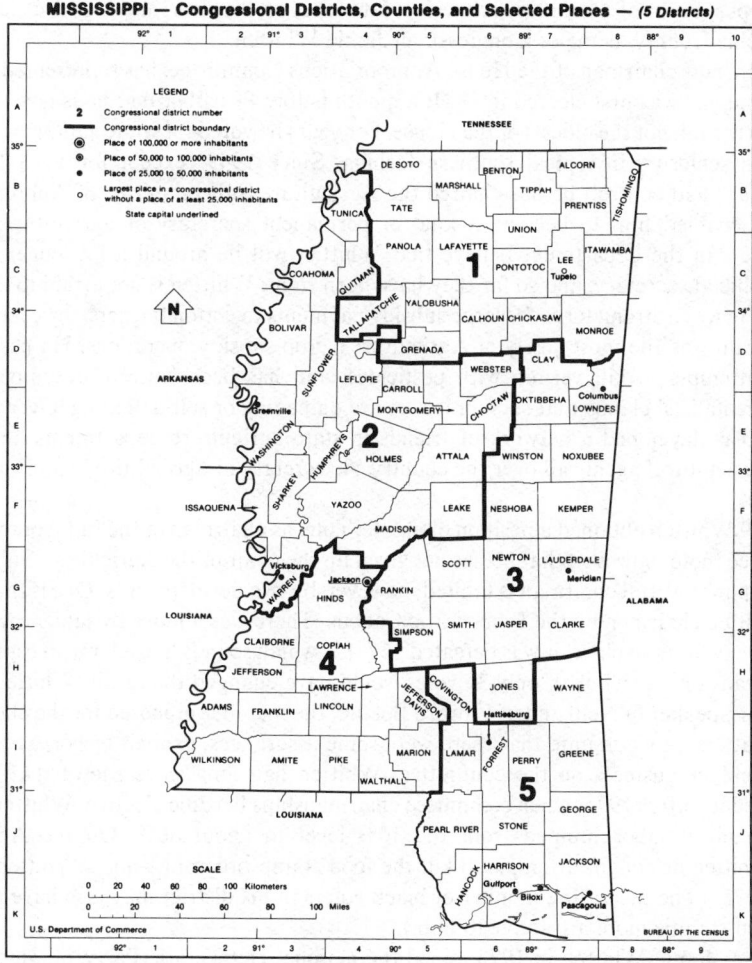

FIRST DISTRICT

The 1st congressional district of Mississippi spans the northernmost section of the state, from the cotton-rich Delta near the Mississippi River to Tishomingo County on the Tennessee River in the state's northeastern corner. The eastern part of the district is about 90% white; these are white farmers whose families have been working these hardscrabble farms for 150 years, and only in the past decade or so have found much affluence or ease. The Tennessee Valley Authority brought electricity here; this is one part of Mississippi where the federal government is not regarded as an evil intruder by articulate white opinion. The western part of the district is Faulkner country; it includes his hometown of Oxford, site of the University of Mississippi, and of his Yoknapatawpha County as well. The district includes the

Mississippi suburbs of Memphis, Tennessee; it touches on the river; and it goes as far west as Tallahatchie County, home of Congressman Jamie Whitten.

Whitten, now chairman of the House Appropriations Committee, has represented this area a long time. He was first elected in 1941, a month before Pearl Harbor; he is now the senior member (though not the oldest) of the House. For years he voted for white supremacy and advanced in seniority, in typical southern fashion. Since 1949 (except for 1953–55, when Republicans had control) he has chaired the Agriculture Subcommittee of Appropriations. This has enabled him to become a kind of permanent secretary of agriculture; the top bureaucrats in the department believe that Whitten will be around a lot longer than the current official secretary; and so far they have been right. Whitten is not afraid to use his influence. He was a strong force for large subsidy payments to cotton farmers; for years the cotton program was the most costly of Agriculture's crop subsidy operations. He has strongly backed attempts to kill vermin with pesticides, and has been entirely unsympathetic to environmentalists' claims that such practices are damaging or self-defeating. Over the years Whitten has developed a network of friends in state agriculture departments and among county agricultural agents all over the country. A secretary of agriculture ignores him at his own peril.

In 1979 Whitten obtained a position of greater note, as chairman of the full Appropriations Committee (note, however, that he has not given up the chair of the Agriculture Subcommittee). His power as full chairman is limited, however, by two developments. One is the election of committee chairmen by the Democratic Caucus. There was a move by junior members in 1979 to deny him the chair; it was defeated 157–88, which sounds like a large margin, but actually means that a switch of only 35 votes would have changed the result. Whitten had the support of Speaker O'Neill and of Edward Boland, the member proposed for the chair by the rebels; but one must assume that there were some assurances, explicit or not, as to how he would conduct business on the committee. Whitten had long since shown that he could accommodate: after 1975, when committee chairmanships became elective, Whitten's rating from organized labor jumped from the 10% level to about 40%. On the Agriculture Subcommittee he fought attempts to kill the food stamp program—not a Whitten favorite before 1975. (The increasing number of black voters in his district may also have helped to make food stamps more attractive to him.)

In effect, Jamie Whitten in 1975 joined the national Democratic Party, of which he has been a valued and useful member ever since. He opposes the Reagan economic programs, fights Reagan cutbacks in the Appropriations Committee, uses his parliamentary skills (despite an accent unintelligible to many members) to good advantage. His power as Appropriations chairman is diminished, however, by a second development: the emergence of the congressional budget process. This was created in large part out of discontent with the appropriations process, which seemed to proceed without regard for revenues and taxes and in which different subcommittees seemed to act—Whitten's is one example—without much regard for the committee or the House as a whole. Whitten naturally resents what he regards as intrusions by the Budget Committee into Appropriations' jurisdiction, and tries to fight them off. That gets him into occasional squabbles with the leadership, and makes life more frustrating than he must have expected 20 years ago, as he looked forward to the chairmanship that was surely to become his.

Whitten has been reelected easily in his district, which, as it happens, moved to the national Democratic Party at about the same time he did. He turns 74 in 1984 and is still in good health and fine shape; he served most of his years on Appropriations under chairmen older than he was in 1982, and there is no reason to expect him to retire.

The People Pop. 1980: 504,714, up 17.7% 1970–80; voting age pop. 344,906; 23% Black, 1% Span. orig. 23% housing units rented. Median owner $30,200; renter $96. Households: 80% family, 46% with children, 67% married couples.

Presidential Vote

1980	Reagan (R)	76,633	(43%)
	Carter (D)	99,085	(55%)
	Anderson (I)	3,073	(2%)

Rep. Jamie L. Whitten (D) Elected 1941; b. Apr. 18, 1910, Cascilla; home, Charleston; U. of MS; Presbyterian.

Career Practicing atty.; School principal; MS House of Reps., 1931; Dist. Prosecuting Atty., 17th Judicial Dist., 1933–41.

Offices 2314 RHOB, 202-225-4306. Also P.O. Bldg., Charleston 38921, 601-647-2413.

Committee *Appropriations* (Chairman). Subcommittee: Agriculture, Rural Development (Chairman).

Group Ratings

	ADA	ACLU	COPE	CFA	LCV	LWV	NTU	NSI	COC	ACA	CSFC
1982	45	21	32	54	43	36	39	100	38	33	43
1981	30	—	30	57	26	—	5	—	22	35	47
1980	28	20	29	29	27	56	35	90	77	57	53

National Journal Ratings

	Economic		Foreign		Cultural	
1982	57%	(LIB)	49%	(LIB)	37%	(LIB)
	43%	(CONS)	51%	(CONS)	63%	(CONS)
1981	66%	(LIB)	3%	(LIB)	33%	(LIB)
	34%	(CONS)	87%	(CONS)	67%	(CONS)

Key Votes

1) Reagan 81 Budget	AGN	5) Incr SS Rtmt Age	AGN	9) Poor Pay Food Stamps	FOR
2) Reagan 81 Tax Cut	AGN	6) Saudi AWACS Sale	FOR	10) Ban Crt Busing Order	FOR
3) Bal Budget Amend	FOR	7) $ for MX Missile	AGN	11) Auto Local Content	FOR
4) Gas & Road Tax	AGN	8) Nerve Gas Prod	AGN	12) Nuclear Arms Freeze	—

Election Results

1982 general	Jamie L. Whitten (D)	79,726	(71%)	($163,819)
	Fran Fawcett (R)	32,750	(29%)	($57,027)
1982 primary	Jamie L. Whitten (D)	21,042	(84%)	
	Jim Richardson (D)	3,936	(16%)	
1980 general	Jamie L. Whitten (D)	104,269	(63%)	($67,794)
	T. K. Moffett (R)	61,292	(37%)	($75,353)

Campaign Contributions and Expenditures

1981-82		Direct Cont. 81-82			PACS brkdwn		
Receipts	$151,754	Indiv	$26,772	Agr	$25,650	Ideo	$3,000
Expend.	$163,819	Party	$100	Bus	$66,690	Lbr	$7,750
Unspent	$53,967	PACS	$114,039	Hlth	$6,250	Prof	$9,600

Indep Expend: For: $749 (NRA) Agn: $6,053 (NCPAC)

SECOND DISTRICT

The 2d congressional district of Mississippi, created by court order in a Voting Rights Act case, is the first black majority congressional district created in Mississippi since blacks became able to vote in significant numbers in 1965. It is essentially a Delta district. The Delta is the incredibly fertile land, criss-crossed by the Mississippi and a dozen tributaries, which was not really settled until well after the Civil War. It was originally swampy land, often flooded; but in the late 19th century the land was drained, the great river lined with levees, and the Illinois Central tracks laid down from Memphis to New Orleans. Wanderers through the Delta wilderness discovered that the topsoil here, accumulated over centuries of Mississippi spring floods, reached depths of 25 feet.

So the Delta became home to the state's largest and most productive cotton producers. Naturally, they needed labor, and they persuaded blacks, now free but still in many ways dependent on whites, to move to the Delta. The patina of graciousness which often covered the brutality of slavery was not apparent in the Delta. The new planters didn't bother to build beautiful mansions of the antebellum type, but lived in more functional, austere houses; they were less likely to feel paternalistic responsibilities for their black laborers. They were capitalists, not cavaliers; and when cotton-picking machines were developed in the 1940s, they did everything they could (perhaps in anticipation of the day when blacks would get the vote) to encourage local blacks to move north to Chicago or Memphis. Welfare payments and aid to the poor are as stingy—or nonexistent—in the Delta as anywhere in the United States.

The 2d district extends almost from Memphis in the north down to Vicksburg in the south; east from the Mississippi it proceeds through the Delta region to a few heavily white hill counties. When it was created, Congressman David Bowen, a 10-year House veteran, announced he would retire; black leaders endorsed state legislator Robert Clark, chairman of the House Education Committee. Clark won the first primary with an absolute majority and had strong backing from Governor William Winter. But the Republicans had been busy even before the new district lines were drawn and Bowen quit. Their candidate, Webb Franklin, was a 41-year-old former Democratic judge, a lawyer from Greenwood whose attitudes toward issues were those conventional among the Delta professional and landowning elite. Naturally there were racial overtones in the campaign, but what was fascinating was the extent to which race hatred was not apparent. Clark campaigned as an experienced legislator who was able to work closely with whites; Franklin campaigned as something approaching a standard Republican.

In the end Franklin won 50%–48%. Clark's 48% looked suspiciously similar to the 48% of the district's adult population who are black. There clearly was some polarization, which reached up even into the Senate race; John Stennis, running with black support and as a supporter of the Voting Rights Act, carried the district with 61%, winning only a small percentage of white votes here, even as he was winning huge majorities from whites in the hill counties. Still, it is apparent from the returns that Clark picked up significant numbers of white votes in several eastern counties and that he ran well ahead of black percentages in some Delta counties. He ran well behind black percentages in others. One reason is that black voter registration has been low in many of these counties; here and there intimidation may still be a factor. Another reason is that Clark, by trying to avoid a campaign based on race, may have failed to arouse enthusiasm in some black voters.

In any case, this seems likely to be a seriously contested district in 1982. In national elections and on economic issues it is basically Democratic; with a slightly different turnout Clark would have won and he may try again. If not, it is possible that either another black or a white candidate could run a strong race.

The People Pop. 1980: 504,654, up 1.3% 1970–80; voting age pop. 327,172; 48% Black, 1% Span. orig. 33% housing units rented. Median owner $27,100; renter $80. Households: 76% family, 46% with children, 57% married couples.

Presidential Vote

1980	Reagan (R)	74,539	(44%)
	Carter (D)	93,044	(55%)
	Anderson (I)	1,997	(1%)

Rep. Webb Franklin (R) Elected 1982; b. Dec. 13, 1941, Greenwood; home, Greenwood; MS State U., B.A. 1963, U. of MS Law Sch., J.D. 1966; Episcopal.

Career U.S. Army Judge Advoc. General's Corps, 1966; Asst. District Atty., 4th Dist., 1972–78; Circuit Judge, 4th Dist., 1978–82.

Offices 508 CHOB, 202-225-5876. Also Federal Bldg., Greenwood 38930, 601-453-0126.

Committees Agriculture (15th). Subcommittees: Cotton, Rice, and Sugar; Department Operations, Research, and Foreign Agriculture; Tobacco and Peanuts. *Merchant Marine and Fisheries* (14th). Subcommittees: Coast Guard and Navigation; Fisheries and Wildlife Conservation and the Environment.

Group Ratings and Key Votes: Newly Elected

Election Results

1982 general	Webb Franklin (R)	74,450	(50%)	($318,376)
	Robert Clark (D)	71,536	(48%)	($208,136)
1982 primary	Webb Franklin (R)	7,166	(99%)	
1980 general	David R. Bowen (D)	96,750	(70%)	($56,912)
	Frank Drake (R)	42,300	(30%)	($21,573)

Campaign Contributions and Expenditures

1981-82		*Direct Cont. 81-82*				*PACS brkdwn*		
Receipts	$316,939	Indiv	$223,043	Agr	$200	Ideo	$6,650
Expend.	$318,376	Party	$28,005	Bus	$42,381	Lbr	$—
Unspent	$4,246	PACS	$58,259	Hlth	$6,000	Prof	$—

Indirect Party Expend: $35,437 *Indep Expend:* For: $891 (NRA)

THIRD DISTRICT

The 3d congressional district of Mississippi is the east central part of the state, a mostly rural area studded with small cities. Blacks are not in the majority today, but some day they may be a much larger percentage than they are today: 27% of this district's adult population and 40% of its children are black. The 3d stretches from Columbus and Starkville, home of Mississippi State University, in the north, to Laurel in the south. Its largest city is Meridian, near the Alabama border, but the district also includes the Rankin County suburbs of Jackson, a relatively high income area and one of the most Republican counties in the state.

The congressman from the 3d district is Sonny Montgomery. He is an exemplar of the traditional southern Democrat: devoted to his work, a delightful companion, dedicated to his principles, but possessed of a fine sense of humor. A veteran of both World War II and Korea, Montgomery serves on the Armed Services and Veterans' Affairs Committee. In 1981 he became chairman of Veterans' Affairs, a body led for years by conservative southerners. Veterans' Affairs bills are traditionally considered on the floor of the House under a closed rule, which means that no amendments are allowed; that means that the bill Montgomery and his allies on the committee report out is the one that passes. Montgomery has been criticized for putting too much emphasis on programs for older veterans and not enough for those of the Vietnam era; he has tended to be skeptical about compensating veterans for exposure to Agent Orange, for example, and has resisted some counseling programs sought by other committee members. But Montgomery may bend on these and similar issues. The major veterans' organizations themselves are changing (the VFW and American Legion endorsed compensation for Agent Orange by 1983), and Montgomery has had to face, and stands to face in the future, challenges for his chair. He was one of the few senior southern Democrats who voted consistently with the Reagan administration (as he has with past Republican administrations)—something that stirs resentment not only among northern liberals but also among southern party loyalists. But by 1983 he was stressing his desire to work with the Democratic leadership, with which he is on friendly personal terms.

So Montgomery is likely to bend on some veterans' issues, and perhaps change positions entirely. He surely will remain, however, an enthusiast for things military; he is Capitol Hill's strongest champion of the Reserves and the National Guard, which have much support in Congress, although they were used sparingly or not at all in the Vietnam war.

Montgomery is regularly reelected without significant opposition and by near-unanimous votes in his district. A considerable change in its boundaries in the 1982 redistricting seems to have made no political difference for him.

The People Pop. 1980: 503,763, up 17.0% 1970–80; voting age pop. 346,476; 27% Black, 1% Span. orig., 1% Am. In. 23% housing units rented. Median owner $31,700; renter $113. Households: 79% family, 45% with children, 64% married couples.

Presidential Vote

1980	Reagan (R)	100,241	(55%)
	Carter (D)	80,348	(44%)
	Anderson (I)	2,197	(1%)

Rep. G. V. (Sonny) Montgomery (D) Elected 1966; b. Aug. 5, 1920, Meridian; home, Meridian; MS St. U., B.S.; Episcopal.

Career Army, WWII and Korea; Owner, Montgomery Ins. Agcy.; V.P., Greater MS Life Ins. Co.; MS Senate, 1956–66.

Offices 2184 RHOB, 202-225-5031. Also P.O. Box 5618, Meridian 39301, 601-693-6681.

Committees *Armed Services* (6th). Subcommittees: Military Installations and Facilities; Military Personnel and Compensation. *Veterans' Affairs* (Chairman). Subcommittees: Compensation, Pension and Insurance; Oversight and Investigations (Chairman).

Group Ratings

	ADA	ACLU	COPE	CFA	LCV	LWV	NTU	NSI	COC	ACA	CSFC
1982	5	0	11	15	25	8	66	100	73	91	62
1981	0	—	11	21	7	—	66	—	83	79	38
1980	0	10	6	14	17	20	55	100	73	58	69

National Journal Ratings

	Economic		Foreign		Cultural	
1982	62	(LIB)	43%	(LIB)	54%	(LIB)
	37%	(CONS)	57%	(CONS)	45%	(CONS)
1981	53%	(LIB)	38%	(LIB)	45%	(LIB)
	46%	(CONS)	61%	(CONS)	55%	(CONS)

Key Votes

1) Reagan 81 Budget	FOR	5) Incr SS Rtmt Age	FOR
2) Reagan 81 Tax Cut	FOR	6) Saudi AWACS Sale	FOR
3) Bal Budget Amend	FOR	7) $ for MX Missile	FOR
4) Gas & Road Tax	FOR	8) Nerve Gas Prod	FOR

9) Poor Pay Food Stamps	FOR
10) Ban Crt Busing Order	FOR
11) Auto Local Content	AGN
12) Nuclear Arms Freeze	AGN

Election Results

1982 general	G. V. (Sonny) Montgomery (D) ...	114,530	(93%)	($61,794)
	James Bradshaw (R)	8,519	(7%)	($0)
1982 primary	G. V. (Sonny) Montgomery (D) ...	26,988	(92%)	
	James E. Parker (D)	2,223	(8%)	
1980 general	G. V. (Sonny) Montgomery (D) ...	128,035	(100%)	($9,909)

Campaign Contributions and Expenditures

1981-82		Direct Cont. 81-82		PACS brkdwn			
Receipts	$92,139	Indiv	$37,824	Agr	$2,200	Ideo	$1,100
Expend.	$61,794	PACS	$42,451	Bus	$33,500	Lbr	$1,000
Unspent	$98,526			Hlth	$4,500	Prof	$250

FOURTH DISTRICT

Mississippi's capital and largest city, Jackson is the center of one of the state's two significant urban concentrations. In the 1960s and 1970s it grew more rapidly, in population and in its economy, than any other part of the state except perhaps the Gulf Coast. It is still only a small city by northern standards, but the boom atmosphere is apparent. On the north side of town, in new subdivisions of pleasant, large colonial houses under huge, overhanging trees, you can get a sense of what growth has meant to Jackson—especially when you consider that at least some of the people in these neighborhoods came from humble houses in rural Mississippi. Even the less well-to-do—people who grew up poor and now make $29,000 a year, more than they ever dreamed of—tend to think of themselves as the new rich, and in fact money goes a good deal further in Jackson than in a large metropolitan area. This kind of growth has helped to make Jackson one of the most Republican parts of the state.

But there are countervailing political forces. One is Jackson's large black community, increasingly involved in politics. Another is the appeal of Governor William Winter. A Democrat with a background in the Jackson establishment, Winter was an early supporter of civil rights who also has an appeal to upper-class whites. Since his election in 1979, he has worked to increase black turnout and black participation in the Democratic Party and to increase the appeal of the party in the wealthy areas as well. As a result, Jackson has been trending Democratic in statewide elections; it is still one of the most Republican parts of the state, but the Republican margins are declining.

That might present difficulties for Senator Thad Cochran, who must run for reelection in 1984; Jackson is his political base, and he served as congressman from the 4th congressional district, which includes Jackson and southwest Mississippi, for six years. Like his successor, Republican Jon Hinson, Cochran first won against split opposition; that will not necessarily happen again. Hinson lost his seat spectacularly in 1981. He announced in 1980 that he had survived a 1977 fire in a Washington homosexual movie house, and said that he had reformed; but in February 1981 he was arrested in a House office building men's room and charged with a sexual offense.

A special election was set for June, and it went quite differently from previous 4th district contests. It was run under a special law, similar to Louisiana's, providing for a runoff between the top two primary candidates, regardless of party; this discouraged a separate black candidacy. The Republican candidate, Liles Williams, head of a Jackson construction business, ran a well-financed campaign. But he lost by 1,027 votes out of more than 100,000 cast to Wayne Dowdy, a Democrat from the small city of McComb. Dowdy combined an appeal to rural whites with strong support from blacks in Jackson; he promised to vote for renewal of the Voting Rights Act—a clear contrast with his opponent. With the help of Governor Winter, he upset Williams and gave the national Democrats—then absorbing loss after loss in the House—a needed tonic. In the 1982 election, Dowdy won again. He still did not carry Hinds County and Jackson, but he came close, and he carried all but one of the smaller counties. An independent black candidate was spurned by black political activists and won only 2% of the vote.

Dowdy has shown political adroitness in Washington as well, winning a coveted seat on the Energy and Commerce Committee. On that body he is likely to support some forms of government regulation and oppose others; it would be surprising if he, as a representative of an oil- and gas-producing district, should oppose deregulation of natural gas. The closeness of the margin in 1982, however, means that Republicans will probably make a serious effort once again in a seat which they did, after all, hold for nine years.

The People Pop. 1980: 503,890, up 12.1% 1970–80; voting age pop. 345,780; 41% Black, 1% Span. orig. 28% housing units rented. Median owner $34,000; renter $127. Households: 76% family, 44% with children, 58% married couples.

Presidential Vote

1980	Reagan (R)	95,760	(50%)
	Carter (D)	93,684	(49%)
	Anderson (I)	2,307	(1%)

Rep. Wayne Dowdy (D) Elected July 7, 1981; b. July 27, 1943, Fitzgerald, GA; home, McComb; Millsaps Col., B.A. 1965, Jackson School of Law, LL.B. 1968; Methodist.

Career Practicing atty., 1968–1981.

Offices 214 CHOB, 202-225-5865. Also P.O. Box 569, Jackson 39205, 601-969-3300; and Commerce Bldg., 521 Main St., Su. C-1, Natchez 39120, 601-446-8628.

Committees *Energy and Commerce* (22d). Subcommittees: Commerce, Transportation, and Tourism; Fossil and Synthetic Fuels. *Veterans' Affairs* (10th). Subcommittees: Compensation, Pension, and Insurance; Hospitals and Health Care.

Group Ratings

	ADA	ACLU	COPE	CFA	LCV	LWV	NTU	NSI	COC	ACA	CSFC
1982	45	—	83	69	51	—	15	80	39	32	37
1981	21	—	73	50	10	—	30	—	31	57	51

National Journal Ratings

	Economic		Foreign		Cultural	
1982	68%	(LIB)	58%	(LIB)	55%	(LIB)
	32%	(CONS)	42%	(CONS)	44%	(CONS)
1981	55%	(LIB)	32%	(LIB)	41%	(LIB)
	45%	(CONS)	68%	(CONS)	59%	(CONS)

Key Votes

1) Reagan 81 Budget	—	5) Incr SS Rtmt Age	AGN	9) Poor Pay Food Stamps	AGN
2) Reagan 81 Tax Cut	AGN	6) Saudi AWACS Sale	AGN	10) Ban Crt Busing Order	FOR
3) Bal Budget Amend	FOR	7) $ for MX Missile	AGN	11) Auto Local Content	FOR
4) Gas & Road Tax	—	8) Nerve Gas Prod	—	12) Nuclear Arms Freeze	FOR

Election Results

1982 general	Wayne Dowdy (D)	79,977	(53%)	($357,109)
	Liles Williams (R)	69,469	(46%)	($980,676)
1982 primary	Wayne Dowdy (D) unopposed			
1981 special	Wayne Dowdy (D)	55,656	(50%)	($277,023)
	Liles Williams (R)	54,744	(50%)	($372,474)
1980 general	Jon C. Hinson (R)	69,321	(39%)	($252,966)
	Lester Burl McLemore (I)	52,959	(30%)	($43,198)
	Britt R. Singletary (D)	52,303	(29%)	($104,871)

Campaign Contributions and Expenditures

1981-82		Direct Cont. 81-82		PACS brkdwn			
Receipts	$377,207	Indiv	$98,173	Agr	$20,750	Ideo	$16,400
Expend.	$357,109	Party	$16,539	Bus	$30,950	Lbr	$95,600
Unspent	$17,744	PACS	$175,393	Hlth	$5,750	Prof	$2,000
		Cand	$80,000				

Indep Expend: For: $1,395 (NRA, AFL-CIO)

FIFTH DISTRICT

The 5th congressional district of Mississippi is the state's Gulf Coast district. About 60% of its residents live on the coastal strip that includes the cities of Biloxi, Gulfport, and Pascagoula—which together form the only significant urban concentration in Mississippi outside Jackson. The remainder live inland, in farm counties or in the medium-sized city of Hattiesburg. Much of this land is piney woods and paper mill country—scrubby land that was not good enough for antebellum plantations. As a result there are relatively few blacks here: only 17% of the district's adults are black, the lowest percentage in Mississippi.

The 5th district has been a boom area economically and one whose residents are pleased to ascribe their success to the free enterprise system. They are mostly from the South, and mostly from less affluent surroundings than they now enjoy. They like to think of themselves as rugged individualists, people who have made their own way. Yet this area owes a fair amount of its prosperity and growth to the federal government. The Pentagon spends about $600 million a year at the Litton Shipyards in Pascagoula, which is the state's largest single employer; it didn't hurt that John Stennis was chairman of the Senate Armed Services Committee and 5th district Congressman William Colmer chairman of the House Rules Committee when the first big contract was awarded here. The 5th district also benefits, as all of Mississippi does, from federal programs like food stamps, which target their dollars to low-income areas.

This federal largesse does not prevent the 5th district from being Mississippi's most Republican seat. It went Republican twice against fellow southerner Jimmy Carter, and in 1972 it gave Richard Nixon his best percentage in any of the 435 congressional districts, a whopping 87%.

The 5th district's congressman, Trent Lott, got his start on Capitol Hill as an assistant to Colmer; when Colmer retired in 1972 he ran for the seat—as a Republican. Some considered that a daring decision then, but in retrospect it seems to have been prudent. A man of Colmer's and Lott's views could never expect to hold a major chairmanship on the Democratic side these days, but Lott is the number-two man in the Republican leadership, the House Minority Whip.

His rise has been rapid. In his first term he served on the Judiciary Committee, where he defended Richard Nixon in the impeachment hearings. In 1975 he got a seat on the Rules Committee, and in 1980 was elected Republican whip.

Lott combines party regularity and dependability with strong views on issues. He is instinctively a loyal party man who does not want to make waves—which is one reason he got the whip post. But he does want to change America in some important ways. As a onetime employee of one of Congress's leading segregationists, he seems to have difficulty understanding how others will perceive racial issues: he was the man who kept urging the Reagan administration to grant a tax exemption to Bob Jones University. But that seems to have caused him little trouble in the House. There he is a crisp speaker, a fluent and competent debater, a solid partisan.

Lott might have run for the Senate in 1982, but he decided not to; the next opening will be in 1988, and he seems unlikely to run after spending 16 years in the House. Besides, by that time he could be House Republican Leader. The succession from the whip post to the minority leadership is by no means automatic; and in all likelihood when Robert Michel retires as leader there will be a serious contest for the post. Lott is a likely and serious contender, though not necessarily the favorite.

Lott has not had any trouble winning reelection in this district since he first won in 1972.

The People Pop. 1980: 503,617, up 22.9% 1970–80; voting age pop. 342,107; 17% Black, 1% Span. orig., 1% Asian orig. 25% housing units rented. Median owner $33,400; renter $155. Households: 78% family, 47% with children, 64% married couples.

Presidential Vote

1980	Reagan (R)	93,916	(59%)
	Carter (D)	63,120	(40%)
	Anderson (I)	2,469	(2%)

Rep. Trent Lott (R) Elected 1972; b. Oct. 9, 1941, Grenada; home, Pascagoula; U. of MS, B.A. 1963, J.D. 1967; Baptist.

Career Practicing atty., 1967–68; A. A. to U.S. Rep. William M. Colmer, 1968–72.

Offices 2400 RHOB, 202-225-5772. Also P.O. Box 1557, Gulfport 39501, 601-864-7670.

Committee *Minority Whip. Rules* (3d). Subcommittees: Rules of the House; The Legislative Process.

Group Ratings

	ADA	ACLU	COPE	CFA	LCV	LWV	NTU	NSI	COC	ACA	CSFC
1982	5	4	16	8	21	8	77	100	70	91	68
1981	0	—	17	14	6	—	79	—	95	86	76
1980	6	13	12	14	17	30	55	100	81	83	81

National Journal Ratings

	Economic		Foreign		Cultural	
1982	25%	(LIB)	25%	(LIB)	34%	(LIB)
	74%	(CONS)	74%	(CONS)	65%	(CONS)
1981	4%	(LIB)	30%	(LIB)	2%	(LIB)
	79%	(CONS)	70%	(CONS)	98%	(CONS)

Key Votes

1) Reagan 81 Budget	FOR	5) Incr SS Rtmt Age	FOR	9) Poor Pay Food Stamps	FOR
2) Reagan 81 Tax Cut	FOR	6) Saudi AWACS Sale	FOR	10) Ban Crt Busing Order	FOR
3) Bal Budget Amend	FOR	7) $ for MX Missile	FOR	11) Auto Local Content	AGN
4) Gas & Road Tax	—	8) Nerve Gas Prod	FOR	12) Nuclear Arms Freeze	AGN

Election Results

1982 general	Trent Lott (R)	82,884	(79%)	($115,857)
	Arlan (Blackie) Coate (D)	224,634	(21%)	($3,013)
1982 primary	Trent Lott (R) unopposed			
1980 general	Trent Lott (R)	131,559	(74%)	($163,118)
	Jimmy McVeay (D)	46,416	(26%)	($73,054)

Campaign Contributions and Expenditures

1981-82		*Direct Cont. 81-82*			*PACS brkdwn*			
Receipts	$226,509	Indiv	$73,073	Agr	$11,200	Ideo	$8,300
Expend.	$115,857	Party	$19,388	Bus	$89,700	Lbr	$6,700
Unspent	$168,295	PACS	$127,220	Hlth	$9,300	Prof	$2,150

MISSOURI

Missouri is the place where north and south, east and west come together. It was the first state created entirely out of territory west of the Mississippi River: admitted to the Union in 1821, as part of the Missouri Compromise. At that time Missouri jutted far out into the frontier: St. Louis was not long removed from the trading post Lewis and Clark passed through; the site of Kansas City was just another lookout point on the bluffs overlooking the Missouri River as it flowed from the northwest. Missouri was the northernmost slave state. It sent proslavery raiders over the border into the Kansas Territory in the 1850s to fight settlers shipped in by abolitionists, and in the 1860s it had its own civil war in the hilly counties along the Missouri River. Missouri was a gateway to the West, an avenue for the great Yankee migrations west from Ohio, Indiana, and Illinois and the southern migration west from Kentucky (Missouri is where Daniel Boone finally came to rest); it was the eastern terminus of the Pony Express and the Transcontinental Railroad. Missouri is almost literally at the center of the country; the geographic center of the coterminous 48 states is not far away in Kansas, and the population center is in Missouri just southwest of St. Louis.

Settled early, with below-average population growth for most of the 20th century, Missouri has kept a civic life and politics akin to what it had around the turn of the century. As in other border states, divisions have fallen on Civil War lines, but the geographical pattern is not what you might expect. Little Dixie, first settled by Virginians, is in the northeast part of the state; the southwest, in the Ozarks, was Union and is Republican country. St. Louis, once a German Republican island in a southern Democratic sea, became heavily Democratic in the 1930s; now metropolitan St. Louis seems to be leaning Republican again. The Kansas City area, less anchored to the state, is the most volatile part politically. So political preference is still a matter of economic divisions superimposed on Civil War regional divides. On cultural and foreign issues there is in Missouri the sort of consensus which obtained nationally 30 years ago. The population here tends to be older than the national average, and lives generally within traditional family patterns.

Missouri's political inclinations are personified in its most famous politician, Harry Truman. Always a strong partisan Democrat, Truman had a grandfather who served in the Confederate army, and his mother, who lived to see her son in the White House, remained a Confederate sympathizer all her life. Truman made his career, however, in the Kansas City area, where he worked his way up with the support of a political machine and learned to deal with the diverse ethnic and racial groups that make up the modern Democratic Party. Truman was in effect torn: the man who integrated the armed forces reacted negatively to the civil rights movement of the 1960s; the man who campaigned as the champion of organized labor also tried to break coal strikes and seized the steel mills; the man who made his career in big cities seemed to many a country boy—which made political sense in a state with two big metropolitan areas, but half its votes cast outside them.

Presidential politics. Near the center of the nation geographically, Missouri is also near the center in partisan preference. Presidential elections here over the last 30 years have always been close and have usually hewed close to the national average; the one time in the 20th century Missouri hasn't supported the winning presidential candidate was in 1956, when it went for Adlai Stevenson. In four of the last eight elections, the winning candidate has carried the state by less than 30,000 votes; Jimmy Carter won here by 70,000 in 1976 and lost by 143,000 in 1980, out of about two million votes cast each time. Carter won in 1976 because of his strength in Missouri's rural counties, which ever since have been more Democratically inclined in statewide races than they were in the 1965–75 period. Missouri is always a hotly contested race, then, in close elections.

Missouri's old-fashioned parties choose their national convention delegates through the party machinery. They are not, however, as centrally controlled or controllable as parties in the culturally and demographically similar state of Indiana.

Senators. Missouri has two well-known senators of two parties whose careers have moved in parallel lines. Both are from prominent families, both were elected attorney general at a very young age, both were first elected to the Senate in unusual circumstances, and both, despite high popularity, were reelected recently by only narrow margins and after experiencing real scares.

The better known nationally is Thomas Eagleton. His father was a prominent lawyer; he was circuit attorney in St. Louis at age 27 and elected attorney general of Missouri in 1960 at 31; lieutenant governor four years later; elected senator when he beat incumbent Edward Long in the primary and Congressman Thomas Curtis in the general in 1968. Then suddenly he became a national figure in 1972: George McGovern selected him to run for vice president; it was revealed that he had undergone shock treatments some years before; he was forced off the ticket. In the short run, that did McGovern more damage than Eagleton; in the long run, it seems to have disqualified this able Missourian for further consideration for national office.

Eagleton, who chaired a minor and now abolished Senate committee (District of Columbia) as a freshman, probably expected to be a considerable power and influence in the Senate in the 1980s. So far he has been disappointed. The Republicans control the Senate; the positions Eagleton would have had have gone to others, and in a Senate pretty well run by

Howard Baker and other Republicans he has little leverage on most issues. Before the 1980 election he must have looked forward to chairing the Governmental Affairs Committee, a post that affords ample chance for publicized investigating, and to holding high ranking seats and subcommittee chairmanships on Labor and Appropriations. He is sometimes part of a committee majority on these bodies, particularly on Labor where two key Republicans often oppose Chairman Orrin Hatch, but he is not in a position to be a leader.

Eagleton is generally counted as a vote for organized labor and for government education and health programs on the Labor Committee. On Appropriations he is the ranking member of the Agriculture Subcommittee and also serves on Defense, where he sometimes joins William Proxmire in supporting cuts but also strongly backs McDonnell–Douglas fighter programs (the company is headquartered in St. Louis and is one of Missouri's largest employers). But to summarize his record this way understates Eagleton's ability as a legislator. He has an original mind, and the capacity to take what others regard as an unorthodox view and to make it the policy of the Senate. At the same time, he is known as a senator other senators can do business with, a man who understands the realities of politics and is willing to accommodate his colleagues even while he pursues his own interests and advances his own views. Some think he is one of the most talented legislators in the Senate, and if the Democrats regain control in 1984, he may have a chance to demonstrate that.

Eagleton had a surprisingly close race in 1980. St. Louis County Executive Gene McNary started with a good base in the St. Louis area and took advantage of the national trend to Republicans. Only in the last weeks did Eagleton turn the campaign around, in large part by running against the National Conservative Political Action Committee (NCPAC) and its tactics. Almost all of Eagleton's margin came from metropolitan Kansas City, the most electorally volatile part of the state—evidence of how closely contested this race was. No one expected Eagleton to be in such trouble, and in a less Republican year he would have won easily; nonetheless, he can no longer count on a free ride and may attract strong competition in 1986.

Missouri's other senator is John Danforth. His family, which started Ralston Purina, is one of the wealthiest in the nation, and very philanthropic; he has a divinity degree, is an ordained minister, and sometimes seems to approach politics with a churchy intensity. Danforth was elected attorney general of Missouri at age 32, in 1968—a very unusual victory for a Republican then—and nearly beat Senator Stuart Symington in 1970. Six years later, he was not a heavy favorite in the Senate race; but the Democratic nominee, Congressman Jerry Litton, died in a plane crash on primary night, and Danforth easily beat the substitute, former Governor Warren Hearnes, in November.

Danforth seems to concentrate on economic issues. He has seats on the Finance and Commerce Committees and important subcommittee chairmanships. He is one Republican who has generally taken the lead on the side of the aging industrial states and in favor of energy consumers rather than producers. He chairs the Subcommittee on Surface Transportation, with jurisdiction over trucking and the railroads. He also chairs the International Trade Subcommittee, potentially one of the most important in Congress. He and Lloyd Bentsen, the ranking Republican, called for restrictions on auto imports from Japan in 1981; whereupon the Reagan administration and the Japanese proceeded to agree on "voluntary" restraints. Danforth seems to have no strong philosophic commitment to either free trade or protection; his vision of Missouri as an aging, energy-consuming state suggests that he may support other forms of protection. His subcommittee could end up as a counterweight to the strongly pro-free trade Trade Subcommittee of Ways and Means in the House. That is ironic, given the free trade views of free market Republicans; it is a reversion, perhaps, to the days when the Republicans were the party of tariffs and the Democrats the party of free trade.

As Danforth's position on trade suggests, he is not philosophically opposed to government interference in the economy. But he is temperamentally disposed to cooperate with presidents of his own party; he believes that Democratic policies put the nation's economy into a mess; he seems to believe that at least some (though surely not all) of the economic discomfort of recent years was necessary to improve the economy in the long run. On foreign policy, he is also inclined to back the administration; only on cultural issues does this Episcopal minister break often with the conservative wing of his party.

Danforth wanted to run a positive campaign in 1982, and win reelection as an endorsement of what he considered his affirmative record. But he did not reckon with his opponent, St. Louis County state Senator Harriett Woods. After an upset victory in the Democratic primary, she ran a strong negative campaign, peppering Danforth with criticisms for supporting Reaganomics, and arguing that she knew what it was like to live on an ordinary income, while Danforth is one of the richest men in the Senate. A former television producer, Woods was able to communicate her message effectively over the medium; by mid-October she was running even with the much better known Danforth. But her campaign ran out of money and pulled its ads for a week; Danforth's well-financed campaign was able to counterattack effectively. Danforth went negative, accusing Woods of demagoguery and distortion. The result—a 51%–49% Danforth victory—was one of the closest in the nation. Interestingly, Danforth carried the once heavily Democratic St. Louis area, even though it is Woods's home; Woods, a TV producer and newspaper reporter from the big city, carried the Kansas City area handily and almost carried rural Missouri. She carried almost every county in southeastern Missouri, carried Little Dixie, did well in the agricultural counties north and west of Kansas City, and even came close to carrying Republican southwest Missouri.

Governor. In his middle 40s, Christopher Bond is approaching the end of his second term as governor; he is ineligible to run in 1984. It will be the first time in a dozen years he hasn't. He was first elected in 1972, at age 33; he lost in an upset to Democrat Joseph Teasdale in 1976; he came back and beat Teasdale in 1980. Like Danforth, Bond is from a rich family and went to Ivy League schools; he returned to Missouri and entered politics as an opponent of the good-old-boy rural Democrats who ran state government, in some cases rather shadily. Most people expect that Bond will be succeeded by the winner of a multi-candidate Democratic primary, but that will not happen automatically. Since Danforth and Bond got into state politics, Republicans have been able to win lower statewide offices in Missouri, and to develop candidates that way; the attorney general currently is a Republican, and may run for governor himself.

Congressional districting. Missouri has nine congressional districts now, one less than in the 1970s. The legislature joined two districts represented by Democrat Ike Skelton and Republican Wendell Bailey. As one might expect, considering the Democratic margins in the legislature, Skelton had the advantage—more of the new territory was his, he had higher percentages there, he had been in longer—and he ended up winning fairly easily. But the new plan did not dislodge the state's other three Republican congressmen, although one was nearly beaten in a district everyone assumed was safely Republican.

The People Est. Pop. 1982: 4,951,000; Pop. 1980: 4,916,686, up 5.1% 1970–80; 2.2% of U.S. total, 15th largest; voting age pop. 3,554,203; 9% Black, 1% Spanish origin. Single ancestry: 13% German, 11% English, 5% Irish, 1% Italian, French, Polish, Dutch. Registered voters (1982): 2,748,726 Total. 14% with 1–3 yrs. col., 13% with 4+ yrs. col. 12.4% below poverty level. 27% housing units rented; median house value: $36,700; median monthly rent: $153. Households: 73% family, 39% with children, 62% married couples.

1982 Share of Federal Tax Burden $11,762,400,000; 1.97% of U.S. total, 17th largest.

1982 Share of Federal Expenditures

	Total		Non-Defense		Defense	
Total Expend	$15,955m	(2.64%)	$9,614m	(2.26%)	$6,341m	(3.55%)
St/Lcl Grants	1,652m	(1.87%)	1,650m	(1.87%)	2m	(5.56%)
Salary/Wages	1,390m	(1.78%)	622m	(2.27%)	768m	(1.52%)
Ind Payments	6,556m	(2.29%)	6,012m	(2.33%)	544m	(1.90%)
Procurement	6,212m	(4.26%)	866m	(2.75%)	5,346m	(4.68%)
Other Programs	145m	(2.68%)	145m	(2.70%)	0m	(0%)
Loan/Insurance	2,123m	(3.32%)	2,100m	(3.40%)	23m	(1.05%)

Political Lineup Governor, Christopher Bond (R). Senators, Thomas F. Eagleton (D) and John C. Danforth (R). Representatives, 9 (6 D and 3 R). State Senate, 34 (22 D and 12 R); State House of Representatives, 163 (110 D and 53 R).

Presidential Vote

1980	Reagan (R)	1,074,181	(51%)
	Carter (D)	931,182	(44%)
	Anderson (I)	77,920	(4%)
1976	Ford (R)	927,443	(47%)
	Carter (D)	998,387	(51%)

SENATORS

Sen. Thomas F. Eagleton (D) Elected 1968, seat up 1986; b. Sept. 4, 1929, St. Louis; home, St. Louis; Amherst Col., B.A. 1950, Harvard U., LL.B. 1953; Roman Catholic.

Career Navy, 1948–49; Practicing atty.; St. Louis Circuit Atty., 1956–60; Atty. Gen. of MO, 1961–65; Lt. Gov. of MO, 1965–69.

Offices 1209 DSOB, 202-224-5721. Also 4039 Fed. Ofc. Bldg., St. Louis 63103, 314-425-5067; and Fed. Bldg., 811 Grand Ave., Rm. 911, Kansas City 64106, 816-374-2747.

Committees *Appropriations* (6th). Subcommittees: Agriculture, Rural Development; Defense; Commerce, Justice, State, the Judiciary; Labor, Health and Human Services, Education; Transportation. *Governmental Affairs* (Ranking Member). Subcommittee: Governmental Efficiency and the District of Columbia. *Labor and Human Resources* (4th). Subcommittees: Education, Arts and Humanities; Family and Human Services; Handicapped; Aging. *Select Committee on Ethics* (3d).

Group Ratings

	ADA	ACLU	COPE	CFA	LCV	LWV	NTU	NSI	COC	ACA	CSFC
1982	85	71	87	80	74	92	12	0	19	10	28
1981	90	—	87	71	89	—	20	—	0	14	29
1980	78	57	89	47	46	75	50	22	39	8	35

National Journal Ratings

	Economic		Foreign		Cultural	
1982	94%	(LIB)	86%	(LIB)	74%	(LIB)
	5%	(CONS)	10%	(CONS)	25%	(CONS)
1981	97%	(LIB)	99%	(LIB)	71%	(LIB)
	2%	(CONS)	0%	(CONS)	27%	(CONS)

Key Votes

1) Reagan 81 Budget AGN	5) $ to El Salvador AGN	9) Poor Pay Food Stamps AGN
2) Reagan 81 Tax Cut AGN	6) Saudi AWACS Sale AGN	10) Ban Crt Busing Order AGN
3) Bal Budget Amend AGN	7) Ban Abortion FOR	11) Clinch Riv Brdr Rctr AGN
4) Gas & Road Tax AGN	8) Nerve Gas Prod AGN	12) Legal Services Corp FOR

Election Results

1980 general	Thomas F. Eagleton (D)	1,074,859	(52%)	($1,272,272)
	Gene McNary (R)	985,399	(48%)	($1,173,161)
1980 primary	Thomas F. Eagleton (D)	553,392	(86%)	
	Two others (D)	91,957	(14%)	
1974 general	Thomas F. Eagleton (D)	735,433	(60%)	($647,143)
	Thomas B. Curtis (R)	480,900	(39%)	($362,804)

Campaign Contributions and Expenditures

1979-80		PACS brkdwn			
Receipts	$1,272,272	Agr	$36,700	Ideo	$20,819
Expend.	$1,390,560	Bus	$112,865	Lbr	$207,450
Unspent	$59,457	Hlth	$22,700	Prof	$9,050

Sen. John C. Danforth (R) Elected 1976, seat up 1988; b. Sept. 5, 1936, St. Louis; home, Flat; Princeton U., A.B. 1958, Yale U., B.D. and LL.B. 1963; Episcopal.

Career Practicing atty., 1963–69; Atty. Gen. of MO, 1969–77; Repub. Nominee for U.S. Senate, 1970.

Offices 460 RSOB, 202-224-6154. Also Railway Exchg. Bldg., 611 Olive St., Su. 1867, St. Louis 63101, 314-425-6381; and Fed. Ofc. Bldg., 811 Grand Ave., Su. 943-945, Kansas City 64106, 816-374-6101.

Committees *Commerce, Science and Transportation* (3d). Subcommittees: Aviation; Consumer; Surface Transportation (Chairman). *Finance* (4th). Subcommittees: Taxation and Debt Management; International Trade (Chairman); Social Security and Income Maintenance Programs. *Governmental Affairs* (8th). Subcommittees: Energy, Nuclear Proliferation and Government Processes; Information Management and Regulatory Affairs (Chairman); Oversight of Government Management.

Group Ratings

	ADA	ACLU	COPE	CFA	LCV	LWV	NTU	NSI	COC	ACA	CSFC
1982	40	43	29	30	24	64	52	80	52	42	66
1981	25	—	32	36	31	—	47	—	89	62	73
1980	50	47	39	20	48	50	44	80	70	48	54

National Journal Ratings

	Economic		Foreign		Cultural	
1982	37%	(LIB)	56%	(LIB)	57%	(LIB)
	62%	(CONS)	43%	(CONS)	42%	(CONS)
1981	34%	(LIB)	40%	(LIB)	53%	(LIB)
	65%	(CONS)	59%	(CONS)	44%	(CONS)

Key Votes

1) Reagan 81 Budget	FOR	5) $ to El Salvador	FOR	9) Poor Pay Food Stamps	AGN
2) Reagan 81 Tax Cut	FOR	6) Saudi AWACS Sale	AGN	10) Ban Crt Busing Order	FOR
3) Bal Budget Amend	FOR	7) Ban Abortion	FOR	11) Clinch Riv Brdr Rctr	FOR
4) Gas & Road Tax	FOR	8) Nerve Gas Prod	AGN	12) Legal Services Corp	FOR

Election Results

1982 general	John C. Danforth (R)	784,876	(51%)	($1,849,025)
	Harriett Woods (D)	758,629	(49%)	($1,193,966)
1982 primary	John C. Danforth (R)	217,162	(74%)	
	Mel Hancock (R)	61,378	(21%)	($35,632)
	Two others (R)	15,289	(5%)	
1976 general	John C. Danforth (R)	1,090,067	(57%)	($741,465)
	Warren E. Hearnes (D)	813,571	(42%)	($660,953)

Campaign Contributions and Expenditures

1979-82		Direct Cont. 79-82		PACS brkdwn			
Receipts	$1,829,501	Indiv	$1,138,122	Agr	$16,100	Ideo	$56,749
Expend.	$1,849,025	Party	$16,368	Bus	$442,876	Lbr	$5,075
Unspent	$9,069	PACS	$573,994	Hlth	$23,500	Prof	$12,125

Indirect Party Expend: $265,608   *Indep Expend:* For: $15,582 (LIFEPAC)

GOVERNOR

Gov. Christopher S. Bond (R) Elected 1980, term expires Jan. 1985; b. Mar. 6, 1939, St. Louis; home, Kansas City; Princeton U., B.A. 1960, U. of VA, J.D. 1963; Presbyterian.

Career Clk. for U.S. Court of Appeals Chf. Judge Elbert P. Tuttle, 5th Ct., Atlanta, GA, 1963–64; Practicing atty., 1964–69; Asst. Atty. Gen. of MO, 1969; MO State Auditor, 1970–72; Gov. of MO, 1973–77; Pres., Great Plains Legal Foundation, 1977–79.

Offices Exec. Ofc., State Capitol Bldg., Jefferson City 65101, 314-751-3222.

Election Results

1980 gen.	Christopher S. Bond (R)	1,098,950	(53%)
	Joseph P. Teasdale (D)	981,884	(47%)
1980 prim.	Christopher S. Bond (R)	223,678	(64%)
	William Phelps (R)	122,867	(35%)
	Two others (R)	5,534	(2%)
1976 gen.	Joseph P. Teasdale (D)	971,184	(50%)
	Christopher S. Bond (R)	958,110	(50%)

MISSOURI — Congressional Districts, Counties, Independent City, and Other Selected Places — (9 Districts)

LEGEND

2   Congressional district number
   Congressional district boundary
◉   Place of 100,000 or more inhabitants
◉   Place of 50,000 to 100,000 inhabitants
●   Place of 25,000 to 50,000 inhabitants
   State capital underlined

Congressional districts established January 7, 1982; all other boundaries are as of January 1, 1980.

FIRST DISTRICT

At the turn of the century St. Louis was the nation's fourth largest city, Chicago's only rival as the transportation and industrial capital of middle America. On the banks of the Mississippi River, just below the point where it is joined by the Missouri, St. Louis was the gateway to the west since the expedition of Lewis and Clark. By 1900, most of the area within the city limits of St. Louis had been built up along the grids of streets and avenues that radiate from downtown St. Louis, mostly in neighborhoods of small, tightly packed brick houses—tightly packed because, in those days before the automobile, people needed to live within walking distance of work, shopping, or horse-drawn trolleys. When the World's Fair (officially the Louisiana Purchase Exposition) was held here in 1904, St. Louis was considered one of the nation's most up-to-date, modern cities.

Now it has a different image. The solidly built neighborhoods which were once so attractive now have little appeal to most Americans. They want space for a yard, trees of their own, and a two-car garage. They fear the crime that has become common in the city—more common as its downtown streets have become deserted at night and its neighborhoods less populated at any time of day. St. Louis, more than any other American city, has become de-populated over the past several decades. In 1930, 821,000 people lived within its city limits;

in 1950, 856,000. By 1980 the figure was down to 453,000—about the same as its population in 1890. Some of the change is accounted for by the aging of its white population and smaller household sizes generally. But some of it represents the abandonment and disappearance of housing units, even public housing projects like Pruitt–Igoe which was demolished several years ago.

In this process of change, St. Louis has become a black majority city. The north side of the city, north of the expressways that feed into downtown, has essentially become all black; the south side has remained all white. Blacks live in suburbs north and west of the city; virtually none have chosen to live on the south side. There is a tendency to ascribe St. Louis's problems to its black majority; but the same demographic and sociological trends are apparent, somewhat different in scope but still apparent, on the south side as well as the north.

Missouri's 1st congressional district includes the north side of St. Louis and adjacent parts of all-suburban St. Louis County. It is a measure of the depopulation of St. Louis that this district, once entirely within the city limits, now has more residents and voters in the suburbs than in the city. Its suburbs include the mostly black towns along St. Charles Rock and Natural Bridge Roads, northwest of the city; high-income Clayton, with its office building developments, and the white-collar suburbs of University City (once mostly Jewish, now 43% black), Richmond Heights, and Maplewood, directly west; and virtually all-white Bellefontaine Neighbors, Spanish Lake, and Black Jack, directly north. The 1st district is the most heavily Democratic in Missouri, by a considerable margin.

Since 1968 this district has been represented by Bill Clay, who got his political start as a union staffer and civil rights activist. When he was first elected, he was considered one of the more militant black members; only five years before, he had served 105 days in jail for participating in a civil rights demonstration. Clay now has more seniority, but has not entirely mellowed. He is one of organized labor's most faithful supporters on the House Education and Labor Committee and on Post Office and Civil Service. From his seat on the latter, he was the House's chief proponent of repealing the Hatch Act's limitations on the political activities of federal employees. He also worked with public employee unions to defeat the Carter administration's civil service reforms. In both efforts he was unsuccessful. In 1981 he was passed over for the chairmanship of the Labor-Management Relations Subcommittee in favor of Phillip Burton, who had less seniority on the subcommittee but was evidently considered by organized labor to be a stronger advocate of its position in what were expected to be tough fights with Republicans bent on changing important labor laws; he got the chairmanship only after Burton's death in early 1983.

Clay has had other problems. In 1976 it was revealed that he had been billing the government for numerous auto trips home, although he was actually purchasing less expensive airline tickets and, presumably, pocketing the difference. The next year he was under investigation for tax fraud. His administrative assistant was sent to jail for falsification of payroll records. Even by Missouri's relaxed standards, this was a seamy record, enough to inspire opposition in the Democratic primary. In 1976 and 1978 six candidates each time held Clay to just over 60% of the primary vote; both times he lost the St. Louis County portion of the district. In 1980 he carried the St. Louis County portion only narrowly and won with huge margins in the city.

The 1st district had to be expanded to meet the population standard in 1982, and there was some talk of eliminating the district altogether. Clay was able to prevent that, but the 1st no longer has a black majority; it is mostly suburban; 52% of the vote in the crucial Democratic primary is cast outside the city. In the 1982 primary Clay was beaten 58%–40% in the suburbs, but he won the city with 83%, enough for a 61% victory overall. Probably the numbers are not there for him to lose, but he is likely to have a serious fight, and if a rival should emerge who can take significant numbers of black votes, there could be a change of representation here.

The People   Pop. 1980: 546,208, dn. 20.7% 1970–80; voting age pop. 393,146; 46% Black, 1% Span. orig., 1% Asian orig. 41% housing units rented. Median owner $31,800; renter $145. Households: 66% family, 36% with children, 45% married couples.

Presidential Vote

1980	Reagan (R)	NA
	Carter (D)	NA
	Anderson (I)	NA

Rep. William (Bill) **Clay** (D) Elected 1968; b. Apr. 30, 1931, St. Louis; home, St. Louis; St. Louis U., B.S. 1953; Roman Catholic.

Career Real estate broker; Life insurance business, 1959–61; St. Louis City Alderman, 1959–64; Business Rep., City Employees Union, 1961–64.

Offices 2470 RHOB, 202-225-2406. Also 5980 Delmar Blvd., St. Louis 63112, 314-725-5770.

Committees *Education and Labor* (6th). Subcommittees: Employment Opportunities; Labor-Management Relations; Labor Standards. *Post Office and Civil Service* (3d). Subcommittees: Postal Operations and Services (Chairman); Postal Personnel and Modernization.

Group Ratings

	ADA	ACLU	COPE	CFA	LCV	LWV	NTU	NSI	COC	ACA	CSFC
1982	65	96	94	85	96	91	15	13	29	0	24
1981	95	—	93	79	99	—	40	—	0	9	25
1980	83	97	89	79	87	100	20	11	53	16	20

National Journal Ratings

	Economic		Foreign		Cultural	
1982	91%	(LIB)	99%	(LIB)	92%	(LIB)
	9%	(CONS)	1%	(CONS)	7%	(CONS)
1981	89%	(LIB)	98%	(LIB)	95%	(LIB)
	3%	(CONS)	1%	(CONS)	1%	(CONS)

Key Votes

1) Reagan 81 Budget	AGN	5) Incr SS Rtmt Age	AGN	9) Poor Pay Food Stamps	AGN
2) Reagan 81 Tax Cut	AGN	6) Saudi AWACS Sale	AGN	10) Ban Crt Busing Order	AGN
3) Bal Budget Amend	AGN	7) $ for MX Missile	AGN	11) Auto Local Content	FOR
4) Gas & Road Tax	FOR	8) Nerve Gas Prod	—	12) Nuclear Arms Freeze	FOR

Election Results

1982 general	William (Bill) Clay (D)	102,656	(66%)	($298,220)
	William E. (Bill) White (R)	52,599	(34%)	($0)
1982 primary	William (Bill) Clay (D)	73,827	(61%)	
	Al Mueller (D)	45,610	(38%)	($143,802)
1980 general	William (Bill) Clay (D)	91,272	(70%)	($102,908)
	William E. (Bill) White (R)	38,667	(30%)	($0)

Campaign Contributions and Expenditures

1981-82		Direct Cont. 81-82		PACS brkdwn			
Receipts	$289,586	Indiv	$119,323	Agr	$2,000	Ideo	$23,400
Expend.	$298,220	Party	$5,000	Bus	$13,700	Lbr	$100,245
Unspent	$8,583	PACS	$147,273	Hlth	$750	Prof	$2,200
		Cand	$350				

Indep Expend: For: $1,479 (Machinists PAC)

SECOND DISTRICT

The 2d congressional district of Missouri is the heart of St. Louis County, the all-suburban county that is not part of, and is more than twice as populous as, the city of St. Louis. The 2d runs the political gamut of suburbs. On its north side, north of Interstate 70, centered on the big McDonnell–Douglas Aircraft plants near the airport, are blue-collar suburbs: Hazelwood, Berkley, St. John, St. Ann, Overland. These are mostly white, filled with people who grew up on the north side of St. Louis, but most of the towns have black residents too, some in large numbers (like Berkley); no one is quite sure whether this represents stable integration or rapid neighborhood change, though it is probably the latter. In the south end of the district are comfortable white-collar suburbs like Kirkwood and Webster Groves, pleasant but not really rich places which remain mostly white but with older populations than they used to have. In the center of the county are high-income Ladue, the home of most of St. Louis's elite, Creve Coeur, and the more Jewish suburb of Olivette. Farther west, you come to new subdivisions, with large, air-conditioned houses which keep their storm doors up all year, and with few trees; they are interspersed among a few crumbling remains of rural houses built higgledy-piggledy by their owners years ago. Out here also is Times Beach, the bedraggled subdivision near a toxic waste dump which was a center of national attention in early 1983; it is worthy of note that Times Beach's population increased substantially in the 1970s, even as the dumping was going on.

Politically, the 2d is a very mixed bag, which often—but not always—produces results similar to the statewide average. The working-class suburbs are Democratic, especially on economic issues, but sometimes leave the party on cultural isusses; the southern suburbs and most of the new subdivisions are pretty solidly Republican, though they look at the world from quite different perspectives; the rich Protestants are heavily Republican, the Jews more Democratic, and both can be attracted to Democrats on liberal cultural issues.

The congressman from the 2d, Bob Young, is a product of the northern part of the district. A pipefitter who represented St. Ann for 20 years in the legislature, he is an old political pro. For a union man, his stands on economic issues have actually been rather cautious, as if he were trying to propitiate some of his more affluent constituents; on cultural and foreign issues he has a mixed record. He is a strong opponent of abortion and a strong backer of Israel. He sits on nuts-and-bolts committees, Public Works and Transportation and Science and Technology, both of which are of some importance to McDonnell–Douglas.

Young has had serious opposition in three out of four elections; oddly, the one time the Republicans didn't give him a real race was in the most Republican year, 1980. Redistricting cost him some Democratic areas, and his opponent spent nearly $250,000 in 1982, and held him to 57% of the vote. That is a percentage that technically takes him out of the marginal category. But he cannot be regarded as completely safe, and this is a district Republicans could win if no incumbent were running.

The People Pop. 1980: 546,039, up 11.4% 1970–80; voting age pop. 386,511; 5% Black, 1% Span. orig., 1% Asian orig. 23% housing units rented. Median owner $53,700; renter $232. Households: 79% family, 44% with children, 68% married couples.

Presidential Vote

1980	Reagan (R)	NA
	Carter (D)	NA
	Anderson (I)	NA

Rep. Robert A. Young (D) Elected 1976; b. Nov. 22, 1923, St. Louis; home, St. Ann; Roman Catholic.

Career Army, WWII; Pipefitter; MO House of Reps., 1957–63; MO Senate, 1963–77.

Offices 2430 RHOB, 202-225-2561. Also 4154 Cypress Rd., St. Ann 63074, 314-425-7200.

Committees *Public Works and Transportation* (10th). Subcommittees: Aviation; Public Buildings and Grounds (Chairman); Water Resources. *Science and Technology* (11th). Subcommittees: Energy Development and Applications; Energy Research and Production.

Group Ratings

	ADA	ACLU	COPE	CFA	LCV	LWV	NTU	NSI	COC	ACA	CSFC
1982	40	54	74	54	42	42	18	70	33	38	37
1981	40	—	75	50	40	—	14	—	28	32	48
1980	50	40	56	57	40	50	20	30	68	33	35

National Journal Ratings

	Economic		Foreign		Cultural	
1982	60%	(LIB)	54%	(LIB)	4%	(LIB)
	39%	(CONS)	46%	(CONS)	87%	(CONS)
1981	56%	(LIB)	56%	(LIB)	51%	(LIB)
	43%	(CONS)	44%	(CONS)	49%	(CONS)

Key Votes

1) Reagan 81 Budget	AGN	5) Incr SS Rtmt Age	AGN	9) Poor Pay Food Stamps	AGN
2) Reagan 81 Tax Cut	AGN	6) Saudi AWACS Sale	AGN	10) Ban Crt Busing Order	FOR
3) Bal Budget Amend	AGN	7) $ for MX Missile	AGN	11) Auto Local Content	FOR
4) Gas & Road Tax	FOR	8) Nerve Gas Prod	FOR	12) Nuclear Arms Freeze	FOR

Election Results

1982 general	Robert A. Young (D)	100,770	(57%)	($241,950)
	Harold L. Dielman (R)	77,433	(43%)	($260,948)
1982 primary	Robert A. Young (D)	51,258	(86%)	
	Edward Phelan Roche (D)	8,069	(14%)	
1980 general	Robert A. Young (D)	148,227	(64%)	($149,633)
	John O. Shields (R)	81,762	(36%)	($94,811)

Campaign Contributions and Expenditures

1981-82		*Direct Cont. 81-82*				*PACS brkdwn*		
Receipts	$251,412	Indiv	$112,200	Agr	$6,650	Ideo	$5,500
Expend.	$241,950	PACS	$108,096	Bus	$36,475	Lbr	$50,998
Unspent	$37,017	Cand	$5,000	Hlth	$5,200	Prof	$600

THIRD DISTRICT

The 3d congressional district of Missouri is the south side of the St. Louis metropolitan area—a slice of pie with its apex in downtown St. Louis, extending outward and getting wider in suburban St. Louis County and finally in Jefferson County, once a rural area alongside the turbulently flowing Mississippi River, now a suburban extension of St. Louis. The south side of St. Louis is almost entirely white, and there are still signs there of the German immigrants who helped make St. Louis one of the nation's most bustling and progressive cities in the late 19th century; the most famous St. Louis German was Carl Schurz, a friend of Lincoln, a Union Army officer in the Civil War, Secretary of the Interior, and U.S. Senator from Missouri. The south side of St. Louis, like the mostly black north side, has lost almost half its population in 30 years; it now comprises only 35% of the 3d district.

About 38% is in St. Louis County, in suburbs which are mostly middle class, but not especially expensive or fashionable. This is where the solid middle class of St. Louis lives, people who keep its offices humming, its stores and warehouses bustling, its schoolchildren instructed and disciplined. In the 1970s many younger people who had grown up here moved farther out, to Jefferson County. The old towns here, sitting near the banks of the Mississippi, are now receiving an infusion of shopping centers, spanking new subdivisions, and apartment complexes, and even a few office buildings.

Carl Schurz was a Republican, and for years St. Louis was a Republican island in a Democratic sea. But with the New Deal, St. Louis became one of our most Democratic cities. That preference has subsided, as racial conflict and cultural issues become more important to some voters in the metropolitan area. But the 3d district, particularly in the city, is an old one; for many of its residents the 1930s remain a vivid memory and the threat of cuts to Social Security was the dominant issue in the 1982 elections. So while the 3d has been trending Republican in presidential elections, it still has Democratic potential in state contests and remains solidly Democratic in local races.

The 3d district has one of the most politically gifted members of the House, Richard Gephardt. Although he was first elected as recently as 1976, Gephardt has already become a force to be reckoned with. This is not just the result of good committee assignments; he got choice seats on Ways and Means and Budget because of his ability. Part of the reason for his rise is that he is an original thinker on substantive issues. He does not simply go along with standard Democratic positions. On health care, for example, he worked with David

Stockman, then in the House, to craft a competition bill, to offer employees choices between different medical insurance plans; he felt this would do more to hold down costs and provide insurance people need than would federally administered national health insurance. On taxes he was open to arguments that taxes should be lowered to encourage investment. He is one of those younger Democrats exploring issues like industrial policy; he is interested less in the redistribution of wealth than he is, at least for the time being, in encouraging its creation.

Gephardt combines this originality of mind with great legislative skill. He is able to get colleagues to work with him on measures he sponsors, and to garner support; and you can do those things only if you've convinced other members that you go out front on an issue only when you're prepared and your position is defensible. Gephardt has managed to be a new thinker and yet be a favorite of the leadership (Missouri's Richard Bolling, former chairman of Rules, thought highly of him); he is one of the Democrats' *de facto* leaders on the Budget Committee.

Gephardt will presumably have to give up his seat on Budget soon, but he will remain influential. He is also one of the young members who could conceivably win a leadership position—and one day even be speaker. Gephardt seems to have settled on a House career: he could have run against Senator John Danforth in 1982, and chose not to. He was politically adept enough that he was not hurt by redistricting, and he was reelected easily: for him the 3d is a safe seat.

The People   Pop. 1980: 546,102, up 0.3% 1970–80; voting age pop. 403,646; 1% Black, 1% Span. orig. 29% housing units rented. Median owner $43,900; renter $151. Households: 72% family, 36% with children, 61% married couples.

Presidential Vote

1980	Reagan (R)	NA
	Carter (D)	NA
	Anderson (I)	NA

Rep. Richard A. Gephardt (D) Elected 1976; b. Jan. 31, 1941, St. Louis; home, St. Louis; Northwestern U., B.S. 1962, U. of MI, J.D., 1965; Protestant.

Career Practicing atty., 1965–76; St. Louis City Alderman, 1971–76.

Offices 1436 LHOB, 202-225-2671. Also 3470 Hampton St., St. Louis 63109, 314-351-5100.

Committees *Budget* (6th). Task Forces: Budget Process; Education and Employment (Chairman). *Ways and Means* (10th). Subcommittee: Social Security.

Group Ratings

	ADA	ACLU	COPE	CFA	LCV	LWV	NTU	NSI	COC	ACA	CSFC
1982	55	33	73	54	59	64	33	90	35	36	36
1981	45	—	73	64	68	—	30	—	11	39	47
1980	56	40	61	43	65	80	30	10	64	33	37

National Journal Ratings

	Economic		Foreign		Cultural	
1982	57%	(LIB)	51%	(LIB)	45%	(LIB)
	43%	(CONS)	49%	(CONS)	55%	(CONS)
1981	68%	(LIB)	32%	(LIB)	47%	(LIB)
	30%	(CONS)	68%	(CONS)	53%	(CONS)

Key Votes

1) Reagan 81 Budget	AGN	5) Incr SS Rtmt Age	AGN
2) Reagan 81 Tax Cut	AGN	6) Saudi AWACS Sale	AGN
3) Bal Budget Amend	AGN	7) $ for MX Missile	AGN
4) Gas & Road Tax	FOR	8) Nerve Gas Prod	FOR

9) Poor Pay Food Stamps	AGN
10) Ban Crt Busing Order	FOR
11) Auto Local Content	FOR
12) Nuclear Arms Freeze	FOR

Election Results

1982 general	Richard A. Gephardt (D)	131,566	(78%)	($345,360)
	Richard Foristel (R)	37,388	(22%)	($2,967)
1982 primary	Richard A. Gephardt (D)	72,882	(100%)	
1980 general	Richard A. Gephardt (D)	143,132	(78%)	($198,785)
	Robert A. Cedarburg (R)	41,277	(22%)	($0)

Campaign Contributions and Expenditures

1981-82		Direct Cont. 81-82		PACS brkdwn			
Receipts	$342,873	Indiv	$140,966	Agr	$13,975	Ideo	$3,850
Expend.	$345,360	Party	$1,000	Bus	$130,125	Lbr	$18,550
Unspent	$900	PACS	$187,514	Hlth	$12,400	Prof	$4,050

FOURTH DISTRICT

The 4th congressional district of Missouri is a slice of basically rural and small-town Missouri, extending from Jefferson City, the state capital, at the center of the state, all the way to Kansas City. Its political attitudes are a vestige of its responses to the Civil War. There are battle sites here, remembrances that the war was fought in Missouri, though it never formally left the Union, as well as in Virginia and Georgia. The district's most famous son, Harry Truman, was born in the town of Lamar, in the southern end of the district, near the Arkansas and Oklahoma borders. His family was Democratic, which means in his mother's case at least that it cherished a lifelong sympathy for the Confederacy. The 4th includes a part of Independence (though not the old Truman home) and some of the fringe of Kansas City; the rest is resolutely nonmetropolitan. And it is by no means all Democratic. Jefferson City, for example, was a solid Union town, and remains very heavily Republican today.

The 4th district's current boundaries were drawn by a Democratic legislature faced with the unpleasant task of reducing the number of the state's congressional districts by one. So in this new 4th district they combined most of the old 4th represented by Democrat Ike Skelton and much of the old 8th district represented by Republican Wendell Bailey. They did so knowing that Skelton would have the advantage, for several reasons. He has been representing most of the new district—64% of its votes. More of the district's counties were traditionally Democratic than Republican. Skelton had been representing his areas longer: he was first elected in 1976, while Bailey was a 1980 freshman. Skelton had a record tailored to his district; Bailey could be attacked as a reflexive supporter of whatever Reagan policies turned out to be unpopular in October.

The contest turned out as planned. The 4th district had seen nothing like this before, but its basic party preferences, forged in the furnace of the Civil War, still held. Skelton got a solid 61% of the vote in the part of the district he had represented. Bailey got just 57% in the counties he (or, in one case, another Republican) had been representing—far less than he needed.

So Skelton continues to serve in the House and on the Armed Services Committee. On economic issues he often, but not always, joins most other Democrats; on cultural and foreign issues he is solidly conservative. On Armed Services he is in line with the committee's pro-Pentagon tilt. He is also well positioned to look after the interests of the Army's Fort Leonard, which is part of the 4th district since redistricting.

The People   Pop. 1980: 546,637, up 19.7% 1970–80; voting age pop. 390,415; 3% Black, 1% Span. orig. 21% housing units rented. Median owner $35,600; renter $141. Households: 77% family, 42% with children, 69% married couples.

Presidential Vote

1980	Reagan (R)	125,477	(57%)
	Carter (D)	90,264	(41%)
	Anderson (I)	5,933	(2%)

Rep. Ike Skelton (D) Elected 1976; b. Dec. 20, 1931, Lexington; home, Lexington; Wentworth Mil. Acad., U. of MO, B.A. 1953, LL.B. 1956, U. of Edinburgh, Scotland, 1956; Disciples of Christ.

Career Lafayette Cnty. Prosecuting Atty., 1957–60; Spec. Asst. Atty. Gen. of MO, 1961–63; Practicing atty., 1964–71; MO Senate, 1971–76.

Offices 2453 RHOB, 202-225-2876. Also 219 Fed. Bldg., 301 W. Lexington, Independence 64050, 816-252-2560.

Committees Armed Services (20th). Subcommittees: Military Personnel and Compensation; Readiness. *Small Business* (11th). Subcommittee: Export Opportunities and Special Small Business Problems.

Group Ratings

	ADA	ACLU	COPE	CFA	LCV	LWV	NTU	NSI	COC	ACA	CSFC
1982	10	29	61	31	51	27	53	100	63	55	53
1981	25	—	63	50	36	—	18	—	37	48	54
1980	17	17	58	29	31	40	31	78	66	42	49

National Journal Ratings

	Economic		Foreign		Cultural	
1982	47%	(LIB)	25%	(LIB)	2%	(LIB)
	53%	(CONS)	75%	(CONS)	98%	(CONS)
1981	56%	(LIB)	18%	(LIB)	33%	(LIB)
	43%	(CONS)	73%	(CONS)	66%	(CONS)

Key Votes

1) Reagan 81 Budget	AGN	5) Incr SS Rtmt Age	AGN	9) Poor Pay Food Stamps	AGN
2) Reagan 81 Tax Cut	AGN	6) Saudi AWACS Sale	AGN	10) Ban Crt Busing Order	—
3) Bal Budget Amend	FOR	7) $ for MX Missile	—	11) Auto Local Content	FOR
4) Gas & Road Tax	FOR	8) Nerve Gas Prod	FOR	12) Nuclear Arms Freeze	—

Election Results

1982 general	Ike Skelton (D)	96,388	(55%)	($459,566)
	Wendell Bailey (R)	79,565	(45%)	($464,385)
1982 primary	Ike Skelton (D)	52,993	(100%)	
1980 general	Ike Skelton (D)	151,459	(68%)	($115,981)
(MO 4)	Bill Baker (R)	71,869	(32%)	($1,921)
1980 general	Wendell Bailey (R)	127,675	(57%)	($254,341)
(MO 8)	Steve Gardner (D)	95,751	(43%)	($138,074)

Campaign Contributions and Expenditures

1981-82		Direct Cont. 81-82			PACS brkdwn		
Receipts	$443,490	Indiv	$233,335	Agr	$28,900	Ideo	$29,450
Expend.	$459,566	Party	$8,500	Bus	$63,423	Lbr	$32,500
Unspent	$10,726	PACS	$184,768	Hlth	$14,300	Prof	$2,500
		Cand	$4,000				

Indirect Party Expend: $113   *Indep Expend:* For: $1,218 (MO LIFEPAC)

FIFTH DISTRICT

The 5th congressional district of Missouri includes the heart of Kansas City—the central portion of the city, including its downtown and most of its industrial area down by the river and the stockyards. This is the focus of the Kansas City metropolitan area, an important manufacturing and commercial hub for the farmlands of western Missouri and most of Kansas—and a city with the air and assurance of one of the nation's major and growing metropolitan areas. "Everything's up to date in Kansas City," goes the song from *Oklahoma!,* which was set in 1907, and Kansas City indeed did have all the modern accoutrements then. It still does today. The 5th district includes the city's downtown skyscrapers sitting on the bluffs above the Missouri River and the Kansas City stockyards. Across a valley, facing them, is the luxurious Crown Center development started by Hallmark, the greeting card company that is one of the major employers, benefactors, and style-setters of the city. Here in the 5th are Kansas City's black neighborhoods and some of its white working-class areas. It goes as far east as Independence, including the old white Truman home on Truman Road. To the south the 5th includes the high-income neighborhoods around the Country Club Plaza—the nation's first shopping center, built in the 1920s—just across the state line from the high-income suburbs of Johnson County, Kansas.

This is a pretty solidly Democratic district, and getting more so, as some of its middle-class Republican voters, or their children, move to farther-out suburban areas. It was represented for 34 years by Richard Bolling, one of the truly creative and effective leaders of the House. A protege of Sam Rayburn who missed out on leadership positions, Bolling wrote trenchant critiques of the House, and pushed reforms that include the election of committee chairmen and the congressional budget process. He is probably more responsible than anyone else for the way the House works—and it does work—today: the fact that it attacks its business in an orderly and timely manner and that leadership responsibilities go only to those who are held accountable by their fellow party members and, ultimately, their constituents. Bolling capped his career by serving as chairman of the House Rules Committee for four years, and as the leading lieutenant of Speaker O'Neill. He decided to retire, while still in the prime of life, in 1982, and to read, study, and write a book on power—something, he says, no one has really done since Machiavelli.

Bolling's successor was determined in the Democratic primary. Much to almost everyone's surprise, he turned out to be a 31-year-old black state legislator, Alan Wheat. The 5th's electorate is only 20% black, but Wheat, running in an eight-candidate Democratic primary, was able to combine solid black support with some white votes and win by a 32%–30% margin over his nearest opponent. With solid support from Bolling in the general election, and a campaign budget raised with help from national Democrats, Wheat was able to win with 58% of the vote. That is below the normal Democratic vote here, but a comfortable margin nonetheless; he essentially split the white vote evenly with his Republican opponent, a pro-labor legislator who stressed his opposition to busing.

Wheat does not sound much like a militant, and his major black-oriented program has been the creation of urban enterprise zones—something entirely palatable to most whites. He has inherited Bolling's seat on the Rules Committee, and can argue to his constituents that he already has clout in the House—and the prospects of being a major national leader some day. If there are to be more black members in the House, they will have to be elected, as Wheat was, in a district where the large majority of voters are white; and while a black candidate can win such a race initially with a minority vote in a multi-candidate primary, he is going to have to be prepared to beat white candidates one-on-one in primaries or general elections. For Wheat, the real threat, now that he is past 1982, is the primary; and he has conducted himself in a way that seems calculated to make him a strong candidate in such a race in 1984. But he probably cannot forestall competition, and he may be spending much of his first term attending to his constituency.

The People Pop. 1980: 546,882, dn. 10.3% 1970–80; voting age pop. 405,263; 20% Black, 2% Span. orig., 1% Asian orig. 37% housing units rented. Median owner $35,100; renter $167. Households: 65% family, 34% with children, 53% married couples.

Presidential Vote

1980	Reagan (R)	89,150	(40%)
	Carter (D)	122,706	(55%)
	Anderson (I)	10,958	(5%)

Rep. Alan Wheat (D) Elected 1982; b. Oct. 16, 1951, San Antonio, TX; home, Kansas City; Grinnell Col., B.A. 1972; Protestant.

Career Economist, Dept. of HUD, Kansas City, 1972–73; Mid-America Regional Cncl., 1973–75; Aide to Jackson Cnty. Exec., Mike White, 1975–76; MO House of Reps., 1977–82.

Offices 1609 LHOB, 202-225-4535. Also U.S. Courthouse, 811 Grand Ave., Rm. 935, Kansas City 64106, 816-842-4545.

Committees *Rules* (9th). Subcommittee: The Legislative Process. *Select Committee on Children, Youth, and Families* (16th).

Group Ratings and Key Votes: Newly Elected

Election Results

1982 general	Alan Wheat (D)	96,059	(58%)	($314,735)
	John A. Sharp (R)	66,664	(40%)	($148,034)
1982 primary	Alan Wheat (D)	21,279	(32%)	
	John Carnes (D)	20,275	(30%)	($192,513)
	Jack L. Campbell (D)	16,197	(24%)	($180,602)
	Five others (D)	10,021	(15%)	($138,382)
1980 general	Richard Bolling (D)	110,957	(70%)	($113,299)
	Vincent E. Baker (R)	47,309	(30%)	($11,388)

Campaign Contributions and Expenditures

1981-82		*Direct Cont. 81-82*			*PACS brkdwn*		
Receipts	$316,791	Indiv	$173,346	Agr	$5,000	Ideo	$31,770
Expend.	$314,735	Party	$7,750	Bus	$21,050	Lbr	$51,454
Unspent	$2,056	PACS	$117,344	Hlth	$2,250	Prof	$900
		Cand	$1,520				

Indirect Party Expend: $3,007   *Non-Cand Loans:* $14,000

SIXTH DISTRICT

Northwest Missouri is mostly farmland, gentle rolling hill country above the bluffs that line the Missouri and other major rivers. In many ways this is a place left behind by the 20th century. The mechanization of the family farm has thinned out the population here, as young people seek a better—or easier—way to make a living elsewhere. All the counties of northwest Missouri, except those in the Kansas City metropolitan area, had more people in 1900 than they do today; in 1900 they had a total population of 508,000 and in 1980, 301,000. Perhaps the most poignant story belongs to St. Joseph, once one of the leading ports of entry to the American West: it was here that the Pony Express riders first saddled up for their transcontinental sprints to Sacramento. In 1900 St. Joseph was a solid commercial competitor of Kansas City, with 102,000 people compared to Kansas City's 163,000. Today metropolitan Kansas City has more than a million people, while St. Joseph's population has dwindled to 72,000 and is diminishing still.

The 6th congressional district covers almost precisely the northwest corner of Missouri, the land north and east of the Missouri River, west of a line drawn north and south through the middle of the state. Although most of the expanse of the 6th is devoted to agriculture, as it was at the turn of the century, most of its residents now live in metropolitan areas. Some are in St. Joseph, but by far the bulk of this population can be found in Clay and Platte Counties in metropolitan Kansas City. To give itself space to grow, Kansas City has been systematically annexing land for 20 years; much of it has been bulldozed for subdivisions or to accommodate Kansas City's giant new airport. Technically, Clay and Platte Counties are mostly part of the central city, but their character is suburban or even rural. Travelers driving into town from Mid-Continent International, the new airport, pass through miles of dairy grazing land and cornfields—inside the corporate limits of Kansas City.

The 6th is one of those Missouri districts that in national and statewide elections trended Republican in the 1960s and 1970s; it didn't like Kennedy's Catholicism, Johnson's Great Society, or Humphrey's or McGovern's liberalism. But there is still a Democratic tradition

"The nation's most respected nonpartisan source of information about how Washington's policy-making machinery really works."

That's how *Newsweek* described NATIONAL JOURNAL. For 14 years, the JOURNAL has reached subscribers with an award-winning weekly magazine noted for its dedication to "facts only" reporting. NATIONAL JOURNAL speaks to people who make it their business to know what's going on in the world's largest business—the United States Government.

Who Reads NATIONAL JOURNAL?

One White House staffer told us he reads NATIONAL JOURNAL religiously . . . to find out what's happening in the White House! But you don't have to work at the White House to subscribe to NATIONAL JOURNAL (although more than 90 subscriptions go to White House staffers).

You don't even have to live in Washington. More than half of our subscribers live somewhere else, and they rely on NATIONAL JOURNAL every week to be their eyes and ears in Washington.

So who are our subscribers? Corporate executives . . . government policy makers . . . public affairs representatives . . . journalists . . . political consultants . . . lobbyists . . . libraries . . . lawyers . . . anyone keenly interested in government and politics. The *Washington Journalism Review* called our subscribers "the *creme de la creme* of American business, government, and journalism." Success is important to them, and they understand that in order to succeed, they have to understand Washington government.

★ ★ ★

But They Don't Just Read NATIONAL JOURNAL

Our subscribers read plenty. They read *The Washington Post, The New York Times,* and *The Wall Street Journal,* along with other publications. Yet they still pay a premium price to read NATIONAL JOURNAL. And they come back for more! We rarely lose a subscriber, because our readers know that they can trust us to provide impartial analysis.

Let's think about what that really means. We don't just report the news, but we look at how each piece of information fits in with everything else we know. We listen to what insiders are saying. In short, we crank massive quantities of information through our reporting system and what comes out are the important facts—analyzed without bias.

★ ★ ★

Now, a Few Words About Our Competition

There is none. Not a single other newspaper, magazine, newsletter, or academic journal. Only NATIONAL JOURNAL provides complete coverage

and analysis of what the government is doing today, what it's going to do tomorrow, and how its actions affect every facet of our lives. Week after week.

★ ★ ★

No risk—your satisfaction is guaranteed!

If at any time you're not pleased with your subscription to NATIONAL JOURNAL, let us know and we will

refund the entire unused portion of your subscription price.

Here's What You'll Find in Each Issue of NATIONAL JOURNAL

In-depth features give you insight into a wide range of topics such as the budget, taxes, defense, health, energy, housing, trade, and all the regulatory issues.

"Focus" presents a series of shorter articles to bring you up-to-date on current, hot issues.

"People" lets you in on the latest job-to-job movements of key policy makers in government, business, labor, interest groups and media.

"At a Glance" catches you up on 20 vital issues confronting Congress and the White House.

"Washington Update" provides you with policy and politics in brief.

"The Numbers Game" reveals the data behind the policy.

"Opinion Outlook" reports on selected polling results to reveal important trends affecting government policy.

"Infofile" directs you to studies, surveys and books of interest.

A convenient cross-reference leads you to other related articles in recent issues.

★   ★   ★

You'll Also Receive
Three Special Subscriber Benefits

1. Your questions, answered. Our research desk is staffed by six professionals, and you can call and ask any one of them about the status of bills or congressional votes. And they can help you locate government documents and previous articles in NATIONAL JOURNAL.

2. Your references, crossed. Twice a year you will receive a cumulative index to all subjects, people and organizations discussed in NATIONAL JOURNAL.

3. Your contacts, listed. You will automatically receive our exclusive White House and Congressional telephone directories . . . absolutely free. (*The New York Times* called the *White House Phone List* the "most intriguing and sought after publication in town.")

★   ★   ★

Special Introductory Offer!
New Subscribers Only . . .

Use the order form above or the postage-paid card in the back of the book!

here, evident in returns from local and state elections, and made manifest in other elections as well. In 1976, when the Democrats nominated a southerner, he carried this district; in 1982, with the economy in distress, Democrat Harriett Woods came within 1,000 votes of beating Senator John Danforth in the 6th.

In congressional representation the 6th has moved from Democrat to Republican, though as much by accident as anything else. Republican Tom Coleman was elected in 1976 when the *Kansas City Star* revealed that Democratic nominee Morgan Maxfield was bragging about fraudulent credentials. Since then Coleman has done a good job of keeping in touch with constituents and handling farm issues on the Agriculture Committee. Against a competent Democratic candidate, in the Democratic year of 1982, Coleman was able to win reelection with 55% of the vote. That makes him one of the more senior members of the youngish Republican Conference; he is ranking Republican on two subcommittees, handling domestic marketing on Agriculture and the other concerned with higher education on Education and Labor. On most issues he is a solid conservative Republican and causes his leadership no problems.

The People Pop. 1980: 546,614, up 7.2% 1970–80; voting age pop. 264,636; 2% Black, 1% Span. orig. 25% housing units rented. Median owner $34,800; renter $151. Households: 74% family, 38% with children, 65% married couples.

Presidential Vote

1980	Reagan (R)	122,231	(52%)
	Carter (D)	102,752	(44%)
	Anderson (I)	8,588	(4%)

Rep. E. Thomas (Tom) **Coleman** (R) Elected 1976; b. May 25, 1943, Kansas City; home, Kansas City; Wm. Jewell Col., B.A. 1965, NYU, M.A. 1969, Washington U., St. Louis, J.D. 1969; Protestant.

Career Asst. Atty. Gen. of MO, 1969–72; MO House of Reps., 1973–76.

Offices 2344 RHOB, 202-225-7041. Also 2701 Rock Creek Pkwy., Kansas City 64116, 816-474-9035.

Committees *Agriculture* (3d). Subcommittees: Conservation, Credit and Rural Development; Domestic Marketing, Consumer Relations and Nutrition. *Education and Labor* (4th). Subcommittees: Employment Opportunities; Human Resources; Postsecondary Education; Select Education.

Group Ratings

	ADA	ACLU	COPE	CFA	LCV	LWV	NTU	NSI	COC	ACA	CSFC
1982	10	8	16	31	34	33	60	100	68	70	54
1981	0	—	14	21	30	—	47	—	94	73	65
1980	6	20	10	7	31	33	49	100	73	87	75

National Journal Ratings

	Economic		Foreign		Cultural	
1982	40%	(LIB)	30%	(LIB)	27%	(LIB)
	60%	(CONS)	70%	(CONS)	73%	(CONS)
1981	21%	(LIB)	3%	(LIB)	27%	(LIB)
	79%	(CONS)	87%	(CONS)	73%	(CONS)

Key Votes

1) Reagan 81 Budget	FOR	5) Incr SS Rtmt Age	FOR	9) Poor Pay Food Stamps	FOR
2) Reagan 81 Tax Cut	FOR	6) Saudi AWACS Sale	FOR	10) Ban Crt Busing Order	FOR
3) Bal Budget Amend	FOR	7) $ for MX Missile	FOR	11) Auto Local Content	FOR
4) Gas & Road Tax	AGN	8) Nerve Gas Prod	—	12) Nuclear Arms Freeze	AGN

Election Results

1982 general	E. Thomas (Tom) Coleman (R) ...	97,993	(55%)	($227,679)
	Jim Russell (D)	79,053	(45%)	($140,536)
1982 primary	E. Thomas (Tom) Coleman (R) ...	25,920	(91%)	
	Robert L. Buck (R)	2,434	(9%)	
1980 general	E. Thomas (Tom) Coleman (R) ...	149,281	(71%)	($188,403)
	Vernon King (D)	62,048	(29%)	($22,751)

Campaign Contributions and Expenditures

1981-82		*Direct Cont. 81-82*				*PACS brkdwn*		
Receipts	$236,752	Indiv	$78,959	Agr	$14,978	Ideo	$1,000
Expend.	$227,674	Party	$9,848	Bus	$52,004	Lbr	$750
Unspent	$56,335	PACS	$80,280	Hlth	$9,000	Prof	$1,000

SEVENTH DISTRICT

Mention the Ozarks and you evoke an image of rural poverty: people with quaint accents living in hillside shacks, cut off from the life of 20th-century America. That was true enough perhaps 50 or 60 years ago, but the Ozark region of southwest Missouri is today very much in the mainstream of American life. Many people from areas that count themselves more sophisticated have in fact been moving to the Ozarks; the landscape here has been transformed in the past dozen years, as migrants from St. Louis and Kansas City and even Chicago build vacation homes or year-round residences in the pleasant green hills, along the large man-made lakes, or on the outskirts of the pleasant middle-sized cities of Springfield and Joplin. The climate here is relatively temperate, and the Ozarks are free from many of the stresses of metropolitan life that so many Americans find unpleasant. The Ozarks, long a backwater, are now one of the fastest-growing parts of the country.

They are also no longer isolated from the political mainstream. For years this part of Missouri has been heavily Republican. Most people in these hills in the 1860s did not share the slaveholding habits or Confederate sympathies of central Missourians, and during the Civil War they became staunch Republicans—and for years stayed that way. Their preference was strengthened by the Democrats' support of Great Society programs. Yet in 1982 the 7th congressional district of Missouri, which includes most of the state's Ozarks area, responded to the recession in much the same way that industrial and metropolitan districts do: it moved sharply to the Democrats.

This surprised almost everyone, and nearly defeated Republican Congressman Gene Taylor. A 10-year veteran of the House, Taylor was expected to have no trouble. But the Democrat, 35-year-old Springfield prosecutor David Geisler, won 49% of the vote. He carried Springfield handily and won most of the adjacent counties; Taylor held on because of his margins farther west, in Joplin and around his home town of Sarcoxie. This was not the result of vast spending; Geisler's budget was modest, much less than Taylor's. Nor was it solely personal popularity; Democratic Senate candidate Harriett Woods, not an Ozark native, was getting 46% of the vote in the 7th district against incumbent Senator John Danforth at the same time.

Taylor presumably will feel compelled to spend more time in the district—and to be thankful for his narrow victory. He is an aggressive, earthy partisan, a solid supporter of the Republican leadership, a member of the Rules Committee, and ranking Republican on the Post Office and Civil Service Committee.

The People Pop. 1980: 545,921, up 22.2% 1970–80; voting age pop. 399,610; 1% Black, 1% Span. orig., 1% Asian orig. 23% housing units rented. Median owner $31,100; renter $135. Households: 75% family, 37% with children, 66% married couples.

Presidential Vote

1980	Reagan (R)	141,329	(61%)
	Carter (D)	85,364	(37%)
	Anderson (I)	6,182	(3%)

Rep. Gene Taylor (R) Elected 1972; b. Feb. 10, 1928, near Sarcoxie; home, Sarcoxie; S.W. MO St. Col.; Methodist.

Career Pub. sch. teacher, 1948–49; Mayor of Sarcoxie, 1954–60; Pres., Gene Taylor Ford Sales, Inc., 1960–72.

Offices 2134 RHOB, 202-225-6536. Also 314A Wilhoit Bldg., Springfield 65806, 417-862-4317.

Committees *Post Office and Civil Service* (Ranking Member). Subcommittee: Investigations. *Rules* (4th). Subcommittees: Rules of the House; The Legislative Process.

Group Ratings

	ADA	ACLU	COPE	CFA	LCV	LWV	NTU	NSI	COC	ACA	CSFC
1982	0	0	13	8	2	17	85	100	95	96	72
1981	0	—	12	14	7	—	49	—	89	83	72
1980	11	0	16	14	17	20	68	100	66	88	82

National Journal Ratings

	Economic		Foreign		Cultural	
1982	10%	(LIB)	21%	(LIB)	4%	(LIB)
	90%	(CONS)	79%	(CONS)	87%	(CONS)
1981	4%	(LIB)	3%	(LIB)	4%	(LIB)
	79%	(CONS)	87%	(CONS)	90%	(CONS)

Key Votes

1) Reagan 81 Budget	FOR	5) Incr SS Rtmt Age	FOR	9) Poor Pay Food Stamps	FOR
2) Reagan 81 Tax Cut	FOR	6) Saudi AWACS Sale	FOR	10) Ban Crt Busing Order	FOR
3) Bal Budget Amend	FOR	7) $ for MX Missile	FOR	11) Auto Local Content	AGN
4) Gas & Road Tax	—	8) Nerve Gas Prod	FOR	12) Nuclear Arms Freeze	AGN

Election Results

1982 general	Gene Taylor (R)	91,391	(51%)	($251,305)
	David A. Geisler (D)	89,549	(49%)	($103,881)
1982 primary	Gene Taylor (R)	58,631	(100%)	
1980 general	Gene Taylor (R)	161,668	(68%)	($99,889)
	Ken Young (D)	76,844	(32%)	($0)

Campaign Contributions and Expenditures

1981-82		*Direct Cont. 81-82*			*PACS brkdwn*		
Receipts	$222,772	Indiv	$99,472	Agr	$3,700	Ideo	$1,350
Expend.	$251,305	Party	$8,992	Bus	$43,010	Lbr	$4,300
Unspent	$159,294	PACS	$60,826	Hlth	$5,050	Prof	$2,350

EIGHTH DISTRICT

The 8th congressional district of Missouri is the southeastern quadrant of the state. The best known part of this district may be the Bootheel, at the extreme southeast. This part of the country was first settled by southerners coming up from Mississippi, looking for more fertile, moist, level land for growing cotton. They found it here, in the late 19th and early 20th centuries, and since then the Bootheel has had more of a Deep South feel to it than any other part of Missouri. The alluvial lands of the Bootheel have shifted mostly from cotton to soybeans in recent years, but the southern heritage still prevails. This is basically a Democratic part of Missouri: it contains the only county in the state which George Wallace carried in the 1968 general election, and it was carried solidly by Jimmy Carter in both 1976 and 1980.

The rest of the district is somewhat different. The 8th goes westward to the Ozarks, although it does not reach the usually Republican counties there; the names of the counties recall prophecies of mineral riches (Iron), Gaelic provenance (Shannon), and westward ambitions (Oregon). The river counties here vary politically. Cape Girardeau is the one solidly Republican part of the district, St. Francois and Ste. Genevieve (pronounced with little hint of their French origin) are more evenly divided. Overall, the 8th is Democratic; in 1982 it gave a solid 53% of the vote to Senate candidate Harriett Woods over Senator John Danforth.

The congressman from the 8th, however, is a Republican, and one who has shown considerable political ability. Bill Emerson had roots in the district, but he was a Washington lobbyist when he spotted the vulnerability, on personal grounds, of Democratic Congressman Bill Burlison. Emerson went back to Missouri, raised a solid campaign fund, and whipped Burlison by a solid 55%–45% margin in 1980. Redistricting removed his home county— Jefferson, an increasingly suburban river county just south of St. Louis—from the district; in 1982 Emerson drew a solid opponent in Cape Girardeau legislator Jerry Ford. Again Emerson raised plenty of money, and outspent Ford 2–1; he ran 8% ahead of Danforth and held onto this Democratic district.

That is a solid performance, although the percentage is low enough that Emerson is almost guaranteed significant opposition again in 1984. He continues to sit on the Agriculture Committee—a good assignment for this agricultural district.

The People Pop. 1980: 546,112, up 14.3% 1970–80; voting age pop. 387,786; 3% Black. 23% housing units rented. Median owner $26,500; renter $105. Households: 76% family, 41% with children, 66% married couples.

Presidential Vote

1980	Reagan (R)	114,807	(54%)
	Carter (D)	94,381	(44%)
	Anderson (I)	4,054	(2%)

Rep. Bill Emerson (R) Elected 1980; b. Jan. 1, 1938, St. Louis; home, De Soto; Westminster Col., B.A. 1959, U. of Baltimore, LL.B. 1964; Presbyterian.

Career Air Force Reserve, 1964–; Spec. Asst. to U.S. Rep. Bob Ellsworth of KS, 1961–67; A. A. to U.S. Rep. Charles Mathias of MD, 1968–69; Dir. of Govt. Relations, Fairchild Indus., 1970–74; Exec. Asst. to Chmn. of Fed. Election Comm., 1975; Dir., Fed. Relations, TRW, Inc., 1976–79.

Offices 418 CHOB, 202-225-4404. Also 339 Broadway, Cape Girardeau 63701, 314-335-0101; and P.O. Box 242, Hillsboro 63050, 314-789-3561.

Committees *Agriculture* (9th). Subcommittees: Cotton, Rice and Sugar; Domestic Marketing, Consumer Relations, and Nutrition; Wheat, Soybeans and Feed Grains. *Interior and Insular Affairs* (12th). Subcommittees: Mining, Forest Management, and BPA; Public Lands and National Parks.

Group Ratings

	ADA	ACLU	COPE	CFA	LCV	LWV	NTU	NSI	COC	ACA	CSFC
1982	10	0	21	23	13	25	87	100	86	83	66
1981	0	—	20	21	14	—	81	—	89	88	74

National Journal Ratings

	Economic		Foreign		Cultural	
1982	20%	(LIB)	45%	(LIB)	4%	(LIB)
	79%	(CONS)	55%	(CONS)	87%	(CONS)
1981	4%	(LIB)	3%	(LIB)	4%	(LIB)
	79%	(CONS)	87%	(CONS)	90%	(CONS)

Key Votes

1) Reagan 81 Budget	FOR	5) Incr SS Rtmt Age	FOR	9) Poor Pay Food Stamps	FOR
2) Reagan 81 Tax Cut	FOR	6) Saudi AWACS Sale	FOR	10) Ban Crt Busing Order	FOR
3) Bal Budget Amend	FOR	7) $ for MX Missile	FOR	11) Auto Local Content	AGN
4) Gas & Road Tax	AGN	8) Nerve Gas Prod	—	12) Nuclear Arms Freeze	AGN

Election Results

1982 general	Bill Emerson (R)	86,493	(53%)	($452,291)
	Jerry Ford (D)	76,413	(47%)	($113,127)
1982 primary	Bill Emerson (R)	22,704	(100%)	
1980 general	Bill Emerson (R)	116,167	(55%)	($282,494)
	Bill D. Burlison (D)	94,465	(45%)	($210,444)

Campaign Contributions and Expenditures

1981-82		Direct Cont. 81-82				PACS brkdwn		
Receipts	$460,803	Indiv	$233,275	Agr	$16,950	Ideo	$11,500
Expend.	$452,291	Party	$31,002	Bus	$133,878	Lbr	$250
Unspent	$9,915	PACS	$185,182	Hlth	$1,850	Prof	$1,600

Indirect Party Expend: $44,164   *Indep Expend*: For: $905 (NRA)

NINTH DISTRICT

The part of rural Missouri that has most faithfully sustained a Democratic tradition is not the southern part of the state; it is the Little Dixie region, north of the Missouri River and across the Mississippi from Yankee-settled Illinois. The land here was settled early in the 19th century mainly by migrants from Kentucky, Tennessee, and Virginia. During the Civil War, some citizens of Little Dixie fought on the Confederate side, and at least one county declared itself independent of the unionist state of Missouri. Since then, not much urbanization has come to this part of the state—so little that Mark Twain would probably recognize his native Hannibal, one of Little Dixie's largest towns, were it not for the tourist traps that use Twain himself for bait. Nor have voting habits changed much. This part of the state continues to be at least as Democratic as the state as a whole.

Little Dixie was once a congressional district unto itself, represented for 40 years by Clarence Cannon, onetime parliamentarian of the House and the longtime crusty chairman of the Appropriations Committee. Now, because of the one-person-one-vote requirement, it dips down into St. Charles County, in the northern reaches of the St. Louis metropolitan area, and it includes Columbia, part of an ancestral Democratic county, but one whose voting habits today are less affected by Civil War allegiance than by the presence of the University of Missouri.

The district remains in Democratic hands. Its congressman, Harold Volkmer, was first elected in 1976; his crucial race was an 11-candidate Democratic primary which he won with 35% of the vote. He did have competition from St. Louis area Republicans in 1976 and 1980, but had margins large enough in Little Dixie to win; in 1982, his Republican opponent was from Columbia and carried the university town. But Volkmer won the St. Louis suburbs and Little Dixie for a solid victory.

That Volkmer was vulnerable in Columbia tells you something about his record. He is not far out of line with most northern Democrats on economic issues, but his record is moderate on cultural issues, and on foreign policy he is very much a hawk. A man of some temper, he is a strong opponent of abortion and gun control. Volkmer serves on the Agriculture Committee, but got his seat there late and is not close to a subcommittee chairmanship; he also serves on Science and Technology and in 1983 became chairman of its Space Science and Applications Subcommittee.

The People   Pop. 1980: 546,171, up 20.6% 1970–80; voting age pop. 391,319; 3% Black, 1% Span. orig. 23% housing units rented. Median owner $35,700; renter $143. Households: 75% family, 41% with children, 66% married couples.

Presidential Vote

1980	Reagan (R)		122,512	(54%)
	Carter (D)		95,235	(42%)
	Anderson (I)		7,258	(3%)

Rep. Harold L. Volkmer (D) Elected 1976; b. Apr. 4, 1931, Jefferson City; home, Hannibal; Jefferson City Jr. Col., St. Louis U., U. of MO, LL.B. 1955; Roman Catholic.

Career Army, 1955–57; Practicing atty., 1957–60; Marion Cnty. Prosecuting Atty., 1960–66; MO House of Reps., 1967–77.

Offices 1230 LHOB, 202-225-2956. Also 316 Fed. Bldg., Hannibal 63401, 314-221-1200.

Committees *Agriculture* (18th). Subcommittees: Department Operations, Research and Foreign Agriculture; Livestock, Dairy and Poultry; Wheat, Soybeans and Feed Grains. *Science and Technology* (12th). Subcommittees: Space Science and Applications (Chairman); Investigations and Oversight.

Group Ratings

	ADA	ACLU	COPE	CFA	LCV	LWV	NTU	NSI	COC	ACA	CSFC
1982	45	50	65	62	62	42	51	70	52	30	42
1981	30	—	65	64	43	—	35	—	26	38	49
1980	39	33	58	36	39	40	29	30	63	29	44

National Journal Ratings

	Economic		Foreign		Cultural	
1982	52%	(LIB)	56%	(LIB)	35%	(LIB)
	48%	(CONS)	44%	(CONS)	65%	(CONS)
1981	56%	(LIB)	18%	(LIB)	51%	(LIB)
	43%	(CONS)	73%	(CONS)	49%	(CONS)

Key Votes

1) Reagan 81 Budget	AGN	5) Incr SS Rtmt Age	AGN	9) Poor Pay Food Stamps	AGN
2) Reagan 81 Tax Cut	AGN	6) Saudi AWACS Sale	AGN	10) Ban Crt Busing Order	FOR
3) Bal Budget Amend	FOR	7) $ for MX Missile	AGN	11) Auto Local Content	FOR
4) Gas & Road Tax	AGN	8) Nerve Gas Prod	FOR	12) Nuclear Arms Freeze	FOR

Election Results

1982 general	Harold L. Volkmer (D)	99,228	(61%)	($185,905)
	Larry E. Mead (R)	63,942	(39%)	($165,592)
1982 primary	Harold L. Volkmer (D)	56,639	(100%)	
1980 general	Harold L. Volkmer (D)	135,905	(56%)	($177,237)
	John W. Turner (R)	104,835	(44%)	($196,790)

Campaign Contributions and Expenditures

1981-82		Direct Cont. 81-82		PACS brkdwn			
Receipts	$187,711	Indiv	$82,889	Agr	$24,790	Ideo	$12,480
Expend.	$185,905	Party	$2,540	Bus	$31,570	Lbr	$17,800
Unspent	$2,201	PACS	$101,102	Hlth	$7,100	Prof	$800
		Cand	$1,000				

Indep Expend: For: $1,156 (NRA)

MONTANA

Montana is a state that is hard for outsiders to comprehend. For one thing, it's vast: the fourth largest state in area, but only 44th in population. Even its name is not entirely accurate. There are plenty of mountains in Montana, rugged chains of Rockies cover the western part of the state; but eastern Montana is almost entirely a brown, treeless plain, rolling upward from the Missouri and Yellowstone Rivers and undergirded, as it turns out, by huge deposits of coal. Montana in some ways is the kind of place most Americans say they would like to live in. The state has no big cities; the largest metropolitan area, Billings, has little more than 100,000 people. Opportunities for hunting, fishing, camping, and boating in unspoiled surroundings are abundant. Wide open spaces, and the famous big sky, are everywhere; you can sometimes drive 40 miles down a road and not see another car. But life in Montana can also be physically harsh. During the winter, winds sweep down unimpeded from the Arctic, and snow is feet thick in the mountains; during the summer, the plains are often baked in heat unrelieved by rain.

Montana's first white settlers were the kind of men willing to go anywhere to get what they were after—they were miners—and they found large deposits of gold, silver, and copper in the mountains of Montana. Raucous mining towns sprang up, complete with outlaws and vigilantes. The largest such town, Butte, sitting on "the richest hill on earth," was for many years the state's largest city—and, aside from Denver, the only recognizably urban center in the Rockies. Butte was known all over the country as a wild place, full of company goons and IWW organizers, a city with a Socialist mayor and with millionaires who bought seats in the U.S. Senate. The early "copper kings," Marcus Daly, William A. Clark, and Augustus Heinze, made millions and feuded with each other. Clark got himself elected to the Senate in 1899 and, after he resigned because of fraud charges, again in 1901; Daly's interests were acquired by the Rockefellers for a time and became the Anaconda Company. Beginning in the early 20th century, Anaconda exerted unparalleled control over the public life of the state. It created the Montana Power Company to suit its needs. It bought up all of Montana's newspapers except the *Great Falls Tribune*. Even so, it did not win all its political battles. Montana elected many notable progressives, even in Anaconda's heyday, Republicans such as Joseph Dixon, Democrats such as Thomas Walsh (who exposed the Teapot Dome scandal); and the young progressive Democrat Burton K. Wheeler. But Anaconda did make sure it escaped significant state taxation and regulation. That increased Anaconda's profits or, as the company might have said, it helped make its metals competitive in world markets and thus created more jobs and prosperity in Montana and the United States.

The old fights between Anaconda and the progressives cut across party lines, but the New Deal tended to organize the state's politics in a partisan manner. On the Republican side were Anaconda (although it became less interested in state politics when it bought copper mines in Chile), Montana Power, the Stockmen's Association of the eastern plains, and the successful farmers of the Farm Bureau. On the Democratic side were most of the old progressives, labor unions (Montana has never passed a right-to-work law and is the most pro-union state in the Rockies), small farmers' groups such as the National Farmers Union, and backers of New Deal programs (for a while in the 1930s Montana received more federal money per capita than almost any other state). Geographically, the eastern plains and Billings typically go Republican, and the western mountains and Butte, Great Falls, and Missoula usually go Democratic. The echoes of class warfare have grown dimmer over the years. Anaconda sold its newspapers in 1959, and after it was acquired by Arco in the 1970s it closed its big smelter in Montana; many of its old enemies would like to have it back. But the divisions in politics remain primarily economic. Butte, now with less than half its 1920 population, and the town of Anaconda, about to become a ghost town like so many mining towns before it, are still heavily Democratic; Billings, riding a local boom based on coal, is heavily Republican.

Presidential politics. Montana is arguably the most marginal of the Rocky Mountain states and yet it never sees much of presidential candidates. The reason is that, even in the airplane age, it takes most of the day just to get up to Montana and touch down, and all for only four electoral votes. For similar reasons, Montana's presidential primary has attracted few campaigners here, although the Democratic contest in 1980, for one, turned out closer than expected.

Senators. In general, Democrats have won the big elections here but seldom by very large margins. Montana has elected a Republican senator only once (in 1946) but came within a few percentage points of doing so half a dozen times. For 16 years it was represented by the Democratic pair of Mike Mansfield, the Senate majority leader from 1961 to 1977, and Lee Metcalf, an old-fashioned liberal and longtime opponent of Montana Power. Mansfield retired in 1976, only to become Ambassador to Japan in both the Carter and Reagan administrations; Metcalf died early in 1978, months before he was expected to retire. The current Democratic senators, John Melcher and Max Baucus, have won impressive election victories. But in the conservative climate of the Rockies—even in this closest thing to an old-fashioned liberal Rocky Mountain state—neither can be said to hold a safe seat.

That was apparent in the 1982 Senate race. John Melcher, to judge just by the numbers, seemed overwhelmingly popular. A veterinarian and local officeholder, he won the House seat in the 2d district (the eastern, plains part of the state, including Billings and Great Falls) in a 1969 special election. The 2d is a vast expanse—the fourth largest district in the nation in area—where cattle ranches stretch as far as the eye can see and towering buttes rise over the magnificently eroded High Plains. This is the agricultural part of the state and the part that has Montana's strip mines; but almost half of its votes are cast in the two urban areas. Melcher became a strong vote-getter in this usually Republican half of Montana, and when Mansfield retired Melcher had no serious opposition for the seat and won with 64%. In the Senate, Melcher seemed to have committee assignments well geared to the state. One is Agriculture, Nutrition and Forestry; the other is Energy and Natural Resources—the old Interior Committee. This has jurisdiction over the federal government's vast landholdings in the West, over grazing and hunting rights, national parks and wilderness areas, Indian tribes and strip mining.

Yet Melcher encountered trouble in the 1982 Senate race. Some Democrats and labor leaders were displeased with his increasingly conservative voting record: he opposed the Panama Canal Treaties and supported President Reagan's economic programs. Republican candidate Larry Williams, who had run against Baucus in 1978, argued that Melcher backed too much federal spending. Melcher's support, though broad, apparently wasn't very deep. He counterattacked Williams, who had problems of his own. An investment counselor and author of *How to Prosper in the Coming Good Years*, Williams had gone through a number of transformations. Baucus in 1978 used a picture Williams once circulated showing him with long hair and a gold chain; Melcher's backers cited a section of Williams's book where he advised investors to buy old people's property with bonds that could be bought heavily discounted from their face value. In a negative year, those attacks, plus Melcher's old home district strength, were enough to give him a 54%–42% victory.

The shape of Melcher's career suggests he is responsive to changes in attitudes and political fashion. He evidently spotted early the conservative trend in the Western states—one that enabled Ronald Reagan to carry Montana against an incumbent president 57%–32%. It will be interesting to see whether his voting record shifts again.

Montana's junior senator is Max Baucus, elected to the House in the 1st district in 1974 and to the Senate in 1978. He came there just as the kind of national Democrats who are his natural allies ran out of steam—and were in the process of losing control of the Senate. More than Melcher, he has specialized in national issues; his major crusade is Health, specifically Medicare. His record on economic issues is somewhat more liberal than Melcher's, but not markedly so; on cultural and foreign issues, he tends to oppose interference by government in personal concerns and to be wary of too aggressive an American military posture in strategic weapons and in the Third World.

Baucus must run for reelection in 1984, and he will probably enter the race the favorite. He is better and more favorably known than any Montana Republican. But the Williams challenges show that there is a solid Republican base and the possibility of building on it. Montana is still a pretty cheap state to campaign in, and most of the 14 Democratic Senate seats up in 1984 seem pretty safe. So a lot of money from both the left and the right could come pouring into Montana to make the election a contest.

1st congressional district. The 1st district seat that Baucus held is basically Democratic; Republicans have won it only four times since the 1920s. There are strong Democratic voting blocs: Butte, Anaconda, and the miners have been 2–1 Democratic for more than 50 years (but their influence is diminishing: they had 27% of the state's population in 1900 and 6% in 1980); Missoula has been usually Democratic since the students at the University of Montana got the vote; mining and Indian counties in various parts of the district produce Democratic margins. The Republican strongholds—the new-rich city of Kalispell, the state capital of Helena, the southwestern corner of the state near Yellowstone National Park and Chet Huntley's Big Sky development—are usually not enough to overcome the Democrats.

The congressman in the 1st is Pat Williams, a teacher and former legislator and Melcher aide. He is an old-fashioned liberal Democrat, close enough to organized labor that the state AFL–CIO director is godfather to one of his children. He serves on Education and Labor—a solid prolabor, proteacher vote—and on Interior and Insular Affairs, whose subject matter is terribly important in western Montana. He won the district smartly in 1978 and has been reelected twice with solid margins against weak oppositions.

Montana has not bothered to redistrict its two congressional seats (the nation's smallest in population) at this writing. Their populations differ only a little, and adjustments needed to get them in line would probably not have any political effect. Apparently no one in the state cares enough to force the issue by filing a lawsuit.

2d congressional district. When Melcher ran for the Senate, the 2d district reverted to the normalcy of a Republican congressman, Ron Marlenee. Marlenee's record seems more directed towards his home district rather than national issues. He serves on the Agriculture and Interior and Insular Affairs Committees—the same assignments Melcher has in the Senate. On farm programs he sometimes supports more generous payments than do other

Republicans—a sensible move, given the fact that this is one of the nation's leading wheat districts. His voting record is largely, but not entirely, conservative; he seems more to be an old-fashioned Main Street Republican, rather than an enthusiast of the New Right.

In 1982 Marlene faced his strongest opponent in six years: Howard Lyman, a farmer who lashed out at him for equivocating over bills to save hard-pressed farmers. Lyman's campaign was set back, however, when his creditors foreclosed on his own ranch and feedlot to secure debts of more than $2 million. Still, Marlenee was held to a 54%–44% victory margin—less than he is used to.

Governor. Few people think that the actions of Montana state government or the policies of the governor of Montana are of much importance to the nation, and in most respects they are not. But the combination of a national energy problem and the presence of major coal deposits in Montana make certain state policies very important indeed. The key policy here is the 30% severance tax Montana places on coal—the highest such tax in the country. Politicians in, of all places, Texas, have complained bitterly that Montana is unfairly stripping consumer states of their wealth for its own greedy purposes and have filed suit to have the tax declared an illegal burden on interstate commerce. Naturally Montanans see it differently. They argue that they are just getting back something they will need for land reclamation and other public purposes in return for giving up a depletable resource. If this appears to reverse Anaconda's old policy of avoiding state taxes, it is in one respect similar: the entity making the decision finds it in the public interest to keep more money for itself. Montana remains a state—one of the very few left—that sees as the centerpiece of its economy the exploitation of nonrenewable resources.

The 30% severance tax was instituted under Governor Thomas Judge, a Democrat with a liberal reputation and a personality that did not, after two terms, wear well. He was defeated in the Democratic primary in 1980 by Ted Schwinden, a more low-key and pleasant politician who won the general election and seems to be a popular governor. He is just as tenacious in sticking to the severance tax, however. Schwinden comes up for reelection in 1984 and seems to be in reasonably good political shape—although a governor's fortunes can always turn.

The People   Est. Pop. 1982: 801,000; Pop. 1980: 786,690, up 1.8% and 13.3% 1970–80; 0.35% of U.S. total, 44th largest; voting age pop. 554,795; 4% American Indian, 1% Spanish origin. Single ancestry: 14% German, 7% English, 5% Irish, Norwegian, 2% Swedish, 1% French, Scottish, Dutch, Italian, Polish. Registered voters (1982): 445,888 Total. 20% with 1–3 yrs. col., 17% with 4+ yrs. col. 12.4% below poverty level. 27% housing units rented; median house value: $46,400; median monthly rent: $165. Households: 72% family, 40% with children, 63% married couples.

1982 Share of Federal Tax Burden $1,855,400,000; .31% of U.S. total, 45th largest.

1982 Share of Federal Expenditures

	Total		Non-Defense		Defense	
Total Expend	$1,782m	(0.30%)	$1,600m	(0.38%)	$182m	(0.10%)
St/Lcl Grants	382m	(0.43%)	382m	(0.43%)	0m	(0%)
Salary/Wages	294m	(0.38%)	190m	(0.69%)	104m	(0.21%)
Ind Payments	938m	(0.33%)	846m	(0.33%)	92m	(0.32%)
Procurement	96m	(0.07%)	59m	(0.19%)	37m	(0.03%)
Other Programs	72m	(1.33%)	72m	(1.34%)	0m	(0%)
Loan/Insurance	1,071m	(1.67%)	1066m	(1.73%)	5m	(0.23%)

Political Lineup   Governor, Ted Schwinden (D). Senators, John Melcher (D) and Max Baucus (D). Representatives, 2 (1 D and 1 R). State Senate, 50 (24 D and 26 R); State House of Representatives, 100 (55 D and 45 R).

Presidential Vote

1980	Reagan (R)	....	206,814	(57%)
	Carter (D)	....	118,132	(32%)
	Anderson (I)	....	29,281	(8%)
1976	Ford (R)	....	173,703	(53%)
	Carter (D)	....	149,259	(45%)

1980 Democratic Presidential Primary			*1980 Republican Presidential Primary*		
Carter	66,922	(51%)	Reagan	68,744	(87%)
Kennedy	47,671	(37%)	Bush	7,665	(10%)
No preference	15,466	(12%)	No preference	3,014	(4%)

SENATORS

Sen. John Melcher (D) Elected 1976, seat up 1988; b. Sept. 6, 1924, Sioux City, IA; home, Forsyth; U. of MN, 1942–43, IA St. U., D.V.M. 1950; Roman Catholic.

Career Army, WWII; Veterinarian, 1950–69; Forsyth City Cncl., 1953–55, Mayor 1955–61; MT House of Reps., 1961–63, 1969; MT Senate, 1963–67; U.S. House of Reps., 1969–77.

Offices 253 RSOB, 202-224-2644. Also 1016 Fed. Bldg., Billings 59102, 406-657-6644; and 12 6th St. South, Great Falls 59401, 406-452-9585.

Committees Agriculture, Nutrition and Forestry (4th). Subcommittees: Agricultural Production, Marketing, and Stabilization of Prices; Nutrition; Soil and Water Conservation. *Energy and Natural Resources* (7th). Subcommittees: Energy Regulation; Energy and Mineral Resources; Public Lands and Reserved Water. *Select Committee on Indian Affairs* (Ranking Member). *Special Committee on Aging* (3d).

Group Ratings

	ADA	ACLU	COPE	CFA	LCV	LWV	NTU	NSI	COC	ACA	CSFC
1982	70	54	79	70	57	45	41	56	44	35	45
1981	55	—	78	43	52	—	30	—	53	53	49
1980	50	50	88	47	44	56	25	50	46	13	38

National Journal Ratings

	Economic		Foreign		Cultural	
1982	70%	(LIB)	79%	(LIB)	62%	(LIB)
	29%	(CONS)	19%	(CONS)	37%	(CONS)
1981	61%	(LIB)	62%	(LIB)	45%	(LIB)
	38%	(CONS)	37%	(CONS)	54%	(CONS)

Key Votes

1) Reagan 81 Budget	FOR	5) $ to El Salvador	AGN	9) Poor Pay Food Stamps	AGN
2) Reagan 81 Tax Cut	FOR	6) Saudi AWACS Sale	FOR	10) Ban Crt Busing Order	FOR
3) Bal Budget Amend	FOR	7) Ban Abortion	AGN	11) Clinch Riv Brdr Rctr	AGN
4) Gas & Road Tax	FOR	8) Nerve Gas Prod	AGN	12) Legal Services Corp	—

Election Results

1982 general	John Melcher (D)	....	174,861	(54%)	($830,892)
	Larry Williams (R)	....	133,789	(42%)	($708,286)
1982 primary	John Melcher (D)	....	83,539	(68%)	
	Mike Bond (D)	....	33,565	(27%)	($67,182)
1976 general	John Melcher (D)	....	206,232	(64%)	($311,101)
	Stanley C. Burger (R)	....	115,213	(36%)	($563,543)

Campaign Contributions and Expenditures

1979-82		*Direct Cont. 79-82*			*PACS brkdwn*		
Receipts	$829,938	Indiv	$313,631	Agr	$43,950	Ideo	$24,300
Expend.	$830,892	Party	$17,500	Bus	$164,560	Lbr	$225,975
Unspent	$3,059	PACS	$481,474	Hlth	$18,400	Prof	$25,650

Indirect Party Expend: $36,881   *Indep Expend:* For: $40,968 (Realtors PAC, LIFEPAC)
Agn: $228,011 (NCPAC)   *Non-Cand Loans:* $17,500

Sen. Max Baucus (D) Elected 1978, seat up 1984; b. Dec. 11, 1941, Helena; home, Missoula; Stanford U., B.A. 1964, LL.B. 1967; United Church of Christ.

Career Staff Atty., Civil Aeronautics Bd., 1967–68; Legal Staff, Securities and Exchange Comm., 1969–71, Legal Asst. to the Chmn., 1970–71; Practicing atty., 1971–75; MT House of Reps., 1973–75; U.S. House of Reps., 1975–78.

Offices 1107 DSOB, 202-224-2651. Also Fed. Bldg., Helena 59601, 406-443-4041.

Committees *Environment and Public Works* (7th). Subcommittees: Water Resources; Nuclear Regulation; Toxic Substances and Environmental Oversight. *Finance* (5th). Subcommittees: Health; International Trade; Taxation and Debt Management. *Judiciary* (7th). Subcommittees: Administrative Practice and Procedure; Courts; Criminal Law; Separation of Power. *Small Business* (5th). Subcommittee: Innovation and Technology.

Group Ratings

	ADA	ACLU	COPE	CFA	LCV	LWV	NTU	NSI	COC	ACA	CSFC
1982	85	75	79	90	69	100	29	10	40	29	38
1981	85	—	80	64	75	—	29	—	39	38	40
1980	72	80	82	60	78	90	29	10	35	16	28

National Journal Ratings

	Economic		*Foreign*		*Cultural*	
1982	76%	(LIB)	90%	(LIB)	72%	(LIB)
	23%	(CONS)	3%	(CONS)	27%	(CONS)
1981	71%	(LIB)	84%	(LIB)	85%	(LIB)
	28%	(CONS)	12%	(CONS)	14%	(CONS)

Key Votes

1) Reagan 81 Budget	FOR	5) $ to El Salvador	AGN	9) Poor Pay Food Stamps	AGN
2) Reagan 81 Tax Cut	FOR	6) Saudi AWACS Sale	AGN	10) Ban Crt Busing Order	AGN
3) Bal Budget Amend	AGN	7) Ban Abortion	AGN	11) Clinch Riv Brdr Rctr	AGN
4) Gas & Road Tax	FOR	8) Nerve Gas Prod	AGN	12) Legal Services Corp	—

Election Results

1978 general	Max Baucus (D)	160,353	(56%)	($653,756)
	Larry Williams (R)	127,589	(44%)	($346,721)
1978 primary	Max Baucus (D)	87,085	(65%)	
	Paul Hatfield (D)	25,789	(19%)	($124,412)
	John Driscoll (D)	18,184	(14%)	($29,720)
	One other (D)	2,404	(2%)	
1972 general	Lee Metcalf (D)	163,609	(52%)	($136,551)
	Henry S. Hibbard (R)	151,316	(48%)	($286,748)

Campaign Contributions and Expenditures

1977-78			*PACS brkdwn*		
Receipts	$668,189	Agr	$14,865	Ideo	$6,637
Expend.	$653,756	Bus	$55,231	Lbr	$92,550
Unspent	$14,434	Hlth	$18,400	Prof	$5,350

GOVERNOR

Gov. Ted Schwinden (D) Elected 1980, term expires Jan. 1985; b. Aug. 31, 1925, Wolf Point; home, Helena; U. of MT, B.A. 1949, M.A. 1950, U. of MN, 1950-54; No religious affiliation.

Career Army, WWII; Grain farmer 1954–; MT House of Reps., 1958; MT Legis. Cncl., 1959–61; Commissioner of State Lands, 1969–76; Lt. Gov. of MT, 1976–80.

Offices State Capitol, Helena 59601, 406-449-3111.

Election Results

1980 gen.	Ted Schwinden (D)	....	199,574	(55%)
	Jack Ramirez (R)	....	160,892	(45%)
1980 prim.	Ted Schwinden (D)	....	69,051	(51%)
	Thomas L. Judge (D)	....	57,946	(42%)
	Two others (D)	....	9,367	(7%)
1976 gen.	Thomas L. Judge (D)	....	195,420	(62%)
	Bob Woodahl (R)	....	115,848	(37%)

FIRST DISTRICT

The People Pop. 1980: 410,071, up 18% 1970–80; voting age pop. 291,809; 3% Am. Ind., 1% Span. orig. 27% housing units rented. Median owner $46,300; renter $161. Households: 72% family, 40% with children, 62% married couples.

Presidential Vote

1980	Reagan (R)	....	107,574	(57%)
	Carter (D)	....	64,393	(34%)
	Anderson (I)	....	16,316	(9%)

Rep. Pat Williams (D) Elected 1978; b. Oct. 30, 1937, Helena; home, Helena; U. of MT, Wm. Jewell Col., U. of Denver, B.A. 1961, W. MT Col.; Roman Catholic.

Career Pub. sch. teacher; MT House of Reps., 1966–68; Exec. Asst. to U.S. Rep. John Melcher, 1968–71; MT State Coord., Family Educ. Prog., 1971–78.

Offices 1512 LHOB, 202-225-3211. Also 306 Steamboat Block, 616 Helena Ave., Helena 59601, 406-443-7878.

Committees *Budget* (16th). Task Forces: Economic Policy and Growth; Education and Employment; Entitlements, Uncontrollables, and Indexing. *Education and Labor* (14th). Subcommittees: Elementary, Secondary and Vocational Education; Employment Opportunities; Human Resources; Select Education.

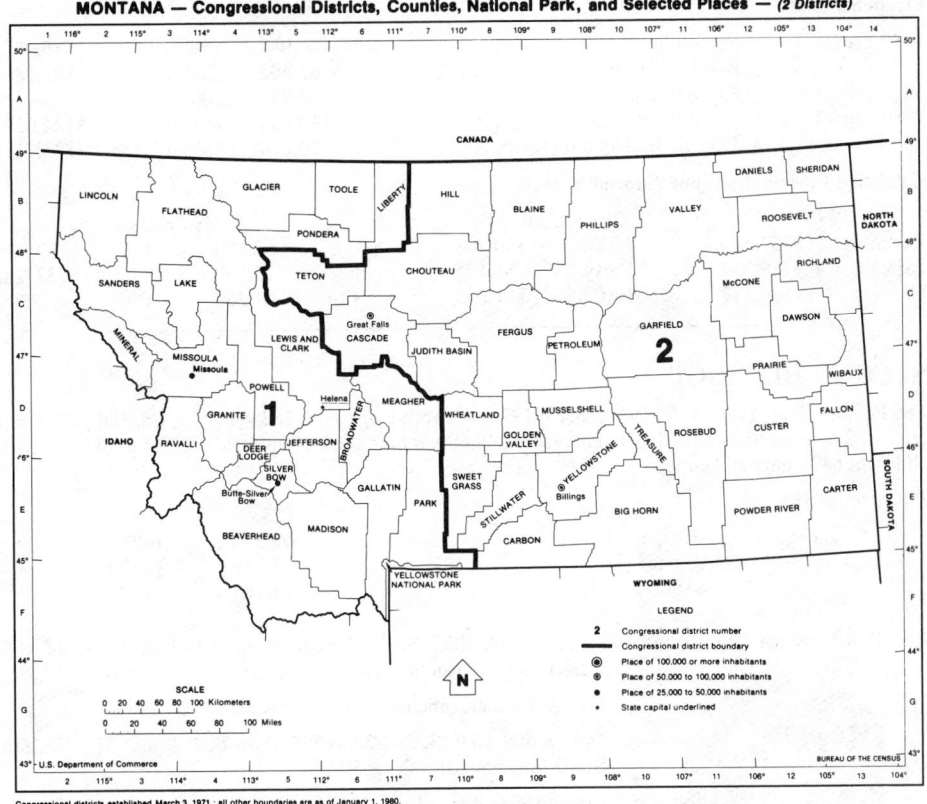

MONTANA — Congressional Districts, Counties, National Park, and Selected Places — *(2 Districts)*

Group Ratings

	ADA	ACLU	COPE	CFA	LCV	LWV	NTU	NSI	COC	ACA	CSFC
1982	85	83	83	85	73	75	27	30	23	13	29
1981	95	—	79	71	79	—	30	—	6	8	30
1980	72	67	67	50	78	67	18	38	66	18	36

National Journal Ratings

	Economic		Foreign		Cultural	
1982	78%	(LIB)	83%	(LIB)	88%	(LIB)
	22%	(CONS)	17%	(CONS)	11%	(CONS)
1981	81%	(LIB)	83%	(LIB)	84%	(LIB)
	15%	(CONS)	16%	(CONS)	15%	(CONS)

Key Votes

1) Reagan 81 Budget	AGN	5) Incr SS Rtmt Age	AGN
2) Reagan 81 Tax Cut	AGN	6) Saudi AWACS Sale	AGN
3) Bal Budget Amend	AGN	7) $ for MX Missile	AGN
4) Gas & Road Tax	AGN	8) Nerve Gas Prod	AGN

9) Poor Pay Food Stamps	AGN
10) Ban Crt Busing Order	AGN
11) Auto Local Content	FOR
12) Nuclear Arms Freeze	FOR

Election Results

1982 general	Pat Williams (D)	100,087	(60%)	($119,052)
	Bob Davies (R)	62,402	(37%)	($83,280)
1982 primary	Pat Williams (D)	55,833	(100%)	
1980 general	Pat Williams (D)	112,866	(61%)	($144,030)
	John K. McDonald (R)	70,874	(39%)	($35,717)

Campaign Contributions and Expenditures

1981-82		*Direct Cont. 81-82*				*PACS brkdwn*		
Receipts	$132,149	Indiv	$50,408	Agr	$2,600	Ideo	$3,525
Expend.	$119,052	Party	$1,195	Bus	$15,100	Lbr	$57,630
Unspent	$20,112	PACS	$81,603	Hlth	$1,250	Prof	$800

SECOND DISTRICT

The People Pop. 1980: 376,619, up 8.5% 1970–80; voting age pop. 262,986; 5% Am. Ind., 1% Span orig. 28% housing units rented. Median owner $46,600; renter $169. Households: 73% family, 41% with children, 64% married couples.

Presidential Vote

1980	Reagan (R)	99,240	(60%)
	Carter (D)	53,639	(32%)
	Anderson (I)	12,965	(8%)

Rep. Ron Marlenee (R) Elected 1976; b. Aug. 8, 1935, Scobey; home, Scobey; MT St. U., U. of MT, Reisch Sch. of Auctioneering; Lutheran.

Career Farmer, rancher, and businessman.

Offices 409 CHOB, 202-225-1555. Also Fed. Bldg., 310 N. 26th St., Billings 59101, 406-585-6753.

Committees *Agriculture* (4th). Subcommittees: Forests, Family Farms and Energy; Wheat, Soybeans, and Feed Grains. *Interior and Insular Affairs* (5th). Subcommittees: Oversight and Investigations; Public Lands and National Parks.

Group Ratings

	ADA	ACLU	COPE	CFA	LCV	LWV	NTU	NSI	COC	ACA	CSFC
1982	5	21	25	23	11	36	77	89	72	80	64
1981	20	—	25	29	22	—	75	—	79	81	66
1980	22	40	32	14	41	38	56	100	68	83	67

National Journal Ratings

	Economic		Foreign		Cultural	
1982	31%	(LIB)	44%	(LIB)	30%	(LIB)
	68%	(CONS)	56%	(CONS)	70%	(CONS)
1981	24%	(LIB)	43%	(LIB)	37%	(LIB)
	68%	(CONS)	57%	(CONS)	63%	(CONS)

Key Votes

1) Reagan 81 Budget	FOR	5) Incr SS Rtmt Age	FOR	9) Poor Pay Food Stamps	FOR
2) Reagan 81 Tax Cut	FOR	6) Saudi AWACS Sale	FOR	10) Ban Crt Busing Order	FOR
3) Bal Budget Amend	FOR	7) $ for MX Missile	FOR	11) Auto Local Content	AGN
4) Gas & Road Tax	—	8) Nerve Gas Prod	FOR	12) Nuclear Arms Freeze	AGN

Election Results

1982 general	Ron Marlenee (R)	79,968	(54%)	($354,351)
	Howard F. Lyman (D)	65,815	(44%)	($189,084)
1982 primary	Ron Marlenee (R)	25,374	(100%)	
1980 general	Ron Marlenee (R)	91,431	(59%)	($214,917)
	Thomas G. Monahan (D)	63,370	(41%)	($36,699)

Campaign Contributions and Expenditures

1981-82		*Direct Cont. 81-82*			*PACS brkdwn*		
Receipts	$331,481	Indiv	$203,201	Agr	$16,100	Ideo	$9,550
Expend.	$354,351	Party	$21,944	Bus	$59,065	Lbr	$800
Unspent	$3,648	PACS	$96,615	Hlth	$9,250	Prof	$200

Indep Expend: For: $2,213 (NRA)

NEBRASKA

Nebraska is a state that sprang suddenly into existence and has changed rather little in the years since. Its beginnings were in the great land rush of the 1880s, when nearly half a million people, most of them from the Midwest states directly east, surged into Nebraska. In 1880 Nebraska had a population of 452,000; by 1890 it reached 1,062,000—not all that far below the 1980 figure of 1,570,000. In the 1880s the patterns of Nebraska life became clear. Most of the state was devoted to farming: corn and hogs in the east, dry-land wheat farming and cattle grazing in the west. Omaha became a major regional center in the 1880s, and Lincoln was established as the state capital. No other major urban centers developed then or exist now.

Many of the people who first settled Nebraska assumed that it would grow as the states to the east did—Missouri, Illinois, Iowa. They thought that Nebraska county seats would become major manufacturing centers and that small Nebraska towns would become rivals of, if not Chicago or St. Louis, at least of Des Moines or Decatur. After all, Chicago itself had grown from nothing to become one of the largest cities in the world in just 30 years. If that were to happen in Nebraska, land values would rise, many original settlers would get very rich, and there would be plenty of work close to home for their children. But Nebraska did not become another Illinois. The 1880s were a time of plentiful rain here; the 1890s were a decade of drought. Nebraska stopped growing: many rural counties and even Omaha lost population. More catastrophic to the Nebraskans of the day was that it became obvious that Nebraska's economy would not support all the children of the people who lived there. Most of Nebraska's settlers, like most migrants into most states, were young people, optimistic and motivated, in search of opportunity, with families full of children. Fully 48% of the one million Nebraskans of 1890 were children, and a very large percentage of them moved elsewhere when they grew up. Since 1890 Nebraska has exported people to the West, the great metropolitan areas of the Midwest, and, more recently, to Texas and the Southwest. Only 28% of Nebraska's 1.6 million residents today are children; there are 60,000 fewer children here than there were 90 years ago. For years Nebraska's population has been elderly (another reason: people live longer here).

The sudden boom of the 1880s and the bust of the 1890s produced the most colorful—and atypical—politics of Nebraska's history, the populist movement and William Jennings Bryan. Nebraska's settlers were mostly from Republican backgrounds, and even early on this was among the most Republican of states. Yet the only serious presidential contender it has ever produced is Bryan, "the silver-tongued orator of the Platte," a man considered radical in his time—so much so that the incumbent Democratic president refused to support him. Bryan was only 36 when he delivered the famous Cross of Gold speech at the 1896 Democratic National Convention, the speech that won him the Democratic nomination and got him achingly close to the White House. Nebraskans supported Bryan, whose program may have been forward-looking, but whose purpose was essentially retrograde: to restore Nebraska to the prosperity and hopes it had enjoyed a few years before. Bryan won the Democratic nomination again in 1900 and 1908 but never came as close to winning as he did the first time. By then Nebraska had already gone back to the Republicans, and Bryan himself eventually moved to Florida. Since Bryan's time, Nebraska's most notable lapse from conservatism was the career of George Norris, congressman (1909–13) and senator (1913–43). During the progressive era Norris led the House rebellion against Speaker Joseph Cannon; during the 1930s he pushed through the Norris-LaGuardia Anti-Injunction Act, the first national pro-union legislation, and the Tennessee Valley Authority.

Presidential politics. Since 1900, 92% of Nebraska's population growth has been in and around Omaha and Lincoln; between them and their suburbs they now contain 43% of the state's people. Most of the immigrants to Omaha, a railroad, meatpacking, and manufacturing center, and Lincoln, the state capital and home of the University of Nebraska, came from the rural Republican hinterland. There is also a sizable Eastern European community on the south side of Omaha which, like the city's small black neighborhood, usually votes Democratic; so too do a few isolated rural counties. But as a whole Nebraska is almost always solidly Republican in national elections. In the close elections of 1960, 1968, and 1976, the Republican nominee carried both big cities and lost only three or four counties out of 93. In 1980, this was Ronald Reagan's second best state: he won with 66% of the vote and carried every county, some by enormous percentages (*e.g.,* 481 to 33).

Nebraska has a presidential primary which, in the middle of the season, used to attract a lot of attention; the whole national press followed Robert Kennedy and Eugene McCarthy out here in 1968. No more. There are too many other primaries, and Nebraska's delegations are small.

Governor. Despite the state's heavy Republican preference, it has a Democratic governor and two Democratic U.S. senators; in fact, it has had Democratic governors in 16 of the last 24 years. At first glance, the reasons for each Democratic victory look idiosyncratic. Take Robert Kerrey, the new Democratic governor. His victory was a triumph of energy over routine, of enthusiasm over plodding. Kerrey ran as a 39-year-old restaurant owner with astonishing credentials. He won the Congressional Medal of Honor in Vietnam and, after convalescing, went around the country denouncing the war. Although he lost his right leg below the knee, he took up running, and now runs the marathon. How can a candidate like that be stopped?

Kerrey applied his enthusiasm to denunciations of the incumbent governor, former Congressman Charles Thone. He charged that Thone was concealing deficits and had mismanaged the state; he tried to make the contest a battle between excellence and mediocrity. The Republicans attacked Kerrey for some of the positions he had taken (supporting homosexual rights in Lincoln, for example) and as one who switched positions. The recession may have contributed to the outcome, but the campaign seems to have been run mostly on state issues, and on the contrast between two personalities. Kerrey won by a small margin; he carried Omaha and Lincoln while Thone won the usually more Republican western part of the state.

Kerrey's charges against Thone were reminiscent of the campaign James Exon, now U.S. senator, waged against the last Republican governor, Norbert Tiemann, when he beat him in 1970. He said that Tiemann was spending too much money, in an undisciplined way. Perhaps there is an endemic problem for Republicans here: dealing with a friendly legislature, they are never subject to the sharp and not entirely friendly scrutiny that a Democratic executive gets here, and so are more likely to be sloppy and undisciplined. Both of Nebraska's Democratic senators had extensive executive experience, and ended up with more respect from the voters than orthodox Republicans: Exon was governor for two terms; Zorinsky was mayor of Omaha for four years, and though he was nominally a Republican he would be a maverick in any party.

Senators. Zorinsky has now won a second Senate term. He ran in 1976 complaining that Republican party leaders passed him over for an Omaha congressman; as the Democratic candidate he beat the man decisively. He considered switching parties when the Republicans took control of the Senate in 1980, but no one offered him a good enough deal. His opponent in 1982, a former Air Force general, never got his campaign off the ground. The election was a referendum on Zorinsky, who is widely popular and carried all but a handful of counties in the state.

Probably the voters like Zorinsky for the same reason he exasperates many of his colleagues: he is an incorrigible maverick. He has been accused of flip-flopping and changing his mind on issues, though other colleagues call him an effective negotiator. He is the one Democrat on the Foreign Relations Committee who didn't vote against the nomination of Kenneth Adelman to a top arms control post; he is more of a hawk than his colleagues. He voted against the Panama Canal Treaties, despite extensive pleas from the Carter administration. He also serves on the Agriculture Committee, and has gone back and forth in his approach there—in response, he would say, to conditions in Nebraska and the nation. A fiscal conservative, his voting record resembles that of northern Republicans more than northern Democrats.

James Exon also has a reputation as a fiscal conservative and a voting record that sometimes looks more Republican than Democratic. But Exon stays with his colleagues more often on both economic and foreign issues; on cultural issues he is solidly conservative. Temperamentally, there is also a difference. Exon is a team player, a man who instinctively works with other members to get a solution. Zorinsky acts that way sometimes, but he is usually ready to go off on his own and announce a position it is unlikely he can get anyone else to agree to. Exon is a member of the Armed Services Committee, where he is by no means a knee-jerk vote either for or against the Pentagon; the Commerce Committee, where he can be a key vote on regulation and deregulation issues; and on the Budget Committee.

Exon was phenomenally popular as governor, and popularity earned after eight years of close exposure to an electorate is unlikely to fade. His seat comes up in 1984, and while the Republicans cannot be expected to let him have it without a contest, they will have a hard time coming up with a candidate who can make a serious race of it.

Congressional districting. Nebraska revised its congressional district lines very slightly after the 1980 Census, with no political effect on any of its three Republican congressmen.

The People   Est. Pop. 1982: 1,586,000; Pop. 1980: 1,569,825, up 1.0% 1980–82 and 5.7% 1970–80; 1.0% of U.S. total, 35th largest; voting age pop. 1,122,655; 3% Black, 1% Spanish origin. Single ancestry: 22% German, 6% English, 4% Irish, 2% Swedish, Polish, 1% French, Italian, Dutch, Norwegian. Registered voters (1982): 832,121 Total. 416,938 R (50%); 362,188 D (44%); 52,995 I (6%). 17% with 1–3 yrs. col., 16% with 4+ yrs. col. 10.4% below poverty level. 29% housing units rented; median house value: $38,000; median monthly rent: $170. Households: 72% family, 38% with children, 63% married couples.

1982 Share of Federal Tax Burden $3,932,100,000; .66% of U.S. total, 35th largest.

1982 Share of Federal Expenditures

	Total		Non-Defense		Defense	
Total Expend	$3,324m	(0.55%)	$2,744m	(0.65%)	$580m	(0.32%)
St/Lcl Grants	524m	(0.59%)	524m	(0.59%)	0m	(0%)
Salary/Wages	487m	(0.62%)	134m	(0.49%)	353m	(0.70%)
Ind Payments	1,880m	(0.66%)	1,719m	(0.67%)	161m	(0.56%)
Procurement	239m	(0.16%)	98m	(0.31%)	141m	(0.12%)
Other Programs	195m	(3.60%)	195m	(3.63%)	0m	(0%)
Loan/Insurance	2,764m	(4.48%)	2,747m	(4.45%)	17m	(0.77%)

Political Lineup   Governor, Bob Kerrey (D). Senators, Edward Zorinsky (D) and J. James Exon (D). Representatives, 3 R. Unicameral Legislature, 49 (32 R, 16 D and 1 I).

Presidential Vote

1980	Reagan (R)	419,214	(66%)
	Carter (D)	166,424	(26%)
	Anderson (I)	44,854	(7%)
1976	Ford (R)	359,705	(59%)
	Carter (D)	233,692	(38%)

1980 Democratic Presidential Primary

Carter	....	72,120	(47%)
Kennedy	....	57,826	(38%)
Two others & write-ins		7,894	(5%)
Uncommitted	....	16,041	(10%)

1980 Republican Presidential Primary

Reagan	....	155,995	(76%)
Bush	....	31,380	(15%)
Anderson	....	11,879	(6%)
Four others & write-ins		5,949	(3%)

SENATORS

Sen. Edward Zorinsky (D) Elected 1976, seat up 1988; b. Nov. 11, 1928, Omaha; home, Omaha; U. of NE, B.S. 1949, Harvard U. Grad. Sch.; Jewish.

Career Tobacco wholesaler; Omaha Pub. Power District, 1968–73; Mayor of Omaha, 1973–77, elected as Repub., switched to Dem. Party, Dec. 1975.

Offices 431 RSOB, 202-224-6551. Also 8311 Fed. Bldg., Omaha 68102, 402-221-4381.

Committees *Agriculture, Nutrition and Forestry* (3d). Subcommittees: Agricultural Credit and Rural Electrification; Agricultural Production, Marketing, and Stabilization of Prices; Foreign Agricultural Policy. *Foreign Relations* (5th). Subcommittees: Arms Control, Oceans and International Operations, and Environment; European Affairs; Western Hemisphere Affairs.

Group Ratings

	ADA	ACLU	COPE	CFA	LCV	LWV	NTU	NSI	COC	ACA	CSFC
1982	20	14	31	50	38	33	64	89	57	71	65
1981	20	—	30	29	12	—	71	—	78	80	62
1980	22	0	31	13	33	20	56	60	79	62	64

National Journal Ratings

	Economic		Foreign		Cultural	
1982	48%	(LIB)	33%	(LIB)	12%	(LIB)
	51%	(CONS)	64%	(CONS)	87%	(CONS)
1981	42%	(LIB)	39%	(LIB)	2%	(LIB)
	57%	(CONS)	60%	(CONS)	82%	(CONS)

Key Votes

1) Reagan 81 Budget	FOR	5) $ to El Salvador	AGN	9) Poor Pay Food Stamps	AGN
2) Reagan 81 Tax Cut	FOR	6) Saudi AWACS Sale	FOR	10) Ban Crt Busing Order	FOR
3) Bal Budget Amend	FOR	7) Ban Abortion	FOR	11) Clinch Riv Brdr Rctr	FOR
4) Gas & Road Tax	AGN	8) Nerve Gas Prod	FOR	12) Legal Services Corp	AGN

Election Results

1982 general	Edward Zorinsky (D)	363,350	(67%)	($523,141)
	Jim Keck (R)	155,760	(29%)	($489,186)
1982 primary	Edward Zorinsky (D)	124,288	(100%)	
1976 general	Edward Zorinsky (D)	313,805	(53%)	($237,613)
	John Y. McCollister (R)	279,284	(47%)	($391,287)

Campaign Contributions and Expenditures

1979-82		Direct Cont. 79-82		PACS brkdwn			
Receipts	$572,983	Indiv	$237,624	Agr	$40,500	Ideo	$12,650
Expend.	$523,141	Party	$26,015	Bus	$173,676	Lbr	$37,100
Unspent	$53,576	PACS	$290,409	Hlth	$19,700	Prof	$2,100

Indirect Party Expend: $40,000   *Indep Expend:* For: $1,720 (NRA)

Sen. J. James Exon (D) Elected 1978, seat up 1984; b. Aug. 9, 1921, Geddes, SD; home, Lincoln; U. of Omaha; Episcopal.

Career Army, WWII; Branch Mgr., Universal Finance Co., 1946–54; Pres., Exon's Inc., office equip. business, 1954–70; Vice Chmn., NE St. Central Comm., 1964–68; Gov. of NE, 1970–78.

Offices 3313 DSOB, 202-224-4224. Also Fed. Bldg., Omaha 68102, 402-221-4665.

Committees *Armed Services* (5th). Subcommittees: Military Construction; Strategic and Theater Nuclear Forces; Manpower and Personnel. *Budget* (10th). *Commerce, Science, and Transportation* (6th). Subcommittees: Aviation; Surface Transportation.

Group Ratings

	ADA	ACLU	COPE	CFA	LCV	LWV	NTU	NSI	COC	ACA	CSFC
1982	40	18	40	70	66	40	45	50	55	58	55
1981	45	—	36	50	38	—	41	—	50	48	51
1980	39	20	37	20	33	40	57	60	50	44	49

National Journal Ratings

	Economic		Foreign		Cultural	
1982	59%	(LIB)	49%	(LIB)	22%	(LIB)
	40%	(CONS)	50%	(CONS)	77%	(CONS)
1981	56%	(LIB)	52%	(LIB)	26%	(LIB)
	43%	(CONS)	47%	(CONS)	73%	(CONS)

Key Votes

1) Reagan 81 Budget	FOR	5) $ to El Salvador	AGN
2) Reagan 81 Tax Cut	FOR	6) Saudi AWACS Sale	FOR
3) Bal Budget Amend	FOR	7) Ban Abortion	FOR
4) Gas & Road Tax	AGN	8) Nerve Gas Prod	FOR

9) Poor Pay Food Stamps	AGN
10) Ban Crt Busing Order	FOR
11) Clinch Riv Brdr Rctr	AGN
12) Legal Services Corp	AGN

Election Results

1978 general	J. James Exon (D)	334,096	(68%)	($234,862)
	Don Shasteen (R)	159,706	(32%)	($218,148)
1978 primary	J. James Exon (D) unopposed			
1972 general	Carl T. Curtis (R)	301,841	(53%)	($250,392)
	Terry Carpenter (D)	265,922	(47%)	($38,629)

Campaign Contributions and Expenditures

1981-82			PACS brkdwn		
Receipts	$262,404	Agr	$4,100	Ideo	$3,000
Expend.	$234,862	Bus	$35,100	Lbr	$8,300
Unspent	$27,539	Hlth	$9,100	Prof	$5,100

GOVERNOR

Gov. Bob Kerrey (D) Elected 1982, term expires Jan. 1987; b. Aug. 27, 1943, Lincoln; home, Lincoln; U. of NE, B.S. 1965; Congregational.

Career Navy, 1966–69; Pharmacist, 1970–72; Restaurant, Sports/ Fitness Enterprises Developer, 1972–82.

Offices State Capitol, Lincoln 68509, 402-471-2244.

Election Results

1982 gen.	Bob Kerrey (D)	277,436	(51%)
	Charles Thone (R)	270,203	(49%)
1982 prim.	Bob Kerrey (D)	87,913	(71%)
	George Bill Burrows (D)	35,426	(29%)
1978 gen.	Charles Thone (R)	275,473	(56%)
	Gerald T. Whelan (D)	216,754	(44%)

FIRST DISTRICT

The 1st congressional district of Nebraska is a band of 26½ counties covering most of the eastern part of the state from South Dakota down to Kansas, except for the Omaha area. Outside of Lincoln, the district's largest city, the economy of the 1st is based almost entirely on agriculture. The political inclination of the region is Republican, but there are a couple of counties with large German Catholic communities that have faithfully supported Democrats of such diverse origins as John Kennedy and Jimmy Carter (in 1976, not 1980). Lincoln, the capital and—more important to people here—home of the University of Nebraska Cornhuskers, is traditionally Republican. But sometimes the large number of state employees with the university community have put Lincoln into the Democratic column, as in the 1982 gubernatorial race.

The 1st district saw a number of close congressional races in the 1960s and 1970s, but seems unlikely to have many in the 1980s. A Democrat actually won the district in 1964, and there were close races in 1966, 1968, 1974, and 1978. But the current incumbent, Doug Bereuter, seems to have made this a safe seat. Bereuter's background and attitudes are a little different from traditional Nebraska Republicans. He served as an aide to Republican

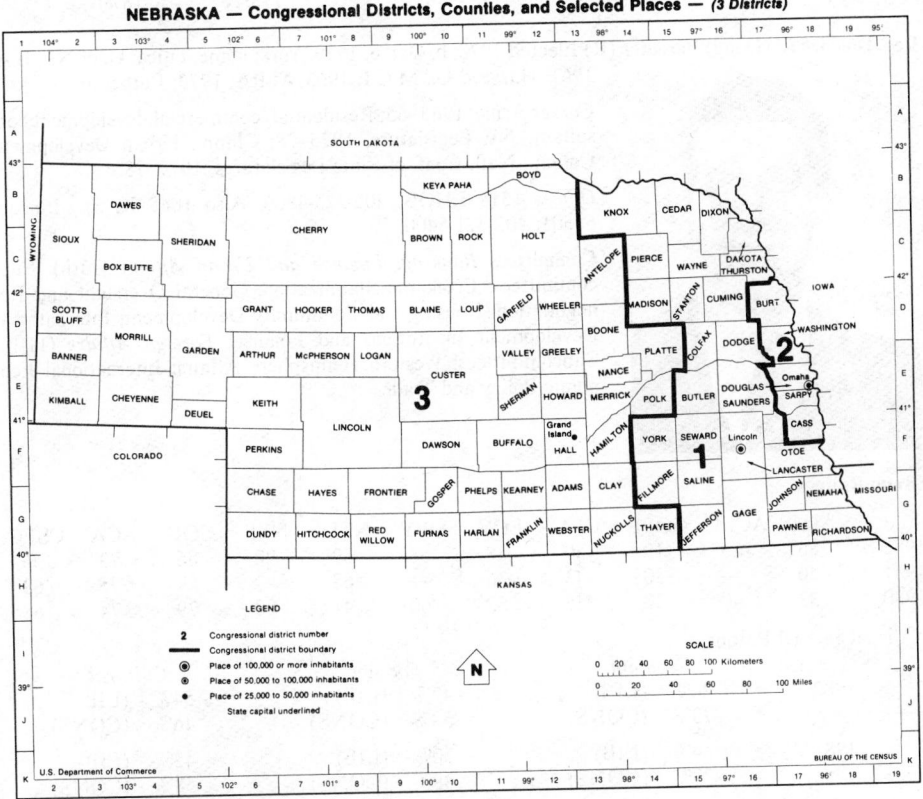

NEBRASKA — Congressional Districts, Counties, and Selected Places — (3 Districts)

LEGEND

2   Congressional district number
—— Congressional district boundary
◉   Place of 100,000 or more inhabitants
◉   Place of 50,000 to 100,000 inhabitants
•   Place of 25,000 to 50,000 inhabitants
State capital underlined

SCALE

N

0 20 40 60 80 100 Kilometers
0 20 40 60 80 100 Miles

BUREAU OF THE CENSUS

U.S. Department of Commerce

Congressional districts established May 26, 1981; all other boundaries are as of January 1, 1980.

Governor Norbert Tiemann, who lost the 1970 election after being attacked as a high-taxer; later Bereuter worked on a committee of the National Council of State Legislators. He seems disposed not so much to denounce government as to study it and try to make it work better.

In 1981 and 1982 that disposition did not give him a record much different from that of other Republicans; Bereuter joined his copartisans in unified support of Reagan administration positions. But he was not solidly conservative on cultural or foreign issues. He serves on the Banking Committee, on Small Business and the Select Committee on Aging, and in 1983 he gave up a seat on the Interior Committee for one on Foreign Affairs. He is interested in promoting exports of American products and, after visiting El Salvador, argued that increased military aid should be used to protect installations and land rather than for launching an offensive campaign.

Bereuter won the 1978 election against a strong, adequately financed opponent; he won huge margins against weak candidates in 1980 and 1982.

The People   Pop. 1980: 523,079, up 6.6% 1970–80; voting age pop. 383,987; 1% Black, 1% Span. orig., 1% Am. Ind. 29% housing units rented. Median owner $38,300; renter $167. Households: 71% family, 36% with children, 63% married couples.

Presidential Vote

1980	Reagan (R)	132,845	(63%)
	Carter (D)	59,434	(28%)
	Anderson (I)	17,612	(8%)

Rep. Douglas K. (Doug) Bereuter (R) Elected 1978; b. Oct. 6, 1939, York; home, Utica; U. of NE, B.A. 1961, Harvard U., M.C.P. 1963, M.P.A. 1973; Lutheran.

Career Army, 1963–65; Residential/commercial development consultant; NE Legislature, 1975–78; Chmn., Urban Development Comm., Natl. Conf. of State Legislatures, 1977–78.

Offices 1314 LHOB, 202-225-4806. Also 1045 K. St., Lincoln 68501, 402-471-5400.

Committees *Banking, Finance and Urban Affairs* (13th). Subcommittees: Economic Stabilization; General Oversight and Renegotiation; Housing and Community Development; International Development Institutions and Finance. *Foreign Affairs* (11th). Subcommittees: Western Hemisphere Affairs; International Economic Policy and Trade.

Group Ratings

	ADA	ACLU	COPE	CFA	LCV	LWV	NTU	NSI	COC	ACA	CSFC
1982	26	25	19	50	38	58	69	90	86	73	56
1981	20	—	20	43	36	—	67	—	89	75	63
1980	33	40	32	36	52	60	41	80	79	74	68

National Journal Ratings

	Economic		Foreign		Cultural	
1982	26%	(LIB)	42%	(LIB)	54%	(LIB)
	73%	(CONS)	58%	(CONS)	46%	(CONS)
1981	4%	(LIB)	50%	(LIB)	42%	(LIB)
	79%	(CONS)	49%	(CONS)	58%	(CONS)

Key Votes

1) Reagan 81 Budget	FOR	5) Incr SS Rtmt Age	FOR	9) Poor Pay Food Stamps	FOR
2) Reagan 81 Tax Cut	FOR	6) Saudi AWACS Sale	FOR	10) Ban Crt Busing Order	AGN
3) Bal Budget Amend	FOR	7) $ for MX Missile	FOR	11) Auto Local Content	AGN
4) Gas & Road Tax	FOR	8) Nerve Gas Prod	AGN	12) Nuclear Arms Freeze	AGN

Election Results

1982 general	Douglas K. (Doug) Bereuter (R) ..	137,675	(75%)	($109,530)
	Curt Donaldson (D)	45,676	(25%)	($7,934)
1982 primary	Douglas K. (Doug) Bereuter (R) ..	63,170	(100%)	
1980 general	Douglas K. (Doug) Bereuter (R) ..	160,705	(79%)	($175,876)
	Rex S. Story (D)	43,605	(21%)	($14,592)

Campaign Contributions and Expenditures

1981-82		Direct Cont. 81-82			PACS brkdwn		
Receipts	$135,304	Indiv	$64,967	Agr	$6,800	Ideo	$1,100
Expend.	$109,530	Party	$17,499	Bus	$37,675	Lbr	$200
Unspent	$42,197	PACS	$48,011	Hlth	$3,950	Prof	$100

SECOND DISTRICT

The 2d congressional district of Nebraska is metropolitan Omaha and a couple of rural counties to the north and south, along the Missouri River. Omaha, like most of Nebraska, sprang into existence suddenly in the 1880s, when it became a regional meatpacking and railroad center of considerable importance. Over the years it has continued to grow with the steadiness that is typical of cities whose economies are based, ultimately, on the processing and transportation of food. However much farm prices and profits may fluctuate—and however loud the cries of protest from farmers—demand for food products continues at a pretty steady level, and a city like Omaha which can supply that demand has a solid base for its way of life.

And that way of life, though it may not strike residents of glamorous parts of big metropolitan areas that way, is pretty close to what most Americans want. Omaha is a small enough city to be readily comprehensible; you don't feel distant, physically or psychologically, from neighborhoods on the other side of town, and you usually know people from a broader range of backgrounds than you would in a large homogeneous neighborhood in a big metropolitan area. At the same time, Omaha has many of the cultural, educational, recreational, religious, and medical facilities which people seek. It has some ethnic and racial diversity, but no really major tensions; economic opportunities, but no vast gulf between the rich and poor. Culturally, it is diverse, but traditional family values do not seem to be under attack, and traditional religions thrive. It is the kind of America many Americans want, the kind of America many Americans in the affluent 1970s left the big metropolitan areas to seek.

Politically, Omaha is on balance a Republican city, which goes Democratic every so often; it elected a Democratic congressman, John Cavanaugh, in 1974, 1976, and 1978; in 1980 he retired at age 35 to spend more time with his family—in Omaha. The current congressman, Hal Daub, is in many ways typical of the Republican congressmen who were elected with Ronald Reagan in 1980. He is young (39 when elected); he has worked in a small business; he was active in Republican Party affairs; he does not have a particularly magnetic personality nor is he a strong speaker. Daub proved to be a solid and faithful Reaganite. His committee assignments in his first term provided him with few opportunities to advance legislation; he was in effect a backbencher, part of the team that gave solid support to administration initiatives. In his second term he moved to the Public Works and Transportation Committee, but it is not in the nature of things, in a House effectively controlled by the Democrats, that he is going to be a leader on issues.

Some observers predicted that Daub would be in trouble in 1982, because of the recession and his pro-Reagan record. But against the same opponent he faced in 1980 he increased his percentage. This is, perhaps, not a perfectly safe Republican seat, but it will be hard for the Democrats to win here.

The People Pop. 1980: 522,919, up 6.2% 1970–80; voting age pop. 364,998; 7% Black, 2% Span. orig., 1% Asian orig. 33% housing units rented. Median owner $40,500; renter $190. Households: 72% family, 42% with children, 60% married couples.

Presidential Vote

1980	Reagan (R)	123,422	(62%)
	Carter (D)	60,819	(30%)
	Anderson (I)	15,780	(8%)

Rep. Harold J. (Hal) **Daub** (R) Elected 1980; b. Apr. 23, 1941, Fort Bragg, NC; home, Omaha; Washington U., St. Louis, B.S. 1963, U. of NE, Lincoln, J.D. 1966; Presbyterian.

Career Army, Korea; Practicing atty., 1968–71; V.P., Gen. Counsel, Standard Chemical Mfg. Co., 1971–80; Douglas Cnty. Repub. Chmn., 1974–77; Repub. Nominee for U.S. House of Reps., 1978.

Offices 1019 LHOB, 202-225-4155. Also 8424 Fed. Bldg., 215 N. 17th St., Omaha 68102, 402-221-4216.

Committees *Public Works and Transportation* (12th). Subcommittees: Surface Transportation; Water Resources. *Small Business* (7th). Subcommittees: SBA and SBIC Authority, Minority Enterprise and General Small Business Problems. *Select Committee on Aging* (10th). Subcommittee: Health and Long-Term Care.

Group Ratings

	ADA	ACLU	COPE	CFA	LCV	LWV	NTU	NSI	COC	ACA	CSFC
1982	10	25	18	23	21	33	77	100	100	74	62
1981	15	—	13	50	29	—	84	—	84	87	69

National Journal Ratings

	Economic		Foreign		Cultural	
1982	15%	(LIB)	42%	(LIB)	4%	(LIB)
	84%	(CONS)	58%	(CONS)	87%	(CONS)
1981	4%	(LIB)	30%	(LIB)	23%	(LIB)
	79%	(CONS)	68%	(CONS)	77%	(CONS)

Key Votes

1) Reagan 81 Budget	FOR	5) Incr SS Rtmt Age	FOR
2) Reagan 81 Tax Cut	FOR	6) Saudi AWACS Sale	FOR
3) Bal Budget Amend	FOR	7) $ for MX Missile	FOR
4) Gas & Road Tax	FOR	8) Nerve Gas Prod	AGN

9) Poor Pay Food Stamps	FOR
10) Ban Crt Busing Order	FOR
11) Auto Local Content	AGN
12) Nuclear Arms Freeze	AGN

Election Results

1982 general	Harold J. (Hal) Daub (R)	92,639	(57%)	($282,268 est.)
	Richard M. Fellman (D)	70,431	(43%)	($190,177)
1982 primary	Harold J. (Hal) Daub (R)	33,047	(100%)	
1980 general	Harold J. (Hal) Daub (R)	107,736	(53%)	($337,833)
	Richard M. Fellman (D)	88,843	(44%)	($153,539)

Campaign Contributions and Expenditures

1981-82		Direct Cont. 81-82			PACS brkdwn			
Receipts	$282,124 (est.)	Indiv	$123,042	Agr	$11,550	Ideo	$8,188
Expend.	$282,268 (est.)	Party	$16,722	Bus	$92,353	Lbr	$3,750
Unspent	$2,445	PACS	$140,174	Hlth	$15,750	Prof	$1,750

Indirect Party Expend: $18,015   *Indep Expend:* For: $737 (NRA)

THIRD DISTRICT

One-third of Nebraska's population is spread out over the western three-fourths of its land area—the 3d congressional district. As you drive west here, the rolling fields of corn and wheat give way to the sand hills and cattle country, much of it devoid of signs of human habitation for miles on end. This is the part of Nebraska to which settlers thronged during the unusually moist 1880s, and which their descendants for years have been leaving, often reluctantly, ever since. Today most of the people here live along the Platte River or near such towns as Grand Island, Hastings, Kearney, and Scottsbluff—none with more than 35,000 people. When people divide the country into regions, they always put Nebraska in the Midwest. But the part of the state that is the 3d congressional district is in many ways more similar to Wyoming, just to the west, than it is to Iowa on the east. Economically, grazing is more important than corn or wheat here; physically, the rainfall is usually low, not much more than on the High Plains of Wyoming or Colorado. Politically, this region seems more western than midwestern as well. Twenty-five years ago western Nebraska was the scene of farm rebellions against Ezra Taft Benson, and Democrats even won House seats in this area. Now western Nebraska is very heavily Republican, like the Rocky Mountain states, and the 3d district is one of the safest Republican seats in the House. Folks here proved to be as hostile to the Carter administration as folks anywhere: fully 74% of the votes here in 1980 were cast for Ronald Reagan and only 21% for the incumbent president.

There was a seriously contested House race here as recently as 1974, however, when no incumbent was running, and a wealthy Democrat came within 737 votes of winning. But the successful Republican, Virginia Smith, has not had any trouble since. In 1980 she won with 84% of the vote—one of the strongest showings in the nation—and in 1982, when there was talk of anti-Republican discontent in farm states, she was unopposed. Mrs. Smith's background suggests party regularity. For 20 years she chaired the American Farm Bureau Women; the Farm Bureau has been one of the pillars of Republican strength in the Farm Belt for many years. In what has become a cohesive Republican bloc Mrs. Smith has been a very reliable Republican vote. She has a seat on the Appropriations Committee and is ranking minority member on the Agriculture Subcommittee. That means she is the opposite number to Jamie Whitten, a shrewd Mississippian who has chaired the subcommittee since 1949 (except for two Republican years). No one imagines that Mrs. Smith is going to dominate Whitten, but her position is nonetheless an important one for Nebraska and this district.

The People Pop. 1980: 523,827, up 4.2% 1970–80; voting age pop. 373,670; 2% Span. orig. 25% housing units rented. Median owner $34,700; renter $142. Households: 73% family, 38% with children, 66% married couples.

Presidential Vote

1980	Reagan (R)	162,947	(74%)
	Carter (D)	46,171	(21%)
	Anderson (I)	11,462	(5%)

Rep. Virginia Smith (R) Elected 1974; b. June 30, 1911, Randolph, IA; home, Chappell; U. of NE, B.A. 1934; Methodist.

Career Natl. Chwmn., Amer. Farm Bureau Women, 1955–74; Chwmn., Pres., Task Force on Rural Development, 1971–72.

Offices 2202 RHOB, 202-225-6435. Also P. O. Bldg., Main Fl., Grand Island 68801, 308-381-0505.

Committee *Appropriations* (12th). Subcommittees: Agriculture, Rural Development and Related Agencies; Energy and Water Development.

Group Ratings

	ADA	ACLU	COPE	CFA	LCV	LWV	NTU	NSI	COC	ACA	CSFC
1982	25	8	10	23	13	33	76	90	86	74	59
1981	10	—	11	36	14	—	81	—	84	79	66
1980	11	20	6	14	26	40	51	100	85	78	72

National Journal Ratings

	Economic		Foreign		Cultural	
1982	28%	(LIB)	55%	(LIB)	4%	(LIB)
	72%	(CONS)	45%	(CONS)	87%	(CONS)
1981	4%	(LIB)	58%	(LIB)	12%	(LIB)
	79%	(CONS)	42%	(CONS)	86%	(CONS)

Key Votes

1) Reagan 81 Budget	FOR	5) Incr SS Rtmt Age	FOR	9) Poor Pay Food Stamps	FOR
2) Reagan 81 Tax Cut	FOR	6) Saudi AWACS Sale	FOR	10) Ban Crt Busing Order	FOR
3) Bal Budget Amend	FOR	7) $ for MX Missile	AGN	11) Auto Local Content	AGN
4) Gas & Road Tax	FOR	8) Nerve Gas Prod	AGN	12) Nuclear Arms Freeze	AGN

Election Results

1982 general	Virginia Smith (R)	171,853	(100%)	($95,915)
1982 primary	Virginia Smith (R)	80,108	(100%)	
1980 general	Virginia Smith (R)	182,887	(84%)	($93,496)
	Stan Ditus (D)	34,967	(16%)	($15,970)

Campaign Contributions and Expenditures

1981-82		Direct Cont. 81-82		PACS brkdwn			
Receipts	$93,124	Indiv	$33,200	Agr	$11,200	Ideo	$425
Expend.	$95,915	Party	$14,657	Bus	$27,200	Lbr	$1,400
Unspent	$18,592	PACS	$46,650	Hlth	$5,775	Prof	$650

NEVADA

The history of Nevada began in 1859 with the discovery of the Comstock Lode—one of those huge mineral finds that triggers a rush of prospectors, speculators, and the usual hangers-on. Suddenly there was a boom town, Virginia City, in empty territory and soon a territorial government in Carson City. There were opera houses, saloons, brothels, and even a United States Mint, to coin some of the silver from the mines. When Civil War Republicans thought (mistakenly, it turned out) they desperately needed electoral votes to reelect Lincoln in 1864, they contrived to make the state of Nevada out of these two towns, plus tens of thousands of square miles of the vacant, arid Great Basin to the north, east, and southeast. The motif runs through Nevada's history: the search for riches, the twist of fortune, the creation of an unexpected new reality.

For years Nevada didn't make much sense as a state. The veins of gold and silver soon petered out. The opera houses closed and the prospectors scattered—to Lead, South Dakota; Bisbee, Arizona; and the Klondike River in the Yukon Territory. Nevada, with fewer than 100,000 residents, was left in economic doldrums for decades. During the Depression of the 1930s the state government was on the verge of bankruptcy. So the legislature liberalized its divorce laws and legalized gambling at just about the same time the federal government was building Hoover Dam near the little crossroads of Las Vegas. Without realizing it, Nevada had tied its economy to what would be one of the leading growth industries 50 years hence: tourism.

During that time, Nevada's population has increased explosively, and demographically the state bears little resemblance to its impermanent origins. Up to the end of World War II, Nevada's population was almost all concentrated around Reno and Carson City. But Reno's position was challenged in 1947, when Bugsy Siegel opened the Flamingo, the first big casino hotel on the Las Vegas Strip. Las Vegas has since become the state's largest city, and more than half of Nevada's residents today live there or in surrounding Clark County. Reno has also grown rapidly, and in the 1970s Nevada's population increased by more than 60%—the highest percentage growth rate in the nation. The state topped the 800,000 mark in 1980, with three-fourths of that population in the two metropolitan areas. The rest of the state, known as the Cow Counties, remains as empty as it always has been, or in ghost towns even emptier.

Politically, Nevada is a state that seems uncomfortable with what it has become. Like most of the Rocky Mountain states, Nevada has voted heavily Republican in recent national elections. It has supported candidates backed by the Moral Majority and gave birth to the Sagebrush Rebellion, the move to force the federal government to give federal lands to the states. Yet Nevada is probably the least family-oriented state: 32% of its households do not contain families (the highest percentage in the nation), while 64% don't have children (a proportion exceeded only in Florida), and 44% aren't occupied by married couples (exceeded only by California and New York). Nevada is filled now with people who came here thinking they were sharper than others, that they had a special angle, that they would could beat the odds—not the steady virtues we associate with traditional morality.

And Nevada's economy is based on two industries the New Right tends to disapprove of—gambling and government (not to mention prostitution, which is legal in some of the Cow

Counties and exists in Las Vegas and Reno as well). The big casinos and the government's atomic proving grounds remain the state's two biggest employers, and the federal government retains title to 87% of Nevada's land. On this base, Nevada has built a buoyant private economy; but underneath, it is based on money that outsiders—gamblers, federal taxpayers—bring in.

Presidential politics. In the 1940s, Nevada was a Democratic state; in the 1960s, it was divided much as the nation was, and now it is heavily Republican. It gave 63% of its votes to Ronald Reagan in 1980 and seems likely to go Republican again in 1984. Nevada has had a presidential primary, predictably ignored by the candidates.

Senators. The leading political figure in Nevada, by any measure, is Senator Paul Laxalt. He is also the Nevadan to have the greatest influence on national policy since Senator Pat McCarran—or maybe ever. Laxalt embodies some of the contradictions of Nevada: a strong believer in traditional morality, he is also divorced and has been a casino owner; a believer in free enterprise, he has spent most of the last 20 years in politics. Laxalt has been an important figure in Nevada since he missed, by exactly 48 votes, beating Senator Howard Cannon in 1964: that was an early signal that, even in the Goldwater landslide, conservative Republican politics had a future in states like Nevada. In 1966 Laxalt was elected governor and, almost as soon as he took office, Howard Hughes moved to Las Vegas and began buying up casinos. Hughes was welcomed to the state, largely because people thought he would buy up interests owned by organized crime figures; Laxalt was the only man outside Hughes's entourage who actually spoke to him. When Laxalt decided not to seek reelection in 1970, Hughes left Nevada.

Laxalt won a Senate seat in 1974, by only 624 votes in that Democratic year. His combination of strong views and easy affability made him a natural leader of the increasingly large and assertive contingent of conservative Republicans. He was a floor leader of the almost successful effort to deny ratification to the Panama Canal Treaties—a campaign that marked his emergence both as a national leader on the right and as a hardworking insider in the Senate. Laxalt and Ronald Reagan were next-door governors for four years and have been personal friends ever since; Laxalt was nominal head of the Reagan campaigns in 1976 and 1980. He had some disappointments: Reagan chose George Bush, not Laxalt, as his vice presidential candidate; Howard Baker moved quickly and became Senate majority leader right after the 1980 elections.

Nonetheless, no one doubts that Laxalt is a man of great influence with the president and in the Senate. He regularly attends leadership meetings, though he holds no regular leadership position; he has evidently worked out a good relationship with Baker. He therefore must be given a good deal of credit for the fact that Senate Republicans have proved to be such a cohesive and effective body—so cohesive that the leadership hasn't had to seek any Democratic votes on many important issues. Laxalt sits on the Appropriations Committee—traditionally a spot where competent insiders can affect the course of government.

But Laxalt has had his disappointments—or has done things which must have disappointed some of his admirers. He went along with the decision made by Baker and Reagan to stress economic and postpone cultural issues in 1981. He opposed the Carter administration's basing mode for the MX missile, which would have required the excavation of much acreage in the Nevada and Utah deserts; his attitude may have influenced the administration in dropping the plan and leaving the MX as an orphan without a home (in early 1983, anyway). After passing a regulatory reform bill through the Senate in 1982, he saw the House refuse to consider it, and dropped the issue in 1983. Politics is, of course, the art of the possible; you can't win all the time. But will Laxalt feel, when he totes up the score for these years, that he won all the points he could?

In 1983 Laxalt became "general chairman" of the Republican Party (a new title designed to avoid a rule forbidding senators to head the party) and installed Nevadan Frank Fahrenkopf as Republican National Chairman; he said he acted on the assumption and with the hope that President Reagan would be a candidate for reelection. Laxalt has been mentioned as a possible presidential candidate if Reagan does not run, and while he has not thrust himself forward he declines to rule himself out of contention. He certainly is not willing to concede the nomination to George Bush, and probably not to Howard Baker either. Laxalt also may be a candidate to succeed Baker as Senate majority (or minority) leader. He has widespread support in the party, and he seems to have many of the same qualities, both temperamental and intellectual, that have made Baker a brilliant leader—even though he and Baker are on opposite sides of some issues.

In Nevada, Laxalt has had the satisfaction in 1982 of seeing proteges win election to the congressional delegation. One was Chic Hecht, elected U.S. senator, defeating Howard Cannon; the other was Barbara Vucanovich, elected to the new 2d district House seat (before 1982, Nevada never had more than one representative). The only blemish is that the 1st district seat was won by Harry Reid, the Democrat who almost beat Laxalt in 1974.

Hecht is probably the least prepossessing member of the Senate. He is short, speaks with a squeaky voice and a lisp, and is anything but a brilliant phrasemaker. He won the Republican primary with only 42% of the vote, mostly thanks to Laxalt operatives. He did beat the last of Nevada's long line of conservative and practical-minded Democratic senators, Howard Cannon. Actually Cannon was in very weak political shape by the time he faced Hecht. He had lost the chairmanships—the Commerce Committee, its Aviation Subcommittee—which enabled him to say he could do great things for Nevada when the Democrats lost control of the Senate. He was 70 years old. He was named in the indictment of Teamsters President Roy Lee Williams and mob figure Allen Dorfman as the object of an attempted bribe; he testified extensively in the trial in Chicago in the month before the election. He had formidable primary opposition from Congressman-at-Large Jim Santini, who combined a conservative record on many issues with a wide appeal to voters in general elections. This was the big time: Santini spent $1,592,094 in the primary contest while Cannon spent $1,657,070 altogether— extraordinary sums for such a small state and a primary in which finally all of 62,046 votes were cast. Santini would have been an easy winner in the general election, but with strong support in Las Vegas, especially from blacks and union members who disliked Santini's record, the senator narrowly won. Cannon couldn't sustain the momentum through November, however. He carried Las Vegas and Clark County again with 55%, but Hecht did well enough in the rest of the state to win. He has seats on the Energy and Commerce and Banking Committees—assignments to complement Laxalt's, and he is expected to follow his senior's lead.

1st congressional district. Nevada's congressional districts are of vastly different physical size; the 1st consists of the southern half, roughly, of Clark County, and the 2d is the whole rest of the state. The 1st includes almost all of Las Vegas, the Strip (actually in a suburb called Paradise Valley), North Las Vegas with its large black population, and the Hoover Dam area. It is a solidly Democratic area, and there was never any doubt that the Democrats would win it. The easy winner of the Democratic primary was Harry Reid, who at age 43 has had a long career in Nevada politics. He was elected lieutenant governor in 1970, lost to Laxalt in 1974, lost a race for mayor of Las Vegas in 1976, and then became head of the Gaming

Commission from 1977 to 1981. That is, of course a powerful position, and one whose incumbent is subjected to severe pressures. After some controversy, Reid made a good record, and, against three other candidates, won 85% of the primary vote. He has seats on the Foreign Affairs and Science and Technology Committees. Quite possibly he is interested in running for the Senate again.

2d congressional district. This is the more Republican district. The 2d's portion of Clark County—about one-sixth of the whole district—is heavily Democratic; most of the Cow Counties and Reno's Washoe County are heavily Republican. The election went to Paul Laxalt's candidate, Barbara Vucanovich. A longtime Republican worker, she managed Laxalt's Reno office after he went to the Senate. He urged her to get into the race, appeared on TV spots for her in the primary, helped her to raise money in the general. The Democratic candidate, Mary Gojack, was Laxalt's opponent in the 1980 election, and got a better-than-expected 37% against him; she did only slightly better against Vucanovich. A strong Reagan supporter, Vucanovich has a seat on the Interior Committee.

Governor. Nevada was the only Rocky Mountain state in 1982 with a Republican governor, and it replaced him with a Democrat. Incumbent Robert List was in trouble because his tax program—reducing property taxes and raising the sales tax—didn't produce as much revenue as expected; the tourist (*i.e.,* gambling) business didn't live up to expectations, whether because of the recession or because of new competition from Atlantic City. The decisive winner was the Democratic Attorney General, Richard Bryan, a former legislator from Las Vegas.

The People   Est. Pop. 1982: 881,000; Pop. 1980: 800,493, up 10.0% 1980–82 and 63.8% 1970–80; 0.37% of U.S. total, 43d largest; voting age pop. 584,694; 1% American Indian, 5% Black, 6% Spanish origin, 2% Asian origin. Single ancestry: 10% English, 7% German, 4% Irish, Italian, 1% French, Polish, Swedish, Scottish, Norwegian, Dutch, Russian. Registered voters (1982): 322,290 Total. 174,470 D (54%); 123,951 R (38%); 1,003 L; 22,866 Ncnpartisan (7%). 20% with 1–3 yrs. col., 15% with 4+ yrs. col. 8.5% below poverty level. 36% housing units rented; median house value: $69,200; median monthly rent: $268. Households: 68% family, 36% with children, 56% married couples.

1982 Share of Federal Tax Burden $2,549,700,000; .43% of U.S. total, 39th largest.

1982 Share of Federal Expenditures

	Total		Non-Defense		Defense	
Total Expend	$2,215m	(0.37%)	$1,749m	(0.41%)	$465m	(0.26%)
St/Lcl Grants	346m	(0.39%)	346m	(0.39%)	0m	(0%)
Salary/Wages	337m	(0.43%)	102m	(0.37%)	235m	(0.46%)
Ind Payments	965m	(0.34%)	788m	(0.31%)	177m	(0.62%)
Procurement	561m	(0.38%)	453m	(1.44%)	109m	(0.10%)
Other Programs	4m	(0.07%)	4m	(0.07%)	0m	(0%)
Loan/Insurance	230m	(0.37%)	205m	(0.33%)	25m	(1.14%)

Political Lineup   Governor, Richard H. Bryan (D). Senators, Paul Laxalt (R) and Jacob (Chic) Hecht (R). Representatives, 2 (1 R and 1 D). State Senate 21, (17 D and 4 R); State Assembly, 42 (23 D and 19 R).

Presidential Vote

1980	Reagan (R)	155,017	(63%)
	Carter (D)	66,666	(27%)
	Anderson (I)	17,651	(7%)
	Other candidates	8,551	(3%)
1976	Ford (R)	101,273	(50%)
	Carter (D)	92,479	(46%)

SENATORS

Sen. Paul Laxalt (R) Elected 1974, seat up 1986; b. Aug. 2, 1922, Reno; home, Carson City; Santa Clara U., 1940–43, U. of Denver, B.S., LL.B. 1949; Roman Catholic.

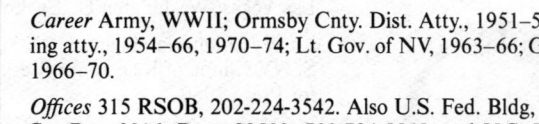

Career Army, WWII; Ormsby Cnty. Dist. Atty., 1951–54; Practicing atty., 1954–66, 1970–74; Lt. Gov. of NV, 1963–66; Gov. of NV, 1966–70.

Offices 315 RSOB, 202-224-3542. Also U.S. Fed. Bldg., 300 Booth St., Rm. 2016, Reno 89502, 702-784-5565; and U.S. Fed. Bldg., 300 Las Vegas Blvd. S., Rm. 4626, Las Vegas 89101, 702-385-6547.

Committees Appropriations (5th). Subcommittees: HUD-Independent Agencies; Interior; Military Construction; Commerce, Justice, State, the Judiciary (Chairman); Treasury, Postal Service, and General Government. *Judiciary* (3d). Subcommittees: Administrative Practice and Procedure; Criminal Law (Chairman); Patents, Copyrights and Trademarks.

Group Ratings

	ADA	ACLU	COPE	CFA	LCV	LWV	NTU	NSI	COC	ACA	CSFC
1982	5	7	11	0	23	27	67	100	76	80	80
1981	5	—	12	7	19	—	71	—	100	80	87
1980	11	27	5	13	16	22	56	100	85	100	84

National Journal Ratings

	Economic		Foreign		Cultural	
1982	18%	(LIB)	16%	(LIB)	8%	(LIB)
	81%	(CONS)	68%	(CONS)	91%	(CONS)
1981	1%	(LIB)	1%	(LIB)	2%	(LIB)
	98%	(CONS)	85%	(CONS)	82%	(CONS)

Key Votes

1) Reagan 81 Budget	FOR	5) $ to El Salvador	FOR	9) Poor Pay Food Stamps	FOR
2) Reagan 81 Tax Cut	FOR	6) Saudi AWACS Sale	FOR	10) Ban Crt Busing Order	FOR
3) Bal Budget Amend	FOR	7) Ban Abortion	FOR	11) Clinch Riv Brdr Rctr	FOR
4) Gas & Road Tax	FOR	8) Nerve Gas Prod	FOR	12) Legal Services Corp	AGN

Election Results

1980 general	Paul Laxalt (R)	144,224	(59%)	($1,126,826)
	Mary Gojack (D)	92,129	(37%)	($285,619)
	Other candidates	3,163	(1%)	
1980 primary	Paul Laxalt (R)	45,857	(90%)	
	Richard Gilster (R)	2,509	(5%)	
	Other candidates	2,501	(5%)	
1974 general	Paul Laxalt (R)	79,605	(47%)	($385,861)
	Harry Reid (D)	78,981	(47%)	($400,553)
	Jack Doyle (Ind. Amer.)	10,887	(5%)	

Campaign Contributions and Expenditures

1979-80		PACS brkdwn			
Receipts	$1,193,284	Agr	$5,658	Ideo	$5,100
Expend.	$1,123,651	Bus	$150,926	Lbr	$—
Unspent	$70,251	Hlth	$12,500	Prof	$6,600

Sen. Jacob (Chic) **Hecht** (R) Elected 1982, seat up 1988; b. Nov. 30, 1928, Cape Girardeau, MO; home, Las Vegas; Washington U., St. Louis, B.S. 1949; Jewish.

Career Counterintelligence; NV Senate, 1966–74, Mnr. Ldr., 1968; S. NV Chmn. of Reagan for Pres., 1976; Dpty. Dir. of NV Reagan for Pres., 1980.

Offices 302 HSOB, 202-224-6244. Also 300 Las Vegas Blvd. S., Las Vegas 89101, 702-385-6606; 300 Booth St., Su. 2016, Reno 89502, 702-784-5007; and 308 N. Curry St., Rm. 201, Carson City 89701, 702-885-9111.

Committees *Banking, Housing, and Urban Affairs* (9th). Subcommittees: Economic Policy; Federal Credit Programs; Insurance (Chairman). *Energy and Natural Resources* (9th). Subcommittees: Energy and Mineral Resources; Public Lands and Reserved Water; Water and Power.

Group Ratings and Key Votes: Newly Elected

Election Results

1982 general	Jacob (Chic) Hecht (R)	....	120,377	(50%)	($1,657,070)
	Howard W. Cannon (D)	....	114,720	(48%)	($1,592,094)
1982 primary	Jacob (Chic) Hecht (R)	....	26,940	(39%)	
	R. Fore (R)	....	17,065	(25%)	($710,828)
	J. Kenney (R)	....	12,191	(18%)	($460,022)
	Two others (R)	....	7,291	(11%)	($380,264)
	Other candidates	....	5,411	(8%)	
1976 general	Howard W. Cannon (D)	....	127,214	(63%)	($405,380)
	David Towell (R)	....	63,471	(31%)	($54,842)

Campaign Contributions and Expenditures

1982		Direct Cont. 1982		PACS brkdwn			
Receipts	$1,025,847	Indiv	$398,655	Agr	$2,000	Ideo	$92,000
Expend.	$981,197	Party	$26,040	Bus	$110,752	Lbr	$—
Unspent	$44,648	PACS	$250,010	Hlth	$1,300	Prof	$1,000
		Cand	$370,000				

Indirect Party Expend: $73,212   *Indep Expend:* For: $469

GOVERNOR

Gov. Richard H. Bryan (D) Elected 1982, term expires Jan. 1987; b. July 16, 1937, Washington DC; home, Carson City; U. of NE, A.B. 1959, U. of CA, Hastings College of Law, LL.B.; Episcopal.

Career Dpty. Dist. Atty., Clark Cnty., 1964–66; Clark Cnty. Public Defender, 1966–68; Counsel to the Clark Cnty. Juv. Ct., 1968–69; NV Assembly, 1968–71; NV Senate, 1973–77; NV Attorney General, 1978–83.

Offices Executive Chamber, Carson City 89701, 702-885-5670.

Election Results

1982 gen.	Richard H. Bryan (D)	128,132	(53%)
	Robert F. List (R)	100,104	(42%)
1982 prim.	Richard H. Bryan (D)	55,261	(51%)
	M.E. Leavitt (D)	34,783	(32%)
	S. Colton (D)	10,830	(10%)
	Three others (D)	2,944	(3%)
	Other candidates	4,418	(4%)
1978 gen.	Robert F. List (R)	108,087	(56%)
	Robert E. Rose (D)	76,361	(40%)

FIRST DISTRICT

The People Pop. 1980: 400,636, up 69.5% 1970–80; voting age pop. 292,870; 8% Black, 7% Span. orig., 2% Asian orig., 1% Am. Ind. 39% housing units rented. Median owner $68,400; renter $267. Households: 67% family, 36% with children, 54% married couples.

Presidential Vote

1980	Reagan (R)	68,627	(62%)
	Carter (D)	34,276	(31%)
	Anderson (I)	7,888	(7%)

Rep. Harry Reid (D) Elected 1982; b. Dec. 2, 1939, Searchlight; home, Las Vegas; UT St. U., B.S. 1961, George Washington Sch. of Law, J.D. 1964; Mormon.

Career Practicing atty., 1963–82; City Atty., Henderson, 1964–66; NV Assembly, 1969–70; Lt. Gov. of NV, 1970–74; Chmn., NV Gaming Comm., 1977–81.

Offices 1711 LHOB, 202-225-5965. Also 300 Las Vegas Blvd. S., Rm. 420, Las Vegas 89101, 702-565-0057.

Committees *Foreign Affairs* (20th). Subcommittees: Africa; Western Hemisphere Affairs. *Science and Technology* (24th). Subcommittees: Investigations and Oversight; Science, Research and Technology. *Select Committee on Aging* (34th). Subcommittee: Housing and Consumer Interests.

Group Ratings and Key Votes: Newly Elected

NEVADA — Congressional Districts, Counties, Independent City, and Other Selected Places — *(2 Districts)*

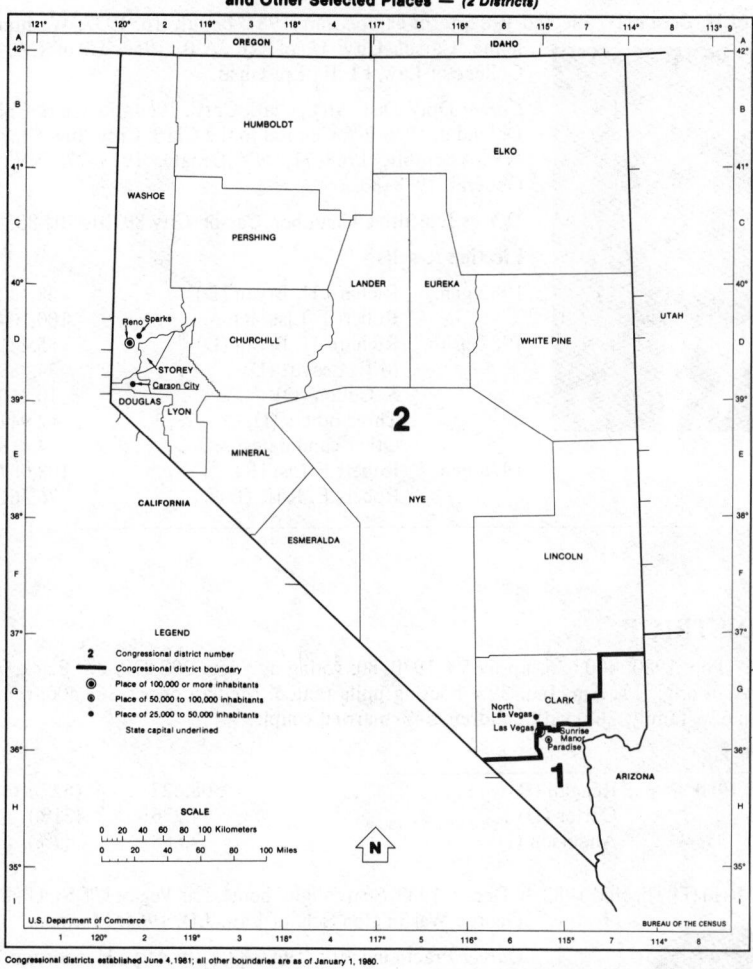

Congressional districts established June 4, 1981; all other boundaries are as of January 1, 1980.

Election Results

1982 general	Harry Reid (D)	61,901	(58%)	($514,048)
	Peggy Cavnar (R)	45,675	(42%)	($96,704)
1982 primary	Harry Reid (D)	41,786	(78%)	
	Three others (D)	7,628	(14%)	
	Other candidates	4,248	(8%)	
1980 general	Jim Santini (D)	165,107	(68%)	($392,583)
	Vince Saunders (R)	63,163	(26%)	($58,760)
	Other candidates	8,558	(3%)	

Campaign Contributions and Expenditures

1981-82		*Direct Cont. 81-82*			*PACS brkdwn*		
Receipts	$543,218	Indiv	$437,207	Agr	$4,500	Ideo	$2,850
Expend.	$514,048	Party	$350	Bus	$44,178	Lbr	$36,750
Unspent	$29,169	PACS	$97,161	Hlth	$8,250	Prof	$500

SECOND DISTRICT

The People Pop. 1980: 399,857, up 58.5% 1970–80; voting age pop. 291,824; 2% Black, 5% Span. orig., 2% Asian orig., 2% Am. Ind. 34% housing units rented. Median owner $70,200; renter $269. Households: 69% family, 37% with children, 58% married couples.

Presidential Vote

	1980	Reagan (R)	86,390	(67%)
		Carter (D)	32,390	(25%)
		Anderson (I)	9,763	(8%)

Rep. Barbara Vucanovich (R) Elected 1982; b. June 22, 1921, Camp Dix, NJ; home, Reno; Manhattanville College; Roman Catholic.

Career Owner, NV franchise of Evelyn Wood Speed Reading Co., 1964–68; Owner, travel agcy., 1968–74; Cmpgn. staffer for Sen. Paul Laxalt, 1974, 1980; District Rep. for Sen. Laxalt, 1974–81.

Offices 507 CHOB, 202-225-6155. Also 300 Booth St., Rm. 1139, Reno 89509, 702-784-5003.

Committees *Interior and Insular Affairs* (14th). Subcommittees: Energy and the Environment; Mining, Forest Management, and BPA; Oversight and Investigations. *Select Committee on Children, Youth, and Families* (9th).

Group Ratings and Key Votes: Newly Elected

Election Results

1982 general	Barbara Vucanovich (R)	70,188	(56%)	($604,624)
	Mary Gojack (D)	52,265	(41%)	($248,865)
1982 primary	Barbara Vucanovich (R)	16,453	(39%)	
	Dean Rhoads (R)	7,684	(18%)	($86,458)
	Paul Prengaman (R)	7,306	(17%)	($6,946)
	Three others (R)	6,533	(16%)	
1980 general	Newly created district			

Campaign Contributions and Expenditures

1981-82		*Direct Cont. 81-82*			*PACS brkdwn*		
Receipts	$634,228	Indiv	$336,836	Agr	$4,600	Ideo	$29,600
Expend.	$604,624	Party	$19,686	Bus	$129,460	Lbr	$—
Unspent	$29,602	PACS	$188,740	Hlth	$7,100	Prof	$2,400
		Cand	$90,000				

Indirect Party Expend: $35,350   *Indep Expend:* For: $15,187 (AMAPAC)

NEW HAMPSHIRE

Once every four years New Hampshire becomes the center of the nation's political attention. Presidential candidates trudge through the melting snow and gooey mud of the state's industrial cities and small New England towns, wooing the votes of about 111,000 Democrats and 147,000 Republicans. New Hampshire's primary is not quite the first event of the presidential campaign season; it was preceded in 1980 by the Iowa caucuses and (although no one paid much attention) the primary in Puerto Rico. But New Hampshire is still the first full-fledged state to hold a full-fledged election, and it is determined to keep things that way. New Hampshire law says that its primary must take place a week before any other state's (it doesn't say what happens if another state passes a law saying its primary is to be on the same day as New Hampshire's); New Hampshire Democrats lobbied the Hunt Commission successfully to allow their primary to be held so early. So it seems that once again, in 1984, this remote and scarcely typical state will once again attract dozens of candidates, hundreds of journalists, and, perhaps, thousands of volunteers, as it has for more than 30 years.

New Hampshire has thus become the main arena of what columnist Mark Shields calls retail politics: a candidate seeking individual votes personally or talking directly to small groups. Even with entourages of press and Secret Service, the candidates still come up here and talk—actually converse—with ordinary voters. It is just about the only place in the nation that candidates seek the views of—and seek to impress—ordinary citizens. Retail campaigning is possible, and expected, here because the electorate is small and the state is a geographically manageable size; more than two-thirds of its citizens live clustered in the southern half of the state, not much more than 90 minutes from the Boston airport. The importance of retail politics tends to hurt incumbent presidential candidates and front-runners, who are burdened with larger entourages; it gives tremendous advantages to the candidate who is not busy tending to the duties of public office—Ronald Reagan in 1976 and 1980, Jimmy Carter in 1976, George Bush in 1980.

Retail politicking in New Hampshire does not involve only candidates. There is a terrific advantage in having a corps of enthusiastic volunteers, as Eugene McCarthy did in 1968 and George McGovern in 1972. There is a premium on novelty as well. New Hampshire voters are aware that they are the first to vote in the process; they seem eager to give little-known candidates a chance, on the theory that if they don't turn out to be good they can be rejected by voters in other states later. Do we really believe that New Hampshire voters were sure in 1976 that Jimmy Carter or in 1972 George McGovern should be president?

In contrast, television advertising is far less important in New Hampshire than in most campaigns. Voters are used to meeting candidates, or at least their volunteers. Buying TV time on Boston stations (the only ones that reach most of New Hampshire) is expensive and counts against the campaign spending limits (although candidates argue that Boston TV expenditures should be allocated to the Massachusetts primary, which is held soon after New Hampshire). Curiously, newspapers may be far more important in New Hampshire voting than elsewhere. The influence of the *Manchester Union Leader* has been noted many times. But analysis of New Hampshire election returns suggests it is limited to Manchester and the towns immediately around it; they turned against the late Governor Hugh Gallen in 1982 when he refused to "take the pledge" against any sales or income tax. In contrast, Gallen carried the cities of Nashua, Concord, Keene, and Portsmouth, where some newspapers supported him and the idea that government might need more revenue. In the long, cold New Hampshire winters, people have time to read their newspapers carefully and compose the letters to the editor that they print in such great numbers. In these circumstances newspapers are what they have been historically in America: communities of like-minded people, conversing and agreeing on common action and decisions.

The importance of retail politics in New Hampshire is one reason voters have time and again fooled the soothsayers. There was the write-in victory of Henry Cabot Lodge, then ambassador in Saigon, in 1964; Eugene McCarthy's 42% against Lyndon Johnson in 1968, which destroyed the myth of the incumbent's invulnerability; George McGovern's startlingly high 37% in 1972. Jimmy Carter's 28% victory here in 1976—achieved with just 23,373 votes—put him on the covers of two newsmagazines and gave him something close to front-runner status, although most voters in the other 49 states knew little or nothing about him. Carter was as good a retail campaigner as New Hampshire has seen, sleeping in the houses of supporters and making his bed, talking quietly with voters and separating himself from the other liberal contenders, sending in his crews of Georgians to campaign. Some observers have argued that retail campaigning ability is a poor test for the presidency, but there are at least some talents it spotlights which are useful in the office. The same talents that gave him his New Hampshire primary victory also helped Carter produce the Camp David agreements. But there are limits to what retail campaigning shows. New Hampshire Democratic primary voters were willing to renominate Carter against Edward Kennedy of nearby Massachusetts in 1980, although they gave the president less than a majority. But in the general election they issued a grim verdict on the man that voters in this state, more than those in any other but Georgia and maybe Iowa, know best; they gave Jimmy Carter just 28% of their votes. Even in normally Republican New Hampshire this is a bad showing for a Democrat, not to mention an incumbent president; it was about as crushing a verdict on the Carter presidency as has been rendered.

About one-fourth of 1% of the nation's general election voters vote in the New Hampshire presidential primaries, and the question arises: is this anything like a representative sample? On the Democratic side, the answer is certainly no. The New Hampshire Democratic electorate is heavily Catholic, with large numbers of French-Canadians, an ethnic group hardly seen in this country outside of New England. It includes many workers in troubled industries like textiles and shoes and is heavily influenced by the right-wing views of the *Manchester Union Leader,* the state's largest newspaper. The numerous Democratic primary voters of Manchester, influenced by the *Union Leader,* usually vote for Republicans in the general election.

The Republican primary can make a better claim to being representative. In fact, one could argue that the Republican electorate in New Hampshire is more representative of the body of people who vote Republican in general elections than are Republican electorates in most other primary states. This is one of five states where there are more registered Republicans than Democrats; and registered Republicans here come from all walks of life and all parts of the state—not just from country-club subdivisions, as in most of the South, or almost entirely from outside the state's major metropolitan area, as in New York or Illinois. And the Republican electorate in New Hampshire has been a pretty accurate prognosticator of the final national Republican outcome. In 1976 Ford led Reagan in New Hampshire 49%—

48%, and they finished about that way in Kansas City; in 1980 Reagan had 50%, far ahead of George Bush's 25%, which is roughly where they ended up in Detroit.

Governor. New Hampshire's primary takes place in late February or early March and, within 24 hours after the returns are in, the politicians, their camp followers, and the media are gone. New Hampshire, which casts only four electoral votes and is safely Republican, seldom sees a national candidate again. Politics in the state returns to normal, featuring fractious politicians and William Loeb's *Union Leader*. Loeb is gone now, and it's not likely that the *Union Leader's* news coverage will be as pointed as it was under his leadership; but the paper has already set an agenda for state government which seems likely to endure many years more. And that is "the pledge." In the early 1960s New Hampshire was only one of several states with no sales or income tax. Liberals and many respectable conservatives argued that state governments needed these broad-based taxes to support necessary or desirable government services. Other states eventually agreed. But New Hampshire, urged on by Loeb, held out. Loeb called on all candidates for governor to take "the pledge," to swear that they would veto any state sales or income tax. Since 1972 no candidate who has refused has won. Thus Meldrim Thomson, a zany conservative, was elected in 1972, 1974, and 1976. Democrat Hugh Gallen beat him in 1978 when he too took "the pledge"; he renewed it again in 1980. But faced with fiscal difficulties, Gallen declined to take "the pledge" again in 1982, and he was defeated by Tufts University professor John Sununu; Gallen died shortly thereafter, just before his term ended.

So there is still no income tax or sales tax in New Hampshire. And the fact, an uncomfortable fact for advocates of government spending programs, is that New Hampshire has grown and prospered like no other state in the East. Its population increased by 25% in the 1970s while that in next-door, heavily taxed Massachusetts increased by 1%; businesses came across the New Hampshire line or started up there; wages and salaries increased and even old factory towns like Manchester and Nashua grew. Massachusetts started cutting its taxes before the end of the decade, and weathered the 1981–83 recession better than any other large state; in this case imitation is flattery.

But not everything is rosy in New Hampshire. The levels of public services are low indeed and, as Massachusetts Governor Michael Dukakis has said, if you have a child with a serious physical handicap, you wouldn't be very happy in New Hampshire. The rapid growth has often spoiled the woodsy environment with ticky-tack subdivision houses and storefronts, and the level of cultural and educational achievement is not high. It may be that we can afford to have tax havens in small states like New Hampshire (which still has less than a million people) but the quality of national life would deteriorate badly if large states, with millions of people who have diverse problems, were to follow the same policies.

Senators. New Hampshire is represented by two Republicans in the Senate. Both defeated incumbent Democrats, but they are very different politicians, with very different backgrounds, and very different impacts on the Senate.

Gordon Humphrey, the senior senator, is not really a politician at all. He was an Allegheny Airlines pilot who, like many pilots, moved to low-tax, pleasant-environment New Hampshire, and became involved in politics. With New Right fund-raising support, he won the not-much-sought-after Republican nomination to oppose veteran Senator Thomas McIntyre. Campaigning on issues like the Panama Canal Treaties and abortion, supported vigorously by the *Union Leader,* Humphrey won the most stunning upset of 1978.

Humphrey does not seem entirely comfortable in the Senate, however. He has important committee assignments, covering issues he cares about—Armed Services, Labor and Human Resources, Energy and Natural Resources. But they may have proven frustrating. Armed Services is a fast track, with very knowledgeable members on all sides of military issues; on the Labor Committee the right is frustrated consistently because two Republicans usually vote with the Democrats; Energy has not been a particularly busy committee.

A number of Democrats were already lined up in 1983 to run against him in 1984. They include former Senator John Durkin, who lost his seat in 1980; 1st district Congressman Norman D'Amours; Governor's Councillor and primary activist Dudley Dudley. Democrats have high hopes of capturing this seat. Yet initial polls showed Humphrey with a large lead. He may not have a list of legislative accomplishments of the kind most senators like to boast of when they run for reelection. But he does seem to be in line (or not far out of line) with the states' voters on most major issues.

New Hampshire's junior senator is a professional politician who, in just two years, has impressed colleagues and observers with his ability and aptitude for the job. Warren Rudman was attorney general of New Hampshire for six years, then a lawyer in private practice; he narrowly edged John Sununu and former Governor Wesley Powell in the 1980 primary to face an old adversary, John Durkin. Durkin resented Rudman's vote against him in the dispute over the deadlocked 1974 Senate race (it was finally run again, in 1975, and Durkin won easily); Rudman resented Durkin's veto of his nomination to be head of the Interstate Commerce Commission. Rudman attacked Durkin as a tool of organized labor and won a 52% victory.

In the Senate, Rudman serves on the Appropriations Committee, typically an insider's assignment. He supported the Reagan administration on major economic policies but is closer in views to Howard Baker or Robert Dole. And he is not unwilling to take on a tough fight. In 1982, he decided to oppose the American Medical Association, which was seeking to exempt doctors from regulation by the Federal Trade Commission. Rudman won that, and by a wide vote, against one of the strongest lobbies and most generous contributors in Washington.

Congressional districting. With only the slightest changes, New Hampshire's two congressional districts have had the same boundaries since 1881. The lines neatly separate the cities of Manchester and Nashua, both mill towns on the Merrimack River. Both have large numbers of Irish, Italian, and French-Canadian mill workers and their offspring, who tend to vote Democratic. The purpose of the 1881 redistricting was to put both districts permanently out of reach of the Democrats, and for the most part it has. Democrats won both districts twice, in 1890 and 1912, and until the 1970s they also won the 1st district on five other occasions.

1st congressional district. The 1st's politics tend to be dominated by Manchester, which together with suburbs casts 41% of its votes. There is also a significant urban concentration around the Portsmouth area, on the Maine border, and along the Massachusetts border as well. But Manchester, and the *Union Leader,* set the tone. Manchester, nominally Democratic, votes heavily against high-tax candidates. Congressman Norman D'Amours, first elected in 1974, has managed to keep Manchester's support and to win reelection by compiling a voting record moderate on cultural issues and conservative on foreign issues. D'Amours sits on the Banking and Merchant Marine Committees, two bodies generally more congenial to practical men of the world than to visionary idealists.

D'Amours's percentage dropped sharply in 1982, despite the national trend and despite the fact that the Republicans had a rather controversial primary. That diminishes some of his luster as a possible Senate candidate in 1984, and it means that he will probably get a

Republican challenge again if he runs for reelection. It also shows how the economy and currents of thought in New Hampshire run independently of the rest of the nation. Still busy attracting new business with its low taxes, boasting a low unemployment rate, New Hampshire has hardly known there is a recession on.

2d congressional district. The 2d district is somewhat less urban and more Yankee than the 1st. It does include Nashua, the state's second city, the capital of Concord, and the fast-growing region around Salem on the Massachusetts border. It is a mistake, incidentally, to think that voters who live near Massachusetts share that commonwealth's views on issues. On the contrary: the reason they came to New Hampshire was to get away from Massachusetts's high taxes and cultural liberalness. Concord and Nashua, led by their papers, supported Governor Hugh Gallen in 1982, as did the towns along the Connecticut River, although Gallen would not take "the pledge" not to allow sales or income taxes. Salem and the nearby towns were strongly for his opponent, the new Governor (who had worked in Massachusetts) John Sununu.

The 2d district's congressman is Judd Gregg, who was first elected in 1980. He is the son of former Governor Hugh Gregg, one of several former Republican governors whose support is anxiously sought by Republican presidential candidates (he was for Reagan in 1976, Bush in 1980). Gregg outcampaigned ten other Republicans in the primary and in the general beat the mayor of Nashua, who carried only his home city and the mill town of Berlin in the far north. He won by an even wider margin in 1982. Gregg is a member of the Government Operations and Science and Technology Committees. No member of the New Right, he nonetheless had a pretty solidly conservative voting record in his first term.

The People   Est. Pop. 1982: 951,000; Pop. 1980: 920,610, up 3.3% 1980–82 and 24.8% 1970–80; 0.41% of U.S. total, 42d largest; voting age pop. 662,528; 1% Spanish origin. Single ancestry: 14% English, 12% French, 6% Irish, 2% German, Italian, Polish, 1% Scottish, Greek, Swedish. Registered voters (1982): 462,457 Total. 17% with 1–3 yrs. col., 15% with 4+ yrs. col. 8.7% below poverty level. 27% housing units rented; median house value: $48,000; median monthly rent: $206. Households: 74% family, 40% with children, 63% married couples.

1982 Share of Federal Tax Burden $2,393,800,000; .40% of U.S. total, 41st largest.

1982 Share of Federal Expenditures

	Total		Non-Defense		Defense	
Total Expend	$2,368m	(0.39%)	$1,451m	(0.34%)	$918m	(0.51%)
St/Lcl Grants	317m	(0.36%)	317m	(0.36%)	0m	(0%)
Salary/Wages	374m	(0.48%)	52m	(0.19%)	322m	(0.64%)
Ind Payments	1,128m	(0.39%)	978m	(0.38%)	150m	(0.52%)
Procurement	538m	(0.37%)	18m	(0.06%)	519m	(0.45%)
Other Programs	11m	(0.20%)	11m	(0.20%)	0m	(0%)
Loan/Insurance	131m	(0.20%)	118m	(0.19%)	13m	(0.59%)

Political Lineup   Governor, John H. Sununu (R). Senators, Gordon J. Humphrey (R) and Warren Rudman (R). Representatives, 2 (1 D and 1 R). State Senate, 24 (12 R, 3 R&D, 4 D, and 5 D&R); State House of Representatives, 399 (182 R, 56 R&D, 136 D, 23 D&R, 1 I and 1 I&R).

Presidential Vote

1980	Reagan (R)	221,705	(58%)
	Carter (D)	108,864	(28%)
	Anderson (I)	49,693	(13%)
1976	Ford (R)	185,935	(55%)
	Carter (D)	147,635	(43%)

1980 Democratic Presidential Primary			*1980 Republican Presidential Primary*		
Carter	52,692	(47%)	Reagan	72,983	(50%)
Kennedy	41,745	(37%)	Bush	33,443	(23%)
Brown	10,743	(10%)	Baker.............	18,943	(13%)
All others..........	6,750	(6%)	Anderson	14,458	(10%)
			All others..........	7,330	(4%)

SENATORS

Sen. Gordon J. Humphrey (R) Elected 1978, seat up 1984; b. Oct. 9, 1940, Bristol, CT; home, Sunapee; Geo. Wash. U., U. of MD, Burnside-Off Aviation Inst. Flight Proficiency, Dallas, TX; Baptist.

Career Air Force, 1958–62; Civilian ferry pilot, 1964–65; Universal Air Transport, Detroit, MI, 1966–67; Pilot, Allegheny Airlines, 1967–78.

Offices 6205 DSOB, 202-224-2841. Also 275 Chestnut St., Rm. 730, Manchester 03103, 603-666-7691.

Committees Armed Services (5th). Subcommittees: Military Construction; Preparedness (Chairman); Manpower and Personnel. *Environment and Public Works* (9th). Subcommittees: Regional and Community Development (Chairman); Toxic Substances and Environmental Oversight; Water Resources. *Labor and Human Resources* (5th). Subcommittees: Alcoholism and Drug Abuse (Chairman); Aging; Family and Human Services.

Group Ratings

	ADA	ACLU	COPE	CFA	LCV	LWV	NTU	NSI	COC	ACA	CSFC
1982	15	29	5	0	54	33	94	100	50	95	82
1981	10	—	7	43	38	—	95	—	83	86	84
1980	6	13	5	0	27	30	74	100	93	96	91

National Journal Ratings

	Economic		Foreign		Cultural	
1982	13%	(LIB)	3%	(LIB)	37%	(LIB)
	86%	(CONS)	84%	(CONS)	62%	(CONS)
1981	37%	(LIB)	1%	(LIB)	29%	(LIB)
	62%	(CONS)	85%	(CONS)	70%	(CONS)

Key Votes

1) Reagan 81 Budget	FOR	5) $ to El Salvador	FOR	9) Poor Pay Food Stamps	FOR
2) Reagan 81 Tax Cut	FOR	6) Saudi AWACS Sale	FOR	10) Ban Crt Busing Order	AGN
3) Bal Budget Amend	FOR	7) Ban Abortion	FOR	11) Clinch Riv Brdr Rctr	AGN
4) Gas & Road Tax	AGN	8) Nerve Gas Prod	FOR	12) Legal Services Corp	AGN

Election Results

1978 general	Gordon J. Humphrey (R)	133,745	(51%)	($357,107)
	Thomas J. McIntyre (D)	127,945	(49%)	($289,628)
1978 primary	Gordon J. Humphrey (R)	35,503	(50%)	
	James Massiello (R)	18,371	(26%)	($75,769)
	Alf E. Jacobson (R)	13,619	(19%)	
	One other (R)	2,885	(5%)	
1972 general	Thomas J. McIntyre (D)	184,495	(57%)	($82,800)
	Wesley Powell (R)	139,852	(43%)	($104,779)

Campaign Contributions and Expenditures

1977-78		*PACS brkdwn*			
Receipts	$366,632	Agr	$4,500	Ideo	$24,126
Expend.	$357,107	Bus	$45,550	Lbr	$1,000
Unspent	$9,522	Hlth	$11,000	Prof	$3,200

Sen. Warren Rudman (R) Elected 1980, seat up 1986; b. May 18, 1930, Boston, MA; home, Nashua; Syracuse U., B.S. 1952, Boston Col., J.D. 1960; Jewish.

Career Army, Korea; Atty. Gen. of NH, 1970–76; Pres., Natl. Assn. of Attys. Gen., 1975.

Offices 4104 DSOB, 202-224-3324. Also Fed. Bldg., 80 Daniels St., Portsmouth 03801, 603-431-5900; 125 N. Main St., Concord 03301, 603-225-7115; and Norris Cotton Fed. Bldg., 275 Chestnut St., Manchester 03101, 603-666-7591.

Committees *Appropriations* (13th). Subcommittees: Defense; Foreign Operations; Interior; Labor, Health and Human Services, Education; Commerce, State, Justice, the Judiciary. *Governmental Affairs* (7th). Subcommittees: Permanent Subcommittee on Investigations (Vice-Chairman); Governmental Efficiency and the District of Columbia; Oversight of Government Management. *Small Business* (7th). Subcommittees: Innovation and Technology (Chairman); Government Procurement.

Group Ratings

	ADA	ACLU	COPE	CFA	LCV	LWV	NTU	NSI	COC	ACA	CSFC
1982	35	57	22	10	46	82	53	100	52	67	66
1981	15	—	21	36	32	—	65	—	94	60	75

National Journal Ratings

	Economic		Foreign		Cultural	
1982	13%	(LIB)	3%	(LIB)	37%	(LIB)
	86%	(CONS)	84%	(CONS)	62%	(CONS)
1981	33%	(LIB)	1%	(LIB)	70%	(LIB)
	66%	(CONS)	85%	(CONS)	29%	(CONS)

Key Votes

1) Reagan 81 Budget	FOR	5) $ to El Salvador	FOR	9) Poor Pay Food Stamps	AGN
2) Reagan 81 Tax Cut	FOR	6) Saudi AWACS Sale	FOR	10) Ban Crt Busing Order	AGN
3) Bal Budget Amend	FOR	7) Ban Abortion	AGN	11) Clinch Riv Brdr Rctr	FOR
4) Gas & Road Tax	FOR	8) Nerve Gas Prod	FOR	12) Legal Services Corp	FOR

Election Results

1980 general	Warren Rudman (R)	195,559	(52%)	($634,264)
	John A. Durkin (D)	179,455	(48%)	($676,150)
1980 primary	Warren Rudman (R)	20,206	(20%)	
	John Sununu (R)	16,885	(17%)	($187,595)
	Wesley Powell (R)	14,861	(15%)	($0)
	Eight others (R)	147,607	(47%)	
1975 special	John A. Durkin (D)	140,778	(54%)	
	Louis C. Wyman (R)	113,007	(43%)	
1974 general	John A. Durkin (D)	110,924	(50%)	($128,389)
	Louis C. Wyman (R)	110,914	(50%)	($138,605)

Campaign Contributions and Expenditures

	1979-80		PACS brkdwn		
Receipts	$635,272	Agr	$—	Ideo	$1,000
Expend.	$634,264	Bus	$3,000	Lbr	$—
Unspent	$1,009	Hlth	$—	Prof	$—

GOVERNOR

Gov. John H. Sununu (R) Elected 1982, term expires Jan. 1985; b. July 2, 1939, Havana, Cuba; home, Salem; MIT, B.S. 1961, M.S. 1962, Ph.D. 1966; Roman Catholic.

Career Cofounder, chief engineer, Astro Dynamics, Inc., 1960–65; Tufts U., Assoc. Dean, 1968–73; Engineering consultant, 1965–82; NH House of Reps., 1973–74; Pres., JHS Engineering, 1965–82.

Offices State House, Concord 03301, 603-271-2121.

Election Results

1982 gen.	John H. Sununu (R)	147,774	(52%)
	Hugh J. Gallen (D)	132,287	(46%)
1982 prim.	John H. Sununu (R)	26,617	(32%)
	Robert Monier (R)	24,823	(30%)
	Louis D'Allesandro (R)	24,163	(29%)
	Six others (R)	7,831	(9%)
1980 gen.	Hugh J. Gallen (D)	226,436	(59%)
	Meldrim Thomson, Jr. (R) ...	156,178	(41%)

FIRST DISTRICT

The People Pop. 1980: 460,863, up 27.4% 1970–80; voting age pop. 332,498; 1% Span. orig. 28% housing units rented. Median owner $49,000; renter $205. Households: 73% family, 40% with children, 62% married couples.

Presidential Vote

1980	Reagan (R)	115,356	(60%)
	Carter (D)	52,611	(28%)
	Anderson (I)	23,122	(12%)

Rep. Norman E. D'Amours (D) Elected 1974; b. Oct. 14, 1937, Holyoke, MA; home, Manchester; Assumption Col., B.A. 1960, Boston U., LL.B. 1963; Roman Catholic.

Career Practicing atty.; Asst. Atty. Gen. of NH, 1966–69; Criminal law instructor, St. Police Trng. Sch., 1967–69; Dir., Manchester Area Sch. for Police Prosecutors, 1970; Manchester City Prosecutor, 1970–72; Instructor, St. Anselm's Col., 1972–73.

Offices 2242 RHOB, 202-225-5456. Also 275 Chestnut St., Manchester 03101, 603-668-6800.

Committees *Banking, Finance and Urban Affairs* (11th). Subcommittees: Economic Stabilization; Financial Institutions Supervision, Regulation and Insurance; Housing and Community Development. *Merchant Marine and Fisheries* (8th). Subcommittees: Fisheries and Wildlife Conservation and the Environment; Oceanography (Chairman).

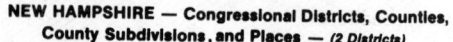

NEW HAMPSHIRE — Congressional Districts, Counties,
County Subdivisions, and Places — (2 Districts)

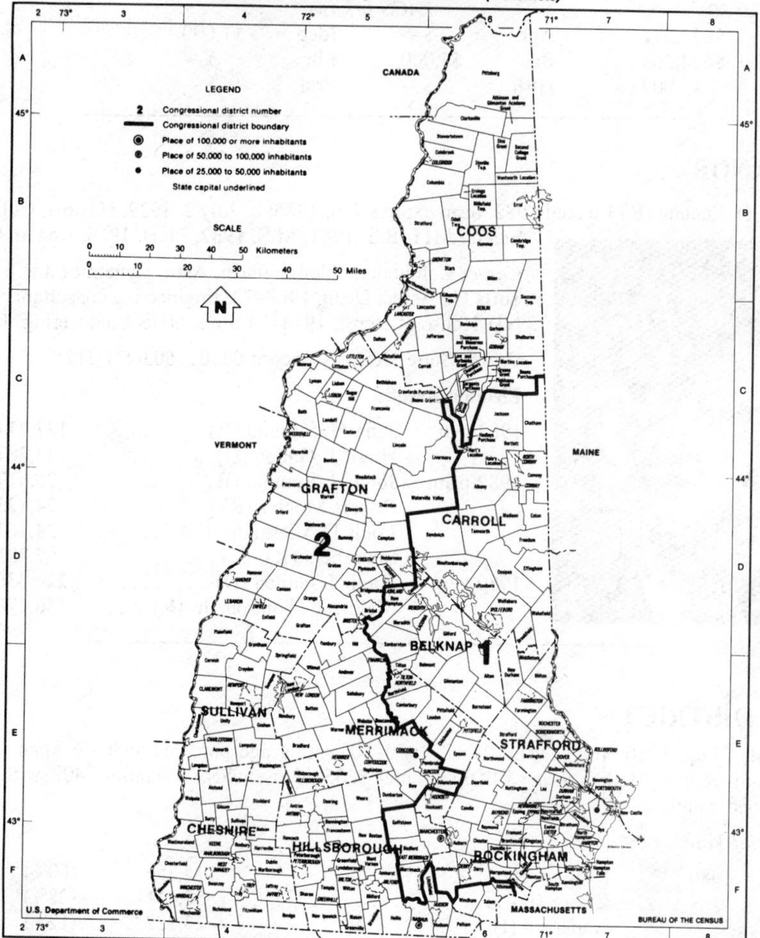

Congressional districts established March 4, 1982 ; all other boundaries are as of January 1, 1980.

Group Ratings

	ADA	ACLU	COPE	CFA	LCV	LWV	NTU	NSI	COC	ACA	CSFC
1982	60	50	77	62	82	70	41	44	53	26	40
1981	70	—	76	86	88	—	33	—	5	27	42
1980	56	30	58	57	72	70	26	40	62	38	46

National Journal Ratings

	Economic		Foreign		Cultural	
1982	64%	(LIB)	64%	(LIB)	43%	(LIB)
	36%	(CONS)	36%	(CONS)	56%	(CONS)
1981	81%	(LIB)	58%	(LIB)	64%	(LIB)
	15%	(CONS)	42%	(CONS)	36%	(CONS)

Key Votes

1) Reagan 81 Budget	AGN	5) Incr SS Rtmt Age	AGN	9) Poor Pay Food Stamps	AGN
2) Reagan 81 Tax Cut	AGN	6) Saudi AWACS Sale	AGN	10) Ban Crt Busing Order	FOR
3) Bal Budget Amend	AGN	7) $ for MX Missile	AGN	11) Auto Local Content	—
4) Gas & Road Tax	FOR	8) Nerve Gas Prod	AGN	12) Nuclear Arms Freeze	FOR

Election Results

1982 general	Norman E. D'Amours (D)	76,281	(55%)	($202,605)
	Robert Smith (R)	61,876	(45%)	($131,822)
1982 primary	Norman E. D'Amours (D)	19,949	(100%)	
1980 general	Norman E. D'Amours (D)	114,061	(61%)	($100,417)
	Marshall W. Cobleigh (R)	73,565	(39%)	($66,062)

Campaign Contributions and Expenditures

1981-82		Direct Cont. 81-82		PACS brkdwn			
Receipts	$186,649	Indiv	$86,970	Agr	$1,700	Ideo	$4,250
Expend.	$202,605	Party	$100	Bus	$41,050	Lbr	$35,350
Unspent	$1,534	PACS	$87,950	Hlth	$2,750	Prof	$500

Indep Expend: For: $274 Agn: $1,861 (NTLPAC)

SECOND DISTRICT

The People Pop. 1980: 459,747, up 22.3% 1970–80; voting age pop. 330,030; 26% housing units rented. Median owner $46,900; renter $208. Households: 74% family, 41% with children, 64% married couples.

Presidential Vote

1980	Reagan (R)	106,349	(56%)
	Carter (D)	56,253	(30%)
	Anderson (I)	26,571	(14%)

Rep. Judd Gregg (R) Elected 1980; b. Feb. 14, 1947, Nashua; home, Greenfield; Columbia U., A.B. 1969, Boston U., J.D. 1972; United Church of Christ.

Career Practicing atty., 1976–80; Chmn., Nashua Repub. Comm., 1976; NH State Exec. Cncl., 1978.

Offices 308 CHOB, 202-225-5206. Also Fed. Bldg., 55 Pleasant St., Concord 03301, 603-228-0315: and 1 Spring St., Nashua 03060, 603-883-0800.

Committees *Government Operations* (8th). Subcommittee: Commerce, Consumer, and Monetary Affairs. *Science and Technology* (6th). Subcommittees: Energy Development and Applications; Science, Research and Technology. *Select Committee on Aging* (8th). Subcommittee: Retirement Income and Employment.

Group Ratings

	ADA	ACLU	COPE	CFA	LCV	LWV	NTU	NSI	COC	ACA	CSFC
1982	35	17	7	8	48	64	94	70	81	78	67
1981	25	—	7	57	53	—	93	—	89	86	72

National Journal Ratings

	Economic		Foreign		Cultural	
1982	15%	(LIB)	60%	(LIB)	41%	(LIB)
	85%	(CONS)	40%	(CONS)	58%	(CONS)
1981	24%	(LIB)	60%	(LIB)	32%	(LIB)
	68%	(CONS)	40%	(CONS)	68%	(CONS)

Key Votes

1) Reagan 81 Budget	FOR	5) Incr SS Rtmt Age	FOR	9) Poor Pay Food Stamps	FOR
2) Reagan 81 Tax Cut	FOR	6) Saudi AWACS Sale	AGN	10) Ban Crt Busing Order	FOR
3) Bal Budget Amend	FOR	7) $ for MX Missile	AGN	11) Auto Local Content	AGN
4) Gas & Road Tax	—	8) Nerve Gas Prod	AGN	12) Nuclear Arms Freeze	FOR

Election Results

1982 general	Judd Gregg (R)	92,098	(71%)	($201,391)
	Bob Dupay (D)	37,857	(29%)	($5,116)
1982 primary	Judd Gregg (R)	36,013	(100%)	
1980 general	Judd Gregg (R)	113,304	(64%)	($122,167)
	Maurice L. Arel (D)	63,350	(36%)	($100,144)

Campaign Contributions and Expenditures

1981-82		Direct Cont. 81-82		PACS brkdwn			
Receipts	$214,261	Indiv	$140,051	Agr	$700	Ideo	$500
Expend.	$201,391	Party	$15,378	Bus	$39,850	Lbr	$3,000
Unspent	$25,560	PACS	$49,350	Hlth	$4,500	Prof	$500
		Cand	$7,000				

Indep Expend: For: $17,139 (AMAPAC)

NEW JERSEY

New Jersey, a much maligned state, is an object of derision for New Yorkers and a place little known by almost everyone else. This fate was evident even in colonial times, when it was remarked that New Jersey was a valley between two mountains of conceit. The reference of course was to Philadelphia and New York, which even then overshadowed what lay between. But New Jersey does have a clear geographic definition, bounded by the Hudson River and the Atlantic Ocean on the east and the Delaware River on the west. It is also a state of some physical beauty: to the west of the grimy New Jersey Turnpike corridor, the part of the state most people know best, are mountains of surprising height and bucolic countryside; to the east are the mysterious Pine Barrens, still as virgin as they were in colonial times, and the kaleidoscopic variety of the resort towns of the Jersey Shore.

New Jersey is the ninth largest state in population, and the most densely populated. It is a manufacturing center of great note and the home of numerous corporations; it housed Thomas Edison's laboratory and gave birth to Frank Sinatra. Yet somehow it failed for years to develop its own identity. In an era of giant metropolitan areas, most residents of New Jersey have thought of themselves as citizens of metropolitan New York or greater Philadelphia. Downtown is across a state line; the local sports teams until recently have been in the big cities, and this is one of two states (Delaware is the other) with no VHF television station of its own. There are some contrary trends: the Meadowlands complex has given New Jersey its own professional sports teams, the legalization of gambling in Atlantic City has made the state distinctive, and the public financing of political campaigns has, at last, made New Jersey politicians well known statewide, if only through television. Still, for many New Jersey is less home than a place of convenience—a good location for a plant, a pleasant suburb with low state income taxes—rather than any kind of promised land.

The lack of state identity is made more apparent by the variety and heterogeneity of the state itself. The outsider's image of New Jersey is of the industrial turnpike corridor and the soot-blackened row houses that you can see before entering the Lincoln or Holland Tunnels on the way to New York. But you can find practically any kind of neighborhood you want in New Jersey. Particularly in northern New Jersey, within 60 miles of New York, there are many high income suburbs, as well as the horse farm country around Far Hills and the university town of Princeton. There are old row-house communities in Hudson County as well—but they are being changed and often renovated by new immigrants, Cubans and other Latins, who have been thronging to these once stagnant entrepots in the 1970s and 1980s. There are old industrial towns, like Paterson with its factories on the old millrace of the Passaic River, and 1950s working class suburbs, like those south of Elizabeth that line both sides of the Turnpike. There are retirement villages and old beach resorts and in south Jersey even a few towns that have the southern atmosphere of Delaware or the Eastern Shore of Maryland.

For years New Jersey's politics was shaped by these factors—by the lack of a real identity in the state and by its heterogeneity. The first left New Jersey vulnerable to boss control and to swings of sudden enthusiasm for one politician or another who seems to be the state's latest savior. The lack of close identification with New Jersey affairs also left the state with congressional delegations many of whose members are pleasant and unobjectionable to their constituents but not very effective in Washington. The second, New Jersey's heterogeneity, left the state's politics in the hands of a small number of county political bosses, who until the 1970s dominated the legislature and usually hand-picked candidates for governor—the only state office that is elective and therefore the one real prize in state politics. Such endorsements were the only way candidates could appeal to the electorate for years, but for television advertisements New Jersey is the second most expensive media state, after California, because it requires buying both New York City and Philadelphia TV. Boss control, plus the obscurity of local politics to many citizens, helped make New Jersey one of the most corrupt of states, with scandals regularly tarring politicians, Democratic and Republican.

Now the evidence is accumulating that all this is changing, and largely because of actions taken by Governor Brendan Byrne—who was, during most of his time in office, acutely unpopular with the states' voters. But it was Byrne who floated the bond issues and arranged the deals that put together the Meadowlands complex. And it was he who pushed through gambling in Atlantic City, and took on the difficult and politically risky task of keeping it honest and out of the hands of the mob. Byrne, after several failed efforts, pushed through an income tax law and added property tax relief, the first check of which was timed to arrive in mailboxes a month before the 1977 election. Byrne and his Democrats pushed through public financing of state elections which, by ensuring that Democratic and Republican gubernatorial nominees each have more than $1 million to spend, has spurred competition in the primaries and ensured that each candidate can get across his message in the general election. The result has been vigorously contested state elections in 1977 and 1981.

Byrne came to office largely because of the corruption issue: in a trial, tapes of a Mafia boss's phone conversations were played in which a don described Byrne, then a judge, as unbuyable. The Democratic bosses slated him as their candidate in 1973, he won the Democratic primary against diverse opposition, and then whipped right-wing Congressman Charles Sandman who had beaten the incumbent in the Republican primary. And he held the office almost by accident too, winning an 11-candidate Democratic primary with 30% and then capitalizing on the Republican nominee's mistakes in 1977. But he did make some major changes in the state, and had a pretty much corruption-free administration as well.

Governor. Byrne's successor, Thomas Kean, is at first glance an improbable governor for a yeastily ethnic state like New Jersey. He is a genuine aristocrat whose family has been prominent in New Jersey since before the Revolution; he speaks with an accent that reminds his listeners of Boston. He had vigorous competition for the office in 1981. In the Republican primary, dominated by conservative-minded voters, he had to live down the moderate reputation he had won in the early 1970s as speaker of the Assembly; he did so in part by arguing for Reagan-style tax cuts. In the general election he faced the upset winner of the Democratic primary, South Jersey Congressman James Florio. If elected, Florio would have been the first governor of Italian descent in a state with a large and politically often frustrated Italian-American population; moreover, he had a genuine and attractive record on issues like disposal of toxic waste (he was the House author of the Superfund law), of considerable importance in New Jersey. And, thanks to public financing, he had the money to run a good campaign. But Kean was running when the initial popularity of the Reagan economic program was still high, and he benefited from the association not just of party but of ideas between his program and the President's. He won by the narrowest of margins, some 1,797 votes of 2.3 million cast.

As governor, Kean was able to do some tax cutting; he eliminated the corporate net worth tax. New Jersey, like other industrial states, was hit hard by the series of recessions in 1979–83; revenues were lower than expected, expenditures higher.

Senators. New Jersey's two senators are Democrats serving their first terms, each of whom has won national distinction in his own way. The more famous is the younger and, in Senate terms, the more senior: Bill Bradley. He is still known to many as the basketball star at Princeton and for the New York Knicks, and for taking two years off in between on a Rhodes Scholarship. During his athletic career, he refused to make commercial endorsements and wrote a thoughtful book about his professional basketball years. Always interested in politics, he ran for the Senate in 1978. It looked like a long shot: the incumbent, liberal Republican Clifford Case, had served 24 years and had won large majorities. But Case was 74, out of touch with New Jersey voters, and far too liberal for Republican primary voters; he was beaten by 34-year-old supply sider Jeffrey Bell in the primary. That gave Bradley an early exposure—and aversion—to supply side economics. He campaigned against Bell's tax cut proposals and beat him, though not by a huge margin.

Senators are often suspicious of new colleagues who are already celebrities. Bradley deftly assuaged those suspicions by deferring to committee chairmen, volunteering for housekeeping tasks, and learning the rules. It paid off. He got outstanding committee assignments—Finance, Energy and Natural Resources—and when he did come forward with a proposal, he won. That was the measure to require a reluctant Carter administration to stock the nation's strategic oil reserve—something Carter later bragged about after the outbreak of the Iran–Iraq war. During the first months of the Reagan administration, Bradley showed himself to be an independent economic thinker by voting for Reagan budget cuts but against the Reagan supply side tax cuts. He was one of two senators to take this position (the other was Dale Bumpers), which, if it had prevailed, would have reduced the deficit to near nothing at a time of still sharp inflation. Bradley also worked closely with Finance Chairman Bob Dole in 1982 on Dole's tax package; although he, like all other Democrats, voted against the bill as a whole, he provided key support for important reforms. Bradley has become a major force on the Finance Committee, probably somewhat to the discomfort of Russell Long, who will chair it if the Democrats regain their majority; but even Long seems to respect Bradley's abilities.

Bradley has been mentioned as a candidate for national office. Up for reelection to the Senate in 1984, he has given no encouragement to such talk. He cannot count on an easy race in New Jersey: this state is balanced closely between the parties, and in each of the last elections for senator and governor has been closely divided as well. At the same time, Bradley brings impressive assets to a campaign: a record of some distinction, even though his party was in the minority; a genuine philosophy on issues different in emphasis, but not very different in substance, from traditional Democratic liberalism.

New Jersey's junior senator, Frank Lautenberg, was one of the big upset winners of 1982. When he entered the Senate race, few thought he had much chance of doing well in the Democratic primary, much less the general election. He was seeking the seat from which Democrat Harrison Williams, after 23 years in the Senate, was expelled after his Abscam conviction, and to which Wall Street investment banker Nicholas Brady was appointed by Governor Kean. The favorite to win the seat was Congresswoman Millicent Fenwick—a septuagenarian with a winning personality, known for smoking her pipe and other eccentricities, but also on occasion a fearless denouncer of wrongdoing, a kind of conscience of the House. The darling of *Doonesbury*, she was out of place in a statewide race in New Jersey. In the Republican primary, dominated by conservative voters, she was nearly beaten by Jeffrey Bell; characteristically, only afterwards did she praise President Reagan and invite him to her state at a time when many other Republicans who had invoked Reagan's name when it was more popular suddenly had no time available to meet him. For the general election, she never raised the sums needed to communicate with the voters in New Jersey. Evidently she thought she was well known and that her charm would be apparent, and perhaps it was; but voters wanted more, wanted some specifics on economic issues, and Frank Lautenberg did a much better job of providing them.

Lautenberg had some advantages in that. Years ago, he started a company called Automatic Data Processing; by 1982 it employed 16,000 people and processed the payroll for one of every 14 non-government workers in the entire country. He spent liberally of his own money in both the primary—where he beat nine other candidates, the most notable of whom were former Congressman Andy Maguire and Barbara Sigmund, daughter of Congresswoman Lindy Boggs—and in the general election, where he heavily outspent Fenwick. And he spent the money on a message: that he, Lautenberg, could help provide the jobs people needed in New Jersey. In a recession, and at a time when practically the entire nation became convinced that the computer business would be the wave of the future, that was an attractive message, and Lautenberg was a credible messenger. He won with 51% of the vote.

What precisely he can do in the Senate to deliver on his program is not entirely clear. But he is no political neophyte. He was a big giver over the years to various Democratic campaigns, notably George McGovern's; and like most big givers he has a pretty shrewd grasp of the issues and the process. He is expected to be a solid economic and cultural issue liberal, and to be a strong supporter of Israel as well.

Congressional districting. New Jersey probably deserves the award for the least aesthetically pleasing redistricting plan of 1981–82. It is, plain and simple, a Democratic gerrymander, passed by the Democratic legislature in the last days of Brendan Byrne's governorship; it has, however, been upheld by courts on the sensible theory that it meets the population requirement, which in turn exerts a substantial discipline over partisan greed. Republicans in fact lost only two districts: one seat that was eliminated because the state lost representation (and they could hardly have expected not to lose this, with the Democrats in control of the process) and one seat in Bergen County in which redistricting played only a minimal role in the outcome.

Presidential politics. Democrats seem to come out on top in most state elections in New Jersey. True, Republican Tom Kean won the governorship, but that was only the second time in 30 years a Republican won; moreover, the margin was very small and the Democrats easily held onto the legislature. New Jersey has two Democratic senators and a Democratic House delegation. Yet in presidential elections, it tilts a little toward the Republicans. To understand that, it helps to recall that New Jersey is basically a suburban state; and if it has had Democratic governors for many years, they taxed and spent much less than Republicans in New York, Pennsylvania, or Massachusetts. New Jersey is basically 1% or 2% more Republican than the national average in most close presidential elections.

New Jersey has a presidential primary, late in the season; and in fact elects rather sizable delegations. Yet turnout is not necessarily high and the contest is usually overshadowed by the simultaneous races in California and Ohio. It costs more to advertise on TV in New Jersey than in Ohio and nearly as much as in California; why not spend the money there where it goes towards electing many more delegates? New Jersey's Republican primary electorate leans conservative, but not as much so as that of, say, Illinois. Its Democratic electorate for years had an affection for candidates who were perceived as choices of the regular party organization, reflecting the general strength then of New Jersey's county political parties. But that strength has waned, and the pro-organization bias is surely much less than it was.

The People Est. Pop. 1982: 7,438,000; Pop. 1980: 7,364,823, up 1.0% 1980–82 and 2.7% 1970–80; 3% of U.S. total, 9th largest; voting age pop. 5,373,962; 11% Black, 6% Spanish origin, 1% Asian origin. Single ancestry: 11% Italian, 6% Irish, German, 4% English, Polish, 1% Russian, Hungarian, Dutch, Ukrainian, Scottish, Portuguese, Greek. Registered voters (1982): 3,681,211 Total. 13% with 1–3 yrs. col., 17% with 4+ yrs. col. 9.7% below poverty level. 35% housing units rented; median house value: $61,400; median monthly rent: $228. Households: 76% family, 39% with children, 61% married couples.

1982 Share of Federal Tax Burden $23,889,000,000; 4.00% of U.S. total, 9th largest.

1982 Share of Federal Expenditures

	Total		Non-Defense		Defense	
Total Expend	$16,619m	(2.75%)	$12,519m	(2.95%)	$4,099m	(2.29%)
St/Lcl Grants	2,718m	(3.08%)	2,718m	(3.08%)	0m	(0%)
Salary/Wages	1,413m	(1.81%)	381m	(1.39%)	1,032m	(2.04%)
Ind Payments	9,170m	(3.21%)	8,620m	(3.35%)	550m	(1.92%)
Procurement	3,275m	(2.25%)	419m	(1.33%)	2,856m	(2.50%)
Other Programs	42m	(0.78%)	42m	(0.78%)	0m	(0%)
Loan/Insurance	795m	(1.24%)	700m	(1.13%)	95m	(4.32%)

Political Lineup Governor, Thomas H. Kean (R). Senators, Bill Bradley (D) and Frank Lautenberg (D). Representatives, 14 (9 D and 5 R). State Senate, 40 (21 D and 19 R); State Assembly, 80 (43 D and 37 R).

Presidential Vote

1980	Reagan (R)	1,546,557	(52%)
	Carter (D)	1,147,364	(39%)
	Anderson (I)	234,632	(8%)
1976	Ford (R)	1,509,688	(50%)
	Carter (D)	1,444,653	(48%)

1980 Democratic Presidential Primary			*1980 Republican Presidential Primary*		
Kennedy	315,109	(56%)	Reagan	225,959	(81%)
Carter	212,387	(38%)	Bush	47,447	(17%)
Uncommitted	19,499	(3%)	Stassen	4,571	(2%)
La Rouche, Jr........	13,913	(2%)			

SENATORS

Sen. Bill Bradley (D) Elected 1978, seat up 1984; b. July 28, 1943, Crystal City, MO; home, Denville; Princeton U., B.A. 1965, Rhodes Scholar, Oxford U., 1965–68; Protestant.

Career U.S. Olympic Team, 1964; Pro basketball player, New York Knicks, 1967–77.

Offices 2107 DSOB, 202-224-3224. Also 1605 Vauxhall Rd., Union 07083, 201-688-0960.

Committees *Energy and Natural Resources* (9th). Subcommittees: Energy Conservation and Supply; Energy and Mineral Resources; Energy Regulation. *Finance* (7th). Subcommittees: International Trade; Energy and Agricultural Taxation; Health. *Special Committee on Aging* (5th).

Group Ratings

	ADA	ACLU	COPE	CFA	LCV	LWV	NTU	NSI	COC	ACA	CSFC
1982	100	93	93	70	77	91	18	22	29	24	31
1981	90	—	93	57	88	—	5	—	13	20	29
1980	72	87	100	80	75	100	17	10	38	0	22

National Journal Ratings

	Economic		Foreign		Cultural	
1982	67%	(LIB)	86%	(LIB)	92%	(LIB)
	32%	(CONS)	10%	(CONS)	7%	(CONS)
1981	93%	(LIB)	77%	(LIB)	86%	(LIB)
	6%	(CONS)	22%	(CONS)	6%	(CONS)

Key Votes

1) Reagan 81 Budget	AGN	5) $ to El Salvador	AGN	9) Poor Pay Food Stamps	AGN
2) Reagan 81 Tax Cut	AGN	6) Saudi AWACS Sale	AGN	10) Ban Crt Busing Order	AGN
3) Bal Budget Amend	AGN	7) Ban Abortion	AGN	11) Clinch Riv Brdr Rctr	AGN
4) Gas & Road Tax	AGN	8) Nerve Gas Prod	AGN	12) Legal Services Corp	FOR

Election Results

1978 general	Bill Bradley (D)	1,082,960	(56%)	($1,688,499)
	Jeffrey Bell (R)	844,200	(43%)	($1,418,931)
1978 primary	Bill Bradley (D)	217,502	(59%)	
	Richard C. Leone (D)	97,667	(26%)	($328,052)
	Alexander Menza (D)	32,386	(9%)	($65,154)
	Three others (D)	21,698	(6%)	
1972 primary	Clifford P. Case (R)	1,743,854	(62%)	($145,275)
	Paul J. Krebs (D)	963,573	(35%)	

Campaign Contributions and Expenditures

	1977-78			PACS brkdwn		
Receipts	$1,689,975	Agr	$2,000	Ideo	$10,226
Expend.	$1,688,499	Bus	$45,750	Lbr	$125,306
Unspent	$1,474	Hlth	$6,800	Prof	$3,700

Sen. Frank R. Lautenberg (D) Elected 1982, seat up 1988; b. Jan. 23, 1924, Paterson; home, Montclair; Columbia U., B.S. 1949; Jewish.

Career Army, WWII; Cofounder, Automatic Data Processing, 1952–82; Commissioner, Port Authority of NY and NJ, 1978–82; Commissioner, NJ Economic Development Council.

Offices HSOB 717, 202-224-4744. Also Fed. Bldg., 970 Broad St., Rm. 939-A, Newark 07102, 201-645-3030.

Committees *Banking, Housing and Urban Affairs* (8th). Subcommittees: Federal Credit Programs; Housing and Urban Affairs; International Finance and Monetary Policy. *Commerce, Science, and Transportation* (8th). Subcommittees: Aviation; Science, Technology and Space; National Ocean Policy Study.

Group Ratings and Key Votes: Newly Elected

Election Results

1982 general	Frank R. Lautenberg (D)	1,117,549	(51%)	($6,435,743)
	Millicent Fenwick (R)	1,047,626	(48%)	($2,606,633)
1982 primary	Frank R. Lautenberg (D)	104,666	(26%)	
	Andy Maguire (D)	92,878	(23%)	($510,815)
	Joseph A. LeFante (D)	81,440	(20%)	($395,981)
	Barbara Boggs Sigmund (D)	45,708	(11%)	($20,691)
	Howard Rosen (D)	28,427	(7%)	($1,318,872)
	Five others (D)	49,840	(12%)	
1976 general	Harrison A. Williams, Jr. (D)	1,681,140	(61%)	($610,090)
	David F. Norcross (R)	1,054,508	(38%)	($73,499)

Campaign Contributions and Expenditures

	1982	Direct Cont. 82			PACS brkdwn		
Receipts	$6,496,088	Indiv	$1,150,766	Agr	$—	Ideo	$13,000
Expend.	$6,435,743	Party	$25,227	Bus	$23,950	Lbr	$91,800
Unspent	$60,343	PACS	$143,899	Hlth	$250	Prof	$—
		Cand	$5,142,812				

Indirect Party Expend: $88,333

GOVERNOR

Gov. Thomas H. Kean (R) Elected 1981, term expires Jan. 1986; b. Apr. 21, 1935, Livingston; home, Livingston; Princeton U., B.A. 1957, Columbia U., M.A. 1965; Episcopal.

Career NJ Assembly, 1966–77, Asst. Major. Leader, 1970–71, Major. Leader, 1972–74, Speaker, 1972–74, Minor. Leader, 1974–77; NJ campaign mgr. for Gerald Ford, 1976; Candidate, Repub. primary for governor, 1977; Chmn. and Pres., Realty Transfer Co., 1977–81.

Offices Governor's Office, State House CN001, Trenton 08625, 609-292-6000.

Election Results

1981 gen.	Thomas H. Kean (R)	1,145,999	(44.77%)
	James J. Florio (D)	1,144,202	(44.70%)
	Eleven others	269,380	(10.5%)
1981 prim.	Thomas H. Kean (R)	122,512	(31%)
	Lawrence F. (Pat) Kramer (R)	83,565	(21%)
	Joseph (Bo) Sullivan (R)	67,651	(17%)
	Jim Wallwork (R)	61,816	(15%)
	Barry T. Parker (R)	26,040	(7%)
	Anthony Imperiale (R)	18,452	(5%)
	Two others (R)	18,323	(4%)
1977 gen.	Brendan T. Byrne (D)	1,184,564	(56%)
	Raymond H. Bateman (R) . . .	888,880	(42%)

FIRST DISTRICT

In no part of the country will you find such an intensive concentration of the petrochemical industry—and the ills attendant upon it—as in the 1st congressional district of New Jersey. This is the part of New Jersey directly opposite Philadelphia's Center City and the flat plains going south and east to the primeval Pine Barrens. At the turn of the century, this was a kind of backwater. The great industries of that era—railroads, steel—had been moving west, through Pennsylvania and to the Great Lakes. They left behind the small industrial city of Camden, across the river from Philadelphia, the home once of Walt Whitman and later of Campbell soups and RCA records; miles of vegetable fields, producing for the huge canneries then coming on line; quiet small towns, like Glassboro, which would become briefly famous when Lyndon Johnson and Alexei Kosygin held a summit meeting there in 1967.

The natural place to process the great product of the first industrial revolution, steel, was where the transportation lines for iron ore and coal intersected—Pittsburgh, Cleveland, Chicago. The natural place to process the great products of the second industrial revolution—chemicals, formed mainly of hydrocarbons—was anywhere you could ship oil cheaply and could find a skilled labor supply. One such place was along the wide, deep Delaware River, a rather lightly populated area then but close to the huge city of Philadelphia. And so vast chemical complexes were built south on the Pennsylvania shore, in Delaware, and across the river in southern New Jersey. In time the ancestral Yankee stock of rural Camden and Gloucester Counties was outnumbered by, or intermarried with, the second-wave immigration stock—Irish and Italian mainly—from Camden, Philadelphia, and elsewhere. Petrochemicals provided these people with well-paying jobs, houses in the suburbs in stable

NEW JERSEY — Congressional Districts, Counties, and Selected Places — *(14 Districts)*

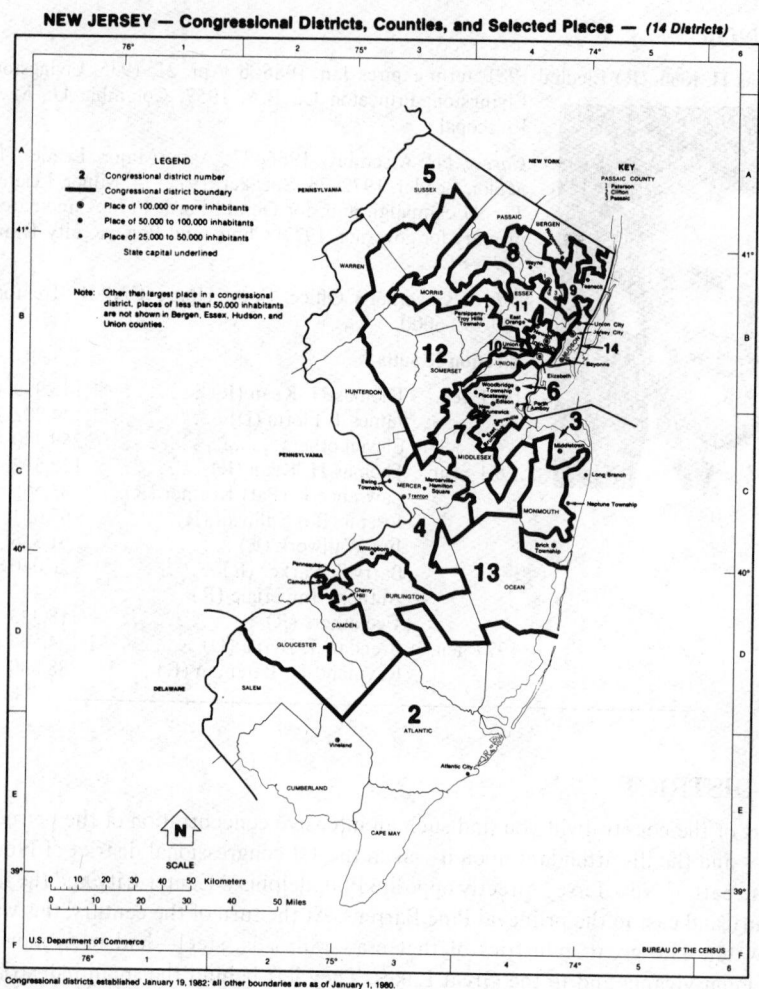

communities, a level of affluence most of their parents never dreamed of. But it also provided problems. Children drifted or lurched away from the ways their parents expected them to follow. And the industries themselves polluted the air, the water, and the land itself, as chemically active hydrocarbons intermixed in the environment with results no one could predict. It is almost certainly no coincidence that this part of New Jersey has the highest incidence of cancer in the nation.

The 1st congressional district includes most of Camden and all of Gloucester County. Near Camden it has a jagged boundary, designed to include in other districts leafy, determinedly middle class suburbs like Collingswood (home of onetime Republican Congressman and Governor William Cahill). Even with them, however, this would have been a pretty solidly

Democratic district in the late 1970s and early 1980s. Although Camden has been losing population for years, most of the 1st's population is clustered within 10 miles of the Delaware River, near the chemical plants, and much of the rest is strung out along a series of modest commuter towns on rail or rapid transit lines from Philadelphia. The old Republican farm towns of the interior are heavily outnumbered.

The congressman from the 1st district, James Florio, has become an important figure in New Jersey and national politics. First elected in 1974, he won a seat on the Energy and Commerce Committee, then a rather obscure body dominated by legislators who were responsive to the lobbyists of regulated businesses. But there was a big turnover in membership in the middle 1970s, and by 1978 he was a subcommittee chairman. Moreover, the subcommittee he chaired—deceptively titled Commerce, Transportation, and Tourism—had jurisdiction over one of the hottest pieces of legislation of the late 1970s, the Superfund law.

The idea was to accumulate money for cleaning up toxic wastes by assessing major chemical companies and other polluters; naturally, great sums of money were at stake in the details, and the bills were heavily lobbied. It was aimed at just the kind of pollution that was becoming obvious in places like the 1st district of New Jersey in the 1970s, where chemical waste dumps turned out, against everyone's expectations, to be poisoning soil and groundwater. Florio is one of the fathers of the Superfund, and one of the members of Congress who knows the critical details of the legislation best; he will be a key figure in any attempts to rewrite the law, and is a force to be reckoned with by anyone who administers it. He was one of the subcommittee chairmen investigating Superfund Administrator Rita Lavelle and EPA Administrator Anne Gorsuch Burford when they were forced out of office and one who will be keeping a close eye on their successors.

Although Florio has become an important and powerful member of Congress, he also has ambitions in New Jersey politics. In 1981 he ran for governor, won the 13-candidate Democratic primary with 26%, and came within 1,797 votes of winning the general election against Thomas Kean. His electoral base is southern New Jersey, which gave him 56% of the votes he won in the primary. He is, however, something of a political loner, without close ties to the fascinating but unscrupulous characters (like Camden Mayor Angelo Errichetti, of Abscam fame) who have dominated local Democratic politics in his district—further evidence of the declining importance of the old county machines in Jersey politics. He raised his own money for the primary and relied on New Jersey's generous public financing of state campaigns for the general. It is pretty widely expected that Florio will run for governor again in 1985, and probably there will be again a large field of Democratic candidates: the prize is so big and the chances of winning in a crowded field good enough to take a chance on. In the meantime, his reelection in the 1st district seems certain.

The People Pop. 1980: 526,057, up 9.4% 1970–80; voting age pop. 366,423; 13% Black, 3% Span. orig., 1% Asian orig. 28% housing units rented. Median owner $40,800; renter $206. Households: 77% family, 44% with children, 60% married couples.

Presidential Vote

1980	Reagan (R)	92,386	(50%)
	Carter (D)	84,622	(46%)
	Other	7,533	(4%)

Rep. James J. Florio (D) Elected 1974; b. Aug. 29, 1937, Brooklyn, NY; home, Camden; Trenton St. Col., B.A. 1962, Columbia U., 1962–63, Rutgers U., J.D. 1967; Roman Catholic.

Career Practicing atty., 1967–74; NJ Gen. Assembly, 1969–75.

Offices 2162 RHOB, 202-225-6501. Also 23 S. White Horse Pike, Somerdale 08083, 609-627-8222.

Committees *Energy and Commerce* (7th). Subcommittees: Commerce, Transportation and Tourism (Chairman); Oversight and Investigations. *Interior and Insular Affairs* (7th). Subcommittees: Energy and the Environment; Oversight and Investigations. *Select Committee on Aging* (7th). Subcommittees: Health and Long-Term Care; Human Services.

Group Ratings

	ADA	ACLU	COPE	CFA	LCV	LWV	NTU	NSI	COC	ACA	CSFC
1982	85	46	89	85	99	83	18	38	33	9	26
1981	40	—	88	50	82	—	3	—	8	24	29
1980	72	50	89	79	81	78	18	44	64	13	29

National Journal Ratings

	Economic		Foreign		Cultural	
1982	85%	(LIB)	81%	(LIB)	89%	(LIB)
	15%	(CONS)	19%	(CONS)	8%	(CONS)
1981	86%	(LIB)	69%	(LIB)	65%	(LIB)
	14%	(CONS)	31%	(CONS)	35%	(CONS)

Key Votes

1) Reagan 81 Budget	AGN	5) Incr SS Rtmt Age	AGN	9) Poor Pay Food Stamps	—
2) Reagan 81 Tax Cut	AGN	6) Saudi AWACS Sale	AGN	10) Ban Crt Busing Order	AGN
3) Bal Budget Amend	AGN	7) $ for MX Missile	AGN	11) Auto Local Content	FOR
4) Gas & Road Tax	AGN	8) Nerve Gas Prod	AGN	12) Nuclear Arms Freeze	FOR

Election Results

1982 general	James J. Florio (D)	110,570	(73%)	($229,042 est.)
	John A. Dramesi (R)	39,501	(26%)	($45,235)
1982 primary	James J. Florio (D)	32,016	(100%)	
1980 general	James J. Florio (D)	147,352	(77%)	($143,463)
	Scott L. Silbert (R)	42,154	(22%)	($23,165)

Campaign Contributions and Expenditures

1981-82		Direct Cont. 81-82				PACS brkdwn		
Receipts	$235,874 (est.)	Indiv	$73,166 (est.)	Agr	$500	Ideo	$2,100
Expend.	$229,042 (est.)	Party	$1,100	Bus	$54,150	Lbr	$33,500
Unspent	$2,954	PACS	$102,908	Hlth	$7,550	Prof	$1,100
		Cand	$52,000				

Indirect Party Expend: $2,163   *Indep Expend:* Agn: $7,101 (NCPAC)

SECOND DISTRICT

The 2d congressional district of New Jersey is the southernmost part of the state. Physically, most of it is taken up with the intensive vegetable farming that gave New Jersey the name of

Garden State and with the seemingly impenetrable wilderness of the Pine Barrens. Here and there amidst this flatness are small towns and gas station intersections, communities in whose eerie calmness in the summer you can hear the mosquitoes buzzing. Most of the people in the 2d district, however, live around its periphery. Some are in industrial towns, around the petrochemical plants on the Delaware River opposite Wilmington; there is the working class community of Vineland, inland among the garden farms; and there is the Jersey shore, north and south of Atlantic City.

The best known of these cities today is, of course, Atlantic City. In the early 1970s, it was as tawdry and threadbare a place as you could find in the United States: a beach resort that started in the late 19th century, when they ran a rail line to this beach from Philadelphia, and whose great heyday ran from the 1920s. Then, as people got their own cars, they went to other beaches, like those up and down the Jersey Shore, where they could live in motels or (as in Cape May, at the south end of the shore) in old Victorian houses rather than in the big hotels, with their small dingy rooms, back of the Atlantic City Boardwalk. Atlantic City, with a large black population (recruited to work in the hotels) and a reputedly corrupt local Republican machine, started to decline rapidly in the years after the Democrats held their 1964 national convention there. Then came gambling. In 1977 New Jersey voters approved gambling in Atlantic City; there was frantic elbowing for licenses; and the city was transformed—to a new kind of tawdriness. In place of dust there was tinsel, in place of grime the kind of veneers motels put up to convince their patrons they are in a classy place. Atlantic City attracted from all over the East people convinced they had some kind of edge and could, against the odds, make the killing which would put them on Easy Street. Politically, the 2d district is a mixed bag. The Delaware River area and Vineland are heavily Democratic; Cape May County is solidly Republican and so, in many elections, is the Atlantic City area. But the latter is also grateful to Democratic Governor Brendan Byrne, the driving force behind the legalization of gambling here. The 2d's portion of Ocean County, north of Atlantic City, is full of comfortable retirement condominiums and is solidly Republican.

The congressman from the district, William Hughes, is a Democrat first elected in 1974. That year he beat Charles Sandman, the most vitriolic defender of Richard Nixon in the House Judiciary Committee impeachment hearings; since then he has held the district by his own talents. Hughes has always been notably more middle-of-the-road than most northern Democrats on a variety of issues. Hughes chairs the Crime Subcommittee and has been one of the workhorses of the Judiciary Committee. One of his pet causes is to keep government appointees from moving directly into jobs in industries they used to oversee, and he has had some success in this regard. Hughes tends carefully to district matters, and has remained highly popular in this varied district. He had a serious challenger in 1980, but still got 57% of the vote—a strong showing for a Democrat that year. The Republicans left him untargeted in 1982, and probably he will remain so for at least several elections to come, though this is a seat a Republican could win if Hughes were not running.

The People   Pop. 1980: 526,279, up 19.5% 1970–80; voting age pop. 381,970; 12% Black, 3% Span. orig. 21% housing units rented. Median owner $43,300; renter $202. Households: 73% family, 37% with children, 58% married couples.

Presidential Vote

1980	Reagan (R)	112,058	(54%)
	Carter (D)	81,155	(39%)
	Other	14,966	(7%)

Rep. William J. Hughes (D) Elected 1974; b. Oct. 17, 1932, Salem; home, Ocean City; Rutgers U., A.B. 1955, J.D. 1968; Episcopal.

Career Practicing atty., 1959–74; Cape May Cnty. Asst. Prosecutor, 1960–70; Ocean City Solicitor, 1970–74.

Offices 341 CHOB, 202-225-6572. Also 2920 Atlantic Ave., Atlantic City 08401, 609-345-4844.

Committees *Judiciary* (8th). Subcommittees: Crime (Chairman); Monopolies and Commercial Law. *Merchant Marine and Fisheries* (10th). Subcommittees: Coast Guard and Navigation; Fisheries and Wildlife Conservation and the Environment; Oceanography. *Select Committee on Aging* (9th). Subcommittee: Human Services. *Select Committee on Narcotics Abuse and Control* (11th).

Group Ratings

	ADA	ACLU	COPE	CFA	LCV	LWV	NTU	NSI	COC	ACA	CSFC
1982	80	67	73	77	92	67	48	60	27	22	38
1981	65	—	71	93	79	—	64	—	24	21	49
1980	61	47	53	50	83	80	37	50	65	42	44

National Journal Ratings

	Economic		Foreign		Cultural	
1982	64%	(LIB)	63%	(LIB)	72%	(LIB)
	36%	(CONS)	36%	(CONS)	27%	(CONS)
1981	67%	(LIB)	61%	(LIB)	80%	(LIB)
	33%	(CONS)	38%	(CONS)	20%	(CONS)

Key Votes

1) Reagan 81 Budget	AGN	5) Incr SS Rtmt Age	AGN	9) Poor Pay Food Stamps	AGN
2) Reagan 81 Tax Cut	AGN	6) Saudi AWACS Sale	AGN	10) Ban Crt Busing Order	AGN
3) Bal Budget Amend	AGN	7) $ for MX Missile	AGN	11) Auto Local Content	FOR
4) Gas & Road Tax	AGN	8) Nerve Gas Prod	AGN	12) Nuclear Arms Freeze	FOR

Election Results

1982 general	William J. Hughes (D)	102,826	(68%)	($157,288)
	John J. Mahoney (R)	47,069	(31%)	($36,385)
1982 primary	William J. Hughes (D)	15,360	(100%)	
1980 general	William J. Hughes (D)	135,437	(57%)	($101,246)
	Beech N. Fox (R)	97,072	(41%)	($141,776)

Campaign Contributions and Expenditures

1981-82		Direct Cont. 81-82		PACS brkdwn			
Receipts	$167,909	Indiv	$92,669	Agr	$1,350	Ideo	$2,752
Expend.	$157,288	Party	$3,337	Bus	$23,355	Lbr	$32,765
Unspent	$19,993	PACS	$63,073	Hlth	$1,750	Prof	$1,100

THIRD DISTRICT

The Jersey Shore has been a retirement area since the late 19th century; President James Garfield came here, to Long Branch, to convalesce after he had been shot in 1881. The first major beach resorts in America were developed here, within easy reach of the great cities of

New York and Philadelphia on the new railroads. There were, for the most part, no older communities to build around: these dunes were bypassed by the original colonial settlers and by the Americans who continually moved west in later years. And so the beach towns took the form most desired by the kinds of people who came there, and each one is somewhat different in character. In some you find grand old clapboard houses, in others little shingled houses clustered on a few blocks on a sand spit, and in some today you find stucco contemporary condominiums, freshly built to attract retiring New Yorkers who are afraid to remain in the city.

The northern and most heavily populated part of the Jersey Shore forms the 3d congressional district of New Jersey. The description should almost be taken literally. The legislature, intent on protecting Democratic Congressman James Howard, drew district lines which run close to the Shore from Ocean County in the south, up and around Sandy Hook, and along Lower New York Bay almost to the industrial town of Perth Amboy. The district juts inward here and there, to pick up Democratic-leaning territory, like Lakewood in the south and Manalapan in the north: the two ends nearly meet like pincers. But the 3d carefully avoids the inland towns which were filling up in the 1960s and 1970s with relatively affluent retirees and others leaving behind things that they disliked—crime, high taxes, minorities— in New York. The district that is left is connected at some points by just a sandspit or an inlet open to the sea, but technically it fulfills the requirements of contiguity and equal population and, it can be argued, assembles a constituency with a community of interest.

Redistricting was one of the things that enabled Congressman James Howard, reelected by a 50%–49% margin in the old 3d district, to win in 1982 against the same well-financed opponent by a 62%–36% margin. But it was not the only factor; it probably increased his share of the vote by 3% or 4%. Also important was the national trend of opinion; the Jersey Shore was not as afflicted by the recession of the early 1980s as some parts of the country, but the basic political thrust of the issue was different. Finally, there was a difference in effort. In 1980 Howard had been caught napping and was nearly outspent by his challenger, Assemblywoman Marie Muhler. In 1982 he spent $699,000 to Muhler's $416,000. Muhler was financed in large part by the national Republican Party. Howard, in contrast, got his financing in primarily because he is chairman of the House Public Works and Transportation Committee—a position which also got him some rather special Republican aid.

Howard became chairman in 1981, at a rather inauspicious time for the committee. His predecessor, Harold Johnson of California, was defeated in 1980, and many colleagues were no longer much interested in the committee's traditional pork barrel functions. In an affluent America, how many voters care whether the community gets a new post office or some road-paving jobs? By 1982, the focus became rather different. The major product of the lame duck session that year was the roads and gas tax bill, passed through Howard's committee. The old conflicts between highway and mass transit advocates were smoothed over in an old-fashioned way: by giving some money to mass transit. The ground was prepared for the bill itself by a lobbying campaign talking about the nation's rotting infrastructure and the need to rebuild bridges and the interstate highways. Howard moved adroitly to compromise some key measures when necessary, although it could be argued that he conceded too much to the truckers, whose vehicles after all have caused the lion's share of the damage that needs to be repaired.

Howard had a valuable ally on this bill and in his 1982 campaign as well: Transportation Secretary Drew Lewis. As shrewd an assessor of power as Washington has seen in some time, Lewis fashioned the roads and gas tax bill, broke the air traffic controllers' strike, and realigned transportation policies generally—all with Howard's help. Lewis breakfasted with

Howard every week, and in the fall campaign he appeared in the 3d district with the congressman—invaluable help to a candidate whose opponent was saying he had no clout. White House political operatives weren't pleased, of course; but that simply made Howard all the more grateful.

All this must seem heady stuff to a man who was a teacher for 12 years in an obscure place on the Jersey Shore until he was elected, at age 37, to Congress in a traditionally Republican seat—and one everyone assumed would go Republican again in two years. Instead, Howard held on in tough years like 1966 and now is in a relatively strong position. But even within the redrawn lines, Howard's position must be considered shaky, and the question is: how long can he continue to exercise heavy responsibilities on issues and tend to the needs of a marginal district?

The People Pop. 1980: 524,825, up 12.1% 1970–80; voting age pop. 379,673; 7% Black, 2% Span. orig., 1% Asian orig. 30% housing units rented. Median owner $59,100; renter $251. Households: 75% family, 40% with children, 62% married couples.

Presidential Vote

1980	Reagan (R)	120,567	(57%)
	Carter (D)	73,732	(35%)
	Other	16,158	(8%)

Rep. James J. Howard (D) Elected 1964; b. July 24, 1927, Irvington; home, Wall Township; St. Bonaventure U., B.A. 1952, Rutgers U., M.Ed. 1958; Roman Catholic.

Career Navy, WWII; Teacher and Acting Principal, Wall Township Sch. Dist., 1952–64.

Offices 2245 RHOB, 202-225-4671. Also 808 Belmar Plaza, Belmar 07719, 201-681-3321.

Committee *Public Works and Transportation* (Chairman).

Group Ratings

	ADA	ACLU	COPE	CFA	LCV	LWV	NTU	NSI	COC	ACA	CSFC
1982	90	75	94	92	90	82	7	50	18	0	25
1981	70	—	93	86	76	—	12	—	17	10	34
1980	83	80	74	79	52	80	12	50	55	14	28

National Journal Ratings

	Economic		Foreign		Cultural	
1982	77%	(LIB)	89%	(LIB)	93%	(LIB)
	22%	(CONS)	10%	(CONS)	3%	(CONS)
1981	89%	(LIB)	66%	(LIB)	82%	(LIB)
	11%	(CONS)	33%	(CONS)	18%	(CONS)

Key Votes

1) Reagan 81 Budget	AGN	5) Incr SS Rtmt Age	AGN	9) Poor Pay Food Stamps	AGN
2) Reagan 81 Tax Cut	AGN	6) Saudi AWACS Sale	AGN	10) Ban Crt Busing Order	AGN
3) Bal Budget Amend	AGN	7) $ for MX Missile	AGN	11) Auto Local Content	FOR
4) Gas & Road Tax	FOR	8) Nerve Gas Prod	AGN	12) Nuclear Arms Freeze	FOR

Election Results

1982 general	James J. Howard (D)	104,055	(62%)	($698,900)
	Marie S. Muhler (R)	60,515	(36%)	($415,843)
1982 primary	James J. Howard (D)	18,628	(100%)	
1980 general	James J. Howard (D)	106,269	(50%)	($208,253)
	Marie S. Muhler (R)	104,184	(49%)	($163,436)

Campaign Contributions and Expenditures

1981-82		*Direct Cont. 81-82*		*PACS brkdwn*			
Receipts	$637,509	Indiv	$286,063	Agr	$1,350	Ideo	$17,250
Expend.	$698,900	Party	$8,311	Bus	$144,002	Lbr	$120,656
Unspent	$7,698	PACS	$293,449	Hlth	$250	Prof	$3,250

Indirect Party Expend: $5,130   *Indep Expend: For:* $18,493 (LCV, NJ Envir. Voters) *Agn:* $308

FOURTH DISTRICT

The 4th congressional district of New Jersey is the middle section of the state, poised between the New York and Philadelphia media markets, centered on the state capital of Trenton. Like most capitals of big states, it is a small city, devoted to little else than state government; its industrial base has been withering away as its population has been moving to its suburbs. Its political persuasion seems to be changing as well, at least a little, away from its ancestral Democratic voting habits and toward more swing voting. The 4th district includes Trenton and all its suburbs (unless you count the fashionable college town of Princeton, which is in the 7th district) and proceeds southward to face Philadelphia across the Delaware River. It was designed by a Democratic legislature to be a Democratic district, and in most elections it is—but not, any more, in congressional contests.

For 26 years the 4th, in various forms, was represented by Frank Thompson, a Democrat who surprised many of his friends and admirers by his involvement—and conviction—in the Abscam case. Now it has twice elected Christopher Smith, a Republican who was widely underestimated—but may not be again. In 1980 Smith was a 27-year-old employed in a family business and a right-to-life activist. On paper, he seemed the kind of sad sack candidate a party dredges up to run in a hopeless district, and that is just what he had been in 1978, when he ran against Thompson, spent $15,000, and won 37% of the vote. But in 1980, with Abscam working against Thompson (he had been indicted, but not tried, as of November) and with national issues breaking toward the Republicans, Smith was able to attract at least a little money and, more importantly, to win 57% of the vote.

But just about everyone figured he was a goner for 1982. He seemed unimpressive in person, he was concerned about an issue (abortion) increasingly peripheral to voters, and he served on two committees with very limited legislative jurisdictions (Small Business, Veterans' Affairs). The Democrats made his district even more Democratic in redistricting, and looked forward to having Joseph Merlino, former state Senate president and longtime Trenton politico, run against him.

But it turned out to be a kind of rerun of the race between the tortoise and the hare. Smith used the advantages of incumbency well, appeared constantly in the district, and was perhaps benefited rather than harmed by the fact that he did not have important committee responsibilities keeping him in Washington. Merlino, meanwhile, was involved in other things. He had major responsibilities in the legislature. He ran for governor in 1981, as a kind of favorite son of Trenton and Mercer County; he carried that and not much else, finishing fourth in a field of 13 with 11% of the vote. Then in 1982, he was challenged in the primary by Craig Yates, a rich businessman who financed much of his own campaign and spent $171,000; the race ended bitterly. Finally, Merlino, for all his competence as a politician, also looked the part: chomping on a cigar, speaking in political lingo. Not only did Smith win, but he won a higher percentage in Trenton and Mercer County—Merlino's home turf and the most Democratic part of the district in most elections—than he did in the industrial suburbs across the river from Philadelphia—new territory to both candidates.

No one would say that Smith is safe for 1984. But he has proven that the Democrats are going to have to come up with a strong candidate, and one tailored to the district and the times, if they want a chance to beat him.

The People   Pop. 1980: 527,472, up 4.0% 1970–80; voting age pop. 382,745; 15% Black, 2% Span. orig., 1% Asian orig. 30% housing units rented. Median owner $43,800; renter $234. Households: 76% family, 41% with children, 60% married couples.

Presidential Vote

1980	Reagan (R)	90,678	(45%)
	Carter (D)	93,581	(47%)
	Other	15,747	(8%)

Rep. Christopher H. Smith (R) Elected 1980; b. Mar. 4, 1953, Rahway; home, Old Bridge; Worcester Col., England, 1974, Trenton St. Col., B.S. 1975; Roman Catholic.

Career Sales exec., family-owned sporting goods business, 1975–80; Exec. Dir., NJ Right to Life, 1977–78; Repub. Nominee for U.S. House of Reps., 1978; Legis. Agent for NJ Senate and Assembly, 1979.

Offices 422 CHOB, 202-225-3765. Also 2333 White Horse, Mercerville Rd., Su. H, Trenton 08619, 609-890-2800; Madison Arms Plaza, 18 Throckmorton La., Rm. 208, Old Bridge 08857, 201-679-7440; 222 High St, Burlington City 08016, 609-386-5534; and 402 E. State St., Rm. 102 A, Trenton 08608, 609-989-2140.

Committees *Small Business* (8th). Subcommittees: Energy, Environment and Safety Issues Affecting Small Business; Tax, Access to Equity Capital and Business Opportunities. *Veterans' Affairs* (6th). Subcommittees: Hospitals and Health Care; Housing and Memorial Affairs.

Group Ratings

	ADA	ACLU	COPE	CFA	LCV	LWV	NTU	NSI	COC	ACA	CSFC
1982	50	25	57	62	75	67	36	60	57	30	45
1981	40	—	40	57	71	—	70	—	79	63	59

National Journal Ratings

	Economic		Foreign		Cultural	
1982	56%	(LIB)	52%	(LIB)	60%	(LIB)
	44%	(CONS)	48%	(CONS)	39%	(CONS)
1981	48%	(LIB)	74%	(LIB)	37%	(LIB)
	51%	(CONS)	26%	(CONS)	62%	(CONS)

Key Votes

1) Reagan 81 Budget	FOR	5) Incr SS Rtmt Age	FOR	9) Poor Pay Food Stamps	AGN
2) Reagan 81 Tax Cut	FOR	6) Saudi AWACS Sale	AGN	10) Ban Crt Busing Order	FOR
3) Bal Budget Amend	AGN	7) $ for MX Missile	AGN	11) Auto Local Content	FOR
4) Gas & Road Tax	FOR	8) Nerve Gas Prod	AGN	12) Nuclear Arms Freeze	FOR

Election Results

1982 general	Christopher H. Smith (R)	85,660	(53%)	($319,212)
	Joseph P. Merlino (D)	75,658	(47%)	($365,435)
1982 primary	Christopher H. Smith (R)	15,295	(100%)	
1980 general	Christopher H. Smith (R)	95,447	(57%)	($79,069)
	Frank Thompson, Jr. (D)	68,480	(41%)	($169,065)

Campaign Contributions and Expenditures

1981-82		Direct Cont. 81-82		PACS brkdwn			
Receipts	$319,745	Indiv	$118,116	Agr	$—	Ideo	$29,590
Expend.	$319,212	Party	$29,161	Bus	$94,176	Lbr	$4,500
Unspent	$569	PACS	$163,603	Hlth	$13,850	Prof	$200
		Cand	$9,173				

Indirect Party Expend: $37,347   *Indep Expend:* For: $2,963 (NRA) Agn: $1,681 (PPAC)

FIFTH DISTRICT

The 5th congressional district of New Jersey may very well be the most grotesquely shaped district in the United States. It follows the northern and western boundaries of the state almost from the Hudson River, near New York, to a point only a few miles from Trenton, on the Delaware River. Yet, with the exception of one fishhook-shaped salient into Morris County, the district goes no farther than a dozen miles inside the state. The district rides up and down each of the ridges that run through northern New Jersey, from northeast to southwest; it includes areas which regard themselves as very close-in suburbs to New York City to places which pride themselves on their rural outlook and which, in terms of cultural attitudes and behavior, could just as easily be in central Iowa. The transparent purpose behind this design was to combine a lot of widely separated Republican territory into a single district—one which, moreover, contained the homes of two of the state's Republican congressmen (that's the reason for the shape of the Morris County salient). The Republicans have a lot to complain about here, except for one thing: for 64 years, when they had control of the redistricting process, they drew a similar shaped district, numbered at various times the 7th and the 6th, for political reasons of their own.

That old 7th district had most of its population, in its later years, in the Bergen County suburbs of New York; the rest of the district was a politically irrelevant appendage. That's not so today with the 5th. Only 36% of its residents live in the by now long-settled suburbs of Bergen County—areas whose populations may decline in the 1980s as young people move out of their parents' homes. The rest live in farther out suburbs, and in most cases also work in offices or factories far out from New York City themselves. It is, in fact, misleading to call much of northern New Jersey a suburb anymore. The communities in this district typically are above the national average in income and education, but they are by no stretch of the imagination or pretention elite communities. On the contrary, their residents are often people who mistrust the elites they see through the media, and who prefer communities where more traditional values do not seem to be under siege. Their Republican voting habits are rooted less in an effort to maintain economic privilege than they are in an expression of support for values and a way of life which a few decades ago were taken for granted and now seem to many people to be vanishing.

This is, in any case, a solidly Republican district, and one in which the choice for congressman is made, for all practical purposes, in the Republican primary. A serious contest was avoided there in 1982 when Millicent Fenwick, a resident of the new 12th district, decided to run for the Senate; at that point, James Courter, the most conservative member of the delegation, decided to run in the 12th himself, leaving the 5th to Republican Marge Roukema.

For her, the easy race she had in 1982 must have seemed like reaching port after days of storms. She had run two strong races against Democrat Andrew Maguire in the old 7th district, losing 52%–47% in 1978 and winning 51%–47% in 1980, and for a while she seemed to be the loser in the musical chairs game necessitated by the fact that New Jersey lost one of its 15 congressional districts. Then suddenly she had negligible opposition in both the primary and general election.

Roukema was well positioned on issues for Bergen County. She was pretty solidly conservative on economic issues, with a record verging toward liberalism on cultural and foreign policy issues. Her committee assignments (Banking, Education and Labor) echoed some of her community activities before she became a political candidate (founding a senior citizens' housing corporation, serving on a local school board). Her record provided a good basis for running against Maguire, who had stressed the ultimately losing issue of oil and gas price controls in his six-year career in Congress. But it provides a weaker basis for carrying this new 5th district should substantial opposition appear. For the moment, however, that seems unlikely.

The People Pop. 1980: 526,367, up 12.2% 1970–80; voting age pop. 371,594; 1% Black, 1% Span. orig., 1% Asian orig. 19% housing units rented. Median owner $76,900; renter $288. Households: 83% family, 46% with children, 73% married couples.

Presidential Vote

1980	Reagan (R)	140,402	(62%)
	Carter (D)	62,901	(28%)
	Other	23,335	(10%)

Rep. Margaret S. (Marge) Roukema (R) Elected 1980; b. Sept. 19, 1929, Newark; home, Ridgewood; Montclair St. Col., B.A. 1951, 1951–53; Reformed Church.

Career High sch. teacher, 1951–55; Ridgewood Bd. of Educ., 1970–73; Cofounder, Ridgewood Sr. Citizens Housing Corp., 1973; Repub. Nominee for U.S. House of Reps., 1978.

Offices 226 CHOB, 202-225-4465. Also 10 Forest Ave., Paramus 07652, 201-845-3335.

Committees *Banking, Finance and Urban Affairs* (11th). Subcommittees: Economic Stabilization; Housing and Community Development; International Development Institutions and Finance; International Trade, Investment and Monetary Policy. *Education and Labor* (6th). Subcommittees: Elementary, Secondary and Vocational Education; Human Resources; Labor-Management Relations; Labor Standards.

Group Ratings

	ADA	ACLU	COPE	CFA	LCV	LWV	NTU	NSI	COC	ACA	CSFC
1982	50	33	29	38	67	67	67	70	68	57	48
1981	35	—	27	71	57	—	87	—	89	63	61

National Journal Ratings

	Economic		Foreign		Cultural	
1982	39%	(LIB)	64%	(LIB)	58%	(LIB)
	61%	(CONS)	35%	(CONS)	42%	(CONS)
1981	35%	(LIB)	62%	(LIB)	63%	(LIB)
	64%	(CONS)	37%	(CONS)	36%	(CONS)

Key Votes

1) Reagan 81 Budget	FOR	5) Incr SS Rtmt Age	FOR	9) Poor Pay Food Stamps	AGN
2) Reagan 81 Tax Cut	FOR	6) Saudi AWACS Sale	AGN	10) Ban Crt Busing Order	FOR
3) Bal Budget Amend	AGN	7) $ for MX Missile	AGN	11) Auto Local Content	AGN
4) Gas & Road Tax	FOR	8) Nerve Gas Prod	AGN	12) Nuclear Arms Freeze	FOR

Election Results

1982 general	Margaret S. (Marge) Roukema (R)	104,695	(65%)	($231,441)
	Fritz Cammerzell (D)	53,659	(33%)	($111,163)
1982 primary	Margaret S. (Marge) Roukema (R)	29,377	(100%)	
1980 general	Margaret S. (Marge) Roukema (R)	108,760	(51%)	($411,986)
	Andrew Maguire (D)	99,737	(47%)	($346,781)

Campaign Contributions and Expenditures

1981-82		Direct Cont. 81-82		PACS brkdwn			
Receipts	$251,790	Indiv	$116,035	Agr	$—	Ideo	$1,700
Expend.	$231,441	Party	$19,092	Bus	$81,027	Lbr	$—
Unspent	$35,810	PACS	$87,503	Hlth	$3,250	Prof	$550
		Cand	$12,600				

Indirect Party Expend: $9,000

SIXTH DISTRICT

South of Newark and New York City, on either side of the New Jersey Turnpike, where it spreads out to ten lanes going each way, is one of the prime industrial areas of the United States. Its factories, as in so much of New Jersey, are based less on steel and coal and more on oil and petrochemicals: the product of a later part of the industrial revolution. This is the country of the 6th congressional district of New Jersey, in Middlesex and Union Counties, from the Elizabeth to the New Brunswick interchanges. Behind the Turnpike are the kind of neighborhoods where ethnic Americans move when they make good, get decent jobs, and can afford something better than the old row houses of Jersey City or Perth Amboy or New Brunswick. This 6th district has the largest concentration of Hungarian-Americans in the nation, in and around New Brunswick; it also has sizeable neighborhoods of Polish-Americans in Woodbridge and Italian-Americans in Perth Amboy. From the old ethnic neighborhoods in these small central cities the children of the original immigrants have moved out into such places as Edison Township, Piscataway Township, and Sayreville, where they live in pleasant subdivisions. Middlesex County had its fastest growth in the 1950s, when New Jersey had a rising number of manufacturing jobs and the second generation of immigrants were having large numbers of babies themselves.

These suburban voters have not forgotten their Democratic heritage, though on occasion they have been willing to ignore it. John Kennedy got 58% in Middlesex County, well above his national average; Jimmy Carter did no better than average here when he ran in 1976 and 1980. As life here has become less distinctive and less visibly different from the experiences of other Americans, its political behavior has been, in the language of political scientists, regressing toward the mean. Middlesex County had a well-known Democratic machine, run for years by David Willentz, who first gained fame in the 1930s as the prosecutor of accused Lindbergh kidnapper Bruno Hauptmann and whose Perth Amboy law office in later years somehow seemed to attract some of the nation's largest corporations as clients.

The Willentz machine has pretty well determined who holds the Middlesex County congressional district since the first one was created in 1962. It has favored experienced and loyal political veterans: in 1962 it picked 57-year-old Edward Patten, then the appointive Secretary of State; in 1980 it favored 59-year-old state Senator Bernard Dwyer. Patten had a couple of seriously contested races—the 1970 primary, the 1978 general. So far Dwyer has had none. His voting record is on the liberal side of the spectrum, and not only on economic issues; he has a seat on the Appropriations Committee. As a member of the Labor-HHS-Education Subcommittee, he is a supporter of relatively generous spending on such programs. He seems likely to have few problems in the next several elections.

The People   Pop. 1980: 523,798, dn. 2.5% 1970–80; voting age pop. 392,465; 7% Black, 5% Span. orig., 2% Asian orig. 33% housing units rented. Median owner $61,200; renter $255. Households: 78% family, 39% with children, 65% married couples.

Presidential Vote

1980	Reagan (R)	105,197	(50%)
	Carter (D)	90,582	(43%)
	Other	14,552	(7%)

Rep. Bernard J. Dwyer (D) Elected 1980; b. Jan. 24, 1921, Perth Amboy; home, Edison; Roman Catholic.

Career Navy, WWII; Insurance exec., 1945–80; Edison Twnshp. Cncl., 1958–70; Mayor, 1970–74; NJ Senate, 1974–80.

Offices 404 CHOB, 202-225-6501. Also Perth Amboy Natl. Bank Bldg., 313 State St., Perth Amboy 08861, 201-826-4610; and P. O. Bldg., 86 Bayard St., New Brunswick 08901, 201-545-5655.

Committee *Appropriations* (31st). Subcommittees: Commerce, Justice, State and Judiciary; Labor-Health and Human Services-Education.

Group Ratings

	ADA	ACLU	COPE	CFA	LCV	LWV	NTU	NSI	COC	ACA	CSFC
1982	90	67	96	77	83	67	1	30	27	13	26
1981	75	—	93	71	57	—	12	—	22	13	31

National Journal Ratings

	Economic		Foreign		Cultural	
1982	98%	(LIB)	69%	(LIB)	82%	(LIB)
	1%	(CONS)	30%	(CONS)	18%	(CONS)
1981	77%	(LIB)	72%	(LIB)	73%	(LIB)
	21%	(CONS)	26%	(CONS)	26%	(CONS)

Key Votes

1) Reagan 81 Budget	AGN	5) Incr SS Rtmt Age	AGN	9) Poor Pay Food Stamps	AGN
2) Reagan 81 Tax Cut	AGN	6) Saudi AWACS Sale	AGN	10) Ban Crt Busing Order	AGN
3) Bal Budget Amend	AGN	7) $ for MX Missile	AGN	11) Auto Local Content	FOR
4) Gas & Road Tax	—	8) Nerve Gas Prod	AGN	12) Nuclear Arms Freeze	FOR

Election Results

1982 general	Bernard J. Dwyer (D)	100,419	(68%)	($70,128)
	Bertram L. Buckler (R)	46,095	(31%)	($29,446)
1982 primary	Bernard J. Dwyer (D)	29,644	(100%)	
1980 general	Bernard J. Dwyer (D)	92,457	(53%)	($149,141)
	William J. O'Sullivan, Jr. (R)	75,812	(44%)	($53,055)

Campaign Contributions and Expenditures

1981-82		Direct Cont. 81-82		PACS brkdwn			
Receipts	$80,019	Indiv	$20,719	Agr	$—	Ideo	$800
Expend.	$70,128	Party	$320	Bus	$28,300	Lbr	$26,300
Unspent	$15,740	PACS	$60,250	Hlth	$3,600	Prof	$500

SEVENTH DISTRICT

The 7th congressional district of New Jersey vies with the 5th for the title of most grotesquely shaped. It is shaped like a giant, misshapen capital letter G, with the top part in the industrial city of Elizabeth, just south of Newark, and the bottom a few miles north of the site of the Revolutionary Battle of Monmouth (the one where Molly Pitcher is supposed to have distinguished herself). There is no way you could drive through this district without passing in or out of its boundaries a couple of times, but if you did set out to do so, and stayed as much within the 7th as possible, you would travel some 85 miles—to cover a distance the crow can fly in 20.

More than half the people here live in Union County, just south of Newark. Elizabeth, its largest city, now has a larger Spanish origin than black community: here are the kind of white working-class neighborhoods which upwardly mobile Cubans and Puerto Ricans favor. Out U.S. 22, once the main highway into New York, with its garish strip culture, you pass through suburbs which once considered themselves WASPy, and are now a little more ethnic in flavor, with Italian and Spanish names and black faces now quite common (a solid majority in Plainfield) where they were seldom seen a generation ago. Union County was once the bellwether of New Jersey and perhaps even the nation: in the close 1960, 1968, and 1976 elections it came close to duplicating the national results for major party candidates.

The district proceeds out U.S. 22, past Plainfield with its black majority, to a corridor along the Green River that connects it with southern Somerset County, traditionally a Republican area; the university town of Princeton, solidly liberal on cultural and foreign issues; some sparsely settled industrial territory in southern Middlesex County; and the area around the county seat of Freehold in Monmouth County. Blue-collar Middlesex is traditionally Democratic; Monmouth, with its new subdivisions for white-collar young marrieds and its fairly affluent New York area retirees, leans Republican. Overall, this is a district pretty closely divided on partisan lines.

But if the Democratic legislature which created it expected it to go Democratic, they reckoned without the vote-getting power of Republican Congressman Matthew Rinaldo. His base is in Union County, where he has been winning public office since 1963. He was popular enough to win a marginal congressional seat by an overwhelming margin in 1972, and to hold it through four subsequent elections without serious challenge. Through most of those years he had a record on most issues close to that of most northern Democrats. In the Reagan years, he has moved to the right, but to a conspicuously lesser degree than many other Republicans. That record helped him to weather a serious challenge in 1982.

It came from Adam Levin, 33-year-old heir to a shopping center fortune, who had run against Rinaldo in 1974 and lost by a wide margin, and who had helped to lobby the legislature to create the district in this form—including several Democratic areas far from Rinaldo's Union County base. The legislature also placed Rinaldo's hometown in the new 12th district, in the hopes that he would run in that safe Republican constituency, but he declined to run against a fellow incumbent in the primary. Levin spent altogether $2,337,000 on this race, most of it his own money, peppering the New York TV stations with ads. Rinaldo spent some $719,000 himself, making this the nation's most expensive House campaign in 1982.

But money did not prove decisive. Levin carried Princeton—the part of the district farthest out of range of New York TV ads—but lost the new Middlesex and Monmouth County portions of the district, although they began the campaign unfamiliar with Rinaldo. And Rinaldo proved his strength in Union County by carrying it 59%–40%. His victory in a Democratic year against such an expensive campaign confirms as conclusively as anything can that he has made this a safe seat—although the Democrats would probably capture it if Rinaldo didn't run.

In the House, Rinaldo is a member of the Energy and Commerce Committee and a member of its Energy Conservation and Power and Telecommunications Subcommittees. He is ranking Republican on the latter, which has jurisdiction over some issues which may have much more effect on life in America 50 years from now than anything you see in today's headlines. The subcommittee is not usually run on partisan lines, and Rinaldo has the opportunity to work with Chairman Tim Wirth to form a consensus on important issues. On many issues before the full committee, however, Rinaldo is a critical key vote: will he support or oppose measures to increase or decrease federal regulation? He will presumably consult the interests of his district but, given his 1982 victory, he can decide with as much independence as any member of Congress. Rinaldo is also ranking Republican on the Select Committee on Aging.

The People   Pop. 1980: 525,563, dn. 0.4% 1970–80; voting age pop. 387,430; 12% Black, 7% Span. orig., 2% Asian orig. 37% housing units rented. Median owner $67,700; renter $247. Households: 76% family, 39% with children, 62% married couples.

Presidential Vote

1980	Reagan (R)	108,032	(51%)
	Carter (D)	84,872	(40%)
	Other	17,707	(8%)

Rep. Matthew J. Rinaldo (R) Elected 1971; b. Sept. 1, 1931, Elizabeth; home, Union; Rutgers U., B.S. 1953, Seton Hall U., M.B.A. 1959, NYU Sch. of Pub. Admin., D.P.A. 1979; Roman Catholic.

Career Pres., Union Twnshp. Zoning Bd. of Adjustment, 1962–63; Union Cnty. Bd. of Freeholders, 1963–64; NJ Senate, 1967–72.

Offices 2338 RHOB, 202-225-5361. Also 1961 Morris Ave., Union 07083, 201-687-4235; 25 E. Main St., Freehold 07728, 201-780-7800; and 220 S. Main St., Manville 08835, 201-725-7373.

Committees *Energy and Commerce* (5th). Subcommittees: Telecommunications, Consumer Protection and Finance. *Select Committee on Aging* (Ranking Member). Subcommittee: Human Services.

Group Ratings

	ADA	ACLU	COPE	CFA	LCV	LWV	NTU	NSI	COC	ACA	CSFC
1982	60	42	79	69	73	60	33	89	38	18	40
1981	20	—	78	57	57	—	57	—	84	52	57
1980	61	47	84	79	57	70	26	90	59	38	49

National Journal Ratings

	Economic		Foreign		Cultural	
1982	61%	(LIB)	58%	(LIB)	44%	(LIB)
	39%	(CONS)	42%	(CONS)	56%	(CONS)
1981	47%	(LIB)	49%	(LIB)	52%	(LIB)
	53%	(CONS)	50%	(CONS)	48%	(CONS)

Key Votes

1) Reagan 81 Budget	FOR	5) Incr SS Rtmt Age	AGN	9) Poor Pay Food Stamps	AGN
2) Reagan 81 Tax Cut	FOR	6) Saudi AWACS Sale	AGN	10) Ban Crt Busing Order	FOR
3) Bal Budget Amend	AGN	7) $ for MX Missile	AGN	11) Auto Local Content	FOR
4) Gas & Road Tax	AGN	8) Nerve Gas Prod	AGN	12) Nuclear Arms Freeze	FOR

Election Results

1982 general	Matthew J. Rinaldo (R)	91,837	(56%)	($719,430)
	Adam K. Levin (D)	70,978	(43%)	($2,337,537)
1982 primary	Matthew J. Rinaldo (R)	21,698	(100%)	
1980 general	Matthew J. Rinaldo (R)	134,973	(77%)	($229,475)
	Rose Zeidwerg Monyek (D)	36,577	(21%)	($0)

Campaign Contributions and Expenditures

1981-82		Direct Cont. 81-82		PACS brkdwn			
Receipts	$591,229	Indiv	$350,092	Agr	$750	Ideo	$5,150
Expend.	$719,430	Party	$24,133	Bus	$98,237	Lbr	$33,900
Unspent	$26,959	PACS	$155,071	Hlth	$11,550	Prof	$3,850

Indirect Party Expend: $35,063   *Indep Expend:* For: $110

EIGHTH DISTRICT

In the late 18th century Alexander Hamilton journeyed to the Great Falls of the Passaic River, some 20 miles west of the Hudson, and predicted that there would be a major industrial development there some day. His prediction made sense: falling water was the main energy source for industry then, and the Great Falls were 72 feet high, the highest in the East except for the Niagara Falls, which were then far away on the frontier. Hamilton died, in a duel in nearby Weehawken, before his prediction was fulfilled, but by the late 19th century Paterson, founded here at the Great Falls and named for New Jersey's Revolutionary War hero, became one of the major manufacturing cities in the United States. It developed major locomotive factories and silk mills and attracted immigrants from England, Ireland, and, after the turn of the century, Italy and Poland. Paterson was a tough town, and even as its fathers were erecting imposing public buildings, its narrow streets were buzzing with rumors of anarchist plots. The great silk strike of 1913 here was led by the revolution-minded Industrial Workers of the World.

Today Paterson is a kind of misfit in its time and place: still a manufacturing center (although neither silk nor locomotives are its mainstay) at a time when manufacturing is no longer considered the nation's prime work, still an old-fashioned central city, though it is surrounded by suburbs of New York and Newark and is an easy freeway ride away from the George Washington Bridge. Paterson is the center of New Jersey's 8th congressional district, which includes most of surrounding Passaic County. To the south there is the old industrial city of Passaic and the larger, more middle-class Clifton, a place with corporate headquarters and companies like Senator Frank Lautenberg's Automated Data Processing. To the north and west are higher-income suburbs of Paterson, notably Wayne Township. The district follows the Passaic River west, through higher and higher hills, and then dips southward to take in the working-class town of Dover in the middle of exurban Morris County.

The political heritage of the 8th district is Democratic, less because of its radical past than because of the allegiances of its immigrant groups. But in the cultural politics of recent years, the district has moved to the right. Although like most of New Jersey its age structure tends to be elderly, it also has very high percentages of married couples and families with children. When economic issues come to the fore, the area can go Democratic, as it did in the 1982 Senate race for Frank Lautenberg (who was kind of a home town candidate here). But it can also go Republican, as it did in the 1980 general election, and by a solid margin.

The 8th district's congressman, Robert Roe, is now one of the most senior Democrats in the New Jersey delegation; he first won in a special election in 1969. One of the highest ranking members of the Public Works Committee, he chairs its Water Resources Subcommittee. This is the unit that handles the traditional pork barrel, the rivers and harbors projects that used to be so important to so many congressmen. Some still are, as was made apparent when Jimmy Carter tried to cancel a raft of water projects in 1977. But for many members, they are of little consequence. Roe, who has extensive experience in state and local government, is aware of the practical importance of these matters, both to congressmen and local governments. He also serves on, and used to chair, the subcommittee with jurisdiction over the Economic Development Agency, which used to provide money to local communities to attract business.

Roe has retained an interest in New Jersey politics, and specifically in the governorship. He ran in 1977 and raised the kind of substantial sums needed to run a media campaign in New Jersey. In an 11-candidate primary field, he won 23% of the vote statewide and 86% in Passaic County. In 1981 he ran again and made a major strategic error: he was the only one of the 13 Democrats running who declined New Jersey's generous public financing. Without that money he had difficulty getting his message across and finished a distant second with

16% of the vote, including 71% in Passaic County. Will Roe try again in 1985? Such decisions are not usually made so long in advance, but he has shown the interest, the ability to raise money, and the strong local base which are useful in running in New Jersey's multicandidate primaries.

The People Pop. 1980: 526,138, dn. 4.1% 1970–80; voting age pop. 383,151; 9% Black, 11% Span. orig., 1% Asian orig. 44% housing units rented. Median owner $68,500; renter $212. Households: 76% family, 40% with children, 60% married couples.

Presidential Vote

1980	Reagan (R)	100,850	(54%)
	Carter (D)	72,666	(39%)
	Other	12,388	(7%)

Rep. Robert A. Roe (D) Elected 1969; b. Feb. 28, 1924, Wayne; home, Wayne; OR St. U., WA St. U.; Roman Catholic.

Career Army, WWII; Wayne Twnshp. Committeeman, 1955–56; Mayor of Wayne, 1956–61; Passaic Cnty. Bd. of Freeholders, 1959–63, Dir., 1962–63; Commissioner, NJ Dept. of Conservation and Econ. Development, 1963–69.

Offices 2243 RHOB, 202-225-5751. Also U.S.P.O., 194 Ward St., Paterson 07510, 201-523-5152.

Committees *Public Works and Transportation* (3d). Subcommittees: Economic Development; Investigations and Oversight; Water Resources (Chairman). *Science and Technology* (2d). Subcommittees: Energy Development and Applications; Energy Research and Production; Investigations and Oversight.

Group Ratings

	ADA	ACLU	COPE	CFA	LCV	LWV	NTU	NSI	COC	ACA	CSFC
1982	75	46	90	85	75	73	3	75	55	13	30
1981	60	—	90	71	61	—	8	—	17	24	38
1980	67	47	85	57	61	70	11	38	59	17	33

National Journal Ratings

	Economic		Foreign		Cultural	
1982	71%	(LIB)	63%	(LIB)	59%	(LIB)
	28%	(CONS)	37%	(CONS)	41%	(CONS)
1981	77%	(LIB)	62%	(LIB)	70%	(LIB)
	21%	(CONS)	38%	(CONS)	30%	(CONS)

Key Votes

1) Reagan 81 Budget	AGN	5) Incr SS Rtmt Age	AGN	9) Poor Pay Food Stamps	AGN
2) Reagan 81 Tax Cut	AGN	6) Saudi AWACS Sale	AGN	10) Ban Crt Busing Order	FOR
3) Bal Budget Amend	AGN	7) $ for MX Missile	AGN	11) Auto Local Content	FOR
4) Gas & Road Tax	FOR	8) Nerve Gas Prod	AGN	12) Nuclear Arms Freeze	FOR

Election Results

1982 general	Robert A. Roe (D)	89,980	(71%)	($159,443)
	Norm Robertson (R)	36,317	(29%)	($32,466)
1982 primary	Robert A. Roe (D)	18,202	(100%)	
1980 general	Robert A. Roe (D)	95,493	(67%)	($244,752)
	William R. Cleveland (R)	44,625	(31%)	($15,894)

Campaign Contributions and Expenditures

1981-82		Direct Cont. 81-82		PACS brkdwn			
Receipts	$156,816	Indiv	$41,965	Agr	$750	Ideo	$1,800
Expend.	$159,443	Party	$4,278	Bus	$52,600	Lbr	$44,350
Unspent	$2,905	PACS	$106,650	Hlth	$2,450	Prof	$4,700

Indirect Party Expend: $212

NINTH DISTRICT

The 9th congressional district of New Jersey occupies most of Bergen County, the suburban county just opposite New York City over the George Washington Bridge. Within its rather irregularly shaped boundaries it takes in three or four distinct areas. The one best known to outsiders is the Meadowlands. This is, or was until very recently, a giant swamp, on both sides of the Hackensack River before it empties into Newark Bay. Driving in on Route 3 to the Lincoln Tunnel you would pass straight through the Jersey Meadows, pocked with gas stations and their giant signs, oil tank farms, truck terminals, and 12 lanes of New Jersey Turnpike. What is astonishing is that so much prime real estate, so near to Manhattan, went undeveloped so long; if people can dredge swamps in Florida, they can in New Jersey. Finally, there was some development during Brendan Byrne's term as governor, notably the construction of the stadium and sports complex—including Giants Stadium, the Meadowlands Racetrack, and the Brendan Byrne Arena—at the intersection of the Turnpike and Route 3. Huddled to the west of the Meadows, on high land overlooking the Passaic River, are towns like Rutherford and Carlstadt, peopled with Polish- and Italian-Americans who usually vote Democratic, extensions really of ethnic communities once rooted in Newark.

The second part of the 9th district, with almost half its population, is a series of towns running along the spine of land which forms the Palisades along the Hudson River. This area, psychologically and almost physically, is part of New York City. The giant apartment complexes in Fort Lee and Cliffside Park advertise what a good view of New York they have and how easy it is to get into the city on an express bus; these are renter and condominium towns where people have only the vaguest sense they are in New Jersey. Farther north, the leafy and pleasantly aged suburbs of Englewood, Tenafly, and Bergenfield have historically been commuter suburbs of New York, especially since the completion of the George Washington Bridge in 1931. Just to the west, on the other side of the ridge, is Teaneck, a predominantly Jewish suburb of somewhat more recent vintage.

The third part of the district, north of the separate old county seat of Hackensack, is the suburbia of the 1950s: Paramus, which has more shopping center parking spaces than residents; Fair Lawn, with a long reputation as a planned town and a large Jewish population; a string of modestly affluent suburbs on either side of northbound Route 17.

All these areas, in their different ways, are excellent examples of the aging of close-in suburbs in the 1970s. There was rapid population growth in most of this area in the 1950s and mild growth in the 1960s; in the 1970s the 9th district's population declined 6%. The reason was not decay: you would have a hard time finding an abandoned house or a dilapidated neighborhood here. A better explanation is empty nest syndrome: the blocks once thronged with children running out of houses to play now are eerily quiet; the parents now live alone, and keep the windows and doors closed to hold in the air conditioning. Young families are moving farther and farther out in New Jersey, to Morris County and beyond; the 9th district increasingly is the home of grandparents.

It is also increasingly Democratic. Bergen County, like Westchester in New York, has a reputation for being Republican which was, in national elections at least, exaggerated. There have always been large Democratic pockets here, in the Meadowlands towns and in Jewish neighborhoods in particular; and Democrats have often carried Bergen. But the 1982 election may have been the first time that a Bergen County Republican was thrown quite so much on the defensive. Congressman Harold Hollenbeck, first elected in 1976, had a voting record generally acceptable to the AFL–CIO and a liberal record on most cultural and foreign issues. But he supported the Reagan economic program in 1981, and in 1982, against strong competition, he was on the defensive.

The competition came from Robert Torricelli, a 31-year-old former aide to Governor Brendan Byrne and Vice President Walter Mondale. Torricelli was politically able enough to have been the resident director of the Carter–Mondale campaign in Illinois six months before the primary and to have been its leading spokesman on the rules at the 1980 Democratic National Convention. In 1982 he returned to his native New Jersey, amassed a substantial campaign treasury, and took on Hollenbeck. He worked hard to find issues he could attack the incumbent on: Reaganomics, gun control, environmental issues. Redistricting helped: the district's jagged boundaries keep out many Republican towns and maximize the Democratic vote. But the fact remains that the heart of Bergen County has become a fairly Democratic district. Torricelli won 53%–46%.

Torricelli took seats on the Foreign Affairs and Science and Technology Committees, bodies seemingly removed from local concerns. But many of his constituents have strong interests in American policy toward particular countries—Israel, Greece, even Korea. And northern New Jersey, though not so glamorous in this respect as Massachusetts or California, remains an important research and development center for the rest of the country; it is the home, most notably, of Bell Labs, perhaps the single most consistently productive research facility in history. Having demonstrated his prowess at the polls in 1982, Torricelli may well be able to avert strenuous competition in 1984.

The People Pop. 1980: 527,349, dn. 6.6% 1970–80; voting age pop. 409,362; 5% Black, 4% Span. orig., 2% Asian orig. 37% housing units rented. Median,owner $71,700; renter $284. Households: 75% family, 33% with children, 63% married couples.

Presidential Vote

1980	Reagan (R)	136,148	(54%)
	Carter (D)	93,755	(37%)
	Other	23,393	(9%)

Rep. Robert G. Torricelli (D) Elected 1982; b. Aug. 26, 1951, Paterson; home, New Milford; Rutgers U., B.A. 1974, J.D., 1977, Kennedy Sch. of Govt., M.P.A. 1979; Methodist.

Career Asst. to Gov. Brendan Byrne, 1975–78; Counsel to V.P. Walter Mondale, 1978–79; IL Carter–Mondale Primary, 1980; Practicing atty., 1981–82.

Offices 317 CHOB, 202-225-5061. Also 27 Warren St., Hackensack 07601, 201-646-1111.

Committees *Foreign Affairs* (17th). Subcommittees: Asian and Pacific Affairs; Europe and the Middle East. *Science and Technology* (25th). Subcommittees: Natural Resources, Agriculture Research and Environment; Science, Research and Technology; Space Science and Applications.

Group Ratings and Key Votes: Newly Elected

Election Results

1982 general	Robert G. Torricelli (D)	99,090	(53%)	($266,401)
	Harold C. Hollenbeck (R)	86,022	(46%)	($194,346)
1982 primary	Robert G. Torricelli (D)	18,612	(100%)	
1980 general	Harold C. Hollenbeck (R)	116,128	(59%)	($145,586)
	Gabriel M. Ambrosio (D)	75,321	(38%)	($182,804)

Campaign Contributions and Expenditures

1981-82		Direct Cont. 81-82		PACS brkdwn			
Receipts	$266,552	Indiv	$181,632	Agr	$2,000	Ideo	$12,550
Expend.	$266,401	Party	$2,450	Bus	$3,914	Lbr	$50,305
Unspent	$150	PACS	$83,287	Hlth	$800	Prof	$100

Indirect Party Expend: $20,960   *Indep Expend:* For: $286 Agn: $72

TENTH DISTRICT

One of the most powerful members of the House in the early 1980s has been Peter Rodino, of the 10th congressional district of New Jersey. As chairman of the Judiciary Committee, he has been the key man on all sorts of legislation—determining the contents of some measures, and killing others. In the first two years of the Reagan administration, he and the Judiciary Committee, which tends to share his views, bottled up proposed constitutional amendments to ban abortions, allow school prayer, and ban school busing. When enough signatures were obtained for a discharge petition, removing the constitutional amendment requiring a balanced budget from Judiciary, Rodino had the satisfaction of seeing it defeated on the floor of the House. He is the House's leading legislator on the important, though largely unheralded, area of bankruptcy, and the main force resisting attempts by big retail creditors to make filing individual bankruptcies more difficult; he resists such attractive-sounding but unwise measures as allowing farmers to reclaim their grain from bankrupt grain elevators ahead of other unsecured creditors; he helped to shape the maritime reform act which passed the House, in ways that promoted competition and reduced incentives for price-fixing. Peter Rodino is a man of resolute views, which tend toward what is called the liberal position on most issues; he knows the legislative process and how to steer it in the direction he wants, or away from a direction he doesn't want; he is widely respected in the House and personally well liked. He is also a man who by chance was called on to play an important part in American history, and he played it well.

That was not what everyone expected. When it became clear that Rodino would chair the hearings on the impeachment of Richard Nixon, some House members were apprehensive. Rodino had been chairman of the Judiciary Committee for only a year, following the primary defeat of New York's Emanuel Celler; and Celler, though 86 when he lost, had been an assertive chairman who let Rodino take little responsibility. But these apprehensions proved unfounded. Relying on the Judiciary staff assembled by Celler as well as on the more publicized services of impeachment counsel John Doar, Rodino was able to master the factual and legal case against Nixon and to get smoothly past the parliamentary difficulties as well. His chairing of the hearings was even-handed and fair; he was careful to give the minority every opportunity to advance its views. But there could be little doubt of where Rodino stood in the face of the massive evidence and, to be a bit cynical about it, in light of the overwhelming sentiments of his constituency; he came out solemnly for impeaching the President.

One strength of the American political system is that it has produced people of extraordinary talent who have happened to find their way into crucial positions at critical times and who have performed far better than their records gave anyone the right to expect. Such leaders have come from the most unlikely places: a Lincoln from the midwestern hick town of Springfield, Illinois; a Franklin Roosevelt from the aristocratic patroon families of the Hudson Valley. In that tradition is Peter Rodino, from Newark, New Jersey—a city which has suffered wrenching difficulties and faces grave problems, and which has not had a reputation for probity or honesty for some time.

A third of a century ago, when Peter Rodino was first elected to Congress, Newark was a fairly prosperous industrial city with a large white-collar employment base. With nearly half a million people, it was the financial center of New Jersey, a city proud of its tree-shaded middle-class neighborhoods. Today the downtown remains, although Prudential Insurance, the biggest employer there, is rapidly but quietly moving much of its operations to the suburbs. Some of the rest of Newark resembles Berlin after the war. With one major exception, the city's middle class—including middle-class blacks—have left Newark in search of nicer lawns and safer streets in the suburbs; houses and apartments have been abandoned, commercial property boarded up or vandalized; most of the people remaining are here because they cannot get out. This is not just a matter of racial change: in fact, the proportion of blacks in Newark in the 1970s barely changed, increasing only from 56% to 58%, because of the rapid abandonment of inner-city neighborhoods by middle-income and working-class blacks. Newark suffered through organized crime control of its city government in the 1960s and a major riot in 1967; it saw the indictment (and acquittal) of its mayor recently, for appointing a no-show officeholder; it saw its population decrease from 438,000 in 1950 to 329,000 in 1980.

The major exception to that pattern is the community Peter Rodino comes from, the Italian-Americans who remain in Newark's North Ward. The Jews who once lived in Philip Roth's Weequahic Park have long since moved to places like Maplewood and Short Hills; the Irish have vanished far beyond the city limits into Livingston or West Orange; the Yankees are now even farther away in Morris or Somerset Counties. But many Italians remain, in close-knit neighborhoods where everyone knows everyone else, there is little crime or violence, and people still speak Italian in the streets and shops. The North Ward has steadily resisted integration, but it is a mistake to see it as a peculiarly racist place; there is something positive here people want to protect and something negative, wholly apart from the race of the people involved, which has happened to other parts of Newark, and which North Ward residents sensibly want to avoid. Blacks have been moving west and south instead of north: to East Orange (now 83% black), Orange (57%), Irvington (38%), Hillside (30%), and high-income South Orange (10%).

Newark makes up just 63% of the population of New Jersey's 10th congressional district now. The district also includes East Orange, Orange, and South Orange on the west; Irvington and Hillside on the south; and two small suburbs, high-income Glen Ridge and working-class Harrison, stuck off on different sides. There was some thought when the district first got a black majority, in 1972, that Rodino would be vulnerable in the Democratic primary. But he won 57% against strong black opposition that year and 62% in 1980: his support from black voters has been rising significantly. The reason is evident from his record. He is a well-placed, effective advocate of positions which black voters believe in—and they know that he was long before he had a black-majority constituency. He is at an age now when most men retire, but he seems to have no appetite for that; his health has been robust, and he seems eager to continue his leadership of Judiciary.

The People　Pop. 1980: 525,832, dn. 8.7% 1970–80; voting age pop. 360,962; 51% Black, 12% Span. orig., 1% Asian orig. 67% housing units rented. Median owner $41,200; renter $196. Households: 69% family, 42% with children, 41% married couples.

Presidential Vote

1980	Reagan (R)	35,452	(27%)
	Carter (D)	90,610	(69%)
	Other	5,800	(4%)

Rep. Peter W. Rodino, Jr. (D) Elected 1948; b. June 7, 1909, Newark; home, Newark; Rutgers U., LL.B. 1937; Roman Catholic.

Career Army, WWII; Practicing atty.

Offices 2462 RHOB, 202-225-3436. Also Fed. Bldg., 970 Broad St., Su. 1435A, Newark 07102, 201-645-3213.

Committees *Judiciary* (Chairman). Subcommittee: Monopolies and Commercial Law (Chairman). *Select Committee on Narcotics Abuse and Control* (2d).

Group Ratings

	ADA	ACLU	COPE	CFA	LCV	LWV	NTU	NSI	COC	ACA	CSFC
1982	100	83	95	85	93	83	27	0	14	9	26
1981	100	—	95	93	100	—	35	—	5	9	25
1980	67	80	95	79	72	90	14	0	52	14	25

National Journal Ratings

	Economic		Foreign		Cultural	
1982	92%	(LIB)	90%	(LIB)	89%	(LIB)
	7%	(CONS)	10%	(CONS)	8%	(CONS)
1981	89%	(LIB)	89%	(LIB)	88%	(LIB)
	3%	(CONS)	10%	(CONS)	12%	(CONS)

Key Votes

1) Reagan 81 Budget	AGN	5) Incr SS Rtmt Age	AGN	9) Poor Pay Food Stamps	AGN
2) Reagan 81 Tax Cut	AGN	6) Saudi AWACS Sale	AGN	10) Ban Crt Busing Order	AGN
3) Bal Budget Amend	AGN	7) $ for MX Missile	AGN	11) Auto Local Content	FOR
4) Gas & Road Tax	FOR	8) Nerve Gas Prod	AGN	12) Nuclear Arms Freeze	FOR

Election Results

1982 general	Peter W. Rodino, Jr. (D)	76,684	(83%)	($93,379)
	Timothy Lee, Jr. (R)	14,551	(16%)	($0)
1982 primary	Peter W. Rodino, Jr. (D)	28,587	(100%)	
1980 general	Peter W. Rodino, Jr. (D)	76,154	(85%)	($212,925)
	Everett J. Jennings (R)	11,778	(13%)	($0)

Campaign Contributions and Expenditures

1981-82		Direct Cont. 81-82		PACS brkdwn			
Receipts	$125,106	Indiv	$36,088	Agr	$500	Ideo	$2,417
Expend.	$93,379	Party	$711	Bus	$39,775	Lbr	$36,450
Unspent	$37,340	PACS	$84,900	Hlth	$1,750	Prof	$84,142
		Cand	$2,500				

ELEVENTH DISTRICT

The 11th congressional district of New Jersey is a strip of suburbs following, roughly, Route 3 and Interstate 280 west, starting at the Jersey Meadowlands and proceeding past several ridges to a Morris County suburb with the ungainly name of Parsippany-Troy Hills, some 25 miles from Manhattan. The Meadowlands communities and the suburbs near Newark have an ethnic flavor: Belleville is heavily Italian, for example, and Orange is mostly black. Farther out, the ethnic identification is less obvious. There are relatively high-income suburbs here, like West Orange and Livingston, as well as many modest ones. This area was fully settled for the most part by 1960, and in some cases much before that; even Parsippany-Troy Hills lost population in the 1970s.

Outsiders would assume that people here feel they are part of metropolitan New York. But many identify more with Newark or with New Jersey generally. Most people here work in New Jersey rather than commute to the city; they enjoy entertainment and cultural events more often at home than in New York; they share much more the traditional cultural outlook you would find in a suburb of Chicago or even Indianapolis rather than the urge to embrace the latest fashion or intellectual trend you find in Manhattan. Ancestrally, this is a Democratic district, but in reality it comes pretty close to the national average in national elections—or leans to the Republican side.

The congressman from the 11th district is Joseph Minish, a Democrat first elected in 1962. Despite his seniority, he has not made a major impact on legislation. As a high-ranking member of the Banking Committee, he chairs a subcommittee with broad jurisdiction (General Oversight and Renegotiation), but has not used it aggressively as many younger members do. Minish's background is in the labor union movement, and his voting record is what you might expect: liberal on economic issues, leaning that way but not invariably on cultural and foreign issues. What is most surprising about Minish's career is that he has not had a significant challenge since he first won the district. His reelection percentages have been large, but it is not clear that his support is as deep as it is broad.

The People   Pop. 1980: 525,290, dn. 7.0% 1970–80; voting age pop. 401,249; 6% Black, 2% Span. orig., 2% Asian orig. 38% housing units rented. Median owner $71,200; renter $261. Households: 76% family, 35% with children, 63% married couples.

Presidential Vote

1980	Reagan (R)	127,164	(54%)
	Carter (D)	86,764	(37%)
	Other	21,010	(9%)

Rep. Joseph G. Minish (D) Elected 1962; b. Sept. 1, 1916, Throop, PA; home, West Orange; Roman Catholic.

Career Army, WWII; Political Action Dir., AFL–CIO Dist. 4, 1953–54; Exec. Secy., Essex W. Hudson Labor Cncl., 1954–61, Treas., 1961–62.

Offices 2109 RHOB, 202-225-5035. Also 308 Main St., Orange 07050, 201-645-6363.

Committees *Banking, Finance and Urban Affairs* (3d). Subcommittees: Consumer Affairs and Coinage; Economic Stabilization; General Oversight and Renegotiation (Chairman). *House Administration* (5th). Subcommittees: Personnel and Police (Chairman); Services.

Group Ratings

	ADA	ACLU	COPE	CFA	LCV	LWV	NTU	NSI	COC	ACA	CSFC
1982	80	46	92	85	92	83	11	50	23	9	30
1981	80	—	91	93	100	—	23	—	11	24	35
1980	72	33	78	71	87	80	24	40	53	23	36

National Journal Ratings

	Economic		Foreign		Cultural	
1982	82%	(LIB)	68%	(LIB)	69%	(LIB)
	18%	(CONS)	32%	(CONS)	30%	(CONS)
1981	80%	(LIB)	72%	(LIB)	67%	(LIB)
	20%	(CONS)	26%	(CONS)	33%	(CONS)

Key Votes

1) Reagan 81 Budget	AGN	5) Incr SS Rtmt Age	AGN
2) Reagan 81 Tax Cut	—	6) Saudi AWACS Sale	AGN
3) Bal Budget Amend	AGN	7) $ for MX Missile	AGN
4) Gas & Road Tax	—	8) Nerve Gas Prod	AGN

9) Poor Pay Food Stamps AGN
10) Ban Crt Busing Order —
11) Auto Local Content FOR
12) Nuclear Arms Freeze FOR

Election Results

1982 general	Joseph G. Minish (D)	105,607	(64%)	($163,614)
	Rey Redington (R)	57,099	(35%)	($47,904)
1982 primary	Joseph G. Minish (D)	27,354	(100%)	
1980 general	Joseph G. Minish (D)	106,155	(63%)	($77,750)
	Robert A. Davis (R)	57,772	(34%)	($17,068)

Campaign Contributions and Expenditures

1981-82		Direct Cont. 81-82			PACS brkdwn		
Receipts	$160,375	Indiv	$64,891	Agr	$—	Ideo	$381
Expend.	$163,614	Party	$1,216	Bus	$23,100	Lbr	$24,676
Unspent	$172,434	PACS	$48,407	Hlth	$250	Prof	$—

Indirect Party Expend: $212

TWELFTH DISTRICT

Most people's image of New Jersey is the one they get from the drive from Newark Airport to Manhattan: factories spewing smoke into the already smoggy air, swampland pocked with truck terminals and warehouses, grim lines of Jersey City row houses, and the docks on the Hudson River. But there is another New Jersey—one that begins 20-odd miles outside Manhattan, past the first ridge of Watchung Mountains west of Manhattan. Out here the high-income suburbs fade into elegant horse farm country around Morristown and Far Hills, Peapack and Bernardsville and Basking Ridge. This is the little-known turf of New Jersey's old Yankee aristocracy, joined by more recent arrivals like the late Charles Engelhard.

New Jersey's 12th congressional district spans the distance between these two New Jerseys. It includes one of the state's most garish strip highways, U.S. 22 in Union, near Elizabeth and Newark; and it has some nondescript rural areas as well, where inexpensively built subdivision houses are going up near broken-down farmhouses with rusted-out cars in the backyard. The horse country is located right in the center of the district, and undoubtedly dominates every politician's view of the unit; but in fact it constitutes only a small part of the district demographically. The 12th is, however, a solidly Republican district, and the election here is determined in the Republican primary.

There was a seriously contested primary here in 1982. Two incumbent congressmen had residences within these lines, drawn by a Democratic legislature. But as it happens, neither decided to run here: Millicent Fenwick ran for the Senate instead, and Matthew Rinaldo ran in the Democrat-leaning 7th district, which contained more of his old territory. The primary instead was between James Courter, who had represented only 25% of the new district, and Rodney Frelinghuysen, a son of Peter Frelinghuysen, who had represented Morris and Somerset Counties—50% of the new district—for 22 years until he retired in 1974. They presented a fine contrast. Frelinghuysen is a member of one of New Jersey's oldest and most aristocratic families: one Frelinghuysen ran for vice president on the Whig ticket in 1844, and another served as secretary of state under Chester Arthur. This Frelinghuysen was enraged when President Reagan endorsed Courter, although that was in line with a general policy of backing Republican incumbents. In the end, Frelinghuysen carried Morris County, but only barely, and lost districtwide by a 63%–37% margin.

Courter was once a Peace Corps volunteer and a legal services lawyer—the sort of background you expect to produce liberal Democrats. Instead, he is the most conservative member of the New Jersey delegation. He defeated Democratic incumbent Helen Meyner in 1978 and won easily in 1980; having survived redistricting and a primary in 1982, he seems solidly entrenched in the 12th district for the 1980s. He is a member of the Armed Services and Post Office and Civil Service Committees—assignments which give him a chance to help increase defense spending and cut back on the scope of domestic government. His views are not always conventional, however. He chairs a bipartisan Military Reform Caucus and is interested in getting more bang out of the government's buck; he is proud of an amendment prohibiting offshore oil and gas drilling in 60 tracts off New Jersey. He seems to have the potential to be one of the more interesting, and perhaps more influential, Republican congressmen.

The People   Pop. 1980: 526,907, up 7.3% 1970–80; voting age pop. 385,868; 3% Black, 1% Span. orig., 1% Asian orig. 22% housing units rented. Median owner $85,300; renter $292. Households: 81% family, 41% with children, 71% married couples.

Presidential Vote

1980			
	Reagan (R)	149,583	(62%)
	Carter (D)	69,963	(29%)
	Other	23,098	(9%)

Rep. James A. (Jim) Courter (R) Elected 1978; b. Oct. 14, 1941, Montclair; home, Hackettstown; Colgate U., B.A. 1963, Duke U., J.D. 1966; Methodist.

Career Peace Corps, Venezuela, 1967–69; Practicing atty., 1969–70; Atty., Union Cnty. Legal Svcs., 1970–71; 1st Asst. Warren Cnty. Prosecutor, 1973–77.

Offices 325 CHOB, 202-225-5801. Also 1 Morris St., Morristown 07960, 201-538-7267; 41 Bridge St., Somerville 08876, 202-772-8200; and 14 River Rd., Summit 07901, 201-273-4855.

Committees *Armed Services* (8th). Subcommittees: Procurement and Military Nuclear Systems; Research and Development. *Post Office and Civil Service* (4th). Subcommittee: Census and Population. *Select Committee on Aging* (14th). Subcommittee: Health and Long-Term Care.

Group Ratings

	ADA	ACLU	COPE	CFA	LCV	LWV	NTU	NSI	COC	ACA	CSFC
1982	10	46	17	23	72	58	61	100	75	77	58
1981	15	—	15	57	45	—	75	—	95	76	69
1980	11	20	16	21	46	40	56	100	61	83	75

National Journal Ratings

	Economic		Foreign		Cultural	
1982	16%	(LIB)	21%	(LIB)	38%	(LIB)
	84%	(CONS)	78%	(CONS)	62%	(CONS)
1981	4%	(LIB)	34%	(LIB)	39%	(LIB)
	79%	(CONS)	63%	(CONS)	61%	(CONS)

Key Votes

1) Reagan 81 Budget	FOR	5) Incr SS Rtmt Age	FOR	9) Poor Pay Food Stamps	FOR
2) Reagan 81 Tax Cut	FOR	6) Saudi AWACS Sale	AGN	10) Ban Crt Busing Order	FOR
3) Bal Budget Amend	FOR	7) $ for MX Missile	FOR	11) Auto Local Content	AGN
4) Gas & Road Tax	—	8) Nerve Gas Prod	FOR	12) Nuclear Arms Freeze	AGN

Election Results

1982 general	James A. (Jim) Courter (R)	117,793	(67%)	($557,896)
	Jeff Connor (D)	57,049	(32%)	($93,114)
1982 primary	James A. (Jim) Courter (R)	39,354	(63%)	
	Rodney P. Freylinghuysen (R)	23,015	(37%)	($289,713)
1980 general	Millicent Fenwick (R)	156,016	(78%)	($32,578)
(NJ 5)	Kieran E. Pillion, Jr. (D)	41,269	(21%)	($7,177)
1980 general	James A. (Jim) Courter (R)	152,862	(72%)	($262,786)
(NJ 13)	Dave Stickle (D)	56,251	(26%)	($18,474)

Campaign Contributions and Expenditures

1981-82		Direct Cont. 81-82			PACS brkdwn		
Receipts	$554,369	Indiv	$412,162	Agr	$2,000	Ideo	$2,350
Expend.	$557,896	Party	$18,380	Bus	$83,711	Lbr	$7,000
Unspent	$86,837	PACS	$102,204	Hlth	$5,000	Prof	$1,200

Indirect Party Expend: $34,975

THIRTEENTH DISTRICT

Girdling southern New Jersey like a belt on a low-slung pair of pants is the state's 13th congressional district. Technically, it does not quite span the state, stopping about a mile short of the Delaware River in the west. But it does reach all the way across the Pine Barrens and swamps to the Atlantic Ocean on the east. There is no unity to this unit, except perhaps in political preference. Nearly half the population is concentrated in the New Jersey suburbs of Philadelphia, and nearly half is spread up and down the Jersey Shore or the towns a few miles inland. In both areas the boundaries are convoluted. In the Philadelphia area, they take in the old Republican suburb of Collingswood and the newer Republican suburb of Cherry Hill, and leave out the more Democratic industrial towns along the Delaware River. On the Shore, the 13th includes the inland townships with their new apartment complexes and the beachfront communities on the Long Beach sand spit facing the ocean. In the middle, relatively unpopulated, are the Barrens and the Army's Fort Dix.

There has been a district roughly of this configuration since 1966. It was created then to accommodate the above average population growth in the Philadelphia suburbs and on the Shore, and since that time has been a solidly Republican district.

Its congressman, Edwin Forsythe, was first elected in 1970; despite his seniority, he has not had a major impact on the legislative process. He does not seem to fit into the usual categories, nor does he seem to have the ambition and drive so evident in most of his colleagues. In 1983 he became ranking Republican on the Merchant Marine and Fisheries Committee, but his clout may be limited by his past skepticism about some of the subsidies whose funneling to the maritime industry is the committee's primary function. He probably won't be entrusted with responsibility for the maritime industry's bill, and there is little chance he will rally dissenting members on the committee or the floor against a committee initiative. He may be able to take more advantage of his ranking minority position on the Fisheries and Wildlife Subcommittee, which has something to say about the wetlands which are so common in the 13th district. Forsythe is also a member, but a rather low ranking one, of the Science and Technology Committee.

On issues, generally, he has a voting record like none other: solidly conservative on economic issues, mixed on cultural issues, solidly liberal on foreign issues. Electorally, he has not been challenged seriously in years, and seems to be in solid shape; but he is one of those congressmen who could be vulnerable in primary or general election should serious competition appear.

The People Pop. 1980: 526,168, up 26.0% 1970–80; voting age pop. 360,671; 4% Black, 2% Span. orig., 1% Asian orig. 17% housing units rented. Median owner $56,000; renter $245. Households: 80% family, 41% with children, 69% married couples.

Presidential Vote

1980			
	Reagan (R)	138,522	(62%)
	Carter (D)	70,924	(32%)
	Other	13,471	(6%)

Rep. Edwin B. Forsythe (R) Elected 1970; b. Jan. 17, 1916, Westtown, PA; home, Moorestown; Quaker.

Career Secy., Moorestown Bd. of Adjustment, 1948–52; Mayor, 1957–62; Chmn., Moorestown Twnshp. Planning Bd., 1962–63; NJ Senate, 1963–69, Asst. Minor. Ldr., 1966, Minor. Ldr., 1967; Sen. Pres. and Acting Gov. of NJ, 1968; Pres. Pro Tem, 1969.

Offices 2210 RHOB, 202-225-4765. Also 3d and Mill Sts., Moorestown 08057, 609-235-6622.

Committees *Merchant Marine and Fisheries* (Ranking Member). Subcommittee: Fisheries and Wildlife Conservation and the Environment. *Standards of Official Conduct* (4th).

Group Ratings

	ADA	ACLU	COPE	CFA	LCV	LWV	NTU	NSI	COC	ACA	CSFC
1982	40	54	26	23	26	33	88	11	73	60	53
1981	35	—	27	21	49	—	81	—	100	50	56
1980	50	57	28	36	70	50	56	25	76	83	63

National Journal Ratings

	Economic		Foreign		Cultural	
1982	13%	(LIB)	71%	(LIB)	43%	(LIB)
	87%	(CONS)	29%	(CONS)	57%	(CONS)
1981	4%	(LIB)	88%	(LIB)	63%	(LIB)
	79%	(CONS)	11%	(CONS)	37%	(CONS)

Key Votes

1) Reagan 81 Budget	FOR	5) Incr SS Rtmt Age	FOR	9) Poor Pay Food Stamps	FOR
2) Reagan 81 Tax Cut	FOR	6) Saudi AWACS Sale	AGN	10) Ban Crt Busing Order	FOR
3) Bal Budget Amend	—	7) $ for MX Missile	AGN	11) Auto Local Content	—
4) Gas & Road Tax	—	8) Nerve Gas Prod	AGN	12) Nuclear Arms Freeze	AGN

Election Results

1982 general	Edwin B. Forsythe (R)	100,061	(59%)	($121,723)
	George S. Callas (D)	65,820	(39%)	($13,338)
1982 primary	Edwin B. Forsythe (R)	28,529	(100%)	
1980 general	Edwin B. Forsythe (R)	125,792	(56%)	($109,593)
	Lewis M. Weinstein (D)	92,227	(41%)	($86,488)

Campaign Contributions and Expenditures

	1981–82		Direct Cont. 81–82			PACS brkdwn		
Receipts	$123,087	Indiv	$75,082	Agr	$2,250	Ideo	$1,600
Expend.	$121,723	Party	$7,216	Bus	$25,624	Lbr	$2,000
Unspent	$16,460	PACS	$37,289	Hlth	$5,550	Prof	$250

Indirect Party Expend: $2,018

FOURTEENTH DISTRICT

"I am the law," Frank Hague used to say, and in Hudson County, New Jersey, he was. Back in the 1930s, when Hague was at the peak of his powers as the boss of the Hudson County Democratic machine, he chose governors and U.S. senators, prosecutors and judges, and even had some influence in the White House of Franklin D. Roosevelt. In Jersey City and other Hudson County towns—then and now the most densely populated part of the United States outside Manhattan—Hague controlled almost every facet of life. He determined who would stay in business and who would fail; he controlled tax assessments and the issuance of parking tickets; he had the support of the workingman and kept the CIO out of town for years (resulting in a major Supreme Court case). Hague's power was firmly anchored in votes. Jersey City and Hudson County had huge payrolls, and every jobholder was expected to produce a certain number of votes on election day. Democratic candidates could expect a 100,000-vote margin in Hudson County and since they often lost the rest of the state by less than that, they were indebted indeed. Hague's power continued into the 1940s, until some of his former allies turned on him and took over the machine. The history of Hudson County politics since then has been a history of entangling alliances, occasional betrayals, indictments, and reform movements whose leaders quickly became the heads of the new machines.

To the naked eye Hudson County has not changed much since Frank Hague's time. It still consists of the same series of towns on the granite Palisades ridge between New York Harbor and the Jersey Meadowlands: Jersey City, Bayonne, Weehawken, Union City, and (below the ridge, entirely on the waterfront) Hoboken. To exploit the view of the Manhattan skyline some luxury high-rise apartments have been built at the northern end of the county, but most of Hudson County's residents live in the same cramped apartments and stone row houses that were aging even before the Great Depression.

Hudson County's function throughout its history has been to absorb some of America's millions of immigrants, to provide them with a community of similar people, to provide them with jobs, whether on the waterfront or in the great factories or on the railroads or in Jersey City's huge City Hall. Physically, it is a kind of island, cut off from New York (some Hudson Countians have never set foot in the city whose skyline they see every day, and which is a short ride away on the PATH tubes) and separated from the rest of New Jersey. It stands apart not only from the bucolic suburbs but, separated by the Meadowlands, also from industrial Newark, which has had a quite different ethnic and political history. Hudson County reached its peak population of 690,000 in 1930, just a few years after most immigration was cut off, when its row houses and apartments were filled with young foreigners who spoke English in broken phrases or with a thick brogue, and raised large families full of children who spoke with the distinctive Jersey City accent. As the children grew up, some stayed in Hudson County, but many moved away, to less distinctive suburban communities, to blend in with the great middle class. Because immigration was restricted, there were fewer young families to replace the ones who grew up, and Hudson County's population aged and fell to 555,000 in 1980.

Now Hudson County seems to be filling up with new immigrants again. Its Irish and Italian populations—there have never been many blacks here—are aging and have nearly as many deaths as births. But there has been a new migration to Hudson County since about 1970, of Spanish-speaking people from Latin America. Union City has become predominantly Cuban (64% Spanish origin, according to the Census Bureau), while there are mixed Latin-American communities in West New York (63%), Hoboken (40%), and Jersey City itself (19%). The new migrants, like those of the earlier 20th century, tend to be young people with many children; if they entered the country illegally, as some have, they are still paying U.S. taxes (through wage withholding) and are raising children who will be U.S. citizens paying taxes to support the 1947–62 baby boomers, who have had small families themselves, when they become Social Security recipients. Altogether 27% of the total population, and 35% of the children, in the 14th district are of Spanish origin.

The Latin migration has had only a limited impact on Hudson County politics so far. Most of the voters here are elderly people from earlier migrations. In Hague's day they almost always voted Democratic (except when Hague was punishing some Democrat); so important was the machine in people's lives that they were happy to help out on election day. By the 1960s the machine had become less important. Prosperity had come to Hudson County; at least people no longer depended on the machine for jobs or coal; service in the machine's cadres came to be more of a burden with fewer rewards; people whose relatives had moved elsewhere no longer felt so confined or helpless. Tussles between local politicos continued, and were written up by outsiders as titanic battles for control of an all-powerful machine. But if the machine could still pick judges and state legislators, and if it still had influence in Democratic gubernatorial primaries, its power to affect votes in general elections became very limited. Hudson County trended Republican. Its traditional Democratic voters, with their faith in church and family, had little use for McGovernish Democrats; terrified of street crime, they were ready to vote for politicians who seemed tough on crime. Many of the new Spanish residents, particularly the Cubans, see their values reflected much more accurately in the Republican than in the Democratic Party. The 100,000-plus Democratic margins in Hudson County have vanished. Jimmy Carter carried the county by only 4,000 votes in 1980, and Senator Frank Lautenberg, in a successful statewide effort, took only a 56,000-vote margin out of Hudson in 1982, and would have won without it.

The Hudson County Democratic machine endorsement does still matter on primary day, however. Frank Guarini, the current congressman from the 14th congressional district, which includes almost all of Hudson County and a couple of towns just to the north, was county Democratic chairman before his election in 1978; he replaced Joseph LeFante, a former Assembly speaker, who was persuaded to retire after just one term in the U.S. House. Guarini appears to be a polished, knowledgeable man with important political credentials, and he obviously has clout in Hudson County. Just before he was elected to Congress, he represented a steelworkers' local in a legal suit where 850 American Can Company workers charged that their exposure to various chemicals caused disabling diseases. The case, according to the *Washington Monthly,* was settled for $2.3 million, with an average of $1,400 going to each of the plaintiffs and legal fees of more than $1 million to Guarini. The size of the fee was much larger than is allowed for class actions and group suits of similar size; evidently Guarini persuaded the court to treat the suit as if it were 850 individual cases. Guarini does not seem eager to be questioned about this; whatever else could be said, it is clear that political success in Hudson County still does not go to the meek or to those who are unable to work the system aggressively for themselves. There is no reason to believe Guarini will have trouble winning reelection.

In the House, Guarini is a member of the Ways and Means Committee, and of its Oversight and Select Revenue Measures Subcommittees. His record on issues is impeccably liberal.

The People   Pop. 1980: 526,778, dn. 8.7% 1970–80; voting age pop. 390,399; 11% Black, 24% Span. orig., 3% Asian orig. 67% housing units rented. Median owner $43,900; renter $188. Households: 69% family, 35% with children, 49% married couples.

Presidential Vote

1980	Reagan (R)	87,155	(47%)
	Carter (D)	90,067	(48%)
	Other	8,445	(4%)

Rep. Frank J. Guarini (D) Elected 1978; b. Aug. 20, 1924, Jersey City; home, Jersey City; Dartmouth Col., Columbia U., NYU, J.D. 1950, LL.M. 1955, Acad. of Internatl. Law, The Hague, Holland; Roman Catholic.

Career Navy, WWII; Practicing atty.; NJ Senate, 1965–72.

Offices 206 CHOB, 202-225-2765. Also 910 Bergen Ave., Jersey City 07306, 201-659-7700.

Committees *Ways and Means* (14th). Subcommittees: Oversight; Select Revenue Measures. *Select Committee on Narcotics Abuse and Control* (7th).

Group Ratings

	ADA	ACLU	COPE	CFA	LCV	LWV	NTU	NSI	COC	ACA	CSFC
1982	90	67	90	77	84	67	7	50	21	19	28
1981	85	—	87	100	84	—	23	—	0	10	33
1980	67	73	68	64	74	80	20	40	59	39	38

National Journal Ratings

	Economic		Foreign		Cultural	
1982	96%	(LIB)	78%	(LIB)	71%	(LIB)
	2%	(CONS)	22%	(CONS)	28%	(CONS)
1981	81%	(LIB)	74%	(LIB)	79%	(LIB)
	15%	(CONS)	25%	(CONS)	21%	(CONS)

Key Votes

1) Reagan 81 Budget	AGN	5) Incr SS Rtmt Age	AGN	9) Poor Pay Food Stamps	AGN
2) Reagan 81 Tax Cut	AGN	6) Saudi AWACS Sale	AGN	10) Ban Crt Busing Order	AGN
3) Bal Budget Amend	AGN	7) $ for MX Missile	AGN	11) Auto Local Content	FOR
4) Gas & Road Tax	FOR	8) Nerve Gas Prod	AGN	12) Nuclear Arms Freeze	FOR

Election Results

1982 general	Frank J. Guarini (D)	94,021	(77%)	($203,973)
	Charles J. Catrillo (R)	28,257	(22%)	($14,980)
1982 primary	Frank J. Guarini (D)	46,003	(100%)	
1980 general	Frank J. Guarini (D)	86,921	(64%)	($182,622)
	Dennis Teti (R)	45,606	(34%)	($59,428)

Campaign Contributions and Expenditures

1981-82		*Direct Cont. 81-82*			*PACS brkdwn*			
Receipts	$178,547	Indiv	$69,920	Agr	$3,250	Ideo	$500
Expend.	$203,973	PACS	$107,025	Bus	$46,325	Lbr	$44,500
Unspent	$11,101			Hlth	$8,250	Prof	$4,200

NEW MEXICO

New Mexico is our most unusual state. The culture of every other state is based primarily on what the first white settlers brought to the land; the native inhabitants (except in Hawaii) have either disappeared or no longer form a substantial part of the population. Not so in New Mexico. The American culture here is superimposed on a society whose written history dates back to 1609, when the Spaniards first established a settlement in Santa Fe, and to centuries long past when the Indians of the various pueblos set up stable agricultural societies on the sandy, rocky lands of northern New Mexico. A very substantial minority of New Mexicans are descendants of these Indians or the Spanish, or both. Nearly one-third of the people in this state speak Spanish in ordinary everyday life, and only a few of them are recent migrants from Mexico. This is the northernmost reach of the great Indian civilizations of the Cordillera, which extend along the mountain chain through Mexico, Central America, to South America as far away as Chile.

The Hispanic-Indian culture dominates most of northern and western New Mexico, except for enclaves—usually related to mining or, in the case of Los Alamos, nuclear energy—where Anglos have settled. In vivid contrast to the Hispanic part of New Mexico is the area called Little Texas. With small cities, plenty of oil wells, vast cattle ranches, and desolate military bases, this region resembles, economically and culturally, the adjacent High Plains of west Texas. Oil is important here but not as vital as the military presence: a couple of Air Force bases and the Army's White Sands Missile Range, near Alamogordo, where the first atomic bomb was detonated.

In the middle of the state is Albuquerque which, with the coming of the air conditioner, grew from a small desert town into a booming Sun Belt city. Albuquerque is also heavily dependent on the military and on the nuclear energy establishment. There are two bases within the city limits and its largest employer is Western Electric's Sandia Laboratories, a nuclear energy contractor. Metropolitan Albuquerque now has almost precisely one-third of the state's population—about the same percentage as the Hispanic areas and Little Texas. By fortunate coincidence, the three regions also coincide quite closely, though not perfectly, with its three congressional districts.

For many years New Mexico politics was a somnolent business. Local bosses—first Republican, later Democratic—controlled the large Hispanic vote. Elections in many counties featured irregularities that would have made a Chicago ward committeeman blush. New Mexico also had for years another evidence of boss-controlled politics, the balanced ticket: one Spanish and one Anglo senator, with the offices of governor and lieutenant governor split between the groups.

In the last few elections, a new pattern has emerged. The Republicans have followed a conservative strategy in statewide contests, in effect conceding the Hispanic areas and hoping for compensating margins in Little Texas and Albuquerque. In the late 1970s it worked, if only by narrow margins. Gerald Ford carried New Mexico in 1976—the first time the state voted for a losing presidential candidate. In 1980, New Mexico went for Ronald Reagan by a solid 55%–37% margin. In 1981, Republicans held the entire New Mexico congressional delegation for the first time since 1917. But by 1982, the pendulum swung toward the

Democrats. Albuquerque, almost alone of Sun Belt cities, has been trending Democratic, and went for the Democratic candidates for senator and governor in 1982. The Hispanic areas went very heavily Democratic, so that even fairly good Republican margins in Little Texas could not save the party's statewide candidates. The Democrats recaptured one Senate seat by a solid margin, won the new House seat, continued to threaten the most veteran Republican congressman, and carried the overall statewide vote for the House. Democrat Toney Anaya won the governorship by 24,000 votes, a solid margin in this small state; the last two Democratic governors won by a combined margin of 7,530 votes.

Part of the reason for the Democratic trend was a unique effort by New Mexico Democrats, assisted by the national party, to organize precincts and register and turn out votes. Another reason is demographic change, of two sorts. First of all, New Mexico's young population is disproportionately Hispanic and Indian; as these young people come of age, and enter the voting stream, they move the state toward the Democrats, the more so because Republicans have been writing off the Hispanic vote. Second, the Sun Belt migration to New Mexico has been different than the migration to other Sun Belt states. With its low wages and living costs, New Mexico is the bargain basement of the Sun Belt; the climate—with cold and sometimes snowy winters in Albuquerque—is not as attractive to most retirees as Phoenix's. So New Mexico tends to attract the least affluent of the migrants, low-skill laborers and retirees who can afford a trailer rather than a Scottsdale condominium. Migrants have made Arizona a Republican state; with a different sort of migrant, New Mexico seems to be getting more Democratic.

Governor. New Mexico has had a succession of Democratic governors since 1970: first Bruce King, an Anglo rancher from near Santa Fe; then Jerry Apodaca, a onetime football star at the University of New Mexico, who left office popular but was later tarred with rumors of scandal; then King again; and now Toney Anaya, the former attorney general who ran a close race against Senator Pete Domenici in 1978. None of these men are allies, to say the least; none has been able to name his successor: Anaya beat King's choice, Aubrey Dunn, by a 57%–39% margin in the 1982 primary.

The election of men like Anaya and Apodaca does lay to rest any charges that non-Hispanic New Mexicans are so prejudiced against Hispanics that they won't vote for them. It has also brought to power one of the nation's most forthrightly liberal governors. Anaya assembled a cabinet of former activists and eagerly took on Interior Secretary James Watt; his policies may enrage some New Mexicans, but they will delight others, and under his leadership New Mexico should prove to be one of those useful laboratories of innovation Brandeis told us state governments could be.

Senators. The most powerful New Mexican in national politics today is Senator Pete Domenici; New Mexico has not had such a powerful senator since the heyday of Clinton Anderson, or maybe ever. Largely unknown outside New Mexico in 1980, not long removed from a time when his major governmental responsibility was superintending the budget of the city of Albuquerque, Domenici suddenly became chairman of the Budget Committee when the Republicans took control of the Senate. Only one of the other Republicans on Budget had any experience on the committee, and none except William Armstrong seemed to have both the knowledge and the drive to compete with Domenici as the Republicans' driving force.

In the years since, Domenici has oscillated between two approaches to the budget. On the one hand, he was sympathetic with the desire of the Reagan administration to cut the size and scope of the federal government's domestic activities and to substantially raise defense spending. Like many Republicans, he looked with some horror on the results of the Carter administration's policies and generally prefers market to government solutions. In 1981 he worked closely with OMB Director David Stockman and with the administration generally, and also with Senate Majority Leader Howard Baker. They persuaded the Senate to pass largely untouched the administration's first and second set of budget cuts.

But in 1982 and early 1983 Domenici, again working with Baker, became an independent force. Domenici had served on Budget at a time when Chairman Edmund Muskie and ranking Republican Henry Bellmon had sought and generally obtained bipartisan agreement on major budget measures. Domenici is the kind of old-fashioned Republican who abhors deficits, and in 1982 he was willing to support revenue increases and defense spending cuts. Much of the struggle in the Senate over the budget in 1982 and early 1983 came not from fights between Republicans and Democrats, but from fights between Domenici, acting with the support of most Budget Committee members, and the Reagan administration, which was unwilling to support a budget that could pass and unwilling to allow a budget to pass which it did not want to support. In early 1983, Domenici seemed particularly inclined toward a bipartisan approach; the new ranking Democrat, Lawton Chiles, was more conciliatory than his predecessor, Ernest Hollings, and he and Domenici have long been good friends.

In all these matters, Domenici has demonstrated a technical competence and strategic sense which his earlier Senate career gave him little opportunity to display. He is a deeply religious and earnest man, and one with a hair-trigger temper on occasion; he has talented but somewhat offbeat top staffers who provide a nice antidote to the inevitable stuffiness of budget briefing charts. Domenici is also on a raft of other important committees: Appropriations, which helps him smooth over the inevitable conflicts between Budget and Chairman Mark Hatfield; Energy and Natural Resources, the old Interior Committee which is so important in western states; and Environment and Public Works, also practically important.

Domenici is up for reelection in 1984. Given his prominence and his competence, Washington observers find it hard to believe he will be seriously challenged. But the Democratic trend in New Mexico suggests he might have problems. In 1978, against Toney Anaya, he won with just 53% of the vote. That was far less than expected, and he might even have lost if Anaya had been able to persuade Democratic fundraisers he had a chance. Domenici will naturally have solid Republican Party support, though he is not a favorite of the New Right; he does not share all its views on cultural issues (though he is very family-oriented and conservative on them personally) and his role in budget matters has not been to its liking. He will be in a good position to argue that he is able to do a great deal for New Mexico, but the force of that argument will be blunted if it appears likely that the Democrats will regain control of the Senate. It is possible that Domenici will have a proven vote-getter as an opponent; 3d district Congressman Bill Richardson probably has ambitions for the seat. Richardson has a solid base in the Hispanic part of the state, but it is not clear whether he will, at age 36, have the stature needed to beat Domenici.

New Mexico's junior senator, Jeff Bingaman, is an unknown quantity in Washington. Young, handsome, rich enough to self-finance some of his campaign, he served four years as New Mexico's attorney general. In the 1982 Democratic primary he beat former Governor Jerry Apodaca, who was reputed to have ties to organized crime figures; he lost only the heavily Hispanic rural counties. In the general election he faced incumbent Republican Harrison Schmitt, who had beaten Joseph Montoya six years before. Schmitt is a geologist who was an astronaut and gathered rocks on the moon; he is a strong supporter of the space program and of higher spending on defense and science as well. But his record of support for Reagan economic programs hurt him in 1982. Ultimately, his loss can be chalked up to negative campaign tactics—his own. He ran TV ads which made damaging—and, it quickly became apparent, misleading—charges against Bingaman. Resentment against these tactics turned some key voters against Schmitt, and he lost by a 53%–47% margin—the only incumbent Republican senator to lose in 1982. Interestingly, despite the talk of resentment by Hispanics against Bingaman's campaign against Apodaca, Bingaman and Anaya, with their quite different backgrounds, got almost identical percentages in every region of the state. Theirs were party, not ethnic, victories.

Bingaman serves now on the Armed Services and Governmental Affairs Committees. On economic issues, he can be expected to join his fellow Democrats pretty faithfully. It will be more interesting to see what he does on military issues. Armed Services is an intellectually distinguished panel, with many points of view ably represented. Will Bingaman, coming from a traditionally strong military state, join other Democrats like Gary Hart, Carl Levin, and Edward Kennedy in their skepticism about too much defense spending? Bingaman is not likely to get much national limelight in his first two years, with Republicans in control of the Senate. This is the time, however, when senators can stake out issues and concerns which can form the basis for a long career.

Congressional districting. New Mexico got a third congressional district out of the 1980 Census and, as predicted, created a new, heavily Hispanic district in the northern part of the state. It is heavily Democratic; the other two seats are, or have been in recent elections, very competitive between the two parties. They correspond quite closely to the major demographic regions of the state: the 1st is the Albuquerque area; the 2d mostly Little Texas; the 3d mostly Hispanic counties.

Presidential politics. As noted, New Mexico has voted for the loser only once in presidential elections since it was admitted to the Union in 1912. Yet its five electoral votes are not a major prize, and its presidential primary has never attracted more than a quick visit from a major candidate. The Democrats' organizational efforts here, in connection with the Democratic trend, make this potentially the most Democratic of the Rocky Mountain states in the 1984 election, and it may again be furiously, if obscurely, contested, as it was in 1960 when John Kennedy carried it by some 2,294 votes.

The People Est. Pop. 1982: 1,359,000; Pop. 1980: 1,302,894, up 4.3% 1980–82 and 28.1% 1970–80; 0.58% of U.S. total, 37th largest; voting age pop. 884,987; 7% American Indian, 2% Black, 33% Spanish origin, 1% Asian origin. Single ancestry: 9% English, 5% German, 3% Irish, 1% Italian, French, Scottish. Registered voters (1982): 582,646 Total. 366,828 D (63%); 176,737 R (30%); 36,247 unaffiliated (6%); 2,834 Minor parties (0%). 17% with 1–3 yrs. col., 17% with 4+ yrs. col. 17.4% below poverty level. 28% housing units rented; median house value: $45,400; median monthly rent: $178. Households: 75% family, 45% with children, 62% married couples.

1982 Share of Federal Tax Burden $2,705,000,000; .45% of U.S. total, 44th largest.

1982 Share of Federal Expenditures

	Total		Non-Defense		Defense	
Total Expend	$5,142m	(0.85%)	$3,963m	(0.93%)	$1,178m	(0.66%)
St/Lcl Grants	727m	(0.82%)	727m	(0.82%)	0m	(0%)
Salary/Wages	824m	(1.06%)	252m	(0.92%)	572m	(1.13%)
Ind Payments	1,562m	(0.55%)	1,285m	(0.50%)	277m	(0.97%)
Procurement	1,994m	(1.37%)	1,539m	(4.88%)	454m	(0.40%)
Other Programs	35m	(0.65%)	34m	(0.63%)	1m	(2.33%)
Loan/Insurance	255m	(0.65%)	247m	(0.40%)	8m	(0.36%)

Political Lineup Governor, Toney Anaya (D). Senators, Peter V. (Pete) Domenici (R) and Jeff Bingaman (D). Representatives, 3 (1 D and 2 R). State Senate, 42 (23 D and 19 R); State House of Representatives, 70 (46 D and 24 R).

Presidential Vote

1980	Reagan (R)	250,779	(55%)
	Carter (D)	167,832	(37%)
	Anderson (I)	29,459	(6%)
1976	Ford (R)	211,419	(51%)
	Carter (D)	201,148	(48%)

1980 Democratic Presidential Primary			*1980 Republican Presidential Primary*		
Kennedy	73,721	(46%)	Reagan	37,982	(64%)
Carter	66,621	(42%)	Anderson	7,171	(12%)
Others	9,288	(6%)	Bush	5,892	(10%)
No preference	9,734	(6%)	Crane	4,412	(7%)
			Two others.........	2,742	(5%)
			Uncommitted delegates	1,347	(2%)

SENATORS

Sen. Peter V. (Pete) Domenici (R) Elected 1972, seat up 1984; b. May 7, 1932, Albuquerque; home, Albuquerque; U. of Albuquerque, 1950–52, U. of NM, B.S. 1954, Denver U., LL.B. 1958; Roman Catholic.

Career Practicing atty., 1958–72; Mbr., Albuquerque City Commission, 1966–68, Mayor Ex-Officio, 1967–68; Repub. Nominee for Gov., 1970.

Offices 4239 DSOB, 202-224-6621. Also New Postal Bldg., Santa Fe 87501, 505-988-6511; and Dennis Chavez New Fed. Bldg., 500 Gold Ave., S.W., Rm. 10013, Albuquerque 87102, 505-766-3481.

Committees *Appropriations* (15th). Subcommittees: District of Columbia; Energy and Water Development; HUD-Independent Agencies; Labor-Health and Human-Services, Education. *Budget* (Chairman). *Energy and Natural Resources* (4th). Subcommittees: Energy Regulation; Energy Research and Development (Chairman); Public Lands and Reserved Water. *Environment and Public Works* (7th). Subcommittees: Nuclear Regulation; Water Resources; Regional and Community Development. *Special Committee on Aging* (2d).

Group Ratings

	ADA	ACLU	COPE	CFA	LCV	LWV	NTU	NSI	COC	ACA	CSFC
1982	15	36	24	10	15	33	72	100	80	62	75
1981	15	—	25	21	25	—	71	—	94	70	82
1980	17	13	22	0	23	33	50	89	88	71	66

National Journal Ratings

	Economic		Foreign		Cultural	
1982	21%	(LIB)	16%	(LIB)	23%	(LIB)
	78%	(CONS)	68%	(CONS)	76%	(CONS)
1981	26%	(LIB)	23%	(LIB)	46%	(LIB)
	73%	(CONS)	74%	(CONS)	52%	(CONS)

Key Votes

1) Reagan 81 Budget	FOR	5) $ to El Salvador	FOR	9) Poor Pay Food Stamps	AGN
2) Reagan 81 Tax Cut	FOR	6) Saudi AWACS Sale	FOR	10) Ban Crt Busing Order	FOR
3) Bal Budget Amend	FOR	7) Ban Abortion	FOR	11) Clinch Riv Brdr Rctr	FOR
4) Gas & Road Tax	FOR	8) Nerve Gas Prod	FOR	12) Legal Services Corp	FOR

Election Results

1978 general	Peter V. (Pete) Domenici (R)	183,442	(53%)	($914,634)
	Toney Anaya (D)	160,045	(47%)	($175,633)
1978 primary	Peter V. (Pete) Domenici (R) unopposed			
1972 general	Peter V. (Pete) Domenici (R)	204,253	(54%)	($517,310)
	Jack Daniels (D)	173,815	(46%)	($496,980)

Campaign Contributions and Expenditures

1977-78			PACS brkdwn		
Receipts	$1,028,500	Agr	$7,550	Ideo	$4,750
Expend.	$1,017,512	Bus	$113,276	Lbr	$4,400
Unspent	$11,336	Hlth	$15,300	Prof	$5,475

Sen. Jeff Bingaman (D) Elected 1982, seat up 1988; b. Oct. 3, 1943, El Paso, TX; home, Santa Fe; Harvard Col., B.A. 1965, Stanford Law Sch., LL.B. 1968; Methodist.

Career Asst. NM Atty. Gen., 1969; Practicing atty., 1970–78; NM Atty. Gen., 1978–80.

Offices 502 HSOB, 202-224-5521. Also Fed. Courthouse, Santa Fe 87501, 505-988-6647.

Committees *Armed Services* (8th). Subcommittees: Manpower and Personnel; Tactical Warfare. *Governmental Affairs* (8th). Subcommittees: Civil Service, Post Office, and General Services; Oversight of Government Management; Permanent Subcommittee on Investigations.

Group Ratings and Key Votes: Newly Elected

Election Results

1982 general	Jeff Bingaman (D)	217,682	(54%)	($1,586,245)
	Harrison H. (Jack) Schmitt (R) ...	187,682	(46%)	($1,692,204)
1982 primary	Jeff Bingaman (D)	91,780	(54%)	
	Jerry Apodaca (D)	66,598	(39%)	($544,067)
	Virginia R. Keehan (D)	10,466	(6%)	($13,035)
1976 general	Harrison H. (Jack) Schmitt (R) ...	234,681	(57%)	($441,309)
	Joseph M. Montoya (D)	176,382	(43%)	($451,111)

Campaign Contributions and Expenditures

1981-82		Direct Cont. 81-82		PACS brkdwn			
Receipts	$1,606,965	Indiv	$480,776	Agr	$8,900	Ideo	$61,725
Expend.	$1,586,245	Party	$17,500	Bus	$15,180	Lbr	$157,250
Unspent	$20,719	PACS	$308,917	Hlth	$6,500	Prof	$7,250
		Cand	$790,941				

Indirect Party Expend: $73,760

GOVERNOR

Gov. Toney Anaya (D) Elected 1982, term expires Jan. 1987; b. Apr. 29, 1941, Moriarty; home, Santa Fe; Highlands U., 1959, Georgetown U., B.A. 1963, American U., J.D. 1967; Roman Catholic.

Career Exec. Asst. to Asst. Sec. of State, 1966; Legis. Counsel to U.S. Sen. Joseph M. Montoya, 1966–69; Practicing atty., 1970, 1973–74, 1975–82; A. A. to NM Gov. Bruce King, 1971–72; NM Atty. Gen., 1975–78.

Offices Executive Legislative Bldg., Santa Fe 87503, 505-827-2221.

Election Results

1982 gen.	Toney Anaya (D)	215,840	(53%)
	John Irick (R)	190,626	(47%)
1982 prim.	Toney Anaya (D)	101,077	(57%)
	Aubrey L. Dunn (D)	60,866	(34%)
	Fabian Chavez, Jr. (D)	11,874	(7%)
1978 gen.	Bruce King (D)	174,631	(51%)
	Joseph R. Skeen (R)	170,848	(49%)

FIRST DISTRICT

The 1st congressional district of New Mexico is, for all practical purposes, the city of Albuquerque and its suburbs. Albuquerque itself accounts for 76% of the district's population, with 21% more in suburban fringe; that leaves just 3% in the three desert counties which have most of the district's land area. In 1940 there were just 35,000 people in Albuquerque; the town was huddled in the blocks around the Old Town and the Indian School, just above the Rio Grande. By 1980 Albuquerque's population had increased to 331,000, with 87,000 more close by; the prosperous part of the city has grown up the gently rising heights to the east, with poorer people concentrated north and south of downtown in the Rio Grande valley. Albuquerque is counted as part of the Sun Belt, but its climate is closer to that of the High Plains of west Texas: hot in the summer, sometimes very cold in the winter, with high winds most of the time. Its growth was stimulated not so much by retirees as by the government: its biggest employers include the Sandia Labs, military bases, and defense contractors.

In the late 1960s, Albuquerque was trending Republican in elections, and was in fact the Republican bastion of the state. But in the late 1970s, the city moved the other way. As partisan elections became a contest between the Democratic Hispanic areas and Republican Little Texas, the Albuquerque area's large Hispanic population gave Democrats larger majorities. This is also not as prosperous an area as many Sun Belt metropolises, and one less disposed to uncritical belief in the free enterprise system.

The congressman from the 1st district is a product of the 1960s Republican upsurge. Manuel Lujan, Jr., is part of a politically prominent Republican family. He was first elected in 1968 and for years won reelection easily. He was prized by national Republicans as their most visible Hispanic elected official. At the same time, he was a reliable party man. Lujan is a vigorous opponent of high government spending and backer of the free enterprise system;

NEW MEXICO — Congressional Districts, Counties, and Selected Places — *(3 Districts)*

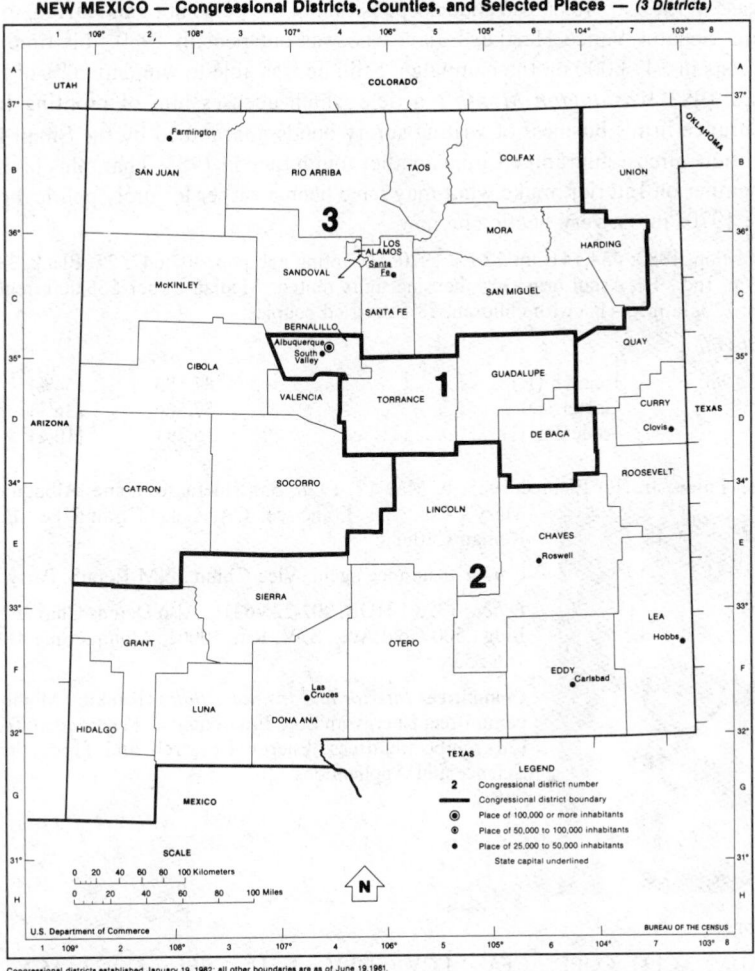

only on noneconomic issues does he dissent much from Republican policy. Since 1981 he has held an important position as ranking Republican on the House Interior Committee. This is a body on which Chairman Morris Udall usually can command a majority. Lujan is more inclined than Udall to relax environmental regulations so as to encourage economic growth, but he is also far from Interior Secretary James Watt's positions on these issues. And there is always the possibility on Interior of persuading key members to dissent from the Udall position, as they have on some issues in recent years.

With his Hispanic background and Republican affiliation, Lujan seemed to be in strong political shape in the old 1st district, which included most of Hispanic northern New Mexico as well as Albuquerque. But in 1980, Democrat Bill Richardson surprised him by spending over $200,000 and winning 49% of the vote. Richardson carried the Hispanic counties, and was an easy winner in the 1982 general election in the new 3d district there. But Lujan did not have surcease in the 1st. He had strenuous opposition in the person of Jan Hartke, son of former Indiana Senator Vance Hartke. Lujan, who was outspent in 1980, this time took no chances: he spent $473,000 on the campaign. Still, he was able to win only 52% of the vote. This, plus a 1983 *Washington Monthly* article which accuses him of profiting from the family insurance firm's business of writing surety bonds guaranteed by the Small Business Administration, almost guarantee Lujan another tough race in 1984. That, plus his duties as ranking member on Interior, make what may have been a rather leisurely political career in the middle 1970s into a very hectic one now.

The People   Pop. 1980: 434,141, up 32.1% 1970–80; voting age pop. 307,647; 2% Black, 33% Span. orig., 2% Am. Ind., 1% Asian orig. 34% housing units rented. Median owner $55,000; renter $202. Households: 72% family, 41% with children, 58% married couples.

Presidential Vote

1980	Reagan (R)	87,583	(54%)
	Carter (D)	57,566	(36%)
	Anderson (I)	15,291	(10%)

Rep. Manuel Lujan, Jr. (R) Elected 1968; b. May 12, 1928, San Ildefonso; home, Albuquerque; St. Mary's Col., San Francisco, CA, Col. of Santa Fe., B.S. 1950; Roman Catholic.

Career Insurance agent; Vice Chmn., NM Repub. Party.

Offices 1323 LHOB, 202-225-6316. Also Dennis Chavez New Fed. Bldg., 500 Gold Ave., S.W., Rm. 10001, Albuquerque 87102, 505-766-2538.

Committees *Interior and Insular Affairs* (Ranking Member). Subcommittee: Energy and the Environment. *Science and Technology* (2d). Subcommittees: Energy Research and Production; Space Science and Applications.

Group Ratings

	ADA	ACLU	COPE	CFA	LCV	LWV	NTU	NSI	COC	ACA	CSFC
1982	10	33	23	31	21	33	75	88	91	90	63
1981	10	—	25	43	14	—	84	—	89	71	54
1980	28	27	26	29	43	33	46	78	73	58	74

National Journal Ratings

	Economic		Foreign		Cultural	
1982	18%	(LIB)	21%	(LIB)	37%	(LIB)
	82%	(CONS)	78%	(CONS)	63%	(CONS)
1981	4%	(LIB)	41%	(LIB)	45%	(LIB)
	79%	(CONS)	58%	(CONS)	54%	(CONS)

Key Votes

1) Reagan 81 Budget	FOR	5) Incr SS Rtmt Age	FOR	9) Poor Pay Food Stamps	AGN
2) Reagan 81 Tax Cut	FOR	6) Saudi AWACS Sale	AGN	10) Ban Crt Busing Order	FOR
3) Bal Budget Amend	FOR	7) $ for MX Missile	FOR	11) Auto Local Content	AGN
4) Gas & Road Tax	FOR	8) Nerve Gas Prod	FOR	12) Nuclear Arms Freeze	AGN

Election Results

1982 general	Manuel Lujan, Jr. (R)	74,459	(52%)	($473,925)
	Jan A. Hartke (D)	67,534	(48%)	($187,488)
1982 primary	Manuel Lujan, Jr. (R)	22,877	(87%)	
	E. G. Martin (R)	3,507	(13%)	
1980 general	Manuel Lujan, Jr. (R)	125,910	(51%)	($178,309)
	Bill Richardson (D)	120,903	(49%)	($230,955)

Campaign Contributions and Expenditures

1981-82		Direct Cont. 81-82		PACS brkdwn			
Receipts	$467,193	Indiv	$300,667	Agr	$4,150	Ideo	$3,050
Expend.	$473,925	Party	$20,688	Bus	$108,986	Lbr	$450
Unspent	$3,397	PACS	$134,419	Hlth	$7,100	Prof	$2,000

Indirect Party Expend: $38,078

SECOND DISTRICT

The 2d congressional district of New Mexico is roughly coincident with the region known as Little Texas. Economically and culturally, this is really an extension of the west Texas counties on the High Plains around Amarillo, Lubbock, Midland, and Odessa. Oil is the mainstay of the economy here; cattle ranching is common; there is even a little cotton farming on irrigated land. There is a considerable Hispanic population—at least 19% in each county—and yet the regional accent is the twang of west Texas, not the lilt of northern Mexico. As you move west from the towns near the Texas border—Clovis, Portales, Lovington, Hobbs—the towns become fewer and agricultural settlement sparser. Around Carlsbad and Roswell the landscape looks to an outsider like desert, with 9,000 foot peaks rising in the crystalline distance.

The southwestern corner of the district, though still near Texas, is a little different in tone. Las Cruces, one of New Mexico's largest towns, is also a majority Spanish community; so are the mining towns in the hills above Silver City and the tiny border town of Columbus, which was raided by Pancho Villa's revolutionary army in 1916.

The 2d district, in somewhat different form, saw one of the roughest and readiest congressional races in the nation in 1980. The incumbent, conservative Democrat Harold Runnels, died in the summer, after having been renominated in the June primary. The Democratic state committee met and nominated David King, then state finance secretary and nephew of then Governor Bruce King. The Republicans had no candidate in the primary, but nonetheless nominated Joe Skeen, who had nearly been elected governor in 1978; the courts quite justifiably ruled that the Republicans had no vacancy to fill and ordered Skeen off the ballot. But the spectacle of the governor's nephew getting the job uncontested was too much: Dorothy Runnels, the congressman's widow, and Joe Skeen both ran write-in campaigns. Skeen won with 38% of the vote.

Skeen was reelected with much less fuss in 1982. He lost the area around Clovis to the Democrat, who had a local base there, and lost the mining counties in the southwest as well. But in the heart of Little Texas he ran strongly and won districtwide with 58%. He has seats on the Agriculture and Science and Technology Committees, both of practical importance to the district; in fact, Science is so important to New Mexico that both its Republican congressmen serve on this committee.

The People Pop. 1980: 436,261, up 17.9% 1970–80; voting age pop. 297,158; 3% Black, 29% Span. orig., 1% Am. Ind., 1% Asian orig. 27% housing units rented. Median owner $33,400; renter $154. Households: 77% family, 45% with children, 66% married couples.

Presidential Vote

1980	Reagan (R)	86,337	(61%)
	Carter (D)	50,472	(36%)
	Anderson (I)	4,843	(3%)

Rep. Joseph R. (Joe) **Skeen** (R) Elected 1980; b. June 30, 1927, Roswell; home, Picacho; TX A&M U., B.S. 1950; Roman Catholic.

Career Navy, WWII; Air Force Res., 1950–51; Sheep rancher, 1950–80; NM Senate, 1961–70; NM Repub. Chmn., 1962–65; Repub. Nominee for Gov. of NM, 1974, 1978.

Offices 1007 LHOB, 202-225-2365. Also Fed. Ofc. Bldg., 200 Griggs, Rm. E-306, Las Cruces 88001, 505-524-8022; Fed. Ofc. Bldg., 300 N. Richardson, Roswell 88201, 505-622-0055; and Kyser Ofc. Complex, 300 Arrington, Farmington 87401, 505-327-4933.

Committees *Agriculture* (10th). Subcommittees: Conservation, Credit, and Rural Development; Livestock, Dairy and Poultry; Tobacco and Peanuts. *Science and Technology* (8th). Subcommittees: Investigation and Oversight; Science, Research and Technology.

Group Ratings

	ADA	ACLU	COPE	CFA	LCV	LWV	NTU	NSI	COC	ACA	CSFC
1982	5	8	14	23	8	16	81	100	82	96	72
1981	0	—	20	7	7	—	59	—	89	75	69

National Journal Ratings

	Economic		Foreign		Cultural	
1982	14%	(LIB)	19%	(LIB)	4%	(LIB)
	85%	(CONS)	80%	(CONS)	87%	(CONS)
1981	4%	(LIB)	33%	(LIB)	4%	(LIB)
	79%	(CONS)	67%	(CONS)	90%	(CONS)

Key Votes

1) Reagan 81 Budget	FOR	5) Incr SS Rtmt Age	FOR	9) Poor Pay Food Stamps	FOR
2) Reagan 81 Tax Cut	FOR	6) Saudi AWACS Sale	FOR	10) Ban Crt Busing Order	FOR
3) Bal Budget Amend	FOR	7) $ for MX Missile	FOR	11) Auto Local Content	AGN
4) Gas & Road Tax	FOR	8) Nerve Gas Prod	FOR	12) Nuclear Arms Freeze	AGN

Election Results

1982 general	Joseph R. (Joe) Skeen (R)	71,021	(58%)	($314,609)
	Caleb J. Chandler (D)	50,599	(42%)	($71,622)
1982 primary	Joseph R. (Joe) Skeen (R)	14,795	(100%)	
1980 general	Joseph R. (Joe) Skeen (R) write-in .	61,564	(38%)	($73,156)
	David King (D)	55,085	(34%)	($91,964)
	Dorothy Runnels, write-in	45,343	(28%)	($167,622)

Campaign Contributions and Expenditures

1981-82		Direct Cont. 81-82		PACS brkdwn			
Receipts	$329,076	Indiv	$232,224	Agr	$6,800	Ideo	$3,050
Expend.	$314,609	Party	$15,159	Bus	$53,937	Lbr	$200
Unspent	$17,067	PACS	$71,387	Hlth	$1,900	Prof	$5,500

Indirect Party Expend: $4,615   *Indep Expend:* For: $18,135 (AMAPAC, NRA)

THIRD DISTRICT

The 3d congressional district of New Mexico is one part of the United States where the political dialogue has been conducted, over the years, much more often in Spanish than in English. It has also been conducted in ways mysterious to Anglos. The district covers most of the northern part of New Mexico, from the High Plains as they rise to the Sangre de Cristo Mountains in the east, through the vast ridges and isolated buttes in the center, to the windy and dusty desert-like plains, dotted occasionally by mountains, with their Indian reservations in the west.

The census figures tell us that this is an area full of minorities: the population is 39% Spanish origin and 21% Indian (there is some overlap between the categories). But here they are not minorities at all. This is their land; their ancestors have been here at least 350, and perhaps 1,350 years. The Spanish conquistadors found a stable civilization here in 1609, and over its Indian customs they erected a thin veneer: the Catholic religion, baroque accents of the adobe buildings, the Spanish language. But if you could go up some of the back roads in Rio Arriba or Santa Fe or Taos or Sandoval Counties, you would find the religion an admixture of Catholicism with adaptations of Indian festivals and old superstitions, the buildings not that much different after all from the pueblos you will find still in use in Taos and elsewhere, the language influenced—as languages always are—by the habits and background of its users.

The political traditions here are more Latin and Indian in some respects than Anglo. For years, there was boss politics in the New Mexico hills. Leading families could deliver the votes of whole communities; ballot boxes were stuffed if need be, and few questions ever asked. Loyalties ran to families and communities, not to parties and principles. That has been changing in recent decades, as television brings the Anglo world into the mountains, and as Santa Fe and Taos have become year-round resorts for affluent young Texans and easterners attracted by ski slopes, summer coolness, and Indian culture. But the future belongs to the products of the old culture: 44% of the children in this district are Hispanic and 27% are Indian. And in the heart of Rio Arriba County, or even in villages on back roads not far from Santa Fe, you can still find more than vestiges of the old communities and old politics—though no one is going to let you in on them much, even if you speak good Spanish.

The creation of the new 3d district gave the Hispanic community here a chance to elect its own congressman; they elected a man named Richardson who was born in Pasadena, California. Actually, Bill Richardson is Hispanic: his mother was Mexican, he was raised in Mexico City, he speaks fluent Spanish. But he came to New Mexico only in 1978 after holding staff jobs on Capitol Hill (the importance of which he exaggerated in 1980 campaign literature). And he worked not in the Hispanic community but as executive director of the state Democratic Party. Richardson lost no time running for office. He won what most observers thought was a worthless nomination to run against Congressman Manuel Lujan, raised over $200,000, and won 49% of the vote. (Only afterward was a $100,000 loan investigated by the Federal Election Commission; Richardson was cleared of wrongdoing.) He did have serious competition in the new 3d district primary, from former Lieutenant Governor Roberto Mondragon, and he lost the counties in the heart of the Hispanic area; but he won enough other territory over the much less well-financed Mondragon to win the nomination with 36% of the vote. In the general election he was subject to some criticism, but won easily with 64% of the vote.

Richardson is obviously a young man in a hurry, and one with a well-developed sense of political strategy. He has done just about everything he would need to to win a Senate seat in New Mexico some day. But for 1984 he must face a tough decision: whether to run against Senator Pete Domenici. The Republican's margin was uninspiring in 1978, but he has gained greatly in prominence since, as chairman of the Senate Budget Committee. Unlike Richardson's other opponents, Domenici will have plenty of money and reason not to be complacent. Moreover, Richardson has very little time in which to establish a genuine record on issues and to give voters some sense of what he really cares about. He has made a good start by winning a much coveted seat on the House Energy and Commerce Committee as well as one on Veterans' Affairs; he sits on subcommittees which handle hot issues like toxic wastes and deregulation of natural gas. Those who want to predict how Richardson might do in a 1984 Senate race would be well advised to consider, not only how he has campaigned, but whether he makes a substantive contribution on these issues; if he wants to be a lifetime senator—and there is every indication he does—then he will have to be something more than a good candidate.

If Richardson decides to seek reelection in the 3d district, he will surely win easily. If he does run for the Senate, there will likely be a free-for-all Democratic primary here which will determine the next congressman.

The People   Pop. 1980: 432,492, up 35.8% 1970–80; voting age pop. 280,182; 1% Black, 37% Span. orig., 17% Am. Ind. 23% housing units rented. Median owner $47,900; renter $166. Households: 77% family, 50% with children, 63% married couples.

Presidential Vote

1980	Reagan (R)	76,859	(53%)
	Carter (D)	59,788	(41%)
	Anderson (I)	9,325	(6%)

Rep. Bill Richardson (D) Elected 1982; b. Nov. 15, 1947, Pasadena, CA; home, Santa Fe; Tufts U., B.A. 1970, Fletcher Sch. of Law and Diplomacy, M.A. 1971; Roman Catholic.

Career State Dept., Ofc. of Congressional Relations, 1973–75; Staff, Senate Subc. on Foreign Relations Assistance, 1975–78; Exec. Dir., NM State Dem. Party, Exec. Dir., Bernalillo Cnty. Dem. Party, 1978; Internatl. business consultant, 1979–82.

Offices 1610 LHOB, 202-225-6190. Also 327 Sandoval St., Su. 210, Santa Fe 87501, 505-988-6177.

Committees *Energy and Commerce* (23d). Subcommittees: Commerce, Transportation, and Tourism; Fossil and Synthetic Fuels. *Veterans' Affairs* (21st). Subcommittees: Education, Training and Employment; Hospitals and Health Care; Housing and Memorial Affairs.

Group Ratings and Key Votes: Newly Elected

Election Results

1982 general	Bill Richardson (D)	84,669	(64%)	($494,767)
	Marjorie Bell Chambers (R)	46,466	(35%)	($124,490)
1982 primary	Bill Richardson (D)	23,123	(36%)	
	Roberto A. Mondragon (D)	19,691	(31%)	($51,661)
	George H. Perez (D)	12,412	(19%)	($100,310)
	Tom Udall (D)	8,619	(13%)	($117,591)
1980 general	Newly created district			

Campaign Contributions and Expenditures

1981-82		Direct Cont. 81-82		PACS brkdwn			
Receipts	$493,482	Indiv	$109,296	Agr	$5,700	Ideo	$13,275
Expend.	$494,767	Party	$365	Bus	$27,181	Lbr	$56,200
Unspent	$1,264	PACS	$124,766	Hlth	$2,250	Prof	$1,850
		Cand	$261,429				

Indirect Party Expend: $9,131

NEW YORK

New York, the state that designed and developed the American version of the welfare state, has spent most of the last decade wondering whether it was such a good idea—and trying to make it work. This was not something New Yorkers wanted to do; they were forced to, by the threatened bankruptcy in 1975 first of the New York City government, and then of the government of New York state. That fiscal crisis caused sharp and painful cuts in government spending, There were layoffs of some of the vast numbers of employees—far more than any other city or state has felt the need to hire. The remaining hundreds of thousands of government employees no longer could look forward to the exceedingly generous gains they had gotten out of collective bargaining over the previous decade. Welfare payments were frozen from 1974 to 1981, despite a rapid rise in the cost of living. Each of these steps was taken agonizingly, by a wide variety of politicians of both political parties and of others—labor leaders, businessmen, the custodians of the huge public employees' pension funds. Interrupted occasionally by elections, they did the unpleasant work of pruning back the welfare state to dimensions New York's private economy could afford. As 1982 ended, it seemed that New Yorkers were not ready to repudiate the welfare state; they elected as their governor a man, Mario Cuomo, who may be the most articulate defender of welfare state policies in American politics. But they also sent a pretty clear signal, by nearly electing businessman Lewis Lehrman, that they wanted the welfare state subject to continued discipline and skeptical scrutiny.

New Yorkers were recognizing, albeit belatedly, that the population and the economy of New York today are no longer the same as the population and the economy the welfare state was created to serve. New York is no longer, as it was up through the 1920s, the nation's leading port of entry for immigrants; today those immigrants are mostly Latin Americans and Asians, whose most popular destination is Los Angeles. But from 1880 to 1924, America's number one immigrant city—and also its richest urban center and one of its economically most creative—was New York. Most of the hundreds of thousands of immigrants who came to the United States every year (except 1914–18) came through New York's Ellis Island, and many stayed in New York. The needs—and demands—of this immigrant population shaped New York politics and the welfare state which that politics produced.

To understand how this happened, consider what New York was like in 1910. Manhattan, swollen with immigrants, had a population of 2.3 million (compared to 1.4 million in the mostly high-status singles Manhattan of today). Large families were packed into old tenements; sanitary conditions were often wretched; working conditions in the lofts and rowhouse factories where so many immigrants worked were dreadful, as the Triangle fire of 1911 demonstrated. The Lower East Side was filled with Jews from eastern Europe, Little Italy with southern Italians, Hell's Kitchen with Irish Catholics, Yorkville with Germans. Manhattan's Yankee, Dutch, and German Jewish aristocrats were squeezed into a few blocks along Fifth Avenue and Central Park and in enclaves like Gramercy Park: most of Manhattan was slums. The outlying boroughs, only recently connected to Manhattan by subway, were still mostly empty; the low-rise apartment complexes which would house so many products of New York's immigration were just beginning to be built.

Politically, the dominant force in New York was the Democratic Party, led mostly by the Irish Catholics of Tammany Hall, though it usually ran Protestants at the top of the ticket. But Tammany was straining under the task of representing the new immigrants. Many of the Italians were Republican (e.g., Fiorello LaGuardia), for the same reasons that many Italians avoided Catholic churches with Irish priests; many of the Jews were Socialists or sympathetic to socialism. Eugene Debs was two years away from winning 900,000 votes in the 1912 presidential election, and it was not apparent then as it is now that the United States would not develop a large socialist party as Britain, France, and Germany had done in the previous decade. Then the Triangle fire of 1911: more than 100 mostly Jewish garment workers were killed when fire broke out in an apparel sweatshop where the fire doors had been barred up. Responding to the demand for regulation was Al Smith, an obscure Tammany assemblyman, the son of an Irish immigrant who more than anyone else created American welfare state politics. Smith combined allegiance to the Democratic machine of the Irish with advocacy of advanced ideas of government regulation and enterprise fostered by Jews and others; he was elected governor four times, and might well have been elected president were he not Catholic. Smith wrote wage and working conditions laws, passed a minimum wage, got New York state into the electric power business, and built the nation's best system of paved roads.

All this was paid for by an affluent and rapidly growing private economy. New York City, with its cheap immigrant labor and rapidly growing class of large and small entrepreneurs, was experiencing explosive economic growth: it was in this period that New York became—it seems inevitable today, but it wasn't then—the center of America's clothing and entertainment industries. Upstate New York was prosperous too. Far from being the home of just a few dairy cows, as some in New York City supposed, Upstate New York had one of the nation's leading industrial corridors, with the New York Central Railroad using the same water-level route the Erie Canal had pioneered. In the 19th century Upstate New York's Yankee communities had been centers of intellectual ferment, the home of such diverse movements as abolitionism, women's rights, and the Mormon Church. By the early 20th century people here, in their sturdy, snug homes kept warm against the frigid Upstate winters, had perhaps the highest standard of living in the nation. They were developing some of the nation's major industries (General Electric, Eastman Kodak, IBM all had their major operations here) and had one of the nation's largest grain ports (Buffalo). New York state as a whole had a per capita income more than 50% ahead of the national figure by the end of Smith's governorship. No wonder they called it the Empire State.

Smith and his Democratic successors carried New York by amassing margins in New York City overwhelming enough to overcome the margins the Republicans almost always had Upstate. Often their margins were small: it is forgotten now, but Franklin Roosevelt carried New York by only small margins in 1940 and 1944, Truman lost it in 1948, and Stevenson ran a strong race in New York in 1952. In New York the key swing voters were the Jews, then as now about one-fourth of New York City's population. Their aversion for Tammany and their affection for vaguely socialist ideas was reflected in the creation of separate American Labor and Liberal Parties, so that Jewish immigrants who didn't read much English could vote for Roosevelt and Mayor LaGuardia's candidates on the same party lever. The welfare state policies of Smith, Roosevelt, and Governor Herbert Lehman attracted these votes and the Democrats held the governorship for 22 of 24 years; the liberal Republican policies—which is to say, acceptance and enlargement of the welfare state—by Thomas Dewey and Nelson Rockefeller helped them win enough of these crucial votes to give their party control of state government for 28 of the next 32 years. Oddly, national strategists took the peculiarities of New York—particularly the presence of a large, leftish Jewish population—as a model for the nation, and built political strategies based on the theory that Republicans couldn't win without appealing to big liberal independent blocs; the persistence of this idea is witnessed by the fact that it is still being articulated by some Republicans after the national victories of Richard Nixon and Ronald Reagan.

And so New York constructed a welfare state, in New York City, Albany, and Washington, where Senator Robert Wagner, Sr., sponsored Social Security and the National Labor Relations Act before FDR endorsed them. In the process, New York itself was changing. Immigration pretty much stopped after the Immigration Act of 1924; and the immigrants of the post-World War II era, blacks from the South and Puerto Ricans, were different from their pre-1924 predecessors: the earlier immigrants were self-selected for initiative and ability to cope with an urban society; the blacks were drawn from a culture that could not be relied on to reward initiative; the Puerto Ricans, as it turns out, in most cases maintained a primary interest in Puerto Rico. The earlier immigrants were diffusing themselves through the New York metropolitan area, filling the potato fields of Long Island with subdivisions, and even Upstate, where you now see as many Italian as Yankee names on store signs. The vast rise in real incomes in the 30 years after 1945 affected New York, although its edge over the rest of the nation has diminished to almost nothing; the decline in ethnic and religious discrimination and distinctiveness has reduced New York's ethnic contentiousness. New York has experienced bouts with a politics of cultural variety, most notably in the vehemence with which different parts of the electorate supported and opposed John Lindsay, the perfect symbol of upper-class radical chic. But that kind of politics seemed suddenly irrelevant when the New York City fiscal crisis hit.

The heyday of New York's welfare state came under two Republicans—Governor Nelson Rockefeller and Mayor John Lindsay (though the latter eventually became a Democrat). Under them taxes rose, the number of public employees increased substantially and their pay and pensions increased explosively, and obligations were incurred that could not be met (Rockefeller's Urban Development Corporation, Lindsay's bonds to pay for current expenditures). They had grand ambitions—Rockefeller was a great builder, with many things to his credit (the State University of New York system, the Empire State Mall in Albany), and Lindsay was vastly sympathetic to the poor and the black. But they also shared what turned out to be a dangerous assumption, shared by many others as well: that New York could afford to pay for whatever its political leaders decreed. The taxes that Rockefeller levied helped keep new industry out of New York and discouraged the state's marginal businesses. Lindsay's tax and racial policies stimulated a vast migration, of as many as a million people, of the middle class out of New York City and state. New York, which had grown more rapidly than the national average in 1880–1940, declined in population by one million in the 1970s. Some of the reasons were benign: an end to migration from the black South and Puerto Rico, as the number of low-wage jobs in New York declined and, after 1975, real welfare payments declined; an aging of the population and the replacement of families by affluent singles in some areas. But some of it represented a real loss of production and wealth to the state. The welfare state, set up as a safety net for a motivated, ambitious class of immigrants, had turned into something which served a mostly affluent, assimilated population and which cost far more than it was worth.

By the early 1980s New York's economic problems seemed at least a little resolved. The state's population rose in 1980–82, and its unemployment rate in the recession of that period was below the national average. New York seemed to be moving toward a future as a stable, solvent high-wage state. Manhattan was booming as an office center; it remained the center of the financial, clothing, entertainment, media, and publishing industries. For all the parochialness of some Manhattanites—the kind Woody Allen's films feature—New York remains the nation's leading center of ideas. The outlying boroughs have attracted a significant migration from Latin America, the eastern Mediterranean, Asia, and even Russia—Colombians and Salvadorians, Koreans and Chinese, Greeks and Russian Jews— injecting vitality and a younger generation into what were aging, listless communities. At the same time the majority of New York City's population is white and middle class; if the city's majority supports measures like rent control, which provides short-run help for the tenant majority but leads to long-run deterioration of the city's housing stock, it also more responsibly has insisted on cutting city payrolls, eliminating racial quotas, and aggressively fighting crime. Under Mayor Edward Koch the profligate and trendy programs of John Lindsay became a thing of the past. That has made Koch a kind of bete noire for *Village Voice* writers and others who, from their high-income apartments, suppose themselves to be the vanguard of the proletariat. But while New York now has a significant leftish vote in Democratic primaries, in general elections its left-wing vote is no larger than those in many other states. In 1980 Jimmy Carter won only 44% of the vote in New York, and John Anderson's independent candidacy took only 8%; New York City, which gave 14% of its votes to Communist-supported Henry Wallace in 1948, gave only 6% to the *Doonesbury*-celebrated Anderson in 1980. The children and grandchildren of the immigrants who made New York a self-consciously liberal state, now dispersed to outer boroughs and suburbs, on many issues embrace the politics of Ronald Reagan.

Upstate New York, like other old industrial areas, has not had substantial economic or population growth, but for the most part has not been plunged into a depression as Detroit and Cleveland were in the early 1980s. Geographically, it has become a kind of backwater: passenger trains no longer run, its freight lines are bankrupt and poorly maintained, and its airports are not very busy. In an air-conditioned age people seek the warmer environment of the Sun Belt and shun Upstate. Its largest city, Buffalo, is one of those Great Lakes metropolises whose economy is visibly sagging; old steel mills are being closed and there is little new investment. Albany, as the headquarters of state government, had a growth industry in 1960–75, but no more. Even Rochester, a corporate headquarters town (Eastman Kodak and formerly Xerox), is not really surging ahead.

Yet Upstate has its assets, which may come into play more in the 1980s than they did in the 1970s. It has a highly skilled labor force. It has a fine physical environment—green hills, majestic mountains, glistening lakes, a plentiful water supply—and its winters are no colder than those in booming Minnesota. For all the talk of this part of the country being doomed to economic stagnation, it sits on Lake Ontario just opposite the most economically productive part of Canada. Upstate's biggest problem may be that it gets little attention: in the state it is overshadowed by New York City; it is not considered an integral part of either the East Coast or the Great Lakes Midwest; its cities do not loom large in the national consciousness. Its history—it was one of America's first frontiers, one of its first industrial workshops—no longer fascinates us; its colleges and cultural institutions do not command national attention.

Presidential politics. The basic constituencies in the New York electorate are now quite different from those in the 1940s which still shape much journalism and analysis. Instead of machine Democrats in New York City, we have their children and grandchildren—Catholic or Jewish, middle income, with a Democratic heritage, but hard-pressed financially, displeased with the cultural liberalism of trendy Manhattan, and interested in disciplining and preserving, but not expanding, the welfare state that was established for their forebears. In place of Yankee Upstate Republicans, we have an Upstate electorate that is heavily Catholic, that retains a Republican identification because of its distrust of New York City, but which is also temperamentally inclined to support incumbents of either party. Instead of a large leftish bloc of Jewish voters, we have very much smaller and dispirited blocs of blacks and Puerto Ricans and many third-wave immigrants who have not yet entered the voting stream. And where there was no significant bloc before, when Upstate started at the northern limits of the Bronx, now we have one-fourth of the electorate in the New York suburbs.

That basic mix adds up to a state that is closer to being, in a close national election, an exceedingly marginal constituency, as Roosevelt and Dewey strategists believed in the 1940s, than the safe Democratic state that analysts in the 1960s and 1970s supposed. It can be expected to run about 2% or 3% more Democratic than the national average, barring special circumstances. One such circumstance was the aid to New York City issue, which probably accounted for Gerald Ford's loss of the state, and the presidency, in 1976; south Georgia peanut farmer Jimmy Carter got a higher percentage in New York City and its suburbs that year than liberal Hubert Humphrey in 1968, Catholic John Kennedy in 1960, or New Yorker Franklin Roosevelt in 1940 and 1944. Balancing that is Upstate's predilection to rally to incumbent presidents of whatever party. Upstate gave above-national-average landslide percentages to Nixon in 1972, Johnson in 1964, and Eisenhower in 1956. Its percentage for Carter declined only from 44% in 1976 to 42% in 1980—one of the lowest drops in the nation. Should Upstate be similarly inclined in 1984, that might give a President Reagan seeking reelection an edge in the race for New York's 36 electoral votes that few analysts are counting on.

If New York's general electorate is closer to the national average than is generally supposed, its primary electorates are very odd indeed. This is a state without primary traditions: Nelson Rockefeller vetoed state primary laws in the 1960s, because he feared, correctly, that his kind of Republican would lose in primaries, and because a convention system allowed Republicans to depict Democratic candidates as the choice of nefarious political bosses. Democratic primary turnout in 1980 was less than one million in a state which casts six million votes in general elections; probably at least one-third of Democratic primary voters are Jewish, and about 80% are in the New York metropolitan area. In Manhattan and in isolated suburban pockets there is an articulate leftish vote which has disproportionate impact, if only because it leads Democratic candidates to take stands on issues from rent control to gay rights which make it hard for them to campaign or to govern later. That leftish bloc gave Edward Kennedy a base for his challenge of Jimmy Carter in 1980. But Kennedy probably would not have won but for the fact that the Carter administration's UN representative voted for a resolution condemning Israel's occupation of the West Bank in terms referring to the crimes of Nazi Germany.

Republican primaries are as heavily tilted toward Upstate as Democratic contests are toward the city. They seem dominated not by laconic Yankees or upscale WASPs, but by Italian-Americans, who indeed form practically the entire Republican primary electorate in New York City. They are not averse to a little government interference in the economy, but on cultural issues their approach is traditional and even on economic issues like rent control they see themselves as adversaries of the great Democratic majority in New York City. In presidential contests, the Republicans elect delegates whose presidential preference is not identified on the ballot; there is no direct vote on the candidates themselves. But no one should have been surprised when Ronald Reagan ended up dominating the 1980 New York delegation. This was no more surprising than Lewis Lehrman's landslide victory in 1982 over a candidate supported by heirs of the old Dewey-Rockefeller organizations or Alfonse D'Amato's defeat of Jacob Javits in 1980.

Any observer of New York politics should be wary of concentrating on the machinations of New York City's Democratic bosses, the county chairmen in each of the four biggest boroughs. It should be apparent to anyone by now that these men have little to do with the outcome of statewide or national elections. They are in a different business, the brokering of judicial patronage; for higher office, a county chairman's endorsement is more often a liability than an asset. The only genuine boss in New York, in the old sense of the word, has been Joseph Margiotta, longtime head of Nassau County's Republican Party. Convicted of steering insurance business to politically favored firms, which seems an unremarkable offense, he nonetheless demanded that Nassau Republicans seek his endorsement publicly; they did, and most of them won anyway. *That* is power. Only after his conviction was upheld by the Supreme Court did he finally resign. As for the state's minor parties, they have some potential influence because they can threaten to run separate candidates, but they no longer seem to move state politics in the direction they want, as the Liberals did in the 1950s and early 1960s and the Conservatives in the late 1960s and 1970s. Even the big fundraisers are no longer necessarily powers here: Mario Cuomo was far outspent by Edward Koch and Lewis Lehrman, and won anyway; Lehrman spent his own money, and Koch won the mayoralty in the first place without much in the way of smart money contributions. The real power brokers may be the media consultants, who prepare TV ads; but the one best known for his successes in the New York area, David Garth, had a poor year in 1982.

Governor. The 1982 campaign for governor provided as vivid a contrast between ideas, brilliantly articulated, as the nation has seen in recent years. This happened almost by accident. Lewis Lehrman, unknown to the public a year before the race and discounted by many politicians, spent some $7 million of the money he made building the Rite-Aid drug chain putting his commercials on TV—and nearly getting himself elected governor. Mario Cuomo, a lieutenant governor seldom consulted by retiring Governor Hugh Carey, upset the heavy favorite in the primary, Edward Koch. Cuomo—a Democrat in a Democratic year, an Italian-American in a state where the large Italian-American vote had been trending Republican—ended up beating Lehrman by a 51%–47% margin. But in the campaign Lehrman set the agenda for state government by calling for cuts in government, and specifically for a 40% cut in state tax rates over eight years, and by calling, in sometimes shrill language, for a stern approach to crime. Lehrman's tax cut sounded like an echo of Kemp-Roth, but differed in one important respect: state governments can't run deficits which have macroeconomic effects.

Cuomo attacked Lehrman's proposal as too drastic, and defended, in often inspiring language, the basic welfare state idea of protecting the helpless. But he was forced to present his own proposals for cutting taxes and scaling back government. The election results show a battle of ideas being translated as a battle of city versus country, New York City versus Upstate. Cuomo grew up and still lives in Queens, in one of the hundreds of urban villages that make up the outer boroughs of New York City, places where welfare state protections, like church and family, are part of the fabric of life. He carried New York City 2–1 and nearly carried the suburban counties. Lehrman, who personally selected sites for Rite-Aid stores all over Upstate New York and nearby Pennsylvania, carried Upstate, with especially large margins in nonmetropolitan counties. Cuomo carried the Jewish vote, Lehrman carried or came close to carrying the Italian vote. There was also in this race a tremendous difference between the sexes. Lehrman, the stern opponent of crime and advocate of fiscal discipline, would be governor now if it were up to only male voters. Cuomo, an opponent of capital punishment and a stirring advocate of government programs to help the helpless, won a solid majority of votes from women.

Cuomo took command in his first months of office, personally handling duties Carey almost entirely delegated to a few trusted aides. In fashioning a budget, Cuomo worked closely with state legislative leaders of both parties, with results everyone agreed to—but which fell short of achieving Cuomo's own ideals. Cuomo has never had a large staff and has always handled details personally; most of his success comes from careful attention to detail. But the governorship under Carey and Rockefeller involved massive delegation of responsibility, and that may cause Cuomo some problems as the months go on. Cuomo has been mentioned as a candidate for national office, and as is sensible for newly installed governors has pooh-poohed such ideas. He is already an attractive candidate—with just the kind of authentic ethnic background Democrats have been seeking for years—but he has still to prove himself a suitable executive.

Senators. New York's senior senator is Daniel Patrick Moynihan, who has had a range of experience in American government as broad as any senator. He worked for Governor Averell Harriman in the 1950s, served as Assistant Secretary of Labor in the Kennedy and Johnson administrations, was chief domestic advisor to President Nixon and his ambassador to India, and was ambassador to the United Nations under President Ford. In all these jobs he displayed a talent for original thinking and a taste for controversy. He still is regarded with hostility by black political activists because of his warning about the breakup of black families in the middle 1960s—although it turns out that his warnings understated the problems to come. He was the strongest advocate for the Nixon administration's Family Assistance Program, which his critics today would be happy to settle for; he saw it scuttled in the Senate Finance Committee, on which he now has a seat. At the United Nations he spoke out against Russia and for Israel and ignored the conventional wisdom that policymakers should accept the premises of Third World and Soviet demands and negotiate quietly for small concessions; his policy is now approaching consensus status, as the Third World itself has been forced by events and stands like Moynihan's to turn away from anti-American rhetoric. Moynihan's prescience, his ability to spot rising issues is almost eerie: in the early 1960s, before Ralph Nader, he was writing about auto safety.

Moynihan showed the same uncanny instinct for spotting issues in the spring of 1981, when he pounced on Reagan administration proposals to cut scheduled future Social Security benefits. As ranking minority member of the Senate's Social Security Subcommittee, he protested vehemently, and he strode forward with a resolution denouncing any benefit cuts which was beaten only by a 49–48 vote; promptly the Senate adopted a resolution by Bob Dole, that said much the same thing, by 96–0. Moynihan's initiative put the kibosh on any attempt to change the Social Security cost of living adjustment, which has persistently overstated inflation, for that Congress; and it helped to preserve for the 1982 election the Social Security issue for the Democrats.

It also helped to put Moynihan in good standing with the liberals who have disproportionate clout in New York's Democratic primaries. Moynihan won his nomination in 1976 over Bella Abzug by only 10,000 votes of 916,000 cast; he did not want to face competition again from a candidate with a similar base, like 1980 Senate nominee Elizabeth Holtzman (elected Brooklyn's District Attorney in 1981). So he underplayed his support of higher defense budgets and emphasized his disagreement with the Reagan administration on issues like Social Security, the Equal Rights Amendment, aid programs to urban areas, and relationships with the Moral Majority. He stressed also his clout as a member of the Senate Finance Committee—its first New Yorker in years—and its practical importance to New York. As a result, Moynihan had only nuisance opposition in the primary and attracted only weak Republican opposition. Elected solidly against then incumbent Senator James Buckley in 1976, he won reelection in a landslide in 1982. It was the largest percentage and the largest plurality won by any senator in New York's history.

Does Moynihan have national ambitions? To a considerable extent, he has already realized them. He has been a figure of national importance for more than a dozen years, and of importance not because of the offices he has held, but because of the ideas he has generated and the policies he has advocated. He continues to write, on subjects ranging from the arms control process to Senate staffs, with an originality and in a style that leaves no doubt that the words are his own. He does not seem suited, except in extraordinary circumstances, for the presidency, which someone described as a place for men with ordinary views and out-of-the-ordinary temperaments. Moynihan has altogether too original a mind for that, and a temperament that prefers originality and controversy to agreement and consensus. He has not the temperament either for the amassing of giant field organizations and constant campaigning that seems necessary to make a presidential race; he is not a man who likes giving the same little speech over and over again. He has made no move to run for president in 1984 and seems an unlikely choice for vice president. His admirers see him as another Churchill—literate, original, patriotic, fervent—but they remember also that Churchill was not summoned to the top office until his nation was on the brink of ruin and the other politicians had no other choice.

New York's other senator, Alfonse D'Amato, cuts less of a national figure, and less of a figure in New York for that matter. Nonetheless, he has made some progress in persuading observers he should be regarded as more than a fluke. In fact, D'Amato showed great foresight in running in 1980 against Senator Jacob Javits; despite a record of brilliant achievement, Javits was too liberal for Republican primary voters and was ailing besides. Then Javits's candidacy on the Liberal line helped D'Amato edge out Democratic nominee Holtzman. D'Amato got the 45% which seems to be the base for a candidate representing the views of the national Republican Party; it was enough to beat Holtzman by 1%.

Much of the impression D'Amato made during the campaign was misleading. He seemed acerbic and unpleasant, particularly in running against Javits; in office, he is jovial and has a good sense of humor—as if he were elbowing erstwhile opponents in the ribs and saying, it's only a game, right? He had made his career in suburban Nassau County as a protege of Republican county boss Joseph Margiotta; right after the campaign he broke with him. That left this former middle-level operative in a patronage-oriented machine in charge of all federal patronage in New York—federal judges, U.S. attorneys, federal marshals, the heads of the New York regional offices of the various federal bureaucracies. Yet he has used that power hesitantly and carefully. He campaigned as a conservative, and yet on occasion he has broken with the Reagan administration. He is unabashed about pursuing the interests of urban areas in general and the New York metropolitan area in particular.

D'Amato has seats on the Appropriations and Banking Committees. In his first years he chaired the District of Columbia Appropriations Subcommittee, and did a workmanlike job to the satisfaction of District residents. In 1983 he chaired a subcommittee with jurisdiction over the SEC—an important agency in New York—and excoriated its leaders for their investigation of White House aide Thomas Reed. No one can be sure now how D'Amato will do when he runs for reelection in 1986; he may start out as the underdog, but he has surprised people before and may do so again.

Mayor. For many years the budget of New York City was bigger than the budget of New York state, and in many ways the mayor of New York sets the tone for public life in New York. Mayor John Lindsay, with his sympathy for blacks and Puerto Ricans and his apparent disdain for middle-income whites, helped stir the resentment among middle-class New Yorkers that led to the election of Senator James Buckley and the development of the Archie Bunker mentality that was so evident in the outer boroughs in the late 1960s and early 1970s. The current mayor, Edward Koch, comes from a liberal background—he once beat Tammany Hall leader Carmine de Sapio for district leader in Greenwich Village—but he was raised in Brooklyn; and his views as mayor seem to be more in accord with his upbringing in the gritty outer boroughs than with his activism in trendy Manhattan. When he ran for mayor in 1977, he attracted attention (and beat Mario Cuomo) by favoring capital punishment, opposing racial quotas, promising tough bargaining with city employees, and advocating cuts in the city budget. In office Koch has antagonized black and Puerto Rican leaders but has been successful in holding the city's budget within the limits of its resources; the one possible exception was the budget concocted while he was running for governor in 1982. That race was uncharacteristic and, perhaps for that very reason, unsuccessful. Koch is book smart and street smart, capable of dazzling urban ethnologists and of giving a heckler the raspberry; he is a sort of quintessential mayor, and belongs in Albany no more than Jimmy Carter belongs in the Bronx. New York City residents gave him such a minuscule plurality in the gubernatorial primary that one can only conclude they preferred to see him stay as mayor—which he probably can do, if he wants, for a long, long time.

Congressional districting. The New York legislature, split in control between the parties, had the unhappy task of reducing the number of New York's congressional districts from 39 to 34 for 1982. Some of their decisions were forced by the numbers: the New York City area, for example, lost four of the five districts, Upstate the other. The losers were political mavericks of varying description and effectiveness, although even some who could be so described survived. Altogether the New York delegation is not as powerful as its numbers might suggest. It has never been a cohesive delegation, and is probably less fractious today than it has ever been. Most important, beyond trying to jimmy federal aid formulas in New York's favor, it shares no common view of the state's interest—which is a problem for New Yorkers generally. The welfare state, though threatened, seems to have been preserved; the state remains more prosperous than the national average, though not by much, even in difficult economic times. New York has talented, in some cases brilliant, public officials, and a level of competence in government appropriate to a state with such a competent private sector. But what does New York go after next?

The People   Est. Pop. 1982: 17,659,000; Pop. 1980: 17,558,072, up 0.6% 1980–82 and dn. 3.7% 1970–80; 7.7% of U.S. total, 2d largest; voting age pop. 12,870,209; 12% Black, 8% Spanish origin, 2% Asian origin. Single ancestry: 11% Italian, 6% Irish, 5% German, English, 3% Polish, 2% Russian, 1% French, Greek, Hungarian. Registered voters (1982): 7,634,992 Total. 14% with 1–3 yrs. col., 19% with 4+ yrs. col. 13.7% below poverty level. 47% housing units rented; median house value: $45,900; median monthly rent: $211. Households: 70% family, 37% with children, 54% married couples.

1982 Share of Federal Tax Burden $48,885,700,000; 8.18% of U.S. total, 2d largest.

1982 Share of Federal Expenditures

	Total		Non-Defense		Defense	
Total Expend	$43,835m	(7.26%)	$34,941m	(8.23%)	$8,894m	(4.97%)
St/Lcl Grants	9,228m	(10.53%)	9,228m	(10.53%)	0m	(0%)
Salary/Wages	2,198m	(2.82%)	1,361m	(4.97%)	837m	(1.65%)
Ind Payments	23,116m	(8.08%)	21,914m	(8.51%)	1,202m	(4.20%)
Procurement	8,816m	(6.05%)	1,060m	(3.36%)	7,800m	(6.83%)
Other Programs	373m	(6.89%)	373m	(6.94%)	0m	(0%)
Loan/Insurance	1,933m	(3.02%)	1,890m	(3.06%)	43m	(1.95%)

Political Lineup   Governor, Mario Cuomo (D). Senators, Daniel Patrick Moynihan (D) and Alfonse M. D'Amato (R). Representatives, 34 (20 D and 14 R). State Senate, 61 (26 D and 35 R); State Assembly, 150 (97 D, 52 R and 1 Vacancy).

Presidential Vote

1980	Reagan (R)	2,893,831	(47%)
	Carter (D)	2,728,372	(44%)
	Anderson (I)	467,801	(8%)
1976	Ford (R)	3,100,791	(47%)
	Carter (D)	3,389,558	(52%)

1980 Democratic Presidential Primary

Kennedy	....	582,757	(59%)
Carter	....	406,305	(41%)

SENATORS

Sen. Daniel Patrick Moynihan (D) Elected 1976, seat up 1988; b. Mar. 16, 1927, Tulsa, OK; home, New York City; CCNY, 1943, Tufts U., B.A. 1948, M.A. 1949, Ph.D. 1961; Roman Catholic.

Career University professor; U.S. Asst. Secy. of Labor, 1963–65; Asst. to the Pres. for Urban Affairs, 1969–70; U.S. Ambassador to India, 1973–74; U.S. Ambassador to the U.N., 1975–76.

Offices 442 RSOB, 202-224-4451. Also 733 3d Ave., New York 10017, 212-661-5150; and Fed Ofc. Bldg., Buffalo 14202, 716-842-3493.

Committees *Budget* (9th). *Environment and Public Works* (5th). Subcommittees: Environmental Pollution; Transportation; Water Resources. *Finance* (4th). Subcommittees: Economic Growth, Employment, and Revenue Sharing; International Trade; Social Security and Income Maintenance Programs. *Select Committee on Intelligence* (Vice-Chairman).

Group Ratings

	ADA	ACLU	COPE	CFA	LCV	LWV	NTU	NSI	COC	ACA	CSFC
1982	95	86	95	80	80	100	12	30	22	25	28
1981	75	—	93	64	92	—	13	—	33	28	31
1980	72	70	100	73	71	75	22	10	33	8	21

National Journal Ratings

	Economic		Foreign		Cultural	
1982	99%	(LIB)	86%	(LIB)	98%	(LIB)
	0%	(CONS)	10%	(CONS)	1%	(CONS)
1981	89%	(LIB)	75%	(LIB)	96%	(LIB)
	10%	(CONS)	24%	(CONS)	2%	(CONS)

Key Votes

1) Reagan 81 Budget	AGN	5) $ to El Salvador	AGN	9) Poor Pay Food Stamps	AGN
2) Reagan 81 Tax Cut	FOR	6) Saudi AWACS Sale	AGN	10) Ban Crt Busing Order	AGN
3) Bal Budget Amend	AGN	7) Ban Abortion	AGN	11) Clinch Riv Brdr Rctr	AGN
4) Gas & Road Tax	—	8) Nerve Gas Prod	AGN	12) Legal Services Corp	—

Election Results

1982 general	Daniel Patrick Moynihan (D–L) ...	3,232,146	(65%)	($2,708,660)
	Florence Sullivan (R–C–RTL)	1,696,766	(34%)	($117,875)
1982 primary	Daniel Patrick Moynihan (D)	922,059	(85%)	
	Melvin Klenetsky (D)	161,012	(15%)	($107,483)
1976 general	Daniel Patrick Moynihan (D)	3,422,594	(54%)	($1,210,796)
	James L. Buckley (R)	2,836,633	(45%)	($2,101,424)

Campaign Contributions and Expenditures

1979-82		Direct Cont. 79-82		PACS brkdwn			
Receipts	$3,093,286	Indiv	$2,415,198	Agr	$3,000	Ideo	$29,450
Expend.	$2,976,639	Party	$18,600	Bus	$160,490	Lbr	$145,370
Unspent	$116,647	PACS	$481,861	Hlth	$13,100	Prof	$12,000

Indirect Party Expend: $62,500   *Indep Expend:* For: $850   Agn: $77,161 (NCPAC, LIFEPAC)

Sen. Alfonse M. D'Amato (R) Elected 1980, seat up 1986; b. Aug. 1, 1937, Brooklyn; home, Island Park; Syracuse U., B.S. 1959, J.D. 1961; Roman Catholic.

Career Island Pk. Atty., Asst. Hempstead Atty., 1965–68; Pub. Admin., Nassau Cnty., 1969; Hempstead Town Receiver of Taxes, 1969, Supervisor, 1971, Presiding Supervisor, 1977.

Offices 432 RSOB, 202-224-6542. Also 420 Leo O'Brian Fed. Bldg., Albany 12207, 518-463-2244; 111 W. Huron, Rm. 620, Buffalo 14202, 716-846-4112; and 1 Penn Plaza, Su. 1632, New York 10001, 212-947-7390.

Committees *Appropriations* (11th). Subcommittees: Defense; Legislative Branch (Chairman); Foreign Operations; HUD-Independent Agencies; Transportation. *Banking, Housing, and Urban Affairs* (5th). Subcommittees: Consumer Affairs; Financial Institutions; Housing and Urban Affairs; Securities (Chairman). *Small Business* (8th). Subcommittees: Small Business: Family Farm; Urban and Rural Economic Development (Chairman). *Joint Economic Committee* (6th). Subcommittees: Economic Goals and Intergovernmental Policy; Investment, Jobs, and Prices.

Group Ratings

	ADA	ACLU	COPE	CFA	LCV	LWV	NTU	NSI	COC	ACA	CSFC
1982	15	25	25	20	54	50	51	100	47	60	68
1981	10	—	22	29	19	—	54	—	94	47	76

National Journal Ratings

	Economic		Foreign		Cultural	
1982	38%	(LIB)	3%	(LIB)	29%	(LIB)
	61%	(CONS)	84%	(CONS)	70%	(CONS)
1981	35%	(LIB)	34%	(LIB)	37%	(LIB)
	64%	(CONS)	65%	(CONS)	62%	(CONS)

Key Votes

1) Reagan 81 Budget	FOR	5) $ to El Salvador	FOR	9) Poor Pay Food Stamps	AGN
2) Reagan 81 Tax Cut	FOR	6) Saudi AWACS Sale	AGN	10) Ban Crt Busing Order	FOR
3) Bal Budget Amend	FOR	7) Ban Abortion	FOR	11) Clinch Riv Brdr Rctr	FOR
4) Gas & Road Tax	FOR	8) Nerve Gas Prod	FOR	12) Legal Services Corp	FOR

Election Results

1980 general	Alfonse M. D'Amato (R–C–RTL) .	2,699,965	(45%)	($1,699,709)
	Elizabeth Holtzman (D)	2,618,661	(44%)	($2,173,056)
	Jacob K. Javits (L)	664,544	(11%)	($1,846,313)
1980 primary	Alfonse M. D'Amato (R)	323,468	(56%)	
	Jacob K. Javits (R)	257,433	(44%)	
1974 general	Jacob K. Javits (R–L)	2,340,188	(45%)	($1,090,437)
	Ramsey Clark (D)	1,973,781	(38%)	($855,576)
	Barbara A. Keating (C)	822,584	(16%)	($192,462)

Campaign Contributions and Expenditures

1981-82		PACS brkdwn			
Receipts	$1,705,786	Agr	$3,100	Ideo	$63,939
Expend.	$1,699,709	Bus	$185,181	Lbr	$8,500
Unspent	$6,071	Hlth	$5,540	Prof	$6,000

GOVERNOR

Gov. Mario M. Cuomo (D) Elected 1982, term expires Jan. 1987; b. June 15, 1932, Queens; home, Queens; St. John's U., B.A. 1953, St. John's U. Sch. of Law, J.D. 1956; Roman Catholic.

Career Confidential Legal Asst. to Judge Adrian T. Burke, NY State Ct. of Appeals, 1956–58; Practicing atty., 1958–74; Professor, St. John's U. Sch. of Law, 1963–73; Secy. of State of NY, 1975–78, Lt. Gov., 1978–82.

Offices Executive Chamber, State Capitol, Albany 12224, 518-474-8390.

Election Results

1982 gen.	Mario M. Cuomo (D–L)	2,675,213	(51%)
	Lewis E. Lehrman (R–C–SI) .	2,494,827	(47%)
1982 prim.	Mario M. Cuomo (D)	678,900	(52%)
	Edward I. Koch (D)	618,356	(48%)
1978 gen.	Hugh L. Carey (D–L)	2,429,272	(51%)
	Perry B. Duryea (R–C)	2,156,404	(45%)

FIRST DISTRICT

The 1st congressional district of New York is the eastern part of Long Island, from 50 to 100 miles east of Times Square. This part of Long Island was settled from two directions, at two very different times. The first settlers came over water, from New England, as early as the 17th century. Yankees from Connecticut and Massachusetts settled the eastern end of Long Island, building little New England fishing villages which, for a brief time in the 19th century, became major whaling ports. Some of these remain picturesque today, for they have become fashionable resort towns—the Hamptons, Montauk, Sag Harbor, Shelter Island—75 to 90 miles away from New York City.

The second wave of migration was much more recent and came from a different direction. It has occurred since 1945, mostly since 1960, and it has come from New York City and its Nassau County suburbs. After World War II some big defense-related operations—the Brookhaven National Laboratory, the Grumman and Republic Aviation plants—were built on Long Island potato fields; the work force followed. Long Island is known to outsiders for its affluent suburbs, but when you get much farther out than Smithtown (the western end of the 1st district) you are in very modest country. The shopping centers on the strip highway feature discount outlets, not designer shops; housing prices are low; landscaping and other amenities are left to homeowners rather than provided by developers. On the north shore there are a couple of old towns, remnants of the New England migration, Port Jefferson and Setauket; but a few miles inland and on the south shore this is very modest country indeed.

It is also, in partisan elections, very Republican and Conservative, with both capital and small Cs. Demographically, the overland migration from New York is much more important than the waterborne migration from New England; and the new residents are mostly young families, with many children, and strong desires in many cases to avoid what they consider the nefarious influences of progressive education and liberalized mores. Those desires are not always fulfilled: you'll find drugs in high schools on the Island just as you will in Brooklyn. There is also, naturally, strong support for defense programs here. The mores and attitudes of

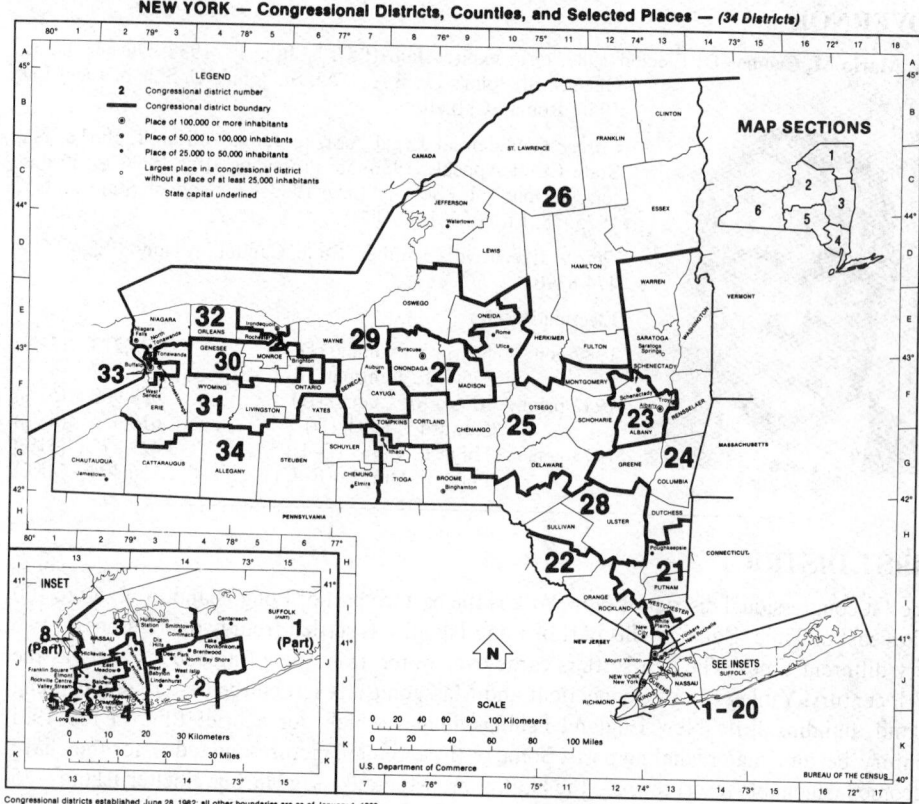

NEW YORK — Congressional Districts, Counties, and Selected Places — *(34 Districts)*

Congressional districts established June 28, 1982; all other boundaries are as of January 1, 1980.

the summer people in the Hamptons are not often shared or admired by the people past whose homes they ride on the Sunrise Highway or Long Island Railroad.

The congressman from the 1st district, William Carney, is a conservative Republican with a record that would surprise no one who knows his constituency. The only surprise is that he should have succeeded a Democrat who represented this area for 18 years and that his margins in his first two elections, in 1978 and 1980, were unimpressive. In 1982, though the national trend was Democratic, he did better: 64% of the vote. His committee assignments— Science and Technology, Merchant Marine and Fisheries—are tailored to the particular interests of this district; he is ranking Republican on two subcommittees, one on Transportation, Aviation, and Materials, the other on the Panama Canal and the Outer Continental Shelf.

The People   Pop. 1980: 516,407, up 36.7% 1970–80; voting age pop. 350,987; 4% Black, 3% Span. orig., 1% Asian orig. 17% housing units rented. Median owner $43,700; renter $281. Households: 81% family, 49% with children, 69% married couples.

Presidential Vote

1980	Reagan (R)	....	NA
	Carter (D)	....	NA
	Anderson (I)	....	NA

Rep. William Carney (R) Elected 1978; b. July 1, 1942, Brooklyn; home, Hauppauge; FL St. U., 1960–61; Roman Catholic.

Career Army, 1961–64; Salesman, heavy equipment business, 1972–76; Suffolk Cnty. Legislature, 1976–79.

Offices 1424 LHOB, 202-225-3826. Also 180 E. Main St., Smithtown 11787, 516-724-4888.

Committees *Merchant Marine and Fisheries* (7th). Subcommittees: Fisheries and Wildlife Conservation and the Environment; Merchant Marine; Panama Canal and the Outer Continental Shelf. *Science and Technology* (4th). Subcommittees: Energy Development and Applications; Transportation, Aviation and Materials.

Group Ratings

	ADA	ACLU	COPE	CFA	LCV	LWV	NTU	NSI	COC	ACA	CSFC
1982	5	21	23	15	33	45	61	89	90	82	61
1981	5	—	21	43	7	—	75	—	89	82	71
1980	11	0	28	21	22	30	51	100	72	83	74

National Journal Ratings

	Economic		Foreign		Cultural	
1982	18%	(LIB)	2%	(LIB)	1%	(LIB)
	82%	(CONS)	98%	(CONS)	98%	(CONS)
1981	35%	(LIB)	34%	(LIB)	12%	(LIB)
	64%	(CONS)	63%	(CONS)	88%	(CONS)

Key Votes

1) Reagan 81 Budget	FOR	5) Incr SS Rtmt Age	FOR	9) Poor Pay Food Stamps	FOR
2) Reagan 81 Tax Cut	FOR	6) Saudi AWACS Sale	AGN	10) Ban Crt Busing Order	FOR
3) Bal Budget Amend	FOR	7) $ for MX Missile	FOR	11) Auto Local Content	AGN
4) Gas & Road Tax	FOR	8) Nerve Gas Prod	FOR	12) Nuclear Arms Freeze	AGN

Election Results

1982 general	William Carney (R–C–RTL)	88,234	(64%)	($149,481)
	Ethan C. Eldon (D)	49,787	(36%)	($62,468)
1982 primary	William Carney (R–C–RTL) unopposed			
1980 general	William Carney (R–C–RTL)	115,213	(56%)	($195,878)
	Thomas A. Twomey (D)	85,629	(42%)	($120,143)

Campaign Contributions and Expenditures

1981-82		Direct Cont. 81-82		PACS brkdwn			
Receipts	$178,105	Indiv	$74,613	Agr	$400	Ideo	$8,950
Expend.	$149,481	Party	$16,821	Bus	$45,880	Lbr	$11,570
Unspent	$29,216	PACS	$75,854	Hlth	$6,550	Prof	$900

Indep Expend: For: $641 (NRA)

SECOND DISTRICT

At the end of World War II, most of the geographical expanse of Suffolk County, which is the eastern half of Long Island, consisted of potato fields. But this mostly flat, only lightly forested sandy land was also directly in the path of one of the major suburban migrations of a generation. On the highways that Robert Moses built to connect his parks to middle-class parts of New York City came tens of thousands of young veterans and their families, forsaking the row-house neighborhoods where they had grown up for the comparatively spacious lots and single-family houses of Levittown and other Long Island subdivisions. The first wave of postwar migration moved into Nassau County, and it was a pretty accurate cross-section of all but the poorest New Yorkers: almost half Catholic, about one-fourth Jewish and one-fourth Protestant. Then, as Long Island developed an employment base of its own, the next wave of migration started, this time far out into Suffolk County. This second wave was more Catholic and less Jewish, more blue collar (aircraft manufacturers are Suffolk County's biggest employers) and less white collar, more Democratic perhaps in ancestral politics but culturally more firmly traditional and conservative in their approach to life.

The 2d congressional district of New York covers a large part of Suffolk County— essentially the South Shore towns of Babylon and Islip, which within them contain dozens of suburbs with different names—one community after another strung out along the Sunrise Highway. With a few exceptions (notably Dix Hills in the north) this is the lowest income part of Long Island, out past the fashionable and expensive suburbs with their minimum acreage zoning, far from the picturesque North Shore and separated by the Great South Bay from the beaches of Fire Island. The area filled up with people in the 1950s and 1960s and has had little population change since; the modest homes are being upgraded by their owners or sometimes left with chipped paint and cracked shingle siding.

Yet there has been change: the district has one of the highest percentages of households with children in New York, and one reason is that young families have been buying here, where decent houses can still be bought for $30,000, and planning to move up to better neighborhoods later. Nor are all these people white. There are black concentrations in North Amityville and Wyandanch, and substantial numbers of blacks and Latin Americans scattered elsewhere to make the district 9% black and 7% Spanish origin.

The congressman from this district, Thomas Downey, is a Democrat who was the youngest member of the large class of 1974. In that race Downey showed the kind of political acumen he has demonstrated since in the House. He was smart enough to spot the weaknesses in an incumbent who had gotten 66% two years before; he was energetic enough to promise credibly that he would give the district more active representation; and he was experienced enough to be able to cite three years' service in the Suffolk County legislature.

In the House Downey has been aggressive, active, a strong partisan, ready to debate big issues. In his first two terms, he was a member of the Armed Services Committee, dovish on policy generally but eager to promote the programs of Long Island's aircraft manufacturers. In 1979 he switched to Ways and Means, and in 1981 he got a seat on Budget. He has spent much time on the latter and is one of the Democrats' chief spokesmen on budget issues: he regularly denounces the Reagan administration for its stinginess on domestic programs and its profligacy on defense. He speaks in tones of sarcasm, but also with the information of one who has done his homework. On Ways and Means, he sits on the Trade Subcommittee. He has been sympathetic to pleas for protection on some occasion, particularly when they come from unions, but cannot be classified as an all-out free trader or protectionist.

The 2d district is not, in state and national elections, a Democratic constituency, though there is a solid Democratic base here, and a Democratic tradition in many households which regularly vote Republican. Downey has been strong enough to hold onto the district, but only in 1982 was he able to crack the 60% barrier. Even so, he is a possible Republican target in some future election. Theoretically, he can look forward to chairing the House Ways and Means Committee some day, since he is considerably younger than any more senior member. But that assumes that he continues to win in this somewhat risky district, doesn't tire of the grind of congressional life, and doesn't run for statewide office—all of which are iffy propositions.

The People   Pop. 1980: 515,595, up 5.1% 1970–80; voting age pop. 351,055; 8% Black, 6% Span. orig., 1% Asian orig. 20% housing units rented. Median owner $41,700; renter $314. Households: 85% family, 53% with children, 71% married couples.

Presidential Vote

1980	Reagan (R)	NA
	Carter (D)	NA
	Anderson (I)	NA

Rep. Thomas J. Downey (D) Elected 1974; b. Jan. 28, 1949, Ozone Park; home, West Islip; Cornell U., B.S. 1970, St. John's U. Sch. of Law, 1972–74; American U., J.D. 1980; Methodist.

Career Personnel mgmt. and labor relations, Macy's Dept. Store, Suffolk Cnty. Legislature, 1971–74.

Offices 303 CHOB, 202-225-3335. Also 4 Udall Rd., West Islip 11759, 516-661-8777.

Committees *Budget* (10th). Task Forces: Education and Employment; Federalism/State-Local Relations; Tax Policy (Chairman). *Ways and Means* (11th). Subcommittee: Trade. *Select Committee on Aging* (6th). Subcommittees: Human Services; Retirement Income and Employment.

Group Ratings

	ADA	ACLU	COPE	CFA	LCV	LWV	NTU	NSI	COC	ACA	CSFC
1982	100	83	89	85	96	80	15	10	18	13	23
1981	80	—	88	100	95	—	23	—	11	9	27
1980	94	100	84	86	94	100	19	10	58	13	24

National Journal Ratings

	Economic		Foreign		Cultural	
1982	98%	(LIB)	85%	(LIB)	93%	(LIB)
	1%	(CONS)	12%	(CONS)	3%	(CONS)
1981	86%	(LIB)	77%	(LIB)	83%	(LIB)
	13%	(CONS)	21%	(CONS)	17%	(CONS)

Key Votes

1) Reagan 81 Budget	AGN	5) Incr SS Rtmt Age	FOR	9) Poor Pay Food Stamps	AGN
2) Reagan 81 Tax Cut	AGN	6) Saudi AWACS Sale	AGN	10) Ban Crt Busing Order	AGN
3) Bal Budget Amend	AGN	7) $ for MX Missile	AGN	11) Auto Local Content	FOR
4) Gas & Road Tax	FOR	8) Nerve Gas Prod	AGN	12) Nuclear Arms Freeze	FOR

Election Results

1982 general	Thomas J. Downey (D–I)	80,951	(64%)	($301,351)
	Paul G. Costello (R–C)	42,790	(34%)	($32,252)
1982 primary	Thomas J. Downey (D–I) unopposed			
1980 general	Thomas J. Downey (D)	84,035	(56%)	($190,889)
	Louis J. Modica (R–C–RTL)	65,106	(44%)	($72,678)

Campaign Contributions and Expenditures

1981-82		Direct Cont. 81-82				PACS brkdwn		
Receipts	$394,749	Indiv	$224,920	Agr	$4,750	Ideo	$12,987
Expend.	$301,351	Party	$4,170	Bus	$48,876	Lbr	$70,300
Unspent	$98,577	PACS	$146,835	Hlth	$3,500	Prof	$2,750
		Cand	$1,000				

Indep Expend: Agn: $4,537 (NCPAC)

THIRD DISTRICT

When F. Scott Fitzgerald set *The Great Gatsby* on the North Shore of Long Island, he was writing about already familiar ground. From the turn of the century, millionaires steamed up Long Island Sound from Manhattan in their yachts and docked them below the bright green lawns rolling up toward their ornate mansions. Sands Point, Port Washington, Glen Cove—the North Shore was populated originally by people there to service the great estates. Only later did suburbanites start coming in: in the 1920s, Jews to Great Neck and WASPs to Manhasset, to settle in more modest mansions, on smaller lots; in the 1940s, middle- and upper-middle-income New Yorkers eager to own their own homes and enjoy their own lawns in the communities that were sprouting up along the Long Island Expressway, Northern State Parkway, and Northern Boulevard. By the 1960s, the North Shore was built up through Syosset in Nassau County and into Huntington in Suffolk County. Since then the population has not changed much. Households have lost people as children have grown up and moved away; new housing units, mostly apartments and condominiums, have been added.

The North Shore of Long Island, from Manhasset, Port Washington, and the New York City line in the west, all the way through Nassau and into Suffolk County, to Smithtown in the west, forms the 3d congressional district of New York. The southern boundary throughout runs near the Long Island Expressway. This is almost entirely affluent country, with the highest housing prices of any New York suburban district, except for the 20th in Westchester County. It tends to go Republican in national and state elections, although its Jewish voters provide a solid liberal base for a Democratic candidate. Yet it is a district which combined most of the constituencies of two Republican congressmen and ended up electing a Democrat—one who has a special place in the heart of Speaker Tip O'Neill.

The central figure in all this is former Congressman John LeBoutillier. He was one of the most distinctive of the freshmen Republicans elected in 1980, both for his achievements (he wrote a book called *Harvard Hates America* and beat a seemingly safe Democratic incumbent) and for his brashness. He was shrewd enough in New York to win the endorsement of Nassau County Republican boss Joseph Margiotta (who got fellow freshman Gregory Carman to retire when their districts were combined) and to raise a big campaign treasury from fellow Harvard alumni. He was also helped by family wealth: he is a descendant of the Vanderbilt and Whitney families, and family money—there were charges it was not his, but a relative's—was crucial to his upset victory in 1980. But in Congress LeBoutillier seemed less than shrewd. Speaker O'Neill, he said early in his term, "is fat, bloated, and out of control—just like the federal budget." That and other cracks earned him the enmity of O'Neill, and not just because they were insults. For O'Neill and others sensed in LeBoutillier a contempt not just for Democrats, but for politics and government generally, a contempt typical of derisive preppies and of the careless rich of the North Shore of whom Scott Fitzgerald wrote.

Local Democrats worked hard and persuaded a candidate with a strong local base, Suffolk County legislator Robert Mrazek, to run in the new 3d. The speaker himself made sure that Mrazek's campaign was well funded; Mrazek spent $310,000 to LeBoutillier's $546,000. But not all of the Republican's money was well spent: one commercial, in which he called for a federal prison in Alaska for hard-core criminals, worked against him. Mrazek in contrast was calm, sober, serious, and hardworking. LeBoutillier carried the Nassau County portion of the district, 50%–48%, but Mrazek got a much bigger margin in the Suffolk County portion, 57%–34%.

Mrazek became the only freshman on the House Appropriations Committee, thanks again to the speaker. His position, his workmanlike approach to government, and his sense of humor—gentler and less acerbic than LeBoutillier's—will presumably be assets when he runs for reelection in 1984. Yet he must also expect a serious Republican challenge in as Republican and affluent a district as this.

The People   Pop. 1980: 518,061, dn. 3.4% 1970–80; voting age pop. 379,111; 3% Black, 2% Span. orig., 1% Asian orig. 20% housing units rented. Median owner $70,500; renter $325. Households: 83% family, 44% with children, 73% married couples.

Presidential Vote

1980	Reagan (R)	NA
	Carter (D)	NA
	Anderson (I)	NA

Rep. Robert J. Mrazek (D) Elected 1982; b. Nov. 6, 1945, Newport, RI; home, Centerport; Cornell U., B.A. 1967; Methodist.

Career Navy, 1967–68; Staff, U.S. Sen. Vance Hartke of IN, 1969–71; Owner, small business, 1971–75; Suffolk Cnty. Legislature, 1975–82.

Offices 509 CHOB, 202-225-5956. Also 143 Main St., Huntington 11743, 516-673-6500.

Committee *Appropriations* (36th). Subcommittees: Commerce, Justice, State, and Judiciary; Transportation.

Group Ratings and Key Votes: Newly Elected

Election Results

1982 general	Robert J. Mrazek (D)	93,846	(52%)	($319,999)
	John LeBoutillier (R–C)	83,238	(46%)	($549,431)
1982 primary	Robert J. Mrazek (D)	15,690	(65%)	
	John O'Shea (D)	8,352	(35%)	($10,757)
1980 general	Gregory W. Carman (R–C)	87,952	(50%)	($1,038,125)
(NY 3)	Jerome A. Ambro, Jr. (D–RTL) ...	83,389	(47%)	($120,061)
1980 general	John LeBoutillier (R–C–RTL)	89,762	(53%)	($490,121)
(NY 6)	Lester L. Wolff (D–L)	80,209	(47%)	($110,221)

Campaign Contributions and Expenditures

1982		Direct Cont. 1982			PACS brkdwn			
Receipts	$322,720	Indiv	$154,403	Agr	$3,000	Ideo	$16,350
Expend.	$319,999	Party	$2,500	Bus	$4,900	Lbr	$106,950
Unspent	$2,721	PACS	$134,897	Hlth	$800	Prof	$2,900

Indirect Party Expend: $15,355   *Non-Cand Loans:* $6,000

FOURTH DISTRICT

At the end of World War II, Nassau County, just beyond the New York City limits, was mostly empty land and potato fields. Here and there, in this flat Long Island county 25 or 35 miles east of Manhattan, a few subdivisions were laid out before the war. On the North Shore and in such places as Old Westbury sat the estates of some of New York's wealthiest families; on the south sand spit were some beach houses. But the vast center of Nassau County lay undeveloped. It did not stay that way for long. Just after the war, a young builder named William Levitt built an entire town full of small tract houses and named it for himself. Soon Levittown came to symbolize Long Island's postwar growth. Young married couples flocked out to the Island and created a new life-style very different from their own Depression childhoods pent up in the city.

So during the 20 years after 1945 Nassau County filled up and became the kind of suburban community that is familiar today but that was largely undreamed of by the veterans who returned to New York after the war. In 1945 Nassau County had a population of about 450,000. By 1960 there were 1,300,000 people here. The number rose slightly to 1,428,000 in 1970 and then dropped back to 1,321,000 in 1980. The reason is not that the area is deteriorating but that the population is aging. The baby-boom babies have grown up, and many of them are not staying in Nassau. Not many houses here are for sale at any one time, so those who like the Long Island life-style move farther out on the Island to Suffolk County, while those who want an urban existence head into New York City. Some who have difficulty finding a job or who like other parts of the country better leave the New York metropolitan area altogether.

In the 1950s there was speculation that the new suburban life-style was creating new political attitudes, that when the postwar young marrieds left New York City they were dropping their Democratic voting habits and becoming Republican. That notion seems wrong, or at least oversimple: people may have changed their party registration in order to participate in the primary that really counted; but the voting habits of the metropolitan area as a whole register no Republican shift during the Eisenhower years that was greater than the national average. Life in the suburbs did, however, make people different from what they were in the city in what have become, some time after the Eisenhower years, salient political characteristics. They became homeowners rather than renters, people more concerned about holding down the property tax than about maintaining rent control. And the young family people of the 1950s, anxious to maintain good public schools and willing to spend money for that purpose, became the empty nesters of the 1970s, less willing to support public spending. Nassau County trended Democratic in the 1960s, electing a Democrat as county executive and several Democratic congressmen (including, once, Allard Lowenstein). But in the 1970s it became more and more Republican and willing to accept the leadership of County Republican leader Joseph Margiotta.

The 4th congressional district of New York lies wholly within Nassau County. It includes most of the original Levittown, its once simple houses now supplemented by countless thousands of additions, and the similar vintage communities of Hicksville, Bethpage, and Plainview. It also includes a string of suburbs along the South Shore of Long Island (actually along the shore of the bay that separates the sand spits of Long Beach and Jones Beach from the main part of the Island) that were tiny separate towns in 1945 but that have long since grown together: East Rockaway, Oceanside, Baldwin, Freeport, Merrick, Bellmore, Wantagh, Seaford, Massapequa. These are today mostly comfortable places of above-average affluence; but they could not be mistaken for elite suburbs. They are the kinds of places where you find Nassau County zoning lawyers and New York City policemen, owners of small businesses and stores, and engineers at Long Island's big aircraft factories. The 4th district is generally counted Republican, although it is actually rather evenly divided in close statewide races.

It has, however, been solidly Republican in congressional races since redistricting helped Norman Lent beat Allard Lowenstein in 1970. Lent is a professional legislator; he represented Nassau County in the state Senate for eight years and now is one of the senior Republicans in the New York delegation. Without attracting much publicity or notice, he holds a high ranking position on the House Energy and Commerce Committee—one of the busiest and most powerful committees in Congress, which handles a host of regulatory and environmental matters. Lent is ranking Republican on the subcommittee that handles the Superfund program. He tends to reflect reasonably accurately the Republican point of view, usually that regulation should not be as stringent as the Democrats want, without being a driving force behind legislation. On other issues, his record is faithful to his party.

Lent had no difficulty winning reelection through the 1970s. In 1982 his percentage dropped from 67% to 60%, a noticeable difference, but one that seems unlikely to threaten his position. If voters here do not get much pizzazz from their congressman, they nonetheless seem satisfied with the kind of representation they have.

The People Pop. 1980: 518,371, dn. 9.0% 1970–80; voting age pop. 377,969; 3% Black, 3% Span. orig., 1% Asian orig. 14% housing units rented. Median owner $55,600; renter $321. Households: 88% family, 46% with children, 77% married couples.

Presidential Vote

1980	Reagan (R)	NA
	Carter (D)	NA
	Anderson (I)	NA

Rep. Norman F. Lent (R) Elected 1970; b. Mar. 23, 1931, Oceanside; home, E. Rockaway; Hofstra Col., B.A. 1952, Cornell U., J.D. 1957; Methodist.

Career Navy, Korea; Practicing atty., 1957–70; Asst. E. Rockaway Police Justice, 1960–62; NY Senate, 1962–70.

Offices 2228 RHOB, 202-225-7896. Also 2280 Grand Ave., Rm. 300, Baldwin 11510, 516-223-1616.

Committees *Energy and Commerce* (2d). Subcommittee: Commerce, Transportation and Tourism. *Merchant Marine and Fisheries* (5th). Subcommittees: Coast Guard and Navigation; Panama Canal and Outer Continental Shelf.

Group Ratings

	ADA	ACLU	COPE	CFA	LCV	LWV	NTU	NSI	COC	ACA	CSFC
1982	35	27	29	46	57	67	50	90	65	70	55
1981	10	—	27	43	29	—	50	—	95	70	63
1980	17	17	33	14	32	25	38	100	70	61	65

National Journal Ratings

	Economic		Foreign		Cultural	
1982	45%	(LIB)	23%	(LIB)	50%	(LIB)
	55%	(CONS)	76%	(CONS)	50%	(CONS)
1981	4%	(LIB)	34%	(LIB)	21%	(LIB)
	79%	(CONS)	63%	(CONS)	79%	(CONS)

Key Votes

1) Reagan 81 Budget	FOR	5) Incr SS Rtmt Age	FOR	9) Poor Pay Food Stamps	FOR
2) Reagan 81 Tax Cut	FOR	6) Saudi AWACS Sale	AGN	10) Ban Crt Busing Order	FOR
3) Bal Budget Amend	FOR	7) $ for MX Missile	AGN	11) Auto Local Content	AGN
4) Gas & Road Tax	FOR	8) Nerve Gas Prod	FOR	12) Nuclear Arms Freeze	AGN

Election Results

1982 general	Norman F. Lent (R–C–RTL)	105,241	(60%)	($344,777)
	Robert P. Zimmerman (D–L)	63,390	(36%)	($126,646)
1982 primary	Norman F. Lent (R–C–RTL) unopposed			
1980 general	Norman F. Lent (R–C–RTL)	117,455	(67%)	($161,941)
	Charles F. Brennan (D–L)	58,270	(33%)	($24,422)

Campaign Contributions and Expenditures

1981-82		Direct Cont. 81-82			PACS brkdwn		
Receipts	$322,720	Indiv	$204,478	Agr	$750	Ideo	$1,650
Expend.	$344,777	Party	$14,805	Bus	$82,834	Lbr	$7,200
Unspent	$66,353	PACS	$103,146	Hlth	$8,200	Prof	$2,450

Indirect Party Expend: $14,898

FIFTH DISTRICT

The 5th congressional district of New York is the part of suburban Long Island closest to New York City. Much of it dates back from before World War II. Garden City, laid out as a model suburb in the 1920s, has spacious streets and large houses. So do the Five Towns—Lawrence, Inwood, Cedarhurst, Hewlett, and Woodmere—at the southwest corner of the district, between Kennedy Airport and the Ocean. But these two communities are quite different politically: Garden City is mostly Protestant and heavily Republican, the Five Towns are mostly Jewish and heavily Democratic. The 5th district has its pockets of black neighborhoods, in Hempstead and Roosevelt. But more typical of the district are suburbs like Valley Stream, nestling against the New York City line, or East Meadow and Uniondale, east of Hempstead. Built up in the years after World War II, these are the homes of typical Long Islanders: homeowners (unlike the renters in the City), parents (unlike the singles of Manhattan), people of above-average education and talents who are struggling to live comfortable, affluent lives in the most expensive, demanding, and exasperating of our metropolitan areas.

Politically, they are inclined to be Republicans, and they have been the voters behind the success of Joseph Margiotta's Nassau County Republican machine in the 1970s and early 1980s. His critics have charged him with various offenses, and he was convicted in federal court on charges of giving insurance contracts to politically favored agents. But why should this be a federal crime? Margiotta made no secret that he rewards political friends and punishes political enemies, and Nassau County residents—literate, well informed—have voted again and again to give his Republicans control of the local government and of Nassau's delegations to Albany, Washington, and Republican national conventions. They may disapprove of some of the machine's methods, but evidently they believe it has provided good local government and has backed the right national policies. Margiotta, though convicted, played an important and visible role in the 1982 elections here, and his party continued to do well; when he lost his appeal in the Supreme Court in 1983 he resigned, but no one should assume that this formidable man's political career is over.

The Margiotta machine's drawing power is evident in elections in the 5th congressional district. Twice now the Democrats have put up very attractive candidates, and twice they have lost to a nondescript Republican, Raymond McGrath, whose one important credential is that he is a faithful follower of the Nassau County Republican organization. In 1980, when the incumbent retired, state Senator Karen Burstein, with a solid base in the Five Towns, could do no better than 42% of the vote against McGrath. In 1982, former Carter White House aide Arnie Miller, a veteran of many political campaigns in Long Island and elsewhere, was able to win only 39%, despite the national Democratic trend. That seems to make it as clear as it can be: this is a district that wants to be represented by a Republican congressman.

And so it is. McGrath's voting record shows no serious departures from Republican policy. He serves quietly on the Government Operations and Science and Technology Committees.

The People Pop. 1980: 513,531, dn. 7.5% 1970–80; voting age pop. 383,910; 10% Black, 3% Span. orig., 1% Asian orig. 25% housing units rented. Median owner $57,000; renter $300. Households: 81% family, 39% with children, 68% married couples.

Presidential Vote

1980	Reagan (R)	NA
	Carter (D)	NA
	Anderson (I)	NA

Rep. Raymond J. McGrath (R) Elected 1980; b. Mar. 27, 1942, Valley Stream; home, Valley Stream; SUNY, Brockport, B.S. 1963, NYU, M.A. 1968; Roman Catholic.

Career High sch. phys. ed. teacher, 1963–65; Hempstead Dpty. Commissioner of Parks and Rec., 1969–76; NY Assembly, 1976–80.

Offices 431 CHOB, 202-225-5516. Also 175 N. Central Ave., Valley Stream 11580, 516-872-9550.

Committees *Government Operations* (7th). Subcommittees: Government Activities and Transportation; Intergovernmental Relations and Human Resources. *Science and Technology* (7th). Subcommittees: Natural Resources, Agriculture Research and Environment; Science, Research and Technology.

Group Ratings

	ADA	ACLU	COPE	CFA	LCV	LWV	NTU	NSI	COC	ACA	CSFC
1982	35	17	29	38	64	64	63	89	73	59	57
1981	15	—	7	57	50	—	64	—	89	79	65

National Journal Ratings

	Economic		Foreign		Cultural	
1982	44%	(LIB)	40%	(LIB)	35%	(LIB)
	56%	(CONS)	60%	(CONS)	64%	(CONS)
1981	24%	(LIB)	34%	(LIB)	20%	(LIB)
	68%	(CONS)	63%	(CONS)	80%	(CONS)

Key Votes

1) Reagan 81 Budget	FOR	5) Incr SS Rtmt Age	FOR	9) Poor Pay Food Stamps	FOR
2) Reagan 81 Tax Cut	FOR	6) Saudi AWACS Sale	AGN	10) Ban Crt Busing Order	FOR
3) Bal Budget Amend	FOR	7) $ for MX Missile	AGN	11) Auto Local Content	AGN
4) Gas & Road Tax	—	8) Nerve Gas Prod	AGN	12) Nuclear Arms Freeze	—

Election Results

1982 general	Raymond J. McGrath (R–C–RTL)	100,485	(58%)	($306,351)
	Arnold J. Miller (D–L)	67,002	(39%)	($143,582)
1982 primary	Raymond J. McGrath (R–C) unopposed			
1980 general	Raymond J. McGrath (R–C–RTL)	105,140	(58%)	($265,777)
	Karen S. Burstein (D–L)	77,228	(42%)	($310,158)

Campaign Contributions and Expenditures

1981-82		Direct Cont. 81-82		PACS brkdwn			
Receipts	$306,027	Indiv	$173,083	Agr	$3,000	Ideo	$6,975
Expend.	$306,351	Party	$19,842	Bus	$74,310	Lbr	$6,500
Unspent	$1,791	PACS	$97,695	Hlth	$8,150	Prof	$4,650

Indirect Party Expend: $17,885   *Indep Expend:* For: $1,034 (NRA)

SIXTH DISTRICT

The 6th congressional district of New York is the southern portion of the borough of Queens—actually two different portions, separated geographically by Kennedy Airport and the swampy island-filled Jamaica Bay. Across the bay, separated from the rest of New York is the Rockaway Peninsula. In Neponsit and Belle Harbor on its western end there are still traces to remind you that this was once a summer resort for high society; Arverne in the middle is a slum; much of the beach, from east to west, is lined with high rises, usually filled with older New Yorkers. The subway ride across the bay is a little far for people who have to commute every day.

The larger part of the district follows a series of linear avenues west from Brooklyn to Nassau County. Closest to Brooklyn are cozy, mostly Catholic communities like Ozone Park, Woodhaven, and Howard Beach; settled long ago, these are filled today mostly with older people. Farther east, you come to the working-class shopping district of Jamaica and, in South Jamaica, some mostly black slums. Farther east, you come to more middle-class neighborhoods—St. Albans, Springfield Gardens, Laurelton—most of whose residents are black. These are younger neighborhoods, with many children; the residents are upwardly mobile, and more likely than residents of black slums to have two-parent families. Altogether, 50% of the 6th district's population is black—a figure exceeded by only one other New York district, the 21st in Brooklyn. For those who despair about the future of blacks in New York, the achievements of the people in these neighborhoods in Queens are a reason for optimism.

Politically, this is not considered a black district, however, and there is no sign that it is discontented in any way with Congressman Joseph Addabbo. First elected in 1960, he is an affable man whose base and home are still in Ozone Park; he has represented many of the black neighborhoods of Queens for a long time, however, and evidently to voters' satisfaction.

Addabbo is an important man in the House. He holds one of the key positions on foreign and military policy, as Chairman of the Defense Appropriations Subcommittee. For years this job was held by George Mahon of Texas, whose approach was friendly cooperation with the Pentagon; Mahon was first elected in 1934, and his attitudes were shaped in World War II, which seemed to validate the course of those congressmen who cooperated with the Executive Branch in arming the country. Addabbo's early congressional career came during the Vietnam years, and he seems to have concluded that the wiser course is to oppose the Executive when its plans seem too expensive or too likely to risk war.

The operation of the seniority system brought Addabbo to his chairmanship in 1979, just as Congress was moving away from the policies he had come to espouse. He was unable to modulate much the strong demands for increased defense spending in the late Carter and early Reagan years. But by 1982 and 1983, he was attracting enough support to prevail on the floor of the House, if not necessarily in his subcommittee or the full Appropriations Committee, with their relatively senior and hawkish memberships. Addabbo is in a good position to prevail now, and to shape a consensus and frame issues in his subcommittee; his major problem is that the defense budget is fiendishly complicated, and everyone is hesitant to cut a specific program (as opposed to an abstract percentage of total spending) when it is singled out. It should be added that Addabbo is careful to look out for the interests of New York's big defense contractors.

In all, Addabbo, who gives the impression of being just another neighborhood politician from a storefront in a slightly shopworn neighborhood in Queens, is one of the most powerful members of the House. It is no wonder he maintains solid support from this constituency. At home he regularly wins the Republican and Liberal as well as Democratic nominations and wins the general election with more than 90% of the vote.

The People Pop. 1980: 516,844, dn. 5.7% 1970–80; voting age pop. 368,903; 47% Black, 8% Span. orig., 1% Asian orig. 42% housing units rented. Median owner $42,800; renter $222. Households: 77% family, 43% with children, 55% married couples.

Presidential Vote

1980	Reagan (R)	NA
	Carter (D)	NA
	Anderson (I)	NA

Rep. Joseph P. Addabbo (D) Elected 1960; b. May 17, 1925, Queens; home, Ozone Park; CCNY, 1942–44, St. John's U. Sch. of Law, LL.B. 1946; Roman Catholic.

Career Practicing atty., 1946–60.

Offices 2365 RHOB, 202-225-3461. Also 96–11 101st Ave., Ozone Park 11416, 212-845-3131.

Committees *Appropriations* (5th). Subcommittees: Defense (Chairman); Military Construction; Treasury-Postal Service-General Government. *Small Business* (3d). Subcommittees: General Oversight and the Economy; SBA and SBIC Authority, Minority Enterprise and General Small Business Problems.

Group Ratings

	ADA	ACLU	COPE	CFA	LCV	LWV	NTU	NSI	COC	ACA	CSFC
1982	85	83	94	92	87	75	13	20	26	0	25
1981	75	—	94	86	61	—	8	—	16	9	28
1980	72	80	100	79	70	88	10	11	54	5	19

National Journal Ratings

	Economic		Foreign		Cultural	
1982	90%	(LIB)	68%	(LIB)	93%	(LIB)
	9%	(CONS)	32%	(CONS)	3%	(CONS)
1981	77%	(LIB)	72%	(LIB)	82%	(LIB)
	23%	(CONS)	26%	(CONS)	18%	(CONS)

Key Votes

1) Reagan 81 Budget	AGN	5) Incr SS Rtmt Age	AGN	9) Poor Pay Food Stamps	AGN
2) Reagan 81 Tax Cut	AGN	6) Saudi AWACS Sale	AGN	10) Ban Crt Busing Order	AGN
3) Bal Budget Amend	AGN	7) $ for MX Missile	AGN	11) Auto Local Content	FOR
4) Gas & Road Tax	—	8) Nerve Gas Prod	AGN	12) Nuclear Arms Freeze	FOR

Election Results

1982 general	Joseph P. Addabbo (D–R–L)	95,483	(96%)	($176,022)
1982 primary	Joseph P. Addabbo (D–R–L) unopposed			
1980 general	Joseph P. Addabbo (D–R–L)	96,137	(95%)	($105,482)
	Francis A. Lees (C–RTL)	4,703	(5%)	($0)

Campaign Contributions and Expenditures

1981-82		*Direct Cont. 81-82*			*PACS brkdwn*		
Receipts	$361,634	Indiv	$221,161	Agr	$250	Ideo	$2,000
Expend.	$176,022	PACS	$124,202	Bus	$73,102	Lbr	$41,050
Unspent	$232,616			Hlth	$5,950	Prof	$750

SEVENTH DISTRICT

Queens is the borough of New York least known to outsiders, though they pass through it on the way into Manhattan from the airports; it is typically of little concern to politicians, though it casts more votes than any other borough. What Queens does not have is a long urban past: much of it was still countryside before World War II, and longtime residents still talk of going into "the city" when they mean Manhattan. In those days the built-up parts of Queens consisted mostly of modest one- and two-family houses, inhabited by Irish, Italian, and German immigrants as well as a considerable number of people of Yankee stock. It was a Republican stronghold that happened, technically, to be part of a much larger Democratic city. After World War II, most of the new housing units in Queens have been in apartment houses, many of them giant, like the units in Lefrak City. Added to its older residents have been a large number of Jews, mostly from Manhattan and Brooklyn. It is an airier place to live and raise a family than Manhattan; there are good public schools; rents are lower, and on the subway Manhattan offices are not so far away.

The 7th congressional district of New York might be called the central part of Queens, with examples of all its various waves of immigration. Near the civic buildings and working-class department stores of Jamaica you can find the pre-Revolution era house of Rufus King, one of New York's first U.S. senators—one of the few reminders of Queen's historic rural era. Off Queens Boulevard in the Elmhurst and Jackson Heights sections you can find the low-rise apartments and two-family houses that were built in the 1920s and now house many of Queens's rapidly increasing numbers of Latin American and Asian residents. Across the Long Island Expressway, between the Forest Hills of tennis fame and Flushing Meadow where two world's fairs were held, are the towers of Lefrak City and Rego Park and a bustling shopping area. This is mostly a Jewish area. Farther out the Grand Central Parkway, near St. John's University, the alma mater of many Queens politicians, are comfortable neighborhoods where successful children and grandchildren of Italian immigrants now live. The 7th district continues out the expressway to the high-rises of Glen Oaks and the homeowner neighborhood of Queens Village by the Nassau County line.

This is a heavily Democratic district in almost all elections; a notable exception was in 1980, when Jewish voters were furious with President Carter over issues like the Middle East and racial quotas. For 20 years most of this territory was represented by Benjamin Rosenthal, who began his career as a typical local Queens politician, but became one of the leaders in the House on several important issues. Sometimes he was successful, particularly on foreign affairs; he was an early opponent of the Vietnam war and a strong supporter of Israel. Sometimes he was not successful; the Consumer Protection Agency bill he once steered through the House never became law. Rosenthal was a man of strong beliefs and a sense of humor and was solidly popular in his district. After a long illness, during most of which he remained active in the House, he died just as the 98th Congress convened.

Governor Mario Cuomo, a resident of the district himself, quickly scheduled a special election March 1. The strongest campaigner was Douglas Schoen, a pollster who spent liberally in his own behalf and bought TV time on New York stations. But he got only 16% of the vote. The easy winner was state Senator Gary Ackerman who, like Rosenthal when he was first elected, had a successful career in local politics. His stands on issues will be similar; the question is whether he will show the drive and the character Rosenthal did.

The People   Pop. 1980: 518,952, dn. 6.5% 1970–80; voting age pop. 409,287; 11% Black, 17% Span. orig., 6% Asian orig. 68% housing units rented. Median owner $56,300; renter $266. Households: 67% family, 29% with children, 50% married couples.

Presidential Vote

1980	Reagan (R)	NA
	Carter (D)	NA
	Anderson (I)	NA

Rep. Gary Ackerman (D) Elected Mar. 1, 1983; b. Nov. 19, 1942, Brooklyn; home, Flushing; Queens Col., B.A. 1965; Jewish.

Career Pub. sch. teacher, 1966–72; Newspaper ed. and publisher, 1970–; Advert. agcy. owner, 1972–; NY Senate, 1979–83.

Offices 1725 LHOB, 202-225-2601. Also 41–65 Main St., U.S. Post Ofc. Bldg., Flushing 11351, 212-939-8200.

Committee *Education and Labor* Subcommittees: Elementary, Secondary and Vocational Education; Employment Opportunities; Postsecondary Education.

Group Ratings and Key Votes: Newly Elected

Election Results

1983 special	Gary Ackerman (D)	18,380	(50%)	($204,939)
	Albert Lemishow (R)	8,303	(22%)	($76,731)
	Douglas Schoen (D)	5,983	(16%)	($352,129)
	Sheldon Leffler (D)	4,347	(12%)	($41,316)
1982 general	Benjamin S. Rosenthal (D–L)	84,013	(77%)	($28,543)
	Albert Lemishow (R–C–RTL)	24,832	(23%)	($0)
1980 general	Benjamin S. Rosenthal (D–L)	84,273	(76%)	($35,765)
	Albert Lemishow (R–C–RTL)	27,156	(24%)	($0)

Campaign Contributions and Expenditures

1983		*Direct Cont. 1983*	
Receipts	$204,976	Indiv	$85,994
Expend.	$204,939	Party	$1,325
Unspent	$36	PACS	$62,630
		Cand	$48,000

PACS Breakdown Not Available

EIGHTH DISTRICT

One of the oldest villages in the borough of Queens is Flushing, named by Dutch settlers after the Dutch town of Vlissingen and then anglicized when the British took Nieuw Amsterdam.

The best evidence of old Flushing today is the crooked street pattern, on which Queens's scheme of numbered names is awkwardly superimposed. Flushing is pretty much the heart of the 8th congressional district of New York, which includes most of northern Queens plus small portions of the Bronx and Nassau County. The Queens portion includes the working-class neighborhoods of Whitestone and College Point, the more affluent double-house neighborhood of Bayside, and higher-income Douglaston, right next to the rich, mostly Jewish suburb of Great Neck in Nassau County, which is also in the district. In Queens the district goes south, below the Long Island Expressway, to pleasant home-owner neighborhoods with names like Utopia, Fresh Meadows, and Oakland Gardens. But even here, far from Manhattan and in relatively affluent areas, there are plenty of high-rises; overall, even in this part of Queens there is a population density not approached, except for a few odd neighborhoods, in other metropolitan areas.

The population in this part of the district includes few blacks or Puerto Ricans; there are more in the Bronx portion of the 8th. This area is a little misleading: it looks like a sliver on the map, but it has 29% of the district's population; its statistics make it sound mostly black (24%) and Spanish origin (30%), but most of the voters here are Jewish. The district's rather jagged boundaries take in several of the Bronx's longstanding Jewish neighborhoods and shopping districts, at least as of 1982, including the Parkchester apartment project, which houses some 40,000 people.

The district as drawn had no incumbent congressman, but much of it was familiar territory to James Scheuer, who now represents it. Scheuer is the flying Dutchman of New York congressmen. Starting off as a resident of Manhattan, since 1964 he has represented in the House parts of the Bronx, Brooklyn, Queens, and a little bit of Nassau County now to boot. He beat an old machine hack in the Bronx in 1964 and survived until his district was combined with Jonathan Bingham's and he lost the resulting primary in 1972; he was elected again in 1974 from a district that included southern portions of Queens and Brooklyn, around Jamaica Bay. He made a point then of establishing a genuine residence in that district, but seemed likely to be a victim of redistricting in 1982. But with support from Queens Borough President Donald Manes, he got the nomination in the new 8th district without opposition. None of it overlapped with his Brooklyn–Queens constituency, but much of the Bronx portion was in his district 10 years before. The general election was a piece of cake; against a conservative candidate he won 90% of the vote. This is a heavily Democratic district and may provide a base to keep Scheuer in Congress another 10 years.

Scheuer's good fortune is all the more remarkable because he is not particularly popular with his fellow politicians or congressmen. He suffered the indignity of seeing Energy and Commerce Committee Chairman John Dingell abolish his subcommittee out from under him in 1981, even though he is the second ranking Democrat on the full committee. He now chairs a Science and Technology subcommittee of considerably less legislative importance, although it did give him a piece of the action in investigating former EPA Administrator Anne Gorsuch Burford and her subordinates in 1982 and 1983. Although Scheuer's record on issues is in line with that of other Democrats on Energy and Commerce—the House's most sought-after committee assignment—it is not entirely clear that he would be elected chairman should Dingell retire; the next ranking members, Richard Ottinger and Henry Waxman, might be able to win more votes for the job.

But Scheuer's problems should not be overstated. He is an active, aggressive legislator who works hard at his job, takes it seriously, and does his homework. He has genuinely idealistic views on issues, although he is not above emphasizing politically useful aspects of them on occasion. He doesn't need the job; he is rich and cannot reasonably be entertaining ambitions for higher office. He was adept enough to win in an almost entirely new district, and he should not be counted out in the House in the future.

The People   Pop. 1980: 512,397, dn. 6.5% 1970–80; voting age pop. 399,706; 9% Black, 12% Span. orig., 4% Asian orig. 61% housing units rented. Median owner $68,400; renter $246. Households: 73% family, 32% with children, 57% married couples.

Presidential Vote

1980	Reagan (R) . . . . NA
	Carter (D) . . . . NA
	Anderson (I) . . . . NA

Rep. James H. Scheuer (D) Elected 1974; b. Feb. 6, 1920, New York City; home, Neponsit; Harvard Business Sch., 1943, Swarthmore Col., A.B. 1945, Columbia U., LL.B. 1948; Jewish.

Career Army Air Corps, WWII; Economist, U.S. Foreign Economic Admin., 1945–46; Mbr., Legal Staff, U.S. Ofc. of Price Stabilization, 1951–52; Pres., NY City Citizens Housing and Planning Cncl.; U.S. House of Reps., 1965–73; Pres., Natl. Housing Conf., 1972–74.

Offices 2402 RHOB, 202-225-5471. Also 1943 Rockaway Pkwy., Brooklyn 11236, 212-251-2222.

Committees *Energy and Commerce* (2d). Subcommittees: Health and the Environment; Oversight and Investigations; Telecommunications, Consumer Protection and Finance. *Science and Technology* (4th). Subcommittees: Energy Development and Applications; Investigations and Oversight; Natural Resources, Agriculture Research and Environment (Chairman). *Select Committee on Narcotics Abuse and Control* (4th). *Joint Economic Committee* (6th). Subcommittees: International Trade, Finance, and Security Economics; Trade, Productivity, and Economic Growth.

Group Ratings

	ADA	ACLU	COPE	CFA	LCV	LWV	NTU	NSI	COC	ACA	CSFC
1982	95	87	92	92	95	83	7	10	14	9	24
1981	90	—	91	93	93	—	18	—	11	4	30
1980	89	83	94	93	65	80	12	25	65	13	23

National Journal Ratings

	Economic		Foreign		Cultural	
1982	99%	(LIB)	82%	(LIB)	89%	(LIB)
	0%	(CONS)	18%	(CONS)	8%	(CONS)
1981	89%	(LIB)	77%	(LIB)	88%	(LIB)
	3%	(CONS)	21%	(CONS)	12%	(CONS)

Key Votes

1) Reagan 81 Budget	AGN	5) Incr SS Rtmt Age AGN	9) Poor Pay Food Stamps AGN
2) Reagan 81 Tax Cut	AGN	6) Saudi AWACS Sale AGN	10) Ban Crt Busing Order AGN
3) Bal Budget Amend	AGN	7) $ for MX Missile AGN	11) Auto Local Content FOR
4) Gas & Road Tax	—	8) Nerve Gas Prod AGN	12) Nuclear Arms Freeze FOR

Election Results

1982 general	James H. Scheuer (D–L)	91,830	(90%)	($126,232)
	John T. Blume (C)	10,741	(10%)	($0)
1982 primary	James H. Scheuer (D–L) unopposed			
1980 general	James H. Scheuer (D–L)	72,798	(74%)	($61,111)
	Andrew E. Carlan (R–C–RTL) ...	25,424	(26%)	($0)

Campaign Contributions and Expenditures

1981-82		*Direct Cont. 81-82*				*PACS brkdwn*		
Receipts	$122,274	Indiv	$25,762	Agr	$—	Ideo	$450
Expend.	$126,232	Party	$100	Bus	$19,575	Lbr	$19,600
Unspent	$3,035	PACS	$43,347	Hlth	$1,700	Prof	$500
		Cand	$57,250				

NINTH DISTRICT

It can be said with some certainty that the durable Archie Bunker lives in the 9th congressional district of New York. The aerial shot taken by TV cameramen of Archie's neighborhood shows the kind of aging, though still neatly maintained, one- and two-family houses that line the streets of Jackson Heights, Astoria, Long Island City, Ridgewood, and Glendale, Queens. Moreover, Archie's views, as modified over the years, are a fairly accurate, if stylized, portrayal of attitudes that are often, though not always, shared in this district. Geographically, the 9th is the Queens district closest to Manhattan's chic and liberal Upper East Side—but it is far away in spirit. People here in Queens refer to Manhattan as "the city," as if it were some alien place; and to many of them it is.

In some ways, though, this part of Queens shares New York's melting pot experience and the tolerance and even appetite for diversity that grew out of it. Most of the people here, Bunker notwithstanding, think of themselves as coming from some sort of immigrant stock. And if they were not eager to share their neighborhoods with low-income blacks in the 1960s and 1970s, they are willing, at least grudgingly, to share them with people who are doing today what their grandparents did 80 years ago. The southern part of this district, in the hilly part of Queens that contains most of New York City's cemeteries, has relatively few immigrants. But north of Queens Boulevard, in Long Island City and Jackson Heights, are increasing numbers of Koreans and other Asians (9% of the district's population in 1980) and of Colombians and other Latins (17% Spanish origin). The small brick row houses and scattered, sometimes battered frame houses of Queens are home to this third wave of American immigration in New York.

In national elections the 9th district has leaned Republican, to varying extents. It rejected George McGovern resoundingly, came close to voting for Jimmy Carter in 1976 when aid to New York City was an issue, and gave Ronald Reagan a large margin in 1980. Its views on economic issues do not follow national party lines: it is wary of welfare, but in fact bellows loudly against most measures dismantling the welfare state, on which people here in many ways rely. On cultural matters this is one of the most conservative parts of New York: its Catholicism is not of the sort that worries about nuclear weapons, but of the kind that mourns the passing of the Latin mass and which sets stern standards of conduct for its followers.

The district is represented in Congress by Geraldine Ferraro. First elected in 1978, when many people expected the Republicans to pick up the seat of retiring Rules Committee

Chairman James Delaney, Ferraro proved a strong campaigner and an attractive candidate. She held the seat in 1980 against a challenge from Vito Battista, a longtime anti-tax crusader popular among some Queens home-owners; she won an overwhelming victory in 1982.

In Washington Ferraro, a former unit chief in the district attorney's office, has gotten credit for solid work on several projects. She became a member of the Budget Committee in 1983, after serving as one of the authors of position papers produced for the House Democratic Caucus. She followed closely the proceedings of the Hunt Commission on Democratic national convention delegate selection and seems likely to continue to be active in national party affairs. With a culturally traditional constituency and background and as a successful career woman herself, she is an interesting figure to watch on cultural issues. Her record on issues generally is toward the liberal side of what her district seems likely to support; she was able to get away with supporting government-financed abortions for the poor.

The People   Pop. 1980: 516,143, dn. 4.5% 1970–80; voting age pop. 407,420; 3% Black, 15% Span. orig., 5% Asian orig. 70% housing units rented. Median owner $57,600; renter $206. Households: 66% family, 29% with children, 50% married couples.

Presidential Vote

1980	Reagan (R)	NA
	Carter (D)	NA
	Anderson (I)	NA

Rep. Geraldine A. Ferraro (D) Elected 1978; b. Aug. 26, 1935, Newburgh; home, Forest Hills; Marymount Col., 1956, Fordham U., J.D. 1960; Roman Catholic.

Career Practicing atty., 1961–74; Chf., Special Victims' Bureau and Confidential Unit, Ofc. of NY Dist. Atty., 1974–78.

Offices 312 CHOB, 202-225-3965. Also 47–02 47th St., Woodside 11377, 212-826-5714.

Committees *Budget* (17th). Task Forces: Capital Resources and Development; Economic Policy and Growth; Entitlements, Uncontrollables, and Indexing. *Public Works and Transportation* (13th). Subcommittees: Aviation; Economic Development; Investigations and Oversight; Water Resources. *Select Committee on Aging* (14th). Subcommittee: Health and Long-Term Care.

Group Ratings

	ADA	ACLU	COPE	CFA	LCV	LWV	NTU	NSI	COC	ACA	CSFC
1982	75	79	91	85	92	91	7	33	19	9	29
1981	85	—	88	93	93	—	19	—	11	17	33
1980	72	60	89	79	72	70	11	33	56	17	27

National Journal Ratings

	Economic		Foreign		Cultural	
1982	80%	(LIB)	73%	(LIB)	86%	(LIB)
	20%	(CONS)	27%	(CONS)	14%	(CONS)
1981	81%	(LIB)	72%	(LIB)	78%	(LIB)
	15%	(CONS)	26%	(CONS)	22%	(CONS)

Key Votes

1) Reagan 81 Budget	AGN	5) Incr SS Rtmt Age	AGN	9) Poor Pay Food Stamps	AGN
2) Reagan 81 Tax Cut	AGN	6) Saudi AWACS Sale	AGN	10) Ban Crt Busing Order	FOR
3) Bal Budget Amend	AGN	7) $ for MX Missile	AGN	11) Auto Local Content	FOR
4) Gas & Road Tax	—	8) Nerve Gas Prod	AGN	12) Nuclear Arms Freeze	FOR

Election Results

1982 general	Geraldine A. Ferraro (D)	75,286	(73%)	($140,557)
	John J. Weigandt (R)	20,352	(20%)	($448)
	Ralph G. Groves (C–RTL)	6,011	(6%)	($0)
1982 primary	Geraldine A. Ferraro (D) unopposed			
1980 general	Geraldine A. Ferraro (D)	63,796	(58%)	($124,743)
	Vito P. Battista (R–C–RTL)	44,473	(41%)	($20,716)

Campaign Contributions and Expenditures

1981-82		*Direct Cont. 81-82*		*PACS brkdwn*			
Receipts	$128,470	Indiv	$50,560	Agr	$1,000	Ideo	$3,000
Expend.	$140,557	Party	$300	Bus	$18,950	Lbr	$41,650
Unspent	$4,705	PACS	$68,872	Hlth	$1,650	Prof	$1,600

TENTH DISTRICT

The 10th congressional district of New York includes the heart of Brooklyn, from Grand Army Plaza at the northern end of Prospect Park to Brighton Beach and Coney Island on the Ocean, following roughly Flatbush Avenue, the main street which runs from downtown Brooklyn to the ocean. This is the part of Brooklyn which most often comes to mind when the borough is mentioned. It is not, however, the Brooklyn that grew up, across the East River, as a separate city from New York; that city was closer to downtown Brooklyn and in the row-house neighborhoods that overlook New York Harbor.

The 10th district is the Brooklyn that grew up along the subway lines in the 1910s and 1920s. Its population is mostly Jewish: this and the next-door 13th district may be the only majority-Jewish congressional districts in the whole United States. In the 1970s blacks began moving in large numbers into Flatbush, formerly a mostly Jewish neighborhood, but most of the blacks are in the neighboring 12th district. And the two- and three-story apartment houses that line Ocean Parkway and Coney Island Avenue seem likely to remain mostly Jewish in the future. There is a renaissance of Orthodox Judaism here, and to some extent a turning away from the goals of secular education and advancement; the Jews here are, in most cases, not tremendously affluent, and they seem more interested in celebrating their traditions than in trying to emulate the dazzling successes of Jews who have long since moved on to Great Neck or Beverly Hills. Similar attitudes, on the part of both Jews and Gentiles, seem to prevail in the two-family house neighborhoods farther out, from Sheepshead Bay near Coney Island to Flatlands and Canarsie.

The 10th district is heavily Democratic country, in partisan terms; but it also has increasingly conservative attitudes on some cultural issues. It is hostile to racial quotas, and it is strongly supportive of Israel, even the combative Israel of Menachem Begin; the Jewish neighborhoods here, after heavily favoring Carter over Ford in 1976, were about evenly split between Carter and Reagan in 1980. In congressional elections, the 10th has been represented by liberal Democrats for about as long as anyone here can remember. For 50 years, this and various hunks of Brooklyn were represented by Emanuel Celler, longtime chairman of the House Judiciary Committee. In 1972 he was upset in the primary by Elizabeth Holtzman, a rather solemn lawyer who won the 1980 Democratic Senate primary but lost the general election to Alfonse D'Amato; in 1982 she was elected Brooklyn's district attorney. Holtzman's successor in the House is Charles Schumer, also young, liberal, serious, and experienced. He served six years in the New York Assembly before he was elected to Congress in 1980 at age 30. He was already strong enough to win a four-candidate primary with 59% of the vote. Schumer is one of the local reformers who have been beating organization-backed candidates in Jewish districts in Brooklyn in the late 1970s; he was well enough connected to survive redistricting with a safe seat.

Schumer's voting record is about as far left as one finds in the House. He serves on three committees: Banking, Judiciary, and Post Office. There he can be counted on to support New York City and Brooklyn interests.

The People Pop. 1980: 513,140, dn. 6.9% 1970–80; voting age pop. 398,815; 4% Black, 7% Span. orig., 2% Asian orig. 64% housing units rented. Median owner $53,500; renter $228. Households: 71% family, 31% with children, 56% married couples.

Presidential Vote

1980	Reagan (R)	NA
	Carter (D)	NA
	Anderson (I)	NA

Rep. Charles E. Schumer (D) Elected 1980; b. Nov. 23, 1950, Brooklyn; home, Brooklyn; Harvard Col., B.A. 1971, Harvard Law Sch., J.D. 1974; Jewish.

Career Practicing atty.; NY Assembly, 1974–80.

Offices 126 CHOB, 202-225-6616. Also 2501 Ave. U, Brooklyn 11229, 212-743-3800.

Committees *Banking, Finance and Urban Affairs* (18th). Subcommittees: Economic Stabilization; Financial Institutions Supervision, Regulation and Insurance; Housing and Community Development. *Judiciary* (16th). Subcommittees: Administrative Law and Governmental Relations; Crime; Monopolies and Commercial Law. *Post Office and Civil Service* (14th). Subcommittees: Census and Population; Investigations.

Group Ratings

	ADA	ACLU	COPE	CFA	LCV	LWV	NTU	NSI	COC	ACA	CSFC
1982	95	96	96	92	93	91	27	0	16	10	26
1981	100	—	93	79	84	—	12	—	6	4	27

National Journal Ratings

	Economic		Foreign		Cultural	
1982	96%	(LIB)	92%	(LIB)	93%	(LIB)
	4%	(CONS)	6%	(CONS)	3%	(CONS)
1981	89%	(LIB)	85%	(LIB)	94%	(LIB)
	3%	(CONS)	13%	(CONS)	6%	(CONS)

Key Votes

1) Reagan 81 Budget	AGN	5) Incr SS Rtmt Age	AGN	9) Poor Pay Food Stamps	AGN
2) Reagan 81 Tax Cut	AGN	6) Saudi AWACS Sale	AGN	10) Ban Crt Busing Order	AGN
3) Bal Budget Amend	AGN	7) $ for MX Missile	AGN	11) Auto Local Content	FOR
4) Gas & Road Tax	FOR	8) Nerve Gas Prod	AGN	12) Nuclear Arms Freeze	FOR

Election Results

1982 general	Charles E. Schumer (D–L)	89,852	(79%)	($187,734)
	Stephen Marks (R–C)	21,726	(19%)	($7,860)
1982 primary	Charles E. Schumer (D–L) unopposed			
1980 general	Charles E. Schumer (D–L)	67,343	(77%)	($199,805)
	Theodore Silverman (R–C)	17,050	(20%)	($23,268)

Campaign Contributions and Expenditures

1981-82		*Direct Cont. 81-82*				*PACS brkdwn*		
Receipts	$501,747	Indiv	$388,874	Agr	$1,000	Ideo	$1,500
Expend.	$187,734	PACS	$74,625	Bus	$33,075	Lbr	$37,100
Unspent	$355,901			Hlth	$1,550	Prof	$300

ELEVENTH DISTRICT

The 11th congressional district of New York includes most of the northern and eastern parts of the borough of Brooklyn, an area which, taken together, has no single personality of its own. It includes most of downtown Brooklyn, with a skyline and a set of civic institutions that would be impressive in most American metropolitan areas but that tend to get lost in New York. It also has the row houses—some of them pleasant, some still wretched slums—of the neighborhoods that fan out in every direction: South Brooklyn and Carroll Gardens to the south, Fort Greene and Clinton Hill to the east. To the north is the center of the old working-class neighborhood of Williamsburg; fanning out southeast are the grid streets of Bushwick. These were old manufacturing areas, where 19th-century Brooklynites produced the most prosaic of commodities—rope, glue, ships, and beer. Almost disconnected with the rest of the district is the East New York neighborhood at the edge of Queens. Once it was mostly Italian; now it has many black and Puerto Rican inhabitants.

The 11th district has a long and varied ethnic history. Its early patricians were Dutchmen and Yankees; its mid-20th century residents were mostly Italian and other Catholics. It still includes some of Brooklyn's Hasidic Jewish community. But it is now what lawyers call a majority minority district. Some 47% of its residents are black and 38% Hispanic; there is, it should be noted, some overlap between these categories. In the process it has not developed much of a civic culture. Part of the reason may be that the civic loyalties of many residents remain elsewhere. Blacks and the Hispanics from the Caribbean often move to Brooklyn intending to stay only a while, to make enough money to set themselves up in a good situation back home. They continue to read newspapers from San Juan or Barbados; they pay U.S. taxes and even become U.S. citizens (if they are not already), but their country is elsewhere.

The 11th district was drawn in part to satisfy the Voting Rights Act; there was controversy between those who wanted the black and the Hispanic percentages higher. Actually, the likely winner in the district, had not non-political circumstances intervened, was Congressman Fred Richmond, a successful Jewish businessman who made no secret of the fact that his main New York residence was an elegant apartment on Manhattan's Sutton Place. Richmond in effect bought a congressional seat in Brooklyn. In 1968 he ran as an insurgent against incumbent John Rooney; the next year he made peace with the organization; in 1973 he got a seat on the City Council; and in 1974 a seat in Congress. Not coincidentally, the Richmond Foundation made generous gifts to community institutions all over the new district—enough to help Richmond win easily in a district with one of the lowest voter turnouts in the country. Richmond was actually an accomplished congressman: one of the leading backers of federal programs for the arts and, as a member of the Agriculture Committee, 'one of the key legislators in the alliance between urban Democrats and Farm Belt legislators which maintained support for both crop subsidies and food stamps. But Richmond had personal weaknesses. In 1978 he was arrested for having sex with a young man. In 1982 it was discovered he had gotten an ex-convict a job in the House under a false name. In August he pleaded guilty to tax and drug charges and resigned from Congress.

That left the 11th district seat to be decided in a Democratic primary with one black and two Hispanic candidates. The black, Edolphus Towns, won. Towns is a social worker who served as Brooklyn's deputy borough president. That is an office with duties more mundane than it sounds, but is nonetheless one which keeps a conscientious incumbent in close touch with organized communities across Brooklyn. Towns evidently succeeded in making himself both popular and non-controversial, and keeping himself from becoming involved in the political feuds that have captivated Bedford-Stuyvesant, a part of which he represents.

In Washington Towns is a member of the Government Operations and Public Works and Transportation Committees. He is likely to be reelected without controversy in the 1980s.

The People   Pop. 1980: 518,165, dn. 26.5% 1970–80; voting age pop. 332,612; 17% Black, 34% Span. orig., 1% Asian orig. 75% housing units rented. Median owner $33,800; renter $174. Households: 69% family, 50% with children, 35% married couples.

Presidential Vote

1980	Reagan (R)	NA
	Carter (D)	NA
	Anderson (I)	NA

Rep. Edolphus Towns (D) Elected 1982; b. July 21, 1934, Chadburn, NC; home, Brooklyn; NC A&T U., B.S. 1956, Adelphi U., MSW 1973; Presbyterian.

Career Army, 1956–58; Professor, Medgar Evers Col., 1959–64; Dpty. hospital administrator, 1965–71; Dem. NY Committeeman; Dpty. Borough Pres. of Brooklyn, 1976–82.

Offices 1009 LHOB, 202-225-5936. Also 93 Prospect Pl., Brooklyn 11217, 212-622-5700.

Committees *Government Operations.* (22d). Subcommittees: Government Information, Justice, and Agriculture; Intergovernmental Relations and Human Resources. *Public Works and Transportation* (26th). Subcommittees: Aviation; Economic Development. *Select Committee on Narcotics Abuse and Control* (16th).

Group Ratings and Key Votes: Newly Elected

Election Results

1982 general	Edolphus Towns (D)	39,357	(84%)	($154,080)
	James W. Smith (R)	4,449	(9%)	($15,423)
1982 primary	Edolphus Towns (D) unopposed			
1980 general	Frederick W. Richmond (D–L)	45,029	(76%)	($392,751)
	Christopher Lovell (R–C)	8,257	(14%)	($1,622)
	Moses S. Harris (New Alliance) ...	4,151	(7%)	($0)

Campaign Contributions and Expenditures

1982		Direct Cont. 1982		PACS brkdwn			
Receipts	$155,093	Indiv	$113,833	Agr	$—	Ideo	$2,750
Expend.	$154,080	Party	$2,700	Bus	$4,250	Lbr	$10,125
Unspent	$193	PACS	$18,375	Hlth	$—	Prof	$—
		Cand	$20,000				

TWELFTH DISTRICT

The largest black community in the New York metropolitan area is not in Harlem or in the South Bronx, but in Brooklyn. Harlem, like other slums in Manhattan before it, has become depopulated as residents move to more spacious neighborhoods in outer boroughs; by 1980 there were more blacks in Queens and in the Bronx than in Manhattan, and nearly twice as many, some 722,000, in Brooklyn. And most of Brooklyn's blacks live in a few square miles in neighborhoods known as Bedford–Stuyvesant, Crown Heights, Brownsville, and East Flatbush, which together form New York's 12th congressional district. There is more variation here than would appear to most whites at first. The rather grim-looking row houses of Bedford–Stuyvesant house many upwardly mobile families, some of them straight from the West Indies; the blacks who have moved recently into once all-white East Flatbush are by no means impoverished. Brownsville, on the other hand, is about as wretched and disorganized a place as there is in America. Once Brooklyn's premier Jewish neighborhood, where young immigrants moved from the Lower East Side and debated socialism and labor unions in streets dense with peddlers and children, Brownsville became all black in the 1950s, and is now a jungle of abandoned buildings, uncontrolled youth gangs, and frequent arson. It is the sort of place anybody with an ability to make his own way will get out of, and so it is the province of the helpess and the vicious, the crippled and the criminal.

The 12th district is 80% black, heavily Democratic, and possessed of a lively political culture which, however, seems to directly touch very few of its citizens. Voter turnout is about as low here as any place in the United States; elections are decided by small groups of hardy civic activists. Their choice for many years, though not always by overwhelming margins, was Shirley Chisholm, elected to the New York Assembly in 1964, to Congress in 1968, and a presidential candidate in 1972. Chisholm in many ways personified the typical voter in the 12th: a woman with a West Indies background, a determined fighter, a strong liberal on issues but with a tough discipline-minded streak as well.

Chisholm decided to retire from Congress in 1982, and the contest to succeed her was bitterly contested. State Senator Vander Beatty was the leading organization Democrat in this area; state Senator Major Owens was considered the leading reformer. What these labels mean exactly is never clear; they are just a clue to a series of complex alliances and relationships. Owens, for example, had the support of Chisholm, but he also was connected to former Councilman and Assemblyman Samuel Wright, who opposed Chisholm in the 1976 primary and was convicted of extortion in 1978. Beatty had the support of a large number of patronage appointees he controlled through his alliance with Brooklyn Democratic organization head Meade Esposito; but the limits of Esposito's power are suggested by the fact that not a single one of Brooklyn's congressmen today is his ally. He does, however, have great influence in local courts, and perhaps that is why a Brooklyn court ordered a rerun of the 12th district's primary after Owens was counted the winner by a margin of some 2,400 votes—more than enough to survive a recount in most states, let alone a congressional district with low turnout. That decision was overturned, however, and Owens became congressman.

He sits now on the Education and Labor and Government Operations Committees, and can be counted on as a solid liberal Democratic vote on national issues. General elections are, of course, no problem for him, but he must always be wary of the primary: even Chisholm, after years of incumbency and national fame, had to worry about primary opposition. Given the closeness of the 1982 result, it seems quite likely there will be another furiously contested primary in the 12th district in 1984, and that much of Owens's attention in 1983 and 1984 will be devoted to it.

The People   Pop. 1980: 516,983, dn. 12.5% 1970–80; voting age pop. 348,549; 78% Black, 9% Span. orig., 2% Asian orig. 77% housing units rented. Median owner $46,200; renter $203. Households: 70% family, 46% with children, 37% married couples.

Presidential Vote

1980	Reagan (R)	NA
	Carter (D)	NA
	Anderson (I)	NA

Rep. Major R. Owens (D) Elected 1982; b. June 28, 1936, Collierville, TN; home, Brooklyn; Moorehouse Col., B.A. 1956, Atlanta U., M.A. 1957; Baptist.

Career Comm. Coord., Brooklyn Pub. Library, 1958–65; Exec. Dir., Brownsville Comm. Cncl., 1966–68; Commissioner, NYC Comm. Development Agcy., 1968–73; Dir., Comm. Media Library Prog., Columbia U., 1974; NY Senate, 1974–82.

Offices 114 CHOB, 202-225-6231. Also 289 Utica Ave., Brooklyn 11213, 212-773-3100.

Committees *Education and Labor* (18th). Subcommittees: Employment Opportunities; Human Resources; Labor Standards; Postsecondary Education. *Government Operations* (21st). Subcommittees: Government Activities and Transportation; Manpower and Housing.

Group Ratings and Key Votes: Newly Elected

Election Results

1982 general	Major R. Owens (D–L)	44,586	(91%)	(*)
	David Katan, Sr. (R)	3,215	(6%)	($0)
1982 primary	Major R. Owens (D–L) unopposed			
1980 general	Shirley Chisholm (D–L)	35,446	(87%)	($31,576)
	Charles Gibbs (R)	3.372	(8%)	($0)

Campaign Contributions and Expenditures
* Candidate has not filed final year-end report with the Federal Election Commission.

PACS brkdwn (declared by PACS)

Agr	$—	Ideo	$2,250
Bus	$1,750	Lbr	$29,850
Hlth	$250	Prof	$750

THIRTEENTH DISTRICT

On the map, the 13th congressional district of New York looks like an egregious example of gerrymandering. It stretches from the northernmost part of Brooklyn, the industrial area of Greenpoint, along most of the Brooklyn waterfront, to the southernmost, the beaches of Coney Island and Brighton Beach. It is seldom more than a mile wide and sometimes only a couple of blocks. Yet it is a district which makes a good deal of demographic sense. This is basically the poor Jewish district, one of the few majority-Jewish districts in the nation and the home of many of the nation's least affluent Jewish communities. This is true despite the fact that the waterfront area was never heavily Jewish; many of its piers now are vacant, and the few waterfront blocks in the 13th district have either been gentrified, as in the case of Brooklyn Heights and its extension to the south, Cobble Hill, or have been substantially depopulated, as is the case with the old Italian neighborhoods of South Brooklyn and Red Hook.

So what emerge as the important voting blocs in the 13th district are these: the Hasidic communities of Greenpoint and Williamsburg, determined to retain old traditions in an often hostile environment; the growing Orthodox communities of Borough Park, in the central part of the district; the new Russian Jewish immigrant communities in Bath Beach; the high rises of Coney Island and Brighton Beach, filled with elderly Jews with modest incomes, the people who can't afford to buy condominiums in Florida. The voters in all these communities have Democratic backgrounds and vote—vote heavily—in Democratic primaries. But they are sternly opposed to crime, suspicious of blacks and opposed to racial quotas, strongly supportive of rent control and housing subsidy programs, but suspicious of welfare. They are very interested in foreign policy: strongly pro-Israel and, increasingly, fiercely anti-Communist. This is the part of the United States, after all, with the highest proportion of immigrants from Communist Russia.

The congressman from the 13th district is Stephen Solarz, an able and ambitious member of the large Democratic class of 1974. Solarz's political and personal background are a little different from that of his present constituency: he was an insurgent against the old Brooklyn machine, a reform assemblyman at age 28, and a victor against an incumbent congressman (tarred with scandal) at age 34. Solarz has solid liberal ratings from most national organizations and lines up usually with the Democratic leadership. He specializes in foreign affairs. For two years he chaired the House's Africa Subcommittee; in 1981 he took over the Asian and Pacific Affairs Subcommittee. Like others whose political careers began during the Vietnam years, he is wary of American military involvement abroad and inclined to judge rather harshly the human rights records of American allies like South Korea. At the same time, his move from Africa to Asia—he had his choice of subcommittees—suggests that he is interested in moving from an area where American choices seem polarized on liberal-conservative lines to where they are less obviously structured and more open to creative influence. Solarz may be responding to the fact that neither side in the Vietnam debate seemed to predict the future: Vietnam's Communism has not spread to other Asian countries, as hawks predicted, nor has the United States been faced with other "national liberation" movements in the Third World, as doves predicted. Also, Solarz may be moving toward reflecting the increasingly militant pro-Americanness of his constituency.

Solarz has other responsibilities as well. He serves on the House Budget Committee, where he tends to favor among options the one most generous in domestic spending. He chairs the Capital Resources and Development Task Force, and is a proponent of the idea of taking capital spending out of the federal budget, and allocating it over the years in which the capital goods are used—the procedure used by almost all state and local governments. Solarz is not a particularly visible congressman, but he is one of those young members with important responsibilities who can change policy and make things happen.

Solarz came through redistricting unscathed, and has ended up with a district at least as heavily Jewish as the one which elected him in the 1970s. Politics in Brooklyn is turbulent, and one cannot rule out primary challenges; but he seems to have a safe seat.

The People Pop. 1980: 518,906, dn. 9.8% 1970–80; voting age pop. 389,944; 6% Black, 13% Span. orig., 2% Asian orig. 74% housing units rented. Median owner $53,700; renter $195. Households: 67% family, 31% with children, 51% married couples.

Presidential Vote

1980	Reagan (R)	NA
	Carter (D)	NA
	Anderson (I)	NA

Rep. Stephen J. Solarz (D) Elected 1974; b. Sept. 12, 1940, New York City; home, Brooklyn; Brandeis U., A.B. 1962, Columbia U., M.A. 1967; Jewish.

Career NY Assembly, 1968–74.

Offices 1536 LHOB, 202-225-2361. Also 1628 Kings Hwy., Brooklyn 11229, 212-965-5100.

Committees *Budget* (3d). Task Forces: Capital Resources and Development (Chairman); Economic Policy and Growth; International Finance and Trade; Tax Policy. *Foreign Affairs* (5th). Subcommittees: Asian and Pacific Affairs (Chairman); Western Hemisphere Affairs; International Operations.

Group Ratings

	ADA	ACLU	COPE	CFA	LCV	LWV	NTU	NSI	COC	ACA	CSFC
1982	95	79	89	85	96	92	10	20	10	13	27
1981	90	—	88	71	86	—	10	—	6	15	30
1980	78	93	89	86	65	90	12	0	52	20	22

National Journal Ratings

	Economic		Foreign		Cultural	
1982	83%	(LIB)	85%	(LIB)	88%	(LIB)
	15%	(CONS)	12%	(CONS)	11%	(CONS)
1981	81%	(LIB)	70%	(LIB)	87%	(LIB)
	15%	(CONS)	30%	(CONS)	13%	(CONS)

Key Votes

1) Reagan 81 Budget	AGN	5) Incr SS Rtmt Age	AGN
2) Reagan 81 Tax Cut	AGN	6) Saudi AWACS Sale	AGN
3) Bal Budget Amend	AGN	7) $ for MX Missile	AGN
4) Gas & Road Tax	FOR	8) Nerve Gas Prod	AGN

9) Poor Pay Food Stamps	AGN
10) Ban Crt Busing Order	AGN
11) Auto Local Content	FOR
12) Nuclear Arms Freeze	FOR

Election Results

1982 general	Stephen J. Solarz (D–L)	68,549	(81%)	($264,790)
	Leon F. Nadrowski (R–RTL)	14,257	(17%)	($0)
1982 primary	Stephen J. Solarz (D–L) unopposed			
1980 general	Stephen J. Solarz (D–L)	81,954	(79%)	($118,916)
	Harry DeMell (R–C)	19,536	(19%)	($0)

Campaign Contributions and Expenditures

1981-82		Direct Cont. 81-82		PACS brkdwn			
Receipts	$669,828	Indiv	$515,143	Agr	$—	Ideo	$2,250
Expend.	$264,790	PACS	$64,697	Bus	$4,075	Lbr	$58,400
Unspent	$605,899			Hlth	$250	Prof	$200

FOURTEENTH DISTRICT

Staten Island is the smallest (pop. 352,000) and by far the least densely populated of the five boroughs of New York City (6,000 people per square mile versus 27,000 for the rest of the city). Geographically, it is off to the side; you could make a good case that it should have been part of New Jersey. Physically, some of it is still rural: yes, cows can actually graze in the nation's largest city. Before 1965, when the Verrazano Narrows Bridge was completed, the only land route from the rest of New York to Staten Island was in New Jersey, and the only water routes were on ferries from Manhattan and Brooklyn. Since then Staten Island's population has increased by more than 50%. Yet it still has a rural atmosphere about it. And it still has a disorganized, random air, as subdivisions do when they are not oriented to a particular center or situated in a recognizable grid.

Most Staten Islanders are quite happy with their comparative isolation. They are in many ways more suburban than real suburbanites. Many are middle-income Italian and Irish Catholics, brought up in Brooklyn and happy to leave the City (as they call it) behind. Politically, Staten Islanders are conservative; Conservative Party candidates have occasionally outpolled Democrats. They are home-owners, not renters; family people, not singles; religious people, not skeptics. They have almost nothing in common with Manhattan. Yet many people here think of themselves as Democrats; they don't have much in common with Upstaters either.

Staten Island forms two-thirds of New York's 14th congressional district. The other one-third is the part of New York City which may be closest to Staten Island in attitudes, as well as in proximity: the Bay Ridge section of Brooklyn. At the eastern terminus of the Verrazano Narrows Bridge, Bay Ridge is mostly Catholic, mostly middle class; there are some large apartment buildings and even high-rises, but 30% of the housing units are owner-occupied, and there are even some large single-family homes overlooking New York Harbor. In heavily Democratic Brooklyn, Bay Ridge consistently votes Republican.

Before 1982, Staten Island shared a congressional district with lower Manhattan, a result that helped to keep Democrat John Murphy in office until his Abscam conviction. Murphy was beaten in 1980 by Republican Guy Molinari; the result might have been different but for the fact that 17% of the vote, mostly from Manhattan, went to Liberal Party candidate Mary Codd. Molinari got some notice in 1981 when he threatened to retire unless President Reagan paid more attention to him on a trip to New York; Reagan did, and Molinari ended his pout.

Actually, the election outcome was pretty well determined by redistricting. Molinari had to face a Democratic incumbent, one with attractive credentials: Leo Zeferetti, former police officer, member of the Rules Committee, chairman of the Select Committee on Narcotics Abuse and Control. On noneconomic issues, these two Italian-American congressmen had similar records; and even on economic issues, Molinari was not quite a solid Reaganite. But Zeferetti no longer had most of the Democratic parts of his old district, and was able to carry the Brooklyn portion of the new 14th by only a 56%-43% margin. Staten Island makes up 68% of the new district, and there Molinari won 62%-37%. So Molinari continues on Public Works and Transportation and Small Business Committees, and seems likely to remain in the House for some years, one of only two Republicans representing the city of New York.

The People   Pop. 1980: 515,863, up 8.7% 1970–80; voting age pop. 379,098; 4% Black, 6% Span. orig., 2% Asian orig. 49% housing units rented. Median owner $62,100; renter $217. Households: 75% family, 38% with children, 60% married couples.

Presidential Vote

1980	Reagan (R)	95,589	(60%)
	Carter (D)	54,443	(34%)
	Anderson (I)	9,487	(6%)

Rep. Guy V. Molinari (R) Elected 1980; b. Nov. 23, 1928, New York City; home, Staten Island; Wagner Col., B.A. 1949, NY Law Sch., LL.B. 1951; Roman Catholic.

Career USMC, 1951–53; Practicing atty., 1953–74; NY Assembly, 1974–80.

Offices 412 CHOB, 202-225-3371. Also 203 Ft. Wadsworth Bldg., Staten Island 10305, 212-981-9800; and 26 Fed. Plaza, 16th Fl., New York 10007, 212-264-9335.

Committees *Public Works and Transportation* (7th). Subcommittees: Investigations and Oversight; Public Buildings and Grounds; Water Reources. *Small Business* (10th). Subcommittee: SBA and SBIC Authority, Minority Enterprise and General Small Business Problems.

Group Ratings

	ADA	ACLU	COPE	CFA	LCV	LWV	NTU	NSI	COC	ACA	CSFC
1982	15	12	27	38	64	75	56	100	67	52	53
1981	25	—	27	57	43	—	66	—	79	65	63

National Journal Ratings

	Economic		Foreign		Cultural	
1982	36%	(LIB)	38%	(LIB)	48%	(LIB)
	64%	(CONS)	62%	(CONS)	52%	(CONS)
1981	41%	(LIB)	52%	(LIB)	53%	(LIB)
	58%	(CONS)	48%	(CONS)	46%	(CONS)

Key Votes

1) Reagan 81 Budget	FOR	5) Incr SS Rtmt Age	AGN	9) Poor Pay Food Stamps	AGN
2) Reagan 81 Tax Cut	FOR	6) Saudi AWACS Sale	AGN	10) Ban Crt Busing Order	FOR
3) Bal Budget Amend	AGN	7) $ for MX Missile	FOR	11) Auto Local Content	AGN
4) Gas & Road Tax	FOR	8) Nerve Gas Prod	AGN	12) Nuclear Arms Freeze	AGN

Election Results

1982 general	Guy V. Molinari (R–C–RTL)	67,626	(56%)	($239,921)
	Leo C. Zeferetti (D)	51,728	(43%)	($313,299)
1982 primary	Guy V. Molinari (R–C–RTL) unopposed			
1980 general	Leo C. Zeferetti (D)	49,684	(50%)	($185,458)
(NY 15)	Paul M. Atanasio (R–C–RTL)	46,467	(47%)	($161,803)
1980 general	Guy V. Molinari (R–C)	69,573	(48%)	($148,993)
(NY 17)	John M. Murphy (D–RTL)	50,954	(35%)	($303,108)
	Mary T. Codd (L)	25,118	(17%)	($50,643)

Campaign Contributions and Expenditures

1981-82		Direct Cont. 81-82		PACS brkdwn			
Receipts	$330,305	Indiv	$159,720	Agr	$—	Ideo	$9,725
Expend.	$239,921	Party	$21,601	Bus	$113,699	Lbr	$5,100
Unspent	$94,242	PACS	$146,269	Hlth	$6,500	Prof	$1,250
		Cand	$2,000				

Indirect Party Expend: $35,170   *Indep Expend:* For: $908 (NRA)

FIFTEENTH DISTRICT

The 15th congressional district of New York is the latest version of a district first created in 1918 and known since at least the 1930s as the Silk Stocking District. The district includes most of the skyscrapers of midtown Manhattan and goes as far south now as City Hall. It includes the Lower East Side, with its high-rise housing for elderly Jews, a reminder of the days, 70 years ago, when these neighborhoods were packed full of young immigrants and their large families. The 15th includes as well the middle-income housing developments of Stuyvesant Town and Peter Cooper Village and the quaint old square of Gramercy Park. The 15th also includes those parts of Manhattan that make it a world-class city, whose only rivals are Paris and London. This is one of the places where the really rich live, shop, and entertain. In apartment buildings overlooking Central Park and above Park Avenue, in the new Fifth Avenue buildings full of Brazilians and French fleeing expropriation and taxes, in Sutton Place townhouses, the world's very richest people live in splendor most people cannot conceive.

Writers have struggled for years to describe this part of New York socially, culturally, even physically. It is easier to describe politically. For, as in all of New York, not everyone votes, and those who do tend to share a set of attitudes which can be described without great difficulty. Most of the voters in this district live in the Upper East Side, from the East 50s to the East 90s, between Central Park and the East River. This is the area we associate with the very rich, and yet they form only a very small share of its population; they huddle along Fifth, Madison, Park, and Sutton Place, just where the very rich lived 70 years ago when the rest of the East Side was filled with factories, breweries, and the German immigrants of Yorkville. Now the factories are torn down and the row houses increasingly replaced with high rises, most in that ugly pale grey brick which must be New York's cheapest building material; and they are filled with highly educated, usually single young professionals and white-collar workers. This is the largest concentration of singles in America. These are the people who make Manhattan the center of the nation's publishing, entertainment, broadcasting, and communications industries. And these are the people who fill Bloomingdale's every Saturday, in ever-hot pursuit of the latest style and fashion. They are the people you see in Woody Allen's *Annie Hall* and *Manhattan*. They are people who love the struggle of New York life— the struggle to keep clean and well dressed in the dirty, gritty New York air, to maintain fashionable hairstyles in the New York wind, to keep themselves going to fashionable vacation places and the latest little restaurants.

In the 1950s these people were only a small part of Manhattan's population, and dominated only one of Manhattan's six congressional districts, the Silk Stocking seat that hugged Central Park on the east. Now Manhattan has lost most of its slumdwellers, and the island has only two districts plus most of one other; the Upper East Side dominates the 15th and the Upper West Side and Greenwich Village, not so different in attitude as they like to suppose, dominate the 17th. Their politics can be summarized as extremely liberal on cultural and foreign issues, and quite cautiously liberal—sometimes maybe a shade conservative—on economic issues. The views of this electorate are probably more important than its numbers, because they are propagated through the media; they are also subject to more change than those of most other places, because there is so much turnover in this district's population. After all, some singles get married and move to the suburbs, some professionals move to other cities; they are replaced by other young, affluent singles, people with similar backgrounds but different experiences and, sometimes, different attitudes.

The Upper East Side and the Silk Stocking District have gone through three political generations in the last 35 years.

• *Herald Tribune* Republicanism. From the days of Franklin Roosevelt to the days of John F. Kennedy, the Silk Stocking District was a bastion of upper-class, Yankee Republicanism in working-class, immigrant New York. It was a Republicanism best articulated by the old *New York Herald Tribune*. It was hostile to New Deal economic measures, but willing to consider the kind of accommodations to the New Deal supported by Thomas Dewey and Dwight Eisenhower. It was firmly internationalist in foreign policy, strongly backing American support of Britain in 1940, entry into World War II, the United Nations, and the Marshall Plan. It looked with some favor on conservationist programs and supported strong civil rights laws. But it firmly opposed national health insurance, federal aid to education, large increases in Social Security, and any strengthening of labor unions.

The *Herald Tribune* looked with some contempt on Democrats, whom it saw as dominated by socialistic labor union bosses and corrupt local machine politicians, and supported by ignorant masses who could not be expected to know what was, in the long run, best for them. People today remember the *Herald Tribune's* sprightly Sunday magazine, which became Clay Felker's *New York,* and forget what a tough partisan the paper was: President Kennedy, in a fit of pique, once banned it from the White House. But whatever else one may say, the Republicanism the *Herald Tribune* fostered was broad in its concerns. The Silk Stocking

District undertook responsibility for the whole world, from beleaguered nations in Europe to victims of discrimination in the South. Its concerns were broadly-gauged and its policies, however they may have helped the direct economic interests of affluent New Yorkers, were designed, and not implausibly, to benefit the great mass of people in good time. The *Herald Tribune* spoke as the voice of people who were in charge of what went on in the world and took their responsibilities seriously.

They discharged those responsibilities, almost always, by being successful in business, contributing to charity, and voting Republican. From 1938 to 1966, the Silk Stocking District voted Republican for president (except in the Goldwater election) and elected congressmen who shared most of these views, the most famous of whom was John V. Lindsay, whose career symbolizes the shift to the next generation.

• Lindsay liberalism. When he was first elected to Congress in 1958, at age 37, there was little to indicate that he was anything but a standard *Herald Tribune* Republican. Educated at St. Paul's and Yale, associate at a big law firm, Lindsay was a personification of tweedy Republican politics. Even his early vote for the Kennedy administration's plan to pack the House Rules Committee was not out of line with the Dewey–Eisenhower tradition. When Lindsay was elected mayor in 1965, he won by sweeping the East Side and Manhattan and by eating into the Jewish vote in the outer boroughs, though he lost New York outside Manhattan.

In his first act as mayor Lindsay at first provoked and then finally capitulated to a strike of transit workers. This personified his term in office: he antagonized the white middle- and working-class of the city, and at the same time so vastly increased public payrolls that the city's budget could not be balanced except by borrowing against next year's revenues. Lindsay was full of sympathy for blacks and Puerto Ricans, but had little but contempt for outer-borough whites. His attitudes were reflected in the Upper East Side. These were the years of radical chic, of fundraising parties for the Black Panthers or the lettuce workers in California, of rallies against the war in Vietnam. There was genuine idealism here, and a demand for redistribution of society's wealth which the old *Herald Tribune* would never have approved of. But the *Herald Tribune* folded in the late 1960s, and was replaced as the organ of Silk Stocking opinion by the more Democratic *New York Times*.

Underneath this attitude was an assumption that society's affluence was unlimited and a dislike—a sort of adolescent rebellion against—the very system which made this affluence possible. There was also a narrowing of focus from the broad concerns of the *Herald Tribune* days. The Silk Stocking District and the Lindsay administration did not seem much interested in issues which would not showcase their moral superiority to the rest of society: Vietnam and civil rights qualified, but crime and education did not quite fit. And despite the rhetorical emphasis on national issues, during the Lindsay years politics increasingly focused on local matters, and especially on the conflicts between the liberalism of Manhattan and the apparent conservatism of the outer boroughs. There was a sort of snobbery operating here, a myopic sense that all whites enjoyed the affluence that East Siders took for granted; sympathy was reserved for minority groups, and Manhattanites became staunch supporters of the Ocean Hill–Brownsville community school board and civilian review boards in the Police Department. In effect affluent Manhattanites were trying to impose their way of life and their vision on the increasingly restive outer boroughs of New York City. Lindsay was re-elected in 1969, again with overwhelming support in Manhattan; but again he lost the outer boroughs and won with only a minority of the citywide vote. The fact that this record made him seem to many writers a plausible presidential candidate only illustrates the centrality of the Silk Stocking District in the lives of journalists.

Lindsay officially turned Democrat in 1971; the Silk Stocking District preceded him and elected a Democratic congressman, Edward Koch, in 1968. Koch came out of the Greenwich Village reform movement, the prototype for a liberal insurgent group in a gentrified neighborhood; and during his first years in Congress he represented opinion in the district accurately. But by the time he was elected mayor in 1977, his origins in the outer boroughs began to show: he ran as a backer of capital punishment and opponent of racial quotas. Earlier in the 1970s, such positions would have made Koch a pariah in Manhattan politics; in today's politics, they cost him votes there, but leave him with enough to carry the area anyway.

• Post-1975 cultural liberalism. New York City's fiscal crisis, which began in 1975, convinced even Upper East Siders that the city did not have the resources to solve all of its residents' problems. At the same time it became apparent that Manhattan and the outer boroughs, full of generously paid civil servants and pensioners, were in the same boat, and the old cultural battles were forgotten. Instead, politics and life on the Upper East Side turned inward. The postponement of childbearing among the baby boom generation raised the age of Manhattan singles, and the booming white-collar economy (symbolized by lawyers' salaries) raised their affluence. And so, amid the pothole-cratered streets and near the decaying bridges of Manhattan, they indulged in the latest clothes and explored the latest restaurants and discotheques: the picture of Galbraith's private affluence amid public squalor. They found in their own pursuit of pleasure the justification for their selfishness: they were practitioners of liberation, whether it was the sexual freedom of the 1970s or gay liberation or simply freedom from the demands of child rearing. They still addressed manifestos to society, but with little care whether they reached beyond the little Manhattans springing up in big cities and resort areas across the country.

Their great cause became not just toleration for, but validation of, their lifestyle; on other issues, especially economics, their opinions became increasingly conventional. The Upper East Side, which in 1972 voted solidly for George McGovern, in the 1977 special election to replace Ed Koch elected a Republican congressman once again. He is S. William Green, a Manhattanite from a rich family with a long record in public life.

Green has one of the most liberal records of any congressional Republican. On cultural and foreign issues, he is to the left of most House Democrats. On economic issues, he supported the Reagan economic program in 1981, and counts himself definitely a supporter of free enterprise; yet he has often voted with the Democrats here too. The Republican leadership probably does not much mind: they understand that without a record like this, Green would have no chance of surviving in this district. And so he has a seat on the Appropriations Committee as well as being one of the leaders of the Northeast–Midwest Coalition. Careful and hardworking, Green does not personify the hedonistic or trend-seeking qualities evident in so many of his constituents.

Even so, Green does not have complete security electorally. He won his first two elections in large part because of splits among Democrats: his first two opponents were Carter Burden, a wealthy onetime councilman who once owned *New York* and the *Village Voice*, and Bella Abzug, the onetime congresswoman from the West Side who lost successive races for senator and mayor. Against Ralph Nader associate Mark Green, the Republican Green won 57% of the vote; against a candidate expected to run weaker, but running in a more Democratic year, he got 53% in 1982. That pretty much guarantees him a vigorous contest in 1984.

The People Pop. 1980: 516,409, dn. 3.2% 1970–80; voting age pop. 444,395; 5% Black, 12% Span. orig., 9% Asian orig. 84% housing units rented. Median owner $185,800; renter $317. Households: 37% family, 14% with children, 28% married couples.

Presidential Vote

1980	Reagan (R)	NA
	Carter (D)	NA
	Anderson (I)	NA

Rep. S. William (Bill) Green (R) Elected Feb. 14, 1978; b. Oct. 16, 1929, New York City; home, New York City; Harvard U., B.A. 1950, J.D. 1953; Jewish.

Career Army, 1953–55; Law Secy., U.S. Court of Appeals for DC Circuit, 1955–56; Practicing atty., 1956–70; NY Assembly, 1965–70; NY Regional Administrator, HUD, 1970–77.

Offices 1110 LHOB, 202-225-2436. Also 137 E. 57th St., New York 10022, 212-826-4466.

Committee *Appropriations* (17th). Subcommittees: District of Columbia; HUD-Independent Agencies.

Group Ratings

	ADA	ACLU	COPE	CFA	LCV	LWV	NTU	NSI	COC	ACA	CSFC
1982	70	92	56	46	83	83	48	10	52	32	41
1981	70	—	54	50	68	—	44	—	72	25	43
1980	94	80	58	86	83	70	20	22	66	29	37

National Journal Ratings

	Economic		Foreign		Cultural	
1982	51%	(LIB)	66%	(LIB)	89%	(LIB)
	49%	(CONS)	33%	(CONS)	8%	(CONS)
1981	50%	(LIB)	77%	(LIB)	91%	(LIB)
	50%	(CONS)	21%	(CONS)	9%	(CONS)

Key Votes

1) Reagan 81 Budget	FOR	5) Incr SS Rtmt Age	FOR	9) Poor Pay Food Stamps	AGN
2) Reagan 81 Tax Cut	FOR	6) Saudi AWACS Sale	AGN	10) Ban Crt Busing Order	AGN
3) Bal Budget Amend	AGN	7) $ for MX Missile	AGN	11) Auto Local Content	AGN
4) Gas & Road Tax	FOR	8) Nerve Gas Prod	AGN	12) Nuclear Arms Freeze	FOR

Election Results

1982 general	S. William (Bill) Green (R–Ind. Neighbors)	66,262	(53%)	($241,019)
	Betty Lall (D–L)	55,483	(45%)	($184,808)
1982 primary	S. William (Bill) Green (R–Ind. Neighbors) unopposed			
1980 general	S. William (Bill) Green (R–Ind. Neighbors)	91,341	(57%)	($330,936)
	Mark J. Green (D–L)	68,786	(43%)	($293,020)

Campaign Contributions and Expenditures

1981-82		Direct Cont. 81-82			PACS brkdwn			
Receipts	$241,193	Indiv	$177,914	Agr	$—	Ideo	$2,250
Expend.	$241,019	Party	$8,988	Bus	$43,036	Lbr	$500
Unspent	$171	PACS	$49,486	Hlth	$3,100	Prof	$600
		Cand	$7,000				

SIXTEENTH DISTRICT

In the 1920s Harlem—originally a tenement district built for white working-class families—became the center of black American culture. These were good years for Harlem, and not only because many Manhattan sophisticates discovered its night spots and jazz music; New York then seemed a land of opportunity and tolerance—no one expected integration then—for blacks. But the Depression of the 1930s hit Harlem hard, and in many ways it never recovered. A few middle-class pockets are still left here, in the apartment complexes built along the Harlem River or at the edge of Morningside Heights. But most of Harlem is very poor and culturally disorganized, plagued by crime and drugs, the kind of place people leave if they get a chance. For all the concentration on Harlem's problems, many of its onetime residents have figured out how to solve them, at least for their families—they got out and moved to more comfortable, spread-out, safer, and socially less disorganized neighborhoods in the outer boroughs or the suburbs. And so there are 200,000 fewer people in Harlem than there were 20 years ago. There are now more blacks in southeast Queens than there are in Harlem, and many more in Brooklyn's large black neighborhoods; nor have Harlem's cultural institutions or places of entertainment retained their central role in black life. Harlem is a place American blacks have outgrown, without entirely replacing.

Harlem has had its own congressional district since 1944—a district whose size has had to expand every 10 years because it has been losing population. The present 16th district, centered on Harlem, includes, on the east, all the Puerto Rican (once Italian) neighborhood of East Harlem and, on the west, dips down into the Upper West Side almost as far as Zabar's delicatessen at 80th Street and includes Columbia University, most of Morningside Heights (an academic neighborhood), virtually all of Washington Heights (once Jewish, now mostly Puerto Rican), and the Inwood neighborhood at the northern tip of Manhattan (still mostly Irish). Less than a majority, 49%, of its residents are black; they are almost outnumbered by the 38% who are of Spanish origin (though many fall into both categories).

In the 40 years it has formed the nucleus of a congressional district, Harlem has had only two congressmen: Adam Clayton Powell and Charles Rangel. Powell was an accomplished legislator, an able chairman of the Education and Labor Committee during the years the Great Society and antipoverty laws were passed through it; he was one of the most eloquent—and most flawed—black leaders of his generation. He was ousted from the House in 1967—the Supreme Court later ruled the procedure illegal—because of outrage over payroll-padding charges. Powell believed, with some justice, that voters were far more outraged when he did such things than when white congressmen did them; still, why did he have to? Powell won two elections afterwards but never really returned to Congress. He lost the 1970 primary to 40-year-old Charles Rangel, a four-year veteran of the New York Assembly.

Rangel is book smart and street smart, an instinctive politician with a New York accent and a good sense of humor. He served on the Judiciary Committee during the Nixon impeachment hearings; a year later he was politically adept enough to get Hugh Carey's seat on Ways and Means when Carey became governor. He now chairs the Oversight Subcommittee. He has solidly liberal voting records and has made constructive contributions to legislation.

If Rangel is not as famous as Powell, he is not as notorious either. You could make the case that he is more powerful than Powell ever was, because he can influence other members; Powell, operating in a House with many racist members (his predecessor as committee chairman never called on him to ask questions at hearings), would have had difficulty doing that as well even if he had had a mellower temperament. Rangel survived the 1982 redistricting fairly well: some 30% of his constituents, mostly non-black, are new to him. But he has never had trouble winning votes in white precincts and seems likely to continue winning with ease.

The People Pop. 1980: 516,405, dn. 16.7% 1970–80; voting age pop. 381,724; 49% Black, 35% Span. orig., 1% Asian orig. 86% housing units rented. Median owner $37,800; renter $169. Households: 58% family, 34% with children, 28% married couples.

Presidential Vote

1980	Reagan (R) . . . . NA
	Carter (D) . . . . NA
	Anderson (I) . . . . NA

Rep. Charles B. Rangel (D) Elected 1970; b. June 11, 1930, New York City; home, New York City; NYU, B.S. 1957, St. John's U. Sch. of Law, LL.B. 1960; Roman Catholic.

Career Army, 1948–52; Asst. U.S. Atty., S. Dist. of NY, 1961; Legal Counsel, NYC Housing and Redevelopment Bd., Neighborhood Conservation Bureau; Gen. Counsel, Natl. Advisory Comm. on Selective Svc., 1966; NY Assembly, 1966–70.

Offices 2330 RHOB, 202-225-4365. Also 163 W. 125 St., New York 10027, 212-663-3900.

Committees *Ways and Means* (4th). Subcommittees: Health; Oversight (Chairman). *Select Committee on Narcotics Abuse and Control* (Chairman).

Group Ratings

	ADA	ACLU	COPE	CFA	LCV	LWV	NTU	NSI	COC	ACA	CSFC
1982	100	96	96	92	96	83	39	10	19	4	23
1981	95	—	93	79	81	—	35	—	6	5	20
1980	78	97	95	79	74	90	15	0	56	14	21

National Journal Ratings

	Economic		Foreign		Cultural	
1982	96%	(LIB)	91%	(LIB)	99%	(LIB)
	2%	(CONS)	8%	(CONS)	1%	(CONS)
1981	89%	(LIB)	92%	(LIB)	92%	(LIB)
	3%	(CONS)	2%	(CONS)	7%	(CONS)

Key Votes

1) Reagan 81 Budget AGN	5) Incr SS Rtmt Age AGN	9) Poor Pay Food Stamps AGN
2) Reagan 81 Tax Cut AGN	6) Saudi AWACS Sale AGN	10) Ban Crt Busing Order AGN
3) Bal Budget Amend AGN	7) $ for MX Missile AGN	11) Auto Local Content FOR
4) Gas & Road Tax FOR	8) Nerve Gas Prod AGN	12) Nuclear Arms Freeze FOR

Election Results

1982 general	Charles B. Rangel (D–R–L)	76,626	(97%)	($124,415)
1982 primary	Charles B. Rangel (D–R–L) unopposed			
1980 general	Charles B. Rangel (D–R–L)	84,062	(96%)	($90,344)

Campaign Contributions and Expenditures

1981-82		Direct Cont. 81-82		PACS brkdwn			
Receipts	$152,651	Indiv	$60,901	Agr	$500	Ideo	$2,950
Expend.	$124,415	PACS	$93,572	Bus	$46,962	Lbr	$25,935
Unspent	$48,883			Hlth	$16,150	Prof	$1,075

SEVENTEENTH DISTRICT

The 17th congressional district of New York follows the Hudson River from the southern tip of Manhattan to the Bronx–Westchester County line, with a salient eastward, across Van Cortlandt Park, to the middle-class Williamsbridge section of the Bronx. It covers most of the West Side of Manhattan, for years the funkiest part of New York City, with such neighborhoods as Hell's Kitchen and Greenwich Village. But now most of the district's residents—and certainly most of its voters—live in gentrified, middle- to upper-income neighborhoods. This is certainly the case with Greenwich Village, once a neighborhood of bohemian artists living uneasily among Italian immigrants. Now the accent is increasingly homosexual, and the professional and creative young singles living here have, thanks to high rents, been colonizing the once industrial or slum neighborhoods to the south—SoHo, Tribeca—living in airy lofts amid newly opening delicatessens and kicky restaurants. Similar gentrification is taking place north of the Village, in Chelsea, and in the Upper West Side blocks between Central Park West's wall of apartments on the Park and the roomy co-ops of West End Avenue and Riverside Drive. Ironically, the gentrification process produces vitriolic complaints from those who are responsible for it and who, if they really had to choose, would not want to live long in pregentrified neighborhoods; still they complain about rising rents, condominium conversions, commercialization of the streets, and the disappearance of the colorful poor people who were one of the attractions of the area in the first place.

Above 90th Street, the 17th district narrows to one block or, in many places, is only as wide as Riverside Park. In effect, this is a thin corridor attaching the portions of the Bronx added onto the district to meet the population requirement. One of these, Riverdale, is most un-Bronxish: a neighborhood of winding streets and mansions overlooking the Hudson. Williamsbridge, connected only by a park to the rest of the district, is one of the dwindling number of middle-class Jewish neighborhoods in the outer Bronx, with one- and two-family houses as well as apartments.

You can get a good idea of the political attitudes and tone that prevail in the 17th district by reading the *Village Voice*. The relatively affluent voters of the West Side pride themselves on their liberalism, or even radicalism; they seem fond of seeing themselves as part of an oppressed proletariat, exploited by greedy corporations, mad generals, and rapacious landlords.

Given their obvious affluence, this view is a little difficult to maintain; but in the 1970s their focus shifted from broad cultural to personal issues, from the nation to New York and finally to themselves. Even as the nation has become culturally more heterogeneous and tolerant, many voters here have a stake in viewing themselves as beleaguered because of their sexual preference or life-style: the *Voice* is filled now with shrieks of outrage from gays and lesbians and women's movement activists. The tolerance they have long been seeking through political means has been achieved to an extent almost no one foresaw; the validation they seem now to be demanding will probably never come. The result is frustration, and a turning away from politics by many voters; and the dominance of politics by quieter, more reflective veterans of the frenzied days of Vietnam war protests and vitriolic Democratic primaries.

That change is reflected in congressional politics. Once the West Side was rent by primary fights that broke up friendships and dominated conversation for months. But the current congressman from the 17th, Theodore Weiss, was first elected in 1976 without a primary at all and has had only nominal opposition from Republicans since. Weiss is a veteran of the reform movement—that political rebellion of gentrifying professionals against the often corrupt hacks who, with the aid of immigrant and stew-bum votes, controlled Manhattan's Democratic Party for years—and was elected to the City Council as long ago as 1961. He ran two unsuccessful races against Leonard Farbstein in 1966 and 1968, and by the time Bella Abzug retired from the House to run for the Senate in 1976, he was well established as the West Side's tribune. Weiss has an impeccably liberal voting record. He is a member of the Education and Labor and Government Operations Committees, a competent congressman but one who, primarily because of his ideological views, seems unlikely to be of major influence in the House. The addition of portions of the Bronx to the district put Weiss in the same district with 18-year Bronx Congressman Jonathan Bingham, but Bingham graciously retired, and Weiss won that election easily. He should have no trouble winning reelection in the 1980s.

The People Pop. 1980: 516,239, up .3% 1970–80; voting age pop. 442,060; 14% Black, 13% Span. orig., 3% Asian orig. 86% housing units rented. Median owner $51,800; renter $271. Households: 39% family, 16% with children, 28% married couples.

Presidential Vote

1980	Reagan (R)	NA
	Carter (D)	NA
	Anderson (I)	NA

Rep. Theodore S. (Ted) Weiss (D) Elected 1976; b. Sept. 17, 1927, Gava, Hungary; home, New York City; Syracuse U., B.A. 1951, LL.B. 1952; Jewish.

Career Army, 1946–47; Practicing atty., 1953–76; Asst. Dist. Atty., NY Cnty., 1955–59; NYC Cncl., 1961–77; Candidate for Dem. Nomination for U.S House of Reps., 1966, 1968.

Offices 2442 RHOB, 202-225-5635. Also 720 Columbus Ave., New York 10025, 212-850-1500.

Committees *Foreign Affairs* (23d). Subcommittees: Africa; Human Rights and International Organizations. *Government Operations* (9th). Subcommittee: Intergovernmental Relations and Human Resources (Chairman). *Select Committee on Children, Youth, and Families* (8th).

Group Ratings

	ADA	ACLU	COPE	CFA	LCV	LWV	NTU	NSI	COC	ACA	CSFC
1982	90	100	92	85	94	90	44	0	24	10	23
1981	100	—	91	86	93	—	46	—	5	8	26
1980	100	100	89	93	87	100	24	0	53	22	20

National Journal Ratings

	Economic		Foreign		Cultural	
1982	89%	(LIB)	88%	(LIB)	93%	(LIB)
	10%	(CONS)	12%	(CONS)	7%	(CONS)
1981	89%	(LIB)	92%	(LIB)	95%	(LIB)
	3%	(CONS)	2%	(CONS)	1%	(CONS)

Key Votes

1) Reagan 81 Budget	AGN	5) Incr SS Rtmt Age AGN
2) Reagan 81 Tax Cut	AGN	6) Saudi AWACS Sale AGN
3) Bal Budget Amend	AGN	7) $ for MX Missile AGN
4) Gas & Road Tax	FOR	8) Nerve Gas Prod AGN

9) Poor Pay Food Stamps AGN
10) Ban Crt Busing Order AGN
11) Auto Local Content   FOR
12) Nuclear Arms Freeze   FOR

Election Results

1982 general	Theodore S. (Ted) Weiss (D–L) ...	113,172	(85%)	($56,613)
	Louis S. Antonelli (R–C–RTL) ...	19,928	(15%)	($0)
1982 primary	Theodore S. (Ted) Weiss (D–L) unopposed			
1980 general (NY 20)	Theodore S. (Ted) Weiss (D–L) ...	86,454	(82%)	($32,092)
	James E. Greene (R)	15,350	(15%)	($0)
1980 general (NY 22)	Jonathan B. Bingham (D–L)	66,301	(84%)	($6,722)
	Robert Black (R)	9,943	(13%)	($0)

Campaign Contributions and Expenditures

1981-82		Direct Cont. 81-82			PACS brkdwn			
Receipts	$71,527	Indiv	$40,007	Agr	$—	Ideo	$3,700
Expend.	$56,613	PACS	$29,197	Bus	$2,200	Lbr	$22,125
Unspent	$21,330			Hlth	$250	Prof	$200

EIGHTEENTH DISTRICT

The 18th congressional district of New York is centered on the South Bronx, which may have become the nation's most famous slum in the 1970s. Presidential candidates trudge through here every four years, their mouths agape as they look at the destroyed buildings and mouth the inevitable comparison with Berlin after the war. The evidence of the arson that has become widespread in the South Bronx is there for all to see; so are abandoned buildings; so are boarded up or vandalized stores. Candidates for president, governor, senator, and mayor all promise to do something for the South Bronx; but nothing much ever gets done. Meanwhile, the people of the South Bronx continue to vote with their feet. During the 1970s, the 18th district lost 37% of its population—the biggest population loss of any congressional district in the country. Social scientists and politicians admonish the rest of the nation that there are South Bronxes all over, waiting to happen. Yet the history of the South Bronx suggests that this is a peculiar New York situation, and that it may not represent as much human misery as first appears.

The South Bronx was settled in a rush. Most of its housing was built in the years between 1906 and 1917, when the newly built subways opened up the Bronx to settlement by the hundreds of thousands of immigrants then jammed into Lower Manhattan. By the late 1960s most of these original Italian, Irish, and Jewish settlers were elderly; their children had long since been dispersed, and they were dying or moving out. Moving in—again in a rush—were blacks and Puerto Ricans who could not find housing in the more stable communities of Harlem or Upper Manhattan. Nearly half the people in the South Bronx in 1970 were under 18, many of them in large fatherless families. With no community institutions and little parental supervision, these teenagers committed hundreds of crimes every day, with relatively little risk of being caught. Arson became an increasingly common crime, committed by kids for kicks or on behalf of landlords who decided they would never get a return on their building any other way. Historically, the South Bronx was a place for New Yorkers in low-wage jobs—the low-wage economy that helped so many immigrants move upward in the years from 1906 to the 1960s. But low-wage jobs largely disappeared from New York City in the 1970s. Union demands, high minimum wages, and high costs of doing business generally in New York have led low-wage employers to take their businesses to the places where the most recent workers have come from, the southeastern states and Puerto Rico. The migrants who had moved to the South Bronx were left to welfare, which tends to split families. In no other part of America have so many low-wage jobs been lost so fast; and nowhere else is there a community as large that was as suddenly depopulated as the South Bronx was in the 1970s.

For this was not an area which showed signs of incipient rapid decline as late as 1970. In the 1960s the population of the area within the current 18th district—which includes the Grand Concourse area up to Fordham University as well as the South Bronx proper—stayed essentially steady; there was lots of movement in and out, but none of the kind of population loss that signals social disorganization and abandonment of a neighborhood to teenage criminals. But in the 1970s the 18th district's population fell from 821,000 to 514,000. What happened? First, most of the elderly immigrants simply moved out, either farther in the Bronx, to the suburbs, or to Florida. Second, many of the blacks and Puerto Ricans moved out as well—or outward from the South Bronx to the Concourse area. Programs which are aimed at revitalizing the South Bronx ignore the fact that most of the people who could help do that have already left the area, for safer and more stable neighborhoods elsewhere. And many poor people seem to have left as well. New York's welfare payments were frozen for seven years after 1974, and it must have occurred to even the most sluggish welfare recipient after a while that they might be better off back in North Carolina or Puerto Rico, where there are more jobs and better living conditions for low-income people. Puerto Ricans, in particular, seem to have moved back to Puerto Rico. It is relatively easy, after all, to get back and forth, on midnight 747s; and Puerto Ricans in the Bronx have always retained their interest in and identification with Puerto Rican culture. The San Juan newspapers have much higher circulation here than do New York's Spanish language newspapers; Puerto Ricans on the mainland follow Puerto Rico politics closely and with considerable fervor, but seldom vote in New York elections. As a result, the 18th district has the lowest voter turnout in the United States—even though the turnout of Puerto Ricans in Puerto Rico is higher than turnout in any American state.

So the depopulation of the South Bronx may make a certain amount of sense: there are no—or not very many—people who want to live here any more. Working-class Americans who make decent livings do not want to live in such close quarters where they have no community ties. No one but criminals want to live where the police are unable to guarantee public safety. The government would probably do well not to build housing here but to help develop sites for light industry and warehousing. The South Bronx is actually well located: right on main trucking lines, with access to rail spurs, not far from airports and port facilities.

The current congressman from the 18th is Robert Garcia, a Democrat first elected in a 1978 special election. Garcia actually lost the Democratic nomination in the special, but won the election as a Republican while making it clear that he would vote as a Democrat in the House. Ironically, in light of his district's population loss, he chairs the Census and Population Subcommittee of the Post Office Committee; he also serves on Foreign Affairs (although apparently only temporarily) and Banking, Finance and Urban Affairs. Garcia's record on most issues is resolutely liberal. He is the primary co-sponsor, with Jack Kemp, of the plan to create urban enterprise zones—one with obvious application to the South Bronx.

Redistricting might have given Garcia trouble; his old district lost literally half its population in the 1970s. But the New York legislature was apparently eager to retain at least one identifiably Puerto Rican seat, and this was it. So they added to the South Bronx the Grand Concourse area and some blocks east of the South Bronx along Bruckner Boulevard— essentially the places where many residents of the South Bronx had been moving. This new 18th district reelected him easily, and he seems likely to hold onto this seat throughout the 1980s.

The People Pop. 1980: 518,106, dn. 37.0% 1970–80; voting age pop. 328,326; 44% Black, 48% Span. orig., 1% Asian orig. 72% housing units rented. Median owner $35,200; renter $177. Households: 70% family, 50% with children, 31% married couples.

Presidential Vote

1980	Reagan (R)	NA
	Carter (D)	NA
	Anderson (I)	NA

Rep. Robert Garcia (D) Elected Feb. 14, 1978; b. Jan. 9, 1933, New York City; home, Bronx; CCNY; Pentecostal.

Career Army, Korea; Computer engineer, 1957–65; NY Assembly, 1965–67; NY Senate, 1967–78.

Offices 223 CHOB, 202-225-4361. Also 840 Grand Concourse, Bronx 10451, 212-860-6200.

Committees *Banking, Finance and Urban Affairs* (16th). Subcommittees: Financial Institutions Supervision, Regulation and Insurance; General Oversight and Renegotiation; Housing and Community Development; International Development Institutions and Finance. *Foreign Affairs* (24th). Subcommittee: Western Hemisphere Affairs. *Post Office and Civil Service* (5th). Subcommittees: Census and Population (Chairman); Compensation and Employee Benefits.

Group Ratings

	ADA	ACLU	COPE	CFA	LCV	LWV	NTU	NSI	COC	ACA	CSFC
1982	95	92	95	77	87	78	44	0	24	5	25
1981	70	—	94	64	79	—	26	—	0	5	20
1980	72	90	94	79	67	100	16	0	46	14	18

National Journal Ratings

	Economic		Foreign		Cultural	
1982	94%	(LIB)	85%	(LIB)	87%	(LIB)
	5%	(CONS)	12%	(CONS)	13%	(CONS)
1981	99%	(LIB)	99%	(LIB)	86%	(LIB)
	1%	(CONS)	1%	(CONS)	14%	(CONS)

Key Votes

1) Reagan 81 Budget	AGN	5) Incr SS Rtmt Age	AGN	9) Poor Pay Food Stamps	AGN
2) Reagan 81 Tax Cut	AGN	6) Saudi AWACS Sale	—	10) Ban Crt Busing Order	AGN
3) Bal Budget Amend	AGN	7) $ for MX Missile	AGN	11) Auto Local Content	FOR
4) Gas & Road Tax	FOR	8) Nerve Gas Prod	AGN	12) Nuclear Arms Freeze	FOR

Election Results

1982 general	Robert Garcia (D–R–L)	57,009	(99%)	($333,631)
1982 primary	Robert Garcia (D–R–L) unopposed			
1980 general	Robert Garcia (D–R–L)	32,173	(98%)	($115,310)

Campaign Contributions and Expenditures

1981-82		Direct Cont. 81-82		PACS brkdwn			
Receipts	$316,204	Indiv	$158,569	Agr	$500	Ideo	$1,745
Expend.	$333,631	PACS	$81,912	Bus	$38,725	Lbr	$35,950
Unspent	$141	Cand	$60,000	Hlth	$1,450	Prof	$1,400

NINETEENTH DISTRICT

The 19th congressional district of New York includes most of the East Bronx (though the boundary is so convoluted it is hard to give the area one name) and most of the city of Yonkers in Westchester County. This is a modest part of New York City, an area usually bypassed by visitors as they speed by on the Thruway or the parkways to Manhattan. The 19th is not a poverty-stricken area, but it is not rich either; about one-quarter of its residents are homeowners, but even renters in two-family houses and small apartments have a kind of pride of ownership which is apparent in the way they maintain their homes. Yet the buildings themselves are, like so many buildings in New York, built in the cheapest way with the cheapest materials possible, occupying the maximum space allowed by the zoning code.

Most of the 19th's neighborhoods are older, occupied by the offspring of Italian and other early 20th-century immigrants; this common background unites the geographically disparate and barely connected areas around Fordham University, in the East Bronx above Eastchester Bay, and in the northern extremity of the borough. Much of its portion of Yonkers is similar. The 19th also includes Co-op City, where 35 35-story towers (that's not a misprint) were erected on landfill surrounded by two limited access highways; the rents are low (and naturally tenants yelped and staged a rent strike when asked to pay for the rise in maintenance costs), the crime of the South Bronx seems far away, and, eventually, the whole area was connected to New York's transportation system. Here came many of the old residents of the Grand Concourse and other parts of the Bronx.

The congressman from the 19th district is, by now, a veteran of the House: Mario Biaggi. His background is similar to that of many of his constituents, except that he has been more accomplished and successful. He was a police officer for 23 years, and when he retired he was the most decorated officer in the New York police force. He was an attorney—he finished law school at night, like so many ambitious city employees in New York—but his real interest was politics. When a Republican congressman from the East Bronx retired, Biaggi was easily elected to succeed him. As a kind of urban populist with a law and order accent, he was the favorite in the 1973 mayor race; he had the Conservative nomination and seemed likely to win the Democratic. But in April 1973 newspapers charged that Biaggi had lied when he said he had not taken the Fifth Amendment before a grand jury. Brazenly Biaggi sued to get some, but not all, of the grand jury records made public; the judge, not to be toyed with, revealed them all. They showed that Biaggi was lying, and his law-and-order candidacy collapsed.

Nevertheless, that episode did not end his congressional career. Indeed, he has not had serious opposition in House elections since then—although the Conservatives, who bent their principles to endorse him in 1973 and then were stuck with him as their candidate in the general election, have not given him their endorsement since. Biaggi is now the number two Democrat on the Merchant Marine and Fisheries Committee, on which he is an enthusiastic supporter of huge subsidies to U.S. shipping companies and members of the tiny maritime unions, some of whom vote in his district. He was the lead sponsor of the maritime bill that passed the House in 1982 and that, if it had been enacted, would have extended the rights of shipping companies to fix prices. Biaggi has a strong ethnic Italian following, and he has also wooed Irish voters by vocally supporting groups sympathetic to the terrorist Irish Republican Army—groups that have been repudiated sternly by Irish-American politicians Tip O'Neill, Edward Kennedy, Daniel Patrick Moynihan, and Hugh Carey.

On the Education and Labor Committee, and on economic issues generally, Biaggi has voted generally against the Reagan administration and on occasion has sternly denounced it. Even on cultural issues his record is fairly liberal, and not far out of line with those of other New York City representatives. He is a leading advocate of banning bullets which can penetrate bullet-proof vests—a measure aimed at protecting policemen, but which is nonetheless opposed by the gun lobby. A question remains whether Biaggi sometimes is just showboating on some issues, hoping to attract public support. Though past 65, he probably thinks wistfully of the year when he seemed on his way to being elected mayor of New York, and perhaps he thinks somehow it can happen again. The more likely prospect is that he will continue his House career, and concentrate on serving the maritime interests which will surely rally to his support should he ever have significant electoral opposition.

The People Pop. 1980: 511,802, up 1.4% 1970–80; voting age pop. 394,974; 11% Black, 13% Span. orig., 1% Asian orig. 71% housing units rented. Median owner $57,800; renter $219. Households: 69% family, 32% with children, 50% married couples.

Presidential Vote

1980	Reagan (R)	NA
	Carter (D)	NA
	Anderson (I)	NA

Rep. Mario Biaggi (D) Elected 1968; b. Oct. 16, 1917, New York City; home, Bronx; NY Law Sch., LL.B. 1963; Roman Catholic.

Career Letter carrier, U.S.P.O., 1936–42; NY City Police Dept., 1942–65; Community Relations Specialist, NY Div. of Housing, 1961–63; Asst. to the NY Secy. of State, 1961–65; Practicing atty., 1966–; Pres., Natl. Police Officers Assn., 1967.

Offices 2428 RHOB, 202-225-2464. Also 2004 Williamsbridge Rd., Bronx 10461, 212-931-0100.

Committees *Education and Labor* (7th). Subcommittees: Elementary, Secondary and Vocational Education; Employment Opportunities; Select Education. *Merchant Marine and Fisheries* (2d). Subcommittees: Coast Guard and Navigation; Merchant Marine (Chairman). *Select Committee on Aging* (3d). Subcommittee: Human Services (Chairman).

Group Ratings

	ADA	ACLU	COPE	CFA	LCV	LWV	NTU	NSI	COC	ACA	CSFC
1982	75	54	86	69	79	60	11	50	20	10	32
1981	45	—	85	64	62	—	14	—	21	24	37
1980	50	47	82	64	34	70	14	67	61	15	29

National Journal Ratings

	Economic		Foreign		Cultural	
1982	92%	(LIB)	64%	(LIB)	64%	(LIB)
	7%	(CONS)	36%	(CONS)	36%	(CONS)
1981	65%	(LIB)	59%	(LIB)	69%	(LIB)
	35%	(CONS)	41%	(CONS)	31%	(CONS)

Key Votes

1) Reagan 81 Budget	AGN	5) Incr SS Rtmt Age	AGN	9) Poor Pay Food Stamps	AGN
2) Reagan 81 Tax Cut	FOR	6) Saudi AWACS Sale	AGN	10) Ban Crt Busing Order	—
3) Bal Budget Amend	AGN	7) $ for MX Missile	AGN	11) Auto Local Content	FOR
4) Gas & Road Tax	—	8) Nerve Gas Prod	AGN	12) Nuclear Arms Freeze	FOR

Election Results

1982 general	Mario Biaggi (D–R–L)	118,803	(94%)	($217,070 est.)
	Michael J. McSherry (C)	7,438	(6%)	($0)
1982 primary	Mario Biaggi (D–R–L) unopposed			
1980 general	Mario Biaggi (D–R–L)	95,322	(94%)	($44,707)

Campaign Contributions and Expenditures

1981-82		Direct Cont. 81-82		PACS brkdwn			
Receipts	$291,940 (est.)	Indiv	$146,070	Agr	$700	Ideo	$1,200
Expend.	$217,070 (est.)	Party	$52,606	Bus	$33,059	Lbr	$53,100
Unspent	$97,742	PACS	$92,181	Hlth	$2,500	Prof	$1,500

TWENTIETH DISTRICT

The conventional wisdom has it that New York's Westchester County is *the* suburb for the wealthy: not only the super-rich like the Rockefellers of Pocantico Hills but also the ordinary rich, the people who own those large, comfortable houses in Scarsdale and White Plains, with their gently sloping lawns shaded by towering trees; or the glassy contemporary houses in the woodsier hills of Harrison, Pound Ridge, Armonk (IBM's headquarters), and Briarcliff Manor. All of these places are in New York's 20th congressional district, which includes most of Westchester County. But the conventional wisdom about Westchester and the 20th district is not entirely accurate. Plenty of rich people do live here. But by no means are all the suburbs here havens for the rich. Most Westchester residents live in rather modest, if pleasant and mellow, houses which date back from before World War II and can be had for prices which a Californian would consider unbelievably low. For Westchester has aged, and if that gives a nice patina to the high-income suburbs, it also means that some of the other towns have problems today which look suspiciously similar to those of many American central cities.

The 20th district includes all of eastern Westchester facing Long Island Sound, from the ethnic neighborhoods of Mount Vernon, through the rich, Catholic, and very conservative suburbs of Pelham, Eastchester, and Bronxville, up through rich, Jewish, and liberal Scarsdale, and the New Haven Railroad commuter towns of New Rochelle, Larchmont, Mamaroneck, and Rye. Just above them is White Plains, the county seat and headquarters of several major companies; the 20th also includes part of the city of Yonkers, on the Hudson. North of White Plains, the county looks more rural, sometimes because of minimum zoning requirements in more higher-income suburbs (Pleasantville, Chappaqua), sometimes because it reaches out to include old towns settled as long ago as New York, like Washington Irving's Tarrytown and the late John Cheever's Ossining.

The 20th district may be the heartland of liberal Republicanism; for a dozen years it was represented by Ogden Reid, heir to the *New York Herald Tribune*. Yet in the 1960s and 1970s it became more Democratic (and Reid himself became a Democrat before he retired to run for governor in 1974). Two different trends produced a similar political effect: the leftward movement of upper-income voters in response to cultural issues like civil rights and foreign issues like Vietnam and the movement into Westchester of blacks, Puerto Ricans, and ethnic New Yorkers who grew up taking Democratic voting habits for granted.

These two trends have helped to fashion the by-now quite lengthy congressional career of Richard Ottinger. Heir to a plywood fortune, Ottinger worked as a Peace Corps regional director during the Kennedy years. He returned to Westchester to run for Congress, and had the good fortune to run in the Goldwater year against a Republican who spent most of his time in California (and later ran for Congress there, in two different districts). He held onto the seat for six years, then ran for the Senate in 1970; spending more than $2 million of family money, he nearly won, but in a three-way race lost to Conservative James Buckley. After an unsuccessful comeback attempt in 1972 (against Peter Peyser, who later turned Democrat and lost in the 22d district in 1982), Ottinger won in 1974 when Reid retired. He has held the seat ever since, never facing really strong challengers but always facing more than nuisance candidates.

Ottinger was one of the earliest environmentalists in Congress and is an important one today. Although his seniority dates only from 1974, he is third ranking Democrat on the Energy and Commerce Committee, the body which sets much regulatory law and which was the most sought-after committee assignment after the 1982 election. He chairs the Energy Conservation and Power Subcommittee, which has jurisdiction over energy conservation programs, solar energy, and nuclear power. On all these Ottinger is an adversary of the Reagan administration: he is a proponent of solar energy and government conservation programs, a skeptic toward nuclear power. As a high-ranking member of the Science and Technology Committee, he is in another good position to advance some of these views, notably his opposition to nuclear power schemes like the Clinch River breeder reactor.

Ottinger has not always been successful in his efforts. He was one of the leading opponents of the deregulation of oil and gas prices—a policy that seems today not only beneficial but necessary. He was beaten for the chairmanship of the Democratic Study Group in 1979. And his margins in his home district have not been huge. A reasonably well-financed Republican held him to 56% of the vote in 1982—less than his 1980 performance, contrary to the national trend. Westchester has moved toward the Democrats, but not enough to give Ottinger a safe seat. Still in his early 50s, he has the potential to be a very important House member indeed—perhaps chairman of Energy and Commerce—but he will always have to tend carefully to his Westchester constituency.

The People Pop. 1980: 521,203, dn. 5.0% 1970–80; voting age pop. 392,174; 14% Black, 5% Span. orig., 2% Asian orig. 48% housing units rented. Median owner $91,900; renter $272. Households: 73% family, 36% with children, 59% married couples.

Presidential Vote

1980	Reagan (R)	104,473	(52%)
	Carter (D)	80,285	(40%)
	Anderson (I)	17,897	(9%)

Rep. Richard L. Ottinger (D) Elected 1974; b. Jan. 27, 1929, New York City; home, Pleasantville; Cornell U., B.A. 1950, Harvard U., LL.B. 1953, International Law Study, Georgetown U., 1960–61; Jewish.

Career Practicing atty., 1955–60, 1972–74; Internatl. corp. contract mgr., 1960–61; Cofounder, 2d Staff Mbr. and Dir., Program for the West Coast of South America, Peace Corps, 1961–64; U.S. House of Reps., 1965–71; Dem. Nominee for U.S. Senate, 1970; Organizer, Grassroots Action, Inc., nonprofit consumer and environmental assistance org., 1971–72.

Offices 2241 RHOB, 202-225-6506. Also 10 Fiske Pl., Mt. Vernon 10550, 914-699-2866.

Committees *Energy and Commerce* (3d). Subcommittees: Energy Conservation and Power (Chairman); Health and the Environment. *Science and Technology* (5th). Subcommittees: Energy Development and Applications; Energy Research and Production; Transportation, Aviation and Materials.

Group Ratings

	ADA	ACLU	COPE	CFA	LCV	LWV	NTU	NSI	COC	ACA	CSFC
1982	95	92	89	100	96	92	36	0	23	4	24
1981	100	—	88	93	100	—	41	—	11	13	25
1980	94	100	95	93	84	89	18	0	58	13	21

National Journal Ratings

	Economic		Foreign		Cultural	
1982	76%	(LIB)	80%	(LIB)	93%	(LIB)
	24%	(CONS)	20%	(CONS)	3%	(CONS)
1981	89%	(LIB)	92%	(LIB)	87%	(LIB)
	3%	(CONS)	2%	(CONS)	12%	(CONS)

Key Votes

1) Reagan 81 Budget AGN	5) Incr SS Rtmt Age AGN	9) Poor Pay Food Stamps AGN
2) Reagan 81 Tax Cut AGN	6) Saudi AWACS Sale AGN	10) Ban Crt Busing Order AGN
3) Bal Budget Amend AGN	7) $ for MX Missile AGN	11) Auto Local Content FOR
4) Gas & Road Tax —	8) Nerve Gas Prod AGN	12) Nuclear Arms Freeze FOR

Election Results

1982 general	Richard L. Ottinger (D)	98,425	(56%)	($224,143)
	Jon S. Fossel (R–C)	72,005	(41%)	($439,226)
1982 primary	Richard L. Ottinger (D) unopposed			
1980 general	Richard L. Ottinger (D)	100,182	(59%)	($69,281)
	Joseph W. Christiana (R–C–RTL)	66,689	(40%)	($32,179)

Campaign Contributions and Expenditures

1981-82		*Direct Cont. 81-82*				*PACS brkdwn*		
Receipts	$235,276	Indiv	$123,999	Agr	$1,000		Ideo	$17,890
Expend.	$224,143	Party	$1,010	Bus	$10,050		Lbr	$51,050
Unspent	$11,133	PACS	$89,499	Hlth	$3,300		Prof	$100
		Cand	$5,000					

TWENTY-FIRST DISTRICT

The 21st congressional district of New York occupies the Lower Hudson Valley, the place where metropolitan New York ends and Upstate New York begins. The boundary is not really clear. The 21st includes northern Westchester County, with its large estates in towns like Bedford Hills and the much more modest subdivisions-*cum*-shopping centers that have sprung up around expressway interchanges there and just to the north, in Putnam County and across the Hudson in Orange County as well. Thus the district houses some of New York's richest and most prominent people, but they are outnumbered increasingly by the offspring of early 20th-century immigrants—white-collar workers in Westchester office headquarters, policemen and firemen in New York City—who have been fleeing the outer borough neighborhoods they grew up in, seeking a quieter place to raise their families, one where their children will be educated in schools where tradition is respected and prohibitions against drug use firmly enforced. These new residents, far from bringing Democratic voting habits from the city, have made the Lower Hudson area one of the most Republican parts of New York state.

Interspersed with this extension of New York City are the old Upstate communities of the Hudson Valley. The Hudson was first settled by Dutch patroons—the Schuylers, the van Rensselaers, the van Cortlandts, the Roosevelts—who owned most of this land in a kind of feudal system even after the Revolution. They prospered in the 19th century by pursuing their business investments in the city on weekdays and steaming up the Hudson to their estates on weekends. Above the point where the river threads its way through a mountain at West Point, the old river towns of the patroon days became small industrial cities in the 19th century: later, Newburgh, Beacon, and Poughkeepsie didn't grow much and they still show their age. These towns and the countryside on either side of the river have always been heavily Republican. Like most of Upstate, they have been suspicious of the financial demands and cultural predilections of the City, and have consistently opposed the Democratic Party which New York City residents have favored since the days of Andrew Jackson.

That makes the 21st a solidly Republican. It is represented today by the holder of a distinguished Hudson Valley name, Hamilton Fish. Hamilton Fishes have been representing New York in Congress since 1842, and one Hamilton Fish was secretary of state under President Grant. The current Hamilton Fish's father served in the House for 24 years, and was one of the most acerbic critics of his longtime constituent, Franklin D. Roosevelt; Fish, Sr., was finally defeated, with the help of redistricting, in 1944.

The current Hamilton Fish fits into a different place on our political spectrum (although both he and his father, who was still alive and active in 1983, were skeptical of U.S. Vietnam policy). Congressman Fish tends to take conservative views on economic issues, though not invariably; he tends to be somewhat liberal on cultural issues. He is now the ranking Republican on the House Judiciary Committee, a body which handles—or refuses to act on—some of the most controversial issues of the 1980s. Undoubtedly many on the New Right dislike the part Fish often takes, for he agrees and cooperates with Chairman Peter Rodino on many of them. He is nonetheless an opponent of abortion, and has introduced his own legislation against it.

Fish was first elected in 1968, after a career in the Foreign Service and service in Dutchess County civic affairs. One of his opponents in the Republican primary, incidentally, was then local Assistant D.A. G. Gordon Liddy, Jr., of Watergate fame; Fish was one of the House Judiciary Committee Republicans who voted to impeach Richard Nixon. Fish had serious opposition in the 1968 general election and, through two redistrictings, has held onto the seat easily ever since.

The People Pop. 1980: 516,778, up 11.3% 1970–80; voting age pop. 365,060; 6% Black, 3% Span. orig., 1% Asian orig. 29% housing units rented. Median owner $56,600; renter $234. Households: 78% family, 45% with children, 66% married couples.

Presidential Vote

1980	Reagan (R)	116,342	(60%)
	Carter (D)	60,257	(31%)
	Anderson (I)	17,147	(9%)

Rep. Hamilton Fish, Jr. (R) Elected 1968; b. June 3, 1926, Washington, DC; home, Millbrook; Harvard U., A.B. 1949, NYU, LL.B. 1957; Episcopal.

Career Navy, WWII; Practicing atty.; Vice Consul, U.S. Foreign Svc., Ireland, 1951–53; Counsel, NY Assembly Judiciary Comm., 1961; Dutchess Cnty. Civil Defense Dir., 1967–68.

Offices 2227 RHOB, 202-225-5441. Also 82 Washington St., Poughkeepsie 12601, 914-452-4220.

Committees *Judiciary* (Ranking Member). Subcommittee: Monopolies and Commercial Law. *Select Committee on Children, Youth, and Families* (2d).

Group Ratings

	ADA	ACLU	COPE	CFA	LCV	LWV	NTU	NSI	COC	ACA	CSFC
1982	45	67	44	54	68	75	44	89	33	55	43
1981	50	—	43	71	71	—	46	—	78	42	50
1980	61	63	41	50	70	70	34	67	68	52	51

National Journal Ratings

	Economic		Foreign		Cultural	
1982	56%	(LIB)	43%	(LIB)	66%	(LIB)
	44%	(CONS)	56%	(CONS)	34%	(CONS)
1981	40%	(LIB)	62%	(LIB)	77%	(LIB)
	59%	(CONS)	37%	(CONS)	23%	(CONS)

Key Votes

1) Reagan 81 Budget	FOR	5) Incr SS Rtmt Age	FOR	9) Poor Pay Food Stamps	AGN
2) Reagan 81 Tax Cut	FOR	6) Saudi AWACS Sale	AGN	10) Ban Crt Busing Order	AGN
3) Bal Budget Amend	FOR	7) $ for MX Missile	FOR	11) Auto Local Content	FOR
4) Gas & Road Tax	—	8) Nerve Gas Prod	AGN	12) Nuclear Arms Freeze	AGN

Election Results

1982 general	Hamilton Fish, Jr. (R–C)	117,460	(75%)	($137,556)
	J. Morgan Strong (D)	38,664	(25%)	($0)
1982 primary	Hamilton Fish, Jr. (R–C) unopposed			
1980 general	Hamilton Fish, Jr. (R–C)	158,936	(81%)	($91,455)
	Gunars M. Ozols (D)	37,369	(19%)	($0)

Campaign Contributions and Expenditures

1981-82		Direct Cont. 81-82		PACS brkdwn			
Receipts	$127,316	Indiv	$74,958	Agr	$500	Ideo	$1,700
Expend.	$137,556	Party	$8,654	Bus	$28,550	Lbr	$4,270
Unspent	$19,295	PACS	$39,770	Hlth	$3,250	Prof	$1,450

TWENTY-SECOND DISTRICT

The 22d congressional district of New York proceeds from a point a few miles from the New York City limit some 120 miles along the state's borders with New Jersey and Pennsylvania. It crosses the Hudson River and is striped by several mountain ridges running from northeast to southwest. Even so, the influence of New York City is never far away. The district includes part of Westchester County—the comfortable, long-settled suburbs along the Hudson where Washington Irving once lived and which he wrote about, Hastings-on-Hudson, Irvington, Dobbs Ferry, and Tarrytown. Across the Tappan Zee Bridge—the name is what the Dutch called the wide part of the Hudson here—is Rockland County, a triangle bounded by the Hudson, New Jersey, and the Ramapo Mountains. Rockland filled up with people in the 30 years after World War II; it has a few elite neighborhoods, but is mostly the home of the comfortable Jewish and Protestant middle class.

Past the Ramapos, you are in Upstate, in Orange County—a part of Upstate whose population has been swelled for 20 years by people from New York City, many of them policemen, firemen, teachers, and other civil servants; they talk of wanting to protect their children from contact with the horrors of the city even as they congratulate themselves quietly for dealing with them. Farther out, past the Shawangunk Mountains, is Sullivan County, the heart of the Catskills Borscht Belt resort district, part of which is in the 22d district. This is one of the few predominantly Jewish non-metropolitan areas in the United States, and has been a Jewish resort area, with huge kosher hotels, since before the turn of the century. Politically, this is a district that usually goes Republican, but not always by huge margins. Westchester has been trending toward the Democrats, Rockland and Sullivan

Counties are usually closely divided in close statewide races. Only Orange County delivers large Republican majorities.

This is one of five New York districts which had two incumbents in 1982, Democrat Peter Peyser and Republican Benjamin Gilman. Both are Jewish, and both were originally elected as liberal Republicans, Peyser in 1970 and Gilman in 1972. But their careers took different courses, and as much, one suspects, because of temperament as because of differences on issues. Peyser left his House seat to run a quixotic primary campaign against Senator James Buckley in 1976, on the grounds that Buckley was insufficiently liberal—though the Republican primary electorate is heavily conservative. Then he became a Democrat and recaptured the seat when the Republican who replaced him ran for lieutenant governor in 1978. In 1981 and 1982 Peyser was one of the most vitriolic critics of the Reagan cutbacks; at a time when many other Democrats were confused and equivocal, Peyser spoke with the fervor of the convert.

Gilman, in contrast, is quieter, easier to get on with, and less likely to make waves. As a member of the Foreign Affairs Committee, he is a strong supporter of Israel; he is ranking Republican on Dante Fascell's International Operations Subcommittee, in 1983 leaving the ranking spot on the more controversial Western Hemisphere Affairs. On foreign affairs he treads a line between the Reagan administration and its critics; on cultural issues his stance has been as liberal as Peyser's. On economic issues he has sometimes dissented from Reaganite orthodoxy.

Gilman had the clear advantage in redistricting: only 18% of the votes in the new 22d were cast in Westchester. Still, Peyser made a race of it, winning 65% in Westchester—far better than he had done in 1978 or 1980. But Gilman won 70% of the vote in Orange County and carried Sullivan and Rockland as well. Given that success, he seems likely to be able to hold this as a safe seat for some time to come.

The People Pop. 1980: 516,625, up 14.4% 1970–80; voting age pop. 363,184; 6% Black, 4% Span. orig., 1% Asian orig. 28% housing units rented. Median owner $63,000; renter $267. Households: 79% family, 45% with children, 68% married couples.

Presidential Vote

1980	Reagan (R)	114,917	(56%)
	Carter (D)	72,132	(35%)
	Anderson (I)	18,694	(9%)

Rep. Benjamin A. Gilman (R) Elected 1972; b. Dec. 6, 1922, Poughkeepsie; home, Middletown; U. of PA, B.S. 1946, NY Law Sch., LL.B. 1950; Jewish.

Career Army Air Corps, WWII; Asst. Atty. Gen. of NY State, 1953; Practicing atty., 1955–72; Atty., NY Temp. Comm. on the Courts, 1956–57; NY Assembly, 1967–72.

Offices 2160 RHOB, 202-225-3776. Also P.O. Bldg., 217 Liberty St., Newburgh 12550, 914-565-6400.

Committees *Foreign Affairs* (3d). Subcommittees: Asian and Pacific Affairs; International Operations. *Post Office and Civil Service* (2d). Subcommittees: Human Resources; Investigations. *Select Committee on Narcotics Abuse and Control* (Ranking Member).

Group Ratings

	ADA	ACLU	COPE	CFA	LCV	LWV	NTU	NSI	COC	ACA	CSFC
1982	50	67	71	77	84	64	47	100	36	45	48
1981	45	—	71	79	50	—	26	—	72	50	49
1980	61	70	83	71	49	75	24	78	63	46	46

National Journal Ratings

	Economic		Foreign		Cultural	
1982	61%	(LIB)	21%	(LIB)	80%	(LIB)
	39%	(CONS)	78%	(CONS)	19%	(CONS)
1981	46%	(LIB)	57%	(LIB)	77%	(LIB)
	53%	(CONS)	43%	(CONS)	23%	(CONS)

Key Votes

1) Reagan 81 Budget	FOR	5) Incr SS Rtmt Age	AGN	9) Poor Pay Food Stamps	AGN
2) Reagan 81 Tax Cut	FOR	6) Saudi AWACS Sale	AGN	10) Ban Crt Busing Order	AGN
3) Bal Budget Amend	AGN	7) $ for MX Missile	FOR	11) Auto Local Content	FOR
4) Gas & Road Tax	FOR	8) Nerve Gas Prod	FOR	12) Nuclear Arms Freeze	AGN

Election Results

1982 general	Benjamin A. Gilman (R)	92,266	(53%)	($432,571)
	Peter A. Peyser (D–L)	73,124	(42%)	($218,605)
1982 primary	Benjamin A. Gilman (R) unopposed			
1980 general	Peter A. Peyser (D)	85,749	(56%)	($70,740)
(NY 23)	Andrew A. Albanese (R–C)	66,771	(44%)	($44,031)
1980 general	Benjamin A. Gilman (R)	137,159	(74%)	($120,100)
(NY 26)	Eugene R. Victor (D–L)	37,475	(20%)	($0)
	Edmond W. Farrell (RTL)	8,766	(5%)	($0)

Campaign Contributions and Expenditures

1981-82		Direct Cont. 81-82		PACS brkdwn			
Receipts	$377,128	Indiv	$232,265	Agr	$9,900	Ideo	$18,850
Expend.	$432,571	Party	$18,656	Bus	$56,719	Lbr	$15,200
Unspent	$1,551	PACS	$106,144	Hlth	$3,950	Prof	$1,400

Indirect Party Expend: $35,198   *Indep Expend:* For: $1,024 (NRA)

TWENTY-THIRD DISTRICT

Albany is one of the oldest cities in America's interior, a city which shows its age and yet continues to be an important political force—and not just because it's New York's state capital. Albany was founded by Dutchmen, on the Hudson River just below its confluence with the Mohawk: this is the natural crossroads for much of Upstate New York. The Hudson is physically an arm of the sea, with tides that are perceptible in Albany. In colonial times and after this was an ocean port even before it became an important junction for boat traffic on the Erie Canal and railroad traffic on the water-level New York Central route. This was one of America's first manufacturing centers. Troy, up the river just a few miles on the other bank, was a steel manufacturing center rivaling Pittsburgh in the 1840s, and later became America's leading producer of detachable collars; the town of Cohoes across the river became one of America's leading textile producers. Schenectady was the site later of Charles Steinmetz's fabled General Electric laboratories and GE is still a major employer there. Albany was a burly factory town as well.

All three of these cities attracted an immigrant labor force, and all were among the nation's largest cities 100 years ago; their industries have not expanded much and they have not had much population growth since 1910. The immigrants made this part of Republican Upstate New York Democratic, and in Albany they became the nucleus of one of the nation's longest-lasting political machines. For more than 50 years this machine had the same boss, Daniel O'Connell, who operated only from his house for much of that time (John Kennedy went there to visit him in 1960); he died finally in 1977 at age 90. From 1941 until his death in 1983 Albany's Mayor was Erastus Corning 2d, a brainy aristocrat who carefully kept in touch with ordinary citizens all that time. Once Governor Dewey tried to wreck the Albany machine; Nelson Rockefeller lived comfortably with it. It was Mayor Corning who arranged the financing, courtesy of Albany County, of the huge South Mall now named for Rockefeller which is his most visible legacy.

The Albany machine is based on jobs: the city has a large payroll for such a small community, and city employees are expected to produce votes on election days. So you will see the lawn in the park across from New York's ornate Victorian Capitol mowed by half a dozen men, each with a tiny hand mower; if you followed them home, you would see row-house neighborhoods where families have lived for generations, always attending Mass and voting Democratic. There is not much suburban development around Albany; this is a city where—if you ignored the Mall—you could easily imagine yourself to be in the 1920s.

The 23d congressional district of New York includes Albany, Troy, Schenectady, the old carpet manufacturing town of Amsterdam on the Mohawk, and the old industrial towns, suburban subdivisions, and rural land in between. Oddly enough it has not been represented by a product of the Albany machine since 1966. Its current congressman, Samuel Stratton, is a Democrat whose original base was in Schenectady, was first elected to the House in 1958. Republicans tried to redistrict him out, and his district once stretched halfway across Upstate New York; but in 1970 they gave up and gave him Albany and Troy, which they expected would elect a Democrat anyway. Since then he has been routinely reelected by margins of 3–1 or better. In 1982 he handily survived opposition from former Democratic colleague John Dow, as outspoken a dove as Stratton is a hawk.

Stratton's major interest today is in defense issues. His experience on Capitol Hill goes back to 1940, when he served as a young aide to Massachusetts Congressman Thomas Eliot, a supporter of FDR's military preparedness program. Those were the days when aid to Britain was highly controversial, when even Britain seemed likely to be conquered by Hitler, and when the draft passed the House a month before Pearl Harbor by just one vote. Roosevelt himself resorted to underhanded tactics to get aid to Britain and to get the United States more involved in the fight against Hitler than most Americans wanted. Those times made a deep impression on many young men in Congress then, including Lyndon Johnson and Henry Jackson, and they seem to have made a lasting impression on Sam Stratton as well.

Stratton sees himself as a Roosevelt and Truman Democrat, reasonably liberal on economic issues, and resolutely in favor of a strong defense and a foreign policy supportive of freedom abroad. He strongly backed the Vietnam war and believes the United States should have made a stronger commitment there. He favors most proposed increases in defense spending and new weapons systems. He is wary of arms control agreements and proposals. He is one of Congress's leading opponents of the nuclear freeze proposal. He is chairman of the Armed Services Subcommittee on Procurement and Military Nuclear Systems, which guarantees him a major voice in most House weapons policy debates. At the beginning of

1983 he was challenged for that post by Charles Bennett of Florida, who has opposed some MX basing modes. But Stratton refused to defer to seniority. He fought back and got a majority of the votes of Armed Services Democrats in secret ballot—an impressive achievement for a onetime maverick.

Stratton wins many of the battles he fights, but he is nonetheless probably a frustrated man. His views command a solid majority on the House Armed Services Committee, on which he is the number three Democrat, and of which he quite possibly will be chairman some time soon; his victory over Bennett may increase that probability. But he himself has not always been a team player in the past and is not regarded as an automatic leader now. Moreover, his views often fail to carry on the House floor. Many younger Democrats seem to regard Stratton as a predictable scold who is invariably wrong; they have little respect for the depth of his knowledge of the breadth of history he has experienced, nor are they willing to acknowledge that sometimes his views have been proved right.

The People   Pop. 1980: 516,943, dn. 4.0% 1970–80; voting age pop. 389,983; 4% Black, 1% Span. orig., 1% Asian orig. 39% housing units rented. Median owner $38,900; renter $169. Households: 67% family, 33% with children, 54% married couples.

Presidential Vote

1980	Reagan (R)	89,801	(40%)
	Carter (D)	109,710	(49%)
	Anderson (I)	22,778	(10%)

Rep. Samuel S. Stratton (D) Elected 1958; b. Sept. 27, 1916, Yonkers; home, Amsterdam; U. of Rochester, B.A. 1937, Haverford Col., M.A. 1938, Harvard U., M.A. 1940; Presbyterian.

Career Secy. to U.S. Rep. Thomas H. Eliot of MA, 1940–42; Navy, WWII and Korea; Dpty. Secy. Gen., Far Eastern Comm., U.S. Dept. of State, 1946–48; Radio and TV news commentator; College lecturer; Schenectady City Cncl., 1950–56, Mayor, 1956–59.

Offices 2205 RHOB, 202-225-5076. Also U.S.P.O., Jay St., Schenectady 12305, 518-374-4547.

Committee *Armed Services* (3d). Subcommittees: Investigations; Procurement and Military Nuclear Systems (Chairman).

Group Ratings

	ADA	ACLU	COPE	CFA	LCV	LWV	NTU	NSI	COC	ACA	CSFC
1982	35	42	79	54	56	75	24	100	45	45	46
1981	30	—	79	57	43	—	3	—	37	26	49
1980	17	23	58	38	27	30	27	90	66	43	45

National Journal Ratings

	Economic		Foreign		Cultural	
1982	66%	(LIB)	28%	(LIB)	41%	(LIB)
	33%	(CONS)	72%	(CONS)	59%	(CONS)
1981	60%	(LIB)	14%	(LIB)	55%	(LIB)
	39%	(CONS)	84%	(CONS)	45%	(CONS)

Key Votes

1) Reagan 81 Budget	AGN	5) Incr SS Rtmt Age	FOR	9) Poor Pay Food Stamps	AGN
2) Reagan 81 Tax Cut	AGN	6) Saudi AWACS Sale	—	10) Ban Crt Busing Order	AGN
3) Bal Budget Amend	AGN	7) $ for MX Missile	FOR	11) Auto Local Content	FOR
4) Gas & Road Tax	FOR	8) Nerve Gas Prod	FOR	12) Nuclear Arms Freeze	AGN

Election Results

1982 general	Samuel S. Stratton (D)	164,427	(76%)	($73,869)
	Frank Wicks (R–NF)	41,386	(19%)	($0)
1982 primary	Samuel S. Stratton (D)	49,089	(73%)	
	John G. Dow (D)	13,495	(27%)	($25,994)
1980 general	Samuel S. Stratton (D)	164,088	(78%)	($30,635)
	Frank Wicks (R)	37,504	(18%)	($0)

Campaign Contributions and Expenditures

1981-82		Direct Cont. 81-82			PACS brkdwn		
Receipts	$77,634	Indiv	$38,404	Agr	$300	Ideo	$700
Expend.	$73,869	Party	$800	Bus	$19,570	Lbr	$6,750
Unspent	$40,039	PACS	$32,420	Hlth	$4,000	Prof	$—

TWENTY-FOURTH DISTRICT

The 24th congressional district of New York might be called the Upper Hudson district. It begins in the south in Dutchess County near Poughkeepsie and proceeds north, bypassing Albany and Troy, to the area around Lake George, where the Hudson narrows from a tidal arm that accommodates oceangoing ships to a rushing mountain stream. This country was settled from two directions: by Dutchmen coming north along the Hudson, and settling on land allowed them by their patroons; and by Yankees, coming overland from Massachusetts and Vermont, in the beginning of what was a major migration that spread west to Iowa and Kansas. In the early 19th century, this caused political turmoil. The Dutchmen were Democrats, and the man who put together Andrew Jackson's Democratic Party was his vice president and successor, Martin Van Buren, of Dutch descent, a native of Columbia County, whose political base was an organization called the Albany Regency. The Yankees, in contrast, backed first the Whig Party and later the Republicans. Their differences on issues were the opposite of what present day politics would lead you to suppose: the Democrats wanted government to stay out of regulating business and banking; the Whigs and Republicans favored government spending on transportation projects and government intervention to promote temperance and discourage slavery.

Now those political divisions are forgotten. People both in the southern half of the district, in the once Dutch counties on either side of the Hudson, and in the northern part, in the small towns around Glens Falls as well as the affluent area around Saratoga Springs which has become a kind of suburb of Albany, all vote heavily Republican. Like most Upstaters, they stand foresquare against the party they associate with New York City.

The 24th district has a Republican congressman, Gerald Solomon, who is one of the most conservative members of the New York delegation. He first won the seat in 1978, defeating a Democrat elected in 1974 who held on, barely, in 1976 and then confessed he had once smoked marijuana. Solomon has been reelected easily since. He switched from the Public Works to the Foreign Affairs Committee in 1983—a recognition, perhaps, that he can afford to spend time on less parochial matters in the 1980s. He can be counted as a solid and enthusiastic supporter of most Reagan administration programs.

The People   Pop. 1980: 515,614, up 15.8% 1970–80; voting age pop. 364,047; 1% Black, 1% Span. orig. 22% housing units rented. Median owner $38,500; renter $174. Households: 76% family, 42% with children, 65% married couples.

Presidential Vote

1980	Reagan (R)	122,479	(55%)
	Carter (D)	76,669	(36%)
	Anderson (I)	19,899	(9%)

Rep. Gerald B. H. Solomon (R) Elected 1978; b. Aug. 14, 1930, Birmingham, AL; home, Glens Falls; Siena Col., St. Lawrence U.; Presbyterian.

Career USMC, Korea; Queensbury Town Supervisor; Chmn., Warren Cnty. Social Svcs. Comm.; NY Assembly, 1972–78.

Offices 227 CHOB, 202-225-5614. Also 33 2d St., Troy 12180, 518-274-3121.

Committees *Foreign Affairs* (10th). Subcommittees: Africa; Asian and Pacific Affairs; Human Rights and International Organizations. *Veterans' Affairs* (4th). Subcommittees: Education, Training and Employment; Hospitals and Health Care; Oversight and Investigations.

Group Ratings

	ADA	ACLU	COPE	CFA	LCV	LWV	NTU	NSI	COC	ACA	CSFC
1982	5	0	19	31	34	20	92	100	76	91	74
1981	5	—	19	36	43	—	95	—	89	88	83
1980	11	3	29	14	37	25	60	100	72	78	81

National Journal Ratings

	Economic		Foreign		Cultural	
1982	21%	(LIB)	9%	(LIB)	31%	(LIB)
	78%	(CONS)	90%	(CONS)	69%	(CONS)
1981	4%	(LIB)	3%	(LIB)	22%	(LIB)
	79%	(CONS)	87%	(CONS)	78%	(CONS)

Key Votes

1) Reagan 81 Budget	FOR	5) Incr SS Rtmt Age	FOR	9) Poor Pay Food Stamps	FOR
2) Reagan 81 Tax Cut	FOR	6) Saudi AWACS Sale	FOR	10) Ban Crt Busing Order	FOR
3) Bal Budget Amend	FOR	7) $ for MX Missile	FOR	11) Auto Local Content	FOR
4) Gas & Road Tax	AGN	8) Nerve Gas Prod	—	12) Nuclear Arms Freeze	AGN

Election Results

1982 general	Gerald B. H. Solomon (R–C–RTL)	140,296	(74%)	($128,030)
	Roy Esiason (D)	49,441	(26%)	($17,866)
1982 primary	Gerald B. H. Solomon (R–C–RTL) unopposed			
1980 general	Gerald B. H. Solomon (R–C–RTL)	141,631	(67%)	($112,581)
	Rodger L. Hurley (D–L)	70,697	(33%)	($40,176)

Campaign Contributions and Expenditures

1981-82		Direct Cont. 81-82		PACS brkdwn			
Receipts	$154,604	Indiv	$72,507	Agr	$6,000	Ideo	$2,650
Expend.	$128,030	Party	$14,315	Bus	$44,700	Lbr	$2,000
Unspent	$31,524	PACS	$62,839	Hlth	$7,400	Prof	$800

Indirect Party Expend: $2,750

TWENTY-FIFTH DISTRICT

During the Revolutionary War, the Mohawk River valley of Upstate New York was the frontier. The Iroquois Indians here were allied with the British, who prohibited new settlements, against the rebels, who coveted the land; this is the background of *Drums Along the Mohawk*. After the Revolution, as the Indians feared, the Mohawk became one of America's main roads west. This river is bounded closely on each side by rolling hills; it was the natural route for the Erie Canal, finished in 1825, and later for the water-level New York Central Railroad. Through the Mohawk New England Yankees moved to settle the west, and the Mohawk Valley in the process; in the other direction came the bulky agricultural products of the Midwest. This route accounted for much of the phenomenal growth in the 19th century of New York City and its port; Boston and Philadelphia, with no similar access inland, were left behind. As migration slowed and trade increased, the Mohawk Valley became one of the early industrial centers of the nation. The little Oneida County hamlets of Utica and Rome grew to become sizable factory towns. First settled by New England Yankees, these towns attracted a new wave of immigration from the Atlantic coast in the early 20th century. Today they are the most heavily Italian- and Polish-American communities between Albany and Buffalo.

The Mohawk Valley area around Utica and Rome, and also a disconnected portion to the east, make up about half of New York's 25th congressional district. The remainder consists of a series of counties to the south which are more sparsely settled. These are hilly areas, not along any major east–west route; the population here remains more Yankee, the area less industrial. The most famous town here is Cooperstown, with 19th-century houses and commercial buildings maintained in better-than-pristine condition, thanks in large part to the money brought in by the Baseball Hall of Fame.

Politically, these counties are heavily Republican, under practically all circumstances. The Mohawk Valley, on the other hand, sometimes goes Democratic: it almost gave a majority to Mario Cuomo in 1982 and it supported Robert Kennedy heavily in 1964; evidently the key factor is the presence of a Democrat with appeal to Italian and other ethnic voters. Usually, however, this is Republican territory, wary of supporting candidates backed by voters in New York City.

The congressional representation of this district is regularly settled in the Republican primary. The winner in 1982 was Sherwood Boehlert, who lost a primary the last time the seat was open, in 1972. Boehlert has been familiar with the job of representing this district for nearly 20 years. He served as an aide to Congressman Alexander Pirnie, who retired in 1972, and to Congressman Donald Mitchell, after Mitchell beat him in the primary. The difficulties of running for Congress from Washington may have persuaded him to move back to Utica, where he was elected Oneida County Executive in 1979. His local strength persuaded incumbent Gary Lee not to run in this district in 1982, though it contained his legal residence. Boehlert won both the Republican primary and general election by respectable, though not overwhelming, margins.

Despite his association with his two predecessors, Boehlert seems inclined to represent the district in a somewhat different way. Pirnie and Mitchell voted pretty much orthodox Republican lines; Boehlert had the support of the state AFL-CIO in 1982, and can be expected to be more liberal on economic issues. Pirnie and Mitchell both served on the Armed Services Committee, in part to protect Rome's Griffiss Air Force Base. Boehlert serves on Science and Technology and Small Business, and appears more interested in building a stronger, new economy in this region which has experienced relatively little economic growth than he does in just protecting what the district already has. But he is like his predecessors in one way: he seems likely to be able to hold this seat easily until he chooses to retire.

The People   Pop. 1980: 515,039, dn. .4% 1970–80; voting age pop. 373,822; 2% Black, 1% Span. orig. 29% housing units rented. Median owner $32,400; renter $155. Households: 73% family, 38% with children, 61% married couples.

Presidential Vote

1980	Reagan (R)	106,127	(51%)
	Carter (D)	82,214	(40%)
	Anderson (I)	17,967	(9%)

Rep. Sherwood L. Boehlert (R) Elected 1982; b. Sept. 28, 1936, Utica; home, New Hartford; Utica Col., B.S. 1961; Roman Catholic.

Career Mgr., pub. relations, Wyandotte Chemicals Corp., 1961–64; A.A. to Rep. A. Pirnie, 1964–72; A.A. to Rep. D. Mitchell, 1972–79; Cnty. Exec., Oneida Cnty., 1979–80.

Offices 1641 LHOB, 202-225-3665. Also 6 Steuben Park, Utica 13501, 315-793-8147.

Committees *Science and Technology* (13th). Subcommittees: Science, Research and Technology; Transportation, Aviation and Materials. *Small Business* (13th). Subcommittees: General Oversight and the Economy; SBA and SBIC Authority, Minority Enterprise and General Small Business Problems.

Group Ratings and Key Votes: Newly Elected

Election Results

1982 general	Sherwood L. Boehlert (R)	93,071	(56%)	($180,586)
	Anita Maxwell (D)	70,793	(42%)	($32,650)
1982 primary	Sherwood L. Boehlert (R)	20,141	(56%)	
	Emlyn I. Griffith (R)	15,604	(44%)	($32,920)
1980 general	Donald J. Mitchell (R–RTL)	135,976	(77%)	($78,925)
	Irving A. Schwartz (D–L)	39,589	(23%)	($6,495)

Campaign Contributions and Expenditures

1982		Direct Cont. 1982			PACS brkdwn			
Receipts	$188,375	Indiv	$101,114	Agr	$3,500	Ideo	$850
Expend.	$180,586	Party	$28,064	Bus	$31,085	Lbr	$6,000
Unspent	$7,788	PACS	$57,110	Hlth	$12,150	Prof	$2,000

Indirect Party Expend: $17,840

TWENTY-SIXTH DISTRICT

The 26th congressional district of New York covers the northernmost reaches of New York state. It includes the counties across the St. Lawrence River from Canada and the ones at the eastern end of Lake Ontario. It dips down as far south as Herkimer, on the Mohawk River. Geographically, much of the 26th is taken up with the Adirondack Forest Preserve, a giant state park that the New York Constitution stipulates must remain "forever wild." This includes Lake Placid, site of the 1980 Winter Olympics. North of the Forest Preserve is Massena, on the St. Lawrence River, which has been blessed with the administrative headquarters of the St. Lawrence Seaway. This project was supposed to give the north country an economic boost. But there have been continual problems: the Seaway freezes over three months a year; its locks are too small for the large containerized ships that have become the rule in most kinds of trade; and the time it takes to negotiate the locks is longer than most shippers want to wait. So despite the Seaway the economy of this part of New York has not grown spectacularly since the days in the early 19th century when it was settled by farmers moving west from northern New England or north from the Mohawk River, to seek their own farms in this agriculturally marginal land.

The large French Canadian population in Clinton and Franklin Counties, just 60 miles south of Montreal, forms the only Democratic voting bloc in the district; as one moves south and west there are fewer French and more Yankees, fewer Democrats and more Republicans. Here in the farm country of the St. Lawrence and in the Adirondacks, where it gets bitterly cold in the winter and not very warm in the summer, the voting preference is decidedly Republican—enough so to make the 26th district Republican in almost every election.

That has been true since the Republican Party began. The prime political celebrity up here was William Wheeler, Vice President under Rutherford B. Hayes, who left office in 1881. The 26th district does not bulk large in the affairs of New York state, and it has elected a series of Republican congressmen who have compiled reliably conservative voting records and not achieved much notice. The current incumbent, David Martin, seems to be following a similar course. First elected in 1980, he was a solid supporter of the Reagan administration in his first two years. He is a member of the Armed Services Committee who supports increased defense spending. A veteran of the New York Assembly, with a base in the north country, he won his 1980 primary with 70% of the vote and has had no trouble in general elections.

The People Pop. 1980: 516,196, up 3.1% 1970–80; voting age pop. 364,170; 1% Black, 1% Span. orig., 1% Am. Ind. 23% housing units rented. Median owner $29,200; renter $144. Households: 74% family, 42% with children, 63% married couples.

Presidential Vote

1980	Reagan (R)	97,185	(51%)
	Carter (D)	79,999	(42%)
	Anderson (I)	14,965	(8%)

Rep. David O'B. Martin (R) Elected 1980; b. Apr. 26, 1944, Ogdensburg; home, Canton; U. of Notre Dame, B.B.A. 1966, Albany Law Sch., J.D. 1973; Roman Catholic.

Career USMC, 1966–70; St. Lawrence Cnty. Legislature, 1973–76; NY Assembly, 1976–80.

Offices 109 CHOB, 202-225-4611. Also 307 Fed. Bldg., Watertown 13601, 315-782-3150; Riverfront Ofc. Bldg., Oswego 13126, 315-342-4688; 104 Fed. Bldg., Plattsburgh 12901, 518-563-1406; and Ogdensburg Mall, Ogdensburg 13669, 315-393-0570.

Committee *Armed Services* (15th). Subcommittees: Investigations; Military Installations and Facilities.

Group Ratings

	ADA	ACLU	COPE	CFA	LCV	LWV	NTU	NSI	COC	ACA	CSFC
1982	15	12	21	23	54	55	66	100	65	83	59
1981	5	—	13	29	36	—	75	—	88	81	73

National Journal Ratings

	Economic		Foreign		Cultural	
1982	29%	(LIB)	19%	(LIB)	42%	(LIB)
	70%	(CONS)	80%	(CONS)	58%	(CONS)
1981	1%	(LIB)	0%	(LIB)	22%	(LIB)
	97%	(CONS)	99%	(CONS)	77%	(CONS)

Key Votes

1) Reagan 81 Budget	FOR	5) Incr SS Rtmt Age	FOR	9) Poor Pay Food Stamps	FOR
2) Reagan 81 Tax Cut	FOR	6) Saudi AWACS Sale	FOR	10) Ban Crt Busing Order	FOR
3) Bal Budget Amend	FOR	7) $ for MX Missile	FOR	11) Auto Local Content	AGN
4) Gas & Road Tax	—	8) Nerve Gas Prod	FOR	12) Nuclear Arms Freeze	AGN

Election Results

1982 general	David O'B. Martin (R–C)	108,962	(72%)	($122,016)
	David P. Landy (D)	43,208	(28%)	($0)
1982 primary	David O'B. Martin (R–C) unopposed			
1980 general	David O'B. Martin (R–C)	111,008	(64%)	($244,377)
	Mary Anne Krupsak (D–L)	54,896	(32%)	($54,837)
	John R. Zagame (RTL)	7,985	(5%)	($118,624)

Campaign Contributions and Expenditures

1981-82		Direct Cont. 81-82		PACS brkdwn			
Receipts	$125,354	Indiv	$37,600	Agr	$6,200	Ideo	$2,175
Expend.	$122,016	Party	$9,855	Bus	$44,095	Lbr	$3,790
Unspent	$10,071	PACS	$65,010	Hlth	$7,750	Prof	$1,000

Indep Expend: For: $130 (NRA)

TWENTY-SEVENTH DISTRICT

Syracuse is close to the geographical center of Upstate New York, and it typifies many of the political and cultural attitudes of this region. Syracuse is an industrial city, and has been one for many years: connected to the Erie Canal, on the New York Central water-level route, it is astride what were for years the nation's major east–west transportation routes. From the time of its settlement in the early 19th century, Syracuse has been a relatively prosperous town: its agricultural hinterland was rich (and still is, with specialty crops like wine grapes), its industrial jobs mostly high skill. Perhaps the weather was a contributing factor. Syracuse gets as much snow as any city in the United States, and if you are going to live up here you are going to have to earn enough money to build a solid, well-insulated house to protect you through the winter.

In another state, where it would have been the center of one of the major metropolitan areas, Syracuse might have been a Democratic city; in New York, where it is vastly overshadowed by the masses of New York City, it is heavily Republican. This partisan preference has survived the glacial ethnic change which has transformed Syracuse from a mostly Protestant Yankee city in 1880 to a mostly Catholic and heavily Italian city in 1980. There is a feeling that New York City, if it ever got the chance, would tax honest, hardworking Upstaters to bankruptcy to support the welfare cheaters and civil service loafers who, in this view, dominate New York City politics. The fiscal collapse of New York City in 1975 showed that there was more to this view than the distrust of the country bumpkin for the city slicker.

Also contributing to Syracuse's Republicanism are the views of its longtime biggest employer, General Electric—propagated in the 1950s and early 1960s by Ronald Reagan. Syracuse does go Democratic on occasion, for attractive Catholic candidates (Robert Kennedy in 1964) or against Republicans it sees as big spenders (Nelson Rockefeller in 1966). But mostly it is solidly Republican.

The 27th congressional district of New York is made up of Syracuse, surrounding Onondaga County, and most of Madison County to the east. This is the eastern end of the Finger Lakes region, and in the old town squares you will see monuments to the enthusiasms of the 19th century—religious revivalism, temperance, abolitionism—which once made this area one of the leading cauldrons of ideas in the country. Now these pleasant, long-settled small towns are solidly Republican.

The congressman from the 27th district, George Wortley, is a Republican who owns a chain of newspapers in suburban Syracuse. He has won two elections now, and in both has had serious primary competition. The first time was in 1980, when a Democrat who had first won in 1964 and had held on with increasingly narrow margins finally retired. The second was in 1982, when redistricting pitted Wortley against fellow Republican Congressman Gary Lee. That produced one of the closest primaries in the nation: Wortley won by 354 votes out of 39,000 cast. In that close an election, anything can be said to have made the difference. But it is interesting to note that Lee was the chief sponsor in the House of the bill to disapprove a Federal Trade Commission rule on used-car dealers, a position that was criticized in the Syracuse newspapers. Did his vehement support of this measure—which usually would make no difference to most voters—cost him his seat?

Wortley's performance in the both primaries and general elections has not been overwhelming, however. Lee, who had his choice of districts, chose to run against him rather than against non-incumbent Sherwood Boehlert in the 25th. And in the general election against a poorly financed anti-nuclear arms activist Wortley won with only 53% of the vote. He has not yet reached the maximum Republican vote in this district. In the House he is a member of the Banking Committee and a reliable conservative Republican.

The People   Pop. 1980: 516,223, dn. 1.1% 1970–80; voting age pop. 372,734; 5% Black, 1% Span. orig., 1% Asian orig., 1% Am. Ind. 34% housing units rented. Median owner $38,100; renter $186. Households: 71% family, 39% with children, 58% married couples.

Presidential Vote

1980	Reagan (R)	108,640	(52%)
	Carter (D)	79,121	(38%)
	Anderson (I)	20,464	(10%)

Rep. George C. Wortley (R) Elected 1980; b. Dec. 8, 1926, Syracuse; home, Fayetteville; Syracuse U., B.S. 1948; Roman Catholic.

Career Navy, WWII; Newspaper publ., 1949–; Repub. Nominee for U.S. House of Reps., 1976; Natl. Comm. on Historical Publications and Records, 1977–80; Fayetteville Sr. Citizens Housing Comm., 1977–80.

Offices 428 CHOB, 202-225-3701. Also 1269 Fed. Bldg., Syracuse 13260, 315-423-5657; and Manley Carriage House, 2 Hayes St., Norwich 13815, 607-334-2211.

Committees *Banking, Finance and Urban Affairs* (10th). Subcommittees: Economic Stabilization; Financial Institutions Supervision, Regulation and Insurance; General Oversight and Renegotiation; Housing and Community Development. *Select Committee on Aging* (9th). Subcommittees: Health and Long-Term Care; Housing and Consumer Interests.

Group Ratings

	ADA	ACLU	COPE	CFA	LCV	LWV	NTU	NSI	COC	ACA	CSFC
1982	15	25	19	32	26	50	69	100	76	77	60
1981	10	—	20	36	29	—	54	—	89	65	65

National Journal Ratings

	Economic		Foreign		Cultural	
1982	35%	(LIB)	37%	(LIB)	42%	(LIB)
	64%	(CONS)	62%	(CONS)	58%	(CONS)
1981	24%	(LIB)	49%	(LIB)	21%	(LIB)
	68%	(CONS)	50%	(CONS)	79%	(CONS)

Key Votes

1) Reagan 81 Budget	FOR	5) Incr SS Rtmt Age	FOR	9) Poor Pay Food Stamps	FOR
2) Reagan 81 Tax Cut	FOR	6) Saudi AWACS Sale	AGN	10) Ban Crt Busing Order	FOR
3) Bal Budget Amend	FOR	7) $ for MX Missile	FOR	11) Auto Local Content	FOR
4) Gas & Road Tax	FOR	8) Nerve Gas Prod	AGN	12) Nuclear Arms Freeze	AGN

Election Results

1982 general	George C. Wortley (R)	95,290	(53%)	($325,100)
	Elaine Lytel (D–L)	79,209	(44%)	($65,234)
1982 primary	George C. Wortley (R)	18,640	(47%)	
	Gary A. Lee (R)	18,286	(46%)	($196,525)
	Peter J. DelGiorno (R)	2,536	(6%)	
1980 general	George C. Wortley (R–C)	108,128	(60%)	($170,106)
(NY 32)	Jeffrey S. Brooks (D–L)	56,535	(32%)	($15,315)
	Peter J. DelGiorno (RTL)	11,978	(7%)	($65,382)
1980 general	Gary A. Lee (R–C)	132,831	(77%)	($128,927)
(NY 33)	Delores M. Reed (D–L)	39,542	(23%)	($5,326)

Campaign Contributions and Expenditures

1981-82		Direct Cont. 81-82		PACS brkdwn			
Receipts	$327,318	Indiv	$164,397	Agr	$4,950	Ideo	$9,450
Expend.	$325,100	Party	$16,781	Bus	$86,095	Lbr	$3,500
Unspent	$5,038	PACS	$112,495	Hlth	$8,300	Prof	$200
		Cand	$30,000				

Indirect Party Expend: $35,254

TWENTY-EIGHTH DISTRICT

New York's 28th congressional district extends along the state's southern border from the Hudson River to the college town of Ithaca, on Lake Cayuga. This spans several parts of Upstate New York. Ulster County, along the Hudson, was first settled by Dutch patroons and their retainers; just above the river are the Catskill Mountains: Rip Van Winkle country. On the other side of the Catskills is the Borscht Belt resort district, part of which is in this district; here a predominantly Jewish clientele has been summering for nearly 100 years. Westward into the fastness of Upstate New York is the Delaware River, the source of much of New York City's excellent water supply. Farther west you come to the beginning of what is called the Southern Tier, along the Pennsylvania border. Here, nestled along a river valley circled by rising hills, are towns like Binghamton, old manufacturing centers with new IBM plants nearby. Off to the north, in the beginning of the Finger Lakes region, is Ithaca and Cornell.

This whole area has had little population growth in the past several decades, but it would be a mistake to see it as economically stagnant. In fact, old industries have been replaced rather steadily by new; low-wage jobs have been replaced by high-wage jobs. Some children choose to leave, to seek opportunities elsewhere; but this part of Upstate New York continues to provide good livings for its frugal, industrious citizens. Politically, they, like most Upstaters, consider themselves Republicans. They are sympathetic to civil rights and became a little skeptical about the Vietnam war; but on economic issues they do not see themselves, as residents of New York City do, as the main beneficiaries of generous federal programs.

Nonetheless, this district has a Democratic congressman, former Ithaca District Attorney Matthew McHugh. He was first elected in 1974, due to a combination of favorable circumstances: the retirement of a popular Republican congressman, a recession, Watergate. He was reelected easily in 1976, but has had tough races in the three elections since then. In each case his Republican opponent has spent liberally, and McHugh has raised and spent even more; in each case he won with 55% or 56% of the vote. Those are decisive victories, but not decisive enough to convince Republican challengers and national strategists that McHugh has made this a safe Democratic seat.

In the House McHugh is a member of the Appropriations Committee and of two subcommittees with a tradition of overseeing closely the operations of the programs they fund. One is Agriculture, ruled for years by Jamie Whitten of Mississippi; Whitten was born in 1910, and McHugh ranks behind just him and Bob Traxler of Michigan. On that McHugh is a key supporter of the food stamp program. He also serves on Foreign Operations, chaired by Clarence Long of Maryland; this has supervision over the foreign aid program and funding for international agencies. It considers dozens of amendments designed to change U.S. policy in various directions. McHugh is considered a workmanlike member of these bodies, more interested in achieving practical results than headlines. These duties, plus his need to tend to his district, which is hard to reach from Washington, gives him one of the heaviest workloads in the Congress.

The People   Pop. 1980: 516,808, up 4.1% 1970–80; voting age pop. 382,593; 3% Black, 2% Span. orig., 1% Am. Ind. 29% housing units rented. Median owner $39,400; renter $185. Households: 71% family, 37% with children, 59% married couples.

Presidential Vote

1980	Reagan (R)	102,040	(50%)
	Carter (D)	78,874	(39%)
	Anderson (I)	22,957	(11%)

Rep. Matthew F. (Matt) McHugh (D) Elected 1974; b. Dec. 6, 1938, Philadelphia, PA; home, Ithaca; Mt. St. Mary's Col., Emmitsburg, MD, B.S. 1960, Villanova U., J.D. 1963; Roman Catholic.

Career Practicing atty., 1964–74; Ithaca City Prosecutor, 1968; Tompkins Cnty. Dist. Atty., 1969–72.

Offices 2335 RHOB, 202-225-6335. Also 201 Fed. Bldg., Binghamton 13902, 607-723-4425.

Committees *Appropriations* (20th). Subcommittees: Agriculture, Rural Development and Related Agencies; Foreign Operations. *Select Committee on Children, Youth, and Families* (5th).

Group Ratings

	ADA	ACLU	COPE	CFA	LCV	LWV	NTU	NSI	COC	ACA	CSFC
1982	100	58	83	77	96	100	15	22	23	17	27
1981	95	—	82	86	86	—	7	—	11	8	31
1980	83	80	72	71	82	90	16	10	64	21	25

National Journal Ratings

	Economic		Foreign		Cultural	
1982	73%	(LIB)	84%	(LIB)	80%	(LIB)
	27%	(CONS)	16%	(CONS)	19%	(CONS)
1981	81%	(LIB)	85%	(LIB)	81%	(LIB)
	15%	(CONS)	13%	(CONS)	18%	(CONS)

Key Votes

1) Reagan 81 Budget	AGN	5) Incr SS Rtmt Age	AGN	9) Poor Pay Food Stamps	AGN
2) Reagan 81 Tax Cut	AGN	6) Saudi AWACS Sale	AGN	10) Ban Crt Busing Order	AGN
3) Bal Budget Amend	AGN	7) $ for MX Missile	AGN	11) Auto Local Content	AGN
4) Gas & Road Tax	FOR	8) Nerve Gas Prod	AGN	12) Nuclear Arms Freeze	FOR

Election Results

1982 general	Matthew F. (Matt) McHugh (D–L)	100,665	(56%)	($454,513)
	David F. Crowley (R–C)	75,991	(43%)	($277,732)
1982 primary	Matthew F. (Matt) McHugh (D–L) unopposed			
1980 general	Matthew F. (Matt) McHugh (D–L)	103,863	(55%)	($288,061)
	Neil Tyler Wallace (R–C)	83,096	(44%)	($199,966)

Campaign Contributions and Expenditures

1981-82		Direct Cont. 81-82				PACS brkdwn		
Receipts	$447,496	Indiv	$271,550	Agr	$17,000	Ideo	$27,242
Expend.	$454,513	Party	$20,028	Bus	$8,550	Lbr	$72,350
Unspent	$4,961	PACS	$136,948	Hlth	$3,000	Prof	$1,100

TWENTY-NINTH DISTRICT

The Finger Lakes of Upstate New York are long, narrow bodies of water, set in trenches—some 40 miles long—excavated by Ice Age glaciers. They are set amid rolling hills and fertile land, with a climate, influenced by the lakes, which permits the growing of fruit trees and wine grapes. This is the land that the settlers of the early 19th century found after making their way through the narrow defile of the Mohawk Valley. Physically, it is the threshold of the bounteous American interior; and from the early 19th century this land, around the Finger Lakes and on the southern shore of Lake Ontario, has been productive both economically and intellectually.

In fact, in the three decades before the Civil War, this area fairly teemed with ideas and enthusiasms. It was the site of religious revivals with feelings so intense it became known as the Burnt-Over District. It provided the strongest abolitionist constituencies in the United States, in a day when even in the North most whites feared and opposed ending slavery. It was the birthplace of the women's suffrage movement; the great 1848 women's convention was held in Seneca Falls, at the head of one of the Finger Lakes. It was the birthplace as well of the temperance movement—and, hard as it may seem for the liberated women of today to believe, the two causes were often linked in those days. It was the birthplace of the Mormon Church: in Palmyra, near the Erie Canal, Joseph Smith had his vision of the Angel Moroni and saw the golden tablets. This part of Upstate New York has always had a taste for learning. It is teeming with small colleges, and some anonymous scholar gave many of its towns classical names: Scipio, Marcellus, Cicero, Ovid, Romulus, Hannibal.

To observers of today's politics, such a history of cultural ferment and issues activism suggests an affiliation with the liberal wing of the Democratic Party. But in the 19th century the same ideas and feelings which produced all these movements also naturally led the Upstate New Yorkers of the Finger Lakes region to join the new Republican Party. The Republicans were the activists of their day: they wanted to use government to restrict slavery and encourage small farmers (through the Homestead Act and land-grant colleges); they wanted to use government lands to finance railroad building and to use government to impose protective tariffs. The way in which their party sprung up and, within months, became the major rival to the Democrats in 1854 suggests the same revivalistic enthusiasm that swept the Burnt-Over District and inspired the early Mormons.

The same sort of crusading spirit animated the Republican Party here until well into the 20th century. Local Republicans saw themselves as the upholders of standards and learning against the immigrant mobs of New York City, and as the conservers of an economic system, which proved vastly productive, against the importers of foreign socialism. But as the American welfare state became a reality rather than a Democratic platform plank, this fervor died down; and today the Republicanism of the Finger Lakes region is a calm credo.

The 29th congressional district of New York includes much of the Finger Lakes region, by-passing Syracuse and Onondaga County; it also includes the southern shore of Lake Ontario from Oswego County west to the city of Rochester. About one-third of the district's population is in Rochester and suburban Monroe County; the district includes the city's east side and the adjacent relatively affluent suburbs of Brighton and Penfield. This was designed to be, and is, a solidly Republican district in most elections.

The congressman from this district is Frank Horton, one of the more senior Republicans in the House and one of the more liberal, particularly on cultural issues. Horton was first elected in 1962, one of a long line of liberal Republicans from the east side of Rochester, which included former Senator Kenneth Keating. Horton is now the ranking Republican on the Government Operations Committee. This is an odd legislative body, in the sense that it does not produce much ongoing legislation, but has tremendous discretion to investigate—and therefore to affect—the conduct of government. That makes it potentially a great weapon for the party out of power, and the chairman today is Jack Brooks of Texas, a partisan Democrat if ever there was one. But Brooks had to spend much of the first two years of the Reagan administration assuring his own reelection, and Gov Ops has not been terribly active during this time. Horton's impulse, should the committee or its subcommittees launch a major, partisan-oriented investigation, would probably be to modulate their approach; he would not be just the Reagan administration's point man.

Horton has had little difficulty winning reelection by wide margins, and the current 29th district, as created by the 1982 redistricting, is more Republican than the constituencies he has had in the past. Indeed, it could even some day give him trouble in a primary, particularly since he did not represent the Finger Lakes or Oswego County before 1982.

The People   Pop. 1980: 516,301, up 2.1% 1970–80; voting age pop. 366,552; 4% Black, 1% Span. orig. 28% housing units rented. Median owner $36,600; renter $190. Households: 72% family, 40% with children, 60% married couples.

Presidential Vote

1980	Reagan (R)	NA
	Carter (D)	NA
	Anderson (I)	NA

Rep. Frank Horton (R) Elected 1962; b. Dec. 12, 1919, Cuero, TX; home, Rochester; LA St. U., B.A. 1941, Cornell U., LL.B. 1947; Presbyterian.

Career Army, WWII; Practicing atty., 1947–62; Rochester City Cncl., 1955–61.

Offices 2229 RHOB, 202-225-4916. Also 314 Fed. Bldg., Rochester 14614, 716-263-6270.

Committee *Government Operations* (Ranking Member). Subcommittee: Legislation and National Security.

Group Ratings

	ADA	ACLU	COPE	CFA	LCV	LWV	NTU	NSI	COC	ACA	CSFC
1982	50	58	66	38	49	60	52	78	35	45	42
1981	35	—	66	57	24	—	50	—	82	37	52
1980	78	70	74	64	39	70	28	75	69	43	42

National Journal Ratings

	Economic		Foreign		Cultural	
1982	55%	(LIB)	62%	(LIB)	58%	(LIB)
	45%	(CONS)	38%	(CONS)	42%	(CONS)
1981	43%	(LIB)	70%	(LIB)	75%	(LIB)
	57%	(CONS)	30%	(CONS)	25%	(CONS)

Key Votes

1) Reagan 81 Budget	FOR	5) Incr SS Rtmt Age	FOR	9) Poor Pay Food Stamps	AGN
2) Reagan 81 Tax Cut	FOR	6) Saudi AWACS Sale	AGN	10) Ban Crt Busing Order	AGN
3) Bal Budget Amend	AGN	7) $ for MX Missile	AGN	11) Auto Local Content	FOR
4) Gas & Road Tax	AGN	8) Nerve Gas Prod	AGN	12) Nuclear Arms Freeze	FOR

Election Results

1982 general	Frank Horton (R)	104,412	(66%)	($37,957)
	William C. Larsen (D)	47,463	(30%)	($0)
1982 primary	Frank Horton (R) unopposed			
1980 general	Frank Horton (R)	133,278	(73%)	($14,669)
	James Toole (D)	37,883	(21%)	($0)

Campaign Contributions and Expenditures

1981-82		Direct Cont. 81-82		PACS brkdwn			
Receipts	$46,995	Indiv	$8,895	Agr	$1,700	Ideo	$200
Expend.	$37,957	Party	$9,005	Bus	$20,700	Lbr	$6,000
Unspent	$36,278	PACS	$30,850	Hlth	$1,500	Prof	$750

THIRTIETH DISTRICT

Rochester is New York's third largest metropolitan area, vastly overshadowed by New York City and, even in its own little corner of New York state, smaller than Buffalo. It is also a city with a very different economic base—and one which might be the prototype for other eastern and Great Lakes cities in the future. For Rochester is essentially a high-tech city. Its great industries include Bausch & Lomb, the lensmakers; Eastman Kodak, a company that continues to thrive due to technological breakthroughs; and Xerox, a company that started here though its headquarters is now in Stamford, Connecticut. Technical innovation, precision workmanship, high reliability, custom service—these are the qualities that have made Rochester a prosperous and pleasant city.

The 30th congressional district of New York includes most of the Rochester metropolitan area plus a swath of rural and small-town Upstate New York to the south along the New York Thruway. It is shaped oddly, with one wide end along Lake Ontario, a narrow pinched waist through downtown Rochester, and then a vast base running along the Thruway. It includes Rochester's highest-income suburb, Pittsford, in hilly country southeast of the city; and it includes the lakefront suburbs, which are quite modest places: Irondequoit, Greece, and Parma. Its southern portion contains the kind of small towns, originally settled by Yankees from New England, which for so many years in Upstate New York and through the Midwest produced the leaders of the Republican Party in the House.

One such man is Barber Conable, congressman from the 30th district. In his first term, back in 1965, he caught the eye of the Republican leadership and won a seat on the Ways and Means Committee. In 1977, he became ranking Republican on that panel. Conable is respected as one of the House's most thoughtful and knowledgeable legislators. He is at one and the same time a thoughtful analyst and critic of what goes on in the House and an aggressive and active partisan for the causes he champions. He has a contemplative bent and an ability to understand and sympathize with the motivations of others even when they are quite different from his own. But, as you would expect from a man who served in the Marines in two wars, he also likes to win, and he fights hard when he has to.

Conable's basic inclinations are mostly in line with classic Republican tradition. He likes balanced budgets, he wants to hold down federal spending, he is skeptical about whether new federal programs are really necessary. He is a strong backer of free trade and almost always a forceful opponent of the latest excuse for protectionism. He believes business needs less onerous taxes and more incentives to be economically productive, and he was the chief congressional sponsor of the 10–5–3 depreciation reform, which cut depreciation periods to those numbers of years on buildings, equipment, and vehicles. Conable was not, however, an enthusiast of the supply-side economics championed by Jack Kemp, whose district adjoins the 30th. Conable did go on record in favor of the Kemp–Roth tax cut, and supported it in committee, but he did so with a notable lack of enthusiasm, and with suggestions that he was considerably more skeptical about where this new policy would lead than were Republicans like Kemp.

Conable is the kind of legislator whose instinct is to compromise and to craft legislation that will pass. But he also is willing to stonewall and to fight when he thinks it necessary. When Democrats refused to confer with Republicans on their tax programs in 1981 and 1982, Conable refused to budge an inch from the Reagan plans, and held the Democrats responsible. He has had an acceptable, but not a particularly warm, working relationship with Ways and Means Chairman Dan Rostenkowski.

Conable has been reelected easily from his district, and redistricting did not hurt him at all in 1982; it rather carefully kept the most Democratic parts of the Rochester area out of his district. A moderate on cultural issues, he does not get the nomination of the Conservative Party, but that makes no difference in the result.

The People Pop. 1980: 516,819, up 3.5% 1970–80; voting age pop. 371,098; 4% Black, 1% Span. orig., 1% Asian orig. 30% housing units rented. Median owner $44,100; renter $211. Households: 74% family, 41% with children, 62% married couples.

Presidential Vote

1980	Reagan (R)	NA
	Carter (D)	NA
	Anderson (I)	NA

Rep. Barber B. Conable, Jr. (R) Elected 1964; b. Nov. 2, 1922, Warsaw; home, Alexander; Cornell U., B.A. 1942, LL.B. 1948; Methodist.

Career USMC, WWII and Korea; Practicing atty., 1949–64; NY Senate, 1963–64.

Offices 237 CHOB, 202-225-3615. Also 311 Fed. Ofc. Bldg., 100 State St., Rochester 14614, 716-263-3156.

Committees *Standards of Official Conduct* (2d). *Ways and Means* (Ranking Member). *Joint Committee on Taxation* (Ranking Member).

Group Ratings

	ADA	ACLU	COPE	CFA	LCV	LWV	NTU	NSI	COC	ACA	CSFC
1982	25	25	16	31	43	55	83	90	70	82	63
1981	25	—	16	29	37	—	87	—	100	81	72
1980	28	43	47	21	47	33	58	38	72	79	69

National Journal Ratings

	Economic		Foreign		Cultural	
1982	38%	(LIB)	47%	(LIB)	61%	(LIB)
	61%	(CONS)	53%	(CONS)	39%	(CONS)
1981	4%	(LIB)	38%	(LIB)	44%	(LIB)
	79%	(CONS)	61%	(CONS)	56%	(CONS)

Key Votes

1) Reagan 81 Budget	FOR	5) Incr SS Rtmt Age	FOR	9) Poor Pay Food Stamps	FOR
2) Reagan 81 Tax Cut	FOR	6) Saudi AWACS Sale	FOR	10) Ban Crt Busing Order	AGN
3) Bal Budget Amend	FOR	7) $ for MX Missile	FOR	11) Auto Local Content	AGN
4) Gas & Road Tax	FOR	8) Nerve Gas Prod	AGN	12) Nuclear Arms Freeze	AGN

Election Results

1982 general	Barber B. Conable, Jr. (R)	119,105	(68%)	($64,613)
	Bill Benet (D)	48,764	(30%)	($38,610)
1982 primary	Barber B. Conable, Jr. (R) unopposed			
1980 general	Barber B. Conable, Jr. (R)	127,623	(72%)	($34,444)
	John M. Owens (D–C)	44,754	(25%)	($0)

Campaign Contributions and Expenditures

1981-82		Direct Cont. 81-82		PACS brkdwn			
Receipts	$61,224	Indiv	$46,833	Agr	$100	Ideo	$150
Expend.	$64,613	Party	$9,112	Bus	$4,320	Lbr	$—
Unspent	$943	PACS	$5,255	Hlth	$185	Prof	$350

THIRTY-FIRST DISTRICT

The 31st congressional district of New York includes most of suburban Erie County, outside Buffalo, plus a swath of Upstate New York stretching east to the Finger Lakes. The district includes most of the more affluent parts of the Niagara Frontier, the heavily industrial Buffalo–Niagara Falls metropolitan area on the Canadian border. Buffalo and its suburbs are the Democratic bastion of Upstate New York and sometimes produce higher Democratic percentages (though many fewer votes) than metropolitan New York City. Buffalo is a place much more like Cleveland or Detroit than like New York, and its residents—many of them Polish, Italian, and black—are not as susceptible to either the city's fashionable liberalism nor to the Archie Bunker reaction to it as are people in the Big Apple. The 31st has the least Democratic part of Erie County, with most of Buffalo's rather scant supply of wealthy suburban enclaves. The regions to the east are ancestrally heavily Republican.

This is the district which elects Jack Kemp, once known chiefly as the former quarterback of the Buffalo Bills but now one of the genuine leaders of the Republican Party, nationally and in the House. He is also one of the genuine intellectual leaders of what became, by the late 1970s, our party of ideas. Kemp has a career that resembles and intersects Ronald Reagan's in many ways. Like Reagan the actor, Kemp the football player was a competent and dependable but not quite top-rank performer; like Reagan, he became head of his fellow workers' union. Unlike Reagan, he grew up in a comfortable background, as the son of a small businessman in southern California. And unlike Reagan, he moved east to pursue his career, though he did work briefly in the 1960s for incoming Governor Reagan in California. Like Reagan, he went through a period where his political ideas changed; unlike Reagan, that change did not lead him to change parties.

Kemp was first elected to Congress in 1970, in part because local Democrats were split between the party's nominee and its incumbent congressman who, having lost a Senate race, tried to run as an Independent. In his first years he was a conventional, little-noticed Republican. But for some reason Kemp, a physical education major in college, began to study economics—and leavened his studies with reflections on the America he knew in Los Angeles and Buffalo. He grew up in an area that had one of the highest economic growth rates in American history, and he represented an area with very little economic growth. He grew up in an environment where government was not a looming presence (though tax rates were not low, and government spent lots of money on schools, freeways, and water) and represented an area more highly taxed than almost any other part of the nation. While Democratic economists seemed concerned about the distribution of wealth, Kemp was concerned about the creation of wealth. He came to believe that government was overtaxing productive (*i.e.,* rich) people—killing the geese that laid the golden eggs. He was the politician who popularized the term supply-side economics and who advanced, and convinced virtually every Republican officeholder to support, the Kemp-Roth plan to cut taxes 10% a year for three years. It had this additional advantage, from the point of view of a representative from the Buffalo area: it would not, in Kemp's view, require cutting many federal programs, for greater economic growth would generate revenues to pay for them.

So to a considerable extent Kemp wrote the agenda and the program for the Reagan economic policy. Kemp–Roth, in modified form, passed the Congress in 1981; Kemp's friend David Stockman became head of the Office of Management and Budget. And if Kemp's supply-side policies have not seemed entirely successful, if they produced far more unemployment than he predicted and far less revenue, the focus of the national debate in 1983 still remained on how to stimulate economic growth, not on how to redistribute the wealth. Kemp's ideas differ in important respects not only from those of conventional Democrats but from those of conventional Republicans. Unlike many other Republicans (including Barber Conable, of the adjoining 30th district), Kemp is not much concerned about the size of deficits, nor is he particularly unfriendly to federal spending programs. He is proud of cosponsoring, with Robert Garcia of the South Bronx, the urban enterprise zones proposal. And he argues that economic growth is what blacks and working-class people, including many in his district, really need. Kemp's policies have not worked out exactly as he predicted—few politicians' policies do. He has even felt it necessary to oppose the president, as in 1982, when he embraced policies to raise revenues. But he has established himself as one of the genuine leaders of his party, intellectually and in the House as well.

His leadership there is formalized by his position as chairman of the House Republican Conference, and he is on the short list of possible minority leaders should Robert Michel relinquish that post. He also has experience in non-economic issues. He used to serve on the Defense Appropriations Subcommittee and chaired the committee drafting the Republicans' defense platform at the 1980 National Convention. He now serves as the ranking Republican on the Foreign Operations Appropriations Subcommittee, which puts him in the uncomfortable position of pushing through the foreign aid appropriation which so many of his colleagues have prided themselves on always voting against and now, with a Republican administration in office, must support. Despite his disagreements with the administration on tax rises, he remains close to at least some parts of the Reagan White House.

Naturally there has been much speculation that Kemp will run for higher office. He could hardly have forced himself onto the Republican national ticket in 1980—a ticket of a former actor and a former football player would not do—and he was not prepared to run for president himself, at age 45, that year. Nor was he willing, when he was rounding up unanimous Republican support, to take on Jacob Javits in the Senate primary and a risky general election race if he won. He stayed clear of the governor's race in 1982. Any statewide race would be chancy for Kemp: he is very popular in the Buffalo area, but it casts only 8% of the state's votes; and New York is still, on balance, a state that believes in the welfare state more than a Democrat would say that Kemp does. Besides, Kemp already has a national platform and important governmental responsibilities as congressman from the 31st district. He is one of the recognized national leaders of his party, and he has to grapple—as none of the leading Democratic candidates in 1983 and 1984 do—with the difficult choices that must be faced in governing. There is no reason why he should not run for president, and be taken as a serious candidate, from the job he now holds.

Kemp remains exceedingly popular in the Buffalo area, which, perhaps coincidentally, seems to have gotten less Democratic in statewide races since he began advancing his supply-side ideas. His reelection is essentially automatic; redistricting added Republican though unfamiliar territory and left him with a safe seat.

The People Pop. 1980: 515,021, up 8.9% 1970–80; voting age pop. 368,360; 1% Black, 1% Span. orig., 1% Asian orig. 23% housing units rented. Median owner $45,300; renter $201. Households: 78% family, 42% with children, 68% married couples.

Presidential Vote

1980	Reagan (R)	115,216	(51%)
	Carter (D)	90,316	(40%)
	Anderson (I)	18,198	(8%)

Rep. Jack F. Kemp (R) Elected 1970; b. July 13, 1935, Los Angeles, CA; home, Hamburg; Occidental Col., B.A. 1957, Long Beach St. U., CA Western U.; Presbyterian.

Career Pro football quarterback, San Diego Chargers and Buffalo Bills, 1957–70; Cofounder and Pres., AFL Players Assn., 1965–70; AFL Most Valuable Player, 1965; Army, 1958; Radio and TV commentator; Special Asst. to Gov. Ronald Reagan of CA, 1967; Special Asst. to Chmn. of Repub. Natl. Comm., 1969.

Offices 2252 RHOB, 202-225-5265. Also 1101 Fed. Bldg., 111 W. Huron St., Buffalo 14202, 716-846-4123.

Committees *Appropriations* (9th). Subcommittee: Foreign Operations. *Budget* (4th). Task Forces: Economic Policy and Growth; Education and Employment; International Finance and Trade; Tax Policy.

Group Ratings

	ADA	ACLU	COPE	CFA	LCV	LWV	NTU	NSI	COC	ACA	CSFC
1982	15	29	19	15	40	56	76	100	74	78	66
1981	10	—	19	36	28	—	86	—	100	82	73
1980	6	33	12	21	51	38	53	100	75	86	72

National Journal Ratings

	Economic		Foreign		Cultural	
1982	36%	(LIB)	4%	(LIB)	52%	(LIB)
	64%	(CONS)	92%	(CONS)	47%	(CONS)
1981	1%	(LIB)	53%	(LIB)	31%	(LIB)
	97%	(CONS)	47%	(CONS)	68%	(CONS)

Key Votes

1) Reagan 81 Budget	FOR	5) Incr SS Rtmt Age	FOR	9) Poor Pay Food Stamps	FOR
2) Reagan 81 Tax Cut	FOR	6) Saudi AWACS Sale	AGN	10) Ban Crt Busing Order	AGN
3) Bal Budget Amend	AGN	7) $ for MX Missile	FOR	11) Auto Local Content	AGN
4) Gas & Road Tax	AGN	8) Nerve Gas Prod	FOR	12) Nuclear Arms Freeze	AGN

Election Results

1982 general	Jack F. Kemp (R–C)	133,462	(75%)	($409,633)
	James A. Martin (D–L)	43,843	(25%)	($6,156)
1982 primary	Jack F. Kemp (R–C) unopposed			
1980 general	Jack F. Kemp (R–C–RTL)	167,434	(82%)	($158,061)
	Gale A. Denn (D–L)	37,875	(18%)	

Campaign Contributions and Expenditures

1981-82		Direct Cont. 81-82		PACS brkdwn			
Receipts	$469,986	Indiv	$337,662	Agr	$850	Ideo	$14,400
Expend.	$409,633	Party	$8,015	Bus	$91,532	Lbr	$5,000
Unspent	$98,348	PACS	$123,782	Hlth	$6,250	Prof	$2,250

THIRTY-SECOND DISTRICT

The 32d congressional district of New York includes Niagara County, site of the falls; part of suburban Erie County, just outside of Buffalo; the southern shore of Lake Ontario, from the Niagara River to the Rochester suburbs; and a swath going into the heart of the city of Rochester itself. Niagara Falls, though a major tourist attraction, is anything but a bucolic spot. Power lines strung on giant pylons fan out in every direction to provide power to the urban Northeast, Midwest, and Ontario; chemical plants emit noxious fumes and liquid wastes; the homes built along Love Canal, polluted by a chemical dump, are now empty and lifeless. The 32d's portion of the Buffalo suburbs, Tonawanda and North Tonawanda, are comfortable bedroom communities, settled three or four decades ago, of working-class and white-collar people. The district's portion of Rochester is almost half black and is the lowest income part of that city. In between the two cities, the country looks rural and is studded with the kind of small towns you find all over Upstate New York. The largest of them is Lockport, home of William Miller, congressman from this district for 14 years and Barry Goldwater's running mate in 1964.

The congressman from this district now is John LaFalce, a Democrat first elected in 1974. He is a product of the Erie County Democratic organization, a veteran of the legislature, a politician who has used his committee assignments—Banking and Small Business—to bring benefits to his district. While Jack Kemp, representing another part of the Niagara Frontier, has experimented with new economic policies, LaFalce remains faithful to what have become traditional Democratic policies. He has a record of solid support of the Democratic leadership and has not advanced any novel ideas for national policies. He chairs the

Economic Stabilization Subcommittee, which handles wage and price controls legislation. But these seem currently in disrepute, and as of early 1983 the Democrats were not interested in authorizing such controls even as a ploy to embarrass the Reagan administration.

This is not a heavily Democratic district in national terms, but it is close enough to one that LaFalce has been able to win reelection by large margins; essentially he has had no serious opposition. If anything the new territory added in the 1982 redistricting made the district more Democratic and LaFalce, without any Republican opponent, won reelection with 91% of the vote. The prospect is for him to continue winning throughout the 1980s.

The People Pop. 1980: 516,387, dn. 6.6% 1970–80; voting age pop. 375,165; 7% Black, 1% Span. orig., 1% Am. Ind. 31% housing units rented. Median owner $37,600; renter $174. Households: 74% family, 39% with children, 61% married couples.

Presidential Vote

1980	Reagan (R)	NA
	Carter (D)	NA
	Anderson (I)	NA

Rep. John J. LaFalce (D) Elected 1974; b. Oct. 6, 1939, Buffalo; home, Tonawanda; Canisius Col., B.S. 1961, Villanova U., J.D. 1964; Roman Catholic.

Career Law Clerk, Ofc. of Gen. Counsel, U.S. Dept. of the Navy, 1963; Practicing atty.; Army, 1965–67; NY Senate, 1971–72; NY Assembly, 1973–74.

Offices 2419 RHOB, 202-225-3231. Also Fed. Bldg., Buffalo 14202, 716-846-4056.

Committees *Banking, Finance and Urban Affairs* (10th). Subcommittees: Economic Stabilization (Chairman); Financial Institutions Supervision, Regulation and Insurance; International Development Institutions and Finance; International Trade; Investment and Monetary Policy. *Small Business* (5th). Subcommittee: SBA and SBIC Authority, Minority Enterprise and General Small Business Problems.

Group Ratings

	ADA	ACLU	COPE	CFA	LCV	LWV	NTU	NSI	COC	ACA	CSFC
1982	85	50	81	92	80	82	24	56	24	22	29
1981	70	—	79	71	71	—	14	—	17	14	37
1980	56	63	82	79	74	80	17	22	65	25	34

National Journal Ratings

	Economic		Foreign		Cultural	
1982	78%	(LIB)	79%	(LIB)	85%	(LIB)
	21%	(CONS)	21%	(CONS)	14%	(CONS)
1981	73%	(LIB)	70%	(LIB)	76%	(LIB)
	26%	(CONS)	30%	(CONS)	24%	(CONS)

Key Votes

1) Reagan 81 Budget	AGN	5) Incr SS Rtmt Age	AGN	9) Poor Pay Food Stamps	AGN
2) Reagan 81 Tax Cut	AGN	6) Saudi AWACS Sale	AGN	10) Ban Crt Busing Order	AGN
3) Bal Budget Amend	AGN	7) $ for MX Missile	AGN	11) Auto Local Content	FOR
4) Gas & Road Tax	—	8) Nerve Gas Prod	AGN	12) Nuclear Arms Freeze	FOR

Election Results

1982 general	John J. LaFalce (D–L)	116,386	(91%)	($80,941)
	Raymond R. Walker (C)	8,638	(7%)	($0)
1982 primary	John J. LaFalce (D–L) unopposed			
1980 general	John J. LaFalce (D–L)	122,929	(72%)	($66,000)
	H. William Feder (R–C–RTL)	48,428	(28%)	($33,088)

Campaign Contributions and Expenditures

1981-82		Direct Cont. 81-82		PACS brkdwn			
Receipts	$136,193	Indiv	$27,607	Agr	$650	Ideo	$500
Expend.	$80,941	Party	$200	Bus	$36,400	Lbr	$16,350
Unspent	$225,614	PACS	$60,475	Hlth	$1,900	Prof	$1,250

THIRTY-THIRD DISTRICT

Buffalo is the second largest city in New York and one of the important industrial centers on the Great Lakes. Huge steel mills line the shores of Lake Erie, as the principal east–west rail lines feed into downtown Buffalo and the industrial areas that circle it. This is the easternmost American port on the Great Lakes, and here giant freighters unload iron ore from the Mesabi Range and grain from the western prairies. Buffalo has long been one of the nation's leading steel producers and rivals Minneapolis as a miller of grain.

At the turn of the century, these basic industries were the fastest-growing, most dynamic sector of the economy. There were flush times in Buffalo then. The city sat on the nation's leading transportation arteries, and tens of thousands of Italian and Polish immigrants moved here, eager to work in its factories. Today the city's steel mills, grain elevators, and docks, along with its downtown and radial avenues, still look like something out of the 1920s, only a little run down and shabby. Buffalo no longer enjoys the advantages it once had. Its basic industries have stopped growing and, in some cases, have shut down. The major transportation routes have shifted to the south, and the great new mode of transportation, the airplane, scarcely touches down in Buffalo at all. In the early part of the century people were willing to put up with the fact that Buffalo receives an unusually heavy snowfall, because of its position at the extreme eastern end of Lake Erie. Now more and more people are trying to get away, to the Sun Belt, and the snow in Buffalo has become a national joke. All of this does not mean that Buffalo is moribund as a city. In the end its economic troubles may help: the price of housing and the cost of labor are now much lower here than in many Sun Belt cities, and it has a vast supply of fresh water. But its economy is not generating enough jobs for its current residents' children—much less any new migrants. The downtown is in trouble, and even the Buffalo branch of the State University of New York has moved to the suburbs.

Virtually all of Buffalo, with the steel mill town of Lackawanna just to the south, the white-collar suburb of Grand Island in the Niagara River to the north, and the blue-collar suburbs of Cheektowaga, Depew, and Lancaster directly to the east, make up the 33d congressional district of New York. This is a very heavily Democratic district—the most Democratic of any in Upstate New York. Republican voters have died or moved to the suburbs, and Buffalo's relatively depressed economy has increased the demand for various kinds of federal aid. The 33d is also the home of a Democratic organization, led by former Democratic State Chairman Joseph Crangle, which has played an important role in winning general elections as well as controlling local nominations.

In 1974 the Erie County Democratic organization elected two new congressmen, both still in their 30s. One was Assemblyman John LaFalce, now congressman from the suburban 32d district which stretches to Rochester, and the other was Erie County Comptroller Henry Nowak, now congressman from the 33d. Both have tended to the practical business of serving their constituencies rather than to the more chancy work of formulating national policy, as suburban Buffalo's Republican congressman, Jack Kemp, has. Nowak is a member of the Public Works and Transportation Committee, and is just one place removed from a subcommittee chairmanship; he has concentrated on programs like the Economic Development Administration, which channels federal aid into deserving local projects. Buffalo, in its days of flushness, did not have to rely on federal aid; now, apparently, it does.

If anyone in Congress has a safe seat, Henry Nowak does. He is a practical politician, one adept at persuading his colleagues to help him on a project; and those qualities seem apparent to his constituents as well. The 1982 redistricting suited him fine, and he won reelection that year, as he has every two years since 1974, with ease.

The People Pop. 1980: 516,392, dn. 17.4% 1970–80; voting age pop. 383,256; 17% Black, 2% Span. orig. 44% housing units rented. Median owner $32,400; renter $138. Households: 67% family, 34% with children, 48% married couples.

Presidential Vote

1980	Reagan (R)	NA
	Carter (D)	NA
	Anderson (I)	NA

Rep. Henry J. Nowak (D) Elected 1974; b. Feb. 21, 1935, Buffalo; home, Buffalo; Canisius Col., B.B.A. 1957, Buffalo Law Sch., J.D. 1961; Roman Catholic.

Career Army, 1957–58, 1961–62; Practicing atty.; Erie Cnty. Asst. Dist. Atty., 1964; Confidential Secy. to NY Supreme Ct. Justice Arthur J. Cosgrove, 1965; Erie Cnty. Comptroller, 1966–75.

Offices 2240 RHOB, 202-225-3306. Also 212 U.S. Courthouse, Buffalo 14202, 716-853-4131.

Committees *Public Works and Transportation* (8th). Subcommittees: Economic Development; Water Resources. *Small Business* (7th). Subcommittee: Tax, Access to Equity Capital and Business Opportunities (Chairman).

Group Ratings

	ADA	ACLU	COPE	CFA	LCV	LWV	NTU	NSI	COC	ACA	CSFC
1982	100	58	88	92	90	82	18	20	23	13	26
1981	75	—	87	100	71	—	26	—	17	13	32
1980	78	53	89	64	70	80	12	10	63	13	28

National Journal Ratings

	Economic		Foreign		Cultural	
1982	86%	(LIB)	90%	(LIB)	85%	(LIB)
	13%	(CONS)	10%	(CONS)	14%	(CONS)
1981	63%	(LIB)	88%	(LIB)	73%	(LIB)
	36%	(CONS)	12%	(CONS)	27%	(CONS)

Key Votes

1) Reagan 81 Budget AGN	5) Incr SS Rtmt Age AGN	9) Poor Pay Food Stamps AGN
2) Reagan 81 Tax Cut AGN	6) Saudi AWACS Sale AGN	10) Ban Crt Busing Order AGN
3) Bal Budget Amend AGN	7) $ for MX Missile AGN	11) Auto Local Content FOR
4) Gas & Road Tax FOR	8) Nerve Gas Prod AGN	12) Nuclear Arms Freeze FOR

Election Results

1982 general	Henry J. Nowak (D–L)	126,091	(84%)	($65,649)
	Walter J. Pillick (R–C)	19,791	(13%)	($1,110)
1982 primary	Henry J. Nowak (D–L) unopposed			
1980 general	Henry J. Nowak (D–L)	94,890	(83%)	($40,515)
	Roger Heymanowski (R–C)	16,560	(14%)	($0)

Campaign Contributions and Expenditures

1981-82		*Direct Cont. 81-82*				*PACS brkdwn*		
Receipts	$81,246	Indiv	$9,866	Agr	$1,000	Ideo	$1,000
Expend.	$65,649	PACS	$41,295	Bus	$17,200	Lbr	$21,150
Unspent	$59,928			Hlth	$—	Prof	$700

THIRTY-FOURTH DISTRICT

The 34th congressional district of New York is the western half of the Southern Tier—the local name for the counties on the northern side of the border between New York and Pennsylvania. Extending from the small city of Elmira to Lake Erie, the district contains the Corning Glass Works in Steuben County, two small Indian reservations, and a point on the western boundary exactly 496 miles from New York City via the Thomas E. Dewey Thruway. The district contains Lake Chautauqua, where the Chautauqua gatherings of the late 19th century were held: in the summer, down by the lake, on wide green lawns and on porches and in gazebos decorated with ornate white Victorian gingerbread, whole families came and listened to educational talks and inspirational lectures from the likes of William Jennings Bryan.

The small cities scattered among the district's valleys—Jamestown, Olean, Hornell, Corning, Penn Yan—and on the shores of Lake Erie—Dunkirk, Fredonia—tend to be Democratic or politically marginal, reflecting the preference of the Irish and Italian Catholics who came to this part of Upstate New York after it had first been settled by New England Yankees. Outside the towns the Yankee Republicans still predominate and overall this is usually a Republican district.

Historically this district has always been Republican; it was represented by Daniel Reed, the last Republican chairman of the House Ways and Means Committee. But it is now represented by a Democrat, Stanley Lundine, who won a special election in March 1976, at a time, in the wake of Watergate and Vietnam, when Democrats seemed to be prevailing in all kinds of historically Republican districts. Lundine had the advantage of being deeply involved in local politics; he was a popular mayor of Jamestown and had a strong base in Chautauqua County. He won that race with a surprising 61%.

Lundine is a member of the Banking and Science and Technology Committees; he is just one seat removed from the chairs of two subcommittees. His record on economic issues is more cautious and less partisan than that of most New York Democrats—which is probably just fine with this district. On cultural issues, he stands with many other Democrats, which is probably not as far out of line with constituents' views here as some would think: this is, after all, territory that left ancestral Republicanism over Watergate and Vietnam. Nonetheless, the changeover is not entirely complete. Lundine has won reelection by decisive, but not overwhelming, margins, but he has not had any really well-financed opposition—and he always could, given the financial capabilities of the national Republican Party. The Southern Tier currently elects two Democratic congressmen, both with strong personal assets; but it would be against the odds if both these districts were still represented by Democrats when it comes time to redistrict again in 1992.

The People Pop. 1980: 517,404, up 1.4% 1970–80; voting age pop. 369,166; 1% Black, 1% Span. orig. 23% housing units rented. Median owner $30,600; renter $152. Households: 74% family, 40% with children, 63% married couples.

Presidential Vote

1980	Reagan (R)	107,617	(55%)
	Carter (D)	73,700	(38%)
	Anderson (I)	13,400	(7%)

Rep. Stanley N. Lundine (D) Elected March 2, 1976; b. Feb. 4, 1939, Jamestown; home, Jamestown; Duke U., B.A. 1961, NYU, LL.B. 1964; Protestant.

Career Chautauqua Cnty. Pub. Defender, 1965–67; Jamestown City Assoc. Corp. Counsel, 1967–69, Mayor, 1969–76.

Offices 2427 RHOB, 202-225-3161. Also Fed. Bldg., Jamestown 14702, 716-484-0252.

Committees *Banking, Finance and Urban Affairs* (12th). Subcommittees: Economic Stabilization; Housing and Community Development; International Trade, Investment and Monetary Policy. *Science and Technology* (14th). Subcommittees: Energy Research and Production; Science, Research and Technology. *Select Committee on Aging* (11th). Subcommittee: Housing and Consumer Interests.

Group Ratings

	ADA	ACLU	COPE	CFA	LCV	LWV	NTU	NSI	COC	ACA	CSFC
1982	80	79	80	69	83	83	47	0	27	5	27
1981	85	—	79	50	76	—	40	—	24	24	30
1980	83	77	79	71	65	70	23	0	57	13	30

National Journal Ratings

	Economic		Foreign		Cultural	
1982	61%	(LIB)	96%	(LIB)	74%	(LIB)
	39%	(CONS)	4%	(CONS)	26%	(CONS)
1981	63%	(LIB)	91%	(LIB)	83%	(LIB)
	37%	(CONS)	9%	(CONS)	16%	(CONS)

Key Votes

1) Reagan 81 Budget	AGN	5) Incr SS Rtmt Age	FOR	9) Poor Pay Food Stamps	—
2) Reagan 81 Tax Cut	FOR	6) Saudi AWACS Sale	AGN	10) Ban Crt Busing Order	AGN
3) Bal Budget Amend	AGN	7) $ for MX Missile	AGN	11) Auto Local Content	FOR
4) Gas & Road Tax	AGN	8) Nerve Gas Prod	AGN	12) Nuclear Arms Freeze	FOR

Election Results

1982 general	Stanley N. Lundine (D)	99,502	(60%)	($195,009)
	James J. Snyder (R–C)	63,972	(39%)	($81,848)
1982 primary	Stanley N. Lundine (D) unopposed			
1980 general	Stanley N. Lundine (D)	93,839	(55%)	($125,269)
	James Abdella (R–C)	75,039	(44%)	($83,315)

Campaign Contributions and Expenditures

1981-82		Direct Cont. 81-82		PACS brkdwn			
Receipts	$218,142	Indiv	$107,302	Agr	$8,250	Ideo	$8,300
Expend.	$195,009	Party	$2,037	Bus	$29,300	Lbr	$41,825
Unspent	$38,355	PACS	$99,657	Hlth	$2,850	Prof	$1,700

Indirect Party Expend: $110   *Indep Expend:* Agn: $5,817 (NCPAC)

NORTH CAROLINA

North Carolina, now the tenth most populous state, still does not bulk large in the national consciousness. It is a place with a feel and a vibrancy of its own, but one which is not much known to outsiders. North Carolina has no major city to establish the state's identity, no well known history or monuments, no major vacation spots—no Atlanta, Mount Vernon, or Disney World. None of North Carolina's metropolitan areas even approaches a population of one million. But, although few Americans are aware of it, North Carolina is one of the most industrialized states in the nation. This does not necessarily mean it is economically advanced; most of its industry is in textiles, a low-wage industry, or furniture-making or tobacco. In these products North Carolina leads the nation; in most others it is not important. The state has a proud political tradition, but one that has not produced a great national leader. That is partly due to the tradition itself: North Carolinians like Sam Ervin and, perhaps, Jesse Helms, have specialized in frustrating what they have seen as overreaching power rather than in exercising power itself.

North Carolina's political development has been affected by its terrain, and yet the state has no clear geographic delineation from its neighbors to the north and south; it is just a slice of land running from coastal barrier islands and the coastal plain up through the rolling Piedmont to the mountains, the highest east of the Rockies. North Carolina was a late-developing colony; it has no major port like Charleston, South Carolina, no inland water route like the rivers that branch off from Chesapeake Bay and reach into Virginia and Maryland. North Carolina's settlers were not as rich as those elsewhere, but they were fiercely independent; they declared independence even before the Declaration in Philadelphia, and they were among the last of the 13 original states to join the Union—because they thought the Constitution might be too constricting. North Carolina was contrary about the Civil War, too. It refused to secede from the Union until Virginia did so, and cut it off from the North; then it contributed more soldiers to the Confederacy than any other state.

This continues to be a state of the common people, not the kind of aristocrats who dominate business and politics in Virginia nor the brash Ted Turnerish tycoons of Georgia's Atlanta. But it has more people than either of these states, and in the last ten years it has been gaining more new jobs than either of them as well. North Carolina has had little in-migration from other states or from abroad—except for slaves brought in before 1808—and North Carolina has always had a lower percentage of blacks than the Deep South states. For many years North Carolina sent migrants elsewhere, from the yeoman farmers (and three presidents, Jackson, Polk, and Andrew Johnson) who were born here and moved to Tennessee, to entire high school classes of young blacks who got on the bus after graduation to go to New York and Philadelphia in the 1950s and 1960s. Today North Carolina remains overwhelmingly Baptist and Methodist (it was one of the last states to allow liquor by the drink, and most counties still do not have it), but it is no longer an exporter of people; there are jobs and boom enough to hold people here.

North Carolina also remains a state with a vigorous two-party politics, built largely around geographical divisions. The coastal lowlands, once strong slave territory, have always been heavily Democratic; the mountains, with virtually no slaves or blacks, have always had a Republican tradition. And even in the days of the solid Democratic South, Republicans won significant minorities of the votes in the Piedmont region. The 1960s backlash against the civil rights movement, and the particular appeal of Jesse Helms to coastal and lowland whites, enabled the Republicans to win significant victories in congressional and state elections from 1966 to 1980—and helped Helms to become a national political figure of great importance. But the Democrats have come charging back, primarily due to the leadership of Jim Hunt, elected governor in 1976 and reelected (after persuading voters, against Ervin's advice, to change their state constitution) in 1980 despite the Republican trend. Since 1980 North Carolina, and a significant part of the political community across the nation, have been waiting for what seems an inevitable clash between these two leaders in the 1984 Senate race. So far Hunt has won the initial skirmishes: he got voters to approve a gas tax rise, despite Helms's campaign against it, in 1981, and Helms's Republicans lost rather than, as they hoped they would, gained House seats in the 1982 elections (in which there were no statewide contests here). The race will be a contrast not only on issues, on which the two have little agreement, but on styles of leadership: Helms is essentially a critic, a Cassandra who decries what he thinks is wrong; Hunt is essentially a doer, a man who puts the force of his personality behind his policies and makes things change. It is also quite likely to be one of the most expensive campaigns ever fought: Helms's Congressional Club raised nearly $10 million through direct mail in 1981–82, and Hunt has already received offers of help from opponents of Helms's New Right policies across the nation, and also has a dense network of financial supporters in every one of the 100 counties in the state. The second most important election in the country—that is what many people in—and out—of North Carolina are calling it—and some of them omit the word second.

Governor. Jim Hunt as governor has done more than most North Carolinians thought possible to change the tone of public life in the state and to make it live up to its traditions of tolerance and progressiveness. He seems to understand that North Carolina cannot continue to grow forever as a low-wage labor state, that it has to upgrade its work force and to attract higher-skill jobs than it has in the past. So Hunt has put together an industrial development program that rivals South Carolina's, and has worked to overcome the hostility many local business owners and officials have toward new businesses that threaten to raise local wages and working conditions. In education, he has done what few northern politicians can do:

gained the support of the teachers' union with higher wages and instituted a program of competency testing, to make sure pupils are actually learning something. On racial issues, Hunt got criticized by some black leaders for refusing to pardon all the defendants in the Wilmington 10 case. But he has appointed blacks to top statewide jobs including the state supreme court, and has helped a black candidate nearly win election to Congress. He is not a liberal on all issues: he strongly backs capital punishment and takes a stern approach to crime; he took on HEW Secretary Joseph Califano in the Carter administration on his attacks on cigarette smoking and on the dispute over racial balance in the state university system.

Hunt has also worked to build a strong Democratic Party in North Carolina, and saw his efforts reach fruition in the 1982 congressional races. He has built a strong organization that, in a typical county, includes leading businessmen and the local labor leader (if there is one; North Carolina has the lowest percentage of union membership in the nation), some of the leading lawyers and all the leaders in the black community, local white liberals and old-time Dixiecrats. He has had important involvement in party affairs at the national level as well. In 1981 he chaired the Hunt Commission on presidential delegate selection, which cut the "window" during which delegate selection could take place and allocated some places at the convention to public officials.

Hunt has shown great strength at the polls. He won his first primary in 1976 without a runoff and won 70% against a former governor in 1980; he won both general elections with more than 60% of the vote, despite the Republican trend in 1980—the highest Democratic percentages in gubernatorial elections since the 1950s. A native of the eastern part of the state, he has carried that area by large margins, and carried both the Piedmont and the western mountains as well. In polls in 1982 and 1983 he led Helms by wide margins, which is not surprising: Helms has won by lesser majorities against weaker candidates, and has a larger percentage of the electorate dead set against him. But Hunt in 1983 had not yet announced as a candidate, and the dynamics of this race have by no means been played out.

The next governor will probably be chosen in the Democratic primary, but no one has any clear idea of who he will be. Prime competitors include Attorney General Rufus Edmisten, Sam Ervin's top aide at the Watergate hearings, and Charlotte Mayor Eddie Knox. The governorship, usually the focus of North Carolina politics, may very well be overshadowed by the Hunt-Helms race.

Senators. Jesse Helms has been an important figure in national politics for eight years, ever since he helped organize the North Carolina primary campaign for Ronald Reagan in 1976, and victory here kept Reagan in the race. He was a top aide to Senator Willis Smith, a conservative who beat University of North Carolina President Frank Graham in 1950; he became well known in the 1960s as a commentator on a Raleigh TV station and on the radio Tobacco Network. He won his first election to the Senate in 1972, against a Democratic congressman with a liberal record on many issues; he won reelection in 1978 against the state insurance commissioner, who had difficulty raising money and articulating positions on national issues.

Helms is a true believer, a vitriolic opponent of policies and trends which he believes are leading America the wrong way. He stands for a hard-line foreign policy, standing by American allies in Taiwan and El Salvador; he is a strong opponent of abortion; he wants to see prayer allowed in schools; he wants to cut back vastly on food stamps and other programs of aid to the poor. He is also a political innovator. He saw the Nixon and Ford administrations taking what he considered the wrong position on many issues; he knew he had few allies in the

Democratic Senate. So he resorted to two unusual tactics. First of all, he sought roll call votes on issues like abortion, not because he hoped to prevail, but to put on record senators he wished to defeat. Then, in campaigns, Helms and his allies could use the roll calls—though many observers claimed they were not always fair tests of the issue.

Helms's other new tactic was direct mail. In effect he created a lobby of thousands of people all over the country who share his views on issues and are willing to part with small and, in some cases, large sums of money to advance them. Helms raised nearly $7 million for his re-election campaign in North Carolina, but very little of it went into his campaign; most was ploughed into building up his mailing lists. By 1980, he was able to use the lists to raise money directly for John East, then the long-shot Republican candidate for senator and now his junior colleague in Washington. In 1981 and 1982 his Congressional Club raised at least $10 million, contributing some to candidates but, more important, making its own independent expenditures in some races. Not all of it was spent effectively that year. But the mere possession of such a fundraising tool makes Helms a force in national politics. It means he can raise very substantial sums should he run for reelection in 1984. And it means he can raise enough to run a visible candidacy for president, in the Republican primaries or as an independent in the general election, should Ronald Reagan not run in 1984.

And yet at the same time as he was raising this money, Helms was becoming a visibly less effective senator. His colleagues resented his tactic of forcing roll calls only to oppose them later in their campaigns. They resented also his use of his seat on the Foreign Relations Committee to block the approval of Reagan nominees who had widespread support in the Senate—though this could not have happened had the administration not submitted to his tactics. They resented his tactics when he finally, in 1982, got the floor and held it for his cherished constitutional amendments to ban abortion and allow school prayer. Helms got so tied up in disputes about procedure, and in debates about which form of anti-abortion measure to advance, that he lost on everything—and by margins that suggested personal repudiation as well as disagreement on the merits.

Most damaging was his management of the farm bill in 1981. When Republicans won a majority in the Senate, Helms became chairman of the Agriculture Committee. The farm bill is one of the politically most sensitive pieces of legislation, and virtually every senator has something important at stake in it; senators rely on a chairman to hold the thing together and see that everyone's interests are protected. Helms instead concentrated on tobacco and peanuts—two of North Carolina's leading crops—and ignored the rest of the bill; things fell apart so badly that Bob Dole had to come in and rescue him by managing the bill himself.

Now the Senate seems poised to attack the tobacco allotment and subsidy program. Tobacco is the number one crop in North Carolina, and one of great importance: it is very labor-intensive, and it is the only crop that enables a family to make a living off as little as 15 acres of land. The economies of dozens of North Carolina counties—the most thickly settled rural part of the country—depend on tobacco. But many senators want to cut tobacco subsidies for health reasons, and others—sometimes backed by tenant tobacco farmers—want to abolish the allotment program which restricts tobacco farming to land devoted to tobacco in the 1930s. It is essentially a subsidy to owners of such land, who include Mrs. Jesse Helms. North Carolina Congressman Charlie Rose, chairman of the Tobacco and Peanuts Subcommittee in the House, wants to change the law to freeze price support levels and to put pressure on non-farmers to give up their allotments; he had the votes to get such a measure through the House in 1982. But Helms desperately wants to avoid any change at all. He can see clearly that his enemies in the Senate, by no means all of them Democrats, would love to embarrass him by hurting his number one crop despite his chairmanship of the Agriculture Committee just before he seeks reelection. Helms has already hurt himself with tobacco interests once, in 1982, when he voted for Bob Dole's tax bill which included a rise in the tax on tobacco. Democrats gleefully labeled Helms and East, who joined him, as "the tobacco tax twins." Actually, this was an act of some political courage, very much in line with Senate tradition; Helms had promised Dole he would give him his vote if he needed it, and he delivered when asked. But it still is likely to hurt him back home.

Such adversity is not new to Jesse Helms. He is not a man who expects political success; when Ronald Reagan was running, Helms was fond of saying that maybe God had given America one more chance—with the implication that it didn't matter much anyway. This is the perfect attitude for direct mail fundraising: the forebodings of imminent doom, the pessimistic outlook, the grim determination to keep fighting for what is right no matter what the odds. But it has not proved a very effective attitude for approaching one's duties as a member of the majority in the Senate. And it leads some observers to believe that Helms, rather than face a difficult reelection campaign, will run for president if he sees any opening at all.

Senator John East operates very much in Helms's shadow. A college professor from East Carolina University, he was elected largely by a campaign financed by the Congressional Club, which raised $600,000 for TV advertising in the last few weeks. East attacked incumbent Democrat Robert Morgan for his support of the Panama Canal Treaties, aid to Sandinist Nicaragua, aid to New York City, and his opposition to the B–1 bomber; he won 50%–49%. In his first two years he attracted notice through hearings he held on a bill to have fetuses be declared persons—an attempt to change a constitutional ruling by a simple law. East's fate seems pretty well tied to Helms's. If Helms does not win reelection in 1984, very few people will expect East to win in 1986; and the competition in the Democratic primary will be correspondingly fierce.

Congressional districting. North Carolina's congressional districting, modified by a federal court to meet the requirements of the Voting Rights Act, was expected to benefit the Republicans. Instead the Democrats won two of the Republicans' four seats. Financed by Helms's Congressional Club, Republicans waged serious campaigns in the 2d, 3d, 4th, and 5th districts; they lost each one, even in the 4th when incumbent Ike Andrews was arrested for drunk driving during the campaign. But the Democrats beat two 1980 freshmen, upsetting one in the 6th who had been strengthened by redistricting and beating another by a narrow margin in the often-marginal, mountainous 11th.

Presidential politics. North Carolina has a relatively early presidential primary. It played a key role in 1976, keeping Ronald Reagan in the race; it has never had much impact on the Democratic side.

In the general election, North Carolina was one of Jimmy Carter's strongest states in 1976, and he nearly won it again in 1980. It is one of the southern states which is likely to be a target for a Democratic presidential candidate in 1984. The state, in presidential elections, breaks much more cleanly on economic lines than do northern states, where cultural attitudes seem more important: in North Carolina blacks vote unanimously Democratic (especially against Helms), lower-income whites vote heavily Democratic, and upper-income whites vote Republican. The key is the blue-collar vote.

The People   Est. Pop. 1982: 6,019,000; Pop. 1980: 5,881,766, up 2.3% 1980–82 and 15.7% 1970–80; 2.6% of U.S. total, 10th largest; voting age pop. 4,224,031; 1% American Indian, 20% Black, 1% Spanish origin. Single ancestry: 23% English, 5% German, 4% Irish, 1% Scottish, French. Registered voters (1982): 2,674,787 Total. 1,924,394 D (72%); 640,675 R (24%); 109,293 unaffiliated (4%). 14% with 1–3 yrs. col., 13% with 4+ yrs. col. 14.6% below poverty level. 28% housing units rented; median house value: $36,000; median monthly rent: $135. Households: 77% family, 43% with children, 63% married couples.

1982 Share of Federal Tax Burden $12,148,200,000; 2.03% of U.S. total, 15th largest.

1982 Share of Federal Expenditures

	Total		Non-Defense		Defense	
Total Expend	$11,527m	(1.91%)	$8,439m	(1.99%)	$3,088m	(1.73%)
St/Lcl Grants	1,852m	(2.10%)	1,851m	(2.10%)	1m	(2.78%)
Salary/Wages	2,163m	(2.77%)	317m	(1.16%)	1,846m	(3.64%)
Ind Payments	6,408m	(2.24%)	5,539m	(2.15%)	869m	(3.04%)
Procurement	1,000m	(0.69%)	167m	(0.53%)	833m	(0.73%)
Other Programs	103m	(1.90%)	103m	(1.92%)	0m	(0%)
Loan/Insurance	3,607m	(5.64%)	3,557m	(5.76%)	50m	(2.27%)

Political Lineup   Governor, James B. Hunt (D). Senators, Jesse A. Helms (R) and John P. East (R). Representatives, 11 (9 D and 2 R). State Senate, 50 (44 D and 6 R); State House of Representatives, 120 (102 D and 18 R).

Presidential Vote

1980	Reagan (R)	915,018	(49%)
	Carter (D)	873,635	(47%)
	Anderson (I)	52,800	(3%)
1976	Ford (R)	741,690	(44%)
	Carter (D)	927,365	(55%)

1980 Democratic Presidential Primary			*1980 Republican Presidential Primary*		
Carter	516,778	(70%)	Reagan	113,854	(68%)
Kennedy	130,684	(18%)	Bush	36,631	(22%)
Brown	21,420	(3%)	Five others.	13,368	(8%)
No preference	68,380	(9%)	No preference	4,538	(3%)

SENATORS

Sen. Jesse A. Helms (R) Elected 1972, seat up 1984; b. Oct. 18, 1921, Monroe; home, Raleigh; Wingate Col., Wake Forest Col.; Baptist.

Career Navy, WWII; City Ed., *Raleigh Times*; A. A. to U.S. Sens. Willis Smith, 1951–53 and Alton Lennon, 1953; Exec. Dir., NC Bankers Assn., 1953–60; Raleigh City Cncl., 1957–61; Exec. V.P., WRAL-TV and Tobacco Radio Network, 1960–72.

Offices 402 DSOB, 202-224-6342. Also Fed. Bldg., Raleigh 27611, 919-755-4630; and Box 2944, Hickory 28601, 704-322-5170.

Committees *Agriculture, Nutrition, and Forestry* (Chairman). Subcommittees: Agricultural Production, Marketing, and Stabilization of Prices; Agricultural Research and General Legislation; Rural Development, Oversight, and Investigations. *Foreign Relations* (3d). Subcommittees: Arms Control, Oceans, International Operations, and Environment; East Asian and Pacific Affairs; Western Hemisphere Affairs (Chairman). *Rules and Administration* (5th). *Select Committee on Ethics* (2d).

Group Ratings

	ADA	ACLU	COPE	CFA	LCV	LWV	NTU	NSI	COC	ACA	CSFC
1982	0	7	9	10	8	8	98	100	95	95	91
1981	0	—	10	14	19	—	96	—	100	95	89
1980	11	20	5	0	23	30	80	100	83	100	97

National Journal Ratings

	Economic		Foreign		Cultural	
1982	34%	(LIB)	3%	(LIB)	0%	(LIB)
	65%	(CONS)	84%	(CONS)	96%	(CONS)
1981	2%	(LIB)	30%	(LIB)	2%	(LIB)
	88%	(CONS)	68%	(CONS)	82%	(CONS)

Key Votes

1) Reagan 81 Budget	FOR	5) $ to El Salvador	FOR	9) Poor Pay Food Stamps	FOR
2) Reagan 81 Tax Cut	FOR	6) Saudi AWACS Sale	FOR	10) Ban Crt Busing Order	FOR
3) Bal Budget Amend	FOR	7) Ban Abortion	FOR	11) Clinch Riv Brdr Rctr	FOR
4) Gas & Road Tax	AGN	8) Nerve Gas Prod	FOR	12) Legal Services Corp	AGN

Election Results

1978 general	Jesse A. Helms (R)	619,151	(55%)	($8,123,205)
	John R. Ingram (D)	516,663	(45%)	($264,088)
1978 primary	Jesse A. Helms (R) unopposed			
1972 general	Jesse A. Helms (R)	795,248	(54%)	($654,246)
	Nick Galifianakis (D)	677,293	(46%)	($470,093)

Campaign Contributions and Expenditures

1977-78		PACS brkdwn			
Receipts	$8,127,522	Agr	$16,900	Ideo	$35,981
Expend.	$8,123,205	Bus	$188,539	Lbr	$—
Unspent	$10,840	Hlth	$25,260	Prof	$5,500

Sen. John P. East (R) Elected 1980, seat up 1986; b. May 5, 1931, Springfield, IL; home, Greenville; Earlham Col., B.A. 1953, U. of IL, J.D. 1959, U. of FL, M.A., Ph.D. 1964; United Methodist.

Career USMC, 1953–55; Practicing atty., 1960; Prof., E. Carolina U., 1964–80; Repub. Natl. Committeeman, 1976, 1980, Platform Comm., 1976; Mbr., Ed. Bd., *Modern Age* and *Political Science Review*.

Offices 553 HSOB, 202-224-3154. Also P.O. Drawer 25009, Raleigh 27611, 919-775-4401; and P.O. Box 8087, Greenville 27834, 919-757-1188.

Committees *Armed Services* (9th). Subcommittees: Manpower and Personnel; Military Construction; Sea Power and Force Projection. *Judiciary* (7th). Subcommittees: Courts; Security and Terrorism; Separation of Powers (Chairman). *Labor and Human Resources* (9th). Subcommittees: Alcoholism and Drug Abuse; Education, Arts and Humanities; Labor.

Group Ratings

	ADA	ACLU	COPE	CFA	LCV	LWV	NTU	NSI	COC	ACA	CSFC
1982	0	11	5	0	0	8	94	100	86	90	92
1981	0	—	11	14	6	—	87	—	100	94	91

National Journal Ratings

	Economic		Foreign		Cultural	
1982	34%	(LIB)	3%	(LIB)	0%	(LIB)
	65%	(CONS)	84%	(CONS)	96%	(CONS)
1981	2%	(LIB)	17%	(LIB)	18%	(LIB)
	88%	(CONS)	82%	(CONS)	81%	(CONS)

Key Votes

1) Reagan 81 Budget	FOR	5) $ to El Salvador FOR	9) Poor Pay Food Stamps FOR
2) Reagan 81 Tax Cut	FOR	6) Saudi AWACS Sale FOR	10) Ban Crt Busing Order FOR
3) Bal Budget Amend	FOR	7) Ban Abortion FOR	11) Clinch Riv Brdr Rctr FOR
4) Gas & Road Tax	AGN	8) Nerve Gas Prod FOR	12) Legal Services Corp —

Election Results

1980 general	John P. East (R)	898,064	(50%)	($1,175,875)
	Robert Morgan (D)	887,653	(49%)	($948,209)
1980 primary	John P. East (R) unopposed			
1974 general	Robert Morgan (D)	633,775	(62%)	($781,201)
	William E. Stevens (R)	377,618	(37%)	($385,527)

Campaign Contributions and Expenditures

1979-80			PACS brkdwn		
Receipts	$1,332,565	Agr	$17,000	Ideo	$36,503
Expend.	$1,297,875	Bus	$129,516	Lbr	$1,000
Unspent	$34,690	Hlth	$4,000	Prof	$—

GOVERNOR

Gov. James B. Hunt, Jr. (D) Elected 1976, term expires Jan. 1985; b. May 16, 1937, Greensboro; home, Raleigh; NC St. U., B.S. 1959, M.S. 1962, J.D. 1964; Presbyterian.

Career Natl. College Dir., Dem. Natl. Comm., 1962–63; Econ. Advisor to State of Nepal, 1964–66; Practicing atty., 1966–72; Asst. NC Dem. Party Chmn., 1969; Lt. Gov. of NC, 1973–77.

Offices The Capitol, Raleigh 27602, 919-733-5811.

Election Results

1980 gen.	James B. Hunt, Jr. (D)	1,143,145	(62%)
	Beverly Lake (R)	691,449	(37%)
1980 prim.	James B. Hunt, Jr. (D)	524,844	(70%)
	Robert W. Scott (D)	217,289	(29%)
	One other (D)	11,551	(2%)
1976 gen.	James B. Hunt, Jr. (D)	1,081,293	(65%)
	David T. Flaherty (R)	564,102	(34%)

FIRST DISTRICT

If you want to know why tobacco farming is still subsidized and encouraged by a federal government that also seeks to discourage smoking, the best place to come to is the eastern coastal plain of North Carolina. This is flat land, not particularly distinguished for its fertility, yet it is among the most thickly settled rural land in the United States. The reason is tobacco. It is a most peculiar crop, one that requires much labor and close tending, since different tobacco

NORTH CAROLINA — Congressional Districts, Counties, and Selected Places — *(11 Districts)*

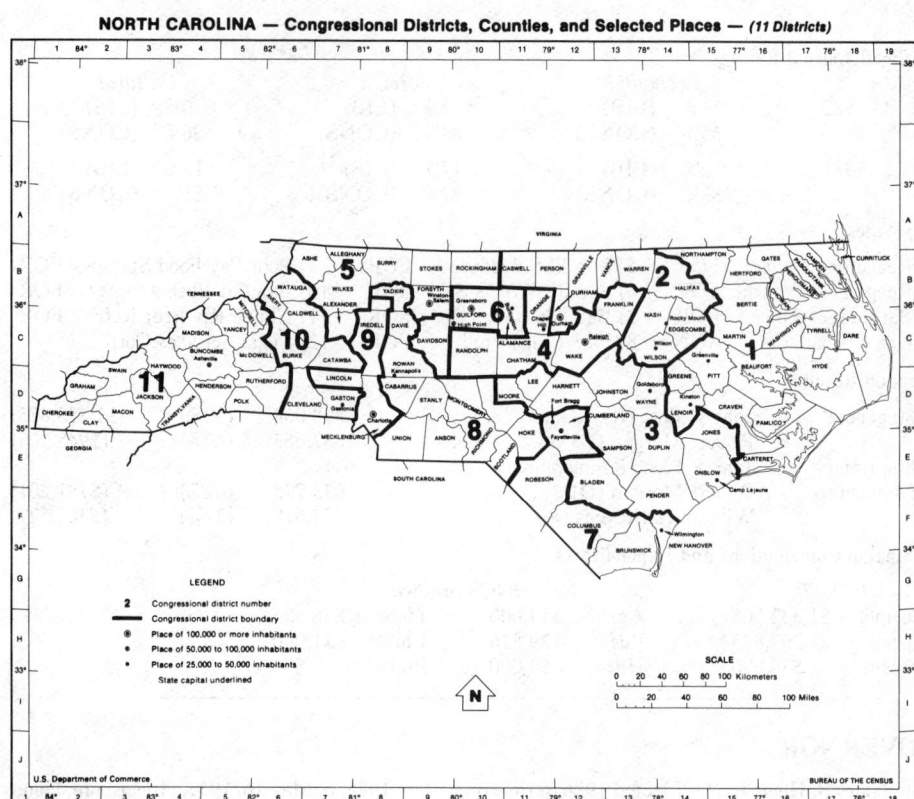

leaves on the same stalk mature at different times. It is also a crop that, acre for acre, can be lucrative. Since slavery tobacco has been grown on small farms, not large plantations, 15 acres of tobacco can produce enough income to support a family. Tobacco production, moreover, is concentrated in a few areas: virtually all of this country's tobacco is grown in North Carolina, South Carolina, and Kentucky. As a result, in these states and in some of their congressional districts there are literally tens of thousands of families whose livelihoods come directly from tobacco. Not surprisingly, their representatives in Congress are not going to allow federal tobacco programs to be cut if there is any way they can help it.

For many years tobacco was the only real mainstay of the economy in eastern North Carolina. Job opportunities were so scarce that eastern North Carolina produced thousands of migrants north; it has always produced high percentages of volunteers for the military services, from the Civil War to the post-Vietnam era. More recently, there have been more jobs: new textile and apparel mills, factories built by European and Japanese companies. But there are virtually no unions here, and wages are still low. Accordingly, tobacco retains its symbolic and most of its economic importance.

North Carolina's 1st congressional district lies entirely within the state's eastern coastal zone. It includes the Outer Banks, the string of coastal islands beyond Pamlico and Albemarle Sounds, where the Wright brothers flew the first airplane. Also here is Cape Hatteras, where the warm Gulf Stream meets the colder currents, creating seas that have sunk countless ships. There is no really good port here (or anywhere else in North Carolina), and most of the people live inland, in small cities like New Bern, Elizabeth City, and Greenville—at 35,000 the district's largest city. Even more live in the countryside, on small farms or in isolated house trailers. Some 32% of the 1st district's adult residents are black, the second highest percentage in North Carolina's 11 congressional districts.

The white voters of the 1st retain a Democratic preference from slaveholding days. They steadfastly supported Democratic presidential candidates until 1968, when they went for George Wallace, and 1972, when they went for Richard Nixon. After Watergate, they reverted to their Democratic habits; even Jesse Helms, who has considerable appeal here, did not carry this district in 1978.

The congressman from the 1st district is Walter Jones, a Democrat first chosen in a 1966 special election. Jones is now the chairman of the Merchant Marine and Fisheries Committee, a position his predecessor in the 1st district also held. Jones supports the elaborate system of subsidies that help the maritime industry and members of the maritime unions escape the rigors of competition. Jones has not, however, been particularly active as committee chairman; he has been ill, and the lead role in the major maritime bill of 1982 was taken by Mario Biaggi, the number two Democrat on the committee.

To get this full committee chairmanship, Jones gave up what is for most of his constituents a more important post, the chairmanship of the Tobacco and Peanuts Subcommittee on Agriculture. However, it was left in good hands: those of Charlie Rose of the 7th district, a politically adept and active Democrat who has been able to pilot his bills through the full committee and on the floor of the House.

Jones, it should be noted, votes quite often with national Democrats on most issues. This may be one example of the effectiveness of the reform requiring all committee chairmen to be elected by the Democratic Caucus; it also reflects the national Democratic orientation of North Carolina's congressional Democrats. Jones has been routinely reelected, though he might choose to retire one of these years.

The People Pop. 1980: 536,219, up 13.2% 1970–80; voting age pop. 382,422; 32% Black, 1% Span. orig. 27% housing units rented. Median owner $33,600; renter $111. Households: 77% family, 43% with children, 61% married couples.

Presidential Vote

1980	Reagan (R)	72,815	(45%)
	Carter (D)	84,207	(53%)
	Anderson (I)	3,337	(2%)

Rep. Walter B. Jones (D) Elected Feb. 5, 1966; b. Aug. 19, 1913, Fayetteville; home, Farmville; NC St. U., B.S. 1934; Baptist.

Career Office supply business, 1934–49; Mayor of Farmville, 1949–53; NC Gen. Assembly, 1955–59; NC Senate, 1965.

Offices 241 CHOB, 202-225-3101. Also 108 E. Wilson St., Farmville 27828, 919-753-3082.

Committees *Agriculture* (3d) Subcommittee: Tobacco and Peanuts. *Merchant Marine and Fisheries* (Chairman).

Group Ratings

	ADA	ACLU	COPE	CFA	LCV	LWV	NTU	NSI	COC	ACA	CSFC
1982	40	50	41	38	41	30	18	71	65	32	34
1981	25	—	39	38	46	—	18	—	36	24	44
1980	22	20	50	36	35	50	30	75	75	38	47

National Journal Ratings

	Economic		Foreign		Cultural	
1982	57%	(LIB)	56%	(LIB)	44%	(LIB)
	42%	(CONS)	44%	(CONS)	56%	(CONS)
1981	64%	(LIB)	—%	(LIB)	61%	(LIB)
	36%	(CONS)	—%	(CONS)	39%	(CONS)

Key Votes

1) Reagan 81 Budget	AGN	5) Incr SS Rtmt Age	FOR	9) Poor Pay Food Stamps	AGN
2) Reagan 81 Tax Cut	AGN	6) Saudi AWACS Sale	—	10) Ban Crt Busing Order	AGN
3) Bal Budget Amend	FOR	7) $ for MX Missile	AGN	11) Auto Local Content	FOR
4) Gas & Road Tax	—	8) Nerve Gas Prod	FOR	12) Nuclear Arms Freeze	AGN

Election Results

1982 general	Walter B. Jones (D)	79,954	(81%)	($45,106)
	James F. McIntyre III (R)	17,478	(18%)	($0)
1982 primary	Walter B. Jones (D)	72,290	(83%)	
	Thomas B. Brandon III (D)	14,952	(17%)	
1980 general	Walter B. Jones (D) unopposed ...	108,738		($29,126)

Campaign Contributions and Expenditures

1981-82		Direct Cont. 81-82		PACS brkdwn			
Receipts	$81,235	Indiv	$11,842	Agr	$2,000	Ideo	$1,500
Expend.	$45,106	Party	$5,100	Bus	$23,524	Lbr	$16,250
Unspent	$112,770	PACS	$45,624	Hlth	$2,000	Prof	$—

SECOND DISTRICT

North of Raleigh and south of the Virginia line, the 2d congressional district of North Carolina is situated on an inland portion of the coastal plain where it rises to become the Piedmont. With one notable exception, this is a rural and small-town district. The largest city in its eastern half is Rocky Mount, with 41,000 people. Tobacco and textiles are the main products; tobacco is marketed in the old courthouse towns, textiles produced in mills scattered here and there, usually near rivers or main highways. The one exception is the city of Durham. After the Civil War, a young Confederate soldier, James B. Duke, returned to his farm where Durham is today. He decided to go into the tobacco business, eventually developed a new product (the cigarette), and founded the American Tobacco Company and one of America's great fortunes. Durham grew up as a tobacco factory town, with a large black population (47% today); it is also the home of Duke University, which the tobacco baron founded, one of America's premier universities. The voting tradition in most of the district is Dixiecratic among the white majority and generally Democratic among the black minority. Durham, however, is a national Democratic town.

The 2d district was the scene in 1982 of a congressional race that, with the shift of a few votes, would have made some history. The district's congressman, L. H. Fountain, a courtly southern gentleman, was retiring after 30 years of service, and among the contenders to replace him was H. M. (Mickey) Michaux, who is black. He also had strong credentials—he served as United States Attorney during the Carter years—and a strong political base in Durham, which he represented in the legislature. These were almost enough to make him the first black elected from a rural district in the South since George White, a Republican, was elected, also from the 2d district of North Carolina, in 1898.

But not quite. Michaux led the first primary with 44% of the vote. But he had respectable opposition in the runoff from former state legislator and state Democratic Chairman Tim Valentine. Mostly the vote split along racial lines, but not completely. Michaux won 59% of the runoff vote in Durham County, far more than the black percentage of voters there. But he ran slightly behind black percentages in Valentine's home area around Rocky Mount. So to some extent racial patterns were supplemented by the hometown loyalties which for years have prevailed in southern Democratic primaries.

In the general election there was a write-in effort for Michaux which, though he repudiated it, won 14% of the vote, including 25% in Durham County and nearly one-third in two rural counties, but virtually none in Valentine's home area. One reason it may not have been more successful is that there was a serious Republican candidate here, former Duke University and Baltimore Bullets basketball player Jack Marin. He was one of several candidates supported by Jesse Helms's Congressional Club; but in this district, within range of the TV station on which Helms was once a commentator, he won only 31% of the vote. Heavy home area support gave Valentine a comfortable, but scarcely unanimous 54% victory.

Valentine's political background suggests he will have a conservative voting record, but other factors may lead him the other way. One is the politics of this district, which has the largest black percentage (40%) in North Carolina and a solid liberal voting base in Durham. Another is the tradition developed in the North Carolina Democratic delegation during the toughest of the Reagan years of staying with the Democratic leadership. It paid off in 1982, and Valentine may choose to stay with it for 1983 and 1984.

The People Pop. 1980: 536,210, up 10.4% 1970–80; voting age pop. 382,220; 36% Black, 1% Span. orig. 36% housing units rented. Median owner $34,700; renter $119. Households: 76% family, 43% with children, 59% married couples.

Presidential Vote

1980	Reagan (R)	65,911	(44%)
	Carter (D)	80,350	(53%)
	Anderson (I)	4,403	(3%)

Rep. I. T. (Tim) Valentine, Jr. (D) Elected 1982; b. March 15, 1926, Nash County; home, Nashville; The Citadel, A.B. 1948, U. of NC, LL.B., 1952; Baptist.

Career Air Force, 1944–46; NC House of Reps., 1955–60; Legal Advisor to the Gov., 1965, Counsel to the Gov., 1967; Chmn., NC Dem. Exec. Comm., 1966–68; Practicing atty., 1952–.

Offices 1107 LHOB, 202-225-4531. Also 207 Foster St., Durham 27701, 919-541-5201; and 219 S. Franklin St., Rocky Mount 27801, 919-446-1147.

Committees *Public Works and Transportation* (25th). Subcommittees: Aviation; Economic Development. *Science and Technology* (23d). Subcommittees: Energy Research and Production; Natural Resources, Agriculture Research and Environment; Science, Research and Technology.

Group Ratings and Key Votes: Newly Elected

Election Results

1982 general	I. T. (Tim) Valentine, Jr. (D)	59,617	(54%)	($368,732)
	John W. Marin (R)	34,293	(31%)	($169,610)
1982 runoff	I. T. (Tim) Valentine, Jr. (D)	58,965	(54%)	
	H. M. Michaux, Jr. (D)	50,949	(46%)	($298,652)
1982 primary	H. M. Michaux, Jr. (D)	47,132	(44%)	
	I. T. (Tim) Valentine, Jr. (D)	34,708	(33%)	
	James Ramsey (D)	24,179	(23%)	($143,254)
1980 general	L. H. Fountain (D)	99,297	(73%)	($18,370)
	Barry L. Gardner (R)	35,946	(27%)	($6,919)

Campaign Contributions and Expenditures

1981-82		Direct Cont. 81-82				PACS brkdwn		
Receipts	$371,618	Indiv	$231,949	Agr	$3,000		Ideo	$9,250
Expend.	$368,732	Party	$8,500	Bus	$70,346		Lbr	$—
Unspent	$2,885	PACS	$102,913	Hlth	$16,750		Prof	$—
		Cand	$20,000					

Indirect Party Expend: $3,500   *Indep Expend:* For: $8,675 (Realtors)

THIRD DISTRICT

The 3d congressional district of North Carolina is one of small farms, small towns, and Atlantic shore landscapes. Lying in the middle of the state's coastal plain, the 3d runs from a point a few miles from Raleigh to the Atlantic Ocean near Wilmington. The district's largest city is Goldsboro, with 31,000 people, but a population concentration just as large can be found in Camp Lejeune, the Marine Corps's giant base at the estuary of the New River. One of the Marines' most important installations, Camp Lejeune looms large in the economy of the region. Also in the 3d is an Air Force base near Goldsboro, and Fort Bragg is just over the line in the 7th and 8th districts.

This is a traditional Democratic area. But with its heavy dependence on the military and its relatively low black percentage (27%), it is usually the most marginal of the coastal North Carolina congressional districts. It gave George Wallace his highest percentage here in the 1972 Democratic presidential primary, and it has gone for Jesse Helms twice in Senate races.

The 3d district House seat has been handed down in a kind of succession for 50 years. From 1934 to 1960 the seat was held by Graham Barden, a stuffy and bigoted conservative. As chairman of the Education and Labor Committee, Barden refused to call on the number two Democrat, Adam Clayton Powell, to ask questions, because he was black. Barden retired in 1960 and was succeeded by David Henderson, who had served on his staff. After 14 years Henderson became chairman of the Post Office and Civil Service Committee, and in 1976 decided to retire. His successor was a member of his staff, Charles Whitley.

Whitley understood that voters wanted more than experience in Washington and, toward the end of Henderson's tenure, he worked in North Carolina; this enabled him to win the primary. He has held onto the district ever since. In 1982 he faced a challenge from an attractive Republican, former prisoner of war Red McDaniel, who was well financed by Jesse Helms's Congressional Club. But though he spent nearly $500,000, he was unable to carry a single county and got only 36% of the vote. Whitley's own popularity and the unpopularity of Helms and the Congressional Club were clearly demonstrated.

Whitley serves on only one House committee, Agriculture, but he has a subcommittee chairmanship (Forests, Family Farms, and Energy) of some importance, for it has jurisdiction over the national forests; and he serves on a subcommittee of vital importance to this district, Tobacco and Peanuts. Its composition is suggestive of how business is done in the House: it is chaired by Charlie Rose of North Carolina's 7th district and has one other North Carolina Democrat as well, a Democrat from a tobacco district in South Carolina, two Democrats from peanut-growing Georgia, and only two Democrats from areas where these crops are not so important (Oklahoma and Texas). The ranking Republican is from tobacco-growing Kentucky, and there is a Republican from peanut-growing Mississippi. The subcommittee wants to maintain support programs for tobacco and peanuts, but it also wants to change the allotment system that, in effect, gives a subsidy to anyone who owns land that grew tobacco in the 1930s, regardless of whether they farm it themselves or lease it out to farmers.

Whitley is also a regional whip, and while that office is not important in some cases, it does seem to be here. The North Carolina Democratic delegation's record in the first two years of the Reagan administration was mostly one of support for the Democratic leadership, and Whitley must take some of the credit (or blame) for this. His own instincts seem solidly conservative, yet on the big votes he stayed with the Democrats and helped persuade others to do so. In effect he, like many southerners of yore, has struck a deal with northern Democrats: he keeps choice committee assignments, of vast importance to his district, and gets support from fellow Democrats on such issues, in return for his own support on their key votes. This alliance between North and South, which Jefferson and Madison made with Aaron Burr in the 1790s and Jackson with Van Buren in the 1830s, is still alive—and, judging from the 1982 election results, quite well—today.

The People Pop. 1980: 535,906, up 13.2% 1970–80; voting age pop. 379,853; 25% Black, 2% Span. orig., 1% Am. Ind. 29% housing units rented. Median owner $31,500; renter $123. Households: 80% family, 47% with children, 65% married couples.

Presidential Vote

1980	Reagan (R)	65,911	(44%)
	Carter (D)	80,350	(54%)
	Anderson (I)	1,935	(1%)

Rep. Charles O. Whitley (D) Elected 1976; b. Jan. 3, 1927, Siler City; home, Mount Olive; Wake Forest U., B.A. 1949, LL.B. 1950, Geo. Wash. U., M.A. 1974; Baptist.

Career Army, WWII; Practicing atty., 1950–60; Mt. Olive Atty., 1961–67; A. A. to U.S. Rep. David Henderson, 1961–76.

Offices 104 CHOB, 202-225-3415. Also Fed. Bldg., Goldsboro 27530, 919-736-1844.

Committee Agriculture (14th). Subcommittees: Cotton, Rice, and Sugar; Forests, Family Farms, and Energy (Chairman); Tobacco and Peanuts.

Group Ratings

	ADA	ACLU	COPE	CFA	LCV	LWV	NTU	NSI	COC	ACA	CSFC
1982	20	42	46	46	34	60	53	100	64	61	51
1981	30	—	45	50	30	—	23	—	39	45	53
1980	28	33	53	50	30	30	32	67	81	39	50

National Journal Ratings

	Economic		Foreign		Cultural	
1982	40%	(LIB)	16%	(LIB)	27%	(LIB)
	59%	(CONS)	82%	(CONS)	72%	(CONS)
1981	56%	(LIB)	1%	(LIB)	48%	(LIB)
	44%	(CONS)	99%	(CONS)	52%	(CONS)

Key Votes

1) Reagan 81 Budget	AGN	5) Incr SS Rtmt Age	FOR	9) Poor Pay Food Stamps	AGN
2) Reagan 81 Tax Cut	AGN	6) Saudi AWACS Sale	FOR	10) Ban Crt Busing Order	AGN
3) Bal Budget Amend	FOR	7) $ for MX Missile	FOR	11) Auto Local Content	AGN
4) Gas & Road Tax	AGN	8) Nerve Gas Prod	FOR	12) Nuclear Arms Freeze	AGN

Election Results

1982 general	Charles O. Whitley (D)	68,936	(64%)	($252,704)
	Eugene McDaniel (R)	39,046	(36%)	($496,279)
1982 primary	Charles O. Whitley (D)	56,456	(88%)	
	Leroy Gibson (D)	7,820	(12%)	
1980 general	Charles O. Whitley (D)	84,862	(68%)	($33,267)
	Larry J. Parker (R)	39,393	(32%)	($10,268)

Campaign Contributions and Expenditures

1981-82		Direct Cont. 81-82		PACS brkdwn			
Receipts	$237,254	Indiv	$139,777	Agr	$10,800	Ideo	$4,750
Expend.	$252,704	Party	$20,389	Bus	$35,445	Lbr	$8,500
Unspent	$15,004	PACS	$68,992	Hlth	$7,800	Prof	$500

FOURTH DISTRICT

One of the fastest-growing metropolitan areas east of the Mississippi is the one centered on Raleigh, North Carolina. For most Americans, this may be a puzzle: why should an old cigarette-manufacturing town experience big growth in a high-tech era? The answer is that Raleigh is part of the high-tech era itself. Between Raleigh and nearby Chapel Hill and Durham lies Research Triangle Park, now a major center of R&D for government and business. It draws on the area's major universities, N.C. State in Raleigh, North Carolina in Chapel Hill, and Duke in Durham; together, they have helped to attract a high-skill, well-educated in-migration. The poorer parts of these cities have grown only a little; the big expansion has been outward from the affluent quadrants, as new neighborhoods of large colonial houses are built to accommodate the increasing number of well-off people here.

The 4th congressional district of North Carolina includes Raleigh, Chapel Hill, and three rural counties, one north of Raleigh and two to the west. The politics in the rural counties are typical of old North Carolina: two are conservative Democratic, the farthest west is solidly Republican. But Chapel Hill and surrounding Orange County vote like a university town in California or the Midwest; and Raleigh in the late 1970s became increasingly Republican as it grew more affluent. The result has been the closest thing in North Carolina to the kind of politics you get outside the South—and some close congressional general elections.

The one with the most surprising outcome was in 1982. When White House aides were looking for a place where the president could campaign for a likely Republican winner in a Democratic district the week before the election, they picked Raleigh. Jesse Helms could be counted on to drum up a good crowd, and Republican challenger Bill Cobey seemed a sure bet to beat incumbent Democrat Ike Andrews. Cobey had carried the district when he ran for lieutenant governor in 1980. He was a popular former athletic director at the University of North Carolina. He had raised more than $600,000 with the help of Helms's Congressional Club. He was running a barrage of ads attacking Andrews as a liberal. Andrews himself, though in Congress 10 years, had never used the advantages of incumbency to become well-known in the district; as an old-time rural Democrat, he seemed out of sync with this affluent, urban district. And there was one more thing: Andrews was arrested October 2 and charged with drunk driving, in a state that did not allow liquor by the drink until 1978.

Governor Jim Hunt's organization, which was running Andrews's campaign even before that, almost gave up hope. But they continued to attack Helms and the Congressional Club and to argue that Cobey was just their puppet. Economic issues did not work for them particularly: Raleigh has one of the lowest unemployment rates in the United States. Nevertheless, Andrews was reelected, with 51% of the vote, an only slightly reduced percentage than he received in 1980.

Can Andrews continue to survive? It would help if he could display a more activist legislative record. He is a fairly high-ranking member of the Education and Labor Committee, and is the only Democrat on it who is not a wholehearted supporter of organized labor; he even chairs the Human Resources Subcommittee. But he has no highly visible accomplishment or goal he can campaign on—in a district which is highly interested in education. Of course he may simply have no significant opposition in 1984; the Republicans, shocked by Cobey's defeat, may be too demoralized to run a strong campaign again. But there is still the threat of a Democratic primary challenge; there are plenty of possible aspirants in this district. Andrews's survival in 1982 does not mean that this is a safe district for him.

The People Pop. 1980: 533,580, up 27.3% 1970–80; voting age pop. 395,635; 18% Black, 1% Span. orig., 1% Asian orig. 33% housing units rented. Median owner $47,000; renter $182. Households: 73% family, 40% with children, 60% married couples.

Presidential Vote

1980	Reagan (R)	87,832	(47%)
	Carter (D)	86,907	(47%)
	Anderson (I)	9,967	(5%)

Rep. Ike F. Andrews (D) Elected 1972; b. Sept. 2, 1925, Bonlee; home, Siler City; Mars Hill Col., U. of NC, B.S. 1950, LL.B. 1952; Baptist.

Career Army, WWII; Practicing atty., 1952–72; NC Senate, 1959–61; NC Gen. Assembly, 1961–63, 1967–72, Major. Ldr., Speaker Pro Tem.

Offices 2201 RHOB, 202-225-1784. Also P.O. Box 12075, Research Triangle Park 27709, 919-541-2981.

Committees *Education and Labor* (8th). Subcommittees: Elementary, Secondary, and Vocational Education; Human Resources (Chairman); Postsecondary Education. *Select Committee on Aging* (4th). Subcommittee: Health and Long-Term Care.

Group Ratings

	ADA	ACLU	COPE	CFA	LCV	LWV	NTU	NSI	COC	ACA	CSFC
1982	30	37	46	46	62	67	41	100	62	43	43
1981	15	—	45	50	37	—	14	—	37	37	47
1980	28	37	38	36	31	33	31	50	83	41	44

National Journal Ratings

	Economic		Foreign		Cultural	
1982	47%	(LIB)	50%	(LIB)	45%	(LIB)
	52%	(CONS)	50%	(CONS)	55%	(CONS)
1981	53%	(LIB)	13%	(LIB)	49%	(LIB)
	47%	(CONS)	87%	(CONS)	51%	(CONS)

Key Votes

1) Reagan 81 Budget	AGN	5) Incr SS Rtmt Age	AGN	9) Poor Pay Food Stamps	AGN
2) Reagan 81 Tax Cut	AGN	6) Saudi AWACS Sale	FOR	10) Ban Crt Busing Order	AGN
3) Bal Budget Amend	FOR	7) $ for MX Missile	AGN	11) Auto Local Content	AGN
4) Gas & Road Tax	—	8) Nerve Gas Prod	AGN	12) Nuclear Arms Freeze	—

Election Results

1982 general	Ike F. Andrews (D)	70,369	(51%)	($205,982)
	William Cobey, Jr. (R)	64,955	(47%)	($690,889)
1982 primary	Ike F. Andrews (D) unopposed			
1980 general	Ike F. Andrews (D)	97,167	(53%)	($72,446)
	Thurman Hogan (R)	84,631	(46%)	($59,634)

Campaign Contributions and Expenditures

1981-82		*Direct Cont. 81-82*		*PACS brkdwn*			
Receipts	$191,829	Indiv	$102,347	Agr	$4,200	Ideo	$3,350
Expend.	$205,982	Party	$10,250	Bus	$22,450	Lbr	$12,900
Unspent	$681	PACS	$54,985	Hlth	$9,075	Prof	$100
		Cand	$16,000				

Indirect Party Expend: $54,985

FIFTH DISTRICT

Perhaps the most scenic part of North Carolina is where the mountains begin to rise from the hilly Piedmont. The land is well watered and green, the weather pleasant most of the year, avoiding the extremes of the snowbound winters of the mountains or the humid, muggy summers of the swampy flatlands to the east. Before the Revolution a group of Mennonites, a religious sect from Pennsylvania and, originally, Germany, made a settlement here and called it Salem. Later it joined with the Southern Presbyterian settlement of Winston, and together they became one of North Carolina's largest cities, Winston-Salem. The city has given its name to two brands of cigarettes manufactured here by the R. J. Reynolds Company; it is also the headquarters of the Wachovia Bank (the name comes from the Moravians), one of the largest in the South.

Winston-Salem shares to some extent the political habits of the hills to the north and west. Here in hollows surrounded by ridges, there lives a Republicanism that grew up in opposition to the domination of the wealthy tobacco farmers on the coastal plain. While recent Republicans in the state, notably Senator Jesse Helms, have styled themselves conservatives, mountain Republicans have been more insurgent in mood. When coastal Republicans talk about law and order, mountain Republicans are likely to think—not entirely with approval—of revenuers driving up into the hills and smashing moonshine stills.

The 5th congressional district of North Carolina extends from Winston-Salem and the industrial town of Eden on the east to the mountains on both sides of the Blue Ridge in the west. The mountain Republican tradition lives on here, particularly in Wilkes County, which only on the most unusual occasions votes Democratic. Winston-Salem shows signs of mountain influence as well. It has never showed much enthusiasm for Helms, though in the Republican sweep of 1980 it did go for his candidates Ronald Reagan and John East.

That sweep also resulted in the near-defeat of Democratic Congressman Stephen Neal. But the pendulum swung back in North Carolina between 1980 and 1982, and Neal beat the same opponent, state Senator Anne Bagnal of Winston-Salem, with 60% of the vote—his largest percentage ever. He even came close to carrying Wilkes County. Redistricting helped him, but only marginally; the chief difference was a pretty uniform swing to the Democrats and against Jesse Helms's Republicans. This has been a closely contested district for many years; perhaps Neal's good showing in 1982 will discourage opposition, but the prospect, sooner or later, is for more seriously contested races here.

Neal has a record fairly close to that of national Democrats, though recognizably different. He is one of the more senior Democrats on the Banking Committee and chairs a subcommittee on International Trade, Investment and Monetary Policy. He also serves on the Government Operations Committee. That is pretty heady stuff; locally, he is more likely to emphasize his success in blocking the building of a dam on the scenic New River.

The People   Pop. 1980: 535,212, up 16.5% 1970–80; voting age pop. 388,006; 15% Black, 1% Am. Ind. 26% housing units rented. Median owner $36,500; renter $136. Households: 77% family, 42% with children, 64% married couples.

Presidential Vote

1980	Reagan (R)	99,410	(54%)
	Carter (D)	84,718	(46%)
	Anderson (I)	4,431	(2%)

Rep. Stephen L. Neal (D) Elected 1974; b. Nov. 7, 1934, Winston-Salem; home, Winston-Salem; U. of CA at Santa Barbara, U. of HI, A.B. 1959; Episcopal.

Career Mortgage banking business, 1959–66; Newspaper business, 1966–74; Pres., Community Press, Inc., Suburban Newspapers, Inc., King Publishing Co., and Yadkin Printing Co., Inc.

Offices 2463 RHOB, 202-225-2071. Also 421 Fed. Bldg., Winston-Salem 27101, 916-761-3125.

Committees Banking, Finance and Urban Affairs (7th). Subcommittees: Domestic Monetary Policy; Financial Institutions Supervision, Regulation and Insurance; International Trade, Investment and Monetary Policy (Chairman). *Government Operations* (11th). Subcommittees: Government Information, Justice, and Agriculture; Legislation and National Security.

Group Ratings

	ADA	ACLU	COPE	CFA	LCV	LWV	NTU	NSI	COC	ACA	CSFC
1982	25	50	48	38	66	75	48	75	50	50	46
1981	55	—	46	64	83	—	14	—	17	50	47
1980	44	23	32	36	73	33	29	44	83	50	46

National Journal Ratings

	Economic		Foreign		Cultural	
1982	45%	(LIB)	45%	(LIB)	53%	(LIB)
	55%	(CONS)	55%	(CONS)	46%	(CONS)
1981	68%	(LIB)	45%	(LIB)	59%	(LIB)
	30%	(CONS)	55%	(CONS)	41%	(CONS)

Key Votes

1) Reagan 81 Budget	AGN	5) Incr SS Rtmt Age	—	9) Poor Pay Food Stamps	AGN
2) Reagan 81 Tax Cut	AGN	6) Saudi AWACS Sale	AGN	10) Ban Crt Busing Order	FOR
3) Bal Budget Amend	FOR	7) $ for MX Missile	AGN	11) Auto Local Content	AGN
4) Gas & Road Tax	AGN	8) Nerve Gas Prod	FOR	12) Nuclear Arms Freeze	FOR

Election Results

1982 general	Stephen L. Neal (D)	87,819	(60%)	($347,080)
	Anne Bagnal (R)	57,083	(39%)	($215,484)
1982 primary	Stephen L. Neal (D)	47,816	(86%)	
	Wallace B. Ray (D)	7,479	(14%)	
1980 general	Stephen L. Neal (D)	99,117	(51%)	($179,450)
	Anne Bagnal (R)	94,894	(49%)	($120,022)

Campaign Contributions and Expenditures

1981-82		Direct Cont. 81-82		PACS brkdwn			
Receipts	$345,581	Indiv	$172,741	Agr	$11,100	Ideo	$23,780
Expend.	$347,080	Party	$11,680	Bus	$58,430	Lbr	$22,750
Unspent	$713	PACS	$138,993	Hlth	$7,550	Prof	$1,250
		Cand	$20,000				

Indirect Party Expend: $8,672　*Indep Expend:* Agn: $7,390 (NCPAC)

SIXTH DISTRICT

Probably the leading furniture manufacturing congressional district in the United States is the 6th district of North Carolina. It includes High Point, with a big furniture mart, and Lexington, another furniture town. It is also a major textile producer, and the town of Burlington here has given its name to one of the nation's textile giants. The 6th district, as currently constituted, stretches along Interstate 85, and its central focus and largest city is Greensboro, which produces furniture, textiles, and many other products. Moving from east to west through the Piedmont on 85, you move from Democratic to Republican territory; Greensboro and High Point, in Guilford County, are almost perfectly balanced politically.

This district was the scene of two close contests—and two upsets of incumbents—in the last two elections. In 1980 millionaire businessman Eugene Johnston outspent incumbent Democrat Richardson Preyer and, capitalizing on the same themes Ronald Reagan was sounding, beat him. It was a result which shocked many Democrats: Preyer was one of the most respected Democrats in the House, a former federal judge and heir to the Richardson–Merrell drug fortune, and a moderate on many issues. But Johnston attacked him for his votes against the B-1 bomber and for food stamps for strikers, and won.

The advantages of incumbency plus redistricting, which removed Preyer's best county from the district and replaced it with the Republican county which includes Lexington, seemed to give Johnston a safe seat for 1982. But Johnston proved to be a sloppy candidate with an undisciplined mouth: when he was challenged for amassing a big hotel bill in San Francisco, he boasted that he was used to traveling first class and would continue to do so. This came from ill grace from a man who spent most of his term voting to cut benefits for poor and middle-income people. The Democratic candidate, Robin Britt, a lawyer who managed one of Preyer's campaigns, emphasized issues of economic fairness and, though outspent 2–1, in the end upset the Republican. Britt carried even the Republican county and got 55% in Guilford County, 5% better than Preyer had in 1980.

Will there be another close race here in 1984? Quite possibly. Britt seems to be concentrating on national issues: he joined the Armed Services Committee, although the 6th district has no major military bases, and also serves on Small Business. Johnston, having failed to hold the district, would not seem a good candidate to win it back; but it is entirely possible the Republicans will make a major effort here again.

The People Pop. 1980: 529,635, up 10.2% 1970–80; voting age pop. 386,301; 19% Black, 1% Am. Ind. 31% housing units rented. Median owner $38,900; renter $144. Households: 76% family, 41% with children, 62% married couples.

Presidential Vote

1980	Reagan (R)	94,162	(54%)
	Carter (D)	74,137	(43%)
	Anderson (I)	5,458	(3%)

Rep. Charles Robin Britt (D) Elected 1982; b. June 29, 1942, San Antonio, TX; home, Greensboro; U. of NC, B.A. 1963, J.D. 1973, NYU., LL.M. 1976; Methodist.

Career U.S. Naval Reserve; Chmn., Guilford Cnty. Dem. Party, 1979–81; Delegate, Dem. Natl. Conv., 1980; Pres. and Chmn., Lawyers of NC, Inc., 1981–82.

Offices 327 CHOB, 202-225-3065. Also P.O. Box 299, Greensboro 27402, 919-378-5005; P.O. Box 864, Lexington 27292, 704-249-7556; P.O. Box 814, Graham 27253, 919-229-0159; and 510 Feindale Blvd., High Point 27260, 919-886-5166.

Committees *Armed Services* (27th). Subcommittees: Investigations; Seapower and Strategic and Critical Materials. *Small Business* (25th). Subcommittees: General Oversight and the Economy; Tax, Access to Equity Capital and Business Opportunities.

Group Ratings and Key Votes: Newly Elected

Election Results

1982 general	Charles Robin Britt (D)	68,696	(54%)	($184,365)
	Eugene Johnston (R)	58,244	(46%)	($380,732)
1982 primary	Charles Robin Britt (D) unopposed			
1980 general	Eugene Johnston (R)	80,275	(51%)	($302,263)
	Richardson Preyer (D)	76,957	(49%)	($214,850)

Campaign Contributions and Expenditures

1981-82		Direct Cont. 81-82		PACS brkdwn			
Receipts	$189,351	Indiv	$93,079	Agr	$1,000	Ideo	$8,000
Expend.	$184,365	Party	$11,455	Bus	$5,100	Lbr	$27,000
Unspent	$4,984	PACS	$55,043	Hlth	$500	Prof	$—
		Cand	$27,500				

Indirect Party Expend: $11,736

SEVENTH DISTRICT

The 7th congressional district of North Carolina is the southern portion of the state's coastal plain, the flat expanse of farmland between the industrialized Piedmont and the Atlantic Ocean. The district has two small urban centers. One is around Wilmington, an old Carolina coastal city that never became a major port—a would-be Charleston or Savannah. The other is around Fayetteville, whose population exceeds only slightly that of the huge Army base of Fort Bragg. Bragg is the home of the Army's 82d Airborne paratroopers and nearby, along the garish highway with its X-rated drive-in movies and topless night clubs, grew up in the 1970s one of the nation's largest concentrations of Vietnamese restaurants.

In between is a rural area with a unique ethnic mix, in and around thickly populated Robeson County. The population there is 40% white, 35% black, and 25% Indian; altogether Indians make up 8% of the district—a larger concentration than any other congressional district east of the Mississippi. Most of the Indians here are Lumbees, and their position in the traditional caste system of the South has always been unclear. In the days of segregation Robeson County maintained three sets of schools. Indians have had their own civil rights demonstrations, but they also have objected to having their children bused to go to school with blacks.

All parts of this district, except sometimes Wilmington, are heavily Democratic; and in most elections this is one of the two or three strongest Democratic districts in North Carolina. Its congressman is a skilled and successful Democratic partisan, and a potential leader of the party, Charlie Rose. He first won the seat in 1972 and has built quite a power base in the House since then. He has a seat on the House Administration Committee, and is the resident expert on the House's computer systems. He has also worked on the problem of protecting individual privacy in an age of computerized records.

Rose got a seat on the Agriculture Committee in his first term, and in 1981 succeeded to the chairmanship of the Tobacco and Peanuts Subcommittee. There could not be a more strategic subcommittee for a congressman from the 7th district. North Carolina's interest in tobacco is no secret: this is the state that produces the most cigarettes and that grows the most tobacco. What is less well known is that tobacco is a crop that receives very little subsidy (there is a program that provides low-interest loans, and hence an interest subsidy) and which is very labor-intensive. A family can live—not well, but live—off 15 acres of tobacco which, however, must be cultivated carefully and picked a little at a time throughout the harvest season. But acreage is not eligible for subsidies and price supports unless it has one of the allotments issued to owners of tobacco lands in the 1930s. North Carolina's tobacco-growing counties, mostly in the eastern part of the state, are among the most thickly populated rural parts of the nation, and whatever people here may think of smoking they are not going to be happy with a member of congress who does not back tobacco.

This is true of peanuts as well. Allotments are critical here, too; there is a whole system, set up after World War II, that makes some farmers rich and keeps others out of the business entirely. Poor growing conditions resulted in a very small crop in 1980 and high prices in 1981—and in pressures for opening up peanut growing to anyone who wants to try it. So in 1981 Congress allowed the production, with price supports, of "additional peanuts" for export and use in domestic markets in time of shortage; but higher price supports and quotas for ordinary domestic sales of peanuts were still confined to those with allotments.

Rose is a strong backer of subsidies and price supports for tobacco and peanuts, and is proud to have pushed through the House bills providing for them. His bills also, however, are designed to pressure holders of tobacco allotments who do not farm the land themselves to relinquish their allotments; there is fierce resentment among many tenant farmers who produce tobacco that the economic benefit of the allotment goes to an absentee landlord. Rose's biggest problem is Senator Jesse Helms, who wants no change in the current tobacco laws, in large part because he fears that the Senate will cut subsidies and supports entirely if it gets the chance. Rose is careful to argue that the personal unpopularity of the Republican senator is jeopardizing the economy of North Carolina. Rose himself has been a close ally of many national Democrats in the House, and he uses that alliance to get support for his tobacco and peanuts bills which pass easily.

Rose is reaching a point where he must choose between options in his political career. He has been mentioned as a candidate for governor of North Carolina in 1984, although he has not spent much time in state politics. He might also be a candidate for John East's Senate seat in 1986, though that is a little far down the road for anything but speculation. Or he could continue on what has been a successful career in the House. He has a reasonably good chance of becoming chairman of the Agriculture Committee sometime soon. And he is a possible candidate for a leadership position as well.

In the 7th district he is reelected routinely, without significant opposition; and no one doubts that he would prevail easily even if he did face a tough challenger.

The People   Pop. 1980: 539,055, up 19.5% 1970–80; voting age pop. 371,808; 25% Black, 7% Span. orig., 2% Am. Ind., 1% Asian orig. 31% housing units rented. Median owner $33,500; renter $148. Households: 79% family, 49% with children, 63% married couples.

Presidential Vote

1980	Reagan (R)	57,184	(45%)
	Carter (D)	70,334	(55%)
	Anderson (I)	2,005	(1%)

Rep. Charles G. (Charlie) **Rose** (D) Elected 1972; b. Aug. 10, 1939, Fayetteville; home, Fayetteville; Davidson Col., A.B. 1961, U. of NC, LL.B. 1964; Presbyterian.

Career Practicing atty., 1964–72; Chf. Dist. Ct. Prosecutor, 12th Judicial Dist., 1967–70.

Offices 2230 RHOB, 202-225-2731. Also P.O. Bldg., Rm. 208, Wilmington 28401, 919-343-4959.

Committees Agriculture (6th). Subcommittees: Cotton, Rice, and Sugar; Livestock, Dairy and Poultry; Tobacco and Peanuts (Chairman). *House Administration* (6th). Subcommittees: Office Systems (Chairman); Personnel and Police.

Group Ratings

	ADA	ACLU	COPE	CFA	LCV	LWV	NTU	NSI	COC	ACA	CSFC
1982	40	54	61	23	61	73	27	56	47	47	37
1981	50	—	60	29	52	—	8	—	29	38	45
1980	44	60	50	43	52	75	19	43	79	38	39

National Journal Ratings

	Economic		Foreign		Cultural	
1982	53%	(LIB)	58%	(LIB)	59%	(LIB)
	47%	(CONS)	41%	(CONS)	41%	(CONS)
1981	70%	(LIB)	32%	(LIB)	56%	(LIB)
	29%	(CONS)	67%	(CONS)	44%	(CONS)

Key Votes

1) Reagan 81 Budget	AGN	5) Incr SS Rtmt Age	AGN	9) Poor Pay Food Stamps	AGN
2) Reagan 81 Tax Cut	AGN	6) Saudi AWACS Sale	FOR	10) Ban Crt Busing Order	AGN
3) Bal Budget Amend	FOR	7) $ for MX Missile	AGN	11) Auto Local Content	FOR
4) Gas & Road Tax	—	8) Nerve Gas Prod	AGN	12) Nuclear Arms Freeze	FOR

Election Results

1982 general	Charles G. (Charlie) Rose (D)	68,529	(71%)	($186,944)
	Edward Johnson (R)	27,015	(28%)	($73,020)
1982 primary	Charles G. (Charlie) Rose (D)	56,614	(80%)	
	T. C. Gibson (D)	14,130	(20%)	($14,887)
1980 general	Charles G. (Charlie) Rose (D)	88,564	(69%)	($65,576)
	Vivian S. Wright (R)	40,270	(31%)	($16,992)

Campaign Contributions and Expenditures

1981-82		Direct Cont. 81-82		PACS brkdwn			
Receipts	$207,836	Indiv	$108,354	Agr	$18,625	Ideo	$1,500
Expend.	$186,944	Party	$5,025	Bus	$34,125	Lbr	$11,550
Unspent	$57,788	PACS	$78,080	Hlth	$6,500	Prof	$200

EIGHTH DISTRICT

The 8th congressional district of North Carolina consists of two areas: a part of the Piedmont textile country and the Sand Hills region of the state's coastal plain. The textile counties lie on both sides of Interstate 85 between Charlotte and Greensboro. Along the roadway you pass through the 8th district towns of Salisbury, Concord, and Kannapolis (a company town, wholly owned by Cannon Mills). Here the textile magnates seem to reign supreme. There is no nonsense about unions or workers' rights—the bosses call the shots. That is true in the mills, it is even true in the streets of Kannapolis, and it almost seems to be true at the polls. For whatever reason, this area is consistently one of the most Republican parts of North Carolina. The textile counties cast two-thirds of the votes in the 8th district; the rest are from the more sparsely populated Sand Hills counties to the east. Here there has always been a traditional Democratic preference—although it tends to be a preference for George Wallace-style Democrats.

The 8th has been represented since 1974 by Democrat Bill Hefner. He used to be a country music disk jockey and radio station owner in Kannapolis, and his campaigns typically have featured a little Democratic oratory and a lot of country music. He beat a Republican incumbent in 1974—a former basketball coach who, improbably, was named governor of American Samoa by President Ford—and he was not seriously challenged in the next three elections. In 1982, when his Republican opponent got financing from Jesse Helms's Congressional Club, Hefner finally had to raise and spend comparable money himself, and to defend himself against charges that he was, by voting for most favored nation treatment for China, allowing cheap competition for North Carolina textiles. Despite the national Democratic trend, the local campaign reduced Hefner's percentage from the 59% he had won in the last two campaigns to 57% in 1982.

Another reason Hefner was, at least a little, on the defensive was his role on the Budget Committee in 1981 and 1982. As the 97th Congress started, Hefner seemed to be in a key position on Budget: would he stick with the Democrats or would he support Reagan? He chose to stick with the Democrats—a decision which helped keep other North Carolina Democrats in line with the leadership. It also had the potential to cause him problems in his district—a greater potential, looking at it from the vantage point of 1981, than was attained, at least in 1982. But one reason Hefner stuck with the Democrats is that they went some distance toward his views. The kind of budget produced by Jim Jones's Budget Committee does not have the defense spending cuts and domestic spending increases that Democratic rhetoric, up to and including the 1980 campaign, would suggest; for that, you would have to look at the Congressional Black Caucus budget. Jones and Speaker O'Neill, who superintends the Budget Committee Democrats' work, know that an increasing number of Democrats are from the South and that if their party is to be unified they must receive some concessions. So Hefner can argue—though perhaps this is too subtle for a 30-second spot—that he has played a key role in modulating the approach of the national Democrats.

Hefner is in fact more inclined than Reagan Republicans to be generous on domestic spending. On defense matters he is more inclined to back large spending increases. And aside from his Budget Committee work, defense is his major preoccupation. He serves on the Defense Appropriations Subcommittee and, after only eight years in the House, became Chairman of the Military Construction Appropriations Subcommittee. This is a key pork barrel committee, which tends to determine which military bases in whose congressional districts get the big spending. The Army's Fort Bragg, partly in the 8th district, and other North Carolina bases presumably will be looked on with favor; it will be interesting to see how Hefner balances his desire for frugality on the one hand with the institutional bias of his chairmanship toward heavy military construction spending on the other.

888 NORTH CAROLINA

The People Pop. 1980: 535,526, up 17.6% 1970–80; voting age pop. 381,299; 18% Black, 1% Span. orig., 1% Am. Ind. 23% housing units rented. Median owner $32,400; renter $106. Households: 79% family, 43% with children, 66% married couples.

Presidential Vote

1980	Reagan (R)	86,311	(52%)
	Carter (D)	76,654	(46%)
	Anderson (I)	3,509	(2%)

Rep. W. G. (Bill) Hefner (D) Elected 1974; b. Apr. 11, 1930, Elora, TN; home, Concord; Baptist.

Career Pres., WRKB Radio, Kannapolis; Mbr., Harvesters Quartet, with weekly TV show on WXII, Winston-Salem; Promoter, "Carolina Sings," gospel music entertainment.

Offices 2161 RHOB, 202-225-3715. Also 2202 S. Cannon Blvd., Kannapolis 28081, 704-933-1615.

Committees *Appropriations* (26th). Subcommittees: Defense; Military Construction (Chairman). *Budget* (9th). Task Forces: Budget Process; Education and Employment; Entitlements, Uncontrollables, and Indexing.

Group Ratings

	ADA	ACLU	COPE	CFA	LCV	LWV	NTU	NSI	COC	ACA	CSFC
1982	20	42	48	46	51	50	50	100	64	50	45
1981	35	—	47	50	29	—	14	—	31	49	49
1980	22	37	47	36	39	22	32	44	81	36	48

National Journal Ratings

	Economic		Foreign		Cultural	
1982	44%	(LIB)	33%	(LIB)	39%	(LIB)
	55%	(CONS)	67%	(CONS)	61%	(CONS)
1981	58%	(LIB)	18%	(LIB)	46%	(LIB)
	41%	(CONS)	73%	(CONS)	54%	(CONS)

Key Votes

1) Reagan 81 Budget	AGN	5) Incr SS Rtmt Age	FOR	9) Poor Pay Food Stamps	AGN
2) Reagan 81 Tax Cut	AGN	6) Saudi AWACS Sale	AGN	10) Ban Crt Busing Order	AGN
3) Bal Budget Amend	FOR	7) $ for MX Missile	—	11) Auto Local Content	AGN
4) Gas & Road Tax	AGN	8) Nerve Gas Prod	FOR	12) Nuclear Arms Freeze	AGN

Election Results

1982 general	W. G. (Bill) Hefner (D)	71,691	(57%)	($264,509)
	Harris D. Blake (R)	52,417	(42%)	($240,429)
1982 primary	W. G. (Bill) Hefner (D)	44,860	(80%)	
	James R. Ellison (D)	11,394	(20%)	
1980 general	W. G. (Bill) Hefner (D)	95,013	(59%)	($79,281)
	L. E. Harris (R)	67,317	(41%)	($18,530)

Campaign Contributions and Expenditures

1981-82		Direct Cont. 81-82		PACS brkdwn			
Receipts	$228,898	Indiv	$73,179	Agr	$9,475	Ideo	$5,250
Expend.	$264,509	Party	$22,982	Bus	$73,275	Lbr	$15,750
Unspent	$7,646	PACS	$114,758	Hlth	$8,375	Prof	$625

Indirect Party Expend: $5,025

NINTH DISTRICT

Charlotte is North Carolina's largest city, a comfortable and prosperous metropolis that has never really been the dominant city in the state. Charlotte has no particular geographical reason for being: it is on no major river, it stands astride no historically important artery of transportation (although Interstate 85, the spinal column of the American textile industry, now runs through it). It is not even in the center of the state, but off to the side, almost in South Carolina. It was not a significant city in colonial times nor even in the period following the Civil War. Charlotte has been described as a town from which traveling salesmen empty out every Monday morning and return every Friday afternoon, and it seems to be a city that has simply outhustled the competition. In blue-collar North Carolina this is a city with a substantial white-collar job base; it provides banking, insurance, and marketing services for many of the textile, furniture, and tobacco factories scattered around North Carolina and much of South Carolina as well. Charlotte likes to think of itself as a modern town—a smaller Atlanta—and a racially progressive place. There was an angry reaction in the early 1970s, when a federal judge, in a landmark case upheld by the Supreme Court, ordered massive busing of schoolchildren in Charlotte and Mecklenburg County to achieve integration. But after a time tempers cooled, the plan worked better than expected, and parents who were still unhappy with it got their children into private schools.

Charlotte and its suburban fringe make up most of North Carolina's 9th congressional district. The district also includes Iredell County, a textile area directly north of Charlotte, and rural Lincoln County, included in the district largely because the longtime congressman from the 9th, Charles Jonas, had his residence there. This seemed like an unusual accommodation by a Democratic legislature, since Jonas was a Republican, first elected in 1952. But Democratic efforts to defeat him proved unavailing, and by the 1960s no one really tried; he retired in 1972 and has been replaced by another Republican, James Martin.

Martin has done well in elections here, even though Charlotte seems to be trending Democratic; Jimmy Carter did almost as well here in 1980 (46%) as in 1976 (50%), in a county that regularly went Republican for almost 30 years. Martin's percentage has been going down; it was 57% in 1982, despite the fact that he had only weak opposition.

Martin is an important member of the House, one of those Republican backbenchers who often plays an important role on issues. He has a seat on the Ways and Means Committee, and is ranking Republican on Charles Rangel's Oversight Subcommittee. Much of his efforts, naturally, are directed to protecting the interests of the textile and apparel industries which, while not the main businesses in Charlotte itself, are the leading industries in the hinterland Charlotte serves. Martin also served one term on the Budget Committee. A onetime chemistry professor at prestigious Davidson College, he is also an effective party spokesman on such unrelated issues as the nuclear freeze. Martin is more interested in promoting free market economics than he is in the cultural agenda about which Jesse Helms is so concerned. In effect he is a kind of classical congressional Republican, conservative but not fanatical, intelligent but not flashy. Whether that continues to be winning politics in this Democratic-trending district is not entirely clear.

The People   Pop. 1980: 536,325, up 15.3% 1970–80; voting age pop. 385,849; 21% Black, 1% Am. Ind., 1% Asian orig. 33% housing units rented. Median owner $44,800; renter $164. Households: 74% family, 42% with children, 60% married couples.

Presidential Vote

1980	Reagan (R)	93,916	(50%)
	Carter (D)	87,500	(46%)
	Anderson (I)	7,512	(4%)

Rep. James G. Martin (R) Elected 1972; b. Dec. 11, 1935, Savannah, GA; home, Davidson; Davidson Col., B.S. 1957, Princeton U., Ph.D. 1960; Presbyterian.

Career Asst. Prof. of Chemistry, Davidson Col., 1960–64, Assoc. Prof., 1964–72; Mecklenburg Cnty. Bd. of Commissioners, 1966–72, Chmn., 1967–68, 1970–71; Founder and First Chmn., Centralina Regional Cncl. of Govts., 1966–69; V.P., Natl. Assn. of Regional Cncls., 1970–72.

Offices 2186 RHOB, 202-225-1976. Also Jonas Fed. Bldg., Rm. 248, Charlotte 28232, 704-372-1976.

Committee *Ways and Means* (7th). Subcommittees: Health; Oversight.

Group Ratings

	ADA	ACLU	COPE	CFA	LCV	LWV	NTU	NSI	COC	ACA	CSFC
1982	5	54	61	23	21	30	88	100	86	96	70
1981	15	—	60	14	33	—	79	—	94	87	73
1980	11	60	11	21	48	40	61	89	77	88	77

National Journal Ratings

	Economic		Foreign		Cultural	
1982	3%	(LIB)	32%	(LIB)	4%	(LIB)
	96%	(CONS)	68%	(CONS)	87%	(CONS)
1981	1%	(LIB)	16%	(LIB)	40%	(LIB)
	97%	(CONS)	83%	(CONS)	60%	(CONS)

Key Votes

1) Reagan 81 Budget	FOR	5) Incr SS Rtmt Age	FOR	9) Poor Pay Food Stamps	FOR
2) Reagan 81 Tax Cut	FOR	6) Saudi AWACS Sale	AGN	10) Ban Crt Busing Order	FOR
3) Bal Budget Amend	FOR	7) $ for MX Missile	FOR	11) Auto Local Content	AGN
4) Gas & Road Tax	AGN	8) Nerve Gas Prod	AGN	12) Nuclear Arms Freeze	AGN

Election Results

1982 general	James G. Martin (R)	64,297	(57%)	($325,915)
	Preston Cornelius (D)	47,258	(42%)	($49,127)
1982 primary	James G. Martin (R) unopposed			
1980 general	James G. Martin (R)	101,156	(59%)	($279,040)
	Randall R. Kincaid (D)	71,504	(41%)	($58,955)

Campaign Contributions and Expenditures

1981-82		Direct Cont. 81-82				PACS brkdwn		
Receipts	$328,375	Indiv	$184,924	Agr	$2,000	Ideo	$2,900
Expend.	$325,915	Party	$9,234	Bus	$95,170	Lbr	$—
Unspent	$3,052	PACS	$124,985	Hlth	$12,100	Prof	$1,250

TENTH DISTRICT

The 10th congressional district of North Carolina is a collection of six counties, plus part of another, in the western Piedmont and the eastern Appalachian Mountains. The southern part of the district, on the South Carolina border, is textile country; Gaston County here may have more textile workers than any other single American county. North of Gastonia, the hills rise to mountains around such towns as Morganton, the home of former Senator Sam Ervin. The nearby hardwood forests provide some of the raw materials for the big furniture factories here, like the Broyhill establishment in the town of Lenoir. Farther north, you reach some of North Carolina's most pleasant vacation country, around Grandfather Mountain.

This district, running from Piedmont to mountains, also spans the gamut of political preferences which date back to the Civil War. Even though there were not many slaves this far west, the lowland areas were pro-Confederate then and are Democratic now, though with a distinct Dixie accent. Gaston County was once a George Wallace stronghold; Cleveland County, next door, years ago produced a string of Democratic governors. In the northern part of the district, far into the hills, you come to some of North Carolina's most heavily Republican counties; Democrats are as scarce up here as big plantation owners were before the war. The counties in the middle are split between the parties; the district as a whole has oscillated between the parties in national elections.

In congressional elections, however, the 10th district has been solidly Republican for 20 years. This is testimony to the popularity and endurance of Congressman James Broyhill. A member of the Broyhill furniture family, he was first elected in 1962, when Republican congressmen were still an oddity in North Carolina—and before opposition to civil rights became a political asset for many southern Republicans. He has concentrated on issues of economic regulation. He is the ranking minority member on the Energy and Commerce Committee, one of the most important committees in Congress. In that position he is almost invariably an advocate of less government regulation and a supporter of positions advanced by the Chamber of Commerce and other business groups. He is the sponsor of the Reagan administration-supported proposal to relax the standards of the Clean Air Act. Yet, although he wants to relax auto emissions standards and otherwise relieve the auto industry, he, unlike Chairman John Dingell of Michigan, was not willing to hold his entire bill hostage until a majority could be assured for the auto provisions. He works to help North Carolina's big industries, of course, but otherwise he talks more of a principled than a parochial approach to regulatory issues. And he has supported his free market principles even when they go against the interests of a specific industry, as when he opposed the measure to prohibit Federal Trade Commission regulation of doctors and other professionals.

Broyhill is in many ways typical of senior House Republicans. He is calm, steady, workmanlike; a faithful advocate of his positions, but not a hyperaggressive legislator, or one who is dazzlingly adept at finding ways to reach his legislative goals. He believes in principles, but also in party regularity; he takes his time before taking positions, and he does not rock the boat.

In the 10th district, he has not encountered significant opposition since at least 1970, when he beat a Democratic incumbent redistricted into the same seat. In 1982 he had no Democratic opposition at all. Presumably this is evidence of his popularity—and of the fact that any opponent knows that Broyhill could, if he had to, raise a huge campaign treasury from the political action committees of the interests he has supported, without much in the way of campaigns contributions, for so many years.

The People   Pop. 1980: 532,954, up 15.6% 1970–80; voting age pop. 379,876; 9% Black, 1% Am. Ind. 25% housing units rented. Median owner $33,400; renter $125. Households: 80% family, 44% with children, 66% married couples.

Presidential Vote

1980	Reagan (R)	93,373	(55%)
	Carter (D)	71,696	(42%)
	Anderson (I)	2,897	(2%)

Rep. James T. Broyhill (R) Elected 1962; b. Aug. 19, 1927, Lenoir; home, Lenoir; U. of NC, B.S. 1950; Baptist.

Career Personnel Executive; Broyhill Furniture Factories of Lenoir, 1945–62.

Offices 2340 RHOB, 202-225-2576. Also Mulberry St., Lenoir 28645, 704-758-4247.

Committee *Energy and Commerce* (Ranking Member). Subcommittee: Oversight and Investigations.

Group Ratings

	ADA	ACLU	COPE	CFA	LCV	LWV	NTU	NSI	COC	ACA	CSFC
1982	10	21	8	31	22	25	93	100	71	100	75
1981	10	—	8	36	30	—	92	—	94	96	74
1980	11	23	11	14	36	22	61	89	78	87	75

National Journal Ratings

	Economic		Foreign		Cultural	
1982	5%	(LIB)	32%	(LIB)	26%	(LIB)
	94%	(CONS)	68%	(CONS)	74%	(CONS)
1981	4%	(LIB)	3%	(LIB)	34%	(LIB)
	79%	(CONS)	87%	(CONS)	65%	(CONS)

Key Votes

1) Reagan 81 Budget	FOR	5) Incr SS Rtmt Age	FOR	9) Poor Pay Food Stamps	FOR
2) Reagan 81 Tax Cut	FOR	6) Saudi AWACS Sale	FOR	10) Ban Crt Busing Order	FOR
3) Bal Budget Amend	FOR	7) $ for MX Missile	FOR	11) Auto Local Content	AGN
4) Gas & Road Tax	AGN	8) Nerve Gas Prod	AGN	12) Nuclear Arms Freeze	AGN

Election Results

1982 general	James T. Broyhill (R)	80,904	(93%)	($168,004)
	John Rankin (L)	6,360	(7%)	($0)
1982 primary	James T. Broyhill (R) unopposed			
1980 general	James T. Broyhill (R)	120,777	(70%)	($248,354)
	James O. Icenhour D)	52,485	(30%)	($18,753)

Campaign Contributions and Expenditures

1981-82		Direct Cont. 81-82		PACS brkdwn			
Receipts	$226,744	Indiv	$84,839	Agr	$2,500	Ideo	$800
Expend.	$168,004	Party	$5,427	Bus	$100,080	Lbr	$1,500
Unspent	$111,327	PACS	$116,808	Hlth	$8,400	Prof	$3,250

Indep Expend: For: $9,849 (AMAPAC)

ELEVENTH DISTRICT

The 11th congressional district of North Carolina occupies the western end of the state. Its main features include Asheville, the place to which Thomas Wolfe couldn't go home again, and the Great Smoky Mountains National Park. The park is the nation's most heavily visited; its roads became so crowded that the National Park Service installed there the first traffic signals ever within a national park. During the summer it is 20° cooler in the mountains than in the lowland towns not far away; the climate and the forested, green, fog-wisped mountains attract some seven million people to the Smokies each year. Over the years, the same elements—the mountains, the cool climate—have made western North Carolina a separate unit from the rest of the state. During the Civil War, it was the part of the state most reluctant to secede. With few slaves (only 5% of the people here today are black), many of the small farmers in the hollows remained loyal to the Union, and those who took up the Confederate cause did so largely because of the efforts of Governor Zebulon Vance, an Asheville native and reluctant secessionist himself.

There are ancestral party loyalties to deal with here, Democratic as well as Republican; this area is nothing like as monolithically Republican as eastern Tennessee, on the other side of the Smokies. The partisan strains are tempered by regional feelings: there is hostility to the segregation-minded Republicanism of eastern North Carolina, and Senator Jesse Helms barely carried this area in his 1972 and 1978 Senate races.

So strong are party loyalties here, on both sides, that this district has had, in the last four congressional elections, some of the closest contests in the nation; there are lots of strong Democrats on one side, lots of strong Republicans on the other, and not very many swing votes in the middle. It is also one of the few districts where presidential coattails demonstrably affected House races. When Jimmy Carter and Jim Hunt carried the mountain area heavily in 1976, Democrat Lamar Gudger won the House seat by a 51%–49% margin. Gudger held on, barely, in 1978, primarily because Jimmy Carter, still popular from the Camp David agreement earlier in the fall, came in and stumped for him just before the election. Then, in 1980, Republican Bill Hendon campaigned in a mule-drawn wagon through the district each day, attacking Gudger as a Carter Democrat; Reagan carried the district and so did Hendon, with 54%. In 1982, Hendon had to carry less attractive baggage: the Reagan economic program did not seem to be working well, and Jesse Helms and the

Congressional Club—which strongly supported Hendon—were now quite unpopular. The result was a 50%–49% victory for Democrat James Clarke.

Clarke is from a family active in local philanthropy and, as administrator of the James Mc-Clure scholarship fund, handed out several dozen college scholarships a year in the area. He also had experience in the state legislature and the strong support of Governor Jim Hunt. Elected at age 65, Clarke is not the kind of active campaigner most young congressmen are; and his electoral fate in 1984 may very well hinge on local attitudes toward the expected Senate race between Jesse Helms and Jim Hunt. He serves on the Interior and Public Works Committees, both of which are of practical importance to this district.

The People   Pop. 1980: 531,144, up 15.6% 1970–80; voting age pop. 390,762; 5% Black, 1% Span. orig., 1% Am. Ind. 20% housing units rented. Median owner $34,300; renter $126. Households: 78% family, 39% with children, 66% married couples.

Presidential Vote

1980	Reagan (R)	98,405	(51%)
	Carter (D)	87,981	(46%)
	Anderson (I)	5,249	(3%)

Rep. James McClure Clarke (D) Elected 1982; b. June 12, 1917, Manchester, VT; home, Fairview; Princeton U., B.A. 1939; Presbyterian.

Career USN, 1942–45; Farmer Fed. Coop., 1939–42, 1945–59; Assoc. Editor, *Asheville Citizen–Times*, 1960–69; Asst. to Pres., Warren Wilson Col., 1969–81; NC House, 1977–80; NC Senate, 1981-82.

Offices 415 CHOB, 202-225-6401. Also One Oak Plaza, Su. 109, Asheville, 28801, 704-253-6065.

Committees *Interior and Insular Affairs* (26th). Subcommittees: Energy and the Environment; Insular Affairs; Public Lands and National Parks. *Public Works and Transportation* (31st). Subcommittees: Economic Development; Public Buildings and Grounds.

Group Ratings and Key Votes: Newly Elected

Election Results

1982 general	James McClure Clarke (D)	85,410	(50%)	($277,890)
	William M. Hendon (R)	84,085	(49%)	($507,213)
1982 primary	James McClure Clarke (D)	50,262	(87%)	
	John Garfield Kleibor (D)	7,223	(13%)	
1980 general	William M. Hendon (R)	104,485	(54%)	($249,389)
	Lamar Gudger (D)	90,789	(46%)	($125,696)

Campaign Contributions and Expenditures

1981–82		Direct Cont. 81-82		PACS brkdwn			
Receipts	$279,312	Indiv	$169,984	Agr	$1,800	Ideo	$8,950
Expend.	$277,890	Party	$18,452	Bus	$1,400	Lbr	$27,300
Unspent	$1,319	PACS	$55,467	Hlth	$2,000	Prof	$—
		Cand	$37,803				

Indirect Party Expend: $5,000

NORTH DAKOTA

North Dakota occupies the northernmost section of our Great Plains—the world's largest expanse of arable land. Most of North Dakota is wheat country: the state produces about one-tenth of the nation's crop, and only Kansas grows more. As the North Dakota plains become more arid toward the west, ranching and livestock grazing—along with strip mining and oil production—tend to replace wheat. Both forms of agriculture are demanding and often discouraging. North Dakota is a hard, treeless land; its winters are cold, with plains open to Arctic blasts from Canada, and its summers are often too short and too dry. Back in 1920 the state had 632,000 people. By 1970 its population had dropped to 617,000, and although it rose to 670,000 in 1982, that may be only partly the result of North Dakota's prosperity; another reason may be the gloomy economic picture in most of the big states where North Dakotans used to move. The demographic history of this state consists of a sudden rush of settlement in the 1890s and the years before World War I, followed by a long period in which many of the state's young people regularly felt forced to move elsewhere. Even in the 1970s there was net outmigration from the state.

About 25% of North Dakotans still live on farms and ranches, the highest percentage of any state. In most states, prosperity depends on the level of wages; but in North Dakota, where farmers are really entrepreneurs, prosperity depends on the level of profits. Profits are inherently volatile and uncertain: the demand for processed food products is always there, but the supply and demand, and therefore the price, can vary widely; and the vagaries of weather are beyond the control of farmers and those whose livings depend on them. Accordingly, this class of numerous entrepreneurs—who always need to anticipate the worst that can happen—seeks a safety net from the government, and government, responsive to their elected representatives, usually complies. But the resulting farm programs are so complicated, and the circumstances of the business so uncertain that there is almost always some sort of raging dissatisfaction with the federal government's farm programs. This has made North Dakota a state temperamentally inclined to vote against incumbent administrations, and was the driving force behind the most interesting episode in the state's politics, its spell of radicalism in the years around World War I.

North Dakota's politics has also been colored by the fact that many of its settlers, during its years of surging growth, were of immigrant stock: Norwegians in the eastern part of the state, Canadians along the northern border, Volga Germans in the west, and native Germans throughout the state. (Volga Germans were people who had migrated to Russia from Germany in the early 19th century, but who retained their German language and character. They are recorded in the U.S. Census figures as Russian stock.) The new North Dakotans lived on lonely, often marginal farms, cut off in many cases from the wider American culture by the barrier of language. Their economic fate seemed to be at the mercy of the grain millers of Minneapolis, the railroads, the banks, and the commodity traders.

These circumstances led A. C. Townley and William Lemke to organize the North Dakota Non-Partisan League (NPL) in 1915. Its program was frankly socialistic—government ownership of the railroads and grain elevators—and, like many North Dakota ethnics, the League opposed going to war with Germany. The positions taken by the NPL won it many adherents in North Dakota, and the League spread to neighboring states. But North Dakota was its bastion. The NPL often determined the outcome of the usually decisive Republican primary and sometimes swung its support to the otherwise heavily outnumbered Democrats. It succeeded in some of its goals in North Dakota, such as establishing a state-owned bank. A particular favorite of the NPL was "Wild Bill" Langer, who served intermittently as governor during the 1930s. He was elected to the Senate in 1940 but was allowed to take his seat only after a lengthy investigation of campaign irregularities. His subsequent career was fully as controversial; Langer was the Senate's most unpredictable maverick until his death in 1959. One of his pet projects was to get a North Dakotan on the Supreme Court, and he filibustered every nomination from 1954 on in an unsuccessful attempt to achieve that goal.

Another NPL favorite was Congressman Usher Burdick, who served from 1935 to 1945 and then again from 1949 to 1959. Burdick, like Langer, was a nominal Republican, but usually voted with the Democrats on economic issues. Burdick's son Quentin, a Democrat, was a member of the House when Langer died. The younger Burdick won a special election to fill the Senate seat after waging a campaign against the inequities of Agriculture Secretary Ezra Taft Benson. The Non-Partisan League of course supported Burdick, and by the 1960s its name had become misleading; it supported Democrats in almost every election.

Presidential politics. North Dakota is historically Republican, but it is competitive in many elections. Currently it has senators of both parties and a Democratic congressman. Republicans hold most of the statewide offices, including the governorship, but it had Democratic governors for 20 years, from 1960 to 1980. In presidential politics North Dakota is usually Republican but has a tendency to move away from the party in power. In 1976 Gerald Ford won by only a 52%–46% margin. In the next four years wheat prices did pretty well and the state's economy was in pretty good shape. But wheat-producing counties across the nation reacted angrily to President Carter's embargo on wheat sales to Russia, and in North Dakota most counties are wheat counties. Ronald Reagan carried North Dakota by a 64%–26% margin. In only two states (Arkansas and Nevada) was there a bigger Republican gain between the two elections, and in only three (Utah, Idaho, and Nebraska) was Reagan's percentage lead larger.

By the middle of Reagan's term, however, no one expected the Republicans to do so well in North Dakota in 1984—even if they do well nationally. There is historic precedent: Dwight Eisenhower's percentage of the vote here declined between 1952 and 1956 from 71% to 62% even while it rose nationally. The recession has not affected farm-belt wages as much as it has those in industrial states, but it has hurt farm profits; and that in turn has caused economic problems—and fears of greater problems—throughout North Dakota. In these circumstances, Republican Senator Mark Andrews has been free with criticism of the administration, which has found few local defenders. Still, no one is predicting the Democrats will carry North Dakota in 1984, any more than Adlai Stevenson did in 1956.

Senators. The political career of Quentin Burdick continues to thrive. In 1982, at age 74, he was able to win reelection over an amply financed challenger by a 62%–34% margin; he lost only three counties. At first, Burdick looked as if he might be vulnerable. The Republican, Gene Knorr, won his party's nomination at a state convention despite the fact that he had spent most of the last 20 years in Washington as a Treasury official and a lobbyist. He had enthusiasm and the capacity to raise money. But against this challenge—as strong as any he has faced—Burdick put together a much more professional campaign organization than ever before. He raised more than $900,000 and spent over $780,000—huge sums in North Dakota. His campaign strategists orchestrated an attack on Knorr as an out-of-state lobbyist, and stressed Burdick's North Dakota roots. Burdick himself campaigned vigorously, and his pleasant personality, complete with rumpled clothes and aw shucks manner, continued to go over well with North Dakota voters. This is a state, after all, where voters have long memories; to them the senator is still "young Burdick." His longtime colleague, Republican Milton Young, who died of cancer on May 31, 1983, won reelection in 1974 at age 77; will Burdick try in 1988, at age 80?

Despite his long incumbency, Burdick is not a real power in the Senate. He has switched committees a number of times, leaving Judiciary and having Post Office and Civil Service abolished out from under him just as he was about to become chairman. He is now the tenth ranking member of the minority party on the Appropriations Committee and the third ranking Democrat on Environment and Public Works. Burdick for many years was a reliable Democratic vote on most issues; by the late 1970s he was sometimes straying, notably on the Panama Canal Treaties. Still, he is usually more interested in getting on with his colleagues than being a maverick. Burdick's lack of clout seems to come down to personal character: he simply does not possess the ambition and desire to dominate that animate so many other senators. And that in turn is what may make him so attractive to North Dakotans, who tend reflexively to be suspicious of people in power.

North Dakota's junior senator, Mark Andrews, was elected in 1980, but he had served a long apprenticeship in Congress, and it was the first time either of the state's Senate seats had changed hands in 20 years. Andrews was first elected to the House in 1963 and as the state's only congressman in the 1970s was reelected with huge margins; his arrival in the Senate may have been postponed by the persistence in office of Milton Young, who resented Andrews in the way many kings of England resented their princes of Wales. The resentment was all the greater because their politics are similar. Andrews is generally a loyal Republican, and can reasonably be classified as a conservative on most issues. But his record on cultural issues is not all that the New Right could wish, and he has shown a tendency to bridle at following blindly administration leads on a number of issues. And on his central preoccupation, farm issues, he is ready to take dictation from no one.

Wheat policy is a major issue for Andrews, and he was careful to get a seat on the Agriculture Committee and on the Agriculture Appropriations Subcommittee. He also sits on the Budget Committee, and in 1982 and 1983 he was not hesitant about criticizing Reagan administration policies, on agriculture and on other issues, with which he disagreed. Tall, with a booming voice and an imposing manner, Andrews looks like a farmer who has become a senator, which is just what he is; he attacks national issues with the confidence of a man with strong and deep support at home. He was elected easily in 1980 and would have won in any year: the strongest young Democratic politician in the state, his successor in the House, Byron Dorgan, took him on in the Democratic year of 1974, and Andrews still won with 56% of the vote. He is likely to do much better in the years ahead.

Congressman. North Dakota's at-large congressional seat was one of four House seats which switched from Republicans to Democrats in 1980. That result, like the result of the Senate race, was due more to the popularity of the winner than any other factor. Byron Dorgan, the congressman-at-large, had been state tax commissioner in North Dakota. That does not sound like an important office, but in this state it is, or can be. Dorgan held the office for 11 years, and his greatest achievement was to force out-of-state corporations to pay more taxes in North Dakota. That is often a technical, legalistic battle, the kind of battle prairie farmers are accustomed to losing to big-city lawyers, but Dorgan won victories that brought back memories of the old Non-Partisan League struggles. Dorgan won the House seat in 1980 with 57% of the vote and was reelected in 1982 with 72%.

Dorgan represents most vividly North Dakota's prairie populism, its distrust of big institutions (especially banks and grain companies) and its concern for the individual family farmer. An opponent of the Vietnam war when that was an issue, he remains a skeptic about defense spending increases. (North Dakota, as it happens, is loaded with missile silos; some residents are a little worried about that, since it never occurred to them before that they would be a target in a nuclear war.) No one should get the impression that Dorgan is unduly earnest, however. On the contrary, he is gifted with a good sense of humor, as well as with an inquiring and interesting mind. Most likely he will not challenge Andrews in 1986, but he seems a sure candidate to succeed Burdick in 1988.

Governor. The Democrats held the governorship here because of the personal popularity of Governor William Guy, elected in 1960, 1962, 1964, and 1968, and the close election victories of Governor Arthur Link in 1972 and 1976. (Link first ran when his congressional district was abolished; it seemed easier than running against Andrews.) The current incumbent, Allen Olson, beat Link in 1980. The North Dakota governorship is important to people outside the state only because the state has substantial coal and other mineral deposits, and state policy helps to determine the conditions under which they can be mined and how they will be taxed—which is to say, how much their energy will cost consumers. Olson stood for a lower severance tax than Link; the Republican didn't want to discourage mining or put what he considered an undue burden on North Dakota coal. So far it appears that Olson has not been so personally popular as to guarantee him an easy reelection in 1984.

The People   Est. Pop. 1982: 670,000; Pop. 1980: 652,717, up 2.6% and up 5.7% 1970–80; 0.29% of U.S. total, 46th largest; voting age pop. 461,726; 2% Black. Single ancestry: 26% German, 15% Norwegian, 2% English, Irish, Swedish, 1% French, Polish. No statewide registration. 20% with 1–3 yrs. col., 15% with 4+ yrs. col. 12.8% below poverty level. 28% housing units rented; median house value: $43,800; median monthly rent: $175. Households: 73% family, 40% with children, 65% married couples.

1982 Share of Federal Tax Burden $1,655,100,000; 0.28% of U.S. total, 48th largest.

1982 Share of Federal Expenditures

	Total		Non-Defense		Defense	
Total Expend	$1,460m	(0.24%)	$1,147m	(0.27%)	$313m	(0.18%)
St/Lcl Grants	301m	(0.34%)	299m	(0.34%)	2m	(5.56%)
Salary/Wages	300m	(0.38%)	75m	(0.27%)	225m	(0.44%)
Ind Payments	628m	(0.22%)	580m	(0.23%)	48m	(0.17%)
Procurement	102m	(0.07%)	33m	(0.10%)	69m	(0.06%)
Other Programs	129m	(2.38%)	129m	(2.40%)	0m	(0%)
Loan/Insurance	2,558m	(4.00%)	2,556m	(4.14%)	2m	(0.09%)

Political Lineup   Governor, Allen I. Olson (R). Senators, Quentin N. Burdick (D) and Mark Andrews (R). Representatives, 1 D. State Senate, 53 (21 D and 32 R); State House of Representatives, 106 (55 D and 51 R).

Presidential Vote

1980	Reagan (R)	193,695	(64%)
	Carter (D)	79,189	(26%)
	Anderson (I)	23,640	(8%)
1976	Ford (R)	153,470	(52%)
	Carter (D)	136,078	(46%)

SENATORS

Sen. Quentin N. Burdick (D) Elected June 28, 1960, seat up 1988; b. June 19, 1908, Munich; home, Fargo; U. of MN, B.A. 1931, LL.B. 1932; United Church of Christ.

Career Practicing atty., 1932–58; Dem. Nominee for Gov., 1946; U.S. House of Reps., 1959–60.

Offices 511 HSOB, 202-224-2551. Also Fed. Bldg., Fargo 58102, 701-237-4000; and Fed. Bldg., Bismarck 58501, 701-255-2553.

Committees *Appropriations* (10th). Subcommittees: Agriculture, Rural Development; Energy and Water Development; Interior; Labor-Health and Human Services-Education. *Environment and Public Works* (3d). Subcommittees: Transportation; Toxic Substances and Environmental Oversight; Regional and Community Development. *Special Committee on Aging* (6th).

Group Ratings

	ADA	ACLU	COPE	CFA	LCV	LWV	NTU	NSI	COC	ACA	CSFC
1982	70	68	84	80	46	58	18	50	50	35	42
1981	75	—	84	50	50	—	27	—	44	29	43
1980	78	77	84	53	33	56	30	50	36	19	32

National Journal Ratings

	Economic		Foreign		Cultural	
1982	71%	(LIB)	69%	(LIB)	65%	(LIB)
	27%	(CONS)	30%	(CONS)	34%	(CONS)
1981	72%	(LIB)	74%	(LIB)	86%	(LIB)
	27%	(CONS)	25%	(CONS)	6%	(CONS)

Key Votes

1) Reagan 81 Budget	FOR	5) $ to El Salvador	AGN	9) Poor Pay Food Stamps	AGN
2) Reagan 81 Tax Cut	FOR	6) Saudi AWACS Sale	AGN	10) Ban Crt Busing Order	AGN
3) Bal Budget Amend	FOR	7) Ban Abortion	AGN	11) Clinch Riv Brdr Rctr	FOR
4) Gas & Road Tax	FOR	8) Nerve Gas Prod	AGN	12) Legal Services Corp	FOR

Election Results

1982 general	Quentin N. Burdick (D)	164,873	(62%)	($783,020)
	Gene Knorr (R)	89,304	(34%)	($406,601)
1982 primary	Quentin N. Burdick (D)	44,835	(100%)	
1976 primary	Quentin N. Burdick (D)	175,772	(62%)	($117,514)
	Robert Stroup (R)	103,466	(37%)	($136,748)

Campaign Contributions and Expenditures

1978-82		Direct Cont. 81-82		PACS brkdwn			
Receipts	$912,059	Indiv	$309,160	Agr	$34,850	Ideo	$72,975
Expend.	$783,020	Party	$17,500	Bus	$137,592	Lbr	$214,150
Unspent	$129,142	PACS	$489,919	Hlth	$12,300	Prof	$7,374

Indirect Party Expend: $73,760   *Indep Expend:* For: $80,014 (LIFEPAC) Agn: $1,039 (NRA)

Sen. Mark Andrews (R) Elected 1980, seat up 1986; b. May 19, 1926, Cass Cnty.; home, Mapleton; U.S. Military Acad., 1944–46, ND St. U., B.S. 1949, Hon. Doctorate 1978; Episcopal.

Career Farmer; Repub. Nominee for Gov., 1962; U.S. House of Reps., 1963–80.

Offices 724 HSOB, 202-224-2043. Also P.O. Box 1915, Bismarck 58502, 701-258-4648; P.O. Box 3004, Fargo 58102, 701-232-8030; Heritage Place, Minot 58701, 701-852-2510; and 106 Fed. Bldg., Grand Forks 58201, 701-775-9601.

Committees *Agriculture, Nutrition, and Forestry* (8th). Subcommittees: Agricultural Credit and Rural Electrification; Agricultural Production, Marketing, and Stabilization of Prices; Agricultural Research and General Legislation; Rural Development, Oversight, and Investigations (Chairman). *Appropriations* (8th). Subcommittees: Agriculture, Rural Development; Defense; Interior; Labor, Health and Human Services, Education; Transportation (Chairman). *Budget* (7th). *Select Committee on Indian Affairs* (Chairman).

Group Ratings

	ADA	ACLU	COPE	CFA	LCV	LWV	NTU	NSI	COC	ACA	CSFC
1982	25	29	37	20	15	58	44	90	42	57	64
1981	30	—	35	14	19	—	52	—	76	52	73

National Journal Ratings

	Economic		Foreign		Cultural	
1982	42%	(LIB)	62%	(LIB)	43%	(LIB)
	57%	(CONS)	37%	(CONS)	56%	(CONS)
1981	38%	(LIB)	38%	(LIB)	62%	(LIB)
	61%	(CONS)	61%	(CONS)	37%	(CONS)

Key Votes

1) Reagan 81 Budget	FOR	5) $ to El Salvador	FOR	9) Poor Pay Food Stamps	FOR
2) Reagan 81 Tax Cut	FOR	6) Saudi AWACS Sale	FOR	10) Ban Crt Busing Order	FOR
3) Bal Budget Amend	FOR	7) Ban Abortion	FOR	11) Clinch Riv Brdr Rctr	FOR
4) Gas & Road Tax	FOR	8) Nerve Gas Prod	AGN	12) Legal Services Corp	FOR

Election Results

1980 general	Mark Andrews (R)	210,347	(70%)	($402,129)
	Kent Johanneson (D)	86,658	(29%)	($139,203)
1980 primary	Mark Andrews (R)	78,833	(100%)	
1974 general	Milton R. Young (R)	114,852	(48%)	($300,121)
	William L. (Bill) Guy (D)	114,675	(48%)	($115,561)

Campaign Contributions and Expenditures

1979-80		PACS brkdwn			
Receipts	$405,975	Agr	$27,450	Ideo	$7,600
Expend.	$402,129	Bus	$178,231	Lbr	$18,500
Unspent	$3,844	Hlth	$11,500	Prof	$5,500

GOVERNOR

Gov. Allen I. Olson (R) Elected 1980, term expires Jan. 1985; b. Nov. 5, 1938, Rolla; home, Bismarck; U. of ND, B.A. 1960, J.D. 1963; Presbyterian.

Career Army, 1963–67; Asst. Dir., ND Legis. Cncl., 1967–69; Practicing atty., 1969–72; ND Atty. Gen., 1972–80.

Offices Executive Office, State Capitol, Bismarck 58505, 701-224-2000.

Election Results

1980 gen.	Allen I. Olson (R)	162,230	(54%)
	Arthur A. Link (D)	140,391	(46%)
1980 prim.	Allen I. Olson (R)	60,016	(76%)
	Orville W. Hagen (R)	19,306	(24%)
1976 gen.	Arthur A. Link (D)	153,309	(52%)
	Richard Elkin (R)	138,321	(46%)

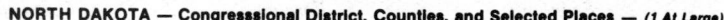

NORTH DAKOTA — Congressional District, Counties, and Selected Places — *(1 At Large)*

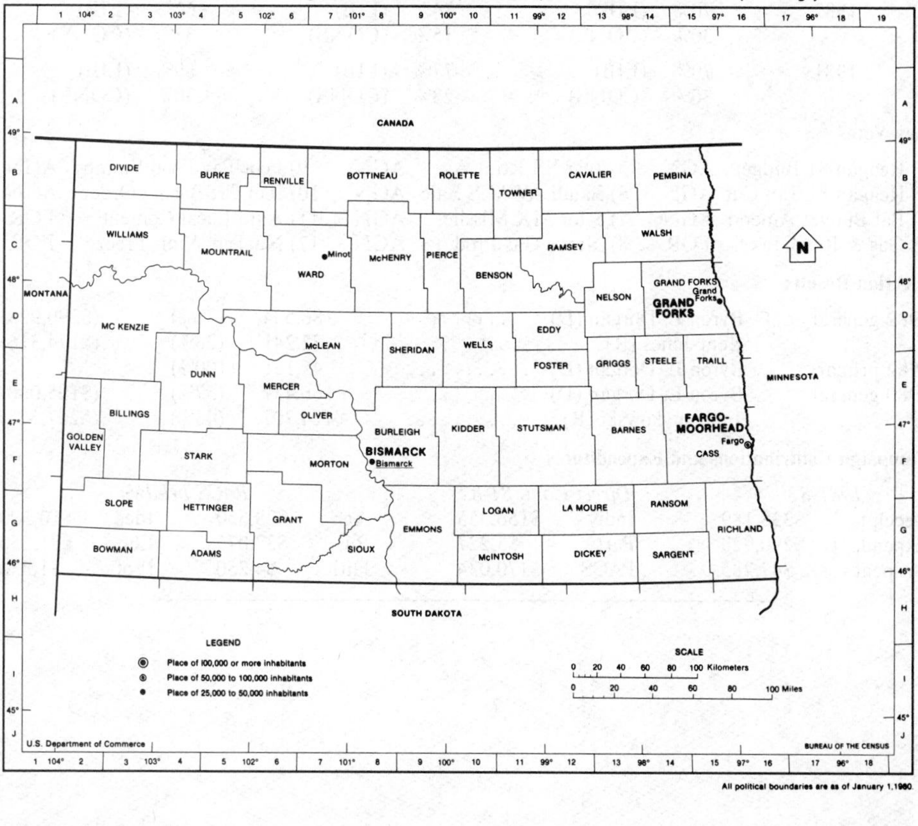

CANADA

DIVIDE, BURKE, RENVILLE, BOTTINEAU, ROLETTE, TOWNER, CAVALIER, PEMBINA

WILLIAMS, MOUNTRAIL, Minot, WARD, McHENRY, PIERCE, BENSON, RAMSEY, WALSH

MC KENZIE, NELSON, GRAND FORKS, Grand Forks

EDDY

MCLEAN, SHERIDAN, WELLS, FOSTER, GRIGGS, STEELE, TRAILL

DUNN, MERCER

BILLINGS, OLIVER, BURLEIGH, KIDDER, STUTSMAN, BARNES, FARGO-MOORHEAD, Fargo

GOLDEN VALLEY, STARK, MORTON, BISMARCK, Bismarck, CASS

SLOPE, HETTINGER, GRANT, EMMONS, LOGAN, LA MOURE, RANSOM, RICHLAND

BOWMAN, ADAMS, SIOUX, McINTOSH, DICKEY, SARGENT

MONTANA, MINNESOTA

SOUTH DAKOTA

LEGEND

◉ Place of 100,000 or more inhabitants
⊛ Place of 50,000 to 100,000 inhabitants
● Place of 25,000 to 50,000 inhabitants

SCALE
0 20 40 60 80 100 Kilometers
0 20 40 60 80 100 Miles

U.S. Department of Commerce

BUREAU OF THE CENSUS

All political boundaries are as of January 1, 1980.

Rep. Byron L. Dorgan (D) Elected 1980; b. May 14, 1942, Dickinson; home, Bismarck; U. of ND, B.S. 1964, U. of Denver, M.A. 1966; Lutheran.

Career Martin-Marietta Exec. Develop. Prog., 1966–67; ND Dpty. Tax Commissioner, 1967–69, Tax Commissioner, 1969–80; Dem. Nominee for U.S. House of Reps., 1974.

Offices 238 CHOB, 202-225-2611. Also P.O. Box 2579, Bismarck 58502, 701-255-4011, ext. 618; and P.O. Box 1664, Fargo 58102, 701-237-5771, ext. 5135.

Committee *Ways and Means* (22d). Subcommittees: Oversight; Select Revenue Measures.

Group Ratings

	ADA	ACLU	COPE	CFA	LCV	LWV	NTU	NSI	COC	ACA	CSFC
1982	85	58	82	85	73	83	27	40	32	17	31
1981	65	—	73	79	71	—	23	—	16	13	37

National Journal Ratings

	Economic		Foreign		Cultural	
1982	70%	(LIB)	84%	(LIB)	62%	(LIB)
	30%	(CONS)	15%	(CONS)	37%	(CONS)
1981	70%	(LIB)	77%	(LIB)	69%	(LIB)
	30%	(CONS)	23%	(CONS)	30%	(CONS)

Key Votes

1) Reagan 81 Budget	AGN	5) Incr SS Rtmt Age	AGN	9) Poor Pay Food Stamps	AGN
2) Reagan 81 Tax Cut	AGN	6) Saudi AWACS Sale	AGN	10) Ban Crt Busing Order	AGN
3) Bal Budget Amend	AGN	7) $ for MX Missile	AGN	11) Auto Local Content	FOR
4) Gas & Road Tax	FOR	8) Nerve Gas Prod	AGN	12) Nuclear Arms Freeze	FOR

Election Results

1982 general	Byron L. Dorgan (D)	186,534	(72%)	($290,928)
	Kent Jones (R)	72,241	(28%)	($174,316)
1982 primary	Byron L. Dorgan (D)	45,131	(100%)	
1980 general	Byron L. Dorgan (D)	166,437	(57%)	($195,068)
	Jim Smykowski (R)	124,707	(43%)	($267,525)

Campaign Contributions and Expenditures

1981-82		Direct Cont. 81-82			PACS brkdwn		
Receipts	$338,189	Indiv	$156,355	Agr	$28,550	Ideo	$10,500
Expend.	$290,928	Party	$3,227	Bus	$37,075	Lbr	$81,250
Unspent	$47,285	PACS	$170,034	Hlth	$4,250	Prof	$1,850

OHIO

If you wanted to send a foreigner to a single state that had within it most of the varying ways of life in America—a state that in its recent history had enjoyed some of the nation's greatest successes and faced some of its most difficult problems—you could not do better than to recommend Ohio. This is a state full of carefully tended farms, God-fearing small towns, and sprawling industrial cities. It has some of the most distressed areas of the United States and some that are booming. That variety stems in part from a history of successive waves of settlement, coming from all different directions. Ohio was the first state from the old Northwest Territory admitted to the Union, in 1803, and within 25 years it was the fourth largest state in population. The first white people here moved down the Ohio River to Marietta or farther down, or up through Kentucky, to Cincinnati. These old-stock Yankees and Virginians were followed by Germans, who fled the failed European revolutions of 1848. By the time of the Civil War, Cincinnati was heavily German and pro-Union and was the fourth largest city of the country; German-born farmers were settling the farmlands and small towns of much of central and northwestern Ohio. The northeastern flatlands, settled mainly by Yankees from Connecticut, remained placid farmland and were the part of the state most receptive to new ideas, like abolitionism, women's suffrage, and the Republican Party.

Then, in the decades after 1880, northeastern Ohio became one of the most rapidly growing industrial parts of the nation. Immigrants from the rural hinterlands of the United States and of central, eastern, and southern Europe poured into Cleveland, the Mahoning Valley, and Toledo to form the gritty ethnic cities which were the most dynamic part of Ohio at the turn of the century. By 1910 Cleveland was larger than Cincinnati and was itself, momentarily, the nation's fourth largest city. Cleveland dreamed then, as Houston does today, of becoming a world-class city; instead, it lost the auto industry to the more venturesome bankers of Detroit and became merely a regional industrial center, thriving through the 1950s, in trouble today as its industries decline.

Ohio has too many parts, too many different regions, for any one generalization to fit. Two statistics suggest its variety. Ohio ranks third in value added by manufacturing, not far behind California and New York, and well ahead of Illinois and Texas which are larger. And Ohio comes very close to ranking third in number of full-time students in institutions of higher education. The colleges that dot Ohio's map in such profusion are the product, mostly, of the waves of Yankee and Catholic migration in the 19th century; unlike Europe, where each country had just one or two universities, or the East Coast, where each state had just a few, every community in Ohio, it seemed, was ambitious enough to have its own college. The manufacturing, of course, results from the wave of industrialization in the late 19th and early 20th century, and shows how productive Ohio is. But these two statistics, in the context of the early 1980s, also suggest Ohio's problems. For this is a state whose number of young people has shrunken even faster than the nation's, and many of its colleges—and its public universities as well—are facing severe fiscal problems. And this is a state whose manufacturing base, all of a sudden, seems to be obsolete and whose factories all seem to be closing down.

The apparent suddenness of these problems has made Ohioans almost panicky about their future. They have survived depression and recession before, and bounced back; but they are not at all sure they will this time—and they have no idea how. Actually, the problems which seem so sudden have been building up for a long time. The last decade in which Ohio grew rapidly enough to gain rather than lose congressional districts was the 1950s (Michigan and New Jersey, two other manufacturing states, gained seats then as well). That was also the last decade in which Ohio's number of young people increased significantly. Since then, its economy, despite publicized attempts by Governor James Rhodes to attract jobs, has grown more slowly than the national average; it has had steady, though slow, outmigration. Moreover, it has failed to do what Ohio did for many Americans and immigrants in the 1830s and in the 1890s—to capture their imaginations, to attract them with a vision of a better to-morrow. That is not necessarily anyone's fault. Ohio is basically a manufacturing state, without the big white-collar and managerial classes you find in New York City or Chicago or Los Angeles or San Francisco; and these have been decades when American manufacturing has not been growing as rapidly as the economy generally. Ohioans, hoping that things will turn up as they have in the past, have not worried much—until the early 1980s—about attracting other kinds of economic activity.

Now Ohioans seem to be abandoning their previous political reflexes. For years Ohio's political leanings have come pretty close to reflecting the nation's, though sometimes in exaggerated form. In the years after the Civil War this was one of the most closely contested partisan states. There were plenty of Confederate-sympathizing copperhead Democrats in the southern part of the state; and as recently as 1976, you could see in the election returns in rural counties below the old National Road (U.S. 40) enough Democratic votes to tip the state to southerner Jimmy Carter by a narrow margin. Then, in the 35 years after William McKinley was elected president, Ohio became a solid Republican state. Some long-settled rural areas remained Democratic, but the big new industrial cities were usually strongholds of the Republican Party, which could claim plausibly that its policies—the protective tariff, antitrust prosecutions, railroad regulation, the gold standard—had enabled private business-men to produce the prosperity which was rapidly raising ordinary people's standard of living.

The Great Depression ushered in a two-party politics, of a bitterness unmatched since the Civil War. In the industrial centers of northern Ohio, labor union members sat down in plants and refused to let their owners throw them out; a Democratic governor declined to evict them. The result was the unionization, in the late 1930s, of the steel, rubber, and auto industries. Workers and management alike assumed that the economy had stopped growing; they were fighting—sometimes in bloody battles in the streets—for bigger shares of the same pie. Conservatives like Senator Robert Taft feared that unions would organize most of the work force and would, through their support of New Deal Democrats, control government and institute something like Marxian Socialism in the United States. He counterattacked with the Taft–Hartley Act, passed in 1947, which was intended to and did end the wave of union organization. It was obviously difficult for Republicans to win elections in a mostly blue-collar state while pursuing such policies. But with the aid of political strategists like Ray Bliss, longtime Ohio Republican chairman, they kept control of the state's congressional delegation; and malapportionment, which swelled the power of the old small towns where McKinley politics was still in vogue, helped them keep control of the legislature. Democrats, in the meantime, were not conveniently concentrated in one metropolitan area, as in New York, Michigan, or Illinois, and their most effective leader, Governor and Senator Frank Lausche, was not so far away from Taft on most issues himself.

So Ohio's politics was pretty closely balanced between the parties: in close presidential elections Ohio sometimes went Republican (1960, 1968) and sometimes went Democratic (1948, 1976). Sometimes it elected Democratic senators and governors, sometimes Republicans. State government, led for 16 out of 20 years by Republican Governor James Rhodes (1963–71, 1975–83), did not grow as large as governments in Illinois or Michigan, but nonetheless got larger than Taft would have liked. Slowly, the Democrats, through organizational strength and good luck, won control of the machinery of state and local government. They have controlled the legislature and most of the statewide offices (three of which redistrict the legislature) since 1970; they were aided that year by a Republican scandal. They have controlled the city governments of the formerly Republican cities of Cincinnati and Columbus for most of that time as well. While retaining a reputation as a Republican state, Ohio has become accustomed to having the Democrats in control of state and local as well as national affairs. And that is wholly apart from the fact that the Republicans have not won a U.S. Senate election here since 1970.

In the 1982 elections Democrats achieved unprecedented victories here. But this is not simply the result of reflex; it is not simply a matter of calling in the Democrats to handle recessions as you call in the Republicans to handle inflation. Those reflexive responses, which worked well in the 1950s and 1960s, have not worked well in the 1970s and 1980s. The most important aspect of the 1982 results was not the Democratic percentage but the vast increase in turnout. Some 3.3 million Ohioans voted in 1982, as compared to 2.8 million in 1978—though the state's population has declined in the 1980s. That turnout is an historic record for Ohio; the state came closest to equaling it in another recession, in 1958. Turnout rose 16% in industrial northeast Ohio, 15% in Dayton's Montgomery County, and 24% in Toledo's Lucas County—even though all of these areas are losing population. In the short run it appears that these are working-class voters, disenchanted with the Democrats in the 1970s, who have decided to vote in the desperate 1980s. Republican nominee Bud Brown, for example, got just 99,000 votes less than James Rhodes did in 1978 when he won the governorship. But Democrat Richard Celeste got 624,000 more votes than he had in losing to Rhodes four years before.

Yet there was not a uniform Democratic trend. The Democrats did pick up the congressional district in Toledo. But they failed to win one in the Mahoning Valley, which had one of the nation's highest unemployment rates, and they lost a seat in the Columbus area. Democrats won the state Senate, but only by the margin of one vote, and they had to scramble to mollify one senator from Cleveland as he threatened to vote to organize with the Republicans. Turnout increased not only in the industrial areas, but in the small towns, and in high-income suburbs as well. The 1980 and 1982 elections, taken together, seem to indicate that Ohioans are looking for some way to adjust to the apparent collapse of their economic world—and are willing to call on either party, regardless of previous voting habits. Among other states, only Michigan—where the Democratic candidate for governor won by a narrower margin—has this kind of desperate uncertainty. But this turbulence suggests that the future of Ohio politics is up for grabs—and will belong to the party and the leaders who can present a plausible way to reinstate the prosperity which the state's citizens for some years had come to take for granted.

Governor. The key race in 1982 was for governor. The two parties nominated two intelligent candidates of sharply contrasting backgrounds and views, and the voters made a decisive choice when they elected Richard Celeste by a 59%–39% margin. No Democrat, and no Republican except Rhodes in 1966, had ever won a victory like that in an Ohio gubernatorial race. Bud Brown represented small-town Ohio in Congress, and helped to deregulate oil and natural gas; he stood for tax cuts and big cuts in public spending. Only by these means, he said, could Ohio hope to stimulate the kind of economic innovation which had made it the inventive workshop of America—and could again. Celeste is from the Cleveland area, and won a tough three-way primary by carrying the industrial northeast, the ailing Dayton area, and the southern Ohio area around the hometown of Speaker Vern Riffe, who supported him. Celeste's background is in government; his father is a successful businessman, who made his living for years as a packager of non-profit, government-assisted housing projects. He has served in the legislature, as lieutenant governor, and as director of the Peace Corps; he knows government and the big lobbying groups which try to affect it. Celeste wants to attract new industry and thinks Ohio has the assets—a skilled labor force, a good water supply, a low standard of living compared to boom areas like California—to do it. He sees government as a facilitator of the process, and he is inclined, as many Ohioans are, to favor protectionist solutions: restrict foreign imports, have the state buy goods made in Ohio.

Celeste's vision seems to be one of protecting what Ohioans have accomplished—businesses and welfare state protections as well. And that seems to be the thrust of his 1983 budget. Rhodes in his last term as governor balanced the budget with rubber bands and baling wire, and with a "temporary" tax increase. Celeste has made that increase permanent. When push came to shove, he decided that maintaining government programs is worth the risk of discouraging economic activity through higher taxes. There is much to say for his choice: government should meet minimal responsibilities, and skimping on education and training in the long run—quite possibly in the short run, too—will hurt the state's economy. But neither Celeste nor his ineffective opposition has a clear answer of how to motivate and encourage the spirit of innovation which once made Ohio an engine of economic growth and not a drag on it. Brown's plans ignored the fact that the statistics suggesting that high-tech employers are shunning Ohio, and its traditional industries in this recession are moving very slowly if at all to innovate. Celeste's policies concede a substantial advantage to other areas, in the United States and beyond, with lower taxes and labor costs. Still, Celeste is one of the ablest new governors elected in 1982 and a man who is entitled to his ambitions, which seem to go beyond the State House in Columbus, no matter how irritating they may be to some journalists. For 1984 he is staunchly backing John Glenn for president, and he has high hopes that Ohio will go Democratic in the next presidential election.

Senators. Ohio's most famous—and most popular—politician today is John Glenn. He is also, in early 1983, a formidable presidential candidate, and something of a national hero. As everyone knows, Glenn got his start in public life as an astronaut, the first American to orbit the earth in space. He was then and is now a small-town boy who radiates all the virtues of his background; he was a brilliant fighter pilot in World War II and Korea; after his service in the military he was a successful businessman in Columbus. His broad smile and "gee whiz" quality have made him a kind of cultural hero to many ordinary Americans; he personifies the virtues of family, God-fearing religion, duty, patriotism, and hard work. He is also, it should be added, shrewd and ambitious; he didn't get into the astronaut program or into the Senate by just letting things happen to him.

Nor did Glenn get into the Senate automatically. He started to run in 1964, then left the race when he was injured in a household accident; ran again in 1970, but was upset in the primary by Howard Metzenbaum, who in turn lost the general election narrowly to Robert Taft, Jr. In 1974 they ran against each other again, in one of the bitterest primaries of recent times, and this time Glenn won. He won the general election easily that year and has had no trouble at all holding the seat. (Metzenbaum won the other Ohio seat in 1976; he and Glenn are the least cordial of Senate colleagues.) He won reelection by a record-breaking 69%–28% margin in 1980, even while Reagan was carrying the state.

The conventional wisdom has it that Glenn is more conservative than most northern Democrats, but that isn't quite right. When he entered the Senate in the middle 1970s, he was less likely than many Democrats to express support for programs like a guaranteed annual income and national health insurance. But as the Carter years showed, the rhetorical support for such measures did not translate into action when the Democrats finally had the votes; and even in the recession year of 1982 you did not hear many Democrats talking about such big government programs. In effect, the national Democrats have moved closer to Glenn's position on economic issues. And he, in turn, has always had a gut commitment to many Democratic economic programs; he comes from a blue-collar background and, despite his business success, seems instinctively to identify with the little guy. On cultural issues, Glenn is also close to most of his Senate Democratic colleagues; he has supported the right to abortion, for example, and opposed the school prayer amendment.

Naturally Glenn is interested in military matters and has a seat on the Foreign Relations Committee. He followed the SALT talks very closely and, despite an obvious desire to support the treaty, hesitated because of concerns about verification (now, he thinks, resolved by technical innovations). He is probably the Senate's most dogged pursuer of the issue of nuclear nonproliferation. He has been criticized as a man who gets too involved in the minutiae of issues and lacks a broad perspective. But he seems to have as sophisticated a perspective as other presidential candidates, and a close knowledge of specifics is not likely to be harmful. As a military man who advanced through channels, Glenn is not particularly sympathetic to the new breed of Pentagon critics, and he tends to support weapons systems recommended by the services. But of course here he has a fund of technical knowledge—and a sense of security about his own military achievements—few others in politics can count on.

For Glenn the Democratic primary has always been harder than the general election in Ohio, and that may be the case nationally too. His very wholesomeness helped ensure that his speech at the 1976 national convention would be overshadowed by Barbara Jordan's; the Democratic delegates love to congratulate themselves for their appreciation of minorities rather than for their love of virtues associated with the majority. Glenn's small-town personality does not translate well to gritty big cities, where a lot of the Democratic primary votes are. But in the presidential race he may have an edge over the competition in the southern primaries, where his virtues may be more valued. As for the general election, at the end of 1982 he was reportedly the candidate Reagan strategists fear most. As a Democrat, he would be well positioned to carry most of the northeastern states; he should be certain of Ohio's 23 electoral votes and those of several other midwestern states besides; and he is a good bet to win in the South. But can he rally the heavy turnout by blacks and working-class whites which was key to the Democrats' 1982 victories in, among other places, Ohio?

Senator Howard Metzenbaum has a background almost entirely different from Glenn's. Metzenbaum is from Cleveland; spent most of his life in business, making a fortune in airport parking lots (not a business one enters for love); has been politically active for years. He was campaign manager for Senator Stephen Young's surprise victories in 1958 at age 74, and against Robert Taft, Jr., in 1964. Then he ran himself, beat Glenn and almost beat Taft in 1970; lost to Glenn in the primary in 1974, after having been appointed to fill a vacancy by Governor John Gilligan; then ran again in 1976, beat Cleveland Congressman William Stanton in the primary and Taft in the general.

Metzenbaum's image, not surprisingly, is one of a fighter. He has one of the most liberal records in the Senate, and in 1980 Republican strategists were putting him high on the list of Democrats they hoped to beat in 1982. But the Reagan administration proved to be a superb foil for Metzenbaum. From the platform of the Senate Budget Committee, he denounced Reagan's economic policy. On the Labor and Human Resources Committee he hammered away at Reagan's budget cuts. On the floor of the Senate, he acted as a kind of Horatius at the bridge, putting holds near the end of the session on dozens of pieces of what he considered special-interest legislation and then filibustering them if they came up. In effect Metzenbaum forced senators backing these bills to negotiate with him, even if they had a large majority and he represented only himself. He first got interested in the possibilities for delay in the Senate rules when he and James Abourezk of South Dakota staged a two-man filibuster against deregulation of oil and gas prices; that failed, but Metzenbaum saw that the possibilities for delay were tremendous, and that at the end of the session delay means death for a bill. So he is ready with amendments (as many as 100 to a single bill) and with extended comment. Metzenbaum himself has proposed changing the rules that allow him to do this; but in the meantime he proposes to take advantage of them.

Metzenbaum's fighting stance was just what Ohio voters, desperate about their state's economic future, wanted in 1982. As it happened, he did not even have strong opposition. Congressman John Ashbrook, a principled conservative who was expected to be the Republican nominee, died in the spring, a month before the primary. The Republican candidate, Paul Pfeifer, was an unknown state senator who was one of the few Republican Senate candidates who could not persuade the national Republican Party to give him the maximum legal funding. Metzenbaum won 57%–41%, a smashing victory.

Presidential politics. Ohio is one of those states that is always a major prize in presidential elections, and always seriously contested. Its reduced number of 23 electoral votes is still too large to be ignored, and in any close race the result here is likely to be close. The 1982 results suggest that the Democrats can regard Ohio as a sure thing, but they surely won't, nor will the Republicans concede it; for one thing, it's not clear that Ohioans will be as ready to accept the Democrats nationally in 1984 as they were to accept them for the state in 1982.

Ohio has its presidential primary in June, late in the season. There was some talk of setting it earlier, to help Glenn, but as of early 1983 that seemed unlikely. Overshadowed by California, the Ohio primary is nonetheless still important and seriously contested because of the large size of the state's delegation.

Congressional redistricting. Congressional redistricting was truly a bipartisan exercise in Ohio in 1982, not because its politicians are altruistic, but because the Democrats controlled the state House of Representatives and the Republicans the state Senate and governorship. The bipartisanship is apparent in the Cincinnati and Columbus areas, where partisans of either side would have drawn the lines differently. It is possible, now that the Democrats won the state Senate and the governorship in 1982, that they will choose to redraw the lines; there is nothing legally to prevent them from doing so. But reopening redistricting, top Democrats are likely to conclude, is probably more trouble than it is worth.

The People   Est. Pop. 1982: 10,791,000; Pop. 1980: 10,797,630, dn. 0.1% 1980–82 and up 1.3% 1970–80; 4.7% of U.S. total, 6th largest; voting age pop. 7,703,310; 9% Black, 1% Spanish origin. Single ancestry: 13% German, 9% English, 4% Irish, 2% Italian, Polish, 1% Hungarian, French. Registered voters (1982): 5,674,128 Total. 1,757,785 D (31%); 1,200,219 R (21%); 2,477,182 unaffiliated (44%). 13% with 1–3 yrs. col., 15% with 4+ yrs. col. 10.5% below poverty level. 29% housing units rented; median house value: $45,100; median monthly rent: $167. Households: 74% family, 41% with children, 62% married couples.

1982 Share of Federal Tax Burden $27,794,800,000; 4.65% of U.S. total, 6th largest.

1982 Share of Federal Expenditures

	Total		Non-Defense		Defense	
Total Expend	$23,282m	(3.86%)	$18,765m	(4.42%)	$4,518m	(2.53%)
St/Lcl Grants	3,612m	(4.09%)	3,612m	(4.09%)	0m	(0%)
Salary/Wages	1,755m	(2.25%)	825m	(3.01%)	930m	(1.84%)
Ind Payments	13,432m	(4.70%)	12,578m	(4.88%)	854m	(2.99%)
Procurement	4,368m	(3.00%)	1,046m	(3.32%)	3,322m	(2.91%)
Other Programs	116m	(2.14%)	115m	(2.14%)	1m	(2.33%)
Loan/Insurance	1,212m	(1.89%)	1,146m	(1.86%)	66m	(3.00%)

Political Lineup   Governor, Richard F. Celeste (D). Senators, John H. Glenn, Jr. (D) and Howard M. Metzenbaum (D). Representatives, 21 (10 D and 11 R). State Senate, 33 (15 D and 18 R); State House of Representatives, 99 (56 D and 43 R).

Presidential Vote

1980	Reagan (R)	2,206,545	(52%)
	Carter (D)	1,752,414	(41%)
	Anderson (I)	254,472	(6%)
1976	Ford (R)	2,000,505	(50%)
	Carter (D)	2,011,621	(50%)

1980 Democratic Presidential Primary				*1980 Republican Presidential Primary*		
Carter	605,744	(51%)		Reagan	692,288	(81%)
Kennedy	523,874	(44%)		Bush	164,485	(19%)
Two others.........	56,792	(5%)				

SENATORS

Sen. John H. Glenn, Jr. (D) Elected 1974, seat up 1986; b. July 18, 1921, Cambridge; home, Columbus; Muskingum Col., B.S. 1939; Presbyterian.

Career USMC, 1942–65; NASA Astronaut, 1959–65, First American to orbit the earth, 1962; Candidate for Dem. Nomination for U.S. Senate, 1964, 1970; V.P., Royal Crown Cola Co., 1966–68, Pres., Royal Crown Internatl., 1967–69.

Offices 2235 HSOB, 202-224-3353. Also 200 N. High St., Su. 600, Columbus 43215, 614-469-6697; and Fed. Court House, Rm. 104, Cleveland 44114, 216-522-7095.

Committees *Foreign Relations* (3d). Subcommittees: European Affairs; East Asian and Pacific Affairs; Near Eastern and South Asian Affairs. *Governmental Affairs* (5th). Subcommittees: Permanent Subcommittee on Investigations; Energy, Nuclear Proliferation, and Government Processes. *Special Committee on Aging* (Ranking Member).

Group Ratings

	ADA	ACLU	COPE	CFA	LCV	LWV	NTU	NSI	COC	ACA	CSFC
1982	70	68	77	80	71	73	4	70	55	35	38
1981	80	—	76	57	56	—	13	—	44	25	33
1980	67	77	72	53	53	90	34	20	38	17	33

National Journal Ratings

	Economic		Foreign		Cultural	
1982	89%	(LIB)	63%	(LIB)	77%	(LIB)
	10%	(CONS)	36%	(CONS)	22%	(CONS)
1981	75%	(LIB)	72%	(LIB)	79%	(LIB)
	24%	(CONS)	27%	(CONS)	19%	(CONS)

Key Votes

1) Reagan 81 Budget	FOR	5) $ to El Salvador	AGN	9) Poor Pay Food Stamps AGN
2) Reagan 81 Tax Cut	FOR	6) Saudi AWACS Sale	AGN	10) Ban Crt Busing Order AGN
3) Bal Budget Amend	AGN	7) Ban Abortion	AGN	11) Clinch Riv Brdr Rctr AGN
4) Gas & Road Tax	FOR	8) Nerve Gas Prod	FOR	12) Legal Services Corp —

Election Results

1980 general	John H. Glenn, Jr. (D)	2,770,786	(69%)	($1,157,965)
	James E. Betts (R)	1,137,695	(28%)	($423,060)
1980 primary	John H. Glenn, Jr. (D)	934,230	(86%)	
	Frances R. Waterman (D)	88,506	(8%)	($1,157)
	Francis Hunstiger (D)	64,270	(6%)	($2,180)
1974 general	John H. Glenn, Jr. (D)	1,930,670	(65%)	($1,149,130)
	Ralph J. Perk (R)	918,133	(31%)	($292,838)

Campaign Contributions and Expenditures

1979-80			PACS brkdwn		
Receipts	$1,229,354	Agr	$7,250	Ideo	$3,000
Expend.	$1,157,965	Bus	$137,713	Lbr	$123,050
Unspent	$125,550	Hlth	$2,800	Prof	$3,200

Sen. Howard M. Metzenbaum (D) Elected 1976, seat up 1988; b. June 4, 1917, Cleveland; home, Shaker Heights; OH State U., B.A. 1939, LL.B. 1941; Jewish.

Career Practicing atty.; Cofounder, Airport Parking Co. of America, ComCorp Communications Corp.; Chmn. of the Bd., ITT Consumer Services Corp.; OH House of Reps., 1943–46; OH Senate, 1947–50; Campaign Mgr. for Sen. Stephen M. Young, 1958, 1964; Dem. Nominee for U.S. Senate, 1970; U.S. Senate, 1974.

Offices 363 RSOB, 202-224-2315. Also 121 E. State St., Rm. 442, Columbus 43215, 614-469-6774.

Committees Budget (7th). *Energy and Natural Resources* (5th). Subcommittees: Energy Conservation and Supply; Energy Regulation; Water and Power. *Judiciary* (4th). Subcommittees: Juvenile Justice; Patents, Copyrights and Trademarks; Security and Terrorism; Separation of Powers. *Labor and Human Resources* (6th). Subcommittees: Employment and Productivity; Aging; Family and Human Services.

Group Ratings

	ADA	ACLU	COPE	CFA	LCV	LWV	NTU	NSI	COC	ACA	CSFC
1982	100	82	92	90	80	100	12	22	11	16	27
1981	85	—	91	71	88	—	13	—	7	22	28
1980	83	87	94	93	71	80	34	10	27	12	24

National Journal Ratings

	Economic		Foreign		Cultural	
1982	77%	(LIB)	79%	(LIB)	99%	(LIB)
	22%	(CONS)	19%	(CONS)	0%	(CONS)
1981	90%	(LIB)	82%	(LIB)	98%	(LIB)
	8%	(CONS)	17%	(CONS)	1%	(CONS)

Key Votes

1) Reagan 81 Budget	—	5) $ to El Salvador	AGN	9) Poor Pay Food Stamps	AGN
2) Reagan 81 Tax Cut	FOR	6) Saudi AWACS Sale	AGN	10) Ban Crt Busing Order	AGN
3) Bal Budget Amend	AGN	7) Ban Abortion	AGN	11) Clinch Riv Brdr Rctr	AGN
4) Gas & Road Tax	AGN	8) Nerve Gas Prod	AGN	12) Legal Services Corp	—

Election Results

1982 general	Howard M. Metzenbaum (D)	1,923,767	(57%)	($2,794,172)
	Paul E. Pfeifer (R)	1,396,790	(41%)	($1,025,595)
1982 primary	Howard M. Metzenbaum (D)	810,785	(83%)	
	Norbert G. Dennerll, Jr. (D)	167,778	(17%)	
1976 general	Howard M. Metzenbaum (D)	1,941,113	(50%)	($1,092,053)
	Robert A. Taft, Jr. (R)	1,823,774	(47%)	($1,304,207)

Campaign Contributions and Expenditures

1979-82		Direct Cont. 81-82		PACS brkdwn			
Receipts	$3,767,625	Indiv	$3,065,814	Agr	$21,600	Ideo	$68,925
Expend.	$2,794,172	Party	$17,500	Bus	$57,844	Lbr	$227,723
Unspent	$970,455	PACS	$404,182	Hlth	$10,500	Prof	$17,050

Indirect Party Expend: $147,606   *Indep Expend:* For: $850 Agn: $30,903 (NCPAC, LIFEPAC)

GOVERNOR

Gov. Richard F. Celeste (D) Elected 1982, term expires Jan. 1987; b. Nov. 11, 1937, Lakewood; home, Cleveland; Yale U., B.A. 1959, Rhodes Scholar, Oxford U., 1960–62, Yale U., 1962; Methodist.

Career Exec. Asst. to U.S. Ambassador to India, 1963–67; Real estate developer, Natl. Housing Corp., 1967–75; OH House of Reps., 1971–75; Lt. Gov. of OH, 1975–79; Dem. Nominee for Gov., 1978; Dir., Peace Corps., 1979–81.

Offices State House, Columbus 43215, 614-466-3555.

Election Results

1982 gen.	Richard F. Celeste (D)	1,981,882	(59%)
	Clarence J. Brown (R)	1,303,962	(39%)
1982 prim.	Richard F. Celeste (D)	436,887	(42%)
	William J. Brown (D)	383,007	(37%)
	Jerry Springer (D)	210,524	(20%)
1978 gen.	James A. Rhodes (R)	1,402,167	(49%)
	Richard F. Celeste (D)	1,354,631	(48%)

FIRST DISTRICT

The 1st congressional district of Ohio is the western part of Cincinnati and Hamilton County. Its boundary falls near, though not precisely along, Mill Creek, along which lies most of

Cincinnati's industrial corridor. Here are the great Procter & Gamble soap factories and many of the city's machine tool makers; Cincinnati is a leader in both industries. The 1st includes some of the oldest and poorest parts of the city, like the Over-the-Rhine area (a name that recalls Cincinnati's German heritage) and some of the city's black slums. But only 16% of its residents are black. More typical are the old neighborhoods, some dating back more than 100 years, of wooden houses tucked in the valleys or ravines between Cincinnati's many hills. Here immigrant Germans moved, commuting to work in the factories on foot or downtown by the early horsecars; in such neighborhoods today you could easily imagine yourself in the America of 50 or even 80 years ago. Cincinnati was one of America's largest cities at the turn of the century, and the comfortable urbanity of that period is still apparent in many of its streets and neighborhoods.

Cincinnati's main ethnic group is German, and its ancestral politics is Republican. As its more prosperous offspring have moved off to the suburbs, the city of Cincinnati itself has become more Democratic; the suburbs in most elections, though not in 1982, are overwhelm-

OHIO — Congressional Districts, Counties, and Selected Places — (21 Districts)

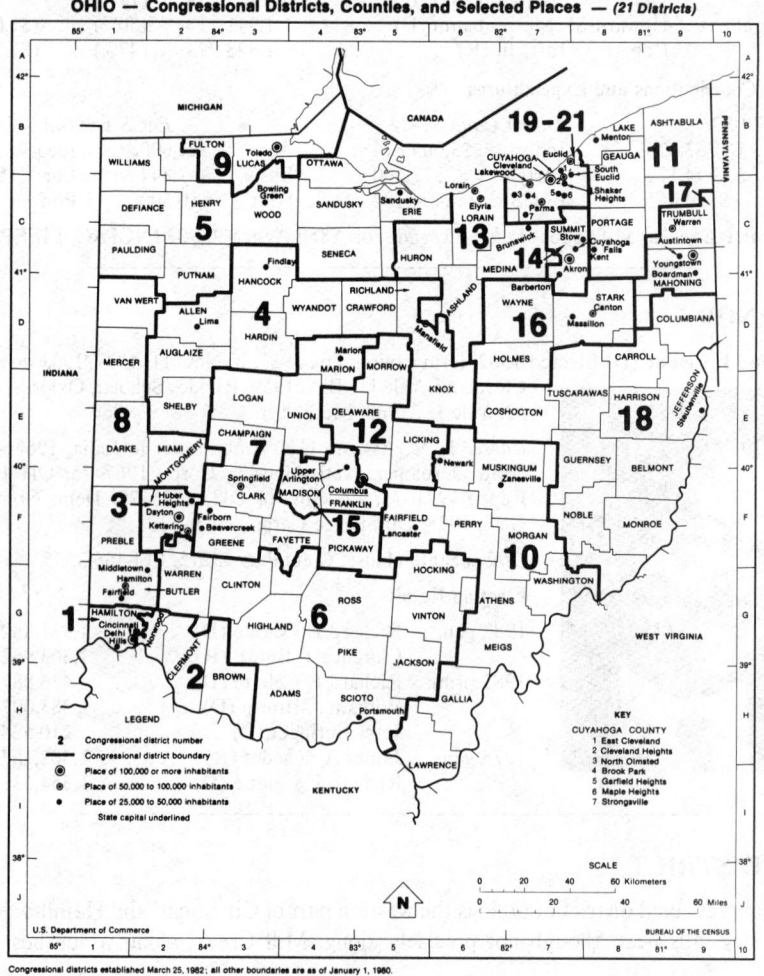

Congressional districts established March 25, 1982; all other boundaries are as of January 1, 1980.

ingly Republican. Nevertheless, this is a district which elects a Democratic congressman. He is Thomas Luken, a veteran of the Cincinnati City Council—a body whose members get so much publicity that they are the strongest candidates in the whole metropolitan area, even though they represent only a fraction of it. In some ways he resembles his district: he is an old-fashioned, not particularly articulate congressman, one who reflects old values and has plodded on with considerable success.

Luken is a member of the Energy and Commerce Committee, and an important one. He has supported measures to relax the Clean Air Act, arguing that its present terms unduly restrict industry; he was the leader in the effort to overturn the Federal Trade Commission's regulations on funeral homes. Overall, his record is notably less liberal on economic issues than those of most northern Democrats, and his approach to cultural issues is traditional; he is a fervent opponent of abortion, for example.

Luken has had an up-and-down career in congressional elections. He was the winner in one of those special elections in 1974 which helped end Richard Nixon's career; he was running in the east Cincinnati district then, and beat Willis Gradison. But Gradison beat Luken in November 1974. Two years later Luken ran in the west Cincinnati district against an incumbent who spent most of his time in Florida. He won that race, and beat a strong opponent again in 1978. In 1980 and 1982 he won easily, against weak opposition. One problem the Republicans have here is that business PACs would probably just as soon keep Luken in; they have few enough votes on the Democratic side of Energy and Commerce, and Luken is usually one of them. So it would be hard for a Republican to raise money in Washington. Redistricting, a bipartisan compromise, neither helped nor hurt Luken much; a weaker or less well-known Democrat, however, would almost certainly lose this district to a Republican.

The People   Pop. 1980: 515,867, dn. 2.3% 1970–80; voting age pop. 365,146; 14% Black, 1% Span. orig. 38% housing units rented. Median owner $47,900; renter $171. Households: 72% family, 40% with children, 57% married couples.

Presidential Vote

1980	Reagan (R)	115,076	(59%)
	Carter (D)	69,262	(36%)
	Anderson (I)	9,198	(5%)

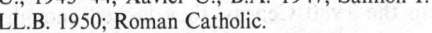

Rep. Thomas A. Luken (D) Elected 1976; b. July 9, 1925, Cincinnati; home, Cincinnati; Bowling Green U., 1943–44, Xavier U., B.A. 1947, Salmon P. Chase Law Sch., LL.B. 1950; Roman Catholic.

Career USMC, WWII; Practicing atty.; Deer Park City Solicitor, 1955–61; U.S. Dist. Atty. for S. Dist. of OH, 1961–64; Cincinnati City Cncl., 1964–67, 1969–74, Mayor, 1971–72; U.S. House of Reps., 1974.

Offices 2342 RHOB, 202-225-2216. Also Fed. Bldg., Rm. 3409, Cincinnati 45202, 513-684-2723.

Committees *Energy and Commerce* (9th). Subcommittees: Energy Conservation and Power; Fossil and Synthetic Fuels; Health and the Environment. *Small Business* (8th). Subcommittee: Antitrust and Restraint of Trade Activities Affecting Small Business (Chairman). *Select Committee on Aging* (13th). Subcommittee: Health and Long-Term Care.

Group Ratings

	ADA	ACLU	COPE	CFA	LCV	LWV	NTU	NSI	COC	ACA	CSFC
1982	65	42	77	62	64	67	13	60	40	17	36
1981	40	—	75	50	57	—	23	—	32	39	50
1980	39	27	68	57	48	22	29	56	61	43	43

National Journal Ratings

	Economic		Foreign		Cultural	
1982	69%	(LIB)	71%	(LIB)	51%	(LIB)
	31%	(CONS)	29%	(CONS)	49%	(CONS)
1981	58%	(LIB)	49%	(LIB)	49%	(LIB)
	42%	(CONS)	50%	(CONS)	51%	(CONS)

Key Votes

1) Reagan 81 Budget	AGN	5) Incr SS Rtmt Age	AGN	9) Poor Pay Food Stamps	AGN
2) Reagan 81 Tax Cut	FOR	6) Saudi AWACS Sale	AGN	10) Ban Crt Busing Order	FOR
3) Bal Budget Amend	AGN	7) $ for MX Missile	AGN	11) Auto Local Content	FOR
4) Gas & Road Tax	—	8) Nerve Gas Prod	AGN	12) Nuclear Arms Freeze	FOR

Election Results

1982 general	Thomas A. Luken (D)	99,143	(65%)	($212,061)
	John E. Held (R)	52,658	(35%)	($11,081)
1982 primary	Thomas A. Luken (D)	27,923	(100%)	
1980 general	Thomas A. Luken (D)	103,423	(59%)	($290,853)
	Tom (Thearon) Atkins (R)	72,693	(41%)	($120,476)

Campaign Contributions and Expenditures

1981-82		Direct Cont. 81-82		PACS brkdwn			
Receipts	$300,218	Indiv	$110,317	Agr	$5,950	Ideo	$1,737
Expend.	$212,061	Party	$500	Bus	$109,480	Lbr	$28,475
Unspent	$92,581	PACS	$172,942	Hlth	$23,050	Prof	$4,250
		Cand	$500				

SECOND DISTRICT

The 2d congressional district of Ohio consists of the east side of Cincinnati and its eastern Hamilton County suburbs, plus two counties along the Ohio River to the east. Since 1852, Cincinnati and Hamilton County have been divided, by a vertical line, into two congressional districts; finally, in the 1980 Census, they lacked enough population for two districts by themselves, and so more territory was added to this district. The addition makes some sense. Clermont County, just to the east, has doubled in population in the last 20 years, filling up with people who moved out from Cincinnati or its close-in suburbs; Brown County, farther up the Ohio River—at the spot where Liza crossed the ice in *Uncle Tom's Cabin*—is still almost entirely rural.

The east side of Cincinnati is, by and large, the more prosperous and fashionable side of the city, which was the cultural and commercial capital of the Midwest even before the Tafts arrived. In some neighborhoods within Cincinnati and in suburbs like Indian Hill are the fashionable estates of the city's elite. The northern suburbs are a mix of shopping centers and high-income subdivisions; within the city itself are the formerly Jewish sections of Avondale and Walnut Hills, now mostly black. Many neighborhoods, such as Norwood, a suburban enclave surrounded by Cincinnati, are inhabited mainly by migrants from the hills of Kentucky and Tennessee. The 2d has most of the city's Jewish population; from its early days as a German river town, Cincinnati has had an important German Jewish community. Politically, it is more conservative and Republican than Jewish communities in other major cities.

Cincinnati has a well-deserved reputation for being a Republican city. Of the nation's 25 largest metropolitan areas, only Dallas–Fort Worth and San Diego turn in Republican margins with greater regularity. That has been the case since before the Civil War, when Cincinnati was a German, pro-Union, and Republican island in a sea of southern Democratic sentiment; it was the home then of Harriet Beecher Stowe, the author of *Uncle Tom's Cabin,* and of other antislavery agitators. In later years Cincinnati did not attract as many southern and eastern European immigrants as did Great Lakes industrial cities like Cleveland, Detroit, and Chicago; its ethnic character (like its physical appearance) and its political preference have remained pretty well fixed. Even many of the Appalachians here are Republicans, from Civil War Republican counties in the hills.

Out of Cincinnati have come several prominent Republicans, including Chief Justice Salmon P. Chase, President and Chief Justice William Howard Taft, Speaker of the House Nicholas Longworth (who married Teddy Roosevelt's daughter Alice), and the late Senator Robert Taft. All were men of urbanity and learning, conservatives who sought to maintain the values and the political system which had allowed the growth and prosperity of places like Cincinnati, the articulate advocates of a system that worked. More recently this district has had a series of prominent congressmen: John Gilligan, later governor of Ohio, and Robert Taft, Jr., later U.S. senator.

The current congressman from the district, Willis Gradison, does not seem to have statewide ambitions, but has made a solid mark in the House. He is a member of both the Ways and Means and the Budget Committees, and one of the most thoughtful and well-informed Republicans on economic issues. His approach is to ask basic questions about programs, to find long-range solutions that make sense; not just to patch things up for the short term. His own temperament seems to favor caution, and he does not quickly embrace the latest nostrum; but when he becomes convinced he can be a tenuous advocate, as he is of income tax indexing, to take one example. He is also a clear-sighted and fair-minded analyst of what is going on, the kind of man members of both parties go to to find out what is happening and what is at stake.

Gradison had to try twice to win this district: he lost to Thomas Luken in a 1974 special election, in which the main issue was Richard Nixon and Watergate; then, with Nixon gone, he beat Luken in November. (Luken went on to win the west Cincinnati district in 1976.) Since his first victory, Gradison has been elected by very large margins and has not attracted serious opposition. His policies and temperament seem to suit the district well, and there is no reason he cannot go on representing it for some time.

The People Pop. 1980: 514,408, dn. 0.5% 1970–80; voting age pop. 370,265; 15% Black, 1% Span. orig. 37% housing units rented. Median owner $49,500; renter $168. Households: 70% family, 39% with children, 57% married couples.

Presidential Vote

1980	Reagan (R)	124,039	(58%)
	Carter (D)	77,435	(36%)
	Anderson (I)	10,723	(5%)

Rep. Willis D. (Bill) **Gradison, Jr.** (R) Elected 1974; b. Dec. 28, 1928, Cincinnati; home, Cincinnati; Yale U., B.A. 1948, Harvard U., M.B.A. 1951, D.C.S. 1954; Jewish.

Career Investment broker; Asst. to U.S. Undersecy. of the Treasury, 1953–55; Asst. to U.S. Secy. of HEW, 1955–57; Cincinnati City Cncl., 1961–74, Vice-Mayor, 1967–71, Mayor, 1971.

Offices 2311 RHOB, 202-225-3164. Also 8008 Fed. Ofc. Bldg., 550 Main St., Cincinnati 45202, 513-684-2456.

Committees Budget (9th). Task Forces: Entitlements, Uncontrollables, and Indexing; Federalism/State-Local Relations; Tax Policy. *Ways and Means* (9th). Subcommittee: Social Security.

Group Ratings

	ADA	ACLU	COPE	CFA	LCV	LWV	NTU	NSI	COC	ACA	CSFC
1982	20	58	17	46	50	58	82	80	73	91	64
1981	35	—	18	57	62	—	72	—	89	60	59
1980	22	40	17	36	52	50	48	89	76	67	68

National Journal Ratings

	Economic		Foreign		Cultural	
1982	25%	(LIB)	43%	(LIB)	58%	(LIB)
	74%	(CONS)	57%	(CONS)	42%	(CONS)
1981	24%	(LIB)	49%	(LIB)	72%	(LIB)
	68%	(CONS)	50%	(CONS)	28%	(CONS)

Key Votes

1) Reagan 81 Budget	FOR	5) Incr SS Rtmt Age	FOR	9) Poor Pay Food Stamps	—
2) Reagan 81 Tax Cut	FOR	6) Saudi AWACS Sale	AGN	10) Ban Crt Busing Order	FOR
3) Bal Budget Amend	FOR	7) $ for MX Missile	AGN	11) Auto Local Content	AGN
4) Gas & Road Tax	FOR	8) Nerve Gas Prod	FOR	12) Nuclear Arms Freeze	AGN

Election Results

1982 general	Willis D. (Bill) Gradison, Jr. (R) ..	97,434	(63%)	($126,233)
	William Luthner (D)	53,169	(34%)	($0)
1982 primary	Willis D. (Bill) Gradison, Jr. (R) ..	27,004	(100%)	
1980 general	Willis D. (Bill) Gradison, Jr. (R) ..	124,080	(75%)	($98,441)
	Donald J. Zwick (D)	38,529	(23%)	($0)

Campaign Contributions and Expenditures

1981-82		*Direct Cont. 81-82*	
Receipts	$122,282	Indiv	$91,036
Expend.	$126,233	Party	$9,891
Unspent	$74,504		

Received no PAC Contributions

THIRD DISTRICT

Dayton, Ohio, is many people's idea of a typical American city. Situated just below the old National Road that spans the Midwest, at a point which was once the center of U.S.

population, and not far from the divide between northern and southern accents. Dayton also illustrates, in exaggerated form, the rise of the American economy and its current problems.

Dayton is a bigger city than most people suppose, with a metropolitan population of some 800,000; it owes its size primarily to the ingenuity of some of its residents in the late 19th and early 20th century. This was the home, for example, of Wilbur and Orville Wright, who manufactured their airplane here and took it down to Kitty Hawk to fly because there were steady high winds there. It was the home of James Ritty, who invented the cash register—that indispensable instrument for large retail trade—and of John Henry Patterson, who made a success of the company that is now National Cash Register. It was the hometown of Charles Kettering, who invented the automatic starters and several other innovations which changed the automobile from a plaything to a practical form of everyday transportation. Dayton at the turn of the century was a town buzzing with mechanical innovations, and with inventors practical enough to turn them into profitable businesses.

Today the atmosphere in Dayton is quite different. Its major businesses seem beleaguered: NCR is determined to compete in the difficult office automation business computer market; Mead Paper is under the shadow of a huge antitrust verdict; companies supplying the Big Three are in severe trouble because of the collapse of the auto industry. The voters of the Dayton area increasingly, and particularly in 1982, voted for Democratic politicians who promise more government aid for the unemployed and continued government programs, even if that means higher taxes. At the same time, the population here is declining: many young people are leaving to find jobs elsewhere. Is the spirit of tinkering and innovation, of practical organization and mechanical dreaming entirely gone now? No one can say for sure. But it does seem clear that the fashionable high-tech industries of the day are not flocking to Dayton, nor, apparently, are the advanced graduates in their disciplines. Perhaps in some research and development office, or huddled over some computer, some young Daytonites are doing what the inventor of the cash register did. But does Dayton have today the large-scale organizations to follow through and make innovations? No one is sure of that today, and people here are now fearful of the future.

The city of Dayton plus most of suburban and rural Montgomery County make up the 3d congressional district of Ohio. This is essentially a Democratic district, and one that has gotten more so. In congressional elections, it has been represented since 1978 by Democrat Tony Hall.

Like many younger members, most of them liberal Democrats, Hall served in the Peace Corps in the 1960s; he went on to be a real estate broker and to serve in the Ohio legislature for 10 years. In the House his record on economic issues is not totally on liberal/labor lines; he seems interested in providing incentives for the kinds of businesses Dayton once developed and now needs again. On cultural issues he is less traditional. Hall is a member of the Rules Committee, and a loyal follower of the Democratic leadership when it comes to procedural matters. In practice, this committee is not so important as it once was, since under Tip O'Neill and Chairmen Richard Bolling and Claude Pepper it has not used its power to obstruct legislation its members don't like.

Hall replaced Charles Whalen, a liberal Republican who retired in 1978 and whose voting record was very close to Hall's. Hall did not win either of his first two elections by overwhelming margins, but in 1982—perhaps in recognition of the Democratic trend in this area of high unemployment—he had no Republican opponent at all. His political outlook for the 1980s is good.

The People   Pop. 1980: 513,588, dn. 7.6% 1970–80; voting age pop. 370,522; 16% Black, 1% Span. orig. 34% housing units rented. Median owner $39,500; renter $159. Households: 72% family, 39% with children, 57% married couples.

Presidential Vote

1980			
	Reagan (R)	89,062	(44%)
	Carter (D)	98,694	(49%)
	Anderson (I)	12,463	(6%)

Rep. Tony P. Hall (D) Elected 1978; b. Jan. 16, 1942, Dayton; home, Dayton; Denison U., B.A. 1964; Presbyterian.

Career Peace Corps, Thailand, 1964–66; Real estate broker, 1966–; OH House of Reps., 1969–73; OH Senate, 1973–79.

Offices 1728 LHOB, 202-225-6465. Also 501 Fed. Bldg., 200 W. 2d St., Dayton 45402, 513-225-2843.

Committee *Rules* (8th). Subcommittee: Rules of the House.

Group Ratings

	ADA	ACLU	COPE	CFA	LCV	LWV	NTU	NSI	COC	ACA	CSFC
1983	70	58	77	54	89	75	47	50	30	33	34
1981	45	—	77	86	86	—	59	—	44	43	46
1980	89	87	79	64	88	88	19	10	68	21	30

National Journal Ratings

	Economic		Foreign		Cultural	
1982	59%	(LIB)	75%	(LIB)	61%	(LIB)
	41%	(CONS)	25%	(CONS)	38%	(CONS)
1981	60%	(LIB)	58%	(LIB)	60%	(LIB)
	40%	(CONS)	41%	(CONS)	40%	(CONS)

Key Votes

1) Reagan 81 Budget	AGN	5) Incr SS Rtmt Age	AGN	9) Poor Pay Food Stamps	AGN
2) Reagan 81 Tax Cut	AGN	6) Saudi AWACS Sale	AGN	10) Ban Crt Busing Order	FOR
3) Bal Budget Amend	AGN	7) $ for MX Missile	AGN	11) Auto Local Content	FOR
4) Gas & Road Tax	—	8) Nerve Gas Prod	AGN	12) Nuclear Arms Freeze	FOR

Election Results

1982 general	Tony P. Hall (D)	119,926	(75%)	($51,945)
	Kathryn E. Brown (L)	16,828	(12%)	($0)
1982 primary	Tony P. Hall (D)	38,307	(100%)	
1980 general	Tony P. Hall (D)	95,558	(57%)	($154,725)
	Albert H. Sealy (R)	66,698	(40%)	($98,305)

Campaign Contributions and Expenditures

1981-82		Direct Cont. 81-82		PACS brkdwn			
Receipts	$101,453	Indiv	$45,642	Agr	$—	Ideo	$1,987
Expend.	$51,945	PACS	$48,131	Bus	$23,750	Lbr	$16,075
Unspent	$64,644			Hlth	$5,100	Prof	$100

FOURTH DISTRICT

The 4th congressional district of Ohio is a group of counties, mostly rural in appearance but with most of the population in small cities and towns, in the western part of the state. Here you can find the home of Neil Armstrong, the first man on the moon, a typically modest and homey place called Wapakoneta. Here also is Lima, an old industrial city with a weak economy of late, and Findlay, the much more prosperous home of Marathon Oil, now a unit of U.S. Steel after a celebrated takeover struggle. Farther to the east is Bucyrus, a town which has given its name to a company producing giant earth-moving equipment, and Mansfield, home of John Sherman, one of Ohio's great Republican statesmen of the 19th century.

This is a deeply Republican area, one of the party's strongholds since the 19th century. Yet recently so wrenching has been Ohio's economic condition that this area has gone Democratic—or come close to it. The first occasion was in June 1981, when a special election was held to fill the vacancy caused by the death of Congressman Tennyson Guyer. The Republican, Michael Oxley, was expected to win; the Reagan economic program was just going through the Congress, and seemed very popular. But the Democratic candidate, state legislator Dale Locker, ran on a conservative platform himself. He may have picked up a few votes from conservatives who were displeased that Oxley, a George Bush backer in 1980, had won the nomination over a local Reaganaut; more likely the result just showed the weakness, even in this part of Ohio, of the Republican Party. Oxley squeaked through by 378 votes out of 83,000 cast in the special election.

As it has turned out, Oxley has compiled a record which any Reagan supporter would be proud of. He supported the President's economic program and, on the key Energy and Commerce Committee, voted to hold down federal regulation. And he worked the district hard enough so that in 1982, despite the Democratic trend, he was able to win the district convincingly. Elected while still in his 30s, Oxley has the potential to hold this seat for many years, and perhaps to become an important voice on major issues.

The People Pop. 1980: 514,696, up 4.5% 1970–80; voting age pop. 360,765; 3% Black, 1% Span. orig. 22% housing units rented. Median owner $39,600; renter $153. Households: 77% family, 42% with children, 67% married couples.

Presidential Vote

1980	Reagan (R)	122,541	(63%)
	Carter (D)	61,521	(32%)
	Anderson (I)	9,024	(5%)

Rep. Michael G. Oxley (R) Elected June 25, 1981; b. Feb. 11, 1944, Findlay; home, Findlay; Miami U. of OH, B.A. 1966, OH State U., J.D. 1969; Lutheran.

Career Spec. Agent of the FBI, 1969–72; OH House of Reps., 1972–81; Practicing atty., 1972–1981.

Offices 1108 LHOB, 202-225-2676. Also 401 W. North St., Rm. 205, Lima 45801, 419-227-6845; 24 W. 3d St., Rm. 314, Mansfield 44902, 419-522-5757; and 110 W. Main Cross, Rm. 212, Findlay 45840, 419-423-3210.

Committees *Energy and Commerce* (14th). Subcommittees: Oversight and Investigations; Telecommunications, Consumer Protection, and Finance. *Select Committee on Narcotics Abuse and Control* (4th).

Group Ratings

	ADA	ACLU	COPE	CFA	LCV	LWV	NTU	NSI	COC	ACA	CSFC
1982	10	—	17	23	16	—	81	100	82	90	65
1981	0	—	20	40	33	—	72	—	92	85	68

National Journal Ratings

	Economic		Foreign		Cultural	
1982	5%	(LIB)	28%	(LIB)	26%	(LIB)
	94%	(CONS)	72%	(CONS)	74%	(CONS)
1981	0%	(LIB)	29%	(LIB)	14%	(LIB)
	99%	(CONS)	70%	(CONS)	86%	(CONS)

Key Votes

1) Reagan 81 Budget —	5) Incr SS Rtmt Age FOR	9) Poor Pay Food Stamps FOR
2) Reagan 81 Tax Cut FOR	6) Saudi AWACS Sale FOR	10) Ban Crt Busing Order FOR
3) Bal Budget Amend FOR	7) $ for MX Missile FOR	11) Auto Local Content AGN
4) Gas & Road Tax —	8) Nerve Gas Prod FOR	12) Nuclear Arms Freeze AGN

Election Results

1982 general	Michael G. Oxley (R)	105,087	(65%)	($181,359)
	Robert Moon (D)	57,564	(35%)	($67,872)
1982 primary	Michael G. Oxley (R)	41,812	(100%)	
1981 special	Michael G. Oxley (R)	41,904	(50%)	($272,562)
	Dale Locker (D)	41,526	(50%)	($138,211)
1980 general	Tennyson Guyer (R)	133,795	(72%)	($41,661)
	Gerry Tebben (D)	51,150	(28%)	($4,832)

Campaign Contributions and Expenditures

1981-82		Direct Cont. 81-82		PACS brkdwn			
Receipts	$195,770	Indiv	$95,949	Agr	$3,260	Ideo	$11,500
Expend.	$181,359	Party	$12,130	Bus	$55,940	Lbr	$1,200
Unspent	$17,620	PACS	$80,110	Hlth	$7,550	Prof	$500

FIFTH DISTRICT

Some 150 years ago, New England Yankees began to settle the flat lands in the northwestern corner of Ohio, joined later by German Protestants. The land here is more fertile and easier to work than the knobby hills of southern Ohio; its flatness and fertility must have amazed the early settlers. It is the beginning of the great corn and hog belt that stretches into Illinois and Iowa, and it has also been one of the heartlands of the Republican Party since it was founded in 1854.

Unlike so much of rural America, northwestern Ohio was not in economic decline in the years after World War II. The fertility of its soil, the industry of its farmers, and, most important, its strategic location prevented the kind of outmigration seen in other rural areas. Northwestern Ohio is encircled by the giant industrial cities of the Midwest and lies on both sides of the nation's major east–west railroads and interstate highways. Taking advantage of the proximity of these major markets, small factories have sprung up in most of the towns and much of the countryside of northwestern Ohio. They have provided jobs for young people here, who otherwise would have migrated to large cities. Even in the 1970s and early 1980s, when the economies of the big industrial cities were in trouble, the economic base here continued to be relatively strong. Labor costs were lower than in the big cities, labor unions less obdurate, taxes lower, and racial tensions largely nonexistent.

The 5th congressional district covers most of northwestern Ohio. Not included is the city of Toledo and most of its suburbs, which make up the 9th district. The 5th has been one of the most solidly Republican districts in the nation over the years, and since 1958 has elected and reelected Congressman Delbert Latta (the name, incidentally, is Welsh, not Italian). Latta is one of those congressmen who labored for years without much public notice. As a member of the Rules Committee he was often part, or even the architect, of the coalition of conservative Republicans and southern Democrats who would kill liberal legislation by refusing to schedule it for debate or by allowing crippling amendments. Always a fierce and aggressive partisan, Latta could be trusted to follow the wishes of the Republican leadership; and within the leadership he usually has been an advocate of hard-line opposition to the Democrats.

In the 1970s, Latta became much more prominent, but his approach remained much the same. His well-deserved reputation for partisanship got him a seat on the Judiciary Committee in 1974; he filled a vacancy just for the hearings on the impeachment of Richard Nixon. Apparently the hope was that Latta would provide a no-holds-barred defense of Nixon, and he did. He made some cheap shots as well, mentioning how much the hearings were costing and attacking a committee counsel for favoring decriminalization of prostitution; the more effective defense of Nixon, made by Charles Wiggins and others, stuck closer to the matter at hand.

When the congressional budget process was established in 1975, Latta again got a key role. He was named the ranking Republican on the Budget Committee, a position he still holds. On the Senate committee in the 1970s there was bipartisan cooperation; on the House there was—and is—partisan struggle. Latta fought for lower domestic spending in the 1970s, and then had the satisfaction after the 1980 election of seeing his Gramm–Latta substitute pass the House in 1981. In 1982 he continued to work against higher taxes, and opposed the 1982 tax increase even though President Reagan endorsed it.

Now Latta seems more likely to be frustrated again. In early 1983 the Republicans chose not to put forward a budget of their own, both because they lacked the votes to pass the Reagan budget and because they were uncomfortable defending a deficit as large as it would show. Latta is also in a small minority on the House Rules Committee now; the nine Democrats, all loyal to the speaker, can easily outvote the four Republicans. That leaves this partisan bulldog in an uncomfortable position: he is unlikely to prevail often in the House, and yet he can be thrown on the defensive when attacks are made on the apparent imperfections in Reagan policies.

Latta may feel additional discomfort back in the 5th district. In the 1982 statewide elections even this Republican stronghold went Democratic, giving 54% of its vote to gubernatorial candidate Richard Celeste. At the same time Latta won with the unaccustomedly low percentage of 55%. One problem was redistricting: he lost one Republican county and picked up areas which went heavily Democratic (59% in his race) in 1982. But there may be a greater problem than year-to-year fluctuations. If the economy of Ohio—and the economy of the big manufacturing cities, on which the economy of northwestern Ohio depends—does not revive soon, will all of Delbert Latta's partisan fervor be able to save him if voters conclude that policies he has favored and played a major part in passing have proved disastrous to their communities?

The People   Pop. 1980: 514,189, up 7.7% 1970–80; voting age pop. 358,629; 2% Black, 2% Span. orig. 22% housing units rented. Median owner $43,200; renter $165. Households: 77% family, 44% with children, 67% married couples.

Presidential Vote

1980	Reagan (R)	118,338	(60%)
	Carter (D)	66,356	(33%)
	Anderson (I)	14,109	(7%)

Rep. Delbert L. Latta (R) Elected 1958; b. Mar. 5, 1920, Weston; home, Bowling Green; OH Northern U., A.B. 1943, LL.B. 1946; Churches of Christ.

Career Practicing atty., 1946–52; OH Senate, 1952–58.

Offices 2309 RHOB, 202-225-6405. Also 100 Fed. Bldg., 280 S. Main St., Bowling Green 43402, 419-353-8871.

Committees *Budget* (Ranking Member). *Rules* (2d).

Group Ratings

	ADA	ACLU	COPE	CFA	LCV	LWV	NTU	NSI	COC	ACA	CSFC
1982	15	0	13	8	25	8	90	100	81	91	74
1981	0	—	13	29	23	—	90	—	95	91	75
1980	17	27	11	7	31	40	70	89	74	88	84

National Journal Ratings

	Economic		Foreign		Cultural	
1982	25%	(LIB)	12%	(LIB)	4%	(LIB)
	75%	(CONS)	84%	(CONS)	87%	(CONS)
1981	34%	(LIB)	3%	(LIB)	10%	(LIB)
	65%	(CONS)	87%	(CONS)	90%	(CONS)

Key Votes

1) Reagan 81 Budget	FOR	5) Incr SS Rtmt Age	FOR	9) Poor Pay Food Stamps	FOR
2) Reagan 81 Tax Cut	FOR	6) Saudi AWACS Sale	FOR	10) Ban Crt Busing Order	FOR
3) Bal Budget Amend	FOR	7) $ for MX Missile	FOR	11) Auto Local Content	FOR
4) Gas & Road Tax	—	8) Nerve Gas Prod	FOR	12) Nuclear Arms Freeze	AGN

Election Results

1982 general	Delbert L. Latta (R)	86,450	(55%)	($131,881)
	James R. Sherck (D)	70,120	(45%)	($47,372)
1982 primary	Delbert L. Latta (R)	39,916	(100%)	
1980 general	Delbert L. Latta (R)	137,003	(70%)	($57,923)
	James R. Sherck (D)	57,704	(30%)	($17,990)

Campaign Contributions and Expenditures

1981-82		Direct Cont. 81-82				PACS brkdwn		
Receipts	$151,357	Indiv	$33,477	Agr	$2,250	Ideo	$3,000
Expend.	$131,881	Party	$14,584	Bus	$59,400	Lbr	$—
Unspent	$97,926	PACS	$81,735	Hlth	$9,300	Prof	$1,450

Indep Expend: For: $180 (OH RTL)

SIXTH DISTRICT

The 6th congressional district of Ohio is a rural district in the southern part of the state. It touches the metropolitan areas of Cincinnati to the southwest and Columbus on the north, and it includes the gritty industrial city of Portsmouth on the Ohio River. But nothing in it has a metropolitan flavor. This is small-town America, where people speak with something very much like a southern accent. The rolling hill country of the valley of the Scioto River, which runs through Columbus, Chillicothe, and Portsmouth, was once Democratic terrain, reflecting the southern origin of the valley's early settlers. But in the 1950s and 1960s this part of Ohio, like much of the South, became more conservative and more Republican. That trend reversed sharply in 1982, when Richard Celeste carried the area solidly. But it remains to be seen whether this was a one-time-only protest against Reagan economic policies or the beginning of a return to ancestral voting patterns. At this point, skepticism is in order.

Until the late 1950s this district, in line with tradition, sent a Democrat to the House. After his death in 1959, the Republican organization carefully selected a candidate, and the district has elected Republicans ever since. The current incumbent, Bob McEwen, was a 1980 Republican freshman. He won the seat at age 30, but with considerable experience, both as an aide to his predecessor and as a state senator in Columbus. His margin was actually a little shaky, and he lost some of his strongest territory (Clermont County, in effect a suburb of Cincinnati) in redistricting; yet he won reelection with a solid 59%. A bigger asset than his solid Republican voting record was his attention to concrete problems, as symbolized by his committee assignments—Public Works and Veterans' Affairs. Having done well in 1982, McEwen seems in good shape to hold onto this seat, even if the Democratic trend here persists.

The People   Pop. 1980: 514,895, up 13% 1970–80; voting age pop. 359,641; 2% Black. 24% housing units rented. Median owner $39,800; renter $143. Households: 79% family, 45% with children, 69% married couples.

Presidential Vote

1980	Reagan (R)	....	106,317	(57%)
	Carter (D)	....	72,918	(39%)
	Anderson (I)	....	6,874	(4%)

Rep. Bob McEwen (R) Elected 1980; b. Jan. 12, 1950, Hillsboro; home, Hillsboro; U. of Miami, FL, B.B.A. 1972; Churches of Christ.

Career Real estate developer; OH House of Reps., 1974–80.

Offices 329 CHOB, 202-225-5705. Also P.O. Bldg., Portsmouth 45662, 614-353-5171; Fed. Bldg., Hillsboro 45133, 513-393-4223; and 190 Main St., Batavia 45103, 513-732-1786.

Committees *Public Works and Transportation* (9th). Subcommittees: Aviation; Economic Development; Water Resources. *Veterans' Affairs* (5th). Subcommittees: Compensation, Pension, and Insurance; Hospitals and Health Care.

Group Ratings

	ADA	ACLU	COPE	CFA	LCV	LWV	NTU	NSI	COC	ACA	CSFC
1982	30	12	29	31	39	17	77	89	86	77	61
1981	0	—	20	29	21	—	84	—	89	83	73

National Journal Ratings

	Economic		Foreign		Cultural	
1982	32%	(LIB)	36%	(LIB)	24%	(LIB)
	68%	(CONS)	63%	(CONS)	76%	(CONS)
1981	4%	(LIB)	33%	(LIB)	4%	(LIB)
	79%	(CONS)	67%	(CONS)	90%	(CONS)

Key Votes

1) Reagan 81 Budget	FOR	5) Incr SS Rtmt Age	FOR	9) Poor Pay Food Stamps	FOR
2) Reagan 81 Tax Cut	FOR	6) Saudi AWACS Sale	FOR	10) Ban Crt Busing Order	FOR
3) Bal Budget Amend	FOR	7) $ for MX Missile	FOR	11) Auto Local Content	FOR
4) Gas & Road Tax	—	8) Nerve Gas Prod	AGN	12) Nuclear Arms Freeze	AGN

Election Results

1982 general	Bob McEwen (R)	92,135	(59%)	($143,149)
	Lynn A. Grimshaw (D)	63,435	(41%)	($79,786)
1982 primary	Bob McEwen (R)	36,810	(100%)	
1980 general	Bob McEwen (R)	101,288	(55%)	($182,388)
	Ted Strickland (D)	84,235	(45%)	($80,608)

Campaign Contributions and Expenditures

1981-82		Direct Cont. 81-82		PACS brkdwn			
Receipts	$143,861	Indiv	$65,728	Agr	$4,500	Ideo	$4,000
Expend.	$143,149	Party	$9,055	Bus	$51,317	Lbr	$1,000
Unspent	$1,182	PACS	$68,017	Hlth	$7,200	Prof	$—

Indep Expend: For: $891 (NRA)

SEVENTH DISTRICT

When the editors of *Newsweek* were looking for a typical American community to profile for their 50th anniversary issue, they chose Springfield, Ohio. It was a good choice, not only to show how America has changed, and how its economy is in trouble, but also to show how the nation has remained stable and steady, even as it has experienced vast economic growth. Springfield is a small industrial city, one which physically resembles the Springfield of the 1920s. Its major industries got their impetus from electrical and mechanical innovations in the first decades of this century. Yet for all its appearance of having stayed the same, Springfield has in fact enjoyed vast economic growth. The working men who exhausted themselves working 60-hour weeks now make much higher real wages working 40 hours; without much notice, factories that once existed have been torn down and others erected in their place.

In the early 1980s Springfield and other Ohio cities were in serious economic distress. Unemployment rose to the highest percentages since the days of Franklin Roosevelt; and if the reality was different, because of unemployment compensation and other benefits, the shock of being out of work was perhaps even greater than it was in the 1930s. Moreover, to many Ohioans the future looks bleak: this manufacturing state no longer seems a beehive of economic innovation; the glamour industries of the future are not locating here. The way of life—vastly improved over 50 years ago—which people worked so hard to build now seems in jeopardy.

Springfield is part of the 7th congressional district of Ohio, an odd-shaped unit which forms a sort of horseshoe some 20 to 50 miles around Columbus. It includes such notable places as Bellefontaine, site of the first concrete street in America, and Marion, where young Socialist-to-be Norman Thomas delivered newspapers edited by President-to-be Warren Harding. Historically this is Republican territory. The policies of the party of William McKinley—tariff protection, railroad regulation, antitrust suits against monopolies, discouragement of labor unions—seemed to work very well to produce economic growth in the years 1900–30; the low tax Republican policies of the 1950s seemed to be working as well, in that last decade in which Ohio had a significant increase in the number of manufacturing jobs. In the 1980s the Republican faith has lost ground here—just how much remains to be seen.

This is the district represented for 17 years by Clarence (Bud) Brown and for 27 years by his father before him. They were both leaders of the Republicans in the House, the younger Brown being one of the heartiest warriors in the ultimately successful battle to deregulate oil and gas. Brown ran for governor in 1982 on a platform similar to the Reagan economic policies he supported—looking to cut taxes, not raise them—but ended up losing badly. He did, however, carry his home district; and the Republican Party, in the person of Michael DeWine, ended up holding onto the seat.

DeWine is an ambitious young politician, elected Greene County prosecutor at age 29 and state senator at 33. He won the Republican nomination easily and in the general election beat a Marine Vietnam veteran confined to a wheelchair by war injuries. He did lose Springfield in the process, but his overall percentage was high enough (56%) to suggest he will have no trouble holding this district in the future, whatever the local trend of opinion.

The People   Pop. 1980: 512,706, up 3.8% 1970–80; voting age pop. 361,162; 5% Black, 1% Span. orig. 26% housing units rented. Median owner $41,500; renter $153. Households: 78% family, 44% with children, 67% married couples.

Presidential Vote

1980	Reagan (R)	103,359	(56%)
	Carter (D)	70,405	(38%)
	Anderson (I)	10,298	(6%)

Rep. Michael DeWine (R) Elected 1982; b. Jan. 5, 1947, Springfield; home, Springfield; Miami U. of OH, B.S. 1969, OH Northern U., J.D. 1972; Roman Catholic.

Career Asst. Prosecuting Atty., Greene Cnty., 1973–75, Prosecuting Atty., 1977–80; OH Senate, 1980–82; Practicing atty., 1973–.

Offices 1407 LHOB, 202-225-4324. Also 150 N. Limestone, Rm. 220, Springfield 45501, 513-325-0474.

Committee *Judiciary* (11th). Subcommittees: Civil and Constitutional Rights; Courts, Civil Liberties, and the Administration of Justice; Criminal Justice.

Group Ratings and Key Votes: Newly Elected

Election Results

1982 general	Michael DeWine (R)	87,842	(56%)	($215,136)
	Roger D. Tackett (D)	65,543	(42%)	($80,475)
1982 primary	Michael DeWine (R)	32,615	(69%)	
	Peter M. Knowlton (R)	6,534	(14%)	
	John F. Evans (R)	4,223	(9%)	($50,170)
	Three others (R)	3,878	(8%)	
1980 general	Clarence J. (Bud) Brown (R)	124,137	(76%)	($205,446)
	Donald Hollister (D)	38,952	(24%)	($6,028)

Campaign Contributions and Expenditures

1981-82		Direct Cont. 81-82			PACS brkdwn		
Receipts	$220,486	Indiv	$83,248	Agr	$2,750	Ideo	$3,950
Expend.	$215,136	Party	$22,455	Bus	$74,306	Lbr	$—
Unspent	$5,349	PACS	$99,541	Hlth	$12,000	Prof	$1,500
		Cand	$10,100				

Indirect Party Expend: $32,716   *Indep Expend:* For: $180 (OH RTL)

EIGHTH DISTRICT

Along the Indiana border, just north of Cincinnati and west of Dayton, is the 8th congressional district of Ohio. Although the suburban sprawl of both Cincinnati and Dayton spills into the 8th, the district's focus is in two manufacturing cities in Butler County, Hamilton and Middletown. In the 8th the hilly Ohio River country slides into the flatter land of the northern part of the state. Over the years, the district has taken most of its settlers from around the Ohio River and farther south, a fact that shows up in the election returns. A southern Democratic heritage exists here, surfacing in the 18% of the vote George Wallace got in the 1968 general election. That was the highest percentage Wallace won in any Ohio district that year and, outside of Oklahoma, the best he did in any district that did not allow slavery at the time of the Civil War.

In general elections the 8th district usually goes Republican. In 1982, however, it went Democratic in statewide contests. This may be evidence of the old southern heritage, but another factor may be unease about the future of Ohio, and especially this part of Ohio, and its manufacturing-based economy. Most of the 8th is in the Dayton media market, and many of its residents work—or worked—in Dayton area factories or offices. The condition of the economy in the Dayton area—not just its present troubles, but its uncertain outlook for the future—seems to be writ large in the 1982 election results here.

But such unease was not apparent in the congressional election. Congressman Thomas Kindness is a Republican who has demonstrated his vote-getting prowess before. He first won the seat in 1974, in a Democratic year; and in a district where Republicans have had difficulty before, he has held it easily ever since. In 1982 his percentage dipped, but only to 66%—an impressive showing.

Kindness's vote-getting ability does not seem related to his committee assignments. He sits on Judiciary and Government Operations, both of which have, for the most part, jurisdictions which must seem abstract and ethereal to most ordinary voters. Kindness may be less interested in committee work, however, than in a Republican leadership position.

The People Pop. 1980: 513,427, up 11.3% 1970–80; voting age pop. 360,843; 3% Black, 1% Span. orig. 25% housing units rented. Median owner $44,800; renter $164. Households: 78% family, 44% with children, 68% married couples.

Presidential Vote

1980	Reagan (R)	119,270	(60%)
	Carter (D)	67,581	(34%)
	Anderson (I)	10,750	(5%)

Rep. Thomas N. Kindness (R) Elected 1974; b. Aug. 26, 1929, Knoxville, TN; home, Hamilton; U. of MD, A.B. 1951, Geo. Wash. U., LL.B. 1953; Presbyterian.

Career Practicing atty., 1954–57; Asst. Counsel, Legal Dept., Champion Internatl. Corp., 1957–73; Hamilton City Cncl., 1964–69, Mayor 1964–67; OH House of Reps., 1971–74.

Offices 2417 RHOB, 202-225-6205. Also 801 High St., Hamilton 45013, 513-895-5656.

Committees *Government Operations* (3d). Subcommittees: Environment, Energy, and Natural Resources; Government Information, Justice and Agriculture. *Judiciary* (4th). Subcommittees: Administrative Law and Governmental Relations; Courts, Civil Liberties, and the Administration of Justice.

Group Ratings

	ADA	ACLU	COPE	CFA	LCV	LWV	NTU	NSI	COC	ACA	CSFC
1982	0	8	13	31	12	8	88	89	81	83	74
1981	10	—	12	7	7	—	81	—	84	78	71
1980	6	20	11	7	41	44	64	100	67	96	83

National Journal Ratings

	Economic		Foreign		Cultural	
1982	9%	(LIB)	24%	(LIB)	21%	(LIB)
	90%	(CONS)	76%	(CONS)	76%	(CONS)
1981	4%	(LIB)	41%	(LIB)	30%	(LIB)
	79%	(CONS)	58%	(CONS)	70%	(CONS)

Key Votes

1) Reagan 81 Budget	FOR	5) Incr SS Rtmt Age	FOR	9) Poor Pay Food Stamps	FOR
2) Reagan 81 Tax Cut	FOR	6) Saudi AWACS Sale	AGN	10) Ban Crt Busing Order	FOR
3) Bal Budget Amend	FOR	7) $ for MX Missile	FOR	11) Auto Local Content	FOR
4) Gas & Road Tax	AGN	8) Nerve Gas Prod	FOR	12) Nuclear Arms Freeze	AGN

Election Results

1982 general	Thomas N. Kindness (R)	98,527	(66%)	($86,471)
	John W. Griffin (D)	49,877	(34%)	($0)
1982 primary	Thomas N. Kindness (R)	30,992	(100%)	
1980 general	Thomas N. Kindness (R)	139,590	(76%)	($58,322)
	John W. Griffin (D)	44,162	(24%)	($0)

Campaign Contributions and Expenditures

1981-82		*Direct Cont. 81-82*				*PACS brkdwn*		
Receipts	$93,040	Indiv	$26,837	Agr	$3,200	Ideo	$3,000
Expend.	$86,471	Party	$9,521	Bus	$42,300	Lbr	$—
Unspent	$8,722	PACS	$53,889	Hlth	$3,850	Prof	$1,500

NINTH DISTRICT

The city of Toledo rises incongruously from the flat plains of northwest Ohio and is different from the surrounding countryside in just about every way you can think of. Situated in the middle of rich agricultural country, Toledo is heavily industrial; set among Anglo-Saxon and German farmers and small-town residents, Toledo is heavily ethnic, with many Polish-Americans; surrounded by what has been some of the nation's staunchest Republican territory, Toledo is solidly Democratic in most elections. Toledo is an important factory town: it produces automobile glass, AMC Jeeps, and other bulky products. It is also a major Great Lakes port and sits on some of the major east–west rail lines. Like Detroit, just 60 miles to the north, Toledo experienced its greatest growth between 1910 and 1930, during the initial expansion of the auto industry. Now, like Detroit, Toledo is suffering from the apparent collapse of that industry. The problem is not simply that unemployment is high—the auto industry has survived recessions before—but that the long-term outlook is anything but bright. The auto business grew more rapidly than the national economy during the years in which it converted American families first to car ownership and then to the two-car family. Now the auto industry, even if it recovers, seems almost certain to lag behind the growth of the economy. So young people move away, and those who stay are uncertain about how to plan for the future.

That uncertainty has shown up in Toledo's congressional politics. Twice in the last two elections the 9th congressional district, which includes Toledo and most of its suburbs, has ousted incumbent congressmen, both times by large margins; and each time it has come as something of a surprise. These changes have been in tandem with changes in the national direction of opinion, but in most districts incumbent congressmen of ability and attractiveness—and both these incumbents fit that description—usually manage to survive such swings. But not in Toledo in the early 1980s.

The first upset was the defeat of Democrat Thomas Ashley in 1980. Ashley had been in trouble in the middle 1970s, but had seemed to recover; he was a leader in the House, the chairman of the ad hoc energy committee Tip O'Neill set up in 1977 to handle President Carter's energy proposals. But Ashley was evidently out of touch with Toledo and allowed himself to be outspent by Republican Ed Weber.

Weber's problem in 1982 was obvious: he had supported the Reagan economic program in 1981, and voters here were not happy with what they considered the results in 1982. But Weber was also a congressman who kept in touch with the district, who had good credentials; such incumbents have survived even in economically troubled districts elsewhere (*e.g.,* Lyle Williams in the Youngstown–Warren district). Weber's position seemed strong enough that Democrat Marcy Kaptur had only token opposition in the Democratic primary. Yet in November she beat Weber by an even bigger percentage than the one he had beaten Ashley by two years before.

Kaptur was a Carter White House aide and returned to Toledo only in 1982 to make the race. But she had genuine roots in the district and political experience there, and she was able to win solid local support from labor unions and the Democratic organization. Turnout was up vastly from 1978, as was true in much of industrial Ohio—another indication of the great uncertainty and unease in the state. Kaptur is now a member of the Banking, Finance and Urban Affairs Committee—as were Ashley and Weber—and of Veterans' Affairs. She has what would be regarded in most circumstances as a safe Democratic seat. But no one can be absolutely sure that that will be the case in Toledo.

The People Pop. 1980: 514,144, dn. 1.1% 1970–80; voting age pop. 364,615; 11% Black, 2% Span. orig. 30% housing units rented. Median owner $42,600; renter $179. Households: 71% family, 39% with children, 57% married couples.

Presidential Vote

1980	Reagan (R)	95,394	(47%)
	Carter (D)	91,716	(45%)
	Anderson (I)	17,884	(9%)

Rep. Marcy Kaptur (D) Elected 1982; b. June 17, 1946, Toledo; home, Toledo; U. of WI, B.A. 1968, U. of MI, M.U.P. 1975, Ph.D Candidate, MIT, 1981–; Roman Catholic.

Career Urban planner, 1969–75; Asst. Dir. of Urban Affairs, Domestic Policy Staff, White House, 1977–80; Dpty. Secy., National Consumer Coop. Bank, 1980–81.

Offices 1630 LHOB, 202-225-4146. Also Fed. Bldg., 234 Summit St., Rm. 719, Toledo 43604, 419-259-7500.

Committees *Banking, Finance and Urban Affairs* (26th). Subcommittees: Economic Stabilization; Housing and Community Development; International Trade, Investment and Monetary Policy. *Veterans' Affairs* (13th). Subcommittees: Education, Training and Employment; Hospitals and Health Care.

Group Ratings and Key Votes: Newly Elected

Election Results

1982 general	Marcy Kaptur (D)	95,162	(58%)	($211,030)
	Ed Weber (R)	64,459	(39%)	($416,552)
1982 primary	Marcy Kaptur (D)	35,824	(78%)	
	John G. Rust (D)	6,122	(13%)	
	Edward Silvio Emery (D)	3,885	(8%)	
1980 general	Ed Weber (R)	96,927	(56%)	($380,673)
	Thomas Ludlow Ashley (D)	68,728	(40%)	($254,264)

Campaign Contributions and Expenditures

1981-82		Direct Cont. 81-82				PACS brkdwn		
Receipts	$216,958	Indiv	$102,790	Agr	$1,000	Ideo	$12,650
Expend.	$211,030	Party	$15,218	Bus	$1,650	Lbr	$81,870
Unspent	$5,928	PACS	$98,985	Hlth	$100	Prof	$900

Indirect Party Expend: $553   *Indep Expend:* For: $600 (BoilerPAC)

TENTH DISTRICT

The 10th congressional district of Ohio is in the southern part of the state; almost all of it is below U.S. 40, the old National Road, which is a rough boundary between northern- and southern-accented Ohio. This is also, though it was the part of Ohio first settled by whites, one of the least thickly populated parts of Ohio today, and one of the least industrialized. Marietta, on the Ohio River, was the site of the first permanent American settlement, in 1788, in the old Northwest Territory, the land north and west of the Ohio River ceded to the new nation by the British after the Revolutionary War. The town's Republican leanings are evidence of the Yankee origins of its first settlers. But many other counties in these rolling hills were settled overland, from Virginia. The voters tend to think of themselves as Democrats and vote for Republicans in most elections. But when there is a Democrat with special appeal to southerners, like Jimmy Carter in 1976, or when the tide of opinion in Ohio turns heavily toward the Democrats, as it did in 1982, this becomes a Democratic district.

Those contrary leanings made this a marginal district in the 1950s and 1960s; party control changed in 1958, 1962, 1964, and 1966. It has stayed the same since then; the district has been represented for nearly 20 years now by Republican Clarence Miller. He has worked to solidify his position in the district and succeeded so that he won with a solid 63% in the Democratic year of 1982.

Miller is an engineer and seems to approach politics seeking precision and orderliness. He established a record of never missing a House roll call vote since he was elected—an example of stern discipline, particularly since many roll calls are demanded for dilatory or mischievous reasons. As a member of the Appropriations Committee in the 1970s he introduced numerous amendments to require across-the-board cuts of specific percentages in departmental spending.

Such measures, if adopted, leave all the hard work to others: evaluating specific programs, finding out where the real fat and real meat are, deciding what goals are important and which are not. They abdicate rather than establish Congress's authority. They in effect confess Congress's inability to set policy; at the best, they are a frustrated cry of anger rather than a reasoned approach to policymaking. The Reagan budget cut proposals, usually, have been much more specific and bottomed on a much more reasoned evaluation of federal programs. But of course Miller's proposals are good politics and, combined with his generally conservative record, provide a good platform from which to win reelection in this district.

The People   Pop. 1980: 513,755, up 12.7% 1970–80; voting age pop. 362,212; 2% Black. 24% housing units rented. Median owner $37,700; renter $150. Households: 77% family, 43% with children, 67% married couples.

Presidential Vote

1980	Reagan (R)	110,588	(56%)
	Carter (D)	77,142	(39%)
	Anderson (I)	8,736	(4%)

Rep. Clarence E. Miller (R) Elected 1966; b. Nov. 1, 1917, Lancaster; home, Lancaster; Internatl. Correspondence Sch.; Methodist.

Career Electrician; Lancaster City Cncl., 1957–63, Mayor, 1964–66.

Offices 2208 RHOB, 202-225-5131. Also 212 S. Broad St., Lancaster 43130, 614-654-5149.

Committee *Appropriations* (6th). Subcommittees: Commerce, Justice, State, and Judiciary; Treasury-Postal Service-General Government.

Group Ratings

	ADA	ACLU	COPE	CFA	LCV	LWV	NTU	NSI	COC	ACA	CSFC
1982	5	0	12	8	42	8	94	90	64	74	67
1981	5	—	12	29	14	—	91	—	84	92	69
1980	11	7	16	14	26	30	70	90	79	75	79

National Journal Ratings

	Economic		Foreign		Cultural	
1982	9%	(LIB)	39%	(LIB)	37%	(LIB)
	90%	(CONS)	60%	(CONS)	62%	(CONS)
1981	4%	(LIB)	30%	(LIB)	12%	(LIB)
	79%	(CONS)	68%	(CONS)	86%	(CONS)

Key Votes

1) Reagan 81 Budget	FOR	5) Incr SS Rtmt Age	AGN	9) Poor Pay Food Stamps	FOR
2) Reagan 81 Tax Cut	FOR	6) Saudi AWACS Sale	FOR	10) Ban Crt Busing Order	FOR
3) Bal Budget Amend	FOR	7) $ for MX Missile	FOR	11) Auto Local Content	FOR
4) Gas & Road Tax	AGN	8) Nerve Gas Prod	FOR	12) Nuclear Arms Freeze	AGN

Election Results

1982 general	Clarence E. Miller (R)	100,044	(63%)	($86,510)
	John M. Buchanan (D)	57,983	(37%)	($13,491)
1982 primary	Clarence E. Miller (R)	40,708	(100%)	
1980 general	Clarence E. Miller (R)	143,403	(74%)	($32,336)
	Jack E. Stecher (D)	49,433	(26%)	($7,647)

Campaign Contributions and Expenditures

1981-82		Direct Cont. 81-82		PACS brkdwn			
Receipts	$80,594	Indiv	$26,212	Agr	$500	Ideo	$500
Expend.	$86,510	Party	$9,425	Bus	$20,480	Lbr	$—
Unspent	$29,270	PACS	$23,580	Hlth	$2,000	Prof	$—
Non-Cand Loans: $12,500							

ELEVENTH DISTRICT

When the original 13 states began thinking about expanding westward after the Revolutionary War, the New England states had a problem: they were blocked from direct expansion by Upstate New York. Nevertheless, they tried to stake out western lands for themselves. Connecticut laid claim to what is now the northeastern corner of Ohio, and called it the Western Reserve. Connecticut's claim didn't last long, but it has its reverberations even today. The Western Reserve name is still used, at least in the names of institutions, in Cleveland and other parts of northeastern Ohio; and the politics of the area still shows some imprint from the Connecticut Yankees who were the first settlers here, and just about the only ones until immigrants, primarily from central, southern, and eastern Europe, began coming here when northeast Ohio began industrializing after 1880.

The Connecticut Yankee migration was dominant in the political leanings here for many years. This was strong antislavery country before the Civil War, the strongest in Ohio; afterward, this was the leading Republican part of the state. Northeastern Ohio produced such outstanding Republican politicians as James Garfield and William McKinley, not the best remembered of our presidents, but among the most effective national politicians of their day. Until the Great Depression of the 1930s, the counties of the old Western Reserve—even after heavy industrialization and immigration—produced heavy Republican majorities in most elections. We find it hard to remember 50 years after the New Deal, but in the 1890–1930 era Republicanism in these parts was considered the credo of progress, of enlightened government assistance to a growing industrial economy, as a program which provided prosperity for the workingman and honest, efficient government for everyone. The Democrats, in contrast, were the party of old feuds—southerners trying to avenge the Civil War, Irishmen trying to get back at the English—and of isolated rural pockets of America, in central and southern Ohio and elsewhere, left behind in the march of industrial progress.

The New Deal changed all that, by destroying the faith of industrial workers in the economic order of the post-McKinley Republicans and by bringing into the voting stream hundreds of thousands of immigrants whose loyalties have ever since gone to what they consider the party of acceptance and toleration. Since then northeastern Ohio has been the leading Democratic part of the state, and particularly in years like 1982 when times are bad. Yet there are still signs here of the older Western Reserve politics. You can see them in the voting returns from places which are still partly rural, like Geauga County: a preference for Republicans generally, but also rather liberal attitudes on many cultural issues. You can see it also in the councils of management, in the downtown lunch clubs and law firm conference rooms, where the leaders of the Republican Party meet and try to devise strategies to win over enough working class and ethnic votes to carry statewide elections. They see politics as a struggle between labor and management, between those who have in the past at least built a more productive economy and those who are trying to build in so many safeguards and safety nets for their workers that they are preventing management from acting for the common good. This produced a bitter politics, a form of class struggle, in the 1930s and 1940s, when Robert Taft was the leading champion of Ohio Republicanism; in the 1950s and 1960s, when Republican State Chairman Ray Bliss of Akron carefully chose candidates to appeal to local electorates, the bitterness was blunted.

The 11th congressional district of Ohio takes in most of the geographical expanse of the Western Reserve; it is the northeast corner of Ohio. It does not, however, include the major industrial cities. Cleveland and Akron lie just to the west, Canton and Youngstown to the south. The 11th does include Cleveland suburbs strung out along Lake Erie, in Lake County; it includes Ashtabula, also on the lake; it includes Kent, site of Kent State University, where students were shot by the National Guard in 1970; and it still includes some rural areas in between the industrial cities, like Hiram, the home of James Garfield, who once (1863–81) represented a very similarly shaped district, then numbered the 19th, when it was the most Republican part of Ohio.

The current 11th district switched from Republican to Democratic representation in 1982, in a rather curious way. The incumbent congressman, William Stanton, could have won reelection easily; redistricting would have cut his margin slightly, but he had plenty to spare. A sometime dissenter from Republican policies, he nonetheless was mostly a party regular and was ranking Republican on the Banking Committee. But Stanton decided to retire in 1982, and reportedly one of the first people he informed was Democratic Congressman Dennis Eckart of the neighboring 22d district. Eckart, a young freshman and one of the few articulate liberals first elected in 1980, had a serious problem. His district was being absorbed by several others, and he was contemplating a difficult primary fight against Ron Mottl, who had represented most of the new 19th district, and for much longer. But Eckart also represented part of the new 11th: his district went into Lake and Geauga Counties. So when Stanton retired, Eckart moved into the new 11th district and ran. His Republican opponent, a fiberglass executive urged into the race by Stanton, had everything going against him. Eckart is a competent campaigner, and in this year of great uncertainty about industrial Ohio's economic future, he was running in an area that went 2–1 Democratic in statewide races. He ended up winning with 61% of the vote, probably enough to deter serious Republican challenges in the future.

Eckart was a freshman whip in the House; he came to Washington from the Ohio legislature with a reputation for being a competent legislator, one ready to express his own views but also willing to go along with the leadership generally. In his second term he got the plum committee assignment of Energy and Commerce; he is on the subcommittees that handle toxic wastes and air pollution laws. This puts Eckart on something of a hot seat. The Democratic leaders of these subcommittees want generally to toughen, not relax, antipollution standards. But the major industries of northeastern Ohio believe strongly that they cannot maintain their current operations, much less expand economically, without some relaxation of current standards and lowering of the large amounts they are required now to spend and invest to stop pollution. These are very basic questions, which must be answered through politics in a generally affluent industrial society; and it will be interesting to watch how a politician as adept and, perhaps, ambitious as Eckart handles them.

The People   Pop. 1980: 512,367, up 10% 1970–80; voting age pop. 354,854; 2% Black, 1% Span. orig. 22% housing units rented. Median owner $55,700; renter $208. Households: 80% family, 46% with children, 70% married couples.

Presidential Vote

1980			
	Reagan (R)	100,571	(52%)
	Carter (D)	77,571	(40%)
	Anderson (I)	13,914	(7%)

Rep. Dennis E. Eckart (D) Elected 1980; b. Apr. 6, 1950, Euclid; home, Euclid; Xavier U., B.A. 1971, John Marshall Law Sch., J.D. 1974; Roman Catholic.

Career OH House of Reps., 1975–80; Chmn., Cuyahoga Cnty. Delegation, 1979–80.

Offices 1221 LHOB, 202-225-6331. Also 9040 Mentor Ave., Mentor 44060, 216-522-2056.

Committees *Energy and Commerce* (21st). Subcommittees: Commerce, Transportation, and Tourism; Health and the Environment. *Small Business* (16th). Subcommittees: SBA and SBIC Authority, Minority Enterprise and General Small Business Problems; Tax, Access to Equity Capital and Business Opportunities.

Group Ratings

	ADA	ACLU	COPE	CFA	LCV	LWV	NTU	NSI	COC	ACA	CSFC
1982	70	62	93	85	88	83	27	30	23	23	30
1981	80	—	87	86	79	—	35	—	11	33	35

National Journal Ratings

	Economic		Foreign		Cultural	
1982	67%	(LIB)	74%	(LIB)	69%	(LIB)
	33%	(CONS)	25%	(CONS)	31%	(CONS)
1981	75%	(LIB)	74%	(LIB)	74%	(LIB)
	24%	(CONS)	26%	(CONS)	26%	(CONS)

Key Votes

1) Reagan 81 Budget	AGN	5) Incr SS Rtmt Age	AGN	9) Poor Pay Food Stamps	AGN
2) Reagan 81 Tax Cut	AGN	6) Saudi AWACS Sale	AGN	10) Ban Crt Busing Order	—
3) Bal Budget Amend	FOR	7) $ for MX Missile	AGN	11) Auto Local Content	FOR
4) Gas & Road Tax	FOR	8) Nerve Gas Prod	AGN	12) Nuclear Arms Freeze	FOR

Election Results

1982 general	Dennis E. Eckart (D)	93,302	(61%)	($371,670)
	Glen W. Warner (R)	56,616	(37%)	($270,033)
1982 primary	Dennis E. Eckart (D)	30,278	(56%)	
	Marcus A. Roberto (D)	12,125	(23%)	($30,808)
	Michael D. Coffey (D)	11,241	(21%)	($22,409)
1980 general	J. William Stanton (R)	128,507	(69%)	($40,501)
	Patrick J. Donlin (D)	51,224	(28%)	($19,871)

Campaign Contributions and Expenditures

1981-82		Direct Cont. 81-82		PACS brkdwn			
Receipts	$375,020	Indiv	$175,469	Agr	$400	Ideo	$19,637
Expend.	$371,670	Party	$8,000	Bus	$20,730	Lbr	$77,260
Unspent	$4,374	PACS	$124,237	Hlth	$4,860	Prof	$850
		Cand	$55,000				

Indirect Party Expend: $350

TWELFTH DISTRICT

In 1960, while campaigning in Columbus, Ohio, John F. Kennedy was greeted by a tumultuous crowd; he was moved to remark that Columbus was the city where he got the loudest cheers and the fewest votes. He was not far off the mark, at least about the votes. The Columbus metropolitan area has been for years a Republican stronghold. That has been changing of late, but only glacially; the basic historic reasons for Columbus's Republicanism still hold. Columbus was settled by migrants of English and German stock, most of them coming overland from Pennsylvania or, as the city grew, moving to Columbus from central Ohio farmlands. Columbus did not attract the eastern and southern European migration that you find even today in Cleveland's cosmo wards; it has a relatively small black population (15% of Franklin County, which includes Columbus and suburbs). Columbus has always been more of a white collar than an industrial town; its major employers include the state government, Ohio State University, and several big banks and insurance companies. Even in the early 1980s, Columbus was still a city with a vibrant private economy, in vivid contrast with the industrial cities of northeastern Ohio and Dayton. Columbus is almost like a bit of the Sun Belt in the heart of Ohio.

True, the city of Columbus is now a Democratic town in most elections. But the suburbs are very heavily Republican, and Franklin County can be counted on for Republican margins in the general elections. Even in the 1982 Democratic sweep, it gave only narrow margins to Richard Celeste and Howard Metzenbaum.

The 12th congressional district of Ohio includes about half the Columbus metropolitan area and some rural areas to the north and east. The 12th includes essentially the east side of Columbus, its downtown, the renovated German Village just to the south, and the affluent suburbs of Bexley and Gahanna to the east. It includes more than half the city's blacks, but none of the academic community around Ohio State University. The counties to the north are among the most Republican in the state.

This is the only district in the United States that ousted a Republican incumbent in the Republican year of 1980 and then ousted a Democratic incumbent in the Democratic year of 1982. The reason, in each case, can be laid to specific circumstances. The defeated Republican incumbent, Samuel Devine, had been in trouble for a long time, despite Columbus's Republican leanings; Democrat Robert Shamansky, not regarded as a strong candidate, caught Devine unaware, put on a strong media campaign attacking his record, and won. But Shamansky proved to be less adept at political infighting than he was at electioneering. In Washington he lost a fight to repeal tobacco subsidies, partly because he refused to yield the floor—an ordinary courtesy—to Carl Perkins, chairman of the Education and Labor Committee and a member of the House since 1948. In Columbus he failed to get a politically more favorable district because he alienated Democratic Speaker Vern Riffe by endorsing gubernatorial candidate William Brown in the primary; since Democrats then controlled only the Ohio House and Republicans the Senate and governorship, he desperately needed Riffe to bargain for him on redistricting. As it turned out, Shamansky carried the Franklin County portion of the new 12th district, suburbs and all. But he lost the rural counties by wide enough margins to lose to Republican John Kasich.

Kasich resembles more closely the Republicans first elected in 1980 than he does his fellow Republicans first elected in 1982. Elected at age 30, his entire adult life has been spent in politics and legislation. He showed his diverse skills by campaigning hard door-to-door and by raising an impressive campaign treasury. On issues Kasich is rated a strong conservative, an opponent of almost every form of government spending (except defense) and of abortion; he backed Philip Crane in the 1980 presidential election. He supports large defense spending increases and has a seat on the Armed Services Committee.

Will this district see another close race in 1984? Probably. Even if Shamansky does not run, there are plenty of other liberals active in Columbus politics who would love to take on Kasich. And it is always possible that the legislature, now in Democratic hands, might decide to change the boundaries of the two Columbus area districts in a way that would help them win the 12th district seat. But that's not too likely: opening up redistricting is a risky business, and Governor Richard Celeste, like Speaker Riffe, is not particularly eager to do something to help Shamansky.

The People Pop. 1980: 512,925, up 14.0% 1970–80; voting age pop. 365,406; 14% Black, 1% Span. orig. 35% housing units rented. Median owner $47,200; renter $179. Households: 72% family, 41% with children, 58% married couples.

Presidential Vote

1980	Reagan (R)	117,080	(56%)
	Carter (D)	82,925	(39%)
	Anderson (I)	10,280	(5%)

Rep. John R. Kasich (R) Elected 1982; b. May 13, 1952, McKees Rocks, PA; home, Columbus; OH State U., B.A. 1974; Roman Catholic.

Career A. A. to State Sen. Donald Lukens, 1975–77; OH Senate, 1979–82.

Offices 1724 LHOB, 202-225-5355. Also Fed. Bldg., 200 N. High St., Columbus 43215, 614-469-7318.

Committee *Armed Services* (16th). Subcommittees: Investigations; Readiness.

Group Ratings and Key Votes: Newly Elected

Election Results

1982 general	John R. Kasich (R)	88,335	(50%)	($373,093)
	Robert N. (Bob) Shamansky (D) ..	82,753	(47%)	($527,700)
1982 primary	John R. Kasich (R)	33,550	(83%)	
	Roy E. Ault (R)	7,086	(17%)	
1980 general	Robert N. (Bob) Shamansky (D) ..	108,690	(53%)	($179,321)
	Samuel L. Devine (R)	98,110	(47%)	($132,072)

Campaign Contributions and Expenditures

1982		*Direct Cont. 1982*			*PACS brkdwn*		
Receipts	$375,519	Indiv	$170,394	Agr	$4,250	Ideo	$28,725
Expend.	$373,093	Party	$19,718	Bus	$118,568	Lbr	$—
Unspent	$2,425	PACS	$169,931	Hlth	$12,250	Prof	$2,000

Indirect Party Expend: $31,826

THIRTEENTH DISTRICT

The 13th congressional district of Ohio, in the north central part of the state, is in many respects like a part of New England dropped into the Midwest. This area, along the southern shore of Lake Erie, was first settled by New England Yankees moving west in the early 19th century, and they brought many of their attitudes with them. Among them was support for education: this district includes Oberlin College, one of Ohio's oldest schools, and numerous other small colleges besides. They also brought the reformist impulse that produced the abolitionist and women's suffrage movements: Oberlin was the first American college to admit blacks and women. In partisan terms, this was naturally Republican territory. The Yankees, with their reformist ideas and dislike of slavery and the South, were the natural Republican base wherever they moved in the young nation, and this was a heavily Republican area for years.

Indeed, the southern part of the district, which remains mostly rural and small town, also remains Republican. But the kind of industrial development which changed the face of Cleveland and the whole shoreline of Lake Erie also affected the northern part of this area. The towns of Lorain and Elyria became, in effect, factory towns, and extensions of the Cleveland metropolitan area; in the 1970s, thousands of Cleveland area residents moved south into once rural Medina County. These new residents, many of them products of post-1880 immigration, became staunch Democrats in the 1930s, and have helped to make this a mostly Democratic district today.

Yet the switch from a Republican to a Democratic congressman did not come until 1976. You could say, however, that it happened in stages: Republican Charles Mosher, of Oberlin, first elected in 1960, had a voting record that increasingly resembled that of a Democrat, especially on cultural issues; it was a metamorphosis typical of that going on at the same time among many New England Yankees. His successor in Congress is Donald Pease, also of Oberlin, who followed Mosher on the *Oberlin News-Tribune* and in the Ohio Senate and in his basic political leanings—although he is a Democrat.

Pease is now a member of the House Ways and Means Committee. On welfare issues he, like other Ohio Democrats, is inclined toward generosity—an inclination that may be strengthened by the troubled outlook of the economy of this manufacturing state. On trade issues, Pease begins as a man who is internationally-minded and instinctively seeks cooperation with other countries. But at the same time he represents an area whose basic industries have been seeking protection against foreign competition with a desperation born of lack of confidence in their own future. His is an important vote on such issues, and it will be interesting to see how he resolves conflicts on them.

Pease has won each of his four congressional elections with more than 60% of the vote, and seems unlikely to encounter a serious Republican challenge soon.

The People   Pop. 1980: 515,346, up 12.5% 1970–80; voting age pop. 351,794; 5% Black, 2% Span. orig. 24% housing units rented. Median owner $50,600; renter $181. Households: 80% family, 47% with children, 69% married couples.

Presidential Vote

1980	Reagan (R)	108,812	(55%)
	Carter (D)	73,714	(38%)
	Anderson (I)	13,545	(7%)

Rep. Donald J. (Don) Pease (D) Elected 1976; b. Sept. 26, 1931, Toledo; home, Oberlin; OH U., B.S. 1953, M.A. 1955, Fulbright Scholar, U. of Durham, England, 1954–55; Protestant.

Career Army, 1955–57; Coeditor and publisher, Oberlin *News Tribune*, 1957–68, Ed., 1968–77; Oberlin City Cncl., 1961–64; OH Senate, 1965–67, 1975–77; OH House of Reps., 1969–75.

Offices 1127 LHOB, 202-225-3401. Also 1936 Cooper Park Rd., Lorain 44053, 216-282-5003.

Committee *Ways and Means* (17th). Subcommittees: Public Assistance and Unemployment Compensation; Trade.

Group Ratings

	ADA	ACLU	COPE	CFA	LCV	LWV	NTU	NSI	COC	ACA	CSFC
1982	90	75	83	85	92	91	24	10	23	26	26
1981	95	—	80	86	86	—	30	—	6	14	32
1980	83	87	81	79	88	89	23	11	62	17	32

National Journal Ratings

	Economic		Foreign		Cultural	
1982	83%	(LIB)	83%	(LIB)	72%	(LIB)
	15%	(CONS)	17%	(CONS)	28%	(CONS)
1981	81%	(LIB)	88%	(LIB)	78%	(LIB)
	15%	(CONS)	12%	(CONS)	22%	(CONS)

Key Votes

1) Reagan 81 Budget	AGN	5) Incr SS Rtmt Age	AGN	9) Poor Pay Food Stamps	AGN
2) Reagan 81 Tax Cut	AGN	6) Saudi AWACS Sale	AGN	10) Ban Crt Busing Order	AGN
3) Bal Budget Amend	AGN	7) $ for MX Missile	AGN	11) Auto Local Content	FOR
4) Gas & Road Tax	FOR	8) Nerve Gas Prod	AGN	12) Nuclear Arms Freeze	FOR

Election Results

1982 general	Donald J. (Don) Pease (D)	92,296	(61%)	($116,031)
	Timothy P. Martin (R)	53,376	(35%)	($70,699)
1982 primary	Donald J. (Don) Pease (D)	36,230	(77%)	
	John M. Ryan (D)	10,669	(23%)	
1980 general	Donald J. (Don) Pease (D)	113,439	(64%)	($61,031)
	David Earl Armstrong (R)	64,296	(36%)	($7,511)

Campaign Contributions and Expenditures

1981-82		*Direct Cont. 81-82*				*PACS brkdwn*		
Receipts	$132,297	Indiv	$50,938	Agr	$2,750	Ideo	$1,762
Expend.	$116,031	Party	$750	Bus	$19,750	Lbr	$43,300
Unspent	$43,068	PACS	$70,791	Hlth	$2,500	Prof	$350

Indirect Party Expend: $410

FOURTEENTH DISTRICT

Akron is the Ohio city most glaringly dependent on a single industry in trouble—the automobile tire industry—and if its troubles have become increasingly apparent, people in Akron worry more and more about the future of their city—and their lives. Akron, like Detroit, is a city that was nothing like its present size at the turn of the century; it was dwarfed then not only by Cleveland to the north but also by Canton to the south. Then, in the years 1910–30, Akron like Detroit had phenomenal growth. From all over unskilled laborers came to work in the rubber plants, many from eastern and southern Europe, many more from the hills of West Virginia, where whole towns migrated almost *en masse* to Akron. In the 1930s and 1940s, when the United Rubber Workers organized the tire companies, there was something like class warfare politics here; management and labor alike doubted that there would be great economic growth in the future, and they fought hard for bigger slices of the pie. The 1950s became more placid: the economy boomed, American families increasingly bought two cars, and Akron achieved its last spurts of growth. Its politics modulated: Akron and Ohio Republican boss Ray Bliss shrewdly realized that workers would always outvote managers, and so he recruited candidates (James Rhodes at the statewide level, Congressman William Ayres in Akron) with appeal to blue-collar voters.

But, in retrospect, the signs of future economic troubles were already apparent. The tire companies in the 1960s began decentralizing their production away from Akron; foreign competition appeared; the American companies shied away from innovations like the radial tire. And the auto market began a long-term sag: families were saturated with cars, and the romance once attendant on getting a new family car began to grow sour. Akron has responded by embracing a kind of politics which, in 1982, triumphed statewide in Ohio: a Democratic politics which emphasizes maintaining the economic positions people have achieved, maintaining public spending programs even at the cost of raising taxes, and encouraging economic development while maintaining environmental protections and anti-pollution programs. Such are the policies of Akron's Congressman John Seiberling, who has represented the 14th congressional district of Ohio, which includes Akron and almost all of Summit County, since he beat Ayres in a hard-fought race in 1970.

Seiberling has achieved notice in the House on several fronts. He was a member of the Judiciary Committee which voted to impeach Richard Nixon, and he is now a senior member of this strongly liberal committee. He devotes more time, however, to the Interior Committee, on which he is now the fourth ranking Democrat. Seiberling was the prime manager in the House of the Alaska Lands Act, the major environmental legislative achievement during the Carter years. This was an immensely complex measure, and one which had the additional disadvantage of being opposed strongly by Alaska's own congressman. Yet Seiberling, with good attention to detail, and with the help of a superb grass-roots lobbying effort, was able to push it through the House with a wide margin.

Seiberling now chairs the Public Lands and National Parks Subcommittee. In that capacity he has reported out no major new parks bills; Phil Burton's bill created a large number of new parks in 1978, and any such effort now would likely be vetoed by the Reagan administration or pigeonholed in the Senate. Nevertheless, Seiberling is one of the main congressional adversaries of Interior Secretary James Watt.

Seiberling is not temperamentally a strident man. A descendant of the founder of one of Akron's rubber companies, he was a management lawyer (a contrast to his Republican predecessor who was a plumber; both parties in effect crossed class lines to find an attractive candidate). He is, however, dogged and determined, in his quiet way, and has one of the most liberal voting records in the House. He has been reelected every time by overwhelming margins, against desultory opposition; in 1982, when Ohioans in less troubled parts of the state than Akron were voting Democratic by large margins, he won easily.

The People Pop. 1980: 514,662, dn. 5.5% 1970–80; voting age pop. 373,723; 10% Black. 29% housing units rented. Median owner $44,700; renter $180. Households: 74% family, 38% with children, 61% married couples.

Presidential Vote

1980	Reagan (R)	89,911	(44%)
	Carter (D)	100,623	(49%)
	Anderson (I)	14,624	(7%)

Rep. John F. Seiberling (D) Elected 1970; b. Sept. 8, 1918, Akron; home, Akron; Harvard U., B.A. 1941, Columbia U., LL.B. 1949; United Church of Christ.

Career Army, WWII; Practicing atty., 1949–53; Atty., Goodyear Tire and Rubber Co., 1954–70.

Offices 1225 LHOB, 202-225-5231. Also Fed. Bldg., 2 S. Main St., Akron 44308, 216-375-5710.

Committees *Interior and Insular Affairs* (4th). Subcommittees: Energy and the Environment; Mining, Forest Management, and BPA; Public Lands and National Parks (Chairman). *Judiciary* (6th). Subcommittees: Criminal Justice; Monopolies and Commercial Law.

Group Ratings

	ADA	ACLU	COPE	CFA	LCV	LWV	NTU	NSI	COC	ACA	CSFC
1982	90	100	89	92	96	92	18	10	14	13	20
1981	100	—	88	93	93	—	41	—	11	4	25
1980	100	100	79	86	91	100	21	0	70	13	25

National Journal Ratings

	Economic		Foreign		Cultural	
1982	86%	(LIB)	92%	(LIB)	79%	(LIB)
	13%	(CONS)	6%	(CONS)	21%	(CONS)
1981	89%	(LIB)	92%	(LIB)	95%	(LIB)
	3%	(CONS)	2%	(CONS)	1%	(CONS)

Key Votes

1) Reagan 81 Budget	AGN	5) Incr SS Rtmt Age	AGN	9) Poor Pay Food Stamps	AGN
2) Reagan 81 Tax Cut	AGN	6) Saudi AWACS Sale	AGN	10) Ban Crt Busing Order	AGN
3) Bal Budget Amend	AGN	7) $ for MX Missile	AGN	11) Auto Local Content	FOR
4) Gas & Road Tax	FOR	8) Nerve Gas Prod	AGN	12) Nuclear Arms Freeze	FOR

Election Results

1982 general	John F. Seiberling (D)	115,629	(70%)	($85,113)
	Louis A. Mangels (R)	48,421	(30%)	($37,778)
1982 primary	John F. Seiberling (D)	50,515	(100%)	
1980 general	John F. Seiberling (D)	103,336	(65%)	($29,143)
	Louis A. Mangels (R)	55,962	(35%)	($46,848)

Campaign Contributions and Expenditures

1981-82		Direct Cont. 81-82		PACS brkdwn			
Receipts	$87,041	Indiv	$50,495	Agr	$250	Ideo	$3,431
Expend.	$85,113	PACS	$36,050	Bus	$6,025	Lbr	$24,665
Unspent	$5,379			Hlth	$1,000	Prof	$200

FIFTEENTH DISTRICT

The 15th congressional district of Ohio includes the west and south sides of Columbus and suburban Franklin County and most of rural Madison County directly to the west. Next to Cincinnati, Columbus is Ohio's most Republican metropolitan area; it is also the state's fastest-growing and most economically buoyant one. The 15th district is, marginally, the more Republican of the two Columbus-area districts. The lines were drawn as part of a compromise between a Democratic House and a Republican Senate and governor; the House speaker was not particularly interested in helping the then-Democratic congressman from the 12th, and the Republicans did not feel they had to do much to help the Republican incumbent in the 15th.

Hence the lines came out looking quite nonpartisan. The 15th district includes some (but not most) of Columbus's black population, some white working-class areas on the south side of the city, and the Ohio State University campus area. But it also includes the heavily Republican suburb of Upper Arlington, across the Olentangy River from Ohio State; and Madison is one of the most heavily Republican counties in Ohio. This is a district that would give a Republican congressman trouble only if he got sloppy, and so far Congressman Chalmers Wylie has not done that.

Wylie has a wealth of experience in Columbus and Ohio politics. He was an assistant attorney general as a young man, as long ago as 1948; he was first elected to Congress when the Columbus area got the second congressional district it had long been entitled to under the population standard, in 1966. Wylie is now the ranking Republican on the House Banking, Finance and Urban Affairs Committee. Like many senior Republicans, he does not take the trouble to make his views known to the world outside the House and his district. He has been a loyal follower of the Republican leadership and of Republican administrations when they are in office; he is a team player and not someone who makes waves. He seems sufficiently convinced of the overall wisdom of Republican policies that he is willing to go along with the party and try to defeat the Democrats even on those rare occasions when he has doubts.

There seems to be an inverse relationship between the current importance of the issues the Banking Committee handles and the publicity they receive. Much ballyhooed issues like aid to New York City (which Wylie opposed), the Chrysler loan guarantee (which he supported), and wage and price controls seemed dormant by the early 1980s. Housing programs have been phased out or reduced in size during the Reagan years, with the committee not doing much about it. The most fiercely lobbied issues on which Wylie may play a major role are fights concerning the regulation of banks and savings institutions. Columbus, as it happens, is the home of some banks which have been pioneers in innovative banking practices; Wylie, seen by many Democrats as a hidebound reactionary, may favor innovation on these issues.

None of this, however, is likely to affect his standing at the polls, nor to impair his ability to amass a big campaign treasury in the unlikely event that a Democrat gives him a serious challenge.

The People   Pop. 1980: 514,697, up 0.9% 1970–80; voting age pop. 377,705; 10% Black, 1% Span. orig. 40% housing units rented. Median owner $47,500; renter $168. Households: 68% family, 37% with children, 54% married couples.

Presidential Vote

1980	Reagan (R)	125,354	(57%)
	Carter (D)	80,779	(37%)
	Anderson (I)	14,238	(6%)

Rep. Chalmers P. Wylie (R) Elected 1966; b. Nov. 23, 1920, Norwich; home, Columbus; Otterbein Col., OH State U., Harvard U., J.D. 1948; Methodist.

Career Army, WWII; Asst. Atty. Gen. of OH, 1948, 1951–54; Asst. Columbus City Atty., 1949–50, City Atty., 1953–56; Admin., OH Bureau of Workmen's Comp., 1957; First Asst. to the Gov. of OH, 1957–58; Practicing atty., 1959–66; OH House of Reps., 1961–67.

Offices 2310 RHOB, 202-225-2015. Also Fed. Bldg., 200 N. High St., Su. 500, Columbus 43215, 614-469-5614.

Committees *Banking, Finance and Urban Affairs* (Ranking Member). Subcommittees: Consumer Affairs and Coinage; Financial Institutions Supervision, Regulation and Insurance; Housing and Community Development. *Veterans' Affairs* (2d). Subcommittees: Compensation, Pension, and Insurance; Education, Training and Employment. *Joint Economic Committee.* Subcommittees: International Trade, Finance, and Security Economics; Monetary and Fiscal Policy (Vice-Chairman).

Group Ratings

	ADA	ACLU	COPE	CFA	LCV	LWV	NTU	NSI	COC	ACA	CSFC
1982	15	25	23	31	48	55	64	75	73	57	53
1981	20	—	22	43	24	—	64	—	94	71	63
1980	28	20	26	21	22	33	49	80	75	65	69

National Journal Ratings

	Economic		Foreign		Cultural	
1982	43%	(LIB)	52%	(LIB)	38%	(LIB)
	57%	(CONS)	48%	(CONS)	62%	(CONS)
1981	32%	(LIB)	42%	(LIB)	44%	(LIB)
	68%	(CONS)	57%	(CONS)	55%	(CONS)

Key Votes

1) Reagan 81 Budget	FOR	5) Incr SS Rtmt Age	FOR	9) Poor Pay Food Stamps	FOR
2) Reagan 81 Tax Cut	FOR	6) Saudi AWACS Sale	FOR	10) Ban Crt Busing Order	FOR
3) Bal Budget Amend	FOR	7) $ for MX Missile	FOR	11) Auto Local Content	FOR
4) Gas & Road Tax	FOR	8) Nerve Gas Prod	AGN	12) Nuclear Arms Freeze	—

Election Results

1982 general	Chalmers P. Wylie (R)	104,678	(66%)	($136,983)
	Greg Kostelac (D)	47,070	(30%)	($6,331)
1982 primary	Chalmers P. Wylie (R)	34,548	(100%)	
1980 general	Chalmers P. Wylie (R)	129,025	(73%)	($93,073)
	Terry Freeman (D)	48,708	(27%)	($0)

Campaign Contributions and Expenditures

1981-82		Direct Cont. 81-82		PACS brkdwn			
Receipts	$138,254	Indiv	$62,035	Agr	$2,500	Ideo	$700
Expend.	$136,983	Party	$9,000	Bus	$58,650	Lbr	$—
Unspent	$22,572	PACS	$65,550	Hlth	$2,500	Prof	$1,100

SIXTEENTH DISTRICT

Canton, Ohio, is known, to the extent it is known at all today, as the home of the Pro Football Hall of Fame. But to American political historians, Canton is most memorable as the home of President William McKinley. It was here that McKinley sat on his front porch and received delegations of voters carefully selected by Republican organizations around the country. And it was here that McKinley received the news that he had been elected president over William Jennings Bryan. Some historians still cling to the notion that factory workers provided McKinley with the votes he needed to win only because their bosses threatened to fire them if they didn't. No more evidence of such coercion exists for this election than for any other in our history. The fact, however unlikely it may seem to two generations brought up after the New Deal, is that McKinley was the heavy choice of northern industrial workers, and they believed that the Republican Party and its policies would provide the full dinner pail he promised.

And the case can be made that McKinley delivered admirably on that promise. For 20 years after his election in 1896 the country experienced a period of prosperity and economic growth. And for 30 years the big northern industrial areas, with only a few exceptions, stayed loyal to the party of McKinley. Canton, Ohio, still does. This is an industrial city which has not had explosive growth in the 20th century; so if it has not experienced the boom that, for example, Akron enjoyed during the growth of the tire market in 1910–30, it also has avoided the bust that Akron has been experiencing lately. Canton, plus the nearby towns of Massillon and Alliance, where some of our current National Football League teams got their start, still retain a basic preference for the Republican Party; even in 1982, they gave Ohio Democrats only small margins. They form the nucleus of the 16th congressional district of Ohio, which also includes the smaller counties of Wayne and Holmes to the west.

McKinley was elected to the House six times in the predecessor of today's district. In those volatile times, he lost the seat twice to Democrats—which didn't prevent him, in the days before the seniority system, from becoming chairman of the House Ways and Means Committee. Much in the mold of McKinley—a principled, yet adaptable professional politician—is the current congressman from the 16th district, Ralph Regula. He is, appropriately, a graduate of the William McKinley School of Law, and in the 1970s he worked to retain the name Mount McKinley for the highest mountain in North America (although Alaska natives did get the surrounding area named Denali National Park). Regula is considered a moderate, a party regular who is thoughtful but no maverick. He is a member of the Appropriations Committee, and ranking Republican on the Military Construction Subcommittee. That has been a kind of pork barrel assignment for many members; but Canton—whose son McKinley declared war on Spain only with the greatest reluctance, when he thought he had no alternative—has no military bases of note nor any big military contractors.

Regula has held this seat with ease. The economy of the Canton area in the early 1980s was not in quite so much visible trouble as many parts of Ohio, and he was able to win reelection easily, against a weak opponent, even in 1982.

The People   Pop. 1980: 513,215, up 5.2% 1970–80; voting age pop. 362,462; 5% Black, 1% Span. orig. 26% housing units rented. Median owner $45,600; renter $167. Households: 78% family, 42% with children, 67% married couples.

Presidential Vote

1980	Reagan (R)	110,809	(57%)
	Carter (D)	73,450	(38%)
	Anderson (I)	10,702	(5%)

Rep. Ralph S. Regula (R) Elected 1972; b. Dec. 3, 1924, Beach City; home, Navarre; Mt. Union Col., B.A. 1948, Wm. McKinley Sch. of Law, LL.B. 1952; Episcopal.

Career Navy, WWII; Practicing atty., 1952–73; OH Bd. of Educ., 1960–64; OH House of Reps., 1965–66; OH Senate, 1967–72.

Offices 2209 RHOB, 202-225-3876. Also 4150 Belden Village St., Canton 44718, 216-456-2869.

Committees *Appropriations* (10th). Subcommittees: Interior; Military Construction. *Select Committee on Aging* (3d). Subcommittee: Health and Long-Term Care.

Group Ratings

	ADA	ACLU	COPE	CFA	LCV	LWV	NTU	NSI	COC	ACA	CSFC
1982	25	25	30	31	60	42	59	100	59	70	54
1981	15	—	30	43	7	—	54	—	89	75	62
1980	28	27	21	29	26	40	45	80	70	63	71

National Journal Ratings

	Economic		Foreign		Cultural	
1982	39%	(LIB)	40%	(LIB)	52%	(LIB)
	61%	(CONS)	59%	(CONS)	48%	(CONS)
1981	4%	(LIB)	50%	(LIB)	36%	(LIB)
	79%	(CONS)	49%	(CONS)	64%	(CONS)

Key Votes

1) Reagan 81 Budget	FOR	5) Incr SS Rtmt Age	AGN	9) Poor Pay Food Stamps	FOR
2) Reagan 81 Tax Cut	FOR	6) Saudi AWACS Sale	FOR	10) Ban Crt Busing Order	FOR
3) Bal Budget Amend	FOR	7) $ for MX Missile	FOR	11) Auto Local Content	FOR
4) Gas & Road Tax	FOR	8) Nerve Gas Prod	AGN	12) Nuclear Arms Freeze	AGN

Election Results

1982 general	Ralph S. Regula (R)	110,485	(66%)	($136,778)
	Jeffrey R. Orenstein (D)	57,386	(34%)	($15,417)
1982 primary	Ralph S. Regula (R)	38,466	(100%)	
1980 general	Ralph S. Regula (R)	149,960	(79%)	($23,914)
	Larry V. Slagle (D)	39,219	(21%)	($6,128)

Campaign Contributions and Expenditures

1981-82		Direct Cont. 81-82	
Receipts	$109,667	Indiv	$83,389
Expend.	$136,778	Party	$8,939
Unspent	$51,096		

Received no PAC Contributions

SEVENTEENTH DISTRICT

The 17th congressional district of Ohio is one of the most heavily industrial districts in the nation—and one of the most economically distressed. The district covers the Mahoning Valley, the area around Youngstown and Warren, a steel manufacturing area halfway between Cleveland and Pittsburgh, where the bumpy hills of western Pennsylvania give way, almost with the suddenness suggested by the dotted line on the map, to the flat plains of northern Ohio. The Mahoning Valley seemed marked for steel: it is halfway between the Lake Erie docks that unload iron ore from Great Lakes freighters and the coalfields of western Pennsylvania and West Virginia. This was an area of rapid growth in the decades after the turn of the century, when the American steel industry was growing rapidly and pioneering the latest technological developments. Now times have changed. Steel has been anything but a growth industry over the last 20 years. Producers in Japan and West Germany—even in South Korea and Brazil—are using new technology and, in some cases, can ship steel cheaper to the American Midwest than can the now-antique furnaces of Youngstown. Steel industry management has concentrated for years on getting presidential permission for wage increases (which price its products above the competition) and governmental protection against imports (which encourages further inefficiency and in turn raises the prices of products made with American steel) rather than improving their product or adapting their business to the imperatives of today's global economy.

The result has been economic disaster for the Mahoning Valley. Several steel plants have closed down altogether, and the sight of these behemoths sitting, quietly and smokelessly, is profoundly disturbing. During the early 1980s metropolitan Youngstown had one of the nation's highest unemployment rates—in some months the highest. And no one is sure what future Youngstown and Warren have. Young people have been leaving since at least 1960, searching for new opportunities; those who have remained seem anchored here by community ties or by an inertia that seems to have been at least partly encouraged by safety nets like unemployment compensation and welfare. Unlike their immigrant grandparents, who came thousands of miles from southern Italy and southern Poland, with no hope of ever returning, today's Mahoning Valley residents are waiting for something to turn up in their backyard.

For everyone, not just the unemployed, this must seem like the collapse of a way of life. People here have worked hard for many years and have seen their standard of living rise in response; now it is falling. They have saved and invested in their homes; now houses in some Youngstown neighborhoods are essentially worthless on the open market. These events have shaken their basic political values and preferences. The Mahoning Valley has been a solidly Democratic area since the United Steelworkers organized the plants after sometimes bloody skirmishes in the late 1930s, and in the past they have responded to hard times by voting even more heavily Democratic. That is not necessarily their response in the early 1980s. They were heavily Democratic in statewide races in 1982. But in 1980 they gave Jimmy Carter no higher a percentage of their votes than they had given George McGovern eight years before. And in the last three congressional elections, this heavily Democratic district has elected a Republican congressman.

He is Lyle Williams, and at first his election seemed a fluke. The Democratic incumbent was old and weak, and did nothing to promote new industry here (his most noteworthy activity was to acquire more than 60,000 surplus books from the Library of Congress). But Williams has managed to keep the seat although he has been challenged by two well-known and popular local legislators. One reason is his own blue-collar background; he was a barber, is the son of a coal miner, and is comfortable talking with blue-collar workers in a way that few Republicans in this onetime scene of class-struggle politics are. Second, Williams does not have a straight-down-the-line Reagan record on economic or other issues; the House Republican leaders know well enough that they can't get his vote on every issue, or they would cost him his seat. Third, Williams can point to some jobs he has helped attract to the Mahoning Valley—which is more than just about anybody else can do.

There seems to be another factor operating here as well. The old political reflexes are simply not operating in a situation in which a whole way of life seems threatened. Voting Democratic in recessions and Republican during inflation has not produced the results for these voters that it produced for Americans generally in the decades after World War II. So there is an opening in economic hard times for the right kind of Republican in a district traditionally as Democratic as this.

The People   Pop. 1980: 515,223, dn. 1.5% 1970–80; voting age pop. 372,845; 10% Black, 1% Span. orig. 25% housing units rented. Median owner $39,300; renter $168. Households: 77% family, 40% with children, 64% married couples.

Presidential Vote

1980	Reagan (R)	88,752	(42%)
	Carter (D)	105,667	(50%)
	Anderson (I)	15,434	(7%)

Rep. Lyle Williams (R) Elected 1978; b. Aug. 23, 1942, Philippi, WV; home, North Bloomfield; Churches of Christ.

Career Army, 1960–61; Barber; Trumbull Cnty. Commissioner, 1972–78.

Offices 1004 LHOB, 202-225-5261. Also 4076 Youngstown Rd., S.E., Su. 204, Warren 44484, 216-369-4378.

Committees *Government Operations* (5th). Subcommittee: Environment, Energy and Natural Resources. *Small Business* (4th). Subcommittee: Tax, Access to Equity Capital and Business Opportunities. *Select Committee on Aging* (15th). Subcommittee: Retirement Income and Employment.

Group Ratings

	ADA	ACLU	COPE	CFA	LCV	LWV	NTU	NSI	COC	ACA	CSFC
1982	50	42	59	46	40	40	47	100	60	48	43
1981	15	—	53	50	21	—	44	—	80	68	60
1980	33	20	68	43	41	40	28	63	69	54	54

National Journal Ratings

	Economic		Foreign		Cultural	
1982	53%	(LIB)	55%	(LIB)	42%	(LIB)
	46%	(CONS)	45%	(CONS)	58%	(CONS)
1981	42%	(LIB)	28%	(LIB)	51%	(LIB)
	58%	(CONS)	71%	(CONS)	48%	(CONS)

Key Votes

1) Reagan 81 Budget	FOR	5) Incr SS Rtmt Age	AGN	9) Poor Pay Food Stamps	AGN
2) Reagan 81 Tax Cut	FOR	6) Saudi AWACS Sale	AGN	10) Ban Crt Busing Order	FOR
3) Bal Budget Amend	FOR	7) $ for MX Missile	AGN	11) Auto Local Content	FOR
4) Gas & Road Tax	—	8) Nerve Gas Prod	AGN	12) Nuclear Arms Freeze	AGN

Election Results

1982 general	Lyle Williams (R)	98,476	(55%)	($306,537)
	George D. Tablack (D)	80,375	(45%)	($90,325)
1982 primary	Lyle Williams (R)	20,805	(100%)	
1980 general	Lyle Williams (R)	107,032	(58%)	($207,760)
	Harry Meshel (D)	77,272	(42%)	($192,887)

Campaign Contributions and Expenditures

1981-82		Direct Cont. 81-82		PACS brkdwn			
Receipts	$311,545	Indiv	$230,260	Agr	$2,000	Ideo	$2,700
Expend.	$306,537	Party	$11,807	Bus	$40,125	Lbr	$2,950
Unspent	$5,127	PACS	$69,705	Hlth	$12,050	Prof	$500

Indep Expend: For: $130 (NRA)

EIGHTEENTH DISTRICT

The 18th congressional district of Ohio, just across the Ohio River from West Virginia, is a land of marginal farms and hills pockmarked by strip mines. The area is part of the great coal and steel belt that stretches from the coal mines of West Virginia to Lake Erie, the destination of the freighters filled with iron ore from Minnesota's Mesabi Range. We tend to think of this steel belt as a series of large cities, but in fact it is one of the most thickly settled nonmetropolitan parts of the United States. The area is filled with small cities, each with their little steel mill or factory, most of them old towns whose storefronts and wooden working class houses, with hills rising behind them, bear the unmistakable imprint of the early 20th century. There is nothing chic or fashionable here: these are gritty places where working people have long toiled long hours at physically demanding work for what pay may be available. For a time the pay was good. But in the late 1970s the coal and steel economy, long in trouble, seemed about to collapse. The impact here was cushioned by continuing demand for coal from electric utilities; but with even union steel wages falling in real dollars, the impact on ordinary people's lives here has been substantial.

The 18th district stretches up and down the Ohio River, beginning in the north just below Youngstown and proceeding almost all the way to Marietta, Ohio, and Parkersburg, West Virginia. Some of the people here are from the Scotch-Irish stock of the first wave of migration over the Appalachians. But more are descended from later immigrants: Italians, Poles, Czechs, Germans. The 18th district, sociologically and politically, is a kind of ethnic working-class neighborhood. Politically, the district is heavily Democratic; it voted for Ronald Reagan in 1980, but in 1982 went 65% for Richard Celeste for governor. Culturally, this is still a place where people believe in, and usually live according to, traditional values, where church, family, home, and hometown are more important than liberation and freedom from restraint. Economically, it is an area that has thrived only occasionally in the last few decades but whose lack of really large factories has made it less vulnerable to the sudden economic dislocation caused by the unexpected closing of a huge factory, which has been so common in much of Ohio.

This is the district that was represented for 28 years by Wayne Hays, the man who built an empire in the House from his positions as chairman of the House Administration and the Democratic campaign committees, and who was forced to resign because of the Elizabeth Ray scandal. The local Democratic Party, forced to name a candidate to replace Hays on the 1976 ballot, chose the man long considered his likely successor, State Senator Douglas Applegate. He has won reelection against nominal, or no, opposition since then.

Applegate is a member of the kind of practical committees—Public Works and Transportation and Veterans' Affairs—that help him do something concrete for his district. He has a liberal voting record on economic issues, according to the AFL-CIO, and is solidly conservative on cultural and foreign issues.

The People   Pop. 1980: 514,012, up 4.1% 1970–80; voting age pop. 367,603; 2% Black. 22% housing units rented. Median owner $34,200; renter $132. Households: 77% family, 41% with children, 67% married couples.

Presidential Vote

1980	Reagan (R)	97,706	(50%)
	Carter (D)	88,245	(45%)
	Anderson (I)	9,663	(5%)

Rep. Douglas Applegate (D) Elected 1976; b. Mar. 27, 1928, Steubenville; home, Steubenville; Presbyterian.

Career Real estate salesman, 1950–56, broker, 1956–76; OH House of Reps., 1961–69; OH Senate, 1969–77.

Offices 2464 RHOB, 202-225-6265. Also 150 W. Main St., St. Clairsville 43950, 614-695-4600; Ohio Valley Tower, Rm. 610, Steubenville 43952, 614-283-3716; 109 W. 3d St., E. Liverpool 43920, 216-385-5921; and 168 W. High Ave., New Philadelphia 44663, 216-343-9112.

Committees *Public Works and Transportation* (12th). Subcommittees: Aviation; Economic Development; Surface Transportation. *Veterans' Affairs* (5th). Subcommittees: Compensation, Pension, and Insurance (Chairman); Housing and Memorial Affairs.

Group Ratings

	ADA	ACLU	COPE	CFA	LCV	LWV	NTU	NSI	COC	ACA	CSFC
1982	45	17	72	62	73	50	48	80	41	18	44
1981	35	—	69	79	64	—	57	—	21	54	58
1980	22	23	63	36	35	30	47	100	59	54	59

National Journal Ratings

	Economic		Foreign		Cultural	
1982	59%	(LIB)	52%	(LIB)	53%	(LIB)
	40%	(CONS)	48%	(CONS)	47%	(CONS)
1981	67%	(LIB)	53%	(LIB)	30%	(LIB)
	32%	(CONS)	45%	(CONS)	69%	(CONS)

Key Votes

1) Reagan 81 Budget	AGN	5) Incr SS Rtmt Age	AGN	9) Poor Pay Food Stamps	AGN
2) Reagan 81 Tax Cut	AGN	6) Saudi AWACS Sale	AGN	10) Ban Crt Busing Order	FOR
3) Bal Budget Amend	FOR	7) $ for MX Missile	AGN	11) Auto Local Content	FOR
4) Gas & Road Tax	FOR	8) Nerve Gas Prod	FOR	12) Nuclear Arms Freeze	FOR

Election Results

1982 general	Douglas Applegate (D)	128,665	(100%)	($50,572)
1982 primary	Douglas Applegate (D)	51,317	(100%)	
1980 general	Douglas Applegate (D)	134,835	(76%)	($44,493)
	Gary L. Hammersley (R)	42,354	(24%)	($24,013)

Campaign Contributions and Expenditures

1981-82		Direct Cont. 81-82		PACS brkdwn			
Receipts	$64,369	Indiv	$22,546	Agr	$500	Ideo	$1,162
Expend.	$50,572	PACS	$33,977	Bus	$18,340	Lbr	$11,725
Unspent	$44,168			Hlth	$2,250	Prof	$—

NINETEENTH DISTRICT

The 19th congressional district of Ohio forms a kind of convoluted U around the city of Cleveland and some of its close-in suburbs, all of which are contained in the 20th and 21st districts. Its current form results from the 1980 Census: not only the city of Cleveland, but

Cuyahoga County as a whole lost population, and instead of four Cuyahoga-based congressional districts, there could be only three. So the districts of maverick Democrat Ron Mottl and freshman Democrat Dennis Eckart were combined; Eckart, however, ran and won in the 11th district vacated by the retirement of Republican William Stanton. Mottl, the only northern Democrat to support the Reagan economic program in 1981, was beaten in the Democratic primary nonetheless by Edward Feighan, a former candidate for mayor of Cleveland and state legislator. To understand how, you need to know the three basic parts of the new 19th district:

• *The southern blue-collar suburbs.* This was Ron Mottl's base. Before he was elected to Congress in 1974, Mottl was a member of the Parma City Council and served in the state legislature. Parma is the largest town here, a working-class suburb which grew rapidly in the 1950s; it is reputed to have the nation's largest concentration of bowling alleys, and accordingly draws more than its share of the nation's political reporters looking for opinion in blue-collar America. The suburbs south of Parma have higher housing prices, largely because their houses and condominiums were built later; this is the home of comfortable blue-collar families, those with skilled workers and two paychecks, prime beneficiaries of the rises in real income in metropolitan Cleveland over the past three decades. These voters liked Mottl's pet causes: his antibusing amendments, his national minimum education standards bill, his support of more spending on veterans' hospitals. Like him, they were inclined to support Ronald Reagan's economic policies in 1981, and if he made a mistake then in doing so, they were willing in 1982 to forgive him.

• *The western white-collar suburbs.* Running west from Cleveland along Lake Erie, but far from railroads and factories, and running south along the Rocky River, whose ravine is lined with parks, not factories, are the western white-collar suburbs. They have the comfortable look of places long settled; their populations tend to be older, often but by no means always of ethnic (or what Clevelanders call cosmo) stock; there is a significant Republican vote here in general elections. This was not Ron Mottl's home territory; he is a little too rough-hewn for these white-collar voters. They may approve of his antibusing initiatives, but they don't feel threatened particularly by busing (there are virtually no blacks on the west side of Cleveland, much less in the west side suburbs), and they didn't like the way he went about making his appeal. They felt more comfortable with Feighan, whose uncle represented the west side of Cleveland in Congress for 28 years and who himself has a west side base.

• *The eastern suburbs.* Ron Mottl had never represented the east side suburbs. There are few blacks here—the district-wide black percentage is just 2%—but there are plenty of Italian-Americans and Jews, two ethnic groups Mottl had little experience with. On cultural issues this is the more liberal side of town; Mottl, with his conservative views and crew cut, did not go over well. Nor did the campaign tactics which worked well in Parma work here. This is the largest part of the new district; with the adjacent Lake County suburbs of Willowick and Wickliffe, it had 43% of the new 19th district's population, as compared to 31% for the western white-collar suburbs and only 26% for Mottl's base in the blue-collar southern suburbs. Feighan worked this side of the district hard and built up a big enough majority to allow him to win the primary by a 49%–47% margin.

Feighan's candidacy was engineered by Cuyahoga County Democratic Chairman Tim Hagan, and supported vehemently by the local AFL-CIO and United Auto Workers, and by the Cleveland newspapers as well. Hagan and his allies had been outraged by Reagan's program and Mottl's support of it, and Mottl's changes of mind in 1982 did not give them any pause. This is one of several Democratic primaries in the spring of 1982 that showed that the Reagan program had little or no appeal in Democratic primaries and that the president's appeal to the white working class in 1980 had largely vanished.

Feighan himself can be counted on to be a solid liberal vote on economic issues, and on other issues as well. He is, however, a member of two committees which have relatively little economic jurisdiction—Judiciary and Foreign Affairs—and will have to satisfy his constituents that he is doing something to improve Cleveland's economic future by something other than committee work. This was by no means his first foray into controversial politics; he ran in 1977, at age 30, for mayor of Cleveland against the terrible-tempered Dennis Kucinich, and almost won. Feighan's tenure in this district seems reasonably safe, although it is possible he will seek some other office someday.

The People Pop. 1980: 514,889, dn. 1.3% 1970–80; voting age pop. 387,390; 1% Black. 25% housing units rented. Median owner $67,300; renter $257. Households: 76% family, 35% with children, 66% married couples.

Presidential Vote

1980	Reagan (R)	NA
	Carter (D)	NA
	Anderson (I)	NA

Rep. Edward F. Feighan (D) Elected 1982; b. Oct. 22, 1947, Lakewood; home, Cleveland; Loyola U., B.A. 1969, Cleveland Marshall Law Sch., J.D. 1977; Roman Catholic.

Career High sch. teacher, 1969–72; OH House of Reps., 1972–78; Cuyahoga Cnty. Commissioner, 1978–82; Practicing atty., 1978–.

Offices 1223 LHOB, 202-225-5731. Also 1240 E. 9th St., Rm. 2951, Cleveland 44199, 216-522-4382.

Committees *Foreign Affairs* (22d). Subcommittees: Africa; International Economic Policy and Trade. *Judiciary* (18th). Subcommittees: Crime; Monopolies and Commercial Law.

Group Ratings and Key Votes: Newly Elected

Election Results

1982 general	Edward F. Feighan (D)	111,760	(59%)	($295,117)
	Richard G. Anter, II (R)	72,682	(38%)	($197,217)
1982 primary	Edward F. Feighan (D)	37,906	(49%)	
	Ronald M. Mottl (D)	36,793	(47%)	($160,344)
1980 general	Dennis E. Eckart (D)	108,137	(55%)	($354,048)
(OH 22)	Joseph J. Nahra (R)	80,836	(41%)	($479,874)
1980 general	Ronald M. Mottl (D)	144,365	(100%)	($62,957)
(OH 23)				

Campaign Contributions and Expenditures

1981-82		Direct Cont. 81-82		PACS brkdwn			
Receipts	$310,067	Indiv	$164,662	Agr	$1,000	Ideo	$9,225
Expend.	$295,117	Party	$250	Bus	$10,600	Lbr	$92,185
Unspent	$14,948	PACS	$116,013	Hlth	$2,500	Prof	$850
		Cand	$25,000				

TWENTIETH DISTRICT

Down the center of Cleveland runs the Cuyahoga River, the industrial heart of the Cleveland metropolitan area, and what has made the city what it is—both good and bad—today. For the Cuyahoga valley holds almost all the giant steel mills and other factories that, since the 1890s, have made Cleveland one of the nation's great manufacturing centers. This is only a narrow, winding stream; and not far beyond its banks the land rises sharply. But it is wide and deep enough to permit the entry of industrial ships, and spacious enough to accommodate most of Cleveland's industrial might. The Cuyahoga is also polluted, though not so badly today as it was when it caught fire some years ago; and the air around it has been polluted by smoke and effluents coming out of the factories. But in the 1980s there was a problem which struck most people here as even more serious: many of the factories were closed, or idle most of the time. Cleveland's smokestack industries, which had made it the nation's fourth largest city in 1910, were now antiquated and inefficient, its products no longer in much demand. Unemployment was high, young people were moving out, local government finances were strained, and, most important, no one in a city built on confidence had much confidence about the city's future any more.

The Cuyahoga River also serves a demographic function in Cleveland: it pretty clearly separates the black and white sections of town. The division is not quite perfect. Just east of the Cuyahoga, along the radial street of Broadway which runs to Garfield Heights, there is still a cosmo (*i.e.,* white ethnic) neighborhood east of the river. It, like all of Cleveland west of the river, with several adjacent suburban areas, makes up the 20th congressional district of Ohio.

The west side of Cleveland has lost population over the last 20 years at what seems, at first glance, an alarming rate; this area had more than 400,000 residents in 1950, and only 265,000 in 1980. But much of this change is benign. It is evidence that young people can afford to buy their own homes in more spacious suburbs. It is evidence as well that older people can afford to live on their own, instead of as unwanted guests in their children's homes. It is evidence not of devastation (almost all of these neighborhoods are still neat and well maintained, though some are full of people frightened of crime) than of affluence. There are some things to be sad about. The cosmo traditions here are, to some extent, being lost. Young people may be showing more interest in the old customs than they were a few years ago, but they are interested in them more as a pleasant form of cultural entertainment than as a way of life; there is no way to preserve these old cultures intact (and of course they are not intact in Europe either any more). Community institutions which once thrived are now in disuse. The congressional district lines, as it happens, have followed many Cleveland families into the suburbs. The city now forms barely half of the 20th district's population, and it extends south into Parma and Seven Hills, southwest to Brookpark, Middleburgh Heights, Berea, Strongsville, and Olmsted Falls, and southeast to Garfield Heights and Maple Heights.

This has been a heavily Democratic district since Franklin Roosevelt inspired the ethnic residents of industrial Cleveland to come to the polls and vote Democratic. The current representative, Mary Rose Oakar, is a product of the Cleveland City Council. She was popular enough to have won a 12-candidate primary with 24% of the vote in 1976; she has not been seriously challenged since. Oakar has a solidly liberal record on economic issues but is more conservative on cultural issues. She is, incidentally, one of an increasing number of politicians of Arab descent—another example of a minority producing high-quality political leaders. She serves on three committees: Banking, Finance and Urban Affairs, Post Office and Civil Service, and House Administration.

The People Pop. 1980: 513,494, dn. 14.7% 1970–80; voting age pop. 382,556; 2% Black, 1% Span. orig. 34% housing units rented. Median owner $45,700; renter $168. Households: 70% family, 34% with children, 56% married couples.

Presidential Vote

1980	Reagan (R)	NA
	Carter (D)	NA
	Anderson (I)	NA

Rep. Mary Rose Oakar (D) Elected 1976; b. Mar. 5, 1940, Cleveland; home, Cleveland; Ursuline Col., B.A. 1962, John Carroll U., M.A. 1966; Roman Catholic.

Career Clerk, Higbee Co., 1956–58; Operator, OH Bell Telephone Co., 1957–62; Instructor, Lourdes Acad., 1963–70; Asst. Prof., Cuyahoga Comm. Col., 1968–75; Cleveland City Cncl., 1973–77.

Offices 2436 RHOB, 202-225-5871. Also 116 Fed. Court Bldg., 215 Superior Ave., Cleveland 44114, 216-522-4927.

Committees *Banking, Finance and Urban Affairs* (13th). Subcommittees: Economic Stabilization; Financial Institutions Supervision, Regulation and Insurance; General Oversight and Renegotiation; Housing and Community Development; International Development Institutions and Finance. *House Administration* (10th). Subcommittees: Accounts; Contracts and Printing. *Post Office and Civil Service* (9th). Subcommittees: Census and Population; Compensation and Employee Benefits (Chairwoman). *Select Committee on Aging* (12th). Subcommittees: Health and Long-Term Care; Retirement Income and Employment.

Group Ratings

	ADA	ACLU	COPE	CFA	LCV	LWV	NTU	NSI	COC	ACA	CSFC
1982	70	50	92	92	88	70	13	38	33	5	31
1981	55	—	91	86	71	—	12	—	0	22	36
1980	67	50	89	86	65	70	12	38	63	13	30

National Journal Ratings

	Economic		Foreign		Cultural	
1982	90%	(LIB)	68%	(LIB)	67%	(LIB)
	9%	(CONS)	32%	(CONS)	33%	(CONS)
1981	89%	(LIB)	67%	(LIB)	58%	(LIB)
	3%	(CONS)	33%	(CONS)	42%	(CONS)

Key Votes

1) Reagan 81 Budget	AGN	5) Incr SS Rtmt Age	AGN	9) Poor Pay Food Stamps	AGN
2) Reagan 81 Tax Cut	AGN	6) Saudi AWACS Sale	AGN	10) Ban Crt Busing Order	FOR
3) Bal Budget Amend	AGN	7) $ for MX Missile	AGN	11) Auto Local Content	FOR
4) Gas & Road Tax	FOR	8) Nerve Gas Prod	AGN	12) Nuclear Arms Freeze	FOR

Election Results

1982 general	Mary Rose Oakar (D)	133,603	(86%)	($90,990)
	Paris T. LeJeune (R)	17,675	(11%)	($0)
1982 primary	Mary Rose Oakar (D)	64,052	(100%)	
1980 general	Mary Rose Oakar (D)	96,217	(100%)	($44,603)

Campaign Contributions and Expenditures

1981-82		Direct Cont. 81-82				PACS brkdwn		
Receipts	$103,188	Indiv	$28,486	Agr	$1,750	Ideo	$1,537
Expend.	$90,990	Party	$100	Bus	$23,400	Lbr	$34,825
Unspent	$30,850	PACS	$71,962	Hlth	$6,600	Prof	$2,650

TWENTY-FIRST DISTRICT

The 21st congressional district of Ohio is the east side of Cleveland, plus several adjacent suburbs to the east and southeast. This area was once a checkerboard of Polish, Czech, Hungarian, Italian, and Jewish neighborhoods, but today it is mostly black. Fully 78% of the 21st's residents of Cleveland, and 62% of all its residents, are black. Media attention is usually focused on the grim suburbs of Hough and other areas not far from Cleveland's downtown; they are additionally visible because they are on the commuting line from the elite suburbs of Shaker Heights and Pepper Pike. But these form only a part of Cleveland's black community. Farther out, blacks live in comfortable working-class neighborhoods, and they have moved out in large numbers to pleasant eastern and southeastern suburbs; in small, but quite significant numbers, they live in the high-income suburbs of Shaker Heights (24% black in 1980) and Cleveland Heights (25%). The boundaries of the 21st district, over successive redistrictings, have followed them.

The changes in the 21st's politics provide an interesting lesson in urban black politics in America today. When Louis Stokes was elected the first black congressman from this district, in 1968, he was following by one year the success of his brother, Carl Stokes, in having been elected mayor of Cleveland. The Stokes brothers were a rags-to-riches story; they were able and successful, and they changed the course of Cleveland politics. Before the Stokeses became powerful, Cleveland's blacks felt excluded from high positions and were unhappy particularly with the city's police department. The Stokes administration changed that. Carl Stokes left the mayor's office in 1971, and Cleveland has not had a black mayor since (Stokes won only with a significant share of the white vote). Yet blacks no longer voice the same complaints or unite as monolithically around candidates for mayor. The political system has become responsive to their interests, as it has to interests of other groups; and electing a black mayor is no longer the only way to get what they want. Cleveland has had some fiercely contested mayoral races since, with both black and white voters taking both sides.

Louis Stokes is now one of the senior, and one of the most accomplished, members of the Congressional Black Caucus. He is a high ranking member of the Appropriations Committee. But he is more important for having taken on a couple of tough assignments and handling them adeptly. One was the chairmanship on the Select Committee on Presidential Assassinations, which he assumed after Henry Gonzalez resigned in 1977. Stokes supervised responsible hearings and the production of a report which has held up as the last word on the subject. In 1981, in the wake of the Abscam scandal, Stokes was called on to chair the Committee on Standards of Official Conduct—the official name of the House Ethics Committee. This is an extremely sensitive assignment, one that typically in the past has been entrusted to a senior southern Democrat of impeccable conservative credentials. Stokes's selection and his performance are both evidence of his fairness, probity, and competence.

Stokes has a safe seat now for the foreseeable future. The only question is whether the leadership will call on him for other sensitive assignments in the future.

The People   Pop. 1980: 514,625, dn. 19.7% 1970–80; voting age pop. 373,272; 58% Black, 1% Span. orig. 48% housing units rented. Median owner $38,000; renter $143. Households: 66% family, 36% with children, 43% married couples.

Presidential Vote

1980	Reagan (R)	NA
	Carter (D)	NA
	Anderson (I)	NA

Rep. Louis Stokes (D) Elected 1968; b. Feb. 23, 1925, Cleveland; home, Cleveland; Western Reserve U., 1946–48, Cleveland Marshall Law Sch., J.D. 1953; Methodist.

Career Practicing atty., 1954–68.

Offices 2465 RHOB, 202-225-7032. Also New Fed. Ofc. Bldg., 1240 E. 9th St., Rm. 2947, Cleveland 44199, 216-522-4900.

Committees *Appropriations* (10th). Subcommittees: District of Columbia; HUD-Independent Agencies; Labor-Health and Human Services-Education. *Standards of Official Conduct* (Chairman). *Permanent Select Committee on Intelligence* (8th). Subcommittee: Legislation.

Group Ratings

	ADA	ACLU	COPE	CFA	LCV	LWV	NTU	NSI	COC	ACA	CSFC
1982	85	100	94	92	92	75	31	0	24	0	23
1981	90	—	94	86	57	—	19	—	11	0	21
1980	78	97	93	93	70	100	14	0	52	10	21

National Journal Ratings

	Economic		Foreign		Cultural	
1982	93%	(LIB)	95%	(LIB)	88%	(LIB)
	6%	(CONS)	4%	(CONS)	11%	(CONS)
1981	87%	(LIB)	99%	(LIB)	95%	(LIB)
	12%	(CONS)	1%	(CONS)	1%	(CONS)

Key Votes

1) Reagan 81 Budget	AGN	5) Incr SS Rtmt Age	AGN	9) Poor Pay Food Stamps	AGN
2) Reagan 81 Tax Cut	AGN	6) Saudi AWACS Sale	AGN	10) Ban Crt Busing Order	AGN
3) Bal Budget Amend	AGN	7) $ for MX Missile	AGN	11) Auto Local Content	FOR
4) Gas & Road Tax	FOR	8) Nerve Gas Prod	AGN	12) Nuclear Arms Freeze	FOR

Election Results

1982 general	Louis Stokes (D)	132,544	(86%)	($138,843)
	Alan G. Shatteen (R)	21,332	(14%)	($0)
1982 primary	Louis Stokes (D)	61,055	(86%)	
	William L. Boyd (D)	9,776	(14%)	
1980 general	Louis Stokes (D)	83,188	(88%)	($57,984)
	Robert L. Woodall (R)	11,103	(12%)	($0)

Campaign Contributions and Expenditures

1981-82		*Direct Cont. 81-82*				*PACS brkdwn*		
Receipts	$156,448	Indiv	$98,081	Agr	$—	Ideo	$3,362
Expend.	$138,843	Party	$1,000	Bus	$10,650	Lbr	$27,930
Unspent	$43,717	PACS	$50,261	Hlth	$5,900	Prof	$200

OKLAHOMA

Oklahoma has one of the odder state histories, memorialized in the Rodgers and Hammerstein musical, an Edna Ferber novel, and half a dozen Hollywood movies. This was at first a land set apart for Indians; the Cherokee and the other Civilized Tribes (as they were called) were herded from their ancestral lands in the South and Midwest and sent here over the Trail of Tears. In 1889 the federal government decided to open what is now Oklahoma to white settlement, long after adjacent Kansas and Texas had been settled. On the morning of the great land rush, thousands of would-be homesteaders drove their wagons across the territorial line, in a moment reenacted on film many times since.

The "Sooners," as they were called (for those who crossed the line sooner than they were supposed to), quickly came to outnumber the Indians. Nonetheless, Oklahoma today has the second largest Indian population of any state, though there are no Indian reservations left; the Indians are about as well assimilated into the rest of the population as they are anywhere in the country. During its first years, Oklahoma held out great promise to its settlers, most of whom were people of modest means from the South. But for many of them the promise of Oklahoma turned as sour as it had for many Indians. The Depression and drought of the 1930s drove thousands of Okies from the Dust Bowl of Oklahoma to the greener fields of California.

Now the movement is, if anything, in the other direction. In the 1970s, as oil prices rose giddily and the economies of most states reeled, Oklahoma thrived. Oklahoma in 1980 was the fifth state in oil production, after Texas, Alaska, Louisiana, and California, and the third in production of natural gas, after Texas and Louisiana. In the early 1980s it was the scene of feverish oil and deep-well gas exploration and of major finds in the Anadarko Basin; the feverishness of the atmosphere is suggested by the collapse of Oklahoma City's Penn Square Bank, which made hundreds of millions of dollars of dubious loans for oil and gas exploration.

In the midst of national recession, Oklahoma had the nation's lowest unemployment rate. Instead of suffering outmigration it saw 95,000 people move into the state from 1980 to 1982.

The boom-and-bust cycle of Oklahoma is mirrored in its population figures. When it was admitted to the Union in 1907, only 18 years after it was opened to settlement, it had 1.5 million people. By 1930 that figure had increased to 2.4 million. Then it stayed basically steady: 2.5 million in 1970, although there was a big shift in that period from the rural counties to Oklahoma City and Tulsa, whose metropolitan areas now have half the state's population. Since then there has been another big jump, to 3.2 million. At the same time, Oklahoma's prosperity has come to people from very modest backgrounds. Its first settlers tended to be people who weren't doing all that well in Kansas or the South. The people who remained after the Dust Bowl years were used to hardship. This is a state without a deeply entrenched elite, or the dense network of civic institutions which comes from hundreds of years of urban settlement. Its major cities rose in quick spurts from the dusty plains; you can see tumbleweed in shopping center parking lots and oil wells on the grounds of the state Capitol.

Presidential politics. Oklahoma's changing economy has changed its political preference. Originally this was a Democratic state: Dixiecrat and populistic settlers from the South outnumbered Republicans coming overland from and via Kansas. Oklahoma became, if anything, more Democratic during the Depression. But later, as prosperity returned, it became more Republican. The voters of the new rich cities were heavily Republican in national elections. And even in the rural areas, the sympathy of national Democrats for cultural liberalism repelled voters whose personal lives are still in the 1980s very much lived along traditional lines. There are no significant national Democratic voting blocs here: there is only a small black population, and no self-conscious Indian vote as there is in states with big reservations like South Dakota and Arizona. Oklahoma went Republican in the 1960 presidential race and in 1968. In 1972 it was Richard Nixon's second best state, after Mississippi (where many of Oklahoma's first settlers came from, as you can tell from place names); in 1980, it was Jimmy Carter's weakest southern state. Oklahoma could conceivably shift toward the national Democrats, especially if the bottom falls out of the oil market. But for the nonce it is one of our more Republican states. It does not have a presidential primary, and its national convention delegations tend to be among the more conservative of both parties.

Senators. Oklahoma has two young first-term senators of quite different backgrounds. Senator David Boren has been in the statewide spotlight for a decade now, and has an even longer experience with Oklahoma politics; his father was a congressman in the 1940s. He owes his political career largely to an astute reading of the temper of the times in 1974. That was the year of Watergate and of the scandal in Oklahoma that ultimately sent Governor David Hall to jail. Boren's campaign prop was a broom, to symbolize his promise to clean up the mess without committing himself to anything specific. That was enough to give him a victory over Hall and a relative of Will Rogers in the Democratic primary and an easy victory in the general election.

Boren had a successful administration, and was an early supporter of President Carter; he later took his distance when he thought Carter was trying to get out of commitments he made in Oklahoma to deregulate oil and gas prices. Incumbent Senator Dewey Bartlett retired in 1978, and Boren campaigned for the seat as a supporter of the Kemp–Roth tax cut; his major problem was charges by a minor candidate that Boren was a homosexual. He swore on the family Bible that they were not true, won the primary runoff, and again won the general election easily.

Boren remains one of the most conservative of young Democratic senators. On economic issues he continues to believe in cutting federal spending, decreasing regulation, and removing energy price controls. He is well positioned to advance these views: he holds the Finance Committee seat that Oklahoma Senator Robert Kerr once used to influence national policy. He is a member of the subcommittees on Social Security and Trade; on the latter he seems export-oriented, which makes sense since Oklahoma exports wheat, other agricultural products, and oil. On cultural issues he is tradition-minded; on foreign policy his record is more mixed. Boren's views might seem to make him odd man out in the Democratic Caucus. But he has a pleasant personality and is on good terms with almost all his colleagues, and even with Senate employees who are usually ignored by senators.

Boren comes up for reelection in 1984. It seems highly unlikely that he will be challenged seriously in the Democratic primary; the primary draws a large segment of the electorate, far larger than the percentage which supports national Democratic candidates, and Boren's stands are closely in line with these voters' views. As for the general election, Boren has demonstrated that, notwithstanding Oklahoma's preference for Republicans in presidential elections, this can be a very Democratic state in statewide contests.

Oklahoma's other senator is one of the more obscure members of this body, and one of the real surprises to come out of the 1980 elections. Nobody gave 31-year-old state Senator Don Nickles much of a chance to win that contest; he campaigned against better-known candidates, without much command over national issues, and his sole asset seemed to be support from fundamentalist church members. But that turned out to be a powerful asset in Oklahoma. If there were polls that could measure intensity of religious feeling, Oklahoma would probably rank near the top of the nation. This is Southern Baptist and evangelical country: Oklahoma still does not allow liquor by the drink, and Tulsa is the headquarters of evangelist Oral Roberts. This helped Nickles to upset two favored Republicans in the primary, and to raise enough money to run a plausible campaign for the general. His victory was along what have become traditional partisan lines in close Oklahoma elections. He carried Tulsa and Oklahoma City and had very wide margins in the wheat-growing country of north central and northwestern Oklahoma; he lost the northeast corner of the state and the southern tiers of counties along the Red River border with Texas.

Nickles was not particularly visible in the Senate in his first two years—a shrewd move, perhaps, given his lack of experience. He is a member of two committees which have not been as active as many conservatives (perhaps including Nickles) would like: Energy and Natural Resources, whose chairman James McClure has been reluctant to tackle deregulation of natural gas, and Labor and Human Resources, whose chairman Orrin Hatch cannot summon a reliable majority. Nickles will undoubtedly be a prime Democratic target in 1986. His problem will be how to convince voters he has addressed effectively the shrill complaints his campaign voiced in 1980.

Governor. Oklahoma's governor is its most experienced officeholder. George Nigh was first elected to the state legislature in 1950, when he was 23; he was elected lieutenant governor of Oklahoma in 1958 and 1966, and served, briefly, as interim governor after the resignation of the incumbent in 1963. He is now the first governor in the state's history to have won two consecutive terms. His first race, against a young football star, was close; his second, against the young state auditor, was a walkaway. He has had advantages: it's easier to be a popular governor when the state treasury is flush and the economy is booming. Nonetheless, Nigh has still shown impressive endurance.

Congressional districting. Oklahoma's congressional districting plan is, to put it bluntly, a

Democratic gerrymander. It was designed to safeguard the seats of the state's five Democratic congressmen and to place the maximum number of Republican voters in the seat of its one Republican House member. The districts do not look grotesque on the map, but when you look at their concentrations of population, particularly in the Republican 5th district, their purpose is evident. So far it has also been successful, though these things seldom remain so for a whole decade.

The People Est. Pop. 1982: 3,177,000; Pop. 1980: 3,025,290, up 5.0% 1980–82 and 18.2% 1970–80; 1.4% of U.S. total, 25th largest; voting age pop. 2,170,406; 6% Black, 5% American Indian, 2% Spanish origin, 1% Asian origin. Single ancestry: 13% English, 6% German, 5% Irish, 1% French, Dutch. Registered voters (1982): 1,485,780 Total. 1,059,349 D (71%); 393,145 R (26%); 33,286 I (2%). 16% with 1–3 yrs. col., 16% with 4+ yrs. col. 13.3% below poverty level. 27% housing units rented; median house value: $35,600; median monthly rent: $164. Households: 74% family, 40% with children, 63% married couples.

1982 Share of Federal Tax Burden $7,650,900,000; 1.28% of U.S. total, 24th largest.

1982 Share of Federal Expenditures

	Total		Non-Defense		Defense	
Total Expend	$6,952m	(1.15%)	$4,972m	(1.17%)	$1,980m	(1.11%)
St/Lcl Grants	991m	(1.12%)	989m	(1.12%)	2m	(5.56%)
Salary/Wages	1,393m	(1.78%)	178m	(0.65%)	1,215m	(2.40%)
Ind Payments	3,802m	(1.33%)	3,247m	(1.26%)	555m	(1.94%)
Procurement	658m	(0.45%)	137m	(0.43%)	521m	(0.46%)
Other Programs	107m	(1.98%)	106m	(1.97%)	1m	(2.33%)
Loan/Insurance	884m	(1.38%)	823m	(1.33%)	61m	(2.77%)

Political Lineup Governor, George P. Nigh (D). Senators, David Lyle Boren (D) and Don Nickles (R). Representatives, 6 (5 D and 1 R). State Senate, 48 (34 D, 13 R and 1 undecided); State House of Representatives, 101 (76 D and 25 R).

Presidential Vote

1980	Reagan (R)	695,570	(60%)
	Carter (D)	402,026	(35%)
	Anderson (I)	38,284	(3%)
1976	Ford (R)	545,708	(50%)
	Carter (D)	532,442	(49%)

SENATORS

Sen. David Lyle Boren (D) Elected 1978, seat up 1984; b. Apr. 24, 1941, Washington, DC; home, Seminole; Yale U., B.A. 1963, Rhodes Scholar, Oxford U., 1965, U. of OK, J.D. 1968; United Methodist.

Career OK House of Reps., 1966–74; Practicing atty.; Gov. of OK, 1975–78.

Offices 442 RSOB, 202-224-4721. Also 621 N. Robinson, Su. 350, Oklahoma City 73102, 405-231-4381.

Committees *Agriculture, Nutrition, and Forestry* (6th). Subcommittees: Agricultural Credit and Rural Electrification; Agricultural Research and General Legislation; Foreign Agricultural Policy. *Finance* (6th). Subcommittees: International Trade; Social Security and Income Maintenance Programs; Estate and Gift Taxation. *Small Business* (9th). Subcommittee: Entrepreneurship and Special Problems Facing Small Business.

Group Ratings

	ADA	ACLU	COPE	CFA	LCV	LWV	NTU	NSI	COC	ACA	CSFC
1982	45	36	36	60	16	25	57	89	65	67	59
1981	30	—	32	21	27	—	59	—	71	76	62
1980	28	17	37	20	6	33	48	80	71	52	57

National Journal Ratings

	Economic		Foreign		Cultural	
1982	57%	(LIB)	59%	(LIB)	40%	(LIB)
	42%	(CONS)	40%	(CONS)	59%	(CONS)
1981	36%	(LIB)	49%	(LIB)	19%	(LIB)
	63%	(CONS)	50%	(CONS)	80%	(CONS)

Key Votes

1) Reagan 81 Budget	FOR	5) $ to El Salvador	AGN	9) Poor Pay Food Stamps	FOR
2) Reagan 81 Tax Cut	FOR	6) Saudi AWACS Sale	FOR	10) Ban Crt Busing Order	FOR
3) Bal Budget Amend	FOR	7) Ban Abortion	—	11) Clinch Riv Brdr Rctr	FOR
4) Gas & Road Tax	AGN	8) Nerve Gas Prod	AGN	12) Legal Services Corp	—

Election Results

1978 general	David Lyle Boren (D)	493,953	(65%)	($751,286)
	Robert B. Kamm (R)	247,857	(33%)	($443,712)
1978 runoff	David Lyle Boren (D)	251,587	(60%)	
	Ed Edmondson (D)	184,175	(40%)	($129,369)
1978 primary	David Lyle Boren (D)	252,560	(46%)	
	Ed Edmondson (D)	155,626	(28%)	
	Gene Stipe (D)	114,423	(21%)	($370,869)
	Four others (D)	28,409	(5%)	
1972 general	Dewey F. Bartlett (R)	516,934	(51%)	($625,095)
	Ed Edmondson (D)	478,212	(48%)	($512,058)

Campaign Contributions and Expenditures

1977-78

Receipts	$779,544
Expend.	$751,286
Unspent	$28,250

Received no PAC Contributions

Sen. Don Nickles (R) Elected 1980, seat up 1986; b. Dec. 6, 1948, Ponca City; home, Ponca City; OK St. U., B.A. 1971; Roman Catholic.

Career Natl. Guard, 1970–76; V.P. and Gen. Mgr., Nickles Machine Corp., 1976–80; OK Senate, 1978–80.

Offices 713 HSOB, 202-224-5754. Also 820 Old P.O. Bldg., Oklahoma City 73102, 405-231-4941; 333 W. 4th., Rm. 3003, Tulsa 74103, 918-581-7651; and 1916 Lake Rd., Ponca City 73601, 405-767-1270.

Committees *Energy and Natural Resources* (8th). Subcommittees: Energy Regulation; Energy Research and Development; Water and Power (Chairman). *Labor and Human Resources* (4th). Subcommittees: Labor (Chairman); Employment and Productivity; Family and Human Services. *Small Business* (6th). Subcommittees: Government Procurement (Chairman); Productivity and Competition.

Group Ratings

	ADA	ACLU	COPE	CFA	LCV	LWV	NTU	NSI	COC	ACA	CSFC
1982	10	0	3	10	15	27	99	90	75	95	85
1981	5	—	5	29	25	—	96	—	94	86	86

National Journal Ratings

	Economic		Foreign		Cultural	
1982	16%	(LIB)	3%	(LIB)	15%	(LIB)
	83%	(CONS)	84%	(CONS)	84%	(CONS)
1981	17%	(LIB)	1%	(LIB)	2%	(LIB)
	79%	(CONS)	85%	(CONS)	82%	(CONS)

Key Votes

1) Reagan 81 Budget	FOR	5) $ to El Salvador	FOR	9) Poor Pay Food Stamps	FOR
2) Reagan 81 Tax Cut	FOR	6) Saudi AWACS Sale	FOR	10) Ban Crt Busing Order	FOR
3) Bal Budget Amend	FOR	7) Ban Abortion	FOR	11) Clinch Riv Brdr Rctr	AGN
4) Gas & Road Tax	AGN	8) Nerve Gas Prod	FOR	12) Legal Services Corp	AGN

Election Results

1980 general	Don Nickles (R)	587,252	(53%)	($828,346)
	Andy Coats (D)	478,283	(44%)	($996,447)
1980 runoff	Don Nickles (R)	81,697	(66%)	
	John Zink (R)	42,818	(34%)	($689,808)
1980 primary	Don Nickles (R)	47,879	(35%)	
	John Zink (R)	45,914	(33%)	
	Ed Noble (R)	39,839	(29%)	($758,329)
	Two others (R)	4,223	(3%)	
1974 general	Henry Bellmon (R)	390,997	(49%)	($622,480)
	Ed Edmondson (D)	387,162	(49%)	($195,429)

Campaign Contributions and Expenditures

1979-80			PACS brkdwn		
Receipts	$925,097	Agr	$4,750	Ideo	$34,956
Expend.	$828,346	Bus	$106,331	Lbr	$1,000
Unspent	$96,751	Hlth	$4,550	Prof	$—

GOVERNOR

Gov. George P. Nigh (D) Elected 1978, term expires Jan. 1987; b. June 9, 1927, McAlester; home, Oklahoma City; Eastern A&M Jr. Col., E. Central St. Teachers Col., B.A. 1950; Baptist.

Career High sch. teacher and grocer; OK House of Reps., 1951–59; Lt. Gov. of OK, 1959–63, 1967–79; Gov. of OK, 1963, 1969.

Offices 212 State Capitol Bldg., Oklahoma City 73105, 405-521-2342.

Election Results

1982 gen.	George P. Nigh (D)	548,159	(62%)
	Tom Daxon (R)	332,207	(38%)
1982 prim.	George P. Nigh (D)	379,301	(82%)
	Howard Bell (D)	79,735	(17%)
1978 gen.	George P. Nigh (D)	402,240	(52%)
	Ron Shotts (R)	367,055	(47%)
1978 runoff	George P. Nigh (D)	269,681	(58%)
	Larry Derryberry (D)	197,457	(42%)

FIRST DISTRICT

Tulsa is a major city built by oil, inspired by religion, and eager to be uplifted by culture. It has been a major regional center of the oil industry almost since Oklahoma gained statehood in 1907. Even today, years after oil was first discovered in these parts, Tulsa is still growing rapidly, fueled not only by oil but by a contagious enthusiasm for new business enterprises and innovations. Although Tulsa's winters are sometimes frigid, it is very much a part of the Sun Belt in spirit. Ordinary people here do not resent or attack the oil companies or the new rich; they identify with them. They see not class conflict, but a coincidence of economic interests. They see government as interfering with efforts to produce goods and services people want and are ready to pay for. Tulsa residents view the liberal cultural values and toleration of diversity they see in government and the media as literally subversive of decent moral values; this is a center not only of the oil business but the home of Oral Roberts University. Tulsa has built some impressive cultural institutions, but it still lacks the confident cosmopolitan style of Dallas and Houston; it is closer in spirit to small Texas boom towns like Midland and Tyler.

Politically, Tulsa is ordinarily heavily Republican. It went 2–1 for Ronald Reagan over

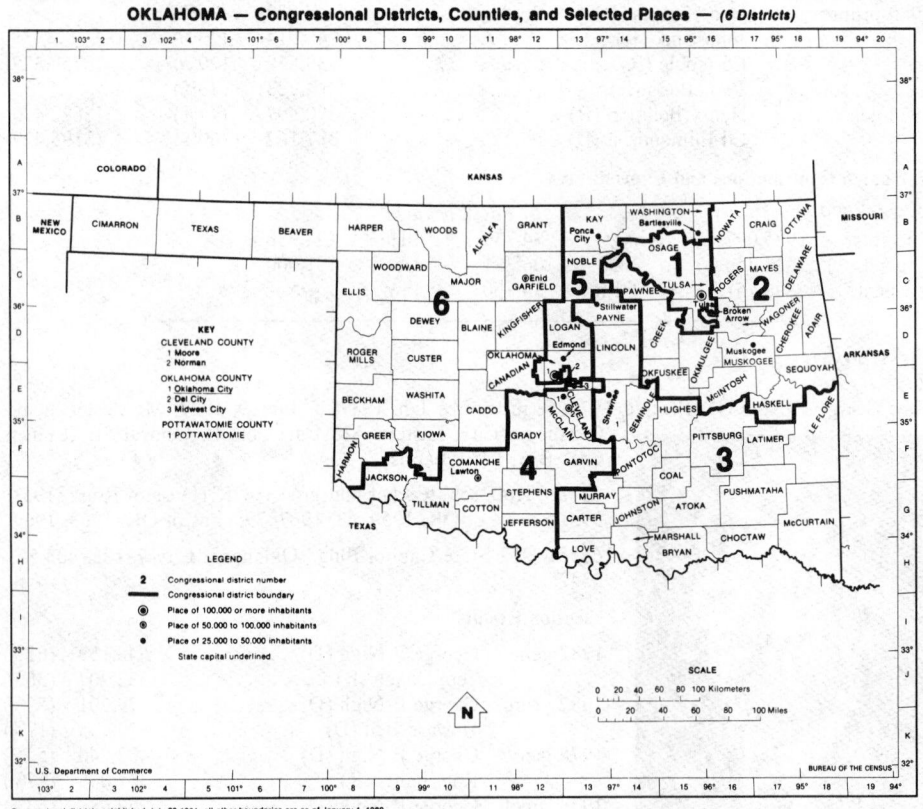

OKLAHOMA — Congressional Districts, Counties, and Selected Places — (6 Districts)

Congressional districts established July 22, 1981; all other boundaries are as of January 1, 1980.

Jimmy Carter in 1980, and gave 79% of its votes to Richard Nixon in 1972. Tulsa forms most of Oklahoma's 1st congressional district; all of the city except for an affluent corner to the south of town are in the 1st. The district also includes some adjacent rural territory, in Osage County, which was once an Indian reservation, in the flat plains north of Tulsa, and in the more heavily settled rural area to the south. These were all added to make the district more Democratic, because despite its basic leanings, the 1st district has a Democratic congressman.

He is James Jones, and he is one of the most important members of the House. Although in his early 40s, he has a wealth of experience: as a congressional aide 20 years ago, as a staff assistant to President Johnson before he turned 30. He was first elected to Congress in 1972, while his party's presidential candidate was getting only a handful of votes in the district. He has held onto the district since, and won a seat on the House Ways and Means Committee. Since 1981, Jones has been Chairman of the House Budget Committee, a post he won despite the misgivings of House Democratic leaders.

Jones has achieved his position by the force of his ideas and by his legislative skills. He has always believed that free market competition produces economic growth more readily than government spending; he has always believed that oil and gas prices—and lots of other things—should be deregulated. He approaches trade issues with a strong belief in free trade and a constituency that generally does not seek protection. Most of these beliefs put Jones very much in the minority in the Democratic Caucus when he first came to Congress, and many members must have wondered why he wasn't a Republican. But in his years on Ways and Means, he attracted some admirers among the younger Democrats who themselves were growing more skeptical of government programs and regulation. While remaining liberal on cultural issues, these Democrats began to support energy price deregulation and lowering of the capital gains tax, and they found themselves working with Jones on Ways and Means. And they provided critical support when Jones beat David Obey of Wisconsin in the Democratic Caucus for the Budget chairmanship. It was a contest between two of the smartest young Democrats, and the Caucus chose the one who tends to favor lower government spending and lower taxes.

As chairman, Jones has not been a liberal/labor Democrat, but he has not acted like a Republican either. Speaker O'Neill evidently does not trust him, and has made sure that old hands like Richard Bolling and Jim Wright watch his work carefully. But the budget resolutions Jones has crafted in 1981 and 1983 have been documents which the large majority of Democrats can support—and that is a formidable achievement in itself. His efforts were not successful in 1981, when there were not enough Democrats to survive the minimal number of Boll Weevil defections, given Republican solidarity; but they seemed more likely to succeed in 1983. Jones's budgets have been criticized by many Democrats as insufficiently generous, but he—and evidently Speaker O'Neill as well—recognizes that the fulcrum point of the Democratic Caucus is not at the point it was when Jones came to Congress. Too many Democrats, even during the recession, no longer have faith that massive government jobs programs, guaranteed incomes, and government health insurance are going to solve the problems they are intended to address. They are more interested, for the moment anyway, in stimulating economic growth than they are in redistributing the wealth.

As for the Republicans, they have attacked Jones's budgets as way too generous, yet too stingy on defense. These attacks have hurt him back in Tulsa. Despite his national responsibilities, Jones keeps in touch with constituents in his home district. But this is a very

Republican district, and probably no other Democrat could hold it; and Jones has had a significant Republican challenge every time he has run—something that is not true of any other House Democrat of similar prominence. Jones substantially outspent his Republican opponent in 1982—and made a point of raising most of his money in Oklahoma—but nevertheless won with only 54% of the vote, and only 53% in Tulsa County. This is an uncomfortably close margin, his closest race since 1976; and it happened despite the fact that redistricting gave him about a 2% premium over what he would have had in a district including all of Tulsa County. This result almost guarantees that Jones will be targeted by the Republicans in 1984.

The People Pop. 1980: 503,739, up 14.1% 1970–80; voting age pop. 365,006; 8% Black, 4% Am. Ind., 1% Span. orig., 1% Asian orig. 32% housing units rented. Median owner $42,500; renter $204. Households: 71% family, 38% with children, 59% married couples.

Presidential Vote

1980	Reagan (R)	NA
	Carter (D)	NA

Rep. James R. Jones (D) Elected 1972; b. May 5, 1939, Muskogee; home, Tulsa; U. of OK, A.B. 1961, Georgetown U., LL.B. 1964; Roman Catholic.

Career Legis. Asst. to U.S. Rep. Ed Edmondson, 1961–64; Army, 1964–65; White House Staff Asst. to Pres. Lyndon B. Johnson, 1965–69; Practicing atty.

Offices 203 CHOB, 202-225-2211. Also 4536 Fed. Bldg., Tulsa 74103, 918-581-7111.

Committees *Budget* (Chairman). *Ways and Means* (6th). Subcommittee: Trade.

Group Ratings

	ADA	ACLU	COPE	CFA	LCV	LWV	NTU	NSI	COC	ACA	CSFC
1982	50	42	44	46	50	50	50	78	53	35	41
1981	35	—	43	43	45	—	41	—	40	38	51
1980	39	63	47	29	26	44	39	50	72	43	44

National Journal Ratings

	Economic		Foreign		Cultural	
1982	54%	(LIB)	59%	(LIB)	46%	(LIB)
	46%	(CONS)	41%	(CONS)	54%	(CONS)
1981	59%	(LIB)	45%	(LIB)	52%	(LIB)
	41%	(CONS)	55%	(CONS)	48%	(CONS)

Key Votes

1) Reagan 81 Budget	AGN	5) Incr SS Rtmt Age	FOR	9) Poor Pay Food Stamps	FOR
2) Reagan 81 Tax Cut	AGN	6) Saudi AWACS Sale	AGN	10) Ban Crt Busing Order	FOR
3) Bal Budget Amend	AGN	7) $ for MX Missile	AGN	11) Auto Local Content	AGN
4) Gas & Road Tax	AGN	8) Nerve Gas Prod	AGN	12) Nuclear Arms Freeze	FOR

Election Results

1982 general	James R. Jones (D)	76,379	(54%)	($635,844)
	Richard C. (Dick) Freeman (R) ...	64,704	(46%)	($200,138)
1982 primary	James R. Jones (D) unopposed			
1980 general	James R. Jones (D)	115,381	(58%)	($239,753)
	Richard C. (Dick) Freeman (R) ...	82,293	(42%)	($153,560)

Campaign Contributions and Expenditures

1981-82		Direct Cont. 81-82			PACS brkdwn			
Receipts	$641,831	Indiv	$279,003	Agr	$13,550	Ideo	$7,150
Expend.	$635,844	PACS	$334,190	Bus	$212,327	Lbr	$29,375
Unspent	$64,049			Hlth	$22,200	Prof	$8,200

Indep Expend: For: $13,266 (NTL) Agn: $127,029 (NCPAC)

SECOND DISTRICT

The 2d congressional district of Oklahoma takes in all the northeast quadrant of the state, except for most of Tulsa and the surrounding area which make up the 1st district. The 2d is where most of Oklahoma's Indians live. Their ancestors were forcibly relocated here from their ancestral lands in the South and Midwest, as early as the 1830s, over the Trail of Tears. This part of Oklahoma remained Indian Territory until it was opened up to white settlement in 1889. Today 12% of the people here report their race as American Indian, and many more claim some percentage of Indian blood. The Indian percentage is highest in the hilly counties just west of the Ozarks of Arkansas, where the county names—Cherokee, Delaware, Sequoyah—recall what were called the Five Civilized Tribes. Much attention nationally is focused on the problems of Indians in states where there are large reservations. But no one seems to be asking whether the experience of the Indians in Oklahoma—where they are now relatively prosperous, assimilated, and living comfortably with the white population—has any useful lessons for Indians and whites in other parts of the country.

The other major cultural influence in this area is the sort of Okie spirit articulated in Merle Haggard's "Okie From Muskogee," a song about attitudes in the largest city in this district. This is a state settled too late for a populist movement, and which never had much of an establishment for ordinary people to rebel against (although there was a big Socialist vote in the 1910s, reflecting hatred of eastern financial interests), and people here have been very positive about traditional cultural values and patriotism, the more so as they see them questioned elsewhere.

The congressman from the 2d district, Mike Synar, is an unusual Oklahoma politician. He was first elected to the House in 1978, at age 28, beating in the Democratic runoff a shaky incumbent accused, by others, of having a heart-shaped waterbed. Synar's record on the issues is about as liberal as that of any Oklahoma congressman. As a young member of the Judiciary Committee, he sponsored a key amendment strengthening the fair housing law the House passed in 1980; Synar's amendment passed by a 205–204 vote. On other Judiciary issues he has generally voted with committee chairman Peter Rodino. In 1981 he got a seat on the Energy and Commerce Committee. There he supports deregulation of energy prices—a position almost unanimously supported in Oklahoma—but sides with most committee Democrats on many regulatory issues.

Until 1982, Synar's hold on this district looked tenuous. He was shrewd enough to challenge a weak incumbent in 1978, and he had the advantage of coming from a rich and politically prominent family in Muskogee County. Under harsh attack from Republican Gary Richardson, he won with less than huge margins in 1978 and 1980; against another candidate with a similar platform he won almost 3–1 in 1982. His one weak spot was the 2d district's portion of Tulsa County, a high-income area almost any Democrat would lose. This does not mean that Synar has an absolutely safe seat; a Democrat with his kind of record risks getting into trouble in a district like this in a year when opinion swings the wrong way. But for the time being, he has proved he is a strong campaigner, with deep roots in the district, and considerable political strength and endurance.

The People   Pop. 1980: 505,149, up 33.6% 1970–80; voting age pop. 353,938; 4% Black, 1% Span. orig., 10% Am. Ind. 20% housing units rented. Median owner $31,500; renter $118. Households: 78% family, 43% with children, 68% married couples.

Presidential Vote

	1980	Reagan (R)	106,508	(57%)
		Carter (D)	81,761	(43%)

Rep. Michael Lynn (Mike) Synar (D) Elected 1978; b. Oct. 17, 1950, Vinita; home, Muskogee; U. of OK, B.A. 1972, J.D. 1977, Northwestern U., M.B.A. 1973; Episcopal.

Career Rancher and real estate broker.

Offices 1713 LHOB, 202-225-2701. Also Fed. Bldg., 125 S. Main, Rm. 2B22, Muskogee 74401, 918-681-2533.

Committees *Energy and Commerce* (17th). Subcommittees: Energy Conservation and Power; Fossil and Synthetic Fuels. *Government Operations* (10th). Subcommittee: Environment, Energy, and Natural Resources (Chairman). *Judiciary* (10th). Subcommittees: Courts, Civil Liberties, and the Administration of Justice; Monopolies and Commercial Law. *Select Committee on Aging* (19th). Subcommittees: Housing and Consumer Interests; Retirement Income and Employment.

Group Ratings

	ADA	ACLU	COPE	CFA	LCV	LWV	NTU	NSI	COC	ACA	CSFC
1982	55	67	61	62	79	100	33	67	50	27	32
1981	80	—	57	69	100	—	19	—	16	17	33
1980	61	87	44	71	63	67	23	40	63	26	36

National Journal Ratings

	Economic		Foreign		Cultural	
1982	55%	(LIB)	66%	(LIB)	67%	(LIB)
	44%	(CONS)	34%	(CONS)	33%	(CONS)
1981	62%	(LIB)	65%	(LIB)	84%	(LIB)
	37%	(CONS)	34%	(CONS)	15%	(CONS)

Key Votes

1) Reagan 81 Budget	AGN	5) Incr SS Rtmt Age	FOR	9) Poor Pay Food Stamps	AGN
2) Reagan 81 Tax Cut	AGN	6) Saudi AWACS Sale	AGN	10) Ban Crt Busing Order	AGN
3) Bal Budget Amend	AGN	7) $ for MX Missile	AGN	11) Auto Local Content	AGN
4) Gas & Road Tax	—	8) Nerve Gas Prod	AGN	12) Nuclear Arms Freeze	—

Election Results

1982 general	Michael Lynn (Mike) Synar (D) ..	111,895	(73%)	($274,149)
	Lou Striegel (R)	42,298	(27%)	($139,599)
1982 primary	Michael Lynn (Mike) Synar (D) unopposed			
1980 general	Michael Lynn (Mike) Synar (D) ..	101,516	(54%)	($270,036)
	Gary Richardson (R)	86,544	(46%)	($205,452)

Campaign Contributions and Expenditures

1981-82		Direct Cont. 81-82				PACS brkdwn		
Receipts	$284,203	Indiv	$257,931	Agr	$—	Ideo	$985
Expend.	$274,149	Party	$4,367	Bus	$10,175	Lbr	$4,320
Unspent	$10,897	PACS	$18,625	Hlth	$—	Prof	$—

THIRD DISTRICT

The southern part of Oklahoma is known as Little Dixie. It was first settled, in the period between 1889 and 1907, by white southerners—some of the county names here (Leflore, Pontotoc) were taken directly from Mississippi. Ever since statehood Little Dixie has been the most Democratic part of Oklahoma. The 3d congressional district of Oklahoma includes most of the Little Dixie counties, and juts up into the center of the state, into the old university town of Stillwater, to include enough people to meet the population standard.

This is the district that for 30 years elected Carl Albert to the House of Representatives. Albert was part of the class of World War II veterans first elected in 1946. Others include John Kennedy and Richard Nixon; none are left in the House today. In his early years, as a loyal Democrat from a southern district, Albert attracted the attention of Speaker Sam Rayburn. He was made majority whip in 1955, and after that his succession to the speakership was, in effect, automatic. Albert's performance as speaker from 1971 to 1977 was a disappointment to those who remembered him as a hard-fighting vote counter in the 1950s and 1960s. He deferred to committee chairmen and to hoary tradition; he had little to say about scheduling and did not establish legislative priorities. He never got close to the younger members who were potential allies for a strong speaker. Albert had been in the leadership for so long, at a time when it was difficult to lead, that he had a hard time taking advantages of opportunities when they did seem to appear. His retirement in 1976 came two years ahead of the date he had set for retirement some years before.

Little Dixie was always proud of Carl Albert and reelected him without difficulty. But he proved unable to hand the 3d district seat on to his administrative assistant. Instead state Senator Wes Watkins won the Democratic primary and captured the district. In his first four years in the House, Watkins had one of the most conservative voting records of any young Democrat. Since 1980, he has joined his fellow Democrats more often, particularly on economic issues. This apparent change took place even before the Reagan economic program became unpopular. It may have something to do with his political ambitions. Before 1980, Watkins considered running for the Senate that year, and in Oklahoma, a Republican state in presidential elections, a conservative record is an asset. But he decided not to make that race. Now he wants to stay in the 3d district, which is the most Democratic district in the state in most elections, and to advance to a position of power in the House, where chairmanships are determined by votes of mostly northern Democrats. He is a member of the Appropriations Committee, and of two subcommittees which can do his district a lot of good: Agriculture and Energy and Water Development. Increasingly he seems to be following the lead and the national Democratic voting records of the chairmen of these two units, Jamie Whitten of Mississippi and Tom Bevill of Alabama.

The People Pop. 1980: 504,268, up 20.1% 1970–80; voting age pop. 365,865; 4% Black, 1% Span. orig., 6% Am. Ind. 25% housing units rented. Median owner $25,100; renter $113. Households: 74% family, 39% with children, 64% married couples.

Presidential Vote

1980	Reagan (R)	95,854	(52%)
	Carter (D)	86,899	(48%)

Rep. Wes Watkins (D) Elected 1976; b. Dec. 15, 1938, DeQueen, AR; home, Ada; OK St. U., B.S. 1960, M.S. 1961, U. of MD, 1961–63; Presbyterian.

Career USDA, 1961–63; Asst. Dir. of Admissions, OK St. U., 1963–66; Exec. Dir., Kiamichi Econ. Develop. Dist. of OK, 1966–68; Realtor and homebuilder, 1968–; OK Senate, 1975–76.

Offices 2440 RHOB, 202-225-4565. Also P.O. Box 1607, Ada 74820, 405-436-1980.

Committee *Appropriations* (29th). Subcommittees: Agriculture, Rural Development; Energy and Water Development.

Group Ratings

	ADA	ACLU	COPE	CFA	LCV	LWV	NTU	NSI	COC	ACA	CSFC
1982	35	33	33	46	39	42	47	90	45	36	47
1981	30	—	28	50	36	—	33	—	26	50	55
1980	33	27	31	43	12	50	36	90	70	46	51

National Journal Ratings

	Economic		Foreign		Cultural	
1982	58%	(LIB)	50%	(LIB)	21%	(LIB)
	42%	(CONS)	50%	(CONS)	76%	(CONS)
1981	56%	(LIB)	18%	(LIB)	45%	(LIB)
	44%	(CONS)	73%	(CONS)	55%	(CONS)

Key Votes

1) Reagan 81 Budget	AGN	5) Incr SS Rtmt Age	FOR	9) Poor Pay Food Stamps	AGN
2) Reagan 81 Tax Cut	AGN	6) Saudi AWACS Sale	AGN	10) Ban Crt Busing Order	FOR
3) Bal Budget Amend	FOR	7) $ for MX Missile	AGN	11) Auto Local Content	FOR
4) Gas & Road Tax	—	8) Nerve Gas Prod	FOR	12) Nuclear Arms Freeze	FOR

Election Results

1982 general	Wes Watkins (D)	121,670	(82%)	($243,247)
	Patrick K. Miller (R)	26,335	(18%)	($0)
1982 primary	Wes Watkins (D)	97,135	(85%)	
	Leland Kelly (D)	16,154	(15%)	
1980 general	Wes Watkins (D) unopposed			($181,666)

Campaign Contributions and Expenditures

1981-82		*Direct Cont. 81-82*		*PACS brkdwn*			
Receipts	$265,015	Indiv	$191,043	Agr	$6,700	Ideo	$1,300
Expend.	$243,247	PACS	$63,725	Bus	$46,075	Lbr	$4,500
Unspent	$103,936			Hlth	$3,500	Prof	$1,650

FOURTH DISTRICT

The 4th congressional district of Oklahoma is part urban and part rural—a combination of different parts of the state and different political orientations. It includes several counties on the Red River border with Texas, an area that has, on both sides of the river, produced heavy Democratic majorities in most elections and some of the nation's most prominent Democratic politicians (including Speakers Sam Rayburn and Carl Albert). The 4th also includes Lawton, a small city whose major industries are oil and the care and maintenance of the Army's Fort Sill. The 4th district's largest urban concentration is around Norman, home of the University of Oklahoma, and in effect a southern extension of the Oklahoma City metropolitan area. And the district also includes a part of Oklahoma City itself, the southeastern corner of the state, where subdivisions give way to rural crossroads and farmland in terrain annexed by the city in anticipation of growth in years hence.

This is a district that is politically marginal in Oklahoma races. The Democratic Red River area is balanced by the Republican leanings of Norman, which votes more like a well-to-do suburb than like a midwestern college town. Republican strategists have been eyeing this district for years, but they lost their best chance in 1980 when they failed to capture it after 32-year incumbent Tom Steed retired.

The winner was Dave McCurdy, a 30-year-old lawyer who won a series of cliffhanger elections. He trailed in the first Democratic primary, 40%–34%, then won 51% in the runoff. In the general election, against former prisoner of war Howard Rutledge, he won with 51% again. McCurdy's career shows what a difference two years of incumbency can make. In 1982 he was reelected with 65% of the vote. Redistricting changed the boundaries of the district, but probably inflated McCurdy's percentage by no more than 2%.

McCurdy's biggest decisions in 1981 were committee assignments and how to vote on the Reagan economic programs. He seems to have made the right decisions. He got on the Armed Services and Science and Technology Committees. The former is of practical importance to the district, and McCurdy's own hawkish policies are in line with district opinion. The latter is a possible political asset in Norman and the Oklahoma City area, where people are aware that, if oil prices drop, they will need some high technology here to continue the advance in their standard of living. On the economic policies, McCurdy went against the Democratic leadership on the budget in 1981, but with it on taxes that year; since 1981 he has generally gone along with fellow Democrats, including fellow Oklahoman James Jones. It seems to have been a popular choice, even in the state with the nation's lowest unemployment rate. After the 1982 election, McCurdy seems firmly entrenched in the House and on the brink of a long career there—unless he should run for the Senate in 1986.

The People Pop. 1980: 505,974, up 17.1% 1970–80; voting age pop. 367,630; 6% Black, 3% Span. orig., 3% Am. Ind., 1% Asian orig. 28% housing units rented. Median owner $37,200; renter $181. Households: 77% family, 44% with children, 67% married couples.

Presidential Vote

1980	Reagan (R)	99,418	(62%)
	Carter (D)	60,533	(38%)

Rep. Dave McCurdy (D) Elected 1980; b. Mar. 30, 1950, Canadian, TX; home, Norman; U. of OK, B.A. 1972, J.D. 1975; Lutheran.

Career OK Asst. Atty. Gen., 1975–77; Practicing atty., 1977–80.

Offices 313 CHOB, 202-225-6165. Also 207 W. Main St., Norman 73069, 405-329-6500; and 103 Fed. Bldg., Lawton 73501, 405-357-2131.

Committees *Armed Services* (18th). Subcommittees: Procurement and Military Nuclear Systems; Readiness. *Science and Technology* (16th). Subcommittees: Energy Development and Applications; Science, Research and Technology. *Permanent Select Committee on Intelligence* (9th). Subcommittee: Program and Budget Authorization.

Group Ratings

	ADA	ACLU	COPE	CFA	LCV	LWV	NTU	NSI	COC	ACA	CSFC
1982	25	42	50	38	54	42	56	100	62	64	53
1981	35	—	60	36	43	—	33	—	37	57	55

National Journal Ratings

	Economic		Foreign		Cultural	
1982	43%	(LIB)	44%	(LIB)	34%	(LIB)
	57%	(CONS)	56%	(CONS)	65%	(CONS)
1981	55%	(LIB)	18%	(LIB)	57%	(LIB)
	45%	(CONS)	73%	(CONS)	43%	(CONS)

Key Votes

1) Reagan 81 Budget	AGN	5) Incr SS Rtmt Age	FOR	9) Poor Pay Food Stamps	AGN
2) Reagan 81 Tax Cut	FOR	6) Saudi AWACS Sale	AGN	10) Ban Crt Busing Order	FOR
3) Bal Budget Amend	FOR	7) $ for MX Missile	AGN	11) Auto Local Content	FOR
4) Gas & Road Tax	AGN	8) Nerve Gas Prod	AGN	12) Nuclear Arms Freeze	AGN

Election Results

1982 general	Dave McCurdy (D)	84,205	(65%)	($326,781)
	Howard Rutledge (R)	44,351	(34%)	($233,043)
1982 primary	Dave McCurdy (D) unopposed			
1980 general	Dave McCurdy (D)	74,245	(51%)	($229,248)
	Howard Rutledge (R)	71,339	(49%)	($159,115)

Campaign Contributions and Expenditures

1981-82		Direct Cont. 81-82		PACS brkdwn			
Receipts	$333,738	Indiv	$213,039	Agr	$12,000	Ideo	$10,800
Expend.	$326,781	Party	$2,887	Bus	$65,490	Lbr	$9,825
Unspent	$10,073	PACS	$111,336	Hlth	$5,800	Prof	$1,650

FIFTH DISTRICT

Oklahoma City is the capital of Oklahoma and its largest city, with a metropolitan population of more than 500,000. During the 1960s the city fathers decided that they would not let the old city limits become a straitjacket, cutting off Oklahoma City from the prosperity and growth of the suburbs. So they annexed so much territory that Oklahoma City spills over into five counties and four congressional districts, and includes hundreds of acres which even today are farm or fallow land. Like Tulsa, Oklahoma City got most of its wealth and growth from oil; on the grounds of the state Capitol are a few wells pumping away. Like most cities in the Southwest, particularly oil cities, Oklahoma City is, on the whole, very hostile to federal regulation and is Republican in national elections.

In the early 1980s, the oil boom here transformed much of Oklahoma City. Its once small downtown is now replete with numerous towering high-rises, and the city's parking lots are full of the luxury cars of its dozens of new—and sometimes temporary—millionaires. Oklahoma City was the scene in 1982 of the collapse of the Penn Square Bank—whose story tells a lot about the boom here. The bank itself was headquartered (and named after) a shopping center; yet a vice president in his early 30s managed to make hundreds of millions of dollars in loans to oil drillers, many of them of dubious creditworthiness, and the bank then sold the loans to some of the nation's largest financial institutions. He was helped by eccentric habits—he was reputed to drink beer out of one of his boots—that evidently convinced the city slickers that they had stumbled onto the real thing. So for awhile you could find in Oklahoma City the atmosphere you always find on a frontier when it seems suddenly very easy to become very rich.

The 5th congressional district of Oklahoma includes most of Oklahoma City, but it is a carefully chosen part: the most Democratic parts of the city, including its black areas, are chopped off and included in Democratic districts. The 5th is intended to be Republican. Besides the prosperous parts of Oklahoma City, it goes north to include wheat-growing counties to the north, the market town of Ponca City, which is as Republican as any similar-sized town in nearby Kansas, and, connected by a strip of mostly uninhabited Osage County, the well-to-do oil town of Bartlesville, headquarters of Phillips Petroleum. This is, in effect, a collection of urban Republican voting precincts stitched together by swaths of thinly populated rural territory.

The direct beneficiary of this is Congressman Mickey Edwards. First elected in 1976, he is one of the leaders of the ideological right in Congress. His career is as a writer and a public relations man rather than as a businessman, but he is one who talks of the importance of private investment; as a sophisticated politician he praises traditional moral and family values. Edwards is Chairman of the American Conservative Union and a spokesman for the New Right. He is less concerned about the details of committee work—he serves on Appropriations—than he is about spreading the ideas which he has, with some success, been advancing since the middle 1970s.

Edwards, who turns 47 in 1984, is the oldest member of the unusually youthful Oklahoma congressional delegation. He had his best chance to run for the Senate in 1980 and passed it by. Don Nickles, a politician of similar views but much less articulateness and experience, won the seat. Perhaps Edwards, who has stirred up controversy in the past, would not have done so well. At any rate, he seems to have a safe seat in the House and as solid a platform as he could hope for.

The People   Pop. 1980: 502,974, up 17.1% 1970–80; voting age pop. 367,630; 5% Black, 2% Span. orig., 3% Am. Ind., 1% Asian orig. 28% housing units rented. Median owner $43,600; renter $199. Households: 71% family, 37% with children, 61% married couples.

Presidential Vote

1980	Reagan (R)	NA
	Carter (D)	NA
	Anderson (I)	NA

Rep. Mickey Edwards (R) Elected 1976; b. July 12, 1937, Oklahoma City; home, Oklahoma City; U. of OK, B.S. 1958, OK City U., J.D. 1969; Episcopal.

Career Practicing atty.; Reporter and editor, *Private Practice* magazine; Pub. rel. exec., 1973–76.

Offices 2434 RHOB, 202-225-2132. Also 215 3d St., N.W., Oklahoma City 73102, 405-231-4541.

Committee *Appropriations* (15th). Subcommittees: Foreign Operations; Military Construction.

Group Ratings

	ADA	ACLU	COPE	CFA	LCV	LWV	NTU	NSI	COC	ACA	CSFC
1982	5	8	7	8	25	33	88	100	81	90	74
1981	5	—	8	29	14	—	91	—	79	88	75
1980	17	27	6	14	31	33	64	100	78	83	79

National Journal Ratings

	Economic		Foreign		Cultural	
1982	5%	(LIB)	31%	(LIB)	20%	(LIB)
	95%	(CONS)	69%	(CONS)	79%	(CONS)
1981	24%	(LIB)	3%	(LIB)	4%	(LIB)
	68%	(CONS)	87%	(CONS)	90%	(CONS)

Key Votes

1) Reagan 81 Budget	FOR	5) Incr SS Rtmt Age	FOR	9) Poor Pay Food Stamps	FOR
2) Reagan 81 Tax Cut	FOR	6) Saudi AWACS Sale	FOR	10) Ban Crt Busing Order	FOR
3) Bal Budget Amend	—	7) $ for MX Missile	FOR	11) Auto Local Content	AGN
4) Gas & Road Tax	AGN	8) Nerve Gas Prod	AGN	12) Nuclear Arms Freeze	AGN

Election Results

1982 general	Mickey Edwards (R)	98,979	(67%)	($232,247)
	Dan Lane (D)	42,453	(29%)	($50,891)
1982 primary	Mickey Edwards (R) unopposed			
1980 general	Mickey Edwards (R)	90,053	(68%)	($300,211)
	David Hood (D)	36,815	(28%)	($50,413)

Campaign Contributions and Expenditures

1981-82		Direct Cont. 81-82		PACS brkdwn			
Receipts	$231,046	Indiv	$149,020	Agr	$1,550	Ideo	$4,050
Expend.	$232,247	Party	$6,830	Bus	$54,656	Lbr	$500
Unspent	$4,107	PACS	$64,606	Hlth	$3,450	Prof	$400

SIXTH DISTRICT

The 6th congressional district of Oklahoma occupies the northwestern and west central parts of the state. It includes the thin panhandle that goes west to touch the borders of Colorado and New Mexico. The 6th is almost entirely small town and rural, with the notable exception of its portion of Oklahoma City. But it has been anything but an unexciting place to live in the late 1970s and early 1980s. For this has been the site of the Anadarko Basin, one of the major natural gas and oil finds of the great mineral exploration that followed OPEC's raising of oil prices in 1973 and 1979. This boom has created almost a mining camp atmosphere in some small towns of this region, like Elk City and Hammon.

The oil and gas boom of this area has fortified the Republican leanings it has had since it was first settled, following the opening up of Oklahoma, in 1889. This was always wheat country, and was settled by farmers moving south from Kansas. They came with large families and high hopes, but the Dust Bowl of the 1930s swept their topsoil into the air and led many families and children to move elsewhere to make a living. From 1907 to 1970, the population of the counties wholly included in the 6th district declined from 360,000 to 282,000. The gas and oil boom has turned that around; in the 1970s there was in-migration and their population was raised to 308,000.

Despite the Republican leanings of most of this district, it elects a Democratic congressman. He has been aided by redistricting, which carefully included a part of Oklahoma City which is 25% black and contains most of the city's white working-class areas; but these Democratic votes were added only in 1982. Before that, the district was kept in the Democratic column by the personal popularity and the conservative issues stands of Congressman Glenn English.

English was once an aide to liberal Democrats in the California Assembly, but you wouldn't know it from his voting record. His Oklahoma credentials are in order: he grew up here and served as executive director of the state Democratic Party before he ran for Congress in 1974. On economic and foreign issues, his profile is quite conservative; on cultural issues, mixed. Perhaps his greatest political achievement so far was to seize a propitious moment—just four days before the showdown on the 1981 Reagan tax cut—and extract from Ronald Reagan, in a letter in his own handwriting, a commitment to veto "with pleasure" any windfall profits tax on natural gas. That promise effectively protected that otherwise vulnerable revenue source in 1982, when Republicans were scrambling around looking for politically painless ways to, in the phrase of the day, enhance revenues.

English serves on the Agriculture Committee, which of course is of great interest to this wheat-growing district. He also serves on Government Operations, and chairs a subcommittee on Government Information, Justice, and (sic) Agriculture. The addition of the "Agriculture" may be an attempt to conceal from his constituents the fact that he has spent considerable time on the difficult and important, but not at all parochial, problems of government computers, individual privacy, and the Freedom of Information Act. National

Republicans, apparently respectful of English's strength, have not really targeted him, and he wins reelection by huge margins.

The People   Pop. 1980: 503,291, up 4.1% 1970–80; voting age pop. 361,309; 9% Black, 2% Span. orig., 3% Am. Ind. 27% housing units rented. Median owner $32,500; renter $152. Households: 73% family, 38% with children, 62% married couples.

Presidential Vote

1980	Reagan (R)	NA
	Carter (D)	NA

Rep. Glenn English (D) Elected 1974; b. Nov. 30, 1940, Cordell; home, Cordell; Southwestern St. Col., B.A. 1964; Methodist.

Career Chf. Asst., Major. Caucus, CA Assembly; Exec. Dir., OK Dem. Party, 1969–73; Petroleum leasing business.

Offices 2235 RHOB, 202-225-5565. Also 410 Maple St., Yukon 73099, 405-354-8638.

Committees *Agriculture* (10th). Subcommittees: Conservation, Credit, and Rural Development; Cotton, Rice, and Sugar; Tobacco and Peanuts; Wheat, Soybeans, and Feed Grains. *Government Operations* (6th). Subcommittee: Government Information, Justice, and Agriculture (Chairman).

Group Ratings

	ADA	ACLU	COPE	CFA	LCV	LWV	NTU	NSI	COC	ACA	CSFC
1982	20	42	27	38	42	33	67	90	77	61	58
1981	25	—	26	43	21	—	54	—	53	58	58
1980	6	13	26	21	22	13	47	100	65	63	59

National Journal Ratings

	Economic		Foreign		Cultural	
1982	46%	(LIB)	33%	(LIB)	21%	(LIB)
	53%	(CONS)	67%	(CONS)	76%	(CONS)
1981	48%	(LIB)	43%	(LIB)	54%	(LIB)
	52%	(CONS)	56%	(CONS)	46%	(CONS)

Key Votes

1) Reagan 81 Budget	AGN	5) Incr SS Rtmt Age	FOR	9) Poor Pay Food Stamps	AGN
2) Reagan 81 Tax Cut	FOR	6) Saudi AWACS Sale	AGN	10) Ban Crt Busing Order	FOR
3) Bal Budget Amend	FOR	7) $ for MX Missile	AGN	11) Auto Local Content	FOR
4) Gas & Road Tax	AGN	8) Nerve Gas Prod	FOR	12) Nuclear Arms Freeze	AGN

Election Results

1982 general	Glenn English (D)	102,811	(75%)	($206,101)
	Ed Moore (R)	33,519	(25%)	($141,382)
1982 primary	Glenn English (D) unopposed			
1980 general	Glenn English (D)	111,694	(65%)	($81,837)
	Carol McCurley (R)	60,980	(35%)	($0)

Campaign Contributions and Expenditures

1981-82		Direct Cont. 81-82		PACS brkdwn			
Receipts	$214,443	Indiv	$99,040	Agr	$22,700	Ideo	$1,250
Expend.	$206,101	Party	$2,515	Bus	$58,815	Lbr	$3,700
Unspent	$80,939	PACS	$94,314	Hlth	$4,900	Prof	$1,500

OREGON

Oregon is a state going through a painful readjustment. People here thought in the 1970s they had developed a distinctive way of life, that Oregon had become a progressive common-wealth, geographically far from the rest of the United States, proud of its special environment and determined to use the wealth it had produced to preserve it. The four-year recessionary period starting in 1979 has changed all that. Oregon was one of the nation's leaders in questioning the value of endless economic growth, and suggesting that growth should be modulated by concern for other things. Its attitudes were suggested by Governor Tom McCall, who served between 1966 and 1974, when he urged people to come to Oregon to visit, "but for heaven's sake don't come to live here." Now migration into Oregon has stopped, but no one is happy about the reasons, and all seek somehow to restore the conditions they used to complain about.

The economic growth which Oregon used to take for granted and no longer enjoys depended, ultimately, on lumber. The moist, damp winds from the Pacific Ocean dump America's heaviest rains over the western mountains and slopes of the Pacific Northwest, and here grow some of America's largest forests. The New England Yankees who came overland on the Oregon Trail and were Oregon's first permanent white settlers wanted to be farmers, and they staked out lands in the fertile Willamette Valley. But it was a long way from Oregon to market, and as a practical matter Oregon's most profitable products for many years were furs and lumber. Even today, lumber companies provide a large percentage of the state's employment, and its whole economy is sensitive to fluctuations in the demand for it. And they can be huge. The demand for the product depends on the level of new construction, which in turn depends on interest rates; and the high interest rates which were the nation's principal defense against inflation during the 1979–83 recession also devastated the housing and lumber industries.

In past recessions, during Republican administrations, the response of Oregon voters was to call in the Democrats. But what is striking is that in 1980 and 1982 they did not do that. Oregon went for Ronald Reagan in 1980, though it gave him his lowest percentage in the western states; and in the same year it ousted the chairman of the House Ways and Means Committee for a Reagan Republican. In 1982 it reelected Governor Victor Atiyeh, long identified as a conservative Republican, by a large margin over a Democrat who had already proven himself attractive to voters. In addition, Oregon Republicans won a new House seat and gave one of Oregon's most talented Democratic officeholders his closest race in years.

One should not conclude from this that Oregon has completely repudiated the politics symbolized by McCall. It remains a culturally liberal state on many issues; there are a relatively large number of young and single voters here, and Oregon tends to look favorably on allowing abortions, on decriminalizing marijuana, on banning throwaway glass bottles and cans. And it remains interested in preserving its environment. What is different is its priorities, and the balance between environmental and economic conditions. Oregon voters now seem to value highly the economic growth they once took for granted—or regarded as a foreboding of incipient California-ization. They are willing to sacrifice a little more of their environment in order to encourage growth. It is partly a matter of changing values, partly just a matter of shifting the balance.

Oregon seems to have reached these conclusions not after dialectical struggle, but through the emergence of a consensus. Unlike most states, it does not have long-standing political differences between different regions. It is true that the coastal areas and the lower Columbia River valley are marginally more Democratic than the rest of the state, and that Salem, the state capital, is usually more Republican than Eugene, the site of the University of Oregon. Also, the low-lying, less affluent sections of Portland east of the Willamette River are usually Democratic, while the more affluent city neighborhoods and suburbs in the hills in the west tend to be Republican. But there is not all that much difference between the areas, and not the kind of contrast in cultural lifestyles you find in California. The longhaired young here like to backpack and think of themselves as middle class; so do blue-collar workers and affluent people in the high-income suburbs.

Governor. In retrospect, the election of Governor Victor Atiyeh in 1978 seems more of a mark of change in Oregon politics than appeared at the time. Atiyeh beat both of his predecessors, men of similar ideas—Republican Tom McCall in the primary, Democrat Bob Straub in the general election. Atiyeh was careful to campaign as a supporter, not an opponent of environmental measures: no James Watt rhetoric here. But he also said he was a proponent of cutting government spending and taxes. As the recession wore on, and Oregon's unemployment rose up past 11%, Atiyeh angrily called on President Reagan and Budget Director Stockman to lower interest rates. And in the fall he campaigned harshly against his Democratic opponent, Ted Kulongoski, claiming that Democratic policies would repel business and discourage economic diversification.

The argument—and Atiyeh's steady, usually calm personality—seemed to be compelling. Kulongoski was a serious candidate, a good campaigner who had held Senator Bob Packwood to a 52%–44% victory in 1980. But Atiyeh won by a 61%–36% margin. It was a bigger victory than McCall, Straub, or Mark Hatfield ever won in a gubernatorial race—the highest margin since 1950, when Oregon was pretty close to being a one-party Republican state.

Senators. Oregon has two longtime Republican senators who chair important committees. But neither operates with the kind of clout some Democrats have exercised in their posts, and neither has won his races in Oregon, when faced with significant opposition, by the kind of overwhelming margins that their personal strengths and issue stands would lead one to suspect. In a pattern common when a state is represented by two senators of the same party and same place in the ideological spectrum, they are not especially close friends nor are they political allies.

The senior senator is Mark Hatfield, Chairman of the Senate Appropriations Committee, and holder of statewide office in Oregon since 1956, when he was only 34 years old. Two years later he was elected governor, and served for eight years; promptly in 1966 he was elected to the Senate, and has been there ever since. The issue that Hatfield has always cared most about is peace. He is a deeply religious man, and as a young serviceman was one of the first

Americans to see Hiroshima after it was bombed. That experience—and deep convictions—have left him as a strong proponent of disarmament and of understandings with our adversaries. He was the cosponsor of the McGovern–Hatfield amendment to end the Vietnam war in the early 1970s; he is an enthusiastic backer of the nuclear freeze in the 1980s. As Appropriations chairman, he uses what leverage he has to hold down defense spending increases. He is no unilateral disarmer, but he is skeptical about the worth of weapons systems and fearful that stockpiles of arms or large conscript armies will be used to make war. Hatfield is not the kind of senator who will use every trick in the book to get his way, and he will let his fellow Republicans have their chance to vote increases he thinks unwise. But he will not be working with the administration on the defense spending increases it believes are so important.

On other issues Hatfield is not so far from the Reagan administration as some believe. He is not an unqualified believer in free market economics, but he has long—long before the current slump in the lumber industry—favored measures to give the lumber companies more access to Oregon's forests than many environmentalists would like. He is not an enthusiast for most domestic spending programs. On cultural issues, his strong religious beliefs do not make him join forces usually with the New Right. But neither is he an enthusiast for the latest form of cultural liberation. As chairman of Appropriations, Hatfield heads the committee which, theoretically, must authorize all federal spending. But in practice the Budget Committee has been encroaching on Appropriations' powers. Hatfield has tried to resist that, and to get Appropriations to do its work in an orderly, timely manner, so that it is less likely to be left out of the process. But the *modus operandi* of the committee under his predecessor, Warren Magnuson of Washington, was to raise the amounts appropriated by the House, especially for projects favored senators were interested in; Hatfield, who would like to keep greater control over spending even if there were no restrictions in the budget process, would not be inclined to operate that way.

Hatfield comes up for reelection in 1984, and with his high position and evident popularity—he was reelected easily in 1978—he would seem to be a shoo-in. But it is not clear that he will run and, if he does, not clear that he will win big. There is some talk that, at 62, and with Republican prospects for maintaining control not good, Hatfield may choose to retire. The pursuit of power does not seem to be an end in itself for him, and he may, as other colleagues have, think it a good idea to start another career while he is still in the prime of life. As for his standing in Oregon, the 1978 result reflected the weakness of his opponent. His position as chairman would surely be an asset in 1984, but he still has the problem most Oregon members of Congress do: it's a long way, at least nine hours on the plane, from Washington, D.C., to Portland, and longer to get to any other part of the state. Hatfield has consistently made 10 to 12 trips home every year, and traveled to all parts of the state; but in a nation that is increasingly used to having its congressmen back in the district 26 to 52 weekends a year 12 trips may not seem like a lot. It may be unfair for voters to expect more: Hatfield has important work to do in Washington and is surely entitled to some leisure time. But he is vulnerable, as most Oregon incumbents are, to attacks by challengers who promise to return more often.

Possible Democratic contenders for this seat include 1st district Congressman Les AuCoin and former Portland Mayor and Transportation Secretary Neil Goldschmidt, now an executive for the Oregon-based Nike shoe company. Both have demonstrated strong vote-getting ability and appeal to the affluent young people who have been the fastest growing part of Oregon's electorate. On the Republican side, if Hatfield doesn't run, one contender might be Attorney General Dave Frohnmayr. Hatfield, however, has had a lucky as well as accomplished political career; and the apparent Republican trend of 1978–82, if it continues, could dim the prospects of possible Democratic opponents and improve his own so much that he might draw only nuisance opposition, as he did last time. This is one of those Senate races whose outcome may depend more on maneuvering and decisions made in late 1983 and early 1984 than in the campaigning that takes place the following fall.

Oregon's junior senator is Bob Packwood. A surprise winner when he ran, at age 32, against four-term incumbent Wayne Morse in 1968, Packwood is now an established fixture in the Senate and a man of some importance in national politics. His most important role in the Senate now is as Chairman of the Commerce, Science, and Transportation Committee, a body with jurisdiction over most federal regulatory agencies and of surpassing interest to many regulated industries. It is not a position Packwood probably expected; in 1977 he was only fifth ranking member of the minority party on the committee, but as the result of retirements, defeats, and Republican capture of the Senate, he became chairman in 1981. To some extent, Commerce is a collection of baronies, with important regional lords (Goldwater on Communications, Danforth on Surface Transportation); it contains two units which once had in the Senate and still have in the House full committee status (Merchant Marine and Science, Technology and Space). Packwood gets along with his barons better than King John did, and he has helped the committee to move toward deregulation in various industries, including some which oppose it (*e.g.,* trucking).

Packwood has other distinctions. In the early 1970s he was the Senate's leading advocate of zero population growth, and in the late 1970s he became its leading opponent of bans on abortion. The Senate still, despite New Right gains, is the branch of government least inclined to restrict abortions; Packwood has proven skillful at using parliamentary devices to rally the majority he has on this issue in the face of attacks from Jesse Helms and others. That issue has also been a major electoral asset to Packwood. Women's rights advocates made his reelection their number one priority in 1980, and they in turn probably were the single biggest bloc of contributors—through a successful direct mail drive—to his campaign, which he won by a smaller-than-expected margin. Packwood also achieved distinction as Chairman of the Republican Senate Campaign Committee, most recently for the 1982 elections; he is one of those who put together the fundraising capability and technical services which have been crucial in giving the Republicans control of the Senate. But he failed in his effort to win another term in 1983, and he was bitter when Richard Lugar, with White House backing, won.

Actually, it is against custom for one senator to chair the campaign committee in two consecutive elections, and the White House had good reason to be peeved with Packwood. While chairman, he made statements sharply critical of the administration and the party for allegedly writing off women, blacks, and Jews; shortly afterwards, the White House ordered the scrapping of eight million fundraising letters featuring favorable mention of Packwood. Later, shortly after losing the chairmanship, Packwood scheduled a tour of New England, purportedly to talk about the future of the Republican Party. Reporters followed him up there, on the theory that he must be considering running for president; he twitted them and said they would only cover what he said if he traveled to New England rather than staying in Washington. Packwood's comments about the need to revitalize the Republican Party by getting support from women and blacks sound a lot like the warmed-over strategic advice of partisans of Nelson Rockefeller, and ignore the fact that Richard Nixon and Ronald Reagan won three of the last four presidential elections while paying that advice no heed. On occasion Packwood has been much more original; he was the real originator of the yearly Tidewater talks, when Republican officeholders from around the country, wearing sweaters and using first names, meet on Maryland's Eastern Shore and try to share the new ideas they have had about policy. There is no doubt about his commitment to the Republican Party, nor to free market economics; he seems ambitious to lead the party rather than ready to leave it.

Packwood is generally considered a popular senator, yet he won reelection in 1974 and 1980 by margins that have to be considered unimpressive. In both elections, particularly the latter, he had the advantage of substantially outspending his opponents, who were not well known statewide to begin with. Yet he won in 1980 over Ted Kulongoski by only a 52%–44% margin. True, Packwood ran ahead of Reagan, who got 48% of the vote in Oregon, but with his reputation and experience one would have expected him to run ahead much further. The distance factor may be playing a part here, and it is possible that Packwood's chairmanship—the ability it gives him to help the state, and to raise money for his campaign—will help him electorally in Oregon. But he can't count on having a free ride in Oregon in 1986 and will probably have to campaign hard to keep his seat.

Congressional districts. Oregon gained a fifth congressional district in 1982; it was one of two districts carried by Republicans. For a while, Democrats held all the seats, through a combination of partisan strength and personal popularity that couldn't last. Again, the distance factor makes it hard for even the most conscientious and attractive congressman to keep winning by the kinds of percentages that members whose districts are within two hours of Washington National Airport can count on.

Presidential politics. Oregon, with seven electoral votes, and geographically closer to Vancouver, British Columbia, than it is to any population concentration in 47 of the states, does not see much of presidential candidates in general elections. It does, however, see some of their ads. The original Yankee settlers made this a Republican state, often the most Republican in the West (it went for Dewey, for example, when most of the West was for Truman). But on the non-economic issues of the Vietnam war and the environment, Oregon shifted left: it was one of George McGovern's best states and came within 2,000 votes of going for Jimmy Carter in 1976. The question for 1984 is whether the increasing importance of economic growth to voters here is going to make Oregon more Republican in presidential elections as it apparently has in state and congressional races. There is that possibility, if national Republicans approach the economic and environmental issues as sensitively as Victor Atiyeh has. But the Democrats will try to identify them with James Watt, and if they do Oregon will probably be one of the most Democratic states in the west.

Oregon's presidential primary, coming in late May, was once one of the nation's most important. It ended Harold Stassen's career as a serious presidential candidate in 1948, when he lost 52%–48% to Thomas Dewey, and it administered to Robert Kennedy his only defeat in 1968. Oregon in those days was part of a West Coast swing, since it came just before the California primary; in a nation when campaigners were not yet used to flying all over the country they, like National Football League teams in the 1950s, scheduled West Coast contests together, to minimize travel time. By 1980 Oregon seemed to come too late in the season and to have too few delegates at stake to earn much attention; and barring some very close races that will be the case in 1984. The Republican primary electorate, incidentally, though far more conservative than it used to be, gave Ronald Reagan one of his lowest percentages in western primaries; the Democratic primary tends to back liberal candidates.

The People   Est. Pop. 1982: 2,649,000; Pop. 1980: 2,633,105, up 0.6% 1980–82 and 25.9% 1970–80; 1.2% of U.S. total, 30th largest; voting age pop. 1,910,048; 2% Spanish origin, 1% American Indian, 1% Black, 1% Asian origin. Single ancestry: 10% English, 9% German, 4% Irish, 2% Norwegian, 1% Swedish, French, Scottish, Italian, Dutch. Registered voters (1982): 1,516,589 Total. 751,100 D (50%); 551,718 R (36%); 213,771 I (14%). 20% with 1–3 yrs. col., 17% with 4+ yrs. col. 11.3% below poverty level. 32% housing units rented; median house value: $59,000; median monthly rent: $212. Households: 70% family, 37% with children, 60% married couples.

1982 Share of Federal Tax Burden $6,566,700,000; 1.10% of U.S. total, 29th largest.

1982 Share of Federal Expenditures

	Total		Non-Defense		Defense	
Total Expend	$5,510m	(0.91%)	$5,003m	(1.18%)	$507m	(0.28%)
St/Lcl Grants	1,168m	(1.32%)	1,168m	(1.32%)	0m	(0%)
Salary/Wages	524m	(0.67%)	395m	(1.44%)	129m	(0.25%)
Ind Payments	3,372m	(1.18%)	3,036m	(1.18%)	336m	(1.18%)
Procurement	395m	(0.27%)	168m	(0.53%)	227m	(0.20%)
Other Programs	52m	(0.96%)	52m	(0.97%)	0m	(0%)
Loan/Insurance	420m	(0.66%)	418m	(0.68%)	2m	(0.09%)

Political Lineup   Governor, Victor G. Atiyeh (R). Senators, Mark O. Hatfield (R) and Robert W. Packwood (R). Representatives, 5 (3 D and 2 R). State Senate, 30 (21 D and 9 R); State House of Representatives, 60 (36 D and 24 R).

Presidential Vote

1980	Reagan (R)	571,044	(48%)
	Carter (D)	456,890	(39%)
	Anderson (I)	112,389	(10%)
1976	Ford (R)	492,120	(48%)
	Carter (D)	490,407	(48%)

1980 Democratic Presidential Primary			*1980 Republican Presidential Primary*		
Carter	208,693	(58%)	Reagan	170,449	(54%)
Kennedy	114,651	(32%)	Bush	109,210	(35%)
Brown	34,409	(10%)	Anderson	32,118	(10%)
			Crane	2,324	(1%)

SENATORS

Sen. Mark O. Hatfield (R) Elected 1966, seat up 1984; b. July 12, 1922, Dallas; home, Newport; Willamette U., B.A. 1943, Stanford U., A.M. 1948; Baptist.

Career Navy, WWII; Assoc. Prof. of Poli. Sci., Willamette U., 1949–56, Dean of Students, 1950–56; OR House of Reps., 1950–54; OR Senate, 1954–56; Secy. of State of OR, 1956–58; Gov. of OR, 1958–66.

Offices 322 HSOB, 202-224-3753. Also 475 Cottage St. N.E., Salem 97301, 503-399-5731; and 105 Pioneer Courthouse, Portland 97204, 503-221-3386.

Committees *Appropriations* (Chairman). Subcommittees: Energy and Water Development (Chairman); Commerce, Justice, State, the Judiciary; Foreign Operations; Labor, Health and Human Services, Education; Legislative Branch. *Energy and Natural Resources* (2d). Subcommittees: Energy Conservation and Supply; Public Lands and Reserved Water; Water and Power. *Rules and Administration* (2d). *Joint Committee on the Library* (2d). *Joint Committee on Printing* (2d).

Group Ratings

	ADA	ACLU	COPE	CFA	LCV	LWV	NTU	NSI	COC	ACA	CSFC
1982	60	71	52	50	29	55	60	10	50	22	54
1981	55	—	53	36	44	—	66	—	88	38	62
1980	50	73	47	33	43	50	36	50	59	65	46

National Journal Ratings

	Economic		Foreign		Cultural	
1982	50%	(LIB)	84%	(LIB)	66%	(LIB)
	49%	(CONS)	15%	(CONS)	33%	(CONS)
1981	44%	(LIB)	71%	(LIB)	74%	(LIB)
	55%	(CONS)	28%	(CONS)	24%	(CONS)

Key Votes

1) Reagan 81 Budget	FOR	5) $ to El Salvador	AGN
2) Reagan 81 Tax Cut	FOR	6) Saudi AWACS Sale	AGN
3) Bal Budget Amend	FOR	7) Ban Abortion	FOR
4) Gas & Road Tax	—	8) Nerve Gas Prod	AGN

9) Poor Pay Food Stamps	AGN
10) Ban Crt Busing Order	AGN
11) Clinch Riv Brdr Rctr	AGN
12) Legal Services Corp	FOR

Election Results

1978 general	Mark O. Hatfield (R)	550,165	(62%)	($223,874)
	Vernon Cook (D)	341,616	(38%)	($38,976)
1978 primary	Mark O. Hatfield (R)	159,617	(66%)	
	Bert W. Hawkins (R)	43,350	(18%)	($64,574)
	Two others (R)	39,922	(16%)	
1972 general	Mark O. Hatfield (R)	494,671	(54%)	($299,626)
	Wayne L. Morse (D)	425,036	(46%)	($251,904)

Campaign Contributions and Expenditures

1977-78		PACS brkdwn			
Receipts	$277,059	Agr	$3,200	Ideo	$6,100
Expend.	$223,874	Bus	$51,883	Lbr	$13,150
Unspent	$53,181	Hlth	$9,700	Prof	$5,200

Sen. Robert W. (Bob) Packwood (R) Elected 1968, seat up 1986; b. Sept. 11, 1932, Portland; home, Portland; Willamette U., B.S. 1954, NYU, LL.B. 1957; Unitarian Universalist.

Career Practicing atty., 1958–68; OR House of Reps., 1962–68.

Offices 259 RSOB, 202-224-5244. Also 1002 N.E. Holladay St., P.O. Box 3621, Portland 97208, 503-233-4471.

Committees *Commerce, Science, and Transportation* (Chairman). Subcommittees: Business, Trade and Tourism; National Ocean Policy Study (Chairman). *Finance* (2d). Subcommittees: Health; Savings, Pensions, and Investment Policy; Taxation and Debt Management (Chairman). *Small Business* (2d). Subcommittees: Capital Formation and Retention (Chairman); Innovation and Technology. *Joint Committee on Taxation* (2d).

Group Ratings

	ADA	ACLU	COPE	CFA	LCV	LWV	NTU	NSI	COC	ACA	CSFC
1982	55	75	44	40	38	58	49	78	52	48	58
1981	35	—	44	29	25	—	54	—	94	50	71
1980	56	63	41	60	75	78	31	80	53	43	46

National Journal Ratings

	Economic		Foreign		Cultural	
1982	44%	(LIB)	61%	(LIB)	82%	(LIB)
	55%	(CONS)	38%	(CONS)	17%	(CONS)
1981	24%	(LIB)	47%	(LIB)	79%	(LIB)
	75%	(CONS)	52%	(CONS)	19%	(CONS)

Key Votes

1) Reagan 81 Budget	FOR	5) $ to El Salvador	FOR	9) Poor Pay Food Stamps	AGN
2) Reagan 81 Tax Cut	FOR	6) Saudi AWACS Sale	AGN	10) Ban Crt Busing Order	AGN
3) Bal Budget Amend	FOR	7) Ban Abortion	AGN	11) Clinch Riv Brdr Rctr	AGN
4) Gas & Road Tax	FOR	8) Nerve Gas Prod	AGN	12) Legal Services Corp	—

Election Results

1980 general	Robert W. (Bob) Packwood (R) ...	594,290	(52%)	($1,534,607)
	Ted Kulongoski (D)	501,963	(44%)	($190,047)
1980 primary	Robert W. (Bob) Packwood (R) ...	191,127	(62%)	
	Brenda Jose (R)	45,973	(15%)	
	Three others (R)	68,809	(22%)	
1974 general	Robert W. (Bob) Packwood (R) ...	420,984	(55%)	($333,004)
	Betty Roberts (D)	338,591	(44%)	($80,193)

Campaign Contributions and Expenditures

1979-80		PACS brkdwn			
Receipts	$1,555,990	Agr	$18,400	Ideo	$27,787
Expend.	$1,534,607	Bus	$211,861	Lbr	$57,394
Unspent	$26,041	Hlth	$27,600	Prof	$5,250

GOVERNOR

Gov. Victor G. Atiyeh (R) Elected 1978, term expires Jan. 1987; b. Feb. 20, 1923, Portland; home, Salem; U. of OR; Episcopal.

Career Pres., Atiyeh Bros., rug business; OR House of Reps., 1959–65; OR Senate, 1965–69.

Offices 207 State Capitol, Salem 97301, 503-378-3100.

Election Results

1982 gen.	Victor G. Atiyeh (R)	639,841	(61%)
	Ted Kulongoski (D)	374,316	(36%)
1982 prim.	Victor G. Atiyeh (R)	208,333	(83%)
	Clif Everett (R)	17,741	(7%)
	Walter Huss (R)	16,892	(7%)
1978 gen.	Victor G. Atiyeh (R)	498,452	(55%)
	Robert W. Straub (D)	409,411	(45%)

FIRST DISTRICT

The 1st congressional district of Oregon occupies the northwestern corner of the state. It includes the area around the mouth of the Columbia River and the coastal counties of Clatsop, Tillamook, and Lincoln. The countryside here still has a frontier ambience to it: rain falls constantly on the weathered frame houses, and men in plaid flannel jackets work in lumber mills and on docks. The towns have an unfinished look to them, as if they were villages in the late 19th century, waiting for a railroad hookup or a new factory to make one of them into one of Oregon's major cities. The 1st district also includes part of the Willamette Valley south of Portland. This has long been farmland, the most fertile land in the state, settled by Yankees in the middle 19th century. But in recent years, areas close to Portland have had an influx of settlers from the metropolitan area, people looking for wider spaces, closer access to the countryside, and, sometimes, a more traditional atmosphere in which to raise their families.

That is the historical 1st district, the descendant of a congressional district first established in 1892. But there is also a newer 1st district, which was largely unsettled then; this is in the

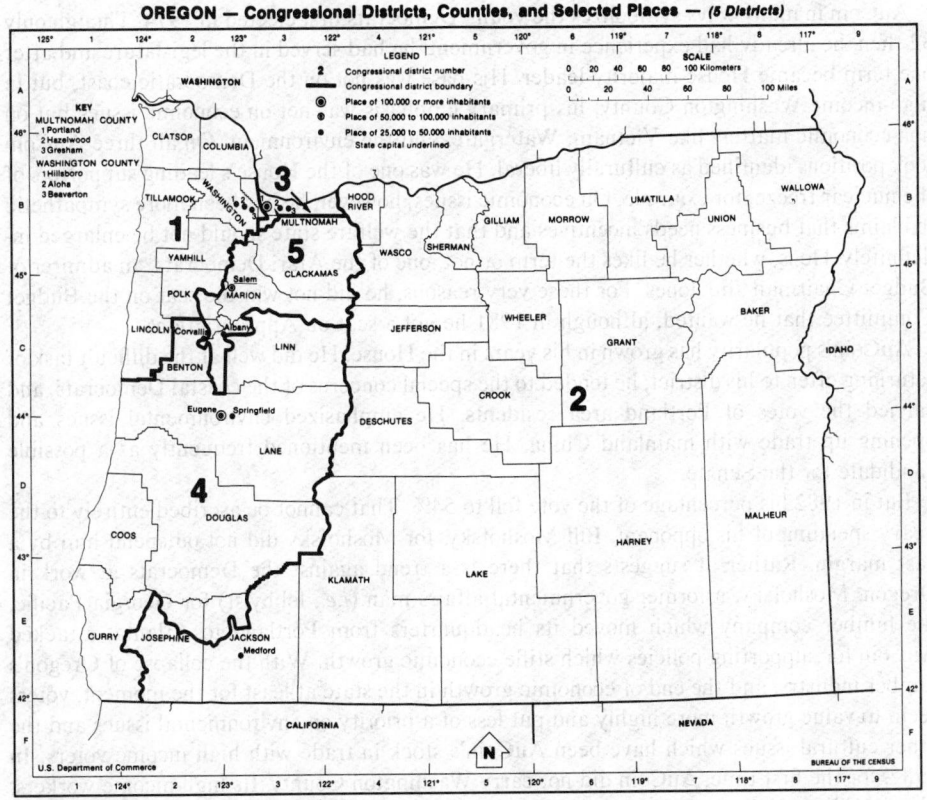

OREGON — Congressional Districts, Counties, and Selected Places — (5 Districts)

Congressional districts established July 26, 1961; all other boundaries are as of January 1, 1980.

Portland metropolitan area, and it includes most of the current 1st district's population. The district includes the part of the city of Portland west of the Willamette River. Geographically it is the smaller part of the city; there is only a little flat land before the hills start to rise. But the district includes both the downtown business section and the affluent neighborhoods in the hills overlooking it.

Nearly half the district's population is in Washington County, directly west of Portland. This was once a valley full of farms, separated from Portland and the Willamette by the hills. In the years since 1945 it has been filling up with comfortable subdivisions and grew rapidly all through the 1970s. This is an affluent, but not an exclusive area; a home for engineers rather than top executives, for middle managers rather than civic leaders. There is developing here a small version of the computer and microchip industry like California's Silicon Valley, and physically this is the same kind of place: at the foot of mountains, woodsy and even rustic, but outfitted with all the comforts and services of modern civilization.

The 1st district was created in 1892, and for 82 years elected only Republican congressmen. For years the Yankee-descended farmers of the Willamette Valley outvoted the lumbermen and fishermen on the coast. But in 1974 this district elected Democrat Les AuCoin, who has held this seat ever since. The question now is whether the 1st district is undergoing another change of attitude, which will result in another party shift in the years ahead.

AuCoin in many ways symbolizes the young Democrats first elected in 1974. Though only 32 then, he already had experience in government: he had served in the legislature and after one term became House majority leader. His base was not on the Democratic coast, but in high-income Washington County; his primary emphasis was not on economic issues but on non-economic matters like Vietnam, Watergate, and the environment. On all three AuCoin took positions identified as culturally liberal. He was one of the House's leading supporters of the nuclear freeze, for example. On economic issues, however, he has been more sympathetic to claims that business needs incentives and that the welfare state should not be enlarged indefinitely. He is, whether he likes the term or not, one of the Atari Democrats, an admirer of Budget Chairman Jim Jones. For those very reasons, he did not win the seat on the Budget Committee that he wanted, although in 1981 he got a seat on Appropriations.

AuCoin's popularity has grown in his years in the House. He did well at the difficult task of returning often to his district; he tended to the special concerns of the coastal Democrats, and carried the votes of Portland area residents. He emphasized environmental issues and opening up trade with mainland China. He has been mentioned frequently as a possible candidate for the Senate.

But in 1982 his percentage of the vote fell to 54%. That cannot be ascribed entirely to the heavy spending of his opponent, Bill Moshofsky, for Moshofsky did not outspend him by a vast margin. Rather, it suggests that there is a trend against the Democrats at work in Oregon. Moshofsky, a former governmental affairs man (*i.e.*, lobbyist) for Georgia Pacific, the lumber company which moved its headquarters from Portland to Atlanta, attacked AuCoin for supporting policies which stifle economic growth. With the collapse of Oregon's lumber industry, and the end of economic growth in the state at least for the moment, voters seem to value growth more highly and put less of a priority on environmental issues and the other cultural issues which have been AuCoin's stock in trade with high income voters. In 1982, for the first time, AuCoin did not carry Washington County. Its high-income workers, like the Silicon Valley voters who elected freshman Congressman Ed Zschau, evidently feel a

Republican can do a better job of handling and facilitating the transition to the computer age we seem to be going through.

Still, AuCoin has the potential to be a strong statewide candidate and continues to be a favorite to win reelection in the 1st district. Statewide, he is well known in three-fourths of the state, because it is covered by Portland media; and having shown he can carry the Republican-leaning 1st district he would likely get a good margin from the Democratic 3d. That makes him a serious candidate for the Senate should Mark Hatfield retire, and a challenger not to be underestimated even if Hatfield does not. In the district, he is almost guaranteed serious Republican competition in 1984, but he still has strong assets. If Oregon's economy should suddenly recover, he would probably be in strong shape; if not, he could have a serious contest.

The People Pop. 1980: 526,840, up 34.2% 1970–80; voting age pop. 387,395; 1% Black, 2% Span. orig., 2% Asian orig., 1% Am. Ind. 34% housing units rented. Median owner $68,100; renter $226. Households: 67% family, 35% with children, 58% married couples.

Presidential Vote

1980	Reagan (R)	118,836	(49%)
	Carter (D)	95,019	(39%)
	Anderson (I)	28,268	(12%)

Rep. Les AuCoin (D) Elected 1974; b. Oct. 21, 1942, Portland; home, Forest Grove; Pacific U., B.A. 1969; Protestant.

Career Army, 1961–64; Newsman, *Portland Oregonian*, 1965–66; Dir. of Pub. Info. and Publications, Pacific U., 1966–73; OR House of Reps., 1971–75, Major. Ldr., 1973–75; Admin., Skidmore, Owings, and Merrill, architectural firm, 1973–74.

Offices 2159 RHOB, 202-225-0855. Also 1716 Fed. Bldg., 1220 S.W. 3d Ave., Portland 97204, 503-221-2901.

Committee *Appropriations* (27th). Subcommittees: Defense; Interior.

Group Ratings

	ADA	ACLU	COPE	CFA	LCV	LWV	NTU	NSI	COC	ACA	CSFC
1982	85	79	68	69	86	91	50	10	26	10	27
1981	70	—	65	43	82	—	57	—	13	14	30
1980	83	80	39	57	72	100	27	0	54	25	37

National Journal Ratings

	Economic		Foreign		Cultural	
1982	63%	(LIB)	92%	(LIB)	81%	(LIB)
	37%	(CONS)	8%	(CONS)	19%	(CONS)
1981	67%	(LIB)	90%	(LIB)	82%	(LIB)
	32%	(CONS)	9%	(CONS)	17%	(CONS)

Key Votes

1) Reagan 81 Budget AGN	5) Incr SS Rtmt Age FOR	9) Poor Pay Food Stamps AGN
2) Reagan 81 Tax Cut AGN	6) Saudi AWACS Sale AGN	10) Ban Crt Busing Order AGN
3) Bal Budget Amend AGN	7) $ for MX Missile AGN	11) Auto Local Content AGN
4) Gas & Road Tax AGN	8) Nerve Gas Prod AGN	12) Nuclear Arms Freeze FOR

Election Results

1982 general	Les AuCoin (D)	118,638	(54%)	($482,176)
	Bill Moshofsky (R)	101,720	(46%)	($585,624)
1982 primary	Les AuCoin (D)	49,337	(82%)	
	Bob Magid (D)	11,094	(18%)	
1980 general	Les Aucoin (D)	203,532	(66%)	($307,477)
	Lynn Engdahl (R)	105,083	(34%)	($61,045)

Campaign Contributions and Expenditures

1981-82		Direct Cont. 81-82		PACS brkdwn			
Receipts	$484,928	Indiv	$188,715	Agr	$3,000	Ideo	$30,935
Expend.	$482,176	Party	$10,150	Bus	$73,795	Lbr	$113,085
Unspent	$8,484	PACS	$238,079	Hlth	$10,590	Prof	$2,400
		Cand	$3,500				

Indep Expend: For: $12,753 (LCV) Agn: $3,011 (NTL)   *Non-Cand Loans:* $27,000

SECOND DISTRICT

The 2d congressional district of Oregon contains 73% of the state's land area and 20% of its population. Most of the land lies east of the Cascade Mountains. This is the thinly settled part of Oregon—much of it is not settled at all. To the south, the terrain is desertlike, and mostly uninhabited. To the east, along the Idaho border, are the irrigated farmlands along the Snake River as it flows northwest to the Columbia. The northern part of eastern Oregon is forested land, with occasional lumber mill towns; settlements are sparse and separated by many miles. There are a few larger towns here—Pendleton in the northeast part of the state, The Dalles on the Columbia River, and Bend, the largest city in the area.

So sparsely populated is this area that almost half the district's population is clustered in the southwestern corner, in an area separated from the rest by the Cascades and the once huge volcano whose blown-off cone is now Crater Lake. This is lumbering country. Most of the people live in and around the towns—Medford, Ashland, Klamath Falls, Grants Pass— but their livelihoods depend on the demand for the trees that, in the early 1980s, were often left just growing on the hillsides.

This is historically a politically marginal area. The old lumber camps sprouted a radical tradition, one often forcibly squelched by management. But in recent years the area east of the mountains has been voting like most of the Rocky Mountain states, which is to say heavily Republican in national elections. Democrat Al Ullman represented this area for 24 years and became Chairman of the House Ways and Means Committee in 1974; despite that—or perhaps because his national duties kept him out of Oregon most of the time, and identified him with national Democratic policies—he was defeated in 1981. The victor in that race, Denny Smith, had the choice of running here or in the more compact 5th, where his legal residence was; he chose the 5th. That in effect made the 2d Oregon's new district, and set up a hotly contested race with no incumbent.

The winner turned out to be Bob Smith, an experienced Oregon legislator from the southeastern part of the state. But he had serious competition. In the primary, he had to beat Mike Fitzgerald, the challenger to the 4th district's Jim Weaver in 1980, who had a base in the southwest; Smith won 63%–37% in a race that split on geographic lines. In the general election he had spirited competition from Larryann Willis, a rancher and high-spirited denouncer of Reagan administration policies. Willis hoped that the depression in the lumber industry would help her, and perhaps it did; she ran ahead of many other Democrats in this area. But, almost uniformly in each county, she ran behind.

Smith, as a onetime speaker of the Oregon House, is likely to be a team player, not a maverick, as a congressman. He is a member of the Public Works Committee, and this is the kind of district that still cares about the projects a seat on that body can help bring in. Having won in what nationally was a Democratic year (although it was rather Republican in Oregon), Smith may not have tough competition in 1984. But this is a district exceedingly hard to keep in touch with, and so the result must always be considered somewhat iffy.

The People Pop. 1980: 526,968, up 34.2% 1970–80; voting age pop. 374,066; 3% Span. orig., 1% Asian orig., 1% Am. Ind. 27% housing units rented. Median owner $49,900; renter $186. Households: 75% family, 39% with children, 65% married couples.

Presidential Vote

1980	Reagan (R)	135,169	(59%)
	Carter (D)	75,944	(33%)
	Anderson (I)	16,239	(7%)

Rep. Robert F. (Bob) Smith (R) Elected 1982; b. June 16, 1931, Portland; home, Burns; Willamette U., B.A. 1953; Presbyterian.

Career Cattle rancher, 1953–; OR House of Reps., 1960–72, Spkr. 1969–72; OR Senate, 1972-82.

Offices 118 CHOB, 202-225-6730. Also 1150 Crater Lake Ave., Medford 97501, 503-776-4646.

Committee *Public Works and Transportation* (15th). Subcommittees: Surface Transportation; Water Resources.

Group Ratings and Key Votes: Newly Elected

Election Results

1982 general	Robert F. (Bob) Smith (R)	106,912	(56%)	($492,808)
	Larryann Willis (D)	85,495	(44%)	($225,762)
1982 primary	Robert F. (Bob) Smith (R)	32,998	(63%)	
	Mike Fitzgerald (R)	19,694	(37%)	($37,011)
1980 general	Newly created district			

Campaign Contributions and Expenditures

1981-82		Direct Cont. 81-82		PACS brkdwn			
Receipts	$494,965	Indiv	$265,342	Agr	$200	Ideo	$8,400
Expend.	$492,808	Party	$20,033	Bus	$114,474	Lbr	$500
Unspent	$2,156	PACS	$141,729	Hlth	$12,200	Prof	$1,000
		Cand	$55,000				

Indirect Party Expend: $33,565

THIRD DISTRICT

Portland is Oregon's big city. About 40% of Oregonians live in its metropolitan area, and more than half live within 60 miles of its downtown. Portland was founded by New England Yankees (they nearly named it Boston) and had its beginnings as a muscular blue-collar town—the place where Oregon loaded its supplies from the east, on the docks or in the railroad yards, and where it shipped out Oregon's products, mainly lumber and fruit. Portland has gained the reputation lately of being a culturally advanced city, where ecology-minded young marrieds jog together in the mornings, eat health food for dinner, and pray at night that no one else moves here.

There is some truth to this picture, but it is an exaggeration that applies to only a rather small segment of the population here. People like this are concentrated in the hills that rise just west of the Willamette River, and in some of the more expensive suburbs. But on the flat plains east of the Willamette, which slope exceedingly gradually into the distance and seem unconnected with the looming presence of Mount Hood, at 11,000 feet looking over the Portland area, Portland has a great many residents and voters who are just plain folks. True, there are more singles in Portland than in any other part of Oregon, and the support for Democrats is higher here than in just about any other part of the state. But many of those singles are elderly people, and much of that Democratic support comes from blue-collar workers who, if they like to fish and hunt in Oregon's wilderness, are still not vastly different in attitudes from their counterparts back east. Values and views in Portland, on the whole, are considerably different from those in, say, Pittsburgh. But they are not the same as those you find in a college town like Eugene.

The 3d congressional district of Oregon takes in all of Portland and Multnomah County east of the Willamette River, plus a couple of suburbs along the Willamette just to the south. These are mostly modest-looking areas, with small houses and rows of commercial buildings on the main streets built in the 1950s. The population begins to thin out as you go east, toward Mount Hood; there is even a little agricultural land there.

The congressman from the 3d district is Ron Wyden, who has had a rather unusual career. He achieved wide notice in Portland, while in his early 30s, as director of the Gray Panthers, a militant organization for the elderly. He was, among other things, the spark behind the successful statewide referendum to reduce the price of dentures. In 1980 he dared to run against an incumbent congressman, Bob Duncan, who was first elected, in another district, in 1962, and who ran two close races for the Senate before going back to the House again in 1974. But Duncan evidently had not kept in touch with Portland—which has no non-stop flights to Washington, D.C.—and Wyden won that race by a solid 60%–40% margin.

Wyden has a pleasant personality and a low-key style which contrasts with the aggressiveness his career has shown. He entered a Congress which was going in a direction very much different from his, but has done well anyway. He won a seat on the Energy and Commerce Committee, which covers all sorts of federal regulatory laws and agencies; he serves on the Health and the Environment Subcommittee, which handles the Clean Air Act as well as health issues, as well as the Energy Conservation and Power Subcommittee. Wyden's victory in a not particularly Democratic year has given him a jump in seniority and experience on the freshmen Democrats elected in 1982. He has the potential to be an active and aggressive legislator.

Wyden's performance at the polls so far suggests he is in strong political shape. He is highly unlikely to lose, or to be challenged in, the general election; this a district that went for George McGovern in 1972 and Jimmy Carter in 1980. He is likely to be vulnerable only in the primary and he, more than anyone, should be alert to any signs of danger there.

The People Pop. 1980: 526,715, up 2.6% 1970–80; voting age pop. 394,345; 5% Black, 2% Span. orig., 2% Asian orig., 1% Am. Ind. 38% housing units rented. Median owner $56,400; renter $220. Households: 65% family, 33% with children, 51% married couples.

Presidential Vote

1980	Reagan (R)	93,975	(41%)
	Carter (D)	110,143	(48%)
	Anderson (I)	23,758	(10%)

Rep. Ron Wyden (D) Elected 1980; b. May 3, 1949, Wichita, KS; home, Portland; U. of CA at Santa

Barbara, 1967–69, Stanford U., A.B. 1971, U. of OR, J.D. 1974; Jewish.

Career Campaign aide to Sen. Wayne Morse, 1972, 1974; Practicing atty., 1974–80; Codir. and Cofounder, OR Gray Panthers, 1974–80; Dir., OR Legal Svcs. for the Elderly, 1977–79.

Offices 1406 LHOB, 202-225-4811. Also 714 BPA Bldg., 1002 N.E. Holladay, P. O. Box 3621, Portland 97208, 503-231-2300.

Committees *Energy and Commerce* (19th). Subcommittees: Energy Conservation and Power; Health and the Environment. *Small Business* (15th). Subcommittees: Export Opportunities and Special Small Business Problems; SBA and SBIC Authority, Minority Enterprise and General Small Business Problems. *Select Committee on Aging* (24th). Subcommittees: Health and Long-Term Care; Housing and Consumer Interests.

Group Ratings

	ADA	ACLU	COPE	CFA	LCV	LWV	NTU	NSI	COC	ACA	CSFC
1982	95	92	93	92	92	100	41	0	18	0	24
1981	100	—	87	100	100	—	52	—	61	21	30

National Journal Ratings

	Economic		Foreign		Cultural	
1982	71%	(LIB)	96%	(LIB)	93%	(LIB)
	29%	(CONS)	1%	(CONS)	3%	(CONS)
1981	81%	(LIB)	89%	(LIB)	80%	(LIB)
	15%	(CONS)	11%	(CONS)	20%	(CONS)

Key Votes

1) Reagan 81 Budget	AGN	5) Incr SS Rtmt Age	AGN	9) Poor Pay Food Stamps	AGN
2) Reagan 81 Tax Cut	AGN	6) Saudi AWACS Sale	AGN	10) Ban Crt Busing Order	AGN
3) Bal Budget Amend	AGN	7) $ for MX Missile	AGN	11) Auto Local Content	AGN
4) Gas & Road Tax	AGN	8) Nerve Gas Prod	AGN	12) Nuclear Arms Freeze	FOR

Election Results

1982 general	Ron Wyden (D)	159,416	(78%)	($121,117)
	Thomas Phelan (R)	44,162	(22%)	($0)
1982 primary	Ron Wyden (D)	63,614	(100%)	
1980 general	Ron Wyden (D)	156,371	(72%)	($183,840)
	Darrell R. Conger (R)	60,940	(28%)	($9,724)

Campaign Contributions and Expenditures

1981-82		Direct Cont. 81-82		PACS brkdwn			
Receipts	$187,061	Indiv	$98,646	Agr	$750	Ideo	$2,650
Expend.	$121,117	PACS	$76,836	Bus	$26,400	Lbr	$34,625
Unspent	$68,479	Cand	$150	Hlth	$10,936	Prof	$1,475

FOURTH DISTRICT

The 4th congressional district of Oregon occupies the southwestern part of the state. Although the district contains about half of Oregon's rocky and picturesque Pacific coastline, most of its people can be found inland, in the southern part of the Willamette Valley and in the valley of the Umpqua River to the south, between the Coast Range and the Cascade Mountains. As in most of the West, relatively few people actually live on farms here, although the area produces much of Oregon's famed fruit crops. Instead, most of the people live in small, well-ordered cities like Roseburg, Coos Bay, Springfield, and the largest in the district, with 104,000 people, Eugene, the home of the University of Oregon.

This is one of the premier lumber districts in the nation. The prevailing winds from the Pacific bring moist air over the mountains, and it is deposited on the hillsides here in the form of almost constant rain. The year-round cool temperatures are conducive to the growth of Douglas firs and other large trees, and they are thick enough in many places that not a ray of sunshine seems to reach the ground. The high interest rates of 1981 and 1982 dried up the housing market and construction industry, and in turn the lumber business experienced a major depression. Mills were shut down, workers laid off, whole communities seemed to be waiting in line for unemployment checks—and wondering what would happen next.

This economic catastrophe, in most cases, seems to have led Oregon voters to shift to the Republicans. But in the 4th district House race they stayed strongly Democratic. The district has a solid Democratic base: Eugene is a Democratic town in all but the oddest elections. But the southern part of the district, which is almost entirely dependent on lumber, historically is more Republican. Yet both were carried by Congressman James Weaver.

This is not because he is not controversial. On the contrary, he is one of the members of Congress who arouses the strongest feelings—pro and con—both inside and outside the district. Nor is Weaver one of those congressmen who fudges issues of major importance to his district. He chairs the Interior Committee's Subcommittee on Mining, Forest Management, and Bonneville Power Administration, and so has more direct influence on lumber policy than any other member of the House. This is an industry the federal government is heavily involved in: much timber is cut on federal lands, under rules established by the federal government. Weaver has not hesitated to antagonize the big lumber companies. He pushed through a timber bill that provides for sustained yields—less than many lumbermen wanted, because of environmental restrictions. He has worked to protect large wilderness areas. He has worked to set aside federal timber lands for small independent loggers, to keep them in business. In a matter less controversial, he moved to cut timber exports to Japan, so that American rather than Japanese mills could convert the logs into lumber. He has clashed has clashed again and again with Interior Secretary James Watt—and even twitted Watt about his belief in an imminent Second Coming.

Weaver also plays a major role on some other issues. His subcommittee has jurisdiction over mining, and he opposes Watt's efforts to open up mining resources on public lands. It also has jurisdiction over the Bonneville Power Administration, which makes Weaver a key player in the fights over financing power generally and nuclear power in particular in the Pacific Northwest. Lower power costs, historically because of the importance of hydroelectric power, have always been one of the major economic assets of the Pacific Northwest. But Weaver's efforts to frustrate the completion of scheduled nuclear plants may add to local power costs, and therefore make the economic growth the region suddenly needs more difficult to achieve.

Weaver infuriates lumber industry leaders. He is openly skeptical about their motives, irreverent, and, in their view, often flaky. They have made it no secret that they would love to defeat him, and they have contributed liberally in pursuit of that goal. In each of the last four elections Weaver has been outspent by a Republican challenger. Yet he has won each of the four in a district which, in the past, was known for ousting even apparently strong incumbents. One reason may have been the distance factor: it takes nine hours to get from Washington, D.C., to Eugene, and so congressmen find it hard to maintain a presence in the district. Weaver's pungent personality may have helped him by enabling him to maintain a vivid presence in a way that would be quite impossible for the sort of bland, pleasant congressman you find in most districts.

Weaver's victory in 1982 was all the more notable because in other Oregon contests it seemed that Democrats were getting more blame than Republicans for the problems afflicting Oregon's lumber economy. This is not to say that Weaver is home free in the future; he seems almost certain to inspire furious opposition even if he is perceived as safe. But he has shown that he has formidable assets for representing this district, and he is likely to remain a major force in lumber policy for some time to come.

The People Pop. 1980: 526,462, up 26.9% 1970–80; voting age pop. 378,675; 2% Span. orig., 1% Asian orig., 1% Am. Ind. 31% housing units rented. Median owner $57,100; renter $208. Households: 73% family, 39% with children, 63% married couples.

Presidential Vote

1980	Reagan (R)	112,766	(49%)
	Carter (D)	91,238	(40%)
	Anderson (I)	19,901	(9%)

Rep. James (Jim) **Weaver** (D) Elected 1974; b. Aug. 8, 1927, Brookings, SD; home, Eugene; U. of OR, B.S. 1952; Protestant.

Career Navy, WWII; Publisher's Rep., Prentice-Hall Co., 1954–58; Staff Dir., OR Legislative Interim Comm. on Agriculture, 1959–60; Builder and apartment complex developer, 1960–75.

Offices 1226 LHOB, 202-225-6416. Also Fed. Bldg., 211 E. 7th Ave., Eugene 97401, 503-687-6732.

Committees *Agriculture* (7th). Subcommittees: Conservation, Credit, and Rural Development; Forests, Family Farms, and Energy. *Interior and Insular Affairs* (6th). Subcommittees: Mining, Forest Management, and BPA (Chairman); Public Lands and National Parks; Water and Power Resources.

Group Ratings

	ADA	ACLU	COPE	CFA	LCV	LWV	NTU	NSI	COC	ACA	CSFC
1982	95	92	86	77	92	80	60	0	5	10	29
1981	90	—	85	86	100	—	89	—	5	23	33
1980	83	87	72	64	93	80	45	0	52	35	40

National Journal Ratings

	Economic		Foreign		Cultural	
1982	70%	(LIB)	99%	(LIB)	98%	(LIB)
	30%	(CONS)	0%	(CONS)	1%	(CONS)
1981	81%	(LIB)	79%	(LIB)	81%	(LIB)
	15%	(CONS)	20%	(CONS)	19%	(CONS)

Key Votes

1) Reagan 81 Budget	AGN	5) Incr SS Rtmt Age	AGN	9) Poor Pay Food Stamps	AGN
2) Reagan 81 Tax Cut	AGN	6) Saudi AWACS Sale	AGN	10) Ban Crt Busing Order	AGN
3) Bal Budget Amend	AGN	7) $ for MX Missile	AGN	11) Auto Local Content	FOR
4) Gas & Road Tax	—	8) Nerve Gas Prod	AGN	12) Nuclear Arms Freeze	FOR

Election Results

1982 general	James (Jim) Weaver (D)	115,448	(59%)	($312,043)
	Ross Anthony (R)	80,054	(41%)	($385,384)
1982 primary	James (Jim) Weaver (D)	51,013	(79%)	
	Gene Arvidson (D)	13,311	(21%)	
1980 general	James (Jim) Weaver (D)	158,745	(55%)	($239,432)
	Michael Fitzgerald (R)	130,861	(45%)	($379,056)

Campaign Contributions and Expenditures

1981-82		Direct Cont. 81-82		PACS brkdwn			
Receipts	$335,210	Indiv	$188,551	Agr	$1,080	Ideo	$32,225
Expend.	$312,043	Party	$6,129	Bus	$9,070	Lbr	$68,895
Unspent	$40,166	PACS	$128,469	Hlth	$750	Prof	$1,250
		Cand	$4,000				

Indep Expend: For: $905 (NRA)

FIFTH DISTRICT

The 5th congressional district of Oregon occupies the heart of the Willamette Valley, south of Portland. This is where Oregon was first settled. It was one of the few valleys which settlers to the West found already suitable for agriculture. California's great valleys depend on irrigation; so does the cultivation of wheat in eastern Washington. But things grow in the Willamette Valley without much difficulty. The soil is fertile, the plain created by the waters of the Willamette sweeping down from the Cascades and the Coast Range are broad, and the rains everyone hears about in Oregon seem pretty much constant. Add to those natural endowments some Yankee ingenuity and ambition, and you have a prosperous agricultural commonwealth—the Willamette Valley from the 1850s to the present day.

The 5th district begins, in the north, where metropolitan Portland tends to thin out. It includes the old pioneer town of Oregon City, and part of the high-income suburb of Lake Oswego. In the south it includes Corvallis, home of Oregon State University. In the center of the district is the state capital of Salem—note the old New England name. This is a district drawn by a Democratic legislature, but which everyone knew would lean Republican. Salem has always been a Republican town, the high-income Portland suburbs here tend to outweigh the more modest Democratic ones, and the student vote in Corvallis is no longer a source of large Democratic majorities.

Nonetheless this was the scene of Oregon's closest congressional election in 1982. Republican Denny Smith, elected in 1982 in a district that included Salem, some of the Willamette Valley, and all of the huge expanse of Oregon east of the Cascades, decided to run in the new 5th district. Smith was elected in part because voters thought Al Ullman, the Chairman of the Ways and Means Committee, had gotten too distant from the district, and partly out of enthusiasm for Smith's own rough-and-ready conservative philosophy. But as the economy deteriorated in 1982, Smith found himself sometimes making angry speeches about Reaganomics, and found himself on the defensive back home in Oregon. State Senator Ruth McFarland, the Democratic nominee, had backing from some of Oregon's liberal activists but, if she could compete with Smith in articulateness she could not compete with him in funding. She carried Corvallis and actually carried the district as a whole outside Salem's Marion County. But Smith's Marion County margin gave him enough for victory.

Smith is a member of the Interior and Veterans' Affairs Committees. On the former, his side is usually outvoted and outmaneuvered by an environmentalist-minded majority. Given the close result here, it is quite likely he will have significant opposition in 1984.

The People Pop. 1980: 526,120, up 41.1% 1970–80; voting age pop. 375,567; 2% Span. orig., 1% Asian orig., 1% Am. Ind. 30% housing units rented. Median owner $62,100; renter $207. Households: 74% family, 40% with children, 63% married couples.

Presidential Vote

1980	Reagan (R)	110,298	(50%)
	Carter (D)	84,546	(39%)
	Anderson (I)	24,223	(11%)

Rep. Denny Smith (R) Elected 1980; b. Jan. 19, 1938, Ontario; home, Salem; Willamette U., B.A. 1961; Baptist.

Career Air Force, 1958–60, 1962–67; Natl. Guard, 1960–62; Pilot Flight Engineer, Pan-Am Airways, 1967–76; Bd. chmn., family newspaper chain, 1968–.

Offices 1213 LHOB, 202-225-5711. Also 4035 12th St. S.E., No. 20, P. O. Box 13089, Salem 97309, 503-399-5756.

Committees *Interior and Insular Affairs* (10th). Subcommittees: Energy and the Environment; Insular Affairs. *Veterans' Affairs* (7th). Subcommittees: Compensation, Pension, and Insurance; Education, Training and Employment.

Group Ratings

	ADA	ACLU	COPE	CFA	LCV	LWV	NTU	NSI	COC	ACA	CSFC
1982	5	0	4	8	12	33	98	100	86	86	85
1981	10	—	0	14	45	—	97	—	88	96	86

National Journal Ratings

	Economic		Foreign		Cultural	
1982	11%	(LIB)	35%	(LIB)	21%	(LIB)
	89%	(CONS)	65%	(CONS)	76%	(CONS)
1981	24%	(LIB)	18%	(LIB)	4%	(LIB)
	68%	(CONS)	73%	(CONS)	90%	(CONS)

Key Votes

1) Reagan 81 Budget	FOR	5) Incr SS Rtmt Age	FOR	9) Poor Pay Food Stamps	FOR
2) Reagan 81 Tax Cut	FOR	6) Saudi AWACS Sale	AGN	10) Ban Crt Busing Order	FOR
3) Bal Budget Amend	FOR	7) $ for MX Missile	AGN	11) Auto Local Content	AGN
4) Gas & Road Tax	—	8) Nerve Gas Prod	FOR	12) Nuclear Arms Freeze	AGN

Election Results

1982 general	Denny Smith (R)	103,906	(51%)	($491,122)
	Ruth McFarland (D)	98,952	(49%)	($205,062)
1982 primary	Denny Smith (R)	37,224	(100%)	
1980 general	Denny Smith (R)	141,854	(49%)	($663,430)
	Al Ullman (D)	138,089	(47%)	($670,390)

Campaign Contributions and Expenditures

1981-82		Direct Cont. 81-82		PACS brkdwn			
Receipts	$495,350	Indiv	$297,150	Agr	$2,166	Ideo	$17,179
Expend.	$491,122	Party	$15,305	Bus	$117,386	Lbr	$6,000
Unspent	$6,044	PACS	$159,941	Hlth	$12,750	Prof	$1,050
		Cand	$700				

Indirect Party Expend: $34,717   *Indep Expend:* For: $3,244 (OR LIFEPAC, NRA, NTL)
Non-Cand Loans: $9,000

PENNSYLVANIA

Pennsylvania is called the Keystone State, and it is an apt name: the commonwealth connects New York and New England with the rest of the nation. Two hundred years ago, the geography of Pennsylvania promised to make it the commercial and transportation hub of the seaboard nation, and it was the most populous state when the Constitution was adopted. But the rugged mountains of central Pennsylvania stalled the early development of transportation arteries west. New York City, not Philadelphia, mushroomed most rapidly in the middle 19th century, thanks to the Erie Canal and the first water-level railroad line which became the New York Central. In 1776 Philadelphia was the nation's capital and largest city. By 1830 it was eclipsed by Washington in government and New York in commerce, and rivaled by Boston in culture. Philadelphia is still the nation's fourth largest metropolitan area and Pittsburgh the 13th (depending on how you define those units), but neither city looms as large in the national consciousness as seemed likely when the Declaration of Independence was signed.

During the 19th century Pennsylvania nonetheless had remarkable growth—but for reasons not anticipated by the founders. It became the energy capital of the United States, much as Texas is today, and the major industrial center as well. The key to all this was coal— Pennsylvania even today probably has enough coal to supply the entire nation's needs for years. Northeastern Pennsylvania was the nation's primary source of anthracite, the hard coal used for home heating; and western Pennsylvania was the major source of bituminous coal, the soft coal used in producing steel and other industrial products. As a result, the area around Pittsburgh became the center of the nation's steel industry by 1890. Immigrants poured into the state to work in the mines and the factories, and the very name Pittsburgh became synonymous with industrial prosperity and was the inspiration behind the civic patriotism that celebrated smoking smokestacks. During this period Pennsylvania was the nation's second largest state and was growing rapidly.

The boom ended conclusively with the Depression of the 1930s, and in much of Pennsylvania good times have never really returned. The coal industry collapsed after World War II, as both home heating and industry switched out of coal; John L. Lewis's United Mine Workers decided to seek higher pay and benefits for fewer workers, and cooperated in sharply cutting the coal work force. Even when coal use rose sharply in the 1970s, the emphasis was on capital-intensive means of extraction, such as strip mines, and there are still far fewer jobs than in the 1940s; the anthracite country now lives on the apparel industry, and has had almost constant outmigration over the past 40 years.

Most important, Pennsylvania steel has long since ceased to be a growth industry. American steel companies dispersed their operations and neglected new technology in their old Pennsylvania plants; steel production abroad increased rapidly, with extremely high capacity (partly because every Third World country wants a steel mill, for prestige reasons) and with greater efficiency than American producers could boast. By 1969, the steel manufacturers and the United Steelworkers—after a series of amicable agreements for ever higher wages—persuaded the federal government to limit steel imports. Further restrictions followed, but have not been accompanied by modernization of local plants nor by adaptation to higher-skill specialty steel production. A century ago the steel producers made Pennsylvania the classic high-tariff state, when they sought protection for what they called infant industries. Now, in the late 20th century, Pennsylvania seems to be seeking protection for industries which have grown senile.

These economic developments have left Pennsylvania in rather sorry shape. People growing up here are as likely to leave the state as stay, and out-of-staters show little interest in moving in. Compared to the growth areas of the Sun Belt, with their garden condominiums and shopping malls, the cities and small towns of Pennsylvania give the traveler a sense of being 40 or 50 years back in time; to judge just from the structure, you would conclude you are in another country altogether. You can see, little changed, the suburb where John Updike lived as a boy and the gritty coal town where John O'Hara grew up. Sometimes the trip is pleasant, as in the spanking clean 1920s downtown of Lancaster, surrounded by early 19th century row houses. Sometimes it is grim, as in the coal towns where houses stand unoccupied and the woods and brush creep up to the edge of neighborhoods built 60 years ago. In 1930, after its last decade of above-national-average economic growth, Pennsylvania had 9.5 million people. In 1982 the number stood at 11.9 million—by far the smallest long-term growth among the nation's biggest states. By the 1980 Census Pennsylvania had slipped behind not only New York and California but also, symbolically important, the nation's new energy capital of Texas. This sluggish growth has political consequences. As recently as 1950, Pennsylvania had 32 seats in the House of Representatives. Today it has 23.

Traditionally Pennsylvania was heavily Republican, the most Republican of all the big states. It was for Lincoln and Union, for the steel industry and the high tariff; in 1932 it was the only big state that stuck with Herbert Hoover and voted against Franklin Roosevelt. Yet it never produced any Republican presidents or national leaders. This was a state where the important people were in business, and politics was left to faintly disreputable leaders like Matthew Quay and Joseph Grundy or, occasionally, to an eccentric and cynical aristocrat like Boies Penrose. Their job was not to build a party which would mobilize one segment of the state enough to make a possible majority (as Tammany Hall mobilized the Irish in New York), but to build a party which would have a place for just about everyone. Back in the days before the New Deal, working-class communities like Pittsburgh and the anthracite country were overwhelmingly Republican, and Philadelphia's City Hall remained in the control of the local Republican machine until 1951. There was a consensus on policy here—the whole state was for the tariff—and the ethnic tensions were not so great. A high proportion of Pennsylvania's immigrants were Welsh, Scottish, Scotch-Irish, and English workingmen, who assimilated fairly easily; also, most of Pennsylvania's immigrants were dispersed into hundreds of little mining and factory towns, almost inaccessibly set into narrow valleys and in clefts between hills; they were not concentrated, as almost all of New York's immigrants were concentrated, into one huge city. Political patronage, similarly, was not concentrated in a single big city, but scattered in jobs in every county of the state.

The men who ran this system believed there was no conflict between the interests of the millionaires who financed this party and the workingmen who voted for it. They had all come to Pennsylvania, after all, to better their economic condition and together were succeeding— some, admittedly, much more than others. Pennsylvania Republicans included within their ranks progressives like Gifford Pinchot (onetime Interior Department official and later governor) and authentic representatives of the working class like James J. Davis (senator and secretary of labor). There was not much idealism, however; politics was a practical business, as indeed it is in Pennsylvania today.

The New Deal seemed to change all this. In partisan terms, it made Pennsylvania one of the most marginal of states. The northern tier of counties along the border with Upstate New York and the central part of the state—the Welsh railroad workers in Altoona and the Pennsylvania Dutch farmers around Lancaster—remained the strongest Republican voting bloc in the East. But Philadelphia became a Democratic city, and Pennsylvania's great blue-collar enclaves—greater Pittsburgh and the whole western end of the state, the northeastern anthracite country—became Democratic bulwarks. Life in these areas changed markedly in the 1930s, when the United Steelworkers organized the mills, against sometimes violent opposition; the old Republican voting habits disappeared quite abruptly.

Now there are some signs that Pennsylvania is changing again—or at least that the glacial pace of demographic change in this aging state is combining with political circumstance to make it more Republican. Pennsylvania has a Republican governor, as it has had during most of the last 20 years; and he, like his predecessors (including maverick Democrat Milton Shapp), has been reducing the number of patronage jobs which used to be the sustenance of the state's political machines. The Republicans are in a strong position in the legislature— something not true in New Jersey or Ohio or Illinois. Republicans have won every U.S. Senate race here since 1962. They held their own in the 1982 elections here, despite the national trend of opinion. Part of the reason is that the Republicans are better organized. They have major candidates who can raise money and a hierarchy that produces strong state tickets. The Democrats, on the other hand, have nothing like central direction and have exceedingly limited financial resources. The old Democratic machines of Philadelphia and Pittsburgh have fallen into desuetude, and concentrate on local matters only; two very different independent mayors in the 1970s, Frank Rizzo in Philadelphia and Peter Flaherty in Pittsburgh, effectively removed the machines from statewide politics. Demographically, the big cities and the coal-and-steel country are declining in population and, sooner or later, in votes. This makes the still-Republican belt of suburbs around Philadelphia, the Pennsylvania Dutch country, and the hills of the central part of the state, which have been gaining population, of greater moment electorally. As the number of blue-collar jobs declines and the number of white-collar jobs stays steady—to oversimplify the picture—the Democratic base is eroded.

And in Pennsylvania the cultural factors which have been moving politics left and right seem to be of less importance than in other large states. This is not only an old state, but one where even the younger people live more in traditional family patterns than the national average. The percentage of wives working is lower in the Pittsburgh area, for example, than in just about any other major metropolitan area in the country. One reason is that the economy doesn't produce many new jobs for anyone; but also contributing to this, probably, is a lingering attitude that wives shouldn't work—an attitude that is reinforced when so many of them do not. There has not been much of a constituency in Pennsylvania for the liberal side of cultural or foreign issues—an oddity, perhaps, in a commonwealth established originally by Quakers (who are now demographically unimportant here), but true.

Presidential politics. All of this is not to say that Pennsylvania could not go Democratic for president in 1984, as it did in the close elections of 1960, 1968, and 1976. But if it does, the pattern will be a little different. Philadelphia cast 915,000 votes in 1960 and gave John Kennedy a 331,000-vote margin. Twenty years later Philadelphia cast 715,000 votes and gave Jimmy Carter a 177,000-vote margin. The vote in Pittsburgh's Allegheny County declined from 750,000 to 621,000, and the Democratic margin practically disappeared, in the same period. Neither big-city bosses nor organized labor seem able to deliver votes automatically; Pennsylvania must be wooed, as other states must, over television. Yet the culturally liberal themes which national Democrats may emphasize—particularly in primary campaigns in Massachusetts, New York, and California—are not likely to go over well in Pennsylvania.

Pennsylvania's presidential primary, in April, has occasionally been a crucial one; this is a major state, and the calendar has been such that it does not compete with many other states' primaries for attention. Jimmy Carter cinched the Democratic nomination in 1976 by beating Henry Jackson and Morris Udall here. The Democratic primary is heavily blue collar; the Republican primary is fairly representative of the state, except for the big cities and some industrial areas.

Senators. Both of Pennsylvania's senators are Republican, but neither comes from a standard partisan background. One is a young man whose political career has been almost entirely successful, the other an older man who has survived a series of political battle wounds.

John Heinz, in his middle 40s, is now Pennsylvania's longest surviving top officeholder. Heir to the H. J. Heinz food fortune, he is one of the richest men in the Senate. He was elected to the House from the Pittsburgh suburbs in 1972 and became very popular in western Pennsylvania. His 1976 Senate race against William Green, then congressman and later mayor of Philadelphia, was a kind of Pirates versus Phillies contest, between two young politicians very popular in the two major parts of the state. The difference was probably money: Heinz spent $2.9 million of his own money, and won.

Heinz was considered a liberal Republican when he was first elected, but he has fit in reasonably well with the Republican majority in the Senate, and even had some part in creating it. That came in the 1980 elections, when he chaired the Senate Republican Campaign Committee. He does not deserve all the credit for the fact that the Republicans won 12 Senate seats that year, but he does deserve some, particularly for the committee's long-sustained fundraising program and for its adroit directing of resources into close races in the last weeks of the campaign. Nonetheless, Heinz is not fully trusted by many of his conservative colleagues. Right after the 1980 triumph, he lost the chairmanship of the Senate Republican Conference to James McClure of Idaho. That loss suggested that he is unlikely to win a leadership post, at least if the composition of the Senate Republicans remains similar to what it is today.

In the Republican Senate Heinz has concentrated on economic issues; and although he supported the Reagan economic policies in 1981 and 1982, he has made at least a different emphasis himself. As Chairman of the Special Committee on Aging, he has been somewhat more skeptical about cutting scheduled future Social Security benefits than many Reaganites, though he supported the 1983 Social Security rescue bill. On the Finance Committee, he has emphasized trade issues. Heinz may very well be the most protection-minded member of the Senate. He pushes for strict enforcement of the antidumping laws, watches closely over the interests of the steel industry, and also looks after smaller Pennsylvania industries threatened by imports, like footwear and mushrooms.

This record proved to be an asset for Heinz in 1982, when he could have faced more political trouble than appeared. Although he stated from the beginning that he didn't intend to spend his own money on this race, the fact is he had demonstrated the ability and willingness to shell out $2.6 million, and that inevitably deterred opposition. Who wants to run against a candidate who can, by writing one check, raise the same amount of money it will take you all year to raise? His opponent turned out to be Cyril Wecht, a local Pittsburgh politico. As a doctor, county commissioner, and county Democratic chairman, he had some following in Pittsburgh, but it was by no means as large or enthusiastic as Heinz's. Elsewhere in the state he was unknown and, since he never raised much money, remained so. The recession, which had much greater impact on western than eastern Pennsylvania, showed up in the election results; Heinz lost votes in the west, as compared to 1976, and gained in the east. That suggests that against a more formidable opponent, Heinz would not have been able to win, as he did against Wecht, the highest percentage of any Republican senator in 1982.

Pennsylvania's other senator is Arlen Specter. A onetime Democrat, and a top staffer for the Warren Commission, Specter was a kind of boy wonder when, as a Republican, he was elected district attorney in Philadelphia in 1965. He won again in 1969, but didn't win another election for 11 years. He lost reelection in an increasingly Democratic city; he lost the 1976 Senate primary to Heinz; he lost the 1978 gubernatorial nomination to Richard Thornburgh. Finally, he beat former Republican state chairman Bud Haabestad in the 1980 Senate primary and then beat former Pittsburgh Mayor Peter Flaherty in the general. Flaherty was a frugal mayor who cut city payrolls and spending, and who refused to spend much money in statewide races; he lost many black votes to Specter and ran poorly outside the Pittsburgh media market where he is well known.

As a senator Specter is considered brainy and competent, if not tremendously well-liked. He was careful not to dissent heavily from Reagan economic policies early in his first term, but his record nonetheless reflects the views of a state that sees itself as needing federal aid of various sorts. Since he is rather liberal on cultural issues, he holds a strategic place on the Judiciary Committee. There is, however, no evidence that he feels terrifically out of place in the Republican Party or that he has been a boat-rocker.

Congressional districting. Pennsylvania's congressional districts were drawn by a Republican legislature and approved by a Republican governor; two seats were lost because of the census, both of them solidly Democratic, one in Philadelphia and the other in the Pittsburgh area. Nevertheless, the House delegation is 13–10 Democratic—a good instance of how the trend of opinion is usually more decisive than redistricting. Pennsylvania's House delegation, not to put too fine a point on it, has long been considered a collection of political hacks; it is somewhat better than that now, but it is not very effective or well-placed. There is some irony in that: Pennsylvania Democrats consider themselves the most practical of men, yet in today's House they are considerably less successful than their more idealistic colleagues from California.

Governor. Pennsylvania's governor, Richard Thornburgh, is a good example of a governor who is both a high-minded chief executive and a tough partisan. He met his most exacting test in his first year in office, reacting to the Three Mile Island nuclear plant incident; he helped to maintain calm without covering up anything that was happening. He is one of the national leaders on federalism issues, and not necessarily an advocate of Reagan administration policies. Nonetheless, Thornburgh has won two elections by close margins, and with the help of luck. In 1978 he faced Pete Flaherty, who deliberately raised and spent little money; Thornburgh, with hefty contributions from, among others, John Heinz's father, prevailed. In 1982 his opponent was Congressman Allen Ertel, whose political base was geographically remote and whose fundraising base was almost nonexistent. Yet Thornburgh won by only a 51%–48% margin. Recession-hit western Pennsylvania went Democratic; Thornburgh was saved by his large majorities in the Philadelphia suburbs, which enabled him to carry metropolitan Philadelphia as a whole.

Thornburgh is one Pennsylvanian who may have national political ambitions; he could conceivably be an attractive running mate for some Republican nominee. But John Heinz has had similar thoughts, and the two are no longer close political allies.

The People Est. Pop. 1982: 11,865,000; Pop. 1980: 11,863,895, no change 1980–82 and up 0.5% 1970–80; 5.2% of U.S. total, 4th largest; voting age pop. 8,740,599; 8% Black, 1% Spanish origin. Single ancestry: 15% German, 6% English, Italian, 5% Irish, 3% Polish, 1% Russian, Dutch, Hungarian, Ukrainian. Registered voters (1982): 5,702,557 Total. 3,035,523 D (53%); 2,357,448 R (41%); and 309,586 Independent or other parties (5%). 11% with 1–3 yrs. col., 14% with 4+ yrs. col. 10.5% below poverty level. 28% housing units rented; median house value: $39,100; median monthly rent: $174. Households: 74% family, 38% with children, 61% married couples.

1982 Share of Federal Tax Burden $30,446,900,000; 5.10% of U.S. total, 5th largest.

1982 Share of Federal Expenditures

	Total		Non-Defense		Defense	
Total Expend	$28,481m	(4.72%)	$23,499m	(5.53%)	$4,982m	(2.79%)
St/Lcl Grants	4,629m	(5.25%)	4,628m	(5.25%)	1m	(2.78%)
Salary/Wages	2,451m	(0.67%)	854m	(3.12%)	1,597m	(3.15%)
Ind Payments	17,260m	(6.03%)	16,250m	(6.31%)	1,010m	(3.53%)
Procurement	3,973m	(2.72%)	922m	(2.92%)	3,051m	(2.67%)
Other Programs	169m	(3.12%)	169m	(3.15%)	0m	(0%)
Loan/Insurance	1,194m	(1.87%)	1,140m	(1.85%)	54m	(2.45%)

Political Lineup   Governor, Richard L. Thornburgh (R). Senators, H. John Heinz III (R) and Arlen Specter (R). Representatives, 23 (13 D and 10 R). State Senate, 50 (24 D and 26 R); State House of Representatives, 203 (103 D and 100 R).

Presidential Vote

1980	Reagan (R)	....	2,261,872	(50%)
	Carter (D)	....	1,937,540	(42%)
	Anderson (I)	....	292,921	(6%)
1976	Ford (R)	....	2,205,604	(48%)
	Carter (D)	....	2,328,677	(50%)

1980 Democratic Presidential Primary			*1980 Republican Presidential Primary*		
Kennedy	736,854	(46%)	Bush	626,759	(52%)
Carter	732,332	(46%)	Reagan	527,916	(44%)
Brown	37,669	(2%)	Baker.............	30,846	(2%)
Others	93,865	(6%)	Others	24,301	(2%)

SENATORS

Sen. H. John Heinz III (R) Elected 1976, seat up 1988; b. Oct. 23, 1938, Pittsburgh; home, Pittsburgh; Yale U., B.A. 1960, Harvard U., M.B.A. 1963; Episcopal.

Career Marketing, H.J. Heinz Co., Pittsburgh, 1965–70; Sales Rep., International Harvester, Australia; Special Asst. to U.S. Sen. Hugh Scott, 1964; U.S. House of Reps., 1971–77.

Offices 227 RSOB, 202-224-6324. Also 9456 Wm. J. Green Fed. Bldg., 4th and Arch Sts., Philadelphia 19106, 215-925-8750; and 2031 Fed. Bldg., Pittsburgh 15222, 412-562-0533.

Committees *Banking, Housing, and Urban Affairs* (3d). Subcommittees: Housing and Urban Affairs; International Finance and Monetary Policy (Chairman); Financial Institutions. *Energy and Natural Resources* (11th). Subcommittees: Energy Conservation and Supply; Energy Research and Development; Energy and Mineral Resources. *Finance* (6th). Subcommittees: International Trade; Economic Growth, Employment and Revenue Sharing (Chairman); Health. *Special Committee on Aging* (Chairman).

Group Ratings

	ADA	ACLU	COPE	CFA	LCV	LWV	NTU	NSI	COC	ACA	CSFC
1982	70	61	67	50	49	83	30	78	29	39	49
1981	35	—	66	36	50	—	37	—	71	32	62
1980	50	90	67	33	67	89	32	80	63	44	52

National Journal Ratings

	Economic		Foreign		Cultural	
1982	54%	(LIB)	57%	(LIB)	67%	(LIB)
	45%	(CONS)	42%	(CONS)	32%	(CONS)
1981	62%	(LIB)	64%	(LIB)	71%	(LIB)
	37%	(CONS)	35%	(CONS)	27%	(CONS)

Key Votes

1) Reagan 81 Budget	FOR	5) $ to El Salvador	AGN	9) Poor Pay Food Stamps	AGN
2) Reagan 81 Tax Cut	FOR	6) Saudi AWACS Sale	AGN	10) Ban Crt Busing Order	AGN
3) Bal Budget Amend	AGN	7) Ban Abortion	AGN	11) Clinch Riv Brdr Rctr	FOR
4) Gas & Road Tax	—	8) Nerve Gas Prod	AGN	12) Legal Services Corp	FOR

Election Results

1982 general	H. John Heinz III (R)	2,136,418	(59%)	($2,952,829)
	Cyril H. Wecht (D)	1,412,965	(39%)	($424,507)
1982 primary	H. John Heinz III (R)	560,102	(100%)	
1976 general	H. John Heinz III (R)	2,318,891	(52%)	($3,004,814)
	William Green (D)	2,216,977	(47%)	($1,269,409)

Campaign Contributions and Expenditures

1979-82		*Direct Cont. 79-82*			*PACS brkdwn*			
Receipts	$3,238,861	Indiv	$2,389,821	Agr	$10,000	Ideo	$41,850	
Expend.	$2,952,829	Party	$22,145	Bus	$416,107	Lbr	$72,200	
Unspent	$524,957	PACS	$589,001	Hlth	$31,600	Prof	$20,900	

Indirect Party Expend: $648,690

Sen. Arlen Specter (R) Elected 1980, seat up 1986; b. Feb. 12, 1930, Wichita, KS; home, Philadelphia; U. of PA, B.A. 1951, Yale U., J.D. 1956; Jewish.

Career Air Force, 1951–53; Practicing atty.; Warren Commission, 1964; Philadelphia Dist. Atty., 1966–74, City Cncl., 1979.

Offices 331 RSOB, 202-224-4254. Also 600 Arch Street, Fed. Bldg., Su. 9400, Philadelphia 19106, 215-597-7200; 2017 Fed. Bldg., Pittsburgh 15222, 412-644-3400; and 118 Fed. Bldg., Erie 16501, 814-433-3010.

Committees *Appropriations* (14th). Subcommittees: Agriculture, Rural Development; Commerce, Justice, State, the Judiciary; District of Columbia (Chairman); Foreign Operations; Labor, Health and Human Services, Education. *Judiciary* (10th). Subcommittees: Administrative Practice and Procedure; Criminal Law; Juvenile Justice (Chairman). *Veterans' Affairs* (5th).

Group Ratings

	ADA	ACLU	COPE	CFA	LCV	LWV	NTU	NSI	COC	ACA	CSFC
1982	70	86	53	50	49	82	32	60	35	40	48
1981	50	—	58	36	39	—	34	—	72	38	61

National Journal Ratings

	Economic		Foreign		Cultural	
1982	52%	(LIB)	66%	(LIB)	90%	(LIB)
	47%	(CONS)	33%	(CONS)	9%	(CONS)
1981	65%	(LIB)	63%	(LIB)	74%	(LIB)
	34%	(CONS)	36%	(CONS)	24%	(CONS)

Key Votes

1) Reagan 81 Budget	FOR	5) $ to El Salvador	AGN	9) Poor Pay Food Stamps	AGN
2) Reagan 81 Tax Cut	FOR	6) Saudi AWACS Sale	AGN	10) Ban Crt Busing Order	AGN
3) Bal Budget Amend	FOR	7) Ban Abortion	AGN	11) Clinch Riv Brdr Rctr	FOR
4) Gas & Road Tax	FOR	8) Nerve Gas Prod	AGN	12) Legal Services Corp	FOR

Election Results

1980 general	Arlen Specter (R)	2,230,404	(50%)	($1,488,588)
	Peter Flaherty (D)	2,122,391	(48%)	($633,861)
1980 primary	Arlen Specter (R)	419,372	(36%)	
	Bud Haabestad (R)	382,281	(33%)	($220,364)
	Six others (R)	350,406	(31%)	
1974 general	Richard S. Schweiker (R)	1,843,317	(53%)	($799,499)
	Peter Flaherty (D)	1,596,121	(46%)	($256,483)

Campaign Contributions and Expenditures

1979-80		PACS brkdwn			
Receipts	$1,512,342	Agr	$11,375	Ideo	$18,615
Expend.	$1,488,588	Bus	$246,721	Lbr	$16,265
Unspent	$23,754	Hlth	$7,250	Prof	$4,200

GOVERNOR

Gov. Richard L. Thornburgh (R) Elected 1978, term expires 1987; b. July 16, 1932, Pittsburgh; home, Harrisburg; Yale U., B.S. 1954; U. of Pitt., LL.B. 1957; Episcopal.

Career Atty. and advisor, ALCOA, 1957–59; Practicing atty., 1959–69; U.S. Atty. for W. PA, 1969–75; Asst. U.S. Atty. Gen., U.S. Dept. of Justice, 1975–77.

Offices Main Capitol, Harrisburg 17120, 717-787-2500.

Election Results

1982 gen.	Richard L. Thornburgh (R) ..	1,872,784	(51%)
	Allen E. Ertel (D)	1,772,353	(48%)
1982 prim.	Richard L. Thornburgh (R) ..	552,386	(100%)
1978 gen.	Richard L. Thornburgh (R) ..	1,966,042	(53%)
	Peter Flaherty (D)	1,737,888	(46%)

FIRST DISTRICT

In 1682 Quakers, acting as agents for William Penn, established the city of Philadelphia. They meant it from the first to be a city; not content with the cowpath street patterns in other North Americans cities, they designed a grid of numbered and named streets which was replicated in dozens of American cities for more than 200 years afterwards. The grid proceeded several miles north and south along the Delaware River, and inland several miles to the Schuylkill; it was interrupted occasionally by the squares which still grace Center City Philadelphia.

Today not many of the structures the Quakers built endure, but there are plenty of buildings here from which you read more than 200 years of history. And not just in the restored townhouses of Society Hill, south of Independence Hall, although these are pleasant enough. A few blocks inward, before you get to Philadelphia's ornate City Hall, the blocks are populated with Federal and Greek Revival buildings, little temples of commerce, built when Philadelphia was the nation's largest city, and left standing because later big buildings in Center City were built around City Hall and farther west.

Then there are Philadelphia's residential districts. Not confined to islands, like New York,

PENNSYLVANIA — **Congressional Districts, Counties, and Selected Places** — *(23 Districts)*

LEGEND

2	Congressional district number
—	Congressional district boundary
◉	Place of 100,000 or more inhabitants
◉	Place of 50,000 to 100,000 inhabitants
●	Place of 25,000 to 50,000 inhabitants
○	Largest place in a congressional district without a place of at least 25,000 inhabitants
	State capital underlined

U.S. Department of Commerce   BUREAU OF THE CENSUS

Congressional districts established March 3, 1982; all other boundaries are as of January 1, 1980.

KEY

ALLEGHENY COUNTY
1 McCandless Township
2 Ross Township
3 Shaler Township
4 Plum
5 Penn Hills
6 Monroeville
7 West Mifflin
8 Mount Lebanon
9 McKeesport
10 Bethel Park

MONTGOMERY COUNTY
1 Upper Moreland Township
2 Norristown
3 Abington Township
4 Upper Merion Township
5 Cheltenham Township
6 Lower Merion Township

BUCKS COUNTY
1 Warminster
2 Falls Township
3 Bristol Township
4 Bensalem Township

PHILADELPHIA COUNTY
1 Philadelphia

DELAWARE COUNTY
1 Radnor Township
2 Haverford Township
3 Upper Darby
4 Springfield
5 Chester
6 Ridley Township

Philadelphia has spread like London over a vast and mostly hilly countryside. Some of the oldest parts of that expansion, plus the older part of Center City, form the 1st congressional district of Pennsylvania. It has all of South Philadelphia, the still resolutely Italian neighborhood directly south of Center City; it has the neighborhood around the University of Pennsylvania. North of Center City it stays east of Broad Street; this leaves it including several black wards, but as you get closer to the river the black presence almost suddenly stops; these remain white neighborhoods, and the pace of racial change in this area is exceedingly slow. The 1st district includes some black precincts, but most of this area is nearly all white. It includes the old Kensington neighborhood, a place along the Delaware River where people of Irish and Italian descent live in rude frame houses, and income levels are lower than in most black neighborhoods; walking around, you feel that you could be back in the 1930s. Overall, the 1st is about one-third black; blacks are just one more minority in the ethnic mix here.

The 1st district is a heavily Democratic district in national elections, although some of its white wards did vote for Ronald Reagan in 1980. It has also been the scene of some rather complicated congressional politics; the current 1st is a combination of two old districts, one of which ten years ago was, in effect, a combination of two more. Such are the political effects of declining population: three congressional districts have essentially been compacted into one. Oddly, the Democratic congressman here, Thomas Foglietta, made most of his career as a

Republican; he ran in 1980 as an Independent, supported by Mayor William Green, against convicted Abscam defendant Ozzie Myers (one of Frank Rizzo's gifts to Congress), and beat him 38%–34%. In 1982 he had a primary against Joseph Smith, another replacement of an Abscam defendant; it was bitterly contested, and Foglietta ended up the winner by a 52%–48% margin. His secret was intense cultivation of the district's Democratic ward and precinct committeemen, plus support from Green and the city's newspapers.

Foglietta is a member of two committees of practical importance to the district: Merchant Marine and Fisheries, and Armed Services. The importance of the first is obvious: Philadelphia is a port, with maritime companies and unions which are subsidized through maritime laws. As for Armed Services, the 1st district is just downriver from the Frankford Arsenal and contains the Philadelphia Navy Yard. The military would like to phase out both facilities, but Pennsylvania politicians, and candidates like Jimmy Carter running in Pennsylvania, fought to retain them. Ironically, the Reagan administration's plans to expand the Navy, fought for by Navy Secretary John Lehman, a Philadelphian, may require the reopening or expansion of naval bases in Philadelphia, Brooklyn, or Newport, Rhode Island. On other issues, Foglietta, despite his Republican background, votes a pretty solidly Democratic line.

The People   Pop. 1980: 515,145, dn. 16.6% 1970–80; voting age pop. 374,046; 29% Black, 7% Span. orig., 2% Asian orig. 38% housing units rented. Median owner $16,800; renter $148. Households: 65% family, 35% with children, 40% married couples.

Presidential Vote

1980	Reagan (R)	67,243	(35%)
	Carter (D)	112,273	(58%)
	Other	14,172	(7%)

Rep. Thomas M. Foglietta (D) Elected 1980; b. Dec. 3, 1928, Philadelphia; home, Philadelphia; St. Joseph's Col., B.A. 1949, Temple U., J.D. 1952; Roman Catholic.

Career Practicing atty., 1952–80; Philadelphia City Cncl., 1955–75; Repub. Nominee for Mayor of Philadelphia, 1975; Regional Dir., U.S. Dept. of Labor, 1976.

Offices 1217 LHOB, 202-225-4731. Also Wm. J. Green Fed. Bldg., 600 Arch St., Philadelphia 19106, 215-925-6840.

Committees *Armed Services* (19th). Subcommittees: Military Installations and Facilities; Readiness; Seapower and Strategic and Critical Materials. *Merchant Marine and Fisheries* (14th). Subcommittees: Coast Guard and Navigation; Merchant Marine; Panama Canal and Outer Continental Shelf.

Group Ratings

	ADA	ACLU	COPE	CFA	LCV	LWV	NTU	NSI	COC	ACA	CSFC
1982	85	75	92	77	90	83	3	22	20	19	28
1981	90	—	87	86	86	—	18	—	11	21	32

National Journal Ratings

	Economic		Foreign		Cultural	
1982	92%	(LIB)	72%	(LIB)	86%	(LIB)
	7%	(CONS)	28%	(CONS)	13%	(CONS)
1981	86%	(LIB)	84%	(LIB)	76%	(LIB)
	14%	(CONS)	15%	(CONS)	24%	(CONS)

Key Votes

1) Reagan 81 Budget	AGN	5) Incr SS Rtmt Age	AGN	9) Poor Pay Food Stamps	AGN
2) Reagan 81 Tax Cut	AGN	6) Saudi AWACS Sale	AGN	10) Ban Crt Busing Order	AGN
3) Bal Budget Amend	AGN	7) $ for MX Missile	AGN	11) Auto Local Content	FOR
4) Gas & Road Tax	FOR	8) Nerve Gas Prod	AGN	12) Nuclear Arms Freeze	FOR

Election Results

1982 general	Thomas M. Foglietta (D)	103,626	(73%)	($430,303)
	Michael Marino (R)	38,155	(27%)	($211,376)
1982 primary	Thomas M. Foglietta (D)	33,683	(52%)	
	Joseph F. Smith (D)	31,277	(48%)	($93,359)
1980 general	Thomas M. Foglietta (I)	58,737	(38%)	($142,835)
(PA 1)	Michael O. Myers (D)	52,956	(34%)	($45,926)
	Robert R. Burke (R)	37,893	(24%)	($37,484)
1980 general	Raymond F. Lederer (D)	67,942	(55%)	($158,026)
(PA 3)	William J. Phillips (R)	40,866	(33%)	($33,580)
	Max Weiner (Consumer)	11,849	(10%)	($9,743)

Campaign Contributions and Expenditures

1980-82		Direct Cont. 81-82		PACS brkdwn			
Receipts	$440,209	Indiv	$278,026	Agr	$800	Ideo	$30,300
Expend.	$430,303	Party	$6,670	Bus	$19,050	Lbr	$86,000
Unspent	$13,165	PACS	$153,700	Hlth	$10,500	Prof	$5,500

SECOND DISTRICT

The 2d congressional district of Pennsylvania is an oddly shaped chunk of the city of Philadelphia. It spans the Schuylkill River, but is not easily connected by any surface street. The shape, however, makes demographic sense: this is Philadelphia's black majority district, and 80% of its residents are black, compared to 32% in the 1st district next door. The 2d includes most of the North Philadelphia and West Philadelphia black neighborhoods; here, in houses mostly built at least 100 years ago, Philadelphia's poorer blacks live in slum and near-slum neighborhoods. Black population movement in Philadelphia has tended to go northwest, so that Germantown, during the Revolutionary War an entirely separate city from Philadelphia and once almost all white, is now almost entirely a black neighborhood. Here in stone houses, in hilly neighborhoods interspersed with parks, you find Philadelphia's black middle class. Farther north are what were once Jewish postwar subdivisions, just within the city line, which are mostly black now too.

This is a heavily Democratic district, the most Democratic in Pennsylvania. There was a day when Philadelphia's black community—a large and well-established one, even before the Civil War—often voted Republican. In some local contests in recent years, large numbers of blacks voted Republican: against Frank Rizzo in 1971, for example, for District Attorney (now Senator) Arlen Specter in 1965 and 1969, and for Governor Richard Thornburgh in

1978. But in presidential and congressional contests, there is not much in the way of a Republican vote here.

In 1978 the district's House seat changed hands, from one of the least active of the Congressional Black Caucus's members to one of its most politically adept. The winner was William Gray III, a young Baptist minister who nearly won the seat in 1976 and returned to beat incumbent Robert Nix two years later. In his first term Gray won a seat on the Budget Committee; in his second he left Budget but got Appropriations, a permanent assignment; now he serves on both Budget and Appropriations. In the process he made some allies by relinquishing seats he could have had and earned some respect by maneuvering.

Gray evidently does not see his job as one simply of articulating black discontent; he shares many of the views but not much of the *modus operandi* of some of the older, more outspoken members of the Black Caucus. Instead, he seems quietly to be building up influence. To exactly what end is not immediately apparent. But legislative craftsmanship does not usually make headlines, and Gray's concentration on seemingly dry budgetary matters and foreign policy has provided his opponents with some ammunition.

Still, Gray's course evidently pleases his constituents. In 1982 he had opposition in the general election from Milton Street, a state senator of extreme verbal militance; Street ran as an Independent, though he is a Republican by virtue of a well-timed and well-rewarded party switch which gave Republicans control of the state Senate. Street is about as well-known and controversial as it is possible to be, and bitterly opposed to Gray; but he was able to win only 22% of the vote to Gray's 76%. To the extent that Gray's victory resulted from the preference of black voters for moderate rather than militant and articulate rather than loud representation, it presaged the emergence of former City Administrator Wilson Goode as the choice for mayor not only of black voters but of enough whites to enable him to beat Frank Rizzo in the 1983 Democratic primary. Goode's victory and Gray's prominence seem to give a new and positive tone to Philadelphia politics.

The People Pop. 1980: 517,215, dn. 17.5% 1970–80; voting age pop. 378,182; 76% Black, 1% Span. orig., 1% Asian orig. 42% housing units rented. Median owner $16,600; renter $157. Households: 61% family, 35% with children, 32% married couples.

Presidential Vote

1980	Reagan (R)	22,999	(11%)
	Carter (D)	177,995	(84%)
	Anderson (I)	10,032	(5%)

Rep. William H. Gray III (D) Elected 1978; b. Aug. 20, 1942, Baton Rouge, LA; home, Philadelphia; Franklin and Marshall Col., B.A. 1963, Drew U. Theological Seminary, M.A. 1966, 1972, Princeton U., M.A. 1970; Baptist.

Career Church history professor; Senior minister, Union Baptist Church, Montclair, NJ, 1966–72; Senior minister, Bright Hope Baptist Church, Philadelphia, 1972–.

Offices 204 CHOB, 202-225-4001. Also 6753 Germantown Ave., Philadelphia 19119, 215-438-6070.

Committees *Appropriations* (30th). Subcommittees: Foreign Operations; Transportation. *Budget* (15th). Task Forces: Economic Policy and Growth; Education and Employment; International Finance and Trade. *District of Columbia* (6th). Subcommittees: Fiscal Affairs and Health; Government Operations and Metropolitan Affairs (Chairman).

Group Ratings

	ADA	ACLU	COPE	CFA	LCV	LWV	NTU	NSI	COC	ACA	CSFC
1982	85	96	97	85	83	80	36	0	26	0	23
1981	90	—	96	79	73	—	26	—	6	0	21
1980	72	97	95	86	81	90	17	0	62	19	24

National Journal Ratings

	Economic		Foreign		Cultural	
1982	94%	(LIB)	99%	(LIB)	79%	(LIB)
	5%	(CONS)	1%	(CONS)	20%	(CONS)
1981	98%	(LIB)	92%	(LIB)	95%	(LIB)
	1%	(CONS)	2%	(CONS)	1%	(CONS)

Key Votes

1) Reagan 81 Budget	AGN	5) Incr SS Rtmt Age	AGN	9) Poor Pay Food Stamps	AGN
2) Reagan 81 Tax Cut	AGN	6) Saudi AWACS Sale	AGN	10) Ban Crt Busing Order	AGN
3) Bal Budget Amend	AGN	7) $ for MX Missile	AGN	11) Auto Local Content	FOR
4) Gas & Road Tax	FOR	8) Nerve Gas Prod	AGN	12) Nuclear Arms Freeze	FOR

Election Results

1982 general	William H. Gray III (D)	120,744	(76%)	($251,494)
	Milton Street (Own party)	35,205	(22%)	($43,657)
1982 primary	William H. Gray III (D)	50,428	(88%)	
	George G. Britt, Jr. (D)	6,964	(12%)	
1980 general	William H. Gray III (D)	127,106	(96%)	($182,192)
	Two others (I, Consumer)	5,865	(4%)	

Campaign Contributions and Expenditures

1981-82		Direct Cont. 81-82		PACS brkdwn			
Receipts	$255,727	Indiv	$118,037	Agr	$500	Ideo	$8,450
Expend.	$251,494	Party	$1,190	Bus	$10,670	Lbr	$86,419
Unspent	$1,191	PACS	$116,562	Hlth	$6,150	Prof	$3,200
		Cand	$8,427				

THIRD DISTRICT

The 3d congressional district of Pennsylvania is northeast Philadelphia, an area with no exact counterpart in any of our other great cities. It includes now almost one-third of the city's population, and in its farther reaches its population is still growing. Some of northeast Philadelphia resembles many other city neighborhoods. The blocks along the Delaware River, with their closely-packed brick row houses and neighborhood bars with neon lights, their mostly Irish and Italian residents and their pungent accents—you expect to see a Democratic (except that in Philadelphia it would have been Republican) ward leader knocking on the doors and distributing coal for the winter. Away from these old neighborhoods, however, you get to the northeast. Out here, 10 to 20 miles from Independence Hall, middle-income tract housing was still going up in the 1960s; more than half the housing units here, in fact, were built after 1950 (as compared to 20% in the rest of the city).

A sizable percentage of northeast Philadelphia's population is Jewish, in neighborhoods that are like neither Brooklyn nor Scarsdale. The houses are pleasant, but modest; the politics Democratic, but not always liberal. Many of these Jews are part of the hard-pressed lower middle class, and can no more afford radical chic than designer clothes. Many voted for Frank Rizzo in his heyday, and many live in fear that blacks will move into their neighborhoods (as they did into Jewish neighborhoods farther west). Northeast Philadelphia also has a sizable Catholic population, which is still pretty conservative on cultural issues. In many ways this is a district out of the 1950s.

The congressional representation of northeast Philadelphia has changed twice in the last three elections. In 1978 Republican Charles Dougherty defeated incumbent Joshua Eilberg, who was charged with accepting $100,000 to help a Philadelphia hospital get a federal grant and was indicted just before the election. Dougherty, a scrappy former Marine, got into a fight with Billy Meehan, the Philadelphia Republican chairman, and was nearly beaten in the 1980 primary, but he won that general election solidly in a Republican year.

In 1982 he was not so fortunate. The legislature, though Republican, did him no favors in redistricting, perhaps on the assumption he didn't need any; the Democrats nominated, in state legislator Robert Borski, an attractive and aggressive young candidate from the older part of the district. Reaganomics did the rest. Dougherty was one of the small number of House Republicans who actually opposed Reagan on some major economic votes. Nevertheless, he supported him on others and, in a recession year in a Democratic district, paid the price on election day.

Borski is now in the fortunate position of a politician who took a chance and saw it pay off; his decision to run against Dougherty was risky, but now he has what should be a safe Democratic seat. He serves on practical-minded committees, Public Works and Merchant Marine, and seems likely to be the kind of politician who will tend closely to district matters and vote with his party on most national issues, except those (like abortion) on which he is strongly committed to particular views.

The People   Pop. 1980: 516,154, dn. 6.6% 1970–80; voting age pop. 391,605; 7% Black, 1% Span. orig., 1% Asian orig. 26% housing units rented. Median owner $32,700; renter $201. Households: 74% family, 34% with children, 59% married couples.

Presidential Vote

1980	Reagan (R)	123,809	(50%)
	Carter (D)	100,673	(41%)
	Other	23,568	(9%)

Rep. Robert A. Borski (D) Elected 1982; b. Oct. 20, 1948, Philadelphia; home, Philadelphia; U. of Baltimore, B.A. 1971; Roman Catholic.

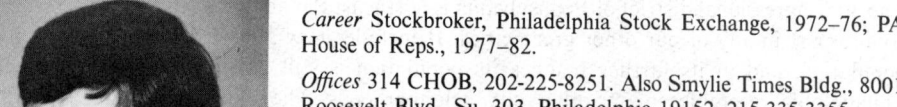

Career Stockbroker, Philadelphia Stock Exchange, 1972–76; PA House of Reps., 1977–82.

Offices 314 CHOB, 202-225-8251. Also Smylie Times Bldg., 8001 Roosevelt Blvd., Su. 303, Philadelphia 19152, 215-335-3355.

Committees *Merchant Marine and Fisheries* (19th). Subcommittees: Coast Guard and Navigation; Merchant Marine; Panama Canal and Outer Continental Shelf. *Public Works and Transportation* (23d). Subcommittees: Economic Development; Investigations and Oversight; Surface Transportation. *Select Committee on Aging* (30th). Subcommittee: Health and Long-Term Care.

Group Ratings and Key Votes: Newly Elected

Election Results

1982 general	Robert A. Borski (D)	97,161	(50%)	($235,326)
	Charles F. Dougherty (R)	94,497	(49%)	($316,992)
1982 primary	Robert A. Borski (D)	30,318	(58%)	
	Malcolm P. Rosenberg (D)	17,628	(33%)	($71,466)
	John R. Fitzpatrick (D)	4,690	(9%)	
1980 general	Charles F. Dougherty (R)	127,475	(63%)	($256,961)
	Thomas J. Magrann (D)	73,895	(37%)	($248,946)

Campaign Contributions and Expenditures

1981-82		Direct Cont. 81-82		PACS brkdwn			
Receipts	$244,533	Indiv	$163,254	Agr	$500	Ideo	$8,050
Expend.	$235,326	Party	$2,496	Bus	$3,500	Lbr	$28,450
Unspent	$9,206	PACS	$61,235	Hlth	$450	Prof	$2,250
		Cand	$8,200				

Indirect Party Expend: $107

FOURTH DISTRICT

The 4th congressional district of Pennsylvania was the scene of one of the nation's most-publicized party switches since John Connally became a Republican and before Phil Gramm became one. In Pennsylvania, if not in either case in Texas, the switch turned out better for the party spurned than for the one embraced. The district's boundaries, ragged and jagged at the edge, were drawn by a Republican legislature to help the new Republican recruit, Congressman Eugene Atkinson, but in vain. The 4th includes the steel towns of Beaver Falls, Aliquippa, and New Castle, all just northwest of Pittsburgh; Butler County, a somewhat more rural and Republican area directly north of Pittsburgh, and the mountainous country northeast of Pittsburgh, including the elite exurb of Ligonier.

President Reagan made quite an impression here when, still recovering from his gunshot wounds, he called Congressman Atkinson on a radio call-in show and asked for his support of his economic program. Atkinson agreed to support it, and then agreed to become a Republican. The Republican legislature cooperated by drawing a favorable district (as a Democrat, Atkinson might have had his district eliminated entirely), and the national Republican Party poured in money and top-level campaigners.

But the strategy failed for two reasons. First, the economy didn't rebound, as Reagan and Atkinson both hoped; the steel country in and around the 4th district was in obvious trouble. Western Pennsylvania trended fairly heavily away from all Republicans, even Senator John Heinz, in 1982. Second, Atkinson was not a strong candidate. He has a history of losing or doing poorly in elections: he lost to Republican Congressman Gary Myers in 1976, a weak candidate in a Democratic district in a Democratic year; he won the 1978 Democratic primary, which admittedly had 11 candidates, with only 25% of the vote; he won the general election that year with less than an absolute majority. He supported Edward Kennedy in 1980 and Ronald Reagan in 1981—a switch that many voters may have thought represented the floundering of a weak politician rather than a principled change of heart. In the 1982 Republican primary, despite the obvious evidence of national Republican support, Atkinson beat a local Republican by an unimpressive 56%–44% margin. So, although Atkinson had more money than his Democratic opponent, there were plenty of reasons to think he would lose in 1982.

And he did, by a 60%–39% margin. In his home area, Beaver County, Atkinson lost 69%–29%. The winner was Joseph Kolter, a state legislator for 14 years. Kolter had solid labor and party support and is considered likely to have a solid labor record in the House. He worked his way up in politics by supporting Democratic policies and making no trouble for Democratic leaders, and that is presumably the course he will continue to take. This district is not quite Democratic enough to say that it is safe for him, but it is close. It has had a series of weak congressmen, and if Kolter works it hard and well, he should be able to hold it for a long time.

The People Pop. 1980: 515,572, up 6.1% 1970–80; voting age pop. 375,245; 2% Black. 22% housing units rented. Median owner $39,400; renter $155. Households: 78% family, 40% with children, 68% married couples.

Presidential Vote

1980	Reagan (R)	89,266	(47%)
	Carter (D)	87,587	(46%)
	Other	12,744	(7%)

Rep. Joseph P. Kolter (D) Elected 1982; b. Sept. 3, 1926, New Brighton; home, New Brighton; Geneva Col., B.S. 1950, Duquesne U., U. of Pittsburgh; Roman Catholic.

Career Accountant, 1950–67; High sch. teacher, 1950, 1965–67; New Brighton Borough Cncl., 1962–66; PA House of Reps., 1969–82.

Offices 212 CHOB, 202-225-2565. Also 1322 7th Ave., Beaver Falls 15010, 412-846-3600.

Committees *Government Operations* (24th). Subcommittees: Environment, Energy, and Natural Resources; Manpower and Housing. *Public Works and Transportation* (24th). Subcommittees: Economic Development; Surface Transportation.

Group Ratings and Key Votes: Newly Elected

Election Results

1982 general	Joseph P. Kolter (D)	100,481	(60%)	($191,200)
	Eugene V. Atkinson (R)	64,539	(39%)	($331,477)
1982 primary	Joseph P. Kolter (D)	17,835	(46%)	
	Peter O. Steege (D)	7,703	(20%)	($55,890)
	John R. Burick (D)	5,915	(15%)	
	Vance Krites (D)	4,738	(12%)	
	Leonard N. Magiocca (D)	2,243	(6%)	
1980 general	Eugene V. Atkinson (D)	119,817	(67%)	($51,196)
	Robert Morris (R)	58,768	(33%)	($89,379)

Campaign Contributions and Expenditures

1981-82		Direct Cont. 81-82		PACS brkdwn			
Receipts	$196,797	Indiv	$52,563	Agr	$2,500	Ideo	$15,150
Expend.	$191,200	Party	$5,250	Bus	$2,750	Lbr	$103,250
Unspent	$5,594	PACS	$132,688	Hlth	$500	Prof	$250
		Cand	$6,000				

Indirect Party Expend: $5,228

FIFTH DISTRICT

The 5th congressional district of Pennsylvania is, technically, part of the Philadelphia metropolitan area—the outer edges of suburban Delaware and Montgomery Counties, plus most of Chester County farther out. In fact, this is country studded with separate settlements with histories and personalities which date back to the times when Philadelphia was a day or so's horse ride away. Chester, a small industrial town on the Delaware River, is really an old city which for years had its own Republican machine; most of its residents are black now. The Chadds Ford area, where the Wyeth family lives and paints, is peaceful countryside far from the brawling tone of Philadelphia public life. Kennett Square nearby is the center of the nation's mushroom industry. Coatesville, at the western edge of the district, is really part of the Pennsylvania Dutch country, although no one is sure just where the boundary is. Not far away is Oxford, home of Lincoln University, one of the nation's oldest black colleges—a symbol of the area's Lincoln Republican heritage and a reminder that there are many blacks scattered over this area. About 5% of the population of all the boroughs and townships is black.

The 5th district is one of the premier Republican congressional districts in the nation. Its Main Line commuters at the Paoli station, its Pennsylvania Dutch country, even the area around Chester—all are heavily Republican. This is one of those heartland Republican districts which for decades has supplied the House Republican Conference with its backbenchers and its most reliable supporters.

The current congressman, Richard Schulze, is a Republican Party loyalist with roots in the richest part of the district. He has taken jobs of sufficient modesty—Chester County register of wills, state representative—to suggest that he was seen as the kind of faithful local functionary who is allowed, by men of great power who commute to offices in the big city, to handle affairs in their small local community.

Schulze has greater responsibilities now, of course, but may still be similarly regarded. He easily won the Republican primary for this seat in 1974 and has been reelected without perceptible difficulty since. His record on major issues is impeccably Republican. He is a member of the Ways and Means Committee and its subcommittees on Select Revenue Measures and Trade. These are not inconsiderable positions. Select Revenue Measures handles all those special tax laws which are usually of minimal fiscal concern but are of great concern to particular taxpayers. Trade handles and monitors most trade legislation. Schulze is considered sympathetic to requests for tax relief, and, as a loyal son of Pennsylvania, is one of the most protection-minded members of the Trade Subcommittee—a strong advocate of strict enforcement of antidumping legislation and supporter of trade barriers, on products from steel to mushrooms.

The People   Pop. 1980: 515,528, up 9.8% 1970–80; voting age pop. 370,556; 10% Black, 1% Span. orig., 1% Asian orig. 29% housing units rented. Median owner $57,300; renter $225. Households: 77% family, 42% with children, 64% married couples.

Presidential Vote

1980	Reagan (R)	107,588	(58%)
	Carter (D)	59,107	(32%)
	Other	18,493	(10%)

Rep. Richard T. Schulze (R) Elected 1974; b. Aug. 7, 1929, Philadelphia; home, Malvern; U. of Houston, 1949–50, Villanova U., 1952; Presbyterian.

Career Army, 1951–53; Proprietor, Home Appliance Ctr., Paoli; Chester Cnty. Register of Wills and Clerk of Orphans Ct., 1967–69; PA House of Reps., 1969–74.

Offices 2421 RHOB, 202-225-5761. Also 2 W. Lancaster Ave., Paoli 19301, 215-648-0555.

Committee *Ways and Means* (8th). Subcommittees: Select Revenue Measures; Trade.

Group Ratings

	ADA	ACLU	COPE	CFA	LCV	LWV	NTU	NSI	COC	ACA	CSFC
1982	15	17	19	31	19	44	77	100	81	57	63
1981	10	—	17	21	14	—	87	—	94	92	77
1980	0	23	17	21	17	22	53	100	75	86	77

National Journal Ratings

	Economic		Foreign		Cultural	
1982	33%	(LIB)	38%	(LIB)	46%	(LIB)
	67%	(CONS)	62%	(CONS)	54%	(CONS)
1981	4%	(LIB)	3%	(LIB)	16%	(LIB)
	79%	(CONS)	87%	(CONS)	83%	(CONS)

Key Votes

1) Reagan 81 Budget	FOR	5) Incr SS Rtmt Age	FOR	9) Poor Pay Food Stamps	FOR
2) Reagan 81 Tax Cut	FOR	6) Saudi AWACS Sale	FOR	10) Ban Crt Busing Order	FOR
3) Bal Budget Amend	FOR	7) $ for MX Missile	FOR	11) Auto Local Content	—
4) Gas & Road Tax	FOR	8) Nerve Gas Prod	FOR	12) Nuclear Arms Freeze	—

Election Results

1982 general	Richard T. Schulze (R)	90,648	(67%)	($207,452)
	Bob Burger (D)	44,170	(33%)	($13,811)
1982 primary	Richard T. Schulze (R)	26,592	(83%)	
	Paul J. McGarvey (R)	3,251	(10%)	
	Bob G. Hill (R)	2,122	(7%)	
1980 general	Richard T. Schulze (R)	148,898	(75%)	($133,815)
	Grady G. Brickhouse (D)	47,092	(24%)	($4,761)

Campaign Contributions and Expenditures

1981-82		Direct Cont. 81-82				PACS brkdwn		
Receipts	$234,376	Indiv	$97,025	Agr	$3,000	Ideo	$1,500
Expend.	$207,452	Party	$19,676	Bus	$84,100	Lbr	$500
Unspent	$145,470	PACS	$95,950	Hlth	$6,100	Prof	$750

SIXTH DISTRICT

The 6th congressional district of Pennsylvania is betwixt and between—a part of eastern Pennsylvania beyond the Philadelphia orbit, south of the center of the anthracite area of northeastern Pennsylvania, and northeast of the Pennsylvania Dutch country. It crosses the barrier between the fertile, rolling plains of southeastern Pennsylvania, and the ridges of mountains which run like corduroy, on a curved diagonal, across the northeastern and central parts of the state. About 60% of the district's population is south of Blue Mountain, on the hilly land around Reading. This is a factory town, famous in the 19th century for its black broad-brimmed hats and in the early 20th century for its ironware manufactures. The Reading Railroad once made this one of the leading railroad centers of the country. It is now a center of light, not heavy, industry, and its old brick factories are used for factory outlet stores that attract bargain hunters from all over the East. The Dutch country is not far away, and the 6th district now includes a small sliver of heavily Dutch Lancaster County.

North of Blue Mountain is the beginning of the anthracite country. Here in Schuylkill County you find the hard-bitten towns that John O'Hara described in so many of his novels, places where the rich people schemed with bootleggers to get a supply of the best smuggled liquor, where people of more modest background tried and usually failed to imitate upper-class manners, and where tough-talking miners and factory workers seemed to stay menacingly in the background unless a character stumbled into the wrong roadhouse at night or diner at dawn. The anthracite mines were humming and the freight cars constantly loaded up in the small, grimy towns of Schuylkill County 50 years ago, when O'Hara's *Appointment in Samarra* shocked people here; there were 235,000 people living here then. Today, with the mines almost entirely closed, and the economy based on wages lower, relative to the national average, there are 160,000.

The 6th district, in national elections, is not as Democratic as you might expect. A lot of the working-class people who would have been good Democratic voters here moved away, long since, looking for jobs. And in Berks County there is a strong Pennsylvania Dutch population, which has been heavily Republican since it split over the slavery issue with local Democrats James Buchanan of Lancaster and his lieutenant, J. Glancy Jones of Reading, chairman of the House Ways and Means Committee, in the 1858 election.

Nevertheless, the congressional representation here has been Democratic since 1948. The current incumbent, Gus Yatron, has been elected since 1968, and continues to win by overwhelming margins. His general voting record in the House is liberal on economic issues, conservative on cultural matters—which seems very much in line with his district. Yet his career in the House has not been placid. In 1981, after four years in the job, he was ousted from the chairmanship of the Inter-American Affairs Subcommittee by a 10–9 vote of Foreign Affairs Committee Democrats, in favor of Michael Barnes of Maryland. That turned out to be a critical vote, since Barnes is both highly articulate and skeptical of the Reagan administration's policies in Nicaragua, El Salvador, Guatemala, and other parts of Latin America, and Yatron is neither.

That loss must have been quite an indignity to Yatron, just as it was a good example of the accountability of committee and subcommittee chairmen, but he did not quit or walk away; perhaps his experience as a professional heavyweight boxer kept him in this political ring. After the 1982 election, he took over the chair of the Human Rights and International Organizations Subcommittee from Don Bonker of Washington, who relinquished it for another chair. Most of Yatron's fellow subcommittee members, even the ranking Republican, probably take a view of human rights closer to that of the Carter administration than their chairman does; he does not have a lot of leeway to enforce his preference. But the primary function of the subcommittee seems to be to receive the reports that Assistant Secretary of State for Human Rights Elliott Abrams is required to file from time to time, and Yatron as chairman is in a good position to see that these reports—which are carefully compiled and are worthy of bipartisan respect—are received in a sober, serious, and not hysterical or partisan way.

The People   Pop. 1980: 515,952, up 3.9% 1970–80; voting age pop. 384,537; 1% Black, 1% Span. orig. 24% housing units rented. Median owner $32,400; renter $154. Households: 75% family, 36% with children, 63% married couples.

Presidential Vote

1980	Reagan (R)	103,705	(57%)
	Carter (D)	65,229	(36%)
	Other	13,262	(7%)

Rep. Gus Yatron (D) Elected 1968; b. Oct. 16, 1927, Reading; home, Reading; Kutztown St. Teachers Col., 1950; Eastern Orthodox.

Career Pro heavyweight boxer; Proprietor, Yatron's Ice Cream, 1950–69; Mbr., Reading Sch. Bd., 1955–60; PA House of Reps., 1956–60; PA Senate, 1960–68.

Offices 2267 RHOB, 202-225-5546. Also U.S.P.O. Bldg., 5th and Washington Sts., Reading 19603, 215-375-4573.

Committees Foreign Affairs (4th). Subcommittees: Human Rights and International Organizations (Chairman); International Operations. *Post Office and Civil Service* (8th). Subcommittees: Human Resources; Investigations.

Group Ratings

	ADA	ACLU	COPE	CFA	LCV	LWV	NTU	NSI	COC	ACA	CSFC
1982	60	33	81	62	70	73	27	90	41	26	36
1981	40	—	80	71	50	—	35	—	28	58	55
1980	39	27	71	29	54	56	34	80	59	50	50

National Journal Ratings

	Economic		Foreign		Cultural	
1982	68%	(LIB)	48%	(LIB)	38%	(LIB)
	32%	(CONS)	52%	(CONS)	61%	(CONS)
1981	62%	(LIB)	28%	(LIB)	35%	(LIB)
	38%	(CONS)	71%	(CONS)	65%	(CONS)

Key Votes

1) Reagan 81 Budget	AGN	5) Incr SS Rtmt Age	AGN	9) Poor Pay Food Stamps	AGN
2) Reagan 81 Tax Cut	FOR	6) Saudi AWACS Sale	AGN	10) Ban Crt Busing Order	FOR
3) Bal Budget Amend	AGN	7) $ for MX Missile	AGN	11) Auto Local Content	FOR
4) Gas & Road Tax	—	8) Nerve Gas Prod	AGN	12) Nuclear Arms Freeze	FOR

Election Results

1982 general	Gus Yatron (D)	108,230	(72%)	($89,400)
	Harry B. Martin (R)	42,155	(28%)	($3,695)
1982 primary	Gus Yatron (D)	29,617	(100%)	
1980 general	Gus Yatron (D)	117,965	(67%)	($66,845)
	George Hulshart (R)	57,844	(33%)	($13,321)

Campaign Contributions and Expenditures

1981-82		Direct Cont. 81-82		PACS brkdwn			
Receipts	$100,622	Indiv	$46,989	Agr	$1,100	Ideo	$1,300
Expend.	$89,400	Party	$50	Bus	$17,450	Lbr	$23,870
Unspent	$35,383	PACS	$48,770	Hlth	$4,600	Prof	$200

SEVENTH DISTRICT

The 7th congressional district of Pennsylvania contains the larger part of Delaware County, a suburban area outside Philadelphia, plus one ward of the city of Philadelphia itself. You might not notice the difference if you drove over the line between the two units: the mostly white working-class neighborhood in Philadelphia looks a lot like the modest, long-settled close-in suburbs nearby, in Upper Darby Township and a dozen or so small incorporated boroughs. They are all, increasingly, the homes of older people whose families are grown, who still treasure traditional cultural values but also feel pinched during the recession and worried about how they will fare, or are faring, in retirement. Farther out, the houses spread out, and housing values rise, in leafy suburbs like Swarthmore; these also are old, but the people are more secure and less anxious. To the north are some of the suburbs of the Main Line—the highest income and highest status communities in the Philadelphia area. Given the fact that many of the suburbs are inhabited by people who grew up in the closely packed neighborhoods of West and South Philadelphia, you might expect most of these to be Democratic suburbs.

But in fact they are the home of one of the nation's oldest Republican organizations, the Delaware County War Board; it continues to dominate local government here, and this part of Delaware County continues to vote Republican in just about every election but its House contest. This may be a reaction, by suburbanites shuddering not far from the border, against the evil big city; you see this sort of thing in the politics of suburbs of Chicago. But it may also be, in some cases, a residual Republicanism, which survived the New Deal. After all, Philadelphia itself had a Republican mayor until 1951 and was solidly enough Republican in 1948 that Pennsylvania went for Dewey over Truman. And the overall Philadelphia metropolitan area—perhaps the appropriate standard of comparison—went Republican not only in the presidential election of 1980 but the senatorial and gubernatorial elections of 1982.

But in congressional elections this district continues to reelect Democrat Bob Edgar. His has been a most improbable career. A Methodist minister who still, as he turns 40, looks to be in his 20s, he was outraged when Richard Nixon fired Archibald Cox, and he ran for Congress just as the national trend of opinion and a local feud between the War Board and other Republicans gave him an opening. He has remained in office not by propitiating the conservative views of his constituents on one or another set of issues, but by compiling one of the most liberal voting records in the country. He sees himself not as an upper-income voters' congressman but as one who represents the working-class from which he himself sprang, and he woos what working-class Democratic base there is here with this theme.

But he has been even more successful in wooing a needed margin of upscale votes by defying the conventional wisdom about how to get along in Congress. He has ruffled his elders in almost every conceivable way. As a member of the Public Works and Transportation Committee, he has led the opposition to the Tennessee–Tombigbee Waterway and once killed $1.4 billion in dams and water projects in 46 states. He delights in challenging the highway, construction, and navigation lobbies; he strongly supports mass transit. He has bucked the leadership of the Veterans' Affairs Committee by calling for more counseling centers and readjustment programs for Vietnam era veterans. He called for formal investigations of fellow Pennsylvania Democrats Daniel Flood and Joshua Eilberg when serious charges were made against them. Edgar does these things coolly, realizing now if he did not early in his career that they will outrage senior colleagues.

But in the House of the 1970s and 1980s his positions have not destroyed his capacity to do useful work. He helped to organize a Northeast–Midwest Caucus of representatives from both parties of these regions, and set up a Northeast–Midwest Institute which has done valuable research on the need for and distribution of federal dollars in the different parts of the country. His fights against what he considers pork barrel projects often win. His viewpoint on Vietnam veterans seemed in 1983 about to carry the day. Flood and Eilberg are gone, and the senior Democrats on the Pennsylvania delegation who dislike and distrust Edgar have no more clout—maybe a little less—in the House than he does.

Still, he is in precarious shape in the 7th district. His 55% victory in 1982 was his best showing since his first election in 1974. It was eked out with a large campaign budget, a substantial volunteer organization, and with help from environmentalists who consider Edgar one of their leading priorities in the country. Although he is rising in seniority and chairs the Veterans' Hospitals and Health Care Subcommittee, he does not see himself remaining in the House forever, and he is probably contemplating a statewide candidacy, for senator or governor, in 1986, after one more House race. His problem—and it is shared by Pennsylvania Democrats of all stripes—is that he has access to neither organization nor money, and this is a big state with an expensive media buy. But perhaps his unconventional positions in the House will help him here, again.

The People   Pop. 1980: 515,766, dn. 8.3% 1970–80; voting age pop. 387,309; 5% Black, 1% Span. orig., 1% Asian orig. 25% housing units rented. Median owner $45,600; renter $233. Households: 75% family, 36% with children, 62% married couples.

Presidential Vote

1980	Reagan (R)	136,454	(56%)
	Carter (D)	83,328	(34%)
	Other	24,156	(10%)

Rep. Robert W. (Bob) Edgar (D) Elected 1974; b. May 29, 1943, Philadelphia; home, Broomall; Lycoming Col., B.A. 1965; Drew U. Theological Seminary, M.Div. 1968; Methodist.

Career Minister; United Protestant Chaplain, Drexel U., 1968–71; Codir., People's Emergency Ctr., 1971–75.

Offices 2352 RHOB, 202-225-2011. Also 204 Long Lane, Upper Darby 19082, 215-352-0790.

Committees *Public Works and Transportation* (9th). Subcommittees: Aviation; Surface Transportation; Water Resources. *Veterans' Affairs* (3d). Subcommittees: Education, Training and Employment; Hospitals and Health Care (Chairman).

Group Ratings

	ADA	ACLU	COPE	CFA	LCV	LWV	NTU	NSI	COC	ACA	CSFC
1982	100	100	88	77	90	92	36	0	24	9	25
1981	100	—	87	93	100	—	46	—	6	14	28
1980	94	93	78	79	93	100	22	0	55	10	27

National Journal Ratings

	Economic		Foreign		Cultural	
1982	99%	(LIB)	92%	(LIB)	89%	(LIB)
	1%	(CONS)	6%	(CONS)	8%	(CONS)
1981	89%	(LIB)	92%	(LIB)	94%	(LIB)
	3%	(CONS)	2%	(CONS)	6%	(CONS)

Key Votes

1) Reagan 81 Budget	AGN	5) Incr SS Rtmt Age	AGN	9) Poor Pay Food Stamps	AGN
2) Reagan 81 Tax Cut	AGN	6) Saudi AWACS Sale	AGN	10) Ban Crt Busing Order	AGN
3) Bal Budget Amend	AGN	7) $ for MX Missile	AGN	11) Auto Local Content	FOR
4) Gas & Road Tax	FOR	8) Nerve Gas Prod	AGN	12) Nuclear Arms Freeze	FOR

Election Results

1982 general	Robert W. (Bob) Edgar (D)	105,775	(55%)	($495,013)
	Steve Joachim (R)	85,023	(45%)	($296,041)
1982 primary	Robert W. (Bob) Edgar (D)	16,425	(82%)	
	Robert E. Moran (D)	3,601	(18%)	
1980 general	Robert W. (Bob) Edgar (D)	99,381	(53%)	($295,529)
	Dennis J. Rochford (R)	87,643	(47%)	($253,406)

Campaign Contributions and Expenditures

1981-82		Direct Cont. 81-82		PACS brkdwn			
Receipts	$493,723	Indiv	$300,552	Agr	$3,700	Ideo	$56,250
Expend.	$495,013	Party	$5,000	Bus	$18,470	Lbr	$92,945
Unspent	$7,289	PACS	$190,229	Hlth	$2,250	Prof	$3,500
		Cand	$560				

Indep Expend: For: $24,762 (LCV) Agn: $8,943 (NCPAC)

EIGHTH DISTRICT

The 8th congressional district of Pennsylvania is one of four suburban Philadelphia districts. It includes a small part of Montgomery County, just about directly north of Philadelphia's Center City, and all of Bucks County, which has 93% of the district's population. Bucks County is one of those place names that have entered our literary imagination. The northwestern or upper part of the county is rolling farmland, easily reached by train from New York as well as Philadelphia. It has long been the residence of well-known writers and artists, who live in stone Quaker farmhouses near such villages as New Hope and Lumberville. Their neighbors are sometimes Pennsylvania Dutch farmers or, more often, comfortably-off people with jobs somewhere closer-in in the Philadelphia area.

But this is not the whole story of Bucks County; Upper Bucks has only about half the district's population. Lower Bucks County is an entirely different place—predominantly industrial and blue collar. Here is U.S. Steel's giant Fairless Works; here also is one of the original Levittowns. In the other suburban Philadelphia counties, most of the blue-collar immigration took place a long time ago, when Philadelphia itself was solidly Republican and the suburban county machines ready to enroll new residents in their party. But in Bucks the blue-collar migration came late, in the 1950s and 1960s, and there is a strong Democratic voting base around Levittown and Bristol in the lower county. The Republican tendencies of Upper Bucks and Montgomery Counties still carry the district in most elections. But there is a sizable Democratic base here too, and sometimes this is the most Democratic of all the suburban Philadelphia districts.

The 8th has switched parties three times in the last four elections, each time somewhat unexpectedly. The beneficiary in two of the three cases, and the loser in the other, is the current congressman, Peter Kostmayer. He was a product of the Democratic politics of the middle 1970s: a press aide to Governor Milton Shapp who, at age 30, won a seat in Congress with some help from national trends, Republican feuds and hard campaigning. Vigorous opposition to corruption—he urged early investigations of Koreagate and of his fellow Pennsylvania Democrats Daniel Flood and Joshua Eilberg—and emphasis on environmental issues (he helped kill the Tocks Island Dam on the Delaware) helped Kostmayer to solidify support in Upper Bucks; and Kostmayer easily won reelection in 1978. But in 1980 the district proved too Republican in a year in which economic issues were the center of attention. Republican James Coyne spent much of his own money, earned in the family chemical business, and eked out a 51% victory.

But Kostmayer never stopped running, and was helped when Coyne demanded that the former congressman cease and desist from helping 8th district residents solve their problems with government. Coyne, a free market and Reaganomics enthusiast on economic issues, had a mixed record on cultural issues; he called for the resignation of Interior Secretary James Watt. But he got in trouble on one non-economic issue, the nuclear freeze. Originally a supporter of the nuclear freeze resolution opposed by the Reagan administration, he switched at the last minute when the administration desperately needed a few votes to win on the issue. They did, but Coyne was put very much on the defensive. Kostmayer won a 50%–49% victory.

Now Kostmayer can tend to environmental issues from the Interior Committee and can use congressional staffers, rather than campaign volunteers, to help solve constituents' problems. But in the 1980s he is spending more time than he used to on economic issues. And on trade issues in particular, he seems to be sticking to Pennsylvania orthodoxy: he vigorously denounced U.S. Steel for importing British steel for finishing instead of fabricating the steel itself in the Fairless works. Kostmayer is one of those congressmen mentioned sometimes as a statewide candidate, and he might run for senator in 1986. But first he must be reelected again from this demonstrably iffy district.

The People Pop. 1980: 516,902, up 14.1% 1970–80; voting age pop. 364,239; 2% Black, 1% Span. orig., 1% Asian orig. 25% housing units rented. Median owner $57,100; renter $255. Households: 80% family, 45% with children, 70% married couples.

Presidential Vote

1980	Reagan (R)	105,253	(56%)
	Carter (D)	60,026	(32%)
	Other	21,963	(12%)

Rep. Peter H. Kostmayer (D) Elected 1982; b. Sept. 27, 1946, New York, NY; home, Solebury; Columbia U., B.A. 1971; Episcopal.

Career Reporter, *The Trentonian*, 1971–72; Press Secy. to the Atty. Gen. of PA, 1972–73; Dpty. Press Secy. to PA Gov. Milton Shapp, 1973–76; U.S. House of Reps., 1977–81; Pub. relations consultant, 1981–82.

Offices 123 CHOB, 202-225-4276. Also 44 East Court St., Doylestown 18901, 215-345-8543.

Committees *Foreign Affairs* (16th). Subcommittees: Human Rights and International Organizations; Western Hemisphere Affairs; International Operations. *Interior and Insular Affairs* (23d). Subcommittees: Energy and the Environment; Public Lands and National Parks.

Group Ratings and Key Votes: Newly Elected

Election Results

1982 general	Peter H. Kostmayer (D)	83,242	(50%)	($553,495)
	James K. Coyne (R)	80,928	(49%)	($607,504)
1982 primary	Peter H. Kostmayer (D)	13,745	(100%)	
1980 general	James K. Coyne (R)	103,585	(51%)	($423,002)
	Peter H. Kostmayer (D)	99,593	(49%)	($222,925)

Campaign Contributions and Expenditures

1981-82		*Direct Cont. 81-82*			*PACS brkdwn*		
Receipts	$555,745	Indiv	$293,743	Agr	$2,000	Ideo	$39,060
Expend.	$553,495	Party	$5,281	Bus	$7,180	Lbr	$137,770
Unspent	$2,829	PACS	$204,378	Hlth	$2,250	Prof	$5,300
		Cand	$39,833				

Indirect Party Expend: $501   *Indep Expend:* For: $22,027 (LCV)   *Non-Cand Loans:* $6,000

NINTH DISTRICT

The Appalachian Mountain chain runs like a series of backbones through central Pennsylvania. Throughout the state's history, the mountains have been a formidable barrier, not so much because of their height, which is unspectacular, but because of their persistence: one rugged chain right after another for 50 to 100 miles. During the 18th century, the mountains provided Quaker Pennsylvania with a rampart against Indian attacks, and allowed this to become the richest and most populous of the colonies. But in the 19th century, when people wanted to open up and trade with the vast interior, the mountains got in the way. They prevented Pennsylvania from ever digging a canal system to compete with New York's Erie Canal, and they delayed, until other states had them, the building of an east–west railroad. Only the aggressive policy of the Pennsylvania Railroad, a relative latecomer to the business, saved the state from branch-line status.

The 9th is the only one of Pennsylvania's congressional districts to lie wholly within these mountains. This part of the Alleghenies (the term is often used interchangeably with Appalachians in Pennsylvania) was first settled by poor Scottish and Ulster Irish farmers just after the Revolutionary War. They were a people of fierce independence and pride, as the Whiskey Rebellion demonstrated. They worked their hardscrabble farms and built their little towns. Sometimes coal was found nearby, and their communities changed. But for the most part the 9th is not really coal country, and the area was denied—or spared—the boom–bust cycles of northeastern Pennsylvania and West Virginia. This was an important area for the Pennsylvania Railroad, however. Near Altoona was the railroad's famous Horseshoe Curve, and in Altoona itself the railroad built the nation's largest car yards. As rail transportation became less important, and the Pennsylvania moved from prosperity to merger to bankruptcy, Altoona's population declined from 82,000 at the end of the 1920s to 57,000 in 1980.

This part of Pennsylvania has been solidly Republican since the election of 1860, and it has not come close to electing a Democrat to Congress for years. The current incumbent, E. G. (Bud) Shuster, is an entrepreneur who made a fortune building up a business and selling it to IBM. He decided to settle in the southern Pennsylvania mountains, became interested in local affairs, decided to run for Congress, and beat the favorite, a local state senator, in the 1972 Republican primary. Shuster has won easily since.

Shuster's solid conservatism and enthusiasm have brought him some notice. He was the House's leading opponent of the air bag, for example, and he served as Chairman of the Republican Policy Committee until 1981. He is now the second ranking Republican on the Budget Committee and a high ranking member of Public Works; he is ranking Republican on the Surface Transportation Subcommittee—an important one for a railroad district. In 1983 he published *Believing in America,* an upbeat book in which he expressed optimism about the basic economic and spiritual strength of the country, and of the sort of policies he has supported in Congress. Like so many men who are successful in business and politics, he seems to have essentially an optimistic temperament, and to assume that difficulties will be overcome and problems solved.

The People   Pop. 1980: 515,430, up 8.5% 1970–80; voting age pop. 368,331; 1% Black. 22% housing units rented. Median owner $32,600; renter $137. Households: 78% family, 41% with children, 67% married couples.

Presidential Vote

1980	Reagan (R)	98,711	(60%)
	Carter (D)	58,199	(35%)
	Other	8,422	(5%)

Rep. E. G. (Bud) Shuster (R) Elected 1972; b. Jan. 23, 1932, Glassport; home, W. Providence Twnshp.; U. of Pitt., B.S. 1954, Duquesne U., M.B.A. 1960, American U., Ph.D. 1967; United Church of Christ.

Career V.P., Radio Corp. of Amer.; Operator, Shuster Farms.

Offices 2455 RHOB, 202-225-2431. Also Penn Alto Hotel, Su. M, Altoona 16603, 814-946-1653.

Committees *Budget* (2d). Task Forces: Budget Process; Education and Employment. *Public Works and Transportation* (3d). Subcommittees: Aviation; Economic Development; Surface Transportation.

Group Ratings

	ADA	ACLU	COPE	CFA	LCV	LWV	NTU	NSI	COC	ACA	CSFC
1982	20	0	15	10	31	18	86	100	93	59	69
1981	0	—	14	14	7	—	75	—	89	88	75
1980	6	10	11	14	17	25	63	100	77	91	84

National Journal Ratings

	Economic		Foreign		Cultural	
1982	27%	(LIB)	44%	(LIB)	17%	(LIB)
	73%	(CONS)	56%	(CONS)	83%	(CONS)
1981	4%	(LIB)	18%	(LIB)	4%	(LIB)
	79%	(CONS)	73%	(CONS)	90%	(CONS)

Key Votes

1) Reagan 81 Budget	FOR	5) Incr SS Rtmt Age	FOR	9) Poor Pay Food Stamps	FOR
2) Reagan 81 Tax Cut	FOR	6) Saudi AWACS Sale	AGN	10) Ban Crt Busing Order	—
3) Bal Budget Amend	FOR	7) $ for MX Missile	—	11) Auto Local Content	—
4) Gas & Road Tax	FOR	8) Nerve Gas Prod	AGN	12) Nuclear Arms Freeze	AGN

Election Results

1982 general	E. G. (Bud) Shuster (R)	92,322	(65%)	($256,825)
	Eugene J. Duncan (D)	49,583	(35%)	($17,042)
1982 primary	E. G. (Bud) Shuster (R)	28,566	(100%)	
1980 general	E. G. (Bud) Shuster (R)	157,241	(100%)	($156,048)

Campaign Contributions and Expenditures

1981-82		Direct Cont. 81-82		PACS brkdwn			
Receipts	$314,732	Indiv	$146,030	Agr	$2,100	Ideo	$850
Expend.	$256,825	Party	$9,240	Bus	$82,420	Lbr	$9,400
Unspent	$69,480	PACS	$102,246	Hlth	$5,650	Prof	$1,050

Non-Cand Loans: $43,000

TENTH DISTRICT

Scranton is the anthracite town par excellence. Back around the turn of the century, anthracite or hard coal was much in demand: it was the fuel used to heat most homes, in furnaces or pot-bellied stoves. Because the only major deposits of anthracite in the United States lie in the Scranton–Wilkes-Barre region of northeastern Pennsylvania, these two cities suddenly came on flush times. Immigrants from Italy, Poland, Austria-Hungary, and Ireland poured in to join the Scots and Welsh already working the mines. Scranton became the third largest city in Pennsylvania, and the region around Scranton and Wilkes-Barre held more than 750,000 people by the end of the 1920s.

Then came the Depression of the 1930s and World War II. Scranton and the anthracite region never really recovered. As the economy began to boom again, Americans were switching from coal to oil or gas furnaces. Demand for anthracite dropped precipitously, and the number of jobs in the mines, and in ancillary businesses, plummeted. In the 1960s and the 1970s there was an influx of textile and apparel mills, bringing low-wage jobs to what had once been a relatively high-wage area. But many people in this area seemed just to be waiting forlornly for the old boom days to return—and many others have simply left. Scranton, which held 143,000 people in 1930, had 87,000 in 1980; the population of all of Lackawanna County fell from 310,000 to 227,000 in the same period. Just a look at the edges of Scranton shows what happened. On one block stand large houses, maintained with care, but obviously built in the 1920s—the city's last prosperous decade. On the next block you find no new suburban housing tract or shopping center, only trees and hills. In few parts of the country can you see such a sudden halt in urban development.

Scranton and Lackawanna County make up almost half of Pennsylvania's 10th congressional district. The rest of it is made up of the kind of territory Scranton was before the anthracite boom: Scots-Irish mountain counties in the Poconos (a favorite resort of many middle-class New Yorkers) and along the northern tier of counties just below Upstate New York. The partisan balance has remained the same in this district for years. The number of votes in Democratic Scranton has declined, but the rural counties are becoming slightly less Republican. So the district has given Republicans margins, though not always large ones, in every presidential election since 1964.

The congressman from this district, Joseph McDade, is now the senior member of the Pennsylvania delegation, a Republican who has mastered the art of remaining popular in this bifurcated district. Even in the Democratic year of 1982, McDade was reelected with 68% of the vote; his closest race in recent years was in 1976, when he got 63% against Democrat Edward Mitchell. McDade was first elected in 1962, succeeding William Scranton, who was elected governor then after one term in Congress; McDade is identified with the same progressive wing of the Republican Party as Scranton. His politics seems to have changed notably in 1980. Before 1980 he had a record that was often pleasing to organized labor; in 1981, like almost every Republican, he supported the basic Reagan economic program in 1981. He still does not support the administration on all economic issues, but he does on many, and his record in the 1980s on cultural and foreign policy issues is definitely on the conservative side as well. McDade is giving House Republican firebrands little reason to deprive him of the high positions to which he is recommended by his seniority.

McDade is in fact one of the most senior Republicans in the House, and the number two minority member of the House Appropriations Committee. He serves as ranking minority member of the Interior Subcommittee, a body sometimes sympathetic to environmental concerns; he also serves on the Defense Subcommittee.

The People   Pop. 1980: 515,442, up 7.1% 1970–80; voting age pop. 376,348. 22% housing units rented. Median owner $34,400; renter $140. Households: 76% family, 38% with children, 64% married couples.

Presidential Vote

1980	Reagan (R)	106,937	(54%)
	Carter (D)	76,795	(39%)
	Other	12,802	(7%)

Rep. Joseph M. McDade (R) Elected 1962; b. Sept. 29, 1931, Scranton; home, Scranton; U. of Notre Dame, B.A. 1953, U. of PA, LL.B. 1956; Roman Catholic.

Career Clerk to Chf. Fed. Judge John W. Murphy, 1956–57; Practicing atty., 1957–62; Scranton City Solicitor, 1962.

Offices 2370 RHOB, 202-225-3731. Also 1223 Northeastern Natl. Bank Bldg., Scranton 18503, 717-346-3834.

Committees *Appropriations* (2d). Subcommittees: Defense; Interior. *Small Business* (Ranking Member). Subcommittee: SBA and SBIC Authority, Minority Enterprise and General Small Business Problems.

Group Ratings

	ADA	ACLU	COPE	CFA	LCV	LWV	NTU	NSI	COC	ACA	CSFC
1982	60	42	66	62	67	42	33	100	32	36	38
1981	25	—	66	50	61	—	46	—	78	55	54
1980	44	47	72	71	32	50	34	89	71	35	53

National Journal Ratings

	Economic		Foreign		Cultural	
1982	60%	(LIB)	47%	(LIB)	63%	(LIB)
	40%	(CONS)	53%	(CONS)	37%	(CONS)
1981	45%	(LIB)	39%	(LIB)	40%	(LIB)
	54%	(CONS)	61%	(CONS)	59%	(CONS)

Key Votes

1) Reagan 81 Budget	FOR	5) Incr SS Rtmt Age	AGN	9) Poor Pay Food Stamps	AGN
2) Reagan 81 Tax Cut	FOR	6) Saudi AWACS Sale	—	10) Ban Crt Busing Order	FOR
3) Bal Budget Amend	AGN	7) $ for MX Missile	AGN	11) Auto Local Content	FOR
4) Gas & Road Tax	—	8) Nerve Gas Prod	AGN	12) Nuclear Arms Freeze	AGN

Election Results

1982 general	Joseph M. McDade (R)	103,617	(68%)	($193,551)
	Robert J. Rafalko (D)	49,868	(32%)	($16,375)
1982 primary	Joseph M. McDade (R)	26,064	(89%)	
	Ervin Hohensee (R)	3,066	(11%)	
1980 general	Joseph M. McDade (R)	145,703	(77%)	($58,582)
	Gene Basalyga (D)	43,152	(23%)	($0)

Campaign Contributions and Expenditures

1981-82		Direct Cont. 81-82				PACS brkdwn		
Receipts	$265,576	Indiv	$161,530	Agr	$2,250	Ideo	$1,450
Expend.	$193,551	Party	$10,487	Bus	$65,150	Lbr	$8,600
Unspent	$90,235	PACS	$84,970	Hlth	$5,750	Prof	$1,650

ELEVENTH DISTRICT

The 11th congressional district of Pennsylvania is centered on Wilkes-Barre and Luzerne County in northeastern Pennsylvania. This is part of America's great anthracite coal district, which was of great importance to the nation in the days when most homes were heated by coal. There was a boom here, and immigrants were attracted to Wilkes-Barre and the string of communities in the narrow flood plain on both sides of the Susquehanna River. There were almost half a million people in Luzerne County in 1930, most of them in this valley, with the rest scattered in mining and manufacturing towns in the hills. But demand for anthracite dropped with the Depression and the conversion to oil and gas heating. Prosperity has never entirely returned to the Wilkes-Barre area. Population has declined (Luzerne County had 343,000 people in 1980), as young people have left to make their livings elsewhere; new industries that have come in, textile and apparel, pay low wages. For many years one of the major economic assets of this district was its congressman, a flamboyant Democrat named Daniel J. Flood, who as Chairman of the Labor–HEW Appropriations Subcommittee brought in lots of federal money to the 11th district.

But in 1978 Flood was charged with accepting money from people who wanted something from the government and, though he was reelected in 1978, he was stripped of his subcommittee chairmanship; in effect his career ended even before he was indicted, convicted, and resigned. Since then the 11th district has had three different elections, with three different winners. State legislator Ray Musto was able to win the April 1980 special election to fill the rest of Flood's term. But he lost in the November landslide to Republican James Nelligan. Nelligan in turn lost the 1982 election to Democrat Frank Harrison. Musto was succeeded, as it happened, by the men who finished second and third in the 1980 special.

Harrison is a Harvard-educated lawyer, with roots in Wilkes-Barre, who campaigned against Reaganomics. Nelligan was able to cite instances when he had opposed some Reagan cutbacks, but he had supported the main part of the program. Harrison lost the outlying counties in the district but carried Luzerne with a solid 55%. He has seats on the Education and Labor and Veterans' Affairs Committees, and can be expected to favor generous spending on their programs. He seems a fairly good bet to win reelection in this district that, on balance, probably leans Democratic; but in the post-Flood years in the Wilkes-Barre area, nothing seems certain.

The People   Pop. 1980: 515,729, up 2.7% 1970–80; voting age pop. 388,822; 1% Black. 26% housing units rented. Median owner $30,100; renter $136. Households: 74% family, 34% with children, 61% married couples.

Presidential Vote

1980	Reagan (R)	102,654	(51%)
	Carter (D)	86,384	(43%)
	Other	11,351	(6%)

Rep. Frank Harrison (D) Elected 1982; b. Feb. 2, 1940, Washington, DC; home, Wilkes-Barre; Kings Col., A.B. 1961, Harvard U. Law Sch., LL.B., 1964; Roman Catholic.

Career Air Force, 1966–69; Practicing atty., 1972–82; Lecturer, Kings Col., 1969–82.

Offices 1541 LHOB, 202-225-6511. Also Ten E. South St. Bldg., S. Main St., Wilkes-Barre 18701, 717-825-2200; 37 W. Main St., Bloomsburg 17815, 717-387-0378; 17 E. Broad St., Hazleton 18201, 717-459-2048; City Hall, Broad St., Pittston 18640, 717-654-8024; and 40 S. Market St., Shamokin 17872, 717-648-2581.

Committees *Education and Labor* (19th). Subcommittees: Employment Opportunities; Health and Safety; Labor Standards; Postsecondary Education. *Veterans' Affairs* (14th). Subcommittees Hospitals and Health Care.

Group Ratings and Key Votes: Newly Elected

Election Results

1982 general	Frank Harrison (D)	90,371	(54%)	($191,306)
	James L. Nelligan (R)	78,485	(46%)	($284,240)
1982 primary	Frank Harrison (D)	15,062	(25%)	
	Thomas F. O'Donnell, Jr. (D)	14,836	(25%)	($81,300)
	Francis P. Bonner (D)	11,424	(19%)	($31,292)
	Edward Mitchell (D)	9,376	(16%)	($30,266)
	Thomas A. Makowski (D)	7,536	(13%)	($18,097)
1980 general	James L. Nelligan (R)	93,261	(52%)	($120,366)
	Raphael Musto (D)	86,703	(48%)	($298,699)

Campaign Contributions and Expenditures

1981-82		*Direct Cont. 81-82*			*PACS brkdwn*			
Receipts	$196,731	Indiv	$122,197	Agr	$—	Ideo	$1,600
Expend.	$191,306	Party	$390	Bus	$—	Lbr	$32,200
Unspent	$5,482	PACS	$38,860	Hlth	$—	Prof	$500
		Cand	$40,150				

TWELFTH DISTRICT

The hills of western Pennsylvania, eastern Ohio, and northern West Virginia, which encircle the Pittsburgh metropolitan area, form the largest industrial section of the country without a major city. The urban focus here is Pittsburgh, though it may be 100 miles away; the economy throughout is based largely on steel and coal. Much of the easternmost part of this area, north of West Virginia and east of Pittsburgh, forms Pennsylvania's 12th congressional district.

It consists of two distinct areas. The largest city in the first is Johnstown, a steel town known best for its disastrous flood; it had 35,000 people in 1980, 67,000 in 1920. This area was first settled by Scots-Irish farmers when it was still the frontier in the 1790s; in the 19th century bituminous coal was discovered here, and immigrants from other parts of Europe were attracted to work the mines and the blast furnaces. The other part of the district, containing about half its population, is almost all of Westmoreland County, just east of Pittsburgh's Allegheny County. Technically, this is a suburban county, which means that many people commute to jobs in Allegheny. Nevertheless, Westmoreland is large—40 miles east to west—and full of separate little industrial communities established on their own long before Pittsburgh's influence reached out this far. Both parts of the district are Democratic in local and congressional elections, and somewhat less reliably in presidential contests. Both, in the politics of 1982, were liberal on economic and conservative on cultural issues.

This was one of two new districts into which the Republican legislature threw together two incumbent Democratic congressmen. The two here were John Murtha, of the Johnstown area, and Don Bailey, of Westmoreland County. They had certain similarities. Both are Vietnam veterans, both are liberal on economic issues and conservative on cultural issues (with Bailey especially hawkish on foreign policy); both see themselves as old-fashioned regular Democrats, uninterested in reforms (although Bailey won his first primary against party politicos). Neither was especially senior (Murtha won a 1974 special election, Bailey first won in 1978), but both had good committee assignments (Appropriations for Murtha, Ways and Means for Bailey). Despite the similarities, however, this was a hard-fought contest: after all, careers were at stake, and these are career-minded politicians.

The winner was Murtha: his old 12th district had 51% of the new district's population, and he had 52% in the primary; two minor Westmoreland candidates probably drained votes from Bailey. Murtha is probably best known, unfairly, because his name was mentioned by federal prosecutors in the Abscam case—even though they admitted that there was never more than a "flimsy" case against him, and despite the fact that he never took or agreed to take any money. That cost Murtha his position on the House Ethics Committee. But he won reelection in 1980 anyway, and is, in his early 50s, the number 14 Democrat on the House Appropriations Committee. He serves on the subcommittees on Defense (where he is a strong supporter of the Marines), Interior (where he supports coal interests), and Legislative. Murtha is the kind of old-style politician who once would have been a real power in the House, and he does have a certain clout as the informal leader of the Pennsylvania regular Democrats and as a buddy of Ways and Means Chairman Dan Rostenkowski. But with the membership of the Democratic Caucus increasingly weighted to suburban and southern districts, Murtha is not nearly so influential as he would have been 20 years ago. Still, he seems to have a safe district in the new 12th district, at least for the 1980s.

The People   Pop. 1980: 515,915, up 4.7% 1970–80; voting age pop. 374,878; 1% Black. 23% housing units rented. Median owner $38,400; renter $153. Households: 78% family, 40% with children, 68% married couples.

Presidential Vote

1980	Reagan (R)	89,878	(50%)
	Carter (D)	82,182	(45%)
	Other	8,760	(5%)

Rep. John P. Murtha, Jr. (D) Elected Feb. 5, 1974; b. June 17, 1932, New Martinsville, WV; home, Johnstown; U. of Pitt., B.A. 1962, Indiana U. of PA; Roman Catholic.

Career USMC, Vietnam; Owner, Johnstown Minute Car Wash; PA House of Reps., 1969–74.

Offices 2423 RHOB, 202-225-2065. Also 226 Fed. Bldg., Johnstown 15901, 814-535-2642.

Committee *Appropriations* (14th). Subcommittees: Defense; Interior; Legislative.

Group Ratings

	ADA	ACLU	COPE	CFA	LCV	LWV	NTU	NSI	COC	ACA	CSFC
1982	45	42	84	54	62	58	3	80	33	43	40
1981	45	—	83	54	36	—	1	—	22	29	41
1980	44	40	78	64	36	44	22	50	65	21	37

National Journal Ratings

	Economic		Foreign		Cultural	
1982	74%	(LIB)	16%	(LIB)	27%	(LIB)
	26%	(CONS)	82%	(CONS)	73%	(CONS)
1981	71%	(LIB)	51%	(LIB)	45%	(LIB)
	29%	(CONS)	49%	(CONS)	55%	(CONS)

Key Votes

1) Reagan 81 Budget	AGN	5) Incr SS Rtmt Age	AGN	9) Poor Pay Food Stamps	AGN
2) Reagan 81 Tax Cut	AGN	6) Saudi AWACS Sale	AGN	10) Ban Crt Busing Order	FOR
3) Bal Budget Amend	AGN	7) $ for MX Missile	FOR	11) Auto Local Content	FOR
4) Gas & Road Tax	FOR	8) Nerve Gas Prod	FOR	12) Nuclear Arms Freeze	AGN

Election Results

1982 general	John P. Murtha, Jr. (D)	96,369	(61%)	($271,441)
	William N. Tuscano (R)	54,212	(34%)	($32,515)
1982 primary	John P. Murtha, Jr. (D)	31,945	(52%)	
	Don Bailey (D)	23,685	(38%)	($178,070)
	Two others (D)	6,161	(10%)	
1980 general	John P. Murtha, Jr. (D)	106,750	(59%)	($133,265)
(PA 12)	Charles A. Getty (R)	72,999	(41%)	($17,675)
1980 general	Don Bailey (D)	112,427	(68%)	($120,891)
(PA 21)	Dirk Matson (R)	51,821	(32%)	($0)

Campaign Contributions and Expenditures

1981-82		Direct Cont. 81-82		PACS brkdwn			
Receipts	$272,915	Indiv	$115,500	Agr	$4,500	Ideo	$6,950
Expend.	$271,441	Party	$1,600	Bus	$92,425	Lbr	$27,150
Unspent	$23,652	PACS	$141,925	Hlth	$4,500	Prof	$4,050
		Cand	$8,000				

Indep Expend: For: $928 (NRA)

THIRTEENTH DISTRICT

The 13th congressional district of Pennsylvania, including most of suburban Montgomery County and two wards in Philadelphia, is the highest income district in the Philadelphia area, or for that matter in Pennsylvania. When you think of Philadelphia suburbs, you probably think of the Main Line, the string of affluent commuter suburbs, with vast comfortable houses and huge overhanging trees, strung out along the main line of the Pennsylvania Railroad. Part of the Main Line is here in the 13th district; probably more of greater Philadelphia's most prominent citizens live in Lower Merion Township, on the lower part of the Main Line, than in any other suburban jurisdiction.

But the Main Line is split between the 13th, 7th, and 5th districts, and most of the suburbs of the 13th district are, while definitely comfortable, still distinctly more modest. And also newer. The Main Line was already built up 60 years ago, as were other older suburbs right on the rail commuter lines that fan out from Philadelphia. But as job sites decentralized and autos became universal, the Philadelphia suburbs filled in, with new subdivisions, the blank spaces between the old commuter towns. Living standards and housing prices are higher out in Montgomery County than in the city, but these are not lavish places. They are, however, in almost every case Republican; even the Jewish suburbs of Cheltenham Township tend to lean Republican. Even the 13th district's portion of Philadelphia sometimes goes Republican; this includes the old Chestnut Hill neighborhood, a posh area with grass tennis courts, and the funkier, more working-class Manayunk area, perched on hills above the Schuylkill River.

The congressman from this district is Lawrence Coughlin, a Republican first elected in 1968 and not seriously challenged since. He is not well known nationally, although he might have been had he not switched off the Judiciary Committee in 1973, just a year before the hearings on the impeachment of Richard Nixon. Coughlin is an active member of the Appropriations Committee and is seventh ranking among the committee's Republicans. He is the ranking minority member on two of its subcommittees—District of Columbia, which is not considered terribly important, and Transportation, which is. Coughlin's voting record can be described as conservative on economic issues, mildly liberal on cultural and foreign issues—which probably matches opinion in the district pretty well.

The People Pop. 1980: 514,346, dn. 2.9% 1970–80; voting age pop. 392,167; 6% Black. 30% housing units rented. Median owner $58,000; renter $269. Households: 74% family, 34% with children, 62% married couples.

Presidential Vote

1980	Reagan (R)	131,442	(55%)
	Carter (D)	81,847	(34%)
	Anderson (I)	26,700	(11%)

Rep. Lawrence Coughlin (R) Elected 1968; b. Apr. 11, 1929, Wilkes Barre; home, Villanova; Yale U., B.A. 1950, Harvard U., M.B.A. 1954, Temple U., LL.B. 1958; Episcopal.

Career USMC, Korea; Practicing atty., 1958–69; PA House of Reps., 1965–66; PA Senate, 1967–68.

Offices 2467 RHOB, 202-225-6111. Also 700 One Montgomery Plaza, Norristown 19401, 215-277-4040.

Committees *Appropriations* (7th). Subcommittees: District of Columbia; HUD-Independent Agencies; Transportation. *Select Committee on Narcotics Abuse and Control* (2d).

Group Ratings

	ADA	ACLU	COPE	CFA	LCV	LWV	NTU	NSI	COC	ACA	CSFC
1982	45	58	33	38	71	58	69	50	59	55	51
1981	35	—	32	43	29	—	61	—	89	61	56
1980	44	43	21	43	67	50	38	78	73	64	60

National Journal Ratings

	Economic		Foreign		Cultural	
1982	42%	(LIB)	54%	(LIB)	73%	(LIB)
	58%	(CONS)	46%	(CONS)	27%	(CONS)
1981	24%	(LIB)	64%	(LIB)	60%	(LIB)
	68%	(CONS)	36%	(CONS)	40%	(CONS)

Key Votes

1) Reagan 81 Budget	FOR	5) Incr SS Rtmt Age	FOR	9) Poor Pay Food Stamps	AGN
2) Reagan 81 Tax Cut	FOR	6) Saudi AWACS Sale	AGN	10) Ban Crt Busing Order	FOR
3) Bal Budget Amend	FOR	7) $ for MX Missile	AGN	11) Auto Local Content	FOR
4) Gas & Road Tax	FOR	8) Nerve Gas Prod	AGN	12) Nuclear Arms Freeze	AGN

Election Results

1982 general	Lawrence Coughlin (R)	109,198	(64%)	($150,151)
	Martin J. Cunningham, Jr. (D)	59,709	(35%)	($14,525)
1982 primary	Lawrence Coughlin (R)	25,256	(78%)	
	Jack D. Gulati (R)	7,304	(22%)	
1980 general	Lawrence Coughlin (R)	138,212	(71%)	($103,457)
	Pete Slawek (D)	57,745	(29%)	($26,533)

Campaign Contributions and Expenditures

1981-82		Direct Cont. 81-82		PACS brkdwn			
Receipts	$156,552	Indiv	$99,781	Agr	$—	Ideo	$1,650
Expend.	$150,151	Party	$5,206	Bus	$36,100	Lbr	$1,400
Unspent	$32,411	PACS	$45,151	Hlth	$4,300	Prof	$1,550

FOURTEENTH DISTRICT

Pittsburgh, Pennsylvania's second largest city, was the first urban center in the American interior. Pittsburgh grew at first because of its propitious site: here the Allegheny and

Monongahela Rivers join to form the Ohio. The place where that happens—the Golden Triangle—remains the city's focal point: it is now surrounded by high-rise buildings, products of a downtown renaissance. When most of the nation's commerce moved over water, Pittsburgh's location was ideal; when traffic switched to railroads, Pittsburgh did nicely. For Pittsburgh became the leading producer of one commodity the railroads needed, steel. With large deposits of coal nearby and ready access to iron ore from across the Great Lakes, Pittsburgh firmly established itself by 1890 as the nation's leading steel producer.

Today Pittsburgh remains the headquarters of many of the nation's largest corporations: U.S. Steel and several other steel companies, Westinghouse, Heinz, and the giant concerns associated with the Mellon family: Alcoa, Gulf Oil, Koppers. But in spite of the city's recent progress—its program of downtown renewal and its rather successful campaign against air pollution—Pittsburgh has been unable to keep pace with other major metropolitan areas. Its major industry, steel, which once grew faster than the economy, now seems to be contracting rather than growing. It does not have the advantage of being a great center of air transportation, like Chicago, Atlanta, or Dallas–Fort Worth. Its climate is cold. It seems to some outsiders physically constricted by its topography: this is very hilly country, not simply punctuated by hills like cities in California but so continuously hilly that it's hard to find a level city block except in the narrow flood plains along the rivers.

For these reasons, Pittsburgh's economy has not grown very rapidly, and its population—not only of the central city, but of the entire metropolitan area—has been declining since 1960. This economic decline has had cultural effects. With so few new jobs, Pittsburgh has one of the lowest percentages among major metropolitan areas of women in its work force. Traditional family patterns, and the attitudes which accompany them, seem more entrenched among the rather old population with its large number of housewives and low number of divorcees.

The 14th congressional district of Pennsylvania includes all of the city of Pittsburgh plus a few adjacent suburbs. It takes in most of the Pittsburgh area's landmarks: the Golden Triangle; the University of Pittsburgh and its skyscraper campus; Carnegie-Mellon University. Not that many of the Pittsburgh area's steel mills lie in the 14th, but many present and former steelworkers do live here, mostly in ethnic neighborhoods nestled in the Pittsburgh hills. The district also includes the Shadyside neighborhood, newly renovated with new shops near some of Pittsburgh's old mansions, and the predominantly Jewish Squirrel Hill neighborhood. Only 24% of Pittsburgh's residents are black, a smaller figure than in most industrial cities because employment opportunities here peaked before the big wave of black migration from the South. Before the 1930s, in the heyday of Henry Clay Frick and Andrew Mellon, Pittsburgh was a solidly Republican town. Since the New Deal the 14th district has been solidly Democratic, in every election.

The congressman from the 14th district, first elected in 1980, is William Coyne. His background is in local politics, and he came to Washington unheralded. He was an ally of Pittsburgh Mayor Richard Caliguiri on the City Council, and demonstrated a strong base by beating the son of his predecessor, William Moorhead, in the 1980 Democratic primary by a 65%–35% margin. In Washington Coyne has made a record much more in line with those of representatives of safe Democratic districts in other states than with those of traditional western Pennsylvania Democrats, and he seems to be well respected and well liked by other Democrats. He serves on the Banking, Finance and Urban Affairs, and the House Administration Committees.

The People Pop. 1980: 516,629, dn. 17.6% 1970–80; voting age pop. 405,532; 19% Black, 1% Span. orig., 1% Asian orig. 44% housing units rented. Median owner $32,500; renter $174. Households: 61% family, 28% with children, 45% married couples.

Presidential Vote

1980	Reagan (R)	73,003	(34%)
	Carter (D)	124,989	(58%)
	Anderson (I)	18,621	(9%)

Rep. William J. Coyne (D) Elected 1980; b. Aug. 24, 1936, Pittsburgh; home, Pittsburgh; Robert Morris Col., B.S. 1965; Roman Catholic.

Career Corporate accountant; PA House of Reps., 1970–72; Pittsburgh City Cncl., 1974–80.

Offices 424 CHOB, 202-225-2301. Also 2005 Fed. Bldg., 1000 Liberty Ave., Pittsburgh 15222, 412-644-2870.

Committees *Banking, Finance and Urban Affairs* (21st). Subcommittees: Economic Stabilization; Housing and Community Development; International Trade, Investment and Monetary Policy. *House Administration* (8th). Subcommittees: Accounts; Contracts and Printing; Services. *Standards of Official Conduct* (6th). *Joint Committee on the Library* (3d).

Group Ratings

	ADA	ACLU	COPE	CFA	LCV	LWV	NTU	NSI	COC	ACA	CSFC
1982	90	83	93	92	71	83	1	10	27	17	53
1981	95	—	87	86	64	—	5	—	16	13	28

National Journal Ratings

	Economic		Foreign		Cultural	
1982	88%	(LIB)	72%	(LIB)	81%	(LIB)
	12%	(CONS)	28%	(CONS)	19%	(CONS)
1981	87%	(LIB)	85%	(LIB)	87%	(LIB)
	12%	(CONS)	13%	(CONS)	12%	(CONS)

Key Votes

1) Reagan 81 Budget	AGN	5) Incr SS Rtmt Age	AGN
2) Reagan 81 Tax Cut	AGN	6) Saudi AWACS Sale	AGN
3) Bal Budget Amend	AGN	7) $ for MX Missile	AGN
4) Gas & Road Tax	FOR	8) Nerve Gas Prod	AGN

9) Poor Pay Food Stamps	AGN
10) Ban Crt Busing Order	AGN
11) Auto Local Content	FOR
12) Nuclear Arms Freeze	FOR

Election Results

1982 general	William J. Coyne (D)	120,980	(75%)	($51,998)
	John R. Clark (R)	32,780	(20%)	($0)
1982 primary	William J. Coyne (D)	45,249	(77%)	
	Robert R. Lansberry (D)	13,205	(23%)	
1980 general	William J. Coyne (D)	102,545	(70%)	($185,071)
	Stan Thomas (R)	44,071	(30%)	($126,150)

Campaign Contributions and Expenditures

1981-82		Direct Cont. 81-82		PACS brkdwn			
Receipts	$86,883	Indiv	$36,288	Agr	$—	Ideo	$250
Expend.	$51,998	Party	$650	Bus	$21,860	Lbr	$23,175
Unspent	$38,348	PACS	$46,255	Hlth	$125	Prof	$800
		Cand	$500				

FIFTEENTH DISTRICT

The 15th congressional district of Pennsylvania covers the industrial Lehigh Valley in the eastern part of the state. Here in Northampton and Lehigh Counties are the adjoining, but quite different, cities of Allentown and Bethlehem and, to the east, the smaller city of Easton. Allentown is a diversified industrial town, one of the nation's leading cement centers (because of local limestone deposits) and the home of Mack Trucks; drawing its labor force from the Pennsylvania Dutch country around it and to the south, it has grown steadily in the 20th century. Bethlehem has a more complex history. It was founded by the Moravian sect in 1741 (the same people who started the Salem of Winston-Salem, North Carolina) and has preserved many 18th-century buildings. Across the Lehigh River there was an iron works in the 19th century, which grew eventually to be the central plant for Bethlehem Steel. As for Easton, it is the home of the companies that make Crayola crayons and Dixie cups.

Allentown, with its steady growth, tends to be Republican or about evenly divided; Bethlehem, with its steelworkers, tends to be Democratic. Overall, the 15th should probably be considered a Democratic district; it has gone Democratic in recent close presidential elections. But it now has a Republican congressman, serving his third term; and in recent contests, while the economically stricken areas of western Pennsylvania have trended Democratic, the Lehigh Valley has if anything trended Republican.

How much credit should go to Congressman Don Ritter is not clear. But probably some: after winning the district by upsetting the incumbent in 1978, Ritter has not followed the usual congressional strategy of propitiating his constituency by voting often against his party. He has, rather, generally stuck by the Republican Party, not only when it was running things in 1981, but when it was on the defensive in 1982 and when it was very much in the minority in 1979 and 1980. One of the few members of Congress with scientific degrees, Ritter believes that free markets almost always allocate goods and services better than government can, and that our government is overregulating and overtaxing us. To judge from the results, increasing numbers of Lehigh Valley voters agree. Not only did Ritter carry the district with a solid 58% in the Democratic year of 1982, but Governor Richard Thornburgh and Senator John Heinz carried it comfortably as well.

Ritter serves on the Energy and Commerce Committee, which governs all kinds of federal regulatory activity. In general, he supports deregulation, but there are complex issues here, and he can be a key vote on many. Limited as all committee Republicans are to one subcommittee assignment, he serves on the unit that has jurisdiction over toxic waste laws.

The People   Pop. 1980: 515,529, up 7.7% 1970–80; voting age pop. 385,814; 1% Black, 2% Span. orig. 27% housing units rented. Median owner $44,600; renter $189. Households: 75% family, 37% with children, 64% married couples.

Presidential Vote

1980			
	Reagan (R)	88,905	(50%)
	Carter (D)	68,288	(39%)
	Other	19,129	(11%)

Rep. Donald L. (Don) **Ritter** (R) Elected 1978; b. Oct. 21, 1940, Bronx, NY; home, Coopersburg; Lehigh U., B.S. 1961, M.I.T., M.S. 1963, Sc.D. 1966; Unitarian.

Career Scientific Exchange Fellow, Moscow, USSR, 1967–78; Asst. Prof., CA Poly. U., 1968–76; Mgr., Research Development Program, Lehigh U., 1976–78.

Offices 124 CHOB, 202-225-6411. Also 212 P. O. Bldg., Allentown 18101, 215-439-8861.

Committee *Energy and Commerce* (10th). Subcommittees: Commerce, Transportation, and Tourism; Energy Conservation and Power.

Group Ratings

	ADA	ACLU	COPE	CFA	LCV	LWV	NTU	NSI	COC	ACA	CSFC
1982	20	17	27	23	42	33	88	90	76	78	65
1981	10	—	26	36	37	—	94	—	84	83	72
1980	22	17	26	36	46	22	56	90	80	74	71

National Journal Ratings

	Economic		Foreign		Cultural	
1982	19%	(LIB)	37%	(LIB)	48%	(LIB)
	81%	(CONS)	63%	(CONS)	52%	(CONS)
1981	24%	(LIB)	45%	(LIB)	21%	(LIB)
	68%	(CONS)	55%	(CONS)	79%	(CONS)

Key Votes

1) Reagan 81 Budget	FOR	5) Incr SS Rtmt Age	FOR	9) Poor Pay Food Stamps	FOR
2) Reagan 81 Tax Cut	FOR	6) Saudi AWACS Sale	AGN	10) Ban Crt Busing Order	FOR
3) Bal Budget Amend	FOR	7) $ for MX Missile	FOR	11) Auto Local Content	FOR
4) Gas & Road Tax	AGN	8) Nerve Gas Prod	FOR	12) Nuclear Arms Freeze	AGN

Election Results

1982 general	Donald L. (Don) Ritter (R)	79,455	(58%)	($339,759)
	Richard J. Orloski (D)	58,002	(42%)	($81,219)
1982 primary	Donald L. (Don) Ritter (R)	15,646	(100%)	
1980 general	Donald L. (Don) Ritter (R)	99,874	(59%)	($318,453)
	Jeanette Reibman (D)	66,626	(40%)	($206,516)

Campaign Contributions and Expenditures

1981-82		*Direct Cont. 81-82*	
Receipts	$339,527	Indiv	$198,657
Expend.	$339,759	Party	$17,845
Unspent	$202	Cand	$10,000

PACS Breakdown Not Available   Indirect Party Expend: $15,184   *Indep Expend:* For: $2,160 (NRA, PA LIFEPAC)

SIXTEENTH DISTRICT

Millions of people know about the Pennsylvania Dutch country: farms scrupulously tended and set amid rolling hills, barns decorated with hex signs, and Amish families clad in black, clattering over the back roads in horse-drawn carriages. Fewer Americans know that the Pennsylvania Dutch are actually German in origin ("Dutch" comes from Deutsch). They are descended from members of Amish, Mennonite, and other pietistic sects who left the principalities of 18th-century Germany for the religious freedom of the Quaker-dominated colony of Pennsylvania. The Quakers were happy to welcome the Germans, but they were not eager to have them in Philadelphia. So they were sent to Germantown, a few miles away, until they could move out to what was then the frontier, where they could protect the pacifist Quakers against the Indians. Thus the Dutch came to the rolling green hills of the part of Pennsylvania centered on Lancaster County. The land was naturally fertile, and careful cultivation by the Dutch increased its productivity. Today farms in Lancaster County continue to produce some of the highest per-acre yields on earth.

The Pennsylvania Dutch are perhaps the most conservative people in America. They are quite unlike Sun Belt conservatives, who seek the reassurance of cultural continuity even as they pursue the economic change inevitably wrought by free-market capitalism. The Pennsylvania Dutch see little need for change of any kind; they believe that they live in a real and present paradise, and aside from some less-than-pleasant tourists much evidence exists to support this belief. Most of the Pennsylvania Dutch, it should be added, are not plain people. But the heritage is important: most people here are of German descent and have a strong work ethic. Small industries have settled in the Lancaster area because of the skills and work habits of the labor force, and agriculture continues to be important economically. The brick townhouses of Lancaster, like the frame farmhouses of the Amish, are sparklingly well kept and seem little different from what they must have looked like 50 years ago.

The Pennsylvania Dutch country has produced one president, James Buchanan, and housed another in his retirement, Dwight Eisenhower, who was himself of Pennsylvania Dutch descent. For most of Buchanan's career the politics of this area was Jeffersonian Democratic. But in the 1850s the Pennsylvania Dutch country, antagonistic to the spread of slavery, became Republican; Lancaster County, once represented by Buchanan, elected as its congressman Thaddeus Stevens, the driving force behind Reconstruction civil rights laws. Today Lancaster County returns 3–1 Republican margins—the largest of any similar-sized area in the East.

The 16th congressional district of Pennsylvania includes almost all of Lancaster County, and mostly Dutch Lebanon County to the north and part of Chester County to the east. Of all the congressional districts in the East, it cast the highest Republican percentages in the last three presidential elections. The district's congressman is Robert Walker, a former congressional aide first elected in 1976. Walker anticipated many of the 1980 freshman Republicans by arguing, loudly and acerbically, that the federal government is too big and needs to be cut back. He seems to be more vocal than influential, however; he is one of those congressmen you will see on snippets of the network newscasts denouncing some helpless witness at a hearing and seething with indignation. This provides steady work for TV cameramen but does not do much to advance the flow of legislation. Given the Republican leanings of his district, Walker is reelected routinely by overwhelming margins.

The People   Pop. 1980: 514,585, up 12.9% 1970–80; voting age pop. 369,823; 2% Black, 2% Span. orig. 29% housing units rented. Median owner $46,400; renter $179. Households: 77% family, 41% with children, 67% married couples.

Presidential Vote

1980			
	Reagan (R)	110,980	(67%)
	Carter (D)	42,603	(27%)
	Other	12,998	(8%)

Rep. Robert S. Walker (R) Elected 1976; b. Dec. 23, 1942, Bradford; home, East Petersburg; Wm. and Mary Col., 1960–61, Millersville St. Col., B.S. 1964, U. of DE, M.A. 1968; Presbyterian.

Career Teacher, 1964–67; A. A. to U.S. Rep. Edwin D. Eshleman, 1967–77.

Offices 2445 RHOB, 202-225-2411. Also Lancaster Cnty. Courthouse, Lancaster 17601, 717-393-0666.

Committees *Government Operations* (4th). Subcommittees: Government Activities and Transportation; Intergovernmental Relations and Human Resources. *Science and Technology* (3d). Subcommittees: Energy Research and Production; Space Science and Applications.

Group Ratings

	ADA	ACLU	COPE	CFA	LCV	LWV	NTU	NSI	COC	ACA	CSFC
1982	15	29	20	0	38	36	96	100	82	83	72
1981	10	—	20	21	36	—	97	—	89	91	78
1980	17	40	10	29	43	40	59	100	76	92	81

National Journal Ratings

	Economic		Foreign		Cultural	
1982	3%	(LIB)	41%	(LIB)	18%	(LIB)
	96%	(CONS)	59%	(CONS)	80%	(CONS)
1981	34%	(LIB)	18%	(LIB)	20%	(LIB)
	65%	(CONS)	73%	(CONS)	79%	(CONS)

Key Votes

1) Reagan 81 Budget FOR	5) Incr SS Rtmt Age FOR	9) Poor Pay Food Stamps FOR
2) Reagan 81 Tax Cut FOR	6) Saudi AWACS Sale AGN	10) Ban Crt Busing Order FOR
3) Bal Budget Amend FOR	7) $ for MX Missile FOR	11) Auto Local Content AGN
4) Gas & Road Tax AGN	8) Nerve Gas Prod AGN	12) Nuclear Arms Freeze AGN

Election Results

1982 general	Robert S. Walker (R)	93,034	(71%)	($60,649)
	Jean D. Mowrey (D)	37,364	(29%)	($15,550)
1982 primary	Robert S. Walker (R)	23,859	(87%)	
	J. Earle Pfoutz, Jr. (R)	3,455	(13%)	
1980 general	Robert S. Walker (R)	129,765	(77%)	($23,719)
	James A. Woodcock (D)	38,891	(23%)	($0)

Campaign Contributions and Expenditures

1981-82		Direct Cont. 81-82		PACS brkdwn			
Receipts	$58,143	Indiv	$24,666	Agr	$100	Ideo	$400
Expend.	$60,649	Party	$9,025	Bus	$24,450	Lbr	$500
Unspent	$5,439	PACS	$26,150	Hlth	$500	Prof	$200

SEVENTEENTH DISTRICT

The 17th congressional district of Pennsylvania is in the geographical center of the state, a series of counties strung along the Susquehanna River. The Susquehanna is the one river strong enough to break through the mountain chains that run, like rugged corduroy, through central Pennsylvania; the 17th district, accordingly, includes several very different kinds of areas. About half its population is in and around the state capital of Harrisburg, an old city with a declining population and a large black community. Just downstream is the site of the Three Mile Island nuclear plant. In the northern extreme of the district, on the upper Susquehanna, is Williamsport, a small manufacturing town that hosts the Little League World Series and has been the home for years of *Grit,* the world's largest family weekly newspaper. In the middle of the district, on the east shore of the Susquehanna, is Northumberland County, a onetime anthracite mining area. On the west shore are three counties reaching inland between the mountain chains. Settled by Scots-Irish farmers, they now house small manufacturing firms.

In most elections this is a solidly Republican district. Harrisburg seems to retain, from the 1860–1930 era of Republican dominance in Pennsylvania, a Republican preference that survives all ethnic and racial change; Williamsport is quintessential Republican country. Northumberland is usually Democratic, but the west shore counties are among the most Republican in the nation; two of the three went for Barry Goldwater in 1964.

Nevertheless the 17th district elected a Democrat to the House in 1976, 1978, and 1980. He was Allen Ertel, the former district attorney in the Williamsport area, who had a liberal record on economics and a moderate record on cultural issues. He doubtless would have won here again in 1982, except that he got into his head what everyone else regarded as the quixotic idea of running for governor. It turned out to be a more Democratic year in Pennsylvania than anyone anticipated, and Ertel won 48% of the vote; in the process, he carried the 17th district.

But there were no coattails in the congressional race. The Republican nominee, George Gekas, was a state senator from Harrisburg who had been trying to construct a favorable seat in the redistricting process. Gekas ran a well-financed campaign that was enough to beat, though not by an overwhelming margin, a candidate backed by Ertel. This is a district which should fairly easily reelect an incumbent Republican who does his homework, except if Ertel runs; then there might be a very seriously contested race.

Gekas specialized in crime legislation as a member of the Pennsylvania legislature, and seems likely to do so again in the House. He is ranking Republican on the Judiciary Subcommittee on Criminal Justice. He is classified as a backer of tough anti-crime measures, but in at least one instance, while testifying on the insanity defense, Gekas won praise from John Conyers, the very liberal chairman of the subcommittee; a good working relationship between these two could prove unusually productive. Gekas's accession to such a position as a freshman is in itself unusual, and an indication that some positive results are expected.

The People Pop. 1980: 515,900, up 7.2% 1970–80; voting age pop. 376,440; 6% Black, 1% Span. orig. 28% housing units rented. Median owner $37,800; renter $164. Households: 74% family, 38% with children, 62% married couples.

Presidential Vote

1980	Reagan (R)	101,956	(60%)
	Carter (D)	56,389	(33%)
	Anderson (I)	10,361	(6%)

Rep. George W. Gekas (R) Elected 1982; b. May 14, 1930, Harrisburg; home, Harrisburg; Dickinson Col., B.A. 1952, Dickinson Law Sch., J.D. 1958; Greek Orthodox.

Career Asst. Dist. Atty., Dauphin Cnty., 1960–66; PA House of Reps., 1967–74; PA Senate, 1976–82.

Offices 1008 LHOB, 202-225-4315. Also The Point, Union Deposit Rd. and Rt. 83, Su. 238, Harrisburg 17111, 717-561-2434.

Committee *Judiciary* (10th). Subcommittees: Civil and Constitutional Rights; Criminal Justice.

Group Ratings and Key Votes: Newly Elected

Election Results

1982 general	George W. Gekas (R)	84,291	(58%)	($178,835)
	Larry J. Hochendoner (D)	61,974	(42%)	($59,587)
1982 primary	George W. Gekas (R)	25,773	(60%)	
	Brian J. McCarthy (R)	14,625	(34%)	($26,050)
	Max Lampenfeld, Jr. (R)	2,528	(6%)	
1980 general	Allen E. Ertel (D)	97,995	(61%)	($97,999)
	Daniel S. Seiverling (R)	63,790	(39%)	($98,130)

Campaign Contributions and Expenditures

1982		*Direct Cont. 1982*				*PACS brkdwn*		
Receipts	$193,235	Indiv	$81,469	Agr	$—		Ideo	$3,000
Expend.	$178,835	Party	$23,185	Bus	$65,805		Lbr	$1,000
Unspent	$14,399	PACS	$82,965	Hlth	$11,060		Prof	$2,100

Indirect Party Expend: $22,983

EIGHTEENTH DISTRICT

The 18th congressional district of Pennsylvania is the suburban Pittsburgh district. It surrounds Pittsburgh like a thick but irregularly shaped doughnut that someone has taken one bite out of; the Republican legislature packed into it just about all the strong Republican suburbs it could find, and connected them using as few Democratic areas as possible. So this district contains most of Pittsburgh's elite, in leafy, secluded suburbs like Fox Chapel and Sewickley. It also includes solid high income, but not elite suburbs like Mount Lebanon and

Upper St. Clair Township, south of the Golden Triangle. But when you go down to the flood plain or over the next hill from these places, you run into much more modest suburban territory, from pleasant tract housing to gritty little factory towns erected 80 or 100 years ago.

This makes the 18th district a mixed bag politically—the most Republican constituency possible in metropolitan Pittsburgh, but still not Republican by any large margin. It elected John Heinz to Congress in 1972 and 1974, but when he ran for the Senate in 1976 it elected Democrat Doug Walgren and has reelected him ever since. Walgren has had some good luck: he had a weak opponent in his first election, and though he has faced a high-spending opponent twice, the man did not run in the most Republican year, 1980.

Walgren is blessed with committee assignments which did not look interesting when he got them but do now. He has a seat on the Science and Technology Committee and chairs a subcommittee on Science, Research and Technology at just the time when most politicians have been convinced that America needs more and better scientific research and engineering talent to build a strong economy. He sits on the Energy and Commerce Committee—the most sought after committee assignment in 1983, because it covers so much federal regulatory law—and has seats on subcommittees on Health, Oversight, and Fossil and Synthetic Fuels. Even so, he has not yet made major news or been credited with major legislative accomplishments. On national issues generally, Walgren has a moderately liberal record.

The People Pop. 1980: 516,050, dn. .8% 1970–80; voting age pop. 382,408; 2% Black, 1% Asian orig. 23% housing units rented. Median owner $57,300; renter $237. Households: 78% family, 38% with children, 68% married couples.

Presidential Vote

1980	Reagan (R)	121,653	(56%)
	Carter (D)	76,657	(35%)
	Other	18,960	(9%)

Rep. Douglas (Doug) Walgren (D) Elected 1976; b. Dec. 28, 1940, Rochester, NY; home, Pittsburgh; Dartmouth Col., B.A. 1963, Stanford U., LL.B. 1966; Roman Catholic.

Career Practicing atty., Asst. Allegheny Cnty. Solicitor, 1971–72; Dem. Nominee for U.S. House of Reps., 1972.

Offices 2441 RHOB, 202-225-2135. Also 2117 Fed. Bldg., 1000 Liberty Ave., Pittsburgh 15222, 412-391-4016.

Committees *Energy and Commerce* (10th). Subcommittees: Fossil and Synthetic Fuels; Health and the Environment; Oversight and Investigations. *Science and Technology* (8th). Subcommittee: Science, Research and Technology (Chairman).

Group Ratings

	ADA	ACLU	COPE	CFA	LCV	LWV	NTU	NSI	COC	ACA	CSFC
1982	80	58	81	69	88	73	36	20	32	18	32
1981	80	—	80	64	79	—	44	—	22	35	37
1980	78	67	79	64	78	80	17	10	71	8	36

National Journal Ratings

	Economic		Foreign		Cultural	
1982	64%	(LIB)	85%	(LIB)	67%	(LIB)
	36%	(CONS)	15%	(CONS)	33%	(CONS)
1981	62%	(LIB)	90%	(LIB)	69%	(LIB)
	38%	(CONS)	9%	(CONS)	31%	(CONS)

Key Votes

1) Reagan 81 Budget	AGN	5) Incr SS Rtmt Age	AGN	9) Poor Pay Food Stamps	FOR
2) Reagan 81 Tax Cut	AGN	6) Saudi AWACS Sale	AGN	10) Ban Crt Busing Order	FOR
3) Bal Budget Amend	AGN	7) $ for MX Missile	AGN	11) Auto Local Content	FOR
4) Gas & Road Tax	—	8) Nerve Gas Prod	AGN	12) Nuclear Arms Freeze	FOR

Election Results

1982 general	Douglas (Doug) Walgren (D)	101,807	(54%)	($267,527)
	Ted Jacob (R)	84,428	(45%)	($240,169)
1982 primary	Douglas (Doug) Walgren (D)	31,021	(100%)	
1980 general	Douglas (Doug) Walgren (D)	126,641	(68%)	($98,136)
	Steven R. Snyder (R)	58,821	(32%)	($77,232)

Campaign Contributions and Expenditures

1981-82		Direct Cont. 81-82		PACS brkdwn			
Receipts	$260,607	Indiv	$112,924	Agr	$2,150	Ideo	$15,325
Expend.	$267,527	Party	$7,110	Bus	$28,775	Lbr	$57,775
Unspent	$10,764	PACS	$128,066	Hlth	$9,325	Prof	$4,800

NINETEENTH DISTRICT

The 19th congressional district of Pennsylvania—Adams and York Counties and half of Cumberland—sits at the western edge of the deeply conservative Pennsylvania Dutch country. This is a land of rolling green farmland extending up to the base of the Appalachian chains that rise at the district's western and northernmost boundaries. The most famous part of this district is also the most sparsely populated, at least by permanent residents: Gettysburg, the tourist-thronged site of the Civil War's northernmost battle. Outside the town itself is the retirement home of President Eisenhower, who was of Pennsylvania Dutch stock himself; his father migrated in the late 19th century with a group of Mennonite brethren out into Kansas and Texas.

The largest city in the district is York, with 44,000 people, which, from September 1777 to June 1778, was the capital of the young nation. When the Continental Congress met at York, it passed the Articles of Confederation, received word from Benjamin Franklin in Paris that the French would help with money and ships, and issued the first proclamation calling for a national day of thanksgiving. The other large population center of the 19th district encompasses the west shore suburbs of Harrisburg, opposite the state capital on the other side of the Susquehanna River. During the past two decades, the west shore has absorbed a considerable white flight away from Harrisburg and has been growing more Republican. Farther west is the town of Carlisle, home of Dickinson College, one of the nation's oldest, and the Army's Carlisle Barracks.

York for some years was more Democratic than other Pennsylvania Dutch areas, and this district was hotly contested by the two major parties for some years; Democrats actually won it in 1954, 1958, and 1964. Except for two years, it has been held by members of the Goodling family since 1961. The current congressman, William Goodling, started off as one of the most conservative members of the Pennsylvania delegation after he was first elected in 1974. But in the ensuing years Goodling, who was a teacher, has been influenced by his work on the Education and Labor Committee and has turned out to support, sometimes rather vehemently, some of those programs slated for extinction or severe cuts by the Reagan administration. This cannot be ascribed entirely to the influence of the committee's dominant liberal Democrats, for it has also had several articulate Republicans who strongly oppose these programs; this seems to be a case, rather, of a legislator being honestly convinced of the worthiness of programs by learning their details. In addition, he seems considerably more liberal than most Republicans on foreign issues. However, on other issues, his record is in line with standard Republican doctrines.

Goodling has become exceedingly popular in this district, and consistently runs well ahead of what have become solid Republican majorities here in any case.

The People   Pop. 1980: 516,605, up 14.4% 1970–80; voting age pop. 376,801; 2% Black, 1% Span. orig. 26% housing units rented. Median owner $46,500; renter $180. Households: 77% family, 40% with children, 67% married couples.

Presidential Vote

1980	Reagan (R)	107,486	(60%)
	Carter (D)	56,185	(32%)
	Anderson (I)	13,982	(8%)

Rep. William F. (Bill) Goodling (R) Elected 1974; b. Dec. 5, 1927, Logansville; home, Jacobus; U. of MD, B.S. 1953, Western MD Col., M.Ed. 1957, PA St. U., 1958–62; Methodist.

Career Army, 1946–48; Pub. sch. teacher and admin., 1957–73.

Offices 2263 RHOB, 202-225-5836. Also Fed. Bldg, 200 S. George St., York 17403, 717-843-8887.

Committees *Education and Labor* (3d). Subcommittees: Elementary, Secondary, and Vocational Education; Employment Opportunities; Postsecondary Education; Select Education. *Permanent Select Committee on Intelligence* (5th). Subcommittees: Legislation; Oversight and Evaluation.

Group Ratings

	ADA	ACLU	COPE	CFA	LCV	LWV	NTU	NSI	COC	ACA	CSFC
1982	25	17	24	31	54	45	81	78	64	59	59
1981	30	—	24	43	53	—	91	—	74	83	66
1980	28	33	28	29	45	44	49	63	73	73	72

National Journal Ratings

	Economic		Foreign		Cultural	
1982	35%	(LIB)	61%	(LIB)	50%	(LIB)
	65%	(CONS)	39%	(CONS)	50%	(CONS)
1981	40%	(LIB)	76%	(LIB)	12%	(LIB)
	59%	(CONS)	24%	(CONS)	88%	(CONS)

Key Votes

1) Reagan 81 Budget	FOR	5) Incr SS Rtmt Age	AGN	9) Poor Pay Food Stamps	FOR
2) Reagan 81 Tax Cut	FOR	6) Saudi AWACS Sale	FOR	10) Ban Crt Busing Order	FOR
3) Bal Budget Amend	FOR	7) $ for MX Missile	AGN	11) Auto Local Content	FOR
4) Gas & Road Tax	FOR	8) Nerve Gas Prod	AGN	12) Nuclear Arms Freeze	—

Election Results

1982 general	William F. (Bill) Goodling (R)	101,163	(71%)	($44,563)
	Larry Becker (D)	41,787	(29%)	($20,092)
1982 primary	William F. (Bill) Goodling (R)	28,962	(100%)	
1980 general	William F. (Bill) Goodling (R)	136,873	(76%)	($40,643)
	Richard P. Noll (D)	41,584	(23%)	($11,274)

Campaign Contributions and Expenditures

1981-82		Direct Cont. 81-82	
Receipts	$46,271	Indiv	$36,023
Expend.	$44,563	Party	$9,916
Unspent	$4,864		

Received no PAC Contributions

TWENTIETH DISTRICT

The 20th congressional district of Pennsylvania is a blue-collar district in the Pittsburgh area. Most of it is a series of towns strung out along the Allegheny and Monongahela Rivers which, just a few miles downstream, join at Pittsburgh's Golden Triangle to form the Ohio. It's important to understand the topography here. This is one of the nation's hilliest metropolitan areas; if you saw it in unsettled form, you would doubt that a city could be built there. Almost the only level spots are on the flood plains, along the rivers; above them banks rise steeply, to the hilly interior land. The great steel mills of the Pittsburgh area were all built along the rivers, mainly on the Monongahela, and the working-class towns or neighborhoods were built on higher land nearby, where frame houses were crowded into narrow streets and almost piled one on top of another. Then, over the next hill, an entirely different, white-collar community might develop, connected to the city by entirely different streets.

Most of the population of the 20th district is strung out along the Monongahela, southwest of Pittsburgh, where the working-class towns have been losing population for 30 or 40 years. There is also a population concentration to the north, on the Allegheny, of similar makeup. Connecting them are modest working-class suburbs, interspersed with a few of higher status. Almost all of this district is heavily Democratic. It is populated by people of almost every ethnic background; the politics of Franklin D. Roosevelt not only gave them hope of economic recovery, but assured them that they were included and valued in America. That Democratic allegiance is sometimes strained by the party's cultural liberalism; this is a place where the population is old and the old patterns remain very much the rule. But in congressional elections it has been solidly Democratic since Roosevelt's time.

The current congressman is Joseph Gaydos, a former state senator and attorney for United Mine Workers District 5. He had Democratic organization and union backing when he first won the seat, in 1968; in Washington he has been a reliable vote for organized labor and, usually, the Democratic leadership. There is no doubt where his loyalties lie as a member of the Education and Labor Committee. He has chaired the Subcommittee on Health and Safety, which has jurisdiction over the Occupational Safety and Health Administration since 1977.

During that time, there have been all manner of controversies over OSHA; the burden of regulations was reduced by Carter-appointed Commissioner Eula Bingham as well as her Reaganite successor Thorne Auchter. In neither case did Gaydos seem to take initiative to monitor the administrative response closely.

By all odds Gaydos should have a safe seat. Yet in 1982 a primary opponent who reported spending nothing won 33% of the vote here. Redistricting added some territory to the district, where voters may have been unfamiliar with Gaydos; nonetheless, this is a danger sign for a longtime incumbent. Gaydos nonetheless should be able to count on solid labor support should he be seriously challenged, which may be enough in itself to deter an opponent.

The People   Pop. 1980: 516,028, dn. 8.0% 1970–80; voting age pop. 390,171; 5% Black. 28% housing units rented. Median owner $37,800; renter $157. Households: 76% family, 35% with children, 62% married couples.

Presidential Vote

1980			
	Reagan (R)	88,489	(40%)
	Carter (D)	116,528	(53%)
	Anderson (I)	16,390	(7%)

Rep. Joseph M. Gaydos (D) Elected 1968; b. July 3, 1926, Braddock; home, McKeesport; Duquesne U., U. of Notre Dame, LL.B. 1951; Roman Catholic.

Career Navy, WWII; Dpty. Atty. Gen. of PA, 1956–57; Asst. Allegheny Cnty. Solicitor, 1958–66; Gen. Counsel, United Mine Workers of Amer., Dist. 5; PA Senate, 1967–68.

Offices 2366 RHOB, 202-225-4631. Also 318 5th Ave., McKeesport 15132, 412-673-7756; and Crown Bldg., 979 4th Ave., Rm. 217, New Kensington 15068, 412-644-2896.

Committees *Education and Labor* (5th). Subcommittees: Health and Safety (Chairman); Select Education. *House Administration* (3d). Subcommittees: Accounts; Contracts and Printing (Chairman). *Joint Committee on Printing* (2d).

Group Ratings

	ADA	ACLU	COPE	CFA	LCV	LWV	NTU	NSI	COC	ACA	CSFC
1982	55	33	91	85	56	60	18	100	19	9	34
1981	40	—	90	57	82	—	14	—	12	39	46
1980	33	33	94	57	26	22	34	60	56	48	45

National Journal Ratings

	Economic		Foreign		Cultural	
1982	72%	(LIB)	49%	(LIB)	63%	(LIB)
	28%	(CONS)	51%	(CONS)	36%	(CONS)
1981	76%	(LIB)	57%	(LIB)	38%	(LIB)
	24%	(CONS)	43%	(CONS)	62%	(CONS)

Key Votes

1) Reagan 81 Budget	AGN	5) Incr SS Rtmt Age	AGN	9) Poor Pay Food Stamps	AGN
2) Reagan 81 Tax Cut	AGN	6) Saudi AWACS Sale	AGN	10) Ban Crt Busing Order	FOR
3) Bal Budget Amend	AGN	7) $ for MX Missile	AGN	11) Auto Local Content	FOR
4) Gas & Road Tax	AGN	8) Nerve Gas Prod	FOR	12) Nuclear Arms Freeze	AGN

Election Results

1982 general	Joseph M. Gaydos (D)	127,281	(76%)	($140,982)
	Terry T. Ray (R)	38,212	(23%)	($0)
1982 primary	Joseph M. Gaydos (D)	39,604	(67%)	
	Ed F. McGivern (D)	19,184	(33%)	
1980 general	Joseph M. Gaydos (D)	122,100	(73%)	($98,430)
	Kathleen M. Meyer (R)	46,313	(27%)	($1,624)

Campaign Contributions and Expenditures

1981-82		Direct Cont. 81-82		PACS brkdwn			
Receipts	$138,350	Indiv	$58,990	Agr	$5,300	Ideo	$1,550
Expend.	$140,982	Party	$1,000	Bus	$21,225	Lbr	$36,950
Unspent	$21,326	PACS	$70,575	Hlth	$3,450	Prof	$—

TWENTY-FIRST DISTRICT

Situated in the northwestern corner of the state, Pennsylvania's 21st congressional district is part of the industrial Great Lakes region. It's a long way overland to the East Coast, and the district has none of metropolitan Philadelphia's eastern ambiance. Erie, with 119,000 people, is the largest city in the district, but not the only urban center. In the southern part of the district Sharon, right on the Ohio border and part of the Youngstown–Warren area, is a major steel-producing town, and so is New Castle, whose suburbs are also part of the district. But there are rural areas, too. Crawford County, between Sharon and Erie, is mostly farming country.

This combination produces a pretty even political balance, with the Democratic majorities of Erie and the steel towns balanced off by the Republican majorities of Crawford County and other rural areas. In the presidential elections of 1976 and 1980, the 21st district virtually mirrored the state's results. In congressional elections, this is one of the classical marginal districts in the country, with exceedingly close results in the last two elections.

The current congressman, Tom Ridge, must be considered something of an upset winner: a Republican who captured an open seat in the economically depressed Great Lakes industrial area in the Democratic year of 1982. He had some important help from the Democrats. In their primary they rejected David DiCarlo, a comparative moderate on economic issues who nearly beat Republican incumbent Marc Lincoln Marks in 1980. Their nominee, state Senator Anthony "Buzz" Andrezeski, campaigned abrasively and raised relatively little money, as if he assumed he were a shoo-in. Ridge, in contrast, proved a shrewd campaigner. He stressed his independence of the Reagan administration (he was a supporter of George Bush in the 1980 primary), his opposition to cuts in Social Security and many aid programs, his own working class (he lived in a housing project for a while as a child) and ethnic background (Slovak and Irish). In a district where Democrats usually vote in lockstep with union leaders and where Republicans are either lackluster choices of local country club denizens or eccentric loners like Marks, Ridge seemed earnest, hardworking, and thoughtful. He did not carry Erie or the steel towns, but did well enough in Crawford County and the rest of the district to win by 729 votes out of nearly 160,000 cast.

Ridge presumably hopes to improve on that margin next time. He has a seat on the Banking, Finance and Urban Affairs Committee, which is of importance to local urban projects. He also has an interest in international trade, an oddity in protectionist Pennsylvania; he points out that Erie, on the St. Lawrence Seaway, is an international seaport. He has a good chance of contrasting favorably with his immediate predecessors: Marks left office with vehement blasts against the Reagan administration, but after having supported its major economic programs in 1981; his predecessor, Democrat Joseph Vigorito, was beaten after he was named by reporter Nina Totenberg as one of the ten dumbest members of Congress. There is a Democratic base here, however, and this may very well be a seriously contested seat again in 1984.

The People Pop. 1980: 516,645, up 5.5% 1970–80; voting age pop. 370,614; 3% Black. 25% housing units rented. Median owner $37,600; renter $156. Households: 76% family, 40% with children, 64% married couples.

Presidential Vote

1980	Reagan (R)	90,029	(49%)
	Carter (D)	77,400	(43%)
	Anderson (I)	14,830	(8%)

Rep. Thomas J. Ridge (R) Elected 1982; b. Aug. 26, 1945, Homestead; home, Erie; Harvard Col., B.A. 1967, Dickinson Sch. of Law, J.D. 1972; Roman Catholic.

Career Practicing atty., 1972–82.

Offices 1331 LHOB, 202-225-5406. Also 108 Fed. Bldg., Erie 16501, 814-456-2308.

Committees *Banking, Finance and Urban Affairs* (16th). Subcommittees: Consumer Affairs and Coinage; Economic Stabilization; Housing and Community Development; International Development Institutions and Finance. *Select Committee on Aging* (17th). Subcommittees: Health and Long-Term Care; Housing and Consumer Interests.

Group Ratings and Key Votes: Newly Elected

Election Results

1982 general	Thomas J. Ridge (R)	80,180	(50%)	($228,140)
	Anthony B. Andrezeski (D)	79,451	(50%)	($158,321)
1982 primary	Thomas J. Ridge (R)	14,211	(48%)	
	Francis G. Vandenberg (R)	8,133	(28%)	
	Keith J. Johnson (R)	3,457	(12%)	
	Edward Hammer (R)	2,254	(8%)	
	Dale N. Sonney (R)	1,372	(5%)	
1980 general	Marc Lincoln Marks (R)	86,687	(50%)	($172,052)
	David C. Dicarlo (D)	86,567	(50%)	($143,032)

Campaign Contributions and Expenditures

1981-82		Direct Cont. 81-82			PACS brkdwn			
Receipts	$237,878	Indiv	$116,963	Agr	$500	Ideo	$8,250
Expend.	$228,140	Party	$24,413	Bus	$62,545	Lbr	$—
Unspent	$9,834	PACS	$80,183	Hlth	$2,850	Prof	$500
		Cand	$18,000				

Indirect Party Expend: $33,121

TWENTY-SECOND DISTRICT

The 22d congressional district of Pennsylvania is the northern tip of Appalachia—the southwestern corner of the state between West Virginia and the Pittsburgh suburbs. This is a region of rugged hills and polluted rivers, lined with steel mills and smaller factories. Industrial towns are huddled around each factory, with frame houses built 70 years ago to house the immigrants from Italy, Poland, Scotland, and what later became Czechoslovakia. There is a small aristocracy here of top management and factory owners, but it lives in the kind of isolation and paranoia you find among the rich in a small Latin American city. This is rough country: it was in a small town here that Joseph Yablonski, the insurgent candidate for president of the United Mine Workers, was found shot to death with his wife and daughters in 1969.

The 22d is one of Pennsylvania's most blue-collar and most Democratic districts. The long slide of the steel industry has made this a kind of depressed area for more than a decade now, and in the early 1980s it was feeling depressed indeed. Both its ethnic composition and its high union membership help to make it Democratic. Even in 1980 this was a Carter, not a Reagan district.

The current congressman here, Austin Murphy, effectively won the seat when he got 29% in a 12-candidate primary in 1976, when 32-year incumbent Thomas Morgan, Chairman of the House Foreign Affairs Committee, retired. Murphy's voting record is solidly Democratic and pro-labor; on cultural issues he is a moderate conservative. He has had no trouble winning reelection, and is not likely to have any in the 1980s.

Murphy has seats on the Interior and Education and Labor Committees, important because they handle strip mining (a major industry in these parts) and labor laws. Murphy chairs the Select Education Subcommittee, a body that does not handle the big-money education bills but has jurisdiction over a number of sensitive programs in which the federal government has been involved, including special education, alcohol and drug abuse, the handicapped, domestic violence, and adoption. Some of these—adoption is a good example— are areas where small, inexpensive programs can improve many people's lives, but where thoughtless federal action could disrupt personal and institutional relationships that have served people's needs for many years.

The People   Pop. 1980: 515,122, up 2.4% 1970–80; voting age pop. 378,475; 3% Black. 25% housing units rented. Median owner $35,500; renter $136. Households: 78% family, 38% with children, 65% married couples.

Presidential Vote

1980				
	Reagan (R)	....	66,607	(38%)
	Carter (D)	....	100,210	(57%)
	Anderson (I)	....	9,050	(5%)

Rep. Austin J. Murphy (D) Elected 1976; b. June 17, 1927, North Charleroi; home, Charleroi; Duquesne U., B.A. 1949, U. of Pitt., J.D. 1952; Roman Catholic.

Career USMC, WWII; Practicing atty., 1952–; Washington Cnty. Asst. Dist. Atty., 1956–57; PA House of Reps., 1959–71; PA Senate, 1971–77.

Offices 2437 RHOB, 202-225-4665. Also 308 Fallowfield Ave., Charleroi 15022, 412-489-4217; 70 E. Beau St., Washington 15301, 412-228-2777; and 365 McClelland Town Rd., Uniontown 15401, 412-438-1490.

Committees *Education and Labor* (11th). Subcommittees: Health and Safety; Labor-Management Relations; Select Education (Chairman). *Interior and Insular Affairs* (11th). Subcommittees: Energy and the Environment; Insular Affairs; Mining, Forest Management, and BPA.

Group Ratings

	ADA	ACLU	COPE	CFA	LCV	LWV	NTU	NSI	COC	ACA	CSFC
1982	55	42	77	46	71	55	33	67	25	19	40
1981	55	—	76	64	53	—	57	—	29	41	52
1980	44	27	68	57	70	50	27	70	59	42	43

National Journal Ratings

	Economic		Foreign		Cultural	
1982	65%	(LIB)	56%	(LIB)	56%	(LIB)
	34%	(CONS)	44%	(CONS)	44%	(CONS)
1981	65%	(LIB)	71%	(LIB)	44%	(LIB)
	34%	(CONS)	29%	(CONS)	56%	(CONS)

Key Votes

1) Reagan 81 Budget	AGN	5) Incr SS Rtmt Age	AGN	9) Poor Pay Food Stamps	—
2) Reagan 81 Tax Cut	AGN	6) Saudi AWACS Sale	AGN	10) Ban Crt Busing Order	AGN
3) Bal Budget Amend	AGN	7) $ for MX Missile	AGN	11) Auto Local Content	FOR
4) Gas & Road Tax	—	8) Nerve Gas Prod	FOR	12) Nuclear Arms Freeze	FOR

Election Results

1982 general	Austin J. Murphy (D)	123,716	(79%)	($92,446)
	Frank T. Paterra (R)	32,176	(20%)	($0)
1982 primary	Austin J. Murphy (D)	51,933	(100%)	
1980 general	Austin J. Murphy (D)	118,084	(70%)	($123,663)
	Marilyn Coyle Ecoff (R)	50,020	(29%)	($788)

Campaign Contributions and Expenditures

1981-82		Direct Cont. 81-82		PACS brkdwn			
Receipts	$121,705	Indiv	$51,592	Agr	$1,250	Ideo	$2,050
Expend.	$92,446	PACS	$58,891	Bus	$22,150	Lbr	$27,120
Unspent	$57,978			Hlth	$3,650	Prof	$1,750

TWENTY-THIRD DISTRICT

The 23d congressional district of Pennsylvania is the rural north central part of the state. The region is the most sparsely populated part of Pennsylvania, and of the entire East. The district's terrain is mountainous, and its valleys have only a few towns here and there; this was a route ignored in the great migrations west, and it contains none of the great historical east–west transportation routes. The only significant concentrations of people are found in the Nittany Valley in the southern part of the district and around Oil City in the extreme west. The Nittany Valley is the home of Pennsylvania State University, commonly called Penn State, long known for its powerful football teams. Oil City is near the site of the nation's first oil well, sunk in 1859. Today Pennsylvania crude—a relatively scarce oil but of higher quality than that found in the Southwest—continues to occupy an important place in the area's economy.

The isolation of this part of Pennsylvania was ended, at least somewhat, by the opening in the early 1970s of the Keystone Shortway, the stretch of Interstate 80 that replaced the Pennsylvania Turnpike as the shortest main road between New York and Chicago. Some people hoped that the Shortway would bring light industrial development to the area; but mainly it seems to have attracted gas stations with 60-foot signs and giant Holiday Inns. The 23d remains a rural and small-town district, populated mainly by descendants of the English stock farmers who moved here in the early 19th century.

The area currently in the 23d district has a long tradition of electing Republican congressmen, a tradition that goes back before the Civil War. But in the 1970s, it trended for a time to the Democrats, and in 1976 even elected a Democratic congressman. He was defeated, however, by the current incumbent, William Clinger, in 1978. In elections since, Clinger has restored old-fashioned Republican majorities; and, while to some extent they represent a shift in opinion on national issues, they also are testimony to Clinger's performance.

He is a mainstream conservative Republican, one who usually but not always sides with the Reagan administration. He is also energetic and active in the propagation of new ideas. One is his proposal for a federal capital budget—that is, having the federal government count capital expenditures as state and local governments do, with just the debt service counting as spending, rather than having the entire expenditure counted in the year in which it is spent. This would have the felicitous effect of coming close to eliminating the federal deficit, and it might also provide a more accurate picture of the federal government's financial status. That is Clinger's main project on Government Operations. On Public Works he is ranking Republican on the Economic Development Subcommittee, one which has fashioned new programs to aid local communities even as the Reagan administration has been trying to zero out old ones.

The People Pop. 1980: 515,976, up 6.1% 1970–80; voting age pop. 378,256; 1% Black. 22% housing units rented. Median owner $34,100; renter $154. Households: 74% family, 39% with children, 64% married couples.

Presidential Vote

1980	Reagan (R)	92,645	(55%)
	Carter (D)	64,222	(38%)
	Anderson (I)	12,083	(7%)

Rep. William F. (Bill) Clinger, Jr. (R) Elected 1978; b. Apr. 4, 1929, Warren; home, Warren; Johns Hopkins U., B.A. 1951, U. of VA, LL.B. 1965; Presbyterian.

Career Adv. Dept., New Process Co., 1955–62; Practicing atty., 1965–75, 1977–78; Chf. Counsel, U.S. Dept. of Commerce, Econ. Develop. Admin., 1975–77.

Offices 1122 LHOB, 202-225-5121. Also 111 S. Allen, State College 16801, 814-238-1776.

Committees *Government Operations* (6th). Subcommittees: Commerce, Consumer and Monetary Affairs; Environment, Energy, and Natural Resources; Legislation and National Security. *Public Works and Transportation* (6th). Subcommittees: Economic Development; Investigations and Oversight; Surface Transportation.

Group Ratings

	ADA	ACLU	COPE	CFA	LCV	LWV	NTU	NSI	COC	ACA	CSFC
1982	25	42	34	23	46	58	58	70	64	61	49
1981	30	—	37	36	43	—	50	—	89	63	60
1980	22	27	26	43	30	60	40	80	74	71	62

National Journal Ratings

	Economic		Foreign		Cultural	
1982	38%	(LIB)	53%	(LIB)	49%	(LIB)
	61%	(CONS)	47%	(CONS)	51%	(CONS)
1981	40%	(LIB)	60%	(LIB)	43%	(LIB)
	59%	(CONS)	40%	(CONS)	57%	(CONS)

Key Votes

1) Reagan 81 Budget	FOR	5) Incr SS Rtmt Age	FOR	9) Poor Pay Food Stamps	FOR
2) Reagan 81 Tax Cut	FOR	6) Saudi AWACS Sale	FOR	10) Ban Crt Busing Order	FOR
3) Bal Budget Amend	FOR	7) $ for MX Missile	AGN	11) Auto Local Content	AGN
4) Gas & Road Tax	FOR	8) Nerve Gas Prod	FOR	12) Nuclear Arms Freeze	AGN

Election Results

1982 general	William F. (Bill) Clinger, Jr. (R) ...	92,424	(65%)	($69,589)
	Joseph J. Calla, Jr. (D)	49,297	(35%)	($906)
1982 primary	William F. (Bill) Clinger, Jr. (R) ...	31,895	(100%)	
1980 general	William F. (Bill) Clinger, Jr. (R) ...	122,855	(74%)	($86,103)
	Peter Atigan (D)	41,033	(25%)	($0)

Campaign Contributions and Expenditures

1981-82		Direct Cont. 81-82		PACS brkdwn			
Receipts	$92,582	Indiv	$31,740	Agr	$2,100	Ideo	$500
Expend.	$69,589	Party	$9,426	Bus	$31,680	Lbr	$3,150
Unspent	$40,523	PACS	$43,230	Hlth	$5,100	Prof	$700

RHODE ISLAND

The state of Rhode Island and Providence Plantations—the full official name—owes its separate existence to a religious schism in the Massachusetts Bay Colony. Roger Williams, as most schoolchildren know, founded Providence in 1636 as a haven for dissident Calvinists fleeing the regime to the north. Williams had a profound—and for that day unusual—belief in religious and political freedom; he was the New World's first civil libertarian. Williams's colony soon attracted a motley gathering of Baptists, Antinomians, and even some Papists (Roman Catholics), along with a few American Indians. Williams, unlike many of his contemporaries and Americans to follow, was kindly disposed toward the Indians and became a scholar of their languages and customs.

Rhode Island's later history has been almost as idiosyncratic. The descendants of Williams's colonists began to prosper and, as people do, grow more conservative. The "triangle trade" out of Newport—rum, sugar, and slaves—was especially lucrative. After the Revolutionary War Rhode Island was the last of the 13 colonies to ratify the Constitution. It had declined to send delegates to the Convention for fear that any proposed union could impose tariffs and cut off the state's oceangoing trade. Only after the new nation threatened to sever commercial relations with Rhode Island did it agree to become the 13th state. As late as 1840, when most other states had given the franchise to all free white males, Rhode Island still allowed only large property owners to vote. This situation led to open revolt, the Dorr Rebellion, during which Rhode Island had two separate state governments, each claiming sovereignty.

In the state's economic history the key event happened in 1793, when Samuel Slater, a British emigre, built the nation's first water-powered cotton mill in Pawtucket and launched America's industrial revolution. During the 19th century the textile industry in Rhode Island boomed, and the tiny state attracted immigrants eager to work the looms and toil on the cutting floor. They came from French Canada, Ireland, and especially from Italy. So by the turn of the century this erstwhile colony of dissident Protestants had become the most heavily Catholic state in the nation. Today an estimated 64% of Rhode Island's citizens are Catholic.

For years the Protestants and Catholics fought out their cultural battles in politics. Long after they had become a numerical minority, the Protestants, through the Republican Party, were able to maintain control of government in Rhode Island. The big switch came in 1928, when thousands of immigrants, especially women, went to the polls for the first time and carried the state for Al Smith. From that time on Rhode Island has been one of our most Democratic states. It has gone Republican for president only three times in 55 years, twice for Eisenhower and once, narrowly, for Nixon; it has elected only one Republican to the U.S. Senate since 1930; it elected no Republicans to the House of Representatives between 1940 and 1978. In 1980, when most of the nation preferred Ronald Reagan, Rhode Island gave him only 37% of its votes—his worst percentage outside the District of Columbia.

Yet the Republicans have won some victories. They won the governorship in 1958, 1962, 1964, and 1966, and have been competitive in four of the last eight elections; they currently hold two of Rhode Island's four seats in Congress. The Democratic machine, only almighty in its primary, has gradually lost its hold. The reason seems to be that this is one state where the local media cover politics closely, and voters have plenty of information about individual candidates—enough often to persuade them to vote against their usual party or to change their minds about particular officeholders. So Senator and former Governor John Chafee has made a successful career, though he is a Republican; so has Congresswoman Claudine Schneider. Voters once very high on Governor Philip Noel and Congressman Edward Beard soured on them both, while the current governor, Joseph Garrahy, who entered office without inspiring much enthusiasm, now has strong support from the large majority of the electorate.

Governor. Garrahy may well be the most popular governor in the nation. The fact that Rhode Island's governors have only two-year terms subjects him to a tough discipline, and to the risk of losing office for a single mistake that a four-year governor would have time to overcome. But Garrahy has won his last two terms by 3–1 margins. On issues he is a mainstream Rhode Island Democrat.

Senators. It must strike anyone as odd that heavily Catholic and ethnic Rhode Island has two blue-blooded Protestant senators—as if the last 60 years had not happened. Actually, both of them, Democrat Claiborne Pell and Republican John Chafee, have had unusual careers. Claiborne Pell, first elected in 1960, is now the state's senior politician. His father was congressman from New York for a term, a friend of Franklin Roosevelt at Groton, and minister to Portugal and Hungary during the outbreak of World War II. Pell himself served as a foreign service officer for several years, then settled near Bellevue Avenue in Newport, where you find the Vanderbilt and Auchincloss "cottages."

Many Washington observers deprecate Pell's political skills, yet he has beaten some of Rhode Island's most popular politicians. In the 1960 Democratic primary he beat former Governor Dennis Roberts and former Governor, Senator, and U.S. Attorney General J. Howard McGrath; it was the first time a candidate endorsed by the Democratic organization was beaten. (All were running for the seat first won by Theodore F. Green in 1936 when he was 69. An entire generation of Rhode Island politicians made plans on the assumption that Green's seat would soon be available. Green, for years the state's aristocratic but domineering political boss, and sometime chairman of the Foreign Relations Committee, finally decided to retire at age 93.) In 1972, one of the few times Rhode Island went Republican, Pell faced John Chafee, then a popular former Governor and Secretary of the Navy. Although Chafee began ahead, Pell turned the campaign around and won again.

In the Senate Pell's main interest is foreign affairs. He is the ranking Democrat on the Foreign Relations Committee and in line to be chairman if the Democrats regain control. Pell's instincts on foreign policy are dovish on most issues; he is generally at odds with the Reagan administration. But he is more civil than aggressive, and seldom takes the lead in opposing administration policy. Sometimes he works closely with Chairman Charles Percy and the committee's bipartisan staff; on other issues, such as the nomination of Kenneth Adelman to head the arms control agency, another Democrat (in this case Alan Cranston, running for president) takes the lead in opposing the administration and Pell goes along. Should Pell become chairman, he seems unlikely to impose his agenda on the committee, as William Fulbright did. He will have some strong-minded Democratic colleagues on the committee—Biden if he is reelected, Glenn if he is not president, Sarbanes, Tsongas, Cranston if he is not president—who will be promoting a more dovish, conciliatory foreign policy.

Pell's other major legislative interest is education. When the Democrats controlled the committee now called Labor and Human Resources, Pell was in charge of education programs. He made a particular mark in setting up a grant program for needy college and university students; they are now called Pell grants, and have been under attack from the Reagan administration. He has also been one of the main promoters of federal aid to the arts, and in the Carter years secured the appointment of his friend Livingston Biddle as chairman of the National Endowment for the Arts.

Will Pell have a difficult race for reelection in 1984? So far, he has had two difficult races in his four terms as senator; he won both. The arguments made against him are that he is ineffective, a dilettante interested in unimportant programs like ocean research (but Rhode Island's license plates call it "Ocean State"), out of touch with the ordinary person. The arguments for him are that he has in fact been effective on some major programs (teachers campaigned strongly for him in 1972) and that he is a good solid Democrat while his opponent, by definition, is not. His toughest opponent would probably be Congresswoman Claudine Schneider; another possibility is Providence Mayor Vincent Cianci, who has become an Independent, though he is currently under indictment. But Schneider did not win overwhelmingly in her district in 1982 and Cianci was beaten badly by Governor Garrahy in 1980.

Senator John Chafee is Rhode Island's most successful Republican politician in the last 50 years. Even so, he has had his setbacks: he was defeated when he sought a fourth term as governor in 1968, and he lost to Pell in 1972. He came back, however, in 1976 when Senator John Pastore retired; he profited when then-Governor Philip Noel was defeated in the Democratic primary by a Cadillac dealer who ran a self-financed campaign but exhausted most of his resources in the primary.

Chafee's popularity comes from a solid, pleasant personality and from his liberal stands on many issues. On economics, while he is not always a solid conservative, he cannot be mistaken for a Democrat either. He supported the Reagan budget and tax cuts in 1981, for example, and he has been lead sponsor of the measure to reduce American regulation of bribery of foreign officials (an absurd law, when you think about it: do we try to enforce ordinary criminal laws against Americans who violate them abroad?). But in 1983 he broke rather conclusively with the Reagan administration, and called for revision of some of its tax cuts, and he has not been a big supporter of energy price controls.

His major legislative role in 1981 and 1982 came on the Environment and Public Works Committee. There he chaired the Environmental Pollution Subcommittee and worked closely with Chairman Robert Stafford, another New England Republican, to reauthorize a strong Clean Air Act. In effect, supporters of the Reaganite idea that such regulations should be greatly relaxed lost out in the Republican Senate, largely because of Stafford and Chafee. And not just because of their votes, but because of their mastery of the subject matter, their thoughtful approach, and their hard work. In return, environmentalists provided critical support, both in money and volunteers, for Chafee in his tough reelection fight in 1982.

Chafee's problem was that the Reagan economic policies were very unpopular in a state that was once one of the nation's leading high-wage states and is no longer, and which gave Reagan only 37% of its votes when he was winning nationwide. The Democratic nominee, Julius Michaelson, was affirmatively popular from his own service as an aggressive state attorney general. General counsel to the state AFL–CIO, Michaelson denounced Reaganomics again and again as heartless and disastrous for the ordinary citizen. He carried Providence, several blue-collar suburbs, and a few mill towns, losing the big, middle-income suburbs; but that was enough to give him 49% of the vote. If the Democrats had had the same ability as the national Republicans to follow each Senate race closely and pump in money as needed, Michaelson might well have won—and the Senate might now be Democratic.

1st congressional district. The 1st congressional district is the eastern half of the state, east of Narragansett Bay, a line that cuts through Providence and then proceeds west and north to the Massachusetts border. There are several Democratic strongholds here: Providence and next-door Pawtucket (although this includes the more prosperous side of Rhode Island's capital and largest city); the onetime textile mill towns of the Blackstone Valley, notably Woonsocket and Central Falls; and, south on the ocean, the old city of Newport, with its restored 18th-century houses, its cottages that are really palaces, and its economy still shattered by the closing of the Navy base here in 1973. Most of the rest of the district is Democratic too; the only real exceptions are the high-income suburb of Barrington and the old Yankee town of Little Compton on the coast.

Rhode Island's only committee chairman these days is Fernand St Germain, congressman from the 1st district and chairman of the House Banking, Finance and Urban Affairs Committee. This is a little-known committee; some of its subject matter is highly technical and very important, while some is rather easily comprehensible but for historical reasons not terribly critical at present. St Germain concentrated for many years on housing programs, and had the happy opportunity to concentrate much of the nation's supply of federally assisted senior citizen housing in eastern Rhode Island. But housing programs have become less important in recent years, even before the coming of the Reagan administration. The private housing market has been increasing the supply more rapidly than the population rises; the cost of federal assistance through interest subsidy has risen astronomically; and Congress has been reluctant to authorize federal mortgage guarantees at high prevailing interest rates lest it be thought to be approving them. Other Banking Committee responsibilities seem dormant. No one wants to consider even an authorization of wage and price controls these days, and no big city or corporation at this writing is seeking a loan guarantee as New York did in 1975 and Chrysler in 1979.

St Germain has switched his attention and his subcommittee chairmanship to banking issues. Here there are simmering disputes between banks and savings institutions to referee; desperate pleas from the savings institutions to attend to; regulations of novel practices to ponder. The problem government faces here is illustrated by the difficulty we encounter in measuring the money supply: banks and other financial institutions are so creative in fashioning new forms of money and credit in a time of high interest that no one can keep track of them—and protect society against a possible collapse of the system and ruin to many citizens. For the politician these problems create an atmosphere fertile with the possibility of raising campaign contributions. St Germain is knowledgeable on all these issues, but he would not be ranked as one of the most idealistic of our politicians. He believes these are matters to be settled by practical men, and as the representative of a seemingly safe district and the chairman of an important technical committee he spends most of his time in Washington dealing with these matters. First elected in 1960, when Democratic organization endorsement was all that mattered, St Germain has never had a challenge tough enough to require him to pull out all the stops and raise all the money he could; against a moderately well-financed Republican in the Democratic year of 1982 he felt safe enough leaving $240,000 of his campaign treasury unspent. Yet there are signs—his rather low percentage in 1978, for example—that St Germain might not be as invulnerable as first appears.

2d congressional district. The 2d congressional district is the western half of the state. While the 1st includes many mill towns, the 2d has most of its population in working- and middle-class suburbs like Cranston and Warwick, which despite their Anglo–Saxon names are inhabited mostly by people with Irish, Italian, French, and Portuguese names. Some of Providence's rich suburbs are also here, and to a very marginal degree this is Rhode Island's more Republican district.

But that is not enough to explain the election and reelection of Republican Congresswoman Claudine Schneider. She owes her election in large part to her predecessor Edward Beard, a house painter who beat an incumbent congressman in the 1974 Democratic primary. At first he captivated Rhode Islanders with his frankness; later he alienated them by his abrasiveness. In 1978 Schneider nearly beat him and in 1980 she came back and won. Schneider has neither roots in Rhode Island nor an ethnic background that is a particular advantage here. She does have a good sense of humor and a strong interest in environmental issues and opposition to nuclear power. On economic issues she was one of the very few—fewer than the fingers on one hand—Republicans who voted against even one of the Reagan economic proposals in 1981, and by the 1982 election she was decrying Reaganomics. On cultural issues she is among the most liberal Republicans in the House, and well to the left of her colleague St Germain.

All these things helped in the 1982 election. Also she was helped by money: she had $360,000 to spend, while her Democratic opponent, a respected state legislator, had $122,000. National Republicans are quite ready to tolerate Schneider's apostasy on some or even many issues because they know she is the only kind of Republican that could be elected from this district. As it is she won with 56%, an impressive performance given the circumstances, but probably not enough to guarantee her against serious competition in the future; anyway, in Rhode Island, any Democratic opponent is serious opposition. If only because any race is risky, Schneider might decide to go statewide and take on Senator Claiborne Pell in 1984.

Presidential politics. You can make a strong case that Rhode Island is the number one Democratic state in presidential elections; if not, it is in the top four. It should be added that the heavy Catholic population here is not invariably swayed by the Church. This is one of the states more tolerant of abortion, for example. One reason is that Catholics, like members of any other group, don't feel beleaguered and forced to stick to all their rules when they form a majority and are not heavily outnumbered. Another is that most of the Catholics have ethnic backgrounds not in Ireland, where the Church was the defender of the people against an alien regime, but in Italy, Portugal, and French Canada, where the Church's dominance of civil as well as religious life made many people, especially men, strong anticlericals; men still call themselves Catholics in many parts of Italy and Rhode Island, but have no more intention of attending Mass regularly or following a priest's orders than they do of wearing a dress.

Rhode Island has had presidential primaries, with the lowest rate of turnout of any state in the nation. In a state of nearly a million people, only 38,000 voted in the Democratic primary and a pathetic 5,000 in the Republican primary in 1980. This is a lower turnout than you get in the Iowa precinct caucuses. Possible reasons: it's a late primary; party registration is not required; people here are used to having the party organizations decide these things.

The People   Est. Pop. 1982: 958,000; Pop. 1980: 947,154, up 1.2% 1980–82 and dn. 0.3% 1970–80; 0.42% of U.S. total, 41st largest; voting age pop. 704,303; 2% Black, 2% Spanish origin, 1% Asian origin. Single ancestry: 13% Italian, 8% French, English, Irish, 7% Portuguese, 2% Polish, 1% German, Scottish, Swedish, Russian. Registered voters (1982): 533,853 Total. 13% with 1–3 yrs. col., 15% with 4+ yrs. col. 10.3% below poverty level. 37% housing units rented; median house value: $47,000; median monthly rent: $158. Households: 72% family, 37% with children, 59% married couples.

1982 Share of Federal Tax Burden $2,457,800,000; .41% of U.S. total, 40th largest.

1982 Share of Federal Expenditures

	Total		Non-Defense		Defense	
Total Expend	$2,538m	(0.42%)	$1,976m	(0.47%)	$562m	(0.31%)
St/Lcl Grants	471m	(0.53%)	469m	(0.53%)	2m	(5.56%)
Salary/Wages	278m	(0.36%)	40m	(0.15%)	238m	(0.47%)
Ind Payments	1,365m	(0.48%)	1,241m	(0.48%)	124m	(0.43%)
Procurement	398m	(0.27%)	127m	(0.40%)	271m	(0.24%)
Other Programs	26m	(0.48%)	26m	(0.48%)	0m	(0%)
Loan/Insurance	71m	(0.11%)	69m	(0.11%)	2m	(0.09%)

Political Lineup   Governor, J. Joseph Garrahy (D). Senators, Claiborne Pell (D) and John H. Chafee (R). Representatives, 2 (1 D and 1 R). State Senate, 50 (45 D and 5 R); State House of Representatives, 100 (85 D and 15 R).

Presidential Vote

1980	Reagan (R)	154,793	(37%)
	Carter (D)	198,342	(48%)
	Anderson (I)	59,814	(14%)
1976	Ford (R)	181,249	(44%)
	Carter (D)	227,636	(55%)

1980 Democratic Presidential Primary			*1980 Republican Presidential Primary*		
Kennedy	26,179	(68%)	Reagan	3,839	(72%)
Carter	9,907	(26%)	Bush	993	(19%)
Two others..........	1,470	(4%)	Uncommitted	348	(6%)
Uncommitted	771	(2%)	Two others..........	155	(3%)

SENATORS

Sen. Claiborne Pell (D) Elected 1960, seat up 1984; b. Nov. 22, 1918, New York, NY; home, Newport; Princeton U., A.B. 1940, Columbia U., A.M. 1946; Episcopal.

Career Coast Guard, WWII; U.S. Foreign Svc. and State Dept., Czechoslovakia and Italy, 1945–52; Exec. Asst. to RI Dem. St. Chmn., 1952, 1954; Consultant, Dem. Natl. Comm., 1953–60; Dir., Internatl. Rescue Comm.; Mbr., U.S. Delegation to U.N., 1970.

Offices 325 RSOB, 202-224-4642. Also 418 Fed. Bldg., Providence 02903, 401-528-4547.

Committees *Foreign Relations* (Ranking Member). *Labor and Human Resources* (3d). Subcommittees: Aging; Education, Arts and Humanities; Employment and Productivity. *Rules and Administration* (2d). *Joint Committee on Printing* (2d).

Group Ratings

	ADA	ACLU	COPE	CFA	LCV	LWV	NTU	NSI	COC	ACA	CSFC
1982	95	68	92	90	85	100	22	0	37	11	31
1981	95	—	92	86	81	—	12	—	17	24	30
1980	78	50	94	60	65	80	28	0	32	10	25

National Journal Ratings

	Economic		Foreign		Cultural	
1982	73%	(LIB)	90%	(LIB)	79%	(LIB)
	26%	(CONS)	3%	(CONS)	20%	(CONS)
1981	94%	(LIB)	83%	(LIB)	73%	(LIB)
	5%	(CONS)	16%	(CONS)	26%	(CONS)

Key Votes

1) Reagan 81 Budget	AGN	5) $ to El Salvador	AGN	9) Poor Pay Food Stamps	AGN
2) Reagan 81 Tax Cut	FOR	6) Saudi AWACS Sale	AGN	10) Ban Crt Busing Order	AGN
3) Bal Budget Amend	AGN	7) Ban Abortion	AGN	11) Clinch Riv Brdr Rctr	AGN
4) Gas & Road Tax	FOR	8) Nerve Gas Prod	AGN	12) Legal Services Corp	FOR

Election Results

1978 general	Claiborne Pell (D)	229,557	(75%)	($373,077)
	James G. Reynolds (R)	76,061	(25%)	($85,614)
1978 primary	Claiborne Pell (D)	69,729	(87%)	
	Two others (D)	10,406	(13%)	
1972 general	Claiborne Pell (D)	221,942	(54%)	($528,347)
	John H. Chafee (R)	188,990	(46%)	($457,409)

Campaign Contributions and Expenditures

1977-78			PACS brkdwn		
Receipts	$398,898	Agr	$550	Ideo	$4,600
Expend.	$373,077	Bus	$22,575	Lbr	$50,820
Unspent	$27,399	Hlth	$9,850	Prof	$250

Sen. John H. Chafee (R) Elected 1976, seat up 1988; b. Oct. 22, 1922, Providence; home, East Greenwich; Yale U., B.A. 1947, Harvard U., LL.B. 1950; Episcopal.

Career USMC, 1942–46, 1950–52; RI House of Reps., 1957–63; Gov. of RI, 1963–69; Secy. of the Navy, 1969–72; Repub. Nominee for U.S. Senate, 1972.

Offices 523 DSOB, 202-224-2921. Also 302 Pastore Bldg., Providence 02903, 401-528-5294.

Committees *Energy and Natural Resources* (10th). Subcommittees: Energy Conservation and Supply; Energy Regulation; Public Lands and Reserved Water. *Environment and Public Works* (3d). Subcommittees: Environmental Pollution (Chairman); Regional and Community Development; Transportation. *Finance* (5th). Subcommittees: Taxation and Debt Management; International Trade; Savings, Pensions, and Investment Policy (Chairman). *Select Committee on Intelligence* (3d). Subcommittees: Legislation and the Rights of Americans; Collection and Foreign Operations (Chairman).

Group Ratings

	ADA	ACLU	COPE	CFA	LCV	LWV	NTU	NSI	COC	ACA	CSFC
1982	80	79	54	40	66	92	41	11	43	14	47
1981	45	—	55	50	75	—	52	—	61	38	62
1980	72	83	63	40	87	100	38	20	55	29	43

National Journal Ratings

	Economic		Foreign		Cultural	
1982	56%	(LIB)	74%	(LIB)	88%	(LIB)
	43%	(CONS)	25%	(CONS)	11%	(CONS)
1981	69%	(LIB)	60%	(LIB)	86%	(LIB)
	30%	(CONS)	39%	(CONS)	6%	(CONS)

Key Votes

1) Reagan 81 Budget	FOR	5) $ to El Salvador	AGN	9) Poor Pay Food Stamps	AGN
2) Reagan 81 Tax Cut	FOR	6) Saudi AWACS Sale	FOR	10) Ban Crt Busing Order	AGN
3) Bal Budget Amend	AGN	7) Ban Abortion	AGN	11) Clinch Riv Brdr Rctr	AGN
4) Gas & Road Tax	FOR	8) Nerve Gas Prod	AGN	12) Legal Services Corp	FOR

Election Results

1982 general	John H. Chafee (R)	175,248	(51%)	($1,065,627)
	Julius C. Michaelson (D)	167,283	(49%)	($438,630)
1982 primary	John H. Chafee (R) unopposed			
1976 general	John H. Chafee (R)	230,329	(58%)	($415,651)
	Richard Lorber (D)	167,665	(42%)	($782,931)

Campaign Contributions and Expenditures

1979-82		Direct Cont. 79-82		PACS brkdwn			
Receipts	$1,117,187	Indiv	$600,799	Agr	$7,500	Ideo	$20,150
Expend.	$1,065,627	Party	$15,838	Bus	$352,950	Lbr	$20,000
Unspent	$53,687	PACS	$421,203	Hlth	$28,500	Prof	$5,850

Indirect Party Expend: $73,758   *Indep Expend:* Agn: $3,297 (NCPAC)

GOVERNOR

Gov. J. Joseph Garrahy (D) Elected 1976, term expires Jan. 1985; b. Nov. 26, 1930, Providence; home, Providence; U. of RI, U. of Buffalo; Roman Catholic.

Career Air Force, Korea; Sales Rep., Narragansett Brewing Co., 1956–62; RI State Senate, 1963–69, Dpty. Major. Ldr., 1967–68; Dem. St. Chmn., 1967–68; Lt. Gov. of RI, 1968–76.

Offices State House, Providence 02903, 401-277-2397.

Election Results

1982 gen.	J. Joseph Garrahy (D)	246,566	(73%)
	Vincent J. Marzullo (R)	79,602	(24%)
1982 prim.	J. Joseph Garrahy (D) unopposed		
1980 gen.	J. Joseph Garrahy (D)	299,174	(74%)
	Vincent (Buddy) Cianci (R) ..	106,729	(26%)

FIRST DISTRICT

The People   Pop. 1980: 474,429, dn. 2.8% 1970–80; voting age pop. 357,096; 2% Black, 2% Span. orig., 1% Asian orig. 42% housing units rented. Median owner $48,600; renter $157. Households: 71% family, 35% with children, 58% married couples.

Presidential Vote

1980	Reagan (R)	74,825	(37%)
	Carter (D)	99,880	(49%)
	Anderson (I)	29,726	(15%)

**RHODE ISLAND — Congressional Districts, Counties,
County Subdivisions (Towns), and Places — *(2 Districts)***

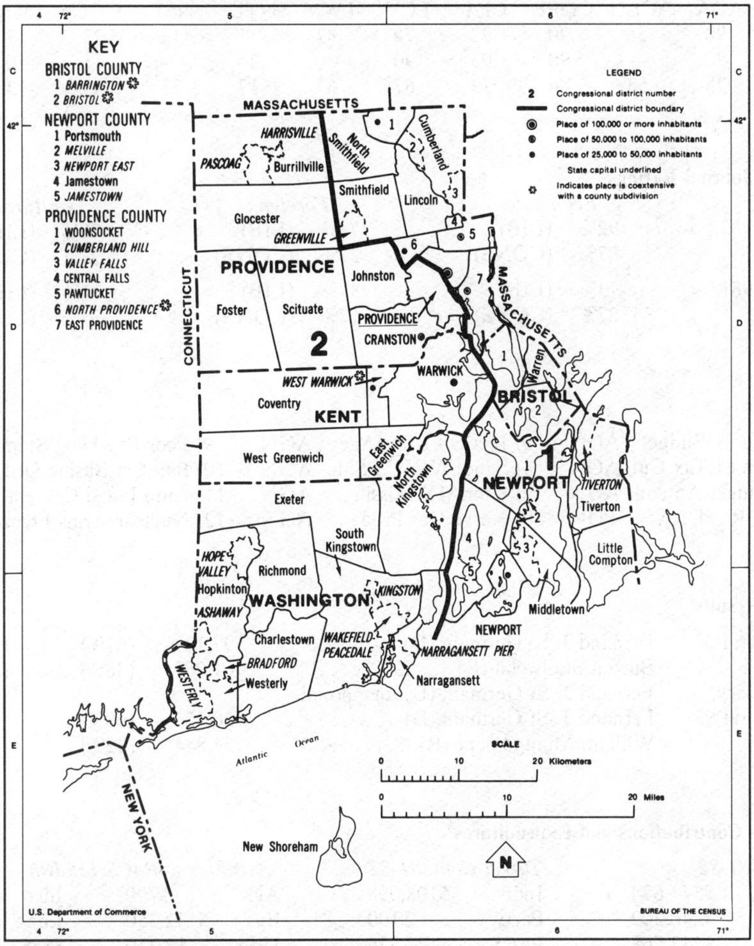

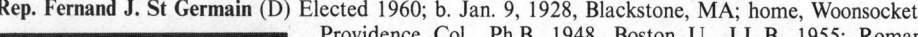

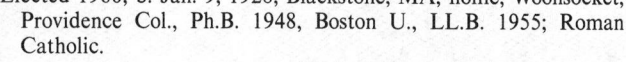

KEY

BRISTOL COUNTY
1 *BARRINGTON* ✿
2 *BRISTOL* ✿

NEWPORT COUNTY
1 Portsmouth
2 *MELVILLE*
3 *NEWPORT EAST*
4 Jamestown
5 *JAMESTOWN*

PROVIDENCE COUNTY
1 WOONSOCKET
2 *CUMBERLAND HILL*
3 *VALLEY FALLS*
4 CENTRAL FALLS
5 PAWTUCKET
6 *NORTH PROVIDENCE* ✿
7 EAST PROVIDENCE

LEGEND

2   Congressional district number
‾‾‾ Congressional district boundary
◉   Place of 100,000 or more inhabitants
◎   Place of 50,000 to 100,000 inhabitants
●   Place of 25,000 to 50,000 inhabitants
     State capital underlined
✿   Indicates place is coextensive
     with a county subdivision

MASSACHUSETTS

CONNECTICUT

PROVIDENCE **2**

KENT

WASHINGTON

NEWPORT **1**

BRISTOL

SCALE

0 ___ 10 ___ 20 Kilometers
0 ___ 10 ___ 20 Miles

New Shoreham

N

U.S. Department of Commerce   BUREAU OF THE CENSUS

Congressional districts established April 9, 1982; all other boundaries are as of January 1, 1960.

Rep. Fernand J. St Germain (D) Elected 1960; b. Jan. 9, 1928, Blackstone, MA; home, Woonsocket; Providence Col., Ph.B. 1948, Boston U., LL.B. 1955; Roman Catholic.

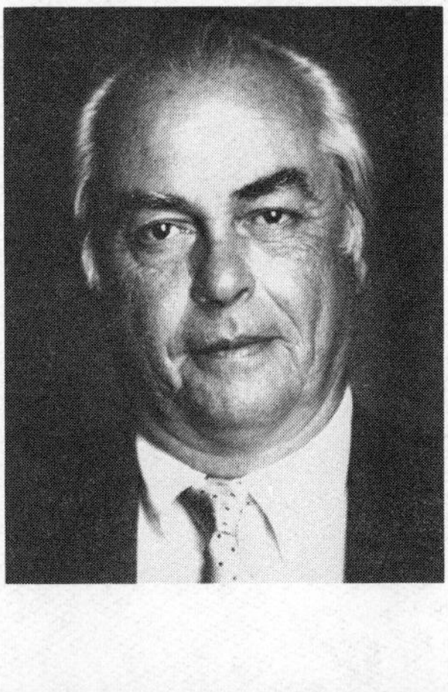

Career Army, 1949–52; RI House of Reps., 1952–60; Practicing atty., 1956–.

Offices 2108 RHOB, 202-225-4911. Also 200 John E. Fogarty Bldg., Providence 02903, 401-528-4323.

Committee *Banking, Finance and Urban Affairs* (Chairman). Subcommittees: Consumer Affairs and Coinage; Financial Institutions Supervision, Regulation and Insurance (Chairman); General Oversight and Renegotiation; Housing and Community Development.

Group Ratings

	ADA	ACLU	COPE	CFA	LCV	LWV	NTU	NSI	COC	ACA	CSFC
1982	90	58	90	92	78	82	1	13	23	17	29
1981	70	—	90	93	90	—	35	—	11	10	37
1980	78	53	84	79	67	67	17	33	45	13	30

National Journal Ratings

	Economic		Foreign		Cultural	
1982	92%	(LIB)	73%	(LIB)	78%	(LIB)
	7%	(CONS)	27%	(CONS)	21%	(CONS)
1981	73%	(LIB)	87%	(LIB)	66%	(LIB)
	27%	(CONS)	12%	(CONS)	34%	(CONS)

Key Votes

1) Reagan 81 Budget	AGN	5) Incr SS Rtmt Age	AGN	9) Poor Pay Food Stamps	AGN
2) Reagan 81 Tax Cut	AGN	6) Saudi AWACS Sale	AGN	10) Ban Crt Busing Order	AGN
3) Bal Budget Amend	AGN	7) $ for MX Missile	AGN	11) Auto Local Content	FOR
4) Gas & Road Tax	FOR	8) Nerve Gas Prod	AGN	12) Nuclear Arms Freeze	FOR

Election Results

1982 general	Fernand J. St Germain (D)	97,181	(61%)	($246,302)
	Burton Stallwood (R)	61,267	(38%)	($167,349)
1982 primary	Fernand J. St Germain (D) unopposed			
1980 general	Fernand J. St Germain (D)	120,756	(68%)	($44,418)
	William Montgomery (R)	57,844	(32%)	($0)

Campaign Contributions and Expenditures

1981-82		Direct Cont. 81-82			PACS brkdwn			
Receipts	$343,674	Indiv	$108,098	Agr	$700	Ideo	$2,250
Expend.	$246,302	Party	$100	Bus	$132,350	Lbr	$1,400
Unspent	$242,568	PACS	$177,326	Hlth	$2,250	Prof	$39,526

SECOND DISTRICT

The People   Pop. 1980: 472,725, up 2.4% 1970–80; voting age pop. 347,207; 3% Black, 2% Span. orig., 1% Asian orig. 33% housing units rented. Median owner $45,700; renter $159. Households: 74% family, 38% with children, 60% married couples.

Presidential Vote

1980	Reagan (R)	79,968	(38%)
	Carter (D)	98,462	(47%)
	Anderson (I)	30,093	(14%)

Rep. Claudine Schneider (R) Elected 1980; b. Mar. 25, 1947, Clairton, PA; home, Narragansett; Rosemont Col., U. of Barcelona, Spain, Windham Col., B.A. 1969; Roman Catholic.

Career Founder, RI Committee on Energy, 1973; Exec. Dir., Conservation Law Foundation, 1973; Repub. Nominee for U.S. House of Reps., 1978; Producer, Pub. Affairs Program on Providence TV, 1979–80.

Offices 1431 LHOB, 202-225-2735. Also 307 Pastore Bldg., Providence 02903, 401-528-4861.

Committees *Merchant Marine and Fisheries* (10th). Subcommittees: Fisheries and Wildlife Conservation and the Environment; Oceanography. *Science and Technology* (9th). Subcommittees: Energy Development and Applications; Investigations and Oversight; Natural Resources, Agriculture Research and Environment. *Select Committee on Aging* (16th). Subcommittee: Human Services.

Group Ratings

	ADA	ACLU	COPE	CFA	LCV	LWV	NTU	NSI	COC	ACA	CSFC
1982	85	75	65	77	92	75	41	10	29	9	32
1981	70	—	47	93	79	—	61	—	63	29	45

National Journal Ratings

	Economic		Foreign		Cultural	
1982	67%	(LIB)	91%	(LIB)	89%	(LIB)
	33%	(CONS)	8%	(CONS)	8%	(CONS)
1981	51%	(LIB)	85%	(LIB)	84%	(LIB)
	48%	(CONS)	13%	(CONS)	16%	(CONS)

Key Votes

1) Reagan 81 Budget	FOR	5) Incr SS Rtmt Age	AGN
2) Reagan 81 Tax Cut	FOR	6) Saudi AWACS Sale	AGN
3) Bal Budget Amend	AGN	7) $ for MX Missile	AGN
4) Gas & Road Tax	FOR	8) Nerve Gas Prod	AGN

9) Poor Pay Food Stamps	AGN
10) Ban Crt Busing Order	AGN
11) Auto Local Content	FOR
12) Nuclear Arms Freeze	FOR

Election Results

1982 general	Claudine Schneider (R)	95,779	(56%)	($349,306)
	James Aukerman (D)	76,769	(44%)	($191,372)
1982 primary	Claudine Schneider (R) unopposed			
1980 general	Claudine Schneider (R)	115,057	(55%)	($289,937)
	Edward P. Beard (D)	92,970	(45%)	($167,559)

Campaign Contributions and Expenditures

1981-82		Direct Cont. 81-82		PACS brkdwn			
Receipts	$360,645	Indiv	$181,924	Agr	$550	Ideo	$25,475
Expend.	$349,306	Party	$26,311	Bus	$78,317	Lbr	$16,200
Unspent	$16,802	PACS	$132,191	Hlth	$9,275	Prof	$1,235

Indirect Party Expend: $17,998   *Indep Expend:* For: $23,877 (AMAPAC)

SOUTH CAROLINA

South Carolina has one of the most distinctive histories of any state, and to understand it you have to go back to the very beginning. While the other Atlantic seaboard colonies were modeled on life in England or based on some religious ideal, the model the first South Carolinians used was Barbados, the sugar-producing island in the West Indies where the very large majority of people were slaves. During the colonial period, South Carolina was the only colony where blacks outnumbered whites massively, and the settlers here were almost all large landholders who could grow their crops—sugar, rice, indigo—only with the labor of vast numbers of slaves. South Carolina produced a planter elite whose most memorable legacies were men like the Pinckneys and John C. Calhoun, and whose gravest fear was that their slaves would revolt, as some did in the Denmark Vesey uprising of 1822. Later South Carolina sparked the Civil War. The young aristocrats who dominated political life here were hotheaded opponents of any action that in any way restricted or reflected negatively on slavery. In early 1861 these rebels opened fire on Fort Sumter in Charleston harbor, and so began the war.

It is not hard to understand why, after the war, the state's white minority was enraged to see blacks take political power. For a time during the 1870s blacks controlled the South Carolina legislature and the state's congressional delegation. Such "outrages" of Reconstruction were soon ended, and the blacks—and most poor whites—lost the vote and all political rights. Meanwhile, as the 19th century wore on, the once booming port of Charleston slipped into economic stagnation, as did the rest of South Carolina. For most of the 20th century this state has been among the lowest in per capita income, level of education, and public health statistics. It has also had one of the lowest levels of political participation: as late as 1948 only 142,000 South Carolinians voted in the presidential election, in a state with more than two million people.

South Carolina no longer has the same economic base or racial mix as it did in the 19th century. Charleston today lives not as a port but largely off the money poured in by numerous military bases, and the coast is studded not with large farms but with huge condominium developments of which the pioneer was Hilton Head. Meanwhile, the economic strength of the state has moved inland. Textiles have become the largest industry here, with the biggest concentration of mills in the Piedmont, along Interstate 85 that passes through Greenville and Spartanburg. South Carolina has been perhaps the most aggressive state in the South in attracting new industry. It has gone over to Europe and enticed French and German firms to set up major operations in the Piedmont, and has seen its standard of living move from one far, far below the national average to one which is, considering differences in costs of living, quite close to the national average indeed—and this during a period when that national average has increased considerably.

As in other southern states, there was a massive outmigration of blacks from the lowlands in the years after World War II; until the middle 1960s they went almost entirely to the North, particularly to New York, Philadelphia, and Baltimore; later some started moving to other parts of South Carolina and the South. South Carolina no longer has a black majority:

30% of its residents were black in 1980; nor does it practice white supremacy: 28% of its voters were black in 1982. And, since these blacks are younger than whites and tend to have more children, the long-term prospect is for the black percentage to increase.

The old South Carolina was solidly Democratic for years: 88% for Franklin Roosevelt in 1944. But it was also the leading Dixiecrat state: Strom Thurmond, then South Carolina's governor, was the Dixiecrat ticket-bearer against Truman in 1948, and he carried his own state easily. The civil rights revolution; the expansion of the electorate to include first lower-income whites and, after the Voting Rights Act of 1965, blacks; the increased prosperity of the state—all these changed the tone and substance of South Carolina politics. For a time it seemed the state might be going Republican: its newly prosperous and anti-civil rights whites went heavily Republican in state as well as national races in the 1960s, and Strom Thurmond became a Republican in 1964. But in retrospect the Republican surge peaked as long ago as 1966. Discontented whites went for George Wallace in 1968, and blacks provided a large vote base for national and state Democrats. By the early 1970s South Carolina had the politics it has today, with an electorate split almost precisely equally between three groups. One are the blacks, who remain heavily Democratic, and attracted to liberal candidates like Charles Ravenel. The second are the country club whites, who are solidly Republican in national and most state contests.

The third are what we might call textile-mill whites. They dislike the national Democratic Party for its liberal stands on cultural issues—not so much racial matters, as on more general attitudes toward religion, patriotism, and traditional family values. They see the national Democrats as endorsing values antithetical to theirs and as smirking at their traditional attitudes as backward and foolish. But on many economic issues they remain New Dealers. They don't like abstract talk about redistributing income, and they don't much care for labor unions. But they are also hostile to tax breaks for the rich, Social Security cuts, and cuts in school lunch and education programs. They seem to understand instinctively that they owe their own advancement—and their hope for more in the future—not only to risks taken by entrepreneurs and their own hard work, but to a government which has provided them not only with a safety net down below but with a hand up as they try to ascend the ladder. The textile-mill whites have broken toward the Democrats here in most elections since 1970. In that year they rejected the quasi-racist appeal of a Republican gubernatorial candidate and elected a Democrat. The Democrats have held the governorship ever since, except in 1974 when James Edwards won it because Democratic nominee Charles Ravenel was ruled off the ballot in October for not meeting a residency requirement. Senator Strom Thurmond, the most durable man in South Carolina politics, has continued to thrive politically, and Republicans have won a fair share of congressional races.

Presidential politics. But in presidential politics, South Carolina, like most of the southeastern states, seems to tilt Democratic. It went solidly for Jimmy Carter in 1976 and was one of seven southern states Carter came within 1% or 2% of carrying in 1980. No one can say for sure that South Carolina will be as Democratic in 1984 if the Democrats nominate a non-southern candidate. But if he manages to avoid antagonizing the state's blue-collar vote on cultural issues, he has a solid chance here.

South Carolina's Democrats did not have a presidential primary in 1980; in 1984 they are likely to be lined up behind Senator Ernest Hollings. The Republicans did have a primary here, and it proved to be the electoral graveyard of John Connally—even though he had the strong support of Senator Strom Thurmond, faithful even when it was apparent that the cause was lost. It was still pretty much a country club electorate, with only 145,000 votes cast.

Senators. South Carolina has two of the most durable and forceful members of the Senate today—or maybe ever. Strom Thurmond was first elected to the legislature in 1932, at age 29; Ernest Hollings first won in 1948, at age 26. Both have been active—and successful—in South Carolina politics ever since.

Thurmond has combined a reputation for firmness and steadfastness with a flexibility and adroitness that has enabled this onetime symbol of racial segregation to prosper politically in an era of integration. Thurmond was elected governor in 1946 and won 39 electoral votes for president in 1948. In 1954 he was elected to the Senate, stunningly, as a write-in candidate; he promised the voters that if he won he would resign and seek election in the ordinary manner, and in 1956 he did. During the 1964 campaign he switched to the Republican Party and supported Barry Goldwater for president; in 1968 he was the key power broker at the Republican National Convention, when he held the South for Richard Nixon. Since then, he has not been so pivotal in presidential politics; he was never an enthusiastic Reagan man, sticking with Ford in 1976 and with Connally in 1980 until Connally himself supported Reagan.

A dozen years ago, many observers were predicting Thurmond's political demise. But he reacted to the enfranchisement of South Carolina's blacks by working as doggedly for them as he had for others: he hired black staffers in the early 1970s, pushed through the appointment of black federal judges, helped black local officials and citizens' groups with federal projects. He still wants to soften the Voting Rights Act and opposes school busing, and he probably gets few black votes. But he has softened black voters' hostility; they don't turn out in large numbers to vote against him.

As the senior Republican senator, Thurmond is president pro tempore of the Senate, and in the theoretical line of succession to the presidency. His leading position of power is as chairman of the Senate Judiciary Committee. No one expected this before 1980, but Thurmond typically laid the groundwork by invoking his seniority two years before and displacing Maryland's Charles Mathias as ranking Republican on the committee. So in 1981 he was able to move quickly to get rid of the liberal staffers accumulated by Edward Kennedy in his two years as chairman. He created an Internal Security Subcommittee and got Alabama's Jeremiah Denton to chair it; but he was also willing to work on a bipartisan basis with Kennedy in an attempt to pass a revised criminal code.

Some people expected Thurmond to work hard for the New Right's agenda of constitutional amendments, but he did not. He has a solidly conservative voting record, but he lacks the conviction of a Jesse Helms that things must be drastically changed or America will be ruined. Helms has spent most of his adult life as a journalist, complaining about the way others are running things; Thurmond has spent most of his adult life as an elected official, running things himself. Having survived all sorts of political and economic changes, he is ready to survive whatever will come next—and by now no one doubts that he will.

Thurmond is now a senior member of the Armed Services Committee. He is a retired general in the Army, an unabashed enthusiast for things military, a supporter of an aggressive and assertive foreign policy. On Armed Services he is very much an Army man. He is also a member of the Veterans' Affairs Committee.

Thurmond's seat comes up in 1984, and a few years ago everyone expected him to retire. But as of early 1983 it looks as if he will run. He has always kept in good physical shape; widowed in his 60s, he married a young beauty queen and fathered the first of his three children when he was nearly 70. Thurmond won reelection in 1978 against an opponent who himself inspires much enthusiasm, Charles Ravenel, and his support continues to be rock-hard. Leading Democrats—Governor Richard Riley, Congressman Butler Derrick, former Lieutenant Governor Nancy Stevenson—have all let it be known they are not interested in the seat if Thurmond runs.

South Carolina's other senator, Ernest Hollings, known widely as Fritz, announced in 1983 that he was running for president. He was elected governor in 1958, when he was 36. He worked carefully and shrewdly to see that South Carolina complied peacefully with desegregation orders, and he began South Carolina's efforts to recruit high-wage industry—efforts which have substantially raised the state's standard of living in the years since. Out of office four years, he won a Senate seat in 1966, beating his successor as governor in the primary and beating a Republican at the height of the party's strength in the state.

Hollings has been for some years one of the key insiders in the Senate, a man who seldom makes headlines but often makes things happen. He was a leading participant on the Budget Committee during the period of bipartisan cooperation between Chairman Edmund Muskie and ranking Republican Henry Bellmon; when Muskie became Secretary of State in 1980, Hollings became chairman. But his tenure was unexpectedly brief; and when the Republicans controlled the Senate, they essentially shut the Democrats out of budget deliberations. In 1981 he was unable to unite Democrats on any approach; one reason may be that Hollings himself is considerably more hawkish and more skeptical of some (but by no means all) domestic spending than most Senate Democrats. In 1982 he advanced the idea of a simultaneous freeze on taxes, domestic spending, and defense spending. It was an attempt to appeal to a sense of common sacrifice, in the World War II spirit, in a nation grown used to candidates promising that great things can be accomplished without discommoding anybody. Hollings's proposal was embraced rhetorically and, to some extent, in practice by the administration and Congress, without much credit going to its originator.

Hollings's main impetus as a presidential candidate comes from his feeling that the United States is falling behind in international competition—and that this need not be so. He believes the government must eliminate its deficit and that it must provide the education and training needed for a high-skill work force. He is contemptuous sometimes when speaking of his rivals; yet he has difficulty getting his message across to voters and to Democratic activists. The problem is not just his Charleston accent—though that is distinctive and difficult for some listeners to understand. It is also that he lacks the instinct for providing capsule summaries of useful ideas—an instinct not much needed when he started his political career in the 1950s but much more useful now in the age of 30-second commercials and TV news squibs.

Hollings gave up his ranking position on Budget to take it on Commerce, Science and Transportation in 1983, to give him more time on the campaign trail. The Commerce post is nonetheless an important one: the committee covers a large part of the federal government's regulatory law. He has also concentrated heavily on nutrition programs; in the late 1960s he discovered that people in South Carolina still suffered from malnutrition, and became the Senate's leading backer of anti-hunger programs. He is one of the Senate's strongest hawks on most military issues, but unwilling to throw money away; in late 1982 he was the leading opponent of the MX missile, on the grounds that the administration, then backing Densepack, had come up with no viable basing mode for it.

Hollings's chances as a presidential candidate are not taken seriously by Washington professionals. In practice, he has to do well in one of the very early tests and in the early southern primaries in order to be a serious factor in the race. His chances for reelection in South Carolina when his term comes up are much better. He has not had serious opposition in his last two races and has won by overwhelming margins.

Governor. South Carolina's governor, Richard Riley, made a name as a reform-minded state senator from the Republican city of Greenville. He upset better-known candidates with more political enemies in the 1978 primary and runoff, and swept the general election. In office he continued South Carolina's efforts to attract high-wage jobs and grappled with the difficult problems of nuclear waste disposal (South Carolina, along with Washington and Nevada, dispose of virtually all the nation's nuclear wastes). South Carolina's voters in 1980 approved a constitutional amendment allowing him to seek a second term; in 1982 they voted him that term by a wide margin.

Congressional districting. South Carolina's congressional districts were changed in only minor ways in redistricting; the Democratic legislature made no major effort to help Democratic candidates. Currently, the Democrats hold only three of the state's six districts; they lost the 4th in 1978, the 1st in 1980, and they haven't held the 2d since its congressman resigned and switched parties in 1965.

The People Est. Pop. 1982: 3,203,000; Pop. 1980: 3,121,820, up 2.6% 1980–82 and 20.5% 1970–80; 1.4% of U.S. total, 24th largest; voting age pop. 2,179,854; 27% Black, 1% Spanish origin. Single ancestry: 19% English, 5% Irish, 4% German, 1% French, Scottish. Registered voters (1982): 1,229,319 Total. 13% with 1–3 yrs. col., 14% with 4+ yrs. col. 15.9% below poverty level. 27% housing units rented; median house value: $35,100; median monthly rent: $133. Households: 78% family, 46% with children, 63% married couples.

1982 Share of Federal Tax Burden $5,945,700,000; 1.00% of U.S. total, 31st largest.

1982 Share of Federal Expenditures

	Total		Non-Defense		Defense	
Total Expend	$7,371m	(1.22%)	$5,102m	(1.20%)	$2,269m	(1.27%)
St/Lcl Grants	1,043m	(1.18%)	1,042m	(1.18%)	1m	(2.78%)
Salary/Wages	1,630m	(2.09%)	124m	(0.45%)	1,506m	(2.97%)
Ind Payments	3,498m	(1.22%)	2,933m	(1.14%)	565m	(1.98%)
Procurement	1,170m	(0.80%)	751m	(2.38%)	419m	(0.37%)
Other Programs	30m	(0.55%)	30m	(0.56%)	0m	(0%)
Loan/Insurance	1,006m	(1.57%)	981m	(1.59%)	25m	(1.14%)

Political Lineup   Governor, Richard W. Riley (D). Senators, Strom Thurmond (R) and Ernest F. Hollings (D). Representatives, 6 (3 D and 3 R). State Senate, 46 (40 D and 6 R); State House of Representatives, 124 (104 D and 20 R).

Presidential Vote

1980	Reagan (R)	441,841	(49%)
	Carter (D)	430,385	(48%)
	Anderson (I)	14,071	(2%)
1976	Ford (R)	346,149	(43%)
	Carter (D)	450,807	(56%)

1980 Republican Presidential Primary

Reagan	79,549	(55%)
Connally	43,113	(30%)
Bush	21,569	(15%)
Five others........	1,270	(1%)

SENATORS

Sen. Strom Thurmond (R) Elected 1956 as Dem., changed party affiliation to Repub., Sept. 16, 1964, seat up 1984; b. Dec. 5, 1902, Edgefield; home, Aiken; Clemson Col., B.S. 1923, studied law at night; Baptist.

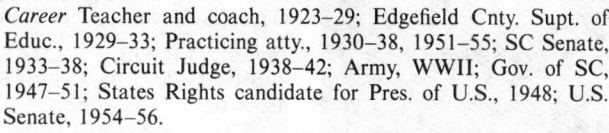

Career Teacher and coach, 1923–29; Edgefield Cnty. Supt. of Educ., 1929–33; Practicing atty., 1930–38, 1951–55; SC Senate, 1933–38; Circuit Judge, 1938–42; Army, WWII; Gov. of SC, 1947–51; States Rights candidate for Pres. of U.S., 1948; U.S. Senate, 1954–56.

Offices 209 RSOB, 202-224-5972. Also 1310 Lady St., Columbia 29201, 803-765-5496; and P.O. Drawer O, Charleston 29402, 803-722-3196.

Committees *Armed Services* (2d). Subcommittees: Military Construction (Chairman); Manpower and Personnel; Strategic and Theater Nuclear Forces. *Judiciary* (Chairman). Subcommittees: Constitution; Courts; Criminal Law. *Veterans' Affairs* (2d).

Group Ratings

	ADA	ACLU	COPE	CFA	LCV	LWV	NTU	NSI	COC	ACA	CSFC
1982	5	4	11	0	15	25	72	100	86	86	84
1981	0	—	11	0	13	—	66	—	100	90	85
1980	17	7	11	0	27	50	63	100	88	88	80

National Journal Ratings

	Economic		Foreign		Cultural	
1982	9%	(LIB)	16%	(LIB)	10%	(LIB)
	90%	(CONS)	68%	(CONS)	89%	(CONS)
1981	2%	(LIB)	1%	(LIB)	2%	(LIB)
	88%	(CONS)	85%	(CONS)	82%	(CONS)

Key Votes

1) Reagan 81 Budget	FOR	5) $ to El Salvador	FOR	9) Poor Pay Food Stamps	FOR
2) Reagan 81 Tax Cut	FOR	6) Saudi AWACS Sale	FOR	10) Ban Crt Busing Order	FOR
3) Bal Budget Amend	FOR	7) Ban Abortion	FOR	11) Clinch Riv Brdr Rctr	FOR
4) Gas & Road Tax	FOR	8) Nerve Gas Prod	FOR	12) Legal Services Corp	AGN

Election Results

1978 general	Strom Thurmond (R)	351,733	(56%)	($2,013,431)
	Charles D. Ravenel (D)	281,119	(44%)	($1,134,168)
1978 primary	Strom Thurmond (R) unopposed			
1972 general	Strom Thurmond (R)	415,806	(63%)	($666,372)
	Eugene N. Zeigler (D)	241,056	(37%)	($167,750)

Campaign Contributions and Expenditures

1977-78		PACS brkdwn			
Receipts	$2,010,073	Agr	$2,950	Ideo	$18,290
Expend.	$2,013,431	Bus	$168,400	Lbr	$—
Unspent	$10,654	Hlth	$22,750	Prof	$5,400

Sen. Ernest F. (Fritz) Hollings (D) Elected 1966, seat up 1986; b. Jan. 1, 1922, Charleston; home, Charleston; The Citadel, B.A. 1942, U. of SC, LL.B. 1947; Lutheran.

Career Practicing atty., 1947–58, 1963–66; SC House of Reps., 1949–55, Speaker Pro Tem, 1951–55; Lt. Gov. of SC, 1955–59; Gov. of SC, 1959–63.

Offices 115 RSOB, 202-224-6121. Also 306 Fed. Bldg., Columbia 29201, 803-765-5731; and 103 Fed. Bldg., Spartanburg 29301, 803-585-3702.

Committees *Appropriations* (5th). Subcommittees: Defense; Energy and Water Development; Labor, Health and Human Services, Education; Legislative Branch; Commerce, Justice, State, the Judiciary. *Budget* (2d). *Commerce, Science and Transportation* (Ranking Member). Subcommittees: Communications; National Ocean Policy Study.

Group Ratings

	ADA	ACLU	COPE	CFA	LCV	LWV	NTU	NSI	COC	ACA	CSFC
1982	55	61	50	80	62	58	28	75	53	50	39
1981	55	—	49	57	46	—	21	—	35	29	52
1980	39	40	22	27	44	44	44	70	62	43	45

National Journal Ratings

	Economic		Foreign		Cultural	
1982	64%	(LIB)	73%	(LIB)	59%	(LIB)
	35%	(CONS)	26%	(CONS)	40%	(CONS)
1981	73%	(LIB)	58%	(LIB)	60%	(LIB)
	26%	(CONS)	41%	(CONS)	39%	(CONS)

Key Votes

1) Reagan 81 Budget	FOR	5) $ to El Salvador	AGN	9) Poor Pay Food Stamps	AGN
2) Reagan 81 Tax Cut	AGN	6) Saudi AWACS Sale	AGN	10) Ban Crt Busing Order	FOR
3) Bal Budget Amend	FOR	7) Ban Abortion	AGN	11) Clinch Riv Brdr Rctr	AGN
4) Gas & Road Tax	—	8) Nerve Gas Prod	—	12) Legal Services Corp	FOR

Election Results

1980 general	Ernest F. (Fritz) Hollings (D)	612,554	(70%)	($723,427)
	Marshall Mays (R)	257,946	(30%)	($62,472)
1980 primary	Ernest F. (Fritz) Hollings (D)	266,796	(81%)	
	Two others (D)	61,072	(19%)	
1974 general	Ernest F. (Fritz) Hollings (D)	356,126	(70%)	($225,678)
	Gwenyfred Bush (R)	146,645	(29%)	($6,754)

Campaign Contributions and Expenditures

1979-80		PACS brkdwn			
Receipts	$810,270	Agr	$11,200	Ideo	$1,200
Expend.	$723,427	Bus	$185,965	Lbr	$29,000
Unspent	$133,668	Hlth	$15,850	Prof	$6,300

GOVERNOR

Gov. Richard W. Riley (D) Elected 1978, term expires Jan. 1987; b. Jan. 2, 1932, Greenville; home, Columbia; Furman U., B.A. 1954, U. of SC, LL.B. 1960; United Methodist.

Career Legal Counsel to U.S. Sen. Olin D. Johnston, 1960–61; Practicing atty., 1961–; SC House of Reps., 1963–67; SC Senate, 1967–77.

Offices State House, 1st Floor West Wing, Box 11450, Columbia 29211, 803-758-3208.

Election Results

1982 gen.	Richard W. Riley (D)	468,819	(70%)
	William D. Workman, Jr.	202,806	(30%)
1982 prim.	Richard W. Riley (D) unopposed		
1978 gen.	Richard W. Riley (D)	385,016	(61%)
	Edward L. Young (R)	236,946	(38%)

FIRST DISTRICT

In the spring the pastel row houses of Charleston are wreathed with flowers of the blossoming trees. There are few, if any, more beautiful urban scenes in America. Charleston, founded in 1670 and blessed with one of the finest harbors on the Atlantic, was one of the South's leading cities up to the Civil War. Across its docks went cargoes of rice, indigo, cotton—all cultivated by black slaves and intended to enrich the white planters and merchants who dominated the state's economic and political life. In the years that followed the Civil War, Charleston became an economic backwater. Today the old part of the city, beautifully preserved and still the home of the city's elite, houses fewer people than it did when it rained out shots on Fort Sumter in 1861.

Charleston has always been the center of life for South Carolina's proud aristocracy. These people are not heard from much today, but once they were a leading force in American political life. The Democrats held their national convention in Charleston in 1860, and the hotheaded dandies in the galleries hooted down the northerners and so disrupted the proceedings that the northerners adjourned and reconvened in Baltimore while the southerners nominated a separate ticket. That split in the Democratic Party made possible Lincoln's 38% victory, which in turn led to war.

Charleston has always had a large black community, one whose history and culture has been memorialized in *Porgy and Bess*. Today politics in the Charleston area is largely a matter of blacks on one side supporting Democrats and whites on the other supporting Republicans. This was not always so. In the 1950s and 1960s there was a white working-class vote in North Charleston, around the Navy Yard, that was particularly strong for Congressman Mendel Rivers, chairman of the House Armed Services Committee. He worked so hard to put military bases in this area that when he died, in 1971, one-third of the payrolls in the Charleston area could be attributed directly or indirectly to the military.

Today the Charleston economy is more diversified and the working class that supported Rivers is more affluent. The 1970s were as healthy a decade as Charleston has seen since the Democrats decamped for Baltimore. Charleston still has plenty of military bases, but it also

SOUTH CAROLINA — Congressional Districts, Counties, and Selected Places — *(6 Districts)*

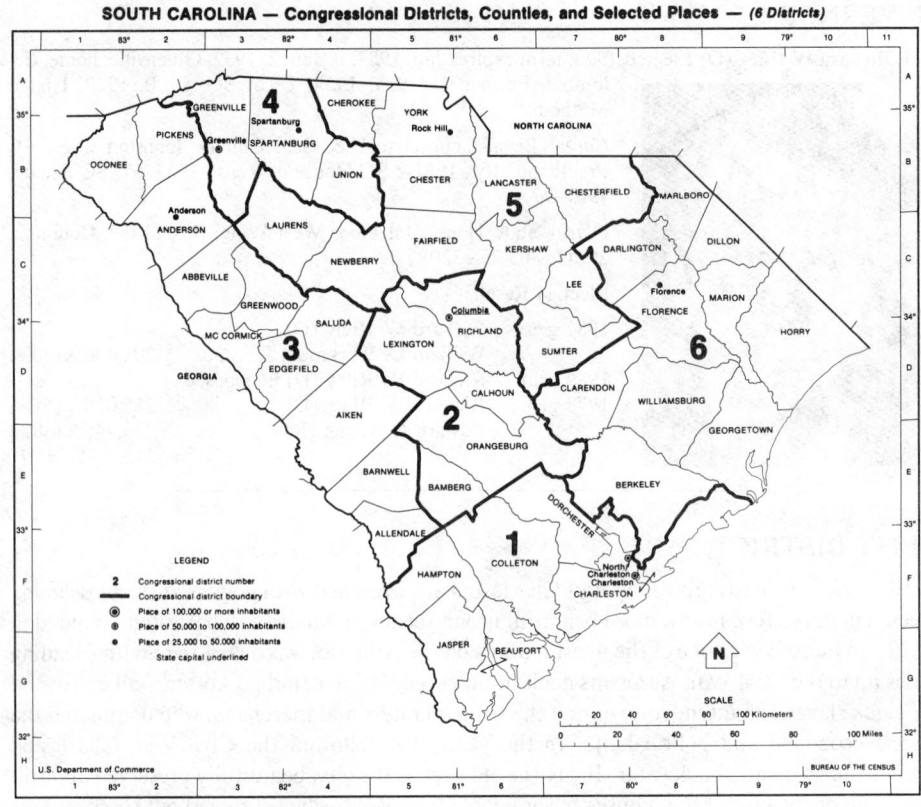

Congressional districts established April 30, 1982; all other boundaries are as of January 1, 1980.

has had considerable commercial expansion. There are not as many new plants as in inland counties, but there have been massive retirement-and-vacation condominium developments on the islands surrounded by tidal inlets and the ocean. The first of these, Hilton Head, was started by Charles Fraser in 1957; it was an untested, risky concept at the time. Nearby were some of the poorest areas in the United States, where lowland blacks lived in poverty and malnutrition; many spoke a distinct dialect called Gullah. Now the blacks are much better off, and practically the entire coast is covered with developments inspired, in varying degrees, by the original.

High-income whites in these new areas, and in the affluent areas of Charleston, both in the old downtown and in new neighborhoods east of the Ashley River and out in the suburbs, have proved to be heavily Republican; blacks, who did not vote in most of this area until after 1965, are even more heavily Democratic. With a small white working class, there is only a small margin of voters who are switchable. The congressman from this district, Republican Tom Hartnett, has been fortunate enough to win just enough of their votes twice. In 1980 he beat Charles Ravenel, who had had a series of misfortunes: after winning the Democratic nomination for governor in 1974, he was taken off the ballot by the courts; four years later he lost to Senator Strom Thurmond. Ravenel also had an enthusiastic following, but it was not quite large enough for him to win. In 1982 Hartnett was helped when his opponent, a former aide to his Democratic predecessor Mendel Davis, was arrested for drunk driving. Hartnett also had a significant financial advantage. Even so, he won with just 54% of the votes.

Hartnett's solid Reaganite voting record pleased upper-income whites and infuriated blacks. He got a seat on the Armed Services—which any congressman from this district would want—and was able to cite some specific military programs he helped to keep in the district. But despite his long experience in the legislature, he seems a less competent and politically adept legislator than some of his southern Republican colleagues, and he will probably keep getting serious opponents in this district, one of whom, if he can avoid problems, might win.

The People   Pop. 1980: 520,338, up 25.3% 1970–80; voting age pop. 362,866; 29% Black, 2% Span. orig., 1% Asian orig. 32% housing units rented. Median owner $41,400; renter $174. Households: 77% family, 47% with children, 61% married couples.

Presidential Vote

1980	Reagan (R)	80,239	(55%)
	Carter (D)	63,430	(43%)
	Other	3,214	(2%)

Rep. Thomas F. Hartnett (R) Elected 1980; b. Aug. 7, 1941, Charleston; home, Mount Pleasant; Col. of Charleston, 1960–62, U. of SC, 1978; Roman Catholic.

Career Air Force, 1963, Reserves, 1963–69; Pres., Hartnett Realty Co.; SC House of Reps., 1965–72; SC Senate, 1973–80.

Offices 228 CHOB, 202-225-3176. Also 263 Hampton St., Walterboro 29488, 803-549-5395; 640 Fed. Bldg., 334 Meeting St., Charlestown 29403, 803-724-4175; and P.O. Box 1538, Beaufort 29902, 803-524-2166.

Committee *Armed Services* (13th). Subcommittees: Military Installations and Facilities; Military Personnel and Compensation; Seapower and Strategic and Critical Materials.

Group Ratings

	ADA	ACLU	COPE	CFA	LCV	LWV	NTU	NSI	COC	ACA	CSFC
1982	10	8	7	8	21	33	92	100	71	100	77
1981	5	—	7	29	36	—	81	—	100	91	76

National Journal Ratings

	Economic		Foreign		Cultural	
1982	22%	(LIB)	8%	(LIB)	1%	(LIB)
	78%	(CONS)	91%	(CONS)	98%	(CONS)
1981	4%	(LIB)	14%	(LIB)	3%	(LIB)
	79%	(CONS)	86%	(CONS)	97%	(CONS)

Key Votes

1) Reagan 81 Budget	FOR	5) Incr SS Rtmt Age	FOR	9) Poor Pay Food Stamps	FOR
2) Reagan 81 Tax Cut	FOR	6) Saudi AWACS Sale	FOR	10) Ban Crt Busing Order	FOR
3) Bal Budget Amend	FOR	7) $ for MX Missile	FOR	11) Auto Local Content	AGN
4) Gas & Road Tax	AGN	8) Nerve Gas Prod	FOR	12) Nuclear Arms Freeze	AGN

Election Results

1982 general	Thomas F. Hartnett (R)	63,945	(54%)	($323,373)
	W. Mullins McLeod (D)	52,916	(45%)	($204,637)
1982 primary	Thomas F. Hartnett (R) unopposed			
1980 general	Thomas F. Hartnett (R)	81,988	(52%)	($226,394)
	Charles D. Ravenel (D)	76,743	(48%)	($179,933)

Campaign Contributions and Expenditures

1981-82		*Direct Cont. 81-82*				*PACS brkdwn*		
Receipts	$362,869	Indiv	$195,903	Agr	$2,250	Ideo	$10,320
Expend.	$323,373	Party	$16,265	Bus	$115,830	Lbr	$8,500
Unspent	$39,497	PACS	$154,285	Hlth	$10,700	Prof	$1,500

Indirect Party Expend: $17,584   *Indep Expend:* For: $1,056 (NRA)

SECOND DISTRICT

Between the coastal swamps and the industrialized Piedmont, square in the middle of the state, is the 2d congressional district of South Carolina. This district has essentially two parts. One is the metropolitan area of Columbia, the state's capital and largest city. This is one of those cities that grew first because it was in the center of the state and had the state government and university; later, because of the Army's huge Fort Jackson; more recently, because it has attracted its share of South Carolina's new industries and offices. As a metropolitan area it has been trending Republican; the city itself, with a large black percentage, sometimes goes Democratic, but the 90% white suburbs of Lexington County, across the Congaree River, are the most heavily Republican part of the state.

Some observers attribute this to an influx of northerners, but census figures show that that migration is rather modest. The Republican trend results instead from the upward mobility of people from the smaller towns and rural areas of the state, moving here to white-collar jobs in the growing private sector, and making more money than they ever thought possible (though their income might look modest to a professional from Manhattan or Beverly Hills). Removed from their traditionally Democratic roots, and convinced that the free enterprise system which made their success possible is threatened by big government programs, they have become enthusiastic conservative Republicans.

The other part of the district, casting about one-fourth of its votes, is part of the South Carolina lowland country around Orangeburg. This was plantation country before 1860, and most of the people who live here now are black. Orangeburg is the site of South Carolina's main black state college, and was the site of a massacre of black students by white state highway patrolmen in 1968. This area is Democratic, with party preference following racial lines pretty closely.

The 2d district has been represented by a Republican since Congressman Albert Watson was denied his committee positions by the Democratic Caucus in 1965 because he had openly supported Goldwater; Watson resigned, ran as a Republican, and won. When he ran for governor in 1970, he was replaced by Floyd Spence, who as a Republican lost to Watson in 1962. Spence has won ever since. By similar majorities he has beaten several strong candidates, including Matthew Perry, a black later made a federal judge by Strom Thurmond, and Jack Bass, a top newspaper reporter and the writer of the definitive work on the Orangeburg massacre. Against weaker opposition in 1982 his percentage hardly rose. Spence won 62% of the vote in the Columbia metropolitan area. But he lost 52%–48% in the lowland counties around Orangeburg. This seems likely to be the pattern in congressional races here indefinitely.

Spence is a high ranking member of the Armed Services Committee and ranking Republican on the Seapower Subcommittee. He is a solid hawk on military affairs, as well as a dependable Reaganite conservative on all issues. He also is ranking Republican on the Committee on Standards of Official Conduct, the House Ethics Committee, a body dormant at this writing but obliged to investigate allegations of scandal. Spence, a pleasant man of great camaraderie, is not as stern with his colleagues as some critics would like, although in some Abscam cases he joined the committee in recommending the ultimate sanction, expulsion.

The People Pop. 1980: 522,688, up 24.6% 1970–80; voting age pop. 372,290; 32% Black, 1% Span. orig., 1% Asian orig. 30% housing units rented. Median owner $40,800; renter $160. Households: 76% family, 45% with children, 60% married couples.

Presidential Vote

1980	Reagan (R)	79,942	(53%)
	Carter (D)	67,766	(45%)
	Other	2,862	(2%)

Rep. Floyd D. Spence (R) Elected 1970; b. Apr. 9, 1928, Columbia; home, Lexington; U. of SC, B.A. 1952, LL.B. 1956; Lutheran.

Career Navy, Korea; Practicing atty., SC House of Reps., 1956–62; SC Senate, 1966–70, Minor. Ldr., 1966–70.

Offices 2466 RHOB, 202-225-2452. Also 2001 Assembly St., Rm. 104, Columbia 29201, 803-765-5871.

Committees *Armed Services* (3d). Subcommittees: Readiness; Seapower and Strategic and Critical Materials. *Standards of Official Conduct* (Ranking Member).

Group Ratings

	ADA	ACLU	COPE	CFA	LCV	LWV	NTU	NSI	COC	ACA	CSFC
1982	0	0	15	8	21	17	49	100	86	87	64
1981	0	—	16	29	21	—	75	—	89	92	74
1980	11	7	16	14	30	40	54	100	79	83	75

National Journal Ratings

	Economic		Foreign		Cultural	
1982	0%	(LIB)	12%	(LIB)	4%	(LIB)
	98%	(CONS)	84%	(CONS)	87%	(CONS)
1981	4%	(LIB)	3%	(LIB)	4%	(LIB)
	79%	(CONS)	87%	(CONS)	90%	(CONS)

Key Votes

1) Reagan 81 Budget	FOR	5) Incr SS Rtmt Age	FOR	9) Poor Pay Food Stamps	FOR
2) Reagan 81 Tax Cut	FOR	6) Saudi AWACS Sale	FOR	10) Ban Crt Busing Order	FOR
3) Bal Budget Amend	FOR	7) $ for MX Missile	FOR	11) Auto Local Content	AGN
4) Gas & Road Tax	AGN	8) Nerve Gas Prod	FOR	12) Nuclear Arms Freeze	AGN

Election Results

1982 general	Floyd D. Spence (R)	71,569	(59%)	($190,265)
	Ken Mosely (D)	50,749	(41%)	($49,780)
1982 primary	Floyd D. Spence (R) unopposed			
1980 general	Floyd D. Spence (R)	92,306	(56%)	($275,010)
	Tom Turnipseed (D)	73,353	(44%)	($72,779)

Campaign Contributions and Expenditures

1981-82		Direct Cont. 81-82		PACS brkdwn			
Receipts	$190,809	Indiv	$89,728	Agr	$2,400	Ideo	$2,936
Expend.	$190,265	Party	$9,224	Bus	$61,875	Lbr	$1,500
Unspent	$2,994	PACS	$74,986	Hlth	$5,125	Prof	$750
		Cand	$875				

Non-Cand Loans: $10,125

THIRD DISTRICT

As you move inland from the South Carolina coast, you see fewer and fewer black people. This is a matter of history and economics. The land along the coast was ideal for growing crops like rice and cotton, which require lots of water and lots of hand labor; so early planters imported thousands of slaves. Inland the terrain is hilly, the rainfall somewhat less plentiful, and the soil less fertile. The tradition here is of family farms, few of which needed or could afford to support slaves. The 3d congressional district of South Carolina, which follows the Savannah River border with Georgia for most of its length, covers the range. Its southernmost point is in the lowlands in Allendale County, which is 62% black; its northernmost point is 3,500-foot Sassafras Mountain, in Pickens County, which is 7% black.

The southern part of this district is Strom Thurmond country. He grew up in Edgefield and as county judge there in the 1930s maintained stern white control of the black majority. He maintains his residence now in Aiken, a prosperous town which has long been a winter haven for New York sportsmen, and which became solidly Republican—as Thurmond did—in the middle 1960s. The northern part of the district is Piedmont upcountry, with almost an Appalachian air. The largest city here is Anderson, a mostly white textile mill town; a strong city for George Wallace in the 1960s, it is now strongly Democratic again.

The congressman from the 3d district is Butler Derrick, a Democrat who won the seat in 1974 and is second in seniority in the oft-changing South Carolina House delegation. He attracted notice in his early years for defying old shibboleths. In 1977 he was a leader in stripping Florida's 37-year veteran Bob Sikes of his chairmanship for financial improprieties; about the same time he supported Jimmy Carter's move to cancel a dam in the 3d district. Derrick has been consistently more favorable to environmental claims than most southern congressmen of either party, and more inclined to support procedural reforms.

More recently he has won less notice, in part because of his committee assignments. He is a member of the Rules Committee, the body which for the most part controls the flow of legislation to the House floor. In that position Derrick is expected to be and is loyal to the Democratic leadership; the leadership, in turn, is loath for historical reasons to use its power over Rules to kill measures it doesn't like. Derrick became a member of the Budget Committee in 1983. He has not yet taken a lead role. But this is a committee on which members can serve only a limited period, and many of the Democratic leaders here will not be on it in 1985 unless the rule is changed. In those circumstances Derrick, as a southerner loyal to the leadership and with a mixed record on economic issues, could be a critical member.

Derrick has been mentioned as a possible candidate for statewide office. He might be interested in the 1984 Senate race, but not if Senator Strom Thurmond seeks reelection. Otherwise there are no openings soon, unless he wants to return to state politics and run for governor in 1986.

The People Pop. 1980: 519,280, up 20.2% 1970–80; voting age pop. 366,318; 20% Black, 1% Span. orig. 23% housing units rented. Median owner $32,000; renter $104. Households: 79% family, 44% with children, 65% married couples.

Presidential Vote

1980	Reagan (R)	69,100	(47%)
	Carter (D)	74,682	(51%)
	Other	2,180	(2%)

Rep. Butler Derrick (D) Elected 1974; b. Sept. 30, 1936, Johnston; home, Edgefield; U. of SC, B.A. 1958, U. of GA, LL.B. 1965; Episcopal.

Career Practicing atty., 1965–74; SC House of Reps., 1969–75.

Offices 201 CHOB, 202-225-5301. Also 315 S. McDuffie St., Anderson 29621, 803-224-7401.

Committees *Budget* (13th). Task Forces: Budget Process; Energy and Technology; Tax Policy. *Rules* (4th). Subcommittee: The Legislative Process. *Select Committee on Aging* (20th). Subcommittee: Health and Long-Term Care.

Group Ratings

	ADA	ACLU	COPE	CFA	LCV	LWV	NTU	NSI	COC	ACA	CSFC
1982	50	50	57	31	80	82	29	70	52	35	40
1981	60	—	56	57	68	—	26	—	37	43	42
1980	56	50	68	50	55	40	27	38	70	50	38

National Journal Ratings

	Economic		Foreign		Cultural	
1982	52%	(LIB)	59%	(LIB)	55%	(LIB)
	47%	(CONS)	41%	(CONS)	45%	(CONS)
1981	54%	(LIB)	46%	(LIB)	69%	(LIB)
	46%	(CONS)	54%	(CONS)	31%	(CONS)

Key Votes

1) Reagan 81 Budget	AGN	5) Incr SS Rtmt Age	AGN	9) Poor Pay Food Stamps	AGN
2) Reagan 81 Tax Cut	AGN	6) Saudi AWACS Sale	FOR	10) Ban Crt Busing Order	AGN
3) Bal Budget Amend	FOR	7) $ for MX Missile	AGN	11) Auto Local Content	AGN
4) Gas & Road Tax	FOR	8) Nerve Gas Prod	AGN	12) Nuclear Arms Freeze	FOR

Election Results

1982 general	Butler Derrick (D)	77,125	(90%)	($95,691)
	Gordon T. Davis (L)	8,214	(10%)	($0)
1982 primary	Butler Derrick (D) unopposed			
1980 general	Butler Derrick (D)	87,680	(60%)	($88,255)
	Marshall Parker (R)	57,840	(39%)	($66,047)

Campaign Contributions and Expenditures

1981-82		Direct Cont. 81-82		PACS brkdwn			
Receipts	$130,223	Indiv	$44,460	Agr	$8,250	Ideo	$850
Expend.	$95,691	PACS	$83,078	Bus	$57,650	Lbr	$7,200
Unspent	$55,158			Hlth	$5,650	Prof	$2,250

FOURTH DISTRICT

The major textile-producing area in the United States is a strip of land along Interstate 85 in North and South Carolina. Two of the biggest textile centers here are Greenville and Spartanburg—the two cities that, with the counties that surround them and one rural county to the east, make up the 4th congressional district of South Carolina. It will probably come as a surprise to many readers that this is one of the most industrialized and blue-collar parts of the nation; that fact surprises even tourists who drive through the South Carolina Piedmont on their way south. For the mills are not concentrated in a few big factories, like giant steel plants, in the inner core of grimy cities. They are all over, in small towns and suburbs, at interchanges on the Interstate as well as in Greenville and Spartanburg themselves. Few blacks live here—19% districtwide, the lowest percentage in South Carolina. And there are even fewer union members: South Carolina has just about the least unionized labor force in the nation, and one reason is the intransigeant opposition of the mill owners to unionization.

These conditions—relatively low wages, no unions, a large and well-motivated work force, increasingly well educated—have helped to make this part of South Carolina one of the boom areas in the South and, in the process, to transform it, or begin to. In the 1960s and 1970s South Carolina moved very aggressively to attract industry, and got many German and

French companies, as well as American concerns, to build installations here. Many are clustered near Interstate 85 and Greenville, to which the Germans have taken a particular liking. These new industries demand higher skill levels than the old textile mills, and their wage level is higher; they are in the process, it seems, of raising this area to a high-skill, high-wage part of the country.

At the same time, what has always been one of the more Republican parts of South Carolina seems to be getting more Republican. Spartanburg has a Democratic tradition, and was the hometown of one of South Carolina's greatest politicians, James Byrnes (senator, Supreme Court justice, secretary of state, and finally governor in the early 1950s), but since his time it has become more Republican in many elections; Greenville, always the premier management town here, has a Republican tradition. The 1970s saw not only a population increase, but an even larger increase in the voting population—a trend quite at odds with that in most other parts of the country. To some extent this marked the entry of many blue-collar workers into the voting stream, and in 1976 this district actually went for Jimmy Carter. But in 1980 the electorate increased still more and switched Republican.

The congressman from the district, Carroll Campbell, is one of those well-groomed young conservative Republicans who got elected all over the nation in 1978 and especially in 1980. Campbell ran here in 1978 when the Democratic incumbent retired, and won in part by stressing that his opponent, the mayor of Greenville and a onetime refugee from Nazi Austria, was Jewish and did not believe in Jesus as his savior. Campbell provided a good forecast of how the freshmen Republicans of 1980 would behave: he voted solidly against expanding government, in favor of more defense spending, and for lower taxes. He bridled at the moderation of the Republican leadership and wanted to attack the Democrats more aggressively.

Campbell won a seat on Appropriations in 1981 and gave it up in 1983 for Ways and Means. It is easy to see why: he is less interested in channeling money to his district than he is in protecting its textile industry against foreign competition; although he doesn't sit on the Trade Subcommittee, he will undoubtedly devote much attention to such issues. He is ranking Republican on Harold Ford's Public Assistance and Unemployment Compensation Subcommittee, a body facing the sticky problem that some states (notably Michigan, Ohio, and Pennsylvania) are hopelessly in debt to the federal unemployment fund. Most of the subcommittee's Democrats are likely to be favorable to them; Campbell, as the representative of a state with low unemployment compensation, is not.

Since 1978 Campbell has had no trouble getting reelected and seems entrenched in this district. The only surprise here is that the Republicans didn't capture and hold this district a long time ago.

The People   Pop. 1980: 520,525, up 17.3% 1970–80; voting age pop. 373,015; 17% Black, 1% Span. orig. 28% housing units rented. Median owner $34,300; renter $132. Households: 78% family, 43% with children, 63% married couples.

Presidential Vote

1980	Reagan (R)	80,182	(54%)
	Carter (D)	66,823	(45%)
	Anderson (I)	2,671	(2%)

Rep. Carroll A. Campbell, Jr. (R) Elected 1978; b. July 24, 1940, Greenville; home, Greenville; U. of SC; Episcopal.

Career Real estate and farming; SC House of Reps., 1970–74; Exec. Asst. to Gov. James B. Edwards, 1975–76; SC Senate 1976–78.

Offices 408 CHOB, 202-225-6030. Also P.O. Box 10011, Greenville 29603, 803-232-1411.

Committee *Ways and Means* (11th). Subcommittees: Oversight; Public Assistance and Unemployment Compensation.

Group Ratings

	ADA	ACLU	COPE	CFA	LCV	LWV	NTU	NSI	COC	ACA	CSFC
1982	0	8	10	0	21	25	55	100	86	95	68
1981	0	—	10	7	14	—	61	—	100	87	74
1980	6	13	11	21	37	44	56	100	87	83	74

National Journal Ratings

	Economic		Foreign		Cultural	
1982	4%	(LIB)	2%	(LIB)	4%	(LIB)
	95%	(CONS)	97%	(CONS)	87%	(CONS)
1981	4%	(LIB)	38%	(LIB)	11%	(LIB)
	79%	(CONS)	61%	(CONS)	89%	(CONS)

Key Votes

1) Reagan 81 Budget	FOR	5) Incr SS Rtmt Age	FOR	9) Poor Pay Food Stamps	—
2) Reagan 81 Tax Cut	FOR	6) Saudi AWACS Sale	FOR	10) Ban Crt Busing Order	FOR
3) Bal Budget Amend	FOR	7) $ for MX Missile	FOR	11) Auto Local Content	AGN
4) Gas & Road Tax	FOR	8) Nerve Gas Prod	FOR	12) Nuclear Arms Freeze	AGN

Election Results

1982 general	Carroll A. Campbell, Jr. (R)	69,802	(63%)	($204,092)
	Marion E. Tyus (D)	40,394	(37%)	($0)
1982 primary	Carroll A. Campbell, Jr. (R) unopposed			
1980 general	Carroll A. Campbell, Jr. (R)	90,941	(93%)	($153,606)
	Thomas Waldenfels (Libertarian) ..	6,984	(7%)	($0)

Campaign Contributions and Expenditures

1981-82		Direct Cont. 81-82		PACS brkdwn			
Receipts	$251,252	Indiv	$99,647	Agr	$7,000	Ideo	$2,690
Expend.	$204,092	Party	$20,619	Bus	$73,450	Lbr	$250
Unspent	$69,967	PACS	$89,481	Hlth	$4,650	Prof	$1,200

Indirect Party Expend: $11,799

FIFTH DISTRICT

The 5th congressional district is one of the most rough-hewn parts of South Carolina. It contains no long-established city like Charleston, no management town like Greenville, no state capital like Columbia. It is a rather oddly shaped collection of counties that look mostly rural on the map but which, in this auto age, are almost a new form of urban area. Many people still live on small farms here, but except for those with tobacco allotments they do not make a living off them; typically, they commute perhaps as much as 50 miles away to work in a textile mill or in one of the new factories South Carolina likes to brag it is attracting. This is an area of fundamentalist religion and stock car racing; it has black majority counties in the lowlands and counties with relatively small black populations in the Piedmont. This was fiercely contested country in the Revolutionary War—the battles of Kings Mountain and Cowpens were fought here—and the fighting spirit has never entirely subsided.

Politically this remains a Democratic district. It has gone Republican on occasion when there was discontent with the national Democrats, but it does not have the large high-income Republican base you can find in several other South Carolina districts. That was illustrated pretty clearly in the 1982 election, when incumbent Congressman Ken Holland announced his retirement a week before filing date. The real contest to succeed him was in the Democratic primary. A Holland aide was able to force a runoff, but the winner was John Spratt, a lawyer and banker who had never held public office.

To some, Spratt seemed an odd representative for such a district. He has degrees from Yale Law and Oxford, is rich, and is part of the small group of wealthy lawyers, bankers, and businessmen who run economic life in small cities and towns in every county of South Carolina. Most such people are very conservative. But those who stuck with the Democratic Party during the difficult years of desegregation and of the national party's unpopularity here were often motivated by a real commitment to at least some of the party's liberal views. And some, like Spratt, were involved in the 1974 gubernatorial campaign of Charles Ravenel, an enterprise unsuccessful in its original intention but successful in involving a large number of highly motivated young people in Democratic politics in this state. The people who run things in places like York and Rock Hill understand that not everybody in these communities is capable of managing civic affairs. But those who are Fritz Hollings–Charles Ravenel Democrats hope and believe they are representing the interests of those ordinary citizens faithfully, however inarticulate they may be and however contrary-minded they may sometimes seem.

Spratt won the general election here by better than a 2–1 margin and seems likely to hold this district with relative ease. He sits on the Armed Services and Government Operations Committees.

The People   Pop. 1980: 519,716, up 12.9% 1970–80; voting age pop. 357,907, 29% Black, 1% Span. orig. 24% housing units rented. Median owner $31,000; renter $104. Households: 80% family, 47% with children, 64% married couples.

Presidential Vote

1980	Reagan (R)	63,518	(45%)
	Carter (D)	74,754	(53%)
	Other	1,766	(1%)

Rep. John M. Spratt, Jr. (D) Elected 1982; b. Nov. 1, 1942, Charlotte, NC; home, York Cnty.; Davidson Col., A.B. 1964, M.A., Oxford U., 1966, Yale U., LL.B. 1969; Presbyterian.

Career Operations, Off. of Asst. Secy. of Defense, 1969–71; Practicing atty., 1971–82; Pres., Bank of Ft. Mill, 1973–82; Pres., Spratt Insurance Agncy., 1973–82.

Offices 1118 LHOB, 202-225-5501. Also Box 272CSS, Rock Hill 29730, 803-327-1114.

Committees *Armed Services* (25th). Subcommittees: Military Installations and Facilities; Military Personnel and Compensation. *Government Operations* (23d). Subcommittees: Commerce, Consumer, and Monetary Affairs; Manpower and Housing.

Group Ratings and Key Votes: Newly Elected

Election Results

1982 general	John M. Spratt, Jr. (D)	69,345	(68%)	($374,714)
	John S. Wilkerson (R)	33,191	(32%)	($235,416)
1982 runoff	John M. Spratt, Jr. (D)	30,859	(55%)	
	John Winburn (D)	25,302	(45%)	($929,723)
1982 primary	John M. Spratt, Jr. (D)	28,388	(38%)	
	John Winburn (D)	19,898	(27%)	
	Ernie Nunnery (D)	19,590	(26%)	($99,083)
	Bill Horne (D)	6,733	(9%)	($65,714)
1980 general	Kenneth L. (Ken) Holland (D)	99,773	(88%)	($89,208)
	Thomas Campbell (Libertarian) ...	14,252	(12%)	($60)

Campaign Contributions and Expenditures

	1982		*Direct Cont. 1982*			*PACS brkdwn*		
Receipts	$380,062	Indiv	$109,761	Agr	$3,650	Ideo	$2,500
Expend.	$374,714	Party	$2,000	Bus	$36,592	Lbr	$6,000
Unspent	$5,345	PACS	$60,236	Hlth	$4,300	Prof	$500
		Cand	$221,500				

Indirect Party Expend: $4,083

SIXTH DISTRICT

The 6th congressional district of South Carolina is part of the state's lowlands, north and east of Charleston, up to the North Carolina border. This is low-lying land; the rivers wind lazily toward the shoreline, where they come upon the barrier islands now developed as South Carolina's Grand Strand. Inland you find tobacco fields; 15 acres can support a family, though not especially well, which helps to explain why tobacco district politicians defend its interests so assiduously. This was once plantation country, and a large percentage of the people here are black; three of the counties have black majorities, and overall the district is 41% black. This is not only the highest black percentage of any South Carolina district; it also is similar to the percentage for 1970. For years blacks from this area lined up after high school graduation and got on the bus to New York (called the chicken bone special, because they packed chicken dinners) to make their livings. Now they remain in South Carolina, and over the long run the black percentage here is likely to rise.

The two places in the district which have the lowest black percentages are those with above-average economic growth which has attracted people from outside the area (though usually from the South). One is Florence, the district's largest city; the other is the Grand Strand area in Horry County, which is only 22% black.

Nonetheless this is a district where black voters have had the satisfaction of influencing congressional politics greatly since the Voting Rights Act of 1965. In 1972 they ousted the chairman of the House District of Columbia Committee, John McMillan, who was often accused of being a racist. In 1974 and 1982 they ousted Republican congressmen who had gotten in under special circumstances. In the latter case, Republican John Napier beat incumbent Democrat John Jenrette in 1980. Jenrette had been convicted for his involvement in Abscam; even so, most blacks stayed with him and he came close to winning.

Napier had a near-impossible assignment in trying to hold onto the district in 1982. He had a near-perfect Reagan voting record and suffered from the recession and from the president's perceived attitude on civil rights issues. He was also hurt when Democratic legislator and clothing chain store owner Robin Tallon finished far ahead in the Democratic primary and won the runoff. Tallon had the same kind of support among blacks that Jenrette did, and concentrated his campaign efforts on turning out the black vote. He ran close to racial percentages in most counties, but won enough white votes in Horry County to win districtwide with 52%. Napier's advantages of incumbency and money were not telling in a district in which most of the votes are committed and Democrats begin with the bigger base.

Tallon has now what Jenrette had until he got into trouble: a district he should be able to hold in fair partisan weather or foul. He sits on the Agriculture Committee, and on its Tobacco and Peanuts Subcommittee—excellent assignments for a congressman from this district. He is expected to support the Democratic leadership often but not invariably.

The People Pop. 1980: 519,273, up 23.6% 1970–80; voting age pop. 347,458; 37% Black, 1% Span. orig. 23% housing units rented. Median owner $33,100; renter $104. Households: 80% family, 49% with children, 63% married couples.

Presidential Vote

1980	Reagan (R)	68,159	(45%)
	Carter (D)	82,043	(54%)
	Anderson (I)	1,600	(1%)

Rep. Robin M. Tallon, Jr. (D) Elected 1982; b. Aug. 8, 1946, Hemingway; home, Florence; U. of SC, 1964–65; Methodist.

Career Owner, Tallon Sales, 1967–82; SC House of Reps., 1980–82.

Offices 128 CHOB, 202-225-3315. Also P.O. Box 6286, Florence 29502, 803-669-9084; and Horry Cnty. Courthouse, Conway 29526, 803-248-6256.

Committees *Agriculture* (20th). Subcommittees: Conservation, Credit, and Rural Development; Tobacco and Peanuts. *Merchant Marine and Fisheries* (22d). Subcommittees: Fisheries and Wildlife Conservation and the Environment; Merchant Marine; Oceanography.

Group Ratings and Key Votes: Newly Elected

Election Results

1982 general	Robin M. Tallon, Jr. (D)	62,582	(53%)	($412,669)
	John L. Napier (R)	56,653	(48%)	($489,456)
1982 runoff	Robin M. Tallon, Jr. (D)	40,836	(71%)	
	Hicks Harwell (D)	17,017	(29%)	($97,739)
1982 primary	Robin M. Tallon, Jr. (D)	35,806	(48%)	
	John Brasington (D)	12,679	(24%)	($65,027)
	Hicks Harwell (D)	17,993	(17%)	
	Charles McGill (D)	8,120	(11%)	
1980 general	John L. Napier (R)	75,964	(52%)	($277,856)
	John W. Jenrette, Jr. (D)	70,747	(48%)	($173,059)

Campaign Contributions and Expenditures

1981-82		Direct Cont. 81-82			PACS brkdwn			
Receipts	$416,746	Indiv	$136,500	Agr	$—	Ideo	$17,500
Expend.	$412,669	Party	$12,728	Bus	$10,750	Lbr	$49,825
Unspent	$4,576	PACS	$92,871	Hlth	$1,100	Prof	$—
		Cand	$181,443				

Indirect Party Expend: $4,315   *Non-Cand Loans:* $8,000

SOUTH DAKOTA

South Dakota was once the heartland of the Sioux Indians, who roamed the plains hunting buffalo. Then the white man came and exterminated the buffalo and, in such places as Wounded Knee, many Indians as well. Those who survived were herded onto reservations. Today South Dakota has one of the highest Indian populations in the nation—7% of the state's population in 1980. Most of the Indians are concentrated in reservations on the arid high plains, west from the Missouri River to where the Black Hills begin. There have been waves of animosity between whites and Indians; the most recent was sparked by the occupation of Wounded Knee in 1973 by American Indian Movement militants, and the trials that followed. Echoes from this episode still reverberate in the state's politics: the chief prosecutor in those trials, William Janklow, is now governor; and the Republican Party, on the defensive before Wounded Knee, has regained its position of political dominance here.

The Plains Indians' economy was based on the buffalo, which provided food, clothing, and shelter. Most of South Dakota was and is good grazing land, and if you could have flown above South Dakota as late as the 1870s you would have seen herds of buffalo like giant dark blots over the plains. The first white men here bypassed the Indians; men like Wild Bill Hickock, America's first dime-novel hero, were out after gold and other minerals, and settled, briefly, in the booming mining towns of Lead and Deadwood in the Black Hills. Later, farmers began moving westward into the eastern edge of the state from Minnesota, Iowa, and Nebraska. Some of them were Scandinavians direct from the old country or coming via Minnesota; many were Germans, coming overland from Wisconsin and Iowa; many were of Yankee stock, moving just a little north of their traditional east–west migration patterns. South Dakota had most of its growth in two decades of agricultural prosperity, 1880–90 and 1900–10. The decade between, the 1890s, was a time of drought, depression, and farm rebellion. By 1910 the state's population reached 85% of the current figure. The difference then is that most South Dakotans were young people with large families; a great many of those children migrated elsewhere, leaving South Dakota today with a comparatively elderly population.

By 1910 the political character of South Dakota had been pretty well set. During the 1890s voters here flirted briefly with the Populists and William Jennings Bryan; but by the 1920s, South Dakota had become almost as monolithically Republican as Nebraska. Voters in South Dakota never had much use for the socialistic ideas of the Non-Partisan League, which caught on in the more Scandinavian soil of North Dakota, and there was never anything here comparable to the Farmer–Labor Party of Minnesota. As in most other Great Plains states, there have been periodic farm revolts against incumbent administrations. Nearly one-fourth of the state's residents live on farms, and its day-to-day economy depends on farmers' profits, not revenues, and hence is subject to wide fluctuations. But South Dakota began with a large enough Republican base that, despite such revolts, the state between 1936 and 1970 had a Democratic governor for only two years and elected only one Democrat to the Senate, George McGovern.

The last dozen years, in contrast, have seen sharp political fluctuations in South Dakota. For a while McGovern's Democrats were on the rise, capturing at various times the governorship, the legislature, both Senate seats, and both House seats, and nearly carrying the state for McGovern's presidential campaign in 1972. This trend owed something to McGovern's personal popularity and something to South Dakotans' revulsion at Vietnam and Watergate. Like other Upper Midwest states, South Dakota tends to be dovish on foreign policy (as it was isolationist before Pearl Harbor) and sternly intolerant of corruption.

Then, around the time of AIM's occupation of Wounded Knee, South Dakota shifted sharply to the right. Republicans picked up one House seat in 1972 and the other in 1974; they won one Senate seat in 1978 and soundly beat McGovern, the symbol of the state's Democratic Party, in 1980. By 1976 the Republicans once again had big margins in the state legislature.

Governor. But the clearest indication in the change of mood was the election of Republican Governor William Janklow in 1978. Janklow had made his career, as special prosecutor and then attorney general, as a vehement opponent of Indian claims. He symbolized his position by carrying a gun himself, and his vehemence is all the more striking since he was once a legal services lawyer on an Indian reservation himself. Elected by a solid margin in 1978, Janklow was reelected by a huge margin in 1982. He promptly got into a controversy with Minnesota Governor Rudy Perpich, arguing that Minnesota deserved to lose businesses to South Dakota because Minnesota's taxes are too high. His latest controversy came in 1983, when he tried to persuade South Dakota bookstores not to carry a volume critical of his role in Indian matters.

Senators. South Dakota's senior senator, though just in his early 40s, is Republican Larry Pressler. He has demonstrated his vote-getting prowess over and over again: he beat an incumbent Democratic congressman in the Democratic year of 1974, he beat a respectable opponent 2–1 in the 1978 Senate race, he is expected to be reelected easily in 1984. He is one of those politicians who came of age in the early 1970s who seems to have an instinct for capitalizing on the latest turn in public opinion. He has a reputation as a liberal Republican; actually, his record shows adroit shifts at politically useful times. You could argue that his shift away from liberal economic policies in the late 1970s was simply evidence that Pressler, like most American voters, had come to understand that they were not working. But you would also have to concede that the shift was politically useful, in South Dakota and in the Senate.

Pressler spent most of his four years in the House running for the Senate and his first months in the Senate launching a preposterous presidential candidacy. He was named by Albert Hunt of the *Wall Street Journal* as a prime example of a congressional show horse (as opposed to workhorse). Now his friends argue that he has become much more active on legislation. He led the drive to get the Senate to overturn an FTC rule regulating used-car dealers—a chore other Commerce Committee Republicans didn't want; they knew the measure would pass because the dealers' PAC had been lobbying and making campaign contributions adroitly, but that there was no political mileage in it back home. Pressler is a strong opponent of grain embargoes—no surprise for a senator from a grain-producing state. He sponsored a successful measure to encourage shelter belts, the rows of trees which helped stop erosion on the Great Plains in the 1930s and could be useful again. On a loftier plane he chairs the Foreign Relations Subcommittee on Arms Control, which also handles the Law of the Sea Treaty and acid rain, and he was the only Republican to vote against arms control agency nominee Kenneth Adelman in 1983. The White House tried to suggest he did this out of pique, but Pressler has been consistently taking arms control stands different from the administration's. His stand is not likely to hurt him in dovish South Dakota.

On dozens of measures Pressler can point to constructive amendments he had advanced; evidently he and his staff do careful detail work. Undoubtedly he has improved, in minor ways which are nonetheless very important to some people, the operations of a vast government. But he has not yet succeeded in establishing his own basic priorities and key issues—the kind which can form the basis of a long senatorial career. The picture you get is of a man responding conscientiously to agendas set by others and to his own short-term political needs.

South Dakota's junior senator has fewer pretentions and the course of his career is not difficult to explicate. He is James Abdnor, a Republican first elected from the western congressional district in 1972. Not especially articulate or ambitious, he nonetheless agreed to take on George McGovern in 1980 when both national issues and local trends worked against the Democrat, and when McGovern seemed plainly tired of returning to the state. Abdnor campaigned doggedly as a supporter of family values, never seeing the irony in the fact that he is a bachelor and McGovern the father of five children. Abdnor's record in both the House and Senate has been faithfully conservative; only on environmental issues does he occasionally surprise observers and vote against the James Watt point of view. He chairs the Water Resources Subcommittee, the old pork barrel committee; South Dakota has been embroiled for some years in disputes over the use of the water of the Missouri River, which flows through the center of the state. Abdnor also has a seat on the Appropriations Committee and chairs its smallest subcommittee, Treasury, Postal Service, and General Government.

Abdnor would be the first to admit that his 1980 victory margin was more a repudiation of McGovern and his policies than it was a personal endorsement of Abdnor. It's easy to construct scenarios in which he is easily reelected in 1986, but there is also one obvious scenario which would give him trouble: opposition from the state's Democratic Congressman-at-Large Thomas Daschle.

Congressman. Until the 1980 Census results came in, South Dakota elected two congressmen; now it has one. That meant that in 1982 there was a musical chairs contest between Democrat Thomas Daschle and Republican Clint Roberts. Daschle represented the eastern edge of the state; it is the more heavily populated part of South Dakota, with lots of farms and few Indians, and most of the state's small cities. Daschle won the seat in 1978 when he campaigned door-to-door and won by all of 139 votes; he won reelection more easily in 1980. Roberts won Abdnor's seat in 1980; his great political assets are a solid conservatism and his resemblance to the Marlboro man—in fact, he posed for one Marlboro ad. His district included some of the agricultural country east of the Missouri, but it also includes South Dakota's High Plains, Black Hills, and most of its Indian reservations in the west; the only significant cities are Mitchell, home of the Corn Palace, and Rapid City, the town nearest Mount Rushmore. Daschle won in 1982 by a 52%–48% vote. Each man carried most of his old district, though not by huge margins; Daschle may have been helped by the Indian vote in the west and by the fact that the Sioux Falls TV stations which cover him heavily also covered much of Roberts's old district, while Rapid City TV does not reach much territory east of the Missouri River. Roberts, aided by national Republicans, could spend more than $500,000. But Daschle, a resourceful politician, raised enough mostly by himself, to enable him to spend even more.

Daschle is an active legislator, a member of the Agriculture and Veterans' Affairs Committees. He is a Vietnam veteran, and on the latter committee he is one of the leading proponents of more counseling programs for Vietnam era veterans and for compensation for injury to health caused by Agent Orange. On Agriculture, he was a lead sponsor of a bill passed by the committee in 1982 increasing emergency price supports and federal loan guarantees. This, like some of Daschle's other agricultural proposals, was not immediately successful, but he has proved he knows the farm issues and is an effective operator on the committee.

Serious, a dogged hard worker, Daschle seems to personify the personal virtues South Dakota values. His record on economic issues is muted enough for the state, and on many of the non-economic issues on which he has liberal opinions he is not out of line with what is, in some respects, a culturally tolerant and liberal state. Daschle is the leading Democratic officeholder in the state, and the odds-on favorite to break the Republican monopoly on Senate seats here, if anyone can.

Presidential politics. South Dakota came close to going Democratic in the 1972 and 1976 presidential elections. No one expects it to do so again soon, though it could, conceivably, if farm discontent rises. With only three electoral votes, it gets little attention. That is true, too, of its presidential primary, held in June and always overshadowed by California and other states. The Democratic primary electorate often favors liberal candidates, including Robert Kennedy in 1968 and Edward Kennedy in 1980; the Republican electorate is pretty solidly conservative.

The People Est. Pop. 1982: 686,000; Pop. 1980: 690,768, dn. 0.7% 1980–82 and up 3.7% 1970–80; .3% of U.S. total, 45th largest; voting age pop. 485,162; 5% American Indian. Single ancestry: 26% German, 7% Norwegian, 4% English, 3% Irish, 2% Dutch, Swedish, 1% French. Registered voters (1982): 426,511 Total. 189,708 D (44%); 200,422 R (47%); 36,381 other (9%). 18% with 1–3 yrs. col., 14% with 4+ yrs. col. 16.1% below poverty level. 27% housing units rented; median house value: $36,600; median monthly rent: $148. Households: 73% family, 40% with children, 64% married couples.

1982 Share of Federal Tax Burden $1,397,000,000; .23% of U.S. total, 50th largest.

1982 Share of Federal Expenditures

	Total		Non-Defense		Defense	
Total Expend	$1,601m	(0.27%)	$1,386m	(0.33%)	$215m	(0.12%)
St/Lcl Grants	325m	(0.37%)	325m	(0.37%)	0m	(0%)
Salary/Wages	262m	(0.34%)	126m	(0.46%)	136m	(0.27%)
Ind Payments	829m	(0.29%)	751m	(0.29%)	78m	(0.27%)
Procurement	110m	(0.08%)	57m	(0.18%)	53m	(0.05%)
Other Programs	76m	(1.40%)	76m	(1.40%)	0m	(0%)
Loan/Insurance	1,097m	(1.72%)	1,095m	(1.77%)	2m	(0.09%)

Political Lineup   Governor, William J. Janklow (R). Senators, Larry Pressler (R) and James Abdnor (R). Representatives, 1 D. State Senate, 35 (26 R and 9 D); State House of Representatives, 70 (54 R and 16 D).

Presidential Vote

1980	Reagan (R)		198,343	(61%)
	Carter (D)		103,855	(32%)
	Anderson (I)		21,431	(7%)
1976	Ford (R)		151,505	(50%)
	Carter (D)		147,068	(49%)

1980 Democratic Presidential Primary			*1980 Republican Presidential Primary*		
Kennedy	33,418	(49%)	Reagan	72,861	(88%)
Carter	31,251	(45%)	Two others..........	4,678	(6%)
Uncommitted	4,094	(6%)	No preference	5,366	(6%)

SENATORS

Sen. Larry Pressler (R) Elected 1978, seat up 1984; b. Mar. 29, 1942, Humboldt; home, Humboldt; U. of SD, B.A. 1964, Rhodes Scholar, Oxford U., 1966, Harvard U., M.A., J.D. 1971; Roman Catholic.

Career Army, Vietnam; U.S. House of Reps., 1975–78.

Offices 415 RSOB, 202-224-5842. Also 102 S. 2d St., Aberdeen 57401, 605-225-0150, ext. 471; 105 Rushmore Mall, Rapid City 57701, 605-341-1185; 334 S. Phillips Ave., Sioux Falls 57102, 605-336-2980, ext. 433; Raymond 57258, 605-532-3549; Buffalo 57720, 605-375-3355; and R.R. 1, Oldham 57051, 605-482-8538.

Committees *Commerce, Science, and Transportation* (5th). Subcommittees: Business, Trade and Tourism (Chairman); Communications; Surface Transportation. *Foreign Relations* (8th). Subcommittees: Arms Control, Oceans and International Operations and Environment (Chairman); Near Eastern and South Asian Affairs; Western Hemisphere. *Small Business* (10th). Subcommittees: Government Regulation and Paperwork; Small Business: Family Farm (Chairman). *Special Committee on Aging* (6th).

Group Ratings

	ADA	ACLU	COPE	CFA	LCV	LWV	NTU	NSI	COC	ACA	CSFC
1982	10	29	37	30	25	58	57	38	70	74	70
1981	30	—	38	21	32	—	59	—	67	55	64
1980	17	50	14	13	65	75	40	100	81	65	63

National Journal Ratings

	Economic		Foreign		Cultural	
1982	43%	(LIB)	46%	(LIB)	9%	(LIB)
	56%	(CONS)	53%	(CONS)	90%	(CONS)
1981	40%	(LIB)	65%	(LIB)	68%	(LIB)
	59%	(CONS)	34%	(CONS)	31%	(CONS)

Key Votes

1) Reagan 81 Budget	FOR	5) $ to El Salvador	AGN	9) Poor Pay Food Stamps	FOR
2) Reagan 81 Tax Cut	FOR	6) Saudi AWACS Sale	FOR	10) Ban Crt Busing Order	FOR
3) Bal Budget Amend	FOR	7) Ban Abortion	FOR	11) Clinch Riv Brdr Rctr	FOR
4) Gas & Road Tax	FOR	8) Nerve Gas Prod	FOR	12) Legal Services Corp	FOR

Election Results

1978 general	Larry Pressler (R)	170,832	(67%)	($449,541)
	Don Barnett (D)	84,767	(33%)	($152,006)
1978 primary	Larry Pressler (R)	66,893	(74%)	
	Ronald F. Williamson (R)	23,646	(26%)	($24,188)
1972 general	James Abourezk (D)	174,773	(57%)	($427,063)
	Robert Hirsch (R)	131,613	(43%)	($300,800)

Campaign Contributions and Expenditures

1977-78		PACS brkdwn			
Receipts	$489,983	Agr	$22,775	Ideo	$13,493
Expend.	$449,541	Bus	$119,327	Lbr	$5,725
Unspent	$40,439	Hlth	$20,100	Prof	$5,650

Sen. James Abdnor (R) Elected 1980, seat up 1986; b. Feb. 13, 1923, Kennebec; home, Kennebec; U. of NE, B.A. 1945; United Methodist.

Career Army, WWII; Farmer-rancher; Sch. teacher and coach; SD Senate, 1956–68, Pres. Pro Tem, 1967–68; Lt. Gov. of SD, 1969–70; U.S. House of Reps., 1972–80.

Offices 309 HSOB, 202-224-2321. Also P.O. Box 492, Aberdeen 57401, 605-225-0250; P.O. Box 873, Sioux Falls 57101, 605-336-2890, ext. 474; 507 Kansas City, Rapid City 57701, 605-343-5000; 375 Dakota S., Huron 57350, 605-352-5117; 113 3d Ave. S., Mitchell 57301, 605-996-3601; and Fed. Bldg., Pierre 57501, 605-224-2891.

Committees *Appropriations* (9th). Subcommittees: Agriculture, Rural Development; Energy and Water Development; HUD-Independent Agencies; Transportation; Treasury, Postal Service, and General Government (Chairman). *Environment and Public Works* (5th). Subcommittees: Toxic Substances and Environmental Oversight; Transportation; Water Resources (Chairman). *Joint Economic Committee* (3d). Subcommittees: Agriculture and Transportation (Chairman); Trade, Productivity, and Economic Growth.

Group Ratings

	ADA	ACLU	COPE	CFA	LCV	LWV	NTU	NSI	COC	ACA	CSFC
1982	10	7	5	20	7	27	67	90	74	67	76
1981	5	—	5	14	25	—	78	—	89	67	79

National Journal Ratings

	Economic		Foreign		Cultural	
1982	32%	(LIB)	16%	(LIB)	13%	(LIB)
	67%	(CONS)	68%	(CONS)	86%	(CONS)
1981	2%	(LIB)	1%	(LIB)	46%	(LIB)
	88%	(CONS)	85%	(CONS)	52%	(CONS)

Key Votes

1) Reagan 81 Budget	FOR	5) $ to El Salvador	FOR	9) Poor Pay Food Stamps	FOR
2) Reagan 81 Tax Cut	FOR	6) Saudi AWACS Sale	FOR	10) Ban Crt Busing Order	FOR
3) Bal Budget Amend	FOR	7) Ban Abortion	FOR	11) Clinch Riv Brdr Rctr	FOR
4) Gas & Road Tax	FOR	8) Nerve Gas Prod	FOR	12) Legal Services Corp	FOR

Election Results

1980 general	James Abdnor (R)	190,594	(58%)	($1,801,653)
	George McGovern (D)	129,018	(39%)	($3,237,669)
1980 primary	James Abdnor (R)	68,196	(73%)	
	Dale Bell (R)	25,314	(27%)	($758,264)
1974 general	George McGovern (D)	147,929	(53%)	($1,172,831)
	Leo K. Thorsness (R)	130,955	(47%)	($528,817)

Campaign Contributions and Expenditures

1979-80				*PACS brkdwn*		
Receipts	$1,814,124	Agr	$17,200	Ideo	$71,079
Expend.	$1,801,653	Bus	$558,762	Lbr	$1,000
Unspent	$20,998	Hlth	$22,150	Prof	$8,125

GOVERNOR

Gov. William J. Janklow (R) Elected 1978, term expires Jan. 1987; b. Sept. 13, 1939, Chicago, IL; home, Pierre; U. of SD, B.S. 1964, J.D. 1966; Lutheran.

Career Staff Atty., Dir. and Chief Officer, SD Legal Svcs. System, Rosebud Indian Reservation, 1966–73; Chief Prosecutor, Ofc. of the Atty. Gen. of SD, 1973–74; Atty. Gen. of SD, 1975–78.

Offices State Capitol Bldg., Pierre 57501, 605-773-3212.

Election Results

1982 gen.	William J. Janklow (R)	197,426	(71%)
	Michael O'Connor (D)	81,136	(29%)
1982 prim.	William J. Janklow (R) unopposed		
1978 gen.	William J. Janklow (R)	147,116	(57%)
	Roger D. McKellips (D)	112,679	(43%)

Rep. Thomas A. Daschle (D) Elected 1978; b. Dec. 9, 1947, Aberdeen; home, Aberdeen; SD St. U., B.A. 1969; Roman Catholic.

Career Air Force, 1969–72; Legis. Asst. to U.S. Sen. James Abourezk, 1973–76, District Aide, 1976–78.

Offices 439 CHOB, 202-225-2801. Also Box 1274, Sioux Falls 57101, 605-334-9596.

Committees *Agriculture* (16th). Subcommittees: Conservation, Credit, and Rural Development; Livestock, Dairy, and Poultry; Wheat, Soybeans, and Feed Grains. *Post Office and Civil Service* (12th). Subcommittees: Human Resources; Postal Operations and Services; Postal Personnel and Modernization. *Veterans' Affairs* (9th). Subcommittees: Compensation, Pension, and Insurance; Hospitals and Health Care.

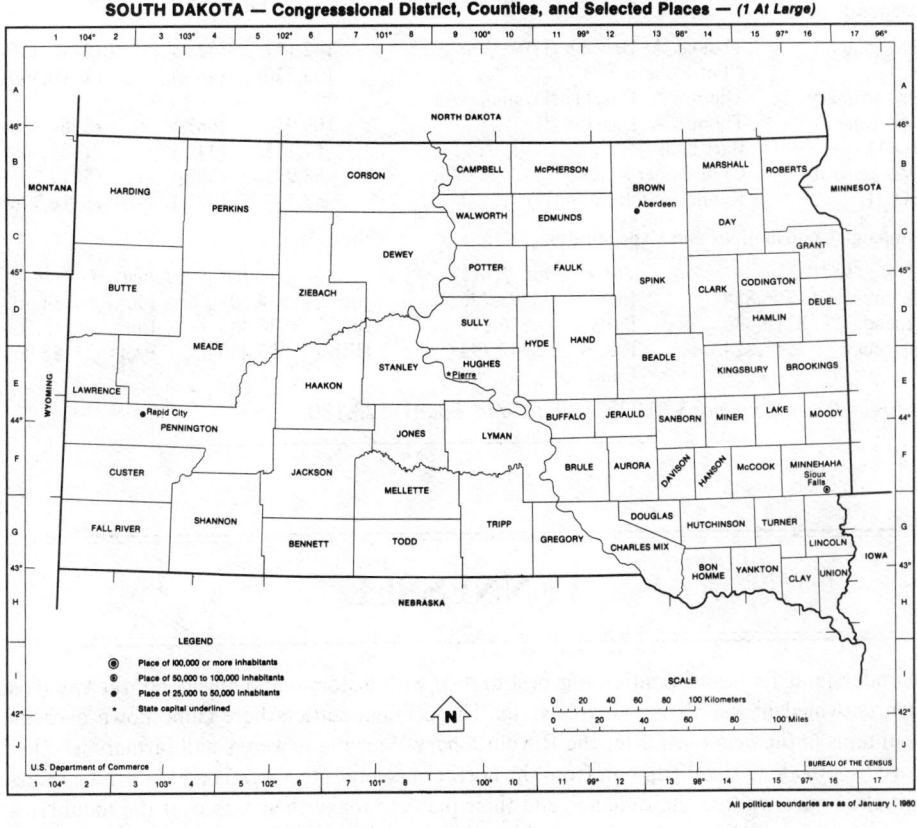

SOUTH DAKOTA — Congressional District, Counties, and Selected Places — *(1 At Large)*

Group Ratings

	ADA	ACLU	COPE	CFA	LCV	LWV	NTU	NSI	COC	ACA	CSFC
1982	80	62	83	92	76	70	41	50	35	23	29
1981	70	—	79	79	86	—	33	—	22	29	39
1980	72	60	74	64	74	67	26	10	68	35	41

National Journal Ratings

	Economic		Foreign		Cultural	
1982	55%	(LIB)	88%	(LIB)	76%	(LIB)
	45%	(CONS)	12%	(CONS)	23%	(CONS)
1981	61%	(LIB)	53%	(LIB)	80%	(LIB)
	38%	(CONS)	45%	(CONS)	19%	(CONS)

Key Votes

1) Reagan 81 Budget	AGN	5) Incr SS Rtmt Age	FOR	9) Poor Pay Food Stamps	AGN
2) Reagan 81 Tax Cut	AGN	6) Saudi AWACS Sale	AGN	10) Ban Crt Busing Order	AGN
3) Bal Budget Amend	FOR	7) $ for MX Missile	AGN	11) Auto Local Content	—
4) Gas & Road Tax	AGN	8) Nerve Gas Prod	AGN	12) Nuclear Arms Freeze	FOR

Election Results

1982 general	Thomas A. Daschle (D)	142,122	(52%)	($716,436)
	Clint Roberts (R)	133,530	(48%)	($570,360)
1982 primary	Thomas A. Daschle (D) unopposed			
1980 general	Thomas A. Daschle (D)	109,910	(66%)	($204,380)
(SD 1)	Bart Kull (R)	57,155	(34%)	($83,909)
1980 general	Clint Roberts (R)	88,991	(58%)	($217,765)
(SD 2)	Kenneth Stofferahn (D)	63,447	(42%)	($116,776)

Campaign Contributions and Expenditures

1981-82		Direct Cont. 81-82			PACS brkdwn		
Receipts	$706,884	Indiv	$398,726	Agr	$34,100	Ideo	$34,600
Expend.	$716,436	Party	$26,877	Bus	$46,485	Lbr	$115,500
Unspent	$11,824	PACS	$242,792	Hlth	$3,450	Prof	$2,800
		Cand	$1,000				

Indirect Party Expend: $30,235   *Non-Cand Loans:* $23,180

TENNESSEE

To understand Tennessee politics, it is best to start with history—and music. For the two have been entwined in the history of this state. The original settlers here came down over the mountains in the years just after the Revolutionary War; many were small farmers who had moved south along the Piedmont, from the northern colonies to Virginia and North Carolina, as if they were waiting their chance and their place to make their way over the mountains. Anglo-American religious folk music followed the same patterns: it originated in the northern colonies in the 18th century, then moved southward and over the mountains by the early 19th, concentrating especially in Tennessee and Kentucky. As the 19th century went on, Tennessee was touched by the issues of slavery and split over the Civil War: the eastern part of the state remained pro-Union (this was the home of Lincoln's vice president and successor, Andrew Johnson), while middle and west Tennessee favored secession. But there were not that many slaves there (the black population now is only 16%, and 45% of the state's blacks are in Memphis), and Tennessee suffered much less destruction than states farther south; Sherman was still getting his provisions from the North by rail when he was here.

Yet Tennessee's divisions remain. East Tennessee still remains a distinctive region politically, and middle Tennessee remains distinctive from the west. Their political personalities—the east is feisty and Republican, middle Tennessee has been devoutly Democratic since the days of Nashville's Andy Jackson, the west is racially polarized—are well known even to ordinary Tennesseeans. Their persistence is matched, and their particular personalities analogous, to the musical traditions which have made Tennessee for many Americans the music capital of the nation. Tennessee is associated with country music, but there are several strains of it. The country music of east Tennessee has been influenced by the bluegrass music and fiddling tradition of the mountains. The country music of Nashville, in contrast, seems to have roots in the gospel music which is also centered in that city—which, as it happens, is also the nation's leading center of religious publishing. Nashville's Grand Ole Opry, broadcast since 1925, remains different from Knoxville's Tennessee Barn Dance, broadcast since 1942; even the names suggest a different focus. As for west Tennessee, the lowlands along the Mississippi River, in and around Memphis, are economically and culturally part of a unit that includes the Mississippi Delta. This is the part of America that gave birth to blues music in the 1890–1920 period. Memphis produced many blues musicians, and others who drew on their tradition, from the jazz musicians of Beale Street in the 1920s to Elvis Presley in his Graceland mansion in the 1950s and 1960s. Blues is a product of black American culture, and west Tennessee remains a heavily black part of the South; it was the one part of Tennessee that heavily favored segregation (many rural blacks couldn't vote then, and the black vote in Memphis was deliverable by the Crump machine until 1948). But whites here have an attraction to, and have been influenced by, black culture, even when they proclaim their superiority to it.

Both the musical traditions and the partisan patterns of the different regions in Tennessee have been remarkably long lasting. So long as middle and west Tennessee remained strongly Democratic, the Republicans could not win a statewide election, no matter how many votes they won in east Tennessee. But when there were defections in the west and middle, Republicans could win: in 1920 Harding carried Tennessee, and the state elected a Republican governor; in 1928 Hoover beat Al Smith here.

The civil rights revolution had a relatively minor effect in the state, but it was enough to make some elections close. Democratic Senators Estes Kefauver and Albert Gore refused to sign the Southern Manifesto denouncing desegregation and both survived politically: Kefauver until his death in 1963, Gore until he was defeated in 1970, and then more for his opposition to the Vietnam war and to Richard Nixon's southern Supreme Court nominees than for his civil rights votes. Tennessee went for Eisenhower over Stevenson twice, but both times by exceedingly narrow margins, and by percentages, not just statewide but in almost every county, remarkably similar to those received by Ronald Reagan and Jimmy Carter in 1980. Tennessee has sent out migrants to other states, most notably to Texas, which was settled primarily by Tennesseeans and is studded with Tennessee place names; but the political divisions of the state endure with a stability unmatched in the rest of the nation.

Presidential politics. Tennessee, heavily for Carter in 1976 and closely divided in 1980, with relatively little population or economic growth in 1980–82, must be considered one of the southern states inclined to go Democratic if there is a close presidential race in 1984. Indeed, the historical patterns of Tennessee voting—and its Democratic preference—which seemed volatile in the late 1960s and through the 1970s, now seem more firmly entrenched than ever. It should be noted that this state is a not inconsiderable prize: it has 11 electoral votes now, only two less than North Carolina, only one less than Indiana, and more than such states as Minnesota, Maryland, and Louisiana.

Tennessee has a presidential primary, which has achieved little notice because of its timing and predictability. Its Democratic voters have behaved much as those in other southern states. Its Republican electorate is drawn from a broader spectrum socioeconomically, if from a rather constricted geographic range; most are in east Tennessee, including blue-collar as well as white-collar voters, and in the affluent suburbs of Memphis.

Senators. Tennessee's senior senator is Howard Baker, the Senate majority leader, certainly the most talented leader of the Senate since Lyndon Johnson, and quite possibly since a long time before him. Howard Baker's roots are in east Tennessee: his father served in

Congress from the Knoxville district, and his stepmother after him. Baker could have had the seat for the asking in 1964. Instead, he ran for the Senate that year, lost narrowly, came back and ran again in 1966, and this time won. He made several false starts for leadership positions, running to succeed his father-in-law, Everett Dirksen, as minority leader in 1969, losing to Hugh Scott, then running against him again in 1970. In 1973 he was suddenly in the national spotlight as ranking Republican on the Senate Watergate Committee. His performance there was careful and yet audacious; he set out from the beginning to judge the president, not necessarily to defend him. Watergate buffs speculated on what kind of double game he was playing, but with the passage of time it seems increasingly clear that he was doing exactly what he said he was: evaluating the evidence, weighing the facts, considering the general implications. He also showed himself to be a natural star on television: his conversational, low-key, but always fluent and articulate style of speaking comes across as well on TV as any politician's style today.

When Watergate was over, Baker returned to committee work, particularly on the Environment and Public Works Committee. He surprised just about everyone when after the 1976 election he was elected minority leader over Robert Griffin. And everyone was even more surprised when in 1980 it became clear that Republicans would control the Senate and he would be Senate majority leader. There was some question—for about two minutes—whether the rather conservative body of senators would elect Baker to that position. But he moved quickly and got Paul Laxalt, the most plausible alternative, to nominate him. All the evidence suggests that he and Laxalt have worked well together since.

This is true despite the fact that Baker is not considered a Reagan Republican by a great many Reaganites and others. After all, he ran against Reagan in the 1980 primaries, though he was knocked out early; he is constantly called a Republican moderate, though his differences with Reagan on issues are actually rather limited. There are differences on priorities with some Reagan backers: Baker gave top priority to economic issues in 1981, and then to defense; the cultural issues like abortion he delayed until late in the 1982 session. He called the Reagan economic program "a riverboat gamble."

But what is more important is that Baker took an unwieldy group of 53 Republican senators and welded them into a solid majority. They were an odd group: most of them freshmen, men and two women of widely differing views and no great trust of one another. None had ever served as part of a Republican majority in Congress; none had ever chaired a congressional committee. As members of a minority, they were used to scoring points; now they were responsible for running a government. Under Howard Baker's leadership they did. Baker profited from the unity Republicans had been developing in the late Carter years, and the attempts Republicans of disparate views were already making, to come up with policies they could all support. He benefited from the leadership of the administration. But finally it was Howard Baker who kept the Republicans all together, voting as a unit, controlling the Senate with their 53 or 54 votes, crafting budgets and pushing through tax cuts and then increases. He did this largely through close individual attention to each Republican senator. Like Lyndon Johnson, he got to know his colleagues, and he relied more on rewards than on threats to get them to do what he wanted.

In 1981 Baker pushed through the administration's program. In 1982, when the administration proposed a budget which could not attract a single Republican vote, he worked with Budget Chairman Pete Domenici to fashion a budget and with Finance Chairman Bob Dole to raise enough revenue to get the budget near balance. After the 1982 election, he negotiated directly with Speaker Tip O'Neill on the road and gas tax bill and on the Social Security rescue plan. Baker has become the balance wheel of government. He succeeds in large part because his senators, and President Reagan, and the speaker as well, trust and like him. There is no evidence of jealousy in his dealings and no evidence of double-dealing. But there is strategy and shrewdness and foresight.

In early 1983 Baker announced he would not run for reelection in 1984. His announcement has been treated as an event in presidential politics: was he trying to force Ronald Reagan out? Or keep his own options open for 1984? More likely, Baker concluded that his work in the Senate was coming to an end. The Democrats have a good chance of gaining control in 1984, and surely Baker doesn't want to be minority leader again. And Baker himself would have to campaign hard to win reelection in basically Democratic Tennessee. In 1978 Jane Eskind, beginning as an unknown, held him to 56% of the vote. True, he has fought hard and, at this writing, successfully for Tennessee projects like the Clinch River breeder reactor and the Tennessee–Tombigbee Waterway. But he might have been vulnerable to charges that he wasn't spending enough time on parochial matters.

As for the presidential race, who else is better qualified? Baker evidently concluded from his melancholy 1980 effort, and the success of non-officeholders Jimmy Carter and Ronald Reagan, that running for the presidency is a full-time job. He now has his options open, as they say, for 1984 and 1988; and surely he is being candid when he says that he doesn't have definite plans for those years because he doesn't know yet all the relevant circumstances. If Baker runs for president, he will be dogged in the Republican primaries by conservative detractors, but he will probably be the Republicans' strongest candidate in the general election. More than that, he has shown as much as any politician in our day that he has the instinctive understanding of how to exercise leadership and how to get others to move things where you want them to go, which was the essence of Franklin Roosevelt's art and probably the art of all great leaders.

Within two months of Baker's announcement of retirement from the Senate, it became likely that his successor would be Democratic Congressman Albert Gore, Jr. He is much more than the bearer of a famous name; he has compiled a thoughtful record not only on issues before his committees (Energy and Commerce, Science and Technology) but also on such distant matters as arms control. The only Democrat at all likely to run against him is Jane Eskind, Baker's 1978 opponent; leading Republicans like Governor Lamar Alexander have already taken themselves out of the race.

Tennessee's junior senator, James Sasser, is far less well known nationally than Baker. He was a junior senator his first four years, a member of the minority his second four. His record is in line with the tradition of Kefauver and Gore, Sr., and much more in line with northern Democrats than most southerners over the years. He owes something as well to an agrarian tradition: his father was an agriculture official who moved all over rural Tennessee, one of those men who make government programs work to help people. Sasser has not voted for all big government programs, but on balance he seems to see government as a friend, not an enemy. Sasser seems to be an insider's senator, working to improve details of complex bills and toiling on the Appropriations and Budget Committees. Currently he is on the minority on both. But should the Democrats win control in 1984, Sasser will move up (because membership is temporary on Budget), and could emerge as one of the most important Democratic spokesmen in Congress.

Sasser was the target of some nasty campaigning in 1982. One ad showed a Fidel Castro lookalike taking a puff on a cigar and saying, "Muchas gracias, Señor Sasser;" he also was the target of tough negative campaigning on the abortion issue. All this seemed, in the end, to help him. The Republican, Congressman Robin Beard, is one of the most bellicose recent members of Congress, and even in a rough-and-ready state like Tennessee there were limits on how aggressive a foreign policy voters wanted. In the end Sasser won 62% of the vote and carried all nine congressional districts.

Governor. At the same time, Republican Governor Lamar Alexander was winning 60% of the vote and carrying eight out of nine districts himself against Knoxville Mayor Randy Tyree. Alexander is an exception to almost all the political rules: he has won twice in a state increasingly Democratic in most races; he has kept the state in sound fiscal condition in difficult economic times; he is a Republican who boasts of raising education spending and seeks, and receives, votes from blacks. He is young, attractive, vigorous, bright, a former aide to Howard Baker with a record of his own.

He has been aided as well by the Democrats' proclivity for scandals and wheeling and dealing, which has helped Republicans win three of the last four gubernatorial races. Democrat John J. Hooker, Jr., lost in 1970 to Winfield Dunn, in large part because Hooker's Minnie Pearl Chicken (renamed, in the style of the day, Performance Systems) went bankrupt; Jake Butcher, Alexander's 1978 opponent, was hurt by his wheeler-dealer image, and his lead bank went into receivership in 1983; Tyree was an associate of Butcher. The only Democrat to win, Ray Blanton in 1974, was even more unsavory; he was convicted of selling gubernatorial pardons. Alexander, whose honesty and devotion to public service are clear, has provided a refreshing contrast.

Congressional districting. Tennessee gained one House seat from the 1980 Census, the same one it lost in 1970. The Democratic legislature tried to gain two seats, and was only half successful. In the new 4th district, which extends from the east Tennessee border with Virginia almost to the west Tennessee border with Mississippi, Democrat Jim Cooper, son of a former governor, beat Cissy Baker, daughter of Howard Baker and granddaughter of Everett Dirksen. But in the restyled 7th, the Democrat Bob Clement, son of another former governor, lost to former Baker aide Don Sundquist, in a seat relinquished by Republican Robin Beard, who ran unsuccessfully for the Senate.

The People Est. Pop. 1982: 4,651,000; Pop. 1980: 4,591,120, up 1.3% 1980–82 and 16.9% 1970–80; 2.0% of U.S. total, 17th largest; voting age pop. 3,292,560; 14% Black, 1% Spanish origin. Single ancestry: 23% English, 5% Irish, 4% German, 1% French, Scottish. Registered voters (1982): 2,272,782 Total. 12% with 1–3 yrs. col., 12% with 4+ yrs. col. 17.0% below poverty level. 29% housing units rented; median house value: $35,600; median monthly rent: $148. Households: 77% family, 42% with children, 63% married couples.

1982 Share of Federal Tax Burden $9,664,200,000; 1.62% of U.S. total, 22d largest.

1982 Share of Federal Expenditures

	Total		Non-Defense		Defense	
Total Expend	$11,359m	(1.88%)	$10,011m	(2.36%)	$1,349m	(0.75%)
St/Lcl Grants	1,607m	(1.82%)	1,605m	(1.82%)	2m	(5.56%)
Salary/Wages	1,518m	(1.95%)	1.127m	(4.12%)	391m	(0.77%)
Ind Payments	5,472m	(1.91%)	4,813m	(0.02%)	609m	(2.13%)
Procurement	2,694m	(1.85%)	2,005m	(6.36%)	689m	(0.60%)
Other Programs	67m	(1.24%)	65m	(1.21%)	2m	(4.65%)
Loan/Insurance	833m	(1.30%)	811m	(1.31%)	22m	(1.00%)

Political Lineup   Governor, Lamar Alexander (R). Senators, Howard H. Baker, Jr. (R) and James R. Sasser (D). Representatives, 9 (6 D and 3 R). State Senate, 33 (22 D and 11 R); State House of Representatives, 99 (60 D, 38 R and 1 I).

Presidential Vote

1980	Reagan (R)	787,761	(49%)
	Carter (D)	783,051	(48%)
	Anderson (I)	35,991	(2%)
1976	Ford (R)	633,969	(43%)
	Carter (D)	825,879	(56%)

1980 Democratic Presidential Primary			*1980 Republican Presidential Primary*		
Kennedy	53,258	(18%)	Reagan	144,625	(76%)
Carter	221,658	(75%)	Bush	35,274	(18%)
Others	17,764	(7%)	Anderson	8,722	(5%)
			Crane	1,574	(1%)

SENATORS

Sen. Howard H. Baker, Jr. (R) Elected 1966, seat up 1984; b. Nov. 15, 1925, Huntsville; home, Huntsville; Tulane U., U. of the South, U. of TN, LL.B. 1949; Presbyterian.

Career Navy, WWII; Practicing atty., 1949–66.

Offices 522 HSOB, 202-224-4944. Also 716 U.S. Courthouse, 801 Broadway, Nashville 37203, 615-749-5129; and 313 P.O. Bldg., Knoxville 37902, 615-546-5486.

Committees *Majority Leader. Environment and Public Works* (2d). Subcommittees: Transportation; Nuclear Regulation; Regional and Community Development. *Foreign Relations* (2d). Subcommittees: European Affairs; East Asian and Pacific Affairs; Near Eastern and South Asian Affairs. *Rules and Administration* (3d). *Joint Committee on Printing* (3d).

Group Ratings

	ADA	ACLU	COPE	CFA	LCV	LWV	NTU	NSI	COC	ACA	CSFC
1982	5	43	24	0	16	36	64	100	74	78	74
1981	20	—	25	7	13	—	59	—	94	67	81
1980	17	40	16	7	25	56	38	75	81	81	70

National Journal Ratings

	Economic		Foreign		Cultural	
1982	10%	(LIB)	16%	(LIB)	42%	(LIB)
	89%	(CONS)	68%	(CONS)	57%	(CONS)
1981	39%	(LIB)	36%	(LIB)	44%	(LIB)
	60%	(CONS)	63%	(CONS)	55%	(CONS)

Key Votes

1) Reagan 81 Budget	FOR	5) $ to El Salvador	FOR	9) Poor Pay Food Stamps	FOR
2) Reagan 81 Tax Cut	FOR	6) Saudi AWACS Sale	FOR	10) Ban Crt Busing Order	—
3) Bal Budget Amend	FOR	7) Ban Abortion	FOR	11) Clinch Riv Brdr Rctr	FOR
4) Gas & Road Tax	FOR	8) Nerve Gas Prod	FOR	12) Legal Services Corp	FOR

Election Results

1978 general	Howard H. Baker, Jr. (R)	642,644	(56%)	($1,922,945)
	Jane Eskind (D)	466,228	(42%)	($1,903,532)
1978 primary	Howard H. Baker, Jr. (R)	205,680	(83%)	
	Five others (R)	40,819	(17%)	
1972 general	Howard H. Baker, Jr. (R)	716,539	(62%)	($830,769)
	Ray Blanton (D)	440,599	(38%)	($224,653)

Campaign Contributions and Expenditures

1977-78			*PACS brkdwn*		
Receipts	$1,946,443	Agr	$21,950	Ideo	$7,700
Expend.	$1,922,945	Bus	$261,093	Lbr	$11,550
Unspent	$24,066	Hlth	$31,500	Prof	$7,950

Sen. James R. (Jim) **Sasser** (D) Elected 1976, seat up 1988; b. Sept. 30, 1936, Memphis; home, Nashville; Vanderbilt U., B.A. 1958, J.D. 1961; United Methodist.

Career Practicing atty.; Chmn., TN State Dem. Comm., 1973–76.

Offices 298 RSOB, 202-224-3344. Also U.S. Courthouse, 801 Broadway, Nashville 37203, 615-251-7353.

Committees Appropriations (12th). Subcommittees: Agriculture, Rural Development; Energy and Water Development; HUD-Independent Agencies; Military Construction. *Banking, Housing and Urban Affairs* (7th). Subcommittees: Federal Credit Programs; Housing and Urban Affairs; International Finance and Monetary Policy. *Budget* (5th). *Governmental Affairs* (6th). Subcommittees: Civil Service, Post Office, and General Services; Permanent Subcommittee on Investigations; Intergovernmental Relations. *Small Business* (4th). Subcommittee: Capital Formation and Retention.

Group Ratings

	ADA	ACLU	COPE	CFA	LCV	LWV	NTU	NSI	COC	ACA	CSFC
1982	55	46	73	90	49	55	24	78	50	48	49
1981	45	—	69	43	12	—	30	—	67	40	48
1980	67	43	68	47	23	50	20	20	43	23	35

National Journal Ratings

	Economic		Foreign		Cultural	
1982	75%	(LIB)	50%	(LIB)	51%	(LIB)
	24%	(CONS)	49%	(CONS)	48%	(CONS)
1981	58%	(LIB)	61%	(LIB)	42%	(LIB)
	41%	(CONS)	38%	(CONS)	57%	(CONS)

Key Votes

1) Reagan 81 Budget	FOR	5) $ to El Salvador	AGN	9) Poor Pay Food Stamps	AGN
2) Reagan 81 Tax Cut	FOR	6) Saudi AWACS Sale	AGN	10) Ban Crt Busing Order	FOR
3) Bal Budget Amend	FOR	7) Ban Abortion	AGN	11) Clinch Riv Brdr Rctr	FOR
4) Gas & Road Tax	AGN	8) Nerve Gas Prod	AGN	12) Legal Services Corp	FOR

Election Results

1982 general	James R. (Jim) Sasser (D)	780,113	(62%)	($2,091,872)
	Robin L. Beard (R)	479,642	(38%)	($1,639,858)
1982 primary	James R. (Jim) Sasser (D)	511,059	(89%)	
	Charles Gordon Vick (D)	63,488	(11%)	
1976 general	James R. (Jim) Sasser (D)	751,180	(52%)	($839,379)
	Bill Brock (R)	673,231	(47%)	($1,301,033)

Campaign Contributions and Expenditures

1979-82		*Direct Cont. 79-82*		*PACS brkdwn*			
Receipts	$2,174,839	Indiv	$1,263,033	Agr	$46,350	Ideo	$75,100
Expend.	$2,091,872	Party	$25,033	Bus	$217,669	Lbr	$241,411
Unspent	$58,064	PACS	$639,720	Hlth	$15,600	Prof	$26,000
		Cand	$40,417				

Indirect Party Expend: $50,000   *Indep Expend*: For: $850 Agn: $5,784 (LIFEPAC, NCPAC)
Non-Cand Loans: $50,000

GOVERNOR

Gov. Lamar Alexander (R) Elected 1978, term expires Jan. 1987; b. July 3, 1940, Maryville; home, Nashville; Vanderbilt U., B.A. 1962, NYU, J.D. 1965; Presbyterian.

Career Newspaper reporter, *Knoxville News-Sentinel,* Nashville *Banner, Maryville Alcoa Daily Times*; Practicing atty., 1965, 1971–; Law Clerk, U.S. Circuit Court of Appeals, 5th Dist., New Orleans, 1965–66; Exec. Asst. to Bryce Harlow, Counselor in charge of congressional relations, 1969; Repub. Nominee for Gov. of TN, 1974.

Offices State Capitol Bldg., Nashville 37219, 615-741-2001.

Election Results

1982 gen.	Lamar Alexander (R)	737,963	(60%)
	Randall Tyree (D)	500,937	(40%)
1982 prim.	Lamar Alexander (R)	259,497	(100%)
1978 gen.	Lamar Alexander (R)	661,959	(56%)
	Jake Butcher (D)	523,495	(44%)

FIRST DISTRICT

The 1st congressional district of Tennessee is the far northeastern corner of the state. Most of it is an extension of the great valley of Virginia which lies between the Blue Ridge and the main ridge of the Appalachians. It is remote from much of Tennessee, farther from Memphis than it is from Richmond, Virginia. This part of Tennessee is not one of the nation's highest income areas, but neither is it the scene of the kind of poverty you can find in some of the hollows of West Virginia or eastern Kentucky. Northeastern Tennessee has not gone through any of the booms and busts of the coal industry. Instead, this has been an industrial area for quite a long time now, and one which, through its modest wage levels and relatively highly skilled labor force, low electric power rates (because of TVA), and good transportation routes (it's on major rail lines), has continued to attract new factories. Its major towns—Johnson City, Kingsport, Bristol—boast major paper and printing plants, and have the look of comfortable,

TENNESSEE — Congressional Districts, Counties, and Selected Places — *(9 Districts)*

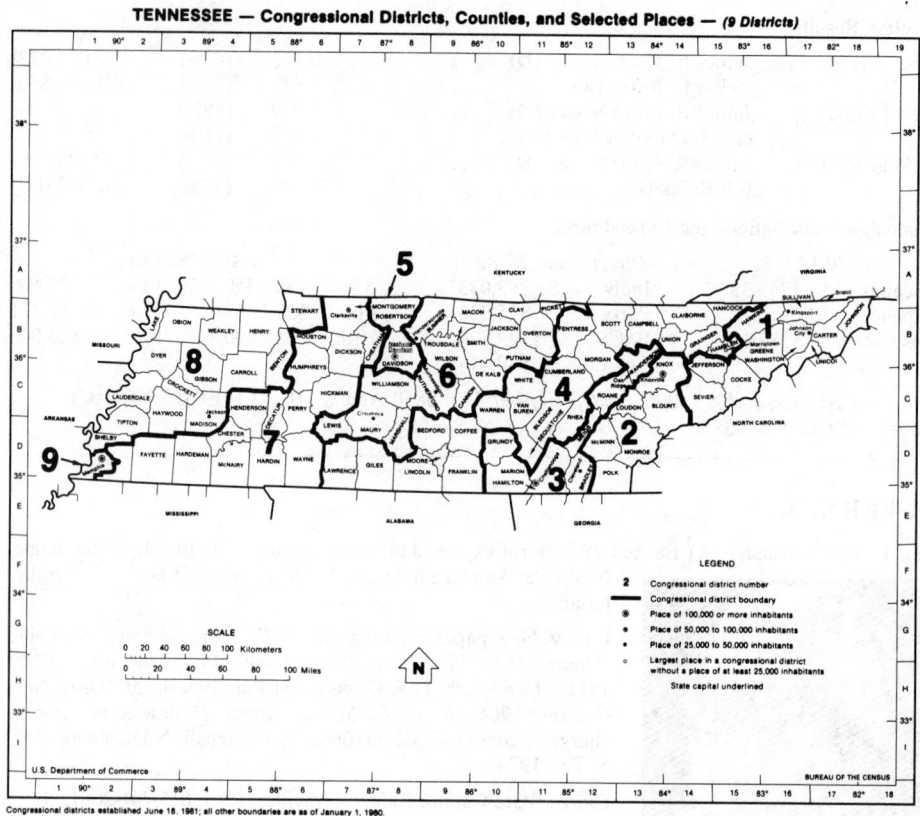

Congressional districts established June 18, 1981; all other boundaries are as of January 1, 1980.

clean 1920s factory towns. This is a part of America where things seem to work, and where the cultural trends of the 1960s and 1970s seem far away or altogether alien.

In Tennessee it seems that changing economic conditions, even in a factory district, don't change political attitudes any more than they change people's religions: there may be a few shifts and some changes in intensity, but for the most part people stick to their beliefs. In this part of Tennessee, those beliefs are usually Republican, as heavily Republican as any part of Kansas or Nebraska. People up here in the mountains never had many slaves, and they had little use for secession in 1861. They stayed loyal to the Union and continued to send congressmen to Washington. Abraham Lincoln picked a local boy, Andrew Johnson, to be his second vice president in 1864. To this day voters in the 1st district continue to support Republican candidates in almost every election.

For 40 years congressional politics in this area was dominated by B. Carroll Reece, a Republican who represented the district for most of the time between 1921 and 1961. Reece's successor, first elected in 1962, is Republican Jimmy Quillen. He is one of the quieter senior members of the House. He has a seat on the Rules Committee and is ranking Republican there. But since the Democrats have a 9–4 majority, and all of their nine members are loyal to the leadership, Republicans don't have much leverage; and in any case, Delbert Latta of

Ohio, the second ranking Republican, is much more aggressive and voluble than Quillen. Quillen is one of those quiet, pleasant Burkean conservatives who for years provided the backbone for the outnumbered Republicans in the House. It is a very different breed from the aggressive, brash crackling-with-ideas young Republicans who dominated their party's ranks when it was in effective control of the House in 1981. Now that they are no longer in ascendance, however, the mantle of leadership may pass back to men like Quillen.

Quillen is routinely reelected by large margins and without significant opposition.

The People Pop. 1980: 512,702, up 18.9% 1970–80; voting age pop. 371,177; 2% Black. 23% housing units rented. Median owner $33,300; renter $128. Households: 80% family, 43% with children, 68% married couples.

Presidential Vote

1980	Reagan (R)	105,474	(61%)
	Carter (D)	62,841	(36%)
	Other	4,623	(3%)

Rep. James H. (Jimmy) **Quillen** (R) Elected 1962; b. Jan. 11, 1916, near Gate City, VA; home, Kingsport; Methodist.

Career Founder and Pub., *Kingsport Mirror*, 1936–39, *Johnson City Times*, 1939–44; Navy, WWII; Pres. and Bd. Chmn., real estate and insurance business, 1946–; Dir., 1st TN Bank, Kingsport; TN House of Reps., 1955–62, Minor. Ldr., 1959–60.

Offices 102 CHOB, 202-225-6356. Also Fed. Bldg., Rm. 157, 1st Flr., Kingsport 37662, 615-247-8161.

Committee *Rules* (Ranking Member).

Group Ratings

	ADA	ACLU	COPE	CFA	LCV	LWV	NTU	NSI	COC	ACA	CSFC
1982	10	12	14	23	7	18	66	89	76	86	62
1981	5	—	14	0	0	—	67	—	100	85	69
1980	17	23	16	14	46	40	46	100	63	57	66

National Journal Ratings

	Economic		Foreign		Cultural	
1982	21%	(LIB)	12%	(LIB)	4%	(LIB)
	79%	(CONS)	84%	(CONS)	87%	(CONS)
1981	4%	(LIB)	0%	(LIB)	17%	(LIB)
	79%	(CONS)	100%	(CONS)	83%	(CONS)

Key Votes

1) Reagan 81 Budget	FOR	5) Incr SS Rtmt Age	FOR	9) Poor Pay Food Stamps	FOR
2) Reagan 81 Tax Cut	FOR	6) Saudi AWACS Sale	FOR	10) Ban Crt Busing Order	FOR
3) Bal Budget Amend	FOR	7) $ for MX Missile	FOR	11) Auto Local Content	AGN
4) Gas & Road Tax	—	8) Nerve Gas Prod	FOR	12) Nuclear Arms Freeze	AGN

Election Results

1982 general	James H. (Jimmy) Quillen (R)	89,497	(74%)	($95,427)
	Jessie J. Cable (D)	27,580	(23%)	($0)
1982 primary	James H. (Jimmy) Quillen (R)	54,451	(100%)	
1980 general	James H. (Jimmy) Quillen (R)	130,296	(86%)	($146,822)
	John Curtis (I)	20,816	(14%)	

Campaign Contributions and Expenditures

1981-82		*Direct Cont. 81-82*			*PACS brkdwn*		
Receipts	$193,435	Indiv	$25,019	Agr	$10,350	Ideo	$10,000
Expend.	$95,427	Party	$14,924	Bus	$84,100	Lbr	$9,250
Unspent	$113,105	PACS	$131,290	Hlth	$11,750	Prof	$3,150
		Cand	$664				

SECOND DISTRICT

You could hardly name a more improbable place for a world's fair than Knoxville, Tennessee. Yet, through the efforts of promoters including banker-politician Jake Butcher and Mayor Randy Tyree, Knoxville was host to a World's Fair in 1982. It was a financially successful enterprise which brought favorable attention to this industrial city in the hills of eastern Tennessee which is the headquarters of the Tennessee Valley Authority and the home of the University of Tennessee. Yet while the fair was, against expectations, a success, it proved a disaster for its promoters: it evidently strained Butcher's financial resources and led to the collapse of his bank in Knoxville in 1983, and Tyree was defeated 60%–40%, and won only 22% of the vote in Knox County, in his race for governor in 1982.

Knoxville has come a long way since John Gunther called it "the ugliest city I ever saw in America." If it is not more beautiful, it is at least much more prosperous than when Gunther saw it in the 1940s; it has higher wages and a better standard of living. People here no longer work six days a week and slave over housework; they have plenty of leisure time to enjoy the lakes TVA dams have created in the mountains or even, if they want to brave the crowds, the Great Smokies National Park.

One thing has not changed in Knoxville, however, and in the nearby counties that make up Tennessee's 2d congressional district, and that is their lopsided preference for the Republican Party. This has been the tradition here since the Civil War, and it is still honored with religious fervor. The 2d district was represented for years by Senator Howard Baker's father and, on his death, by his widow; Baker could have had it in 1964, but decided to run for the Senate instead. That left the job to then-Knoxville Mayor John Duncan. He won by a comfortable margin in that Democratic year and has represented the district ever since.

Duncan does not make much noise around the Capitol. He blends quietly into the ranks of old-style conservative Republicans, the ones for whom "conservative" means not rocking the boat rather than making radical changes. He is the second ranking Republican on the House Ways and Means Committee, but in no way overshadows ranking member Barber Conable. He is also ranking member on the Select Revenue Measures Subcommittee, which considers all sorts of special tax laws. His legislative output seems limited to technical matters, perfecting sloppy pieces of legislation and preventing unintended application of new laws.

The People   Pop. 1980: 510,197, up 17.3% 1970–80; voting age pop. 375,709; 6% Black, 1% Span. orig. 30% housing units rented. Median owner $37,000; renter $152. Households: 75% family, 39% with children, 63% married couples.

Presidential Vote

1980	Reagan (R)	106,979	(58%)
	Carter (D)	71,287	(39%)
	Anderson (I)	6,026	(3%)

Rep. John J. Duncan (R) Elected 1964; b. Mar. 24, 1919, Scott Cnty.; home, Knoxville; Presbyterian.

Career Army, WWII; Asst. Atty. Gen. of TN, 1947–56; Knoxville Law Dir., 1956–59; Pres., Knoxville Pro Baseball Club, 1956–59; Mayor of Knoxville, 1959–64.

Offices 2458 RHOB, 202-225-5435. Also 318 P. O. Bldg., Knoxville 37902, 615-546-5686.

Committees *Ways and Means* (2d). Subcommittees: Health; Oversight; Select Revenue Measures. *Joint Committee on Taxation* (2d).

Group Ratings

	ADA	ACLU	COPE	CFA	LCV	LWV	NTU	NSI	COC	ACA	CSFC
1982	10	25	18	23	29	36	56	100	73	74	57
1981	5	—	17	23	0	—	54	—	94	64	65
1980	17	20	16	7	35	40	41	100	68	67	67

National Journal Ratings

	Economic		Foreign		Cultural	
1982	23%	(LIB)	16%	(LIB)	13%	(LIB)
	77%	(CONS)	82%	(CONS)	86%	(CONS)
1981	22%	(LIB)	29%	(LIB)	25%	(LIB)
	77%	(CONS)	71%	(CONS)	75%	(CONS)

Key Votes

1) Reagan 81 Budget	FOR	5) Incr SS Rtmt Age	FOR	9) Poor Pay Food Stamps	FOR
2) Reagan 81 Tax Cut	FOR	6) Saudi AWACS Sale	AGN	10) Ban Crt Busing Order	—
3) Bal Budget Amend	FOR	7) $ for MX Missile	FOR	11) Auto Local Content	AGN
4) Gas & Road Tax	AGN	8) Nerve Gas Prod	FOR	12) Nuclear Arms Freeze	AGN

Election Results

1982 general	John J. Duncan (R)	109,045	(100%)	($131,658)
1982 primary	John J. Duncan (R)	44,456	(100%)	
1980 general	John J. Duncan (R)	147,947	(76%)	($109,305)
	David H. Dunnaway (D)	46,578	(24%)	($38,018)

Campaign Contributions and Expenditures

1981-82		Direct Cont. 81-82		PACS brkdwn			
Receipts	$202,728	Indiv	$33,329	Agr	$5,750	Ideo	$5,750
Expend.	$131,658	Party	$14,154	Bus	$75,800	Lbr	$1,500
Unspent	$172,884	PACS	$115,020	Hlth	$25,600	Prof	$1,600
		Cand	$7,629				

THIRD DISTRICT

The 3d congressional district of Tennessee includes two significant urban areas plus several rural counties. The larger of the urban areas, with half the district's population is Chattanooga. Set where the Tennessee River cuts through an Appalachian chain, leaving stark cliffs overlooking the river, Chattanooga was the site of several Civil War battles (Lookout Mountain, Chickamauga), though it was then only a village. It is one of those southern cities, like Birmingham and Atlanta, which grew into an industrial city during the New South years after the Civil War. Chattanooga does not seem to have a political preference as deeply rooted in Civil War history as the rest of Tennessee: this is a nominally Democratic town that often goes Republican in national and sometimes in state contests. It was marginal enough to provide a base for Bill Brock when he was first elected as a young congressman in 1962; it is adaptable enough to provide a base now for the Democrat who represents the district, Marilyn Lloyd.

The other urban area here accounts for much of Lloyd's workload. This is Oak Ridge, the town the government built from scratch in World War II to be one of its centers for nuclear power research. Set in the east Tennessee hills above Knoxville and north of Chattanooga, it has a population heavy with scientists who are married to women with advanced degrees; it does not always fit in politically with the surrounding area. Some atomic scientists are known for their opposition to nuclear weapons, but Oak Ridge is pretty enthusiastic about nuclear power; here is where many of the plans are made, and enthusiasm generated, for the Clinch River breeder reactor scheduled to be built in east Tennessee. Lloyd, as a member of the Science and Technology Committee, and chairwoman of the Energy Research and Production Subcommittee, has as her job every year the defense of the breeder reactor against its critics, who include environmentalist opponents of nuclear power and fiscal conservatives who argue that the project will never pay off. She has been very much on the defensive and the House voted 217–196 to kill the Clinch River breeder reactor in 1982; it was saved only through the efforts of Senator Howard Baker and a 49–48 margin in the Senate. Voters may not immediately blame Lloyd, who has fought hard for Clinch River, but if she does not win, their wounded pride may lead them to react against her sooner or later.

The Clinch River breeder reactor is not all there is to representing this district. It is a TVA district, one with many dams; all these things require congressional tending. Lloyd, as a member of the Public Works Committee, is in a good position to do that. On other issues, she is not a Boll Weevil, but not much of a liberal either; she generally goes along with the leadership, but is quite cautious on cultural and foreign issues.

Lloyd won this district in 1974 after her husband, the Democratic nominee, was killed in a plane crash in August; she was given the nomination, and defeated a weak Republican incumbent in November. She has held the district since, by comfortable margins. She remarried later and became known politically as Marilyn Lloyd Bouquard; now that marriage has ended, and she prefers to be known as Marilyn Lloyd again.

The People   Pop. 1980: 516,692, up 17.1% 1970–80; voting age pop. 370,457; 11% Black, 1% Span. orig. 29% housing units rented. Median owner $35,400; renter $149. Households: 78% family, 42% with children, 64% married couples.

Presidential Vote

1980	Reagan (R)	101,094	(56%)
	Carter (D)	74,677	(41%)
	Other	4,202	(2%)

Rep. Marilyn Lloyd (D) Elected 1974; b. Jan. 3, 1929, Ft. Smith, AR; home, Chattanooga; Shorter Col., 1967–70; Churches of Christ.

Career Co-owner and Mgr., WTTI Radio, Dalton, GA; Family agriculture flight service business.

Offices 2334 RHOB, 202-225-3271. Also 230 P. O. Bldg., Chattanooga 37401, 615-483-8611.

Committees *Armed Services* (22d). Subcommittees: Procurement and Military Nuclear Systems; Seapower and Strategic and Critical Materials. *Science and Technology* (7th). Subcommittees: Energy Development and Applications; Energy Research and Production (Chairwoman). *Select Committee on Aging* (10th). Subcommittee: Health and Long-Term Care.

Group Ratings

	ADA	ACLU	COPE	CFA	LCV	LWV	NTU	NSI	COC	ACA	CSFC
1982	25	37	57	46	34	55	31	100	52	50	48
1981	30	—	56	57	22	—	26	—	37	50	54
1980	22	30	53	29	22	40	40	90	72	54	54

National Journal Ratings

	Economic		Foreign		Cultural	
1982	48%	(LIB)	40%	(LIB)	4%	(LIB)
	51%	(CONS)	60%	(CONS)	87%	(CONS)
1981	53%	(LIB)	18%	(LIB)	47%	(LIB)
	46%	(CONS)	73%	(CONS)	53%	(CONS)

Key Votes

1) Reagan 81 Budget	AGN	5) Incr SS Rtmt Age	FOR
2) Reagan 81 Tax Cut	FOR	6) Saudi AWACS Sale	AGN
3) Bal Budget Amend	FOR	7) $ for MX Missile	AGN
4) Gas & Road Tax	AGN	8) Nerve Gas Prod	FOR

9) Poor Pay Food Stamps	AGN
10) Ban Crt Busing Order	FOR
11) Auto Local Content	AGN
12) Nuclear Arms Freeze	—

Election Results

1982 general	Marilyn Lloyd (D)	84,967	(62%)	($226,661)
	Glen Byers (R)	49,885	(36%)	($75,384)
1982 primary	Marilyn Lloyd Bouquard (D)	48,002	(82%)	
	Stephen L. Roberts (D)	10,437	(18%)	($20,821)
1980 general	Marilyn Lloyd Bouquard (D)	117,355	(61%)	($159,440)
	Glen Byers (R)	74,761	(39%)	($43,236)

Campaign Contributions and Expenditures

1981-82		Direct Cont. 81-82		PACS brkdwn			
Receipts	$221,313	Indiv	$109,807	Agr	$5,750	Ideo	$2,000
Expend.	$226,661	Party	$500	Bus	$52,125	Lbr	$17,400
Unspent	$3,354	PACS	$88,245	Hlth	$6,700	Prof	$2,950
		Cand	$15,000				

FOURTH DISTRICT

The 4th congressional district of Tennessee is a district newly created after the 1980 Census, the first new district entirely in rural Tennessee in many years. Its lines were drawn by a Democratic legislature, and it was intended to be a Democratic district, although it went for Ronald Reagan over Jimmy Carter narrowly in 1980. It did end up Democratic in 1982, and by a large margin, but only after a fiercely fought campaign between two young members of politically prominent families.

Geographically, the district is really a monstrosity. It extends from Virginia almost all the way to Mississippi; more than 250 miles from one end to the other, yet the district is seldom more than 20 miles wide. It can be divided into two almost equal parts topographically and politically, at the same point. The eastern counties are part of the Appalachian chain; successive ridges go up and down the state, from northeast to southwest, like corduroy. Some of this area is heavily Republican, the result of Civil War allegiance to the Union, and in the rest Republican sentiment is strong enough that each of these counties went for Ronald Reagan in 1980. After the last ridge in the west, the mountains give way to the Cumberland Plateau, a hilly but far from mountainous area that has been the home of small farmers since Andrew Jackson's day. This area is heavily Democratic: all the counties but one here went for Jimmy Carter in 1980. It should be added that this area, though pro-Confederate, never had large numbers of slaves and has few black residents today. These are white Democrats here, and ones which stayed pretty faithful to their party in years when white Democrats elsewhere in the South were becoming Republicans.

The two competitors in this race were Jim Cooper, son of former (1939–45) Governor Prentice Cooper, and Cissy Baker, daughter of Senator Howard Baker. Baker got most of the publicity, but Cooper ended up with almost two-thirds of the votes. In retrospect, Baker's campaign was ill-advised: this is a Democratic district, which her father carried by only 14,000 votes in 1978. It contains the Baker family's home county, but Cissy Baker was raised in Washington, went to school and held jobs there, and worked for Ted Turner's Cable News Network there before returning to Tennessee specifically to run for Congress. She tried to assert her roots here by spending nights in every county in the district, but evidently it didn't take. Baker raised huge sums of money—more than $1.2 million by November—but she was still not able to do particularly well at the polls. She had two Republican primary opponents, from opposite ends of the district, and won with only 55% of the vote. In the general election, she got 34% and carried only one county, and even lost the Baker family's usually Republican home county. It must have been a disheartening loss for her and her family.

And an exhilarating victory for Cooper. While Baker was under attack in the primary, Cooper was easily beating a former opponent. While Baker was attacked as an out-of-stater, Cooper was able to parry such attacks on him easily by pointing out that he had been practicing law in Nashville, although admittedly he went to secondary schools and university elsewhere (including two years at Oxford as a Rhodes Scholar). While Baker was peppered with questions about whether she was accepting help from her father (why shouldn't she?), Cooper was coolly amassing a campaign treasury of nearly $900,000 himself.

Cooper's large margin is testimony to his political competence. He entered the House as its youngest member, and one with a bright political future. His politics are probably not so close to those of national Democrats as is his neighbor, Albert Gore, Jr.; but Cooper is no Boll Weevil either. He is a member of the Banking and Small Business Committees—moderately useful assignments in this district; he will have time to switch later if he wants to. After a campaign in which over $2 million was spent, the 4th district will probably see little politicking in 1984; Cooper is likely to win reelection without serious competition.

The People   Pop. 1980: 510,732, up 22.2% 1970–80; voting age pop. 359,160; 4% Black, 1% Span. orig. 22% housing units rented. Median owner $29,000; renter $109. Households: 81% family, 45% with children, 70% married couples.

Presidential Vote

1980	Reagan (R)	81,664	(50%)
	Carter (D)	80,216	(49%)
	Anderson (I)	2,566	(2%)

Rep. Jim Cooper (D) Elected 1982; b. June 19, 1954, Nashville; home, Shelbyville; U. of NC, B.A. 1975, Rhodes Scholar, Oxford U., B.A., M.A. 1977, Harvard Law School, J.D. 1980; Episcopal.

Career Practicing atty., 1980–81.

Offices 425 CHOB, 202-225-6831. Also 116 Depot St., P.O. Box 725, Shelbyville 37160, 615-684-1114; City Hall, 7 S. High St., Winchester 37398, 615-967-4150.

Committees *Banking, Finance and Urban Affairs* (25th). Subcommittees: Domestic Monetary Policy; Economic Stabilization; Financial Institutions Supervision, Regulation and Insurance; Housing and Community Development; International Trade, Investment and Monetary Policy. *Small Business* (23d). Subcommittees: General Oversight and the Economy.

Group Ratings and Key Votes: Newly Elected

Election Results

1982 general	Jim Cooper (D)	93,453	(66%)	($905,474)
	Cynthia (Cissy) Baker (R)	47,865	(34%)	($1,225,458)
1982 primary	Jim Cooper (D)	52,682	(69%)	
	Buddy Perry (D)	24,185	(31%)	($206,261)
1980 general	Newly created district			

Campaign Contributions and Expenditures

1981-82		Direct Cont. 81-82		PACS brkdwn			
Receipts	$905,522	Indiv	$180,357	Agr	$2,500	Ideo	$5,750
Expend.	$905,474	Party	$5,346	Bus	$12,240	Lbr	$54,600
Unspent	$48	PACS	$81,397	Hlth	$500	Prof	$500
		Cand	$616,307				

Indirect Party Expend: $149   *Non-Cand Loans*: $18,906

FIFTH DISTRICT

Nashville is Tennessee's capital and second largest city; after its consolidation with surrounding Davidson County in the 1960s, it reached the impressive population of 450,000. Because of its location near the center of the state, Nashville is in many ways—especially politically— more important to Tennessee than its larger rival, Memphis. The two Nashville newspapers reflect neatly the state's two-party politics: the *Banner* is so resolutely Republican that when it withdrew its endorsement of Senate candidate Robin Beard in 1982 it was assumed the race was over, and the *Tennesseean* is determinedly Democratic. Nashville is also a center of businesses like printing and insurance. But what sets the tone here are its cultural influences. You could make the case that Nashville is the center of the Bible Belt; it is the nation's leader in Bible and religious publishing. It has its own version of the Parthenon (featured in Robert Altman's movie *Nashville*), Vanderbilt University, major black institutions like Fisk University and Meharry Medical College, and several religious schools. And of course Nashville is the national center of country music. That music has its roots in the religious folk songs brought over the mountains and, like them, it speaks directly to the most important concerns of ordinary people. It is also a hugely successful business. Nashville is the home of the Grand Ole Opry and of some of the nation's technically most sophisticated recording studios.

Nashville was also the home of Andrew Jackson, the first president to call himself a Democrat and the founder of what has been called continuously since the Democratic Party. Nashville's favorite shrine is still the Hermitage, Jackson's mansion. Old Hickory moved to Nashville from the Carolinas when Tennessee was still very much the frontier. He made a small fortune, won election to the House when George Washington was still president, and was elected to the Senate, where he served briefly just after he turned 30. It was only after this youthful political career, and after some financial setbacks, that Jackson made his national reputation as a merciless Indian fighter, the scourge of the British at the Battle of New Orleans, and the common man's candidate for president. Jackson was a Democrat, and Nashville has remained a Democratic city in most of the years since; it dallied with the Whig Party in the 1850s but, occupied by Union troops, it became Democratic again in the 1860s and has remained that way ever since.

The 5th congressional district of Tennessee includes all of Nashville and Davidson County and one rural and partly suburban county to the north. The 5th is usually a reliable Democratic district in statewide elections, and it always elects Democrats to Congress. They are, moreover, usually pretty liberal Democrats, who vote with most of their copartisans from the North on most issues. Racial divisions have played less of a part in voting here than in most southern cities; blacks are 22% of the population, but even in the 1960s Nashville's Congressman (and now Mayor) Richard Fulton voted for civil rights laws and had no trouble winning votes from Nashville whites.

The current congressman from Nashville is Bill Boner, who first won the seat by a fluke. In 1976 he was the only primary opponent of incumbent Clifford Allen, who died between the filing deadline and the primary. Boner had Independent as well as Republican opposition in the general election, and won with just 51%. But he has solidified his position since. His record is not quite as liberal on either economic or cultural issues as were Fulton's or Allen's, but they are enough so to protect him from primary opposition to the left; he was not a Boll Weevil and has a strong labor voting record. In 1983 Boner won a seat on the Appropriations Committee and on its Energy and Water Development and HUD–Independent Agencies Subcommittees.

The People Pop. 1980: 514,832, up 7.9% 1970–80; voting age pop. 384,057; 20% Black, 1% Span. orig. 39% housing units rented. Median owner $44,300; renter $193. Households: 71% family, 37% with children, 56% married couples.

Presidential Vote

1980	Reagan (R)	69,332	(37%)
	Carter (D)	111,122	(60%)
	Anderson (I)	4,961	(3%)

Rep. William Hill (Bill) Boner (D) Elected 1978; b. Feb. 14, 1945, Nashville; home, Nashville; Middle TN St. U., B.S. 1967, Peabody Col., M.A. 1969, YMCA Night Law Sch., Nashville, J.D. 1978; Methodist.

Career College basketball coach, 1969–71; TN House of Reps., 1970–72, 1974–76; Sr. Staff Asst., Nashville Mayor's Ofc., 1971–72; Asst. V.P. and Dir. of Pub. Rel., 1st Amer. Natl. Bank, Nashville; Law Clerk, 1976–77; TN Senate, 1976–78.

Offices 107 CHOB, 202-225-4311. Also 552 U.S. Courthouse, 801 Broadway, Nashville 37203, 615-251-5296.

Committees Appropriations (33d). Subcommittees: Energy and Water Development; HUD-Independent Agencies. *Select Committee on Aging* (27th). Subcommittee: Housing and Consumer Interests.

Group Ratings

	ADA	ACLU	COPE	CFA	LCV	LWV	NTU	NSI	COC	ACA	CSFC
1982	40	42	81	62	56	50	27	90	40	32	42
1981	35	—	81	64	57	—	33	—	28	39	51
1980	39	27	79	43	37	33	29	50	73	38	46

National Journal Ratings

	Economic		Foreign		Cultural	
1982	58%	(LIB)	49%	(LIB)	52%	(LIB)
	42%	(CONS)	51%	(CONS)	48%	(CONS)
1981	58%	(LIB)	43%	(LIB)	53%	(LIB)
	42%	(CONS)	56%	(CONS)	47%	(CONS)

Key Votes

1) Reagan 81 Budget	AGN	5) Incr SS Rtmt Age	AGN	9) Poor Pay Food Stamps	AGN
2) Reagan 81 Tax Cut	FOR	6) Saudi AWACS Sale	AGN	10) Ban Crt Busing Order	FOR
3) Bal Budget Amend	FOR	7) $ for MX Missile	AGN	11) Auto Local Content	FOR
4) Gas & Road Tax	—	8) Nerve Gas Prod	FOR	12) Nuclear Arms Freeze	FOR

Election Results

1982 general	William Hill (Bill) Boner (D)	109,282	(80%)	($249,238)
	Laurel Steinhice (R)	27,061	(20%)	($0)
1982 primary	William Hill (Bill) Boner (D)	63,293	(88%)	
	Nick Cupido (D)	8,410	(12%)	
1980 general	William Hill (Bill) Boner (D)	118,506	(65%)	($237,908)
	Mike Adams (R)	62,746	(35%)	($208,944)

Campaign Contributions and Expenditures

1981-82		Direct Cont. 81-82		PACS brkdwn			
Receipts	$324,274	Indiv	$185,823	Agr	$6,150	Ideo	$400
Expend.	$249,238	Party	$200	Bus	$44,945	Lbr	$46,000
Unspent	$120,733	PACS	$106,711	Hlth	$6,400	Prof	$400

SIXTH DISTRICT

The 6th congressional district of Tennessee is part of the Cumberland Plateau, the hilly and fertile land just west of the Appalachian chains, inside the U formed by the Tennessee River as it begins in the mountains, flows through northern Alabama, and then goes back up north again through Tennessee to meet the Ohio River near Paducah, Kentucky. Middle Tennessee, as this area is called, is one of the heartlands of the Democratic Party. It was the political home base of Andrew Jackson and supported him nearly unanimously; during the Civil War, though it had precious few slaves, it resented the invading Union armies, and has voted solidly Democratic ever since. It is neither particularly rich nor particularly poor; its farmers suffered during the Depression and have seen their land values rise somewhat as people fanned out in the 1970s from Nashville and from the other, much smaller cities in this region, to live in the small towns and the countryside so many of their parents had felt forced to leave. Through all this, their Democratic allegiance has remained, almost magically, intact. In the 17 counties here east and south of Nashville that make up Tennessee's 6th congressional district, Jimmy Carter got 65% of the vote in 1976 and won again easily in 1980. Even George McGovern got 33% in 1972, and in a district where only 7% of the people are black. The counties that make up the current 6th district have elected congressmen who have become national leaders of the Democratic Party: James K. Polk (1825–39), speaker of the House and later president; Cordell Hull (1907–21, 1923–31), later senator and secretary of state; Albert Gore (1939–53), later senator.

The district's current congressman, Albert Gore, Jr., promises to continue in the same tradition. A Harvard graduate and Vietnam veteran, Gore returned to Tennessee and made a living there for five years before Joe Evins, who succeeded his father in the House, retired. Gore ran for the seat and won rather easily. It should not be assumed that this happened automatically. Voters in the dusty courthouse towns of middle Tennessee and even in the shopping center crossroads that are springing up in the countryside 50 miles from Nashville expect to meet their political candidates, and sometimes the offspring of famous fathers do not measure up (while Gore in 1976 and Jim Cooper in 1982 won House seats, Cissy Baker and Bob Clement both lost in the latter year). Gore has held onto the seat easily ever since and has made such a mark in the House that when he indicated an interest in running for the Senate seat being vacated by Howard Baker in 1984, other notable politicians lost interest in the seat. The toughest potential competitor, Republican Governor Lamar Alexander, declared in 1983 that he would not be a candidate; the strongest potential primary opposition is Baker's 1978 opponent Jane Eskind.

Gore has a seat on the Energy and Commerce Committee—the most sought-after committee assignment in the early 1980s, because it has jurisdiction over most federal regulatory laws. He is not a subcommittee chairman, but has nonetheless made important contributions on several issues. On the Science and Technology Committee he does chair a subcommittee, Investigations and Oversight. He has shown the ability to resist cheap shots and to probe thoughtfully into difficult policy areas. And in areas not covered by his committees he has also made a contribution. He studied arms control issues intensively for months, and came forward with a proposal—to de-MIRV missiles, that is, remove their multiple warheads—which was echoed by none less than Henry Kissinger.

So in early 1983 Gore, at age 35, seems to have all the qualifications to be a senator, and an important leader for the national Democratic Party too. Like his father he is a Democrat in line with his national party, but independent enough in temperament not to be a lockstep follower. He seems to lack the inclination his father had in his last Senate term to respond to pressure by further irritating his constituents. No one has thought much about which members of Gore's political generation will be serious presidential candidates, but he has shown enough intellect, temperament, and political skill already to suggest that he could, if he continues to grow, end up on the short list.

Gore's successor as 6th district congressman will be determined in the Democratic primary. There is no single population center in this district, and Tennessee does not have a runoff primary. This means that there are likely to be many candidates running, on the theory that even a small local base could produce a large enough percentage to win, and a lifetime congressional seat.

The People Pop. 1980: 511,805, up 37.0% 1970–80; voting age pop. 362,322; 7% Black, 1% Span. orig. 23% housing units rented. Median owner $40,400; renter $151. Households: 81% family, 46% with children, 70% married couples.

Presidential Vote

1980	Reagan (R)	72,526	(43%)
	Carter (D)	92,485	(55%)
	Anderson (I)	3,209	(2%)

Rep. Albert Gore, Jr. (D) Elected 1976; b. Mar. 31, 1948, Washington, DC; home, Carthage; Harvard U., B.A. 1969, Vanderbilt U.; Baptist.

Career Army, Vietnam; Homebuilding and subdivision business operator, 1971–76.

Offices 1131 LHOB, 202-225-4231. Also U.S. Courthouse, Carthage 37030, 615-735-0173.

Committees *Energy and Commerce* (11th). Subcommittees: Energy Conservation and Power; Oversight and Investigations; Telecommunications, Consumer Protection, and Finance. *Science and Technology* (10th). Subcommittees: Investigations and Oversight (Chairman); Transportation, Aviation and Materials. *Permanent Select Committee on Intelligence* (7th). Subcommittee: Oversight and Evaluation.

Group Ratings

	ADA	ACLU	COPE	CFA	LCV	LWV	NTU	NSI	COC	ACA	CSFC
1982	70	67	81	100	71	83	3	50	18	26	30
1981	70	—	79	64	57	—	3	—	11	14	34
1980	50	47	79	71	35	40	16	40	67	29	36

National Journal Ratings

	Economic		Foreign		Cultural	
1982	66%	(LIB)	60%	(LIB)	67%	(LIB)
	34%	(CONS)	40%	(CONS)	32%	(CONS)
1981	76%	(LIB)	65%	(LIB)	70%	(LIB)
	23%	(CONS)	35%	(CONS)	30%	(CONS)

Key Votes

1) Reagan 81 Budget	AGN	5) Incr SS Rtmt Age	AGN	9) Poor Pay Food Stamps	AGN
2) Reagan 81 Tax Cut	AGN	6) Saudi AWACS Sale	AGN	10) Ban Crt Busing Order	AGN
3) Bal Budget Amend	AGN	7) $ for MX Missile	AGN	11) Auto Local Content	AGN
4) Gas & Road Tax	—	8) Nerve Gas Prod	FOR	12) Nuclear Arms Freeze	FOR

Election Results

1982 general	Albert Gore, Jr. (D)	104,094	(100%)	($19,416)
1982 primary	Albert Gore, Jr. (D)	74,303	(100%)	
1980 general	Albert Gore, Jr. (D)	137,612	(79%)	($74,422)
	James Beau Seigneur (R)	35,954	(21%)	($13,870)

Campaign Contributions and Expenditures

1981-82		Direct Cont. 81-82				PACS brkdwn		
Receipts	$32,846	Indiv	$3,210	Agr	$—		Ideo	$3,000
Expend.	$19,416	Party	$50	Bus	$5,800		Lbr	$4,250
Unspent	$64,050	PACS	$16,874	Hlth	$1,500		Prof	$1,600
		Cand	$350					

SEVENTH DISTRICT

The 7th congressional district of Tennessee stretches from the heart of middle Tennessee to the heart of west Tennessee, from the city limits of Nashville to inside the city limits of Memphis. Politically, it contains several distinct areas. The counties nearest Nashville and along the lower Tennessee River are part of the heavily Democratic bloc which has existed in this part of the state almost uninterrupted since the time of Andrew Jackson. In the southern part of the district, just across the Tennessee River, are several rural counties which have been mostly Republican since the Civil War. Farther west are two counties just north of Mississippi with black majorities—just about the only heavily black rural part of Tennessee. And then the district includes 171,000 people in Memphis's Shelby County, 92% of them white, the large majority of them affluent.

In political analysis these two sections of the district are usually collapsed into two: the rural counties, with two-thirds of the population, generally preferring country-based Democratic candidates; Shelby County, with one-third of the population, strongly preferring conservative Republicans. Voting here in the Memphis area is heavily polarized by race: blacks are almost unanimously Democratic; whites, especially affluent whites, go Republican by percentages nearly as high. Despite the relative populations, the Shelby County portion has prevailed in every election here since 1972 (the district's precise boundaries, but not its basic character, were changed in 1982). For 10 years it elected Robin Beard, a pugnacious Republican who ran for the Senate against James Sasser in 1982.

The contest to succeed him was hard fought. Bob Clement, son of former Governor Frank Clement and former state public service commissioner himself, was the favorite. But he had significant opposition and lost three counties, including Shelby, to state legislator Harold Byrd in the primary. In the general election he faced Don Sundquist, a former aide to Senator Howard Baker, who could afford a serious television campaign and banked on a big Shelby County margin. It came through. Clement carried the rural counties with 65% of the vote. But Sundquist got 75% in Shelby County, and carried the district by 1,476 votes. That is a margin small enough to almost guarantee him significant opposition in 1984; Harold Byrd, for one, is said to be interested in running.

Sundquist is a member of the Public Works and Veterans' Affairs Committee. With his background as a Baker Republican, he is expected to follow the Republican congressional leadership faithfully on most issues.

The People Pop. 1980: 503,611, up 47.4% 1970–80; voting age pop. 351,201; 11% Black, 1% Span. orig., 1% Asian orig. 24% housing units rented. Median owner $42,200; renter $184. Households: 81% family, 47% with children, 70% married couples.

Presidential Vote

1980	Reagan (R)	104,480	(57%)
	Carter (D)	75,945	(41%)
	Other	3,876	(2%)

Rep. Don Sundquist (R) Elected 1982; b. Mar. 15, 1936, Moline, IL; home, Memphis; Augustana Col., B.A. 1957; Lutheran.

Career USN, 1957–59; Jostins Inc., 1961–72; Partner, Graphic Sales of Amer., 1972, Pres., 1973–82.

Offices 515 CHOB, 202-225-2811. Also 5905 Shelby Oaks Dr., Su. 112, Memphis 38134, 901-382-5811.

Committees *Public Works and Transportation* (16th). Subcommittees: Economic Development; Investigations and Oversight. *Veterans' Affairs* (10th). Subcommittees: Housing and Memorial Affairs; Oversight and Investigations.

Group Ratings and Key Votes: Newly Elected

Election Results

1982 general	Don Sundquist (R)	73,835	(50%)	($508,451)
	Robert N. Clement (D)	72,359	(50%)	($373,530)
1982 primary	Don Sundquist (R)	21,846	(100%)	
1980 general	Robin L. Beard, Jr. (R)	127,945	(100%)	($146,038)

Campaign Contributions and Expenditures

1981-82		Direct Cont. 81-82		PACS brkdwn			
Receipts	$515,688	Indiv	$227,074	Agr	$3,250	Ideo	$23,100
Expend.	$508,451	Party	$21,000	Bus	$95,912	Lbr	$—
Unspent	$7,237	PACS	$156,441	Hlth	$7,540	Prof	$250
		Cand	$111,509				

Indirect Party Expend: $35,033

EIGHTH DISTRICT

The 8th congressional district of Tennessee takes in the northwestern part of the state. The district extends from the TVA lakes of the Tennessee and Cumberland Rivers at the Kentucky state line to the northern part of the city of Memphis. Physically and politically the 8th resembles the flat lands of eastern Arkansas and the Mississippi Delta. Rivers flow lazily through the flat land toward the Mississippi; cotton and, increasingly, soybeans are the main crops; many of the blacks who worked these fields before mechanization have long since left, but enough remain to give this district the highest black percentage of any rural district in Tennessee. Outside of Memphis and Shelby County, the district's largest city is Jackson, with a population of 49,000.

Most of the counties here are traditionally Democratic, but in the era of the civil rights revolution they switched parties regularly, and in the late 1960s and early 1970s rural west Tennessee was the critical part of the state in close elections. Now they seem to have stabilized again, in line with historic patterns: there is one Republican Civil War county here, and Jackson sometimes goes Republican, but the other counties remain Democratic, even when the Democrats, as in the 1982 gubernatorial race, are losing big. Shelby County is another matter. The 8th includes the northern fringes of Memphis and its suburbs, a not particularly elite or affluent area where 22% of the residents are black. But partisan preferences in the Memphis area are so polarized on racial lines that this area goes Republican in most national and statewide elections.

This is a district that has had only one substantial general election contest in the last 20 years. That was in 1969, in a special election after the incumbent died. This corner of Tennessee suddenly became the proving ground for various southern strategies. Richard Nixon's Republicans campaigned heavily for their candidate, and George Wallace came in and supported an American Party nominee. But the winner, with 51% of the vote, was Democrat Ed Jones. A former state agriculture commissioner, he did without national endorsements and ran as a folksy local Democrat.

In the House Jones is one of the most senior members of the Agriculture Committee. He chairs the subcommittee on Conservation, Credit, and Rural Development, which governs all sorts of programs. Most urban Americans have little idea of how many safety nets and assistance programs there are for farmers, and how many ways the federal government regulates farming and the food business. All this goes against the rhetoric of the early 1980s, which suggests that all these things should be left to free enterprise; and the initiative which is left to the individual farmer-entrepreneur goes against the impulse of political liberals toward some form of economic planning. Practical politicians like Ed Jones know, however, that there is something important to be said in favor of this hybrid system: it works. American agriculture is the most productive in the world, and, for all the problems farmers have, more Americans run their own businesses in agriculture than in all the other sectors of the economy together. Jones has proved a workmanlike and steady Agriculture Committee member, a man who understands the programs and fine-tunes them competently.

Jones has had only one significant electoral challenge in his years in the House, in the 1976 primary. The return to Democratic allegiance in west Tennessee makes his seat safer, and he shows no more sign of retiring, though he is past 70, than does Speaker Tip O'Neill, who is the same age.

The People   Pop. 1980: 504,957, up 12.2% 1970–80; voting age pop. 358,805; 18% Black, 1% Span. orig. 28% housing units rented. Median owner $30,400; renter $119. Households: 78% family, 43% with children, 65% married couples.

Presidential Vote

1980	Reagan (R)	79,874	(47%)
	Carter (D)	87,547	(52%)
	Anderson (I)	2,300	(1%)

Rep. Ed Jones (D) Elected Mar. 25, 1969; b. Apr. 20, 1912, Yorkville; home, Yorkville; U. of TN, B.S. 1934; Presbyterian.

Career Inspector, TN Dept. of Agric., 1934–41; Sprvsr., TN Dairy Products Assn., 1941–43; Agric. Rep., IL Central R.R., 1943–48, 1952–69; TN Commissioner of Agric., 1949–52.

Offices 108 CHOB, 202-225-4714. Also P.O. Box 27190, 3179 N. Watkins St., Memphis 38127, 901-358-4094.

Committees *Agriculture* (4th). Subcommittees: Conservation, Credit, and Rural Development (Chairman); Cotton, Rice, and Sugar; Livestock, Dairy, and Poultry. *House Administration* (4th). Subcommittees: Contracts and Printing; Services (Chairman). *Joint Committee on Printing* (3d).

Group Ratings

	ADA	ACLU	COPE	CFA	LCV	LWV	NTU	NSI	COC	ACA	CSFC
1982	30	42	60	62	53	50	44	100	50	25	40
1981	25	—	60	50	36	—	18	—	39	45	51
1980	22	23	63	29	17	22	32	50	63	45	47

National Journal Ratings

	Economic		Foreign		Cultural	
1982	54%	(LIB)	55%	(LIB)	59%	(LIB)
	46%	(CONS)	45%	(CONS)	41%	(CONS)
1981	55%	(LIB)	43%	(LIB)	48%	(LIB)
	44%	(CONS)	56%	(CONS)	52%	(CONS)

Key Votes

1) Reagan 81 Budget	AGN	5) Incr SS Rtmt Age	AGN
2) Reagan 81 Tax Cut	FOR	6) Saudi AWACS Sale	AGN
3) Bal Budget Amend	FOR	7) $ for MX Missile	AGN
4) Gas & Road Tax	—	8) Nerve Gas Prod	—

9) Poor Pay Food Stamps	AGN
10) Ban Crt Busing Order	FOR
11) Auto Local Content	FOR
12) Nuclear Arms Freeze	—

Election Results

1982 general	Ed Jones (D)	93,945	(75%)	($259,059)
	Bruce Benson (R)	31,527	(25%)	($36,727)
1982 primary	Ed Jones (D)	67,092	(68%)	
	Larry Bates (D)	31,904	(32%)	($106,810)
1980 general	Ed Jones (D)	133,606	(77%)	($76,919)
	Daniel H. Campbell (R)	39,227	(23%)	($0)

Campaign Contributions and Expenditures

1981-82		Direct Cont. 81-82		PACS brkdwn			
Receipts	$239,662	Indiv	$115,986	Agr	$52,700	Ideo	$500
Expend.	$259,059	Party	$800	Bus	$53,075	Lbr	$9,950
Unspent	$31,355	PACS	$119,725	Hlth	$2,750	Prof	$500

NINTH DISTRICT

Memphis, Tennessee's largest city, with more than 600,000 people, is set in the far southwestern corner of the state. Memphis is the major financial and commercial center of much of the lower Mississippi Valley; as such, it looks as much south to Mississippi and west to Arkansas as it does north and east to Tennessee. Memphis, like eastern Arkansas and the Delta of Mississippi, has always had a large black population. This was plantation and slave country before the Civil War, and for a century after that conflict Memphis remained a Democratic city. For more than 20 years, until Estes Kefauver destroyed its power in 1948, the political machine run by Ed Crump could deliver the Memphis vote *en bloc,* particularly in the Democratic primary, and Crump was the *de facto* political boss of the state. Even so, Memphis never seemed much interested in the rest of Tennessee; its economic ties went up and down the Mississippi, and those were what mattered.

West Tennessee's separateness is symbolized by its musical tradition as well. Beale Street, near downtown Memphis, gave birth to jazz in the 1920s; and jazz, in turn, came from the blues music which is the product of the lower Mississippi Valley, particularly the Delta. Memphis and New Orleans were the natural conduits of the Delta's music, as they were of its cotton, to the outside world. Elvis Presley, Memphis's later musical hero, was born in Mississippi and drew much of his inspiration from black music.

The racial patterns of the Delta also seemed replicated in Memphis. This city likes to think of itself as an all-American town, the place that gave us the first supermarket in the 1920s, the first Holiday Inn in the 1950s, and Federal Express in the 1970s. But it also was an obdurately segregationist city when other parts of Tennessee and the South were adapting to new patterns. Voting patterns in Memphis, even today, in both nonpartisan and partisan elections, are firmly polarized on racial lines. Forty-eight percent of Memphis's residents, and 42% of the residents of all of Shelby County, are black, and nearly all black voters support Democrats. The white majority, in contrast, almost exclusively supports Republicans. This is particularly true in the affluent suburban tracts east and south of downtown Memphis, but even in white working-class areas you typically will find large Republican majorities in elections.

The 9th congressional district of Tennessee consists of most of the city of Memphis, with 505,000 people, 57% of them black in 1980. The percentage will undoubtedly rise in the 1980s, as blacks move farther outward and whites move farther out in response. These facts make this a solidly Democratic district in all elections.

The current congressman, Harold Ford, first won this district a little ahead of schedule. It didn't quite have a black majority in 1974, but it was close enough that, with the votes of some anti-Watergate whites, he was able to beat a Republican incumbent and become the first black congressman from Tennessee. Ford is part of a politically prominent Memphis family: his older brother is a state legislator, and he has shown plenty of political savvy. He makes few concessions to Memphis-area whites, either in his personal style or his voting record, which is the most liberal in the Tennessee delegation. He has no trouble winning reelection.

Ford is a member of the Ways and Means Committee and in 1983 became chairman of the Public Assistance and Unemployment Compensation Subcommittee. This governs the rules of the basic welfare programs (which haven't been changed much lately; the real fight is over levels of funding, which is handled elsewhere) and the financing of the increasingly precarious unemployment compensation system. This assignment sounds as though it will give Ford a lot of opportunities to do things that will please his constituents; more likely, it means a lot of hard technical work if some of the problems these systems face are to be resolved.

The People   Pop. 1980: 505,592, dn. 9.4% 1970–80; voting age pop. 359,672; 51% Black, 1% Span. orig. 43% housing units rented. Median owner $32,300; renter $136. Households: 69% family, 38% with children, 46% married couples.

Presidential Vote

1980	Reagan (R)	69,769	(34%)
	Carter (D)	128,962	(63%)
	Anderson (I)	4,279	(2%)

Rep. Harold E. Ford (D) Elected 1974; b. May 20, 1945, Memphis; home, Memphis; TN St. U., B.S. 1967, John Gupten Col., L.F.D., L.E.D. 1969; Baptist.

Career Mortician, 1969–75; TN House of Reps., 1971–74.

Offices 2305 RHOB, 202-225-3265. Also 369 Fed. Bldg., Memphis 38103, 901-521-4131.

Committees *Ways and Means* (8th). Subcommittees: Health; Public Assistance and Unemployment Compensation (Chairman). *Select Committee on Aging* (8th). Subcommittee: Health and Long-Term Care.

Group Ratings

	ADA	ACLU	COPE	CFA	LCV	LWV	NTU	NSI	COC	ACA	CSFC
1982	80	87	91	69	80	75	24	0	30	12	25
1981	85	—	91	64	57	—	12	—	11	0	24
1980	83	83	89	64	58	75	17	11	60	19	25

National Journal Ratings

	Economic		Foreign		Cultural	
1982	85%	(LIB)	91%	(LIB)	76%	(LIB)
	14%	(CONS)	9%	(CONS)	24%	(CONS)
1981	87%	(LIB)	92%	(LIB)	94%	(LIB)
	12%	(CONS)	2%	(CONS)	6%	(CONS)

Key Votes

1) Reagan 81 Budget	AGN	5) Incr SS Rtmt Age	AGN	9) Poor Pay Food Stamps	AGN
2) Reagan 81 Tax Cut	AGN	6) Saudi AWACS Sale	AGN	10) Ban Crt Busing Order	AGN
3) Bal Budget Amend	AGN	7) $ for MX Missile	AGN	11) Auto Local Content	FOR
4) Gas & Road Tax	—	8) Nerve Gas Prod	AGN	12) Nuclear Arms Freeze	FOR

Election Results

1982 general	Harold E. Ford (D)	112,143	(72%)	($223,826)
	Joe Crawford (R)	40,812	(26%)	($0)
1982 primary	Harold E. Ford (D)	63,330	(84%)	
	Mark F. Flanagan (D)	11,733	(16%)	
1980 general	Harold E. Ford (D)	110,139	(100%)	($187,385)

Campaign Contributions and Expenditures

1981-82		Direct Cont. 81-82		PACS brkdwn			
Receipts	$233,514	Indiv	$104,109	Agr	$8,500	Ideo	$900
Expend.	$223,826	PACS	$123,195	Bus	$52,650	Lbr	$40,800
Unspent	$9,981			Hlth	$11,750	Prof	$1,450

TEXAS

Texas politics—the big victories of conservative Republicans in 1978 and 1980, the big Democratic sweep of 1982—can only be understood if you understand that in several ways Texas is like a developing country. It is, to be sure, economically advanced, but it is still in large measure unformed, its future not determined. Texas politics is an arena in which several visions of the future are contending furiously for people's allegiance. Texas is torn between faith in the free market and a desire for government safety nets, between the traditional culture of the rural South and the self-consciously modern culture of the rapidly growing cities, between Texas's traditional image of ethnic uniformity and its increasingly heterogeneous population.

These are not the problems, posed by economic contraction, that Ohio and Michigan face; they are the choices presented by rapid—unexpectedly rapid—economic growth. They are nonetheless agonizing. And they seem certain to split this state, which prides itself on its local patriotism, down the middle. There is, after all, quite a bit to fight for in Texas politics; here you are not just talking about how to apportion budget cuts and tax rises; you are talking about how to structure a new and affluent society. State and local governments' powers are limited, of course, and Texas can't hope to set the course for the federal government alone (though it has been known to try). But no one, least of all those involved in Texas's public life, doubts that Texas matters.

Like Mexico and Venezuela, Indonesia and Nigeria, Texas grew rapidly in the 1970s because of the rise in oil prices. That is apparent from the population figures (up from 11.2 million to 14.2 million in the 1970s, or almost as much in the 20-year period before 1970) and in economic terms (incomes in Texas for years were about 80% of the national level, but rose to 100% by 1980). But the mechanism in Texas was not quite the same as in these developing countries, and the drop in oil prices in the early 1980s seems not to be having anything like as disastrous effect here as it did there. Back in the 1930s and 1940s Texas benefited from geological dumb luck (it turned out to have lots of oil) and political clout (Sam Rayburn and others persuaded the Roosevelt administration to let Texas limit production and prop up prices). But by the time of the first oil shock in 1973, Texas was much more than a producing state; it was becoming the corporate and operational center of the oil industry for the entire world. Texas has literally thousands of specialized companies that can find oil in all kinds of places or produce custom oil bits or put out oil well fires or construct pipelines.

And Texas has other things besides the oil business. It is a great agricultural state; it has sophisticated financial and insurance companies; it has major petrochemical installations; it has high-tech companies led by Texas Instruments. It has excellent transportation facilities. It has a class and culture of risk-taking entrepreneurs who seem more venturesome and more aggressive than their counterparts in the Northeast or Midwest, and rivaled in the United States only by those of California.

It also has, as developing countries do, a very wide range of incomes and living standards. Texas's blacks, who are 12% of the population, tend to have low incomes; even lower are the incomes of the 21% whom the Census counted as Spanish origin. Almost all are Mexican-American, or simply Mexicans living here illegally or on a sojourn; Texas's rapid economic growth has attracted many Mexicans, and the existence of this large, low-wage, highly motivated labor force has in turn spurred certain kinds of economic growth that simply are not seen in uniformly high-wage economies like those in Massachusetts or Michigan. Texas has one of the lowest rates of unionization in the country, and is the only major state with a right to work law; there are, for all practical purposes, no unions to push up wages here. You can drive just a few minutes on the freeway from the wealthy west side of Houston, where house sales of $750,000 are not considered worthy of comment, and find neighborhoods of tiny, drafty frame houses which are little better than tarpaper shacks. One's natural reaction is to say that income should be distributed more evenly here, and a little of the wealth that Texas has produced should be allowed to trickle down to people in such obvious need. But they in turn are better off than they were when they were growing up in rural Mexico or east Texas, and overly generous welfare programs might simply attract too many immigrants, who would sop up the existing wealth and produce none of their own.

The men who ruled Texas politics for 40 years, known sometimes as the Tory Democrats, were unable to adapt to the new environment created by vast economic growth—even though they claimed credit, with some justice, for fostering much of that growth. Their basic philosophy was to have government sit tight and keep the lid on, and let the economy grow by itself, without regulation and interference. But to do that they felt they needed federal protection of Texas's oil industry, which for years was vulnerable to cheaper foreign competition; and they got that by staying Democratic, and letting Texas's senior Democratic congressmen play a major role in the national Democratic Party. So Speaker Sam Rayburn saw that there was always a pro-oil majority on the House Ways and Means Committee; Senate Majority Leader and President Lyndon Johnson always kept sight of Texas's interests. The mechanisms for keeping control of Texas elections were simple: huge amounts of money for the right candidates, and the open primary in which those who voted Republican in national elections could nonetheless help nominate Tory Democrats for state and congressional office. The incendiary approach of Texas liberals, their association with the national Democratic Party on issues like civil rights, and their inability to raise money made them easy to beat.

But the strength of the Tory Democrats faded as Texas changed from a rural to an urban state. High-income urban voters became solid Republicans. Blacks and Mexican-Americans supported liberals. And the Tories produced a series of weak candidates. The 1978 election signaled the change. Governor Dolph Briscoe, a conservative rancher, was beaten by Attorney General John Hill in the primary. Then Hill was beaten in the general election by Republican William Clements, the founder of an offshore drilling platform company, who spent $7 million of his own money on the campaign.

Clements's victory, and the almost identical reelection victory of Senator John Tower that year, symbolized the success of Texas's high-income electorate. Clements and Tower carried the west side of Houston, north Dallas, southwest Fort Worth, north San Antonio, and very little else—scattered Republican rural counties, the oil towns of Midland, Lubbock, Tyler, and Longview. But turnout in these affluent areas was extremely high, and so was esprit. These Texans, buoyed by the economic success of the 1970s, had the kind of confidence in the future that most affluent Americans had in the 1950s but lost in the next decade. There is no apology or guilt about wealth here, no notion that it is evil unless it is given away to foundations. The feeling is that it is the God-given reward for building productive businesses and creating a thriving economy where none existed before. So there is very little radical chic and not much noblesse oblige in Texas. People here, like the rich in developing countries, do not feel defensive because others are still poor; they have grown up in a society in which most people are poor, and they believe, probably rightly, that if you waited until everybody got affluent before you let the rich keep their money, there wouldn't be any affluence at all. It would be hard to find more solidly Republican neighborhoods than the burgeoning high-income neighborhoods in Texas's cities. The west Houston and north Dallas congressional districts have been among the top five Republican districts in the nation in recent presidential elections.

For a time it appeared that this small but influential and enthusiastic segment of the Texas electorate would carry all before it. It produced not one but two formidable presidential candidacies in 1980, even if John Connally never made it to Texas and George Bush finished a close second to Ronald Reagan in the state's presidential primary. It led the state in giving Ronald Reagan a thumping 55%–41% margin in a state that had gone Democratic in the close presidential elections of 1960, 1968, and 1976. It helped to persuade more ordinary Texans, in modest urban neighborhoods and in small towns and rural areas, to abandon the party of their ancestors and vote for the party that seemed to express Texas's values and Texas's hopes. But by 1982 the Republican elan had begun to fade. As it became apparent that Reaganomics was not producing instant recovery, and as even the economy of Texas seemed to sag, many affluent Texans must have lost faith in the cures which seemed so certain in the Carter years. You can see the enthusiasm factor in turnout. In 1978 and 1980 the affluent areas turned out much more heavily than the rest of the state, and turnout in black and Mexican areas was extremely low. In 1982 turnout in affluent areas was not much above the state average, and turnout in black and Mexican areas was much higher than before. The result was that Clements was beaten, though by a Democrat, Mark White, whose ties were to the Tories rather than the liberals; and liberal Democrats were elected attorney general, land commissioner, and agriculture commissioner.

Texas's affluent Republicans appeal in their campaigns to voters' sense of Texas tradition. They are strongly hawkish on military issues in this state that remembers the Alamo and are ready to denounce liberal Democrats for interfering with the family and community. But the fact is that it is economic growth, championed by these laissez-faire Republicans, which is changing Texas's families and communities more rapidly than anything the liberals dare to propose. Houston and Dallas–Fort Worth in 1980 had the nation's highest percentage of working wives, about 75%, the same level as in the trendy metropolises of Denver and Minneapolis–St. Paul. Women in Texas's big cities are working, getting divorced, having far fewer children than they expected, not attending church regularly or at all; people are living very different lives from what they expected when they were growing up in rural areas or even in the much smaller and less cosmopolitan cities Houston and Dallas were 30 years ago. These people may, in most cases, call themselves conservative, and vote for candidates like Ronald Reagan who preach free market economics and traditional family values. But those two goals, in their own lives, tend to work against each other.

Not all those changes, of course, are for the worse. But as in many developing countries, so in Texas, those who would let the free market make all economic decisions find themselves opposed again and again by those who would have traditional arrangements or moral principles govern instead. In much of Latin America the Catholic Church, with its historic prejudice against the free market and economic mechanisms like interest and its belief in the notion of a just price, is the strongest opponent of political dictators whose economic instinct is to trust the free market. American commentators see the Church as an advocate of a welfare state, but you could just as well say that it is expressing a theological preference for an economically static society.

In Texas the situation is rather different. But the Democrats, traditionally the party of the small farmer and the small town, seem to be the advocates of modulating economic change, whether through environmental protection, regulation of wages and working conditions, or restriction of immigration (although this is unpopular with Mexican-American organizations, and few politicians take a clear stand on the issue).

The Republicans and the high-income voters, in contrast, sometimes seem contemptuous of traditional values and of the ordinary people who still cherish them. Men who have achieved great economic success in the ethnically stratified Northeast instinctively assume that many others could have done as well if they had had similar advantages. But men like Clements who become very rich in the ethnically homogeneous and egalitarian climate of Texas seem sometimes to assume that people who are not as rich are simply stupid. There was an element of contempt in Clements's bearing, and even in the unexpectedly good grace with which he took his defeat—as if he were relieved of a duty that was really below him anyway. There may be a resentment among many ordinary Texans of the rich who shop in the Galleria, with its shops selling chocolates from Switzerland and Gucci shoes from Italy. National Democratic leaders, who tend to live the same grand lifestyle, will find it hard to capitalize on such feelings, but Texas Democrats, if they consult some of their state's traditions, may be able to do so.

Presidential politics. All this flux makes Texas one of the hardest states to predict for the outcome in Texas of the 1984 presidential election. It is also one of the biggest prizes, with 29 electoral votes now, and is sure to be seriously contested. And it will also be one of the largest sources of campaign funds, especially for Republicans.

Texas has produced a series of presidential candidates over the past 20 years. The first of them, and still the only success, was Lyndon Johnson—who certainly can't be summed up in half a sentence. John Connally, his protege, long cherished national ambitions; after his spectacular stint in the Nixon cabinet, he became a national figure. But the same personality which so impresses corporate chief executive officers turns off ordinary voters. They may sense that Connally has made his career being an efficient, tough number two man (to oil man Sid Richardson, Johnson, Nixon) and has some of the unpalatable qualities we associate with courtiers.

The other presidential candidate from the west side of Houston in 1980, and a likely national candidate in 1984 and 1988 is Vice President George Bush. Actually, he is not an indigenous Texan, but a transplanted New Englander, and despite all the talk about inmigration by northerners, the large majority of new Texans are from the South. Bush actually hasn't shown all that much appeal in Texas: he lost two Senate races, one to liberal Ralph Yarborough in 1964, one to the man who beat Yarborough in the primary, Lloyd Bentsen, in 1970; he came close but did not carry the state in the Republican presidential primary. In a state where virtually every Republican identifies himself as a hard right conservative, Bush is seen as a moderate, not so much because of his issue positions, but because of his accent and carriage. At this stage of his career, and really for many years, Bush is more a national politician than a local one, and talk about his having a local base here is not particularly enlightening.

Governor. The current governor of Texas, Mark White, is a man with no clear philosophy—which, for the moment anyway, may be an advantage for him. Nor does he have the sort of pungent and brutally frank personality of his predecessor. He was secretary of state, an appointive position, under Governor Dolph Briscoe; he was elected attorney general in 1978, over James Baker, who later managed George Bush's campaign and Ronald Reagan's White House. White is in a different position, however, from previous governors associated with Tory Democrats. He owes far less to the big money interests, who tended to support Clements, and more to the liberals, who supported him gamely in the general election. Nevertheless, it would be a mistake to expect him to increase vastly state spending or to do anything to help labor unions; for one thing, the huge surpluses that enabled Texas to cut state taxes in the 1970s have now pretty much disappeared.

Senators. Texas's senior senator is John Tower, a Republican who has proved more durable than anyone expected. He was first elected to the Senate in 1961, after a gadfly race the year before against Lyndon Johnson; he beat, by not large margins, three very different kinds of Democrats in 1966, 1972, and 1978. Now he is one of the longest-serving senators in Texas history and chairman of the Senate Armed Services Committee. This is a body crammed full of first-class intellects, years of experience on military issues, and a wide variety of views. Tower nonetheless manages to run a tight ship. His own views are unambiguous: he supports defense spending increases, the larger the better; he tends to back Pentagon decisions, though not mechanically; he has consolidated control of the committee staff, which used to be used in a kind of collegial manner by his courtly predecessor John Stennis.

Tower is not courtly, nor particularly congenial. He does not suffer fools. He does not sway other senators by charm or humor. However, he is effective, because he is brainy, usually well prepared, and always ready to take maximum advantage of circumstances. And he is nobody's patsy. When the Reagan administration couldn't decide on a basing mode for the MX missile, and after Tower had loyally supported its earlier decisions, he moved that funds for development of the missile be deleted until the administration came up with a basing mode Congress accepted. Tower is diligent in looking after Texas's interests in military contracts. He is also a high ranking member of the Banking Committee, but he has devoted most of his attention in recent years to military policy.

Tower was reelected by some 12,000 votes out of 2.2 million cast in 1978; his seat can be regarded as anything but safe. Democrats lining up to run against him include his 1978 opponent Bob Krueger, a former congressman and English professor who came as close as anyone has to getting the House to deregulate natural gas; Congressman Kent Hance, who has a West Texas geographical and an independent oil fundraising base, and who, after cosponsoring the Reagan tax cut in 1981, has stressed his support of Democratic programs; former Governor Dolph Briscoe; and Austin state Senator Lloyd Doggett, a bright, young, hardworking, and earnest member of the usually outnumbered liberal bloc in the legislature. Both the primary and the general election must be regarded as unpredictable.

Texas's other senator, Lloyd Bentsen, has also had a long congressional career characterized by competence and hard work. His roots are in the Tory Democrat tradition. He is from a big landowning family in the lower Rio Grande valley and was first elected to the House in 1948 at age 27. He left Congress after six years to make money in business, and returned successfully to challenge Senator Yarborough in the 1970 primary. In that contest he ran ads featuring footage of the riots outside the Democratic National Convention in Chicago in 1968; in the general election, however, he sought labor, black, and Mexican-American endorsements, and beat George Bush.

As senator, Bentsen has toed a careful line between mainstream Democrats and conservatives. He has devoted much attention to complex legislation, such as the pension reform act and the oil depletion allowance (retained, on his motion, for small producers). He combines an ability to deal with complex government regulation with a commitment to free market capitalism. In 1979 and 1980, Bentsen chaired the Joint Economic Committee and produced its first unanimous report, calling for lower taxes on capital gains and greater incentives for investment. He serves now on the Finance Committee, where he is ranking Democrat on the International Trade Subcommittee. Generally he supports free trade; Texas, after all, is a major exporter of everything from cotton to oil drilling equipment to military airplanes. But he also has worked with the subcommittee's chairman, John Danforth, to persuade the Japanese to restrict auto imports voluntarily.

Bentsen is a Texas Democrat in the tradition of Jesse Jones, the Houston banker who was FDR's secretary of commerce and RFC head. Jones was never much of a New Dealer, but he believed strongly in government acting in partnership with business—especially Texas business—to build a stronger economy; and he was never troubled if such activities helped to make certain people very rich. Bentsen, like Jones, is not a free market ideologue; and if he no longer shares Jones's vision of Texas as an underdeveloped country that needs help, he nonetheless sees a real need for government assistance to the private economy around the nation. He is likely to be a senator of major importance if the Democrats recapture the Senate.

Bentsen has proved to be a strong vote-getter in Texas. In his toughest race he beat George Bush in 1970, with the help of a big outpouring of rural Baptists who turned out to vote against a liquor by the drink referendum. Since then he has beaten two Dallas congressmen: in 1976 Alan Steelman, who was something of a liberal on environmental issues but who couldn't raise much money; in 1982 James Collins, a solid conservative and successful businessman who raised plenty of money but couldn't avoid errors. Bentsen's success is all the more striking because he has a rather cold demeanor: he is a cerebral man who makes decisions carefully and is not comfortable communicating the vision which seems to animate him. His biggest disappointment in politics must have been his 1976 presidential race. He was correct in calculating that voters might want a middle-of-the-road southerner, but wrong in supposing that they wanted one with Washington experience.

Congressional districting. Texas has traditionally had a formidable congressional delegation. Today, thanks to its growth in the 1970s, it has the largest delegation in its history, with 27 members; thanks to the persistence of political tradition, 21 of those members are Democrats. They include House majority leader Jim Wright of Fort Worth and such senior Democrats as Jack Brooks and Jake Pickle. But Texas was not able to dominate the Democratic committee selection process in 1983, as Wright wanted; California did instead. And Texas no longer has many committee chairmen; in 1978 six of its 24 congressmen retired and it lost 190 years of seniority. Texas is the home state of several of the Boll Weevils, who gave crucial support to the Reagan administration economic policies; most came back to the Democrats in 1982, however, and the one who conspicuously declined to do so, Phil Gramm, resigned his seat and then won it back as a Republican in early 1983.

Congressional districting, like many other governmental matters in Texas, has gotten gummed up in the federal courts; one judge in particular has taken it upon himself to right all wrongs, even when a legal theory cannot be cited to support doing so. He overturned the boundaries of seven of the state's congressional districts in 1982, rearranging two Mexican-American districts (the 15th and 27th) and changing the Dallas area districts around. The legislature had gone along with Governor Clements and produced a plan which would create a 24th district with a large black percentage and a 5th which would be virtually all-white and heavily Republican. The court said that this would be unfair to blacks, and substituted a plan which would produce a 24th with a lower black percentage and a 5th with enough blacks and working-class whites to be safely Democratic, on the theory that the election results from this plan—two Democrats where there had been one before—would be more to the liking of black voters. Of course this principle means that the Voting Rights Act requires redrawing all district lines across the country to benefit Democrats—an absurd result, and one that was overturned by the Supreme Court, but not in time for the 1982 election. For 1984, the legislature, now with a Democratic governor, can draw new lines which will protect the Democrats elected now in the two districts.

The People Est. Pop. 1982: 15,280,000; Pop. 1980: 14,229,191, up 7.3% 1980–82 and 27.1% 1970–80; 6.4% of U.S. total, 3d largest; voting age pop. 9,923,085; 3% American Indian, 11% Black, 18% Spanish origin, 1% Asian origin. Single ancestry: 12% English, 5% German, 4% Irish, 1% French, Italian. Registered voters (1982): 6,414,988 Total. No party registration. 17% with 1–3 yrs. col., 16% with 4+ yrs. col. 15% below poverty level. 32% housing units rented; median house value: $39,100; median monthly rent: $213. Households: 75% family, 43% with children, 63% married couples.

1982 Share of Federal Tax Burden $41,233,100,000; 6.90% of U.S. total, 3d largest.

1982 Share of Federal Expenditures

	Total		Non-Defense		Defense	
Total Expend	$32,114m	(5.32%)	$20,424m	(4.81%)	$11,690m	(6.54%)
St/Lcl Grants	3,725m	(4.22%)	3,724m	(4.22%)	1m	(2.78%)
Salary/Wages	4,894m	(6.27%)	1,321m	(4.83%)	3,573m	(7.05%)
Ind Payments	14,987m	(5.24%)	12,505m	(4.86%)	2,482m	(8.68%)
Procurement	7,919m	(5.43%)	1,213m	(3.85%)	6,707m	(5.87%)
Other Programs	589m	(10.88%)	588m	(10.95%)	1m	(2.33%)
Loan/Insurance	4,273m	(6.68%)	3,890m	(6.30%)	383m	(17.41%)

Political Lineup Governor, Mark W. White, Jr. (D). Senators, John G. Tower (R) and Lloyd Bentsen (D). Representatives, 27 (21 D and 6 R). State Senate, 31 (26 D and 5 R); State House of Representatives, 150 (114 D and 36 R).

Presidential Vote

1980	Reagan (R)	2,510,705	(55%)
	Carter (D)	1,881,417	(41%)
	Anderson (I)	111,613	(2%)
1976	Ford (R)	1,953,300	(48%)
	Carter (D)	2,082,319	(51%)

1980 Democratic Presidential Primary			*1980 Republican Presidential Primary*		
Carter	769,390	(56%)	Reagan	268,798	(51%)
Kennedy	314,129	(23%)	Bush	249,819	(47%)
Brown	35,529	(2%)	Uncommitted	8,162	(2%)
Uncommitted	256,723	(19%)			

SENATORS

Sen. John G. Tower (R) Elected May 27, 1961, seat up 1984; b. Sept. 29, 1925, Houston; home, Wichita Falls; Southwestern U., B.A. 1948, U. of London, 1952, SMU, M.A. 1953; United Methodist.

Career Navy, WWII; Prof. of Govt., Midwestern U., 1951–61.

Offices 179 RSOB, 202-224-2934. Also 961 Fed. Ofc. Bldg., 300 E. 8th St., Austin 78701, 512-397-5933; and Fed. Bldg., 1114 Commerce St., Dallas 75202, 214-749-7525.

Committees *Armed Services* (Chairman). Subcommittees: Sea Power and Force Projection; Strategic and Theater Nuclear Forces; Tactical Warfare. *Banking, Housing, and Urban Affairs* (2d). Subcommittees: Housing and Urban Affairs (Chairman); Financial Institutions; Rural Housing and Development. *Budget* (6th).

Group Ratings

	ADA	ACLU	COPE	CFA	LCV	LWV	NTU	NSI	COC	ACA	CSFC
1982	10	43	9	0	0	18	70	100	80	74	76
1981	10	—	9	0	6	—	66	—	100	72	84
1980	6	20	12	0	11	25	58	80	94	91	83

National Journal Ratings

	Economic		Foreign		Cultural	
1982	23%	(LIB)	16%	(LIB)	20%	(LIB)
	76%	(CONS)	68%	(CONS)	79%	(CONS)
1981	0%	(LIB)	1%	(LIB)	24%	(LIB)
	99%	(CONS)	85%	(CONS)	75%	(CONS)

Key Votes

1) Reagan 81 Budget	FOR	5) $ to El Salvador	FOR	9) Poor Pay Food Stamps	FOR
2) Reagan 81 Tax Cut	FOR	6) Saudi AWACS Sale	FOR	10) Ban Crt Busing Order	FOR
3) Bal Budget Amend	FOR	7) Ban Abortion	AGN	11) Clinch Riv Brdr Rctr	FOR
4) Gas & Road Tax	AGN	8) Nerve Gas Prod	FOR	12) Legal Services Corp	AGN

Election Results

1978 general	John G. Tower (R)	....	1,151,376	(50%)	($4,359,365)
	Robert Krueger (D)	....	1,139,149	(49%)	($2,428,666)
1978 primary	John G. Tower (R)	....	142,202	(100%)	
1972 general	John G. Tower (R)	....	1,822,877	(53%)	($2,301,870)
	Barefoot Sanders (D)	....	1,511,985	(44%)	($629,008)

Campaign Contributions and Expenditures

1977-78		PACS brkdwn			
Receipts	$4,298,779	Agr	$12,150	Ideo	$11,503
Expend.	$4,359,365	Bus	$318,751	Lbr	$0
Unspent	$15,120	Hlth	$318,751	Prof	$13,900

Sen. Lloyd Bentsen (D) Elected 1970, seat up 1988; b. Feb. 11, 1921, Mission; home, Houston; U. of TX, LL.B. 1942; Presbyterian.

Career Army Air Corps, WWII; Judge, Hidalgo Cnty., 1946; U.S. House of Reps., 1949–55; Pres., Lincoln Consolidated, financial holding co. 1955–.

Offices 703 HSOB, 202-224-5922. Also Fed. Bldg., Rm. 912, Austin 78701, 512-397-5834; and Fed. Bldg., Houston 77002, 713-226-5496.

Committees *Environment and Public Works* (2d). Subcommittees: Regional and Community Development; Water Resources, Transportation. *Finance* (2d). Subcommittees: Taxation and Debt Management; International Trade; Energy and Agricultural Taxation. *Select Committee on Intelligence* (7th). Subcommittees: Budget Authorization; Analysis and Production. *Joint Economic Committee* (Ranking Minority Member). Subcommittees: Agriculture and Transportation, Economic Goals and Intergovernmental Policy (Vice-Chairman). *Joint Committee on Taxation* (2d).

Group Ratings

	ADA	ACLU	COPE	CFA	LCV	LWV	NTU	NSI	COC	ACA	CSFC
1982	40	43	48	40	27	64	43	80	65	65	58
1981	25	—	46	36	19	—	39	—	57	57	58
1980	39	47	39	13	31	44	39	44	43	43	43

National Journal Ratings

	Economic		Foreign		Cultural	
1982	63%	(LIB)	32%	(LIB)	44%	(LIB)
	36%	(CONS)	67%	(CONS)	55%	(CONS)
1981	50%	(LIB)	51%	(LIB)	48%	(LIB)
	49%	(CONS)	48%	(CONS)	51%	(CONS)

Key Votes

1) Reagan 81 Budget	FOR	5) $ to El Salvador	AGN	9) Poor Pay Food Stamps	FOR
2) Reagan 81 Tax Cut	FOR	6) Saudi AWACS Sale	AGN	10) Ban Crt Busing Order	FOR
3) Bal Budget Amend	FOR	7) Ban Abortion	AGN	11) Clinch Riv Brdr Rctr	AGN
4) Gas & Road Tax	FOR	8) Nerve Gas Prod	FOR	12) Legal Services Corp	FOR

Election Results

1982 general	Lloyd Bentsen (D)	1,818,223	(59%)	($5,097,445)
	James M. Collins (R)	1,256,759	(40%)	($4,285,377)
1982 primary	Lloyd Bentsen (D)	987,967	(78%)	
	Joe Sullivan (D)	276,453	(22%)	
1976 general	Lloyd Bentsen (D)	2,199,956	(57%)	($1,237,910)
	Alan Steelman (R)	1,636,370	(42%)	($665,058)

Campaign Contributions and Expenditures

1979-82		Direct Cont. 79-82		PACS brkdwn			
Receipts	$5,083,557	Indiv	$3,679,289	Agr	$27,907	Ideo	$38,250
Expend.	$5,097,445	Party	$17,500	Bus	$604,220	Lbr	$47,250
Unspent	$12,801	PACS	$826,593	Hlth	$37,300	Prof	$65,400
		Cand	$75,000				

Indirect Party Expend: $156,576   *Indep Expend*: Agn: $225,119 (NCPAC, LIFEPAC)

GOVERNOR

Gov. Mark W. White, Jr. (D) Elected 1982, term expries Jan. 1987; b. Mar. 17, 1940, Henderson; home, Austin; Baylor U., B.B.A. 1962, LL.B. 1965; Baptist.

Career Asst. Atty. Gen. of TX for Insurance, Banking and Securities Div., 1966–69; TX Secy. of State, 1973–1977; Atty. Gen. of TX, 1979–82.

Offices P.O. Box 12428 Capitol Station, Austin 78711, 512-475-4101.

Election Results

1982 gen.	Mark W. White, Jr. (D)	1,697,527	(53%)
	William (Bill) Clements (R) .	1,465,952	(46%)
1982 prim.	Mark W. White, Jr. (D)	592,658	(45%)
	Buddy Temple (D)	402,693	(31%)
	Bob Armstrong (D)	262,189	(20%)
1978 gen.	William (Bill) Clements (R) ..	1,183,839	(50%)
	John Hill (D)	1,166,979	(49%)

TEXAS — Congressional Districts, Counties, and Selected Places — (27 Districts)

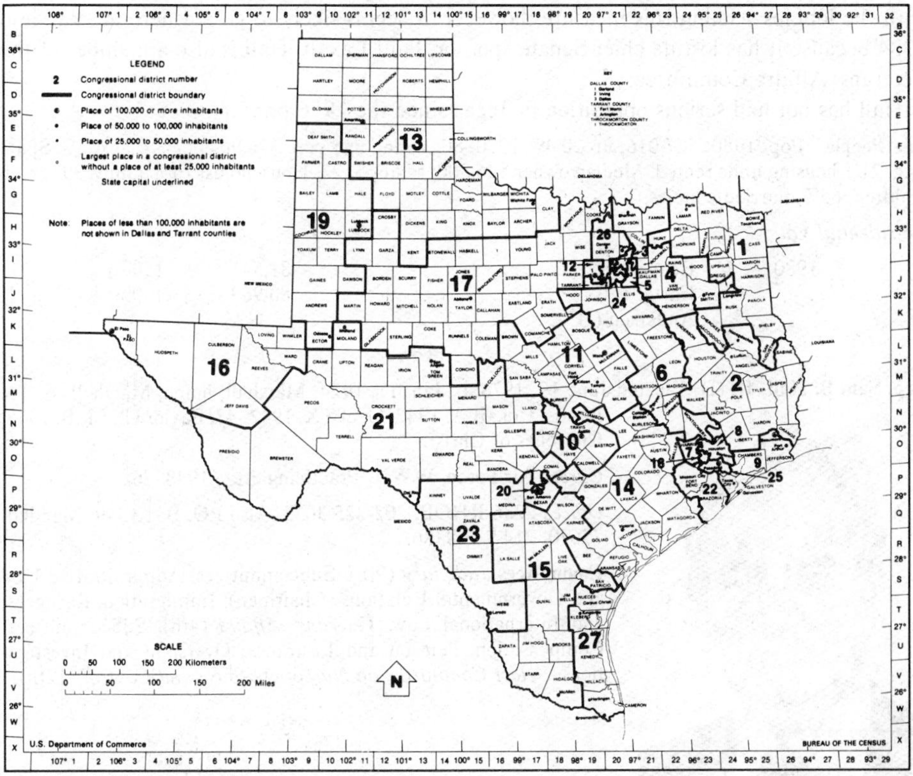

LEGEND

2 Congressional district number

—— Congressional district boundary

● Place of 100,000 or more inhabitants

● Place of 50,000 to 100,000 inhabitants

• Place of 25,000 to 50,000 inhabitants

● Largest place in a congressional district without a place of at least 25,000 inhabitants

State capital underlined

Note: Places of less than 100,000 inhabitants are not shown in Dallas and Tarrant counties

SCALE

0 50 100 150 200 Kilometers

0 50 100 150 200 Miles

U.S. Department of Commerce

BUREAU OF THE CENSUS

Congressional districts established February 25, 1982; all other boundaries are as of January 1, 1980.

FIRST DISTRICT

The 1st congressional district of Texas is the northeastern corner of the state. This is not part of the new, glittering urban Texas. The land here is green and only mildly undulating, overrun it seems with vegetation; the towns are no longer the dusty crossroads they were in the days before roads were paved, but they are pretty plain places still. The largest city here is Texarkana, with its city hall so squarely on the Texas–Arkansas line that different wings serve Texarkana, Texas, and Texarkana, Arkansas. Geographically, this is the part of the state closest to the Deep South; demographically, this is also true: 20% of the people here are black, the largest figure for a nonurban Texas district. The boundaries of the district are weirdly misshapen, the result of a redistricting engineered by state Senator William Patman (now 14th district congressman) for his father, Wright Patman, who represented this district for nearly 50 years. Patman, a scourge of bankers, chaired the Banking Committee for several years, lost his chairmanship in 1974 and died in 1976.

His successor, Sam Hall, does not continue this Texas populist tradition and in fact has one of the most conservative records of Texas Democrats. Hall is a member of the Judiciary Committee and chairman of the subcommittee rather grandly named Administrative Law and Governmental Relations. This is the body which has handled the regulatory reform bills sought by business organizations and denounced, rather tepidly, by others as changes in substantive laws rather than mere reforms of procedure. Hall might be inclined to go along with the lobbies seeking this measure; however, it seems likely to go nowhere in 1983 and 1984 because it has lost its chief Senate sponsor, Paul Laxalt. Hall is also a member of the Veterans' Affairs Committee.

Hall has not had serious opposition in Texas since the 1976 primary.

The People Pop. 1980: 527,016, up 20.4% 1970–80; voting age pop. 376,964; 17% Black, 1% Span. orig. 21% housing units rented. Median owner $26,300; renter $123. Households: 76% family, 39% with children, 65% married couples.

Presidential Vote

1980	Reagan (R)	81,541	(50%)
	Carter (D)	80,969	(50%)
	Anderson (I)	NA	

Rep. Sam B. Hall, Jr. (D) Elected June 19, 1976; b. Jan. 11, 1924, Marshall; home, Marshall; E. TX Baptist Col., B.A. 1942, U. of TX, 1942–43, Baylor U., LL.B. 1948; Churches of Christ.

Career Air Force, WWII; Practicing atty., 1948–76.

Offices 2236 RHOB, 202-225-3035. Also P.O. Box 1349, Marshall 75670, 214-938-8386.

Committees *Judiciary* (9th). Subcommittees: Administrative Law and Governmental Relations (Chairman); Immigration, Refugees, and International Law. *Veterans' Affairs* (4th). Subcommittees: Compensation, Pension and Insurance; Oversight and Investigations. *Select Committee on Narcotics Abuse and Control* (12th).

Group Ratings

	ADA	ACLU	COPE	CFA	LCV	LWV	NTU	NSI	COC	ACA	CSFC
1982	5	8	23	31	38	8	64	90	67	78	57
1981	15	—	24	21	7	—	86	—	79	87	67
1980	0	13	22	7	17	30	55	89	84	73	67

National Journal Ratings

	Economic		Foreign		Cultural	
1982	33%	(LIB)	23%	(LIB)	21%	(LIB)
	67%	(CONS)	77%	(CONS)	76%	(CONS)
1981	45%	(LIB)	30%	(LIB)	23%	(LIB)
	55%	(CONS)	68%	(CONS)	76%	(CONS)

Key Votes

1) Reagan 81 Budget	FOR	5) Incr SS Rtmt Age	FOR
2) Reagan 81 Tax Cut	FOR	6) Saudi AWACS Sale	FOR
3) Bal Budget Amend	FOR	7) $ for MX Missile	FOR
4) Gas & Road Tax	—	8) Nerve Gas Prod	AGN

9) Poor Pay Food Stamps	AGN
10) Ban Crt Busing Order	FOR
11) Auto Local Content	FOR
12) Nuclear Arms Freeze	AGN

Election Results

1982 general	Sam B. Hall, Jr. (D)	100,685	(97%)	($110,821 est.)
1982 primary	Sam B. Hall, Jr. (D)	82,384	(86%)	
	Jim Zorn (D)	13,364	(14%)	($6,792)
1980 general	Sam B. Hall, Jr. (D)	137,665	(100%)	($83,698)

Campaign Contributions and Expenditures

1981-82		Direct Cont. 81-82		PACS brkdwn			
Receipts	$188,472 (est.)	Indiv	$119,964	Agr	$3,000	Ideo	$1,800
Expend.	$110,821 (est.)	PACS	$55,645	Bus	$42,950	Lbr	$—
Unspent	$115,100			Hlth	$5,200	Prof	$1,950

SECOND DISTRICT

During the 1930s, east Texas was a busy place—and one of the few parts of the United States where this decade was something other than a dreary one. The reason was oil; for it was during the 1930s that the really big oil discoveries were made in east Texas. Oil drilling had started here as early as 1901, and there were some producing wells. But the big oil companies' geologists pooh-poohed the idea that there was any great field here. That left it to oddball wildcatters to prove that it did, and one of them, H. L. Hunt, did so, and found enough oil to build the foundation of a billion dollar fortune.

The 2d congressional district of Texas, a collection of rural and small town counties in east Texas, includes the site of Hunt's discovery. Yet oil riches have never seemed to stick to this part of Texas. It includes no wealthy little oil cities. The big money taken out from under this soil has mostly gone to men who chose to live in Dallas or Houston or to investors from all over the world. Settled by small farmers and a few slaves from the Deep South, this was long one of the poorest parts of the state; it is much more prosperous now, but still humble. It is full of stands of cheap, quick-growing pine, and is one of the leading lumber- and paper pulp-producing areas of the United States.

The 2d district elects one of the most flamboyant members of Congress, Charles Wilson. He has been known since his days in the Texas Senate as a liberal; his voting record on economic issues is often in accord with northern liberals. On oil matters he is, of course, a loyal

Texan. On cultural issues, his record is mixed; on foreign policy he is something of a hawk. Aggressiveness is probably Wilson's most noticeable trait; he also has a sly wit and a willingness to use it on just about everybody. The best example is his comment after President Carter fired HEW Secretary Joseph Califano and others in 1979: "Good grief! He's cut down the tall trees and left the monkeys."

Wilson has pushed himself forward, first when he ran for Congress in 1972, later in shoving aside a fellow Texan and getting a seat on the Appropriations Committee; later, in getting a seat on the Defense Subcommittee. He also sits on the Foreign Operations Subcommittee, which gives him a potentially broad view of the whole range of foreign policy. Yet Wilson seems more interested in promoting, aggressively, the interests of Texas defense contractors.

Wilson's voting record has not gotten him into trouble with his constituents. He has seldom had significant opposition, and the changing tide of opinion in Texas in the early 1980s seemed to help him. In 1982 redistricting also helped him, by removing most of Montgomery County, once a rural area but now an affluent, and Republican, suburban area outside Houston. He was dogged in 1983 by an investigation of charges that he had used cocaine—charges made by an old political enemy and which never seemed credible. But political opposition did not seem to arise, and his reputation for effectiveness seemed likely to sustain him.

The People Pop. 1980: 526,772, up 35.4% 1970–80; voting age pop. 372,792; 14% Black, 3% Span. orig. 21% housing units rented. Median owner $31,300; renter $155. Households: 78% family, 43% with children, 67% married couples.

Presidential Vote

1980	Reagan (R) .... NA
	Carter (D) .... NA
	Anderson (I) .... NA

Rep. Charles Wilson (D) Elected 1972; b. June 1, 1933, Trinity; home, Lufkin; Sam Houston St. U., U.S. Naval Acad., B.S. 1956; Methodist.

Career Navy, 1956–60; Mgr., retail lumber store; TX House of Reps., 1961–66; TX Senate, 1967–72.

Offices 2265 RHOB, 202-225-2401. Also 40005 S. Medford Dr., Su. 9 West, Lufkin 75901, 713-634-8247.

Committee *Appropriations* (17th). Subcommittees: Defense; District of Columbia; Foreign Operations.

Group Ratings

	ADA	ACLU	COPE	CFA	LCV	LWV	NTU	NSI	COC	ACA	CSFC
1982	25	46	62	31	26	36	27	90	56	65	44
1981	20	—	63	36	22	—	10	—	58	62	50
1980	17	47	59	29	28	44	30	89	67	43	40

National Journal Ratings

	Economic		Foreign		Cultural	
1982	50%	(LIB)	0%	(LIB)	32%	(LIB)
	50%	(CONS)	99%	(CONS)	68%	(CONS)
1981	52%	(LIB)	14%	(LIB)	50%	(LIB)
	48%	(CONS)	86%	(CONS)	50%	(CONS)

Key Votes

1) Reagan 81 Budget	AGN	5) Incr SS Rtmt Age	FOR	9) Poor Pay Food Stamps	—
2) Reagan 81 Tax Cut	AGN	6) Saudi AWACS Sale	FOR	10) Ban Crt Busing Order	FOR
3) Bal Budget Amend	FOR	7) $ for MX Missile	FOR	11) Auto Local Content	FOR
4) Gas & Road Tax	FOR	8) Nerve Gas Prod	—	12) Nuclear Arms Freeze	AGN

Election Results

1982 general	Charles Wilson (D)	91,762	(94%)	($264,197)
	Ed Richbourg (L)	5,584	(6%)	($0)
1982 primary	Charles Wilson (D)	66,492	(74%)	
	William Baxter (Bill) Duncan (D) .	23,286	(26%)	($61,636)
1980 general	Charles Wilson (D)	142,496	(69%)	($239,766)
	F. H. Pannill, Sr. (R)	60,742	(30%)	($5,698)

Campaign Contributions and Expenditures

1981-82		Direct Cont. 81-82		PACS brkdwn			
Receipts	$268,944	Indiv	$87,892	Agr	$10,000	Ideo	$500
Expend.	$264,197	PACS	$124,914	Bus	$82,234	Lbr	$11,600
Unspent	$10,782	Cand	$41,000	Hlth	$5,500	Prof	$13,500

Non-Cand Loans: $15,000

THIRD DISTRICT

The 3d congressional district of Texas is the north side of Dallas, the most affluent part of this metropolitan area, the place where caricatures of rich Texans, from H. L. Hunt to J. R. Ewing, are most likely to feel at home. The district begins in the south in the enclaves of University Park and Highland Park, old suburbs (which in the Dallas area means most of the houses date back to the 1950s) which have long been the home of much of Dallas's elite. It extends in the north beyond the Dallas County line to where Dallas and the suburb of Richardson cross over into Collin County. Affluent Dallas has been marching north for some time now. The land in between, which not so long ago was rolling hillsides with occasional trees and a little scrub, is now given over to subdivisions and condominium developments, each enclosed by its own little wall, with occasional office parks rising high into the sky.

Dallas is the older of Texas's two largest cities, and the one with the more diversified economy. Its wealth was originally based not on oil, which was not discovered until the turn of the century, but on cotton. Dallas was where the first railroad in Texas stopped, because its builders did not want to scale the Balcones Escarpment which rises between Dallas and Fort Worth; that geological line also marks the boundary between east Texas, which is humid and green and where the view of the sky is blocked by trees, and west Texas, which is arid and brown and where the sky seems very high and wide. By 1900 Dallas was the banking, finance, and insurance center for Texas, and to a considerable extent it still is. Of course it has a large number of oil-related businesses. But it has also spawned companies like Texas Instruments.

This district is one of the most heavily Republican in the United States. Affluent people on the north side of Dallas, unlike many rich people in the Northeast, do not feel that they have done something bad because they are rich. They are people who, despite the disappointments of the early 1980s, still believe that things in this country are getting better, and that technology and free enterprise can produce a better life for all, and particularly for people like them. That, after all, has been their experience. They have seen their part of the world advance from a small and provincial city in the 1950s to a world capital of industry and finance in the 1980s. The role government has played in this—by providing education, infrastructure, defense contracts, a secure world market, and a very large consumer class—is largely invisible from their perspective; what they have seen is entrepreneurs going out and fighting against the forces of inertia and mishap which keep most enterprises from succeeding. In this view, government is an impediment, its regulations a nuisance and an extra expense, its taxes a drain on capital that could be put to much better use.

So this part of Texas has always been a right-wing stronghold; it is not only Republican but at times its politics has had a bitter, almost hysterical edge to it. That was symbolized when Dallas Republican Congressman Bruce Alger led a group shoving Lyndon and Lady Bird Johnson in a Dallas hotel in the 1960 campaign. Dallas has settled down somewhat since; Congressman James Collins, who served from 1968 until he ran for the Senate in 1982, was known for his personal philanthropies and solid conservative record.

Now the district is represented by a new generation of Republicans. The real contest here is in the Republican primary, and the winner in 1982 was Steve Bartlett, a 35-year-old Dallas councilman. Bartlett finished second in the first primary to former state legislator Kay Hutchinson. But he won the support of several of the other candidates and campaigned heavily on the abortion and gun control issues in the runoff, and won. His background as the owner of a tool and plastics company and his committee assignments—Banking and Education and Labor—suggest he will be concentrating on economic issues. He will almost certainly be a solid conservative. Reelection should be no problem, barring a serious challenge in the Republican primary.

The People   Pop. 1980: 526,925, up 47.8% 1970–80; voting age pop. 394,610; 3% Black, 6% Span. orig., 1% Asian orig. 39% housing units rented. Median owner $77,800; renter $292. Households: 65% family, 34% with children, 56% married couples.

Presidential Vote

1980	Reagan (R)	NA
	Carter (D)	NA
	Anderson (I)	NA

Rep. Steve Bartlett (R) Elected 1982; b. Sept. 19, 1947, Los Angeles; home, Dallas; U. of TX at Austin, B.A. 1971; Presbyterian.

Career Real estate broker, 1971–76; Founder, Chmn. of Bd., Meridian Products Corp., 1976–; Mbr., City Cncl. of Dallas, 1977–81.

Offices 1233 LHOB, 202-225-4201. Also 6600 LBJ Freeway, Su. 4190, Dallas 75240, 214-392-2622.

Committees *Banking, Finance and Urban Affairs* (17th). Subcommittees: General Oversight and Renegotiation; Housing and Community Development; International Development Institutions and Finance. *Education and Labor* (8th). Subcommittees: Elementary, Secondary, and Vocational Education; Employment Opportunities; Labor-Management Relations; Select Education.

Group Ratings and Key Votes: Newly Elected

Election Results

1982 general	Steve Bartlett (R)	99,852	(77%)	($792,324)
	James L. McNees, Jr. (D)	28,223	(22%)	($39,792)
1982 runoff	Steve Bartlett (R)	18,159	(57%)	
	Kay Bailey Hutchinson (R)	13,715	(43%)	($503,392)
1982 primary	Kay Bailey Hutchinson (R)	15,820	(37%)	
	Steve Bartlett (R)	12,170	(28%)	
	Jim Jackson (R)	9,494	(22%)	($140,150)
	Dee Travis (R)	4,154	(10%)	($119,408)
1980 general	James M. (Jim) Collins (R)	218,228	(79%)	(303,229)
	Earle Stephen Porter (D)	49,667	(18%)	($0)

Campaign Contributions and Expenditures

1981-82		Direct Cont. 81-82		PACS brkdwn			
Receipts	$792,188	Indiv	$518,441	Agr	$7,600	Ideo	$20,950
Expend.	$792,324	Party	$24,505	Bus	$125,625	Lbr	$—
Unspent	$138	PACS	$177,163	Hlth	$6,450	Prof	$1,600
		Cand	$47,500				

Indirect Party Expend: $8,932

FOURTH DISTRICT

The 4th congressional district of Texas is part of the Red River Valley. This land was settled, on the Texas side, more than a century ago, and soon became thickly populated; it has some of the best farmland in the state. The agricultural areas, however, reached their maximum population more than 50 years ago. Mechanization reduced manpower needs on the farm, and ever since the young people here have been moving into Texas's big urban areas, especially the Dallas–Fort Worth metroplex, as it is called.

In turn, metropolitan growth has reached out here, beyond the limits of Dallas County. Now Rockwall and Collin Counties find their populations swelled by affluent newcomers from over the line; behind the fences that used to protect farmland are now new subdivisions and condominium developments. Towns like Sherman and Greenville, even farther out, which have not seen much change since the main streets were paved in the 1920s, are now seeing the beginnings of metropolitan growth, although they are 40 or 50 miles from downtown Dallas. Far in the eastern part of the district are the small oil cities of Tyler and Longview, affluent Republican strongholds in Democratic east Texas.

The old rural areas of the 4th district are Democratic, in fact some of the most solidly Democratic counties in the country for most of their existence. The Red River Valley has produced some of the national Democratic Party's leaders: Speaker Carl Albert comes from the Oklahoma side of the river, and Speaker Sam Rayburn came from the town of Bonham in the 4th district. Rayburn represented the district for nearly 50 years, from 1913 to 1961; his service saw Texas change from a poor, agricultural, populist state to a considerably more affluent, metropolitan, and conservative one. The change was not much to his liking, but he managed to serve the interests of Texas and of the national Democratic Party at one and the same time: he never allowed the oil depletion allowance to be tampered with, but his last great victory was the packing of the Rules Committee to allow Kennedy administration legislation to come to the floor.

Since Rayburn's death the 4th district has been represented by men of mild demeanor and conservative instincts, neither of which Rayburn shared. The current congressman, Ralph Hall, was first elected in 1980 after a long career in business and state and local politics; he had strong competition both in the Democratic primary and the general election. Hall got good committee assignments: Energy and Commerce and Science and Technology. On the former he is on the subcommittee which handles deregulation of natural gas; he can be counted on to favor that, although the interests get so tangled up that he may be torn in two directions on some particulars. Hall can't be a particular favorite of the Democratic leadership: after getting such good assignments, he voted with the Boll Weevils in 1981 for the Reagan budget and tax cuts. He was reelected comfortably in 1982, and has a good chance to remain in the Congress for some time. A serious Republican challenge, however, can't be ruled out, as affluent young conservatives continue to extend the metroplex out into Sam Rayburn's old territory.

The People Pop. 1980: 526,991, up 25.8% 1970–80; voting age pop. 377,899; 13% Black, 2% Span. orig. 25% housing units rented. Median owner $32,500; renter $159. Households: 76% family, 40% with children, 66% married couples.

Presidential Vote

1980	Reagan (R)	103,330	(58%)
	Carter (D)	73,460	(42%)
	Anderson (I)	NA	

Rep. Ralph M. Hall (D) Elected 1980; b. May 23, 1923, Rockwall Cnty.; home, Rockwall; U. of TX, TCU, SMU, J.D. 1951; Methodist.

Career Navy, WWII; Rockwall Cnty. Judge, 1950–62; TX Senate, 1962–72; Pres. and CEO, Texas Aluminum Corp.; Gen. Counsel, Texas Extrusion Co., Inc.

Offices 1224 LHOB, 202-225-6673. Also 104 San Jacinto St., Rockwall 75087, 214-722-9118; 201 Fed. Bldg., Sherman 75090, 214-892-1112; and 211 Fed. Bldg., Tyler 75702, 214-597-3729.

Committees *Energy and Commerce* (20th). Subcommittees: Energy Conservation and Power; Fossil and Synthetic Fuels. *Science and Technology* (15th). Subcommittees: Energy Development and Applications; Energy Research and Production; Space Science and Applications.

Group Ratings

	ADA	ACLU	COPE	CFA	LCV	LWV	NTU	NSI	COC	ACA	CSFC
1982	5	17	25	23	29	17	63	100	64	57	57
1981	5	—	27	29	0	—	54	—	74	67	66

National Journal Ratings

	Economic		Foreign		Cultural	
1982	32%	(LIB)	34%	(LIB)	21%	(LIB)
	68%	(CONS)	65%	(CONS)	76%	(CONS)
1981	38%	(LIB)	16%	(LIB)	29%	(LIB)
	62%	(CONS)	83%	(CONS)	70%	(CONS)

Key Votes

1) Reagan 81 Budget	FOR	5) Incr SS Rtmt Age	FOR	9) Poor Pay Food Stamps	—
2) Reagan 81 Tax Cut	FOR	6) Saudi AWACS Sale	AGN	10) Ban Crt Busing Order	FOR
3) Bal Budget Amend	FOR	7) $ for MX Missile	FOR	11) Auto Local Content	FOR
4) Gas & Road Tax	AGN	8) Nerve Gas Prod	FOR	12) Nuclear Arms Freeze	AGN

Election Results

1982 general	Ralph M. Hall (D)	94,134	(74%)	($168,959)
	Pete Collumb (R)	32,221	(25%)	($22,544)
1982 primary	Ralph M. Hall (D)	40,812	(100%)	
1980 general	Ralph M. Hall (D)	102,787	(52%)	($347,903)
	John Wright (R)	93,915	(48%)	($159,152)

Campaign Contributions and Expenditures

1981-82		*Direct Cont. 81-82*			*PACS brkdwn*		
Receipts	$264,957	Indiv	$143,205	Agr	$8,200	Ideo	$1,550
Expend.	$168,959	PACS	$114,511	Bus	$85,387	Lbr	$250
Unspent	$98,762			Hlth	$14,250	Prof	$2,750

FIFTH DISTRICT

The 5th congressional district of Texas includes the central and eastern parts of the city of Dallas. It includes Dallas's booming downtown, the affluent apartment neighborhood just to the north, and the warehouse and hospital area to the northwest, along the Trinity River and Elm Fork. But most of this part of Dallas is a decidedly modest place, with none of the glitter and sheen you find on the north side of town. Here people live in modest frame houses, commute to unexciting office and factory jobs, try to make ends meet and keep their neighborhoods up. The district includes the mostly black neighborhoods east of downtown Dallas, and the white working-class areas farther east, along the eastern loop of the LBJ Freeway, and in the modest suburbs of Mesquite and Garland. Some 20% of the people here are black and 12% Mexican-American, but the minority percentages are higher in the 24th district, south and west of the Trinity River. But generally this is Dallas's white working-class district.

The 5th district's current boundaries were drawn by a federal court which wanted to maximize Democratic representation in the Dallas area on the theory that that was the way to fulfill the mandates of the Voting Rights Act—a cockamamie theory if ever there was one. The Supreme Court has overruled that decision, but the new lines if any will be drawn by the Democrats, and will probably be similar. The district was so obviously Democratic that when the court set these lines, Republican Steve Bartlett left the race here; he ran in the north side 3d district and won. The Democratic nomination was won by John Bryant, an eight-year veteran of the legislature at age 35; he had the warm endorsement of incumbent Jim Mattox, who had decided to run for attorney general when he saw the lines the legislature drew (he ultimately won that office).

Bryant has shown many signs of political astuteness. He won his Democratic primary with 65% of the vote against a well-known opponent. He won the general election by a 2–1 margin. He came within two votes of being elected the freshman member on the Democratic Steering and Policy Committee, which hands out committee assignments; he was beaten by Howard Berman of California. This was a battle between Jim Wright of Fort Worth, the majority leader, who supported Bryant, and Phil Burton and Henry Waxman of California, who supported Berman; the Californians won, but Bryant acquitted himself well enough that he got a much-coveted seat on the House Energy and Commerce Committee—a plum he will still be able to enjoy when the memory of the Steering Committee fight fades.

Bryant, like his predecessor Mattox, promises to be an urban Texas liberal, not wholly unsympathetic to oil interests, but by no means a believer in pure free market economics. He is likely to be a key member of Energy and Commerce on closely divided issues. Given his performance in 1982, his chances of reelection—barring a truly unfavorable redistricting—seem excellent.

The People   Pop. 1980: 526,633, up .8% 1970–80; voting age pop. 374,926; 18% Black, 10% Span. orig., 1% Asian orig. 37% housing units rented. Median owner $35,500; renter $222. Households: 68% family, 39% with children, 53% married couples.

Presidential Vote

1980	Reagan (R)	72,348	(51%)
	Carter (D)	69,560	(49%)
	Anderson (I)	NA	

Rep. John Bryant (D) Elected 1982; b. Feb. 22, 1947, Lake Jackson; home, Dallas; SMU, B.A. 1969, SMU Sch. of Law, J.D. 1972; Methodist.

Career Practicing atty., 1972–82; TX House of Reps., 1974–82; Chief counsel, TX Senate Subcom. on Consumer Affairs, 1973–74, A.A., TX Senate, 1973.

Offices 506 CHOB, 202-225-2231. Also 8035 East R. L. Thorton Hwy., Su. 520, Dallas 75228, 214-767-6554.

Committees *Energy and Commerce* (26th). Subcommittees: Energy Conservation and Power; Telecommunications, Consumer Protection, and Finance. *Veterans' Affairs* (20th). Subcommittees: Education, Training and Employment; Hospitals and Health Care; Housing and Memorial Affairs.

Group Ratings and Key Votes: Newly Elected

Election Results

1982 general	John Bryant (D)	52,214	(65%)	($280,137)
	Joe Devany (R)	27,121	(34%)	($66,307)
1982 primary	John Bryant (D)	14,571	(67%)	
	Bill Blackburn (D)	4,756	(22%)	($76,675)
1980 general	Jim Mattox (D)	70,892	(51%)	($529,743)
	Tom Pauken (R)	67,848	(49%)	($265,248)

Campaign Contributions and Expenditures

1982		Direct Cont. 1982		PACS brkdwn			
Receipts	$282,272	Indiv	$76,532	Agr	$6,200	Ideo	$8,550
Expend.	$280,137	Party	$256	Bus	$16,436	Lbr	$75,300
Unspent	$1,261	PACS	$117,007	Hlth	$1,500	Prof	$2,000
		Cand	$83,700				

SIXTH DISTRICT

On the map, the 6th congressional district of Texas looks like a rural and small town district, the sort that for so many years sent conservative Democrats back to Washington, where they accumulated seniority and became committee chairmen. But appearances are deceiving: the 6th is not exactly such a district, and it certainly does not elect that kind of congressman.

The 6th extends literally from the Houston city limit to one mile south of the Dallas city limit. About 20% of its population is in Montgomery County, just north of Houston; this once rural and countrified county has been overrun now with fairly affluent and politically quite conservative Houstonians, in search of reasonably priced subdivisions and condominiums, people who don't mind the scruffy roadside stands and stores which are evidence of its previous inhabitants. About 30% of the 6th is part of the Dallas–Fort Worth metroplex, including a small part of southern Dallas County and the two counties, Ellis and Johnson, directly south of Dallas and Fort Worth. These, too, were once primarily rural farming country, and now are increasingly metropolitan; in their southern portions you can still see the expanses of ranch and farming land which make them attractive to many unwilling urbanites.

The middle part of the district is a series of small towns and rural areas. Its largest population concentration is around College Station—the home of Texas A&M University and its famous Aggies—and also of the district's congressman, Phil Gramm.

First elected as recently as 1978, Gramm has already become a national figure of considerable importance and, for a time, power. That could not have happened in more placid times when people were confident about the workings of the economy; few people then would pay much attention to an economics professor who believes in free markets and very little government, and advocates his positions with a fervor and a disregard for his own political interest that would ordinarily repel practical politicians. But the late 1970s and early 1980s were not ordinary economic times, and the old economic policies, of right and left, did not seem to be working.

Phil Gramm, a man of irrepressible energy, believed he had the answer, and he was not shy about making his views known. In 1979 and 1980 he had a solidly conservative, anti-Carter voting record. Nevertheless, in 1980 he asked for and got, thanks largely to the efforts of Majority Leader Jim Wright of Fort Worth, a seat on the Budget Committee. There Gramm was the intellectual leader of the Boll Weevils, and more. He not only voted with the Republicans; he attended Democratic strategy sessions, and then told the Republicans what the Democrats were planning—something no one else on the Budget Committee did. His name was ultimately placed on the Reagan administration budget plans, Gramm–Latta and Gramm–Latta II. He had the satisfaction of seeing his budget resolutions adopted, and of seeing the liberals he had long opposed vanquished. And when the economy turned sour in 1982, Gramm had no regrets, except perhaps that he had not worked harder to trim the budget more.

That unrepentance—and his betrayal of confidence—led the Democrats to kick Gramm off the Budget Committee as the new Congress began. He bellowed his displeasure and complained of boss rule, but it's hard to see how a party which claims any right to secure its members' allegiance could continue to reward Gramm with a high position, one which is elective and not due anyone automatically, after he had betrayed secrets to the opposition. Gramm immediately turned Republican, and did what was honorable: he resigned, and let his constituents vote on whether they wanted him as a Republican congressman.

It was a principled move, and one not entirely without risk. Gramm had faced opposition in the Democratic primary in 1982, and although he beat John Olin Teague, the son of his predecessor, by a 62%–28% margin, he clearly had some detractors; and the national Democrats were ready to run a campaign against him. But Gramm was ready too. He had raised over $800,000 for his 1980 campaign and had more than $200,000 left over after the election; outgoing Governor William Clements called a quick special election, so the Democrats would have little time to raise money or campaign. So Gramm was able to win by a comfortable margin. The Republicans have put him back on the Budget Committee, and he is sure to continue to make his peppery contributions to the debate. But he is less likely to be a major force in this Congress. Rather than being a pivotal vote, he is now part of an outnumbered minority; he is back again to the position conservatives held in the middle 1970s, when they were critics rather than doers. That is a congenial mode intellectually for Gramm, however, and probably politically too. He has all but announced that he will be a Senate candidate any time there is an opening. That might happen if John Tower does not run for reelection in 1984. If Tower runs, Gramm might run for governor in 1986 or might wait for 1988 and a chance to run again against Senator Lloyd Bentsen, against whom he got 28% of the vote in the 1976 Democratic primary, when he was still an unknown economics professor. Whatever else he is, he is not that any more.

The People Pop. 1980: 527,393, up 56.6% 1970–80; voting age pop. 375,239; 10% Black, 5% Span. orig. 25% housing units rented. Median owner $40,900; renter $189. Households: 76% family, 42% with children, 66% married couples.

Presidential Vote

1980	Reagan (R)	NA
	Carter (D)	NA
	Anderson (I)	NA

Rep. Phil Gramm (R) Elected 1978 as a Dem., elected 1983 in special election as a Repub.; b. July 8, 1942, Ft. Benning, GA; home, College Station; U. of GA, B.B.A. 1964; Ph.D. 1967; Episcopal.

Career Prof., TX A&M U., 1967–78.

Offices 1116 LHOB, 202-225-2002. Also 216 W. 26th St., Bryan 77801, 713-846-0687; and 210 W. 5th Ave, Corsicana 75110, 214-872-4411.

Committees *Budget* (6th). Task Forces: Budget Process; Economic Policy and Growth; Entitlements, Uncontrollables, and Indexing. *Veterans' Affairs* (8th).

Group Ratings

	ADA	ACLU	COPE	CFA	LCV	LWV	NTU	NSI	COC	ACA	CSFC
1982	10	8	12	15	16	17	97	100	73	100	81
1981	0	—	15	14	7	—	91	—	89	88	76
1980	0	7	10	7	2	25	63	100	78	71	71

National Journal Ratings

	Economic		Foreign		Cultural	
1982	5%	(LIB)	4%	(LIB)	40%	(LIB)
	94%	(CONS)	92%	(CONS)	60%	(CONS)
1981	4%	(LIB)	3%	(LIB)	11%	(LIB)
	79%	(CONS)	87%	(CONS)	88%	(CONS)

Key Votes

1) Reagan 81 Budget	FOR	5) Incr SS Rtmt Age	FOR	9) Poor Pay Food Stamps	FOR
2) Reagan 81 Tax Cut	FOR	6) Saudi AWACS Sale	FOR	10) Ban Crt Busing Order	—
3) Bal Budget Amend	FOR	7) $ for MX Missile	FOR	11) Auto Local Content	AGN
4) Gas & Road Tax	AGN	8) Nerve Gas Prod	FOR	12) Nuclear Arms Freeze	AGN

Election Results

1983 special	Phil Gramm (R)	46,334	(55%)	($751,083)
	Dan Kubiak (D)	33,162	(39%)	($126,009)
	Nine others (8 D and 1 L)	4,566	(5%)	
1982 general	Phil Gramm (D)	91,546	(95%)	($811,714)
	Ron Hard (L)	5,288	(5%)	($0)
1982 primary	Phil Gramm (D)	41,150	(62%)	
	John O. Teague (D)	18,923	(28%)	($70,951)
	Wayne Sadberry (D)	3,987	(6%)	($6,322)
1980 general	Phil Gramm (D)	144,816	(71%)	($21,215)
	Dave (Buster) Haskins (R)	59,503	(29%)	($0)

Campaign Contributions and Expenditures

1981-Feb. 83		Direct Cont. 1981-Feb. '83			PACS brkdwn*		
Receipts	$1,778,122	Indiv	$1,291,810	Agr	$4,650	Ideo	$4,900
Expend.	$1,562,797	Party	$1,793	Bus	$214,278	Lbr	$—
Unspent	$407,101	PACS	$433,335	Hlth	$15,950	Prof	$6,500

Indep Expend: For: $1,880 (NRA)
PACS brkdwn does not include $164,445 figure for 1983 special election.

SEVENTH DISTRICT

In the ten years after the oil shock of 1973, Houston was the nation's most visibly booming city. It became the center of the American oil industry, indeed of the whole world's oil business, and not just because some of the Seven Sisters moved their headquarters here. More important, Houston is the home of hundreds of businesses that serve and aid the exploration for, production, transportation, and refining of oil and natural gas—and of the lawyers who write out contracts and figure their way through the maze of government regulations.

The signs of Houston's prosperity are instantly and readily apparent to any visitor. There are new skyscrapers, both downtown and strewn in various places on the west side, new hotels, new apartment buildings, and countless new residential subdivisions. There is traffic congestion, quite possibly the nation's worst. Houston is proud that it has attracted some of the world's luxury stores—at the Galleria shopping mall you can find Tiffany's, Gucci, and so forth—but even more impressive is the wide range of upper- and upper-middle-income stores and services that are thriving there. Yet even amid the glitter, as oil prices fell in the early 1980s, signs of doubt began to appear. Is Houston so dependent on the oil industry that it will decline whenever oil does, like another Detroit or Pittsburgh? Or has Houston built a diversified economic base, as Los Angeles did in the 1950s and Chicago did in the 1880s, that will enable it to become a true world city?

Most of the visible boom in Houston is on the west side of the city. The downtown sits separately, between a marginal residential area and slums; and to the east are the great refineries and the Houston Ship Channel. The west and southwest sides are where most of Houston's high-income people live. The commercial streets here do not look special: Houston has no zoning laws, and next to a pleasant garden apartment you may find a U-Totem store or a drive-in restaurant. But the neighborhoods behind the main streets preserve their character through protective covenants, and use the lush greenery that thrives in humid Houston to compensate for the uninteresting flatness of the land. The visitor may marvel at the high prices commanded by the mansions in River Oaks or on guarded streets off Memorial Drive. But there are literally hundreds of newly built subdivisions on the west side of Houston—the city has been expanding its city limits, but still falls short of keeping up with their growth— where prices are, by the standards of some other large metropolitan areas, quite reasonable.

The growth of the west side of Houston mirrors the growth of Houston's entrepreneurial and professional sectors. There were about 150,000 people living on the west side in 1960; by 1980 there were 900,000 in the same area. About half this area forms the present-day 7th congressional district of Texas—a constituency that did not exist 20 years ago. The 7th district covers the area west of Memorial Park, on both sides of the Katy Freeway; generally it stays north of Westheimer, one of the main business streets here. It takes in the vast, flat, still empty expanse of the western part of Harris County, a place once dotted with tiny towns amid a part of Texas with a high proportion of blacks. Now the affluent part of Houston is advancing relentlessly into this empty quarter, conquering new square miles every year.

The 7th district is one of the two or three most Republican congressional districts in the United States. People here believe strongly in free enterprise; they see the federal government as an impediment to salutary business and economic growth. You can attack this position as selfish, and it does serve people's short-term interests. But they can see in Houston in their own lifetimes, how capitalism has transformed a sleepy, backward community into a thriving, exceedingly productive metropolis whose goods and services have improved the lives of people around the world. Government, in their experience, has done little to help and a lot to hinder this process. The conservatism here is more economic than cultural; many of these people, after all, have moved far from their original roots and they are not particularly interested in influencing other people's lifestyles. But few voters here are aggressive liberals on cultural issues, and very few dissent from the hawkish consensus on foreign policy. You won't find many Democrats in these precincts; about three-fourths of the votes here regularly go to Republican presidential candidates.

The 7th district produced two Republican presidential candidates in 1980: John Connally, who lives in River Oaks and practiced law in downtown Houston; and George Bush, who lived off Woodway Drive, and was elected the 7th district's congressman in 1966 and 1968. Bush's later successes have come more in Washington and various primary states than in Texas; he lost two Senate races here, in 1964 and 1970, and he failed, barely, to win the 1980 Texas presidential primary.

The district's current congressman is Bill Archer, Bush's successor and one of the *de facto* leaders of the Republican Party in the House. Born and brought up in Texas—as are most people here, despite the talk of northern migrants and Bush's example—Archer was elected to the legislature as a Democrat and then became a Republican. He has been a member of the Ways and Means Committee for 10 years, and there he has been an articulate and effective spokesman for positions backed by the oil industry. Archer serves as ranking Republican on the Social Security Subcommittee, and with Chairman Jake Pickle he spent several years trying to reach a compromise on Social Security refinancing. He is heedful enough of principle, however, that he refused to support the compromise reached in 1983, on the grounds it imposed too high a tax burden on the economy. Still, it did end up doing some of the things he suggested: addressing (though not necessarily as he would like) the long-term problems of the system, and raising the retirement age and cutting some scheduled future benefits rather than simply raising taxes. His position has much to say for it, and despite the safeness of his seat he has shown considerable political courage in advancing it.

Archer is bright, articulate, and principled enough that he could be on any short list of possible future Republican leaders. He has the additional advantage of coming from a district where he cannot possibly lose and is in the South.

The People Pop. 1980: 527,083, up 103.6% 1970–80; voting age pop. 375,483; 3% Black, 6% Span. orig., 3% Asian orig. 33% housing units rented. Median owner $79,200; renter $302. Households: 72% family, 42% with children, 62% married couples.

Presidential Vote

1980	Reagan (R)	NA
	Carter (D)	NA
	Anderson (I)	NA

Rep. Bill Archer (R) Elected 1970; b. Mar. 22, 1928, Houston; home, Houston; Rice U., 1946–47, U. of TX, B.B.A., L.L.B. 1951; Roman Catholic.

Career Air Force, Korea; Pres., Uncle Johnny Mills, Inc., 1953–61; Hunters Creek Village Cncl. and Mayor Pro Tem, 1955–62; TX House of Reps., 1966–70; Dir., Heights State Bank, Houston, 1967–70; Practicing atty., 1968–71.

Offices 1135 LHOB, 202-225-2571. Also 5108 Fed. Bldg., 515 Rusk St., Houston 77002, 713-226-4941.

Committee *Ways and Means* (3d). Subcommittees: Social Security; Trade.

Group Ratings

	ADA	ACLU	COPE	CFA	LCV	LWV	NTU	NSI	COC	ACA	CSFC
1982	0	0	6	8	16	17	96	100	86	91	80
1981	5	—	6	36	36	—	93	—	89	88	83
1980	6	7	11	14	32	11	73	100	68	96	88

National Journal Ratings

	Economic		Foreign		Cultural	
1982	9%	(LIB)	26%	(LIB)	4%	(LIB)
	91%	(CONS)	74%	(CONS)	87%	(CONS)
1981	4%	(LIB)	18%	(LIB)	12%	(LIB)
	79%	(CONS)	73%	(CONS)	86%	(CONS)

Key Votes

1) Reagan 81 Budget	FOR	5) Incr SS Rtmt Age	FOR	9) Poor Pay Food Stamps	FOR
2) Reagan 81 Tax Cut	FOR	6) Saudi AWACS Sale	AGN	10) Ban Crt Busing Order	FOR
3) Bal Budget Amend	FOR	7) $ for MX Missile	FOR	11) Auto Local Content	AGN
4) Gas & Road Tax	AGN	8) Nerve Gas Prod	FOR	12) Nuclear Arms Freeze	AGN

Election Results

1982 general	Bill Archer (R)	108,718	(85%)	($193,449)
	Dennis G. Scoggins (D)	17,866	(14%)	($281)
1982 primary	Bill Archer (R)	24,555	(100%)	
1980 general	Bill Archer (R)	242,810	(82%)	($124,687)
	Robert L. Hutchings (D)	48,594	(16%)	($3,877)

Campaign Contributions and Expenditures

1981-82		*Direct Cont. 81-82*	
Receipts	$279,509	Indiv	$180,373
Expend.	$193,449	Party	$70
Unspent	$411,241		

Received no PAC Contributions

EIGHTH DISTRICT

The 8th congressional district of Texas is the northeast part of Houston and surrounding Harris County. Most of it is situated north of the Houston Ship Channel, as it makes its murky way from Houston's industrial area out to Galveston Bay and the Gulf of Mexico, and directly north of the city. About one-third of the people here live within the city of Houston, and about a third of these are black; these are modest working-class precincts on the city's east side. To the north, the district includes what was once countryside, dotted by roadside stores and jerry-built houses, and what is now the home of Houston's Intercontinental Airport, and the glassy high-rise office buildings and glittery subdivisions that are being built nearby. At the far eastern end of the district is Baytown, an industrial refinery town where the Ship Channel empties out into the bay.

This is part of the working-class side of Houston, a part you won't see on tours of the city except as you're coming in from the airport. But it is also a part of the city that exemplifies Houston's upward mobility. Most of the people here are probably from modest, countrified backgrounds, in Houston or more likely elsewhere in Texas or the rural South. They came here to find opportunity and have found it; and they are building a new way of life literally on top of buildings reminiscent of the places they came from. This is a district that believes more deeply in traditional personal values than do the rich people on the west side of town, but which clings to a belief like theirs in the free enterprise system and the deregulation of oil prices. In elections this is generally Republican territory, although there are plenty of Democratic precincts here, and the right Democrats have been known to carry it.

The current congressman is Jack Fields, a young Republican who engineered one of the biggest upsets of 1980 by beating scholarly liberal Democrat Bob Eckhardt. Fields was a favorite of the Republican Party and of oil and business PACs; he spent nearly $800,000 in that race and harped on the themes Ronald Reagan used. But his victory cannot be ascribed to money or to coattails: Eckhardt spent close to $500,000 himself, on top of the advantages he had from 14 years of incumbency, and Fields ran ahead of Reagan: Carter carried the 8th district as it existed then. Since 1980, the legislature moved the district outward, giving Fields something pretty close to a safe seat; but the configuration also meant that the new 25th district in the Houston area would be solidly Democratic.

Fields was in many ways typical of the 1980 Republican freshmen: young, ambitious, attractive in a way that is unthreatening to those with traditional values. He has genuine roots in the district (which not many of its voters do). Democrats see him as plastic and unthinking; Republicans see him as a talented and attractive fighter for sound principles. His constituents evidently view him favorably: in a Democratic year he won reelection with 57% of the votes. In 1983 Fields won a seat on the Energy and Commerce Committee, and on the subcommittee that deals with energy price deregulation; that puts him on the front lines in the internecine battles between various natural gas interests. In the crunch, however, he is likely to come out for deregulation.

The People   Pop. 1980: 527,531, up 65.7% 1970–80; voting age pop. 347,798; 15% Black, 11% Span. orig., 1% Asian orig. 27% housing units rented. Median owner $46,700; renter $256. Households: 81% family, 52% with children, 69% married couples.

Presidential Vote

1980	Reagan (R)	NA
	Carter (D)	NA
	Anderson (I)	NA

Rep. Jack Fields (R) Elected 1980; b. Feb. 3, 1952, Humble; home, Humble; Baylor U., B.A. 1974, J.D. 1977; Baptist.

Career Practicing atty., 1977–; Exec. V.P., Rosewood Memorial Park, family business, 1977–79; TX Governor's Small Business Advisory Assistance Cncl., 1979–80.

Offices 413 CHOB, 202-225-4901. Also 12605 E. Freeway, Su. 320, First State Bank Bldg., Houston 77015, 713-451-6334.

Committees Energy and Commerce (13th). Subcommittee: Fossil and Synthetic Fuels. *Merchant Marine and Fisheries* (9th). Subcommittees: Merchant Marine; Panama Canal and Outer Continental Shelf.

Group Ratings

	ADA	ACLU	COPE	CFA	LCV	LWV	NTU	NSI	COC	ACA	CSFC
1982	5	4	4	8	21	17	96	100	86	91	80
1981	0	—	7	21	14	—	93	—	95	91	79

National Journal Ratings

	Economic		Foreign		Cultural	
1982	9%	(LIB)	10%	(LIB)	21%	(LIB)
	91%	(CONS)	89%	(CONS)	76%	(CONS)
1981	4%	(LIB)	18%	(LIB)	0%	(LIB)
	79%	(CONS)	73%	(CONS)	99%	(CONS)

Key Votes

1) Reagan 81 Budget	FOR	5) Incr SS Rtmt Age	FOR	9) Poor Pay Food Stamps	FOR
2) Reagan 81 Tax Cut	FOR	6) Saudi AWACS Sale	AGN	10) Ban Crt Busing Order	FOR
3) Bal Budget Amend	FOR	7) $ for MX Missile	FOR	11) Auto Local Content	AGN
4) Gas & Road Tax	AGN	8) Nerve Gas Prod	FOR	12) Nuclear Arms Freeze	AGN

Election Results

1982 general	Jack Fields (R)	50,630	(57%)	($604,539)
	Henry E. Allee (D)	38,041	(43%)	($59,201)
1982 primary	Jack Fields (R)	5,713	(100%)	
1980 general	Jack Fields (R)	72,856	(52%)	($794,870)
	Bob Eckhardt (D)	67,921	(48%)	($457,630)

Campaign Contributions and Expenditures

1981-82		Direct Cont. 81-82		PACS brkdwn			
Receipts	$615,210	Indiv	$385,154	Agr	$6,550	Ideo	$4,100
Expend.	$604,539	Party	$8,370	Bus	$122,874	Lbr	$1,750
Unspent	$16,046	PACS	$159,096	Hlth	$12,750	Prof	$8,550

Indirect Party Expend: $196   *Indep Expend:* For: $2,360 (NRA)   *Non-Cand Loans:* $42,000

NINTH DISTRICT

The 9th congressional district of Texas is the eastern end of the state's Gulf Coast—an area of big refineries, petrochemical plants, and other factories. This is not the place for the delicate: it is dominated by heavy industry and has one of the highest concentrations of blue-collar workers in Texas. There are two main urban areas here. One is around Galveston Bay. The city of Galveston, built on a sand spit, was one of Texas's original main cities; but it was devastated by a hurricane in 1900, and even venturesome Texans decided it was better to build the big city (which became Houston) on swamps rather than on a sand spit scarcely above sea level. So Galveston has expanded inland: to the oil port of Texas City and north to Clear Lake City, around the NASA's Lyndon B. Johnson Space Center, which Johnson and former longtime Houston Congressman Albert Thomas located here. The other major population center is in the southeastern corner of the state, centered on Beaumont and Port Arthur. These were for years the main outlets for much of the oil from the east Texas fields, and they have huge refineries today. There are large black populations here—each city is close to half black—and, because Louisiana is just a few miles away, there is a significant Cajun population as well.

Politically, this is one of Texas's few solidly liberal districts on economic issues. There is a significant union movement here, more united because it does not have a huge membership; there are many blacks; the smaller numbers of Cajuns and Mexican-Americans tend to be liberals too. On most cultural issues they are anything but fashionably leftish; yet on civil rights the 9th not only tolerated but gladly reelected as its congressman a man who supported civil rights bills. This was a solid Carter district in 1976 and an even one in 1980.

The congressman from this district is Jack Brooks. He was first elected to the House in 1952, before he was 30. He is undeniably brainy and even more undeniably forceful; he has a record on a variety of issues which commands respect. He is probably the current member of Congress who most closely resembles Lyndon Johnson, in both his virtues and his faults. Brooks is extremely partisan, profane, knowledgeable, witty, effective. He is also a member who is comfortable doing business with lobbyists; he is the chief House sponsor, for example, of the heavily lobbied bill to allow beer distributors to get exclusive territories.

Brooks is generally a liberal on economic issues, out of conviction but also because he believes in going along with the Democratic leadership on important matters; he is no maverick. He has supported civil rights bills since he came to Congress, which may not sound awesome today, but which in east Texas required great political courage in the 1950s and 1960s. He could not have been sure that his positions would be as easily accepted by his constituents as they were. His positions recently on foreign issues have been more liberal than they were when he supported Johnson on the Vietnam war; on cultural issues his record is mixed.

Brooks is the number two Democrat on Judiciary, and will be chairman if Peter Rodino retires; he serves now as chairman of the Government Operations Committee. This body has a charter which allows it to investigate most government agencies. But it passes relatively little legislation, and much of that deals with government reorganization—which seldom turns out to be as important as its advocates claim. Brooks, to his credit, was skeptical of the worth of the Carter administration's reorganization proposals and fought them on constitutional grounds; but his lack of success did not increase his reputation for effectiveness. Periodically Government Operations is singled out by reformers of some stripe as a committee which could, in the right hands, make a bigger difference in the way government works. But the fact that the committee has had several able chairmen, including Brooks, without satisfying these expectations suggests that the problem is more basic. Archimedes said that if you gave him a long enough lever and a place to stand, he could move the world; but Gov Ops is not a long enough lever, usually, to move the government. Brooks is a potentially powerful legislator, but because of his talent, not his position.

Despite that, Brooks has had problems at the polls in the last two elections. Democratic primary opponents have charged that he is too liberal. In 1980 he edged challenger Bubba Pate by a 50%–43% margin; in 1982 he won with 53% against Pate and three other challengers. These are uncomfortably close margins; if just a few votes had gone the other way, he would have been forced into a runoff, and in those contests the momentum is often with the challenger. Brooks was caught by surprise in 1980, but in 1982 he campaigned hard and spent over $700,000; he could have another tough fight in 1984. He has not had, nor is he likely to have, any trouble in general elections in this solidly Democratic district.

The People Pop. 1980: 526,443, up 17.5% 1970–80; voting age pop. 370,362; 20% Black, 7% Span. orig., 1% Asian orig. 28% housing units rented. Median owner $39,300; renter $209. Households: 76% family, 43% with children, 63% married couples.

Presidential Vote

1980	Reagan (R)	NA
	Carter (D)	NA
	Anderson (I)	NA

Rep. Jack Brooks (D) Elected 1952; b. Dec. 18, 1922, Crowley, LA; home, Beaumont; Lamar Jr. Col., 1939–41, U. of TX, B.J. 1943, J.D. 1949; Methodist.

Career USMC, WWII; TX House of Reps., 1946–50; Practicing atty., 1949–52.

Offices 2449 RHOB, 202-225-6565. Also 230 Fed. Bldg., Beaumont 77701, 713-838-0271.

Committees *Government Operations* (Chairman). Subcommittee: Legislation and National Security (Chairman). *Judiciary* (2d). Subcommittees: Courts, Civil Liberties, and the Administration of Justice; Monopolies and Commercial Law.

Group Ratings

	ADA	ACLU	COPE	CFA	LCV	LWV	NTU	NSI	COC	ACA	CSFC
1982	50	46	73	46	59	56	10	70	40	33	38
1981	45	—	73	29	43	—	41	—	33	38	47
1980	28	57	50	50	13	13	21	43	69	21	32

National Journal Ratings

	Economic		Foreign		Cultural	
1982	65%	(LIB)	52%	(LIB)	54%	(LIB)
	35%	(CONS)	47%	(CONS)	46%	(CONS)
1981	57%	(LIB)	71%	(LIB)	53%	(LIB)
	42%	(CONS)	28%	(CONS)	47%	(CONS)

Key Votes

1) Reagan 81 Budget	AGN	5) Incr SS Rtmt Age	FOR	9) Poor Pay Food Stamps	—
2) Reagan 81 Tax Cut	AGN	6) Saudi AWACS Sale	—	10) Ban Crt Busing Order	FOR
3) Bal Budget Amend	AGN	7) $ for MX Missile	AGN	11) Auto Local Content	FOR
4) Gas & Road Tax	FOR	8) Nerve Gas Prod	FOR	12) Nuclear Arms Freeze	FOR

Election Results

1982 general	Jack Brooks (D)	78,969	(68%)	($701,007)
	John W. Lewis (R)	35,422	(30%)	($28,740)
1982 primary	Jack Brooks (D)	37,264	(53%)	
	W. L. (Bubba) Pate (D)	15,230	(22%)	($77,246)
	E. Douglas McLeod (D)	8,573	(12%)	($179,362)
	Tom Combs (D)	7,812	(11%)	($74,634)
1980 general	Jack Brooks (D)	103,225	(100%)	($113,569)

Campaign Contributions and Expenditures

1981-82		Direct Cont. 81-82		PACS brkdwn			
Receipts	$634,348	Indiv	$257,986	Agr	$6,900	Ideo	$4,667
Expend.	$701,007	Party	$5,000	Bus	$137,375	Lbr	$67,700
Unspent	$5,445	PACS	$240,305	Hlth	$3,150	Prof	$19,980
		Cand	$125,000				

TENTH DISTRICT

The 10th congressional district of Texas is the LBJ district. Here in the central Texas hills the towns are farther apart and trees less common than in east Texas; the land is less fertile, and there is less rain. Lyndon Johnson was born and raised and went to college and began his political career among the rolling hills of central Texas, when most residents were farmers and only with difficulty eked out a living. The poverty of its people—with no electricity, only rudimentary transportation, cut off in so many ways from the outside world—affected Johnson, and he in turn changed the way of life in the district. Even a disapproving biographer concedes that Johnson was "the best congressman ever": within a few years of his election to the House in 1937, at age 29, he had cinched a dam for the area and brought electricity to the hills. Johnson grew up in a Texas that was segregated, although racial barriers and tensions were not so great here as they were farther east; as Senate majority leader he passed the civil rights acts of 1957 and 1960 and as president helped pass the civil rights acts of 1964 and 1965.

Johnson also changed the way of life here more subtly and indirectly than by just building a dam and introducing electricity. His Great Society programs, the vast increase in the scope and size of government that he sponsored, have in turn helped to make Austin the metropolis it currently is. In 1930, when Johnson was contemplating a political career, Austin was a town of 53,000. It contained the state Capitol—appropriately the largest in the nation—an office building or two, the University of Texas, the old Driskill Hotel, and not a whole lot else. Today metropolitan Austin is a city of 400,000, with what may well be the world's largest university campus, the LBJ Library, and pleasant residential neighborhoods that are overflowing into the hills around it. Its cost of living is one of the lowest in the country; its quality of life, according to many enthusiasts, one of the highest.

Austin remains a government, university, and white-collar town; the oil business is not important here, nor really are any of the free enterprises which seem so dominant in so much of the rest of Texas. Austin is a kind of observer of the rest of Texas, sometimes proud, sometimes bemused, sometimes dismayingly solemn and superior, and sometimes just delighted. It is the headquarters of the *Texas Monthly,* probably the most successful—editorially and financially—of the nation's regional magazines and of the persistently, peskily liberal *Texas Observer.* Politically, Austin is Democratic. The affluent neighborhoods go Republican, but not by margins as one-sided as in other Texas cities; the college and the rather small number of black and Mexican-American precincts go heavily for liberal Democrats. Austin totally dominates 10th district politics these days; the city plus surrounding Travis County have become so large that they account for 80% of the district's population.

The congressman from the 10th district is Jake Pickle, first elected in 1963, just after

Johnson became president. Pickle may be characterized as a Johnson Democrat: his first governmental experience was in the National Youth Administration in 1930s, in which Johnson also made his mark. He has a voting record which is probably what Johnson's would be like if he were still in the House. That leaves Pickle rather mixed on the issues, as far as rating groups are concerned; on both economic and non-economic issues Pickle does not always side with liberals or conservatives. Like Johnson, he has an instinct to help the poor and helpless. But unlike Johnson, he is also concerned about paying for the services he votes for, and conservative in his estimates of what is possible.

Pickle lacks Johnson's aggressiveness and ruthlessness; he is a gentle and pleasant man. Yet he has also shown that he can be persistent—and successful—when he feels he needs to be. He is the third ranking Democrat on the House Ways and Means Committee now, and chairman of the Social Security Subcommittee. He was worried, even before Ronald Reagan took office, about the solvency of the system, and he insisted on trying to attack both its short-term and long-term financial problems. He was dubious about the breezy predictions some Democrats and Social Security experts made that the system would pull through with nothing more than a temporary tax in the 1980s, and he was dubious that too great a tax increase would put too great a burden on the economy. In 1981 he was working with Republicans to find some compromise solution when Speaker O'Neill called him off: Social Security was the Democrats' only strong issue against Reagan Republicans then, and he didn't want to lose it before 1982. Pickle was also prevailed upon not to serve on the 15-member presidential commission charged to come up with a solution for Social Security.

That decision denied Pickle visibility and credit for the solution which was ultimately achieved. When the commission did produce a recommendation in early 1983, he speeded it through his subcommittee and shepherded it to the floor. But he himself favored an amendment which would raise the basic retirement age in the 21st century—a rather simple change that, announced now, gives those affected plenty of notice, and that makes a world of difference in Social Security's financial soundness. That amendment passed, and O'Neill hurried the resulting bill through the House and on to passage, before too many people noticed that a change opposed by most Democrats had been made. Claude Pepper got the publicity as the leading Social Security legislator, but Jake Pickle was the one who got the bill he wanted.

Since college students got the vote, Pickle has had a potential political problem: he is not the kind of stylish liberal such voters in the early 1970s preferred. There are some in Austin though: State Senator Lloyd Doggett for one, and former state Representative Sarah Weddington. But Pickle was not seriously challenged in the Democratic primary then, and by the 1970s the student mood had become quiescent or even conservative. As for the general election, this is basically a Democratic district, and unlikely ever to elect a Republican.

The People   Pop. 1980: 527,181, up 41.0% 1970–80; voting age pop. 390,909; 9% Black, 15% Span. orig., 1% Asian orig. 40% housing units rented. Median owner $47,800; renter $222. Households: 65% family, 35% with children, 53% married couples.

Presidential Vote

1980	Reagan (R)	NA
	Carter (D)	NA
	Anderson (I)	NA

Rep. J. J. (Jake) **Pickle** (D) Elected Dec. 17, 1963; b. Oct. 11, 1913, Big Spring; home, Austin; U. of TX, B.A. 1938; Methodist.

Career Area Dir., Natl. Youth Admin., 1938–41; Navy, WWII; Coorganizer, KVET Radio, Austin; Adv. and pub. rel. business; Dir., TX State Dem. Exec. Comm., 1957–60; Mbr., TX Employment Commission, 1961–63.

Offices 242 CHOB, 202-225-4865. Also 763 Fed. Bldg., Austin 78701, 512-397-5921.

Committees *Ways and Means* (3d). Subcommittees: Oversight; Social Security (Chairman). *Joint Committee on Taxation* (3d).

Group Ratings

	ADA	ACLU	COPE	CFA	LCV	LWV	NTU	NSI	COC	ACA	CSFC
1982	30	50	51	46	43	70	39	90	58	59	43
1981	40	—	51	43	43	—	23	—	58	33	46
1980	22	53	42	43	30	33	35	67	79	33	39

National Journal Ratings

	Economic		Foreign		Cultural	
1982	51%	(LIB)	48%	(LIB)	46%	(LIB)
	49%	(CONS)	52%	(CONS)	54%	(CONS)
1981	51%	(LIB)	58%	(LIB)	57%	(LIB)
	49%	(CONS)	41%	(CONS)	43%	(CONS)

Key Votes

1) Reagan 81 Budget AGN	5) Incr SS Rtmt Age FOR	9) Poor Pay Food Stamps AGN
2) Reagan 81 Tax Cut AGN	6) Saudi AWACS Sale AGN	10) Ban Crt Busing Order FOR
3) Bal Budget Amend FOR	7) $ for MX Missile AGN	11) Auto Local Content AGN
4) Gas & Road Tax FOR	8) Nerve Gas Prod FOR	12) Nuclear Arms Freeze AGN

Election Results

1982 general	J. J. (Jake) Pickle (D)	121,030	(90%)	($79,157)
	William G. Kelsey (L)	8,735	(7%)	($0)
1982 primary	J. J. (Jake) Pickle (D)	55,303	(100%)	
1980 general	J. J. (Jake) Pickle (D)	135,618	(59%)	($308,661)
	John Biggar (R)	88,940	(39%)	($77,586)

Campaign Contributions and Expenditures

1981-82		Direct Cont. 81-82		PACS brkdwn			
Receipts	$196,001	Indiv	$112,826	Agr	$—	Ideo	$700
Expend.	$79,157	PACS	$41,450	Bus	$30,650	Lbr	$750
Unspent	$262,011			Hlth	$2,750	Prof	$6,600

ELEVENTH DISTRICT

The 11th congressional district is deep in the heart of Texas. Made up of all or part of 13 counties, it sits slightly off the geographic center of the state, but just about at the center of its population. It is not, however, within the orbit of greater Houston or the Dallas–Fort Worth metroplex, or even of Austin: it is betwixt and between, a part of Texas whose farm fields and small towns recall the state as it was half a century ago, before the growth of the oil industry transformed this rural backwater into one of the centers of western capitalism.

This part of Texas has been changed, too, of course. It is much more affluent than it was even 10 years ago, and less insular. But some things have remained the same. Cotton is a major crop here; in fact, Texas is one of the largest cotton producers. The Army's giant Fort Hood continues not only to be a mainstay of the area, but its presence seems to bolster the hawkish instincts of Texans. Politically, this part of Texas is filled with ancestral Democrats. There are not all that many blacks here and not many Mexican-Americans, not many labor unions or universities. But Waco, the largest city here, Killeen, near Fort Hood, and the other parts of the district have been solidly Democratic since the Civil War. They were not deterred by the national Democrats' support of civil rights: they gave Hubert Humphrey an absolute majority of their votes in 1968. In 1980 the 11th district did shift and give Ronald Reagan a slight plurality. But by 1982 it was roaring back Democratic.

Despite this record of supporting national Democratic candidates, the 11th has always elected very conservative Democratic congressmen. The current incumbent, Marvin Leath, was elected in 1978 when Bob Poage, longtime House Agriculture Committee chairman (but ousted from that position in 1974) retired after 42 years in the House. Poage had a solid conservative record on most issues, but favored government farm programs. Leath is just as conservative on most things, but specializes in things military: he sits on Armed Services and Veterans' Affairs. He was one of those Texas Democrats who provided critical support to the Reagan administration in 1981.

Leath had serious competition both in the Democratic primary and the general election in 1978. Since then he has had nuisance opposition or none at all, and seems well entrenched in the district.

The People   Pop. 1980: 527,382, up 25.3% 1970–80; voting age pop. 381,013; 13% Black, 8% Span. orig., 1% Asian orig. 32% housing units rented. Median owner $30,400; renter $162. Households: 75% family, 41% with children, 65% married couples.

Presidential Vote

1980	Reagan (R)	NA
	Carter (D)	NA
	Anderson (I)	NA

Rep. J. Marvin Leath (D) Elected 1978; b. May 6, 1931, Rusk Cnty.; home, Marlin; U. of TX, B.A. 1954; Presbyterian.

Career Army, 1954–56; High sch. teacher and coach, 1956–58; Banker, 1962–72; Spec. Asst. to U.S. Rep. Bob Poage, 1972–75.

Offices 336 CHOB, 202-225-6105. Also 205 Fed. Bldg., Waco 76701, 817-752-9609.

Committees *Armed Services* (17th). Subcommittees: Investigations; Procurement and Military Nuclear Systems; Readiness. *Veterans' Affairs* (6th). Subcommittees: Compensation, Pension, and Insurance; Education, Training and Employment (Chairman).

Group Ratings

	ADA	ACLU	COPE	CFA	LCV	LWV	NTU	NSI	COC	ACA	CSFC
1982	10	21	21	8	21	33	73	100	67	81	63
1981	0	—	22	21	14	—	72	—	78	82	70
1980	0	10	19	0	1	29	62	100	73	71	76

National Journal Ratings

	Economic		Foreign		Cultural	
1982	23%	(LIB)	9%	(LIB)	0%	(LIB)
	77%	(CONS)	91%	(CONS)	99%	(CONS)
1981	38%	(LIB)	3%	(LIB)	20%	(LIB)
	61%	(CONS)	87%	(CONS)	80%	(CONS)

Key Votes

1) Reagan 81 Budget	FOR	5) Incr SS Rtmt Age	FOR	9) Poor Pay Food Stamps	AGN
2) Reagan 81 Tax Cut	FOR	6) Saudi AWACS Sale	FOR	10) Ban Crt Busing Order	FOR
3) Bal Budget Amend	FOR	7) $ for MX Missile	FOR	11) Auto Local Content	AGN
4) Gas & Road Tax	AGN	8) Nerve Gas Prod	FOR	12) Nuclear Arms Freeze	AGN

Election Results

1982 general	J. Marvin Leath (D)	83,236	(96%)	($126,771)
	Thomas B. Kilbride (L)	3,136	(4%)	($0)
1982 primary	J. Marvin Leath (D)	52,029	(82%)	
	Jay P. Larsen (D)	11,383	(18%)	
1980 general	J. Marvin Leath (D)	128,520	(100%)	($171,978)

Campaign Contributions and Expenditures

1981-82		Direct Cont. 81-82		PACS brkdwn			
Receipts	$213,155	Indiv	$112,208	Agr	$3,200	Ideo	$1,000
Expend.	$126,771	PACS	$56,152	Bus	$44,100	Lbr	$1,000
Unspent	$173,151			Hlth	$450	Prof	$3,050

TWELFTH DISTRICT

Between Fort Worth and Dallas, through the new Dallas–Fort Worth Regional Airport and near the Freeway Stadium and Six Flags Over Texas theme park in the suburb of Arlington, runs a not always visible line marking the geological divide known as the Balcones Escarpment. This is a rim of land, sometimes hovering above the eastern plain, sometimes smoothed or paved over by civilization. It divides dry west Texas from humid east Texas; it separates the treeless grazing lands that run west from Fort Worth from the green croplands that run east from Dallas. Fort Worth and Dallas are only 30 miles apart, but they are very different cities, from their geology to their recent development and their politics. As the old saying goes, Dallas is the end of the East and Fort Worth is the beginning of the West.

Fort Worth got its start as a cattle town. Dallas was once the western end of the railroad, but Fort Worth built its own line, the Texas Pacific, and its own stockyards, the largest in Texas. So cowboys drove their herds into Fort Worth to have them shipped east. While Dallas was concentrating on cotton and banking, Fort Worth was concentrating on railroads and meat-packing. Fort Worth developed more as a blue-collar town, although of course it had its management class and town fathers; Dallas had its factories, but as time went on became even more white collar. The difference even extended to defense contracts. Dallas tends to produce high-technology items; Fort Worth has the General Dynamics assembly plant that produces many of the nation's military aircraft. Dallas residents sometimes look down on Fort

Worth and call it Cowtown. But Fort Worth has its own strong civic culture and a set of art museums far superior to any others in Texas. Among them is the Amon Carter Museum of Western Art, the premier collection of its kind; looking west from one of Fort Worth's hills, toward the treeless skyline in the distance, you can almost see some of the scenes again on the high plains.

As the differences between Fort Worth and Dallas suggest, Fort Worth tends to be more Democratic and Dallas more Republican. But the differences have tended to become muted in recent years, as Fort Worth sprouts high-tech businesses of its own (Tandy Radio Shack) and Dallas has a larger low-income population, and as Fort Worth sprouts more affluent suburbs in Tarrant County and some of Dallas County's affluent population moves to counties north and east. Thus in 1980 there was not much difference between the margin by which Dallas County went for Reagan (59%–37%) and Tarrant Couty did (57%–40%). The difference was a little greater in 1982: Dallas was 54% for Republican William Clements in the gubernatorial race and Tarrant 51% for Democrat Mark White. The 12th congressional district, which includes most of Fort Worth and the Tarrant County suburbs to the north, is somewhat more Democratic; the most affluent parts of Fort Worth and the high-income suburb of Arlington are not included in it.

This is the district that elects Congressman Jim Wright, the House majority leader. He was first elected in 1954, and has spent much of his career in uncomfortable straddling positions as he finds himself torn in two directions. In the 1950s he was considered the most liberal member of the Texas delegation, a young national Democrat among a group of old and mostly conservative nominal members of the party. He had statewide ambitions, but was frustrated in them. In 1961 he ran for the Senate seat vacated by Lyndon Johnson, and just missed making the runoff; if he had made it, he might very well have beaten John Tower and might still be in the Senate today. In 1966 he wanted to run again but was unable to raise money from the state's big economic interests. He went on television and asked for $10 contributions, and got a lot of them—but not enough for a Senate race in Texas.

So Wright settled in for a long career in the House. In the days when Great Society bills were being passed, he was a strong supporter of national Democratic economic policies and generally had a good labor voting record. But on other issues, he sometimes parted company with many other Democrats. He remained a strong supporter of American policy in Vietnam. As a high-ranking member of the Public Works Committee, he favored roadbuilding and dam projects on the traditional Democratic theory that they helped needy communities and created jobs; he didn't think much of the arguments that they hurt the environment. Wright sees a positive role for government, but he was never one who wanted national economic planning; government in his view should work closely with business to create jobs and help the ordinary person. This is classic centrist Democratic politics in Texas, the beliefs that animated Sam Rayburn, Jesse Jones, and Lyndon Johnson. But in the middle 1970s, Wright found himself at odds with many Texas and southern Democrats, who considered him too liberal, and with many younger northern Democrats, who considered him too unsympathetic to their views on non-economic issues.

In that light, Wright's election as majority leader in 1976 was a startling event, and one that owed much to the liabilities of his opponents. He began the race with support from the Texas delegation and some, but not all, southerners. On the second ballot he edged out Richard Bolling by two votes; on the third he beat Phillip Burton 148–147 on the secret ballot. A reform-minded group of Democrats elected the one candidate without distinguished reform credentials.

Since then Wright has been a national figure, summoned regularly to the White House, speaking regularly for his party on national television. In general even his adversaries would grant that he has performed his duties competently. He knows parliamentary procedure, and works closely with Speaker O'Neill on keeping the flow of work in the House orderly. Wright was given a seat on the Budget Committee, in large part to help the Speaker oversee the work of Chairman James Jones. Wright seems to fancy himself an old-time orator, and he has a gift for a turn of phrase, sometimes eloquent, sometimes homey. But he may come off a little too practiced and hot on the colloquial and cool medium of television. He has made some mistakes along the way. His initial response to Reagan budget cuts was to make the top Democratic priority the full funding of the synfuels program; that is perhaps a defensible strategy, and it is certainly in line with Wright's predilection for government–business partnerships. But many Democrats thought he should have been addressing some of the cuts in benefits for the poor and middle class, and ultimately in 1982 the Democrats emphasized Social Security. He sought good committee assignments for some young Texans in 1981, which was fair enough; but one of those was Phil Gramm, whom he singlehandedly placed on the Budget Committee. Gramm not only made common cause to the Republicans; he attended Democratic strategy meetings and reported all their conclusions to the Republicans. A shrewder understanding of Gramm—for whom the principles of free market economics are more important than personal commitments—would have avoided this mistake.

For all that, however, there is no overwhelming discontent with Wright, and if an election were held tomorrow for the office, the House Democrats would almost surely elect him speaker. Of his competitors from 1976, Bolling has retired and Burton is dead. House majority whip Thomas Foley, appointed by O'Neill and Wright, does not seem the type to run an insurgent campaign. Other younger Democrats have a ways to go before they would be credible candidates for speaker. Wright is technically competent, and, if he veers from Democrats' positions on some issues, overall he does not veer too far. This Democratic Caucus is less liberal on economic issues than its counterpart of 10 years ago, and not much more liberal on cultural issues; on balance, it is not too far from Wright. Nonetheless, the succession is not automatic, as it was for Tip O'Neill in 1976, Carl Albert in 1970, John McCormack in 1962, and Sam Rayburn in 1940. Wright will have to fight for the post, and may well have some competition. That possibility has almost certainly made him a more competent and responsive majority leader—and so may end up improving his chances in the end.

Wright won reelection in the 12th district for years without serious opposition. Then in 1980 Jim Bradshaw, the mayor pro tem of Fort Worth, waged an enthusiastic Republican campaign. National Republicans and oil interests poured in money (although Wright has never been unfriendly to oil), but Wright outdid them, raising and spending more than $1.2 million. Wright also won votes. He took a solid 60% of the votes and squelched, probably for good, any ideas Republicans might have of taking this seat. Bradshaw himself ran in the new 26th district, in suburban Tarrant County, in 1982, and lost narrowly; Wright won overwhelmingly. Now that it seems clear, again, that the Democrats will hold onto their majority in the House, why would Fort Worth want to oust the likeliest candidate to be the next speaker?

The People   Pop. 1980: 527,074, up 5.8% 1970–80; voting age pop. 374,579; 15% Black, 9% Span. orig., 1% Asian orig. 33% housing units rented. Median owner $34,000; renter $204. Households: 73% family, 41% with children, 59% married couples.

Presidential Vote

1980	Reagan (R)	NA
	Carter (D)	NA
	Anderson (I)	NA

Rep. Jim Wright (D) Elected 1954; b. Dec. 22, 1922, Ft. Worth; home, Ft. Worth; Weatherford Col., U. of TX; Presbyterian.

Career Army Air Corps, WWII; Partner, trade extension and adv. firm; TX House of Reps.; Mayor of Weatherford; Pres., TX League of Municipalities, 1953.

Offices 1236 LHOB, 202-225-5071. Also 9A–10 Lanham Fed. Bldg, Ft. Worth 76102, 817-334-3212; and 536 B Seminary Dr., Ft. Worth 76115, 817-334-4845.

Committees *Majority Leader. Budget* (2d).

Group Ratings

	ADA	ACLU	COPE	CFA	LCV	LWV	NTU	NSI	COC	ACA	CSFC
1982	55	42	74	62	51	56	0	89	38	39	34
1981	30	—	74	43	30	—	0	—	29	28	44
1980	39	33	71	50	31	56	14	38	73	29	30

National Journal Ratings

	Economic		Foreign		Cultural	
1982	72%	(LIB)	45%	(LIB)	33%	(LIB)
	28%	(CONS)	54%	(CONS)	66%	(CONS)
1981	60%	(LIB)	33%	(LIB)	50%	(LIB)
	39%	(CONS)	66%	(CONS)	50%	(CONS)

Key Votes

1) Reagan 81 Budget	AGN	5) Incr SS Rtmt Age	FOR	9) Poor Pay Food Stamps	AGN
2) Reagan 81 Tax Cut	AGN	6) Saudi AWACS Sale	AGN	10) Ban Crt Busing Order	—
3) Bal Budget Amend	AGN	7) $ for MX Missile	AGN	11) Auto Local Content	FOR
4) Gas & Road Tax	FOR	8) Nerve Gas Prod	FOR	12) Nuclear Arms Freeze	FOR

Election Results

1982 general	Jim Wright (D)	78,913	(69%)	($498,898)
	Jim Ryan (R)	34,879	(30%)	($42,816)
1982 primary	Jim Wright (D)	27,677	(100%)	
1980 general	Jim Wright (D)	99,104	(60%)	($1,256,142)
	Jim Bradshaw (R)	65,005	(40%)	($645,289)

Campaign Contributions and Expenditures

1981-82		Direct Cont. 81-82		PACS brkdwn			
Receipts	$558,636	Indiv	$309,688	Agr	$20,000	Ideo	$18,802
Expend.	$498,898	PACS	$254,130	Bus	$148,991	Lbr	$49,625
Unspent	$69,152			Hlth	$5,750	Prof	$10,962

Indep Expend: Agn: $217,115 (NCPAC)

THIRTEENTH DISTRICT

The 13th congressional district of Texas is an entity that is totally the creation of politics, an amalgam of two old congressional districts that, because of the equal population rule, had to be combined, but that had always been separate and rather different regions. The old 13th district, which forms the eastern part of the current seat, is part of the agricultural land of the Red River Valley; like all of that valley, on both the Texas and the Oklahoma sides, it is traditionally heavily Democratic. It is dusty land, with empty skylines; it only grudgingly yields a living. Almost all the people here are white Anglos; few blacks got this far west and few Mexican-Americans go this far north. Population has been declining here not only in the rural counties, but also in the district's second largest city, Wichita Falls, whose population fell below 100,000 in 1980.

The other half of the 13th district was the old 18th, situated on the high plains of the Texas Panhandle. This land is drier and less fertile than that in the Red River Valley. West of the 100° meridian, the countryside is full of dry gullies that swell to floods when it rains. But it seldom does; instead, the wind blows as hard and unremittingly here as anywhere in the United States. Over the years, most of the Panhandle's farmers and ranchers have moved into town, many to Amarillo, the district's largest city and the helium capital of the world, others into smaller towns like Pampa and Borger. First settled by people from neighboring northwest Oklahoma and western Kansas, the Panhandle has always been one of the most Republican parts of Texas. Opposition to energy price regulation has strengthened this area's Republicanism, and in national elections it almost seethes hostility toward the Democrats.

The result is a pretty even balance between Democrats and Republicans in close elections; when they're not close, as in 1980, the 13th is heavily Republican. The congressman is Jack Hightower, a Democrat first elected in 1974, when low morale cut Republican turnout in the Panhandle and enabled him to beat an incumbent. Like most incumbents, he has used the advantages of office to bolster his position in the district. He also has maintained a mostly unobjectionably conservative voting record. He has specialized in farming issues, serving first on the Agriculture Committee, then on Appropriations and its Agriculture Subcommittee. Today he serves on that and on the Defense Subcommittee as well.

Hightower, like many incumbents, has won reelection easily several times. But in 1980 he ran into unexpected trouble from Republican Ron Slover, an Amarillo salesman and broker, who spent only $67,000 but held him to 55% of the vote. He evidently was only a beneficiary of a Republican trend, however; in 1982 he ran again and this time Hightower won easily, carrying all but a few Panhandle counties.

The People Pop. 1980: 526,840, up 7.7% 1970–80; voting age pop. 376,878; 5% Black, 7% Span. orig., 1% Asian orig. 27% housing units rented. Median owner $28,800; renter $166. Households: 75% family, 39% with children, 66% married couples.

1152   TEXAS

1980	Reagan (R)	117,716	(63%)
	Carter (D)	68,648	(37%)
	Anderson (I)	NA	

Rep. Jack Hightower (D) Elected 1974; b. Sept. 6, 1926, Memphis; home, Vernon; Baylor U., B.A. 1949; LL.B. 1951; Baptist.

Career Navy, WWII; Practicing atty., 1951–74; TX House of Reps., 1953–54; TX Dist. Atty., 1955–61; TX Senate, 1965–74.

Offices 2348 RHOB, 202-225-3706. Also Box F13207, 205 E. 5th St., Amarillo 79101, 806-376-2381; 208 P. O. Bldg., Wichita Falls 76301, 817-767-0541; and P.O. Box 1720, Vernon 76384, 817-553-4321.

Committee *Appropriations* (22d). Subcommittees: Agriculture, Rural Development and Related Agencies; Defense; Legislative.

Group Ratings

	ADA	ACLU	COPE	CFA	LCV	LWV	NTU	NSI	COC	ACA	CSFC
1982	30	46	34	38	33	45	44	70	64	57	44
1981	15	—	33	36	21	—	52	—	74	61	57
1980	17	17	33	21	15	25	36	60	82	43	51

National Journal Ratings

	Economic		Foreign		Cultural	
1982	47%	(LIB)	31%	(LIB)	21%	(LIB)
	53%	(CONS)	68%	(CONS)	76%	(CONS)
1981	42%	(LIB)	3%	(LIB)	42%	(LIB)
	57%	(CONS)	87%	(CONS)	58%	(CONS)

Key Votes

1) Reagan 81 Budget	FOR	5) Incr SS Rtmt Age	FOR	9) Poor Pay Food Stamps	AGN
2) Reagan 81 Tax Cut	FOR	6) Saudi AWACS Sale	FOR	10) Ban Crt Busing Order	FOR
3) Bal Budget Amend	FOR	7) $ for MX Missile	FOR	11) Auto Local Content	AGN
4) Gas & Road Tax	—	8) Nerve Gas Prod	AGN	12) Nuclear Arms Freeze	AGN

Election Results

1982 general	Jack Hightower (D)	86,376	(64%)	($325,997)
	Ron Slover (R)	47,877	(35%)	($82,625)
1982 primary	Jack Hightower (D)	49,248	(100%)	
1980 general	Jack Hightower (D)	98,779	(55%)	($145,292)
	Ron Slover (R)	80,819	(45%)	($67,863)

Campaign Contributions and Expenditures

1981-82		Direct Cont. 81-82		PACS brkdwn			
Receipts	$335,506	Indiv	$199,651	Agr	$17,450	Ideo	$7,450
Expend.	$325,997	Party	$13,000	Bus	$80,738	Lbr	$5,795
Unspent	$15,320	PACS	$126,441	Hlth	$10,000	Prof	$2,600

FOURTEENTH DISTRICT

The afternoon heat shimmers up from the pavement and the flat fields, only occasionally marked by a tree and extending for miles to the horizon, appear to be wavering slightly in the heat. Suddenly, a thundercloud seems to dominate the sky; then, marked by a line as sharp as the edge of a piece of scissors-cut paper, the driving rain starts, so heavy you can hardly see ten feet ahead. After ten minutes it is, suddenly, gone. The humidity returns, soaking your shirt; the heat shimmers as before, distorting vision again. This is the climate you find in the summers in south Texas, in the cotton lands west and southwest of Houston. Settled late in the 19th century, after the more temperate-climated northeast Texas, these have always been dedicated to market-oriented rather than subsistence farming; the lifeline here is the railroad, with the cotton gin beside it. The coastline, though it has plenty of inlets, never had any important ports in this stretch between Houston and Corpus Christi, until the discovery of oil in this part of Texas made it worthwhile to build channels to ship the oil out.

This is the land of the 14th congressional district of Texas, an area made up almost entirely of rural areas and small towns, even though it is situated between Houston and Austin and San Antonio and Corpus Christi. These cotton lands, settled well after the Civil War, don't have very many blacks (11% districtwide); the percentage of Mexican-Americans (20% districtwide) is only average for Texas. You don't find many Mexicans until you get down to Victoria and to the south. This is mostly white-Anglo country, ancestrally Democratic except for a couple of counties settled by Texas Germans, who were pro-Union in the Civil War and have remained Republican ever since.

Representing the 14th is William Patman, son of Wright Patman who served 48 years as congressman from Texarkana and who was a lifelong adversary of big bankers; the younger Patman moved to a small town in this part of Texas, practiced law, and served 20 years in the state Senate. There he was one of the beleaguered group of economic populists, almost always foiled by the big lobbyists; he was one of the leaders of the "killer bees," a group of state senators who absented themselves from the chamber and prevented a quorum being formed in order to stop a bill that would have put Texas's presidential and state primaries on different days, thus enabling Reagan and Connally presidential primary voters to vote for conservative Democrats in state elections.

Despite all the enemies he accumulated, Patman became one of the handful of liberals in the tradition of rural populism elected to replace conservatives in 1980. The seat fell open because Joe Wyatt, an ultraconservative elected in 1978, was retiring, after being arrested on homosexual charges in 1979 and entering an alcohol rehabilitation program. Patman had tough competition in the primary, the runoff, and the general election; he had to spend $665,000 altogether. Oddly, the toughest part of the district for him was Corpus Christi, with its large Mexican-American population; he did much better in the rural Anglo counties, many of which he represented in Austin. For 1982, Corpus Christi was removed from the district. His opponent was none other than Joe Wyatt, this time running as a Republican. But Wyatt carried only Victoria, an affluent Republican town; Patman took every other county and won handily. Wyatt's personal problems may have contributed to the result, although he ran close to William Clements's performance in the district.

Patman, like his father, is a member of the Banking Committee and of Interior as well. As a junior member, and one who in his first term seemed to have a shaky seat, he has not been

1154   TEXAS

greatly influential. He is, however, steadfast in times of adversity (there are many of those for a Texas liberal) and willing to stand up to opposition, however forbidding the odds seem.

The People Pop. 1980: 526,920, up 26.0% 1970–80; voting age pop.368,619; 11% Black, 17% Span. orig. 24% housing units rented. Median owner $34,900; renter $153. Households: 77% family, 42% with children, 67% married couples.

Presidential Vote

1980	Reagan (R)	98,335	(59%)
	Carter (D)	69,596	(41%)
	Anderson (I)	NA	

Rep. William N. (Bill) Patman (D) Elected 1980; b. Mar. 26, 1927, Texarkana; home, Ganado; U. of TX, B.B.A. 1953, J.D. 1953; Methodist.

Career USMC, WWII; Air Force Reserve, 1953–56; Dipl. Courier, U.S. Foreign Svc., 1949–50; Practicing atty., 1955–80; TX Senate, 1961–81.

Offices 1408 LHOB, 202-225-2831. Also U.S.P.O. & Court House, Rm. 218, Victoria 77901, 512-578-9954.

Committees *Banking, Finance and Urban Affairs* (20th). Subcommittees: Consumer Affairs and Coinage; Domestic Monetary Policy; Financial Institutions Supervision, Regulation and Insurance; International Trade, Investment and Monetary Policy. *Interior and Insular Affairs* (22d). Subcommittees: Energy and the Environment; Water and Power Resources.

Group Ratings

	ADA	ACLU	COPE	CFA	LCV	LWV	NTU	NSI	COC	ACA	CSFC
1982	15	8	44	31	29	42	53	90	73	70	57
1981	20	—	57	43	29	—	40	—	37	61	56

National Journal Ratings

	Economic		Foreign		Cultural	
1982	36%	(LIB)	16%	(LIB)	4%	(LIB)
	63%	(CONS)	82%	(CONS)	87%	(CONS)
1981	60%	(LIB)	1%	(LIB)	21%	(LIB)
	39%	(CONS)	99%	(CONS)	78%	(CONS)

Key Votes

1) Reagan 81 Budget	AGN	5) Incr SS Rtmt Age	AGN	9) Poor Pay Food Stamps	AGN
2) Reagan 81 Tax Cut	AGN	6) Saudi AWACS Sale	FOR	10) Ban Crt Busing Order	FOR
3) Bal Budget Amend	FOR	7) $ for MX Missile	FOR	11) Auto Local Content	AGN
4) Gas & Road Tax	FOR	8) Nerve Gas Prod	FOR	12) Nuclear Arms Freeze	AGN

Election Results

1982 general	William N. (Bill) Patman (D)	76,851	(61%)	($406,020)
	Joe Wyatt, Jr. (R)	48,942	(39%)	($375,520)
1982 primary	William N. (Bill) Patman (D)	44,382	(100%)	
1980 general	William N. (Bill) Patman (D)	93,884	(57%)	($665,984)
	C. L. Concklin (R)	71,495	(43%)	($182,572)

Campaign Contributions and Expenditures

1981-82		Direct Cont. 81-82		PACS brkdwn			
Receipts	$406,587	Indiv	$79,973	Agr	$8,400	Ideo	$2,800
Expend.	$406,020	Party	$3,600	Bus	$21,124	Lbr	$17,175
Unspent	$1,980	PACS	$58,369	Hlth	$7,400	Prof	$1,150
		Cand	$248,825				

Indirect Party Expend: $470   *Indep Expend:* For: $885 (NRA)

FIFTEENTH DISTRICT

The Rio Grande is the southern border of Texas. It is a shallow stream most of the year, and even when it is high it is not a serious barrier to immigration; and in many senses of the word it is not really a boundary at all. In the south Texas counties along the Rio Grande, some 90% of the people—the number is not quite certain, because it is hard to conduct an absolutely accurate census here—are of Mexican descent or origin, and no one can—or will—say exactly how many of them are legally in this country. Spanish is the language commonly spoken in the streets and in the stores, and the talk of politics may revolve as much around events in Mexico as elections in the United States.

Life in south Texas is intimately affected by what happens in Mexico. When Mexico was flush with oil earnings in the early 1980s, south Texas was a huge emporium for Mexican shoppers; goods were much cheaper in the United States, and there are perhaps a million Mexicans living along the border, plus at least two million more 150 miles away in the industrial city of Monterrey. Then, when the Mexican economy and the peso collapsed in 1982, the movement went back in the other direction; it was suddenly much cheaper to live and shop in Mexico, and south Texas seemed to wither. Population figures, border lines, economic projections, all the standard data here do not mean much; the large population increase in the 1970s tells us more about exchange rates than about permanent patterns of living. People make use of the standard categories in order to make their own way, but do not feel bound by them. To most Americans the wage levels and standard of living in the lower Rio Grande valley look shamefully low. But if you grew up in a Mexican subsistence farming village, they may look luxuriously high; and a few years' work there may be enough to make a man's fortune when he goes back home. Culturally, economically, in almost every way but politically, this is really part of Mexico rather than the United States.

Political affairs and public life in the lower Rio Grande Valley have historically been the province of the Anglo minority. It is almost like something out of the feudal age. Giant landowners farm and ranch huge territories with low-wage Mexican labor; some of them deliver their workers' votes with regularity on election day. With irrigation the fields here produce good crops of cotton, fruits, and vegetables. The towns in the lower Rio Grande Valley—Brownsville, Harlingen, McAllen—have developed some of the shops and accoutrements for high-income Texans that you see elsewhere, but most of the people living in the side streets are of Mexican origin.

The 15th congressional district of Texas includes much of the Lower Rio Grande Valley, including McAllen and Harlingen, and Hidalgo, Starr, and Zapata Counties along the river. It also goes north, almost as far as San Antonio, although 60% of its population in the 1980 Census was along the border. Inland there is Duval County, long the fiefdom of the Parr family. Its most famous performance came in the 1948 Senate runoff. After some delay, Duval reported 4,622 votes for Lyndon Johnson and 40 for his opponent. Inasmuch as the county had gone the other way, by almost the same margin, in the first primary a few weeks before, there were some suspicions about the result; but it was certified, and "Landslide Lyndon" won the Democratic nomination, then tantamount to election, by 87 votes. George Parr, the last "Duke of Duval," killed himself in 1975. But the same kind of power is now exerted by a Mexican-American family that used to be allied with the Parrs.

The House seat here used to be within the gift of the big Anglo families. One congressman was Lloyd Bentsen. His father had made a fortune in land in the valley (and was accused of selling parcels without water and sewers to northern retirees); young Lloyd, after returning from the war, was elected county judge at 25 and congressman at 27, in 1948. Bentsen retired from the House in 1954 to go into business; his successor was Joe M. Kilgore, a pillar of the Connally Tory Democratic establishment. Kilgore wanted to run against Ralph Yarborough in the 1964 Senate primary, in furtherance of a feud John Kennedy had gone to Dallas in 1963 to help settle; Johnson persuaded Kilgore not to run, but he quit the House anyway, and six years later Yarborough was beaten in the primary by Bentsen.

When Kilgore retired from the House in 1964, someone apparently decided it was time the 15th had a Mexican-American congressman. Accordingly, Eligio (Kika) de la Garza was elected. He had shown his reliability through 12 years in the legislature; he was never a favorite of the militant Chicanos and generally voted like other rural Texas Democrats. His voting record has moved a little to the left over the intervening years. But he evidently remains convinced that the country cannot afford too lavish a welfare state; on foreign affairs he is generally hawkish. But no one claims de la Garza is a vastly original thinker. He is an amiable practical politician who represents an unusual constituency sufficiently satisfactory to its electorate that he has never had serious opposition for reelection.

De la Garza is now chairman of the House Agriculture Committee. He got that job in 1981 when Chairman Thomas Foley was selected as House majority whip; Foley relinquished the chair and, although there was some opposition to de la Garza, no rival candidacy materialized. One reason is that no one expected de la Garza to be an overbearing chairman, and he apparently hasn't been. Agriculture programs are technical, and the farm bill represents a balancing of interests which is highly complex; interests are regional and in many cases bipartisan; yet at the same time farm programs plus food stamps, which are in Agriculture's purview, are the glue that holds the Democratic Party together. By and large de la Garza seems to have relied on several strong subcommittee chairmen to tend their commodities in committee and help manage the farm bill on the floor. There have been some cuts: the Reagan administration has sliced into dairy price supports and threatened the peanut subsidy, and tobacco is under attack in the Senate from Jesse Helms's many enemies. But overall the farm bill has held together pretty well in the House. De la Garza weathered 1981, when Republicans seemed to be in working control; in 1983 and 1984, with the Democrats evidently having enough votes for working control, he should be able to stay out of trouble.

The People Pop. 1980: 527,203, up 38.4% 1970–80; voting age pop. 329,023; 1% Black, 66% Span. orig. 24% housing units rented. Median owner $23,100; renter $126. Households: 84% family, 54% with children, 71% married couples.

Presidential Vote

1980	Reagan (R)	58,846	(43%)
	Carter (D)	79,221	(57%)
	Anderson (I)	NA	

Rep. E (Kika) **de la Garza** (D) Elected 1964; b. Sept. 22, 1927, Mercedes; home, Mission; Edinburg Jr. Col., St. Mary's U., San Antonio, LL.B. 1952; Roman Catholic.

Career Navy, WWII; Army, Korea; Practicing atty., 1952–64; TX House of Reps., 1952–64.

Offices 1401 LHOB, 202-225-2531. Also 1418 Beach St., La Posada Village, McAllen 78501, 512-682-5545.

Committee *Agriculture* (Chairman).

Group Ratings

	ADA	ACLU	COPE	CFA	LCV	LWV	NTU	NSI	COC	ACA	CSFC
1982	25	33	55	46	50	55	11	90	42	38	38
1981	45	—	54	43	36	—	19	—	32	50	49
1980	22	37	40	43	8	30	30	57	71	52	49

National Journal Ratings

	Economic		Foreign		Cultural	
1982	52%	(LIB)	31%	(LIB)	47%	(LIB)
	48%	(CONS)	69%	(CONS)	53%	(CONS)
1981	59%	(LIB)	53%	(LIB)	47%	(LIB)
	40%	(CONS)	45%	(CONS)	52%	(CONS)

Key Votes

1) Reagan 81 Budget	AGN	5) Incr SS Rtmt Age	FOR	9) Poor Pay Food Stamps	AGN
2) Reagan 81 Tax Cut	FOR	6) Saudi AWACS Sale	AGN	10) Ban Crt Busing Order	AGN
3) Bal Budget Amend	FOR	7) $ for MX Missile	FOR	11) Auto Local Content	AGN
4) Gas & Road Tax	—	8) Nerve Gas Prod	FOR	12) Nuclear Arms Freeze	AGN

Election Results

1982 general	E (Kika) de la Garza (D)	76,544	(96%)	($84,038)
1982 primary	E (Kika) de la Garza (D)	47,322	(100%)	
1980 general	E (Kika) de la Garza (D)	105,325	(70%)	($66,324)
	Robert L. McDonald (R)	45,090	(30%)	($17,639)

Campaign Contributions and Expenditures

1981-82		Direct Cont. 81-82		PACS brkdwn			
Receipts	$93,379	Indiv	$26,880	Agr	$22,275	Ideo	$400
Expend.	$84,038	PACS	$60,425	Bus	$29,600	Lbr	$1,900
Unspent	$51,171			Hlth	$6,250	Prof	$—

SIXTEENTH DISTRICT

El Paso is a city almost entirely cut off from the rest of America and, in some ways, even from the rest of Texas. It is the only part of Texas on Mountain Time, because it is so far west; its metropolitan area, with well over a million people, overshadows anything in nearby New Mexico. It is separated by hundreds of miles of arid desert and mountains from the nearest metropolitan area its size. It was founded because the Rio Grande here passes through a couple of mountains towering 2,000 feet above it, and until after World War II it was a sleepy town of about 100,000, with another 100,000 or so in the sleazy border town of Juarez across the river.

El Paso and Juarez still have a symbiotic relationship, but they are much larger. The 1980 Census counted 425,000 people in El Paso and 50,000 more in outlying parts of the county; the Mexican government estimated that there were 570,000 people in Juarez in 1977. But these are hard figures to pin down. A lot of Mexicans living in El Paso may not have wanted to be counted; but then El Paso's work force is swelled every day by commuters from Juarez. The relative cost of living on each side of the border changed sharply when the peso was devalued in 1982, and so presumably did migration patterns—but no one is sure just how. This is the part of the country that gave us the word "wetback," and no one has any real idea of how many times and by how many people the border is crossed. This is, after all, the border with the widest difference in the world in living standards on either side.

El Paso lives off low-wage labor: it has lots of apparel factories and assembly lines where low-skill people assemble components of all kinds; some work also is farmed out to Juarez, under laws that leave it free of duty. Several years ago there was a much publicized strike against the Farah slacks company, and it was supported by the Catholic archbishop. Most Americans would like to see higher wages and better working conditions here, but it's not easy to see how this can be done. The labor force doesn't have skills that would command high wages on the open market, and even if it did there would still be an onrush of lower-wage workers from somewhere in Mexico seeking their fortune. The sad fact is that, for all Mexico's economic growth in the 1960s and 1970s, its wages and living standards are far below those of the United States, and there is not enough money in the world to bring them instantly up to our level.

The 16th congressional district of Texas is made up of El Paso and several counties to the east. These are mostly desert. They extend east to the Pecos River and beyond; in this area you find Loving County, the smallest of Texas's 254 counties with only 91 people in 1980, and the town of Langtry, where Judge Roy Bean once held court as the only law west of the Pecos. But politically these count for very little. El Paso County has 91% of the district's population and 87% of its votes.

The congressional seat was opened up here in 1982 when 18-year incumbent Richard White, a cautious conservative, retired. The new congressman seems different, temperamentally and ideologically: he is unabashedly liberal and he is a risk-taker. Ron Coleman spent 10 years in the Texas House, where he was not a favorite of the usually conservative leadership; he was the attorney for the Farah strikers. Electorally, he had to count on the Mexican-American vote, but that is a terribly iffy thing in El Paso. According to the Census Bureau, 60% of the people here are of Spanish origin. But an unknown number are not U.S. citizens, and many more are at best marginal voters. In effect elections in El Paso are really battles of turnout, with the more enthusiastic side winning.

Coleman's task was complicated by the presence of a Mexican-American candidate in the initial Democratic primary. But Coleman had a strong enough base to lead with 33% in the first primary, and he had enough Mexican-American turnout to beat a conservative Democrat in the runoff and a Republican heavily supported by the national party in the general.

He is still not in risk-free territory. He has a seat on the Armed Services Committee—a local asset, since the Fort Bliss Military Reservation is one of the mainstays of El Paso's economy. But he is likely to take stands which will infuriate many conservative Anglo voters in El Paso. In 1980 Ronald Reagan carried this area solidly; should turnout turn against him, Coleman could face trouble in this polarized and economically troubled district in 1984.

The People Pop. 1980: 527,401, up 29.9% 1970–80; voting age pop. 341,560; 4% Black, 55% Span. orig., 15% Asian orig. 37% housing units rented. Median owner $36,800; renter $158. Households: 81% family, 53% with children, 66% married couples.

Presidential Vote

1980	Reagan (R)	62,134	(58%)
	Carter (D)	45,785	(42%)
	Anderson (I)	NA	

Rep. Ronald D. Coleman (D) Elected 1982; b. Nov. 29, 1941, El Paso; home, El Paso; U. of TX, El Paso, B.A. 1963; U. of TX Sch. of Law, J.D. 1967; U. of Kent, England, 1981; Methodist.

Career Army, 1967–69; Asst. El Paso Cnty. Atty., 1969; First Asst. El Paso Cnty. Atty., 1971; TX House of Reps., 1973–82.

Offices 1017 LHOB, 202-225-4831. Also U.S. Courthouse, Rm. 146, El Paso 79901, 915-541-7650.

Committees *Armed Services* (29th). Subcommittees: Military Personnel and Compensation; Research and Development. *Government Operations* (15th). Subcommittees: Commerce, Consumer, and Monetary Affairs; Government Activities and Transportation; Government Information, Justice, and Agriculture.

Group Ratings and Key Votes: Newly Elected

Election Results

1982 general	Ronald D. Coleman (D)	44,024	(54%)	($374,821)
	Patrick B. Haggerty (R)	36,064	(44%)	($318,180)
1982 runoff	Ronald D. Coleman (D)	20,537	(55%)	
	T. Udell Moore (D)	17,003	(45%)	($222,335)
1982 primary	Ronald D. Coleman (D)	14,668	(33%)	
	T. Udell Moore (D)	10,335	(23%)	
	Danny Anchondo (D)	9,294	(21%)	($29,062)
	Jim Scherr (D)	6,100	(14%)	($54,098)
	Ronald P. McCluskey (D)	4,002	(9%)	($39,268)
1980 general	Richard C. White (D)	104,734	(85%)	($49,964)
	Catherine McDivitt (Libertarian) ..	19,010	(15%)	($0)

Campaign Contributions and Expenditures

1981-82		Direct Cont. 81-82				PACS brkdwn		
Receipts	$374,841	Indiv	$125,992	Agr	$200	Ideo	$23,250
Expend.	$374,821	Party	$10,444	Bus	$14,400	Lbr	$84,700
Unspent	$18	PACS	$135,192	Hlth	$3,550	Prof	$5,250
		Cand	$15,829				

Indirect Party Expend: $6,148   *Non-Cand Loans*: $76,400

SEVENTEENTH DISTRICT

The 17th congressional district is the geographical heart of Texas. Here are thousands and thousands of acres of arid farming and grazing land stretching west from Fort Worth to the horizon. The 17th is primarily cattle country, although there is some oil here and some raising of cotton and grain. Its largest city is Abilene, with 98,000 people. As is usually the case in Texas, the town is more conservative than the countryside; all the bankers, lawyers, and professionals are concentrated in the town, as well as all the men who congregate in the local Petroleum Club, where they discuss the state of the world while watching the sunset out the window of one of Abilene's few several-storied buildings. Like most of central Texas, this area was settled originally by southerners who brought their Democratic politics with them, and it remained pretty solidly Democratic up through 1978. In 1980 it shifted sharply to the Republicans. In 1982, it shifted back again; at this point, the move toward Reaganism seems temporary.

The 1980 shift had little effect on congressional politics here. The district was open, for the first time in 32 years, in 1978; and the winner was Charles Stenholm, a conservative young Democrat with a background in farming. From his first term Stenholm was ready to complain whenever he felt Democrats like him were slighted. He was unhappy that southern conservatives were not getting good committee assignments in 1978; he was right, since the best posts were reserved for those who were in agreement with most Democrats. In 1980 he was one who pressured for the appointment of, among others, Phil Gramm on the Budget Committee. Stenholm was also the co-founder of the Conservative Democratic Forum, the group commonly referred to as the Boll Weevils. There is not a perfect congruence between CDF and the Democrats who voted for the Reagan budget and tax cut plans in 1981; Stenholm himself sternly disclaims any role as the boss of the group, and says he is only a spokesman. He was, however, an articulate and attractive spokesman, and he did cast well-publicized and decisive votes in favor of both Reagan initiatives.

In Stenholm's view it is the other Democrats who have left the party, not him. But in 1982 and 1983 he seemed to be pursuing a less confrontational strategy. This makes sense in the long term. He is pretty well committed to remaining a Democrat—it makes great political sense in this district, among other reasons—and if he wants to advance to positions of power, he will need the votes of other Democrats to do so. So it is better to emphasize areas of agreement than issues on which he dissents. Stenholm has a good committee for that, Agriculture; on farm policy northern and southern Democrats have long been able to make mutually beneficial deals. And Stenholm's objections to high government spending are more prudent than they are based on unyielding principle, as in the case of Phil Gramm.

Stenholm's only real contest in this district was in the 1978 Democratic primary and runoff. He polished off a Republican contender easily in that general election, and the only opponent he has faced since was the Libertarian candidate in 1982. It would probably be different if he were a Republican: the district is full of ambitious local Democrats, and so any Republican congressman here would probably have significant opposition almost every time, and in a district with a strong long-term partisan tilt toward the Democrats.

The People Pop. 1980: 526,913, up 9.3% 1970–80; voting age pop. 380,499; 3% Black, 9% Span. orig. 23% housing units rented. Median owner $25,900; renter $144. Households: 76% family, 38% with children, 67% married couples.

Presidential Vote

1980	Reagan (R)	102,033	(55%)
	Carter (D)	82,171	(45%)
	Anderson (I)	NA	

Rep. Charles W. Stenholm (D) Elected 1978; b. Oct. 26, 1938, Stamford; home, Stamford; Tarleton St. Jr. Col., 1959, TX Tech. U., B.S. 1961; Lutheran.

Career Vocational agriculture teacher, 1962–64; Farm mgr., 1961–

Offices 1232 LHOB, 202-225-6605. Also 903 E. Hamilton, Stamford 79553, 915-773-3623; and 341 Pine St, Rm. 2102, Abilene 79604, 915-673-7221.

Committees *Agriculture* (17th). Subcommittees: Conservation, Credit, and Rural Development; Cotton, Rice, and Sugar; Livestock, Dairy and Poultry; Tobacco and Peanuts. *Small Business* (11th). Subcommittee: Export Opportunities and Special Small Business Problems.

Group Ratings

	ADA	ACLU	COPE	CFA	LCV	LWV	NTU	NSI	COC	ACA	CSFC
1982	5	17	15	15	21	25	91	90	86	82	71
1981	0	—	17	36	7	—	87	—	84	82	70
1980	0	7	11	7	4	0	68	100	75	74	75

National Journal Ratings

	Economic		Foreign		Cultural	
1982	12%	(LIB)	10%	(LIB)	4%	(LIB)
	88%	(CONS)	89%	(CONS)	87%	(CONS)
1981	36%	(LIB)	3%	(LIB)	29%	(LIB)
	62%	(CONS)	87%	(CONS)	71%	(CONS)

Key Votes

1) Reagan 81 Budget	FOR	5) Incr SS Rtmt Age	FOR	9) Poor Pay Food Stamps	AGN
2) Reagan 81 Tax Cut	FOR	6) Saudi AWACS Sale	FOR	10) Ban Crt Busing Order	FOR
3) Bal Budget Amend	FOR	7) $ for MX Missile	FOR	11) Auto Local Content	AGN
4) Gas & Road Tax	AGN	8) Nerve Gas Prod	FOR	12) Nuclear Arms Freeze	AGN

Election Results

1982 general	Charles W. Stenholm (D)	109,359	(97%)	($110,303)
1982 primary	Charles W. Stenholm (D)	58,198	(100%)	
1980 general	Charles W. Stenholm (D)	130,465	(100%)	($98,134)

Campaign Contributions and Expenditures

1981-82		Direct Cont. 81-82				PACS brkdwn		
Receipts	$209,473	Indiv	$107,054	Agr	$9,450	Ideo	$3,000
Expend.	$110,303	PACS	$78,873	Bus	$56,820	Lbr	$—
Unspent	$145,809			Hlth	$6,500	Prof	$2,950

EIGHTEENTH DISTRICT

The 18th congressional district of Texas covers the central part of the city of Houston. It includes within its boundaries most of the city's blacks and many of its Mexican-Americans. In 1980, 41% of its residents were black and 31% of Spanish origin, with very little overlap between the categories. The number of Mexican-Americans has been rising in the inner-city neighborhoods, as a result of heavy immigration in the 1970s; blacks have moved outward, and in redistricting the 18th grew tentacles to take in some of the north side neighborhoods which were mostly white in 1970 and are mostly black now. This is a very different part of Houston from the gleaming west side, although the districts are right next to each other. Like many rapidly growing cities in developing countries, Houston seems to have great disparities of income and wealth. While entrepreneurs are getting rich in the oil business and living in $750,000 houses off Westheimer and Memorial Drive, many black and Mexican-American residents live east and south of downtown in unpainted frame houses replete with cracks wide enough to let in Houston's humid, smoggy air. The Houston slums look like something out of the sharecropper 1930s, and they remind us that although this is one of our fastest-growing cities, its growth is based in large part on the availability of cheap labor. Houston has had a strong developing economy, and perhaps in time everyone will benefit; you can even argue that many blacks and Mexican-Americans in these slums are better off than they were where they came from. But even so, it is apparent that in this city the wealth is trickling down to some people a whole lot faster than it is to others.

Not all of Houston's black and Mexican neighborhoods, it should be added, are so grim. As one moves north in the 18th district, one finds solid working- and middle-class neighborhoods, some even with a touch of grandeur from when their houses were built many years ago. All of Houston's black neighborhoods cast higher Democratic percentages—on the order of 98%—than any other part of the United States. The voting habits here in the 18th district are thus a considerable contrast to the 7th district, immediately to the west, which is one of the most Republican districts in the country. The real question in Houston is who will outvote whom? In 1978 and 1980 the rich turned out in large numbers and with great enthusiasm and swept Texas for the Republicans. In the 1981 mayor's race blacks and Mexican-Americans turned out and voted for liberal Kathy Whitmire; in 1982 they turned out heavily and helped elect Democratic Governor Mark White and reelect Senator Lloyd Bentsen. The difference is apparent from congressional results. In his first congressional race in 1978 Congressman Mickey Leland got 36,000 votes in the general election. In 1982, in a district expanded by some 23%, he got 68,000 votes, nearly twice as many. And virtually all those votes went for Democratic candidates up and down the line.

Leland is less famous than his predecessor, Barbara Jordan, who quit a prominent political career and now teaches at the LBJ School in Austin. Leland is also different temperamentally. He is more militant, less interested in getting along with the power structure; but then the power structure in the House is interested in getting along with members like Leland, which wasn't always the case a decade or two ago. He has one choice committee assignment,

Energy and Commerce, the most sought-after committee assignment in the House; he serves on the Telecommunications and Health Subcommittees. His record on virtually every issue is solidly liberal. He has not had significant opposition since his first election.

The People Pop. 1980: 527,393, dn. 5.9% 1970–80; voting age pop. 366,424; 39% Black, 27% Span. orig., 1% Asian orig. 51% housing units rented. Median owner $31,900; renter $185. Households: 65% family, 39% with children, 46% married couples.

Presidential Vote

1980	Reagan (R)	NA
	Carter (D)	NA
	Anderson (I)	NA

Rep. Mickey Leland (D) Elected 1978; b. Nov. 27, 1944, Lubbock; home, Houston; TX St. U., B.S. 1970; Roman Catholic.

Career Instructor, TX St. U., 1970–71; Dir. of Spec. Development Projects, Hermann Hosp., 1971–78; TX House of Reps., 1972–79.

Offices 419 CHOB, 202-225-3816. Also 4101 San Jacinto Ctr., Su. 101, Houston 77004, 713-527-9692.

Committees *District of Columbia* (5th). Subcommittee: Fiscal Affairs and Health. *Energy and Commerce* (14th). Subcommittees: Health and the Environment; Telecommunications, Consumer Protection, and Finance. *Post Office and Civil Service* (6th). Subcommittees: Census and Population; Compensation and Employee Benefits; Postal Personnel and Modernization (Chairman). *Select Committee on Children, Youth, and Families* (10th).

Group Ratings

	ADA	ACLU	COPE	CFA	LCV	LWV	NTU	NSI	COC	ACA	CSFC
1982	90	92	94	85	81	91	33	0	19	10	25
1981	95	—	92	71	84	—	30	—	6	10	25
1980	83	87	100	71	81	89	17	0	67	5	21

National Journal Ratings

	Economic		Foreign		Cultural	
1982	99%	(LIB)	92%	(LIB)	89%	(LIB)
	0%	(CONS)	6%	(CONS)	11%	(CONS)
1981	89%	(LIB)	92%	(LIB)	86%	(LIB)
	3%	(CONS)	2%	(CONS)	14%	(CONS)

Key Votes

1) Reagan 81 Budget	AGN	5) Incr SS Rtmt Age	AGN	9) Poor Pay Food Stamps	AGN
2) Reagan 81 Tax Cut	AGN	6) Saudi AWACS Sale	AGN	10) Ban Crt Busing Order	AGN
3) Bal Budget Amend	FOR	7) $ for MX Missile	AGN	11) Auto Local Content	FOR
4) Gas & Road Tax	AGN	8) Nerve Gas Prod	AGN	12) Nuclear Arms Freeze	FOR

Election Results

1982 general	Mickey Leland (D)	68,104	(83%)	($204,489)
	C. Leon Pickett (R)	12,104	(15%)	($18,315)
1982 primary	Mickey Leland (D)	22,119	(84%)	
	Harrel Tillman (D)	4,117	(16%)	($15,153)
1980 general	Mickey Leland (D)	71,985	(80%)	($132,490)
	C. L. Kennedy (R)	16,128	(18%)	($0)

Campaign Contributions and Expenditures

	1981-82		Direct Cont. 81-82			PACS brkdwn		
Receipts	$196,688	Indiv	$94,534	Agr	$1,500	Ideo	$6,425
Expend.	$204,489	PACS	$92,019	Bus	$25,925	Lbr	$37,700
Unspent	$835			Hlth	$7,350	Prof	$7,925

Indirect Party Expend: $152

NINETEENTH DISTRICT

The 19th congressional district of Texas, along the New Mexico border, includes much of the high plains of west Texas. It is on the high side of the incline, as Texas slants up toward the Rocky Mountains. Originally this was flat, dusty land, eroded into giant gullies, swept by constant winds. But much of it has been irrigated, with waters captured from the mountains as they come down from the stream, or from the giant (but perhaps dangerously depleted) Ogallala Aquifer. Thus much of this part of Texas is a sort of green island in a vast brown sea of arid grazing land, on the east, west, north, and south. It was settled relatively late, with much growth in recent decades. The biggest city here is Lubbock, a rough-and-ready town which is both an oil and an agricultural center.

The southern part of the district covers much of the Permian Basin, whose oil and gas reserves were first developed in the 1950s and which remains highly productive today. The 19th district does not include Midland, the town where the rich oil investors live, but it does include Odessa, a similar-sized town one county west, which houses many of the technically skilled men who do the gritty, sweaty work of making the oil rigs work and getting the oil to the surface.

Politically, this is essentially a Republican district. Lubbock, like many fast-growing cities in the Southwest, is considerably more Republican than the rural area around it—or the places where the people who live here now came from. People here are upwardly mobile, but not fashionable in the way those who shop the boutiques of Midland are; they tend to stick strongly to traditional religion and family patterns. That is true of Odessa as well; and its Republicanism is strengthened by an intense anger at the federal government's regulation of oil prices in the 1970s. There is a significant Mexican-American population here, but many of these residents are not citizens, and many who are do not vote as automatically for Democrats as liberal strategists assumed they would. And few of the rural counties here are as heavily Democratic as those in central and east Texas.

Nevertheless, the 19th district has had nothing but Democratic congressmen. For 42 years this district was represented by George Mahon, an austere man who was chairman of the House Appropriations Committee. When he retired—two years after receiving his first tough challenge—he was succeeded by Democrat Kent Hance. Hance profited in that election from the contrast in cultural backgrounds between the candidates. The Republican was George W. Bush, 32-year-old son of our current vice president, a resident of Midland (then in the district) as his father once was, a graduate of an eastern prep school and Harvard and Yale. Hance, in contrast, comes from a modest middle-class background near Lubbock, attended Texas Tech there, and then went on to the University of Texas Law School. He won an upset victory for the Texas Senate in 1974 and staked his all on winning the House seat. Bush carried Midland, and Hance won almost everything else.

Within three years of that victory Hance had become a national political figure. He won a seat on the House Ways and Means Committee, with the help of Majority Leader Jim Wright, and there naturally represents the interests of small oil operators (which are sometimes counter to those of the big oil companies). But in 1981 the big issue before Ways and Means was the Reagan tax cut. Hance supported it, and became the Democratic name cosponsor. This naturally caused some friction with other Democrats, though presumably it was popular in the district, which went 70% for Reagan in 1980 and which, even in 1982, went Republican in the gubernatorial race.

Over the next year, Hance took a very different course from that of his fellow Texas Boll Weevil, Phil Gramm, who was the name sponsor of the Reagan budget cut. Gramm, as a committed free market ideologue, continued to work with the Republicans, and by early 1983 was a Republican himself. Hance, in contrast, feels a sense of identification with the Democratic Party and, though he supports few of its big government programs, still sees it— and himself—as representing the little guy against the sleek, arrogant rich people in the East and the fashionable neighborhoods in the big cities of Texas. He worked hard, using his contacts among independent oil men, to raise money for Democrats around the country in 1982, and on Ways and Means he also worked to cement his relations with the party's leadership. By 1983, he was pretty much welcomed back—while Gramm lost his Budget Committee post and left the party altogether.

Hance has been mentioned as a possible candidate for John Tower's Senate seat in 1984; such a race, involving a primary, a runoff, and a tough general election, would be a real test of his mettle as a fundraiser. His standing in the 19th district seems solid. In 1982, while the district remained Republican on the top of the ticket, it gave Hance a near-unanimous percentage of its votes. Should he choose, he can go on representing this district for as long as he wants.

The People Pop. 1980: 527,805, up 15.2% 1970–80; voting age pop. 360,942; 5% Black, 20% Span. orig., 15% Asian orig. 31% housing units rented. Median owner $33,200; renter $191. Households: 77% family, 45% with children, 68% married couples.

Presidential Vote

1980	Reagan (R)	113,606	(70%)
	Carter (D)	47,739	(30%)
	Anderson (I)	NA	

Rep. Kent Hance (D) Elected 1978; b. Nov. 14, 1942, Dimmitt; home, Lubbock; TX Tech. U., B.B.A. 1965, U. of TX, LL.B. 1968; Baptist.

Career Practicing atty., 1968–; TX Senate, 1974–78.

Offices 1214 LHOB, 202-225-4005. Also 611 Fed. Ofc. Bldg., 1205 Texas Ave., Lubbock 79401, 806-763-1611.

Committee *Ways and Means* (18th). Subcommittees: Public Assistance and Unemployment Compensation; Trade.

Group Ratings

	ADA	ACLU	COPE	CFA	LCV	LWV	NTU	NSI	COC	ACA	CSFC
1982	30	37	30	38	53	56	67	88	52	74	54
1981	15	—	28	29	22	—	72	—	81	65	63
1980	11	30	26	21	12	43	42	100	83	43	54

National Journal Ratings

	Economic		Foreign		Cultural	
1982	43%	(LIB)	26%	(LIB)	42%	(LIB)
	56%	(CONS)	73%	(CONS)	58%	(CONS)
1981	38%	(LIB)	1%	(LIB)	52%	(LIB)
	61%	(CONS)	99%	(CONS)	48%	(CONS)

Key Votes

1) Reagan 81 Budget	FOR	5) Incr SS Rtmt Age	FOR
2) Reagan 81 Tax Cut	FOR	6) Saudi AWACS Sale	FOR
3) Bal Budget Amend	FOR	7) $ for MX Missile	FOR
4) Gas & Road Tax	FOR	8) Nerve Gas Prod	FOR

9) Poor Pay Food Stamps	AGN
10) Ban Crt Busing Order	FOR
11) Auto Local Content	AGN
12) Nuclear Arms Freeze	AGN

Election Results

1982 general	Kent Hance (D)	89,702	(82%)	($244,461)
	E. L. Hicks (R)	19,062	(17%)	($0)
1982 primary	Kent Hance (D)	43,614	(100%)	
1980 general	Kent Hance (D)	126,632	(94%)	($106,573)
	J. D. Webster (Libertarian)	8,792	(6%)	($0)

Campaign Contributions and Expenditures

1981-82		Direct Cont. 81-82		PACS brkdwn			
Receipts	$444,995	Indiv	$282,617	Agr	$7,950	Ideo	$4,550
Expend.	$244,461	Party	$100	Bus	$109,534	Lbr	$200
Unspent	$233,841	PACS	$141,825	Hlth	$11,350	Prof	$6,200

TWENTIETH DISTRICT

San Antonio was the most important town in Texas when the state was part of Mexico. It was here that Santa Ana and his troops wiped out Davy Crockett, Jim Bowie, and 184 others at the Alamo in 1836. (Crockett was a Tennessee congressman in 1827–31 and 1833–35; if he had not lost his bid for reelection in 1835, he never would have left Tennessee for Texas.) Today San Antonio is Texas's third largest city, with 785,000 people and a metropolitan population over one million. Metropolitan San Antonio is thus only one-third the size of metropolitan Dallas–Fort Worth or Houston; it has never been a center of the oil or electronics business. But it is not a withering city, either, and in the 1980s its low wages and low cost of living have been attracting more new industry than it has ever had before. It also helps that San Antonio has, from its Spanish and Mexican days, its own special atmosphere. It is most apparent along the banks of the San Antonio River, as it wanders through the center of town; they are lined with huge overhanging trees and with pleasant shops and restaurants below street traffic. You can see it as well in the bare-tabled Mexican restaurants in the market area; just 150 miles from the border, this is the closest thing the United States has to a large Mexican city.

Yet it is also fiercely American too, in one respect, and that is militarily. Long ago, San Antonio was chosen, perhaps because of its closeness to the border, to be a site for major military bases, and they remain one of the city's economic mainstays, and perhaps its largest employer, to this day. San Antonio has Fort Sam Houston, with 10,000 men; the Brooks Aero Medical Center, the major medical facility of the Air Force; and no less than three Air Force bases either within the city limits or just outside them.

In its population, too, San Antonio is a Mexican-American city. In the 1980 Census 54% of its population described themselves as of Spanish origin. Of course not all of them are citizens or voters; and San Antonio has had for years a divisive ethnic politics, with most Mexican-Americans voting for liberals and most white Anglos for conservatives. That seems to have ended, however, at least in city elections. In 1981 the city elected its first Mexican-American mayor, Henry Cisneros. But he is not a stereotyped militant: he wants to create a good climate for growth of business and investment, and sees that as the best way to create a vibrant economy that will raise everyone up as a rising tide lifts all ships.

The 20th congressional district includes the central part of San Antonio, leaving the mostly Anglo northern fringes and suburbs as part of the 21st district and the southern fringes and suburbs on three sides as part of the 23d. More than 60% of the residents of the current 20th, according to the 1980 Census, are Mexican-American, and probably a higher percentage of them are citizens and voters than in the Lower Rio Grande valley districts. As a result, the 20th is a national Democratic district in every election—indeed, a district that probably stands to the left of the national Democratic Party, at least on economic issues.

The congressman here is Henry B. Gonzalez, first elected in 1961, when Mexican-American politicians were far less common than they are now; in those days he was the patron saint of Texas liberalism. But he alienated many liberals and young Chicano activists in the late 1960s and early 1970s by supporting the Vietnam war effort and by heaping scorn on them. His stubbornness—or adherence to principle—seems vindicated now: our abandonment of the Vietnam war produced a result few of its opponents are proud of, and Gonzalez's policies, rather than the separatist impulses of the activists of the 1960s, assimilation rather than polarization, seem to be the wave of the future. Mexican-Americans are rapidly becoming a part—and a successful part—of the larger American society, bringing some of their traditions with them but embracing the wider tradition. People from other parts of the country still find it odd, but most Mexican-Americans here speak with a Texas accent.

Gonzalez is the second ranking Democrat on the Banking, Finance and Urban Affairs Committee, and chairman of its Housing and Community Development Subcommittee. This must be a frustrating assignment, especially for this proud and stubborn man who backs many of the housing programs which are being phased out by common consent of national administrations and most members of Congress. Gonzalez is prickly and quick to take offense, as he showed in the fight he got into when he quit as chairman of the House committee investigating the Kennedy and King assassinations; he does not find it easy to compromise or wheel and deal. A possible reason is that he may have vivid memories of the days when, as a junior congressman in the 1960s or a state senator in the 1950s, none of the good old boys from Texas were interested in being civil to him, much less wheeling and dealing with him.

Gonzalez has had no trouble winning reelection. The militants who once criticized him were wise enough never to challenge him in a Democratic primary, and he is essentially unopposed every two years.

The People Pop. 1980: 526,350, dn. 5.8% 1970–80; voting age pop. 358,812; 8% Black, 56% Span. orig., 15% Asian orig. 40% housing units rented. Median owner $23,500; renter $142. Households: 75% family, 45% with children, 56% married couples.

Presidential Vote

1980	Reagan (R)	NA
	Carter (D)	NA
	Anderson (I)	NA

Rep. Henry B. Gonzalez (D) Elected 1961; b. May 3, 1916, San Antonio; home, San Antonio; San Antonio Col., U. of TX, St. Mary's U., San Antonio, LL.B. 1965; Roman Catholic.

Career Army, WWII; Bexar Cnty. Chf. Probation Ofcr., 1946; Work with bilingual publications; Teacher, San Antonio Night Sch.; San Antonio City Cncl., 1953–56, Mayor Pro Tem, 1955–56; TX Senate, 1956–61.

Offices 2413 RHOB, 202-225-3236. Also B-124 Fed. Bldg., 727 E. Durango, San Antonio 78205, 512-229-6199.

Committees *Banking, Finance and Urban Affairs* (2d). Subcommittees: Consumer Affairs and Coinage; General Oversight and Renegotiation; Housing and Community Development (Chairman). *Small Business* (4th). Subcommittees: Antitrust and Restraint of Trade Activities Affecting Small Business; General Oversight and the Economy.

Group Ratings

	ADA	ACLU	COPE	CFA	LCV	LWV	NTU	NSI	COC	ACA	CSFC
1982	60	92	90	77	63	73	11	67	27	22	32
1981	70	—	91	71	56	—	0	—	0	17	33
1980	72	80	79	79	35	60	11	33	56	17	23

National Journal Ratings

	Economic		Foreign		Cultural	
1982	63%	(LIB)	51%	(LIB)	75%	(LIB)
	37%	(CONS)	48%	(CONS)	25%	(CONS)
1981	98%	(LIB)	40%	(LIB)	87%	(LIB)
	1%	(CONS)	60%	(CONS)	13%	(CONS)

Key Votes

1) Reagan 81 Budget	AGN	5) Incr SS Rtmt Age	AGN	9) Poor Pay Food Stamps	AGN
2) Reagan 81 Tax Cut	AGN	6) Saudi AWACS Sale	AGN	10) Ban Crt Busing Order	AGN
3) Bal Budget Amend	AGN	7) $ for MX Missile	AGN	11) Auto Local Content	FOR
4) Gas & Road Tax	AGN	8) Nerve Gas Prod	AGN	12) Nuclear Arms Freeze	FOR

Election Results

1982 general	Henry B. Gonzalez (D)	68,544	(91%)	($66,571)
	Roger V. Gary (L)	4,163	(6%)	($0)
1982 primary	Henry B. Gonzalez (D)	36,387	(100%)	
1980 general	Henry B. Gonzalez (D)	84,113	(82%)	($51,385)
	Merle Nash (R)	17,725	(17%)	($17,190)

Campaign Contributions and Expenditures

1981-82		Direct Cont. 81-82		PACS brkdwn			
Receipts	$67,552	Indiv	$54,423	Agr	$1,500	Ideo	$—
Expend.	$66,571	Party	$3,680	Bus	$6,730	Lbr	$—
Unspent	$1,862	PACS	$11,830	Hlth	$—	Prof	$3,400

TWENTY-FIRST DISTRICT

A series of modern urban settlements across ranges of arid hills and miles of rugged desert—this is the 21st congressional district of Texas. This is by a considerable margin Texas's largest congressional district in area, and most of it is vacant as far as the eye can see. Actually, it is a collection of rather different constituencies. They include:

• *The Big Bend territory west of the Pecos River.* Few people know it, but Texas has 7,000-foot peaks where the Rio Grande makes a big bend. This land is virtually uninhabited on both sides of the border.

• *Midland.* This small city is a spot of rich suburbia out in the middle of the desert. It is the headquarters of the people who run the Permian Basin, rich oil and gas terrain where George Bush made his fortune in the 1950s and which continue to make Midland prosperous. Blue-collar people live 25 miles down the road in Odessa, in the 19th district; Midland has one of the highest income levels in the country, and is one of the nation's most heavily Republican places. It may well supply more big Republican contributors per capita than anywhere else in the United States.

• *San Angelo.* This is an older town, a center of cattle ranching as well as oil. It is ancestrally Democratic, in practice Republican.

• *The Texas German country.* In the hills north and northwest of San Antonio, refugees from the failed German revolutions of 1848 settled in Texas. They made good livings, even off barren soil, but they found the Texans unappealing. They disliked slavery, instinctively favored the Union, and when Texas became one of the most heavily Democratic states in the Union after the Civil War they insisted on voting Republican in every election. They still do. The hill country around Fredericksburg and Kerrville got electricity back in the 1930s, thanks to Lyndon Johnson,whose LBJ Ranch is just at the edge of German country; and the hill country now is the site of condominium developments, for prosperous Texans who want a second home in a pleasant, quiet environment.

• *The north side of San Antonio.* There are few Mexican-Americans on the north side of San Antonio, where most of the city's affluent people live; and most of this area is in the 21st district. Altogether 26% of the 21st's residents live in San Antonio and surrounding Bexar County. Affluent Anglos in San Antonio have voted heavily Republican since 1961, when Congressman Henry Gonzalez was elected to replace Paul Kilday, the conservative Democrat whose machine controlled city politics.

This all adds up to a Republican district, yet it didn't go Republican until 1978. It was represented for 32 years by an ultraconservative Democrat who retired in 1974; his successor was Bob Krueger, a wealthy former English professor, who dazzled the House and almost persuaded it to deregulate natural gas in the 1970s. He ran for the Senate in 1978 and nearly beat John Tower; he might run again in 1984.

The 21st's current congressman is Tom Loeffler. He comes from the German country and worked as a congressional lobbyist in the Ford White House, while still in his 20s. In winning the seat he showed a sturdy loyalty to conservative principles, expressing reservations about bilingual education in a district with a significant Spanish-speaking minority and questioning federal aid to schools in an area loaded with military bases. In his first election he won by a large majority in Bexar County. The balance of the district was changed after the 1980 Census, and Bexar casts a smaller share of its votes now; but Loeffler seems firmly entrenched and wins overwhelmingly.

In the House he has shown impressive legislative skills. He served on the Energy and Commerce Committee in his first term, and then got a seat on Appropriations. After the 1982 election he became a member of the Budget Committee. He makes a point of keeping in touch with conservative Democrats in the Texas delegation, and he was one of the key links in the fruitful alliance between the Reagan administration and junior conservative Democrats like Phil Gramm, Kent Hance, and Charles Stenholm. With a safe seat, sound principles, and political agility, he is just the kind of member the Republicans should be considering for a future leadership position.

The People Pop. 1980: 527,044, up 31.9% 1970–80; voting age pop. 377,612; 3% Black, 18% Span. orig., 1% Asian orig. 26% housing units rented. Median owner $45,300; renter $211. Households: 75% family, 39% with children, 66% married couples.

Presidential Vote

1980	Reagan (R)	NA
	Carter (D)	NA
	Anderson (I)	NA

Rep. Thomas G. (Tom) **Loeffler** (R) Elected 1978; b. Aug. 1, 1946, Fredericksburg; home, Hunt; U. of TX, B.B.A. 1968, J.D. 1971; Lutheran.

Career Practicing atty. and rancher; Chf. Legis. Counsel to U.S. Sen. John Tower, 1972-74; Spec. Asst. for Legis. Affairs, Fed. Energy Admin., 1974–75; Spec. Asst. for Legis. Affairs to Pres. Gerald Ford, 1975.

Offices 1212 LHOB, 202-225-4236. Also B-209 Fed. Bldg., 727 E. Durango, San Antonio 78205, 512-229-5880.

Committees *Appropriations* (18th). Subcommittees: Interior; Military Construction. *Budget* (10th). Task Forces: Budget Process; Energy and Technology.

Group Ratings

	ADA	ACLU	COPE	CFA	LCV	LWV	NTU	NSI	COC	ACA	CSFC
1982	0	92	9	8	8	25	87	100	82	91	76
1981	0	—	11	7	7	—	70	—	100	83	74
1980	0	80	10	7	26	10	65	100	73	92	83

National Journal Ratings

	Economic		Foreign		Cultural	
1982	0%	(LIB)	12%	(LIB)	4%	(LIB)
	98%	(CONS)	84%	(CONS)	87%	(CONS)
1981	4%	(LIB)	34%	(LIB)	4%	(LIB)
	79%	(CONS)	63%	(CONS)	90%	(CONS)

Key Votes

1) Reagan 81 Budget	FOR	5) Incr SS Rtmt Age	FOR	9) Poor Pay Food Stamps	FOR
2) Reagan 81 Tax Cut	FOR	6) Saudi AWACS Sale	AGN	10) Ban Crt Busing Order	FOR
3) Bal Budget Amend	FOR	7) $ for MX Missile	FOR	11) Auto Local Content	AGN
4) Gas & Road Tax	AGN	8) Nerve Gas Prod	FOR	12) Nuclear Arms Freeze	AGN

Election Results

1982 general	Thomas G. (Tom) Loeffler (R)	106,515	(75%)	($149,500)
	Charles S. Stough (D)	35,112	(25%)	($6,953)
1982 primary	Thomas G. (Tom) Loeffler (R)	19,810	(100%)	
1980 general	Thomas G. (Tom) Loeffler (R)	196,424	(76%)	($344,199)
	Joe Sullivan (D)	58,425	(23%)	($45,382)

Campaign Contributions and Expenditures

1981-82		Direct Cont. 81-82		PACS brkdwn			
Receipts	$383,687	Indiv	$214,641	Agr	$5,100	Ideo	$6,000
Expend.	$149,500	Party	$3,662	Bus	$87,850	Lbr	$—
Unspent	$384,809	PACS	$110,680	Hlth	$6,500	Prof	$4,450

TWENTY-SECOND DISTRICT

The 22d congressional district of Texas moves from the west side of Houston across the sprouting subdivisions of the coastal plain to the Brazosport area on the Gulf of Mexico. Most of this territory was empty not so long ago: there were 526,000 people here in 1980, just under 300,000 in 1970, and less than 200,000 in 1960. Like so much of the Sun Belt, it would not exist in its present form without the air conditioner. The sun beats down on these flat and swampy plains most of the year; the humidity is insufferable for about half the year. Yet an advanced civilization has sprung up here, in air-conditioned offices, air-conditioned shopping malls, air-conditioned houses and cars. Outside is the shimmering heat and an almost eerie silence.

The 22d district begins, you could say, at the intersection of Post Oak and Westheimer, the site of Houston's most fashionable shopping centers: this is the 5th Avenue and 57th Street of the oil kingdom. The district follows the Southwest Freeway southwest out through a prosperous section of west side Houston. The biggest political landmark here is the Sharpstown Shopping Center, put up by a local wheeler-dealer whose financial collapse and political dealings brought down a governor and likely future governor in 1972. The Southwest Freeway proceeds outward into Fort Bend County, past what were once cottonfields and are now prime residential land. By the time you get to the old county seat of Rosenberg, you think you are in rural Texas, although this is now becoming commuting country for Houstonians. South, toward the Gulf of Mexico, is Brazoria County, where the Brazos River empties into the Gulf. An artificial port has been established here, around Freeport and Lake Jackson, to ship out the area's oil production.

This is basically a Republican district. Its portion of west side Houston is heavily Republican. Fort Bend County, with its Houston suburbanites, is now Republican enough to balance off the Democratic margins from industrial, roughneck Brazoria. But if the 22d district is fairly conventionally Republican, its congressman is not.

He is Ron Paul, and he is probably the closest thing to a libertarian member of Congress. A physician from Lake Jackson, he is a believer that government should enforce contracts, patrol the streets, maintain a currency convertible to gold—and not do much else. He is probably Congress's most enthusiastic advocate of the gold standard; he may be, for a time, elbowed out of the spotlight by supply siders advocating the same thing, but when they move on to something else, you can bet Paul will keep the faith. He does so on other issues. He does not join Reagan Republicans in many of their crusades to uphold personal morality: that's government interference. Nor does he support an aggressive or even an active foreign policy: no entangling alliances, no foreign wars.

His one committee assignment is Banking. He is ranking Republican on the Consumer Affairs and Coinage Subcommittee, chaired by Chicago's Frank Annunzio, a practical-minded politician if there ever was one; he also ranks second to George Hansen (evidently a silver rather than a gold bug) on the Domestic Monetary Policy Subcommittee chaired by the District of Columbia's Walter Fauntroy. Theoretically, these assignments should give Paul a chance to air and advance his views; in practice, they don't give him much influence or leverage.

It should be added that these stands have been to Paul's political detriment. In the previous 22d district, which included many black precincts in Houston, Paul had some close races. He won a 1976 special election by 8,000 votes, but lost the 1976 general by 236 votes to Bob Gammage, the same candidate he beat by 1,200 votes in 1978. In 1980, he beat Mike Andrews, now the congressman from the new 25th district, by 5,703. His 1978 and 1980 victories occurred even though he was outspent significantly by the Democrats both times. In 1982 he had an easier time: token primary opposition and no Democratic opponent. Drawing on likeminded contributors, he raised $465,000 and had nearly $300,000 in the bank after the election. But even in this new, more Republican district, he still may find himself with formidable opposition accusing him of being an oddball. Of course, in his view, it's the rest of the nation's politicians, with their devotion to an inherently inflationary currency and to self-defeating government programs, who are the oddballs.

The People   Pop. 1980: 526,602, up 76.9% 1970–80; voting age pop. 381,492; 13% Black, 12% Span. orig., 3% Asian orig. 42% housing units rented. Median owner $64,200; renter $271. Households: 67% family, 38% with children, 57% married couples.

Presidential Vote

1980	Reagan (R)	NA
	Carter (D)	NA
	Anderson (I)	NA

Rep. Ron Paul (R) Elected Apr. 6, 1976; b. Aug. 20, 1935, Pittsburgh, PA; home, Lake Jackson; Gettysburg Col., B.A. 1957; Duke U., M.D. 1961; Episcopal.

Career Flight Surgeon, U.S. Air Force, 1963–65; Practicing physician, 1965–.

Offices 1234 LHOB, 202-225-5951. Also 4545 Bissonnet, Su. 220, Bellaire 77401, 713-669-0503.

Committee *Banking, Finance and Urban Affairs* (5th). Subcommittees: Consumer Affairs and Coinage; Domestic Monetary Policy; Economic Stabilization.

Group Ratings

	ADA	ACLU	COPE	CFA	LCV	LWV	NTU	NSI	COC	ACA	CSFC
1982	35	21	6	8	30	27	99	10	70	74	78
1981	25	—	7	29	48	—	99	—	76	79	76
1980	22	27	5	7	47	20	94	60	58	92	89

National Journal Ratings

	Economic		Foreign		Cultural	
1982	2%	(LIB)	74%	(LIB)	57%	(LIB)
	97%	(CONS)	26%	(CONS)	42%	(CONS)
1981	32%	(LIB)	77%	(LIB)	23%	(LIB)
	67%	(CONS)	23%	(CONS)	77%	(CONS)

Key Votes

1) Reagan 81 Budget	FOR	5) Incr SS Rtmt Age	FOR
2) Reagan 81 Tax Cut	FOR	6) Saudi AWACS Sale	AGN
3) Bal Budget Amend	FOR	7) $ for MX Missile	AGN
4) Gas & Road Tax	—	8) Nerve Gas Prod	AGN

9) Poor Pay Food Stamps	FOR
10) Ban Crt Busing Order	FOR
11) Auto Local Content	AGN
12) Nuclear Arms Freeze	AGN

Election Results

1982 general	Ron Paul (R)	66,536	(99%)	($254,794)
1982 primary	Ron Paul (R)	14,679	(88%)	
	Jerry Ford (R)	2,094	(12%)	($9,024)
1980 general	Ron Paul (R)	106,797	(51%)	($359,558)
	Mike Andrews (D)	101,094	(48%)	($750,836)

Campaign Contributions and Expenditures

1981-82		Direct Cont. 81-82				PACS brkdwn		
Receipts	$464,960	Indiv	$371,835	Agr	$—	Ideo	$2,160
Expend.	$254,794	Party	$5,505	Bus	$35,955	Lbr	$—
Unspent	$287,359	PACS	$45,365	Hlth	$7,250	Prof	$—

TWENTY-THIRD DISTRICT

From San Antonio south, you are in the border country: a part of the United States which is neither entirely American nor entirely Mexican, but a mixture—and a volatile and constantly changing mixture—of the two. There are desert-like rural counties here where big landowners continue to rule the lives—and cast the votes—of their Mexican-American field hands. There are other small counties where "brown power" movements have taken over local government, only to find that holding office does not automatically give one leverage to change the world. Then there are the border towns, like Laredo. More than 90% of the people here on the U.S. side are of Spanish origin, according to the Census; and most of the business done here would not exist were it not for the border. On the U.S. side, shops and department stores specialized in selling consumer goods to Mexicans; that trade, however, collapsed along with the Mexican economy and the peso in 1982.

The 23d congressional district of Texas extends from the south side of San Antonio south to Laredo and west to Eagle Pass, both on the Rio Grande. Most of the land area is in the border counties, which in most elections are among the most heavily Democratic counties in the nation. But some 62% of the population is in San Antonio and surrounding Bexar County (pronounced with something like the soft Spanish X, which sounds like an H to English-speakers). The district includes the southern fringes of San Antonio, working-class neighborhoods near big military bases where nearly half the residents are Mexican-Americans. But the district also includes suburban territory east, west, and north of the city. This takes in some of the most affluent precincts in Bexar County, where historically mistrust of Mexicans and Democrats is high.

Much of the suburban territory was added to the district for 1982, and caused problems for Democratic Congressman Abraham Kazen. Of Lebanese descent, his political base is in Laredo and he has always been popular with Mexican-American voters. But he had tough Republican opposition for the first time in memory, in the person of Jeff Wentworth, who outspent Kazen nearly 2–1. It was a Democratic year, with good turnout in Mexican areas, and Kazen carried all the small counties in the district. But in some his margins were small. And he lost Bexar County, which cast 63% of the district's votes, by a 54%–46% margin. That's not a strong showing, and suggests that Kazen may get serious opposition again—particularly if there's population growth in the San Antonio suburbs.

Kazen has a mildly liberal voting record on economic issues, coupled with a more conservative approach to environmental issues and a hawkish approach to military matters. First elected in 1966, he has plenty of seniority, but he has not been a particularly influential figure. He has not made major initiatives, nor does he seek to dominate proceedings. He is now the second ranking Democrat on the House Interior Committee, but even so he is not the clear heir to Chairman Morris Udall; House Democrats might well pass him over for someone closer to their views on Interior's issues, like third ranking John Seiberling. Even a significant subcommittee chairmanship (Water and Power Resources) has not made Kazen a major power. He also sits on Armed Services, where he does not disturb the consensus, but looks after the interests of San Antonio's many military bases. Like most congressmen, he can say he has done things for the immediate needs of his district and constituents. But his lack of a readily advertisable record may make it hard for him to win if he is seriously challenged again.

The People   Pop. 1980: 526,531, up 57.9% 1970–80; voting age pop. 336,355; 4% Black, 48% Span. orig., 1% Asian orig. 28% housing units rented. Median owner $35,200; renter $184. Households: 83% family, 54% with children, 69% married couples.

Presidential Vote

1980			
	Reagan (R)	81,338	(56%)
	Carter (D)	63,378	(44%)
	Anderson (I)	NA	

Rep. Abraham (Chick) **Kazen, Jr.** (D) Elected 1966; b. Jan. 17, 1919, Laredo; home, Laredo; U. of TX, 1937–40, Cumberland U. Sch. of Law, 1941; Roman Catholic.

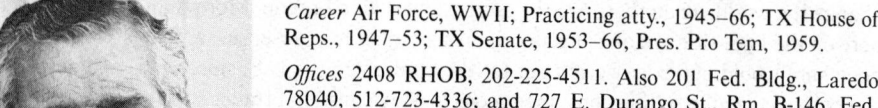

Career Air Force, WWII; Practicing atty., 1945–66; TX House of Reps., 1947–53; TX Senate, 1953–66, Pres. Pro Tem, 1959.

Offices 2408 RHOB, 202-225-4511. Also 201 Fed. Bldg., Laredo 78040, 512-723-4336; and 727 E. Durango St., Rm. B-146, Fed. Bldg., San Antonio 78205, 512-229-6191.

Committees *Armed Services* (10th). Subcommittees: Investigations; Military Installations and Facilities. *Interior and Insular Affairs* (2d). Subcommittees: Mining, Forest Management, and BPA; Water and Power Resources (Chairman).

Group Ratings

	ADA	ACLU	COPE	CFA	LCV	LWV	NTU	NSI	COC	ACA	CSFC
1982	20	33	53	62	33	50	39	100	64	48	50
1981	35	—	52	50	36	—	10	—	26	54	54
1980	22	23	44	50	31	33	27	75	62	30	44

National Journal Ratings

	Economic		Foreign		Cultural	
1982	49%	(LIB)	12%	(LIB)	4%	(LIB)
	50%	(CONS)	84%	(CONS)	87%	(CONS)
1981	60%	(LIB)	3%	(LIB)	47%	(LIB)
	39%	(CONS)	87%	(CONS)	52%	(CONS)

Key Votes

1) Reagan 81 Budget	AGN	5) Incr SS Rtmt Age	FOR	9) Poor Pay Food Stamps	AGN
2) Reagan 81 Tax Cut	AGN	6) Saudi AWACS Sale	FOR	10) Ban Crt Busing Order	FOR
3) Bal Budget Amend	FOR	7) $ for MX Missile	FOR	11) Auto Local Content	AGN
4) Gas & Road Tax	AGN	8) Nerve Gas Prod	FOR	12) Nuclear Arms Freeze	AGN

Election Results

1982 general	Abraham (Chick) Kazen, Jr. (D) ..	51,690	(55%)	($220,527)
	Jeff Wentworth (R)	41,363	(44%)	($396,588)
1982 primary	Abraham (Chick) Kazen, Jr. (D) ..	34,023	(100%)	
1980 general	Abraham (Chick) Kazen, Jr. (D) ..	104,595	(70%)	($317,815)
	Bobby Locke (R)	45,139	(30%)	($8,516)

Campaign Contributions and Expenditures

1981-82		Direct Cont. 81-82		PACS brkdwn			
Receipts	$216,854	Indiv	$124,419	Agr	$9,550	Ideo	$5,076
Expend.	$220,527	Party	$6,100	Bus	$41,427	Lbr	$11,475
Unspent	$1,223	PACS	$83,106	Hlth	$11,500	Prof	$3,258

Indirect Party Expend: $4,000

TWENTY-FOURTH DISTRICT

Downtown Dallas is situated on high land overlooking the Trinity River; on the other side of the river, on high land also, is the old part of the city called Oak Cliff. Traveling its back streets, you can find old Victorian gingerbread houses; there is more evidence here than on the north side of the river of the kind of city Dallas was before steel-and-glass skyscrapers towered over downtown and were scattered around freeway interchanges on the north side of the city. The river forms a clean dividing line; because of floods, the bottomlands are maintained as parkland, and there are not all that many bridges across. The south side of Dallas, from Oak Cliff on south, is where most of the city's black residents live and most of its much smaller number of Mexican-Americans.

This is the heart of the 24th congressional district of Texas, the strongest national Democratic district in the Dallas–Fort Worth metroplex. Its population is 32% black and 13% Spanish origin, according to the 1980 Census; its housing prices are relatively inexpensive. It does include some suburban territory, however: the modest suburb of Grand Prairie and somewhat higher-income Irving, home of the Dallas Cowboys' Texas Stadium, and a part of Arlington, over the border in Tarrant County. The 24th district's boundaries were the key issue in the partisan fights over Texas's redistrictings. The Republicans wanted to put more blacks into this district and make it even more Democratic, in order to create a less black and less Democratic 5th district next door. Governor William Clements persuaded the legislature to pass such a plan, but it was overthrown by an intervention-minded federal court, on the specious theory that the Voting Rights Act requires a maximization of the number of Democratic districts, since most blacks vote Democratic.

That decision was supposed to have been crucial to the political survival of Congressman Martin Frost. Actually, he probably would have survived anyway. Frost won the district, which had different contours but included Oak Cliff, in 1978 by beating conservative incumbent Dale Milford in the Democratic primary (he had lost the same race four years before). In those contests, and later, he campaigned door-to-door in black areas and won huge majorities there. He had a much more liberal voting record than the Texas freshmen elected that year from rural districts; he is well within the range of national Democrats. Majority Leader Jim Wright helped him get a seat on the House Rules Committee, where he has almost always supported the House leadership. So Frost was well positioned to win votes even against a black primary opponent in a black majority district; he could argue that he worked for blacks when it wasn't necessarily to his political advantage.

As it happened, Frost did have a black opponent, in the 1982 general election. This was something of a coup for the national Republican Party: Lucy Patterson, a member of the Dallas City Council for six years, switched parties. She received help from the Republican Party but not the PAC money that usually accompanies it. But Frost ended up winning with a solid 59% of the vote and winning more than 90% of black votes—testimony to his popularity among black voters. Frost's chief worry for 1984 must be redistricting: the legislature will have a chance to act, and, if he is lucky, will choose about the same lines as at present. But even if it doesn't, he has strong appeal and will be hard to beat in any district.

The People Pop. 1980: 526,677, up 7.6% 1970–80; voting age pop. 357,187; 29% Black, 11% Span. orig., 15% Asian orig., 1% Am. Ind. 41% housing units rented. Median owner $35,400; renter $220. Households: 75% family, 46% with children, 57% married couples.

Presidential Vote

1980			
	Reagan (R)	72,156	(48%)
	Carter (D)	76,914	(52%)
	Anderson (I)	NA	

Rep. Martin Frost (D) Elected 1978; b. Jan. 1, 1942, Glendale, CA; home, Dallas; U. of MO, B.A., B.J. 1964, Georgetown U., LL.B. 1970; Jewish.

Career Practicing atty., 1970–.

Offices 1238 LHOB, 202-225-3605. Also Oakcliff Bank Tower, Su. 1319, Dallas 75208, 214-941-6032; and Grand Prairie Tower, 801 West Freeway, Su. 720, Grand Prairie 75051, 214-262-1503.

Committees *Budget* (19th). Task Forces: Education and Employment; Energy and Technology; Tax Policy. *Rules* (6th). Subcommittee: The Legislative Process.

Group Ratings

	ADA	ACLU	COPE	CFA	LCV	LWV	NTU	NSI	COC	ACA	CSFC
1982	70	50	71	69	71	80	3	60	23	30	29
1981	50	—	65	43	73	—	7	—	24	40	41
1980	50	57	58	50	17	63	18	60	67	23	37

National Journal Ratings

	Economic		Foreign		Cultural	
1982	96%	(LIB)	65%	(LIB)	52%	(LIB)
	2%	(CONS)	35%	(CONS)	47%	(CONS)
1981	70%	(LIB)	48%	(LIB)	64%	(LIB)
	30%	(CONS)	51%	(CONS)	35%	(CONS)

Key Votes

1) Reagan 81 Budget	AGN	5) Incr SS Rtmt Age	AGN	9) Poor Pay Food Stamps	—
2) Reagan 81 Tax Cut	AGN	6) Saudi AWACS Sale	AGN	10) Ban Crt Busing Order	AGN
3) Bal Budget Amend	AGN	7) $ for MX Missile	AGN	11) Auto Local Content	FOR
4) Gas & Road Tax	—	8) Nerve Gas Prod	AGN	12) Nuclear Arms Freeze	FOR

Election Results

1982 general	Martin Frost (D)	33,857	(59%)	($618,258)
	Lucy Patterson (R)	22,798	(40%)	($129,018)
1982 primary	Martin Frost (D)	18,496	(100%)	
1980 general	Martin Frost (D)	93,690	(61%)	($406,096)
	Clay Smothers (R)	59,172	(39%)	($126,092)

Campaign Contributions and Expenditures

1981-82		Direct Cont. 81-82				PACS brkdwn		
Receipts	$621,090	Indiv	$380,356	Agr	$18,950	Ideo	$21,750
Expend.	$618,258	PACS	$235,540	Bus	$89,590	Lbr	$76,650
Unspent	$2,830	Cand	$5,000	Hlth	$16,450	Prof	$12,150

TWENTY-FIFTH DISTRICT

The 25th congressional district of Texas is one of three new districts created after the 1980 Census. It consists of the south side of Houston and Harris County. The district includes just a bit of west side Houston, north and west of Main Street; it has Rice University, the Texas Medical Center, the Houston Astrodome, and one of the few Jewish sections of the city. But to the east, separated by factories and swamp, is the rest of the district. Here you find frame houses, with air conditioners chugging noisily in windows. That, combined with the rush of traffic on nearby highways, makes conversation on the streets hard to hear.

On the east side of Houston is Pasadena, a suburb of similar size but very different character from its genteel California namesake. This Pasadena is the home of Gilley's, the bar in *Urban Cowboy* where young men and women, who have moved to Houston from rural towns to find work, dress and act like cowboys and ride the mechanical bull each night. The district proceeds eastward from here, following the Houston Ship Channel, past subdivisions some of which are subsiding back into the earth, toward Galveston Bay. It stops just short of the Johnson Space Center.

The new 25th district was 25% black and 14% Spanish origin. Its blacks are concentrated in all-black neighborhoods directly south of Houston's downtown; the Mexican-Americans are more dispersed. These two groups, however, tend to make this a Democratic district; blacks cast almost no Republican votes in Houston, and Mexicans don't cast very many. Their margins more than cancel out the Republican margins from the west side or the suburbs between Pasadena and the bay.

Nevertheless there were serious contests and runoffs in both the Republican and the Democratic primaries. The Republicans, perhaps, could not forget how they had won the 8th district for Jack Fields in 1980; the 8th contained a lot of working-class territory, including some precincts included in the new 25th. But the ultimate winner turned out to be Mike Andrews, the same candidate who nearly beat Republican Ron Paul in the old 22d district in 1980. Andrews was billed then as the candidate of downtown businessmen, and he spent some $750,000 in 1980 and $647,000 in 1982—sums that suggest he had a lot of smart-money backing in both contests. It made a certain amount of sense: Paul is a libertarian, heedless of local business interests; and Mike Faubion, the ultimate Republican nominee in the 25th, never really had a chance.

Andrews is now a member of the Public Works and Science and Technology Committees. These are associated with the programs which have done so much to develop Houston: Public Works authorizes projects like the dredging of the Houston Ship Channel, which made this swampy inland county seat one of the nation's great seaports; Science authorized the Johnson Space Center, and Houston Congressman Albert Thomas was the man who got it here. Whether Andrews has Thomas's political skill is not yet clear, but he may well have; he has already shown he can raise a lot of money and beat a lot of competitors for a congressional seat he can probably hold easily, now that he's got it, for many years.

The People   Pop. 1980: 526,801, up 20.4% 1970–80; voting age pop. 366,175; 23% Black, 12% Span. orig., 1% Asian orig. 38% housing units rented. Median owner $46,700; renter $261. Households: 74% family, 44% with children, 60% married couples.

Presidential Vote

1980	Reagan (R)	80,426	(53%)
	Carter (D)	71,622	(47%)
	Anderson (I)	NA	

Rep. Mike Andrews (D) Elected 1982; b. Feb. 7, 1944, Houston; home, Houston; U. of TX at Austin, B.A. 1967, SMU Sch. of Law, J.D. 1970; Methodist.

Career Practicing atty., 1970–82.

Offices 1039 LHOB, 202-225-7508. Also 7707 Fannin, Houston 77054, 713-791-1877.

Committees *Public Works and Transportation* (28th). Subcommittees: Investigations and Oversight; Public Buildings and Grounds; Surface Transportation. *Science and Technology* (21st). Subcommittees: Natural Resources, Agriculture Research and Environment; Space Science and Applications; Transportation, Aviation and Materials.

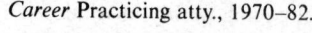

Group Ratings and Key Votes: Newly Elected

Election Results

1982 general	Mike Andrews (D)	63,974	(60%)	($647,677)
	Mike Faubion (R)	40,112	(38%)	($330,611)
1982 runoff	Mike Andrews (D)	11,011	(58%)	
	John Ray Harrision (D)	8,029	(42%)	($136,006)
1982 primary	Mike Andrews (D)	10,651	(43%)	
	John Ray Harrision (D)	7,500	(30%)	
	Tom Bass (D)	6,582	(27%)	($45,070)
1980 general	Newly created district			

Campaign Contributions and Expenditures

1981-82		Direct Cont. 81-82		PACS brkdwn			
Receipts	$646,350	Indiv	$414,295	Agr	$7,500	Ideo	$9,750
Expend.	$647,677	Party	$3,500	Bus	$87,807	Lbr	$30,050
Unspent	$693	PACS	$164,330	Hlth	$4,450	Prof	$15,650
		Cand	$56,500				

Indep Expend: For: $985

TWENTY-SIXTH DISTRICT

The 26th congressional district of Texas is one of three new districts created after the 1980 Census. This one, it was clear from the population figures, would have to be constructed in the Dallas–Fort Worth metroplex; and the odds were that it would lean Republican. Three of the four other districts in this metropolitan area turned out to be Democratic, although the area as a whole usually goes Republican. The new 26th is of irregular shape, and shows every sign of having been constructed of materials representatives of the other districts did not particularly want.

The largest part of the district is in Tarrant County, including the southwest, south, southeast, and east sections of the county. They all have this in common: they are more affluent, and generally more Republican, than average. The 26th includes the most affluent parts of Fort Worth, which is otherwise represented by House Majority Leader Jim Wright; it includes most of the city of Arlington, a burgeoning suburb halfway between Fort Worth and Dallas; it also includes the affluent and growing area of Grapevine, near the Dallas–Fort Worth Regional Airport. To the north, the district takes in all of Denton County, once a rural and Democratic place, but now with its southern portion taken over completely and its northern portion partly by affluent young metroplex workers seeking comfortable housing a little farther out from the cities. The district goes even farther north, into Cooke County, and east, into Collin County, which like Denton is being suburbanized.

Almost everyone predicted the district would go Republican—except, they all added, if Tom Vandergriff ran. Vandergriff held no public office at the time, and had never been a legislator. Nevertheless he is a legend in these parts. He served as mayor of Arlington for 26 years, from 1951 to 1977, and converted it from a town of 8,000—hardly more than a gas station crossroads—into a city with municipal pride and institutions which many central cities would kill for. Vandergriff got the Washington Senators baseball team to move here in 1969 and become the Texas Rangers; he got Turnpike Stadium built; he got Six Flags Over Texas built here. By 1980 there were 160,000 people in Arlington—a large population, but not a huge one by metroplex standards. Nevertheless, this town is not overshadowed, in people's minds, by either Fort Worth or Dallas. And everyone knows that Vandergriff made Arlington what it is.

Vandergriff had the Democratic nomination unopposed. His opponent was Jim Bradshaw, the former mayor pro tem of Fort Worth who had run an expensive, but losing, campaign against Jim Wright in 1980. Bradshaw was no more lucky this time. He trumpeted his support of President Reagan. But everyone knew Vandergriff is conservative too, except that he is not bound to support aspects of the Reagan program not popular here. This turned out to be one of the closest races in the country: Vandergriff, who spent more personal funds than any House member in 1982, won by 344 votes.

In the House Vandergriff is a member of the Public Works and Small Business Committees. It hardly seems likely that he can duplicate his feats in creating Arlington, but perhaps he will try. On national issues, he is a likely dissenter from Democratic positions. This remains, after all, a Republican district, where a good Republican challenger could still give Vandergriff trouble, and where any other Democrat almost surely would be soundly beaten.

The People Pop. 1980: 527,299, up 87.3% 1970–80; voting age pop. 367,421; 3% Black, 3% Span. orig., 1% Asian orig. 25% housing units rented. Median owner $63,200; renter $260. Households: 79% family, 47% with children, 71% married couples.

Presidential Vote

1980	Reagan (R)	138,472	(69%)
	Carter (D)	60,945	(31%)
	Anderson (I)	NA	

Rep. Tom Vandergriff (D) Elected 1982; b. Jan. 29, 1926, Carrollton; home, Arlington; USC, B.A. 1947; Methodist.

Career Mayor of Arlington, 1951–77; family automobile business.

Offices 1529 LHOB, 202-225-7772. Also 1141 W. Pioneer Pkwy., Su. 105, Arlington 76103, 817-461-3334; P.O. Box 1816, Denton 76201, 817-383-2616; A105 Fed. Bldg., McKinney 75069, 214-542-2617; and 2821 W. Parker Rd., Plano 75203, 214-985-0025.

Committees *Public Works and Transportation* (29th). Subcommittees: Aviation; Surface Transportation. *Small Business* (22d). Subcommittees: Export Opportunities and Special Small Business Problems; Tax, Access to Equity Capital and Business Opportunities. *Select Committee on Aging* (36th). Subcommittee: Retirement Income and Employment.

Group Ratings and Key Votes: Newly Elected

Election Results

1982 general	Tom Vandergriff (D)	69,782	(50%)	($948,024)
	Jim Bradshaw (R)	69,438	(50%)	($516,781)
1982 primary	Tom Vandergriff (D)	16,553	(100%)	
1980 general	Newly created district			

Campaign Contributions and Expenditures

1982		Direct Cont. 1982			PACS brkdwn		
Receipts	$953,564	Indiv	$87,119	Agr	$7,500	Ideo	$8,600
Expend.	$948,024	Party	$3,000	Bus	$29,150	Lbr	$9,350
Unspent	$5,539	PACS	$59,454	Hlth	$200	Prof	$500
		Cand	$800,500				

TWENTY-SEVENTH DISTRICT

The 27th congressional district of Texas is one of three new districts created after the 1980 Census. This one, it was clear, would be created in south Texas, and, after a court intervened, the current lines were drawn. The result is a district that follows the Gulf of Mexico from Corpus Christi south to the Mexican border at Brownsville. In front of the Gulf is the sand spit of Padre Island, which extends almost the whole distance. For most of its length it is a national seashore; this area, where the hot sands meet the almost steamy waters of the summertime Gulf, cannot be developed. At the south end of the island, however, there are extensive high-rise developments now, where residents can sit high in air conditioning and watch the beach shimmer in the heat.

Demographically, the population of this district is concentrated in its two ends. Exactly 50% of its residents live in Corpus Christi and surrounding Nueces County. Corpus, as it is familiarly called, is an oil port, the most important south of Houston. About half its residents are Mexican-Americans, but they do not set the tone of life or culture here: many are not citizens, and shy away from any form of public life; Corpus is mostly an Anglo, blue-collar town. Politically, it has always been Democratic, favoring national as well as local Democrats. But there are a lot of local political currents here, and in city politics some increasing tension between Anglos and Mexicans as the Mexican voting population grows.

At the other extreme, geographically, of the district, containing 40% of its residents, is Cameron County. The main cities here are Brownsville and Harlingen. This is part of the Lower Rio Grande Valley: 77% of the residents here are Mexican-American; income levels are exceedingly low by U.S. standards; the area has been hurt as well by the collapse of the Mexican economy and the peso in 1982. This is the southernmost point of the mainland United States, and a part of the country that seems only contingently American.

In between is a vast expanse of land which is exceedingly sparsely inhabited. There you will find the headquarters, but not quite all the acreage, of the Kleberg family's King Ranch. This is famous for its size and wealth; politically, it is important since the vote in Kleberg County is still pretty deliverable.

This is an overwhelmingly Democratic district, and the real contest for it was in the Democratic primary. There were five main candidates, and in the first primary their votes fell in the narrow range between 14% and 26%. The high figure was won by Solomon Ortiz, the sheriff of Nueces County. He was known as a tough law enforcer; it's a mistake to suppose that south Texas Mexican-Americans share all the views of Mexican-American organization representatives in Washington or Los Angeles. His major opponent was former Corpus Christi legislator Joe Salem. But Ortiz outmaneuvered him for support in Cameron County; by making a local alliance there he cinched the runoff. The general election was anticlimactic: the Republican candidate had the impressive-sounding credential of having been mayor of Corpus Christi, but he had not been active recently and his party label was a handicap impossible to overcome.

Ortiz now has a safe seat, barring serious primary competition. His committee assignments suggest he does not regard himself as part of the left wing of his party. He is one of several Texans on the Armed Services Committee, almost all of them strong supporters of increased military spending. And of course his seat there gives him a chance to look after the interests of the military bases in the district. His other assignment is Merchant Marine and Fisheries, a committee dedicated to maintaining the elaborate system of subsidies to U.S. shipbuilders, shipping companies, and maritime unions.

The People Pop. 1980: 526,988, up 23.7% 1970–80; voting age pop. 341,512; 3% Black, 55% Span. orig. 34% housing units rented. Median owner $31,000; renter $171. Households: 80% family, 50% with children, 66% married couples.

Presidential Vote

1980	Reagan (R)	NA
	Carter (D)	NA
	Anderson (I)	NA

Rep. Solomon P. Ortiz (D) Elected 1982; b. June 3, 1937, Robstown; home, Corpus Christi; Del Mar Col., 1969, Natl. Sheriffs' Inst., 1977; Methodist.

Career Nueces Cnty. Constable, 1955–68, Commissioner, 1969–76, Sheriff, 1977–82.

Offices 1524 LHOB, 202-225-7742. Also 303 Fed. Courthouse, 521 Starr St., Corpus Christi 77401, 512-888-3381.

Committees *Armed Services* (28th). Subcommittees: Military Personnel and Compensation; Seapower and Strategic and Critical Materials. *Merchant Marine and Fisheries* (25th). Subcommittees: Fisheries and Wildlife Conservation and the Environment; Merchant Marine; Panama Canal and Outer Continental Shelf. *Select Committee on Narcotics Abuse and Control* (14th).

Group Ratings and Key Votes: Newly Elected

Election Results

1982 general	Solomon P. Ortiz (D)	66,604	(64%)	($304,668)
	Jason Luby (R)	35,209	(34%)	($1,500)
1982 runoff	Solomon P. Ortiz (D)	24,539	(52%)	
	Joe Salem (D)	23,082	(48%)	($206,409)
1982 primary	Solomon P. Ortiz (D)	19,497	(26%)	
	Joe Salem (D)	18,984	(25%)	
	Jorge Rangel (D)	14,008	(18%)	($227,853)
	Arnold Gonzales (D)	13,072	(17%)	($18,358)
	Ruben M. Torres (D)	10,302	(14%)	($7,555)
1980 general	Newly created district			

Campaign Contributions and Expenditures

1982		*Direct Cont. 1982*			*PACS brkdwn*		
Receipts	$309,960	Indiv	$142,031	Agr	$4,000	Ideo	$6,625
Expend.	$304,668	Party	$1,200	Bus	$54,800	Lbr	$10,700
Unspent	$5,082	PACS	$89,074	Hlth	$10,000	Prof	$—
		Cand	$74,250				

UTAH

In 1827 Joseph Smith, a young Palmyra, New York, farmer, experienced a vision in which the Angel Moroni appeared to him. Moroni was a prophet of the lost tribe of Israel (the American Indians) that had presumably found its way to the New World some 600 years before the birth of Christ. Moroni told Smith where to unearth several golden tablets inscribed with hieroglyphic writings. With the aid of special spectacles, Smith translated the tablets and published them as the Book of Mormon in 1831. He then declared himself a prophet and founded a religious group he called the Church of Jesus Christ of Latter Day Saints.

The group was just one wave in a wash of religious revivalism, prophecy, and utopianism that swept across Upstate New York in the 1830s; the region was so alive with religious enthusiasm that it was known as the "burnt-over district." Very quickly the prophet's new sect attracted hundreds of converts. Persecuted for their beliefs, these Mormons, as they were called, moved west to Ohio, Missouri, and then Illinois. In 1844 the Mormon colony at Nauvoo, Illinois, had some 15,000 members, all living under the strict theocratic rule of Joseph Smith. In secular Illinois politics Nauvoo—then the largest city in the state—held the balance of power between contending Democrats and Whigs. It was here that Smith received a revelation sanctioning the practice of polygamy, which led to his death at the hands of a mob in 1844.

After the murder, the new president of the church, Brigham Young, decided to move the faithful, "the saints," farther west into territory that was still part of Mexico and far beyond the pale of white settlement. Young led a well-organized march across the Great Plains and into the Rocky Mountains. In 1847 the prophet and his followers stopped on the western slope of the Wasatch Range and, as Brigham Young gazed over the valley of the Great Salt Lake spread out below, he uttered the now famous words, "This is the place."

The place was Utah. It is today the only state that continues to live by the teachings of the church responsible for its founding. Throughout the 19th century and even today "Zion" has attracted thousands of converts from the Midwest, the north of England, and Scandinavia. The object of religious fear, prejudice, and perhaps some envy, Utah was not granted statehood until 1896, after the church renounced polygamy. Today about 70% of all Utah citizens are members of the LDS (Latter Day Saints) Church.

The Church dominates life in Utah in many ways. It owns one of the two leading newspapers in Salt Lake City and a TV station there; it has holdings in an insurance company, several banks, and real estate, and owns ZCMI, the largest department store in Salt Lake City. The Mormon hierarchy also takes stands on secular political matters: it supports Utah's right-to-work law and came out against the racetrack basing mode for the MX missile which the Carter administration proposed to build in Utah and Nevada. One doctrine which particularly embarrassed many Mormons—blacks were denied the "priesthood," *i.e.,* full church membership—was changed when LDS Church President Spencer Kimball had a revelation in 1978. The president is the most senior member of the Church's ruling body, and is therefore usually elderly—but also, in the case of Kimball and others, active and energetic. The man next in line for the post is Ezra Taft Benson, secretary of agriculture in the Eisenhower administration and a very conservative Republican.

Outsiders tend to sneer at the Church and its leadership, accusing them of being old-fashioned and out of line with trends in society today. But whatever progress secularism and liberation from traditional morality has made in other places, it has not advanced in Utah. On the contrary, all the evidence is that most Utahns enthusiastically endorse the attitudes of the Church. And their numbers are growing rapidly. Utah's population shot up 38% in the 1970s, both because of high birth rates here and because of heavy in-migration.

The moral code of the Mormons seems to provide a good basis for building a productive and confident society; in Utah, at least, the Mormon way of life works. It carries to their logical extremes the virtues celebrated in early 19th-century Upstate New York, virtues which only recently have been found to have beneficial side effects. Mormons are still forbidden to consume alcohol, tobacco, or caffeine; their cancer rates are significantly lower than the national average. They are supposed to live according to traditional sexual moral standards; they have large families and productive breadwinners. Young Mormons are asked to give two years of their lives to "missions" at home and in some of the unlikeliest places overseas, to win new converts to the faith; they come back with some knowledge of a different culture. Members are required to pledge 10% of their income, a tithe, to the Church; the Church remains solvent, and Mormons are extremely hardworking, and do well in business and the professions. National statistics—per capita statistics particularly—understate how well Utahns are doing economically: so many Utahns are children, and there are fewer two-paycheck families here than in big metropolitan areas.

So in Utah the 1950s American ideal is still alive—and thriving. Utah has the nation's highest percentage of households that are families and households with children and married couples. It also has an economy which was below the national average during the New Deal years and considered itself colonial then, and in need of federal assistance, but which now is probably above the national average and sees itself as successful. But Utah is also uncomfortably aware that it is living in a nation where the lessons its own experience seems so vividly to be teaching seem increasingly to be ignored. Utah's increasing economic prosperity transformed it from a Democratic state in the Roosevelt–Truman years to a pretty solidly Republican one by the middle 1960s. In the years since, the success of its own traditional values at home—and their waning influence in the rest of America—have made Utah probably our most conservative state on cultural issues. As a result, Utah has become the most Republican of states. In 1960 Richard Nixon carried Utah with 55% of the vote; by 1972 he won with 72%. In 1980 Ronald Reagan won 73% of Utah's votes and Jimmy Carter only 21%. The result was almost as one-sided as the Democrats' typical lead in the District of Columbia.

Governor. Still, Utah will elect an occasional Democrat, and in fact has had Democratic governors since 1964. Not surprisingly, they have been men of considerable ability and conservative attitudes. The current incumbent, Scott Matheson, was a Salt Lake City lawyer whose clients included the Union Pacific Railroad and Anaconda, and who in his first term repeatedly jousted with the federal government. He claimed credit for saving the Central Utah (water) Project during the Carter administration and fought plans for storing nerve gas bombs and locating an MX missile racetrack system in Utah. He cut spending and taxes; he was out of line with local opinion most notably in his support of the Equal Rights Amendment.

Matheson was first elected in 1976 and reelected against a not particularly strong Republican in 1980. Why do the Rocky Mountain states, so Republican in national politics, all have Democratic governors, some of whom are extremely bright? (Examples include Matheson, Bruce Babbitt of Arizona, Dick Lamm of Colorado.) One reason may be that in these economically dynamic states, really bright Republicans who believe in free enterprise are busy practicing it, and leave the uncongenial work of government to caretaker politicians. That leaves the field open for really bright Democrats, who may be conservative by national standards but still believe government has a positive role.

Senators. Utah has two Republican senators who are both chairmen of important committees and, more important, are men with a force of character and conviction who have had considerable effect, in quite different ways, on the course of government. The senior senator is Jake Garn, who has been an important person in Utah's public life since he became mayor of Salt Lake City in 1971. Garn was elected to the Senate in 1974, and since 1981 he has chaired the Banking, Housing, and Urban Affairs Committee. Garn is bright, aggressive, and strongly committed, a man with some sense of humor but also with a noted temper. As a former mayor, he is familiar with many of the housing programs the Banking Committee superintends. He has also stepped confidently into the technical and arcane world of banking regulation, and played a key role in the reappointment of Federal Reserve Chairman Paul Volcker in 1983. Garn does not have a solid majority on his committee, both because of differences of opinion and because of some fights he has had with fellow conservative Republicans. He also chairs the HUD–Independent Agencies Appropriations Subcommittee, which makes him a virtual czar of the Department of Housing and Urban Development.

Garn seems to reserve much of his interest and drive for foreign and defense issues. He is by most measures a hawk, and he was heard from frequently during the Carter administration, denouncing its SALT II and Panama Canal Treaties. Now, and not just on foreign and defense issues, he is less voluble, a politician who makes his influence felt from the inside. He and Nevada's Paul Laxalt, for example, probably had some role in killing the racetrack basing mode for the MX missile, which would have required tearing up a considerable part of Utah's and Nevada's desert; but both men as longtime defense advocates seemed a little uncomfortable about their positions. Garn was easily reelected in 1980, and no one doubts that he will be in 1986 too.

Orrin Hatch is a different sort of senator: Mr. Outside to Garn's Mr. Inside. Where Garn is happy to pursue his ends in the quiet of an Appropriations Committee meeting, Hatch seems happier in a crowded hearing room full of hostile witnesses and jostling reporters. During his first years in the Senate, Hatch seemed almost feverish in his advocacy of New Right and free market causes, and many of his colleagues regarded him as a bit of a fanatic. One of the bogies the Democrats used in the 1980 campaigns was the specter of Hatch as chairman of the Labor and Human Resources Committee.

Well, he has been chairman for two years, and the Republic still stands. One reason is that Hatch has not been terribly successful: on many of his former causes he has either lost or has declined to fight at all. Thus he did not bring forward in 1981 the subminimum wage for teenagers (the McDonald's exemption to its detractors) which he championed in the 1970s. Then he was strong for repealing the Davis–Bacon Act, and tried to do so in ingenious ways; once chairman, he also shelved that project. He did not advance any major change of labor laws. On abortion, he let the battle be carried by Jesse Helms, with disastrous results.

One reason Hatch hesitated on so many issues was that it was clear he did not command a majority on his committee. Republicans Robert Stafford and Lowell Weicker supported organized labor positions and voted with Democrats on many issues (and were suitably rewarded in their tough 1982 reelection races), which meant that if anyone had a majority it was ranking minority member Edward Kennedy. Another problem was that it became apparent that Hatch does not command as much respect as he does attention. No one denies that he is smart and energetic, but somehow he does not strike other senators as a heavy hitter. He is like an earnest professor who uses fancy words and ornate phrases, and gets them just a little wrong.

That, apparently, is how he struck many Utah voters when he stood for reelection in 1982. He was a surprise senator, a recent migrant to Utah (and bishop in the Mormon Church) who filed to run against Democratic Senator Frank Moss on the last day after serving as a Reagan volunteer. Hatch ran a tough, negative issues campaign and upset Moss; even so, he personally was not yet well known to Utah voters. By 1982 he was, and he was being closely pressed by Ted Wilson, the Democratic mayor of Salt Lake City, a man with moderate views and a pleasant, modest personality. Wilson ran nearly even in some polls, and labor put in some money, hoping to upset Hatch. But this is too Republican a state; it would be hard to find a major issue on which Hatch is far out of line with majority opinion in the state. Eventually Hatch won by a solid enough margin to indicate that, whatever his clout in the Senate, he probably has a safe seat in Utah.

Congressional districting. In 1982 Utah got its third congressional district, and the lines were drawn by the Republican legislature pretty much as predicted. The 2d district, which includes most of Salt Lake County, is the least Republican of the three, but is not a district you would refer to as Democratic in any other state. The 3d district, whose big population center is around Provo and Brigham Young University, can probably be called the most Republican congressional district in the nation.

Presidential politics. Utah is not likely to see many presidential candidates in 1984. It will probably be the most Republican state in the nation again in the general election, and for the national conventions its relatively few delegates are chosen by party officials.

The People Est. Pop. 1982: 1,554,000; Pop. 1980: 1,461,037, up 6.3% 1980–82 and 37.9% 1970–80; 0.66% of U.S. total, 36th largest; voting age pop. 920,932; 4% Spanish origin, 1% American Indian, 1% Black, 1% Asian origin. Single ancestry: 28% English, 4% German, 2% Irish, 1% Swedish, Scottish, Dutch, Italian, French, Norwegian. Registered voters (1982): 748,730 Total. No party registration. 24% with 1–3 yrs. col., 20% with 4+ yrs. col. 10.7% below poverty level. 27% housing units rented; median house value: $60,000; median monthly rent: $190. Households: 78% family, 50% with children, 69% married couples.

1982 Share of Federal Tax Burden $2,993,600,000; .50% of U.S. total, 36th largest.

1982 Share of Federal Expenditures

	Total		Non-Defense		Defense	
Total Expend	$3,710m	(0.61%)	$2,467m	(0.58%)	$1,243m	(0.70%)
St/Lcl Grants	605m	(0.69%)	604m	(0.68%)	1m	(2.78%)
Salary/Wages	875m	(1.12%)	257m	(0.94%)	618m	(1.22%)
Ind Payments	1,375m	(0.48%)	1,232m	(0.48%)	143m	(0.50%)
Procurement	822m	(0.56%)	273m	(0.87%)	549m	(0.48%)
Other Programs	33m	(0.61%)	33m	(0.61%)	0m	(0%)
Loan/Insurance	211m	(0.33%)	204m	(0.33%)	7m	(0.32%)

Political Lineup   Governor, Scott M. Matheson (D). Senators, Jacob (Jake) Garn (R) and Orrin G. Hatch (R). Representatives, 3 R. State Senate, 29 (5 D and 24 R); State House of Representatives, 75 (16 D and 59 R).

Presidential Vote

1980	Reagan (R)	. . . .	439,687	(73%)
	Carter (D)	. . . .	124,266	(21%)
	Anderson (I)	. . . .	30,284	(5%)
1976	Ford (R)	. . . .	337,908	(62%)
	Carter (D)	. . . .	182,110	(34%)

SENATORS

Sen. Jacob (Jake) **Garn** (R) Elected 1974, seat up 1986; b. Oct. 12, 1932, Richfield; home, Salt Lake City; U. of UT, B.S. 1955; Mormon.

Career Navy, 1956–69; Asst. Mgr., Salt Lake City Ofc. of Home Life Insurance Co. of NY, 1961–66; Salt Lake City Commissioner, 1967–71; Mayor of Salt Lake City, 1971–74.

Offices 505 DSOB, 202-224-5444. Also 4225 Fed. Bldg., 125 S. State St., Salt Lake City 84138, 801-524-5933; and Fed. Bldg., Ogden 84401, 801-399-6208.

Committees *Appropriations* (6th). Subcommittees: Defense, Energy and Water Development; HUD-Independent Agencies (Chairman); Interior; Military Construction. *Banking, Housing, and Urban Affairs* (Chairman). Subcommittees: Housing and Urban Affairs; Financial Institutions; International Finance and Monetary Policy. *Select Committee on Intelligence* (2d). Subcommittees: Budget Authorization; Legislation and the Rights of Americans; Collection and Foreign Operations.

Group Ratings

	ADA	ACLU	COPE	CFA	LCV	LWV	NTU	NSI	COC	ACA	CSFC
1982	5	0	10	10	15	33	72	100	67	81	76
1981	0	—	11	14	31	—	80	—	94	90	86
1980	17	27	10	7	13	22	68	100	88	96	87

National Journal Ratings

	Economic		Foreign		Cultural	
1982	22%	(LIB)	16%	(LIB)	5%	(LIB)
	77%	(CONS)	68%	(CONS)	94%	(CONS)
1981	21%	(LIB)	1%	(LIB)	2%	(LIB)
	78%	(CONS)	85%	(CONS)	82%	(CONS)

Key Votes

1) Reagan 81 Budget	FOR	5) $ to El Salvador	FOR	9) Poor Pay Food Stamps	FOR
2) Reagan 81 Tax Cut	FOR	6) Saudi AWACS Sale	FOR	10) Ban Crt Busing Order	FOR
3) Bal Budget Amend	FOR	7) Ban Abortion	FOR	11) Clinch Riv Brdr Rctr	FOR
4) Gas & Road Tax	AGN	8) Nerve Gas Prod	FOR	12) Legal Services Corp	AGN

Election Results

1980 general	Jacob (Jake) Garn (R)	434,675	(74%)	($1,113,061)
	Dan Berman (D)	151,454	(26%)	($237,882)
1980 primary	Jacob (Jake) Garn (R) unopposed			
1974 general	Jacob (Jake) Garn (R)	210,299	(50%)	($363,162)
	Wayne Owens (D)	185,377	(44%)	($445,400)
	Bruce Bangerter (Amer.)	24,966	(6%)	($1,488)

Campaign Contributions and Expenditures

1979-80		*PACS brkdwn*			
Receipts	$1,121,563	Agr	$17,000	Ideo	$12,323
Expend.	$1,113,061	Bus	$223,036	Lbr	$10,000
Unspent	$9,132	Hlth	$15,175	Prof	$8,375

Sen. Orrin G. Hatch (R) Elected 1976, seat up 1988; b. Mar. 22, 1934, Pittsburgh, PA; home, Salt Lake City; Brigham Young U., B.S. 1959, U. of Pittsburgh, J.D. 1962; Mormon.

Career Practicing atty., 1962–77.

Offices 125 RSOB, 202-224-5251. Also Fed. Bldg., 125 S. State St., Salt Lake City 84138, 801-524-4380.

Committees *Agriculture, Nutrition and Forestry* (10th). Subcommittees: Agricultural Research and General Legislation; Nutrition; Soil and Water Conservation. *Budget* (5th). *Judiciary* (4th). Subcommittees: Constitution (Chairman); Security and Terrorism; Patents, Copyrights and Trademarks. *Labor and Human Resources* (Chairman). Subcommittees: Education, Arts and Humanities; Labor; Employment and Productivity. *Small Business* (3d). Subcommittees: Capital Formation and Retention; Government Regulation and Paperwork (Chairman).

Group Ratings

	ADA	ACLU	COPE	CFA	LCV	LWV	NTU	NSI	COC	ACA	CSFC
1982	5	0	8	10	32	25	77	100	70	95	80
1981	0	—	10	21	31	—	84	—	100	85	85
1980	17	57	10	7	17	33	60	100	90	96	80

National Journal Ratings

	Economic		Foreign		Cultural	
1982	6%	(LIB)	3%	(LIB)	6%	(LIB)
	93%	(CONS)	84%	(CONS)	93%	(CONS)
1981	2%	(LIB)	1%	(LIB)	2%	(LIB)
	88%	(CONS)	85%	(CONS)	82%	(CONS)

Key Votes

1) Reagan 81 Budget	FOR	5) $ to El Salvador	FOR	9) Poor Pay Food Stamps	AGN
2) Reagan 81 Tax Cut	FOR	6) Saudi AWACS Sale	FOR	10) Ban Crt Busing Order	FOR
3) Bal Budget Amend	FOR	7) Ban Abortion	FOR	11) Clinch Riv Brdr Rctr	FOR
4) Gas & Road Tax	AGN	8) Nerve Gas Prod	FOR	12) Legal Services Corp	AGN

Election Results

1982 general	Orrin G. Hatch (R)	309,547	(58%)	($3,838,335)
	Ted Wilson (D)	218,895	(41%)	($1,703,170)
1982 primary	Orrin G. Hatch (R) unopposed			
1976 general	Orrin G. Hatch (R)	290,221	(54%)	($370,517)
	Frank E. Moss (D)	241,948	(45%)	($343,598)

Campaign Contributions and Expenditures

1979-82		Direct Cont. 79-82		PACS brkdwn			
Receipts	$3,925,739	Indiv	$2,893,371	Agr	$15,950	Ideo	$67,037
Expend.	$3,838,335	Party	$32,313	Bus	$772,821	Lbr	$2,500
Unspent	$97,122	PACS	$930,420	Hlth	$48,525	Prof	$16,750

Indirect Party Expend: $69,093 *Indep Expend:* For: $22,081 (NRA) Agn: $85,964 (NOWPAC, PROPAC, CCSND) *Non-Cand Loans:* $40,000

GOVERNOR

Gov. Scott M. Matheson (D) Elected 1976, term expires Jan. 1985; b. Jan. 8, 1929, Chicago, IL; home, Salt Lake City; U. of UT, B.S. 1950, Stanford U., J.D. 1952; Mormon.

Career Practicing atty., 1953–54, 1956–68; Parowan City Atty. and Iron Cnty. Dpty. Atty., 1953–54; Law Clerk for U.S. Dist. Judge, Salt Lake City, 1954–56; Salt Lake Cnty. Dpty. Atty., 1956–57; Atty., Union Pacific R.R., 1958–69; Gen. Solicitor, 1972–76; Counsel, Anaconda Cnty., 1969–70, Asst. Gen. Counsel, 1970–72.

Offices 210 State Capitol, Salt Lake City 84114, 801-533-5231.

Election Results

1980 gen.	Scott M. Matheson (D)	330,974	(55%)
	Bob Wright (R)	266,578	(44%)
1980 prim.	Scott M. Matheson (D) unopposed		
1976 gen.	Scott M. Matheson (D)	280,606	(52%)
	Vernon B. Romney (R)	248,027	(46%)

FIRST DISTRICT

The 1st congressional district of Utah is the western part of the state, from the Idaho border in the north to where the Colorado River flows through Glen Canyon into Arizona in the south. This is a vast area; national parks (Zion, Bryce Canyon) in the south, mining country in the center, the vast Bonneville Salt Flats and the Great Salt Lake Desert west of Salt Lake City, and the expanse of Great Salt Lake in the north. That expanse has been growing: the lake has no outlet, and heavier than usual rains lately have raised its levels to a point that shoreline industries and vacation attractions are threatened. The legislature passed a law forbidding the lake to rise above a certain level, but it has been violated, and no one has a remedy.

For all its expanse, most of the population of the 1st district is clustered into a small area. Fully 78% of the people here live in a section of the narrow Wasatch Front, the flat land just west of the Wasatch Mountains and east of the Great Salt Lake. Ogden is an old working-class town on the Union Pacific line, the nearest station stop to Promontory Point, where the golden spike connecting the transcontinental railroad was laid in 1869 (the railroad is now, incidentally, threatened by the rising lake). The land here is given over to agriculture, and the towns north of Ogden—Brigham City and Logan—are mainly farm centers, almost entirely Mormon and heavily conservative. To the south is Davis County, with some high income spillover from Salt Lake City. Ogden has a Democratic past, but any Democratic votes it casts today (it did give a small margin against Senator Orrin Hatch in 1982) are overcome by Davis's Republican majorities.

Another 9% of the district's residents live around Cedar City and St. George in the southern part of the state, not far from Las Vegas, Nevada, but some 335 miles from Ogden. These are very strong Mormon communities, and very heavily Republican. So are most of the scattered communities in the rest of the district.

So it should be no surprise that this district is Republican; what is odd is that its predecessor, which included even more heavily Republican territory, was represented by a

UTAH — Congressional Districts, Counties, and Selected Places — *(3 Districts)*

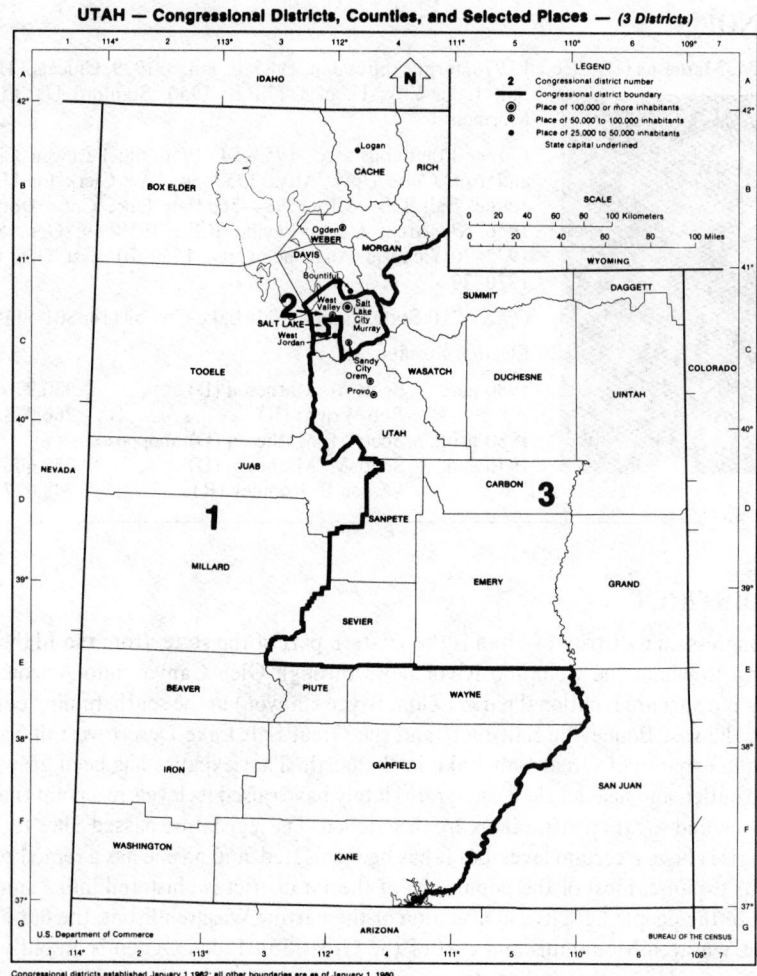

Congressional districts established January 1, 1982; all other boundaries are as of January 1, 1980.

Democrat for 10 years. He was finally beaten in 1980 by James Hansen, the current congressman. A speaker of the Utah House, he has fit in quietly, and is a member of the Interior Committee (as is the 2d district's Dan Marriott). He is respected enough to have been named to Standards of Official Conduct, the House's Ethics Committee, in his first term. His voting record has been impeccably conservative. He was reelected by a comfortable margin in 1982, even carrying Ogden's Weber County.

The People   Pop. 1980: 487,833, up 31% 1970–80, voting age pop. 303,406; 4% Span. orig., 1% Black, 1% Asian orig., 1% Am. Ind. 24% housing units rented. Median owner $58,200; renter $177. Households: 81% family, 51% with children, 72% married couples.

Presidential Vote

1980	Reagan (R)	158,837	(77%)
	Carter (D)	39,968	(19%)
	Other	7,723	(4%)

Rep. James V. Hansen (R) Elected 1980; b. Aug. 14, 1932, Salt Lake City; home, Farmington; U. of UT, B.A. 1960; Mormon.

Career Navy, 1951–53; Farmington City Cncl., 1962–72; UT House of Reps., 1972–80, Speaker, 1978–80.

Offices 1113 LHOB, 202-225-0453. Also 1017 Fed. Bldg., 324 25th St., Ogden 84401, 801-626-2151; and West Park Bldg., 750 N. 200 West, Su. 204, Provo 84601, 801-375-0370.

Committees *Interior and Insular Affairs* (11th). Subcommittees: Insular Affairs; Oversight and Investigations; Public Lands and National Parks. *Standards of Official Conduct* (6th).

Group Ratings

	ADA	ACLU	COPE	CFA	LCV	LWV	NTU	NSI	COC	ACA	CSFC
1982	0	4	8	0	12	18	94	100	81	85	76
1981	0	—	8	21	7	—	93	—	94	100	80

National Journal Ratings

	Economic		Foreign		Cultural	
1982	2%	(LIB)	27%	(LIB)	25%	(LIB)
	98%	(CONS)	73%	(CONS)	75%	(CONS)
1981	1%	(LIB)	3%	(LIB)	1%	(LIB)
	97%	(CONS)	87%	(CONS)	98%	(CONS)

Key Votes

1) Reagan 81 Budget	FOR	5) Incr SS Rtmt Age	FOR	9) Poor Pay Food Stamps	FOR
2) Reagan 81 Tax Cut	FOR	6) Saudi AWACS Sale	FOR	10) Ban Crt Busing Order	FOR
3) Bal Budget Amend	FOR	7) $ for MX Missile	FOR	11) Auto Local Content	AGN
4) Gas & Road Tax	—	8) Nerve Gas Prod	FOR	12) Nuclear Arms Freeze	AGN

Election Results

1982 general	James V. Hansen (R)	....	111,416	(63%)	($258,103)
	A. Stephen Dirks (D)	....	66,006	(17%)	($103,339)
1982 primary	James V. Hansen (R) unopposed				
1980 general	James V. Hansen (R)	....	157,111	(52%)	($232,206)
	K. Gunn McKay (D)	....	144,459	(48%)	($275,313)

Campaign Contributions and Expenditures

1981-82		Direct Cont. 81-82		PACS brkdwn			
Receipts	$268,966	Indiv	$144,626	Agr	$1,500	Ideo	$5,400
Expend.	$258,103	Party	$8,834	Bus	$93,624	Lbr	$2,500
Unspent	$10,864	PACS	$106,934	Hlth	$10,600	Prof	$2,700

Indirect Party Expend: $34,756   *Indep Expend*: For: $333 (RTL)

SECOND DISTRICT

Salt Lake City is the center of the state of Utah and of the Mormon Church. The Church's Tabernacle is there, home of the famous choir, and the Temple which is entered only by

1192   UTAH

Church members. Salt Lake City is also the home of the Church's business enterprises. It is an impressive city in any terms, its skyscrapers rising against a background of magnificent mountains; the Great Salt Lake can be seen out of high windows, shimmering in the waning light of day. Salt Lake City is also, ironically, the part of Utah which least resembles the kind of commonwealth the Church has been so successful generally in persuading its members to establish. This is, after all, a city; it has a tiny slum, and a street well enough known for prostitution that when a congressman was arrested here (Democrat Allan Howe, in 1976), most people assumed that he was up to no good.

Utah's 2d congressional district, which includes most of Salt Lake County, has lower percentages of families, children, and married couples per household than the other two Utah districts: in and around Salt Lake City is where you will find most of Utah's young singles and a disproportionate number of its "gentiles" (non-Mormons). The 2d district includes most of Utah's most affluent people, living in Salt Lake City and suburbs like East Millcreek, Holladay, and Cottonwood, right next to the Wasatch Mountains which rise, right there, to 9,000 feet. It is just an easy drive over the mountain, as recruiters for businesses here like to tell prospects, to the ski slopes at Park City and Alta. The district also includes some of the more modest suburbs on the flat land just south of Salt Lake City and east toward the Lake. On the salty flat land by the Lake there is some industry but virtually no residential development.

The 2d district is the closest thing to a Democratic district in Utah. In the early 1970s the Salt Lake City-based district elected Democrat Wayne Owens who, on the House Judiciary Committee, voted to impeach Richard Nixon. He lost the 1974 Senate election to Jake Garn and was later asked by the LDS Church to do missionary work in Montreal. The current congressman, Dan Marriott, had the political good fortune to be running against Allan Howe when he was arrested; he was one of two Republicans who beat a 1974 freshman Democrat in 1976.

Marriott's record is solidly conservative. He serves on the Interior and Small Business Committees, and has considerable seniority now. He is ranking minority member of the Mining, Forest Management, and Bonneville Power Administration Subcommittee, which is chaired by James Weaver of Oregon, a legislator with a very different voting record and cultural attitude. Utah doesn't have much in the way of forests, but it is still an important mining state, and some of Salt Lake City's economy is based on mining.

Marriott had an uncomfortably close race in 1982. He was challenged by Frances Farley, a state senator from Salt Lake City who held him to 54% of the vote. That is not a particularly impressive result for the Republican, and he may get tough competition again.

The People Pop. 1980: 487,475, up 21.3% 1970–80; voting age pop. 325,863; 4% Black, 2% Asian orig., 1% Span. orig., 1% Black. 34% housing units rented. Median owner $63,100; renter $200. Households: 72% family, 43% with children, 61% married couples.

Presidential Vote

1980	Reagan (R)	137,282	(67%)
	Carter (D)	48,693	(24%)
	Other	17,568	(9%)

Rep. Dan Marriott (R) Elected 1976; b. Nov. 2, 1939, Bingham; home, Salt Lake City; U. of UT, B.S. 1967, Amer. Col. of Life Underwriters, C.L.U. 1968; Mormon.

Career Pres., Marriott Associates, corp. benefit planners and business consultants, 1976–77.

Offices 1133 LHOB, 202-225-3011. Also 2311 Fed. Bldg., 125 S. State St., Salt Lake City 84138, 801-524-4394.

Committees *Interior and Insular Affairs* (4th). Subcommittees: Energy and the Environment; Mining, Forest Management, and BPA. *Select Committee on Children, Youth, and Families* (Ranking Member).

Group Ratings

	ADA	ACLU	COPE	CFA	LCV	LWV	NTU	NSI	COC	ACA	CSFC
1982	10	25	18	31	21	30	63	100	75	82	60
1981	5	—	16	21	7	—	61	—	94	83	67
1980	17	37	7	14	40	44	44	100	81	74	68

National Journal Ratings

	Economic		Foreign		Cultural	
1982	29%	(LIB)	19%	(LIB)	30%	(LIB)
	71%	(CONS)	80%	(CONS)	70%	(CONS)
1981	21%	(LIB)	3%	(LIB)	16%	(LIB)
	78%	(CONS)	87%	(CONS)	83%	(CONS)

Key Votes

1) Reagan 81 Budget	FOR	5) Incr SS Rtmt Age	FOR	9) Poor Pay Food Stamps	FOR
2) Reagan 81 Tax Cut	FOR	6) Saudi AWACS Sale	FOR	10) Ban Crt Busing Order	FOR
3) Bal Budget Amend	FOR	7) $ for MX Missile	FOR	11) Auto Local Content	AGN
4) Gas & Road Tax	—	8) Nerve Gas Prod	FOR	12) Nuclear Arms Freeze	AGN

Election Results

1982 general	Dan Marriott (R)	92,109	(54%)	($414,300)
	Frances Farley (D)	78,981	(46%)	($234,319)
1982 primary	Dan Marriott (R) unopposed			
1980 general	Dan Marriott (R)	194,885	(67%)	($352,435)
	Arthur L. Monson (D)	87,967	(30%)	($27,669)

Campaign Contributions and Expenditures

1981-82		Direct Cont. 81-82		PACS brkdwn			
Receipts	$380,251	Indiv	$197,292	Agr	$2,850	Ideo	$7,250
Expend.	$414,300	Party	$20,126	Bus	$122,231	Lbr	$—
Unspent	$533	PACS	$149,509	Hlth	$12,050	Prof	$2,500

Indirect Party Expend: $34,916   *Indep Expend:* For: $2,855 (NTL, RTL)

THIRD DISTRICT

The heart of Utah's 3d congressional district, a vast stretch of land from the northwestern to the southern borders of the state, is in a strip of land about 10 miles wide and less than 40 miles long, east of the Great Salt Lake and Utah Lake, in the valley of the Jordan River that runs between them. Nearly three-fourths of this district's population is here. It includes the southwestern part of the Salt Lake City metropolitan area, a series of modest and even working-class suburbs on the flat lands looking west to the horizon over the Great Salt Lake. And it goes south to the communities of Provo and Orem, on Utah Lake, in Utah County.

Here, in a valley geographically isolated from the rest of America, the Mormon way of life thrives. This is the home of Brigham Young University, an institution long known for the rigorous and conservative views of its faculty and the old-fashioned moral standards of its students. It is also the home of the Osmond family and of their superb recording studio. Mormonism has always welcomed, and not been hostile to, technological innovation. The Mormon commonwealth, after all, started off with a terrific labor shortage and was willing to use any reasonable means—labor-saving devices, polygamy—to overcome it and prosper. This is an optimistic area, and one with an historical warrant for its optimism: you have only to look at the beautiful but forbidding terrain to understand how much the early Mormon settlers here banked on their own efforts and how much they accomplished.

The 3d congressional district spans far and wide. Its northernmost point is near Wyoming's Overthrust Belt, site of the greatest American oil strikes of the late 1970s, and it includes the uranium country in the eastern part of the state around Moab. The Canyonlands zone in the southeast is almost uninhabited; although it does include part of the Navajo reservation, there are very few Indians living in Utah. But the spirit of the 3d district is pretty well summed up in the Provo area. This was the nation's most Republican congressional district in the 1980 presidential election, and it would surprise no one if it were again in 1984.

The 3d district was created when Utah gained a third seat in the 1980 Census, and so the congressman here is new too. He is former Utah House Speaker Howard Nielson. His real contest was in the Republican primary which he won by a small margin and by virtue of his majority in his home base, Utah County; in the rest of the district he ran even. In the general election he faced an independent running with Democratic endorsement and won 77% of the vote—not far from the standard Republican percentage here. He got a seat on the House Energy and Commerce Committee—a coveted post—and on the Health and the Environment Subcommittee, where he can be expected to resolve conflicts in favor of encouraging economic growth and taking some risk, in situations where the extent of dangers of environmental pollution can't be known for years. It will be interesting to see how he votes on PSD—the current provision of the Clean Air Act that prevents significant deterioration of air quality in pristine areas (like much of the West) even when such pollution meets national standards. That provision was designed in large part to discourage coal-fired electric plants like those in the Four Corners area, which is part of the 3d district; most of their benefits go not to people in the area, but to electric customers in southern California or somewhere back East.

The People   Pop. 1980: 485,729, up 70% 1970–80; voting age pop. 291,663; 3% Span. orig., 2% Am. Ind., 1% Asian orig. 22% housing units rented. Median owner $58,600; renter $183. Households: 83% family, 57% with children, 75% married couples.

Presidential Vote

1980	Reagan (R)	143,457	(78%)
	Carter (D)	35,581	(19%)
	Other	4,963	(3%)

Rep. Howard C. Nielson (R) Elected 1982; b. Sept. 12, 1924, Richfield; home, Provo; U. of UT, B.A. 1947; U. of OR, M.S. 1949, Stanford U., M.B.A. 1956, Ph.D. 1958; Mormon.

Career Statistician, 1949–51, 1963–64; Research economist and analyst, Stanford Res. Inst., 1951–57; Brigham Young U., Assoc. Prof., 1957–61, Chmn., Dept. of Statistics, 1960–63, Prof., 1961–82, Dir., Cntr. for Econ. Res., 1971–73; Economic consultant, 1957–82.

Offices 1229 LHOB, 202-225-7751. Also 88 W. 100, N.S. 105, Provo 84601, 801-377-1776.

Committee *Energy and Commerce* (15th). Subcommittee: Health and the Environment.

Group Ratings and Key Votes: Newly Elected

Election Results

1982 general	Howard C. Nielson (R)	108,478	(77%)	($234,630)
	Henry A. Huish (I)	32,661	(23%)	($61,977)
1982 primary	Howard C. Nielson (R)	28,097	(54%)	
	Ray Beckham (R)	23,698	(46%)	
1980 general	Newly created district			

Campaign Contributions and Expenditures

1982		*Direct Cont. 1982*				*PACS brkdwn*		
Receipts	$237,708	Indiv	$82,333	Agr	$3,000	Ideo	$9,100
Expend.	$234,630	Party	$26,000	Bus	$33,250	Lbr	$10,000
Unspent	$3,077	PACS	$69,250	Hlth	$4,650	Prof	$1,650
		Cand	$40,322				

Indirect Party Expend: $35,385   *Non-Cand Loans*: $19,975

VERMONT

You can spend a lot of time in Vermont and feel that you're still in the 19th century. The classic New England town squares are still there; the cows graze on the hillsides; the taciturn Yankee farmers still tap sugar maple trees in early spring; and the autumn foliage is perhaps the most magnificent in the world. Vermont remains, by census definition, our most rural state, with two-thirds of the population living outside urban areas. But even so, the 1960s and 1970s brought change here. There are now large **IBM** and **General Electric** complexes around Burlington, the state's largest city; its metropolitan population has passed 100,000 and in the last two elections the city has elected a frankly socialist mayor, Bernard Sanders, of Vermont's own Liberty Union Party. The ski resort and summer home industries have boomed so much that the price of land has skyrocketed far above what most Vermonters can afford to pay. And so the very things that have attracted people to Vermont threaten to vanish. From 1850 to 1960 Vermont's population hovered between 300,000 and 400,000; only in 1963 were there more people than cows in the state. But in 1970 there were 444,000 people living in Vermont, and in 1982, 516,000.

There have also been massive political changes here—massive enough that this state, long the most Republican in the nation, now has a genuine two-party politics. Vermont today has one Democratic senator—the first in its history—and for most of the 1960s and 1970s had Democratic governors. Before 1960 the only areas of Democratic strength were the small Irish and French Canadian communities in Burlington and other towns near the Canadian border; it was almost as if the entire Catholic minority were Democrats and the entire Protestant majority Republicans. As long as that was the case, there was no suspense in general election campaigns. This is one part of New England that still has a Yankee majority, and Democrats have won only when they cracked the Yankee vote. The Democrats have on occasion been split between their culturally traditional Catholic base and the culturally liberal newcomers who are enthusiastic about Vermont's physical environment. In terms of registration and also in terms of most election results this is still a Republican state, and the most successful politicians here are Republicans, particularly those Republicans who identify themselves with Vermont's lifestyle and environmental issues.

Presidential politics. James A. Farley had a good laugh on Vermont in 1936 when he updated an adage to say "As goes Maine, so goes Vermont." Those were the only two states Franklin Roosevelt lost that year. Vermont still has gone Democratic for president only once, in 1964, but it would be a mistake to regard this locally Republican state as inevitably Republican in national elections. Vermont has shown resistance to Republicans who take conservative stands on cultural issues. Ronald Reagan won this state in 1980, but with only 44% of the vote; in only six states was his percentage lower. This was also John Anderson's best state (15%), and he did well in the Republican presidential primary, too (29%).

Vermont's presidential primary is early in the season, and the state has tried (but, at this writing, not yet succeeded) in getting it scheduled for the same day as New Hampshire's. But it seems impossible that anything is going to get the national press up to Vermont for more than a day: this is a smaller state and, if anything, one less typical of the rest of the country than New Hampshire—not to mention any other states which might compete with it for attention.

Senators. Vermont's most durable and successful politician is Robert Stafford; nevertheless, he had a close call in 1982. Stafford has held statewide office since 1954. He was elected governor in 1958 and to Congress in 1960; he was appointed senator when the incumbent died in 1971. Stafford is a taciturn Yankee, neither aggressive nor overbearing; he does not look like a natural politician. Yet in 1981 and 1982 he showed enough political adroitness, on Capitol Hill and in Vermont, to put to shame the cleverest pol from South Boston. In the Senate Stafford chaired the Environment and Public Works Committee, which had to handle one of the hottest of potatoes—renewal of the Clean Air Act. The Reagan administration, and powerful industrial interests (steel, autos, electric utilities, coal) wanted certain terms of the Act relaxed; environmental activists and, presumably, voters in Vermont wanted it strengthened, particularly against the threat of acid rain; environmental lobbyists in Washington simply wanted it reauthorized as is. Stafford took a sharply divided committee and by 1982 came up with a bill which reauthorized the Act and added tough acid rain provisions which almost every member supported. Although this did not become law, it changed the terms on which the Clean Air Act battle was fought. Stafford also proved a roadblock, as a member of the Labor and Human Resources Committee, to many of the changes in labor and welfare laws conservative Republicans wanted. With Lowell Weicker, he prevented Chairman Orrin Hatch from having a majority on many issues.

These positions were not an advantage, however, in the Republican primary. Stafford was 69 in 1982, and had not won by an impressive margin in 1976; he drew strong opposition in both primary and general election. The anti-Stafford vote in the primary was split between Stewart Ledbetter, the nearly successful Republican nominee against Patrick Leahy in 1980, and John McClaughry, a Reagan White House aide with a base in the Northeast Kingdom around St. Johnsbury. Stafford, with support from environmentalist and labor groups, won with 46%. Then, in the general, he faced opposition from James Guest, the unpaid head of Consumers Union, who self-financed much of his campaign. Guest also got labor and environmentalist support, especially from Vermont-based groups; Washington-based groups, on the other hand, tended to support Stafford. In the end Stafford won reelection 50%–47%—not an inspiring margin, but enough to keep him in the Senate for another six years and in the chair of the Environment Committee for at least another two.

Vermont's other senator, and the only Democratic senator in its history, is Patrick Leahy. He first won the seat in 1974, when that quintessential Vermont Yankee George Aiken retired after 34 years in the Senate. Leahy had made a name for himself as a Burlington area prosecutor who tried all cases personally and attacked the big oil companies during the gasoline price crisis of 1974. He had a solid base in Democratic, Catholic Burlington, plus the kind of quiet, thoughtful temperament Yankee Vermonters like in their public officials. Elected by a narrow margin in 1974, he won again by a narrow margin in 1980.

Why has this Democrat been able to keep his seat in a Republican state? The main reason is that Leahy established, not just in campaign periods but over the long haul of nearly ten years, that he shared many of the values of most Vermonters. His basic instincts are parsimonious, as residents of Washington, D.C., learned when he chaired the District of Columbia Appropriations Subcommittee. He was attacked in 1980 for opposing certain weapons systems but argued convincingly in often dovish Vermont that they were bad buys. On the Agriculture Committee he is one of the leading advocates of the interests of dairy farmers—a numerous and economically important group in Vermont. Faced with a sophisticated campaign by Republican Stewart Ledbetter in the Republican year of 1980, Leahy was one of the few Senate Democrats to survive. He returned to a Republican Senate with less clout but more experience and earned a reputation as a critic of cheap-shot tactics by the majority.

Congressman. Vermont's congressman-at-large is James Jeffords, a Republican with one of the most liberal records in his party. Even in 1981, when Republicans were voting lockstep for the Reagan economic policies, Jeffords was dissenting occasionally, as often as any Republican. By 1982 he was a pretty vocal critic of Reagan budget cuts. Jeffords has a long involvement in politics and public life in Vermont, and he is one Republican who comes not from an affluent background, but who represents the large middle class of his constituency. He is vocal and ready to back many popular projects and is one of the dairy farmers' few Congressional partisans, but his legislative output is limited. Perhaps that is inevitable, as he is a member of the minority party; his Democratic colleagues on Education and Labor are unlikely to let him take credit for anything, although Agriculture, his other committee, is run on a more bipartisan basis. First elected in 1974, Jeffords has won reelection by large margins. He is one of several politicians in Vermont—Governor Richard Snelling and former Lieutenant Governor Madeleine Kunin are others—popular enough to win a Senate seat, if they don't run against each other.

Governor. Actually, Snelling and Kunin did run against each other in 1982. Snelling saw his percentage trimmed from 59% to 55%; Kunin saw her unbeaten streak broken. Snelling is at one and the same time businesslike and generous on many programs. Although Vermont is a small state and he is a Republican, he is the spokesmen often for all the nation's governors on issues of federalism—and has often been a stern critic of Reagan administration proposals. His popularity seems such that he can be reelected indefinitely if he wants. He did, however, announce he would retire in 1982—after which Kunin entered the race—and then changed his mind. Kunin, a liberal Democrat on most issues, who emphasized her support of the nuclear freeze in the gubernatorial race, remains highly popular; she is one Democrat with a demonstrated ability to hold the Catholics and break into the Yankee vote.

The People　Est. Pop. 1982: 516,000; Pop. 1980: 511,456, up 0.9% 1980–82 and 15% 1970–80; 0.23% of U.S. total, 49th largest; voting age pop. 366,138; 1% Spanish origin. Single ancestry: 15% English, 11% French, 5% Irish, 2% German, Italian, 1% Scottish, Polish. Registered voters (1982): 318,832 Total. No party registration. 15% with 1–3 yrs. col., 20% with 4+ yrs. col. 11% below poverty level. 25% housing units rented; median house value: $42,300; median monthly rent: $176. Households: 72% family, 40% with children, 61% married couples.

1982 Share of Federal Tax Burden　$1,068,000,000; .18% of U.S. total, 51st largest.

1982 Share of Federal Expenditures

	Total		Non-Defense		Defense	
Total Expend	$1,155m	(0.19%)	$907m	(0.21%)	$248m	(0.14%)
St/Lcl Grants	271m	(0.31%)	271m	(0.31%)	0m	(0%)
Salary/Wages	66m	(0.08%)	41m	(0.15%)	25m	(0.05%)
Ind Payments	594m	(0.21%)	536m	(0.21%)	58m	(0.20%)
Procurement	213m	(0.15%)	11m	(0.03%)	202m	(0.18%)
Other Programs	12m	(0.22%)	11m	(0.20%)	1m	(2.33%)
Loan/Insurance	92m	(0.14%)	90m	(0.15%)	2m	(0.09%)

Political Lineup　Governor, Richard A. Snelling (R). Senators, Robert T. Stafford (R) and Patrick J. Leahy (D). Representatives, 1 R at large. State Senate, 30 (17 R and 13 D); State House of Representatives, 150 (83 R, 65 D, 1 I, 1 contested).

Presidential Vote

1980	Reagan (R)	....	94,628	(44%)
	Carter (D)	....	81,952	(38%)
	Anderson (I)	....	31,761	(15%)
1976	Ford (R)	....	100,387	(55%)
	Carter (D)	....	78,789	(43%)

1980 Democratic Presidential Primary			*1980 Republican Presidential Primary*		
Kennedy	10,135	(26%)	Reagan	19,720	(30%)
Carter	29,015	(73%)	Anderson	19,030	(29%)
Others	553	(1%)	Bush	14,226	(22%)
			Baker	8,055	(12%)
			Three others & scattering	4,580	(7%)

SENATORS

Sen. Robert T. Stafford (R) Appointed Sept. 1971, elected Jan. 1972, seat up 1988; b. Aug. 8, 1913, Rutland; home, Rutland; Middlebury Col., B.S. 1935, U. of MI, Boston U., LL.B. 1938; United Church of Christ.

Career Rutland City Prosecuting Atty., 1938–42; Navy, WWII and Korea; Rutland Cnty. States Atty., 1947–51; Dpty. Atty. Gen. of VT, 1953–55; Atty. Gen. of VT, 1955–57; Lt. Gov. of VT, 1957–59; Gov. of VT, 1959–61; U.S. House of Reps., 1961–71.

Offices 133 HSOB, 202-224-5141. Also 501 Fed. Bldg., Burlington 05401, 802-951-6707; and 27 S. Main St., Rutland 05701, 802-775-5446.

Committees *Environment and Public Works* (Chairman). Subcommittee: Transportation. *Labor and Human Resources* (2d). Subcommittees: Labor; Education, Arts, and Humanities (Chairman); Handicapped. *Veterans' Affairs* (3d).

Group Ratings

	ADA	ACLU	COPE	CFA	LCV	LWV	NTU	NSI	COC	ACA	CSFC
1982	65	71	62	10	54	91	39	60	45	32	53
1981	35	—	64	36	47	—	47	—	75	47	71
1980	61	77	58	33	71	80	35	44	62	38	44

National Journal Ratings

	Economic		Foreign		Cultural	
1982	40%	(LIB)	60%	(LIB)	73%	(LIB)
	59%	(CONS)	39%	(CONS)	26%	(CONS)
1981	55%	(LIB)	46%	(LIB)	64%	(LIB)
	44%	(CONS)	53%	(CONS)	35%	(CONS)

Key Votes

1) Reagan 81 Budget	FOR	5) $ to El Salvador	FOR	9) Poor Pay Food Stamps	AGN
2) Reagan 81 Tax Cut	FOR	6) Saudi AWACS Sale	FOR	10) Ban Crt Busing Order	AGN
3) Bal Budget Amend	FOR	7) Ban Abortion	AGN	11) Clinch Riv Brdr Rctr	AGN
4) Gas & Road Tax	AGN	8) Nerve Gas Prod	AGN	12) Legal Services Corp	AGN

Election Results

1982 general	Robert T. Stafford (R)	83,259	(51%)	($407,340)
	James A. Guest (D)	78,447	(48%)	($282,600)
1982 primary	Robert T. Stafford (R)	26,323	(46%)	
	Stewart M. Ledbetter (R)	19,743	(35%)	($263,851)
	John McClaughry (R)	10,692	(19%)	($68,658)
1976 general	Robert T. Stafford (R)	94,481	(50%)	($157,927)
	Thomas P. Salmon (D)	85,682	(45%)	($169,296)

Campaign Contributions and Expenditures

1977-82		Direct Cont. 77-82		PACS brkdwn			
Receipts	$401,685	Indiv	$97,512	Agr	$18,500	Ideo	$31,199
Expend.	$407,340	Party	$15,811	Bus	$136,320	Lbr	$58,300
Unspent	$3,887	PACS	$295,532	Hlth	$22,000	Prof	$7,300

Indirect Party Expend: $72,379 *Indep Expend:* For: $17,003 (LCV) Agn: $3,297 (NCPAC)

Sen. Patrick J. Leahy (D) Elected 1974, seat up 1986; b. Mar. 31, 1940, Montpelier; home, Burlington; St. Michael's Col., Winooski, B.A. 1961, Georgetown U., J.D. 1964; Roman Catholic.

Career Practicing atty., 1964–74; Chittenden Cnty. States Atty., 1966–74.

Offices 433 RSOB, 202-224-4242. Also Box 2, Burlington 05401, 802-863-2525.

Committees *Agriculture, Nutrition, and Forestry* (2d). Subcommittees: Agricultural Production, Marketing, and Stabilization of Prices; Rural Development, Oversight, and Investigations; Nutrition. *Appropriations* (11th). Subcommittees: District of Columbia; Foreign Operations; HUD-Independent Agencies; Interior. *Judiciary* (6th). Subcommittees: Constitution; Patents, Copyrights, and Trademarks; Security and Terrorism. *Select Committee on Intelligence* (6th). Subcommittees: Budget Authorization; Legislation and the Rights of Americans (Vice-Chairman).

Group Ratings

	ADA	ACLU	COPE	CFA	LCV	LWV	NTU	NSI	COC	ACA	CSFC
1982	90	79	89	90	85	91	22	10	45	19	29
1981	95	—	81	71	99	—	5	—	6	5	32
1980	83	77	83	53	90	80	30	0	43	16	27

National Journal Ratings

	Economic		Foreign		Cultural	
1982	83%	(LIB)	90%	(LIB)	80%	(LIB)
	16%	(CONS)	3%	(CONS)	19%	(CONS)
1981	96%	(LIB)	88%	(LIB)	84%	(LIB)
	3%	(CONS)	9%	(CONS)	15%	(CONS)

Key Votes

1) Reagan 81 Budget	AGN	5) $ to El Salvador	AGN	9) Poor Pay Food Stamps	AGN
2) Reagan 81 Tax Cut	AGN	6) Saudi AWACS Sale	AGN	10) Ban Crt Busing Order	AGN
3) Bal Budget Amend	AGN	7) Ban Abortion	AGN	11) Clinch Riv Brdr Rctr	AGN
4) Gas & Road Tax	AGN	8) Nerve Gas Prod	AGN	12) Legal Services Corp	—

Election Results

1980 general	Patrick J. Leahy (D)	104,176	(50%)	($434,644)
	Stewart M. Ledbetter (R)	101,421	(49%)	($532,904)
1980 primary	Patrick J. Leahy (D)	27,548	(100%)	
1974 general	Patrick J. Leahy (D)	70,629	(49%)	($152,817)
	Richard W. Mallary (R)	66,223	(46%)	($90,617)

Campaign Contributions and Expenditures

1979-80		PACS brkdwn			
Receipts	$525,547	Agr	$35,308	Ideo	$30,332
Expend.	$434,644	Bus	$30,670	Lbr	$112,950
Unspent	$95,656	Hlth	$3,100	Prof	$1,400

GOVERNOR

Gov. Richard A. Snelling (R) Elected 1976, term expires Jan. 1985; b. Feb. 18, 1927, Allentown, PA; home, Montpelier; U. of Havana, Cuba, Lehigh U., Harvard U., A.B. 1948; Unitarian Universalist.

Career Army, WWII; Founder and Chmn., Shelburne Industries, Inc.; VT House of Reps., 1959–60, 1973–76, Major. Ldr., 1975–76.

Offices Governor's Office, Montpelier 05602, 802-828-3333.

Election Results

1982 gen.	Richard A. Snelling (R)	92,588	(55%)
	Madeleine M. Kunin (D)	74,304	(44%)
1982 prim.	Richard A. Snelling (R) unopposed	47,872	
1980 gen.	Richard A. Snelling (R)	123,229	(59%)
	M. Jerome Diamond (D)	77,363	(37%)

Rep. James M. Jeffords (R) Elected 1974; b. May 11, 1934, Rutland; home, Montpelier; Yale U., B.S. 1956, Harvard U., LL.B. 1962; United Church of Christ.

Career Navy, 1956–59; Law Clerk to U.S. Dist. Ct. Judge Ernest W. Gibson, 1962; Practicing atty., 1963–75; Chmn., Rutland Cnty. Bd. of Property Tax Appeals, 1964–66; VT Senate, 1967–68; Atty. Gen. of VT, 1969–73.

Offices 2431 RHOB, 202-225-4115. Also P.O. Box 676, Fed. Bldg., Montpelier 05602, 802-223-5274.

Committees *Agriculture* (2d). Subcommittees: Conservation, Credit, and Rural Development; Livestock, Dairy and Poultry. *Education and Labor* (2d). Subcommittees: Employment Opportunities; Labor-Management Relations; Postsecondary Education. *Select Committee on Aging* (6th). Subcommittee: Retirement Income and Employment.

Group Ratings

	ADA	ACLU	COPE	CFA	LCV	LWV	NTU	NSI	COC	ACA	CSFC
1982	65	62	46	38	80	83	53	20	53	39	39
1981	60	—	46	71	68	—	41	—	53	24	41
1980	67	87	18	57	91	80	32	56	79	30	50

National Journal Ratings

	Economic		Foreign		Cultural	
1982	53%	(LIB)	76%	(LIB)	84%	(LIB)
	47%	(CONS)	23%	(CONS)	16%	(CONS)
1981	55%	(LIB)	77%	(LIB)	79%	(LIB)
	45%	(CONS)	21%	(CONS)	21%	(CONS)

Key Votes

1) Reagan 81 Budget	FOR	5) Incr SS Rtmt Age	FOR	9) Poor Pay Food Stamps	AGN
2) Reagan 81 Tax Cut	AGN	6) Saudi AWACS Sale	AGN	10) Ban Crt Busing Order	AGN
3) Bal Budget Amend	AGN	7) $ for MX Missile	AGN	11) Auto Local Content	AGN
4) Gas & Road Tax	FOR	8) Nerve Gas Prod	AGN	12) Nuclear Arms Freeze	FOR

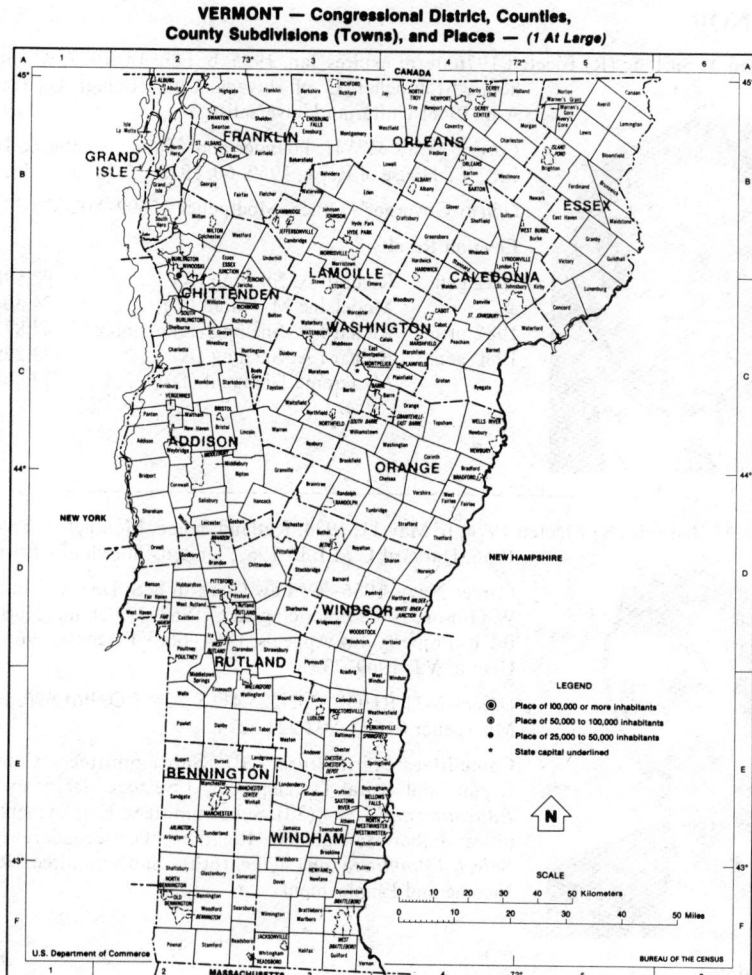

VERMONT — Congressional District, Counties,
County Subdivisions (Towns), and Places — (1 At Large)

Election Results

1982 general	James M. Jeffords (R)	114,191	(69%)	($78,102)
	Mark A. Kaplan (D)	38,296	(23%)	($47,056)
1982 primary	James M. Jeffords (R)	43,090	(78%)	
	William K. Tufts (R)	12,030	(22%)	($7,557)
1980 general	James M. Jeffords (R)	154,274	(79%)	($58,781)
	Robin Lloyd (D)	24,758	(13%)	($0)
	Peter Isaac Diamondstone (LU) ...	15,218	(8%)	($0)

Campaign Contributions and Expenditures

1981-82		Direct Cont. 81-82				PACS brkdwn		
Receipts	$101,175	Indiv	$38,771	Agr	$27,650	Ideo	$1,450
Expend.	$78,102	Party	$13,969	Bus	$20,510	Lbr	$1,400
Unspent	$37,409	PACS	$54,360	Hlth	$2,350	Prof	$1,000

VIRGINIA

The enduring puzzle in Virginia politics is why this commonwealth, which contributed so many leaders of dazzling brilliance to the Revolutionary era of American politics, has had such uninspiring and mostly mediocre political leadership since. One generation of Virginians included George Washington, Patrick Henry, Thomas Jefferson, George Mason, James Madison, and James Monroe. The next generation, and generations after that, were full of names seldom remembered today; the one exception, Robert E. Lee, was never a politician and only reluctantly rallied to Virginia's cause in 1861. Succeeding generations of Virginia leaders have seen themselves quite clearly as the successors of the Founders, but have also seen their mission as preventing change and keeping their system exactly as it is. So Virginia's leaders before the Civil War championed slavery, though never with the force and lucidity of a John C. Calhoun. Virginia's leaders after the Civil War in few cases sought industry, though not with any abstract defense of agrarianism.

Virginia's political leaders from 1930 to 1970—which is to say, the members of the so-called Byrd machine, led by Senator Harry Byrd, Sr.—set themselves the task of opposing the welfare state and racial equality in all their forms. Although they won virtually every significant election in the state for 40 years, they ultimately failed in their purposes. A makeshift welfare state was established by politicians in Washington despite all Byrd's efforts as chairman of the Senate Finance Committee. Integration was ordered by the courts, and Virginia's Massive Resistance program—of closing public schools when they were ordered integrated—collapsed in the late 1950s. Finally, the Byrd machine itself got into political trouble. The Richmond and small-town lawyers and bankers which were its bulwark were increasingly unable to deliver votes as the electorate grew vastly larger. Areas never friendly to the Byrd machine grew in importance: the Washington suburbs were 5% of the state in 1940 and 21% in 1970; the Tidewater area around Norfolk was 13% in 1940 and 22% in 1970. Senator Byrd resigned in 1965, and was succeeded by his son, who retained the seat only by a narrow margin; the elder Byrd's longtime colleague, A. Willis Robertson, was beaten in the 1966 Democratic primary. The line of Byrd governors ended abruptly when Linwood Holton, a Republican and a believer in integration, was elected in 1969. Harry Byrd, Jr., never sought to impose his will on the rest of the state or lead an organization. He ran for reelection in 1970 and 1976 as an Independent (thus avoiding a potentially difficult Democratic primary but keeping his Democratic seniority in the Senate), and after he retired in 1982 none of the top positions in the state was held by Byrd machine members or by the kind of staid, sober, locally prominent conservatives the Byrd machine put into office.

For about a decade the Republican Party carried all before it in Virginia. It endorsed old Byrd stalwarts like Mills Godwin, elected as a Byrd machine governor in 1965 and a Republican governor in 1973. It endorsed the offspring of old insurgent mountain Republicans, like Governor John Dalton, elected in 1977. But it was a Republican Party built less on local notables and more on the politics of ideology, mass mailings, and television advertising which is the backbone of organized Republicanism anywhere. It took its candidates whence they came, electing the socialite husband of Elizabeth Taylor to the Senate in 1978, nominating for governor in 1981 a young man who seemed to lack the staidness and steadiness of old Byrd retainers, electing as senator in 1982 a young man brought up outside Virginia who ran for Congress two years after moving into his district and ran for the Senate just six years later. The contrast between the old Byrd officeholders and these new Republicans was almost as sharp as the contrast between the Founding Fathers and the generation of Virginia politicians who succeeded them.

In terms of personal background—though not on issues—the Democrats were more like the Byrd men. Their last two Senate candidates, both unsuccessful, were the son of an old Virginia aristocrat-politician and a businessman and mortgage banker who served as mayor of his city. You could argue that these men are better Burkean conservatives than the Republicans: in accepting the welfare state and integration, they accept the organic relationships on which people rely when they make the major decisions of their lives. But they differ sharply from the old Byrd conservatives, who could plausibly think of themselves as Burkeans too, not only because of differences on specific issues, but also because they lacked the hard-edged bitterness that characterized the Byrd leaders. Politics in most states is full of stories about warm-hearted and good-humored conservatives. Not in Virginia: the Byrd leaders were mean, tough, humorless, and unwilling to give their opponents a scrap of consolation. They treated them with the ruthlessness with which, perhaps, they imagined that their ancestors had been treated by the conquering Union armies after Appomattox.

This leaves Virginia with political divisions which, oddly, resemble those of the New Deal era more than those in most of the rest of America today. Outside the Washington suburbs, where political allegiance seems based on cultural attitudes more than anything else, political choices in Virginia seem to be a matter of economics. Black voters go heavily Democratic; white working-class voters, as the 1982 elections show, will often give Democrats large margins too. Upper-income voters, as in the rest of the South, are heavily Republican. The old idea which the Byrd machine fostered, that it was somehow un-Virginian to vote against the candidates supported by your local banker, lawyer, and big landowner, seems to be dying out. The result is that Virginia has a viable if not thriving two-party system at last.

Presidential politics. Beginning in 1952, Senator Byrd used to maintain what was called a "golden silence" about the presidential campaign. As a Democrat, he could not endorse the Republican candidate; but he wouldn't endorse the Democrat either, and voters got the idea. Virginia has voted Republican in every presidential election since except 1964, when it went for Lyndon Johnson (who courted Senator Byrd shamelessly). In 1976 and 1980 it was the most Republican southern state except Oklahoma, and that is likely to be the case again in 1984, despite the Democrats' capture of the governorship in 1981. The biggest urban areas of the state—the Washington suburbs, Tidewater, and the Richmond area—do not reliably produce Democratic majorities; Southside Virginia and the Shenandoah Valley are now solidly Republican in national contests. Virginia's parties select their national convention delegates through caucus systems. They are to the right of both parties' spectrums.

Governor. The governor of Virginia, Charles Robb, is the first Democrat elected to the post since 1965 and the first non-Byrd Democrat since Harry Byrd, Sr., won the office in 1925. He was elected lieutenant governor in 1977; he was best known then as Lyndon Johnson's son-in-law. But Robb is very much his own man, a ramrod-straight Marine officer who is not sympathetic with much of the cultural liberalism of his time; a parsimonious man who is fiscally very cautious. He is a departure for Virginia, however, in his appointments. Instead of appointing tested, elderly men with roots deep in local elites, he has appointed women and blacks to top cabinet positions and a black to the Virginia Supreme Court. Robb has been mentioned, occasionally, as a candidate for the Senate, and he might be, but only after his term expires; he has been mentioned also, less plausibly, as a national candidate.

Robb is ineligible to run again in 1985; Virginia, Kentucky, and Mississippi are the last states to prohibit consecutive terms. The most prominent candidates now are Lieutenant Governor Dick Davis and, less likely, Attorney General Gerald Baliles; both are Democrats, with politics similar to Robb's. The Republicans undoubtedly will have a well-financed candidate, though two years ahead of the election no one was sure who.

Senators. Virginia is represented in the Senate by two Republicans with solid conservative records, but with political backgrounds which the late Senator Byrd would have considered odd indeed. Senator John Warner has been fortunate in his marriages: his first wife was a Mellon, one of the world's richest families; his second wife, Elizabeth Taylor, was an effective campaigner for him in 1978. Warner did not actually win the Senate nomination at the Republican convention that year—a gigantic affair, with some 9,000 delegates, probably the largest political convention in American history. But he campaigned hard enough to come in second; and when Richard Obenshain, the nominee and longtime Republican state chairman, was killed in a plane crash, there was no way his supporters could keep from substituting Warner, who had been working hard raising money for the man who beat him. Warner won a hairsbreadth victory in the general election over Democrat Andrew Miller, without convincing Washington observers that he was anything more than a dilettante.

Warner has been something more than that. He served as Secretary of the Navy in the Ford administration and serves on the Armed Services Committee now—a panel with an intellectually distinguished membership and an agenda of the greatest difficulty. Warner plugs away, working hard to master the issues. He is, as almost every Virginia congressman tends to be, a Navy man; Virginia's Tidewater region is the East Coast headquarters of the Navy. Warner is the fourth ranking Republican on this panel, which means he could be chairman some time soon; the current chairman, John Tower, faces a tough race in 1984, and the next two Republicans, Strom Thurmond and Barry Goldwater, are much older than Warner. Warner also serves on the Energy and Natural Resources Committee, where he supports deregulation of energy prices.

Warner's secret in politics and the Senate has been hard work; Elizabeth Taylor reportedly complained (they are now divorced) that he spent too much time on dull things. Not an original man, he is prone to the most egregious cliches, but he is loyal, and he causes little trouble for his colleagues or his constituents. It is easy to see how he could win reelection in 1984. His conservative views are not that far from those of most Virginia voters; he is generally well liked; the Democrats had a hard time coming up with a candidate who could unify their party in 1982, and may again.

The result of the Democrats' difficulty was the election, at age 35, of Senator Paul Trible. He is the unlikeliest of Virginia politicians. He grew up in an affluent suburb of Scranton, Pennsylvania, and after law school worked as an assistant federal prosecutor in the Virginia suburbs of Washington. But his family does have roots there, he attended college and law school in the state, and after his Washington area experience he moved to his family's ancestral home area in the Northern Neck of Virginia—the part of the state northeast of Richmond, and laced with broad estuaries off Chesapeake Bay—and became local prosecutor. From there his upward progress was more rapid than he could have expected. The local congressman retired, unexpectedly, in 1976; Trible ran as a Republican for the seat, and drew an overconfident Democratic opponent; in his first term in the House he was able to make a big issue of Carter administration plans to renovate the *Saratoga* in Philadelphia, to pay off a political debt, rather than in Newport News, the population center of the district. He went around the state for a year before 1982, anticipating that Senator Byrd might retire; Byrd, against most of his friends' expectations and even after publicly reconsidering at their behest, decided to quit.

Trible then benefited from the Democrats' problems. Their original consensus choice was Owen Pickett, a Tidewater legislator with a conservative record. But state Senator Douglas Wilder, the *de facto* leader of Virginia's black politicians, threatened to run as an independent if Pickett were the Democratic nominee; and in that case Pickett obviously couldn't win. So Pickett withdrew from the race and the Democrats, after some agonizing, picked Lieutenant Governor Dick Davis to run. In many ways he was an ideal candidate: a successful mortgage banker and mayor of Portsmouth, with a fine head of white hair, his experience in community affairs was as deep and his Virginia accent as thick as Trible's were shallow and flat. But Trible had started earlier and raised much more money, and Davis lacked the ambition and drive needed to run a strong campaign; his personal goal seems to be the governorship. The campaign degenerated into a series of charges and countercharges about Trible's attendance record, since Davis did not want to talk much about most national issues and Trible didn't want to contrast their personalities. The low point came when Trible, who never served in the military, ran an ad showing himself in a uniform about to get into a plane.

Trible has spent only a few years of his life concentrating on the duties of his present job rather than seeking the one that comes after. Now he has the chance to settle down. In the Senate he serves on the Banking and Commerce Committees—important assignments, but not of great parochial interest to Virginia. It is too early to speculate on his chances for reelection in 1988.

Congressional districting. In 1980 Virginia elected nine Republican congressmen and only one Democrat, and he is a strong conservative; it was the most conservative delegation in the nation. In 1982 Democrats won three seats here, even without winning either in the usually marginal Washington metropolitan area. Redistricting played no part in these victories; the districts' boundaries were changed only slightly, and in politically unimportant ways.

The People Est. Pop. 1982: 5,491,000; Pop. 1980: 5,346,818, up 2.7% 1980–82 and 15% 1970–80; 2.4% of U.S. total, 13th largest; voting age pop. 3,872,484; 17.5% Black, 1% Spanish origin, 1% Asian origin. Single ancestry: 15% English, 5% German, 4% Irish, 1% Italian, French, Scottish, Polish. Registered voters (1982): 2,232,985 Total. No party registration. 15% with 1–3 yrs. col., 19% with 4+ yrs. col. 12% below poverty level. 32% housing units rented; median house value: $48,100; median monthly rent: $207. Households: 75% family, 42% with children, 62% married couples.

1982 Share of Federal Tax Burden $13,945,200,000; 2.33% of U.S. total, 11th largest.

1982 Share of Federal Expenditures

	Total		Non-Defense		Defense	
Total Expend	$21,865m	(3.62%)	$9,737m	(2.29%)	$12,128m	(6.78%)
St/Lcl Grants	1,623m	(1.84%)	1,623m	(1.84%)	0m	(0%)
Salary/Wages	6,474m	(8.30%)	883m	(3.23%)	5,591m	(11.03%)
Ind Payments	7,181m	(2.51%)	5,889m	(2.29%)	1,292m	(4.52%)
Procurement	6,531m	(4.48%)	875m	(2.77%)	5,655m	(4.95%)
Other Programs	56m	(1.03%)	55m	(1.02%)	1m	(2.33%)
Loan/Insurance	1,403m	(2.19%)	1,251m	(2.03%)	152m	(6.91%)

Political Lineup Governor, Charles S. Robb (D). Senators, John W. Warner (R) and Paul S. Trible, Jr. (R). Representatives, 10 (6 R and 4 D). State Senate, 40 (31 D and 9 R); State House of Delegates (66 D, 33 R and 1 I).

Presidential Vote

1980	Reagan (R)	989,609	(53%)
	Carter (D)	752,174	(40%)
	Anderson (I)	95,418	(5%)
1976	Ford (R)	836,554	(49%)
	Carter (D)	813,896	(48%)

SENATORS

Sen. John W. Warner (R) Elected 1978, seat up 1984; b. Feb. 18, 1927, Washington DC; home, Middleburg; Wash. & Lee U., B.S., U. of VA, LL.B. 1953; Episcopal.

Career Navy, WWII; Law Clerk to U.S. Ct. of Appeals Chf. Judge E. Barrett Prettyman, 1953–54; Practicing atty., 1954–56, 1960–69; Asst. U.S. Atty., 1956–60; Cattle farm owner and operator, 1961–; U.S. Secy. of Navy, 1972–74; Dir., Am. Rev. Bicenten. Comm., 1974–77.

Offices 405 RSOB, 202-224-2023. Also Fed. Bldg., Rm. 8000, Richmond 23240, 804-782-2579.

Committees *Armed Services* (4th). Subcommittees: Military Construction; Tactical Warfare; Strategic and Theater Nuclear Forces (Chairman). *Energy and Natural Resources* (6th). Subcommittees: Energy Research and Development; Energy and Mineral Resources (Chairman); Energy Conservation and Supply. *Rules and Administration* (6th). *Joint Committee on Library* (3d).

Group Ratings

	ADA	ACLU	COPE	CFA	LCV	LWV	NTU	NSI	COC	ACA	CSFC
1982	5	14	11	7	15	25	81	100	81	86	82
1981	5	—	12	14	19	—	66	—	100	80	84
1980	22	7	21	13	27	20	51	80	86	77	74

National Journal Ratings

	Economic		Foreign		Cultural	
1982	7%	(LIB)	16%	(LIB)	11%	(LIB)
	92%	(CONS)	68%	(CONS)	88%	(CONS)
1981	2%	(LIB)	18%	(LIB)	33%	(LIB)
	88%	(CONS)	80%	(CONS)	66%	(CONS)

Key Votes

1) Reagan 81 Budget	FOR	5) $ to El Salvador	FOR	9) Poor Pay Food Stamps	FOR
2) Reagan 81 Tax Cut	FOR	6) Saudi AWACS Sale	FOR	10) Ban Crt Busing Order	FOR
3) Bal Budget Amend	FOR	7) Ban Abortion	FOR	11) Clinch Riv Brdr Rctr	FOR
4) Gas & Road Tax	FOR	8) Nerve Gas Prod	FOR	12) Legal Services Corp	AGN

1208 VIRGINIA

Election Results

1978 general	John W. Warner (R)	613,232	(50%)	($2,897,237)
	Andrew P. Miller (D)	608,511	(50%)	($832,773)
1978 primary	John W. Warner (R) nominated by Republican Party			
	Richard Obenshain (R) nominated by convention			
1972 general	William Lloyd Scott (R)	718,337	(51%)	($619,908)
	William B. Spong, Jr. (D)	643,963	(46%)	($380,921)

Campaign Contributions and Expenditures

Expend. 77-78		*PACS brkdwn*			
Receipts	$2,907,073	Agr	$2,420	Ideo	$9,823
Expend.	$2,897,237	Bus	$83,267	Lbr	$0
Unspent	$9,835	Hlth	$11,200	Prof	$ 5,550

Sen. Paul S. Trible, Jr. (R) Elected 1982, seat up 1988; b. Dec. 29, 1946, Baltimore, MD; home, Tappahannock; Hampden-Sydney Col., B.A. 1968, Wash. & Lee U., J.D. 1971; Episcopal.

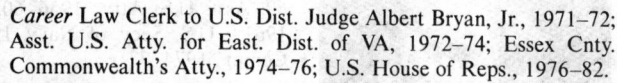

Career Law Clerk to U.S. Dist. Judge Albert Bryan, Jr., 1971–72; Asst. U.S. Atty. for East. Dist. of VA, 1972–74; Essex Cnty. Commonwealth's Atty., 1974–76; U.S. House of Reps., 1976–82.

Offices 517 HSOB, 202-224-4024. Also 823 E. Main St., 6th Floor, Richmond 23219, 804-771-2221; P.O. Box 869, Roanoke 24005, 703-892-4676; Tower Box 59, 2101 Executive Dr., Hampton 23666, 804-838-3309; and 105 S. Union St., Rm. 514, Danville 24541, 804-792-5444.

Committees *Banking, Housing, and Urban Affairs* (10th). Subcommittees: Federal Credit Programs (Chairman); Housing, and Urban Affairs; Securities. *Commerce, Science, and Transportation* (9th). Subcommittees: Aviation; Merchant Marine; Science, Technology, and Space; National Ocean Policy Study.

Group Ratings and Key Votes: Newly Elected

Election Results

1982 general	Paul S. Trible, Jr. (R)	724,571	(51%)	($2,170,961)
	Richard J. Davis (D)	690,839	(49%)	($1,192,203)
1982 primary	Paul S. Trible, Jr. (R) nominated by convention			
1976 general	Harry F. Byrd, Jr. (I)	890,778	(57%)	($802,928)
	Elmo R. (Bud) Zumwalt (D)	596,009	(38%)	($443,107)
	Martin H. Perper (I)	70,559	(5%)	

Campaign Contributions and Expenditures

1982		*Direct Cont. 82*			*PACS brkdwn*		
Receipts	$2,228,848	Indiv	$1,414,441	Agr	$14,200	Ideo	$71,225
Expend.	$2,170,961	Party	$33,788	Bus	$523,990	Lbr	$13,714
Unspent	$57,891	PACS	$652,551	Hlth	$20,900	Prof	$10,650
		Cand	$75,000				

Indirect Party Expend: $295,334 *Indep Expend*: For: $23,678 (NTL)

GOVERNOR

Gov. Charles S. Robb (D) Elected 1981, term expires Jan. 1986; b. June 26, 1939, Phoenix, AZ; home, Richmond; Cornell U., U. of WI, B.A. 1961; U. of VA, J.D. 1973; Episcopal.

Career USMC, 1961–70; Law Clerk to Judge John D. Butzner, Jr., U.S. Ct. of Appeals, 1973–74; Practicing atty., 1974–77; Lt. Gov. of VA, 1978–82.

Offices Office of the Governor, State Capitol, Richmond 23219, 804-786-2211.

Election Results

1981 gen.	Charles S. Robb (D)	760,357	(54%)
	J. Marshall Coleman (R)	659,398	(46%)
1981 prim.	Charles S. Robb (D) nominated by convention		
1977 gen.	John N. Dalton (R)	699,302	(56%)
	Henry Howell (D)	541,319	(43%)

FIRST DISTRICT

The 1st congressional district of Virginia is part of Tidewater Virginia. This is the name given to the low-lying parts of the state separated by the wide tidal estuaries off Chesapeake Bay. The district includes the southern tip of the Delmarva Peninsula, site of the annual roundup of wild Chincoteague ponies and the rural Northern Neck counties that in some ways have changed little since the times of native sons George Washington and Robert E. Lee. The district's population is not concentrated in these areas, but in the metropolitan Tidewater area, across Hampton Roads from Norfolk, where 64% of the 1st district's residents live. This area includes the cities of Newport News and Hampton plus adjacent suburbs, including the restored colonial capital of Williamsburg. There is a large black population in all parts of this district; there were big plantations here before the Civil War, and many blacks moved into the industrial Tidewater to find good jobs. Altogether 31% of the residents of the 1st are black—the second highest percentage in Virginia.

This part of Tidewater Virginia owes much of its growth and prosperity to the federal government. Hampton Roads is one of the best natural harbors on the Atlantic Coast and is the headquarters of the Navy's Atlantic Fleet. Most of the naval bases are on the south side of the Roads, but here in the 1st is Tenneco's Newport News Shipbuilding and Dry Dock Company, for years one of the nation's largest shipbuilders, and the largest employer (except for the federal government) in the Tidewater area. It is also, as you might expect, heavily dependent on Navy business. An understanding of that relationship was crucial to the success of Paul Trible as congressman from this district. Trible spent much of his time and efforts urging the Navy to do more work at Newport News, and he was always ready to shake hands with the workers at 6 a.m. and tell them about his success.

Trible's election in this district seemed something of an upset; he is a Republican and the district, historically, is Democratic. Moreover, the industrial Tidewater area long went for national Democrats. But when Trible ran for the Senate in 1982, the district was nevertheless kept by the Republicans. The Republican candidate, Herbert Bateman, was an old Byrd

VIRGINIA — Congressional Districts, Counties, Independent Cities, and Other Selected Places — *(10 Districts)*

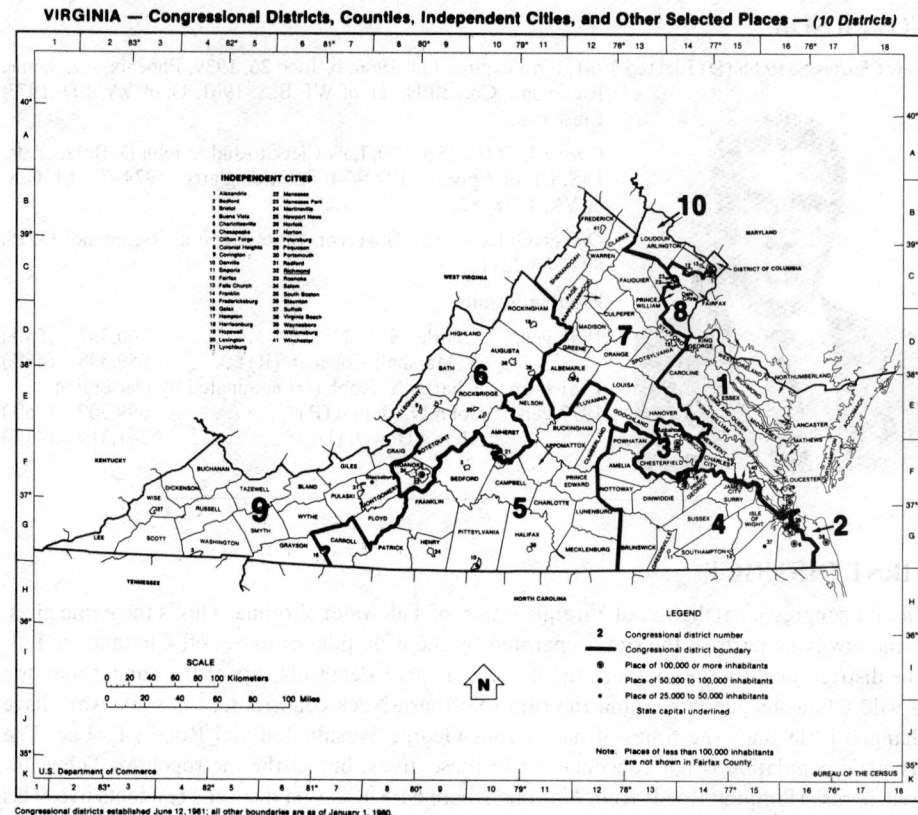

Congressional districts established June 12, 1981; all other boundaries are as of January 1, 1980.

Democrat who represented Newport News in the Virginia Senate for 15 years. He does not seem particularly aggressive; he was outmaneuvered by Trible for the congressional nomination in 1976 and failed to get the Republican lieutenant governor nomination in 1981. But Bateman was nominated easily in 1982, and his Democratic opponent, Williamsburg legislator George Grayson, withdrew from the race in June. The Democrats substituted another young William and Mary professor, but he never became a serious candidate. Only the Democratic trend of national opinion kept Bateman's percentage down.

Bateman now has seats on the Science and Technology and Merchant Marine and Fisheries Committees, both of which are of some importance to the district—though much less than Armed Services. If he uses the advantages of incumbency well, he is likely to make this a safe Republican seat, as it was for Trible.

The People　Pop. 1980: 535,092, up 11.3% 1970–80; voting age pop. 384,328; 29% Black, 1% Span. orig., 1% Asian orig. 30% housing units rented. Median owner $41,600; renter $180. Households: 76% family, 43% with children, 62% married couples.

Presidential Vote

1980			
	Reagan (R)	90,093	(51%)
	Carter (D)	80,434	(45%)
	Anderson (I)	7,440	(4%)

Rep. Herbert H. Bateman (R) Elected 1982; b. Aug. 7, 1928, Elizabeth City, NJ; home, Newport News; William and Mary Col., B.A. 1949, Georgetown U. Sch. of Law, LL.B. 1956; Presbyterian.

Career Teacher, Hampton Sch., 1949–51; USAF, 1951–53; Law Clerk to Judge W. Bastian, 1956–57; Practicing atty., 1957–82; VA Senate, 1968–82.

Offices 1518 LHOB, 202-225-4261. Also 739 Thimble Shoals Blvd., Newport News 23606, 804-877-5832; P.O. Box 1183, Tappahannock 22560, 804-443-4740; and P.O. Box 188, Tasley, 23441, 804-787-7836.

Committees *Merchant Marine and Fisheries* (12th). Subcommittees: Fisheries and Wildlife Conservation and the Environment; Merchant Marine; Oceanography. *Science and Technology* (12th). Subcommittees: Energy Development and Applications; Science, Research and Technology; Space Science and Applications.

Group Ratings and Key Votes: Newly Elected

Election Results

1982 general	Herbert H. Bateman (R)	76,926	(54%)	($257,335)
	John J. McGlennon (D)	62,379	(44%)	($101,798)
1982 primary	Herbert H. Bateman (R) nominated by convention			
1980 general	Paul S. Trible, Jr. (R)	130,130	(90%)	($38,697)
	Sharon D. Grant (I)	13,688	(10%)	($0)

Campaign Contributions and Expenditures

1982		*Direct Cont. 82*		*PACS brkdwn*			
Receipts	$260,789	Indiv	$136,396	Agr	$2,500	Ideo	$9,250
Expend.	$257,335	Party	$18,898	Bus	$68,031	Lbr	$—
Unspent	$3,451	PACS	$100,189	Hlth	$13,500	Prof	$1,000
		Cand	$3,000				

Indirect Party Expend: $37,234

SECOND DISTRICT

Norfolk, Virginia, is the headquarters of the Navy's Atlantic Fleet. Within its city limits are one of the world's largest naval bases and more than half a dozen other naval installations, not to mention the dozen or so military facilities in nearby Portsmouth, Virginia Beach, Hampton, and Newport News. The naval buildup during and after World War II made Norfolk what it is today. Before the war it was a city of 144,000 with perhaps another 100,000 in adjacent areas. Today Norfolk is the center of an urban area of nearly a million people. Suburban homes have been built in low-lying land near the wide inlets off the bay, and shopping centers have sprouted up at freeway interchanges. During the 1960s and 1970s the fastest growth in this area was in the east, in the former swamplands which, filled up with subdivisions, now overshadow the beachfront area and form most of the city of Virginia Beach. Norfolk and Virginia Beach together form Virginia's 2d congressional district.

Politically Norfolk is a working-class town. Most Navy personnel don't vote here, a fact which shows up in low turnout figures. The Norfolk voter is likely to be a blue-collar worker, who moved here from a small town in Southside Virginia or eastern North Carolina looking for a job. In Norfolk 35% of the people are black; residential segregation remains very high, but so far elections have not come down to a contest between black and white. One reason: some of Virginia's most powerful (and liberal) state legislators come from Norfolk and other Tidewater cities. They have kept each city an at-large constituency, electing several legislators, mostly whites; they fear that their politics would cost them the white vote and their race the black vote in a smaller single-member district. In any case, Norfolk is a national Democratic town.

But Norfolk's voters are now outnumbered by those in Virginia Beach. This is quite a different town politically: an affluent suburb. Only 10% of its residents are black, and its housing values are the highest in the Hampton Roads area. If Norfolk, with its rowdy bars and burly downtown, appeals to the enlisted man, Virginia Beach caters to officers—and their families. The atmosphere here is comfortably suburban; even the area's swampiness is an advantage because many of its old trees have been retained in construction. The Navy has become staffed increasingly with experts and officers and less with manual laborers and enlisted men, and that change is reflected in the changed balance of Norfolk and Virginia Beach. Not only does it cast more votes than Norfolk, but its Republican margins usually overcome Norfolk's Democratic edges. So a congressional district which went for Hubert Humphrey in 1968 now leans Republican.

That transformation was anticipated by the election of a Republican congressman here as long ago as 1968. He is William Whitehurst, a former college professor and television commentator. He is one of those congressmen who has returned often to his district and used the advantages of incumbency to the maximum. As a result, he often has no opposition at all and, when he does, he is easily elected.

Whitehurst has had a seat on the Armed Services Committee since his first term, and he is currently the second ranking Republican on the committee. As one might expect, he generally favors increased defense spending, and he looks out for the interests of Norfolk and the Navy. But he also has served as one of the chairmen of a bipartisan group of conservatives and liberals interested in military reform. Whitehurst is ranking Republican on the Readiness Subcommittee, and one of the things some reformers have criticized is the Pentagon's (and Congress's) tendency to skimp on readiness in order to spend heavily on exotic and often impractical weapons systems. What is a senior Republican doing in a group like this? A cynic might say that Whitehurst is being a good Navy man: many reformers want a more mobile Navy and would slash spending on the Air Force. But more than that, Whitehurst seems genuinely perturbed about problems which are among the most vexing—and imponderable—any public officeholder is called on to ponder.

The People   Pop. 1980: 529,178, up 10.2% 1970–80; voting age pop. 383,036; 21% Black, 2% Asian orig., 2% Span. orig. 43% housing units rented. Median owner $50,000; renter $202. Households: 74% family, 43% with children, 58% married couples.

Presidential Vote

1980	Reagan (R)	75,442	(53%)
	Carter (D)	60,013	(42%)
	Anderson (I)	8,163	(6%)

Rep. G. William Whitehurst (R) Elected 1968; b. Mar. 12, 1925, Norfolk; home, Virginia Beach; Wash. & Lee U., B.A. 1950, U. of VA, M.A. 1951, WV U., Ph.D. 1962; Methodist.

Career Navy, WWII; Prof. of History, Old Dominion Col., 1950–68, Dean of Students, 1963–68; News analyst, WTAR-TV, Norfolk, 1962–68.

Offices 2469 RHOB, 202-225-4215. Also Fed. Bldg., Rm. 815, Norfolk 23510, 804-441-3340.

Committees *Armed Services* (2d). Subcommittees: Military Installations and Facilities; Readiness. *Permanent Select Committee on Intelligence* (2d). Subcommittee: Legislation.

Group Ratings

	ADA	ACLU	COPE	CFA	LCV	LWV	NTU	NSI	COC	ACA	CSFC
1982	5	17	16	23	16	20	67	90	76	87	65
1981	10	—	15	43	36	—	67	—	100	82	70
1980	0	20	12	7	13	22	54	89	74	87	73

National Journal Ratings

	Economic		Foreign		Cultural	
1982	28%	(LIB)	12%	(LIB)	15%	(LIB)
	72%	(CONS)	84%	(CONS)	85%	(CONS)
1981	4%	(LIB)	13%	(LIB)	28%	(LIB)
	79%	(CONS)	86%	(CONS)	72%	(CONS)

Key Votes

1) Reagan 81 Budget	FOR	5) Incr SS Rtmt Age	FOR	9) Poor Pay Food Stamps	FOR
2) Reagan 81 Tax Cut	FOR	6) Saudi AWACS Sale	—	10) Ban Crt Busing Order	FOR
3) Bal Budget Amend	FOR	7) $ for MX Missile	FOR	11) Auto Local Content	AGN
4) Gas & Road Tax	—	8) Nerve Gas Prod	FOR	12) Nuclear Arms Freeze	AGN

Election Results

1982 general	G. William Whitehurst (R)	78,108	(100%)	($67,996)
1982 primary	G. William Whitehurst (R) nominated by convention			
1980 general	G. William Whitehurst (R)	97,319	(90%)	($43,672)
	Kenneth P. Morrison (I)	11,003	(10%)	

Campaign Contributions and Expenditures

1981-82		*Direct Cont. 81-82*		*PACS brkdwn*			
Receipts	$76,896	Indiv	$37,759	Agr	$250	Ideo	$1,000
Expend.	$67,996	Party	$157	Bus	$21,950	Lbr	$3,500
Unspent	$28,676	PACS	$32,365	Hlth	$2,250	Prof	$100

THIRD DISTRICT

Richmond, the capital of the Confederacy, remains the capital of Virginia and a major tobacco-producing center. In many ways Richmond is Virginia's most important city, although it is eclipsed in size by the Washington suburbs and by the Tidewater area around Norfolk. Richmond is not just the seat of government; it is a center of the ideas that for years have governed Virginia. It is the home of the Virginia Electric and Power Company, which has long gotten its way from state regulators. It is the home of the state's largest banks and of the major law firm which produced U.S. Supreme Court Justice Lewis Powell. It is the home of newspapers which present an aggressive articulation and defense of the status quo and free enterprise. During the 1950s they provided the most intellectually phrased defense of racial segregation and defiance of federal desegregation orders; even today they are unremittingly hostile to black politicians and civil rights leaders. In the words of columnist Mark Shields, Richmond is a famous center of social rest.

This is true even though Richmond today has a black majority and has on occasion elected a black mayor. However, he lost the post in 1982, and in any case the people who run things in Virginia were not going to let a black-majority city government make too many big decisions. And if you take the whole Richmond metropolitan area, blacks are still heavily outnumbered by whites. Richmond was 51% black in 1980, but the 3d congressional district, which includes suburban Henrico and Chesterfield Counties as well as the city, is only 28% black. While Richmond usually goes Democratic in elections, even for national candidates these days, the 3d district is solidly Republican. For this is a place where partisan voting is heavily polarized by race; only a rather small percentage of whites vote Democratic.

Yet Republicans have elected the congressman here only since 1980. His predecessor was a conservative Democrat, David Satterfield, who voted with Republicans so often that he was passed over for an important subcommittee chairmanship in 1979, and without comment; his retirement soon followed. The current incumbent, Thomas Bliley, was a nominal Democrat while mayor of Richmond between 1970 and 1977; in 1980 he captured the Republican nomination without a primary and easily won the general election. Bliley is a member of the Energy and Commerce and the District of Columbia Committees. He seems to be competent and conscientious, and reliably conservative. His reelection in 1982 went according to form: he carried the two suburban counties, lost Richmond, and won easily.

The People   Pop. 1980: 533,668, up 12% 1970–80; voting age pop. 394,810; 27% Black, 1% Span. orig., 1% Asian orig. 37% housing units rented. Median owner $47,000; renter $203. Households: 71% family, 38% with children, 55% married couples.

Presidential Vote

1980	Reagan (R)	121,797	(58%)
	Carter (D)	80,943	(38%)
	Anderson (I)	8,640	(4%)

Rep. Thomas J. Bliley, Jr. (R) Elected 1980; b. Jan. 28, 1932, Chesterfield Cnty.; home, Richmond; Georgetown U., B.A. 1952; Roman Catholic.

Career Navy, 1952–55; Owner, funeral home, 1955–80; Richmond City Cncl., 1968, Vice Mayor, 1968–70, Mayor, 1970–77.

Offices 213 CHOB, 202-225-2815. Also 510 E. Main St., Richmond 23219, 804-771-2809.

Committees *District of Columbia* (3d). Subcommittees: Fiscal Affairs and Health; Judiciary and Education. *Energy and Commerce* (12th). Subcommittees: Health and the Environment; Oversight and Investigations. *Select Committee on Children, Youth, and Families* (4th).

Group Ratings

	ADA	ACLU	COPE	CFA	LCV	LWV	NTU	NSI	COC	ACA	CSFC
1982	0	0	11	15	21	17	81	100	91	96	74
1981	0	—	13	14	21	—	66	—	100	79	72

National Journal Ratings

	Economic		Foreign		Cultural	
1982	6%	(LIB)	4%	(LIB)	4%	(LIB)
	94%	(CONS)	92%	(CONS)	87%	(CONS)
1981	4%	(LIB)	34%	(LIB)	4%	(LIB)
	79%	(CONS)	63%	(CONS)	90%	(CONS)

Key Votes

1) Reagan 81 Budget	FOR	5) Incr SS Rtmt Age	FOR	9) Poor Pay Food Stamps	FOR
2) Reagan 81 Tax Cut	FOR	6) Saudi AWACS Sale	AGN	10) Ban Crt Busing Order	FOR
3) Bal Budget Amend	FOR	7) $ for MX Missile	FOR	11) Auto Local Content	AGN
4) Gas & Road Tax	FOR	8) Nerve Gas Prod	FOR	12) Nuclear Arms Freeze	AGN

Election Results

1982 general	Thomas J. Bliley, Jr. (R)	92,928	(59%)	($290,846)
	John A. Waldrop, Jr. (D)	63,946	(41%)	($65,428)
1982 primary	Thomas J. Bliley, Jr. (R) nominated by convention			
1980 general	Thomas J. Bliley, Jr. (R)	96,524	(52%)	($259,131)
	John A. Mapp (D)	60,962	(33%)	($0)
	Howard H. Carwile (I)	19,549	(10%)	($0)
	James B. Turney (I)	9,852	(5%)	($10,432)

Campaign Contributions and Expenditures

1981-82		Direct Cont. 81-82		PACS brkdwn			
Receipts	$290,418	Indiv	$178,496	Agr	$1,400	Ideo	$1,450
Expend.	$290,846	Party	$9,940	Bus	$78,200	Lbr	$—
Unspent	$3,074	PACS	$96,490	Hlth	$13,150	Prof	$1,500

Indirect Party Expend: $1,580   *Indep Expend:* For: $487 (NRA)

FOURTH DISTRICT

The 4th congressional district of Virginia, in the southeastern part of the state, stretches from the industrialized Tidewater region west to the sparsely populated counties where Robert E. Lee's troops made their last march before surrendering at Appomattox. The Tidewater region—the industrial city of Portsmouth, its blue-collar suburb of Chesapeake, the suburb of Suffolk to the west—has half the population of this district. The other urban population center is around the old industrial town of Petersburg, a railroad center and battle prize of importance in the Civil War, and not all that much larger today. In between are the flat lands of Southside Virginia fanning south from the James River. These were tobacco lands when the English first settled them, in the 17th century, and they produce some tobacco today. They also produce much of Virginia's peanut crop, and its special Smithfield hams.

Beginning in the 17th century, planters brought in African slaves to work these fields. Today the population of the 4th district is 40% black—the highest percentage of any district in Virginia. For years the district's public life, economically and politically, has been dominated by whites, and by the rather small number of whites who own large amounts of land, who own and run the banks and law practices in town, who are the first to learn of any business opportunities. These people see themselves as having paternal responsibilities to the community—to help people who are in trouble and, more important to many in Virginia, to keep the community from changing.

Such a person was Robert Daniel, congressman from the 4th district for 10 years. A large landholder, and former CIA agent, he ran as the Republican candidate in this newly drawn district in 1972 and won the election with a minority of the vote in a six-candidate field. His hold was tenuous ever after. A serious man with little charm, he compiled a solidly conservative voting record which made not a concession to the presumed views of the large black population in the district. He served on the Armed Services Committee, supported high defense budgets, and tended to the business of local military bases. He won reelection against weak or divided opposition.

In 1982 he was finally defeated. The large size of the base against him, combined with the trend in national opinion, put the seat at risk; and for once he was faced with an opponent who could outspend him. This was Norman Sisisky, a Pepsi-Cola distributor from Petersburg, and a state legislator with a majority black district. Sisisky had the additional advantage of a mixed record on the issues and a vivid personality. He carried the Tidewater portion of the district and the Southside counties just to the west with 56% of the vote; he broke even in the Petersburg area (carrying the city, losing the mostly white suburbs); he lost only in the sparsely populated western counties. Sisisky, who is Jewish, did not find his religion a political handicap, although Daniel did try to make school prayer an issue.

Sisisky is well positioned to be reelected in this district. House Democrats assigned him to the Armed Services Committee, which is of clear importance here. And his willingness to spend his own money, plus the district's large black percentage, may be enough to deter the Republicans' natural candidates—local aristocrats like Daniel—from emerging from their mansions decorated with Williamsburg reproductions out into the hurly-burly of 4th district politics.

The People　Pop. 1980: 535,703, up 7.1% 1970–80; voting age pop. 377,071; 37% Black, 1% Span. orig., 1% Asian orig. 31% housing units rented. Median owner $38,900; renter $145. Households: 79% family, 46% with children, 63% married couples.

Presidential Vote

1980	Reagan (R)	83,956	(47%)
	Carter (D)	91,715	(51%)
	Anderson (I)	4,589	(3%)

Rep. Norman Sisisky (D) Elected 1982; b. June 9, 1927, Baltimore, MD; home, Petersburg; VA Commonwealth U., B.S. 1949; Jewish.

Career Businessman, 1949–82; Pres., Petersburg Pepsi-Cola Bottling Co.

Offices 1429 LHOB, 202-225-6365. Also Chamber of Commerce Bldg., 322 S. Main St., Emporia 23847, 804-634-5575; VA First Sav. and Loan Bldg., Franklin and Adams St., Rm. 607, Petersburg 23803, 804-732-2544; and 801 Water St., Portsmouth 23704, 804-393-2068.

Committees *Armed Services* (23d). Subcommittees: Military Installations and Facilities; Seapower and Strategic and Critical Materials. *Small Business* (19th). Subcommittees: Export Opportunities and Special Small Business Problems; General Oversight and the Economy. *Select Committee on Aging* (35th). Subcommittee: Retirement Income and Employment.

Group Ratings and Key Votes: Newly Elected

Election Results

1982 general	Norman Sisisky (D)	80,695	(54%)	($525,304)
	Robert W. (Bob) Daniel, Jr. (R) ...	67,708	(46%)	($328,382)
1982 primary	Norman Sisisky (D) nominated by convention			
1980 general	Robert W. (Bob) Daniel, Jr. (R) ...	92,557	(61%)	($186,334)
	Cecil Y. Jenkins (D)	59,930	(39%)	($84,109)

Campaign Contributions and Expenditures

1982		Direct Cont. 82			PACS brkdwn		
Receipts	$528,141	Indiv	$119,732	Agr	$—	Ideo	$12,950
Expend.	$525,304	Party	$2,350	Bus	$19,009	Lbr	$19,550
Unspent	$2,835	PACS	$56,201	Hlth	$—	Prof	$250
		Cand	$349,183				

Indirect Party Expend: $5,844

FIFTH DISTRICT

The 5th congressional district of Virginia covers about half of Southside Virginia, which is more a state of mind than a location. Southside is the Virginia name for those counties in the southern part of the state where support for racial segregation, among whites, was always very strong; it includes everything from Richmond south and from the Tidewater west to the Blue Ridge, and perhaps a little more here and there. The 5th district is, roughly, the western half of Southside. Its eastern counties, those nearest Richmond, are flat and humid; they were the frontier in the late colonial period and were plantation country by 1800. Currently about 40% of their residents are black. As you go west, slowly the land gets hillier. This is land which, in North Carolina and states further south, is called the Piedmont. Here you find the textile and furniture manufacturing centers of Danville and Martinsville. Farther west, getting nearer the mountains, you find more livestock and less tobacco, more whites with mountain accents and fewer blacks; the black percentage is about 10%. Altogether the 5th district is 25% black—significantly less than the 40% in the 4th district just to the east.

This is a part of Virginia where politics is still racially polarized. Before the Voting Rights Act of 1965, it was a stronghold of Byrd Democrats, and its public life was firmly in the hands of big landholders, local bankers, and courthouse lawyers, almost all of whom remembered the Civil War and were dedicated to retaining racial segregation. Even today, the blacks here almost all vote Democratic, and a large preponderance of the whites vote Republican. In national elections and in most statewide contests, this part of Southside Virginia has become reliably Republican.

In congressional elections, however, it is represented by the last survivor in the Virginia delegation of the Byrd Democratic tradition. Dan Daniel, a former executive at Danville's Dan River Mills, was first elected in 1968, when the Byrd machine was already in disarray in most parts of Virginia. He had Republican and Independent opposition that year, but managed to win anyway. Since that time, he has either won easily or been unopposed. He seems likely to remain in the House for as long as he wants, even though he turns 70 in 1984.

Daniel is a senior member now of the House Armed Services Committee, ranking fifth in seniority. There are no big military installations in the 5th district, but there are in most parts of Virginia; Daniel, like other Virginians, tends to be fond of the Navy, which is of especially great importance in the state. He is chairman of the Readiness Subcommittee, on which the Norfolk area's William Whitehurst is ranking Republican. Daniel is a believer in a strong defense and large increases in defense spending; he seems to be temperamentally disposed to accept the recommendations of Defense Department officials and to take for granted their good faith when they assure members of Congress that weapons systems work properly and costs no more money than forecast.

The People   Pop. 1980: 531,308, up 13.7% 1970–80; voting age pop. 382,312; 22% Black, 1% Span. orig. 21% housing units rented. Median owner $32,600; renter $109. Households: 80% family, 43% with children, 67% married couples.

Presidential Vote

1980	Reagan (R)	97,717	(56%)
	Carter (D)	73,563	(42%)
	Anderson (I)	3,630	(2%)

Rep. W. C. (Dan) **Daniel** (D) Elected 1968; b. May 12, 1914, Chatham; home, Danville; Baptist.

Career Asst. to Bd. Chmn., Dan River Mills, Inc., and various other business positions, 1939–68; VA House of Delegates, 1959–68.

Offices 2368 RHOB, 202-225-4711. Also 315 P.O. Bldg., Danville 24541, 804-792-1280.

Committee *Armed Services* (5th). Subcommittees: Investigations; Readiness (Chairman).

Group Ratings

	ADA	ACLU	COPE	CFA	LCV	LWV	NTU	NSI	COC	ACA	CSFC
1982	5	0	10	8	16	17	75	100	71	77	70
1981	0	—	10	21	14	—	81	—	89	83	73
1980	6	7	10	7	17	11	61	100	82	92	73

National Journal Ratings

	Economic		Foreign		Cultural	
1982	14%	(LIB)	18%	(LIB)	3%	(LIB)
	86%	(CONS)	82%	(CONS)	97%	(CONS)
1981	36%	(LIB)	3%	(LIB)	4%	(LIB)
	62%	(CONS)	87%	(CONS)	90%	(CONS)

Key Votes

1) Reagan 81 Budget	FOR	5) Incr SS Rtmt Age	FOR	9) Poor Pay Food Stamps	FOR
2) Reagan 81 Tax Cut	FOR	6) Saudi AWACS Sale	FOR	10) Ban Crt Busing Order	FOR
3) Bal Budget Amend	—	7) $ for MX Missile	FOR	11) Auto Local Content	AGN
4) Gas & Road Tax	—	8) Nerve Gas Prod	FOR	12) Nuclear Arms Freeze	AGN

Election Results

1982 general	W. C. (Dan) Daniel (D)	88,293	(100%)	($35,610)
1982 primary	W. C. (Dan) Daniel (D) nominated by convention			
1980 general	W. C. (Dan) Daniel (D)	112,143	(100%)	($7,747)

Campaign Contributions and Expenditures

1981-82		*Direct Cont. 81-82*				*PACS brkdwn*		
Receipts	$77,489	Indiv	$13,931	Agr	$2,000	Ideo	$2,500
Expend.	$35,610	PACS	$49,150	Bus	$40,900	Lbr	$500
Unspent	$68,071			Hlth	$3,000	Prof	$250

Indirect Party Expend: $546   *Non-Cand Loans:* $2,000

SIXTH DISTRICT

In Thomas Jefferson's time, Virginians were just beginning to settle the vast valley west of the Blue Ridge. This was still frontier country in 1776, and the big planters, including Jefferson and George Washington, while they may have invested in this land for speculation, had not yet established plantations and imported slaves into this territory. Jefferson hoped they never would and, as it turned out, his hopes were realized. The lands east of the Blue Ridge were planted mainly in tobacco, a labor-intensive crop; those in the valley were planted mostly in wheat, a crop which an individual farmer and his family could handle. So the valley, and the mountains to the west, became an almost entirely all-white part of Virginia, and one which was suspicious of the planter elite on the other side of the Blue Ridge.

These suspicions made much of the valley pro-Union during the Civil War; and of course the counties that now make up West Virginia split off from Virginia entirely during that time. Following the war, a mountain Republicanism took root in the southern part of the valley, around Roanoke. It was an insurgent faith, not one which celebrated the status quo; a credo hospitable to economic assistance to the little guy, not one wedded to doctrines of laissez-faire. Mountain Republicans ran brave campaigns against Harry Byrd's Democrats from time to time; some of them became federal judges during Republican administrations. And, beginning in 1952, some of them became congressmen, in the 6th congressional district centered on Roanoke, in the southern part of the valley.

Now that district, which extends from Roanoke north to Harrisonburg and west to the West Virginia border and which includes one county and most of the city of Lynchburg east of the Blue Ridge, is represented by a Democrat. He is James Olin, a retired vice president of General Electric, elected in 1982. And his victory represents almost a complete reversal of the role and strength of the parties here. For it was Olin who was running as an insurgent, a critic of the Reagan administration's policies. And it was his opponent, Republican Kevin Miller, who called for acceptance of the status quo. Even the geographic bases switched. Olin carried the historically Republican Roanoke area heavily, as well as the area in the hills around Covington and Clifton Forge. Miller carried the area east of the Blue Ridge and the northern part of the valley. Historically this is Byrd Democratic country; the Byrd family still owns the newspaper in Harrisonburg.

The retiring 6th district congressman, Caldwell Butler, was the essence of the mountain Republican tradition: a party loyalist on many issues, but a brilliant country lawyer with a peppery command of the facts, who voted for the impeachment of Richard Nixon. He is a legal craftsman who was the House's leading expert on bankruptcy and other arcane corners of the law. Butler retired at age 57 to return to law practice; Olin won the seat at age 62 to start another career. Olin, though critical of Reagan economic policies, is not likely to be a left-wing Democrat, and may end up with a record like Butler's. What he will have a hard time doing is winning the district as easily as Butler usually did. This is not a district the Republicans will likely give up without returning to fight another day.

The People   Pop. 1980: 538,360, up 8.6% 1970–80; voting age pop. 401,356; 10% Black, 1% Span. orig. 28% housing units rented. Median owner $38,600; renter $153. Households: 75% family, 39% with children, 62% married couples.

Presidential Vote

1980	Reagan (R)	103,147	(55%)
	Carter (D)	76,202	(41%)
	Anderson (I)	7,352	(4%)

Rep. James R. (Jim) **Olin** (D) Elected 1982; b. Feb. 28, 1920, Chicago, IL; home, Roanoke; Deep Springs Col., CA, B.S. 1941, Cornell U., B.E.E. 1943; Unitarian.

Career U.S. Army Signal Corps., WWII; Plant manager, V.P. and Gen. Mgr., Industrial Electronics Div., G.E., 1946–82.

Offices 1207 LHOB, 202-225-5431. Also First Fed. Sav. & Loan Bldg., 406 First St., Rm. 706, Roanoke 24011, 703-982-4672.

Committees *Agriculture* (25th). Subcommittees: Department Operations, Research, and Foreign Agriculture; Domestic Marketing, Consumer Relations, and Nutrition; Livestock, Dairy, and Poultry. *Small Business* (24th). Subcommittees: General Oversight and the Economy; Tax, Access to Equity Capital and Business Opportunities.

Group Ratings and Key Votes: Newly Elected

Election Results

1982 general	James R. (Jim) Olin (D)	68,192	(50%)	($245,708)
	Kevin G. Miller (R)	66,537	(49%)	($260,976)
1982 primary	James R. (Jim) Olin (D) nominated by convention			
1980 general	M. Caldwell Butler (R)	123,125	(100%)	($114,929)

Campaign Contributions and Expenditures

1982		*Direct Cont. 82*			*PACS brkdwn*			
Receipts	$249,988	Indiv	$109,333	Agr	$—	Ideo	$8,500
Expend.	$245,708	Party	$3,475	Bus	$6,100	Lbr	$30,450
Unspent	$4,278	PACS	$48,950	Hlth	$—	Prof	$1,200
		Cand	$85,777				

Indirect Party Expend: $4,517

SEVENTH DISTRICT

East and west of the Blue Ridge Mountains in northern Virginia is some of the most beautiful countryside in the United States. Away from the tidal flatlands, the climate is cool and salubrious; the flowering bushes and trees in the spring provide an even greater riot of color than the turning leaves in the fall; the mountains to the west protect against icy blasts. The Piedmont, on the eastern side of the Blue Ridge, was once the property of large landowners, like Lord Fairfax, George Washington's patron; much of the land here now is the property of some of the nation's wealthiest families, who spend their winters riding to the hunt. West of the Blue Ridge is the Shenandoah Valley, once the granary of the Confederacy and still marvelously fertile land, although now more often given over to orchards than to grain. The region's major towns—Winchester in the valley, Charlottesville and Fredericksburg in the Piedmont, none with a population as large as 40,000—still retain an old-fashioned air at least in the narrow streets of their downtowns, although a McDonald's culture has developed on the bypass roads of their outskirts.

This is the land of the 7th congressional district of Virginia—the northern part of the state beyond the Washington metropolitan area. It was the home of three presidents (Jefferson, Madison, and Monroe) and the scene of more carnage in the Civil War than any other area of comparable size in the nation. The district is also the home turf of Virginia's Byrd dynasty. The late Senator Harry Byrd, Sr., developed one of the world's largest and most productive apple orchards in the Shenandoah Valley and also acquired newspapers in Winchester and Harrisonburg; Harry Byrd, Jr., who retired as senator in 1982, continues to oversee these interests. The 7th district continues to be solid Byrd country in most elections, which means that it has shifted from conservative Democrats to conservative Republicans over the past 15 years.

It has done precisely that in congressional elections. Back in 1970 the district's congressman, John Marsh, declined to seek another term—this was the first year in which Byrd, Jr., ran as an Independent—because it seemed he might lose the Democratic primary to a liberal. His replacement was a Republican, Kenneth Robinson, who also replaced Harry Byrd, Jr. in the Virginia Senate. Robinson is now one of the more senior Republicans in the House. He is fifth ranking Republican on the Appropriations Committee, and heir apparent to that position on the Defense Subcommittee. He is also ranking Republican on Edward Boland's Select Committee on Intelligence. Robinson's record on foreign and defense policy is one of supporting increased defense spending and an assertive foreign policy; his instinct seems to be to trust the Executive Branch and the Pentagon, particularly during Republican administrations.

Robinson has not faced a tough challenge in the 7th district since 1974. In 1982, when Republicans were on the defensive on economic issues in the mountain districts, Robinson was not troubled by them in what is a much more prosperous part of the state.

The People Pop. 1980: 535,147, up 31% 1970–80; voting age pop. 383,878; 12% Black, 1% Span. orig. 28% housing units rented. Median owner $48,700; renter $190. Households: 77% family, 43% with children, 65% married couples.

Presidential Vote

1980	Reagan (R)	108,471	(59%)
	Carter (D)	66,580	(36%)
	Anderson (I)	9,286	(5%)

Rep. J. Kenneth Robinson (R) Elected 1970; b. May 14, 1916, Winchester; home, Winchester; VA Polytech. Inst., B.S. 1937; Quaker.

Career Family fruit growing and packing business, 1937–42; Army, WWII; Dir., Winchester Cold Storage, R&T Packing Corp., Inc., Winchester Apple Growers Assn., and Green Chemical Co.; VA Senate, 1965–70.

Offices 2233 RHOB, 202-225-6561. Also P.O. Box 136, 112 N. Cameron St., Winchester 22601, 703-667-0990; P.O. Box 741, 100 Court Square Annex, Charlottesville 22902, 804-295-2106; and P.O. Box 336, 904 Princess Anne St., Su. 305, Fredericksburg 22404, 703-373-0536.

Committees *Appropriations* (5th). Subcommittees: Agriculture, Rural Development and Related Agencies; Defense. *Permanent Select Committee on Intelligence* (Ranking Member). Subcommittee: Program and Budget Authorization.

Group Ratings

	ADA	ACLU	COPE	CFA	LCV	LWV	NTU	NSI	COC	ACA	CSFC
1982	5	8	10	8	8	17	82	90	82	87	73
1981	5	—	10	0	7	—	75	—	95	78	75
1980	6	13	10	7	13	20	59	100	82	92	80

National Journal Ratings

	Economic		Foreign		Cultural	
1982	10%	(LIB)	12%	(LIB)	4%	(LIB)
	89%	(CONS)	88%	(CONS)	87%	(CONS)
1981	4%	(LIB)	3%	(LIB)	18%	(LIB)
	79%	(CONS)	87%	(CONS)	82%	(CONS)

Key Votes

1) Reagan 81 Budget	FOR	5) Incr SS Rtmt Age	FOR	9) Poor Pay Food Stamps	FOR
2) Reagan 81 Tax Cut	FOR	6) Saudi AWACS Sale	FOR	10) Ban Crt Busing Order	FOR
3) Bal Budget Amend	FOR	7) $ for MX Missile	FOR	11) Auto Local Content	AGN
4) Gas & Road Tax	AGN	8) Nerve Gas Prod	FOR	12) Nuclear Arms Freeze	AGN

Election Results

1982 general	J. Kenneth Robinson (R)	76,752	(60%)	($117,052)
	Lindsay G. Dorrier, Jr. (D)	46,514	(36%)	($61,753)
1982 primary	J. Kenneth Robinson (R) nominated by convention			
1980 general	J. Kenneth Robinson (R)	139,957	(100%)	($33,173)

Campaign Contributions and Expenditures

1981-82		Direct Cont. 81-82		PACS brkdwn			
Receipts	$124,450	Indiv	$41,850	Agr	$6,600	Ideo	$1,750
Expend.	$117,052	Party	$4,290	Bus	$43,600	Lbr	$—
Unspent	$85,261	PACS	$60,147	Hlth	$7,500	Prof	$—

Indep Expend: For: $1,055 (NRA)

EIGHTH DISTRICT

The 8th congressional district of Virginia covers the southern part of the Virginia suburbs of Washington, D.C. Just across the Potomac from Washington is Alexandria, whose Old Town section recalls the tobacco port George Washington once frequented. Today, it is more significant politically that Alexandria has a large black population and that about two-thirds of its households are in multi-family structures, usually high-rise apartments. These two groups make Alexandria the most Democratic part of northern Virginia. Beyond Alexandria, in Fairfax County, are the suburbs of Springfield, Annandale, and Mount Vernon. These are affluent places, with large colonial or, occasionally, contemporary houses built for large families; voters here are wary both of new developments and of higher taxes, and they have the cautious and sometimes reactionary impulses you find in parents of teenage children. South of Fairfax is Prince William County, most of which is in the 8th district. Here zoning restrictions are less stringent and there are fewer and lower minimum acreage requirements. You could not call this a poor area, but it is where blue-collar and lower-paid federal workers are moving; the cheapest new housing in metropolitan Washington is in places like this, 30 miles from the White House.

The 8th district was one of the fastest-growing congressional districts in the 1960s and, despite the efforts of some Fairfax County officials, it was one of the fastest-growing on the Eastern seabord, and the fastest-growing in Virginia in the 1970s. The primary reason for this is that there is a growth industry here, the federal government. Federal paychecks have more than doubled since 1960, and here in the 8th about 30% of all wage earners take home each payday the familiar green government check.

The 8th district, despite the high education and income levels of its residents, has been the scene of some of the least edifying congressional campaigns of recent years. It is the district that gave us William Lloyd Scott, the congressman and later senator who, when named the dumbest man in Congress by an article in an obscure magazine, promptly called a press conference and struggled to refute the charge. More recently, the district has seen three races between Democrat Herb Harris and Republican Stanford Parris which have been models of what congressional campaigns ought not to be.

Harris is an experienced local politician whose basic credo is that enough cannot be promised the federal worker; he has also promised to fight against any efforts to make federal employees accountable for what they do. He beat Parris in 1974, the Watergate year when so many Republican incumbents fell; Harris beat other Republicans in 1976 and 1978. In 1980 the two faced each other again, with Parris running as the fervent opponent of excessive federal spending; this time he won, by a little more than 1,000 votes. In 1982 these two men who dislike each other—they both have good reasons—ran against each other again, with an even more excessive barrage of charges and countercharges. Intellectually, the race was a scoreless tie; in votes, Parris came out slightly ahead.

Parris is a member of the Banking Committee and of the District of Columbia Committee. He is of the old school which believes that officials elected by the black majority in the District cannot be trusted to manage their own affairs. There is sure to be another furiously contested battle for this seat in 1984, although it is not clear whether Washington area voters will have the treat of watching Harris battle Parris again.

The People Pop. 1980: 534,366, up 26% 1970–80; voting age pop. 376,074; 10% Black, 3% Span. orig., 3% Asian orig. 35% housing units rented. Median owner $86,000; renter $312. Households: 74% family, 44% with children, 63% married couples.

Presidential Vote

1980	Reagan (R)	102,416	(56%)
	Carter (D)	61,289	(34%)
	Anderson (I)	17,744	(10%)

Rep. Stanford E. Parris (R) Elected 1980; b. Sept. 9, 1929, Champaign, IL; home, Woodbridge; U. of IL, B.S. 1950, Geo. Wash. U., J.D. 1958; Episcopal.

Career Air Force; Commercial pilot; Practicing atty., Fairfax Cnty. Bd. of Sprvsrs., 1964–67; VA House of Delegates, 1969–72; U.S. House of Reps., 1972–74; Secy., Commonwealth of VA, 1978; Dir., VA Fed. Liaison Ofc., 1978–80.

Offices 230 CHOB, 202-225-4376. Also 6901 Old Keene Mill Rd., Su. 101, Springfield 22150, 703-644-0004.

Committees *Banking, Finance and Urban Affairs* (8th). Subcommittees: Economic Stabilization; General Oversight and Renegotiation; International Trade, Investment and Monetary Policy. *District of Columbia* (2d). Subcommittees: Fiscal Affairs and Health; Government Operations and Metropolitan Affairs. *Select Committee on Narcotics Abuse and Control* (6th).

Group Ratings

	ADA	ACLU	COPE	CFA	LCV	LWV	NTU	NSI	COC	ACA	CSFC
1982	16	8	30	25	25	25	56	100	67	62	56
1981	5	—	29	29	30	—	57	—	94	83	69

National Journal Ratings

	Economic		Foreign		Cultural	
1982	36%	(LIB)	30%	(LIB)	3%	(LIB)
	64%	(CONS)	69%	(CONS)	97%	(CONS)
1981	38%	(LIB)	3%	(LIB)	24%	(LIB)
	62%	(CONS)	87%	(CONS)	76%	(CONS)

Key Votes

1) Reagan 81 Budget	FOR	5) Incr SS Rtmt Age	FOR	9) Poor Pay Food Stamps	FOR
2) Reagan 81 Tax Cut	FOR	6) Saudi AWACS Sale	FOR	10) Ban Crt Busing Order	FOR
3) Bal Budget Amend	FOR	7) $ for MX Missile	FOR	11) Auto Local Content	AGN
4) Gas & Road Tax	AGN	8) Nerve Gas Prod	AGN	12) Nuclear Arms Freeze	AGN

Election Results

1982 general	Stanford E. Parris (R)	69,620	(50%)	($722,302 est.)
	Herbert E. Harris II (D)	68,071	(49%)	($416,624)
1982 primary	Stanford E. Parris (R) nominated by convention			
1980 general	Stanford E. Parris (R)	95,624	(49%)	($410,291)
	Herbert E. Harris II (D)	94,530	(48%)	($238,680)

Campaign Contributions and Expenditures

1981-82		*Direct Cont. 81-82*		*PACS brkdwn*			
Receipts	$748,609 (est.)	Indiv	$377,637	Agr	$4,500	Ideo	$23,600
Expend.	$722,302 (est.)	Party	$22,404	Bus	$205,206	Lbr	$10,000
Unspent	$27,695	PACS	$275,983	Hlth	$13,250	Prof	$5,400
		Cand	$30,000				

Indirect Party Expend: $35,069   *Indep Expend:* For: $25,510 (Realtors, NRA)

NINTH DISTRICT

The southwestern corner of Virginia is perhaps the only part of the nation sometimes known in ordinary discourse by the number of its congressional districts. Part of the Appalachian mountain country, the 9th probably has more in common with neighboring eastern Kentucky and Tennessee than with the rest of Virginia. Except for a few counties, the area has never been as dependent on coal as southern West Virginia; and it has benefited over past decades from the economic development in the valley of Virginia that extends from the Shenandoah to Knoxville, Tennessee, along Interstate 81. The mountain area of southwestern Virginia is a place with its own cultural traditions, where the federal government can still mean the hated revenuers, and where the kind of music most favored is still what is heard from bluegrass banjo pickers and the participants at the Galax Old Time Fiddlers' Convention.

The Fighting Ninth never did much cotton to the Byrd organization. Its mountain Republican tradition goes back to the Civil War, when the virtually all-white mountains had little use for slavery and the Confederacy. The local breed of Democrat dates mostly from New Deal days, and a devotion to Franklin D. Roosevelt was mutually exclusive here with devotion to Harry Byrd, Sr. This is an area which has had close two-party competition, with both parties approximating, on economic issues at least, the positions of their national leaders; most voters are strongly committed to one or the other party, and elections are a spirited contest for the relatively few voters in the middle—and to stir up enthusiasm and spur turnout among one's own partisans. The Fighting Ninth has a taste for raucous, noisy politics: it favored the loud conservatism of William Lloyd Scott, the yahooing populism of Henry Howell, and in 1976 the southern accent of Jimmy Carter.

The Fighting Ninth has changed partisan hands four times in 30 years—in 1952 and 1954, in 1966, and again in 1982—and each time William Wampler, "the bald eagle of the Cumberlands," played a role. As a young Republican Wampler captured the district in 1952 and lost it two years later; he returned to win it again in 1966, and held it until he lost it to Democrat Rick Boucher in 1982. Economic conditions played a major role in the last result: the coal counties on the Kentucky border had high unemployment, and they were just about the only part of the district Boucher carried. He did well enough everywhere else, however, to win a narrow victory.

Boucher seems likely to have a record on issues basically in line with national Democratic positions. He is, however, not likely to get too far out of line with his district; though young, and appearing even younger, he has had seven years' experience in the Virginia Senate. In the House he has seats on the Education and Labor, and Science and Technology Committees— assignments that suggest an interest in retraining and "human capital" issues. Boucher cannot expect to win this district without serious competition in 1984, but he appears to be the kind of politician who will do the maximum possible to strengthen his position for that contest.

The People   Pop. 1980: 538,871, up 19.2% 1970–80; voting age pop. 388,333; 2% Black, 1% Span. orig. 23% housing units rented. Median owner $32,700; renter $137. Households: 79% family, 44% with children, 68% married couples.

Presidential Vote

1980	Reagan (R)	86,251	(49%)
	Carter (D)	84,218	(48%)
	Anderson (I)	4,573	(3%)

Rep. Frederick C. (Rick) Boucher (D) Elected 1982; b. Aug. 1, 1946, Abingdon; home, Abingdon; Roanoke Col., B.A. 1968, U. of VA, J.D. 1971; Methodist.

Career Practicing atty., 1971–82; VA Senate, 1975–1982.

Offices 1723 LHOB, 202-225-3861. Also 180 E. Main St., Abingdon 24210, 703-628-1145; 321 Shawnee Ave. E., Big Stone Gap 24219, 703-523-5450; and Rt. 1, Box T19, Dublin 24084, 703-674-8378.

Committees *Education and Labor* (20th). Subcommittees: Elementary, Secondary, and Vocational Education; Human Resources; Postsecondary Education. *Science and Technology* (26th). Subcommittees: Energy Development and Applications; Science, Research and Technology. *Select Committee on Aging* (30th). Subcommittee: Retirement Income and Employment.

Group Ratings and Key Votes: Newly Elected

Election Results

1982 general	Frederick C. (Rick) Boucher (D) ..	76,205	(50%)	($238,373)
	William C. Wampler (R)	75,082	(50%)	($316,900)
1982 primary	Frederick C. (Rick) Boucher (D) nominated by convention			
1980 general	William C. Wampler (R)	119,196	(69%)	($89,461)
	Roosevelt Ferguson (D)	52,636	(31%)	($17,198)

Campaign Contributions and Expenditures

	1982	Direct Cont. 82			PACS brkdwn		
Receipts	$241,113	Indiv	$174,735	Agr	$—	Ideo	$11,870
Expend.	$238,373	Party	$1,875	Bus	$1,700	Lbr	$39,150
Unspent	$2,739	PACS	$63,573	Hlth	$500	Prof	$1,250
		Cand	$10,200				

Indirect Party Expend: $11,787

TENTH DISTRICT

The 10th congressional district of Virginia includes the northern half of the commonwealth's suburbs of Washington, D.C. Twenty years ago, the bulk of this area's population was in Arlington, the portion of Virginia which was originally part of the District of Columbia but which was ceded back to Virginia in 1846 on the grounds that the capital would never need it. In the years after World War II Arlington filled up with suburbanites, young marrieds with large families, many people who had left racially changed neighborhoods; with rising government salaries and local economic growth, they began to live in affluence that many had never anticipated. Now this population has grown older, and the children have moved away. Arlington has seen, instead, huge high-rise apartment developments, to the point that most of its residents now are renters, and it has also a substantial Vietnamese community living in what used to be a decaying white neighborhood.

The kind of young marrieds who used to fill Arlington now move farther out, in Fairfax County. Some live in tony subdivisions in McLean; others more modestly in Annandale or in more contemporary accents in the "new town" of Reston. Those with lower incomes tend to live farther out, in subdivisions in Chantilly or Sterling which have sprung up in treeless land next to the four-lane highways which lead to the Blue Ridge.

Historically, the 10th district has been a Republican seat. The newfound affluence of its residents, combined with their fear of Washington's black majority, helped reelect Congressman Joel Broyhill for 22 years after the district was first created in 1952. Now attitudes have changed, and even in Fairfax County most residents don't worry about Washington's blacks. Instead the conflict is between voters with different cultural attitudes—between colonial and contemporary subdivisions, as someone put it. Democratic voters want more money spent on local services and strict limits on development; Republican voters have no great aesthetic or moral problems with more development—Fairfax continues to grow rapidly in the 1980s— and are more parsimonious on spending. In congressional races, the district elected for six years Democrat Joseph Fisher, an economist who was a veteran of the movement for national economic planning in the New Deal years. The disappointing economic results of Carter administration policy evidently eroded his prestige, and he was beaten in 1980.

The current congressman, Frank Wolf, is a serious man whose personal attitudes are those of a churchgoing family man of the 1950s. He has seats on the Post Office and Civil Service, and the Public Works and Transportation Committees—one covers the problems the many government employees here have, the other has jurisdiction over federal funding for Washington's Metro subway lines. His voting record shows little difference from Virginia's Republican orthodoxy. But he is hardworking enough and listens hard enough to others on local and even some national issues that he was able to win reelection over a longtime liberal activist and officeholder in 1982. This can hardly be considered a safe Republican seat, however. No one has ever won as much as 60% of the vote in this district, and any incumbent is guaranteed serious opposition because both parties have a core of dedicated and politically competent activists.

The People   Pop. 1980: 535,125, up 15% 1970–80; voting age pop. 401,276; 6% Black, 4% Span. orig., 4% Asian orig. 42% housing units rented. Median owner $92,900; renter $317. Households: 66% family, 35% with children, 55% married couples.

Presidential Vote

1980	Reagan (R)	120,328	(54%)
	Carter (D)	76,676	(35%)
	Anderson (I)	23,999	(11%)

Rep. Frank R. Wolf (R) Elected 1980; b. Jan. 30, 1939, Philadelphia, PA; home, Vienna; PA St. U., B.A. 1961; Georgetown U., J.D. 1965; Presbyterian.

Career Army, 1962–63; Army Reserve, 1963–; Practicing atty., 1965–; Legis. Asst. to U.S. Rep. Edward Biester of PA, 1968–71; Asst. to Secy. of Interior Rogers Morton, 1971–74; Dpty. Asst. Secy., Cong./Legis. Affairs, Dept. of Interior, 1974–75.

Offices 130 CHOB, 202-225-5136. Also 1651 Old Meadow Rd., Su. 115, McLean 22102, 703-734-1500; and 19 E. Market St., Rm. 4B, Leesburg 22075, 703-777-4422.

Committees *Post Office and Civil Service* (8th). Subcommittees: Civil Service; Postal Personnel and Modernization. *Public Works and Transportation* (10th). Subcommittees: Aviation; Surface Transportation. *Select Committee on Children, Youth, and Families.*

Group Ratings

	ADA	ACLU	COPE	CFA	LCV	LWV	NTU	NSI	COC	ACA	CSFC
1982	10	8	14	15	43	58	56	100	82	62	53
1981	10	—	0	36	29	—	57	—	100	79	66

National Journal Ratings

	Economic		Foreign		Cultural	
1982	30%	(LIB)	11%	(LIB)	18%	(LIB)
	70%	(CONS)	88%	(CONS)	80%	(CONS)
1981	4%	(LIB)	48%	(LIB)	4%	(LIB)
	79%	(CONS)	51%	(CONS)	90%	(CONS)

Key Votes

1) Reagan 81 Budget	FOR	5) Incr SS Rtmt Age	FOR
2) Reagan 81 Tax Cut	FOR	6) Saudi AWACS Sale	AGN
3) Bal Budget Amend	FOR	7) $ for MX Missile	FOR
4) Gas & Road Tax	FOR	8) Nerve Gas Prod	FOR

9) Poor Pay Food Stamps	FOR
10) Ban Crt Busing Order	FOR
11) Auto Local Content	AGN
12) Nuclear Arms Freeze	AGN

Election Results

1982 general	Frank R. Wolf (R)	86,506	(53%)	($557,553)
	Ira M. Lechner (D)	75,361	(46%)	($418,044)
1982 primary	Frank R. Wolf (R) nominated by convention			
1980 general	Frank R. Wolf (R)	110,840	(51%)	($460,504)
	Joseph L. Fisher (D)	105,883	(49%)	($279,920)

Campaign Contributions and Expenditures

1981-82		Direct Cont. 81-82		PACS brkdwn			
Receipts	$563,637	Indiv	$294,698	Agr	$6,925	Ideo	$5,275
Expend.	$557,553	Party	$21,604	Bus	$180,104	Lbr	$4,500
Unspent	$6,082	PACS	$222,765	Hlth	$15,050	Prof	$3,650

Indirect Party Expend: $35,008   *Indep Expend:* For: $963 (NRA)

WASHINGTON

In the far northwestern corner of the continental United States is the state of Washington. Someone once said that if the nation had been settled from the Pacific rather than from the Atlantic, almost everyone would have remained on the West Coast. Conditions of life in Washington—and in Oregon and California as well—make that speculation plausible. True, it rains a lot in the Pacific Northwest; but that very rain is one of the things which makes an advanced civilization possible here. It provides the moisture necessary for Washington's greatest crop, lumber, and for the fruits and vegetables which are produced in the bright green valleys you find nestled here and there amid mountains and inlets. The geology here sometimes seems hostile: the Pacific Northwest, it became clear when Mount St. Helens exploded in 1980, sits atop a whole range of volcanoes that could become active any time; we thought they were dormant only because we hadn't been observing them very long.

But the terrain has been very helpful to building an affluent society. The inlets of Puget

Sound provide several excellent natural ports. The Cascades themselves, as a series of peaks rather than a ridge, do not cut off the interior. And Washington is well watered in addition by the Columbia River. Its waters come from far north in Canada, and are plenteous and powerful enough to charge through the arid, eerie-looking terrain of eastern Washington and to plunge through the Cascades; they have long provided cheap hydroelectric power for the Pacific Northwest, and have augmented a plentiful water supply. Even so, most of Washington is not thickly settled. About two-thirds of the people live in a thin strip of land 50 miles long on the east shore of Puget Sound, from Everett south through Seattle to Tacoma and the small state capital of Olympia.

When white men first arrived here, the hills along the Sound were covered with green firs, the result of what sometimes seems a constant drizzle. To an extent that is not generally appreciated, Seattle and its environs are still picturesque: the hills, covered with colorful houses, dive down toward the Sound or the inland lakes not far away; ferries ply from Seattle to harbors on the other side of the Sound or as far away as Victoria, British Columbia. The valleys are dense with factories, warehouses, railroad yards; for railroads made the Puget Sound economy. This is the closest continental U.S. port to Alaska and the Orient, a major point for exports (wheat from Washington's Inland Empire and the Great Plains) and imports (Japanese goods, Alaskan oil) as well as a major fishing area (salmon). The railroads reached the Sound in the 1880s, and it was not clear immediately which port—Seattle, Tacoma, or Everett—would emerge dominant, until Seattle grew, in a flash, with the 1898 Alaska gold strike. It quickly became and remains the major city of the Northwest.

In that booming, young, lusty Seattle there developed a turbulent politics. This was the major center of the Industrial Workers of the World (the IWW or Wobblies) in the years before World War I; Seattle's business and civic leaders decided to exterminate the movement and in brutal fashion did so. Adding to the distinctiveness of the area were its large numbers of Scandinavian immigrants. They rode the Great Northern or Northern Pacific west from Minneapolis after the long trip from Bergen or Goteborg. The Scandinavians brought with them attitudes favorable to cooperative enterprises (Washington has more businesses owned by workers than any other part of the country). They had no reluctance to encourage public power growth, and Washington, blessed with the hydroelectric resources of the Columbia, became the leader in public power in the United States in the 1930s. Also, despite the experience of the IWW, Washington proved hospitable to the trade union movement from the 1930s on; today it has one of the largest percentages of workers in unions of any state.

Washington was a New Deal state, and Franklin D. Roosevelt piled up especially large margins in the Puget Sound counties. For a period of 50 years, with only one exception, Washington elected only Democrats to the U.S. Senate. But since World War II, Washington has been a two-party state. Republicans have held the governorship most of this time, primarily because they have offered more respectable and less eccentric candidates. The legislature is usually closely divided. Republicans are competitive in congressional elections.

During most of the 1960s and 1970s Washington attracted many migrants. Its wage levels are well above the national average, and its quality of life is attractive, particularly to many highly educated young people. Yet the state also suffers from its economic dependence on just a few industries. One is lumber. This is an industry sensitive to high interest rates; they discourage homebuilding and construction, and sharply reduce the demand for lumber. Exactly this happened in the early 1980s; parts of Washington had very high unemployment rates, and the state's economy suffered generally. The other major industry here is aircraft, which is to say Boeing, which has long been the state's number one employer. Boeing has been superbly managed over the years, and its products are a prime example of the mass production of high-technology instruments. But the fact is that unit sales of airliners are very low; if you lose an order for a few dozen planes, you can go out of business. In 1970 Boeing's Washington payroll fell from 101,000 to 38,000 when the federal government refused to finance Boeing's supersonic transport. Boeing has been careful not to build up its work force so much again. Nevertheless, the slump the airlines experienced in the early 1980s held down orders for Boeing's new 757 and 767 planes. That slump, with the lumber industry depression, pushed Washington's unemployment rate up to 11% in 1982, and slowed its economic growth and in-migration.

Presidential politics. Will this economic slump, if it continues, affect Washington's attitudes in national politics? Perhaps it will make the state more Democratic. But this is already a state where cultural attitudes seem to have replaced economic status as the main force behind voting behavior. Seattle, once a Democratic stronghold, has grown more white collar and more prosperous, and shifts much more between the two parties than it used to; the same development can be seen in the late 1970s and early 1980s in more heavily blue-collar areas like Tacoma and Everett. Young voters here tend to be strong environmentalists, opposed to the policies and attitudes represented by James Watt; they are also strongly opposed to nuclear power, one reason for the defeat in 1980 of Governor Dixy Lee Ray, a strong nuclear power advocate. Migration into Washington continued in the early 1980s, despite the recession—a sign that the affluence which provides the bedrock for cultural issue politics remains.

So Washington's responses to national candidates are not necessarily the same as the nation's. In the last three close presidential elections, Washington's electoral votes have been determined by close margins—and the state has gone for the loser each time. This is a state far from the rest of the United States—the nearest big city to Seattle is Vancouver, British Columbia—and Washington's political rhythms are not necessarily those of the rest of the country.

Governor. Washington's current governor, elected in 1980, is Republican John Spellman, the kind of moderate Republican the state seems to call in to manage its local affairs after the turbulence of a Democratic administration. He succeeded Dixy Lee Ray, as controversial a governor as any state has had in recent years. Spellman is likely to meet serious opposition in 1984, although it is too early to say from whom and with what result.

The biggest problem facing Washington—and it preoccupies not only state and local officials, but the congressional delegation as well—is the condition of the Washington Public Power Supply System (WPPSS, pronounced "whoops"). For years it provided cheap public hydroelectric power to most of the Pacific Northwest. But by the 1960s Washington had exhausted most of its hydroelectric capacity (the Columbia falls only so far), and it is a long way here to ready coal supplies. So WPPSS decided to go nuclear. Just about everything possible went wrong. Lawsuits delayed construction. Technical problems resulted in vast cost overruns. Sloppy management, apparently, resulted in even greater cost overruns. Interest rates rose. Then, because of energy conservation, demand for electric power fell. The upshot is that Washington power users are faced with having to pay vastly increased rates for electricity to meet the construction costs of nuclear plants whose construction has been cancelled. There is even the possibility that WPPSS may declare bankruptcy. Naturally, people are not particularly pleased about this; and the effects on the Northwest's long-term economic growth are not likely to be good. But no one has a simple solution, or even a convenient scapegoat.

Senators. For many years Washington had two of the nation's most powerful senators. Warren Magnuson chaired the Commerce Committee, Henry Jackson the Interior Committee; but these two canny politicians got their power from more than chairmanships. They knew their issues, and they knew how to get things done—and everyone knew it. They were also—and this is unusual for senators of the same party—amiable colleagues in the Congress for 40 years. Magnuson was first elected to the House in 1936 and the Senate in 1944; Jackson was first elected to the House in 1940 and the Senate in 1952. But it could not go on forever. Magnuson was defeated in 1980, a year when his New Deal style of politics seemed out of fashion, at age 75; and even if he had won, he and Jackson would have been far less powerful in a Republican Senate.

Jackson remains an important senator, reelected in 1982, but far less powerful than he will be if the Democrats regain control in 1984. What is striking, looking back over Jackson's career, is the wide range of his interests. As chairman of Interior (now Energy and Natural Resources), he was a sort of czar over the Interior Department and its many activities in the West; he was also the writer of the Environmental Protection Act and the creator of EPA. Jackson, with a career that spanned the Depression and the prosperous 1960s, had a sense that the goals of environmental protection and economic growth need to be balanced—a sense that many environmentalists and conservatives of the James Watt stripe grievously lack.

Jackson was also a major force on defense issues. Leading a group of senators skeptical about arms control, he negotiated arms control agreements with administrations: he extracted concessions from the Nixon administration on SALT I and vocally opposed SALT II. He authored the Jackson–Vanik Amendment, cutting off the Soviet Union from most-favored-nation trade status if it did not allow free emigration of Jews. Jackson's constants are a deep mistrust of the Soviet Union, strong support of Israel, and a European and NATO orientation; he never joined conservatives in their romance with Chiang Kai-shek or liberals in their romance with Mao Tse-tung. A backer of the Vietnam war, though he had misgivings about the strategy, Jackson sees himself as following the Roosevelt–Truman–Kennedy–Johnson policy, and he sees his adversaries on Vietnam and arms control as following the discredited policies of Neville Chamberlain and the Midwestern isolationists.

A superb legislator, Jackson proved to be less than a brilliant presidential candidate when he ran in 1976. He won the Massachusetts and New York primaries, but ran out of money and was beaten by Jimmy Carter in Pennsylvania. He had the misfortune to be an insider running when voters wanted a new face. Evidently he has no interest in running again, although he seems as plausible a candidate as his contemporaries Alan Cranston and Ronald Reagan. Jackson has had better political fortune in his home state. He has regularly won reelection by overwhelming margins, and in 1982, at age 70, he was reelected with 69% of the vote. On completing that term, he will have served in Congress for 48 years.

In the transition period before the Reagan administration took office, Jackson was mentioned as a possible secretary of defense. But once in office, neither the administration nor the Republican leadership in the Senate has consulted him much. His old Interior Committee, under James McClure of Idaho, has been inactive, as has been the Permanent Investigations Subcommittee he once chaired. On Armed Services he remains an important, but not necessarily dominant, voice. In superb health and physical condition, Jackson seems to be waiting until circumstances allow him to play a bigger role again. That will likely happen if the Democrats regain control of the Senate in 1984 or 1986. He will not only regain his chairmanship, but his will be an important vote again, and one carrying weight with his colleagues, instead of just another vote among a powerless minority.

Jackson's current colleague is only the second Republican senator the state has elected in the last 50 years. He is Slade Gorton, former attorney general of the state. He ran a campaign in 1980 which contrasted his own vigor (he jogged down to Olympia with his nominating petitions) with Magnuson's age, and which was by no means entirely negative—his slogan was "the next great senator." A cerebral man with the image of a moderate, Gorton may represent the Washington electorate's self-image today better than the burly Magnuson with his working-class roots. Gorton is in fact something of an aristocrat, from the Gorton's of Gloucester fish products family; he is liberal on environmental matters, on consumer issues, and on some procedural issues; but throughout his career he has been unsympathetic to unions despite their large membership in the state. If he is not entirely at home in Ronald Reagan's Washington, he has not been entirely out of place either. On the Budget Committee he is one of the few Republicans, besides Chairman Pete Domenici and conservative leader Bill Armstrong, who plays a significant role in reaching decisions. His power derives not from a great ability to swing votes, but simply from a sound understanding of the issues and hard work. Gorton tended to back the Reagan budget and tax cuts in 1981, but has had some doubts about them in 1982 and 1983. He serves also on the Commerce Committee and on Environment and Public Works. His major legislative feat in the 97th Congress was steering through the Senate the revised Maritime Act, a complex piece of legislation supported by the shipping companies and maritime unions.

Congressional districting. Washington gained one House seat in the 1980 Census, and went through a good deal of hassle drawing new district lines. Republicans controlled the legislature and the governorship, but when the legislature passed a partisan plan devised by the conservative Rose Institute, Governor Spellman vetoed it. It would have jeopardized the seats of several Democrats and one Republican congressman, and it was passed just after the delegation, led by Democrat Norman Dicks, had turned the House around and gotten it to approve Export-Import Bank loans for foreign purchases of American airplanes—the key method of financing which accounted for many of Boeing's sales. Practical men of business in the state let the governor know that they were more interested in keeping a savvy delegation that could do that sort of thing in a Democratic House than they were in getting one or two more Republican congressmen out of 435.

The plan the legislature did pass ended up giving the Republicans the new seat, which made sense demographically anyway, since the biggest population growth was in affluent Puget Sound suburbs. It was declared to exceed the population limits by a federal court, but for 1984 needs to be revised only slightly.

The People   Est. Pop. 1982: 4,245,000; Pop. 1980: 4,132,156, up 2.7% 1980–82 and 21% 1970–80; 1.8% of U.S. total, 20th largest; voting age pop. 2,992,796; 2% Black, 2% Asian origin, 2% Spanish origin, 1% American Indian. Single ancestry: 9% English, 8% German, 3% Irish, Norwegian, 2% Swedish, 1% French, Italian, Dutch, Scottish, Polish. Registered voters (1982): 2,105,563 Total. No party registration. 20% with 1–3 yrs. col., 19% with 4+ yrs. col. 10% below poverty level. 31% housing units rented; median house value: $60,700; median monthly rent: $220. Households: 70% family, 38% with children, 59% married couples.

1982 Share of Federal Tax Burden $12,540,200,000; 2.10 % of U.S. total, 13th largest.

1982 Share of Federal Expenditures

	Total		Non-Defense		Defense	
Total Expend	$13,010m	(2.16%)	$8,038m	(1.89%)	$4,971m	(2.78%)
St/Lcl Grants	1,580m	(1.79%)	1,580m	(1.79%)	0m	(0%)
Salary/Wages	2,123m	(2.72%)	534m	(1.95%)	1,589m	(3.14%)
Ind Payments	5,193m	(1.82%)	4,403m	(1.71%)	790m	(2.76%)
Procurement	3,987m	(2.73%)	1,083m	(3.43%)	2,904m	(2.54%)
Other Programs	126m	(2.33%)	126m	(2.35%)	0m	(0%)
Loan/Insurance	1,064m	(1.66%)	1,007m	(1.63%)	57m	(2.59%)

Political Lineup Governor, John D. Spellman (R). Senators, Henry M. Jackson (D) and Slade Gorton (R). Representatives, 8 (5 D and 3 R). State Senate, 49 (26 D and 23 R); State House of Representatives, 98 (54 D and 44 R).

Presidential Vote

1980	Reagan (R)	865,244	(50%)
	Carter (D)	650,193	(37%)
	Anderson (I)	185,073	(11%)
1976	Ford (R)	777,732	(50%)
	Carter (D)	717,323	(46%)

SENATORS

Sen. Henry M. (Scoop) Jackson (D) Elected 1952, seat up 1988; b. May 31, 1912, Everett; home, Everett; U. of WA, LL.B. 1935; Presbyterian.

Career Practicing atty., 1936–38; Snohomish Cnty. Prosecuting Atty., 1938–40; U.S. House of Reps., 1941–53.

Offices 711 HSOB, 202-224-3441. Also 802 U.S. Courthouse, Seattle 98104, 206-442-7476.

Committees Armed Services (Ranking Member). Subcommittees: Military Construction; Strategic and Theater Nuclear Forces; Preparedness. *Energy and Natural Resources* (2d). Subcommittees: Energy Research and Development; Public Lands and Reserved Water; Water and Power. *Governmental Affairs* (2d). Subcommittees: Permanent Subcommittee on Investigations; Energy, Nuclear Proliferation and Government Processes; Information Management and Regulatory Affairs. *Select Committee on Intelligence* (5th). Subcommittees: Budget Authorization; Analysis and Production (Vice-Chairman); Collection and Foreign Operations.

Group Ratings

	ADA	ACLU	COPE	CFA	LCV	LWV	NTU	NSI	COC	ACA	CSFC
1982	75	79	94	78	38	75	1	80	42	29	34
1981	60	—	94	71	50	—	8	—	33	24	41
1980	72	60	84	87	33	80	21	30	38	19	26

National Journal Ratings

	Economic		Foreign		Cultural	
1982	93%	(LIB)	54%	(LIB)	78%	(LIB)
	6%	(CONS)	45%	(CONS)	21%	(CONS)
1981	81%	(LIB)	56%	(LIB)	69%	(LIB)
	18%	(CONS)	43%	(CONS)	30%	(CONS)

Key Votes

1) Reagan 81 Budget	FOR	5) $ to El Salvador	AGN	9) Poor Pay Food Stamps	AGN
2) Reagan 81 Tax Cut	FOR	6) Saudi AWACS Sale	AGN	10) Ban Crt Busing Order	AGN
3) Bal Budget Amend	AGN	7) Ban Abortion	AGN	11) Clinch Riv Brdr Rctr	FOR
4) Gas & Road Tax	FOR	8) Nerve Gas Prod	AGN	12) Legal Services Corp	FOR

Election Results

1982 general	Henry M. (Scoop) Jackson (D)	870,307	(69%)	($1,379,110)
	Doug Jewett (R)	306,522	(24%)	($241,695)
1982 primary	Henry M. (Scoop) Jackson (D)	450,580	(95%)	
	Four others (D)	24,035	(5%)	
1976 general	Henry M. (Scoop) Jackson (D)	1,071,219	(72%)	($198,375)
	George M. Brown (R)	361,546	(24%)	($10,841)

Campaign Contributions and Expenditures

1979-82		Direct Cont. 79-82		PACS brkdwn			
Receipts	$2,093,837	Indiv	$1,557,298	Agr	$4,100	Ideo	$27,600
Expend.	$1,379,110	Party	$17,500	Bus	$129,500	Lbr	$115,100
Unspent	$767,822	PACS	$282,460	Hlth	$1,500	Prof	$5,860

Indirect Party Expend: $42,090   *Indep Expend:* For: $1,850   Agn: $683 (NCPAC)

Sen. Slade Gorton (R) Elected 1980, seat up 1986; b. Jan. 8, 1928, Chicago, IL; home, Olympia; Dartmouth Col., B.A. 1950, Columbia U., LL.B. 1953; Episcopal.

Career Army, WWII; Air Force, 1953–56; Air Force Res., 1956–; Practicing atty., 1956–68; WA House of Reps., 1958–68; Atty. Gen. of WA, 1968–76.

Offices 3327 DSOB, 202-224-2621. Also 2988 Fed. Ofc. Bldg., 915 2d Ave., Seattle 98174, 206-442-5545; and U.S. Courthouse, Rm. S770, W. 920 Riverside Dr., Spokane 99201, 509-456-6816.

Committees *Banking, Housing and Urban Affairs* (6th). Subcommittees: Consumer Affairs; Economic Policy (Chairman); Housing and Urban Affairs; International Finance and Monetary Policy. *Budget* (12th). *Commerce, Science, and Transportation* (6th). Subcommittees: Merchant Marine; Science, Technology, and Space (Chairman); Communications; National Ocean Policy Study. *Small Business* (5th). Subcommittees: Export Promotion and Market Development; Productivity and Competition (Chairman). *Select Committee on Indian Affairs* (3d).

Group Ratings

	ADA	ACLU	COPE	CFA	LCV	LWV	NTU	NSI	COC	ACA	CSFC
1982	45	64	14	28	31	67	53	80	62	43	62
1981	10	—	6	43	38	—	59	—	94	67	76

National Journal Ratings

	Economic		Foreign		Cultural	
1982	36%	(LIB)	52%	(LIB)	63%	(LIB)
	63%	(CONS)	47%	(CONS)	36%	(CONS)
1981	49%	(LIB)	26%	(LIB)	63%	(LIB)
	50%	(CONS)	73%	(CONS)	36%	(CONS)

Key Votes

1) Reagan 81 Budget	FOR	5) $ to El Salvador	FOR	9) Poor Pay Food Stamps	FOR
2) Reagan 81 Tax Cut	FOR	6) Saudi AWACS Sale	FOR	10) Ban Crt Busing Order	FOR
3) Bal Budget Amend	AGN	7) Ban Abortion	AGN	11) Clinch Riv Brdr Rctr	FOR
4) Gas & Road Tax	FOR	8) Nerve Gas Prod	AGN	12) Legal Services Corp	FOR

Election Results

1980 general	Slade Gorton (R)	936,317	(54%)	($896,532)
	Warren G. Magnuson (D)	792,052	(46%)	($1,614,999)
1980 primary	Slade Gorton (R)	313,560	(57%)	
	Lloyd Cooney (R)	229,178	(42%)	($277,035)
1974 general	Warren G. Magnuson (D)	611,811	(61%)	($463,116)
	Jack Metcalf (R)	363,626	(36%)	($63,153)

Campaign Contributions and Expenditures

1979-80		*PACS brkdwn*			
Receipts	$930,567	Agr	$5,250	Ideo	$14,304
Expend.	$896,532	Bus	$127,147	Lbr	$1,000
Unspent	$6,566	Hlth	$2,237	Prof	$100

GOVERNOR

Gov. John D. Spellman (R) Elected 1980, term expires Jan. 1985; b. Dec. 29, 1926, Bellevue; home, King Cnty.; Seattle U., B.S.S. 1949, Georgetown U., J.D. 1953; Roman Catholic.

Career Navy, WWII; Practicing atty., 1954–67; King Cnty. Commissioner, 1967–69, Cnty. Exec., 1969–77; 1st V.P. and Bd. of Dirs., Natl. Assn. of Counties, 1969–80.

Offices Legislative Bldg., Olympia 98504, 206-753-6780.

Election Results

1980 gen.	John D. Spellman (R)	981,083	(57%)
	Jim McDermott (D)	749,813	(43%)
1980 prim.	John D. Spellman (R)	162,426	(41%)
	Duane Berentson (R)	154,724	(39%)
	Bruce K. Chapman (R)	70,875	(18%)
1976 gen.	Dixy Lee Ray (D)	821,787	(53%)
	John D. Spellman (R)	687,017	(44%)

FIRST DISTRICT

The 1st congressional district of Washington includes most of the northern part of the Seattle metropolitan area, running along Puget Sound from just north of Elliott Bay, Seattle's harbor, all the way to the old paper mill town of Everett. If you were sailing up the Sound 40 years ago, much of this shore would have looked undeveloped to you: stands of Douglas firs and pines on the hills overlooking the water. Since that time, the shoreline, and the area inland for perhaps 20 miles, has pretty well filled with subdivisions and people. White-collar families who used to live in small houses in cramped neighborhoods in Seattle have seen their incomes rise and have moved out to more spacious quarters or to a bluff with a view of the

WASHINGTON — Congressional Districts, Counties, and Selected Places — *(8 Districts)*

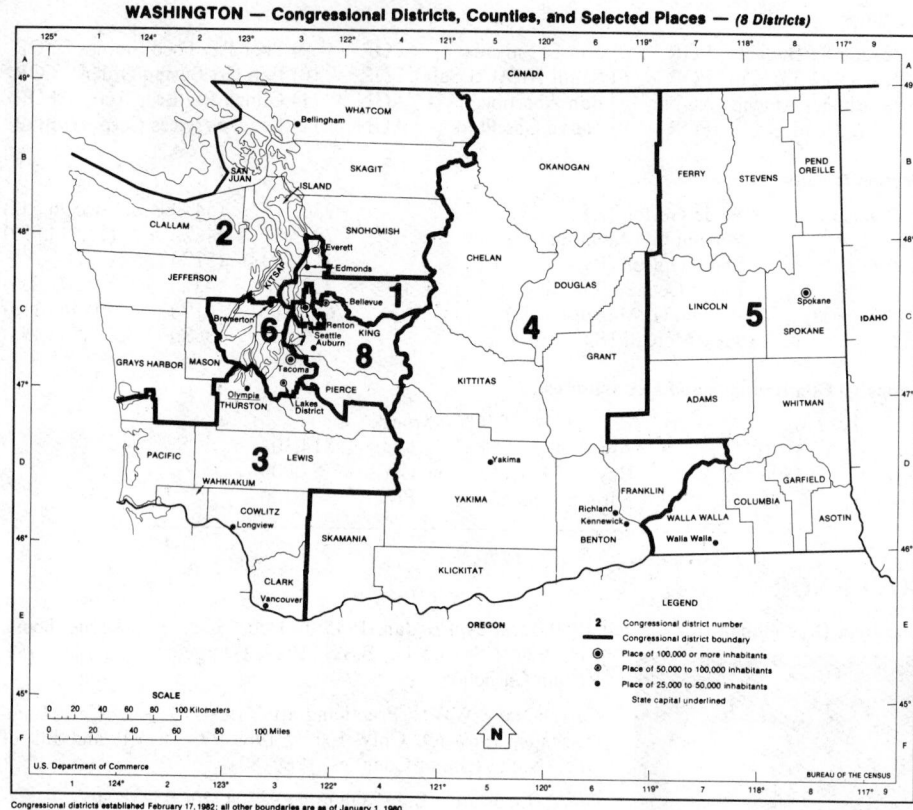

Congressional districts established February 17, 1982; all other boundaries are as of January 1, 1980.

Sound or of Lake Washington. Inland they have filled in some of the agricultural lands where you can find even vineyards and wineries.

The boundaries of this district are rather tortuous; they are designed to take in most of the Republican precincts in this part of Washington and to exclude most of the Democratic territory. Accordingly, they include the shoreline neighborhoods of the north side of Seattle, but not the more modest and lower-priced neighborhoods a few miles inland. On the eastern shore of Lake Washington the 1st district includes most of the modest suburbs of Redmond and Kirkland; in the middle of Puget Sound, it includes Bainbridge Island, a rustic high-income area, where conservatively dressed commuters go into downtown Seattle every day by ferry and then return to don flannel shirts and L. L. Bean trousers. On environmental issues this may well be the most liberal district in the state.

It is a constituency quite well suited to its incumbent congressman, Joel Pritchard. He is a Republican whose record on economic issues has been moderately conservative and whose record on environmental issues has been moderately liberal. Pritchard serves on the Foreign Affairs Committee where he is by no means a reliable supporter of Reagan administration policies; he is ranking Republican on the Asian and Pacific Affairs Subcommittee. He also serves on the Merchant Marine and Fisheries Committee, a body of some import to this area. Not only are there merchant seamen and big shipowners in the Seattle area, but there are commercial fishermen up and down Puget Sound.

First elected in 1972, Pritchard has been reelected easily every two years; redistricting seemed to cause him no trouble. The only thing that might prevent him from winning in 1984 is that when he was first elected he said he thought members of Congress should serve no more than 12 years. Should he retire, there undoubtedly will be a strongly contested Republican primary here, and the Democrats may very well seriously contest the district as well, although it would be a long shot for them to win.

The People Pop. 1980: 518,829, up 22% 1970–80; voting age pop. 379,960; 2% Asian orig., 1% Black, 1% Span. orig., 1% Am. Ind. 28% housing units rented. Median owner $74,100; renter $282. Households: 72% family, 38% with children, 62% married couples.

Presidential Vote

1980	Reagan (R)	NA
	Carter (D)	NA
	Anderson (I)	NA

Rep. Joel Pritchard (R) Elected 1972; b. May 5, 1925, Seattle; home, Seattle; Marietta Col., 1946–48; Presbyterian.

Career Army, WWII; Griffin Envelope Co., 1948–72, Pres., 1970–72; WA House of Reps., 1958–66; WA Senate, 1966–70.

Offices 2268 RHOB, 202-225-6311. Also 2888 Fed. Bldg., 915 2d Ave., Seattle 98174, 206-442-4220.

Committees *Foreign Affairs* (5th). Subcommittees: Asian and Pacific Affairs; International Operations. *Merchant Marine and Fisheries* (3d). Subcommittees: Coast Guard and Navigation; Fisheries and Wildlife Conservation and the Environment; Oceanography. *Select Committee on Narcotics Abuse and Control* (5th).

Group Ratings

	ADA	ACLU	COPE	CFA	LCV	LWV	NTU	NSI	COC	ACA	CSFC
1982	55	37	39	23	71	67	58	56	47	48	42
1981	25	—	40	50	59	—	54	—	82	48	54
1980	72	73	33	29	62	67	30	25	82	42	48

National Journal Ratings

	Economic		Foreign		Cultural	
1982	49%	(LIB)	72%	(LIB)	69%	(LIB)
	51%	(CONS)	28%	(CONS)	31%	(CONS)
1981	43%	(LIB)	64%	(LIB)	68%	(LIB)
	57%	(CONS)	36%	(CONS)	32%	(CONS)

Key Votes

1) Reagan 81 Budget	FOR	5) Incr SS Rtmt Age	FOR	9) Poor Pay Food Stamps	FOR
2) Reagan 81 Tax Cut	FOR	6) Saudi AWACS Sale	FOR	10) Ban Crt Busing Order	AGN
3) Bal Budget Amend	AGN	7) $ for MX Missile	AGN	11) Auto Local Content	AGN
4) Gas & Road Tax	—	8) Nerve Gas Prod	AGN	12) Nuclear Arms Freeze	FOR

Election Results

1982 general	Joel Pritchard (R)	123,956	(68%)	($127,960)
	Brian Long (D)	59,444	(32%)	($23,994)
1982 primary	Joel Pritchard (R)	51,567	(83%)	
	Dick Patten (R)	9,908	(16%)	($15,826)
1980 general	Joel Pritchard (R)	180,475	(78%)	($40,045)
	Robin Drake (D)	41,830	(18%)	($21,573)

Campaign Contributions and Expenditures

1981-82		Direct Cont. 81-82		PACS brkdwn			
Receipts	$123,506	Indiv	$66,872	Agr	$750	Ideo	$1,800
Expend.	$127,960	Party	$9,150	Bus	$24,425	Lbr	$2,750
Unspent	$17,957	PACS	$37,314	Hlth	$6,250	Prof	$200

SECOND DISTRICT

The 2d congressional district of Washington occupies the far northwestern corner of the contiguous 48 states. The dominant fact of life in this part of the nation is that it rains almost constantly. On the Olympic Peninsula, where the wet air off the Pacific Ocean collides with cold air coming off the massive mountains, you will find the nation's heaviest rainfall (except for one isolated spot in Hawaii); and in just about every part of the 2d district the rainfall is, by national standards, exceedingly high. The mountains here therefore are green, the trees that line the inlets off Puget Sound towering, and the evenness of the climate makes the way of life here steadier and less subject to violent surprise than it can be on the tornado-swept plains of Kansas or the hurricane coasts of Florida.

And so over the last couple of decades the coastlines here have become more thickly settled than one might expect. Most of the 2d district's population lives in a narrow strip of land just east of Puget Sound, in or near Bellingham, in Everett with its paper mills and giant Boeing plant, and in the agricultural Skagit Valley. But another 10% here live on the islands in Puget Sound and the Strait of Juan de Fuca, and 34% live along the coast of the Olympic Peninsula and down the Pacific to the lumber mill and fishing town of Hoquiam. This land has attracted some counterculture veterans and many young people looking for a more natural, less metropolitan life; and there is little hint here of the sophistication of downtown Seattle. This is blue-collar country, where men go out to work at 6 a.m. in air cold enough to see your breath year round, and where there remains a certain surly independence and suspicion of authority. Convicted spy Robert Boyce spent several months in Port Angeles here after escaping from jail and, although some people suspected he was a fugitive, no one turned him in.

The political tradition in most of the lumbering and fishing areas here is Democratic; in the agricultural areas it is sometimes more Republican. That can change, however, when some important local issue arises, as happened in the late 1970s over Indian fishing rights. A federal judge ruled that Indians had a right to half the salmon catch in some of Washington's waterways. Commercial fishermen were faced with bankruptcy; sports fishermen worried that the supply of salmon would be depleted. In 1976 this issue nearly defeated, and in 1978 led to the retirement of, Democratic Congressman Lloyd Meeds; he was unwilling to support a law entirely overturning the decision.

But in the end the Indian fishing rights issue was settled on a basis reasonably satisfactory to everyone, and the current congressman has a more difficult issue to contend with. This is the huge debt, and threatened bankruptcy, of the Washington Public Power Supply System (WPPSS), because of huge debts it incurred to build nuclear plants, most of which have been cancelled. Congressman Al Swift, a former aide to Meeds elected in his own right in 1978, is second ranking Democrat on the House Energy and Commerce Subcommittee on Energy Conservation and Power. What all that verbiage means is that the House has given him the responsibility for doing whatever Congress can do to clean up the mess and maintain the electric power system in the Pacific Northwest. This is a deadly serious business, and evidently so far Swift has performed to voters' satisfaction; he has been reelected twice by wide margins since initially winning the seat narrowly. Swift also serves on the House Administration Committee, which may have another hot potato to handle, campaign finance reform.

The People Pop. 1980: 518,753, up 40% 1970–80; voting age pop. 370,223; 2% Span. orig., 2% Am. Ind., 1% Black, 1% Asian orig. 24% housing units rented. Median owner $59,700; renter $208. Households: 74% family, 40% with children, 65% married couples.

Presidential Vote

1980	Reagan (R)	NA
	Carter (D)	NA
	Anderson (I)	NA

Rep. Al Swift (D) Elected 1978; b. Sept. 12, 1935, Tacoma; home, Bellingham; Whitman Col., 1953–55, Central WA U., B.A. 1957; Unitarian.

Career Broadcaster and Dir. of Pub. Affairs, KVOS-TV, Bellingham, 1957–62, 1969–77; A. A. to U.S. Rep. Lloyd Meeds, 1965–69, 1977.

Offices 1502 LHOB, 202-225-2605. Also Fed. Bldg., Rm. 201, 3002 Colby, Everett 98201, 206-252-3188.

Committees *Energy and Commerce* (13th). Subcommittees: Energy Conservation and Power; Telecommunications, Consumer Protection, and Finance. *House Administration* (7th). Subcommittees: Accounts; Office Systems; Services. *Joint Committee on the Library* (2d).

Group Ratings

	ADA	ACLU	COPE	CFA	LCV	LWV	NTU	NSI	COC	ACA	CSFC
1982	85	83	79	77	75	92	18	40	23	22	27
1981	85	—	74	79	71	—	10	—	21	8	34
1980	94	93	58	71	70	90	14	22	64	17	26

National Journal Ratings

	Economic		Foreign		Cultural	
1982	68%	(LIB)	88%	(LIB)	72%	(LIB)
	31%	(CONS)	11%	(CONS)	27%	(CONS)
1981	68%	(LIB)	65%	(LIB)	89%	(LIB)
	30%	(CONS)	35%	(CONS)	10%	(CONS)

Key Votes

1) Reagan 81 Budget	AGN	5) Incr SS Rtmt Age	AGN	9) Poor Pay Food Stamps	AGN
2) Reagan 81 Tax Cut	AGN	6) Saudi AWACS Sale	AGN	10) Ban Crt Busing Order	AGN
3) Bal Budget Amend	AGN	7) $ for MX Missile	AGN	11) Auto Local Content	FOR
4) Gas & Road Tax	FOR	8) Nerve Gas Prod	AGN	12) Nuclear Arms Freeze	FOR

Election Results

1982 general	Al Swift (D)	....	101,383	(60%)	($189,483)
	Joan Houchen (R)	....	68,622	(40%)	($114,218)
1982 primary	Al Swift (D)	....	54,951	(88%)	
	Zell A. Young (D)	....	7,834	(12%)	
1980 general	Al Swift (D)	....	162,002	(64%)	($143,100)
	Neal Snider (R)	....	82,639	(33%)	($15,003)

Campaign Contributions and Expenditures

1981-82		Direct Cont. 81-82		PACS brkdwn			
Receipts	$191,402	Indiv	$70,760	Agr	$9,275	Ideo	$1,098
Expend.	$189,483	Party	$375	Bus	$49,200	Lbr	$43,565
Unspent	$6,141	PACS	$113,123	Hlth	$4,000	Prof	$2,000
		Cand	$150				

THIRD DISTRICT

Lumber is one of Washington's most important industries. And nowhere in the state is lumber more important to the local economy than in the damp, mountainous region along the Pacific Coast and the lower Columbia River. This is Washington's 3d congressional district, which touches on the Seattle–Tacoma and Portland metropolitan areas, but whose atmosphere is generally more like that of a sawmill town. The 3d's main concentrations of population are in Vancouver, a working-class town just across the Columbia from Portland, Oregon; Olympia, the tiny state capital set on a promontory overlooking an arm of Puget Sound; and a string of lumber towns—Centralia, Chehalis, Longview—on the rail and Interstate highway lines between Olympia and Vancouver.

The political atmosphere in the 3d has not changed much since the turn of the century, when the lumberjacks first attacked the firs and sawmill towns sprang up along rivers and in bays off Puget Sound and the ocean. It is an atmosphere that retains a kind of rough-hewn populism, reminiscent of the days when the Industrial Workers of the World were trying to organize the lumber camps. People usually vote Democratic here, and have since the New Deal, for basic economic reasons: they think the Republicans are on the side of the bosses and the Democrats are on the side of the little guy. Politics here has sometimes been radical, but it has never been chic.

Lumber issues have tended to favor the Democrats here as well. Congressman Don Bonker won his seat in 1974, in large part because he favored limiting timber exports to Japan; he wanted the logs milled into lumber, in the 3d district, before it was sent out. In 1982 the depression in the lumber industry helped Bonker win reelection against the best-financed and most serious Republican he has faced. J. T. Quigg had proved his ability to win a legislative race from a Democratic district, but he was not able to get close to Bonker. High interest rates had closed down the construction and homebuilding industries, which in turn closed down the lumber mills; voters here did not buy Quigg's argument that this was because the Democrats' policies have discouraged investment and job creation. Bonker's solid margin makes it pretty clear this is a safe seat for him.

The economic problems here also help to explain why Bonker switched subcommittee chairmanships in 1983. He used to chair the Foreign Affairs Subcommittee on Human Rights and International Organizations, and there he was a critic of Reagan administration policies. But he yielded that post, to a less critical and active Democrat, in order to chair the International Economic Policy and Trade Subcommittee. This is not the body that directly handles U.S. trade law; that is the Trade Subcommittee of Ways and Means. But Bonker's subcommittee gives him, at the very least, a platform and a voice in what is an issue of exceedingly great importance. His own proclivities, to judge from his record and the experiences of his district, are toward allowing at least some protectionism to preserve American jobs.

The People Pop. 1980: 516,468, up 40% 1970–80; voting age pop. 359,783; 1% Black, 1% Span. orig., 1% Am. Ind., 1% Asian orig. 29% housing units rented. Median owner $55,300; renter $202. Households: 74% family, 41% with children, 63% married couples.

Presidential Vote

1980	Reagan (R)	NA
	Carter (D)	NA
	Anderson (I)	NA

Rep. Donald L. (Don) Bonker (D) Elected 1974; b. Mar. 7, 1937, Denver, CO; home, Olympia; Clark Col., Vancouver, WA, A.A. 1962, Lewis & Clark Col., B.A. 1964, American U., 1964–66; Protestant.

Career Coast Guard, 1955–59; Research Asst. to U.S. Sen. Maurine B. Neuberger of OR, 1964–66; Clark Cnty. Auditor, 1966–74; Candidate for Secy. of State of WA, 1972.

Offices 434 CHOB, 202-225-3536. Also 209 Fed. Bldg., Olympia 98501, 206-753-9528.

Committees *Foreign Affairs* (6th). Subcommittees: Human Rights and International Organizations; International Economic Policy and Trade (Chairman). *Merchant Marine and Fisheries* (7th). Subcommittees: Fisheries and Wildlife Conservation and the Environment; Merchant Marine. *Select Committee on Aging* (5th). Subcommittee: Housing and Consumer Interests (Chairman).

Group Ratings

	ADA	ACLU	COPE	CFA	LCV	LWV	NTU	NSI	COC	ACA	CSFC
1982	70	46	84	85	77	80	18	30	33	14	30
1981	75	—	83	71	99	—	19	—	17	19	36
1980	83	67	67	71	77	89	16	0	70	30	31

National Journal Ratings

	Economic		Foreign		Cultural	
1982	64%	(LIB)	77%	(LIB)	70%	(LIB)
	36%	(CONS)	22%	(CONS)	30%	(CONS)
1981	73%	(LIB)	81%	(LIB)	64%	(LIB)
	26%	(CONS)	18%	(CONS)	36%	(CONS)

Key Votes

1) Reagan 81 Budget	AGN	5) Incr SS Rtmt Age	AGN	9) Poor Pay Food Stamps	AGN
2) Reagan 81 Tax Cut	AGN	6) Saudi AWACS Sale	—	10) Ban Crt Busing Order	FOR
3) Bal Budget Amend	AGN	7) $ for MX Missile	AGN	11) Auto Local Content	AGN
4) Gas & Road Tax	FOR	8) Nerve Gas Prod	AGN	12) Nuclear Arms Freeze	FOR

Election Results

1982 general	Donald L. (Don) Bonker (D)	97,323	(60%)	($246,463)
	J. T. Quigg (R)	59,686	(37%)	($348,343)
1982 primary	Donald L. (Don) Bonker (D)	48,985	(100%)	
1980 general	Donald L. (Don) Bonker (D)	155,906	(63%)	($96,112)
	Rod Culp (R)	92,872	(37%)	($32,871)

Campaign Contributions and Expenditures

1981-82		Direct Cont. 81-82		PACS brkdwn			
Receipts	$246,477	Indiv	$125,718	Agr	$2,950	Ideo	$13,600
Expend.	$246,463	Party	$1,000	Bus	$24,025	Lbr	$66,650
Unspent	$8,347	PACS	$114,375	Hlth	$5,850	Prof	$1,300
		Cand	$500				

Indirect Party Expend: $564

FOURTH DISTRICT

For most of its length in Washington, the Columbia River flows either within or along the borders of the state's 4th congressional district. To the west the district follows the river down almost to Vancouver, across the river from Portland, Oregon. Upriver the 4th cuts through the Cascade Mountains at Bonneville Dam, past McNary Dam, to the "Tri-Cities" of Richland, Pasco, and Kennewick. This is the site of one of the major nuclear power areas in the United States; the Hanford Works here house government nuclear projects and one of the nation's three significant nuclear disposal sites. Jobs and the area's recent growth depend on the health of the nuclear industry, which has been fading, and few parts of the country are so ardently in favor of nuclear power—and bitter about the successes of nuclear opponents. Farther upriver you come to the Yakima River, along which thrives one of Washington's most fertile agricultural valleys, the producer of so many of the famous Washington apples. Still farther upriver, past Wenatchee, is the Grand Coulee Dam, one of the greatest federal construction projects of the New Deal, one that produced cheap hydroelectric power and plentiful irrigation water for much of this Inland Empire of interior Washington.

This is an area of the country much indebted to the federal government: for Grand Coulee and the other dams, for subsidies to the nuclear industry, for government support of agriculture. Yet the 4th district is one of those constituencies consistently sour and negative in its attitude toward government generally. One reason may be that some of government's projects themselves have gone sour: electric power is much more expensive now, because a Washington agency made several mistakes on safety criteria for the licensing of nuclear plant construction; the nuclear industry generally is doing poorly; farming is always subject to crises. Another reason for the sourness is that people don't like to acknowledge their benefactors. People here like to attribute their success to their own efforts and, if you look at it from most perspectives, that makes sense. They just don't want to acknowledge any view of things that points out the help government gave them.

This is basically a Republican district, usually the most Republican in the state in national elections. Throughout the 1970s it elected a Democratic congressman, Mike McCormack, an outspoken supporter of nuclear power. But he seemed to be losing his battles, and on other issues voters preferred Republicans. So in 1980 they dumped him for Republican Sid Morrison. A veteran state legislator with a base in the Yakima Valley, he serves on the Agriculture Committee. Apparently he has been able to avoid close identification with the issues the district is upset about—nuclear power and public power supply—although he is correctly positioned on them. At any rate, Morrison was able to avoid strong Democratic opposition in 1982 and won reelection by a large margin. All signs say this is a safe seat for him.

The People   Pop. 1980: 511,961, up 26% 1970–80; voting age pop. 356,411; 1% Black, 1% Asian orig. 29% housing units rented. Median owner $48,000; renter $185. Households: 74% family, 41% with children, 64% married couples.

Presidential Vote

1980	Reagan (R)	113,840	(58%)
	Carter (D)	64,820	(33%)
	Anderson (I)	14,612	(7%)

Rep. Sid Morrison (R) Elected 1980; b. May 13, 1933, Yakima; home, Zillah; WA St. U., B.S. 1954; Methodist.

Career Army, 1954–56; Orchardist, Morrison Fruit Co., Inc., 1956–; WA House of Reps., 1966–74; WA Senate, 1974–80.

Offices 208 CHOB, 202-225-5816. Also 212 E. E St., Yakima 98901, 509-575-5891; 3311 W. Clearwater, Su. 105, Kennewick 99336, 509-376-9702; and Morris Bldg., 23 W. Wenatchee, Su. 210, Wenatchee 98801, 509-662-4294.

Committee *Agriculture* (11th). Subcommittees: Conservation, Credit, and Rural Development; Forests, Family Farms, and Energy.

Group Ratings

	ADA	ACLU	COPE	CFA	LCV	LWV	NTU	NSI	COC	ACA	CSFC
1982	10	17	18	31	29	42	60	100	73	74	58
1981	5	—	7	29	14	—	54	—	100	79	66

National Journal Ratings

	Economic		Foreign		Cultural	
1982	35%	(LIB)	28%	(LIB)	37%	(LIB)
	65%	(CONS)	71%	(CONS)	62%	(CONS)
1981	4%	(LIB)	14%	(LIB)	25%	(LIB)
	79%	(CONS)	84%	(CONS)	75%	(CONS)

Key Votes

1) Reagan 81 Budget	FOR	5) Incr SS Rtmt Age	FOR
2) Reagan 81 Tax Cut	FOR	6) Saudi AWACS Sale	FOR
3) Bal Budget Amend	FOR	7) $ for MX Missile	FOR
4) Gas & Road Tax	—	8) Nerve Gas Prod	FOR

9) Poor Pay Food Stamps	FOR
10) Ban Crt Busing Order	FOR
11) Auto Local Content	AGN
12) Nuclear Arms Freeze	AGN

Election Results

1982 general	Sid Morrison (R)	112,148	(70%)	($173,926)
	Charles D. Kilbury (D)	45,990	(29%)	($9,312)
1982 primary	Sid Morrison (R)	54,883	(100%)	
1980 general	Sid Morrison (R)	134,691	(57%)	($402,884)
	Mike McCormack (D)	100,114	(43%)	($250,728)

Campaign Contributions and Expenditures

1981-82		Direct Cont. 81-82			PACS brkdwn		
Receipts	$171,415	Indiv	$89,928	Agr	$6,550	Ideo	$700
Expend.	$173,926	Party	$6,141	Bus	$43,000	Lbr	$3,000
Unspent	$1,414	PACS	$58,529	Hlth	$5,950	Prof	$250
		Cand	$7,000				

Indirect Party Expend: $58,879

FIFTH DISTRICT

The 5th congressional district of Washington is the easternmost part of the state. Centered on Spokane, Washington's second largest city, this has been called the Inland Empire. Here the Columbia, Spokane, and Snake Rivers wind through and beneath vast plateaus, bringing vast amounts of water from the American and Canadian Rockies to this low-rainfall land. Much of it has been irrigated to produce good crops; other parts, like the Palouse in the southeast corner of the state, are so fertile (the topsoil is said to be 200 feet deep) that it can produce huge yields just on the rain it gets each year. These rivers are not hospitable streams; they are fast flowing, and in some places lie in great clefts, far below the rest of the landscape. Getting the water out to where it would be useful was a major task, one achieved in large part by New Deal projects like the Grand Coulee Dam.

Yet eastern Washington is not particularly enamored of the federal government. This was Reagan country in the 1980 presidential election. He carried not only isolated agricultural counties, but also Spokane County, which contains 66% of the district's population, and the county which contains Pullman and Washington State University. Historically and today, voting habits here have been more like those in neighboring Rocky Mountain states than they have been like those in the urbanized Puget Sound area—which makes some sense, since this part of Washington is physically and economically much more a part of the intermountain basin than of the Pacific coast.

In congressional elections, however, the 5th district has elected Democrat Thomas Foley since 1964, and gave him a margin in 1982 that suggested that the problems he had had here in the three preceding elections had been overcome. Foley was an example of the phenomenon, seen in a number of western districts in particular, where a congressman who had maintained strong popularity by attention to local problems and personal cultivation of his constituency suddenly found himself in political trouble back home when he became a leader of national prominence in Washington.

Foley as one of several dozen Democratic freshmen—and one whose chances of political survival didn't seem particularly good—attracted little notice in Washington in the 1960s. But his workmanlike attitude combined with his liberal views attracted the notice of men like Phillip Burton; and Foley became chairman of the Democratic Study Group, when it was something of an insurgent group, after the 1972 election. Foley is not an insurgent by temperament; he seems much more comfortable operating as part of a reasonably unified Democratic Party. But unbeknownst to many observers, the DSG was in the process of unifying and making the Democratic Party stronger in those years. Two years later Foley, after only 10 years in the House, was chairman of the House Agriculture Committee. He got that position partly by luck: in 1970 he ranked eighth in seniority on the committee; in 1972 three senior Democrats retired and two more were defeated; another was beaten in his 1974 primary; and the incumbent Chairman Bob Poage, though an expert on agricultural legislation, was such a bleak reactionary on every other issue that the post-1974 Democratic Caucus was unwilling to back him, even though Foley himself supported him.

Foley's prominence as Agriculture Chairman made him a natural target for discontent over farm issues. But more than that, as a Democrat who made no effort to separate himself from his party's leadership, he suffered from the disenchantment of voters here with the Carter administration. Once that was gone, his standing improved, to the point that he won reelection with 64% of the vote in 1982 against the same man who had held him to 52% in 1980.

Despite that close call, Foley was chosen by Speaker O'Neill and Majority Leader Wright to be House Democratic Whip—the number three position in the leadership—in 1981. It is not necessarily a position he would have won had it been elective; Foley might not have thrust himself forward, and he would not necessarily be the first choice of many factions. But he would have been a strong affirmative choice of almost all. He is widely respected as a parliamentarian who is knowledgeable (in itself a feat, given the complexity of the Rules of the House), careful in his rulings, and scrupulously fair. If he is a stickler for detail, those who are irritated by that usually end up admitting he was right. He is trusted by Tip O'Neill and by Jim Wright, and by Wright's rivals Richard Bolling, now retired, and the late Phil Burton. He is probably one of the best natural legislators in the House, a man who is respectful of the opinions of others even as he is forceful in the advocacy of his own.

He is a possible speaker of the House himself some day, because of his position and because of his talents. The very fact that he does not seem possessed by great ambition may work for him. Also working for him is the fact that he can make an excellent impression on the cool medium of television—something that has proved very difficult for other Democratic leaders of otherwise vast talents. He does not panic: despite his tenuous position in his district, he never waffled on issues or tried to persuade constituents he was a crypto-Republican. He has that essential quality of a good leader, of being willing to risk losing when he is pretty sure he is right. Still, the speakership these days is a position that must be sought actively. Tip O'Neill, when he announced in early 1983 that he would run again in 1984, put a stop to speculation on whether Foley would oppose Wright for the speakership—but probably only temporarily. There will probably be some major candidate against Wright, and while Foley could probably be elected majority leader pretty easily in those circumstances, he might find himself blocked off from the speakership. That sort of thing doesn't seem to trouble him much, though. He has useful work, which he is good at, and he would probably be happy if he could just keep working at it.

The People Pop. 1980: 518,962, up 19% 1970–80; voting age pop. 375,183; 2% Span. orig., 1% Black, 1% Am. Ind., 1% Asian orig. 30% housing units rented. Median owner $46,300; renter $181. Households: 70% family, 38% with children, 59% married couples.

Presidential Vote

1980	Reagan (R)	120,364	(56%)
	Carter (D)	73,239	(34%)
	Anderson (I)	17,164	(8%)

Rep. Thomas S. Foley (D) Elected 1964; b. Mar. 6, 1929, Spokane; home, Spokane; U. of WA, B.A. 1951, LL.B. 1957; Roman Catholic.

Career Practicing atty., Spokane Cnty. Dpty. Prosecuting Atty., 1958–60; Instructor, Gonzaga U. Sch. of Law, 1958–60; Asst. Atty. Gen. of WA, 1960–61; Asst. Chf. Clerk and Spec. Counsel, U.S. Sen. Comm. on Interior and Insular Affairs, 1961–63.

Offices 1201 LHOB, 202-225-2006. Also E. 12929 Sprague, Spokane 99216, 509-926-4434; and 28 W. Main, Walla Walla 99362, 509-529-6111.

Committees *Majority Whip. Agriculture* (2d). Subcommittees: Department Operations, Research, and Foreign Agriculture; Domestic Marketing, Consumer Relations, and Nutrition; Forests, Family Farms, and Energy; Wheat, Soybeans, and Feed Grains (Chairman). *House Administration* (9th). Subcommittees: Accounts; Office Systems.

Group Ratings

	ADA	ACLU	COPE	CFA	LCV	LWV	NTU	NSI	COC	ACA	CSFC
1982	65	67	81	69	60	73	3	67	33	25	29
1981	55	—	81	64	48	—	3	—	32	18	37
1980	61	60	72	64	49	60	15	11	73	17	30

National Journal Ratings

	Economic		Foreign		Cultural	
1982	63%	(LIB)	66%	(LIB)	62%	(LIB)
	37%	(CONS)	34%	(CONS)	38%	(CONS)
1981	60%	(LIB)	58%	(LIB)	66%	(LIB)
	39%	(CONS)	41%	(CONS)	34%	(CONS)

Key Votes

1) Reagan 81 Budget	AGN	5) Incr SS Rtmt Age	AGN	9) Poor Pay Food Stamps	AGN
2) Reagan 81 Tax Cut	AGN	6) Saudi AWACS Sale	AGN	10) Ban Crt Busing Order	—
3) Bal Budget Amend	AGN	7) $ for MX Missile	AGN	11) Auto Local Content	AGN
4) Gas & Road Tax	FOR	8) Nerve Gas Prod	AGN	12) Nuclear Arms Freeze	FOR

Election Results

1982 general	Thomas S. Foley (D)	109,549	(64%)	($428,953)
	John Sonneland (R)	60,816	(36%)	($163,991)
1982 primary	Thomas S. Foley (D)	61,842	(93%)	
	Kerry Dean Pinard (D)	4,875	(7%)	
1980 general	Thomas S. Foley (D)	120,530	(52%)	($361,234)
	John Sonneland (R)	111,705	(48%)	($213,853)

Campaign Contributions and Expenditures

1981-82		Direct Cont. 81-82		PACS brkdwn			
Receipts	$466,125	Indiv	$161,400	Agr	$39,075	Ideo	$30,450
Expend.	$428,953	Party	$150	Bus	$133,382	Lbr	$73,000
Unspent	$90,132	PACS	$286,757	Hlth	$4,300	Prof	$6,550

Indep Expend: For: $981 (NRA) Agn: $6,048 (NCPAC)

SIXTH DISTRICT

Tacoma, the second largest city on Puget Sound, has always lived in the shadow of its larger neighbor, Seattle. In 1900, just before the state's most explosive decade of growth, Tacoma was still a credible rival—it had 37,000 people to Seattle's 80,000. But in the years that followed, Seattle's growth continued, while Tacoma got itself embroiled in an unsuccessful attempt to rewrite history and change the name of Mount Rainier (which is in Pierce County, like the city) to Mount Tacoma. Seattle was diversifying, adding white-collar employment to its basic industries of shipping, fishing, lumber, and railroading. Tacoma remained primarily a lumber town, headquarters of the giant Weyerhaeuser firm, with only about one-fourth the population of its larger neighbor. Tacoma sits today on the hills rising from Commencement Bay, not as grim an environment as many mill towns, but not the city it hoped it would become.

Tacoma is the heart of Washington's 6th congressional district, which includes the city and virtually all of its suburbs. The 6th also crosses the Puget Sound Narrows (where the Tacoma Straits Bridge collapsed in 1940) to include most of Kitsap County and its major city, Bremerton, which lies across the Sound from Seattle. Kitsap is bristling with several Navy installations and is the home port of several nuclear submarines; it is one of the major military bases on the West Coast.

The 6th is Democratic in most elections. There are white-collar neighborhoods in high lands overlooking the waters, but most of the Tacoma and Bremerton area is blue-collar territory, quite liberal on economic issues, but somewhat more conservative than Seattle on cultural issues, and decidedly hawkish on military issues. In many elections this is the most Democratic congressional district in Washington. But in 1980 it swung heavily to Ronald Reagan and went for Republicans up and down the line, and cutting the margin of its Democratic congressman, Norman Dicks.

Dicks is a product of the staff of Senator Warren Magnuson, which may have been one of the most competent staffs ever seen on Capitol Hill. He returned back home to Kitsap County to run for Congress in 1976, when the 6th district incumbent finally got the judgeship he had been hankering after for 12 years. Dicks was elected easily that year and reelected easily in 1978 and 1982; in 1980 he was held to 54% of the vote as the district swung sharply toward the Republicans.

Dicks's positions on issues match his district's inclinations pretty closely. And his progress in the House shows some of the political savvy associated with Magnuson and his staff. He became a member of the Appropriations Committee early, and after only six years in Congress ranked 19th out of the committee's 36 Democrats. He has a seat on the Interior Subcommittee, which handles a raft of environmental issues; and he sits as well on the Defense Subcommittee. There his is a key vote. The subcommittee is chaired by dovish Joseph Addabbo of New York, and has several other similarly inclined members; three of its four Republicans and several Democrats are reliable hawks. This leaves Dicks in a strong position. It can be taken for granted that he looks after the interests of 6th district and Washington military bases and defense contractors.

Dicks has also shown that he can play a major role on other issues. One of the few aid-to-business programs the Reagan administration proposed to cut was Export-Import Bank loans. But these are what finance the purchase of many airplanes from Boeing, Washington's largest employer. The House voted in 1981 to cut the loans. But Dicks organized the Washington delegation and led an effort which turned around some 80 votes literally overnight and changed the result. That kind of ability *is* clout in the House today. Dicks has been mentioned as a candidate for the Senate, and he might conceivably run in 1986 or 1988; meanwhile, he remains an important member of the House.

The People Pop. 1980: 515,970, up 15% 1970–80; voting age pop. 374,471; 6% Black, 3% Asian orig., 2% Span. orig., 1% Am. Ind. 35% housing units rented. Median owner $53,400; renter $208. Households: 71% family, 39% with children, 59% married couples.

Presidential Vote

1980	Reagan (R) .... NA
	Carter (D) .... NA
	Anderson (I) .... NA

Rep. Norman D. Dicks (D) Elected 1976; b. Dec. 16, 1940, Bremerton; home, Port Orchard; U. of WA, B.A. 1963, J.D. 1968; Lutheran.

Career Staff Mbr., Ofc. of U.S. Sen. Warren G. Magnuson, Legis. Asst., 1968–73, A. A., 1973–76.

Offices 2429 RHOB, 202-225-5916. Also Security Bldg., Su. 604, Tacoma 98402, 206-593-6536; and 900 Pacific Ave., Su. 3, Bremerton 98310, 206-479-4011.

Committee *Appropriations* (19th). Subcommittees: Defense; Interior; Military Construction.

Group Ratings

	ADA	ACLU	COPE	CFA	LCV	LWV	NTU	NSI	COC	ACA	CSFC
1982	65	62	84	85	79	67	3	70	23	30	27
1981	50	—	83	57	53	—	7	—	42	26	43
1980	67	63	76	57	44	67	18	33	71	26	35

National Journal Ratings

	Economic		Foreign		Cultural	
1982	83%	(LIB)	61%	(LIB)	71%	(LIB)
	15%	(CONS)	38%	(CONS)	29%	(CONS)
1981	59%	(LIB)	48%	(LIB)	68%	(LIB)
	41%	(CONS)	51%	(CONS)	32%	(CONS)

Key Votes

1) Reagan 81 Budget	AGN	5) Incr SS Rtmt Age	AGN	9) Poor Pay Food Stamps	AGN
2) Reagan 81 Tax Cut	FOR	6) Saudi AWACS Sale	AGN	10) Ban Crt Busing Order	AGN
3) Bal Budget Amend	AGN	7) $ for MX Missile	AGN	11) Auto Local Content	FOR
4) Gas & Road Tax	FOR	8) Nerve Gas Prod	FOR	12) Nuclear Arms Freeze	FOR

Election Results

1982 general	Norman D. Dicks (D)	89,985	(63%)	($271,250)
	Ted Haley (R)	47,720	(33%)	($197,365)
1982 primary	Norman D. Dicks (D)	48,088	(90%)	
	Gus Schwartz (D)	5,439	(10%)	
1980 general	Norman D. Dicks (D)	122,903	(54%)	($234,650)
	James E. Beaver (R)	106,236	(46%)	($165,330)

Campaign Contributions and Expenditures

1981-82		Direct Cont. 81-82				PACS brkdwn		
Receipts	$293,579	Indiv	$135,698	Agr	$4,050	Ideo	$5,050
Expend.	$271,250	PACS	$146,847	Bus	$83,025	Lbr	$48,850
Unspent	$42,739	Cand	$10,000	Hlth	$3,850	Prof	$1,300

SEVENTH DISTRICT

Seattle, like most American cities, has its own personality. If its high-rise buildings could be in almost any large American city—although they are impressive for a metropolitan area with less than two million people—then the city's setting is not. It rises on steep hills, almost as precipitous as San Francisco's, from a crescent-shaped harbor, and behind the city you can see on a clear day, from almost anywhere, the nimbus of Mount Rainier. Right on the waterfront, below the gleaming high rises, is the Pike Place market, where you can get fresh salmon and Dungenesse crab; nearby is Pioneer Square, where stores and warehouses from the turn of the century have been restored and renovated. Seattle's upper class, like San Francisco's, continues to be anchored downtown and has kept residential quarters not too far away; but people here are less obsessed with their aristocracy, and many may not realize it exists at all. Seattle's working class has maintained many comfortable neighborhoods of frame houses on steep hillsides. The old ethnic groups are not very distinctive to the untrained eye, because so many people are of Scandinavian ancestry; but Seattle is now getting a significant, although not huge, influx of newcomers of Asian and Mexican background.

Like every city, Seattle is divided into neighborhoods. Its topography—with lots of hills, bays, and lakes—prevents it from having the huge miles-long expanses of homogeneous neighborhoods you find in such cities as Detroit or Houston; there is plenty of variety in almost every mile of Seattle. Generally blue-collar workers live on the south side of the city and in valleys or midway between Puget Sound and Lake Washington; the factories, warehouses, and railroad yards are concentrated in a flat plain near Puget Sound and south of downtown. The big Boeing factories are in the plain farther south, and younger blue-collar workers have followed them into the suburban areas directly south of the city: Burien, Tukwila, and Renton, which lies at the southern end of Lake Washington. More affluent, white-collar workers, and better-educated people tend to live on hills and near the water, and are more likely to be found on the north than the south side.

The 7th congressional district of Washington includes most of the city of Seattle and many of its suburbs directly to the south. Its boundaries were drawn artfully, however, to corral most of its Democratic voters into this district, to keep them from contaminating the Republican 1st and 8th districts. So the 7th district doesn't include the north Seattle shores of Puget Sound or Lake Washington, nor the high-income suburb of Mercer Island; it does include the city's small black community (the only significant concentration of blacks in the state) and some of its recent communities of Asian immigrants. Overall, this is a solidly Democratic district and may prove to be the most Democratic district in the state in the 1980s.

The creation of the district in this form ended any worries about reelection that Congressman Mike Lowry might have had. He won this district in 1978 by beating a Republican, a right-winger who had won a special election to succeed Brock Adams when he became secretary of transportation. Lowry's background is in local and state government; he seems to be not so much an intellectual as he is a doer, one who gets to know his way around capitals and city halls and get things done. His voting record is, however, the most liberal in the Washington delegation. Lowry now has medium-level seniority on the Banking, Finance and Urban Affairs Committee, and in 1983 won a seat on the Budget Committee.

The People   Pop. 1980: 514,040, dn. 7% 1970–80; voting age pop. 415,596; 8% Black, 7% Asian orig., 2% Span. orig., 1% Am. Ind. 48% housing units rented. Median owner $62,400; renter $285. Households: 53% family, 24% with children, 41% married couples.

Presidential Vote

1980	Reagan (R)	NA
	Carter (D)	NA
	Anderson (I)	NA

Rep. Michael E. (Mike) Lowry (D) Elected 1978; b. Mar. 8, 1939, St. John; home, Mercer Island; WA St. U., B.A. 1962; Baptist.

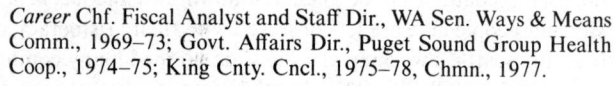

Career Chf. Fiscal Analyst and Staff Dir., WA Sen. Ways & Means Comm., 1969–73; Govt. Affairs Dir., Puget Sound Group Health Coop., 1974–75; King Cnty. Cncl., 1975–78, Chmn., 1977.

Offices 1206 LHOB, 202-225-3106. Also 107 Prefontaine Pl. S., Seattle 98104, 206-442-7170.

Committees *Banking, Finance and Urban Affairs* (17th). Subcommittees: Consumer Affairs and Coinage; Housing and Community Development; International Development Institutions and Finance; International Trade, Investment and Monetary Policy. *Budget* (12th). Task Forces: Education and Employment; Federalism/State-Local Relations; International Finance and Trade (Chairman).

Group Ratings

	ADA	ACLU	COPE	CFA	LCV	LWV	NTU	NSI	COC	ACA	CSFC
1982	95	100	81	77	83	100	18	0	14	13	69
1981	100	—	78	79	100	—	35	—	11	9	26
1980	100	93	68	79	87	100	16	20	59	17	28

National Journal Ratings

	Economic		Foreign		Cultural	
1982	87%	(LIB)	92%	(LIB)	87%	(LIB)
	13%	(CONS)	6%	(CONS)	12%	(CONS)
1981	89%	(LIB)	99%	(LIB)	89%	(LIB)
	3%	(CONS)	0%	(CONS)	10%	(CONS)

Key Votes

1) Reagan 81 Budget	AGN	5) Incr SS Rtmt Age	AGN
2) Reagan 81 Tax Cut	AGN	6) Saudi AWACS Sale	—
3) Bal Budget Amend	AGN	7) $ for MX Missile	AGN
4) Gas & Road Tax	FOR	8) Nerve Gas Prod	AGN

9) Poor Pay Food Stamps	AGN
10) Ban Crt Busing Order	AGN
11) Auto Local Content	AGN
12) Nuclear Arms Freeze	FOR

Election Results

1982 general	Michael E. (Mike) Lowry (D)	126,313	(71%)	($161,692)
	Bob Dorse (R)	51,759	(29%)	($31,686)
1982 primary	Michael E. (Mike) Lowry (D)	68,998	(100%)	
1980 general	Michael E. (Mike) Lowry (D)	112,848	(57%)	($236,351)
	Ron Dunlap (R)	84,218	(43%)	($221,223)

Campaign Contributions and Expenditures

1981-82		Direct Cont. 81-82		PACS brkdwn			
Receipts	$184,887	Indiv	$92,795	Agr	$2,450	Ideo	$1,650
Expend.	$161,692	Party	$2,762	Bus	$28,920	Lbr	$42,860
Unspent	$31,803	PACS	$79,122	Hlth	$1,100	Prof	$1,250

Indep Expend: For: $769 (NRA)

EIGHTH DISTRICT

The 8th congressional district of Washington is the new seat granted by reapportionment following the 1980 Census and created by the legislature. Washington was one of the few states in which Republicans controlled the redistricting process in 1981 and 1982, and to no one's surprise this turned out to be a Republican district. It includes essentially two geographically separate suburban sections of Seattle. One, which accounts for about 60% of the district's population, consists of the suburbs on the ridges and valleys that run up and down the land just east of Puget Sound, south of Seattle from Tacoma. The 8th district includes the small industrial cities of Kent and Auburn, set in the valleys and, between them and the Sound, the hillier suburbs starting with Burien and Normandy Park in the north, near Seatac Airport, down to the city limits of Tacoma. This is pleasant middle-income territory, on the average. Politically, Republican and Democratic suburbs seem to alternate, leaving a pretty even balance overall.

The second part of the district, with about 30% of the people, is directly east of Seattle, across Lake Washington. (The other 10% live in mostly agricultural country, which rises up to Mount Rainier National Park.) The largest city here is Bellevue, a high-income suburb; the most prominent suburb is Mercer Island, where contemporary homes are set among the woods on hills overlooking Lake Washington; this town is connected to Seattle by a once-famous pontoon bridge across the lake. This part of the district is heavily Republican. People here are solidly conservative on economic issues; on cultural matters, particularly environmental issues, they may be more liberal.

The new congressman from this district is Rod Chandler, a former television anchorman and eight-year veteran of, and leader in, the Washington legislature. He ran as a self-described centrist Republican in a multi-candidate primary, and was fortunate enough to have the conservative vote split between two significant opponents. In the general election he ran against Beth Bland, the mayor of Mercer Island, who might have been a formidable candidate against one of the conservatives; against Chandler her candidacy did not get off the ground. Chandler, like many Republicans first elected in 1982, cannot be taken as an automatic vote for Reagan administration programs, although he should not be regarded as a crypto-Democrat either. He is the sort of Republican who should be able to hold this district without great difficulty—barring a strong conservative primary challenge.

The People   Pop. 1980: 517,173, up 29% 1970–80; voting age pop. 361,169; 2% Asian orig., 1% Black, 1% Span. orig., 1% Am. Ind. 25% housing units rented. Median owner $76,100; renter $285. Households: 77% family, 45% with children, 67% married couples.

Presidential Vote

1980	Reagan (R)	NA
	Carter (D)	NA
	Anderson (I)	NA

Rep. Rodney Chandler (R) Elected 1982; b. July 13, 1942, LaGrande, OR; home, Redmond; OR St. U., B.S. 1968; Protestant.

Career Corresp. and Anchorman, KOMO-TV, 1968–73; Asst. V.P. for Mktg., WA Mutual Savings Bank, 1973–77; WA House of Reps., 1975–82; Partner, pub. rel. firm, 1977–82.

Offices 216 CHOB, 202-225-7761. Also 3350 161st Ave. S.E., Bellevue 98008, 206-442-0116.

Committees *House Administration* (7th). Subcommittees: Personnel and Police; Services. *Science and Technology* (11th). Subcommittees: Energy Research and Production; Natural Resources, Agriculture Research and Environment; Space Science and Applications. *Joint Committee on the Library* (2d). *Joint Committee on Printing* (2d).

Group Ratings and Key Votes: Newly Elected

Election Results

1982 general	Rodney Chandler (R)	79,209	(57%)	($344,614)
	Beth Bland (D)	59,824	(43%)	($175,930)
1982 primary	Rodney Chandler (R)	20,374	(41%)	
	Bob Eberle (R)	15,342	(31%)	($325,618)
	Paul Barden (R)	12,477	(25%)	($57,628)
1980 general	Newly created district			

Campaign Contributions and Expenditures

1982		Direct Cont. 1982		PACS brkdwn			
Receipts	$347,313	Indiv	$208,182	Agr	$1,000	Idec	$3,250
Expend.	$344,614	Party	$24,287	Bus	$59,420	Lbr	$3,000
Unspent	$2,700	PACS	$84,325	Hlth	$9,750	Prof	$1,200
		Cand	$10,000				

Indirect Party Expend: $24,322

WEST VIRGINIA

West Virginia lies in the middle of the Appalachian chain that separates the East Coast from the vast interior of America. This is a state with scarcely a square mile of level ground, and it has been said that if all the mountains were ironed out, its surface area would cover the entire nation. The mountains and the narrow, twisting roads that wind through them give West Virginia an isolation and a sense of distance from the rest of the country. This is not a state that thinks of itself as part of the East or Midwest or even the South; the term Appalachian is heard occasionally, but people here really think of themselves as West Virginians.

It is an identity hard won. Until 1863 these mountain counties were a part, a misfit part, of the commonwealth of Virginia. There were few slaves here; in the late 1820s legislators from the mountain counties teamed up with Jeffersonian aristocrats and almost abolished slavery in Virginia. But the specter of slave rebellions and the increasing profitability of breeding slaves for sale in the cotton belts of the Deep South strengthened the peculiar institution east of the Blue Ridge, and the mountain counties went their own way. They opposed secession; they stayed part of the Union and continued to send congressmen to Washington. In 1863, after a dispute over the name (the new state was nearly called Kanawha), West Virginia was admitted to the Union.

The new state contained about one-fourth of the residents of old Virginia. But in the years that followed the Civil War, West Virginia grew much more rapidly than its parent. The reason was simple: coal. Buried under virtually all the mountains here, and often near the surface, are rich veins of bituminous coal, the essential fuel for industry in the late 19th and the first half of the 20th centuries. The hills and hollows of West Virginia in the years 1880–1920 were a kind of frontier. Men from all over the Appalachian region, the South, and the East, and even some immigrants from southern and eastern Europe came to work the booming mines.

The working conditions in the mines were never very good and were sometimes deadly. Lovers of country music know something of life in the coal company towns and the credit practices of company stores, where workers and their families had to buy everything. Immigrant communities in the big cities of the time had some geographical proximity and exposure to other kinds of American life. The coal mining communities of West Virginia, often literally up a creek or a hollow, were connected to the rest of the world only by a rail line that carried coal cars only. Conditions were bad enough that a union movement developed, and during the 1930s John L. Lewis's United Mine Workers organized most of West Virginia's mines—so successfully that for years since West Virginia has been the most heavily unionized state in the nation. But just as unionization was complete, the coal industry entered a decades-long decline. The railroads switched from coal-powered steam engines to oil-powered diesels. Homes switched from messy coal to cleaner oil or gas. In 1950 Lewis agreed with the companies to allow mechanization of the industry in return for much higher wages and fringe benefits. This program was in many ways a vast success but was a disaster for West Virginia. In 1950 the state's population was more than 2 million; by 1970, after thousands had left to look for work elsewhere, it was down to 1.7 million. Almost a whole generation of young people found themselves forced to leave the state, leaving behind an elderly population and a sense of hopelessness about the state's future.

That mood, and the state's economy, changed in the 1970s; but it was hit hard by the recession of the early 1980s and it is not clear to what extent it will recover. The 1973 oil shock helped to revive the coal industry. It didn't bring back the coal furnace in homes, but it did persuade many electric utilities to switch to—or stay with—coal, and it allowed coal prices to rise substantially at the same time. The result was a vast increase in mining, especially in strip mining. This is capital-intensive work, and doesn't provide as many jobs directly as underground mining; it also can leave ugly scars on the landscape. For those reasons politicians like Jay Rockefeller opposed strip mining in the early 1970s; by 1976 Rockefeller, about to be elected governor, and others changed their minds.

The fact is that the coal boom did help to improve the state's economy; other industries came in, attracted by West Virginia's low energy costs and relatively low-cost, but high-skill labor force. In other ways West Virginia changed. The United Mine Workers, torn by factionalism and hurt by erratic leadership, lost much of its clout, and by the late 1970s represented a much smaller percentage of the coal labor force than it once had. And the old-line Democratic political leadership of the state, which was often corrupt, lost its clout as well. Men it did not control—Republican Arch Moore, Democrat Jay Rockefeller—held the governorship for 16 years, and insurgents won a variety of other elections. Neither West Virginia's unions nor its political parties have, over the years, had inspiring leadership; while faraway liberals like to imagine that leaders springing from poor people will represent poor people's interests altruistically, all too often they are interested in representing their own interests first. So the weakness of these institutions has probably elevated the quality of West Virginia's public life.

The question now is how, and whether, West Virginia will rebound from the 1979–83 recession. Its unemployment rate just before the 1982 election was the highest in the nation. This is a steel as well as a coal state, and much of West Virginia's coal is used in steel production; the demand for coal for many utilities in the Great Lakes region was far less than expected. But West Virginians had gotten out of the habit of leaving the state, and instead found their way onto the unemployment rolls. Governor Jay Rockefeller prided himself on attracting jobs to West Virginia; by early 1983 he must have felt like Sisyphus, with heavy labor ahead of him.

Presidential politics. West Virginia's partisan preferences are the legacy of two searing decades, the 1860s and 1930s. Although West Virginia stayed with the Union, parts of the state were more sympathetic to it than others, and there are Republican strongholds today—sparsely populated counties in the mountains, cities and towns along the Ohio River—dating from that period. There are also rural Democratic counties as well, like the one around Harpers Ferry, where John Brown was convicted and hanged for storming the arsenal and trying to incite a local slave rebellion. The 1930s saw the coal-mining counties not only unionized, but made heavily Democratic, to the point that the coal counties south of Charleston are one of the most Democratic parts of the nation. But Charleston and Kanawha County, a heavily industrialized area and the most populous part of the state, still go Republican as often as they do Democratic—the Civil War legacy lives on.

Nevertheless, West Virginia now is among the most Democratic of states; in 1980 it was Jimmy Carter's best state after Georgia. It was solidly Democratic in the close elections of 1948, 1960, 1968, and 1976. The presidential primary was important here only once, in 1960, when John Kennedy seized on it as an opportunity to prove he could beat Hubert Humphrey ın an all-Protestant state, spending money freely and in ways that would not be legal today. Otherwise, West Virginia sees little presidential campaigning.

Governor. The governor of West Virginia, Jay Rockefeller, has a household name and, by now, a long political career in his adopted state. Rockefeller was an expert in Asian affairs when he moved to West Virginia in 1964 to work in an antipoverty program. He decided to stay and to enter politics but—unlike his uncles, the governors of New York and Arkansas, as a Democrat rather than as a Republican. He was elected to the legislature in 1966 and to statewide office in 1968. He received his one setback in 1972, when incumbent Governor Arch Moore—one of the wiliest and most talented politicians of our times—beat him and won a second term. Moore got mileage out of calling Rockefeller a carpetbagger (one ad showed people on a New York street being asked whether they would elect as governor an outsider from West Virginia), but he won primarily because the state was prosperous and he had done a good job attracting industry and building roads. When Rockefeller was elected in 1976, that was pretty much his program too: West Virginia's needs, however ably its public officials address them, remain pretty much constant. Rockefeller used his national celebrity to promote coal and remove the sales tax on food. In 1980 he faced Moore again, and this time won. It was an affirmative endorsement of Rockefeller's record, and it also helped that he was able and willing to spend $9 million of his own money on his campaign.

Rockefeller has been mentioned as a possible presidential candidate almost from the time he ran for House of Delegates in Kanawha County. He has done very little to encourage such speculation; in 1980 he did run ads on Washington TV stations (they are the TV market for three or four West Virginia counties), but in 1982 he did not even show up at, much less try to impress the delegates at, the 1982 Democratic mid-term conference in Philadelphia. Rockefeller's project for 1984 is to run for the Senate seat being vacated by Jennings Randolph; he is likely to win if only because no one—certainly not Moore again—wants to run against a man who is popular, a member of the state's majority party, and can afford to spend $9 million on his campaign.

Senators. It was not a surprise when Jennings Randolph announced in early 1983 that he would retire from the Senate. He turned 80 in 1982, and he had won in 1978, over the ubiquitous Arch Moore, by less than 5,000 votes. Randolph has had a distinguished and successful career. He was first elected to Congress in 1932, and he was the last member of Congress to remember having served during Franklin Roosevelt's Hundred Days. Defeated for reelection in 1946, he became a lobbyist, and then was elected to the Senate in 1958. He won his last term 20 years later, with his first major media campaign; but the themes were familiar: Randolph building roads, helping West Virginia, doing something for the little guy.

For many years Randolph was chairman of the Environment and Public Works Committee. Under its old name, Public Works, this was the key pork barrel committee, and its chairman doled out dams and post offices and other federal projects to his colleagues. This was a role Randolph found congenial. A generous and amiable man, he was pleased to help his friends. An old-fashioned New Dealer, he delighted in creating jobs and helping little people. Beginning in the late 1960s, Public Works became the key Senate committee on air and water pollution laws. Randolph naturally championed the interests of West Virginia coal, and while Edmund Muskie was winning the headlines he was still careful to keep Randolph satisfied. Since the 1930s Randolph has been Congress's leading backer of projects to help the handicapped; it was he who wrote the law requiring candy stands in federal buildings to be run by blind persons. When he announced his retirement, more than 50 years after beginning his service in Congress, he was still vigorous, active, and with nary a gray hair—a happy warrior who has seen and made a lot of history.

West Virginia's most powerful politician is Senator Robert Byrd. Unhappy still to be minority, rather than majority, leader, he is nonetheless a figure of considerable importance and influence in Congress. If you look back to the beginning of his career, his rise seems most improbable. He was once a Ku Klux Klan member (he quit in 1945), he voted against civil rights laws in the House and the Senate, he was not exactly well connected with the Washington establishment. There is only one secret behind his success: hard work. He cultivated constituents in West Virginia assiduously; he still keeps card files with thousands of names and telephone numbers and calls constituents every night, to ask their opinions on issues and to find out what is happening back home. In 1969 and 1970, when Edward Kennedy was Senate majority whip, Byrd was secretary of the Senate Democratic Conference. After Kennedy was distracted from his duties by Chappaquiddick, Byrd paid meticulous attention to the petty details that can make the lives of senators easier: keeping them informed of the pace of floor debate and the scheduling of upcoming votes, helping them to get amendments before the Senate, arranging pairs, and even getting taxis. He showed his colleagues elaborate courtesy, writing them thank-you notes on the slightest pretext. It all paid off in 1971, when Byrd suddenly challenged Kennedy and, with the help of Richard Russell's deathbed proxy, beat him.

Byrd has continued to attend to details to this day. That helped him win the Senate majority leadership after Mike Mansfield retired in 1976; although Byrd obviously had the votes to beat Hubert Humphrey, he continued to seek the votes of every senator every day, even those strongly supporting Humphrey. He was less than pleased when the Democrats lost their majority in 1980, although his successor as majority leader, Howard Baker, let Byrd keep his old office. Byrd has also, from time to time, played important roles on substantive issues, usually when he has plugged away and learned the details more thoroughly than any of his colleagues. He played a critical role in unraveling the Watergate scandal: it was Byrd who got L. Patrick Gray to admit that John Dean "probably lied" about the affair, an admission that sparked Dean's determination to tell the truth.

But Byrd has not proved to be as successful a strategist as he has been a detail man. He became majority leader in a Senate where Democrats thought their majority was eternal and saw no reason to take common action on anything. Byrd, like Tip O'Neill, waited for the incoming Carter administration to establish a legislative agenda, as previous Democratic administrations had. What he got was an agenda full of issues that divided the Democrats, like energy, or were simply non-starters, like welfare reform and tax reform. After 1978, the 41 Republicans, united, could filibuster at will; Byrd, under the rules, could not stop them. The Carter administration has been criticized for its lack of conviction on issues, which led it to emphasize too many too weakly; the same criticism is sometimes made of Byrd. But it has to be added that probably no one could have led a united Democratic Party in the Senate in the years before the 1980 election, or the years after. In 1981 Byrd was unwilling to forge a common Democratic budget or tax policy, as the House Democratic leadership did; Democratic senators were too ornery, too panicked, and, finally, too obviously powerless in a Senate where Howard Baker deftly commanded a united Republican majority. Byrd made serious efforts to unite the Democrats in the early 1980s, but with varying results.

Byrd, so well suited to the mechanics of leading a disunited majority party, had great difficulty creating a united opposition. By 1983 there was talk that he might be opposed for the majority leadership if Democrats captured the majority in the 1984 elections. But no one should underestimate Byrd's talent as a vote-counter in these matters, nor his desire to win. For a while, it looked as though Byrd would have a close race in 1982. NCPAC ran TV ads against him, charging that he had no residence in West Virginia and was out of touch with the state; Congressman Cleveland Benedict spent freely in a campaign harshly critical of Byrd. But none of these attacks rang true. Instead, they boomeranged against Benedict to the point that he became one of the most unpopular figures in the state. Before Robert Byrd, no one had ever carried every county in West Virginia. In 1970, 1976, and once again in 1982, he carried every one—even though Benedict spent more than $1 million against him. Some of Byrd's Democratic colleagues may grouse about him, but the voters, who know him best, gave him a rousing endorsement.

Congressional districting. West Virginia surprised almost everyone by electing two Republican congressmen in its four districts in 1980. It surprised very few people by electing four Democrats in 1982. Benedict's Senate race gave the Democrats an easy win in his district, and in the 3d district, centered on Charleston, religious fundamentalist Mick Staton was beaten by poor people's lawyer Bob Wise. Redistricting changed the districts' boundaries slightly, but played no role in the outcome of any race.

The People Est. Pop. 1982: 1,948,000; Pop. 1980: 1,949,644, dn. 0.1% 1980–82 and up 12% 1970–80; 0.85% of U.S. total, 34th largest; voting age pop. 1,390,008; 3% Black, 1% Spanish origin. Single ancestry: 20% English, 7% German, 5% Irish, 2% Italian, 1% Dutch, Polish, French. Registered voters (1982): 948,329 Total. 631,989 D (67%); 295,419 R (31%); 20,862 other (2%). 10% with 1–3 yrs. col., 10% with 4+ yrs. col. 14.5% below poverty level. 24% housing units rented; median house value: $38,500; median monthly rent: $137. Households: 77% family, 42% with children, 65% married couples.

1982 Share of Federal Tax Burden $3,970,300,000; .66% of U.S. total, 34th largest.

1982 Share of Federal Expenditures

	Total		Non-Defense		Defense	
Total Expend	$3,998m	(0.66%)	$3,769m	(0.89%)	$229m	(0.13%)
St/Lcl Grants	772m	(0.88%)	772m	(0.88%)	0m	(0%)
Salary/Wages	257m	(0.33%)	199m	(0.73%)	58m	(0.11%)
Ind Payments	2,792m	(0.98%)	2,579m	(1.00%)	213m	(0.75%)
Procurement	168m	(0.12%)	61m	(0.19%)	106m	(0.09%)
Other Programs	9m	(0.17%)	8m	(0.15%)	1m	(2.33%)
Loan/Insurance	180m	(0.28%)	175m	(0.28%)	5m	(0.23%)

Political Lineup Governor, John D. Rockefeller IV (D). Senators, Jennings Randolph (D) and Robert C. Byrd (D). Representatives, 4 (4 D). State Senate, 34 (31 D and 3 R); State House of Delegates, 100 (87 D and 13 R).

Presidential Vote

1980	Reagan (R)	334,206	(45%)
	Carter (D)	367,462	(50%)
	Anderson (I)	31,691	(4%)
1976	Ford (R)	314,726	(42%)
	Carter (D)	435,864	(58%)

1980 Democratic Presidential Primary			*1980 Republican Presidential Primary*		
Carter	197,687	(62%)	Reagan	115,407	(84%)
Kennedy	120,247	(38%)	Bush	19,509	(14%)
			Others	3,100	(2%)

SENATORS

Sen. Jennings Randolph (D) Elected 1958, seat up 1984; b. Mar. 8, 1902, Salem; home, Elkins; Salem Col., B.A. 1924; Seventh-day Adventist.

Career Ed. Staff, *Clarksburg Daily Telegram*, 1924–25; Assoc. Ed., WV *Review*, 1925–26; Prof. and Athletic Dir., Davis & Elkins Col., 1926–32; Instructor and Business Col. Dean, Southeastern U.; U.S. House of Reps., 1933–47; Asst. to the Pres. and Dir. of Pub. Rel., Capital Airlines, 1947–48.

Offices 302 DSOB, 202-224-6472. Also Fed. Bldg., 300 3d St., Rm. 328-329, Elkins 26241, 304-636-5100.

Committees *Environment and Public Works* (Ranking Member). Subcommittee: Transportation. *Labor and Human Resources* (2d). Subcommittees: Labor; Education, Arts and Humanities; Handicapped. *Veterans' Affairs* (2d).

Group Ratings

	ADA	ACLU	COPE	CFA	LCV	LWV	NTU	NSI	COC	ACA	CSFC
1982	70	29	77	57	62	58	4	30	48	29	42
1981	60	—	77	50	56	—	18	—	33	44	41
1980	72	47	89	60	49	40	28	67	38	12	31

National Journal Ratings

	Economic		Foreign		Cultural	
1982	88%	(LIB)	64%	(LIB)	36%	(LIB)
	11%	(CONS)	35%	(CONS)	63%	(CONS)
1981	74%	(LIB)	68%	(LIB)	53%	(LIB)
	25%	(CONS)	31%	(CONS)	44%	(CONS)

Key Votes

1) Reagan 81 Budget	AGN	5) $ to El Salvador	AGN	9) Poor Pay Food Stamps	AGN
2) Reagan 81 Tax Cut	FOR	6) Saudi AWACS Sale	FOR	10) Ban Crt Busing Order	FOR
3) Bal Budget Amend	AGN	7) Ban Abortion	FOR	11) Clinch Riv Brdr Rctr	AGN
4) Gas & Road Tax	FOR	8) Nerve Gas Prod	FOR	12) Legal Services Corp	FOR

Election Results

1978 general	Jennings Randolph (D)	249,034	(50%)	($684,605)
	Arch A. Moore, Jr. (R)	244,317	(50%)	($458,823)
1978 primary	Jennings Randolph (D) unopposed			
1972 general	Jennings Randolph (D)	486,310	(66%)	($133,670)
	Louise Leonard (R)	245,531	(34%)	($45,513)

Campaign Contributions and Expenditures

	1977-78		*PACS brkdwn*		
Receipts	$732,484	Agr	$2,850	Ideo	$2,650
Expend.	$684,605	Bus	$105,450	Lbr	$120,400
Unspent	$47,876	Hlth	$5,500	Prof	$5,800

Sen. Robert C. Byrd (D) Elected 1958, seat up 1988; b. Nov. 20, 1917, North Wilkesboro, NC; home, Sophia; Beckley Col., Concord Col., Morris Harvey Col., Marshall Col., American U., JD; Baptist.

Career WV House of Reps., 1946–50; WV Senate, 1950–52; U.S. House of Reps., 1953–59; U.S. Sen. Major. Whip, 1971–77, Major. Ldr. 1978–80.

Offices 311 HSOB, 202-224-3954. Also Fed. Bldg., 500 Quarrier St., Rm. 1006, Charleston 25301, 304-342-5855.

Committees *Minority Leader. Appropriations* (2d). Subcommittees: Agriculture, Rural Development; Energy and Water Development; Interior; Labor, Health and Human Services, Education; Transportation. *Judiciary* (3d). *Rules and Administration* (3d).

Group Ratings

	ADA	ACLU	COPE	CFA	LCV	LWV	NTU	NSI	COC	ACA	CSFC
1982	60	43	67	71	69	58	9	40	48	48	44
1981	70	—	66	64	75	—	25	—	39	29	43
1980	56	47	57	53	23	30	34	30	33	15	33

National Journal Ratings

	Economic		Foreign		Cultural	
1982	68%	(LIB)	33%	(LIB)	56%	(LIB)
	31%	(CONS)	64%	(CONS)	43%	(CONS)
1981	77%	(LIB)	76%	(LIB)	41%	(LIB)
	22%	(CONS)	23%	(CONS)	58%	(CONS)

Key Votes

1) Reagan 81 Budget	FOR	5) $ to El Salvador	AGN	9) Poor Pay Food Stamps	AGN
2) Reagan 81 Tax Cut	FOR	6) Saudi AWACS Sale	AGN	10) Ban Crt Busing Order	FOR
3) Bal Budget Amend	FOR	7) Ban Abortion	AGN	11) Clinch Riv Brdr Rctr	AGN
4) Gas & Road Tax	AGN	8) Nerve Gas Prod	FOR	12) Legal Services Corp	AGN

Election Results

1982 general	Robert C. Byrd (D)	387,170	(69%)	($1,792,573)
	Cleveland K. (Cleve) Benedict (R) .	173,910	(31%)	($1,098,218)
1982 primary	Robert C. Byrd (D)	210,523	(100%)	
1976 general	Robert C. Byrd (D)	338,444	(100%)	($94,335)

Campaign Contributions and Expenditures

1979-82		Direct Cont. 81-82			PACS brkdwn		
Receipts	$1,869,580	Indiv	$980,858	Agr	$33,000	Ideo	$102,000
Expend.	$1,792,573	Party	$17,500	Bus	$277,875	Lbr	$260,200
Unspent	$225,313	PACS	$707,641	Hlth	$10,250	Prof	$18,100

Indirect Party Expend: $80,000   *Indep Expend:* For: $10,034 (NRA) Agn: $270,168 (NCPAC)

GOVERNOR

Gov. John D. (Jay) **Rockefeller IV** (D) Elected 1976, term expires Jan. 1985; b. June 18, 1937, New York, NY; International Christian U., Tokyo, 1957–60, Harvard U., B.A. 1961; Baptist.

Career Natl. Advisory Cncl. of Peace Corps, 1961, Asst. to Peace Corps Dir., R. Sargent Shriver, 1962; Staff Mbr., Pres. Comm. on Juvenile Delinquency and Youth Crime, 1964–66; WV House of Delegates, 1966–68; Secy. of State for WV, 1968–72; Pres., WV Wesleyan Col., 1972–76.

Offices Charleston 25305, 304-348-2000.

Election Results

1980 gen.	John D. (Jay) Rockefeller IV (D) . . .	401,863	(54%)
	Arch A. Moore, Jr. (R)	337,240	(45%)
1980 prim.	John D. (Jay) Rockefeller IV (D) . . .	240,550	(78%)
	H. John Rogers (D)	70,452	(22%)
1976 gen.	John D. (Jay) Rockefeller IV (D) . . .	495,600	(66%)
	Cecil H. Underwood (R)	253,398	(34%)

FIRST DISTRICT

West Virginia's northern panhandle is part of the troubled steel belt of western Pennsylvania and northeastern Ohio; in fact, the panhandle sticks straight in between the two states. This is probably the least isolated part of West Virginia. The terrain here is hilly rather than mountainous, and not far away from Pittsburgh, Cleveland, and Columbus. Along the Ohio River here are giant blast furnaces in Wheeling and Weirton, now mostly cold; workers in 1983 were trying to buy the Weirton works. With the Pittsburgh area, the panhandle is one of the leading glassmaking areas of the country as well. In the early 1970s people here worried about pollution; the air by some measures was the dirtiest in the country. In the early 1980s they worried about the economy, and what they were going to do for a living; the factories were quiet, and it began to appear to people that the props underneath their communities and their personal lives had been kicked out.

The panhandle forms about one-third of West Virginia's 1st congressional district. Another third is in the industrialized Monongahela valley, directly south of Pittsburgh, around Clarksburg and Fairmont. This also is coal, steel, and glassmaking country. Finally, about one-third live in the more rural and less industrial hills along the Ohio River, or in the city of Parkersburg. The Panhandle and the Monongahela valley are ordinarily Democratic, though vestiges of Civil War Republicanism remain; the area along the Ohio tends to be Republican.

The incumbent congressman here, Alan Mollohan, is one of two sons of previous West Virginia congressmen who won seats themselves in 1982. His father, Robert Mollohan, was elected in 1952 and 1954, defeated by Arch Moore in 1956, then won the seat again when Moore was elected governor in 1968, and kept it until his retirement at age 73 in 1982. He was an old-time Democrat with a liberal record on economic issues and a record as a supporter of military spending increases on the House Armed Services Committee. Alan Mollohan did not win the seat automatically. His main problem was that from 1973 to 1982 he was a Washington, D.C., lawyer, working for, among others, Consolidation Coal. He

WEST VIRGINIA — Congressional Districts, Counties, and Selected Places — (4 Districts)

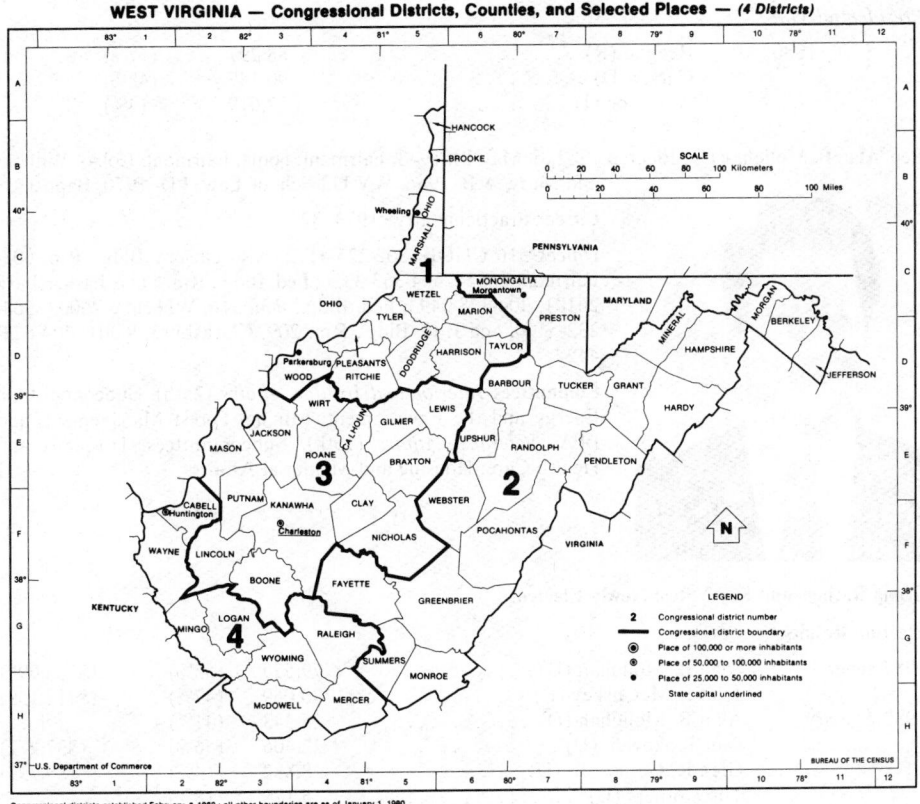

Congressional districts established February 8, 1982 ; all other boundaries are as of January 1, 1980.

returned to Fairmont and established a base in the Monongahela valley, but primary opponent Dan Tonkovich carried the southern panhandle and the Ohio River counties.

Mollohan had a game opponent in the general election, John McCuskey, a 34-year-old state legislator and former Republican state chairman who had considerable support in the United Mine Workers. McCuskey carried his home county around Clarksburg, but the Democratic trend in the rest of the district was too much for him; Mollohan carried Clarksburg, the panhandle, ran even in Parkersburg, and even carried one Ohio River county.

This is one congressman for whom the first term should be very important. The breaks were with him in 1982; to establish a long congressional career, he now needs to make breaks of his own. He got a seat on the Interior Committee and on subcommittees on Energy and the Environment and on Mining, Forest Management, and Bonneville Power Administration. He will be working to sew up the support of the United Mine Workers and to try to demonstrate some ability to help the ailing economy of this district.

The People Pop. 1980: 488,568, up 6% 1970–80; voting age pop. 353,283; 2% Black, 1% Span. orig. 24% housing units rented. Median owner $38,200; renter $137. Households: 76% family, 40% with children, 65% married couples.

Presidential Vote

1980	Reagan (R)	88,297	(47%)
	Carter (D)	90,147	(48%)
	Anderson (I)	7,619	(4%)

Rep. Alan B. Mollohan (D) Elected 1982; b. May 14, 1943, Fairmont; home, Fairmont; Col. of William and Mary, A.B. 1966, WV U., Sch. of Law, J.D. 1970; Baptist.

Career Practicing atty., 1973–82.

Offices 516 CHOB, 202-225-4172. Also Deveny Bldg., Rm. 603, Fairmont 26554, 304-363-3356; Fed. Bldg., Rm. 1117, Parkersburg 26101, 304-428-0493; Fed. Bldg., Rm. 316, Wheeling 26003, 304-232-5390; and P. O. Bldg., Rm. 209, Clarksburg 26301, 304-623-4422.

Committees *Interior and Insular Affairs* (25th). Subcommittees: Energy and the Environment; Mining, Forest Management, and BPA. *Veterans' Affairs* (15th). Subcommittees: Hospitals and Health Care; Housing and Memorial Affairs.

Group Ratings and Key Votes: Newly Elected

Election Results

1982 general	Alan B. Mollohan (D)	79,529	(53%)	($202,099)
	John F. McCuskey (R)	70,069	(47%)	($213,159)
1982 primary	Alan B. Mollohan (D)	25,543	(41%)	
	Dan Tonkovich (D)	22,406	(36%)	($37,272)
	Glen R. Gainer, Jr. (D)	8,882	(14%)	($9,797)
	Three others (D)	5,175	(8%)	
1980 general	Robert H. Mollohan (D)	107,471	(64%)	($57,941)
	Joe Bartlett (R)	61,438	(36%)	($60,925)

Campaign Contributions and Expenditures

1981-82		*Direct Cont. 81-82*			*PACS brkdwn*			
Receipts	$206,009	Indiv	$92,541	Agr	$5,750	Ideo	$2,500
Expend.	$202,099	Party	$11,395	Bus	$22,000	Lbr	$38,300
Unspent	$3,909	PACS	$78,119	Hlth	$2,750	Prof	$1,500
		Cand	$18,050				

SECOND DISTRICT

The 2d congressional district of West Virginia occupies the eastern part of the state and contains the most mountainous and sparsely populated counties of West Virginia. The district extends from Harpers Ferry, not far from Washington, D.C., where John Brown's raiders seized the arsenal and tried to free the slaves in 1859, south and west to Fayette County, near the state capital of Charleston, and not all that far from the Kentucky line. In the northwestern part of the district, not far from Pittsburgh, is the 2d's only significant city, Morgantown, with a population of just 27,000—part of the industrial Monongahela valley and home of West Virginia University.

This part of West Virginia has some of the loveliest scenery in the United States: gentle hills and rugged mountains, stands of green trees and vistas that stretch to far horizons—"almost heaven," in the words of the song. Yet in most counties you will find, amid scenery primeval and rural, sudden evidence of industrialization: a pulp mill or charcoal factory in a clearing scraped out of the forest; a small factory town, built close to a river in a cleft bordered with hills, its houses built in the same 1910s style as in the factory towns of Pittsburgh; the entrance to an underground coal mine or the exposed brown earth of a strip mine scar. All this looks ugly to the eye used to Sierra Club calendars, but we should remember what these towns looked like to the people who first lived in them, when they were built rapidly, or to those who have been living there in the prosperous 1970s. For these people, these towns and mines represented a chance to live better than they could have off a farm in the West Virginia hills, and at the same time to remain in the hills they loved rather than move to Akron or Detroit or Pittsburgh to make a living. The recession of the early 1980s has brought difficult times, and difficult choices, back to these hills again.

Politically, the 2d congressional district is a patchwork quilt of partisan preferences. Coal counties have generally been Democratic since the 1930s; counties with relatively few miners trace their partisan ancestry back to the Civil War. The balance generally favors the Democrats, but not overwhelmingly; in many elections, this is the least Democratic of West Virginia's four districts.

The current congressman, Harley Staggers, Jr., is the son of the man who represented this district from 1948 to 1980, and who for more than a decade chaired what now is the House Energy and Commerce Committee. The succession was not automatic, however. When Staggers, Sr., retired in 1980, his son lost the Democratic primary to state Senator Pat Hamilton, who in turn lost the general election to Republican Cleveland Benedict. Benedict, a Procter & Gamble heir, could afford to spend liberally on his races, and he might have held onto the district; but he ran for the Senate, and was devastatingly defeated by Senator Robert Byrd. In the meantime, Harley Staggers, Jr., sought and won a state Senate seat, and when it came time to file for the 2d district in 1982, he had no competition for the Democratic nomination.

That turned out to be tantamount to victory. The Republicans again had a rich self-financing candidate, but he was unable to carry a single one of the district's 20 counties. Staggers is a member of the Agriculture Committee; he was unable to get on his father's old committee, which is now the most sought after committee assignment in the House. Nevertheless, Staggers seems to be in good shape for reelection. Conceivably, Benedict could run here again, but the dimensions of his defeat by Byrd suggest a personal repudiation over and above a partisan loss.

The People   Pop. 1980: 487,438, up 21% 1970–80; voting age pop. 350,168; 3% Black, 1% Span. orig. 23% housing units rented. Median owner $36,600; renter $134. Households: 76% family, 41% with children, 64% married couples.

Presidential Vote

1980	Reagan (R)	89,481	(47%)
	Carter (D)	90,639	(48%)
	Anderson (I)	8,954	(5%)

Rep. Harley O. Staggers, Jr. (D) Elected 1982; b. Feb. 22, 1951, Washington, DC; home, Keyser; Harvard U., B.A. 1974, WV U., J.D. 1977; Roman Catholic.

Career WV Asst. Atty. Gen., 1977–79; WV Senate, 1980–82; Practicing atty., 1980–82.

Offices 1504 LHOB, 202-225-4331. Also P.O. Box 1096, Keyser 26726, 304-788-6311.

Committees Agriculture (21st). Subcommittees: Department Operations, Research, and Foreign Agriculture; Domestic Marketing, Consumer Relations, and Nutrition; Forests, Family Farms, and Energy. *Veterans' Affairs* (17th). Subcommittees: Hospitals and Health Care; Oversight and Investigations.

Group Ratings and Key Votes: Newly Elected

Election Results

1982 general	Harley O. Staggers, Jr. (D)	87,904	(64%)	($158,806)
	J. D. Hinkle, Jr. (R)	49,413	(36%)	($535,796)
1982 primary	Harley O. Staggers, Jr. (D)	40,194	(100%)	
1980 general	Cleveland K. (Cleve) Benedict (R) .	102,805	(56%)	($231,377)
	Pat R. Hamilton (D)	80,940	(44%)	($447,450)

Campaign Contributions and Expenditures

1981-82		Direct Cont. 81-82		PACS brkdwn			
Receipts	$159,493	Indiv	$28,751	Agr	$4,500	Ideo	$1,500
Expend.	$158,806	Party	$6,500	Bus	$11,975	Lbr	$67,900
Unspent	$685	PACS	$92,857	Hlth	$1,500	Prof	$1,500
		Cand	$28,171				

THIRD DISTRICT

Charleston is West Virginia's capital, the center of its largest metropolitan area, and the state's leading commercial center. Along the banks of the Kanawha River (pronounced "kan-AW" locally) stands the Capitol, one of the largest and most beautiful in the country. But a little more typical of Charleston are the large Union Carbide plants a little farther downriver. Like most West Virginia cities, Charleston is situated in a narrow river valley, hemmed in by mountains; so situated, the city is a victim of smog that can rival that of Los Angeles. It is primarily an industrial city, with large chemical plants. Although there are a few skyscrapers here, the country atmosphere still prevails; there are not a lot of management personnel here, and the elite of West Virginia public life form a small surface layer over a larger population which, while often liberal on economic issues, is ordinarily very conservative on cultural issues.

Charleston and surrounding Kanawha County are the population centers and political pivot of West Virginia's 3d congressional district. Upriver in the mountains is coal mining country, the kind of hollows where Jay Rockefeller lived when he first came to West Virginia as an antipoverty worker. The territory below Charleston, down to the Ohio River, is less mountainous and less densely populated. The coal counties are usually heavily Democratic; the Ohio River counties retain Republican leanings which go back to the days when West

Virginia became a state during the Civil War. Charleston itself often leans a little more Republican than Democratic. In 1980, for example, when West Virginia was one of the six states to give a plurality to Jimmy Carter, Kanawha County was almost dead even.

This was a solidly Democratic district for many years—from 1926 to 1980—and may very well be again. The one time it went Republican, in 1980, the result may have been produced less by Republican strength (Carter carried the district) than by the problems of the Democratic incumbent. After he won a 1980 special election he took a vacation, while Congress was in session; after he fired one attractive aide, his wife was revealed to have written a memo insisting that he hire only homely women. The Republican, Mick Staton, got his start in politics campaigning against allegedly pornographic textbooks, and liked to say that he and President Reagan were called by God to help lead the country. In Staton's case, the call turned out to be temporary; in 1982 he won only 42% of the vote here, and carried only two of 14 counties.

The new congressman, Bob Wise, has quite a different style. Well connected and well educated, he has nevertheless had the career of an insurgent. He ran a law firm geared to low- and middle-income clients; led a movement to force coal companies to pay higher taxes; unseated the state Senate president in the 1980 Democratic primary; and beat the House majority leader and the former Kanawha County sheriff in the 1982 congressional primary. Running in a bleak recession year, he captured the attention and the imagination of voters here in an area where politics is populated mostly by dull hacks and cynical careerists.

How will an insurgent like Wise fare in the House? Pretty well, if he picks his fights as carefully as he has in West Virginia. He has a seat on the Public Works Committee, which other West Virginians might use to get local projects for the district and defend the interests of the coal industry; Wise may do these things, but he also seems the type to try to upset someone else's pet project as well. With this district, and his politics, and after winning at age 34, Wise has the potential for a long and notable career in Congress.

The People   Pop. 1980: 486,112, up 10% 1970–80; voting age pop. 347,147; 3% Black, 1% Span. orig. 25% housing units rented. Median owner $43,500; renter $150. Households: 78% family, 42% with children, 67% married couples.

Presidential Vote

1980	Reagan (R)	89,359	(47%)
	Carter (D)	93,700	(49%)
	Other	8,863	(5%)

Rep. Robert E. (Bob) Wise (D) Elected 1982; b. Jan. 6, 1948, Washington, DC; home, Charleston; Duke U., B.A. 1970, Tulane Sch. of Law, J.D. 1975; Episcopal.

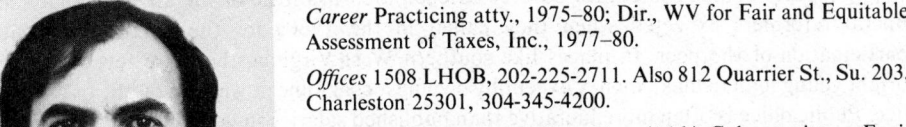

Career Practicing atty., 1975–80; Dir., WV for Fair and Equitable Assessment of Taxes, Inc., 1977–80.

Offices 1508 LHOB, 202-225-2711. Also 812 Quarrier St., Su. 203, Charleston 25301, 304-345-4200.

Committees *Government Operations* (16th). Subcommittees: Environment, Energy, and Natural Resources; Government Activities and Transportation; Government Information, Justice, and Agriculture. *Public Works and Transportation* (32d). Subcommittees: Economic Development; Investigations and Oversight. *Select Committee on Aging* (37th). Subcommittee: Housing and Consumer Interests.

Election Results

1982 general	Robert E. (Bob) Wise (D)	84,619	(58%)	($137,299)
	David Michael (Mick) Staton (R) .	60,844	(42%)	($254,056)
1982 primary	Robert E. (Bob) Wise (D)	26,016	(45%)	
	Roger W. Tompkins (D)	16,600	(29%)	
	G. Kemp Melton (D)	15,351	(26%)	
1980 general	David Michael (Mick) Staton (R) .	94,583	(53%)	($155,579)
	John G. Hutchinson (D)	84,980	(47%)	($246,961)

Campaign Contributions and Expenditures

1982		Direct Cont. 1982				PACS brkdwn		
Receipts	$138,163	Indiv	$44,048	Agr	$—	Ideo		$17,500
Expend.	$137,299	Party	$4,500	Bus	$550	Lbr		$53,800
Unspent	$861	PACS	$82,716	Hlth	$2,000	Prof		$1,000
		Cand	$3,000					

Indirect Party Expend: $1,198

FOURTH DISTRICT

The 4th congressional district of West Virginia is the southern part of the state. This is coal country. The eight counties of the 4th district have produced more bituminous coal over the years than any other single congressional district in the United States. Not quite all the district is mining country, however; it also contains Huntington, with 63,000 people one of the state's largest cities, a railroad junction and manufacturing center on the Ohio River. But from the banks of the Ohio the mountains rise steeply, and the heart of the 4th is in the small coal towns sitting in clefts and along rivers between the mountainsides. This was a boom area around the turn of the century, with lots of in-migration, mostly from the South. But after World War II employment in the mines declined drastically, and continued to do so for 20 years. The population of the counties now in the 4th declined from 579,000 in 1950 to 437,000 in 1970. In the 1970s the economy in this area rebounded somewhat, as coal prices rose and mining—at least strip mining—actively increased, and by 1980 the population was up to 487,000. But even then the number of coal mining jobs was still far from its old peak, and of existing jobs an increasing proportion are non-union. Then in the early 1980s the lengthy recession began to affect the coal counties, resulting in high unemployment again here, and reviving worries that this area might again be in pervasive decline.

The politics of this sometimes poverty-stricken area has little of the altruism that some liberal reformers expected when they called in the 1960s for the maximum feasible participation of the poor. In places like southern West Virginia, there are few ways for a bright young man to make money except by owning a coal mine or winning public or union office. Public office is often more lucrative than published salaries suggest; corruption has been common here, and there are still counties where one is still supposed to be able to buy votes. Poor people see politics less as a way of helping poor people generally—who can abolish poverty in West Virginia?—than as a way of advancing themselves personally. In the struggle to get ahead, the ordinary politician here has little concern for matters like unsafe mine conditions, black lung disease, or air and water pollution.

That is not the kind of representation the 4th district has had in Congress for some time, however. For 18 years its congressman was Ken Hechler, a former professor who shopped around for a safe district, found one, and had the courage to, among other things, oppose the leadership of United Mine Workers president Tony Boyle after his opponent, Joseph Yablonski, was murdered. The current congressman, Nick Joe Rahall II, is scion of a family that owns radio and television stations in such widely dispersed locales as Beckley, West Virginia, and St. Petersburg, Florida. Rahall has been willing to spend his own money in campaigns; that helped him win the 1976 primary (when Hechler was running for governor) and the general election (in which Hechler ran as an Independent). Since then Rahall has won with ease: in 1982 he got 81% of the vote.

In the House Rahall is a member of the Interior and Public Works Committees. He is solidly liberal on economic and foreign issues; on cultural matters, and particularly on environmental issues, his record is mixed. He wants to see lots of West Virginia coal mined, but he is not totally insensitive to the demands of the environment either. With the three other West Virginia seats held by freshmen, he became the dean of the state's House delegation at 33. He is close to a Public Works subcommittee chairmanship: on Surface Transportation he is outranked only by Glenn Anderson of California (who turns 71 in 1984) and Bob Edgar (who has announced he'll seek other office that year). Rahall is also a member of Standards of Official Conduct, the House Ethics Committee. With an utterly safe seat, he will likely remain in the House for years, unless he runs for the Senate.

The People Pop. 1980: 487,526, up 11% 1970–80; voting age pop. 339,410; 6% Black, 1% Span. orig. 25% housing units rented. Median owner $36,000; renter $135. Households: 79% family, 45% with children, 66% married couples.

Presidential Vote

1980	Reagan (R)	67,069	(40%)
	Carter (D)	92,976	(56%)
	Other	6,255	(4%)

Rep. Nick Joe Rahall II (D) Elected 1976; b. May 20, 1949, Beckley; home, Beckley; Duke U., B.A. 1971, Geo. Wash. U., 1973; Presbyterian.

Career Sales Rep. and Mbr. of the Bd., Rahall Communications Corp.; Pres., Mountaineer Tour and Travel Agency.

Offices 440 CHOB, 202-225-3452. Also Bair Bldg., Main and N. Fayette Sts., Beckley 25801, 304-252-5000.

Committees *Interior and Insular Affairs* (12th). Subcommittees: Energy and the Environment; Mining, Forest Management, and BPA. *Public Works and Transportation* (11th). Subcommittees: Aviation; Surface Transportation; Water Resources. *Standards of Official Conduct* (2d).

Group Ratings

	ADA	ACLU	COPE	CFA	LCV	LWV	NTU	NSI	COC	ACA	CSFC
1982	70	62	84	69	56	50	18	11	25	6	25
1981	75	—	82	71	53	—	10	—	11	30	34
1980	67	50	94	64	41	70	21	33	70	13	31

National Journal Ratings

	Economic		Foreign		Cultural	
1982	77%	(LIB)	76%	(LIB)	65%	(LIB)
	23%	(CONS)	24%	(CONS)	34%	(CONS)
1981	80%	(LIB)	83%	(LIB)	60%	(LIB)
	20%	(CONS)	17%	(CONS)	39%	(CONS)

Key Votes

1) Reagan 81 Budget	AGN	5) Incr SS Rtmt Age	AGN	9) Poor Pay Food Stamps	AGN
2) Reagan 81 Tax Cut	AGN	6) Saudi AWACS Sale	FOR	10) Ban Crt Busing Order	AGN
3) Bal Budget Amend	AGN	7) $ for MX Missile	AGN	11) Auto Local Content	FOR
4) Gas & Road Tax	FOR	8) Nerve Gas Prod	AGN	12) Nuclear Arms Freeze	FOR

Election Results

1982 general	Nick Joe Rahall II (D)	91,184	(81%)	($192,414)
	Homer L. Harris (R)	22,054	(19%)	($0)
1982 primary	Nick Joe Rahall II (D)	53,440	(100%)	
1980 general	Nick Joe Rahall II (D)	117,595	(77%)	($155,285)
	Winton G. Covey, Jr. (R)	36,020	(23%)	($0)

Campaign Contributions and Expenditures

1981-82		Direct Cont. 81-82		PACS brkdwn			
Receipts	$199,694	Indiv	$94,338	Agr	$7,450	Ideo	$1,450
Expend.	$192,414	Party	$100	Bus	$43,925	Lbr	$44,000
Unspent	$34,996	PACS	$95,447	Hlth	$1,850	Prof	$1,190

WISCONSIN

Wisconsin is a state of political anomalies. It spawned both Bob LaFollette and the Progressive movement and Joe McCarthy and his campaign against communism in high places. Richard Nixon carried Wisconsin, the state where the Republican Party was founded, three times; yet in the 1970s this became one of the most heavily Democratic states at all levels. It provided 11 crucial electoral votes for Jimmy Carter in 1976 and came close to supporting him in 1980 as well. Wisconsin is heavily industrial, although it is also the nation's leading producer of dairy products; a heavily urban state, yet one whose lake and forest country has been its fastest-growing area since 1970.

Wisconsin owes much of its uniqueness to the German and Scandinavian immigrants who comprised the majority of its early settlers. Here, as in Minnesota and North Dakota, the immigrants left a distinctive political stamp; but while those states seem heavily Scandinavian, Wisconsin was and is profoundly German—a kind of lake-dotted Mitteleuropa in the Middle West. Wisconsin was admitted to the Union in 1848, and the failed revolutions in German-speaking Europe that year led many young Germans to migrate to the United States, and a lot of them found their way to Wisconsin. They found the Republican Party of the 1850s and 1860s attractive. They too abhorred slavery; they welcomed the free lands the Republicans were promising in the Homestead Act, the free educations they were promising in setting up land grant colleges, the transportation routes (now called infrastructure) they were building by subsidizing railroad builders.

Yet when the Republican Party began to represent stand-patism, the Germans of Wisconsin were ready for an alternative. One was provided by "Fighting Bob" LaFollette. Elected governor in 1900, he completely revamped the state government before going to the Senate in 1906. LaFollette was a national figure by 1912; he wanted to run for president that year as a Progressive, but was shoved aside by Theodore Roosevelt. In the Senate he led insurgent reformers and vitriolically opposed American entry into World War I. In 1924 he ran for president under the banner of the Progressive Party and won 18% of the nation's votes. It was the best third-party showing of the last 60 years, and the assemblage of a constituency (he was strongest in the northern tier from Wisconsin to Washington, along the West Coast, and in some hitherto Republican factory towns like Cleveland).

LaFollette's sons maintained the traditions of Wisconsin's progressivism. Robert LaFollette, Jr., served in the Senate from 1925 to 1947, and Philip LaFollette was governor of Wisconsin from 1935 to 1939. During the 1930s the LaFollettes ran on the Progressive Party line in Wisconsin and dreamed of forming a national third party. But the onset of World War II destroyed the plans of these isolationist reformers. In 1946 Senator LaFollette, busy with congressional reorganization in Washington, was upset in the Republican primary by one Joseph McCarthy.

How did the same state produce such different politicians at about the same time? Part of the answer lies in Wisconsin's German heritage. As Samuel Lubell once pointed out, much of the impetus for isolationism before Pearl Harbor and for anticommunism after 1945 came from German-Americans who dreaded a war against Germany and—although they supported the war when it did come—still felt underneath that we ought to have been fighting Communist Russia instead. The LaFollettes articulated strong opposition to war with Germany; when they declined to be articulate anticommunists, the Wisconsin electorate sought other politicians who would be. The strength of these underlying beliefs and voters' reluctance to acknowledge them produced the sort of bitterness and sense of betrayal that animated McCarthy's followers (although McCarthy himself seems to have been simply an opportunist, seeking his political fortune where he could). In retrospect, what is surprising about that era is not the vitriolic tone that dominated our politics in the early 1950s, but how quickly it dissipated after the war in Korea ended in 1953 and McCarthy himself was censured by the Senate in 1954. When McCarthy died in 1957, he was no longer the leader of a movement, but an ailing politician facing defeat in the next off-year election; as it happened, his seat was won, and has been held ever since, by Democrat William Proxmire.

Proxmire was one member of a group of liberal Democrats, headquartered in Madison and associated in some vague way with the University of Wisconsin, the *Progressive,* and the *Madison Capital-Times.* The Democrats all ran for various offices in the early and middle 1950s, and were beaten badly; then, after 1957, they came to dominate the state's politics. Proxmire was the first to win a major race, when he beat former Governor Walter Kohler in the special election to replace McCarthy. Gaylord Nelson was elected governor in 1958 and won the first of three Senate terms in 1962. Patrick Lucey was elected governor in 1970 and 1974; Robert Kastenmeier won the 2d district House seat in 1958 and has held it ever since. They have lost some elections since then, but only a few—the governorship in 1964, 1966, 1968, and 1978; a Senate race in 1980—and in the 1970s seemed to cinch solid control of the legislature.

Why has Wisconsin moved slowly to the left in years when the nation has, if anything, moved to the right? One reason is that its own economic base, which left the state rather smugly satisfied with the status quo in the 1950s, now is not quite so secure. It used to seem so: Wisconsin specialized in providing the nation with basic beverages like milk and beer, commodities like cheese and paper, and basic machinery like that engineered in big factories in Milwaukee and the other smaller cities along Lake Michigan. But these industries have not grown as fast as the economy as a whole in an America which has become more upscale (boosting wine sales while beer holds even), less family-oriented (producing fewer children and less demand for milk), and more high tech (making the old factories obsolete or inefficient). Now Wisconsin residents are worried, at least a little, about their state's economic future, and are more inclined to believe they need government aid, assistance, and guidance.

The other reason for the shift in attitudes here has been the shift in cultural patterns of living. Wisconsin is part of that northern tier of states which have been willing to accept, and sometimes eager to embrace, new lifestyles. It has been strongly in favor of protecting the environment, since Gaylord Nelson began stressing that issue in the 1950s; environmentalists here typically are not rich aristocrats seeking to preserve the habitats of rarely seen birds, but people who, like Nelson himself, are hunters and fishermen who love the outdoors and want to keep it available to all. Wisconsin has also been skeptical about American military involvements abroad and about government attempts to enforce traditional morality at home. It remains, statistically, a rather family-oriented state, but seems comfortable with untraditional attitudes—perhaps because here, out in this cold midwestern state, no one seems quite so closely threatened by the singles lifestyles of Manhattan or the Sunset Strip. In 1972 Wisconsin was one of the few states to shift toward, rather than away from, the Democratic candidacy of George McGovern; in 1976 it went Democratic, for the first time in the last four close presidential elections; even in 1980 Democrats remained competitive here at all levels.

Governor. Wisconsin's basic views on issues are shared by its new governor, Anthony Earl. He is a product of the state's 1970s politics, a former state legislator who narrowly won a three-candidate Democratic primary, beating in the process Martin Schreiber, the acting governor after Lucey moved to Mexico, and then winning the general election with ease. Earl ran explicitly on a platform of big government and more taxes. He believes that the things government does for people, particularly education and helping the helpless, are worth the cost. And he believes that Wisconsin does not have to have the lowest levels of taxes to get new jobs. The state already has major assets—a high-skill work force, good transportation, an excellent educational system, and plentiful access to fresh water—which in his view make its higher wages and taxes worth the cost to many investors. That view is shared, evidently, by most voters here, and by the legislature; and it will have a fair chance to be tested during Earl's governorship.

Senators. Wisconsin's senior official now is William Proxmire; indeed, he is now one of the senior members of the Senate. This is not a result many of his colleagues of 20 years ago would have greeted with equanimity; Proxmire was seen then as an uncooperative maverick with a penchant for lost causes. But his hard work, and perhaps his very maverick ways, have turned some of his lost causes into sacred cows. The turning point in his career probably came in 1970, when he took on the Nixon administration proposal to finance a supersonic transport. His opponents were the administration, Boeing, and the two powerful and savvy senators from Washington, Warren Magnuson and Henry Jackson, and he beat them all. The vast cost overruns and huge losses of the British-French Concorde seem to justify Proxmire's instinct that the SST was a loser. Since then he has taken on defense contractors and social scientists, the Pentagon and HHS, even the Congress itself. His monthly "golden fleece" award for wasting federal money has become a Washington tradition.

Since 1970 Proxmire has served six years as chairman of the Banking Committee, a practical-minded body with a very practical jurisdiction; he served two years as ranking Democrat on the Appropriations Committee before John Stennis decided in 1983 to exercise his right to that position under the seniority system, making Proxmire ranking Democrat on Banking. If the Democrats regain control of the Senate, Proxmire will chair one of these committees and, in the end, perhaps both.

Proxmire has a reputation in some quarters as a liberal; actually, he is more of a pinchpenny. He is consistently rated one of the best senators by the National Taxpayers Union, which simply notes whether members vote for or against every spending issue. In his private life he prizes discipline and hard work. He runs four miles from his home to the Capitol every morning, and prefers to stand rather than sit at a desk. He is in superb health and looks years younger than his age. He has an utter disdain for the camaraderie that most politicians enjoy, and is ready to irk the most powerful colleague over the slightest principle; he makes himself exceedingly unpopular by fighting against salary increases (he is independently wealthy himself) and against the proposed gymnasium in the new Hart Senate Office Building (after Proxmire won, Howard Baker closed a small shower room where Proxmire dressed after running to work).

On non-spending issues Proxmire is not necessarily liberal either. On cultural issues, he is a conservative—against busing, for example. On foreign policy issues, he lines up usually with liberals, but in large part because he opposes spending by the Pentagon. In his committee areas, Proxmire has not been a force for increased spending on housing, and he was a initial skeptic rather than supporter of federal loan guarantees to New York City and the Chrysler Corporation. On Appropriations he is less effective in shaping an overall budget than he might be, because he concentrates on opposing just about every spending item, regardless of importance. (The major exception, naturally, is on dairy price supports: Proxmire is solidly for them.) And this is the major criticism that can be made of his career: that he is a nitpicker, not a man who can move government in a major way in the direction he wants.

At home Proxmire remains one of the most popular and invincible senators. With his incredible energy, he has continued to work the state hard; the saying is that you can't get into a Green Bay Packers' football game without shaking Proxmire's hand. His reputation as a budget-cutter is helpful in the frugal Upper Midwest and his skepticism about defense budgets has not hurt in a state that has virtually no defense industry or military bases. The numbers suggest, however, that Proxmire's appeal is fading a little: in 1982, at age 67, he was reelected with 64% of the vote—an outstanding percentage but below the 71% and 72% he received in the two preceding elections. That's still an excellent performance, and just about everyone in Wisconsin assumes that Proxmire wants to and will win another six-year term in 1988.

Wisconsin's other senator, although still far less well known, has won his own upset victories, both in Wisconsin and in Washington. He is Robert Kasten, a Republican elected to the House in 1974 and 1976, the loser in the gubernatorial primary in 1978, and the conqueror of Senator Gaylord Nelson in 1980. Kasten owed that victory to his espousal of the Republican ideas that were popular and in the air that year; he was helped by the fact that

Nelson had little of the personal ambition and motivation that keeps so many candidates working overtime.

In the Senate Kasten sits on the Budget and Appropriations Committees; after a rather brief apprenticeship in government, he became potentially one of the key shapers of macroeconomic policy in the richest nation in the world. Actually, Kasten was more a follower than a leader on many budget and spending issues, but he did not always follow the same lead. Initially he tended to go along with Budget Chairman Pete Domenici and Majority Leader Howard Baker; sometimes, however, he would go along with conservative Bill Armstrong.

But Kasten has also proved himself a notable leader. In 1982 Kasten was the leading opponent of withholding from savings and brokerage accounts, and lost to Bob Dole on the issue. But he worked closely with the banking lobby and in 1983 emerged in control of the Senate on this issue. The bankers inspired, with misleading propaganda, an outpouring of thousands of letters to Capitol Hill, and Kasten had the commitment of a majority of senators on the issue. He tied up the Senate in early 1983 and seemed to hold the Social Security reform bill as hostage; he agreed to let it pass for a promise of a vote on his measure in April. There was some more face-saving compromise—not only Dole, but President Reagan came out against Kasten's position—but Kasten essentially won. Withholding was put off until 1987, and most senators would bet that it will never happen at all.

Kasten has shown solid political skills, including the ability to stand up under heavy pressure. His own political past, however, is limited. He won his first offices by running well-organized campaigns, with good financing and lots of volunteers, in Republican primaries. But he is very much the product of a country club atmosphere. He comes from the richest suburbs, and got involved in a civil suit over some investments he made. On the savings withholding issue, he was able to make a connection between the lives of ordinary people and the concerns you hear voiced when people in expensive vacation condominiums begin talking about tax shelters and federal regulators. But can he do so on a broad range of issues, in a way that will be attractive or even comprehensible to Wisconsin voters? Kasten is, evidently, willing to take considerable risks to advance what he believes in, and some of those risks may make it more difficult for him to hold onto this seat when it comes up in 1986.

Congressional districting. Wisconsin's congressional district lines were drawn according to a bipartisan plan agreed to by Democrat David Obey and Republican James Sensenbrenner. Interestingly, Obey and Sensenbrenner, at different times, have helped their colleagues and given the hard tasks to themselves: Obey put himself in the same district with a 30-year Republican veteran in 1972, and Sensenbrenner added the Democratic city of Sheboygan to his district in 1982. Both survived handily.

Presidential politics. Even as Wisconsin has become more Democratic in national elections, it has become less influential in Democratic pre-convention politics. Its primary in early April used to be one of the nation's earliest showcases; now more than a dozen states have primaries before it, most notably Illinois, which is also in the Midwest and is much larger. The last time Wisconsin was at all important was in 1976 when Morris Udall was barely edged out by Jimmy Carter, but it was overshadowed even then by the New York primary the same day. For 1984, the national Democratic Party threatens to refuse to seat Wisconsin's delegation unless the state abandons its open primary. Wisconsin is reluctant: the lack of party registration was one of the LaFollette reforms, and the open primary has the quite sensible justification that voters, very few of whom feel the strong allegiance that party registration implies, should be free to vote for the candidate they want regardless of party. But this was one of the few issues which Democratic reformers and regulars of the 1970s could agree on, and so Wisconsin may have to change.

The People Est. Pop. 1982: 4,765,000; Pop. 1980: 4,705,767, up 1.3% 1980–82 and up 6.5% 1970–80; 2.1% of U.S. total, 16th largest; 3.2% Black, 1% Spanish origin, 1% American Indian. Single ancestry: 24% German, 4% Polish, 3% English, Norwegian, 2% Irish, 1% Italian, Swedish, Dutch, French. Registered voters (1982): 1,787,799 Total. No party registration. 15% with 1–3 yrs. col., 15% with 4+ yrs. col. 8.5% below poverty level. 28% housing units rented; median house value: $48,600; median monthly rent: $186. Households: 73% family, 40% with children, 63% married couples.

1982 Share of Federal Tax Burden $11,312,600,000; 1.89% of U.S. total, 18th largest.

Share of Federal Expenditures

	Total		Non-Defense		Defense	
Total Expend	$8,879m	(1.47%)	$7,792m	(1.83%)	$1,087m	(0.61%)
St/Lcl Grants	1,894m	(2.15%)	1,893m	(2.15%)	1m	(2.78%)
Salary/Wages	378m	(0.48%)	235m	(0.86%)	143m	(0.28%)
Ind Payments	5,454m	(1.91%)	5,125m	(1.99%)	329m	(1.15%)
Procurement	1,073m	(0.74%)	221m	(0.70%)	852m	(0.75%)
Other Programs	79m	(1.46%)	77m	(1.43%)	2m	(4.65%)
Loan/Insurance	1,103m	(1.72%)	1,074m	(1.74%)	29m	(1.32%)

Political Lineup Governor, Anthony S. Earl (D). Senators, William Proxmire (D) and Robert W. Kasten, Jr. (R). Representatives, 9 (5 D and 4 R). State Senate, 33 (19 D and 14 R). State House of Representatives, 99 (59 D and 40 R).

Presidential Vote

1980	Reagan (R)	1,088,845	(48%)
	Carter (D)	981,584	(43%)
	Anderson (I)	160,657	(7%)
1976	Ford (R)	1,004,987	(48%)
	Carter (D)	1,040,232	(49%)

1980 Democratic Presidential Primary				*1980 Republican Presidential Primary*			
Carter	353,662	(56%)		Reagan	364,898	(40%)
Kennedy	189,520	(30%)		Bush	276,164	(30%)
Brown	74,496	(12%)		Anderson	248,623	(27%)
Others	11,941	(2%)		Others	18,168	(2%)

SENATORS

Sen. William Proxmire (D) Elected Aug. 1957, seat up 1988; b. Nov. 11, 1915, Lake Forest, IL; home, Madison; Yale U., B.A. 1938, Harvard U., M.B.A. 1940, M.P.A. 1948; Episcopal.

Career WI House of Reps., 1951; Dem. Nominee for Gov. of WI, 1952, 1954, 1956; Pres., Artcraft Press, 1953–57.

Offices 5241 DSOB, 202-224-5653. Also Rm. 301, 30 W. Mifflin St., Madison 53703, 608-252-5338; and Fed. Court Bldg., 517 E. Wisconsin Ave., Milwaukee 53202, 414-272-0388.

Committees *Appropriations* (3d). Subcommittees: Defense; HUD-Independent Agencies; Labor, Health and Human Services, Education; Treasury, Postal Service, and General Government. *Banking, Housing, and Urban Affairs* (Ranking Member). Subcommittees: Housing and Urban Affairs; Financial Institutions; International Finance and Monetary Policy. *Joint Economic Committee* (2d). Subcommittees: International Trade, Finance, and Security Economics (Vice-Chairman); Trade Productivity.

Group Ratings

	ADA	ACLU	COPE	CFA	LCV	LWV	NTU	NSI	COC	ACA	CSFC
1982	75	36	71	100	69	42	94	0	24	43	51
1981	55	—	72	50	56	—	99	—	61	71	59
1980	56	80	52	73	93	50	87	60	36	54	44

National Journal Ratings

	Economic		Foreign		Cultural	
1982	65%	(LIB)	86%	(LIB)	60%	(LIB)
	34%	(CONS)	10%	(CONS)	39%	(CONS)
1981	64%	(LIB)	96%	(LIB)	27%	(LIB)
	35%	(CONS)	2%	(CONS)	72%	(CONS)

Key Votes

1) Reagan 81 Budget	FOR	5) $ to El Salvador	AGN	9) Poor Pay Food Stamps	FOR
2) Reagan 81 Tax Cut	FOR	6) Saudi AWACS Sale	AGN	10) Ban Crt Busing Order	FOR
3) Bal Budget Amend	FOR	7) Ban Abortion	FOR	11) Clinch Riv Brdr Rctr	AGN
4) Gas & Road Tax	AGN	8) Nerve Gas Prod	AGN	12) Legal Services Corp	AGN

Election Results

1982 general	William Proxmire (D)	983,311	(64%)	($0)
	Scott McCallum (R)	527,355	(34%)	($119,924)
1982 primary	William Proxmire (D)	467,214	(86%)	
	Marcel Dandeneau (D)	75,258	(14%)	
1976 general	William Proxmire (D)	1,396,970	(72%)	($697)
	Stanley York (R)	521,902	(27%)	($62,210)

Campaign Contributions and Expenditures

Received no campaign contributions and had no expenditures.

Sen. Robert W. Kasten, Jr. (R) Elected 1980, seat up 1986; b. June 19, 1942, Milwaukee; home, Milwaukee; U. of AZ, B.A. 1964, Columbia U., M.A. 1966; Episcopal.

Career Air Force, 1967; WI Air Natl. Guard; WI Senate, 1972; U.S. House of Reps., 1974–78.

Offices 110 HSOB, 202-224-5323. Also 120 Bishops Way, Brookfield 53005, 414-784-5315.

Committees *Appropriations* (10th). Subcommittees: Agriculture, Rural Development; Defense; Energy and Water Development; Foreign Operations (Chairman); Transportation. *Budget* (10th). *Commerce, Science, and Transportation* (8th). Subcommittees: Consumer (Chairman); Merchant Marine; Surface Transportation; National Ocean Policy Study. *Small Business* (9th). Subcommittee: Entrepreneurship and Special Problems Facing Small Business.

Group Ratings

	ADA	ACLU	COPE	CFA	LCV	LWV	NTU	NSI	COC	ACA	CSFC
1982	5	7	14	43	38	33	85	90	70	86	77
1981	10	—	16	36	19	—	80	—	83	70	79

National Journal Ratings

	Economic		Foreign		Cultural	
1982	39%	(LIB)	3%	(LIB)	17%	(LIB)
	60%	(CONS)	84%	(CONS)	82%	(CONS)
1981	16%	(LIB)	29%	(LIB)	38%	(LIB)
	83%	(CONS)	70%	(CONS)	60%	(CONS)

Key Votes

1) Reagan 81 Budget	FOR	5) $ to El Salvador	FOR	9) Poor Pay Food Stamps	FOR
2) Reagan 81 Tax Cut	FOR	6) Saudi AWACS Sale	AGN	10) Ban Crt Busing Order	FOR
3) Bal Budget Amend	FOR	7) Ban Abortion	FOR	11) Clinch Riv Brdr Rctr	FOR
4) Gas & Road Tax	AGN	8) Nerve Gas Prod	FOR	12) Legal Services Corp	AGN

Election Results

1980 general	Robert W. Kasten, Jr. (R)	1,106,311	(50%)	($686,758)
	Gaylord A. Nelson (D)	1,065,487	(48%)	($897,774)
1980 primary	Robert W. Kasten, Jr. (R)	134,586	(37%)	
	Terry J. Kohler (R)	106,270	(29%)	($524,929)
	Douglass Cofrin (R)	84,355	(23%)	($1,497,508)
	One other (R)	40,823	(11%)	
1974 general	Gaylord A. Nelson (D)	740,700	(62%)	($247,555)
	Thomas E. Petri (R)	429,327	(36%)	($80,590)

Campaign Contributions and Expenditures

1979-80		PACS brkdwn			
Receipts	$725,281	Agr	$9,450	Ideo	$36,482
Expend.	$686,758	Bus	$228,501	Lbr	$1,200
Unspent	$38,522	Hlth	$6,000	Prof	$5,200

GOVERNOR

Gov. Anthony S. Earl (D) Elected 1982, term expires Jan. 1987; b. April 12, 1936, Lansing, MI; home, Madison; MI St. U., B.A. 1958, U. of Chicago Sch. of Law, J.D. 1961; Roman Catholic.

Career U.S. Navy, 1962–65; Asst. Dist Atty., Marathon Cnty., 1965, City Atty., Wausau; Assemblyman, 1969–75, Major. Flr. Ldr., 1971–75; Practicing atty., 1969–74, 80–82; WI State Secy. of Dept. of Admin., 1974, Secy. of Dept. of Natural Resources, 1975–80.

Offices State Capitol, P.O. Box 7863, Madison 53702, 608-266-1212.

Election Results

1982 gen.	Anthony S. Earl (D)	896,812	(57%)
	Terry J. Kohler (R)	662,838	(42%)
1982 prim.	Anthony S. Earl (D)	268,857	(46%)
	Martin J. Schreiber (D)	245,952	(42%)
	James B. Wood (D)	71,282	(12%)
1978 gen.	Lee Sherman Dreyfus (R) ...	816,056	(54%)
	Martin J. Schreiber (D)	673,813	(45%)

WISCONSIN — Congressional Districts, Counties, and Selected Places — (9 Districts)

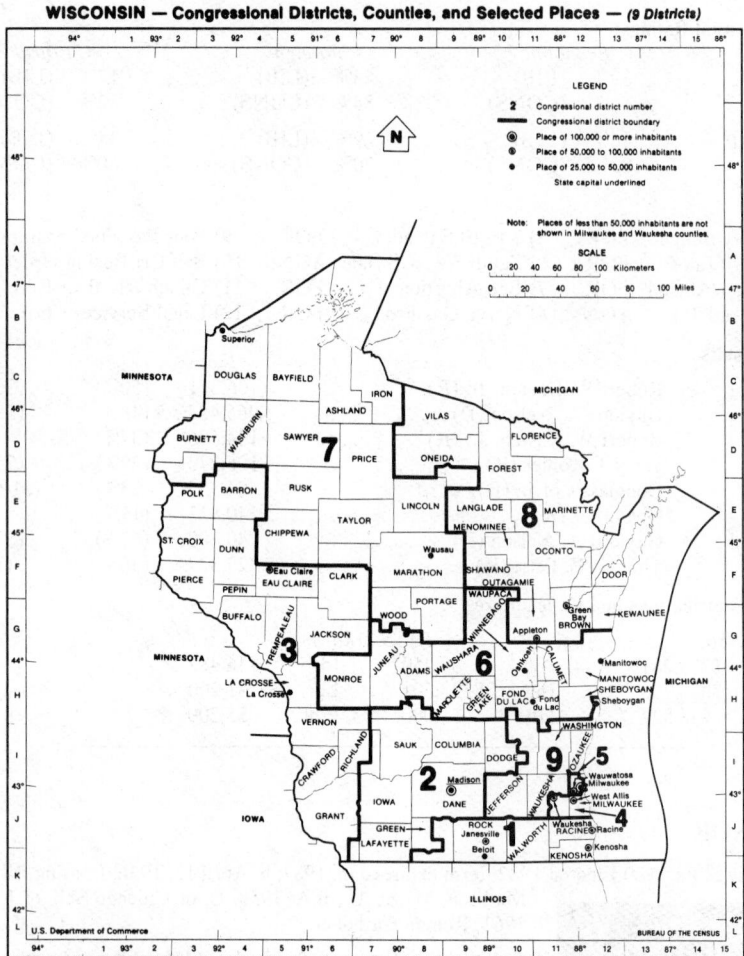

Congressional districts established March 31,1982; all other boundaries are as of January 1, 1980.

FIRST DISTRICT

The 1st congressional district of Wisconsin is the southeastern corner of the state. It contains a fair cross-section of Wisconsin, from the industrial cities along Lake Michigan to the verdant dairying country inland. In the eastern part of the 1st, along the lake, are Racine and Kenosha, the homes respectively of firms like Johnson's Wax and American Motors (now mostly owned by Renault). Here you still find vestiges of the old political struggles between management and labor, and on balance they are usually Democratic. Not too far inland is the high-income resort town of Lake Geneva, which attracts some of the richest people in Chicago; this is one of the most Republican parts of Wisconsin. To the west are the cities of Janesville and Beloit, industrial like the lakefront towns but less ethnic and more Anglo-

Saxon in their ethnic composition. The surrounding territory is dairying country, settled 140 years ago by Yankee and German farmers; their descendants still live there in considerable comfort and prosperity. This part of the district on balance leans Republican in most elections.

This combination produces a pretty close partisan balance, and in the 1960s this was one of the most marginal congressional districts in the country. But since 1970 the 1st district has consistently gone Democratic in House races, since Les Aspin was first elected.

Aspin was one of the first of what might be called the post-Vietnam Democrats. He is in the vanguard of that generation whose initiation into public events came long after World War II and who were skeptical of the justifications for American policies in Vietnam. His resume is distinctive, and is more typical of young politicians today than it was when he got started: he worked on Senator Proxmire's staff, for Walter Heller when he was chairman of the President's Council of Economic Advisers, and (while he was in the Army) for Defense Secretary Robert McNamara in the Pentagon. After two years as an economics professor in Wisconsin, he ran for Congress in 1970 against a weak Republican and won, with a stunningly large percentage.

Aspin is today one of the active leaders of House Democrats on difficult issues, but when he entered Congress, he was very much the outsider. Back in the early 1970s top committee positions were still held by men born in the 19th century; virtually the entire House membership supported the Vietnam war; the House as a whole was sympathetic to the Nixon administration, whose real problem was the Senate. Aspin got a seat on the Armed Services Committee and proceeded to legislate by press release. As one of the few doves and supporters of McNamara management techniques, Aspin found plenty to ridicule and attack in the Pentagon, and he became expert at feeding stories to reporters—and getting credit.

By the late 1970s this gadfly posture had become obsolete. The House was less hawkish and more liberal; even Armed Services contained a few more Pentagon critics. Aspin began writing articles setting forth his own military strategy and advancing his own views on the floor of the House. As a strategist Aspin has none of that adolescent spirit, so apparent in some leftish writers, of rooting against the older generation in his own country; he writes sometimes puckishly but always from the perspective of one responsible for advancing human dignity by defending the interests of the United States. He is one of the brainiest and most original members of the House, and one of the few liberals of his generation who devotes close attention to strategic military and foreign policy—to the problems of advancing American interests rather than restraining American aggressiveness.

By 1983 Aspin had become the *de facto* leader of the House on major military issues. He supported the nuclear freeze resolution and led the debate when others (including Wisconsin's Clement Zablocki) stumbled. Then he was a leading supporter of the Scowcroft Commission recommendations for the MX missile. On both issues Aspin took a leading role, even though he acknowledged intellectual weaknesses in both positions. He took his stands because he believed that they made the best sense, given the imperfect choices, in advancing American interests in arms control and strong defense. This was a legislative bravura performance; most of Aspin's allies on the nuclear freeze opposed his position on the MX. But he proved he can swing the key votes in the House on these issues.

At the same time Aspin also became for the first time a subcommittee chairman on Armed Services; despite speculation Armed Services Democrats did not block his elevation to the head of the Military Personnel and Compensation Subcommittee. Since he has looked with some favor on reviving the draft, his taking that post could be important. But otherwise in today's House, that kind of triumph is no longer terribly significant. Aspin may be outvoted on many issues in committee, but he has the votes on the floor to make national policy. That's more than the orthodox members of the Armed Services Committee can say; there could be strong pressure again for a draft—and Aspin's post would be a hot seat.

Aspin won reelection by large percentages into the middle 1970s. But in 1978 he was held to 54% of the vote, and in 1980 some Republicans wanted to target him. His association with dovish views, in the era of Iran and Afghanistan, seemed a liability rather than an asset. But by 1982 he was winning strongly again, with no sign of strong opposition in what had been one of the most marginal districts in the country in the 1960s.

The People   Pop. 1980: 522,838, up 5.1% 1970–80; voting age pop. 366,924; 4% Black, 2% Span. orig. 27% housing units rented. Median owner $47,900; renter $188. Households: 75% family, 43% with children, 64% married couples.

Presidential Vote

1980	Reagan (R)	117,711	(51%)
	Carter (D)	98,911	(42%)
	Anderson (I)	16,391	(7%)

Rep. Les Aspin (D) Elected 1970; b. July 21, 1938, Milwaukee; home, Racine; Yale U., B.A. 1960, Oxford U., M.A. 1962, M.I.T., Ph.D. 1965; Episcopal.

Career Staff Asst. to U.S. Sen. William Proxmire, 1960; Staff Asst. to Walter Heller, Pres. Cncl. of Econ. Advisers, 1963; Army, 1966–68; Asst. Prof. of Econ., Marquette U., 1969–70.

Offices 442 CHOB, 202-225-3031. Also 1661 Douglas Ave., Racine 52404, 414-632-4446; and 210 Dodge St., Janesville 53545, 608-752-9074.

Committees *Armed Services* (7th). Subcommittees: Investigations; Military Personnel and Compensation (Chairman). *Budget* (8th). Task Forces: Budget Process; Capital Resources and Development; Economic Policy and Growth (Chairman); Tax Policy.

Group Ratings

	ADA	ACLU	COPE	CFA	LCV	LWV	NTU	NSI	COC	ACA	CSFC
1982	85	75	82	85	87	82	24	22	24	30	33
1981	75	—	82	79	93	—	26	—	7	17	34
1980	67	53	61	64	85	100	21	10	61	25	29

National Journal Ratings

	Economic		Foreign		Cultural	
1982	68%	(LIB)	70%	(LIB)	77%	(LIB)
	31%	(CONS)	30%	(CONS)	23%	(CONS)
1981	85%	(LIB)	75%	(LIB)	73%	(LIB)
	14%	(CONS)	25%	(CONS)	27%	(CONS)

Key Votes

1) Reagan 81 Budget	AGN	5) Incr SS Rtmt Age	AGN	9) Poor Pay Food Stamps	AGN
2) Reagan 81 Tax Cut	AGN	6) Saudi AWACS Sale	AGN	10) Ban Crt Busing Order	AGN
3) Bal Budget Amend	AGN	7) $ for MX Missile	AGN	11) Auto Local Content	FOR
4) Gas & Road Tax	FOR	8) Nerve Gas Prod	AGN	12) Nuclear Arms Freeze	FOR

Election Results

1982 general	Les Aspin (D)	95,005	(61%)	($180,258)
	Peter N. Jansson (R)	59,309	(38%)	($114,647)
1982 primary	Les Aspin (D)	45,253	(100%)	
1980 general	Les Aspin (D)	126,222	(56%)	($152,364)
	Kathryn H. Canary (R)	96,047	(43%)	($75,766)

Campaign Contributions and Expenditures

1981-82		Direct Cont. 81-82			PACS brkdwn		
Receipts	$199,735	Indiv	$102,078	Agr	$14,000	Ideo	$5,300
Expend.	$180,258	Party	$1,000	Bus	$16,413	Lbr	$52,746
Unspent	$4,153	PACS	$94,233	Hlth	$2,450	Prof	$200

Indep Expend: Agn: $6,054 (NCPAC)

SECOND DISTRICT

Madison is Wisconsin's second largest city, with nearly 200,000 people, and the state capital. It is also one of the nation's most important university communities—home of the University of Wisconsin and its 30,000 students. The university was a factor in Wisconsin politics long before the 18-year-old vote of the early 1970s. Back in 1900, Robert LaFollette, a Madison native, was elected governor. Once in office, he called on professors from the university to set up the Wisconsin Tax Commission and to draft a workmen's compensation law—both firsts in the nation. Wisconsin's progressive movement, including the *Progressive* magazine, which is published in Madison, has always relied heavily on the university community. As a result Madison, not the much bigger city of Milwaukee, has always been the center of Wisconsin liberalism.

In the early 1950s, when LaFollette progressives had completely lost control of the Republican Party here, Madison became the center of a new liberal movement in the minority and moribund Democratic Party. Today the city remains the home base of Senator William Proxmire and of former Governor Patrick Lucey, who was John Anderson's running mate in the 1980 presidential election. Anderson carried Madison heavily, though he lost the rest of Wisconsin, in the 1980 Republican presidential primary; students vote in large numbers here, and Wisconsin has always had an open primary, with no party registration, on the sensible theory that voters ought to be able to support whom they like, and not be constrained by the fiction that they are faithful followers of one party or the other. Nonetheless, that theory may not be allowed to operate in 1984; the national Democrats have banned letting open primaries elect delegates to their conventions, largely because it was one of the few changes reformers and regulars could agree on in the 1970s.

Madison is the center of Wisconsin's 2d congressional district; Madison and surrounding Dane County casts 65% of the district's votes. Since the 1958 election the 2d district has been represented by Robert Kastenmeier, one of the youngest members of the group of Madison liberals of the 1950s. With a rural background, Kastenmeier was nonethelesss one of the most liberal members of the House in the early 1960s; he was not able to win reelection by a wide margin until after the redistricting of 1964.

Until 1974 Kastenmeier was little known outside his district, climbing slowly to a high seniority position on the House Judiciary Committee. Suddenly the impeachment hearings focused national attention on the committee and its members. Kastenmeier, as fourth-ranking Democrat, was considered the most senior member absolutely sure to vote for impeachment. He made an important contribution to the proceedings by insisting that each article of impeachment be voted on separately, after evidence pertaining to it was discussed. Some of the Republicans and conservative Democrats favoring impeachment wanted to wait and hold all the roll calls at the end, as if somehow people wouldn't notice then. But Kastenmeier's rule ensured an orderly procedure and kept the evidence and the voting closely tied together in people's minds.

That was typical of Kastenmeier's method of operating: he is quiet and not at all fiery, seemingly more concerned with details than he is with the big picture. He has spent much of the time since impeachment on copyright law—a seemingly mundane area, but one with vast implications for the lively arts and the entertainment industry. But despite his apparently languid style and his sense of humor, he has a habit of coming out on the winning side and getting what he wants.

The 2d is one of the most polarized districts in the nation: surrounding liberal Dane County are some of the most heavily Republican rural counties in Wisconsin. Republican candidates, spotting this natural Republican base, ran vigorous campaigns against Kastenmeier in 1978 and especially in 1980. But his Dane County margins remained very solid (61%–38%). Kastenmeier's 54% victory that year thus demonstrated not his weakness but his strength. He was not seriously challenged in 1982, and won reelection with 61% overall, and 67% in Dane County.

The People   Pop. 1980: 523,011, up 9.8% 1970–80; voting age pop. 383,086; 1% Black, 1% Span. orig., 1% Asian orig. 35% housing units rented. Median owner $53,900; renter $211. Households: 68% family, 37% with children, 59% married couples.

Presidential Vote

1980	Reagan (R)	105,752	(41%)
	Carter (D)	124,141	(49%)
	Anderson (I)	25,601	(10%)

Rep. Robert W. Kastenmeier (D) Elected 1958; b. Jan. 24, 1924, Beaver Dam; home, Sun Prairie; U. of WI, LL.B. 1952; No religious affiliation.

Career Practicing atty., 1952–58.

Offices 2232 RHOB, 202-225-2906. Also 119 Monona Ave., Madison 53703, 608-252-5206.

Committee *Judiciary* (3d). Subcommittees: Civil and Constitutional Rights; Courts, Civil Liberties, and the Administration of Justice (Chairman).

Group Ratings

	ADA	ACLU	COPE	CFA	LCV	LWV	NTU	NSI	COC	ACA	CSFC
1982	90	92	89	85	99	83	33	0	20	9	23
1981	95	—	89	93	100	—	41	—	5	13	24
1980	100	97	79	79	91	100	24	0	58	13	23

National Journal Ratings

	Economic		Foreign		Cultural	
1982	83%	(LIB)	92%	(LIB)	81%	(LIB)
	17%	(CONS)	6%	(CONS)	19%	(CONS)
1981	89%	(LIB)	89%	(LIB)	95%	(LIB)
	3%	(CONS)	10%	(CONS)	1%	(CONS)

Key Votes

1) Reagan 81 Budget	AGN	5) Incr SS Rtmt Age	AGN	9) Poor Pay Food Stamps	AGN
2) Reagan 81 Tax Cut	AGN	6) Saudi AWACS Sale	AGN	10) Ban Crt Busing Order	AGN
3) Bal Budget Amend	AGN	7) $ for MX Missile	AGN	11) Auto Local Content	FOR
4) Gas & Road Tax	FOR	8) Nerve Gas Prod	AGN	12) Nuclear Arms Freeze	FOR

Election Results

1982 general	Robert W. Kastenmeier (D)	112,677	(61%)	($334,590)
	Jim Johnson (R)	71,989	(39%)	($264,330)
1982 primary	Robert W. Kastenmeier (D)	64,920	(100%)	
1980 general	Robert W. Kastenmeier (D)	142,037	(54%)	($225,706)
	James A. Wright (R)	119,514	(45%)	($282,348)

Campaign Contributions and Expenditures

1981-82		Direct Cont. 81-82		PACS brkdwn			
Receipts	$319,052	Indiv	$185,642	Agr	$13,435	Ideo	$6,800
Expend.	$334,590	Party	$6,409	Bus	$33,840	Lbr	$47,185
Unspent	$4,354	PACS	$111,037	Hlth	$600	Prof	$1,100

THIRD DISTRICT

It's hard to think of another industry as benign as dairy farming. Its products have long been regarded as healthful, and carefully regulated to guard against spoilage; they are necessities for most babies and growing children. The industry's waste products are nontoxic and biodegradable; its business is conducted in pleasant surroundings, away from crowded cities; it does not withdraw land from other productive activities, since dairy cattle generally graze on land that is not useful for growing other, higher-dollar-yield crops.

Yet the dairy industry in America is in terrible trouble, for three reasons. First, there are fewer children in this country today than in the 1950s; hence the demand for milk has declined. Second, people have much higher incomes, in real dollars, than they did in the 1950s. Hence they use much less powdered milk and other dairy solids, which used to be one of the major products of the dairy industry. Third, the dairy industry itself has gotten much more productive. It takes fewer cows and fewer dairy farmers to produce the same amount of total dairy output as it did in the 1950s—which is about what we produce today.

Given these problems, dairy farmers have done what any other organized group in the United States does in similar circumstances: they have come to the government for aid. Dairy farmers and processors have long been organized in cooperatives, and these dairy coops became brilliant lobbyists and campaign contributors by the 1970s; they worked Democrats and Republicans alike to increase dairy subsidies and price supports. As a result, by the early 1980s the government had mountains of cheese and powdered milk it literally could not give away.

The 3d congressional district of Wisconsin is probably the nation's number-one dairy district. It stretches along the Mississippi River and one or two counties eastward from the Illinois border in the south up past the Wisconsin outposts of the Minneapolis–St. Paul metropolitan area in the north. This is a place north of the main paths of westward migration and of intensive cultivation; it was settled largely by German and Scandinavian immigrants, and, because the growing season was short and the soil stony with debris left behind by receding glaciers, it was given over mostly to dairy farming. In partisan terms, the district is rather evenly divided: the more German counties in the south tend to be Republican, the more Scandinavian counties north of LaCrosse tend to be Democratic. But the biggest issue here since the dairy industry became dependent on federal help is dairy policy, and it is not one which splits local Democrats and Republicans on party lines.

This is illustrated by the career of Congressman Steven Gunderson, a Republican first elected in 1980 at age 29. Gunderson upset Democratic incumbent Al Baldus, who had become chairman of the subcommittee handling the dairy program, and he ran as a supporter of the Reagan economic programs. He did support Reagan's budget and tax cut measures in 1981. But he also distanced himself very quickly from administration proposals to cut dairy price supports. And he was able to get himself a place on the Agriculture Committee and on the Livestock, Dairy and Poultry Subcommittee, a body stocked with dairy program lovers.

Gunderson is patently ambitious, a hardworking campaigner who beat a tough incumbent one year and fended off another serious Democrat in the Democratic year of 1982. He ran ahead of Ronald Reagan in 1980 and won despite Reagan's attempts to dismantle the dairy programs in 1982. He probably has statewide ambitions—he said he ran for the House in 1980 because he was too young to serve in the Senate—but he had the good sense not to take Senator William Proxmire on in 1982. In the meantime, the 3d district is a tough one to hold, a demanding constituency on dairy issues and a volatile one in general party preference.

The People   Pop. 1980: 522,909, up 13.4% 1970–80; voting age pop. 383,086; 25% housing units rented. Median owner $41,700; renter $162. Households: 73% family, 40% with children, 64% married couples.

Presidential Vote

1980	Reagan (R)	123,610	(49%)
	Carter (D)	109,701	(44%)
	Anderson (I)	18,629	(7%)

Rep. Steven Gunderson (R) Elected 1980; b. May 10, 1951, Eau Claire; home, Pleasantville; U. of WI, B.A. 1973, Brown Sch. of Broadcasting, 1974; Lutheran.

Career WI Assembly, 1974–79.

Offices 416 CHOB, 202-225-5506. Also 438 N. Water St., Black River Falls 54615, 715-284-7431.

Committees *Agriculture* (12th). Subcommittees: Conservation, Credit, and Rural Development; Department Operations, Research, and Foreign Agriculture; Livestock, Dairy and Poultry. *Education and Labor* (7th). Subcommittees: Elementary, Secondary, and Vocational Education; Employment Opportunities; Health and Safety; Postsecondary Education.

Group Ratings

	ADA	ACLU	COPE	CFA	LCV	LWV	NTU	NSI	COC	ACA	CSFC
1982	45	25	26	31	46	58	76	60	64	64	59
1981	30	—	20	43	43	—	79	—	84	75	60

National Journal Ratings

	Economic		Foreign		Cultural	
1982	45%	(LIB)	69%	(LIB)	46%	(LIB)
	55%	(CONS)	30%	(CONS)	54%	(CONS)
1981	24%	(LIB)	46%	(LIB)	44%	(LIB)
	68%	(CONS)	54%	(CONS)	56%	(CONS)

Key Votes

1) Reagan 81 Budget	FOR	5) Incr SS Rtmt Age	FOR	9) Poor Pay Food Stamps	AGN
2) Reagan 81 Tax Cut	FOR	6) Saudi AWACS Sale	FOR	10) Ban Crt Busing Order	FOR
3) Bal Budget Amend	FOR	7) $ for MX Missile	AGN	11) Auto Local Content	AGN
4) Gas & Road Tax	FOR	8) Nerve Gas Prod	AGN	12) Nuclear Arms Freeze	FOR

Election Results

1982 general	Steven Gunderson (R)	99,304	(57%)	($338,643)
	Paul Offner (D)	75,132	(43%)	($217,780)
1982 primary	Steven Gunderson (R)	36,517	(100%)	
1980 general	Steven Gunderson (R)	132,001	(51%)	($177,782)
	Alvin Baldus (D)	126,859	(49%)	($136,320)

Campaign Contributions and Expenditures

1981-82		Direct Cont. 81-82		PACS brkdwn			
Receipts	$329,538	Indiv	$177,275	Agr	$18,850	Ideo	$6,850
Expend.	$338,643	Party	$31,055	Bus	$71,309	Lbr	$3,000
Unspent	$5,407	PACS	$107,009	Hlth	$7,000	Prof	$—

Indirect Party Expend: $34,936

FOURTH DISTRICT

The 4th congressional district of Wisconsin is the south side Milwaukee district, including the southern part of the city of Milwaukee plus suburban territory going inland from Lake Michigan some 30 miles. The Milwaukee River splits the city into two different sections; traditionally, the north side has been German and the southern Polish. But these are oversimplifications, and with the aging and emptying out of central city neighborhoods—a phenomenon quite apparent in the south side, although there has been none of the increase in the black population to which it is often attributed—there aren't that many people, German or Polish, left in the old neighborhoods. Just 39% of the residents of this 4th district live inside Milwaukee; the rest may have grown up here, or have parents who did, but they live in the suburbs. These range from working-class suburbs with basic, unadorned houses, to newish, pleasant suburbs southwest of the city, like Greendale and New Berlin.

The south side of Milwaukee had a Democratic tradition before the rest of Wisconsin developed one. Its current congressman, Clement Zablocki, was first elected in 1948, and his attitudes over the years have been closer to those of big-city machine Democrats than to the ideological liberals in the rest of the Wisconsin delegation. He was the only Wisconsin Democrat to support the Vietnam war policies of the Johnson and Nixon administrations, and he is considerably more conservative on cultural issues than these colleagues.

Zablocki holds a position that sounds impressive: he is chairman of the House Foreign Affairs Committee. The reality is more mundane. Foreign Affairs has never been as important as its Senate counterpart, because the House's approval is not required for treaties and nominations. Foreign Affairs was for many years dominated by Democrats from working-class districts who simply wanted to cooperate with the administration in power. Now the committee is more important: its real movers are the young subcommittee chairmen, most of them strong opponents of Reagan administration policies in their areas; they have power because they can cut off American funds or put restrictions on their use.

In these matters Zablocki plays a delicate role. His natural instincts are quite different from those of his subcommittee chairmen: he is strongly anti-Communist, inclined to believe rather than disbelieve the incumbent administration, skeptical about aiding Israel. The subcommittee chairmen have the votes, usually, to prevail on the whole committee; Zablocki accordingly tends to go along too. But he does not always do so enthusiastically or effectively. In 1983, speaking as a major sponsor of the nuclear freeze resolution, he was unable to answer questions in line with pro-freeze orthodoxy, and the issue had to be put over to another day. Zablocki is a pleasant and decent man, well-intentioned but not particularly aggressive; and he is not the only full committee chairman who has let his subcommittee chairmen take the initiative. But it cannot be a happy situation for him.

Zablocki had serious primary opposition in 1982. Part of suburban Waukesha County was added to the district, and with that the 4th also received Lynn Adelman, an aggressive state legislator who ran a strong race as the Democratic candidate in the 9th district in 1974. In 1982 he ran against Zablocki in the primary and won 67% of the vote in Waukesha County. Zablocki still carried Milwaukee County 2–1, and won the race with 61%. But that is not an impressive percentage for a longtime incumbent, and it would not be shocking to see Zablocki seriously challenged—or decide to retire—in 1984.

The People Pop. 1980: 522,880, dn. 1.3% 1970–80; voting age pop. 381,822; 3% Span. orig., 1% Am. Ind., 1% Asian orig. 37% housing units rented. Median owner $59,900; renter $210. Households: 73% family, 38% with children, 61% married couples.

Presidential Vote

1980	Reagan (R)	NA
	Carter (D)	NA
	Anderson (I)	NA

Rep. Clement J. Zablocki (D) Elected 1948; b. Nov. 18, 1912, Milwaukee; home, Milwaukee; Marquette U., Ph.B. 1936; Roman Catholic.

Career Organist and choir dir., 1932–48; High sch. teacher, 1938–40; WI Senate, 1942–48.

Offices 2183 RHOB, 202-225-4572. Also 4302 W. Forest Home Ave., Milwaukee 53219, 414-327-2525; and 112 W. Broadway, Waukesha 53186, 414-549-5565.

Committees *Foreign Affairs* (Chairman). Subcommittee: International Security and Scientific Affairs (Chairman). *Permanent Select Committee on Intelligence* (2d). Subcommittee: Program and Budget Authorization.

Group Ratings

	ADA	ACLU	COPE	CFA	LCV	LWV	NTU	NSI	COC	ACA	CSFC
1982	70	46	92	85	68	67	1	78	30	22	32
1981	50	—	92	64	37	—	0	—	12	30	41
1980	61	37	83	71	43	80	10	22	65	13	31

National Journal Ratings

	Economic		Foreign		Cultural	
1982	83%	(LIB)	57%	(LIB)	58%	(LIB)
	15%	(CONS)	43%	(CONS)	42%	(CONS)
1981	72%	(LIB)	39%	(LIB)	58%	(LIB)
	27%	(CONS)	60%	(CONS)	42%	(CONS)

Key Votes

1) Reagan 81 Budget	AGN	5) Incr SS Rtmt Age	AGN
2) Reagan 81 Tax Cut	AGN	6) Saudi AWACS Sale	FOR
3) Bal Budget Amend	AGN	7) $ for MX Missile	AGN
4) Gas & Road Tax	FOR	8) Nerve Gas Prod	AGN

9) Poor Pay Food Stamps	AGN
10) Ban Crt Busing Order	FOR
11) Auto Local Content	FOR
12) Nuclear Arms Freeze	FOR

Election Results

1982 general	Clement J. Zablocki (D)	129,557	(95%)	($181,311)
	Two others (L and I)	6,485	(5%)	
1982 primary	Clement J. Zablocki (D)	56,047	(61%)	
	Lynn S. Adelman (D)	36,102	(39%)	($196,249)
1980 general	Clement J. Zablocki (D)	146,437	(70%)	($14,592)
	Elroy C. Honadel (R)	61,027	(30%)	($10,201)

Campaign Contributions and Expenditures

1982		Direct Cont. 1982		PACS brkdwn			
Receipts	$182,193	Indiv	$57,264	Agr	$12,500	Ideo	$6,000
Expend.	$181,311	Party	$2,100	Bus	$34,845	Lbr	$39,100
Unspent	$12,756	PACS	$97,700	Hlth	$2,000	Prof	$450
		Cand	$25,000				

Indep Expend: For: $726

FIFTH DISTRICT

The 5th congressional district of Wisconsin is made up of the northern side of the city of Milwaukee and Milwaukee County. Some 82% of the people here live in the city, some in the poor black neighborhoods not far from downtown, but more in the pleasant, 1950s-ish subdivisions in the far northwest part of Milwaukee. Others live in the middle-income suburb of Wauwatosa, west of Milwaukee, or in some of the high-income suburbs along the lake shore, north of downtown. The north side is the traditionally German half of Milwaukee, and this may very well be the most heavily German congressional district in the United States. Thanks to the advertisements of the many beers now or once brewed in Milwaukee, we have some notion of the gemutlichkeit atmosphere of this old German city.

Not as well known is the unique brand of politics Milwaukee has had for many years, a politics with roots deep in the German tradition. During the years Robert LaFollette and his progressive Republicans were governing the rest of Wisconsin, Milwaukee was governed by a series of Socialist mayors and represented by Socialist congressmen. The most notable of the latter was Victor Berger, who served in the House from 1911 to 1913 and 1923 to 1929. After the 1918 and 1920 elections Berger was denied his seat because of his opposition to American entry into World War I. Those who think that the prosecution of antiwar dissenters is a phenomenon new to the 1960s should know that Berger was sentenced in 1919 to 20 years in prison for having written antiwar articles. The prosecution was brought by the Wilson administration and, after the conviction was reversed by the Supreme Court, all charges were dropped by the "return to normalcy" Harding administration. It is a measure of the strength of German Milwaukee's opposition to the war against Germany that Berger was reelected to Congress while his case was on appeal and after he had been denied his seat.

Today many of the original German neighborhoods are mostly black. Blacks made up just 28% of the population of this district in 1980, but they accounted for 81% of the black population of Wisconsin. The descendants of the German immigrants have moved to the west, north, and northwest; what were once rural townships are now part of the Milwaukee area. The more prosperous of them tend to be out in the 9th district; the 5th remains heavily Democratic, as it has been since the 1950s.

The 5th district was the scene of a congressional race in 1982 that illustrated that Wisconsin is *not* a political machine state. The incumbent congressman, Henry Reuss, retired after 28 years of service; a scholarly liberal, he chaired the Banking Committee for six years and ended his service by chairing the Joint Economic Committee, enunciating skepticism about Reaganomics even as it was sweeping all before it. The Democratic primary to succeed him contained no less than 11 candidates, six of whom finished in close range of each other. A black candidate came in second; the winner was state Senator Jim Moody, a Ph.D. economist who has made his political career by campaigning door to door and has no major alliances.

Moody serves now on the Interior and Public Works Committees, assignments which suggest a concentration on environmental issues. Barring major mistakes, he should have a safe district here. It is solidly Democratic in general elections; the only threat can come in a primary, but an incumbent as energetic as Moody's vote-getting record suggests he is should be able to discourage primary opposition without difficulty.

The People Pop. 1980: 522,854, dn .10% 1970–80; voting age pop. 381,248; 22% Black, 2% Span. orig., 1% Asian orig. 50% housing units rented. Median owner $50,700; renter $190. Households: 64% family, 34% with children, 46% married couples.

Presidential Vote

1980	Reagan (R)	NA
	Carter (D)	NA
	Anderson (I)	NA

Rep. Jim Moody (D) Elected 1982; b. Sept. 2, 1935, Richlands, VA; home, Milwaukee; Haverford Col., B.A. 1957, JFK Sch. of Govt., Harvard U., M.P.A. 1967, U. of CA at Berkeley, Ph.D. 1973; Protestant.

Career Field Rep., CARE, Yugoslavia, 1958–60, Iran, 1960; Country Dir., Peace Corps, Pakistan, 1961; Economist, D.O.T., 1967, 1969; Prof., U. of WI, Milwaukee, 1973–82; WI Assembly, 1977–78; Small businessman 1979–; WI Senate, 1979–82.

Offices 1721 LHOB, 202-225-3571. Also 135 W. Wells St., Su. 618, Milwaukee 53202, 414-291-1331.

Committees *Interior and Insular Affairs* (24th). Subcommittees: Energy and the Environment; Mining, Forest Management, and BPA; Public Lands and National Parks. *Public Works and Transportation* (22d). Subcommittees: Surface Transportation; Water Resources.

Group Ratings and Key Votes: Newly Elected

Election Results

1982 general	Jim Moody (D)	99,713	(64%)	($253,204)
	Rod K. Johnston (R)	54,824	(35%)	($208,313)
1982 primary	Jim Moody (D)	17,073	(19%)	
	Frederick P. Kessler (D)	15,804	(17%)	($147,892)
	Orville E. Pitts (D)	15,264	(17%)	($50,806)
	Warren D. Braun (D)	13,320	(14%)	($73,263)
	Marty Aronson (D)	11,799	(13%)	($96,249)
	Kevin D. O'Connor (D)	10,368	(11%)	($94,525)
	Four others (D)	8,578	(9%)	
1980 general	Henry Reuss (D)	129,574	(77%)	($36,250)
	David Bathke (R)	37,267	(22%)	($1,107)

Campaign Contributions and Expenditures

1982		Direct Cont. 1982		PACS brkdwn			
Receipts	$256,475	Indiv	$49,253	Agr	$—	Ideo	$3,250
Expend.	$253,204	Party	$5,035	Bus	$7,050	Lbr	$29,953
Unspent	$3,268	PACS	$50,603	Hlth	$1,000	Prof	$700
		Cand	$170,160				

SIXTH DISTRICT

The 6th congressional district of Wisconsin is a rectangular cross-section of the central part of the state, from Lake Michigan almost all the way to the Mississippi River. The heart of the district, geographically and demographically, is the area around Lake Winnebago and the Fox River valley. Here the different rural sections of Wisconsin meet: the dairying country of the south and the west, and the lumber country of the north. The small cities around the lake—Fond du Lac, Oshkosh, Menasha, Neenah, and Appleton (though most of the last is in the 8th district) are major paper-milling centers more than dairying market towns; yet the surrounding area is very good dairy country.

This area includes about half the district's population. About one-fourth is along Lake Michigan, in and near the industrial city of Manitowoc; the other one-fourth is dairying country, with small towns, west of Oshkosh. In the heart of the district is Ripon, where the Republican Party is said to have been founded in 1854. (Jackson, Michigan, claims the same distinction.)

The politics here is Republican, and has been since the area was first settled, by some Yankee farmers and woodsmen, but mostly by German immigrants. Wisconsin was admitted to the Union in 1848, and many of the Germans left Europe then; they were disappointed by the failure of the revolutions in what was not yet a united Germany in that year. They found the Republican Party, with its abhorrence of slavery and encouragement of agriculture (the Homestead Act), education (land grant colleges), and economic growth (the tariff, financing railroads) congenial; around the turn of the century they became LaFollette progressives. That allegiance was strengthened by the LaFollettes' opposition to war with Germany in 1917 and 1940. The New Deal did not really convert people here. The farmers were comparatively comfortable and the factory workers were not signed up in militant CIO unions. In the 1960s and 1970s the Democrats became more competitive here in some elections, but this is still one of the most Republican districts in Wisconsin.

It has been represented by Republicans with moderate reputations. One was William Steiger, an expert on the party's rules, leading opponent of the draft, and backer of the successful bill to cut capital gains taxes in 1978. After his untimely death late that year, the district had a special election, and chose, by only 1,223 votes, a Republican with similar politics, Thomas Petri. He serves on the Education and Labor and Public Works Committees; he has a reputation as a thoughtful moderate. He is rather conservative on cultural issues, more liberal on foreign policy—points of view in line with the Wisconsin electorate. He has been reelected by wide margins in 1980 and 1982 and seems now to have a safe seat.

The People Pop. 1980: 522,477, up 7.5% 1970–80; voting age pop. 370,486; 1% Span. orig. 22% housing units rented. Median owner $41,100; renter $158. Households: 75% family, 41% with children, 67% married couples.

Presidential Vote

1980	Reagan (R)	135,204	(55%)
	Carter (D)	94,598	(39%)
	Anderson (I)	14,759	(6%)

Rep. Thomas E. Petri (R) Elected Apr. 9, 1979; b. May 28, 1940, Marinette; home, Fond du Lac; Harvard Col., A.B. 1962, Harvard Sch. of Law, J.D. 1965; Lutheran.

Career Instructor, Kennedy Institute of Politics; Peace Corps, 1966–67; Practicing atty., 1972–.

Offices 1024 LHOB, 202-225-2476. Also 14 Western Ave., Fond du Lac 54935, 800-242-4883 and 414-922-1180.

Committees *Education and Labor* (5th). Subcommittees: Employment Opportunities; Human Resources; Labor Standards; Postsecondary Education. *Public Works and Transportation* (11th). Subcommittees: Aviation; Economic Development.

Group Ratings

	ADA	ACLU	COPE	CFA	LCV	LWV	NTU	NSI	COC	ACA	CSFC
1982	35	25	32	23	71	58	77	60	64	70	58
1981	40	—	31	50	64	—	97	—	83	68	68
1980	39	33	44	36	44	33	55	56	59	57	73

National Journal Ratings

	Economic		Foreign		Cultural	
1982	31%	(LIB)	50%	(LIB)	47%	(LIB)
	69%	(CONS)	50%	(CONS)	53%	(CONS)
1981	24%	(LIB)	67%	(LIB)	36%	(LIB)
	68%	(CONS)	32%	(CONS)	64%	(CONS)

Key Votes

1) Reagan 81 Budget	FOR	5) Incr SS Rtmt Age	FOR	9) Poor Pay Food Stamps	FOR
2) Reagan 81 Tax Cut	FOR	6) Saudi AWACS Sale	AGN	10) Ban Crt Busing Order	FOR
3) Bal Budget Amend	FOR	7) $ for MX Missile	AGN	11) Auto Local Content	AGN
4) Gas & Road Tax	FOR	8) Nerve Gas Prod	FOR	12) Nuclear Arms Freeze	AGN

Election Results

1982 general	Thomas E. Petri (R)	111,348	(65%)	($152,510)
	Gordon E. Loehr (D)	59,922	(35%)	($28,709)
1982 primary	Thomas E. Petri (R)	46,423	(100%)	
1980 general	Thomas E. Petri (R)	143,980	(59%)	($524,122)
	Gary R. Goyke (D)	98,628	(41%)	($234,563)

Campaign Contributions and Expenditures

1981-82		Direct Cont. 81-82		PACS brkdwn			
Receipts	$192,872	Indiv	$104,142	Agr	$16,000	Ideo	$600
Expend.	$152,510	Party	$11,574	Bus	$41,625	Lbr	$1,850
Unspent	$42,709	PACS	$67,619	Hlth	$1,900	Prof	$1,000
		Cand	$2,160				

SEVENTH DISTRICT

Northern Wisconsin is a land of forests and lakes and mines. Two natural resources are of key importance here, the dairy cow and the tree; without them, there would be few people here at all. This is the land of Wisconsin's 7th congressional district, which stretches from a point near Green Bay in the southeast up to the city limits of Duluth, Minnesota, in the northwest. Superior, the Wisconsin town next to Duluth, is like its neighbor an iron port, with scarcely any other reason to exist there on the icy fastness of Lake Superior. In contrast, most of the jobs in towns like Wausau, Stevens Point, and Wisconsin Rapids, in the southern part of the district, depend on the lumber and paper mills. All these places were off the beaten track of east–west migration; they attracted their own unusual ethnic groups, like the Finns of Superior and the Poles of Stevens Point. The politics of northern Wisconsin and the 7th district has always had a rough-hewn quality about it, a certain populist flavor; although this is an ancestrally Republican area, it is also part of the state that always favored the progressivism of the LaFollettes.

The current congressman from the 7th, however, is a Democrat. He is David Obey, who in his middle 40s has spent a decade and a half in the House already. He was elected in something of an upset in a 1969 special election, in the seat vacated by Defense Secretary Melvin Laird. Obey showed signs of political talent early. He won election to the Wisconsin legislature when he was 24. He won his House seat at age 30 and proceeded to make himself strong enough that, by 1972, when he was placed in the same district as a 30-year incumbent Republican with a liberal record, he won with 63% of the vote. Obey is reelected every two years by wide margins, and seems to be widely popular in this district.

Obey is now one of the leading legislators in the House, one of the dozen or so members who can really make a difference on major issues. To some extent he owes his prominence to committee position. He got a seat on the Appropriations Committee early and is now the eighth-ranking Democrat of 36, and he is 13 years younger than the youngest more senior Democrat. He does not yet chair an Appropriations subcommittee, but he is number two on Foreign Operations and number three on Labor–HHS–Education, and on quite a few occasions effectively takes the lead on their bills.

The way the House used to work, these committee positions would have made Obey powerful, but his prominence would still be far in the future. But in the House of the 1970s power moved more fluidly to those who understood how to exercise it—and had something in mind to do with it. Obey was one of the younger members called on by the leadership to handle difficult assignments, and he performed ably on all of them. In 1977 and 1978 he chaired a special committee on ethics and came up with a new code that was backed by reformers and passed by the House—a substantial achievement, and one virtually without precedent. In 1979 he was elected head of the liberal Democratic Study Group, at a time when many of its principles seemed under fire. After the 1980 elections, he came within a few votes of becoming Budget Committee chairman; he finally lost to James Jones of Oklahoma on the third ballot by a 121–116 margin.

Obey remained a member of the Budget Committee one more term, however; and he prepared a substitute budget and tax plan in 1982 which presented the clearest Democratic alternative to Reagan economic policies. Obey has become the effective leader of traditional liberal Democrats in the House. They no longer comprise necessarily a majority of even the Democratic Caucus; that now includes not only conservative southerners, but many northern Democrats representing economically conservative districts and/or with doubts about traditional government programs themselves. Obey himself is anything but a bleeding heart in temperament, and there is nothing sloppy about his generosity. He takes pride in being thoroughly prepared and will not be backed into taking a position before he has become convinced that it is right and that he can stand up and defend it. But he is also capable of acting quickly, and of assembling a position that a large number—perhaps a majority—of House members will support. Obey's term on the Budget Committee has expired, but he is still likely to play a major role on macroeconomic issues, and may some day seek the Budget chairmanship again.

Obey is also the House's leader on legislation to improve the reforms of the campaign finance laws. Before the 1980 election he was almost successful in passing a law to put a limit on the total amount of contributions a candidate for Congress could accept from political action committees. In 1983 he is again sponsoring a major measure to limit what a candidate can get from PACs; it would also limit personal contributions further and would give candidates free radio and TV time to respond to independent expenditure campaigns against them. Obey has not come out in favor of complete public financing of congressional elections; he does, however, believe that under the present system business PACs are too powerful and too important in the campaign process. In early 1983 chances for passage of such a law in the 98th Congress seemed less than 50–50. But Obey is a legislator with a long time frame who is willing to take on causes which seem, at first, impossibly difficult.

The People   Pop. 1980: 522,623, up 12% 1970–80; voting age pop. 366,683; 1% Am. Ind. 19% housing units rented. Median owner $38,100; renter $158. Households: 75% family, 41% with children, 66% married couples.

Presidential Vote

1980	Reagan (R)	116,207	(46%)
	Carter (D)	118,215	(47%)
	Anderson (I)	16,108	(6%)

Rep. David R. Obey (D) Elected Apr. 1, 1969; b. Oct. 3, 1938, Okmulgee, OK; home, Wausau; U. of WI, Marathon, U. of WI, Madison, M.A. 1960; Roman Catholic.

Career WI House of Reps., 1962–68.

Offices 2217 RHOB, 202-225-3365. Also Fed. Bldg., Wausau 54401, 715-842-5606.

Committees *Appropriations* (8th). Subcommittees: Foreign Operations; Labor-Health and Human Services-Education; Legislative. *Joint Economic Committee* (Ranking Member). Subcommittees: Investment, Jobs, and Prices; Monetary and Fiscal Policy.

Group Ratings

	ADA	ACLU	COPE	CFA	LCV	LWV	NTU	NSI	COC	ACA	CSFC
1982	100	67	85	85	99	83	41	30	9	13	29
1981	85	—	84	93	100	—	44	—	11	21	30
1980	94	70	75	79	78	100	23	0	58	15	26

National Journal Ratings

	Economic		Foreign		Cultural	
1982	89%	(LIB)	89%	(LIB)	83%	(LIB)
	11%	(CONS)	10%	(CONS)	17%	(CONS)
1981	89%	(LIB)	83%	(LIB)	82%	(LIB)
	3%	(CONS)	17%	(CONS)	18%	(CONS)

Key Votes

1) Reagan 81 Budget	AGN	5) Incr SS Rtmt Age	AGN
2) Reagan 81 Tax Cut	AGN	6) Saudi AWACS Sale	AGN
3) Bal Budget Amend	AGN	7) $ for MX Missile	AGN
4) Gas & Road Tax	FOR	8) Nerve Gas Prod	AGN

9) Poor Pay Food Stamps	AGN
10) Ban Crt Busing Order	AGN
11) Auto Local Content	FOR
12) Nuclear Arms Freeze	FOR

Election Results

1982 general	David R. Obey (D)	122,124	(68%)	($141,319)
	Bernard A. Zimmermann (R)	57,535	(32%)	($27,575)
1982 primary	David R. Obey (D)	60,677	(100%)	
1980 general	David R. Obey (D)	164,340	(65%)	($134,287)
	Vinton A. Vesta (R)	89,745	(35%)	($38,835)

Campaign Contributions and Expenditures

1981-82		Direct Cont. 81-82			PACS brkdwn		
Receipts	$165,305	Indiv	$65,098	Agr	$18,000	Ideo	$2,000
Expend.	$141,319	Party	$588	Bus	$10,100	Lbr	$52,250
Unspent	$71,913	PACS	$85,677	Hlth	$2,050	Prof	$350

EIGHTH DISTRICT

The 8th congressional district of Wisconsin could be called the Packers' district. Centered on the midwestern metropolis of Green Bay, with less than 100,000 people, it is the home of the Green Bay Packers and the smallest city with any kind of big-time athletic franchise in the United States. That the team is here is a reminder of the early days of pro football, when the National Football League included teams from towns like Green Bay and Canton, Ohio. During the late 1960s "the Pack" under Vince Lombardi was the first team to dominate the NFL during the Super Bowl era. The Packers in the swirling snows of Lambeau Field are the aspect of the 8th district best known to the outside world, although this 13-county district in northeastern Wisconsin has other features of note. It includes, in the same Fox River Valley as Green Bay, the city of Appleton, the hometown of Senator Joe McCarthy. It includes one county, Menominee, founded when an Indian reservation was terminated during the 1950s. It includes northwoods vacation and logging country and the gentler woods dotted with lakes of Door County, a peninsula jutting out into Lake Michigan.

There are some heavily Republican counties here, and a couple that usually go Democratic, but the real political balance is cast in the Fox River valley, around Green Bay and Appleton. This is a heavily German Catholic area: it went for John Kennedy in 1960 and came fairly close to going for Jimmy Carter in 1976. It seemed to react against the military policies of the Vietnam era (vestigial isolationism?) and against the cultural liberalism of the Carter administration. During most of the 1970s it was a marginal district in congressional elections. But the current congressman, Toby Roth, seems to have made it a safe Republican district again.

This is not because of any great legislative accomplishments. Roth, like most House Republicans, has little opportunity to stage-manage major legislation, and his committees (Foreign Affairs, Small Business) afford few opportunities for legislative productivity. His record on issues generally is solidly conservative; he is in effect a foot soldier rather than a general in Ronald Reagan's congressional army. Roth seems simply to work hard at keeping in touch with the district and handling constituency problems—the standard formula for incumbents' success. He had a well-known opponent in 1982, Ruth Clusen, former League of Women Voters president; but she could raise little money. Roth far outspent her and won, in a Democratic year, by a comfortable 57%–42% margin.

The People   Pop. 1980: 523,225, up 12% 1970–80; voting age pop. 362,554; 2% Am. Ind. 19% housing units rented. Median owner $43,800; renter $169. Households: 76% family, 42% with children, 67% married couples.

Presidential Vote

1980	Reagan (R)	139,698	(56%)
	Carter (D)	93,714	(38%)
	Anderson (I)	14,723	(6%)

Rep. Toby Roth (R) Elected 1978; b. Oct. 10, 1938; home, Appleton; Marquette U., B.A. 1961; Roman Catholic.

Career Realtor, WI House of Reps., 1972–78.

Offices 215 CHOB, 202-225-5665. Also 325 E. Walnut, Rm. 202, Green Bay 54305, 414-465-3931.

Committees *Foreign Affairs* (7th). Subcommittees: Africa; International Economic Policy and Trade. *Small Business* (11th). Subcommittees: Energy, Environment and Safety Issues Affecting Small Business; Export Opportunities and Special Small Business Problems.

Group Ratings

	ADA	ACLU	COPE	CFA	LCV	LWV	NTU	NSI	COC	ACA	CSFC
1982	10	12	13	15	42	25	75	100	68	87	62
1981	10	—	12	57	41	—	81	—	88	96	71
1980	22	23	10	14	48	30	62	90	67	75	80

National Journal Ratings

	Economic		Foreign		Cultural	
1982	28%	(LIB)	24%	(LIB)	21%	(LIB)
	71%	(CONS)	76%	(CONS)	76%	(CONS)
1981	22%	(LIB)	30%	(LIB)	28%	(LIB)
	77%	(CONS)	68%	(CONS)	72%	(CONS)

Key Votes

1) Reagan 81 Budget	FOR	5) Incr SS Rtmt Age	FOR	9) Poor Pay Food Stamps	FOR
2) Reagan 81 Tax Cut	FOR	6) Saudi AWACS Sale	FOR	10) Ban Crt Busing Order	FOR
3) Bal Budget Amend	FOR	7) $ for MX Missile	FOR	11) Auto Local Content	FOR
4) Gas & Road Tax	AGN	8) Nerve Gas Prod	AGN	12) Nuclear Arms Freeze	AGN

Election Results

1982 general	Toby Roth (R)	101,379	(57%)	($157,873)
	Ruth C. Clusen (D)	74,436	(42%)	($64,238)
1982 primary	Toby Roth (R)	43,273	(100%)	
1980 general	Toby Roth (R)	169,664	(68%)	($144,146)
	Michael R. Monfils (D)	81,043	(32%)	($20,233)

Campaign Contributions and Expenditures

1981-82		Direct Cont. 81-82		PACS brkdwn			
Receipts	$201,306	Indiv	$100,887	Agr	$15,050	Ideo	$3,250
Expend.	$157,873	Party	$15,520	Bus	$45,050	Lbr	$3,050
Unspent	$43,433	PACS	$75,444	Hlth	$4,250	Prof	$200

Indep Expend: For: $2,985 (NTL)

NINTH DISTRICT

The 9th congressional district of Wisconsin forms a kind of arc north and west of Milwaukee, around the outer edge of that metropolitan area. Redistricting in 1982 moved the district outward from Milwaukee—reflecting population movement in the 1960s and 1970s. Those were years when Milwaukeeans and residents of the close-in suburbs moved in large numbers to new subdivisions in what were not so long ago agricultural townships 20 or even 30 miles from Milwaukee. They have incorporated now, and some of them—Mequon and Brookfield—are among Milwaukee's highest-priced suburbs; the district also includes some of the high-income suburbs just north of Milwaukee on the lake. The 9th proceeds west and northwest into dairying country, taking in the city of West Bend, which has given its name to the appliance company there, and going as far north along Lake Michigan as the industrial city of Sheboygan. About two-thirds of the population is technically within the Milwaukee metropolitan area; but its actual boundary is hazy, and probably a larger percentage than one-third of the residents of this district think of themselves as residents of rural and small-town Wisconsin.

This is Wisconsin's most Republican district. It is the descendant of a district first created in 1964, and drawn to take Republican territory out of the 2d and 5th districts. Both its high-income and its dairying country are heavily Republican.

The current congressman, James Sensenbrenner, was first elected in 1978 when incumbent Robert Kasten ran for governor. Kasten lost that race in the primary, but was elected to the Senate in 1980. Sensenbrenner's only tough race was the 1978 primary, in which he barely beat a moderate candidate; since then he has won easily. Sensenbrenner is a solid conservative on issues in the House; the one exception is on some foreign policy issues, on which he, like other Wisconsinites, tends to be a little dovish.

Sensenbrenner is now the ranking minority member of the Judiciary subcommittee on Civil and Constitutional Rights. This is a hair-shirt assignment for a man of his beliefs; committee chairman Don Edwards holds a solid 5–3 margin and is not going to let measures he opposes out of the committee if he can help it. These include constitutional amendments to ban abortion and require a balanced budget, to allow prayer in schools and ban busing to achieve integration. Should these measures come to the floor, Sensenbrenner will likely be one of the leading speakers in their behalf.

The People   Pop. 1980: 522,950, up 15% 1970–80; voting age pop.; 1% Span. orig. 22% housing units rented. Median owner $66,900; renter $206. Households: 81% family, 46% with children, 73% married couples.

Presidential Vote

1980	Reagan (R)	150,995	(59%)
	Carter (D)	88,156	(34%)
	Anderson (I)	18,044	(7%)

Rep. F. James Sensenbrenner, Jr. (R) Elected 1978; b. June 14, 1943, Chicago, IL; home, Shorewood; Stanford U., A.B. 1965, U. of WI, J.D. 1968; Episcopalian.

Career Staff of U.S. Rep. Arthur Younger of CA, 1965; Asst. to WI Senate Minor. Ldr., 1967; Practicing atty., 1968–; WI Assembly, 1968–76.

Offices 315 CHOB, 202-225-5101. Also 120 Bishops Way, Brookfield 53005, 414-784-1111.

Committees *Judiciary* (7th). Subcommittees: Civil and Constitutional Rights; Crime. *Science and Technology* (5th). Subcommittees: Energy Development and Applications; Science, Research and Technology.

Group Ratings

	ADA	ACLU	COPE	CFA	LCV	LWV	NTU	NSI	COC	ACA	CSFC
1982	25	33	13	23	67	42	95	67	73	83	70
1981	20	—	11	43	57	—	98	—	84	92	76
1980	22	33	5	14	48	30	67	90	63	79	83

National Journal Ratings

	Economic		Foreign		Cultural	
1982	20%	(LIB)	42%	(LIB)	57%	(LIB)
	80%	(CONS)	58%	(CONS)	42%	(CONS)
1981	24%	(LIB)	53%	(LIB)	21%	(LIB)
	68%	(CONS)	45%	(CONS)	79%	(CONS)

Key Votes

1) Reagan 81 Budget	FOR	5) Incr SS Rtmt Age	FOR
2) Reagan 81 Tax Cut	FOR	6) Saudi AWACS Sale	AGN
3) Bal Budget Amend	FOR	7) $ for MX Missile	AGN
4) Gas & Road Tax	AGN	8) Nerve Gas Prod	AGN

9) Poor Pay Food Stamps	FOR
10) Ban Crt Busing Order	FOR
11) Auto Local Content	AGN
12) Nuclear Arms Freeze	AGN

Election Results

1982 general	F. James Sensenbrenner, Jr. (R) ...	111,503	(100%)	($99,631)
1982 primary	F. James Sensenbrenner, Jr. (R) ...	43,693	(100%)	
1980 general	F. James Sensenbrenner, Jr. (R) ...	206,227	(78%)	($143,524)
	Gary C. Benedict (D)	56,838	(22%)	($2,678)

Campaign Contributions and Expenditures

1981-82		Direct Cont. 81-82		PACS brkdwn			
Receipts	$141,516	Indiv	$76,721	Agr	$6,500	Ideo	$1,000
Expend.	$99,631	Party	$9,665	Bus	$31,365	Lbr	$—
Unspent	$75,375	PACS	$41,370	Hlth	$1,150	Prof	$1,300

WYOMING

Wyoming is the closest thing we have to the Old West—and also one of the closest we have to a state whose economy is driven by technological innovation and economic creativity. In Wyoming cattle ranchers, organized in the Wyoming Stock Growers' Association, and a railroad, the Union Pacific, remain important political powers. But the most important force in the life of the state today is the exploration for oil, gas, and other minerals which has transformed Wyoming's economy, substantially increased its population, and raised its income levels up near the nation's highest. Those changes have also transformed this state politically. In national politics it was a closely divided state for many years, with Republicans getting increasingly stronger in the 1960s. The minerals boom, however, has made Wyoming one of the nation's most heavily Republican states.

The old partisan divisions were based on something like class warfare, western style. The big ranchers who sponsored the first major white settlement consolidated their power in the Johnson County land war of the 1890s, a far from gentle affair. The railroad's clout came from the land it received for building the first transcontinental line across southern Wyoming in the 1860s. The railroad workers, who for years comprised a large percentage of the residents of Wyoming's southern tier of counties, tended to vote Democratic; the ranchers who populated the more sparsely populated central and northern counties tended to vote Republican. This was the basic partisan split which made Wyoming a closely contested state from the 1930s to the 1960s. On top of that, personal campaigning always plays an important role in Wyoming politics. Even today there are no cities with as many as 50,000 people here, and Wyoming voters expect to talk with—not just shake hands with, but actually exchange views with—their governor, senators, and congressman every couple of years or so.

Despite the national recession, Wyoming in the early 1980s continued to find itself in the midst of a boom the likes of which it had never seen before. There has been strip mining of coal in the northeastern part of the state, minerals in Johnson County and around Rock Springs (uranium, coal, soda ash), oil exploration centering around Casper, and, most important, the oil discoveries in the Overthrust Belt in southwestern Wyoming. Recent Census estimates tell the story: there are more than 500,000 Wyomingites now, and the state's population increased more in the dozen years after 1970 than in the 50 years between 1920 and 1970.

Such explosive growth obviously transforms the public life—and the quality of life generally—in such a sparsely settled place. Lots of people in Wyoming today have gotten quite rich. They see their wealth as a fair reward for developing oil and minerals the nation needs. Others are disturbed at the ticky-tacky growth at the edge of Wyoming's towns or near its mineral sites. Many who have flocked here live in grimy trailers, linked precariously to civilization's utilities and unprotected against the winds and snows that come out of the enormous sky. Wyoming simply does not have the infrastructure to protect itself against the pollution that even a small influx of people brings. There is another kind of pollution as well: the mining-camp atmosphere that builds around suddenly sprung-up camps near drilling rigs or mines. Wyoming is one of the few states that has always had more men than women—a sure sign that it never got far from a frontier atmosphere (and also the reason it was the first part of the United States, back in 1869, to give women the vote). In the 1970s around towns like Rock Springs there grew a subculture of prostitution, gambling, and violent crime, which would have been familiar to anyone acquainted with Virginia City, Nevada, or Cripple Creek, Colorado, in their heydays.

Presidential politics. Wyoming is one state where, in the 1970s, deregulation of oil and natural gas was a policy with genuine popular support. People here felt that federal price controls were hobbling their efforts to find new energy sources, just as they complained that federal regulations, backed by environmentalists living in Oregon or San Francisco, prevented them from poisoning the coyotes that were killing their sheep. As a result, this has become one of the most Republican states in the nation in presidential elections and in congressional elections as well—although in the latter the Republicans have done well at least in part because they have offered excellent candidates.

Governor. Rapid growth has changed Wyoming's state politics beyond recognition. This state, increasingly Republican in national politics, has had a Democratic governor since 1974. Ed Herschler won his first election in 1974 largely because he opposed a slurry pipeline—a device to mix coal with water and pump it out of the state to market for use in highway and street surfacing. Coal operators wanted the slurry pipeline, but the railroads, environmentalists, and ranchers, fearful of depleting the state's scarce water supplies, were all opposed. In 1978 Herschler was reelected despite controversy over law enforcement in Rock Springs; at one point the governor fired his own attorney general and ousted the state party chairman.

But he shifted the focus to his proposal to increase Wyoming's severance tax on minerals by 5%, and criticized his Republican opponent's dealings with a mining company.

By 1982 Herschler was widely popular and was reelected by a wide margin over a Casper oil man and former state House speaker. Herschler is not an environmentalist in the Sierra Club sense, but evidently voters see him as a balancer of interests, all of which they would like served. He has been mentioned as a Senate candidate, but has shown no inclination to run; his issues are state issues, and his popularity is based on his performance at the state level.

Senators. Wyoming's congressional delegation does not have much seniority, but man for man it is one of the most talented delegations any state can boast. Its senior member is Malcolm Wallop, first elected in 1976 and reelected in 1982. Wallop is a solid part of the mainstream of Senate Republicans. On issues he is inclined to go with the right on most but not all matters; temperamentally, he is inclined to go along with the Republican leadership. He is a believer in the free market as an allocator of resources, and he opposes what he sees as intrusive federal regulations. He does, however, take pains to say that he is an environmentalist, or at least one who takes into account environmental considerations when setting public policy.

His committee assignments are very closely related to matters of great importance to Wyoming. He is a member of the Finance Committee, and chairs the subcommittee on Energy and Agricultural Taxation; he is a member of the Energy and Natural Resources Committee, and chairs the subcommittee on Public Lands and Reserved Water. Before 1982, he chaired the Senate's Ethics Committee, an assignment which made him the leading advocate of the expulsion of convicted Abscam defendant Harrison Williams; that post was one he happily relinquished.

Wallop is perhaps the least firmly established of Wyoming's three members in Congress. He surprised and upset 18-year Democratic Senator Gale McGee in 1976, and he faced a spirited challenge from Democrat Rodger McDaniel in 1982. But McDaniel was 34, managed Edward Kennedy's Wyoming campaign in 1980, favored a lot of national policies which most people in Wyoming oppose, and had far less money to spend than Wallop; and the recession, strong as it was in most of the country, was not really depressing the living standards of most voters here. Wallop won with 57% of the vote, a solid victory, but not an overwhelming one. He still lost the Union Pacific counties which other Republicans have carried.

Wyoming's junior senator is Alan Simpson, who though still in his first term has played an important role on several national issues, and with great success. He is a member of the Environment and Public Works Committee, and chairs the subcommittee on Nuclear Regulation. This is a sensitive assignment; Simpson has proved to be a cautious but convinced advocate of nuclear power. He is chairman as well of the full Veterans' Affairs Committee, and there also is a voice of caution against what he considers jumping to conclusions on issues like Agent Orange.

But Simpson's most important assignment has been on the Judiciary Committee. Here, after two years in the Senate, he inherited the chairmanship of the Immigration and Refugee Policy Subcommittee, and the right to handle one of the hottest potatoes before Congress, the immigration bill. On this Simpson has done what even his critics must concede is a brilliant job. Working with his counterpart in the House, Romano Mazzoli of Kentucky, Simpson constructed a bipartisan bill which compromised some of the main issues. It did not fudge, however; it provided for sanctions against employers of illegal aliens, for increases in the quotas allowed Latin countries, and for an amnesty for illegal aliens admitted before a certain date. It was criticized from all sides. But in a Senate where opponents of any measure can choose from a dazzling array of procedural devices to kill it, Simpson was able to steer his bill through to passage with 80 votes. He did it, moreover, without the support of the ranking Democrat on the subcommittee (and chief sponsor of the 1965 law), Edward Kennedy. Simpson is expected to repeat his feat again in 1983 or 1984; the bill was stopped in the House, in the 1982 lame duck session, but was moved forward by its sponsors there in early 1983.

Simpson was able to do this in large part because he has earned the respect of most senators in almost record time. Part of the reason is his sense of humor: he has one of the best repertoires of jokes, and some of the most brilliant timing and delivery, that the Senate has seen for a long time. But he also studies his issues hard and thoughtfully—he knew little about immigration when he came to the Senate in 1979—and supports his conclusions strenuously but without cheap shots. It's fairly easy to predict where he'll come out on an issue; he's a solid conservative on most matters. But he is nonetheless one of those senators whose support for a particular measure or an argument can sway colleagues' votes.

Simpson is ultimately a doer, not a critic. That was one reason he exploded at Jesse Helms for his delaying tactics during the lame duck session. Helms has specialized in procuring roll call votes with which he can run direct mail campaigns against his colleagues; he failed signally to accomplish his primary legislative agenda in 1982 and muffed the farm bill in 1981. Temperamentally and historically, Helms is part of a minority; Simpson thinks like a member of the majority, which in Wyoming he certainly is, and he fulfills his responsibilities accordingly. So Simpson, proud of his work on the immigration bill and frustrated because it was being delayed to death in the House, was able to articulate the low opinion most senators, and perhaps most Republican senators, have of Helms and his tactics.

Simpson is not just part of the majority in Wyoming; he is part of one of its leading political families. His father, Milward Simpson, served as governor and senator. Al Simpson jumped from the state House of Representatives to the U.S. Senate in 1978 with wonderfully little competition when Senator Clifford Hansen retired. Simpson is expected to be reelected without much trouble in 1984; this should be one of the Republicans' safest seats.

Congressman-at-large. Wyoming's one and only congressman is Richard Cheney, who brings to the office an unusual credential: he was White House chief of staff under President Ford. Cheney achieved that distinction in his middle 30s as a protege of Donald Rumsfeld; and in the ordinary course of things he could have been expected to live a comfortable life in Washington, earning a good living as a lobbyist. Instead he went home to Wyoming and ran for the House of Representatives in 1978. His race was not easy: he had a serious Republican opponent and suffered a mild heart attack during the campaign. Nevertheless he won convincingly.

It looked as if Cheney were moving from a position near the center of power to one very far out on the periphery, as a junior member of the minority party in a House which in general seemed rather disorganized. But it has worked out quite differently. In 1981 and for much of 1982, the Republican leadership in effect controlled the House with a solid working majority. Cheney, elected after one term as chairman of the House Republican Policy Committee, was a member of that leadership. House Democrats have to wait much longer for leadership positions, because there is so much more competition. House Republicans, much fewer in

WYOMING 1299

number and with far less seniority (most House Republicans today were first elected in 1978 or later), can reward a talented newcomer right away.

Despite his background in the Ford White House, Cheney was a solid supporter of the Reagan economic program. He believed—and experience in the White House can fortify this—that government had gotten too large, and was growing larger absent strong countervailing forces; he shared also the president's feeling that American defenses were too weak and the nation's resolve too dubious. Though only in his third term, Cheney has good prospects for becoming Republican leader in the House some day. He has the resume to be the natural candidate of moderates who viscerally prefer a Ford to a Reagan and the record on issues to be the first choice of a great many Reaganites; he has the ability to lead the party ably in the House, and the calm and crisply articulate demeanor needed to be an able spokesman for it on television. He has, moreover, the respect of the national press, which sees most House Republicans as yahoos but respects Cheney because of his high-level experience.

Cheney serves on the Interior Committee, and is ranking Republican on the Water and Power Resources Subcommittee. He tends to Wyoming problems, and has been reelected by very large margins. Washington observers presume that he must be hungering to run for the Senate, but he seems on his way to being a very important member of the House, and one with a safe seat. Moreover, both of Wyoming's senators are comparatively young, politically strong, and philosophically compatible with Cheney, who is doing quite nicely where he is.

The People Est. Pop. 1982: 502,000; Pop. 1980: 467,557, up 6.8% 1980–82 and 41.3% 1970–80; .21% of U.S. total, 50th largest; voting age pop. 324,004; 1% American Indian, 1% Black, 4% Spanish origin. Single ancestry: 13% German, 11% English, 5% Irish, 2% Swedish, 1% Norwegian, French, Scottish, Italian, Dutch, Polish. Registered voters (1982): 230,074 Total. No party registration. 20% with 1–3 yrs. col., 17% with 4+ yrs. col., 8% below poverty level. 27% housing units rented; median house value: $60,400; median monthly rent: $220. Households: 73% family, 43% with children, 65% married couples.

1982 Share of Federal Tax Burden $1,536,700,000; .26% of U.S. total, 49th largest.

1982 Share of Federal Expenditures

	Total		Non-Defense		Defense	
Total Expend	$1,048m	(0.17%)	$873m	(0.21%)	$174m	(0.10%)
St/Lcl Grants	349m	(0.40%)	348m	(0.39%)	1m	(2.78%)
Salary/Wages	182m	(0.23%)	100m	(0.37%)	82m	(0.16%)
Ind Payments	407m	(0.14%)	357m	(0.14%)	50m	(0.17%)
Procurement	103m	(0.07%)	37m	(0.12%)	66m	(0.06%)
Other Programs	8m	(0.15%)	8m	(0.15%)	0m	(0%)
Loan/Insurance	199m	(0.31%)	186m	(0.30%)	13m	(0.59%)

Political Lineup Governor, Ed Herschler (D). Senators, Malcolm Wallop (R) and Alan K. Simpson (R). Representatives, 1 R at large. State Senate, 30 (11 D and 19 R), State House of Representatives, 63 (25 D and 38 R).

Presidential Vote

1980	Reagan (R)	110,700	(63%)
	Carter (D)	49,427	(28%)
	Anderson (I)	12,072	(7%)
1976	Ford (R)	92,717	(59%)
	Carter (D)	62,239	(40%)

SENATORS

Sen. Malcolm Wallop (R) Elected 1976, seat up 1988; b. Feb. 27, 1933, New York, NY; home, Big Horn; Yale U., B.A. 1954; Episcopal.

Career Rancher; Army, 1955–57; WY House of Reps., 1969–73; WY Senate, 1973–77; Candidate for Repub. Nomination for Gov. of WY, 1974.

Offices 210 RSOB, 202-224-6441. Also 2201 Fed. Bldg., Casper 82601, 307-266-3240; and 2009 Fed. Ctr., Cheyenne 82001, 307-634-0626.

Committees *Energy and Natural Resources* (5th). Subcommittees: Energy and Mineral Resources; Water and Power; Public Lands and Reserved Water (Chairman). *Finance* (7th). Subcommittees: Taxation and Debt Management; International Trade; Energy and Agricultural Taxation (Chairman). *Select Committee on Intelligence* (5th). Subcommittees: Budget Authorization (Chairman); Analysis and Production.

Group Ratings

	ADA	ACLU	COPE	CFA	LCV	LWV	NTU	NSI	COC	ACA	CSFC
1982	10	32	9	0	16	38	85	100	75	74	79
1981	10	—	11	14	25	—	75	—	100	70	85
1980	22	23	5	0	28	30	63	100	95	92	80

National Journal Ratings

	Economic		Foreign		Cultural	
1982	3%	(LIB)	16%	(LIB)	19%	(LIB)
	96%	(CONS)	68%	(CONS)	80%	(CONS)
1981	15%	(LIB)	15%	(LIB)	20%	(LIB)
	84%	(CONS)	84%	(CONS)	76%	(CONS)

Key Votes

1) Reagan 81 Budget	FOR	5) $ to El Salvador	FOR	9) Poor Pay Food Stamps	FOR
2) Reagan 81 Tax Cut	FOR	6) Saudi AWACS Sale	FOR	10) Ban Crt Busing Order	FOR
3) Bal Budget Amend	FOR	7) Ban Abortion	AGN	11) Clinch Riv Brdr Rctr	FOR
4) Gas & Road Tax	AGN	8) Nerve Gas Prod	FOR	12) Legal Services Corp	AGN

Election Results

1982 general	Malcolm Wallop (R)	94,690	(57%)	($1,139,082)
	Rodger McDaniel (D)	72,453	(43%)	($389,511)
1982 primary	Malcolm Wallop (R) unopposed ...	46,834		
1976 primary	Malcolm Wallop (R)	84,810	(55%)	($301,595)
	Gale McGee (D)	70,558	(45%)	($181,028)

Campaign Contributions and Expenditures

1979–82		Direct Cont. 79–82		PACS brkdwn			
Receipts	$1,151,531	Indiv	$592,636	Agr	$14,600	Ideo	$31,700
Expend.	$1,139,082	Party	$29,125	Bus	$379,044	Lbr	$2,500
Unspent	$19,080	PACS	$472,290	Hlth	$16,750	Prof	$15,000
		Cand	$7,000				

Indirect Party Expend: $73,760   *Indep Expend:* For: $1,706 (NRA) Agn: $41,922 (CCSND)

Sen. Alan K. Simpson (R) Elected 1978, seat up 1984; b. Sept. 2, 1931, Denver, CO; home, Cody; U. of WY, B.S. 1954, J.D. 1958; Episcopal.

Career Practicing atty., 1958; Cody City Atty., 1959–69; WY House of Reps., 1964–78, Major. Whip, 1973–75, Major. Ldr., 1975–77, Speaker Pro Tem, 1977.

Offices 709 HSOB, 202-224-3424. Also 1731 Sheridan Ave., Cody 82414, 307-587-5323.

Committees *Environment and Public Works* (4th). Subcommittees: Environmental Pollution; Nuclear Regulation (Chairman); Toxic Substances and Environmental Oversight. *Judiciary* (6th). Subcommittees: Courts; Immigration and Refugee Policy (Chairman); Separation of Powers. *Veterans' Affairs* (Chairman).

Group Ratings

	ADA	ACLU	COPE	CFA	LCV	LWV	NTU	NSI	COC	ACA	CSFC
1982	15	39	3	7	16	55	77	80	76	85	75
1981	5	—	2	21	38	—	80	—	100	86	83
1980	17	33	5	0	45	50	64	100	88	91	80

National Journal Ratings

	Economic		Foreign		Cultural	
1982	4%	(LIB)	16%	(LIB)	34%	(LIB)
	94%	(CONS)	68%	(CONS)	65%	(CONS)
1981	2%	(LIB)	33%	(LIB)	20%	(LIB)
	88%	(CONS)	66%	(CONS)	76%	(CONS)

Key Votes

1) Reagan 81 Budget	FOR	5) $ to El Salvador	FOR	9) Poor Pay Food Stamps	FOR
2) Reagan 81 Tax Cut	FOR	6) Saudi AWACS Sale	FOR	10) Ban Crt Busing Order	FOR
3) Bal Budget Amend	FOR	7) Ban Abortion	AGN	11) Clinch Riv Brdr Rctr	FOR
4) Gas & Road Tax	AGN	8) Nerve Gas Prod	FOR	12) Legal Services Corp	AGN

Election Results

1978 general	Alan K. Simpson (R)	82,908	(62%)	($439,805)
	Raymond B. Whitaker (D)	50,456	(38%)	($142,749)
1978 primary	Alan K. Simpson (R)	37,332	(55%)	
	Hugh Binford (R)	20,768	(30%)	($245,064)
	Two others (R)	10,203	(15%)	
1972 general	Clifford P. Hansen (R)	101,314	(71%)	($169,878)
	Mike M. Vinich (D)	40,753	(29%)	($10,411)

Campaign Contributions and Expenditures

1977-78		PACS brkdwn			
Receipts	$442,484	Agr	$4,300	Ideo	$7,905
Expend.	$439,805	Bus	$90,380	Lbr	$1,000
Unspent	$2,677	Hlth	$16,500	Prof	$5,500

GOVERNOR

Gov. Ed Herschler (D) Elected 1974, term expires Jan. 1987; b. Oct. 27, 1918, Lincoln Cnty.; home, Cheyenne; U. of CO, U. of WY, LL.B. 1949; Episcopal.

Career USMC, WWII; Practicing atty., 1949–74; Kemmerer Town Atty., 1949–74; Lincoln Cnty. Prosecuting Atty., WY House of Reps., 1960–69.

Offices Capitol Bldg., Cheyenne 82002, 307-777-7434.

Election Results

1982 gen.	Ed Herschler (D)	106,424	(63%)
	Warren A. Morton (R)	62,119	(37%)
1982 prim.	Ed Herschler (D)	44,396	(85%)
	Pat McGuire (D)	7,720	(15%)
1978 gen.	Ed Herschler (D)	69,972	(51%)
	John C. Ostlund (R)	67,595	(49%)

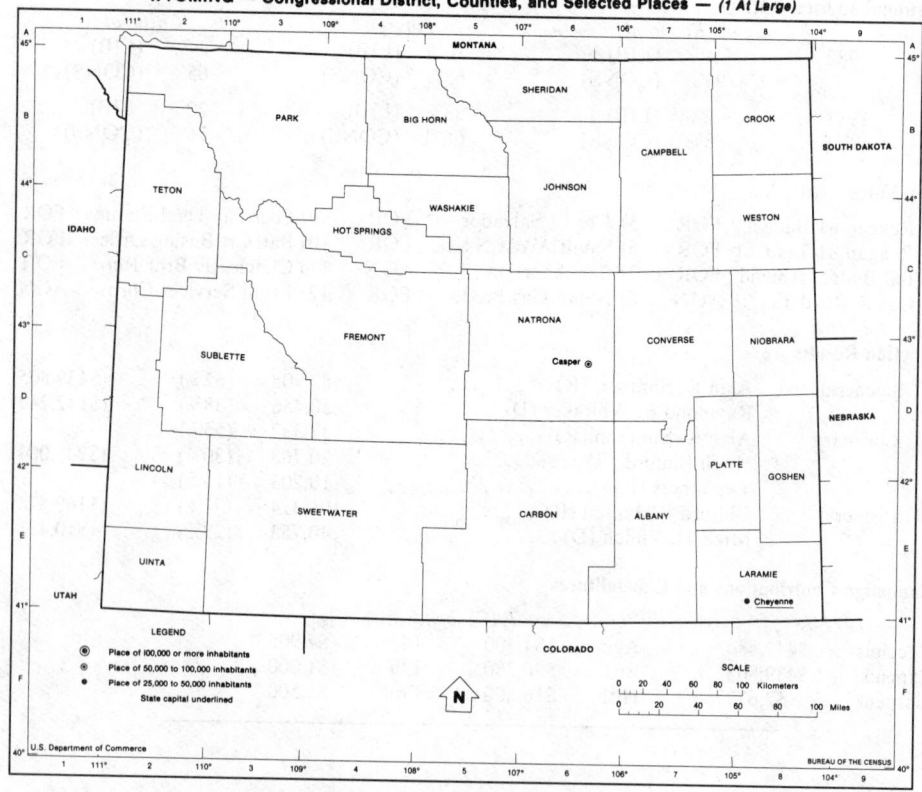

WYOMING — Congressional District, Counties, and Selected Places — *(1 At Large)*

LEGEND

Place of 100,000 or more inhabitants
Place of 50,000 to 100,000 inhabitants
Place of 25,000 to 50,000 inhabitants
State capital underlined

SCALE

U.S. Department of Commerce

BUREAU OF THE CENSUS

All political boundaries are as of January 1, 1980

Rep. Richard Bruce (Dick) **Cheney** (R) Elected 1978; b. Jan. 30, 1941, Lincoln, NE; home, Casper; U. of WY, B.A. 1965, M.A. 1966, U. of WI, 1968; Methodist.

Career Spec. Asst. to the Dir. of OEO; Dpty. to White House Pres. Counselor Donald Rumsfeld; Asst. Dir. for Operations, Cost of Living Cncl.; V.P., Bradley, Woods & Co., investment advisors, 1973–74, 1976–78; Asst. to Pres. Gerald Ford, 1974–76.

Offices 225 CHOB, 202-225-2311. Also Fed. Bldg., Rm. 4005, Casper 82601, 307-265-5550.

Committee *Interior and Insular Affairs* (6th). Subcommittees: Water and Power Resources; Public Lands and National Parks.

Group Ratings

	ADA	ACLU	COPE	CFA	LCV	LWV	NTU	NSI	COC	ACA	CSFC
1982	5	0	7	0	3	25	93	100	80	100	79
1981	5	—	9	21	6	—	87	—	82	79	73
1980	6	13	10	21	12	22	64	100	70	95	80

National Journal Ratings

	Economic		Foreign		Cultural	
1982	5%	(LIB)	2%	(LIB)	4%	(LIB)
	94%	(CONS)	97%	(CONS)	87%	(CONS)
1981	4%	(LIB)	39%	(LIB)	27%	(LIB)
	79%	(CONS)	60%	(CONS)	73%	(CONS)

Key Votes

1) Reagan 81 Budget	FOR	5) Incr SS Rtmt Age	FOR	9) Poor Pay Food Stamps	FOR
2) Reagan 81 Tax Cut	FOR	6) Saudi AWACS Sale	FOR	10) Ban Crt Busing Order	FOR
3) Bal Budget Amend	FOR	7) $ for MX Missile	FOR	11) Auto Local Content	AGN
4) Gas & Road Tax	AGN	8) Nerve Gas Prod	FOR	12) Nuclear Arms Freeze	AGN

Election Results

1982 general	Richard Bruce (Dick) Cheney (R) .	113,236	(71%)	($111,631)
	Ted Hommel (D)	46,041	(29%)	($5,921)
1982 primary	Richard Bruce (Dick) Cheney (R) .	67,093	(89%)	
	Michael Dee (R)	8,453	(11%)	
1980 general	Richard Bruce (Dick) Cheney (R) .	116,361	(69%)	($97,959)
	Jim Rogers (D)	53,338	(31%)	($0)

Campaign Contributions and Expenditures

1981-82		Direct Cont. 81-82		PACS brkdwn			
Receipts	$110,730	Indiv	$28,230	Agr	$1,100	Ideo	$2,516
Expend.	$111,631	Party	$5,000	Bus	$57,711	Lbr	$—
Unspent	$23,882	PACS	$70,027	Hlth	$7,700	Prof	$1,000

DISTRICT OF COLUMBIA

Washington, D.C., is a political paradox: the capital of a great democracy and a city that, until 1974, was not allowed to choose its own mayor or city council for 100 years; a black-majority capital in a white-majority nation; a city whose most prominent citizens make their livings in public affairs but know little or nothing of the public affairs of their own city. It is probably true that those involved in national politics in any great nation know or care little about the local politics of the capital. But in the United States the phenomenon is more noticeable and pronounced than in Britain or France, because our capital is a city whose only significant business is government; it is not a commercial or cultural center like London or Paris. And the separation between national and local politics is particularly notable in Washington because of race.

For Washington, from the days before the Civil War, has been a special city for blacks. The slave trade was abolished here as part of the Compromise of 1850, and the city became a haven for free Negroes, who heavily outnumbered the slaves by the time Lincoln became president. Blacks formed more than one-fourth of the electorate that installed Governor Alexander Shepherd, the last elected head of the D.C. government in the 19th century, whose profligate spending led Congress to revoke the city's system of home rule. And blacks held high office in the District during the rest of the 19th century under Republican administrations. At the northern edge of the South, Washington always had a higher percentage of blacks than most major American cities; and when the city's metropolitan population ballooned in the years after the New Deal and World War II, it was inevitable that, with the suburbs restricted to whites, the District would have a black majority. It was fear of this majority, more than anything else, that kept Congress from granting the District self-government, even though the same Congress had helped establish some of the institutions—Howard University, Freedmen's Hospital—that made Washington so important to blacks all over the nation.

Washington officially got its black majority in the 1960 census; by 1970 the District was 71% black, a figure that has remained the same in the 1980 counts. Washington is now our only major city without a white working class. Its affluent whites live mostly in areas west of Rock Creek Park, in such redeveloped (or "gentrified") neighborhoods as Capitol Hill, and other neighborhoods (e.g., Adams-Morgan and Mount Pleasant) that are fast being gentrified but for the moment are very proud of what some citizens call their Third World atmosphere (to which many illegal immigrants from Latin America contribute). The white population is almost entirely highly educated and high income; the poor elderly whites who once lived in fear in newly black neighborhoods are now almost all gone. There are many well-to-do blacks in the District too, although the outmigration of middle-income blacks to Prince Georges County, Maryland, and less frequently, to other suburbs, has deprived the city of an important segment of its black middle class.

The development of electoral politics in the District was delayed by the long time it took to gain home rule. Not until 1964 could the residents of the District vote for president; not until 1968 could they elect their own school board; not until 1971 did Washington get a non-voting delegate in the House of Representatives. Only in 1974 was the District able to elect its mayor and city council. Until home rule, control of the District's budget and lawmaking processes were in the hands of Congress, and for 22 years (1949–53, 1955–73) that meant mostly in the hands of South Carolina Congressman John McMillan, chairman of the House District of Columbia Committee. McMillan and his fellow Dixiecrats on the House Committee were considered implacably hostile to the District's black majority and provided the city with many of the worst aspects of colonial government. Their power collapsed suddenly in 1972, when McMillan was defeated in his primary in South Carolina (in a district with a large black percentage) and several other southern committee members retired.

Yet even today Congress inevitably retains much power over the District. It is the power of the purse—Congress every year votes the District a federal payment, in lieu of the taxes federal buildings might pay if they were not tax exempt. The question is how much the federal payment should be. For years the federal payment gave Congress the same kind of power over Washington that most state legislatures get from the aid they provide large city governments; and while most big-city mayors are used to going up to the capital with hat in hand, local Washington politicians assumed those days would be over when home rule came. By the early 1980s, the determination of the formula became a largely automatic matter, but even so there is always the threat that some politician—a suburban congressman angry over some local matter, a congressman angry about a traffic ticket—will try to hold the federal payment hostage for some trivial demand. But for the most part Congress has let the District do what it wants, even when members have had some serious doubts, as they did on the D.C. lottery, for example. The height of intervention in recent years came when the District's council amended its rape and sexual offense laws in ways that most House members thought foolish; but the city council itself changed its mind before Congress could take final action.

At the head of the District government today is Mayor Marion Barry, who not so long ago was known as a militant who started an organization called Pride, Inc. He ran for the school board and got citywide recognition. In 1978 he won a close three-way primary over incumbent Walter Washington and City Council President Sterling Tucker; in 1982 he won a second term by defeating his main challenger, former HUD and HEW/HHS Secretary Patricia Harris. One thing that is fascinating about Washington's electoral politics is that support for candidates does not differ much by race: the percentage in both 1974 and 1978 mayoral primaries among whites and blacks differed by only a few points, and in the 1982 primary by not much more. Age and cultural attitudes are more important in determining choices, and Washington has never had an electoral struggle here of the kind seen in so many cities between blacks and whites for control of the city government. Many blacks see in gentrification the possibility of a rise in the white percentage in the city, a white takeover of its government. But whites in Washington think that blacks ought to be in control here and are less than eager to take over a government that does not much impinge on their lives anyway.

Before the 1982 election, many observers thought Barry would be in trouble, and he attracted a field of serious competitors. There had been some serious fiscal problems, and some allegations of financial irregularities in Pride, Inc., including some involving the mayor's former wife. But Barry seemed to hit his stride in late 1981, and his confidence was increased by his fundraising success: he raised something like $1 million, more than the District had ever seen in a campaign before. There was an ugly side to this, a sense that this administration, like those in many other cities, was hitting all the smart money contributors who would be asking for something in return sooner or later. But Harris was unable to persuade voters that Barry's work had been ineffective or that he was an inappropriate choice for the job, and so her own credentials never became the focus of debate.

Barry had the advantage of running for reelection in a city that was thriving, for reasons many of which had nothing to do with local government. Economically much of Washington is booming. People are renovating houses and apartments; the business district is thriving and moving eastward into territory land developers once shunned; property values are still climbing not only in affluent white areas but in many of the city's comfortable black neighborhoods as well. But the city government tends to operate at the edge of fiscal solvency; some departments remain bloated with civil servants (some a legacy of the McMillan era), while others provide deficient services. The District government performs many services better than it is given credit for. But voters in Washington are getting used to the fact that there are no longer any good alibis for the failings of local government here.

The District has one member of Congress, Delegate Walter Fauntroy, who necessarily spends a lot of time on District affairs. Like other nonvoting members, he can vote in committee, and he is now the number two Democrat on the House District of Columbia Committee. He first won his seat in a special 1971 election, and the real contest was in the Democratic primary; he has had no serious opposition since. Fauntroy gets on fairly well now with Mayor Barry, although he supported Tucker in the last election. He seems not to have any ambition to run for mayor himself. A minister with a proud past in the civil rights movement, he is also a fine tenor and does a fine rendition of "The Impossible Dream."

Fauntroy has not had particularly good fortune when he has ventured beyond local matters, however. In 1979, when Andrew Young was fired as Ambassador to the United Nations, for negotiating with PLO members, Fauntroy was one of the black leaders who made a great show of interest in and support for the PLO—although it became painfully obvious that he knew virtually nothing about Middle East policy. He seems inclined to take any negative incident involving a black politician—even the issuing of a traffic ticket to a black congressman—as evidence of racism; this seems more likely the result of naivete than of any demagogic instinct.

When he does take constructive action, it is not always successful. In 1978 he got the Congress to approve a constitutional amendment giving the District full representation in the Congress, which in practical terms would mean the addition of two senators and a vote as well as a voice for the city's congressman. Fauntroy himself would obviously have a good chance to be elected to the Senate if this were passed. But as of early 1983 far fewer states than needed had ratified the amendment, and some—prompted by a right-wing movement interested in squelching both this measure and the Equal Rights Amendment—have explicitly disapproved it. It seems almost certain to join the list of constitutional amendments that have never been passed.

Fauntroy is a member of the Banking Committee, in which he was probably first interested because of its jurisdiction over housing programs. Now he is chairman of the subcommittee on Domestic Monetary Policy. This is potentially an important pressure point, a place where Congress can exert pressure on the technically autonomous Federal Reserve System. Fauntroy, however, perhaps unjustly, is probably not taken very seriously by central bankers; and any tendency they might have to underestimate the subcommittee is strengthened by the identity of its ranking Republican, George Hansen of Idaho.

The People Est. Pop. 1982: 631,000; Pop. 1980: 638,333, dn. 1.1% 1980–82 and 15.6% 1970–80; .28% of U.S. total, 47th largest; voting age pop. 494,842; 66% Black, 3% Spanish origin, 1% Asian origin. Registered voters (1982): 368,803 Total. 283,876 D (77%); 32,424 R (9%); 50,216 other (14%). 14% with 1–3 yrs. col., 28% with 4+ yrs. col. 18.9% below poverty level. 59% housing units rented; median house value: $70,700; median monthly rent: $208. Households: 53% family, 29% with children, 30% married couples.

1982 Share of Federal Tax Burden $2,145,800,000; .36% of U.S. total, 43d largest.

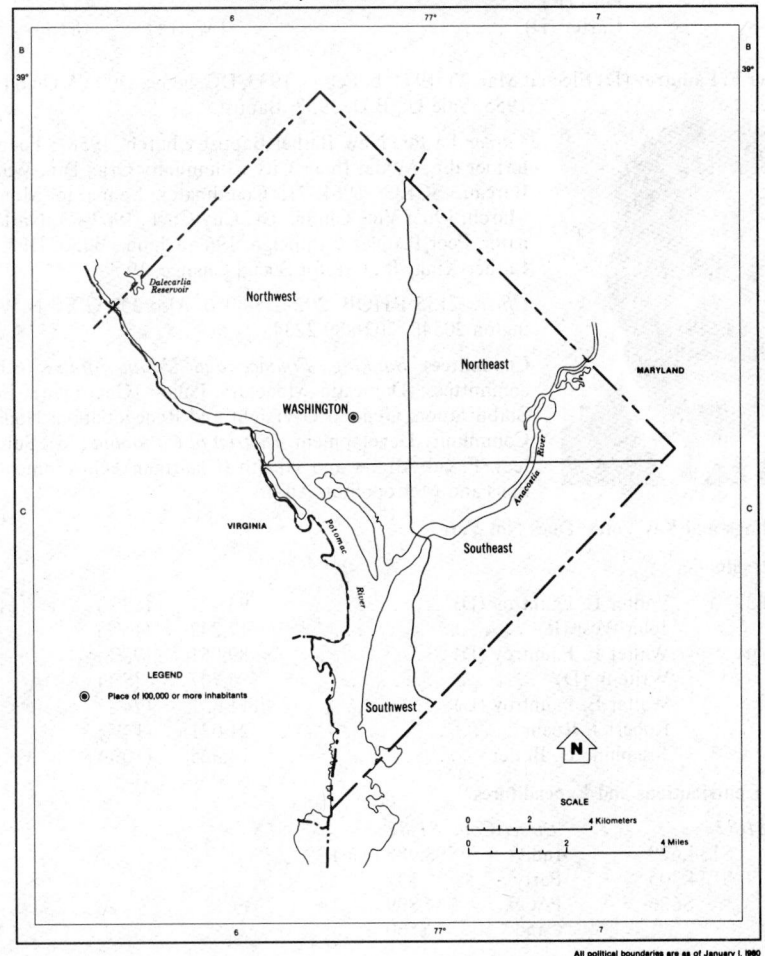

DISTRICT OF COLUMBIA — Delegate District,
Quadrants, and Place — *(1 Delegate At Large)*

1982 Share of Federal Expenditures

	Total		Non-Defense		Defense	
Total Expend	$10,807m	(1.79%)	$9,046m	(2.13%)	$1,761m	(0.98%)
St/Lcl Grants	1,295m	(1.47%)	1,295m	(1.47%)	0m	(0%)
Salary/Wages	6,058m	(7.76%)	5,284m	(19.31%)	774m	(1.53%)
Ind Payments	1,539m	(0.54%)	1,365m	(0.53%)	174m	(0.61%)
Procurement	1,874m	(1.29%)	1,013m	(3.21%)	861m	(0.75%)
Other Programs	42m	(0.78%)	42m	(0.78%)	0m	(0%)
Loan/Insurance	87m	(0.14%)	83m	(0.13%)	4m	(0.18%)

Political Lineup   Representative, 1 D at large.

Presidential Vote

1980	Reagan (R)	23,313	(13%)
	Carter (D)	130,231	(75%)
	Anderson (I)	16,131	(9%)
1976	Ford (R)	27,873	(17%)
	Carter (D)	137,818	(82%)

Rep. Walter E. Fauntroy (D) Elected Mar. 23, 1971; b. Feb. 6, 1933, DC; home, DC; VA Union U., A.B. 1955, Yale U., B.D. 1958; Baptist.

Career Pastor, New Bethel Baptist Church, 1958–; Founder and former dir., Model Inner City Community Org.; Dir., Washington Bureau, SCLC, 1961–71; Coordinator, Selma to Montgomery March, 1965; Vice Chmn., DC City Cncl., 1967–79; Natl. Coordinator, Poor Peoples Campaign, 1969; Chmn., Bd. of Dirs., Martin Luther King, Jr., Ctr. for Social Change, 1969–.

Offices 2135 RHOB, 202-225-8050. Also 350 G St. N.W., Washington 20548, 202-889-2234.

Committees *Banking, Finance and Urban Affairs* (6th). Subcommittees: Domestic Monetary Policy (Chairman); Economic Stabilization; General Oversight and Renegotiation; Housing and Community Development. *District of Columbia* (2d). Subcommittees: Fiscal Affairs and Health (Chairman); Government Operations and Metropolitan Affairs.

Group Ratings and Key Votes: Does Not Vote

Election Results

1982 general	Walter E. Fauntroy (D)	93,422	(83%)	($134,305)
	John West (R)	17,242	(15%)	($0)
1982 primary	Walter E. Fauntroy (D)	89,051	(95%)	
	Write-in (D)	4,707	(5%)	
1980 general	Walter E. Fauntroy (D)	111,631	(74%)	
	Robert J. Roehr	21,021	(14%)	
	Josephine D. Butler	14,325	(10%)	

Campaign Contributions and Expenditures

1981-82		*Direct Cont. 81-82*	
Receipts	$134,629	Indiv	$98,988 (est.)
Expend.	$134,305	Party	$32
Unspent	$626	PACS	$34,809
		Cand	$500

No PAC breakdown recorded.

PUERTO RICO, VIRGIN ISLANDS, GUAM, AMERICAN SAMOA

Four American insular territories are represented in Congress by elected delegates who—like the District of Columbia representative—have floor privileges and votes on committees but may not vote on the floor. They are Puerto Rico, the Virgin Islands, Guam, and American Samoa, and they are a diverse lot.

The largest by far is Puerto Rico, a Caribbean island with more than three million people. (It has about the same population as Connecticut, South Carolina, or Oklahoma.) Puerto Rico was one of Spain's last colonial possessions; the United States gained it in the Spanish-American War of 1898. Until the 1940s it was desperately poor: heavily populated, devoted almost entirely to sugar cultivation. Then in the 1940s, 1950s, and early 1960s Puerto Rico was transformed by Governor Luis Munoz Marin and his Popular Democratic Party. Munoz initiated Operation Bootstrap, a program to lure businesses to Puerto Rico with promises of low-wage labor and government assistance; it took advantage of the fact that Puerto Rico is within the United States for trade purposes but is not subject to federal taxes. Munoz also developed what is known in English as the Commonwealth form of government (in Spanish it is estado liberado associado, free associated state). Under Commonwealth, Puerto Rico is part of the United States for purposes of international trade, foreign policy, and war, but has its own separate laws, taxes, and representative government. Puerto Rico has also developed its own political parties: Munoz's Popular Democrats, the New Progressives (originally associated with the mainland Republicans), and two independence parties. Munoz himself could have been reelected president for life. Instead, in 1964 he retired, like George Washington; his death in 1979 was an occasion for an islandwide outpouring of emotion.

Puerto Rico has developed a vibrant politics in the years since Munoz's retirement. The central question, to which Puerto Ricans always return, is status. Some mainlanders suppose that Puerto Ricans yearn for independence, but in fact in the several referenda on status that have taken place over the years, independence has been the choice of fewer than 10% of the voters. (Nor is there any large number of independence-minded abstentions. Voter turnout is much higher in Puerto Rico than on the mainland.) The big argument is between Commonwealth and statehood. In crafting Commonwealth, Munoz artfully preserved a way for Puerto Rico to retain its Hispanic culture and the advantages of its association with the United States. But many Puerto Ricans, particularly the younger and more highly educated people, and residents of the growing San Juan metropolitan area, are proud of their American citizenship and want to be part of a state. Statehood has always had fewer backers than Commonwealth, however. In the 1976 election, the New Progressive candidate, Carlos Romero Barcelo carefully downplayed the status issue; he won election over Popular Democratic incumbent Rafael Hernandez Colon largely on economic issues. In 1980, Romero was expected to beat Hernandez easily. But actually the election was very close. One reason was that Romero had promised, if reelected, to stage a referendum on status, and there was no question that he was going to push statehood hard. But he was nearly defeated (there was a lengthy recount) and his party lost control of the Puerto Rican legislature;

Romero in turn promised not to push statehood during the next four years. That promise is a good indication of where Puerto Ricans stand on this issue today.

The other major issue in Puerto Rico is the state of the economy. The island's rapid growth during the Operation Bootstrap period gave it the highest-income level in Latin America—even higher than oil-producing Venezuela. But the 1970s were difficult years. Much of the island's prosperity was based on oil refining (because of quirks in the U.S. laws) which required cheap energy; the rise in energy prices hurt Puerto Rico badly. Romero Barcelo during his first term, on the advice of the same supply-side economists who advise the Reagan administration, systematically lowered tax rates and claimed that the economy was, as a result, growing rapidly. His opponents claimed that all people were seeing was more inflation. The truth is that no one knows for sure. Economic measurements are not so well developed here; there may be traces left of a subsistence economy and, because of high taxes, perhaps a cash economy as well. More than half of Puerto Ricans receive food stamps because eligibility is based on mainland income standards; the cupones, as the stamps are called, presumably reduce work incentives and are part of the reason for the very high unemployment rate. Things cannot be too bad, though; during the 1970s the net migration of Puerto Ricans was away from the mainland (particularly New York) and toward Puerto Rico.

Puerto Rico's delegate (his official title is resident commissioner) to the House of Representatives is Baltasar Corrada, elected in 1976 and 1980 (the term is for four years) as the candidate of Romero's New Progressive Party. Romero was a political ally of Jimmy Carter, and Corrada votes as a Democrat on congressional committees. Like two others of the four insular delegates, he is a member of the Interior and Insular Affairs Committee, which handles most of the specialized legislation concerning Puerto Rico. He is also on Education and Labor.

The United States' other insular area in the Caribbean is the Virgin Islands, a very different sort of place. It is much smaller than Puerto Rico, with a population under 100,000. Puerto Rico is multiracial and not self-conscious about it; most of the Virgin Islanders are black, and there is a pretty clear divide between the races, much resented by the blacks. Puerto Rico has attracted all kinds of light industry; the Virgin Islands lives off tourism and refineries (although the major refinery on St. Croix is in trouble). The Virgin Islands has had an elected governor only since 1976; before that he was appointed by the president. The delegate from the Virgin Islands is Ron de Lugo, who votes with the Democrats; in 1980 he defeated Melvin Evans, who voted with the Republicans. De Lugo serves on the Interior and Insular Affairs Committee and two others—Post Office and Civil Service, and Public Works and Transportation.

It takes some 19 hours to fly from Washington, D.C., to Guam, the place where, as every viewer of political conventions knows, America's day begins. Guam lies just west of the International Date Line, and it is indeed the early hours of Tuesday there when the rest of us are just trying to get through Monday afternoon. Guam is geographically in the center of the Marianas, but judicially it is separate; Guam is an integral part of the United States, while the Marianas and the islands around them were for years United Nations territories administered by the United States. With a population just over 100,000, Guam is a more advanced society than the Marianas, but economically it is not yet self-supporting. More than two-thirds of the workers are employed by the federal government (there are big defense bases here) or by the Guamanian government. The people are of mixed ethnic stock (Spanish and Pacific Islander), their religion is almost always Catholic, and they speak English, Spanish, and a local language called Chamorro.

Guam's delegate to the House is a Democrat: Antonio Borja Won Pat, first elected in 1972 and the senior insular delegate in Congress. He was a close ally of the late Phillip Burton, the San Francisco Democrat who for years chaired the Insular Affairs Subcommittee. "The sun never sets on the Burton empire," the saying went, and Burton labored hard to help the insular areas. He persuaded Congress to allow food stamps and other aid programs to be distributed with the same income cutoffs in the insular possessions as on the mainland, with the result that in Guam, as in Puerto Rico, a very large percentage of the population has come to depend on food stamps. Some argue that these programs are too generous, that they make the islanders too dependent and reduce their incentive to work at either traditional or modern tasks. Burton, Won Pat, and other defenders of the programs would argue that they are simple justice, just a matter of seeing that hungry people get food.

Won Pat is chairman of the Insular Affairs Subcommittee—as important a position as there is in Congress for a representative from Guam. He is reelected by overwhelming if not unanimous margins.

In 1981, for the first time, American Samoa had representation in Congress. This Southern Pacific Island, unlike Guam, has been little influenced by western settlers; it is almost as Polynesian as it was when the United States took possession in 1900. The new delegate is Fofo I.F. Sunia, who served eight years in the American Samoa legislature and for ten years in public office before that. He votes as a Democrat on the Merchant Marine and Fisheries, and Public Works and Transportation Committees. As might be expected, he concentrates on legislation affecting American Samoa. He has sponsored bills to extend housing projects, to establish a National Guard unit, and to authorize the American Samoa legislature to draft a constitution for local self-government.

GUIDE TO USAGE

The *Almanac of American Politics* is designed to be self-explanatory. However, the following pages are designed to put the figures into a better overall perspective. Information that does not come from a public source is so noted.

Demographics and References

Population. All population figures come from the Bureau of the Census, U.S. Department of Commerce. Publications used include: Characteristics of the Population, Number of Inhabitants, PC80-1-A; Characteristics of the Population, General Population Characteristics, PC80-1-B; and Characteristics of Housing Units, General Housing Characteristics, HC80-1-A. Contact Data User Services Division, Bureau of the Census, Washington, DC 20233, for further information.

Figures for 1970 and 1980 are final Census population counts as of April 1 of those years; 1982 figures are provisional estimates. Using two component methods, administration records method and multiple regression, the 1982 estimate measures everything from net internal migration to elementary school enrollment. Since they are estimates, the 1982 figures are rounded off to the nearest thousandth. The national population increase between 1970 and 1980 was 11.4%. Chart I shows total U.S. population and total voting age population for 1982 (provisional estimate), 1980 and 1970.

Voting Age Population. A tally of persons over eighteen years of age who are eligible to vote, the voting age population is a measurement of the voter potential in a district. (Chart I).

Chart I

Total U.S. Population		Total U.S. Voting Age Population	
July 1, 1982	231,531,000 (est.)	April 1, 1982	168,769,000 (est.)
April 1, 1980	226,545,805	April 1, 1980	163,997,000
April 1, 1970	203,302,031	April 1, 1970	135,290,000

Chart II indicates the range of highest and lowest state population changes in percentage growth and raw numeric change for 1970–80. The District of Columbia is included in all of the following charts as a state.

Chart II

1970–80 Population Change
(National Avg.: 11.4%)

State	Highest		State	Lowest	
Nevada	63.8%	(311,755)	Dist. of Columbia	−15.6%	(−118,355)
Arizona	53.1	(942,816)	New York	−3.7	(−683,319)
Florida	43.5	(2,954,906)	Rhode Island	−0.3	(−2,569)
Wyoming	41.3	(137,141)			
Utah	37.9	(401,764)			

Chart III illustrates the highest net in-migration and outmigration for the recession years of 1980 through 1982. Twenty states grew faster than the 2.2% national increase. New

Hampshire (up 3.3%) and North Dakota (up 2.6%) were the only northern states to grow faster than the national average.

Chart III

1980–82 Population Change
(National Avg.: 2.2%)

State	Highest		State	Lowest	
Nevada	10.0%	(80,000)	Michigan	-1.7%	(-153,000)
Alaska	8.9	(36,000)	Dist. of Columbia	-1.1	(-7,000)
Texas	7.4	(1,051,000)	Indiana	-0.4	(-20,000)
Florida	6.9	(669,000)	Iowa	-0.3	(-9,000)
Wyoming	6.8	(32,000)	Ohio	-0.1	(-6,000)

Chart IV shows the ten highest as well as the ten lowest state populations.

Chart IV

1982 U.S. Population: Ten Highest and Lowest States
(as of April 1, 1982)

State	Highest	State	Lowest
California	24,724,000	Alaska	438,000
New York	17,659,000	Wyoming	502,000
Texas	15,280,000	Vermont	516,000
Pennsylvania	11,865,000	Delaware	602,000
Illinois	11,448,000	Dist. of Columbia	631,000
Ohio	10,791,000	North Dakota	670,000
Florida	10,416,000	South Dakota	691,000
Michigan	9,109,000	Montana	801,000
New Jersey	7,438,000	Nevada	881,000
North Carolina	6,019,000	New Hampshire	951,000

Ethnic Breakdown. The ethnic breakdown illustrates the potential ethnic vote as opposed to the overall population. The concept of race as used by the Census reflects self-identification and not clear cut biological or scientific definition. Any one of the four ethnic classifications are noted only if the ethnic percentage in relation to the overall population rounds off to one percent or more. Chart V lists the minority populations overall and their voting age populations.

Chart V

1980 Total Minority Population and Voting Age Population

	Total pop.	% of pop.	Voting age pop.	% of voting age pop.
Black	26,495,025	11.7%	17,099,113	10.4%
Spanish Origin	14,608,673	6.4	8,980,717	5.5
American Indian	1,364,033	0.60	830,718	0.5
Asian/Pacific Islander	3,500,439	1.5	2,455,838	1.5

Black: Black ethnic classification refers to those persons who indicated their race as Black or Negro on the Census questionnaire, and includes entries such as Jamaican, Black Puerto Rican, West Indian, Haitian or Nigerian. Chart VI lists states with black voting age populations well above the national average of 10.9%. The total black population also listed illustrates the relative amount of black voters-to-be, children under eighteen years of age.

Chart VI

1980 Black Population: Total State and Voting Age Population

State	% of voting age pop.	% of total state pop.	State	% of voting age pop.	% of total state pop.
Dist. of Columbia	65.8%	70.3%	Tennessee	14.2%	15.8%
Mississippi	31.0	35.2	Delaware	14.1	16.1
South Carolina	27.3	30.4	Arkansas	14.0	16.3
Louisiana	26.7	29.4	Illinois	12.9	14.7
Georgia	24.3	26.8	New York	12.4	13.7
Alabama	22.9	25.6	Michigan	11.7	12.9
Maryland	20.8	22.7	Florida	11.3	13.8
North Carolina	20.3	22.4	Texas	11.1	12.0
Virginia	17.5	18.9			

Spanish Origin: The Spanish classification includes three specific categories—Mexican, Puerto Rican and Cuban, as well as those persons from Spain or the Spanish speaking countries of Central or South America. Persons of Spanish origin may be of any race. Chart VII illustrates voting age and total population figures of the ten states with the highest Spanish concentrations.

Chart VII

1980 Spanish Origin: Total State and Voting Age Population

State	% of voting age pop.	% of total state pop.
New Mexico	33.1%	36.6%
Texas	17.7	21.0
California	16.1	19.2
Arizona	13.3	16.2
Colorado	9.8	11.8
Florida	8.5	8.8
New York	8.3	9.5
Hawaii	6.0	6.7
Nevada	5.8	6.7
New Jersey	5.7	7.4

American Indian: The American Indian classification includes those persons reporting under the general category American Indian or who give a specific tribe. Chart VIII includes all states with an American Indian concentration above one percent.

Chart VIII

1980 American Indian: Total State and Voting Age Population

State	% of voting age pop.	% of total state pop.
Alaska	13.7%	16.0%
New Mexico	6.6	8.1
Oklahoma	4.8	5.6
South Dakota	4.7	6.5
Arizona	4.3	5.6
Montana	3.7	4.7

Asian/Pacific Islander: The Asian/Pacific Islander classification includes those persons who indicate their race as Japanese, Chinese, Filipino, Korean, Vietnamese, Asian Indian, Hawaiian, Guamanian, Samoan and those classifying themselves as some Asian/Pacific Island group such as Laotian, Pakastani or Fiji Islander. Chart IX includes all states with an Asian/Pacific Islander concentration above one percent.

Chart IX

1980 Asian/Pacific Islander: Total State and Voting Age Population

State	% of voting age pop.	% of total state pop.
Hawaii	59.9%	60.5%
California	5.2	7.0
Washington	2.4	2.5
Alaska	2.1	2.0
Nevada	1.4	1.7

Households. Percentage of housing units rented is determined by relating figures for all renter-occupied units to the total amount of housing units. In Census definition, a housing unit is a "separate living quarter" whether occupied or vacant, if intended for occupancy. Tents, caves, boats, vans and the like are included only if occupied.

Median Owner or Median House Value. Owner-occupied housing units in this category includes one one-family house on less than ten acres of land without a commercial establishment on the premises. This figure does not include condominiums, mobile homes, trailers or boats. Value is determined through usual residence costs including mortgage payments, deeds or trusts, real estate taxes, fire and hazard insurance, utilities and fuels. Chart X indicates the highest and lowest median housing unit values.

Chart X

1980 Median Housing Unit Value
(National Avg.: $47,300)

State	Highest	State	Lowest
Hawaii	$119,300	Arkansas	$31,300
California	84,700	Mississippi	31,400
Alaska	75,200	Alabama	33,900
Dist. of Columbia	70,700	Kentucky	34,200
Nevada	69,200	South Carolina	35,100

Monthly Rent or Median Monthly Rent. Renter-occupied housing units include all contract rentals except for one-family houses on ten or more acres. Contract rent includes the monthly rent agreed to, or contracted for, even if furnishings, utilities or services are part of the package. Chart XI lists the states with the highest and lowest monthly contract unit values.

Chart XI

1980 Median Monthly Contract Rent
(National Avg.: $199)

State	Highest	State	Lowest
Alaska	$338	Mississippi	$113
Hawaii	273	Alabama	119
Nevada	268	Arkansas	129
California	253	South Carolina	133
Arizona	229	North Carolina	135

Family Households. A family consists of a head of house and one or more individuals related by birth, marriage or adoption to the head of house. Chart XII lists the states with the highest and lowest average percentages of family households.

Chart XII

1980 Family Households
(National Avg.: 73%)

State	Highest	State	Lowest
Kentucky, South Carolina, Utah	78%	Dist. of Columbia	53%
		Nevada	68
Alabama, Arkansas, Hawaii, North Carolina, Tennessee, West Virginia	77	California	69
		Colorado, New York, Oregon, Washington	70

Households with Children. These households contain persons under eighteen years of age who are related to the head of house by birth, marriage or adoption. Chart XIII illustrates the states with the highest and lowest average percentages of households with children.

Chart XIII

1980 Households with Children
(National Avg.: 40%)

State	Highest	State	Lowest
Utah	50%	Dist. of Columbia	29%
Alaska	49	Florida	33
South Carolina	46	Nevada, Massachusetts	36
Hawaii, Louisiana, New Mexico	45	California, New York, Oregon	37

Married-Couple Households. These households are families where the head of house and spouse are counted as members of the same household. Chart XIV illustrates the states with the highest and lowest average percentages of married-couple households.

Chart XIV

Married-Couple Households
(National Avg.: 60%)

State	Highest	State	Lowest
Utah	69%	Dist. of Columbia	30%
Idaho	67	New York	54
Arkansas, Kentucky, North	65	California	55
Dakota, West Virginia,		Nevada	56
Wyoming		Massachusetts	57

Education. The national average for high school graduates is 66.3%. States range from 82.8% (Alaska) to 55.3% (North Carolina). Chart XV illustrates the state spread of high school graduates.

Chart XV

1980 National Spread of % of High School Graduates
(National Avg.: 66.3%)

Above 75%	7 states
70–75%	14 states
65–70%	15 states
60–65%	5 states
Below 60%	10 states

The level of higher education is measured from persons over 25 years of age who have attended vocational, public or private forms of college education not necessarily leading to graduation. Chart XVI illustrates states with the highest and lowest percentages of citizens completing four or more years of higher education.

Chart XVI

4+ yrs. College
(National Avg.: 16.3%)

State	Highest	State	Lowest
Dist. of Columbia	28%	Arkansas, West Virginia	10%
Colorado	23	Kentucky	11
Alaska	22	Indiana, Tennessee	12
Hawaii, Utah	20	Alabama, Louisiana, Missis-sippi, North Carolina	13

Poverty Level. The poverty level of families and unrelated individuals is determined by a poverty index that provides a range of income cutoffs or "poverty thresholds." Updated annually to reflect the changes in the Consumer Price Index, the thresholds vary in relation to size of family, number of children and the age of the head of house or unrelated individual. Chart XVII illustrates the 1979 average poverty thresholds. Chart XVIII indicates the spread of highest and lowest state percentages of persons below the poverty level.

Chart XVII

Average Poverty Thresholds for 1979

	Under 65 yrs.	65+ yrs.
1 person	$3774	$3479
2 persons	4876	4389
4 persons		7,412
8 persons		12,484

Chart XVIII

Persons Living Below Poverty Level
(National Avg.: 12.5%)

State	Highest	State	Lowest
Mississippi	24.5%	Wyoming	8.0%
Dist. of Columbia	18.9	Wisconsin	8.5
Louisiana	18.9	Nevada	8.5
Arkansas	18.7	New Hampshire	8.7
Kentucky	18.4	Connecticut	8.7
Alabama	17.9	Minnesota	9.3
New Mexico	17.4	New Jersey	9.7

Share of Federal Tax Burden. The federal tax burden is determined by the Tax Foundation, Inc., a non-partisan, non-profit organization located at 1875 Connecticut Avenue, N.W., Washington, DC 20009, 202-328-4500. The Tax Foundation uses federal-fund taxes (individual, corporate, alcohol, tobacco, etc.) and trust-fund taxes as bases to determine a more accurate picture of the tax burden than Treasury Department tax collection data. The total federal tax burden for 1983 is $578.7 billion. Chart XIX shows the overall national averages for total tax and per capita burden. Chart XX gives a source breakdown of federal tax collections for 1981–83.

Chart XIX

Total and Per Capita Federal Tax Burdens
(Fiscal Years 1981–83)

Total burden (in millions)				Per capita burden			
1981	1982	1983	1984	1981	1982	1983	1984
$581,595	$597,472	$578,702	$640,203	$2,542	$2,587	$2,482	$2,720

Chart XX

Federal Tax Collections by Type of Tax
(Fiscal Years 1981–83[a])

Tax	1981	1982	1983
	(in billions)		
Individual income	$285.9	$298.6	$304.5
Corporation income	61.1	46.7	65.3
Employment	163.0	185.5	199.5
Unemployment	15.8	16.4	18.5
Estate and gift	6.8	7.2	5.9
Excise	40.8	43.0	41.7
All other taxes	8.2	9.0	9.5
Total	$581.6	$606.4	$644.9

[a] For 1981, data are actual; for 1982 and 1983, as estimated in the budget presented February 1982.
Source: Office of Management and Budget.

Chart XXI shows the highest and lowest state spenders; predictably, states with the highest populations pay the most.

Chart XXII shows the highest and lowest per capita federal tax burdens; states with relatively high average incomes tend to shoulder the most.

Chart XXI

1983 Total Federal Tax Burden
(in billions)

Highest		Lowest	
California	$68.4	Vermont	$1.0
New York	47.2	South Dakota	1.4
Texas	39.8	Wyoming	1.5
Illinois	33.6	North Dakota	1.6
Pennsylvania	29.6	Alaska	1.6
Ohio	26.9		
Florida	24.9		
Michigan	23.3		
New Jersey	23.2		
Massachusetts	15.5		

Chart XXII

1983 Per Capita Federal Tax Burden

Highest		Lowest	
Alaska	$3,832	Mississippi	$1,626
DC	3,334	Arkansas	1,746
Connecticut	3,330	South Carolina	1,797
New Jersey	3,115	Vermont	1,827
Illinois	2,921	Alabama	1,871
Wyoming	2,846		
Washington	2,807		
Maryland	2,796		
Delaware	2,751		
California	2,744		

Federal Expenditures by State. For fiscal year 1982, the Census Bureau compiled statistics on federal expenditures amounting to $604 billion. Not included in this figure is interest on federal debts, international payments and foreign aid, and expenditures for selected federal agencies (*i.e.*, CIA and National Security Agency). Federal Expenditures by State for Fiscal Year 1982 (February 1983) by the Department of Commerce contains an in-depth discussion of the categories composing the total federal expenditure. The raw numbers are in millions of dollars; the percentages indicate per capita spending when contrasted to the state percentage of U.S. population total found in The People section. Chart XXIII shows the highest and lowest federal expenditures for defense and non-defense by state.

Chart XXIII

Federal Expenditures for Defense
(National Avg.: $3,311)

	Highest				Lowest		
State	$ (in millions)	% dis-tribution	$ per capita	State	$ (in millions)	% dis-tribution	$ per capita
California	$32,329	18.1%	$1,336.11	Wyoming	$174	0.1%	$353.98
Virginia	12,128	6.8	2,233.51	Montana	182	0.1	229.57
Texas	11,690	6.6	791.67	South Dakota	215	0.1	313.57
New York	8,894	5.0	505.30	West Virginia	229	0.1	117.11
Connecticut	6,309	3.5	2,013.06	Idaho	236	0.1	245.89

Federal Expenditures for Non-Defense
(National Avg.: $8,155)

	Highest				Lowest		
State	$ (in millions)	% dis-tribution	$ per capita	State	$ (in millions)	% dis-tribution	$ per capita
California	$42,685	10.0%	$1,764.13	Wyoming	$873	0.2%	$1,775.22
New York	34,941	8.2	1,985.04	Vermont	907	0.2	1,758.01
Pennsylvania	23,499	5.5	1,979.54	Alaska	1006	0.2	2,442.59
Florida	20,730	4.9	2,035.71	Delaware	1059	0.2	1,770.41
Texas	20,424	4.8	1,383.20	North Dakota	1147	0.3	1,742.58

Chart XXIV shows the highest and lowest per capita expenditures for defense and non-defense.

Chart XXIV

Per Capita Federal Expenditures for Defense
(National Avg.: $781.64)

	Highest		Lowest	
State	$ per capita	State	$ per capita
Dist. of Columbia	$2,790.59	West Virginia	$117.11
Virginia	2,233.51	Iowa	165.47
Alaska	2,090.67	Oregon	191.25
Connecticut	2,013.06	Wisconsin	229.18
Hawaii	1,969.18	Montana	229.57

Per Capita Federal Expenditures for Non-Defense
(National Avg.: $2,101.67)

	Highest		Lowest	
State	$ per capita	State	$ per capita
Dist. of Columbia	$14,336.36	Indiana	$1,375.69
New Mexico	2,984.30	Texas	1,383.20
Alaska	2,442.59	North Carolina	1,417.63
Maryland	2,336.62	Louisiana	1,494.77
Tennessee	2,170.55	New Hampshire	1,549.79

Elected Officials. This section lists the date each Senator, Representative and Governor was first elected, when the Governor's and Senator's seats are up, their residence, and relevant facts about their personal background. Also listed is a brief outline of the politician's career, and his or her district and capitol offices—complete with telephone numbers. The zip code for the House of Representatives is 20515; the Senate is 20510.

Chart XXV shows the average ages of Democratic and Republican members of Congress.

Chart XXV

98th Congress: Average Ages
(1/1/83)

	Senate	House	All Members
Democrats	54.9	44.4	45.8
Republicans	52.2	47.6	48.7

Religious affiliation was compiled by the Americans United for Separation of Church and State located at 8120 Fenton Street, Silver Spring, MD 20910, 301-589-3707. Chart XXVI lists all religious denominations used throughout the text, total number and change from the last congressional session.

Chart XXVI

98th Congress: Religious Affiliations

Affiliation	Members	Change
Apostolic Christian	1	0
Armenian Church of America	1	0
Baptist	46	−8
Bible Church	1	0
Churches of Christ	7	+2
Christian Reformed	1	0
Christian Science	2	−2
Disciples of Christ	4	−2
Episcopal	61	−10
Eastern Orthodox	7	+2
Friends (Quaker)	2	0
Free Methodist	1	0
Jewish	38	+5
Latter Day Saints (Mormon)	13	+2
Lutheran	25	+3
United Methodist	73	+3
Presbyterian	54	−1
Pentecostal	1	0
Protestant (no denomination)	24	+5
Reformed Church	1	0
Roman Catholic	142	+6
Seventh-day Adventist	1	0
Seventh-day Baptist	1	0
Unitarian Universalist	10	0
United Church of Christ	14	−2
No Affiliation	5	0

Rating Groups. The congressional rating statistics of 11 lobby groups are used to provide an idea of a legislator's general ideology and the degree to which the legislator represents different groups' interest. Not just a record of liberal/conservative voting behavior, these ratings come from a range of groups concerned with everything from single issues (defense spending) to those that focus on the political and economic interests of a particular group (consumers). The order of the groups are such that the more "liberal" ones are on the left and the more "conservative" on the right with the single issue groups in the middle. Three groups, ACLU, LWV and NSI, rate only every two years, the time of one full congressional session. Following is a general description of each organization along with addresses and telephone numbers for reference.

ADA   Americans for Democratic Action, 1411 K Street, N.W., Su. 850, Washington, DC 20005, 202-638-6447.

Liberal: Since its founding in 1947, ADA members have pushed for economic legislation designed to reduce inequality, curtail rising defense spending, prevent encroachments on civil liberties, and promote international human rights. The ADA uses a broad spectrum of issues for its vote analysis. (Votes used: 1982—House 20; Senate 20).

FOR: Voting Rights Act extension; Public service jobs program; leaving food stamp program intact; school busing; nuclear freeze; not banning abortion.

AGN: Balanced Budget Amendment; Clinch River breeder reactor; binary gas development; funding for MX; B-1 Bomber; amendment prohibiting financial aid payment to men failing to register for the draft.

ACLU   American Civil Liberties Union, 600 Pennsylvania Avenue, S.E., Washington, DC 20003, 202-544-1681.

Pro-individual liberties: ACLU members have fought to protect individuals from legal, executive and congressional infringement on their basic rights guaranteed by the Bill of Rights. The ratings are published for every congress; the 1982 ratings include the years 1981 as well as 1982. (Votes used: 1982—House 12; Senate 14).

FOR: Medicaid payment for abortion of rape and incest victims; Legal Services Corporation; Voting Rights Act.

AGN: School prayer; Immigration Reform and Control Act; stripping courts of their rights to bus.

COPE   Committee on Political Education of the AFL-CIO, 815 16th Street, N.W., Washington, DC 20006, 202-637-5101.

Liberal-Labor: As the powerful and well-funded arm of the AFL-CIO, COPE is concerned with the economic interests of the American worker. While COPE covers a broad spectrum of issues, it monitors few votes on foreign policy and defense spending. (Votes used: 1982—House 13; Senate 18).

FOR: Davis-Bacon Act; food stamps; restore mine safety; public service jobs program; medicare and medicaid; Voting Rights Act; maintaining pensions for retired federal workers.

AGN: Immigration and Reform Act; Balanced Budget Amendment.

CFA   Consumer Federation of America, 1314 14th Street, N.W., Washington, DC 20005, 202-387-6121.

Pro-Consumer: CFA is a group spawned in the mid-sixties as a pro-consumer counter-weight to various business-oriented lobbies. Areas of pro-consumer interest include food, banking, communications, energy and low-income consumer issues. (Votes used: 1982—House 14; Senate 14).

FOR: Food Stamps; Legal Services Corporation; sugar and tobacco price supports; reducing government regulation of intercity bus industry.

AGN: Infant formula; oil company merger; Gramm-Latta budget program.

LCV   League of Conservation Voters, 317 Pennsylvania Avenue, S.E., Washington, DC 20003, 202-547-7200.

Environmental: Formed in 1970, LCV lobbies for legislation and executive action favoring the environment and opposing those who despoil it. A steering committee composed of leaders from major national environmental groups determine the key votes for LCV's ratings. (Votes used: 1982—House 24; Senate 13).

FOR: Superfund; increase EPA budget; against federal irrigation subsidies; Gas and Road Tax; Clean Air Act; hazardous waste regulation.

AGN: Clinch River breeder reactor; federal subsidies for temporary nuclear waste storage; federal coal lease sales.

LWV   League of Women Voters of the United States, 1730 M Street, N.W., Washington, DC 20036, 202-296-1770.

Liberal: Founded in 1920 after the suffragette movement, the LWV lobbies for social welfare in the form of equal access to education, government spending on low-income public housing, no ceiling on food stamps, strong windfall profits tax, and limiting non-tariff barriers to trade.

NTU   National Taxpayers Union, 713 Maryland Avenue, N.E., Washington, DC 20002, 202-543-1300.

Anti-governmental spending: Founded in 1969 as a sort of closet libertarian group, NTU sets its goals to fight big government by curbing government spending and promoting a balanced federal budget. Their vote selection includes every roll-call vote that affects the amount of federal spending.

NSI   National Security Index of the American Security Council, 499 S. Capitol Street, S.W., Su. 500, Washington, DC 20003, 202-484-1676.

Pro-strong defense: Founded in 1965, the Council feels that American security is best preserved by developing and maintaining large weapons systems to achieve strategic military superiority. The NSI rates members on their support of defense and foreign policy issues that affect their strategy of peace through strength. (Votes used: 1982—House 10; Senate 10).

FOR: Military construction of binary gas plant; neutron weapon development; MX missile; F/A-18 fighter; B-1 Bomber; aid to El Salvador and Chile.

AGN: Nuclear freeze.

COC   Chamber of Commerce of the United States, 1615 H Street, N.W., Washington, DC 20062, 202-659-6143.

Pro-business: Founded in 1912 as a voice for organized business, COC represents local, regional and state chambers of commerce in addition to trade and professional organizations. (Votes used: 1982—House 22; Senate 21)

FOR: Balanced budget; Clinch River breeder reactor; Gas and Road tax; easing sanctions on employer-hiring of illegal aliens; federal subsidies for temporary nuclear waste storage.

AGN: Davis-Bacon Act; public service jobs program.

ACA Americans for Constitutional Action, 955 L'Enfant Plaza N., S.W., Su. 1000, Washington, DC 20024, 202-484-5525.

Conservative: Founded in 1958 by conservative senators, ACA is concerned about the movement of American society toward socialism. The group is as conservative as the ADA is liberal. ACA focuses primarily on economic, foreign and defense issues. (Votes used: 1982—House 23; Senate 21).

FOR: MX missile; balanced budget; amendment prohibiting financial aid payment to men failing to register for the draft.

AGN: Busing; Davis-Bacon; FTC used-car rule; nuclear freeze.

CFSC The Committee for the Survival of a Free Congress, 721 Second Street, N.E., Washington, DC 20002, 202-546-3000.

Conservative: Founded in 1974, the CSFC lobbies for free enterprise, limited government, strong national defense and traditional family mores. (Votes used: 1982—House 260; Senate 295).

FOR: Saudi AWACS sale; school prayer; money to El Salvador; tax cuts and income tax indexing.

AGN: Legal Services Corporation; federal subsidized housing; federal funding for abortions.

National Journal Ratings. *National Journal* initiated its rating system in an attempt to establish an objective method of analyzing congressional voting patterns that avoid the value judgments characteristic of interest-group ratings. Editors from *National Journal* and *The Baron Report* canvassed a wide variety of organizations that provide members of Congress with ratings based on their voting records. In the second session of the 97th Congress (1982), 49 key Senate votes and 42 key House votes were chosen to illustrate the voting behavior of all members on economic, foreign and cultural policy issues. The votes were subjected to a statistical procedure called principal components analysis that weighted all the votes to the degree they fit a common pattern. All members of Congress who voted or actively paired on at least half of the selected votes received ratings; those who missed more than half were given dashes. Absences or abstentions were not counted in the final scores.

Members of Congress were rank ordered according to relative liberalism or conservatism. Finally, they were assigned percentiles showing their rank relative to others in their chamber. Suppose that a Senator received a rating of 94% (LIB) and 5% (CONS) on economic issues. His or her voting behavior is 94% more liberal and 5% more conservative than all the other senators. Often the numbers do not add up to 100%; the difference is the percentage of senators who are tied at that same rank. In this case, the senator was tied with 1% of the body (one other senator). Chart XXVII illustrates both the Senate and House overall averages of the three subjects by party and the averages broken down by geographic and political classifications.

Chart XXVII
National Journal Ratings: Senate Averages

	Overall			*Geographic*	
	Democrats	**Republicans**			**Average**
	L/C	L/C			L/C
Economic	75/24	28/71	Liberal (34)		
Social	63/36	38/61	Eastern Democrats (10)		86/13
Foreign	68/30	30/62	Western Democrats (9)		75/23
			Midwestern Democrats (15)		67/31
			Swing (24)		
			Southern Democrats (12)		52/47
			Eastern Republicans (12)		50/48
			Conservative (42)		
			Midwestern Republicans (15)		35/62
			Western Republicans (17)		25/71
			Southern Republicans (10)		17/79

National Journal Ratings: House Averages

	Overall			*Geographic*	
	Democrats	**Republicans**			**Average**
	L/C	L/C			L/C
Economic	69/31	26/74	Liberal (173)		
Social	63/36	32/66	Eastern Democrats (65)		78/22
Foreign	63/36	32/67	Western Democrats (39)		77/22
			Midwestern Democrats (69)		71/28
			Swing (118)		
			Eastern Republicans (48)		45/54
			Southern Democrats (70)		41/58
			Conservative (144)		
			Midwestern Republicans (69)		32/67
			Western Republicans (37)		18/80
			Southern Republicans (38)		18/81

Key Votes. The Key Votes section is an attempt to illustrate a legislator's stance on important votes where he or she must vote for or against a national issue. The process grossly oversimplifies the legislative system where months of debate, amendment, pressure, persuasion, and compromise go into a final floor vote. However, the voting record remains the best indication of a member's position on specific issues and his or her general ideological persuasions. Depending on how an issue is framed legislatively, a member may vote for the motion but against the concept. For example, House vote #12 (Nuclear Freeze) is worded so that a vote for the motion is a vote against the nuclear freeze. The resolution was constructed giving only lip service to the idea of a freeze, and effectively prevented more aggressive and immediate action on the institution of a freeze.

Following is a list of House and Senate key votes used. Paired votes have been included. When a legislator wants to vote on a bill but cannot attend the roll call vote, he or she will sometimes call a colleague who takes an opposing position and both will agree not to vote. A pair in favor is considered a FOR vote and a pair against is AGN. A member who was absent or who was not elected in time to vote received a dash.

House Votes:

1) **Reagan 81 Budget**
   HR 3982, June 25, 1981. Rule substitutes permitting a single vote on the Reagan reconciliation savings program. Adopted 216–212.

2) **Reagan 81 Tax Cut**
   HR 4242, July 29, 1981. Amendment reducing individual income tax by 25% over three years, index tax rates starting in 1985, and supply business and investment tax incentives. Adopted 238–195.

3) **Bal Budget Amend**
   H J Res 350, October 1, 1982. Amendment to the Constitution requiring Congress to adopt a balanced budget every year, except in wartime or if a three-fifths congressional majority votes for deficit spending. Rejected 187–236.

4) **Gas & Road Tax**
   HR 6211, December 21, 1982. Bill authorizing an increase in gas and highway tax, and a $71.3 billion fiscal 1983–86 budget for highway construction and repairs, and mass transit. Adopted 180–87.

5) **Incr SS Rtmt Age**
   HR 1900, March 9, 1983. Amendment raising social security retirement age from age 65 to 67 after the year 2000 and raise payroll taxes in 2015. Adopted 228–202.

6) **Saudi AWACS Sale**
   H Con Res 194, October 14, 1981. Resolution disapproving the sale of Airborne Warning and Control System radar planes to Saudi Arabia. Adopted 301–111.

7) **$ for MX Missile**
   HR 7355, December 7, 1982. Amendment to delete $988 million for procurement of five MX missiles. Adopted 245–176.

8) **Nerve Gas Prod**
   HR 6030, July 22, 1982. Amendment prohibiting use of funds for binary chemical munitions. Adopted 232–181.

9) **Poor Pay Food Stamps**
   HR 3603, October 22, 1981. Amendment requiring food stamp recipients to pay for a portion of their stamps. Rejected 147–251.

10) **Ban Crt Busing Order**
   HR 6957, December 9, 1982. Amendment preventing use of Justice Department funds, either directly or indirectly to require busing of students beyond the school nearest a student's home. Adopted 243–153.

11) **Auto Local Content**
   HR 5133, December 15, 1982. Bill requiring automakers to use certain percentages of U.S. labor and parts in motor vehicles sold in U.S. Passed 215–188.

12) **Nuclear Arms Freeze**
   H J Res 521, August 5, 1982. Substitute, supported by the President, to call for a superpower nuclear freeze at equal and substantially reduced rates, instead of calling for the two nations to decide when and how to implement an immediate freeze. Adopted 204–202.

Senate Votes:

1) **Reagan 81 Budget**
   S 1377, June 25, 1981. Bill revising existing laws to achieve fiscal 1982–1984 budget savings according to fiscal 1982 budget resolution. Passed 80–15.

2) **Reagan 81 Tax Cut**
   H J Res 266, July 29, 1981. Amendment reducing income tax by 25% over three years, index tax rates starting in 1985, and supply business and investment tax incentives. Adopted 89–11.

3) **Bal Budget Amend**
   S J Res 58, August 4, 1982. Amendment to the Constitution requiring Congress to adopt a balanced budget every year, except in wartime or if a three-fifths congressional majority votes for deficit spending. Passed 69–31.

4) **Gas & Road Tax**
   HR 6211, December 20, 1982. Bill authorizing an increase in gas and highway tax, and a $71.3 billion fiscal 1983–1986 budget for highway construction and repairs, and mass transit. Passed 56–34.

5) **$ to El Salvador**
   S 1196, September 24, 1981. Helms (R-NC) amendment transforming proposed conditions on U.S. military aid to El Salvador into a statement of the sense of Congress that aid should be used to encourage a democratic solution to the civil war. Rejected 47–51.

6) **Saudi AWACS Sale**
   H Con Res 194, October 28, 1982. Resolution disapproving sale of Airborne Warning and Control System radar planes to Saudi Arabia. Rejected 48–52.

7) **Delay MX Missile**
   H J Res 631, December 16, 1982. Amendment barring funding of MX missile until Congressional approval of a basing mode. Adopted 56–42.

8) **Nerve Gas Prod**
   S 2248, May 13, 1982. Motion to table amendment that would delete $54 million for production of binary chemical munitions, and to earmark $54 million for materials to defend against chemical warfare. Agreed to 49–45.

9) **Poor Pay Food Stamps**
   S 1007, June 10, 1981. Amendment requiring food stamp recipients to pay their own money in exchange for a larger purchase value. Rejected 33–66.

10) **Ban Crt Busing Order**
    S 951. February 4, 1982. Amendment preventing Justice Department from bringing any legal action that could lead to court-ordered busing. Adopted 58–38.

11) **Clinch Riv Brdr Rctr**
    H J Res 631, December 16, 1982. Amendment dropping House provision that would eliminate construction funds for the Tennessee nuclear breeder reactor. Adopted 49–48.

12) **Legal Services Corp**
    HR 4169, November 13, 1981. Weicker (D-CT) motion to table amendment that would have cut the current funding level of the Legal Services Corporation from $321 million to $100 million. Passed 48–33.

Election Results. Listed for each member of Congress are the results of the 1982 general, primary, runoff and special elections, as well as the 1980 general elections. Votes and percentages are included, indicating the margin of victory. Dollar amounts listed to the right of the vote totals are campaign expenditures as reported by the candidate to the Federal Election Commission. Expenditures are listed only once for each particular candidate and include all previous campaign races for that particular seat. Candidates reporting no expenses are listed as ($0). When no figure appears, the candidate has not filed a report with the FEC. The FEC does not require a statement if the receipts and expenditures are under $5,000.

Presidential Vote. As a result of the 1980 Census, many congressional district boundaries have been redrawn to conform to the new population statistics. Recalculation of the 1980 presidential vote has been difficult in many urban areas and states where counties have been split. In many instances, the redistricting plan originated by a partisan state legislature has been challenged in court. Districts in California, Maine, New Jersey and Washington have been redrawn. Cases are pending in Ohio, Texas, Mississippi, Georgia and Louisiana. Data not available as of this printing has been noted with an NA. ABC News and the Republican National Committee provided most of the raw statistical data. The notation, Other, includes John Anderson and other third party candidates such as Ed Clark (Libertarian) and Barry Commoner (Citizen's Party) if they ran.

Campaign Finance

All data is derived from candidate reports and official studies available from the Federal Election Commission (FEC) located at 1325 K Street, N.W., Washington, DC 20463, 800-424-9530.

Receipts and disbursement activity covers the period beginning January 1, 1981, and ending December 31, 1982, for members of the House of Representatives unless otherwise indicated. Additional receipts and expenditures of significance during the years 1978–80 are included for senators elected or reelected in 1982. Totals for senators elected in 1978 and 1980 are calculated only for periods beginning January 1st of the year preceding their election.

Receipts, Expenditures and Cash-on-Hand. As a package, the three figures, receipts, expenditures and unspent, give a good overall indication of a winning candidate's campaign finances in the 1982 elections. These figures only refer to financial activity during the 1982 primary, runoff and general election campaigns. Funds raised and spent for special elections to fill a vacancy caused by death or resignation are not included. However, expenditures for such races are listed chronologically in the section on election results for each seat. The financial activity of those committees maintained solely to pay off debts on past elections has been included to provide a more accurate overall picture. Transfer payments by affiliates have not been included. Chart XXVIII gives an overview of total receipts, expenditures, cash-on-hand (unspent) and contributions from political action committees (PACs) for all 1982 congressional candidates.

Chart XXVIII

1981–82 Total Senate Financial Activity: Winners/Losers
(in dollars)

	Number Cands.	Total Receipts	Total Expend.	Cash-on-Hand	Total PAC Contrib.
Democrats	121	$69,224,477	$67,116,705	$3,568,536	$11,042,149
Republicans	104	72,987,883	71,842,660	1,428,378	11,302,403
Others	58	402,567	391,821	11,966	12,503
Incumbents	30	$56,136,377	$53,886,056	$4,200,408	$14,221,894
Challengers	192	48,156,231	47,744,123	436,767	5,174,880
Open Seats	61	38,322,319	37,721,007	371,705	2,960,281

1981–82 Total House Financial Activity: Winners/Losers
(in dollars)

	Number Cands.	Total Receipts	Total Expend.	Cash-on-Hand	Total PAC Contrib.
Democrats	903	$109,147,861	$103,236,111	$12,624,128	$34,057,918
Republicans	742	104,611,440	101,029,085	9,538,195	26,689,578
Others	311	304,213	301,188	5,850	9,607
Incumbents	402	$111,911,080	$103,707,661	$20,576,553	$40,586,115
Challengers	1089	53,516,762	52,911,247	823,043	10,849,126
Open Seats	465	48,635,672	47,947,476	768,577	9,321,862

Chart **XXIX** shows the increase in total financial activity for Senate and House winners since 1975.

Chart XXIX

1975–82 Senate/House Winners: Financial Activity*
(in millions)

	Senate				House			
	1981–82	1979–80	1977–78	1975–76	1981–82	1979–80	1977–78	1975–76
Receipts	$71.3	$41.7	$43.0	$21.0	$124.4	$86.0	$60.0	$42.5
Expend.	68.8	40.0	42.3	20.1	115.9	78.0	55.6	38.0
PAC Contrib.	15.6	10.2	6.0	3.1	42.6	27.0	17.0	10.9

*Figures for 1981–82 include transfers from authorized committees which are not included for previous years. Figures for 1975–76 have been reduced for refunds, rebates, and loan repayments.

Receipts. The receipt category is composed of all incoming funds as reported by the candidate for the 1982 campaign. Candidate-authorized committees report on a quarterly basis in election years, direct contributions in the form of individual, party, PACs and candidate contributions (see Direct Contributions). Totals also include incoming funds in the form of interest, dividends and rebates. Adjustments have not been made to net out refunds of previously received contributions, refunds and rebates of expenditures, buying and selling of investment securities, loan repayments, or contributions to other candidates' committees.

Expenditures. The expenditures category is composed of all outgoing funds spent by the candidate or candidate-authorized committee. Chart XXX shows the members of the Senate and House elected in 1982 with the highest receipts and expenditures over their reporting period.

Chart XXX

1981–82 Senate Winners: Top Ten Raisers		1981–82 Senate Winners: Top Ten Spenders	
1. Pete Wilson (R-CA)	$7,190,985	1. Pete Wilson (R-CA)	$7,082,651
2. Frank Lautenberg (D-NJ)	6,496,088	2. Frank Lautenberg (D-NJ)	6,435,743
3. Lloyd Bentsen (D-TX)	5,083,557	3. Lloyd Bentsen (D-TX)	5,097,445
4. David Durenberger (R-MN)	4,268,602	4. David Durenberger (R-MN)	4,189,619
5. Orrin Hatch (R-UT)	3,925,739	5. Orrin Hatch (R-UT)	3,838,335
6. Howard Metzenbaum (D-OH)	3,767,625	6. Richard Lugar (R-IN)	2,987,573
7. John Heinz (R-PA)	3,238,861	7. Daniel Moynihan (D-NY)	2,976,639
8. Daniel Moynihan (D-NY)	3,093,286	8. John Heinz (R-PA)	2,952,829
9. Richard Lugar (R-IN)	3,041,685	9. Howard Metzenbaum (D-OH)	2,794,172
10. Edward Kennedy (D-MA)	2,609,514	10. Edward Kennedy (D-MA)	2,470,473

1981–82 House Winners: Top Twenty Raisers		1981–82 House Winners: Top Twenty Spenders	
1. Barney Frank (D-MA4)	$1,509,239	1. Barney Frank (D-MA4)	$1,502,581
2. Thomas Lantos (D-CA11)	1,220,529	2. Thomas Lantos (D-CA11)	1,192,394
3. Tom Vandergriff (D-TX26)	953,564	3. Tom Vandergriff (D-TX26)	948,024
4. Ronald Dellums (D-CA8)	944,089	4. James Cooper (D-TN4)	905,474
5. James Cooper (D-TN4)	905,522	5. Ronald Dellums (D-CA8)	868,705 est.*
6. Phil Gramm (D-TX6)	822,101	6. Morris Udall (D-AZ2)	850,142
7. Morris Udall (D-AZ2)	794,533	7. Phil Gramm (D-TX6)	811,714
8. Steve Bartlett (R-TX3)	792,188	8. Steve Bartlett (R-TX3)	722,324
9. Timothy Wirth (D-CO2)	791,458	9. Richard Durbin (D-IL20)	777,043
10. Richard Durbin (D-IL20)	780,052	10. Anthony Coelho (D-CA15)	767,953
11. Stanford Parris (R-VA8)	748,609	11. Timothy Wirth (D-CO2)	750,295
12. Anthony Coelho (D-CA15)	744,808	12. Buddy Roemer (D-LA4)	732,825
13. Buddy Roemer (D-LA4)	741,311	13. Stanford Parris (R-VA8)	722,302
14. Thomas Daschle (D-SD1)	706,884	14. Matthew Rinaldo (R-NJ7)	719,430
15. Tom Loeffler (R-TX21)	699,551	15. Thomas Daschle (D-SD1)	716,436
16. Robert Michel (R-IL18)	697,084	16. Jack Brooks (D-TX9)	701,007
17. Stephen Solarz (D-NY13)	669,828	17. James Howard (D-NJ3)	698,900
18. Edwin Zschau (R-CA12)	647,780	18. Robert Michel (R-IL18)	687,875
19. James Jones (D-OK1)	641,831	19. Michael Andrews (D-TX25)	647,677
20. James Howard (D-NJ3)	637,509	20. James Jones (D-OK1)	635,844

*As of 5/1/83, candidate had not filed with F.E.C.

Chart XXXI shows a range of receipts and expenditures for primary and general election races, including winning and losing campaigns.

Chart XXXI

1982 Senate Incumbent/Challenger: Financial Activity for Primary and General Elections

	Receipts	Expend.
$5,000,000 +	5	5
3,000,000 - 5,000,000	7	3
2,000,000 - 3,000,000	10	14
1,000,000 - 2,000,000	27	26
500,000 - 1,000,000	18	18
250,000 - 500,000	18	19
100,000 - 250,000	18	17

1982 House Incumbent/Challenger: Financial Activity for Primary and General Elections

	Receipts	Expend.
$1,000,000 +	6	5
750,000 - 1,000,000	15	15
500,000 - 750,000	53	47
400,000 - 500,000	52	47
300,000 - 400,000	105	95
200,000 - 300,000	182	171
100,000 - 200,000	255	260
50,000 - 100,000	151	168
10,000 - 50,000	270	276

Unspent Funds. Unspent funds refers to a campaign's leftover cash-on-hand as of December 31, 1982. Excluding any debts unpaid by the candidate for whatever reason, this amount can be regarded as a "war chest" of surplus funds to help finance subsequent campaigns. Unless a member was first elected after January 8, 1980, he or she may convert such surplus funds to personal use after leaving congressional service.

In most cases, this figure does not represent the difference between listed receipts and expenditures over the reporting period. Re-elected incumbents often have cash-on-hand from their previous campaigns along with the interest it has accrued (see Interest and Dividends). Chart XXXII shows 1982 Senate and House winners with the highest reported cash-on-hand as of January 1983.

Chart XXXII

1981–82 Senate Winners: Top Ten Cash-on-Hand (1/1/83)

1.	Howard Metzenbaum (D-OH)	$970,455
2.	Henry Jackson (D-WA)	767,822
3.	John Heinz (R-PA)	524,957
4.	Spark Matsunaga (D-HI)	338,524
5.	Donald Riegle (D-MI)	274,240
6.	Robert Byrd (D-WV)	225,313
7.	Edward Kennedy (D-MA)	139,041
8.	Quentin Burdick (D-ND)	129,142
9.	Daniel Moynihan (D-NY)	116,647
10.	Pete Wilson (R-CA)	108,080

1981–82 House Winners: Top Twenty Cash-on-Hand (1/1/83)

1.	Stephen Solarz (D-NY13)	$605,899
2.	Dan Rostenkowski (D-IL8)	494,894
3.	William Archer (R-TX7)	411,241
4.	Tom Loeffler (R-TX21)	384,809
5.	Charles Schumer (D-NY10)	355,901
6.	W. Henson Moore (R-LA6)	331,562
7.	Gillis Long (D-LA8)	311,426
8.	Ronald Paul (R-TX22)	287,359
9.	J.J. Pickle (D-TX10)	262,011
10.	Fernand St Germain (D-RI1)	242,568
11.	Robert Livingston (R-LA1)	241,537
12.	Kent Hance (D-TX19)	233,841
13.	Joseph Addabbo (D-NY6)	232,616
14.	John LaFalce (D-NY32)	225,614
15.	Thomas Huckaby (D-LA5)	217,698
16.	Phil Gramm (D-TX6)	202,163
17.	Philip Crane (R-IL12)	201,592
18.	Carlos Moorhead (R-CA22)	196,958
19.	William Broomfield (R-MI18)	193,929
20.	Tom Bevill (R-AL4)	185,865

Chart XXXIII shows the range of cash-on-hand for all candidates for congressional office. The vast majority of those listed are incumbents.

Chart XXXIII

1982 Senate Incumbent/Challenger: Cash-on-Hand (1/1/83)		1982 House Incumbent/Challenger: Cash-on-Hand (1/1/83)	
$500,000 - 1,000,000	3	$300,000 +	7
100,000 - 500,000	8	200,000 - 300,000	9
50,000 - 100,000	8	100,000 - 200,000	44
25,000 - 50,000	10	50,000 - 100,000	69
10,000 - 25,000	5	25,000 - 50,000	79
		10,000 - 25,000	82
		5,000 - 10,000	86

Direct Contributions. Breakdown of campaign contributions are obtained from a wide variety of sources at the Federal Election Commission. The candidate's own reports filed quarterly with the FEC in election years, major political party contribution itemizations and political action committee (PAC) information forms the basis of the middle chart of the Direct Contributions section. The sum total of all the categories do not add up to the total receipts since they do not include interest, dividend income and refunds and rebates from contributions and expenditures. Breakdown of direct contributions are not included for senators elected in 1978 and 1980.

Individual Contributions. This figure is taken from the candidate reports and represents the amount received in personal contributions from individual donors.

Major Party Contributions. This figure represents direct donations of funds or in-kind contributions of goods and services to a campaign from "party committees." Party committees can be any political party organization formed at local, state or national levels that has registered under the Federal Election Campaign Act. Party expenditures spent on behalf of a candidate (*i.e.*, not directly contributed to a candidate committee) are not included in the *Almanacs'* section on Direct Contributions (see Indirect Party Contributions). However, these figures are included in the following two charts.

Chart XXXIV illustrates the party financial activity of the Republicans ($214.9 million) and the Democrats ($39 million) .

Chart XXXIV

1981–82 Party Financial Activity: Republican/Democratic
(in dollars)

Republican	Total receipts minus trans.	Total Expend. minus trans.	Latest C.O.H.	Debts owed	Contrib. to cands.	Indep. Exp.
National Committees	$ 84,032,188	$ 85,028,777	$ 309,977	$1,075,663	$1,648,767	$ 229,127
Senatorial	48,879,354	47,680,853	1,341,006	3,495,798	548,826	8,707,537
Congressional	58,041,972	57,056,101	5,034,725	69,633	2,554,863	4,943,249
Presidential Conventions	2,967	87,246	30,151	29,687	0	0
State/Local	23,948,726	24,079,995	731,944	627,002	401,213	401,213
Totals	$214,905,207	$213,932,972	$7,447,803	$5,297,783	$5,553,250	$14,281,126

Democratic	Total receipts minus trans.	Total Expend. minus trans.	Latest C.O.H.	Debts owed	Contrib. to cands.	Indep. Exp.
National Committees	$16,235,129	$16,481,622	$ 200,047	$2,972,674	$ 83,198	$ 144,742
Senatorial	5,622,254	5,568,306	156,019	112,838	530,000	1,877,245
Congressional	6,525,419	6,481,665	114,966	544,354	560,605	197,936
Assoc. of St. Dem. Chair	3,065,988	2,644,847	580,499	0	0	0
Presidential Conventions	20,035	1,193,709	0	0	0	0
State/Local	7,558,084	7,677,280	327,604	467,855	546,660	1,071,950
Totals	$39,026,909	$40,047,429	$1,379,135	$4,097,721	$1,720,463	$3,291,873

Chart XXXV shows the total direct and indirect party funds donated to 1982 Senate winners. House recipients of the maximum party assistance are too numerous to list.

Chart XXXV

1981–82 Senate Winners:
Direct and Indirect Party Funds
(over $75,000 during 1979–82)

1.	Pete Wilson (R-CA)	$1,340,068
2.	John Heinz (R-PA)	670,835
3.	Richard Lugar (R-IN)	342,602
4.	Paul Trible (R-VA)	329,122
5.	John Danforth (R-MO)	281,976
6.	David Durenberger (R-MN)	245,378
7.	Lowell Weicker (R-CT)	208,678
8.	Lloyd Bentsen (D-TX)	174,076
9.	Howard Metzenbaum (D-OH)	165,106
10.	Frank Lautenberg (D-NJ)	117,260
11.	Donald Riegle (D-MI)	108,168
12.	Malcolm Wallop (R-WY)	102,885
13.	Orrin Hatch (R-UT)	101,406
14.	Chic Hecht (R-NV)	99,252
15.	Robert Stafford (R-VT)	98,190
16.	Robert Byrd (D-WV)	97,500
17.	John Stennis (D-MS)	95,000
18.	William Roth (R-DE)	91,826
19.	Jeff Bingaman (D-NM)	91,260
20.	Quentin Burdick (D-ND)	91,260
21.	John Chafee (R-RI)	89,596
22.	George Mitchell (D-ME)	86,179
23.	James Sasser (D-TN)	75,035

Candidate Contributions. These figures represent direct candidate contributions and candidate-secured loans. Most contributions take the form of loans which may be subsequently repaid from other fundraising sources. Chart XXXVI shows personal contributions and loans of Senators elected in 1982. Chart XXXVII lists House members contributing over $75,000 to their campaigns.

Chart XXXVI

1981–82 Senate Winners: Personal Contributions and Loans

1.	Frank Lautenberg (D-NJ)	$5,142,812
2.	Jeff Bingaman (D-NM)	790,941
3.	Chic Hecht (R-NV)	370,000
4.	Lowell Weicker (R-CT)	236,000
5.	Lloyd Bentsen (D-TX)	75,000
6.	Paul Trible (R-VA)	75,000
7.	David Durenberger (R-MN)	50,000
8.	John Stennis (D-MS)	50,000
9.	James Sasser (D-TN)	40,417
10.	Malcolm Wallop (R-WY)	7,000

Chart XXXVII

1981–82 House Winners: Personal Contributions and Loans (over $75,000)

1.	Tom Vandergriff (D-TX26)	$800,500
2.	Jim Cooper (D-TN4)	609,994
3.	Bill Richardson (D-NM3)	261,429
4.	Lindy Boggs (D-LA2)	257,000
5.	William Patman (D-TX14)	248,825
6.	John Spratt (D-SC5)	221,500
7.	Buddy Roemer (D-LA4)	200,000
8.	Robin Tallon (D-SC6)	181,443
9.	James Moody (D-WI5)	170,160
10.	John McGain (R-AZ1)	167,100
11.	Richard Ray (D-GA3)	135,000
12.	Jack Brooks (D-TX9)	125,000
13.	Pete Stark (D-CA9)	116,158
14.	Donald Sundquist (R-TN7)	111,509
15.	Barbara Vucanovich (R-NV2)	90,000
16.	James Olin (D-VA6)	85,777
17.	John Bryant (D-TX5)	83,700
18.	Lindsay Thomas (D-GA1)	81,000
19.	Ron Packard (R-CA43)	80,925
20.	Wayne Dowdy (D-MS4)	80,000
21.	Dan Burton (R-IN6)	76,072

Indirect Party Expenditures and Independent Expenditures. Contributions to a campaign can be given indirectly by a source who spends money or resources on behalf of the candidate instead of giving directly. These figures are hard to quantify but play an important role in the overall politics of campaign finance.

Indirect Party Expenditures. These figures include expenditures at the national level by Republican and Democratic National, Senatorial, and Congressional Party Committees to congressional campaigns. Since these are independent of the candidate committees, they are not included in the party totals under direct contributions. (See also section on Major Party Contributions).

Independent Expenditures. These are independent expenditures spent without candidate cooperation or consultation. Unlike direct contributions, independent expenditures are not limited by amount, and can be spent either to elect or defeat a candidate. These figures are marked either FOR or AGN throughout the *Almanac*; the abbreviations are found in the Guide to Abbreviations. Chart XXXVIII shows the highest independent expenditures for and against 1982 Senate and House candidates. Chart XXXIX identifies the top ten political action committee contributors.

Chart XXXVIII

1981–82 Independent Spending For and Against Senate Races: Top Ten
(in dollars)

Member	Total $	For	Against
1. Edward Kennedy (D-MA)	$1,079,784	$ 1,350	$1,078,434
2. Paul Sarbanes (D-MD)	728,114	30,351	697,763
3. Robert Byrd (D-WV)	280,202	10,034	270,168
4. John Melcher (D-MT)	268,979	40,968	228,011
5. Lloyd Bentsen (D-TX)	225,119	0	225,119
6. Lowell Weicker (R-CT)	221,756	21,248	200,508
7. Howard Cannon (D-NV)	192,801	0	192,801
8. Edmund Brown (D-CA)	174,658	9,482	165,176
9. Orrin Hatch (R-UT)	108,045	22,081	85,964
10. Harrison Schmitt (R-NM)	85,449	5,682	79,767

1981–82 Independent Spending For and Against House Races: Top Ten
(in dollars)

Member	Total $	For	Against
1. Thomas P. O'Neill (D-MA8)	$301,055	$ 0	$301,055
2. Jim Wright (D-TX12)	217,115	0	217,115
3. James Jones (D-OK1)	140,295	13,266	127,029
4. Dan Rostenkowski (D-IL8)	57,507	0	57,507
5. Bob Edgar (D-PA7)	33,705	24,762	8,943
6. Jim Dunn (R-MI6)	32,705	24,013	8,692
7. William Chappell (D-FL4)	30,332	30,332	0
8. John Kasich (R-OH12)	27,294	27,294	0
9. James Coyne (R-PA8)	26,700	25,019	1,681
10. Edward Weber (R-OH9)	26,134	17,442	8,692

Chart XXXIX

1981–82 Independent Spending on Congressional Races
(total $5.7 million dollars–143% increase over 1980)

Independent PAC Spending: Top Ten

1. National Conservative Political Action Committee	$3,177,210
2. Fund for a Conservative Majority	390,170
3. Citizens Organized to Replace Kennedy	349,199
4. Life Amendment PAC	255,188
5. NRA Political Victory Fund	234,516
6. American Medical Association PAC	211,624
7. Realtors PAC	188,060
8. Progressive PAC	142,885
9. Independent Action, Inc.	132,920
10. League of Conservation Voters	129,163

Interest and Dividend Earnings. Incumbents who have previously raised large campaign chests and maintain surplus cash-on-hand often have high investment earnings from interest and dividends. Chart XL shows the amount of members' earnings on campaign funds, the total expenditures for the 1982 campaign, and the percentage of expenditures represented by this income. Also included is the final cash-on-hand as of January 1, 1983; the future war chests that are continually gaining interest.

Chart XL
1981–82 Senate Winners: Interest and Dividend Earnings
(over $25,000 on campaign funds)

Candidate	Interest and Dividends	Total Expend.	Interest/Dividend % of Expend.	C.O.H. (1/1/83)
1. Lloyd Bentsen (D-TX)	$443,329	$5,097,445	8.7%	$ 12,801
2. Henry Jackson (D-WA)	225,941	1,379,110	16.4	767,822
3. Howard Metzenbaum (D-OH)	225,380	2,794,172	8.1	970,455
4. John Danforth (R-MO)	183,809	1,849,025	9.9	9,069
5. John Heinz (R-PA)	159,719	2,952,829	5.4	524,957
6. Dennis DeConcini (D-AZ)	131,245	2,086,401	6.3	107,324
7. Robert Byrd (D-WV)	121,377	1,792,573	6.8	225,313
8. Richard Lugar (R-IN)	118,345	2,987,573	4.0	53,814
9. Spark Matsunaga (D-HI)	86,631	655,713	13.2	338,524
10. Donald Riegle (D-MI)	78,913	1,585,439	5.0	274,240
11. John Chafee (R-RI)	74,646	1,065,627	7.0	53,687
12. James Sasser (D-TN)	63,474	2,091,872	3.0	58,064
13. Orrin Hatch (R-UT)	61,914	3,838,335	1.6	97,122
14. David Durenberger (R-MN)	52,877	4,189,619	1.3	89,846
15. Quentin Burdick (D-ND)	43,030	1,783,020	5.5	129,142
16. William Roth (R-DE)	41,796	797,516	5.2	48,019
17. Paul Sarbanes (D-MD)	35,603	1,623,533	2.2	8,637
18. Malcolm Wallop (R-WY)	33,419	1,139,032	2.9	19,080
19. Jeff Bingaman (D-NM)	31,576	1,586,245	2.0	20,719

1981–82 House Winners: Interest and Dividend Earnings
(over $20,000 on campaign funds)

Candidate	Interest and Dividends	Total Expend.	Interest/Dividend % of Expend.	C.O.H. (1/1/83)
1. William Archer (R-TX7)	$97,260	$193,449	50.3%	$411,241
2. Stephen Solarz (D-NY13)	92,341	264,790	34.9	605,899
3. Gillis Long (D-LA8)	80,717	516,321	15.6	311,426
4. Dan Rostenkowski (D-IL8)	64,364	248,744	25.9	494,894
5. W. Henson Moore (R-LA6)	56,846	233,096	24.4	331,562
6. Gene Taylor (R-MO7)	51,856	251,305	20.6	159,294
7. Matthew Rinaldo (R-NJ7)	50,543	719,430	7.0	26,959
8. Phil Gramm (D-TX6)	48,049	811,714	6.0	202,163
9. Fernand St Germain (D-RI1)	47,309	246,302	19.2	242,568
10. Tom Loeffler (R-TX21)	46,909	465,364	10.1	384,809
11. John LaFalce (D-NY32)	45,860	809,417	56.7	225,614
12. Joseph Minish (D-NJ11)	44,189	163,614	27.0	172,434
13. J.J. Pickle (D-TX10)	41,675	79,157	52.6	262,011
14. Gene Snyder (R-KY4)	40,495	303,653	13.3	155,845
15. Bill Frenzel (R-MN3)	37,512	243,611	15.4	176,695
16. Philip Crane (R-IL12)	35,174	334,720	10.5	201,592
17. Eldon Rudd (R-AZ4)	34,510	248,536	13.9	159,347
18. William Broomfield (R-MI18)	33,693	62,599	58.8	193,929
19. John Duncan (R-TN2)	29,350	131,658	22.3	172,884
20. Ronnie Flippo (D-AL5)	29,317	197,401	14.9	139,348
21. Richard Schulze (R-PA5)	28,216	207,452	14.0	145,470
22. Tom Bevill (D-AL4)	28,181	63,927	44.1	185,865
23. Robert Livingston (R-LA1)	26,110	138,464	18.9	241,537
24. Jerry Lewis (R-CA35)	25,368	86,679	29.3	138,674
25. Doug Barnard (D-GA10)	25,253	69,764	36.2	175,646
26. John Breaux (D-LA7)	22,471	171,244	13.1	179,534

Political Action Committees–(PACs). Political Action Committees are groups that are not affiliated directly with a candidate or political party. PAC figures represent donations of money or in-kind goods and services to a congressional campaign. Total PAC contributions listed under the Direct Contributions section constitute the amount declared by the PACs themselves in their reports to the FEC as of December 31, 1982. PAC growth within the last four years has been phenomenal, not only in total amount of contributions but in the growth of the total number of committees. Chart XLI shows total Senate/House PAC contribution growth from 1978–82. Chart XLII reveals the tremendous growth of PACs in total number of committees from 1974–82.

Chart XLI

1978–82 Financial Activity: PAC Contributions to Senate/House
(in millions)

	1982	1980	1978
Senate/House	$87.3	$50.7	$31.2
Senate	24.9	15.5	8.5
House	62.2	35.2	22.7
Democrat	47.0	27.4	17.4
Republican	40.1	23.3	13.7
Incumbent	58.2	31.7	18.2
Challenger	16.6	12.5	6.6
Open Seat	12.4	6.5	6.2

Chart XLII

1974–82 PAC Growth
(in number of committees)

Committee type	1974	1975	1976	1977	1978	1979	1980	1981	1982
Business	89	139	433	550	784	949	1,204	1,327	1,467
Labor	201	226	224	234	217	240	297	318	380
Trade/Member- ship/Health	*318	*357	*489	438	451	512	574	608	628
Ideological	—	—	—	110	165	250	378	539	746
Agricultural	—	—	—	8	12	17	42	41	47

* Group breakdown not available for these years. Number indicates total for all 3 groups.

Chart XLIII indicates the total 1981–82 PAC financial activity. (See following section on PACs Breakdown for definition of committee type.) The FEC breakdown of PAC categories are similar to Common Cause with the exception that the Common Cause Health and Professional groups are included under the FEC heading of Trade/Membership/Health.

Chart XLIII

1981–82 PAC Financial Activity

Committee type	Total receipts minus trans.	Total Expend. minus trans.	Latest C.O.H.	Debts owed	Contrib. to cands.	Indep. Expend.
Business	$47,157,663	$43,214,855	$10,311,431	$ 346,561	$29,270,815	$ 21,190
Labor	37,439,179	35,040,569	8,180,963	241,518	20,824,227	41,629
Trade/Member-ship/Health	43,238,569	41,707,751	6,617,164	392,402	22,834,099	807,703
Ideological	64,673,561	64,567,739	3,522,511	4,071,576	11,060,171	372,136
Agricultural	4,045,650	3,752,976	1,805,776	0	2,188,668	5,968

Chart XLIV lists the top 10 1981–82 Senate PAC recipients. Chart XLV lists the top 20 1981–82 House PAC recipients.

Chart XLIV

1981–82 Senate Winners: PAC $ Recipients
(over $500,000)

1.	Pete Wilson (R-CA)	$1,182,432
2.	David Durenberger (R-MN)	1,078,954
3.	Orrin Hatch (R-UT)	930,420
4.	Lloyd Bentsen (D-TX)	826,593
5.	Richard Lugar (R-IN)	715,139
6.	Robert Byrd (D-WV)	706,891
7.	Paul Trible (R-VA)	652,551
8.	James Sasser (D-TN)	639,720
9.	Donald Riegle (D-MI)	610,646
10.	John Heinz (R-PA)	589,001

Chart XLV

1981–82 House Winners: Top Twenty PAC $ Recipients

1.	Robert Michel (R-IL18)	$476,637
2.	James Jones (D-OK1)	334,190
3.	Anthony Coelho (D-CA15)	305,765
4.	Thomas P. O'Neill (R-MA8)	301,212
5.	James Howard (D-NJ3)	293,449
6.	Dan Rostenkowski (D-IL8)	290,425
7.	Thomas Foley (D-WA5)	284,442
8.	William Chappell (D-FL4)	284,416
9.	Stanford Parris (R-VA8)	275,983
10.	Phil Gramm (D-TX6)	269,190
11.	Jim Wright (D-TX12)	253,065
12.	Thomas Daschle (D-SD1)	242,792
13.	Jack Brooks (D-TX9)	240,305
14.	Les AuCoin (D-OR1)	238,079
15.	James Coyne (D-PA14)	237,199
16.	Thomas Evans (D-IA3)	236,574
17.	Martin Frost (D-TX24)	233,414
18.	Barney Frank (D-MA4)	223,266
19.	Frank Wolf (R-VA10)	222,765
20.	Timothy Wirth (D-CO2)	220,629

Chart XLVI shows the range of PAC contributions received by Senate and House winners and losers for primary and general election races.

Chart XLVI

1981–82 Senate Winners/Losers: PAC Contributions

	PAC Contributions
$1,000,000 +	2
500,000 - 1,000,000	13
250,000 - 500,000	24
100,000 - 250,000	15
50,000 - 100,000	6
10,000 - 50,000	12

1981–82 House Winners/Losers: PAC Contributions

	PAC Contributions
$200,000 +	32
100,000 - 200,000	209
50,000 - 100,000	122
10,000 - 25,000	110
5,000 - 10,000	66

PACS Breakdown. PACs breakdowns come from Common Cause, 2030 M Street, N.W., Washington, DC 20036, 202-833-1200, who broke down PAC contributions by type of donor based on November 22, 1982, FEC information. The five week lag between the PAC total and the sum of the PACs breakdown accounts for the discrepancy often found between the two. Other inconsistencies arise since FEC figures are largely unaudited and can often differ greatly from the amount of PAC contributions reported by the candidate committee. Following is a definition of the six categories Common Cause chose to define as PAC donors.

AGR   Agriculture. Includes PACs of farmer organizations, commodity exchanges, and specific agriculture groups (cotton, tobacco, sugar, dairy, grains, etc.) Chart XLVII.

Chart XLVII

1981–82 Agricultural PACs: Top Five Raisers and Spenders

Raisers

1. Committee for Thorough Agricultural Pol. Education of Associated Milk Producers Inc. (C-TAPE)	$1,757,638
2. Dairymen Inc.—Special Political Agricultural Community Education (DI-SPACE)	847,523
3. Mid-American Dairymen Inc. Agricultural & Dairy Educational Pol. Trust (ADEPT)	721,906
4. CF Industries, Inc. Political Action Committee	79,808
5. Diamond Walnut Growers Inc. Political Action Committee	69,147

Spenders

1. Committee for Thorough Agricultural Pol. Education of Associated Milk Producers Inc. (C-TAPE)	$1,611,630
2. Dairymen Inc.—Special Political Agricultural Community Education (DI-SPACE)	690,519
3. Mid-America Dairymen Inc. Agricultural & Dairy Educational Pol. Trust (ADEPT)	667,383
4. Farmland Industries Political Action Committee	65,698
5. Diamond Walnut Growers Inc. Political Action Committee	60,365

BUS   Business. Includes general business association groups (National Assn. of Manufacturers, U.S. Chamber of Commerce, etc.) as well as specific corporate PACs involved in energy, finance, insurance, and transportation. Chart XLVIII.

Chart XLVIII

1981–82 Business PACs: Top Ten Raisers and Spenders

Raisers

1. Tenneco Employees Good Government Fund (Tenneco Inc.)	$499,294
2. Amoco Political Action Committee (Standard Oil Company—Indiana)	455,589
3. Sunbelt Good Government Committee of Winn-Dixie Stores (Winn-Dixie Stores, Inc.)	442,756
4. Bear, Stearns & Co. Political Campaign Committee (Bear, Stearns & Co.)	435,000
5. American Family Political Action Committee (American Family Corporation)	328,694

6. Signal Companies, Inc.   325,118
   (Wheelabrator-Frye, Inc.)
7. Fluor Corporation Public Affairs Committee   323,478
   (Fluor Corporation)
8. Harris Corporation—Federal Political Action Committee   306,168
   (Harris Corporation)
9. General Dynamics Corporation Voluntary Pol. Contributions   304,758
   (General Dynamics Corporation)
10. Grumman Political Action Committee   304,601
   (Grumman Corporation)

Spenders

1. Tenneco Employees Good Government Fund $499,651
   (Tenneco Inc.)
2. Amoco Political Action Committee   445,899
   (Standard Oil Company—Indiana)
3. Bear, Stearns & Co. Political Campaign Committee   439,153
   (Bear, Stearns & Co.)
4. American Family Political Action Committee   335,613
   (American Family Corporation)
5. Sunbelt Good Government Committee of Winn-Dixie Stores   319,863
   (Winn-Dixie Stores, Inc.)
9. General Dynamics Corporation Voluntary Pol. Contributions   315,392
   (General Dynamics Corporation)
7. Grumman Political Action Committee   307,064
   (Grumman Corporation)
8. Non-Partisan Pol. Support Committee for G.E. Co. Employees   290,038
   (General Electric Co.)
9. Harris Corporation—Federal Political Action Committee   272,134
   (Harris Corporation)
10. Rockwell International Corporation Good Government Committee   266,688
   (Rockwell International Corporation)

HLTH   Health. Includes PACs for doctors, dentists, nurses, other health professionals, and hospitals. The Common Cause Health PACs breakdown is included along with the Professional in the FEC Trade/Membership/Health category. Chart XLIX.

Chart XLIX

1981–82 Trade/Membership/Health PACs: Top Ten Raisers and Spenders

Raisers

1. Realtors Political Action Committee $2,991,732
2. American Medical Association Political Action Committee   2,466,425
3. NRA Political Victory Fund   2,026,801
   (National Rifle Association of America)
4. Build Political Action Committee of the National   1,318,750
   Association of Home Builders
5. League of Conservation Voters   1,254,661
6. Automobile and Truck Dealers Election Action Committee   1,167,395
7. Texas Medical Association PAC-TEXPAC   1,089,046
8. California Medical Political Action Committee   1,075,168
9. National Association of Life Underwriters PAC   1,065,042
10. Gun Owners of America Campaign Committee   932,329

Spenders

1.	Realtors Political Action Committee	$3,144,475
2.	American Medical Association Political Action Committee	2,491,214
3.	California Medical Political Action Committee	1,369,171
4.	NRA Political Victory Fund	1,349,726
	(National Rifle Association of America)	
5.	League of Conservation Voters	1,255,082
6.	Automobile and Truck Dealers Election Action Committee	1,202,475
7.	Build Political Action Committee of the National	1,197,738
	Association of Home Builders	
8.	National Association of Life Underwriters PAC	1,085,638
9.	Texas Medical Association PAC-TEXPAC	1,061,845
10.	American Bankers Association BANKPAC	1,042,095

IDEO   Ideological/Other. Includes a broad range of interest group PACs (*i.e.*, arms control, liberal/conservative), PACs of former Presidents, presidential candidates, members of Congress, non-connected PACs and all PACs that remain unclassified. Chart L.

Chart L

1981–82 Ideological PACs: Top Ten Raisers and Spenders

Raisers

1.	National Conservative Political Action Committee	$9,990,931
2.	National Congressional Club	9,742,494
3.	Fund for a Conservative Majority	2,945,874
4.	National Committee for an Effective Congress	2,430,886
5.	Citizens for the Republic	2,415,720
6.	Committee for the Survival of a Free Congress	2,359,477
7.	Fund for a Democratic Majority	2,307,605
8.	Committee for the Future of America, Inc.	2,190,264
9.	Republican Majority Fund	1,967,119
10.	Independent Action, Inc.	1,189,059

Spenders

1.	National Congressional Club	$10,404,521
2.	National Conservative Political Action Committee	10,118,891
4.	Fund for a Conservative Majority	2,945,883
5.	National Committee for an Effective Congress	2,512,682
7.	Citizens for the Republic	2,480,629
8.	Committee for the Survival of a Free Congress	2,394,782
9.	Fund for a Democratic Majority	2,207,305
3.	Committee for the Future of America, Inc.	2,170,295
6.	Republican Majority Fund	2,023,794
10.	Independent Action, Inc.	1,182,516

LBR   Labor. Includes unions and teacher organizations. Chart LI.

Chart LI

1981–82 Labor PACs: Top Ten Raisers and Spenders

Raisers

1. UAW-V-CAP (United Auto Workers)	$1,956,578
2. Machinists Non-Partisan Political League	1,609,674
3. Transportation Political Education League	1,472,222
4. Seafarers Political Activity Donation (SPAD)	1,426,508
5. National Education Association PAC	1,322,215
6. Active Ballot Club (United Food & Commercial Workers)	1,220,393
7. AFL-CIO COPE Political Contributions Committee	1,152,019
8. ILGWU Campaign Committee (Int. Ladies Garment Workers Union)	1,082,897
9. United Steelworkers of America Political Action Fund	1,032,160
10. Voice of Teachers for Education (Amer. Fed. of Teachers)	1,020,612

Spenders

1. UAW-V-CAP (United Auto Workers)	$2,204,645
2. Machinists Non-Partisan Political League	1,613,118
3. National Education Association PAC	1,442,722
4. Transportation Political Education League	1,348,236
5. AFL-CIO COPE Political Contributions Committee	1,156,805
6. ILGWU Campaign Committee (Int. Ladies Garment Workers Union)	1,119,776
7. Active Ballot Club (United Food & Commercial Workers)	1,072,099
8. Seafarers Political Activity Donation (SPAD)	1,042,485
9. United Steelworkers of America Political Action Fund	1,031,046
10. CWA-COPE Political Contributions Committee	919,710

PROF   Professional. Includes non-health/educational/professional groups, such as lawyers, accountants, engineers and social workers. The Common Cause Professional PACs breakdown is included along with Health in the FEC Trade/Membership/Health category listed in Chart XLIX.

ABBREVIATIONS

AA	Administrative Assistant
ACA	Americans for Constitutional Action
ACLU	American Civil Liberties Union
ACU	American Conservative Union
ADA	Americans for Democratic Action
ADEPT	Mid-America Dairymen Inc. Agricultural & Dairy Educational Political Trust
Admin.	Administration
Adv.	Advertising
Agcy.	Agency
Agr.	Agriculture
AMAPAC	American Medical Association Political Action Committee
Amer.	American
Asst.	Assistant
Atty.	Attorney
BANKPAC	American Bankers Association Political Action Committee
Bd.	Board
Bldg.	Building
Boiler PAC	Boiler Makers Local 85 Federal Political Action Committee
Bus	Business
C	Conservative Party (New York)
CA	Carroll Arms Building
CACPAC	Citizens Action Coalition Political Action Committee
Cand.	Candidate
CCSND	Citizens for Common Sense in National Defense
CFA	Consumer Federation of America
CG	Coast Guard
Chf.	Chief
Chmn.	Chairman
CHOB	Cannon House Office Building
Chwmn.	Chairwoman
Cncl.	Council
Cnty.	County
Co.	Company
COC	Chamber of Commerce of the United States
COH	Cash-On-Hand
Col.	College
Com.	Committee
COPE	Committee on Political Education (AFL-CIO)

Corp.	Corporation
CSFC	Committee for the Survival of a Free Congress
Ct.	Court
Ctr.	Center
D	Democrat
Dem.	Democratic
Dem80s	Democrats for the 80s
Dept.	Department
Develop.	Development
DFL	Democratic–Farmer–Labor Party (Minnesota)
Dir.	Director
Dpty.	Deputy
DSOB	Dirksen Senate Office Building
Econ.	Economic
EPA	Environmental Protection Agency
Expend.	Expenditure/s
FCM	Fund for a Conservative Majority
Fed.	Federal
FreezePAC	Nuclear Freeze Political Action Committee
GOA	Gun Owners of America Campaign Committee
H	Capitol Building Room, House side
Hlth	Health
HSOB	Hart Senate Office Building
I, Indep.	Independent
Ideo	Ideological
Indiv.	Individual
Internatl.	International
IR	Independent-Republican Party (Minnesota)
Jt. Com.	Joint Committee
L	Liberal Party (New York)
Lbr	Labor
LCV	League of Conservation Voters
LHOB	Longworth House Office Building
LIFEPAC	Life Amendment Political Action Committee
LU	Liberty Union Party (Vermont)
LWV	League of Women Voters
MA Citiz. for Life	Massachusetts Citizens for Life
MA LIFEPAC	Massachusetts Life Amendment Political Action Committee
MI LIFEPAC	Michigan Life Amendment Political Action Committee
MIRTL	Michigan Right to Life
MO LIFEPAC	Missouri Life Amendment Political Action Committee
Natl.	National

NCFC	National Coalition for a Free Cuba
NCPAC	National Conservative Political Action Committee
NRA	National Rifle Association Political Victory Fund
NSI	National Security Index of the American Security Council
NTL	National Tax Limitation Political Action Committee
NTLRTL	National Right to Life Political Action Committee
NTU	National Taxpayers Union
PAC	Political Action Committee
PPAC	Progressive Political Action Committee
Pres.	President
Prof	Professional
Pub.	Public
Publ.	Publisher
R, Repub.	Republican
Realtors	Realtors Political Action Committee
Rep.	Representative
Reps.	Representatives
RHOB	Rayburn House Office Building
RSOB	Russell Senate Office Building
S	Capitol Building Room, Senate side
Sch.	School
Sel. Com.	Select Committee
Sheet Metal Workers PAL	Sheet Metal Workers Political Action League
Sp. Com.	Special Committee
SSSPAC	Save Social Security Political Action Committee
Subcom.	Subcommittee
Su.	Suite
U.	University
UAW	United Auto Workers Political Action Committee
USAF	United States Air Force
USAFR	United States Air Force Reserve
USMC	United States Marine Corps
VA	Veterans Administration

SENATE COMMITTEES

STANDING COMMITTEES

AGRICULTURE, NUTRITION, AND FORESTRY 328A RSOB, 42035

Majority (10 R): Helms (NC), Chmn.; Dole (KS), Lugar (IN), Cochran (MS), Boschwitz (MN), Jepsen (IA), Hawkins (FL), Andrews (ND), Wilson (CA), Hatch (UT).
Minority (8 D): Huddleston (KY), Leahy (VT), Zorinsky (NE), Melcher (MT), Pryor (AR), Boren (OK), Dixon (IL), Heflin (AL).

Subcommittees

[Messrs. Helms and Huddleston are ex officio members of all subcommittees of which they are not regular members.]

AGRICULTURAL CREDIT AND RURAL ELECTRICATION

Majority (3 R): Hawkins, Chmn.; Jepsen, Andrews.
Minority (3 D): Zorinsky, Heflin, Boren.

AGRICULTURAL PRODUCTION, MARKETING, AND STABILIZATION OF PRICES

Majority (5 R): Cochran, Chmn.; Dole, Boschwitz, Andrews, Helms.
Minority (5 D): Leahy, Huddleston, Zorinsky, Melcher, Dixon.

AGRICULTURAL RESEARCH AND GENERAL LEGISLATION

Majority (5 R): Lugar, Chmn.; Hatch, Wilson, Andrews, Helms.
Minority (4 D): Boren, Heflin, Huddleston, Pryor.

FOREIGN AGRICULTURAL POLICY

Majority (7 R): Boschwitz, Chmn.; Wilson, Lugar, Cochran, Jepsen, Dole, Hawkins.
Minority (4 D): Dixon, Zorinsky, Boren, Huddleston.

AGRICULTURE, NUTRITION, AND FORESTRY

Majority (5 R): Dole, Chmn.; Hawkins, Lugar, Boschwitz, Hatch.
Minority (4 D): Pryor, Melcher, Leahy, Dixon.

RURAL DEVELOPMENT, OVERSIGHT, AND INVESTIGATIONS

Majority (2 R): Andrews, Chmn.; Helms.
Minority (2 D): Pryor, Leahy.

SOIL AND WATER CONSERVATION

Majority (4 R): Jepsen, Chmn.; Hatch, Wilson, Cochran.
Minority (2 D): Melcher, Heflin.

APPROPRIATIONS 118 DSOB, 43471

Majority (15 R): Hatfield (OR), Chmn.; Stevens (AK), Weicker (CT), McClure (ID), Laxalt (NV), Garn (UT), Cochran (MS), Andrews (ND), Abdnor (SD), Kasten (WI), D'Amato (NY), Mattingly (GA), Rudman (NH), Specter (PA), Domenici (NM).

Minority (14 D): Stennis (MS), Byrd (WV), Proxmire (WI), Inouye (HI), Hollings (SC), Eagleton (MO), Chiles (FL), Johnston (LA), Huddleston (KY), Burdick (ND), Leahy (VT), Sasser (TN), DeConcini (AZ), Bumpers (AR).

Subcommittees
[Messrs. Hatfield and Stennis are nonvoting members of all subcommittees of which they are not regular members.]

AGRICULTURE, RURAL DEVELOPMENT AND RELATED AGENCIES
Majority (7 R): Cochran, Chmn.; McClure, Andrews, Abdnor, Kasten, Mattingly, Specter.
Minority (6 D): Eagleton, Stennis, Byrd, Chiles, Burdick, Sasser.

COMMERCE, JUSTICE, STATE, THE JUDICIARY, AND RELATED AGENCIES
Majority (6 R): Laxalt, Chmn.; Stevens, Weicker, Rudman, Hatfield, Specter.
Minority (5 D): Hollings, Inouye, DeConcini, Bumpers, Eagleton.

DEFENSE
Majority (9 R): Stevens, Chmn.; Weicker, Garn, McClure, Andrews, Kasten, D'Amato, Rudman, Cochran.
Minority (8 D): Stennis, Proxmire, Inouye, Hollings, Eagleton, Chiles, Johnston, Huddleston.

DISTRICT OF COLUMBIA
Majority (3 R): Specter, Chmn.; Mattingly, Domenici.
Minority (2 D): Leahy, Bumpers.

ENERGY AND WATER DEVELOPMENT
Majority (8 R): Hatfield, Chmn.; McClure, Garn, Cochran, Abdnor, Kasten, Mattingly, Domenici.
Minority (7 D): Johnston, Stennis, Byrd, Hollings, Huddleston, Burdick, Sasser.

FOREIGN OPERATIONS
Majority (5 R): Kasten, Chmn.; Hatfield, D'Amato, Rudman, Specter.
Minority (4 D): Inouye, Johnston, Leahy, DeConcini.

HUD—INDEPENDENT AGENCIES
Majority (6 R): Garn, Chmn.; Weicker, Laxalt, D'Amato, Abdnor, Domenici.
Minority (5 D): Huddleston, Stennis, Proxmire, Leahy, Sasser.

INTERIOR AND RELATED AGENCIES
Majority (8 R): McClure, Chmn.; Stevens, Laxalt, Garn, Cochran, Andrews, Rudman, Weicker.
Minority (7 D): Byrd, Johnston, Huddleston, Leahy, DeConcini, Burdick, Bumpers.

LABOR, HEALTH AND HUMAN SERVICES, EDUCATION, AND RELATED AGENCIES
Majority (8 R): Weicker, Chmn.; Hatfield, Stevens, Andrews, Rudman, Specter, McClure, Domenici.
Minority (7 D): Proxmire, Byrd, Hollings, Eagleton, Chiles, Burdick, Inouye.

LEGISLATIVE BRANCH

Majority (3 R): D'Amato, Chmn.; Hatfield, Stevens.
Minority (2 D): Bumpers, Hollings.

MILITARY CONSTRUCTION

Majority (3 R): Mattingly, Chmn.; Laxalt, Garn.
Minority (2 D): Sasser, Inouye.

TRANSPORTATION AND RELATED AGENCIES

Majority (5 R): Andrews, Chmn.; Cochran, Abdnor, Kasten, D'Amato.
Minority (4 D): Chiles, Stennis, Byrd, Eagleton.

TREASURY, POSTAL SERVICE, AND GENERAL GOVERNMENT

Majority (3 R): Abdnor, Chmn.; Laxalt, Mattingly.
Minority (2 D): DeConcini, Proxmire.

ARMED SERVICES
222 RSOB, 43871

Majority (10 R): Tower (TX), Chmn.; Thurmond (SC), Goldwater (AZ), Warner (VA), Humphrey (NH), Cohen (ME), Jepsen (IA), Quayle (IN), East (NC), Wilson (CA).
Minority (8 D): Jackson (WA), Stennis (MS), Nunn (GA), Hart (CO), Exon (NE), Levin (MI), Kennedy (MA), Bingaman (NM).

Subcommittees

MANPOWER AND PERSONNEL

Majority (5 R): Jepsen, Chmn.; Thurmond, Humphrey, Cohen, East.
Minority (4 D): Exon, Nunn, Kennedy, Bingaman.

MILITARY CONSTRUCTION

Majority (5 R): Thurmond, Chmn.; Warner, Humphrey, Quayle, East.
Minority (4 D): Hart, Jackson, Stennis, Exon.

PREPAREDNESS

Majority (4 R): Humphrey, Chmn.; Goldwater, Jepsen, Wilson.
Minority (3 D): Levin, Jackson, Kennedy.

SEA POWER AND FORCE PROJECTION

Majority (5 R): Cohen, Chmn.; Tower, Quayle, East, Wilson.
Minority (4 D): Nunn, Stennis, Hart, Levin.

STRATEGIC AND THEATER NUCLEAR FORCES

Majority (6 R): Warner, Chmn.; Tower, Thurmond, Goldwater, Cohen, Quayle.
Minority (5 D): Jackson, Stennis, Nunn, Hart, Exon.

TACTICAL WARFARE

Majority (5 R): Goldwater, Chmn.; Tower, Warner, Jepsen, Wilson.
Minority (3 D): Kennedy, Levin, Bingaman.

1350   SENATE COMMITTEES

BANKING, HOUSING, AND URBAN AFFAIRS   534 DSOB, 47391

Majority (10 R): Garn (UT), Chmn.; Tower (TX), Heinz (PA), Armstrong (CO), D'Amato (NY), Gorton (WA), Hawkins (FL), Mattingly (GA), Hecht (NV), Trible (VA).
Minority (8 D): Proxmire (WI), Cranston (CA), Riegle (MI), Sarbanes (MD), Dodd (CT), Dixon (IL), Sasser (TN), Lautenberg (NJ).

Subcommittees
COMSUMER AFFAIRS

Majority (3 R): Hawkins, Chmn.; D'Amato, Gorton.
Minority (2 D): Dodd, Dixon.

ECONOMIC POLICY

Majority (3 R): Gorton, Chmn.; Hecht, Armstrong.
Minority (2 D): Dodd, Cranston.

FEDERAL CREDIT PROGRAMS

Majority (3 R): Trible, Chmn.; Armstrong, Hecht.
Minority (2 D): Sasser, Lautenberg.

FINANCIAL INSTITUTIONS

Majority (6 R): Armstrong, Chmn.; Garn, Tower, Heinz, D'Amato, Hecht.
Minority (4 D): Cranston, Dixon, Proxmire, Riegle.

HOUSING AND URBAN AFFAIRS

Majority (7 R): Tower, Chmn.; Garn, Heinz, D'Amato, Gorton, Hawkins, Trible.
Minority (6 D): Riegle, Sasser, Lautenberg, Proxmire, Cranston, Sarbanes.

INSURANCE

Majority (2 R): Hecht, Chmn.; Hawkins.
Minority (1 D): Sarbanes.

INTERNATIONAL FINANCE AND MONETARY POLICY

Majority (5 R): Heinz, Chmn.; Garn, Armstrong, Mattingly, Gorton.
Minority (4 D): Proxmire, Dixon, Sasser, Lautenberg.

RURAL HOUSING AND DEVELOPMENT

Majority (2 R): Mattingly, Chmn.; Tower.
Minority (1 D): Cranston.

SECURITIES

Majority (4 R): D'Amato, Chmn.; Hawkins, Mattingly, Trible.
Minority (3 D): Sarbanes, Riegle, Dodd.

BUDGET
                                                          203 CA, 40642

Majority (12 R): Domenici (NM), Chmn.; Armstrong (CO), Kassebaum (KS), Boschwitz (MN), Hatch (UT), Tower (TX), Andrews (ND), Symms (ID), Grassley (IA), Kasten (WI), Quayle (IN), Gorton (WA).

Minority (10 D): Chiles (FL), Hollings (SC), Biden (DE), Johnston (LA), Sasser (TN), Hart (CO), Metzenbaum (OH), Riegle (MI), Moynihan (NY), Exon (NE).

No Subcommittees

COMMERCE, SCIENCE, AND TRANSPORTATION   508 DSOB, 45115

Majority (9 R): Packwood (OR), Chmn.; Goldwater (AZ), Danforth (MO), Kassebaum (KS), Pressler (SD), Gorton (WA), Stevens (AK), Kasten (WI), Trible (VA).
Minority (8 D): Hollings (SC), Long (LA), Inouye (HI), Ford (KY), Riegle (MI), Exon (NE), Heflin (AL), Lautenberg (NJ).

Subcommittees
[The chairman and the ranking minority member of the full committee are members ex officio of all subcommittees.]

AVIATION

Majority (5 R): Kassebaum, Chmn.; Goldwater, Danforth, Stevens, Trible.
Minority (4 D): Exon, Inouye, Ford, Lautenberg.

BUSINESS, TRADE, AND TOURISM

Majority (2 R): Pressler, Chmn.; Packwood.
Minority (1 D): Riegle.

COMMUNICATIONS

Majority (4 R): Goldwater, Chmn.; Pressler, Stevens, Gorton.
Minority (3 D): Hollings, Inouye, Ford.

CONSUMER

Majority (2 R): Kasten, Chmn.; Danforth.
Minority (1 D): Ford.

MERCHANT MARINE

Majority (4 R): Stevens, Chmn.; Gorton, Kasten, Trible.
Minority (3 D): Inouye, Long, Heflin.

SCIENCE, TECHNOLOGY, AND SPACE

Majority (4 R): Gorton, Chmn.; Goldwater, Kassebaum, Trible.
Minority (3 D): Heflin, Riegle, Lautenberg.

SURFACE TRANSPORTATION

Majority (4 R): Danforth, Chmn.; Pressler, Kassebaum, Kasten.
Minority (3 D): Long, Riegle, Exon.

NATIONAL OCEAN POLICY STUDY

Majority (5 R): Packwood, Chmn.; Stevens, Vice Chmn.; Gorton, Kasten, Trible.
Minority (4 D): Hollings, Long, Inouye, Lautenberg.

ENERGY AND NATURAL RESOURCES   360 DSOB, 44971

Majority (11 R): McClure (ID), Chmn.; Hatfield (OR), Weicker (CT), Domenici (NM), Wallop (WY), Warner (VA), Murkowski (AK), Nickles (OK), Hecht (NV), Chafee (RI), Heinz (PA).

Minority (9 D): Johnston (LA), Jackson (WA), Bumpers (AR), Ford (KY), Metzenbaum (OH), Matsunaga (HI), Melcher (MT), Tsongas (MA), Bradley (NJ).

Subcommittees
[Messrs. McClure and Johnston are ex officio members of all subcommittees.]

ENERGY AND MINERAL RESOURCES

Majority (5 R): Warner, Chmn.; Heinz, Wallop, Murkowski, Hecht.
Minority (4 D): Melcher, Bumpers, Matsunaga, Bradley.

ENERGY CONSERVATION AND SUPPLY

Majority (5 R): Weicker, Chmn.; Hatfield, Chafee, Warner, Heinz.
Minority (4 D): Matsunaga, Metzenbaum, Tsongas, Bradley.

ENERGY REGULATION

Majority (5 R): Murkowski, Chmn.; Weicker, Nickles, Domenici, Chafee.
Minority (4 D): Metzenbaum, Ford, Melcher, Bradley.

ENERGY RESEARCH AND DEVELOPMENT

Majority (5 R): Domenici, Chmn.; Warner, Heinz, Weicker, Nickles.
Minority (4 D): Ford, Jackson, Bumpers, Tsongas.

PUBLIC LANDS AND RESERVED WATER

Majority (5 R): Wallop, Chmn.; Hatfield, Hecht, Chafee, Domenici.
Minority (4 D): Bumpers, Jackson, Matsunaga, Melcher.

WATER AND POWER

Majority (5 R): Nickles, Chmn.; Hatfield, Wallop, Murkowski, Hecht.
Minority (4 D): Tsongas, Jackson, Ford, Metzenbaum.

ENVIRONMENT AND PUBLIC WORKS　　　　410 DSOB, 46176

Majority (9 R): Stafford (VT), Chmn.; Baker (TN), Chafee (RI), Simpson (WY), Abdnor (SD), Symms (ID), Domenici (NM), Durenberger (MN), Humphrey (NH).
Minority (7 D): Randolph (WV), Bentsen (TX), Burdick (ND), Hart (CO), Moynihan (NY), Mitchell (ME), Baucus (MT).

Subcommittees
ENVIRONMENTAL POLLUTION

Majority (4 R): Chafee, Chmn.; Simpson, Symms, Durenberger.
Minority (3 D): Mitchell, Hart, Moynihan.

NUCLEAR REGULATION

Majority (4 R): Simpson, Chmn.; Baker, Domenici, Symms.
Minority (3 D): Hart, Mitchell, Baucus.

REGIONAL AND COMMUNITY DEVELOPMENT

Majority (4 R): Humphrey, Chmn.; Baker, Domenici, Symms.
Minority (3 D): Hart, Mitchell, Baucus.

TOXIC SUBSTANCES AND ENVIRONMENTAL OVERSIGHT

Majority (4 R): Durenberger, Chmn.; Simpson, Abdnor, Humphrey.
Minority (3 D): Baucus, Burdick, Hart.

TRANSPORTATION

Majority (5 R): Symms, Chmn.; Stafford, Baker, Chafee, Abdnor.
Minority (4 D): Bentsen, Randolph, Burdick, Moynihan.

WATER RESOURCES

Majority (4 R): Abdnor, Chmn.; Domenici, Durenberger, Humphrey.
Minority (3 D): Moynihan, Bentsen, Baucus.

FINANCE   221 DSOB, 44515

Majority (11 R): Dole (KS), Chmn.; Packwood (OR), Roth (DE), Danforth (MO), Chafee (RI), Heinz (PA), Wallop (WY), Durenberger (MN), Armstrong (CO), Symms (ID), Grassley (IA).
Minority (9 D): Long (LA), Bentsen (TX), Matsunaga (HI), Moynihan (NY), Baucus (MT), Boren (OK), Bradley (NJ), Mitchell (ME), Pryor (AR).

Subcommittees

ECONOMIC GROWTH, EMPLOYMENT AND REVENUE SHARING

Majority (2 R): Heinz, Chmn.; Roth.
Minority (2 D): Mitchell, Moynihan.

ENERGY AND AGRICULTURAL TAXATION

Majority (3 R): Wallop, Chmn.; Symms, Durenberger.
Minority (3 D): Bradley, Pryor, Bentsen.

ESTATE AND GIFT TAXATION

Majority (2 R): Symms, Chmn.; Grassley.
Minority (1 D): Boren.

HEALTH

Majority (4 R): Durenberger, Chmn.; Dole, Packwood, Heinz.
Minority (3 D): Baucus, Bradley, Mitchell.

INTERNATIONAL TRADE

Majority (8 R): Danforth, Chmn.; Roth, Chafee, Heinz, Wallop, Armstrong, Grassley, Symms.
Minority (7 D): Bentsen, Matsunaga, Boren, Bradley, Mitchell, Moynihan, Baucus.

OVERSIGHT OF THE INTERNAL REVENUE SERVICE

Majority (2 R): Grassley, Chmn.; Dole.
Minority (1 D): Long.

SAVINGS, PENSIONS, AND INVESTMENT POLICY

Majority (3 R): Chafee, Chmn.; Packwood, Roth.
Minority (2 D): Pryor, Matsunaga.

SOCIAL SECURITY AND INCOME MAINTENANCE PROGRAMS

Majority (4 R): Armstrong, Chmn.; Durenberger, Danforth, Dole.
Minority (4 D): Moynihan, Boren, Pryor, Long.

TAXATON AND DEBT MANAGEMENT

Majority (5 R): Packwood, Chmn.; Danforth, Chafee, Wallop, Armstrong.
Minority (4 D): Matsunaga, Bentsen, Baucus, Long.

FOREIGN RELATIONS
427 DSOB, 44651

Majority (9 R): Percy (IL), Chmn.; Baker (TN), Helms (NC), Lugar (IN), Mathias (MD), Kassebaum (KS), Boschwitz (MN), Pressler (SD), Murkowski (AK).
Minority (8 D): Pell (RI), Biden (DE), Glenn (OH), Sarbanes (MD), Zorinsky (NE), Tsongas (MA), Cranston (CA), Dodd (CT).

Subcommittees

[The chairman and ranking minority member of the full committee are ex officio members of each subcommittee.]

AFRICAN AFFAIRS

Majority (3 R): Kassebaum, Chmn.; Mathias, Percy.
Minority (2 D): Tsongas, Dodd.

ARMS CONTROL, OCEANS, INTERNATIONAL OPERATIONS, AND ENVIRONMENT

Majority (3 R): Pressler, Chmn.; Helms, Kassebaum.
Minority (2 D): Cranston, Zorinsky.

EAST ASIAN AND PACIFIC AFFAIRS

Majority (3 R): Murkowski, Chmn.; Baker, Helms.
Minority (2 D): Glenn, Cranston.

EUROPEAN AFFAIRS

Majority (5 R): Lugar, Chmn.; Mathias, Boschwitz, Baker, Percy.
Minority (4 D): Biden, Glenn, Sarbanes, Zorinsky.

INTERNATIONAL ECONOMIC POLICY

Majority (4 R): Mathias, Chmn.; Lugar, Boschwitz, Murkowski.
Minority (3 D): Dodd, Biden, Sarbanes.

NEAR EASTERN AND SOUTH ASIAN AFFAIRS

Majority (4 R): Boschwitz, Chmn.; Baker, Percy, Pressler.
Minority (3 D): Sarbanes, Glenn, Tsongas.

WESTERN HEMISPHERE AFFAIRS

Majority (5 R): Helms, Chmn.; Lugar, Kassebaum, Pressler, Murkowski.
Minority (4 D): Zorinsky, Tsongas, Cranston, Dodd.

GOVERNMENTAL AFFAIRS

346 DSOB, 44751

Majority (10 R): Roth (DE), Chmn.; Percy (IL), Stevens (AK), Mathias (MD), Cohen (ME), Durenberger (MN), Rudman (NH), Danforth (MO), Cochran (MS), Armstrong (CO).
Minority (8 D): Eagleton (MO), Jackson (WA), Chiles (FL), Nunn (GA), Glenn (OH), Sasser (TN), Levin (MI), Bingaman (NM).

Subcommittees

CIVIL SERVICE, POST OFFICE, AND GENERAL SERVICES

Majority (3 R): Stevens, Chmn.; Mathias, Armstrong.
Minority (2 D): Bingaman, Sasser.

ENERGY, NUCLEAR PROLIFERATION AND GOVERNMENT PROCESSES

Majority (4 R): Percy, Chmn.; Durenberger, Cohen, Danforth.
Minority (3 D): Glenn, Jackson, Levin.

GOVERNMENTAL EFFICIENCY AND THE DISTRICT OF COLUMBIA

Majority (3 R): Mathias, Chmn.; Rudman, Cochran.
Minority (2 D): Eagleton, Chiles.

INFORMATION MANAGEMENT AND REGULATORY AFFAIRS

Majority (3 R): Danforth, Chmn.; Percy, Durenberger.
Minority (2 D): Chiles, Jackson.

INTERGOVERNMENTAL RELATIONS

Majority (4 R): Durenberger, Chmn.; Stevens, Cochran, Armstrong.
Minority (3 D): Sasser, Nunn, Levin.

OVERSIGHT OF GOVERNMENT MANAGEMENT

Majority (3 R): Cohen, Chmn.; Rudman, Danforth.
Minority (2 D): Levin, Bingaman.

PERMANENT SUBCOMMITTEE ON INVESTIGATIONS

Majority (7 R): Roth, Chmn.; Rudman, Vice Chmn.; Percy, Mathias, Cohen, Armstrong, Cochran.
Minority (6 D): Nunn, Jackson, Chiles, Glenn, Sasser, Bingaman.

JUDICIARY

224 DSOB, 45225

Majority (10 R): Thurmond (SC), Chmn.; Mathias (MD), Laxalt (NV), Hatch (UT), Dole (KS), Simpson (WY), East (NC), Grassley (IA), Denton (AL), Specter (PA).
Minority (8 D): Biden (DE), Kennedy (MA), Byrd (WV), Metzenbaum (OH), DeConcini (AZ), Leahy (VT), Baucus (MT), Heflin (AL).

Subcommittees

ADMINISTRATIVE PRACTICE AND PROCEDURE

Majority (3 R): Grassley, Chmn.; Laxalt, Specter.
Minority (2 D): Heflin, Baucus.

CONSTITUTION

Majority (3 R): Hatch, Chmn.; Thurmond, Grassley.
Minority (2 D): DeConcini, Leahy.

COURTS

Majority (4 R): Dole, Chmn.; Thurmond, Simpson, East.
Minority (3 D): Heflin, Baucus, DeConcini.

CRIMINAL LAW

Majority (4 R): Laxalt, Chmn.; Thurmond, Specter, Dole.
Minority (3 D): Biden, Baucus.

IMMIGRATION AND REFUGEE POLICY

Majority (3 R): Simpson, Chmn.; Grassley, Mathias.
Minority (2 D): Kennedy, Heflin.

JUVENILE JUSTICE

Majority (3 R): Specter, Chmn.; Denton, Mathias.
Minority (2 D): Metzenbaum, Kennedy.

PATENTS, COPYRIGHTS AND TRADEMARKS

Majority (4 R): Mathias, Chmn.; Laxalt, Hatch, Dole.
Minority (3 D): Metzenbaum, Leahy, DeConcini.

SECURITY AND TERRORISM

Majority (3 R): Denton, Chmn.; Hatch, East.
Minority (2 D): Leahy, Metzenbaum.

SEPARATION OF POWERS

Majority (3 R): East, Chmn.; Denton, Simpson.
Minority (2 D): Baucus, Metzenbaum.

LABOR AND HUMAN RESOURCES   428 DSOB, 45375

Majority (10 R): Hatch (UT), Chmn.; Stafford (VT), Quayle (IN), Nickles (OK), Humphrey (NH), Denton (AL), Weicker (CT), Grassley (IA), East (NC), Hawkins (FL).
Minority (8 D): Kennedy (MA), Randolph (WV), Pell (RI), Eagleton (MO), Riegle (MI), Metzenbaum (OH), Matsunaga (HI), Dodd (CT).

Subcommittees
[Mr. Hatch, chairman of the full committee, is an ex officio member of all subcommittees of which he is not a member.]

AGING

Majority (4 R): Grassley, Chmn.; Hawkins, Humphrey, Denton.
Minority (3 D): Eagleton, Pell, Metzenbaum.

ALCOHOLISM AND DRUG ABUSE

Majority (3 R): Humphrey, Chmn.; Quayle, East.
Minority (2 D): Matsunaga, Riegle.

EDUCATION, ARTS, AND HUMANITIES

Majority (6 R): Stafford, Chmn.; Hatch, Quayle, Denton, Weicker, East.
Minority (5 D): Pell, Kennedy, Randolph, Eagleton, Dodd.

EMPLOYMENT AND PRODUCTIVITY

Majority (5 R): Quayle, Chmn.; Hawkins, Hatch, Nickles, Grassley.
Minority (4 D): Metzenbaum, Pell, Riegle, Kennedy.

FAMILY AND HUMAN SERVICES

Majority (5 R): Denton, Chmn.; Humphrey, Nickles, Weicker, Grassley.
Minority (3 D): Dodd, Eagleton, Metzenbaum.

HANDICAPPED

Majority (4 R): Weicker, Chmn.; Stafford, Hawkins, Nickles.
Minority (3 D): Randolph, Eagleton, Matsunaga.

LABOR

Majority (6 R): Nickles, Chmn.; East, Grassley, Hatch, Stafford, Denton.
Minority (4 D): Riegle, Kennedy, Randolph, Matsunaga.

RULES AND ADMINISTRATION   309 RSOB, 46352

Majority (7 R): Mathias (MD), Chmn.; Hatfield (OR), Baker (TN), McClure (ID), Helms (NC), Warner (VA), Dole (KS).
Minority (5 D): Ford (KY), Pell (RI), Byrd (WV), Inouye (HI), DeConcini (AZ).

No Subcommittees

SMALL BUSINESS   428A RSOB, 45175

Majority (10 R): Weicker (CT), Chmn.; Packwood (OR), Hatch (UT), Boschwitz (MN), Gorton (WA), Nickles (OK), Rudman (NH), D'Amato (NY), Kasten (WI), Pressler (SD).
Minority (9 D): Nunn (GA), Huddleston (KY), Bumpers (AR), Sasser (TN), Baucus (MT), Levin (MI), Tsongas (MA), Dixon (IL), Boren (OK).

Subcommittees
[The chairman and the ranking minority member of the full committee are ex officio members of all subcommittees.]

CAPITAL FORMATION AND RETENTION

Majority (3 R): Packwood, Chmn.; Hatch, Boschwitz.
Minority (2 D): Bumpers, Sasser.

ENTREPRENEURSHIP AND SPECIAL PROBLEMS FACING SMALL BUSINESS

Majority (2 R): Kasten, Chmn.; Weicker.
Minority (1 D): Boren.

EXPORT PROMOTION AND MARKET DEVELOPMENT

Majority (2 R): Boschwitz, Chmn.; Gorton.
Minority (1 D): Huddleston.

GOVERNMENT PROCUREMENT
Majority (3 R): Nickles, Chmn.; Rudman, Kasten.
Minority (2 D): Levin, Bumpers.

GOVERNMENT REGULATION AND PAPERWORK
Majority (2 R): Hatch, Chmn.; Pressler.
Minority (1 D): Huddleston.

INNOVATION AND TECHNOLOGY
Majority (2 R): Rudman, Chmn.; Packwood.
Minority (1 D): Baucus.

PRODUCTIVITY AND COMPETITION
Majority (2 R): Gorton, Chmn.; Nickles.
Minority (1 D): Tsongas.

SMALL BUSINESS: FAMILY FARM
Majority (2 R): Pressler, Chmn.; D'Amato.
Minority (1 D): Nunn.

URBAN AND RURAL ECONOMIC DEVELOPMENT
Majority (2 R): D'Amato, Chmn.; Weicker.
Minority (1 D): Dixon.

VETERANS AFFAIRS   414 RSOB, 49126

Majority (7 R): Simpson (WY), Chmn.; Thurmond (SC), Stafford (VT), Murkowski (AK), Specter (PA), Denton (AL), Boschwitz (MN).
Minority (5 D): Cranston (CA), Randolph (WV), Matsunaga (HI), DeConcini (AZ), Mitchell (ME).

No Subcommittees

SELECT COMMITTEES

SELECT COMMITTEE ON ETHICS   113 CA, 42981

Majority (3 R): Stevens (AK), Chmn.; Helms (NC), Durenberger (MN).
Minority (3 D): Heflin (AL), Vice Chmn.; Pryor (AR), Eagleton (MO).

No Subcommittees

SELECT COMMITTEE ON INDIAN AFFAIRS   640 DSOB, 42251

Majority (4 R): Andrews (ND), Chmn.; Goldwater (AZ), Gorton (WA), Murkowski (AK).
Minority (3 D): Melcher (MT), Inouye (HI), DeConcini (AZ).

No Subcommittees

SELECT COMMITTEE ON INTELLIGENCE
G50 DSOB, 41700

[Mr. Baker, majority leader, and Mr. Byrd, minority leader of the Senate, are ex officio members of the committee.]

Majority (8 R): Goldwater (AZ), Chmn.; Garn (UT), Chafee (RI), Lugar (IN), Wallop (WY), Durenberger (MN), Roth (DE), Cohen (ME).

Minority (7 D): Moynihan (NY), Vice Chmn.; Huddleston (KY), Biden (DE), Inouye (HI), Jackson (WA), Leahy (VT), Bentsen (TX).

Subcommittees

[Mr. Goldwater, Committee Chairman, and Mr. Moynihan, Committee Vice Chairman, are ex officio members on all subcommittees.]

ANALYSIS AND PRODUCTION

Majority (3 R): Lugar, Chmn.; Wallop, Roth.
Minority (2 D): Jackson, Vice Chmn.; Bentsen.

BUDGET AUTHORIZATION

Majority (5 R): Wallop, Chmn.; Garn, Durenberger, Roth, Cohen.
Minority (4 D): Inouye, Vice Chmn.; Jackson, Leahy, Bentsen.

COLLECTION AND FOREIGN OPERATIONS

Majority (4 R): Chafee, Chmn.; Garn, Lugar, Cohen.
Minority (4 D): Huddleston, Vice Chmn.; Biden, Inouye, Jackson.

LEGISLATION AND THE RIGHTS OF AMERICANS

Majority (4 R): Durenberger, Chmn.; Garn, Chafee, Cohen.
Minority (3 D): Leahy, Vice Chmn.; Huddleston, Biden.

SPECIAL COMMITTEE

SPECIAL COMMITTEE ON AGING
G37 DSOB, 45364

Majority (8 R): Heinz (PA), Chmn.; Domenici (NM), Percy (IL), Kassebaum (KS), Cohen (ME), Pressler (SD), Grassley (IA), Wilson (CA).

Minority (7 D): Glenn (OH), Chiles (FL), Melcher (MT), Pryor (AR), Bradley (NJ), Burdick (ND), Dodd (CT).

No Subcommittees

JOINT COMMITTEES OF THE CONGRESS

JOINT ECONOMIC COMMITTEE
G01 DSOB, 45171

Senate (10): Jepsen (IA), Chmn.; Roth (DE), Abdnor (SD), Symms (ID), Mattingly (GA), D'Amato (NY), Bentsen (TX), Proxmire (WI), Kennedy (MA), Sarbanes (MD).

House (10): Hamilton (IN), Vice Chmn.; Long (LA), Mitchell (MD), Hawkins (CA), Obey (WI), Scheuer (NY), Wylie (OH), Holt (MD), Lungren (CA), Snowe (ME).

JOINT COMMITTEE ON THE LIBRARY   309 RSOB, 40299

Senate (5): Mathias (MD), Chmn.; Hatfield (OR), Warner (VA), Inouye (HI), DeConcini (AZ)
House (5): Hawkins (CA), Vice Chmn.; Chmn.; Swift (WA), Coyne (PA), Gingrich (GA), Chandler (WA).

No Subcommittees

JOINT COMMITTEE ON PRINTING   151 S, 45241

Senate (5): Mathias (MD), Vice Chmn.; Gaydos (PA), Jones (TN), Martin (IL), Chandler (WA).
House (5): Hawkins (CA), Chmn.; Hatfield (OR), Baker (TN), Ford (KY), Pell (RI).

No Subcommittees

JOINT COMMITTEE ON TAXATION   1015 LHOB, 43621

Senate (5): Dole (KS), Vice Chmn.; Gibbons (FL), Pickle (TX), Conable (NY), Duncan (TN).
House (5): Rostenkowski (KS), Chmn.; Packwood (OR), Roth (DE), Long (LA), Bentsen (TX).

No Subcommittees

HOUSE COMMITTEES

STANDING COMMITTEES

AGRICULTURE

Majority (26 D): de la Garza (TX), Chmn.; Foley (WA), Jones (NC), Jones (TN), Brown (CA), Rose (NC), Weaver (OR), Harkin (IA), Bedell, (IA), English (OK), Panetta, (CA), Huckaby (LA), Glickman (KS), Whitley (NC), Coelho (CA), Daschle (SD), Stenholm (TX), Volkmer, (MO), Hatcher, (GA), Tallon, (SC), Staggers (WV), Durbin (IL), Evans (IL), Thomas (GA), Olin, (VA), Penny (MN).

Minority (15 R): Madigan (IL), Jeffords (VT), Coleman (MO), Marlenee (MT), Hopkins (KY), Hansen (ID), Stangeland (MN), Roberts (KS), Emerson (MO), Skeen (NM), Morrison (WA), Gunderson (WI), Evans (IA), Chappie (CA), Franklin (MS).

Subcommittees

[The chairman and ranking minority member are ex officio members of all subcommittees.]

CONSERVATION, CREDIT, AND RURAL DEVELOPMENT

Majority (10 D): Jones (TN), Chmn.; Weaver, Bedell, English, Glickman, Daschle, Stenholm, Tallon, Durbin, Evans.
Minority (5 R): Coleman, Jeffords, Skeen, Morrison, Gunderson.

COTTON, RICE, AND SUGAR

Majority (8 D): Huckaby, Chmn.; Coelho, Jones (TN), Rose, English, Whitley, Stenholm, Hatcher.
Minority (4 R): Stangeland, Emerson, Chappie, Franklin.

DEPARTMENT OPERATIONS, RESEARCH, AND FOREIGN AGRICULTURE

Majority (8 D): Brown, Chmn.; Staggers, Penny, Panetta, Foley, Coelho, Volkmer, Olin.
Minority (4 R): Roberts, Gunderson, Evans, Franklin.

DOMESTIC MARKETING, CONSUMER RELATIONS, AND NUTRITION

Majority (6 D): Panetta, Chmn.; Olin, Huckaby, Glickman, Staggers, Foley.
Minority (3 R): Emerson, Coleman, Hansen.

FORESTS, FAMILY FARMS, AND ENERGY

Majority (8 D): Whitley, Chmn.; Foley, Brown, Weaver, Huckaby, Staggers, Bedell, Panetta.
Minority (4 R): Hansen, Marlenee, Morrison, Chappie.

LIVESTOCK, DAIRY, AND POULTRY

Majority (10 D): Harkin, Chmn.; Volkmer, Olin, Jones (TN), Rose, Coelho, Stenholm, Hatcher, Penny, Daschle.
Minority (5 R): Jeffords, Hopkins, Hansen, Skeen, Gunderson.

TOBACCO AND PEANUTS

Majority (8 D): Rose, Chmn.; Jones (NC), Hatcher, Thomas, Whitley, Tallon, English, Stenholm.
Minority (4 R): Hopkins, Roberts, Skeen, Franklin.

WHEAT, SOYBEANS, AND FEED GRAINS

Majority (10 D): Foley, Chmn.; Harkin, Bedell, English, Glickman, Daschle, Volkmer, Durbin, Evans (IL), Thomas.

Minority (5 R): Marlenee, Stangeland, Roberts, Emerson, Evans (IA).

APPROPRIATIONS

218 H, 52771

Majority (36 D): Whitten (MS), Chmn.; Boland (MA), Natcher (KY), Smith (IA), Addabbo (NY), Long (MD), Yates (IL), Obey (WI), Roybal (CA), Stokes (OH), Bevill (AL), Chappell (FL), Alexander (AR), Murtha (PA), Traxler (MI), Early (MA), Wilson (TX), Boggs (LA), Dicks (WA), McHugh (NY), Lehman (FL), Hightower (TX), Sabo (MN), Dixon (CA), Fazio (CA), Hefner (NC), AuCoin (OR), Akaka (HI), Watkins (OK), Gray (PA), Dwyer (NJ), Ratchford (CT), Boner (TN), Hoyer (MD), Carr (MI), Mrazek (NY).

Minority (21 R): Conte (MA), McDade (PA), Edwards (AL), Myers (IN), Robinson (VA), Miller (OH), Coughlin (PA), Young (FL), Kemp (NY), Regula (OH), O'Brien (IL), Smith (NE), Rudd (AZ), Pursell (MI), Edwards (OK), Livingston (LA), Green (NY), Loeffler (TX), Lewis (CA), Porter (IL), Rogers (KY).

Subcommittees

[The chairman and ranking minority member are ex officio members of all subcommittees on which they do not hold a regular assignment.]

AGRICULTURE, RURAL DEVELOPMENT AND RELATED AGENCIES

Majority (9 D): Whitten, Chmn.; Traxler, McHugh, Natcher, Akaka, Watkins, Hightower, Smith, Alexander.

Minority (4 R): Smith, Robinson, Myers, Rogers.

COMMERCE, JUSTICE, STATE, AND JUDICIARY

Majority (6 D): Smith, Chmn.; Alexander, Early, Dwyer, Mrazek, Carr.

Minority (3 R): O'Brien, Miller, Porter.

DEFENSE

Majority (8 D): Addabbo, Chmn.; Chappell, Murtha, Dicks, Wilson, Hefner, Hightower, AuCoin.

Minority (4 R): Edwards, Robinson, McDade, Young.

DISTRICT OF COLUMBIA

Majority (6 D): Dixon, Chmn.; Natcher, Stokes, Wilson, Lehman, Sabo.

Minority (3 R): Coughlin, Green, Rogers.

ENERGY AND WATER DEVELOPMENT

Majority (6 D): Bevill, Chmn.; Boggs, Chappell, Fazio, Watkins, Boner.

Minority (3 R): Myers, Smith, Rudd.

FOREIGN OPERATIONS

Majority (8 D): Long, Chmn.; Obey, Yates, McHugh, Lehman, Wilson, Dixon, Gray.

Minority (4 R): Kemp, Edwards, Livingston, Lewis.

HUD—INDEPENDENT AGENCIES

Majority (6 D): Boland, Chmn.; Traxler, Stokes, Boggs, Sabo, Boner.
Minority (3 R): Green, Coughlin, Lewis.

INTERIOR

Majority (6 D): Yates, Chmn.; Murtha, Dicks, Ratchford, Boland, AuCoin.
Minority (3 R): McDade, Regula, Loeffler.

LABOR—HEALTH AND HUMAN SERVICES—EDUCATION

Majority (8 D): Natcher, Chmn.; Smith, Obey, Roybal, Stokes, Early, Dwyer, Hoyer.
Minority (5 R): Conte, O'Brien, Pursell, Porter, Young.

LEGISLATIVE

Majority (6 D): Fazio, Chmn.; Obey, Murtha, Traxler, Boggs, Hightower.
Minority (4 R): Lewis, Conte, Myers, Porter.

MILITARY CONSTRUCTION

Majority (8 D): Hefner, Chmn.; Bevill, Long, Alexander, Addabbo, Chappell, Dicks, Fazio.
Minority (4 R): Regula, Edwards, Loeffler, Livingston.

TRANSPORTATION

Majority (6 D): Lehman, Chmn.; Sabo, Gray, Ratchford, Carr, Mrazek.
Minority (4 R): Coughlin, Conte, Edwards, Pursell.

TREASURY—POSTAL SERVICE—GENERAL GOVERNMENT

Majority (6 D): Roybal, Chmn.; Addabbo, Akaka, Hoyer, Bland, Long.
Minority (3 R): Miller, Rudd, Rogers.

ARMED SERVICES   2120 RHOB, 54151

Majority (29 D): Price (IL), Chmn.; Bennett (FL), Stratton (NY), Nichols (AL), Daniel (VA), Montgomery (MS), Aspin (WI), Dellums (CA), Schroeder (CO), Kazen (TX), Won Pat (GU), McDonald (GA), Byron (MD), Mavroules (MA), Hutto (FL), Skelton (MO), Leath (TX), McCurdy (OK), Foglietta (PA), Dyson (MD), Hertel (MI), Bouquard (TN), Sisisky (VA), Ray (GA), Spratt (SC), McCloskey (IN), Britt (NC), Ortiz (TX), Coleman (TX).
Minority (16 R): Dickinson (AL), Whitehurst (VA), Spence (SC), Holt (MD), Hillis (IN), Badham (CA), Stump (AZ), Courter (NJ), Hopkins (KY), Davis (MI), Kramer (CO), Hunter (CA), Hartnett (SC), Crane, D. (IL), Martin (NY), Kasich (OH).

Subcommittees

INVESTIGATIONS

Majority (9 D): Nichols, Chmn.; Kazen, Mavroules, Leath, Ray, Britt, Stratton, Daniel, Aspin.
Minority (5 R): Hopkins, Stump, Crane, Martin, Kasich.

MILITARY INSTALLATIONS AND FACILITIES

Majority (9 D): Dellums, Chmn.; Montgomery, Kazen, Won Pat, Hutto, Foglietta, Hertel, Sisisky, Spratt.
Minority (5 R): Kramer, Whitehurst, Dickinson, Hartnett, Martin.

MILITARY PERSONNEL AND COMPENSATION

Majority (9 D): Aspin, Chmn.; Montgomery, Schroeder, Byron, Skelton, Spratt, McCloskey, Ortiz, Coleman.
Minority (5 R): Hillis, Holt, Hunter, Hartnett, Dickinson.

PROCUREMENT AND MILITARY NUCLEAR SYSTEMS

Majority (9 D): Stratton, Chmn.; Byron, Mavroules, Skelton, Leath, McCurdy, Dyson, Bouquard, Ray.
Minority (5 R): Holt, Badham, Courter, Kramer, Davis.

READINESS

Majority (8 D): Daniel, Chmn.; McDonald, Hutto, Leath, McCurdy, Foglietta, Hertel, Nichols.
Minority (4 R): Whitehurst, Spence, Crane, Kasich.

RESEARCH AND DEVELOPMENT

Majority (10 D): Price, Chmn.; Schroeder, Won Pat, McDonald, Hutto, Hertel, McCloskey, Coleman, Bennett, Dellums.
Minority (6 R): Dickinson, Courter, Badham, Davis, Stump, Hopkins.

SEAPOWER AND STRATEGIC AND CRITICAL MATERIALS

Majority (8 D): Bennett, Chmn.; Foglietta, Dyson, Bouquard, Sisisky, Britt, Ortiz, Price.
Minority (4 R): Spence, Hartnett, Hillis, Hunter.

BANKING, FINANCE AND URBAN AFFAIRS
2129 RHOB, 54247

Majority (30 D): St Germain (RI), Chmn.; Gonzalez (TX), Minish (NJ), Annunzio (IL), Mitchell (MD), Fauntroy (DC), Neal (NC), Patterson (CA), Hubbard (KY), LaFalce (NY), D'Amours (NH), Lundine (NY), Oakar (OH), Vento (MN), Barnard (GA), Garcia (NY), Lowry (WA), Schumer (NY), Frank (MA), Patman (TX), Coyne (PA), Roemer (LA), Lehman (CA), Morrison (CT), Cooper (TN), Kaptur (OH), Erdreich (AL), Levin (MI), Carper (DE), Torres (CA).
Minority (17 R): Wylie (OH), McKinney (CT), Hansen (ID), Leach (IA), Paul (TX), Bethune (AR), Shumway (CA), Parris (VA), McCollum (FL), Wortley (NY), Roukema (NJ), Lowery (CA), Bereuter (NE), Dreier (CA), Hiler (IN), Ridge (PA), Bartlett (TX).

Subcommittees

CONSUMER AFFAIRS AND COINAGE

Majority (9 D): Fauntroy, Chmn.; Neal, Barnard, Hubbard, Patman, Roemer, Morrison, Cooper, Carper.
Minority (5 R): Hansen, Paul, McCollum, Lowery, Hiler.

ECONOMIC STABILIZATION

Majority (16 D): LaFalce, Chmn.; Lundine, Vento, D'Amours, Oakar, Minish, Fauntroy, Schumer, Coyne, Roemer, Morrison, Cooper, Kaptur, Erdreich, Levin, Torres.
Minority (9 R): Shumway, McKinney, Paul, Bethune, Parris, Wortley, Roukema, Bereuter, Ridge.

FINANCIAL INSTITUTIONS SUPERVISION, REGULATON AND INSURANCE

Majority (17 D): St Germain, Chmn.; Annunzio, Hubbard, D'Amours, Barnard, LaFalce, Oakar, Vento, Garcia, Schumer, Patman, Neal, Frank, Lehman, Cooper, Erdreich, Carper.

Minority (10 R): Wylie, Hansen, Leach, Bethune, McKinney, Shumway, McCollum, Lowery, Wortley, Dreier.

GENERAL OVERSIGHT AND RENEGOTIATION

Majority (10 D): Minish, Chmn.; Gonzalez, Annunzio, Mitchell, Barnard, Fauntroy, Oakar, St Germain, Garcia, Roemer.
Minority (6 R): Parris, Wortley, Bereuter, Dreier, Hiler, Bartlett.

HOUSING AND COMMUNITY DEVELOPMENT

Majority (23 D): Gonzalez, Chmn.; St Germain, Fauntroy, Patterson, Lundine, Oakar, Vento, Garcia, Lowry, Mitchell, Hubbard, D'Amours, Schumer, Frank, Coyne, Lehman, Morrison, Cooper, Kaptur, Erdreich, Levin, Carper, Torres.
Minority (13 R): McKinney, Wylie, Leach, Bethune, Roukema, Wortley, McCollum, Lowery, Bereuter, Dreier, Hiler, Ridge, Bartlett.

INTERNATIONAL DEVELOPMENT INSTITUTIONS AND FINANCE

Majority (7 D): Patterson, Chmn.; LaFalce, Oakar, Lowry, Garcia, Levin, Torres.
Minority (4 R): Bereuter, Roukema, Ridge, Bartlett.

INTERNATIONAL TRADE, INVESTMENT AND MONETARY POLICY

Majority (13 D): Neal, Chmn.; Lundine, Barnard, Patterson, LaFalce, Lowry, Patman, Coyne, Roemer, Lehman, Kaptur, Cooper, Levin.
Minority (7 R): Leach, Hansen, Shumway, Parris, Dreier, McCollum, Roukema.

BUDGET

214 HOB Anx. 1, 57200

Majority (20 D): Jones (OK), Chmn.; Wright (TX), Solarz (NY), Wirth (CO), Panetta (CA), Gephardt (MO), Nelson (FL), Aspin (WI), Hefner (NC), Downey (NY), Donnelly (MA), Lowry (WA), Derrick (SC), Miller (CA), Gray (PA), Williams (MT), Ferraro (NY), Wolpe (MI), Frost (TX), Fazio (CA).
Minority (11 R): Latta (OH), Shuster (PA), Frenzel (MN), Kemp (NY), Bethune (AR), Gramm (TX), Martin (IL), Fiedler (CA), Gradison (OH), Loeffler (TX), Mack (FL).

Task Forces

[The chairman, ranking majority and minority members are ex officio members of all task forces on which they do not hold a regular assignment.]

BUDGET PROCESS

Majority (7 D): Panetta, Chmn.; Gephardt, Aspin, Hefner, Donnelly, Derrick, Miller.
Minority (5 R): Shuster, Frenzel, Bethune, Gramm, Loeffler.

CAPITAL RESOURCES AND DEVELOPMENT

Majority (4 D): Solarz, Chmn.; Aspin, Ferraro, Wolpe.
Minority (2 R): Fielder, Martin.

ECONOMIC POLICY AND GROWTH

Majority (5 D): Aspin, Chmn.; Solarz, Gray, Williams, Ferraro.
Minority (3 R): Bethune, Kemp, Gramm.

EDUCATION AND EMPLOYMENT

Majority (11 D): Gephardt, Chmn.; Wirth, Panetta, Hefner, Downey, Lowry, Miller, Gray, Williams, Wolpe, Frost.
Minority (4 R): Martin, Shuster, Kemp, Mack.

ENERGY AND TECHNOLOGY

Majority (5 D): Wirth, Chmn.; Nelson, Derrick, Frost, Fazio.
Minority (2 R): Loeffler, Mack.

ENTITLEMENTS, UNCONTROLLABLES, AND INDEXING

Majority (5 D): Donnelly, Chmn.; Hefner, Williams, Ferraro, Fazio.
Minority (3 R): Gramm, Gradison, Mack.

FEDERALISM/STATE-LOCAL RELATIONS

Majority (4 D): Nelson, Chmn.; Downey, Lowry, Wolpe.
Minority (2 R): Frenzel, Gradison.

INTERNATIONAL FINANCE AND TRADE

Majority (5 D): Lowry, Chmn.; Solarz, Wirth, Gray, Fazio.
Minority (3 R): Frenzel, Kemp, Fiedler.

TAX POLICY

Majority (7 D): Downey, Chmn.; Solarz, Aspin, Donnelly, Derrick, Miller, Frost.
Minority (5 R): Kemp, Frenzel, Martin, Fiedler, Gradison.

DISTRICT OF COLUMBIA   1310 LHOB, 54457

Majority (8 D): Dellums (CA), Chmn.; Fauntroy (DC), Mazzoli (KY), Stark (CA), Leland (TX), Gray (PA), Barnes (MD), Dymally (CA).
Minority (4 R): McKinney (CT), Parris (VA), Bliley (VA), Holt (MD).

Subcommittees

FISCAL AFFAIRS AND HEALTH

Majority (5 D): Fauntroy, Chmn.; Dellums, Stark, Leland, Gray.
Minority (3 R): Holt, Parris, Bliley.

GOVERNMENT OPERATIONS AND METROPOLITAN AFFAIRS

One majority member, one minority member to be appointed.
Majority (5 D): Gray, Chmn.; Stark, Barnes, Fauntroy, one vacancy.
Minority (3 R): Parris, McKinney, one vacancy.

JUDICIARY AND EDUCATION

(Two majority members, one minority member to be appointed.)
Majority (5 D): Dymally, Chmn.; Mazzoli, Barnes, two vacancies.
Minority (3 R): Bliley, Holt, one vacancy.

EDUCATION AND LABOR

(One majority member, two minority members to be appointed.)

Majority (21 D): Perkins (KY), Chmn.; Hawkins (CA), Ford (MI), Gaydos (PA), Clay (MO), Biaggi (NY), Andrews (NC), Simon (IL), Miller (CA), Murphy (PA), Corrada (PR), Kildee (MI), Williams (MT), Kogovsek (CO), Martinez (CA), Owens (NY), Harrison (PA), Boucher (VA), one vacancy.

Minority (11 R): Erlenborn (IL), Jeffords (VT), Goodling (PA), Coleman (MO), Petri (WI), Roukema (NJ), Gunderson (WI), Bartlett (TX), Packard (CA), two vacancies.

Subcommittees

[The chairman is an ex officio member of all subcommittees. The ranking minority member, or his designee, is an ex officio voting member of all subcommittees. Designees will be indicated by an asterisk (*).]

ELEMENTARY, SECONDARY, AND VOCATIONAL EDUCATION

One majority and one minority member to be appointed.)

Majority (12 D): Perkins, Chmn.; Ford, Andrews, Miller, Corrada, Kildee, Williams, Hawkins, Biaggi, Boucher, Martinez.

Minority (6 R): Goodling, Packard, Roukema, Gunderson, Bartlett, one vacancy.

EMPLOYMENT OPPORTUNITIES

One majority and one minority member to be appointed.)

Majority (11 D): Hawkins, Chmn.; Clay, Corrada, Simon, Martinez, Biaggi, Williams, Kogovsek, Owens, Harrison.

Minority (7 R): Jeffords, Gunderson, Goodling, Coleman, Petri, Bartlett, one vacancy.

HEALTH AND SAFETY

Majority (4 D): Gaydos, Chmn.; Murphy, Ford, Harrison
Minority (2 R): Gunderson, one vacancy.

HUMAN RESOURCES

Majority (6 D): Andrews, Chmn.; Corrada, Williams, Owens, Boucher, Miller.
Minority (3 R): Petri, Coleman, Roukema.

LABOR-MANAGEMENT RELATIONS

(One majority member to be appointed.)

Majority (6 D): Clay, Chmn.; Ford, Kildee, Murphy, Martinez, one vacancy.
Minority (3 R): Roukema, Bartlett, Jeffords.

LABOR STANDARDS

(One majority member to be appointed.)

Majority (7 D): Miller, Chmn.; Kildee, Clay, Martinez, Owens, Harrison.
Minority (4 R): Erlenborn, Petri, Roukema, Packard.

POSTSECONDARY EDUCATION

Majority (7 D): Simon, Chmn.; Ford, Andrews, Kogovsek, Harrison, Boucher, Owens.
Minority (6 R): Coleman, Gunderson, Jeffords, Goodling, Petri, Packard.

SELECT EDUCATION

Majority (7 D): Murphy, Chmn.; Mille, Biaggi, Simon, Gaydos, Williams, Corrada.
Minority (3 R): Bartlett, Goodling, Coleman.

ENERGY AND COMMERCE

2125 RHOB, 52927

Majority (27 D): Dingell (MI), Chmn.; Scheuer (NY), Ottinger (NY), Waxman (CA), Wirth (CO), Sharp (IN), Florio (NJ), Markey (MA), Luken (OH), Walgren (PA), Gore (TN), Mikulski (MD), Swift (WA), Leland (TX), Shelby (AL), Collins (IL), Synar (OK), Tauzin (LA), Wyden (OR), Hall (TX), Eckart (OH), Dowdy (MS), Richardson (NM), Slattery (KS), Sikorski (MN), Bryant (TX), Bates (CA).

Minority (15 R): Broyhill (NC), Lent (NY), Madigan (IL), Moorhead (CA), Rinaldo (NJ), Corcoran (IL), Dannemeyer (CA), Whittaker (KS), Tauke (IA), Ritter (PA), Coats (IN), Bliley (VA), Fields (TX), Oxley (OH), Nielson (UT).

Subcommittees

[The chairman and ranking minority member are ex officio members, with vote, of all subcommittees.]

COMMERCE, TRANSPORTATION, AND TOURISM

Majority (6 D): Florio, Chmn.; Mikulski, Tauzin, Eckart, Dowdy, Richardson.
Minority (2 R): Lent, Ritter.

ENERGY CONSERVATION AND POWER

Majority (8 D): Ottinger, Chmn.; Swift, Synar, Wyden, Hall, Bryant, Luken, Gore.
Minority (3 R): Moorhead, Ritter, Coats.

FOSSIL AND SYNTHETIC FUELS

Majority (12 D): Sharp, Chmn.; Synar, Tauzin, Hall, Dowdy, Richardson, Slattery, Markey, Luken, Walgren, Shelby, Collins.
Minority (5 R): Corcoran, Coats, Fields, Dannemeyer, Tauke.

HEALTH AND THE ENVIRONMENT

Majority (12 D): Waxman, Chmn.; Scheuer, Luken, Walgren, Mikulski, Shelby, Wyden, Eckart, Sikorski, Ottinger, Wirth, Leland.
Minority (5 R): Madigan, Dannemeyer, Whittaker, Bliley, Nielson.

OVERSIGHT AND INVESTIGATIONS

Majority (9 D): Dingell, Chmn.; Gore, Slattery, Sikorksi, Bates, Scheuer, Florio, Markey, Walgren.
Minority (4 R): Broyhill, Whittaker, Bliley, Oxley.

TELECOMMUNICATIONS, CONSUMER PROTECTION, AND FINANCE

Majority (10 D): Wirth, Chmn.; Markey, Swift, Collins, Gore, Leland, Bryant, Bates, Scheuer, Waxman.
Minority (4 R): Rinaldo, Moorhead, Tauke, Oxley.

FOREIGN AFFAIRS

2170 RHOB, 55021

(One majority member to be appointed.)

Majority (24 D): Zablocki (WI), Chmn.; Fascell (FL), Hamilton (IN), Yatron (PA), Solarz (NY), Bonker (WA), Studds (MA), Ireland (FL), Mica (FL), Barnes (MD), Wolpe (MI), Crockett (MI), Gejdenson (CT), Dymally (CA), Lantos (CA), Kostmayer (PA), Torricelli (NJ), Smith (FL), Berman (CA), Reid (NV), Levine (CA), Feighan (OH), Weiss (NY), one vacancy.

Minority (13 R): Broomfield (MI), Winn (KS), Gilman (NY), Lagomarsino (CA), Pritchard (WA), Leach (IA), Roth (WI), Snowe (ME), Hyde (IL), Solomon (NY), Bereuter (NE), Siljander (MI), Zschau (CA).

Subcommittees

[Note: The chairman and ranking minority member of the full committee may attend the meetings and participate in the activities of all subcommittees except for voting and being counted for a quorum.]

AFRICA

Majority (6 D): Wolpe, Chmn.; Crockett, Berman, Reid, Feighan, Weiss.
Minority (3 R): Solomon, Roth, Zschau.

ASIAN AND PACIFIC AFFAIRS

Majority (7 D): Hamilton, Chmn.; Lantos, Ireland, Dymally, Torricelli, Smith, Levine.
Minority (3 R): Winn, Siljander, Zschau.

HUMAN RIGHTS AND INTERNATIONAL ORGANIZATIONS

Majority (6 D): Yatron, Chmn.; Bonker, Levine, Weiss, Lantos, Kostmayer.
Minority (3 R): Leach, Zschau, Solomon.

WESTERN HEMISPHERE AFFAIRS

Majority (7 D): Barnes, Chmn.; Studds, Gejdenson, Kostmayer, Reid, Garcia, Solarz.
Minority (3 R): Lagomarsino, Hyde, Bereuter.

INTERNATIONAL ECONOMIC POLICY AND TRADE

Majority (7 D): Bonker, Chmn.; Mica, Berman, Feighan, Barnes, Wolpe, Gejdenson.
Minority (3 R): Roth, Snowe, Bereuter.

INTERNATIONAL OPERATIONS

Majority (6 D): Fascell, Chmn.; Crockett, Yatron, Kostmayer, Smith, Solarz.
Minority (3 R): Gilman, Siljander, Pritchard.

INTERNATIONAL SECURITY AND SCIENTIFIC AFFAIRS

Majority (5 D): Zablocki, Chmn.; Fascell, Hamilton, Studds, Mica.
Minority (2 R): Broomfield, Hyde.

GOVERNMENT OPERATIONS   2157 RHOB, 55051

Majority (25 D): Brooks (TX), Chmn.; Fascell (FL), Fuqua (FL), Conyers (MI), Collins (IL), English (OK), Levitas (GA), Waxman (CA), Weiss (NY), Synar (OK), Neal (NC), Barnard (GA), Frank (MA), Lantos (CA), Coleman (TX), Wise (WV), Boxer (CA), Levin (MI), MacKay (FL), Levine (CA), Owens (NY), Towns (NY), Spratt (SC), Kolter (PA), Erdreich (AL), one vacancy.
Minority (14 R): Horton (NY), Erlenborn (IL), Kindness (OH), Walker (PA), Williams (OH), Clinger (PA), McGrath (NY), Gregg (NH), Burton (IN), McKernan (ME), Lewis (FL), McCandless (CA), Craig (ID), Schaefer (CO).

Subcommittees

[The chairman and ranking minority member are ex officio members of all subcommittees on which they do not hold a regular assignment.]

COMMERCE, CONSUMER, AND MONETARY AFFAIRS

Majority (6 D): Barnard, Chmn.; Coleman, Spratt, Conyers, Levitas, Waxman.
Minority (3 R): Gregg, Clinger, Lewis.

ENVIRONMENT, ENERGY, AND NATURAL RESOURCES

Majority (6 D): Synar, Chmn.; Wise, Boxer, Levine, Kolter, Lantos.
Minority (3 R): Williams, Clinger, Kindness.

GOVERNMENT ACTIVITIES AND TRANSPORTATION

Majority (6 D): Collins, Chmn.; Owens, Boxer, Lantos, Coleman, Wise.
Minority (4 R): McGrath, McCandless, Walker, Schaefer.

GOVERNMENT INFORMATION, JUSTICE, AND AGRICULTURE

Majority (6 D): English, Chmn.; Neal, Coleman, Wise, MacKay, Towns.
Minority (3 R): Kindness, Lewis, Burton.

INTERGOVERNMENTAL RELATIONS AND HUMAN RESOURCES

Majority (6 D): Weiss, Chmn.; Conyers, Levin, MacKay, Towns, Erdreich.
Minority (3 R): Walker, McCandless, McGrath.

LEGISLATION AND NATIONAL SECURITY

Majority (7 D): Brooks, Chmn.; Fascell, Fuqua, Levitas, Waxman, Neal, Lantos.
Minority (4 R): Horton, Erlenborn, Clinger, Burton.

MANPOWER AND HOUSING

Majority (6 D): Frank, Chmn.; Levine, Owens, Spratt, Kolter, Erdreich.
Minority (4 R): McKernan, Burton, Erlenborn, Schaefer.

HOUSE ADMINISTRATION
326 H, 52061

Majority (12 D): Hawkins (CA), Chmn.; Annunzio (IL), Gaydos (PA), Jones (TN), Minish (NJ), Rose (NC), Swift (WA), Coyne (PA), Foley (WA), Oakar (OH), Coelho (CA), Bates (CA).
Minority (7 R): Frenzel (MN), Dickinson (AL), Badham (CA), Gingrich (GA), Thomas (CA), Martin (IL), Chandler (WA).

Subcommittees
ACCOUNTS

Majority (8 D): Annunzio, Chmn.; Swift, Coyne, Foley, Oakar, Coelho, Bates, Gaydos.
Minority (4 R): Badham, Thomas, Martin, Frenzel.

CONTRACTS AND PRINTING

Majority (4 D): Gaydos, Chmn.; Jones, Oakar, Coyne.
Minority (2 R): Gingrich, Martin.

OFFICE SYSTEMS

Majority (4 D): Rose, Chmn.; Foley, Bates, Swift.
Minority (2 R): Thomas, Dickinson.

PERSONNEL AND POLICE

Majority (4 D): Minish, Chmn.; Annunzio, Rose, Coelho.
Minority (2 R): Chandler, Gingrich.

SERVICES

Majority (4 D): Jones, Chmn.; Minish, Swift, Coyne.
Minority (2 R): Dickinson, Chandler.

INTERIOR AND INSULAR AFFAIRS   1324 LHOB, 52761

(One majority member to be appointed.)
Majority (28 D): Udall (AZ), Chmn.; Kazen (TX), Seiberling (OH), Won Pat (GU), Weaver (OR), Florio (NJ), Sharp (IN), Markey (MA), Corrada (PR), Murphy (PA), Rahall (WV), Vento (MN), Huckaby (LA), Patterson (CA), Kogovsek (CO), Kildee (MI), Coelho (CA), Byron (MD), de Lugo (VI), Gejdenson (CT), Patman (TX), Kostmayer (PA), Moody (WI), Mollohan (WV), Clarke (NC), McNulty (AZ), Lehman (CA), one vacancy.
Minority (14 R): Lujan (NM), Young (AK), Lagomarsino (CA), Marriott (UT), Marlenee (MT), Cheney (WY), Pashayan (CA), Craig (ID), Brown (CO), Smith (OR), Hansen (UT), Emerson (MO), McCain (AZ), Vucanovich (NV).

Subcommittees

[The chairman and ranking minority member are nonvoting ex officio members of all subcommittees on which they do not hold a regular assignment.]

ENERGY AND THE ENVIRONMENT

Majority (16 D): Udall, Chmn.; Seiberling, Florio, Sharp, Markey, Murphy, Rahall, Vento, Huckaby, Patterson, Gejdenson, Patman, Kostmayer, Moody, Mollohan, Clarke.
Minority (8 R): Lujan, Smith, Marriott, McCain, Vucanovich, Brown, Craig, Pashayan.

INSULAR AFFAIRS

(One majority member to be appointed.)
Majority (7 D): Won Pat, Chmn.; Corrada, Murphy, Kildee, de Lugo, Clarke, one vacancy.
Minority (4 R): Lagomarsino, Smith, Hansen, Brown.

MINING, FOREST MANAGEMENT, AND BONNEVILLE POWER ADMINISTRATION

Majority (12 D): Weaver, Chmn.; Udall, Kazen, Seiberling, Murphy, Rahall, Huckaby, Kogovsek, Byron, Moody, Mollohan, McNulty.
Minority (6 R): Marriott, Vucanovich, Young, Craig, Emerson, McCain.

OVERSIGHT AND INVESTIGATIONS

Majority (4 D): Markey, Chmn.; Florio, Sharp, Gejdenson.
Minority (3 R): Marlenee, Hansen, Vucanovich.

PUBLIC LANDS AND NATIONAL PARKS

(One majority member to be appointed.)
Majority (16 D): Seiberling, Chmn.; Won Pat, Weaver, Vento, Patterson, Kogovsek, Kildee, Coelho, Byron, de Lugo, Gejdenson, Kostmayer, Moody, Clarke, Lehman, one vacancy.
Minority (8 R): Young, Marlenee, Craig, Hansen, Emerson, Lagomarsino, Cheney, Pashayan.

WATER AND POWER RESOURCES

Majority (8 D): Kazen, Chmn.; Udall, Weaver, Kogovsek, Coelho, Patman, McNulty, Lehman.
Minority (4 R): Cheney, Pashayan, Brown, McCain.

JUDICIARY 2137 RHOB, 53951

Majority (20 D): Rodino (NJ), Chmn.; Brooks (TX), Rostenmeier (WI), Edwards (CA), Conyers (MI), Seiberling (OH), Mazzoli (KY), Hughes (NJ), Hall (TX), Synar (OK), Schroeder (CO), Glickman (KS), Frank (MA), Crockett (MI), Schumer (NY), Morrison (CT), Fieghan (OH), Smith (FL), Berman (CA), one vacancy.
Minority (11 R): Fish (NY), Moorhead (CA), Hyde (IL), Kindness (OH), Sawyer (MI), Lungren (CA), Sensenbrenner (WI), McCollum (FL), Shaw (FL), Gekas (PA), DeWine (OH).

Subcommittees

ADMINISTRATIVE LAW AND GOVERNMENTAL RELATIONS

Majority (5 D): Hall, Chmn.; Mazzoli, Frank, Schumer, Berman.
Minority (3 R): Kindness, McCollum, Shaw.

CIVIL AND CONSTITUTIONAL RIGHTS
(One majority member to be appointed.)
Majority (5 D): Edwards, Chmn.; Kastenmeier, Conyers, Schroeder, one vacancy.
Minority (3 R): Sensenbrenner, Gekas, DeWine.

COURTS, CIVIL LIBERTIES, AND THE ADMINISTRATION OF JUSTICE

Majority (9 D): Kastenmeier, Chmn.; Brooks, Mazzoli, Synar, Schroeder, Glickman, Frank, Morrison, Berman.
Minority (5 R): Moorhead, Hyde, DeWine, Kindness, Sawyer.

CRIME

Majority (5 D): Hughes, Chmn.; Schumer, Morrison, Feighan, Smith.
Minority (3 R): Sawyer, Shaw, Sensenbrenner.

CRIMINAL JUSTICE
(One majority member to be appointed.)
Majority (5 D): Conyers, Chmn.; Edwards, Seiberling, Berman, one vacancy.
Minority (3 R): Gekas, McCollum, DeWine.

IMMIGRATION, REFUGES, AND INTERNATIONAL LAW

Majority (5 D): Mazzoli, Chmn.; Hall, Frank, Crockett, Smith.
Minority (3 R): Lungren, McCollum, Fish.

MONOPOLIES AND COMMERCIAL LAW

Majority (9 D): Rodino, Chmn.; Brooks, Edwards, Seiberling, Hughes, Synar, Crockett, Schumer, Feighan.
Minority (5 R): Fish, Moorhead, Hyde, Sawyer, Lungren.

MERCHANT MARINE AND FISHERIES 1334 LHOB, 54047

(One majority member to be appointed.)
Majority (26 D): Jones (NC), Chmn.; Biaggi (NY), Anderson (CA), Breaux (LA), Studds (MA), Hubbard (KY), Bonker (WA), D'Amours (NH), Oberstar (MN), Hughes (NJ), Mikulski (MD), Hutto (FL), Tauzin (LA), Foglietta (PA), Sunia (AS), Hertel (MI), Dyson (MD), Lipinski (IL), Borski (PA), Carper (DE), Bosco (CA), Tallon (SC), Thomas (GA), Boxer (CA), Ortiz (TX), one vacancy.

Minority (14 R): Forsythe (NJ), Snyder (KY), Pritchard (WA), Young (AK), Lent (NY), Davis (MI), Carney (NY), Shumway (CA), Fields (TX), Schneider (RI), Sawyer (MI), Bateman (VA), McKernan (ME), Franklin (MS).

Subcommittees

[The chairman and ranking minority member are ex officio members, with vote, of all subcommittees of which they are not designated as chairman or ranking minority member.]

COAST GUARD AND NAVIGATION

Majority (13 D): Studds, Chmn.; Hughes, Tauzin, Biaggi, Oberstar, Mikulski, Hutto, Foglietta, Borski, Carper, Thomas, Hubbard, Boxer.
Minority (7 R): Young, Snyder, Pritchard, Lent, Davis, Sawyer, Franklin.

FISHERIES AND WILDLIFE CONSERVATION AND THE ENVIRONMENT
(One majority member to be appointed.)

Majority (18 D): Breaux, Chmn.; Bonker, Oberstar, Hutto, Dyson, Carper, Bosco, Thomas, Ortiz, Anderson, Studds, D'Amours, Hughes, Tauzin, Sunia, Hertel, Tallon, one vacancy.
Minority (10 R): Forsythe, Pritchard, Young, Carney, Shumway, Schneider, Sawyer, Bateman, McKernan, Franklin.

MERCHANT MARINE
(One majority member to be appointed.)

Majority (16 D): Biaggi, Chmn.; Anderson, Mikulski, Foglietta, Hertel, Lipinski, Borski, Tallon, Boxer, Hubbard, Bonker, Dyson, Ortiz, Breaux, Thomas, one vacancy.
Minority (9 R): Snyder, Young, Davis, Carney, Shumway, Fields, Sawyer, Bateman, McKernan.

OCEANOGRAPHY

Majority (9 D): D'Amours, Chmn.; Sunia, Tallon, Boxer, Studds, Hughes, Mikulski, Tauzin, Lipinski.
Minority (4 R): Pritchard, Shumway, Schneider, Bateman.

PANAMA CANAL AND OUTER CONTINENTAL SHELF

Majority (11 D): Hubbard, Chmn.; Breaux, Bosco, Anderson, Tauzin, Foglietta, Sunia, Hertel, Borski, Ortiz, Mikulski.
Minority (5 R): Carney, Young, Lent, Davis, Fields.

POST OFFICE AND CIVIL SERVICE   309 CHOB, 54054
(Five majority members to be appointed.)

Majority (16 D): Ford (MI), Chmn.; Udall (AZ), Clay (MO), Schroeder (CO), Garcia (NY), Leland (TX), Albosta (MI), Yatron (PA), Oakar (OH), Hall (IN), Sikorski (MN), five vacancies.
Minority (9 R): Taylor (MO), Gilman (NY), Corcoran (IL), Courter (NJ), Pashayan (CA), Dannemeyer (CA), Crane, D. (IL), Wolf (VA), Mack (FL).

Subcommittees

[The chairman and ranking minority member are ex officio voting members of all legislative subcommittees on which they do not hold a regular assignment].

CENSUS AND POPULATION
(One majority member to be appointed.)

Majority (4 D): Garcia, Chmn.; Leland, Oakar, one vacancy.
Minority (2 R): Courter, Dannemeyer.

CIVIL SERVICE
Majority (4 D): Schroeder, Chwmn.; Udall, Hall, Sikorski.
Minority (2 R): Pashayan, Wolf.

COMPENSATION AND EMPLOYEE BENEFITS
(One majority member to be appointed.)
Majority (4 D): Oakar, Chwmn.; Leland, Garcia, one vacancy.
Minority (2 R): Dannemeyer, Mack.

HUMAN RESOURCES
(Two majority members to be appointed.)
Majority (4 D): Albosta, Chmn.; Yatron, two vacancies.
Minority (2 R): Crane, Gilman.

INVESTIGATIONS
(One majority member to be appointed.)
Majority (4 D): Ford, Chmn.; Udall, Yatron, one vacancy.
Minority (2 R): Taylor, Gilman.

POSTAL OPERATIONS AND SERVICES
(Two majority members to be appointed.)
Majority (5 D): Clay, Chmn.; Hall, Sikorski, two vacancies.
Minority (3 R): Corcoran, Pashayan, Mack.

POSTAL PERSONNEL AND MODERNIZATION
(One majority member to be appointed.)
Majority (4 D): Leland, Chmn.; Clay, Albosta, one vacancy.
Minority (2 R): Wolf, Crane.

PUBLIC WORKS AND TRANSPORTATION   2165 RHOB, 54472

Majority (32 D): Howard (NJ), Chmn.; Anderson (CA), Roe (NJ), Breaux (LA), Mineta (CA), Levitas (GA), Oberstar (MN), Nowak (NY), Edgar (PA), Young (MO), Rahall (WV), Applegate (OH), Ferraro (NY), Donnelly, (MA), Albosta (MI), de Lugo (VI), Savage (IL), Sunia (AS), Hall (IN), Bosco (CA), McNulty (AZ), Moody (WI), Borski (PA), Kolter (PA), Valentine (NC), Towns (NY), Lipinski (IL), Andrews (TX), Vandergriff (TX), Rowland (GA), Clarke (NC), Wise (WV).
Minority (18 R): Snyder (KY), Hammerschmidt (AR), Shuster (PA), Stangeland (MN), Gingrich (GA), Clinger (PA), Molinari (NY), Shaw (FL), McEwen (OH), Wolf (VA), Petri (WI), Daub (NE), Martin (IL), Weber (MN), Smith (OR), Sundquist (TN), Johnson (CT), Packard (CA).

Subcommittees
[The chairman and ranking minority member of the committee are ex officio members of all subcommittees.]

AVIATION
Majority (17 D): Mineta, Chmn.; Levitas, de Lugo, Hall, Valentine, Towns, Lipinski, Vandergriff, Anderson, Oberstar, Edgar, Young, Rahall, Applegate, Donnelly, Bosco, Ferraro.
Minority (9 R): Hammerschmidt, Shuster, Stangeland, Gingrich, McEwen, Wolf, Petri, Weber, Packard.

ECONOMIC DEVELOPMENT

Majority (14 D): Oberstar, Chmn.; Nowak, Applegate, Ferraro, Hall, Bosco, Borski, Kolter, Valentine, Towns, Clarke, Wise, Sunia, Roe.
Minority (7 R): Clinger, Shuster, McEwen, Petri, Martin, Sundquist, Johnson.

INVESTIGATIONS AND OVERSIGHT

Majority (10 D): Levitas, Chmn.; Roe, Andrews, Rowland, Wise, Breaux, Ferraro, Albosta, Borski, Lipinski.
Minority (6 R): Molinari, Gingrich, Clinger, Shaw, Sundquist, Johnson.

PUBLIC BUILDINGS AND GROUNDS

Majority (7 D): Young, Chmn.; Clarke, Levitas, Savage, Hall, Andrews, Rowland.
Minority (3 R): Shaw, Stangeland, Molinari.

SURFACE TRANSPORTATION

Majority (19 D): Anderson, Chmn.; Edgar, Rahall, Donnelly, Savage, Sunia, McNulty, Moody, Lipinski, Andrews, Vandergriff, Breaux, Mineta, Applegate, Albosta, Bosco, Borski, Kolter, de Lugo.
Minority (9 R): Shuster, Hammerschmidt, Gingrich, Clinger, Shaw, Wolf, Daub, Martin, Smith.

WATER RESOURCES

Majority (17 D): Roe, Chmn.; Breaux, Albosta, de Lugo, Rowland, Anderson, Oberstar, Nowak, Edgar, Young, Rahall, Ferraro, Donnelly, Savage, Sunia, McNulty, Moody.
Minority (8 R): Stangeland, Hammerschmidt, Molinari, McEwen, Daub, Weber, Smith, Packard.

RULES
312 H, 59486; Minority 305 H, 56991

Majority (9 D): Pepper (FL), Chmn.; Long (LA), Maokley (MA), Derrick (SC), Beilenson (CA), Frost (TX), Bonior (MI), Hall (OH), Wheat (MO).
Minority (4 R): Quillen (TN), Latta (OH), Lott (MS), Taylor (MO).

Subcommittees
RULES OF THE HOUSE

Majority (4 D): Moakley, Chmn.; Beilenson, Bonior, Hall.
Minority (2 R): Taylor, Lott.

THE LEGISLATIVE PROCESS

Majority (4 D): Long, Chmn.; Derrick, Frost, Wheat.
Minority (2 R): Lott, Taylor.

SCIENCE AND TECHNOLOGY
2321 RHOB, 56371

Majority (26 D): Fuqua (FL), Chmn.; Roe (NJ), Brown (CA), Scheuer (NY), Ottinger (NY), Harkin (IA), Bouquard (TN), Walgren (PA), Glickman (KS), Gore (TN), Young (MO), Volkmer (MO), Nelson (FL), Lundine (NY), Hall, (TX), McCurdy (OK), Dymally (CA), Simon (IL), Mineta (CA), Durbin (IL), Andrews (TX), MacKay (FL), Valentine (NC), Reid (NV), Torricelli (NJ), Boucher (VA).

Minority (15 R): Winn (KS), Lujan (NM), Walker (PA), Carney (NY), Sensenbrenner (WI), Gregg (NH), McGrath (NY), Skeen (NM), Schneider (RI), Lowery (CA), Chandler (WA), Bateman (VA), Boehlert (NY), McCandless (CA), Lewis (FL).

Subcommittees
[The chairman and ranking minority member are ex officio members, with vote, of all subcommittees.]

ENERGY DEVELOPMENT AND APPLICATIONS

Majority (13 D): Fuqua, Chmn.; Ottinger, Harkin, Hall, Simon, Boucher, Roe, Scheuer, Bouquard, Young, Nelson, McCurdy, Mineta.
Minority (7 R): Sensenbrenner, Schneider, Lowery, Bateman, Lewis, Carney, Gregg.

ENERGY RESEARCH AND PRODUCTION

Majority (7 D): Bouquard, Chmn.; Roe, Young, Lundine, Ottinger, Hall, Valentine.
Minority (4 R): Walker, Chandler, Lujan, Lowery.

INVESTIGATIONS AND OVERSIGHT

Majority (6 D): Gore, Chmn.; Reid, Volkme, Roe, Durbin, Scheuer.
Minority (3 R): Skeen, McCandless, Schneider.

NATURAL RESOURCES, AGRICULTURE RESEARCH AND ENVIRONMENT

Majority (7 D): Scheuer, Chmn.; Valentine, Harkin, Andrews, MacKay, Torricelli, Brown.
Minority (4 R): McGrath, Schneider, Chandler, Lewis.

SCIENCE, RESEARCH AND TECHNOLOGY

Majority (13 D): Walgren, Chmn.; Brown, McCurdy, Dymally, Mineta, MacKay, Torricelli, Lundine, Simon, Durbin, Valentine, Reid, Boucher.
Minority (6 R): Gregg, Boehlert, Sensenbrenner, McGrath, Skeen, Bateman.

SPACE SCIENCE AND APPLICATIONS

Majority (9 D): Volkmer, Chmn.; Nelson, Andrews, Brown, Hall, Dymally, Mineta, MacKay, Torricelli.
Minority (5 R): Lujan, Lowery, Chandler, Bateman, Walker.

TRANSPORTATION, AVIATION AND MATERIALS

Majority (6 D): Glickman, Chmn.; Gore, Dymally, Ottinger, Harkin, Andrews.
Minority (3 R): Carney, Boehlert, McCandless.

SMALL BUSINESS   2361 RHOB, 55821

Majority (26 D): Mitchell (MD), Chmn.; Smith (IA), Addabbo (NY), Gonzalez (TX), LaFalce (NY), Bedell (IA), Nowak (NY), Luken (OH), Ireland (FL), Skelton (MO), Stenholm (TX), Mazzoli (KY), Mavroules (MA), Hatcher (GA), Wyden (OR), Eckart (OH), Savage (IL), Roemer (LA), Sisisky (VA), McCloskey (IN), Torres (CA), Vandergriff (TX), Cooper (TN), Olin (VA), Britt (NC), Ray (GA).
Minority (15 R): McDade (PA), Conte (MA), Broomfield (MI), Williams (OH), Hiler (IN), Weber (MN), Daub (NE), Smith (NJ), Dreier (CA), Molinari (NY), Roth (WI), Chappie (CA), Boehlert (NY), Bilirakis (FL), one vacancy.

ANTITRUST AND RESTRAINT OF TRADE ACTIVITIES AFFECTING SMALL BUSINESS

Majority (4 D): Luken, Chmn.; Gonzalez, Mazzoli, McCloskey.
Minority (2 R): Weber, Chappie.

ENERGY, ENVIRONMENT AND SAFETY ISSUES AFFECTING SMALL BUSINESS

Majority (5 D): Skelton, Chmn.; Mavroules, Hatcher, Torres, Bedell.
Minority (3 R): Hiler, Smith, Roth.

EXPORT OPPORTUNITIES AND SPECIAL SMALL BUSINESS PROBLEMS

Majority (7 D): Ireland, Chmn.; Stenholm, Wyden, Savage, Sisisky, Torres, Vandergriff.
Minority (4 R): Broomfield, Roth, Chappie, Bilirakis.

GENERAL OVERSIGHT AND THE ECONOMY

Majority (8 D): Bedell, Chmn.; Sisisky, Cooper, Olin, Ray, Addabbo, Gonzalez, Britt.
Minority (4 R): Conte, Dreier, Boehlert, Bilirakis.

SBA AND SBIC AUTHORITY, MINORITY ENTERPRISE AND GENERAL SMALL BUSINESS PROBLEMS

Majority (8 D): Mitchell, Chmn.; Smith, Addabbo, LaFalce, Wyden, Eckart, Savage, Luken.
Minority (4 R): McDade, Daub, Molinari, Boehlert.

TAX, ACCESS TO EQUITY CAPITAL AND BUSINESS OPPORTUNITIES

Majority (6 D): Nowak, Chmn.; Roemer, Vandergriff, Britt, Eckart, Olin.
Minority (3 R): Williams, Smith, Dreier.

STANDARDS OF OFFICIAL CONDUCT   2360 RHOB, 57103

Majority (6 D): Stokes (OH), Chmn.; Rahal (WV), Jenkins (GA), Dixon (CA), Fazio (CA), Coyne (PA).
Minority (6 R): Spence (SC), Conable (NY), Myers (IN), Forsythe (NJ), Brown (CO), Hansen (UT).

No Subcommittees

VETERANS' AFFAIRS   335 CHOB, 53527

Majority (21 D): Montgomery (MS), Chmn.; Edwards (CA), Edgar (PA), Hall (TX), Applegate (OH), Leath (TX), Shelby (AL), Mica (FL), Daschle (SD), Dowdy (MS), Martinez (CA), Evans (IL), Kaptur (OH), Harrison (PA), Mollohan (WV), Penny (MN), Staggers (WV), Rowland (GA), Slattery (KS), Bryant (TX), Richardson (NM).
Minority (12 R): Hammerschmidt (AR), Wylie (OH), Hillis (IN), Solomon (NY), McEwen (OH), Smith (NJ), Smith (OR), Gramm (TX), Burton (IN), Sundquist (TN), Bilirakis (FL), Johnson (CT).

Subcommittees
[The chairman and ranking minority member are ex officio members of all subcommittees.]

COMPENSATION, PENSION, AND INSURANCE

Majority (9 D): Applegate, Chmn.; Hall, Daschle, Martinez, Montgomery, Leath, Shelby, Mica, Dowdy.
Minority (5 R): McEwen, Wylie, Hammerschmidt, Smith, Burton.

EDUCATION, TRAINING AND EMPLOYMENT

Majority (7 D): Leath, Chmn.; Edgar, Evans, Kaptur, Slattery, Bryant, Richardson.
Minority (3 R): Solomon, Wylie, Smith.

HOSPITALS AND HEALTH CARE

Majority (14 D): Edgar, Chmn.; Mica, Dowdy, Evans, Kaptur, Harrison, Mollohan, Penny, Staggers, Rowland, Slattery, Bryant, Richardson, Daschle.
Minority (7 R): Hammerschmidt, Hillis, Solomon, McEwen, Smith, Bilirakis, Johnson.

HOUSING AND MEMORIAL AFFAIRS

Majority (6 D): Shelby, Chmn.; Applegate, Mollohan, Mica, Bryant, Richardson.
Minority (3 R): Smith, Sundquist, Bilirakis.

OVERSIGHT AND INVESTIGATIONS

Majority (7 D): Montgomery, Chmn.; Edwards, Hall, Penny, Staggers, Rowland, Evans.
Minority (5 R): Hillis, Solomon, Burton, Sundquist, Johnson.

WAYS AND MEANS   1102 LHOB, 53625

Majority (23 D): Rostenkowski (IL), Chmn.; Gibbons (FL), Pickel (TX), Rangel (NY), Stark, (CA), Jones (OK), Jacobs (IN), Ford (TN), Jenkins (GA), Gephardt (MO), Downey (NY), Heftel (HI), Fowler (GA), Guarini (NJ), Shannon (MA), Russo (IL), Pease (OH), Hance (TX), Matsui (CA), Anthony (AR), Flippo (AL), Dorgan (ND), Kennelly (CT).
Minority (12 R): Conable (NY), Duncan (TN), Archer (TX), Vander Jagt (MI), Crane (IL), Frenzel (MN), Martin (NC), Schulze (PA), Gradison (OH), Moore (LA), Campbell (SC), Thomas (CA).

Subcommittees

HEALTH

Majority (5 D): Jacobs, Chmn.; Rangel, Ford, Shannon, Russo.
Minority (3 R): Moore, Duncan, Martin.

OVERSIGHT

Majority (7 D): Rangel, Chmn.; Gibbons, Pickle, Guarini, Anthony, Flippo, Dorgan.
Minority (4 R): Martin, Duncan, Campbell, Thomas.

PUBLIC ASSISTANCE AND UNEMPLOYMENT COMPENSATION

Majority (7 D): Ford, Chmn.; Stark, Pease, Hance, Matsui, Fowler, Kennelly.
Minority (4 R): Campbell, Moore, Frenzel, Thomas.

SELECT REVENUE MEASURES

Majority (7 D): Stark, Chmn.; Heftel, Guarini, Flippo, Dorgan, Kennelly, Jenkins.
Minority (4 R): Duncan, Schulze, Vander Jagt, Moore.

SOCIAL SECURITY

Majority (7 D): Pickle, Chmn.; Jacobs, Gephardt, Shannon, Fowler, Matsui, Anthony.
Minority (4 R): Archer, Gradison, Crane, Thomas.

TRADE

Majority (9 D): Gibbons, Chmn.; Rostenkowski, Jones, Jenkins, Downey, Pease, Hance, Heftel, Russo.
Minority (5 R): Vander Jagt, Archer, Frenzel, Schulze, Crane.

SELECT COMMITTEES

SELECT COMMITTEE ON AGING   712 HOB Anx. 1, 63375

Majority (38 D): Roybal (CA), Chmn.; Pepper (FL), Biaggi (NY), Andrews (NC), Bonker (WA), Downey (NY), Florio (NJ), Ford (TN), Hughes (NJ), Bouquard (TN), Lundine (NY), Oakar (OH), Luken (OH), Ferraro (NY), Byron (MD), Ratchford (CT), Mica (FL), Waxman (CA), Synar (OK), Derrick (SC), Vento (MN), Frank (MA), Lantos (CA), Wyden (OR), Albosta (MI), Crockett (MI), Boner (TN), Skelton (MO), Hertel (MI), Borski (PA), Boucher (VA), Erdreich (AL), MacKay (FL), Reid (NV), Sisisky (VA), Vandergriff (TX), Wise (WV), Richardson (NM).
Minority (22 R): Rinaldo (NJ), Hammerschmidt (AR), Regula (OH), Shumway (CA), Snowe (ME), Jeffords (CT), Tauke (IA), Gregg (NH), Wortley (NY), Daub (NE), Craig (ID), Roberts (KS), Evan (IA), Courter (NJ), Williams (OH), SChneider (RI), Ridge (PA), McCain (AZ), Biliradkis (FL), Gekas (PA), Siljander (MI), Smith (NJ).

Subcommittees
[The chairman and ranking minority member are ex officio members of all subcommittees.]

HEALTH AND LONG-TERM CARE

Majority (16 D): Pepper, Chmn.; Florio, Ford, Bouquard, Oakar, Luken, Ratchford, Derrick, Wyden, Ferraro, Waxman, Vento, Skelton, Hertel, Borski.
Minority (10 R): Regula, Tauke, Wortley, Daub, Craig, Roberts, Courter, Ridge, McCain, Bilirakis.

HOUSING AND CONSUMER INTERESTS

Majority (9 D): Bonker, Chmn.; Lundine, Byron, Crockett, Boner, Reid, Wise, Synar, Wyden.
Minority (5 R): Hammerschmidt, Wortley, Ridge, Gekas, Siljander.

HUMAN SERVICES

Majority (9 D): Biaggi, Chmn.; Hughes, Albosta, Lantos, Erdreich, MacKay, Richardson, Downey, Florio.
Minority (5 R): Snowe, Rinaldo, Schneider, Bilirakis, Smith.

RETIREMENT INCOME AND EMPLOYMENT

Majority (9 D): Roybal, Chmn.; Downey, Synar, Frank, Mica, Boucher, Sisisky, Vandergriff, Oakar.
Minority (5 R): Shumway, Jeffords, Gregg, Evans, Williams.

SELECT COMMITTEE ON CHILDREN, YOUTH, AND FAMILIES 385 H2, 67660

Majority (16 D): Miller (CA), Chmn.; Lehman (FL), Schroeder (CO), Boggs (LA), McHugh (NY), Patterson (CA), Mikulski (MD), Weiss (NY), Anthony (AR), Leland (TX), Boxer (CA), Levin (MI), Morrison (CT), Rowland (GA), Sikorski (MN), Wheat (MO).
Minority (9 R): Marriott (UT), Fish (NY), Coats (IN), Bliley (VA), Wolf (VA), Burton (IN), Johnson (CT), McKernan (ME), Vucanovich (NV).

PERMANENT SELECT COMMITTEE ON INTELLIGENCE   405 H, 54121

Majority (9 D): Boland (MA), Chmn.; Zablocki (WI), Mazzoli (KY), Mineta (CA), Fowler (GA), Hamilton (IN), Gore (TN), Stokes (OH), McCurdy (OK).
Minority (5 R): Robinson (VA), Whitehurst (VA), Young (FL), Stump (AZ), Goodling (PA).

Subcommittees
[The chairman is a member of all subcommittees.]

LEGISLATION

Majority (3 D): Mazzoli, Chmn.; Fowler, Stokes.
Minority (2 R): Whitehurst, Goodling.

OVERSIGHT AND EVALUATION

Majority (3 D): Fowler, Chmn.; Hamilton, Gore.
Minority (2 R): Young, Goodling.

PROGRAM AND BUDGET AUTHORIZATION

Majority (4 D): Boland (MA), Chmn.; Zablocki, Mineta, McCurdy.
Minority (3 R): Robinson, Young, Stump.

SELECT COMMITTEE ON NARCOTICS ABUSE AND CONTROL 234 H2, 63040

Majority (16 D): Rangel (NY), Chmn.; Rodino (NJ), Stark (CA), Scheuer (NY), Collins (IL), Akaka (HI), Guarini (NJ), Matsui (CA), Fascell (FL), Fauntroy (DC), Hughes (NJ), Hall (TX), Levine (CA), Ortiz (TX), Smith (FL), Towns (NY).
Minority (9 R): Gilman (NY), Coughlin (PA), Shaw (FL), Oxley (OH), Pritchards (WA), Parris (VA), Chappie (CA), Hunter (CA), Lewis (FL).

INDEX OF TOPICS

INDEX OF PEOPLE

Names appearing in bold face refer to current Governors and Members of Congress. Page numbers appearing in bold face refer to profiles of current Governors and Members of Congress.

INDEX OF PLACES

First page number refers to each state's map; page numbers appearing in bold face refer to state chapters. Counties are listed in italic form.

THE AUTHORS

MICHAEL BARONE is a senior writer on the editorial staff of *The Washington Post*. He has been senior vice president of a public opinion research firm and a consultant to CBS news. He is a graduate of Harvard College and Yale Law School and is a native of the Detroit area. He lives in Washington, D.C. with his wife Joan and their daughter Sarah.

GRANT UJIFUSA, a Japanese-American, is a native of Worland, Wyoming, and a graduate of Harvard College. An editor at Random House, he lives in New York City with his wife Amy and their two young sons Steven and Andrew.

Photographs by Shepard Sherbell. Mr. Sherbell is a freelance photographer living in Washington, D.C.

1984 Almanac Order Form

		Amount	Item
YES!	____ Hardcover ALMANAC(s) @ $35.00 each	_____	HC84
Send me:	____ Softcover ALMANAC(s) @ $22.50 each	_____	SC84
	For D.C. orders: Add 6% sales tax	_____	
	Shipping & Handling @ $2.50 per book	_____	
	TOTAL	_____	

☐ I enclose a check (payable to ALMANAC 1984)

☐ Charge my: ☐ Visa ☐ MasterCard ☐ American Express

Account_____ Expiration_____

Signature_____

(required if using credit card)

Name_____

Address_____

City_____ State_____ Zip_____

MAIL TO:
ALMANAC 1984, P.O. Box 33727
Washington, D.C. 20033

Please allow 4-6 weeks for delivery.
Interested in ordering more than 2 copies?
Call 1-800-424-2921 for special discounts!
(In D.C. call: 857-1491)   **E01**

▲   ▲   ▲   ▲   ▲   ▲

Use this card to order more copies of the 1984 ALMANAC.

Use this card to subscribe to NATIONAL JOURNAL.

▼   ▼   ▼   ▼   ▼   ▼

Special Introductory Offer! New Subscribers Only . . .

National Journal
Subscription Order Form

☐ **YES!** I want to subscribe to NATIONAL JOURNAL

Sign me up for:

Best Value! ☐ 13 weeks for $88—you save $25!
☐ 6 months (26 issues) for $198—you save $29!
☐ 1 year (52 issues) for $395—you save $60!

Name_____

Organization_____

Address_____

City_____ State_____ Zip_____

☐ Bill Me. ☐ I prefer to enclose a check (payable to NATIONAL JOURNAL).

Mail to: NATIONAL JOURNAL, Department A, 1730 M Street, N.W.,
Washington, D.C. 20036.

For even faster service, call Toll Free: 800-424-2921. (In D.C. call 857-1400.)

ALM

Mail in an envelope to:

ALMANAC 1984
Post Office Box 33727
Washington, D.C. 20033

Social Theory and the Urban Question

Second Edition

Peter Saunders

Professor of Sociology and Urban Studies,
School of Cultural and Community Studies,
University of Sussex

London
UNWIN HYMAN
Boston   Sydney   Wellington

Published by the Academic Division of

Unwin Hyman Ltd
15/17 Broadwick Street, London W1V 1FP, UK

Unwin Hyman Inc.,
8 Winchester Place, Winchester, Mass. 01890, USA

Allen & Unwin (Australia) Ltd,
8 Napier Street, North Sydney, NSW 2060, Australia

Allen & Unwin (New Zealand) Ltd in association with the
Port Nicholson Press Ltd,
60 Cambridge Terrace, Wellington, New Zealand

First published in 1987
Second edition 1986
Second impression 1989

British Library Cataloguing in Publication Data

Saunders, Peter, *1950–*
    Social theory and the urban question. —
    2nd ed.
    1. Sociology, Urban
    I. Title
    307.7′6   HT151
ISBN 0 04 445371 X

Printed in Great Britain by Billing & Son Ltd, Worcester

Contents

6 *Contents*

Introduction to the second edition

As a final year undergraduate student back in 1970, I chose to follow an option in urban sociology. I had very little idea of what to expect, and the course proved to be very varied. One week we would be looking at voluntary organizations in West African towns; the next at the power structure of Atlanta, Georgia. Extended families in Bethnal Green jostled for our attention with taxi-dance hall customers in Al Capone's Chicago. Ancient cities, medieval cities and modern cities, cities in capitalist countries, cities in socialist countries and cities in Third World countries, all were included in our broad intellectual sweep. Urban sociology, it soon transpired, could be about anything and everything – if you could find it happening in cities, then you could find it discussed somewhere in the urban sociology literature.

One major problem with all this was that none of the authors we considered seemed to be very clear about what a city was. To be sure, cities are places where large numbers of people live and work, but even this rudimentary definition is problematic. In North America and Australia, settlements which in Britain might be referred to as small towns, suburbs or even villages rejoice in a formally-designated city status. Just how big does a settlement have to be before it becomes urban?

Reflection on this problem immediately leads us into another, for in western capitalist countries, the boundaries between city and countryside, urban and rural, are generally indistinct. It is not just that we live in an age of the metropolis where cities have effectively 'joined up' as they have sprawled across the spaces which once divided them. It is also that we live in an age where people commute from outlying areas to work in city centres, and where, irrespective of their location, they tend to go to the same sorts of schools, to buy the same sorts of goods, to receive the same sorts of television programmes, to vote for the same sorts of political parties, and to lead much the same sorts of lives. Most of what we find going on in cities can, in a society like Britain, be found going on outside them too, and this makes it virtually impossible to identify any specific aspect of social life which is distinctive to cities – still less to focus on the city as an explanatory variable in the sense of identifying some causal factor or mechanism which may be said to generate particular kinds of social arrangements.

In the years since I did that urban sociology option, the subject itself has changed enormously. The attempt to trace and explain contrasts between 'urban' and 'rural' ways of life has now been recognized as largely futile. Other attempts to identify social processes which are distinctive to the particular spatial form of cities have been explored, but in my view, these too have been unsuccessful. By the late 1970s, when the first edition of this book was written, urban sociology had reached a point where it no longer seemed either possible or worthwhile to seek to identify any particular social process in western capitalist industrial societies as a phenomenon of cities. 'Urbanism' was everywhere, with the result that a sociology of urbanism was about everything.

Given such a conclusion, one might have expected the subject to disappear for there seems little point in continuing to offer courses, pursue research or write books in a field of study which has no distinctive object of analysis. In fact, however, urban sociology, and urban studies generally, have continued to grow. Not only this, but the field has arguably become one of the most stimulating and vibrant areas of the social sciences in the contemporary period. The explanation for this apparent paradox is, in my view, that urban studies has, in its long search for specifically 'urban' social phenomena, stumbled upon a distinctive and crucial research agenda. This agenda has little, if anything, to do with cities, but it has a lot to do with pressing problems of contemporary social organization in society as a whole. Urban sociology, in short, has developed into a sociology of consumption.

The first edition of this book was written in 1979–80 and published in 1981. In the final chapter of that edition, I outlined the bare bones of what this sociology of consumption might consist of. This was, however, little more than a conceptual skeleton, a first attempt to chart the contours of a newly-emerging research paradigm. In the years since then, a lot of things have happened and a lot of things have changed, and it is these changes and developments which have prompted me to revise and update the book.

One major change, of course, is that the political and economic conditions in most western societies, and certainly in Britain, have altered dramatically since the late 1970s. The economic recession has deepened with the result that in Britain, the officially-recorded unemployment rate has trebled to record levels while traditional industries have collapsed. This has coincided with the election in 1979, and re-election in 1983, of a 'radical right' Conservative government which has sought to reorganize the whole basis of state provision for consumption by cutting welfare expenditure, privatizing services and pursuing a market ideology which is the very antithesis of the corporatism and neo-Keynesianism which had grown up during the preceding period. It has also coincided with a stark polarization of British society which is expressed in a number of forms – the division between north and south, between inner city and suburb, between black and white, between unemployed and employed – and which has undoubtedly contributed to the sense of anger and frustration which spilled into the streets in 1981, when riots flared in London, Liverpool and other large cities, and again in 1985, when Handsworth in Birmingham and Tottenham in London were the scenes of widespread arson, looting, vandalism and violence.

These social changes inevitably mean that some of the concerns addressed in the first edition of this book (e.g. the focus on corporatism) have at the very least to be reconsidered, while other issues which were not discussed there (e.g. the privatization of consumption) must now be given more prominence. Inevitably, social research takes its cue from the problems and developments of the time, and this new edition provides the opportunity to trace out a new research agenda which is relevant to the changed conditions of the mid 1980s.

A second change which has occurred since the first edition of this book was published has taken place within urban studies itself. The dominance achieved just a few years ago by the structuralist Marxist paradigm has now been shattered, not least as a result of the publication by one of its leading figures, Manuel Castells, of a book which overturns most of the philosophical, theoretical and political arguments which he had himself done so much to develop during the 1970s. Taken together with the publication of other major works by writers such as David Harvey, Ray Pahl, Anthony Giddens and Doreen Massey, this has shifted the whole agenda of urban studies by introducing new substantive concerns and by opening up new theoretical and methodological perspectives. In retrospect, it is now clear that the first edition of this book appeared at a pivotal time in the development of urban social theory, for while the old paradigm was visibly crumbling, the new had yet to develop. In this second edition, I have therefore been able to move beyond mere critique of structuralist Marxism (which was effectively where the first edition ended) and to address the problems and potential of new and exciting directions of theoretical research.

As I have already suggested, the most significant of these 'new directions' has been the growth of work exploring sociological aspects of consumption. Work such as that by Dunleavy (on consumption sector cleavages) and Pahl (on domestic self-provisioning) has been enormously significant in helping to establish this new research agenda. In addition, I have myself been able to put some empirical and theoretical flesh on the conceptual bones presented in the first edition of this book, and the results are assembled in Chapter 8.

Taken as a whole, the book has been thoroughly and fundamentally revised. Chapters 7 and 8, together with the major part of Chapter 6, are completely new and bear little resemblance to the chapters they have replaced, but the first five chapters too have been amended to a greater or lesser extent, and the appendix has been extended.

Chapter 1 considers the way Weber, Durkheim and Marx and Engels came to address the urban question in their historical works and in their analyses of contemporary capitalism. This chapter also provides the opportunity to outline the essentials of their different methodological approaches to social explanation, for it is basically these methodologies which form the basis of the various theories and approaches discussed in later chapters. My revisions to this chapter mainly consist of an attempt to simplify the discussion of Marx's method, although I have also revised the section which deals with Weber's difficult but important essay on the city.

The next five chapters cover what I see as the four main attempts this century to identify a sociological process which is distinctive to cities in the modern period. Chapter 2 discusses the theories of human ecology from Robert Park through to Amos Hawley, and this remains virtually unchanged from the first edition. In Chapter 3, I consider the various cultural theories of urbanism, concentrating in particular on the work of Georg Simmel and Louis Wirth, although in this edition I have also tried to give more careful consideration in addition to the well-known but rarely-read work of Ferdinand Tönnies. This is followed in Chapter 4 by a discussion of the Weberian urban sociology of John Rex and Ray Pahl, and the text here includes a substantial revision of the treatment of urban managerialist and corporatist theories in the light of the changed circumstances in Britain since 1979.

Chapters 5 and 6 consider some of the Marxist analyses of urbanism which developed from the late 1960s onwards. Chapter 5 compares the very different approaches of Henri Lefebvre and Manuel Castells, and here I have introduced various amendments, both in the light of a growing secondary literature on Lefebvre's work, and of subsequent changes in Castells's position. The shift in Castells's approach in recent years has necessitated a major re-write of Chapter 6 which not only traces this development, but also attempts to come to some conclusions regarding the methodological and theoretical arguments generated by his work over the years.

Chapters 7 and 8 have been written anew. Following a summary of the argument which has developed through preceding chapters, Chapter 7 considers two bodies of literature which attempt to theorize the social significance of space in contemporary capitalist or industrial societies. The first, associated with the Marxist geography of writers such as Soja, Harvey and Massey, basically explores the importance of space as a factor which helps to structure the opportunities for future capital accumulation. The second, associated more with sociologists such as Urry and Giddens, seeks to establish the importance of space in constituting social relations in the sense of enabling or constraining the development of social processes. The chapter concludes that, while space is important as an inherent feature of all social relations, it cannot itself form an object of theoretical analysis.

This then clears the way for the discussion in the final chapter of how urban sociology, stripped of its traditional preoccupation with spatial units such as cities or regions, may be developed through a substantive focus on the question of consumption. Beginning with an analysis of the politics of state consumption provision, in which the so-called 'dual politics thesis' is outlined and defended against its critics, the chapter goes on to analyse the implications of the current transition from a 'socialized' to a 'privatized' mode of consumption, arguing that a major social cleavage is now opening up between a relatively secure majority of the population and an increasingly marginalized minority. The chapter ends by considering how this division may be overcome and how consumption provision could be reorganized so as to extend the degree of autonomy and control which ordinary people may be able to assert in key areas of their everyday lives.

There have been times as I have been revising this book for this new edition when I have thought that it might have been easier to have started again from scratch. There is, I think, an analogy here with the argument developed by David Harvey in his analysis of contemporary capitalism, for just as, according to Harvey, capitalist firms encounter a major problem in reconciling their new requirements with existing patterns of investment, so too I have constantly encountered the problem of how to organize and present new materials and new ideas while all the time being constrained by a form of analysis and a framework laid down some years ago. That I have ended up with a revised edition of an existing book, rather than with a totally new work, reflects two fundamental elements of continuity between this and the first edition.

The first element concerns the core theme which ripples through most of these chapters. I suggested in the first edition, and I repeat with even more conviction here, that urban sociology, through its distinctive substantive focus on questions of consumption, has an enormous and as yet largely unrealized potential. The main reason why this potential has not been realized lies in the lingering and obstructive concern with relating urban social theory to the analysis of cities and/or space. It was my argument in 1981 and (despite considerable criticism) it remains my argument today that the traditional attempt to define urban sociology, or urban studies generally, in spatial terms (e.g. as the study of cities, regions or social-spatial interrelations) is both futile and diversionary. Urban sociology, like any other branch of social science, will address the peculiarities of space, just as it does those of time, but this cannot and must not be taken as its specific focus. Conceived as a sociology of consumption, urban sociology goes to the heart of some of the most significant questions regarding social organization in a country like Britain in the present period; conceived as a sociology of space, however, it is largely tangental to them.

The second source of continuity between this edition and the first is that it is still intended that this should be both a work *of* theory and a text *on* theory. In the chapters that follow, I have attempted not only to contribute to current debates and thinking in urban studies, but also to reflect on the tradition of urban social theory from the nineteenth century through to the present. A 'textbook' does not, I believe, have to limit itself to a dry and dispassionate reporting of existing ideas, for inevitably, while trying to discuss all approaches sympathetically, one is drawn into a critical engagement with them in the course of outlining them. What follows, therefore, is simultaneously an outline of, and an intervention in, what I believe is a fascinating and potentially very significant theoretical research tradition.

In the first edition, I acknowledged the help and influence of a number of friends and colleagues who had contributed in one way or another to my work on the book, and I am pleased to repeat those acknowledgements – to Jenny Backwell, Colin Bell, Alan Cawson, John Lloyd, Ray Pahl and Andrew Sayer – in this new edition. In the intervening years, of course, I have accumulated further intellectual debts, not least to other colleagues at Sussex University where the Urban and Regional Studies group remains an enormously stimulating context in which to work, but also to all those in Britain, North America, Australia and New Zealand with whom I have had the opportunity to discuss and exchange ideas over this period.

It is also usual to acknowledge the patience and understanding of the typist who painstakingly prepared the manuscript. In the present case, this is not appropriate since I prepared the manuscript myself on a home computer (a further example, perhaps, of the move to self-provisioning and privatized consumption which I discuss in Chapter 8). I will, however, thank Claire and Michael for the forbearance they have shown in watching me monopolize the machine while they have been waiting to play 'Beach-head' and 'The Staff of Karnath'. The least I can do is to dedicate this new edition to them.

Brighton
September 1985

1 Social theory, capitalism and the urban question

Most areas of sociology today are characterized by a certain degree of theoretical and methodological pluralism, and urban sociology is no exception. Thus there are distinctive Marxist urban sociologies, Weberian urban sociologies and so on, each differing according to the questions they pose and the criteria of adequacy or validity they adopt. What seems to be peculiar to urban sociology, however, is that these various approaches have rarely paid much attention to what the so-called 'founding fathers' of the discipline actually wrote about the urban question. Contemporary Marxist urban theories, for example, make considerable references to Marx's discussions of the method of dialectical materialism, the theory of class struggle and the capitalist state and so on, but rarely pay much attention to his discussions of the town–country division or the role of the city in the development of capitalism. Similarly, Weberian urban sociology has tended simply to ignore Weber's essay on the city and to concentrate instead on his discussions of bureaucracy and social classes. Whereas other branches of the discipline have generally developed directly out of the substantive concerns of key nineteenth- and early twentieth-century European social theorists (for example, the debates within industrial sociology over alienation and anomy, the concern with the question of bureaucracy in organizational sociology, the discussions of the state and political power in political sociology, the recurrent concern with secularization in the sociology of religion and with ideology in the sociology of knowledge), urban sociology has continually underemphasized the work of these writers on the city, and has tended instead to take as its starting point the theory of human ecology developed at the University of Chicago in the years following the First World War.

The reason for this is not hard to find, for it is not that Marx, Weber, Durkheim and other significant social theorists had little to say about the city (far from it, for as Nisbet (1966)* has suggested, this was in some ways a key theme in the work of all these writers), but rather that

*Full references quoted in the text are contained in the References beginning on p. 369.

what they did say tends to suggest that a distinctive urban sociology cannot be developed in the context of advanced capitalist societies. The central concern of all of these writers was with the social, economic and political implications of the development of capitalism in the West at the time when they were writing. The rapid growth of cities was among the most obvious and potentially disruptive of all social changes at that time. In England and Wales, for example, the 'urban population' (administratively defined) nearly trebled in the second half of the nineteenth century with the result that over 25 million people (77 per cent of the total population) lived in 'urban' areas at the turn of the century (see Hall *et al*. 1973, p. 61). This sheer increase in size was startling enough, but it also came to be associated in the minds of many politicians and commentators with the growth of 'urban' problems – the spread of slums and disease, the breakdown of law and order, the increase in infant mortality rates and a plethora of other phenomena – all of which attracted mounting comment and consternation on the part of the Victorian middle classes.

Of course, Marx, Weber and Durkheim were each fully aware of the scale and significance of these changes, yet it is clear from their work that none of them considered it useful or necessary to develop a specifically urban theory in order to explain them. In other words, all three seem to have shared the view that, in modern capitalist societies, the urban question must be subsumed under a broader analysis of factors operating in the society as a whole. While cities could provide a vivid illustration of fundamental processes such as the disintegration of moral cohesion (Durkheim), the growth of calculative rationality (Weber) or the destructive forces unleashed by the development of capitalist production (Marx), they could in no way explain them. For all three writers, what was required was not a theory of the city but a theory of the changing basis of social relations brought about through the development of capitalism, and it was to this latter task that they addressed themselves.

When they did discuss the city, they did so only in one of two ways. First, all three saw the city as an historically important object of analysis in the context of the transition from feudalism to capitalism in western Europe. In his essay on the city, for example, Weber showed how in the Middle Ages the towns played a highly significant role in breaking the political and economic relations of feudalism and establishing a new spirit of rationality which was later to prove crucial for the development of capitalist entrepreneurship and democratic rights of citizenship. Similarly, Durkheim showed how the medieval towns helped break the bonds of traditional morality and foster the growth of the division of labour in society, while Marx and Engels saw the division between town and country in the Middle Ages as the expression of the antithesis between the newly developing capitalist mode of production and the old feudal mode in this period. However, it is clear that all three writers agree that the city was significant only at a specific period in history, and that neither the ancient city nor the modern capitalist city can be analysed in these terms. The city in contemporary capitalism is no longer the basis for human association (Weber), the locus of the division of labour (Durkheim) or the expression of a specific mode of production (Marx), in which case it is neither fruitful nor appropriate to study it in its own right.

The second context in which the city appears in the work of these writers is as a secondary influence on the development of fundamental social processes generated within capitalist societies. The city, in other words, is analysed not as a cause, but as a significant condition, of certain developments. The clearest example here concerns the argument found in the work of Marx and Engels to the effect that, although the city does not itself create the modern proletariat, it is an important condition of the self-realization of the proletariat as a politically and economically organized class in opposition to the bourgeoisie. This is because the city concentrates the working class and renders more visible the stark and growing antithesis between it and capital. In rather different vein, Durkheim's concern with the effects of an advanced division of labour on the moral cohesion of modern societies similarly takes urbanization as an important precondition of the development of functional differentiation. In both cases, therefore, a developmental theory (the growth of class struggle, the growth of new forms of social solidarity) is made conditional upon the growth of towns.

We can now appreciate why urban sociology has tended to pay so little attention to what Marx, Weber and Durkheim had to say about the city, for it is apparent in their work that the city in contemporary capitalism does not itself constitute a theoretically significant area of study. It is hardly surprising, then, that subsequent attempts to establish an urban sociology have drawn upon other aspects of their work while generally bypassing their discussion of the urban question. We shall see in later chapters, for example, how Durkheim's work on the social effects of the division of labour came to be incorporated into ecological theories of city growth and differentiation in the 1920s, how Weber's writings on political domination and social stratification formed the basis for a conceptualization of the city as a system of resource allocation in the 1960s, and how in the 1970s Marx's analysis of social reproduction and class struggle was developed as the foundation for a new political economy of urbanism. The influence of these three writers over the development of urban sociology has been pervasive yet selective.

The aim of this chapter is to retrace the way in which Weber, Durkheim and Marx and Engels all came to the conclusion that the city in contemporary capitalism was not a theoretically specific object of analysis. The paths followed by their respective analyses are divergent, yet the end-point is the same. In other words, although these writers differed radically in their methods, their theories and their personal political commitments and persuasions, their application of their different perspectives and approaches nevertheless resulted in conclusions that are broadly compatible. In each case, therefore, we shall consider first the methodological principles that guided their work, and second the results of the application of these principles to an analysis of the urban question.

Marx and Engels: the town, the country and the capitalist mode of production

Marx's method of analysis has been debated long and hard by subsequent generations. It is clear that Marx himself believed that his was a 'scientific' method in the sense that it led to the discovery of the forces which shaped the development of the social world, just as, for example, Darwin's work had led to the discovery of the forces shaping the evolution of the natural world. The problem, however, is that Marx did not devote much of his writing explicitly to elaborating this method, and it has therefore been left to later philosophers and theorists to specify precisely how such scientific discoveries could be accomplished.

Although Marx himself never used the term, his approach has often been designated by the label 'dialectical materialism'. The phrase is useful as it points to the two basic principles upon which Marx's method of analysis was based.

The principle of the dialectic is essentially that any 'whole' is comprised of a unity of contradictory parts, such that it is impossible to understand any one aspect of reality without first relating it to its context. We cannot, for example, understand the plight of wage labour under capitalism without also understanding the process leading to the augmentation of the wealth and power of capital, for capital and wage labour are tied together in an inescapable yet inherently antagonistic relation of mutual interdependence. A method of analysis which is dialectical, therefore, is a method which holds that no single aspect of reality can be analysed independently of the totality of social relations and determinations of which it forms a necessary part. Put another way, any explanation of the part can only be accomplished through an analysis of the whole. As Swingewood suggests, 'The dialectical approach in Hegel and Marx is preeminently a method for analysing the interconnections of phenomena, of grasping facts not as isolated, rigid and external data but as part of an all-embracing process' (1975, p. 33).

It is this claim to be able to analyse the totality of things which has helped to make Marxism so attractive to so many contemporary social scientists. In contrast to so-called 'bourgeois' social science with its irksome and petty disciplinary boundaries, Marxism holds out the promise of an all-embracing explanation which can relate the processes studied by the political scientist to those analysed by the economist or the sociologist. Its first claim to superiority, therefore, lies in its purported ability to transcend the inevitably partial and stunted knowledge of the specialist disciplines by means of an analysis of the totality of social relations in which changes in one sphere of life are explained with reference to changes in another.

There is, moreover, a second claim advanced on behalf of a Marxist method, and this had to do with Marx's 'materialism'. The term 'materialism' in this context is generally used in contra-distinction to 'idealism', and it basically refers to the principle that the material world exists prior to our conceptions or ideas about it. Marx recognizes that the prevailing ideas which we share about what the world is like and how it works must bear some relation to the actual reality, for it is inconceivable that generations of people should collectively delude themselves entirely about the nature of a reality which daily confronts them in various forms and manifestations. Nevertheless, Marx also argues that reality may rarely be directly reflected in consciousness. The way the world appears to us, in other words, may conceal or distort its essential character. Indeed, if this were not the case, there would be no need for science since all knowledge of reality would be immediately available to us through our everyday unmediated experience of living in the world. What science does, according to Marx, is to penetrate the forms of appearance in which reality cloaks itself in order to discover the essential causal relations which lie behind and give rise to such appearances. As Derek Sayer puts it, 'Unlike phenomenal forms, Marx holds, essential relations need not be transparent to direct experience. Phenomenal forms may be such as to mask or obscure the relations of which they are the forms of manifestation' (1979, p. 9).

We are now in a position to understand Marxism's claims relative to 'bourgeois' social science. First, a Marxist method will understand the total context of interrelations and mutual determinations which shape the social world, whereas bourgeois approaches will remain partial and thus fail to achieve any clear overall understanding of the causes of the changes they are studying. And second, a Marxist method will penetrate the phenomenal forms of appearance in which the world presents itself to our consciousness while bourgeois approaches will remain stuck at the level of these appearances and fail to analyse the underlying essential relations which generate them. It was precisely in these terms that Marx attacked the bourgeois economists of his day, for in his view, any theory which fails to relate the operation of the economy to processes taking place in society as a whole (e.g. as in economists' fascination with Robinson Crusoe models of economic life), and which adopts as its tools of analysis the categories of everyday experience (e.g. land, labour and capital as three 'factors of production' which exchange freely as equivalents) while failing to analyse the processes which underpin these experiences (i.e. the creation of value by labour and its expropriation by capitalists and landowners) will simply end up reproducing in more elaborate terminology the existing and muddy conceptions characteristic of any given period. Such theories, in other words, are no more than ideologies. It is the task of science to go beyond the world of common-sense experience: 'The forms of experience are reproduced directly and spontaneously, as current and usual modes of thought; the essential relation must first be discovered by science' (Marx 1976, p. 682).

All of this, of course, raises the obvious question of how Marx's method of dialectical materialism can analyse the totality and come to discover its essential features when all other methods are doomed to remain partial in their scope and superficial in their insight. How do we get from our existing knowledge, which is inevitably partial and superficial, to a scientific knowledge which claims to be holistic and essential? And (just as important), having made this transition from common sense to science, how are we to know that the totality is as the theory tells us, and that the essential determinations which it has discovered are actually present and operating, when all that we can ever 'see' are the 'parts' and the 'appearances'?

It is clear from Marx's own writings that he believed that scientific understanding derived both from theoretical critique and development of existing ideas and from empirical investigation of existing conditions. There is, in other words, a dialectical interplay between theory and observation, the development of generalizations and a concern with specifics, the elaboration of abstractions and the analysis of concrete cases. Seen in this way, Marx's science is a product both of his mulling over musty texts in the British Museum and of his observation of conditions in the European capitalist countries of his time. McBride summarizes this method as, 'A movement from broad generalizations to endless specifics to generalities qualified by facts' (1977, p. 56).

Now this is all very well, but it does not take us very far. The problem still remains: *how* is the scientific knowledge produced and *how* is it to be evaluated? If the scientific knowledge is a product first and foremost of Marx's theorizing, then why should we accept his ideas as in any way more insightful or valid than anyone else's? Are we to accept, for example, that Marx had some privileged insight into reality, an 'inside track' denied to other mortals who, in their reflections on the world, fail to get beyond partiality and phenomenal forms of appearance? If, on the other hand, the knowledge is primarily a function of observation and experience, then how was Marx able to construct valid and all-embracing generalizations out of his own selective and partial biographical experience? How, for example, could he derive his theoretical constructs and abstractions directly and necessarily from his observations when, as he himself argues, such observations necessarily obscure or even invert the essential reality which lies behind them?

Despite the manifold attempts over the last hundred years to demonstrate the epistemologically superior starting point of Marxist analysis, it is clear that any approach which attempts to analyse the whole when all that can be experienced are the parts, and which attempts to discover essential causes when all that can be experienced are phenomenal forms, can never be more than conjectural. What Marx offers, in other words, is not a special insight into the truth, but a distinctive approach based upon what Sayer has termed a 'method of retroduction'.

Sayer resolutely denies the claims which have often been advanced by Marxists that a Marxist method starts from theoretical abstraction.

As he points out, any mode of investigation that began with a battery of abstractions would have to be premised on the assumption of some prior magical or privileged insight into the essence of reality, yet it is precisely this essence which the method is supposed to discover. It follows, therefore, that the starting point for investigation must be empirical:

> Marx's historical categories ... are generated neither from 'simple abstractions' in general, nor from transhistorical categories in particular. They are emphatically *a posteriori* constructs, arrived at precisely by abstraction from the 'real and concrete'. Marx had no mysteriously privileged starting point (D. Sayer 1979, p. 102).

This then raises the question of how Marx derives his abstractions from observation of 'concrete' conditions. How does he penetrate the phenomenal forms of appearance to reveal the essential relations which lie behind them? Sayer's answer is that he only ever develops conjectural knowledge of the essential relations. In other words, the logic of Marx's approach is to suppose the existence of certain relations which, *if they did exist*, would account for the observed phenomenal forms. 'The "logic" of Marx's analytic', says Sayer, 'is essentially a logic of hypothesis formation, for what he basically does is to *posit* mechanisms and conditions which would, if they existed, respectively explain how and why the phenomena we observe come to assume the forms they do' (p. 114). This method is neither deductive (since there are no *a priori* covering laws or transhistorical generalizations from which essential relations can be deduced), nor inductive (since the discovery of regularities in the phenomena under investigation cannot itself imply the existence of certain essential causes). Rather, it is a 'retroductive' method.

The logic of retroductive explanation involves the attempt to explain observable phenomena by developing hypotheses about underlying causes. It cannot support *any* conjecture, since the hypothesized causes must be able to explain evidence at the level of appearances, but it is equally a weak form of inference since the hypotheses can never be directly tested. In other words, it is never possible finally to demonstrate that a posited 'law' of capitalist development is actually true since such a law refers to processes which, even if they do exist, remain hidden. Furthermore, it is never possible to demonstrate that the essential relations posited by the theory are the correct ones since there is always the possibility that other essences could be put forward which could explain phenomenal forms equally as well.

Marx's method, understood as a method of retroduction, thus carries no guarantees of truth and no privileged insight into the inner workings of society. There is no warrant in this method for dismissing alternative theories that can also explain phenomenal appearances, nor for claiming a monopoly over the 'correct' scientific mode of analysis. Equally, of course, it makes no sense to attack this method on the grounds that its results cannot be directly tested against experience, since its very purpose is to theorize processes that by definition cannot be amenable to direct observation. The results of the application of such a method must be evaluated on its own terms (for example, does the posited essence explain phenomenal forms? are the predictions – as opposed to the prophecies – that arise out of this method borne out historically? how well does the theory explain comparative variations between societies? and so on). As Sayer concludes,

If we require all the propositions in a scientific explanation to be open to empirical refutation, we must conclude that Marx was no scientist. If, on the other hand, we demand merely that it must be possible to provide independent empirical evidence which bears on its truth or falsity, then we may reasonably regard *Capital* as a paradigm of scientific research (D. Sayer 1979, p. 141).

In short, Marx's method can be used fruitfully to generate theories that are plausible to a greater or lesser extent but can never finally be demonstrated, and it follows that there is no necessary and compelling reason to accept such theories other than one's own political values and purposes. Marxism, in other words, is as much a guide to political practice as a method of scientific analysis.

The distinction drawn in Marxist methodology between phenomenal appearances and the essential relations of which they are an expression is crucial to any understanding of how Marx and Engels themselves analysed the phenomenon of urbanism. Both writers argued that the division between town and country had characterized all human societies from antiquity to modern capitalism. Historically this separation was second only to the division between men and women as the cornerstone of social organization, and for Marx, it was thus a primordial expression of the social division of labour: 'The foundation of every division of labour which has attained a certain degree of development, and has been brought about by the exchange of commodities, is the separation of town from country. One might well say that the whole economic history of society is summed up in the movement of this antithesis' (1976, p. 472). Yet having said this, the essence of the relation between city and countryside was different in different periods of human history. The town–country antithesis is, in other words, a phenomenon which has to be analysed in the context of the underlying mode of production which sustains and is sustained through it in any given period of human history. The analysis of the city and its relation to the countryside is thus premised on the analysis of class relations inscribed within specific modes of production, for urbanism assumes a different significance in different social contexts.

According to Marx, the first real class society was that of the ancient city (notably Rome). Roman society was based on a slave mode of production in which the wealth of the ruling class was founded on agricultural land ownership. Ownership of the means of production became increasingly concentrated into great estates – the *latifundiae* – as a result of the progressive collapse of the independent peasantry, but although the great landowners lived in the city itself, the mode of production remained rural: 'Ancient classical history is the history of cities, but cities based on landownership and agriculture' (Marx 1964, p. 77).

In antiquity, therefore, the city never became the locus of a new mode of production. The relation of Rome to its provinces was entirely political; the city was nothing more than an administrative centre superimposed upon a slave–agriculture mode of production. It followed from this that internal struggles could destroy this political bond but that there was no basis in this society for the development of a qualitatively new mode of production out of the ruins of the old: 'Rome, indeed, never became more than a city; its connection with the provinces was almost exclusively political and could, therefore, easily be broken again by political events' (Marx and Engels 1970, p. 90). Rome collapsed, it was not transcended, and this is because the tension between town and country, centre and periphery, was never more than political. Ancient society disappeared 'without producing a different mode of production, a different society . . . Why? Because the town in antiquity consisted of a closed system. Internal struggle could only harm it from the inside without being able to open up another practical reality' (Lefebvre 1972, p. 40). With the collapse of Rome, the break-up of the *latifundiae* and the fall of a slave mode of production, all that happened was a return to individual peasant agriculture.

The history of human societies up to the Middle Ages is therefore a history of the countryside. In the feudal or Germanic period, however, this begins to change: 'The middle ages (Germanic period) starts with the countryside as the locus of history, whose further development then proceeds through the opposition of town and country; modern history is the urbanization of the countryside, not, as among the ancients, the ruralization of the city' (Marx 1964, pp. 77–8). In other words, in the feudal era, for the first time, the division between town and country comes to express an *essential contradiction* which eventually brings about the transcendence of feudalism itself.

According to Marx, the growth of a merchant class in the established towns during the Middle Ages had the important effect of extending trading links between different areas, thereby facilitating a division of labour between different towns and stimulating the growth of new industries: 'The towns enter into relations with one another, new tools are brought from one town into the other, and the separation between production and commerce soon calls forth a new division of production between the industrial towns, each of which is soon exploiting a predominant branch of industry' (Marx and Engels 1970, p. 72). However, the development of industrial capital was hindered by the existing relations of production in the established towns, for the guild system both restricted entry into manufacture and regulated the movement of labour. Capitalist manufacture, based originally on weaving, was thus propelled out of the corporate towns and was at the same time attracted into the countryside where there was water power to drive the new machinery and labour power to work it:

The money capital formed by means of usury and commerce was prevented from turning into industrial capital by the feudal organization of the countryside and the guild organization of the towns. These fetters vanished with the dissolution of the feudal band of retainers, and the expropriation and partial eviction of the rural population. The new manufacturers were established at sea-ports, or at points in the countryside which were beyond the control of the old municipalities and their guilds (Marx 1976, p. 915).

The new system of capitalist manufacture, facilitated by merchants' capital in the medieval towns, thus took root in the countryside, and the great cities of the Industrial Revolution grew up around it. Whereas the towns of antiquity had represented a closed system, these new industrial towns represented an opposition to the mode of production that had spawned them. The hierarchical obligations of feudalism and the corporate regulation of the medieval towns were here replaced by relations based entirely on the cash nexus. The new social relations of capitalism thus became established as the antithesis to the old social relations of feudalism, and the contradictions between them, expressed in the class antagonism between industrial bourgeoisie and feudal landowners, came to be represented directly and vividly in the conflict between town and country.

In the feudal period, therefore, the division between town and country not only reflected the growing division of labour between manufacture and agriculture, but was also the phenomenal expression of the antithesis between conflicting modes of production. Although the new industrial towns were not themselves the cause of the transcendence of feudalism, they were the form it took. In this sense, the town was at this time an historical subject:

For Marx, the dissolution of the feudal mode of production and the transition to capitalism is attached to a *subject*, the town. The town breaks up the medieval system (feudalism) while transcending itself . . . the town is a 'subject' and a coherent force, a partial system which attacks the global system and which simultaneously shows the existence of this system and destroys it (Lefebvre 1972, p. 71).

The stark contrast between town and country is, of course, in no way overcome by the establishment of a capitalist mode of production. Indeed, Engels suggests that this contrast is 'brought to its extreme point by present-day capitalist society' (1969b, p. 333). However, the significance of this division changes with the development of capitalism, for the essential contradiction within the capitalist mode of production (that between capital and labour) no longer corresponds to the phenomenal forms of town and country in the way in which that between capital and feudal landownership once did. Once capitalism has become established, it permeates throughout social production, and (in time) agriculture becomes characterized by capitalist social relations just as manufacturing industry does. The town and the country are thus no longer the real subjects of analysis or of political struggle, for although the separation between them becomes ever more vivid, it does not itself set the parameters within which the struggle for socialism is to be waged. Put another way, the struggle between proletariat and bourgeoisie extends across urban–rural boundaries as workers in town and countryside are increasingly drawn into the capital relation.

Having said that, it is nevertheless the case that Marx and Engels look to the *urban* proletariat to lead the struggle for socialism. As Williams (1973) has pointed out, there is something of an ambivalence in their analysis of the role of the city in capitalist societies, for they argue on the one hand that the city expresses most vividly the evils of capitalism, and on the other that it is within the city that the progressive forces of socialism are most fully developed. What this indicates is not so much an 'emotional confusion' (as Williams 1973, p. 37, suggests) as a dual focus in their work on capitalist urbanization. In other words, Marx and Engels study the capitalist city in two ways: first as an illustration or a microcosm of processes occurring at a different rate throughout capitalist society, and second as an important condition of the development of certain specific processes within that society.

When they discuss the city as a microcosm, their concern is not with the city *per se* but with capitalist processes that are most clearly revealed in an urban context: 'From this perspective, seen in this light, the town provides the backcloth; on that backcloth lots of events and notable facts come to pass which analysis detaches from their relatively unimportant decor' (Lefebvre 1972, p. 106). It is, in other words, not the city that is held responsible for the poverty and squalor of the urban proletariat, but the capitalist mode of production. Engels makes this abundantly clear both in his early work on the condition of the English working class, where he argues that 'the great cities really only secure a more rapid and certain development for evils already existing in the germ' (1969a, p. 150), and in his later essay on the housing question. In both works the city is portrayed as the hothouse of capitalist contradictions, the exaggerated expression of essential tendencies within capitalism itself, and in both Engels leaves us in no doubt that urban poverty can be overcome only through a transformation of the society as a whole.

As his work developed, so his treatment of the urban question became every more firmly grounded in a critique of capitalism. In his essay on the housing question (written some thirty years after his discussion of the condition of the English working class), he states explicitly that 'The housing shortage from which the workers and part of the petty bourgeoisie suffer in our modern big cities is one of the innumerable *smaller* secondary evils which result from the present day capitalist mode of production' (Engels 1969b, p. 305). And whereas in his earlier work, written before he met Marx, he had been tempted to suggest that the 'Big Whigs' of Manchester were perhaps in part responsible for perpetuating the pattern of urban deprivation in that city (see Engels 1969a, pp. 80–1), he is clear in his later essay that it is the capitalist system itself, and not the conscious and deliberate actions of individual capitalists, that explains the deplorable conditions under which large sections of the proletariat are obliged to live. Indeed, he argues that the bourgeoisie has sometimes attempted (out of self-interest) to alleviate these conditions, but that such attempts necessarily fail as the logic of capitalism constantly reasserts itself:

Capitalist rule cannot allow itself the pleasure of generating epidemic diseases among the working class with impunity. ... Nevertheless the capitalist order of society reproduces again and again the evils to be remedied, and does so with such inevitable necessity that even in England the remedying of them has hardly advanced a single step (Engels 1969b, p. 324).

This notion of an 'inevitable necessity', an inexorable capitalist logic, recurs throughout this essay. There is, according to Engels, no possibility of resolving the housing question within capitalist society. Every attempt at what today would be termed 'urban renewal' results in the eradication of slums in one area and their simultaneous reappearance in another:

The breeding places of disease, the infamous holes and cellars in which the capitalist mode of production confines our workers night after night, are not abolished; they are merely shifted elsewhere! The same economic necessity which produced them in the first place produces them in the next place also! As long as the capitalist mode of production continues to exist it is folly to hope for an isolated settlement of the housing question or of any other social question affecting the lot of the workers. The solution lies in the abolition of the capitalist mode of production (Engels 1969b, pp. 352–3).

The city is not, however, only a reflection of the logic of capitalism, for Marx and Engels also see in the development of urbanization the necessary condition for the transition to socialism. This is not because the city is the locus of a new mode of production, as was the case in the medieval period, but because it is in the city that the revolutionary class created by capitalism, the proletariat, achieves its 'fullest classic perfection' (Engels 1969a, p. 75). Precisely because the tendencies within capitalism are most fully developed in the great cities, it is there that the conditions for effective struggle against capital reach their maturity:

Since commerce and manufacture attain their most complete development in these great towns, their influence upon the proletariat is also most clearly observable here. Here the centralization of property has reached the highest point . . . there exist here only a rich and a poor class, for the lower middle class vanishes more completely with every passing day (Engels 1969a, p. 56).

The tendencies for capital to become concentrated and for the classes to polarize develop in the cities, and it is therefore in the cities that the concentration and common deprivation of the proletariat is most likely to result in the growth of class consciousness and revolutionary organization:

If the centralization of population stimulates and develops the property-holding class, it forces the development of the workers yet more rapidly. The workers begin to feel as a class, as a whole. . . . The great cities are the birthplaces of labour movements; in them the workers first began to reflect upon their own condition and to struggle against it; in them the opposition between proletariat and bourgeoisie first made itself manifest. . . . Without the great cities and their forcing influence upon the popular intelligence, the working class would be far less advanced than it is (Engels 1969a, p. 152).

Here, then, is the source of the ambivalence noted by Williams, for although the city represents a concentration of the evils of capitalism, it also constitutes the necessary conditions for the development of the workers' movement that will overthrow it. The conditions of life in the countryside cannot sustain a coherent class challenge to the bourgeoisie because 'the isolated dwellings, the stability of the surroundings and occupations, and consequently of the thoughts, are decidedly unfavourable to all development' (Engels 1969a, p. 291). This is why Marx and Engels develop the well-known argument in the *Communist Manifesto* to the effect that the bourgeoisie has rendered a service to the workers' movement by creating large cities which have 'rescued a considerable part of the population from the idiocy of rural life' (1969, p. 112).

It is important to recognize, however, that it is not urbanization itself that forges a revolutionary working class any more than it is urbanization that gives rise to poverty, squalor and disease. The development of potentially revolutionary conditions is a tendency inherent within the development of capitalism, and the growth of cities is a contingent condition influencing whether and how such conditions come to be acted upon by the working class. The city is only of secondary significance in Marx's analysis of capitalism and the transition to socialism.

What this means, of course, is that there is no basis in the work of Marx and Engels for the development of a specific theory of urbanism in capitalist societies. The city may illustrate the manifestations of essential tendencies within capitalism, and it may even influence the way in which these manifestations come to be articulated in political struggle, but it is not the essential cause of such developments, nor is it the phenomenal form of an underlying contradiction as was the case in feudal society. A Marxist analysis that seeks to go beyond the level of appearances and to posit the existence of essential relations will not take the city as an object of analysis, but will rather consider the phenomena that become manifest in cities in terms of the underlying relations and determinations of which they are but one manifestation.

From a Marxist perspective, then, there seems little basis for developing a theory of urbanism. Even Marx's analysis of the role of the cities in fostering a nascent capitalism during the medieval period has been challenged by writers such as Abrams (1978) and Holton (1984) who argue that the cities were generally part of the feudal system rather than antithetical to it, and that the transition to capitalism took place as much in the countryside (through the struggle between serfs and their lords) as in the towns (where the burghers often enjoyed the patronage of the feudal landed nobility). Whether or not the medieval city represents what Lefebvre calls an 'historical subject', however, it is clear from Marx's work that the capitalist city does not. For Marx and Engels, it is capitalism rather than urbanism which constitutes the essential object of analysis in the contemporary period. Any analysis which seeks to attribute causal powers to the city (e.g. through explanations couched in terms of 'urban problems' or 'urban processes') is thus little more than an ideology, for in the context of modern capitalism, the urban is a common-sense category with no scientific status.

Max Weber: the city and the growth of rationality

Weber's approach to sociological explanation represents almost a total reversal of Marx's method. While Marx emphasized totality, the need to relate everything to everything else, Weber argues that only partial and one-sided accounts are ever possible. Where Marx seeks to identify essential causes behind phenomena, Weber's concepts represent logical purifications of phenomenal forms. Marx's notion of praxis, the inherent fusion of scientific analysis and political struggle, is directly opposed to Weber's insistence on the separation of science and politics, facts and values. And while Marx is interested in individuals only in so far as they are personifications of objective relations, Weber sees individual actions and individual consciousness as the very base of sociological analysis.

The basic concept in Weber's sociology is that of the human subject endowed with free will who, in interaction with others, attempts to realize certain values or objectives. He recognizes that not all human actions are rational since individuals may be unaware of certain possibilities for realizing their aims, and their actions may in any case be contaminated by habit or emotion. Sociology in his view can therefore perform a technical service by clarifying what people want to achieve (e.g. by pointing to inconsistencies between different sets of values to which they are committed), and by indicating which strategies are most likely to result in the required effects.

At the heart of Weber's sociological enterprise, therefore, is the attempt to relate subjective motives to particular courses of action. It follows from this that the explanation of social action will be premised upon an understanding of the subjective meaning that that action has for the individual concerned. Hence Weber's well-known definition of sociology as 'A science concerning itself with the interpretative understanding of social action and thereby with a causal explanation of its course and consequences' (1968, p. 4). By social action, Weber means human action which is subjectively meaningful and which takes account of the actions of others.

Implied in this definition is a rejection of any attempt to explain social phenomena as the result of anything other than subjectively meaningful human actions:

Action in this sense of subjectively understandable orientation of behaviour exists only as the behaviour of one or more *individual* human beings . . . collectivities must be treated as *solely* the resultants and modes of organization of the particular acts of individual persons, since these alone can be treated as agents in the course of subjectively understandable action (Weber 1968, p. 13).

Thus, when using collective concepts such as 'social class', or 'state', the sociologist should always remember that it is not a class or a state that acts, but rather the individuals who comprise it.

The explanation of social action involves two stages. First, the sociologist must attempt to provide a plausible account of the actors' motives. This is possible because certain types of subjective meanings are generally attached to certain types of actions in certain types of situations (e.g. chopping wood on a cold day may be indicative of a desire to light a fire). There is, of course, no guarantee that the posited motive is the actual motive (the more rational the action, the greater is the likelihood that we will understand it correctly), and having adduced a possible motive, the sociologist must then go on to show that this individual tends to act in similar ways in other similar situations. In other words, an adequate sociological explanation must attempt both to understand the meaning of a given action for those involved, and to demonstrate the probability of its occurrence in particular types of situations. As Weber puts it,

If adequacy with respect to meaning is lacking, then no matter how high the degree of uniformity and how precisely its probability can be numerically determined, it is still an incomprehensible statistical probability, whether we deal with overt or subjective processes. On the other hand, even the most perfect adequacy on the level of meaning has causal significance from a sociological point of view only insofar as there is some kind of proof for the existence of a probability that action in fact normally takes the course which has been held to be meaningful (Weber 1968, p. 12).

Correlations and generalizations explain nothing if we fail to understand what lies behind them, just as understanding of subjective meanings is useless if we cannot predict typical patterns of action.

Two points in particular should be noted about this argument. The first is that Weber only ever talks of *adequate* explanations; even when the attribution of meaning is successfully combined with an analysis of probability, we can never be certain that the explanations we put forward are correct. Furthermore, the element of free will in social life means that there must always be an element of uncertainty in the explanation of social action, for if individual actions are not determined then the most that sociology can achieve is statements of probability regarding the likely occurrence of certain types of actions in certain types of situations. It follows from this that laws of social life (including Marxist laws) are impossible, since each action is a unique (though often predictable) event. The so-called 'laws' of the social sciences (for example, the law of supply and demand) are in fact statements of typical probability regarding the likelihood of certain types of action occurring in certain types of situations.

The second point is that, although all social events are historically unique, there is clearly a need for some means whereby social phenomena can be classified in general terms, for only in this way is it possible to understand typical motives and to recognize typical patterns of action. It is, in other words, necessary to generalize in order to explain unique events. In Weber's sociology, this function of generalization is fulfilled through the construction of *ideal types*. These are mental constructs which serve to specify the theoretically most significant aspects of different classes of social phenomena. They may be either 'individual' types (Calvinism, capitalism, bureaucracy, etc.) or generic types (such as the four different types of social action). As Burger has pointed out, individual types clearly refer to numerous empirical cases (for example, there are many different capitalist societies): 'This type of ideal type is not called "individual" because it refers to one individual phenomenon, but because the occurrence of the constellation of elements decribed in it characterizes, from the point of view adopted by the historian, a class of phenomena occurring in a distinct unique, i.e. individual, historical epoch' (1976, pp. 131–2). Generic types, on the other hand, are ahistorical and serve to specify the elements from which individual types are constructed. One of the defining features of Weber's ideal type of the spirit of capitalism, for example, is goal-oriented rational action (one of four generic types of social action). As Torrance suggests, 'On the whole, Weber's position appears to be that types are constructed out of general conceptual elements, but may be additionally defined by a specific historical reference to times, places or persons' (1974, p. 136).

Weber insists that ideal types are indispensable in sociological explanation and that we constantly construct and use them whether or not we realize it. Whenever we refer to 'capitalist societies', for example, we are employing an ideal type construct, for there are many variations between, say, France and the United States which we choose to ignore for the purposes of classification while emphasizing those aspects that they have in common and that appear most relevant for our theoretical purposes. Social reality is infinite, and we can never know all there is to know about a given phenomenon. When we come to study some aspect of social life, therefore, we are immediately confronted with a chaotic complexity of sense impressions, and the only way to impose order on this chaos in order to distinguish that which is relevant to our concerns from that which is not is through the application of conceptually pure types. Ideal types are the yardsticks by means of which empirical reality can be rendered accessible to analysis. In the absence of such constructs we would be left only with an infinite range of different unique cases, each with its own history and characteristics, and we would lack any criteria for determining which of these characteristics are significant for our theoretical purposes.

Although they are mental constructs, ideal types are not simply conjured up out of nothing in the mind of the researcher, but are developed on the basis of existing empirical knowledge of actual phenomena. They involve the logical extension of certain aspects of reality into a pure, artificial yet logically possible type against which existing phenomena can be measured and compared. While their basis lies in empirical reality, ideal types do not express that reality but rather exaggerate certain aspects of it while thinking away others. The only test of an ideal type consists in the assessment of its logical coherence. Since its purpose is to clarify reality in order to facilitate the development of hypotheses, it clearly makes no sense to criticize an ideal type on the grounds that it fails to reproduce the real world in all its bewildering complexity. Ideal types are not intended as descriptions. Indeed, it is quite possible to construct any number of different ideal types of the 'same' phenomenon according to which aspects of it are deemed most significant for any given purpose. While these different types may vary in their fruitfulness for research, they cannot be evaluated against each other in terms of their empirical validity since they will each involve extensions of different aspects of the phenomenon in question. Ideal types, in other words, are always partial: 'There is no absolutely "objective" scientific analysis of culture or ... of "social phenomena" independent of special and "one-sided" viewpoints according to which – expressly or tacitly, consciously or unconsciously – they are selected, analysed and organized for expository purposes' (Weber 1949, p. 72).

Now it has often been suggested that this emphasis on the onesidedness of sociological constructs leads Weber into a hopeless relativism in which any one account is as good as any other. Hindess (1977), for example, finds in Weber's approach a 'systematic epistemological relativism' and concludes in relation to the ideal type method that 'There is no reason why the social scientist should not let his imagination run wild. He has nothing to lose but the chains of reason' (p. 38). Such arguments, however, ignore the fact that for Weber ideal types are simply the means of analysis, not its end product. It does not follow that a partial account cannot be objective, for although ideal types are subjective constructs and cannot be tested, the hypotheses developed on the basis of them can and must be: 'Essentially, all that Weber meant by objectivity was that, within the limits of the inescapably one-sided viewpoint, it is both possible and necessary to validate one's substantive propositions' (Dawe 1971, p. 50). All explanations are partial, but not all are valid (or to be more precise, adequate). Any sociological account must be demonstrated through historical and comparative evidence.

Where Weber does endorse relativism is not in the realm of facts but in the realm of values. Thus, although he argued that scientific explanations had to be evaluated in terms of their empirical adequacy, he denied that ethical judgements could ever be evaluated in the same way. For him, the moral realm necessarily consists of fundamental dilemmas which individuals must resolve for themselves. 'The ultimately possible attitudes toward life are irreconcilable, and hence their struggle can never be brought to a final conclusion' (Weber 1948a, p. 152). Science, therefore, can never legislate on moral questions, and the basic reason for this is that, as we have seen, science is itself partial in that the ideal types that it employs are constructed according to the relevance of particular aspects of reality for the scientist's own moral and practical concerns: 'The problems of the social sciences are selected by the value-relevance of the phenomena treated . . . cultural (i.e. evaluative) interests give purely empirical scientific work its direction' (Weber 1949, pp. 21–2). Sociology is therefore grounded in ethical concerns from the very outset: 'An attitude of moral indifference has no connection with scientific "objectivity" ' (1949, p. 60).

It follows from this, as Dawe suggests, that, 'Weber is arguing for the centrality of value to social science, not merely as a "principle of selection of subject matter", but as the *sine qua non of all meaningful knowledge of social reality*. Without the attribution of value, knowledge of social phenomena is inconceivable' (Dawe 1971, p. 42). This being the case, sociology clearly cannot be used to justify a particular value position, since, 'If sociology is shaped by value, it cannot become the justification for that value; the argument would be entirely circular' (pp. 55–6). Weber's concern is not to create a dry and morally indifferent social science, but rather to ensure that the inherently one-sided accounts of social science are not used to provide a spurious resolution to fundamental moral questions which individuals must confront for themselves: 'Weber is more concerned with defending the value sphere against the unfounded claims of science than with protecting the scientific process from valuational distortions' (Bruun 1972, p. 54).

Hindess suggests that Weber's method gives rise to 'plausible generalizations and plausible stories, nothing more' (1977, p. 48). This is true in the sense that, for Weber, there can be no final guarantee of truth (his criterion of science is one of adequacy, not truth), and there are many different sides to any one question. But as we saw in the previous section, Marx's logic of retroduction is similarly unable to offer guarantees of truth, and despite its emphasis on dialectical totality, it too may be seen as partial and one-sided (for example in the emphasis it places on economic factors). The significance of Weber's method is precisely that it recognizes the partiality of sociological explanations and thus takes account of the theoretical pluralism that has always characterized the social sciences. For Weber, no one approach ever enjoys a monopoly over 'correct' scientific knowledge of social reality. As we shall see in Chapter 5, attempts by Marxists to argue otherwise appear entirely unconvincing.

Weber's ideal type method is clearly evident in his study of the city; indeed, one commentator has suggested that this study contains 'the most fully worked out typology' in his economic sociology (see Freund 1968, p. 168). As we shall see later (p. 95), Weber begins by rejecting the idea found in Simmel and others that size constitutes an adequate basis for conceptualizing the city, and he goes on to suggest that questions of economic and political organization are much more significant. As regards the former, he suggests that cities are defined by the existence of an established market system: 'Economically defined, the city is a settlement the inhabitants of which live primarily off trade and commerce rather than agriculture . . . the city is a market place' (Weber 1958, pp. 66–7). He then distinguishes between consumer, producer and commercial cities on the basis of this economic criterion, adding that 'It hardly needs to be mentioned that actual cities nearly always represent mixed types' (p. 70) and that these are therefore ideal constructions that enable classification.

As regards the political dimension, he suggests that partial political autonomy is a key criterion: 'The city must . . . be considered to be a partially autonomous association, a "community" with special political and administrative arrangements' (p. 74). On this basis, he distinguishes the 'patrician city', run by an assembly of notables, and the 'plebeian city', run by an elected assembly of citizens. He further suggests that, in its pure form, political autonomy entails some independent basis of military power in the form of a fortress or garrison, although he recognizes at various points in the study that, in the Middle Ages, the political autonomy of the cities in northern Europe was achieved on the basis of economic rather than military power.

Taking these two dimensions together, Weber then constructs his ideal type city:

To constitute a full urban community a settlement must display a relative predominance of trade-commercial relations with the settlement as a whole displaying the following features. 1. a fortification; 2. a market; 3. a court of its own and at least partially autonomous law; 4. a related form of association; and 5. at least partial autonomy and autocephaly, thus also an administration by authorities, in the election of whom the burghers participated (Weber 1958, pp. 80–1).

Clearly this is an ideal type which is useful only in the analysis of the city at particular historical periods. This reflects Weber's concerns in this study which are basically to trace the significance of the medieval European city in the development of western capitalism, and to show why cities in ancient times and those in other parts of the world in the Middle Ages failed to create these conditions. As Bendix (1966) recognizes, this study is therefore an essential complement to Weber's earlier work on the Protestant ethic, and it reflects the same historical interest in the question of the peculiar origins of western capitalism.

Essentially, Weber's essay sets out to show how the medieval cities in western Europe sustained a fundamental challenge to the feudal system which surrounded them, and thus paved the way for the subsequent development of a rational–legal, capitalistic social order. This challenge emanated partly from the erosion of traditional values and the development of new forms of individualism, and partly from the usurpation of traditional powerful landed interests and their replacement by new forms of domination on the part of wealthy merchants and the urban nobility (as in the 'patrician cities') or later (and especially in Italy), on the part of entrepreneurs and artisans organized through urban guilds (as in the 'plebeian cities'). As Elliott and McCrone suggest, the essay 'depicts the medieval cities as places of revolution, as centres in which legitimate forms of political authority were challenged and overthrown, as places where new classes and strata appeared and contrived first to usurp power and subsequently to establish some legitimation for their own system of rule. These struggles...represented the piecemeal efforts to transform the economic and political systems that we call feudalism' (1982, p. 37). It is this concern with the struggle for political hegemony and the break from traditional values and patterns of domination which explains Weber's emphasis in his ideal type on the military, economic, legal, social and political autonomy and distinctiveness of western medieval urbanism, and his dismissal as insignificant of factors such as demographic structure or physical layout, for his concern throughout is not to develop a theory of urbanism, but to generate an historical understanding of the roots of modern capitalism.

Having developed this ideal type, Weber notes that general approximations to it are found only in the Occident. Thus, although there are many similarities between East and West, both in antiquity and in the Middle Ages, it was only in the West in the medieval period that the city came to be the basis of human association. In other places and in previous times, urban residents formed associations on the basis of kinship and estate, but in the western city in the Middle Ages, they came together for the first time as *individuals*:

Here, in new civic creations burghers joined the citizenry as single persons. The oath of citizenship was taken by the individual. Personal membership, not that of kin groups or tribe, in the local association of the city supplied the guarantee of the individual's personal legal position as a burgher (Weber 1958, p. 102).

This contrasts with both the ancient city, where 'the individual could be a citizen . . . but only as a member of his clan' (p. 101), and with the Oriental and Asiatic city, where 'when the urban community appears at all it is only in the form of a kin association which also extends beyond the city' (p. 104).

Weber argues that a major factor explaining this difference was Christianity, for it helped dissolve clan associations while other religions such as Islam reinforced clan and tribe structures: 'By its very nature the Christian community was a confessional association of believing individuals rather than a ritualistic association of clans' (p. 103). It was also significant that there was no centralized hierarchical bureaucracy in the West as there was, for example, in China, for this meant that there were no religious or political barriers to the development of the city as an association of individuals.

The main form of association that emerged in the western medieval cities was the guild (and, later, the corporation). As time went on, the guilds became less and less associated with particular crafts and businesses, and more and more associated with the *de facto* political control of the city. Citizenship rights became dependent upon guild membership, and non-urban, non-industrial classes such as the large nobles and bishops had therefore to join the guilds in order to achieve access to political power: 'The English guild often bestowed the civic rights. ... Nearly everywhere the guild was actually, though not legally, the governing association of the city' (Weber 1958, p. 134). Like Marx, therefore, Weber sees the city in the Middle Ages as highly significant in the break with feudalism and the foundation of the conditions for the development of capitalism: 'Neither modern capitalism nor the modern state grew up on the basis of the ancient cities while medieval urban development, though not alone decisive, was carrier of both phenomena and an important factor in their origin' (p. 181).

This significance was both economic and political. Economically, the guilds laid the basis for the development of economic rationality: 'Under the domination of the guild the medieval city was pressed in the direction of industry on a rational economic model in a manner alien to the city of antiquity' (p. 223). This is not to suggest that capitalist industry developed within the guild system, for Weber agrees with Marx that 'the new capitalistic undertakings settled in new locations' (p. 189) away from the traditional forms of enterprise and the constricting organization of labour represented by the city guilds and corporations. The economic importance of the western medieval city was not, therefore, that it spawned capitalist industry, but that it created the ideological and institutional legacy that 'formed the urban population of medieval Europe into a "ready-made" audience for the doctrines of the great Reformers' (Bendix 1966, p. 79). In other words, the development of the spirit of capitalism from the sixteenth century onwards, which Weber traces to the influence of puritanism, can be seen as the germination of a seed sown some 400 years earlier in the medieval city.

Just as important as the development of a rational and individualistic ethos in economic affairs was the development of new legal and political forms. Weber shows, for example, how rational codes of law came to be drawn up and administered by a formally-disinterested class of specialist administrators whose job it was to arbitrate between feuding factions within the patrician ruling class. Not only did this enable disputes to be settled according to some set of 'objective' criteria, rather than by force of arms or personal decree from on high, but it also facilitated the spread of common legal institutions between different cities, thereby underpinning inter-urban trade and contacts.

Furthermore, as power shifted from the military might of the nobility to the economic power of the entrepreneurial class, so new forms of political representation developed, based on the guilds and later the corporations, in which a rudimentary form of democratic self-government came to be established: 'In the Middle Ages resident citizen entrepreneurs and small capitalistic craftsmen played the politically central role. Such strata had no significant role within the ancient citizenry' (p. 204). In this way, the medieval city in Europe was the place where the crucial political as well as economic break from feudalism was accomplished.

Weber is clear that the city became the basis of human association and the spearhead of social transformation only at a specific historical period. In antiquity the basis of association, even within the cities, was kinship; in the modern period it is the nation-state. As Elliott and McCrone suggest, Weber's concern is thus directed at a fleeting yet crucial period of urban autonomy sandwiched between the city's subordination to feudal lords prior to the thirteenth century and its subordination to the absolute monarchies of the newly-emerging nations from the sixteenth century. Like Marx, therefore, Weber shows no interest in analysing the city in modern capitalist societies, and there is no basis in his work for developing a theory of urbanism as such. Just as Marx denies the theoretical significance of contemporary urbanism on the grounds that the town–country division no longer expresses an underlying class contradiction, so Weber denies it on the grounds that the city is no longer a meaningful and autonomous unit of economic and political association. Both writers thus cast a long shadow of doubt over the possibility or fruitfulness of developing an urban theory in the context of modern capitalist societies.

Émile Durkheim: the city, the division of labour and the moral basis of community

Durkheim's method provides a direct contrast to the approaches of both Marx and Weber. Like Marx, he accepts that the essence of social reality may be hidden and distorted by everyday common-sense ideas about it, but unlike Marx he suggests that the appearance of phenomena can nevertheless be taken as the expression of their essence if such phenomenal appearances are directly observed without conceptual encumbrances. In other words, Durkheim rejects the Marxist method of theorizing essences, and argues instead that essences can be directly ascertained through pure observation of appearances. Like Weber, therefore, Durkheim assumes that reality is given in observation, but unlike Weber he denies the necessity for any conceptual abstraction of partial aspects of that reality and he asserts the ability of sociology to penetrate to the essence of social phenomena. Put simply, it is Durkheim's commitment to empiricism that most sharply separates his approach from that of the other two writers discussed in this chapter, for what is specific to his method is the assertion of observation as the basis of knowledge and the consequent denial of any *a priori* theorization or conceptualization as a condition of knowledge.

Durkheim's firm commitment to empiricism has often led commentators to suggest that his is a positivist sociology. To some extent this is correct, for his endorsement of a purely experiential basis for knowledge, his equation of the logic of explanation between the natural and social sciences and his rejection of actors' ideas about the world as an important aspect of sociological explanation are all commonly associated with sociological positivism (see Giddens 1974). Against this, however, Durkheim rejects the positivist prescription of value-freedom and ethical neutrality of science, arguing that if science cannot prescribe ends then it loses all point, and that valuations of good and bad can be derived from observation of normal and pathological forms of phenomena. He also rejects individualistic explanations in favour of those that seek the causes of phenomena in collective forces which are not themselves directly observable. As Keat and Urry argue, it is therefore too simple to summarize his method as positivist since 'there are in Durkheim elements of both positivist and realist conceptions of science' (1975, p. 81). As we shall see, it is precisely the strain between these two conceptions that results in the final internal incoherence of his approach.

Basic to Durkheim's method is his argument that reality cannot be known through ideas about it. Science must address itself to the facts themselves if it is to avoid the ideological contamination of common-sense ideas, and this entails the eradication of all preconceptions: 'We must, therefore, consider social phenomena in themselves as distinct from the consciously formed representations of them in the mind; we must study them objectively as external things' (Durkheim 1938, p. 28). Science thus begins with 'a complete freedom of mind' (1933, p. 36) in which the objectivity of social facts can impress itself upon the senses. Only then is it possible to develop definitions of social facts which can identify their essential and inherent qualities: 'In order to be objective, the definition must obviously deal with phenomena not as ideas but in terms of their inherent properties. It must characterize them by elements essential to their nature' (1938, p. 35).

Sociological definitions are thus built up inductively, for it is only by observing a range of cases that the common elements essential to them all can be ascertained. Theory, in other words, plays no part in the definition, identification and classification of phenomena, but rather is developed on the basis of prior empirical observation. The classic problem of induction, of course, is that we can never be sure that we have identified an element common to all cases since the next empirical observation may prove to be an exception. Durkheim, however, denies that this is a problem for his method, and argues explicitly that there is no need even to aim for completeness of observation:

A satisfactory method must, above all, aim at facilitating scientific work by substituting a limited number of types for the indefinite multiplicity of individuals. . . . But for this purpose it must be made not from a complete inventory of all the individual characteristics but from a small number of them, carefully chosen (Durkheim 1938, p. 80).

The reason why exhaustiveness is not required (and, incidentally, why this method is far removed from the conceptual partiality of Weber's ideal types) is that, for Durkheim, observable cases provide the means for identifying the common essence that lies behind them. The inductive analysis of a small number of cases is therefore sufficient to establish the common essential element of which each case is an expression.

Durkheim is careful to argue that the initial definition of social facts does not itself penetrate to their essence. All that is possible at this first stage is the identification of the surface features of phenomena: 'Since the definition in question is placed at the beginnings of the science, it cannot possibly aim at a statement concerning the essence of quality; that must be attained subsequently. The sole function of the definition is to establish contact with things' (1938, p. 42). Social facts, in other words, leave visible traces which provide indications of their essence; different types of social solidarity, for example, give rise to and are therefore indicated by different types of law, so that it becomes possible to distinguish the moral basis of different societies by means of an initial definition of legal forms (see below, pp. 45–6). Sociology therefore relies on observable phenomena as indicators of the essence of social facts, just as, say, the physicist relies on observation of the movement of mercury in a thermometer to indicate temperature.

This argument, of course, assumes that there is a direct causal link between indicator and essence – that what we can observe is the direct expression of social facts that remain hidden. In order to establish such a link, Durkheim advances two principles of causality. The first is that social phenomena have social causes: 'The determining cause of a social fact should be sought among the social facts preceding it and not among the states of the individual consciousness' (1938, p. 110). The explanation of social facts cannot therefore be reduced to an analysis of individual actions any more than the explanation of biological facts can be found in the analysis of the chemical composition of living organisms. Social facts, the collective phenomena of social life, have an existence external to individuals, and individual actions are constrained by them in various ways (for instance by the moral authority of laws, by the determinacy of socialization, by the 'currents' generated in collective life, and so on). It follows that there exists a distinct social reality which sociology alone can study, and that the causes of social phenomena cannot be sought through psychology or any other science: 'Products of group life, it is the nature of the group which alone can explain them' (1933, p. 350).

The second principle of causality is that any social fact has only one social cause: 'A given effect can maintain this relationship with only one cause, for it can express only one single nature' (1938, p. 127). If there appear to be several causes, then this can only mean that there are, in fact, several different phenomena to be explained. For example, if, as Durkheim (1952) suggests, there are three principal causes of suicide, then there must be three types of suicide corresponding to them. The morphological classification of social facts can therefore be followed by analysis of the causes of each of the facts identified.

Taken together, the argument that social phenomena are *sui generis*, and that single facts have single causes, enables Durkheim to assert the inherent connection between visible indicators and the essences of which they are a function. To return to our previous example, if there are two types of law then there must be two distinct types of social phenomena that have given rise to them. The question then is how are these social causes to be discovered?

Durkheim's answer is that the discovery of causes proceeds through the method of 'concomitant variation': 'We have only one way to demonstrate that a given phenomenon is the cause of another, viz., to compare the cases in which they are simultaneously present or absent, to see if the variations they present in these different combinations of circumstances indicate that one depends on the other (1938, p. 125). If a consistent correlation is found in a number of different cases, then a real relationship is to be assumed between them: 'As soon as one has proved that, in a certain number of cases, two phenomena vary with one another, one is certain of being in the presence of a law' (p. 133). Observable correlations therefore point to the existence of an essential causal relation.

It is only at this point that theory plays a part in the analysis, for having demonstrated concomitant variation, the sociologist must attempt to explain it:

> When two phenomena vary directly with each other, this relationship must be accepted. . . . The results to which this method leads need, therefore, to be interpreted. . . . We shall first investigate, by the aid of deduction, how one of the two terms has produced the other; then we shall try to verify the result of this deduction with the aid of experiments, i.e., new comparisons. If the deduction is possible and if the verification succeeds, we can regard the proof as completed (Durkheim 1938, p. 132).

The example given by Durkheim concerns the statistical relationship between levels of education and suicide rates. Since education cannot itself explain an increase in the tendency to suicide, we must attempt to identify some common factor that can account for both. Such a factor is the break-down of traditional religion, which increases both the desire for knowledge and the tendency towards suicide, and the task is then to show that wherever such religions have been eroded, both education and suicide increase accordingly. If this is demonstrated, then a sociological proof has been established.

The major question that must be posed to Durkheim's method, however, is whether theory really is limited to the secondary role that he attributes to it, and thus whether he has in fact developed an objective empirical science freed from contaminating preconceptions. The first point to be noted is that the initial process of classification and identification of visible phenomena is itself dependent upon theoretically derived criteria. The identification of 'facts' is theoretically derived:

> 'Facts', supposedly, can be identified and classified on the basis of 'experience' and 'observation' alone, without prior theory or interpretation.

Classification is, however, a theory-dependent exercise. It requires observation and comparison, of course, but it also requires a knowledge of its field of operation, criteria of identity, difference and relevance for characteristics of the 'objects' classified (Benton 1977, p. 89).

Durkheim's phenomenalism thus reveals the classic weakness of positivist approaches which rest on the assumption of a purely experiential basis of knowledge.

There is, however, also a second problem which derives from his attempt to assert this postulate of phenomenalism while at the same time drawing the distinction between observable phenomena and their hidden essences. The point, quite simply, is that, far from discovering essences through the method of concomitant variation and theoretical deduction, Durkheim's method assumes their existence from the outset. The existence of essences, and their relation to observable phenomena, is therefore pre-established in the assumptions on which the method is premised. Thus Durkheim's starting point, that observable phenomena are significant as expressions and embodiments of an essential reality to which they are causally linked, depends upon a prior theory of essences and their relation to appearances which is, according to his own prescriptions for eradicating preconceptions, illegitimate. As Hirst shows, he can only assert the phenomenal as the basis of knowledge by positing an essence theoretically: 'Durkheim's sociology . . . is a theoretical mechanism for the reproduction of the "given". It is a device for "saving" the phenomena of immediate experience: at one and the same time it promotes these phenomena to primacy ("the given") and it installs an essence behind their groundless existence' (Hirst 1975, p. 103). The result of the application of such a method is, as Hirst suggests, self-confirming, since Durkheim's sociology begins by identifying 'social facts' on the basis of unacknowledged theoretical criteria, and then asserts the necessity of these facts by 'discovering' essential causes which are similarly the product of prior theoretical assumptions: 'The essence to which we refer tells us nothing but what we already know' (p. 101).

This problem of the prior role of theory in positing the existence of an underlying essence as the basis for phenomenal forms is, in fact, explicitly recognized by Durkheim in his study of suicide (1952). There he argues that the method of morphological classification cannot be followed since it is not possible to identify different types of suicide on the basis of the empirical study of individual cases (i.e. the official records do not distinguish different types of suicide). He therefore proposes to reverse the order of study and to proceed from a *theoretical* identification of the different causes of suicide (anomy, egoism and altruism) to an empirical classification of the different types (see pp. 145–7). In other words, he assumes that his theory, which argues for three causes of suicide, is correct in order to identify different types of cases on the basis of which the theory can be tested. While he apparently sees this problem as specific to this particular analysis (in that available data are inadequate for the purposes of classification), it is clear that his procedure in this study is in fact entailed in his very method, the difference being that the theory-dependency of classification and of the identification of the essential causes of phenomena is here made explicit.

To summarize, then, Durkheim's method is inherently contradictory. If he wishes to assert the theoretical neutrality of observation of social facts as the basis for subsequent sociological explanation, then there is no ground in his method for the identification of essences causally linked to such facts. If, on the other hand, he wishes to assert the existence of an essential social reality to account for phenomenal appearances, then there is no basis in his method for rejecting the role of theory in constituting knowledge. This dilemma between phenomenalism and realism is irresolvable within the terms of Durkheim's method, and as we shall see in Chapter 2, it is a dilemma that recurs in the work of the Chicago school of human ecology whose exponents, like Durkheim, attempted to hold to a positivist approach to the source of knowledge while at the same time explaining observed phenomena as the result of unobservable hidden forces in human society.

Durkheim's method was set out most explicitly in *The Rules of Sociological Method* (1938), but as Giddens notes, this work 'explicates the methodological suppositions already applied in *The Division of Labour*' (Giddens 1971, p. 82). This latter text, Durkheim's first major work, is the most significant of his writings as regards our present concern with the role of the city in Durkheim's sociology.

The theme of the book concerns the moral basis of social solidarity, that is the social origins and foundation of the social cohesion of collective life. In it, Durkheim is concerned to show that social solidarity may be a function of either homogeneity or heterogeneity, of similarly between the 'parts' comprising the social whole or of the complementary differences between them. The problem, however, is that the moral basis of social life is not itself directly observable. The resolution to this problem, in line with his methodological prescriptions, is to identify an observable indicator that reveals it:

Social solidarity is a completely moral phenomenon which, taken by itself, does not lend itself to exact observation nor indeed to measurement. To proceed to this classification and this comparison, we must substitute for this internal fact which escapes us an external index which symbolizes it and study the former in the light of the latter. This visible symbol is law (Durkheim 1933, p. 64).

His argument, therefore, is that different types of law, which can (he suggests) be classified directly through observation, are the effects of different types of solidarity: 'Since law reproduces the principal forms of social solidarity, we have only to classify the different types of law to find therefrom the different types of social solidarity which correspond to it' (p. 68).

The two types of law he identifies are 'repressive' (the imposition of punishment through suffering or loss) and 'restitutive' (the restoration of normality to counterbalance an infraction). Both are social in origin but their forms are different (indicating that they arise from different social conditions).

Repressive law is indicative of the existence of strong, generalized collective sentiments in society – a strong 'collective conscience' – to which all normal members of the society subscribe. An offence against this collective morality is thus not merely an offence against an individual, but is a transgression of something that is felt to be sacred and above any individual. Repressive law is thus the means by which the collectivity avenges itself: 'Since these sentiments are collective it is not us they represent in us, but society. Thus, in avenging them, it is surely society and not ourselves that we avenge, and moreover, it is something superior to the individual' (p. 101). Clearly, such a law based on a generalized collective morality can derive only from a society based on 'essential social likenesses' (p. 105), for it is only in such a society that a high degree of moral conformity and collective sentiment can be sustained. Repressive law, in other words, is both a product of and indicative of what Durkheim terms social bonds of 'mechanical solidarity'. Such a society is maintained and perpetuated on the basis of the similarity between its members, and challenges to this solidarity meet with a strong collective response through the use of repressive sanctions.

Restitutive law, by contrast, does not reflect a strong collective conscience (although its origin remains social) in that an offence against such law does not provoke a generalized moral outrage but merely an attempt to rectify the wrong that has been done. The only collective sentiment expressed in restitutive law relates to the ethic of individualism: 'The only collective sentiments that have become more intense are those which have for their object, not social affairs, but the individual' (p. 167). This type of law, therefore, is indicative of a society that derives its solidarity from the complementary differences between individuals and in which mechanical bonds of similarity have been replaced by 'organic' relations of interdependence. In such a society, the force of collective sentiments has given way to a positive union of co-operation brought about by the social division of labour: 'It is the division of labour which, more and more, fills the role that was formerly filled by the common conscience. It is the principal bond of social aggregates of higher types' (p. 173). The bonds of interdependence forged by the growth of the division of labour are infinitely stronger than the mechanical bonds of similarity, and the development of advanced societies is the history of the transition from the latter to the former.

Having classified the two types of social solidarity, Durkheim then considers the causes of the growth of the division of labour which brings about the transition from one to the other. It is at this point that the analysis of the city becomes important.

His argument is that two factors give rise to an increased division of labour in society: 'material density' (by which he means density of population in a given area) and 'moral density' (which refers to the increased density of interaction and social relationships within a population). In *The Division of Labour* (1933) he argues that the two are in practice inseparable and that 'it is useless to try to find out which has determined the other' (p. 257), although he later revised this view, arguing that social concentration cannot simply be deduced from physical concentration (since this would be to admit to the origins of a social fact in a physical rather than a social cause), and that the key cause of the division of labour was therefore an increase in moral density (see 1938, p. 115).

The increase in moral density of a society is expressed through urbanization: 'Cities always result from the need of individuals to put themselves in very intimate contact with others. There are so many points where the social mass is contracted more strongly than elsewhere' (1933, p. 258). In simple segmental societies characterized by only the most rudimentary division of labour and by mechanical bonds of solidarity, cities do not exist. The history of the advanced societies, on the other hand, reveals a continuous expansion of urban life which, 'Far from constituting a sort of pathological pheno-menon...comes from the very nature of higher social species' (p. 259). Urbanization, together with the associated development of new means of transportation and communication, is the cause of the division of labour. The reason is simple; a concentrated human population can survive only through differentiation of functions: 'In the same city, different occupations can co-exist without being obliged mutually to destroy one another, for they pursue different objects . . . all condensation of the social mass, especially if it is accompanied by an increase in population, necessarily determines advances in the division of labour' (pp. 267–8). As we shall see in the next chapter, this explicit application of Darwinian principles to the analysis of functional differentiation in human societies is one of the principal themes that later urban sociologists abstracted from Durkheim's work.

There is, however, no guarantee that an increase in moral density will result in increased division of labour, since it may simply lead to, say, the collapse of the society or to the elimination of weaker competitors within it. Moral density is, in other words, a necessary but not a sufficient condition. What is necessary in addition is that the moral weight of the collective conscience be weakened, since 'the progress of the division of labour will be as much more difficult and slow as the common conscience is vital and precise' (p. 284). Here too, however, the development of the city performs an important role. This is because cities grow principally through immigration rather than through natural increase and thus attract new residents from surrounding areas whose attachment to traditional beliefs and values is thereby weakened: 'Nowhere have the traditions less sway over minds. Indeed, great cities are the uncontested homes of progress . . . When society changes, it is generally after them and in imitation . . . no ground is more favourable to evolutions of all sorts. This is because the collective life cannot have continuity there' (p. 296).

Durkheim's characterization of the city as a force for change presents what has since become a very familiar analysis of the nature of urban life. His argument that the city undermines traditional controls, that the collectivity cannot possibly impose a single code of moral conduct over the diverse spheres of action in which the urbanite becomes involved, that the individual enjoys freedom as a result of the necessary anonymity of the city, that small moral communities may develop in different parts of the city but that their sphere of influence over the individual is circumscribed, that the city extends its influence over the surrounding countryside and thus 'urbanizes' the society as a whole – all of this is reflected in the work of the Chicago school of urban ecology (Chapter 2), in Wirth's essay on urbanism as a way of life (Chapter 3) and in countless community study monographs up to the present day. And what these subsequent developments have also taken over from Durkheim is the recognition that, while the city is undoubtedly a force for progress and individual freedom, it may also become associated in the most vivid way with the pathological aspects of modern society.

It is Durkheim's concern to show that, while the development of the division of labour contains within it the possibility for a new and stronger basis of social solidarity, it may nevertheless come to be expressed through 'abnormal' forms. In other words, the erosion of collective morality that it entails may, in certain circumstances, result not in a new organic solidarity of interdependence, but in a state of moral deregulation or anomy. Where this occurs (i.e. where the division of labour has not become sufficiently institutionalized as the moral basis of social life), the moral cohesion of society itself is threatened, and according to Durkheim this was the explanation of the malaise of the advanced societies at the time when he was writing. Given the role of the city as the primary force for change, it is naturally in the cities themselves that the anomic character of modern societies becomes most evident: 'The average number of suicides, of crimes of all sorts, can effectively serve to mark the intensity of immorality in a given society. . . . Far from serving moral progress, it is in the great industrial centres that crimes and suicides are most numerous' (pp. 50–1). This is why (as we noted at the start of this chapter) the cities tend to be associated with social 'problems', for they are the most developed expression of the pathology generated as a result of moral deregulation in the society as a whole.

Given his commitment to a science of ethics, Durkheim attempts in *The Division of Labour* to diagnose the causes of this social malaise and to prescribe a remedy. The latter he finds in the establishment of a modern form of occupational guild system, nationally organized. His argument here is particularly relevant to our present concern with the urban question, for he suggests that the medieval guilds and corporations were at that time the 'normal mould' for the organization of economic interests (p. 20) and that the town was thus the cornerstone of medieval society. However, as large-scale capitalist industry developed, so the urban corporation of merchants and traders became less and less suited to its organizational needs:

While, as originally, merchants and workers had only the inhabitants of the city or its immediate environs for customers, which means as long as the market was principally local, the bodies of trades, with their municipal organization, answered all needs. But it was no longer the same once great industry was born. As it had nothing especially urban about it, it could not adapt itself to a system which had not been made for it . . . An institution so entirely wrapped up in the commune as was the old corporation could not then be used to encompass and regulate a form of collective activity which was so completely foreign to the communal life (Durkheim 1933, p. 22).

The erosion of the corporation of the Middle Ages (which in France was finally completed in the Revolution of 1789) has, however, left a vacuum precisely at the time in history when economic life has become central to collective existence. This vacuum cannot be filled by the state, for it is too remote from individuals and is ill-equipped to regulate the complexity of modern economic relations. Nor can it be filled by a resurrection of the medieval guild system, since this is totally inappropriate to a society in which the advanced division of labour has become extended far beyond the locality:

There are not many organs which may be completely comprised within the limits of a determined district, no matter how far it extends. It almost always runs beyond them. . . . The manner of human grouping which results from the division of labour is thus very different from that which expresses the partition of the population in space. The occupational environment does not coincide with the territorial environment any more than it does with the familial environment (Durkheim 1933, pp. 189–90).

It can, therefore, be filled only by nationally organized occupational corporations which alone can regulate the moral basis of economic life and thereby overcome the anomic condition of modern industrial societies.

It is clear from this argument that, like Marx and Weber, Durkheim does not consider the modern city relevant to the key concerns of social theory in advanced capitalist societies. Like them, he argues that it is only in the Middle Ages that the city was significant in itself since it was only during that period that it provided the organizational expression for functional economic interests. Just as Marx and Weber see the city in antiquity as theoretically unimportant, so too does Durkheim, arguing that 'Rome was essentially an agricultural and military society' (p. 19), and that the basis of association was familial rather than urban. And just as Marx and Weber deny the theoretical significance of the modern city (since for Marx it no longer expresses essential class relations, and for Weber it is no longer the basis for human association), so too Durkheim argues that the distinction between the city and the society as a whole in the modern period is no longer meaningful, that the society itself can now be likened to one great city (p. 300), and that localism has been undermined by the extension of the occupational and social division of labour. As he puts it,

As advances are made in history, the organization which has territorial groups as its base (village or city, district, province, etc.) steadily becomes effaced. . . . These geographic divisions are, for the most part, artificial and no longer awaken in us profound sentiments. . . . Our activity is extended quite beyond these groups which are too narrow for it, and, moreover, a good deal of what happens there leaves us indifferent (Durkheim 1933, pp. 27–8).

Like the other two theorists discussed in this chapter, Durkheim therefore addresses the urban question in two ways. First, he sees the city as an historically significant condition for the development of particular social forces (that is to say, it creates a social concentration which stimulates the division of labour, while at the same time it facilitates this development by breaking down the bonds of traditional morality); second, he sees in the modern city the expression of the current (abnormal) development of these forces (pathological disorganization reflecting the anomic state of modern society). What appears as the most striking (and, given the divergences in their methods, astonishing) feature of any comparative reading of the works of Marx, Weber and Durkheim in relation to the urban question is thus their unanimity in their approach to the city, for all three see the medieval city as historically significant while addressing the modern city simply as the most visible expression of developments in the society as a whole.

The lesson from these three writers should be clear. There may or may not be a case for treating the city as an object of analysis in historical context. Even here, it is apparent that caution is needed, for in most places and at most times, the city has not functioned autonomously of the society of which it forms a part. The image of medieval urban autonomy is one which has been disputed (e.g. by Abrams (1978) who recommends that urban sociologists and historians alike 'get rid of the concept of the town' from their disciplines – p.10), and to the extent that it is valid, it applies (as Weber recognized) only to certain western cities over just a few hundred years. As Sjoberg notes in his classic study of feudal urbanism, 'Such a generalization, except perhaps for a narrow time period and a restricted locale in western Europe, is untenable for feudal societies in general . . . the city, shaped as it is by the enfolding socio-cultural system, whether preindustrial or industrial, must be taken as a *dependent* rather than an independent variable' (1960, p. 15). But if caution is needed in the field of urban history, then the lesson from Marx, Weber and Durkheim is surely even stronger in the case of urban sociology, for there appears to be no coherent rationale for studying cities as such in the context of modern industrial societies where cities have seemingly lost all sociological significance. As we shall see in the following chapters, urban sociologists over most of this century have ignored this lesson in their attempts to conceptualize contemporary urbanism. The result has, in most cases, been conceptual confusion and a series of theoretical dead-ends.

2 The urban as an ecological community

In his review of various attempts by sociologists to develop a specifically urban theory, Leonard Reissman suggests that the ecological perspective advanced between the wars by Robert Park and his colleagues at the University of Chicago remains 'the closest we have come to a systematic theory of the city' (1964, p. 93). Certainly human ecology was the first comprehensive urban social theory, and in the United States it has some claim to have been the first comprehensive sociological theory, for it developed at a time when American sociology was gaining institutional recognition as a discipline but lacked an indigenous body of theory. As Hawley observes, 'The reformist phase of sociology was drawing to a close and the subject was gaining acceptance as a respected discipline in the curricula of American universities. . . . Ecology opportunely provided the necessary theory' (1968, p. 329).

From its very inception, therefore, human ecology exhibited a certain tension as regards the scope of its applicability. On the one hand, it was represented as a theory of the city and thus as an attempt to develop an explanation of patterns of city growth and urban culture. In this sense, human ecology could be seen as a sub-discipline within sociology with its own object of study; while some sociologists studied education and others studied the family, those interested in human ecology studied the city. On the other hand, however, it claimed to be a discipline in its own right with its own distinctive body of theory. Indeed, the human ecologists argued that the ecological perspective addressed a problem that could not be subsumed under any other discipline, including sociology. Human biology studied the individual organism, human psychology the individual psyche, human geography the organization of space, and the various social sciences the different aspects, economic, political or cultural, of social organization. In contrast with all of these, human ecology was concerned with the specific theoretical problem of how human populations adapted to their environment. As we shall see, it then followed from this formulation that human ecology was the basic social science that established the framework within which economic, political and moral phenomena could be investigated. As one of Park's students was later to suggest, 'Human ecology, as Park conceived it, was not a branch of sociology but rather a perspective, a method, and a body of knowledge essential for the scientific study of social life and hence, like social psychology, a general discipline basic to all the social sciences' (Wirth 1945, p. 484).

This tension between human ecology as an approach within urban sociology, and human ecology as a distinct and basic discipline within the social sciences, runs throughout the work of the Chicago school. It is basically a tension between defining the perspective in terms of a concrete, physical, visible object of study – the community – and defining it in terms of a theoretically specific problem – the adaptation of human populations to their environment. Whenever Park addressed himself to such methodological questions (which was not very often), he adopted, as Wirth suggests, the latter position, arguing that a science was defined by the theoretical problem it posed rather than the concrete object it studied. Yet throughout his writings, Park nevertheless emphasized the ecological concern with the community as a visible and real entity. This confusion, which lies at the heart of the problems associated with human ecology, is reflected in, and was exacerbated by, the ambiguity inherent in Park's concept of 'community', for this term is employed to refer both to the physical community and to the ecological process. In the former case it refers to an empirical object of analysis, in the latter to a theoretical one.

Community and society

Many different intellectual influences can be discerned through an examination of Park's writings, among them those of Simmel, Comte, Spencer and W. I. Thomas. However, it does appear that two writers were especially significant. At risk of some oversimplification, it may be suggested that it was from Émile Durkheim that Park derived his methodological framework, and from Charles Darwin that he derived his theory.

Durkheim's influence can be found first in Park's ontological assumptions regarding 'human nature' and the relationship between the individual and society. In his first important statement of the ecological perspective in 1916, for example, Park wrote, 'The fact seems to be that men are brought into the world with all the passions, instincts and appetites uncontrolled and undisciplined. Civilization, in the interests of the common welfare, demands the suppression sometimes, and the control always, of these wild, natural dispositions' (1952, p. 49). Just as Durkheim sought the conditions for social stability and cohesion in the subordination of the individual to the moral authority of society, so Park takes as his starting point the tension between individual freedom and social control. Like Durkheim, Park explains personal and social disorganization in terms of the erosion of moral constraints, for *Homo ecologicus* is an inherently egoistical and unsocial creature who needs to be kept in check by society for his or her own good and for the good of others.

Of course, Park recognized that the social control of human nature was not, and never could be, total. Indeed, in the same way that Durkheim noted that social disorganization (within limits) was the necessary price to be paid for human progress, and that too much moral constraint was as bad as too little since it resulted in individual fatalism and social stagnation, so Park found in the break-down of traditional moral controls a cause for both concern and celebration. On the one hand, he saw that the growth of the cities had undermined the social cohesion once maintained by the family, the church and the village, and he pointed to the threat of the mob 'swept by every new wind of doctrine, subject to constant alarms' (1952, p. 31). Yet on the other, he saw the potential for individual freedom and self-expression that the city represented, and he noted how disorganization could be seen as a prelude to reorganization at a new level of human organization involving new modes of social control.

Human nature and moral constraint thus constantly confronted each other, and it followed that any form of human organization was necessarily an expression of both. This was certainly true of the city, for despite the regular geometrical form of many American cities, which suggested artificial rather than natural causes, Park maintained that 'The structure of the city . . . has its basis in human nature, of which it is an expression', and that, because of this, 'There is a limit to the arbitrary modifications which it is possible to make (1) in its physical structure and (2) in its moral order' (1952, p. 16). In other words, the city is as much a manifestation of natural and invariant forces as it is of political and conscious choices, and it is no more possible to abolish the ghettos and the dens of iniquity than it is to programme people's passions or eliminate their instincts.

For Park, then, human society involves a double aspect. On the one hand, it is an expression of human nature, and this is revealed in the competition for survival in which relationships with others are entirely utilitarian (a view that Park finds in the work of Herbert Spencer). On the other, it is an expression of consensus and common purpose (a view that he traces to Comte). On one level individual freedom is supreme; on the other individual will is subordinated to the 'collective mind' of society as a superorganism (to what Durkheim termed the *conscience collective*). The first level Park terms 'community', and the second 'society'; 'The word community more accurately describes the social organism as Spencer conceived it. Comte's conception, on the other hand, comes nearer to describing what we ordinarily mean by society' (1952, p. 181).

As we shall see later, this distinction between community as the biotic level of social life and society as its cultural level proved highly problematic. In particular, Park's writings on the subject exhibit some inconsistency as regards the methodological status of the dichotomy, for on some occasions he refers to community and society as analytical categories, while on others he treats them as empirical realities. The distinction is, however, basic to his ecological approach, for it enables Park to identify the peculiar concerns of human ecology in relation to the other social science disciplines. 'Ecology', he writes, 'is concerned with communities rather than societies, though it is not easy to distinguish between them' (1952, p. 251). The ecological approach to social relations, therefore, was characterized by an emphasis on the biotic as opposed to the cultural aspect of human interaction, the Spencerian rather than the Comtean view of social relations. This did not mean that human ecology denied the relevance of consensus and culture in the study of social life; only that it concentrated on the unconscious and asocial aspects as its specific area of interest.

By thus delimiting the field of ecological inquiry, Park was able to draw upon the work of Darwin in order to show how the forces that shape plant and animal communities also play a significant role in the evolution of human communities. Central to Darwin's thesis was the notion of a 'web of life' through which all organisms were related to all others in ties of interdependence or 'symbiosis'. This balance of nature was a product of the tooth and claw struggle for survival which served to regulate the population size of different species and to distribute them among different habitats according to their relative suitability. Competition for the basic resources of life thus resulted in the adaptation of different species to each other and to their environment and hence to the evolution of a relatively balanced ecological system based upon competitive co-operation among differentiated and specialized organisms. Needless to say, this was an entirely natural and spontaneous process.

It was Park's contention that the same process operated in the human community: 'Competition operates in the human (as it does in the plant and animal) community to bring about and restore the communal equilibrium when, either by the advent of some intrusive factor from without or in the normal course of its life history, that equilibrium is disturbed' (1952, p. 150). Competition between individuals, he argued, gave rise to relations of competitive co-operation through differentiation of functions (division of labour) and the orderly spatial distribution of these functions to the areas for which they are best suited. His analysis, in other words, is both functional and spatial: 'The main point is that the community so conceived is at once a territorial and a functional unit' (1952, p. 241).

His discussion of the development of functional differentiation and interdependence in the human community draws heavily on Durkheim's analysis of the origins of the division of labour. Just as Durkheim argues that the transition from a relatively homogeneous to a relatively differentiated society is effected by an increase in material and moral density, so too Park suggests that an increase in population size within a given area, together with an extension of transport and communication networks, results in greater specialization of functions (and thus stronger ties of interdependence). Park then goes on to argue, however, that this functional differentiation is also expressed spatially, for competition not only stimulates a division of labour, but also distributes the different economic groups to different niches in the urban environment. The pattern of land use in the city therefore reveals the pattern of economic interdependence.

The ecological concept that explains the congruence between spatial and economic differentiation is that of dominance. Again with reference to Darwin, Park suggests that 'In every life community there is always one or more dominant species' (1952, p. 151). The beech tree, for example, has achieved dominance over its natural habitat in the sense that only those plants, such as bluebells, that flower at a time when the tree has no leaves can flourish under its branches. In the human community, analogously, industry and commerce are dominant, for they can outbid other competitors for strategic central locations in the city. The pressure for space at the centre therefore creates an area of high land values, and this determines the pattern of land values in every other area of the city, and thus the pattern of land use by different functional groups. As Park puts it, 'The struggle of industries and commercial institutions for a strategic location determines in the long run the main outlines of the urban community ... the principle of dominance ... tends to determine the general ecological pattern of the city and the functional relation of each of the different areas of the city to all others' (1952, pp. 151–2). Differences in land values are thus the mechanism by which different functional groups are distributed in space in an orderly, efficient yet unplanned manner.

It follows from all this that the natural state of the ecological community, be it human or otherwise, is one of equilibrium. Change, which may result either from internal expansion or from external disruption, is represented as basically a cyclical and evolutionary process involving, first, a destabilization of the existing equilibrium; second, a renewed outburst of competition; and, finally, the development of a new (and 'higher') stage of adaptation. Basic to this conception are two assumptions. The first is that, having reached a 'climax' stage (an optimal point at which population size and differentiation is most closely adapted to environmental conditions), a community will remain in a state of balance unless some new element emerges to disturb the *status quo*. The second is that the process of community change involves an evolution from the simple to the complex through the adaptive process of differentiation of functions. This theory of community change was most explicitly set out by one of Park's colleagues at the University of Chicago, Roderick McKenzie.

McKenzie (1967) argued that the size of any human community is limited by what it can produce and by the efficiency of its mode of distribution. Thus a primary service community (such as one based on agriculture) cannot grow beyond a population of around 5000, whereas an industrial town can grow to many times that size provided its industries are serviced by an efficient system of market distribution. It was McKenzie's contention that any particular type of community tended to increase in size until it reached its climax point at which the size of population was most perfectly adjusted to the capacity of the economic base to support it. The community would then remain in this state of equilibrium until some new element (e.g. a new mode of communication or a technological innovation) disturbed the balance, at which point a new cycle of biotic adjustment would begin involving movement of population, differentiation of functions, or both of these processes. Competition, in other words, would again sift and sort the population functionally and spatially until a new climax stage was reached.

Drawing again on Darwin's work, the human ecologists referred to this process of structural community change as succession – 'that orderly sequence of changes through which a biotic community passes in the course of its development from a primary and relatively unstable to a relatively permanent or climax stage' (Park 1952, p. 152). Just as in nature one species succeeds another as the dominant life form in a particular area, so too in the human community the pattern of land use changes as areas are invaded by new competitors which are better adapted to the changed environmental conditions than the existing users. Such a process of invasion and succession is reflected in the human community in changes in land values with the result that competition for desirable sites forces out the economically weaker existing users (e.g. residents) who make way for economically stronger competitors (e.g. business). Following a successful invasion, a new equilibrium is then established and the successional sequence comes to an end.

It is these related processes of competition, dominance, succession and invasion that provide the basis for the well-known model of community expansion proposed by Burgess (1967). He suggested that the city could be conceptualized ideally as consisting of five zones arranged in a pattern of concentric circles. The expansion of the city occurred as a result of the invasion by each zone of the next outer zone, so that the central business district tended to expand into the surrounding inner-city zone of transition, which in turn tended to expand into the zone of working-class housing around it, and so on. This physical process of succession therefore results in the segregation of different social groups in different parts of the city according to their suitability: 'In the expansion of the city, a process of distribution takes place which sifts and sorts and relocates individuals and groups by residence and occupation. . . . Segregation offers the group, and thereby the individuals who compose the group, a place and a role in the total organization of city life' (pp. 54 and 56).

This constant process of change and adjustment, invasion and succession, disorganization and reorganization, is especially marked in the inner-city zone of transition. The outward pressure of the central business district accelerates the deterioration of the area around it by increasing the value of surrounding land while threatening the existing housing stock, and existing inhabitants progressively move out while their place is taken by new migrants into the city who find their niche in the decaying properties. In time, these migrants themselves move out and are replaced by later arrivals, and so the process of physical expansion and social turnover goes on. Burgess recognizes that mobility is therefore most pronounced in the inner-city areas that are in an almost constant state of flux, and he sees this as the explanation for the social disorganization (crime, vice, poverty, etc.) that tends to characterize these area. Mobility, in other words, is a source of change and of personal and social disorganization, and where mobility is greatest, so too is the lack of social cohesion and the demoralization of the human spirit.

All of these processes that we have described so far involve the natural and spontaneous response of human populations to changes in the environment in which they live. However, we noted earlier that Park and his colleagues recognized that human populations had certain characteristics that were not shared by plant and animal communities. In particular, human beings enjoyed scope for mobility which plants did not possess, and they had a capacity for consciously changing their environment which had no parallel in the plant and animal worlds. As McKenzie observed, 'The human community differs from the plant community in the two dominant characteristics of mobility and purpose, that is, in the power to select a habitat and in the ability to control or modify the conditions of the habitat' (1967, pp. 64–5). Human beings, in other words, shared a culture.

According to the Chicago ecologists, the cultural aspect of human organization, which they associated with the concept of society as opposed to community, developed at the point where the biotic struggle for existence had established a natural equilibrium. Competition led naturally to one form of human organization by forcing increased functional and spatial differentiation and thereby creating utilitarian ties of mutual interdependence (symbiosis). Once distributed functionally and territorially, however, the members of a human population were then in a position to develop new and qualitatively different bonds of cohesion based not on the necessities of the division of labour but on common goals, sentiments and values. From its origins in unconscious competition, human organization thus developed a new basis in consensus and conscious co-operation, for while competition resulted in specialization and individuation, consensus involved communication and the subordination of the individual's primordial instincts to the collective consciousness. As Park writes,

It is when, and to the extent that, competition declines that the kind of order which we call society may be said to exist. In short, society, from the ecological point of view, and in so far as it is a territorial unit, is just the area within which biotic competition has declined and the struggle for existence has assumed higher and more sublimated forms (Park 1952, pp. 150–1).

There are therefore two types of human association: the symbiotic, brought about by competition, and the social, brought about by consensus:

The distinction is that in the community, as in the case of the plant and animal community, the nexus which unites individuals of which the community is composed is some kind of symbiosis or some form of division of labour. A society, on the other hand, is constituted by a more intimate form of association based on communication, consensus and custom (Park 1952, p. 259).

This does not mean, however, that at the level of society there is no competition or conflict, for although he never defines the term it is clear that for Park consensus refers to shared orientations rather than shared objectives, to a common frame of reference for action rather than universal agreement over what that action should be (see Weber 1968, appendix I, for a similar formulation of the concept). Thus Park suggests that, on the social level, competition takes the form of conflict (1952, p. 152), by which he means that competition becomes conscious and collectively organized (for example through political parties) and thereby patterned by cultural norms: 'In human as contrasted with animal societies, competition and the freedom of the individual is limited on every level above the biotic by custom and consensus' (1952, p. 156). Competition is therefore mediated by culture, but the cultural form does not fundamentally alter the underlying biotic process.

This distinction between the biotic and the cultural, community and society, is fundamental to the classical perspective of human ecology, for as we have seen it is on the basis of this dichotomy that Park identifies the specific area of concern that is peculiar to this approach. The methodological basis of this crucial distinction is, however, never clearly established.

On some occasions, Park refers to communities and societies as empirical categories and thus as real entities which can be distinguished (albeit with some difficulty) in empirical research. Following Durkheim, he designates communities and societies as 'things' which can be directly studied and which exist independently of our ideas and conceptualizations of them. Communities are in this sense identified as locally based functional systems which are irreducible to the elements (that is, to human individuals) from which they are composed. Communities are therefore visible objects which can be studied in their own right: 'The community is a visible object. One can point it out, define its territorial limits, and plot its constituent elements, its population and its institutions on maps' (1952, p. 182). Empirical research can therefore begin with the study of communities because community is the framework within which society develops, and because it is more immediately visible than society and thus more amenable to statistical analysis. From such a starting point, it should be possible to discover empirical regularities between different communities, and thereby inductively to develop plausible hypotheses and scientific generalizations.

Elsewhere, however, Park treats the community–society dichotomy as an analytical construct. This follows from his argument that a science is distinguished not by a specific object of study but by the theoretical problem it poses in relation to some aspect of that object: 'What things are for any special science or for common sense, for that matter, is determined largely by the point of view from which they are looked at' (1952, p. 179). This suggests that human ecology is defined, not by its empirical concern with communities, but by its mode of conceptualizing 'community'. In this sense, community refers to a specific aspect of human organization which is identified theoretically as the unorganized and unconscious process whereby human populations adjust to their environment through unrestricted competition. Community here is not a thing but a process, not a separate and visible area of human existence but a distinct perspective on human existence. Seen in this way, the concept of community is merely a shorthand term for the biotic forces operating in human society, in which case it is clearly not possible to distinguish it from society in any empirical research setting.

Of these two approaches, the latter appears to achieve more prominence in Park's writings. Like Durkheim, he is concerned to analyse the complexity of society by first tracing the simplest and most basic unit of human organization, and this he finds in the concept of community. Only through exhaustive analysis of the impact of biotic forces on human society is it possible to begin to identify the significance of cultural factors. As Wirth (1945) explained it, the basic physical and natural forces at work in human society establish the framework and the context within which people act, and human ecology is therefore basic and complementary to the analysis of social organization and social psychology: 'Human ecology is not a substitute for, but a supplement to, the other frames of reference and methods of social investigation' (p. 438).

Having first established the scope of the biotic in human affairs, Park then attempts to reconstruct the complexity of social reality by taking into account the additional significance of human technology and cultural values. While conceptually distinct, he therefore recognizes that the biotic and the cultural are empirically interrelated:

Human ecology has, however, to reckon with the fact that in human society competition is limited by custom and culture. The cultural superstructure imposes itself as an instrument of direction and control upon the biotic substructure. Reduced to its elements the human community, so conceived, may be said to consist of a population and a culture, including in the term culture (1) a body of customs and beliefs and (2) a corresponding body of artifacts and technological devices. To these three elements or factors – (1) population, (2) artifact (technological culture), (3) custom and beliefs (non-material culture) – into which the social complex resolves itself, one should, perhaps, add a fourth, namely, the natural resources of the habitat. It is the interaction of these four factors that maintain at once the biotic balance and the social equilibrium when and where they exist (Park 1952, p. 158).

Having torn asunder the biotic and the cultural at the conceptual level, Park therefore reunites them at the level of empirical reality, for his four elements of the 'social complex' include ecological and cultural factors as inherently interrelated aspects.

Clearly, then, Park recognizes the mutual interdependence of the biotic and the cultural in the 'real' social world. Indeed, he takes the analysis further by suggesting that it is possible to conceptualize a hierarchy of constraints on the individual in terms of the operation of the ecological, economic, political and moral orders, such that the freedom of the individual is progressively restricted beyond the biotic level: 'The individual is more free upon the economic level than upon the political, more free on the political than the moral' (1952, p. 157). Such a formulation can be understood only analytically, and such an interpretation is reinforced in one of the last essays Park published where he developed a model of human society 'as a kind of cone or triangle, of which the basis is the ecological organization of human beings' (1952, p. 260). Furthermore, in this essay he added that on this basic ecological level 'the struggle for existence may go on, will go on, *unobserved* and relatively unrestricted' (p. 260; my emphasis), thereby demonstrating beyond doubt that the ecological community is not a thing but a theoretically defined aspect of social organization.

How, then, can a view of community as an empirical category – an observable and measurable object – be reconciled with the parallel view of community as an analytical construct? That both views are present in Park's writings cannot be doubted. That he never explicitly recognized their incompatibility is also apparent. His essays on human ecology span twenty-three years, yet in all that time he seemingly never felt obliged to address what appears as an obvious and fundamental confusion surrounding the dichotomy on which his entire approach was based.

The source of the confusion lies in the methodology that Park derived from Durkheim. As we saw in Chapter 1, this is basically an empiricist methodology, in that Durkheim (and Park) argues that knowledge is derived directly from the sense experiences and that phenomena must therefore be defined solely in terms of their external characteristics. It is for this reason that Park emphasizes community as an empirical and visible object. However, both Durkheim and Park are also committed to an holistic view of social collectivities in the sense that they wish to avoid reducing such collectivities to their individual components. Community (for Park) and society (for Durkheim) are therefore objects of study *sui generis*. There is an evident tension between these two postulates of phenomenalism and holism, for when we actually observe human communities and societies all we ever actually see are individuals. In other words, the very apprehension of a social collectivity as a thing is necessarily conceptual rather than phenomenal. The commitment to holism thus necessarily undermines the empiricist methodology by postulating a reality beyond direct experience. As Keat and Urry observe, 'When positivists seek to put into operation their methodology they often find themselves employing realist arguments or positing realist-type entities, albeit in an unsystematic and confused way' (1975, p. 82).

Such was the case with Durkheim in his study of the suicidogenic current which he saw as the underlying yet unobservable cause of the social suicide rate. Such is also the case with Park in his study of biotic forces as the underlying yet unobservable cause of functional and spatial organization. The way in which Durkheim side-stepped this problem was by reversing his own prescriptions as regards causal analysis. Because he was unable to observe the variations in the suicidogenic current, Durkheim inferred them from their supposed consequences in the suicide statistics (in other words, rather than tracing the effect of the current on the suicide rate,he deduced these effects from variations in the suicide rate, thereby developing an entirely tautological analysis). The way in which Park attempted to resolve what was essentially the same problem as regards the biotic forces behind human organization was by eliding an empirical category – community – which he argued could be observed, with an analytical one – the biotic level – which could not. In this way, he tried to fuse a phenomenal form with a realist concept. The way in which he did this was through the development of perhaps the most important concept of all in the ecological dictionary – that of 'natural area'.

We have seen that both Park and McKenzie argued that the biotic forces of competition always tend to produce a natural equilibrium at the point where the population is optimally adjusted to its environment. At this climax stage, the community is functionally and spatially differentiated such that different functional groups are located in different areas according to their relative suitability. As this unstable biotic equilibrium develops, so too do distinctive cultural forms corresponding to the different areas: 'The general effect of the continuous processes of invasions and accommodations is to give to the developed community well-defined areas, each having its own peculiar selective and cultural characteristics' (McKenzie 1967, p. 77). These different areas within the city, fashioned by competition and characterized by both functional and cultural differentiation, are termed 'natural areas'.

The significance of the concept of natural area for the Chicago school's human ecology is twofold. First, it overcomes the empirical problem associated with the biotic–cultural division by specifying an observable object – the ghetto, the red light district, the suburb or whatever – in which these two aspects of human organization have become fused. A natural area, that is, is also a cultural area. It is on the one hand an area characterized by division of labour and competitive co-operation, while on the other it is a moral area characterized by consensus and communication. It therefore represents an object, a 'thing', which can be studied both ecologically and sociologically, as a natural unit or as a social unit. Human ecology is therefore provided with an object of analysis in the sense that visible natural areas constitute a laboratory in which biotic processes of population change and adaptation can be studied.

The second point is related to this, for the natural area not only provides a concrete object of study, but also represents the conceptual framework within which such studies can be developed. Because natural areas are seen as the manifestations of natural forces operating in any and every human settlement, it follows that the different regions of one city should be directly comparable with those of another. Categories such as the ghetto or the suburb are treated generically, so that, for example, the cultural form of one ghetto should be similar to that of all others. Park writes,

The natural areas of the city . . . serve an important methodological function. They constitute, taken together, what Hobson has described as 'a frame of reference', a conceptual order within which statistical facts gain a new and more general significance. They not only tell us what the facts are in regard to conditions in any given region, but in so far as they characterize an area that is natural and typical, they establish a working hypothesis in regard to other areas of the same kind. . . . Most facts that can be stated statistically, once they have been plotted in this conceptual scheme – this ecological frame of reference – can be made the basis of general statements which may be eventually reduced to abstract formulae and scientific generalizations (Park 1952, p. 198).

Empirical research is thus situated within a framework that enables the development of inductive generalizations (i.e. what Park sees as the transition from concrete fact to conceptual knowledge). Because biotic forces are assumed to be at work, the hidden causes of visible phenomena in natural areas, it is possible to develop scientific knowledge about them by studying their effects in different comparable locations: 'The result of every new specific enquiry should reaffirm or redefine, qualify or extend, the hypotheses upon which the original enquiry was based. The results should not merely increase our fund of information, but enable us to reduce our observations to general formulae and quantitative statements true for all cases of the same kind' (1952, p. 198).

Faced with the same methodological problems as Durkheim (how to develop knowledge of an underlying force in human society when the only valid knowledge is that grounded in experience of 'concrete facts'), Park therefore resorts to much the same solution (assume the existence of the force and search empirically for phenomena that are deemed to be manifestations of that force). Implicitly, however, Park seems to recognize that such an approach is hardly consistent with his positivist methodology, and it is for this reason that he also suggests that the natural area is itself an object of study in which the biotic as well as the cultural may be directly analysed.

This, then, is the source of the confusion referred to earlier between community as an empirical category and as an analytical construct. For Park it has to be both a thing that can be observed directly, and a force in human organization which can be theorized on the basis of such observation. The natural area concept is pressed into service to perform this dual function as both an observable object and a manifestation of an unobservable force. Once we recognize this uneasy tension in Park's methodology between positivism and realism, the analysis of communities and the theorization of the biotic forces that are at work within them, we can understand how it is that human ecology itself exhibits a dual identity, as on the one hand a sociological method for studying the city, and on the other a distinct discipline within the human sciences. Park's human ecology was from the very beginning set upon two stools. It was only a matter of time before the critics kicked them apart.

Human ecology is dead ...

'By 1950, the ecological approach as developed by Park, his colleagues and students at the University of Chicago was virtually dead' (Berry and Kasarda 1977, p. 3). The demise was gradual and cumulative, brought about by a combination of essentially misguided criticisms (which nevertheless served to call the approach into question) and fundamental critiques.

What I term the 'misguided criticisms' fell into three categories. The first, stated most forcibly by Davie (1937), accepted the basic assumptions of human ecology – that city growth was the product of 'automatic forces' involving competition and selection – but took issue with Burgess's application of these ideas through the hypothesis of a concentric zone pattern. In a study of New Haven, Davie showed that patterns of residential location were largely a function of patterns of industrial location, and that industry located near lines of communication which exhibited no uniform pattern. Recognizing that Burgess's model was conceived as an ideal type, Davie nevertheless concluded that 'There is no universal pattern, not even of an "ideal type" ' (p. 161). His study then stimulated a series of other projects on other cities in which various authors engaged in increasingly elaborate mapping exercises, but this whole line of research and criticism inevitably led up a cul-de-sac since it was addressed only to the descriptive question of urban form. The theoretical problems of the ecological analysis of such forms remained unexamined. In retrospect it does seem that Burgess's famous paper has received disproportionate attention over the years, and this has resulted in widespread concern with the question of spatial distribution to the neglect of the more basic question of functional differentiation (a tendency which, as we shall see, was later 'corrected' by Hawley).

The second misconceived (yet in a different context very significant) criticism concerned the mode of statistical analysis in ecological research. Robinson (1950) drew a distinction between ecological correlations (correlations between aggregate phenomena such as that between the proportion of blacks in a population and the rate of illiteracy) and individual correlations (correlations between indivisible units). He then pointed to the fallacy of using an ecological correlation as evidence for an individual one, for the fact that there may be a strong correlation between the illiteracy rate and the proportion of blacks in a given population does not necessarily justify the deduction that it is the blacks who are illiterate. Indeed, Robinson showed that ecological correlations invariably overemphasized (and occasionally even reversed) individual ones.

Robinson's paper represents an important criticism of research which does aim to deduce individual statistical relationships from correlations based on aggregate data (one famous example being Durkheim's *Suicide*). This was not, however, the intention of the Chicago ecologists, for as Menzel (1950) pointed out, ecological correlations in their research were used to demonstrate 'a common underlying cause inherent not in the individuals as such but in inter-individual differences and relationships – properties of areas as such' (p. 674). Indeed, we saw in the previous section that Park was concerned to emphasize the irreducibility of the ecological community to its individual components. Thus a correlation between, say, divorce rates and crime rates would not be used to imply that divorcees are criminals, but as evidence of how the characteristics of a particular area (and in particular a high level of mobility) generate high levels of social disorganization which are reflected in the divorce rate, the crime rate and so on. Ecological correlation thus performed the same function as Durkheim's concomitant variation (which was discussed above, pp. 41–2).

The third criticism that is basically misguided is one developed by Alihan (1938), among others, to the effect that there is a disjuncture between the theoretical and the empirical products of the Chicago school. Reviewing the research monographs of those like Anderson (on the hobo) and Zorbaugh (on the slum), Alihan suggests that they invariably fail to distinguish biotic and cultural forces, and that they are no more than sociological studies in which territorial distribution is taken into account on a descriptive level: 'If we take a territorially demarcated unit as a basis of study, we do not discriminate between certain activities carried on within the area as those of "society" and others which are those of "community" (p. 82). Alihan's argument here is true but irrelevant, for while it certainly is the case that the various Chicago monographs do not draw this distinction, it is equally the case that it was never intended that they should. As we saw in the last section, such studies were premised on the assumption that the areas under investigation had been created by biotic forces, and their objective was to study the cultural forms that had developed as a result with a view to developing theoretical generalizations. The biotic–cultural division, in other words, provided the initial framework for such studies rather than their object of analysis. Thus Alihan's comment that Park and his colleagues 'waver between the complete scission of the two concepts on the one hand, and their fusion on the other' (pp. 69–70) cannot in itself be deemed a criticism, since it was precisely Park's intention to separate the two analytically and to fuse them empirically.

This line of attack was, nevertheless, pursued with much enthusiasm by critics of the Chicago school, and most notably by Firey (1945). He suggested that human ecology explained locational activity purely in terms of economic maximization, and argued against this that space may have a symbolic as well as economic value, and that locational activity may therefore reflect sentiment as much as economic rationality. Reporting his study of land use in Boston, he then showed how upper-class residents had remained in Beacon Hill for 150 years because of their sentimental attachment to the area and despite the economic advantages of selling up and moving out; how 'sacred sites' such as the common and civil war burial grounds had been preserved from development even though they occupied the most valuable ground in the city and caused economically wasteful traffic congestion; and how, even in an Italian slum, the first generation immigrants were loath to leave the area owing to their commitment to the values of family and *paesani* which were upheld in the slum but were threatened outside it. It followed from all this that cultural values and intersubjective meanings were clearly crucial variables in the explanation of patterns of land use, and that the ecological concern with biotic forces had therefore to be modified.

Park, however, never denied the empirical significance of cultural factors. Indeed, as we have seen, he included both technology and 'non-material' cultural factors as two of the four elements of the 'social complex'. In terms of empirical research, he and his colleagues never intended that community could be analysed separately from society (as Alihan's critique suggested), nor that distributional patterns should be explained solely in terms of ecological forces (as Firey claims). The most that can be said about the difference between Park and Firey is that they are primarily interested in different questions: for Firey, the interesting question is why and how Beacon Hill has resisted invasion from business uses for a century and a half; for Park, it would be why and how Beacon Hill came to be associated with the upper class in the first place.

Where the work of writers such as Alihan and Firey *does* pose an important challenge to human ecology is not in their atacks on the biotic–cultural dichotomy, but in the implications that their arguments have for the fundamental methodological division (which underpins this dichotomy) between the community as a visible object and the community as an analytical construct. These implications are in fact brought out by Alihan, who suggests in relation to the Chicago ecologists that

One of their main difficulties lies in the confusion between abstraction and reality. Some of this confusion might have been avoided if the school had been familiar with the 'ideal type' method of investigation. The concept 'community' is approached in a way that denies its social attributes. In its very definition it is an abstraction of the asocial aspect of human behaviour. Yet the ecologists find themselves compelled in many ways to take account of the social factors which in reality are intrinsically related to and bound up with the asocial community. Had ecologists persisted in dealing with the concept of the 'natural order' as an abstraction, or as an 'ideal type', for the purposes of study these social factors could be treated apart from 'community', as conditioning, concomitant and intrusive phenomena of the 'natural order'. We would then have only the problem of the validity and scientific utility of a particular classification and of the particularistic philosophical ideology underlying the delimitation of the category 'community'. But ecologists do not pursue this course consistently; what is to them an abstraction at one time becomes a reality at another (Alihan 1938, pp. 48–9).

Alihan here summarizes the main point at issue. If Park had consistently approached the concept of 'community' solely as an abstraction, an heuristic device for analysis, then his approach would have been methodologically (though not necessarily theoretically)

valid. We may still have wished to argue that it was not useful to approach human society from such a naturalistic perspective, and that to do so was to resort to unwarranted biological determinism (see Gettys 1940), but there would be no methodological grounds for disputing the biotic–cultural distinction. The fact that Park did not, and could not, limit the concept in this way was due to his commitment to the positivist postulate of phenomenalism. In other words, for him any abstraction had to have a direct empirical reference. He could no more accept the idealism implicit in Alihan's reference to ideal types than he could the realism inherent in the alternative view of abstractions as referring to a level of reality beyond the senses. Following Durkheim, the ecologists were concerned above all with things: 'Their universe of discourse became limited to externalities and the interpretation of social life hinged upon its most concrete aspects. Reducing social behaviour to a common denominator of the tangible and the measurable ... human ecologists became the expounders of the socially "given" ' (Alihan 1938, p. 6).

In the light of this critique, human ecology was confronted with two options. Either it could retain its foundation in a positivist methodology while rejecting attempts to theorize the underlying forces determining the mode of human organization, or it could attempt to develop and justify the concept of the ecological community as an abstraction while rejecting the search for an observable and physical reference point. Human ecology could no longer have its cake and eat it, and the two questions of spatial form and functional process, which Park had attempted to unite, had at last to be severed.

Different analysts, faced with this dilemma, chose different options. Those who chose the first continued to undertake research on the observable and external characteristics of human communities, but this was now divorced from any rigorous theoretical framework, and what Mills (1959) refers to as 'abstracted empiricism' was too often the result. Basically these studies fell into two categories: those concerned with statistical analyses of urban populations (tracing patterns of migration, mapping social phenomena, etc.) and those concerned with descriptive accounts of cultural forms (for example the tradition of community studies). Neither of these categories has provided coherent and cumulative data, for while the former merely amasses figures and trends, the latter provides a long series of non-comparable case studies on individual localities. Neither, in fact, can any longer be termed 'ecological', for while the first has disintegrated into the most descriptive demography, the second appears little different from cultural anthropology (see Hannerz 1980, ch. 2). In both, the theoretical specificity of the urban has disappeared. Those analysts who chose the second option have fared somewhat better. This approach was first spelt out by Hawley (1944), who asserted (against the contemporary line of argument at that time) that human ecology was a viable theoretical perspective, but that it had been distorted by the Chicago school's emphasis on spatial distributions of social phenomena. Hawley sought to relocate human ecology in the mainstream of ecological thought, and in doing so he argued that space, far from being central, was incidental to the ecological problem. The traditional concern of the Chicago ecologists with the physical distribution of social phenomena (which, as we have seen, was the product of their commitment to the principle of phenomenalism) was, for Hawley, indicative not of a genuinely ecological framework but of a geographical one. Space, he suggested, was merely a factor that had to be taken into account by human ecology, just as it had to be taken into account by any other science. What was specific to human ecology was not, therefore, its concern with the physical human community, but rather its interest in a particular process; that of the adaptation of human populations by means of functional differentiation.

Six years after this article appeared, Hawley published a book which set out an ecological framework that has guided research in human ecology ever since. In the words of Berry and Kasarda, 'Hawley reformulated the ecological approach and initiated its present revival within the field of sociology' (1977, p. 3). So it was that human ecology re-emerged during the 1950s as a more modest, but methodologically more secure, approach than that first outlined by Park thirty-four years before.

. . . Long live human ecology!

Like Park, Hawley began from the position that a science should be distinguished according to its perspective rather than its object of study: 'A science is delimited by what it does rather than by any *a priori* definition of its field . . . it must bring into focus a set of problems not included within the scope of other disciplines to which scientific techniques can be, and are in fact being, applied' (1950, p. 10). The perspective that was specific to ecology was that which sought to explain how populations adapted collectively and unconsciously to their environment. This struggle to adapt was seen as a central problem for all species, including human beings, for although human beings had developed cultural artefacts which enabled them to adapt more efficiently and effectively than other species, the difference between them was quantitative rather than qualitative: 'The difference between men and other organisms in adaptive capacity, though great, seems to be a matter of degree rather than kind' (1950, p. 32). There was therefore no reason why the principles of ecological theory as a whole should not be applied to the analysis of adaptation by human communities in particular, and this is what Hawley set out to do.

It is important to recognize that Hawley does not suggest that an ecological approach to the human community is in any way exhaustive, for he argues that such communities are comprised of psychological and moral as well as functional relations, and that human ecology is concerned only with the latter. Nor does he suggest that these different aspects of social relationships can be empirically distinguished, for 'Sustenance activities and relationships are inextricably interwoven with sentiments, value systems and other ideational constructs' (1950, p. 73). Hawley never seeks to deny that values and individual motivations may play an important part in the development of human communities, but rather seeks to assert that this is irrelevant to the ecological problem. The theoretical objective of human ecology, he states, 'is to develop a description of the morphology or form of collective life under varying external conditions. With its problem stated in that manner, the irrelevance of the psychological properties of individuals is self-evident' (1950, p. 179). It is because human ecology is concerned with how human populations adapt collectively to their environment that questions of individual values and motivations have no place within it.

Hawley's analysis of adaptation is developed around the four ecological principles of interdependence, key function, differentiation and dominance. These principles are themselves derived and justified from certain 'cardinal assumptions' concerning the invariant conditions in which human populations are situated (see Hawley 1968). For example, every human population must afford some means whereby its members can achieve access to the environment in order to live; every human population develops some form of interdependence between its members; and so on. From such simple and seemingly non-contentious assertions, Hawley develops a complex and highly contentious theory. (It is worth noting here that Hawley's 'cardinal assumptions' are not dissimilar from those identified by Marx, for both writers emphasize the primacy of material production in society, and both stress the necessity for a system of social relations through which this can be accomplished. What is interesting about this is that, while both writers start from similar *a priori* assumptions regarding the conditions for social existence, they go on to develop very different theories, and this would tend to suggest that neither ecological nor Marxist theory can be justified simply in terms of logical deduction from general principles. As we saw in the discussion of Marx's methodology in Chapter 1, such abstract transhistorical generalizations are in fact very limited, and it follows from this that Hawley's claim to have 'deduced' the principles of ecological organization from such generalizations should be approached with some caution.)

The first of Hawley's ecological principles is interdependence, and he suggests that a major difference between his approach and that of earlier human ecologists concerns the relative emphasis on interdependence as opposed to competition. In any human population, the process of adaptation to the environment involves the development of interdependence among its members. This may take the form either of symbiotic relations (i.e. complementary relations between functionally dissimilar groups) or commensalistic relations (i.e. aggregation of functionally similar groups). In both cases, the combination of individual units increases their collective capacity for action beyond what would have been possible had they remained isolated. Thus a symbiotic union enhances the creative powers of human groups (for it enables specialization), while a commensalistic union enhances their defensive powers (for it increases numerical strength). Symbiotic unions are therefore productive while commensalistic unions are protective. Hawley terms the former 'corporate groups' and the latter 'categoric groups'. The main corporate groups in modern society are familial, associational and territorial, while the main categoric groups are those based on common occupation (for instance the trade unions).

The pattern of ecological organization of a given population within a given territory is therefore determined by the two axes of symbiosis and commensalism. The pattern will be far from simple, however, for Hawley recognizes that corporate groups (based on symbiotic interdependence) may sometimes function as categoric units (for example when responding to some external threat), while categoric groups (based on commensalistic aggregation) may sometimes develop corporate characteristics (for example by developing a specialized leadership stratum). Furthermore, the relations between various units may take either a symbiotic or commensalistic form, so that, for example, corporate units may establish categoric combinations while categoric units may develop symbiotic ties between them as a result of differentiation between their functions. Any human population therefore exhibits a complex pattern of interdependence between different units, but this complexity can nevertheless be analysed by means of the simple formal dichotomy between symbiosis and commensalism. For Hawley, in other words, the ecological community, which constitutes the object of analysis for human ecology, is the system of symbiotic and commensalistic relationships which enables a human population to carry on its daily life. As a system of interdependent relations, the ecological community is therefore irreducible to the units that comprise it: 'It is, in fact, the least reducible universe within which ecological phenomena may be adequately observed. ... The community, then, is the basic unit of ecological investigation' (1950, p. 180).

Having thus identified the ecological community in terms of a system of functional and interdependent relationships, Hawley is then in a position to develop three further ecological principles. The first of these is the principle of the 'key function', by which he means that certain units within the system will tend to perform a more significant function in adapting the population to its environment than others: 'In every system of relationships among diverse functions, the connection of the system to its environment is mediated primarily by one or a relatively small number of functions' (1968, p. 332). Because the fundamental problem faced by human populations is that of adapting to the external environment, it follows that those units most centrally involved in this process must be the key functional units in the system. Although Hawley does not spell out the implications of this argument, it is clear from his work that the key function is therefore performed in a capitalist society by private enterprise firms which mediate both between the population and its natural environment (through material production) and between the population and its surrounding social environment (through trade).

The performance of the key function is crucial to the two remaining ecological principles identified by Hawley. The first of these is functional differentiation, the extent of which depends upon the productivity of the key function. Thus, while the low productivity of hunting and gathering societies inhibits the development of functional differentiation and specialization, the high productivity of societies organized around the key function of industry means that there is in principle no upper limit on the extent to which differentiation may proceed. This is significant because differentiation, involving an increasingly complex mode of social organization, is the principal way in which human populations adapt to their environment. In other words, given adequate productivity of the key function, differentiation restores the balance between population and environment where this is disturbed by competition (in the way Park suggested) or by improvements in transport and communications (in the way Durkheim suggested in his discussion of moral density).

The final ecological principle – that of dominance – is similarly dependent upon the key function, for the dominant positions within the ecological system are assumed by those units that contribute most to the key function: 'Dominance attaches to the unit that controls the conditions necessary to the functioning of other units. Ordinarily that means controlling the flow of sustenance into the community' (1950, p. 221). Interestingly, Hawley recognizes that one implication of this view is that the dominant units in a human population are likely to be economic rather than political:

It is commonly assumed that government assumes the dominant position. . . . Yet its dominance is not without qualification . . . government, especially in the United States, plays a passive part in the sustenance flow to the community. In effect, government shares and is in competition for the dominant position with associational units whose functions enable them to exert a decisive influence on the community's sustenance supply (Hawley 1950, p. 229).

The functional dominance of business within the ecological system is therefore expressed politically through business influence over community decision-making; a conclusion that Hawley later re-affirmed (1963) in a study of concentrated business power in relation to urban renewal programmes.

The functional dominance of business is expressed not only politically, but also spatially and temporally. It is expressed spatially through centrality, for the centre of human settlements is the point at which functional interdependence is integrated and administered. Dominant units performing the key function therefore occupy central sites, while other units performing lesser functions are distributed according to their relative contributions: 'In general, units performing key functions have the highest priority of claim on location. Other units tend to distribute themselves about the key function units, their distances away corresponding to the number of degrees of removal separating their functions from direct relation with the key function'

(Hawley 1968, p. 333). The functional hierarchy is thus expressed in the form of a spatial gradient, and although Hawley notes that the spatial distribution of different functional units may be affected by factors such as topography and transport routes, his analysis nevertheless results in a very familiar conclusion: 'A noticeable tendency appears for each class of land use to become segregated in a zone situated at an appropriate distance from the centre. The resulting series of more or less symmetrical concentric zones represents in general outline a universal community pattern' (1950, p. 264). Burgess's famous description of the pattern of land use is therefore reaffirmed by Hawley, but his analysis is not, for Hawley explains this pattern as the result of *functional* dominance rather than central dominance *per se*. Where business performs the key function in the system, it will be found at the centre of human settlements, but where other units (e.g. household units in pre-industrial societies) perform the key function, they will occupy the central locations. Thus, while evidence relating to the spatial pattern of pre-industrial cities appears to refute Burgess's model, it is entirely consistent with Hawley's.

The temporal dimension of dominance is revealed in the way in which the rhythm of the principal sustenance unit in the community becomes imposed upon other activities. Just as business dominance is expressed spatially in the pattern of land use, so it is expressed temporally in the rhythm of community activities, the most obvious example of this being the rush-hour.

The significance of these four principles of interdependence, key function, differentiation and dominance is that together they explain how it is that human populations exhibit a constant tendency towards functional equilibrium in their relationship with their environment. Thus Hawley suggests that these four factors tend to bring about a situation where 'development has terminated in a more or less complete system that is capable of sustaining a given relationship to environment indefinitely' (1968, p. 334). In such a closed system, differentiation of functions has been maximized (relative to the productivity of the key function) and organized in terms of corporate and categoric units; the performance of the key function itself has been concentrated in just one unit (or a categoric grouping of units) in order to maximize efficient control of other units of the system; all functions are mutually complementary and are organized at maximum efficiency so that the number of individuals involved in performing each function is just enough to maintain it adequately; and the different functional units have been arranged in space and time so that accessibility is directly proportional to the frequency of exchanges between them.

The tendency towards such an optimally adjusted and maximally efficient system is, however, only a tendency. The fact that such systems are never actually realized is due first to 'immanent change' (that is, change in the environment, such as a decline in non-replaceable natural resources, which necessitates constant readjustment of the ecological system), and second to 'cumulative change' (expansion of the system itself consequent upon the growing productivity of the key function). Because the ecological system is never static it never attains a state of closure, but the underlying tendency within the ecological community is nevertheless always towards the re-establishment of equilibrium. System change is thus fundamentally an evolutionary process involving expansion and readjustment of the ecological system.

This emphasis on evolutionary change lies at the heart of contemporary ecological theory. It is found, for example, in the work of Otis Dudley Duncan, one of the leading exponents of Hawley's approach to human ecology, who writes, 'The most fundamental postulates of human ecology still are best elucidated in an evolutionary framework' (1964, p. 45). Like Hawley, Duncan conceptualizes the ecological community as 'equilibrium-seeking' (Duncan 1959). He suggests that the ecological system may be understood as a functionally interdependent 'ecological complex' consisting of population, environment, human technology and human organization. All four of these variables interact upon each other, although in general population and organization tend to be dependent while environment and technology are independent. In other words, just as Hawley traces the source of system change to external environmental conditions or to internal expansion of productivity, so too Duncan emphasizes the significance of environmental and technological changes in the evolution of the ecological complex as a whole. Changes in these two factors, together with associated changes in population size and organizational capacity, bring about the expansion of the system as a whole: 'Ecological expansion . . . may be characterized by a formula, the four terms in which have been called the "ecological complex": technological accumulation at an accelerated rate; intensified exploitation of environment; demographic transition (now popularly known as "population explosion"); and organizational revolution' (Duncan 1964, p. 75).

Contemporary human ecology is thus characterized above all by its emphasis on the tendency to equilibrium (homeostasis) and the evolutionary nature of system change. In both respects, it has come very close to the functionalist paradigm in sociology. Indeed, there are other parallels between ecological and functionalist perspectives, for not only do they both address themselves to the same problems of the maintenance of equilibrium and the evolutionary development of social systems, but both are oriented towards the analysis of system features rather than individual values and motivations (see Beshers 1962, ch. 2), and both attach considerable significance to patterns of functional interdependence between different units in social systems and to the process of cybernetic feedback within systems (for example through the mutual interaction of the four elements in Duncan's ecological complex). Duncan himself has recognized this close affinity between the two approaches, and has even argued that the ecological perspective may help to clarify some of the areas of confusion within functionalist sociology as a whole (see Duncan and Schnore 1959).

Given this affinity between ecological and functionalist approaches, it is not surprising that many of the familiar criticisms made against functionalist theory have also been made against post-war human ecology. Two in particular deserve mention. The first concerns the problem of teleology and tends to involve the argument that analysis of social systems cannot be accomplished without reference to the subjectively meaningful purposive actions of individual members. The second concerns the question of ideology and tends to involve the assertion that theories that are addressed to the problem of system maintenance are grounded in inherently conservative postulates.

The problem of teleology is that collectivities do not act purposefully, which renders problematic any explanation of a given phenomenon couched in terms of the social purpose, or function, it serves. According to Hawley, however, human ecology does not encounter the problem of teleology found in structural functionalism because it theorizes the control and regulation mechanism within ecological systems: 'As an organization attains completeness it acquires the capacity for controlling change and for retaining its form through time (1968, p. 331). In other words, as the ecological community develops towards a closed system, so there evolves a centralized and concentrated key function which effectively controls the development of other units within the system.

What remains unclear in this analysis, however, is how this control and integration on the part of the key functional unit is achieved. Thus according to Robson (1969), any such analysis of the functional role of institutions must implicitly resort to an analysis of the purposive actions of the individuals within them: 'A viewpoint which emphasizes the functional role of social institutions, as does Hawley's, makes assumptions as to motivations, attitudes, sentiments and values which must at least be recognized and considered' (p. 23). Hawley, however, seeks to develop a theoretical perspective which can put to one side questions of individual motives and values, yet according to Robson he conspicuously fails to demarcate the line between the cultural aspects which he does not wish to study and the ecological aspects which he does. Robson's argument is precisely that this line cannot be drawn and that any ecological analysis must take account of the subjective values and purposes of individual actors.

This sort of criticism is at one and the same time both profound and irrelevant. It is profound because it points to a basic problem in urban sociology in particular (see Chapter 4 on urban managerialism and Chapter 6 on the state and the urban system) and in sociology in general; namely, the division between the 'two sociologies' of system and action discussed by Dawe (1970).

Yet it is also irrelevant for the same reason, for it fails to articulate theoretically with the ecological perspective. As Castells (1977a, ch. 8) has suggested, criticisms of the ecological perspective that are grounded in a commitment to an action frame of reference represent less of a critique and more of an inversion. Human ecology is criticized not for what it is, but for what it is not. The debate between voluntaristic action theorists and deterministic systems theorists is as old as sociology itself, and it does not therefore appear particularly useful to criticize human ecology on these grounds.

The argument that human ecology is ideological is one that has more often been made in relation to the pre-war than the post-war literature. Alihan (1938), for example, suggested that the Chicago school's emphasis on competition as 'the process basic to all other processes' (p. 91) was little more than an ideological judgement reflecting the core competitive ethic of American capitalism at the time when Park and his colleagues were writing. Similarly Gettys (1940) pointed to the biologistic and naturalistic claims of the Chicago school as fundamentally misrepresenting and mystifying what were essentially social processes – a criticism that has subsequently been developed more fully by Castells (1977a), who has suggested that the apparently 'natural' forces identified by Park must rather be explained as forces specific to the capitalist mode of production (see Chapter 5).

With the work of Hawley and Duncan, however, the emphasis on competition as a basic process in human organization has been replaced by an emphasis on interdependence, while assertions about the natural basis of ecological processes have become blurred as a result of the attempt to dispense with the biotic–cultural dichotomy. Nevertheless, post-war human ecology is still open to the charge of ideology for much the same reason as the work of the Chicaco school was, for fundamental to the claims of contemporary ecological theory is the view that certain processes are constant and invariant. Human ecology, in other words, is still concerned to identify transhistorical generalities – forces and processes that invariably operate in all human societies.

We noted earlier that the range of transhistorical generalizations that can safely be made concerning necessary features of all societies appears very limited, and that Hawley's set of cardinal assumptions (that individuals must have access to the environment; that this access must involve some degree of interdependence; that individuals are time-bound; and so on) do not take us very far. The problem is that Hawley believes that other principles can logically be deduced from these initial assumptions (for example principles of dominance and the key function) and that these principles are also invariant. It is in this respect that his work can be attacked as ideological, for there appear no necessary logical grounds for arguing that, for example, certain groups must exercise a dominant function and must therefore attain political, spatial and temporal dominance in society, or that dominant groups must always occupy central locations from which they can control the whole system. Although Hawley avoids discussion of natural biotic forces, the whole thrust of his analysis is nevertheless towards the conclusion that centralized power and extreme division of labour are natural and necessary. Indeed, his conceptualization of the closed ecological system, towards which all systems are said to exhibit a constant tendency, appears as much a political as a theoretical 'ideal', and it is one that, with its implications of extensive corporate power and all-embracing political control, many people are concerned to work and fight against.

Like structural functionalism, therefore, human ecology has tended to develop theoretical explanations (and hence, implicitly, justifications) for a particular mode of political and economic organization. It is a theory of the *status quo* that supports arrangements by explaining them as the outcome of invariant principles. Its concerns are the concerns of the dominant groups in society – it talks of maximizing efficiency but has nothing to say about increasing accountability, it talks of maintaining equilibrium through gradual change and readjustment and rules out even the possibility of fundamental restructuring. In one sense, the ecological perspective can be enlightening in that it points to the processes that need to be addressed by those seeking social change. But in another sense it is totally restricting and inhibiting in that it denies the possibility of acting on these processes. At best it is mildly reformist; at worst it is fatalistic in its conservatism.

Whether all this is sufficient to dismiss human ecology as ideological depends on how ideology is conceptualized, and this in turn depends on whether it is possible to distinguish science and ideology. This is a question that is taken up in Chapter 5. For the moment, the least that can be said is that this body of theory presents a picture of the social world that is likely to prove particularly unattractive to those who are committed to working for change.

As regards its contribution to the development of a specifically 'urban' social theory, however, we are in a position to draw more definite conclusions regarding the claims and achievements of human ecology. It is clear from Duncan's work that the application of the ecological perspective to the urban question is now problematic. For a start, Duncan (1959) argues convincingly against Hawley's claim that the community represents a microcosm which can be studied in its own right as the smallest indivisible ecological unit, for he points out that the scope of the interdependency between the four elements of the ecological complex now extends far beyond the community to the 'supra-local'. Indeed, it may be suggested that, given the interdependency of localities, regions and states in the world today, the only viable ecological unit is the world system! Clearly urban sociology loses its specificity entirely when the theoretical processes in which it is interested, and the objects of study that it is concerned to analyse, can only be represented quite literally as the world and its entire contents.

Second, it is also clear from Duncan's work that ecology has become a theoretical perspective which has no necessary connection with urban analysis. In a defence of the ecological perspective, for example, Duncan and Schnore (1959) suggest that it can fruitfully be applied to the study of any aggregate phenomenon, and they cite as examples the analysis of bureaucracy and stratification as well as urbanization. The distinctiveness of the ecological approach, in other words, lies solely in its emphasis on the problem of how human aggregates adapt to changing conditions, and there is nothing specifically 'urban' about that.

Appreciation of this point enables us to situate human ecology more precisely in terms of its relationship to structural functionalism, for it is apparent that ecology has become merely one specialized area of study *within* the functionalist paradigm. The problem that it poses is one of the four key functional problems identified by Parsons in his famous 'AGIL' scheme, the other three being goal definition (which on a societal level refers to the political system), integration (which refers to institutions performing social control functions) and latency or pattern maintenance (which refers to the process of socialization) (see Parsons, Bales and Shils 1953). For Parsons, adaptation, the fourth cell in the typology, is achieved by the economic system, for this mediates between the social system as a whole and its external non-social environment.

It is interesting in the light of this to note that, in his attempt to distinguish the theoretical concerns of human ecology from those of other social science disciplines, Hawley (1950, ch. 4) encounters the greatest difficulty in distinguishing it from economics, and he resolves his problem only by claiming that ecology is broader than economics in that it focuses on interdependencies beyond those grounded in mere exchange values. It may be, therefore, that the ecological system should replace the economic system in Parson's AGIL typology, for what is clear is that Parsons's theoretical identification of the problem of adaptation coincides exactly with the theoretical concerns of the postwar human ecology.

Once human ecology is located as a sub-discipline within structural–functionalism, its significance for urban analysis can more readily be evaluated. We have seen in this chapter that, as originally developed by the Chicago school, human ecology represented an attempt to generate both a distinct theoretical approach to human society and a specific theory of the city, and that the irreconcilable tension between these two resulted eventually in its collapse. Hawley was able to resurrect human ecology only by jettisoning its specific relevance to the city, and his development of the ecological approach as a sociological perspective rather than as an urban theory was then taken further by Duncan with the result that the relation between ecological theory and urban theory became purely contingent. Now that ecology has found its niche within the functionalist paradigm, we may debate its validity and its usefulness in that context, but irrespective of the conclusions we draw from such a debate, it is clear that human ecology is no longer essentially an urban theory and that it cannot provide a conceptual framework within which a specifically urban social theory can be developed.

3 The urban as a cultural form

There is in Anglo-Saxon culture a deep and enduring tension between the image of the town and that of the countryside. The imagery is that of opposites, for the virtues of rural life – family, traditional morality, community – are mirrored in the vices of the city – egoism, materialism, anonymity – while the advantages of urban living are similarly reflected in the disadvantages of rural existence. As Raymond Williams observes,

On the country has gathered the idea of a natural way of life: of peace, innocence and simple virtue. On the city has gathered the idea of an achieved centre: of learning, communication, light. Powerful hostile associations have also developed: on the city as a place of noise, worldliness and ambition; on the country as a place of backwardness, ignorance, limitation. A contrast between country and city, as fundamental ways of life, reaches back into classical times (Williams 1973, p. 1).

While the prevailing image of the city, which can be traced in literature and, more recently, in film, includes both positive and negative aspects – progress as well as pollution, liberty as well as loneliness – it does appear that evaluation is more often hostile than favourable: 'Life in the countryside is viewed as one of harmony and virtue. The town is disorganized; the countryside is settled. The town is bad; the countryside is good' (Newby 1977, p. 12). In part this may be the legacy of the fear of the town by the dominant classes in the nineteenth century, for as Glass (1968) has argued, the expanding Victorian cities represented a concentration of the industrial proletariat which the guardians of the *status quo* viewed with some apprehension. Then as now, industrialists, philanthropists and visionary planners sought to re-establish the moral bonds of the small community by developing company towns and new model communities which would reintegrate the individual into society and demobilize the mob (see Dennis 1968, Heraud 1975). Yet this is far from a complete explanation for the durability and pervasiveness of anti-urban sentiment in western cultures, for as Williams demonstrates, the tendency to compare the urban present with an idyllic version of a rural past has been in evidence for centuries. We shall consider Williams's own explanation for this later in this chapter.

Not surprisingly, the tension between the urban and the rural and between the values that each represents has found expression not only in cultural forms, but also in social theory and philosophy, where it is revealed most clearly in the concept of community. Nisbet (1966) has suggested that community constitutes 'the most fundamental and far-reaching of sociology's unit-ideas' (p. 47), and this is the case because it is indicative of what appear to be some of the most basic dilemmas in social relationships. If, as Nisbet suggests, community encompasses relationships of personal intimacy, depth, commitment and continuity, then, either implicitly or explicitly, it represents a vivid contrast with other types of relationships which are characterized by indifference, superficiality, segmentalism and brevity. It is the contrast between emotion and intellect, altruism and egoism, affection and instrument-alism, and so on.

Such contrasts are basic to sociological analysis for they help to define the range of types of action in which people may engage in different situations. When we come to study the social relationships involved in families, street gangs, factories, churches or state bureaucracies, we inevitably make use of such ideal type conceptual contrasts in order to describe and analyse the patterns of social interaction which we find there. Herein lies the usefulness of such well-known conceptual schema as Parsons's 'pattern variables'. Parsons (1951) identifies a series of dilemmas which confront actors when they enter a given situation. Should they, for example, display emotion towards others or should they maintain emotional indif-ference? Should they accept a wide range of obligations towards others or should their concern be more specific? Should they apply universal criteria when evaluating other people's actions or are the particular qualities of others more relevant in determining how to behave towards them? And should they relate to others in terms of what they do or in terms of who they are?

According to Parsons, such dilemmas are usually resolved for us as a result of our socialization – we 'know' in most situations what the appro-priate role behaviour should be. Indeed, these dilemmas tend to cluster into typical patterns – within the family, for example, we will normally be expected to act emotionally, to accept a wide range of obligations, to be concerned with the particular qualities of other family members and to relate to each other in terms of ascribed rather than achieved characteristics, whereas such a pattern of action would normally be entirely inappropriate within, say, a formal bureaucratic organization.

Parson's pattern variables represent an elaboration and refinement of a fundamental dualism which runs through much social theory over the last hundred years or more. We see it, for example, in Durkheim's contrast between mechanical and organic solidarity, or in Weber's distinction between traditional and rational action. Such contrasts have often been used in one or both of two ways: either as a basis for developing a theory of social change in which human societies are said to 'evolve' from one typical pattern to the other over time, or as a basis for developing a theory of social geography in which different types of human settlements are distinguished according to their conformity to one or other typical pattern. In the first case, the contrasts are ranged at either end of a time continuum – societies are said to change (or often 'develop') from traditionalistic, affectual, homogenous and undifferentiated structures at one time to modern, rational, heterogenous and highly differentiated structures at another. In the second, the contrasts are ranged at either end of a space continuum in which human settlements are said to vary between generally small-scale units where interaction takes place at a face-to-face level and is governed by strong bonds of communality and tradition, and much larger human aggregates where intimacy has been replaced by formal role requirements and personal modes of social regulation and obligation have given way to impersonal systems of social control and to communities of limited liability in which egoism and self-interest come to the fore.

Often, the time and space continua have been combined into a single theory. Such is the case, for example, in Tönnies's classic study of *gemeinschaft* and *gesellschaft*, originally published in 1890 and republished with a new introduction in 1931.

Tönnies described it as his purpose 'to study the sentiments and motives which draw people to each other, keep them together, and induce them to joint action' (1955, p. 3). To this end, he drew a basic distinction between what he termed 'natural will' (the sensations, feelings and instincts which derive from physiological and psychological processes and which he believed to be 'inborn and inherited' – p. 121) and 'rational will' (the deliberate, goal-oriented and calculative product of the use of intellect). In common parlance, the distinction is that between the heart and the head. While recognizing that the two types can never be totally disentangled in empirical situations, Tönnies argued that it was possible to distinguish predominant tendencies in human affairs towards one or the other. To the extent that social relationships were governed mainly by natural will, he spoke of '*gemeinschaft*'; to the extent that they were governed by rational will, he designated them as '*gesellschaft*'.

It was Tönnies's fundamental thesis that human societies had changed over time from forms of association based on *gemeinschaft* to those based on *gesellschaft*, and that the factor which had more than any other produced this shift had been the extension of trade and the development of capitalism. Indeed, at one point he characterizes *gesellschaft* as 'bourgeois society' (p. 87). The unity of sentiment which characterizes *gemeinschaft* and which flows from the 'natural' bonds of blood, neighbourhood and religious belief is disrupted by the growth of industrial capitalism which puts in its place a precarious unity based on monetary calculation and the resolute pursuit of self-interest: 'The possibility of a relation in the Gesellschaft assumes no more than a multitude of mere persons who are capable of delivering something and consequently of promising something . . . In Gesellschaft every person strives for that which is to his own advantage and affirms the actions of others only insofar as and as long as they can further his interest' (p. 88). In such a context, the only source of unity is the state, but the modern state lacks the natural authority which characterizes the paternalistic rule of fathers, village elders or clerics in the *gemeinschaft*. Instead, it serves the interests of the propertied class by exercising a formal, legalistic authority which comes to be experienced by ordinary people as alien.

What Tönnies is outlining in his book is a rudimentary evolutionary theory of social change. Indeed, like Marx, he tries to extrapolate his theory of change into the future, for while he recognizes that a return to *gemeinschaft* is impossible, he nevertheless suggests that the association of *gesellschaft* which characterizes modern day capitalism may be developed into a more cohesive and less alienative union of *gesellschaft* through the emergence of worker co-operatives and similar structures which may transcend the individualistic era of competitive capitalism.

There is, however, in this work also a rudimentary theory of social geography (what Bell and Newby, 1976, rightly see as his most mischievous legacy). Thus, not only do *gemeinschaft* and *gesellschaft* appear at opposite ends of a time continuum, but they also appear by the end of the book at opposite ends of a space continuum. *Gemeinschaft*, we are told, is physically located in the house, the village and the town, and it is 'almost entirely lost' with the development of the city (which is 'typical of Gesellschaft in general') and the metropolis (the 'highest form' of *gesellschaft*). As the urban centres grow, so the *gemeinschaft* of the rural hinterland is eclipsed and undermined. Family life and village communalism are replaced by urban individualism and state power which itself carries the seeds of a future development of socialist union.

By the end of the book, it is impossible to disentangle the effects of capitalism from those of urbanism. Change over time has become inextricably interwoven with change over space, for the *gemeinschaft/ gesellschaft* dualism is applied equally to both. The significance of Tönnies's work as regards the later development of urban sociology is that it blended and confused these two dimensions and thereby opened up the possibility of developing theories of urbanism around the classic polarities of nineteenth-century evolutionary social thought. Concepts which had previously been applied to the analysis of different types of societies at different points in time could hereon equally be applied to different types of settlement within the same society at different points in space. The potential for confusion was, needless to say, considerable, and the confusion began shortly after the publication of Tönnies's book when the German sociologist, Georg Simmel, published an essay on metropolitan life which, for all its undoubted insights, hopelessly muddled up the analysis of the effects of modern capitalism with that of the effects of urban concentration. It was to take urban sociology some sixty years to sort out the difference.

The metropolis and mental life

It has often been suggested that Simmel's sociology is highly personal, wilfully eclectic and internally incoherent. However, the wide diversity of his writings does reveal a certain methodological unity and a degree of substantive continuity. The methodological unity is a function of his commitment to formalistic analysis and to the principle of the dialectic (the unity of opposites), while the substantive continuity is revealed in his recurring concern with the questions of individuality and freedom, modernity and the division of labour, and intellectual rationality and the money economy. All of these concerns are expressed in his essay on the metropolis and mental life.

Simmel's methodology was fundamentally neo-Kantian. Like Weber, he believed that knowledge of the world could be achieved only through the active mediation of a knowing subject – that is, through a prior mental process of selection of relevant aspects of concrete reality and of classification of these aspects through analytical constructs. The sociologist, in other words, imposed a conceptual order upon the world in order to understand it.

For Simmel, this order was achieved through the analytical separation of form and content. While the content of specific human actions could be explained only psychologically (the question of why certain individuals choose to embark upon certain courses of action was for Simmel a psychological question), the social form through which they were expressed was a sociological phenomenon. For example, in his analysis of the triad (the forms taken by three-person interaction), he identified three different forms that interaction between the parties could take. One party could adopt the role of referee or mediator between the other two, or could attempt to profit from the conflict between the other two while remaining non-aligned, or could adopt a strategy of divide and rule. These formal possibilities are inscribed in the properties of triadic interaction and may appear in a wide variety of contexts (e.g. interaction within families, within legislatures, between nations, and so on). While sociologists cannot explain why one party chooses to adopt one strategy rather than another (for the mainsprings of action lie in the spontaneity of individual personality), they can analyse the forms which action may take – forms which both facilitate and constrain action and which in a sense take on a life of their own. In this way, it becomes possible to generalize about cultural forms divorced from their specific historical contexts.

Sociology, therefore, is the science of the forms of human association as abstracted from real-world interaction. Just as grammar studies the forms of language rather than what is actually said, and epistemology studies the forms of knowledge rather than what is actually theorized, so sociology studies the forms of interaction rather than what is actually done (see Levine 1971, introduction). Sociology is the geometry of social forms, for its relationship to the content of social action is 'like that of geometry with regard to physico-chemical sciences of matter: it considers form, thanks to which matter generally takes an empirical shape – consequently a form that exists in itself only as an abstraction' (Simmel, quoted in Freund 1978, p. 160).

Simmel's commitment to dialectical analysis emerges out of his methodological formalism, for he suggests that social forms are at one and the same time the means whereby individual actions come to be expressed and the source of constraint upon them. Not only is the individual in society, but society is in the individual. Society (in the sense of the forms of human association) is both the source and the negation of individuality:

Social man is not partially social and partially individual; rather his existence is shaped by a fundamental unity which cannot be accounted for in any other way than through the synthesis or coincidence of two logically contradictory determinations: man is both social link and being for himself, both product of society and life from an autonomous centre (Simmel; quoted in Coser 1965, p. 11).

Social life is thus founded in an irresolvable paradox, for the expansion of society is both the condition of and the challenge to the growth of individuality.

This analysis becomes clearer in Simmel's discussion of the sociological significance of number. As we have seen, the difference between a group of two and a group of three is, according to Simmel, qualitative as well as quantitative. In the dyad, each partner can rely on only one other, and this results in intense commitment to the relationship and to the knowledge that no superpersonal level of constraint is operating. In the triad, however, it becomes possible for the first time for the group to prevail over the individual, for the individual can be outnumbered. 'Simmel put his finger on a fundamental sociological phenomenon: series really begin only with the number three' (Freund 1978, p. 163); for the transition from two to three is qualitative, whereas transitions thereafter are quantitative.

There is, however, another qualitative shift at the indeterminate point at which a small group becomes a large group. In the large aggregate, new phenomena are needed that are not necessary in smaller groupings:

It will immediately be conceded on the basis of everyday experiences that a group upon realising a certain size must develop forms and organs which serve its maintenance and promotion but which a small group does not need. On the other hand, it will also be admitted that smaller groups have qualities, including types of interaction among their members, which inevitably disappear when the groups grow larger (Simmel; in Wolff 1950, p. 87).

The unity of the group is no longer preserved by direct interaction among its members, and the personal and emotional commitments of members of small groups are replaced by formal means of control such as agencies of the law. If custom is characteristic of small groups, law is characteristic of large ones. In the large group, therefore, the individual is more restricted by the operation of superpersonal agencies that confront him and are seemingly beyond his control. However, the individual's commitment to the large group is correspondingly less, for as groups expand, so different social circles begin to intersect and the individuals spread their commitments across each. The result is that the increasing constraint within large groups is offset by the growing area of individual freedom across them: 'The increased restriction is more bearable for the individual because, outside of it, he has a sphere of freedom which is all the greater' (in Wolff 1950, p. 102).

An increase in the size of a social group has implications not only for the scope of individual freedom, however, but also for the degree of individual distinctiveness. As a group expands, so it threatens to immerse the individual within the mass: 'It pulls the individual down to a level with all and sundry' (in Wolff 1950, p. 31). The intellect of the individual is eroded by the emotion of the masses, and social interaction is debased as social life becomes grounded in the lowest common denominator. The larger the group, the more impersonal group interaction becomes, and the less concerned members become with the unique personal qualities of others. Faced with this assault on their individuality, people in the metropolis come to emphasize their own subjectivity, both to others (e.g. by distancing themselves from the crowd by exaggerating their particular attributes or displays) and to themselves (e.g. by adopting a blasé attitude of indifference or antipathy towards others which highlights the distinctiveness of self). In the large group, the individual stands alone – isolated yet rejoicing in the privacy which the metropolis affords. 'When the individual's relations begin to exceed a certain extensiveness, he becomes all the more thrown back upon himself' (in Levine 1971, p. 290). In the large group, the individual increasingly stands alone.

Simmel's work on the social effects of size thus leads to the conclusion that, in a large group (such as the modern city), custom is replaced by formal social control mechanisms, the individual's commitments become extended across a number of different social circles, the scope of individual freedom is increased, the character of social relations is highly impersonal, and the individual's consciousness of self is heightened. Exploration of the significance of number for social life is, however, only one theme in Simmel's sociology, and it is complemented by a second major concern which relates to the analysis of the social effects of modernity. Of particular significance here is the development of an advanced division of labour in society, together with the establishment of a money economy.

The growth of the division of labour in modern societies has three main effects for the forms of human association. First, it fragments and segmentalizes social life. In small-scale relatively homogeneous societies, the individual's group memberships form a concentric pattern; the individual belong to a guild, which belongs to a confederation, etc. Individuals are therefore vertically integrated into their society, and the pattern of association becomes total, enveloping all aspects of their lives. With an advanced division of labour, however, the social circles in which individuals move become tangential to each other, and their involvement in any one of them is partial and specific. As Simmel puts it, 'The point at which the individual momentarily touches the totality or the structure of the whole no longer pulls parts of his personality into the relationship that do not belong there' (in Levine 1971, p. 293).

Second, the division of labour reinforces the self-consciousness engendered by an increase in size. This is because, in a highly differentiated society, the individual is constantly exposed to an infinite variety of changing situations and sensations in which his or her own unique personality is the only constant factor:

The more uniformly and unwaveringly life progresses, and the less the extremes of sensate experience depart from an average level, the less strongly does the sensation of personality arise; but the farther apart they stretch, and the more energetically they erupt, the more intensely does a human being sense himself as a personality (in Levine 1971, p. 291).

The division of labour therefore encourages egoism and individualism.

Third, the development of the division of labour in society fosters an alienation of individuals from the cultural world which they have created. For Simmel, such alienation is unavoidable in modern life (see Mellor 1977, p. 185), for it is the division of labour (and not simply capitalism) which leads to the reification of all humanly-created cultural products.

The world of things that individuals have created thus confronts them as an objective spirit, while the essential creativity of individuals is increasingly impoverished. Increasingly, the objective spirit comes to dominate the subjective spirit: 'The price of the objective perfection of the world will be the atrophy of the human soul' (Coser 1965, p. 23).

These characteristics of modernity are expressed in, and reinforced by, the development of a money economy. Money is totally depersonalized, for its exchange leaves no trace of the personality of its previous owner. It is a leveller, for it reduces all qualitative values to a common quantitative base. It is a source of individual freedom and independence, for the development of a cash economy enables social expansion upon a world level on the one hand, yet individual freedom of choice on the other. It confronts the individual as an objective power. It is, in short, the finest expression of the rationality of the modern world.

We find in Simmel's work, therefore, a recurrent concern with three core themes: size, division of labour and money/rationality. At the risk of some oversimplification, it may be suggested that these three constitute the 'independent variables' of his analysis of the forms of human association in the modern world. It is for this reason that the metropolis assumes a central significance for Simmel, for it is here that the effects of size, differentiation and the money economy on social relationships are most immediately visible and most intensely felt. As Nisbet observes, 'The direction of history is toward metropolis, which for Simmel is the structure of modernism, performing for his thought the role that democracy does for Tocqueville, capitalism for Marx, and bureaucracy for Weber' (1966, p. 308). The metropolis is the crystallization of the objective spirit.

These three variables are prominent in his essay on the metropolis and mental life. According to Simmel, the sheer *size* of the metropolis is significant because it gives rise to 'one of the few tendencies for which an approximately universal formula can be discovered' (in Wolff 1950, p. 416). As we have seen this formula is that larger social circles increase the scope of individual freedom while reducing the quality of relationships with others:

The reciprocal reserve and indifference and the intellectual life conditions of large circles are never felt more strongly by the individual in their impact upon his independence than in the thickest crowd of the big city. This is because the bodily proximity and narrowness of space makes the mental distance only the more visible. It is obviously only the obverse of this freedom if, under certain circumstances, one nowhere feels as lonely and lost as in the metropolitan crowd. For here as elsewhere it is by no means necessary that the freedom of man be reflected in his emotional life as comfort (Wolff 1950, p. 418).

Similarly, the effects of *differentiation* are most pronounced in the metropolis, for 'cities are, first of all, seats of the highest economic division of labour' (Wolff 1950, p. 420). This extreme differentiation is itself a function of size, for Simmel argues (consistently with Spencer and Durkheim) that only large human aggregates give rise to and can support a wide variation of services. Because of this close association between the city and the economic division of labour, the effects of division of labour in terms of individuality and alienation are most clearly revealed there. Individuals are driven constantly to exaggerate their own uniqueness and to 'adopt the most tendentious peculiarities, that is, the specifically metropolitan extravagances of mannerism, caprice and preciousness' (p. 421) in order to gain attention and assert their personality. The change and flux that characterize city life intensify nervous stimulation and lead to greater consciousness of self: 'The city sets up a deep contrast with small town and rural life with reference to the sensory foundations of psychic life. The metropolis extracts from man as a discriminating creature a different amount of consciousness than does rural life' (p. 410). Yet precisely because new sensations become the norm in the metropolis, the individual develops a blasé attitude towards them. As nerves are blunted by continual stimulation, we become incapable of reacting to new sensations with the appropriate enthusiasm and energy. We become 'sophisticated' as a defence against the assault on our senses: 'The finite psyche becomes overloaded with mental images' (Smith 1980, p. 108).

This devaluation of the world 'in the end drags one's own personality down into a feeling of the same worthlessness' (p. 415). Art, technology, science and other aspects of human culture all become devalued and grow increasingly distant from the individual whose creation they are: 'The individual has become a mere cog in an enormous organization of things and powers which tear from his hands all progress, spirituality and value in order to transform them from their subjective form into the form of a purely objective life' (p. 422). Other individuals, too, are devalued and urbanites develop an aversion and antipathy towards others as a shield against others' indifference towards them. Metropolitan life thus becomes impersonal and calculative, and again Simmel points to the contrast with small-town life.

This impersonality is reinforced by the third defining feature of the metropolis, the *money economy*. 'The metropolis', argues Simmel, 'has always been the seat of the money economy' (in Wolff 1950, p. 411). Money is both the source and the expression of metropolitan rationality and intellectualism, for both money and intellect share a matter-of-fact attitude towards people and things and are indifferent to genuine individuality. Metropolities are guided by their heads rather than their hearts, by calculation and intellect, not affection and emotion. 'Throughout the whole course of English history, London has never acted as England's heart, but often as England's intellect and always as her moneybag!' (p. 412). Money also contributes to urbanites' devaluation of the things and people around them, for it is the 'most frightful leveller' in its capacity to express all variations in terms of a single measure of equivalence: 'Money expresses all qualitative differences of things in terms of "how much?" Money, with all its colourlessness and indifference, becomes the common denominator of all values' (p. 414).

In the metropolis, therefore, are found the basic dilemmas of social life. It is here that the struggle is waged by the individual 'to preserve the autonomy and individuality of his existence in the face of overwhelming social forces (p. 409). It is here that the tension is most clearly revealed between the eighteenth-century ideal of the freedom of the individual from traditional bonds, and the nineteenth-century ideal of individuality in the face of the mass. The metropolis is for Simmel the crucible of modern life.

Many aspects of Simmel's work have attracted considerable criticism over the years. He has been attacked for his formalism, for his exclusive concern with the minutiae of social life, for his empiricism and for his assumption of the inevitability of the patterns of social relationships that he identifies (see, for example, Mellor 1977, ch. 5). His claims regarding the invariant relation between size and the quality of social relationships (his so-called 'universal formula') have been challenged, not least by Weber, who argued in the opening paragraph of his essay on the city that 'various cultural factors determine the size at which "impersonality" tends to appear' (1958, p. 65). From our present perspective, however, the basic question to which we must address ourselves is how far Simmel's work constitutes a specific theory of the city as opposed to a theory of social relations in modern industrial capitalist societies. Leaving aside questions of its empirical validity, its theoretical consistency and its methodological adequacy, therefore, we need to consider the extent to which Simmel's approach to the analysis of the metropolis provides the framework for a distinctive urban sociological theory.

Clearly it is a different approach from that adopted by Weber, Durkheim or even Tönnies, for the contrasts drawn by these theorists relate mainly to changes in patterns of social relations over time following on the growth of rationality, the expansion of the division of labour, or whatever in society as a whole. This is not the case with Simmel, for although the distinction between cause and effect is far from clear in his analyses, it does seem that he sees in the metropolis itself the source of at least some of the features of modern life. He does not refer to the city merely as an illustration of the rationality, impersonality and the like that characterize social relationships in the modern era, but rather sees it as a causal factor in its own right in the explanation of such social forms. What is crucial here, and what separates Simmel from the other writers discussed, is his unique emphasis on the sociology of number. The metropolis is above all a large human agglomeration, and according to Simmel's writings on the sociological significance of size, this fact alone should be expected to create different patterns of human association from those found in small settlements such as rural villages. With regard to his emphasis on size, therefore, Simmel's essay does represent an attempt to theorize the city *per se*.

Equally clearly, however, Simmel draws on other factors apart from size (namely, the division of labour and the money economy) to explain the depersonalized and utilitarian character of social relationships in the city, and although these additional factors are, according to his argument, historically associated with the metropolis, they are not peculiar to it or explained by it. They are, in other words, features of the mode of organization of society as a whole. It is because his theory of metropolis includes factors that are 'social' rather than specifically 'metropolitan' that Simmel is obliged to define the city in other than merely geographical or numerical terms: 'A city consists of its total effects which extend beyond its immediate confines' (in Wolff 1950, p. 419). But applying this definition, we soon end up with an equation between the concepts of metropolis and society, in which case the arguments about the effect of size become irrelevant (since society includes both small and large settlements) and the use of the term 'metropolis' becomes redundant. With regard to his emphasis on the effects of division of labour and the money economy, therefore, Simmel's essay cannot be represented as a specifically urban theory.

This latter interpretation of Simmel's essay lies behind Becker's assertion that

Simmel never thought of urbanization as an explanatory formula. . . . On the contrary, the cities that he had in view were exclusively of the kind manifesting an elaborate division of labour, a money economy, a wage system, marked industrialization and other characteristics peculiar to the western world from the fifteenth century until very recent times (Becker 1959, p. 230-1).

But Becker's argument that Simmel was 'really' writing about a particular type of society rather than a particular type of settlement pattern ignores the central significance accorded to the fact of size in his work. When we consider Simmel's essay on the metropolis, therefore, we are confronted with a classic (though unintended) Simmelian dualism, for it is on the one hand an analysis of the city, and on the other an analysis of modern western society.

These two dimensions must be treated separately, yet in Simmel's work they are inextricably confused. As it stands, Simmel's essay on the metropolis appears highly plausible as a description, yet hopelessly muddled as an analysis. Any attempt to develop a theory of the city must be able to include the common essential features of all cities, irrespective of the mode of production in which they are located. As Louis Wirth observed, 'It is particularly important to call attention to the danger of confusing urbanism with industrialism and modern capitalism' (1938, p. 7). It was precisely such a confusion that characterized Simmel's approach, and it was just this confusion that Wirth, thirty-five years later, set out to correct.

Urbanism and ruralism as ways of life

Wirth's paper, 'Urbanism as a way of life' (1938) is arguably the most famous article ever to have been published in a sociology journal. Its intellectual pedigree is explicit, for it reflects on the one hand the influence of Simmel and on the other that of Park. Having said that, it should be noted that it is therefore the product of rather intense inbreeding, for Park was himself a student of Simmel's at Berlin, and his sociology was strongly (though by no means entirely) influenced by Simmel's work (see the introduction to Levine 1971 for a discussion of the connections and disjunctions between Park and Simmel). As is often the case with the products of inbreeding, the essay reflects the weaknesses of its parentage.

In many ways, Wirth's essay can be seen as an extension, modification and development of Simmel's paper on the metropolis (a paper that Wirth described as 'the most important single article on the city from the sociological standpoint' – 1967, p. 219). From

Simmel he derives a concern with the forms of human association in the city, with the dualism between town and country, and with the subjective experience of urban life. Like Simmel, he identifies size as a key explanatory variable, although Simmel's analysis of the division of labour is replaced in Wirth's paper by an analysis of heterogeneity, while the effects of a money economy are dropped from the analysis altogether.

As a student of Park's, on the other hand, Wirth also drew upon some of the insights developed by the Chicago human ecologists as regards the effects of density on human organization and the dominance achieved by the city over its hinterland. He saw human ecology as one of three significant perspectives on the city (the other two being organizational and socio–psychological, concerned respectively with forms of social relationships and personality characteristics), and argued that all three should complement each other: 'Human ecology is not a substitute for, but a supplement to, the other frames of reference and methods of social investigation' (Wirth 1945, p. 488). It was his intention, therefore, to develop a theory of the city that could account for the ecological, organizational and social–psychological characteristics of urbanism. Put another way, he set out to synthesize Park's human ecology and Simmel's analyses of the forms of association and the development of urban personality.

Wirth believed that such a systematic theory of the city was possible but had yet to be achieved (Weber and Park had, in his view, come closest to fulfilling this objective, but neither of their essays on the city provided an ordered or coherent framework for analysis). He was highly critical of contemporary work, which proceeded on the basis of arbitrary classifications of urban settlements – usually that employed by the American census, which defined an urban area as one of a certain population size – for he argued that such classifications were mechanical and unsophisticated and in no way correspond with actual entities. 'What we look forward to', he wrote in a paper shortly before he died, 'is not the piling up of a vast body of reliable, continuous information if this labour is to be largely wasted on a basic system of classification such as we have used up to now. The factor-by-factor analysis of any problem in terms of which rural and urban settlements have shown significant differences . . . leads to sterile results' (Wirth 1964, p. 224). The size of settlement was not in itself of any sociological interest unless it could be shown to affect forms of association: 'As long as we identify urbanism with the physical entity of the city, viewing it merely as rigidly delimited in space, and proceed as if urban attitudes abruptly ceased to be manifested beyond an arbitrary boundary line, we are not likely to arrive at any adequate conception of urbanism as a mode of life' (1938, p. 4).

For Wirth, therefore, the urban–rural dichotomy referred to two ideal types of human community, two basic patterns of human association that characterized the modern age. Different types of settlements were thus more or less urban or more or less rural: 'We should not expect to find abrupt and discontinuous variation between urban and rural types of personality. The city and the country may be regarded as two poles in reference to one or the other of which all human settlements tend to arrange themselves' (1938, p. 3). There is, in other words, a continuum between the urban and the rural, and the differences between any two existing settlements are differences in degree along this continuum (Wirth 1964, p. 224). The important point to note about this is that differences between different settlements have therefore to be determined empirically. The role of Wirth's ideal types is to provide a framework for such analysis which (unlike government census classifications) is relevant to sociological concerns and which can provide the basis for hypothesis formation: 'To set up ideal–typical polar concepts such as I have done, and many others before me have done, does not prove that city and country are fundamentally and necessarily different. . . . Rather it suggests certain hypotheses to be tested' (1964, p. 223).

The hypothesis that Wirth advances is that variations in patterns of human association may be explained as the effects of three factors – size, density and heterogeneity. These three constitute the parameters of his conceptualization of the urban: 'For sociological purposes a city may be defined as a relatively large, dense and permanent settlement of socially heterogeneous individuals' (1938, p. 8). The task for urban sociology is then to analyse the extent to which each of these three variables gives rise to definite forms of social relationships: 'We may expect the outstanding features of the urban social scene to vary in accordance with size, density and differences in the functional type of cities' (p. 7).

It is important to recognize, however, that Wirth emphasizes that 'folk' ways of life may still be found in cities, for previously dominant patterns of human association are not completely obliterated by urban growth, and also to recognize that 'urban' ways of life are likely to spread beyond the boundaries of the city, given the ecological dominance of the city over its hinterland. Furthermore, he notes that technological developments in transport and communications have led to the spillover of the city into the countryside and to a new accessibility of the city to rural dwellers, and that the pace of such changes has 'made such notions as we have about rural and urban likenesses and differences obsolete' (1964, p. 221). All this merely reinforces his argument that the designation of different localities as more urban or more rural is a conceptual exercise, and that while we should expect larger, denser and more heterogeneous settlements to exhibit more urban characteristics than smaller, more scattered and more homogeneous ones, this remains an empirical question which should not be 'resolved' by the *a priori* identification of urbanism with particular physical locations.

Wirth's analysis of the social effects of *size* closely reflects that of Simmel. Thus he develops the familiar argument that larger size means greater variation, and then draws upon the ecological tradition to suggest that this in turn will be reflected in the spatial segregation of different groups according to ethnicity, race, status, occupation and so on. He also suggests, *pace* Simmel, that an increase in size reduces the chances of any two individuals knowing each other personally, and that this leads to segmentalism in social relationships, an emphasis on secondary rather than primary contacts, and a corresponding indifference towards others:

The contacts of the city may indeed be face to face, but they are nevertheless impersonal, superficial, transitory and segmental. The reserve, the indifference and the blasé outlook which urbanites manifest in their relationships may thus be regarded as devices for immunising themselves against the personal claims and expectations of others (Wirth 1938, p. 12).

It is important to note that Wirth does not claim that primary relationships disappear in the city; in his earlier study of a Jewish ghetto in Chicago, for example, he concluded that it formed a 'cultural community' with a communal way of life (1927, p. 71). Nor does he suggest that the urbanite knows fewer people than the country dweller; the reverse may well be the case. All that he is arguing here, therefore, is that in a large settlement, the individual will be personally acquainted with a smaller proportion of those with whom he or she interacts, and that this fact alone explains the development of the social distance that characterizes urban life.

Like Simmel, Wirth recognizes that size engenders a tension between individuality and individual freedom, for a large human group undermines the former while encouraging the latter: 'Whereas the individual gains, on the one hand, a certain degree of emancipation or freedom from the personal and emotional controls of intimate groups, he loses, on the other hand, the spontaneous self-expression, the morale and the sense of participation that comes with living in an integrated society' (1938, pp. 12–13). Life in large groups thus tends to become anomic, and moral deregulation is countered by the development of more formal agencies of control and participation such as the mass media.

The effects of *density* on social relationships are a function of the growth of differentiation. Wirth follows Durkheim and the Chicago ecologists in arguing that differentiation is the way in which any population responds to an increase in numbers in a given area. The effects of an increase in density are therefore clearly related to those of size, and Wirth notes that 'Density thus reinforces the effect of numbers in diversifying men and their activities and in increasing the complexity of the social structure' (1938, p. 14).

Complex differentiation of functions within a human aggregate creates forms of interaction in which people relate to each other on the basis of their specific roles rather than their personal qualities: 'We see the uniform which denotes the role of functionaries, and are oblivious to the personal eccentricities hidden behind the uniform' (p. 14). It therefore fosters an instrumental attitude towards others who are treated merely in terms of the role they perform, and the resulting spirit of mutual exploitation has therefore to be regulated by law and other mechanisms of formal control. However, Wirth also notes that homogeneous sub-groups created in the process of differentiation tend to congregate together in different parts of the city, forming what Park and his colleagues termed 'natural areas'. Predatory relationships within the city as a whole may therefore come to be mediated within different parts of the city by the development of more personal and emotional ties: 'Persons of homogeneous status and needs unwittingly drift into, consciously select, or are forced by circumstances into the same area. The different parts of the city acquire specialized functions and the city consequently comes to resemble a mosaic of social worlds in which the transition from one to the other is abrupt' (p. 15).

If Wirth's discussion of density relies heavily on Park, his analysis of the effects of *heterogeneity* leads him to return once again to Simmel. The analysis of social heterogeneity is couched largely in terms of Simmel's geometry of social circles. Individuals participate in many different circles, none of which can command their undivided allegiance. These circles are tangential and intersecting (in contrast to the concentric totality of the rural community), and individuals enjoy a different status, and perhaps even a different identity, in each of them with the result that instability and personal insecurity becomes a norm. The urban personality easily becomes disorganized, and rates of mental illness, suicide and so on increase accordingly.

Heterogeneity also leads to a process of social levelling in which the individual is subordinated to the mass: 'If the individual would participate at all in the social, political and economic life of the city, he must subordinate some of his individuality to the demands of the larger community and in that measure immerse himself in mass movements' (p. 18). Action, to be effective, has to be collective, and political participation is achieved through representation. The individual is 'reduced to a state of virtual impotence' (p. 22), and official agencies assume responsibility for a wide range of provisions and services on which the urbanite increasingly depends.

Wirth's description of urbanism as a way of life, and in particular his diagnosis of the urban personality, is overwhelmingly bleak, yet neither he nor Simmel could be described as rural romantics. Wirth was as aware of the positive aspects of city life as he was of the negative aspects of the countryside. Nevertheless, his work did serve to bring social theory closer to the rural nostalgia and virulent anti-urbanism that has been so characteristic of western culture, for his description of urban life as anonymous, impersonal, superficial, instrumental and so on was entirely consistent with the imagery portrayed in English novels and poetry for generations. The difference, of course, is that Wirth deduced these characteristics from an analysis of the sociological significance of three variables, and thereby established the traditional imagery of the city in the form of a hypothesis: 'The deductive inferences sound plausible, principally because they point to the characteristics that have for so long been accepted as typically urban' (Reissman 1964, p. 143). As with Simmel's work. Wirth's essay appears intuitively plausible as a description of city life, but the question, as we shall see, is whether his simple explanation in terms of the necessary effects of size, density and heterogeneity does in fact account for the phenomena he describes.

Support for Wirth's thesis came just three years after the publication of his essay from another of Park's students, Robert Redfield. Redfield (1941) studied four communities in the Yucatan peninsula of Mexico, ranging from the small, homogeneous and very isolated settlement at Tusik to the largest town in the region, Merida.

On the basis of this study, he argued that the less isolated and more heterogeneous the settlement, the more it became characterized by cultural disorganization, secularization and the growth of individualism. On the basis of this and other studies, Redfield (1947) then proceeded to develop an ideal type of the 'folk society' which complemented Wirth's analysis by identifying the cultural characteristics of communities at the other end of the rural–urban continuum.

According to Redfield, 'Folk societies have certain features in common which enable us to think of them as a type – a type which contrasts with the society of the modern city' (1947, p. 293). He saw the city as a 'vast complicated and rapidly changing world' (p. 306), and contrasted this with the folk society as 'small, isolated, non-literate and homogeneous with a strong sense of group solidarity' (p. 297). The ideal type folk society was small, isolated, intimate, immobile, pre-literate, homogeneous and cohesive. It had only a rudimentary division of labour based mainly on a rigid differentiation of sex roles; the means of production were shared; and economic activity was contained within the community. The culture of the folk society was strongly traditional and uncritical. It was grounded in social bonds based upon kinship and religion, and its internal coherence derived from custom rather than formal law. Patterns of interaction were based on ascribed status, and social relationships were personal and diffuse. In such relationships, added Redfield somewhat wistfully, 'There is no place for the motive of commercial gain' (p. 305).

Taken together, the work of Wirth and Redfield exhibits two main themes. The first is that patterns of human relationships can be conceptualized in terms of a pair of logically opposite ideal types (the contents of which are open to discussion) such that any empirical case can be located at some point between them and compared with other cases against some purely conceived yardstick of urbanism or ruralism. It should be noted that the characterization of the ideal types themselves is variable, for some researchers may choose to emphasize one aspect while others may select other aspects. It is not a valid criticism of Wirth's approach to suggest that cities exhibit certain features that are different from those he identified in his paper, for Wirth's characterization of urbanism is a logical construct, not an empirical description. It is a construct designed to facilitate empirical research on actual cities by providing a conceptual criterion of urbanism, and like all ideal types, it may therefore be evaluated in terms of its usefulness but not its empirical validity.

Wirth's paper, of course, attempts to go beyond a simple exercise in conceptualization and to develop an explanation of empirical variations in ways of life between different settlements. This provides the second theme to emerge out of his and Redfield's work: namely that variations in patterns of human relationships between different communities are to be explained in terms of differences in their size and density, their degree of internal homogeneity, and the extent of their isolation from other centres of population.

The first of these themes is therefore a concern with conceptualization, while the second is an attempt at explanation. It follows that this line of work has to be evaluated on two levels, for the exercise in conceptualization may be assessed only in terms of its logical consistency and its fruitfulness for empirical research, while the attempt at explanation has to be examined in terms of its theoretical adequacy. Unfortunately, as we shall now see, much of the subsequent work that has claimed to refute Wirth has failed to recognize this distinction.

'Real but relatively unimportant'

Just as the critics of the Chicago school in the 1930s were led up an empiricist blind alley by attempting to refute Burgess's concentric zone model of urban growth while ignoring the theoretical adequacy of the ecological postulates that lay behind it, so too much of the debate over Wirth's thesis since the war has been theoretically sterile. There is now, as Pahl points out, 'an almost overwhelming body of evidence that the central areas of cities differ from what Wirth and many others have suggested' (Pahl 1968, p. 267). Yet such evidence is of only marginal relevance to an evaluation of Wirth's theory, for it has generally been cited as part of an ultimately misguided and futile attempt to refute an ideal type with empirical data.

Such evidence falls mainly into two categories. The first concerns those studies (e.g. Young and Willmott 1957, Gans 1962, Abu-Lughod 1961) that have documented the existence of 'rural' ways of life (such as close kinship links or personal friendships among neighbours) in the centre of large cities (in the case of these writers, London, Boston and Cairo respectively). There is now a lot of evidence from a lot of different cities which indicates that what Gans terms 'urban villages' are fairly common, and that Wirth's description of urban ways of life in terms of anonymity, impersonality and so on is not applicable to them.

The second category of evidence concerns studies that have documented 'urban' ways of life in the countryside. Mann (1965, p. 106) provides one such example when he suggests that the residents of the small Sussex village of Forest Row exhibit more 'urban' characteristics in terms of sophistication and a blasé attitude than do the inhabitants of a northern town such as Huddersfield. More pertinently, Lewis (1951) studied the same Mexican village of Tepoztlan that Redfield had studied twenty years earlier (and from which he had derived many of his original conceptions regarding folk society) and found not 'rural' harmony, tranquility and consensus, but rather a 'pervading quality of fear, envy and distrust in inter-personal relations' (p. 429).

Two points need to be made about these and other similar studies. The first is that, despite the claims often made for them, they are not necessarily inconsistent with Wirth's characterization of urban and rural types. Evidence on the existence of urban villages and what Abu-Lughod terms the 'ruralization of the city' is encompassed by Wirth's argument that one effect of increased density is precisely the creation of a 'mosaic of social worlds' in which groups of similar race, class, status, etc., congregate. Similarly, studies of rural areas that find elements of urban culture can readily be explained in Wirth's approach as the result of the dominance achieved by the city over its hinterland. It is a source of some surprise, therefore, that evidence like this has so often been used in an attempt to counter the description of city life that Wirth provides.

The second point is that, even if such data were not consistent with the image of urban life that Wirth presents, they would not constitute a refutation of his theory, but only a criticism of the usefulness of his concepts. As Sjoberg has recognized, 'We must not confuse an analytical distinction with empirical reality' (1964, p. 131). To repeat once again, Wirth did not argue that ways of life in cities were necessarily anonymous, superficial, transitory and segmental; only that it was in terms of such characteristics that he wished to conceptualize the notion of urbanism. If Bethnal Green is not like that then, from this perspective, Bethnal Green is not highly urban (though from another perspective, such as one that conceptualized urbanism in terms of atmospheric pollution or mileage of made-up roads, it clearly would be).

This, however, does raise the first significant question-mark against Wirth's approach, in that we may validly ask how useful or fruitful such a conceptualization of the urban really is. We cannot disprove an ideal type, but if we doubt its relevance to empirical research we are most certainly justified in ignoring it.

One problem with his conceptualization of the urban, and with the very notion of a continuum between two ideal types of urban and rural, is that it is indiscriminate. This has been recognized both by those who defend an approach based on rural–urban distinctions (e.g. Miner 1952, Jones 1973) and by those, such as Lewis, who attack it. The problem is that many different variables are clustered together at each pole of the continuum, but it cannot be assumed that they are all interdependent and that they will all vary consistently with each other. Lewis, for example, suggests that it is logically and empirically possible for a society to exist with both a high degree of homogeneity and of individualism, and he concludes that 'The concept "urban" is too much of a catchall to be useful for cultural analysis' (1951, p. 434). This argument was subsequently reinforced by Duncan (1957), who showed not only that 'urban' and 'rural' characteristics did not always vary consistently with each other, but also that they did not even exhibit a continuous gradation.

A second problem with this mode of conceptualization, also noted by Lewis, is that it appears too narrow to be useful. Thus Lewis accounted for much of the difference between his and Redfield's descriptions of Tepoztlan in terms of the limitations imposed upon the scope of Redfield's observation by his commitment to the organizing principle of the folk–urban continuum. According to him, the process of change in Mexican society is far too complex to be reduced to a single principle: 'There is no single formula which will explain the whole range of phenomena' (Lewis 1951, p. 445). Of course, Weber argued when he developed the ideal type as the distinctive method of sociological analysis that an all-embracing view of the social world was impossible, and that it was precisely the function of an ideal type to identify and isolate those aspects of reality that the researcher found most relevant to his or her concerns. Lewis's argument is that the use of urban and folk types fails to identify the most significant aspects for study.

A third criticism concerns not so much the usefulness of the concepts of urban and rural as their evaluative character. To quote Lewis's critique of Redfield once again, 'Again and again in Redfield's writings there emerges the value judgement that folk societies are good and urban societies bad. It is assumed that all folk societies are integrated while urban societies are the great disorganizing force' (1951, p. 435). This is a common criticism made against those who employ rural–urban contrasts, although it appears less applicable in the case of Wirth (who was careful to point to the positive aspects of urbanism, especially the growth of individual freedom, as well as its negative side) than it does to Redfield. Without wishing to enter the long debate over value-freedom in the social sciences (which I have discussed briefly in Saunders 1979, pp. 338–46), it should nevertheless be noted that the ideal type method is inherently evaluative (see Chapter 1). The decision to emphasize certain aspects of 'urbanism' and to ignore others is a decision that is necessarily grounded in value, and while we may wish to take issue with the values that guide and interpret work such as that by Redfield or Wirth, it is hardly a valid criticism to attack them for an evaluative bias *per se*.

Despite these various criticisms, therefore, it may be suggested that the main problems with Wirth's approach concern not his mode of conceptualization but the adequacy of his theoretical explanation. The problem here is that Wirth fails to demonstrate that size, density and heterogeneity are the key determinants of the ways of life he describes; both Morris (1968) and Reissman (1964) argue that the same characteristics could be deduced from many other variables that are similarly commonly associated with cities (for example technology, economic rationality and so on). This line of criticism has been developed most fully by Gans and Pahl.

Gans levels three fundamental criticisms against Wirth's analysis:

First, the conclusions derived from a study of the inner city cannot be generalised to the entire urban area. Second, there is as yet not enough evidence to prove – nor, admittedly, to deny – that number, density and heterogeneity result in the social consequences which Wirth proposed. Finally, even if the causal relationship could be verified, it can be shown that a significant proportion of the city's inhabitants were, and are, isolated from these consequences by social structures and cultural patterns which they either brought to the city, or developed by living in it (Gans 1968, pp. 98–9).

Of these three points, the third is ultimately most significant.

Gans illustrates his first point, concerning Wirth's spurious generalization from statements about the inner city to a theory of the city as a whole, by citing evidence on social relationships in outer city and suburban areas which shows that ways of life in these areas, though not entirely intimate, are nevertheless not entirely anonymous and impersonal either. Gans then coins the term 'quasi-primary' to describe these relationships in which 'interaction is more intimate

than a secondary contact, but more guarded than a primary one'
(1968, p. 104).

His second point, which relates to the dubious adequacy of size,
density and heterogeneity as explanatory variables in those cases
where ways of life do approximate Wirth's ideal type of urbanism, is
developed by arguing that the key characteristic of parts of the inner
city is their residential instability, and that this factor (which itself
gives rise to heterogeneity) constitutes a more adequate explanation
than Wirth's three variables:

> Under conditions of transience and heterogeneity, people interact only in
> terms of the segmental roles necessary for obtaining local services. Their
> social relationships thus display anonymity, impersonality and superficiality.
> The social features of Wirth's concept of urbanism seem therefore to be a
> result of residential instability, rather than of number, density or heterogeneity
> (Gans 1968, p. 103).

The important implication of this argument is that 'urban' ways of life
may be expected to develop wherever there is residential instability,
irrespective of whether it occurs in the city or in the countryside.
Gans's second point therefore throws into doubt the validity of any
attempt to develop a theory of the city in order to account for ways of
life found within it, and it is this theme that is developed more fully by
his third point.

His third argument is that, even if Wirth's three variables could be
shown to affect the quality of social relationships, this can be the case
only where certain social and cultural factors obtain. To illustrate this
point, he distinguishes between five types of inner city residents, all
of whom live in densely populated and socially heterogeneous
surroundings. The cosmopolites, such as students, intellectuals and
professionals, choose to live in the inner city because of its proximity
to the cultural centre. Young unmarrieds and childless couples, on the
other hand, tend to live there until they start a family, at which point
they remove to the suburbs. Both of these first two groups therefore
reside in the inner city by choice but are largely detached from it,
either because their interests lie outside their immediate environment,
or because they are located there only temporarily. The third group is
the urban villagers, who are in, but not of, the city, and who form a
relatively self-contained and homogeneous enclave within which
ways of life continue relatively unaffected by the surrounding urban
environment. Like the first two groups, therefore, they too remain
virtually immune from the effects Wirth described. Only the last two

groups – the deprived (who are forced by their material circumstances to live in inner-city slum areas) and the trapped (usually elderly people who remain behind in deteriorating inner neighbourhoods) – are susceptible to the sorts of factors Wirth analysed, for they are not detached from their surrounding environment.

What emerges from this argument is that, even in the inner city, many residents enjoy a choice as regards their physical location and the way of life they adopt, and that, the greater the choice available, the less significant do Wirth's three variables become. Gans therefore shifts analysis of social relationships in the city from identification of the determinants of ways of life to the study of choice as a way of life. In this way, he suggests that the most significant factors explaining variations in social relationships are the sociological variables of class and life-cycle: 'If people have an opportunity to choose, these two characteristics will go far in explaining the kinds of housing and neighbourhoods they will occupy and the ways of life they will try to establish within them' (p. 111).

For Gans, then, where people do not enjoy choice their ways of life will reflect the degree of residential instability of their neighbourhoods, and where they do social patterns will be a function of factors such as class and life-cycle. In neither case will size, density and heterogeneity appear as particularly significant explanatory variables. It follows from this that the explanation of social and cultural forms in the city cannot be accomplished through an analysis of inherent characteristics of the city: 'If ways of life do not coincide with settlement types, and if these ways are functions of class and life-cycle stage rather than of the ecological attributes of the settlement, a sociological definition of the city cannot be formulated. ... The sociologist cannot, therefore, speak of an urban or suburban way of life' (pp. 114–15).

This conclusion is reasserted by Pahl, who argues that the explanation of social patterns in any given locality can be achieved only through analysis of social structure. Concepts of urban and rural thus appear of little value as analytical frameworks, and are positively misleading when used as explanatory variables: 'It is clear it is not so much communities that are acted upon as groups and individuals at particular places in the social structure. Any attempt to tie particular patterns of social relationships to specific geographical milieux is a singularly fruitless exercise' (Pahl 1968, p. 293).

Pahl therefore agrees with Gans that social relationships have to be explained with reference to sociological factors, and that geographical and environmental theories are essentially misconceived. However, he also takes Gans's argument several stages further, first by pointing to factors other than class and life-cycle which must be taken into account in any analysis (e.g. divisions between traditional residents and newcomers and the different patterns of social networks between locals and cosmopolitans), and second by indicating the direction in which urban sociology should develop. For Pahl, local social processes are important in affecting people's lives, and what Stacey (1969) later termed 'local social systems' are therefore an important area of study. But both Pahl and Stacey emphasize that the analysis of localities must take into account the relationship that exists between them and the wider society, for 'in any locality study some of the social processes we shall want to consider will take us outside the locality' (Stacey 1969, p. 145). It follows from this that the important distinction around which research should be oriented concerns not whether a particular locality is 'urban' or 'rural', but rather the relationship between the local and the national: 'I can find little universal evidence of a rural–urban continuum, which even as a classificatory device seems to be of little value. Of much greater importance is the notion of a fundamental distinction between the local and the national' (Pahl 1968, p. 285). As we shall see in Chapter 4, this distinction lies at the heart of Pahl's subsequent attempt to specify a distinctive area of interest for urban sociology, for he argues that 'Since people will always have their lives shaped by a combination of national and local influences and processes, a sub-discipline will continue – and this implies a convergence between rural and urban sociology – under whatever name' (p. 287). It is Pahl's view, in other words, that while an urban sociology cannot be founded upon the notion of a distinctive urban culture, there is nevertheless a conceptual space for a sub-discipline which focuses upon the combination of local and national processes and their effects on individuals' life chances.

Before we proceed to consider this claim in the next chapter, we should however pause to consider two final questions regarding the arguments discussed in this. The first is why, if the rural–urban distinction is essentially spurious, it nevertheless occupies such a central place in western culture? Ideas like this cannot achieve dominance in people's conceptions of their world unless they are in some way related to aspects of their everyday experience of that world. So we must ask to what, if anything, does the urban–rural dichotomy refer? Second, and in part related to this, we should also consider whether physical factors such as the size of human settlements are really totally irrelevant to an understanding of different patterns of social relationships, for there is a danger in following the critiques offered by writers such as Gans and Pahl that we throw the (albeit small) baby out with the bathwater.

On the question of why rural–urban imagery remains so pervasive in western culture, we can do no better than refer to Williams's argument in the final chapter of *The Country and the City* (1973). Williams suggests that the resilience of this imagery points to a real division in our experience and to a fundamental need which that division creates: 'Clearly the contrast of country and city is one of the major forms in which we become conscious of a central part of our experience and of the crises of our society ... the persistence indicates some permanent or effectively permanent need, to which the changing interpretations speak' (1973, p. 289). It is through reference to the physical forms of the country and the city that 'experience finds material which gives body to the thoughts' (p. 291).

According to Williams, the experience from which this imagery derives and to which it relates is that of social relationships in a capitalist society. Capitalism divorces a necessary materialism from a necessary humanity, and this division is expressed, not only in the dichotomy of work and leisure, week and weekend, society and individual, but also in that between town and country:

> The pull of the idea of the country is towards old ways, human ways, natural ways. The pull of the idea of the city is towards progress, modernisation, development. In what is then a tension, a present experienced as tension, we use the contrast of country and city to ratify an unresolved division and conflict of impulses, which it might be better to face on its own terms (Williams 1973, p. 297).

Leading our everyday lives in the context of a capitalist mode of production, we come to accept as normal the 'modes of detached, separated, external perception and action: modes of using and consuming rather than accepting and enjoying people and things' (p. 298). Alienation is the accepted condition. Yet elements of the suppressed humanity remain – in childhood memories, in occasional communality when collectively we are threatened, and so on. It is this recurring sense that 'one is not necessarily a stranger and an agent, but can be a member, a discoverer, in a shared source of life' (p. 298) which becomes displaced into the representation of the country and the subsequent antithesis between it and the town: 'Unalienated experience is the rural past and realistic experience is the urban future' (p. 298). The rural–urban contrast is therefore the ideology through which we live and interpret our alienated existence under capitalism. It follows from this, of course, that those sociological theories that are premised upon this contrast are themselves in their function 'ideological' (see Chapter 5).

This need not imply, however, that these theories have no basis in reality. It is one thing to argue that differences in the size and density of human settlements cannot provide an adequate explanation for variations in ways of life, but quite another to conclude from that that they are therefore irrelevant. Simmel's analysis of the changes wrought by an increase in the size of any human aggregate undoubtedly has some validity, and Gans appears to recognize this when he notes that social differences between residents cannot entirely account for variations in social patterns which 'must therefore be attributed to features of the settlement' (Gans 1968, p. 112). Similarly Pahl (1968, p. 273) notes that status group interaction will tend to be more marked in a small settlement, while elsewhere (1975, p. 91) he lists some of the significant differences in life chances (e.g. in terms of availability of local services, the range of occupational choice and so on) between urban and rural areas which follow directly from the differences between them in terms of population density. While we are surely right to reject the division between rural and urban cultures as the basis for an urban social theory, it does nevertheless appear that there are certain differences between them that can be explained in terms of factors such as size and density.

What is basically at fault with the theories of Simmel, Wirth, Redfield and other similar writers is not that they chose to focus their attention on, say, the question of how size affects the pattern of social relationships, but that they failed to recognize the very limited scope of such an approach and in consequence attempted to explain a wide range of culturally variable phenomena through an illegitimate physical reduction. As Dewey recognized some years ago, 'The inclusion of both population and cultural bases in the term "urbanism" renders it useless except for labelling time-bound phenomena' (1960, p. 64).

Dewey argues that, other things being equal, variations in the size of human settlements do tend to be reflected in the degree of anonymity, differentiation, heterogeneity, impersonality and universalism of social relationships within them, but that the sorts of cultural factors that have been identified by various writers as 'urban' or 'rural' have nothing to do with size:

There is no such thing as urban culture or rural culture, but only various culture contents somewhere on the rural–urban continuum. The movement of zoot suits, jass and antibiotics from city to country is no more a spread of urbanism than is the transfer or diffusion of blue jeans, square dancing and tomatoes to the cities a movement of ruralism to urban centres (Dewey 1960, p. 65).

If Dewey's argument is accepted, then it does seem that we should draw back a little from Pahl's somewhat sweeping assertion that the analysis of social relationships in terms of physical location is a singularly fruitless exercise. The size and density of settlement does have some effect on patterns of social relationships and, indeed, on the distribution of life chances. However, it also follows from Dewey's analysis that the scope of these effects is limited, for it does not take us very far to suggest that anonymity is more characteristic of life in cities than of life in small rural settlements, or that social differentiation tends to be more marked in large towns than in small villages. As Dewey observes, 'No evidence suggests that these concepts can acquire more than incidental importance in the understanding of the complexities of human relations in cities or hamlets' (1960, p. 66). Furthermore, 'It may occur to one that, if this be all that there is to the rural–urban continuum, it is of minor importance for sociology. He would be quite correct' (p. 66).

The most judicious conclusion, then, would appear to be that, while there is no distinctively urban culture and thus no basis in the work of Simmel or Wirth for development of a specifically urban social theory, it is nevertheless possible to identify a small range of questions in which the issue of population size and density remains pertinent. It is, however, doubtful whether such questions can constitute the basis for a specific theory or sub-discipline, for not only are the social implications of size very limited, but it may also be suggested that any attempt to analyse them will involve not an urban theory but a social–psychological theory in which spatial factors are taken into account as one among several variables. In other words, the size of human settlements is just one factor among many which may have some effect on the pattern of social relationships, and there appears little justification for isolating it as the object of intensive and specialized study. It is for this reason that we may endorse Dewey's argument that the effects identified by cultural theories of urban–rural differences are 'real but relatively unimportant'.

4   The urban as a socio-spatial system

For many years following the Second World War, urban sociology was unmistakably in decline as it became increasingly isolated from developments within the discipline as a whole. Following the demise of Chicago ecology and the lingering but finally inevitable collapse of the rural–urban continuum, urban sociology staggered on as an institutionally recognized sub-discipline within sociology departments, yet its evident lack of a theoretically specific area of study resulted in a diverse and broad sweep across a range of concerns that shared nothing in common save that they could all be studied in cities. Urban sociology became the study of everything that happened in 'urban' areas – changing patterns of kinship, political controversies over land use, educational deprivation among the working class, social isolation in council tower blocks – and it therefore became indistinct from the sociological analysis of advanced, industrial capitalist societies. The 'urban' was everywhere and nowhere, and the sociology of the urban thus studied everything and nothing. As Pahl observed, 'It is as if sociologists cannot define urban without a rural contrast: when they lose the peasant they lose the city too' (1975, p. 199).

Given this context, it is not surprising that urban sociologists (in Britain at least) reacted with considerable enthusiasm and not a little gratitude to the publication in 1967 of a book that aimed partly to contribute to the sociology of race relations, but which also set out to develop a new sociological approach to the analysis of the city. *Race, Community and Conflict*, written by John Rex and Robert Moore, reported a study of housing and race relations in an inner-city area of Birmingham called Sparkbrook. In it they developed a theoretical framework which represented a fusion between Burgess's work in Chicago on the zone of transition and Weber's sociological emphasis on the meaningful actions of individuals, and in this way they laid the foundations for an urban sociology which could retain its distinctive concern with the spatial dimension to social relationships while at the same time drawing upon a body of theory located within mainstream sociology in order to analyse such relationships.

Spatial structure and social structure

For Rex and Moore, the significance of the Chicago school in general, and of the work of Burgess in particular, lies in their recognition that, in the course of its historical development, the city becomes differentiated into distinct sub-communities which are spatially segregated into various zones or sectors, and which are associated with particular types of residents who collectively exhibit particular kinds of culture. Rex and Moore take this insight as the starting point for their theory of the city, and they suggest that 'In the initial settlement of the city, three different groups, differentially placed with regard to the possession of property, become segregated from one another and work out their own community style of life' (1967, p. 8). These three groups are, first, the upper middle-class, who own relatively large houses located near the cultural and business centre but away from the factories and other negative urban amenities; second, the working class, who rent small terraced cottages and whose common experience of economic adversity generates a strong sense of collective identity and mutual support; and, third, the lower middle class, who rent their houses but who aspire to the way of life of the bourgeois home-owners.

Like Park and Burgess, Rex and Moore suggest that the process of city growth involves the migration of population from central to outlying areas. In part this is due to the expansion of the central business district, but it is also due to the widespread pursuit of a middle-class way of life which becomes associated with the newly developing suburbs. Thus, while the professionals and the 'captains of industry' move out to detached houses in the inner suburbs, the lower middle class (who can gain access to credit for house purchase) move further out to semi-detached suburbia, and the working class (whose growing political muscle comes to be reflected in the provision of state housing) similarly relocate to a 'new public suburbia' (p. 9). As a result of this 'great urban game of leapfrog' (Rex 1968, p. 213), the various types of nineteenth-century housing around the city centre are abandoned to new users. The imposing homes of the bourgeoisie become swallowed up by the encroaching central business district, while the houses once occupied by the lower middle class are bought up and sublet as lodging houses accommodating new migrants into the city. In this way, inner-city zones like Sparkbrook are gradually transformed into 'twilight areas', characterized by physical decay of short-life properties and by growing concentrations of immigrant populations.

Central to Rex and Moore's theory is their assertion that 'the city does to some extent share a unitary status-value system' (1967, p. 9) in the sense that the move to the suburbs is an aspiration that is general among all groups of residents: 'The persistent outward movement which takes place justifies us in saying and positing as central to our model that suburban housing is a scarce and desired resource' (Rex 1968, p. 214). If suburban housing is widely desired, however, it is clear that it is not widely available. It is a scarce resource, and access to it is unequally distributed among the population. Two key points follow directly from this. First, if desirable housing is in short supply, then the means whereby it is allocated to different sections of the population become crucial to an understanding of the distribution of life chances in the city. Second, it is clear that the pattern of housing distribution constitutes the basis for at least potential conflict between different groups demanding access to the same resource. It was by pointing to the significance of these two questions of access and conflict that Rex and Moore provided urban sociology with a new orientation to the analysis of urban processes; an orientation that was inherently political in the fundamental concerns it raised.

Their analysis of the question of access to scarce and desirable housing indicated the importance of two principal criteria. The first was size and security of income, for it was largely on this basis that those institutions (e.g. the building societies) that controlled the allocation of credit for house purchase determined whether or not individuals could achieve access to the private owner-occupied housing sector. In general, the income criterion could be expected to operate in favour of middle class and relatively well paid skilled manual workers. The second criterion related to 'housing need' and length of residence, for need and residence qualifications were laid down by local authorities as conditions of access to good standard public housing. Thus, in Birmingham at the time of the research, the housing department operated a five-year residence rule which effectively rendered recent immigrants from the West Indies and the Indian sub-continent ineligible for council housing. Furthermore, even those immigrants who could satisfy the local authority's criteria then had to negotiate a further hurdle represented by the housing visitor whose job it was to grade applicants according to their suitability for different qualities of council accommodation, and this often resulted in black families being offered sub-standard short-life housing in inner-city clearance areas. The only other means of access to council housing was by being rehoused as part of a local authority slum clearance programme, and even this channel was often closed off to immigrants as a result of the council's apparent policy of clearing predominantly white areas while leaving areas of black concentration to continue deteriorating.

Rex and Moore's analysis of access to desirable housing thus suggested that, while the white middle class could generally gain entry to the owner-occupied sector in the suburban areas through the market mode of allocation, and while the white working class could usually secure access to council housing on suburban estates via the bureaucratic mode of allocation, there was nevertheless a residual group in the population (in which immigrants were heavily over-represented) that was effectively deprived entry to either of these desirable housing tenures. This third category could not therefore fulfil the general aspiration for suburban life, and was instead obliged to seek accommodation in the inner-city zone of transition.

According to Rex and Moore, the first cohort of immigrants to arrive in the city, faced with their effective exclusion from both the owner-occupied and local authority sectors, were forced either to seek private rented accommodation or to purchase the large deteriorating houses in areas like Sparkbrook which had been vacated owing to the middle-class flight to the suburbs. Because such purchases could not be arranged through building societies, however, they had therefore to turn to alternative sources of finance which entailed their accepting short-term loans at high rates of interest. The high repayments on such loans in turn necessitated sub-division and multi-occupation of the houses: 'Buying a house of this kind was possible only if the owner proceeded to let rooms. Once he did this he found himself meeting a huge demand from other immigrants' (1967, p. 30). Certain areas thus soon became characterized by multi-occupation, and the housing stock began to deteriorate even more quickly. Furthermore, as more immigrants moved into an area, so more indigenous families moved out. In Birmingham, as elsewhere, particular inner-city areas thus swiftly became associated with large concentrations of minority groups living in poor quality lodging houses.

In contrast to suburban owner-occupation, which is legitimated by the core values of a 'property-owning democracy', and purpose-built council housing, which is legitimated by values of welfare statism, such lodging house areas are, according to Rex and Moore, deemed to be illegitimate forms of tenure by radicals and conservatives alike:

'Both unite . . . in condemning the "bad landlords" who operate the system, and also the tenants for their failure to obtain better housing' (p. 40). The response of the local authority is therefore to insulate such areas in an attempt to stop them spreading into surrounding neighbourhoods, and thus to consolidate the formation of ghettos. The local authority therefore acts against the very group – the lodging house landlords – who provide housing for those (like themselves) who fall between the two stools of market and bureaucratic allocation: 'The city, having failed to deal with its own housing problem, turns on those upon whom it relies to make alternative provision, and punishes them for its own failure' (p. 41). Immigrant landlords, who were forced into landlordism because of the lack of alternative strategies for achieving accommodation, thus become convenient scapegoats for the inadequacies of the housing system.

It follows from Rex and Moore's analysis that the twilight zones of the city come to be populated by four distinct housing groups: tenants of nineteenth-century working-class housing, inhabitants of short-life slum property (often owned by the local authority) awaiting demolition, lodging-house landlords, and lodging-house tenants. While there are obvious sources of conflict between these groups (for instance between tenants and landlords over rents, repairs, etc.), all four appear disadvantaged as compared with suburban owner-occupiers and council tenants on purpose-built estates. All four are frustrated in their general desire for suburban living. The effect of local authority planning and public health policies, which are designed to restrict the growth of the twilight areas, and of its housing policies, which function to prevent certain groups from gaining access to more desirable forms of housing, is to exacerbate this comparative disadvantage and to foster the conditions for more intense conflict over the housing issue: 'Any attempt to segregate the inhabitants of this area permanently is bound to involve conflict. The long term destiny of a city which frustrates the desire to improve their status by segregationist policies is some sort of urban riot' (Rex and Moore 1967, p. 9).

The basic social processes within the city therefore relate to the allocation of scarce and desirable housing, both through the market and by bureaucratic means, and to the resulting struggle over housing by different groups located at different points in the housing hierarchy. As we shall see later, Rex and Moore suggested that this struggle over housing could be analysed as a class struggle over the distribution of life chances in the city. In other words, just as class struggles occurred in the world of work with respect to the distribution of life chances, so too they occurred in the realm of consumption of housing.

The significance of Rex and Moore's study is twofold. First, by emphasizing housing as an important, and analytically distinct, area in which individuals' life chances were determined, they located the theoretical concerns of urban sociology firmly within the traditional concerns of mainstream sociology with the sources of inequality and class conflict (see Harloe 1975, p. 2). Second, they showed how the spatial structure of the city articulated with its social organization through the system of housing allocation: 'The housing market represents, analytically, a point at which the social organisation and the spatial structure of the city intersect' (Haddon 1970, p. 118). In this way they laid the foundations for a new approach to urban sociology, although it was left to Pahl to draw out a conceptualization of the urban system which remained largely implicit in their study.

Like Rex and Moore, Pahl argues that the city is a source of new inequalities over and above those generated in the world of work, although like them he also recognizes that wage inequalities are an important factor determining urban inequalities. His argument is that individuals' life chances are affected by their relative access to sources of indirect, as well as direct, income; those who have to travel long distances to work (such as central city service workers who cannot afford to live in central areas) are therefore worse off than those who can choose to live near their employment, just as those who live near to positive public resources such as shops, parks and so on are better off than those who live near to negative ones such as gasworks or motorways. While high wages enable people to buy privileged access to positive urban resources, it is also the case that, in a country like Britain, allocation of public resources by the state is also important in distributing life chances. The task of urban sociology, therefore, is to study the distributional patterns of urban inequalities as these are affected by both market and bureaucratic processes: 'Urban sociologists are concerned with the basic constraints which affect people's life chances in urban areas, in so far as these fall into a pattern' (Pahl 1970, p. 53).

For Pahl, as for Rex and Moore, the city can be conceptualized as a relatively discrete local social system (see Elliott and McCrone 1975, p. 32). This does not imply that the city can be studied independently of the wider society of which it forms a part (the fact that Pahl recognizes that people's position in the occupational structure strongly influences their position in the urban system indicates his awareness of the need to understand the relationship between city and society). Indeed, Pahl has criticized traditional urban sociology for making precisely this assumption: 'Paradoxically, the fundamental error of urban sociology was to look to the city for an understanding of the city. Rather, the city should be seen as an arena, an understanding of which helps in the understanding of the overall society which creates it' (1975, pp. 234-5). Like Stacey (discussed above, page 110), therefore, Pahl's position is that, while the urban system cannot be divorced from the wider society, there are nevertheless important processes within it which can be identified and analysed in their own right.

The most fundamental of these processes concerns the distribution of scarce urban resources. Thus Pahl defines the city as 'A given context or configuration of reward-distributing systems which have space as a significant component' (1975, p. 10). There are three main implications of this approach.

First, space remains an important factor in Pahl's analysis. It has consistently been a basic feature of his approach that space is inherently unequal since no two people can occupy the same location in relation to the provision of any facility. This is why, according to his definition, an urban resource must have a spatial component. Urban sociology does not, therefore, study all allocative or distributive systems: 'Housing and transportation are elements in my view of the city; family allowances and pension schemes are not' (p. 10). The specificity of urban sociology lies in its concern with the patterns of distribution of those resources that are inherently unequal owing to their necessary location in a spatial context.

Given that inequalities in the distribution of urban resources are inevitable, it follows that spatial constraints on life chances will always operate to some extent independently of the mode of economic and political organization in society: 'It is central to my argument that these spatial constraints on the distribution of resources operate to a greater or lesser degree independently of the economic and political order. . . . These constraints can be ameliorated by political intervention but such intervention cannot totally negate their effects' (Pahl 1975, p. 249). Both capitalist and socialist societies are confronted with the operation of this spatial logic, and both may therefore encounter similar problems with regard to the distribution of urban facilities: 'The process of resource allocation has certain common elements no matter what the scale of organization or the specific mode of production with which we are concerned' (Pahl 1979, p. 34). It is for this reason that the results of state intervention in the urban system may be similar in very different types of society, and that the actual effects of policies may fall far short of the original intentions behind them' (see Pahl 1977a, p. 154).

Pahl does not, however, argue for a spatial or ecological determinism, for the second implication of this approach is that, although urban resources will always be unequally distributed, the question of *how* they are distributed is largely a function of the actions of those individuals who occupy strategic allocative locations in the social system. A pattern of social distribution is thus superimposed upon an underlying spatial logic. In the urban system, there are various 'gatekeepers' whose decisions determine degrees of access of different sections of the population to different types of crucial urban resources, and the task of urban sociology is therefore to study their goals and values in order to explain resulting patterns of distribution: 'We agree that certain urban resources will always be scarce and that social and spatial constraints will mutually reinforce one another whatever the distribution of power in society may be, However, given that certain managers are in a position to determine goals, what are these goals and on what values are they based? (Pahl, p. 208).

The third implication of Pahl's approach is that conflict over the distribution of urban resources is inevitable in any society. This is because such resources are crucial in the determination of individuals' life chances, yet are inevitably scarce and unequally distributed: 'Fundamental life chances are affected by the type and nature of access to facilities and resources and this situation is likely to create conflict in a variety of forms and contexts' (Pahl 1975, p. 204). Whether or not this conflict becomes manifest through conscious and politically organized struggles is for Pahl an open question, for distinct patterns of urban inequalities are not always immediately visible, and different groups may appear to be relatively more privileged in respect of the allocation of one type of resource and less privileged in relation to another. However, Pahl does suggest that, in future years, consciousness of common urban deprivations may develop, in which case conflicts between the managers and the managed in the urban system will increase: 'I am not certain whether a distinctive class struggle over the means of access to scarce urban resources and facilities could emerge ... but increasingly political pressure may be less to reduce inequalities at the work place than to reduce inequalities at the place of residence' (1975, p. 257).

These three elements – spatial constraints on, social allocation of, and conflict over, the distribution of life chances in the urban system – together constitute Pahl's framework for urban sociological analysis. For Pahl, the urban is to be conceptualized as a socio-spatial system which generates patterns of inequality in the distribution of life chances over and above the inequalities generated in the sphere of production. He summarizes his perspective in the following terms:

(a) There are fundamental *spatial* constraints on access to scarce urban resources and facilities. Such constraints are generally expressed in time/cost distance. (b) There are fundamental *social* constraints on access to scarce urban facilities. These reflect the distribution of power in society and are illustrated by: bureaucratic rules and procedures [and] social gatekeepers who help to distribute and control urban resources. (c) . . . The situation which is structured out of (a) and (b) may be called a socio-spatial or socio-ecological system. Populations limited in this access to scarce urban resources and facilities are the *dependent* variable; those controlling access, the *managers* of the system, would be the independent variable. (d) Conflict in the urban system is inevitable (Pahl 1975, p. 201).

Taken together, the work of Rex and Moore and Pahl provides a distinctive focus for urban sociology which combines an emphasis on the sociological significance of spatial distribution of population and resources with the familiar Weberian concerns with the goals and values of individual actors and the distribution of life chances in society. In particular, this body of work has served to focus attention within urban sociology on two questions: first, the significance of urban managers as allocators of life chances, and, second, the significance of patterns of urban resource distribution for the development of new forms of class struggle. It is to an examination of these two themes that the remainder of this chapter is devoted.

Urban managers: independent, dependent or intervening variables?

We have seen that, in his original conception, Pahl saw urban managers as the independent variables of analysis. In other words, the explanation of any given pattern of resource distribution could be achieved through analysis of the goals and values of strategically placed allocators and controllers of the stock of scarce and desired urban facilities. Thus: 'A truly *urban* sociology should be concerned with the social and spatial constraints on access to scarce urban resources and facilities as dependent variables and the managers or controllers of the urban system, which I take as the independent variable' (Pahl 1975, p. 210). This position was, of course, entirely consistent with that of Rex and Moore, who identified the actions of housing managers, housing visitors, planners, building society managers and so on as the source of the inequalities of opportunity in Birmingham's housing system.

As regards the identification of crucial urban managers, Pahl's original work suggested that a wide range of individuals, working in both the private and the public sectors, controlled access to key urban resources such as housing, and that the task for research was to discover the extent to which these different gatekeepers shared common ideologies and therefore acted consistently with each other in generating and perpetuating definite patterns of bias and disadvantage in respect to different sections of the population:

The crucial urban types are those who control or manipulate scarce resources and facilities such as housing managers, estate agents, local government officers, property developers, representatives of building societies and insurance companies, youth employment officers, social workers, magistrates, councillors and so on. These occupations and professions should be studied comparatively to discover how far their ideologies are consistent, how far they conflict with each other and how far they help to confirm a stratification order in urban situations (Pahl 1975, p. 206).

This perspective stimulated and encompassed much fruitful research (see Williams 1978 for a brief summary). Some studies focused on gatekeepers in the private sector; Ford (1975), for example, showed how building society managers were socialized into a value system that defined certain types of applicants for mortgages as bad risks; Elliott and McCrone (1975) analysed the motives and values of private landlords in Edinburgh; and so on. Other research concentrated on the actions of political leaders and state employees in local government; Davies (1972), for example, showed how planners in the Rye Hill area of Newcastle imposed their values in the name of the client population; Young and Kramer (1978) showed how the ideologies of suburban political elites in London led them to frustrate attempts by the Greater London Council to decentralize council housing; and so on. Some research (notably that by Harloe, Issacharoff and Minns 1974) took up Pahl's call for comparative research and engaged in analysis of both private and public sector gatekeepers in order to discover how far a comprehensive housing policy was possible.

Increasingly, however, such research encountered two problems on which Pahl's urban managerialism thesis provided little effective guidance. The first concerned the identification of urban managers. Should research address itself to the values and goals of those in the top positions in bureaucratic hierarchies who were formally responsible for deciding policies, or should it focus instead on lower-level employees who actually worked at the interface with the client population? Furthermore, should studies of urban managerialism consider the actions of public sector gatekeepers as more significant than those of individuals in private sector agencies or vice versa? What such problems pointed to was the fact that, although he had urged sociologists to consider the actions of crucial urban managers, Pahl had failed to provide any theoretically rigorous criteria by means of which the relative significance of different types of managers could be assessed. As Norman (1975) pointed out, his identification of urban managers was achieved descriptively rather than analytically. Research grounded in this perspective could thus easily degenerate into mindless empiricism, studying one set of empirically determined urban managers after another with no coherent theoretical rationale other than some vague recognition that they all appeared to enjoy some degree of control over allocation of some resource.

The second problem concerned the autonomy of those managers who were selected for study. Pahl did, of course, recognize that, although they could be treated as independent variables in analysis, urban managers were nevertheless constrained to some degree by the operation of a spatial logic which contained its own inherent inequalities. Later research, however, indicated that the context of constraint was much broader than this. Harloe *et al.* (1974), for example, found that, while the ideologies of those involved in the supply of housing were important in determining their actions, so too were the organizational constraints upon them, in terms both of the availability of resources such as land and finance, and of the limitations imposed on their choice of action by other organizations with which they interacted. What this and other studies tended to suggest, therefore, was that urban managers in the public sector at least were restricted in their actions by the operation of market processes in the private sector (for example, land for public housing had to be purchased at current market prices, finance for such schemes had to be raised from the private capital market at current rates of interest, and so on), and by the organizational structure in which they were located (for example, many areas of policy were strictly regulated by higher-level governmental agencies). Given such constraints, the designation of urban managers as independent variables began to look somewhat dubious.

These two problems of identification and autonomy led Pahl to introduce two important refinements in his later work on urban managerialism. First, he distinguishes between managers in the private sector and those in the local state sector and restricts his definition of urban managers to those in the latter category. Second, he recognizes that local state bureaucrats have to operate under the constraints imposed by their relations with the private sector and central government. In this way, he moves from an analysis of urban managers as independent variables to one that conceptualizes them as intervening variables mediating between, on the one hand, the contradictory pressures of private sector profitability and social needs, and on the other the demands of central government and the local population:

It seems to me that one set of urban managers and technical experts must play crucial *mediating roles* both between the state and the private sector and between central state authority and the local population. Another set of private managers control access to capital and other resources. ... The attempt to focus on the relationship between market distributive systems and 'rational' distributive systems, seeing the urban managers as the essential mediators between and manipulators of the two systems, is extremely interesting (Pahl 1977c, p. 55).

This shift in Pahl's approach is a significant one, for while he continues to see the analysis of the goals, values and actions of local state employees as a valid and useful area of research, he does so only in so far as such an analysis is situated in a broader theoretical framework in which the key variables are the state and the capitalist economy. Thus he criticizes his own earlier formulation for its focus on the 'middle dogs' to the exclusion of the 'top dogs', and for its neglect of the constraints imposed upon public policy by the operation of national and international capitalism. At best, he suggests, local authority officers 'only have slight, negative influence over the deployment of private capital, and their powers of bargaining with central government for more resources from public funds are limited' (Pahl 1975, p. 269). To locate responsibility for urban inequalities and the urban crisis in the actions of local state employees is, he argues, 'rather like the workers stoning the house of the chief personnel manager when their industry faces widespread redundancies through the collapse of world markets' (1975, p. 284). Clearly we have moved a long way from an analysis of urban managers as the independent variables of the subject.

In this revised formulation, therefore, urban managers are significant as allocators of resources, but it is recognized that the initial availability of such resources depends upon decisions made by central government and by those who control investment in the private sector. It follows from this that an adequate explanation of the distribution of life chances in the urban system can be achieved only by combining an analysis of the process of allocation at the local level with an analysis of the production of resources in society as a whole. Put another way, if urban managers are no longer the independent variables, then it is necessary to identify those individuals or groups that are. For Pahl, this entails analysis of the changing role of the state in an advanced capitalist society like Britain.

Pahl's argument is that, in Britain at least (for he denies the possibility of developing a single theory of *the* capitalist state given the wide variations between different capitalist societies), lack of investment in the private sector, coupled with the growing intensity of international competition, has increasingly resulted in a qualitative change in the relation between the state and private capital. Britain, he suggests, is developing into a corporatist society:

In general it could certainly be argued until fairly recently that the state was subordinating its intervention to the interests of private capital. However, there comes a point when the continuing and expanding role of the state reaches a level where its power to control investment, knowledge and the allocation of services and facilities gives it an autonomy which enables it to pass beyond its previous subservient and facilitative role. The state manages everyday life less for the support of private capital and more for the independent purposes of the state. . . . Basically the argument is that Britain can best be understood as a corporatist society (Pahl 1977a, p. 161).

His discussion of the role of the state in the new corporatist society is located firmly within the Weberian tradition of political sociology. In particular it reflects three basic themes in Weber's writings: namely, a conceptualization of the state as an apparatus controlled by individuals with definite aims and motivations; a view of the state's mode of operation in which officials and technical experts are deemed to prevail against elected political leaders; and a commitment to a theory of politics as a realm autonomous of economic class relations.

We saw in Chapter 1 that Weber's approach to sociological explanation rests on the analysis of the goals and values that guide individuals' actions in relation to others. We also noted his ontological commitment to a view of the social world as a moral realm in which individual actors are constantly confronted with choices between irreconcilable values (Weber's 'warring gods'). From these two basic orientations, it is clear that the question of power was central to Weber's entire sociology, for as soon as individuals attempt to achieve transcendent goals (that is, to impose their objectives against those of others), conflict becomes inevitable and power becomes crucial. Thus in Weber's view, power involves the ability of any one actor within a social relationship to realize his or her will, if necessary against the opposition of others. It is, in other words, a function of the relationship between individuals. When the power of one actor in relation to others becomes sufficiently well established that there is a recurring probability that his or her commands will be obeyed by them as a matter of course, Weber identifies a relationship based on domination.

Domination over others may be achieved on the basis of economic power (through control of goods and services in demand by others) or of political power. Weber insisted that these two spheres of domination in society were analytically distinct. He denied the Marxist claim that there was a necessary correspondence between them, for although he recognized that historically those who controlled economic resources often also controlled the instruments of state power, he argued that this did not reveal any historical necessity. While economic power is achieved through control of commodity or labour markets, political power is achieved through control of the state and therefore refers to 'the leadership, or the influencing of the leadership, of a political association, hence today of a state' (Weber 1948b, p. 77). Political power, in other words, entails the pursuit of given goals or values by those individuals who are in a position to control or influence state policies. Thus we arrive at the first of Weber's key principles that is carried over into Pahl's analysis: political domination is autonomous of economic class domination.

The second principle develops directly out of this, for it is apparent that, for Weber, the state is a 'thing' to be controlled by individuals. More accurately, it is a particular type of political association which is characterized by a legally sanctioned monopoly over the use of physical coercion:

Ultimately one can define the modern state sociologically only in terms of the specific means peculiar to it, as to every political association, namely the use of physical force. . . . Of course, force is certainly not the normal or the only means of the state – nobody says that – but force is a means specific to the state . . . a state is a human community that (successfully) claims the monopoly of the legitimate use of physical force within a given territory (1948b, pp. 77–8).

Political domination is therefore achieved by individuals through privileged access to the instruments of state power. In order to understand state policies, therefore, it is necessary to understand the goals and values of certain key individuals. This is reflected in Pahl's argument that the state today manages society according to its own independent purposes. It is also, of course, the logic behind his search for crucial urban managers.

The third aspect of Weber's work that recurs in Pahl's analysis concerns the role of state officials. We saw earlier that, in his reformulation of the concept of urban managers, Pahl came to focus exclusively on the actions of bureaucrats and technical experts who are in the employment of the state. Similarly in his discussion of corporatism, it is clear that Pahl traces the 'independent purposes' of the state to the objectives set by the state bureaucracy through the establishment of various agencies of social and economic planning. This emphasis on the role of the bureaucracy reflects Weber's argument that the growing rationalization and complexity of modern capitalist (or socialist) societies must increasingly be reflected in the rationalization of the state's administration of these societies: 'The question is always who controls the existing bureaucratic machinery. And such control is possible only in a very limited degree to persons who are not technical specialists' (Weber 1968, p. 224).

Weber is resolutely sceptical as regards the claims made on behalf of modern representative democracy, for he argues that direct democratic control over a large and complex state is impossible. Representative assemblies perform just two functions: they are the means for mobilizing the consent of the masses to their own subordination, and they provide the means whereby new political leaders can emerge. Weber therefore rejects the notion of parliaments representing the 'will of the people', and argues instead that the masses vote for leaders rather than policies, and out of emotion rather than calculation. The most successful political leaders are those who have mastered the art of demagogy: 'Democratisation and demagogy belong together' (1968, p. 1450). Elected on the basis of plebiscitary democracy, it is then the task of strong political leaders to attempt to counter the deadening hand of bureaucracy by introducing a spark of creativity into the political process. Political administration in modern society thus exhibits a recurring tension between the official and the charismatic leader, the ethic of responsibility and the ethic of conviction, bureaucracy and democracy, rational administration and value-commitments, in which the power of expertise generally prevails over the power of ideals.

The picture that emerges from Weber's political writings is that of a centralized state imposing goals of efficiency in its administration of ever-widening areas of social and economic life. It is precisely this picture that is developed in Pahl's work on the development of a corporatist society in Britain and which underpins his more recent discussions of the role of urban managers.

Pahl's work on corporatism is contained mainly in two articles (Pahl 1977a and b), although it resonates through much of his writing in the late 1970s (e.g. 1977c, 1979) and should be read in conjunction with papers by Winkler (1976, 1977) who was originally responsible for developing the key elements of the theory to which Pahl refers. Taking all this work together, we may discuss the corporatism thesis in terms of the three questions of the causes, functions and mode of operation of the new corporatist state.

There are basically four factors that explain the increased role of the state in managing the British economy. The first is the growing concentration of capital into a small number of large oligopolies such that the fate of the economy as a whole is now bound up with the fate of a handful of companies. The state must therefore act to ensure that these companies continue to generate an adequate rate of return on investment, but in underwriting their profits it must also ensure that it does not create a 'licence to plunder'. Profits, in other words, must be both guaranteed and regulated. Second, the falling rate of profit in the economy as a whole (which the theory does not itself explain) has resulted in private companies seeking state financial aid as alternative sources of investment dry up. In providing capital (for example through the National Enterprise Board), the state has therefore been able to exert its influence over patterns of investment in the private sector. Third, new technological developments, which have themselves spurred on the process of industrial concentration, have generated new problems which have necessitated further state regulation of, and participation in, the private sector. Research and development costs, for example, have escalated to a point where even the largest companies require state aid, while the social implications of new technology in terms of pollution, public safety, levels of employment and so on have necessarily led to increased state involvement. Finally, as we have already seen, the growing intensity of international competition has led private sector firms to seek the support and protection of the state in their search for new markets and their need to consolidate existing ones.

These four factors have not only resulted in a quantitative increase in state economic activity, but have provoked a qualitative shift in its role in relation to the private sector: 'Stripped to its essentials, corporatism is principally defined by one particularly important qualitative change, the shift from a supportive to a directive role for the state in the economy' (Winkler 1976, p. 103). It is fundamental to Pahl's and Winkler's position that the developing corporatist society represents a mode of political and economic organization that is different from that of both capitalism and socialism: while capitalism entails the private control of private property, and socialism entails state control of collective property, corporatism 'is an economic system of private ownership and state control' (ibid., p. 109).

The change in the state's role from the support to the direction of the private sector thus involves a new set of state functions which to some extent challenge some of the basic principles of capitalism. Corporatism replaces the 'anarchy' of the free market with the order of the rational plan; it substitutes predictability for profit maximization; and it undermines traditional elements of capitalist property rights by dictating uses (such as investment) and restricting benefits. In place of the principles of free enterprise and competition, the corporatist state imposes four principles of its own: unity (collaboration and co-operation between the functional interests of capital and labour), order (stability and discipline in, for example, industrial relations), nationalism (defence of the national interest both domestically, against sectional interests, and internationally, against foreign competitors) and success (the dominance of the principle of means by the pragmatism of ends – notably in ensuring efficiency). Not only, therefore, does the state extend its sphere of economic influence and control, but it increasingly directs the economy according to its own non-capitalist criteria.

The mode of corporatist control is hierarchical but essentially non-bureaucratic in the sense that a premium is placed upon flexibility of administration. The state dictates policy but attempts to find others to carry it out, preferably on a 'voluntary' basis. Thus, for example, agreements are reached with the trade union leadership over wages policy, and it is then left to the union bureaucracies to impose or sell the policy to the rank-and-file. Similarly, planning agreements are secured with the largest companies as the means of controlling the economy as a whole. As Winkler puts it,

What appears to be happening is a formalisation of interest group politics; an institutionalisation of pluralism. And, indeed, within co-optive institutions, the state will have to bargain and make compromises. But the ultimate purpose of such institutions is to give the state some measure of control over what were previously autonomous private organisations (Winkler 1977, p. 54).

The corporatist state is therefore centralized, hierarchical and co-optive.

It is in this context that the role of urban managers – local state officials – has to be analysed. On the one hand, they are agents of a centralized corporatist state, and this leads Pahl to reject the view that they are responsible for the policies that they carry out: 'The previous work on local decision-makers "running" a town overtly or covertly seems curiously inadequate and dated' (Pahl 1979, p. 42). On the other hand, however, it is in his view inevitable that the peripheral agents of a centralized state must enjoy a certain degree of discretion in determining how policies are to be carried out: 'Those who administer these systems of allocation we may term the managers, and generally they have considerable discretion either in determining the rules or in administering the rules determined elsewhere' (1979, p. 39). It follows from this that, while they are certainly not the independent variables in any analysis of the pattern of urban resource distribution, they must be taken into account as significant intervening variables: 'The urban managers remain the allocators of this surplus; they must remain, therefore, as central to the urban problematic' (1975, p. 285).

The argument that Pahl continually emphasizes is that the state, both at national and local levels, cannot be studied merely in terms of the 'needs' of capital. In other words, state policies do not always or necessarily reflect the interests of capital but are rather the outcome of 'managerial bargaining' between agents representing different types of organizations. Like Weber, therefore, he is concerned to stress, first, that political power is not simply a reflection or derivation of economic power but can be and is used to direct, control and influence key economic interests, and, second, that such power has ultimately to be analysed as a function of relationships between individuals:

'Specific *agents* ultimately control and allocate resources' (1979, p. 43). Analysis of political outcomes must therefore begin with the goals, values and practical purposes of those individuals who control access to key resources, and then must attempt to identify the constraints that limit the potential scope of their actions.

In the case of urban managers, this necessitates carrying the analysis beyond and outside the urban system: 'It is no longer possible to consider "urban" problems and "urban" studies separately from the political economy of the society as a whole' (Pahl 1975, p. 6). Thus, by arguing that urban managers perform a dual mediating role between the private sector and the welfare sector on the one hand, and between the central state and the local population on the other (see page 125), Pahl identifies the context of political and economic constraints within which the allocators of resources within the urban system must operate. In other words, not only are their actions limited by the operation of an inequitable spatial logic within the urban system (for throughout his work Pahl has consistently reiterated his argument that territorial inequalities are inevitable in any society), but they are also constrained by the power of a centralized interventionist state and by decisions taken by private sector firms outside it. None of these three factors – ecological, governmental and economic processes – can be said to *determine* the pattern of urban resource distribution (theories that deny the relevance of urban managers are therefore every bit as inadequate as those that assert their autonomy), but all three together constitute the system of constraints within which the actions of urban managers must be studied and understood.

Williams has pointed out that 'Urban managerialism is not a theory, nor even an agreed perspective. It is instead a framework for study' (1978, p. 236). The question, therefore, is how useful this framework appears for empirical study.

The first point to make is that Pahl's whole approach was very much a product of its time. The concern with urban managers was a clear reflection of the context of the 1960s and early 1970s – a period of enormous expansion in state spending on consumption provisions such as housing, health and education, and a time when public sector bureaucracies were growing and professional autonomy and power was expanding. These were the years of massive urban renewal projects when millions of people saw their homes designated as 'slums' and were forcibly removed to system-built high-rise flats by zealous 'evangelistic bureaucrats'; when public services in Britain were fundamentally restructured and 'modernized' through managerial upheavals affecting local government, personal social services, health and the schools and higher education; and when the rediscovery of poverty and the growing fear of racial disturbances led to a variety of interventionist programmes designed to break the so-called 'cycle of deprivation' in the inner-city areas. Against such a context, a focus on urban managers – on the people who seemingly had it in their power to allocate millions of pounds of public money and to determine policy priorities and outputs – appeared not only plausible but crucial if the pattern of urban inequalities of life chances was to be analysed.

Similarly, Pahl's interest in corporatist state theories in the later 1970s also reflected important economic and political developments in British society at that time. Under the 1974–9 Labour government, for example, attempts were made to draw big capital and organized labour into regular negotiation and consultation with government, and the Industry Acts of 1972 and 1975, taken together with the so-called 'Social Contract' governing wages, investment and public spending, seemed to many to herald the consolidation of an irreversible shift towards public sector regulation of private sector economic activity.

Much of this context against which the managerialist and corporatist theses were developed has subsequently changed. The onset of a sustained recession from the mid 1970s, coupled with the election in 1979, and re-election in 1983, of a radical-right Conservative government, led in a few short years to dramatic reductions in certain areas of welfare spending (notably housing), a resurgence of economic liberalism coupled with an outright attack on state planning agencies, and an unprecedented erosion of local state autonomy from the centre. In the light of such changed conditions, we may indeed ask how useful Pahl's framework has been for empirical analysis.

It has immediately to be said that the strong corporatist thesis developed by Pahl and Winkler has been disproved in so far as any social science theory can be disproved. Winkler's brave but, in retrospect, foolhardy prediction in 1977 that 'Corporatist institutions should be reasonably well established in Britain by around the end of the 1980s' (p. 57) now seems faintly ludicrous, but even back in the 1970s, there was probably little evidence to sustain such confident futurology. As various critics pointed out at the time, the planning agreements system introduced in the 1975 Industry Act was effectively toothless from the start, price controls were mainly cosmetic and incomes policies soon foundered on the inability of the union leaderships to police their own rank-and-file. As Westergaard (1977), Hill (1977) and others pointed out, the supposedly new 'corporatist' society did not look very different from the old 'capitalist' one it was said to be replacing. 'Why', asked Hill rhetorically, 'call Britain corporatist rather than state capitalist?' (p. 42).

While rejecting the claim that Britain is developing into a corporatist society, however, it is important to recognize that a somewhat weaker version of corporatist theory may still be extremely useful in contemporary political analysis. In this version (e.g. Cawson 1982, Jessop 1982) corporatism is understood, not as a type of society or even type of state system, but rather as one among several modes through which particular functional interests may achieve privileged access to state power and themselves take on specific responsibilities for administering policies agreed with government. Corporatism as a distinct mode of interest representation and mediation has, it seems, survived the ravages of recession and the anti-planning ideology of successive governments, and flourishes in particular areas of the state system including land use planning (Flynn 1981, Simmie 1981, Reade 1984). The growth of non-elected urban service agencies such as the water authorities, the health authorities and the urban development corporations in Britain from the 1970s onwards has also facilitated the emergence of exclusive corporatist forms. In London's derelict docklands, for example, local residents and trade union groups were kept at arms length by the Development Corporation set up by the government to redevelop and 'revitalize' the area, while various business and professional interests seem to have been closely involved in formulating and executing the redevelopment strategy (see Duncan and Goodwin 1985). Similarly, the non-elected regional water authorities, which took over responsibility for water services from local councils in 1974, have developed clear corporatist strategies in their relations with key users such as farmers, industrialists and developers while participation on the part of domestic and other consumers (e.g. amenity groups) has been little more than token and ritualistic (see Saunders 1985a).

Evidence like this suggests that a modified concept of corporatism may still have a place in the lexicon of urban studies. However, it is clearly important not to over-extend the concept, for not all urban services are managed and provided in this way. In the British health authorities, for example, there is little evidence of corporatist forms, the prevailing pattern here being that of managerial and professional domination within a strongly centralized system in which central government controls the purse strings. And in other areas of urban policy, especially those under the control of elected local authorities, it is still possible for, say, residents, tenants, trade unions or other voluntary citizens' groups to achieve some input and influence. Furthermore, services characterized by one form of control and mediation at one point in time may shift to another pattern at another time, just as the pattern found in one country may vary from that found in another. The point is, then, that corporatism, managerialism and pluralism represent three possible systems for determining urban policy outputs, and we should be wary of any general theory which claims that any one of these is general or universal across all services at all times in all places (I return to this issue in Chapter 8).

Where does all this leave Pahl's urban managerialism thesis? The importance of the thesis in my view lies in its recognition that the state, whether at central or local level, now plays a crucial role in a country like Britain in shaping or influencing people's life chances. Precisely because we are so familiar with its presence in so many aspects of our everyday lives, it is easy to forget just how pervasive the state has become. One-third of British households live in accommodation rented from the state; nineteen out of every twenty children in Britain are educated (compulsorily) in state schools; the vast majority of people rely on the state health service when they fall ill; millions rely on the state-run bus and train services to get them to work, to the shops or wherever; and everyone relies on the state to provide roads and other aspects of physical infrastructure such as water, sewerage, gas and electricity, and so on. In addition, some 7 million people rely on the state for their employment (in local government, the public services, the nationalized industries, etc.) while millions more rely on it for cash benefits such as housing allowances, family allowances, pensions, unemployment benefits, supplementary benefits and the rest. It is the essential strength of an urban managerialist perspective that it asks who, if anyone, controls this vast resource system, how they seek to direct it, and to whose benefit?

Now it is clear that Pahl's initial answer to such questions – namely that the managers of the services represent the 'independent variables' – is crude and naïve. However, his later formulation, in which local state bureaucrats and professionals are seen as playing a crucial mediating role at the intersection of strong cross-cutting pressures – those between the central authority and the local population, and between the private sector and the welfare system – seems altogether more fruitful in that it avoids what Pahl himself came to term the 'managerial heresy' (1975, p. 7). It is no longer true, for example, that 'The managerialist approach, in concentrating on studying the allocation and distribution of "scarce resources", fails to ask why resources are in scarce supply' (Gray 1976, p. 81), for the actions of urban managers are now to be seen in the wider context of relations between government and the private sector. Similarly, the argument developed by Lambert and his colleagues (1978) to the effect that the importance of urban managers lies not in the content of their policies but in the style with which they administer them is not entirely inconsistent with Pahl's later formulation in which managers are seen as juggling the pressures and expectations imposed from above against the demands and aspirations coming up from below.

Yet having said all this, there remains a fundamental problem with this whole approach, and that concerns the limits to managerial autonomy and discretion. Pahl's claim that the allocation of 'urban'. resources can do much to ameliorate or exacerbate existing inequalities arising out of the operation of the labour market represents a seemingly 'obvious' yet nevertheless crucial insight. Sociology has long been preoccupied with the significance of occupational class and labour market situation in shaping people's lives, yet the majority of people in a country like Britain do not engage in waged work (e.g. school students, the retired, 'housewives', the unemployed, the sick and so on), and of those that do, many are still in receipt of significant state support in cash or in kind. Clearly, then, the use of state power and the allocation of state resources is likely to be as, if not more, significant in determining patterns of inequality and life chances as the operation of market power in the formal economic system. Furthermore, Pahl's additional claim that the 'logic' dictating the way this state power is used may be different from that underpinning the operation of the economic system is also crucial and incontrovertible. As Weber recognized, economic or market power and political or state power are analytically distinct bases of domination in the modern world, and although each may influence and set limits upon the other, it is surely fascile to assume that we can simply read off from one the logic which dictates the other. While one is necessarily subject to the operation of what Marxists term 'the law of value' (simply, nothing can or will be produced in the long run which does not generate a normal rate of profit), the other is to some extent subject to political will and human volition (simply, governments may and frequently do commit themselves to providing certain things irrespective rather than because of cost or profitability calculations). In so far as the urban managerialist perspective serves to direct our attention to these often neglected principles, it represents an enormously significant corrective to those approaches which all too often forget that the system of power and domination analysed by Marx over a hundred years ago has been dramatically modified by an unprecedented extension of state power into every nook and cranny of people's lives.

The problem, however, remains that this approach gives no indication of where the power of state managers to shape resource distribution ends and the logic of the capitalist market system takes over. For all its faults, the original managerial thesis was at least clear in the assertions which it was making. But once Pahl recognized (mainly under pressure from Marxist critics) that managers were constrained by the political–economic system in which they were obliged to function, the thesis effectively lost its analytical cutting edge. As Pickvance suggests:

Pahl's starting point was a strong statement that urban managers could be seen as independent variables. . . . But in response to Marxist critics he abandoned this claim and introduced two typologies. The outcome of urban management could now be to narrow, reflect or widen income inequalities . . . and resource allocation might be carried out by urban managers, central government, capitalists or some combination. . . . Whereas there was an underlying logic to the initial claim, viz. that it was the professional ideologies of urban managers that led them to reduce income inequalities, this coherence disappears as soon as the typologies are introduced since they cater for every eventuality (1984, p. 43).

Putting the same point another way, the more realistic the thesis became, the less it explained. Thus it is undoubtedly true that the state at both national and local level is hedged in by constraints, many of which derive from the operation of a capitalist logic in the markets for land, finance, labour and so on, just as it is also true (as we have seen) that state managers may play important roles in allocating some resources while being virtually insignificant in allocating others. But having recognized all this, we end up with an extremely weak form of theory in which virtually everything is found to be contingent. That managers may enjoy *some* autonomy from the dictates of central government and the constraints imposed by the need to safeguard capital accumulation may be taken as axiomatic: the problem then still remains to theorize how far and in which situations this autonomy may be exercised.

This Pahl fails to do. To the extent that he offers an answer to the problem, it is that it is an empirical question to be resolved by empirical research. This, however, is inadequate, for it is a recipe for extremely dubious inductive generalization, the conclusion to which is likely to be no more than the observation that things are different in different places at different times. If we start out on an empirical investigation merely on the assumption that managers are constrained to some extent, then not only will we lack any criteria for determining where to begin looking for the origins of any given policy, but we shall also lack the theoretical means for explaining variations between the different cases we observe. Indeed, Pahl's revised urban managerialism thesis will simply open up without resolving the familiar problem of the receding locus of power: the actions of urban managers can only be understood in the context of national state policy; national state policy can only be understood in the context of the operation of a complex mixed economy; the operation of the economy can only be understood in the context of the world economic system. In this way, the researcher who starts out by trying to explain, say, housing inequalities in Birmingham swiftly ends up by trying to analyse the determination of Middle Eastern oil prices or the impact of American budgetary strategies on the international terms of trade.

The point of this example is not to deny that such 'wider' factors are important – of course they are – but to show how, in an attempt to meet the criticisms made against his original formulation, Pahl's later revisions effectively undermined the distinctiveness of his focus on the urban system as a resource and power system. It was therefore no accident that, having shifted his position on urban managers, he soon ended up studying, not the urban system, but the national political economy. His work on corporatism, in which he attempted (wrongly as it turned out) to analyse what he saw as a fusion of private ownership and state control in the national economy, was the inevitable end-point of what began, much less ambitiously, as a concern with the actions of local authority housing managers, social workers and other strategically-placed professionals and bureaucrats at the local level.

In this transition, any notion of the 'urban' as a distinct object of analysis was irretrievably lost. The simple yet compelling idea which stimulated Pahl's initial approach – that inequalities generated in the operation of the capitalist economy could be modified in crucial ways through processes operative in the urban system – was inexorably eclipsed as he fatally pursued the logic of his own thinking into the intellectual minefield of political economy. In this way, his work met the same fate as that of Park and McKenzie, Simmel and Wirth, before him, as the initial focus on the city crumbled into an indistinct and inevitably confused concern to understand the wider social processes which enveloped it.

The concern with urban management was, of course, just one aspect of the reformulation of the urban question which developed out of Rex and Moore's work in the 1960s. The other, complementary, aspect concerned the new and distinct patterns of social and political cleavages which were seen to arise around the process of urban resource allocation – cleavages which Rex and Moore themselves sought to analyse through their concept of a 'housing class' struggle. If the focus on urban managers eventually collapsed, it is now necessary to trace what happened to this second and related concern with the distinctively urban bases of class formation.

Housing distribution and class struggle

We saw in the first section of this chapter that the fundamental argument developed by Rex and Moore in their attempt to reformulate a sociology of the city was that the distribution of scarce and desired housing resources created new patterns of inequality of life chances that were analytically separate from those arising out of the occupational system. Drawing on Weber's analysis of class and class conflict, they then suggested that, just as struggles over access to wages could be seen in terms of class struggle, so too could competition over access to housing. The central principle of their urban sociology, therefore, was that

There is a class struggle over the use of houses and that this class struggle is the central process of the city as a social unit. In saying this we follow Max Weber who saw that class struggle was apt to emerge wherever people in a market situation enjoyed differential access to property, and that such class struggles might therefore arise not merely around the use of the means of industrial production, but around the control of domestic property. . . . There will therefore be as many potential housing classes in the city as there are kinds of access to the use of housing (Rex and Moore 1967, pp. 273–4).

For Weber, the concept of class, like any other collective concept in sociology, can be understood only as referring to an aggregate of individual subjects. Class is a sociological construct which is imposed upon reality in order to clarify analysis – in reality there are only individuals, not classes, who act – although Weber did recognize that class may, in certain situations, become a meaningful concept for groups of individuals who may therefore come to designate themselves as a class and act accordingly. For Weber, therefore, it is fallacious to argue that classes exist and that 'the individual may be in error concerning his interests but that the "class" is "infallible" about its interests' (1968, p. 930), and this is the first of two crucial differences between his and Marxist approaches. Marx's distinction between a class in and for itself is alien to Weber's sociology; for Weber, class is ultimately only an idea, whether it be an idea used in sociological analysis or one to which groups of individuals orient their actions.

The second major difference between Weber's and Marx's analysis is that for Weber, the concept of class may usefully be applied to the analysis of any situation in which groups of individuals share roughly common life chances as a result of their economic power in labour or property markets. The relationship between employer and employee was therefore only one among several different class situations in which individuals may find themselves, and Weber drew a basic distinction between commercial classes, which referred to groups of individuals who typically shared common life chances as a result of their possession or non-possession of marketable skills, and property classes, which could be identified among groups whose life chances were a function of the ownership or non-ownership of resources that could be used to generate income. Unlike Marx, who analysed classes in terms of the relationship between those who owned and controlled the means of production in society and those who did not, Weber therefore located class analysis in the sphere of distribution rather than production relations, in the market rather than in the mode of production.

In arguing that competition over housing could be conceptualized in terms of a class struggle, Rex and Moore thus drew upon Weber's distinction between commercial and property classes by suggesting that, while power in the labour market was clearly an important factor in determining an individual's power in the housing market (including the mode of bureaucratic allocation), the distribution of housing nevertheless created a situation in which an individual could occupy one class situation in respect of the power to command a wage and another in respect of the power to command access to a desirable house. The formation of commercial classes in the world of work would not therefore necessarily be reflected in the formation of property classes in the city, in which case the task for urban sociology was, first to analyse the distribution of life chances consequent upon the differential power of different groups in the housing system and, second, to study the extent to which these groups come to recognize their common market situation and to mobilize politically in order to defend or improve it.

There was, however, a problem with this approach which was apparent from the outset and which derived directly from Rex and Moore's commitment to Weber's view of classes as distributionally defined aggregates of individuals. This concerned the identification of the main types of access to housing, and thus of the major housing class categories. It is an inescapable implication of Weber's formulation that, if classes are to be defined in terms of common degrees of market power among different individuals, then the number of potential classes that may be identified is almost infinite since no two individuals will ever share an exactly identical market situation. As Weber recognized, 'A uniform class situation prevails only when completely unskilled and propertyless persons are dependent on irregular employment' (1968, p. 302). The problem is thus to construct ideal types of different class situations which are mutually exclusive and relatively unambiguous. This was what Weber attempted to achieve with his concept of 'social class' which referred to a cluster of different market situations between which individuals could move relatively easily. As Giddens (1971) shows, he was then able to develop a model of the class system in which three main social classes were identified, consisting of an upper class with privileged access to property and skills, a lower class with little or no property and skills, and a middle class, comprising those with property but few skills and those with marketable skills but little property. Quite apart from the question of the usefulness of such a formal taxonomy in empirical research where the allocation of different individuals to different class categories is likely to remain a hazardous and somewhat arbitrary process, this mode of conceptualizing the class structure also left unexamined the problem of how the three social classes related to one another. Weber's work on class is descriptive rather than analytical, static rather than dynamic, positional rather than relational.

The same problems recur in the work of Rex and Moore (1967). For a start, it is never clear how the different housing classes are to be identified. At the beginning of *Race, Community and Conflict*, they suggest that the system of housing allocation gives rise to five housing classes: owner-occupiers, council house tenants, tenants of private landlords, owners of lodging houses and lodging house tenants (p. 36). By the end of the book (p. 274), however, they have added a sixth, namely those buying a house on mortgage, and have subdivided the 'class' of council tenants into those in long-life accommodation and those in slum stock. This subdivision was then subsequently represented as a distinct class division (Rex 1968, p. 215), bringing the total number of housing classes to seven, and in a still later study, Rex elaborated on this schema to identify four more classes or subclasses, thereby bringing the grand total to eleven (Rex and Tomlinson 1979, p. 132). Yet there is no reason why taxonomic innovation should end there; for Moore (1977, p. 106) has suggested that two more classes could have been analysed in the Sparkbrook study, Rex (1977, p. 21) has argued that any group (such as one-parent families) that is discriminated against in housing may constitute a housing class, and Pahl (1975, pp. 242–3) has pointed out that the framework fails to take account of large landowners or of local authorities (who are, after all, more significant providers of housing than lodging house owners), both of which could, given the logic of Rex and Moore's approach, be included. There are, it seems, dozens of potential housing classes.

Part of the problem here derives not so much from the inherent pluralism of any Weberian class analysis as from a confusion, noted by Haddon (1970), between the conceptualization of housing classes and their empirical identification. While Rex and Moore's conceptual model stresses inequalities in *access* to scarce housing resources, their various taxonomies all refer to differences in current housing tenure: 'They equate this typology of housing with "housing classes" assuming that, analytically at least, people who are *at the present moment* in the same type of housing accommodation constitute a housing class' (Haddon 1970, p. 128).

In one sense, this criticism does not appear particularly cogent, for although there undoubtedly are some people who continue to live in relatively undesirable housing despite their ability to gain access to a more favoured type (for example the inner-city intellectuals and urban villagers identified by Gans – see page 108), these would appear to be in a small minority, in which case current housing situation may be taken as a reasonable indicator of potential power in the system of housing allocation. This, in fact, is how Rex and

Tomlinson counter Haddon's criticism: 'This seems on reflection to be an unreasonable criticism since the type of housing occupied is a very good indicator of the strength of its occupants in the housing market' (1979, pp. 20–1). Yet in another sense the criticism is highly pertinent, and Rex and Tomlinson's response to it misses the significant point. This is that the theoretical emphasis on inequalities of access to housing should lead in empirical research not to concern with housing groups as the units of analysis, but rather to a concern with different types of social groups. When Rex, for example, argues that fatherless families may constitute a housing class, he is clearly resorting to a very different mode of conceptualization from that employed when he identifies, say, council tenants in slum property as a housing class; single-parent families may be found in owner-occupied housing, on council estates, in rented rooms in the inner city and so on, and they cannot therefore be equated with a particular type of housing in the way in which council tenants obviously can be. Rex and Moore's application of the housing class concept is therefore confused. Indeed, it may be argued that their theoretical concern lies not with *housing* classes, but with different groupings within *social* classes (for instance, blacks, women, one-parent families, etc.) who, because of their peculiar *status* characteristics, experience greater difficulty in achieving access to certain types of housing than do other people who are in a similar market position with regard to the distribution of other types of resources in society. This is a crucial point, for it suggests that analysis of differential access to housing does not involve a sociology of the city at all, but rather entails analysis of the sources of inequality in society as a whole, in which case the distinctiveness of urban sociology disappears. This is the point to which we shall return at the end of this chapter.

A second problem with Rex and Moore's analysis concerns their assumption of a unitary value system in the city in which owner-occupation is valued above renting, council tenancies are valued above private tenancies, and suburban locations are valued above inner-city locations. This assumption was, it will be recalled, central to their theory of the city, since it was the foundation of their argument that the basic urban process was one of conflict between different classes desiring the same type of housing.

Subsequent research has, however, called this assumption into question. Davies and Taylor (1970), for example, report that in Newcastle ownership of lodging houses is positively desired by many Asians as a means of upward social mobility through property ownership. Indeed, no less than 75 per cent of the Asian population who owned the property in the Rye Hill area were landlords, and most of these were absentee landlords (indicating that, far from being pushed into lodging house ownership through lack of alternatives, many recent immigrants were opting for it as a means of capital accumulation). Furthermore, Davies (1972) went on to show that rented accommodation was generally despised by Asians to the extent that none of those interviewed had made any attempt to gain access to council housing and many had resisted attempts by the local authority to move them from inner-city clearance areas into council accommodation. He suggested that renting was rejected as a vulnerable form of tenure and that property ownership was embraced because of the security and opportunities for capital gains that it offered. He also claimed that few immigrants experienced unusual difficulties in gaining access to funds for house purchase: 'I have no evidence at all that the question of colour intruded into the economics of house buying in such a way as to *force* the immigrant into unwanted and oppressive methods of finance' (p. 32).

Further evidence against Rex and Moore's assumption is provided in a study of housing in the city of Bath by Couper and Brindley (1975). They show that one-third of all applicants for council housing in Bath would prefer a central to a suburban location, that one-quarter of all tenants in the city were in privately rented accommodation and would not apply for a council tenancy under any circumstances, and, perhaps most surprisingly of all, that 'There appear to be many people, not necessarily on low incomes, who prefer renting to owning' (p. 567) – indeed, one-half of all tenants in unfurnished accommodation said that they preferred to rent rather than to buy.

Such evidence appears very damaging to Rex and Moore's thesis, although, as Couper and Brindley themselves recognize, there is a methodological problem in such research in that the preferences that people articulate may reflect their (scaled-down) realistic aspirations as much as their ideal choices. Rex (1971), for example, criticizes the Davies and Taylor findings by suggesting that immigrant landlords may claim to have chosen this form of tenure even though they were in fact forced into it, although in the same article he concedes that 'multiple value systems do exist' (p. 297). He then argues, somewhat obscurely, that there may be a dominant value system among the competing value systems in the city, but this does little to rescue the original analysis since it appears that it is precisely those groups living in the supposedly 'undesirable' housing who do not subscribe to the dominant value system on which Rex and Moore founded their hierarchy of desirable housing types. Indeed, in his later research in the Handsworth area of Birmingham, he and Tomlinson have recognized that the desire to move to the suburbs is not prevalent among blacks living in the inner city, and they argue (rather lamely) that this 'does not alter the fact of the existence of housing classes (at least in themselves) since access is in effect denied to those who do wish to move' (Rex and Tomlinson 1979, p. 132). The point is however that, while this may not invalidate an ideal type model of housing classes, it does remove the very factor – competition over scarce resources desired by virtually all city dwellers – that made this model useful in urban research. By conceding that many of those in apparently disadvantaged housing conditions do not aspire to suburban living, Rex has therefore removed the grounds for arguing that the housing classes he identifies are in conflict with one another. As with Weber's ideal types of social classes, we are therefore left with a static positional description rather than a dynamic relational analysis.

In their Handsworth study, Rex and Tomlinson effectively attempted to rectify this by shifting the emphasis of their analysis of distribution of life chances in the city from an exclusive focus on access to housing to one that encompasses education and employment as well as housing opportunities. Their argument is that blacks in areas like Handsworth constitute a distinct 'underclass' in British society owing to the systematic inequalities they experience in competition with whites for jobs and for educational success, and that it is this broad area of disadvantage rather than discrimination in housing *per se* that creates the conditions for conflict. The significance of discriminatory housing policies is that they have created black concentrations in particular inner-city areas which enable the development of political organization separate from the white labour movement. In other words, the process of segregation in housing has produced the conditions – neighbourhood-based ethnic and kin ties – by means of which blacks can mobilize as an 'underclass-for-itself':

Just as exploitation in industry gave rise to the trade union movement and more widely to the Labour movement amongst native British workers, so the fact of discrimination in housing has given rise to partially segregated areas, and to locally-based and relatively effective communal and ethnic organisations which are useful as a means of protecting the rights of minority groups. (Rex and Tomlinson 1979, p. 157).

In this later study, therefore, Rex and Tomlinson argue that situations of common housing deprivation are the means rather than the cause of conflict, and they document the growth in militancy of the West Indian organizations that are based in neighbourhoods like Handsworth. However, although this argument provides a convincing explanation of the sources of conflict, it does so largely at the expense of the housing class concept, for when Rex and Tomlinson discuss housing class mobilization, they are in fact referring to the mobilization of a black underclass on the basis of neighbourhood organization. Indeed, their emphasis on the common situation of disadvantage experienced by blacks in Handsworth in the job market and the educational system leads Rex and Tomlinson to deny the significance of tenure divisions among them, yet such divisions were the very basis of Rex's original housing-class concept. Thus they write: 'Private property owners and renters on the one hand, and immigrant council tenants on the other, have tended to be much the same sort of individual and, to all intents and purposes, we found very little differences in the observed attributes of those housed in the public and private sectors' (p. 144). The key factor, then, is not housing but race, and the focus of concern turns out not to be urban inequality but racial inequality. Once again, therefore, we find that the housing class concept does not constitute the basis for urban analysis but rather points to the need to understand sources of inequality in the society as a whole.

The third major criticism that can be levelled against Rex and Moore's discussion of housing classes is that it rests on a misinterpretation of Weberian class analysis. As we have seen, Weber applied the concept of class to the analysis of groups of individuals who share roughly common life chances as a result of their power in labour or commodity markets (that is, as a result of their ability to realize income from the sale of their skills or their property). He then distinguished between classes and status groups, defining the latter in terms of the distribution of social honour or prestige in society as reflected in different styles of life, and he argued that, while social honour (like political power) was often empirically closely related to patterns of economic inequality, it was nevertheless analytically separated and 'need not necessarily be linked with a class situation' (Weber 1968, p. 932). It followed from this that groups of individuals may come to act either as classes or as status groups, and that collective action on the basis of shared status characteristics could cross-cut class divisions.

Weber summarized the distinction between classes and status groups as basically that between the situation of individuals with respect to the distribution of life chances through the market, and their situation with respect to the distribution of life-styles through the process of consumption of goods and services. Seen in this way, it is clear that the groups that Rex and Moore identify as 'housing classes' are not classes at all but housing status groups. Different types of housing tenure are simply different modes of consumption of housing which may be differently evaluated according to the life-styles associated with them. The class situation of the council tenant with respect to the ability to realize returns in the housing market is the same as that of the private tenant, for both are, in Weber's terms, 'negatively-privileged' in the sense that neither owns property that can be used to generate income. The difference between them is a difference in their style of life – in other words, a status difference – rather than a difference in their market power. As Haddon puts it, 'Use of housing is an index of achieved life chances, not primarily a cause' (1970, p. 132).

This does not mean that a Weberian analysis of housing classes is not possible – Weber himself sees the ownership of domestic buildings as one type of property that may differentiate the market situation of various property classes (1968, p. 928) – but it does mean that Rex and Moore's emphasis on forms of tenure has to be replaced by an analysis grounded in the question of ownership and non-ownership of those types of housing that, potentially at least, may generate economic returns. This is the logic behind Pahl's reconceptualization of housing classes in which he distinguishes between large property owners (public or private), smaller landlords, owners of capital sufficient to buy their own houses, and those who lack property and are obliged to rent (Pahl 1975, p. 245). Similarly, I suggested in earlier works (1978 and 1979 ch. 2) that the application of a Weberian framework could lead to the identification of three housing classes according to whether people used housing as capital (e.g. landlords), as a pure means of consumption (e.g. tenants), or as both (e.g. in the case of owner-occupiers who may achieve considerable capital gains from ownership at the same time as they enjoy the use value of the house).

A major problem with all such formulations, however, is that they fail to explain the relationship between the 'housing class system' and the overall class structure. How, for example, does the class situation of a working-class owner-occupier differ from that of a comparable working-class council tenant? Furthermore, it is by no means clear why the exclusive focus should be on housing, for if it is the case that people's life chances are influenced by differential access to resources such as education, health care, personal transport and so on as well as to housing, then it would seem more fruitful to develop a mode of analysis which takes all such relations into account. As we shall see in Chapter 6, this is precisely what has happened with the development by Dunleavy (1979) and others of the concept of 'consumption sectors' – a concept which identifies a major cleavage in the modern period between those who are able to provide for their basic consumption needs through the market (e.g. by buying their house, running their own car, purchasing pre-school education for their children, paying into private pension schemes or whatever) and those who remain reliant on state provision. Seen in this way, the crucial basis of urban alignment is not housing tenure as such, but is the division between those with private property rights in key commodities or services (including housing) and those without.

Rex, however, remains resolutely sceptical about any attempt to reformulate the housing class concept around the question of property ownership, for, as we have seen, in his work with Tomlinson he argues both that owner-occupation among immigrants in the inner city may be no less a disadvantaged form of tenure than renting, and that the original conception of housing classes, suitably expanded to encompass groups such as homeless families and tenants of housing associations, remains a useful framework for analysis.

Such an assertion, however, simply ignores Haddon's argument that the housing class concept derives from a misreading of Weber and that the various groups that Rex identifies are in fact differentiated by status rather than by class situation. Rex has never answered this most fundamental criticism, yet it is crucial since it leads to the conclusion that housing struggles between different tenure groups can be understood only as status group conflicts, which may cross-cut and obscure more basic economic class divisions. It is but a short step from here to much of the contemporary Marxist literature on housing, which argues that divisions grounded in different forms of housing consumption are important only at the level of ideology in that the working class is fragmented by different types of provision, none of which alters the basic underlying class division between wage labour and capital. This sort of analysis (see Saunders 1979, ch. 2 for a resumé) totally ignores or devalues the significance of, for example, the capital gains which may accrue to owner-occupying households or the differential power and control experienced by those who buy commodities like housing as compared with those who rent from a public or private landlord. As we shall see in Chapter 8, such divisions arising out of patterns of consumption of crucial goods and services cannot simply be dismissed as 'superficial' or 'irrelevant', for their significance in influencing the quality of people's lives and the way they view their world can be enormous. There is a lot more of sociological significance in the spread of mass home ownership than simply the 'ideological partitioning' of the working class, but Rex's failure to reconceptualize the problem of housing cleavages around the issue of property ownership as opposed to tenure effectively closes off this avenue of analysis. Rex's Marxist critics are surely right when they dismiss tenure divisions as an important factor in reshaping the class system, but what both they and he apparently fail to consider is the deeper significance of the division between private and state provisioning.

The inescapable conclusion that suggests itself as a result of our discussion of the three major problems with Rex and Moore's work on housing classes is that the attempt to found a sociology of the city on this concept has now collapsed. Rex virtually admits as much in his book with Tomlinson, when he suggests that 'It was never claimed that the housing classes which seemed more relevant to explaining ethnic political conflict in Sparkbrook in the mid-1960s could be taken as a kind of inductive generalization covering all cases at all times' (Rex and Tomlinson 1979, p. 128). In other words, he now suggests that housing class is not a generic concept, yet this is clearly a retreat from his earlier position, in which he suggested that 'The *basic process* underlying urban social interaction is competition for scarce and desired types of housing', and that 'What is *common to all urban situations* is that housing, and especially certain kinds of desirable housing, is a scarce resource', for which different groups are in competition (Rex 1968, pp 214 and 216; emphases added). In his work with Moore (1967) Rex clearly saw the concept of housing classes as the basis for a new approach to the sociology of the city; in his work twelve years later with Tomlinson (1979) he equally clearly did not.

We have seen that there are three main reasons why a specifically urban sociology cannot be based upon the concept of housing class. First, the focus on access to housing means that housing classes cannot be equated with housing tenure groups and that analysis must focus not on a theory of the city but on a theory of social stratification which explains why different groups enjoy different degrees of access to the housing system. Second, the work by Rex and Tomlinson (1979) clearly demonstrates that the lack of a common value system with respect to desirable types of housing undermines an analysis of housing class conflict unless the application of the concept is restricted to particular groups (i.e. the black 'underclass') whose situation in other areas of life (namely the occupational and educational systems) creates the potential for conflict. In other words, the analysis of housing class struggles becomes merely a part of a sociological theory of race relations rather than the basis for a distinctive urban sociology. Third, the fact that, even from a Weberian perspective, the housing classes that Rex and Moore identify are not classes but status groups indicates that the analysis of housing divisions can be accomplished only through the attempt to theorize the significance of patterns of consumption for class relations, in which case what is needed is not a theory of the city but a sociological analysis of consumption as it affects class relations. In all three cases, therefore, we see that what appears to be the concern of urban sociology with housing class conflict is in fact the concern of a sociology of stratification, and that urban research premised upon this concept collapses into an analysis of questions of class structure, the relation between ethnicity and class, and the problem of consumption divisions and ideology.

Taking together the related concepts of housing class and urban managerialism, we can only endorse the conclusion reached by Lambert *et al.* (1978) in their study of housing allocation in Birmingham that we should 'reject the former notion and substantially redefine the latter' (p. 171). As they stand, neither concept provides a satisfactory foundation for a specifically urban sociology. A focus on urban managerialism soon leads beyond the city and into the complexities of national and international economic and political systems, while a focus on housing classes equally soon collapses into a more general concern with the system of social stratification in society as a whole in which the relation between social classes and consumption sectoral divisions appears central. But having said this, it obviously remains the case that the general themes addressed by writers such as Rex and Pahl through the 1960s and 1970s are of major significance for sociology. Unlike the legacy of the human ecologists and the cultural urbanists, that of Weberian urban sociology does contain within it the seeds of a coherent and important theoretical programme. At the heart of such a programme is the focus on the question of consumption in the context of contemporary capitalist societies where the state has come to play a central role in shaping people's lives. As we shall see, this concern with consumption became the focus for an important development in Marxist urban theory through the 1970s – a development which was to prove crucial in redefining urban sociology's object of analysis.

5 The urban as ideology

Since the late 1960s, there has been a tendency for western Marxist theory to broaden its traditional horizons in order to take account of various radical movements that have developed outside the process of production and which cannot simply be analysed in terms of the wage labour–capital relation. The growth of the feminist movement, for example, has spawned a considerable literature on the role of women and the family in capitalist societies and on the relationship between the women's movement and the labour movement. Similarly, the rise of black movements in the West and in the Third World and (to a lesser extent) the explosion of student radicalism in the 1960s both helped to undermine narrow conceptions of Marxist theory and political practice which sought to reduce all political struggles to that between bourgeoisie and proletariat.

It is in this context that Marxist theory has rediscovered the problem of the city, a problem that has been posed by the development of radical movements in the cities addressed to issues such as the decline of urban public services, environmental desecration and so on. The argument of Marx and Engels (discussed in Chapter 1) to the effect that the capitalist city is not in itself theoretically significant has therefore been reconsidered in recent years.

This reconsideration has involved two steps. The first is the critique of existing urban theories (such as human ecology) and urban practice (for instance, planning) as 'ideological'. The term 'ideology' has, however, meant different things for different writers, and this reflects two distinct (though related) meanings of the concept in Marx's work. Thus some writers have emphasized the notion of ideology as a means of legitimating class domination, and in this they have taken their cue from arguments such as that advanced in the *Communist Manifesto* that 'The ruling ideas of each age have ever been the ideas of its ruling class' (Marx and Engels 1969, p. 125). Current conceptions of urbanism and current explanations of urban problems are then termed ideological on the grounds that they reflect and are subordinated to the class interests of the bourgeoisie. Other writers, however, have seen this as too limited a conception of ideology and have attempted to develop a conception (also found in Marx) that contrasts 'theoretical ideologies' with 'scientific practice'. In other words, current theories are criticized on the grounds that they fail to break with the ideological appearances of material reality and thus reproduce ideological modes of thought in an elaborated theoretical form which is justified by a spurious claim to scientific status.

Having established the critique of existing conceptions of urbanism as ideological, the second step is to develop a theory that is not subordinate to dominant class interests or does not simply formalize existing ideological representations. Again, however, there are intense disagreements between different writers, and these tend to reflect a major division between humanist and determinist interpretations of Marxism. Thus, while one approach addresses the urban question in terms of the limitations and potential of 'urban society' for human liberation and individual self-realization, another is openly contemptuous of socialist humanism and rejects notions of the individual human subject as metaphysical. While the first conception sees the 'urban crisis' as central to advanced capitalism, the second sees it as secondary to the basic class struggle in industry. And while the former focuses on the question of the production of space (that is, on the way in which capitalist organization becomes extended and imprinted upon all aspects of everyday life), and hence on the need to develop new forms of struggle against capitalist domination of space, the latter sees the urban question as significant only in so far as urban crisis enables an extension of the traditional struggle against capitalist domination of industrial production.

It should be noted that these disagreements are not merely academic but reflect very different views regarding Marxist political strategy. As we shall see, the humanist approach seeks fundamentally to reorientate the workers' movement towards what it sees as the central question of the quality of everyday life, while the determinist approach seeks rather to encompass urban struggles within the existing workers' movement. The theoretical gulf between these two approaches cannot therefore be fully understood except in the context of recent debates within the European (and notably the French) communist parties regarding socialist strategy in the conditions of advanced capitalism. It is, in other words, no accident that the literature that we shall be discussing in this and the following chapter is almost entirely French and Italian in origin, for it is precisely in these countries that the question of communist strategy has been posed in its most practical terms since 1968.

In this chapter we focus on the way in which two Marxist theorists – Henri Lefebvre and Manuel Castells – sought to refashion the field of urban studies through the critique of existing approaches to and conceptions of 'the urban'. Although Castells has subsequently rejected much of his earlier work, his writings during this period were enormously influential in laying the basis for what became known as 'the new urban sociology', and it is difficult to over-estimate the significance of his legacy for the later development of the field.

Henri Lefebvre: the humanist critique of urbanism

Lefebvre's work on urbanism is not widely known in the English-speaking world. In part this appears to be due to the relative inaccessibility of his relevant work, for little of it exists in English translation. It is also due in part to the fact that Castells's text, *The Urban Question*, has been widely read and discussed, and this includes a heavily critical chapter on Lefebvre's theories. In other words, not only have the terms of academic Marxist debate (in Britain at least) been set largely by reference to Castells's framework, but also there has been little stimulus to examine Lefebvre's ideas since these were apparently demolished and transcended by Castells's work. In recent years, Lefebvre has begun to receive more attention through the work of Marxist urban geographers such as Harvey and Soja (discussed in Chapter 7), but his impact on urban sociology remains somewhat peripheral. This is probably due to its highly speculative, self-consciously 'utopian' character. Lefebvre's writings appear lively but also (sometimes at least) lacking in academic rigour. In places he clearly contradicts himself; the development of his argument often seems more arbitrary than logical; and the sense of spontaneity that pervades his writing stands in stark contrast to the painstaking formalism of a text such as *The Urban Question*. It is perhaps this difference in style (which itself clearly reflects a difference in their approaches to Marxism) that more than any other factor explains the differential response in Britain to Lefebvre and Castells, for the British intellectual tradition within and outside Marxism is one that has bred an extreme suspicion of academic speculation and spontaneity.

Lefebvre's critique of existing urban theories is premised on the argument that any theoretical system that guides human actions in such a way that they serve to maintain the existing system of social relations may be termed ideological: 'Any representation is ideological if it contributes either immediately or "mediately" to the reproduction of the relations of production. Ideology is therefore inseparable from practice' (1976, p. 29). He cites as an example the traditional ideology in capitalist societies that the system reproduces itself naturally, without the purposive interventions of human agents, for this not only serves to legitimate the system (what is natural is acceptable), but also denies the possibility of radical interventions to change it (what is natural is inevitable). Already, therefore, we see here the basis of Lefebvre's rejection of deterministic Marxist as well as of 'bourgeois' theories, for both have the practical effect of stunting the development of revolutionary action (that is to say, a deterministic Marxism that denies the effectivity of conscious human subjects denies also the potential for radical action and thus performs the same function as 'bourgeois' theories in undermining the practical struggle against capitalist domination).

Ideologies, therefore, are general social theories that have the practical effect of maintaining the dominance of particular class interests: 'It is the role of ideologies to secure the assent of the oppressed and exploited' (1968a, p. 76). This is achieved by masking the true interests of the dominated classes and thus curtailing their political struggle against the source of their domination. Marxism is not therefore ideological in this sense since it enables and facilitates such struggles; in other words, it is revolutionary in its practical effects: 'It discloses – not by some power of "pure" thought but by deeds (the revolutionary praxis) – the conditions under which ideologies and works of man generally . . . are produced, run their course and pass away' (1968a, p. 86).

In arguing that Marxism is not an ideology, Lefebvre does not seek to imply that it is therefore a science with a privileged insight into 'truth' and 'reality'. Far from it; for all theory, he suggests, is a mixture of truth and error, and there is no sharp distinction between science and ideology, truth and falsity. His discussion of ideology is not premised on the science/ideology distinction but on the distinction between those theories that have revolutionary practical effects and those that secure political consensus and containment. Lefebvre's views are echoed by Harvey, who criticizes 'the rather trivial view that there is one version of some problem that is scientific and a variety of versions which are purely ideological', and who asserts on the contrary that 'The principles of scientific method (whatever they may be) are normative and not factual statements. The principles cannot therefore be justified and validated by appeal to science's own methods . . . the use of a particular scientific method is of necessity founded in ideology' (Harvey 1974, p. 214). This reveals a crucial distinction between Lefebvre's view of Marxism and that of Castells, since for Lefebvre Marxism is not a science but a political theory of socialist practice. This is a view that the argument developed in the final section of this chapter will strongly endorse.

Given this view of Marxist theory, it follows that the development of radical ideas is crucial, not because ideas can wish away the material reality of capitalism, but because practical activity by individuals is guided and informed by the ideas that they have of that reality. This leads Lefebvre to designate himself as a 'utopian' on the grounds that 'Today more than ever there are no ideas without a utopia. Otherwise a person is content to state what he sees before his eyes' (1977, p. 349). Lefebvre's project, therefore, is to develop a set of ideas about urbanism that can stimulate radical action against what he sees as a new and all-embracing mode of capitalist domination of everyday life.

It is in this context that he develops his critique of urban planning and of the theory that underpins it. This is a theory that represents space as a purely scientific object and gives rise to a planning 'science' that claims to be as precise and objective as mathematics. It is a technocratic theory, in that spatial forms are taken as given and planning is conceived as a technical intervention which can bring about particular effects on the basis of a scientific understanding of a purely spatial logic. Urban theory and planning practice are thus premised on a denial of the inherent political character of space – politics are conceived as an irrational element that intrudes upon the spatial system from outside it rather than as an essential element in the constitution and perpetuation of spatial forms. This theory is thus ideological, for it sustains the *status quo* by depoliticizing the question of space and its use, and as an ideology it permeates throughout the society with the effect that political struggles over the use of urban space are defused:

Urbanism, almost as a system, is now fashionable. Urban questions and reflections emanate from technical circles, from specialists and intellectuals who think of themselves as *avant garde*. They pass to the public sphere via newspaper articles and writings with various aims and objectives. Simultaneously, urbanism becomes ideology and praxis. Yet questions concerning the city and urban reality are not yet well understood or recognized, they have not yet assumed a *political* importance in the same way as they exist in *thoughts* (in ideology) or in *practice* (Lefebvre 1968b, p. 9).

The task for a critical theory is to explode this urban ideology by showing how spatial forms and organization are the product of a specific mode of production – capitalism – and how they contribute to the reproduction of the relations of domination on which that mode of production depends:

Space is political. Space is not a scientific object removed from ideology or politics; it has always been political and strategic. . . . Space, which seems homogeneous, which seems to be completely objective in its pure form such as we ascertain it, is a social product. The production of space can be likened to the production of any particular type of merchandise (Lefebvre 1977, p. 341).

It is precisely because space is a product of capitalism, and that it is therefore infused with the logic of capitalism (production for profit and exploitation of labour), that the urban ideology of space as a pure and non-political object is so crucial.

What is required, according to Lefebvre, is not therefore a science of space *per se*, but rather a theory of how space is produced in capitalist societies and of the contradictions that this process of production generates: 'We are not speaking of a science of space, but of a knowledge (a theory) of the production of space' (1976, p. 18). Such a theory will involve not a logical and physical theory of structures and systems, but rather a dialectical theory of contradictory processes which provide the basis for political struggle over the urban question. The basic contradiction in the production of space is that between the necessity for capital to exploit it for profit and the social requirements of those who consume it; in other words, the contradiction between profit and need, exchange value and use value. The political expression of this contradiction is found in the constant political struggle between individualistic and collectivistic strategies. It is this contradiction and this struggle that lies at the heart of Lefebvre's concern with the urban question.

Lefebvre argues that the contradiction identified by Marx between the forces and relations of capitalist production has been overcome in the advanced capitalist societies by spatial expansion. The development of capitalism, in other words, has not encountered its limits because capital has transformed space itself into a commodity: 'We now come to a basic and essential idea: capitalism is maintained by the conquest and integration of space. Space has long since ceased to be a passive geographical milieu or an empty geometrical one. It has become instrumental' (1970, p. 262). From a system where commodities are produced in a spatial setting capitalism has evolved into a system where space itself is produced as a scarce and alienable resource. Space, that is, is created as an homogeneous and quantifiable commodity:

Space, e.g. volume, is treated in such a way as to render it homogeneous, its parts comparable, therefore exchangeable. . . . The subordination of space to money and capital implies a quantification which extends from the monetary evaluation to the commercialization of each plot of the entire space. . . . Space now becomes one of the new 'scarcities', together with its resources, water, air and even light (Lefebvre 1970, pp. 261–2).

In this new era of capitalism, manufacturing industry is replaced by the construction and leisure industries as the pivotal points of the capitalist system of production:

Capitalism has not just integrated existing space, it has extended into completely new sectors. Leisure is becoming an industry of prime importance. We have conquered for leisure the sea, mountains and even deserts. The leisure industry and the construction industry have combined to extend the towns and urbanization along coastlines and in mountain regions . . . this industry extends over all space not already occupied by agriculture and the traditional production industries (Lefebvre 1970, p. 265).

In this way, the capitalist production of space has become integral both in generating surplus value (for these industries employ an immense and low-paid labour force and are characterized by a low organic composition of capital) and in realizing profits (since the commodification of space has created vast new markets). It is this gradual transition from an industrial to an urban base of modern capitalist production that Lefebvre refers to as 'the urban revolution', and he likens it to the earlier industrial revolution in which the main basis of production shifted from agriculture to manufacturing.

It is apparent from Lefebvre's concept of an urban revolution that he does not intend to equate the concept of the urban with the physical object of the city. It is precisely his argument that the urban revolution creates an urban society, in which case the physical separation of city and countryside becomes of less and less significance. Rather, the urban for Lefebvre consists of three related concepts, namely space, everyday life and reproduction of capitalist social relations. The urban, that is, is the global spatial context through which the relations of production are reproduced in people's everyday experience. Capitalist social relations are reproduced through the everyday use of space because space has itself been captured by capital and subordinated to its logic:

The reproduction of the relations of production cannot be localized in the enterprise. . . . Reproduction (of the relations of production, not just the means of production) is located not simply in society as a whole but in space as a whole. Space, occupied by neo-capitalism, sectioned, reduced to homogeneity yet fragmented, becomes the seat of power (Lefebvre 1976, p. 83).

Because space bears the imprint of capitalism, it imposes the form of capitalist relations (individualism, commodification, etc.) on the whole of everyday life. The architecture of our cities symbolizes capitalist relations ('The Phallic unites with the political: verticality symbolizes power' (1976, p. 88)), our leisure space reflects capitalist relations (since it commercializes our non-work lives in line with our working lives), the dispersal of our homes in far-flung suburbs is a product of capitalist relations (central areas are taken over by commercial functions while residential use of space is relegated to the periphery), and so on. The organization of space – the essential similarity of different places, the fragmentation of life (e.g. work and home) between different places, and the hierarchy of control between dominant and subordinate places – thus carries within it the inner logic of capitalist hegemony. Capitalist social relations are reproduced in everyday life through this spatial patterning.

Lefebvre's analysis is by no means inherently pessimistic, however, for he argues that the urban revolution that overcomes one set of problems for capital gives rise to another. This is because the colonization of space by capital can proceed only by fragmenting and decentralizing the population: 'The centre attracts those elements which constitute it (commodities, capital, information, etc.) but which soon saturate it. It excludes those elements which it dominates (the "governed", "subjects" and "objects") but which threaten it' (1976, p. 18). This creates a political problem in so far as the city has traditionally been the cultural centre of the society – the principal source and location of the reproduction of social relations. If the city is fragmented and dispersed leaving only the economic and political offices of administration at the centre, then, while political power becomes centralized, cultural hegemony will necessarily become weakened:

The spread of urban tissue is accompanied by the fragmentation of the town. And it is this that gives rise to one of the deepest contradictions of space. For the town not only represents a colossal accumulation of wealth, it is also the centre of birth and learning, the point of reproduction of all social relations. But it also becomes the place where these relations are threatened. . . . Should it be sacrificed, letting the urban tissue proliferate in disorder and chaos but thereby strengthening the decision-making centres? It is an unsettling contradiction for the reproduction of social relations (Lefebvre 1976, p. 28).

The effect of the progressive extension of the capitalist production of space is therefore to concentrate the decision-making centre while creating dependent colonies on the periphery: 'Around the centres there are nothing but subjugated, exploited and dependent spaces: neo-colonial spaces' (1976, p. 85). In France, for example, Paris presides over a system of internal colonialization in which the disparities between the underdeveloped regions of Brittany and the south and the over-urbanized metropolitan centre become ever more stark (see 1970, p. 258). Thus, while capitalism is consolidated through the exploitation of space, this very process engenders at the same time a contradiction which threatens to undermine capitalist domination: 'If space as a whole has become the place where reproduction of the relations of production is located, it has also become the terrain for a vast confrontation' (1976, p. 85). The political power of the centre is strengthened as key decision-making functions become concentrated there, yet at the same time the cohesion of the society is weakened as everyday life becomes dispersed to the periphery: 'Power suffers, as in Shakespearian tragedy: the more it consolidates, the more afraid it is. It occupies space, but space trembles beneath it' (1976, p. 86). The result, potentially at least, is a crisis of the reproduction of capitalist social relations.

This is a crisis that the bourgeoisie attempts to regulate and mediate by means of its control of the decision-making centres, and notably the state. Yet it is ultimately an irresolvable crisis, since the more capitalism becomes extended in space, the more it undermines the reproduction of the social relations on which its continuation depends. Lefebvre neatly summarizes the paradox by distinguishing between the extension of capitalist organization and the fragmentation of the organization of capitalism that results from it. The capacity of the productive forces to produce space on a large scale, and thus to extend capitalist organization into every corner of life, increasingly confronts the need to reproduce the relations of production, and thus to maintain the organization of capitalism. The hegemony of the bourgeoisie is threatened by the growing fragmentation of space and of everyday life, and the increasing power of the centre is challenged by the reaction of the periphery. It is in this way that Lefebvre explains the trend towards regional devolution in the advanced capitalist countries, for such a strategy involves the attempt by the ruling class 'to offload some of their responsibilities on to local and regional organisms while preserving the mechanisms of power intact' (1976, p. 87).

This basic contradiction in the new urban society is not only revealed in political struggles between centre and periphery, however, but is also expressed in a broadening concern with the quality of life. The traditional assumption that the development of the productive forces of capitalism would automatically involve an improvement in the qualitative conditions of everyday life has been undermined:

This is what is new . . . that economic growth and social development can no longer be confused, as they have been before, by thinking that growth would bring development, that the quantitative would sooner or later bring the qualitative. . . . The ideology of growth has been mortally wounded. The vast ideological construct crumbles slowly but surely. Why? Because of the urban malaise, of the destruction of nature and its resources, because of blockages of all kinds which paralyze social development while enabling economic growth (Lefebvre 1970, p. 260).

The penetration of everyday life by capitalist organization has therefore revealed more clearly than before the contradiction between private profit and social need, between capitalist domination and social life. It is for this reason that Lefebvre sees the urban crisis as the central and fundamental crisis of advanced capitalism, for the struggle over the use of space and the control of everyday life goes to the heart of the conflict between the requirements of capital and social need.

The practical political implications of Lefebvre's analysis are clear; the workers' movement must organize in order to harness the productive forces to social needs, and this will involve a strategy that links the periphery (meaning not only the regions, but also 'urban peripheries' such as black city ghettos and migrant worker shanty towns, and international peripheries in the Third World) to the labour movement and organizes both production and everyday life in terms of self-management. However, he recognizes that the existing strategies of the French Communist Party represent the very antithesis of such a programme. This is because, first, the party is still waging the industrial battle in the urban era; that is, it interprets all political struggles in terms of a basic economic orientation to questions of the workplace, and thus fails to address the fundamental issue of advanced capitalism concerning the control of space and everyday life. The result is that it lacks a strategy for confronting the bourgeoisie over the most crucial question of advanced capitalism, and it approaches urban struggles armed with only the most 'infantile' concepts which seek to reduce such struggles to the traditional and superseded categories of the Marxist analysis of a century ago.

The second source of divergence between Lefebvre's position and that of orthodox Marxism is that he totally rejects the Leninist view of the role of the party and criticizes the Communists for their inherent conservatism in seeking merely to 'take over the baton' from the bourgeoisie. Against their orientation towards an appropriation of the power centres of the existing society, Lefebvre asserts the need for self-management which necessarily entails the abolition of central domination altogether. As Castells (1977a, p. 89) suggests, Lefebvre's position thus appears not only humanist but anarchist.

For Lefebvre, then, the critical struggle in the urban phase of capitalist development is the struggle to free everyday life from capitalist organization and to bring about the management of space by and for the masses. This is what he means by the title of one of his books, *The Right to the Town* (1968b), for the concentration of the power of capital in the centres and the consequent expulsion of the people to the periphery most vividly symbolizes the subordination of need to profit in the contemporary period. The potential offered by urban society for human liberation is immense, but this potential can be realized only through the struggle against the capitalist domination of space, and hence by transcending the technocratic ideology of space of the bourgeoisie and the narrow economistic ideology of the existing Marxist parties.

Manuel Castells: science, ideology and the urban question

Like Lefebvre, Castells has developed a critique of existing theories of urbanism as ideological. Unlike Lefebvre, however, he does not rest this argument on the identification of the functions of such theories in sustaining capitalist class relations, but rather explains this functional aspect of 'theoretical ideologies' as itself due to the failure of existing theories to transcend the ideological relations through which individuals live their relation to the real world. In other words, existing theories (and Castells includes Lefebvre's work in this category) are ideological in that they merely elaborate rather than break with the ideological forms of capitalist society, and therefore fail to establish the basis for a scientific analysis of the reality of that society. As Walther suggests, 'For Castells, the fact that urban sociology and its dispersed fields had bowed to social demand is not sufficient grounds to refute it as ideology. His critique of ideology in urban sociology delves to a more subtle level; it is essentially an *epistemological critique*' (1982, p. 16). Castells's critique of existing theories as ideological is thus premised on the argument that there is a scientific mode of analysis by means of which it is possible to identify ideological discourses.

It should be noted at the outset that, in the course of the development of his work, Castells had cause to amend his initial epistemological position quite considerably. In this section, however, we shall be concerned principally with his earlier work, since it is here that he develops his critique of urban sociology as ideological. The subsequent revisions to his epistemology were developed as a result of his attempt to apply his approach in empirical research, and this experience appears to have led him to reconsider his earlier conceptions of science and its relation to ideology. As we shall see, this reconceptualization has the effect of undermining any attempt at maintaining such a distinction and thus throws into question his earlier critique of alternative theories, although Castells himself has never explicitly re-examined his initial attack on these alternative theories in the light of his changed epistemological stance. The original critique of urban social theories was grounded in a relatively uncritical application of the Marxist philosophy of Louis Althusser to the urban question. Of particular significance was Althusser's argument that science develops out of an 'epistemological break' with existing ideological discourses – in other words that science involves a theoretical transformation of ideological concepts into scientific ones – for it was this that led Castells to engage in a critique of existing theories as the first step in developing a framework through which the 'real' question to which such theories were oriented could be identified and explored. As Althusser put it, 'The theoretical practice of a science is always completely distinct from the ideological theoretical practice of its prehistory: this distinction takes the form of a "qualitative" theoretical and historical discontinuity which I shall follow Bachelard in calling an "epistemological break"' (1969, pp. 167–8).

According to Althusser, the procedure whereby scientific practice comes to transcend prescientific ideological theories is implicit in Marx's own work, but is only ever made explicit in the 1857 Introduction in the *Grundrisse*. His argument is that Marx succeeded in breaking with ideology and founding a science of social formations when he developed his method of dialectical materialism, but that he never actually came to write the theory of this method. This is the task that Althusser takes upon himself and which he designates the Theory of Theoretical Practice.

The argument, which is derived mainly from a reading of the 1857 Introduction, begins by suggesting that the production of theory takes the same form as material production in society – that it involves the 'transformation of a determinate given raw material into a determinate product, a transformation effected by a determinate human labour, using determinate means (of production)' (Althusser 1969, p. 166). What this means is that scientific practice begins with certain raw materials of thought which it sets out to transform. These raw materials are existing general concepts, which may themselves be ideological or the products of earlier scientific practice. Althusser therefore endorses Marx's argument in the *Grundrisse* that science begins with abstractions, not with concrete reality itself: 'A science never works on an existence whose essence is pure immediacy and singularity ("sensations" or "individuals"). It always works on something "general" . . . a science always works on existing concepts. . . . It does not "work" on a purely objective "given", that of pure and absolute "facts"' (1969, pp. 183–4). Althusser's argument here reflects his resolute rejection of empiricist philosophy, for in his view, knowledge can never be derived directly from experience. It therefore follows that science starts out, not from observation, but from existing conceptual generalities (which he calls 'Generalities I').

These general concepts are transformed through the application of theoretical means of production (Generality II). Just as production in society involves the application of certain tools to certain raw materials, so too theoretical production involves the application of theoretical tools to prescientific concepts. This does not mean that theorists simply apply their own subjective ideas in order to produce scientific knowledge, for the theorist is seen by Althusser as the agent by means of which theoretical 'tools' come to be applied to a problem, just as the worker is the agent through which machines come to be applied in the production of commodities. Althusser is as opposed to idealism (the view that knowledge is a product of the individual human consciousness) as he is to empiricism (the view that knowledge is a reflection of concrete reality on to consciousness). Science involves neither the direct analysis of a given reality, nor the imposition of subjective constructs on to reality: 'The act of abstraction whereby the pure essence is extracted from concrete individuals is an ideological myth' (Althusser 1969, p. 191).

What this means, of course, is that the product of scientific practice (Generality III, knowledge) is the result of a theoretical transformation of existing concepts rather than of any direct articulation with the reality it claims to explain. For Althusser, it seems, there are two 'realities'; the reality that exists outside of thought, and remains unaffected by theoretical practice, and the reality that exists as a product of theoretical practice. There are, he says, 'two different concretes: the concrete-in-thought which is a knowledge, and the concrete-reality which is its object. The process which produces the concrete-knowledge takes place wholly in the theoretical practice' (1969, p. 186).

At this point, the obvious question concerns the relationship, if any, between the concrete reality and the concrete in thought. Althusser, however, rejects the premise on which such a question is based since the question makes sense only if we hold to an epistemology that distinguishes a knowing subject from the object of knowledge. His epistemology rejects this dualism since it rejects the notion of the knowing subject; as we have seen, the theorist is merely an agent of the theoretical transformation that takes place in scientific practice. This practice is itself *real* in that it involves a real transformation of ideology into knowledge:

The critique which, in the last instance, counterposes the abstraction it attributes to theory and to science and the concrete it regards as the real itself, remains an ideological critique since it denies the reality of scientific practice, the validity of its abstractions and ultimately the reality of that theoretical 'concrete' which is a knowledge (Althusser 1969, p. 187).

In other words, Althusser defines scientific knowledge as the product of theoretical practice since it cannot be the product of pure experience, and further suggests that to deny the validity of such knowledge is to deny the validity of science itself and thus to collapse into ideology. As we shall see later, however, this all too neat solution to the problem still begs the question as to why dialectical materialism should provide the only correct guide to scientific practice – that is, why we should accept Althusser's epistemological legislation of scientific investigation in the first place.

It will be clear from this short exposition that, when Althusser turns to consider the question of ideology, his epistemology obliges him to reject the traditional argument that ideology involves the distortion of reality through ideas, since to argue thus would be to accept that knowledge is the product of the consciousness of human subjects (idealism), or to accept that reality is reflected in some way in our ideas about it (empiricism). Ideology is no more capable of distorting concrete reality than science is of representing it. Ideology, therefore, is not an ideal representation of reality, but is rather the way in which individuals relate to reality in their everyday lives: 'It is not their real conditions of existence, their real world, that "men represent to themselves" in ideology, but above all it is their relation to those conditions of existence which is represented to them there' (Althusser 1971, p. 154). Because the real relations in which individuals enter cannot themselves be directly known, individuals relate to their world by means of an imaginary relation. Thus, just as the product of scientific practice (the 'concrete-in-thought') is distinct from the concrete-reality, so too is the product of ideological practice (the 'imaginary lived relation').

One implication of this argument is that, although particular ideologies may change through history, ideology in general remains ever-present. Even in a communist society ideology would remain essential as the means whereby individuals lived their everyday lives, since reality itself will never become apparent. Ideology, therefore, is an inherent feature of social organization: in Althusser's terms, it is one 'instance' of the social totality (the concept of the social totality is considered in Chapter 6). It is also important to emphasize that, like science, ideology is a practice since it refers not to ideas about reality but to the very way in which we live that reality. Put another way, ideology is not ideal but material: 'Men "live" their ideologies as the Cartesian "saw" or did not see – if he was not looking at it – the moon two hundred paces away: not at all as a form of consciousness, but as an object of their "world" – as their "world" itself' (Althusser 1969, p. 233).

The most significant function of ideology, and one that serves to illustrate Althusser's argument, concerns what he terms the 'interpellation" of concrete individuals as subjects. By this he means simply that it is through our imaginary lived relation to the real world that we come to recognize ourselves and others as acting human subjects. In everyday life we act towards others, and others act towards us, as if we were subjects; that is, it is through ideological practices that we become constituted as subjects. The notion of the human subject, generating his/her own ideas from his/her own unique consciousness and imposing these ideas on the external world, is therefore a product of ideological practice in that subjects are constituted only through such practice: 'All ideology has the function (which defines it) of "constituting" concrete individuals as subjects. ... Like all obviousnesses ... the obviousness that you and I are subjects – and that that does not cause any problems – is an ideological effect, the elementary ideological effect' (Althusser 1971, pp. 160–1).

If the very notion of human subjectivity (with its related notions of human consciousness, human essence and so on) is a product of ideological practice, of our *imaginary* lived relation to the world, then it follows, of course, that scientific practice must involve a break with the category of the subject if it is to produce a knowledge that transcends ideology. For as long as theory retains the ideological concept of the human subject, it will remain incapable of developing a scientific knowledge of real, as opposed to 'imaginary', relations. Put somewhat crudely, such a theory will fail to see the wood (the totality of objective social relations) for the trees ('human subjects' constituted by such relations). Such a theory will be 'closed' in the sense that it will fail to open up the question of how the imaginary relation is itself constituted and is therefore destined merely to reproduce ideology in elaborated form. It is only when science breaks with ideology and becomes autonomous from it that it becomes possible to recognize ideology for what it is:

Those who are in ideology believe themselves by definition outside ideology: one of the effects of ideology is the practical denegation of the ideological character of ideology by ideology: ideology never says, 'I am ideological'. It is necessary to be outside ideology, i.e. in scientific knowledge, to be able to say: I am in ideology (a quite exceptional case) or (the general case): I was in ideology (Althusser 1971, pp. 163–4).

It is now possible to understand the Althusserian critique of humanism as ideology, for it is not that humanist theories (those which set human subjects at the centre of the theoretical stage and endow them with consciousness and effectivity) are in some way false, but rather that they take categories constituted through ideological practice as the basic and unquestioned categories of analysis and thus preclude the possibility of explaining them: 'When I say that the concept of humanism is an ideological concept (not a scientific one), I mean that while it really does designate a set of existing relations, unlike a scientific concept it does not provide us with a means of knowing them' (Althusser 1969, p. 223). It is precisely this argument that Castells employs against Lefebvre.

Castells sets out to demolish Lefebvre's utopian concept of an urban society which he sees as in some ways a left version of Wirth's culturalist conception of urbanism (in that both see the city as structuring social relations rather than the reverse (Lebas 1980)). The demolition is effected, however, through an epistemological rather than theoretical critique, for Castells argues that Lefebvre's whole analysis stands or falls on the validity of his humanistic assumptions. Lefebvre's analysis, he suggests,

indicates that space, like the whole of society, is the ever-original work of that freedom of creation that is the attribute of Man, and the spontaneous expression of his desire. It is only by accepting this absolute of Lefebvrian humanism (a matter of philosophy or religion) that the analysis might be pursued in this direction: it would always be dependent on its metaphysical foundation (Castells 1977a, p. 92).

Lefebvre's analysis is therefore little more than a theoretical ideology, since it is grounded in ideological (or 'metaphysical') categories which it simply elaborates. The consequence of this is that it prevents any breakthrough to science through its failure to recognize the determinate conditions of social life. Despite its radical flavour, therefore, it effectively hinders rather than aids scientific critique: 'This new urban ideology may thus serve noble causes . . . while masking fundamental phenomena that theoretical practice still finds difficult to grasp' (Castells 1977a, p. 94).

Castells develops much the same argument against other, less radical, urban theories which similarly seek to explain urban processes in terms of the actions of individual subjects. The (mainly American) community power literature, which is concerned to trace which individuals or groups at the local level enjoy the greatest power to determine policies, is one obvious example, since for Castells power cannot be conceptualized in terms of individual attributes or individual relationships (see Chapter 6). Another equally obvious example concerns the urban managerialist literature discussed in Chapter 4:

This perspective which, by virtue of the ease with which it responds to the concrete problems that face the 'decision-makers', is assuming increasing importance . . . rests entirely on an ideological base, for it is based on a metaphysical postulate, without which it becomes purely empirical description. This postulate is that 'ultimately one must place the accent on the freedom of man who remains, whatever his situation, an autonomous agent capable of negotiating his cooperation' (Castells 1977a, p. 250).

As we saw in Chapter 4, the basic problem encountered but not resolved in the urban managerialism approach concerns the need to theorize the limits on the autonomy of significant actors. Castells's analysis suggests that this problem must necessarily remain unresolved for as long as theory begins with the (ideological) category of individual subjects rather than with the question of the social totality that constitutes them as subjects: 'It is by situating the elements of social structure in a prior theoretical context that one will succeed in making significant the practices concretely observed and then, and only then, can one rediscover this supposed "autonomy" of the "actors"' (p. 251). For as long as analysis retains the actor as its focus of concern, it is doomed merely to reproduce but never to explain the imaginary relation of individuals to the real world:

The analysis that sets out from the concrete actors and their strategies necessarily ends up in an impasse: if these actors are simply empirical objects, the analysis becomes a mere description of particular situations; if they are first realities, therefore essences, the analysis is dependent on a metaphysics of freedom (Castells 1977a, p. 251).

For Castells, as for Althusser, the notion of the human subject consciously constituting his or her world must therefore be abandoned to the realm of prescience. He states his position most clearly in one of his earlier essays where he writes,

To identify the production of forms with their origin in action presupposes acceptance of the notion of actor-subjects, constructing their history in terms of their own values and aims. . . . This requires that one take as a starting point actors and combinations of actors, and thus that one accept the existence of primary essences, not deduced from social structures. . . . The theoretical issue is this: historical actors founding society through their action, or support-agents expressing particular combinations of the social structure through their practice. We will take for granted that the first approach belongs to the philosophy of history, and that only the second is capable of founding a science of society (Castells 1976b, pp. 77–8).

The practices of individuals thus can be explained only through a scientific theory of structure.

This emphasis on a theory of structure and of its elements explains the ironic feature of Castells's critique of urban sociology; namely that he is most implacably opposed to the most radical theories (for example those of Lefebvre and the elite theorists of community power) while finding much that is commendable in the most conservative theory (namely human ecology) and its later derivatives (mainly Wirth's theory of urbanism). As regards the ecological approach he writes, 'The attempt to explain territorial collectivities by the notion of an ecological system constitutes the most serious attempt to give urban sociology a specific theoretical field in conjunction with the functionalist approach' (1976b, p. 71); and he later extended the compliment to Wirth's work, which he sees as 'the most serious theoretical attempt ever made within sociology to establish a theoretical object (and consequently a domain of research) specific to urban sociology' (1977a, p. 77). The significance of Park and Wirth is that they not only avoided explanations couched in terms of human subjects (neither Park's biotic forces nor Wirth's size, density and heterogeneity made reference to the purposive actions of individuals in bringing about certain effects), but they also attempted to explain urban reality by developing a theory of determinate processes. In other words, their theoretical practice sought to identify a theoretically specific problem (what Castells terms a 'theoretical object') as the precondition for developing a scientific explanation of a concrete reality (the 'real object'). For them, as for Castells, the city or space cannot be known and explained directly but must be analysed in terms of a theoretically produced object. Park's theoretical object was integration (that is, the urban system was theorized in terms of the biotic forces operating to bring about social and system integration), while Wirth's was a specific cultural content (the urban was theorized in terms of the causal effect of demographic factors in bringing about anonymity, superficiality, etc.).

The problem with both of these theories, however, was that their theoretical objects, while valid in themselves, could not provide the basis for a distinctively urban theory that could be applied to the empirical study of the city. The problem of integration, for example, necessarily involved analysis of factors that bore no necessary relationship to urbanism: 'As soon as the urban context is broken down even into such crude categories as social class, age or "interests", processes which seemed to be peculiar to particular urban areas turn out to be determined by other factors' (1976a, p. 40). This resulted in the tension diagnosed in Chapter 2 between human ecology as a theory of the city and human ecology as a theory of adaptation, for there was no reason why the theoretical object of biotic processes of integration and adaptation should be confined to analysis of the city. Similarly, Wirth's problem of urban culture turned out on closer inspection to be a theory of the cultural forms of capitalism, for not only did research demonstrate that the cultures of pre-industrial and non-capitalist cities differ from that identified by Wirth, but the sorry history of the rural–urban continuum demonstrated that the factors that he took as adequate for explaining cultural differences between town and country in capitalist societies were in fact inadequate.

Neither of these theories therefore succeeded in producing a theoretical object by means of which the real object (urbanism, space) could be analysed. Rather, by equating a concept of urbanism with what was in fact a theorization of capitalism, they succeeded only in representing capitalist processes (competition, individualism, etc.) as inherent to the nature of cities: 'An urban sociology founded on urbanism is an ideology of modernity ethnocentrically identified with the crystallization of the social forms of liberal capitalism' (1976b, p. 70). In this way, these theories served an ideological function by providing a naturalistic explanation for people's everyday experiences: 'Such a "theory" is extremely useful to ruling political elites inasmuch as it conceptualizes social organization as depending less on social data, in particular class relations, than on natural, spatial, technical and biological data' (1977b, p. 62).

By this stage of his argument, Castells has effectively demolished the whole of urban sociology as ideological. The problem with previous work is twofold. First, theories such as those developed in the urban managerialist literature or that advanced by Lefebvre are grounded in the ideological category of the human subject and are therefore incapable of sustaining a scientific analysis (since such an analysis must be derived from a theory of the system and of its interrelated elements). Second, theories such as human ecology that avoid such categories have failed to develop a means of relating their real object of study (urbanism) to their overall theories of adaptation, and have therefore resulted in ideological effects (since they equate the effects of overall social processes within capitalism with the specific effects of urban processes). What is required, therefore, is a radical reformulation which can identify what is to be studied (the real object) and can provide a theoretical framework by means of which this real object can be studied in the context of its relationship to the system as a whole (a theoretical object).

As the first step towards such a reformulation, Castells suggests that, among the plurality of real objects which urban sociology has studied in the past, it is possible to identify two that, when taken together, constitute a legitimate focus for scientific concern. The first of these is space: 'The sociological analysis of space appears to us to be a quite legitimate field of study. However, it is not a theoretical object but a real object, since space is a material element and not a conceptual unit' (1976b, p. 70). Concern with space is, of course, the common feature of all previous approaches, but none of them has succeeded in demonstrating the coincidence of spatial units with social units. Thus spatial units do not coincide with distinctive cultural units (Wirth), with distinctive political units (Pahl), and so on, and this is why previous approaches have collapsed into a nonspecific concern with culture in general, politics in general or whatever. It is therefore a precondition for any scientific reformulation of the 'urban question' that we establish the coincidence of a real spatial unit with a real social unit: 'What we would like to examine . . . is under what conditions a sociology could be defined as urban from the point of view of its scientific object. In our opinion this possibility exists when there is a coincidence between a spatial unit and a social unit' (1976a, p. 57).

The only candidate among the various social phenomena that have been studied by urban sociologists which can fulfil this requirement is what Castells terms 'collective consumption' units. As we shall see in the next chapter, his definition of collective consumption is by no means clear, and it undergoes various metamorphoses as his work develops, but in the early essays this term refers simply to 'consumption processes whose organization and management cannot be other than collective given the nature and size of the problems' (1976b, p. 75). The examples provided by Castells include housing, social facilities and leisure provisions. The basic assertion in his reformulation of the urban question is that, unlike units of production, which are organized on a regional (or even national or international) scale, units of consumption are socially organized and provided within the context of a spatially bounded system. The coincidence between a spatial unit and a social unit which has so often eluded urban sociology is therefore identified as that between spatial organization and the organization of collective consumption facilities. This is a relationship that has often been implicit in urban analysis but has never been made explicit as the definition of the urban real object: 'Urban sociology has in fact tended to tackle two types of problem: (1) relationships to space and (2) what may be termed the process of collective consumption. . . . Thus, as well as ideological themes and highly diverse real objects, the urban sociology tradition includes a sociology of space and a sociology of collective consumption' (1976b, pp. 74–5).

Having identified the real object as a (spatial) unit of collective consumption, Castells has prepared the ground for the rise of a new theoretical Phoenix with a secure scientific foundation from the ashes of the old urban sociology. It only remains for him to apply his ready-constituted theory of the total social system (a theory that he finds in Althusserian Marxism) in order to identify the theoretical element in that system to which collective consumption corresponds. As we shall see in Chapter 6, this is a relatively simple process since the theory breaks down the social totality into three analytical levels (the economic, the political and the ideological), and further breaks down the economic level into its constitutive elements of production, consumption and exchange. Each of these elements is defined through its functions within the system as a whole such that production entails the application of human labour to the material environment in order to create commodities; exchange involves the circulation of these commodities and thus (in capitalism) the realization of exchange value; and consumption involves the final utilization of these commodities by individuals as their means of life and sustenance. It is through the process of consumption, in other words, that individuals reproduce their labour-power (for example by consuming food, housing, recreation, education and so on) which then re-enters the system as a resource to be used in the process of producing new commodities. Consumption is therefore defined within this theoretical system in terms of its function in reproducing labour-power, and in this way its relation to the other elements (production, exchange) and levels (political and ideological) of the total system is established.

Castells, therefore, is now in possession of both a real object (the concrete reality of spatial units of collective consumption) and a theoretical object (the process of consumption as a functional element within the total social system involving the reproduction of the most fundamental resource in that system – labour-power). He is then in a position to analyse the real object by analysing the role of the theoretical object to which it corresponds within the total theoretical system. But before we consider the analysis that he offers, it is necessary to examine critically his claim that this new approach to the urban question is set upon a secure scientific basis which distinguishes it from the ideological character of all previous theories.

Epistemological imperialism and the new urban sociology

In choosing to attack existing approaches on epistemological grounds, by asserting their 'ideological' character in contrast to his own 'scientific' method, Castells clearly engaged in a very dangerous game, for it was then possible for others to criticize his perspective on exactly the same basis! As Lebas notes in a trend report on the new urban sociology, 'Contemporary discussion is truffled with allegations of bourgeois empiricism, ideal type classifications, not to mention rampant positivism, and such criticisms are more often directed at studies which claim to be Marxist in flavour if not in intent' (1982, p. 34). The problem with epistemological critique is that it encourages dismissal of people's work, not through addressing their arguments, but through the application of prior and inevitably arbitrary yardsticks of 'acceptable' scientific procedure. Castells was particularly vulnerable in this respect given that, first, his application of Althusser's epistemology was always somewhat inconsistent, second, the Althusserian distinction which he employed between 'science' and 'ideology' was ultimately unjustifiable, and, third, his work in any case developed in such a way as to undermine his initial epistemological principles. The remainder of this chapter will elaborate these three points.

The inconsistency in Castells's early work concerns his discussion of the real and the theoretical object. The latter appears relatively unproblematic within the context of the Althusserian schema, for it evidently refers to Althusser's notion of the 'concrete-in-thought' or scientific knowledge (which does not imply some 'final' state of knowledge or some absolute truth, but rather means that it is the foundation for the further development of scientific, as opposed to ideological, discourse). But what of the 'real object'? There appear to be two possibilities.

The first is that Castells intends this term to refer to what Althusser calls the 'concrete reality'. In this sense, spatial units of collective consumption exist in the real world but can never be directly known, either through experience or through ideal abstractions. But if this is what Castells means by a real object, then it would appear illogical to suggest, as he does on several occasions, that a science may be said to exist if it possesses *either* a real *or* a theoretical object: 'A scientific discipline is built either by a certain conceptual cutting up of reality, i.e. through the definition of a *scientific object*, or by a specific field of observation, i.e. through the choice of a *real object*' (Castells 1977b, pp. 61-2). Yet it is precisely Althusser's argument that the concrete reality can never itself be known, and Castells echoes this view when he warns that 'There is no such thing as a direct relationship between researcher and real object. All thought is more or less consciously shaped by a pre-existing theoretico-ideological field' (1976b, p. 83). The necessary consequence of this argument is that a science cannot be constituted through its possession of a real object, a 'specific field of observation', but rather constitutes itself through its theoretical practice. If we assume that Castells is following Althusser in his early work, then we must assume that the real object does not refer to the concrete reality, since for Althusser a science cannot be defined in terms of its empirical concern with some aspect of reality. Thus it will be recalled that he argues explicitly that 'The act of abstraction whereby the pure essence is extracted from concrete individuals is an ideological myth' (Althusser 1969, p. 191).

The second possibility is that Castells intends the real object to refer to the ideological raw materials of thought (Generalities I) which scientific practice transforms into theoretical knowledge. In this sense, the real object is not the concrete reality itself but the existing representations of the imaginary relation to the concrete. This is the interpretation of Castells offered by Pickvance when he suggests that 'The real object refers to some aspect of reality, ready-wrapped in preconceptions which are usually "ideological", while the science seeks knowledge in the form of a theoretical object' (Pickvance 1976a, p. 4). But if this is indeed what Castells means by the term, then it follows that spatial units of collective consumption are merely existing categories through which urban sociologists have conceptualized the real world, and that science will involve the transformation of these categories and hence their supersession. Clearly this is not what Castells intends, for he claims to have identified both a theoretical and a real object for his new scientific approach. His aim is not to transcend the real object but to study it. Collective consumption is not a prescientific category in his analysis but a constitutive category of his analysis.

We are forced to the conclusion that Castells's notion of the real object has no reference in Althusser's philosophy of scientific practice. Indeed, despite his protestations to the contrary, it is apparent that the whole thrust of Castells's critique of human ecology and of his subsequent reformulation of the field is premised upon an epistemology that Althusser himself rejects. Put simply, when Castells criticizes human ecology for failing to develop a theory specific to an urban real object, he has to assume that such a real object exists and can be known outside of theory, for how else can the lack of correspondence between the theory and the object be established? Similarly, when he sets out to identify a new real object (the coincidence of units of collective consumption with spatial units), he has first to assume that this can be identified unproblematically through observation before he can go on to show how it can be studied by means of his theoretical object. In short, both the critique and the reformulation are based on the argument that there must be a *correspondence* between some aspect of reality termed 'urban' and the theory that relates to it. Castells, in other words, has effectively re-introduced the knowing subject/object of knowledge dichotomy which Althusser sought to reject. By defining his science in terms of the relation between theory and reality, a theoretical object and a real object, he has fallen into what Althusser sees as the ideological trap of empiricism–humanism and has thereby re-opened the question of how a correspondence can be demonstrated between them. As we shall see in Chapter 6, Castells can therefore be criticized on precisely the same grounds as he criticized others; namely that his conceptualization of the urban does not 'fit' the reality observed. Thus Harloe has rightly noted the 'remarkable similarity between Castells's actual approach, as opposed to his intentions, and that of the bourgeois theorists he has criticized', for he ends up by imposing his theoretical categories on to reality in an attempt to relate the reality of the city to his pre-existing conceptual system (see Harloe 1979, p. 128).

As I shall suggest later (p. 223) Castells's approach actually owed more to Weber's method of ideal type construction than it did to Althusser's theoretical practice, for what it entailed was basically a one-sided conceptualization of one aspect of reality (the process of collective consumption) as the relevant object of study. That this procedure was wrapped up in Althusserian clothing perhaps reflects the fact that there is no warrant in Weber's sociology for drawing the distinction which Castells sought to employ between scientific and ideological modes of discourse. This is why Castells resorts to the formal structure of Althusserian scientific practice in his critique of urban sociology, even though his own method has little relation to this practice. Thus he begins with a critique of current conceptions of urbanism (the 'ideological' raw materials of thought); he then applies the theoretical tools of Marxist analysis to these conceptions (the theory of structure); and he ends up by producing a new scientific knowledge of the urban question (in terms of the function of collective consumption in reproducing labour-power). The move from Generalities I to Generalities III is reproduced in formal terms in his work, for it is only by means of this schema that he can claim to have developed a scientific knowledge that transcends ideological conceptions through an epistemological break with them.

There is, however, an irony in this attempt to hang on to the appearance of an Althusserian method, for even if Castells's approach had been consistent with that of Althusser, we should still have to reject the claim that it can distinguish between scientific and ideological theories. The reason for this, quite simply, is that no epistemology can legislate on the question of correct scientific method *per se*. The role of epistemology (as Castells was later to recognize in his article written jointly with Ipola) is to aid the clarification and subsequent resolution of problems confronted *within* particular discourses, not to referee what are basically irresolvable disputes over method *between* different discourses. It can, for example, point to obstacles of empiricism that may arise within approaches that seek to reject empiricism, but it cannot lay down with any final authority that empiricism is itself an 'incorrect' or 'invalid' approach to scientific knowledge (still less that it is inherently ideological).

My argument here closely reflects that developed in the work of Paul Hirst (1979). He has provided a detailed critique of Althusser's theory of ideology (including its later revisions) in the course of which he emphatically restates the critique of epistemological imperialism which he first developed in his work with Hindess. Basically, his argument is that no epistemology can establish a general principle, to be applied to all discourses, regarding the relation between theory and reality. This is because the relationship of any discourse to reality is defined within the discourse itself: 'Outside of epistemology what it is discourses and practices construct and refer to has no necessary common attributes; equally these constructions and referents are unintelligible except in and as discourse ... we deny any non-discursive level of "experience" or "consciousness"' (p. 20). It follows that epistemological principles that lay down the means of developing scientific knowledge cannot exist outside the theories that adopt and apply them, in which case Althusser's epistemology is applicable only within Althusser's theory (or, to put the same point in a different way, it has no general applicability and is not therefore an epistemology, in the sense of a general theory of the production of knowledge, at all).

If we abandon epistemology, then it follows that criteria of valid knowledge are always internal to theoretical systems:

We would argue that discourses and practices *do* employ the criteria of appropriateness or adequacy (not of epistemological validity) but these are specific to the objectives of definite bodies of discourse and practice. None will pass muster as a general criterion of validity, but there is no knowledge process in general and, therefore, no necessity for such a criterion (Hirst 1979, p. 21).

This argument does not represent a collapse into relativism, both because relativism itself is only a problem within debates over general epistemological principles, and because different discourses may share common criteria of adequacy (in other words, criteria may be dependent upon, but not exclusively determined by, specific theories – see Andrew Sayer (1979, p. 9)).

The effect of this argument is to undermine any claim to epistemological privilege on the part of Marxist theories, and thus to demolish the division between science and ideology that such theories assert: 'Marxism is not a "science" (equally it is not a "non-science", science-ideology is an epistemological distinction), it has no privileged knowledge' (Hirst 1979, p. 6). This conclusion, of course, relates back to the discussion of Marx's method in Chapter 1, for there we noted that Marx has no privileged starting-point for analysing reality and that his method consists in hypothesizing certain relations as a means of providing a plausible explanation for the phenomena he identified in the real world. This is a perfectly acceptable method on its own terms, but it contains no means for asserting itself as the general and only scientific method for analysing social reality, nor does it establish any general criteria of scientificity against which other approaches may cavalierly be dismissed as ideological.

Even if Castells had remained faithful to the Althusserian position, therefore, there would be no warrant in his work for his epistemological distinction between scientific and ideological theories of the urban question. Yet, as we have already noted, in his later work he came to reject certain crucial elements of that position and thereby himself to undermine his original critique.

Of considerable significance here was a joint article originally published in 1972 and translated into English four years later. In this paper, Castells sought to retain Althusser's critique of humanism and subjectivism and his concept of the epistemological break while rejecting any general theory of science and ideology: 'We do refuse the abstract general thesis of an absolute and universal opposition between science and ideology and the consequences such a distinction entails' (Castells and Ipola 1976, p. 117). The authors went on to suggest that epistemology is limited in the scope of its intervention in scientific practice to clearing obstacles that are themselves epistemological; that is, it cannot determine the principles of scientific practice themselves but is rather an aid to clear analysis: 'A materialist epistemological intervention cannot be reduced to the application of pre-established rules according to a theoretical system: its relevance must be assessed after its effects and not after its ability to conform to any "principle" whatsoever' (p. 139). It followed from this that, rather than looking to epistemology to determine criteria of scientific truth, Marxism should develop its theories through concrete political struggles as the means of elaborating and realizing them.

The Castells and Ipola paper appears somewhat ambivalent towards Althusser's position (it is by no means clear, for example, how the epistemological break can be retained without a general theory of science and ideology), but Castells's drift away from Althusser became more marked in later work. The experience of applying the method in empirical research in the Dunkerque region was undoubtedly a chastening one, for in their theoretical and methodological introduction to this study he and Godard recognize the dangers of applying a preconstituted theoretical system to particular concrete cases: 'To fix a certain mode of theoretical analysis and to hold on to its internal logic and to the validity of the social laws already established by the general theoretical framework from which this mode of analysis derives is a considerable risk, or if you like, a gamble on its applicability' (Castells and Godard 1974, p. 14). Such a method would result simply in an unfounded attempt to reduce the complexity of the observed reality to the pre-existing system of concepts, and the authors reject such a sterile approach in favour of one that attempts to establish a correspondence between theory and reality:

We have not 'operationalized' each concept as an indicator, following a one-to-one correspondence which would be perfectly illusory in the analysis of dynamic social processes, but we have traced the correspondence between a 'theoretical chain', through their logical articulation, such that the totality of facts becomes illuminated and interpreted in a coherent and theoretically significant way (Castells and Godard 1974, pp. 15–16).

Empirical research, in other words, is guided by and interpreted through theory, but theory is in turn itself developed and amended in the course of such research.

One year later, in his Afterword to *The Urban Question* (1977a), Castells underlined the significance of this break with Althusser's theoretical practice by explicitly rejecting the argument that knowledge involves a movement from the abstract to the concrete and arguing instead that the development of theory must be grounded in analysis of concrete cases from the very outset:

What is involved is the very style of the theoretical work, the epistemological approach in question. One must choose between, on the one hand, the idea of a 'Great Theory' (even a Marxist one) which one then verifies empirically, and, on the other hand, the proposition of a theoretical work that produces concepts and their historical relations within a process of discovery of the laws of society given in their specific modes of existence. It is not only a question of 'carrying out empirical research'. It is a question rather of the fact that *'theory' is not produced outside a process of concrete knowledge* (Castells 1977a, p. 438; emphasis added).

This rethinking of his own method then led him to criticize his own theoretical work in this book as formalistic. He had, he reflected, simply 'coded' empirical reality by fitting aspects of the world into ready-made conceptual boxes, and this coding exercise had taken the place of any concrete analysis. As he explained in a later essay, 'The theoretical coding has been too rapid, too formal, the reality analysed was more complex than the models used' (Castells 1978, p. 12).

By 1983, when Castells published his major study of urban social movements, *The City and the Grassroots*, the shift away from his Althusserian origins had been completed. In the introduction to the book, he made plain his distrust of 'former experiences involving the useless construction of abstract grand theories' and he asserted his commitment to grounding 'theory-building on reliable research' in order to 'rectify the excesses of theoretical formalism that have flawed . . .our earlier work' (1983a, p. xvii). In contrast with the method and style of *The Urban Question*, this book sets up various tentative hypotheses which are to be evaluated, refined and developed through the comparative empirical study of urban movements across several different countries. In place of the painstaking discussions of epistemology, the book includes over fifty pages of methodological appendices setting out interview schedules, data sources and statistical profiles in order to show how 'All the facts had to be empirically established', and how 'All the relationships between these facts had to be empirically verified' (p. 341). And in place of the confident faith in the epistemological superiority of Marxist claims to knowledge, Castells launches a bitter assault on the Marxist tradition in urban research culminating in an attack on the 'Shameful pattern of constructing theories according to the party line' (p. 297).

Another notable feature of this dramatic change in Castells's whole approach is his endorsement of the role of human agency and subjectivity as central to social analysis and explanation. A major theme of the book lies in the exploration of how cities are created and transformed in response to the pursuit by people of their various values and objectives, and Castells even goes so far as to conceptualize the city in terms of the meanings which come to be assigned to it at different periods in history by different groups engaged in a struggle with one another. In this way, urban form is explained as the symbolic expression of social meanings imposed by various groups through struggle, while urban change is seen in terms of a successful redefinition of the meaning of the city consequent upon such struggles. In terms highly reminiscent of Lefebvre, Castells argues that:

Spatial forms, at least on our planet, will be produced by human action, as are all other objects, and will express and perform the interests of the dominant class according to a given mode of production and to a specific mode of development. They will express and implement the power relationships of the state in a historically defined society. They will be realized and shaped by gender domination and by state-enforced family life. At the same time, spatial forms will also be marked by resistance from exploited classes, oppressed subjects and abused women (1983a, pp. 311–12).

Not surprisingly, perhaps, Lefebvre himself, dismissed in *The Urban Question* as a 'millenarist utopian', is now reinstated as 'a great Marxist philosopher' (p. 15).

All of this raises an obvious question. If there are, after all, no epistemologically-privileged starting points, and if empirical research is an essential component of the development of scientific knowledge, and if grand *a priori* theories are to be dismissed as 'useless' or even 'shameful' while approaches grounded in the subjectivity of human actors are defended, then where does all this leave the original attack on urban social theories as 'ideological'? Castells has never really returned to this issue in the light of his later work (although some indication of his thoughts on this can be found in his 1985 paper), but it seems obvious enough that the logic of his argument has to be that such an epistemological mode of critique can no longer be sustained. Thus, while theories may be termed 'ideological' in the sense that they appear to reflect particular views of the world associated with particular kinds of interests, they cannot be dismissed scientifically through appeal to such criteria. Human ecology, for example, may be seen as 'ideological' in the sense that its concerns with competition and integration reflect the values and goals inscribed in American society at the time when the theory was developed, but even if such a label is applied, this tells us nothing of the theory's validity. Theories which appear to serve the interests of dominant groups may have some validity, just as those born of a sympathy with the oppressed may turn out to be worthless. As Giddens (1979, ch. 5) suggests, ideology is thus a matter of political theory, not epistemology.

Castells himself seems to recognize this when he argues that theories and perspectives can be justified in social science 'only by the fecundity of the research results acquired as a result of these new bases' (1977a, p. 450). The acid test of any urban theory, in other words, is its 'explicative capacity' (p. 454). It is to the question of this explicative capacity of recent Marxist analyses of the urban question that we now turn.

6 The urban as a spatial unit of collective consumption

Althusser's influence on Castells's reformulation of urban sociology was both epistemological and theoretical. We saw in the preceding chapter that the epistemological inheritance that provided the basis for Castells's critique of previous theories must be rejected on the grounds that no epistemology can be self-evident and self-justifying. We also saw that Castells himself was in any case never fully committed to this epistemology and that, as his work developed, so the separation between his and Althusser's method became increasingly explicit. The consequence of this is that the philosophical foundation of his work is now far from clear (for example, the notion of establishing a correspondence between 'chains of observation' and 'chains of theory' begs many familiar questions), and that his early critique of urban sociology as ideological has been undermined.

The rejection of Althusserian epistemology, however, does not in itself entail a rejection of the theoretical framework that Castells derived from Althusser and from other theorists (notably Nicos Poulantzas) influenced by his writings. This follows from the argument developed in the last chapter that theories must be evaluated on their own terms and cannot be upheld or rejected by reference to some set of external and eternal epistemological principles. Thus, while the critique of Althusser's attempt to legislate science and ideology necessarily leads us to reject the basis on which Castells attacked previous theories, it leaves open the question of the theoretical fruitfulness of Castells's own approach to the urban question.

Just as in the last chapter we saw how Castells moved away from his initial (half-hearted) endorsement of Althusser's method, so too we shall see in this chapter that his work has involved a progressive shift away from an initial commitment to Althusser's theoretical framework. In particular, we shall see how (in common with many other Marxist theorists) he has come to reject the uncompromising structural determinacy which characterized Althusser's position, and how he has attempted to take account of the various social interests and identities other than class which enter into social relations in the contemporary period. Central to this discussion will be the continuing focus in Castells's work on problems of consumption – a focus which has proved contentious yet which arguably provides the basis for a coherent urban sociology.

The urban system and the capitalist mode of production

Althusser's single most important contribution to the development of Marxist theory is arguably his critique of traditional interpretations of Marx's dialectic. Basically he suggests that the orthodox view that Marx 'inverted' Hegel's dialectic, thereby substituting a materialist theory of social development for an idealist one, is a gross over-simplification and misunderstanding of Marx's approach. Such a simple inversion would have led Marx to develop a theory of historical change based entirely on the development of the economic forces and relations of production and on the contradiction between them, just as Hegel's dialectic resulted in a theory based entirely on the development of a universal idea or spirit embodied in the state. Such an economistic theory does not, according to Althusser, bear any approximation to the theory of historical materialism that Marx did actually produce (although many later Marxist theorists have themselves interpreted Marx in such a way).

According to Althusser, Marx argued that the economic contra-diction between the forces and relations of production (which in capitalism takes the form of the contradiction between capital and wage labour) was a necessary but not sufficient condition for historical transformations from one mode of production to another. What was necessary in addition was the development of other, secondary contradictions within the 'superstructure' of political and ideological relations, contradictions that could then act back upon the basic contradiction. In other words, although political and ideological relations derived out of the mode of economic organization, they developed to some extent independently of economic relations and generated their own effects within the system as a whole. The development of the economic contradiction thus takes place within the context of a unified system of contradictions and cannot be isolated from this system as a single motive force in history, for its development and effectivity is contingent upon the autonomous and uneven development of secondary contradictions elsewhere in the system (and, indeed, on the international context within which the system as a whole is situated). In Althusser's terminology, the basic economic contradiction is 'overdetermined' by contradictions developing at other points or 'instances' of the system, and the transformation from one mode of production to another is dependent upon the development of a 'ruptural fusion' of these different contradictions at a particular point in time ('historical conjucture'). It is in this way that Althusser explains the revolution in Russia in 1917, although it should be noted in passing that such a theory will always be *a posteriori* since, as Walton and Gamble (1972, p. 133) point out, it lacks any criteria by means of which we can identify a ruptural fusion of contradictions before a revolution takes place.

Althusser's theoretical framework constitutes a rejection of traditional Marxist concepts of an economic base determining a political and ideological superstructure. In its place he conceptualizes a complex system of three levels – the economic, political and ideological – in which contradictions develop both within and between each level. The system as a whole represents a specific mode of production in its pure form (that is, existing societies or 'social formations' always involve elements of different pure modes of production with the result that further contradictions develop between as well as within the different modes). Within any given mode of production, one of the three levels will perform the dominant role (for example, in a feudal mode of production the dominant level is the ideological, since religion performs the crucial function in maintaining the unity of the whole; in competitive capitalism the dominant level is the economic, because of the self-perpetuating character of commodity production; in ancient societies such as Rome the dominant level was the political, for the state was the crucial factor in maintaining the unity of the system as a whole). The system as a whole is thus termed by Althusser a 'structure in dominance' since it is a system that achieves its (contradictory) unity by means of a dominant level: 'The unity discussed by Marxism is the unity of the complexity itself . . . the complex whole has the unity of a structure articulated in dominance' (1969, p. 202).

The question of which of the three levels is to perform the dominant function in any particular mode of production is determined by the nature of the economic relations pertaining in that mode (feudal economic relations, for example, necessitated a dominant role for religion in maintaining the unity of the system; capitalist economic relations necessitate a dominant role for the economy itself; and so on). In other words, although the economic is not always dominant, it is always determinate in the sense that it determines the nature of the relations between the three levels and hence which is to perform the dominant role. This is what Althusser means by economic determinancy 'in the last instance'.

It is important to recognize that this ambiguous term should be understood analytically rather than temporally. Thus, when Althusser writes that 'From the first moment to the last, the lonely hour of the "last instance" never comes' (1969, p. 113), he does not mean (as interpreters have suggested) that economic determinacy never actually asserts itself, but rather that, while the economic *always* determines which level is to be dominant, it *never* determines how this level (or the other levels) is to develop. In other words, within a structure of dominance, the different levels develop in different ways and at different rates, and in the process they each affect the development of the others. Each level, that is, is *relatively autonomous* of each other level (only relatively so, since each level is necessarily affected by the specific effects of each other level; they exist only within a unified system, in which case total autonomy clearly becomes impossible). As we shall see later, this concept of relative autonomy has become crucial for Castells's application of the Althusserian system in his own theory.

Both in his early essays and in *The Urban Question*, Castells makes clear his theoretical debt to Althusser (e.g. Castells 1976c, pp. 149–50; 1977a, p. 125), and the development of his theory is premised upon a prior acceptance of Althusser's theory of the structure in dominance. Castells's starting point is therefore given in a theory of which the key elements are (a) the distinction between mode of production and social formation; (b) a concept of mode of production as constituted by three relatively autonomous levels; (c) a recognition of the dominance of one level, this being determined 'in the last instance' by the economic; and (d) an explanation of system change in terms of the identification of structural contradictions which are expressed in and through class practices. Taking this theory of structure as given, Castells then confronts the question of how the urban system relates to this structure.

He begins by arguing that the urban system is not something separate from the total system but is one aspect of it. It is, in other words, the specific expression of that system within a spatial unit of collective consumption: 'We shall use the term spatial structure (or "urban system" to conform to tradition) to describe the particular way in which the basic elements of the social structure are spatially articulated' (1976b, p. 78). The way in which the different levels of the total system articulate with one another must therefore correspond to their articulation in the urban system, and any change in the total system must be reflected in a similar change within the urban system: 'The urban system is not external to the social structure; it specifies that social structure, it forms part of it' (1977a, p. 263).

The first step in Castells's analysis therefore involves the application of the theory of the total system to the urban system. The urban system is thus to be constituted by three levels – the economic, the political and the ideological. The political level corresponds to urban administration (local government and other locally based agencies of the state) which performs the dominant function within the urban system of regulating the relations between the different levels in order to maintain the cohesion of the system. The ideological level corresponds to the 'urban symbolic' (the meanings emitted by socially produced spatial forms). Finally, the economic level is broken down into its three elements of production, consumption and exchange, each of which corresponds to different elements in the urban system (such as factories and offices, housing and recreation facilities, and means of transportation respectively).

The urban system thus contains all the levels and elements of the social system of which it forms a part, and these levels and elements are all structured in the same way as in the wider system. However, as we saw in Chapter 5, Castells argues that this system within a system is a theoretically significant object of study; it is not merely a microcosm of the total system but performs a specific function in relation to that system. As he puts it, 'It is necessary to refer back to the overall social structure (as a concept) to be able to define the urban system and give it a historical content' (1976b, p. 79). The way in which he identifies the theoretically important specific function that the urban system performs within the total social structure is by a process of elimination.

The urban system cannot be specified as a cultural unit (that is, with reference to the ideological level of the social structure), for as Castells's critique of Wirth demonstrated, there is no urban culture as such. Nor can it be specified as a political unit, for although (as we saw in Chapter 1) the medieval city was indeed a unit of political organization, the capitalist city cannot be so defined since political boundaries appear somewhat arbitrary and do not correspond to the contours of social units. It follows that its specific function within the total system must be economic.

As we have seen, the economic level consists of two main elements, production and consumption, which are mediated by a third, exchange. Castells argues that the urban system cannot refer to the production element since capitalist production is organized on a regional scale (for example, different stages in the production process may be located at different centres, factories in one town are administered from offices in another, and so on). It follows from this that it cannot be a specific system of exchange either. The function of the urban system must therefore lie in the process of consumption. Consumption, of course, performs a number of functions within the total capitalist system. It is, for example, the necessary end point of commodity production: 'Without production, no consumption; but also, without consumption, no production; since production would then be purposeless' (Marx 1973, p. 91). However, the principal function of consumption is that it is the means whereby the human labour-power expended in the production of commodities comes to be replaced. In other words, it is only by consuming socially necessary use values (housing, food, leisure facilities, etc.) that the work-force is able to reproduce its capacity for labour which it sells afresh each day.

The specific function of the urban system thus lies in the reproduction of labour-power. This is performed on a daily basis (through the reproduction of the labour-power of existing workers) and on a generational basis (through the production of new generations of workers to replace the existing one), and it entails both simple reproduction (recreation of expended labour-power) and extended reproduction (development of new capacities of labour-power). The means whereby such reproduction is realized are the means of consumption – housing and hospitals, social services and schools, leisure facilities and cultural amenities, and so on. Unlike the means of production, these means of consumption are specific to urban spatial units: '"The urban" seems to me to connote directly the processes relating to labour-power other than in its direct application to the production process. . . . The urban units thus seem to be to the process of reproduction what the companies are to the production process' (Castells 1977a, pp. 236–7).

Castells's justification for identifying the consumption process through which labour-power is reproduced as 'urban' is twofold. First, he suggests (somewhat tentatively) that the growing concentration of capital in advanced capitalist societies is paralleled by a growing concentration of the labour force, with the result that the processes of everyday life through which labour-power is reproduced (eating, sleeping, playing, etc.) are spatially delimited. Second, he argues that such spatial units of everyday life are increasingly structured by the requirements for the reproduction of labour-power within the capitalist system as a whole. For reasons that we shall consider in the next section, the provision of necessary means of consumption within advanced capitalist societies is a contradictory process, and the state has increasingly intervened and then taken responsibility for such provision upon itself. The result is that the means of consumption have not only become concentrated within specific spatial units, but have also become more and more collectivized, and it is this growing significance of the collective provision of the means of consumption that enables Castells to equate the urban system with the process of consumption since it gives rise to increased concentration and centralization:

> The organization of a process will be all the more concentrated and centralized, and therefore structuring, as the degree of objective socialization of the process is advanced, as the concentration of the means of consumption and their interdependence is greater, as the administrative unity of the process is more developed. It is at the level of collective consumption that these features are most obvious (Castells 1977a, p. 445).

Castells's argument may therefore be summarized as follows. (a) The urban system is an expression of the total system of which it forms a part, and it therefore consists of the same levels and elements, interrelated in the same way, as in the total system. (b) It nevertheless performs a significant and specific function within the total system, namely the reproduction of labour-power through the process of consumption. (c) The reproduction of labour-power within the social system as a whole is increasingly achieved within specific spatial units. (d) This is because the process of consumption is becoming concentrated as the population itself becomes concentrated, and as the state assumes increasing responsibility for the provision of crucial consumption facilities. (e) Urban space and the reproduction of labour-power are thus increasingly dependent upon and influenced by the level and form of state provision of necessary means of consumption. It follows from this that, to the extent that consumption becomes collectivized, the urban question becomes a political question.

Urban politics and the crisis of collective consumption

We have seen that Althusser's concept of a 'structure in dominance' indicates the potential development of a multitude of contradictions within any given capitalist society – contradictions internal to each of the three levels of the capitalist mode of production, contradictions between each of these levels, and contradictions between overlapping modes of production within the same society. Given Castells's argument that the urban system is a part of this social structure, it follows that the contradictions that develop in the whole will also develop in the part. To the extent that this is the case, they become manifest as 'urban problems' such as disjunctures between local labour availability and local labour requirements, planning failures, traffic congestion, shortages of building land and so on (see Castells 1976c, pp. 152–3).

For Castells, however, the urban system is not simply one part of the total social structure but is also a specific functional unit within it; it is the subsystem within which labour-power is reproduced. This means that, in addition to reflecting the contradictions within the system as a whole, it is the locus of a specific contradiction or set of contradictions that develops between the process of consumption and other key processes within the total system. Of particular significance here, according to Castells, is the contradiction between consumption and production; that is, between the need to reproduce labour-power and the need to produce commodities at the maximum possible profit.

The argument, quite simply, is that, although the capitalist system must secure the adequate reproduction of labour-power as a prerequisite of continued production and accumulation, individual capitalist producers find it less and less profitable to invest in the production of those commodities that are necessary for such reproduction to take place. The reason for this concerns not the inherent nature of the products concerned (housing, hospitals, educational facilities, etc.) but rather the peculiar character of the firms and industries involved. As one example, Castells cites the French house-building industry (1977a, pp. 149–69).

According to Castells, French capital has found it increasingly unprofitable to invest in the production of low-cost working-class housing, even though there is a desperate need for such housing from the point of view of both workers and industrial capital as a whole (the former because they need somewhere to live, the latter because labour-power must be reproduced cheaply and efficiently). Part of the reason for this is that this widespread need cannot be translated into 'solvent demand' (in other words, housing is an extremely expensive commodity which most workers cannot afford to buy), and to build housing to rent involves a long-term commitment of capital (and firms cannot afford to wait for many years before getting a return on capital). In addition to these problems of realizing profits, there are also problems of generating surplus value through house production. This is because the building industry is fragmented among many small producers, each employing only a few workers, and because of the lack of technological innovation in the industry as a whole.

Castells recognizes that the French case cannot be generalized across all capitalist societies at all points in time. He notes, for example, that the inadequate provision of working-class housing by the private sector is less marked in the United States than it is in France because of a more advanced level of building technology (for instance, factory-based prefabrication), easier availability of building land, a higher level of solvent demand (owing to the higher standard of living), and so on. Nevertheless, he does suggest that the French case is by no means unique: 'The housing question in France is not an exception, but a typical case, within the developed capitalist economy, at a certain phase of its evolution' (1977a, p. 158).

As Duncan (1978) has suggested, there is clearly a danger of drawing unwarranted generalizations from particular cases. Historical and comparative evidence suggests that different types of consumption facilities may fall short of social requirements in different societies at different points in time, and the question of whether and how such situations occur is necessarily contingent upon a range of specific factors which cannot be encompassed within a general theory. However, what is implicit in Castells's argument is that the *potential* for a crisis in the provision of commodities necessary for the reproduction of labour-power is inherent in the nature of capitalist commodity production. The reason for this is simply that production is concerned with exchange values while consumption is concerned with use values. There is, in other words, no necessary reason why what it is most profitable to produce should coincide with what is most socially necessary to consume, since the investment of capital is dictated by rates of return rather than need.

It is Castells's argument that this potential disjuncture between profit and need, exchange value and use value, production and consumption, has become increasingly manifest in different ways throughout the western capitalist world, and that this has resulted in 'lacunae in vast areas of consumption which are essential to individuals and to economic activity' (1978, p. 18). Left to itself, in other words, private capital has shown a marked inability to produce socially necessary facilities.

If this growing contradiction, which becomes manifest in housing shortages, inadequate medical care, lack of social facilities and so on, is not regulated in some way, then it must necessarily create new sources of political tension and strife. Resorting to Althusserian terminology, Castells suggests that 'Any fundamental contradiction unregulated by the system leads finally to an overdetermined contradiction within the political system' (1977a, p. 270). The regulation of system contradictions is, as we saw earlier, the function specific to the political level. It therefore falls to the state as the agency of social cohesion and the regulator of the total system to intervene in the process of reproduction of labour-power in an attempt to plug the gaps. This is why consumption becomes more and more collectivized and why the urban system as a whole is increasingly structured by state intervention.

Such an explanation for state intervention and the growth of collective consumption does, of course, appear strongly functionalist (system needs provoke system responses), although it is a central feature of this analysis that, while state intervention may overcome one set of contradictions, it necessarily generates another (i.e. the system is not a dynamic equilibrium, as in Parsonian sociology, but is inherently contradictory – see below, p. 199). Nevertheless, the functionalist assumptions on which this analysis necessarily rests clearly disturbed Castells as his work developed over the years, and increasingly he came to place greater emphasis on the analysis of the direct causes of state intervention (which he traces to the development of class struggle and urban social movements) than on the functional requirements which it is said to fulfil. This shift (which represents a move away from Althusser's theoretical structuralism in that it emphasizes the effectivity of people's actions) is not, however, as profound as may first appear, for the theory of the state which Castells employs has always contained both aspects. In other words, the theory entails two different kinds of explanations, one having to do with practices (the state does what it does as a response to class struggle), and the other having to do with structures (the state does what it does because of its structurally-determined role in the mode of production). Thus, as Castells increasingly emphasized the role of class struggle and urban social movements in shaping the pattern of state intervention, he was not so much breaking with his initial theory as shifting the emphasis between its two constituent dimensions. The problem, however, was always how to relate these two causal elements of the theory to each other, for it was by no means clear why or how the state's actions in response to class struggle should necessarily be consistent with its structurally-defined role in safeguarding the interests of the capitalist class and reproducing the relations of capitalist domination. Is it not possible that political pressures may dictate one course of action while system needs dictate another? How is it possible to hold both that the state responds to the (unequal) power exerted by different classes, and that its interventions are the expression of the structural needs of the system at any given time? Is it political power or structural requirements which shape the interventions of the state?

The theory of the state which lies behind all of Castells's work was derived originally from the work of Poulantzas (1973) who attempted to theorize the 'political instance' in its relation to the other levels of the capitalist mode of production. Poulantzas it was who attempted to introduce the analysis of class practices into structuralist theory:

The originality of Poulantzas's work lies in his attempt to transcend the integrationist perspective of functionalist sociology. He does this by trying to graft the Marxist proposition that the class struggle is the motor of history onto Althusser's structural-functionalist conception of society. The theory of class is inserted between the structure and the state, so that the state is subject to a double determination. In the first place, it is determined directly by the structure as a specific functional level of that structure. Secondly, its functioning in practice, within limits determined by its place in the structure, is subject to the conditions of the class struggle, which are in turn determined, at least partially, by the structure (Clarke 1977, p. 11).

In terms of its *structural determination*, Poulantzas analyses the function of the state as its role in regulating the articulation of the different levels of the system as a whole: 'Inside the structure of several levels dislocated by uneven development, the state has the particular function of constituting the factor of cohesion between the levels of a social formation' (1973, p. 44). In other words, its location in the system is such that it must perform this function of system regulation. On the other hand, as a part of the system, it must also necessarily reflect the contradictions that develop within and between the other levels; indeed, it is precisely within the state (namely at the political level) that these contradictions come together and are manifested and 'condensed'. As Castells (1977a, p. 243) suggests, it is therefore at the political level that 'one may map the indices of change'.

In terms of its *determination by class struggle*, Poulantzas argues that the state is a condensation of the class struggle. In other words, while it is certainly not a neutral instrument of political administration as pluralist theory suggests, it is not a tool of any one class as is often claimed by economistic Marxist theories. Poulantzas's argument is basically that contradictions within the system give rise to class struggles, and that the state's response to these contradictions through its interventions is determined by such struggles. Thus, while its function is necessarily to maintain the system in the interests of dominant class interests, the way it achieves this is by responding to the political balance of class forces at any one time. Quite simply, the state cannot possibly perform its (structurally determined) function of maintaining system cohesion without responding to the political pressures exerted upon it from dominated as well as dominant classes, for to remain aloof from working-class claims would be to fail to intervene on the contradictions that have provoked such claims.

It follows from this argument that the state does not itself have power, but rather reflects through its interventions the political relations between different classes. Power, in other words, is a function of class relations and is revealed through class practices: 'The concept of power is constituted in the field of class practices. . . . Class relations are relations of power' (Poulantzas 1973, p. 99). The various institutions of the state are merely the organizations that express the relative power of different classes in any given 'conjuncture'. It also follows from the argument that class practices are constituted at all three levels of the social formation; Poulantzas is heavily critical of the familiar dichotomy in Marxist analysis between classes in and for themselves, arguing instead that classes are constituted through their practices and that such practices develop (albeit unevenly) through economic, political and ideological struggles simultaneously. Political struggles are thus an inherent aspect of class practices (that is, classes do not first constitute themselves as economic categories and then engage in political struggles), although the political groupings (for example, parties) through which they are expressed cannot be directly reduced to economic categories owing to the relative autonomy between the levels. In other words, we do not find wage-labour and capital necessarily confronting each other directly at the political level, but this does not mean that the groups that do confront each other there are not engaged in class struggle.

It is evident from all of this that class practices bring about system change (since they are reflected in state intervention), but that such practices are in turn determined to some extent by the development of system contradictions. Class struggle is in this sense the link in the causal chain between contradictions in the system and state intervention which attempts to resolve them. The greater the contradictions, the greater will be the intensity of political struggle, and the more the state will intervene as a result. However, both Poulantzas and Castells then go on to argue that class practices are determined by the structure only *to some extent.* Thus, not only is there a relative autonomy between the different levels of the structure (the political is relatively autonomous from the economic), but there is also a relative autonomy between the levels of the structure and the practices to which they correspond (political struggles are not merely the expression of contradictions condensed at the political level). This is because practices do not simply express contradictions but bring them together and articulate them. Contradictions in the structure exist only through practices, and (as we saw in the last chapter with reference to the notion of theoretical practice) the very concept of practice entails the production of qualitatively new effects. This is why Poulantzas insists on 'conceiving of practice as a production, i.e. a work of transformation. It is important to see that in this sense a structural instance does not as such directly constitute a practice' (1973, p. 87). Similarly, Castells argues that political practice 'is not simply a vehicle of structured effects: it produces new effects. However, these new effects proceed not from the consciousness of men, but from the specificity of the combinations of their practices, and this specificity is determined by the state of the structure' (1977a, p. 125; see also p. 244). Practices are therefore determined by the structure in the sense that structural contradictions give rise to them, but they generate new effects within the system according to how they articulate these contradictions. The state thus performs its functional task in regulating the system by responding to the particular way in which different classes mobilize around system contradictions.

But if class struggle arising out of system contradictions is the immediate cause of state intervention, how does this enable the state to fulfil its regulative function in the system? Poulantzas's answer is twofold. First, the state organizes and unifies the divergent interests of different fractions of the capitalist class under the hegemony of the dominant fraction (monopoly capital): 'It takes charge, as it were, of the bourgeoisie's political interests and realizes the function of political hegemony which the bourgeoisie is unable to achieve. But in order to do this, the capitalist state assumes a relative autonomy with regard to the bourgeoisie' (1973, pp. 284–5). In other words, by reflecting in its policies the different interests of different fractions of capital (even if, on occasion, this necessitates the pursuit of a policy that is against the interests of the dominant fraction in the short term), the state maintains the unity of the capitalist 'power block' and thus acts in the long-term interests of monopoly capital which dominates the power bloc.

Second, while unifying an inherently fragmented capitalist class, the state also fragments the dominated classes. This it does in two ways. First, the legal system, the electoral system and so on produce and sustain an ideology of the individual through which members of these classes come to conceive of themselves and to live their lives as atomized individual subjects rather than as class agents (an argument that closely reflects Althusser's concept of the interpellation of individual subjects discussed in Chapter 5). Having created isolated individuals out of objective social relations, the state can then function 'to represent the unity of isolated relations founded in the body politic' (Poulantzas 1973, p. 134) – e.g. by representing the 'public interest'. Second, and more significantly from our present perspective, the state fragments the lower classes in the very process of responding to their political class practices. Precisely because the state is relatively autonomous of any one class, it is quite possible for it to cede concessions to dominated classes at the economic level provided this does not threaten the domination of capital at the political level: 'Within these limits it can effectively satisfy some of the economic interests of certain dominated classes. . . . While these economic sacrifices are real and so provide the ground for an equilibrium, they do not as such challenge the political power which sets precise limits to this equilibrium (p. 192). This, according to Poulantzas, is the explanation for the growth of the capitalist welfare state.

This argument is fundamental to Castells's analysis, for it explains how it is that the state may come to respond to working-class pressure, increase its spending on social items that benefit this class (even though this may not be in the immediate interests of the dominant class – for instance since it raises taxation), and yet still function in the long-term interests of monopoly capital by maintaining social cohesion. As he puts it,

The state apparatus not only exercises class domination, but also strives, as far as possible, to regulate the crises of the system in order to preserve it. It is in this sense that it may, sometimes, become reformist. Although reforms are always imposed by the class struggle and, therefore, from outside the state apparatus, they are no less real for that: their aim is to preserve and extend the existing context, thus consolidating the long-term interests of the dominant classes, even if it involves infringing their privileges to some extent in a particular conjuncture (Castells 1977a, p. 208).

In the particular case of collective consumption provisions, state intervention performs this function of system maintenance in at least four different ways. First, it is essential to the reproduction of labour-power required by the various fractions of capital. Second, it regulates the class struggle by appeasing lower-class groups with economic concessions while leaving the relations of political domination intact. Third, it stimulates demand in the economy both directly (for example through state purchases from the private sector) and indirectly (through the multiplier effect), thereby combating crises of under-consumption/over-production. And fourth, by investing in unprofitable areas, the state counters the falling rate of profit in the private sector:

Public investment, as we know, is an essential form of 'devaluation of social capital', a major recourse for counteracting the tendency toward a lowering of the profit margin. By investing 'at a loss', the general rate of profit in the private sector holds steady or increases in spite of the lowering of profit relative to social capital as a whole. In this sense, 'social' expenditures of the state not only thus favour big capital, but they are also indispensable to the survival of the system (Castells 1978, pp. 18–19).

So it is that the growth of collective consumption, brought about by the development of working-class struggle (which itself reflects the development of the contradiction within the system between profit and need, production and consumption), functions in the long-term interests of monopoly capital and allied fractions by aiding the reproduction of labour-power, regulating class conflict, orchestrating new solvent demand and countering the tendency for the rate of profit to fall in the private sector.

Two further points should be made about this argument. First, as we noted earlier, Castells has tended to shift the emphasis of his analysis between his earlier and later writings. This is revealed most clearly in the way in which he has applied his theory of state intervention to the specific question of urban planning (the political level within the urban system). In his earlier essays, urban planning is explained almost entirely in terms of its necessary function within the structure of regulating system contradictions: 'If one accepts the idea of the political system as regulating the system (concrete social formation) as a whole, according to the structural laws on which it is based, then urban planning is its intervention on a given reality in order to counteract the dislocations expressed' (1976c, p. 166). In his later work, however, and in the light of his empirical research in Dunkerque, much greater emphasis comes to be placed on planning as the expression and mediation of class relations: 'The political role of urban planning is due essentially to its capacity to act as an instrument of mediation and negotiation between the different fractions of the dominant class and between the various requirements necessary to the realization of their overall interests, as well as *vis-à-vis* the pressures and demands of the dominated classes' (1977b, p. 77).

As we have already seen, this shift represents more a modification of his earlier theoretical position than a fundamental break with it. It is true, of course, that the earlier emphasis on the functional determination of the state by its location in the structure assumes a general theory of the capitalist state whereas the later emphasis on the determinate role of class struggle recognizes that the character of state intervention will vary across different societies in different historical periods (hence Castells's call in his later writings for a 'theorized history of states' (1978, p. 181)). However, it is equally clearly the case that, just as the earlier formulation recognizes that class struggle is the means whereby structurally determined functions are achieved, so the later formulation recognizes that the state performs a regulatory role within the system as a result of its mediation between the demands of different classes and class fractions. The emphasis has changed but the components of the analysis remain the same, for both formulations necessarily include the elements of structure and function on the one hand, and practice and class struggle on the other. As we shall see in the next section, the tension between these two necessary aspects of the theory is in no way resolved by switching the primary focus of attention from one to the other.

The second point to be noted is that, although Castells argues that the growth of state intervention in the sphere of collective consumption has produced a number of positively functional effects (reproduction of labour-power, appeasement of class struggle, etc.), he then goes on to suggest that it nevertheless also generates a new set of contradictions within the system. These basically derive from the 'dislocation between the private control of labour-power and of the means of production and the collective character of the (re)production of these two elements' (1977, p. 279). In other words, the state pays the increasing cost of reproducing labour-power while private capital retains the profits created by this labour-power. The more the state is driven to increase its social provisions, the wider the gap becomes between its expenditure and its revenues. The result is a fiscal crisis of the state which, in the United States at least, has dramatically been reflected in a fiscal crisis of the cities (the most celebrated example being the near bankruptcy of New York City), and which has become manifest in other countries to a greater or lesser degree (for example through massive rate increases in British cities). As Castells puts it, 'The fiscal crisis of the inner cities was a particularly acute expression of the overall fiscal crisis of the state, that is, of the increasing budgetary gap created in public finance in advanced capitalist countries because of the historical process of socialization of costs and privatization of profits' (1977a, p. 415).

Although taxation may be increased in response to fiscal crisis, such a policy cannot resolve the problem, for taxation on profits would undermine the profitability of the private sector which the state must act to sustain, while taxation on wages (which Castells suggests has increased) (1978, p. 21) is limited and, in the long run, counter-productive (since it will tend to result in demands on capital for higher wages together with a heightened level of working-class mobilization):

State intervention in the maintenance of essential but unprofitable public services has effectively been carried out at the cost of an inflationary and growing public debt, for the financing of these growing and indispensable public expenses could not be achieved through an imposition on capital (which refused to yield part of its profits) or, completely, through increased taxation – the eventual social struggles and political oppositions spelled out the limits of such a strengthening of state power at the expense of wage earners (Castells 1978, pp. 175–6).

Faced with an inflationary spiral and encroaching recession, the state reacts by cutting its level of expenditure and redirecting resources from the support of labour-power to the direct support of capital. The result is a crisis in the provision of collective consumption.

The basic problems – lack of housing, poor health care, inadequate schooling, poor transportation facilities, shortage of cultural amenities and so on – that led the state to intervene in the process of consumption in the first place thus reappear. What is different, however, is that the whole area of consumption has now become politicized; the more the state assumes responsibility for the provision of social resources, the more centrally involved it becomes in the organization of everyday life and the more everyday life is politicized as a result. If one function of this increased level of collective provision has been the appeasement of the lower classes, then it follows that a reduction in the level of such provision carries with it the possibility of a strong and politically organized lower-class reaction against the state itself (and hence against the political dominance of monopoly capital).

Castells is careful to argue that the politicization of the urban question does not necessarily result in an intensification of class struggle. This is because, as we saw earlier, system contradictions do not determine class practices but are rather articulated through such practices. Thus Castells writes:

> The permanent and ever extending intervention of the state apparatus in the area of the processes and units of consumption makes it the real source of order in everyday life. This intervention of the state apparatus, which we call urban planning in the broad sense, involves an almost immediate politicization of the whole urban problematic. ... However, the politicization thus established is not necessarily a source of conflict or change, for it may also be a mechanism of integration and participation: *everything depends on the articulation of the contradictions and practices* (Castells 1977a, p. 463; emphasis added).

The factor that determines how these contradictions will be articulated in terms of class practices and how effective these practices will be in terms of fundamental social change is political organization. Without socialist organization, contradictions will be reflected in an uncoordinated, fragmented and ultimately ineffective way:

> The role of the organization (as a system of means specific to an objective) is fundamental for ... it is the organization that is the locus of fusion or articulation with the other social practices. When there is no organization,

urban contradictions are expressed either in a refracted way, through other practices, or in a 'wild' way, a pure contradiction devoid of any structural horizon (Castells 1977a, pp. 271–2).

The role of political organization is to link contradictions in practice. This means not only bringing together different urban struggles (e.g. housing struggles, education campaigns and so on), but also locating urban struggles as a whole within the wider context of class struggle. A failure to achieve the first will result in the perpetuation of divisions between different groups such that concessions gained by one group will be won at the expense of another, and this can only result in the reproduction of the system rather than an effective challenge to it. A failure to achieve the second will limit any popular movement to reformism. This is because urban contradictions are secondary: 'Whatever the level and the content of the various "urban issues", they can all be characterized as secondary structural issues, that is to say, ones not directly challenging the production methods of a society nor the political domination of the ruling classes' (Castells 1977a, p. 376). It follows that urban struggles cannot themselves provoke fundamental social change, but can only effect limited changes within the confines of the urban system: 'a municipal revolution and nothing more' (p. 360).

Castells's thinking on the role and significance of urban movements has, like so many other areas of his work, changed considerably over the years. Basically, his ideas have developed through three distinct phases.

In his earliest writings, he was clear that to be effective, urban movements must be assimilated into the wider working-class movement (which he took to be synonymous with the Communist Party). On its own, urban protest will always be limited in its political effectiveness, but if it can be harnessed to the Communist Party, with its strong base in industrial class struggles, then it can come to play a crucial role in bringing about social change. This is because 'the working class cannot on its own . . . pose a socialist alternative in western Europe' (1978, p. 172). It has to forge popular alliances with other classes such as the 'new petty bourgeoisie', and urban issues facilitate the formation of such alliances in that the movements which develop around the crisis of collective consumption draw upon a wide range of social interests. Polluted air does not stop at the boundaries of middle-class suburbs; cuts in school budgets do not discriminate between working-class and middle-class students; the shortage of hospital beds affects professional workers as much as manual workers; and so on. Urban contradictions, in other words, are 'pluri-class' in their impact, and the protests which they generate thus provide the basis on which to build new, anti-capitalist and anti-state alliances.

In this first phase of his work, Castells saw the significance of such alliances (somewhat implausibly) as being realized in popular insurrection. As the urban crisis deepened, so the fusion of industrial muscle and popular protest represented by the development of 'urban social movements' would shake the system of class domination to its foundations. 'Urban power', claimed Castells, 'lies in the streets', and these new alliances would 'reopen the roads to revolution' (1977a, p. 378). The events in Paris in 1968 seem to have provided the model which Castells had in mind.

In the second phase of his work, he continued to argue that urban protest had to be channelled through the wider political struggle for socialism, but he came to see the role of urban social movements less in terms of popular insurrection and more as a means of widening the electoral base of the socialist and communist parties:

The articulation of new social struggles with alternative democratic politics can lead to a Left-wing electoral victory based on a programme opening the way to socialism. For such a victory to be possible and not to get bogged down in the administrative underground of the bougeois state, it must not support itself on a coalition of dissatisfactions, but on the political and ideological hegemony of the socialist forces at the mass level. We know that this hegemony must necessarily depend on a transformation of mass conscious-ness, and that this transformation will not be brought about by televised electoral speeches but by and in struggle. In our historical conditions, the revolutionary's essential task consists above all in winning the masses. The battle for the masses replaces the battle of the Winter Palace (1978, p. 60).

This endorsement of an electoral strategy obviously reflected the influence of 'Eurocommunism' within the French Communist Party in the 1970s, but it was also consistent with the deeper shifts within Castells's overall theory. The Castells of the early essays could only theorize change in terms of insurrection given his emphasis on the structural determinations of the state's role and functions, for no matter who ran the system, the outputs would always necessarily be the same. As his work came to emphasize the causal significance of practices relative to structures, however, so the possibility was opened up for endorsing a parliamentary strategy in which people could have some effect on outcomes. The democratic road to socialism, in other words, came to be seen as viable only when the theory made room for human actors.

In the third and most recent phase of his work, however, much of this theory of urban social movements has been jettisoned. Following a study of tenants protest movements in two municipal housing estates in Paris, Castells came to the conclusion that urban movements should maintain some distance between themselves and left political parties if they were to stand any chance of maintaining their vitality and pursuing their particular concerns. Moreover, he went on to argue that the labour movement is itself effectively powerless to bring about social transformation in a world where the levers of economic control are globally organized, and that its narrow economistic concerns with workplace issues prevent it from addressing the wider concerns regarding the quality of life which lie at the heart of the urban question.

Following a wide ranging analysis of urban movements in the USA, South America and Spain as well as France, he concluded that to be successful, such movements needed to focus not simply on collective consumption issues (what he termed 'consumer trade unionism'), but also on the political question of state power and the cultural question of urban meaning. In Paris, for example, the tenants' movement was limited by its failure to address wider community and political issues; in San Francisco, the gay movement succeeded in transforming neighbourhoods around its own cultural identity and in challenging for power in City Hall, but failed to address the problem of collective consumption provision; and in the South American shanty towns, the squatters' movement exerted demands for urban services and established new cultural communities, but at the expense of political subordination to state power and patronage. Only in Madrid during the Franco regime did Castells find an example (in the Citizens' Movement) of an urban social movement which successfully combined all three dimensions of the urban question; for here, demands for urban services were coupled up with a challenge to authoritarian state power and the development of new urban cultural forms which emphasized the city as a use value for people rather than as a speculative playground for big capital.

Given the inherent weakness and limitations of the labour movement in the contemporary period, Castells concludes by arguing that urban social movements are the only channel through which popular pressures for change can be expressed. However, they too are ultimately powerless to transform the conditions of oppression which give rise to them, for they lack the means to change the economic system, to control the production and dissemination of dominant culture, and to challenge the might of the modern nation state. They are, in the last analysis, 'local utopias' which keep alive the challenge to domination and exploitation but which cannot themselves overcome it: 'Urban movements do address the real issues of our time, although neither on the scale nor terms that are adequate to the task. And yet they do not have any choice since they are the last reaction to the domination and renewed exploitation that submerges our world' (1983a, p. 331). They are, to paraphrase Marx, the sigh of the oppressed creature and the soul of souless conditions. We have come a long way from the events of May 1968.

Production, consumption and the city

Thus far in this chapter, I have concentrated almost exclusively on outlining the core theoretical propositions developed by just one writer in the neo-Marxist tradition, Manuel Castells. This emphasis is justified given the enormous impact of Castells's early writing on the reshaping of urban sociology in the 1970s, especially in Britain. As Harloe has observed, 'It would be an exaggeration to say that Castells's approach monopolised the development of the "new" urban sociology in Britain in the mid-1970s. . . . Nevertheless, the citations to his work, as well as the attention paid to a critical examination of it, indicate that Castells's writings were of central importance' (1981, p. 4). The centrality of Castells's work during this period was partly a reflection of the fact that his key papers, and his key book, were translated into English quite early on while foreign-language works by other writers remained relatively inaccessible. For much of this period, many of us in Britain remained largely ignorant of the political and intellectual context which had spawned Castells's theories and had little knowledge of the alternatives being proposed by other European Marxists, nor of the debates to which Castells's work was addressed (see Lebas 1982). But having said that, it remains the case that Castells's early writings succeeded in pinpointing many of the core issues and problems in urban studies at that time, and that (rather like Rex and Moore's work in the mid 1960s) they generated intense interest and argument mainly because they challenged existing orthodoxies and assumptions while pointing the way forward to a new research agenda.

By the mid 1980s, however, Castells's work was no longer so dominant. Gradually, the English-speaking audience became familiar with other European theorists as well as itself generating critiques of, and alternatives to, Castells's proposed paradigm. Furthermore, as we have seen, Castells himself criticized many basic aspects of his own earlier work, while (as we shall go on to see in the next two chapters) other writers began to develop new agendas for urban studies which reflected the changed conditions brought about by deepening economic recession, new patterns of political conflict and, most crucially, a sustained attack by radical right governments in Britain, the USA and other advanced capitalist countries on the very system of collective consumption which lay at the heart of Castells's theoretical concerns.

For the remainder of this chapter, therefore, I wish to broaden the discussion to go beyond mere exegisis and critique of Castells's writings and to focus in more general terms on some of the issues and problems which are raised in his work but which are not necessarily resolved there. I shall therefore take various key themes and ideas from Castells's writings as springboards for discussion of certain methodological and theoretical issues which have attracted argument and debate among other writers in recent years, and in this way the chapter will lay the foundations for an analysis of the questions surrounding space (Chapter 7) and consumption (Chapter 8) which remain central to much work within urban studies in the contemporary period.

Let us begin with problems of methodology, following which we may go on to consider issues concerning his substantive concern with analysing collective consumption.

Methodological questions

According to many of his critics, Castells's approach as exemplified in *The Urban Question* was (a) ahistorical, (b) ethnocentric, and (c) functionalist (see, for example, Duncan 1981, Harloe 1981, Mingione 1981).

The charge of ahistoricism was undou.,edly valid, for it was a feature of the Althusserian structuralist paradigm that it not only ignored history but resolutely set its face against historical explanations in which social causality is traced to specific events (the shooting of an Archduke, a sealed train through Germany, a famine, a battle or whatever) rather than being established in terms of the necessary outcome of structural conjunctures. Historical explanation was for

Althusser fatally tied to the problematic of the human subject (for it explains change as the product of human actions) and to the methods of empiricism (for its claims to knowledge are grounded in historical evidence), both of which his approach had already ruled out; history, in other words, directly contradicted the 'scientific' method of theoretical practice.

We need not dwell on this issue, for Althusser's dismissal of history has been widely criticized elsewhere (see especially Thompson 1978), while Castells has himself come to reject this recipe for theoretical formalism and to emphasize the need for what he terms 'theorised histories' (1978, p. 181). As we have seen, he recognized quite early on the barrenness of an approach which led to the application of pre-existing (and empirically-untestable) theoretical generalities while ignoring historical variations, and he criticized the tendency in his own earlier work towards 'coding' observations into conceptual categories without ever understanding the specific conditions which give rise to them. Along with most other urban researchers, therefore, Castells now argues for a theoretically-sensitive historical method.

The issue raised by this in terms of current debates, however, is how an historical method focusing on the specific conditions arising in specific times and places can be combined with the generalizing claims of theoretical explanation. As we saw in Chapter 1, this was precisely the problem addressed by Max Weber in his methodology of ideal types when he argued that sociological explanation entailed generalization through the identification and understanding of typical probabilities of action. Notwithstanding the infinite number of factors which could and did give rise to any given phenomenon, it was possible in his view to develop adequate though partial explanations by focusing on those features which were relevant to the concerns of the researcher, and by showing how people typically responded in subjectively meaningful ways to them. Ideal types were thus the tools by which general concepts could be applied to the analysis of historically specific conditions.

In contemporary urban studies, however, Weber's methodology has not been widely endorsed. Rather, with the collapse of the Althusserian paradigm, Marxist theorists have attempted to reconcile the search for general theories with a recognition of the significance of specific conditions by developing what has come to be known as a 'realist' method. I have discussed this methodology elsewhere (Saunders 1983) and I consider it again in the appendix to this book.

Briefly, it differs from Weber's approach to explanation by rejecting a notion of causality as a sequence of events (as in, for example, the claim that Calvinism helped to create the conditions in which capitalism could develop), and focusing instead on causality as an inherent property of things themselves. Causal explanation is in this way achieved when analysis reveals how the capacity of something to behave in a certain way has been realized (or has been prevented from being realized) by the conditions in which it is operating. Thus, to revert to a physical analogy developed by Sayer (1984a), a length of copper wire has the inherent capacity to conduct an electric current, but this capacity will only be realized under certain contingent conditions (dampness, for example, may hinder conductivity). The task of scientific explanation lies not in analysing the peculiar events leading up to this result (e.g. the fact that it had rained), but rather in identifying the inherent mechanism (in this case, the ionic structure of copper) which necessarily generates a given tendency (i.e. the capacity to conduct electricity), irrespective of whether this tendency is actually realized in any given case. Whereas Weberian ideal type analysis identifies one factor as important while ignoring others on the basis of the researcher's own concerns and interests, a realist methodology thus distinguishes what it sees as the 'necessary' properties of things from the 'contingent' factors which may affect their operation. Its concern is not so much whether things happen but how they happen.

Despite the claims of its adherents to the contrary, this methodology is not that different in its practical applications to research from the Althusserian approach. Where the Althusserians came to a problem already armed with their theory of an underlying structure and simply 'coded' their empirical observations in terms of this theory, social realists come to their research similarly equipped with a theory which purports to explain the necessary tendencies of things, and they then proceed to explain what they find by pinpointing effects as the realization of these tendencies, modified where appropriate by the intrusion of contingent factors. What is deemed 'necessary' is thus determined by the theory while the actual observations are accounted for by reference to the peculiar effects of contingencies which no theory could or should generalize about. Theory, in other words, tells you about the generalities of how things necessarily work, while empirical and historical research tells you why these things may not work as theorized in actually-observed reality. In this way (just as for Althusserianism) the theory is safeguarded from empirical disconfirmation (since theorized tendencies may or may not reveal themselves according to contingent historical conditions), but unlike Althusserianism, this approach has the attraction of enabling empirical study so as to identify the operation of contingent conditions, and therefore of taking account of the fact that, for example, not all capitalist societies look the same even though they are said to operate according to the same inherent logic.

Here then is the response of urban studies to Castells's call for 'theorized histories'. Yet it is a response which still asserts the primacy of theoretical over empirical knowledge, which still facilitates the development of theories which are in principle unfalsifiable (since the controlled experiment in which all contingent events are held constant is not usually feasible in social science), and which still enables claims to epistemological privilege to be put forward against other perspectives which can safely be dismissed as 'empiricist' because they fail to theorize the necessities which are held to underpin the operation of real world events. The collapse of Althusserian epistemology has encouraged the growth of empirical research, but the findings of such research (while worthwhile in themselves) are never allowed to intrude upon the initial theory which is meant to explain them. Thus it becomes possible, for example, to analyse the important differences between housing provision in two different capitalist countries – differences which reflect the organization of the building industry, the role of the state, the pattern of class relations and so on – while still concluding that these differences are the products of contingent historical events which do nothing to undermine a theoretical explanation which is held to apply equally to both (see, for example, Dickens *et al.* 1985). If you study the contingencies, the theoretical necessities can safely be left undisturbed to look after themselves.

It is important to emphasize that Castells himself has avoided such an approach in his later work. His analysis of urban social movements in *The City and the Grassroots*, for example, is developed on the basis of observation of different cases in order to derive tentative theoretical generalizations (e.g. regarding the significance of different types of demands and strategies exemplified by different types of movements). These theoretical insights are then applied and amended through further empirical investigation – a methodology of grounded theory which explicitly sets out to avoid the prior imposition of general theories and which enables an inter-penetration of theory and empirical research which is effectively precluded by the adoption of a realist methodology. This is a very different notion of 'theorized history' from that employed in realist social science, and it is one which owes more to the methodology of ideal type generalization than it does to this alternative approach. Unfortunately, however, a new 'realist' orthodoxy does seem to be taking root in urban studies at this time, and although this will not preclude empirical investigation in the way that Althusserianism did, it does carry familiar dangers of theoretical non-falsifiability and epistemological claims to privileged knowledge.

I shall return to this issue in the appendix, but for now we may go on to consider the second, and related, criticism which has been levelled against Castells's earlier methodology: namely, that it was ethnocentric.

An approach grounded in a Weberian methodology of ideal types is, in a sense, inherently ethnocentric, not simply because the concepts employed will reflect the value-conditioned interests of a given researcher at a particular time in a particular place, but also because the 'individual types' employed are always partial and one-sided and will thus always reflect one aspect of the phenomenon in question while ignoring others. This is not, however, a serious problem within Weberian sociology since ideal types can always be amended or developed in the light of new observations, and it is always open to other researchers to develop other pure types reflecting conditions in other social contexts.

Althusserian methodology is, however, very different. Its concepts are developed as generalities without content. Rather like Weber's generic as opposed to individual types, they are timeless and spaceless for they are held to apply to all societies in all periods. Thus, they are total rather than partial in their scope and, furthermore, because of the exclusive claim to scientificity, they are the only generalities which can be employed. There is no room in such an approach for the development of alternative conceptualizations of the world, for these are dismissed as 'ideological'. There is only one road to scientific truth.

In practice, of course, the generalities which Althusserian researchers employed were not derived mysteriously from some privileged theoretical insight into the inner workings of human society, but inevitably reflected specific conditions pertaining in particular places and times. Castells was no exception. Abstract and formalistic concepts developed on the basis of Althusser's three 'levels' within a mode of production were invested with content and meaning by Castells by drawing upon concrete and specific historical instances and elevating them to the status of timeless generalities. As Duncan pointed out, 'The concepts employed, such as the urban question, the housing crisis, the state, are at once ahistorical generalizations and highly specific historically' (1981, p. 239). Thus Duncan showed how the conception of the state (the 'political instance' within a 'capitalist mode of production') developed by Castells in fact owed much to the particular form of state power which was characteristic of French society at the time when he was writing. Similarly, the emphasis on the contradiction between capital accumulation and the reproduction of labour power culminating in a tendency to fiscal crisis, which was seen by Castells as inherent to capitalism, was very much a peculiar feature of particular western European capitalist countries during the 1970s. Yet these essentially individual concepts were put forward as generic, despite the fact that in other countries (Duncan gives the example of Sweden) they simply did not apply.

Duncan, incidentally, claims that this is a problem shared in common by Althusserian and Weberian methodologies, and he sees this tendency in Castells's earlier work as 'surprisingly reminiscent of the Weberian method of formulating ideal types' (p. 248). This, of course, is not the case, for although ideal types may similarly be partial in their scope, there is no attempt in this methodology to apply them as if they were general across all times and places. As we saw in Chapter 1, for example, Weber's ideal type of the city was grounded in an analysis of western European cities during a specific period of their history, and neither he nor anyone else ever tried to suggest that the emphasis he placed on fortification, autonomous legal systems and the rest was generalizable across all cities at all times. The reason why ethnocentrism was such a crucial problem in Castells's work, therefore, was not so much that he was arguing on the basis of a distinctive experience (France in the late 1960s) but that he was elevating this experience to the status of an all-encompassing generality.

What, then, of his later work? As we have seen, his theory of urban social movements has now been developed, not on the basis of prior generalizations, but through empirical studies in the USA, Latin America and Europe, plus secondary analysis of historical materials ranging from studies of the Comunidades of sixteenth-century Castilla to the black ghetto riots of 1960s America. Only as a result of such wide-ranging empirical analysis does he then propose a general theory which is said to apply 'across different cultures of the capitalist-informational mode of production and in our epoch' (1983a, p. 322) – a claim which is certainly broad, but which in specifying a time period is still rather more modest than that characteristic of his earlier theory.

There are, however, still problems in so far as Castells continues to underplay the specific context within which his observations are set. Pickvance (1985) has pinpointed the problem clearly, for he shows the way in which Castells takes urban movements in a very peculiar situation (Franco's Spain) to exemplify successful grass-roots mobilization and thereby generalizes from what the Madrid Citizen's movement did to develop a general theory while failing to appreciate the peculiar conditions in which they did it (notably the ban on political parties which meant that urban movements became an important substitute as vehicles for expressing popular demands and opposition). For Pickvance, it is not so much the nature of the movement (e.g. whether or not it encompasses the three concerns with collective consumption, state power and urban meaning) that is important in explaining its success or failure as the character of the times and places in which it appears, and he goes on to suggest that, for all the apparent changes in Castells's methodology over the years, his latest work is still marred by the tendency to abstract from specific contexts while ignoring the importance of variations between contexts: 'Referring back to Castells's earlier model . . . one can in fact see a striking *formal* parallel with the new model despite the change of content. In each case a single model is advanced, and an exemplar of an urban social movement pointed to in order to illustrate it. . . . In both cases contextual features were played down or ignored' (p. 36).

Duncan's criticism of the early Castells and Pickvance's criticism of the later work are both pointing to the same problem – namely, the tendency to establish generalizations through reference (in the first case tacit, in the second explicit) to specific cases with their own specific contextual conditions which render such generalizations highly problematic. Castells has not been alone in this, for as Szelenyi (1981a) recognized in an influential paper reviewing the problems in the 'new urban sociology', there was a strong tendency in much of the work conducted through the 1970s to take western capitalist cities as *the* paradigm of contemporary urbanism, and to ignore variations both between capitalist and non-capitalist (Third World or eastern European) societies, and within different western capitalist countries. It is precisely the growing recognition of this problem which has led researchers, whether wedded to a realist or ideal type methodology, to emphasize the need for comparative research in which historical and empirical differences are identified and explained rather than subsumed under general and all-embracing theories. In particular, it is clear that any conceptualization of 'the urban question' will need to be sensitive to the temporal and spatial context, for as Castells has himself argued, 'A city (and each type of city) is what a historical society decides the city (and each city) will be. Urban is the social meaning assigned to a particular spatial form by a historically defined society' (1983a, p. 302). This indicates that the meaning of urbanism will differ over different times and places as different interests struggle to realize the expression of their own values and aspirations. There can thus be no generic concept of urbanism.

The third area of criticism levelled against Castells's original methodology concerned its inherent functionalism. Again, Castells has himself agreed with this criticism (1985, p. 7), although the issues involved here are complex, and it is important to unravel them if we are to derive any lessons for the future.

Functionalist forms of explanation in the social sciences seek to account for the existence and persistence of social phenomena by analysing their effects. Phenomena are explained by pointing to the beneficial consequences which they have for social groups or social systems, such that once a social 'need' has been identified and it has been shown how this need is met by the existence of the phenomenon in question, the phenomenon itself is said to have been explained. The problem in such a logic of explanation is not that it analyses phenomena to discover their hidden or intended consequences, but that it takes these consequences as adequate grounds for the existence of the phenomena in the first place. There are two faults in this logic. The first is that social systems do not have 'needs' as such which have to be fulfilled. It is quite possible to argue that if something is not done (e.g. if capital does not make profit) then something will change in the system (e.g. firms will go bankrupt, people will lose their jobs and all sorts of pressures will mount for political and economic change), but this is quite a different proposition from that which says that capital *must* make profit. Unlike biological organisms which do have system needs and which die if those needs are not fulfilled, societies do not die, they change. The second fault in the logic is that, in deducing a cause from a consequence, functionalist explanations invert the temporal sequence of causality. Put another way, the tacit assumption is built into functionalism that someone or something is capable of recognizing system needs and of organizing social affairs so that these needs are met; for as Mennell, among others, has pointed out, 'Collectivities have no group mind, and therefore cannot merely be assumed to be goal-directed and purposive' (1974, p. 157). A teleological explanation thus normally depends upon the recognition of human agency in social affairs (e.g. the argument that the people running the government see a problem looming and act to forestall it), yet even explanations of this sort tend to be dubious given the limited capacity of any one group of actors either to anticipate problems or to act effectively to resolve them. Even the most powerful groups in our society, whether they be governments, big companies, banks, unions or professions tend to respond to short-term problems with little idea of the long-term consequences, and their actions generally have unanticipated results which may turn out to be quite different from those intended.

Both flaws in the functionalist logic can be found in the structuralist Marxism of the 1970s, but the problem of teleology is especially marked in this perspective given that it rules out any explanation involving conscious and purposive human agency. Castells's original analysis of collective consumption, and the theory of the state which this analysis entailed, was a case in point, for the growth of collective consumption in advanced capitalist societies was explained in terms of the functions which it performed in reproducing labour-power, and this argument itself rested on a theory of the state which saw it as necessarily performing certain functions on behalf of the dominant class, yet all of this was held to occur in the absence of any deliberate human intent.

As we saw earlier, the theory of the state which Castells employed was basically that developed by Poulantzas (1973). According to this theory, the capitalist state 'must' perform a regulative role within the mode of production of which it forms an integral part – this is the function of the political level. State intervention serves the purpose of fragmenting the working class while unifying the different fractions of the capitalist class within a 'power bloc' under the hegemony of monopoly capital. The long-term hegemony of monopoly capital is ensured by making short-term concessions to other classes as and when this is necessary, but the state 'cannot' pursue policies which fundamentally threaten the monopoly fraction's interests. This is what Castells meant when he argued in an early essay that, 'Not every conceivable intervention . . . is possible, because it must take place within the *limits* of the capitalist mode of production, otherwise the system would be *shaken* rather than regulated' (1976c, p. 166).

Although the state functions on behalf of monopoly capital, however, it is not subject to its dictates. There is a 'relative autonomy' between the economic and political levels of the system which means that, although big capitalist interests are hegemonic, they do not dictate what the state does. This, of course, follows from the structuralist foundations of the theory, for to argue that certain capitalists control or influence the state according to their own purposes (a so-called 'instrumentalist' conception of the state) would be to admit human agency into the heart of the explanation. Thus the state functions in certain necessary ways, but no one – not the capitalist class, nor the agents within the state system, nor any other interest in society – acts to ensure that it does so.

How, then, are these functions discharged and maintained? The answer given by Poulantzas and adopted by Castells is that the causal agency in the system is class struggle. Quite simply, the balance of class forces at any one time is reflected in state intervention (for example, the extension of collective consumption provisions to the working class at times when it is relatively strong) which then has the effect of damping down unrest and hence reproducing the hegemony of the dominant class fraction. Thus system contradictions generate an intensification of class struggle which in turn generates a state response which regulates the original contradictions. There is (to borrow a concept from Parsons's systems theory) a cybernetic process at work whereby the system regulates itself through perpetual feedback and adjustment. As Mennell observes, such cybernetic loops can provide a logical solution within functionalist theories to the teleology problem, for they explain how systems adjust to meet new needs without conscious human direction. However, as Mennell also observes, 'Empirical evidence for the existence of feedback has to be produced and explained in the usual way and the logical requirements for doing so extremely stringent' (1974, p. 160). In the case of Castells and Poulantzas, these requirements are not met on at least two counts.

First, it is by no means clear in their work why the cause of state intervention (class struggle) should *necessarily* result in functional effects (system regulation). Why is it not possible, as Szelenyi (1981b) suggested, for the state to be driven by an escalation of popular demands and mobilization to pursue policies that have a directly deleterious effect on the long-term profitability of monopoly capital? In their discussion of Poulantzas's state theory, Gold and his colleagues suggested that 'Although there is a fairly rich discussion of *how* the relative autonomy of the state protects the class interests of the dominant class, and of the functional *necessity* for such a state structure, there is no explanation of the social mechanisms which guarantee that the state will in fact function in this way' (1975, p. 38). The same criticism can be made against Castells, for his functional theory of the state rested wholly on the assumption that reform is always ameliorative as regards the working class and non-threatening as regards the long-term interests of monopoly capital. This argument always was dubious theoretically (for it can be argued that system change raises rather than regulates aspirations for further change (see Runciman 1966)) and unsubstantiated historically (for radicalism is often more intense during periods of reform than during periods of stability or retrenchment). Castells's assumption that political zeal varies inversely with political concessions rested on an astounding ignorance (sustained by his methodology) of how people typically understand and interpret their situations.

Second, it is impossible in this theory to disentangle empirically the cause and the effect. The only way we have of knowing that the working class is strong (and hence that the state should be responding with reforms) is when we see the state introducing reforms which benefit that class! The theory, in other words, rests on a classic tautology. Furthermore, as Pahl (1977b) suggests, it is immune to empirical evaluation since, no matter how far the state goes in supporting the interests of the working class, the theory always ensures in advance (a) that such interventions must be because the working class is strong at that time, and (b) that they must be in the interests of monopoly capital in that they will ensure system stability in the long run. The lack of any counterfactual condition in the theory means that, no matter what the state does, the theory will be able to cover it. As Lefebvre suggests, 'This structural (non-dialectical) analysis is not false. It is not true either. It is trivial. It bears no date. It can be true or false anywhere and everywhere' (1976, p. 66).

It is not clear how far in his later work Castells breaks with this functionalist mode of theorizing. He has claimed that the theory of the state which underpins the analysis in *The City and the Grassroots* is 'a total revision' of what was basically a Leninist theory employed in his earlier work. The basis for this claim is first, that the theory recognizes axes of domination other than class (Castells cites in addition autonomous state power, gender domination and cultural domination around ethnicity or nationality), and second that it sees the state less as the automatic pilot of monopoly capital and more as 'the crystallisation of class and other social struggles, that is both of processes of dominance of certain classes and groups and genders but also as the expression of the process of resistance to dominance by classes and social groups and genders'. Planning, he now says, is 'a battlefield which is, to some extent biased by the political domination imbedded in the state apparatus but at the same time wide open to whatever struggles develop in society' (1985, p. 8).

This formulation has not so much resolved the problems of the earlier theory as sidestepped them. To define the state as a battlefield in which the capitalist class and other dominant social interests command the high ground is to beg all the familiar questions of the relationship between state power and economic power on the one hand, and between structural necessities and political practices on the other. Castells seems to recognize the analytical weaknesses of his earlier theory, yet still seeks to apply its essential insights as if mere recognition of the problems is enough to overcome them. In *The City and the Grassroots*, for example, he asserts that 'The state is present in the capitalist mode of production, having a major repressive function and tending to represent the interests of the capitalist class' (p. 306), but how this function is maintained and how capitalist interests come to be represented is never examined. We are told that, 'The management of urban services by state institutions, while demanded by the labour movement as part of the social contract reached through class struggle, has been one of the most powerful and subtle mechanisms of social control and institutional power over everyday life in our societies' (p. 317), but this familiar argument still fails to explain the cybernetic feedback whereby services demanded by one class come to serve the interests of another. Similarly, in *The Economic Crisis and American Society*, published three years earlier, we again find the claim that, 'The intervention of the state is required by capital (in its process of accumulation and legitimization) and forced by labor (which demands a larger share of the product through forced socialized consumption)' (1980, p. 125), yet the necessary connection between functional effect and immediate cause is never explicated. We are told that, 'The intervention of the state takes place within the structural rules of capitalism for the purpose of overcoming the historical contradictions that arise during the latter stages of its development' (p. 130), yet the relation between structural constraints and political practices is never theorized, while the problem of attributing a 'purpose' to state intervention when the state itself is not an agent but a battleground is never considered. And we are warned that, 'The state cannot be seen as a pure instrument of the ruling class', nor is it 'an even mirror of the class struggle', but that, 'It is the product of a historical process characterized, in a capitalist society, by the continuous domination of capital' such that 'The state is the crystallization of this class domination, and its institutions will reflect fundamentally the interests of the bourgeoisie' (p. 153), yet nowhere in this essentially descriptive outline can we find an explanation of how class struggle comes to be refracted in such a way that economic domination is automatically translated into political domination in the absence of direct capitalist control of the state apparatus.

What I am suggesting, then, is that while much else has changed in Castells's work, the theory of the state has remained in its essentials very much the same. It is still basically a functionalist theory, and as such it still falls down on the fundamental problem of relating the structurally-necessary functions which the state is said to perform to the causes which are said to bring them about. It is not that such a theory is empirically false, for at a descriptive level it seems plausible to suggest that capitalist states do often respond to diverse interests while at the same time attempting to safeguard capital accumulation. The point, however, is that the theory employed by Castells, Poulantzas and others simply does not and cannot explain how this happens.

There is a crucially important lesson to be drawn from this. If it is true, as seems to be the case, that capitalist states do respond to the ebb and flow of political struggles, then simple instrumentalist theories which explain state outputs as the product of exclusive control by dominant class interests need to be rejected (as Poulantzas and Castells argue). Equally, if it is also true that such a response is uneven, and that some interests enjoy an 'inside track' within the state system, then simple pluralist theories which explain state outputs as the product of popular political pressures need also to be rejected (as Poulantzas and Castells also argue). This suggests that we need a perspective which explains both types of outcome – both the prevalence of key economic interests and the partial effects achieved by less powerful groups – yet this cannot be achieved by a single theory such as that proposed by Poulantzas and Castells since such an approach constantly collapses back into functionalism. Rather, we need to develop a mode of analysis which recognizes the crucial role of human agency in shaping state policy (as both instrumentalism and pluralism – and, for that matter, managerialism – do), but which also recognizes the potential and limitations of the different kinds of demands, interests and preferences which come to be expressed by different kinds of groups through different parts of the state system. Rather than choosing between theories such as instrumentalism, pluralism and managerialism as if they were mutually exclusive, we need in other words to understand their complementarity in the sense of tracing the contexts in which each of them is most likely to apply. This, in my view, is the only way out of the recurring problems which beset Castells's attempt to escape from functionalist teleology, and it is the logic behind the development of a 'dual theory of politics' in which the forces shaping the collective provision of consumption are seen as different from those shaping other aspects of state intervention and regulation. What such a dualistic theory might look like, and its relevance for understanding the activities of the state in a country like Britain in the contemporary period, are matters which are examined in Chapter 8.

This extended discussion of some of the methodological issues arising out of Castells's work over the years can usefully be drawn together by summarizing the three lessons which can be learned as regards future work in urban sociology. First, we saw that the development of general theories must be sensitive to the peculiarities of time in the sense that causal explanations must relate historical specificities to theoretical generalities. Both realist and ideal type methodologies provide means for doing this, the former through the distinction between contingency and necessity, the latter through the construction of partial 'individual types' which generalize from specific historical patterns of social organization. However, we also saw the dangers in a realist methodology of asserting untestable theories which remain immune to, and divorced from, historical analysis, and we concluded by reasserting the value of an ideal type methodology as the basis for hypothesis construction.

Second, we saw the importance of sensitivity to the peculiarities of space. Social relations vary, not only historically, but also geographically, and it is important to guard against a form of ethnocentrism in which generalizations built up on the basis of just one or two places are then extended to encompass all others. There is, in this sense, no general theory of 'the' capitalist state, but rather theories of capitalist states (see Duncan 1981, Jessop 1982, Paris 1983). Similarly, there can be no generic specification of 'the' urban question, but rather conceptualizations of the urban question as it appears in different places at different times.

Third, we saw the importance of guarding against functionalist forms of explanation by insisting on the pivotal role of human agency in any theory. As regards a theory of state power, this implies that we need to start, not by identifying the functions performed and then working backwards to discover their causes, but rather with an analysis of the pressures and demands being exerted by different groups, which will then enable us to work forwards in order to trace how these interests are realized or constrained within any particular system of state power. This implies an endorsement of theoretical pluralism (in that different theories may be seen, not as incommensurable, but as complementary) which in turn takes us back to a methodology of ideal types in which different aspects of reality may be identified and explained in terms of different complexes of causality.

These three themes – the use of ideal types in historical explanation, the dangers of confusing historically individual types with ahistorical and aspatial generic ones, and the need to combine types in any overall theory of state power – form the methodological guidelines for the argument developed in Chapter 8. The substance of that argument, however, is developed not from a critical analysis of Castells's methodology, but from reflections on and developments of his theoretical ideas concerning collective consumption, and it is to these that I now turn.

Substantive questions

In his earlier work, Castells specified 'the urban question' in terms of the organization of, and struggles over, collective consumption. In his later work, the urban is still conceptualized in this way, although two further dimensions are added – namely, state power (i.e. urban struggles are struggles against centralized, bureaucratic domination), and cultural meaning (i.e. urban struggles are struggles to impose new cultural forms in the face of domination by the mass media and the various centres of information control). In his later view, therefore, the focus on collective consumption is valid but partial and its essentially economic focus has to be complemented by an equal concern with political and cultural issues (1985, p. 7).

How useful or legitimate is it to conceptualize the urban in this way? In particular, how far can we follow Castells in seeing the issue of collective consumption as a necessary (if no longer sufficient) factor in the analysis of urbanism? The critical literature has focused on four related issues: the relation if any between cities as spatial units and the organization of collective consumption; the analytical separation of 'consumption' from 'production'; the distinction between 'individual' and 'collective' forms of consumption; and the significance of consumption as regards an understanding of class structure.

The first of these problems refers to the key theme of this book – namely the question of whether it is possible to identify some social process or object which corresponds to the spatial entity of the contemporary city. As we saw in Chapter 5, Castells believes that this is indeed possible, for cities in advanced capitalist countries represent the containers within which labour-power is produced and reproduced. They are spatial units for the reproduction of labour-power, and in so far as capitalist states have found it 'necessary' to socialize the costs of such reproduction through the development of welfare provisions, cities can thus be seen as units of collective consumption:

'What is an 'urban area'? A production unit? Not at all, insofar as the production units are placed on another scale (on a regional one at least). An institutional unit? Certainly not, since we are aware of the almost total lack of overlap between the 'real' urban units and the administrative segmentation of space. An ideological unit, in terms of a way of life proper to a city or to a spatial form? This is meaningless as soon as one rejects the culturalist hypothesis of the production of ideology by the spatial context. . . . What is, then, what is called an urban unit? . . . It is, in short, the everyday space of a delimited fraction of the labour force . . . it is a question of the process of reproduction of labour-power' (1977a, pp. 44–5).

This formulation has provoked two types of criticisms. One is that such a definition ignores other crucial processes which occur in cities and which 'must' be taken into account in any definition of urbanism (e.g. Lojkine 1977). The other is that it does not encompass the range of collective consumption in advanced capitalism, much of which is either aspatial or spatially organized on a scale beyond that of the city. In my view, the first of these criticisms is irrelevant while the second is profound.

The first criticism contains an obvious truth – cities are more than mere units of consumption. As we shall see in Chapter 7, for example, there is a very different tradition of Marxist urban research which sees the primary importance of the city, not in terms of consumption, but in terms of the production and circulation of capital. When we look at any major city and see the office blocks housing the headquarters of major companies, the factories producing all sorts of commodities, the road and rail links transporting these goods to their markets, the banks and retail outlets which speed up the circuit of capital between its money and commodity form, then it would indeed be fatuous to argue that all that is important about cities is the housing, schools, hospitals and other provisions which aid the reproduction of labour-power.

This, of course, is not what Castells is saying. As he makes clear in the afterword to *The Urban Question*, 'A concrete city (or an urban area, or a given spatial unit) is not only a unit of consumption. It is, of course, made up of a very great diversity of practices and functions. It expresses, in fact, society as a whole, though through the specific historical forms it represents. Therefore, whoever wishes to study a city (or series of cities) must also study capital, production, distribution, politics, ideology, etc.' (1977a, p. 440). His argument is not that collective consumption is the only important urban process, but is that it is the only specifically urban process. The acid test of this claim is not whether things other than consumption happen in cities, but is whether collective consumption is spatially limited to cities in the way Castells suggests.

Here the critics are on stronger ground. Mingione, for example, writes that, 'It is impossible to isolate "urban" needs from "non-urban" ones. The consumption process itself is not definable in a purely territorial context, it does not correspond to any "urban question" but is rather an important part of the general social question' (1981, p. 67). It is not just that consumption occurs in many different types and scales of spaces – in inner cities, in suburbia, in agricultural villages – but that its organization through the state takes two crucially different forms – namely, provision in kind (council housing, schools, old people's homes, children's homes) and provision in cash (housing allowances, student grants, pensions, family allowances). Provisions in kind are necessarily spatial in the sense that all objects entail spatial location and extension, but provisions in cash are not. Both, however, involve the state in providing the resources whereby people can reproduce themselves (albeit with different implications; as I shall argue in Chapter 8, provision in kind carries within it a potential for state control and direction which is not inherent in a system of money transfers). If the object is to focus on collective consumption and the reproduction of labour power then there seems little coherent rationale for analysing those forms of consumption which happen to be provided in kind within a given spatial setting, and those which take alternative forms.

Castells's definition of an object of analysis is, in fact, remarkably similar to Pahl's. Thus for Pahl, 'I tend to use the word "city" as shorthand for "a given context of configuration of reward-distributing systems which have space as a significant component". Thus housing and transportation are elements in my view of a city, family allowances and pension schemes are not. An *urban* resource or facility must have a spatial component' (1975, p. 10). The problem with both formulations is that what is a 'spatial resource' actually varies over time and between different countries. For example, in Britain the sale of council houses has resulted in a shift from state provision of spatial resources in kind (the construction and letting of housing) to state provision of non-spatial resources in cash (the growth of tax concessions on mortgage interest payments). The amount of public money going into housing is as great, if not greater, as before, yet on the Castells/Pahl definition, state support for urban consumption has declined dramatically. Similarly, recent moves by health authorities away from institutional and towards community-based care for the elderly, the handicapped and other such groups would qualify on this criterion as a reduction in collective consumption provision, yet the people themselves may be receiving more adequate support than before! At the heart of this sort of specification of the urban question, therefore, lies a taken for granted acceptance of current (ethnocentric) forms of state provision and budgeting as in some way the 'real' basis for urban studies; as governments shift between benefits in cash and benefits in kind, so urban sociology adjusts its research agenda accordingly!

It is clear from this that collective consumption is not an urban 'real object'. Rather, Castells's focus on spatial units of collective consumption as the object of urban research reflects his particular (and quite legitimate) interests. The reason why he is only interested in state provisions in kind is that the spatial dimension to such provisions carries with it the possibility of collective mobilization. When people are spatially concentrated on municipal housing estates, or when their children are brought together in the same place to be educated, or when they all rely on the same bus route to get them to work, or on the same local hospital when they are ill, a capacity exists for common organization which is not present among those who receive tax concessions through their pay packets or Giro cheques through the post. This is essentially the same point as was made in Chapter 1 regarding Marx's analysis of the city as an aid to the development of class organization and consciousness. Such a focus on spatial forms of consumption is fair enough, as long as it is recognized that this is only one aspect of the consumption question. What Castells has done, implicitly, is to set up an ideal type conceptualization of urban processes which excludes both non-consumption processes and consumption processes with no spatial component, for in this way he is able to focus on that slice of social reality which interests him most – namely, city-based movements oriented to welfare issues. As he himself recognizes at one point, 'The urban system is only a concept and, as such, has no other use than that of elucidating social practices and concrete historical situations in order both to understand them and to discover their laws' (1977a, p. 241).

It should come as no surprise to find that Castells's identification of the urban question is, notwithstanding his own claims to have discovered a 'real object', grounded in an ideal type construct. As Weber observed, 'All specifically Marxian "laws" and developmental constructs – insofar as they are theoretically sound – are ideal types' (1949, p. 103). Seen in this light, however, it is clear that there are no compelling grounds why we should accept this conceptualization of the urban question, for how we respond to Castells's research agenda will depend upon how we view its usefulness. For myself, I would argue that the restricted focus on spatial units of consumption precludes analysis of what are precisely some of the most interesting and pertinent issues regarding the sociology of consumption in the current period. In particular, it fails to address the question of why consumption provisions take the form they do (cash or kind) at particular periods (e.g. the growth of direct provision in kind through the 1960s as compared with the privatization of services in the 1980s), and what the implications are of any shift in this balance of provision. In other words, the problem with Castells's definition of the urban question lies in my view not in his focus on consumption, but in his concern to link this to spatial forms. As he himself recognizes, 'A "sociology of space" can only be an analysis of social practices given in a certain space. . . . Of course there is the "site", the "geographical" conditions, but they concern analysis only as the support of a certain web of social relations' (1977a, p. 442). As I read this, it is saying that the specification of sociological objects of inquiry entails a concern with objects and processes rather than with the spatial relations between these objects or the spatial location of these processes. If that is the case (and as we shall see in Chapter 7, such a view has been disputed), then the concern with consumption should not be hedged in and constrained by a lingering concern to locate it in the specific spatial context of the city.

Some writers have argued that the impossibility of correlating consumption (or any other process) with the city as a spatial unit makes it futile to search for a definition of urbanism (cf. Mingione 1981, p. 70, Paris 1983, p. 94). Others have been more positive in the sense that they have adopted Castells's focus on collective consumption as the basis for urban analysis while stripping it of any necessary spatial connotations. Dunleavy, for example, defines urban politics as 'the study of decision processes involved in areas of collective consumption' while stressing that, 'My usage of "urban" applies to collective consumption processes in any area of the country, without any specific spatial reference' (1980, pp. 2 and 3). In previous work, I too have suggested that the urban may be equated with collective consumption as the basis for a 'non-spatial urban sociology' (Saunders 1985b). The question of the social significance of space, and whether urban studies or any other social science can proceed in this way, will be considered in more detail in the next chapter. For the moment, however, we may simply note that whether or not we choose to designate collective consumption as 'urban' is merely now a matter of convention. What matters is not the label which we apply to the analysis of consumption issues, but how we proceed to study them, and this brings us on to the second area of criticism of Castells's substantive focus – the analytical split between consumption and production.

Where some critics have denied that collective consumption can form an object of analysis for urban sociology because it is not specific to cities, others have rejected it on the grounds that it reflects and perpetuates an artificial or even ideological division between two processes – production and consumption – which cannot be understood in isolation from one another. Castells, in other words, is said to have broken the fundamental methodological rule of dialectical materialism which, as we saw in Chapter 1, emphasizes the contradictory unity of the parts within the wider whole and hence denies the possibility of partial scientific analyses.

There is no shortage of such criticisms. For Mingione, 'The consumption process is only a partial aspect of the general production process. Production (in a strictly technical sense), distribution and consumption relations are highly interdependent and together form the social relations of production, i.e. the social structure. One cannot consider consumption processes separately from the other two aspects of the capitalist reproduction process' (1981, p. 66). Harloe's point is similar: 'It seems quite unhelpful to place a special emphasis on consumption considered in isolation from production, for they are inseparabie in the Marxist analysis of capitalism' (1979, p. 136), and Lojkine too is critical of any attempt to 'reduce policy simply to the "management of the reproduction of labour-power" (housing and social infrastructure) and exclude its economic dimension' (1977b, p. 142). Indeed, Lojkine it is who attacks the production/consumption division as 'ideological', arguing that it reproduces 'the ideological split – imposed by the ruling class – between factory life and life in the city' (1984, p. 219). Harvey too echoes this argument that the division between a sphere of work (production) and a sphere of community (consumption) is an artificial separation imposed by capitalism, and that analysis must go beyond such ideological appearances to uncover the essential unity of oppression which gives rise to struggles in both spheres: 'The separation between working and living is at best a surficial estrangement, an apparent tearing asunder of what can never be kept apart. And it is at this deeper level too that we can more clearly see the underlying unity between work-based and community-based conflicts' (1978b, p. 35). Some Marxist urban researchers – most notably Katznelson (1981) in the USA – have attempted to document the way this division between work and home, production and consumption, was brought about in the early development of capitalism, while a number of feminist researchers (e.g. McDowell 1983, MacKenzie and Rose 1983) have pointed to the significance of patriarchy and gender relations of domination in generating and sustaining it, and have tried to trace the 'underlying links' between the two spheres of domestic and industrial life (both of which, they point out, involve women in productive activity).

What, in the face of all this, can be said in defence of the sort of analytical distinction drawn by Castells between production and consumption? Is it useful or even possible to sustain an analysis of one without at the same time focusing on the other?

The first point to make about this is that Castells recognizes that production and consumption are interrelated. As Dunleavy points out, 'Castells has never suggested that the inter-relationships between production and consumption activity should be ignored' (1980, p. 47). As we have seen, his original concept of the urban system identified the three economic elements of production, consumption and exchange, together with the political and ideological levels, as all interrelating within the system. His focus on the consumption element as that aspect which was specific to the urban system was, furthermore, premised upon the recognition of its importance for capitalist production, not only through its role in reproducing labour-power, but also as a source of demand for the products of capitalist firms (e.g. the drug companies which supply the health service, or the builders who erect public housing) and as a means of counteracting falling profit rates by socializing costs which would otherwise be incurred by the private sector. Both in his work with Godard or Dunkerque (Castells and Godard 1974), where collective consumption was analysed precisely in terms of the contradiction between economic and social priorities which followed the development of two large industrial complexes, and in his subsequent work on the role of the state in the American economy (Castells 1980), he demonstrated a clear awareness of the wider economic and political significance of collective consumption provision.

Criticisms to the effect that Castells ignores the link between production and consumption are thus clearly unfounded. What really seems to be at issue in such criticisms, however, is how this link is theorized. It is my contention that what many of Castells's Marxist critics really find objectionable in his work is the recognition that consumption may generate its own effects, notably as regards the formation of social cleavages and political movements which cannot be theorized as mere phenomena of class power arising out of the organization of production. In other words, Castells's specific focus on consumption, while all the time relating it to production, class power and the role of the state in a capitalist economy, also opens up the possibility of identifying non-class bases of power and popular mobilization (as in his analysis of urban social movements) and non-class forms of popular aspiration and identity. In asserting the interrelation of production and consumption, what the critics are really asserting is the primacy of production and hence the centrality of a conventional class analysis. Castells recognizes the links between production and consumption, but what the critics seek to do is to reduce the analysis of consumption to the analysis of production. The way they do this is by equating consumption with reproduction.

Castells himself, of course, theorizes collective consumption in terms of its role in reproducing labour-power. The analysis is grounded in Marx's theory of value according to which 'The value of labour-power is the value of the means of subsistence necessary for the maintenance of its owner' (Marx 1976, p. 274). Marx argues that the 'necessary' level of such subsistence is determined socially, by what is considered 'normal' in any given society at any given time, rather than biologically, and that unlike other commodities, the value of labour-power therefore 'contains a historical and moral element' (p. 275). Thus, for example, the value of an unskilled worker's labour-power in England is higher than that of a similar worker in India precisely because working-class living standards are different in the two countries.

The obvious problem with this formulation is that it rules out even the possibility that a gap may develop between the level of subsistence necessary to reproduce labour-power and the level of provision for workers' consumption needs. Whatever the working class achieves in raising its living standards is automatically deemed necessary if its labour-power is to be reproduced satisfactorily from the point of view of capitalist employers. If it is in the long-term interests of the capitalist class that labour-power be reproduced adequately, and if the criterion for this is that workers must be in a position to consume up to the normal standards prevailing in their society at that time, then it follows that whatever workers receive in the way of wages or state services 'must' be necessary if the capitalist system of production is to continue to function properly. This proposition lays the basis for the logically impeccable yet historically absurd thesis that, say, centrally-heated council houses with garages and gardens, or the teaching of foreign languages and social studies in schools, or the provision of free meals in hospitals, or an increase in the level of old age pensions, must all in fact be necessary if capitalist firms are to continue to exploit labour-power and accumulate profits. Every working-class gain short of a fundamental transformation of the whole capitalist system thus turns out on closer inspection to be in the interests of the capitalist class (although each gain may also hasten the development of contradictions which threaten the system).

There has been growing dissatisfaction with this kind of reasoning in recent years. In his review of reproduction theories, Connell (1983, ch. 8) takes issue with the static conception which seems to be built into them – the assumption that time is simply a succession of repeated patterns and that human agency can do little to bring about system change. As he observes:

If dynamics are not recognised, we have functionalism. . . . It is, I suggest, a problem embedded in the very language of 'social reproduction'. Reproduction analysis, to put it in the most general way, is based methodologically on a bracketing of history which, unless the most strenuous efforts are made to prevent it, must suppress the agency of people in creating history, in creating the very structures whose reproduction is being examined (1983, p. 148).

The insistence on theorizing 'consumption' as 'reproduction' reflects the basic premise of any Marxist urban theory that the organization of production plays a determinate role in shaping social processes. Consumption, therefore, has to be analysed in terms of its contribution to the production system – whether in terms of providing labour-power (as in Castells's original formulation) or more generally in underpinning the class relations around which production is structured. It is this initial starting point which leads to the functionalist arguments criticized by Connell, for although subsequent writers have attempted to avoid a simple reduction of consumption to production, and hence to recognize the specific effects which are associated with particular 'modes of consumption', such analyses continue to be flawed by their claims that production is both primary and determinate.

The clearest example of this can be found in a study by Preteceille and Terrail which explicitly sets out to avoid any simple reduction of consumption to production while at the same time retaining a notion of production as the determining factor. As they explain the problem with earlier formulations, 'A proper insistence on the determining character of the social relations of production has overshadowed not only the necessary analysis of the specific structure of modes of consumption, but also an analysis of the relations between the two spheres, which has been reduced to a single, mechanistic determination' (1985, p. 4). Yet as their analysis proceeds, so they too inevitably develop a strongly functionalist model which ultimately collapses back into precisely the sort of 'mechanistic reduction' which they set out to avoid.

Preteceille and Terrail begin by criticizing 'bourgeois theories' which, they say, take consumer preferences and demands as given without explaining their origins. In their view, needs expressed in the sphere of consumption can only be explained by analysing the way capitalist production is organized. To explain why people have certain needs as consumers, it is necessary first to understand the 'needs' of the production system – the need to renew labour power, to create new skills, to slot people into their work roles and to perpetuate the existing form of social organization. Although these needs are not necessarily met (which enables the authors to claim that their's is not a functionalist theory), they do tend to generate forms of consumption which are appropriate to their resolution. This is achieved when individuals 'internalize' system needs as their own – e.g. when they demand forms of education which will enable them to secure employment, or when they ask their doctors for medicines which will overcome depression or fatigue and thus enable them to continue to function as productive workers. Preteceille and Terrail never really explain how this process of internalization is accomplished, for as they themselves recognize, they lack a theory of social psychology, but it is evident from their argument that state provision is important in this process (i.e. the state provides for needs in a form which is consistent with those required by the production system – by laying down educational standards and curriculum contents, for example, or by emphasizing curative rather than preventative forms of health care), as is the 'ideological message' encoded in commodity exchange in the private sector (e.g. the image of the consumer as sovereign which is perpetuated despite the obvious real limits on consumers imposed by the limited purchasing power which reflects the wage system in the sphere of production).

In advanced capitalism, both individual and collective consumption has expanded, but it is crucial to the Preteceille/Terrail thesis that this has done little to meet people's real needs. Rather, as the intensity of production has been stepped up, so the need to consume has increased as a result: 'The need for an increase in consumption, and of new forms of consumption, is only a response to the demands of this increasing wearing out of the labour force, and its consequences. Thus in order to achieve the same result, the reproduction of the same labour power, it is necessary to have a higher level of consumption, and thus a higher real income' (1985, p. 107). If households can now buy vacuum cleaners, dishwashers and other such commodities, this is simply to facilitate the increased exploitation of female labour which is released to work more hours outside the home while still performing the necessary level of domestic duties within it. If car ownership has expanded, this is simply a reflection of the need for workers to travel greater distances in shorter times to their place of employment. If millions of working-class people can now afford foreign holidays, this is simply because their need for recuperation has intensified as a result of changes in the organization of their working lives.

This increased pressure has also led to increased demands for state provision – for nursery schools to allow mothers to return to employment, for public transport to whisk workers to and from their office and factories, and so on. Such provisions invariably fall short of people's real (but perhaps not consciously realized) needs. As they expand, so their costs begin to erode private sector profitability while their inadequacies foster resentment and stimulate yet further demands. Preteceille and Terrail recognize that different consumers will press for different kinds of demands and hence that the consumption sphere generates cleavages rather than alliances (as had been supposed in Castells's original theory), but again these divisions are explained by relating them back to production relations. Thus different groups of workers experience different material conditions in employment which then generate different needs as expressed through consumption:

> The low attendance by workers in theatres . . . is not only because of tiredness and lack of time, but is also the outcome of a lack of interest, of cultural distance, of a profound feeling that this is something for 'them', not 'us'. The same statement can be made about education and training, reading, health care or exercise. Capital weighs down on the dominated class and shapes its needs by constricting them. But this is not a 'purely' ideological process: it is a process with a material basis in the conditions of daily life (p. 175).

The political challenge facing the left is therefore seen as breaking down these restricted notions of need and generating new needs (hence new demands) among working people through changing their material practices (e.g. by radical innovations in local politics, by encouraging and supporting self-management schemes in industry, and so on).

The importance of this approach is that it recognizes that consumption generates some independent effects. As Preteceille (1985) makes clear in a later paper, one's position in the organization of production does not totally determine one's consumption pattern (inheritance of material and cultural capital, for example, varies widely between different people in the same class location), and consumption can act back upon the social relations of production (e.g. divisions between different groups of consumers expressing different needs may fragment a social class). Nevertheless, he continues to assert that production is determining in the sense that divisions expressed through consumption can only be explained in terms of the divisions generated through production. This argument directly reflects a functionalist theory of system needs.

Preteceille and Terrail deny that their's is a functionalist theory on the grounds that they recognize that system needs may not be met. Yet no sophisticated functionalist theory would claim that all system needs are inevitably met (see, for example, Merton 1968, on functions and dysfunctions). In fact, their analysis, which is centrally concerned to show how the needs expressed by individuals through consumption are the product of system needs created in the organization of production, not only begs all the familiar questions about how system needs are to be identified, but also directly mirrors more conservative functionalist theories in its emphasis on the internalization by individuals of system imperatives. As they put it, 'Social needs are, *essentially*, no more than the objective demands of the mode of production with regard to its agents' (p. 58). What is entailed here is a strong version of functionalist socialization theory in which individuals somehow learn to express in their everyday practices desires and preferences which are consistent with those required by a capitalist economy. How this is done remains a mystery, however, for (unlike Parsonian systems theory) we are offered no theory of the personality and cultural 'systems', nor of how they interrelate with the social, economic and political systems.

The result, predictably, is tautology: as in Castells's earlier formulations, so too in Preteceille and Terrail's analysis, any apparent improvement in the conditions of working-class life is explained simply as a reflection of changed system needs. The possibility that capitalism may be able increasingly to meet people's needs is ruled out from the start: the growth of car ownership, home ownership, foreign travel, educational opportunities and the rest is explained simply as the response of the system (mediated through the demands of its socialized members) to increased exploitation in production.

Now it has, of course, to be accepted that the social organization of consumption relates to, and to some extent reflects, the way production in society is organized. But then, every aspect of social life obviously relates in some way to every other aspect. It is certainly the case, for example, that people's location in the organization of production sets limits upon their range of action as consumers (we cannot buy a house, for example, if we lack a regular household income of the appropriate size), but this does not mean that consumption has to be analysed as functional to production (as in Castells's focus on the reproduction of labour-power), or as a response to production (as in Preteceille and Terrail's focus on the creation and intensification of needs). Every position we occupy and role we play sets limits upon our capacity for action in some other role, but this does not mean that we cannot analyse particular aspects of social life without all the time relating them back to some prior, holistic conception of the total 'system' of which they form a part.

There are, in short, no necessary grounds for asserting that consumption is determined by production, and that a sociological analysis of consumption must always proceed by way of an analysis of production. The fact that the two spheres are related does not mean that both are subject to the same logic, nor that one is necessarily a function of the other. It is therefore quite legitimate to identify consumption as a specific area for study (as Castells does), and thus to investigate the specific patterns of inequalilty, political struggle and cultural identity which develop there. Indeed, it is my contention that the repeated attempts by Marxist urban theorists to relate such inequalities, struggles and identities back to a more 'fundamental' class analysis grounded in a concern with production have not only led inevitably into functionalist culs-de-sac, but have also obscured our understanding of some crucial changes which are located in, and derive from, the organization of consumption itself, and which are having the most profound effects on our society as a whole, and on class relations in particular.

At the heart of these changes is the growing economic, political and cultural significance of the division between collective and individual forms of consumption. As I shall argue below and in Chapter 8, the basic class division between those who own and control the means of production and those who do not is today increasingly being overlaid by an equally important division between those who own and control crucial means of consumption and those who do not – i.e. a division, which cuts right across the class structure, between those with access to individual forms of consumption and those who are reliant on collective provision. This distinction between individual and collective consumption is basic to any sociological analysis of consumption in the contemporary period. Like the division between production and consumption, it derives out of Castells's work, and it too has been the subject of some critical argument and refinement.

The main problem is simply to determine what is designated by the term 'collective'. As Mingione suggests, 'If we add the adjective "collective" to the word "consumption" we raise a number of questions which French neo-Marxist urban sociology scholars have not answered. What can be called collective consumption and what individual consumption?' (1981, pp. 66–7). At first sight, this may look like academic semantic quibbling, but the implications of different definitions of collective and individual consumption can be significant.

In his earliest formulations, Castells took collective consumption to refer to 'consumption processes whose organization and management cannot be other than collective given the nature and size of the problems' (1976b, p. 75). In later works, however, he specified the term more clearly as referring to 'processes which are largely determined by state activity' (1978, p. 179). It is not always clear, therefore, whether consumption is 'collective' because it is communal (a view also found in Lojkine 1976) or because it is socialized. Many communally-consumed resources are supplied by the private sector (theatres, coaches, etc.) while many resources provided by the state are not communally-consumed (housing being the clearest example). Furthermore, there appears to be some confusion over whether 'collective consumption' is inherently collective given factors like size, accessibility and 'neighbourhood effects' (e.g. roads or city parks – see Friedman 1962, ch. 2), or is historically variable (as in the 'privatization' of certain aspects of consumption by the Thatcher governments in the 1980s in Britain).

These sorts of issues have been widely discussed in the literature (see Pahl 1977a and 1978, Saunders 1979, ch. 3), and as Harloe (1979) suggests, Castells himself seems to have settled on a definition which limits collective consumption to social provisions provided and managed by the state, irrespective of whether they are consumed individually or collectively. Even so, problems remain with such a formulation, for some goods or services may be provided by the private sector and dispensed or managed by the state (e.g. public housing or drugs), others will be provided and dispensed by the private sector yet subsidised or regulated by the state (e.g. owner-occupied housing or private medicine), and yet others will be provided and managed wholly within the public sector (e.g. state schooling or social work services). Such variations may have significant economic, political and ideological implications such that their subsumption under a single and all-embracing category is likely to prove unhelpful.

The clearest and most useful attempt to clarify the concept of collective consumption, and to distinguish it from individual consumption, has been made by Dunleavy. In his initial formulation (1980, ch. 2), he established five criteria for determining collective consumption. The concept, he argued, precluded money transfers, referred to services rather than commodities, and covered only those services which were collectively organized and managed, allocated on non-market criteria, and paid for at least partially out of taxation. In a later paper (1983), he then developed these ideas more rigorously in the form of a typology of consumption.

Following Castells, Dunleavy defines 'consumption' as 'the final appropriation of products by people'. This enables him to rule out of his analysis both the consumption by firms of raw materials which are transformed into some other commodity, and the provision by the state of transfer payments in cash (since money is not itself consumed but is used to buy objects which people then 'appropriate').

The next step in the analysis is to distinguish 'autonomous consumption' (where people consume what they have themselves produced) from 'commodified consumption' (where they consume things provided either by private firms through the market, or by professional interests through bureaucratic systems of allocation), and the latter category is then itself subdivided into 'individualized' and 'socialized' forms. For Dunleavy, individualized consumption refers to those goods and services marketed without state subsidy, while socialized consumption covers those provided either with subsidies or through non-market channels. Socialized consumption is then itself broken down into 'quasi-individualized consumption' (private goods marketed with a subsidy – e.g. owner-occupied housing), 'quasi-collective consumption' (private services provided with a subsidy, such as the theatre, or provided outside the market, such as voluntary welfare services), and 'collective consumption' proper (which is thus limited to public services which are either non-marketed – e.g. schools and health care – or marketed with a subsidy – e.g. public transport).

Dunleavy argues that 'socialized consumption' as conceptualized in this paper 'provides a clear analytical solution to the problems of delimiting a field of urban studies' (1983, p. 9). Urban sociology, therefore, is concerned with more than just collective consumption (for it encompasses quasi-individual and quasi-collective forms of provision) but with less than consumption as a whole, since it precludes analysis of individualized consumption (i.e. the consumption of unsubsidized private goods and services through the market), or of autonomous consumption (i.e. self-provisioning), or of cash payments made by the state in order to facilitate consumption. As I shall argue in Chapter 8, such a limited specification of urban studies seems arbitrary and unnecessarily restrictive, but the typology itself is enormously useful in clarifying the different forms of consumption, each of which may have very different implications in terms of patterns of inequality and political domination in contemporary capitalist societies.

The key implication, which Dunleavy himself traces in this and in other work, concerns the development of new forms of political cleavage arising out of the organization of consumption and cutting across the vertical lines of class cleavage generated in the production sphere. Even more than Castells, Dunleavy recognizes that consumption may be crucial in influencing political alignments.

As we have already noted, Castells recognized from his earliest writings that political mobilization around issues of collective consumption rarely occurred on straight class lines. His initial theory of urban social movements, for example, held that waged workers, professionals, white-collar workers and even petty-bourgeois small traders and capitalists could mobilize in common over consumption issues, and that this could enable socialist or communist parties to build broad, popular alliances in support of an overall challenge to the capitalist system despite the separation and antagonism of these different classes in respect of workplace politics.

This theory has been criticized and largely discredited. Pickvance (1977b), for example, took issue with what he called the 'urban fallacy' of assuming that groups which may share common interests in particular consumption issues will as a result be willing to join in a radical anti-monopoly capital alliance whose main aim is to transform the social organization of production. The idea that individuals whose economic situations (wages, conditions of work, standard of living, etc.) were in all other respects totally divergent may nevertheless somehow be forged into a unified political bloc fighting together for socialism simply because a local hospital was threatened with closure or a neighbourhood bus route was withdrawn was clearly little more than wishful thinking. Such an argument could only be entertained by totally ignoring the subjective dimension of the actors' own views of their situations, for while it is true that consumption issues can result in a willingness on the part of the middle classes to join with less privileged groups in limited protests over specific consumption issues, it is also obvious that this is unlikely to eclipse actors' awareness of the other factors which divide them.

Rather than assuming that consumption issues can unite classes which are normally opposed, it is empirically and theoretically more plausible to suggest that such issues may be expected to fragment classes which are normally unified. For every example of an urban movement which draws on a pluri-class social base, there are probably many more of consumption cleavages cutting through a single class and setting its members against each other. Like gender, ethnicity and nationality, consumption location tends to be class-divisive, and this is especially the case in a context (such as that in Britain since the late 1970s) where collective consumption provisions are being selectively cut back. As Harloe and Paris (1984) recognize, a government strategy of reducing public expenditure on consumption provision and of privatizing consumption wherever feasible is unlikely to generate any unified opposition because of the cross-cutting pressures which such a strategy generates. A 'crisis of collective consumption', far from provoking broad and radical opposition (as Castells originally assumed), is thus more likely to create political confusion, fragmentation and ineffectiveness.

In a later paper, Pickvance (1985) has made the further and crucially important point that consumption issues do not necessarily stimulate 'progressive' or socialistic popular responses. A policy of privatization, for example, may represent a threat to some working-class people while providing an opportunity for others. The sale of council houses may be experienced as an attack by those on the waiting list for council accommodation, but for those existing tenants who aspire to buy their homes, it represents an unprecedented chance to realize their personal objectives. Similarly, privatization of certain municipal services may hit those workers who provide the service (e.g. by reducing wage levels) while benefiting working-class ratepayers (e.g. by reducing charges). Again, therefore, we see the tendency to fragmentation rather than fusion, polarization rather than unification, associated with the politics of consumption.

This political fragmentation has been documented in the case of Britain by Patrick Dunleavy (1979, 1980) who explains the growing 'class dealignment' in voting patterns as in large part a product of the increasing significance of the division between the public and private sectors in areas such as housing and transport. Controlling for social class, he shows that home ownership and car ownership appear to be highly significant variables associated with conservative voting (home owners, for example, are almost twice as likely to vote for the Conservative Party as council tenants), and he argues from this that 'consumption location' is a major factor, equivalent to occupational class location, in shaping political alignments.

Dunleavy's analysis has received considerable empirical support from other sources. Work in Greater Manchester by Duke and Edgell, for example, shows a high degree of working-class political fragmentation consequent upon variations in consumption patterns, and concludes that 'Political party alignment is influenced more by overall consumption location than by social class' (1984, p. 195). Analysis of the 1983 general election result indicates the political significance of housing tenure as a major consumption cleavage, for among manual workers, the Labour Party attracted only 5 per cent more support than the Conservatives, and the major factor associated with working-class Conservative voting was home ownership. Indeed, among those who had purchased their council houses, no fewer than 56 per cent voted Conservative compared with just 18 per cent who voted Labour (Crewe 1983). Case study evidence, such as my own work in the London Borough of Croydon (Saunders 1979), also tends to support the view that public/private divisions, at least as regards housing, are a major basis of political alignment and mobilization in local politics, while cross-cultural research (e.g. Kemeny 1980) has suggested that high rates of privatized consumption of housing can generate a strongly conservatizing influence as regards people's orientation to the welfare state and collective provision generally. Furthermore, more recent work by Dunleavy himself suggests that consumption sector cleavages, which come into being as a result of increased state involvement in the provision of consumption, may react back upon state programmes as the public/private sector division assumes increasing ideological significance (Dunleavy 1985).

Such evidence must, of course, be treated with some caution. Dunleavy's analysis has, for example, been questioned by Franklin and Page (1984) who cite evidence to suggest that consumption issues such as housing policy do not figure centrally in voters' minds at election times, and who argue that political socialization is still far more significant in affecting voting behaviour than consumption location. Clearly more research is needed into the relation between consumption sector cleavages and political alignments before any clear evaluation of Dunleavy's thesis is possible, and such work will need to go beyond mere studies of voting to consider other (arguably more significant) indicators of political alignment and political ideology.

More important than this, however, is the need to extend Dunleavy's analysis of consumption sectors beyond the political context. Again taking housing as the example, it is now irrefutable that home owners in Britain have often been able to generate large and real material gains from their housing – gains which have not been available to public sector tenants (see, for example, Farmer and Barrell 1981). It is also highly plausible to suggest that home owners may experience much more control and autonomy in their everyday lives outside of the formal workplace than is possible for those who rent their accommodation from the state (see, for example, Ward 1985). Such economic and cultural aspects of consumption location are just as crucial for a sociological analysis of consumption sector cleavages as the political effects in terms of party alignment, but they receive scant attention in Dunleavy's work. As we shall see in Chapter 8, the significance of social relations of consumption for an understanding of class and inequality in a society like Britain goes beyond mere political realignment, for as Mingione (1981) suggests, we are witnessing a process of 'social disgregation' and 'social restratification' within society as a whole in which the changing organization of consumption is playing a pivotal role.

Such considerations have taken us a long way from Castells's original analysis of collective consumption. We have seen in this chapter that Castells's initial focus has to be reconceptualized. In particular, it is clear that the analysis of collective consumption has to be made more sensitive to the different patterns of state management, subsidy and provision, that a focus on consumption should be alert to the fragmentation and restratification of class relations in the contemporary period, and that consumption effects can and must be analysed on their own terms without constantly seeking to explain them in terms of the 'functions' they are held to perform for a system of capitalist production. We have also seen that Castells's attempt to conceptualize the city as a unit of consumption is unhelpful, and that a sociology of consumption can only be developed once we break with the specific spatial orientation which has characterized urban studies up to the present day.

Unlike most of the other approaches to the 'urban question' discussed in previous chapters, Castells's focus on issues of consumption does at least open up the possibility of a coherent research agenda. To adopt such an agenda, however, means dropping the hitherto distinctive focus on the city as an object of analysis, for the organization of consumption is no more spatially delimited than any of the other processes identified in earlier urban theories. Paradoxically, however, we reach this conclusion at a time when some urban theorists have begun to reassert the specific significance of spatial organization in social and economic life. Before developing a framework for the sociological analysis of consumption in Chapter 8, it is thus necessary to address head-on the issue which has rippled through the whole of this book so far of whether spatial forms in general, and the city in particular, can constitute a significant object of analysis for urban studies in the context of advanced capitalist societies. This is the concern of Chapter 7.

7   A non-spatial urban sociology?

One of the most important legacies of Castells's assault on urban sociology in his early work has been the recognition that theorists and practitioners alike have tended to identify phenomena as 'urban' when their causes lie not in the existence of cities, but in the organization of society as a whole. Although Castells's critique of such approaches was grounded in an epistemology which he and many others have subsequently come to reject, it is notable that, among all the changes in his work over the years since then, he has remained consistent in his view that such formulations are fundamentally flawed. In his reflections on *The Urban Question*, for example, he states that he still stands by the critique of urban sociology developed there: 'It contains some mistakes but basically I would not change much' (1985, p. 6).

One of the puzzles surrounding his work, however, is that having demolished urban sociology, he then set about rebuilding it around the concept of collective consumption. As we saw in the last chapter, this concept can, when suitably clarified and revised, provide the basis for a sociological research programme which is both coherent and pertinent to the analysis of key aspects of contemporary capitalist societies, but Castells's attempt to tie it to the analysis of cities was unsuccessful. State provision of means of consumption is not specific to cities, nor to any other spatial units save for the space bounded by nation-states themselves. Indeed, this is implicitly recognized by Castells himself in so far as his analyses of collective consumption, while located in cities, have not generally explored the significance of this spatial context. Even in *The City and the Grassroots*, it is apparent that his focus is on the social processes which he finds going on in urban areas rather than on the areas themselves. Andrew Sayer makes the point clearly when he suggests:

Castells . . . repeatedly refers to space and 'urban space', but these turn out to be references to objects whose spatial structure and setting is then ignored. Certainly, when we talk about housing and factories we are referring to things which could not possibly be aspatial, but this hardly justifies the claim that space is being discussed properly, for we are told nothing about the internal spatial organisation of these objects or their spatial relations with other objects. . . . What Castells offers is more in the nature of classification of objects, activities and social relations in 'urban space' rather than an analysis of their spatial form (1979, pp. 65–6).

Now it is important to clarify at the outset just what is at stake in the issues raised by this sort of criticism. Sayer is not claiming that Castells's analysis is *aspatial*, but that it is to all intents and purposes *non-spatial*. The distinction is crucial, for as we saw in Chapter 1, it is quite possible to argue that in the modern period spatial units below the level of the nation state have lost their social significance without also arguing that space is therefore totally irrelevant to social scientific analysis. Weber, Durkheim and Marx and Engels all believed that the city had been eclipsed as a significant economic, political or cultural unit, but they also all recognized that the spatial context of social action could and did still play an important role in sustaining or inhibiting the development of particular kinds of action. Their analyses, in other words, were not aspatial, for they understood how spatial proximity could, for example, help foster a sense of class consciousness among city-based factory workers, or could aid the erosion of a powerful collective morality, but they were non-spatial, in the sense that the explanations for such phenomena were located in changes current in the society as a whole which were not specific to cities or any other form of human settlement. Much the same point can be made in respect of Castells's work, for as we saw in Chapter 6, his focus on urban-based collective consumption provisions took space into account as a factor tending to promote or inhibit collective political mobilization, but his primary focus was on the contradiction between consumption and production within the economy as a whole. In short, a non-spatial social science does not preclude the possibility of analysing spatial organization as a secondary factor, but it does deny the relevance of spatial form as an object of study in itself.

In this chapter, we shall consider some of the contemporary theoretical work in geography and sociology which claims that space cannot be analysed simply as a secondary factor, and which thus develops a critique of non-spatial social science. Throughout this discussion, however, it is important to bear in mind that what is at issue is not whether, as one recent influential book repeatedly asserts, 'space matters' (Massey 1984), but how much it matters. No one is arguing for an aspatial sociology any more than an ahistorical sociology: the issue is simply whether space is so crucial to sociological explanation that it must be a central and primary constitutive element of any sociological analysis.

In this chapter we shall consider two streams of thought which assert the centrality of space to social analysis. The first, associated mainly with the Marxist geography of writers such as David Harvey and Doreen Massey, attempts to theorize space in terms of its role in the process of capital accumulation, circuits of capital and capitalist restructuring. The second, associated principally with the sociological theory of Anthony Giddens and with the realist sociology of writers such as John Urry, has connections with the first approach, but its focus is wider than simply the operation of the capitalist economy, and it attempts to theorize space as a constitutive element of social interaction. Both approaches are rich with theoretical insight, and both amply demonstrate the inadequacy of an aspatial social science, but neither in my view establishes the much more problematic case for placing 'space' (still less 'urban space' or the 'city') at the centre of social scientific inquiry.

As a prelude to this discussion, and by way of a summary of the core theme which has developed in earlier chapters, this chapter begins with a brief résumé of the problem of relating spatial categories to social processes – a problem which has been explicitly addressed by various different traditions within urban sociology during the twentieth century but which has thus far eluded a solution.

Beyond a sociology of the city

We saw in Chapter 1 that, despite their very different methodological approaches and substantive concerns, Marx, Weber and Durkheim all came to very similar conclusions as regards the analysis of urban questions. All agreed that the city played an historically specific role in the development of western capitalism (although as we also saw, even this has been disputed by later historians), but they all also argued that once capitalism had become established, the city ceased to be a theoretically significant entity. This was because it was no longer the expression and form of a new mode of production (Marx), or because it ceased to be the basis of human association, social identity and political domination (Weber), or because it no longer corresponded to the geographical boundaries within which the division of labour was integrated (Durkheim). To the extent that these writers discussed the city in the context of their analyses of capitalist-industrial societies, they treated it either as an illustration of the most developed tendencies within such societies (class polarization, bureaucratic rationality, anomic social disorganization), or as a secondary condition of the development of certain tendencies (notably, class struggle or the erosion of the collective conscience). The city, in other words, was not treated as a significant object of analysis in its own right, nor were spatial units other than the nation state itself invested with any great sociological importance. Urban questions were addressed only in so far as they could contribute to a wider understanding of certain processes associated with modernity.

The development of urban sociology as a distinct sub-discipline with its own journals, departments, associations and professional chairs changed all this, for urban sociology was premised on the assumption that cities were theoretically important in their own right, that certain social phenomena were characteristic of and peculiar to urban areas, and that it was therefore possible and necessary to generate specific theories of urbanism in order to explain distinctively urban phenomena. These assumptions were reinforced academically by a judicious, selective and generally uncritical reading of certain key works by writers such as Tönnies and Simmel, and were sustained practically by the willingness of governments and certain private foundations to fund work which would generate explanations if not solutions for problems which were generally manifested in large cities, be they poverty, crime, mental stress, racial tension or whatever. In confronting such problems through empirical work and through participation in the fledgling town planning movement, sociologists were inevitably led to the basic problem of how the city was to be conceptualized, for only by resolving this question was it possible to identify the specific problems that urban sociology could analyse and the range of factors which it might identify in its search for explanations.

So it was that the search began for an 'urban' object of analysis. Other sociological sub-disciplines each had their own specific object – the family, crime, organizations, religion or whatever – and although all of these could be observed in cities, none of them could be colonized by this new sub-discipline as objects distinctively of cities. What was needed, and what was to prove so elusive, was the specification of some social process or phenomenon which could be related to a physically-bounded area within the confines of the nation state. The subsequent theoretical history of urban sociology has been the history of a search for a sociological entity corresponding to the physical entity of the city. It has been the history of an institutionalized sub-discipline in search of a rationale for its own existence.

We have seen that four principal 'solutions' have been put forward in response to this problem. None of them has been successful, although each of them has contributed much by way of empirical work (as in the Chicago school ethnographies – see Hannerz 1980, ch. 2) or through analysing processes which, while not distinctively 'urban', are nevertheless crucial to other areas of sociological research. The problems encountered within each approach, together with the empirical or theoretical legacy which they left behind, are summarized in Figure 1.

The first attempt to develop a distinctive conceptual framework for urban sociology was Robert Park's theory of human ecology. However, as we saw in Chapter 2, this approach was from its very inception torn between a concern to explain processes of city growth and differentiation on the one hand, and processes of human adaptation to environmental changes within society as a whole on the other. In terms of the former, Chicago human ecology was a theory of the city, but in terms of the latter it was a theory of unconscious processes of competition and adaptation which occur in any human aggregate.

This division was the product of a methodological confusion, for like Durkheim, Park sought both to ground knowledge in observation of the world and to discover underlying causal processes which could not be observed directly. This logical contradiction lay at the heart of the contradiction in the theory itself. As a theory of the (observable) city, there was no reason to limit analysis to the biotic level of human organization, for as Firey, Alihan and other critics pointed out, the city was as much a product of cultural processes as of biotic ones. As a theory of adaptation, by contrast, there was no reason to limit its empirical reference to cities, for as Hawley, Duncan and others went on to show, such processes could equally be analysed in relation to any social groups, organizations or institutions. Increasingly, therefore, a split developed within the ecological tradition. One set of researchers held on to the city as the empirical object of analysis but jettisoned the theoretical focus on biotic struggles, and in this way they continued the Chicago school ethnographic tradition but lost any coherent theoretical framework through which to order and situate their observations. The result was a long series of demographic mapping exercises produced by quantitative researchers, and a tradition of community studies produced by qualitative ones, but both

Definition of 'urban'	Analytical tension			Legacy
Ecological system	(a) theory of the city (observable processes) versus			(a) community studies/ ethnographies
	(b) theory of adaptation (non-observable biotic forces)			(b) functionalist sociology
Cultural form	(Simmel)	(a) sociology of number versus		(a) theories of moral density
		(b) sociology of modernity		
	(Wirth)	(a) demographic analysis versus		(b) cultural theories of capitalism
		(b) class/life cycle analysis		
Socio-spatial system	(Pahl)	(a) sociology of spatial inequality versus sociology of the state		(a) corporatist state theory/studies of bureaucratic and professional domination
	(Rex)	(b) sociology of the city versus analysis of social stratification		(b) focus on consumption cleavages
Spatial unit of collective consumption	(a) theory of capitalist urbanism versus			(a) political economy of space
	(b) analysis of state functions in reproducing labour-power			(b) sociology of consumption (non-spatial 'urban' sociology)

Figure 1   Sociological conceptualizations of urbanism

proved essentially non-cumulative and atheoretical. Meanwhile, a different set of researchers, following Hawley, held on to processes of adaptation as the theoretically specific problem for analysis, but severed this from the concern with the city or other spatial forms. This second approach increasingly drew upon and became integrated with functionalist systems theories which likewise focused upon adaptation as one of the basic functional prerequisites of human societies, and as it did so, so the initial concern with the city was eclipsed and finally abandoned. Today, therefore, we are confronted with a schism between atheoretical descriptions of city life and theoretical analyses of processes which have no necessary relation to cities.

A second attempt to develop a coherent basis for urban sociology is represented by the work of Tönnies, Simmel and, most significantly, Louis Wirth. Here, some causal relation is posited between demographic features of human settlements and the cultural patterns thought to be associated with them, yet as we saw in Chapter 3, the familiar tension between a concern with the city and a focus on specific sociological phenomena which were not specific to urban space soon resurfaced.

In the case of Simmel, this tension reflected the distinct concerns in his work with a sociology of number or size, and a sociology of modernity. The first led to an analysis of the social implications of the growth of large-scale forms of human association, while the second was more concerned with the significance of factors such as the development of monetary systems and the intensification of the division of labour. In his essay on the metropolis, Simmel ran these two areas of analysis together with the result that factors inherent to cities (i.e. population size) became confused with factors inherent to capitalist societies (e.g. the alienation born of the division of labour and monetary relationships). Metropolis was thus neither urbanism nor capitalism; it was both.

Wirth's essay was an attempt to clarify this distinction. He was careful to theorize urbanism in terms of just three variables (size, density and heterogeneity), none of which was inherently associated with any particular economic or social form of organization, and he then went on to hypothesize that an increase in these three variables would tend to generate an increase in distinctively urban patterns of social relations as identified in his ideal type of urbanism (i.e. anonymous, superficial, transitory and segmental relations). The problem with this approach is not (as is often suggested) that it is empirically false (i.e. that social relationships in cities are not as Wirth characterized them), for such a criticism fails to understand Wirth's project and rests on a misinterpretation of the ideal type method. Rather, the problem is that the three key variables appear not to be the principal ones in explaining variations in patterns of social life. As the work of Pahl, Gans and others revealed, factors such as people's class situation, their ethnic culture, and their stage in the family life cycle appear to be much stronger determinants of ways of life than are the demographic factors identified by Wirth. Once again, therefore, we are forced beyond the city, to a study of social relations in society as a whole, in order to explain what we find going on in the city.

Both ecological and cultural theories of urbanism thus appear inadequate as the basis for a distinctively urban social theory, although both have left some residues. Human ecology has spawned a community study tradition which has been rich descriptively despite its theoretical weaknesses. The main problems with such studies, however, are first, that the very lack of a theoretical framework has hindered comparison and hence generalization (they are, as Bell and Newby 1971, suggest, essentially non-cumulative), and second, that it is always unclear to what extent the findings from one community can be taken as common to all. As we shall see later in this chapter, the 'locality' as an object of analysis has recently reappeared in urban studies research, but such studies today are premissed on a rejection of the notion that localities are microcosms of the wider society, for their rationale is precisely to understand how and why social processes vary between different places. In any event, it is clear that community/locality cannot itself constitute a theoretical object for urban sociology, for what is of interest is not the place *per se* but the social processes which are generated or mediated through different places. We return to this issue below in the discussion of work by Massey, Urry and Giddens.

The residue from cultural theories of urbanism is a theoretical concern with the effects of size, spatial form and what Durkheim termed 'moral density' on social relationships. As we saw in Chapter 3, these effects cannot entirely be dismissed, although once we take account of more specifically sociological variables such as class, life cycle and sub-culture, they often turn out, in Dewey's phrase, to be 'relatively unimportant'. Nevertheless, some interesting and fruitful work has been done on the social implications of different spatial arrangements, and such research can prove of practical relevance to those concerned with city design and planning practices. Newman's analysis of *Defensible Space* (1972), for example, has been influential in documenting the possibilities of and constraints upon criminal activity which follow from different types of site planning and architectural design. More broadly, Hillier and Hansen's *The Social Logic of Space* (1984) shows how the physical layout of buildings, both internally and in relation to each other, functions to structure the social use of space and hence to order the social relationships between people. Nevertheless, it can still be argued that sociological variables should probably take precedence in any explanation of such phenomena. Human behaviour in formally similar spatial settings can vary widely according to the socio-economic and cultural characteristics of those involved (consider, for example, the dramatic changes documented by Ward (1985) when council-owned flats were sold into owner-occupation in Liverpool), and the tendency to physical reductionism and spatial determinism should always be resisted by analysing the diverse meanings which different social groups may invest in similar spaces. What this work does show, however, is that spatial arrangements (including factors such as size and density as well as layout) cannot be ignored in sociological analysis. As we shall see below, spatial arrangements can inhibit or facilitate certain types of social phenomena, in which case it is important to avoid an aspatial social science. Nevertheless, it is a giant step from here to an acceptance of the idea that spatial variables determine social phenomena in the way that Wirth tried to suggest.

In Chapter 4 we considered a third approach to urban theory. This was based on the three main propositions that space is inherently unequal, that different social groups use such power as they command in the market or through the state to achieve favourable locations and access to resources, and that the decisions made by strategically-placed gatekeepers are crucial in influencing the distribution of such resources among these different groups. Urban sociology was then defined in terms of its theoretical concern with the distributive consequences of urban managerial decisions and with conflicts between different 'housing classes' over the allocation of scarce and desirable resources. Subsequent analysis of these two questions, however, has indicated that neither urban managerialism nor the housing class concept can adequately specify peculiarly 'urban' processes, although the legacy of this approach is again of some interest.

The initial problem with Pahl's focus on urban managers was that it lacked clear criteria for determining which sorts of people were significant in shaping resource allocation and how far they were responsible for the pattern of distribution which resulted. This led to a reconceptualization of urban managers as local state bureaucrats mediating between the private sector, central government and the local population. Although this formulation resolved the problem of identification, it failed to clarify the question of managerial autonomy and discretion. Inevitably, Pahl himself was driven by the logic of his own analysis to investigate national political and economic processes and hence to undermine his original concern with the city as a system of resource allocation. So developed the all too familiar tension between the empirical focus on the city and the theoretical analysis of processes located outside and beyond it, for the ensuing investigation of national-level corporatism clearly had little to do with Pahl's initial interest in theorizing specifically urban processes.

The housing class concept fared even worse. The main reason for this was the confusion in Rex's work between empirical and conceptual criteria of identification and classification. Thus we saw in Chapter 4 that Rex sometimes identifies housing classes in terms of current housing tenure (owner-occupiers, council tenants, landlords, etc.) yet at other times identifies them in terms of the potential power of different social groups when they enter the housing market (blacks, one-parent families, etc.). There is, in other words, a tension in his work between an interest in housing tenure as a basis of inequality and political mobilization outside of the sphere of production, and a concern to demonstrate how access to a crucial consumption resource such as housing depends upon factors such as racial status. Clearly his theoretical interest is in the latter, but this means that the social divisions he draws correspond not to 'urban' classes but to strata and classes in society as a whole, and that his work leads not to a theory of the city but to a theory of social stratification in which race and ethnicity play a major role. This becomes clear in his later work with Sally Tomlinson where he argued that the major source of conflict in inner Birmingham was not housing, but education and jobs – i.e. resources which have nothing inherently to do with cities as such, but which form the basis for conflict between different groups which live, in the main, in the large conurbations. Just as the study of urban managers leads us beyond the city to an analysis of political power in society as a whole, so too the question of housing classes takes us away from an initial urban spatial focus into an analysis of class structure and its relation to divisions grounded in race, gender or whatever. Neither concept thus establishes the basis for a sociology of the city.

The legacy of this work is nonetheless important. The key point to emerge from Pahl's work in this period is that the state is today a crucial factor in determining people's life chances, and that it does not necessarily operate according to a strict capitalist logic. It follows from this that sociological analyses of class and market power grounded in the study of relations of production must be complemented by analyses of inequalities generated and sustained through bureaucratic systems of allocation. We do not have to endorse Pahl and Winkler's somewhat overblown theory of corporatism to recognize that the state is today a major 'actor' intervening in many aspects of people's lives, and that the interests shaped by its interventions may not correspond to the neat lines of cleavage between capital and labour which are still the basis of so many sociological analyses of power and inequality.

The legacy of Rex's housing class analysis is similar, for it too was premissed on the recognition that inequalities and political struggles over consumption resources were distinct from the class inequalities and class struggles arising out of relations of production in society. Although Rex's analysis was muddled, the focus on housing tenure as one major aspect of consumption-based inequalities was fruitful, for it stimulated a protracted (and currently unresolved) debate within urban studies over the significance of home ownership as a factor tending to fragment or even restructure the class relations arising out of a capitalist organization of production. As we shall see in Chapter 8, housing tenure is a key feature of consumption sector cleavages in the contemporary period, and Rex's initial formulation of the housing class concept, while flawed, did much to alert later researchers to the significance of such divisions. For our present purposes, however, the main point remains that analysis of such cleavages and divisions cannot be contained within an empirical focus on the city as an object of study.

The concern with the state and with the related issue of consumption, which ran through the neo-Weberian work of the 1960s and 1970s, became the explicit focus of the fourth attempt to theorize the city – that by Castells. Indeed, it was Castells who for the first time directly pointed to the problem in urban sociology of identifying an urban 'theoretical object', and in his early work he criticized previous approaches (including the Marxist analysis developed by Lefebvre) for fetishizing space by attributing causal properties to urbanism which were in fact aspects of the organization of capitalism. In his reformulation of the urban question, he argued that the city is theoretically significant as the spatial container within which labour-power is reproduced through state provision of necessary consumption resources, although in his later writings he expanded this conception by arguing that cities are sites of struggle where different groups seek to realize their goals, interests and values, not only in respect of state consumption provisions, but also in relation to questions of political power and cultural identity.

Clearly, although Castells included the spatial dimension within his definition of urbanism, space actually played a very minor role within his analysis. As Gottdiener (1984) suggests, once he had fastened on to collective consumption (and latterly, urban social movements) as his substantive focus, he was 'no longer interested in a theory of space per se, but rather in a theory of urban problems' (p. 203). This does not mean that he ignored space, for as he made clear in a paper in 1983, 'From the critique of the "spatialist theory" of social crises, it does not follow that space is unimportant and that the spatial dimension of the crisis should be ignored' (1983b, p. 3). Indeed, in this paper he went on (in terms somewhat reminiscent of his old adversary, Lefebvre) to argue that the spatial implications of the use of new technology were crucial in, for example, reinforcing hierarchical relations between different specialized locations and thus in separating centres of control and domination from the places of everyday life. Space, he argues, is inseparable from society, and the use of space is a product of struggles between dominant groups (capital, the state and men) and oppressed sections of society (workers, citizens, women) pursuing alternative projects and blueprints. As Kirby suggests, the image of space which Castells is proposing is analogous to that of a chessboard:

Space thus becomes the chessboard upon which each and every person is located. The moves that the pieces make take place within the spatial constraints of the board and the directions that are permitted. Most importantly, if we remove the board, we can no longer understand the logic of the pieces that remain. In fact, this is at the heart of Castells's account: namely, that swift changes within the contemporary capitalist mode of production are dissolving the form of the chessboard (1985, pp. 9–10).

Nevertheless, what interests Castells is not the board but the pieces, not the city but the struggles which occur within it. Neither his original focus on collective consumption, nor his later interest in urban-based movements challenging for material resources, political power and cultural self-determination have any inherent connection to the city as an object of analysis. For him, the city is a space within which interesting things happen, but as we saw in Chapter 6, there seems little reason for restricting either the analysis of consumption, or the study of non-class political and cultural movements, to an exclusive focus on this space.

Like the other three approaches, therefore, Castells's analysis results in something of a dilemma. If it is to be understood as a theory of the city, then the focus on consumption is too narrow for it ignores the significance of other processes which also unfold in major urban centres, for consumption (or, indeed, state power and cultural domination) is no more specifically centred on the city than retailing, banking, manufacturing, transportation, recreation or any other core social processes. Indeed, Castells recognized as much when he argued at the end of *The City and the Grassroots* that urban social movements are ultimately utopian since they address problems, the solutions to which extend beyond the boundaries of their local areas. As he graphically puts it, 'When people find themselves unable to control the world, they simply shrink the world to the size of their community' (1983a, p. 331).

If, on the other hand, Castells's project is to be understood as a theory of consumption, then the focus on urban space is too restrictive, for it ignores any aspect of consumption and state provision which is either non-spatial (as is the case with the many subsidies and tax concessions associated with the 'hidden welfare state') or which is organized at a higher spatial scale (e.g. the various regional state bodies involved in areas like health care, training, transportation, and the like; clearly, the equation which Castells draws between consumption and the city, and production and the region, is both arbitrary and unconvincing, for both processes may be organized at both levels).

Just as human ecology split apart some fifty years ago into its constituent yet irreconcilable elements (the focus on the city and the focus on adaptation), so urban studies has today split along a very similar fault line. Notwithstanding the commitment to a dialectical method, Marxist as well as non-Marxist urban researchers are now to be found working in two distinct fields. One group has basically forgotten about the city as an object of analysis and has devoted itself to the analysis of issues concerning consumption. This group is to be found working, for example, on the welfare state and the inequalities associated with it, on studies of fiscal strain in state budgets, on analyses of local government services and the increasing conflicts between central and local government in the current period, on local political struggles around consumption issues, on the growth of the 'self-service economy' and domestic self-provisioning in the face of unemployment and welfare cut-backs, on privatization and its implications for class relations and social inequality, and so on.

Another group, by contrast, has held on to the city and other spatial forms as its distinctive object of inquiry but has foresaken any attempt to theorize the city in terms of a specific social phenomenon or process. This group is interested in cities and regions as spatial forms which in some way reflect, influence or help constitute wider economic and social changes and processes. Some researchers, for example, see spatial organization as important as an element in the system through which a capitalist mode of production operates (like Lefebvre, they therefore see the analysis of space as integral to the analysis of modern capitalism). Others focus on spatial organization as important in enabling and constraining the development of social processes generally (i.e. they see the analysis of space as integral to the development of any sociological explanation of why, how and when things happen in the way they do).

The first group is engaged in developing what we may term a 'sociology of consumption', or a 'non-spatial urban sociology', and we shall consider the main elements in such work in Chapter 8. The second group is engaged in developing a 'political economy of space' or, more generally, a mode of social analysis in which space plays a central role. It is with this second group that we shall be concerned for the remainder of this chapter.

The spatial aspect of economic organization

The attempt by some Marxist theorists from the 1970s onwards to develop a political economy of space was premised on the unequivocal rejection of Castells's claim that urbanism constituted neither a 'real' nor a 'scientific' object. The point was made forcibly by Dear and Scott in setting out a framework for such work:

A specifically *urban question* does indeed exist. It is structured around the particular and indissoluble geographical and land-contingent phenomena that come into existence as capitalist social and property relations are mediated through the dimension of urban space. . . . The city *is* a definite object of theoretical enquiry (1981, p. 6).

For them, the urban question therefore refers to the problem of how land comes to be used and managed through the interplay of classes and the state in modern capitalist societies. Put another way, the focus for research is to be the explanation of how the organization of socially-created space comes to reflect, express, mediate or influence the social organization of capitalism with all the contradictions which that mode of production is said to entail. Just as Marxist analysis has long recognized that time is socially produced as history, so too it must come to recognize how space is socially produced as geography. An early example of this sort of approach was an influential paper in which Roweis and Scott (1978) set out to show how spatial organization may enter into the process of capital accumulation as a factor inhibiting the most economically rational pattern of investment. In particular, the private ownership of urban land may thwart the optimal use of space as individuals seek to maximize their locational advantages in ignorance of the overall effects which their decisions are having. Furthermore, having invested in plant and equipment in one place, capitalist firms are then to some extent committed to staying put, even though the original factors which drew them to that place are soon likely to be eroded as a result of the self-interested locational decisions of other capitalists. As Roweis and Scott summarize the problem: 'Capitalist social and property relations create two major contradictory tendencies around the issue of urban land. On the one hand, the logic of commodity production and the private appropriation of profit call for functionally efficient urban land-use patterns. On the other, the private ownership and control of urban land lead to a tendency away from such efficiency' (p. 63).

It is in this context that the state tries to organize its interventions in the urban land system. Lipietz (1980), for example, argues that state planning and regulation involves the attempt to organize space in the interests of capital, both by providing collective infrastructure and other resources which each individual firm needs but cannot or is not willing to provide itself, and by forcibly imposing a logic of capital against private landowners through, for example, the compulsory purchase of land for redevelopment or by means of zoning and other measures. As Lamarche (1976, p. 104) suggests, state planning clears and prepares the land in order for private capital to sow and harvest the best fruit. Yet as Roweis and Scott go on to point out, the state is always limited in what it can achieve by the fact of private property ownership. It cannot direct investment in any coherent and rational way and it cannot lay down an efficient spatial pattern which all capitalist firms are obliged to follow. Even the British land use planning system is essentially a system of negative planning, for when the local and strategic plans have been established, it is still the private sector which decides whether and where to develop (see, for example, Ambrose and Colenutt 1975).

There is, at the heart of the urban land question, a 'contradiction between the socialized production of urban land in its totality, on the one hand, and the privatization of concomitant benefits on the other' (Roweis and Scott, p. 72). This contradiction is expressed in class struggles, not only between capital and labour, but also between different branches of capital itself, with the state centrally embroiled in the ensuing conflicts while being unable to resolve them. Capital accumulation, therefore, does not simply take place across space, but is essentially tied up with, and affected by, the organization of space.

The key implication of such an approach is that space is much more than a mere 'container' within which certain social or economic processes work out. In the view of those committed to developing a political economy of space, the attempt by Castells and others to find a social process which is limited to a particular organization of space is wrong-headed, for the task is rather to see how particular spatial forms are produced by, and react back upon, processes embedded within a particular organization of production. Putting the point somewhat oversimply, while Castells sought to locate social processes in a spatial setting, these writers seek to locate spatial processes in their wider societal and economic context.

That this is putting things oversimply is due to the fact that most of those who have attempted to develop a political economy of space reject the idea that space and society are separate entities which have to be related theoretically, one to the other. As Smith suggests, an approach which sees space and society 'interacting', or which analyses one as a 'reflection' of the other, is too crude, for it assumes that we are dealing with two distinct objects when, in fact, social organization is inherently and necessarily spatial. As material beings in a material world, we do not simply inhabit spatial locations, but we actively create them and have to live with the consequences: 'We do not live, act and work "in" space so much as by living, acting and working we produce space' (Smith 1984, p. 85).

In one respect, the space which is produced in a capitalist society will itself be an expression of capitalist social relations. As Lamarche puts it, 'The city is necessarily made in the image of the society which builds it' (1976, p. 117). Thus, when capitalism is reproduced, so too is its spatial form, and when capital restructures in response to mounting crisis, so too space is restructured. However, existing spatial arrangements also constrain and shape the way in which capitalism is reproduced or restructured, for space is already to some extent 'fixed' or congealed in forms which may have expressed previous patterns of economic activity. As Lipietz observes, 'Society recreates its space on the basis of a concrete space, always already provided, established in the past' (1980, p. 61). If and when capital restructures, therefore, it is immediately confronted by an existing spatial form which constrains and mediates any changes. If space changes when capitalism changes, then it is also the case that capitalism changes in and through an existing geographical landscape which cannot simply be reshaped by an act of will. Any change in the organization of capitalism thus not only carries with it an inherent change in the way space is used, but it also reflects existing spatial arrangements. Capitalist crises are spatial phenomena, not only in the sense that they are expressed in geographical unheavals (the creation of industrial wastelands in one place, the exacerbation of problems of rapid growth and concentration in another), but also in that material space may shape or intensify them by the constraints that it imposes on possible 'solutions'.

Here, then, is the 'urban question' reformulated in terms of what Soja (1980, 1985) has termed a 'socio-spatial dialectic': 'The structure of organized space is not a separate structure with its own autonomous laws of construction and transformation, nor is it simply an expression of the class structure emerging from the social (i.e. aspatial) relations of production. It represents, instead, a dialectically defined component of the general relations of production, relations which are simultaneously social and spatial' (1980, p. 208). The argument here is that there is a homology between the social structure with its division between dominant and exploited classes, and the spatial structure, with its division between centres and peripheries, for both arise from the same common cause (the organization of capitalism), are expressions of the same thing, and simultaneously shape each other.

At the heart of this dialectic is the assertion that, 'The spatiality of social life is society materially constituted' (Soja 1985, p. 177). Problems which manifest themselves in space (e.g. uneven development between countries or regions) are the inherent expressions of the contradictions within a capitalist mode of production, contradictions which are mediated by existing spatial arrangements and which are exacerbated by the tension between the inertia of current patterns and the dictates of new economic imperatives. Similarly, the conflicts which arise over the use of space are the mediated expressions of the class conflict within capitalism itself between capitalists, workers and other strata and fractions. There can be no theory of space as such, but nor can there be an aspatial theory of capitalist society, for, to adapt a well-worn aphorism, capital does not accumulate, nor classes struggle, nor the state intervene on the head of a pin.

As Soja himself acknowledges, this sort of approach to space and urbanism owes much to the theories of Henri Lefebvre. As we saw in Chapter 5, Lefebvre argues that the use of space has become integral to the survival of capitalism. The contradictions identified by Marx and Engels in the nineteenth century have been managed by ensuring the reproduction of capitalism through the domination of space – both by opening up new areas of accumulation outside and within the capitalist core countries (e.g. through exploitation of the Third World and through new investment in the core countries in property development and the provision for mass consumption – the so-called 'second circuit' dominated by finance capital), and by organizing space as a hierarchical structure which can ensure continued capitalist hegemony in every nook and cranny of everyday life as well as within the system of production. For Lefebvre, it is no longer enough to transform the social relations of production, for what is needed in addition is a reappropriation of urban space itself (an argument which, as we saw in Chapter 6, has now been taken up to some extent in Castells's revised theory of urban social movements as attempts to impose alternative meanings and uses on to the city).

According to Soja, Marxist theory has for too long ignored these sorts of insights into the spatiality of capitalism. For him, Lefebvre's work provides the basis for a retheorization of space which places 'the production of space and its control over the reproduction of social relations at the center of the survival of modern capitalism' (Soja and Hadjimichalis 1979, p. 9). The theorist who, more than any other, has critically taken up the sorts of issues raised in Lefebvre's work and who has attempted to develop Marxist theory in order to analyse the ways in which space is produced and reproduced under capitalism is David Harvey. In a series of articles and in two key books (*Social Justice and the City*, published in 1973, and *The Limits to Capital*, published in 1982), Harvey has developed what one commentator calls, 'The most systematic attempt to relate the theory of accumulation to the specific geography of capitalism' (Smith 1984, p. 125). He has since the 1970s become to Marxist urban geography what Castells became to Marxist urban sociology. How then does Harvey seek to put theoretical flesh on the conceptual bones of the socio-spatial dialectic?

Although Harvey's work has undoubtedly been influenced by

Lefebvre's writings (e.g. in the emphasis on the central role played by finance capital in producing space and in the concern with tracing the circuit of capital through the production of the built environment), it by no means accepts the whole of Lefebvre's research programme. Indeed, Soja (1980) bemoans the fact that Harvey fails to follow Lefebvre in placing space at the centre of the analysis of contemporary capitalism. Thus, although both writers see space as crucial in capitalism's ever-more pressing search for a means to ensure its own reproduction, Harvey from the outset rejected Lefebvre's view (expressed in his concept of an 'urban revolution') that the organization of space has become the fulcrum around which the whole system balances or collapses:

To say that urbanism now dominates industrial society is to say that contradictions between urbanism as a structure in the process of transformation and the internal dynamic of the older industrial society are usually resolved in favour of the former. I do not believe this claim is realistic. In certain important and crucial respects industrial society and the structures which comprise it continue to dominate urbanism (1973, p. 311).

For Harvey, the industrial sector is still the motor of capitalist development and the major source of change in capitalist societies. The urban system has therefore to be analysed in this context. Thus, the creation of space is largely a function of where big firms choose to site their head offices, their research and development centres, their assembly plants and so on; the money which flows into land and property development is governed by rates of profitability in the industrial sector; and the key role of the urban system lies in its significance as a means for realizing profits for industrial capital (e.g. through the increased demand for cars and other individual consumer goods consequent upon the spread of suburbanization). In short, the creation of the built environment is a product of the relentless drive for profitability on the part of capitalist industry.

Harvey argues that, just as individual firms try to establish a comparative advantage over their competitors by investing in new and more productive technology, so too they also attempt to secure a competitive edge by locating in relatively advantageous places (e.g. those nearest to sources of supply or to markets). Like many of the other writers discussed above, he recognizes that physical relocation is limited by the pattern of existing investment in 'fixed capital' (i.e. plant and machinery whose value is only gradually exhausted through each round of accumulation), and that current spatial arrangements thus represent a fetter on the possibility of adjusting to changing conditions. Firms, that is, have to weigh up the relative advantages of a new location against the devaluation of existing assets in the old one, and this may prevent them from moving, at least in the short run. Nevertheless, the drive to maximize returns results in a constant pressure on firms to close down in one place and open up in another, and dogged resistance to such pressures is likely to lead eventually to falling profits and ultimate bankruptcy as competitors reap ever-increasing advantages of location. It is in this sense that uneven geographical development is inherent to and necessary for capitalism. Every time the conditions of production and circulation change (e.g. with the introduction of new technologies, new transportation systems and the like), so a process of 'musical chairs' is sparked off in which certain places are abandoned to their fate:

The social geography which evolves is not...a mere reflection of capital's needs, but the locus of powerful and potentially disruptive contradictions. The social geography shaped to capital's needs at one moment in history is not necessarily consistent with later requirements. Since that geography is hard to change and often the focus of heavy long-term investment, it then becomes the barrier to be overcome. New social geographies have to be produced, often at great cost to capital and usually accompanied by not a little human suffering (1982, p. 403).

Capitalist relocation – the restructuring of space – is thus an essential feature of capitalist restructuring in periods of crisis. However, Harvey goes on to argue that this continuing search for relative locational advantage is ultimately self-defeating, for given the private ownership of land (which he sees as an essential and necessary feature of any capitalist society), temporary advantages which enable firms to make excess profits will soon disappear in increased rent payments to private landowners. In other words, no sooner do industrial firms move to an area and begin to reap greater returns (e.g. through savings in transportation costs, labour costs or whatever) than these returns are whittled away through rising rents and land prices.

Harvey has devoted much of his work over the years to an analysis of the role of rent in capitalist economies. In his view, rent is the concept which links the analysis of capitalist production to that of space and the built environment: 'Rent is that theoretical concept through which political economy (of whatever stripe) traditionally confronts the problem of spatial organization' (1982, p. 337). Rent (which includes both regular rental payments and capitalized one-off purchase payments for the use of land) is an example of 'fictitious capital' in that it represents a claim over future revenue. Land, in other words, does not produce value, but as an essential condition of production, it enables those who hold title to it to demand a slice of the value created by those who produce on it. Rent, in other words, is a deduction from the surplus value created in industrial production.

Broadly following Marx, Harvey identifies four categories of rent. *Monopoly rent* is that which accrues to a landowner as a result of the ability of the user of the land to sell his or her commodities at a monopoly price. In agriculture, for example, a particular plot of land may be used to produce wine of a unique quality which can command a high price, and in this case, the landlord will be able to raise the rent accordingly. Similarly, according to Harvey, the owner of a central location in a city will be able to command a high monopoly rent given the unique advantages of that location for, say, offices or retail outlets.

Absolute rent, by contrast, is the return which a landlord can demand before even the worst quality land is released. In Marx's analysis of agricultural rents, absolute rent is significant since it represents a barrier to investment in farming and thus prevents the equalization of profit rates between agriculture and other sections of industry. Thus higher rates of profit in agriculture, consequent upon a lower than average organic composition of capital, will result not in the attraction of new investment (and hence a raising of the organic composition and a reduction of profits to the average level), but rather in a creaming off by private landlords. Applied by Harvey to the urban context, the concept of absolute rent refers to the ability of landowners and property developers to extract money through the maintenance of artificial scarcity. Aided by state agencies (which restrict land availability for various uses through zoning) and by financial institutions (which determine lending policies in relation to house purchase and industrial investment), landlords as a class are able to maintain scarcity and thus to extract artificially high rents from people who have no alternative but to pay them.

The other two types of rent are forms of *differential rent*. The first of these refers to the difference between the returns which a producer can achieve on a given site and the returns which can be achieved on the worst land. In agriculture, for example, the owner of a high fertility field can extract the surplus profit which can be made on this land relative to that which is possible on land at the economic margin of cultivation, and this has the effect of reducing surplus profits to an average level pertaining throughout the farming industry. The second type of differential rent accrues as a result of previous investment in the land which raises its productivity, for here too, the owner will attempt to claw back the increased profits which can thereby be achieved. Differential rent therefore functions to equalize profit rates among producers on different quality sites at differentially-advantageous locations. The better the site, in terms of the advantages it provides in reducing costs and increasing returns, the higher the rent will be (although as Ball (1977), points out, the exact level or rent charged and paid will reflect specific struggles between landowners and users and cannot be generalized theoretically).

Now this analysis of rent leads Harvey to what he terms an 'extraordinary' conclusion. As we saw above, the competitive struggle to achieve surplus profits involves both the search for improved technology and the search for advantageous location. However, the search for excess profits through new technology is ultimately self-defeating since short-run advantages are soon wiped out as all other competitors also invest in the new machinery, thus raising the organic composition of capital and lowering the average rate of profit in the system as a whole. All that happens is that the same number of producers now manufacture a larger number of commodities of a lower value, hence depressing rates of profit and hastening the onset of a crisis of over-accumulation which can only be overcome by driving some firms to the wall. What Harvey now adds to this classic Marxist analysis of crisis is that spatial relocation follows much the same sort of pattern, for the pursuit of excess profits in new locations simply results in increased rents and hence in a reduction of rates of return back to the average level. Individual firms have no option but to relocate in order to seize competitive advantage, yet having done so, they find that this advantage promptly disappears! Industry is thus perpetually chasing its own tail while wreaking havoc across different regions and countries as it abandons existing investments in a futile attempt to improve profit rates:

Individual capitalists, acting in their own self-interest and striving to maximise their profits under the coercive pressures of competition, tend to expand production and shift locations up to the point where the capacity to produce further surplus value disappears. There is, it seems, a spatial version of Marx's falling rate of profit thesis (1982, pp. 389–90).

It is this insight which lies behind Harvey's attempt to develop Marx's analysis of crisis by integrating the question of space into the investigation of capital accumulation. Like Lefebvre, he argues that Marxist theory has to be developed to take account of the way in which crises of capitalist production have been overcome by opening up new possibilities of accumulation, but unlike Lefebvre, he goes on to demonstrate how each successive 'solution' has set in motion a new set of contradictions – contradictions which represent the unavoidable 'limits to capital' and which ultimately threaten the very future of humankind.

The analysis begins by identifying as a basic contradiction of capitalism the fact that competition between individual capitalists results in aggregate effects which run counter to their own individual and collective interests. For Harvey, this is demonstrated by Marx's analysis of the tendency for unbridled competition to result in a falling rate of profit and an over-accumulation of capital in the system as a whole. Harvey here closely follows Marx's own analysis in arguing that the drive to invest in new technology necessarily results in a crisis of over-accumulation which becomes manifest in gluts on the market, falling prices, idle productive capacity and rising unemployment:

Here we can clearly see the contradictions which arise out of the tendency for individual capitalists to act in a way which, when aggregated, runs counter to their own class interest. This contradiction produces a tendency towards over-accumulation – too much capital is produced in aggregate relative to the opportunities to employ that capital (1978a, pp. 104–6).

Harvey describes this analysis as a 'first cut' at crisis theory. This does not mean that the analysis is in some way wrong or even approximate, for in his view it succeeds in pinpointing the basic reason for the chronic instability of capitalist economies. What he does mean is rather that the analysis is incomplete in the sense that it fails to appreciate how the capitalist system has come to terms with this inherent tendency to a crisis of over-accumulation. What is involved here is a 'switching' of investment at times of impending crisis out of the 'primary circuit' of industrial production and into a 'secondary circuit' involving investment by financial institutions in 'fixed capital' and what he terms 'the consumption fund'.

As we saw above, fixed capital refers to that portion of investment which does not offer an immediate return but which gives up its value gradually through successive periods of productive activity. The most obvious examples are assets such as factories and offices. The consumption fund is in some ways analogous in that it consists of those items which are not directly consumed but are rather used over a long period of time to facilitate consumption. Examples here include housing and various consumer durables.

It is Harvey's argument that, faced with falling rates of return in industry, capital responds by increasing investment in this secondary circuit, much of which entails investing in the built environment. Sometimes this takes the form of investment in fixed capital such as office blocks. It is for this reason that bouts of property speculation (such as the office boom of the early 1970s) so often occur at times of industrial decline, for the development of urban physical infra-structure represents an alternative channel of investment when rates of return in the primary circuit begin to fall. Alternatively, it may involve investment in the consumption fund. The explosion of suburbanization in the United States after 1945, for example, is explained by Harvey (1977) as a massive switch into the secondary circuit, facilitated by the state (through tax concessions to home-buyers and construction firms) and by financial institutions (through special credit arrangements), which not only opened up new investment possibilities, but also helped stimulate demand for the products of industry such as cars and petroleum. Furthermore, such investment in the consumption fund had the additional advantage of maintaining political stability by creating 'a large wedge of debt-encumbered home owners' (1977, p. 125) intent on working all hours to pay off their mortgages while all the time believing that they had a 'stake in the system' which was worth defending.

Such switches of investment are themselves problematic, however. For a start, new investment in fixed capital commits enormous sums to physical infrastructure which may prove inappropriate to capital's future needs. Furthermore, the ability to switch investment into the secondary circuit is dependent upon a massive increase in the power of financial institutions which, together with the state, become the effective co-ordinators and managers of the whole system through their control of credit. Yet this only adds to the chronic instability of the system as large sums of fictitious capital are directed into various secondary forms of investment which may or may not show a return and which may or may not prove necessary for future capitalist growth. The collapse of various banks following the end of the office boom in the early 1970s was just one example of how speculative investment in the secondary circuit may relieve the pressure of over-accumulation only to exacerbate the crisis at a later date when falling rates of return can trigger off financial panic and mad lurches in commodity and currency markets.

The problem, therefore, is that switching into the secondary circuit displaces rather than resolves the basic contradiction. Just as the scope for employing capital profitably in the primary circuit dries up, so too the secondary circuit soon becomes saturated:

As the pressure builds, either the accumulation process grinds to a halt or new investment opportunities are found as capital flows down various channels into the secondary and tertiary [i.e. investment in research and development] circuits. This movement may start as a trickle and become a flood as the potential for expanding the production of surplus value by such means becomes apparent. But the tendency towards over-accumulation is not eliminated. It is transformed rather into a pervasive tendency towards over-investment in the secondary and tertiary circuits (1978a, pp. 111–12).

Just as the onset of crisis demands the mass devaluation of industrial capital, so too it results in the devaluation of fixed capital and the consumption fund. Empty office blocks and bankrupt cities are just as much a mocking reminder of the basic contradictions of capitalism as are industrial wastelands and failed companies.

Here, then, is Harvey's 'second cut' theory of crisis. Yet as with the first cut theory, a potential solution is apparently at hand. This is what Harvey refers to as the 'spatial fix', by which he means the search for new areas of the globe in which capital can invest. And it is here that the earlier argument about the functional necessity of uneven spatial development comes back into the analysis. The spatial fix involves movement across territory in an attempt to bolster rates of return on new investment, but this proves problematic in practice. For a start, it is hindered by territorial coalitions of workers, politicians and small businesses which exert pressure on big firms seeking to abandon one area in favour of another. 'People who live in the communities being "obsolesced" resist and resent the process for the most part. Community activism arises as a response to the pressures for change' (1977, p. 137). Yet the more successful such coalitions are, the more dramatic is the collapse when the firms eventually do leave or close down.

More significant than popular resistance, however, is the problem that redirection of investment into underdeveloped regions or countries, far from resolving the basic crisis of over-accumulation, simply exacerbates it by reproducing it on a wider scale. Capital in the new areas grows up and intensifies the competition which was at the heart of the problem in the first place, for it too begins to encounter the limits of over-accumulation and it too starts to search for its own spatial fix. Geographical space has thus become central to the survival of capitalism, for the opening up of new areas of investment is necessary to keep the machine going yet the more this is done, the more pressing the problems become. It is in this way that Harvey explains the outbreak of the Second World War as the product of imperialistic rivalries as Britain sought to close off the Commonwealth, Japan expanded into Manchuria, Italy looked for space in Africa and Germany pushed eastwards into Czechoslovakia and Poland. It is also in this way that he comes to the apocolyptic conclusion that the continuing search for a spatial fix today has set the world on a course of nuclear destruction. The 'third cut' theory of crisis, in other words, ends up in obliteration, for the use of the credit system and territorial expansion to put off the effects of the growing crisis of capital accumulation has now brought us to the point where only wholesale destruction on a massive scale could achieve the devaluation necessary for capital to re-establish the conditions of profitable investment.

Harvey's 'second cut' and 'third cut' theories of crisis represent a major attempt to demonstrate the significance of space for an analysis of how capitalism has responded to the over-accumulation problem. For him, space is far from incidental to the concerns of political economy, for the creation and recreation of the built environment (through investment switches into the secondary circuit) and the attempt to exploit uneven geographical development for profitable investment (through the 'spatial fix') represent the strategies by which impending crisis has at one and the same time been staved off and intensified. Yet Harvey's concern to relate the analysis of space to the theory of political economy is ultimately unconvincing. Three problems in particular arise out of his work.

The first is simply that his work is pitched at such a high level of abstraction that it is often difficult both to pin down the precise propositions which are being made and to see how his ideas can be related to concrete analysis. He himself admits, in the introduction to *Limits to Capital*, that the book represents 'the theory as an abstract conception, without reference to the history' (p. xiv), and it is noticeable that many of the reviews of this book commend it for its sophisticated treatment of Marxist theory while noting the failure to relate this theory to the specific issues of the built environment and the space economy. As Ball suggests, the discussion of space is the 'least satisfactory' part of the whole book: 'sweeping generalisations are presented on a take-it-or-leave-it basis, including the announcement of the next world war. Here the author seems to forget that there are limits to abstract theorising as well as to capital' (1983, p. 494).

Harvey tells us in the introduction to *Limits to Capital* that he set out to write a theory of urbanization under capitalism but ended up writing a general treatise on the capitalist mode of production itself. The explanation he gives for this slippage is that the use of a Marxist dialectical method necessitates a theoretical understanding of the whole prior to analysis of what he calls the 'bits and pieces'. Yet as we saw in our earlier discussion of the structuralist methodology of Castells, it is precisely this emphasis on theorizing the totality of social relations which in the end tends to inhibit understanding of specifics. The emphasis on holism and dialectics inevitably pitches analysis at such a level of abstraction that it becomes virtually impossible to translate the theoretical focus into empirically or historically relevant categories: 'This impasse is tied in part to the abstract realms of Hegelian philosophy and its holistic argument where such terms as totality and essence square uncomfortably with empirical analysis. It is precisely this philosophy of structure and holism that Harvey . . . and others adhere to . . . which frustrates the empirical examination of advanced societies by Marxist geographers' (Duncan and Ley 1982, p. 31).

The first problem with Harvey's work, therefore, is essentially a methodological one. Rather like the early Castells, his analysis is abstract, formalistic and ultimately untestable. The theory is not evaluated against historical evidence (indeed, Harvey argues that validity is to be sought in political practice rather than empirically) but is selectively illustrated with reference to historical examples (Duncan and Ley 1982, p. 50). Indeed, the generality of the approach 'makes the transition to historical analysis virtually impossible' (Ball 1983, p. 495), for having identified 'contradictions' theoretically, these are simply mapped on to the empirical world with little or no concern for the specific features of particular historical conditions. In short, the theory has its own existence apart from the world it is intended to explain, and the two rarely articulate with each other.

The second problem, which is also reminiscent in many ways of Castells's earlier work, is that Harvey almost entirely neglects the historical role of human agency in producing and reproducing social relations. Indicative of this is the way in which human agents always appear in Harvey's work in the guise of reified categories (he talks, for example, not of 'capitalists' but of 'capital': capital 'does' things, 'encounters' problems, 'responds' to crises) such that, 'substance, power, activity, and sometimes intentionality' come to be attributed not to people, but to abstract concepts (Duncan and Ley 1982, p. 37). As is so often the case in such teleological reasoning, it is but a short step from here to unwarranted functionalist explanation in which things happen because 'capital' requires them to (one example being the explanation of suburban expansion as a response to capital's need to find new outlets for its surplus capacity).

Even more striking, however, is the fact that many social categories do not appear in the analysis at all. Harvey's explanations revolve entirely around what 'capital' does: the labour movement, the women's movement, community action, not to mention politicians, administrators and the professions, have no historical role to play. The whole thrust of the analysis is taken up with the logic of capital accumulation and the problems which arise from it. Amazingly for a Marxist, class struggle is a mere postscript to the theory (crises may provoke some working-class response – e.g. in territorial movements which try to prevent 'capital' from relocating elsewhere) but is in no way central to it, for the major contradiction which drives the whole system forward towards its impending demise is not brought about by class action (or any other form of action) but is simply the result of competition between 'capitals' producing an unintended and dysfunctional aggregate effect. From Harvey's perspective, the inevitable crisis of capitalism is self-engendered; the working class stands by on the sidelines of history and at most plays a reactive role while 'capital' inflicts its own wounds as a result of the incessant drive to accumulate.

Furthermore, when Harvey does discuss class relations, his analysis is crude in the extreme. Although he does recognize that classes are often divided against themselves (1978b, p. 12), his analysis proceeds as if late twentieth-century America (for most of his empirical examples come from observations of Baltimore) were no different from mid nineteenth-century England. There is no cognizance of the problem posed by the growth of the middle class, or of the significance of the expansion of state employment, or of the importance of sources of collective identity outside of the workplace. The wage labour–capital relation is taken as fundamental to all social relations, reverberating 'to every corner of the social totality' (1978a, p. 125). Urban conflicts, such as those discussed in Castells's later work on grass-roots movements, are all simply 'displaced' class struggles, just as urban problems are simply displaced problems of over-accumulation. The state is simply an appendage or tool of 'finance capital', the junior partner in 'an almost conspiratorial tie-up between government and finance capital' (Bassett and Short 1980, p. 200). The whole analysis of class relations and political power is, as Mingione (1981, p. 69) suggests, 'oversimplified' and 'mechanical'.

The third, and from our present perspective most significant, problem in Harvey's analysis is that the theory ultimately fails to demonstrate what it sets out to prove – namely, that space is now central to the reproduction of capitalism. As we have seen, Harvey tries to demonstrate this in two ways: first, by relating the function of the built environment to the process of switching investment into the secondary circuit, and second, by emphasizing the 'spatial fix' as a major strategy for avoiding crises of over-accumulation. Neither argument is convincing.

The problem with the first is that the empirical object of the built environment does not correspond to the theoretical categories of 'fixed capital' and the 'consumption fund'. As Harvey himself recognizes, fixed capital need not be spatially 'fixed' (he gives the examples of ships and locomotives), and productive investment in the built environment thus represents just one example of investment in the secondary circuit of capital. Furthermore (as Harvey does not seem to recognize), much of the 'consumption fund' is not spatially fixed either (e.g. 'cutlery and kitchen utensils, refrigerators, television sets and washing machines', to take his own illustrations (1982, p. 229)). The equation of the creation of the built environment with the switching of investment into the secondary circuit is thus something of a sleight of hand, for what is being demonstrated is not the centrality of the built environment as an outlet for over-accumulation, but rather the need to find some new investment outlets which may or may not involve new geographical arrangements.

The only grounds which Harvey offers for focusing specifically on the significance of investment in new built forms is that, unlike investments in other types of fixed capital or consumption fund items, the construction of offices, factories, motorways, houses and the like physically constrains future patterns of investment change. As we have seen, this is a point which is repeated throughout the spatial political economy literature, but how significant is it as a major contradiction of advanced capitalism? Certainly there is no *inherent* reason to believe that what is built today will prove obsolescent, a barrier to further accumulation, tomorrow. Most of the physical infrastructure laid down in a country like Britain – the roads, railways, sewers, houses, schools, hospitals and even factories and office blocks – is intensively used over several generations and much of it, built in the Victorian period, is still in use today and has repaid the initial investment several times over. Nor does Harvey demonstrate why investment in this secondary circuit necessarily reaches saturation (see Gottdiener, 1985, p. 97). Clearly there is no necessary contradiction entailed in investing in the built environment. Some investments will prove short-lived and some will be abandoned as 'capital' searches for more favourable locations, but to elevate these cases to a generalized theoretical 'contradiction' around which an entire political economy of space can be woven seems somewhat ingenuous. Harvey's work demonstrates how Marxist theory can be applied to an analysis of the creation of the built environment, but it does not in any way demonstrate that analysis of the built environment is a central or even necessary feature of a political economy of contemporary capitalism.

Much the same can be said of his discussion of the so-called 'spatial fix'. Indeed, here even the application of the theory is tenuous, for as Forbes, Thrift and Williams observe, the analysis 'tails off as Harvey addresses the spatial dimension' owing precisely to the problems of applying a general and abstract theory of crisis tendencies to the specific issue of spatial forms (1983, p. 356). The discussion of the space economy at the end of *Limits to Capital* is fragmentary, consisting of one or two scattered insights and half-developed hunches, and it certainly does not add up to a coherent political economy of space. Harvey does succeed in demonstrating the inherent geographical unevenness of capitalist development, and he does point to some of the problems which this creates (e.g. the problems faced by the core regions of selling to the periphery when the latter cannot afford to buy, and the tendency for investment in peripheral regions to create problems later when these areas begin to compete with the core areas for markets for their goods), but the analysis hardly represents a coherent basis for Harvey's claim that geography has to be integrated into overall theories of crisis (1982, p. 425). Indeed, there is a tendency in all of this to fetishize space by treating such concepts as 'core' and 'periphery' as entities in themselves. As Browett points out in an interesting review of the spatial political economy literature, it is one thing to recognize that economic processes unavoidably develop unevenly across space, but it is quite another to argue from this that uneven development is 'functional', still less that space therefore represents an object of analysis. It is precisely the absence of *people* from this sort of analysis, of course, which creates the void which is filled in these theories by *places*:

The consideration of spatial relationships and spatial conflicts whereby regions develop, have social relations with, and do things to, each other is at best mystifying. . . . If one is to personify space in terms of exploiting and exploited regions, then why not greedy, or lazy, or clever regions? (Browett 1984, p. 164).

Analysis of spatial categories can conceal more than it reveals. There are some very affluent areas, and some very prosperous people, in the 'depressed regions' of Britain, just as some of the poorest areas and most desperate people can be found in the 'soft underbelly' of the south-east. Indeed, when we move away from geographical categories to sociological ones, we often find that it is not areas which are affluent or depressed, but certain social groups who may be more concentrated in one type of area than another. Cameron's review of the evidence on deprivation in Britain's major conurbations, for example, found that particular groups – the elderly, blacks, unskilled workers and so on – were often in a similar situation irrespective of their location (Cameron 1980). While it is obviously true that recession and economic restructuring has different implications for different places, it is all too easy to forget that most people in Merseyside or Tyneside are not chronically unemployed, just as most people in Berkshire or Cambridge do not work as highly skilled computer programmers. It is people, not places, who become redundant, and it is people, not places, who enter into new technology industries. The danger in seeking to develop a political economy of space is that we resurrect the ecological fallacy (see Chapter 2) by focusing on aggregate spatial configurations while overlooking the social variability that exists within them.

This conclusion leads us to something of a paradox. On the one hand, we have seen that space is more than simply a passive backdrop or 'container' within which social processes occur, for spatial arrangements evidently influence and affect how these processes develop. Yet on the other hand, we have also seen that space is not a 'thing' with its own materiality and causal properties, for ultimately it has no independent existence other than as the relation between objects. The problem with concepts such as Soja's 'socio-spatial dialectic' is that they posit society and space as two distinct entities which interact, and such an approach thus ends up by fetishizing space as an active component in social relations.

Evidently what is required is an approach which rejects both the 'relationist' position, in which space is said to consist of nothing more than the relations between objects, and the 'absolutist' position, in which space is said to possess its own distinctive causal properties (for a discussion of these two positions, see Smith 1984, ch. 3, and Urry 1985). Such an approach will need to go beyond the mere repetition of the sorts of platitudes which abound in the spatial political economy literature (e.g. the constant insistence that space is created and that it acts back upon social organization) in order to identify *how* new forms of economic organization shape new spatial patterns, and *how* spatial reorganization may structure social relations.

A significant start in this direction has been made by the British Marxist geographer, Doreen Massey. In various books and articles, but most notably in her *Spatial Divisions of Labour*, Massey sets out to show, not simply that 'space matters', but how it matters.

Her starting point is a familiar one:

Geography matters. The fact that processes take place over space, the facts of distance or closeness, of geographical variation between areas, of the individual character and meaning of specific places and regions – all these are essential to the operation of social processes themselves. Just as there are no purely spatial processes, neither are there any non-spatial social processes. . . . Geography . . . is not a constraint on a pre-existing non-geographical social and economic world. It is constitutive of that world (1984, pp. 52–3).

Similarly, she goes on to argue, in terms reminiscent of much of the spatial political economy literature, that space is socially constructed and that social processes are constructed over space: 'The reproduction of social and economic relations and of the social structure takes place over space, and that conditions its nature' (p. 58). But what is distinctive about Massey's analysis is that she then proceeds to demonstrate how social relations are affected by spatial location – how it is that location shapes whether and how things happen – and she achieves this through concrete historical and comparative analysis.

Her analysis focuses primarily on class relations. Her thesis is that class relations develop differently in different places according to the peculiarities of past and present forms of economic organization. It is therefore misleading to talk of, say, 'the' working class in a country like Britain as if all workers in comparable forms of employment were homogeneous, for class relations are geographically structured and class capacities vary across different places. The point is obvious enough – one has only to compare, say, miners in the Nottinghamshire and Yorkshire coal fields to realize that apparently common work situations may generate very different kinds of social and political practices in different locations, and that a blanket term such as 'traditional–proletarian workers' (Lockwood 1966) is somewhat inadequate when it comes to understanding such variations. Similarly, Massey herself shows how an apparently similar national-level change (decentralization of assembly plants employing a high proportion of female labour) can in fact work out very differently in different parts of the country according to the existing social character of the areas concerned.

Why, then, do things happen differently in different areas? Massey argues that specific local histories mediate the effects of contemporary changes. Successive rounds of investment in an area (reflecting the part played by the local economy in the wider national and international division of labour) lay down 'layers of activity' and establish distinctive social, political and cultural legacies which then affect how later changes work out. The closure of a coal mine does not wipe out the pattern of social relations built up over generations, just as a shift from an agricultural to a manufacturing base does not eclipse the cultural traditions of the old farming communities. Such historical variations in local 'civil societies' are enormously significant in affecting the locational decisions of capitalist firms (e.g. the decision to establish a new assembly plant in an area of 'green' labour where there is no history of trade union organization) and in shaping the response of an area to local economic restructuring or 'deindustrialization' (see also Murgatroyd and Urry 1983). They also help to explain how it is that one working-class area sustains a radical local political culture while another does not (see Duncan and Goodwin 1982).

Having established that different areas with different histories generate different patterns of class organization with different capacities for action, Massey then goes on to consider the significance of contemporary patterns of capitalist investment across space. Unlike Harvey, she stresses that capital does not roam free across the landscape, investing in one place and pulling out of another, for such decisions reflect struggles and conflicts involving management, workers and the state: 'The establishment of a spatial structure . . . is not just a matter of a simple calculation on the part of capital. Its success or failure can be a function of workers' own attitudes and strategies. .... "The requirements of capital" do not always have it their own way' (p. 90). However, she also recognizes that new patterns of spatial organization of firms are emerging, and that these are having a significant effect on local class and gender relations.

She distinguishes three main spatial patterns in contemporary capitalist production which she terms 'part-process', 'cloning' and 'single location'. The part-process spatial structure entails the establishment of different functions of the firm in different locations (e.g. the headquarters in one place, research and development in another, and assembly in a third). In this case, both the hierarchy of control and that of the technical division of labour are spatially organized. In the cloning structure, by contrast, the whole production process is located in each different plant, but the headquarters is concentrated is just one of them. In this case, the hierarchy of control is spatially organized but the technical division of labour is not. Finally, many firms of course carry out all their functions in a single location, and in these cases there is no spatial hierarchy of control or division of labour.

This very simple schema enables Massey to detect an important tendency in current patterns of investment – namely the move towards part-process systems in which large firms are likely to locate their head offices in London (which now contains between 80 and 90 per cent of the total office value in the UK (Urry 1985)), their prestigious and well-paid research and development functions in areas (normally in the south-east) where they can attract scarce, highly-skilled professional workers, and their routine assembly plants in other (often 'depressed') regions of the country (or sometimes overseas) where it is possible to find pools of relatively cheap, often 'green', and predominantly female labour.

This emerging geographical pattern demonstrates three crucial points. First, it exposes the fallacy in broad-brush spatial theories which assume that 'capital' (conceptualized as a homogeneous thing) simply deserts one area in favour of another, for what is happening is rather that different functions are gravitating to different areas. Second, it also shows how new investment is occurring in all sorts of areas, including to some extent the 'declining regions', but that the different kinds of investment going into different types of areas is producing a spatial hierarchy of control in which London and the south-east is coming to dominate the rest of the country. And third, it shows how the spatial reorganization of capitalist production involves at one and the same time a recomposition of local social relations. The old heartlands of male-dominated trade unionism are being broken up and new reserves of labour (whether in old industrial areas, where women are taking up unskilled jobs as men lose their traditional skilled occupations, or in newer and smaller towns) are being tapped with enormous implications for traditional class and gender relations in these areas. It is not just capital, but the working class as well, which is undergoing geographical reorganization, and this spatial factor is therefore crucial to any understanding of contemporary class and gender relations.

Massey's work overcomes many of the problems in Harvey's analysis – notably in its recognition of how people help structure the future of places, and in its attempt to relate a general Marxist theory of capital accumulation and class struggle to the historically specific conditions of different locations. Yet we are still some way away from establishing a theoretical understanding of the social significance of space. Massey shows that places vary in significant ways and that 'general' processes in society 'as a whole' are actively constituted and mediated through locally-specific conditions. It is clear from her work, for example, that an aspatial analysis of, say, class or gender relations cannot be sustained in that such social relations vary in important ways according to local historical factors. But although her work shows the need to take account of spatial variations in any social analysis, it is still not clear how – or even why – a distinctive concern with space should be integrated into the heart of social theory. Space has been shown to matter empirically, but the question for social theory remains, so what?

The spatial aspect of social organization

Mainstream social science has never denied the significance of space to social analysis (see Harris 1983). Although the community study tradition did in the past sometimes fall into the fallacy of assuming that one place was just like any other, and that a study of one locality could therefore be generalized to the society as a whole, sociology and related disciplines have more usually been acutely aware of the distinctiveness of place and, in empirical research, have normally taken great care to select areas for study with reference to the peculiar features they exhibit. Rex and Moore, for example, did not just happen to select Birmingham for their study of housing and race relations (any more than I myself simply chanced upon Croydon for my work on community power). It comes as no real surprise, then, to learn that things happen differently in different places with different histories, for location is one of a number of variables routinely addressed in any adequate social scientific inquiry.

When reading through the literature discussed in the previous section, the suspicion arises that Marxist geographers have in recent years been busy constructing theoretical mountains out of conceptual molehills. Of course, space matters, just as time matters, and it makes no more sense to attempt to practice an aspatial social science than it does an ahistorical one. The question, however, is why identify space as peculiarly significant for social analysis? What makes location something more than simply one variable among many which need to be taken into account when developing explanations of why and how social phenomena develop as they do?

The most sophisticated response to this question has come from sociologists and geographers working within a realist epistemology. As we shall see in the appendix, realism seeks explanations for how things happen by positing the existence of necessary and inherent causal properties in things which may or may not be realized (or which may be realized in one form rather than another) according to the contingent conditions in which they occur. An adequate explanation for some social phenomenon will thus entail both a theoretical identification of its inherent causal powers (e.g. the inherent capacity of the working class to organize itself as a political force) and an empirical identification of the relevant contingent conditions which in a particular case have enabled or constrained the expression of such powers (e.g. the existence of radical parties, the growth of full employment, the fragmentation of the work process, or whatever).

It is this crucial distinction between (theoretically identified) necessities and (empirically variable) contingencies which has been employed by writers such as Sayer (1984a and b) and Urry (1981, 1985) to specify the social significance of space. These writers reject both the relational and absolutist conceptions of space and argue instead that space is a contingent feature of social organization.

Put simply, the argument is that things have causal properties which, to be realized, depend upon an interrelation with other things with other causal properties. The inherent tendencies of things to act in certain ways will thus only become manifest when they come into particular spatially-conjunctural relations with other things. Gunpowder has the inherent capacity to explode, but it will not do so unless it coincides in its spatial and temporal location with, say, a dry atmosphere and a lighted match. So too, it is with social relations. Class relations, for example, will develop in different ways and take on different forms according to the presence or absence in a given place of, say, large companies, public sector employers, service employment, and so on (see Urry 1981). Seen in this way, space is neither a container of social relations, nor an object which interacts with social processes, but is the expression of contingent relations between social objects.

This sort of approach rules out the possibility of a theory or political economy of space, for if space is the contingent conjuncture of objects which enables causal powers to be realized but which does not itself have such powers, then it is impossible to develop a general theory of how space operates:

Because spatial terms are contentless abstractions, until we specify what kinds of object with what kinds of causal powers actually constitute spatial relations, there can be no abstract general theory of space that is applicable to all objects (Sayer 1984b, p. 282).

It is impossible and incorrect to develop a general science of the spatial. The latter cannot be separated from the social in such a manner that a general set of distinct laws can be devised. This is because space *per se* has no *general* effects. The significance of spatial relations depends upon the particular character of the social objects in question (Urry 1981, p. 458).

This, of course, is precisely what is wrong with the notion of a 'socio-spatial dialectic', and it also explains why Harvey ultimately failed to develop his abstract and general crisis theory in the context of a specific concern with space. From this perspective, abstract and general theory is appropriate to an understanding of the causal properties of objects, but the analysis of how and whether these properties are realized through specific spatial conjunctures can only ever be empirical.

One crucially important point arises out of all this, and that is that if space is to be analysed in terms of the contingent interrelation of things, then general theories about the things themselves need not be spatial. As Sayer (1984a, p. 134) recognizes, it is quite possible and legitimate to have a non-spatial social theory – indeed, given that abstract theory cannot generalize about spatially-contingent conditions, this is not only possible and legitimate but inevitable. While empirical analysis of concrete social phenomena must take the spatial context (i.e. the coexistence of other phenomena) into account if it is to explain what is happening in a particular case (hence Massey's dictum that 'geography matters'), the development of general social theory need not and cannot do this.

Here, then, is the epistemological justification for what most sociologists have been doing all the time! When you engage in empirical research, it is crucial to take account of the peculiar combinations of phenomena which arise in any given place, for these affect how and whether particular processes develop. But when you seek to generalize theoretically about such processes, you do so without worrying too much about the spatially variable contexts in which they may occur. We have, it seems, rediscovered the *ceteris paribus* clause – theory suggests that certain things will tend to happen, other things being equal, while empirical research shows how such things do not happen in this way owing to other things being far from equal in particular spatial contexts.

I am not suggesting that social theory is necessarily aspatial, in the sense that theory should totally disregard the fact that social phenomena have a spatial existence and location, but in following the logic of Sayer's argument, I am suggesting that it is necessarily non-spatial in the sense that space is not and cannot be an object of theoretical inquiry. The search for a political economy theory of space, or a sociological theory of space, is a non-starter. As we saw in Chapter 1 in the discussion of Marx, Weber and Durkheim, general theories of social organization are not inherently spatial, but spatial forms become relevant to them as secondary factors affecting the ways in which particular processes (e.g. the growth of working-class consciousness or the erosion of collective morality) develop in particular situations.

It has taken a long and roundabout route to arrive at a very simple conclusion! Here, however, we could let matters rest and turn to more substantial and theoretically interesting questions were it not for the fact that the theoretical waters, already murky with concepts such as 'the socio-spatial dialectic', have in recent years been muddied still further by the intervention of a leading social theorist, Anthony Giddens. In a widely read, and even more widely cited, series of books, Giddens has sought to place a concern with space in general, and the city in particular, at the heart of modern social theory, and in doing so he has breathed new life into the corpse of spatial sociology. It is, therefore, necessary to conclude this chapter with a critical discussion of Giddens's theoretical position, for those who seek to emphasize the social significance of space and to deny the possibility of a non-spatial sociology have tended to use his work to justify their arguments (see, for example, Paris 1983, p. 221, and Kirby 1985, p. 8).

Giddens's theoretical interest in space arises out of his concern to develop what he calls a 'theory of structuration' which can transcend the long-standing dualism in social theory between action and structure. In essence, the theory of structuration holds that structures consist of rules and material resources which represent the conditions of action in the sense that they both enable and constrain action. Individuals are conscious, acting subjects who understand these conditions without necessarily consciously acknowledging them, and who draw upon these rules and resources in living their everyday lives. In doing so, their actions reproduce them, although normally unintentionally, and often not with the results which they anticipated. In this way, the structural properties of social systems are routinely reproduced and changed over time through the unintended consequences of the (consciously or unconsciously motivated) actions of human agents. As Giddens puts it, 'The structural properties of social systems are both medium and outcome of the practices they recursively organize' (1984, p. 25).

How, then, does space (still less the city) enter into this analysis? The answer, in terms of the earliest versions of the theory, is hardly at all! In *New Rules of Sociological Method* (1976), for example, Giddens first explicitly outlined the key concepts of his theory of structuration, concepts which still constitute the foundations of his theoretical work today, but nowhere in this book is space taken to be in any sense central to an understanding of social reproduction. In the third chapter there is a passing reference to what Giddens sees as the 'obvious' point that interaction is situated in a spatial, as well as a temporal, context, yet this is evidently considered to be so insignificant an observation that it is never picked up in the concluding chapter where he summarizes the key elements of the theory of structuration.

This neglect of the spatial dimension in the early formulation of the theory is significant, for it is clear that whereas Giddens was from the outset sensitized by the logic of his analysis to the importance of time (since the reproduction of social systems is essentially an historical process), the concern with space only emerged later. It is my contention that this later interest in space is simply a corollary to the interest in time and is not a necessary feature of the theory of structuration. Even in the later works, the treatment of space seems almost gratuitous, an appendage to the theory rather than an essential component of it.

This appendage was grafted on to the theory in his 1979 work, *Central Problems in Social Theory*. Here, like so many other advocates of the crucial importance of space, he begins by taking sociology to task for its neglect of the spatial dimension in social life:

Most forms of social theory have failed to take seriously enough *not only the temporality of social conduct but also its spatial attributes*. At first sight, nothing seems more banal and uninstructive than to assert that social activity occurs in time and in space. But neither time nor space have been incorporated into the centre of social theory; rather they are ordinarily treated more as 'environments' in which social conduct is enacted (1979, p. 202)

Against this view of space as a passive environment, Giddens argues that space forms part of the 'setting' of interaction. A setting, he tells us, 'is not just a spatial parameter, and physical environment, in which interaction "occurs": it is these elements mobilised as part of the interaction' (1979, p. 207).

He illustrates the point with reference to the structuration of classes. In an argument not dissimilar from that of Massey and Urry, he holds that spatial separation is a 'major feature' of class differentiation, and that the geographical separation of classes helps foster and reproduce regionalized class cultures which constitute different constraints and possibilities as regards individual and collective action. It is thus impossible to explain how and why any particular class acts as it does in particular situations without understanding the specifics of time and place in which it acts. Put another way, we cannot theorize, say, 'the working class' without first appreciating that the people designated by this term act in a physical and social context which affects and reflects what they do by structuring the rules and resources available to them. It is therefore a mistake to theorize class aspatially since class relations are constituted and reproduced in varying spatial settings. Where something happens is thus central to the explanation of how and why it happens.

This argument leads Giddens in his later books (notably *A Contemporary Critique of Historical Materialism, volume I* and *The Constitution of Society*, published in 1981 and 1984 respectively) to suggest that urban sociology is 'not merely one branch of sociology among others' (1984, p. 366), but is pivotal to the entire discipline. This is because urban sociology is that part of the discipline which has articulated most closely with geography and which has recognized most explicitly the interrelation of social and spatial organization. This elevation of urban sociology from its status as a somewhat neglected backwater of the discipline to a position of eminence within the social sciences and social theory reflects Giddens's belief that a concern with space in general, and with urban space (i.e. cities) in particular, is crucial to the 'problem of order' which lies at the heart of all social analysis.

As he sees it, the problem of order can be conceptualized as the problem of how social systems are bound or integrated over time and across space. Following familiar terminology, he distinguishes between 'social integration' (which arises out of face-to-face interaction in situations of 'co-presence' or 'high presence availability'), and 'system integration' (which refers to the integration of social systems across temporal and spatial distance where social relations are maintained between people who are not physically 'co-present' – i.e. in conditions of high 'time-space distanciation').

Giddens argues that space is crucial to both social and system integration. As regards the former, he suggests that integration is routinely reproduced by actors moving through familiar 'time–space paths' which intersect with other actors moving along their time–space paths, with the result that particular 'regions' of our lives assume a pattern in terms of recurring sets of social relationships. This accomplishment of routine interaction within spatial–temporal settings is, according to Giddens, enormously significant as a factor making for a sense of 'ontological security', for it means that in most aspects of our lives, we do not have to think too much about what to do or how to behave, but simply get on with the business of doing whatever it is we do in particular places at particular times in interaction with others whom we routinely expect to encounter there.

This regionalization of everyday life within particular 'locales' then helps build up system integration. Because time–space paths are repetitive, action is channelled through, and itself reproduces, regions of life which become institutionalized:

Social integration has to do with interaction in contexts of co-presence. The connections between social and system integration can be traced by examining the modes of regionalisation which channel, and are channelled by, the time–space paths that members of a community or society follow in their day-to-day activities. Such paths are strongly influenced by, and also reproduce, basic institutional parameters of the social systems in which they are implicated (1984, pp. 142–3).

In traditional or 'tribal' societies, most of this routine activity takes place within a single physical setting in a situation of high co-presence. In such a situation, the accomplishment of social integration is simultaneously the accomplishment of system integration since there are few, if any, social relationships to be maintained and reproduced beyond the everyday face-to-face level.

As human beings extend their control over nature (what Giddens calls 'allocative resources') and hence expand their capacity for organizing themselves socially (through the use of 'authoritative resources'), so the social system is progressively 'stretched' over time and space as reliance on face-to-face interaction diminishes. It is then that the problem of system integration emerges, and it is then that the city develops as the means for ensuring it.

Giddens argues that a society's control over allocative and authoritative resources can only grow to any significant extent when the means for storing them has developed. The concept of 'storage' is self-explanatory when applied to allocative resources, for it refers to the means for keeping, say, grain and cattle for extended time periods. Applied to authoritative resources, it means primarily the ability to collate and keep information (e.g. through the development of writing). Such storage capacity is a source of power in social life, for Giddens defines power as control over rules and resources (both allocative and authoritative). The place where resources are stored thus becomes the dominant place in such 'class-divided' societies, and this place is the city. Thus the city in class-divided societies represents a 'power container', a centre of economic, military and political strength and intelligence, which both depends upon and dominates its rural hinterland. So it is that the city–country relation emerges as the key structuring principle of class-divided societies where the social system has been 'stretched' and where system integration rests upon the relations of domination and interdependence forged between cities and their hinterlands.

With the development of capitalism in western Europe from the eighteenth century onwards, this stretching develops further and the social system bursts out of the city–countryside relation as trade is extended to a world level. Time–space distanciation is thereby massively increased with innovations in transport, communications, systems of monetary exchange and so on. In such a situation, system integration now depends upon ties of economic interdependency between people who rarely, if ever, even know of each other's existence, let alone meet face-to-face. In these 'class societies', therefore, the link between social relationships and spatial location becomes ever more tenuous, and natural space itself, which once represented a major constraint on social life (e.g. through people's inability to cross water, to settle in infertile regions and so on), is now subordinated to a social logic. Space is commodified (land is bought and sold like any other commodity) and is socially created with little reference to its natural form (e.g. as in the city block pattern of north American urbanization).

The extension of allocative and authoritative resources in modern class societies enhances the power of the nation state which displaces the city as the crucible of power in society as it expands its sophisticated methods of surveillance and information storage. In a world system of nation states, the old city–country relation all but disappears and the city itself ceases to constitute a significant 'locale' or setting of action:

> With the advent of capitalism, the city is no longer the dominant time–space container or crucible of power: this role is assumed by the territorially-bounded nation state. . . . The development of capitalism has not led to the consolidation of the institutions of the city, but rather to its eradication as a distinct social form (1981, pp. 147–8).

This last point is particularly important for our present purposes, for it certainly qualifies (and arguably undermines) much of what Giddens says about the centrality of urban space to social theory. Like Marx, Weber and Durkheim, Giddens here recognizes that, while cities were crucial units of organization in pre-capitalist, pre-industrial 'class-divided' societies where the city–country relations was fundamental, they have ceased to be so in contemporary capitalist 'class societies'. Today, that is, the city has ceased to be a significant unit of social, economic or political life.

In class societies, according to Giddens, the principal 'locale' or setting of social relations is the 'created environment'. 'The old city-countryside relation', he says, 'is replaced by a sprawling expansion of a manufactured or "created environment" ' (1984, p. 184). Yet the created environment is everywhere! The countryside, with its fields, hedgerows, woodlands and national parks, has been created just as the cities have. While it is true that action tends to be situated in particular locales, it is also the case that the substantive content of that action is little influenced by the environment in which it is placed. Just as social life has to a large extent transcended the temporal dimension (e.g. we may work at night as well as in the day, and the rhythm of social life does not vary much between winter and summer), so too it has transcended the spatial dimension. What happens in a particular place is largely determined, not by the character of the place itself, but by the operation of the land market and the intervention of the state. Where there is no natural harbour we build one; where the land is of poor quality we raise its fertility with artificial chemicals; where a hill blocks our path we force a cutting or drive a tunnel; and where there is no sun to tan our bodies we construct a solarium.

Now Giddens is obviously right to insist that none of this renders space insignificant in the modern period. Particular 'locales' (which may 'range from a room in a house, a street corner, the shop floor of a factory, towns and cities, to the territorially demarcated areas occupied by nation-states' (1984, p. 118)) are still associated with particular routinized patterns of everyday interaction, and the way space is 'packaged' may be important in facilitating information storage and surveillance and hence in reproducing relations of power and domination. Nevertheless, our relative transcendence of space in modern social life does seem to suggest that where something happens may not be as crucial as Giddens believes to an explanation of why and how it happens.

His discussion of the created environment seems to revolve around two key points. First, he recognizes that geographical divisions are not as marked as they once were – every town centre looks much the same, every housing estate has a similar design, every workplace is organized in much the same pattern, and so on. Second, he also accepts that we are much less tied to specific areas than was the case in the past – physical transportation is more readily available, geographical mobility is common, and electronic communications have freed us from the constraints of space. Taken together, these two points indicate that for most of us most of the time, where we happen to do something is relatively unimportant in affecting how we do it. Yet this conclusion flies in the face of Giddens's theoretical insistence on the centrality of space to social theory.

The source of the problem lies in Giddens's use of the concept of 'locale'. I would agree with Kirby (1985, p. 9) that this concept is 'poorly articulated' in Giddens's theory, and that the use he makes of it is 'idiosyncratic'. In 'class-divided' (i.e. pre-industrial, pre-capitalist) societies, locale refers primarily to the city–country cleavage in that these were the principal settings of social life which affected how you lived and whose relation structured the pattern of system integration in the society as a whole. But, as Giddens recognizes, this structural principle of organization has now been eroded. The city is no longer the power container of the society, for this role has passed to the nation state, and the division between the city and its rural hinterland has dissolved. This means that Giddens's statement that, 'The city cannot be regarded as merely incidental to social theory but belongs at its very core' (1981, p. 140) is actually rather misleading, for like Marx, Weber and Durkheim before him, Giddens knows full well that the city has long since ceased to be a sociologically significant locale in class societies. Today, the fundamental 'locale' is, according to Giddens, the created environment, yet as we have seen, the created environment is everywhere. Giddens's argument is thus tantamount to saying that place has lost its significance, for if the locale which sets the meaningful context of action is anywhere and everywhere, then specific locations would seem to have become virtually irrelevant.

It is as a result of his attempt to avoid this conclusion that Giddens's analysis becomes confused and confusing. To save his new-found commitment to space, he introduces yet another concept – that of the 'region'. Regions are, in a sense, mini-locales – places like the home, the street or (still more confusing given his earlier argument) the city – where social relations are routinely constituted and reproduced. As Thrift (1983) suggests, the region is thus the place where social structure and human agency meet – regions are the nodes through which social systems are structured.

But what does all this actually mean? In what sense are these regions crucial in structuring social relations? How exactly does the home, the street or the city work as a setting of reflexive action? What is at issue here is the specification of the process whereby physical places enter into the constitution of social life.

Giddens's analysis at this point is very weak. If we consider what he says about the home, for example, his argument consists simply of demonstrating how even this mini-locale is itself regionalized such that different rooms are associated with different life activities at different points in the day. Space within the home, he says, is structured into core and periphery regions (e.g. the kitchen and the spare bedroom) and this is analogous to the regionalization of other, larger-scale, locales such as the division of the city into the core business district and the peripheral suburbs, or that of the world into metropolitan core countries and the less developed nations. But this is a highly formalistic analysis, identifying formal similarities of spatial organization in different locales while abstracting from their contents. It is also very unclear what we as sociologists are meant to make of it. That we move through the home in definable time–space paths, washing in the bathroom in the morning, eating in the dining room in the evening, and sleeping in the bedroom at night, is indisputable. But so what?

Notwithstanding Giddens's conclusions to the contrary, I believe that it follows from the logic of his own analysis that social theory, in so far as it has addressed contemporary industrial societies, has been quite right to treat space as a 'backdrop' against which social processes develop. Unlike time, which is inherently caught up in, and thus constitutive of, the reproduction of social life, space only enters into the 'constitution of society' in a contingent way. It is notable that many commentators on Giddens's recent work have pointed out that his theoretical discussion of time is far more developed than his treatment of space (see, for example, Urry 1985). This is not, in my view, a weakness or lacuna which can be filled through further theoretical work, for the concern with space does not derive necessarily from the theory of structuration, but is tacked on to it from outside. This is inevitably the case given that (as Sayer recognizes) spatial arrangements, and the presence or absence of phenomena in space, are contingent and their effects can only be analysed empirically. Of course social science should not ignore space, for it is one factor (among others) which will need to be addressed when seeking explanations for specific empirical processes. We cannot afford an aspatial social science, for social processes do work out differently in different places according to the specific conjuncture of relations which occur there, but nor can we countenance a social theory of space which seeks to make location and positioning a key factor in the analysis. Location is a contingent variable and to fetishize it is as dangerous as ignoring it.

The fact that space is not central to the theory of structuration as developed by Giddens becomes clear when we consider the theory's applications. Giddens himself cites Paul Willis's study, *Learning to Labour* (1977), as an illustration of how his theoretical ideas can be translated into empirical research (although as Giddens himself admits, the study was actually accomplished without benefit of the theory (1984, p. 326)). This study exemplifies Giddens's own concerns with how system integration is routinely and unconsciously accomplished through meaningful action which is enabled and constrained by the rules and resources available to people in their everyday lives, and which gives rise to consequences (in this case, continued working class subordination) which are often unanticipated, unintended and unwelcome to the actors themselves. Yet it is notable that neither Willis nor Giddens, when discussing this research, feel it necessary to focus explicitly on the issue of space. Nowhere does Giddens demonstrate, or even ask, how space enters into this process whereby working-class 'lads' reproduce the conditions of their own subordination. Indeed, he does not even question whether 'lads' from other parts of 'Hammertown', or from other towns elsewhere in the country, engage in different sorts of practices as a result of their different geographical locales and time–space trajectories. The fact that Willis clearly believes that his in-depth study of just twelve adolescent boys in one town can to some extent be generalized to thousands of other working-class boys in dozens of other towns, and that he explicitly argues that Hammertown represents 'an archetypal industrial town' with 'all the classic industrial hallmarks' (1977, p. 6), is all accepted without comment in Giddens's discussion of the study. Not only, therefore, did Willis carry out this research without drawing upon the abstract theory of structuration, but he also did it without elevating space to a central position within the analysis, and Giddens himself seems to accept and endorse this as entirely adequate!

The point is, of course, that Willis was quite justified in stressing the similarities and generalities between Hammertown and other industrial towns and cities in Britain. Spatial considerations obviously did enter into his study at a very early stage, for as in any other empirical research, he needed to select a site where he would be able to study the particular people and processes in which he was interested. Hammertown is not Cheltenham, and he presumably chose the former rather than the latter precisely because he needed an area characterized by particular kinds and combinations of phenomena – e.g. working-class concentration, reliance on heavy manual forms of employment, etc. – not found in certain other places. But having selected his 'locale', what he found when he went on to study the lads' subculture was not a product of their living in Hammertown; rather, it was a product of their *social* location as working-class youth living in a capitalist society. What was going on does not happen in the same way in every other place, but the theoretical explanation for it has little, if anything, to do with space.

Giddens is, I believe, right to emphasize the centrality of recent urban sociology to the core concerns of social theory, but he asserts this centrality for the wrong reasons. The promise of urban sociology lies not in its traditional concerns with space and cities, which Giddens seeks to resurrect, but in its substantive focus on particular processes which Giddens in his discussion totally overlooks. Theoretical attempts to generalize about space, whether in terms of a 'socio-spatial dialectic' or a theory of 'locale', always end up either in the repeated assertions of banal observations (e.g. that space is socially created, that things happen differently in different places, or that we routinely do different things and interact with different people in different locations), or in a theoretical impasse where the general theory fails to articulate with the analysis of space (as in Harvey's failure to relate the theory of capital accumulation and crisis to the question of spatial form, or Giddens's failure to demonstrate the centrality of space to the process of social reproduction).

Here, then, is the case for what I term a 'non-spatial' urban sociology. What I mean by this is that urban sociology, like all other branches of the discipline, is essentially concerned with particular social relations and processes. Like every other branch of sociology, it must, when analysing these relations and processes, take into account their spatial setting, for particular combinations of presence and absence in particular places will have an affect on how and whether these processes occur. Urban sociology cannot therefore be aspatial, any more than industrial sociology, the sociology of education or the sociology of deviance can. But like every other branch of sociology, it will not focus on these spatial arrangements as its object of study. What is distinctive to urban sociology is not a particular concern with space, still less with the city as a particular spatial entity, but a specific focus on one aspect of social organization inscribed in space. Work by writers such as Pahl and Castells over the last few years has been enormously suggestive in terms of its substantive focus, but has ultimately collapsed in the face of the attempt to tie social processes to spatial forms. Ever since the work of Robert Park early this century, urban sociologists have been developing theoretical insights which have been undermined by the insistent attempt to mould them to a concern with space. It is time to rid ourselves of this theoretical straitjacket. It is time to put space in its place as a contingent factor to be addressed in empirical investigations rather than as an essential factor to be theorized in terms of its generalities. It is time for urban social theory to develop a distinctive focus on some aspect of social organization in space rather than attempting to sustain a futile emphasis on spatial organization in society. It is time, in short, to develop a non-spatial urban sociology which, while recognizing the empirical significance of spatial arrangements, does not seek to elevate these arrangements to the status of a distinct theoretical object.

8 From urban social theory to a sociology of consumption

We have seen that urban social theory cannot be constituted around the object of the city or the problem of space. This then leaves us with the question of what, if anything, urban sociology is about, and what it has to contribute to an understanding of contemporary social problems and processes.

In Chapter 6, we saw that much of urban sociology in recent years has come to focus on a range of issues concerning processes of consumption in advanced capitalist (and to some extent, state socialist) societies. This focus on consumption is, I suggested, crucial to the analysis of social inequality and political alignments in the current period, and it provides a distinctive object of analysis for urban studies. Whether or not the analysis of consumption, divorced from the traditional concern with cities and urban space, can still be termed 'urban' is simply a matter of convention, though like Dunleavy, I believe it is useful to retain this designation so as to maintain the intellectual continuity of the field. For the remainder of this chapter, therefore, I shall refer to 'urban sociology' and 'the sociology of consumption' as interchangeable labels for the same set of theoretical and substantive concerns.

It is necessary to make one point of clarification at the outset. We saw in Chapter 6 that Dunleavy seeks to restrict 'urban analysis' to the study of specific types of consumption. In particular, he rules out any concern with what he calls 'autonomous consumption' (where people service their own consumption needs and preferences) and 'individual consumption' (where people consume goods and services marketed without state subsidy). He also wishes to exclude analysis of those state provisions made in cash rather than kind on the grounds that money transfers enhance consumer spending power but do not themselves function as means of consumption. In this chapter, I shall suggest that this specification of the problem is too narrow and restrictive, and I shall attempt to demonstrate how a sociological analysis of the different patterns of consumption – state provision in kind, state provision in cash, self-provisioning and marketed or privatized provisioning – is in fact central to an understanding of certain key features of contemporary social organization and the way it is changing.

The chapter is arranged as three sections. In the first I seek to identify what is distinctive to the forms of politics which arise around state consumption provision. I do this by developing a typology which contrasts the politics of consumption with the politics of production. Although these two spheres are obviously related, I suggest that they tend to vary in terms of the types of interests which mobilize around them, the forms of state institutions through which they are organized, the level of the state at which they are located, and the dominant ideologies and values which surround them. It also follows from this that different kinds of political theory may be appropriate to the explanation of different aspects of state intervention in the modern period.

The second section then develops this analysis by considering the sociological significance of the division between private and socialized forms of consumption. Drawing on the literature on 'housing classes' (discussed in Chapter 4) and 'consumption sectors' (discussed in Chapter 6), it is suggested that a major fault line is opening up in countries like Britain between a majority of people who can service their key consumption requirements through the market and a minority who remain reliant on an increasingly inadequate and alienative form of direct state provision. This division, arising out of the social relations of consumption, is, it is argued, becoming as if not more significant than the more familiar class divisions arising out of the social relations of production, for it is fundamentally influencing not only political alignments, but also material life chances and cultural identities.

This conclusion then leads into the final section of the chapter where I consider some of the recent literature on the 'informal economy', domestic self-provisioning, and alternatives to state control of consumption. Drawing on work from within (e.g. Gans and Castells) and outside (e.g. Gorz and Ward) the urban social theory tradition, I suggest that the experience of domination and alienation which inevitably characterizes the organization of production in the modern period may to some extent be countered in the realm of consumption where there is a real potential for people to exert some degree of control over their everyday lives. This potential can, however, only be realized if the state's role in consumption is fundamentally restructured so as to enable rather than constrain individual and collective self-determination.

The politics of socialized consumption

We begin by trying to establish what, if anything, is distinctive to the forms of politics which tend to develop around the provision by the state of means of consumption. Two points, arising out of the discussion in Chapter 6, need to be made by way of introduction.

The first is that an analytical focus on consumption does not imply that consumption and production are unrelated. As we saw in Chapter 6, production influences and sets limits upon consumption, both in the sense that we cannot consume what has not been produced, and in that the social organization of productive life generates different capacities for consumption among different groups of people. To take an obvious example, a low-paid or unemployed worker will be unlikely to be able to afford to buy a house, run a car, pay for private medical insurance, and so on.

Having said this, however, it is also obviously the case that consumption influences and sets limits upon production, both in the sense that we cannot go on producing goods or services which are not consumed (hence Harvey's concern with problems of 'over-accumulation' in late capitalism), and that consumption generates different capacities for production among different groups of people (hence Castells's concern with the role of consumption in reproducing labour-power). There is, therefore, an interrelation between the two spheres, not a one-way determination.

More important than this, however, is the fact that in most contemporary capitalist societies, the capacity to consume is not entirely governed by one's location in the process of production. As we noted in the discussion of Pahl's work in Chapter 4, the enhanced role of the state in providing for basic consumption needs such as housing, education, health care and transportation has created a distinct pattern of consumption in the modern period which need not, and often does not, directly reflect the organization of production. Today, that is, most households depend for part of their consumption capacity on earnings from employment of one or more members, but their overall consumption also reflects their use of state provisions as well as their own home-based activities. Household consumption capacity is thus shaped by three key factors – the ability to earn, the right to state services, and the capacity to self-provision. Leaving discussion of the last of these to later in the chapter, it is clear that determination of household consumption capacity cannot be read off from members' participation in the formal system of production, for state provision is subject, in part at least, to a political logic which does not necessarily reflect the economic logic of the market.

In the modern period, therefore, people's life chances reflect the articulation of two systems of power – the operation of labour and commodity markets on the one hand, and the operation of the state on the other. As most contemporary political theorists, including Marxists, recognize, these are not reducible to each other. It therefore follows, if people's consumption is determined partly by participation in the market and partly by dependence on the state, that analysis of their place in the organization of production (i.e. their class location) cannot by itself be adequate for an understanding of their place in the organization of consumption. Put another way, although production and consumption are interrelated, they are also distinct processes shaped to some extent by different factors. This is why it is both possible and fruitful to distinguish them analytically.

Some critics of the approach to be outlined here have nevertheless continued to assert that the distinction between production and consumption cannot be sustained, and that a dualistic analysis based on this distinction must therefore be rejected. Duncan and Goodwin, for example, suggest that, 'There seems little historical argument for so rigid a separation between production and consumption. Much state activity . . . [is] clearly connected with both' (1982, p. 87). Similarly, Harrington argues of such an approach that, '. . . by splitting up the empirical objects of the explanation, it draws attention away from any connection between them. For example, the relation between "production" and "consumption" emphasised in Marxist analysis becomes deemphasised when using a dualist model' (1983, p. 215). Such arguments are, of course, reminiscent of those developed by Mingione, Preteceille and others against Castells's work (see Chapter 6). But as we saw when we discussed this work, a specific focus on consumption does not negate the relation to production, but simply denies that the former is reducible to the latter or that both are subject to the same logic.

What is really at issue here is a question of methodology. What critics like Duncan and Goodwin and Harrington seem to be suggesting is that a focus on consumption must be rejected because it is not holistic (which in contemporary social science is tantamount to saying it is not Marxist). It is, of course, nonsense to suggest, as

Harrington does, that a conceptual distinction between production and consumption necessarily obliterates the relation between them. The crucial point is that, in order to analyse this relation empirically, it is necessary first to draw the distinction conceptually. Those who deny this do so because, armed with their holistic framework, they already 'know' what the relation is, for their Marxist theory tells them that consumption is a function of production, that the two 'apparently' separate spheres are actually 'moments of one process in which production is the real point of departure and hence also the predominant moment' (Marx 1973, p. 94). These theorists thus proceed from the whole to the parts knowing in advance what the interrelation of the parts will be.

The approach outlined here, by contrast, proceeds by developing partial understandings of aspects of the social world, and thus gradually builds up a picture of how the different 'parts' affect each other. If we take this route, then it is essential that we have a clear idea of how the aspects of reality in which we are interested are to be identified and distinguished from other aspects. It also follows that knowledge of the interrelation of the parts will be derived, not from *a priori* theory, but from empirical research in different places at different times. This is the logic of a Weberian ideal type methodology, and it is this logic which informs the analytical distinction between production and consumption.

This brings me on to the second basic introductory point arising out of the discussion in Chapter 6, and this concerns the generalizability of the approach to be developed here.

We saw in Chapter 6 that a major problem with much recent urban social theory is that it has sought to establish as theoretical generalities insights gleaned from specific countries at specific periods. At first sight, an approach grounded in a methodology of ideal types would seem destined to reproduce this ethnocentrism and ahistoricism, for ideal types are constructed on the basis of observation of concrete social phenomena in particular times and places. The framework developed below, for example, clearly reflects the political arrangements pertaining in Britain in the contemporary period, and various critics have argued that it does not apply to this country at other points in its history (Duncan and Goodwin 1982, p. 85), or to other countries (e.g. Australia (Paris 1983, Badcock 1984) or Scandinavian (Kalltorp 1984)) in the current period.

More careful consideration of an ideal type methodology, however, leads to the recognition that ideal types may be either 'generic' or 'individual' (see Chapter 1). Individual types, such as Weber's concepts of the city or bureaucracy, are not intended to be generalizable beyond the times and places to which they refer, but they are constructed on the basis of generic types (e.g. Weber's four types of social action) which are taken to be timeless and spaceless. So it is with the framework developed here. This consists of an individual type, referring to the contemporary British context, but is built up on the basis of certain core elements (of which production and consumption are two) which may be taken as generic. The elements of the framework are thus generalizable, but the specific relation posited between them is not. To say, therefore, that the framework does not apply to the nineteenth century, or to other countries today, is to miss the point, for a major objective of this approach is to develop a set of concepts which, in different combinations, may enable the development of historical and comparative hypotheses by identifying which aspects of this or that state system are similar and which are different. Given that I have myself used this framework in an analysis of municipal politics in Melbourne (Saunders 1984a) and in a study of different forms of state intervention in the Australian Capital Territory (Saunders 1984b), the charge of ethnocentrism brought by Australian-based critics such as Badcock and Paris is particularly galling!

Let us, then, proceed to develop the framework itself. This entails identifying some of the main dimensions on which political interventions in the two spheres of production and consumption may typically differ. There are, I suggest, four such dimensions which relate to (a) the kinds of interests or 'social base' mobilized, (b) the mode through which these interests mobilize, (c) the level of the state system at which they mobilize, and (d) the sorts of values and ideologies which inform the state's activity in each sphere. Let me stress again that what is being proposed is not an empirical model designed to replicate any given reality in all its messy complexity, but an ideal type framework which logically purifies and exaggerates certain tendencies found in reality but which is itself a one-sided abstraction which does not actually exist in this pure form at any time or in any place. The purpose of this framework is to clarify concepts as an aid to hypothesis construction rather than to replicate or represent some concrete situation, and having outlined the framework, I will go on to develop a key hypothesis about the nature of consumption politics in the contemporary period.

The social base

The distinction between a 'politics of production' and a 'politics of consumption' derives partly from the work of Castells, but more especially from developments within German 'critical' theory. The key writers here are Jürgen Habermas and Claus Offe.

From the 1960s onwards, Habermas has been arguing that Marx's political economy is inadequate for an understanding of late capitalism. This is partly because the increased significance of science in revolutionizing the forces of production has in his view undermined the labour theory of value, and partly due to the crucial role that the state now plays in managing the economy. In *Legitimation Crisis* (1976), Habermas brought together many of the themes explored in his earlier works by suggesting that the 'steering problems' in late capitalist societies have been displaced from the economic sphere of the market to the political sphere of the state. In taking upon itself the responsibility for directing and managing the future development of the society, the state has undermined traditional laissez-faire ideologies while at the same time creating enormous 'rationality problems' as regards how to secure and direct economic growth. Failure to resolve these problems threatens both the legitimacy of the system (which now rests mainly on the ability of the state to deliver on its promises) and the motivation of individuals to participate fully within it.

These ideas were taken up and explored by Claus Offe in his influential 1975 paper and in various other essays (many of which are reprinted in Offe 1984). He distinguished between two aspects of the state's role – its traditional 'allocative' functions (in which the conditions of capital accumulation are maintained in a purely authoritative way through, for example, control of the money supply or regulation of working conditions), and its newer 'productive' functions (in which the state directly provides the resources required for further capital accumulation by, for example, nationalizing key but unprofitable sectors of the economy or by providing welfare to support the reproduction of the labour force). Offe argued that while allocative functions could be discharged according to the relative pressure brought upon the state by outside interests, this was not possible in the case of productive functions which had in some way to be insulated from competitive political pressures if they were to achieve their necessary effect. Offe discusses various possible strategies through which such insulation could be achieved, but concludes that none can ensure that productive interventions do in fact accord with the requirements of the system. For him, therefore, the 'rationality problem' confronting the modern capitalist state is irresolvable.

Offe's distinction between two sets of state functions (allocation and production), each of which is determined in a different way, was reflected in various works published outside of Germany through the 1970s. Of particular significance was James O'Connor's *The Fiscal Crisis of the State*, published in 1973. Like Offe, O'Connor believed that the primary task of the capitalist state lay in supporting capital accumulation, and that this was achieved (to the extent that it was possible to achieve it) by different kinds of interventions. He distinguished two main types of state expenditure designed to realize this objective – 'social expenses' (i.e. spending on items such as law and order or social security which are necessary to maintain social order and legitimacy but which are unproductive and thus constitute a drain on profitability) and 'social capital' which contributes to capital accumulation either directly (in the form of 'social investment' designed to lower the costs of constant capital – e.g. spending on economic infrastructure) or indirectly (in the form of 'social consumption' which lowers the costs of variable capital by supplementing workers' living standards and thus reducing the necessary level of wages – e.g. spending on housing or health care). In O'Connor's view, escalating demands on all three areas of the state budget result in a fiscal crisis as the state attempts in vain to maintain profitability and suppress social unrest during a long-term economic decline.

O'Connor's distinctions, and in particular that between 'social investment' and 'social consumption' functions, are useful in pointing to the different kinds of interventions made by modern capitalist states, but are ultimately flawed by the functionalist assumptions which lie behind them. For O'Connor, all state spending serves the interests of capital in one way or another, yet as we saw in Chapter 6, spending on 'social consumption' in most western countries has arguably gone far beyond anything which can seriously be designated as 'necessary' from the point of view of capitalist firms. This is not to deny that welfare provisions may contribute in some way to private sector profitability, for as Castells and others have noted, they not only reduce necessary wage costs but also sustain demand for the commodities produced by drug companies, building firms and the like. Nevertheless, the primary beneficiaries of (and often, though not always, the driving force behind the growth of) such provisions are not generally capitalist enterprises, but are the people who consume the services (public sector tenants, patients, students or whatever) and/or the people employed by the state to provide them (social workers, doctors, teachers, etc.). These groups have gained in real material terms from the expansion of social consumption spending, and they have done so to some extent at the expense of private capital (see, for example, Bacon and Eltis 1978).

It is this insight which leads us, not only to distinguish between interventions of the state which directly support capital accumulation (e.g. provision of physical infrastructure such as road and rail links, provision of raw materials and energy such as steel, coal and gas and electricity, provision of financial grants and incentives, and so on) and those which directly support people's consumption requirements (e.g. provision of public housing, health services, schooling, public transport, and so on), but also to recognize that different kinds of interests are likely to be mobilized around these different types of intervention. Where the state intervenes in the organization or production, it is class-based organizations such as, in Britain, the Confederation of British Industry and the Trades Union Congress which respond, for such organizations are constituted in terms of the social relations of production. Where, on the other hand, the state is involved in direct provision for consumption, the typical pattern of mobilization is not generally class-based but arises out of the organization of sectoral interests which may (depending to some extent on the service in question) cut across classes according to the specific constituency of interests affected by the policy.

The distinction between different aspects of the state's role can thus be said to coincide, to some extent at least, with the distinction between political cleavages based on class and those based on consumption location. It is of course important to avoid any mechanistic reduction of political action to an objectively-defined social base. As Franklin and Page (1983) point out, sectoral interests do not automatically produce political cleavages but are mediated through people's political consciousness. Or as Pickvance (1977a) argued in relation to Castells's work, we should not simply assume that, having identified a 'social base', it will necessarily be mobilized into a social force. Nevertheless, we can suggest that, when and if people do mobilize or align themselves around consumption questions, their class interests (e.g. as workers organized through trade unions, professionals organized through credentialist associations, employers, managers and entrepreneurs organized through industrial federations, etc.) will tend to figure less centrally than their sectoral interests (e.g. as home buyers, as parents of schoolchildren, or as ratepayers). Typically, we would no more expect, say, owner-occupiers to mobilize around the issue of import controls than we would car firms to exert pressure over the issue of mortgage interest tax relief.

The mode of interest mediation

The next step in the analysis lies in the recognition that different kinds of interests not only mobilize around different aspects of the state's role, but they also organize their relationship to the state in different ways. Thus, while class-based producer interests typically participate in corporatist forms of state institutions, consumer interests generally have little option but to organize (to the extent that they organize at all) in the more public arena of competitive or pluralistic politics.

My argument here derives mainly from work in Britain from the late 1970s on the question of corporatism. As we saw in Chapter 4, the strong corporatist thesis developed by Pahl and Winkler was certainly over-ambitious, but later writers have attempted to refine and develop the concept by specifying more carefully the sorts of relations and processes involved, and by limiting its applications to certain particular areas of state activity.

Of particular relevance here is Cawson's work (1978, 1982), where he suggests that the division between monopolistic and competitive sectors of the economy has a parallel in the division within the polity between a relatively closed corporatist sector and a more open competitive sector. His notion of corporatism owes much to the approach of Philippe Schmitter (1974) who defines it, not as a new societal or state system (in the way Pahl and Winkler suggest), but as a distinctive way of organizing key interests within advanced capitalist countries. For Schmitter, as for Cawson, corporatism is thus a mode of interest mediation characterized by functional rather than territorial representation of interests, and by the participation of such functional interests in both the development and implementation of state policy. Although it often takes the form of tripartite arrangements involving capital, organized labour and the state, Cawson stresses that this is not a necessary feature, for corporatist mediation can and does develop in bipartite relations and may encompass various other producer interests (notably the professions such as the doctors) besides industry and the unions.

There is still considerable debate in the literature about the nature of existing corporatist relations. Mercer (1984), for example, argues that Cawson is mistaken when he cites the doctors as a major interest involved in corporatist arrangements in the British health care system. Similarly, where Jessop (1978, 1979) sees organized labour as very much a 'junior partner' in corporatist economic policy-making which is dominated by the relation between capital and the state, Middlemas (1979) detects the growth of a 'corporate bias' in British economic policy since the First World War in which organized labour has played the key role at the expense of capital. Such disputes are important, but they represent disagreements over the content of corporatist relations rather than over their existence. All of these writers agree that a new system of functional representation and mediation of interests has emerged side-by-side with the more traditional elective aspect of the state system and that effective power has increasingly shifted from the latter to the former. They also agree that it is producer (class) interests which have come to participate in these new arrangements (though which producer interests remains unclear) while other social interests have been excluded.

Summarizing all this, we may agree with Jessop that, in Britain at least, the political system has become 'bifurcated' between a sphere of electoral-democratic politics (the world of parliament, petitions and pressure groups) and a more closed sphere of corporatist mediation in which key producer interests come to be directly represented and involved in the making and implementation of state policy. This split tends to coincide with that between the politics of consumption and the politics of production. The modern state, in other words, is not a homogeneous entity, but consists of various institutions which tend to operate in different ways in different policy areas and which are differentially accessible to different kinds of interests. Furthermore, as we shall now see, these variations tend also to coincide with the different levels on which state intervention is organized.

The level of intervention

We saw in Chapter 4 that Pahl's concept of urban managerialism collapsed as he came to realize that local bureaucrats were not autonomous agents but were operating in a context of constraint in which the pressures from central government on the one hand, and from the local population on the other, were a major factor. The concept which eventually displaced that of urban managerialism in urban studies from the late 1970s was that of the 'local state', first coined by Cockburn (1977) in her study of the London Borough of Lambeth. Cockburn both dismissed the idea of local autonomy and argued (in terms strongly reminiscent of Poulantzas) against analysing urban politics in terms of the goals and values of individual managers or politicians. For her, the 'local state' (by which she really meant little more than local government – see Duncan and Goodwin 1982) could only be understood as part of a unified capitalist state, and the provision of services at the local level simply reflected the requirements of capital as a whole. In this way, she equated 'local state' with 'capitalist state' (thereby denying any degree of local discretion or autonomy), and 'capitalist state' with 'the interests of capital as a whole' (thereby denying any effective degree of state autonomy from capital).

In the shift from urban managerialism to the local state, urban studies in Britain lurched from frying pan to fire. Where Pahl had over-emphasised local discretion and political autonomy, Cockburn now denied them! Clearly, as Boddy (1983) has argued, what is needed is some approach which can combine the strengths of Marxist state theory with the insights of mainstream political science which has long recognized that local government is more than simply a passive agent of central authority (e.g. see Rhodes 1980). To achieve this, it is necessary to return briefly to Jessop's discussion of the bifurcation of politics between corporatist and competitive sectors.

To the extent that Jessop's analysis is correct, it seems that the state today operates in two different ways. On the one hand, the traditional institutions of representative democracy (elections, lobbying, demonstrations, petitions and all the other paraphernalia of liberal-democratic systems) provide a forum for non-incorporated interests such as small business, welfare clients and consumers generally to press their demands; on the other, the corporatist sector, which is exclusive to representatives of functional producer interests such as industry, organized labour and the professions, operates mainly to develop policies which are consistent with the requirements of these key groups and which can therefore overcome to some extent the 'rationality' or 'steering' problem identified by writers such as Habermas and Offe.

The problem, however, is that according to Jessop there exists a 'contradictory unity' between these two modes of interest mediation, for popular pressures exerted through the democratic sector tend to undermine the commitments negotiated in the corporatist arena. There is, in other words, a recurring tension between rational planning and democratic accountability (a point which has also been noted by so-called 'new right' theories which seek to explain what they see as 'the ungovernability of Britain' – see Dearlove and Saunders 1984, for a review). This tension is overlaid by that between economic and social expenditure priorities identified in O'Connor's work, for the question of how to reconcile the demands of key producer interests with those of consumers is at one and the same time the question of how to reconcile corporatist economic strategies with electoral pressures on social spending.

One way in which these tensions may be mediated is through the location of different types of intervention, involving different modes of interest mediation, at different levels of the state system. As Friedland and his co-authors have noted, the more local the organization of state intervention, the more susceptible it is likely to be to popular mobilization and pressure:

The electoral-representative arrangements which underpin municipal govern-ments make them vulnerable to popular discontent . . . local governments are often important loci for popular political participation because they are structurally accessible, the point of daily contact between citizen and state. The relative visibility of local government policies and the relative accessibility of local government agencies make them a more susceptible target of political opposition than other levels of the state (1977, pp. 449, 451).

This crucial insight suggests that one way in which the tensions between different aspects of the state's role may be managed (whether intentionally or not) is through the removal of key services relating to production to higher levels of the state system. Certainly there is no doubt that producer interests generally find it easier to organize effectively on a regional or national level while consumer interests are most effective at a local level (I have demonstrated this both in respect of health and water services in England (Saunders 1985a) and through an analysis of the mobilization of bias in land use planning questions following the removal of municipal government in Melbourne (Saunders 1984a)). I am not here suggesting that local level politics are always open and pluralistic (what Cochrane has dismissively termed the 'pluralist and institutionalist myth that local government is more responsive than central government' (1984, p. 282)); only that consumers of state services are likely to find it less difficult to make their voices heard the closer to home the agency which is responsible for providing them. Put another way, if popular, non-class, interests cannot organize effectively at the local level, then it is unlikely that they will be able to organize effectively anywhere.

Two other points should also be emphasized about this argument. First, notwithstanding the criticisms advanced by Harrington (1983, p. 209) and Duncan and Goodwin (1982, p. 85), I am not here positing a new form of functionalist state theory in which the level at which a service is provided is explained in terms of the need to insulate it from, or tailor it to, this or that interest or pressure. The explanation for *why* particular aspects of policy are located at particular levels of the state system involves an historical analysis of various factors, and does not imply that there was some functional necessity impelling this pattern of distribution. One factor has undoubtedly been the deliberate and conscious intention on the part of governments to remove 'contentious', 'strategic' or 'expensive' aspects of public policy from the local level (this, for example, seems to have been the motive for nationalizing the social security system in Britain between the wars, for regionalizing water services in 1974, and for eroding local government autonomy since 1979; it was also the major motive behind the dismissal of the Melbourne City Council in 1981 when a residents/socialist coalition began to block new commercial developments in the central area). But other factors have also played their part. Furthermore, even where key powers have been relocated to higher levels of the state in a deliberate attempt to safeguard the interests of capitalist or other major producer groups, this has not guaranteed that the strategy has been successful. As Giddens notes in his theory of structuration, even purposive action has a nasty habit of producing unintended and undesired consequences. The 'steering problems' faced by the modern interventionist state are such that there can be no simple safeguard against failure, and when it comes to directing the use of state monopoly power, the clearest of intentions may turn out to have the most disastrous of consequences (see Hayek 1960). The argument outlined here is thus neither functionalist in the explanations it offers, nor functionalist in its expectations of outcomes.

The second point to note is that the tendency for consumption interventions to be focused on local, electoral levels of the state while production interventions gravitate towards higher level corporatist institutions, obviously takes different forms in different places at different times and is nowhere as clear-cut as the ideal type suggests. There is no country in the world where the national/local division corresponds neatly to that between production and consumption, or corporatism and pluralism, or class politics and sectoral politics. In America and in Norway, studies of business and union involvement in local affairs suggest that, 'Corporatism should not be restricted to the analysis of national politics' (Villadsen 1983, p. 22), and in Britain, studies of local planning (e.g. Flynn 1981 and 1983, Reade 1984, Simmie 1981) have claimed to find some evidence of local corporatist initiatives. Sharpe, too, argues that, 'There may now be emerging something that looks like a corporate dimension at the local level' (1984, p. 37), while other commentators have suggested that local political action 'may involve an important social class component as well as a consumption sectoral component' (Duke and Edgell 1984, p. 196). Cooke (1982) goes further in suggesting that the local arena has often been crucial in generating and sustaining class-based political cultures, and he argues that the relation between capital and labour is constantly surfacing at all levels of the state system.

Much of this work is valid and significant, and it would be foolish to deny that corporatist initiatives may emerge at local level or that people may organize around their class interests at this level. However, the crucial question is whether such patterns are *typical*, for in Britain at least, I believe they are not. Thus, when corporatist initiatives are launched at local level (e.g. in various contemporary local economic strategies) they not only prove very limited in scope, but they also tend to be largely ineffectual in anything other than propaganda terms. Similarly, the history of class mobilization at local level is generally one of short-term action and highly fragmented organization (hence the conspicuous absence in Britain of fully-fledged 'urban social movements'). The framework outlined here does not deny the possibility that elements of the politics of production may appear at local level, but it does rest on strong theoretical and empirical grounds for believing that such patterns are not typical and are rarely enduring.

The only significant exception to this pattern concerns the tendency for state consumption provisions in cash (i.e. the social security system) to be located centrally in most countries (see Dunleavy 1984, and Sharpe 1984). This is an important exception. As Sharpe suggests, it is partly a reflection of the fact that monetary payments are much more easily centralized than are services in kind. I would add to this the observation that the state has less inherent control over people when it gives them money than when it provides them with specific services or goods (a point I shall explore in the final section of this chapter), in which case the centralization of cash transfer payments (which in Britain followed the rebellion of the Poplar councillors over Poor Law payments in the 1920s) may represent an attempt to increase surveillance over that aspect of consumption which is least easily monitored and controlled.

The ideology

Thus far, we have been examining the external environment in which the state operates – the types of interests it encounters, the ways in which it articulates with them and the levels at which it deals with them. However, as Harrington notes, 'The influence of external forces will to some extent be modified by the attempt of professional groups within the state to assert their own interests' (1983, p. 214; see also Flynn 1986). We need, in other words, to return to the sorts of issues addressed in Pahl's work on urban managerialism, for although professionals and bureaucrats within the state do not generally operate in a political vacuum, nor are they normally totally insignificant in determining what the state does and how it does it.

The problem with Pahl's urban managerialism thesis was ultimately that he failed to theorize managerial discretion. To some extent, of course, this cannot be theorized, for the scope for action in any given case will depend on a range of empirically variable factors. However, we can take the theoretical analysis further than Pahl took it by first identifying in more detail the relations which managers are called upon to mediate, second, recognizing the sorts of professional/managerial ideologies and values which are likely to emerge in different situations, and third specifying under what conditions these values and ideologies are likely to prove paramount in shaping state outcomes.

The first point is self-evident from the foregoing analysis. Urban managers stand at the intersection of the politics of production and the politics of consumption. To the extent that these different spheres relate to different types of state intervention organized in different ways at different levels in respect of different kinds of interests, urban managers can be seen as mediating the tensions between economic and social priorities, corporatist and democratic strategies, central and local initiatives and class and sectoral interests.

The way they mediate these various cross-cutting pressures will depend upon their own values and interests, which are often technocratic and supposedly 'apolitical' (see, for example, Reade 1984), but whose content is likely to vary along a continuum from 'capitalistic' values at one extreme to 'public service' values at the other. In my work on health and water authorities in England

(Saunders 1985a), for example, it was apparent that the managers and professionals involved in the water authorities tended to reveal a commitment to a view of water as a commodity rather than a service (thus reflecting the significance of water as a means of production for private sector interests such as farmers, developers and industry), whereas health professionals and administrators stressed their role in providing for social need (albeit in a rather paternalistic way). Different types of ideology are thus appropriate to different types of state provision, and these ideologies and values are likely to permeate the policy-making processes within these different state institutions.

The significance of professional and managerial values will, however, depend upon the context in which the managers are operating. Managerial autonomy, I would argue, is a function of two key factors – the degree to which strategic producer interests are content to permit it, and the extent to which consumer interests can be held at arm's length. In national level corporate institutions, for example, it is likely to be highly circumscribed given the integration of producer interests into the policy process. In local level competitive institutions it may be more pronounced, though will be limited to the extent that the consumers of the service in question are able to force their views and demands on to the political agenda. Managerial autonomy is probably most developed in situations where, as in the English Regional Health Authorities, the service in question is of little interest to producers while the scale or level at which it operates (reinforced in this case by the absence of electoral mechanisms at the regional level in England) is beyond the scope of consumers to influence.

All of this reinforces the argument that the state in the modern period cannot be analysed as a single, cohesive entity. It is fragmented into different 'branches' (see, for example, Miliband 1969, ch. 3), each of which is internally differentiated into different levels and departments. Some parts of the system are elected, some are open to domination by bureaucratic or professional employees, and some effectively function as the mouthpiece of particular private interests. The different bits and pieces of the system operate according to different logics, are accountable to different publics and are responsible for managing different types of problems. The sheer organizational complexity of the state apparatus makes it virtually impossible for any one group to impose any single, transcendent strategy culminating in any one set of desired outcomes (hence the 'rationality problem' identified by Habermas and Offe). Theories of *the* state, which attempt to explain its overall operation in terms of a single general theory, should clearly be treated with some scepticism, for the possibility that any one group (be it the elected government or the capitalist class) or any one logic could dominate such a system seems highly implausible.

This, then, is the case for what may be termed a 'dualistic theory of politics'. By distinguishing the social base, mode of interest mediation, level of intervention and affinitive ideology typically associated respectively with the politics of production and the politics of consumption, it is possible to identify different aspects of politics which may best be explained by different political theories. In other words, we can move from the construction of an ideal type framework (summarized in Figure 2) to the development of specific hypotheses by recognizing that theories which have often been counterposed to each other as incompatible may in fact be complementary in the sense that they are appropriate to an understanding of different aspects of the political process.

	Politics of production	*Politics of consumption*
Social Base	Class interests	Consumption sector interests
Mode of interest mediation	Corporatist	Competitive
Level	Central state	Local state
Dominant ideology	Capitalistic (private property rights)	Public service (citizenship rights)
State theory	Instrumentalism (class theory)	Imperfect pluralism (interest group theory)

Figure 2   The dual politics thesis

What is being suggested here is not that all of these elements necessarily always line up with each other in all times and in all places, but that there is a tendency for the different elements to correspond in this way, and that (most crucially) to the extent that they do, the greater will be the relative applicability of one or other theory to understanding and explaining them. The dual politics thesis, in other words, is above all else an attempted solution to the relative autonomy problem discussed in Chapter 6, for it sets out to identify the different mechanisms which, in aggregate, result in the state both supporting the interests of dominant classes and responding to the demands of less powerful groups.

The basic hypothesis is very simple and may be stated in the form of two propositions. First, the state will operate in the interests of dominant classes the more its interventions are directed at the process of production, the more corporatist its organizational forms, the more centralized its operations and the more those in key positions are predisposed to support the principles of allocation grounded in rights of private property. Second, the state will be more responsive to the weight of popular opinion and various demands articulated by different sections of the population the more its interventions are directed towards provision for consumption, the more competitive or democratic its organizational forms, the more localized its operations and the more those in key positions are predisposed to support principles of allocation grounded in concepts of citizenship rights and notions of social need.

The first pattern is thus best explained in terms of instrumentalist theories which see the state as operating in the interests of dominant classes due to (a) the fact that key individuals and groups recognize that primacy must be accorded to capital accumulation in order to maintain all other state activity, (b) the fact that dominant class interests will often achieve direct access to key state institutions, and (c) the fact that most strategic state personnel at this level will be ideologically predisposed to support the rights of private property (see, for example, Miliband 1977). The second pattern, by contrast, is best explained by theories of imperfect pluralism which emphasize the relative openness and responsiveness of elected authorities to the pressures brought upon them by their constituencies, while also recognizing that the competition for the ear of government is unequal, and that political pressures will be mediated through the values of those responsible for managing the services in question (see, for example, Dahl 1963).

The framework outlined here can be used to develop other, more specific, hypotheses (e.g. it can be applied to the development of a theory of central–local state relations – see Saunders 1984c). It has been applied with some success in various empirical studies of urban politics, not only in my own work on Australian city government and on English regional authorities, but also in work such as that by Blowers (1984) on a planning conflict between industrial and environmentalist interests in Bedfordshire. And as we shall see in the next section, it can also provide the basis for a retheorization of social stratification in the modern period. In addition, however, this framework can help to clarify two fundamental issues which have been at the centre of recent debates in urban studies; namely, the problem of specifying an object of study, and the problem of explaining the relative autonomy of the state.

I have already suggested that urban studies may fruitfully be defined in terms of an interest in questions of consumption. We are now in a position to specify this object of study more rigorously, for we have seen that the analysis of consumption will generally entail a concern with the four dimensions identified in Figure 2. This specification of the object of study is, interestingly, broadly consistent with the proposition arrived at by Castells in *The City and the Grassroots*, for as we saw in Chapter 6, Castells now argues that the urban question relates to the issues of collective consumption, political power and cultural meaning. Castells's focus on collective consumption is reflected here in the division between producer and consumer interests, his focus on cultural meaning is reflected in the division between values of need and values of profit, and his focus on political power is broken down into its two constitutive elements of scale – local/non-local – and mode – democratic/non-democratic.

Seen in this way, the 'urban question' may be defined in terms of the tensions which arise in the contemporary period between consumption and production based interests, competitive and corporatist forms of politics, local and central levels of state power, and values of need or social rights as against values of profit or private property rights. Taken together, this cluster of related issues defines, not simply a coherent research agenda for urban studies, but also a set of problems which go to the heart of the issues facing modern industrial societies in the late twentieth century. The significance of the tension between producer interests and consumer interests is revealed in, for example, the battles of trade unions to save jobs even at the expense of higher prices or taxes, the concerns of the professions to preserve their legal monopolies even at the expense of consumer choice, the concerted attempts by capitalist firms and capitalist governments to bolster profits even at the expense of welfare provisions, environmental quality or (as in the case of the defence industry) growing threats to world peace. The significance of the tension between competitive and corporatist modes is revealed in the growing problems of secrecy and closure – the demands for freedom of information, the demands for greater political accountability, the mounting frustration with bureaucratic insensitivity and non-responsiveness. The significance of the tension between local and central state levels is revealed in the mounting chaos surrounding relations between central and local authorities in a country like Britain, in initiatives such as the 'new federalism' in the USA or the decentralization programme in France, and in the spread of local participatory, co-operative or self-help movements designed to claw back some degree of control and autonomy in an increasingly centralized system of power and domination. And the significance of the tension between values of need or social rights as against values of profit or property rights is revealed in the breakdown of the post-war ideological consensus, in the growing polarization of politics and society between collectivistic and individualistic solutions, in the divisions between the 'new left' with its attempts to rethink the socialist project and the 'new right' with its assertion of neo-liberal values, and in the widening gulf (discussed in the next section) between those who can service their needs through the market and those who must rely on the state.

These, then, are the sorts of issues addressed by urban studies when it takes consumption as its object of analysis, and they are issues which are central in determining the future shape of the society as a whole. It is for this reason that I suggested in Chapter 7 that Giddens is right when he claims that urban sociology has a place at the very core of social theory and social analysis, but this position reflects not its concern with the abstract problem of space, but rather its substantive concerns with a set of crucial contemporary themes.

The second major issue in urban studies which the framework developed here may help to resolve is the problem of how to explain the 'relative autonomy' of the state. As we saw in Chapter 6, structuralist Marxism was undoubtedly right in its observation that the modern capitalist state tends to operate in the long-term interests of dominant classes while responding in the short term to various popular interests, but the theory advanced to explain this was seen to be inadequate. The dual politics thesis can, however, explain how this happens, and it can do so in a way which is in principle testable. Thus, if a situation could be found in which productive interventions at central level organized through corporatist initiatives and managed by individuals supportive of private property were nevertheless determined by pluralistic competition between different interest groups (the acid test of general pluralist theories), or in which consumption interventions at local level organized through elective or participatory agencies and managed by progressive individuals were determined by the influence of dominant economic class interests (the acid test of general instrumentalist theories), then the thesis would be refuted. Unlike structuralist Marxist theories of relative autonomy, then, this approach specifies counterfactual conditions and hence recognizes the empirical criteria of its own invalidation. It also allows for further development and modification in the light of new empirical research findings.

This proposed solution to the relative autonomy problem reflects an explicit commitment in the dual politics thesis to theoretical pluralism – i.e. to the view that different theories can be applied in a complementary way to the analysis of different aspects of political processes. Such an approach has, however, been criticized by some commentators as 'eclecticism'. Paris, for example, describes the approach as 'unashamedly eclectic' and attacks it for taking 'analytical categories out of context from different and mutually contradictory theoretical frameworks' (1983, pp. 225 and 223). Similarly, Kalltorp is critical of the attempt to 'unite very different theoretical elements into one single framework', and he suggests that 'these theoretical perspectives to some extent contradict each other if their full ramifications are elaborated' (1984, p. 63).

Such criticisms must be refuted, for it is clear that this approach is not eclectic. It does not rip theories from their contexts and cobble together the various bits and pieces, but rather applies theories as integral wholes while also recognizing that their applicability is limited to particular aspects of the political process. Only if one denies the possibility that different kinds of processes may be subject to different kinds of social determinations will it make sense to attack the thesis as eclectic. This of course is precisely what many (though not all) Marxist theorists do deny through their assertion that one single theory must explain all aspects of the social totality. Yet as the failure of Marxist relative autonomy theories indicates, such an holistic approach collapses once it is recognized that an institution seen as a unity (i.e. the state in its entirety) may in fact be engaged in two or more different courses of action at the same time, for it then becomes necessary to break the apparent unity down in order to see how different factors are influencing different parts of the system in different ways. To accept the dual politics thesis, at least as a possible starting point, is to accept that Marx was not the fountainhead of all wisdom (and, similarly, that the liberal–democratic tradition is also partial in its applicability). The criticism of 'eclecticism', if taken seriously, would simply return us to the intellectually stagnant theoretical trenches of the 1970s when different schools of thought were able to seek shelter from their opponents rather than having to engage with alternative ideas which threatened to disturb their precarious ontological security. After all, some of the most exciting developments in twentieth-century social theory have come when writers have broken out of such trenches and have sought to combine insights from different traditions (e.g. as in German critical theory's attempt to relate Marx to Weber and Freud, or in Parsons's early development of a theory of action out of the ideas of Weber, Durkheim and Marshall).

Some critics (notably Pickvance 1982 and 1984) have accepted the need for theoretical pluralism but have argued that different approaches are best integrated by distinguishing levels of abstraction rather than types of processes, thereby enabling micro-level theories (he gives the example of urban managerialism) to 'nest' inside macro-level ones (such as structural Marxism). I would reject such a formulation, partly because the micro/macro distinction is in my view unsustainable (see, for example, Giddens 1984, ch. 3), and partly because I suspect that such an approach would simply result in a reduction of the 'micro' theory to the 'macro' one. However, Pickvance's argument does have the merit of emphasizing that some processes are more general or more powerful than others. Thus, referring back to Figure 2, it is clear that the various elements identified as constituting the 'politics of production' tend to set limits on the elements constituting the 'politics of consumption', for the concern to safeguard capital accumulation takes priority over the concern to cater for social need, the corporate bias tends to prevail over demands expressed through democratic institutions, the centre tends to extend its control over the locality, and the ideologies of private property tend to take precedence over ideologies of citizenship, both in law and in cultural forms of everyday life. That there is an unequal relationship between the left and right hand columns in Figure 2 is undeniable, for consumer interests are subordinated to producer interests on all dimensions, and current patterns of social and political change (e.g. the continuing erosion of local government powers) seem only to exacerbate this power imbalance. I shall address this particular issue again in the final section.

Consumption sector cleavages and social restratification

Just as the main social division arising out of the organization of production in capitalist societies is that between those who own and control the means of production and those who do not, so the main division arising out of the process of consumption in these societies is that between those who satisfy their main consumption requirements through personal ownership (e.g. through purchase of a house, a car, nursery schooling, dental treatment, medical insurance, pension schemes and so on) and those who are excluded from such forms of ownership and who thus remain reliant on collective provision through the state. And just as, in the sphere of production, the division between owners and non-owners is pertinent, not only in shaping the distribution of economic power and life chances, but also in influencing political alignments and cultural–ideological forms of life and consciousness, so too the division between owners and non-owners in the sphere of consumption is crucial politically and culturally as well as economically.

The growing significance of relations of consumption in countries like Britain reflects an historical process of political and economic change in which the prevailing 'mode of consumption' has shifted over the last 150 years or so from a 'market', through a 'socialized', to a 'privatized' mode, each of which is distinguished by the dominant form of property relations inscribed in the process of consumption.

In the first of these phases (dating in Britain to the period up to the mid nineteenth century), consumption was organized primarily through the market. In 1860, for example, there was no state system of income security other than that offered by the Poor Law, no state medical care (apart from lunatic asylums, vaccination and environmental health controls), no state education apart from grants to religious schools, no system of state housing, and no state-run public transport (see Mishra 1977, p. 92). This did not, of course, mean that there was no system of social support, but it did mean that people's consumption needs were met (to the extent that they were met) by a patchwork combination of private charity, self-help initiatives such as the friendly societies and building societies, and market purchase.

As Marxist theorists from Engels to Castells have argued, the basic problem in this market mode of consumption lay in the contradiction between low wages and high consumption costs. Housing provides the clearest example of this, for it is an inherently expensive commodity which could only be afforded by many people through gross overcrowding in shoddily-constructed and insanitary dwellings. In the nineteenth century, labour represented a major cost of production in most industries, and relatively low productivity meant that labour costs had to be kept to a minimum if profits were to be maintained, yet this in turn meant that many (though by no means all) workers could not afford to buy the provisions they and their families desperately needed.

Gradually – first by regulating the symptoms, and later by itself taking responsibility for rectifying the causes – the state intervened in the sphere of consumption. It is important to recognize that a number of factors contributed to this growth of intervention – ruling-class paternalism, fear of insurrection, and economic self-interest among them – but that pressure from the working class itself is probably not a major explanation. Popular hostility towards the state, fostered by the cynical operation of the Poor Law and sustained by a widespread view of the state as the instrument of the wealthy, led many working-class people and their leaders in the fledgling trade union and labour movement to suspect and distrust many attempts at social reform. The Housing Acts, for example, often resulted in the clearance of working-class areas with little or no provision for replacement, the early Education Acts forced working-class parents to send their children to school yet levied fees which were a burden on many, the Factory Acts inhibited the earning capacities of working-class households by limiting child and female labour, and even as late as 1911, the National Insurance Act obliged certain categories of workers to pay a compulsory weekly sum which many resented (not least because this undermined the voluntary and collective forms of security provision which they had built up through the friendly societies (see Green 1982)). It is not therefore surprising that, even with the extension of the franchise to working-class males in 1886, there was no popular thrust for reform, and none of the elections from then until the turn of the century were fought on social welfare issues (see Pelling 1968). To assert, as so many theories of the welfare state do, that collective provision emerged as a response to working class or popular agitation, pressure or mobilization is, in the case of Britain at any rate, a rewriting of history.

As state intervention was stepped up from the early, faltering steps taken by the Disraeli and Gladstone ministries, via the reforms of the pre-war Liberals under Lloyd George, through to the pragmatism of the inter-war governments in responding to the growing problems posed to the creaking Poor Law system by the onset of mass unemployment, so the market mode of consumption was slowly undermined and there emerged in its place the seeds of a new socialized mode which came to fruition with the Beveridge reforms following the end of the Second World War. The comprehensive system of national insurance introduced in 1946, coupled with far-reaching reforms in health care, housing, town planning and education, created a socialized system of support consisting on the one hand of cash payments (e.g. unemployment benefits, old age pensions, family allowances and supplementary benefits) and on the other of provision in kind. So it was that this new socialized mode of consumption to a large extent overcame the contradiction between low wages and high consumption costs by supplementing the former and lowering the latter.

Yet, as Marxist theorists have also argued, this system itself gave rise to a new contradiction – that between the socialized costs of welfare provision and the limited revenues available to pay for it. It was this contradiction which O'Connor pinpointed in his theory of fiscal crisis, and it is this which has sparked off a further change in the organization of consumption from a socialized to a privatized mode.

The origins of this transition in the British case go back to shortly after the war, while the transition itself is even now still in progress. Like the socialized mode which it is replacing, the privatized mode has a long gestation period and develops fitfully and unevenly across different aspects of consumption.

The first steps in this transition, which occurred very early on, involved the abandonment by governments and parties of the left of the universalistic welfare principle. In housing, health, education and pensions, the coexistence of private and public sectors came to be tolerated and, in some cases (such as the shift in Labour Party policy towards owner-occupation during the 1950s and 1960s) actively supported. This step was then followed swiftly by the abandonment of the free welfare principle as user charges were introduced into various welfare services (e.g. the battles in the post-war Labour governments over the introduction of prescription charges and charges for spectacles). The third step was to raise user charges to notional 'market' or commercial levels (e.g. as in the imposition of so-called 'fair rents' in the public housing sector in the early 1970s, or the erosion of subsidies to public transport in the early 1980s), and the final step lies in the transfer of ownership from the state to individual consumers (e.g. through the drive to sell off council houses or to privatize the State Earnings Related Pension Scheme) which is only possible when the service in question has been reorganized on commercial costing principles.

Two points should be emphasized about this transition. The first is that the move to privatized consumption may, and often does, still involve considerable state subsidy (e.g. tax relief on mortgage interest payments or school fees, discounted prices on council house sales, the use of public sector equipment in the private medical sector, and so on). Whether or not the aggregate level of state spending declines or increases as a result of such changes is therefore an open question, but what is clear is that there is no sign of a return to the nineteenth-century market mode in which the state played an insignificant role. It is not therefore the case, as Harloe has argued, that my analysis assumes that 'privatization involves withdrawal of state support with, eventually at least, a wholly free and private market' (1984, p. 229), for what is entailed in these changes is mainly a shift from one form of state support (provision in kind) to another (financial subsidy). It is quite likely that this will enable a reduction in the overall level of state spending, if only because it reduces the costs involved in managing and distributing resources in kind, but this is by no means certain.

The second point to emphasize is that there is nothing 'necessary' or 'inevitable' about these developments. I am not positing an historical evolutionary theory of consumption to match some of the cruder theories of social change in the sphere of production which have been associated with economistic Marxist theories over the years, for such tendencies can to some extent be checked, changed or perhaps even reversed as a result of changing economic and political conditions. Nevertheless, there are, I believe, strong grounds for arguing that a transition from a predominantly socialized to a predominantly privatized mode of consumption is now well under way in Britain (and possibly in other countries too), and that this transition is more likely to continue, albeit with various hiccups and diversions, than to be halted or reversed.

There are four factors that lead me to this conclusion, and these have to do with the crisis of socialized provision, the demand for privatized provision, the changed standard of living since the nineteenth century, and the momentum already gathered by the changes which have occurred. Taken together, these four factors suggest that, 'Collective consumption is proving to be not a permanent feature of advanced capitalism but an historically specific phenomenon' (Rose 1979, p. 23). The socialized mode of consumption will in the future, I suspect, come to be seen as having represented a period of transition between the decline of a market mode and the rise of a privatized mode – a period when the state performed a 'holding operation' in order to cover people's basic consumption needs until such time as they were able to reclaim responsibility for providing for these needs themselves.

The first factor which supports such an argument is that the welfare state is in crisis. Demands on state budgets are rising while the capacity to meet them is falling. The contradiction of the market mode has thus reappeared within the public sector in the form of a fiscal crisis, and the results are much the same as they were in the nineteenth century as the quality of welfare services dwindles and the services themselves begin to collapse. Even when the level of spending is increased, this tends not to enhance the quality of the service, for much of the money is syphoned off into administration and staff costs (see Bacon and Eltis 1978), while the primary beneficiaries of much welfare spending are in any case not the poor but the middle class, for it is they who make most use of the health services, of further and higher education, of commuter train services, and so on. As social expenditure has increased, so too has deprivation (Townsend 1979). The welfare state has reached saturation point.

Second, although popular support for certain aspects of the welfare system in Britain (notably the National Health Service) remains high, it is also ambivalent (Taylor-Gooby 1985). This reflects partly the worsening experiences suffered by many people when they come into contact with state consumer agencies (the long queues at the hospitals, the intrusions into one's privacy by the social security office, the bureaucratic insensitivity of the housing department and the irregularity of the local bus service) and partly the escalating costs incurred through local and national taxation required to keep these services going, but most of all it is a function of the increased popularity of, and aspirations for, private ownership solutions in the sphere of consumption. Where they can, most people today prefer to buy a car rather than rely on public transport, to buy a house rather than rent from the local authority, and so on. I shall explore the reasons for this later in this chapter, but here we may simply note that the shift to a privatized mode of consumption is in part a response to a shift in people's values.

Such a change in values would, of course, be of little consequence if people did not also have the financial means to realize such objectives. The third major factor behind the growth of a privatized mode of consumption is that, since the war, real incomes have been rising and, with the growth in the numbers of women employed, real household incomes have for many risen dramatically. The contradiction between low wages and high costs which characterized the nineteenth-century market mode of consumption is thus for many people no longer operative, for they can now afford many of the items which were out of the reach of their parents' or grandparents' generations. In Britain (and it happened somewhat earlier in the USA, somewhat later in some other European countries), car ownership became more common among working class and middle class alike through the first twenty years after the war while house ownership spread through these strata in the 1960s and 1970s to a point where today, 62 per cent of all households (and 40 per cent of working-class households) own or are buying their homes. Private pension schemes too have spread to many sections of the population (more than 11 million subscribers by 1975), and although schooling and health care are still predominantly state-provided, aspects of these services too have begun to shift from public to private sectors (e.g. the growth of private pre-school education, the increased fees for specialist tuition within the state system, parental purchases of educational capital equipment such as home computers, the growth in corporate subscriptions – by trade unions among others – to private medical insurance schemes, the spread of private 'fringe' medicine, the growth of private dental treatment, and so on). Nevertheless, with some 95 per cent of British children still attending state schools, and with less than 10 per cent of the population covered by private health insurance, these remain the two bulwarks of the socialized mode, and if the shift to a privatized mode is to proceed in the future, it is in these two areas that it will have to occur. As I shall suggest in the final section of this chapter, this is by no means inconceivable.

The final factor which suggests that the tendency to a privatized mode is more than simply an empirical trend which may be reversed at any time is that, once set in motion, it seems to take on a momentum of its own. The raising of public transport fares to cover reduced subsidies serves to encourage private car ownership; the raising of school meal charges to commercial levels serves to encourage private forms of catering; the raising of council house rents serves to enhance the attractiveness of house purchase; and the increased charges and lengthening waiting lists in the health service serve to encourage private health insurance. In all these cases, the more users who opt for a private solution, the poorer becomes the quality and the higher the price for those who remain in the dwindling socialized sector. This is what Hirschmann (1970) has referred to as the 'exit phenomenon', and as welfare services crumble, charges rise and more and more people seek alternative solutions, we may expect all those who can to exit from the system with increasing haste.

What all this suggests is that we are moving towards a dominant mode of consumption in which the majority will satisfy most of its consumption requirements through private purchase (subsidized where appropriate by the state through income transfers, discounts, tax relief or whatever), while the minority is cast adrift on the water-logged raft of what remains of the welfare state. If this is the case, then the division between the privatized majority and the marginalized and stigmatized minority, which is already evident in respect of housing (Forrest and Williams 1980), is likely to grow wider and deeper as a fault line opens up in British society, not along the lines of class, nor even along the lines of gender or ethnicity (although race does coincide to a high degree with this division), but around the ownership and non-ownership of key resources for consumption.

Some urban analysts have begun to recognize the implications of this. Mingione (1981), for example, has discussed the 'disgregation' of the traditional class system and has identified a process of 'social restratification' in advanced capitalist societies in which class boundaries have become blurred and class allegiances fractured as new divisions have emerged around questions of consumption (or what he terms 'reproduction'). 'The main axis of the contradictions of modern societies', he writes, 'is progressively shifting from the economic sphere of production relationships to the social sphere of complex reproduction relationships' (1981, p. 11). Unfortunately, Mingione then attempts to reduce the consumption cleavages he has identified to a more traditional Marxist class analysis by arguing that exploitation by capital in the workplace spills over into consumption. As we saw in Chapter 6, such arguments are unhelpful and unnecessary, for what we are facing here is not a reflection of familiar relations of exploitation and domination, but the emergence of new ones. The key difference betwen the two, of course, is that whereas the class system is constituted in such a way that a minority excludes a majority from its power and privileges, the divisions arising out of consumption reveal an inverted pattern. The implications of this for an understanding of the distribution of life chances and the development of future lines of social conflict and cleavage are enormous, for the more important the consumption sphere becomes in people's lives, the more likely they are to see themselves as part of a majority with something to defend rather than (as in the class system) part of a majority with nothing to lose. The familiar metaphor of the 'triangle' of power and privilege is thus slowly turning upside down, for as regards consumption cleavages, the 'haves' are becoming a majority while the 'have-nots' – those who, by virtue of age, education, gender, race or religion cannot achieve private access to key consumption resources – are coming to form a small, fragmented, alienated and isolated minority whose response to their marginalization may vary from morose acceptance to violent and inarticulate reaction.

But how significant are these consumption cleavages? Is it realistic to suggest, as I have done, that they are becoming as important in shaping people's lives and in determining the pattern of social relations and conflicts as the more traditional class cleavages? My grounds for arguing thus, and for asserting that what Mingione calls a process of restratification is indeed taking place (and with crucial implications), are threefold. Consumption cleavages are, I suggest, important in shaping material life chances, in structuring political alignments, and in shaping cultural experiences and identities.

Back in the nineteenth century, when the market mode of consumption was dominant (and, incidentally, when most of our current theories of social stratification were first developed), people's class location was fundamental in determining their material well-being. If your wages were low, then your consumption capacity was stunted and many of your basic needs or requirements were therefore inadequately met. Certainly in Marx's day, but also to a large extent in Weber's, class power was therefore basic to an understanding of social inequality and domination.

Since then, as we have seen, the state has intervened directly and massively in both the production and consumption spheres. With around 7 million people in Britain employed in the public sector, and with millions more reliant on state provision of services such as education, health care, housing and general welfare, it is no longer axiomatic that class location is the fundamental basis of material life chances. As we saw in our discussion of Pahl's work (Chapter 4), resources today are allocated not only on the basis of market power, but also according to a political logic determined by the exercise of state power. Yet the significance of this change has not generally been recognized in theories of social stratification, for whether Marxist or Weberian, they continue to employ essentially nineteenth-century ideas to analyse late twentieth-century conditions. As we saw in Chapter 6, the cleavages which arise out of the use of allocative state power cannot be reduced to a Marxist class analysis, but neither are they examples of Weber's status groups (for they reflect differences in material life chances as much as attributions of prestige and 'social honour') or parties (for they do not necessarily organize in an attempt to control or influence the direction of state power). They are, rather, a distinct phenomenon of the distribution of power in the modern period, and as such they generate qualitatively different economic, political and cultural effects.

Some contemporary writers recognize this, but only up to a point. As we saw above, Mingione (1981), for example, accepts that a process of 'restratification' has occurred through changes in the organization of consumption, but he then tries to integrate these changes back into a conventional Marxist class theory by generalizing the concept of 'exploitation' from the sphere of production into the sphere of 'reproduction'. Similarly, Preteceille (1985) accepts that state provision of consumption goods and services can and does generate new inequalities and social divisions over and above those generated within the class system, but he too then suggests that such divisions are essentially derivative and secondary. This is because, first, people's class position fundamentally structures their access to state consumption resources just as it does when these resources are distributed through the market, and second, because consumption sectors are internally fragmented such that different consumers derive different benefits or incur different costs from state provisions according to their class position.

Preteceille's argument here is on the face of it a strong one, for there is now considerable evidence (including that which he himself presents on the basis of research in Paris) to support his contention that access to, and benefit from, state services often tends to reflect pre-existing class inequalities. Nevertheless, the conclusion which he draws from such evidence neglects two crucial points.

The first is that, as we have already seen, class is often a poor guide to a household's consumption location. Private cars, private superannuation schemes and insurance policies, home ownership and aspects or private health and education provision are commonly purchased in many capitalist societies (and sometimes in state socialist societies too (see Ward 1983, p. 187, on housing policy in Romania)) by large sections of the population including many working-class people. Indeed, as Pahl's recent work (discussed in the final section of this chapter) has shown, the key factor structuring access to consumption may often have less to do with class than with whether or not people have *any* form of paid employment, and whether or not households are able to draw on more than one income.

Seen in this way, class divisions *per se* are probably less salient in the explanation of differential patterns of consumption than divisions between the employed and the unemployed, or between single and multi-earner households (see Pahl 1984).

The second point to note in response to the sort of analysis offered by Preteceille is that, notwithstanding their internal fragmentation (and it is worth remembering here that classes too are internally fragmented), consumption sectors still share certain fundamental material interests in common. It may well be, to take his own example, that working-class children tend to get less out of the same state system of schooling than their middle-class counterparts, and even that working-class and middle-class parents seek different things from the school system (although this is less certain, and Preteceille's argument here rests less on empirical evidence than on the dubious theoretical determination of people's different 'needs' which we discussed and dismissed in Chapter 6), but the fact remains that, as public sector consumers, both sets of people share a common interest in, say, keeping state schools open, maintaining good quality and high levels of staffing, ensuring adequate provision of books and equipment, and so on. It is true that they may also differ among themselves in their views on syllabus content, disciplinary codes, patterns of assessment or whatever, but this does nothing to undermine their common and shared interest as state sector consumers, nor does it erode the significance of the major fissure between them and those other parents who send their children to private schools and whose interests lie in reducing levels of expenditure in the state sector, increasing state subsidies to the private sector, and so on. Furthermore, the relative distribution of resources between these two sectors will have a crucial bearing on the relative material life chances of each group. In other words, the initial pattern of educational advantage or disadvantage bequeathed on children by their position in the class system can be modified according to the allocation of resources within and between the two sectors. It may be, as Bernstein (1970) puts it, that 'education cannot compenste for society', but it is also clearly the case that it can influence and mediate patterns of inequality. One has only to think of the significance for the children of many skilled working-class families of the decision to expand higher education in Britain during the 1960s to see that the use of state power in the sphere of consumption can be significant in modifying the horizons of opportunity imposed by the class system in the sphere of production.

Much the same argument can be made in respect of other aspects of consumption such as housing. Here again it is undoubtedly true (as Rex and Moore's work indicated) that households on the same side of the public/private sector division nevertheless vary in their material well-being, and that these variations to some extent reflect their prior class situation. Council tenants in well-built houses with their own gardens are in a different situation from those living on the fourteenth floor of a crumbling, damp and vandalized tower block, just as owners occupying detached houses in their own grounds experience a different quality of life from those struggling to meet the mortgage repayments on a two-up, two-down inner city Victorian terraced property. Nevertheless, the different circumstances of people within each sector cannot undermine the interests that they share in common by virtue of their location in the organization of consumption. All owner-occupiers, for example, have a common interest in maintaining domestic property values, reducing interest rates, increasing state subsidies through tax relief, grants or other channels, and so on, and in this they come into conflict with the interests of all public sector tenants in reducing rents and improving maintenance and repair services through increased state spending on the public sector.

As in the case of education, furthermore, we can see how consumption location in respect of housing generates new patterns of material privilege and inequality over and above those deriving out of the organization of production. This reflects a number of factors. Owner-occupiers, for example, can raise additional money through loans secured on their property or through second mortgages which are often spent on other consumer items (it is estimated that up to half of the mortgage money advanced by British building societies in 1984 was actually spent on non-housing-related consumption such as cars, holidays and consumer durables). They also have the ability, within the limits of what they can afford, to choose their location, and this enables them to maximize benefits from spatially-fixed public goods such as schools or parks in a way that is not normally possible for public sector tenants. And in general, owner-occupiers do not have to worry too much about their financial viability as they approach old age, for not only is the mortgage then paid off (unlike the rental payments of the tenant), but the capital value of the house is an insurance which can substitute for the need to pay out large sums in insurance and pension payments through the working life (see, in relation to this, Kemeny's interesting work on the way privatized consumption of housing affects people's orientation to collective provision in other areas of consumption (Kemeny 1980)).

The major factor, however, which creates differential life chances between owners and non-owners of housing, and which can be of such significance that consumption location may actually come to outweigh class location in its economic effects, is the capacity of private house buyers to accumulate capital. This is one of the reasons in my view why, despite the obvious and crucial importance of other aspects of consumption provision such as education and health care, housing is the most basic element in the analysis of consumption relations (the other reason has to do with its cultural significance, discussed below).

I have discussed the issue of capital gains in housing at some length elsewhere (Saunders 1978), and I shall not repeat those arguments here. Suffice it to say that real gains can be and are made by owner-occupiers as a result of house price inflation (which tends to outstrip inflation of wages or of other commodity prices), favourable rates of interest on housing loans, government subsidies on house purchase (e.g. tax relief, improvement grants, discounts, first-time-buyer grants and all the other instruments developed by various governments to support private home ownership over the years) and the opportunity that owners have to use their own labour to increase the value of their dwellings. Farmer and Barrell (1981) estimate in the case of Britain that owner-occupiers achieved a staggering *real* annual rate of return on their capital of between 11.7 per cent (for those who stayed in the same house) and 15.7 per cent (for those who 'traded up') in the period from 1965 to 1979, and as they point out, no other form of investment could come anywhere near matching this rate of return over the same period.

Now it is true that this period was to some extent exceptional and that, in other periods, gains are likely to be less spectacular (see Edel 1982 and Williams 1982). It is also true, as Thorns (1982) has shown through comparative work in Britain and New Zealand, and as Edel and his colleagues (1984) have demonstrated historically in work on Boston, that those who gain most tend to be those who have most in the first place, and that some people during some periods may actually lose as a result of a relative decline in the value of their housing. Nevertheless, even Edel and his co-authors have to admit that the overall historical pattern for the last hundred years has been one of uneven but moderate gains, and when we consider that these have been secured in addition to the enjoyment by owner-occupiers of the use value of their houses (one cannot live in stocks and shares), and that owners can reap the full capital gain even though they probably only advanced a fraction of the initial purchase price (receiving the rest as a mortgage advance), it is clear that we are dealing here with a resource of immense economic significance.

The owner-occupied sector in Britain accounts for over 60 per cent of households (in countries like the USA and Australia, this figure is considerably higher). This suggests that a majority of the population today is in a position to accumulate some capital gains simply by virtue of its particular mode of consuming housing. It also indicates that, for the first time in our history, we are approaching a situation where millions of working people stand at some point in their lives to inherit a capital sum which (even if realized from a small terraced house and divided among several children) is likely to exceed anything they could hope to save through earnings from employment.

The sociological significance of this development cannot be overstated. Even seventy years ago, when Weber was writing, such large-scale inheritance of property would have been inconceivable. Today, however, it is starting to happen. As this process unfolds, so it will force social scientists to reconsider their nineteenth-century conceptions of class and inequality as simply phenomena of the organization of production. Taken together with the other material advantages enjoyed by owner-occupiers, and in the context of the significance of the public/private division in generating material inequalities in other areas of consumption such as education, pensions or health care, the inheritance factor is likely to demonstrate ever more clearly the significance of people's consumption location. Any analysis which continues to insist, in the face of these developments, on the primacy of class or the derivative nature of consumption is likely to prove less and less relevant to an understanding of patterns of power and privilege as the years go by.

What, then, of the political and cultural significance of these consumption-based cleavages? We have already considered their political significance in the discussion of Dunleavy's work in Chapter 6. There we saw that the public/private split (notably in respect of housing) has had a major bearing on political alignments, not only as regards voting behaviour, but also in relation to people's overall attitudes towards public spending and cuts in state services (see Duke and Edgell 1984). Dunleavy (1985) himself has suggested in a carefully argued paper that the sectoral divisions created by increased state welfare provision tend to react back on to the political process by changing the social basis of support for political parties, such that parties of the left increasingly draw their support not from the working class, but from a coalition of state sector workers and state sector consumers, while parties of the right come to represent a private sector constituency which similarly cuts across traditional class lines. This in turn fragments the working class and establishes a political agenda which is structured around the issue of state intervention such that the expansion of state spending in one period tends to provoke a backlash in another.

Other writers have come to similar conclusions. Drawing on a range of British empirical data, for example, Newby and his co-authors suggest:

Those most dependent on state provision are most supportive of state spending in these areas, and vice-versa. The Labour Party thus appears to be representing a smaller and smaller minority rather than a clear majority of the working class. Post-war patterns of consumption (in particular housing) have thus served to integrate workers into capitalism as individuals: and in a directly economic (rather than simply ideological) way, providing them with a stake in the system of financial and property markets which in turn undermines their sense of class identity and hence their participation in class politics (1984, p. 23).

The crucial point here is that these political divisions are not simply the product of ideological determinations, but reflect in mediated form divisions based on real, economic interests. As I suggested at the start of this section, consumption sector cleavages are essentially expressions of specific sets of property relations, for just as social classes are distinguished first and foremost by the division between owners and non-owners of key means of production, so consumption sectors are distinguished above all else by the division between owners and non-owners of key means of consumption. It is the nature of property rights in means of consumption which gives rise to new patterns of economic inequality and new clusters of political alignment, and it is here too that we find the source of the cultural significance of consumption-based cleavages.

Two points need to be made about this. The first is, as Harloe (1984) rightly points out, that property rights in means of consumption may still be facilitated or underpinned by the intervention of the state. Home ownership, for example, is subsidized in most capitalist countries by one or another form of state support. As I emphasized earlier, the emergence of a privatized mode of consumption is not tantamount to a return to the nineteenth-century market mode. Nevertheless, with or without state subsidies, it does represent a fundamental break with the socialized mode in that property rights are transferred from the state to the consumer.

The second point is that the type of property represented in consumption is fundamentally different from that represented in production. Prouhdon recognized this when he argued in the latter case that 'property is theft', and in the former that 'property is freedom' (see Ward 1983, pp. 186–7). It has long been recognized in the more subtle traditions of socialist and libertarian thought that ownership of what Lafargue called 'property of personal appropriation' (defined as 'the food one eats . . . and the articles of clothing and objects of luxury . . . with which one covers and decks oneself' (no date, p. 4)) entails very different sorts of power and sets of social relations from those associated with capitalist private property in means of production. Thus Williams, for example, notes that, 'The legal institution of property covers a wide range of situations. . . . But clearly not all property has the same significance. . . . The spread of home ownership does not confer economic power in the sense of the rights to those properties giving a say in the direction of the British economy' (1982, pp. 19–20). Similarly, Ward writes that, 'Most of us . . . make a distinction between real property and personal property . . . the owner-occupied house, like the peasant's private plot, is personal property like clothing, not real property like the landlord's estate' (1983, p. 187).

Clearly, then, it is important to distinguish different types of private property ownership. Equally, however, it is also important to distinguish between individual and collective ownership within each of these types. For example, while agreeing with Williams that the rights and capacities of the home owner are qualitatively different from those of the factory owner, we should also recognize that they are also qualitatively different from those of the public sector tenant. The variations in types of property rights and relations thus include both the dimension of economic power (i.e. the capacity to accumulate and to dominate others by virtue of an exclusive control of resources) and that of individual autonomy, (i.e. the capacity to control, direct, benefit from the use of, and dispose of resources). Seen in this way, the person who owns a house lacks the economic power of the person who owns a factory but shares with the factory owner the individual control and autonomy which is denied to the tenant (for an extended discussion of these issues, see Newby *et al.* 1978).

These distinctions are of crucial importance, both for political argument over the consumption question, and for sociological analysis of the growth in the privatized mode. As regards the former, it is clear that current socialist thinking has largely forgotten the sorts of distinctions drawn by writers such as Proudhon and Lafargue, for the socialist attack on private property has too often been generalized across both production and consumption. One reason for this is that socialism evolved at a time when, under a market mode of consumption, few people enjoyed property rights in key means of production or consumption, and there seemed little likelihood, given the level of wages prevailing at that time, that mass ownership of either could be achieved other than by collective means. As Stretton has observed:

It was a tragedy that socialism had to be born between the first industrial revolution and the second, when working families had scarcely any private resources and an appalling proportion of all private property was used by the few who owned it to exploit the labour of the many who didn't. . . . It is a terrible mistake to let the abuse of capitalist property discredit the idea of family property or to confuse commercial capital with the home capital which really has opposite possibilities (1974, p.76).

This 'terrible mistake' has, however, been further compounded in socialist thought by a traditional intellectual distaste for all forms of 'petty property' and the ways of thinking and acting associated with it. As Keat notes, 'For many socialists, capitalism is to be condemned not only as a system based on the exploitation of one class by another . . . but also for the individualistic character of its social relationships' (1981, p. 127). Owner-occupation, in particular, seems to provoke the same sorts of reactions among socialists today as the French peasantry did among Marxists a century or more ago, for personal property rights in a house are seen (as in Harvey's work, for example) as seducing the occupant into a hopelessly conservative support for the status quo. Every display of personal attachment to the home – the gnomes in the garden, the stone-cladding on the walls, the name on the garden gate – provides a further wincing reminder of the 'petty bourgeois' mentality thought to be associated with ownership of personal property. As Ward again acutely observes, the socialist antipathy to such forms of property is based on 'the fear that "the workers" will be at home papering the parlour when they ought to be out in the streets making a revolution' (1983, p. 186).

It is, however, not only important for socialist theory to rediscover the distinctions between different types of property rights, for this is also obviously crucial to the future sociological analysis of privatized consumption. We know surprisingly little about *why* people so often opt, when given the effective choice, for a private form of consumption, nor about how people experience privatized as against socialized provision. It is true, as Dunleavy (1983) suggests, that privatized consumption is sometimes effectively forced on to people (e.g. cut-backs in state provision of buses, day nurseries or dentists may leave those who can afford it with little option but to turn to private solutions). But it is surely also the case that people often actively seek out private solutions even where (as in the case of council house sales) the object of ownership remains unchanged. There is, it seems, something about private ownership and possession which itself is important to people, irrespective of the nature of the service or object in question.

This cultural dimension to the consumption question (which, precisely because it is a *cultural* phenomenon rather than something inherent to the objects themselves, is likely to vary in form and significance between different societies at different times) is as fascinating as it is under-researched. Here, we may simply float two points deserving of further consideration.

The first is that private ownership seems often to be associated with personal identity. Work by social psychologists, for example, suggests that adults as well as children depend upon their personal possessions as externalizations of self and as means of expressing their identity to themselves and to others (see, for example, Trasler 1982). Similarly, Goffman (1961), in his work on the way 'total institutions' attempt to mould their inmates through a process of 'mortifying the self', points to the significance of stripping people of their possessions as the first step in stripping them of their identities. As Bryant puts it, 'Human beings live in symbolic universes and they vest something of themselves in their personal belongings' (1978, p. 63).

It would seem plausible to suggest, therefore, that the opportunity to extend the scope of objects in one's environment in which one can claim some right of personal and exclusive possession may represent one means of asserting the self against the enveloping intrusions of 'mass society'. This, however, is only part of the story, for what ownership also offers, in principle at least, is an extension of the individual's capacity to *control* those objects.

Here, then, is the second aspect to the cultural dimension of privatized consumption; that private ownership entails exclusive rights of control, benefit and disposal, and thus represents a capacity for asserting personal autonomy in key areas of everyday life. As I shall argue in the next section, few of us can ever realistically aspire to asserting effective control over that part of our lives devoted to formal productive activity, but private consumption can offer an alternative outlet. Access to a car, for example, entails a certain degree of freedom of mobility for many people today and releases them from reliance on the pre-set routes and timetables of public transport. The purchase of private medical care or private schooling (which unlike private transport is not today generally available to most people in a country like Britain) would in principle similarly enhance the range of options available to people and would (if some means could be found for making it universally available) enable consumers to break out of the relationship of dependency and clientalism so often nurtured by state agencies such as hospitals and schools, and to assert a degree of control as purchasers enforcing property rights, rather than as clients relying on citizenship rights (just as in the nineteenth century, working-class members of friendly societies were able to exert control over the doctors, pharmacists and other professional producers whom they collectively employed and collectively dismissed (see Green 1982)).

Most significant, however, are the possibilities for control opened up by private ownership of dwellings. This is because home ownership represents rights of control over an everyday personal space of crucial significance. As Porteous observes, the home 'is the locus at which individual control of fixed physical space is paramount' (1976, p. 384).

We saw in Chapter 7 how Giddens argues that the 'stretching' of social systems across time and space has created a sense of 'ontological insecurity' in the modern world. Social relations, he suggests, have been displaced from their traditional spatial and temporal settings with the result that people have sought to re-establish some degree of autonomy, familiarity and inter-subjective meaning within the private realm. The popular desire for home ownership, I would suggest, is indicative of this response, for 'a home of one's own' is above all else a property right which ensures both a physical (spatially-rooted) and permanent (temporally-rooted, in perpetuity and across subsequent generations) location in the world where the owner can feel, both literally and metaphorically, 'at home'.

As autonomy has been eroded in the sphere of production, so it has been asserted through the desire for home ownership in the sphere of consumption. Ever since the nineteenth century, working-class people have responded to the intrusions into their lives of an uncontrollable world capitalist system of production by seeking to carve out 'a separate sphere in the sense of seeking out, in and through the fabric of everyday life, a distinct cultural space for gaining as much control as possible over the purpose and direction of our lives' (Rose 1981, p. 32). Whether or not this search for a separate sphere has been successful in re-asserting control and autonomy, and whether or not it is feasible in the modern world of multinational corporations and powerful nation states to continue to seek it through a private realm of consumption, are issues I shall take up in the next section.

Before that, however, it is necessary to draw this discussion to a conclusion by making four important points about what I have suggested as regards the capacity for control through private property rights in the sphere of consumption.

First, it is obviously the case that exclusive property rights may be vested in individuals or in groups of individuals. The privatization of consumption does not necessarily therefore entail the individualization of consumption. Assuming that my analysis is correct, and that the tendency to privatized consumption continues, this does not mean that individuals may not come together – e.g. in housing cooperatives, car pools, or even (as in the fledgling communal education initiatives currently developing in Britain among certain middle-class and Asian communities) in neighbourhood schooling arrangements – to form collective organizations for the provision of members' consumption needs. The point here is that individual property rights can be pooled in collective endeavours in a way that collective rights granted through national citizenship cannot easily be disaggregated. Collectivism may in this sense be an outgrowth of privatized consumption rather than (as is so often assumed) its antithesis. Certainly the future, as regards the emerging forms of consumption, is by no means predictable and need not result in a society of individualized and home-centred family units huddled around the video machine (although, of course, this is one possible pattern).

Second, the capacity of different social groups to exert control through private ownership is uneven. As consumption is currently organized, women, in particular, are often disadvantaged as compared with men. Freedom of mobility through car ownership, for example, is more often characteristic of the male than the female experience in most households. Similarly, the private home may represent a sphere of personal control for men, while it represents a place of work and subordination for their wives. Privatization of health care, too, can result (in the absence of any other changes) in an increase in the domestic burden for women who may be called upon to nurse aged relatives, tend to sick children, and so on. The point, then, is that the different modes of consumption offer different capacities for control, but that the ability to take advantage of these reflects other dimensions of power and inequality in our society, of which gender is one. And as Weber was well aware, a change in one dimension of power has no necessary implications as regards a change in any other.

Third, and related to this last point, the privatization of consumption only offers opportunities for control, self-expression and so on if consumers themselves have the financial capacity to service their requirements through purchasing the goods and services they need. At present, in a country like Britain, this clearly is not the case. Many households still cannot afford to buy a car, still less a house, a private pension, private medical insurance and the rest. It is for this reason that I have argued in this section that a major cleavage is opening up in the sphere of consumption between those who can afford to take advantage of the emerging privatized mode, and those who must remain reliant on the dwindling socialized mode. Most Marxist writers assume that such a division is inherent within a capitalist society – that the organization of production inevitably generates such inequalities and incapacities in the sphere of consumption. I have argued here and in Chapter 6 that this is not necessarily the case, and in the next section I shall try to suggest how a change in the form of state provisioning may overcome it. Nevertheless, for the moment it is important to remember that, like gender, class remains a factor in influencing access to key items of private consumption.

Fourth and finally, it is necessary to recognize that, if and as private means of consumption come to be generally available, so the rights of control and benefit associated with them may themselves be reduced. This is essentially the phenomenon referred to by Edel and his colleagues (1984) as 'partial mobility', or the process of going up the down escalator. Thus, as these writers point out, the more car ownership spreads, the more congested the roads become, and the less advantage there is to be had from running a car. Similarly, the more educational opportunities are opened up, the better qualified the population becomes, and the more any given credential becomes devalued. However, there is no 'iron law' which suggests that this will always be the case in every extension of consumption capacity. Furthermore, even if there were, it would only mean that enhanced consumption provision left people no better off in relative terms, for they would still have benefited in absolute terms. Sitting in one's car in a traffic jam may still be preferable to standing in the rain waiting for a bus, just as the opportunity to have twelve years schooling may still represent an improvement on six years, even if one is offered the same sort of job at the end. If, indeed, such enhanced consumption capacities entail, not only material improvements (i.e. more of this or that good or service), but also a change in the form in which consumption is achieved (i.e. more control over the goods or services in question), then these changes may be of much greater significance than the concept of 'partial mobility' allows. After all, tenants who buy their council houses experience no change in the material object which they consume (i.e. the house remains the same), but may experience an enormous change in the possibilities which open up in terms of how they can consume it. In sociological analyses of consumption, the quantitative question of how much people benefit must never be allowed to eclipse the equally important qualitative question of how they benefit. Put another way, as for production, so for consumption, analysis of social relations is as central as analysis of material means.

Privatized consumption, self-provisioning and the dual society

The various urban theories which we have explored in this book are to a large extent products of the time when they were developed. The human ecology of the Chicago school, for example, reflects the conditions of market capitalism in America in the period before the Great Depression and the growth of state intervention ushered in by the New Deal. The focus by Pahl and others on urban managerialism was in many ways the product of post-war welfare state capitalism in Britain at a time when the economy was still growing and when state social expenditures were rising rapidly. And the growth of Marxist urban theory during the 1970s reflected the onset of a new recession in the West which brought with it a crisis of state consumption provision and which seemed, in the context of the 1968 events in Paris, to offer the prospect of new forms of political struggle and new paths to a socialist transformation.

Writing in the context of the mid 1980s, none of these approaches any longer seems relevant. As we have seen, the market mode of consumption, on which human ecology theories were largely based, has long since disappeared, and the socialized mode, which generated theories of urban management, is now similarly in decline. Furthermore, the recession has deepened, the crisis of the welfare state has been exacerbated, but urban social movements have, in most western capitalist countries, all but disappeared (see Pickvance 1985). The neo-Marxist work of the 1970s thus seems to have been appropriate (within its own theoretical limitations) to an understanding of a particular transitional period in which the socialized mode was in crisis and the privatized mode was still in its infancy; but fifteen years on, it seems to have less and less analytical purchase on the new social forms which are emerging. Not for the first time, social change seems to be proceeding in advance of our theoretical capacity to understand it.

Most of the developed capitalist world has been in recession, now marked, now less so, since at least 1974. The reasons for this sustained recession and the high levels of unemployment associated with it are various – the end of the post-war 'long wave' of accumulation, the development of new capital-intensive technologies, the restructuring of the international division of labour, the saturation of the credit system, the fiscal crisis generated by 'unproductive' state expenditures, and so on – but irrespective of how they explain it, few commentators see any serious prospect of a return to the levels of economic growth and full employment which characterized the quarter-century after the war. In Britain, the recession has been more severe than in most other countries, and again this reflects a number of specific factors, which include the legacy of historically low levels of investment, the haemorrhaging of capital overseas, the peculiarities of the class sytem, and the impact of successive disastrous government policies culminating in the last-ditch return to neo-liberalism after 1979 (see Gamble 1981, and Dearlove and Saunders, 1984, ch. 8). Yet in Britain, as much if not more than in other western countries, the sustained slump cannot really be said to have resulted in a crisis of the society. Sporadic rioting in a few inner city areas in 1981, and again in 1985, an increasing bitterness in industrial relations (as exemplified by the miners' strike of 1984–5), and a growing polarization of party politics (with a new 'centre party alliance' coming through the middle) are all indicators of the severity of the country's economic decline, but what is striking about the current period is less the overt conflicts which have arisen than the sense of hopeless resignation which now pervades so much of social and economic life.

What this seems to suggest is that British society (and almost certainly other western capitalist societies too) is in some way 'adjusting', fitfully and with some difficulty, to changed economic conditions rather than 'collapsing' or 'transforming' in the face of them. Capitalist firms are adjusting through mergers and take-overs, through diversification and relocation, through shedding labour and reorganizing labour relations and the hierarchy of control. The state is adjusting through institutional reforms designed to block off popular aspirations (e.g. in the local government system), through stepping up social control and surveillance while backing out of a range of economic and social commitments, and through engineering a new political culture in which the 'legitimation crisis' prophesied by Habermas is to be averted through the denial of public responsibility for what are defined as individual problems. And the culture of everyday life is adjusting too as people seek to defend what they've got rather than assert what they want, and as they learn to trim their aspirations and to lower their hopes for the future. The prevailing mood of the time is fatalism, and no radical transformation of society was every born out of that.

There is, however, a paradox in all of this. Real earnings in Britain have continued to rise even as the recession has bitten deeper. At a time of record unemployment, when conditions in cities like Liverpool or Glasgow have degenerated to become among the worst in Europe, and when the per capita GNP of the country has fallen to a level around that of Portugal, Eire or Italy, the country has witnessed a spectacular and sustained consumer spending boom (much of it financed by mortgage credit). Ownership per head of consumer durables such as video machines is higher in Britain then anywhere else in the world. For many households, the 1980s must seem more like a boom than a slump.

It is not difficult to explain this apparent paradox. As Prime Minister Thatcher never ceased to remind her audiences, even with 15 per cent unemployment, over eight in ten people who could and wished to have paid employment did so. The 1980s, in other words, have been a period of massive social polarization in Britain in which perhaps three-quarters or more of all households have remained virtually untouched by mass unemployment (for as Urry notes, 'The majority of the labour force is rarely unemployed while a small but growing proportion bears much of the impact' (1983, p. 36), while a

marginalized minority has either suffered chronic long-term unemployment (e.g. older workers made redundant and school-leavers
who fail to find work), or has lurched from one insecure job to another.
This polarization is expressed along a number of divisions – between
different parts of the country, between different types of workers
with different levels of skills or in different sectors of the economy,
between the old, the young and the middle-aged, and between certain
categories of male and female workers – but in every case it cuts
through the traditional class system. It is not only the middle class
who have been buying the video recorders and home computers, nor is
it only the middle class who have been borrowing on the strength of
home ownership to finance foreign holidays and car purchase.

Like the division between those who can increasingly afford
privatized consumption and the marginalized minority which is being
left reliant on a residualized state system of support, this major
cleavage thus takes the form of a split between a majority of
households which, at the very least, are 'getting by', and a minority
which is struggling to cope in the face of negligible employment
opportunities and declining state services. Those who are suffering
the full impact of the recession are not the working class as such, but
are fragments of the population, what Mingione (1985) calls the
'surplus population', groups such as the elderly, one-parent families
and young blacks. The rest of us continue on our spending spree while
(just occasionally) Toxteth burns.

The wave of consumer spending (which is generally directed at
imported domestic goods and which therefore does little to stimulate
demand for indigenous industry) is part of a process identified some
years ago by Gershuny (1978) as the emergence of a 'self-service
economy'. Gershuny's thesis is that the traditional, evolutionary
model of socio-economic development, in which societies are said to
'progress' from primary production, through manufacturing, to a
reliance on service industries, is over-simple. He recognizes that in
Britain, employment in manufacturing has been falling while service
employment has (until recently) been rising, but he also shows for a
number of European countries including Britain that since the 1970s,
people's expenditure on services has been falling while their
purchases of goods have been rising! He explains this partly in terms
of a proportion of service employment being consumed by industry
rather than households (e.g. industrial cleaning or accounting
services), and partly in terms of differential productivity in manufacturing and service industries (Gershuny 1985). Thus, he shows

that productivity in the service sector (whether private or state) has lagged behind that in manufacturing with the result that households have found it increasingly expensive to buy, say, bus journeys, laundry services or cinema seats, but increasingly cheaper to purchase the cars, washing machines or videos which will enable them to provide equivalent services for themselves.

All of this led Garshuny to propose that work in what he termed the 'informal sector' of the economy was expanding at the same time as employment in the formal economy was contracting. People were no longer buying services for final consumption, but were buying the goods – televisions, power tools, freezers – which they could use as means of consumption (to entertain themselves, to refurbish their own houses, to store their own produce). Hence, what is developing is a self-service economy in which domestic work or self-provisioning is not only raising people's living standards (by enabling them to consume more services more cheaply), but is also expanding the scope for people to realize the potential of their own labour.

Now, all of this would seem to have considerable implications for an analysis of both the newly-emerging privatized mode of consumption, and the division associated with it between the majority of 'haves' and the residualized minority of 'have-nots'. In particular, it would seem but a short step from Gershuny's analysis of self-servicing to the argument that the decline of paid work is in some sense being compensated by the growth of self-provisioning in which workers, freed from the burdens of formal employment, are liberated into an alternative form of work characterized by greater autonomy, control and self-sufficiency. This is what Pahl, for example, seems to have had in mind in one of his early contributions to this literature when he suggested that reduced demands for paid labour, coupled with continuing state support for the surplus population, could actually prove beneficial for those who have more usually been defined as the marginal and the dispossessed:

The formal economy appears to have shrinking manpower requirements both as its productivity increases and as the informal economy flourishes, growing, as it does, at a faster rate than the formal economy. Released from the realm of necessity by capitalism's inevitable desire to continue accumulation and to maintain rates of profit, and protected in the realm of freedom by the need of the state to maintain social control, it seems as though some workers are slipping out of their chains and walking out of the system's front door (1980, p. 17).

Gershuny, too, seemed attracted by the same sort of argument, for he tentatively suggested that the decline in paid work was being counter-balanced by the rise of the informal sector, and thereby held out the prospect of transforming people's whole experience of work.

Today, however, few (least of all Pahl himself) would hold to this view. The debate over the so-called 'informal economy' (a term which Pahl himself now rejects) has today developed into a dispute between, on the one hand, those who believe that it is a hopeless coping strategy which the non-employed are forced to adopt in order to ensure some degree of subsistence, and on the other, those who suggest that the non-employed are effectively excluded from informal work just as they are excluded from paid employment.

The first position is exemplified by the analysis developed by Mingione (1983, 1985). He sees the growth of informal activities (in which category he includes moonlighting, non-registered employment, informal self-employment, criminal activity, do-it-yourself, reciprocal exchanges and the like) as the way in which working-class people have attempted to ensure their own survival at a time when capitalism is in sustained recession and the state is under pressure to cut its spending. The responsibility for reproducing the surplus population has thus been shifted, for households must now carry more of the costs (in terms of time, money or both) which were once covered by wages or by welfare provisions. Drawing on his work in Italy, he suggests that this growth of informal activity not only fails to meet the needs of the surplus population (for they must now work longer hours for lower rates of subsistence), but also reproduces and perpetuates their subordination and poverty. Children, for example, are withdrawn early from school to help augment the family income, and this ensures that they remain unqualified, semi-literate and (in terms of the formal economy) virtually unemployable. Furthermore, self-provisioning on a subsistence level reduces demand for the products of local industry and thus gives an added twist to the crisis of formal waged employment, while at the same time it also reduces the state's tax revenue thereby whittling away the capacity of the welfare system to bolster household incomes.

For Mingione, then, the expansion of domestic self-provisioning is a phenomenon, not of choice, but of coercion, not of hope but of despair. It is 'a forced response of families to the situation of inflation and of crisis of the public or collective service industry sector' (1983, p. 323). The only grounds he can detect for possible optimism are that informalized consumption may foster a sense of communal solidarity and neighbourhood co-operation which could provide a basis for a political challenge and alternative to be mounted against the existing system of mass consumerism and social reproduction (an argument which would seem to echo Castells's hopes in the 1970s in regard to the crisis of collective consumption, and which in my view is just as utopian).

A rather different approach has been developed by Pahl (1984) as a result of his research in the Isle of Sheppey in Kent. This research leads Pahl both to reject his earlier speculative ideas concerning informal work as a substitute for paid employment, and to develop an alternative view of domestic self-provisioning to that advanced by Mingione. Basically, Pahl's conclusion is that informal work such as moonlighting is relatively rare, that home-based self-servicing on the Gershuny model is common among certain categories of households but not others, and that neither strategy is generally available to those members of households which are not locked into the formal economy of paid employment.

He argues that full-time paid work is indeed in decline, although he also notes that the full employment years of the 1950s and 1960s were probably somewhat unique. Thus, he shows historically that most households have relied upon a variety of work strategies by their various members, that they have not generally depended solely on the wages brought in by one 'breadwinner', and that periods of unemployment have been common. The post-war years, however, effectively incapacitated many households in the sense that they came to rely entirely on waged work while the resources which were necessary to sustain other work activities disappeared:

In retrospect, the years when it was said they never had it so good, in the period of recovery after the Second World War, were the years of incapacitation. The messy back streets with their potential premises for small workshops were knocked down as part of slum clearance. The factories were rebuilt and rationalized. The unions got stronger and led their members to believe that collective solidaristic action would lead to a permanent position in the rising escalator of incomes. . . . The physical and social infrastructure of the post-war period was developed on an assumption of smooth and continuing growth. Households with a limited and narrow view of work as factory employment . . . had, perhaps for the first time in English history, lost the means of getting by with a household work strategy (1984, pp. 56–7).

Nevertheless, Pahl also shows that, with the onset of the recession, household self-provisioning has been increasing again. In terms reminiscent of Gershuny, he cites figures to show what have been quite spectacular increases in the sales of tools, home decorating products, and DIY equipment (up by 19 per cent between 1974 and 1980 compared with a rise in GDP over that period of 8 per cent), and he explains this in terms of the growth of home ownership, the increased costs of marketed services and the reduced hours spent in paid employment (1984, pp. 101–2). He also notes that those households which have been busy renovating their houses, repairing their cars or growing their own vegetables have often derived considerable personal satisfaction in the process – they are certainly not the cowed and coerced informal sector workers described by Mingione. Nor, however, are they the unemployed, for Pahl's key finding is that the households engaged in 'informal' or domestic work are also those with access to paid employment: 'Employment and self-provisioning go together, rather than one being a substitute for another' (1984, p. 236).

This point is crucial, for it underscores the argument developed here that the division between the employed and the unemployed tends to coincide with that between privatized and non-privatized consumers. Indeed, as Pahl goes on to point out, the same people who work in paid employment and who also work most in the home are also those who make most use of formal services purchased through the market. The line of exclusion is, it seems, drawn at around the same point no matter which aspect of resources we focus on. The households which earn money are the households which provide for themselves are the households which buy private sector services. They are also, as Pahl emphasizes, normally the households which own their own homes.

The reason, of course, is that money from paid employment (as well as the contacts and skills which may be built up there) is a condition of engaging in other forms of work (which require outlays of capital on materials) and of purchasing marketed consumption services. The unemployed 'are too poor to work informally' (p. 96). Furthermore, given that the house is the major focus of informal work, home ownership, too, would seem to be a condition of its development, for on the Isle of Sheppey at least, house purchase and renovation was a major strategy for acquiring capital (p. 183).

It is important to emphasize that none of this supports a class-reductionist thesis, for Pahl clearly establishes that it is household structure (i.e. the number of earners and the stage in the life cycle) rather than class which is (and in his view has always been) the key factor in shaping patterns of work. What his study establishes is the growth of a social polarization, not on class lines, but between households that can work (formally and informally) and those that cannot. There is, he says, a 'growing middle mass' (p. 324), and the fundamental cleavage in contemporary British society lies between it and the marginalized, residualized 'underclass':

A process of polarization is developing, with households busily engaged in all forms of work at one pole and households unable to do a wide range of work at the other. ... The division between the more affluent home-owning households of ordinary working people and the less advantaged under-class households is coming to be more significant than conventional divisions based on the manual/non-manual distinction (1984, p. 314).

For the remainder of this chapter I shall take this polarization thesis as given, for the evidence and arguments which have been marshalled in support of it in this and the previous section are, I believe, overwhelming. I shall therefore turn to consider what might realistically be done about it. How, in other words, could changes be instituted which might break down this depressing and frightening cleavage in British society between the new privileged majority and the marginalized minority?

The solution, obviously, lies in somehow enhancing the consumption capacity of those at the bottom. At present, they are at the butt end of declining state services from which the majority are fast 'exiting', and they are excluded not only from what Dunleavy (1983) terms 'individual consumption' (i.e. the purchase of marketed goods and services), but also from what he calls 'autonomous consumption' (i.e. effective self-provisioning).

One way of doing this, of course, would be to bolster the state welfare sector – to build more council houses, increase staff in schools, pump more money into the National Health Service, raise subsidies to public transport, and so on. Yet not only is this probably the least realistic strategy given the availability of state revenues, it is also arguably the least attractive one. Most commentators with eyes to see recognize that, as Castells puts it, the demand for enhanced consumption provisions 'is too often understood in terms of more public housing and more social services. It is crucial to consider it in terms of different kinds of services and urban amenities' (1983b, p. 15). I would also add to this that it is crucial to consider it in terms of what people as consumers actually seem to want. 'When we build again', pleads Colin Ward, 'we need not a plan for housing, but an attitude that will enable millions of people to make their own plans' (1985, p. 120). And so of course it is with other consumption resources. Could not socialized consumption provisions be democratized, then, to take account of consumer opinion? The dual politics thesis would suggest, for example, that welfare services can be made more accountable and controllable if they are locally organized and administered by elected bodies. The tendency in Britain is, of course, in the other direction, towards regional or national non-elected bodies such as the health authorities and the metropolitan public transport agencies; but even if local democratization could be brought about, its impact would be limited. As we saw when we discussed the dual politics thesis, consumer interests tend always to be subordinated to producer interests within the state system. Furthermore, the experience of local democratic initiatives suggests that most people pay them little heed, for no matter how much the housing department decentralizes its management offices, or the health authority delegates to its community councils, the consumers themselves still experience the services passively, as clients, and they act accordingly, grumbling here, grateful there, but never asserting control.

If the aim really is to make consumption provisions more accountable to people – i.e. to shift power from those (whether they be politicians, urban managers, state-employed professionals, public sector workers or private sector producers) who currently control these services to those who use them – then this implies a transfer of responsibility from the former to the latter. Effectively, this can only mean a transfer of property rights – rights to control and dispose of, as well as to use and benefit from, the resources in question. It implies, in other words, an extension (to all aspects of consumption, and to all sections of the population) of the privatized consumption mode. In practical terms, this could only be achieved through a move from state provision in kind to state provision in cash.

There tends to be a curious knee-jerk reaction on the left when this sort of proposal is floated. Ward (1985, p. 28) notes how concepts such as 'self-help' and 'mutual aid' have somehow become 'dirty words' for socialists, and Pahl (1984, p. 325) similarly despairs of the way collectivistic solutions have come to dominate socialist thinking as regards consumption as well as production. 'For a time', he says, 'ordinary people were prepared to go along with solidaristic collectivism as perhaps the only way to get major advances into citizenship. Now, it seems, the citizens of the middle mass are asserting themselves in their private lives' (p. 326).

As I suggested in the previous section, this 'middle mass' has been able to pursue a privatized solution to its consumption requirements owing to the increase in real household income which has taken place over the last hundred years. Bolstered in many cases by the 'hidden welfare state' of tax allowances and other financial benefits, its income from work is now enough to support purchase of the most expensive household consumption item – the house itself – and the time is probably fast approaching when, individually or corporately (e.g. through trade union or company subscription), it will be able to finance most elements of its health care needs too. The minority of households which do not enjoy regular wage income cannot, however, aspire to the private ownership solution under current arrangements. They cannot 'assert themselves in their private lives', either by purchasing services or by self-provisioning through purchasing means of consumption, but instead remain locked into dependency on whatever the state chooses to dispense.

State spending on consumption provisions in Britain accounts for around 25 per cent of the country's Gross National Product, or 60,000 million pounds in 1981–2 prices (see Le Grand and Robinson 1984). Of this, nearly half goes on transfer payments – mainly pensions, but also supplementary, child and unemployment benefits. The rest is distributed among provisions in kind, with education and health and personal services accounting for about 80 per cent of it, and housing and transport taking up the rest. Now suppose (leaving aside the question of any addition to the overall budget which may be deemed desirable) the money which currently goes to finance provisions in kind were reallocated, gradually over a period of years, to enhance people's ability to buy the goods and services they want. Such a redistribution of money would take account of variations in household needs and incomes and could take the form of 'negative' income tax payments, earmarked benefits such as increased child allowances, specific voucher schemes, or some combination of all three. This would generate, on average, an extra £2000 per household per year at 1981–2 prices, although some households would in practice receive very little extra (for as we have seen, many multi-earner households can already afford to finance most of their consumption needs without additional support), while others, including those who currently make up the marginalized minority of our society, would receive a large increase. In any event, such a system would have to establish a minimum income level so as to ensure that everyone could purchase at least that level of services to which they are currently entitled under the existing system of provision in kind. Judging by figures calculated by Patrick Minford and cited in Green (1986, ch. 6), this should not be too difficult to achieve.

The first effect of such a gradual transition in the mode of state spending would be to bring about a substantial redistribution of income in favour of the worst off. Under Minford's scheme, for example, people would pay for health insurance, schooling and pension arrangements, but the lower paid would receive in negative income tax and child benefits more than the total cost of such payments and would therefore be better off than they are under existing arrangements. Furthermore, a shift away from provision in kind would mean that lower income earners would no longer be compelled to pay through their taxes for services which they tend to under-use and from which more affluent people extract the most benefit.

A second effect of such a change would almost certainly be a reduction in the costs of most services. Privatization of consumption can, of course, increase costs since economies of scale may be lost, provisions may be duplicated by competing suppliers, and prices obviously include a profit component. Against this, however, administration costs could certainly be cut by overcoming the need to maintain the current levels of monitoring and surveillance entailed in a state system of allocation in kind. As Ward suggests, there is an 'appalling difficulty about the expensive business of looking after people. They would be better off if they simply had the cash to look after themselves' (1985, p. 94). Furthermore, competition between suppliers of services can be expected to reduce prices and costs as compared with a state system of monopoly provision which contains no mechanism for ensuring that service producers pursue the most cost-effective strategies. Not only this, but the individual and co-operative forms of control which would replace state provision are almost certainly less wasteful. As Ward notes in relation to public housing, for example, accommodation which is rented to tenants by the state tends to deteriorate much more rapidly than the equivalent sorts of buildings sold to equivalent sorts of people through the market sector: 'The transfer of council houses to their occupants is the best guarantee of their survival' (1985, p. 50). Much the same logic would seem to apply to other aspects of consumption provision as well.

A third and vitally important effect would be to break down the stark division which is now emerging between net recipients and net donors in the welfare system. My argument here is premised on Dunleavy's recognition that consumption sector cleavages tend only to arise around the provision of resources in kind. As he notes, in the case of 'generalized income transfers which are not tied to the consumption of specific commodities . . . we should find that the overall importance of consumption sector effects . . . is reduced' (1985, p. 10). The reason for this is simple. An integrated tax/benefit system of income transfers leaves no visible trace of who is reliant upon the state and who is not, for everyone appears in the market to purchase their consumption requirements as customers rather than as clients, and no one need feel stigmatized. As Simmel noted long ago, money carries no trace of its origins and is no respecter of status.

Fourth, such a change should enable all households to participate more fully than they can at present in informal modes of work. As Pahl suggests, 'Money is necessary to do all the other forms of work. . . . If there were a national minimum wage instead of the present system of benefits and allowances, the total amount of work done would almost certainly increase' (1984, p. 336). Not only, therefore, would the extension of transfer payments to cover health, education and so on enable people to assert themselves more effectively through the selection of the particular services they wished to purchase, but it would also enable them to develop, where feasible, their own modes of self-provisioning and mutual aid. People could, if they chose, form consumer co-operatives to organize for their children to be educated and they could come together in modern forms of the nineteenth-century friendly societies to employ doctors and dentists who would be made accountable to them. Or, if they preferred, they could instead purchase services on an individual basis, selecting the type of schooling they most preferred and the level of medical insurance which best suited their personal requirements. Either way, their capacity for controlling key aspects of their lives would be enormously enhanced.

The major effect of such a change, however, would be to bring about a fundamental redistribution of power in society – something which the existing welfare system has conspicuously failed to achieve. As the (socialist) theorist, Alec Nove, has recognized in his stimulating analysis of markets and state planning, 'With a given distribution of income (as egalitarian as the given society chooses it to be), *there is no better way* of enabling citizens to register their preferences than to allow them freely to spend their "money" (tokens) or their money. If this is denounced by the fundamentalist [Marxist] as a "market", so be it. .... [N]o voting system can be a substitute because, first, the huge variety of preferences makes it an impossibly unwieldy task, and secondly ... because this is not a matter of majority vote anyhow, since a minority is entitled to be supplied also (1983, p. 54, emphasis in original). Customers can exert power (albeit limited) within a market through their purses, pockets and pouches, but this is denied to the client within a system of state provision. Clients can complain, can vote, can demand, but in the end they have nowhere else to go, and no choice but to accept what is offered. They are, in short, *dependent* in a way that is never true of customers in a competitive market.

There is a tendency among conservatives and state socialists alike to doubt people's ability to take over such a degree of control and responsibility for their own lives. In one sense, such doubts are justified, for a century of escalating state control has undoubtedly eroded our capacities for making our own decisions about crucial aspects of our own lives. It is precisely because the system they defend has made us dependent that such conservative and socialist thinkers can argue that it would be folly now to bring about a shift in effective power from producers and state managers to consumers. But against this, a change of the kind envisaged here could be expected to revolutionize people's aspirations and expectations and to break through the grudging deference and hopeless fatalism which pervades so much of the state welfare system. After all, people already make decisions in their everyday lives which have a crucial bearing on their health and well-being – decisions about the food that they purchase, the shoes and clothing they dress their children in, and (in the case of the 'middle mass') the home that they will live in and the kind of pension and insurance arrangements that they require. A shift in other areas of consumption from state provision in kind to a policy designed to enable people to exert their own effective demand for what they want would extend the scope of such responsibilities, and there is no reason to assume that people who already make decisions and choices in one area would not also be able to make them in another.

Those who often deny this most vociferously tend to be those responsible for managing and providing the services in question, the 'professional hierarchies' of the welfare institutions who 'have convinced society that their ministrations are morally necessary' (Illich 1971, p. 12). These, of course, are the interests which stand to lose from any increase in effective consumer power, for they would lose their captive client constituency and would, for the first time since the socialized mode of consumption developed, have to address themselves to the demands of the consumers of their services.

Such a shift in power from producers to consumers is in my view the moral and political rationale which lies behind the future development of urban sociology as a sociology of consumption. In a recent and stimulating contribution, Herbert Gans has outlined what he terms a 'third paradigm' for urban sociology, which goes beyond the anti-collectivism of neo-ecology and the anti-individualism of neo-Marxism. What distinguishes this third paradigm is its emphasis on consumers rather than producers, an emphasis (exemplified in different ways in the writings of Pahl and Ward discussed above) on understanding what people want and on analysing how best they might achieve it. For Gans, 'Producers of goods and services probably have more power than consumers in all societies, because they play a central role in a communist economy, and because they have the incentives and resources to put pressure on government in a capitalist economy' (1984, p. 295). This producer power goes unchallenged by both neo-ecology (which speaks for private sector corporations) and neo-Marxism (which, despite its sympathy for 'an imagined coalition of the poor and the working class' actually resists the expressed aspirations of these groups and speaks mainly for academics who are themselves, of course, part of the public sector producer interest). The task, therefore is to develop an urban sociology:

... beginning from the perspective of the users (be these customers or clients or constituents) and tracing the relationships and problems with the public bodies. This sociology would pay less attention than current ones on how public bodies are structured and function, or how they produce and reproduce – or reach users. Instead, the analysis begins with the interests of users, as perceived and felt by them, looking at producers and suppliers of services in terms of their ability and willingness to pay attention to, or ignore or manipulate, user demands and preferences (1984, p. 305).

Such a research agenda cannot, of course, ignore producers, for as we saw in Chapter 6, modes of consumption are related to modes of production, and a change in one will carry implications as regards change in the other. If, for example, a policy was adopted in which, wherever practicable, state provisions in kind were replaced by cash payments in one form or another, then this would certainly change the character and organization of agencies producing goods and services. Just as consumer co-operatives could develop, so too, for example, could producer co-operatives (e.g. teachers who share a particular ethos of education could come together to offer a particular kind of schooling). Furthermore, the redistribution of spending power away from state monopolies and towards those sections of the population who currently lack financial power in consumer markets would clearly create new patterns of demand and would (provided the minimum level of household income were established at a point sufficient to ensure that everyone could participate effectively in the market) bring forth new forms of supply to meet them.

Given this interrelation of production and consumption, it may well be asked why this 'third paradigm' in urban sociology should focus primarily on the latter. Why analyse people's experience as consumers rather than as producers? Why seek to liberate people through their use of goods and services rather than through their production of these goods and services? Why, in short, elevate consumption above production?

The answer is that, in the conditions pertaining in advanced industrial societies, liberation through the formal production sphere is almost certainly impractical. The sphere of consumption is as important and crucial as it is precisely because it is here that the potential exists for extending people's control over their own lives. In general, this potential does not exist in the sphere of production.

My argument here has much in common with that developed by André Gorz in his two books, *Farewell to the Working Class* (1982) and *Paths to Paradise* (1985). Both books start out from the assumption, shared by Pahl and many others, that the era of full employment in a single, paid job has finished. Technological developments have brought us to a point in the West where only 20,000 hours of labour are necessary in any one lifetime in order to produce all the items we need to consume. In such a situation, it is ludicrous to continue to assert that formal paid employment constitutes people's central life activity and identity: 'There can no longer be full-time waged work for all, and waged work cannot remain the centre of gravity or even the central activity in our lives. Any politics which denies this, whatever its ideological pretensions, is a fraud' (1985, p. 34). Gorz also argues that the Marxist project of liberating people in and through their labour is similarly fraudulent, since for most workers, labour is necessarily experienced as alienative. This, he says, is not simply because of the way capitalist production is organized, but is because of the inherent character of advanced production methods which are too large in scale and too diversified and fragmented in nature for anyone to experience creativity through their work or to seek to control the overall process. It follows from this that:

> For workers, it is no longer a question of freeing themselves *within* work, putting themselves in control of work, or seizing power within the framework of their work. The point now is to free oneself *from* work by rejecting its nature, content, necessity and modalities. But to reject work is also to reject the traditional strategy and organisational forms of the working class movement. It is no longer a question of winning power as a worker, but of winning the power no longer to function as a worker (1982, p. 67).

It is on the basis of such arguments that Gorz distinguishes two spheres within what he terms a future 'dual society'. One sphere is the realm of compulsion and necessity, what he terms the 'sphere of heteronomy'. It is here that the goods and services are produced which are conditions of the exercise of 'practical autonomy' in the other sphere of life. People, he suggests, could contribute 20,000 hours of labour to working in a planned and programmed system of production, in return for which they would earn sufficient to claim access to the various goods and services they required in order to pursue their other and more central life activities.

What is of interest in Gorz's work as regards our current concerns is less his futuristic blueprint than the arguments which lie behind it. Two points appear to be crucial. First, Gorz is clear that, even with the decline in paid employment, some necessary work remains to be done and this will always be experienced by most people as alienative and coercive:

> The division of labour is thus inevitably depersonalising. . . . There can never be effective self-management of a big factory, an industrial combine or a bureaucratic department. It will always be defeated by the rigidity of technical constraints. . . . It is thus impossible to abolish the depersonalisation, standardisation and trivialisation of socially determined labour without abolishing the division of labour through a return to craft production and the village economy. This is out of the question. . . . The point, then, is not to abolish heteronomous work, but only to use the goods it supplies and the way in which they are produced in order to enlarge the sphere of autonomy (1982, pp. 100–1).

It follows from this that, whether organized through a market or a planning system, the sphere of formal production cannot today offer the prospect of popular liberation or autonomous control.

The second argument is that personal liberation and control is nevertheless an essential feature of popular aspirations (one which has generally gone unrecognized in socialist movements), and that it can potentially be realized outside of people's formal working lives. Provided they have the necessary means (which they gain through work in the heteronomous sphere of production), people can therefore achieve control and self-determination away from formal work in what I have called the sphere of consumption.

It is important to emphasize that Gorz does not limit this sphere of autonomy simply to passive consumption of goods and services, but includes in it all the activities in which people may choose to engage other than through instrumental–economic necessity. 'The sphere of individual sovereignty', he notes, 'is not based upon a mere desire to consume, nor solely upon relaxation and leisure activities. It is based, more profoundly, upon activities unrelated to any economic goal which are an end in themselves' (1982, p. 80). It thus includes both passive and active consumption, or what Dunleavy terms 'individual' and 'autonomous' consumption. It includes, in other words, the use of means of consumption in 'informal work' and self-provisioning as well as consumption as an end in itself, DIY as well as TV.

Given his view that paid employment is no longer the central life activity (if, indeed, it ever was) and that self-management, identity and control can only be expressed outside of the formal production sphere, it is clearly crucial for Gorz that the realm of autonomy should determine the realm of heteronomy rather than vice versa. As he puts it:

There can be neither morality nor relations informed by morality unless two conditions are fulfilled. First, there must exist a sphere of autonomous activity in which the individual is the sovereign author of actions carried out without recourse to necessity, alibis or excuses. Secondly, this sphere must be prevalent rather than subordinate (1982, p. 93).

Here, then, is the case for concentrating our attentions on the sphere of consumption prior to the sphere of production, and for attempting to expand the capacity for people to control their own lives in the consumption sphere by limiting the power of producers to control it. This also provides the justification for attempting as far as possible to limit state determination of human activities to the sphere of production while keeping state monopoly power away from the sphere of consumption. As Gorz says, 'There is no "good" government, "good" state or "good" form of power, and . . . society can never be "good" in its own form of organisation but only by virtue of the space for self-organisation, cooperation and voluntary exchange which that organisation offers to individuals' (1982, p. 118).

Here, too, is the case for Gans's attempt to forge a new sociology which goes beyond both the anti-collectivism of the right and the anti-individualism of the left, for it is clear that individualistic solutions in the sphere of consumption are not inconsistent with, and may to some extent require, collectivistic solutions in the sphere of production. Just as we saw earlier in this chapter that different social scientific theories which have generally been seen as incompatible may in fact be complementary in so far as they apply to the different spheres of production and consumption, so now we see that this is also the case with different political and moral philosophies. As Gorz recognizes, 'Economic liberalism gives rise to demands for state control and . . . state control provokes demands for liberalisation. The point, however, is not to choose one or the other; but to define the field in which both can be cogently put into effect' (1982, p. 114). The privatized mode of provision is thus appropriate to the sphere of consumption, but the state may still have a crucial role to perform in the sphere of production in order to ensure that the conditions of autonomy in the former are maintained and reproduced.

Just how state power could or should be used in the production sphere in order to safeguard the autonomy of the consumption sphere is, however, a problem requiring further consideration and analysis. Gorz himself fails to provide a satisfactory answer, for having argued at the beginning of his analysis that the modern system of production does not allow for any effective popular control, he is forced at the end (e.g. 1985, pp. 57–8) to posit the existence of a social consensus as the basis for determining collective decisions as to what needs to be produced and how. The possibility that such a consensus could ever exist is, to say the least, dubious, as is his belief that it is possible to retain a technical division of labour without perpetuating a hierarchy of authority and stratification (1985, p. 77).

Various of Gorz's critics (and there have been many, for his analysis strikes at the heart of traditional Marxist theory and practice) have suggested that the partial liberation which he offers does not go far enough. Production, they assert in familiar vein, remains primary and determinant over consumption, in which case Gorz's attempt to carve out a niche of personal autonomy in respect of the latter is doomed. Ignoring his tightly-argued demonstration that freedom in the sphere of formal work is a chimera, for example, Godard concludes his critical discussion of Gorz's work by asking with a rhetorical flourish, 'Is this not to prescribe the hopelessness of significantly changing the logic (of functioning) of the large-scale apparatuses of production and control of the state machine? Can we change ways of life without also changing the ways of producing and governing?' (1985, p. 335).

In contrast to these critics, I would suggest that Gorz probably goes too far. What is wrong with his analysis is not that it seeks to establish autonomy in only one sphere, for this is entirely realistic, but that he fails to show how the other sphere will accommodate and adjust to this. It is for this reason that I have outlined an altogether more modest proposal – namely, a reform of the state's role in consumption involving a shift from direct provision to cash transfers – for while this will not usher in a new age of freedom and self-determination, it will enormously enhance people's capacity for controlling and determining certain core aspects of their lives, and it does appear to be an attainable goal.

Such issues and arguments are, of course, open to further debate, elaboration and critical analysis. As Pahl notes, 'The sociology of consumption is not well developed' (1984, p. 106; see also Moorhouse 1983). But provided we can shake off the legacy of a long strain of intellectual thought which asserts that consumption is simply a derivative of production, then such a sociology does hold out considerable promise. As Gans suggests, 'If citizens want anything from sociology, it is informational help in escaping exploitation and domination, and in maximising their control over their own lives' (1984, p. 306). Urban sociology, understood as a sociology of consumption, can, I believe, help provide such information and point the way to such control. In focusing on that sphere of life which provides the greatest potential for the expression of individual autonomy, urban sociology is uniquely equipped to chart a path out of the 'iron cage' which Weber believed was encompassing the whole of modern society. In the problem of consumption, therefore, urban sociology has not only at long last discovered an object of analysis; it has helped identify one of the core questions of the modern age.

Appendix A note on the empirical testing of theories

It has been suggested at various points in this book that empirical testability is one important criterion of theoretical adequacy. We saw in Chapter 6, for example, that Marxist theories of the relative autonomy of the state ultimately fail to explain what they describe because they are essentially tautologies which are immune to empirical evaluation. The reason for this is that the concept of relative autonomy combines two opposing principles into a single general statement which cannot support counterfactual conditions, for to argue that the state both supports the long-term interests of monopoly capital and responds to the interests of non-capitalist classes without specifying the conditions under which these two contradictory tendencies become operative is simply to provide a self-confirming theory which is descriptively accurate but devoid of explanatory power. It was for this reason that it was suggested in Chapter 8 that a dualistic perspective may prove fruitful, for by distinguishing those situations in which capitalist interests are dominant from those in which the state responds to different interests engaged in competitive struggles with one another, it is possible to develop a range of hypotheses that may be assessed in the light of empirical research.

One possible objection to this whole argument, however, is that it betrays a naive view of the relation between theory and empirical evidence. Thus social scientists have increasingly come to recognize that the traditional assumption behind positivist research that 'facts' can be assembled through direct experience of the social world must be treated with some caution. It is now generally agreed that knowledge cannot be the product of unmediated experience through the senses, but that the way in which we come to 'see' the world is in some way dependent upon the theoretical assumptions and conceptual frameworks that we apply to it. As we saw in Chapter 1 when discussing the problems with Durkheim's sociological method, what we take to be 'facts', and thus 'evidence' and 'proof' for our assertions, will depend upon the way we conceptualize the world. There is no 'pure' observation, no neutral body of evidence, no 'facts' that are independent of prior conceptual assumptions.

If observation is theory-dependent, then resort to empirical evidence to arbitrate between competing theoretical explanations is clearly problematic. As Hindess suggests in relation to Popper's arguments regarding the need for empirical falsification in science, 'If all observation is to some extent theoretical, then how is it possible to maintain that all knowledge is reducible to observation and that theory is to be tested against the "facts" of observation?' (1977, p. 18). The point is not simply that theory determines where we look, but that it to some extent governs what we find.

The theory dependency of empirical research findings does not, however, undermine my earlier argument that empirical testability is an essential condition of theoretical adequacy. Three points need to be considered.

The first is that theory dependency does not imply theory determinacy. There is, in other words, no reason to suggest that different theoretical perspectives cannot agree on common areas of conceptualization and common criteria of empirical evidence. To argue otherwise would be to suggest that different theorists always talk past one another, never engage in meaningful debate and mutual criticism, and never concur over what is actually happening in the world; yet this is clearly not the case. For example, although they certainly disagree over the explanations they offer, and sometimes disagree over criteria of adequate or valid empirical evidence, conflict and consensus theorists nevertheless broadly agree on the sort of evidence that may indicate the perpetuation or break-down of social order. Similarly, while we may doubt, say, Castells's reasons for predicting the growth of urban social movements, and we may criticize the very concept of an urban social movement, none of this precludes the possibility of Castells and his critics agreeing on the existence or non-existence of such movements in a particular place at a particular time on the basis of the criteria which Castells himself puts forward.

The point is, therefore, that any theory employs both relatively high- and relatively low-level concepts, and that there is always likely to be a fairly broad conceptual 'lower common denominator' between different perspectives. As Andrew Sayer notes in his defence of Marxist methodology, ' "Looking at the evidence" need not imply an empiricist notion of observation as theory-neutral, but in relation to concepts like "socialization of consumption", those employed in observation are liable to be of a "*lower order*". That is, they are unlikely to be exclusive to Marxism' (A. Sayer 1979, p. 48). Thus Sayer distinguishes between the (correct) view that evidence is theory-laden and the (incorrect) view that it is therefore theory-determined. Different theories share a broad (though low-level) area of agreement regarding their conceptualization of the world and their criteria of empirical evidence, and, this being the case, the theory dependency of empirical research need not rule out some degree of empirical evaluation of different theories, nor need it result in a collapse into cognitive relativism (see also A. Sayer 1984a, Ch. 2).

Before leaving this point, and as a prelude to the second point, it is important to take issue with one aspect of Sayer's argument concerning his critique of Hirst's rejection of epistemology which we discussed briefly in Chapter 5. It will be recalled that, in criticizing Althusser's epistemological imperialism, Hirst came to the conclusion that there are no epistemological principles divorced from particular discourses that can determine the correct mode of scientific analysis. We cannot, that is, criticize any given perspective simply on epistemological grounds, although different perspectives can be attacked on criteria internal to their own discourse. While himself rejecting Althusser's position, Sayer also rejects Hirst's argument as 'fatuous' and 'silly' on the grounds that it assumes that 'all observation is completely theory-determined' (A. Sayer 1979, p. 73). For Sayer, in other words, a rejection of epistemology is tantamount to an endorsement of cognitive relativism (despite the fact that Hirst has stressed that his is not a relativist – or, indeed, any other epistemological – position).

Given our endorsement of Hirst's argument in Chapter 5, it is clearly necessary to answer this criticism, for we have seen that Sayer is quite justified in arguing against the theory determinacy view of observation. The point is, however, that Hirst's argument does not entail such a view. Hirst and his various co-authors do not necessarily deny that different discourses may agree on epistemological principles; only that any one epistemology can be taken as self-evident and thus as the basis for rejecting alternative approaches grounded in alternative methodologies. His critique of epistemology suggests simply that no approach can be dismissed on the grounds that it is epistemologically invalid because no general epistemology can be self-justifiable. This does not, however, imply that different discourses cannot engage in mutual criticism based on common agreement regarding what is to count as a valid mode of analysis or adequate empirical evidence.

Neither Sayer nor other like-minded critics of Hirst's position have been able to demonstrate the superiority of one epistemological position over others. In his critique, for example, Collier suggests that, for knowledge to be possible, it must be assumed that reality is structured in a certain way:

If our faculties of knowledge depend for their possibility on the structure of the world outside them in this way, why should we not assume that the world really has that structure and hence makes them possible, rather than that they have the additional magic ability to force the world into a knowable form which it doesn't have in itself? (Collier 1978, p. 16).

The answer, of course, is that there is no reason why we should not *assume* that our concepts develop in such a way as progressively to map and hence reveal the real structure of the world, and that dialectical materialism is the method that is most appropriate to such a voyage of discovery since 'its result depends on the structure of external reality, not on us' (Collier 1978, p. 19), provided we always remember that this is a starting assumption which is not an *a priori* truth (as Althusser seems to believe), and which cannot in itself justify the rejection of other approaches based on other initial assumptions. It is not Hirst and his colleagues who must 'come clean', as Sayer and Collier both suggest at the end of their respective papers, but rather those Marxist theorists who claim to work with a privileged epistemology yet who have failed to demonstrate the source of its superiority. It does seem that the hostility shown by many academic Marxists towards Hirst's arguments is born of a fear of losing the 'scientific' basis of their political analyses, the paradox being (as Hirst himself has shown) that it is precisely this claim to scientific privilege that has so consistently weakened rather than strengthened the political impact of Marxism over the last hundred years.

What is specific to the Marxist method is, as we saw in Chapter 1, the distinction that it draws between essence and phenomenal appearance, and hence its claim to be able to explain the latter through the discovery of the former. This leads us to consider the second point relating to the question of empirical testability; namely, that Marxist laws cannot and should not be tested through any simple notion of empirical falsification. Sayer's paper is again relevant here.

Sayer argues, quite justifiably, that the Marxist method involves the attempt to discover necessary tendencies (such as the tendency within capitalism for the rate of profit to fall), and that the question of whether or not these tendencies are realized is contingent on a variety of empirical conditions (for example the mobilization of counter-acting tendencies to prevent the rate of profit from falling). Drawing an analogy with the natural sciences, he argues that, just as the chemical laws of combustion are not falsified if a particular pile of gunpowder fails to explode when a flame is applied (since, for example, it may be damp), and just as the law of gravity is not falsified whenever aeroplanes fail to drop from the sky, so too Marxist laws cannot be rejected as false simply because they fail to become manifest in particular situations. He then argues on the basis of this that Marxist theories cannot be subject to the test of empirical falsification (since this ignores the question of counteracting tendencies), or even to the test of their success in guiding political practice (since political intervention changes the situation to which they refer). He concludes that 'In social science there are no "tests", only applications' (A. Sayer 1979, p. 33).

This argument reflects Sayer's commitment to what has become known as 'realist' philosophy. As we saw in Chapter 6, this is an approach to social scientific explanation which seeks to identify the inherent capacities of things to act in certain ways. Unlike empiricist approaches, which see causality in terms of correlation between events (whenever A occurs, then so too does B), realist philosophy argues for a conception of causality in terms of generative mechanisms. Theoretical progress thus entails identification of the 'necessary' mechanisms which tend to produce given tendencies. The fact that such tendencies may not become manifest in observation is due to the operation of contingent factors which obviously cannot be theorized, but whose effects can be examined in given empirical cases. Thus, for example, it may be held that there is a necessary and inherent tendency in capitalism for the rate of exploitation of labour to increase. This will itself tend to generate an intensification of class struggle between labour and capital, but the form that such struggles take (e.g. worker absenteeism, industrial sabotage, strikes, demon-strations, revolutions), and, indeed, whether or not they occur at all, will reflect the particular historical conditions pertaining at any given time in any given place (e.g. the character of the labour movement, the nature of dominant ideologies, the strength of state coercion, etc.). The important point about all this is that, even if events do not seem to bear out the theory, this does not invalidate it, for events reflect contingent conditions while theory is concerned with necessary mechanisms which exist irrespective of whether they become manifest.

One confusing aspect of this approach which is immediately apparent concerns the distinction between 'necessities' and 'contingencies', for what is a necessity (and thus capable of being theorized) from one point of view may be a 'contingency' (and thus incapable of being theorized) from another. Thus, taking the above example, the 'contingent' factor of the nature of the labour movement can itself be re-translated into a 'necessary' one by a simple shift in the types of research questions we set ourselves. We could presumably develop an argument to the effect that placid labour movements are necessarily generated by, say, the tendency for real wages to rise as capitalism develops, and the contingent condition in this case would be that factors sometimes arise (e.g. the quadrupling of oil prices in the early 1970s) which depress living standards and which therefore prevent this placidity from becoming manifest. There are, in other words, no obvious guidelines (other than the researcher's own value-conditioned interests) for determining what is necessary and what is contingent.

There is, however, an even more thorny problem with this whole approach which is basically that it becomes possible to posit virtually anything as a 'real' and 'necessary' tendency, given that contingent events or 'counteracting tendencies' can always be appealed to in order to save the theory. What is to stop us identifying through our theories all sorts of causal mechanisms which may or may not exist?

Realist philosophy attempts to guard against this by stipulating three steps in the construction of any explanation. The first is observation in which we detect empirical regularities in the world (e.g. all swans are white, apples fall downwards, capitalist economies lurch into crisis every few years). The second step is then to develop plausible explanations relating to the mechanism which may be generating these regularities (e.g. that the genetic make-up of swans inhibits pigmentation in the feathers, that a gravitational force exists which draws all objects to the centre of the earth, or that competition between capitalists tends to drive overall rates of profit downwards). As we saw when we discussed Derek Sayer's notion of 'retroduction' in Chapter 1, this second stage is necessarily conjectural, for we are not and cannot be sure that the mechanisms we have posited are the real ones. It is for this reason that the third step – experimental checking – is so crucial, for it is here that contingent conditions are as far as possible held constant so as to identify the causal mechanisms which are actually generating the observed effects.

The problem when we come to apply this method to the social world, however, is that this third experimental stage is not normally possible. There are many reasons why this is so – among them, the fact that there are too many variables to hold constant, that sociological experiments in controlled conditions destroy the situation which is being studied, and that enormous ethical problems are raised in any attempt to experiment with people's lives. Realists generally accept this. One of the leading realist philosophers, for example, admits that the crucial third stage of experimental verification cannot be carried through in social explanation:

The central argument of this study ... has turned on the possibility of experimental activity. . . . [I]t is clear that experimental activity is impossible in the social sciences ... there is a general problem of confirmation (or corroboration) and falsification in the non-experimental sciences (Bhaskar 1978, pp. 244–5).

This would seem to throw considerable doubt over the application of a realist methodology in the explanation of social phenomena, for while we may be in a position to observe regularities and to conjure up various plausible explanations for them in terms of the operation of 'necessary tendencies', we cannot follow through to the crucial third stage of examining whether or not these tendencies actually exist when contingent conditions are held constant. We never know, for example, whether there is, as Marxist theory tells us, a real tendency in capitalist societies for the rate of profit to fall, for the contingent events which operate in the opposite direction (e.g. increased investment in 'Department I' industries, or increased rates of exploitation of labour in 'Department II' industries) occur simultaneously, and it is impossible to examine the effects of a rise in the ratio of constant to variable capital independently of these 'counteracting tendencies'.

What then is to stop us developing any theory of necessity when we know that it cannot be checked through controlled experimental conditions? Andrew Sayer (1984 a) provides two checks. First, he says that it is normally possible, though by no means easy, to find independent corroborative evidence for the existence of a necessary tendency. Second, he suggests that fanciful theories can be eliminated by exposing the weaknesses in the explanations which they offer of the generative mechanisms at work. Thus, for example, my pet theory that there are no elephants in Surrey because I go round the county once a month scattering mustard seed which keeps them away can be rejected first, by seeking independent evidence (e.g. were there elephants in Surrey before I began my monthly ritual?), and second, by demonstrating the inadequacy of the mechanism (e.g. by looking at the effect which mustard seed has on elephants) (see Sayer 1984a, pp. 198–200). This, however, does not really answer the problem. For a start, the refutation of the theory rests on a controlled experiment (testing the effects of mustard seed on elephants) which we have already seen is not possible in the case of social theories. And second, the independent corroboration (e.g. evidence that Surrey has never had elephants) can simply be dismissed as itself the result of other contingent conditions (e.g. the effects of climate) which do nothing to undermine the theorized necessary mechanism regarding the inherent tendencies of mustard seed as an elephant deterrent.

My theory concerning the inherent tendencies of mustard seed is, as Sayer says, trivial, but the lessons to be learned from it are not. In my view, the growth of realist approaches in urban studies during the 1980s is effectively leading to a repeat of the sorts of claims being advanced by Althusserian philosophy in the 1970s.

As we saw in Chapter 5, Althusserianism gained its adherents through its claim that there was but one scientific method and that alternative approaches were essentially ideological. This brash assertiveness eventually collapsed as researchers came to realize, not only that this method hindered empirical work (in that it denied the possibility of knowing the world other than through theory), but also that (as Hirst showed) there could be no meta-epistemology which could possibly justify Althusser's claims to a privileged insight into reality.

Liberated from the yoke of Althusserian epistemology, many people (among them, Castells) began to discuss the need for more empirical research, and a few actually began to do it. In particular, they began to assert the importance of historical analysis as the means for explaining how and why things came to be as they are. This tendency, however, carried the clear danger of heresy against some cherished Marxist principles (as is obvious in Castells's later work), for to argue that history could explain causality was to undermine a belief in scientific laws governing human affairs. Various neologisms were coined in an attempt to resolve these difficulties. What was required, we were told, was not a return to 'empiricism' (bad), but the development of 'theoretically-informed empirical research' (good);

not 'bourgeois history' (bad) with its preoccupations with unique events and key individuals, but 'theorized histories' (good) which would situate these events and individuals within the laws and universal tendencies of which they were but an expression. What all this amounted to was a call for selective empirical and historical research which would not produce new knowledge so much as illustrate and 'confirm' existing knowledge gleaned through a thorough grounding in Marxist theory. The theory, in other words, was to be preserved while allowing empirical research to develop within its boundaries. What was needed was an approach which would subordinate history to theory and which would guarantee the immunity of the latter from the results of the former. Realism was the epistemology which was seized upon to fulfil this requirement.

Part of the attraction of realism has been that it seems to offer many of the old epistemological certainties which disappeared with the collapse of Althusserianism. Just as Althusser distinguished his 'science' from everybody else's 'ideology', so now realists such as Bhaskar (and in urban studies, Sayer or Urry) distinguish their knowledge of 'real' causal mechanisms from everybody else's 'superficial' knowledge of the manifest pattern of events. As the very name implies, to be a 'realist' is to distinguish oneself from others who by definition have only a tenuous grasp of 'reality'.

Realism's atttraction also lies in its offer of an approach which justifies the desire to hold history at arm's length from theory. This is achieved through the basic distinction between necessary causes and contingent conditions. As we have seen, necessary causes are identified by means of theory while contingent conditions are identified empirically (even though in practice, the distinction between what is necessary and what is contingent seems to hinge entirely on what it is the researcher is interested in looking at). This means that realism accords to empirical and historical research the task of identifying the contingencies which are mediating the real motive forces which have already been identified through the theory.

What we have here is a revised and more subtle form of Althusserianism. Unlike Althusserianism, realism does make room for empirical work – indeed, it demands it. Like its predecessor, however, it accords explanatory primacy to causes which can only be identified theoretically and which, in the absence of controlled experiments, remain effectively immune to falsification even though there may be no evidence that they are operating or even that they exist. The 'necessities' are simply asserted while the catch-all category of 'contingency' takes care of all the problems. In this way, awkward empirical or historical 'events' play second fiddle to theoretical certainties (for as Urry (1985) suggests, echoing Harré, realism involves not an 'event ontology' but a 'thing ontology'), and these certainties are invariably derived from Marxism (for there are, as far as I know, no examples in contemporary social science of non-Marxist realist work).

The growing attraction of realism is that it not only makes existing theories immune from falsification while still enabling empirical research, but it also carries the added bonus that other people's theories (which may be objected to on political grounds) can be dismissed as methodologically unsound. Non-Marxist approaches can all be condemned as superficial – as looking only at manifest events while failing to appreciate the deeper real causes which have brought them about. Monetarist economics can be dismissed in this way because it lacks an understanding of the 'real' value movements which underpin price movements; pluralist political theory can be dismissed because it fails to understand how 'real' class relations underpin the superficial cleavages and alliances which arise over particular issues; and Weberian sociology can be dismissed because it fails to understand how the values, beliefs and motives which give direction to people's actions are simply the expression of 'real' material forces operating in a given mode of production. Realism, in short, provides a spurious intellectual justification for asserting a left orthodoxy and discounting alternative approaches by presenting political and moral values and beliefs as if they were scientifically derived. The irony, of course, is that this was precisely the complaint voiced by earlier generations of radicals against positivism!

The third main point I wish to make about the problem of empirical testability concerns the question of testing within as opposed to between theories, for it follows from our earlier discussion of Hirst's critique of epistemology that the specification of counterfactuals and of the criteria by which they can be identified empirically will be specific to particular discourses.

My insistence on the importance of counterfactuality refers only to the necessity of any theory to support the possibility of disconfirming instances and to stipulate the criteria by which such instances may be recognized in empirical research. Theories should not be merely self-confirming tautologies, but should be open to empirical test in accordance with conditions that they themselves lay down. To the extent that different approaches can agree on these conditions, they can be evaluated empirically against each other; to the extent that they cannot so agree, they can be evaluated empirically only on their own terms. But to the extent that they fail to provide such conditions, they cannot be evaluated empirically at all, in which case any claim they make to scientific knowledge can safely be ignored.

It is on this basis that I would justify the dualistic approach developed in Chapter 8, for as we saw there, such an approach can sustain counterfactual testing in terms of the argument that different types of political strategies tend to be associated with different aspects of the state's role performed at different levels of its organization. It was not, of course, suggested that this is universally the case, but only that this may be taken as an ideal-typical framework within which empirical research on a variety of different cases may fruitfully proceed. The significance of this approach, in other words, is that it enables the development of hypotheses that are not true by definition but that can be amended, developed, further specified or even abandoned in the light of empirical evidence from different studies of different aspects of state activity in different countries at different times. It therefore facilitates the development of Castells's call for a 'theorized history of states' in a way that Castells's own use of the concept of relative autonomy did not.

One final point should be made in conclusion, and this concerns the possible criticism that an insistence on counterfactuality and empirical testability is inconsistent with a rejection of general epistemological principles. Such a criticism would appear valid in the sense that my argument does point to a universal principle (internal testability) by means of which all perspectives are to be evaluated, and this reflects my assertion that sociological explanations that are inherently immune from empirical evaluation, even on their own terms, in effect explain nothing. Those who remain content to accept such 'explanations' will obviously reject my emphasis on counterfactuality. However, for those approaches that seek to go beyond tautology and resolute faith, an insistence on counterfactuality does not represent an unwarranted epistemological intrusion since it does not attempt to impose external and general principles regarding correct procedure or universal criteria of empirical adequacy (for such questions are determined within discourses), but merely holds that some such criteria must be specified. This is a minimal epistemological principle, yet it is one that much of the literature discussed in the later chapters of this book fails to address.

Further reading

General texts

Martin Slattery's *Urban Sociology* (Causeway Press 1985) provides in ch. 2 probably the most basic and introductory review of urban social theory which is currently available, while *Structures and Processes of Urban Life* (Longman 1983), written by Ray Pahl, Rob Flynn and Nick Buck, discusses various key theories in the context of historical and empirical evidence. More detailed, but also more dated, discussions of approaches prior to the development of the 'new urban sociology' in the 1970s can be found in Leonard Reissman's *The Urban Process* (1964) and Rosemary Mellor's *Urban Sociology in an Urbanised Society* (1977). More recently, Les Kilmartin, David Thorns and Terry Burke have published *Social Theory and the Australian City* (George Allen and Unwin 1985) which contains useful reviews of ecological, Weberian and Marxist perspectives, as does Keith Bassett and John Short, *Housing and Residential Structure* (Routledge & Kegan Paul 1980). The Open University's D202 course on *Urban Change and Conflict* is also a valuable source (see especially Dunleavy's contribution in units three and four). For those who wish to follow up specific approaches in more detail, I identify below a few key references in respect of each chapter.

Chapter 1: Social theory, capitalism and the urban question

Marx's discussions of the urban question are scattered and fragmented, although an important reference is undoubtedly part 1c of Marx and Engels (1970), in which the town–country division is considered in the context of the development of the division of labour in society. This may usefully be read alongside some of the later chapters of the first volume of *Capital* (1976– notably chs. 26, 27 and 30–32), which also contains a short discussion of the causes and effects of capitalist urbanization (pp. 811–18 in the 1976 edition), although this latter theme is more fully elaborated in Engels (1969a, b). The best secondary source on all this is Lefebvre (1972), although this is unfortunately not available in English translation. Giddens (1971, ch. 2) is, however, a useful and readily accessible source.

Weber's essay on the city can be found in Weber (1968, ch. 16) or in a separate publication edited and introduced by Martindale (Weber 1958). As was suggested in Chapter 1, this essay has suffered some neglect within sociology – even Martindale's introduction focuses more on work by other writers such as Park and Wirth than it does on Weber – but there are short, useful discussions of it in Mellor (1977, pp. 189–94) and Bendix (1966, pp. 70–9). In my view, however, by far the best discussion of Weber's essay can be found in ch. 2 of *The City: Patterns of domination and conflict* (Macmillan 1982) by Brian Elliott and David McCrone. Philip Abrams's essay (1978) is also important, not only for its discussion of Weber, but also for its review of Marxist historical debates over the city in the feudal period.

The principal reference with regard to Durkheim's discussion of urbanization is Durkheim (1933, see especially pp. 1–10, 18–28, 181–90 and 256–301). This work has rarely been discussed in the context of its contribution to urban sociology, although S. Lukes, *Emile Durkheim: His Life and Work* (Allen Lane 1973, ch. 7) provides a thorough and critical review of its main arguments while J. Eldridge, *Sociology and Industrial Life* (Nelson 1973, pp. 73–91) is useful on the concept of anomie and its relation to Durkheim's discussion of a new nationally organized guild system.

Chapter 2:   The urban as an ecological community

Probably the most concise statement of Park's theory is his essay on human ecology which was first published in the *American Journal of Sociology*, vol. 42, 1936, and which is contained in Park (1952, ch. 12). This collection of Park's essays should also be consulted for ch. 15 (in which he discusses the concept of natural areas in the context of his sociological method) and ch. 19 (a paper originally written in 1939 in which he comes to his final conclusions on the biotic–cultural distinction). His original essay on the city is also included in this collection, and can also be found in Park and Burgess, *The City* (University of Chicago Press 1925; re-issued in 1967), which contains other important contributions by Burgess (his famous paper on concentric rings) and McKenzie.

Of the avalanche of critical discussions of the Chicago school, the most important is probably that by Alihan (1938, especially chs. 2, 3 and 4), part of which is reprinted in G. Theodorson, *Studies in Human Ecology* (New York: Harper Row 1961). The Theodorson collection also contains papers or excerpts by Wirth, Robinson, Firey, Hawley and others, in addition to short summaries of the various papers by the editor. Hawley's reformulation of human ecology is summarized in his 1968 paper, although this should be read in conjunction with his earlier book (Hawley 1950, especially ch. 4). Brief and useful résumés of the ecological tradition can be found in Robson (1969, pp. 8–15 and 35–8) and Berry and Kasarda (1977, ch. 1); and further critical commentaries are provided by Reissman (1964, ch. 5), Mellor (1977, ch. 6) and Castells (1977a, ch. 8). Chapter 2 of Hannerz (1980) is also well worth consulting, not only for a summary of Chicago school theory, but also for a very readable review of much of its ethnography.

Chapter 3:   The urban as a cultural form

Simmel's essay on the metropolis and mental life first appeared in English translation in Wolff (1950), though it has subsequently been reprinted elsewhere (e.g. in K. Thompson and J. Tunstall, *Sociological Perspectives* (Penguin 1971)). Wirth's 1938 essay on urbanism as a way of life has also subsequently appeared in a number of edited collections including P. Hatt and A. Reiss, *Cities and Society*, 2nd edn. (New York: Free Press 1957) and A. Reiss, *Louis Wirth on Cities and Social Life* (University of Chicago Press 1964). The Reiss collection also contains Wirth's essays on the ghetto (1927) and human ecology (1945), as well as his unfinished but important article on rural–urban differences. Useful supplementary reading on Simmel includes his essay 'On the significance of numbers for social life' (in Wolff 1950, Pt II, ch. 1) and the piece on 'Group expansion and the development of individuality' included in Levine (1971). Levine's introduction to this latter collection is also useful on Simmel's formalism, his sociological emphasis on number, and his relation to Park's later work.

The history of urban–rural dichotomies in sociology is discussed and summarized in Pahl (1968), which is also an important article in its own right for the critique that it develops of any attempt to relate cultural patterns to spatial locations. The other major contribution to this debate is by Gans (1968) who shows that, at most, Wirth's theory of urbanism applies only to deprived groups in inner-city areas of high population turnover. See also Dewey (1960) for an evaluation of the effects of location on cultural patterns, and the final chapter in Lewis (1951) for a critique of Redfield's work on folk culture. Mellor (1977, ch. 5) provides a critical overview of this whole tradition, while Williams (1973) develops a fascinating argument regarding the ideological significance of rural and urban imagery in western capitalism (see especially chs. 1 and 25; also his article on 'Literature and the city' in the *Listener*, vol. 78, 1967, pp. 653–6). M. P. Smith's *The City and Social Theory* (1980) contains exhaustive chapters on Wirth and Simmel which can also be recommended.

Chapter 4:   The urban as a socio-spatial system

The original concept of a socio-spatial system is set out in Pahl (1970, ch. 4) and in ch. 7 of the second edition of *Whose City?* (Pahl 1975). The latter is a collection of Pahl's essays which clearly documents the shift in his thinking on urban managerialism from the earlier conception of managers as independent variables (as in ch. 10) to the later recognition of their mediating role in a context of economic and political constraint (ch. 13). This shift is clarified and discussed in Williams (1978) and Norman (1975). Its relation to Pahl's later writings on corporatism is never made entirely clear in Pahl's own work, although his 1979 article perhaps comes closest to spelling out the common methodological and theoretical position that lies behind his approach to both urban managerialism and corporate state strategies (cf. his argument on p. 34 that 'The process of resource allocation has certain common elements no matter what the scale of organization. . . . '). His discussions of corporatism can be found in Pahl (1977b, c), and these should be read alongside the two articles by Winkler (1976, 1977).

On the concept of housing classes, see Rex and Moore (1967, chs. 1 and 12), Rex (1968), and, for the various amendments made in the light of later criticisms, Rex (1971), on the problem of multiple value systems, Rex (1977) where the emphasis shifts from current tenure to potential access, and Rex and Tomlinson (1979, pp. 20–4 and chs. 5 and 8). This last reference also contains a methodological appendix in which recent Marxist work is attacked for its metaphysical assumptions and a Weberian emphasis on meaningful action and the use of ideal types is asserted and defended. The most important critique of the housing class model remains Haddon (1970), but see also Davies (1972, chs. 3 and 4), Couper and Brindley (1975) and C. Bell, 'On Housing Classes', *Australian and New Zealand Journal of Sociology*, vol. 13, pp. 36–40. Lambert *et al.* (1978) provide a useful evaluation of both the managerialist and housing class concepts in chs. 1 and 7, while my work on urban politics (Saunders 1979) also provides a fairly comprehensive review in chs. 2 and 3.

Chapter 5:   The urban as ideology

Most of the relevant work by Lefebvre is still unavailable in English, although the flavour of his arguments can be sampled in Lefebvre (1976), especially ch. 1, section 7 (which contains an attack on Althusserian Marxism). Lefebvre's ideas are discussed in the final chapter of Harvey (1973) and in Castells (1977a, ch. 6).

Perhaps the most useful secondary sources, however, are Soja and Hadjimichalis (1979), Soja (1980), Martins (1982) and Gottdiener (1984 and 1985, ch. 4). Soja is one of Lefebvre's strongest advocates, while Martins and Gottdiener provide very useful accounts contrasting Lefebvre's approach with that of Castells.

Castells's critique of urban sociology (including the work of Lefebvre) is contained in two early papers (1967a, b) and in *The Urban Question* (1977a, chs. 5–8). These should be read in the light of Althusser's papers on Marxist methodology, especially chs. 3, 6 and 7 in Althusser (1969), and his discussion of ideology in his 1971 paper. A useful guide to Althusser's arguments can be found in A. Callinicos, *Althusser's Marxism* (Pluto Press 1976), especially chs. 2 and 3, while his approach has been subjected to a merciless critique from a humanist position by E. Thompson in his essay on 'The poverty of theory', which is contained in a book of the same title published in 1978 by the Merlin Press.

The key chapter in *The Urban Question* as regards Castells's formal conceptualization of his object of analysis is ch. 10, and much of his later work represents a gradual retreat from the position set out there. Significant milestones in this retreat include the 1975 Afterword to the English edition (which is important both for the auto-critique of his earlier formalism and for its clarification of the conceptualization of urbanism in terms of collective consumption) and ch. 1 in Castells (1978).

Chapter 6: The urban as a spatial unit of collective consumption

A simple introduction to the earlier Marxist work in urban sociology can be found in M. Harloe, 'The New Urban Sociology' (*New Society*, 5 October 1978). Mellor's article 'Marxism and the Urban Question' (in M. Shaw, ed., *Marxist Sociology Revisited*, Macmillan 1985) and Lebas's trend report (*Current Sociology* 1982) provide more detailed and critical overviews.

Castells provided useful summaries of his earlier position in ch. 2 of his 1978 collection and in two other papers – 'The class struggle and urban contradictions' (in J. Cowley *et al.*, *Community or class struggle?*, Stage 1 1977), and 'The wild city' (*Kapitalistate*, no. 4/5, 1976, pp. 2–30). For the later work, the key reference is, of course, *The City and the Grassroots*, although his retrospective reflections in Castells (1985) are also interesting.

Marxist approaches to theorizing the capitalist state are discussed and reviewed in Gold *et al* (1975), in Saunders (1979, ch. 4), and Dearlove and Saunders (1984, ch. 7). The problem encountered by structuralist Marxism in relating structures to practices, and in explaining the relative autonomy of the state is ably diagnosed by Clarke (1977) and Hirst (1977), while the specific problems in Castells's initial treatment of urban social movements are discussed by Pickvance (1976b, 1977a). Pickvance's 1985 paper addresses Castells's more recent work on such movements, as does ch. 1 of S. Lowe's *Urban Social Movements* (Macmillan 1985). The conceptualization of collective consumption is discussed by Pahl (1977a) and Dunleavy (1980, 1983); the latter, of course, is also the key source on the political significance of consumption sector cleavages – a concept which is developed in his 1979 article and his 1980 book, and which is applied in, among others, his 1985 paper.

Chapter 7: A non-spatial urban sociology?

For general discussions of the production of space from a Marxist standpoint, see N. Smith, *Uneven Development* (Basil Blackwell 1984), and M. Dunford and D. Perrons, *The Arena of Capital* (Maxmillan 1983). Soja's 1980 and 1985 papers are important for the discussion of the 'socio-spatial dialectic', which he claims to derive from a reading of Lefebvre. Harvey's work is not always as coherent and consistent as it might be, although his 1978a paper is probably a good place to start. Useful secondary accounts of Harvey's work are contained in Gottdiener (1985) and Bassett and Short's *Housing and Residential Structure* (1980), although neither addresses the arguments in *Limits to Capital*. Duncan and Ley (1982) provide a good critique.

Urry's approach can best be gauged by his 1981 and 1985 papers – the latter appears in a collection, edited by Gregory and Urry, which also contains important contributions by, among others, Sayer, Thrift and Giddens. Gregory interviews Giddens in *Society and Space* (vol. 2, 1984, pp. 123–32), but the key references on Giddens on space can be found in his 1979 (ch. 6), 1981 (especially pp. 140–50) and 1984 (especially ch. 3 and pp. 355–68) books. The latter is given an extended review by Thrift in *Sociology* (vol. 19, 1985), while I elaborate my arguments against Giddens's treatment of space in 'Anthony Giddens: Urban space man' (in D. Held and J. Thompson, eds., *Critical Theory of the Industrial Societies*, Cambridge University Press 1986).

Chapter 8:   From urban social theory to a sociology of consumption

The dual politics thesis is set out and elaborated in a number of places, but see especially my paper with Alan Cawson ('Corporatism, competitive politics and class struggle') in R. King's edited collection, *Capital and Politics* (Routledge & Kegan Paul 1983), and my 'Reflections on the dual politics thesis: the argument, its origins and its critics' (in M. Goldsmith, ed., *Urban Political Theory and the Management of Fiscal Stress*, Gower 1986). This latter reference discusses the eight major criticisms which have been made against this approach (for examples, see Duncan and Goodwin 1982; Harrington 1983; Sharpe 1984; and Dunleavy 1984).

The discussion of socialized and privatized consumption is based mainly on my 1984 paper, 'Beyond housing classes' (*International Journal of Urban and Regional Research*, vol. 8, pp. 202–7). The same issue of the journal contains an empirical evaluation of the consumption sector cleavage argument by Duke and Edgell, and a critique of my paper by Harloe. Obviously, Dunleavy's various papers are central to much of this discussion (for a critique see Franklin and Page 1984), as is Mingione's 1981 discussion of restratification.

The further reading relating to the final section of the chapter suggests itself. Pahl (1984) is probably the key reference on the 'informal economy', though Gershuny's work is also important, as is Mingione's rather different approach. All three have contributions in N. Redclift and E. Mingione, eds., *Beyond Employment* (Basil Blackwell 1985). Gorz's ideas on the 'dual society' and the liberation from work appear mainly in his 1982 book, and are developed in Gorz (1985). Ward's libertarian anarchist approach to housing is set out in a number of essays collected together in Ward (1983), though his *When we build again* (1985) is a more polished statement of his position. Also to be recommended in his study of the inter-war plotlands, *Arcadia for All*, jointly authored with D. Hardy, and published by Mansell (1984), for not only does this demonstrate the strong popular desire to exert autonomy through personal property, but it also shows the extraordinary lengths to which the state will go to thwart such aspirations.

References

Abrams, P. (1978), 'Towns and economic growth: some theories and problems', in P. Abrams and E. Wrigley (eds.), *Towns in Societies*, Cambridge University Press

Abu-Lughod, J. (1961), 'Migrant adjustment to city life: the Egyptian case', *American Journal of Sociology*, **67**, pp. 22–32

Alihan, M. (1938), *Social Ecology: A Critical Analysis*, New York: Columbia University Press

Althusser, L. (1969), *For Marx*, Allen Lane

Althusser, L. (1971), 'Ideology and ideological state apparatuses', in L. Althusser, *Lenin and Philosophy and Other Essays*, New Left Books

Ambrose, P. and Colenutt, B. (1975), *The Property Machine*, Penguin

Bacon, R. and Eltis, W. (1978), *Britain's Economic Problem: Too Few Producers*, Macmillan

Badcock, B. (1984), *Unfairly Structured Cities*, Basil Blackwell

Ball, M. (1977), 'Differential rent and the role of landed property', *International Journal of Urban and Regional Research*, **I**, pp. 380–403

Ball, M. (1983), Review of 'Limits to Capital', *Society and Space*, *1*, pp. 494–5

Bassett, K. and Short, J. (1980), *Housing and Residential Structure*, Routledge & Kegan Paul

Becker, H. (1959), 'On Simmel's "Philosophy of Money"', in K. Wolff (ed.), *Georg Simmel 1858–1918*, Columbus: Ohio State University Press

Bell, C., and Newby, H. (1971), *Community Studies*, Allen & Unwin

Bell, C., and Newby, H. (1976), 'Community, communion, class and community action', in D. Herbert and R. Johnson (eds.), *Social Areas in Cities*, John Wiley

Bendix, R. (1966), *Max Weber: An Intellectual Portrait*, Methuen

Benton, T. (1977), *Philosophical Foundations of the Three Sociologies*, Routledge & Kegan Paul

Bernstein, B. (1970), 'Education cannot compensate for society', *New Society*, 26 February, pp. 344–7

Berry, B., and Kasarda, J. (1977), *Contemporary Urban Ecology*, Collier Macmillan

Beshers, J. (1962), *Urban Social Structure*, New York: Free Press

Bhaskar, R. (1978), *A Realist Theory of Science*, Harvester Press

Blowers, A. (1984), *Something in the Air: Corporate Power and the Environment*, Harper and Row

Boddy, M. (1983), 'Central-local government relations: theory and practice',

Political Geography Quarterly, **2**, pp. 119–38

Browett, J. (1984), 'On the necessity and inevitability of uneven spatial development under capitalism', *International Journal of Urban & Regional Research*, **8**, pp. 155–76

Bruun, H. (1972), *Science, Values and Politics in Max Weber's Methodology*, Copenhagen: Munksgaard

Bryant, C. (1978), 'Privacy, privatisation and self-determination', in J. Young (ed.), *Privacy*, Chichester and New York: Wiley

Burger, T. (1976), *Max Weber's Theory of Concept Formation*, Chapel Hill, North Carolina: Duke University Press

Burgess, E. (1967), 'The growth of the city: an introduction to a research project', in R. Park and E. Burgess, *The City*, University of Chicago Press

Cameron, G. (1980), 'The future of the conurbations', in G. Cameron (ed.), *The Future of the British Conurbations*, Longman

Castells, M. (1976a), 'Is there an urban sociology?' in C. Pickvance (ed.), *Urban Sociology: Critical Essays*, Tavistock

Castells, M. (1976b), 'Theory and ideology in urban sociology', in Pickvance (ed.), *Urban Sociology*

Castells, M (1976c), 'Theoretical propositions for an experimental study of urban social movements', in Pickvance (ed.), *Urban Sociology*

Castells, M (1977a), *The Urban Question*, Edward Arnold

Castells, M (1977b), 'Towards a political urban sociology', in M. Harloe (ed.), *Captive Cities*, John Wiley

Castells, M (1978), *City, Class and Power*, Macmillan

Castells, M (1980), *The Economic Crisis and American Society*, Basil Blackwell

Castells, M (1983a), *The City and the Grassroots*, Edward Arnold

Castells, M (1983b), 'Crisis, planning and the quality of life: managing the new historical relationships between space and society', *Society and Space*, **1**, pp. 3–21

Castells, M (1985), 'From the urban question to the city and the grassroots', Urban and Regional Studies *Working Paper*, no. 47, University of Sussex

Castells, M., and Godard, F. (1974), *Monopolville: l'enterprise, l'état, l'urbain*, Paris: Mouton

Castells, M., and Ipola, E. (1976), 'Epistemological practice and the social sciences', *Economy and Society*, **5**, pp. 111–44

Cawson, A. (1978), 'Pluralism, corporatism and the role of the state', *Government and Opposition*, **13**, pp. 178–98

Cawson, A. (1982), *Corporatism and Welfare*, Heinemann

Clarke, S. (1977), 'Marxism, sociology and Poulantzas' theory of the state', *Capital and Class*, **2**, pp. 1–31

Cochrane, A. (1984), Review of 'Corporatism and welfare', *International Journal of Urban & Regional Research*, **8**, pp. 281–2

Cockburn, C. (1977), *The Local State*, Pluto Press

Collier, A. (1978), 'In defence of epistemology', *Radical Philosophy*, 20, pp. 8–21

Cooke, P. (1982), 'Class interests, regional restructuring and state formation in Wales', *International Journal of Urban & Regional Research*, 6, pp. 187–204

Connell, R. (1983), *Which Way Is Up?*, George Allen and Unwin

Coser, L., (1965), *Georg Simmel*, Englewood Cliffs, NJ: Prentice-Hall

Couper, M., and Brindley, T. (1975), 'Housing classes and housing values', *Sociological Review*, 23, pp. 563–76

Crewe, I. (1983), 'The disturbing truth behind Labour's rout', *The Guardian*, 13 June, p. 5

Dahl, R. (1963), *Modern Political Analysis*, Englewood Cliffs, NJ: Prentice-Hall

Davie, M. (1937), 'The pattern of urban growth', in G. Murdock (ed.), *Studies in the Science of Society*, New Haven, Conn., Yale University Press

Davies, J. (1972), *The Evangelistic Bureaucrat*, Tavistock

Davies, J., and Taylor, J. (1970), 'Race, community and no conflict', *New Society*, 9, pp. 67–9

Dawe, A. (1970), 'The two sociologies', *British Journal of Sociology*, 21, pp. 207–18

Dawe, A. (1971), 'The relevance of values', in A. Sahay (ed.), *Max Weber and Modern Sociology*, Routledge & Kegan Paul

Dear, M. and Scott, A. (1981), 'Towards a framework for analysis', in M. Dear and A. Scott (eds.), *Urbanization and Urban Planning in Capitalist Society*, London and New York: Methuen

Dearlove, J. and Saunders, P. (1984), *Introduction to British Politics*, Polity Press

Dennis, N. (1968), 'The popularity of the neighbourhood community idea', in R. Pahl, *Readings in Urban Sociology*, Pergamon Press

Dewey, R. (1960), 'The rural–urban continuum: real but relatively unimportant', *American Journal of Sociology*, 66, pp. 60–6

Dickens, P., Duncan, S., Goodwin, M. and Gray, F. (1985), *Housing, States and Localities*, Methuen

Duke, V. and Edgell, S. (1984), 'Public expenditure cuts in Britain and consumption sectoral cleavages', *International Journal of Urban & Regional Research*, 8, pp. 177–201

Duncan, J. and Ley, D. (1982), 'Structural marxism and human geography: critical assessment', *Annals of the Association of American Geographers*, 72, pp. 30–59

Duncan, O. (1957), 'Community size and the rural–urban continuum', in P. Hatt and A. Reiss, (eds.), *Cities and Society* (2nd edn), New York: Free Press

Duncan, O. (1959), 'Human ecology and population studies', in P. Hauser and O. Duncan (eds.), *The Study of Population*, Chicago: Chicago University Press

Duncan, O. (1964), 'Social organization and the ecosystem', in R. Faris (ed.), *Handbook of Modern Sociology*, Chicago: Rand McNally

Duncan, O., and Schnore, L. (1959), 'Cultural, behavioural and ecological perspectives in the study of social organization', *American Journal of Sociology*, **65**, pp. 132–46

Duncan, S. (1981), 'Housing policy, the methodology of levels and urban research: the case of Castells', *International Journal of Urban & Regional Research*, **5**, pp. 231–54

Duncan, S. and Goodwin, M. (1982), 'The local state: functionalism, autonomy and class relations in Cockburn and Saunders', *Political Geography Quarterly*, **1**, pp. 77–96

Duncan, S. and Goodwin, M. (1985), 'The local government crisis in Britain, 1979–84: Part 2, Centralising local policy', *Geography Discussion Papers*, new series, no. 14, London School of Economics

Dunleavy, P. (1980), *Urban Political Analysis*, Macmillan

Dunleavy, P. (1983), 'Socialised consumption and economic development', paper presented at the Anglo-Danish seminar on Local State Research, University of Copenhagen (September); revised version forthcoming in *International Journal of Urban & Regional Research*

Dunleavy, P. (1984), 'The limits to local government', in M. Boddy and C. Fudge (eds.), *Local Socialism?*, Macmillan

Dunleavy, P. (1985), 'The growth of sectoral cleavages and the stabilization of state expenditures', paper presented at the Fifth Urban Change and Conflict Conference, University of Sussex (April); revised version forthcoming in *Society and Space*

Durkheim, É. (1933), *The Division of Labour in Society*, Toronto: Macmillan

Durkheim, É. (1938), *The Rules of Sociological Method*, New York: Free Press

Durkheim, É. (1952), *Suicide: A Study in Sociology*, Routledge & Kegan Paul

Edel, M. (1982), 'Home ownership and working class unity', *International Journal of Urban & Regional Research*, **6**, pp. 205–22

Edel, M., Sclar, E. and Luria, D. (1984), *Shaky Palaces: Homeownership and Social Mobility in Boston's Suburbanization*, New York: Columbia University Press

Elliott, B., and McCrone, D. (1975), 'Landlords as urban managers: a dissenting opinion', in M. Harloe (ed.), *Proceedings of the Conference on Urban Change and Conflict*, Centre for Environmental Studies

Elliott, B. and McCrone, D. (1982), *The City: Patterns of Domination and Conflict*, Macmillan

Engels, F. (1969a), *The Condition of the Working Class in England*, Panther Books

Engels, F. (1969b), 'The housing question', in K. Marx and F. Engels, *Selected Works*, vol. 2, Moscow: Progress Publishers

Farmer, M. and Barrell, R. (1981), 'Entrepreneurship and government policy: the case of the housing market', *Journal of Public Policy*, 2, pp. 307–32

Firey, W. (1945), 'Sentiment and symbolism as ecological variables', *American Sociological Review*, 10, pp. 140–8

Flynn, R. (1981), 'Managing consensus: strategies and rationales in policy-making', in M. Harloe (ed.), *New Perspectives in Urban Change & Conflict*, Heinemann

Flynn, R. (1983), 'Co-optation and strategic planning in the local state', in R. King (ed.), *Capital and Politics*, Routledge & Kegan Paul

Flynn, R. (1986), 'Urban politics, the local state and consumption', in M. Goldsmith (ed.), *Urban Political Theory and the Management of Fiscal Stress*, Gower

Forbes, D., Thrift, N. and Williams, P. (1983), 'Social relations in space: books in 1982', *Society and Space*, 1, pp. 355–64

Ford, J. (1975), 'The role of the building society manager in the urban stratification system', *Urban Studies*, 12, pp. 295–302

Forrest, K. and Williams, P. (1980), 'The commodification of housing', *Working Paper*, no. 73, Centre for Urban and Regional Studies, University of Birmingham

Franklin, M. and Page, E. (1984), 'A critique of the consumption cleavage approach in British voting studies', *Political Studies*, 32, pp. 521–36

Freund, J. (1968), *The Sociology of Max Weber*, Allen Lane

Freund, J. (1978), 'Émile Durkheim', in T. Bottomore and R. Nisbet (eds.), *A History of Sociological Analysis*, Heinemann

Friedland, R., Fox Piven, F., and Alford, R. (1977), 'Political conflict, urban structure and the fiscal crisis', *International Journal of Urban and Regional Research*, 1, pp. 447–71

Friedman, M. (1962), *Capitalism and Freedom*, University of Chicago

Gamble, A. (1981), *Britain in Decline*, London, Macmillan

Gans, H. (1962), *The Urban Villagers*, New York: Free Press

Gans, H. (1968), 'Urbanism and suburbanism as ways of life', in R. Pahl, *Readings in Urban Sociology*, Pergamon

Gans, H. (1984), 'American urban theories and urban areas: some observations on contemporary ecological and marxist paradigms', in I. Szelenyi: (ed.), *Cities in Recession: Critical responses to the urban policies of the New Right*, Sage

Gershuny, J. (1978), *After Industrial Society: The emerging self-service economy*, Macmillan

Gershuny, J. (1985), 'Economic development and change in the mode of provision of services', in N. Redclift and E. Mingione (eds.), *Beyond Employment*, Basil Blackwell

Gettys, W. (1940), 'Human ecology and social theory', *Social Forces*, 17, pp. 469–76

Giddens, A. (1971), *Capitalism and Modern Social Theory*, Cambridge University Press

Giddens, A. (1974), 'Introduction' to A. Giddens (ed.), *Positivism and Sociology*, Heinemann

Giddens, A. (1976), *New Rules of Sociological Method*, Hutchinson

Giddens, A. (1979), *Central Problems in Social Theory*, Macmillan

Giddens, A. (1981), *A Contemporary Critique of Historical Materialism*, vol. I, Macmillan

Giddens, A. (1984), *The Constitution of Society*, Polity Press

Godard, F. (1985), 'How do ways of life change?', in N. Redclift and E. Mingione (eds.), *Beyond Employment*, Basil Blackwell

Goffman, E. (1961), *Asylums*, New York: Doubleday Anchor Books

Gold, D., Lo, C., and Wright, E. (1975), 'Recent developments in Marxist theories of the capitalist state', *Monthly Review*, **27**, pp. 37–51

Gorz, A. (1982), *Farewell to the Working Class: An Essay on Post-Industrial Socialism*, Pluto Press

Gorz, A. (1985), *Paths to Paradise: On the Liberation from Work*, Pluto Press

Gottdiener, M. (1984), 'Debate on the theory of space: toward an urban praxis', in M. Smith (ed.), *Cities in Transformation*, Sage

Gottdiener, M. (1985), *The Social Production of Urban Space*, Austin: University of Texas Press

Gray, F. (1976), 'The management of local authority housing', in Conference of Socialist Economists Political Economy of Housing Workshop, *Housing and Class in Britain*, Conference of Socialist Economists

Green, D. (1982), 'The welfare state: For rich and for poor?', *Institute of Economic Affairs Papers*, no. 63

Green, D. (1986), *The New Right*, Harvester Press

Habermas, J. (1976), *Legitimation Crisis*, Heinemann

Haddon, R. (1970), 'A minority in a welfare state society', *New Atlantis*, **2**, pp. 80–133

Hall, P., Gracey, H., Drewitt, R., and Thomas, R. (1973), *The Containment of Urban England*, vol. 1, George Allen and Unwin

Hannerz, U. (1980), *Exploring the City*, New York: Columbia University Press

Harloe, M. (1975), 'Introduction' to M. Harloe (ed.), *Proceedings of the Conference on Urban Change and Conflict*, Centre for Environmental Studies

Harloe, M. (1977), 'Introduction' to M. Harloe (ed.), *Captive Cities*, John Wiley

Harloe, M. (1979), 'Marxism, the state and the urban question: critical notes on two recent French theories', in C. Crouch (ed.), *State and Economy in Contemporary Capitalism*, Croom Helm

Harloe, M. (1981), 'New perspectives in urban and regional research:

Progress and problems', in M. Harloe (ed.), *New Perspectives in Urban Change and Conflict*, Heinemann

Harloe, M. (1984), 'Sector and class: A critical comment', *International Journal of Urban & Regional Research*, 8, pp. 228–37

Harloe, M., Issacharoff, R., and Minns, R. (1974), *The Organization of Housing*, Heinemann

Harloe, M. and Paris, C. (1984), 'The decollectivisation of consumption', in I. Szelenyi (ed.), *Cities in Recession*, Sage

Harrington, T. (1983), 'Explaining state policy-making: a critique of some recent "dualist" models', *International Journal of Urban & Regional Research*, 7, pp. 202–18

Harris, R. (1983), 'Space and class: a critique of Urry', *International Journal of Urban & Regional Research*, 7, pp. 115–21

Harvey, D. (1973), *Social Justice and the City*, Edward Arnold

Harvey, D. (1974), 'Class monopoly rent, finance capital and the urban revolution, *Regional Studies*, 8, pp. 239–55

Harvey, D. (1977), 'Government policies, financial institutions and neighbourhood change in United States cities', in M. Harloe (ed.), *Captive Cities*, John Wiley

Harvey, D. (1978a), 'The urban process under capitalism: a framework for analysis', *International Journal of Urban and Regional Research*, 2, pp. 101–31

Harvey, D. (1978b), 'Labour, capital and class struggle around the built environment in advanced capitalist societies', in K. Cox (ed.), *Urbanization and Conflict in Market Societies*, Methuen

Harvey, D. (1982), *The Limits to Capital*, Basil Blackwell

Hawley, A. (1944), 'Ecology and human ecology', *Social Forces*, 22, pp. 144–51

Hawley, A. (1950), *Human Ecology: A Theory of Community Structure*, New York: Ronald Press

Hawley, A. (1963), 'Community power and urban renewal success', *American Journal of Sociology*, 68, pp. 422–31

Hawley, A. (1968), 'Human ecology', *International Encyclopedia of Social Science*, 4, Macmillan and Free Press

Hayek, F. (1960), *The Constitution of Liberty*, Routledge & Kegan Paul

Heraud, B. (1975), 'The new towns: a philosophy of community', in O. Leonard (ed.), *The Sociology of Community Action*, Sociological Review Monograph, no. 21

Hill, R. (1977), 'Two divergent theories of the state', *International Journal of Urban and Regional Research*, 1, pp. 37–44

Hillier, B. and Hanson, J. (1984), *The Social Logic of Space*, Cambridge University Press

Hindess, B. (1977), *Philosophy and Methodology in the Social Sciences*, Harvester Press

Hindess, B. (1978), 'Class and politics in Marxist theory', in G. Littlejohn,

B. Smart, J. Wakeford and N. Yuval-Davis (eds.), *Power and the State*, Croom Helm

Hirschmann, A. (1970), *Exit, Voice and Loyalty*, Cambridge, Mass.: Harvard University Press

Hirst, P. (1975), *Durkheim, Bernard and Epistemology*, Routledge & Kegan Paul

Hirst, P. (1976), *Social Evolution and Sociological Categories*, George Allen and Unwin

Hirst, P. (1977), 'Economic classes and politics', in A. Hunt (ed.), *Class and Class Structure*, Lawrence & Wishart

Hirst, P. (1979), *On Law and Ideology*, Macmillan

Holton, R. (1984), 'Cities and the transitions to capitalism and socialism', *International Journal of Urban & Regional Research*, 8, pp. 13–37

Illich, I. (1971), *Deschooling Society*, New York: Harper & Row

Jessop, B. (1978), 'Capitalism and democracy: the best possible political shell?', in G. Littlejohn, B. Smart, J. Wakeford and N. Yuval-Davis (eds.), *Power and the State*, Croom Helm

Jessop, B. (1979), 'Corporatism, parliamentarism and social democracy', in P. Schmitter and G. Lehmbruch (eds.), *Trends Toward Corporatist Intermediation*, Sage

Jessop, B. (1982), *The Capitalist State*, Martin Robertson

Jones, G. (1973), *Rural Life*, Longman

Kalltorp, O. (1984), Review of 'Social Theory and the Urban Question', *Scandinavian Housing and Planning Research*, 1, pp. 61–4

Katznelson, I. (1981), *City Trenches: Urban Politics and the Patterning of Class in the United States*, University of Chicago Press

Keat, R. (1981), 'Individualism and community in socialist thought', in J. Mepham and D. Ruben (eds.), *Issues in Marxist Philosophy*, vol. 4: *Social and Political Philosophy*, Harvester press

Keat, R., and Urry, J. (1975), *Social Theory as Science*, Routledge & Kegan Paul

Kemeny, J. (1980), 'Home ownership and privatisation', *International Journal of Urban & Regional Research*, 4, pp. 372–88

Kirby, A. (1985), 'Pseudo-random thoughts on space, scale and ideology in political geography', *Political Geography Quarterly*, 4, pp. 5–18

Lafargue, P. (no date), *Evolution of Property from Savagery to Civilization*, Calcutta: Sreekali Prakasalaya

Lamarche, F. (1976), 'Property development and the economic foundations of the urban question', in C. Pickvance (ed.), *Urban Sociology: Critical Essays*, Methuen

Lambert, J., Paris, C., and Blackaby, B. (1978), *Housing Policy and the State*, Macmillan

Lebas, E. (1982), 'Urban and regional sociology in advanced industrial societies', *Current Sociology*, 30, pp. 7–130

Lebas, E. (1980), 'Some comments on a decade of marxist urban and regional research in France', in Political Economy of Housing Workshop, *Housing, Construction and the State*, London, Conference of Socialist Economists

Lefebvre, (1968a), *The Sociology of Marx*, Allen Lane

Lefebvre, (1968b), *Le droit à la ville*, Paris: Anthropos

Lefebvre, (1970), *La révolution urbaine*, Paris: Gallimard

Lefebvre, (1972), *La pensée marxiste et la ville*, Paris: Castermann

Lefebvre, (1976), *The Survival of Capitalism*, Allison & Busby

Lefebvre, (1977), 'Reflections on the politics of space', in R. Peet (ed.), *Radical Geography*, Chicago: Maaroufa Press

Le Grand, J. and Robinson, R. (1984), 'Privatisation and the welfare state: An introduction', in J. Le Grand and R. Robinson (eds.), *Privatisation and the Welfare State*, Allen and Unwin

Levine, D. (1971), *Georg Simmel on Individuality and Social Forms*, University of Chicago Press

Lewis, O. (1951), *Life in a Mexican Village: Tepozilán Restudied*, Urbana: University of Illinois Press

Lipietz, A. (1980), 'The structuration of space, the problem of land and spatial policy', in J. Carney, R. Hudson and J. Lewis (eds.), *Regions in Crisis*, Croom Helm

Lockwood, D. (1966), 'Sources of variation in working class images of society', *Sociological Review*, **14**, pp. 249–67

Lojkine, J. (1977), 'Big firms' strategies, urban policy and urban social movements', in M. Harloe (ed.), *Captive Cities*, John Wiley

Lojkine, J. (1984), 'The working class and the state: the French experience in socialist and communist municipalities', in I. Szelenyi (ed.), *Cities in Recession*, Sage

McBride, W. (1977), *The Philosophy of Marx*, Hutchinson

McDowell, L. (1983), 'Towards an understanding of the gender division of urban space', *Society and Space*, **1**, pp. 59–72

McKenzie, R. (1967), 'The ecological approach to the study of the human community', in R. Park and E. Burgess (eds.), *The City*, University of Chicago Press

MacKenzie, S. and Rose, D. (1983), 'Industrial change, the domestic economy and home life', in J. Anderson, S. Duncan and R. Hudson (eds.), *Redundant Spaces in Cities and Regions?*, Academic Press

Mann, P. (1965), *An Approach to Urban Sociology*, Routledge & Kegan Paul

Martins, M. (1982), 'The theory of social space in the work of Henri Lefebvre', in R. Forrest, J. Henderson and P. Williams (eds.), *Urban Political Economy and Social Theory*, Gower

Marx, K. (1964), *Pre-capitalist Economic Formations*, New York: International Publishers

Marx, K. (1969), 'Preface to "A contribution to the critique of political economy"', in K. Marx and F. Engels, *Selected Works*, vol. 1, Moscow:

Progress Publishers

Marx, K. (1973), *Grundrisse*, Penguin

Marx, K. (1976), *Capital*, vol. 1, Penguin

Marx, K., and Engels, F. (1969), 'Manifesto of the Communist Party', in K. Marx and F. Engels, *Selected Works*, vol. 1, Moscow: Progress Publishers

Marx, K., and Engels, F. (1970), *The German Ideology*, Lawrence & Wishart

Massey, D. (1984), *Spatial Divisions of Labour: Social Structures and the Geography of Production*, Macmillan

Mellor, J. (1977), *Urban Sociology in an Urbanized Society*, Routledge & Kegan Paul

Mennell, S. (1974), *Sociological Theory: Uses and Unities*, Nelson

Menzel, H. (1950), 'Comment on Robinson's "Ecological correlations and the behaviour of individuals"', *American Sociological Review*, 15, p. 674

Mercer, G. (1984), 'Corporatist ways in the NHS?', in M. Harrison (ed.), *Corporatism and the Welfare State*, Gower

Merton, R. (1968), *Social Theory and Social Structure*, New York: Free Press

Middlemas, K. (1979), *Politics in Industrial Society*, Andre Deutsch

Miliband, R. (1969), *The State in Capitalist Society*, Weidenfeld & Nicolson

Miliband, R. (1977), *Marxism and Politics*, Oxford University Press

Mills, C. (1959), *The Sociological Imagination*, Oxford University Press

Milner, H. (1952), 'The folk–urban continuum', *American Sociological Review*, 17, 529–37

Mingione, E. (1981), *Social Conflict and the City*, Basil Blackwell

Mingione, E. (1983), 'Informalization, restructuring and the survival strategies of the working class', *International Journal of Urban & Regional Research*, 7, pp. 311–39

Mingione, E. (1985), 'Social reproduction of the surplus labour force: the case of southern Italy', in N. Redclift and E. Mingione (eds.), *Beyond Employment*, Basil Blackwell

Mishra, R. (1977), *Society and Social Policy*, Macmillan

Moore, R. (1977), 'Becoming a sociologist in Sparkbrook', in C. Bell and H. Newby (eds.), *Doing Sociological Research*, George Allen and Unwin

Moorhouse, H. 'American automobiles and workers dreams', *Sociological Review*, 31, pp. 403–26

Morris, R. (1968), *Urban Sociology*, George Allen and Unwin

Murgatroyd, S. and Urry, J. (1983), 'The restructuring of a local economy: the case of Lancaster', in J. Anderson, S. Duncan and R. Hudson, (eds.), *Redundant Spaces in Cities and Regions?*, Academic Press

Newby, H. (1977), *The Deferential Worker*, Allen Lane

Newby, H., Bell. C, Rose, D. and Saunders, P. (1978), *Property, Paternalism and Power*, Hutchinson

Newby, H., Vogler, C., Rose, D. and Marshall, G. (1984), 'From class structure to class action: British working class politics in the 1980s', paper presented at seminar on Geographical Aspects of Social Stratification, University of London (September)

Newman, O. (1972), *Defensible Space: Crime Prevention Through Urban Design*, New York: Collier

Nisbet, R. (1966), *The Sociological Tradition*, New York: Basic Books

Norman, P. (1975), 'Managerialism: a review of recent work', in M. Harloe (ed.), *Proceedings of the Conference on Urban Change and Conflict*, Centre for Environmental Studies

Nove, A. (1983), *The Economics of Feasible Socialism*, George Allen & Unwin

O'Connor, J. (1973), *The Fiscal Crisis of the State*, New York: St Martin's Press

Offe, C. (1975), 'The theory of the capitalist state and the problem of policy-formation', in L. Lindberg, R. Alford, C. Crouch and C. Offe (eds.), *Stress and Contradiction in Modern Capitalism*, Lexington Books

Offe, C. (1984), *Contradictions of the Welfare State*, Hutchinson

Pahl, R. (1968), 'The rural–urban continuum', in R. Pahl (ed.), *Readings in Urban Sociology*, Pergamon

Pahl, R. (1970), *Patterns of Urban Life*, Longman

Pahl, R. (1975), *Whose City?* (2nd edn), Penguin

Pahl, R. (1977a), 'Collective consumption and the state in capitalist and state socialist societies', in R. Scase (ed.), *Industrial Society: Class, Cleavage and Control*, Tavistock

Pahl, R. (1977b), 'Stratification, the relation between states and urban and regional development', *International Journal of Urban and Regional Research*, 1, pp. 6–17

Pahl, R. (1977c), 'Managers, technical experts and the state', in M. Harloe (ed.), *Captive Cities*, John Wiley

Pahl, R. (1977d), 'A rejoinder to Mingione and Hill', *International Journal of Urban and Regional Research*, 1, pp. 340–3

Pahl, R. (1978), 'Castells and collective consumption', *Sociology*, 12, pp. 309–15

Pahl, R. (1979), 'Socio-political factors in resource allocation', in D. Herbert and D. Smith (eds.), *Social Problems and the City*, Oxford University Press

Pahl, R. (1980), 'Employment, work and the domestic division of labour', *International Journal of Urban & Regional Research*, 4, pp. 1–20

Pahl, R. (1984), *Divisions of Labour*, Basil Blackwell

Paris, C. (1983), 'Whatever happened to urban sociology?' *Society and Space*, 1, pp. 217–25

Park, R. (1952), *Human Communities*, New York: Free Press

Parsons, T. (1951), *The Social System*, New York: Free Press
Parsons, T., Bales, R., and Shils, E. (1953), *Working Papers in the Theory of Action*, New York: Free Press
Pelling, H. (1968), *Popular Politics and Society in Late Victorian Britain*, Macmillan
Pickvance, C. (1976a), 'Introduction: historical materialist approaches to urban sociology', in C. Pickvance (ed.), *Urban Sociology: Critical Essays*, Tavistock
Pickvance, C. (1976b), 'On the study of urban social movements', in Pickvance (ed.), *Urban Sociology*
Pickvance, C. (1977a), 'From social base to social force; some analytical issues in the study of urban protest', in M. Harloe (ed.) *Captive Cities*, John Wiley
Pickvance, C. (1977b), 'Marxist approaches to the study of urban politics', *International Journal of Urban and Regional Research*, 1, pp. 218–55
Pickvance, C. (1982), Review of 'Social Theory and the Urban Question' and 'City, Class and Capital', *Critical Social Policy*, 2, pp. 94–8
Pickvance, C. (1984), 'The structuralist critique in urban studies', in M. Smith (ed.), *Cities in Transformation: Class, capital and the state*, Sage
Pickvance, C. (1985), 'The rise and fall of urban movements and the role of comparative analysis', *Society and Space*, 3, pp. 31–54
Porteous, J. (1976), 'Home: the territorial core', *Geographical Review*, 66, pp. 383–90
Poulantzas, N. (1973), *Political Power and Social Classes*, New Left Books
Preteceille, E. (1985), 'Collective consumption, urban segregation, social classes', paper presented at the Fifth Urban Change and Conflict conference, University of Sussex (April); to be published in *Society and Space*
Preteceille, E. and Terrail, J. (1985), *Capitalism, Consumption and Needs*, Basil Blackwell
Reade, E. (1984), 'Town and country planning', in M. Harrison (ed.), *Corporatism and the Welfare State*, Gower
Redfield, E. (1941), *The Folk Culture of Yucatan*, University of Chicago Press
Redfield, R. (1947), 'The folk society', *American Journal of Sociology*, 52, pp. 293–308
Reissman, L. (1964), *The Urban Process*, Collier Macmillan
Rex, J. (1968), 'The sociology of a zone of transition', in R. Pahl (ed.), *Readings in Urban Sociology*, Pergamon
Rex, J. (1971), 'The concept of housing class and the sociology of race relations', *Race*, 12, pp. 293–301
Rex, J. (1977), 'Sociological theory and the city', *Australian and New Zealand Journal of Sociology*, 13, pp. 218–23

Rex, J., and Moore, R. (1967), *Race, Community and Conflict*, Oxford University Press

Rex, J., and Tomlinson, S. (1979) *Colonial Immigrants in a British City*, Routledge & Kegan Paul

Rhodes, R. (1980), 'Analysing inter-governmental relations', *European Journal of Political Research*, **8**, pp. 289–322

Robinson, W. (1950), 'Ecological correlations and the behaviour of individuals', *American Sociological Review*, **15**, pp. 351–7

Robson, B. (1969), *Urban Analysis*, Cambridge University Press

Rose, D. (1979), 'Toward a re-evaluation of the political significance of home ownership in Britain', paper presented at CSE Housing Workshop, University of Manchester (February); subsequently published in revised form in Political Economy of Housing Workshop, *Housing, Construction and the State*, Conference of Socialist Economists

Rose, D. (1981), 'Home ownership and industrial change: the struggle for a separate sphere', *Urban and Regional Studies Working Paper*, no. 25, University of Sussex

Roweis, S., and Scott, A. (1978), 'The urban land question', in K. Cox (ed.), *Urbanization and Conflict in Market Societies*, Methuen

Runciman, W. (1966), *Relative Deprivation and Social Justice*, Routledge & Kegan Paul

Saunders, P. (1978), 'Domestic property and social class', *International Journal of Urban and Regional Research*, **2**, pp. 233–51

Saunders, P. (1979), *Urban Politics: A Sociological Interpretation*, Hutchinson

Saunders, P. (1983), 'On the shoulders of which giant? The case for Weberian political analysis', in P. Williams (ed.), *Social Process and the City*, Sydney: Allen and Unwin

Saunders, P. (1984a), 'The crisis of local government in Melbourne', in J. Halligan and C. Paris (eds.), *Australian Urban Politics*, Sydney: Longman

Saunders, P. (1984b), 'The Canberra tea party: bureaucracy, corporatism and pluralism in the administration of the Australian Capital Territory', in P. Williams (ed.), *Policy, Politics and the City*, Sydney: Allen and Unwin

Saunders, P. (1984c), 'Rethinking local politics', in M. Boddy and C. Fudge (eds.), *Local Socialism?*, Macmillan

Saunders, P. (1985a), 'The forgotten dimension of central-local relations: Theorising the regional state', *Government and Policy*, **3**, pp. 149–62

Saunders, P. (1985b), 'Space, the city and social theory', in D. Gregory and J. Urry (eds.), *Social Relations and Spatial Structures*, Macmillan

Sayer, A. (1979), 'Theory and empirical research in urban and regional political economy: a sympathetic critique', *Urban and Regional Studies Working Papers*, no. 14, University of Sussex

Sayer, A. (1984a), *Method in Social Science*, Hutchinson

Sayer, A. (1984b), 'Defining the urban', *Geojournal*, **9**, pp. 279–85

Sayer, D. (1979), *Marx's Method*, Harvester Press

Schmitter, P. (1974), 'Still the century of corporatism?' *Review of Politics*, **36**, pp. 85–131

Sharpe, J. (1984), 'Functional allocation in the welfare state', *Local Government Studies*, **10**, pp. 27–45

Simmie, J. (1981), *Power, Property and Corporatism*, Macmillan

Sjoberg, G. (1960), *The Pre-Industrial City*, New York: Free Press

Sjoberg, G. (1964), 'The rural–urban dimensions in pre-industrial transitional and industrial societies', in R. Faris (ed.), *Handbook of Modern Sociology*, Chicago: Rand McNally

Smith, M. (1980), *The City and Social Theory*, Basil Blackwell

Smith, N. (1984), *Uneven Development*, Basil Blackwell

Soja, E. (1980), 'The socio-spatial dialectic', *Annals of the Association of American Geographers*, **70**, pp. 207–25

Soja, E. (1985), 'Regions in context: spatiality, periodicity and the historical geography of the regional question', *Society and Space*, **3**, pp. 175–90

Soja, E. and Hadjimichalis, C. (1979), 'Between geographical materialism and spatial fetishism: Some observations on the development of marxist spatial analysis', *Antipode*, **11**, pp. 3–11

Stacey, M. (1969), 'The myth of community studies', *British Journal of Sociology*, **20**, pp. 134–45

Stretton, H. (1974), *Housing and Government*, Sydney: Australian Broadcasting Commission

Swingewood, A. (1975), *Marx and Modern Social Theory*, Macmillan

Szelenyi, I. (1981a), 'Structural changes of and alternatives to capitalist development in the contemporary urban and regional system', *International Journal of Urban & Regional Research*, **5**, pp. 1–14

Szelenyi, I. (1981b), 'The relative autonomy of the state or state mode of production?', in M. Dear and A. Scott (eds.), *Urbanization and Urban Planning in Capitalist Society*, Methuen

Taylor-Gooby, P. (1985), *Public Opinion, Ideology and Social Welfare*, Routledge & Kegan Paul

Thompson, E. (1978), *The Poverty of Theory*, Merlin Press

Thorns, D. (1982), 'Industrial restructuring and change in the labour and property markets in Britain', *Environment and Planning 'A'*, **14**, pp. 745–63

Thrift, N. (1983), 'On the determination of social action in space and time', *Society and Space*, **1**, pp. 23–58

Tönnies, F. (1955), *Community and Society*, New York, Harper & Row

Torrance, J. (1974), 'Max Weber: methods and the man', *European Journal of Sociology*, **15**, pp. 127–65

Townsend, P. (1979), *Poverty in the United Kingdom*, Penguin

Trasler, G. (1982), 'The psychology of ownership and possessiveness', in P. Hollowell (ed.), *Property and Social Relations*, Heinemann

Urry, J. (1981), 'Localities, regions and social class', *International Journal of Urban & Regional Research*, 5, pp. 455–74

Urry, J. (1983), 'De-industrialisation, classes and politics', in R. King (ed.), *Capital and Politics*, Routledge & Kegan Paul

Urry, J. (1985), 'Social relations, space and time', in D. Gregory and J. Urry (eds.), *Social Relations and Spatial Structures*, Macmillan

Villadsen, S. (1983), 'Urban Politics: central control versus local demands', University of Copenhagen, Institute of Political Studies, *Central Control, Local Communities and Local Politics*, report no. 10

Walther, U. (1982), 'The making of a new urban sociology', in R. Forrest, J. Henderson and P. Williams (eds.), *Urban Political Economy and Social Theory*, Gower

Walton, P. and Gamble, A. (1972), *From Alienation to Surplus Value*, Sheed & Ward

Ward, C. (1983), *Housing: An Anarchist Approach*, Freedom Press

Ward, C. (1985), *When We Build Again*, Pluto Press

Weber, M. (1948a), 'Science as a vocation', in H. Gerth and C. Mills (eds.), *From Max Weber: Essays in Sociology*, Routledge & Kegan Paul

Weber, M. (1948b), 'Politics as a vocation', in Gerth and Mills, *From Max Weber*, Routledge & Kegan Paul

Weber, M. (1949), *The Methodology of the Social Sciences*, New York: Free Press

Weber, M. (1958), *The City*, Chicago: Free Press

Weber, M. (1968), *Economy and Society*, New York: Bedminster Press

Westergaard, J. (1977), 'Class inequality and corporatism', in A. Hunt, (ed.), *Class and Class Structure*, Lawrence & Wishart

Williams, P. (1978), 'Urban managerialism: a concept of relevance?', *Area*, 10, pp. 236–40

Williams, P. (1982), Property, power and politics: home ownership and social relations', paper presented at the Association of American Geographers annual conference, San Antonio, Texas (April)

Williams, R. (1973), *The Country and the City*, Chatto & Windus

Willis, P. (1977), *Learning to Labour*, Saxon House

Winkler, J. (1975), 'Corporatism', *European Journal of Sociology*, 17, pp. 100–36

Winkler, J. (1977), 'The corporate economy: theory and administration', in R. Scase (ed.), *Industrial Society: Class, Cleavage and Control*, George Allen and Unwin

Wirth, L. (1927), 'The ghetto', *American Journal of Sociology*, 33, pp. 57–71

Wirth, L. (1938), 'Urbanism as a way of life', *American Journal of Sociology*, 44, pp. 1–24

Wirth, L. (1945), 'Human ecology', *American Journal of Sociology*, 50, pp. 483–8

Wirth, L. (1964), 'Rural–urban differences', in A. Reiss (ed.), *Louis Wirth on Cities and Social Life*, University of Chicago Press

Wirth, L. (1967), 'A bibliography of the urban community', in R. Park and E. Burgess, *The City*, University of Chicago Press

Wolff, K. (1950), *The Sociology of Georg Simmel*, Glencoe, Ill.: Free Press

Young, K., and Kramer, J. (1978), 'Local exclusionary policies in Britain: the case of suburban defence in a metropolitan system', in K. Cox (ed.), *Urbanization and Conflict in Market Societies*, Methuen

Young, M., and Willmott, P. (1957), *Family and Kinship in East London*, Routledge & Kegan Paul

Index

Social Theory and the
Urban Question

Second Edition